BIG LONDON

Published by Geographers' A-Z Map Company Limited
An imprint of HarperCollins Publishers
Westerhill Road
Bishopbriggs
Glasgow G64 2QT
www.az.co.uk
a-z.maps@harpercollins.co.uk

14th edition 2020

A catalogue record for this book is available from the British Library.

ISBN 978-0-00-838800-3

10 9 8 7 6 5 4 3 2 1

Printed in China

REFERENCE

Motorway	M1
A Road	A2
B Road	B408
Dual Carriageway	
One-way Street Traffic flow on A Roads is also indicated by a heavy line on the drivers' left.	
Road Under Construction Opening dates are correct at the time of publication.	
Proposed Road	
Junction Name	MARBLE ARCH
Restricted Access	
Pedestrianized Road	
Track / Footpath	
Residential Walkway	
Congestion Charging Zone See inside Front Cover for information	Zone edge. Within Zone.
Low Emission Zone Visit www.tfl.gov.uk/modes/driving for more information on London's driving zones.	Zone edge. Within Zone.

Railway — Level Crossing — Tunnel

Stations: Large Scale Map Pages

National Rail Network	⇄	⇄
Crossrail	✕	✕
Docklands Light Railway	DLR	DLR
Overground	⊖	⊖
Underground	●	⊖

London Tramlink   Tunnel
The boarding of Tramlink trams at stops may be limited to a single direction, indicated by the arrow.   Stop

Built-up Area   EXHIBITION   ROAD

Postcode Boundary

Map Continuation	▲ 82 Large Scale Map Pages ▲ 10
Airport	✈
Car Park (selected)	P
Church or Chapel	†
Fire Station	■
Hospital	H
House Numbers (A & B Roads only)	20 163
Information Centre	i
National Grid Reference	^{5}30
Police Station	▲
Post Office	★
River Bus Stop	R
Toilet	▽
Educational Establishment	▢
Hospital or Healthcare Building	▢
Industrial Building	▢
Leisure or Recreational Facility	▢
Place of Interest	▢
Public Building	▢
Shopping Centre or Market	▢
Other Selected Buildings	▢

SCALE

Map Pages 4-19   1:7,454

0   ⅛   ¼ Mile

0   100   200   300   400   500 Metres

8½ inches (21.59 cm) to 1 mile   13.4 cm to 1 km

Map Pages 20-174   1:14,908

0   ¼   ½ Mile

0   250   500   750 Metres   1 Kilometre

4¼ inches (10.79 cm) to 1 mile   6.71 cm to 1 km

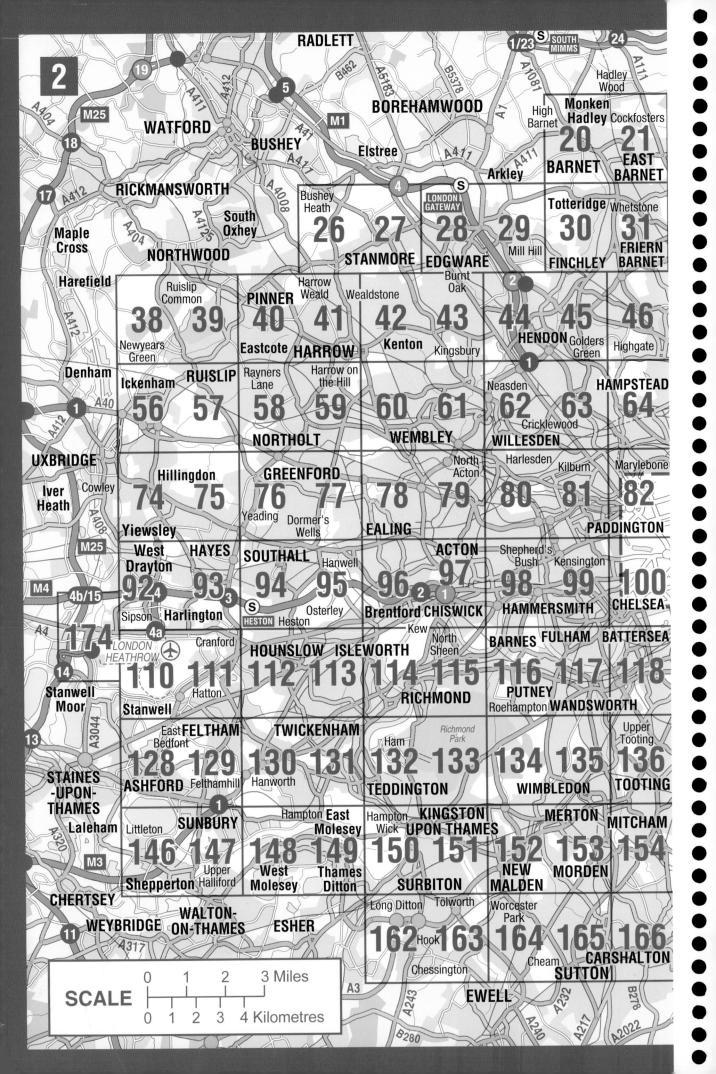

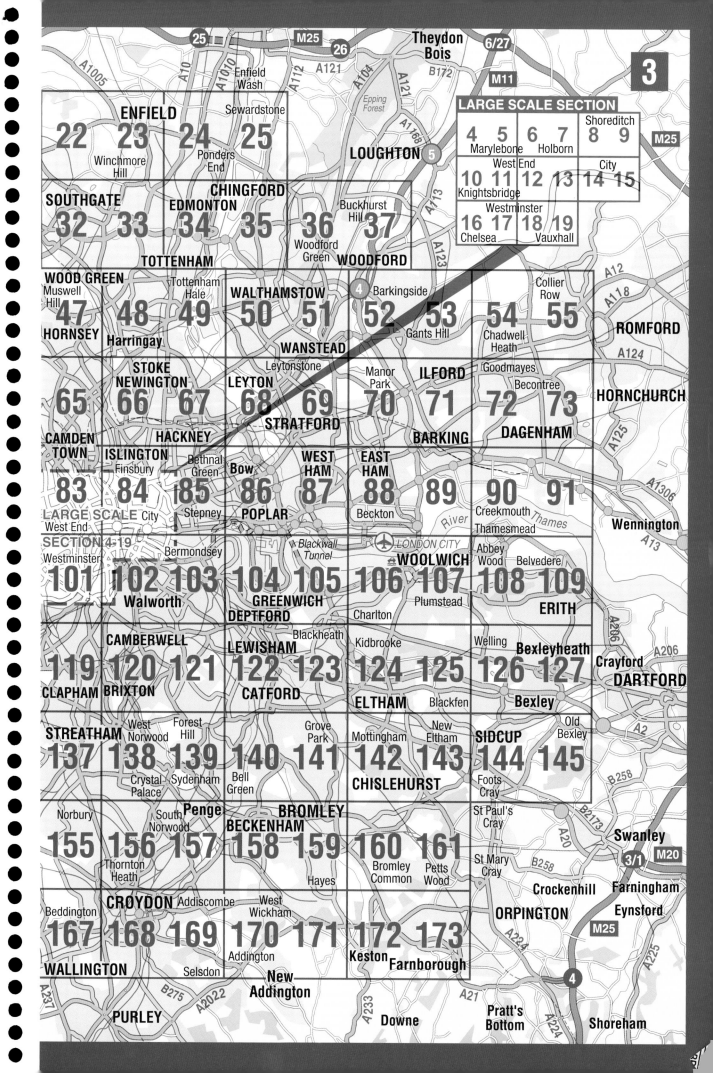

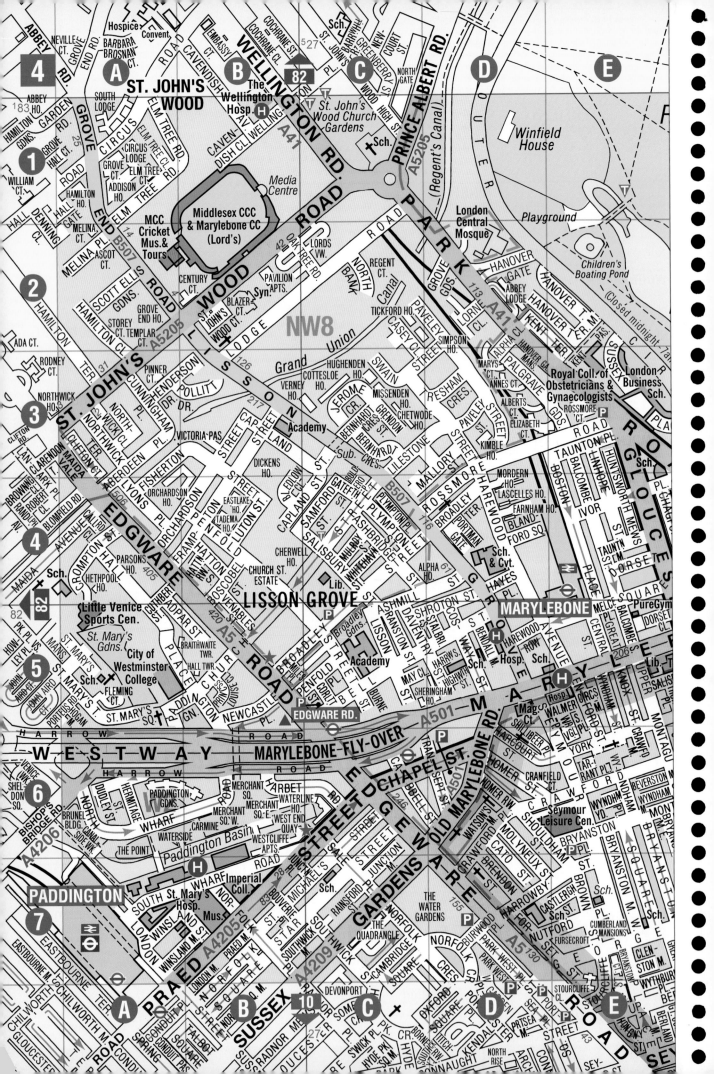

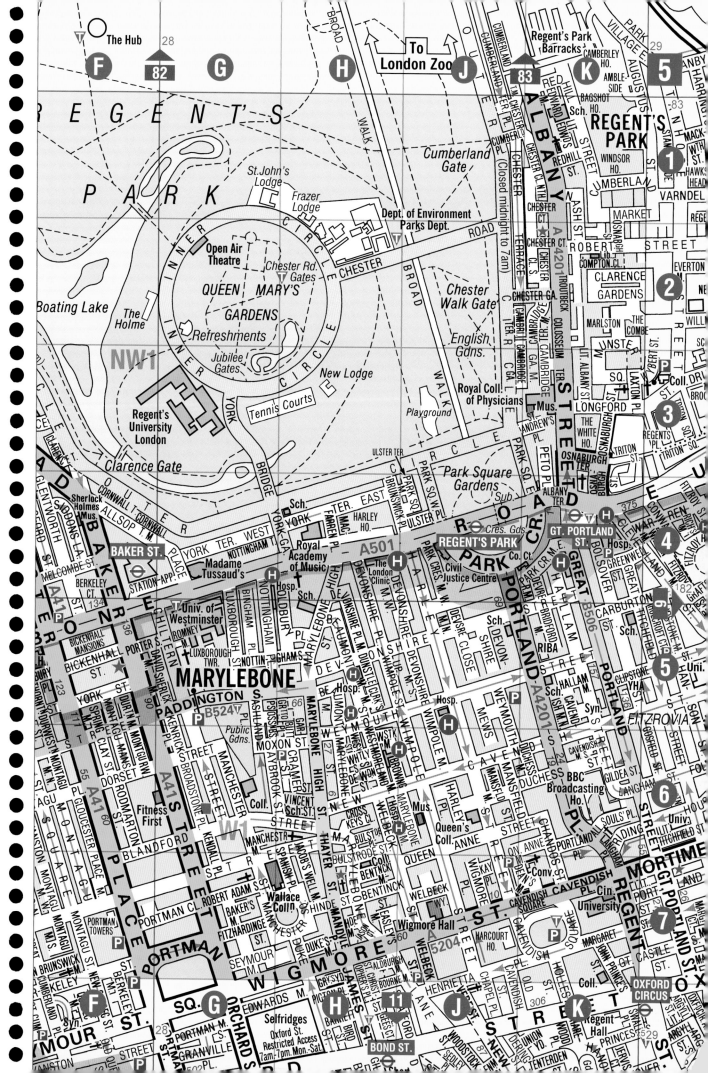

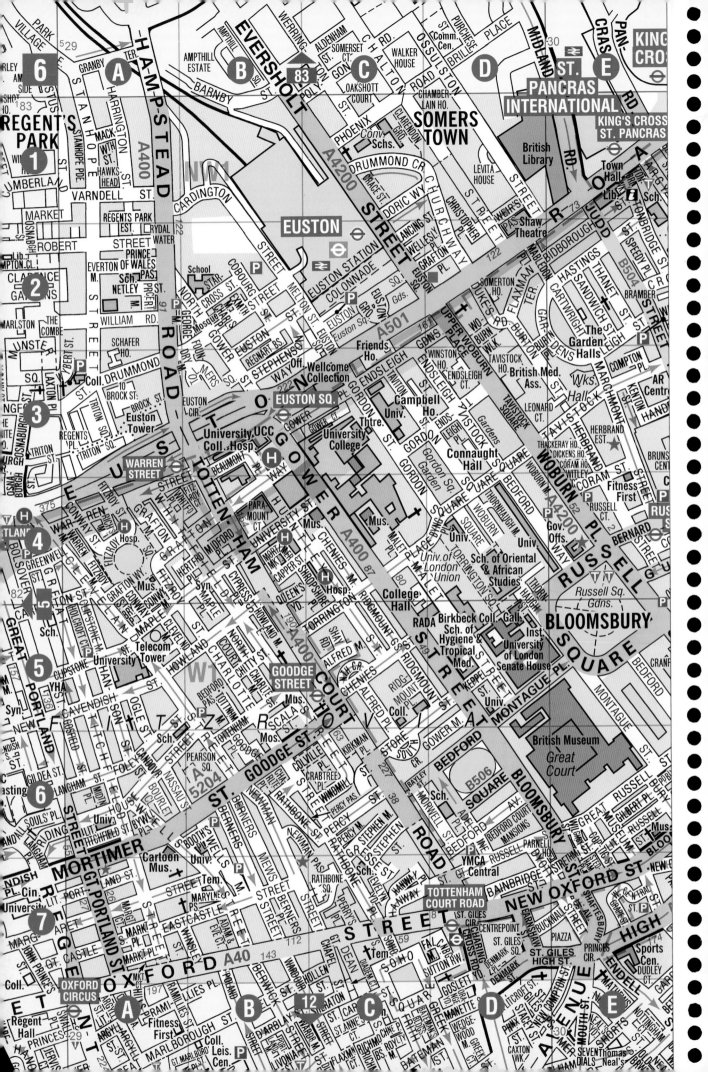

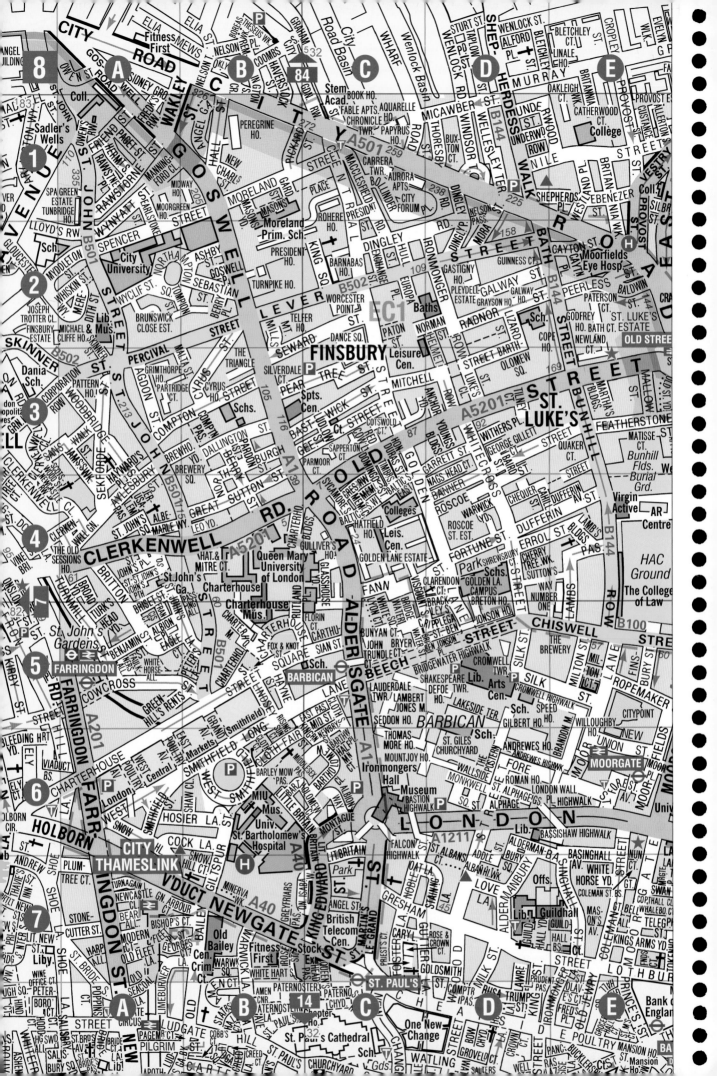

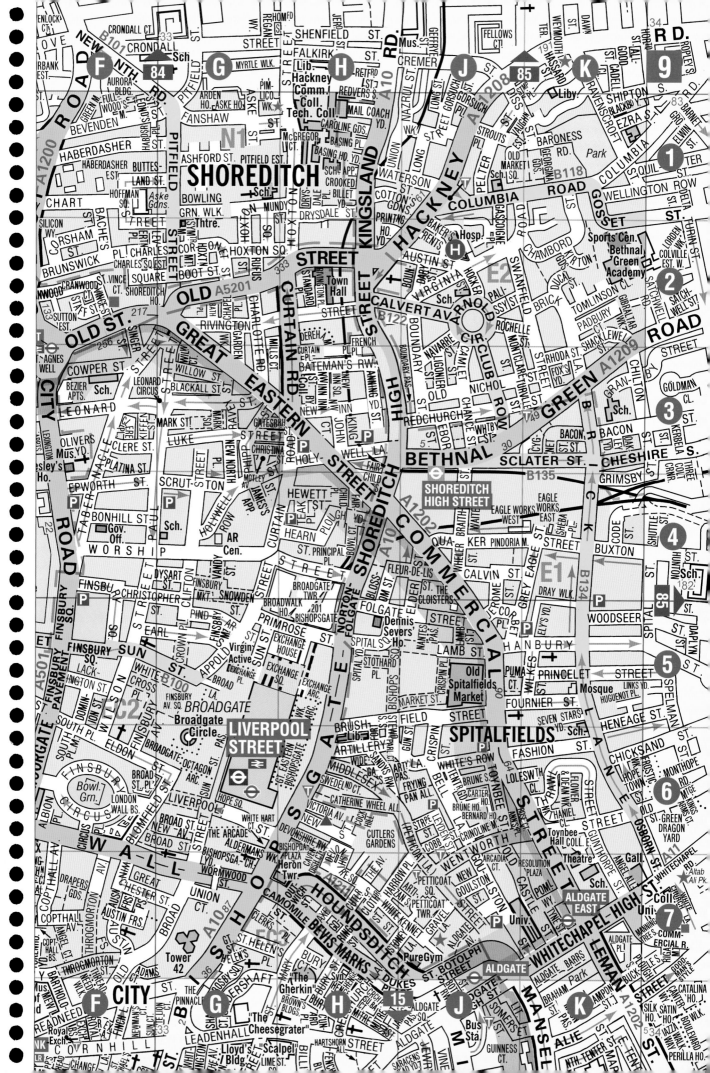

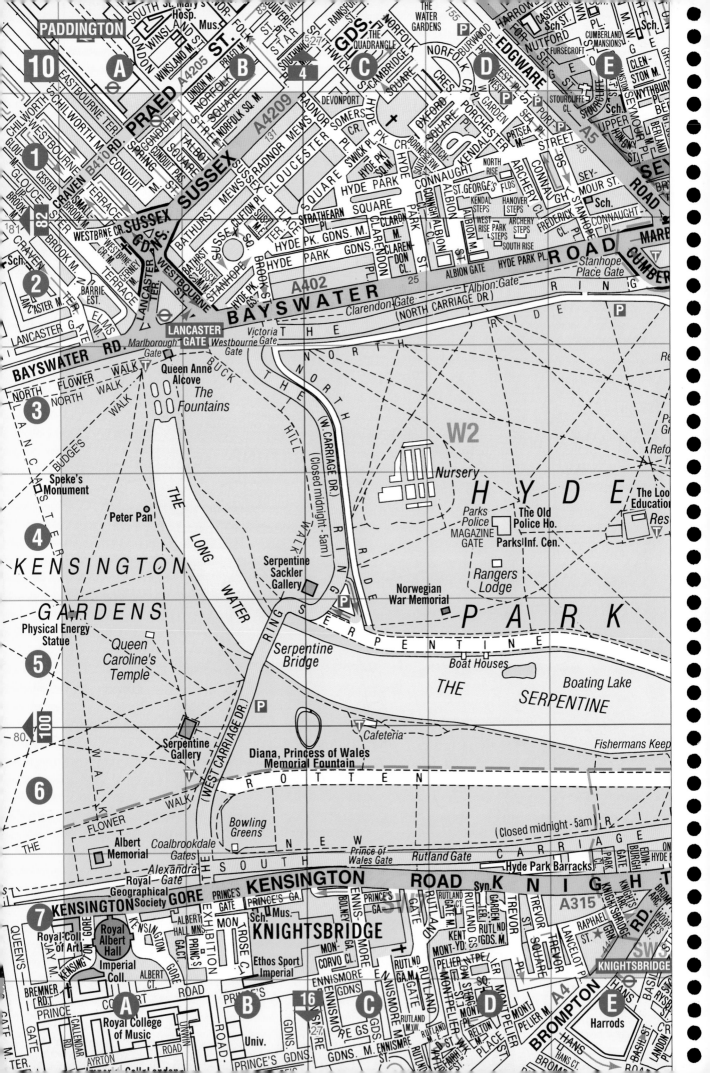

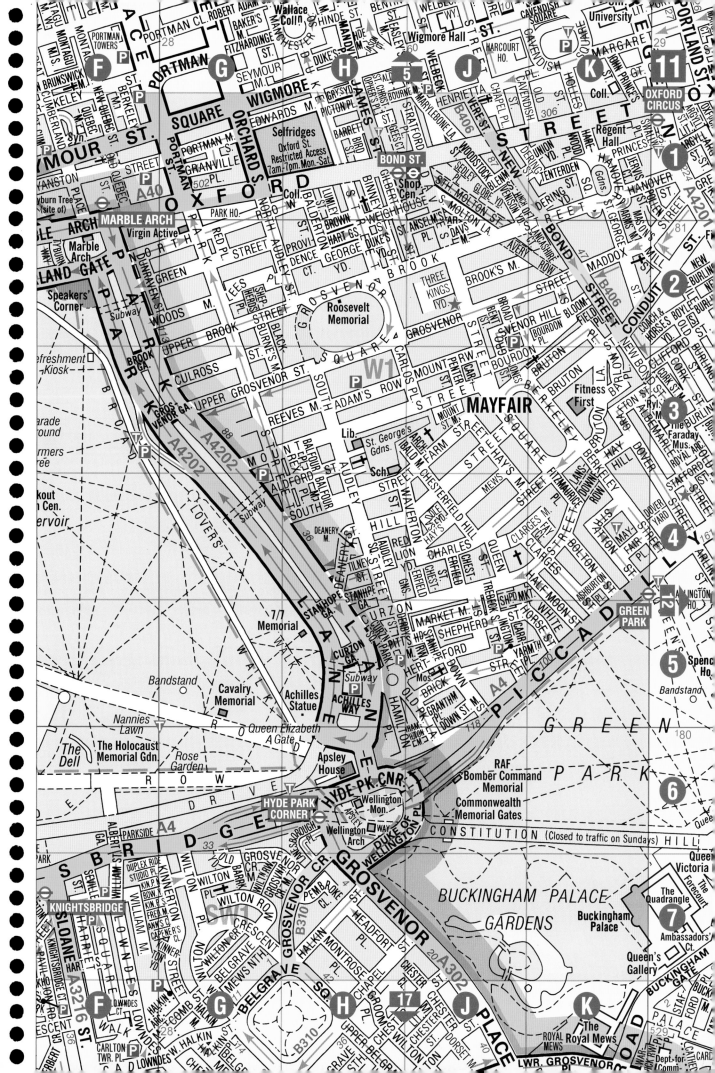

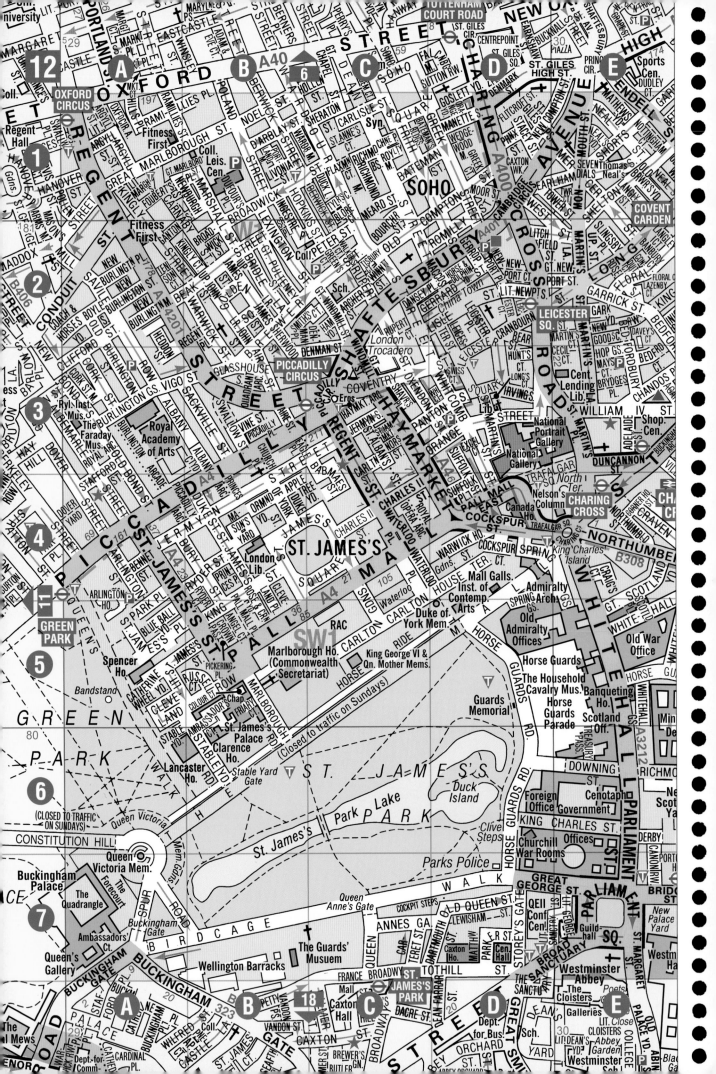

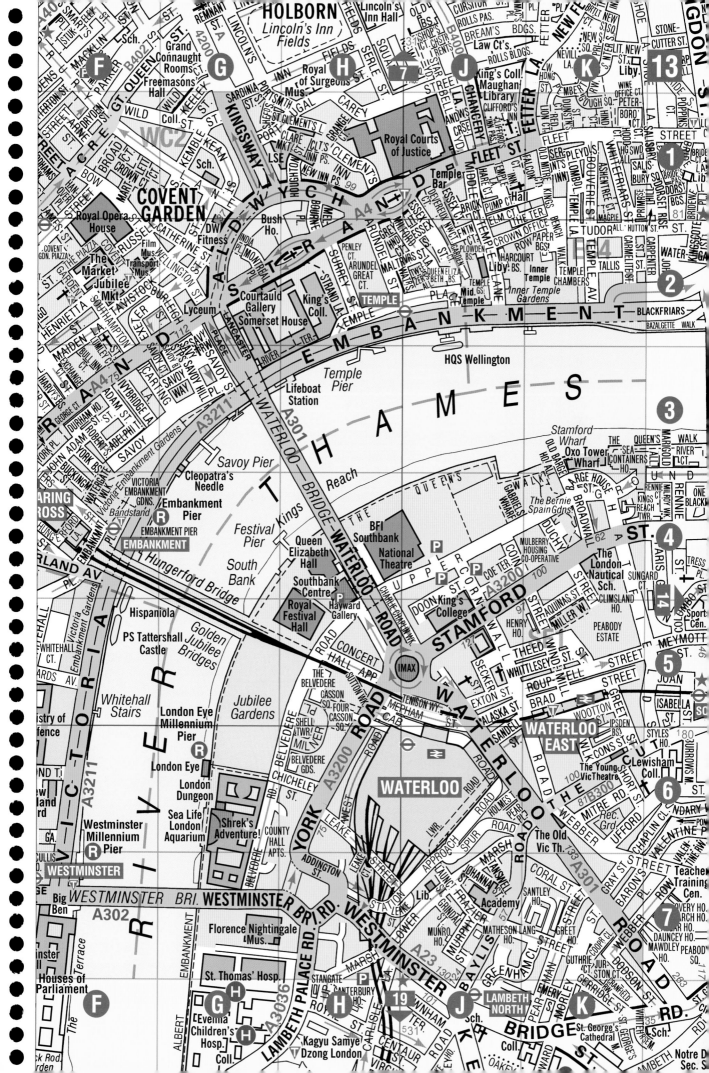

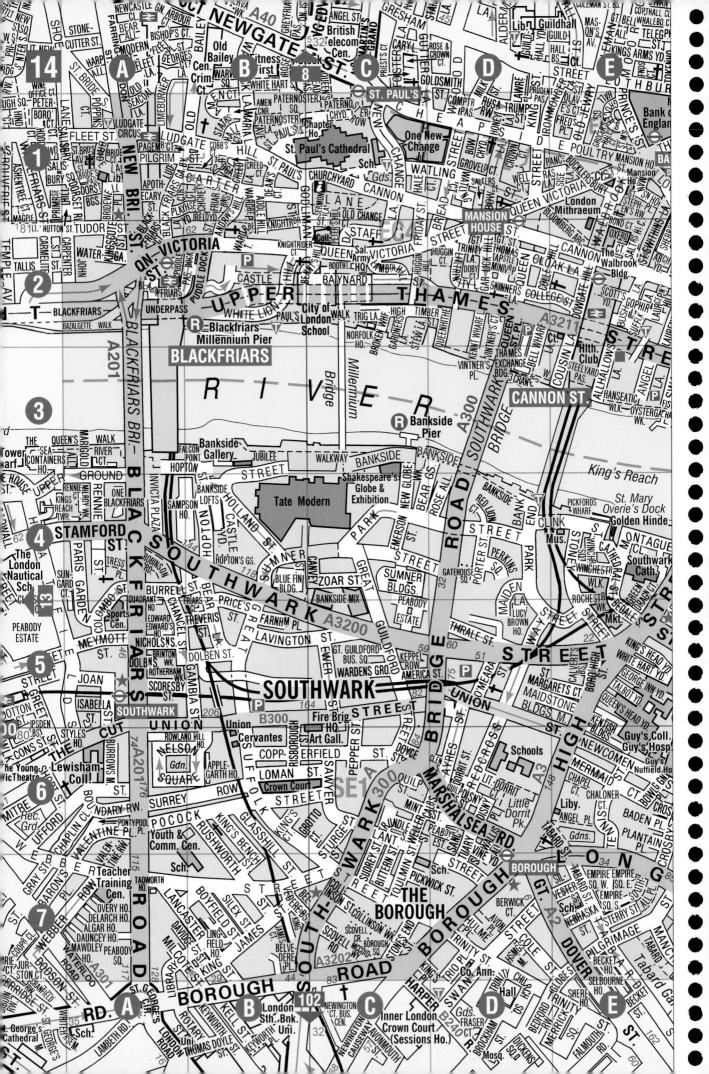

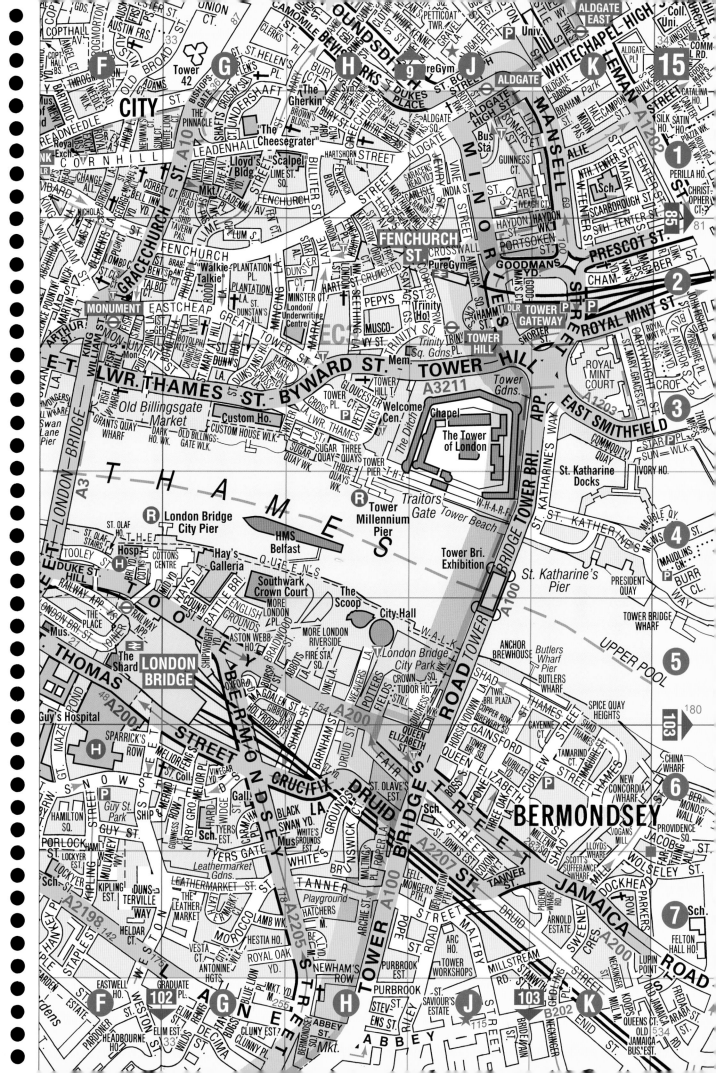

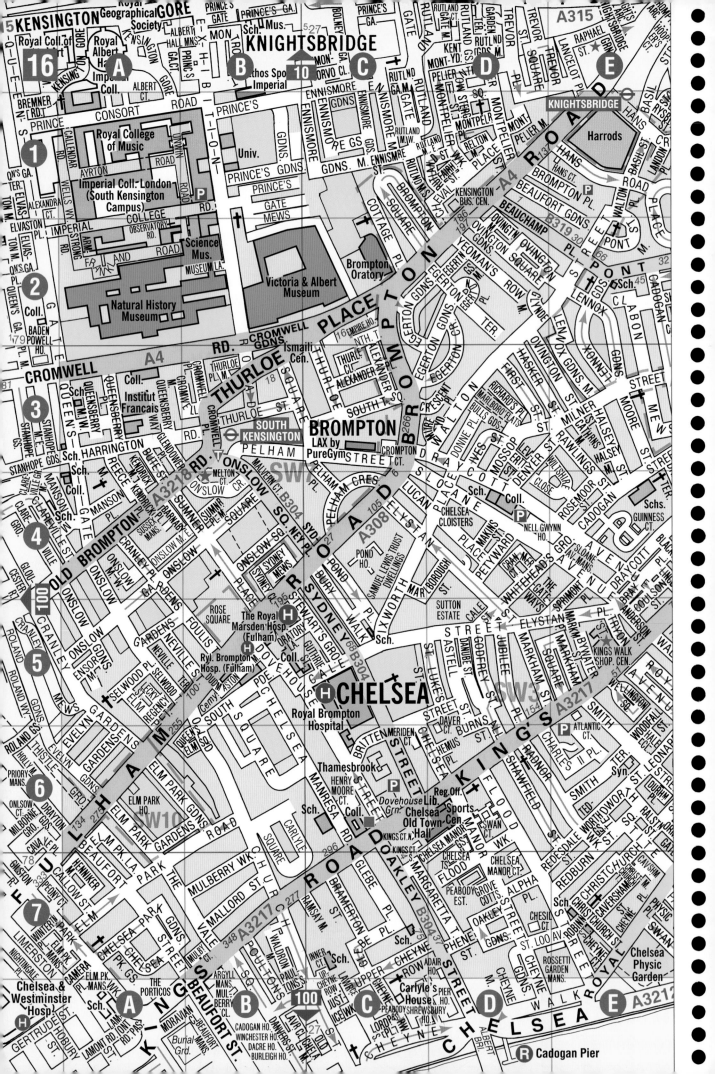

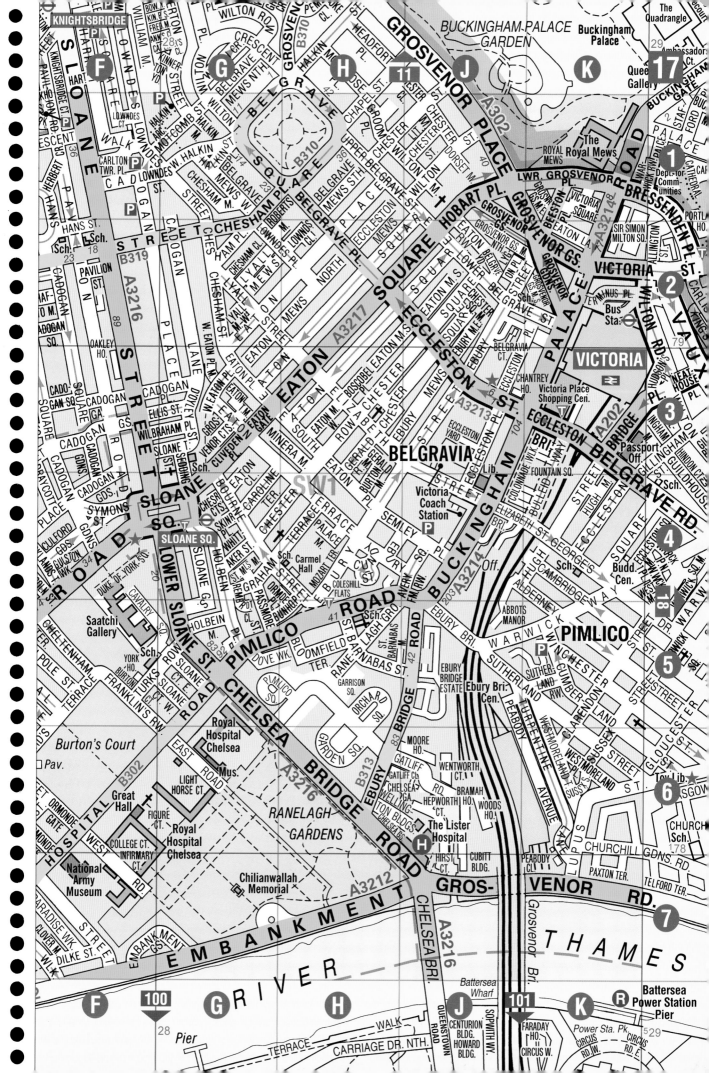

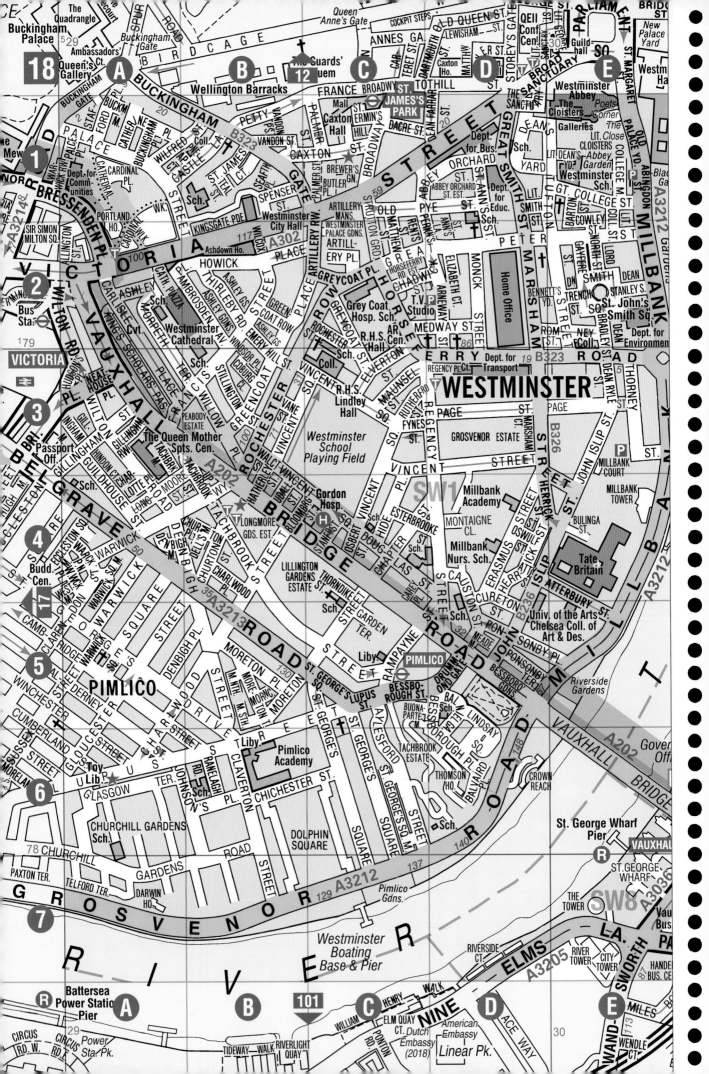

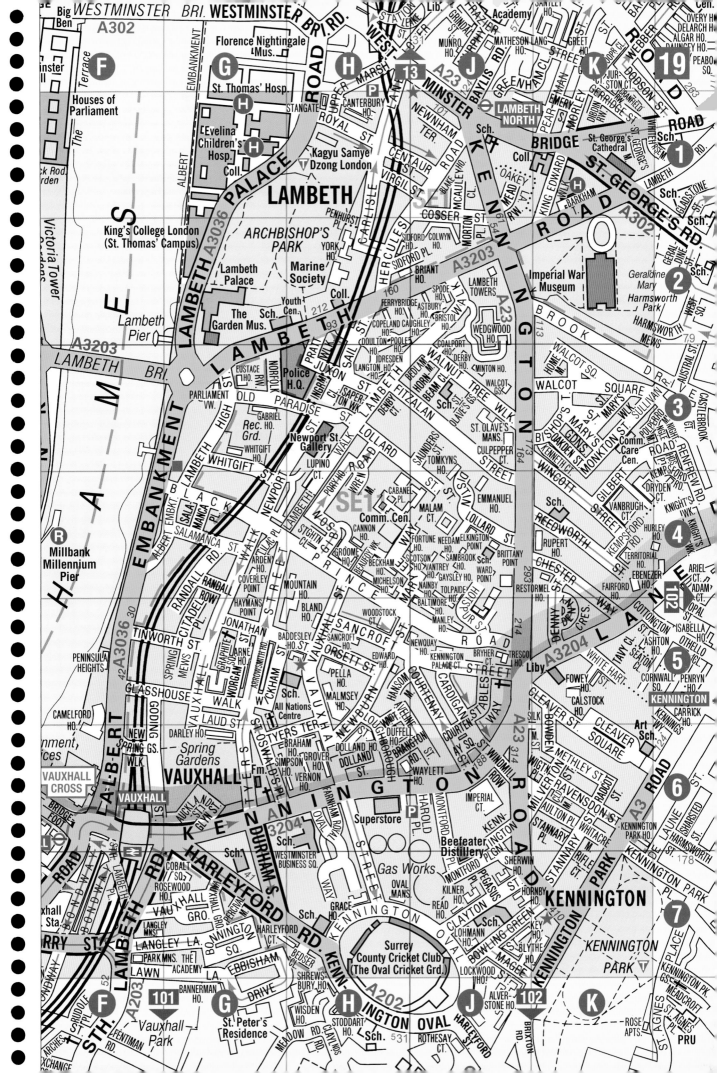

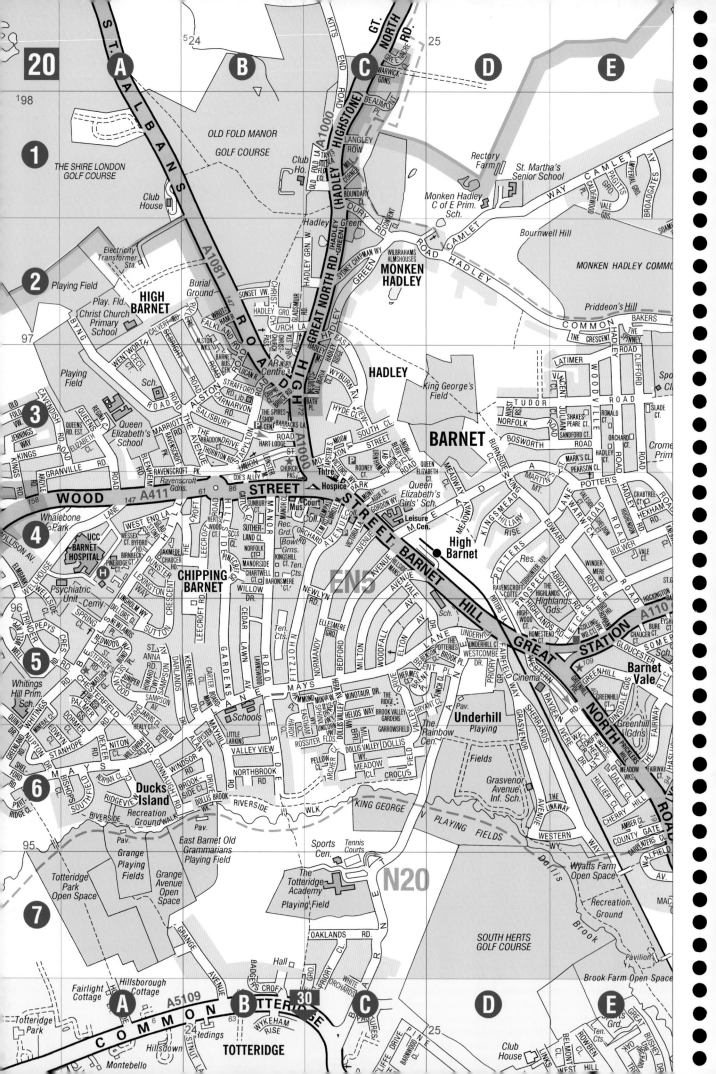

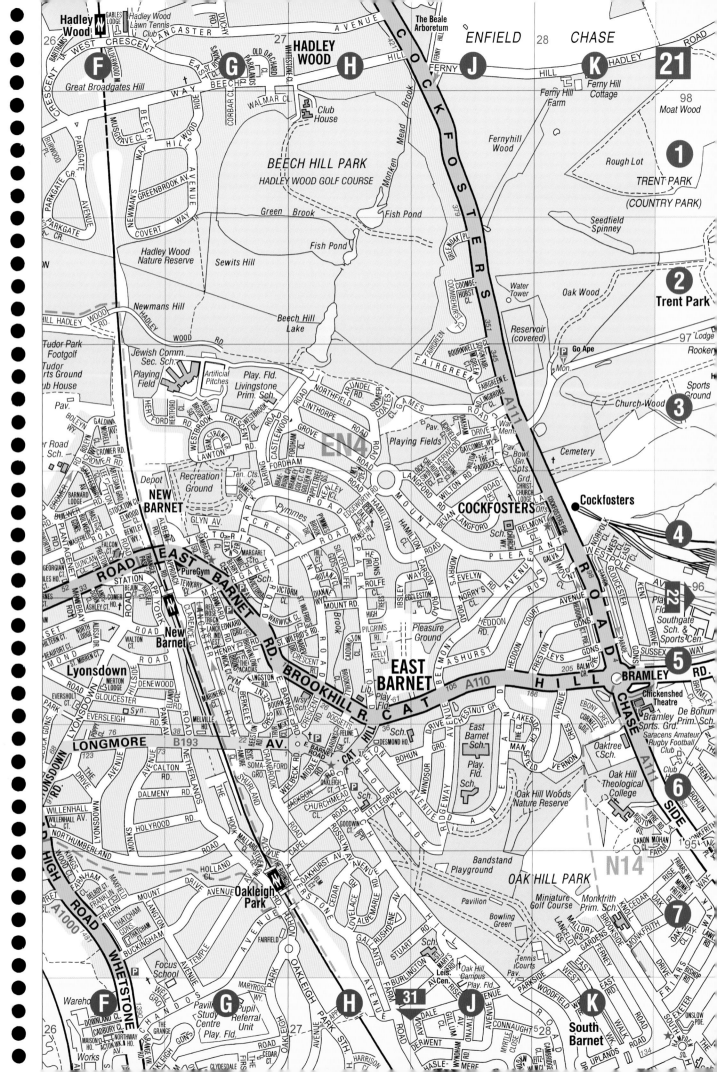

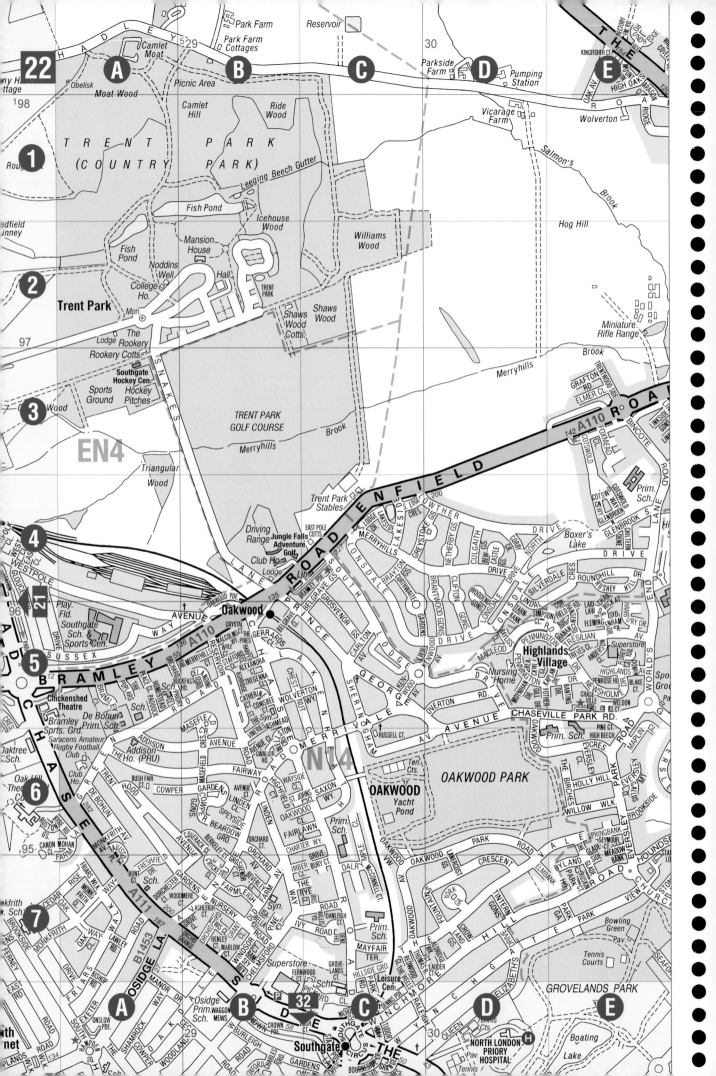

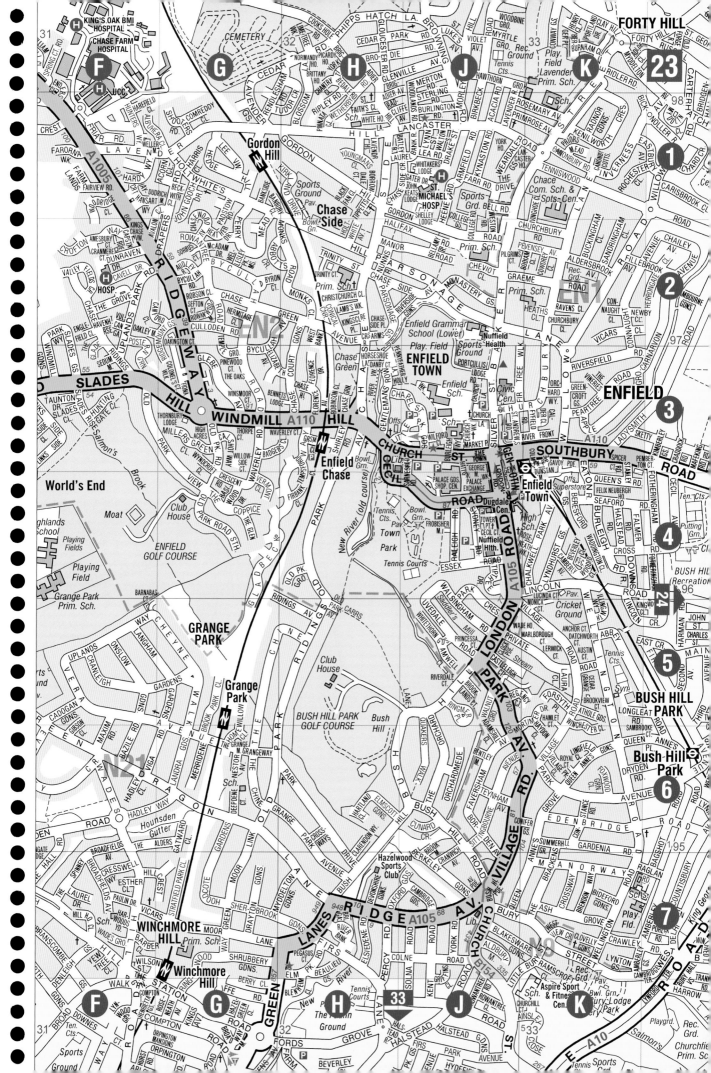

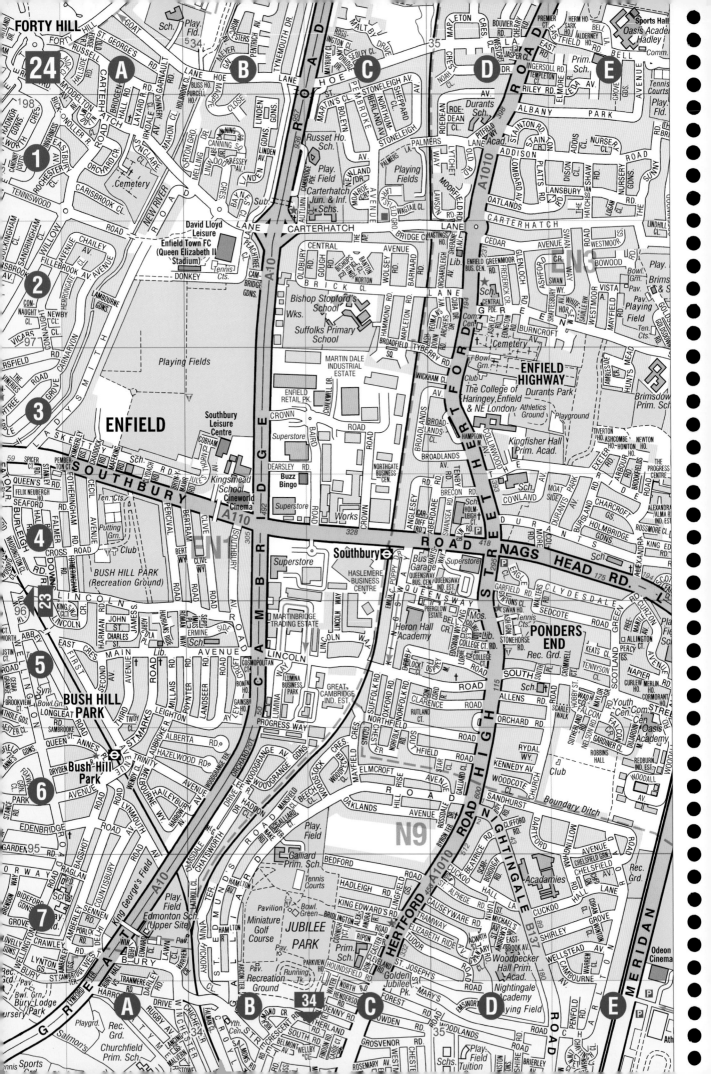

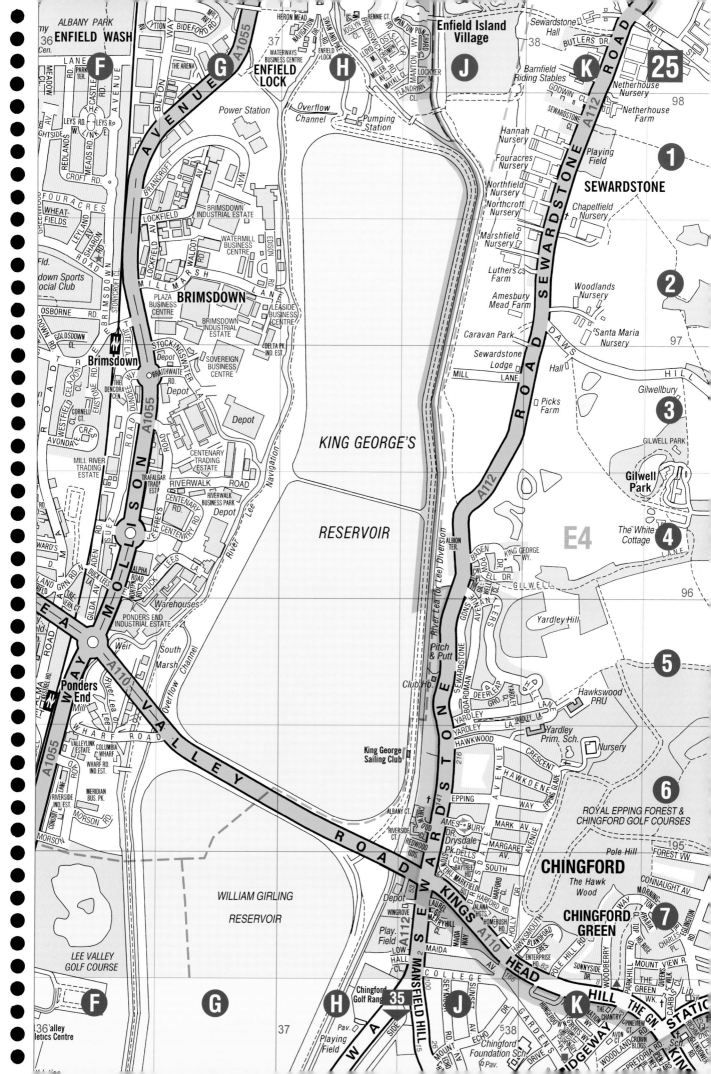

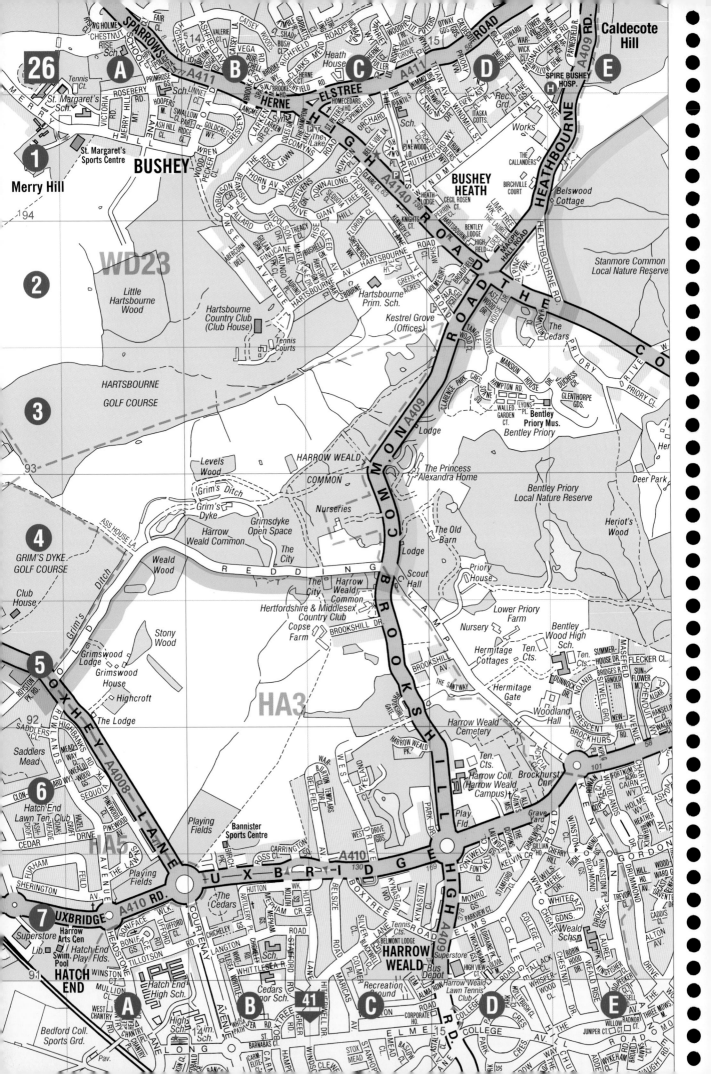

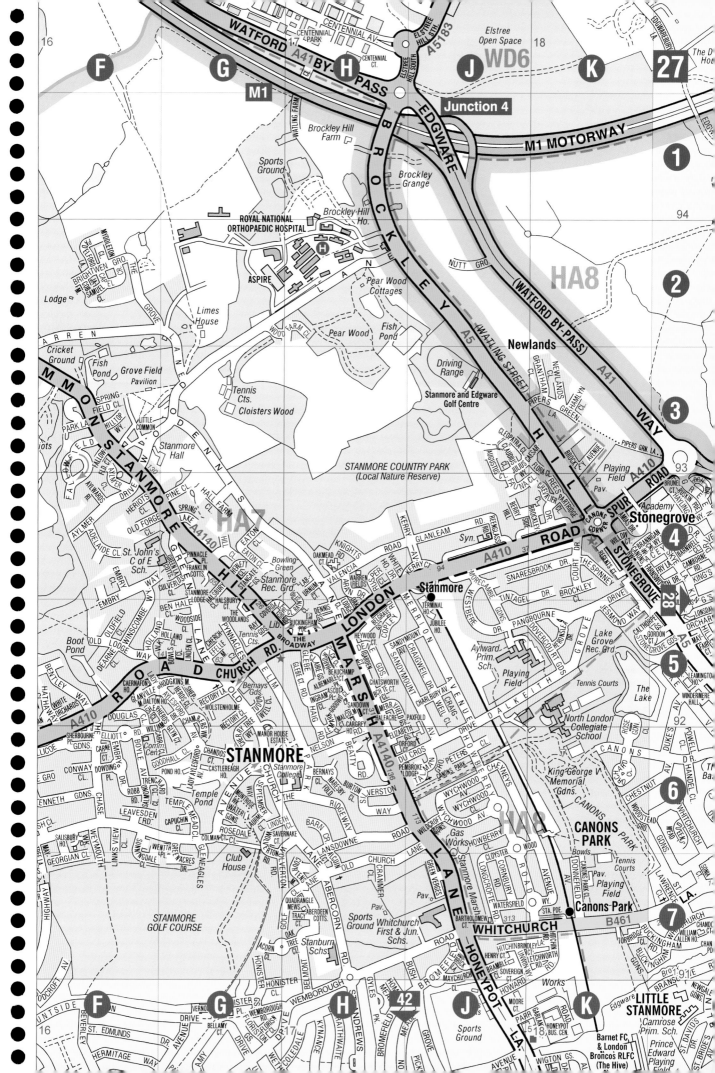

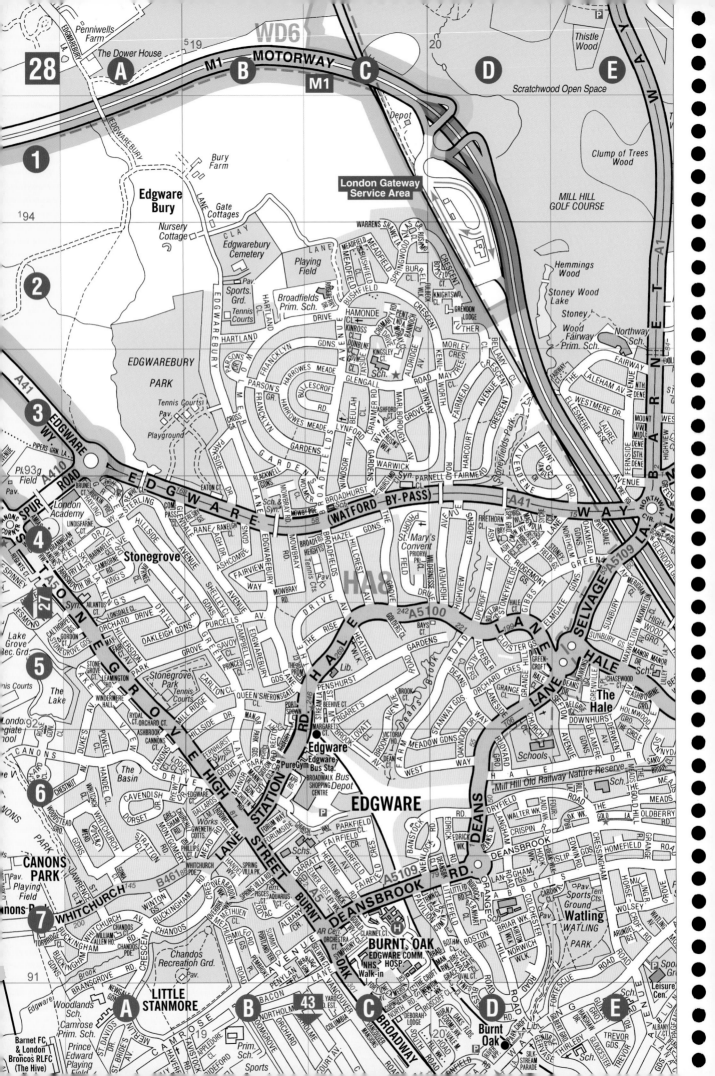

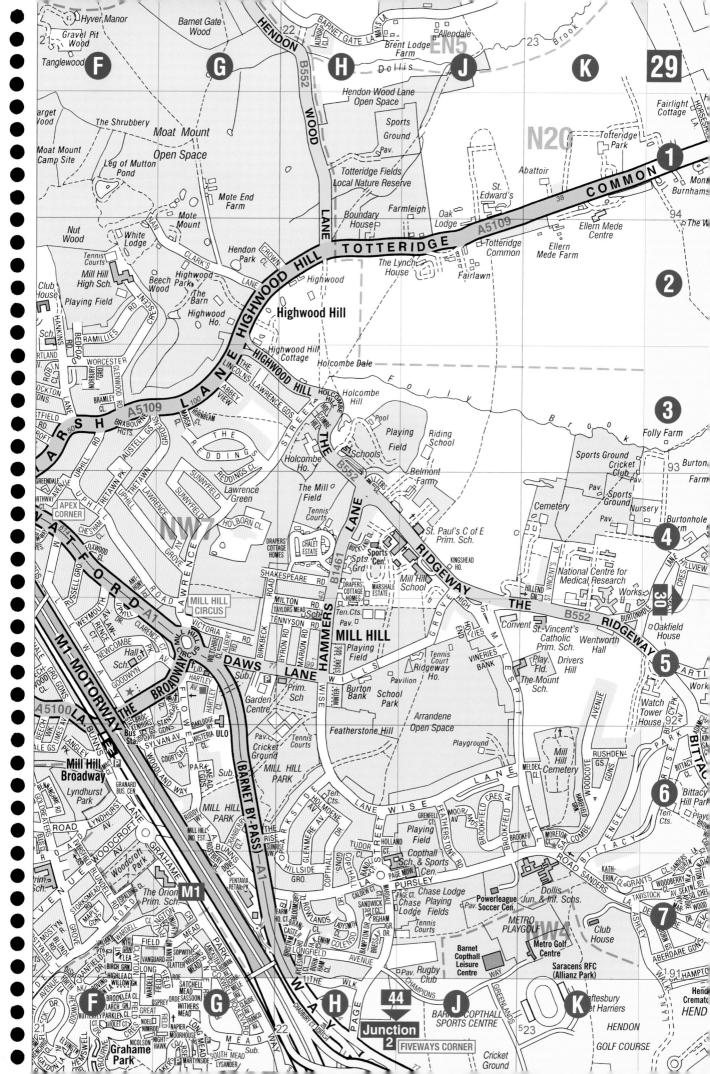

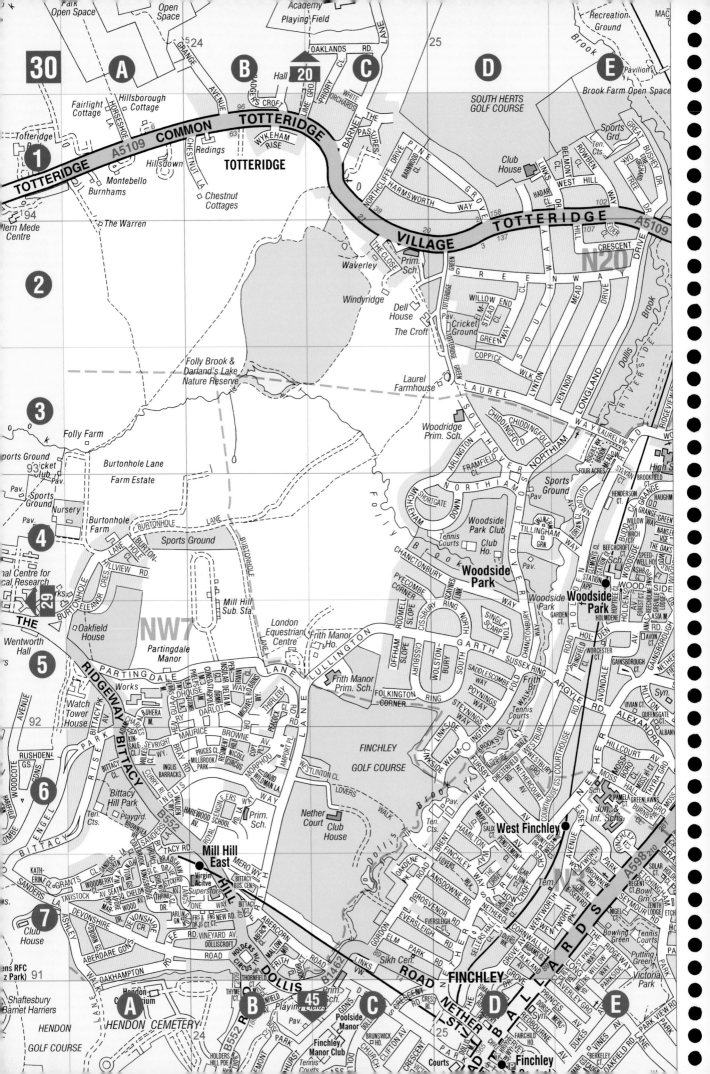

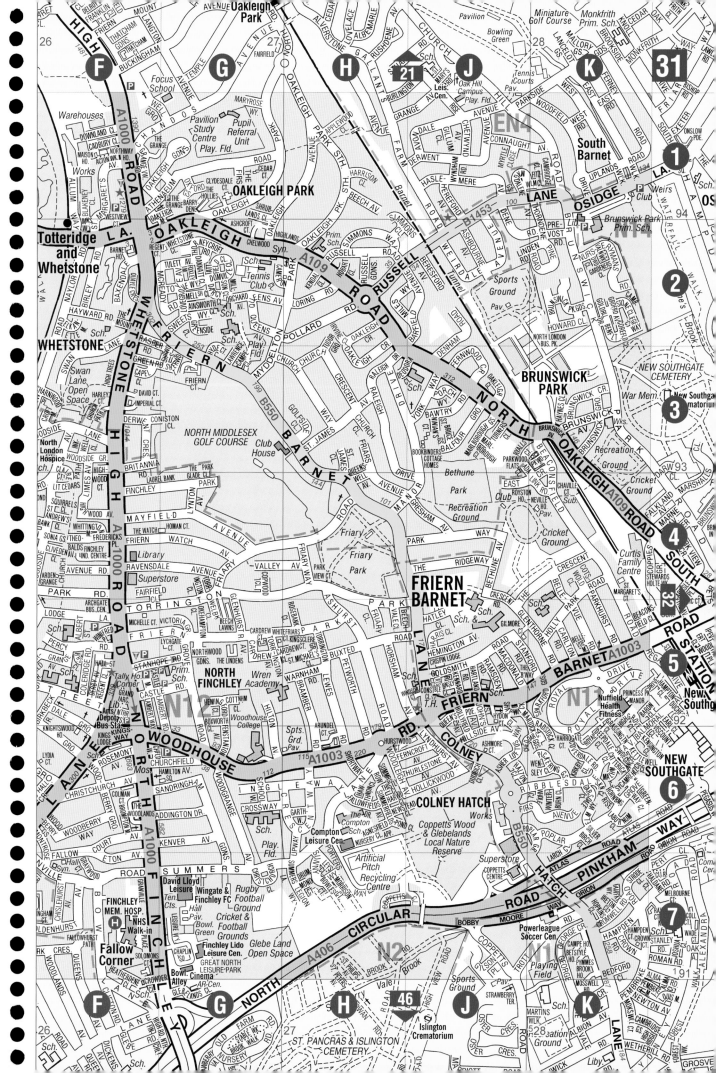

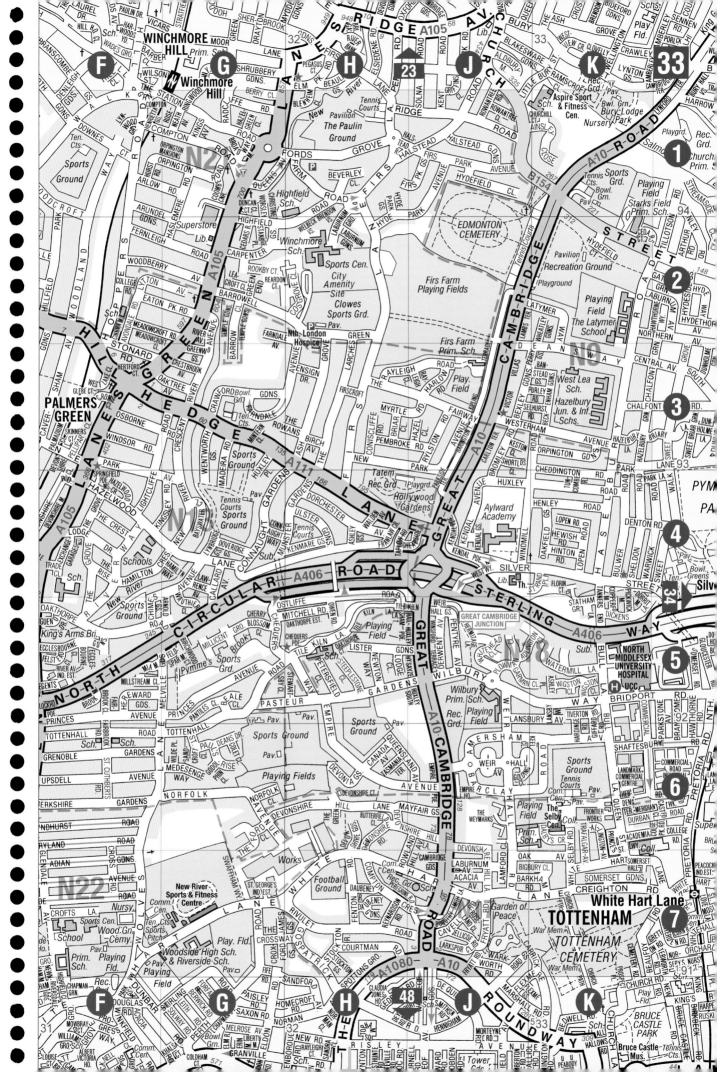

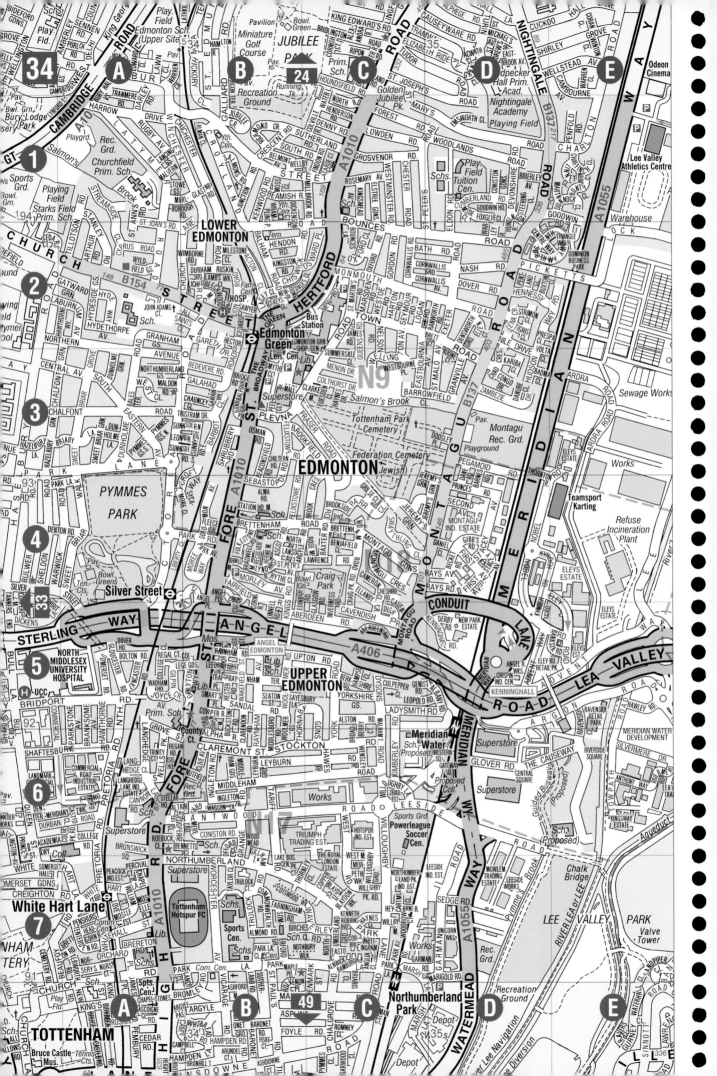

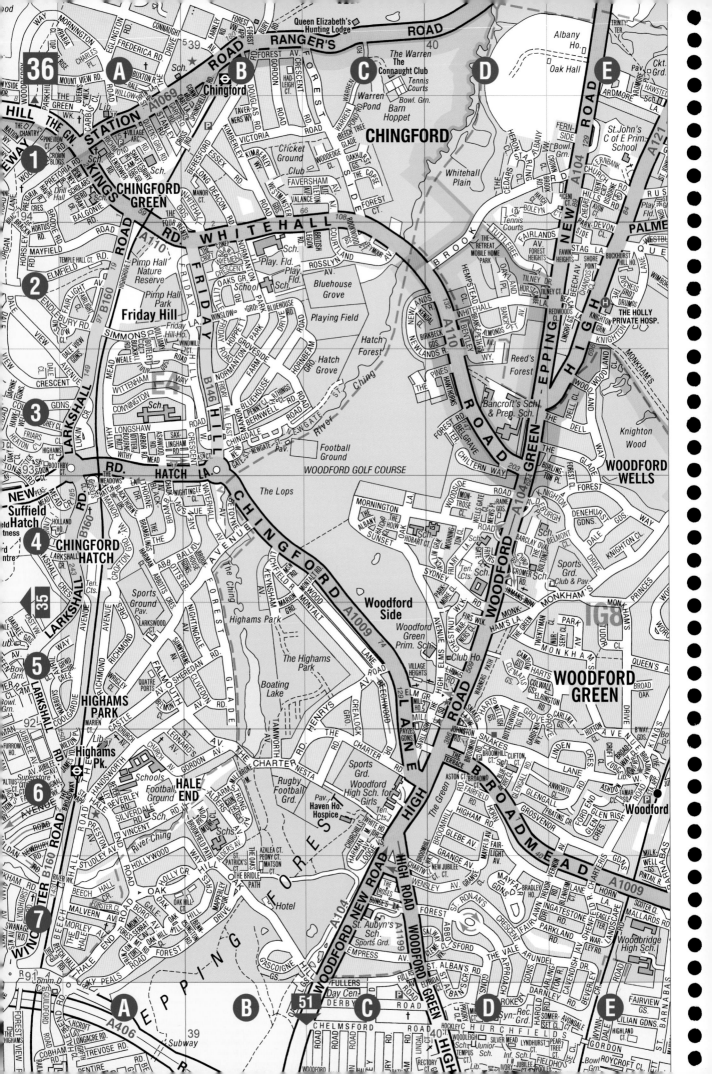

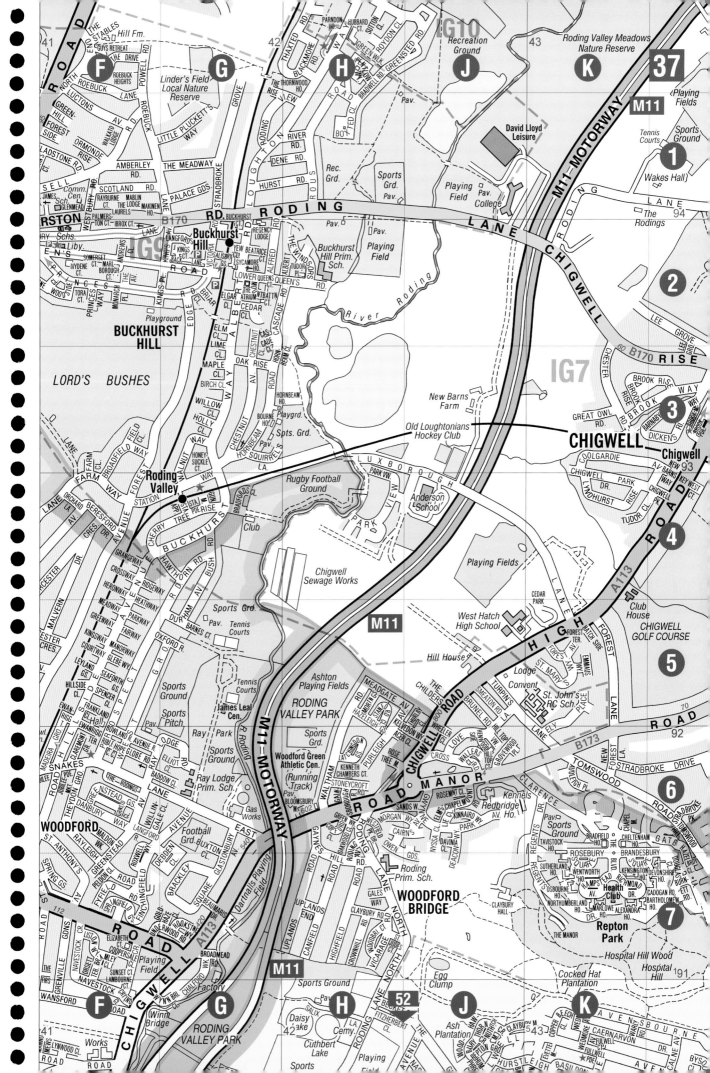

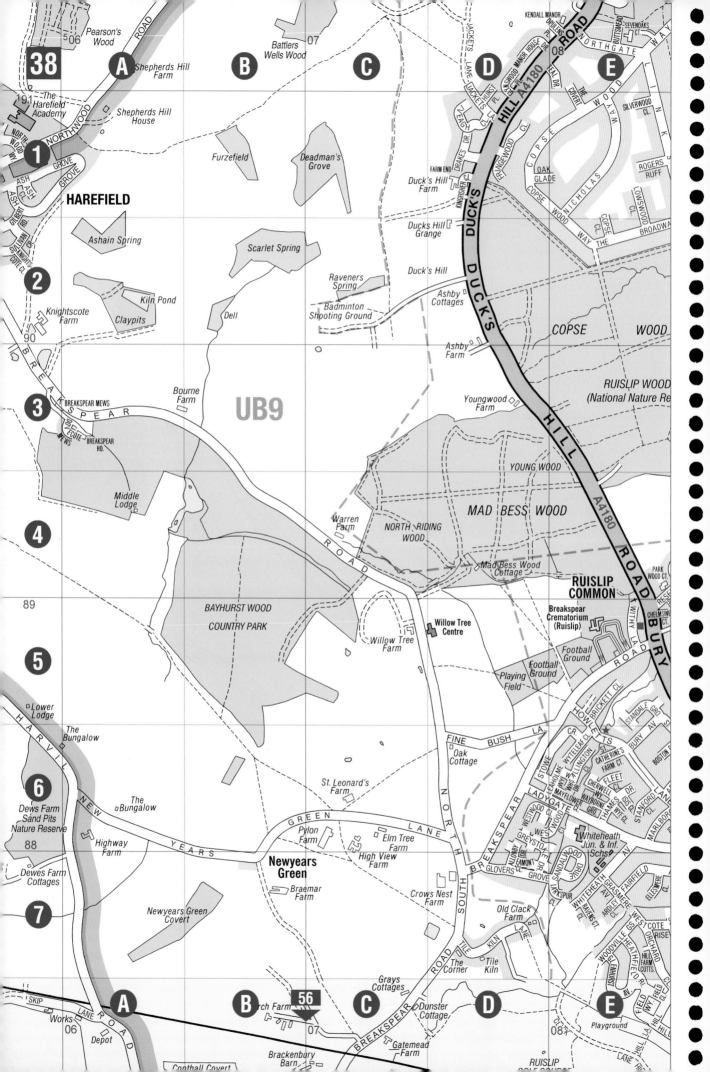

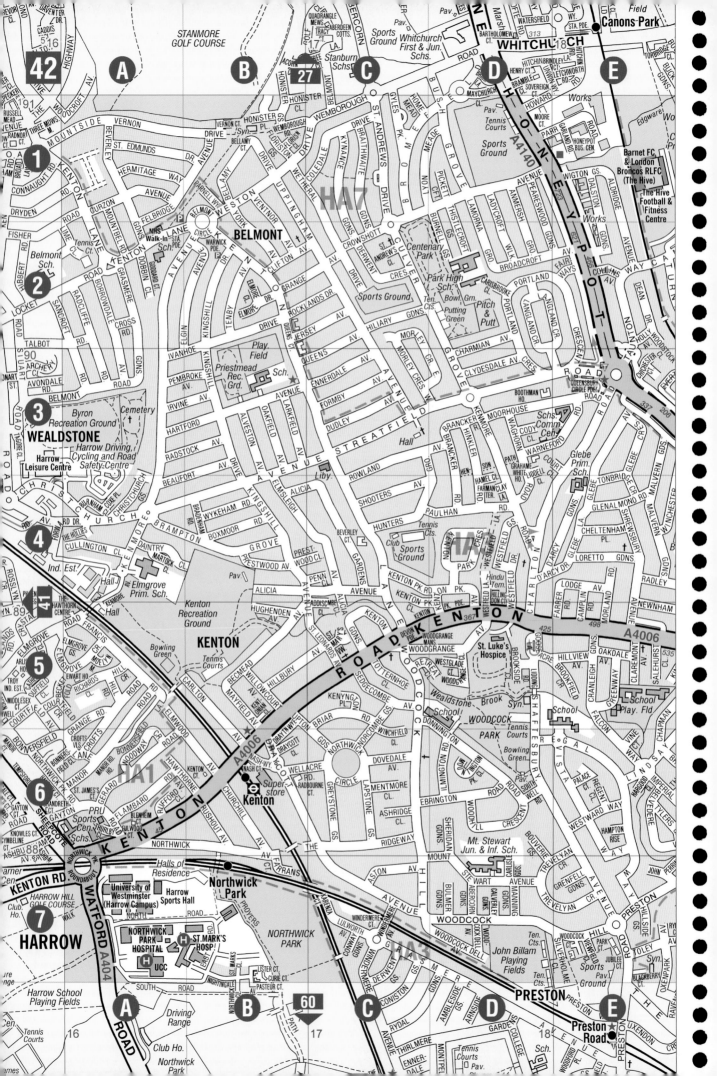

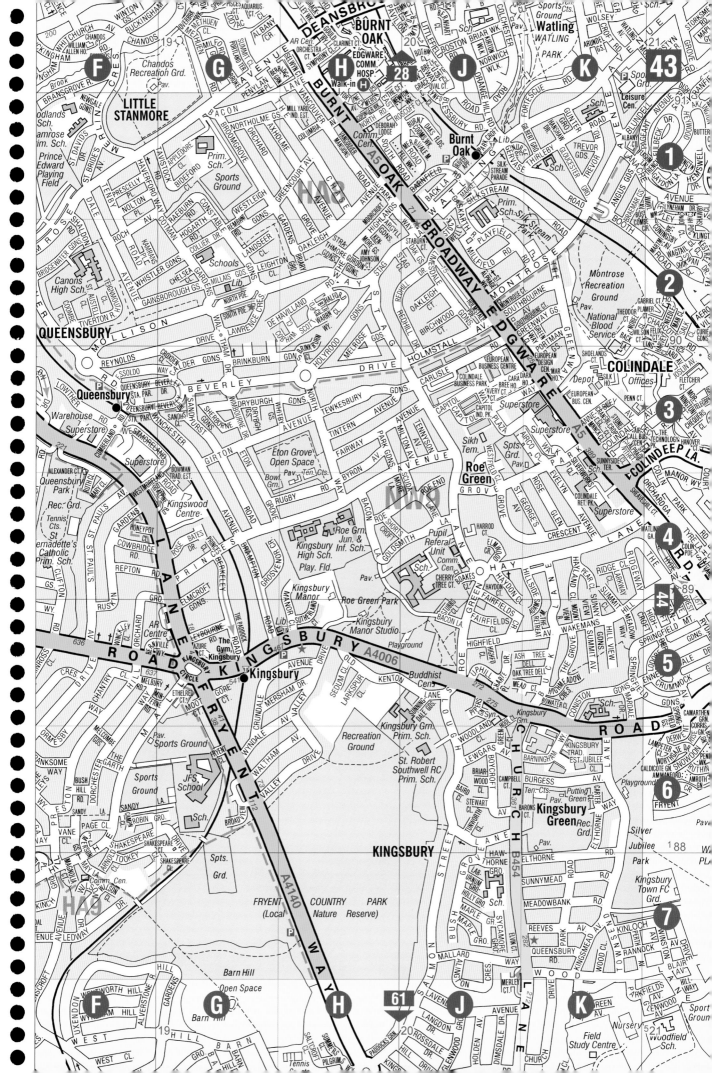

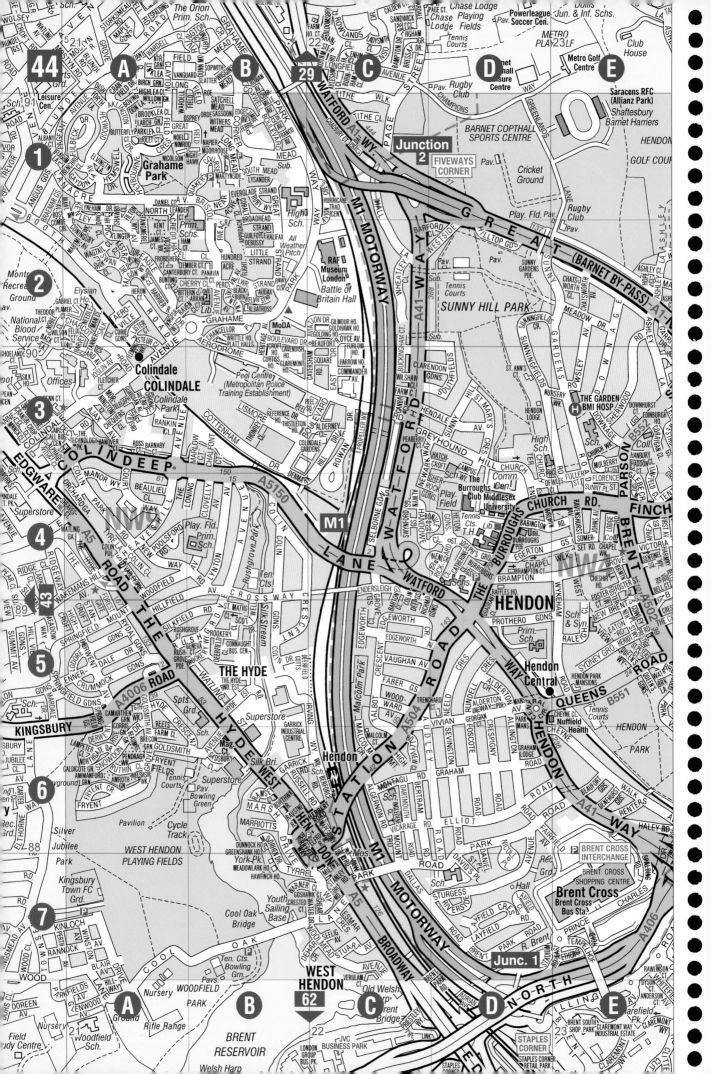

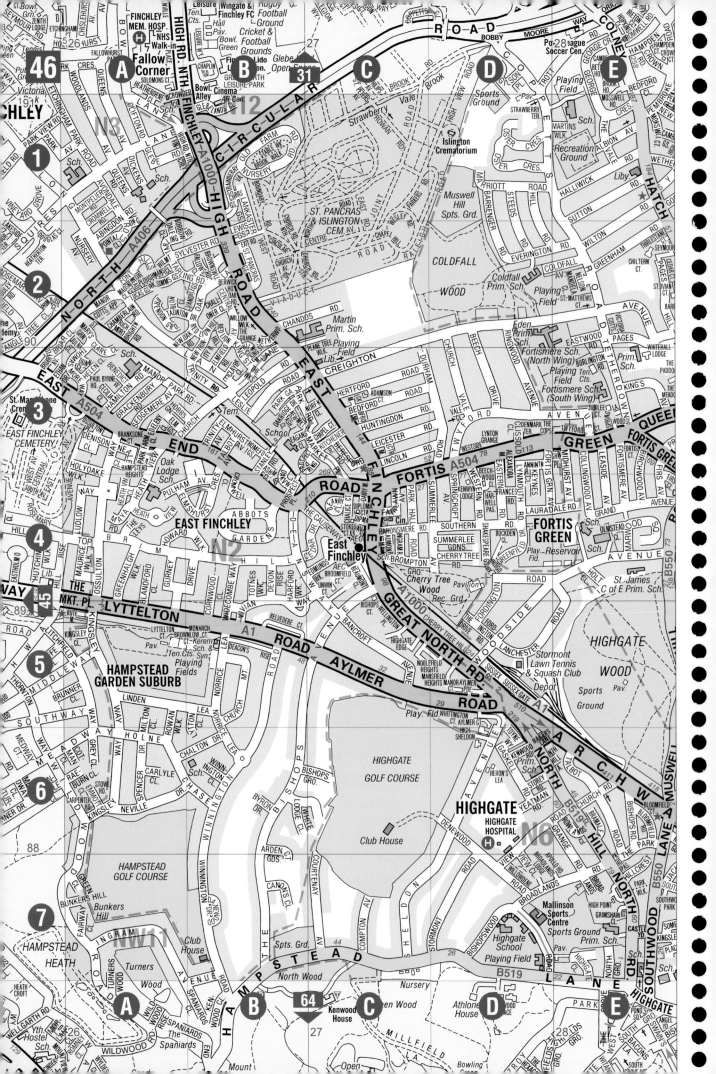

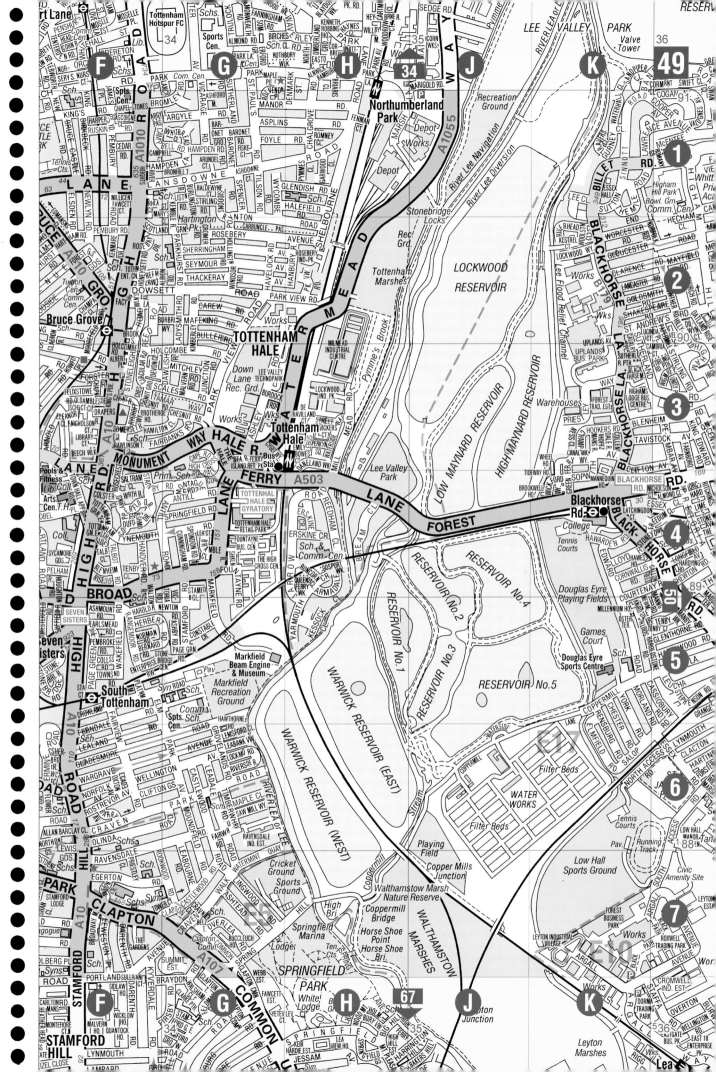

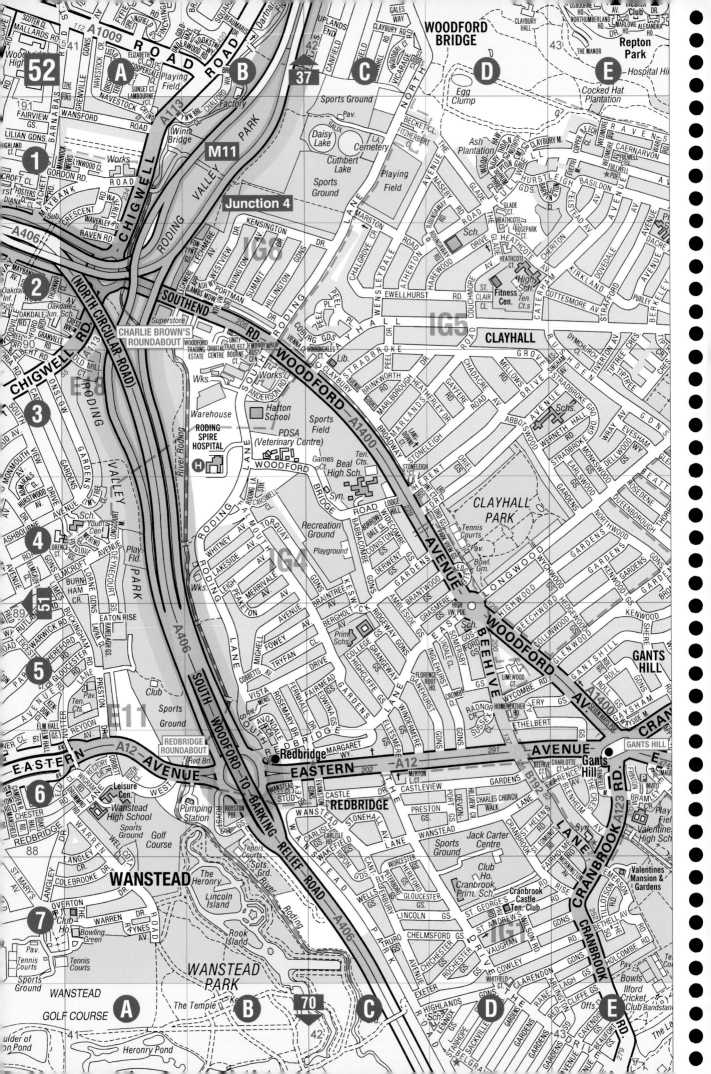

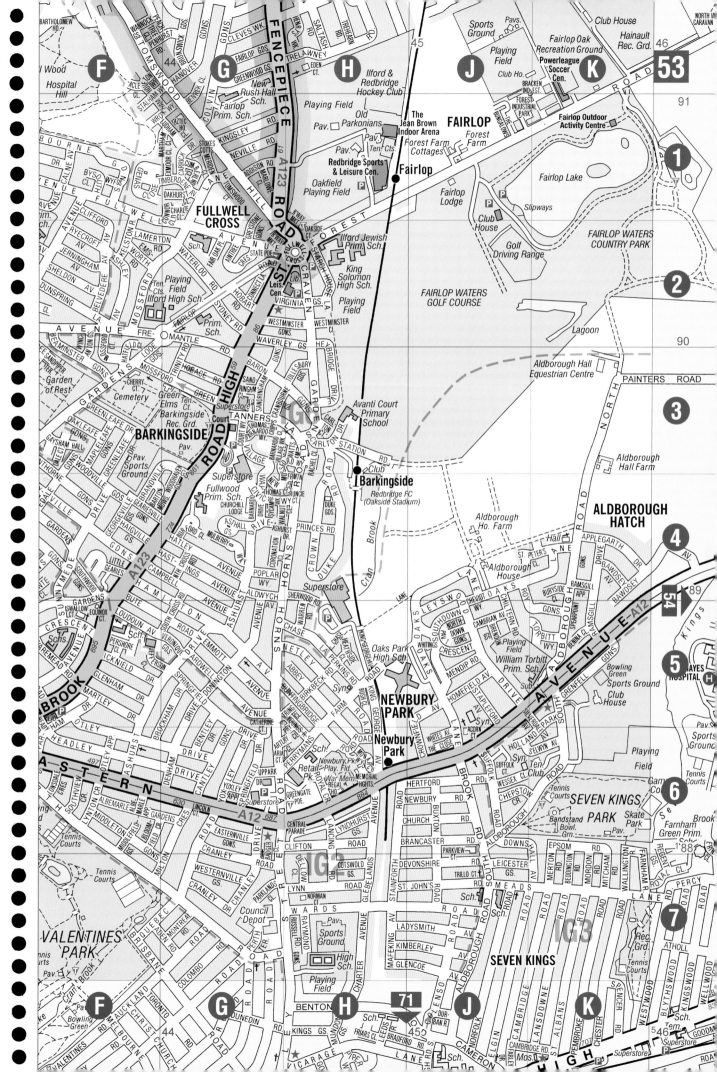

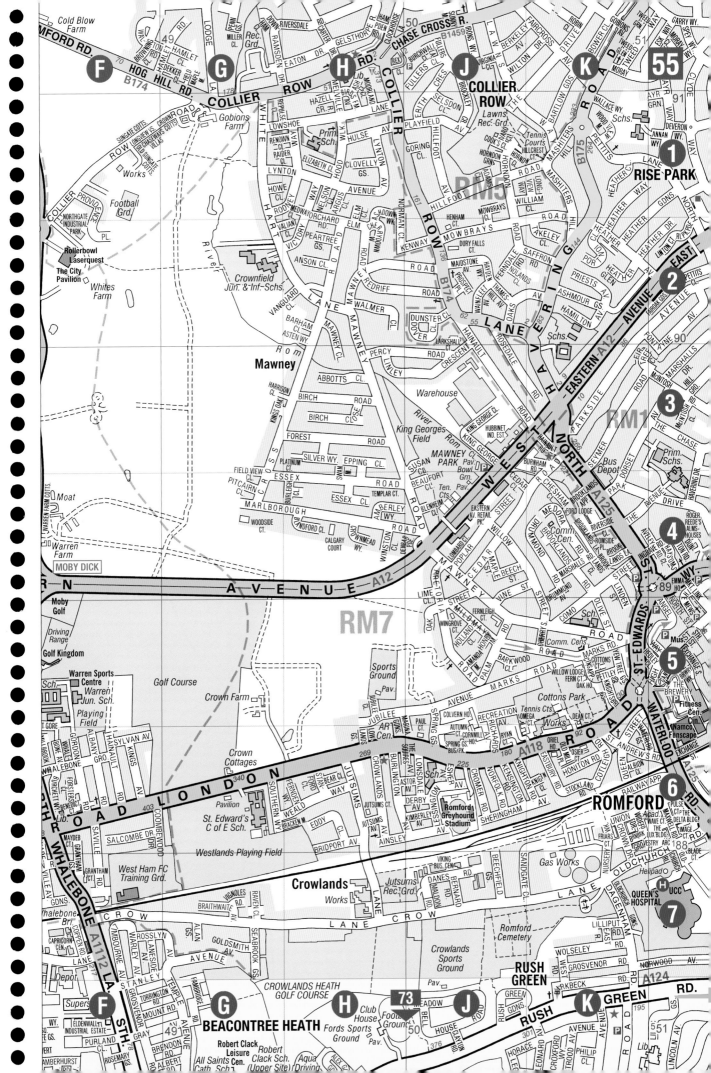

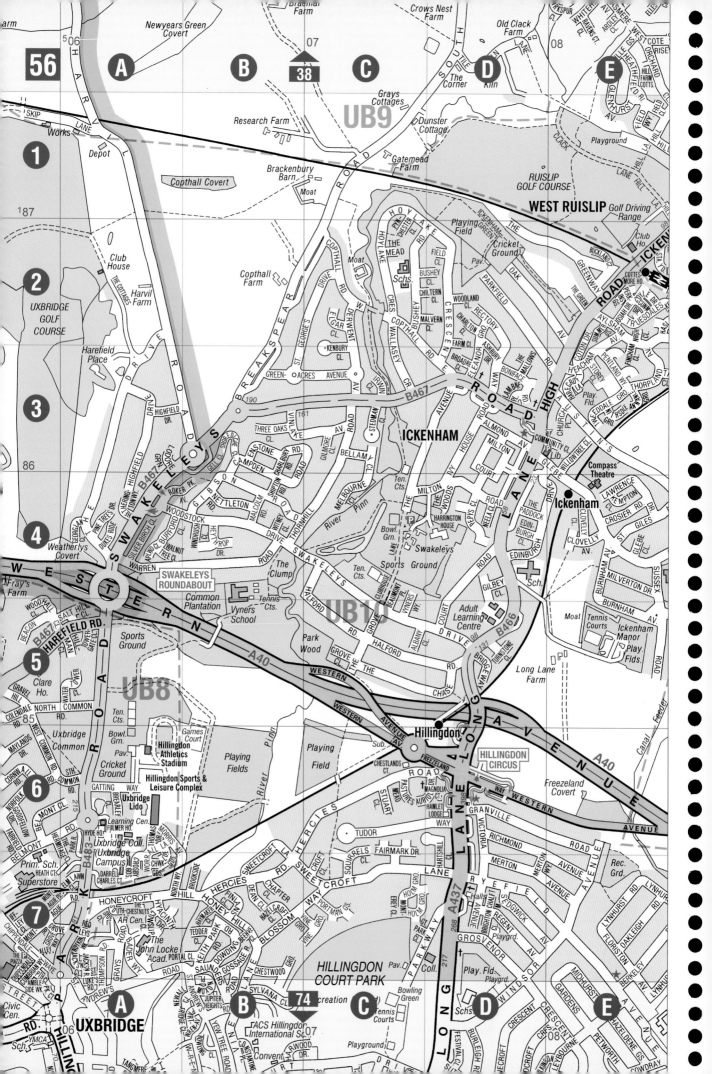

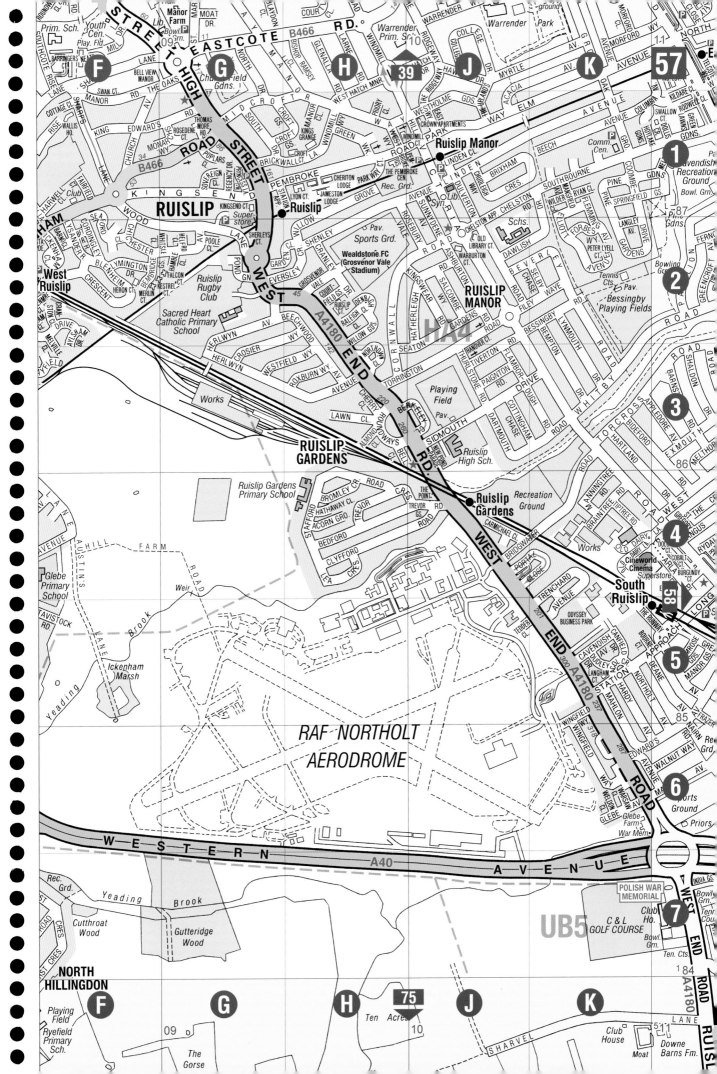

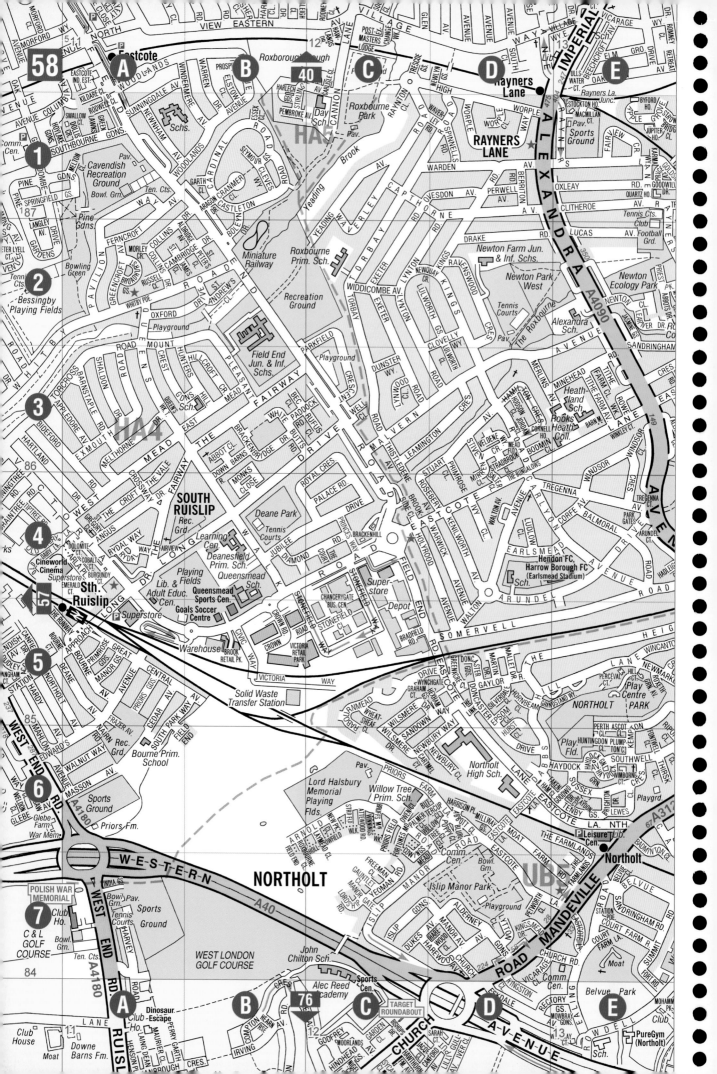

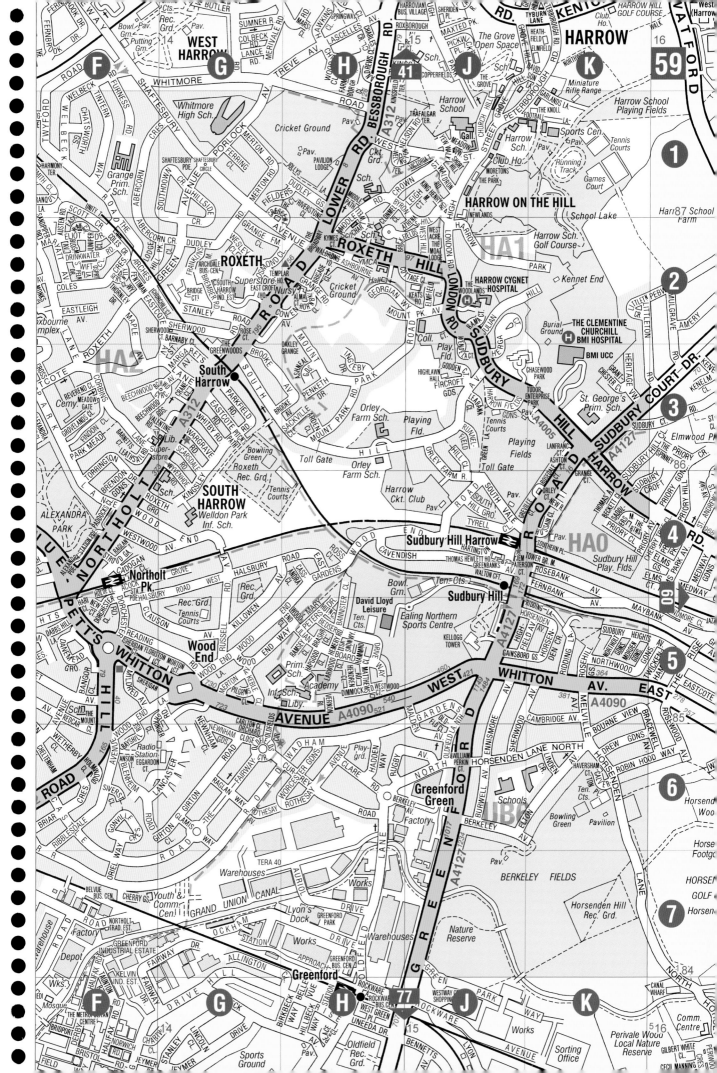

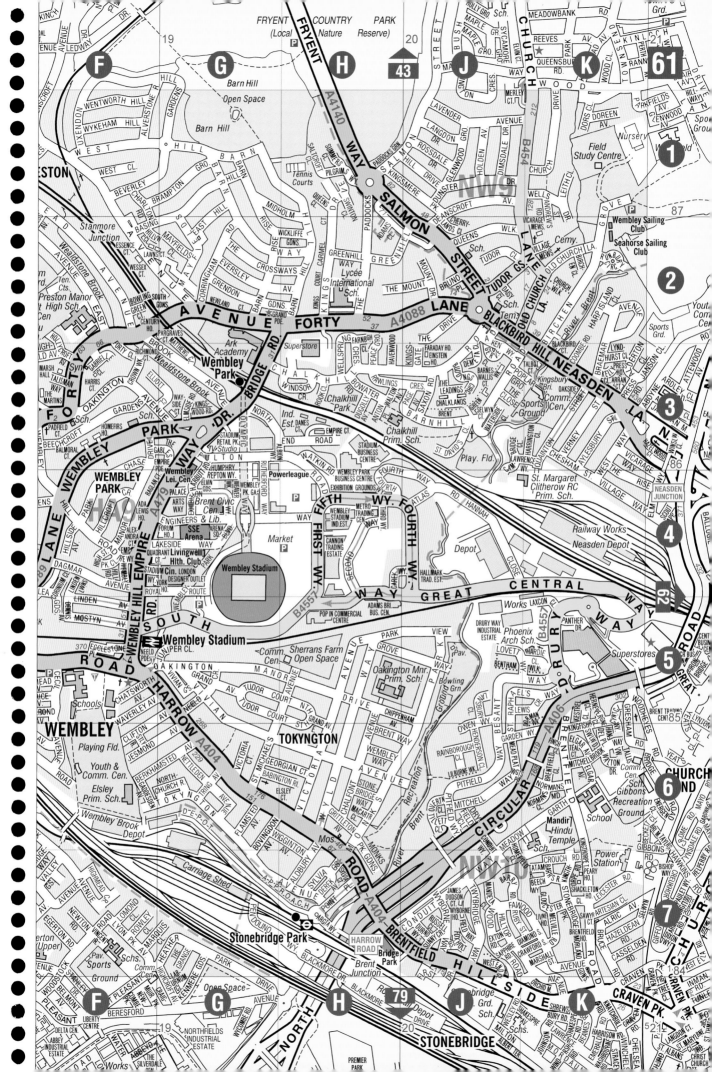

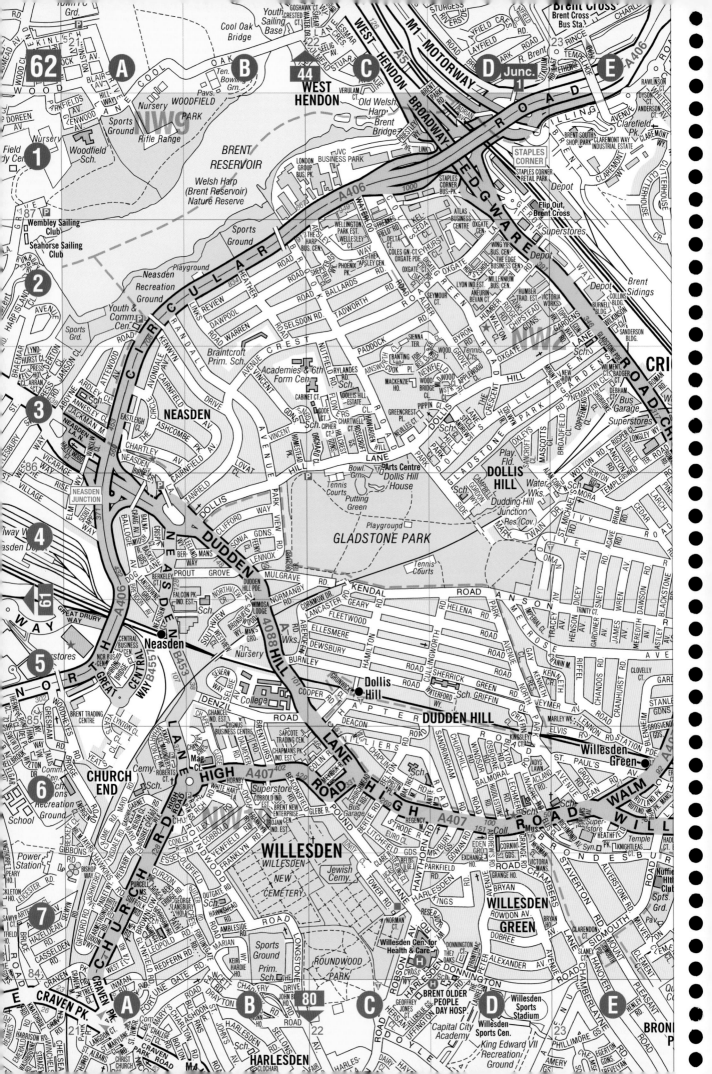

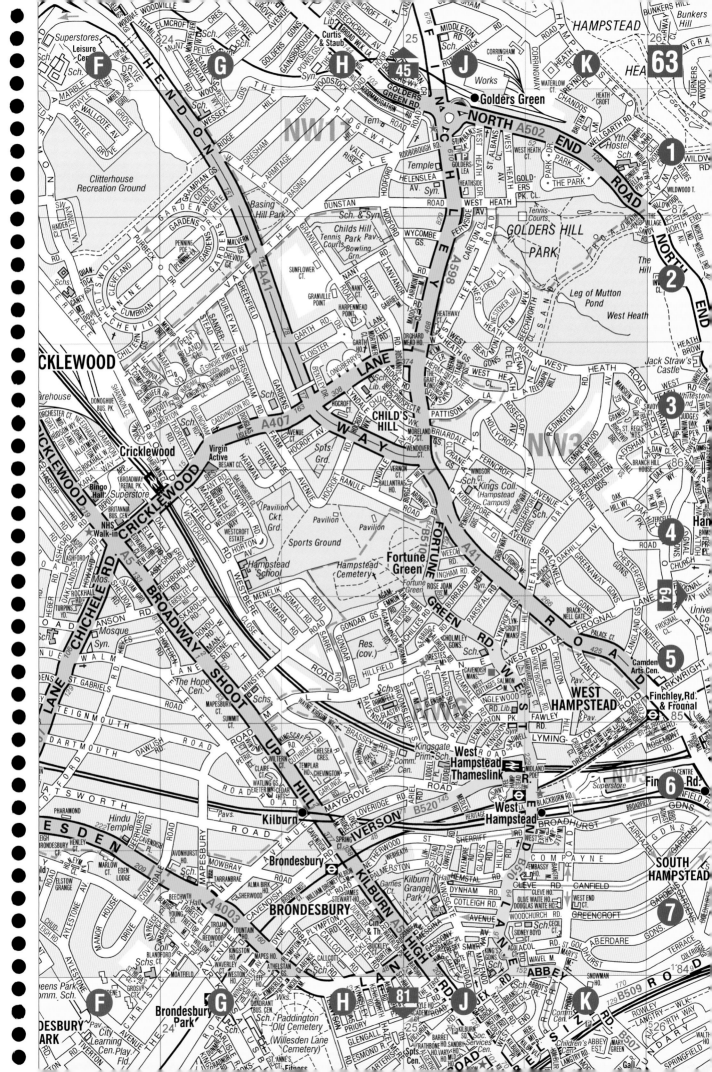

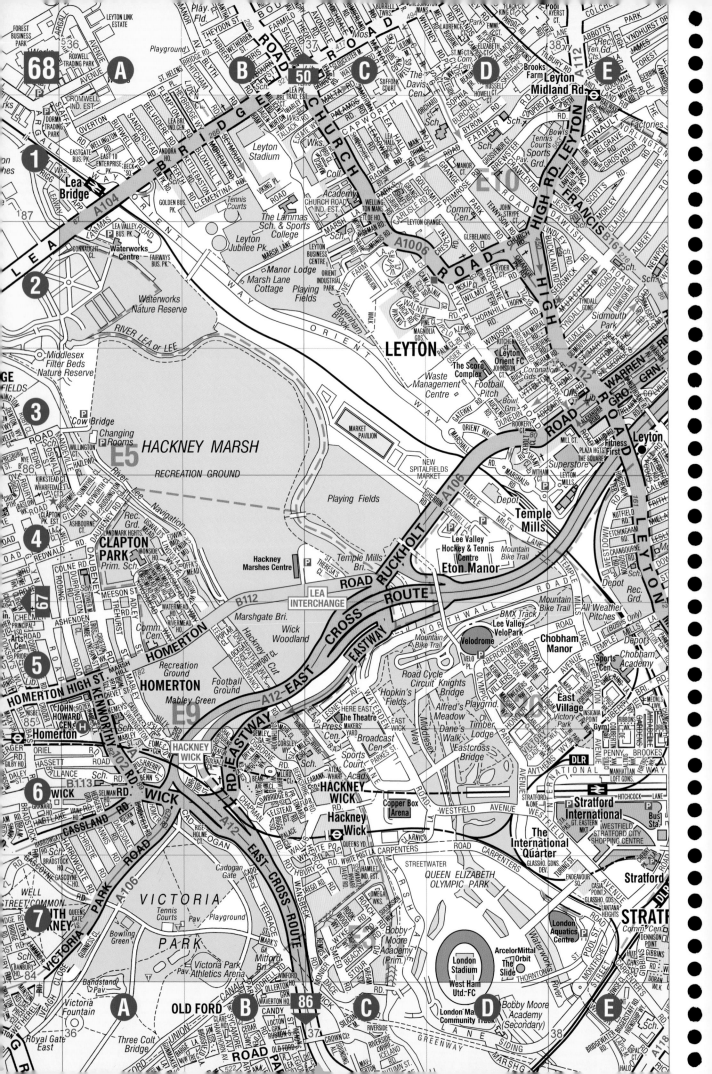

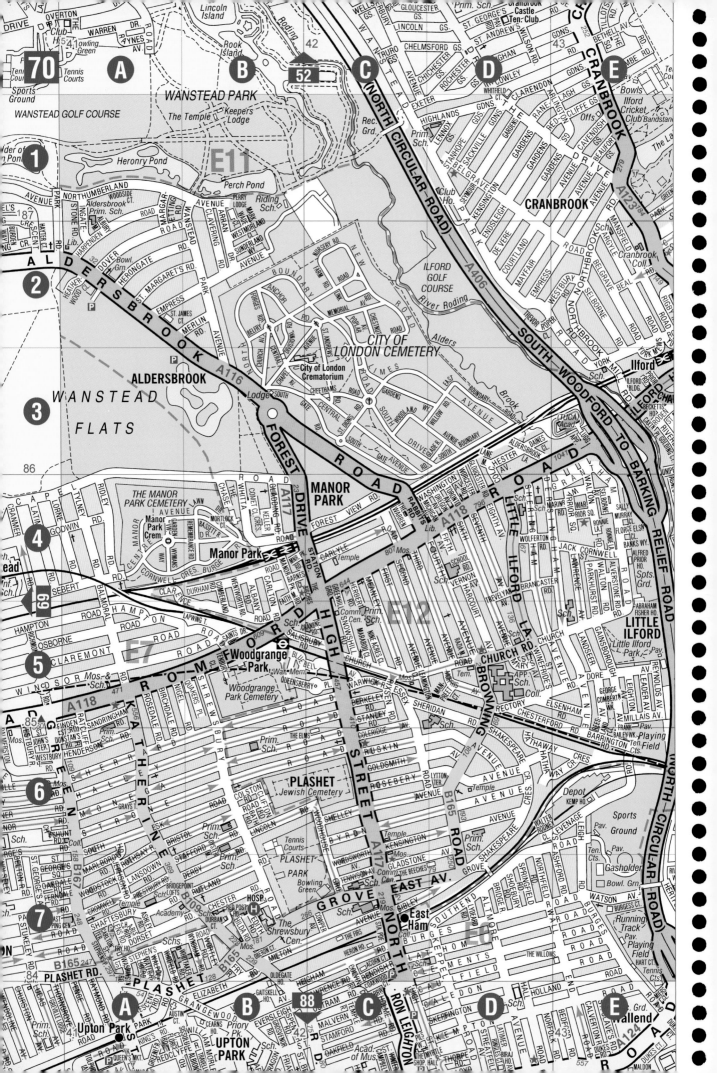

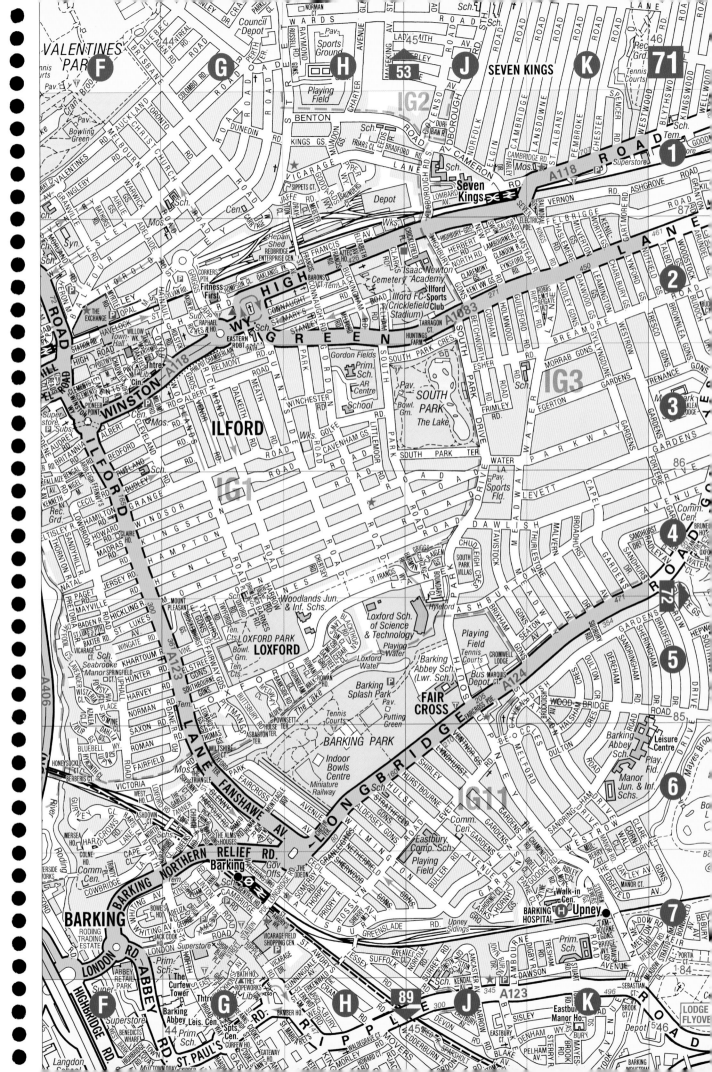

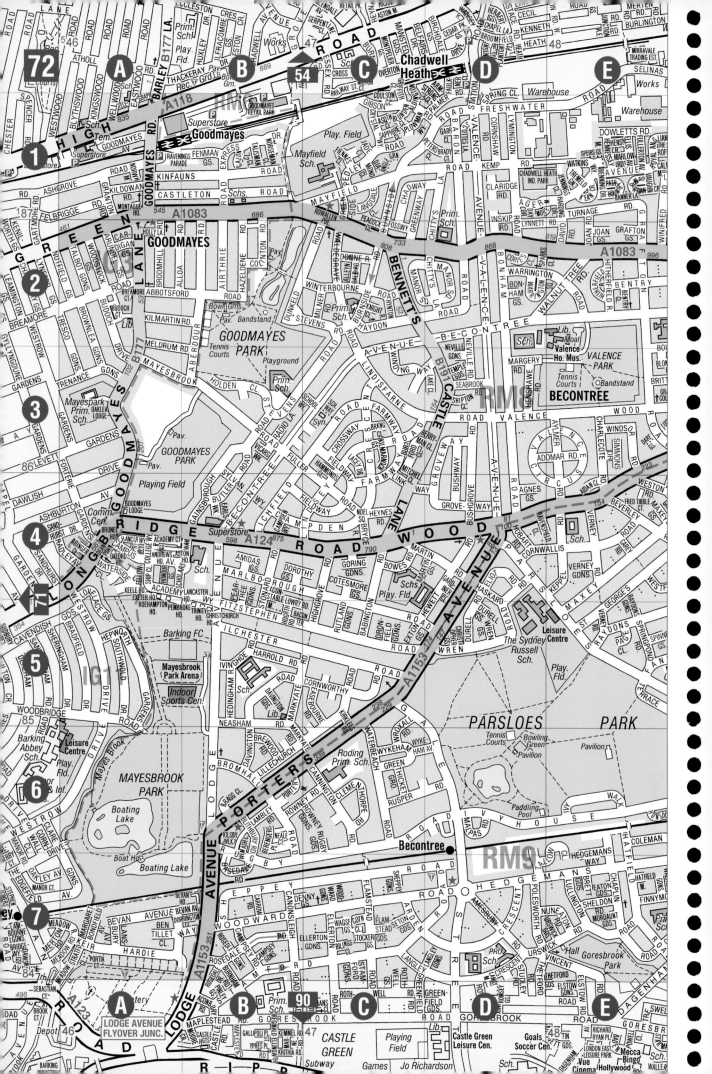

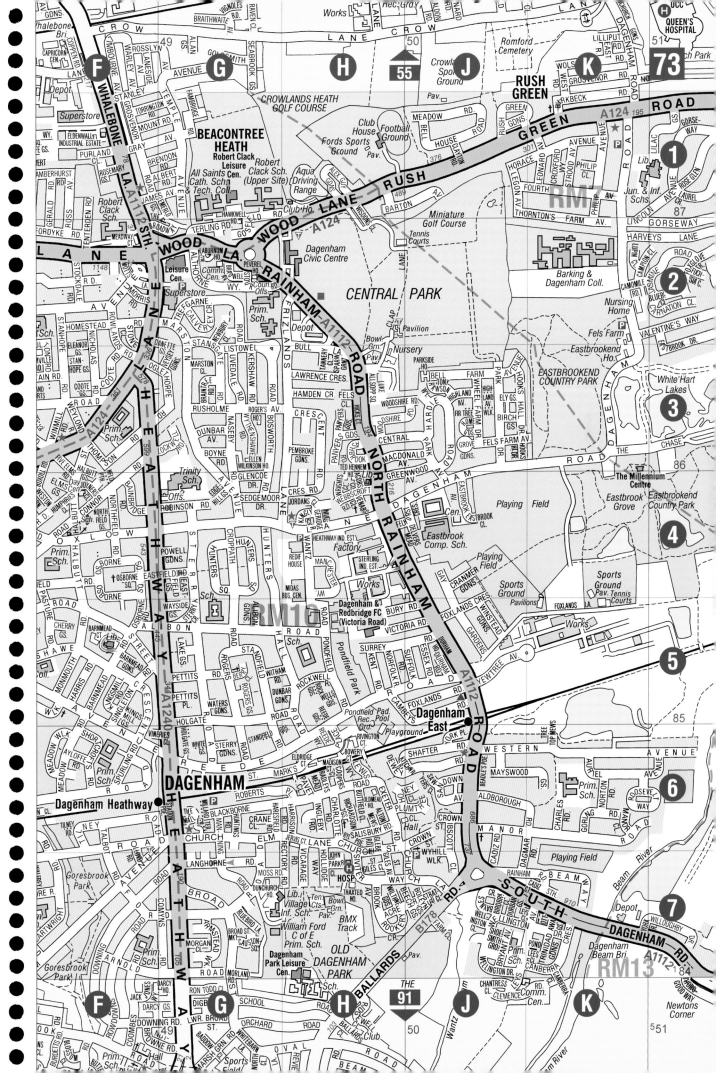

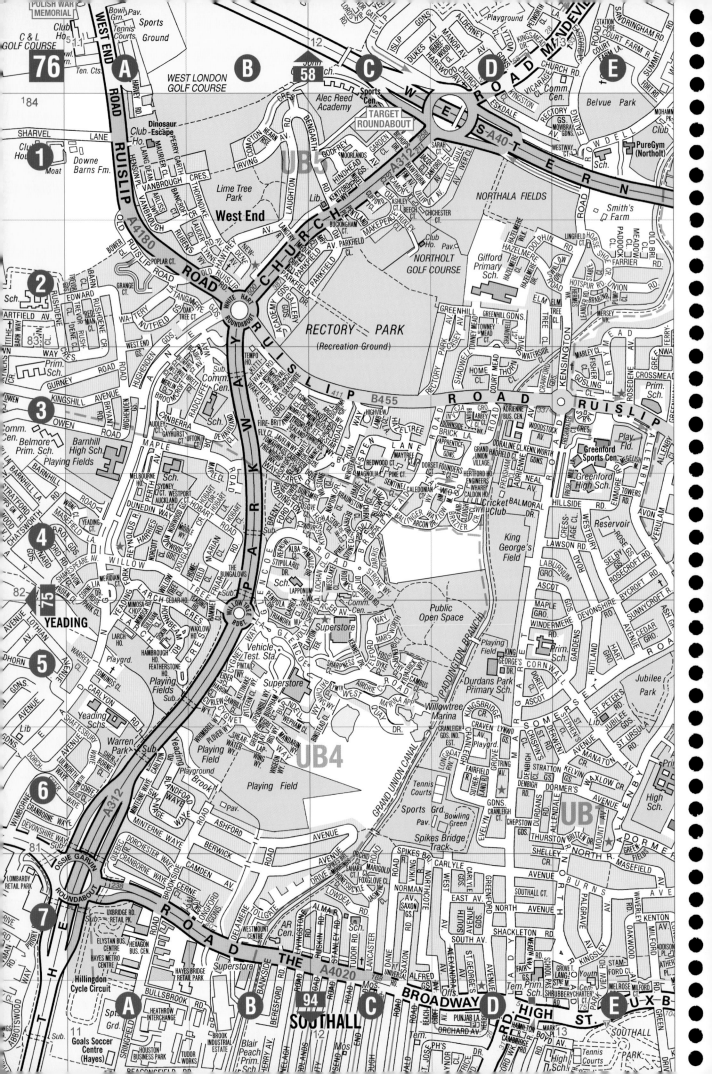

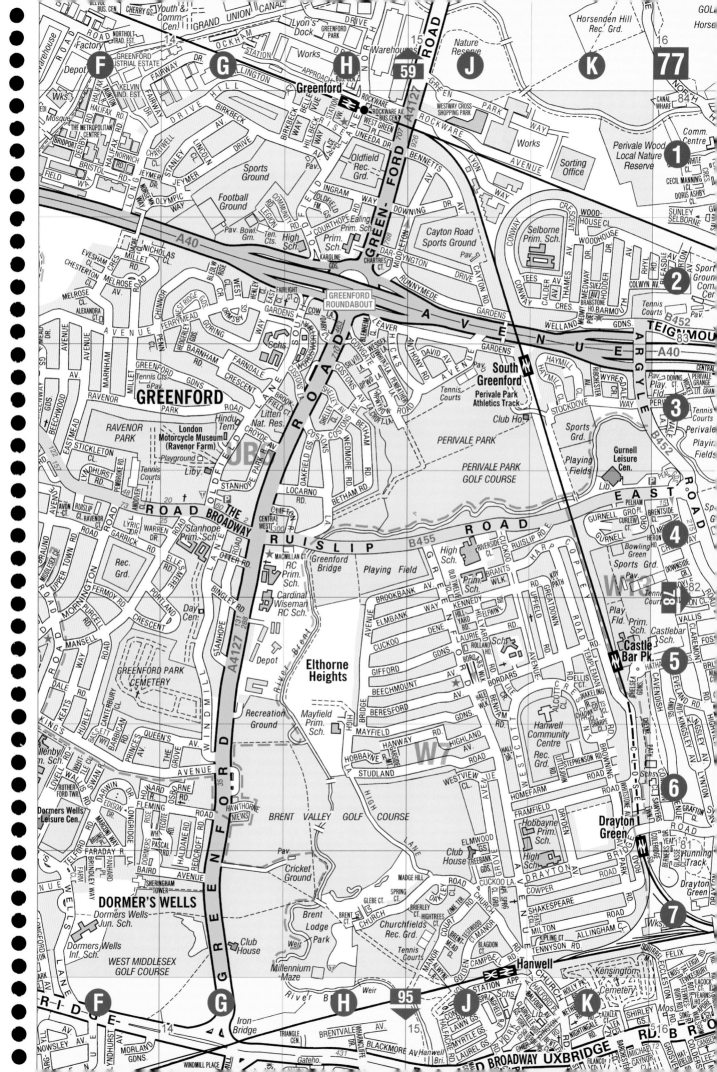

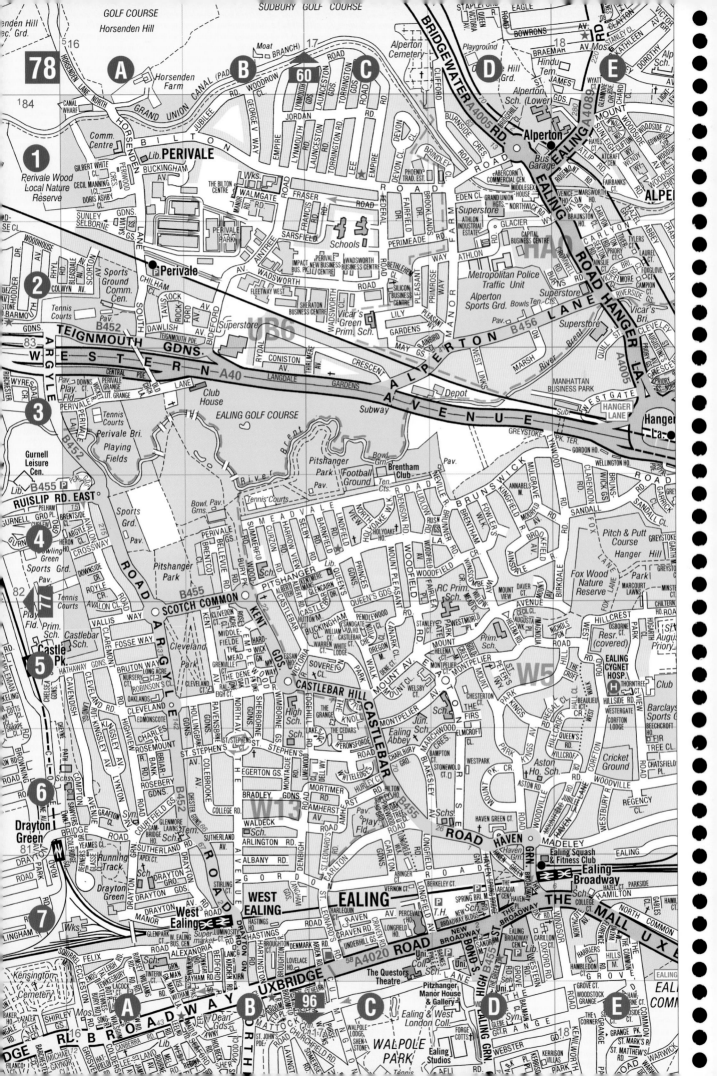

79
61
97
80
F
G
H
J
K
1
2
3
4
5
6
7
Stonebridge Park
HARROW ROAD
Brent Junction
Royal Mail Depot
Stonebridge Rec. Grd.
STONEBRIDGE
HILLSIDE
CRAVEN PK.
A404
Harlesden
Open Space
NORTHFIELDS INDUSTRIAL ESTATE
PARK ROYAL JUNCTION
A406
NORTH CIRCULAR ROAD
PREMIER PARK
TOWNSEND INDUSTRIAL ESTATE
Lower Place
GRAND UNION CANAL (Paddington Branch)
Power Station
Twyford Abbey Prim. Sch.
PARK ROYAL
PARK ROYAL CEN.
CENTRAL MIDDLESEX HOSPITAL
UCC
NW10
FROGMORE INDUSTRIAL ESTATE
B4492
PARK ROYAL ROAD
NORTH ACTON ROAD
Playing Field
Sports Grd.
WESTERN AVENUE
A40
London Shootfighters Gym
Park Royal
Hanger Hill
Tenpin Cinema
ROYALE LEISURE PARK
NORTH ACTON Cemetery
North Acton
VICTORIA RD.
A4000
WESTWOOD BUS. CEN.
GYPSY CORNER
WALES FARM RD.
West Acton
NORTH ACTON PLAYING FIELDS
Sports Ground
Acton Main Line
W3
Nth. Ealing
HANGER LANE
A406
LYNTON ROAD
Japanese Sch. London
HORN LANE
EAST ACTON
The Park Club
Cricket Grd.
ACTON
Twyford Spts. Cen.
Ealing Common
Acton Central
ACTON PARK
HIGH STREET
CHURCHFIELD
GUNNERSBURY
A4020
UXBRIDGE ROAD

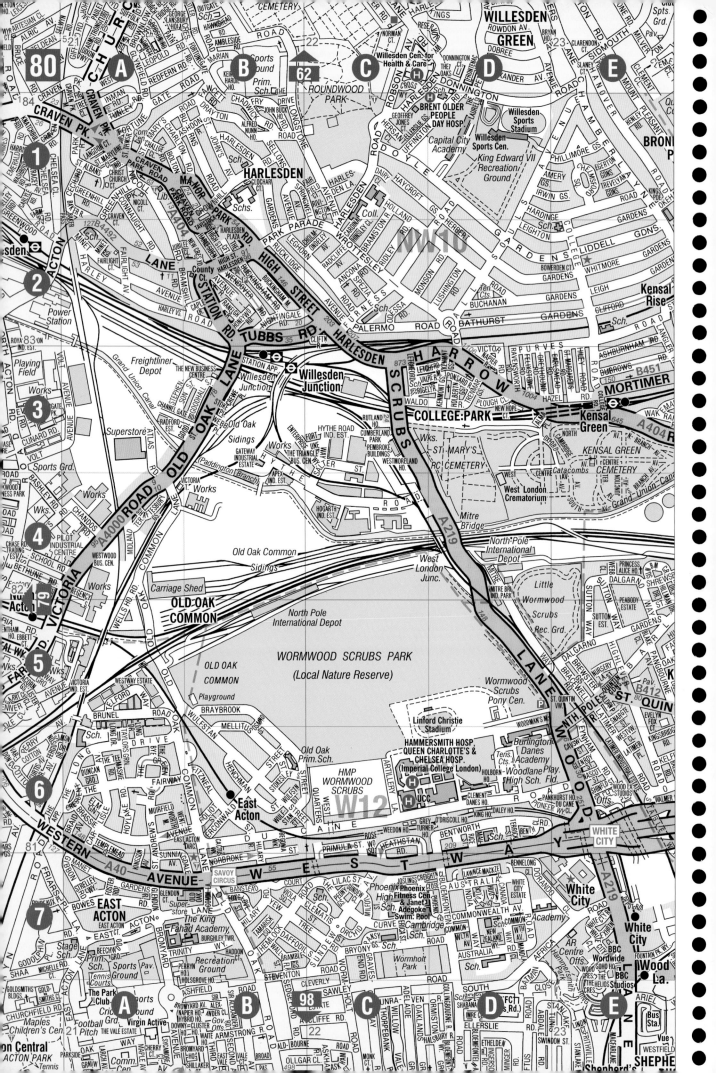

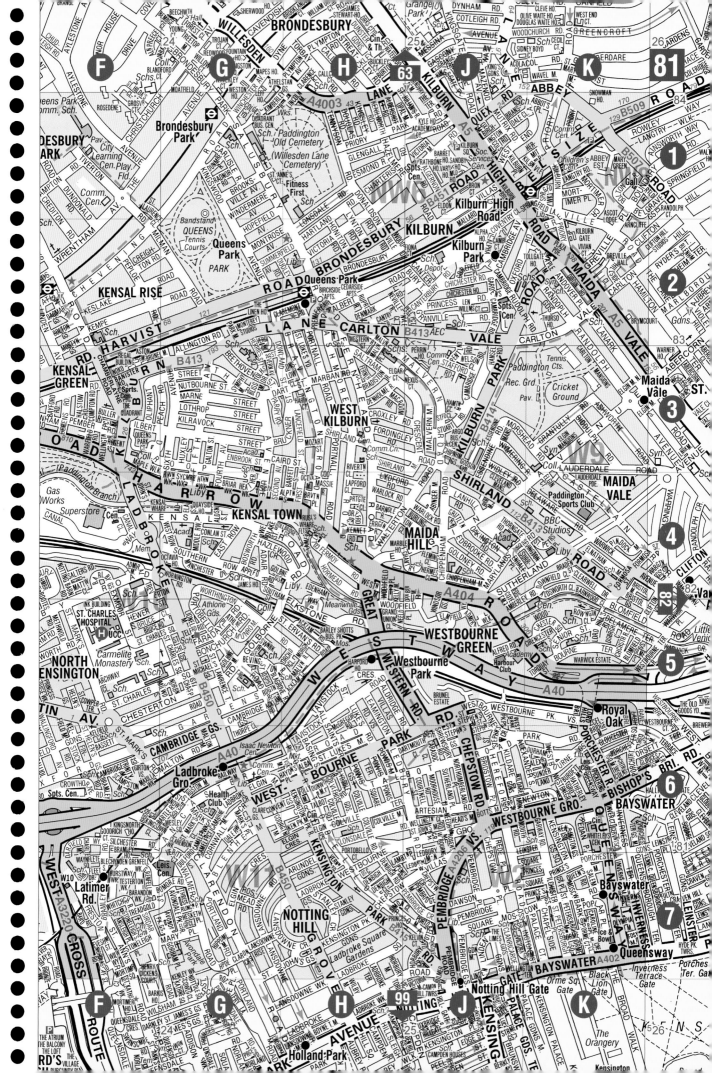

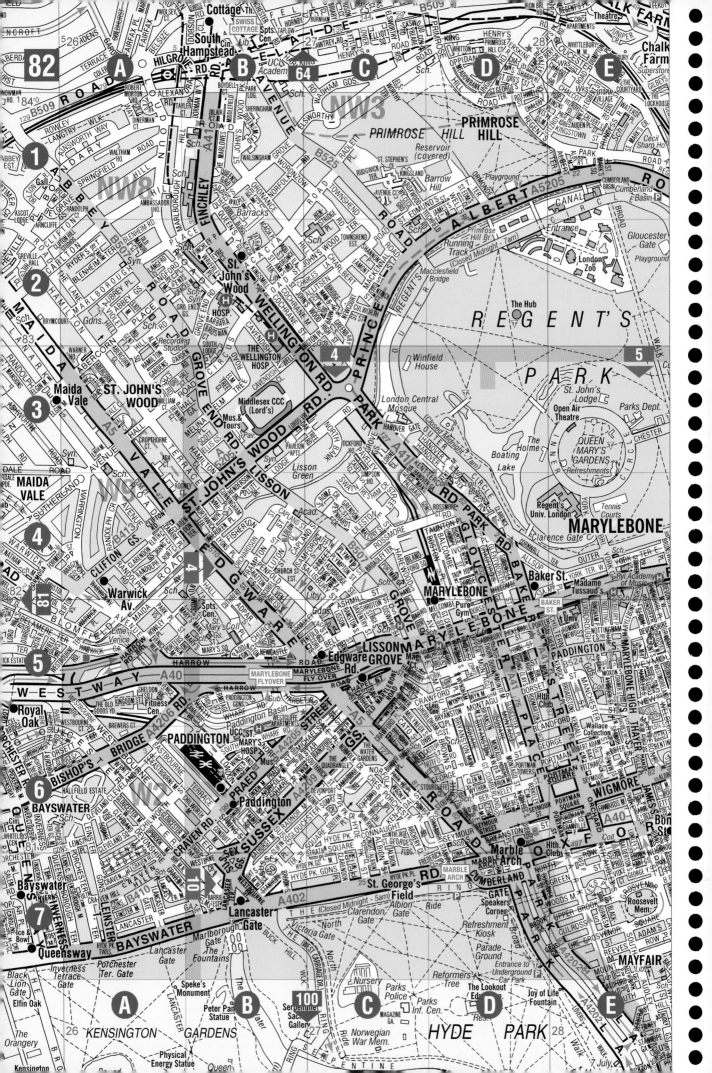

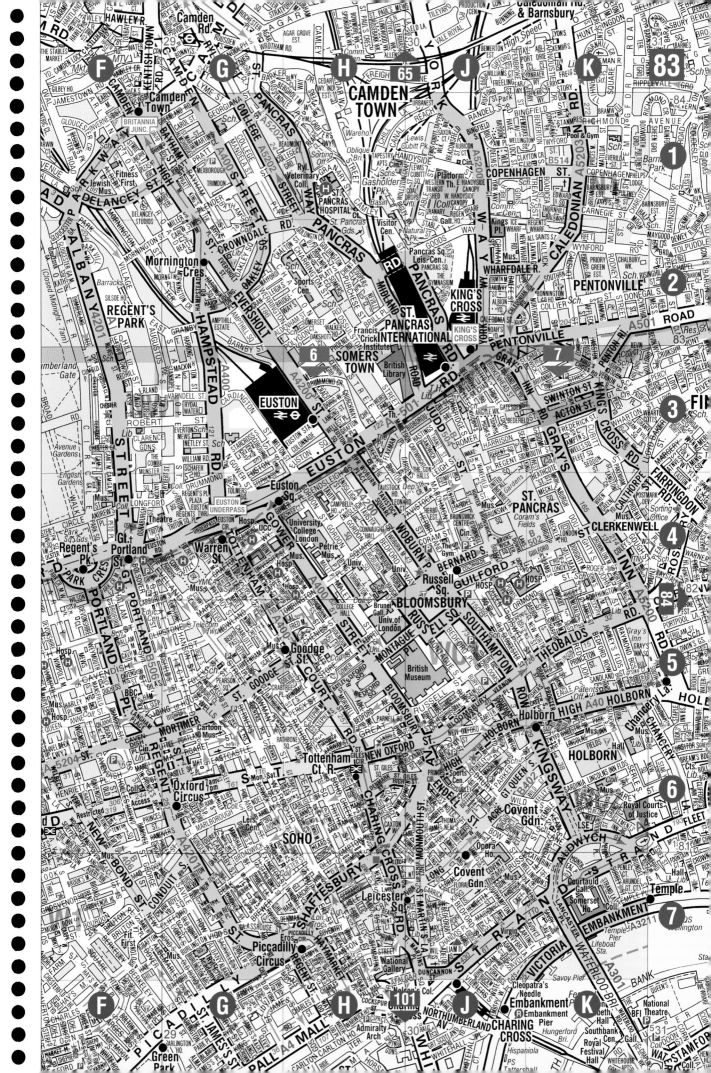

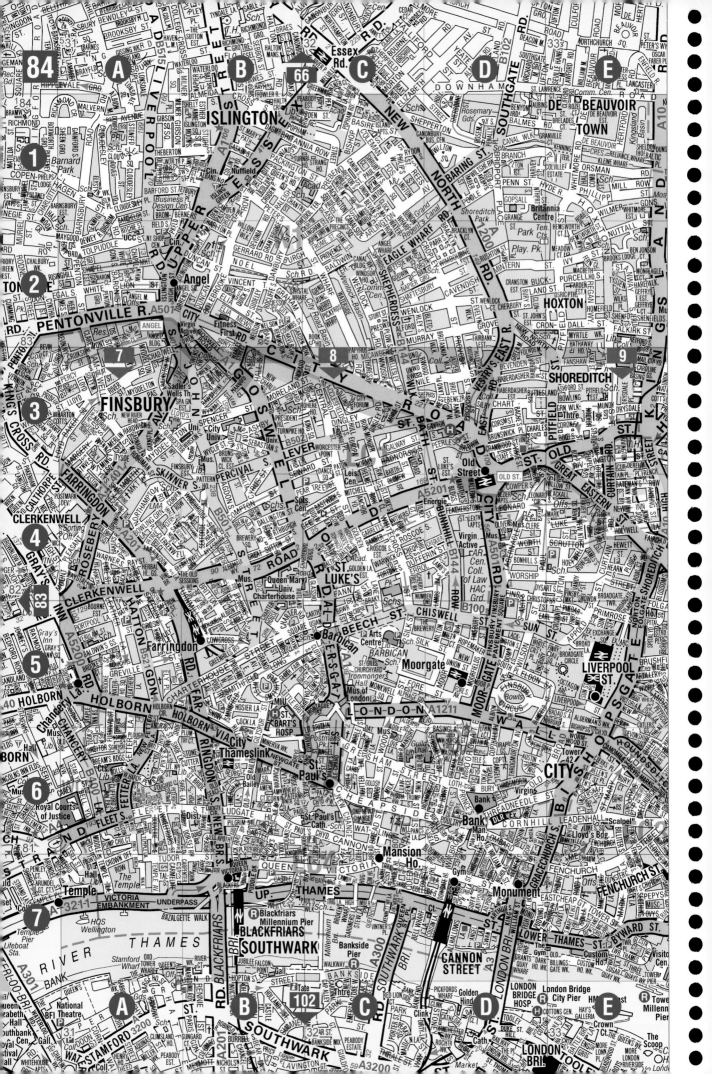

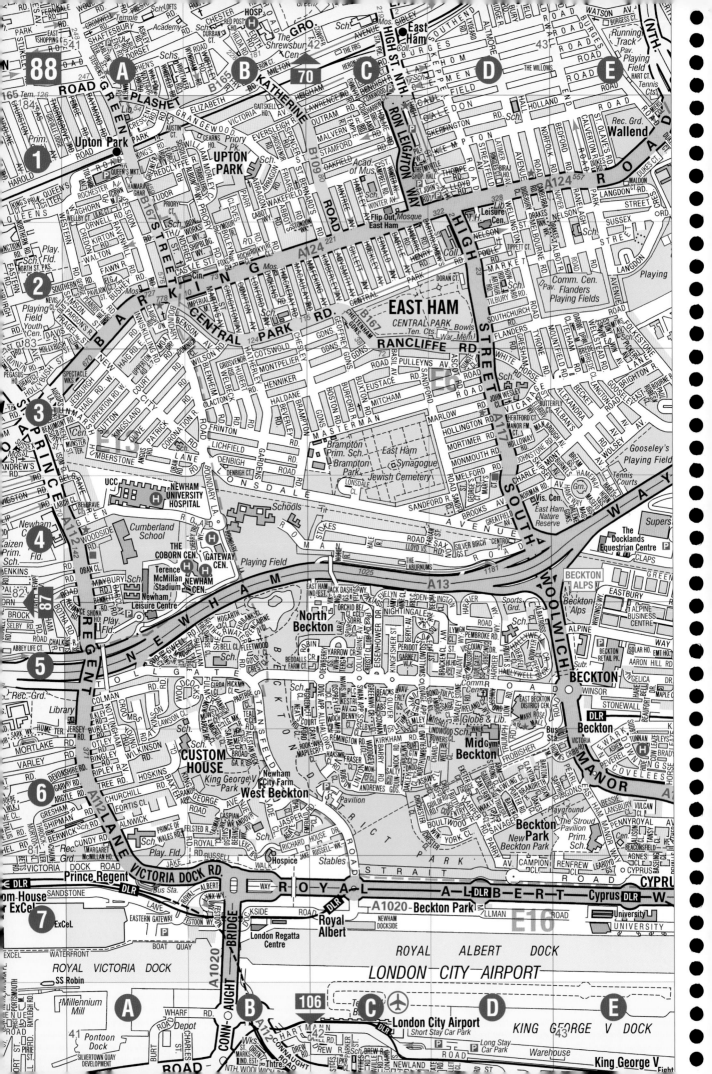

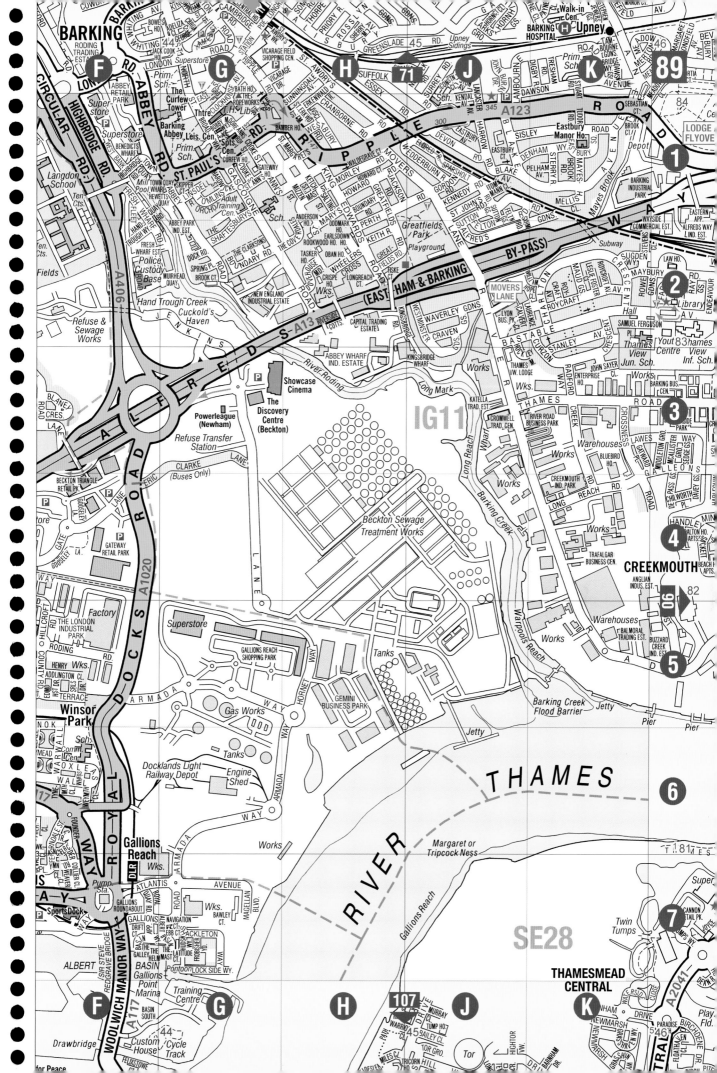

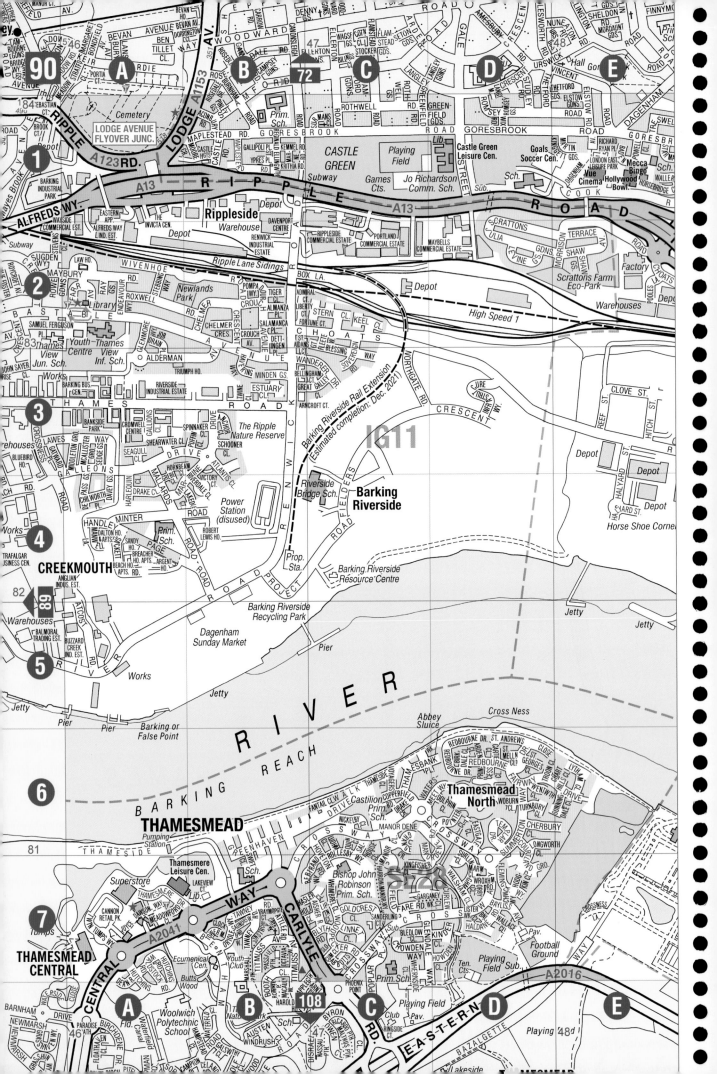

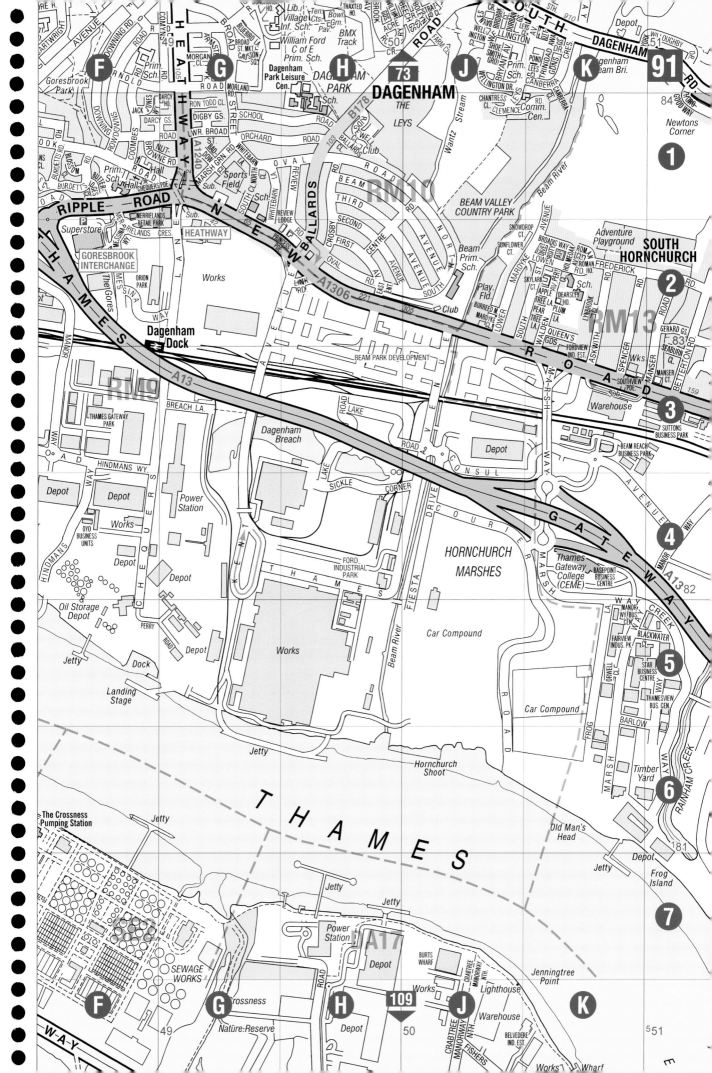

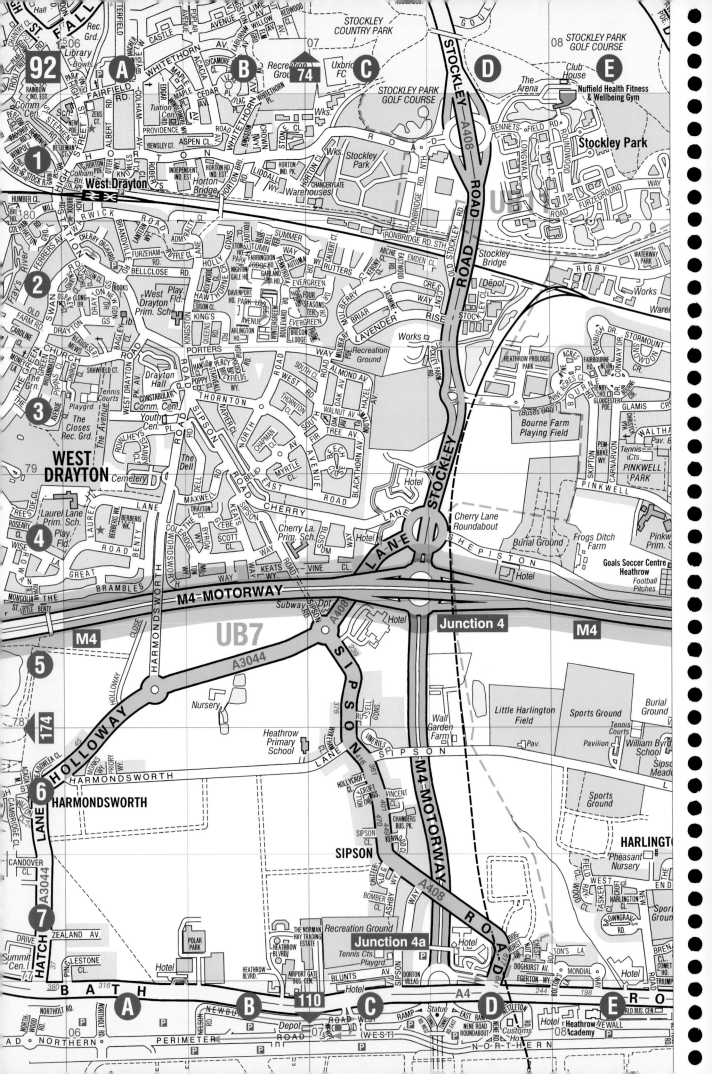

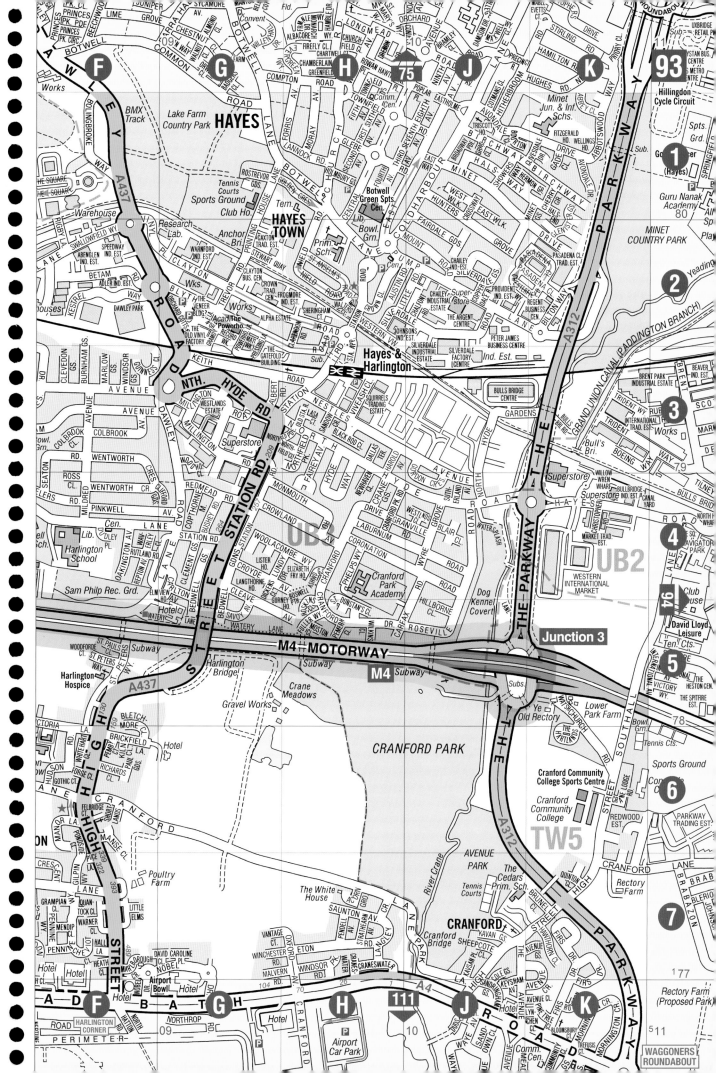

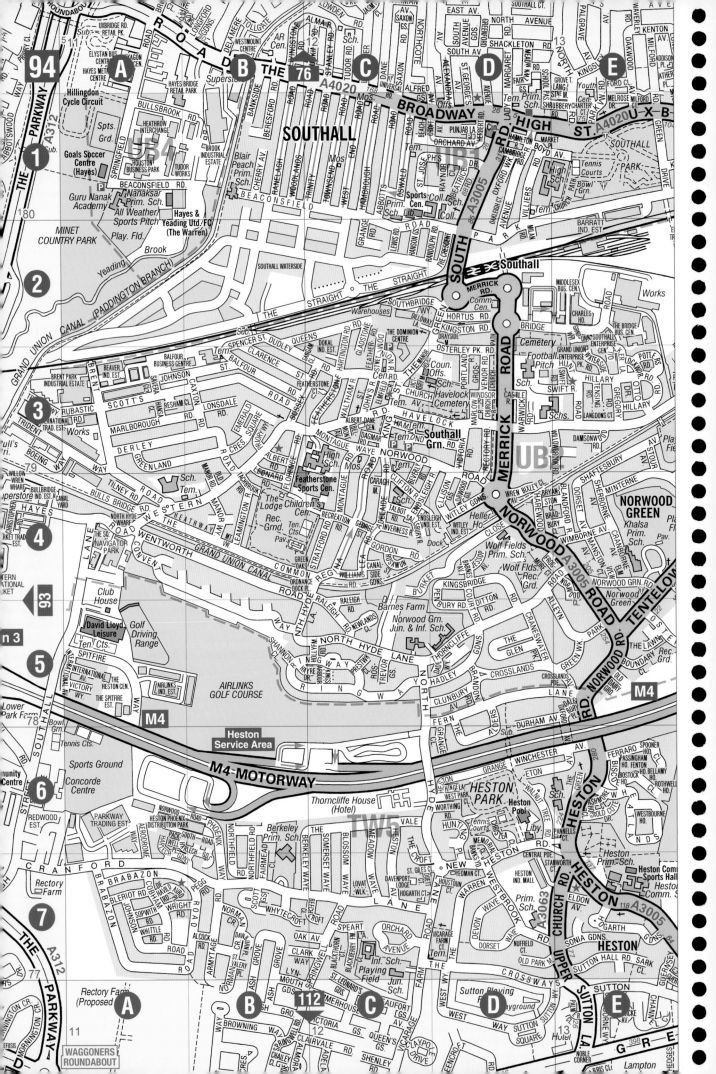

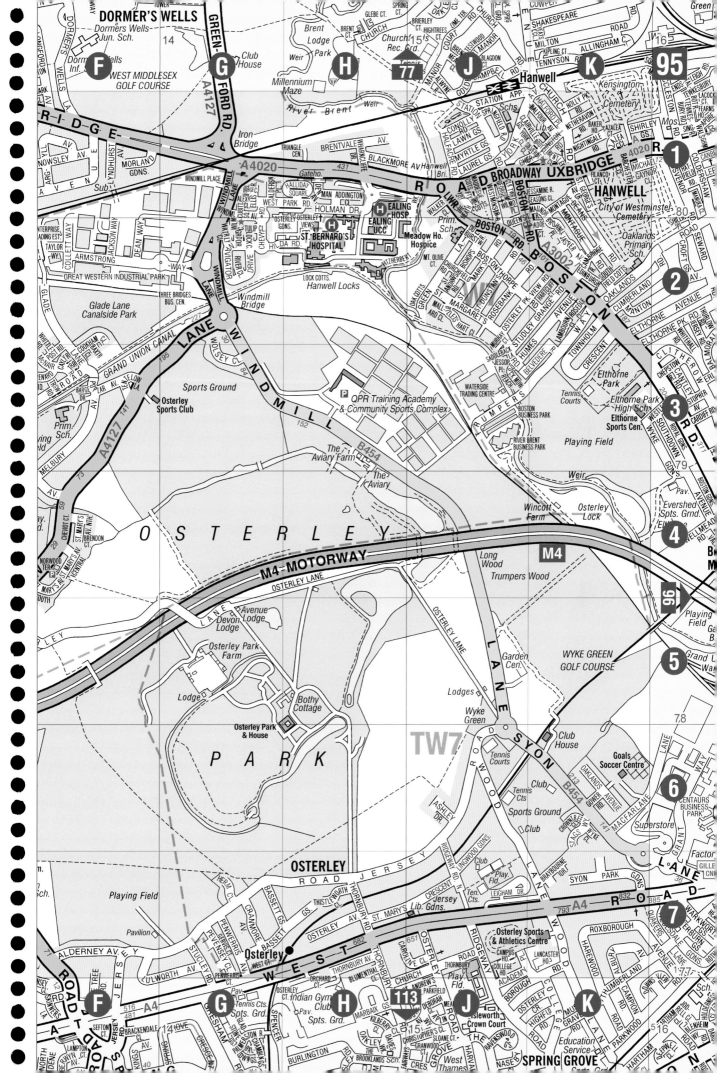

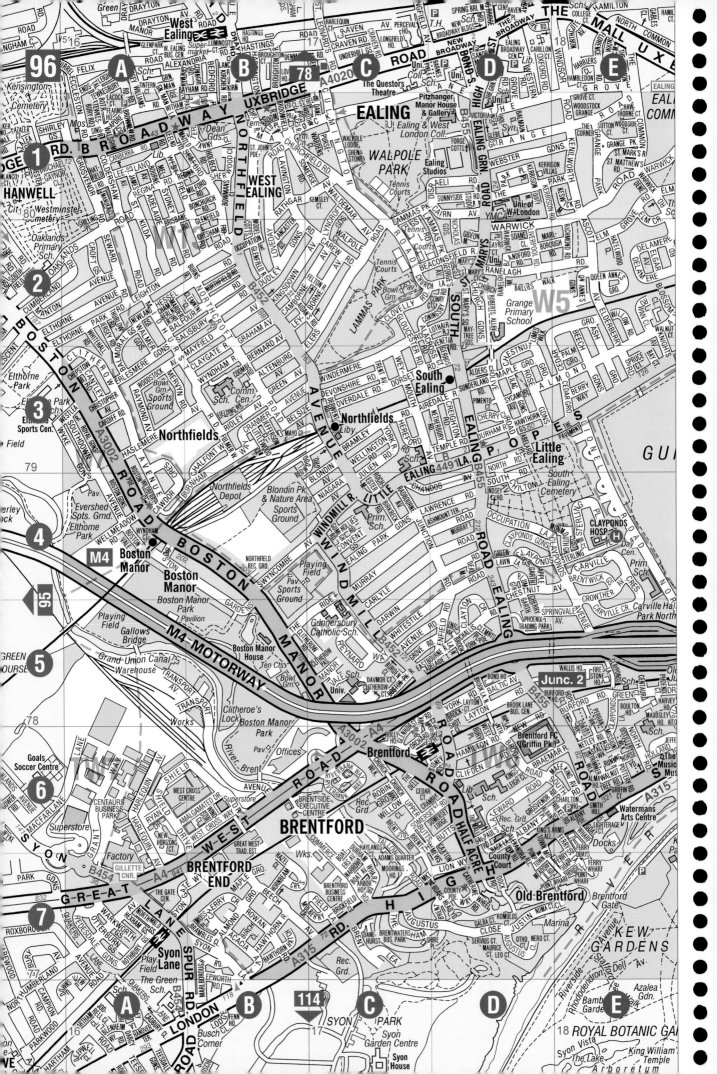

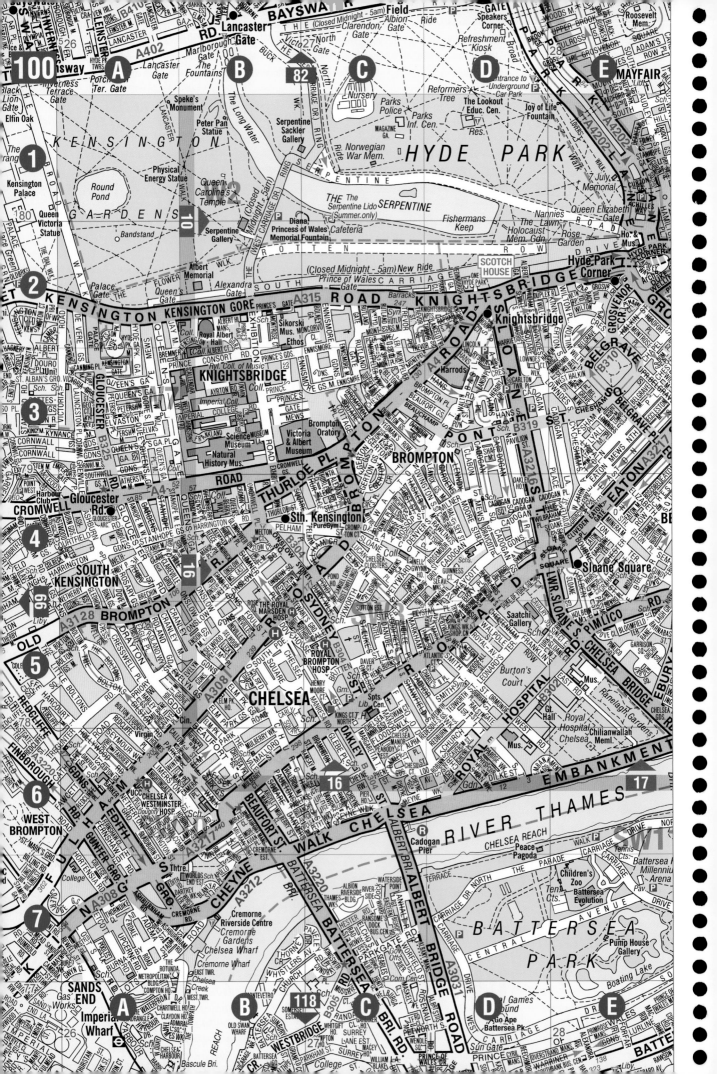

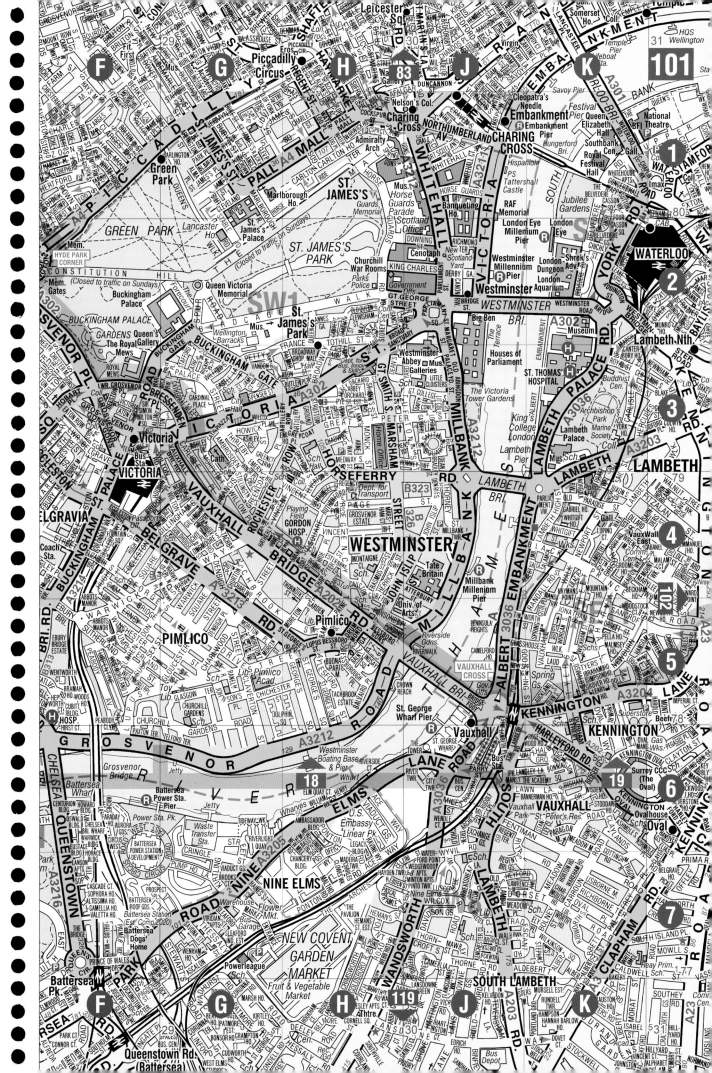

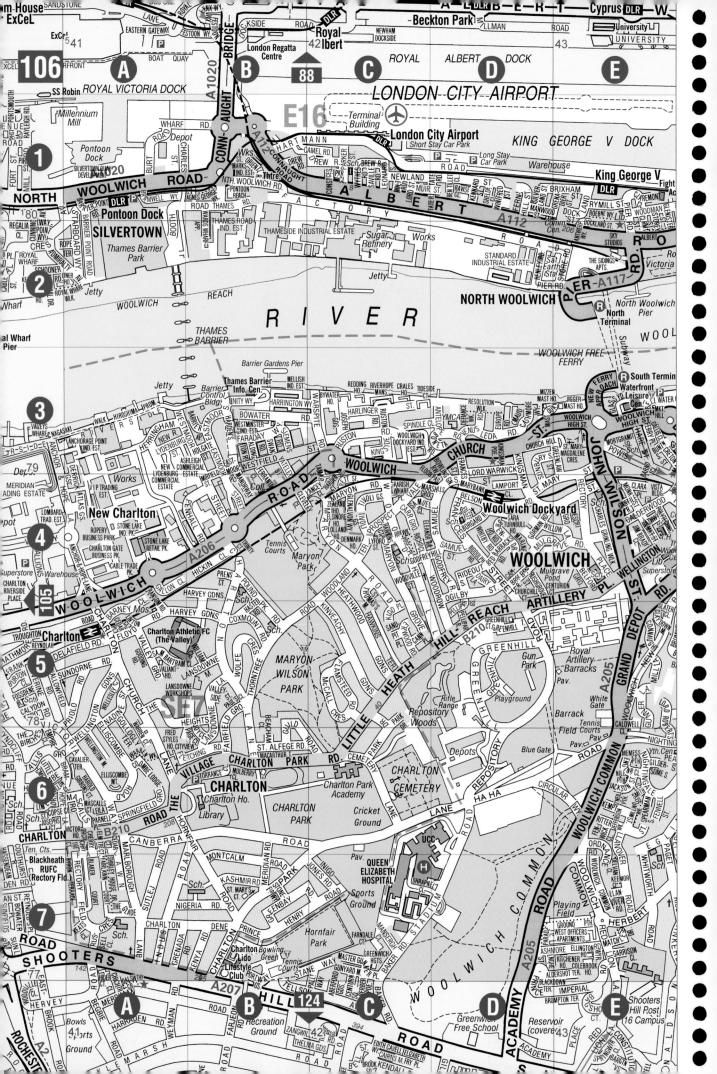

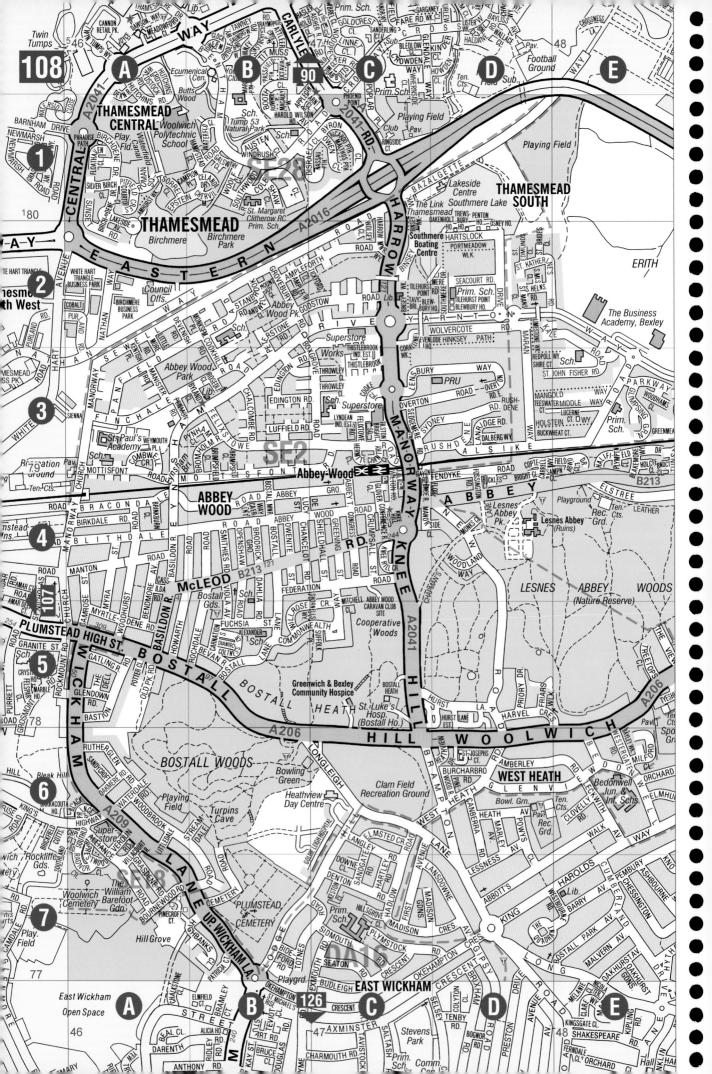

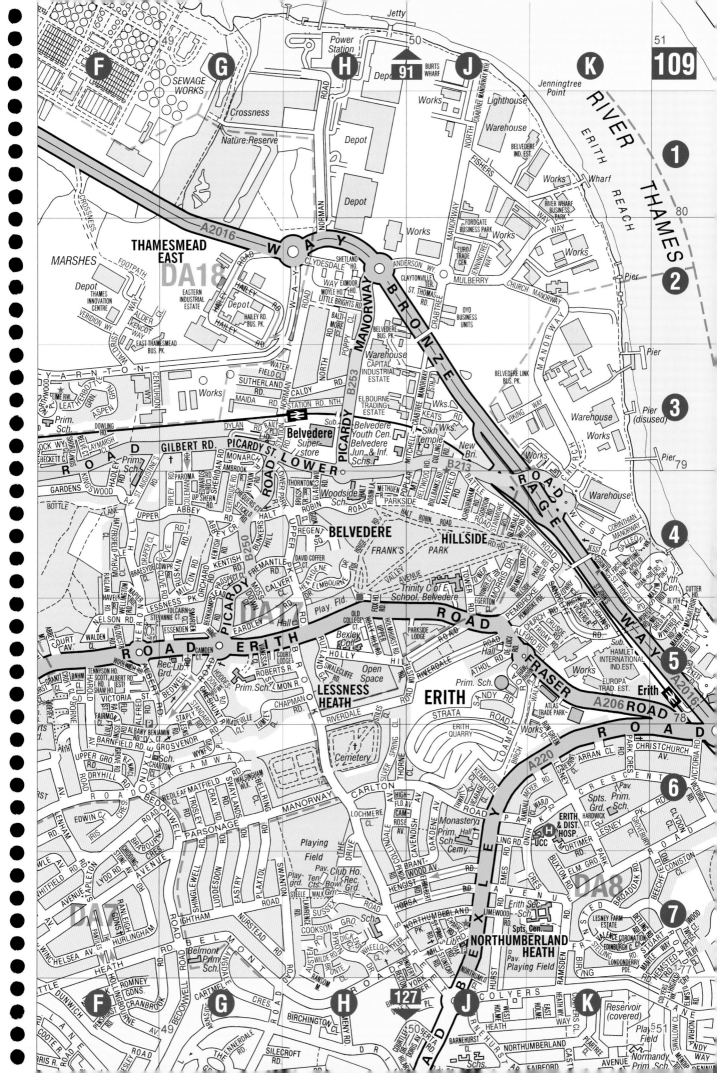

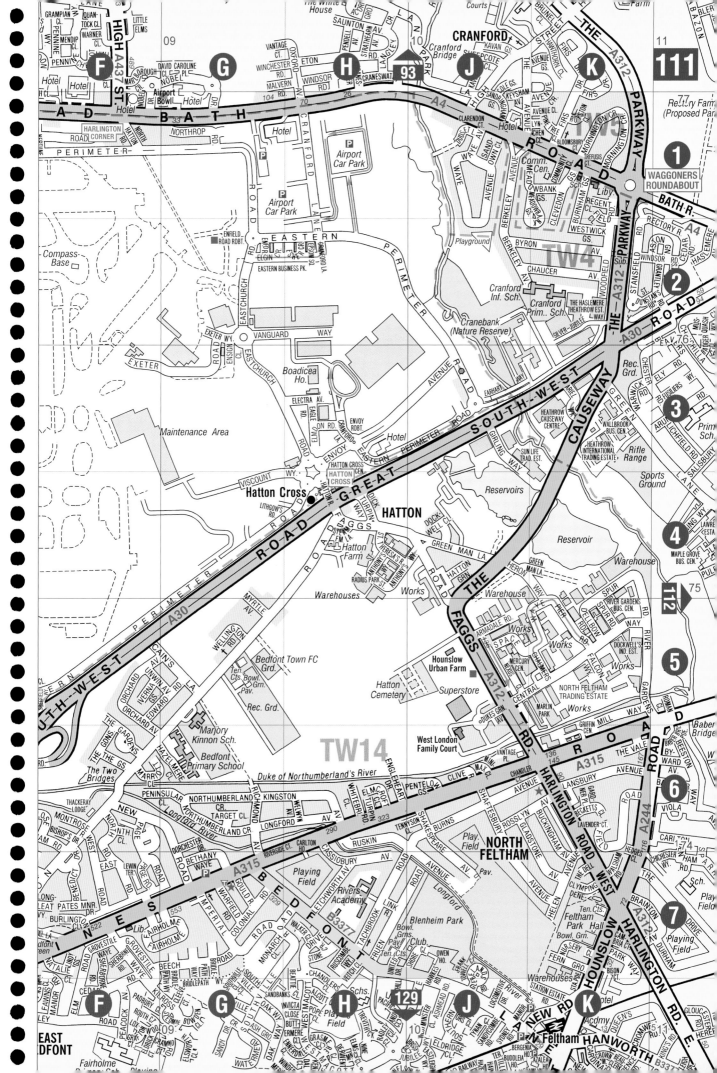

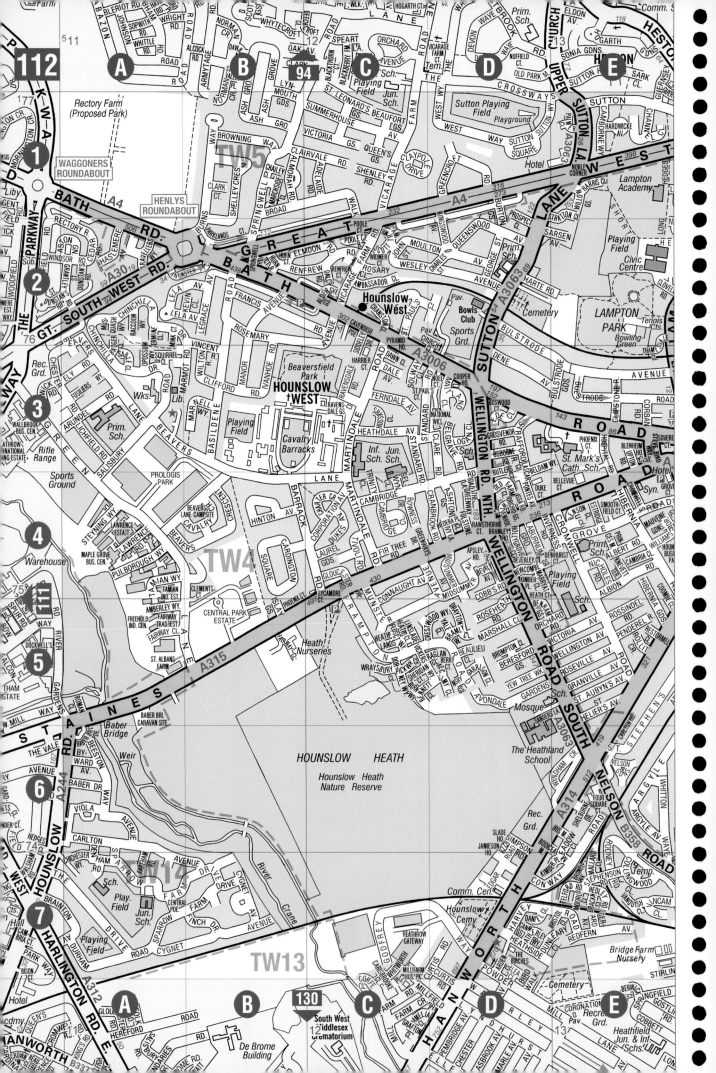

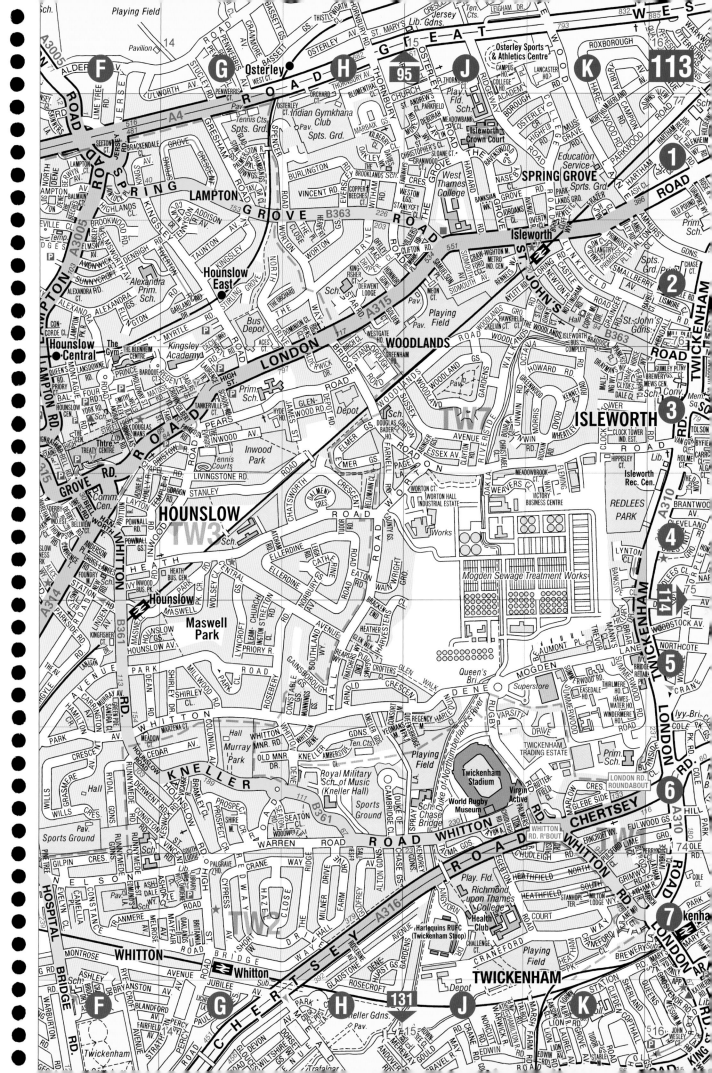

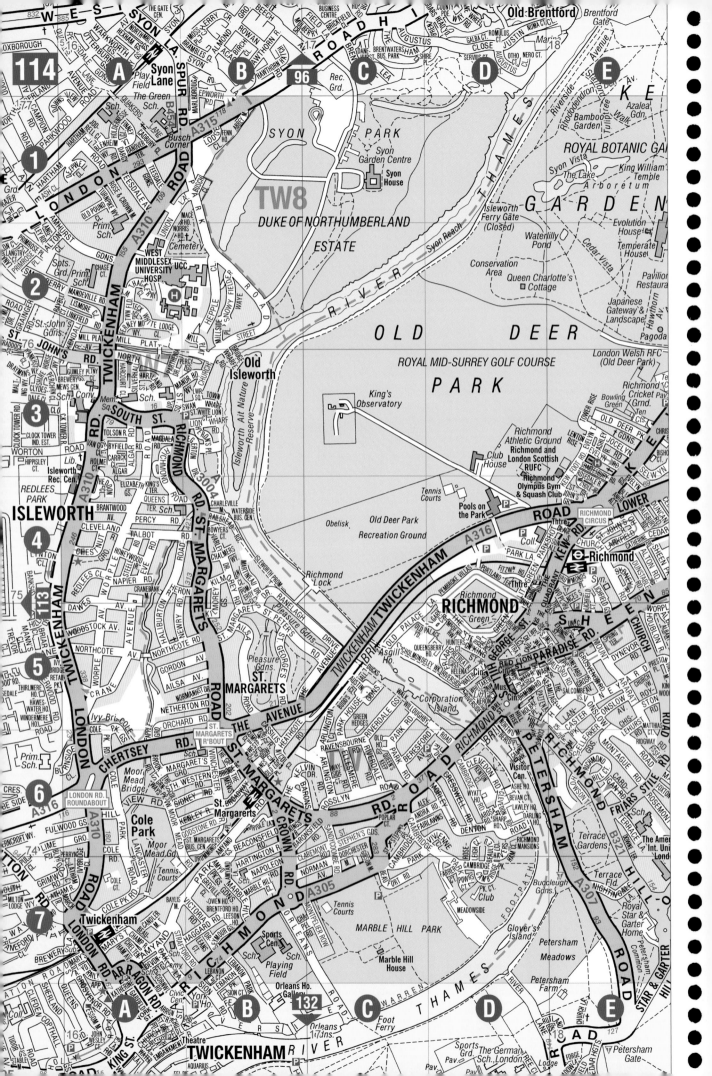

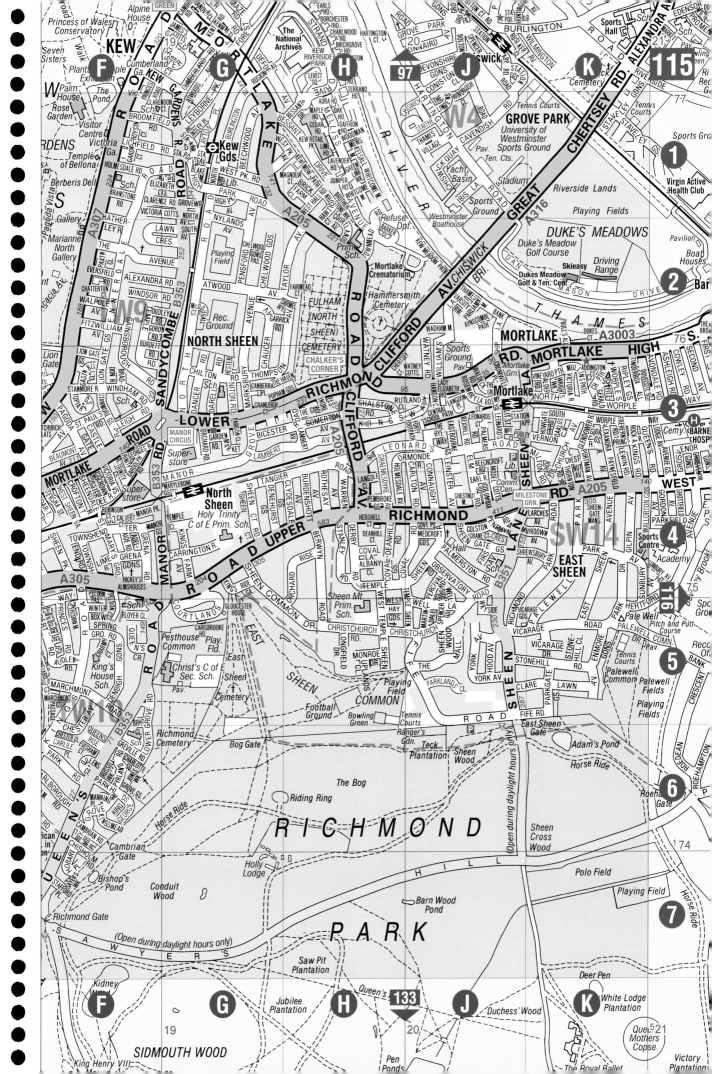

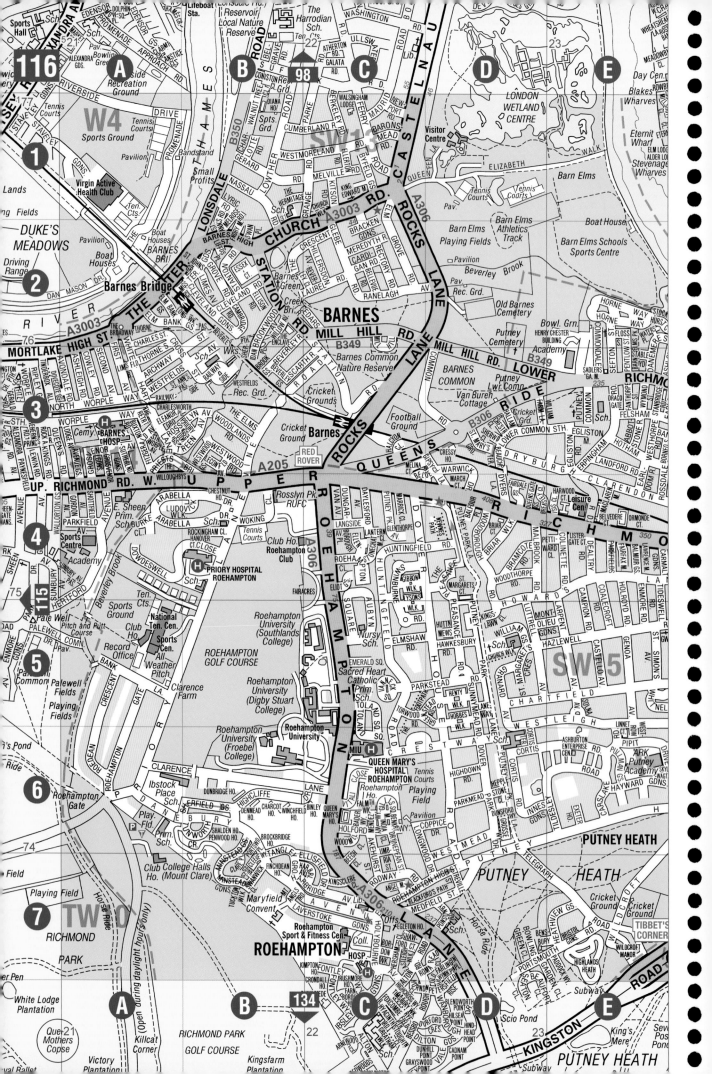

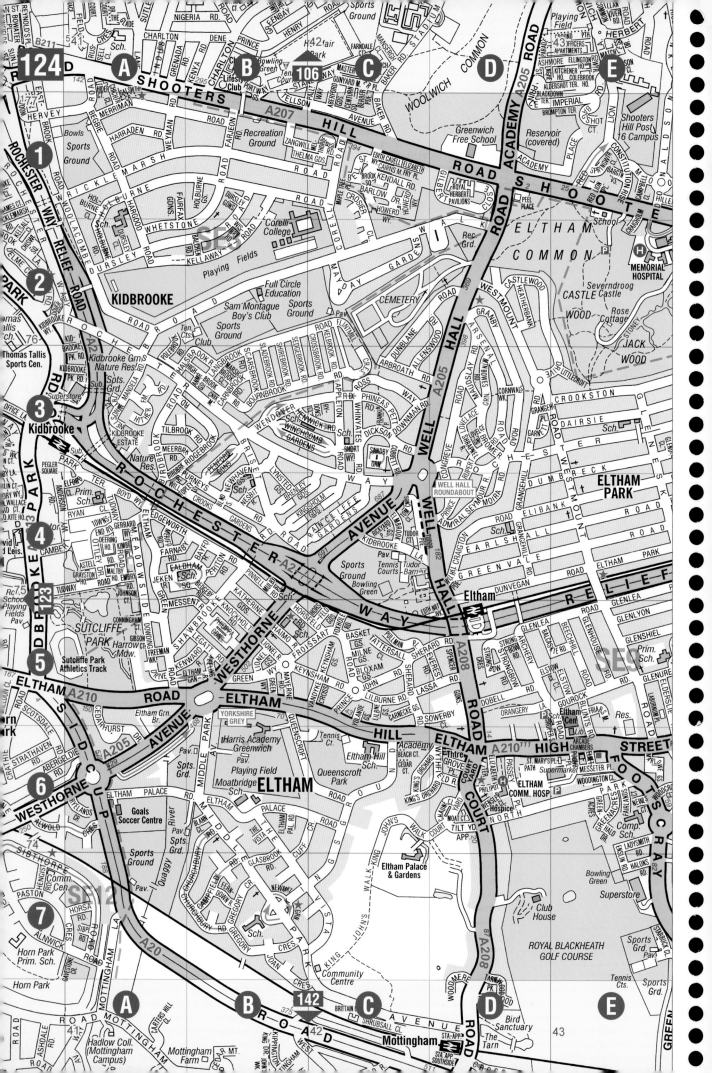

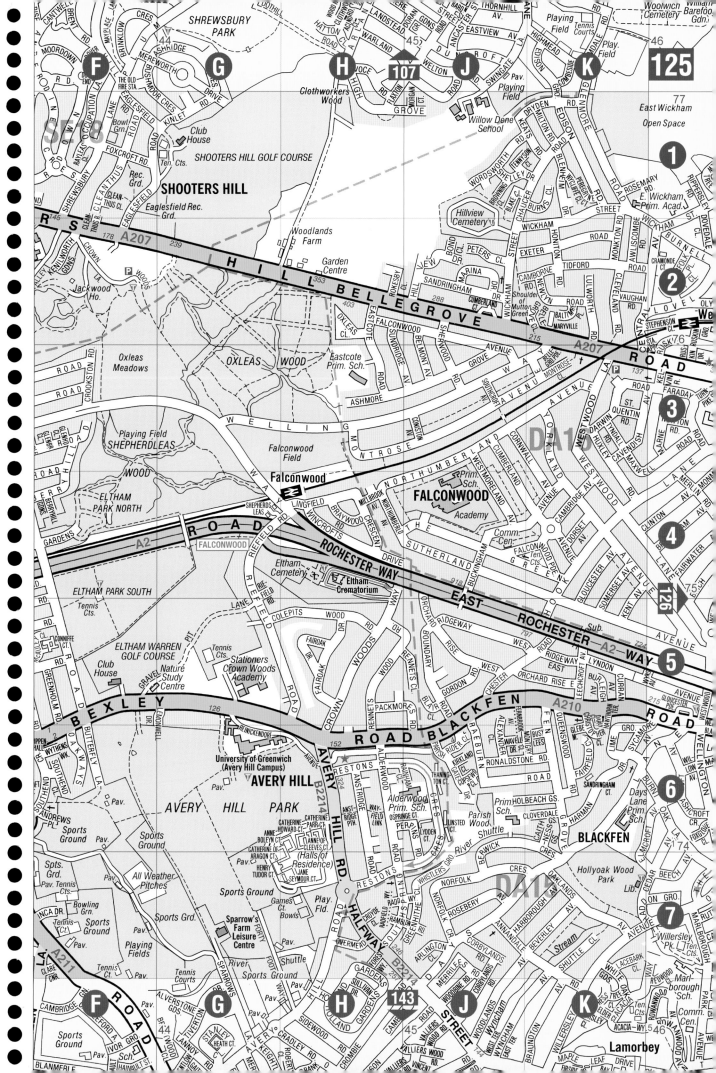

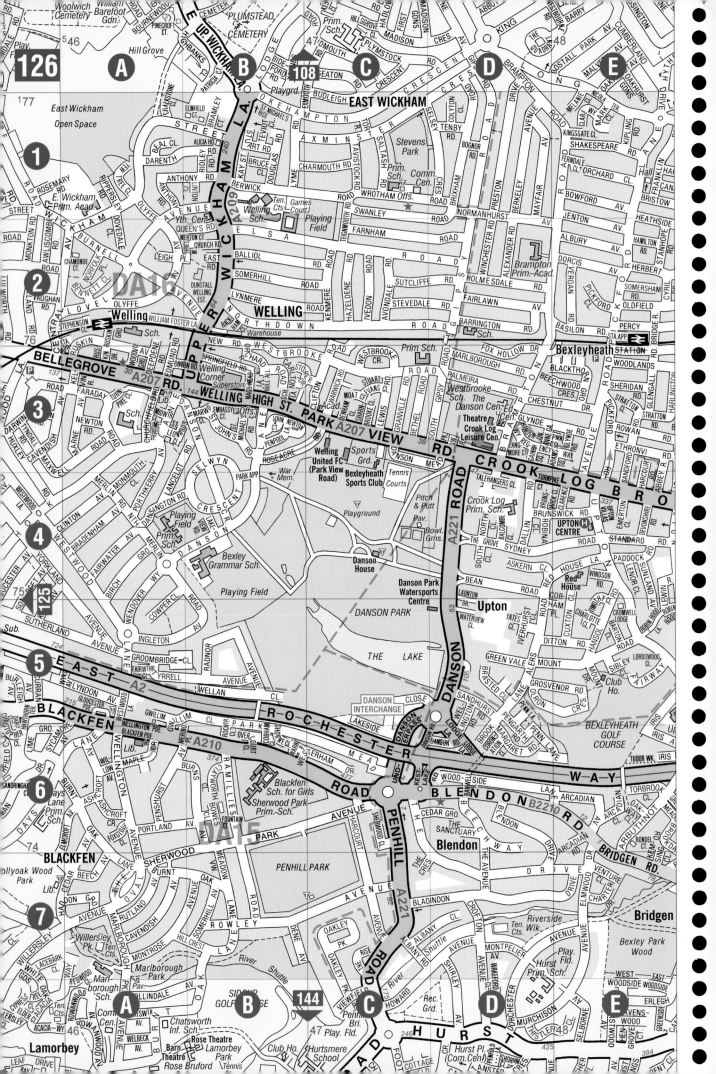

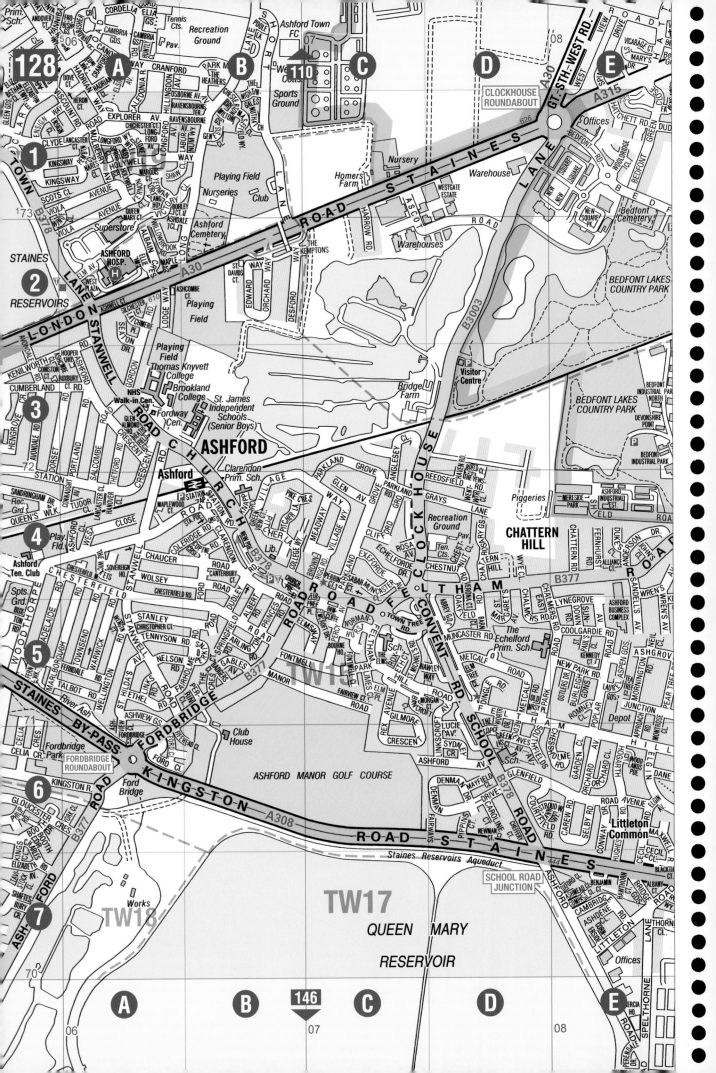

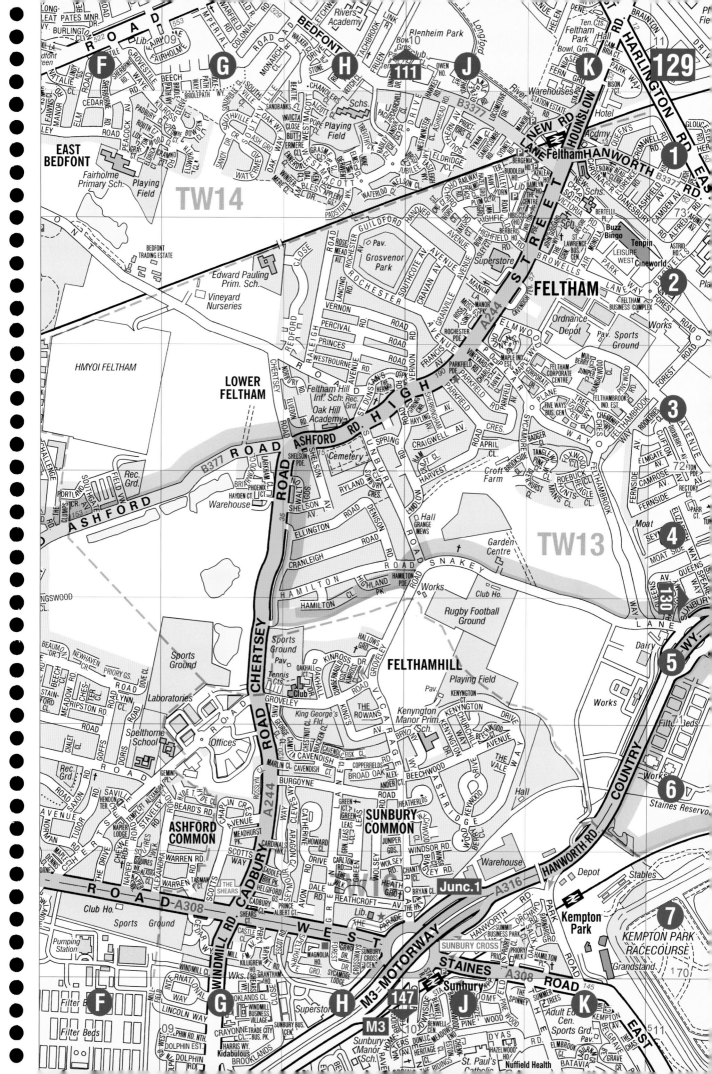

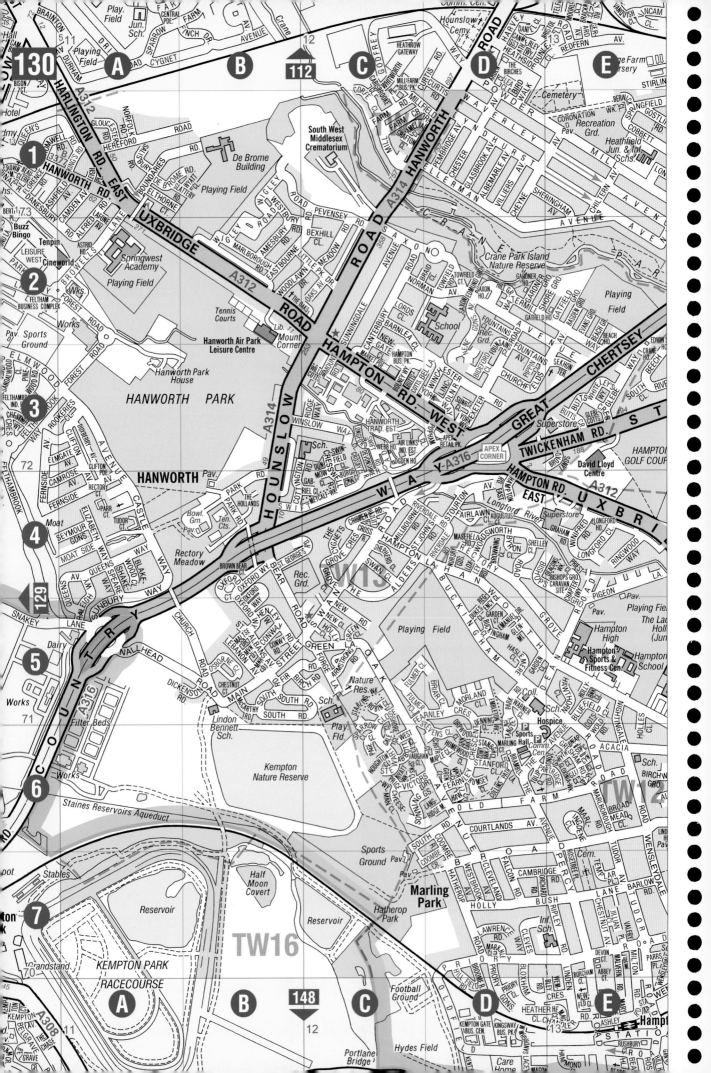

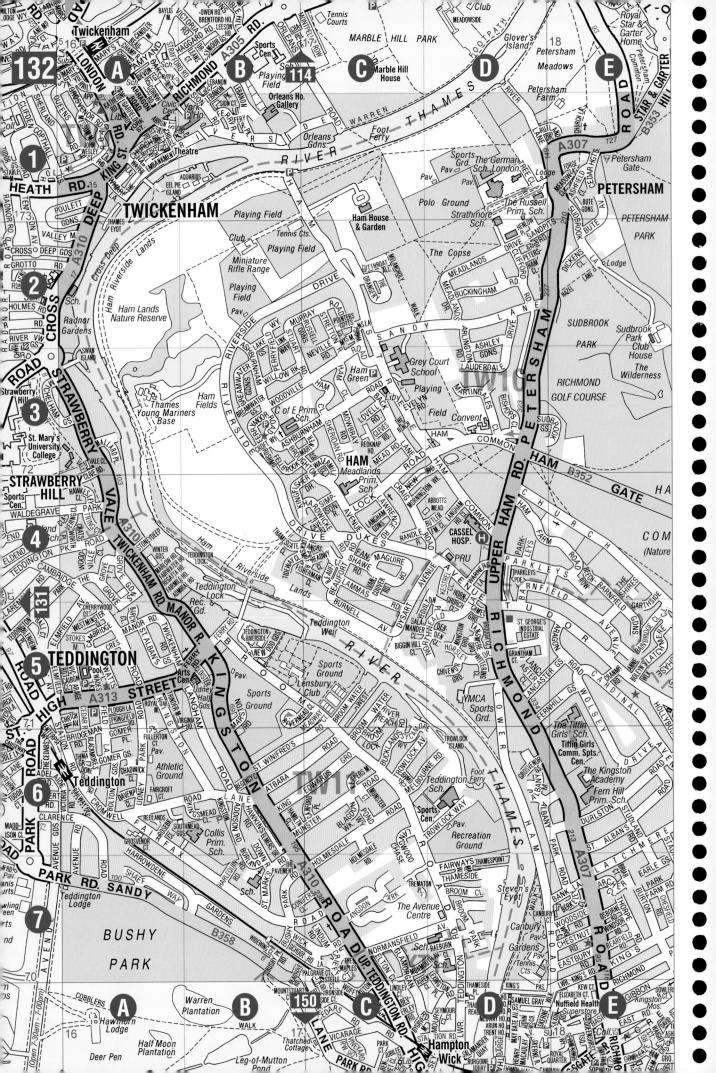

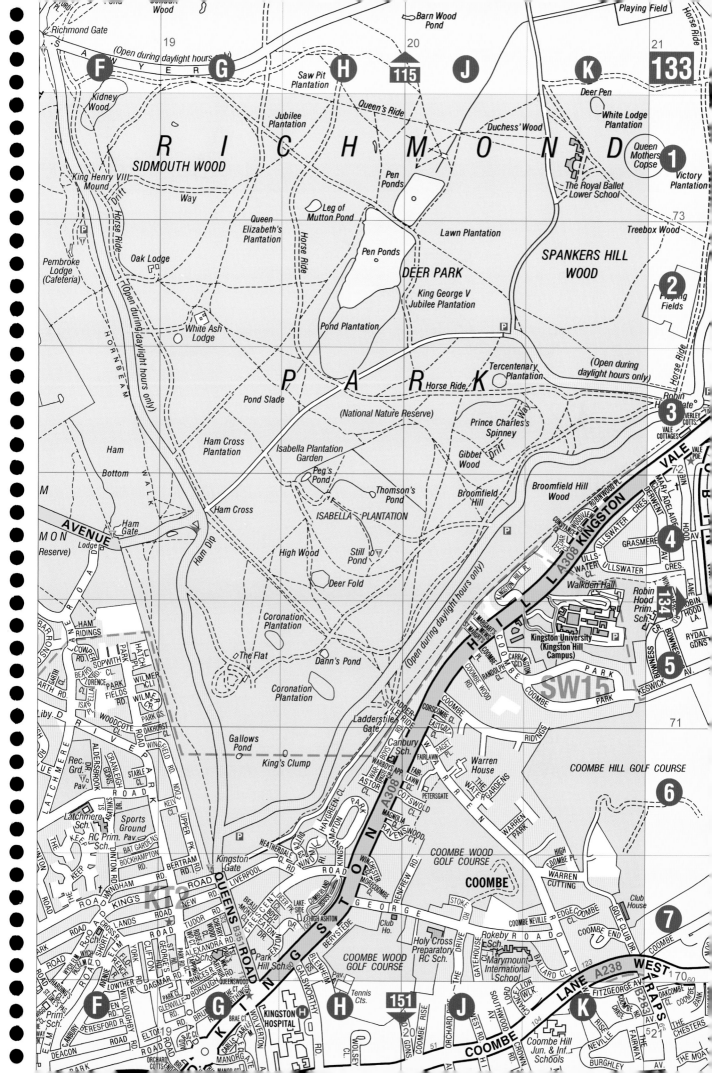

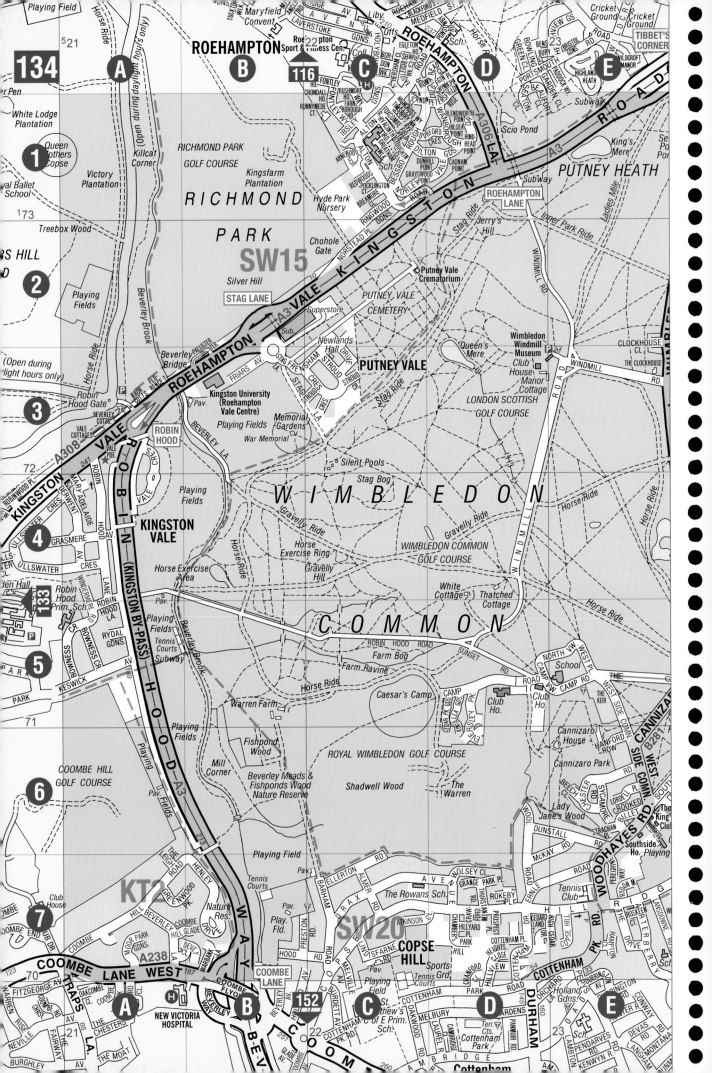

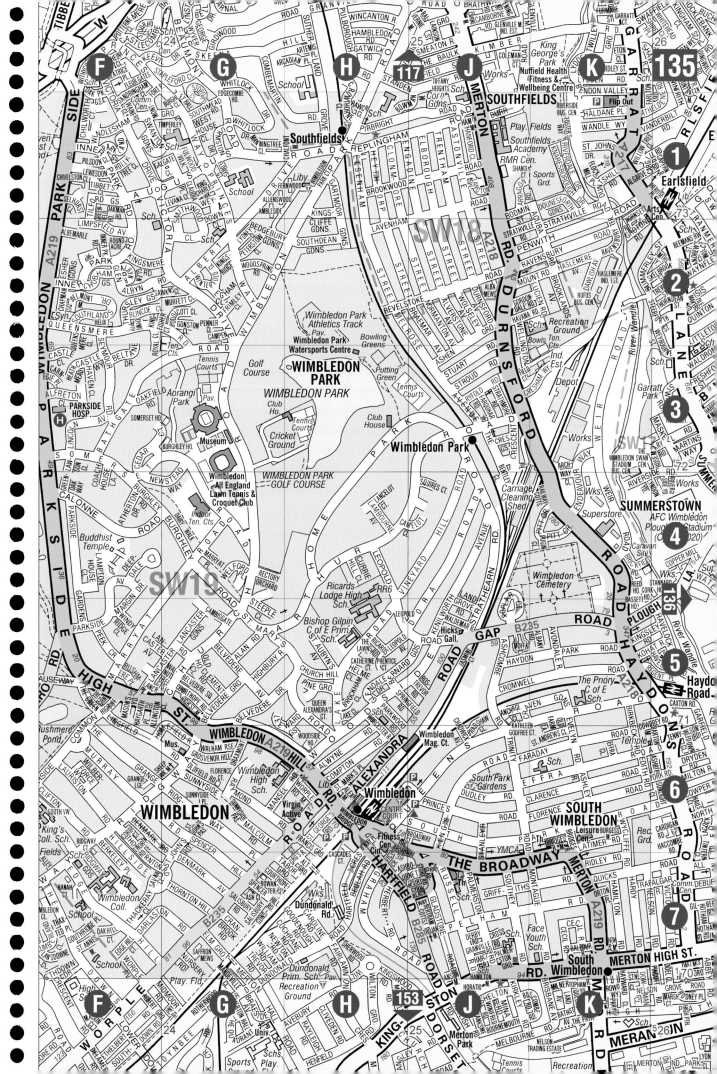

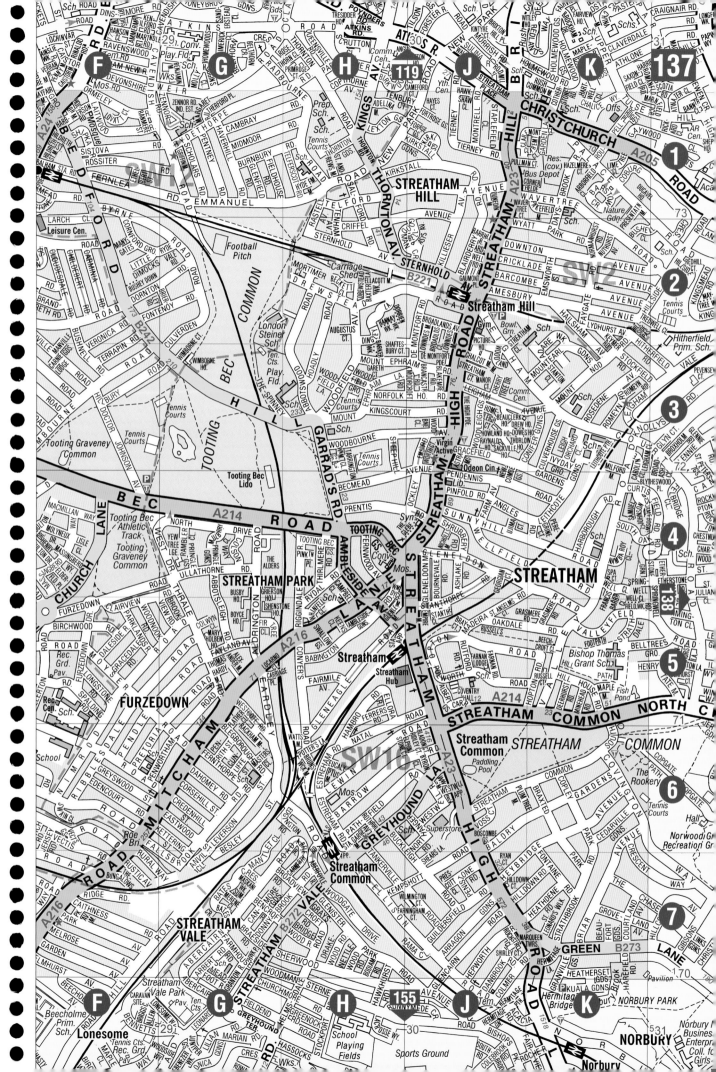

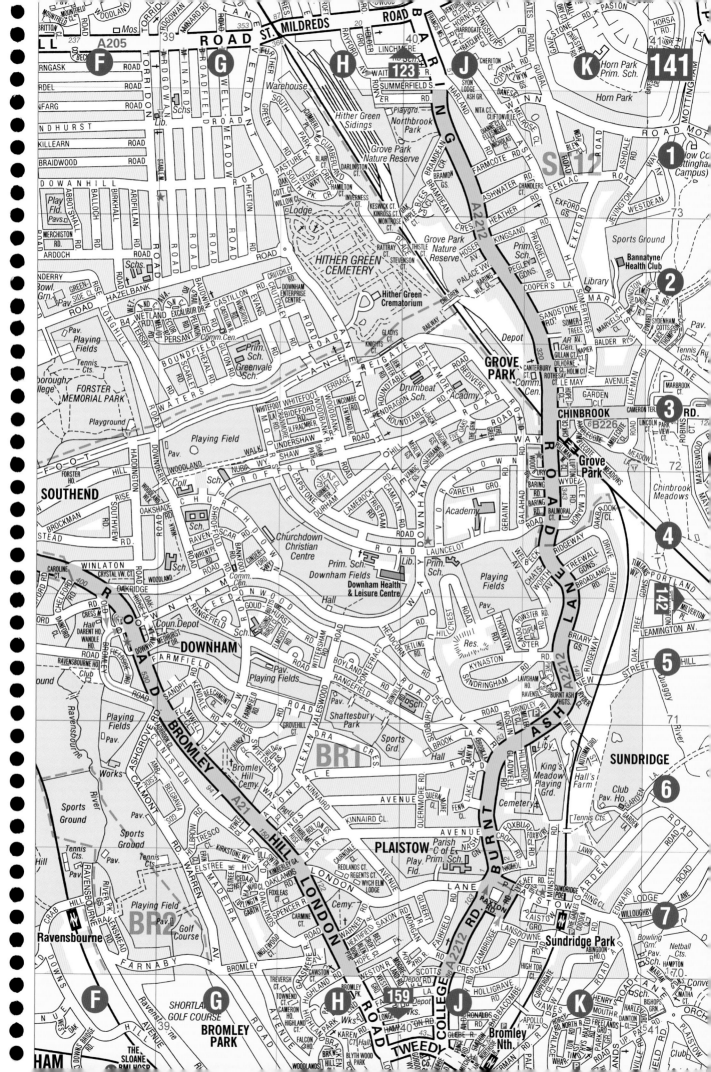

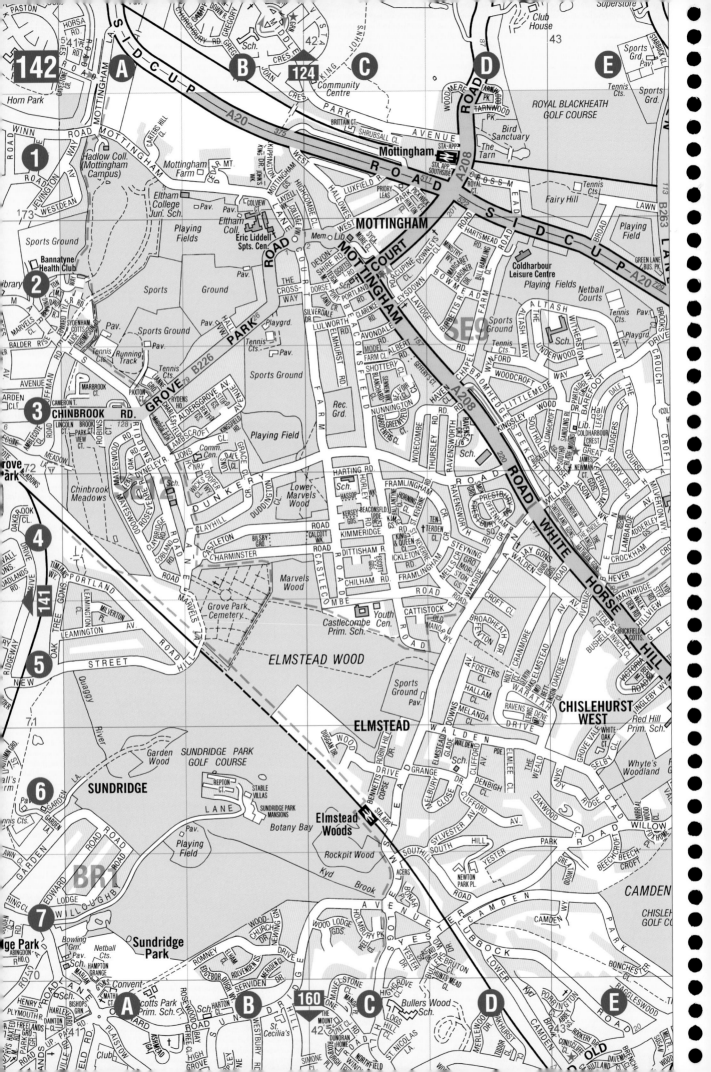

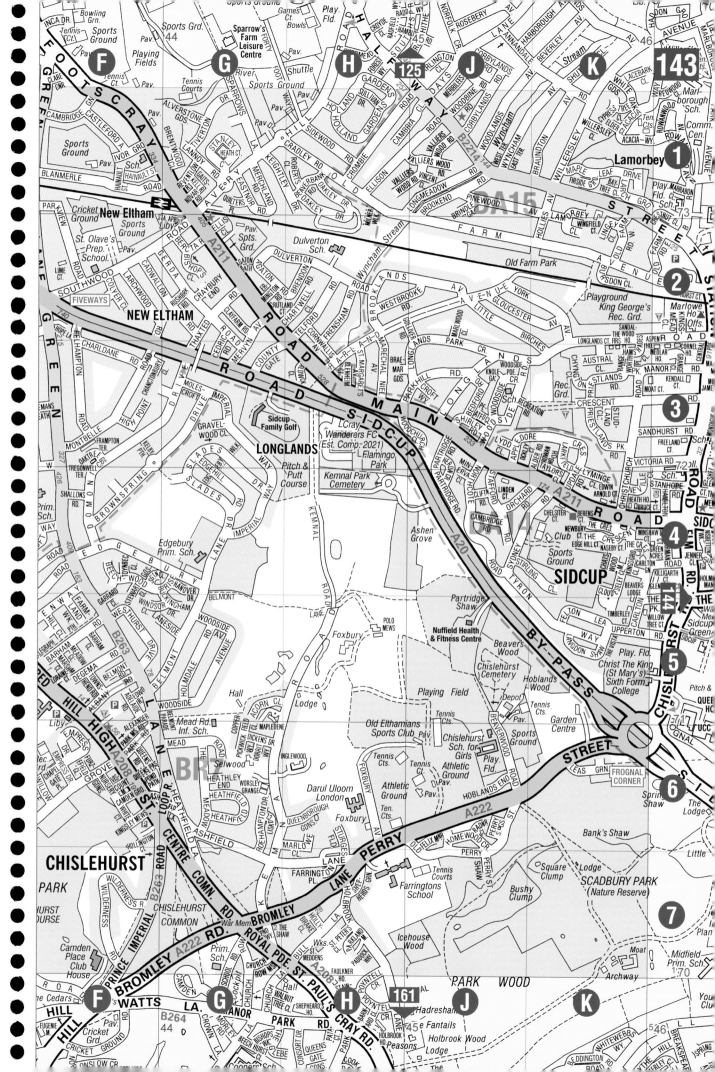

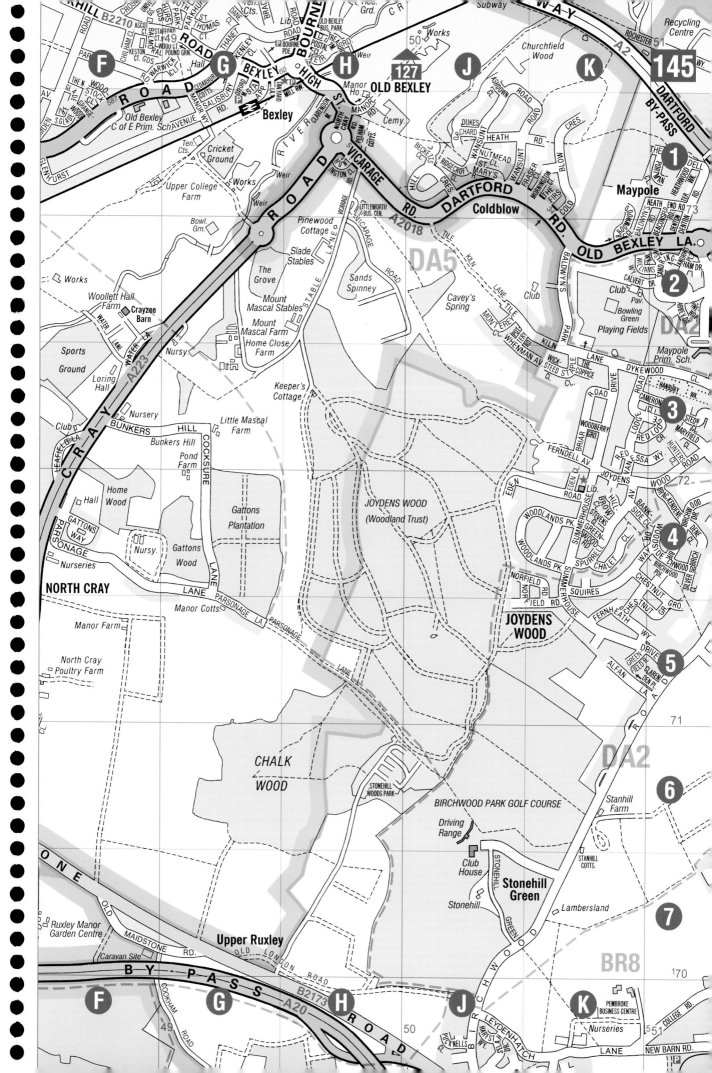

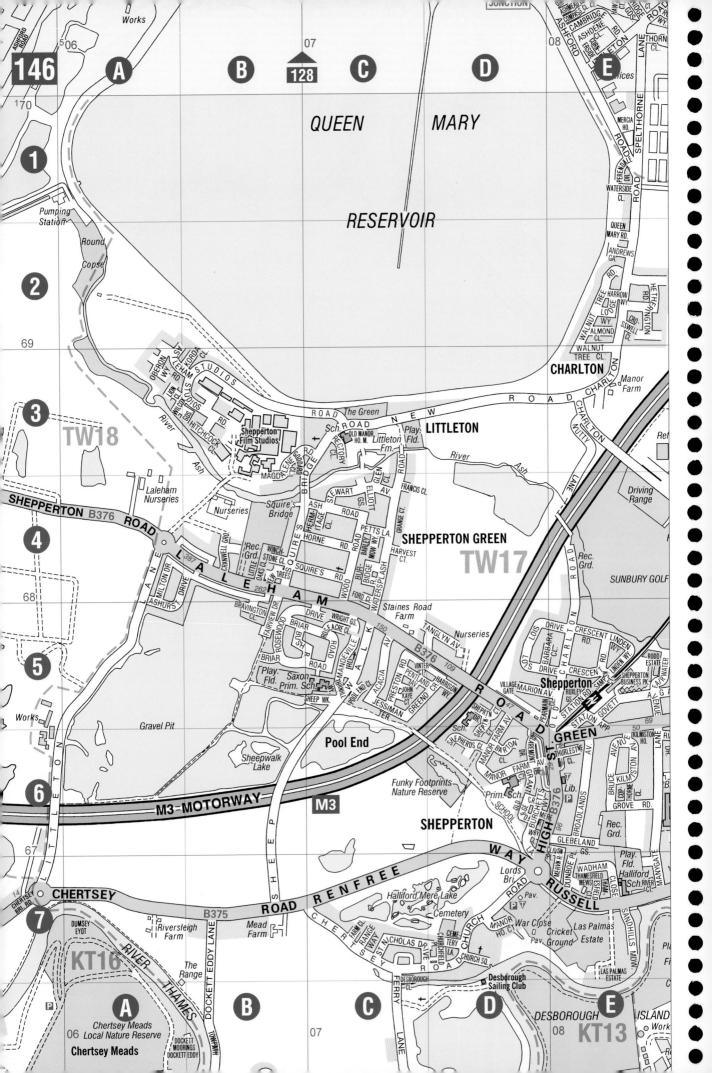

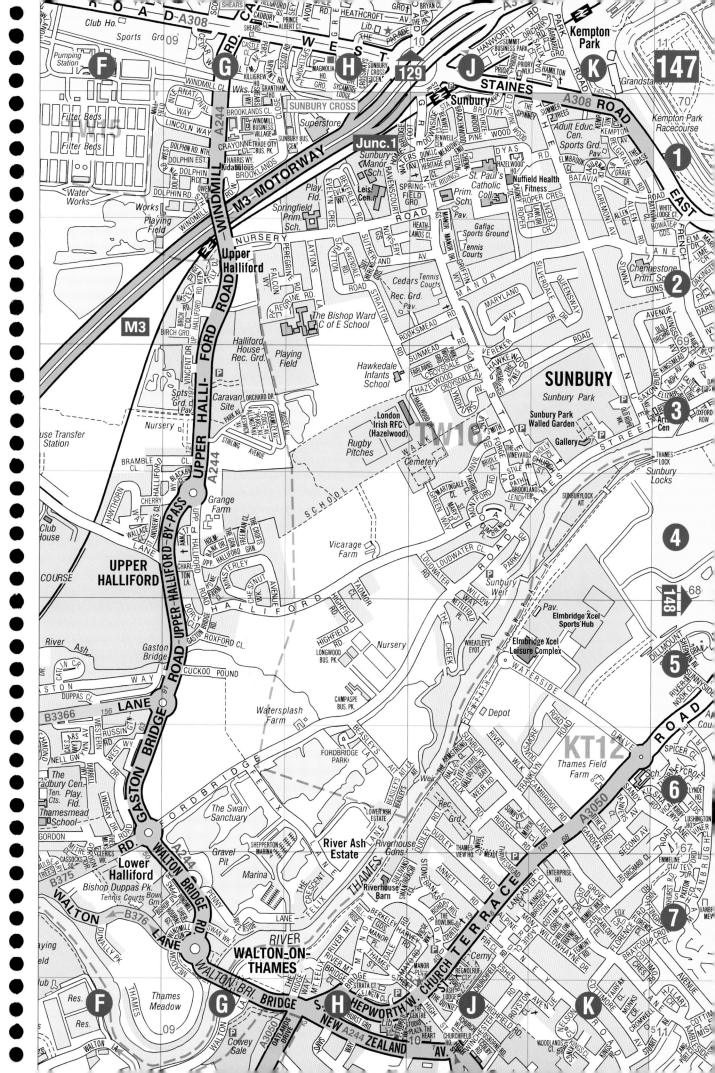

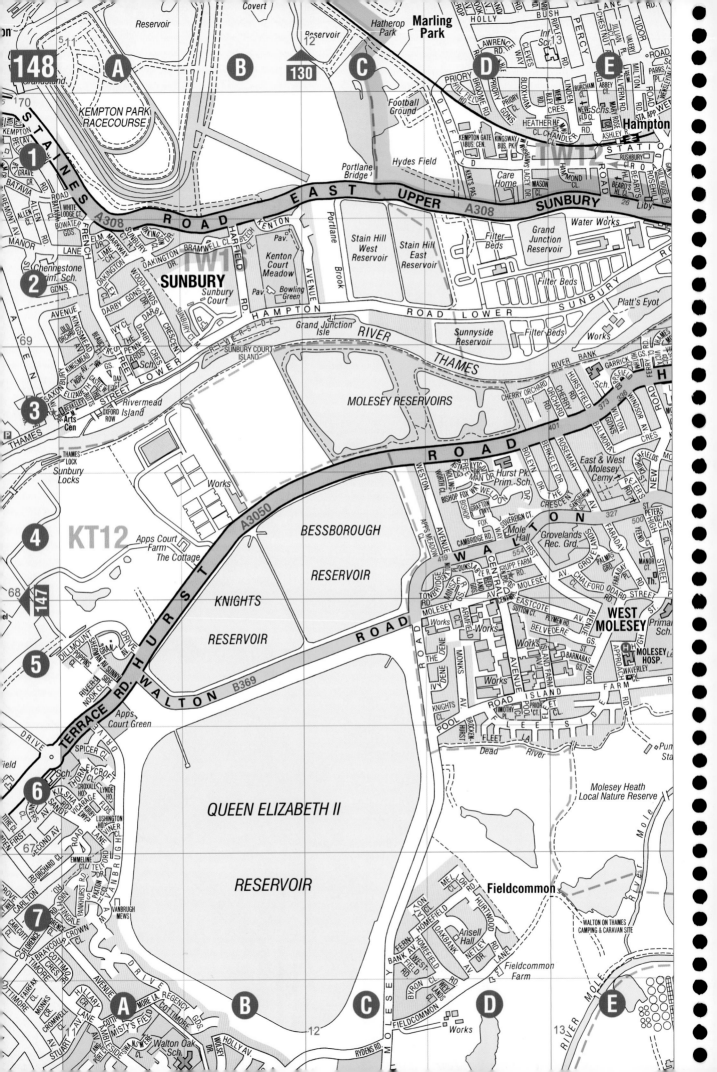

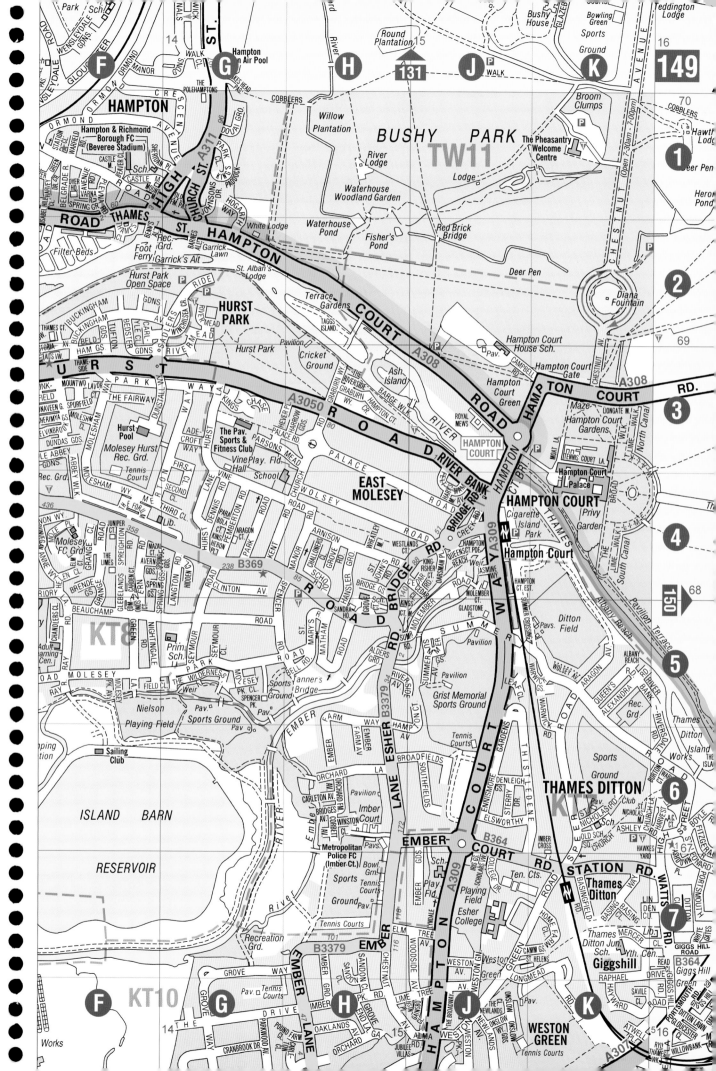

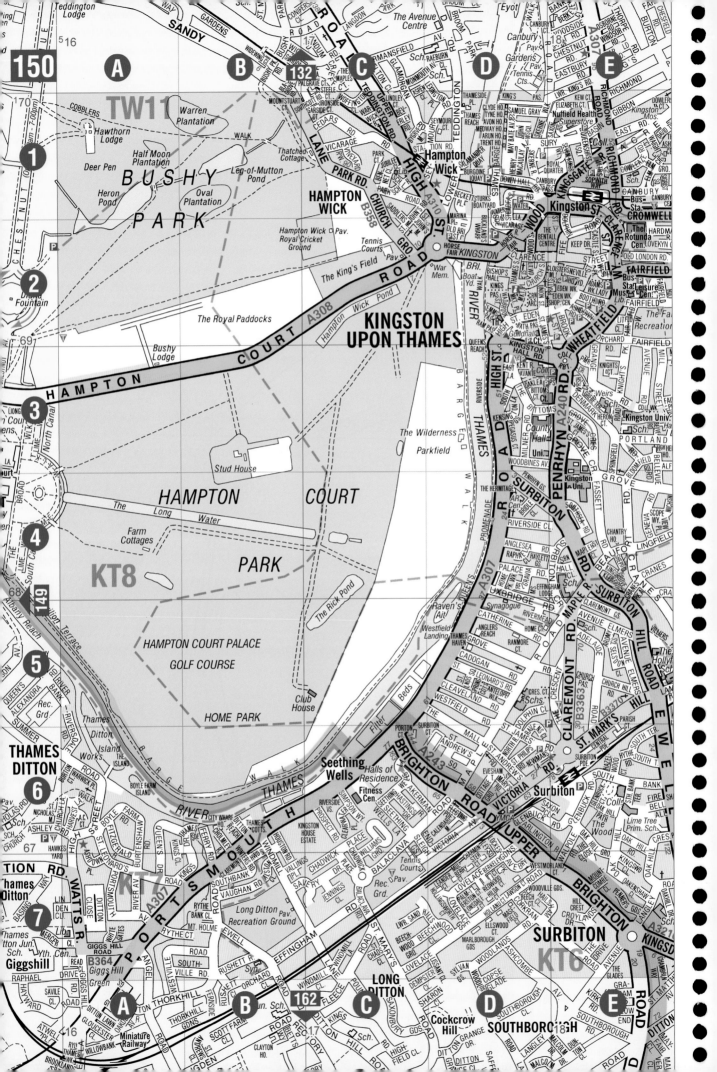

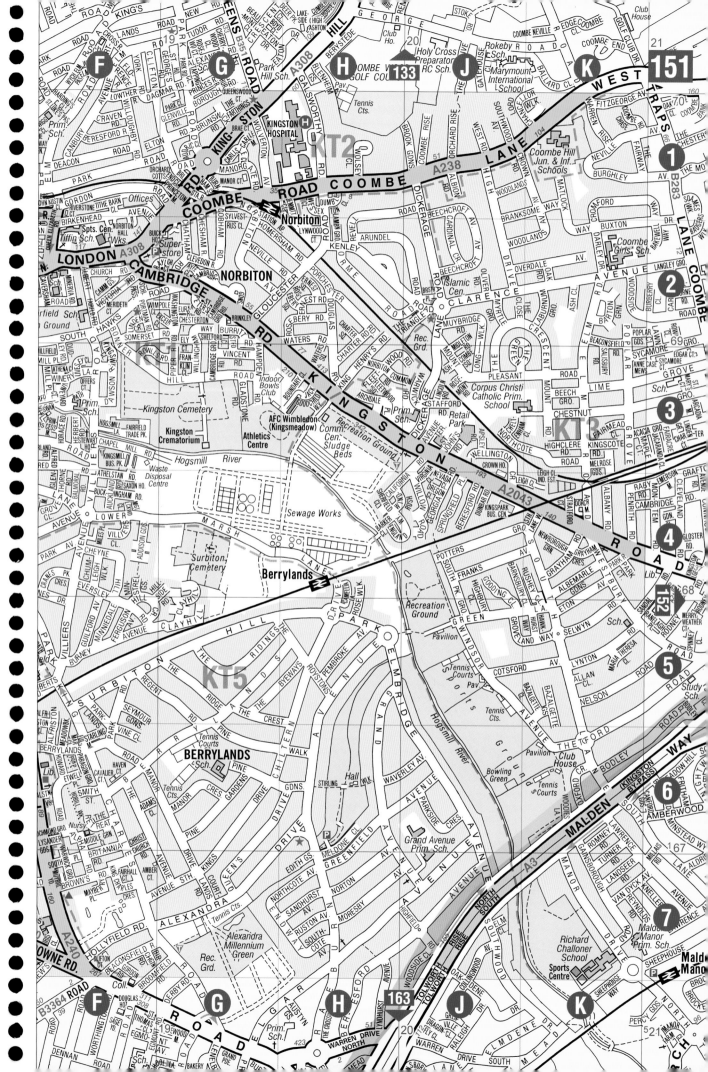

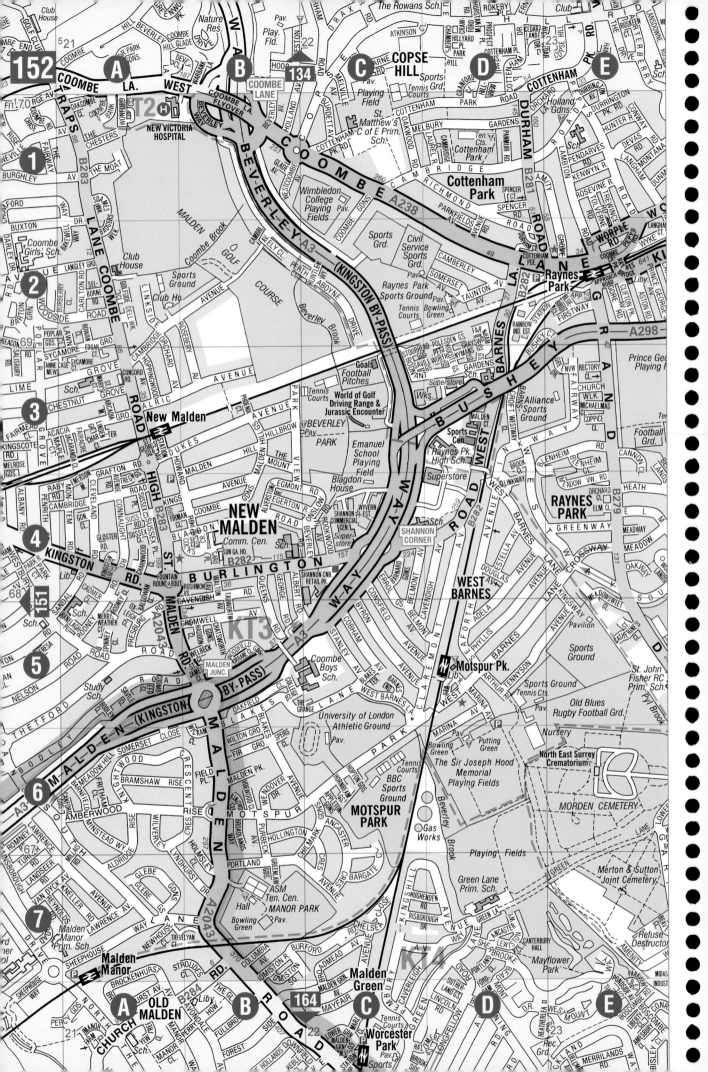

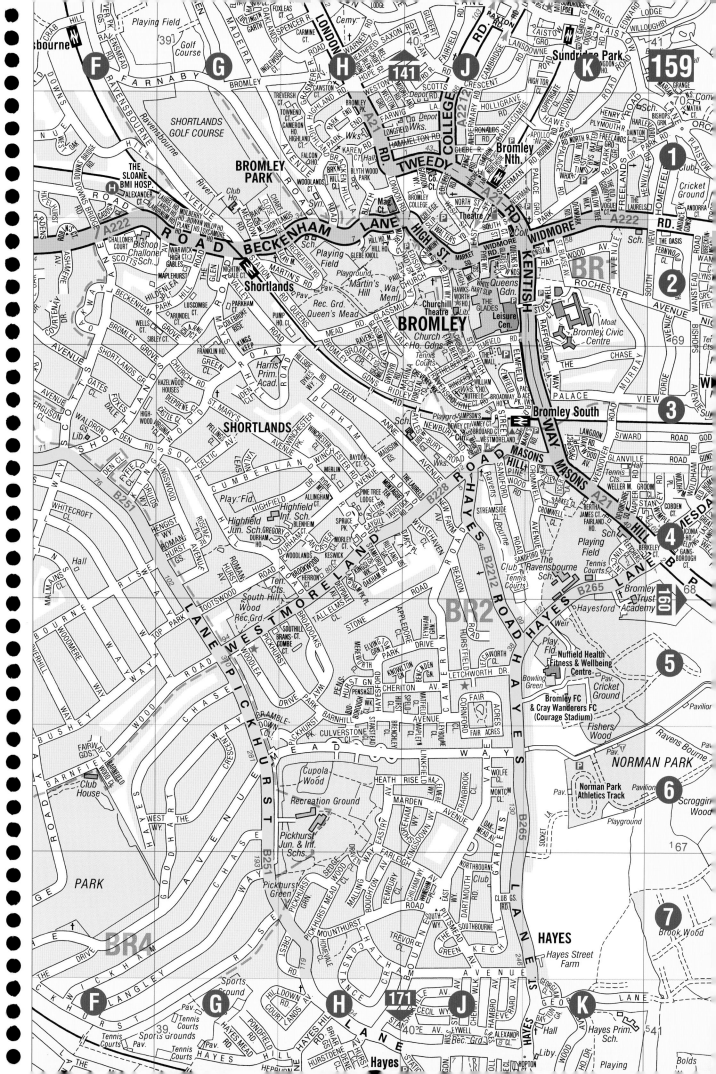

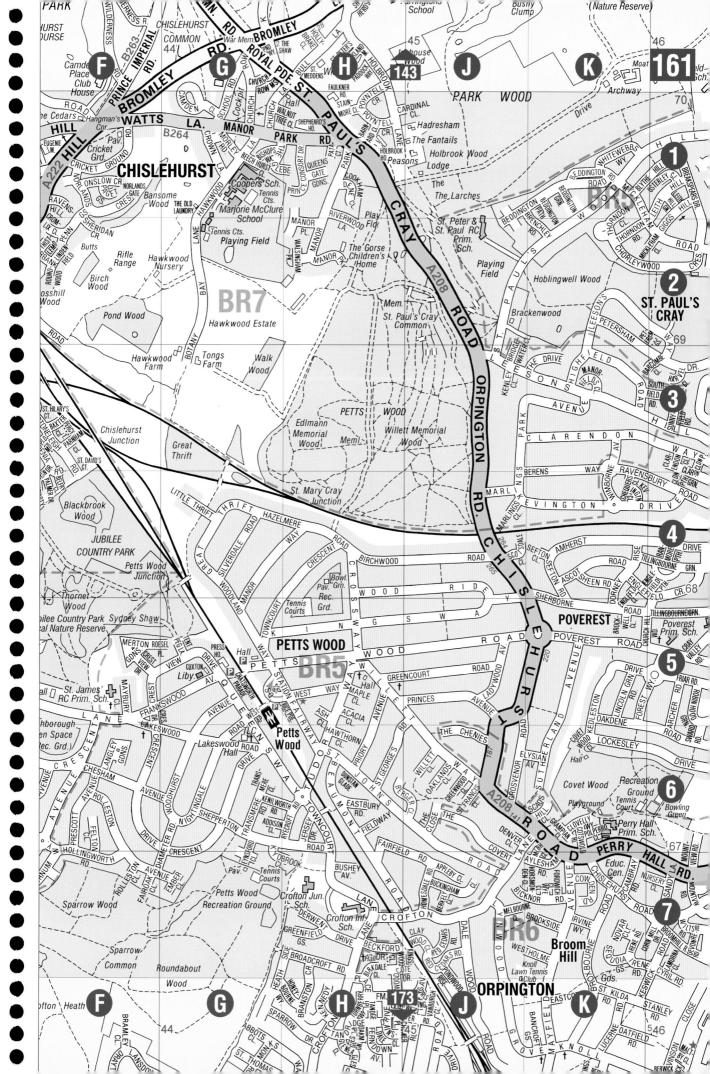

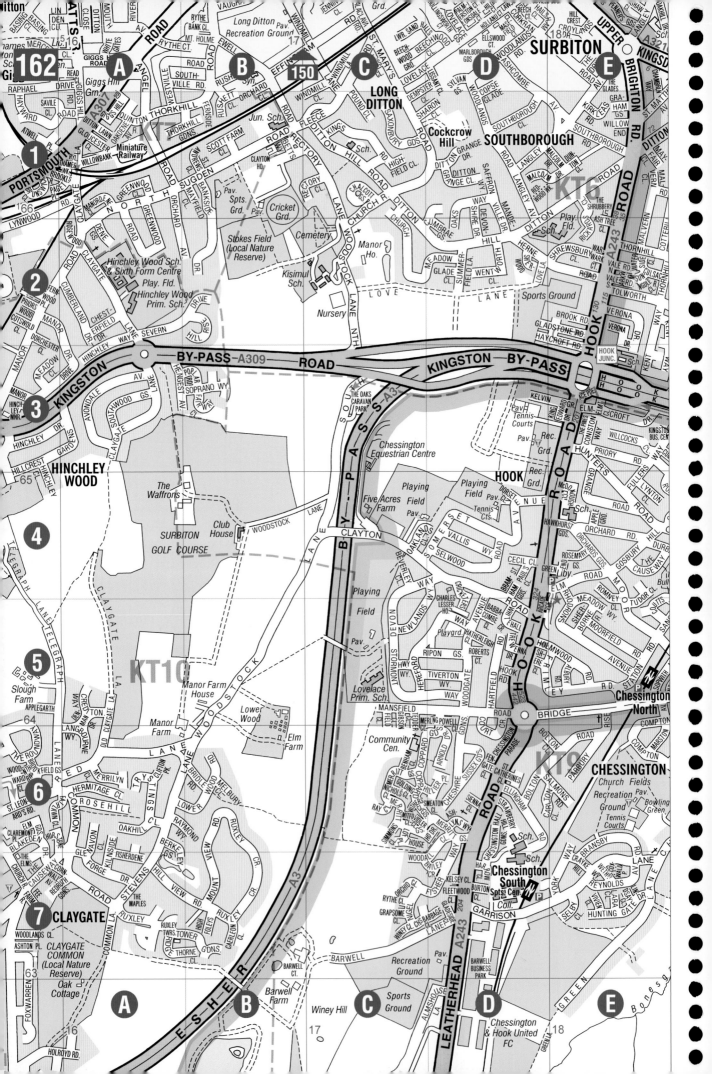

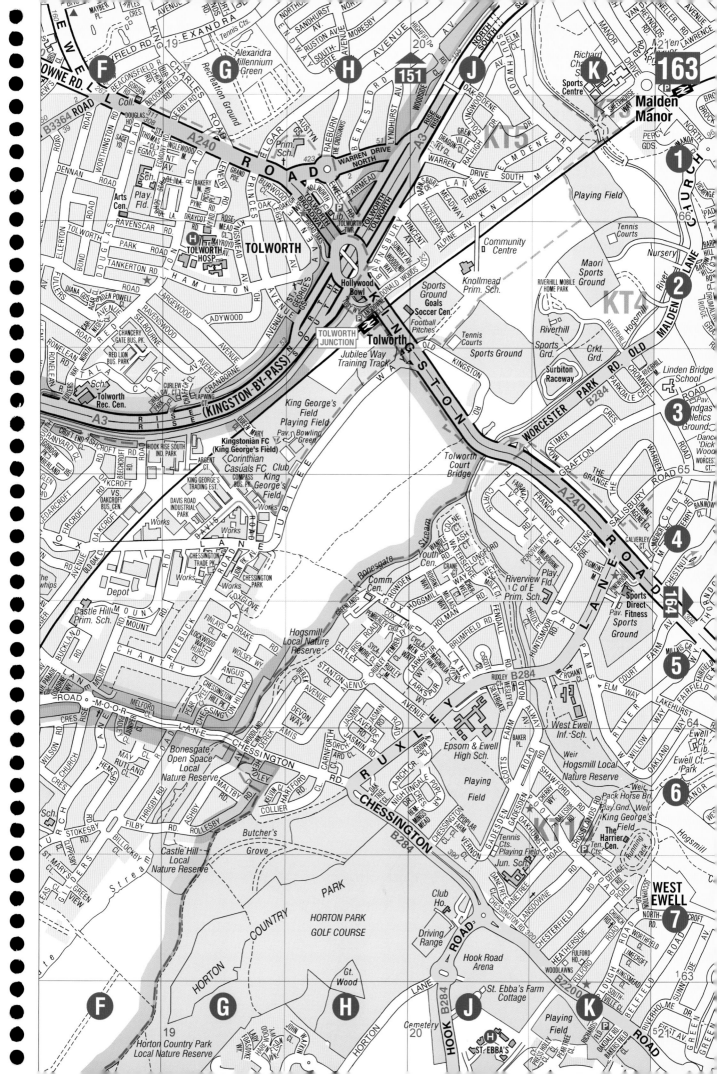

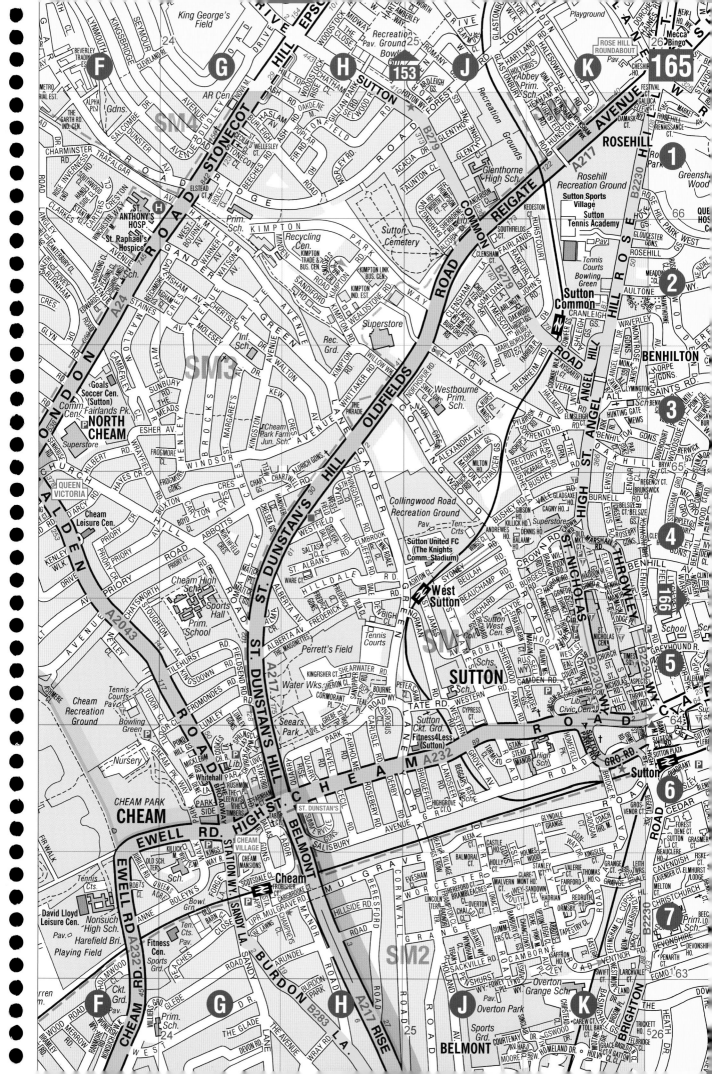

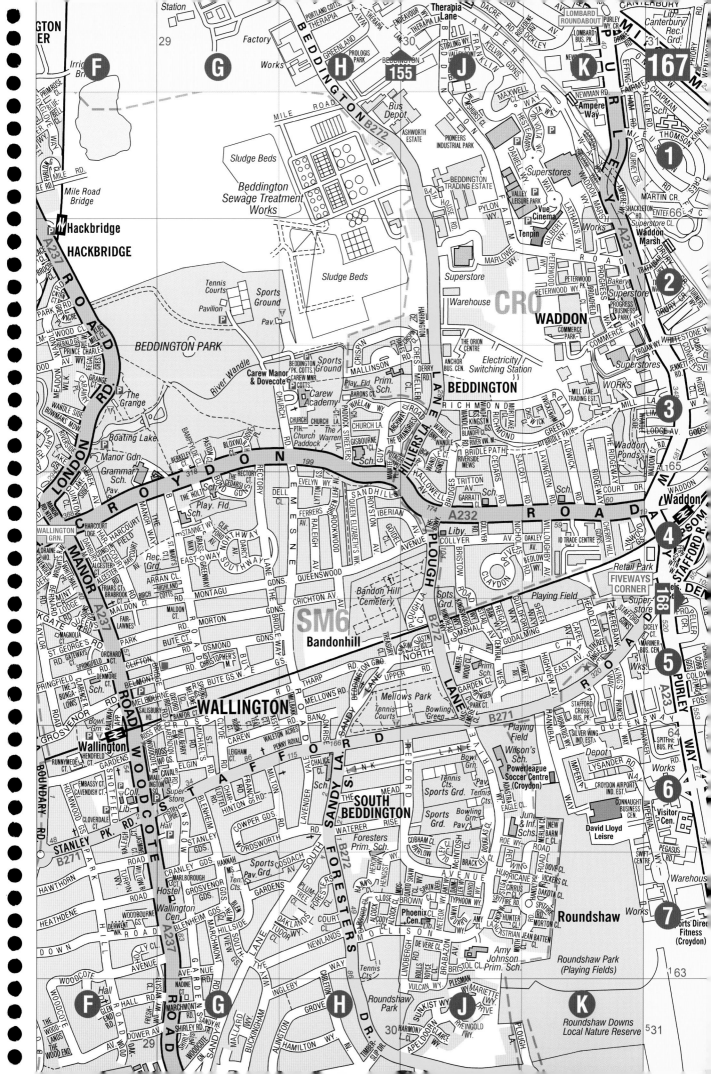

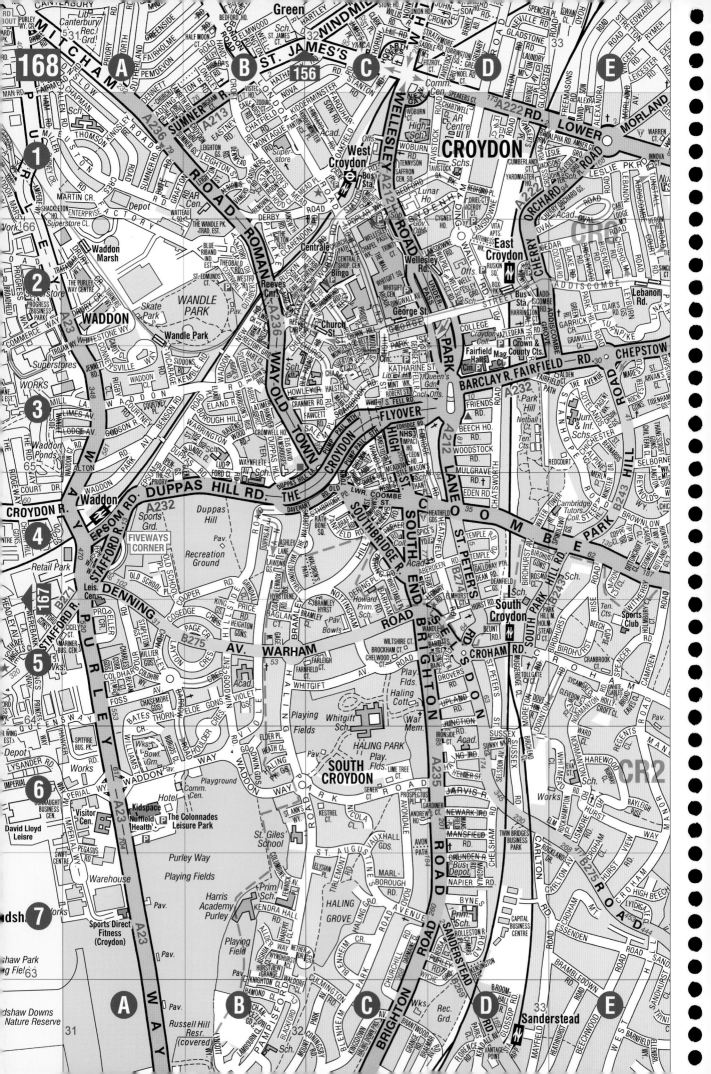

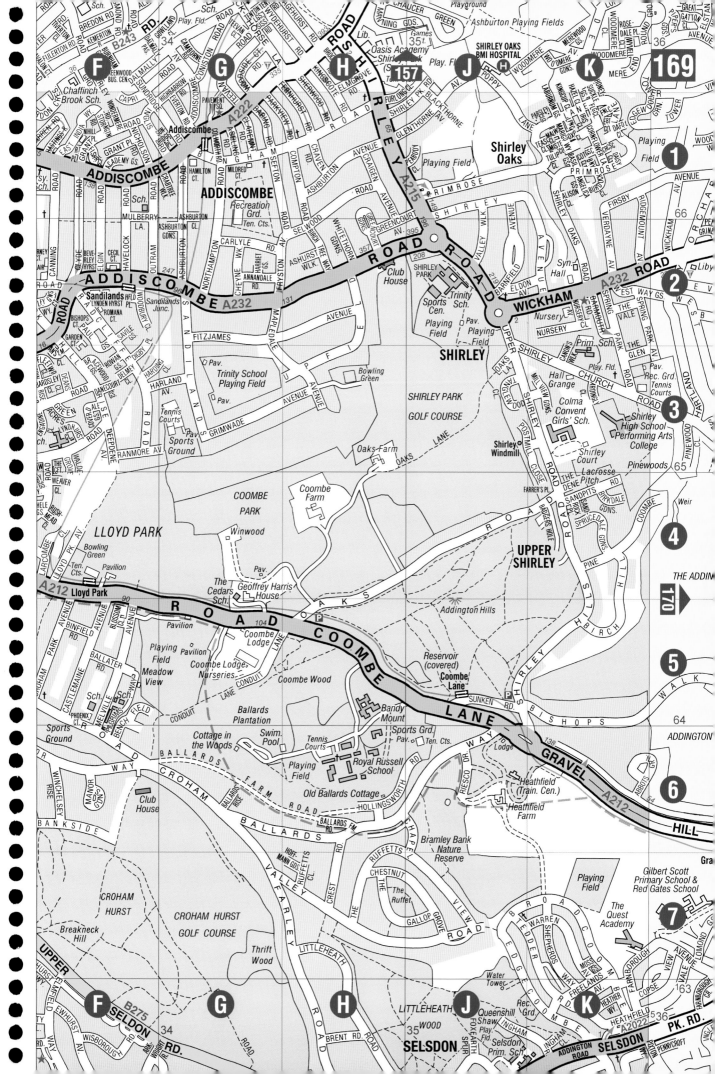

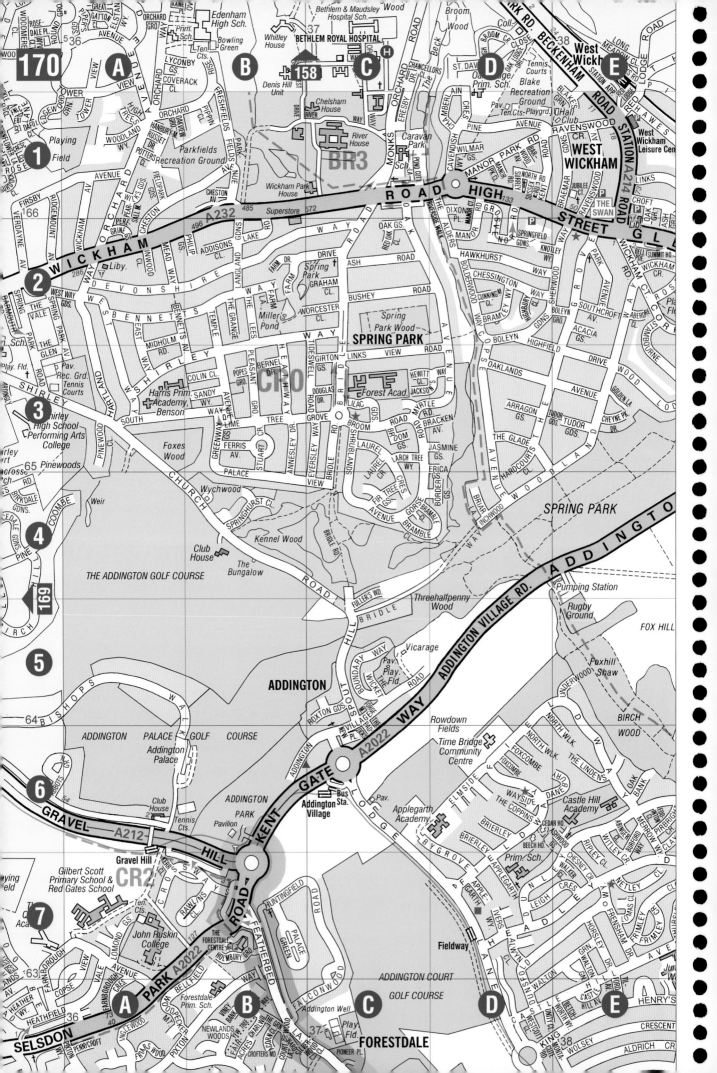

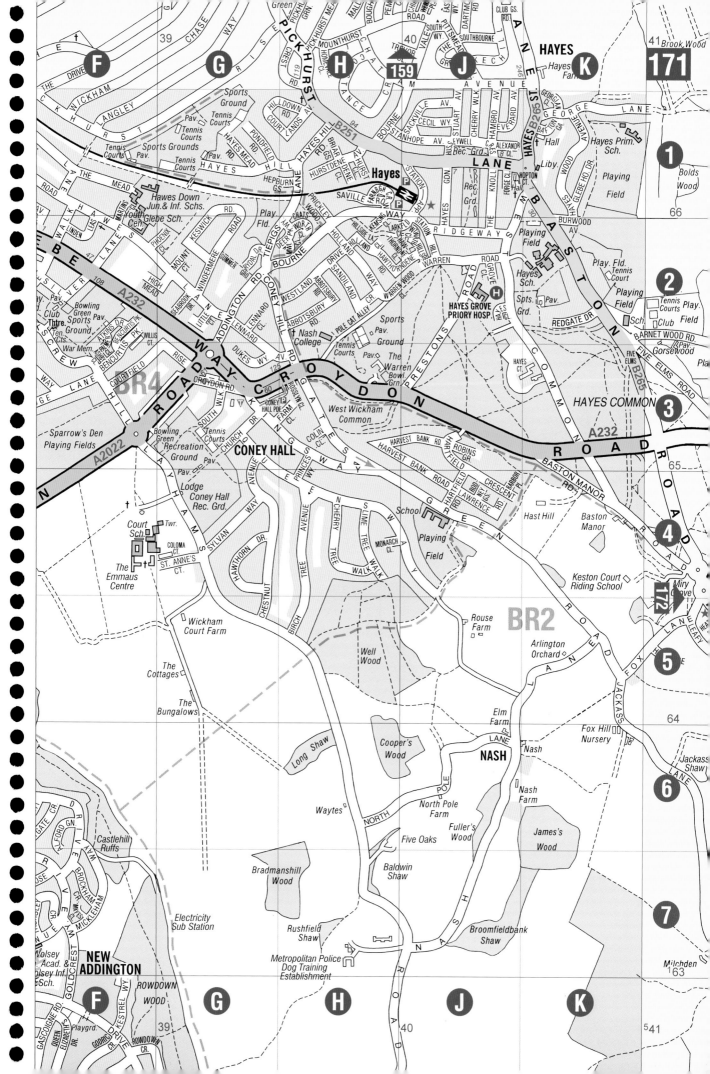

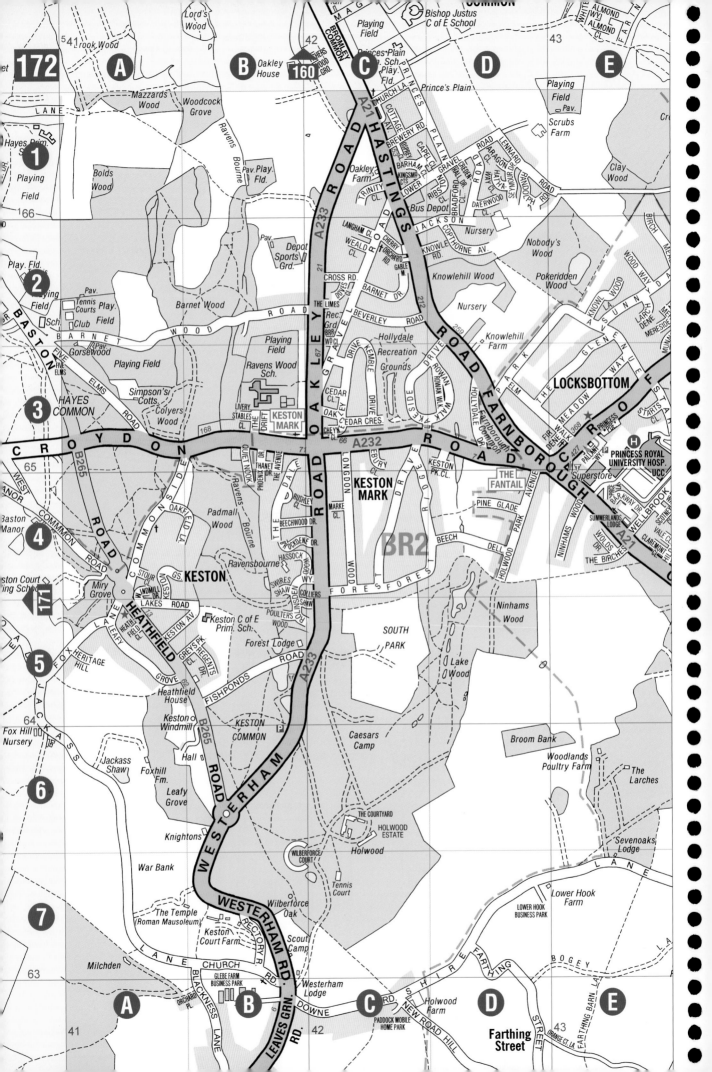

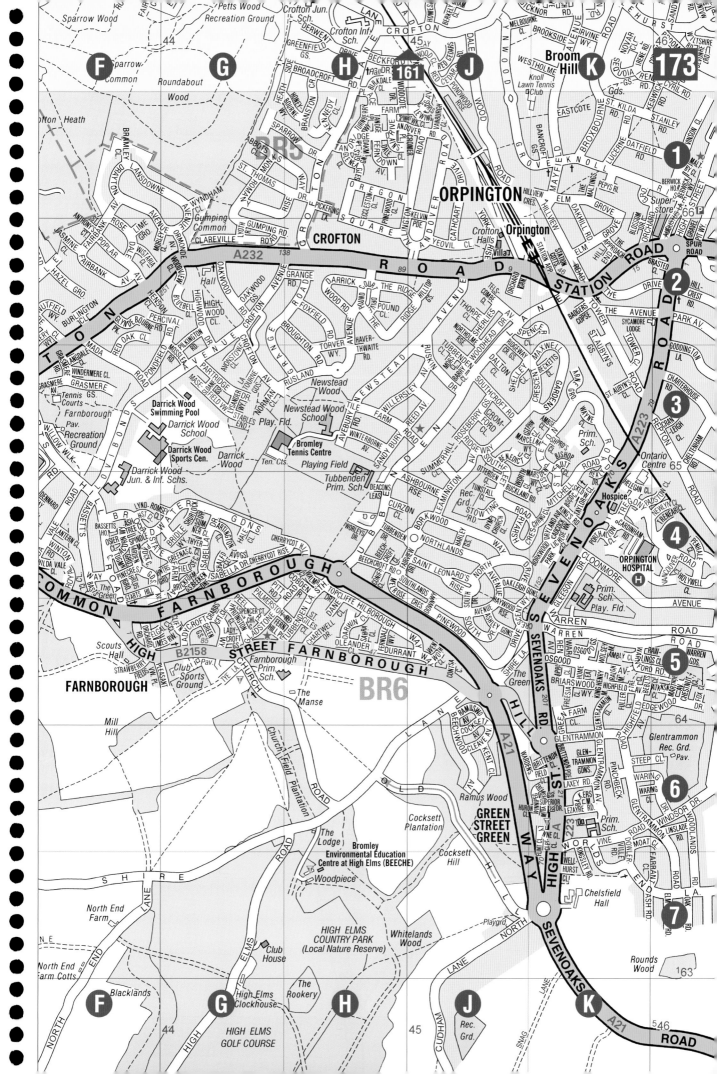

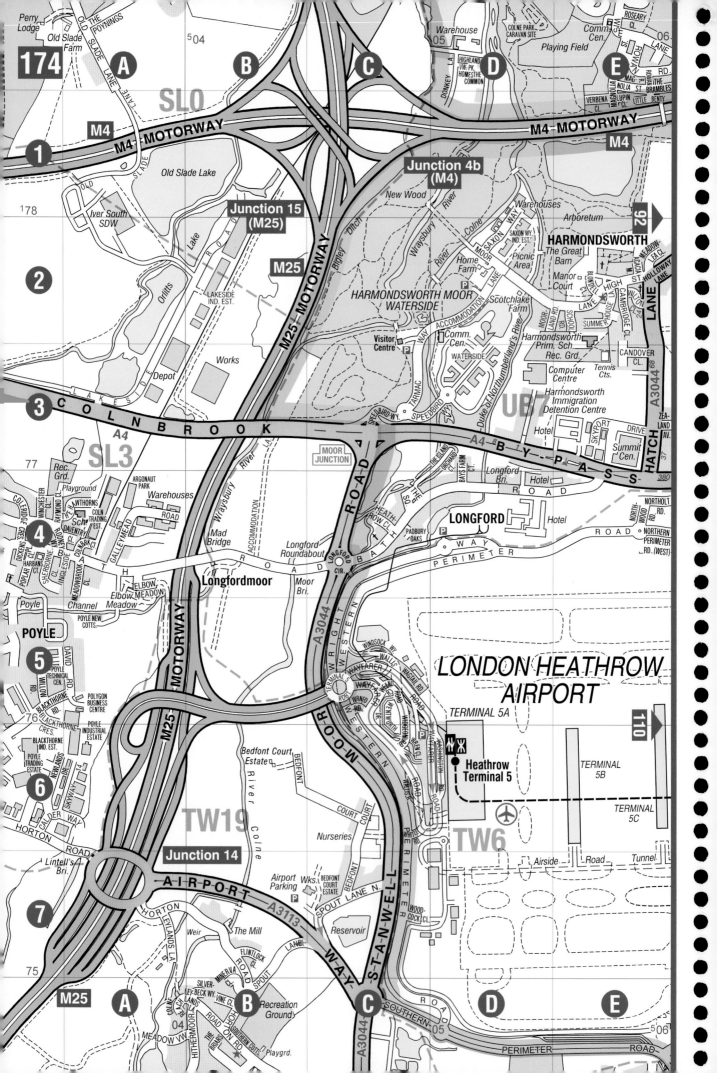

INDEX

Including Streets, Places & Areas, Industrial Estates, Selected Flats & Walkways, Park & Rides, Junction Names & Service Areas and Selected Places of Interest.

HOW TO USE THIS INDEX

1. Each street name is followed by its Postcode District (or, if outside the London Postcodes, by its Locality Abbreviation(s)) and then by its map reference; e.g. **Abbey Av.** HA0: Wemb . . . .2E **78** is in the HA0 Postcode District and the Wembley locality and is to be found in square 2E on page **78**. The page number being shown in bold type.

2. A strict alphabetical order is followed in which Av., Rd., St., etc. (though abbreviated) are read in full and as part of the street name; e.g. **Alder M.** appears after **Aldermary Rd.** but before **Aldermoor Rd.**

3. Streets and a selection of flats and walkways that cannot be shown on the mapping, appear in the index with the thoroughfare to which they are connected shown in brackets; e.g. **Abady Ho.** *SW1 . . . .3D 18 (off Page St.)*

4. Addresses that are in more than one part are referred to as not continuous.

5. Places and areas are shown in the index in **BLUE TYPE** and the map reference is to the actual map square in which the town centre or area is located and not to the place name shown on the map; e.g. **ABBEY WOOD 4C 108**

6. An example of a selected place of interest is **Barnet Mus. 4B 20**

7. Junction names and Service Areas are shown in the index in **BOLD CAPITAL TYPE**; e.g. **ANGEL EDMONTON 5B 34**

8. Map references for entries that appear on large scale pages **4-19** are shown first, with small scale map references shown in brackets; e.g. **Abbey St.** SE1 . . . .7H **15** (3E **102**)

GENERAL ABBREVIATIONS

All. : Alley
Apts. : Apartments
App. : Approach
Arc. : Arcade
Av. : Avenue
Bk. : Back
Blvd. : Boulevard
Bri. : Bridge
B'way. : Broadway
Bldg. : Building
Bldgs. : Buildings
Bus. : Business
Cvn. : Caravan
C'way. : Causeway
Cen. : Centre
Chu. : Church
Circ. : Circle
Cir. : Circus
Cl. : Close
Coll. : College
Comn. : Common
Cnr. : Corner
Cott. : Cottage
Cotts. : Cottages
Ct. : Court
Ctyd. : Courtyard
Cres. : Crescent
Cft. : Croft
Dpt. : Depot
Dr. : Drive
E. : East
Emb. : Embankment
Ent. : Enterprise
Est. : Estate
Fld. : Field
Flds. : Fields
Gdn. : Garden
Gdns. : Gardens
Gth. : Garth
Ga. : Gate
Gt. : Great
Grn. : Green
Gro. : Grove
Hgts. : Heights
Ho. : House
Ho's. : Houses
Ind. : Industrial
Info. : Information
Intl. : International
Junc. : Junction
La. : Lane
Lit. : Little
Lwr. : Lower
Mnr. : Manor
Mans. : Mansions
Mkt. : Market
Mdw. : Meadow
Mdws. : Meadows
M. : Mews
Mt. : Mount
Mus. : Museum
Nth. : North
No. : Number
Pal. : Palace
Pde. : Parade
Pk. : Park
Pas. : Passage
Pav. : Pavilion
Pl. : Place
Pct. : Precinct
Prom. : Promenade
Quad. : Quadrant
Ri. : Rise
Rd. : Road
Rdbt. : Roundabout
Shop. : Shopping
Sth. : South
Sq. : Square
Sta. : Station
St. : Street
Ter. : Terrace
Twr. : Tower
Trad. : Trading
Up. : Upper
Va. : Vale
Vw. : View
Vs. : Villas
Vis. : Visitors
Wlk. : Walk
W. : West
Yd. : Yard

LOCALITY ABBREVIATIONS

Addington: BR4,CR0 . . . . Addtn
Arkley: EN5 . . . . Ark
Ashford: TW15 . . . . Ashf
Banstead: SM2 . . . . Bans
Barking: IG3,IG11,RM8-9 . . . . Bark
Barnet: EN4-5 . . . . Barn
Beckenham: BR3 . . . . Beck
Beddington: CR0,SM6 . . . . Bedd
Bedfont: TW14 . . . . Bedf
Belvedere: DA7,DA17-18 . . . . Belv
Bexley: DA1,DA5,DA15 . . . . Bexl
Bexleyheath: DA5-7 . . . . Bex
Brentford: TW7-8 . . . . Bford
Brimsdown: EN3 . . . . Brim
Bromley: BR1-2 . . . . Broml
Buckhurst Hill: IG8-9 . . . . Buck H
Bushey: WD23 . . . . Bush
Bushy Heath: WD23 . . . . B Hea
Carshalton: CR4,SM4-5 . . . . Cars
Chadwell Heath: RM6-7 . . . . Chad H
Cheam: SM2-3 . . . . Cheam
Chelsfield: BR6 . . . . Chels
Chertsey: KT16 . . . . Chert
Chessington: KT9 . . . . Chess
Chigwell: IG6-7 . . . . Chig
Chislehurst: BR7 . . . . Chst
Claygate: KT10 . . . . Clay
Cockfosters: EN4-5 . . . . Cockf
Collier Row: RM5-7 . . . . Col R
Colnbrook: SL3 . . . . Coln
Cowley: UB8 . . . . Cowl
Cranford: TW4-6,UB3 . . . . Cran
Crayford: DA1 . . . . Cray
Croydon: CR0 . . . . C'don
Dagenham: IG11,RM6,RM8-10 . . . . Dag
Dartford: DA1,DA5 . . . . Dart
Downe: BR6 . . . . Downe
East Barnet: EN4 . . . . E Barn
Eastcote: HA4-5 . . . . Eastc
East Molesey: KT1,KT8,TW12 . . . . E Mos
Edgware: HA8 . . . . Edg
Elstree: WD6 . . . . E'tree
Enfield: EN1-2 . . . . Enf
Enfield Highway: EN3 . . . . Enf H
Enfield Lock: EN3 . . . . Enf L
Enfield Wash: EN3 . . . . Enf W
Epsom: KT19 . . . . Eps
Erith: DA7-8,DA17-18 . . . . Erith
Esher: KT10 . . . . Esh
Ewell: KT17,KT19 . . . . Ewe
Farnborough: BR5-6 . . . . Farnb
Feltham: TW13-14 . . . . Felt
Greenford: UB6 . . . . G'frd
Hadley Wood: EN4 . . . . Had W
Ham: TW10 . . . . Ham
Hampton: TW12 . . . . Hamp
Hampton Hill: TW12 . . . . Hamp H
Hampton Wick: KT1,TW11 . . . . Hamp W
Hanworth: TW13 . . . . Hanw
Harefield: UB9 . . . . Hare
Harlington: UB3,UB7 . . . . Harl
Harmondsworth: UB7 . . . . Harm
Harrow: HA1-3 . . . . Harr
Harrow Weald: HA3 . . . . Hrw W
Hatch End: HA5 . . . . Hat E
Havering-Atte-Bower: RM1 . . . . Have B
Hayes: BR2,BR4,UB3-4 . . . . Hayes
Hersham: KT12 . . . . Hers
Heston: TW5 . . . . Hest
Hextable: BR8 . . . . Hext
Hillingdon: UB4,UB8,UB10 . . . . Hil
Hinchley Wood: KT10 . . . . Hin W
Hounslow: TW3-4,TW7,TW14 . . . . Houn
Ickenham: UB10 . . . . Ick
Ilford: IG1-6,IG8,RM6 . . . . Ilf
Isleworth: TW1,TW3,TW5,TW7 . . . . Isle
Kenton: HA3,HA7,HA9 . . . . Kenton
Keston: BR2 . . . . Kes
Kew: TW9 . . . . Kew
Kingston upon Thames: KT1-2 . . . . King T
Laleham: TW18 . . . . Lale
Langley: SL3 . . . . L'ly
London Heathrow Airport: TW6 . . . . H'row A
Longford: TW6,UB7 . . . . Lford
Loughton: IG9-10 . . . . Lough
Mawney: RM7 . . . . Mawney
Mitcham: CR0,CR4 . . . . Mitc
Morden: SM4 . . . . Mord
New Addington: CR0 . . . . New Ad
New Barnet: EN5 . . . . New Bar
New Malden: KT3 . . . . N Mald
Northolt: UB4-5 . . . . N'olt
Northwood: HA6 . . . . Nwood
Orpington: BR5-6 . . . . Orp
Petts Wood: BR5-6 . . . . Pet W
Pinner: HA5-6 . . . . Pinn
Ponders End: EN3 . . . . Pond E
Poyle: SL3 . . . . Poyle
Pratts Bottom: BR6 . . . . Prat B
Purley: CR8 . . . . Purl
Rainham: RM9,RM13 . . . . Rain
Richings Park: SL0,SL3 . . . . Rich P
Richmond: TW9-10 . . . . Rich
Romford: RM1,RM5,RM7 . . . . Rom
Ruislip: HA4 . . . . Ruis
Rush Green: RM7,RM10 . . . . Rush G
St Mary Cray: BR5-6 . . . . St M Cry
St Pauls Cray: BR5 . . . . St P
Sanderstead: CR2 . . . . Sande
Selsdon: CR0,CR2 . . . . Sels
Shepperton: TW17-18 . . . . Shep
Sidcup: DA14-15,SE9 . . . . Sidc
Sipson: UB7 . . . . Sip
Southall: UB1-2 . . . . S'hall
South Croydon: CR2 . . . . S Croy
Staines: TW18-19 . . . . Staines
Stanmore: HA3,HA7 . . . . Stan
Stanwell: TW6,TW19 . . . . Stanw
Stanwell Moor: TW19 . . . . Stanw M
Stockley Park: UB11 . . . . Stock P
Sunbury: TW16 . . . . Sun
Surbiton: KT1,KT5-6,KT10 . . . . Surb
Sutton: SM1-3 . . . . Sutt
Swanley: BR8,DA14 . . . . Swan
Teddington: TW1,TW11 . . . . Tedd
Thames Ditton: KT7,KT10 . . . . T Ditt
Thornton Heath: CR7 . . . . Thor H
Twickenham: TW1-2,TW7,TW13 . . . . Twick
Uxbridge: UB8,UB10 . . . . Uxb
Waddon: CR0 . . . . Wadd
Wallington: SM5-6 . . . . W'gton
Walton-on-Thames: KT12 . . . . Walt T
Wealdstone: HA3 . . . . W'stone
Welling: DA16 . . . . Well
Wembley: HA0,HA9,NW10 . . . . Wemb
Wennington: RM13 . . . . Wenn
West Drayton: UB7 . . . . W Dray
West Molesey: KT8 . . . . W Mole
West Wickham: BR4 . . . . W W'ck
Weybridge: KT13 . . . . Weyb
Whitton: TW2 . . . . Whitt
Wilmington: DA2 . . . . Wilm
Woodford Green: IG4,IG8-9 . . . . Wfd G
Worcester Park: KT4,SM3 . . . . Wor Pk
Yeading: UB4 . . . . Yead
Yiewsley: UB7 . . . . Yiew

2 Temple Place *2J 13*
(off Temple Pl.)
2 Willow Rd. 4C 64
7 July Memorial 5H 11 (1E 100)
10 Brock St. NW1 . . . . 3A **6**
18 Stafford Terrace *3J 99*
(off Stafford Ter.)
60 St Martins La. *WC2* *2E* ***12***
(off St Martin's La.)
198 Contemporary Arts & Learning *6B 120*
(off Railton Rd.)
201 Bishopsgate EC2 . . . . 5H **9**

A

Aaron Hill Rd. E6 . . . . 5E **88**
Abady Ho. *SW1* *3D* ***18***
(off Page St.)
Abberley M. SW4 . . . . 3F **119**
Abbess Cl. E6 . . . . 5C **88**
SW2 . . . . 1B **138**
Abbeville M. SW4 . . . . 4H **119**
Abbeville Rd. N8 . . . . 5H **47**
SW4 . . . . 6G **119**
Abbey Av. HA0: Wemb 2E **78**
Abbey Cl. E5 . . . . 4G **67**
HA5: Pinn 3K **39**
SW8 . . . . 1H **119**
UB3: Hayes 1K **93**
UB5: N'olt 3D **76**
Abbey Ct. *NW8* *2A* ***82***
(off Abbey Rd.)
SE6 . . . . 6C **122**
SE17 . . . . *5C* ***102***
(off Macleod St.)
TW12: Hamp 7E **130**
Abbey Cres. DA17: Belv 4G **109**
Abbeydale Rd. HA0: Wemb 1F **79**
Abbey Dr. DA2: Wilm 2K **145**
SW17 . . . . 5E **136**
Abbey Est. NW8 . . . . 1K **81**
Abbeyfield Cl. CR4: Mitc 2C **154**
Abbeyfield Est. SE16 . . . . 4J **103**
Abbeyfield Rd. SE16 . . . . 4J **103**
(not continuous)
Abbeyfields Cl. NW10 . . . . 3G **79**
Abbey Gdns. BR7: Chst 1E **160**
NW8 . . . . 2A **82**
SE16 . . . . 4G **103**
SW1 . . . . *1E* ***18***
(off Great College St.)
TW15: Ashf 5D **128**
W6 . . . . 6G **99**
Abbey Gro. SE2 . . . . 4B **108**
Abbeyhill Rd. DA15: Sidc 2C **144**
Abbey Ho. *E15* *2G* ***87***
(off Baker's Row)
NW8 . . . . 1A **4**
Abbey Ind. Est. CR4: Mitc 5D **154**
HA0: Wemb 1F **79**
Abbey La. BR3: Beck 7C **140**
E15 . . . . 2E **86**
(not continuous)
Abbey La. Commercial Est. E15 . . . . 2G **87**
Abbey Leisure Cen. 1G 89
Abbey Life Ct. E16 . . . . 5K **87**
Abbey Lodge NW8 . . . . 2D **4**
Abbey Mansion M. SE24 . . . . 5B **120**
Abbey M. E17 . . . . 5C **50**
TW7: Isle 1B **114**
Abbey Mt. DA17: Belv 5F **109**
Abbey Orchard St.
SW1 . . . . 1D **18** (3H **101**)
Abbey Orchard St. Est.
SW1 . . . . 1D **18** (3H **101**)
(not continuous)
Abbey Pde. *SW19* *7A* ***136***
(off Merton High St.)
W5 . . . . 3F **79**
Abbey Pk. BR3: Beck 7C **140**
Abbey Pk. Ind. Est. IG11: Bark 2G **89**
Abbey Retail Pk. 7F **71**
Abbey Rd. CR0: C'don 3B **168**
DA7: Bex 4E **126**
DA17: Belv 4D **108**
E15 . . . . 2F **87**
EN1: Enf 5K **23**
IG2: Ilf 5H **53**
IG11: Bark 1F **89**
NW6 . . . . 7K **63**
NW8 . . . . 1A **4** (7K **63**)
NW10 . . . . 1H **79**
SE2 . . . . 4D **108**
SW19 . . . . 7A **136**
Abbey Rd. Apts. *NW8* *2A* ***82***
(off Abbey Rd.)
Abbey Sports Cen. 1G 89
Abbey St. E13 . . . . 4J **87**
SE1 . . . . 7H **15** (3E **102**)
SE16 . . . . 7H **15** (3G **103**)
Abbey Ter. SE2 . . . . 4C **108**
Abbey Trad. Est. SE26 . . . . 5B **140**
Abbey Vw. NW7 . . . . 3G **29**
Abbey Wlk. KT8: W Mole 3F **149**
Abbey Wharf Ind. Est. IG11: Bark 3H **89**
ABBEY WOOD 4C 108
Abbey Wood Cvn. Club Site 4C **108**
Abbey Wood Rd. SE2 . . . . 4B **108**
Abbot Cl. HA4: Ruis 3B **58**
Abbot Ct. *SW8* *7J* ***101***
(off Hartington Rd.)
Abbot Ho. *E14* *7D* ***86***
(off Smythe St.)
Abbotsbury *NW1* *7H* ***65***
(off Camley St.)
Abbotsbury Cl. E15 . . . . 2E **86**
W14 . . . . 2G **99**
Abbotsbury Gdns. HA5: Eastc 7A **40**
Abbotsbury Ho. W14 . . . . 2G **99**
Abbotsbury M. SE15 . . . . 3J **121**
Abbotsbury Rd. BR2: Hayes 2H **171**
SM4: Mord 5K **153**
W14 . . . . 2G **99**
Abbots Cl. BR5: Farnb 1G **173**
Abbots Ct. *W8* *2K* ***99***
(off Thackeray St.)
Abbots Dr. HA2: Harr 2E **58**
Abbotsford Av. N15 . . . . 4C **48**
Abbotsford Gdns. IG8: Wfd G 7D **36**
Abbotsford Rd. IG3: Ilf 2A **72**
Abbots Gdns. N2 . . . . 4B **46**
Abbots Grn. CR0: Addtn 6K **169**
Abbotshade Rd. SE16 . . . . 1K **103**
Abbotshall Av. N14 . . . . 3B **32**
Abbotshall Rd. SE6 . . . . 1F **141**
Abbot's Ho. *W14* *3H* ***99***
(off St Mary Abbot's Ter.)
Abbots Lane SE1 . . . . 5H **15**
Abbots La. SE1 . . . . 1E **102**
Abbotsleigh Cl. SM2: Sutt 7K **165**
Abbotsleigh Rd. SW16 . . . . 4G **137**
Abbots Mnr. SW1 . . . . 5J **17** (4F **101**)
(not continuous)
Abbots Pk. SW2 . . . . 1A **138**
Abbot's Pl. NW6 . . . . 1K **81**
Abbot's Rd. E6 . . . . 1B **88**
Abbots Rd. HA8: Edg 7D **28**
Abbots Ter. N8 . . . . 6J **47**
Abbotstone Rd. SW15 . . . . 3E **116**
Abbot St. E8 . . . . 6F **67**
Abbots Wlk. W8 . . . . 3K **99**
Abbots Way BR3: Beck 5A **158**
Abbotswell Rd. SE4 . . . . 5B **122**
Abbotswood Cl. DA17: Belv 3E **108**
Abbotswood Gdns. IG5: Ilf 3D **52**
Abbotswood Rd. SE22 . . . . 4E **120**
SW16 . . . . 3H **137**
Abbotswood Way UB3: Hayes 1K **93**
Abbott Av. SW20 . . . . 1F **153**
Abbott Cl. TW12: Hamp 6C **130**
UB5: N'olt 6D **58**
Abbott Rd. E14 . . . . 5E **86**
(not continuous)
Abbott's Cl. UB8: Cowl 5A **74**
Abbotts Cl. N1 . . . . 6C **66**
RM7: Mawney 3H **55**
SE28 . . . . 7C **90**
Abbotts Cres. E4 . . . . 4A **36**
EN2: Enf 2G **23**
Abbotts Dr. HA0: Wemb 2B **60**
Abbotts Ho. *SW1* *6C* ***18***
(off Aylesford St.)
Abbotts Mead TW10: Ham 4D **132**
Abbottsmede Cl. TW1: Twick 2K **131**
Abbotts Pk. Rd. E10 . . . . 7E **50**
Abbotts Rd. CR4: Mitc 4G **155**
EN5: New Bar 4E **20**
SM3: Cheam 4G **165**
UB1: S'hall 1C **94**
Abbott's Wlk. DA7: Bex 7D **108**
Abbott's Wharf *E14* *6C* ***86***
(off Stainsby Pl.)
Abbotts Wharf Moorings *E14* *6C* ***86***
(off Stainsby Rd.)
Abchurch La. EC4 . . . . 2F **15** (7D **84**)
(not continuous)
Abchurch Yd. EC4 . . . . 2E **14** (7D **84**)
Abdale Rd. W12 . . . . 1D **98**
Abelard Pl. W5 . . . . 3D **96**
Abel Ho. *SE11* *7K* ***19***
(off Kennington Rd.)
Abenglen Ind. Est. UB3: Hayes 2F **93**
Aberavon Rd. E3 . . . . 3A **86**
Abercairn Rd. SW16 . . . . 7G **137**
Aberconway Rd. SM4: Mord 4K **153**
Abercorn Cl. NW7 . . . . 7B **30**
NW8 . . . . 3A **82**
Abercorn Commercial Cen.
HA0: Wemb 1D **78**
Abercorn Cotts. *NW8* *3A* ***82***
(off Abercorn Pl.)
Abercorn Cres. HA2: Harr 1F **59**
Abercorn Dell WD23: B Hea 2B **26**
Abercorn Gdns. HA3: Kenton 7D **42**
RM6: Chad H 6B **54**
Abercorn Gro. HA4: Ruis 4F **39**
Abercorn Mans. *NW8* *2A* ***82***
(off Abercorn Pl.)
Abercorn M. TW10: Rich 5F **115**
Abercorn Pl. NW8 . . . . 3A **82**

A-Z Big London 175

Abercorn Rd.—Aird Ho.

Abercorn Rd. HA7: Stan 7H 27
NW7 7B 30
Abercorn Wlk. NW8 3A 82
Abercorn Way SE1 5G 103
Abercrombie Dr. EN1: Enf 1B 24
Abercrombie Rd. E20 5D 68
Abercrombie St. SW11 2C 118
Aberdale Ct. SE16 2K 103
(off Garter Way)
Aberdare Cl. BR4: W W'ck 2E 170
Aberdare Gdns. NW6 7K 63
NW7 7A 30
Aberdare Rd. EN3: Pond E 4D 24
Aberdeen Cotts. HA7: Stan 7H 27
Aberdeen Ct. W9 4A 4
(off Maida Vale)
Aberdeen La. N5 5C 66
Aberdeen Mans. WC1 3E 6
(off Kenton St.)
Aberdeen Pde. N18 5C 34
(off Aberdeen Rd.)
Aberdeen Pk. N5 5C 66
Aberdeen Pl. NW8 4A 4 (4B 82)
Aberdeen Rd. CR0: C'don 4C 168
HA3: W'stone 2K 41
N5 4C 66
N18 5B 34
(not continuous)
NW10 5B 62
Aberdeen Sq. E14 1B 104
Aberdeen Ter. SE3 2F 123
Aberdeen Wharf E1 1H 103
(off Wapping High St.)
Aberdour Rd. IG3: Ilf 3B 72
Aberdour St. SE1 4E 102
Aberfeldy Ho. SE5 7B 102
(not continuous)
Aberfeldy St. E14 5E 86
(not continuous)
Aberford Gdns. SE18 1C 124
Aberfoyle Rd. SW16 6H 137
(not continuous)
Abergeldie Rd. SE12 6K 123
Abernethy Ho. EC1 6C 8
(off Bartholomew Cl.)
Abernethy Rd. SE13 4G 123
Abersham Rd. E8 5F 67
Abery St. SE18 4J 107
Abid M. SE15 2G 121
Ability Pl. E14 2D 104
Ability Plaza E8 7F 67
(off Arbutus St.)
Ability Towers EC1 1C 8
(off Macclesfield Rd.)
Abingdon W14 4H 99
(off Kensington Village)
Abingdon Cl. KT4: Wor Pk 3D 164
NW1 6H 65
SE1 4F 103
(off Bushwood Dr.)
SW19 6A 136
UB10: Hil 1B 74
Abingdon Ct. W8 3J 99
(off Abingdon Vs.)
Abingdon Gdns. W8 3J 99
Abingdon Ho. BR1: Broml 7K 141
E2 3J 9
(off Boundary St.)
Abingdon Lodge BR2: Broml 2H 159
(off Beckenham La.)
W8 3J 99
Abingdon Mans. W8 3J 99
(off Pater St.)
Abingdon Rd. N3 2A 46
SW16 2J 155
W8 3J 99
Abingdon St. SW1 1E 18 (3J 101)
Abingdon Vs. W8 3J 99
Abinger Cl. BR1: Broml 3C 160
CR0: New Ad 6E 170
IG11: Bark 4A 72
SM6: W'gton 5J 167
Abinger Ct. SM6: W'gton 5J 167
(off Abinger Cl.)
W5 7C 78
Abinger Gdns. TW7: Isle 3J 113
Abinger Gro. SE8 6B 104
Abinger Ho. SE1 7E 14
(off Gt. Dover St.)
Abinger M. W9 4J 81
Abinger Rd. W4 3A 98
Ablett St. SE16 5J 103
Abney Gdns. N16 2F 67
Abney Pk. Cemetery
Local Nature Reserve 2E 66
Abney Pk. Ter. N16 2F 67
(off Cazenove Rd.)
Aborfield NW5 5G 65
Aboyne Dr. SW20 2C 152
Aboyne Rd. NW10 3A 62
SW17 3B 136
Abraham Fisher Ho. E12 5E 70
Abyssinia Cl. SW11 4C 118
Abyssinia Ct. N8 5K 47
Abyssinia Rd. SW11 4C 118
Acacia Av. HA4: Ruis 1J 57
HA9: Wemb 5E 60
N17 7J 33
TW8: Bford 7B 96
TW17: Shep 5C 146
UB3: Hayes 6H 75
UB7: Yiew 7B 74
Acacia Bus. Cen. E11 3G 69
Acacia Cl. BR5: Pet W 5H 161
HA7: Stan 6D 26
SE8 4A 104
SE20 2G 157
Acacia Ct. HA1: Harr 5F 41
Acacia Dr. SM3: Sutt 1H 165
Acacia Gdns. BR4: W W'ck 2E 170
NW8 2B 82
Acacia Gro. KT3: N Mald 3K 151
SE21 2D 138
Acacia Ho. N22 1A 48
(off Douglas Rd.)
Acacia M. UB7: Harm 2E 174
Acacia Pl. NW8 2B 82
Acacia Rd. BR3: Beck 3B 158
CR4: Mitc 3E 154
E11 2G 69
E17 6A 50
EN2: Enf 1J 23
N22 1A 48
NW8 2B 82
Acacia Rd. SW16 1J 155
TW12: Hamp 6E 130
Acacia Rd. W3 7J 79
The Acacias EN4: E Barn 5G 21
Acacia Wlk. SW10 7A 100
(off Tadema Rd.)
Acacia Way DA15: Sidc 1K 143
Academia Way N17 6K 33
The Academy
Middlesex County Cricket Club
2K 45
The Academy SW8 7G 19 (6K 101)
Academy Apts. E8 5H 67
(off Dalston La.)
Academy Bldgs. N1 1G 9
(off Fanshaw St.)
Academy Ct. DA5: Bexl 2K 145
(off Beaconsfield Rd.)
E2 3J 85
(off Kirkwall Pl.)
NW6 1J 81
RM8: Dag 4A 72
Academy Gdns. CR0: C'don 1F 169
UB5: N'olt 2B 76
W8 2J 99
Academy Ho. E3 5D 86
(off Violet Rd.)
Academy Pl. SE18 1D 124
TW7: Isle 1J 113
Academy Rd. SE18 1D 124
Academy Way E17 1C 50
RM8: Dag 4A 72
Acanthus Dr. SE1 5G 103
Acanthus Rd. SW11 3E 118
Accommodation La.
UB7: Harm 2D 174
UB7: Lford 4B 174
Accommodation Rd. E4 3A 36
(off Ashwood Rd.)
KT17: Ewe 5C 164
NW11 1H 63
AC Court KT7: T Ditt 6A 150
Ace Pde. KT9: Chess 3E 162
Acer Av. UB4: Yead 5C 76
Acer Cl. IG8: Wfd G 6H 37
Acer Ct. EN3: Enf H 3F 25
(off Enstone Rd.)
Acer Rd. E8 7F 67
Acers BR7: Chst 7C 142
Aces Ct. TW3: Houn 2G 113
Ace Way SW11 7D 18 (6H 101)
Acfold Rd. SW6 1K 117
Achilles Cl. SE1 5G 103
Achilles Ho. E2 2H 85
(off Old Bethnal Grn. Rd.)
Achilles Rd. NW6 5J 63
Achilles Statue 5H 11 (1E 100)
Achilles St. SE14 7A 104
Achilles Way W1 5H 11 (1E 100)
Acklam Rd. W10 5G 81
(not continuous)
Acklington Dr. NW9 1A 44
Ackmar Rd. SW6 1J 117
Ackroyd Dr. E3 5B 86
Ackroyd Rd. SE23 7K 121
Acland Cl. SE18 7H 107
Acland Cres. SE5 3D 120
Acland Ho. SW9 1K 119
Acland Rd. NW2 6D 62
Acle Cl. IG6: Ilf 1F 53
Acme Studios E14 5E 86
(Gillender St.)
E14 5E 86
(off Leven Rd.)
Acock Gro. UB5: N'olt 4F 59
Acol Ct. NW6 7J 63
Acol Cres. HA4: Ruis 5K 57
Acol Rd. NW6 7J 63
Aconbury Rd. RM9: Dag 1B 90
Acorn Cl. BR7: Chst 5G 143
E4 5J 35
EN2: Enf 1G 23
HA7: Stan 7G 27
TW12: Hamp 6F 131
Acorn Ct. E3 2C 86
(off Morville St.)
E6 7C 70
IG2: Ilf 6J 53
Acorn Gdns. SE19 1F 157
W3 5K 79
Acorn Gro. HA4: Ruis 4H 57
UB3: Harl 7H 93
Acorn Pde. SE15 7H 103
Acorn Production Cen. N7 7J 65
Acorn Wlk. SE16 1A 104
Acorn Way BR3: Beck 5E 158
BR6: Farnb 4F 173
SE23 3K 139
Acqua Ho. TW9: Kew 7H 97
Acre Dr. SE22 4G 121
Acrefield Ho. NW4 4F 45
(off Belle Vue Est.)
Acre La. SM5: Cars 4E 166
SM6: W'gton 4E 166
SW2 4J 119
Acre Path UB5: N'olt 6C 58
(off Arnold Rd.)
Acre Rd. KT2: King T 1E 150
RM10: Dag 7H 73
SW19 6B 136
Acre Way HA6: Nwood 1H 39
Acris St. SW18 5A 118
Acropolis Ho. KT1: King T 3F 151
(off Winery La.)
Actaeon Mews SE18 6F 107
ACTON 1J 97
Acton Apts. N1 1D 84
(off Branch Pl.)
Acton Central Ind. Est. W3 1H 97
Acton Cl. N9 2B 34
ACTON GREEN 3J 97
Acton Hill M. W3 1H 97
Acton Ho. E8 1F 85
(off Lee St.)
W3 6J 79
Acton La. NW10 3J 79
W3 2J 97
W4 4J 97
(not continuous)
Acton M. E8 1F 85
Acton Pk. Est. W3 2K 97
Acton St. WC1 2G 7 (3K 83)
Acton Swimming Baths 1J 97
(off Salisbury St.)
Acton Va. Ind. Pk. W3 2B 98
Acton Wlk. N20 1G 31
Acuba Rd. SW18 2K 135
Acworth Cl. N9 7D 24
Acworth Ho. SE18 6F 107
(off Barnfield Rd.)
Ada Cl. N11 3J 31
Ada Ct. N1 1C 84
(off Packington St.)
W9 2A 4 (3A 82)
Ada Gdns. E14 6F 87
E15 1H 87
Adagio Point SE8 6D 104
(off Copperas St.)
Ada Ho. E2 1G 85
(off Ada Pl.)
Adair Cl. SE25 3H 157
Adair Ho. SW3 7D 16
Adair Rd. W10 4G 81
Adair Twr. W10 4G 81
(off Appleford Rd.)
Ada Kennedy Ct. SE10 7E 104
(off Greenwich Sth. St.)
Ada Lewis Ho. HA9: Wemb 4F 61
Adam & Eve Ct. W1 7B 6
Adam & Eve M. W8 3J 99
Ada Maria Ct. E1 6H 85
(off James Voller Way)
Adam Cl. NW7 6A 30
SE6 4B 140
Adam Ct. SE11 4K 19
SW7 4A 100
(off Gloucester Rd.)
Adamfields NW3 7B 64
(off Adamson Rd.)
Adam Rd. E4 6G 35
Adams Bri. Bus. Cen. HA9: Wemb 5H 61
Adams Cl. KT5: Surb 6F 151
N3 7D 30
NW9 2H 61
RM5: Col R 1J 55
Adams Ct. E17 6A 50
EC2 7F 9 (6E 84)
Adams Gdns. Est. SE16 2J 103
Adams Ho. E14 6F 87
(off Aberfeldy St.)
Adams M. N22 7E 32
SW17 2D 136
Adamson Ct. N2 3C 46
Adamson Rd. E16 6J 87
NW3 7B 64
Adamson Way BR3: Beck 5E 158
Adams Pl. E14 1D 104
(off The Nth. Colonnade)
N7 5K 65
Adams Quarter TW8: Bford 7C 96
Adamsrill Cl. EN1: Enf 6J 23
Adamsrill Rd. SE26 4K 139
Adams Rd. BR3: Beck 5A 158
N17 2D 48
Adam's Row W1 3H 11 (7E 82)
Adams Sq. DA6: Bex 3E 126
Adams Ter. E3 3C 86
(off Rainhill Way)
Adam St. WC2 3F 13 (7J 83)
Adams Wlk. KT1: King T 2E 150
Adams Way CR0: C'don 6F 157
SE25 5H 157
Adam Wlk. SW6 7E 98
Adana SE13 2E 122
Ada Pl. E2 1G 85
Adare Wlk. SW16 3K 137
Ada Rd. HA0: Wemb 3D 60
SE5 7E 102
Adastral Ho. WC1 5G 7
(off Harpur St.)
Adastra Way SM6: W'gton 6J 167
Ada St. E8 1H 85
Adcock Wlk. BR6: Orp 4K 173
Adderley Gdns. SE9 4E 142
Adderley Gro. SW11 5E 118
Adderley Rd. HA3: W'stone 1K 41
Adderley St. E14 6E 86
Addey Ho. SE8 7B 104
ADDINGTON 5C 170
Addington Cl. UB2: S'hall 1H 95
Addington Ct. SW14 3K 115
Addington Court Golf Course 7C 170
Addington Dr. N12 6G 31
The Addington Golf Course 4B 170
Addington Gro. SE26 4A 140
Addington Ho. SW9 2K 119
(off Stockwell Rd.)
Addington Lofts SE5 7C 102
(off Bethwin Rd.)
Addington Palace Golf Course 6A 170
Addington Rd. BR4: W W'ck 4E 170
CR0: C'don 1A 168
CR2: Sande, Sels 7K 169
E3 3C 86
E16 4G 87
N4 6A 48
Addington Sq. SE5 6D 102
(not continuous)
Addington St. SE1 7H 13 (2K 101)
Addington Village Rd.
CR0: Addtn 6B 170
(not continuous)
Addis Cl. EN3: Enf H 1E 24
ADDISCOMBE 1G 169
Addiscombe Av. CR0: C'don 1G 169
Addiscombe Cl. HA3: Kenton 5C 42
Addiscombe Ct. Rd. CR0: C'don 1E 168
Addiscombe Gro. CR0: C'don 2E 168
Addiscombe Rd. CR0: C'don 2D 168
(not continuous)
Addis Ho. E1 5J 85
(off Lindley St.)
Addisland Ct. W14 2G 99
(off Holland Vs. Rd.)
Addison Av. N14 6A 22
TW3: Houn 1G 113
W11 1G 99
Addison Bri. Pl. W14 4H 99
Addison Cl. BR5: Pet W 6G 161
HA6: Nwood 1J 39
Addison Ct. NW6 1J 81
(off Brondesbury Rd.)
Addison Cres. W14 3G 99
(not continuous)
Addison Dr. SE12 5K 123
Addison Gdns. KT5: Surb 4F 151
W14 3F 99
Addison Gro. W4 3A 98
Addison Ho. NW8 1A 4
Addison Pk. Mans. W14 3F 99
(off Richmond Way)
Addison Pl. SE25 4G 157
UB1: S'hall 7E 76
W11 1G 99
Addison Rd. BR2: Broml 5A 160
E11 6J 51
E17 5D 50
EN3: Enf H 1D 24
IG6: Ilf 1G 53
SE25 4G 157
TW11: Tedd 6B 132
W14 2G 99
Addisons Cl. CR0: C'don 2B 170
Addison Ter. W4 4J 97
(off Chiswick Rd.)
Addison Way HA6: Nwood 1H 39
NW11 4H 45
UB3: Hayes 6J 75
Addle Hill EC4 1B 14 (6B 84)
Addlestone Ho. W10 5E 80
(off Sutton Way)
Addle St. EC2 7D 8 (6C 84)
Addy Ho. SE16 4J 103
Adecroft Way KT8: W Mole 3G 149
Adela Av. KT3: N Mald 5D 152
Adela Ho. W6 5E 98
(off Queen Caroline St.)
Adelaide Av. SE4 4B 122
Adelaide Cl. EN1: Enf 1K 23
HA7: Stan 4F 27
SW9 4A 120
Adelaide Community Gdn. 7D 64
(off Adelaide Rd.)
Adelaide Ct. BR3: Beck 7C 140
E9 5A 68
(off Kenworthy Rd.)
NW8 2A 82
(off Abbey Rd.)
W7 2K 95
Adelaide Gdns. RM6: Chad H 5E 54
Adelaide Gro. W12 1C 98
Adelaide Ho. E15 2H 87
E17 2B 50
SE5 2E 120
W11 6H 81
(off Portobello Rd.)
Adelaide Rd. BR7: Chst 5F 143
E10 3D 68
IG1: Ilf 2F 71
KT6: Surb 5E 150
NW3 7B 64
SW18 5J 117
TW5: Hest 1C 112
TW9: Rich 4F 115
TW11: Tedd 6K 131
TW15: Ashf 5A 128
UB2: S'hall 4C 94
W13 1A 96
Adelaide St. WC2 3E 12 (7J 83)
(not continuous)
Adelaide Ter. TW8: Bford 5D 96
Adela St. W10 4G 81
Adelina Gro. E1 5J 85
Adelina M. SW12 1H 137
Adelina Yd. E1 5J 85
(off Adelina Gro.)
Adeline Pl. WC1 6D 6 (5H 83)
Adeliza Cl. IG11: Bark 7G 71
Adelphi Ct. E8 7F 67
(off Celandine Dr.)
SE16 2K 103
(off Garter Way)
W4 6K 97
Adelphi Cres. UB4: Hayes 3G 75
Adelphi Ter. WC2 3F 13 (7J 83)
Adelphi Theatre 3F 13
(off Strand)
Adelphi Way UB4: Hayes 3H 75
Adeney Cl. W6 6F 99
Aden Gro. N16 4D 66
Adenmore Rd. SE6 7C 122
Aden Rd. EN3: Brim 4F 25
IG1: Ilf 7G 53
Aden Ter. N16 4D 66
Adeyfield Ho. EC1 2F 9
(off Cranwood St.)
Adie Rd. W6 3E 98
Adine Rd. E13 4K 87
Adler Ind. Est. UB3: Hayes 2F 93
Adler St. E1 6G 85
Adley St. E5 5A 68
Adlington Cl. N18 5J 33
Admaston Rd. SE18 7G 107
Admiral Ct. IG11: Bark 2B 90
SE5 1E 120
(off Havil St.)
SM5: Cars 1C 166
SW10 1A 118
(off Admiral Sq.)
W1 6G 5
(off Blandford St.)
Admiral Ho. SW1 3B 18
(off Willow Pl.)
TW11: Tedd 4A 132
Admiral Hyson Ind. Est. SE16 5H 103
Admiral M. SW19 7A 136
W10 4F 81
Admiral Pl. N8 4B 48
SE16 1A 104
Admirals Cl. E18 4K 51
Admirals Ct. E6 6F 89
(off Trader Rd.)
SE1 5J 15
(off Horselydown La.)
Admiral Seymour Rd. SE9 4D 124
Admiral's Ga. SE10 1D 122
Admiral Sq. SW10 1A 118
Admiral's Twr. SE10 6D 104
(off Dowells St.)
Admiral St. SE8 2C 122
Admirals Wlk. NW3 3A 64
Admirals Way E14 2C 104
Admiralty & Commercial Court
7J 7 (6A 84)
Admiralty Arch 4D 12 (1H 101)
Admiralty Av. E16 2K 105
Admiralty Bldg. KT2: King T 1D 150
(off Down Hall Rd.)
Admiralty Cl. SE8 7C 104
UB7: W Dray 2A 92
Admiralty Ho. E1 7G 85
(off Vaughan Way)
Admiralty Rd. TW11: Tedd 6K 131
Admiralty Way TW11: Tedd 6K 131
Admiral Wlk. W9 5J 81
Adolf St. SE6 4D 140
Adolphus Rd. N4 2B 66
Adolphus St. SE8 7B 104
Adomar Rd. RM8: Dag 3E 72
Adpar St. W2 5A 4 (5B 82)
Adrian Av. NW2 1D 62
Adrian Boult Ho. E2 3H 85
(off Mansford St.)
Adrian Cl. EN5: Barn 6A 20
Adrian Ho. E15 7F 69
(off Jupp Rd.)
N1 1K 83
(off Barnsbury Est.)
SW8 7J 101
(off Wyvil Rd.)
Adrian M. SW10 6K 99
Adriatic Apts. E16 7J 87
(off Western Gateway)
Adriatic Bldg. E14 7A 86
(off Horseferry Rd.)
Adriatic Ho. E1 4K 85
(off Ernest St.)
Adrienne Av. UB1: S'hall 4D 76
Adrienne Bus. Cen.
UB1: S'hall 3D 76
Adron Ho. SE16 4J 103
(off Millender Wlk.)
Adstock Ho. N1 7B 66
(off The Sutton Est.)
Advance Rd. SE27 4C 138
Adventure Kingdom 2K 159
(off Stockwell Cl.)
Adventurers Ct. E14 7F 87
(off Newport Av.)
Advent Way N18 5D 34
Adys Lawn NW2 6D 62
Ady's Rd. SE15 3F 121
Aegean Apts. E16 7J 87
(off Western Gateway)
Aegon Ho. E14 3D 104
(off Lanark Sq.)
Aerodrome Rd. NW9 2B 44
Aerodrome Way TW5: Hest 6A 94
Aeroville NW9 2A 44
AFC Wimbledon 3G 151
AFC Wimbledon Plough La. Stadium
4A 136
Affleck St. N1 1G 7 (2K 83)
Afghan Rd. SW11 2C 118
Afsil Ho. EC1 6K 7
(off Viaduct Bldgs.)
Aftab Ter. E1 4H 85
(off Tent St.)
Agamemnon Rd. NW6 4H 63
Agar Cl. KT6: Surb 2F 163
Agar Gro. NW1 7G 65
Agar Gro. Est. NW1 7H 65
Agar Ho. KT1: King T 3E 150
(off Denmark Rd.)
Agar Pl. NW1 7G 65
Agar St. WC2 3E 12 (7J 83)
Agate Cl. E16 6B 88
NW10 3G 79
Agate Rd. W6 3E 98
Agatha Cl. E1 1H 103
Agaton Path SE9 2G 143
Agaton Rd. SE9 2G 143
Agave Rd. NW2 4E 62
Agdon St. EC1 3A 8 (4B 84)
Ager Av. RM8: Dag 1D 72
Agincourt Rd. NW3 4D 64
Agnes Av. IG1: Ilf 4E 70
Agnes Cl. E6 7E 88
Agnesfield Cl. N12 6H 31
Agnes Gdns. RM8: Dag 4D 72
Agnes George Wlk. E16 1B 106
Agnes Ho. W11 7F 81
(off St Ann's Rd.)
Agnes Rd. W3 1B 98
Agnes St. E14 6B 86
Agnew Rd. SE23 7K 121
Agricola Ct. E3 1B 86
(off Parnell Rd.)
Agricola Pl. EN1: Enf 5A 24
The Ahoy Cen. 5C 104
(off Stretton Mans.)
Aidan Cl. RM8: Dag 4E 72
Aigburth Mans. SW9 7A 102
(off Mowll St.)
Ailantus Ct. HA8: Edg 5A 28
Aileen Wlk. E15 7H 69
Ailsa Av. TW1: Twick 5A 114
Ailsa Ho. E16 7E 88
(off University Way)
Ailsa Rd. TW1: Twick 5B 114
Ailsa St. E14 5E 86
Ainger M. NW3 7D 64
(off Ainger Rd.)
Ainger Rd. NW3 7D 64
Ainsdale NW1 1A 6
(off Harrington St.)
Ainsdale Cl. BR6: Orp 1H 173
Ainsdale Cres. HA5: Pinn 3E 40
Ainsdale Dr. SE1 5G 103
Ainsdale Rd. W5 4D 78
Ainsley Av. RM7: Rom 6H 55
Ainsley Cl. N9 1K 33
Ainsley St. E2 3H 85
Ainslie Ct. HA0: Wemb 2E 78
Ainslie Wlk. SW12 7F 119
Ainslie Wood Cres. E4 5J 35
Ainslie Wood Gdns. E4 4J 35
Ainslie Wood
Local Nature Reserve 5J 35
Ainslie Wood Rd. E4 5H 35
Ainsty Est. SE16 2K 103
Ainsty St. SE16 2J 103
Ainsworth Cl. N20 2G 31
NW2 3C 62
SE15 2E 120
Ainsworth Ct. NW10 3D 80
(off Plough Cl.)
Ainsworth Ho. NW8 1K 81
(off Ainsworth Way)
W10 3G 81
(off Kilburn La.)
Ainsworth Rd. CR0: C'don 1B 168
E9 7J 67
Ainsworth Way NW8 1A 82
Aintree Av. E6 1C 88
Aintree Cl. UB8: Hil 6D 74
Aintree Cres. IG6: Ilf 2G 53
Aintree Est. SW6 7G 99
Aintree Rd. UB6: G'frd 2B 78
Aintree St. SW6 7G 99
Airbourne Ho. SM6: W'gton 4G 167
(off Maldon Rd.)
Air Call Bus. Cen. NW9 3K 43
Airco Cl. NW9 3K 43
Aird Ho. SE1 3C 102
(off Rockingham St.)

Aird Point—Alfoxton Av.

Aird Point E16 7G 89
(off Lock Side Way)
Airdrie Cl. N1 7K 65
UB4: Yead 5C 76
Airedale Av. W4 4B 98
Airedale Av. Sth. W4 5B 98
Airedale Rd. SW12 7D 118
W5 3C 96
Airlie Gdns. IG1: Ilf 1F 71
W8 1J 99
Airlinks Golf Course 5A 94
Air Links Ind. Est. TW13: Hanw 3C 130
Airlinks Ind. Est. TW5: Cran 5A 94
Air Pk. Way TW13: Felt 2K 129
Airport Bowl 1G 111
Airport Ga. Bus. Cen. UB7: Sip 7B 92
Airport Way TW19: Stanw M 7A 174
Air Sea M. TW2: Twick 2H 131
Air St. W1 3B 12 (7G 83)
Airthrie Rd. IG3: Ilf 2B 72
Aisgill Av. W14 5H 99
(not continuous)
Aisher Rd. SE28 7C 90
Aislibie Rd. SE12 4G 123
Aiten Pl. W6 4C 98
Aithan Ho. E14 6B 86
(off Copenhagen Pl.)
Aitken Cl. CR4: Mitc 7D 154
E8 1G 85
HA4: Eastc 6J 39
Aitken Rd. SE6 2D 140
Aitman Dr. TW8: Bford 5G 97
Aitons Ho. TW8: Bford 5E 96
Aits Vw. KT8: W Mole 3F 149
Ajax Av. NW9 3A 44
Ajax Ho. E2 2H 85
(off Old Bethnal Grn. Rd.)
Ajax Rd. NW6 4H 63
Akabusi Cl. CR0: C'don 6G 157
Akbar Ho. E14 4D 104
(off Cahir St.)
Akehurst St. SW15 6C 116
Akenside Rd. NW3 5B 64
Akerman Rd. KT6: Surb 6C 150
SW9 2B 120
Akintaro Ho. SE8 6B 104
(off Alverton St.)
Alabama St. SE18 7H 107
Alacia Ct. W3 3J 97
(off Bassington Rd.)
Alacross Rd. W5 2C 96
Alamaro Lodge SE10 3H 105
(off Teal St.)
Alameda Pl. E3 2B 86
Alana Hgts. E4 7J 25
Alan Coren Cl. NW2 4E 62
Alandale Dr. HA5: Pinn 1K 39
Aland Ct. SE16 3A 104
Alander M. E17 4E 50
Alan Dr. EN5: Barn 6B 20
Alan Gdns. RM7: Rush G 7G 55
Alan Hocken Way E15 2G 87
Alan Preece Ct. NW6 7F 63
Alan Rd. SW19 5G 135
Alanthus Cl. SE12 6J 123
Alaska Apts. E16 7J 87
(off Western Gateway)
Alaska Bldg. SE13 1D 122
(off Deal's Gateway)
Alaska Bldgs. SE1 3F 103
Alaska St. SE1 5J 13 (1A 102)
Alastor Ho. E14 3E 104
(off Strattondale Ho.)
Alba Cl. UB4: Yead 4B 76
Albacore Cres. SE13 6D 122
Albacore Way UB3: Hayes 7H 75
Alba Gdns. NW11 6G 45
Albain Cres. TW15: Ashf 2A 128
Alba M. SW18 2J 135
Alban Highwalk EC2 7D 8
(not continuous)
The Albany 7C 104
Albany N12 6E 30
W1 3A 12 (7G 83)
The Albany IG8: Wfd G 4C 36
Albany Cl. DA5: Bexl 7C 126
N15 4B 48
SW14 4H 115
UB10: Ick 5C 56
Albany Ct. E1 6G 85
(off Plumber's Row)
E4 6H 25
(Chelwood Cl.)
E4 5G 35
(Westward Rd.)
E10 7C 50
HA8: Edg 1K 43
NW8 1A 4
(off Abbey Rd.)
NW10 3D 80
(off Trenmar Gdns.)
TW15: Ashf 7E 128
Albany Ctyd. W1 3B 12 (7G 83)
Albany Cres. HA8: Edg 7B 28
Albany Mans. SW11 7C 100
Albany M. BR1: Broml 6J 141
KT2: King T 6D 132
N1 7A 66
SE5 6C 102
SM1: Sutt 5K 165
Albany Pde. TW8: Bford 6E 96
Albany Pk. Av. EN3: Enf W 1D 24
Albany Pk. Rd. KT2: King T 6D 132
Albany Pas. TW10: Rich 5E 114
Albany Pl. TW8: Bford 6D 96
Albany Reach KT7: T Ditt 5K 149
Albany Rd. BR7: Chst 5F 143
DA5: Bexl 7C 126
DA17: Belv 6F 109
E10 7C 50
E12 4B 70
E17 6A 50
KT3: N Mald 4K 151
N4 6A 48
N18 5D 34
RM6: Chad H 6F 55
SE5 6C 102
SW19 5K 135
TW8: Bford 6D 96
TW10: Rich 5F 115
W13 7B 78
Albany St. NW1 1K 5 (2F 83)
Albany Ter. NW1 4K 5
TW10: Rich 5F 115
(off Albany Pas.)
Albany Vw. IG9: Buck H 1D 36
Albany Works E3 1A 86
(off Gunmakers La.)
Alba Pl. W11 6H 81
Albatross NW9 2B 44
Albatross Cl. E6 5D 88
Albatross St. SE18 7J 107
Albatross Way SE16 2K 103
Albemarle SW19 2F 135
Albemarle App. IG2: Ilf 6F 53
Albemarle Av. TW2: Whitt 1D 130
Albemarle Ct. N17 3H 49
(off Perkyn Sq.)
Albemarle Gdns. IG2: Ilf 6F 53
KT3: N Mald 4K 151
Albemarle Ho. SE8 4B 104
(off Foreshore)
Albemarle Pk. BR3: Beck 1D 158
HA7: Stan 5H 27
Albemarle Rd. BR3: Beck 1D 158
EN4: E Barn 7H 21
Albemarle St. W1 3K 11 (7F 83)
Albemarle Wlk. SW9 3A 120
Albemarle Way EC1 4A 8 (4B 84)
Alberon Gdns. NW11 4H 45
Alberta Av. SM1: Sutt 4G 165
Alberta Est. SE17 5B 102
(off Alberta St.)
Alberta Ho. UB4: Yead 3K 75
(off Ayles Rd.)
Alberta Rd. DA8: Erith 1J 127
EN1: Enf 6A 24
Alberta St. SE17 5B 102
Albert Av. E4 4H 35
SW8 7K 101
Albert Barnes Ho. SE1 3C 102
(off New Kent Rd.)
Albert Basin 7F 89
Albert Basin Way E16 7G 89
Albert Bigg Point E15 2E 86
(off Godfrey St.)
ALBERT BRI. 7D 16 (6C 100)
Albert Bri. Rd. SW11 7C 100
Albert Carr Gdns. SW16 5J 137
Albert Cl. E9 1H 85
N22 1H 47
Albert Cotts. E1 5G 85
(off Deal St.)
Albert Ct. E7 4J 69
SW7 7A 10 (3B 100)
Albert Ct. Ga. SW1 7E 10
(off Knightsbridge)
Albert Cres. E4 4H 35
Albert Dane Cen. UB2: S'hall 3C 94
Albert Dr. SW19 2G 135
Albert Emb. SE1 6F 19 (5J 101)
(Kennington La.)
SE1 1G 19 (3K 101)
(Lambeth Pal. Rd.)
Albert Gdns. E1 6K 85
Albert Ga. SW1 6F 11 (2D 100)
Albert Gray Ho. SW10 7B 100
(off Worlds End Est.)
Albert Gro. SW20 1F 153
Albert Hall Mans.
SW7 7B 10 (2B 100)
Albert Ho. E18 3K 51
(off Albert Rd.)
SE28 3G 107
Albert Mans. CR0: C'don 1D 168
(off Lansdowne Rd.)
SW11 1D 118
(off Albert Bri. Rd.)
Albert Memorial 6A 10 (2B 100)
Albert M. E14 7A 86
(off Northey St.)
N4 1K 65
SE4 4A 122
W8 3A 100
Albert Pal. Mans. SW11 1F 119
(off Lurline Gdns.)
Albert Pl. N3 1J 45
N17 3F 49
W8 3K 99
Albert Rd. BR2: Broml 5B 160
CR4: Mitc 3D 154
DA5: Bexl 6G 127
DA17: Belv 5F 109
E10 2E 68
E16 1C 106
E17 5C 50
E18 3K 51
EN4: E Barn 4F 21
HA2: Harr 3G 41
IG1: Ilf 3F 71
IG9: Buck H 2G 37
KT1: King T 2F 151
KT3: N Mald 4B 152
N4 1K 65
N15 6E 48
N22 1G 47
NW4 4F 45
NW6 2H 81
NW7 5G 29
RM8: Dag 1G 73
SE9 3C 142
SE20 6K 139
SE25 4G 157
SM1: Sutt 5B 166
TW1: Twick 1K 131
TW3: Houn 4E 112
TW10: Rich 5E 114
TW11: Tedd 6K 131
TW12: Hamp H 5G 131
TW15: Ashf 5B 128
UB2: S'hall 3B 94
UB3: Hayes 3G 93
UB7: Yiew 1A 92
W5 4B 78
Albert Rd. Est. DA17: Belv 5F 109
Alberts Ct. NW1 3D 4
Albert Sleet Ct. N9 3C 34
(off Colthurst Dr.)
Albert Sq. E15 5G 69
SW8 7K 101
Albert Starr Ho. SE8 4K 103
(off Haddonfield)
Albert St. N12 5F 31
NW1 1F 83
Albert Studios SW11 1D 118
Albert Ter. IG9: Buck H 2H 37
NW1 1E 82
NW10 1J 79
W5 4B 78
W6 5C 98
(off Beavor La.)
Albert Ter. M. NW1 1E 82
Albert Victoria Ho. N22 1A 48
Albert Wlk. E16 2E 106
Albert Way SE15 7H 103
Albert Westcott Ho. SE17 5B 102
Albert Whicher Ho. E17 4E 50
Albert Yd. SE19 6F 139
Albery Ct. E8 7F 67
(off Middleton Rd.)
Albion Av. N10 1E 46
SW8 2H 119
Albion Bldgs. N1 2J 83
(off Albion Yd.)
Albion Cl. RM7: Rom 6K 55
W2 2D 10 (7C 82)
Albion Ct. SE10 4G 105
(off Azof St.)
SM2: Sutt 7B 166
W6 4D 98
(off Albion Pl.)
Albion Dr. E8 7F 67
Albion Est. SE16 2K 103
Albion Gdns. W6 4D 98
Albion Ga. W2 2D 10
(not continuous)
Albion Gro. N16 4E 66
Albion Ho. E16 1F 107
(off Church St.)
SE8 7C 104
(off Watsons St.)
Albion M. N1 1A 84
NW6 7H 63
W2 2D 10 (7C 82)
W6 4D 98
Albion Pde. N16 4D 66
Albion Pl. EC1 5A 8 (5B 84)
EC2 6F 9 (5D 84)
W6 4D 98
Albion Riverside Bldg. SW11 7C 100
Albion Rd. DA6: Bex 4F 127
E17 3E 50
KT2: King T 1J 151
N16 4D 66
N17 2G 49
SM2: Sutt 6B 166
TW2: Twick 1J 131
TW3: Houn 4E 112
UB3: Hayes 6G 75
Albion Sq. E8 7F 67
(not continuous)
Albion St. CR0: C'don 1B 168
SE16 2J 103
W2 1D 10 (6C 82)
Albion Ter. E4 4J 25
E8 7F 67
Albion Vs. Rd. SE26 3J 139
Albion Wlk. N1 1F 7
(off York Way)
Albion Way E6 1B 88
EC1 6C 8 (5C 84)
HA9: Wemb 3G 61
SE13 4E 122
Albion Yd. E1 5H 85
N1 2J 83
Albon Ho. SW18 6K 117
(off Neville Gill Cl.)
Albrighton Rd. SE22 3E 120
Albuhera Cl. EN2: Enf 1F 23
Albuhera M. NW7 5A 30
Albury Av. DA7: Bex 2E 126
TW7: Isle 7K 95
Albury Cl. TW12: Hamp 6F 131
Albury Ct. CR0: C'don 4C 168
(off Tanfield Rd.)
CR4: Mitc 2B 154
SE8 6C 104
(off Albury St.)
SM1: Sutt 4A 166
UB5: N'olt 3A 76
(off Canberra Dr.)
Albury Dr. HA5: Pinn 1A 40, 1C 40
Albury Ho. SE1 7B 14
(off Boyfield St.)
Albury M. E12 2A 70
Albury Rd. KT9: Chess 5E 162
Albury St. SE8 6C 104
Albyfield BR1: Broml 4D 160
Albyn Rd. SE8 1C 122
Alcester Ct. SM6: W'gton 4F 167
Alcester Cres. E5 2H 67
Alcester Rd. SM6: W'gton 4F 167
Alcock Cl. SM6: W'gton 7H 167
Alcock Rd. TW5: Hest 7B 94
Alconbury DA6: Bex 5H 127
Alconbury Rd. E5 2G 67
Alcorn Cl. SM3: Sutt 2J 165
Alcott Cl. TW14: Felt 1H 129
W7 5K 77
Alcuin Ct. HA7: Stan 7H 27
Aldam Pl. N16 2F 67
Aldborough Ct. IG2: Ilf 5K 53
(off Aldborough Rd. Nth.)
Aldborough Hall Equestrian Cen. 3K 53
ALDBOROUGH HATCH 4K 53
Aldborough Rd. RM10: Dag 6J 73
Aldborough Rd. Nth. IG2: Ilf 5K 53
Aldborough Rd. Sth. IG3: Ilf 1J 71
Aldbourne Rd. W12 1B 98
Aldbridge St. SE17 5E 102
Aldburgh M. W1 7H 5 (6E 82)
Aldbury Av. HA9: Wemb 7H 61
Aldbury Ho. SW3 5C 16
(off Cale St.)
Aldbury M. N9 7J 23
Aldebert Ter. SW8 7J 101
Aldeburgh Cl. E5 2H 67
Aldeburgh Pl. IG8: Wfd G 4D 36
SE10 4J 105
(off Aldeburgh St.)
Aldeburgh St. SE10 5J 105
Alden Av. E15 3H 87
Alden Ct. CR0: C'don 3E 168
Aldenham Dr. UB8: Hil 4D 74
Aldenham Ho. NW1 1B 6
(off Aldenham St.)
Aldenham St. NW1 1C 6 (2G 83)
Alden Ho. E8 1H 85
(off Duncan Rd.)
Aldensley Rd. W6 3D 98
Alderbrook Rd. SW12 6F 119
Alderbury Rd. SW13 6C 98
Alder Cl. DA18: Erith 2F 109
SE15 6F 103
Alder Ct. E7 5J 69
N11 6B 32
Alder Gro. NW2 2C 62
Aldergrove Gdns. TW3: Houn 2C 112
Alder Ho. E3 1B 86
(off Hornbeam Sq.)
NW3 6D 64
SE4 3C 122
SE15 6F 103
(off Alder Cl.)
Alder Lodge SW6 1E 116
Alderman Av. IG11: Bark 3A 90
Aldermanbury EC2 7D 8 (6C 84)
Aldermanbury Sq. EC2 6D 8 (5C 84)
Alderman Judge Mall
KT1: King T 2E 150
(off Eden St.)
Aldermans Hill N13 4D 32
Aldermans Ho. E9 5A 68
(off Ward La.)
Aldermans Wlk. EC2 6G 9 (5E 84)
Aldermary Rd. BR1: Broml 1J 159
Alder M. N19 2G 65
Aldermoor Rd. SE6 3B 140
Alderney Av. TW5: Hest, Isle 7F 95
Alderney Cl. NW9 3C 44
Alderney Ct. SE10 6F 105
(off Trafalgar Rd.)
Alderney Gdns. UB5: N'olt 7D 58
Alderney Ho. EN3: Enf W 1E 24
N1 6C 66
(off Arran Wlk.)
Alderney M. SE1 3D 102
Alderney Rd. E1 4K 85
Alderney St. SW1 4K 17 (4F 101)
Alder Rd. DA14: Sidc 3K 143
SW14 3K 115
The Alders BR4: W W'ck 1D 170
N21 6F 23
SW16 4G 137
TW5: Hest 6D 94
TW13: Hanw 4C 130
Alders Av. IG8: Wfd G 6B 36
ALDERSBROOK 2K 69
Aldersbrook Av. EN1: Enf 2K 23
Aldersbrook Dr. KT2: King T 6F 133
Aldersbrook La. E12 3D 70
Aldersbrook Rd. E11 2K 69
E12 2K 69
Alders Cl. E11 2K 69
HA8: Edg 5D 28
W5 3D 96
Aldersey Gdns. IG11: Bark 6H 71
Aldersford Cl. SE4 5K 121
Aldersgate Ct. EC1 6C 8
(off Bartholomew Cl.)
Aldersgate St. EC1 5C 8 (5C 84)
Alders Gro. KT8: E Mos 5H 149
Aldersgrove Av. SE9 3B 142
Aldershot Rd. NW6 1H 81
Aldershot Ter. SE18 7E 106
Aldersmead Av. CR0: C'don 6K 157
Aldersmead Rd. BR3: Beck 7A 140
Alderson Pl. UB2: S'hall 1G 95
Alderson St. W10 4G 81
Alders Rd. HA8: Edg 5D 28
Alderton Cl. NW10 3K 61
Alderton Ct. KT8: W Mole 4D 148
(off Dunstable Rd.)
Alderton Cres. NW4 5D 44
Alderton Rd. CR0: C'don 7F 157
SE24 3C 120
Alderton Way NW4 5D 44
Alderville Rd. SW6 2H 117
Alder Wlk. IG1: Ilf 5G 71
Alderwick Ct. N7 6K 65
(off Cornelia St.)
Alderwick Dr. TW3: Houn 3H 113
Alderwood M. EN4: Had W 1F 21
Alderwood Rd. SE9 6H 125
Aldford Ho. W1 4G 11
(off Park St.)
Aldford St. W1 4H 11 (1E 100)
ALDGATE 7J 9
Aldgate E1 6F 85
(off Whitechapel High St.)
EC3 1J 15 (6F 85)
Aldgate Av. E1 7J 9 (6F 85)
Aldgate Barrs E1 7K 9
Aldgate High St. EC3 1J 15 (6F 85)
Aldgate Pl. E1 7K 9 (6F 85)
Aldgate Sq. EC3 1J 15 (6F 85)
Aldgate Twr. E1 6F 85
Aldham Ho. SE4 2B 122
(off Malpas Rd.)
Aldine Ct. W12 2E 98
(off Aldine St.)
Aldine Pl. W12 2E 98
Aldine St. W12 2E 98
Aldington Cl. RM8: Dag 1C 72
Aldington Ct. E8 7G 67
(off London Flds. W. Side)
Aldington Rd. SE18 3B 106
Aldis M. SW17 5C 136
Aldis St. SW17 5C 136
Aldred Rd. NW6 5J 63
Aldren Rd. SW17 3A 136
Aldrich Cres. CR0: New Ad 7E 170
Aldriche Way E4 6K 35
Aldrich Gdns. SM3: Cheam 3H 165
Aldrich Ter. SW18 2A 136
Aldrick Ho. N1 1K 83
(off Barnsbury Est.)
Aldridge Av. HA4: Ruis 2A 58
HA7: Stan 1E 42
HA8: Edg 3C 28
Aldridge Ct. W11 5H 81
(off Aldridge Rd. Vs.)
Aldridge Ri. KT3: N Mald 7A 152
Aldridge Rd. Vs. W11 5H 81
Aldridge Wlk. N14 7D 22
Aldrington Rd. SW16 5G 137
Aldsworth Cl. W9 4K 81
Aldwick Cl. SE9 3H 143
Aldwick Rd. CR0: Bedd 3K 167
Aldworth Gro. SE13 6E 122
Aldworth Rd. E15 7G 69
Aldwych WC2 2G 13 (6K 83)
Aldwych Av. IG6: Ilf 4G 53
Aldwych Bldgs. WC2 7F 7
(off Parker M.)
Aldwych Ct. E8 7F 67
(off Middleton Rd.)
Aldwych Theatre 1G 13
(off Aldwych)
Aldwyn Ho. SW8 7J 101
(off Davidson Gdns.)
Alers Rd. DA6: Bex 5D 126
Alesia Cl. N22 7D 32
Alestan Beck Rd. E16 6B 88
Alexa Ct. SM2: Sutt 6J 165
W8 4J 99
Alexander Av. NW10 7D 62
Alexander Cl. BR2: Hayes 1J 171
DA15: Sidc 6J 125
EN4: E Barn 4G 21
TW2: Twick 2J 131
UB2: S'hall 1G 95
Alexander Ct. BR3: Beck 1F 159
HA7: Stan 3F 43
TW16: Sun 6H 129
Alexander Evans M. SE23 2K 139
Alexander Fleming Laboratory Mus.
7B 4 (6B 82)
Alexander Ho. E14 3C 104
(off Tiller Rd.)
KT2: King T 1E 150
(off Seven Kings Way)
SE15 2H 121
(off Godman Rd.)
Alexander M. SW16 5G 137
W2 6K 81
Alexander Pl. SW7 3C 16 (4C 100)
Alexander Rd. BR7: Chst 6F 143
DA7: Bex 2D 126
N19 3J 65
Alexander Sq. SW3 3C 16 (4C 100)
Alexander St. W2 6J 81
Alexander Studios SW11 4B 118
(off Haydon Way)
Alexander Ter. SE2 5B 108
Alexandra Av. HA2: Harr 1D 58
N22 1H 47
SM1: Sutt 3J 165
SW11 1E 118
UB1: S'hall 7D 76
W4 7K 97
Alexandra Cl. HA2: Harr 3E 58
SE8 6B 104
TW15: Ashf 7F 129
Alexandra Cotts. SE14 1B 122
Alexandra Ct. HA9: Wemb 4F 61
N14 5B 22
SE5 6C 102
(off Urlwin St.)
SW7 1A 16
TW3: Houn 2F 113
TW15: Ashf 6F 129
UB6: G'frd 2F 77
W2 7K 81
(off Moscow Rd.)
W9 4A 82
(off Maida Vale)
Alexandra Cres. BR1: Broml 6H 141
Alexandra Dr. KT5: Surb 7G 151
SE19 5E 138
Alexandra Gdns. N10 4F 47
SM5: Cars 7E 166
TW3: Houn 2F 113
W4 7A 98
Alexandra Gro. N4 1B 66
N12 5E 30
Alexandra Ho. E16 1K 105
(off Wesley Av.)
IG8: Wfd G 7K 37
W6 5E 98
(off Queen Caroline St.)
Alexandra Mans. SW3 7A 16
(off King's Rd.)
W12 1E 98
(off Stanlake Rd.)
Alexandra M. N2 3D 46
N4 2B 66
SW19 6H 135
Alexandra Palace 2H 47
Alexandra Palace Ice Rink 2H 47
Alexandra Palace Theatre 2H 47
Alexandra Pal. Way N8 4G 47
N22 4G 47
Alexandra Pde. HA2: Harr 4F 59
Alexandra Pk. Rd. N10 2F 47
N22 1G 47
Alexandra Pl. CR0: C'don 1E 168
NW8 1A 82
SE25 5D 156
Alexandra Rd. CR0: C'don 1E 168
CR4: Mitc 7C 136
E6 3E 88
E10 3E 68
E17 6B 50
E18 3K 51
EN3: Pond E 4E 24
KT2: King T 7G 133
KT7: T Ditt 5K 149
N8 3A 48
N9 7C 24
N10 7A 32
N15 5D 48
NW4 4F 45
NW8 1A 82
RM6: Chad H 6E 54
SE26 6K 139
SW14 3K 115
SW19 6H 135
TW1: Twick 6C 114
TW3: Houn 2F 113
TW8: Bford 6D 96
TW9: Kew 2F 115
TW15: Ashf 7F 129
W4 2K 97
Alexandra Rd. Ind. Est.
EN3: Pond E 4E 24
Alexandra Sq. SM4: Mord 5J 153
Alexandra St. E16 5J 87
SE14 7A 104
Alexandra Ter. E14 5D 104
(off Westferry Rd.)
Alexandra Wlk. SE19 5E 138
Alexandra Wharf E2 1H 85
(off Darwen Pl.)
Alexandra Yd. E9 1K 85
Alexandria Apts. SE17 4E 102
(off Townsend St.)
Alexandria Rd. W13 7A 78
Alex Guy Gdns. RM8: Dag 1H 73
Alexia Sq. E14 3D 104
Alexis St. SE16 4G 103
Alfan La. DA2: Wilm 5K 145
Alfearn Rd. E5 4J 67
Alford Ct. N1 1D 8
(off Shepherdess Wlk.)
Alford Grn. CR0: New Ad 6F 171
Alford Ho. N6 6G 47
Alford Pl. N1 1D 8 (2C 84)
Alford Rd. DA8: Erith 5J 109
Alfoxton Av. N15 4B 48

A-Z Big London 177

Alfreda St.—Anchor Bus. Cen.

Alfreda St. SW11 . . . . .1F **119**
Alfred Cl. W4 . . . . .4K **97**
Alfred Ct. *SE16 . . . . .4H 103*
(off Bombay St.)
Alfred Dickens Ho. *E16 . . . . .6H 87*
(off Hallsville Rd.)
Alfred Finlay Ho. N22 . . . . .2B **48**
Alfred Gdns. UB1: S'hall 7C **76**
Alfred Ho. *E9 . . . . .5A 68*
(off Homerton Rd.)
E12 . . . . .7C 70
(off Tennyson Av.)
Alfred M. W1 . . . . .5C **6** (5H **83**)
Alfred Nunn Ho. NW10 . . . . .1B **80**
Alfred Pl. WC1 . . . . .5C **6** (5H **83**)
Alfred Prior Ho. E12 . . . . .4E **70**
Alfred Rd. DA17: Belv 5F **109**
E15 . . . . .5H **69**
IG9: Buck H 2G **37**
KT1: King T 3E **150**
SE25 . . . . .5G **157**
SM1: Sutt 5A **166**
TW13: Felt 2A **130**
W2 . . . . .5J **81**
W3 . . . . .1J **97**
Alfred Salter Ho. *SE1 . . . . .4F 103*
(off Fort Rd.)
Alfred's Gdns. IG11: Bark 2J **89**
Alfred St. E3 . . . . .3B **86**
Alfreds Way IG11: Bark 3F **89**
Alfreds Way Ind. Est. IG11: Bark 2A **90**
Alfred Vs. E17 . . . . .4E **50**
Alfreton Cl. SW19 . . . . .3F **135**
Alfriston KT5: Surb 6F **151**
Alfriston Av. CR0: C'don 7J **155**
HA2: Harr 6E **40**
Alfriston Cl. KT5: Surb 5F **151**
Alfriston Rd. SW11 . . . . .5D **118**
Algar Cl. HA7: Stan 5E **26**
TW7: Isle 3A **114**
Algar Ho. SE1 . . . . .7A **14**
Algar Rd. TW7: Isle 3A **114**
Algarve Rd. SW18 . . . . .1K **135**
Algernon Rd. NW4 . . . . .6C **44**
NW6 . . . . .1J **81**
SE13 . . . . .4D **122**
Algiers Rd. SE13 . . . . .4C **122**
Alibon Gdns. RM10: Dag 5G **73**
Alibon Rd. RM9: Dag 5F **73**
RM10: Dag 5F **73**
Alice Cl. *EN5: New Bar 4F 21*
(off Station App.)
Alice Gilliatt Ct. *W14 . . . . .6H 99*
(off Star Rd.)
Alice La. E3 . . . . .1B **86**
Alice M. TW11: Tedd 5K **131**
Alice Owen Technology Cen. *EC1 . . . .1A 8*
(off Goswell Rd.)
Alice Shepherd Ho. *E14 . . . . .2E 104*
(off Manchester Rd.)
Alice St. SE1 . . . . .3E **102**
(not continuous)
Alice Thompson Cl. SE12 . . . . .2A **142**
Alice Walker Cl. SE24 . . . . .4B **120**
Alice Way TW3: Houn 4F **113**
Alicia Av. HA3: Kenton 4B **42**
Alicia Cl. HA3: Kenton 4C **42**
Alicia Gdns. HA3: Kenton 4B **42**
Alicia Ho. DA16: Well 1B **126**
Alie St. E1 . . . . .1K **15** (6F **85**)
Alington Cres. NW9 . . . . .7J **43**
Alington Gro. SM6: W'gton 7G **167**
Alison Cl. CR0: C'don 1K **169**
E6 . . . . .6E **88**
HA5: Eastc 6K **39**
Alissa Dr. EN5: New Bar 5F **21**
Aliwal M. SW11 . . . . .4C **118**
Aliwal Rd. SW11 . . . . .4C **118**
Alkerden Rd. W4 . . . . .5A **98**
Alkham Rd. N16 . . . . .2F **67**
Allan Barclay Cl. N15 . . . . .6F **49**
Allan Cl. KT3: N Mald 5K **151**
Allandale Av. N3 . . . . .3G **45**
Allanson Ct. *E10 . . . . .2C 68*
(off Leyton Grange Est.)
Allan Way W3 . . . . .5J **79**
Allard Cres. WD23: B Hea 1B **26**
Allard Gdns. SW4 . . . . .5H **119**
Allard Ho. *NW9 . . . . .2B 44*
(off Boulevard Dr.)
Allardyce St. SW4 . . . . .4K **119**
Allbrook Cl. TW11: Tedd 5J **131**
Allcroft Rd. NW5 . . . . .5E **64**
Allder Way CR2: S Croy 7B **168**
Allenby Cl. UB6: G'frd 3E **76**
Allenby Rd. SE23 . . . . .3A **140**
SE28 . . . . .3G **107**
UB1: S'hall 3E **76**
Allen Cl. CR4: Mitc 1F **155**
TW16: Sun 1K **147**
Allen Ct. *E17 . . . . .6C 50*
(off Yunus Khan Cl.)
Allendale Av. UB1: S'hall 6E **76**
Allendale Cl. SE5 . . . . .2D **120**
SE26 . . . . .5K **139**
Allendale Rd. HA0: Wemb 6B **60**
UB6: G'frd 6B **60**
Allen Edwards Dr. SW8 . . . . .1J **119**
Allenford Ho. *SW15 . . . . .6B 116*
(off Tunworth Cres.)
Allen Ho. *W8 . . . . .3J 99*
(off Allen St.)
Allen Mans. *W8 . . . . .3J 99*
(off Allen St.)
Allen Rd. BR3: Beck 2K **157**
CR0: C'don 1A **168**
Allen Rd. E3 . . . . .2B **86**
N16 . . . . .4E **66**
TW16: Sun 1K **147**
Allensbury Pl. NW1 . . . . .7H **65**
Allens Rd. EN3: Pond E 5D **24**
Allen St. W8 . . . . .3J **99**
Allenswood SW19 . . . . .1G **135**
Allenswood Rd. SE9 . . . . .3C **124**
Allerford Ct. HA2: Harr 5G **41**
Allerford Rd. SE6 . . . . .3D **140**
Allerton Ho. *N1 . . . . .1E 8*
(off Provost St.)
Allerton Rd. N16 . . . . .2C **66**
Allerton St. N1 . . . . .1E **8** (3D **84**)
Allerton Wlk. N7 . . . . .2K **65**
Allestree Rd. SW6 . . . . .7G **99**
Alleyn Cres. SE21 . . . . .2D **138**
Alleyndale Rd. RM8: Dag 2C **72**
Alleyn Ho. *SE1 . . . . .3D 102*
(off Burbage Cl.)
Alleyn Pk. SE21 . . . . .2D **138**
UB2: S'hall 5E **94**
Alleyn Rd. SE21 . . . . .3D **138**
Alley Way UB8: Uxb 7A **56**
Allfarthing La. SW18 . . . . .6K **117**
Allgood Cl. SM4: Mord 6F **153**
Allgood St. E2 . . . . .1K **9** (2F **85**)
All Hallows by the Tower Church
. . . . .3H **15** (7E **84**)
Allhallows La. EC4 . . . . .3E **14** (7D **84**)
All Hallows Rd. N17 . . . . .1E **48**
Allhallows Rd. E6 . . . . .5C **88**
Alliance Cl. HA0: Wemb 4D **60**
TW4: Houn 5D **112**
Alliance Ct. TW15: Ashf 4E **128**
W3 . . . . .5H **79**
Alliance Rd. E13 . . . . .5A **88**
SE18 . . . . .6A **108**
W3 . . . . .4H **79**
Allianz Park .7K **29**
Allied Ct. *N1 . . . . .7E 66*
(off Enfield Rd.)
Allied Ind. Est. W3 . . . . .2A **98**
Allied Way W3 . . . . .2A **98**
Allingham Cl. W7 . . . . .7K **77**
Allingham Ct. BR2: Broml 4H **159**
Allingham M. *N1 . . . . .2C 84*
(off Allingham St.)
Allingham Rd. SW4 . . . . .6H **119**
Allingham St. N1 . . . . .2C **84**
Allington Av. N17 . . . . .6K **33**
TW17: Shep 3G **147**
Allington Cl. SW19 . . . . .5F **135**
UB6: G'frd 7G **59**
Allington Ct. *CR0: C'don 6J 157*
(off Chart Cl.)
EN3: Pond E 5E **24**
SW8 . . . . .2G **119**
Allington Rd. BR6: Orp 2H **173**
HA2: Harr 5G **41**
NW4 . . . . .5D **44**
W10 . . . . .3G **81**
Allington St. SW1 . . . . .2A **18** (3F **101**)
Allison Cl. SE10 . . . . .1E **122**
Allison Gro. SE21 . . . . .1E **138**
Allison Rd. N8 . . . . .5A **48**
W3 . . . . .6J **79**
Alliston Ho. *E2 . . . . .2K 9*
(off Gibraltar Wlk.)
Allitsen Rd. NW8 . . . . .2C **82**
(not continuous)
All Nations Ho. *E8 . . . . .7H 67*
(off Martello St.)
Allnutt Way SW4 . . . . .5H **119**
Alloa Rd. IG3: Ilf 2A **72**
SE8 . . . . .5K **103**
Allom Ho. *W11 . . . . .7G 81*
(off Clarendon Rd.)
Allonby Dr. HA4: Ruis 7D **38**
Allonby Gdns. HA9: Wemb 1C **60**
Allotment Way NW2 . . . . .3F **63**
Alloway Rd. E3 . . . . .3A **86**
Alloy Ho. *SE14 . . . . .6B 104*
(off Moulding La.)
Allport Ho. *SE5 . . . . .3D 120*
(off Champion Pk.)
Allport M. *E1 . . . . .4J 85*
(off Hayfield Pas.)
All Saints Cl. N9 . . . . .2B **34**
SW8 . . . . .1J **119**
All Saint's Ct. *TW5: Hest 1B 112*
(off Springwell Rd.)
All Saints Ct. *E1 . . . . .7J 85*
(off Johnson St.)
SW11 . . . . .7F 101
(off Prince of Wales Dr.)
All Saints Dr. SE3 . . . . .2G **123**
(not continuous)
All Saints Ho. *W11 . . . . .5H 81*
(off All Saints Rd.)
All Saints M. HA3: Hrw W 6D **26**
All Saints Pas. SW18 . . . . .5J **117**
All Saints Rd. SM1: Sutt 3K **165**
SW19 . . . . .7A **136**
(not continuous)
W3 . . . . .3J **97**
W11 . . . . .5H **81**
All Saints St. N1 . . . . .2K **83**
All Saints Wlk. SE15 . . . . .7F **103**
Allsop Pl. NW1 . . . . .4F **5** (4D **82**)
All Souls Av. NW10 . . . . .2D **80**
All Souls' Pl. W1 . . . . .6K **5** (5F **83**)
Allum Way N20 . . . . .1F **31**
Alluvium Ct. *SE1 . . . . .7G 15*
(off Long La.)
Allwood Cl. SE26 . . . . .4K **139**
Alma Av. E4 . . . . .7K **35**
Alma Birk Ho. NW6 . . . . .7G **63**
Almack Rd. E5 . . . . .4J **67**
Alma Cl. N10 . . . . .1F **47**
Alma Ct. HA2: Harr 2H **59**
Alma Cres. SM1: Sutt 5G **165**
Alma Gro. SE1 . . . . .4F **103**
Alma Ho. N9 . . . . .4B **34**
TW8: Bford 6E **96**
Almanza Pl. IG11: Bark 2B **90**
Alma Pl. CR7: Thor H 5A **156**
NW10 . . . . .3D **80**
SE19 . . . . .7F **139**
Alma Rd. DA14: Sidc 3A **144**
EN3: Enf H, Pond E 5F **25**
KT10: Esh 7J **149**
N10 . . . . .7A **32**
SM5: Cars 5C **166**
SW18 . . . . .4A **118**
UB1: S'hall 7C **76**
Alma Rd. Ind. Est.
EN3: Pond E 4E **24**
Alma Row HA3: Hrw W 1H **41**
Alma Sq. NW8 . . . . .2A **82**
Alma St. E15 . . . . .6F **69**
NW5 . . . . .6F **65**
Alma Ter. *E3 . . . . .1B 86*
(off Beale Rd.)
SW18 . . . . .7B **118**
W8 . . . . .3J **99**
Almeida St. N1 . . . . .1B **84**
Almeida Theatre 1B **84**
(off Almeida St.)
Almeric Rd. SW11 . . . . .4D **118**
Almer Rd. SW20 . . . . .7C **134**
Almington St. N4 . . . . .1K **65**
Almond Av. SM5: Cars 2D **166**
UB7: W Dray 3C **92**
UB10: Ick 3D **56**
W5 . . . . .3D **96**
Almond Cl. BR2: Broml 7E **160**
E17 . . . . .4A **50**
HA4: Ruis 3H **57**
SE15 . . . . .2G **121**
TW13: Felt 1J **129**
TW17: Shep 2E **146**
UB3: Hayes 7G **75**
Almond Gro. TW8: Bford 7B **96**
Almond Ho. *E15 . . . . .3G 87*
(off Teasel Way)
Almond Rd. N17 . . . . .7B **34**
SE16 . . . . .4H **103**
Almonds Av. IG9: Buck H 2D **36**
Almond Way BR2: Broml 7E **160**
CR4: Mitc 5H **155**
HA2: Harr 2F **41**
Almorah Rd. N1 . . . . .7D **66**
TW5: Hest 1B **112**
Almshouse La. KT9: Chess 7C **162**
The Alms Ho's. IG11: Bark 6G **71**
Al-Nehar Mosque 2K **83**
(off Caledonian Rd.)
Alnmouth Ct. *UB1: S'hall 6G 77*
(off Fleming Rd.)
Alnwick N17 . . . . .7C **34**
Alnwick Gro. SM4: Mord 4K **153**
Alnwick Rd. E16 . . . . .6A **88**
SE12 . . . . .6K **123**
ALPERTON .2E **78**
Alperton La. HA0: Wemb 3C **78**
UB6: G'frd 3C **78**
Alperton St. W10 . . . . .4H **81**
Alphabet Gdns. SM5: Cars 6B **154**
Alphabet M. SW9 . . . . .1A **120**
Alphabet Sq. E3 . . . . .5C **86**
Alpha Cl. NW1 . . . . .2D **4** (4C **82**)
Alpha Est. UB3: Hayes 2G **93**
Alpha Gro. E14 . . . . .2C **104**
Alpha Ho. NW6 . . . . .2J **81**
NW8 . . . . .4D **4**
SW4 . . . . .4K **119**
Alpha Pl. NW6 . . . . .2J **81**
SM4: Mord 1F **165**
SW3 . . . . .7D **16** (6C **100**)
Alpha Rd. CR0: C'don 1E **168**
E4 . . . . .3H **35**
EN3: Pond E 4F **25**
KT5: Surb 6F **151**
N18 . . . . .6B **34**
SE14 . . . . .1B **122**
TW11: Tedd 5H **131**
UB10: Hil 4D **74**
Alpha St. SE15 . . . . .2G **121**
Alphea Cl. SW19 . . . . .7C **136**
Alpine Av. KT5: Surb 2J **163**
Alpine Bus. Cen. E6 . . . . .5E **88**
Alpine Cl. CR0: C'don 3E **168**
KT19: Ewe 5J **163**
Alpine Copse BR1: Broml 2E **160**
Alpine Gro. E9 . . . . .7J **67**
Alpine Rd. E10 . . . . .2D **68**
KT12: Walt T 7J **147**
NW9 . . . . .4G **43**
SE16 . . . . .5K **103**
Alpine Vw. SM5: Cars 5C **166**
Alpine Wlk. HA7: Stan 2D **26**
Alpine Way E6 . . . . .5E **88**
Alric Av. KT3: N Mald 3A **152**
NW10 . . . . .7K **61**
Alroy Rd. N4 . . . . .7A **48**
Alsace Rd. SE17 . . . . .5E **102**
Alscot Rd. SE1 . . . . .4F **103**
Alscot Way SE1 . . . . .4F **103**
Alsike Rd. DA18: Erith 3D **108**
SE2 . . . . .3D **108**
Alsom Av. KT4: Wor Pk 4C **164**
Alston Cl. KT6: Surb 7B **150**
Alston Rd. EN5: Barn 3B **20**
N18 . . . . .5C **34**
SW17 . . . . .4B **136**
Alston Works EN5: Barn 2B **20**
Altair Cl. N17 . . . . .6A **34**
Altash Way SE9 . . . . .2D **142**
Altenburg Av. W13 . . . . .3B **96**
Altenburg Gdns. SW11 . . . . .4D **118**
Alt Gro. SW19 . . . . .7H **135**
Altham Ct. HA2: Harr 1F **41**
Altham Rd. HA5: Pinn 1C **40**
Althea St. SW6 . . . . .2K **117**
Althorne Gdns. E18 . . . . .4H **51**
Althorne Way RM10: Dag 2G **73**
Althorp Cl. EN5: Ark 1H **29**
Althorpe M. SW11 . . . . .1B **118**
Althorpe Rd. HA1: Harr 5G **41**
Althorp Rd. SW17 . . . . .1D **136**
Altima Ct. *SE22 . . . . .4G 121*
(off E. Dulwich Rd.)
Altior Ct. N6 . . . . .6G **47**
Altissima Ho. SW11 . . . . .7F **101**
Altitude Apts. *CR0: C'don 3D 168*
(off Altyre Rd.)
Altitude Point *E1 . . . . .6G 85*
(off Alie St.)
Altius Apts. *E3 . . . . .2C 86*
(off Wick La.)
Altius Ct. E4 . . . . .6K **35**
Altius Wlk. E20 . . . . .6E **68**
Altmore Av. E6 . . . . .7D **70**
Alton Av. HA7: Stan 7E **26**
Alton Cl. DA5: Bexl 1E **144**
TW7: Isle 2K **113**
Alton Gdns. BR3: Beck 7C **140**
TW2: Whitt 7H **113**
Alton Ho. *E3 . . . . .3D 86*
(off Bromley High St.)
Alton Rd. CR0: Wadd 3A **168**
N17 . . . . .3D **48**
SW15 . . . . .1C **134**
TW9: Rich 4E **114**
Alton St. E14 . . . . .5D **86**
Altura Twr. SW11 . . . . .2B **118**
Altus Ho. SE6 . . . . .4E **140**
Altyre Cl. BR3: Beck 5B **158**
Altyre Rd. CR0: C'don 2D **168**
Altyre Way BR3: Beck 5B **158**
Aluna Ct. SE15 . . . . .3J **121**
Alvanley Gdns. NW6 . . . . .5K **63**
Alverstone Av. EN4: E Barn 7H **21**
SW19 . . . . .2J **135**
Alverstone Gdns. SE9 . . . . .1G **143**
Alverstone Ho. SE11 . . . . . .7J **19** (6A **102**)
Alverstone Rd. E12 . . . . .4E **70**
HA9: Wemb 1F **61**
KT3: N Mald 4B **152**
NW2 . . . . .7E **62**
Alverston Gdns. SE25 . . . . .5E **156**
Alverton St. SE8 . . . . .5B **104**
(not continuous)
Alveston Av. HA3: Kenton 3B **42**
Alveston Sq. E18 . . . . .2J **51**
Alvey St. SE17 . . . . .5E **102**
Alvia Gdns. SM1: Sutt 4A **166**
Alvington Cres. E8 . . . . .5F **67**
Alway Av. KT19: Ewe 5K **163**
Alwold Cres. SE12 . . . . .6K **123**
Alwyn Av. W4 . . . . .5K **97**
Alwyn Cl. CR0: New Ad 7D **170**
Alwyne La. N1 . . . . .7B **66**
Alwyne Pl. N1 . . . . .6C **66**
Alwyne Rd. N1 . . . . .7C **66**
SW19 . . . . .6H **135**
W7 . . . . .7J **77**
Alwyne Sq. N1 . . . . .6C **66**
Alwyne Vs. N1 . . . . .7B **66**
Alwyn Gdns. NW4 . . . . .4C **44**
W3 . . . . .6H **79**
Alyth Gdns. NW11 . . . . .6J **45**
Alzette Ho. *E2 . . . . .2K 85*
(off Mace St.)
Amalgamated Dr. TW8: Bford 6B **96**
Amanda Ct. *TW15: Ashf 2B 128*
(off Edward Way)
Amanda M. RM7: Rom 5J **55**
Amar Ct. SE18 . . . . .4K **107**
Amar Deep Ct. SE18 . . . . .5K **107**
Amarelle Apts. *CR0: C'don 1D 168*
(off Cherry Orchard Rd.)
Amazon Bldg. N8 . . . . .4K **47**
Amazon St. E1 . . . . .6G **85**
Ambassador Bldg. SW11 . . . . .6H **101**
Ambassador Cl. TW3: Houn 2C **112**
Ambassador Gdns. E6 . . . . .5D **88**
Ambassador Ho.
CR7: Lon, Thor H 4C 156
(off Brigstock Rd.)
NW8 . . . . .1A **82**
Ambassadors Court 7A **12**
Ambassador's Ct. SW1 . . . . .5B **12**
Ambassadors Ct. *E8 . . . . .7F 67*
(off Holly St.)
Ambassador Sq. E14 . . . . .4D **104**
Ambassadors Theatre 1D **12**
(off West St.)
Amber Av. E17 . . . . .1A **50**
Amber Cl. EN5: New Bar 6E **20**
Amber Ct. CR0: C'don 1E **168**
E15 . . . . .1E 86
(off Warton Rd.)
KT5: Surb 7F **151**
N7 . . . . .6A 66
(off Bride St.)
SW17 . . . . .4E 136
(off Brudenell Rd.)
Amberden Av. N3 . . . . .3J **45**
Ambergate St. SE17 . . . . .5B **102**
Amber Gro. NW2 . . . . .1F **63**
Amber Ho. *E1 . . . . .6K 85*
(off Aylward St.)
Amberley Cl. BR6: Chels 5K **173**
HA5: Pinn 3D **40**
Amberley Ct. BR3: Beck 7B **140**
DA14: Sidc 5C **144**
Amberley Gdns. EN1: Enf 7K **23**
KT19: Ewe 4B **164**
Amberley Gro. CR0: C'don 7F **157**
SE26 . . . . .5H **139**
Amberley Rd. E10 . . . . .7C **50**
EN1: Enf 7A **24**
IG9: Buck H 1F **37**
N13 . . . . .2E **32**
SE2 . . . . .6D **108**
W9 . . . . .5J **81**
Amberley Way RM7: Mawney 4H **55**
SM4: Mord 7H **153**
TW4: Houn 5A **112**
UB10: Uxb 2A **74**
Amberlith Ho. *CR7: Thor H 5A 156*
(off Thornton Rd.)
Amber M. *N22 . . . . .3A 48*
(off High Rd.)
Amberside Cl. TW7: Isle 6H **113**
Amber Way W3 . . . . .2A **98**
Amber Wharf *E2 . . . . .1F 85*
(off Nursery La.)
Amberwood Cl. SM6: W'gton 5J **167**
Amberwood Ri. KT3: N Mald 6A **152**
Amblecote Cl. SE12 . . . . .3K **141**
Amblecote Mdws. SE12 . . . . .3K **141**
Amblecote Rd. SE12 . . . . .3K **141**
Ambler Rd. N4 . . . . .3B **66**
Ambleside BR1: Broml 6F **141**
NW1 . . . . .1K **5**
SW19 . . . . .1G **135**
Ambleside Av. BR3: Beck 5A **158**
KT12: Walt T 7A **148**
SW16 . . . . .4H **137**
Ambleside Cl. E9 . . . . .5J **67**
E10 . . . . .7D **50**
N17 . . . . .3F **49**
Ambleside Cres. EN3: Enf H 3E **24**
Ambleside Dr. TW14: Felt 1H **129**
Ambleside Gdns.
HA9: Wemb 1D **60**
IG4: Ilf 4C **52**
SM2: Sutt 6A **166**
SW16 . . . . .5H **137**
Ambleside Point *SE15 . . . . .7J 103*
(off Tustin Est.)
Ambleside Rd. DA7: Bex 2G **127**
NW10 . . . . .7B **62**
Ambleside Wlk. UB8: Uxb 1A **74**
Ambrook Rd. DA17: Belv 3G **109**
Ambrosden Av. SW1 . . . . . .2B **18** (3G **101**)
Ambrose Av. NW11 . . . . .7G **45**
Ambrose Cl. BR6: Orp 3K **173**
E6 . . . . .5D **88**
Ambrose Ct. *N18 . . . . .6A 34*
(off Cannon Rd.)
Ambrose Ho. *E14 . . . . .5C 86*
(off Selsey St.)
Ambrose M. SW11 . . . . .2D **118**
Ambrose St. SE16 . . . . .4H **103**
Ambrose Wlk. E3 . . . . .2C **86**
Ambulance Rd. E11 . . . . .5F **51**
AMC Bus. Cen. NW10 . . . . .3H **79**
Amelia Cl. TW4: Houn 1C **130**
W3 . . . . .1H **97**
Amelia Ho. *E14 . . . . .6G 87*
(off Lyell St.)
NW9 . . . . .2B 44
(off Boulevard Dr.)
TW9: Kew 7H **97**
Amelia Ho. *W6 . . . . .5E 98*
(off Queen Caroline St.)
Amelia Mans. *E20 . . . . .6D 68*
(off Olympic Pk. Av.)
Amelia St. SE17 . . . . .5C **102**
Amen Cnr. EC4 . . . . .1B **14** (6B **84**)
SW17 . . . . .6D **136**
Amen Ct. EC4 . . . . .1B **14** (6B **84**)
Amenity Way SM4: Mord 7E **152**
The American International
University in London
Kensington Campus,
Ansdell Street 3K 99
(off Ansdell St.)
St Albans Grove 3K **99**
Young Street 2K **99**
Richmond Hill Campus 7E **114**
The American University of London
. . . . .3K **65**
America Sq. EC3 . . . . .2J **15** (7F **85**)
America St. SE1 . . . . .5C **14** (1C **102**)
Amerland Rd. SW18 . . . . .5H **117**
Amersham Av. N18 . . . . .6J **33**
Amersham Gro. SE14 . . . . .7B **104**
Amersham Rd. CR0: C'don 6C **156**
SE14 . . . . .1B **122**
Amersham Va. SE14 . . . . .7B **104**
Amery Gdns. NW10 . . . . .1E **80**
Amery Ho. *SE17 . . . . .5E 102*
(off Kinglake St.)
Amery Rd. HA1: Harr 2A **60**
Amesbury Av. SW2 . . . . .2J **137**
Amesbury Cl. KT4: Wor Pk 1E **164**
Amesbury Ct. EN2: Enf 2F **23**
Amesbury Dr. E4 . . . . .6J **25**
Amesbury Rd. BR1: Broml 3B **160**
RM9: Dag 7D **72**
TW13: Felt 2B **130**
Amesbury Twr. SW8 . . . . .2G **119**
Ames Cotts. *E14 . . . . .5A 86*
(off Maroon St.)
Ames Ho. *E2 . . . . .2K 85*
(off Mace St.)
Amethyst Cl. N11 . . . . .7C **32**
Amethyst Ct. *BR6: Chels 5J 173*
(off Farnborough Hill)
EN3: Enf H 3F 25
(off Enstone Rd.)
Amethyst Rd. E15 . . . . .4F **69**
Amherst Av. W13 . . . . .6C **78**
Amherst Dr. BR5: St M Cry 4K **161**
Amherst Gdns. *W13 . . . . .6C 78*
(off Amherst Rd.)
Amherst Ho. *SE16 . . . . .2K 103*
(off Wolfe Cres.)
Amherst Rd. W13 . . . . .6C **78**
Amhurst Gdns. TW7: Isle 2A **114**
Amhurst Pde. *N16 . . . . .7F 49*
(off Amhurst Pk.)
Amhurst Pk. N16 . . . . .7D **48**
Amhurst Pas. E8 . . . . .4G **67**
Amhurst Rd. E8 . . . . .5H **67**
N16 . . . . .4F **67**
Amhurst Ter. E8 . . . . .4G **67**
Amhurst Wlk. SE28 . . . . .1A **108**
Amias Dr. HA8: Edg 4K **27**
Amias Ho. *EC1 . . . . .3C 8*
(off Central St.)
Amidas Gdns. RM8: Dag 4B **72**
Amiel St. E1 . . . . .4J **85**
Amies St. SW11 . . . . .3D **118**
Amigo Ho. *SE1 . . . . .1K 19*
(off Morley St.)
Amina Way SE16 . . . . .3G **103**
Amiot Ho. *NW9 . . . . .2B 44*
(off Heritage Av.)
Amis Av. KT19: Ewe 6H **163**
Amisha Ct. *SE1 . . . . .3F 103*
(off Grange Rd.)
Amity Gro. SW20 . . . . .1D **152**
Amity Rd. E15 . . . . .7H **69**
Ammanford Grn. NW9 . . . . .6A **44**
Ammonite Ho. E15 . . . . .7H **69**
Amner Rd. SW11 . . . . .6E **118**
Amor Rd. W6 . . . . .3E **98**
Amory Ho. *N1 . . . . .1K 83*
(off Barnsbury Est.)
Amott Rd. SE15 . . . . .3G **121**
Amoy Pl. E14 . . . . .7C **86**
(not continuous)
Ampere Way CR0: Wadd 7J **155**
Ampleforth Rd. SE2 . . . . .2B **108**
Amport Pl. NW7 . . . . .6B **30**
Ampthill Est. NW1 . . . . .1B **6** (2G **83**)
Ampthill Sq. NW1 . . . . .1B **6** (2G **83**)
Ampton Pl. WC1 . . . . .2G **7** (3K **83**)
Ampton St. WC1 . . . . .2G **7** (3K **83**)
Amroth Cl. SE23 . . . . .1H **139**
Amroth Grn. NW9 . . . . .6A **44**
Amstel Ct. SE15 . . . . .7F **103**
Amsterdam Rd. E14 . . . . .3E **104**
Amundsen Ct. *E14 . . . . .5C 104*
(off Napier Av.)
Amundsen Ho. *NW10 . . . . .7K 61*
(off Stonebridge Pk.)
Amwell Cl. EN2: Enf 5J **23**
Amwell Ct. Est. N4 . . . . .2C **66**
Amwell Ho. *WC1 . . . . .1J 7*
(off Cruikshank St.)
Amwell St. EC1 . . . . .1J **7** (3A **84**)
Amyand Cotts. TW1: Twick 6B **114**
Amyand La. TW1: Twick 7B **114**
Amyand Pk. Gdns. TW1: Twick 7B **114**
Amyand Pk. Rd. TW1: Twick 7A **114**
Amy Cl. SM6: W'gton 7J **167**
Amy Johnson Ct. HA8: Edg 2H **43**
Amyruth Rd. SE4 . . . . .5C **122**
Amy Warne Cl. E6 . . . . .4C **88**
Anastasia M. N12 . . . . .5E **30**
Anatola Rd. N19 . . . . .2G **65**
Anayah Apts. *SE8 . . . . .5K 103*
(off Trundleys Rd.)
Ancaster Cres. KT3: N Mald 6C **152**
Ancaster M. BR3: Beck 3K **157**
Ancaster Rd. BR3: Beck 3K **157**
Ancaster St. SE18 . . . . .7J **107**
Anchor SW18 . . . . .4K **117**
Anchorage Cl. SW19 . . . . .5J **135**
Anchorage Ho. *E14 . . . . .7F 87*
(off Clove Cres.)
Anchorage Point *E14 . . . . .2B 104*
(off Cuba St.)
Anchorage Point Ind. Est. SE7 . . . . .3A **106**
Anchor & Hope La. SE7 . . . . .3K **105**
Anchor Brewhouse SE1 . . . . .5J **15** (1F **103**)
Anchor Bus. Cen. CR0: Bedd 3J **167**

178 A-Z Big London

Anchor Cl.—Arcon Dr.

Anchor Cl. IG11: Bark 3B 90
Anchor Ct. EN1: Enf 5K 23
SW1 4C 18
(off Vauxhall Bri. Rd.)
Anchor Dr. N15 4E 48
Anchor Ho. E16 5H 87
(off Barking Rd.)
E16 6A 88
(off Prince Regent La.)
EC1 3C 8
(off Old St.)
SW10 6B 100
(off Cremorne Est.)
Anchor Iron Wharf SE10 5F 105
Anchor M. N1 6E 66
SW12 6F 119
Anchor Retail Pk. 4J 85
Anchor St. SE16 4H 103
Anchor Ter. E1 4J 85
SE1 4D 14
(off Southwark Bri. Rd.)
Anchor Wharf E3 5D 86
(off Yeo St.)
Anchor Yd. EC1 3D 8 (4C 84)
Ancill Cl. W6 6G 99
Ancona Rd. NW10 2C 80
SE18 5H 107
Andace Pk. Gdns. BR1: Broml 1A 160
Andalus Rd. SW9 3J 119
Ander Cl. HA0: Wemb 4D 60
Anderson Cl. N21 5E 22
SM3: Sutt 1J 165
W3 6K 79
Anderson Ct. NW2 1E 62
Anderson Dr. TW15: Ashf 4E 128
Anderson Hgts. SW16 2K 155
Anderson Ho. E14 7E 86
(off Woolmore St.)
IG11: Bark 1H 89
SW17 5B 136
Anderson Pl. TW3: Houn 4F 113
Anderson Rd. E9 6K 67
IG8: Wfd G 3B 52
SE3 4K 123
Anderson Sq. N1 1B 84
(off Gaskin St.)
Anderson St. SW3 5E 16 (5D 100)
Anderson Way DA17: Belv 2H 109
Anderton Cl. SE5 3D 120
Anderton Ct. N22 2H 47
Andora Ct. NW6 7G 63
(off Brondesbury Pk.)
Andora Ho. E10 1A 68
Andorra Ct. BR1: Broml 1A 160
Andover Av. E16 6B 88
Andover Cl. TW14: Felt 1H 129
UB6: G'frd 4F 77
Andover Ct. E2 4H 85
(off Thee Colts La.)
TW19: Stanw 7A 110
Andover Pl. NW6 2K 81
Andover Rd. BR6: Orp 1H 173
N7 2K 65
TW2: Twick 1H 131
Andoversford Ct. SE15 6E 102
(off Bibury Cl.)
Andover Ter. W6 4D 98
(off Raynham Rd.)
Andreck Ct. BR3: Beck 2E 158
(off Crescent Rd.)
Andre St. E8 5G 67
Andrew Cl. DA1: Cray 5K 127
Andrew Ct. SE23 2K 139
Andrewes Gdns. E6 6C 88
Andrewes Highwalk EC2 6D 8
Andrewes Ho. EC2 6D 8
SM1: Sutt 4J 165
The Andrew Gibb Memorial 1H 123
Andrew Pl. SW8 7H 101
Andrew Reed Ho. SW18 7G 117
(off Linstead Way)
Andrews Cl. HA1: Harr 7H 41
IG9: Buck H 2F 37
KT4: Wor Pk 2E 164
Andrews Crosse WC2 1J 13
Andrews Ga. TW17: Shep 2E 146
Andrew's Ho. CR2: S Croy 6C 168
Andrews Ho. NW3 7D 64
(off Fellows Rd.)
Andrews Pl. DA2: Wilm 2K 145
SE9 6F 125
Andrew's Rd. E8 1H 85
Andrew St. E14 6E 86
Andrews Wlk. SE17 6B 102
Andringham Lodge BR1: Broml 1K 159
(off Palace Gro.)
Andrula Ct. N22 1B 48
Andwell Cl. SE2 2B 108
ANERLEY 1H 157
Anerley Gro. SE19 7F 139
Anerley Hill SE19 6F 139
Anerley Pk. SE20 7G 139
Anerley Pk. Rd. SE20 7H 139
Anerley Rd. SE19 7G 139
SE20 7G 139
Anerley Sta. Rd. SE20 1H 157
Anerley St. SW11 2D 118
Anerley Va. SE19 7F 139
Aneurin Bevan Ct. NW2 2D 62
Aneurin Bevan Ho. N11 7C 32
Anfield Cl. SW12 7G 119
ANGEL 2A 84
Angela Carter Cl. SW9 3A 120
Angela Davies Ind. Est.
SE24 4B 120
Angela Hooper Pl. SW1 1B 18
(off Victoria St.)
Angel All. E1 7K 9
Angel Bldg. N1 1K 7 (2A 84)
Angel Cl. N18 5A 34
TW12: Hamp H 5G 131
Angel Cnr. Pde. N18 4B 34
Angel Ct. E15 6F 69
EC2 7F 9 (6D 84)
SW1 5B 12 (1G 101)
ANGEL EDMONTON 5B 34
Angelfield TW3: Houn 4F 113
Angel Ga. EC1 1B 8 (3B 84)
(not continuous)
Angel Hill SM1: Sutt 3K 165
Angel Hill Dr. SM1: Sutt 3K 165
Angel Ho. E3 3C 86
(off Campbell Rd.)
Angelica Cl. UB7: Yiew 6A 74
Angelica Dr. E6 5E 88
Angelica Gdns. CR0: C'don 1K 169
Angelica Ho. E3 1B 86
(off Sycamore Av.)
Angelina Ho. SE15 1G 121
(off Goldsmith Rd.)
Angelis Apts. N1 1B 8
(off Graham St.)
Angel La. E15 6F 69
EC4 3E 14 (7D 84)
UB3: Hayes 5F 75
Angell Pk. Gdns. SW9 3A 120
Angell Rd. SW9 3A 120
ANGELL TOWN 1A 120
Angell Town Est. SW9 2A 120
Angel M. E1 7H 85
N1 2A 84
SW15 7C 116
Angelo M. SW16 3K 155
Angel Pl. N18 4B 34
SE1 6E 14 (2D 102)
Angel Rd. HA1: Harr 7F 41
KT7: T Ditt 7A 150
N18 5B 34
Angel Rd. Works N18 5D 34
Angel Sq. EC1 2B 84
Angel St. EC1 7C 8 (6C 84)
Angel Wlk. W6 4E 98
Angel Way RM1: Rom 5K 55
Angel Wharf N1 2C 84
Angel Yd. N6 1E 64
Angerstein Bus. Pk. SE10 4J 105
Angerstein La. SE3 1H 123
Anglais M. NW9 4A 44
(off Colin Cl.)
Anglebury W2 6J 81
(off Talbot Rd.)
Angle Cl. UB10: Hil 1C 74
Angle Grn. RM8: Dag 1C 72
The Anglers KT1: King T 3D 150
(off High St.)
Anglers Cl. TW10: Ham 4C 132
Angler's La. NW5 6F 65
Anglers Reach KT6: Surb 5D 150
Anglesea Av. SE18 4F 107
Anglesea Ho. KT1: King T 4D 150
(off Anglesea Rd.)
Anglesea M. SE18 4F 107
Anglesea Rd. KT1: King T 4D 150
SE18 4F 107
Anglesea Ter. W6 3D 98
(off Wellesley Av.)
Anglesey Cl. TW15: Ashf 3C 128
Anglesey Ct. Rd. SM5: Cars 6E 166
Anglesey Gdns. SM5: Cars 6E 166
Anglesey Ho. E14 6C 86
(off Lindfield St.)
Anglesey Rd. EN3: Pond E 4C 24
Anglesmede Cres. HA5: Pinn 3E 40
Anglesmede Way HA5: Pinn 3E 40
Angles Rd. SW16 4J 137
Anglia Cl. N17 7C 34
Anglia Ct. RM8: Dag 1D 72
(off Spring Cl.)
Anglia Ho. E14 6A 86
(off Salmon La.)
Anglian Ind. Est. IG11: Bark 4K 89
Anglian Rd. E11 3F 69
Anglia Wlk. E6 1E 88
(off Napier Rd.)
Anglo Rd. E3 2B 86
Angora Cl. SM6: W'gton 2E 166
Angrave Ct. E8 1F 85
(off Scriven St.)
Angrave Pas. E8 1F 85
Angus Cl. KT9: Chess 5G 163
Angus Dr. HA4: Ruis 4A 58
Angus Gdns. NW9 1K 43
Angus Ho. SW2 7H 119
Angus Rd. E13 3A 88
Angus St. SE14 7A 104
Anhalt Rd. SW11 7C 100
Ankerdine Cres. SE18 7F 107
Anlaby Rd. TW11: Tedd 5J 131
Anley Rd. W14 2F 99
Anmersh Gro. HA7: Stan 1D 42
Annabel Cl. E14 6D 86
Annabels M. W5 4D 78
Anna Cl. E8 1F 85
Annandale Gro. UB10: Ick 3E 56
Annandale Rd. CR0: C'don 2G 169
DA15: Sidc 7J 125
SE10 6H 105
W4 5A 98
Anna Neagle Cl. E7 4J 69
Annan Way RM1: Rom 1K 55
Anne Boleyn Ct. SE9 6G 125
Anne Boleyn's Wlk. KT2: King T 5E 132
SM3: Cheam 7F 165
Anne Case M. KT3: N Mald 3K 151
Anne Compton M. SE12 7H 123
Anne Goodman Ho. E1 6J 85
(off Jubilee St.)
Anne Matthews Ct. E14 5C 86
(off Selsey St.)
Anne M. IG11: Bark 7G 71
Anne of Cleeves Ct. SE9 6H 125
Annes Ct. NW1 3D 4
Annesley Apts. E3 5C 86
(off Gresham Pl.)
Annesley Av. NW9 3K 43
Annesley Cl. NW10 3A 62
Annesley Dr. CR0: C'don 3B 170
Annesley Ho. SW9 1A 120
Annesley Pl. BR2: Broml 6C 160
Annesley Rd. SE3 1K 123
Annesley Wlk. N19 2G 65
Annesmere Gdns. SE3 3B 124
Anne St. E13 4J 87
Anne Sutherland Ho. BR3: Beck 7K 139
Annett Cl. TW17: Shep 5G 147
Annette Cl. HA3: W'stone 2J 41
Annette Cres. N1 7C 66
Annette Rd. N7 3K 65
(not continuous)
Annett Rd. KT12: Walt T 7J 147
Anne Way KT8: W Mole 4F 149
Annexe Mkt. E1 5J 9
(off Spital Sq.)
Annie Besant Cl. E3 1B 86
Annie Taylor Ho. E12 4E 70
(off Walton Rd.)
Anning St. EC2 3H 9 (4E 84)
Annington Rd. N2 3D 46
Annis Rd. E9 6A 68
Ann La. SW10 6B 100
Ann Moss Way SE16 3J 103
Ann's Cl. SW1 7F 11
Ann's Pl. E1 6J 9
Ann St. N1 1C 84
SE18 5G 107
(not continuous)
Ann Stroud Ct. SE12 5J 123
Annsworthy Av. CR7: Thor H 3D 156
Annsworthy Cres. SE25 2D 156
Ansar Gdns. E17 5B 50
Ansdell Rd. SE15 2J 121
Ansdell St. W8 3K 99
Ansdell Ter. W8 3K 99
Ansell Gro. SM5: Cars 1E 166
Ansell Ho. E1 5J 85
(off Mile End Rd.)
Ansell Rd. SW17 3C 136
Anselm Cl. CR0: C'don 3F 169
Anselm Rd. HA5: Hat E 1D 40
SW6 6J 99
Ansford Rd. BR1: Broml 5E 140
Ansleigh Pl. W11 7F 81
Anson Cl. RM7: Mawney 2H 55
Anson Ho. E1 4A 86
(off Shandy St.)
SW1 7A 18
(off Churchill Gdns.)
Anson M. SW19 7J 135
Anson Pl. SE28 2H 107
Anson Rd. N7 4G 65
NW2 4D 62
Anson Ter. UB5: N'olt 6F 59
Anstey Ct. W3 2H 97
Anstey Ho. E9 1J 85
(off Templecombe Rd.)
Anstey Rd. SE15 3G 121
Anstey Wlk. N15 4B 48
Anstice Cl. W4 7A 98
Anstridge Path SE9 6H 125
Anstridge Rd. SE9 6H 125
Antelope Rd. SE18 3D 106
Antelope Wlk. KT6: Surb 5D 150
Antenor Ho. E2 2H 85
(off Old Bethnal Grn. Rd.)
Anthems Way E20 6D 68
Anthony Cl. NW7 4F 29
Anthony Cope Ct. N1 1F 9
(off Chart St.)
Anthony Ct. W3 2A 98
Anthony Ho. NW8 4C 4
(off Ashbridge St.)
Anthony Rd. DA16: Well 1A 126
SE25 6G 157
UB6: G'frd 3J 77
Anthony St. E1 6H 85
Anthony Way N18 6E 34
Antigua M. E13 3K 87
Antigua Wlk. SE19 5D 138
Antila Ct. E1 3K 9
(off Sclater St.)
Antilles Bay E14 2E 104
Antill Rd. E3 3A 86
N15 4G 49
Antill Ter. E1 6K 85
Antlers Hill E4 5J 25
Antoinette M. NW2 6C 62
Anton Cres. SM1: Sutt 3J 165
Antoneys Cl. HA5: Pinn 2B 40
Antonine Hgts. SE1 7G 15
Anton Pl. HA9: Wemb 3H 61
Anton St. E8 5G 67
Antony Ho. SE16 4J 103
(off Raymouth Rd.)
Antrim Gro. NW3 6D 64
Antrim Rd. NW3 6D 64
Antrobus Cl. SM1: Sutt 5H 165
Antrobus Rd. W4 4J 97
Antwerp Way E16 2E 106
Anvil Cl. SW16 7G 137
Anvil Rd. TW16: Sun 3J 147
Anworth Cl. IG8: Wfd G 6E 36
Apeldoorn Dr. SM6: W'gton 7J 167
Apelles St. SE18 1C 124
(off Tellson Av.)
Apex Cl. BR3: Beck 1D 158
APEX CORNER
(Feltham) 3D 130
(Mill Hill) 4F 29
Apex Ct. W13 7A 78
Apex Ho. E1 3K 9
(off Bacon St.)
Apex Ind. Est. NW10 4B 80
Apex Pde. NW7 4E 28
(off Selvage La.)
Apex Retail Pk. 3D 130
Aphrodite Ct. E14 4C 104
(off Homer Dr.)
E15 1E 86
(off Warton Rd.)
Aplin Way TW7: Isle 1J 113
Apollo Av. BR1: Broml 1K 159
Apollo Bldg. E14 4C 104
Apollo Bus. Cen. SE8 5K 103
Apollo Ct. E1 7G 85
(off Thomas More St.)
E15 1E 86
(off High St.)
SW9 1A 120
(off Southey Rd.)
Apollo Ho. E2 2H 85
(off St Jude's Rd.)
E3 2C 86
(off Garrison Rd.)
N6 7D 46
SW10 7B 100
(off Milman's St.)
Apollo Pl. E11 3G 69
SW10 7B 100
Apollo Theatre 2C 12
(off Shaftesbury Av.)
Apollo Victoria Theatre 2A 18
(off Wilton Rd.)
Apollo Way DA8: Erith 4K 109
SE28 3H 107
Apostle Ct. SE20 7K 139
The Apostles SE23 2K 139
(off Church Ri.)
Apostle Way CR7: Thor H 2B 156
Apothecary St. EC4 1A 14 (6B 84)
Appach Rd. SW2 5A 120
Appian Ct. E3 2B 86
(off Parnell Rd.)
Apple Blossom Ct. SW8 7H 101
(off Pascal St.)
Appleby Cl.
BR5: Pet W 7J 161
E4 6K 35
N15 5D 48
Appleby Cl. TW2: Twick 2H 131
UB8: Hil 6E 74
Appleby Ct. SE6 6C 122
W3 2J 97
(off Newport Rd.)
Appleby Gdns. TW14: Felt 1H 129
Appleby Rd. E8 7G 67
E16 6H 87
Appleby St. E2 2F 85
Appledore Av. DA7: Bex 1J 127
HA4: Ruis 3K 57
Appledore Cl. BR2: Broml 5H 159
HA8: Edg 1G 43
SW17 2D 136
Appledore Cres. DA14: Sidc 3J 143
Appledore Way NW7 7A 30
Appleford Ho. W10 4G 81
(off Bosworth Rd.)
Appleford Rd. W10 4G 81
Apple Gth. TW8: Bford 4D 96
Applegarth CR0: New Ad 7D 170
(not continuous)
KT10: Clay 5A 162
Applegarth Dr. IG2: Ilf 4K 53
Applegarth Ho. SE1 6B 14
SE15 7G 103
(off Bird in Bush Rd.)
Applegarth Rd. SE28 1B 108
W14 3F 99
Applegate Ho. E20 5E 68
(off Victory Pde.)
Apple Gro. EN1: Enf 3K 23
HA2: Harr 1E 58
KT9: Chess 4E 162
TW1: Twick 6A 114
Apple Mkt. KT1: King T 2D 150
(off Market Pl.)
Apple Rd. E11 3G 69
Appleshaw Ho. SE5 3E 120
Appleton Cl. DA7: Bex 2J 127
Appleton Gdns. KT3: N Mald 6C 152
Appleton Rd. SE9 3C 124
Appleton Sq. CR4: Mitc 1C 154
Apple Tree Av. UB7: Yiew 5B 74
UB8: Hil 5B 74
Appletree Cl. SE20 1H 157
Appletree Gdns. EN4: E Barn 4H 21
Apple Tree La. RM13: Rain 2K 91
APPLE TREE RDBT. 6B 74
Apple Tree Yd. E1 3K 85
(off Longnor Rd.)
SW1 4B 12 (1G 101)
Applewood Cl. N20 1H 31
NW2 3D 62
UB10: Ick 4A 56
Applewood Dr. E13 4K 87
Apple Yd. SE20 1G 157
Appold St. EC2 5G 9 (5E 84)
Apprentice Gdns. UB5: N'olt 3D 76
Apprentice Way E5 4H 67
The Approach BR6: Orp 2K 173
EN1: Enf 2C 24
NW4 5F 45
W3 6K 79
Approach Cl. N16 4E 66
Approach Rd. E2 2J 85
EN4: E Barn 4G 21
HA8: Edg 6B 28
KT8: W Mole 5E 148
SW20 2E 152
TW15: Ashf 6E 128
Apps Mdw. Cl. KT8: W Mole 4D 148
Aprey Gdns. NW4 4E 44
April Cl. BR6: Chels 5K 173
TW13: Felt 3J 129
W7 7J 77
April Ct. E2 2G 85
(off Teale St.)
April Glen SE23 3K 139
April St. E8 4F 67
The Apsley Cen. NW2 2C 62
Apsley Cl. HA2: Harr 5G 41
Apsley House 6H 11 (2E 100)
Apsley Ho. E1 5J 85
(off Stepney Way)
NW8 2B 82
(off Finchley Rd.)
SW15 6C 116
(off Holford Way)
TW4: Houn 4D 112
Apsley Rd. KT3: N Mald 3J 151
SE25 4H 157
Apsley Way NW2 2C 62
W1 6H 11 (2E 100)
(not continuous)
Aqua Ho. NW10 3G 79
Aquarelle Ho. EC1 1C 8
Aquarius TW1: Twick 1B 132
Aquarius Bus. Pk. NW2 1C 62
(off Priestley Way)
Aquarius Ct. HA8: Edg 7B 28
Aquarius Golf Course 6J 121
Aqua Vista Sq. E3 5C 86
(off Bow Comn. La.)
Aquila St. NW8 2B 82
Aquinas St. SE1 5K 13 (1A 102)
Arabella Ct. NW8 2A 82
(off Marlborough Pl.)
Arabella Dr. SW15 4A 116
Arabella St. SE16 7K 15 (3G 103)
Arabia Cl. E4 7K 25, 1A 36
Arabian Ho. E1 4A 86
(off Ernest St.)
Arabin Rd. SE4 4A 122
Arado Ho. NW9 2B 44
(off Boulevard Dr.)
Aragon Av. KT7: T Ditt 5K 149
Aragon Cl. BR2: Broml 1D 172
EN2: Enf 1E 22
TW16: Sun 6H 129
Aragon Ct. KT8: E Mos 4G 149
SE11 5J 19
(off Hotspur St.)
Aragon Dr. HA4: Ruis 1B 58
Aragon Ho. E16 1J 105
(off Capulet M.)
Aragon Pl. SM4: Mord 7G 153
Aragon Rd. KT2: King T 5E 132
SM4: Mord 6F 153
Aragon Twr. SE8 4B 104
Aral Ho. E1 4K 85
(off Ernest St.)
Arandora Cres. RM6: Chad H 7B 54
Aran Dr. HA7: Stan 4H 27
Aran Lodge NW6 7J 63
(off Woodchurch Rd.)
Aran M. N7 7A 66
(off St Clements St.)
Arapiles Ho. E14 6F 87
(off Blair St.)
Arbery Rd. E3 3A 86
Arbon Ct. N1 1C 84
(off Linton St.)
Arbor Cl. BR3: Beck 2D 158
Arbor Ct. N16 2D 66
Arboretum Ct. N1 6D 66
(off Dove Rd.)
Arboretum Pl. IG11: Bark 7G 71
(off Clockhouse Av.)
Arborfield Cl. SW2 1K 137
Arborfield Ho. E14 7C 86
(off E. India Dock Rd.)
Arbor Ho. BR6: Orp 2K 173
(off Orchard Gro.)
SE14 6B 104
TW8: Bford 7C 96
Arbor Rd. E4 3A 36
Arbot Ho. SE10 4G 105
(off Manilla Wlk.)
Arbour Ho. E1 6K 85
(off Arbour Sq.)
Arbour Rd. EN3: Pond E 3E 24
Arbour Sq. E1 6K 85
Arbroath Rd. SE9 3C 124
Arbury Ter. SE26 3G 139
Arbus Crescent HA2: Harr 3G 41
Arbuthnot La. DA5: Bexl 6E 126
Arbuthnot Rd. SE14 2K 121
SM4: Mord 4A 154
Arbutus St. E8 1F 85
Arcade CR0: C'don 2C 168
The Arcade CR0: C'don 3C 168
(off High St.)
E20 6E 68
(within Westfield Shop. Cen.)
EC2 6G 9
N7 4J 65
(off Macready Pl.)
SE9 6E 124
(off High St.)
Arcade Chambers SE9 6E 124
Arcade Pde. KT9: Chess 5D 162
Arcadia Av. N3 2J 45
The Arcadia Cen. 7D 78
Arcadia Cl. SM5: Cars 4E 166
Arcadia Ct. E1 7J 9
Arcadia M. KT3: N Mald 3A 152
Arcadian Av. DA5: Bexl 6E 126
Arcadian Cl. DA5: Bexl 6E 126
Arcadian Gdns. N22 7E 32
Arcadian Pl. SW18 7H 117
Arcadian Rd. DA5: Bexl 6E 126
Arcadia St. E14 6C 86
Arc Ct. N11 5A 32
RM7: Rush G 6K 55
ArcelorMittal Orbit 7D 68
Archangel St. SE16 2K 103
Archbishop Lanfranc School
Sports Cen. 6J 155
Archbishop's Pl. SW2 7K 119
Archdale Bus. Cen. HA2: Harr 2G 59
Archdale Ct. W12 1D 98
Archdale Ho. SE1 7G 15
(off Long La.)
Archdale Pl. KT3: N Mald 3H 151
Archdale Rd. SE22 5F 121
Archel Rd. W14 6H 99
Archer Apts. N1 2E 84
(off Fern Cl.)
Archer Cl. EN5: Barn 6C 20
KT2: King T 7E 132
Archer Ho. N1 1E 84
(off Whitmore Est.)
SE14 1A 122
SW11 1B 118
W11 7H 81
(off Westbourne Gro.)
W13 1B 96
(off Sherwood Cl.)
Archer M. SW9 3J 119
TW12: Hamp H 6G 131
Archer Rd. BR5: St M Cry 5K 161
SE25 4H 157
Archers Ct. CR2: S Croy 5C 168
(off Nottingham Rd.)
Archers Dr. EN3: Enf H 2D 24
Archers Lodge SE16 5G 103
(off Culloden Cl.)
Archer Sq. SE14 6A 104
Archer St. W1 2C 12 (7H 83)
Archer Ter. UB7: Yiew 7A 74
Archery Cl. HA3: W'stone 3K 41
W2 1D 10 (6C 82)
Archery Flds. Ho. WC1 1H 7
(off Wharton St.)
Archery La. BR2: Broml 6B 160
Archery Rd. SE9 5D 124
Archery Steps W2 2D 10
Arches SW8 7F 19 (6J 101)
The Arches E16 4G 87
HA2: Harr 2F 59
NW1 7F 65
SE8 6A 104
SW8 7H 101
WC2 4F 13
(off Villiers St.)
The Arches Bus. Cen. UB2: S'hall 2D 94
(off Merrick Rd.)
Arches La. SW11 6F 101
Archgate Bus. Cen. N12 5F 31
Archibald M. W1 3J 11 (7F 83)
Archibald Rd. N7 4H 65
Archibald St. E3 3C 86
Archie Cl. UB7: W Dray 2C 92
Archie St. SE1 7H 15 (2E 102)
Arc Ho. SE1 7J 15
Arch St. SE1 3C 102
ARCHWAY 2G 65
Archway Bus. Cen. N19 3H 65
Archway Cl. SM6: Bedd 3H 167
SW19 3K 135
W10 5F 81
Archway Leisure Cen. 2G 65
Archway Mall N19 2G 65
Archway M. SW15 4G 117
(off Putney Bri. Rd.)
Archway Rd. N6 6E 46
N19 6E 46
Archway St. SW13 3A 116
Arcola St. E8 5F 67
Arcola Theatre 5F 67
Arcon Dr. UB5: N'olt 4C 76

Arcon Ter.—Ashdown Wlk.

Arcon Ter. N9 7B 24
Arctic Ho. NW9 2B 44
(off Heritage Av.)
Arctic St. NW5 5F 65
Arcus Rd. BR1: Broml 6G 141
Ardbeg Rd. SE24 5D 120
Arden Cl. HA1: Harr 3H 59
SE28 6D 90
TW2: Whitt 7D 112
UB4: Yead 4K 75
Arden Ct. Gdns. N2 6B 46
Arden Cres. E14 4C 104
RM9: Dag 7C 72
Arden Est. N1 2E 84
Arden Grange N12 4F 31
Arden Gro. BR6: Farnb 4F 173
Arden Ho. N1 1G 9
SE11 4G 19
SE13 3D 122
(off Thurston Rd.)
SW9 2J 119
(off Grantham Rd.)
Arden M. E17 5D 50
Arden Mhor HA5: Eastc 4K 39
Arden Rd. N3 3H 45
W13 7C 78
Ardent Cl. SE25 3E 156
Ardent Ho. E3 2A 86
(off Roman Rd.)
Ardfern Av. SW16 3A 156
Ardfillan Rd. SE6 1F 141
Ardgowan Rd. SE6 7G 123
Ardilaun Rd. N5 4C 66
Ardingly Cl. CR0: C'don 3K 169
Ardleigh Ct. BR1: Broml 7H 141
(off London Rd.)
Ardleigh Gdns. SM3: Sutt 7J 153
Ardleigh Ho. IG11: Bark 1G 89
(off Cooke St.)
Ardleigh M. IG1: Ilf 3F 71
Ardleigh Rd. E17 1B 50
N1 6E 66
Ardleigh Ter. E17 1B 50
Ardley Cl. HA4: Ruis 7E 38
NW10 3A 62
SE6 3A 140
Ardlui Rd. SE27 2C 138
Ardmay Gdns. KT6: Surb 5E 150
Ardmere Rd. SE13 6F 123
Ardmore La. IG9: Buck H 1E 36
Ardmore Pl. IG9: Buck H 1E 36
Ardoch Rd. SE6 2F 141
Ardra Rd. N9 3E 34
Ardrossan Gdns. KT4: Wor Pk 3C 164
Ardshiel Cl. SW15 3F 117
Ardwell Av. IG6: Ilf 5G 53
Ardwell Rd. SW2 2J 137
Ardwick Rd. NW2 4J 63
The Arena EN3: Enf L 1G 25
Arena Bus. Cen. N4 6C 48
Arena Ho. E3 2C 86
(off Lefevre Wlk.)
Arena Shop. Pk. 6B 48
Arena Sq. HA9: Wemb 4G 61
Arena Twr. E14 2D 104
Ares Ct. E14 4C 104
(off Homer Dr.)
Arethusa Ho. E14 4C 104
(off Cahir St.)
Argali Ho. DA18: Erith 3E 108
(off Kale Rd.)
Argall Av. E10 7K 49
Argall Way E10 1K 67
Argan Cl. EN5: Barn 3C 20
Argenta Way NW10 7H 61
The Argent Cen. UB3: Hayes 2J 93
Argent Ct. E14 5C 86
(off Thomas Rd.)
EN5: New Bar 4F 21
(off Leicester Rd.)
KT6: Surb 3G 163
Argent Ho. IG11: Bark 4A 90
Argenton Twr. SW18 6K 117
(off Mapleton Cres.)
Argo Apts. E16 6H 87
(off Sylvia Pankhurst St.)
Argo Bus. Cen. NW6 3J 81
Argonaut Pk. SL3: Poyle 4A 174
Argon M. SW6 7J 99
Argon Rd. N18 5D 34
Argos Ct. SW9 1A 120
(off Caldwell St.)
Argos Ho. E2 2H 85
(off Old Bethnal Grn. Rd.)
Argosy Ho. SE8 4A 104
Argosy La. TW19: Stanw 7A 110
Argus Cl. RM7: Mawney 1H 55
Argus Way UB5: N'olt 3C 76
Argyle Av. TW3: Houn 6E 112
Argyle Cl. W13 4A 78
Argyle Ho. E14 3E 104
Argyle Pas. N17 1F 49
Argyle Pl. W6 4D 98
Argyle Rd. E1 4K 85
E15 4G 69
E16 6K 87
EN5: Barn 4A 20
HA2: Harr 6F 41
IG1: Ilf 2E 70
N12 5E 30
N17 1G 49
N18 4B 34
TW3: Houn 5F 113
UB6: G'frd 3K 77
W13 5A 78
Argyle Sq. WC1 1F 7 (3J 83)
(not continuous)
Argyle St. WC1 1E 6 (3J 83)
Argyle Wlk. WC1 2F 7 (3J 83)
Argyle Way SE16 5G 103
Argyll Av. UB1: S'hall 1F 95
Argyll Cl. SW9 3K 119
Argyll Ct. SW2 7J 119
(off New Pk. Rd.)
Argyll Gdns. HA8: Edg 2H 43
Argyll Mans. SW3 7B 16 (6B 100)
W14 4G 99
(off Hammersmith Rd.)
Argyll Rd. SE18 3G 107
W8 2J 99
Argyll St. W1 1A 12 (6G 83)
Argyll Ter. SW19 7F 117
Aria Ct. IG2: Ilf 6G 53
Arica Ho. SE16 3H 103
(off Slippers Pl.)
Arica Rd. SE4 4A 122
Ariel Apts. E16 6J 87
Ariel Ct. SE11 4K 19 (4B 102)
Ariel Ho. E1 7G 85
(off Vaughan Way)
Ariel Rd. NW6 6J 63
Ariel Way TW4: Houn 3K 111
W12 1E 98
Aristotle Rd. SW4 3H 119
Arizona Bldg. SE13 1D 122
(off Deal's Gateway)
The Ark W6 5F 99
(off Talgarth Rd.)
Arkell Gro. SE19 7B 138
Arkindale Rd. SE6 3E 140
Arklay Cl. UB8: Hil 4B 74
Arkley Cres. E17 5B 50
Arkley Rd. E17 5B 50
Arklow Ho. SE17 6D 102
Arklow M. KT6: Surb 2E 162
Arklow Rd. SE14 6B 104
Arkwright Rd. CR2: Sande 7F 169
NW3 5A 64
Arla Pl. HA4: Ruis 4A 58
Arlesey Cl. SW15 5G 117
Arlesford Rd. SW9 3J 119
Arlidge Ho. EC1 5K 7
(off Kirby St.)
Arlingford Rd. SW2 5A 120
Arlington N12 3D 30
Arlington Av. N1 2C 84
Arlington Bldg. E3 2C 86
Arlington Cl. DA15: Sidc 7J 125
SE13 5F 123
SM1: Sutt 2J 165
TW1: Twick 6C 114
Arlington Ct. W3 2H 97
(off Mill Hill Rd.)
Arlington Dr. HA4: Ruis 6F 39
SM5: Cars 2D 166
Arlington Gdns. IG1: Ilf 1E 70
W4 5J 97
Arlington Grn. NW7 7A 30
Arlington Ho. EC1 1K 7
(off Arlington Way)
SE8 6B 104
(off Evelyn St.)
SW1 4A 12 (1G 101)
TW9: Kew 7H 97
UB7: W Dray 2B 92
W12 1D 98
(off Tunis Rd.)
Arlington Lodge SW2 4K 119
Arlington M. SE13 5F 123
Arlington Pk. Mans. W4 5J 97
(off Sutton La. Nth.)
Arlington Pas. TW11: Tedd 4K 131
Arlington Pl. SE10 7E 104
Arlington Rd. IG8: Wfd G 1J 51
KT6: Surb 6D 150
N14 2A 32
NW1 1F 83
TW1: Twick 6C 114
TW10: Ham 2D 132
TW11: Tedd 4K 131
TW15: Ashf 5B 128
W13 6B 78
Arlington Sq. N1 1C 84
Arlington St. SW1 4A 12 (1G 101)
Arlington Way EC1 1K 7 (3A 84)
Arliss Ho. HA1: Harr 5K 41
Arliss Way UB5: N'olt 1A 76
Arlow Rd. N21 1F 33
Armada Ct. SE8 6C 104
Armadale Cl. N17 4H 49
Armadale Rd. SW6 7J 99
TW14: Felt 5J 111
Armada St. SE8 6C 104
Armada Way E6 5F 89
Armagh Rd. E3 1B 86
Arments Ct. SE5 6D 102
(off Albany Rd.)
Armfield Cl. KT8: W Mole 5D 148
Armfield Cres. CR4: Mitc 2D 154
Armfield Rd. EN2: Enf 1J 23
Arminger Rd. W12 1D 98
Armistice Gdns. SE25 3G 157
Armitage Ho. NW1 5D 4
(off Lisson Gro.)
Armitage Rd. NW11 1G 63
SE10 5H 105
Armour Cl. N7 6K 65
The Armoury 4C 64
(off Pond St.)
Armoury Ho. E3 1A 86
(off Gunmakers La.)
Armoury Rd. SE8 2D 122
Armoury Way SW18 5J 117
Armsby Ho. E1 5J 85
(off Stepney Way)
Armstead Wlk. RM10: Dag 7G 73
Armstrong Av. IG8: Wfd G 6B 36
Armstrong Cl. BR1: Broml 3C 160
E6 6D 88
HA5: Eastc 6J 39
KT12: Walt T 6J 147
RM8: Dag 7D 54
SE3 4K 123
Armstrong Cres. EN4: Cockf 3G 21
Armstrong Ho. E14 6A 86
(off Commercial Rd.)
Armstrong Rd. NW10 7A 62
SE18 3G 107
SW7 2A 16 (3B 100)
TW13: Hanw 5C 130
W3 1B 98
Armstrong Way UB2: S'hall 2F 95
Armytage Rd. TW5: Hest 7B 94
Arnal Cres. SW18 7G 117
Arncliffe NW6 2K 81
Arncliffe Cl. N11 6K 31
Arncroft Ct. IG11: Bark 3B 90
Arndale Wlk. SW18 5K 117
Arne Gro. BR6: Orp 3K 173
Arne Ho. SE11 5G 19
Arne St. WC2 1F 13 (6J 83)
Arnett Sq. E4 6G 35
Arne Wlk. SE3 4H 123
Arneways Av.
RM6: Chad H 3D 54
Arneway St. SW1 2D 18 (3H 101)
Arnewood Cl. SW15 1C 134
Arneys La. CR4: Mitc 6E 154
Arngask Rd. SE6 7F 123
Arnhem Pl. E14 3C 104
Arnhem Way SE22 5E 120
Arnhem Wharf E14 3B 104
Arnison Rd. KT8: E Mos 4H 149
Arnold Bennett Way N8 3A 48
Arnold Cir. E2 2J 9 (3F 85)
Arnold Cl. HA3: Kenton 7F 43
Arnold Ct. N22 7D 32
Arnold Cres. TW7: Isle 5H 113
Arnold Dr. KT9: Chess 6D 162
Arnold Est. SE1 7K 15 (2F 103)
(not continuous)
Arnold Gdns. N13 5G 33
Arnold Ho. SE3 7A 106
(off Shooters Hill Rd.)
SE17 5B 102
(off Doddington Gro.)
Arnold Mans. W14 6H 99
(off Queen's Club Gdns.)
Arnold Rd. E3 3C 86
N15 3F 49
RM9: Dag 7F 73
RM10: Dag 7F 73
SW17 7D 136
UB5: N'olt 6B 58
Arnold Ter. HA7: Stan 5E 26
Arnos Gro. N14 4C 32
Arnos Gro. Ct. N11 5B 32
(off Palmer's Rd.)
Arnos Rd. N11 5B 32
Arnos Swimming Pool 5C 32
Arnot Ho. SE5 7C 102
(off Comber Gro.)
Arnott Cl. SE28 1C 108
W4 4K 97
Arnould Av. SE5 4D 120
Arnsberg Way DA6: Bex 4G 127
DA7: Bex 4G 127
Arnside Gdns. HA9: Wemb 1D 60
Arnside Ho. SE17 6D 102
(off Arnside St.)
Arnside Rd. DA7: Bex 1G 127
Arnside St. SE17 6D 102
Arnulf St. SE6 4D 140
Arnulls Rd. SW16 6B 138
Arodene Rd. SW2 6K 119
Arona Ho. BR3: Beck 2E 158
Arora Twr. SE10 1F 105
Arosa Rd. TW1: Twick 6D 114
Arpley Sq. SE20 7J 139
(off High St.)
Arragon Gdns. BR4: W W'ck 3D 170
SW16 7J 137
Arragon Rd. E6 1B 88
SW18 1J 135
TW1: Twick 7A 114
Arran Cl. DA8: Erith 6K 109
SM6: W'gton 4F 167
Arran Ct. NW9 2B 44
NW10 3K 61
Arran Dr. E12 1B 70
Arran Ho. E14 1E 104
(off Raleana Rd.)
Arran M. W5 1F 97
Arran Rd. SE6 2D 140
Arran Wlk. N1 7C 66
Arras Av. SM4: Mord 5A 154
Arrival Sq. E1 7G 85
Arrol Ho. SE1 3C 102
Arrol Rd. BR3: Beck 3J 157
Arrow Ct. SW5 4J 99
(off W. Cromwell Rd.)
Arrowhead Quay E14 2C 104
Arrow Ho. N1 1E 84
(off Wilmer Gdns.)
Arrow Rd. E3 3D 86
Arrowscout Wlk. UB5: N'olt 3C 76
(off Argus Way)
Arrows Ho. SE15 7J 103
(off Clifton Way)
Arrowsmith Ho. SE11 5G 19
Arsenal FC 4A 66
Arsenal Rd. SE9 2D 124
Arsenal Way SE18 3G 107
Arta Ho. E1 6J 85
(off Devonport St.)
Artbrand Ho. SE1 7G 15
(off Leathermarket St.)
Artemis Ct. E14 4C 104
(off Homer Dr.)
Artemis Pl. SW18 7H 117
Arterberry Rd. SW20 7E 134
Artesian Cl. NW10 7K 61
Artesian Gro. EN5: New Bar 4F 21
Artesian Ho. SE1 3F 103
(off Grange Rd.)
Artesian Rd. W2 6J 81
Artesian Wlk. E11 3G 69
Arthaus Apts. E8 6H 67
(off Richmond Rd.)
Arthingworth St. E15 1G 87
Arthouse 5J 47
Arthur Ct. CR0: C'don 3E 168
(off Fairfield Path)
SW11 1E 118
W2 6K 81
(off Queensway)
W10 6F 81
(off Silchester Rd.)
Arthur Deakin Ho. E1 5K 9
(off Hunton St.)
Arthurdon Rd. SE4 5C 122
Arthur Gro. SE18 4G 107
Arthur Henderson Ho. SW6 2H 117
(off Fulham Rd.)
Arthur Horsley Wlk. E7 5H 69
(off Tower Hamlets Rd.)
Arthur Ho. N1 1E 84
(off Halcomb St.)
Arthur Lovell Ct. E14 6B 86
(off Lovat Cl.)
Arthur Newton Ho. SW11 3B 118
(off Winstanley Est.)
Arthur Rd. E6 2D 88
KT2: King T 7G 133
KT3: N Mald 5D 152
N7 4K 65
N9 2A 34
RM6: Chad H 6C 54
SW19 5H 135
Arthur St. EC4 2F 15 (7D 84)
Arthur Wade Ho. E2 1K 9
(off Baroness Rd.)
Arthur Wallis Ho. E12 3E 70
(off Grantham Rd.)
Artichoke Hill E1 7H 85
Artichoke M. SE5 1D 120
(off Artichoke Pl.)
Artichoke Pl. SE5 1D 120
Artichoke Wlk. TW9: Rich 5D 114
(off Red Lion St.)
The Artillery Bldg. E1 6H 9
(off Artillery La.)
Artillery Cl. IG2: Ilf 6G 53
Artillery Ho. E3 1A 86
(off Barge La.)
E15 6G 69
SE18 5E 106
(off Connaught M.)
Artillery La. E1 6H 9 (5E 84)
W12 6C 80
Artillery Mans. SW1 1C 18
Artillery Pas. E1 6J 9
Artillery Pl. HA3: Hrw W 7B 26
SE18 4D 106
SW1 2C 18 (3G 101)
Artillery Row SW1 2C 18 (3G 101)
Artillery Sq. SE18 3F 107
Artington Cl. BR6: Farnb 4G 173
Artisan Cl. E6 6F 89
Artisan Ct. E8 6G 67
Artisan M. NW10 3F 81
(off Warfield Rd.)
Artisan Pl. HA3: W'stone 2J 41
Artisan Quarter NW10 3F 81
(off Wellington Rd.)
Artizan St. E1 7J 9
Arts Depot 5F 31
Arts La. SE16 3F 103
Arts Sq. E1 4A 86
Arts Theatre 2E 12
(off Gt. Newport St.)
Arun Ct. SE25 5G 157
Arundale KT1: King T 4D 150
(off Anglesea Rd.)
Arundel Av. SM4: Mord 4H 153
Arundel Bldgs. SE1 3E 102
Arundel Cl. CR0: Wadd 3B 168
DA5: Bexl 6F 127
E15 4G 69
SW11 5C 118
TW12: Hamp H 5F 131
Arundel Ct. BR2: Broml 2G 159
HA2: Harr 4E 58
N12 6H 31
N17 1G 49
SE16 5H 103
(off Verney Rd.)
SW3 5D 16
(off Jubilee Pl.)
SW13 6D 98
(off Arundel Ter.)
W11 7H 81
(off Arundel Gdns.)
Arundel Dr. HA2: Harr 4D 58
IG8: Wfd G 7D 36
Arundel Gdns. HA8: Edg 7E 28
IG3: Ilf 2A 72
N21 1F 33
W11 7H 81
Arundel Gt. Ct. WC2 2H 13 (7K 83)
Arundel Gro. N16 5E 66
Arundel Ho. CR0: C'don 5D 168
(off Heathfield Rd.)
E17 1B 50
Arundel Ho. W3 2H 97
(off Park Rd. Nth.)
Arundel Mans. SW6 1H 117
(off Kelvedon Rd.)
Arundel Pl. N1 6A 66
Arundel Rd. CR0: C'don 6D 156
EN4: Cockf 3H 21
KT1: King T 2H 151
SM2: Cheam, Sutt 7H 165
(not continuous)
TW4: Houn 3A 112
Arundel Sq. N7 6A 66
Arundel St. WC2 2H 13 (7K 83)
Arundel Ter. SW13 6D 98
Arun Ho. KT2: King T 1D 150
Arvon Rd. N5 5A 66
(not continuous)
Asa Ct. UB3: Harl 3H 93
Asbaston Ter. IG1: Ilf 6G 71
Asbridge Ct. W6 3D 98
(off Dalling Rd.)
Asbury Ct. N21 5D 22
(off Pennington Dr.)
Ascalon Ho. SW8 7G 101
(off Thessaly Rd.)
Ascalon St. SW8 7G 101
Ascensis Twr. SW18 4A 118
Ascent Ho. NW9 2B 44
(off Boulevard Dr.)
Ascham Dr. E4 7J 35
Ascham End E17 1A 50
Ascham St. NW5 5G 65
Aschurch Rd. CR0: C'don 7F 157
Ascot Cl. UB5: N'olt 5E 58
Ascot Ct. DA5: Bexl 7F 127
NW8 2A 4
Ascot Gdns. UB1: S'hall 4D 76
Ascot Ho. NW1 1K 5
(off Redhill St.)
W9 4J 81
(off Harrow Rd.)
Ascot Lodge NW6 1K 81
Ascot Pl. HA7: Stan 5H 27
Ascot Rd. BR5: St M Cry 4K 161
E6 3D 88
N15 5D 48
N18 4B 34
SW17 6E 136
TW14: Bedf 1C 128
Ascott Av. W5 2E 96
Ascott Cl. HA5: Eastc 4J 39
Ashanti M. E8 5J 67
Ash Av. SE17 4C 102
Ashbee Ho. E2 3J 85
(off Portman Pl.)
Ashbourne Av. DA7: Bex 7E 108
E18 4K 51
HA2: Harr 2H 59
N20 2J 31
NW11 5H 45
Ashbourne Cl. N12 4E 30
W5 5G 79
Ashbourne Ct. E5 4A 68
N12 4E 30
(off Ashbourne Cl.)
Ashbourne Gro. NW7 5E 28
SE22 4F 121
W4 5A 98
Ashbourne Pde. NW11 4H 45
W5 4F 79
Ashbourne Ri. BR6: Orp 4J 173
Ashbourne Rd. CR4: Mitc 7E 136
W5 4F 79
Ashbourne Ter. SW19 7H 135
Ashbourne Way NW11 4H 45
Ashbridge Rd. E11 7G 51
Ashbridge St. NW8 4C 4 (4C 82)
Ashbrook HA8: Edg 6A 28
Ashbrook Rd. N19 1H 65
RM10: Dag 3H 73
Ashburn Gdns. SW7 4A 100
Ashburnham Av. HA1: Harr 6K 41
Ashburnham Cl. N2 3B 46
Ashburnham Ct. BR3: Beck 2E 158
Ashburnham Gdns. HA1: Harr 6K 41
Ashburnham Gro. SE10 7D 104
Ashburnham Mans. SW10 7A 100
(off Ashburnham Rd.)
Ashburnham M. SW1 3D 18
(off Regency St.)
Ashburnham Pl. SE10 7D 104
Ashburnham Retreat SE10 7D 104
Ashburnham Rd. DA17: Belv 4J 109
NW10 3E 80
SW10 7A 100
TW10: Ham 3B 132
Ashburnham Twr. SW10 7B 100
(off Worlds End Est.)
Ashburn Pl. SW7 4A 100
Ashburton Av. CR0: C'don 1H 169
IG3: Ilf 5J 71
Ashburton Cl. CR0: C'don 1G 169
Ashburton Ent. Cen. SW15 6E 116
Ashburton Gdns. CR0: C'don 2G 169
ASHBURTON GROVE 4A 66
Ashburton Ho. W9 4H 81
(off Fernhead Rd.)
Ashburton Memorial Homes
CR0: C'don 7H 157
Ashburton Pl. W1 4K 11 (1F 101)
Ashburton Rd. CR0: C'don 2G 169
E16 6J 87
HA4: Ruis 2J 57
Ashburton Ter. E13 2J 87
Ashburton Triangle N5 4A 66
Ashbury Dr. UB10: Ick 3D 56
Ashbury Gdns. RM6: Chad H 5D 54
Ashbury Pl. SW19 6A 136
Ashbury Rd. SW11 3D 118
Ashby Av. KT9: Chess 6G 163
Ashby Cl. BR4: W W'ck 3F 171
Ashby Ct. NW8 3B 4
(off Pollitt Dr.)
Ashby Gro. N1 7C 66
(not continuous)
Ashby Ho. N1 7C 66
(off Essex Rd.)
SW9 2B 120
UB5: N'olt 4D 76
(off Waxlow Way)
Ashby M. SE4 2B 122
SW2 5J 119
(off Prague Pl.)
Ashby Rd. N15 5G 49
SE4 2B 122
Ashbys Ct. E3 2B 86
(off Centurion La.)
Ashby St. EC1 2B 8 (3B 84)
Ashby Wlk. CR0: C'don 6C 156
Ashby Way UB7: Sip 7C 92
Ashchurch Gro. W12 3C 98
Ashchurch Pk. Vs. W12 3C 98
Ashchurch Ter. W12 3C 98
Ash Cl. BR5: Pet W 5H 161
DA14: Sidc 3B 144
HA7: Stan 6F 27
HA8: Edg 4D 28
KT3: N Mald 2K 151
RM5: Col R 1H 55
SE20 2J 157
SM5: Cars 2D 166
TW7: Isle 1K 113
UB9: Hare 1A 38
Ashcombe Av. KT6: Surb 7D 150
Ashcombe Cl. TW15: Ashf 3A 128
Ashcombe Ct. TW15: Ashf 2B 128
Ashcombe Gdns. HA8: Edg 4B 28
Ashcombe Ho. E3 3D 86
(off Bruce Rd.)
EN3: Pond E 3E 24
Ashcombe Pk. NW2 3A 62
Ashcombe Rd. SM5: Cars 6E 166
SW19 5J 135
Ashcombe Sq. KT3: N Mald 3J 151
Ashcombe St. SW6 2K 117
Ash Ct. KT19: Ewe 4A 164
N11 6B 32
SW19 7G 135
Ashcroft HA5: Hat E 6A 26
N14 2C 32
Ashcroft Av. DA15: Sidc 6A 126
Ashcroft Ct. N20 2G 31
Ashcroft Cres. DA15: Sidc 6A 126
Ashcroft Ho. SW8 1G 119
(off Wadhurst Rd.)
Ashcroft Rd. KT9: Chess 3F 163
Ashcroft Sq. W6 4E 98
Ashcroft Theatre 3D 168
(within Fairfield Halls)
Ashdale Cl. TW2: Whitt 7G 113
TW19: Stanw 2A 128
Ashdale Gro. HA7: Stan 6E 26
Ashdale Ho. N4 7D 48
Ashdale Rd. SE12 1K 141
Ashdale Way TW2: Whitt 7F 113
Ashdene HA5: Pinn 3A 40
SE15 7H 103
Ashdene Cl. TW15: Ashf 7E 128
Ashdon Cl. IG8: Wfd G 6E 36
Ashdon Rd. NW10 1B 80
Ashdown W13 5B 78
(off Clivedon Ct.)
Ashdown Cl. BR3: Beck 2D 158
DA5: Bexl 7J 127
Ashdown Ct. E17 2E 50
IG11: Bark 6F 71
SM2: Sutt 6A 166
Ashdown Cres. NW5 5E 64
Ashdown Ct. N17 1G 49
Ashdown Pl. KT7: T Ditt 7A 150
KT17: Ewe 7B 164
Ashdown Rd. EN3: Enf H 2D 24
KT1: King T 2E 150
UB10: Hil 2C 74
Ashdown Wlk. E14 4C 104
RM7: Mawney 1H 55

180 A-Z Big London

Ashdown Way—Auriol Rd.

Ashdown Way SW17 2E 136
Ashe Ho. TW1: Twick 6D 114
Ashen E6 6E 88
Ashenden Rd. E5 5A 68
Ashen Gro. SW19 3J 135
Ashentree Ct. EC4 1K 13
Asher Loftus Way N11 6J 31
Asher Way E1 7G 85
Ashfield Av. TW13: Felt 1K 129
WD23: Bush 1B 26
Ashfield Cl. BR3: Beck 7C 140
TW10: Ham 1E 132
Ashfield Ct. SW9 2J 119
(off Clapham Rd.)
Ashfield Ho. W14 5H 99
(off W. Cromwell Rd.)
Ashfield La. BR7: Chst 6F 143
(not continuous)
Ashfield Pde. N14 1C 32
Ashfield Rd. N4 6C 48
N14 3B 32
W3 1B 98
Ashfield St. E1 5H 85
(not continuous)
Ashfield Yd. E1 5J 85
ASHFORD 4B 128
Ashford Av. N8 4J 47
TW15: Ashf 6D 128
UB4: Yead 6B 76
Ashford Bus. Complex TW15: Ashf 5E 128
Ashford Cl. E17 6B 50
TW15: Ashf 4A 128
ASHFORD COMMON 7F 129
Ashford Ct. HA8: Edg 3C 28
NW2 4F 63
Ashford Cres. EN3: Enf H 2D 24
TW15: Ashf 3A 128
Ashford Ho. SE8 6B 104
SW9 4B 120
Ashford Ind. Est. TW15: Ashf 4E 128
Ashford Manor Golf Course 6B 128
Ashford M. N17 1G 49
Ashford Pas. NW2 4F 63
Ashford Rd. E6 7E 70
E18 2K 51
NW2 4F 63
TW13: Felt 4F 129
TW15: Ashf 7E 128
TW18: Lale, Staines 7A 128
Ashford St. N1 1G 9 (3E 84)
Ashford Tennis Club 4A 128
Ash Gro. BR4: W W'ck 2E 170
E8 1H 85
(not continuous)
EN1: Enf 7K 23
HA0: Wemb 4A 60
N10 4F 47
N13 3H 33
NW2 4F 63
SE12 1J 141
SE20 2J 157
TW5: Hest 1B 112
TW14: Felt 1G 129
UB1: S'hall 5E 76
UB3: Hayes 7F 75
UB7: Yiew 7B 74
UB9: Hare 1A 38
W5 2E 96
Ashgrove Ct. W9 5J 81
(off Elmfield Way)
Ashgrove Ho. SW1 5D 18
(off Lindsay Sq.)
Ashgrove Rd. BR1: Broml 6F 141
IG3: Ilf 1K 71
TW15: Ashf 5E 128
Ash Hill Cl. WD23: Bush 1A 26
Ash Hill Dr. HA5: Pinn 3A 40
Ash Ho. E14 2E 104
(off E. Ferry Rd.)
SE1 4F 103
(off Longfield Est.)
W10 4G 81
(off Heather Wlk.)
Ashingdon Cl. E4 3K 35
Ashington Ho. E1 4H 85
(off Barnsley St.)
Ashington Rd. SW6 2H 117
Ash Island KT8: E Mos 3H 149
Ashlake Rd. SW16 4J 137
Ashland Pl. W1 5G 5 (5E 82)
Ashlar Pl. SE18 4F 107
Ashleigh Commercial Est. SE7 3A 106
Ashleigh Ct. N14 7B 22
W5 4D 96
(off Murray Rd.)
Ashleigh Gdns. SM1: Sutt 2K 165
Ashleigh M. SE15 3F 121
(off Oglander Rd.)
Ashleigh Point SE23 3K 139
Ashleigh Rd. SE20 3H 157
SW14 3A 116
Ashley Av. IG6: Ilf 2F 53
SM4: Mord 5J 153
Ashley Cl. HA5: Pinn 2K 39
NW4 2E 44
Ashley Ct. E3 3E 86
(off Bolinder Way)
EN5: New Bar 5F 21
NW4 2E 44
SW1 2A 18
(off Morpeth Ter.)
UB5: N'olt 1C 76
Ashley Cres. N22 2A 48
SW11 3E 118
Ashley Dr. TW2: Whitt 7F 113
TW7: Isle 6J 95
Ashley Gdns. BR6: Orp 5J 173
HA9: Wemb 2E 60
N13 4H 33
SW1 2B 18 (3G 101)
(not continuous)
TW10: Ham 2D 132
Ashley La. CR0: Wadd 4B 168
NW4 2E 44
Ashley Pl. SW1 2A 18 (3G 101)
(not continuous)
Ashley Rd. CR7: Thor H 4K 155
E4 6H 35
E7 7A 70
EN3: Enf H 2D 24
KT7: T Ditt 6K 149
N17 3G 49
N19 1J 65
SW19 6K 135
TW9: Rich 3E 114
TW12: Hamp 1E 148
Ashleys Alley N15 4C 48
Ashley Wlk. NW7 7K 29
Ashling Rd. CR0: C'don 1G 169
Ashlin Rd. E15 4F 69
Ash Lodge KT12: Walt T 7J 147
TW16: Sun 7H 129
(off Forest Dr.)
Ashlone Rd. SW15 3E 116
Ashlyns Way KT9: Chess 6D 162
Ashmead N14 5B 22
Ashmead Bus. Cen. E16 4F 87
Ashmead Cl. TW15: Ashf 7E 128
Ashmead Ga. BR1: Broml 1A 160
Ashmead Ho. E9 5A 68
(off Homerton Rd.)
W13 1A 96
(off Tewkesbury Rd.)
Ashmead M. SE8 2C 122
Ashmead Rd. SE8 2C 122
TW14: Felt 1J 129
Ashmere Av. BR3: Beck 2F 159
Ashmere Cl. SM3: Cheam 5F 165
Ashmere Gro. SW2 4J 119
Ash M. NW5 5G 65
Ashmill St. NW1 5C 4 (5C 82)
Ashmole Pl. SW8 6K 101
Ashmole St. SW8 6K 101
Ashmore NW1 7H 65
(off Agar Gro.)
Ashmore Cl. SE15 7F 103
Ashmore Ct. N11 6J 31
TW5: Hest 6E 94
Ashmore Gro. DA16: Well 3H 125
Ashmore Ho. W14 3G 99
(off Russell Rd.)
Ashmore Rd. SE18 7D 106
W9 2H 81
Ashmount Est. N19 7H 47
Ashmount Rd. N15 5F 49
N19 7G 47
Ashmount Ter. W5 4D 96
Ashmour Gdns. RM1: Rom 2K 55
Ashneal Gdns. HA1: Harr 3H 59
Ashness Gdns. UB6: G'frd 6B 60
Ashness Rd. SW11 5D 118
Ashpark Ho. E14 6B 86
(off Norbiton Rd.)
Ashridge Cl. HA3: Kenton 6C 42
N3 3J 45
Ashridge Ct. N14 5B 22
UB1: S'hall 6G 77
(off Redcroft Rd.)
Ashridge Cres. SE18 7G 107
Ashridge Gdns. HA5: Pinn 4C 40
N13 5C 32
Ashridge Way SM4: Mord 3H 153
TW16: Sun 6J 129
Ash Rd. BR6: Chels 7K 173
CR0: C'don 2C 170
E15 5G 69
SM3: Sutt 7G 153
TW17: Shep 4C 146
Ash Row BR2: Broml 7E 160
Ashtead Rd. E5 7G 49
Ashton Cl. SM1: Sutt 4J 165
Ashton Ct. E4 3B 36
HA1: Harr 3K 59
Ashton Gdns. RM6: Chad H 6E 54
TW4: Houn 4D 112
Ashton Hgts. SE23 1J 139
Ashton Ho. SE11 5K 19
SW9 7A 102
Ashton Pl. KT10: Clay 7A 162
Ashton Reach SE16 4A 104
Ashton Rd. E15 5F 69
Ashton St. E14 7E 86
Ashtree Av. CR4: Mitc 2B 154
Ash Tree Cl. BR6: Farnb 4F 173
CR0: C'don 6A 158
KT6: Surb 2E 162
Ash Tree Ct. TW15: Ashf 5D 128
(off Feltham Hill Rd.)
Ash Tree Dell NW9 5J 43
Ash Tree Ho. SE5 7C 102
(off Pitman St.)
Ash Tree Way CR0: C'don 5K 157
Ashurst Cl. SE20 1H 157
Ashurst Dr. IG2: Ilf 6F 53
IG6: Ilf 5G 53
TW17: Shep 5A 146
Ashurst Gdns. SW2 1A 138
Ashurst Rd. EN4: Cockf 5J 21
N12 5H 31
Ashurst Wlk. CR0: C'don 2H 169
Ashvale Ct. E3 2C 86
(off Matilda Gdns.)
Ashvale Rd. SW17 5D 136
Ashview Apts. N4 7C 48
(off Katherine Cl.)
Ashview Cl. TW15: Ashf 5A 128
Ashview Gdns. TW15: Ashf 5A 128
Ashville Rd. E11 2F 69
Ash Wlk. HA0: Wemb 4C 60
Ashwater Rd. SE12 1J 141
Ash Way IG8: Wfd G 2B 52
The Ashway Cen. KT2: King T 1E 150
Ashwell Cl. E6 6C 88
Ashwell Ct. TW15: Ashf 2A 128
Ashwin St. E8 6F 67
Ashwood Av. UB8: Hil 6C 74
Ashwood Gdns. CR0: New Ad 6E 170
UB3: Harl 4H 93
Ashwood Ho. NW4 4E 44
(off Belle Vue Est.)
Ashwood Rd. E4 3A 36
Ashworth Cl. SE5 2D 120
Ashworth Est. CR0: Bedd 1J 167
Ashworth Mans. W9 3K 81
(off Elgin Av.)
Ashworth Rd. W9 3K 81
Aske Ho. N1 1G 9
Asker Ho. N7 4J 65
Askern Cl. DA6: Bex 4D 126
Aske St. N1 1G 9 (3E 84)
The Askew Bldg. EC1 6C 8
(off Bartholomew Cl.)
Askew Cres. W12 2B 98
Askew Rd. W12 2B 98
Askham Ct. W12 1C 98
Askham Rd. W12 1C 98
Askill Dr. SW15 5G 117
Askwith Rd. RM13: Rain 3K 91
Asland Rd. E15 1G 87
Aslett St. SW18 7K 117
Asman Ho. N1 2B 84
(off Colebrooke Rd.)
Asmara Rd. NW2 5G 63
Asmuns Hill NW11 5J 45
Asmuns Pl. NW11 5H 45
Asolando Dr. SE17 4C 102
Aspect Ct. E14 2E 104
(off Manchester Rd.)
SW6 2A 118
Aspects SM1: Sutt 5K 165
Aspen Cl. KT1: Hamp W 1C 150
N19 2G 65
UB7: Yiew 1B 92
W5 2F 97
Aspen Copse BR1: Broml 2D 160
Aspen Ct. NW4 2G 45
Aspen Dr. HA0: Wemb 3A 60
Aspen Gdns. CR4: Mitc 5E 154
TW15: Ashf 5E 128
W6 5D 98
Aspen Grn. DA18: Erith 3F 109
Aspen Gro. HA5: Eastc 3H 39
Aspen Ho. DA15: Sidc 2A 144
E15 3G 87
(off Teasel Way)
SE15 6J 103
(off Sharratt St.)
Aspen La. UB5: N'olt 3C 76
Aspenlea Rd. W6 6F 99
Aspen Lodge W8 3K 99
(off Abbots Wlk.)
Aspen M. SE20 6J 139
Aspen Pl. WD23: B Hea 1D 26
Aspen Way E14 7D 86
TW13: Felt 3K 129
Aspern Gro. NW3 5C 64
Aspinall Rd. SE4 3K 121
(not continuous)
Aspinden Rd. SE16 4H 103
ASPIRE National Training Cen. 2G 27
Aspire Sport & Fitness Cen. 1K 33
Aspland Gro. E8 6H 67
(off Amhurst Rd.)
Aspley Rd. SW18 5K 117
Asplins Rd. N17 1G 49
Asprey M. BR3: Beck 5B 158
Asprey Pl. BR1: Broml 2C 160
Asquith Cl. RM8: Dag 1C 72
Asquith Ho. SW1 2D 18
(off Monck St.)
Assam St. E1 6G 85
(off White Church La.)
Assata M. N1 6B 66
Assembley Ho. SE14 6B 104
(off Arklow Rd.)
Assembly Apts. SE15 1J 121
(off York Gro.)
Assembly Pas. E1 5J 85
Assembly Wlk. SM5: Cars 7C 154
Ass Ho. La. HA3: Hrw W 4A 26
Astall Cl. HA3: Hrw W 1J 41
Astbury Bus. Pk. SE15 1J 121
Astbury Ho. SE11 2J 19
Astbury Rd. SE15 1J 121
Astell Ho. E14 6G 87
(off Lyell St.)
SW3 5D 16
(off Astell St.)
Astell Rd. SE3 4A 124
Astell St. SW3 5D 16 (5C 100)
Asten Way RM7: Mawney 2H 55
Aster Ct. E5 2J 67
(off Woodmill Rd.)
Asterid Hgts. E20 5E 68
(off Liberty Bri. Rd.)
Aster Pl. E9 7J 67
(off Frampton Pk. Rd.)
Aste St. E14 2E 104
Astey's Row N1 7C 66
Asthall Gdns. IG6: Ilf 4G 53
Astins Ho. E17 4D 50
Astleham Rd. TW17: Shep 3A 146
Astle St. SW11 2E 118
Astley Av. NW2 5E 62
Astley Ho. SE1 5F 103
(off Rowcross St.)
SW13 6D 98
(off Wyatt Dr.)
W2 5J 81
(off Alfred Rd.)
Aston Av. HA3: Kenton 7C 42
Aston Cl. DA14: Sidc 3A 144
Aston Ct. IG8: Wfd G 6D 36
Aston Grn. TW4: Cran 2A 112
Aston Ho. EC4 6J 7
(off Furnival St.)
RM8: Dag 4A 72
SW8 1H 119
W11 7H 81
(off Westbourne Gro.)
Aston M. RM6: Chad H 7C 54
W10 3F 81
Aston Pl. SW16 6B 138
Aston Rd. SW20 2E 152
W5 6D 78
Aston St. E14 5A 86
Aston Ter. SW12 6F 119
Astonville St. SW18 1J 135
Aston Webb Ho. SE1 5G 15
Astor Av. RM7: Rom 6J 55
Astor Cl. KT2: King T 6H 133
Astor Coll. 5B 6
(off Charlotte St.)
Astor Ct. E16 6A 88
(off Ripley Rd.)
SW6 7A 100
(off Maynard Cl.)
Astoria Ct. E8 7F 67
(off Queensbridge Rd.)
Astoria Ho. NW9 2B 44
(off Boulevard Dr.)
Astoria Mans. SW16 3J 137
Astoria Wlk. SW9 3A 120
Astra Ho. E3 3B 86
(off Alfred St.)
SE14 6B 104
(off Arklow Rd.)
Astral Ho. E1 6H 9
(off Middlesex Rd.)
SE6 4E 140
Astrid Ho. TW13: Felt 2A 130
Astrop M. W6 3E 98
Astrop Ter. W6 2E 98
Astwood Dr. HA7: Stan 2D 26
Astwood M. SW7 4A 100
Asylum Rd. SE15 7H 103
Atalanta St. SW6 7F 99
Atbara Rd. TW11: Tedd 6B 132
Atcham Rd. TW3: Houn 4G 113
Atcost Rd. IG11: Bark 5A 90
Atcraft Cen. HA0: Wemb 1E 78
Atelier Ct. SE8 7C 104
(off Watson's St.)
Atelier Ct. Central E14 5E 86
(off Leven Rd.)
Atelier Ct. Nth. E14 5E 86
(off Leven Rd.)
Atelier Ct. Sth. E14 5E 86
(off Leven Rd.)
Atheldene Rd. SW18 1K 135
Athelney St. SE6 3C 140
Athelstane Gro. E3 2B 86
Athelstane M. N4 1A 66
Athelstan Gdns. NW6 7G 63
Athelstan Ho. E9 5B 68
(off Homerton Rd.)
KT1: King T 4F 151
(off Athelstan Rd.)
Athelstan Pl. TW2: Twick 1J 131
Athelstan Rd. KT1: King T 4F 151
Athelstone Rd.
HA3: W'stone 2H 41
Athena Cl. HA2: Harr 2H 59
KT1: King T 3F 151
Athena Ct. SE1 7G 15
(off City Wlk.)
Athenaeum Ct. N5 4C 66
Athenaeum Lawn Tennis Club 6K 53
Athenaeum Pl. N10 3F 47
Athenaeum Rd. N20 1F 31
Athena Pl. HA6: Nwood 1H 39
Athene Pl. EC4 7K 7
(off Thavie's Inn)
Athenia Ho. E14 6F 87
(off Blair St.)
Athenlay Rd. SE15 5K 121
Athens Gdns. W9 4J 81
(off Harrow Rd.)
Atherden Rd. E5 4J 67
Atherfold Rd. SW9 3J 119
Atherley Way TW4: Houn 7D 112
Atherstone Ct. W2 5K 81
(off Delamere Ter.)
Atherstone M. SW7 4A 100
Atherton Dr. SW19 4F 135
Atherton Hgts. HA0: Wemb 7C 60
Atherton Leisure Cen. 6H 69
Atherton M. E7 6H 69
Atherton Pl. HA2: Harr 3H 41
UB1: S'hall 7E 76
Atherton Rd. E7 6H 69
IG5: Ilf 2C 52
SW13 7C 98
Atherton St. SW11 2C 118
Athlone Cl. E5 5H 67
Athlone Ct. E17 3F 51
Athlone Ho. E1 6J 85
(off Sidney St.)
Athlone Pl. W10 5G 81
Athlone Rd. SW2 7K 119
Athlone St. NW5 6E 64
Athlon Ind. Est. HA0: Wemb 1D 78
Athlon Rd. HA0: Wemb 2D 78
Athol Cl. HA5: Pinn 1K 39
Athole Gdns. EN1: Enf 5K 23
Athol Gdns. HA5: Pinn 1K 39
Atholl Ho. W9 3A 82
(off Maida Vale)
Atholl Rd. IG3: Ilf 7A 54
Athol Rd. DA8: Erith 5J 109
Athol Sq. E14 6E 86
Athol Way UB10: Hil 3C 74
Atkin Bldg. WC1 5H 7
(off Raymond Bldgs.)
Atkins Ct. E3 1B 86
(off Willow Tree Cl.)
Atkins Dr. BR4: W W'ck 2F 171
Atkins Lodge W8 2J 99
(off Thornwood Gdns.)
Atkinson Cl. BR6: Chels 5K 173
SW20 7C 134
Atkinson Ct. E10 7D 50
(off Kings Cl.)
Atkinson Ho. E2 2G 85
(off Pritchards Rd.)
E13 4H 87
(off Sutton Rd.)
SE17 4D 102
(off Catesby St.)
SW11 1E 118
(off Austin Rd.)
Atkinson Morley Av. SW17 3B 136
Atkinson Rd. E16 5A 88
Atkins Rd. E10 6D 50
SW12 7G 119
Atkins Sq. E8 5H 67
Atlanta Bldg. SE13 1D 122
(off Deal's Gateway)
Atlanta Ct. CR7: Thor H 3C 156
Atlanta Ho. SE16 3A 104
(off Brunswick Quay)
Atlantic Apts. E16 7J 87
(off Seagull La.)
Atlantic Bldg. E15 5F 69
(off Property Row)
Atlantic Ct. E14 7F 87
(off Jamestown Way)
SW3 5E 16 (5D 100)
Atlantic Rd. SW9 4A 120
Atlantic Wharf E1 7K 85
Atlantis Av. E16 7F 89
Atlantis Cl. IG11: Bark 3B 90
Atlas Bus. Cen. NW2 1D 62
Atlas Cres. HA8: Edg 2C 28
Atlas Gdns. SE7 4A 106
Atlas M. E8 6F 67
N7 6K 65
SE13 4F 123
Atlas Rd. E13 2J 87
HA9: Wemb 4J 61
N11 7K 31
NW10 3A 80
Atlas Trade Pk. DA8: Erith 5K 109
Atlas Wharf E9 6C 68
Atlip Rd. HA0: Wemb 1E 78
Atney Rd. SW15 4G 117
The Atrium IG9: Buck H 2G 37
W12 1F 99
Atrium Apts. N1 1D 84
(off Felton St.)
Atrium Hgts. SE8 6D 104
(off Creekside)
Atrium Ho. SE8 7B 104
Atterbury Rd. N4 6A 48
Atterbury St. SW1 4D 18 (4J 101)
Attewood Av. NW10 3A 62
Attewood Rd. UB5: N'olt 6C 58
Attfield Cl. N20 2G 31
Attfield Ct. KT1: King T 2F 151
(off Albert Rd.)
Attilburgh Ho. SE1 7J 15
(off St Saviour's Est.)
Attleborough Ct. SE23 2G 139
Attle Cl. UB10: Hil 2C 74
Attlee Cl. CR7: Thor H 5C 156
UB4: Yead 3K 75
UB5: N'olt 3K 75
Attlee Rd. SE28 7B 90
UB4: Yead 3J 75
Attlee Ter. E17 4D 50
Attneave St. WC1 2J 7 (3A 84)
Attock M. E17 5D 50
Attwood La. SE10 4G 105
Atunbi Ct. NW1 7G 65
(off Farrier St.)
Atwater Cl. SW2 1A 138
Atwell Cl. E10 6D 50
Atwell Pl. KT7: T Ditt 7K 149
Atwell Rd. SE15 2G 121
Atwood Av. TW9: Kew 2G 115
Atwood Ho. W14 4H 99
(off Beckford Cl.)
Atwood Rd. W6 4D 98
Atwoods All. TW9: Kew 1G 115
Aube Ho. SE6 4E 140
Aubers Ridge Ct. E3 2B 86
(off Festubert Pl.)
Aubert Ct. N5 4B 66
Aubert Pk. N5 4B 66
Aubert Rd. N5 4B 66
Aubrey Beardsley Ho. SW1 4B 18
(off Vauxhall Bri. Rd.)
Aubrey Mans. NW1 5C 4
(off Lisson St.)
Aubrey Moore Point E15 2E 86
(off Abbey La.)
Aubrey Pl. NW8 2A 82
Aubrey Rd. E17 3C 50
N8 5J 47
W8 1H 99
Aubrey Wlk. W8 1H 99
Aubrey Way E17 4D 50
Auburn Cl. SE14 7A 104
Aubyn Hill SE27 4C 138
Aubyn Sq. SW15 5C 116
Auckland Cl. SE19 1F 157
Auckland Ct. UB4: Yead 4A 76
Auckland Gdns. SE19 1E 156
Auckland Hill SE27 4C 138
Auckland Ho. W12 7D 80
(off White City Est.)
Auckland Ri. SE19 1E 156
Auckland Rd. E10 3D 68
IG1: Ilf 1F 71
KT1: King T 4F 151
SE19 1F 157
SW11 4C 118
Auckland St. SE11 6G 19 (5K 101)
Audax NW9 2B 44
Auden Pl. NW1 1E 82
SM3: Cheam 4E 164
Audleigh Pl. IG7: Chig 6K 37
Audley Cl. N10 7A 32
SW11 3E 118
Audley Ct. E18 4H 51
HA5: Pinn 2A 40
TW2: Twick 3H 131
UB5: N'olt 3A 76
Audley Dr. E16 1K 105
Audley Gdns. IG3: Ilf 2K 71
Audley Pl. SM2: Sutt 7K 165
Audley Rd. EN2: Enf 2G 23
NW4 5C 44
TW10: Rich 5F 115
W5 5F 79
Audley Sq. W1 4H 11 (1E 100)
Audrey Cl. BR3: Beck 6D 158
Audrey Gdns.
HA0: Wemb 2B 60
Audrey Rd. IG1: Ilf 3F 71
Audrey St. E2 2G 85
Audric Cl. KT2: King T 1G 151
Augurs La. E13 3K 87
Augusta Cl. KT8: W Mole 3D 148
Augusta Rd. TW2: Twick 2G 131
Augustas La. N1 7A 66
Augusta St. E14 6D 86
Augusta Wlk. W5 5D 78
Augustine Bell Twr. E3 2C 86
(off Pancras Way)
Augustine Rd. HA3: Hrw W 1F 41
W14 3F 99
Augustus Bldg. E1 6H 85
(off Tarling St.)
Augustus Cl. HA7: Stan 3J 27
TW8: Bford 7C 96
W12 2D 98
Augustus Ct. SE1 4E 102
(off Old Kent Rd.)
SW16 2H 137
TW13: Hanw 4D 130
Augustus Ho. NW1 1A 6
(off Augustus St.)
Augustus La. BR6: Orp 2K 173
Augustus Rd. SW19 1F 135
Augustus St. NW1 1K 5 (2F 83)
Aulay Ho. SE16 3F 103
Aultone Way SM1: Sutt 2K 165
SM5: Cars 3D 166
Aultone Yd. Ind. Est.
SM5: Cars 3D 166
Aulton Pl. SE11 6K 19 (5A 102)
Aumonier M. N2 4C 46
Aura Ct. SE15 4H 121
Aura Ho. TW9: Kew 1H 115
Aurelia Gdns. CR0: C'don 5K 155
Aurelia Ho. E20 5E 68
(off Sunrise Cl.)
Aurelia Rd. CR0: C'don 6J 155
Auriel Av. RM10: Dag 6K 73
Auriga M. N1 5D 66
Auriol Cl. KT4: Wor Pk 3A 164
Auriol Dr. UB6: G'frd 7H 59
UB10: Hil 6C 56
Auriol Ho. W12 1D 98
(off Ellerslie Rd.)
Auriol Mans. W14 4G 99
(off Edith Rd.)
Auriol Pk. Rd. KT4: Wor Pk 3A 164
Auriol Rd. W14 4G 99

Aurora Apts. EC1 1C 8
SW18 5J 117
(off Buckhold Rd.)
Aurora Bldg. E14 1E 104
(off Blackwall Way)
The Aurora Bldg. N1 1F 9
Aurora Gdns. 6F 101
Aurora Ho. E14 6D 86
(off Kerbey St.)
SE6 4E 140
Aurora Point SE8 4B 104
(off Grove St.)
Austell Gdns. NW7 3F 29
Austell Hgts. NW7 3F 29
(off Austell Gdns.)
Austen Apts. SE20 2H 157
Austen Cl. SE28 1B 108
Austen Ho. NW6 3J 81
(off Cambridge Rd.)
SW17 3B 136
(off St George's Gro.)
Austen Rd. DA8: Erith 7H 109
HA2: Harr 2F 59
Austin Av. BR2: Broml 5C 160
Austin Cl. SE23 7A 122
TW1: Twick 5C 114
Austin Ct. E6 1A 88
EN1: Enf 5K 23
SE15 3G 121
(off Peckham Rye)
Austin Friars EC2 7F 9 (6D 84)
Austin Friars Pas. EC2 7F 9
Austin Friars Sq. EC2 7F 9
(off Austin Friars)
Austin Ho. SE14 7B 104
(off Achilles St.)
Austin Rd. SW11 1E 118
UB3: Hayes 2H 93
Austin's La. HA4: Ruis 4F 57
UB10: Ick 3E 56
Austin St. E2 2J 9 (3F 85)
Austin Ter. SE1 1K 19
(off Morley St.)
Austral Cl. DA15: Sidc 3K 143
Australia Ho. WC2 1H 13
(off Aldwych)
Australian War Memorial 2E 100
Australia Rd. W12 7D 80
Austral St. SE11 3K 19 (4B 102)
Austyn Gdns. KT5: Surb 1H 163
Autumn Cl. EN1: Enf 1B 24
SW19 6A 136
Autumn Ct. RM7: Rom 6J 55
Autumn Gro. BR1: Broml 6K 141
Autumn Lodge CR2: S Croy 4E 168
(off South Pk. Hill Rd.)
Autumn St. E3 1C 86
Autumn Way UB7: W Dray 2B 92
Avalon Cl. EN2: Enf 2F 23
SE6 2G 141
SW20 2G 153
W13 5A 78
Avalon Ct. CR0: C'don 7F 157
Avalon Rd. SW6 1K 117
W13 4A 78
Avante KT1: King T 3D 150
Avantgarde Pl. E1 3K 9
(off Sclater St.)
Avantgarde Twr. E1 3J 9
(off Sclater St.)
Avard Gdns. BR6: Farnb 4G 173
Avarn Rd. SW17 6D 136
Avebury Ct. N1 1D 84
(off Imber St.)
Avebury Ct. SE16 4J 103
(off Debnams Rd.)
Avebury Pk. KT6: Surb 7D 150
Avebury Rd. BR6: Orp 3H 173
E11 1F 69
SW19 1H 153
Avebury St. N1 1D 84
Avedon Cl. HA2: Harr 2G 41
Aveley Mans. IG11: Bark 7F 71
(off Whiting Av.)
Aveley Rd. RM1: Rom 4K 55
Aveline St. SE11 5H 19 (5A 102)
Aveling Pk. Rd. E17 2C 50
Ave Maria La. EC4 1B 14 (6B 84)
Avenell Mans. N5 4B 66
Avenell Rd. N5 3B 66
Avenfield Ho. W1 2F 11
(off Park La.)
Avening Rd. SW18 7J 117
Avening Ter. SW18 7J 117
Avenir Ho. E15 6F 69
(off Forrester Way)
Avenons Rd. E13 4J 87
Aventine Av. CR4: Mitc 3F 155
The Avenue BR1: Broml 3B 160
BR2: Kes 4B 172
BR3: Beck 1D 158
BR4: W W'ck 7E 158
BR5: St P 7B 144
BR6: Orp 2K 173
CR0: C'don 3E 168
DA5: Bexl 7D 126
E3 4D 86
(off Devas St.)
E4 6A 36
E11 6K 51
EC2 7H 9 (6E 84)
EN5: Barn 3B 20
HA3: Hrw W 1K 41
HA5: Pinn 6D 40
HA9: Wemb 1E 60
IG9: Buck H 2F 37
KT4: Wor Pk 2B 164
KT5: Surb 7F 151
KT17: Ewe 7D 164
N3 2J 45
N8 3A 48
N10 2G 47
N11 5A 32
N17 3D 48
NW6 1F 81
RM1: Rom 4K 55
SE10 7F 105
SM2: Cheam 7G 165
SM5: Cars 7E 166
SW4 4E 118
SW18 7C 118
TW1: Twick 5B 114
TW3: Houn 5F 113
TW5: Cran 7J 93
TW9: Kew 2F 115
TW12: Hamp 6D 130
The Avenue TW16: Sun 1K 147
UB10: Ick 4C 56
W4 3A 98
W13 6B 78
Avenue Cl. N14 6B 22
NW8 1C 82
(not continuous)
TW5: Cran 1K 111
UB7: W Dray 3A 92
Avenue Ct. IG5: Ilf 3C 52
N14 6B 22
NW2 3H 63
SW3 4E 16
(off Draycott Av.)
Avenue Cres. TW5: Cran 1K 111
W3 2H 97
Avenue Elmers KT6: Surb 5E 150
Avenue Gdns. SE25 2G 157
SW14 3A 116
TW5: Cran 7K 93
TW11: Tedd 7K 131
W3 2H 97
Avenue Ho. NW6 7G 63
(off The Avenue)
NW8 2C 82
(off Allitsen Rd.)
NW10 2D 80
(off All Souls Av.)
Avenue Ind. Est. E4 6H 35
Avenue Lodge NW8 7B 64
(off Avenue Rd.)
Avenue Mans. NW3 5K 63
(off Finchley Rd.)
Avenue M. N10 3F 47
Avenue Pde. N21 7J 23
TW16: Sun 3K 147
Avenue Pk. Rd. SE27 2B 138
Avenue Rd. BR3: Beck 2K 157
DA7: Bex 3E 126
DA8: Erith 7J 109
DA17: Belv, Erith 4J 109
E7 4K 69
HA5: Pinn 3C 40
IG8: Wfd G 6F 37
KT1: King T 3E 150
KT3: N Mald 4A 152
N6 7G 47
N12 4F 31
N14 7B 22
N15 5D 48
NW3 7B 64
NW8 7B 64
NW10 2B 80
RM6: Chad H 7B 54
SE20 1J 157
SE25 2F 157
SM6: W'gton 7G 167
SW16 2H 155
SW20 2D 152
TW7: Isle 1K 113
TW8: Bford 5C 96
TW11: Tedd 7A 132
TW12: Hamp 1F 149
TW13: Felt 3H 129
UB1: S'hall 1D 94
W3 2H 97
Avenue Sth. KT5: Surb 7G 151
Avenue Studios SW3 4B 16
(off Sydney Cl.)
Avenue Ter. KT3: N Mald 3J 151
Averil Gro. SW16 6B 138
Averill St. W6 6F 99
Avern Gdns. KT8: W Mole 4F 149
Avern Rd. KT8: W Mole 4F 149
Avershaw Ho. SW15 5F 117
Avery Cl. BR3: Beck 6B 140
Avery Ct. NW9 3J 43
Avery Farm Row SW1 4J 17 (4E 100)
Avery Gdns. IG2: Ilf 5D 52
AVERY HILL 6H 125
Avery Hill Rd. SE9 6H 125
Avery Row W1 2J 11 (7F 83)
Avery Wlk. SW11 3E 118
Aviary Cl. E16 5H 87
Aviation Dr. NW9 2C 44
Aviemore Cl. BR3: Beck 5B 158
Aviemore Way BR3: Beck 5A 158
Avigdor M. N16 2D 66
Avignon Rd. SE4 3K 121
Avingdor Ct. W3 1J 97
(off Horn La.)
Avington Ct. SE1 4E 102
(off Old Kent Rd.)
Avington Gro. SE20 7J 139
Avion Cres. NW9 1C 44
Avis Sq. E1 6K 85
Avoca Rd. SW17 4E 136
Avocet Cl. SE1 5G 103
Avocet M. SE28 3H 107
Avon Cl. KT4: Wor Pk 2C 164
SM1: Sutt 4A 166
UB4: Yead 4A 76
Avon Ct. E4 1K 35
IG9: Buck H 1E 36
N12 5E 30
SW15 5G 117
UB6: G'frd 4F 77
W9 5J 81
(off Elmfield Way)
Avondale Av. EN4: E Barn 1J 31
KT4: Wor Pk 1B 164
KT10: Hin W 3A 162
N12 5E 30
NW2 3A 62
Avondale Ct. E11 1G 69
E16 5G 87
E18 1K 51
SM2: Sutt 7A 166
(off Brighton Rd.)
Avondale Cres. EN3: Enf H 3F 25
IG4: Ilf 5B 52
Avondale Dr. UB3: Hayes 1J 93
Avondale Gdns. TW4: Houn 5D 112
Avondale Ho. SE1 5G 103
(off Avondale Sq.)
Avondale Mans. SW6 1H 117
(off Rostrevor Rd.)
Avondale Pk. Gdns. W11 7G 81
Avondale Pk. Rd. W11 7G 81
Avondale Pavement SE1 5G 103
Avondale Ri. SE15 3F 121
Avondale Rd. BR1: Broml 6G 141
CR2: S Croy 6C 168
DA16: Well 2C 126
E16 5G 87
E17 7C 50
Avondale Rd. HA3: W'stone 3K 41
N3 1A 46
N13 2F 33
N15 5B 48
SE9 2C 142
SW14 3A 116
SW19 5K 135
TW15: Ashf 3A 128
Avondale Sq. SE1 5G 103
Avonfield Ct. E17 3F 51
Avongrove Ct. EC1 1D 8
(off Bollinder Pl.)
Avon Ho. KT2: King T 1D 150
W8 3J 99
(off Allen St.)
W14 4H 99
(off Kensington Village)
Avonhurst Ho. NW2 7G 63
Avonley Rd. SE14 7J 103
Avon M. HA5: Hat E 1D 40
Avonmore Gdns. W14 4H 99
Avonmore Mans. W14 4G 99
(off Avonmore Rd.)
Avonmore Pl. W14 4G 99
Avonmore Rd. W14 4G 99
Avonmouth Apts. SW11 4C 118
(off Monarch Sq.)
Avonmouth St. SE1 7C 14 (3C 102)
Avon Path CR2: S Croy 6C 168
Avon Pl. SE1 7D 14 (2C 102)
Avon Rd. E17 3F 51
SE4 3C 122
TW16: Sun 7H 129
UB6: G'frd 4E 76
Avonstowe Cl. BR6: Farnb 3G 173
Avon Way E18 3J 51
Avonwick Rd. TW3: Houn 2F 113
Avril Way E4 5K 35
Avro Ct. E9 5A 68
(off Mabley St.)
Avro Ho. NW9 2B 44
(off Boulevard Dr.)
SW8 7F 101
(off Havelock Ter.)
Avro Pl. TW5: Hest 7A 94
Avro Way SM6: W'gton 7J 167
Awlfield Av. N17 1D 48
Awliscombe Rd. DA16: Well 2K 125
Axe St. IG11: Bark 1G 89
(not continuous)
Axholme Av. HA8: Edg 1G 43
Axiom Apts. BR2: Broml 4K 159
(off Masons Hill)
Axio Way E3 5C 86
Axis Apts. E1 3J 9
(off Sclater St.)
Axis Ct. SE10 6G 105
(off Woodland Cres.)
SE16 2G 103
(off East La.)
Axis Ho. SE13 4E 122
(off Lewisham High St.)
Axminster Cres. DA16: Well 1C 126
Axminster Rd. N7 3J 65
Axon Pl. IG1: Ilf 2G 71
Aybrook St. W1 6G 5 (5E 82)
Aycliffe Cl. BR1: Broml 4D 160
Aycliffe Ho. SE17 6D 102
(off Portland St.)
Aycliffe Rd. W12 1C 98
Ayerst Ct. E10 7E 50
Aylands Cl. HA9: Wemb 2E 60
Aylesbury Cl. E7 6H 69
Aylesbury Ct. SM1: Sutt 3A 166
Aylesbury Ho. HA0: Wemb 1E 78
(off Hatton Rd.)
SE15 6G 103
(off Friary Est.)
Aylesbury Rd. BR2: Broml 3J 159
SE17 5D 102
Aylesbury St. EC1 4A 8 (4B 84)
NW10 3K 61
Aylesford Av. BR3: Beck 5A 158
Aylesford Ho. SE1 7F 15
(off Long La.)
Aylesford St. SW1 5C 18 (5H 101)
Aylesham Cen. 1G 121
Aylesham Cl. NW7 7H 29
Aylesham Rd. BR6: Orp 7K 161
Ayles Rd. UB4: Yead 3K 75
Aylestone Av. NW6 7F 63
Aylett Rd. SE25 4H 157
TW7: Isle 2J 113
Ayley Cft. EN1: Enf 5B 24
Ayliffe Cl. KT1: King T 2G 151
Aylmer Cl. HA7: Stan 4F 27
Aylmer Ct. N2 5D 46
Aylmer Dr. HA7: Stan 4F 27
Aylmer Ho. SE10 5F 105
Aylmer Pde. N2 5D 46
Aylmer Rd. E11 1H 69
N2 5C 46
RM8: Dag 3E 72
W12 2B 98
Ayloffe Rd. RM9: Dag 6F 73
Aylsham Dr. UB10: Ick 2E 56
Aylton Est. SE16 2J 103
Aylward Rd. SE23 2K 139
SW20 2H 153
Aylwards Ri. HA7: Stan 4F 27
Aylward St. E1 6J 85
(Jamaica St.)
E1 6J 85
(Jubilee St.)
Aylwin Est. SE1 3E 102
Aynhoe Mans. W14 4F 99
(off Aynhoe Rd.)
Aynhoe Rd. W14 4F 99
Aynscombe Path SW14 2J 115
Ayr Ct. W3 5G 79
Ayres Cl. E13 3J 87
Ayres St. SE1 6D 14 (2C 102)
Ayr Grn. RM1: Rom 1K 55
Ayrsome Rd. N16 3E 66
Ayrton Gould Ho. E2 3K 85
(off Roman Rd.)
Ayrton Rd. SW7 1A 16 (3B 100)
Ayr Way RM1: Rom 1K 55
Aysgarth Ct. SM1: Sutt 3K 165
Aysgarth Rd. SE21 7E 120
Ayston Ho. SE16 4K 103
(off Plough Way)
Aytoun Pl. SW9 2K 119
Aytoun Rd. SW9 2K 119
Azalea Cl. IG1: Ilf 5F 71
W7 1K 95
Azalea Ct. IG8: Wfd G 6B 36
W7 1K 95
Azalea Ho. SE14 7B 104
(off Achilles St.)
TW13: Felt 1K 129
Azalea Wlk. HA5: Eastc 5K 39
Azania M. NW5 6F 65
Azenby Rd. SE15 2F 121
Azof St. SE10 4G 105
Azov Ho. E1 4A 86
(off Commodore St.)
Aztec Ho. IG1: Ilf 2H 71
IG6: Ilf 1G 53
Azura Ct. E15 1E 86
(off Warton Rd.)
Azure Bldg. E15 7F 69
(off Gt. Eastern Rd.)
Azure Ct. NW9 5G 43
Azure Ho. E2 3G 85
(off Buckfast St.)
Azure Pl. TW3: Houn 4F 113

B

Baalbec Rd. N5 5B 66
Babbacombe Cl. KT9: Chess 5D 162
Babbacombe Gdns. IG4: Ilf 4C 52
Babbacombe Ho. BR1: Broml 1J 159
(off Babbacombe Rd.)
Babbacombe Rd. BR1: Broml 1J 159
Babbage Ct. SE17 6B 102
(off Cook's Rd.)
Babbage Point SE10 6D 104
(off Norman Rd.)
Babell Ho. N1 6B 66
(off Canonbury Rd.)
Baber Bri. Cvn. Site 5A 112
Baber Bri. Pde. TW14: Felt 6A 112
Baber Dr. TW14: Felt 6A 112
Babington Ct. WC1 5G 7
Babington Ho. SE1 6D 14
(off Disney St.)
Babington Ri. HA9: Wemb 6G 61
Babington Rd. NW4 4D 44
RM8: Dag 5C 72
SW16 5H 137
Babmaes St. SW1 3C 12 (7H 83)
Bache's St. N1 2F 9 (3D 84)
Back All. EC3 1H 15
Bk. Church La. E1 6G 85
Bk. Hill EC1 4K 7 (4A 84)
Backhouse Pl. SE17 4E 102
Back La. DA5: Bexl 7G 127
HA8: Edg 1J 43
IG9: Buck H 2G 37
N8 5J 47
NW3 4A 64
NW9 2K 43
RM6: Chad H 7D 54
TW8: Bford 6D 96
TW10: Ham 3C 132
Backley Gdns. SE25 6G 157
Back Rd. DA14: Sidc 4A 144
E11 6G 51
E17 4E 50
TW11: Tedd 7J 131
Bacon Gro. SE1 3F 103
Bacon La. HA8: Edg 1G 43
NW9 4H 43
(not continuous)
Bacon's College Sports Cen. 1A 104
Bacons La. N6 1E 64
Bacon St. E1 3K 9 (4F 85)
E2 3K 9 (4F 85)
Bacon Ter. RM8: Dag 5B 72
Bacton NW5 5E 64
Bacton St. E2 3J 85
Baddeley Ho. KT8: W Mole 5E 148
(off Down St.)
Baddesley Ho. SE11 5H 19
Baddow Cl. IG8: Wfd G 6F 37
RM10: Dag 1G 91
Baden Dr. E4 4J 25
Baden Pl. SE1 6E 14 (2D 102)
Baden Powell Cl. KT6: Surb 2F 163
RM9: Dag 1E 90
Baden Powell Ho. 2A 16
Baden Powell Ho. DA17: Belv 3G 109
(off Ambrooke Rd.)
Baden Rd. IG1: Ilf 5F 71
N8 4H 47
Bader Ct. NW9 2B 44
(off Runway Cl.)
Bader Way SW15 6C 116
UB10: Uxb 7A 56
Badger Cl. IG2: Ilf 6G 53
TW4: Houn 3A 112
TW13: Felt 3K 129
Badger Ct. NW2 3E 62
Badgers Cl. EN2: Enf 3G 23
HA1: Harr 6H 41
TW15: Ashf 5B 128
UB3: Hayes 7G 75
Badgers Copse BR6: Orp 2K 173
KT4: Wor Pk 2B 164
Badgers Cft. N20 7B 20
SE9 3E 142
Badgers Hole CR0: C'don 4K 169
Badgers Wlk. KT3: N Mald 2A 152
Badlis Rd. E17 3C 50
Badma Cl. N9 3D 34
Badminton Cl. HA1: Harr 4J 41
UB5: N'olt 6E 58
Badminton M. E16 1J 105
Badminton Rd. SW12 6E 118
Badric Ct. SW11 2B 118
Badsworth Rd. SE5 1C 120
Baffin Way E14 1E 104
Bafton Ga. BR2: Hayes 1K 171
Bagley Cl. UB7: W Dray 2A 92
Bagley's La. SW6 1K 117
Bagleys Spring RM6: Chad H 4E 54
Bagley Wlk. N1 1H 83
Bagnigge Ho. WC1 2J 7
(off Margery St.)
Bagshot Ct. SE18 1E 124
Bagshot Ho. NW1 1K 5
Bagshot Rd. EN1: Enf 7A 24
Bagshot St. SE17 5E 102
Bahram Ct. E2 4H 85
(off Three Colts La.)
Baildon E2 2J 85
(off Cyprus St.)
Baildon St. SE8 7B 104
Bailes Pl. BR3: Beck 1A 158
Bailey Cl. E4 4K 35
N11 7C 32
SE28 1J 107
Bailey Cotts. E14 5A 86
(off Maroon St.)
Bailey Ct. NW9 3A 44
(off Lingard Av.)
Bailey Cres. KT9: Chess 7D 162
Bailey Ho. E3 3D 86
(off Talwin St.)
SW10 7K 99
(off Coleridge Gdns.)
Bailey M. SW2 5A 120
W4 6H 97
Bailey Pl. N16 5E 66
SE26 6K 139
Baileys Ho. SW11 7H 101
(off Charles Clowes Wlk)
Bailey St. SE8 4A 104
Bailey Twr. E1 7H 85
Baillies Wlk. W5 2D 96
Bainbridge Cl. TW10: Ham 5E 132
Bainbridge Court SE10 3J 105
(off Rennie Street)
Bainbridge Rd. RM9: Dag 4F 73
Bainbridge St. WC1 7D 6 (6H 83)
Baines Cl. CR2: S Croy 5D 168
Baird Av. UB1: S'hall 7F 77
Baird Cl. E10 1C 68
NW9 6J 43
Baird Gdns. SE19 4E 138
Baird Ho. W12 7D 80
(off White City Est.)
Baird Memorial Cotts. N14 2C 32
(off Balaams La.)
Baird Rd. EN1: Enf 3C 24
Baird St. EC1 3D 8 (4C 84)
Bairny Wood App. IG8: Wfd G 6E 36
Baizdon Rd. SE3 2G 123
Bakehouse M. TW12: Hamp 7E 130
Baker Beal Ct. DA7: Bex 3H 127
Baker Ho. E3 3D 86
(off Bromley High St.)
W7 1K 95
WC1 4F 7
(off Colonnade)
Baker La. CR4: Mitc 2E 154
Baker Pas. NW10 1A 80
Baker Pl. KT19: Ewe 6J 163
Baker Rd. NW10 1A 80
SE18 7C 106
Bakers Av. E17 6D 50
Bakers Ct. SE25 3E 156
Bakers End SW20 2G 153
Baker's Fld. N7 4H 65
Bakers Field Cl. KT19: Ewe 7K 163
Bakers Gdns. SM5: Cars 2C 166
Bakers Hall Ct. EC3 3G 15
Bakers Hill E5 1J 67
EN5: New Bar 2E 20
Bakers Ho. W5 1D 96
(off The Grove)
Bakers La. N6 6D 46
Baker's M. W1 7G 5 (6E 82)
Bakers M. BR6: Chels 6K 173
Bakers Pas. NW3 4A 64
(off Heath St.)
Baker's Rents E2 2J 9 (3F 85)
Baker's Row E15 2G 87
EC1 4J 7 (4A 84)
BAKER STREET 5D 82
Baker St. EN1: Enf 3J 23
NW1 4F 5 (4D 82)
W1 4F 5 (4D 82)
Baker's Yd. EC1 4J 7
Bakery Cl. RM6: Chad H 3E 54
SW9 7K 101
Bakery M. KT6: Surb 1G 163
Bakery Path HA8: Edg 5C 28
(off St Margaret's Rd.)
Bakery Pl. SW11 4D 118
Bakery St. SE16 3F 103
Bakewell Way KT3: N Mald 2A 152
Balaam Ho. SM1: Sutt 4J 165
Balaam Leisure Cen. 4J 87
Balaams La. N14 2C 32
Balaam St. E13 4J 87
Balaclava Rd. KT6: Surb 7C 150
SE1 4F 103
Bala Grn. NW9 6A 44
(off Ruthin Cl.)
Balboa Court E14 5A 86
(off Pechora Way)
Balcaskie Rd. SE9 5D 124
Balchen Rd. SE3 2B 124
Balchier Rd. SE22 6H 121
Balcombe Cl. DA6: Bex 4D 126
Balcombe Ho. NW1 3E 4
(off Taunton Pl.)
Balcombe St. NW1 3E 4 (4D 82)
Balcon Ct. W5 6F 79
The Balcony W12 1F 99
Balcorne St. E9 7J 67
Balder Ri. SE12 2K 141
Balderton Flats W1 1H 11
(off Balderton St.)
Balderton St. W1 1H 11 (6E 82)
Baldewyne Ct. N17 1G 49
Baldock St. E3 2D 86
Baldrey Ho. SE10 5H 105
(off Blackwall La.)
Baldry Gdns. SW16 6J 137
Baldwin Cres. SE5 1C 120
Baldwin Gdns. TW3: Houn 1G 113
Baldwin Ho. SW2 1A 138
Baldwin Rd. SW11 6E 118
Baldwins Gdns. EC1 5J 7 (5A 84)
Baldwin St. EC1 2E 8 (3D 84)
Baldwin Ter. N1 2C 84
Baldwyn Gdns. W3 7K 79
Baldwyn's Pk. DA5: Bexl 2K 145
Baldwyn's Rd. DA5: Bexl 2K 145
Balearic Apts. E16 7J 87
(off Western Gateway)
Bale Rd. E1 5A 86
Bales Ter. N9 3A 34
Balfern Gro. W4 5A 98
Balfern St. SW11 2C 118
Balfe St. N1 2J 83
Balfour Av. W7 1K 95
Balfour Bus. Cen. UB2: S'hall 3A 94
Balfour Gro. N20 3J 31
Balfour Ho. SW11 1E 118
(off Forfar Rd.)
W10 5F 81
(off St Charles Sq.)

Balfour M.—Baron Ho.

Balfour M. N9 3B 34
W1 4H 11 (1E 100)
Balfour Pl. SW15 4D 116
W1 3H 11 (7E 82)
Balfour Rd. BR2: Broml 5B 160
HA1: Harr 5H 41
IG1: Ilf 2F 71
N5 4C 66
SE25 5G 157
SM5: Cars 7D 166
SW19 7K 135
TW3: Houn 3F 113
UB2: S'hall 3B 94
W3 5J 79
W13 2A 96
Balfour St. SE17 4D 102
Balfour Ter. N3 2C 45
Balfron Twr. E14 6E 86
Balgonie Rd. E4 1A 36
Balgove Ct. NW10 6D 62
(off Eden Gro.)
Balgowan Cl. KT3: N Mald 5A 152
Balgowan Rd. BR3: Beck 3A 158
Balgowan St. SE18 4K 107
BALHAM 1E 136
Balham Gro. SW12 7E 118
Balham High Rd. SW12 3E 136
SW17 3E 136
Balham Hill SW12 7F 119
Balham Leisure Cen. 2F 137
Balham New Rd. SW12 7F 119
Balham Pk. Rd. SW12 1D 136
Balham Rd. N9 2B 34
Balham Sta. Rd. SW12 1F 137
Balin Ho. SE1 6E 14
(off Long La.)
Balladier Wlk. E14 5D 86
Ballamore Rd. BR1: Broml 3J 141
Ballance Rd. E9 6K 67
Ballantine St. SW18 4A 118
Ballantrae Ho. NW2 4H 63
Ballantyne Cl. SE9 4C 142
Ballard Cl. KT2: King T 7K 133
Ballard Ho. SE10 6D 104
(off Thames St.)
Ballards Cl. RM10: Dag 1H 91
Ballards Farm Rd. CR0: C'don 6G 169
CR2: S Croy 6G 169
Ballards La. N3 1J 45
N12 1J 45
Ballards M. HA8: Edg 6B 28
Ballards Ri. CR2: Sels 6G 169
Ballards Rd. NW2 2C 62
RM10: Dag 2H 91
Ballards Way CR0: C'don 6G 169
CR2: Sels 6G 169
Ballast Quay SE10 5F 105
Ballater Rd. CR2: S Croy 5F 169
SW2 4J 119
Ball Ct. EC3 1F 15
(off Birchin La.)
Balletica Apts. WC2 1F 13
(off Long Acre)
Ball Ho. NW9 3B 44
(off Aerodrome Rd.)
Ballie Apts. E16 7G 89
(off Lock Side Way)
Ballina St. SE23 7K 121
Ballin Ct. E14 2E 104
(off Stewart St.)
Ballingdon Rd. SW11 6E 118
Ballinger Point E3 3D 86
(off Bromley High St.)
Ballinger Way UB5: N'olt 4C 76
Balliol Av. E4 4B 36
Balliol Rd. DA16: Well 2B 126
N17 1E 48
W10 6E 80
Balloch Rd. SE6 1F 141
Ballogie Av. NW10 4A 62
Ballow Cl. SE5 7E 102
Balls Pond Pl. N1 6D 66
Balls Pond Rd. N1 6D 66
Balmain Cl. W5 1D 96
Balmain Ct. TW3: Houn 1F 113
Balmain Lodge KT5: Surb 4E 150
(off Cranes Pk. Av.)
Balman Ho. SE16 4K 103
(off Rotherhithe New Rd.)
Balmer Rd. E3 2B 86
Balmes Rd. N1 1D 84
Balmoral Apts. W2 6C 4
(off Praed St.)
Balmoral Av. BR3: Beck 4A 158
N11 6K 31
Balmoral Cl. SW15 6F 117
Balmoral Ct. BR3: Beck 1E 158
(off The Avenue)
HA9: Wemb 3F 61
KT4: Wor Pk 2D 164
NW8 2B 82
(off Queen's Ter.)
SE12 4K 141
SE16 1K 103
(off King & Queen Wharf)
SE17 5D 102
(off Merrow St.)
SE27 4C 138
SM2: Sutt 7J 165
Balmoral Cres. KT8: W Mole 3E 148
Balmoral Dr. UB1: S'hall 4D 76
UB4: Hayes 4G 75
Balmoral Gdns. DA5: Bexl 7F 127
IG3: Ilf 1K 71
W13 3A 96
Balmoral Ho. E14 3D 104
(off Lanark Sq.)
E16 1K 105
(off Keats Av.)
SE1 1F 103
(off Duchess Wlk.)
W14 4G 99
(off Windsor Way)
Balmoral M. W12 3B 98
Balmoral Rd. E7 4A 70
E10 2D 68
HA2: Harr 4E 58
KT1: King T 4F 151
KT4: Wor Pk 3D 164
NW2 6D 62
Balmoral Trad. Est. IG11: Bark 5K 89
Balmore Cl. E14 6E 86
Balmore Cres. EN4: Cockf 5K 21
Balmore St. N19 2F 65
Balmuir Gdns. SW15 4E 116
Balnacraig Av. NW10 4A 62
Balniel Ga. SW1 5D 18 (5H 101)
Balsam Ho. E14 7D 86
(off E. India Dock Rd.)
Baltic Apts. E16 7J 87
(off Western Gateway)
Baltic Av. TW8: Bford 5D 96
Baltic Cl. SW19 7B 136
Baltic Ct. E1 1J 103
(off Clave St.)
SE16 2K 103
Baltic Ho. SE5 2C 120
Baltic Pl. N1 1E 84
Baltic St. E. EC1 4C 8 (4C 84)
Baltic St. W. EC1 4C 8 (4C 84)
Baltimore Cl. DA17: Belv 2H 109
Baltimore Ct. SW1 4C 18
(off Vauxhall Bri. Rd.)
Baltimore Ho. SE11 5J 19
SW18 3A 118
Baltimore Pl. DA16: Well 2K 125
Baltimore Wharf E14 3D 104
Balvaird Pl. SW1 6D 18 (5H 101)
Balvernie Gro. SW18 7H 117
Balvernie M. SW18 7J 117
Bamber Ho. IG11: Bark 1G 89
Bamber Rd. SE15 1F 121
Bamboo Ct. E5 2J 67
(off Woodmill Rd.)
Bamborough Gdns. W12 2E 98
Bamburgh N17 7C 34
Bamford Av. HA0: Wemb 1F 79
Bamford Rd. BR1: Broml 5E 140
IG11: Bark 6G 71
Bampfylde Cl. SM6: W'gton 3G 167
Bampton Ct. W5 6D 78
Bampton Dr. NW7 7H 29
Bampton Rd. SE23 3K 139
Banavie Gdns. BR3: Beck 1E 158
Banbury Cl. EN2: Enf 1G 23
Banbury Ct. SM2: Sutt 7J 165
WC2 2E 12
Banbury Ho. E9 7K 67
Banbury Rd. E9 7K 67
E17 7E 34
Banbury St. SW11 2C 118
Banbury Wlk. UB5: N'olt 2E 76
(off Brabazon Rd.)
Banchory Rd. SE3 7K 105
Bancroft Av. IG9: Buck H 2D 36
N2 5C 46
Bancroft Cl. TW15: Ashf 5C 128
Bancroft Ct. SW8 7J 101
(off Allen Edwards Dr.)
UB5: N'olt 1A 76
Bancroft Gdns. BR6: Orp 1K 173
HA3: Hrw W 1G 41
Bancroft Ho. E1 4J 85
(off Cephas St.)
Bancroft Rd. E1 3J 85
HA3: Hrw W 2G 41
Bandon Cl. UB10: Uxb 2B 74
BANDONHILL 5H 167
Bandon Ri. SM6: W'gton 5H 167
Banfield Rd. SE15 3H 121
Banfor Ct. SM6: W'gton 5G 167
Bangalore St. SW15 3E 116
Bangla Ho. E8 1F 85
(off Clarissa St.)
Bangor Cl. UB5: N'olt 5F 59
Banim St. W6 4D 98
Banister Ho. E9 5K 67
SW8 1G 119
(off Wadhurst Rd.)
W10 3G 81
(off Bruckner St.)
Banister M. NW6 7K 63
Banister Rd. W10 3F 81
The Bank N6 1F 65
Bank Av. CR4: Mitc 2B 154
Bank Bldgs. E4 6A 36
(off The Avenue)
Bank Ct. E17 4E 50
Bank End SE1 4D 14 (1C 102)
Bankfoot Rd. BR1: Broml 4G 141
Bankhurst Rd. SE6 7B 122
Bank La. KT2: King T 7E 132
SW15 5A 116
Bank M. SM1: Sutt 6A 166
Bank of England 1E 14 (6D 84)
Bank of England Museum 1F 15
Bank of England Sports Cen. 5A 116
Banks Ho. SE1 3C 102
(off Rockingham St.)
Banksian Wlk. TW7: Isle 1J 113
Banksia Rd. N18 5E 34
Bankside CR2: S Croy 6F 169
EN2: Enf 1G 23
SE1 3C 14 (7C 84)
(not continuous)
UB1: S'hall 1B 94
Bankside Av. SE13 3E 122
UB5: N'olt 2J 75
Bankside Cl. DA5: Bexl 4K 145
SM5: Cars 6C 166
TW7: Isle 4K 113
Bankside Dr. KT7: T Ditt 1B 162
Bankside Gallery 3B 14 (7B 84)
Bankside Lofts SE1 4B 14
Bankside Mix 4C 14 (1C 102)
Bankside Pk. IG11: Bark 3A 90
Bankside Pl. N4 6C 48
Bankside Rd. IG1: Ilf 5G 71
Bankside Way SE19 6E 138
Banks La. DA6: Bex 4F 127
Bank St. E14 1D 104
Banks Way E12 4E 70
Banks Yd. TW5: Hest 6D 94
Bankton Rd. SW2 4A 120
Bankwell Rd. SE13 4G 123
Bannatyne Health Club
Chingford 6H 35
Grove Park 2K 141
Maida Vale 2K 81
(off Greville Rd.)
Orpington 7D 144
Russell Square 3D 6
(off Woburn Pl.)
Banner Ct. SE16 4J 103
(off Rotherhithe New Rd.)
Banner Ho. EC1 4D 8
(off Roscoe St.)
Banner La. RM8: Dag 1E 72
Bannerman Ho.
SW8 7G 19 (6K 101)
Banner St. EC1 4D 8 (4C 84)
Banning St. SE10 5G 105
Bannister Cl. SW2 1A 138
UB6: G'frd 5H 59
Bannister Ho. HA3: W'stone 3J 41
(off Headstone Dr.)
SE14 6K 103
(off John Williams Cl.)
Bannister Sports Cen. 6B 26
Bannockburn Rd. SE18 4J 107
Bannon Ct. SW6 1K 117
(off Michael Rd.)
Bannow Cl. KT19: Ewe 4A 164
Banqueting House 5E 12 (1J 101)
Banstead Ct. W12 7B 80
Banstead Gdns. N9 3K 33
Banstead Rd. SM5: Cars 7B 166
Banstead Rd. Sth. SM2: Sutt 7B 166
Banstead St. SE15 3J 121
Banstead Way SM6: W'gton 5J 167
Banstock Rd. HA8: Edg 6C 28
Bantam Ho. NW9 2B 44
(off Heritage Av.)
Banting Dr. N21 5E 22
Banting Ho. NW2 3C 62
Bantock Ho. W10 3G 81
(off Third Av.)
Banton Cl. EN1: Enf 2C 24
Bantry Ho. E1 4K 85
(off Ernest St.)
Bantry St. SE5 7D 102
Banwell Rd. DA5: Bexl 6D 126
Banyan Court E16 1K 105
(off Regalia Close)
Banyard Rd. SE16 3H 103
Baptist Gdns. NW5 6E 64
Baquba SE13 2D 122
Barandon Rd. W11 7F 81
(off Grenfell Rd.)
Barandon Wlk. W11 7F 81
Barbanel Ho. E1 4J 85
(off Cephas St.)
Barbara Brosnan Ct. NW8 1A 4 (2B 82)
Barbara Castle Cl. SW6 6H 99
Barbara Cl. TW17: Shep 7D 146
Barbara Hucklesby Cl. N22 2B 48
Barbauld Rd. N16 3E 66
Barber Beaumont Ho. E1 3K 85
(off Bancroft Rd.)
Barber Cl. N21 7F 23
Barberry Ct. E15 6G 69
Barbers All. E13 3K 87
Barbers Rd. E15 2D 86
Barbican EC2 5D 8
Barbican Art Gallery 5C 84
Barbican Arts Centre 5D 8 (5C 84)
Barbican Cinema 1 5D 8
(within Arts Cen.)
Barbican Cinema 2 & 3 5D 8
(off Whitecross St.)
Barbican Rd. UB6: G'frd 6F 77
Barbican Theatre 5D 8
(within Arts Cen.)
Barb M. W6 3E 98
Barbon Cl. WC1 5F 7 (5K 83)
Barbot Cl. N9 3B 34
Barchard St. SW18 5K 117
Barchester Cl. W7 1K 95
Barchester Rd. HA3: Hrw W 2H 41
Barchester St. E14 5D 86
Barclay Cl. SW6 7J 99
Barclay Ho. E9 7J 67
(off Well St.)
Barclay Oval IG8: Wfd G 4D 36
Barclay Path E17 5E 50
Barclay Rd. CR0: C'don 3D 168
E11 1H 69
E13 4A 88
E17 5E 50
N18 6J 33
SW6 7J 99
Barcombe Av. SW2 2J 137
Barcombe Cl. BR5: St P 3K 161
Bardell Ho. SE1 7K 15
(off Parkers Row)
Barden St. SE18 7J 107
Bardfield Av. RM6: Chad H 3D 54
Bardney Rd. SM4: Mord 4K 153
Bardolph Rd. N7 4J 65
TW9: Rich 3F 115
Bard Rd. W10 7F 81
Bardsey Pl. E1 4J 85
Bardsey Wlk. N1 6C 66
(off Douglas Rd. Nth.)
Bardsley Cl. CR0: C'don 3F 169
Bardsley Ho. SE10 6E 104
(off Bardsley La.)
Bardsley La. SE10 6E 104
Barents Ho. E1 4K 85
(off White Horse La.)
Barfett St. W10 4H 81
Barfield Av. N20 2J 31
Barfield Rd. BR1: Broml 3E 160
E11 1H 69
Barfleur La. SE8 4B 104
Barford Cl. NW4 2C 44
Barford Ho. E3 2B 86
(off Tredegar Rd.)
Barford St. N1 1A 84
Barforth Rd. SE15 3H 121
Barfreston Way SE20 1H 157
Bargate Cl. KT3: N Mald 7C 152
SE18 5K 107
Barge Dr. UB2: S'hall 3F 95
Barge Ho. Rd. E16 2F 107
Barge Ho. St. SE1 4K 13 (1A 102)
Barge La. E3 1A 86
Bargery Rd. SE6 1D 140
Barge Wlk. KT1: Hamp W 3D 150
KT2: King T 1D 150
KT8: E Mos 6A 150
(Boyle Farm Island)
KT8: E Mos 3H 149
(Hampton Ct. Cres.)
SE10 3H 105
Bargrove Cl. SE20 7G 139
Bargrove Cres. SE6 2B 140
Barham Cl. BR2: Broml 1C 172
BR7: Chst 5F 143
HA0: Wemb 6B 60
RM7: Mawney 2H 55
Barham Ct. CR2: S Croy 4C 168
(off Barham Rd.)
Barham Ho. SE17 5E 102
(off Kinglake Est.)
Barham Rd. BR7: Chst 5F 143
CR2: S Croy 4C 168
SW20 7C 134
Baring Cl. SE12 2J 141
Baring Ct. N1 1D 84
(off Baring St.)
Baring Ho. E14 6C 86
(off Canton St.)
Baring Rd. CR0: C'don 1G 169
EN4: Cockf 4G 21
SE12 7J 123
Baring St. N1 1D 84
Baritone Ct. E15 1H 87
(off Church St.)
Barker Cl. HA6: Nwood 1H 39
KT3: N Mald 4H 151
TW9: Kew 2H 115
Barker Dr. NW1 7G 65
Barker Ho. SE17 4E 102
(off Congreve St.)
Barker M. SW4 4F 119
Barker's Arc. 2K 99
Barker St. SW10 6A 100
Barker Wlk. SW16 3H 137
Barkham Rd. N17 7J 33
Barkham Ter. SE1 1K 19
BARKING 7G 71
Barking Abbey 1G 89
Barking Abbey School
Leisure Cen. 6A 72
Barking Bus. Cen. IG11: Bark 3A 90
Barking Ind. Pk. IG11: Bark 1K 89
Barking Northern Relief Rd.
IG11: Bark 7F 71
Barking Park Miniature Railway 6H 71
BARKING RIVERSIDE 3B 90
Barking Rd. E6 2A 88
E13 4J 87
E16 5G 87
BARKINGSIDE 3G 53
Barking Splash Pk. 5H 71
Barkis Ho. W11 1F 99
Bark Pl. W2 7K 81
Barkston Gdns. SW5 4K 99
Barkway Ct. N4 2C 66
Barkway Dr. BR6: Farnb 4E 172
Barkwith Ho. SE14 6K 103
(off Cold Blow La.)
Barkwood Cl. RM7: Rom 5J 55
Barkworth Rd. SE16 5H 103
Barlborough St. SE14 7K 103
Barlby Gdns. W10 4F 81
Barlby Rd. W10 5E 80
Barley Cl. HA0: Wemb 4D 60
Barleycorn Way E14 7B 86
(not continuous)
Barley Ct. E5 2J 67
RM13: Rain 2K 91
(off Lwr Mardyke Av.)
Barleyfields Cl. RM6: Chad H 6B 54
Barley La. IG3: Ilf 7A 54
RM6: Chad H 7A 54
Barley Mow Pas. EC1 6B 8
W4 5K 97
Barley Mow Way TW17: Shep 4C 146
Barley Shotts Bus. Pk. W10 5H 81
Barley Wlk. SW18 5K 117
Barling NW1 6F 65
(off Castlehaven Rd.)
Barlow Cl. SM6: W'gton 6J 167
Barlow Dr. SE18 1C 124
Barlow Ho. N1 1E 8
(off Provost Est.)
SE16 4H 103
(off Rennie Est.)
W11 7G 81
(off Walmer Rd.)
Barlow Pl. W1 3K 11 (7F 83)
Barlow Rd. NW6 6H 63
TW12: Hamp 7E 130
W3 1H 97
Barlow St. SE17 4D 102
Barlow Way RM13: Rain 5K 91
Barmeston Rd. SE6 2D 140
Barmor Cl. HA2: Harr 2F 41
Barmouth Av. UB6: G'frd 2K 77
Barmouth Rd. CR0: C'don 2K 169
SW18 6A 118
Barnabas Ct. EN2: Enf 4F 23
Barnabas Ho. EC1 2C 8
Barnabas Lodge SW8 1J 119
(off Guildford Rd.)
Barnabas Rd. E9 5K 67
Barnaby Cl. HA2: Harr 2G 59
Barnaby Ct. NW9 3A 44
SE16 2G 103
(off Scott Lidgett Cres.)
Barnaby Ho. SE15 6J 103
Barnaby Pl. SW7 4A 16
Barnaby Way IG7: Chig 3K 37
Barnard Cl. BR7: Chst 1H 161
SE18 3E 106
SM6: W'gton 7H 167
TW16: Sun 7K 129
Barnard Gdns. KT3: N Mald 4C 152
UB4: Yead 4K 75
Barnard Gro. E15 7H 69
Barnard Hill N10 1F 47
Barnard Ho. E2 3H 85
(off Ellsworth St.)
Barnard Lodge EN5: New Bar 4F 21
W9 5J 81
(off Admiral Wlk.)
Barnard M. SW11 4C 118
Barnardo Dr. IG6: Ilf 4G 53
Barnardo Gdns. E1 7K 85
Barnardo St. E1 6K 85
Barnardo Village Wlk. IG6: Ilf 3G 53
Barnard Rd. CR4: Mitc 3E 154
EN1: Enf 2C 24
SW11 4C 118
Barnards Ho. SE16 2B 104
(off Wyatt Cl.)
Barnard's Inn EC1 6J 7
Barnbrough NW1 1G 83
(off Camden St.)
Barnby Sq. E15 1G 87
Barnby St. E15 1G 87
NW1 1B 6 (2G 83)
Barn Cl. NW5 5H 65
(off Torriano Av.)
TW15: Ashf 5D 128
UB5: N'olt 2A 76
Barn Cres. HA7: Stan 6H 27
Barncroft Cl. UB8: Hil 5D 74
Barneby Cl. TW2: Twick 1J 131
BARNEHURST 3J 127
Barnehurst Av. DA7: Bex 1J 127
DA8: Erith 1J 127
Barnehurst Cl. DA8: Erith 1J 127
Barnehurst Golf Course 3K 127
Barnehurst Rd. DA7: Bex 2J 127
Barn Elms Athletics Track 2D 116
Barn Elms Cl. KT4: Wor Pk 3B 164
Barn Elms Pk. SW15 3E 116
BARNES 2B 116
Barnes All. TW12: Hamp 2G 149
Barnes Av. SW13 7C 98
UB2: S'hall 4D 94
BARNES BRI. 2A 116
Barnes Cl. E12 4B 70
HA8: Edg 4A 28
Barnes Common Nature Reserve
3C 116
Barnes Ct. CR7: Thor H 3C 156
E16 5A 88
EN5: New Bar 4E 20
IG8: Buck H, Wfd G 5G 37
N1 7A 66
Barnes End KT3: N Mald 5C 152
Barnes High St. SW13 2B 116
Barnes Ho. E2 2J 85
(off Wadeson St.)
NW1 7F 65
(off Camden Rd.)
SE14 6K 103
(off John Williams Cl.)
Barnes Pikle W5 7D 78
Barnes Rd. IG1: Ilf 5G 71
N18 4D 34
Barnes St. E14 6A 86
Barnes Ter. SE8 5B 104
Barnes Wallis Ct. HA9: Wemb 3J 61
BARNET 3B 20
Barnet Burnt Oak Leisure Cen. 1K 43
Barnet Bus. Cen. EN5: Barn 3B 20
Barnet By-Pass NW7 6G 29
Barnet Copthall Leisure Cen. 7J 29
Barnet Copthall Sports Cen. 1D 44
Barnet Dr. BR2: Broml 2C 172
Barnet FC 1E 42
Barnet Ga. La. EN5: Ark 1H 29
Barnet Gro. E2 1K 9 (3G 85)
Barnet Hill EN5: Barn 4C 20
Barnet Ho. N20 2F 31
Barnet La. EN5: Barn 1C 30
N20 1C 30
Barnet Mus. 4B 20
Barnetts Ct. HA2: Harr 3F 59
Barnett St. E1 6H 85
BARNET VALE 5E 20
Barnet Way NW7 3E 28
Barnet Wood Rd. BR2: Broml 2A 172
Barney Cl. SE7 5A 106
Barn Fld. NW3 5D 64
Barnfield KT3: N Mald 6A 152
Barnfield Av. CR0: C'don 2J 169
CR4: Mitc 4F 155
KT2: King T 4D 132
Barnfield Cl. N4 7J 47
SW17 3B 136
Barnfield Gdns. KT2: King T 4E 132
SE18 6F 107
Barnfield Pl. E14 4C 104
Barnfield Rd. CR2: Sande 7E 168
DA17: Belv 6F 109
HA8: Edg 1J 43
SE18 6F 107
(not continuous)
W5 4C 78
Barnfield Wood Cl. BR3: Beck 6F 159
Barnfield Wood Rd. BR3: Beck 6F 159
Barnham Dr. SE28 1K 107
(not continuous)
Barnham Rd. UB6: G'frd 3G 77
Barnham St. SE1 6H 15 (2E 102)
Barn Hill HA9: Wemb 1G 61
Barnhill HA5: Eastc 5A 40
Barnhill Av. BR2: Broml 5H 159
Barnhill La. UB4: Yead 3K 75
Barnhill Rd. HA9: Wemb 3J 61
UB4: Yead 3K 75
Barningham Way NW9 6K 43
Barnlea Cl. TW13: Hanw 2C 130
Barnmead Ct. RM9: Dag 5F 73
Barnmead Gdns. RM9: Dag 5F 73
Barnmead Rd. BR3: Beck 1K 157
RM9: Dag 5F 73
Barn M. HA2: Harr 3E 58
Barn Ri. HA9: Wemb 1G 61
BARNSBURY 7K 65
Barnsbury Cl. KT3: N Mald 4J 151
Barnsbury Cres. KT5: Surb 1J 163
Barnsbury Est. N1 1K 83
(not continuous)
Barnsbury Gro. N7 7K 65
Barnsbury Ho. SW4 6H 119
Barnsbury La. KT5: Surb 2H 163
Barnsbury Pk. N1 7A 66
Barnsbury Rd. N1 2A 84
Barnsbury Sq. N1 7A 66
Barnsbury St. N1 7A 66
Barnsbury Ter. N1 7K 65
Barnscroft SW20 3D 152
Barnsdale Av. E14 4D 104
Barnsdale Rd. W9 4H 81
Barnsley St. E1 4H 85
Barnstaple Ho. SE10 7D 104
(off Devonshire Dr.)
SE12 5H 123
(off Taunton Rd.)
Barnstaple La. SE13 4E 122
Barnstaple Rd. HA4: Ruis 3A 58
Barnston Wlk. N1 1C 84
(off Popham St.)
Barn St. N16 2E 66
The Barn Theatre
Sidcup 1A 144
West Molesey 4E 148
Barn Way HA9: Wemb 1G 61
Barnwell Cl. HA8: Edg 4A 28
Barnwell Ho. SE5 1E 120
(off St Giles Rd.)
Barnwell Rd. SW2 5A 120
Barnwood Cl. HA4: Ruis 2F 57
N20 1C 30
W9 4K 81
Baron Cl. N1 2A 84
N11 5K 31
Baroness Rd. E2 1K 9 (3F 85)
Baronet Gro. N17 1G 49
Baronet Rd. N17 1G 49
Baron Gdns. IG6: Ilf 3G 53
Baron Gro. CR4: Mitc 4C 154
Baron Ho. SW19 1B 154

Baron Rd. RM8: Dag 1D 72
The Barons TW1: Twick 6B 114
Baronsclere Ct. N6 . . . . .7G 47
BARONS COURT 5G 99
Barons Ct. IG1: Ilf 2H 71
   NW9 .6K 43
   SM6: Bedd 3H 167
Baron's Ct. Rd. W14 . . . . .5G 99
Barons Court Theatre 5G 99
(off Comeragh Rd.)
Baronsfield Rd. TW1: Twick 6B 114
Barons Ga. EN4: E Barn 6H 21
   W4 . . . . .3J 97
Barons Keep W14 . . . . .5G 99
Barons Lodge E14 . . . . .4F 105
(off Manchester Rd.)
Barons Mead HA1: Harr 4J 41
Baronsmead Rd. SW13 . . . . .1C 116
Baronsmede W5 . . . . .2F 97
Baronsmere Rd. EN5: Barn 4B 20
Baronsmere Rd. N2 . . . . .4C 46
Baron's Pl. SE1 . . . . . . .7K 13 (2A 102)
Baron St. N1 . . . . .2A 84
Baron's Wlk. CR0: C'don 6A 158
Baron Wlk. CR4: Mitc 4C 154
   E16 . . . . .5H 87
Baroque Ct. TW3: Houn 3F 113
Baroque Gdns. SE8 . . . . .4A 104
(off Grand Canal Av.)
Barque M. SE8 . . . . .6C 104
Barquentine Hgts. SE10 . . . . .3J 105
Barrack Rd. TW4: Houn 4B 112
Barracks La. EN5: Barn 3B 20
Barracouta Ho. SE18 . . . . .6K 107
Barra Hall Cir. UB3: Hayes 7G 75
Barra Hall Rd. UB3: Hayes 7G 75
Barrat Av. N22 . . . . .2K 47
Barratt Ho. N1 . . . . .7B 66
(off Sable St.)
Barratt Ind. Est. UB1: S'hall 2E 94
Barratt Ind. Pk. E3 . . . . .4E 86
Barratt Way HA3: W'stone 2H 41
Barra Wood Cl. UB3: Hayes 6G 75
Barrenger Rd. N10 . . . . .1D 46
Barret Ho. NW6 . . . . .1J 81
   SW9 .3K 119
(off Benedict Rd.)
Barrett Ct. SE5 . . . . .7D 102
(off Dobson Wlk.)
Barrett Ho. SE17 . . . . .5C 102
(off Browning St.)
Barrett Pl. UB10: Uxb 1A 74
Barrett Rd. E17 . . . . .4E 50
Barrett's Grn. Rd. NW10 . . . . .3J 79
Barrett's Gro. N16 . . . . .5E 66
Barrett St. W1 . . . . .1H 11 (6E 82)
Barrhill Rd. SW2 . . . . .2J 137
Barrie Ct. EN5: New Bar 5F 21
(off Lyonsdown Rd.)
Barriedale SE14 . . . . .2A 122
Barrie Est. W2 . . . . .2A 10 (7B 82)
Barrie Ho. NW8 . . . . .1C 82
(off St Edmund's Ter.)
   W2 . . . . .7A 82
(off Lancaster Ga.)
Barrier App. SE7 . . . . .3B 106
Barrier Point Rd. E16 . . . . .1A 106
Barringers Ct. HA4: Ruis 7F 39
Barringer Sq. SW17 . . . . .4E 136
Barrington Cl. IG5: Ilf 1D 52
   NW5 . . . . .5E 64
Barrington Ct. N10 . . . . .2E 46
   SW4 .2J 119
   W3 . . . . .2H 97
(off Cheltenham Pl.)
Barrington Rd. DA7: Bex 2D 126
   E12 . . . . .6E 70
   N8 . . . . .5H 47
   SM3: Sutt 2J 165
   SW9 .3B 120
Barrington Vs. SE18 . . . . .1E 124
Barrington Wlk. SE19 . . . . .6E 138
Barrons Chase TW10: Ham 5F 133
Barrow Av. SM5: Cars 7D 166
Barrow Cl. N21 . . . . .3G 33
Barrow Ct. SE6 . . . . .1H 141
(off Cumberland Pl.)
Barrowdene Cl. HA5: Pinn 2C 40
Barrowell Grn. N21 . . . . .2G 33
Barrowfield Cl. N9 . . . . .3C 34
Barrowgate Rd. W4 . . . . .5J 97
Barrow Hedges Cl. SM5: Cars 7C 166
Barrow Hedges Way
   SM5: Cars 7C 166
Barrow Hill KT4: Wor Pk 2A 164
Barrow Hill Cl. KT4: Wor Pk 2A 164
Barrow Hill Est. 2C 82
(off Barrow Hill Rd.)
Barrow Hill Rd. NW8 . . . . . .1C 4 (2C 82)
Barrow Point Av. HA5: Pinn 2C 40
Barrow Point La. HA5: Pinn 2C 40
Barrow Rd. CR0: Wadd 5A 168
   SW16 . . . . .6H 137
Barrow Store Ct. SE1 . . . . .7G 15
(off Decima St.)
Barrow Wlk. TW8: Bford 6C 96
Barrs Rd. NW10 . . . . .7K 61
Barry Av. DA7: Bex 7E 108
   N15 . . . . .6F 49
Barry Blandford Way E3 . . . . .4D 86
Barry Cl. BR6: Orp 3J 173
Barrydene N20 . . . . .1G 31
Barry Ho. SE16 . . . . .4H 103
(off Rennie Est.)
Barry Pde. SE22 . . . . .5G 121
Barry Rd. E6 . . . . .6C 88
   NW10 .7J 61
   SE22 .6G 121
Barry Ter. TW15: Ashf 2B 128
(off Orchard Way)
Barset Rd. SE15 . . . . .3J 121
(not continuous)
Barson Cl. SE20 . . . . .7J 139
Barston Rd. SE27 . . . . .3C 138
Barstow Cres. SW2 . . . . .1K 137
Barter St. WC1 . . . . .6F 7 (5J 83)
Barters Wlk. HA5: Pinn 3C 40
Barth M. SE18 . . . . .4J 107
Bartholomew Cl. EC1 . . . . .6B 8 (5C 84)
(not continuous)
   SW18 .4A 118
Bartholomew Ct. E14 . . . . .7E 87
(off Newport Av.)
   EC1 . . . . .3D 8
(off Old St.)
   HA8: Edg 7J 27

Bartholomew Ho.
   IG8: Wfd G 1F 53, 7K 37
   W10 . . . . .4G 81
(off Appleford Rd.)
Bartholomew La. EC2 . . . . .1F 15 (6D 84)
Bartholomew Pl. EC1 . . . . .6C 8
Bartholomew Rd. NW5 . . . . .6G 65
Bartholomew Sq. E1 . . . . .4H 85
   EC1 . . . . .3D 8 (3C 84)
Bartholomew St. SE1 . . . . .3D 102
Bartholomew Vs. NW5 . . . . .6G 65
Barth Rd. SE18 . . . . .4J 107
Bartle Av. E6 . . . . .2C 88
Bartle Rd. W11 . . . . .6G 81
Bartlett Cl. E14 . . . . .6C 86
Bartlett Ct. EC4 . . . . .7K 7 (6A 84)
Bartlett Ho. KT4: Wor Pk 2B 164
(off The Avenue)
Bartlett Ho's. RM10: Dag 7H 73
(off Vicarage Rd.)
Bartlett M. E14 . . . . .5D 104
(off The Avenue)
Bartletts Pas. EC4 . . . . .7K 7
(off Fetter La.)
Bartlett St. CR2: S Croy 5D 168
Bartlow Gdns. RM5: Col R 1K 55
Bartok Ho. W11 . . . . .1H 99
(off Lansdowne Wlk.)
Barton Av. RM7: Rush G 1H 73
Barton Cl. DA6: Bex 5E 126
   E6 . . . . .6D 88
   E9 . . . . .5J 67
   NW4 . . . . .5C 44
   SE15 .3H 121
   TW17: Shep 6D 146
Barton Ct. W14 . . . . .5G 99
(off Baron's Ct. Rd.)
Barton Grn. KT3: N Mald 2K 151
Barton Ho. E3 . . . . .2C 86
(off Bow Rd.)
   N1 . . . . .7B 66
(off Sable St.)
   SW6 . . . . .3K 117
(off Wandsworth Bri. Rd.)
Barton Mdws. IG6: Ilf 4F 53
Barton M. E14 . . . . .2D 104
   SW9 .6A 136
Barton Rd. DA14: Sidc 6E 144
   W14 . . . . .5G 99
Barton St. SW1 . . . . . .1E 18 (3J 101)
Bartonway NW8 . . . . .1B 82
(off Queen's Ter.)
Bartram Cl. UB8: Hil 4D 74
Bartram Rd. SE4 . . . . .5A 122
Bartrams La. EN4: Had W 1F 21
Bartrip St. E9 . . . . .6B 68
Barts & The London School of
  Medicine & Dentistry
   Whitechapel Campus 5H 85
(off Turner St.)
Barts Cl. BR3: Beck 5C 158
Barville Cl. SE4 . . . . .4A 122
Barwell Bus. Pk. KT9: Chess 7D 162
Barwell Ct. KT9: Chess 7B 162
Barwell Ho. E2 . . . . .4G 85
(off Menotti St.)
Barwell La. KT9: Chess 7C 162
Barwick Dr. UB8: Hil 5D 74
Barwick Ho. W3 . . . . .2J 97
(off Strafford Rd.)
Barwick Rd. E7 . . . . .4K 69
Barwood Av. BR4: W W'ck 1D 170
Bascombe Gro. DA1: Bexl, Cray . . .7K 127
Bascombe St. SW2 . . . . .6A 120
Basden Gro. TW13: Hanw 2E 130
Basden Ho. TW13: Hanw 2E 130
Baseing Cl. E6 . . . . .7E 88
Baseline Bus. Studios W11 . . . . . . .7F 81
(off Barandon Wlk.)
Basepoint Bus. Cen. RM13: Rain . . .4K 91
Basevi Way SE8 . . . . .6D 104
Bashley Rd. NW10 . . . . .4K 79
Basil Av. E6 . . . . .3C 88
Basildene Rd. TW4: Houn 3B 112
Basildon Av. IG5: Ilf 1E 52
Basildon Cl. SM2: Sutt 7K 165
Basildon Ct. W1 . . . . .5H 5
(off Devonshire St.)
Basildon Rd. SE2 . . . . .5A 108
Basil Gdns. CR0: C'don 1K 169
   SE27 .5C 138
Basil Ho. E1 . . . . .6G 85
(off Henriques St.)
   SW8 . . . . .7J 101
(off Wyvil Rd.)
Basilica M. SW12 . . . . .6E 118
Basilica Pl. E3 . . . . .2B 86
Basil Mans. SW3 . . . . .7E 10
(off Basil St.)
Basilon Rd. DA7: Bex 2E 126
Basil Spence Ho. N22 . . . . .1K 47
Basil St. SW3 . . . . .1E 16 (3D 100)
Basin App. E14 . . . . .6A 86
   E16 . . . . .7F 89
Basing Cl. KT7: T Ditt 7K 149
Basing Ct. SE15 . . . . .1F 121
Basingdon Way SE5 . . . . .4D 120
Basing Dr. DA5: Bexl 6F 127
Basingfield Rd. KT7: T Ditt 7K 149
Basinghall Av. EC2 . . . . . . .7E 8 (6D 84)
Basinghall Gdns. SM2: Sutt 7K 165
Basinghall St. EC2 . . . . . . .7E 8 (6D 84)
Basing Hill HA9: Wemb 2F 61
   NW11 .1H 63
Basing Ho. Yd. E2 . . . . .1H 9
Basing Pl. E2 . . . . .1H 9 (3E 84)
Basing St. W11 . . . . .6H 81
Basing Way KT7: T Ditt 7K 149
   N3 . . . . .3J 45
Basin Mill Apts. E2 . . . . .1F 85
(off Laburnum St.)
Basin Sth. E16 . . . . .1F 107
Basire St. N1 . . . . .1C 84
Baskerville Gdns. NW10 . . . . .4A 62
Baskerville Rd. SW18 . . . . .7C 118
Basket Gdns. SE9 . . . . .5C 124
Baslow Cl. HA3: Hrw W 1H 41
Baslow Wlk. E5 . . . . .4K 67
Basnett Rd. SW11 . . . . .3E 118
Basque Ct. SE16 . . . . .2K 103
(off Garter Way)
Bassano St. SE22 . . . . .5F 121
Bassant Rd. SE18 . . . . .6K 107
Bass Ct. E15 . . . . .1H 87
(off Plaistow Rd.)
Bassein Pk. Rd. W12 . . . . .2B 98

Bassett Gdns. TW7: Isle 7G 95
Bassett Ho. SW19 . . . . .5K 135
Bassett Rd. W10 . . . . .6F 81
Bassett's Cl. BR6: Farnb 4F 173
Bassetts Ho. BR6: Farnb 4F 173
Bassett St. NW5 . . . . .6E 64
Bassett's Way BR6: Farnb 4F 173
Bassett Way UB6: G'frd 6F 77
Bassingbourn Ho. N1 . . . . .7J 83
(off The Sutton Est.)
Bassingham Rd. HA0: Wemb 6D 60
   SW18 .7A 118
Bassishaw Highwalk EC2 . . . . .6E 8
Basswood Cl. SE15 . . . . .3H 121
Bastable Av. IG11: Bark 2J 89
Baste M. SE22 . . . . .4G 121
Basterfield Ho. EC1 . . . . .4C 8
(off Golden La. Est.)
Bastion Highwalk EC2 . . . . .6C 8
Bastion Ho. EC2 . . . . .6D 8
(off London Wall)
Bastion Rd. SE2 . . . . .5C 108
Bastwick St. EC1 . . . . .3C 8 (4C 84)
Basuto Rd. SW6 . . . . .1J 117
Batavia Cl. TW16: Sun 1K 147
Batavia Ho. SE14 . . . . .7A 104
(off Batavia Rd.)
Batavia M. SE14 . . . . .7A 104
Batavia Rd. SE14 . . . . .7A 104
   TW16: Sun 1K 147
Batchelor St. N1 . . . . .1A 84
Bate M. SW19 . . . . .7G 137
Bateman Cl. IG11: Bark 6G 71
Bateman Ho. SE17 . . . . .6B 102
(off Otto St.)
Bateman M. SW4 . . . . .6H 119
Bateman Rd. E4 . . . . .6H 35
Bateman's Bldgs. W1 . . . . .1C 12
Bateman's Row EC2 . . . . . .3H 9 (4E 84)
Bateman St. W1 . . . . . .1C 12 (6H 83)
Bates Cres. CR0: Wadd 5A 168
   SW16 .7G 137
Bateson St. SE18 . . . . .4J 107
Bat Gdns. KT2: King T 6F 133
Bath Cl. SE15 . . . . .7H 103
Bath Ct. EC1 . . . . .2E 8
(St Luke's Est.)
   EC1 . . . . .4J 7
(Warner St.)
   SE26 . . . . .3G 139
(off Droitwich Cl.)
Bathgate Ho. SW9 . . . . .1B 120
(off Lothian Rd.)
Bathgate Rd. SW19 . . . . .3F 135
Bath Gro. E2 . . . . .2G 85
Bath Ho. E2 . . . . .4G 85
(off Ramsey St.)
   IG11: Bark 7G 71
   SE1 . . . . .3C 102
(off Bath Ter.)
Bath Ho. Rd. CR0: Bedd 1J 167
Bath Pas. KT1: King T 2D 150
Bath Pl. EC2 . . . . .2G 9 (3E 84)
   EN5: Barn 3C 20
   W6 . . . . .5E 98
(off Peabody Est.)
Bath Rd. E7 . . . . .6B 70
   N9 . . . . .2C 34
   RM6: Chad H 6E 54
   SL3: Coln, Poyle 4A 174
   TW3: Houn 3F 113
   TW4: Houn 2B 112
   TW5: Cran 1G 111
   TW6: H'row A 1G 111
   UB3: Harl 1G 111
   UB7: Lford, Harm, Sip 4C 174
   W4 . . . . .4A 98
Baths Ct. W12 . . . . .2D 98
Baths Rd. BR2: Broml 4B 160
Bath St. EC1 . . . . .2D 8 (3C 84)
Bath Ter. SE1 . . . . .3C 102
Bathurst Av. SW19 . . . . .1K 153
Bathurst Gdns. NW10 . . . . .2D 80
Bathurst Ho. W12 . . . . .7D 80
(off White City Est.)
Bathurst M. W2 . . . . .2B 10 (6B 82)
Bathurst Rd. IG1: Ilf 1F 71
Bathurst Sq. N15 . . . . .4E 48
Bathurst St. W2 . . . . . . .2B 10 (7B 82)
Bathway SE18 . . . . .4E 106
Batley Cl. CR4: Mitc 7D 154
Batley Pl. N16 . . . . .3F 67
Batley Rd. EN2: Enf 1H 23
   N16 . . . . .3F 67
Batman Cl. W12 . . . . .1D 98
Batoum Gdns. W6 . . . . .3E 98
Batsford Ho. SW19 . . . . .4K 135
(off Durnsford Rd.)
Batson Ho. E1 . . . . .6G 85
(off Fairclough St.)
Batson St. W12 . . . . .2C 98
Batsworth Rd. CR4: Mitc 3B 154
Battalion Ho. NW9 . . . . .2B 44
(off Heritage Av.)
Battenberg Wlk. SE19 . . . . .6E 138
Batten Cl. E6 . . . . .6D 88
Batten Cotts. E14 . . . . .5A 86
(off Maroon St.)
Batten Ho. SW4 . . . . .5G 119
   W10 . . . . .3G 81
(off Third Av.)
Batten St. SW11 . . . . .3C 118
BATTERSEA 1E 118
Battersea Arts Cen. 3D 118
(off Lavender Hill)
BATTERSEA BRI. 7B 100
Battersea Bri. Rd. SW11 . . . . .7C 100
Battersea Bus. Cen. SW11 . . . . . . .3E 118
Battersea Bus. Pk. SW11 . . . . .1B 118
Battersea Church Rd. SW11 . . . . . .1B 118
Battersea Dogs' Home 7F 101
Battersea Evolution 7E 100
Battersea High St. SW11 . . . . .1A 118
(not continuous)
BATTERSEA PARK 7F 101
Battersea Pk. Children's Zoo 7E 100
Battersea Pk. Millennium Arena . .7E 100
Battersea Pk. Rd. SW8 . . . . .1E 118
   SW11 .2C 118

Battersea Power Stn. Development
   SW11 .6F 101
Battersea Ri. SW11 . . . . .5C 118
Battersea Roof Gdns. SW11 . . . . . .7F 101
Battersea Sports Cen. 3B 118
Battersea Sq. SW11 . . . . .1B 118
Battery Rd. SE28 . . . . .2J 107
Battishill St. N1 . . . . .7B 66
Battlebridge Ct. N1 . . . . .2J 83
(off Wharfdale Rd.)
Battle Bri. La. SE1 . . . . . .5G 15 (1E 102)
Battle Cl. SW19 . . . . .6A 136
Battledean Rd. N5 . . . . .5B 66
Battle Rd. DA8: Erith 4J 109
   DA17: Belv, Erith 4J 109
Battle Rd. SE15 . . . . .6G 103
(off Haymerle Rd.)
Batty St. E1 . . . . .6G 85
Batwa Ho. SE16 . . . . .5H 103
Baudwin Rd. SE6 . . . . .2G 141
Baugh Rd. DA14: Sidc 5C 144
The Baulk SW18 . . . . .7J 117
Bavant Rd. SW16 . . . . .2J 155
Bavaria Rd. N19 . . . . .2J 65
Bavdene M. NW4 . . . . .4D 44
(off The Burroughs)
Bavent Rd. SE5 . . . . .2C 120
Bawdale Rd. SE22 . . . . .5F 121
Bawdsey Av. IG2: Ilf 4K 53
Bawley Ct. E16 . . . . .7G 89
(off Rick Roberts Way)
Bawtree Rd. SE14 . . . . .7A 104
   UB8: Uxb 3J 31
Baxendale N20 . . . . .2F 31
Baxendale St. E2 . . . . .3G 85
Baxter Cl. BR1: Broml 3F 161
   UB2: S'hall 3F 95
   UB10: Hil 3D 74
Baxter Ho. E3 . . . . .3D 86
(off Bromley High St.)
Baxter Rd. E16 . . . . .6A 88
   IG1: Ilf .5F 71
   N1 . . . . .6D 66
   N18 . . . . .4C 34
Baxter Wlk. SW16 . . . . .2H 137
Bayard Ct. DA6: Bex 4H 127
Bay Ct. E1 .4K 85
(off Frimley Way)
   W5 . . . . .3E 96
Baycroft Cl. HA5: Eastc 3A 40
Baydon Ct. BR2: Broml 3H 159
Bayer Ho. EC1 . . . . .4C 8
(off Golden La. Est.)
Bayes Cl. SE26 . . . . .5J 139
Bayes Ct. NW3 . . . . .7D 64
(off Primrose Hill Rd.)
Bayes Ho. N1 . . . . .7A 66
(off Augustas La.)
Bayfield Ho. SE4 . . . . .4K 121
(off Coston Wlk.)
Bayfield Rd. SE9 . . . . .4B 124
Bayford M. E8 . . . . .7H 67
(off Bayford St.)
Bayford Rd. NW10 . . . . .3F 81
Bayford St. E8 . . . . .7H 67
Bayford St. Bus. Cen. E8 . . . . .7H 67
(off Sidworth St.)
Baygrove M. KT1: Hamp W 1C 150
Bayham Pl. NW1 . . . . .1G 83
Bayham Rd. SM4: Mord 4K 153
   W4 . . . . .3K 97
   W13 . . . . .7B 78
Bayham St. NW1 . . . . .1G 83
Bay Ho. SE16 . . . . .3A 104
Bayhurst Wood Country Pk. 5B 38
Bayleaf Cl. TW12: Hamp H 5H 131
Bayley St. WC1 . . . . .6C 6 (5H 83)
Bayley Wlk. SE2 . . . . .6E 108
Baylis Hgts. SE10 . . . . .4J 105
(off Horn Link Way)
Baylis M. TW1: Twick 7A 114
Baylis Rd. SE1 . . . . .7J 13 (2A 102)
Bayliss Av. SE28 . . . . .7D 90
Bayliss Cl. N21 . . . . .5D 22
   UB1: S'hall 6F 77
Baynard Ho. EC4 . . . . .2B 14
(off Queen Victoria St.)
Bayne Cl. E6 . . . . .6D 88
Baynes Cl. EN1: Enf 1B 24
Baynes Cres. RM10: Dag 7J 73
Baynes M. NW3 . . . . .6B 64
Baynes St. NW1 . . . . .7G 65
Bayonne Rd. W6 . . . . .6G 99
Bays Cl. HA8: Edg 5C 28
Bayscourt Ho. N16 . . . . .3F 67
Bayston Rd. N16 . . . . .3F 67
BAYSWATER 7A 82
Bayswater Cl. N13 . . . . .4G 33
Bayswater Rd. W2 . . . . . . .3A 10 (7K 81)
     (off Acklam Rd.)
Bay Tree Cl. BR1: Broml 1B 160
   IG6: Ilf .1F 53
Baytree Cl. DA15: Sidc 1K 143
   SE13 .2C 122
Bay Tree Ho. EC1 . . . . .4J 7
(off Baker's Row)
Baytree Ho. E4 . . . . .7J 25
Baytree M. SE17 . . . . .4D 102
Baytree Rd. SW2 . . . . .4K 119
Baywillow Av. SM5: Cars 1D 166
Bazalgette Cl. KT3: N Mald 5K 151
Bazalgette Gdns. KT3: N Mald 5K 151
Bazalgette Ho. NW8 . . . . .3B 4
(off Orchardson St.)
Bazalgette Wlk. EC4 . . . . .7A 84
Bazalgette Way SE2 . . . . .1C 108
Bazeley Ho. SE1 . . . . .7A 14
(off Library St.)
Bazely St. E14 . . . . .7E 86
Bazile Rd. N21 . . . . .6F 23
BBC Broadcasting House . . .6K 5 (5F 83)
BBC Maida Vale Studios 4K 81
BBC Studios 1E 98
BBC Worldwide 7E 80
BDA Dental Mus. 6J 5 (5F 83)

Beacham Cl. SE7 . . . . .5B 106
Beachborough Rd. BR1: Broml 4E 140
Beach Ct. SE9 . . . . .6C 124
Beachcroft Av. UB1: S'hall 1C 94
Beachcroft Way N19 . . . . .1H 65
Beach Gro. TW13: Hanw 2E 130
Beach Ho. SW5 . . . . .5J 99
(off Philbeach Gdns.)
   TW13: Hanw 2E 130
Beachy Rd. E3 . . . . .7C 68
Beacon Bingo
   Cricklewood 4F 63
Beacon Cl. SE14: Uxb 3K 121
Beacon Ga. SE14 . . . . .3K 121
Beacon Gro. SM5: Cars 4E 166
Beacon Hill N7 . . . . .5J 65
Beacon Ho. E14 . . . . .4F 105
(off Burrells Wharf Sq.)
   SE5 . . . . .7E 102
(off Southampton Way)
Beacon Pl. CR0: Bedd 3J 167
Beacon Point SE10 . . . . .6D 104
(off Dowells St.)
Beacon Rd. SE13 . . . . .6F 123
   TW6: H'row A 6C 110
Beacons Cl. E6 . . . . .5C 88
Beaconsfield WC1 . . . . .6G 7
(off Red Lion St.)
Beaconsfield Cl. N11 . . . . .5K 31
   SE3 . . . . .6J 105
   W4 . . . . .5J 97
Beaconsfield Pde. SE9 . . . . .4C 142
Beaconsfield Pde. BR1: Broml 3B 160
   CR0: C'don 6D 156
   DA5: Bexl 2K 145
   E10 . . . . .2E 68
   E16 . . . . .4H 87
   E17 . . . . .6C 50
   KT3: N Mald 2K 151
   KT5: Surb 7F 151
   N9 . . . . .3B 34
   N11 . . . . .4E 48
   N15 . . . . .4E 48
   NW10 .7C 62
   SE3 . . . . .7H 105
   SE9 . . . . .2C 142
   SE17 .5D 102
   TW1: Twick 6B 114
   UB1: S'hall 1A 94
   UB4: Yead 1A 94
   W4 . . . . .3K 97
   W5 . . . . .2C 96
Beaconsfield St. N1 . . . . .1J 83
Beaconsfield Ter. RM6: Chad H 6D 54
Beaconsfield Ter. Rd. W14 . . . . . . .3G 99
Beaconsfield Wlk. E6 . . . . .6E 88
   SW6 . . . . .1H 117
BEACONTREE 2C 72
BEACONTREE HEATH 1G 73
Beacontree Av. E17 . . . . .1F 51
Beacontree Rd. E11 . . . . .1H 69
Beadle's Pde. RM10: Dag 6J 73
Beadlow Cl. SM5: Cars 6B 154
Beadman Pl. SE27 . . . . .4B 138
Beadman St. SE27 . . . . .4B 138
Beadnell Ct. E1 . . . . .7G 85
(off Cable St.)
Beadnell Rd. SE23 . . . . .1K 139
Beadon Rd. BR2: Broml 4J 159
   W6 . . . . .4E 98
Beaford Gro. SW20 . . . . .3G 153
Beagle Cl. TW13: Felt 4K 129
Beak St. W1 . . . . .2B 12 (7G 83)
Beal Cl. DA16: Well 1A 126
The Beale Arboretum 1G 21
Beale Cl. N13 . . . . .5G 33
Beale Pl. E3 . . . . .2B 86
Beale Rd. E3 . . . . .1B 86
Beal Rd. IG1: Ilf 2E 70
Beam Av. RM10: Dag 1H 91
Beames Rd. NW10 . . . . .1K 79
Beaminster Gdns. IG6: Ilf 2F 53
Beaminster Ho. SW8 . . . . .7K 101
(off Dorset Rd.)
Beamish Dr. WD23: B Hea 1B 26
Beamish Ho. SE16 . . . . .4H 103
(off Rennie Est.)
Beamish Rd. N9 . . . . .1B 34
Beam Pk. Development RM9: Dag . .3H 91
Beam Reach Bus. Pk. RM13: Rain . .3K 91
Beam Valley Country Pk. 1J 91
Beamway RM10: Dag 7K 73
Beanacre Cl. E9 . . . . .6B 68
Bean Rd. DA6: Bex 4D 126
Beanshaw SE9 . . . . .4E 142
Beansland Gro. RM6: Chad H 3E 54
Bear All. EC4 . . . . .7A 8 (6B 84)
Bear Cl. RM7: Rom 6H 55
Beardell St. SE19 . . . . .6F 139
Bearder Gro. N14 . . . . .6B 22
Beardsfield E13 . . . . .2J 87
Beardsley Ter. RM8: Dag 5B 72
(off Stonard Rd.)
Beardsley Way W3 . . . . .2K 97
Bearfield Rd. KT2: King T 7E 132
Bear Gdns. SE1 . . . . .4C 14 (1C 102)
Bear La. SE1 . . . . .4B 14 (1B 102)
Bear Pit Apts. SE1 . . . . .4C 14
(off New Globe Wlk.)
Bear Rd. TW13: Hanw 4B 130
Bearstead Ri. SE4 . . . . .5B 122
Bearsted Ter. BR3: Beck 1C 158
Bear St. WC2 . . . . .2D 12 (7H 83)
Beasley's Ait TW16: Sun 6H 147
Beasley's Ait La. TW16: Sun 6H 147
Beaton Cl. SE15 . . . . .1F 121
Beatrice Av. HA9: Wemb 5E 60
   SW16 .3K 155
Beatrice Cl. E13 . . . . .4J 87
   HA5: Eastc 4J 39
Beatrice Ct. IG9: Buck H 2G 37
Beatrice Ho. W6 . . . . .5E 98
(off Queen Caroline St.)
Beatrice Pl. SW19 . . . . .7F 117
Beatrice Rd. E17 . . . . .5C 50
   N4 . . . . .7A 48
   N9 . . . . .7D 24
   SE1 . . . . .4G 103
   TW10: Rich 5F 115
   UB1: S'hall 1D 94

Beatrice Webb Ho.—Belitha Vs.

Beatrice Webb Ho. *E3* 2A 86
(off Chisenhale Rd.)
Beatrix Apts. *E3* 4B 86
(off English St.)
Beatrix Ho. *SW5* 5K 99
(off Old Brompton Rd.)
Beatson Wlk. SE16 1A 104
(not continuous)
Beattie Cl. TW14: Felt 7H 111
Beattie Ho. SW8 1G 119
Beattock Ri. N10 4F 47
Beatty Ho. *E14* 2C 104
(off Admirals Way)
SW1 6B 18
(off Dolphin Sq.)
Beatty Rd. HA7: Stan 6H 27
N16 4E 66
Beatty St. NW1 2G 83
Beattyville Gdns. IG6: Ilf 4E 52
Beauchamp Cl. W4 3J 97
Beauchamp Ct. *EN5: Barn* 4C 20
(off Victors Way)
HA7: Stan 5H 27
Beauchamp Pl. SW3 1D 16 (3C 100)
Beauchamp Rd. E7 7K 69
KT8: W Mole, E Mos 5F 149
SE19 1D 156
SM1: Sutt 4J 165
SW11 4C 118
TW1: Twick 7A 114
Beauchamp St. EC1 6J 7 (5A 84)
Beauchamp Ter. SW15 3D 116
Beauclerc Ct. TW16: Sun 2A 148
Beauclerc Rd. W6 3D 98
Beauclere Ho. SM2: Sutt 6A 166
Beauclerk Cl. TW13: Felt 1K 129
Beauclerk Ho. SW16 3J 137
Beau Ct. *HA7: Stan* 7J 27
(off Hitchin La.)
Beaudesert M. UB7: W Dray 2A 92
Beaufort E6 5E 88
Beaufort Av. HA3: Kenton 4A 42
Beaufort Cl. E4 6J 35
RM7: Mawney 4J 55
SW15 7D 116
W5 5F 79
Beaufort Ct. *E14* 2C 104
(off Admirals Way)
EN5: New Bar 5F 21
N11 5A 32
(off The Limes Av.)
SW6 6J 99
TW10: Ham 4C 132
Beaufort Dr. NW11 4J 45
Beaufort Gdns. E1 5K 85
IG1: Ilf 1E 70
NW4 6E 44
SW3 1D 16 (3C 100)
SW16 7K 137
TW5: Hest 1C 112
Beaufort Ho. *E16* 1K 105
(off Fairfax M.)
SW1 6C 18
(off Aylesford St.)
SW3 7B 16
(off Beaufort St.)
Beaufort Mans. SW3 7B 16 (6B 100)
Beaufort M. SW6 6H 99
Beaufort Pk. NW11 4J 45
Beaufort Rd. HA4: Ruis 2F 57
KT1: King T 4E 150
TW1: Twick 7C 114
TW10: Ham 4C 132
W5 5F 79
Beaufort Sq. NW9 2C 44
Beaufort St. SW3 7A 16 (6B 100)
Beaufort Ter. *E14* 5E 104
(off Ferry St.)
Beaufort Way KT17: Ewe 7C 164
Beaufoy Ho. SE27 3B 138
SW8 7K 101
(off Rita Rd.)
Beaufoy Rd. N17 7K 33
(not continuous)
Beaufoy Wlk. SE11 4H 19 (4K 101)
Beaulieu Av. E16 1K 105
SE26 4H 139
Beaulieu Cl. CR4: Mitc 1E 154
NW9 4A 44
SE5 3D 120
TW1: Twick 6D 114
TW4: Houn 5D 112
Beaulieu Ct. W5 5E 78
Beaulieu Dr. HA5: Pinn 6B 40
Beaulieu Gdns. N21 7H 23
Beaulieu Hgts. SE25 1E 156
Beaulieu Lodge *E14* 3F 105
(off Schooner Cl.)
Beaulieu Pl. W4 3J 97
Beaumanor Gdns. SE9 4E 142
Beaumanor Mans. *W2* 7K 81
(off Queensway)
Beaumans Dr. E17 1B 50
Beaumaris Dr. IG8: Wfd G 7G 37
Beaumaris Gdns. SE19 7C 138
Beaumaris Grn. NW9 6A 44
Beaumaris Twr. *W3* 2H 97
(off Park Rd. Nth.)
Beaumont *W14* 4H 99
(off Kensington Village)
Beaumont Av. HA0: Wemb 5C 60
HA2: Harr 6F 41
TW9: Rich 3F 115
W14 5H 99
Beaumont Bldgs. *WC2* 1F 13
(off Martlett Ct.)
Beaumont Cl. KT2: King T 7G 133
N2 4C 46
Beaumont Ct. E1 3K 85
E5 3H 67
HA0: Wemb 5C 60
NW1 1H 83
NW9 2B 44
(off Cherry Cl.)
W1 5H 5
(off Beaumont St.)
W4 5J 97
Beaumont Cres. W14 5H 99
Beaumont Dr. KT4: Wor Pk 7D 152
TW15: Ashf 5F 129
Beaumont Gdns. NW3 3J 63
Beaumont Gro. E1 4K 85
Beaumont Ho. *E10* 7D 50
(off Skelton's La.)
W9 3H 81
(off Fernhead Rd.)
Beaumont Lodge *E8* 6G 67
(off Greenwood Rd.)
Beaumont M. HA5: Pinn 3C 40
NW5 5H 65
(off Charlton King's Rd.)
W1 5H 5 (5E 82)
Beaumont Pl. EN5: Barn 1C 20
TW7: Isle 5K 113
UB10: Ick 5C 56
W1 3B 6 (4G 83)
Beaumont Ri. N19 1H 65
Beaumont Rd. BR5: Pet W 6H 161
E10 7D 50
(not continuous)
E13 3K 87
SE19 6C 138
SW19 7G 117
W4 3J 97
Beaumont Sq. E1 5K 85
Beaumont St. W1 5H 5 (5E 82)
Beaumont Ter. *SE13* 7G 123
(off Wellmeadow Rd.)
Beaumont Wlk. NW3 7D 64
Beauvais Ter. UB5: N'olt 3B 76
Beauvale *NW1* 7E 64
(off Ferdinand St.)
Beauval Rd. SE22 6F 121
The Beaux Arts Bldg. N7 3J 65
Beaverbank Rd. SE9 1H 143
Beaver Cl. SE20 7G 139
SM4: Mord 7E 152
TW12: Hamp 1F 149
Beaver Ct. BR3: Beck 7D 140
Beaver Gro. UB5: N'olt 3C 76
Beaver Ind. Est. UB2: S'hall 3A 94
Beavers Cres. TW4: Houn 4A 112
Beavers La. TW4: Houn 2A 112
Beavers La. Campsite 4B 112
Beavers Lodge DA14: Sidc 4K 143
Beaverwood Rd. BR7: Chst 6J 143
Beavor Gro. *W6* 5C 98
(off Beavor La.)
Beavor La. W6 5C 98
Bebbington Rd. SE18 4J 107
Beblets Cl. BR6: Chels 5K 173
Beccles Dr. IG11: Bark 6J 71
Beccles St. E14 6B 86
Bec Cl. HA4: Ruis 3B 58
Bechervaise Ct. *E10* 1D 68
(off Leyton Grange Est.)
Bechtel Ho. *W6* 4F 99
(off Hammersmith Rd.)
Beck Cl. SE13 1D 122
Beck Ct. BR3: Beck 3K 157
BECKENHAM 2C 158
Beckenham Bus. Cen. BR3: Beck 6A 140
Beckenham Crematorium 3J 157
Beckenham Gdns. N9 3K 33
Beckenham Gro. BR2: Broml 2F 159
Beckenham Hill Est. BR3: Beck 5D 140
Beckenham Hill Rd. BR3: Beck 6D 140
SE6 6D 140
Beckenham La. BR2: Broml 2G 159
Beckenham Place Park 6E 140
Beckenham Pl. Pk. BR3: Beck 7D 140
Beckenham Rd. BR3: Beck 1K 157
BR4: W W'ck 7D 158
The Beckenham Theatre Cen. 2D 158
The Beckers N16 4G 67
Becket Av. E6 3E 88
Becket Cl. IG8: Wfd G 1C 52
SE25 6G 157
SW19 1K 153
(off High Path)
Becket Fold HA1: Harr 5K 41
Becket Ho. *E16* 1K 105
(off Constable Av.)
SE1 7E 14
WC1 3F 7
Becket Rd. N18 4D 34
Becket St. SE1 7E 14 (3D 102)
Beckett Cl. DA17: Belv 3F 109
NW10 6A 62
SW16 2H 137
Beckett Ho. *E1* 5J 85
(off Jubilee St.)
SW9 2J 119
Becketts Cl. BR6: Orp 3K 173
DA5: Bexl 1J 145
TW14: Felt 6K 111
Becketts Ho. IG1: Ilf 3E 70
Becketts Pl. KT1: Hamp W 1D 150
Becketts Wharf *KT1: Hamp W* 1D 150
(off Lwr. Teddington Rd.)
Beckett Wlk. BR3: Beck 6A 140
Beckfoot *NW1* 1B 6
(off Ampthill Est.)
Beckford Cl. W14 4H 99
Beckford Dr. BR5: Orp 7H 161
Beckford Ho. N16 5E 66
Beckford Pl. SE17 5C 102
Beckford Rd. CR0: C'don 6F 157
Beckham Ho. SE11 4H 19 (4K 101)
Beckhaven Ho. *SE11* 4K 19
(off Gilbert Rd.)
Beck Ho. *N18* 5C 34
(off Upton Rd.)
Beck La. BR3: Beck 3K 157
Beckley Ho. *E3* 4B 86
(off Hamlets Way)
Becklow Gdns. *W12* 2C 98
(off Becklow Rd.)
Becklow M. *W12* 2C 98
(off Becklow Rd.)
Becklow Rd. W12 2B 98
Beck River Pk. BR3: Beck 1B 158
Beck Rd. CR4: Mitc 6D 154
E8 1H 85
Beck Sq. E10 1A 68
Becks Rd. DA14: Sidc 3A 144
The Beck Theatre 6H 75
BECKTON 5E 88
BECKTON ALPS 4D 88
BECKTON PARK 6D 88
Beckton Retail Pk. 5E 88
Beckton Rd. E16 5H 87
Beckton Triangle Retail Pk. 4F 89
Beck Way BR3: Beck 3B 158
Beckway Rd. SW16 2H 155
Beckway St. SE17 4E 102
(not continuous)
Beckwith Cl. EN2: Enf 1G 23
Beckwith Ho. *E2* 2H 85
(off Wadeson St.)
Beckwith Rd. SE24 5D 120
Beclands Rd. SW17 6E 136
Becmead Av. HA3: Kenton 5B 42
SW16 4H 137
Becondale Rd. SE19 5E 138
BECONTREE 4D 72
Becontree Av. RM8: Dag 4B 72
Becontree Heath Leisure Cen. 2G 73
Becquerel Ct. *SE10* 3H 105
(off West Parkside)
Bective Pl. SW15 4H 117
Bective Rd. E7 4J 69
SW15 4H 117
Becton Pl. DA8: Erith 7H 109
Bedale Rd. EN2: Enf 1H 23
Bedale St. SE1 5E 14 (1D 102)
Beddalls Farm Ct. E6 5B 88
BEDDINGTON 4J 167
BEDDINGTON CORNER 7E 154
Beddington Cross CR0: Bedd 7H 155
Beddington Farm Rd.
CR0: Bedd, Wadd 7J 155
Beddington Gdns. SM5: Cars 6E 166
SM6: W'gton 6E 166
Beddington Grn. BR5: St P 1K 161
Beddington Gro. SM6: W'gton 5H 167
Beddington La.
CR0: Bedd, C'don 5G 155
Beddington Pk. 3F 167
Beddington Pk. Cotts.SM6: Bedd 3H 167
Beddington Path BR5: St P 1K 161
Beddington Rd. BR5: St P 2J 161
IG3: Ilf 7K 53
Beddington Ter. CR0: C'don 7K 155
Beddington Trad. Est. CR0: Bedd 1J 167
Bede Cl. HA5: Pinn 1B 40
Bedefield WC1 2F 7 (3J 83)
Bede Ho. *SE14* 1B 122
(off Clare Rd.)
Bedens Rd. DA14: Sidc 6E 144
Bede Rd. RM6: Chad H 6C 54
Bede Sq. *E3* 4B 86
(off Joseph St.)
Bedevere Rd. N9 3B 34
Bedfont Cl. CR4: Mitc 2E 154
TW14: Bedf 6E 110
Bedfont Ct. TW19: Stanw M 6B 174
Bedfont Ct. Est. TW19: Stanw M 7C 174
Bedfont Grn. Cl. TW14: Bedf 1E 128
Bedfont Ind. Pk. TW15: Ashf 1E 128
Bedfont Ind. Pk. Nth.
TW15: Ashf 3E 128
Bedfont Lakes Country Pk. 2E 128
Bedfont Lakes Country Pk.
Vis. Cen. 3D 128
Bedfont La. TW13: Felt 5G 111
TW14: Felt 7G 111
Bedfont Rd. TW13: Felt 1E 128
TW14: Bedf 1E 128
TW19: Stanw 6A 110
Bedfont Trad. Est. TW14: Bedf 2F 129
Bedford Av. EN5: Barn 5C 20
UB4: Yead 6K 75
WC1 6D 6 (5H 83)
Bedfordbury WC2 2E 12 (7J 83)
(not continuous)
Bedford Cl. N10 7K 31
W4 6A 98
Bedford Cnr. *W4* 4A 98
(off South Pde.)
Bedford Ct. *CR0: C'don* 1D 168
(off Tavistock Rd.)
WC2 3E 12 (7J 83)
Bedford Ct. Mans. WC1 6D 6
Bedford Gdns. W8 1J 99
Bedford Gdns. Ho. *W8* 1J 99
(off Bedford Gdns.)
Bedford Hill SW12 1F 137
SW16 1F 137
Bedford Ho. CR0: C'don 7B 156
SW4 4J 119
(off Solon New Rd. Est.)
Bedford M. N2 3C 46
SE6 2D 140
BEDFORD PARK 3K 97
Bedford Pk. CR0: C'don 1C 168
Bedford Pk. Cnr. W4 4A 98
Bedford Pk. Mans. W4 4K 97
Bedford Pas. *SW6* 7G 99
(off Dawes Rd.)
W1 5B 6 (5G 83)
Bedford Pl. CR0: C'don 1D 168
WC1 5E 6 (5J 83)
Bedford Rd. DA15: Sidc 3J 143
E6 1E 88
E17 2C 50
E18 2J 51
HA1: Harr 6G 41
HA4: Ruis 4H 57
IG1: Ilf 3F 71
KT4: Wor Pk 2E 164
N2 3C 46
N8 6H 47
N9 7C 24
N15 4E 48
N22 2J 47
NW7 2F 29
SW4 4J 119
TW2: Twick 3H 131
W4 3K 97
W13 7B 78
Bedford Row SE1 7D 14 (3C 102)
WC1 5H 7 (5K 83)
Bedford Sq. WC1 6D 6 (5H 83)
Bedford St. WC2 2E 12 (7J 83)
Bedford Ter. SM2: Sutt 6A 166
SW2 5J 119
Bedford Way WC1 4D 6 (4H 83)
Bedgebury Ct. E17 2E 50
Bedgebury Gdns. SW19 2G 135
Bedgebury Rd. SE9 4B 124
Bedivere Rd. BR1: Broml 3J 141
Bedlam M. SE11 3J 19
Bedlow Way CR0: Bedd 4K 167
Bedmond Ho. *SW3* 5C 16
(off Cale St.)
Bedonwell Rd.
DA7: Belv, Bex, Erith 6F 109
DA17: Belv 6E 108
SE2 6E 108
Bedser Cl. CR7: Thor H 3C 156
SE11 7H 19 (6K 101)
Bedser Dr. UB6: G'frd 5H 59
Bedster Gdns. KT8: W Mole 2F 149
Bedwardine Rd. SE19 7E 138
Bedwell Cl. CR0: C'don 5D 156
Bedwell Ct. *RM6: Chad H* 7D 54
(off Chapel La.)
Bedwell Gdns. UB3: Harl 5G 93
(not continuous)
Bedwell Ho. SW9 2A 120
Bedwell Rd. DA17: Belv 5G 109
N17 1E 48
Beeby Rd. E16 5K 87
Beech Av. DA15: Sidc 7A 126
HA4: Ruis 1K 57
IG9: Buck H 2E 36
N20 1H 31
TW8: Bford 7B 96
W3 1A 98
Beech Cl. N9 6B 24
SE8 6C 104
SM5: Cars 2D 166
SW15 7C 116
SW19 6E 134
TW15: Ashf 5F 129
TW16: Sun 2B 148
UB7: W Dray 3C 92
Beech Copse BR1: Broml 1D 160
CR2: S Croy 5E 168
Beech Ct. *BR1: Broml* 1H 159
(off Blyth Rd.)
BR3: Beck 7B 140
E17 3F 51
IG1: Ilf 3E 70
(off Riverdene Rd.)
KT6: Surb 7D 150
UB5: N'olt 1C 76
W9 5J 81
(off Elmfield Way)
Beech Cres. Ct. N5 4B 66
Beechcroft BR7: Chst 7E 142
Beechcroft Av. DA7: Bex 1K 127
HA2: Harr 7E 40
Beechcroft Av. KT3: N Mald 1J 151
NW11 7H 45
Beechcroft Cl. BR6: Orp 4H 173
SW16 5K 137
TW5: Hest 7C 94
Beechcroft Ct. N12 4E 30
NW11 7H 45
(off Beechcroft Av.)
Beechcroft Gdns. HA9: Wemb 3F 61
Beechcroft Ho. W5 5E 78
Beechcroft Lodge SM2: Sutt 7A 166
Beechcroft Rd. BR6: Orp 4H 173
E18 2K 51
KT9: Chess 3F 163
SW14 3J 115
SW17 2C 136
Beechdale N21 2E 32
Beechdale Rd. SW2 6K 119
Beech Dell BR2: Kes 4D 172
Beechdene *SE15* 1H 121
(off Carlton Gro.)
Beech Dr. N2 2D 46
Beechen Cliff Way TW7: Isle 2K 113
Beechen Gro. HA5: Pinn 3D 40
Beechen Pl. SE23 2K 139
The Beeches *CR2: S Croy* 5D 168
(off Blunt Rd.)
E12 7C 70
TW3: Houn 1F 113
Beeches Av. SM5: Cars 7C 166
Beeches Cl. SE20 1J 157
Beeches Rd. SM3: Sutt 1G 165
SW17 3C 136
Beeches Wlk. SM5: Cars 7B 166
Beechey Ho. *E1* 1H 103
(off Watts St.)
Beechfield Cotts. BR1: Broml 1A 160
Beechfield Ct. *CR2: S Croy* 4C 168
(off Bramley Hill)
Beechfield Gdns. RM7: Rush G 7J 55
Beechfield Rd. BR1: Broml 2A 160
DA8: Erith 7K 109
N4 6C 48
SE6 1B 140
Beech Gdns. *EC2* 5C 8
(off Beech St.)
RM10: Dag 7J 73
W5 2E 96
Beech Gro. CR4: Mitc 5H 155
KT3: N Mald 3K 151
Beech Hall Cres. E4 7A 36
Beech Hall Rd. E4 7K 35
Beech Haven Ct. *DA1: Cray* 5K 127
(off London Rd.)
Beech Hill EN4: Had W 1G 21
Beech Hill Av. EN4: Had W 1F 21
Beechhill Rd. SE9 5E 124
Beech Ho. CR0: New Ad 6D 170
SE16 2J 103
(off Ainsty Est.)
Beech Ho. Rd. CR0: C'don 3D 168
Beech Hurst Cl. BR7: Chst 1G 161
Beeching Ct. *W3* 6J 79
(off Bollo Bri. Rd.)
Beech La. IG9: Buck H 2E 36
Beech Lawns N12 5G 31
Beechmont Cl. BR1: Broml 5G 141
Beechmore Gdns.
SM3: Cheam 2F 165
Beechmore Rd. SW11 1D 118
Beechmount Av. W7 5H 77
Beecholme N12 5E 30
Beecholme Av. CR4: Mitc 1F 155
Beecholme Est. E5 3H 67
Beech Rd. N11 6D 32
SW16 2J 155
TW14: Bedf 7G 111
Beechrow TW10: Ham 4E 132
Beech St. EC2 5C 8 (5C 84)
RM7: Rom 4J 55
Beech Tree Cl. HA7: Stan 5H 27
N1 7A 66
Beech Tree Glade E4 1C 36
Beech Tree Pl. SM1: Sutt 5K 165
Beechvale Cl. N12 5H 31
Beech Wlk. N17 3F 49
NW7 6F 29
Beech Way NW10 7K 61
TW2: Twick 3E 130
Beechway DA5: Bexl 6D 126
Beechwood Av. BR6: Chels 5J 173
CR7: Thor H 4B 156
HA2: Harr 3F 59
HA4: Ruis 2H 57
N3 3H 45
TW9: Kew 1G 115
TW16: Sun 6J 129
UB3: Hayes 7F 75
UB6: G'frd 3F 77
UB8: Hil 6C 74
The Beechwood Cen.
BR2: Broml 1D 172
(off Lwr. Gravel Rd.)
Beechwood Circ. HA2: Harr 3F 59
Beechwood Cl. KT6: Surb 7C 150
N2 3D 46
NW7 5F 29
Beechwood Ct. SM5: Cars 4D 166
TW16: Sun 6J 129
W4 6K 97
Beechwood Cres. DA7: Bex 3D 126
Beechwood Dr. BR2: Kes 4B 172
IG8: Wfd G 5C 36
Beechwood Gdns. HA2: Harr 3F 59
IG5: Ilf 5D 52
NW10 3F 79
Beechwood Gro. KT6: Surb 7C 150
W3 7A 80
Beechwood Hall N3 3H 45
Beechwood Ho. *E2* 2G 85
(off Teale St.)
Beechwood M. N9 2B 34
Beechwood Pk. E18 3J 51
Beechwood Pl. SE10 1E 122
Beechwood Ri. BR7: Chst 4F 143
Beechwood Rd. CR2: Sande 7E 168
E8 6F 67
N8 4H 47
Beechwoods Ct. SE19 5F 139
Beechworth NW6 7G 63
Beechworth Cl. NW3 2J 63
Beecroft La. SE4 5A 122
Beecroft M. SE4 5A 122
Beecroft Rd. SE4 5A 122
Beefeater Distillery 6J 19 (5A 102)
Beehive Cl. E8 7F 67
UB10: Uxb 7B 56
Beehive Ct. HA8: Edg 5C 28
IG1: Ilf 6D 52
Beehive La. IG1: Ilf 5D 52
IG4: Ilf 5D 52
Beehive Pl. SW9 3A 120
Beeken Dene BR6: Farnb 4G 173
Beeleigh Rd. SM4: Mord 4K 153
Beemans Row SW18 2A 136
Beeston Cl. E8 5G 67
Beeston Ho. *SE1* 3D 102
(off Burbage Cl.)
Beeston Pl. SW1 1K 17 (3F 101)
Beeston Rd. EN4: E Barn 6G 21
Beeston Way TW14: Felt 6A 112
Beethoven St. W10 3G 81
Beeton Cl. HA5: Hat E 1E 40
Beeton Way SE27 4D 138
Begbie Rd. SE3 1A 124
BEGGAR'S HILL 6B 164
Beggar's Hill KT17: Ewe 7B 164
Beggars Roost La. SM1: Sutt 6J 165
Begonia Cl. E6 5D 88
Begonia Pl. TW12: Hamp 6E 130
Begonia Wlk. W12 6B 80
Beirach Moshe Sq. E5 2H 67
Beira St. SW12 7F 119
Bejun Ct. EN5: New Bar 4F 21
Bekesbourne St. E14 6A 86
Belcroft Cl. BR1: Broml 7H 141
Beldam Way TW3: Houn 3D 112
Beldanes Lodge NW10 7C 62
Beldham Gdns. KT8: W Mole 2F 149
Belfairs Dr. RM6: Chad H 7C 54
Belfast Rd. N16 2F 67
SE25 4H 157
Belfield Rd. KT19: Ewe 7K 163
Belfont Wlk. N7 4J 65
(not continuous)
Belford Gro. SE18 4E 106
Belford Ho. E8 1F 85
Belfort Rd. SE15 2J 121
Belfry Cl. BR1: Broml 4F 161
SE16 5H 103
Belgrade Rd. N16 4E 66
TW12: Hamp 1F 149
Belgrave Cl. N14 5B 22
NW7 5E 28
W3 2H 97
Belgrave Ct. *E2* 2H 85
(off Temple St.)
E13 4A 88
E14 7B 86
(off Westferry Cir.)
SW8 7G 101
(off Ascalon St.)
W4 5J 97
Belgrave Cres. TW16: Sun 1K 147
Belgrave Gdns. HA7: Stan 5H 27
N14 5C 22
NW8 1K 81
Belgrave Hgts. E11 1J 69
Belgrave Ho. SW9 7A 102
Belgrave Mans. *NW8* 1K 81
(off Belgrave Gdns.)
Belgrave M. Nth. SW1 7G 11 (2E 100)
Belgrave M. Sth.
SW1 1H 17 (3E 100)
Belgrave M. W. SW1 1G 17 (3E 100)
Belgrave Pl. SW1 1H 17 (3E 100)
Belgrave Rd. CR4: Mitc 3B 154
E10 1E 68
E11 2J 69
E13 4A 88
E17 5C 50
IG1: Ilf 1D 70
SE25 4F 157
SW1 3K 17 (4F 101)
SW13 7B 98
TW4: Houn 3D 112
TW16: Sun 1K 147
Belgrave Sq. SW1 1G 17 (3E 100)
Belgrave St. E1 5K 85
Belgrave Ter. IG8: Wfd G 3D 36
Belgrave Wlk. CR4: Mitc 3B 154
Belgrave Yd. SW1 2J 17
BELGRAVIA 2H 17 (3E 100)
Belgravia Cl. EN5: Barn 3C 20
Belgravia Ct. SW1 2J 17
Belgravia Gdns. BR1: Broml 6G 141
Belgravia Ho. *SW1* 1G 17
(off Halkin Pl.)
SW4 6H 119
Belgravia M. KT1: King T 4D 150
Belgravia Workshops *N19* 2J 65
(off Marlborough Rd.)
Belgrove St. WC1 1F 7 (3J 83)
Belham Wlk. SE5 1D 120
Belinda Rd. SW9 3B 120
Belitha Vs. N1 7K 65

A-Z Big London 185

THE BELL 3C 50
Bella Best Ho. *SW1* 5K 17
(off Westmoreland Ter.)
Bellamy Cl. E14 2C 104
HA8: Edg 2D 28
UB10: Ick 3C 56
W14 5H 99
Bellamy Ct. HA7: Stan 1B 42
Bellamy Dr. HA7: Stan 1B 42
Bellamy Ho. SW17 4B 136
TW5: Hest 6E 94
Bellamy Rd. E4 6J 35
EN2: Enf 2J 23
Bellamy's Ct. *SE16* 1K 103
(off Abbotshade Rd.)
Bellamy St. SW12 7F 119
Bel La. TW13: Hanw 3C 130
Bellarmine Cl. SE28 1K 107
Bellasis Av. SW2 2J 137
Bell Av. UB7: W Dray 4B 92
Bell Brook Ri. N11 4A 32
Bell Cl. HA4: Ruis 3H 57
HA5: Pinn 2A 40
Bellclose Rd. UB7: W Dray 2A 92
Bell Ct. NW4 4E 44
Bell Dr. SW18 7G 117
Bellefields Rd. SW9 3K 119
Bellegrove Cl. DA16: Well 2K 125
Bellegrove Pde. DA16: Well 3K 125
Bellegrove Rd. DA16: Well 2H 125
Bellenden Rd. SE15 1F 121
Bellenden Rd. Retail Pk. 1G 121
Bellestaines Pleasaunce E4 2H 35
Belleville Ho. *SE10* 7D 104
(off Norman Rd.)
Belleville Rd. SW11 5C 118
Belle Vue UB6: G'frd 1H 77
Bellevue Ct. TW3: Houn 4E 112
Belle Vue Est. NW4 4F 45
Belle Vue La. WD23: B Hea 1C 26
Bellevue M. N11 5K 31
Bellevue Pde. SW17 1D 136
Belle Vue Pk. CR7: Thor H 3C 156
Bellevue Pl. E1 4J 85
Belle Vue Rd. E17 2F 51
NW4 4E 44
Bellevue Rd. DA6: Bex 5F 127
KT1: King T 3E 150
(not continuous)
N11 4K 31
SW13 2C 116
SW17 1C 136
W13 4B 78
Bellew St. SW17 3A 136
Bell Farm Av. RM10: Dag 3J 73
Bellfield CR0: Sels 7A 170
Bellfield Av. HA3: Hrw W 6C 26
Bellfield Cl. SE3 7K 105
Bellflower Cl. E6 5C 88
Bell Gdns. *E10* 1C 68
(off Church Rd.)
Bellgate M. NW5 4F 65
BELL GREEN 4B 140
Bell Grn. SE26 4B 140
Bell Grn. La. SE26 5B 140
Bell Grn. Retail Pk. 3B 140
Bell Grn. Trade City SE6 3B 140
Bellhaven E15 6F 69
Bell Hill CR0: C'don 2C 168
Bell Ho. HA9: Wemb 3E 60
SE10 6E 104
(off Haddo St.)
Bellhouse Cotts. UB3: Hayes 7G 75
Bell Ho. Rd. RM7: Rush G 1J 73
Bellina M. NW5 4F 65
Bell Ind. Est. W4 4J 97
Belling Cres. EN3: Pond E 5D 24
BELLINGHAM 3D 140
Bellingham *N17* 7C 34
(off Park La.)
Bellingham Ct. IG11: Bark 3B 90
Bellingham Grn. SE6 3C 140
Bellingham Leisure & Lifestyle Cen. 3D 140
Bellingham Rd. SE6 3D 140
Bellingham Trad. Est. SE6 3D 140
Bell Inn Yd. EC3 1F 15 (6D 84)
Bell La. E1 6J 9 (5F 85)
E16 1H 105
EN3: Enf H, Enf W 1E 24
HA9: Wemb 2D 60
NW4 4F 45
TW1: Twick 1A 132
TW14: Bedf 7F 111
Bellmaker Ct. E3 5C 86
Bell Mdw. SE19 5E 138
Bell Moor NW3 3A 64
Bello Cl. SE24 7B 120
Bellot Gdns. *SE10* 5G 105
(off Bellot St.)
Bellot St. SE10 5G 105
Bell Pde. BR4: W W'ck 2E 170
Bellring Cl. DA17: Belv 6G 109
Bell Rd. EN1: Enf 1J 23
KT8: E Mos 5H 149
TW3: Houn 3F 113
Bells All. SW6 2J 117
Bells Hill EN5: Barn 5A 20
Bellsize Ct. NW3 5B 64
Bell St. NW1 5C 4 (5C 82)
SE18 1C 124
Belltrees Gro. SW16 5K 137
Bellview Ct. TW3: Houn 4F 113
Bell Vw. Mnr. HA4: Ruis 7F 39
Bell Water Ga. SE18 3E 106
Bellwether La. *SW18* 5K 117
(off Ryland Blvd.)
Bell Wharf La. EC4 3D 14 (7C 84)
Bellwood Rd. SE15 4K 121
Bell Yd. WC2 1J 13 (6A 84)
Bell Yd. M. SE1 7H 15 (2E 102)
Belmarsh Rd. SE28 2J 107
BELMONT
HA3 2A 42
SM2 7J 165
Belmont Av. DA16: Well 3J 125
EN4: Cockf 5J 21
HA0: Wemb 1F 79
KT3: N Mald 5C 152
N9 1B 34
N13 5E 32
N17 3C 48
UB2: S'hall 3C 94
Belmont Circ. HA3: Kenton 1B 42
Belmont Cl. E4 5A 36
EN4: Cockf 4J 21
Belmont Cl. IG8: Wfd G 4E 36
N20 1E 30
SW4 3G 119
UB8: Uxb 6A 56
Belmont Ct. N5 4C 66
NW11 5H 45
Belmont Gro. SE13 3F 123
W4 4K 97
Belmont Hall Ct. SE13 3F 123
Belmont Hill SE13 3F 123
Belmont La. BR7: Chst 5G 143
HA7: Stan 1C 42
Belmont Lodge HA3: Hrw W 7C 26
Belmont M. SW19 2F 135
Belmont Pde. BR7: Chst 5G 143
NW11 5H 45
Belmont Pk. SE13 4F 123
Belmont Pk. Cl. SE13 4G 123
Belmont Pk. Rd. E10 6D 50
Belmont Ri. SM2: Sutt 6H 165
Belmont Rd. BR3: Beck 2A 158
BR7: Chst 5F 143
DA8: Erith 7G 109
HA3: W'stone 3K 41
IG1: Ilf 3G 71
N15 4C 48
N17 4C 48
SE25 5H 157
SM6: W'gton 5F 167
SW4 3G 119
TW2: Twick 2H 131
UB8: Uxb 7A 56
W4 4K 97
Belmont St. NW1 7E 64
Belmont Ter. W4 4K 97
Belmore Av. UB4: Hayes 6J 75
Belmore Ho. N7 5H 65
Belmore La. N7 5H 65
Belmore St. SW8 1H 119
Beloe Cl. SW15 4C 116
Belsham St. E9 6J 67
Belsize Av. N13 6E 32
NW3 6B 64
W13 3B 96
Belsize Ct. SM1: Sutt 4K 165
Belsize Ct. Garages *NW3* 5B 64
(off Belsize La.)
Belsize Cres. NW3 5B 64
Belsize Gdns. SM1: Sutt 4K 165
Belsize Gro. NW3 6C 64
Belsize La. NW3 6B 64
Belsize M. NW3 6B 64
Belsize Pk. NW3 6B 64
Belsize Pk. Gdns. NW3 6B 64
Belsize Pk. M. NW3 6B 64
Belsize Pl. NW3 5B 64
Belsize Rd. HA3: Hrw W 7C 26
NW6 1K 81
Belsize Sq. NW3 6B 64
Belsize Ter. NW3 6B 64
Belson Rd. SE18 4D 106
Beltane Dr. SW19 3F 135
Belthorn Cres. SW12 7G 119
Belton Rd. DA14: Sidc 4A 144
E7 7K 69
E11 4G 69
N17 3E 48
NW2 6C 62
Belton Way E3 5C 86
Beltran Rd. SW6 2K 117
Beltwood Rd. DA17: Belv 4J 109
BELVEDERE 4G 109
The Belvedere SE1 1K 101
SW10 1A 118
(off Chelsea Harbour)
Belvedere Av. IG5: Ilf 2F 53
SW19 5G 135
Belvedere Bldgs. SE1 7B 14 (2B 102)
Belvedere Bus. Pk. DA17: Belv 2H 109
Belvedere Cl. TW11: Tedd 5J 131
Belvedere Ct. DA17: Belv 3F 109
N1 1E 84
(off De Beauvoir Cres.)
N2 5B 46
NW2 6F 63
(off Willesden La.)
SW15 4E 116
Belvedere Dr. SW19 5G 135
Belvedere Gdns. KT8: W Mole 5D 148
SE1 6H 13 (2K 101)
Belvedere Gro. SW19 5G 135
Belvedere Ho. *TW13: Felt* 1J 129
(off Lemon Gro.)
Belvedere Ind. Est. DA17: Belv 1J 109
Belvedere Link Bus. Pk.
DA8: Erith 3J 109
Belvedere M. SE3 7K 105
SE15 3J 121
Belvedere Pl. SE1 7B 14 (2B 102)
SW2 4K 119
Belvedere Rd. DA7: Bex 3F 127
E10 1A 68
SE1 7G 13 (2K 101)
SE19 7F 139
W7 3K 95
Belvedere Row Apartments *W12* 7E 80
(off Fountain Park Way)
Belvedere Sq. SW19 5G 135
Belvedere Strand NW9 2B 44
Belvedere Way HA3: Kenton 6E 42
Belvoir Cl. SE9 3C 142
Belvoir Ho. SW1 4G 101
Belvoir Rd. SE22 7G 121
Belvue Bus. Cen. UB5: N'olt 7F 59
Belvue Cl. UB5: N'olt 7E 58
Belvue Rd. UB5: N'olt 7E 58
Belz Dr. N15 4E 48
Belz Ter. E5 7G 49
Bembridge Cl. NW6 7G 63
Bembridge Gdns. HA4: Ruis 2F 57
Bembridge Ho. *KT2: King T* 2G 151
(off Coombe Rd.)
SE8 4B 104
(off Longshore)
SW18 6K 117
(off Iron Mill Rd.)
Bemersyde Point *E13* 3K 87
(off Dongola Rd. W.)
Bemerton Est. N1 7J 65
Bemerton St. N1 1K 83
Bemish Rd. SW15 3F 117
Bempton Dr. HA4: Ruis 2K 57
Bemsted Rd. E17 3B 50
Benares Rd. SE18 4K 107
Benbow Ct. *W6* 3E 98
(off Benbow Rd.)
Benbow Ho. *SE8* 6C 104
(off Benbow St.)
Benbow M. *E3* 3B 86
(off Tredegar Sq.)
Benbow Rd. W6 3D 98
Benbow St. SE8 6C 104
Benbury Cl. BR1: Broml 5E 140
Bence Ho. *SE8* 4A 104
(off Rainsborough Av.)
The Bench TW10: Ham 3C 132
Bench Fld. CR2: S Croy 6F 169
Bencroft Rd. SW16 7G 137
Bencurtis Pk. BR4: W W'ck 3F 171
Bendall Ho. *NW1* 5D 4
(off Penfold St.)
Bendall M. NW1 5D 4
Bendemeer Rd. SW15 3F 117
Benden Ho. *SE13* 5E 122
(off Monument Gdns.)
Bendish Point SE28 2G 107
Bendish Rd. E6 7C 70
Bendmore Av. SE2 5A 108
Bendon Valley SW18 7K 117
Benedict Cl. BR6: Orp 3J 173
DA17: Belv 3E 108
Benedict Ct. RM6: Chad H 6F 55
Benedict Dr. TW14: Bedf 7F 111
Benedict Rd. CR4: Mitc 3B 154
SW9 3K 119
Benedicts Wharf IG11: Bark 1F 89
Benedict Way N2 3A 46
Benedict Wharf CR4: Mitc 3C 154
Benenden Grn. BR2: Broml 5J 159
Benenden Ho. *SE17* 5E 102
(off Mina Rd.)
Benett Gdns. SW16 2J 155
Ben Ezra Ct. *SE17* 4C 102
(off Asolando Dr.)
Benfleet Cl. SM1: Sutt 3A 166
Benfleet Ct. E8 1F 85
Benfleet Way N11 2K 31
Bengal Ct. *EC3* 1F 15
(off Birchin La.)
Bengal Rd. IG1: Ilf 4F 71
Bengarth Dr. HA3: Hrw W 2H 41
Bengarth Rd. UB5: N'olt 1C 76
Bengeo Gdns. RM6: Chad H 6C 54
Bengeworth Rd. HA1: Harr 2A 60
SE5 3C 120
Ben Hale Cl. HA7: Stan 5G 27
Benham Cl. KT9: Chess 6C 162
SW11 3B 118
Benham Gdns. TW4: Houn 5D 112
Benham Ho. *SW10* 7K 99
(off Coleridge Gdns.)
Benham Rd. W7 5J 77
Benham's Pl. NW3 4A 64
Benhill Av. SM1: Sutt 4K 165
(not continuous)
Benhill Rd. SE5 7D 102
SM1: Sutt 3A 166
Benhill Wood Rd. SM1: Sutt 3A 166
BENHILTON 2K 165
Benhilton Gdns. SM1: Sutt 3K 165
Benhurst Ct. SW16 5A 138
Benhurst La. SW16 5A 138
Benina Cl. IG2: Ilf 5K 53
Benin Ho. *WC1* 6G 7
(off Procter St.)
Benin St. SE13 7F 123
Benjafield Cl. N18 4C 34
Benjamin Cl. E8 1G 85
Benjamin Ct. DA17: Belv 6F 109
TW15: Ashf 7E 128
Benjamin Franklin House 4E 12
(off Craven St.)
Benjamin M. SW12 7G 119
Benjamin St. EC1 5A 8 (5B 84)
Benjamin Truman Cl. E1 4G 85
Ben Jonson Ct. N1 2E 84
Ben Jonson Ho. EC2 5D 8
Ben Jonson Pl. EC2 5D 8
Ben Jonson Rd. E1 5K 85
Benkart M. SW15 6C 116
Benledi Rd. E14 6F 87
Benlow Works *UB3: Hayes* 2H 93
(off Silverdale Rd.)
Bennelong Cl. W12 7D 80
Bennerley Rd. SW11 5C 118
Bennet Cl. KT1: Hamp W 1C 150
Bennet M. *N19* 3H 65
(off Wedmore St.)
Bennets Ctyd. SW19 1A 154
Bennets Fld. Rd. UB11: Stock P 1D 92
Bennet's Hill EC4 2B 14 (7C 84)
Bennets Lodge EN2: Enf 3G 23
Bennet St. SW1 4A 12 (1G 101)
Bennett Cl. DA16: Well 2A 126
HA6: Nwood 1H 39
TW4: Houn 5C 112
Bennett Ct. N7 3K 65
Bennett Gro. SE13 1D 122
Bennett Ho. *SW1* 3D 18
(off Page St.)
Bennett Pk. SE3 3H 123
Bennett Rd. E13 4A 88
N16 4E 66
RM6: Chad H 6E 54
SW9 2A 120
Bennetts Av. CR0: C'don 2A 170
UB6: G'frd 1J 77
Bennett's Castle La. RM8: Dag 2C 72
Bennetts Cl. CR4: Mitc 1F 155
N17 6A 34
Bennetts Copse BR7: Chst 6C 142
Bennett St. W4 6A 98
Bennetts Way CR0: C'don 2A 170
Bennett's Yd. SW1 2D 18 (3H 101)
Benning Dr. RM8: Dag 1E 72
Benningholme Rd. HA8: Edg 6F 29
Bennington Cl. CR7: Thor H 4C 156
Bennington Rd. IG8: Wfd G 7B 36
N17 1E 48
Benn's All. TW12: Hamp 2F 149
Benn St. E9 6A 68
Benns Wlk. *TW9: Rich* 4E 114
(off Michelsdale Dr.)
Benrek Cl. IG6: Ilf 1G 53
Bensbury Cl. SW15 7D 116
Bensham Cl. CR7: Thor H 4C 156
Bensham Gro. CR7: Thor H 2C 156
Bensham La. CR0: C'don 7B 156
CR7: Thor H 5B 156
Bensham Mnr. Rd. CR7: Thor H 4C 156
Bensham Mnr. Rd. Pas.
CR7: Thor H 4C 156
Bensley Cl. N11 5J 31
Ben Smith Way SE16 3G 103
Benson Av. E6 2A 88
Benson Cl. EN5: Barn 5C 20
TW3: Houn 4E 112
UB8: Hil 5A 74
Benson Ct. *SW8* 1J 119
(off Hartington Rd.)
Benson Ho. *E2* 3J 9
(off Ligonier St.)
SE1 5K 13
(off Hatfields)
W14 4H 99
(off Radnor Ter.)
Benson Mews BR7: Chst 5E 142
Benson Quay E1 7J 85
Benson Rd. CR0: Wadd 3A 168
SE23 1J 139
The Bentall Cen. 2D 150
Bentfield Gdns. SE9 3B 142
Bentfield Ho. *NW9* 3B 44
(off Heritage Av.)
Benthal Rd. N16 2G 67
Bentham Ct. *N1* 7C 66
(off Ecclesbourne Rd.)
Bentham Ho. *SE1* 3D 102
(off Falmouth Rd.)
SE18 3F 107
Bentham Rd. E9 6K 67
SE28 7B 90
Bentham Wlk. NW10 5J 61
Ben Tillet Cl. E16 1D 106
IG11: Bark 7A 72
Ben Tillet Ho. N15 3B 48
Bentinck Cl. NW8 2C 82
Bentinck Ho. *SW1* 2D 18
(off Monck St.)
W12 7D 80
(off White City Est.)
Bentinck Mans. *W1* 7H 5
(off Bentinck St.)
Bentinck M. W1 7H 5 (6E 82)
Bentinck Rd. UB7: Yiew 1A 92
Bentinck St. W1 7H 5 (6E 82)
Bentley Cl. SW19 3J 135
W7 1K 95
Bentley Ct. *SE13* 4E 122
(off Whitburn Rd.)
Bentley Dr. IG2: Ilf 6G 53
NW2 3H 63
Bentley Ho. *E3* 4C 86
(off Wellington Way)
SE5 1E 120
(off Peckham Rd.)
Bentley Lodge WD23: B Hea 2D 26
Bentley M. EN1: Enf 6J 23
Bentley Priory
Local Nature Reserve 4D 26
Bentley Priory Mus. 3D 26
Bentley Rd. N1 6E 66
Bentley Way EN5: New Bar 4F 21
HA7: Stan 5F 27
IG8: Buck H, Wfd G 2D 36
Benton Rd. IG1: Ilf 1H 71
Bentons La. SE27 4C 138
Benton's Ri. SE27 5D 138
Bentry Cl. RM8: Dag 2E 72
Bentry Rd. RM8: Dag 2E 72
Bentworth Ct. *E2* 3K 9
(off Granby St.)
Bentworth Rd. W12 6D 80
Ben Uri Gallery 1K 81
Benville Ho. *SW8* 7K 101
(off Dorset Rd.)
Benwell Cen. TW16: Sun 1J 147
Benwell Ct. TW16: Sun 1J 147
Benwell Rd. N7 4A 66
Benwick Cl. SE16 4H 103
Benwick M. SE20 1J 157
Benwood Ct. SM1: Sutt 3A 166
Benworth St. E3 3B 86
Benyon Ct. *N1* 1E 84
(off De Beauvoir Est.)
Benyon Ho. *EC1* 1K 7
(off Myddelton Pas.)
Benyon Rd. N1 1D 84
Benyon Wharf *E8* 1E 84
(off Kingsland Rd.)
Berberis Ct. IG1: Ilf 6F 71
Berberis Ho. *E3* 5C 86
(off Gale St.)
TW13: Felt 2J 129
Berberis Wlk. UB7: W Dray 4A 92
Berber Pde. SE18 1C 124
Berber Pl. E14 7C 86
Berber Rd. SW11 5D 118
Berberry Cl. HA8: Edg 4D 28
Bercta Rd. SE9 2G 143
Berebinder Ho. *E3* 2B 86
(off Tredegar Rd.)
Beregaria Ct. *SE11* 7K 19
(off Kennington Pk. Rd.)
Berengers Ct. *RM6: Chad H* 7F 55
(off Whalebone La. Sth.)
Berengers Pl. RM9: Dag 6B 72
Berenger Twr. *SW10* 7B 100
(off Worlds End Est.)
Berenger Wlk. *SW10* 7B 100
(off Worlds End Est.)
Berens Ct. DA14: Sidc 4K 143
Berens Rd. NW10 3F 81
Berens Way BR7: Chst 3K 161
Beresford Av. HA0: Wemb 1F 79
KT5: Surb 1H 163
N20 2J 31
TW1: Twick 6C 114
W7 5H 77
Beresford Ct. *E9* 5A 68
(off Mabley St.)
Beresford Dr. BR1: Broml 3C 160
IG8: Wfd G 4F 37
Beresford Gdns. EN1: Enf 4K 23
RM6: Chad H 5E 54
TW4: Houn 5D 112
Beresford Rd. E4 1B 36
E17 1D 50
HA1: Harr 5H 41
KT2: King T 1F 151
KT3: N Mald 4J 151
N2 3C 46
N5 5D 66
N8 5A 48
SM2: Sutt 7H 165
UB1: S'hall 1B 94
Beresford Sq. SE18 4F 107
Beresford St. SE18 3F 107
Beresford Ter. N5 5C 66
Berestede Rd. W6 5B 98
Bere St. E1 7K 85
Bergen Ho. *SE5* 2C 120
(off Carew St.)
Bergenia Ho. TW13: Felt 1J 129
Bergen Sq. SE16 3A 104
Berger Cl. BR5: Pet W 6H 161
Berger Ct. *E3* 3E 86
(off Bolinder Way)
Berger Rd. E9 6K 67
Berghem M. W14 3F 99
Bergholt Av. IG4: Ilf 5C 52
Bergholt Cres. N16 7E 48
Bergholt M. NW1 7H 65
Berglen Ct. E14 6A 86
Bergman Ho. *E17* 4C 50
(off Hoe St.)
Bering Sq. E14 5C 104
Bering Wlk. E16 6B 88
Berisford M. SW18 6A 118
Berkeley Av. DA7: Bex 1D 126
IG5: Ilf 2E 52
RM5: Col R 1J 55
TW4: Cran 1J 111
UB6: G'frd 6H 59
(not continuous)
Berkeley Cl. BR5: Pet W 7J 161
HA4: Ruis 3J 57
KT2: King T 7E 132
Berkeley Ct. BR2: Broml 4K 159
CR0: C'don 4D 168
(off Coombe Rd.)
KT6: Surb 7D 150
N3 1K 45
N14 6B 22
NW1 4F 5
NW10 4A 62
NW11 7H 45
(off Ravenscroft Av.)
SM6: W'gton 3G 167
W5 7C 78
Berkeley Cres. EN4: E Barn 5G 21
Berkeley Dr. KT8: W Mole 3D 148
Berkeley Gdns. KT10: Clay 6A 162
KT12: Walt T 7H 147
N21 7J 23
W8 1J 99
Berkeley Ho. *E3* 3C 86
(off Wellington Way)
SE8 5B 104
(off Grove St.)
TW8: Bford 6D 96
(off Albany Rd.)
Berkeley M. TW16: Sun 3A 148
W1 1F 11 (6D 82)
Berkeley Pl. SW19 6F 135
Berkeley Rd. E12 5C 70
N8 5H 47
N15 6D 48
NW9 4G 43
SW13 1C 116
UB10: Hil 7E 56
The Berkeleys SE25 4G 157
Berkeley Sq. W1 3K 11 (7F 83)
Berkeley St. W1 3K 11 (7F 83)
Berkeley Twr. *E14* 1B 104
(off Westferry Cir.)
Berkeley Wlk. *N7* 2K 65
(off Durham Rd.)
Berkeley Waye TW5: Hest 6B 94
Berkhampstead Rd. DA17: Belv 5G 109
Berkhamsted Av. HA9: Wemb 6F 61
Berkley Cl. *TW2: Twick* 3J 131
(off Wellesley Rd.)
Berkley Gro. NW1 7E 64
Berkley Rd. NW1 7D 64
Berkshire Ct. *W7* 4K 77
(off Copley Cl.)
Berkshire Gdns. N13 6F 33
N18 5C 34
Berkshire Ho. SE6 4C 140
Berkshire Rd. E9 6B 68
Berkshire Way CR4: Mitc 4J 155
Berley Rd. E17 1B 50
Berlin Ter. E15 5G 69
Bermans Way NW10 4A 62
BERMONDSEY 7K 15 (2G 103)
Bermondsey Exchange *SE1* 7H 15
(off Bermondsey St.)
Bermondsey Sq. SE1 7H 15 (3E 102)
Bermondsey St. SE1 5G 15 (1E 102)
Bermondsey Trad. Est. SE16 5J 103
Bermondsey Wall E. SE16 2G 103
Bermondsey Wall W.
SE16 6K 15 (2G 103)
Bermuda Way *E1* 5A 86
(off Dongola Rd.)
Bernal Cl. SE28 7D 90
Bernard Angell Ho. *SE10* 6F 105
(off Trafalgar Rd.)
Bernard Ashley Dr. SE7 5K 105
Bernard Av. W13 3B 96
Bernard Cassidy St. E16 5H 87
Bernard Gdns. SW19 5H 135
Bernard Hegarty Lodge *E8* 7G 67
(off Lansdowne Dr.)
Bernard Ho. E1 6J 9
Bernard Mans. *WC1* 4E 6
(off Bernard St.)
Bernard Myers Ho. *SE5* 7E 102
(off Havil St.)
Bernard Rd. N15 5F 49
RM7: Rush G 7J 55
SM6: W'gton 4F 167
Bernard Shaw Ct. *NW1* 7G 65
(off St Pancras Way)
Bernard Shaw Ho. *NW10* 1K 79
(off Knatchbull Rd.)
Bernard St. WC1 4E 6 (4J 83)
Bernard Sunley Ho. *SW9* 7A 102
(off Sth. Island Pl.)
Bernays Cl. HA7: Stan 6H 27
Bernays Gro. SW9 4K 119
Bernel Dr. CR0: C'don 3B 170
Berne Rd. CR7: Thor H 5C 156
Berners Dr. W13 7A 78
Berners Ho. *N1* 2A 84
(off Barnsbury Est.)
Berners M. W1 6B 6 (5G 83)
Berners Pl. W1 7B 6 (6G 83)
Berners Rd. N1 1B 84
N22 1A 48
Berners St. W1 6B 6 (5G 83)
Berner Ter. *E1* 6G 85
(off Fairclough St.)

Berney Ho.—Birtwhistle Ho.

Berney Ho. BR3: Beck ... 5A 158
Berney Rd. CR0: C'don ... 7D 156
Bernhard Baron Ho. E1 ... 6G 85
(off Henriques St.)
Bernhardt Cres. NW8 ... 3C 4 (4C 82)
Bernhart Cl. HA8: Edg ... 7D 28
Bernie Grant Arts Cen. ... 4F 49
Bernville Way HA3: Kenton ... 5F 43
Bernwell Rd. E4 ... 3B 36
Berridge Grn. HA8: Edg ... 7B 28
Berridge M. NW6 ... 5J 63
Berridge Rd. SE19 ... 5D 138
Berriman Rd. N7 ... 3K 65
Berrington Ho. W2 ... 7J 81
(off Herrington Rd.)
Berriton Rd. HA2: Harr ... 1D 58
Berrybank Cl. E4 ... 2K 35
Berry Cl. N21 ... 1G 33
RM10: Dag ... 5G 73
Berry Cotts. E14 ... 6A 86
(off Maroon St.)
Berry Ct. TW4: Houn ... 5D 112
Berrydale Rd. UB4: Yead ... 4C 76
Berryfield Cl. BR1: Broml ... 1C 160
E17 ... 4D 50
Berryfield Rd. SE17 ... 5B 102
Berry Hill HA7: Stan ... 4J 27
Berryhill SE9 ... 4F 125
Berryhill Gdns. SE9 ... 4F 125
Berry Ho. E1 ... 4H 85
(off Headlam St.)
SW11 ... 2D 118
(off Culvert Rd.)
BERRYLANDS ... 6G 151
Berrylands KT5: Surb ... 6F 151
SW20 ... 3E 152
Berrylands Rd. KT5: Surb ... 6F 151
Berry La. SE21 ... 4D 138
Berryman Cl. RM8: Dag ... 3C 72
Berryman's La. SE26 ... 4K 139
Berrymead Gdns. W3 ... 1J 97
Berrymede Rd. W4 ... 3K 97
Berry Pl. EC1 ... 2B 8 (3B 84)
Berryside Apts. N4 ... 1C 66
(off Swan La.)
Berry St. EC1 ... 3B 8 (4B 84)
Berry Way W5 ... 3E 96
Bertal Rd. SW17 ... 4B 136
Bertelli Pl. TW13: Felt ... 1K 129
Bertha Hollamby Ct. DA14: Sidc ... 5C 144
(off Sidcup Hill)
Bertha James Ct. BR2: Broml ... 4K 159
Berthons Gdns. E17 ... 5F 51
(off Wood St.)
Berthon St. SE8 ... 7C 104
Bertie Rd. NW10 ... 6C 62
SE26 ... 6K 139
Bertram Cotts. SW19 ... 7J 135
Bertram Rd. EN1: Enf ... 4B 24
KT2: King T ... 7G 133
NW4 ... 6C 44
Bertram St. N19 ... 2F 65
Bertrand Ho. E16 ... 6K 87
(off Russell Rd.)
SW16 ... 3J 137
(off Leigham Av.)
Bertrand St. SE13 ... 3D 122
Bertrand Way SE28 ... 7B 90
Bert Rd. CR7: Thor H ... 5C 156
Bert Way EN1: Enf ... 4A 24
Berwick Av. UB4: Yead ... 6B 76
Berwick Cl. HA7: Stan ... 6E 26
TW2: Whitt ... 1E 130
Berwick Ct. SE1 ... 7D 14
Berwick Cres. DA15: Sidc ... 7J 125
Berwick Gdns. SM1: Sutt ... 3A 166
Berwick Ho. BR6: Orp ... 1K 173
N2 ... 2B 46
Berwick Rd. DA16: Well ... 1B 126
E16 ... 6K 87
N22 ... 1B 48
Berwick St. W1 ... 7B 6 (6G 83)
Berwick Way BR6: Orp ... 1K 173
Berwyn Av. TW3: Houn ... 1F 113
Berwyn Rd. SE24 ... 1B 138
TW10: Rich ... 4H 115
Beryl Av. E6 ... 5C 88
Beryl Ho. SE18 ... 5K 107
(off Spinel Cl.)
Beryl Rd. W6 ... 5F 99
Berystede KT2: King T ... 7H 133
Besant Cl. NW2 ... 3G 63
Besant Ct. N1 ... 5D 66
SE28 ... 1B 108
(off Titmuss Av.)
Besant Ho. NW8 ... 1A 82
(off Boundary Rd.)
Besant Pl. SE22 ... 4F 121
Besant Rd. NW2 ... 4G 63
Besant Wlk. N7 ... 2K 65
Besant Way NW10 ... 5J 61
Besford Ho. E2 ... 2G 85
(off Pritchard's Rd.)
Besley St. SW16 ... 6G 137
Bessant Dr. TW9: Kew ... 1H 115
Bessborough Gdns. SW1 ... 5D 18 (5H 101)
Bessborough Pl. SW1 ... 5D 18 (5H 101)
Bessborough Rd. HA1: Harr ... 1H 59
SW15 ... 1C 134
Bessborough St. SW1 ... 5C 18 (5H 101)
Bessemer Ct. NW1 ... 7G 65
(off Rochester Sq.)
Bessemer Pk. Ind. Est. SE24 ... 4B 120
Bessemer Pl. SE10 ... 3H 105
Bessemer Rd. SE5 ... 2C 120
Bessie Lansbury Cl. E6 ... 6E 88
Bessingby Rd. HA4: Ruis ... 2K 57
Bessingham Wlk. SE4 ... 4K 121
(off Aldersford Cl.)
Besson St. SE14 ... 1J 121
Bessy St. E2 ... 3J 85
Bestwood St. SE8 ... 4K 103
Beswick M. NW6 ... 6K 63
Beta Ct. CR0: C'don ... 1D 168
(off Sydenham Rd.)
Betam Rd. UB3: Hayes ... 2F 93
Beta Pl. SW4 ... 4K 119
Betchworth Cl. SM1: Sutt ... 5B 166
Betchworth Rd. IG3: Ilf ... 2J 71
Betchworth Way CR0: New Ad ... 7E 170
Betham Rd. UB6: G'frd ... 3H 77
Bethany Waye TW14: Bedf ... 7G 111
Bethecar Rd. HA1: Harr ... 5J 41
Bethel Cl. NW4 ... 5F 45
Bethell Av. E16 ... 4H 87
IG1: Ilf ... 7E 52
Bethel Rd. DA16: Well ... 3C 126
Bethersden Cl. BR3: Beck ... 7B 140
Bethersden Ho. SE17 ... 5E 102
(off Kinglake Est.)
Bethlehem Cl. UB6: G'frd ... 2C 78
Bethlehem Ho. E14 ... 7B 86
(off Limehouse C'way.)
BETHNAL GREEN ... 3H 85
Bethnal Green Cen. for Sports & Performing Arts ... 2K 9 (3F 85)
Bethnal Grn. Rd. E1 ... 3J 9 (4F 85)
E2 ... 3J 9 (4F 85)
Bethune Av. N11 ... 4J 31
Bethune Rd. N16 ... 7D 48
NW10 ... 4K 79
Bethwin Rd. SE5 ... 7B 102
Betjeman Cl. HA5: Pinn ... 4E 40
Betjeman Ct. UB7: Yiew ... 1A 92
Betjeman M. N5 ... 4C 66
Betony Cl. CR0: C'don ... 1K 169
Betoyne Av. E4 ... 4B 36
Betsham Ho. SE1 ... 6E 14
(off Newcomen St.)
BETSTYLE CIR. ... 4A 32
Betstyle Ho. N10 ... 7K 31
Betstyle Rd. N11 ... 4A 32
Bettenson Cl. BR7: Chst ... 5D 142
Better Gym
East Village ... 6E 68
Greenwich ... 2G 105
Harrow ... 6J 41
(within St George's Shop. & Leisure Cen.)
Pinner ... 3B 40
Woolwich ... 3F 107
Betterton Dr. DA14: Sidc ... 2E 144
Betterton Ho. WC2 ... 1F 13
(off Betterton St.)
Betterton Rd. RM13: Rain ... 3K 91
Betterton St. WC2 ... 1E 12 (6J 83)
Bettons Pk. E15 ... 1G 87
Bettridge Rd. SW6 ... 2H 117
Betts Cl. BR3: Beck ... 2A 158
Betts Ho. E1 ... 7H 85
(off Betts St.)
Betts M. E17 ... 6B 50
Betts Rd. E16 ... 7K 87
Betts St. E1 ... 7H 85
Betts Way KT6: Surb ... 1B 162
SE20 ... 1H 157
Betty Brooks Ho. E11 ... 3F 69
Betty May Gray Ho. E14 ... 4E 104
(off Pier St.)
Beulah Av. CR7: Thor H ... 2C 156
Beulah Cl. HA8: Edg ... 3C 28
Beulah Cres. CR7: Thor H ... 2C 156
Beulah Gro. CR0: C'don ... 6C 156
Beulah Hill SE19 ... 6B 138
Beulah Path E17 ... 5E 50
Beulah Rd. CR7: Thor H ... 3C 156
E17 ... 5D 50
SM1: Sutt ... 4J 165
SW19 ... 7H 135
Bevan Av. IG11: Bark ... 7A 72
Bevan Ct. CR0: Wadd ... 5A 168
E3 ... 2C 86
(off Tredegar Rd.)
TW1: Twick ... 6D 114
Bevan Ho. IG11: Bark ... 7B 72
N1 ... 1E 84
(off Halcomb St.)
WC1 ... 5F 7
(off Boswell St.)
Bevan M. W12 ... 2C 98
Bevan Rd. EN4: Cockf ... 4J 21
SE2 ... 5B 108
Bevans Ho. SW18 ... 4A 118
(off Eltringham St.)
Bevan St. N1 ... 1C 84
Bev Callender Cl. SW8 ... 3F 119
Bevenden St. N1 ... 1F 9 (3D 84)
Bevercote Wlk. DA17: Belv ... 6F 109
(off Osborne Rd.)
Beveree Stadium ... 1F 149
Beveridge Ct. N21 ... 5D 22
(off Pennington Dr.)
SE28 ... 7B 90
(off Saunders Way)
Beveridge M. E1 ... 5J 85
Beveridge Rd. NW10 ... 7A 62
Beverley Av. DA15: Sidc ... 7K 125
SW20 ... 1B 152
TW4: Houn ... 4D 112
Beverley Cl. EN1: Enf ... 4K 23
KT9: Chess ... 4C 162
N21 ... 1H 33
SW11 ... 4B 118
SW13 ... 2C 116
Beverley Cotts. SW15 ... 3A 134
Beverley Ct. HA2: Harr ... 3H 41
HA3: Kenton ... 4C 42
N2 ... 4D 46
(off Western Rd.)
N14 ... 7B 22
NW6 ... 7A 64
(off Fairfax Rd.)
SE4 ... 3B 122
(not continuous)
TW4: Houn ... 4D 112
W4 ... 5J 97
Beverley Cres. IG8: Wfd G ... 1K 51
Beverley Dr. HA8: Edg ... 3G 43
Beverley Gdns. HA7: Stan ... 1A 42
HA9: Wemb ... 1F 61
KT4: Wor Pk ... 1C 164
NW11 ... 7G 45
SW13 ... 3B 116
Beverley Ho. BR1: Broml ... 5F 141
(off Brangbourne Rd.)
Beverley Hyrst CR0: C'don ... 2F 169
Beverley La. KT2: King T ... 7A 134
SW15 ... 3B 134
Beverley Meads & Fishponds Wood Nature Reserve ... 6B 134
Beverley M. E4 ... 6A 36
Beverley Path SW13 ... 2B 116
Beverley Rd. BR2: Broml ... 2C 172
CR4: Mitc ... 4H 155
DA7: Bex ... 2J 127
E4 ... 6A 36
E6 ... 3B 88
HA4: Ruis ... 2J 57
KT1: Hamp W ... 1C 150
KT3: N Mald ... 4C 152
KT4: Wor Pk ... 2E 164
RM9: Dag ... 4E 72
SE20 ... 2H 157
Beverley Rd. SW13 ... 3B 116
TW16: Sun ... 1H 147
UB2: S'hall ... 4C 94
W4 ... 5B 98
Beverley Trad. Est. SM4: Mord ... 7F 153
Beverley Way KT3: N Mald ... 1B 152
SW20 ... 1B 152
Beversbrook Rd. N19 ... 3H 65
Beverstone Rd. CR7: Thor H ... 4A 156
SW2 ... 5K 119
Beverston M. W1 ... 6E 4
Bevill Allen Cl. SW17 ... 5D 136
Bevill Cl. SE25 ... 3G 157
Bevin Cl. SE16 ... 1A 104
Bevin Ct. WC1 ... 1H 7 (3K 83)
Bevington Path SE1 ... 7J 15
Bevington Rd. BR3: Beck ... 2D 158
W10 ... 5G 81
Bevington St. SE16 ... 2G 103
Bevin Ho. E2 ... 3J 85
(off Butler St.)
E3 ... 3C 86
(off Alfred St.)
Bevin Rd. UB4: Yead ... 3J 75
Bevin Sq. SW17 ... 3D 136
Bevin Way WC1 ... 1J 7 (2A 84)
Bevis Marks EC3 ... 7H 9 (6E 84)
Bevis Marks Synagogue ... 7H 9 (6E 84)
Bewcastle Gdns. EN2: Enf ... 4D 22
Bew Ct. SE22 ... 7G 121
Bewdley St. N1 ... 7A 66
Bewick M. SE15 ... 7H 103
Bewick St. SW8 ... 2F 119
Bewley Ho. E1 ... 7H 85
(off Bewley St.)
Bewley St. E1 ... 7J 85
SW19 ... 6A 136
Bewlys Rd. SE27 ... 5B 138
Bexhill Cl. TW13: Felt ... 2C 130
Bexhill Rd. N11 ... 6C 32
SE4 ... 6B 122
SW14 ... 3J 115
Bexhill Wlk. E15 ... 1G 87
BEXLEY ... 7G 127
Bexley Gdns. N9 ... 3J 33
RM6: Chad H ... 5B 54
BEXLEYHEATH ... 4G 127
Bexleyheath Golf Course ... 5E 126
Bexleyheath Sports Club ... 4C 126
Bexley High St. DA5: Bexl ... 7G 127
Bexley Ho. SE4 ... 4A 122
Bexley La. DA1: Cray ... 5K 127
DA14: Sidc ... 4C 144
Bexley Lawn Tennis, Squash & Racketball Club ... 7G 127
Bexley Local Studies & Archive Cen. ... 4G 127
(off Townley Rd.)
The Bexley Mus. Collection ... 6J 127
Bexley Music & Dance Cen. ... 4A 144
(off Station Rd.)
Bexley Rd. DA8: Erith ... 1J 127
SE9 ... 5F 125
Bexley Tourist Information Centre ... 4F 127
Beynon Rd. SM5: Cars ... 5D 166
Bezier Apts. EC2 ... 3F 9 (4D 84)
BFI Southbank ... 4H 13
Bianca Ho. N1 ... 1G 9
(off Crondall St.)
Bianca Rd. SE15 ... 6G 103
Bibsworth Rd. N3 ... 2H 45
Bibury Cl. SE15 ... 6E 102
(not continuous)
Bicester Rd. TW9: Rich ... 3G 115
Bickels Yd. SE1 ... 2E 102
Bickenhall Mans. W1 ... 5F 5
(not continuous)
Bickenhall St. W1 ... 5F 5 (5D 82)
Bickersteth Rd. SW17 ... 6D 136
Bickerton Rd. N19 ... 2G 65
BICKLEY ... 3C 160
Bickley Cres. BR1: Broml ... 4C 160
Bickley Pk. Rd. BR1: Broml ... 3C 160
Bickley Rd. BR1: Broml ... 2B 160
E10 ... 7D 50
Bickley St. SW17 ... 5C 136
Bicknell Ho. E1 ... 6G 85
(off Ellen St.)
Bicknell Rd. SE5 ... 3C 120
Bicknoller Rd. EN1: Enf ... 1K 23
Bicknor Rd. BR6: Orp ... 7J 161
Bicycle M. SW4 ... 3H 119
Bidborough Cl. BR2: Broml ... 5H 159
Bidborough St. WC1 ... 2E 6 (3J 83)
Biddenden Way SE9 ... 4E 142
Biddenham Ho. SE16 ... 4K 103
(off Plough Way)
Bidder St. E16 ... 5G 87
(not continuous)
Biddesden Ho. SW3 ... 4E 16
(off Cadogan St.)
Biddestone Rd. N7 ... 4K 65
Biddulph Ho. SE18 ... 4D 106
Biddulph Mans. W9 ... 3K 81
(off Elgin Av.)
Biddulph Rd. W9 ... 3K 81
Bideford Av. UB6: G'frd ... 2B 78
Bideford Cl. HA8: Edg ... 1G 43
TW13: Hanw ... 3D 130
Bideford Gdns. EN1: Enf ... 7K 23
Bideford Rd. BR1: Broml ... 3H 141
DA16: Well ... 7B 108
EN3: Enf L ... 1G 25
HA4: Ruis ... 3K 57
Bidwell Gdns. N11 ... 7B 32
Bidwell St. SE15 ... 1H 121
Big Ben ... 7F 13 (2J 101)
Bigbury Cl. N17 ... 7J 33
Biggerstaff Rd. E15 ... 1E 86
Biggerstaff St. N4 ... 2A 66
Biggin Av. CR4: Mitc ... 1D 154
Biggin Hill SE19 ... 7B 138
Biggin Hill Cl. KT2: King T ... 5C 132
Biggin Way SE19 ... 7B 138
Bigginwood Rd. SW16 ... 7B 138
Biggs Ct. NW9 ... 2A 44
(off Harvey Cl.)
Biggs Row SW15 ... 3F 117
Biggs Sq. E9 ... 6B 68
Big Hill E5 ... 1H 67
Bigland St. E1 ... 6H 85
Bignell Rd. SE18 ... 5F 107
Bignold Rd. E7 ... 4J 69
Bigsworth Ct. SE20 ... 1H 157
Bigwood Ct. NW11 ... 5K 45
Bigwood Rd. NW11 ... 5K 45
Bilberry Ho. E3 ... 5C 86
(off Watts Gro.)
Billet Cl. RM6: Chad H ... 3D 54
Billet Rd. E17 ... 1K 49
RM6: Chad H ... 3B 54
Billets Hart Cl. W7 ... 2J 95
Bill Hamling Cl. SE9 ... 2D 142
Billingford Cl. SE4 ... 4K 121
Billing Ho. E1 ... 6K 85
(off Bower St.)
Billinghurst Way SE10 ... 3J 105
Billingley NW1 ... 1G 83
(off Pratt St.)
Billing Pl. SW10 ... 7K 99
Billing Rd. SW10 ... 7K 99
Billings Cl. RM9: Dag ... 7C 72
Billingsgate Market ... 1D 104
Billing St. SW10 ... 7K 99
Billington M. W3 ... 1H 97
(off High St.)
Billington Rd. SE14 ... 7K 103
Billinton Hill CR0: C'don ... 2D 168
Billiter St. EC3 ... 1H 15 (6E 84)
Bill Nicholson Way N17 ... 7A 34
(off High Rd.)
Billockby Cl. KT9: Chess ... 6F 163
Billson St. E14 ... 4E 104
Bill Voisey Ct. E14 ... 6A 86
(off Repton St.)
Bilsby Gro. SE9 ... 4B 142
Bilsby Lodge HA9: Wemb ... 3J 61
(off Chalklands)
The Bilton Cen. UB6: G'frd ... 1B 78
Bilton Rd. UB6: G'frd ... 1A 78
Bilton Towers W1 ... 1F 11
(off Gt. Cumberland Pl.)
Bilton Way EN3: Enf L ... 1F 25
UB3: Hayes ... 2K 93
Bina Gdns. SW5 ... 4A 100
Binbrook Ho. W10 ... 5E 80
(off Sutton Way)
Bincote Rd. EN2: Enf ... 3E 22
Binden Rd. W12 ... 3B 98
Bindon Grn. SM4: Mord ... 4K 153
Binfield Rd. CR2: S Croy ... 5F 169
SW4 ... 1J 119
Bingfield St. N1 ... 1J 83
(not continuous)
Bingham Ct. N1 ... 7B 66
(off Halton Rd.)
Bingham Pl. W1 ... 5G 5 (5E 82)
Bingham Point SE18 ... 4F 107
(off Wilmount St.)
Bingham Rd. CR0: C'don ... 1G 169
Bingham St. N1 ... 6D 66
Bingley Rd. E16 ... 6A 88
TW16: Sun ... 7J 129
UB6: G'frd ... 4F 77
Binley Ho. SW15 ... 6C 116
Binnacle Ho. E1 ... 1H 103
(off Cobblestone Sq.)
Binney St. W1 ... 1H 11 (6E 82)
Binnie Ho. SE1 ... 3C 102
(off Bath Ter.)
Binnington Twr. BR2: Broml ... 6C 160
Binns Rd. W4 ... 5A 98
Binns Ter. W4 ... 5A 98
Binsey Wlk. SE2 ... 2C 108
(not continuous)
Binstead Cl. UB4: Yead ... 6C 76
Binyon Cres. HA7: Stan ... 5E 26
Bioko Ct. E1 ... 5A 86
(off Ocean Est.)
Biraj Ho. E6 ... 1D 88
Birbetts Rd. SE9 ... 2D 142
Bircham Path SE4 ... 4K 121
(off Aldersford Cl.)
Birchanger Rd. SE25 ... 5G 157
Birch Av. N13 ... 3H 33
UB7: Yiew ... 6B 74
Birch Cl. E16 ... 5G 87
IG9: Buck H ... 3G 37
N19 ... 2G 65
RM7: Mawney ... 3H 55
SE15 ... 2G 121
TW3: Houn ... 2H 113
TW8: Bford ... 7B 96
TW11: Tedd ... 5A 132
TW17: Shep ... 2G 147
Birch Ct. N12 ... 4E 30
RM6: Chad H ... 6C 54
SM1: Sutt ... 4A 166
SM6: W'gton ... 4F 167
Birch Cres. UB10: Uxb ... 1B 74
Birchdale Gdns. RM6: Chad H ... 7D 54
Birchdale Rd. E7 ... 5A 70
Birchdene Dr. SE28 ... 1A 108
Birchdown Ho. E3 ... 3D 86
(off Rainhill Way)
Birchen Cl. NW9 ... 2K 61
Birchend Cl. CR2: S Croy ... 6D 168
Birchen Gro. NW9 ... 2K 61
The Birches BR2: Broml ... 4H 159
(off Durham Rd.)
BR6: Farnb ... 4E 172
E12 ... 4C 70
N21 ... 6E 22
SE5 ... 2E 120
SE7 ... 6K 105
TW4: Houn ... 7D 112
Birches Cl. CR4: Mitc ... 3D 154
HA5: Pinn ... 5C 40
N17 ... 7B 34
Birchfield Ct. KT12: Walt T ... 7K 147
(off Grove Cres.)
Birchfield Ho. E14 ... 7C 86
(off Birchfield St.)
Birchfield St. E14 ... 7C 86
Birch Gdns. RM10: Dag ... 3J 73
Birch Grn. NW9 ... 7F 29
Birch Gro. DA16: Well ... 4A 126
E11 ... 4G 69
SE12 ... 7H 123
TW17: Shep ... 2G 147
W3 ... 1G 97
Birchgrove Ho. TW9: Kew ... 7H 97
Birch Hill CR0: C'don ... 5K 169
Birch Ho. N22 ... 1A 48
(off Acacia Rd.)
SE14 ... 1B 122
SW2 ... 6A 120
UB7: W Dray ... 2B 92
(off Park Lodge Av.)
W10 ... 4G 81
(off Droop St.)
Birchington Cl. DA7: Bex ... 1H 127
Birchington Ct. NW6 ... 1K 81
(off West End La.)
Birchington Ho. E5 ... 5H 67
Birchington Rd. KT5: Surb ... 7F 151
N8 ... 6H 47
NW6 ... 1J 81
Birchin La. EC3 ... 1F 15 (6D 84)
Birchlands Av. SW12 ... 7D 118
Birch Mead BR6: Farnb ... 2E 172
Birchmead Av. HA5: Pinn ... 4A 40
Birchmere Bus. Pk. SE28 ... 2A 108
Birchmere Lodge SE16 ... 5H 103
(off Sherwood Gdns.)
Birchmere Row SE3 ... 2H 123
Birchmore Hall N5 ... 3C 66
Birchmore Wlk. N5 ... 3C 66
(not continuous)
Birch Pk. HA3: Hrw W ... 7B 26
Birch Rd. RM7: Mawney ... 3H 55
TW13: Hanw ... 5B 130
Birch Row BR2: Broml ... 7E 160
Birchside Apts. NW6 ... 2H 81
Birch Tree Av. BR4: W W'ck ... 5K 171
Birch Tree Way CR0: C'don ... 2H 169
Birch Va. Ct. NW8 ... 3B 4
(off Pollitt Dr.)
Birch Vw. HA1: Harr ... 5H 41
Birchville Ct. WD23: B Hea ... 1D 26
Birch Wlk. CR4: Mitc ... 1F 155
DA8: Erith ... 6J 109
IG3: Ilf ... 4J 71
(off Loxford La.)
Birchway UB3: Hayes ... 1J 93
Birchwood Apts. N4 ... 7C 48
(off Woodberry Gro.)
Birchwood Av. BR3: Beck ... 4B 158
DA14: Sidc ... 2B 144
N10 ... 3E 46
SM6: W'gton ... 3E 166
Birchwood Cl. SM4: Mord ... 4K 153
Birchwood Ct. HA8: Edg ... 2J 43
N13 ... 5G 33
Birchwood Dr. DA2: Wilm ... 4K 145
NW3 ... 3K 63
Birchwood Gro. TW12: Hamp ... 6E 130
Birchwood Pde. DA2: Wilm ... 4K 145
Birchwood Pk. Golf Course ... 7J 145
Birchwood Rd. BR5: Pet W ... 4H 161
BR8: Swan ... 7J 145
DA2: Wilm ... 7J 145
SW17 ... 5F 137
Birdbrook Cl. RM10: Dag ... 7J 73
Birdbrook Ho. N1 ... 7C 66
(off Popham Rd.)
Birdbrook Rd. SE3 ... 4A 124
Birdcage Wlk. SW1 ... 7A 12 (2G 101)
Birdham Cl. BR1: Broml ... 5C 160
Birdhurst Av. CR2: S Croy ... 4D 168
Birdhurst Ct. SM6: W'gton ... 7G 167
(off Woodcote Av.)
Birdhurst Gdns. CR2: S Croy ... 4D 168
Birdhurst Ri. CR2: S Croy ... 5E 168
Birdhurst Rd. CR2: S Croy ... 5E 168
SW18 ... 5A 118
SW19 ... 6C 136
Bird in Bush BMX Track ... 7H 103
(off Bird in Bush Rd.)
Bird in Bush Rd. SE15 ... 7G 103
Bird in Hand La. BR1: Broml ... 2B 160
Bird in Hand M. SE23 ... 2J 139
(off Bird-in-Hand Pas.)
Bird in Hand Pas. SE23 ... 2J 139
Bird in Hand Yd. NW3 ... 4A 64
Birdsall Ho. SE5 ... 3E 120
Birds Farm Av. RM5: Col R ... 1H 55
Birdsfield La. E3 ... 1B 86
Birdsmouth Ct. N15 ... 4E 48
(off Bathurst Sq.)
Bird St. W1 ... 1H 11 (6E 82)
Bird Wlk. TW2: Whitt ... 1D 130
Birdwood Av. SE13 ... 6F 123
Birdwood Cl. TW11: Tedd ... 4J 131
Birkbeck Av. UB6: G'frd ... 1G 77
W3 ... 7J 79
Birkbeck Ct. W3 ... 1K 97
Birkbeck Gdns. IG8: Wfd G ... 2D 36
Birkbeck Gro. W3 ... 2K 97
Birkbeck Hill SE21 ... 1B 138
Birkbeck M. E8 ... 5F 67
W3 ... 1K 97
Birkbeck Pl. SE21 ... 2C 138
Birkbeck Rd. BR3: Beck ... 2J 157
DA14: Sidc ... 3A 144
E8 ... 5F 67
EN2: Enf ... 1J 23
IG2: Ilf ... 5H 53
N8 ... 4J 47
N12 ... 5F 31
N17 ... 1F 49
NW7 ... 5G 29
RM7: Rush G ... 1K 73
SW19 ... 5K 135
W3 ... 1K 97
W5 ... 4C 96
Birkbeck St. E2 ... 3H 85
Birkbeck Way UB6: G'frd ... 1H 77
Birkdale Av. HA5: Pinn ... 3E 40
Birkdale Cl. BR6: Orp ... 7H 161
SE16 ... 5H 103
SE28 ... 6D 90
Birkdale Ct. UB1: S'hall ... 6G 77
(off Redcroft Rd.)
Birkdale Gdns. CR0: C'don ... 4K 169
Birkdale Ho. E14 ... 6B 86
(off Keymer Pl.)
Birkdale Rd. SE2 ... 4A 108
W5 ... 4E 78
Birkenhead Av. KT2: King T ... 2F 151
Birkenhead St. WC1 ... 1F 7 (3J 83)
Birkhall Rd. SE6 ... 1F 141
Birkwood Cl. SW12 ... 7H 119
Birley Lodge NW8 ... 2B 82
(off Acacia Rd.)
Birley Rd. N20 ... 2F 31
Birley St. SW11 ... 2E 118
Birling Rd. DA8: Erith ... 7K 109
Birnam Rd. N4 ... 2K 65
Birnbeck Ct. EN5: Barn ... 4A 20
NW11 ... 5H 45
Birrell Ho. SW9 ... 2K 119
(off Stockwell Rd.)
Birse Cres. NW10 ... 3A 62
Birstall Rd. N15 ... 5E 48
Birtwhistle Ho. E3 ... 1B 86
(off Parnell Rd.)

Biscay Ho.—Blyth Ho.

Biscay Ho. E1 4K 85
(off Mile End Rd.)
Biscayne Av. E14 1F 105
Biscay Rd. W6 5F 99
Biscoe Cl. TW5: Hest 6E 94
Biscoe Way SE13 3F 123
Biscott Ho. E3 4D 86
Bisenden Rd. CR0: C'don 2E 168
Bisham Cl. SM5: Cars 1D 166
Bisham Gdns. N6 1E 64
Bishop Butt Cl. BR6: Orp 3K 173
Bishop Ct. TW9: Rich 3E 114
Bishop Duppas Pk. TW17: Shep 7G 147
Bishop Fox Way KT8: W Mole 4D 148
Bishop Ken Rd. HA3: W'stone 2K 41
Bishop King's Rd. W14 4G 99
Bishop Ramsey Cl. HA4: Ruis 7H 39
Bishop Rd. N14 7A 22
Bishop's Av. E13 1K 87
SW6 2F 117
Bishops Av. BR1: Broml 2A 160
RM6: Chad H 6C 54
The Bishops Av. N2 7B 46
Bishop's Bri. Rd. W2 6A 4 (6K 81)
Bishop's Cl. N19 3G 65
SE9 2G 143
SM1: Sutt 3J 165
Bishops Cl. E17 4D 50
EN1: Enf 2C 24
EN5: Barn 6A 20
TW10: Ham 3D 132
UB10: Hil 2C 74
W4 5J 97
Bishop's Ct. EC4 7A 8
WC2 7J 7
Bishops Ct. CR0: C'don 2F 169
HA0: Wemb 4B 60
N2 5C 46
W2 6K 81
(off Bishop's Bri. Rd.)
Bishopsdale Ho. NW6 1J 81
(off Kilburn Vale)
Bishop's Dr. TW14: Bedf 6F 111
Bishops Dr. UB5: N'olt 1C 76
Bishopsford Ho. SM5: Cars 6C 154
Bishopsford Rd. SM4: Mord 7A 154
Bishopsgate EC2 1G 15 (6E 84)
Bishopsgate Arc. EC2 6H 9
Bishopsgate Churchyard
EC2 7G 9 (5E 84)
Bishopsgate Plaza EC3 6H 9
Bishops Grn. BR1: Broml 1A 160
Bishop's Gro. TW12: Hamp 4D 130
Bishops Gro. N2 6C 46
Bishops Gro. Cvn. Site 4E 130
Bishop's Hall KT1: King T 2D 150
Bishops Hill KT12: Walt T 7J 147
Bishops Ho. SW8 7J 101
(off Sth. Lambeth Rd.)
Bishop's Mans. SW6 2F 117
Bishops Mead SE5 7C 102
(off Camberwell Rd.)
Bishop's Pk. Rd. SW6 2F 117
Bishops Pk. Rd. SW16 1J 155
Bishops Pl. SM1: Sutt 5A 166
Bishop's Rd. CR0: C'don 7B 156
SW11 7C 100
UB3: Hayes 6E 74
Bishops Rd. N6 6E 46
SW6 1G 117
W7 2J 95
Bishops Sq. E1 5H 9 (5E 84)
Bishop's Ter. SE11 3K 19 (4A 102)
Bishopsthorpe Rd. SE26 4K 139
Bishop St. N1 1C 84
Bishops Vw. Ct. N10 4F 47
Bishops Wlk. BR7: Chst 1G 161
CR0: Addtn 5K 169
HA5: Pinn 3C 40
Bishop's Way E2 2H 85
Bishops Wharf Ho. SW11 7C 100
(off Parkgate Rd.)
Bishops Wood Almshouses E5 4H 67
(off Lwr. Clapton Rd.)
Bishopswood Rd. N6 7D 46
Bishop Way NW10 7A 62
Bishop Wilfred Wood Cl. SE15 2G 121
Bishop Wilfred Wood Ct. E13 2A 88
(off Pragel St.)
Bisley Cl. KT4: Wor Pk 1E 164
Bisley Pl. TW3: Houn 2F 113
Bison Ct. TW14: Felt 7K 111
Bispham Rd. NW10 3F 79
Bissagos Ct. E1 5A 86
(off Ocean Est.)
Bissextile Ho. SE13 2D 122
Bisson Rd. E15 2E 86
Bisterne Av. E17 3F 51
Bittacy Bus. Cen. NW7 7B 30
Bittacy Cl. NW7 6A 30
Bittacy Ct. NW7 7B 30
Bittacy Hill NW7 6A 30
Bittacy Pk. Av. NW7 5A 30
Bittacy Ri. NW7 6K 29
Bittacy Rd. NW7 6A 30
Bittern Cl. UB4: Yead 5B 76
Bittern Ct. NW9 2A 44
SE8 6C 104
Bittern Ho. SE1 7C 14
(off Gt. Suffolk St.)
Bittern Pl. N22 2K 47
Bittern St. SE1 7C 14 (2C 102)
The Bittoms KT1: King T 3D 150
Bittoms Ct. KT1: King T 3D 150
Bixley Cl. UB2: S'hall 4D 94
Blackall St. EC2 3G 9 (4E 84)
Blackberry Cl. E17 3D 50
TW17: Shep 4G 147
Blackberry Ct. HA3: Kenton 7E 42
Blackberry Farm Cl. TW5: Hest 7C 94
Blackberry Fld. BR5: St P 7A 144
Blackbird Ct. NW9 3K 61
Blackbird Hill NW9 2J 61
Blackbird Yd. E2 1K 9 (3F 85)
Blackborne Rd. RM10: Dag 6G 73
Blackborough Ho. IG9: Buck H 2G 37
(off Beatrice Ct.)
Black Boy La. N15 5C 48
Blackbrook La. BR1: Broml 5E 160
BR2: Broml 5E 160
Black Bull Yd. EC1 5K 7
(off Hatton Wall)
Blackburn NW9 2B 44
Blackburne's M. W1 2G 11 (7E 82)
Blackburn Rd. NW6 6K 63
Blackburn Trad. Est. TW19: Stanw 6B 110
Blackburn Way TW4: Houn 5C 112
Blackbush Av. RM6: Chad H 5D 54
Blackbush Cl. SM2: Sutt 7K 165
Blackdown Cl. N2 2A 46
Blackdown Ter. SE18 1D 124
Blackett Apts. E3 4B 86
(off Hamlets Way)
Blackett St. SW15 3F 117
Black Fan Cl. EN2: Enf 1H 23
BLACKFEN 6A 126
Blackfen Pde. DA15: Sidc 6A 126
Blackfen Rd. DA15: Sidc 5J 125
Blackford Cl. CR2: S Croy 7B 168
Blackford's Path SW15 7C 116
Blackfriars Bri. EC4 2A 14 (7B 84)
Blackfriars Ct. EC4 2A 14
Black Friars La. EC4 2A 14 (6B 84)
(not continuous)
Blackfriars Pas. EC4 2A 14 (7B 84)
Blackfriars Rd. SE1 4A 14 (2B 102)
Blackfriars Underpass EC4 2A 14 (7A 84)
Black Gates HA5: Pinn 3D 40
BLACKHEATH 2H 123
Blackheath Av. SE10 7F 105
Blackheath Bus. Cen. SE10 1E 122
Blackheath Bus. Est. SE10 1E 122
(off Blackheath Hill)
Blackheath Concert Halls 3H 123
Blackheath Gro. SE3 2H 123
Blackheath Hill SE10 1E 122
BLACKHEATH PARK 3J 123
Blackheath Pk. SE3 3H 123
Blackheath Ri. SE13 2E 122
(not continuous)
Blackheath Rd. SE10 1D 122
Blackheath RUFC 7K 105
BLACKHEATH VALE 2H 123
Blackheath Va. SE3 2G 123
Blackheath Village SE3 2H 123
Black Horse Ct. SE1 3D 102
Blackhorse La. CR0: C'don 7G 157
E17 2K 49
Blackhorse M. E17 3K 49
Black Horse Pde. HA5: Eastc 5K 39
BLACKHORSE ROAD 4K 49
Blackhorse Rd. DA14: Sidc 4A 144
E17 4K 49
SE8 6A 104
Blacklands Dr. UB4: Hayes 4E 74
Blacklands Rd. SE6 4E 140
Blacklands Ter. SW3 4E 16 (4D 100)
Black Lion La. W6 4C 98
Black Lion M. W6 4C 98
Blackmans Yd. E2 4G 85
Blackmore Av. UB1: S'hall 1H 95
Blackmore Dr. NW10 7H 61
Blackmore Ho. N1 1K 83
(off Barnsbury Est.)
Blackmore Rd. IG9: Buck H 1H 37
Blackmore's Gro. TW11: Tedd 6A 132
Blackness La. BR2: Kes 7B 172
Black Path E10 7A 50
Blackpool Gdns. UB4: Hayes 4G 75
Blackpool Rd. SE15 2H 121
BLACK PRINCE INTERCHANGE 6H 127
Black Prince Rd. SE1 4G 19 (4K 101)
SE11 4G 19 (4K 101)
Black Prince St. SE18 6A 108
Black Rod Cl. UB3: Hayes 3H 93
Blackshaw Rd. SW17 4A 136
Blacksmith Cl. RM6: Chad H 6C 54
TW16: Sun 3J 147
Blacksmiths Ho. E14 6F 87
(off Valencia Cl.)
E17 4C 50
(off Gillards M.)
Blacks Rd. W6 5E 98
Blackstock M. N4 2B 66
Blackstock Rd. N4 2B 66
N5 2B 66
Blackstone Est. E8 7G 67
Blackstone Ho. SW1 6A 18
(off Churchill Gdns.)
Blackstone Rd. NW2 5E 62
Black Swan Yd. SE1 6H 15 (2E 102)
Blackthorn Av. N7 6A 66
UB7: W Dray 4C 92
Blackthorn Ct. E15 4F 69
(off Hall Rd.)
TW5: Hest 7C 94
Blackthorne Av. CR0: C'don 1J 169
Blackthorne Ct. SE15 7F 103
(off Cator St.)
TW15: Ashf 7E 128
UB1: S'hall 1F 95
(off Dormer's Wells La.)
Blackthorne Cres. SL3: Poyle 5A 174
Blackthorne Dr. E4 4A 36
Blackthorne Ind. Est.
SL3: Poyle 6A 174
Blackthorne Rd. SL3: Poyle 5A 174
Blackthorn Gro. DA7: Bex 3E 126
Blackthorn Ho. SE16 2A 104
(off Blondin Way)
Blackthorn Rd. IG1: Ilf 5H 71
Blackthorn St. E3 4C 86
Blacktree M. SW9 3A 120
BLACKWALL 1E 104
Blackwall La. SE10 5G 105
Blackwall Trad. Est. E14 5F 87
BLACKWALL TUNNEL 1F 105
Blackwall Tunnel App. E14 7E 86
Blackwall Tunnel Northern App.
E3 2C 86
Blackwall Tunnel Southern App.
SE10 3G 105
Blackwall Way E14 1E 104
Blackwater Cl. E7 4H 69
RM13: Rain 5K 91
Blackwater Ho. NW8 5B 4
(off Church St.)
Blackwater St. SE22 5F 121
Blackwell Cl. E5 4K 67
HA3: Hrw W 7C 26
N21 5D 22
Blackwell Gdns. HA8: Edg 4B 28
Blackwell Ho. SW4 6H 119
Blackwood Ho. E1 4H 85
(off Collingwood St.)
Blackwood St. SE17 5D 102
Blade M. SW15 4H 117
Bladen Ho. E1 6K 85
(off Dunelm St.)
Blades Ct. SW15 4H 117
W6 5D 98
(off Lower Mall)
Blades Ho. SE11 7J 19
(off Kennington Oval)
Bladindon Dr. DA5: Bexl 7C 126
Bladon Ct. SW16 6J 137
Bladon Gdns. HA2: Harr 6F 41
Blagdens Cl. N14 2C 32
Blagdens La. N14 2B 32
Blagdon Ct. W7 7J 77
Blagdon Rd. KT3: N Mald 4B 152
SE13 6D 122
Blagdon Wlk. TW11: Tedd 6C 132
Blagrove Cres. HA4: Eastc 6K 39
Blagrove Rd. TW11: Hamp W 7B 132
W10 5G 81
Blair Av. NW9 7A 44
Blair Cl. DA15: Sidc 5J 125
N1 6C 66
UB3: Harl 4J 93
Blair Ct. BR3: Beck 1D 158
NW8 1B 82
SE6 1H 141
Blairderry Rd. SW2 2J 137
Blairgowrie Ct. E14 6F 87
(off Blair St.)
Blair Ho. SW9 2K 119
Blair St. E14 6E 86
Blake Av. IG11: Bark 1J 89
Blake Bldg. N8 3K 47
Blake Cl. DA16: Well 1J 125
SM5: Cars 1C 166
UB4: Hayes 2F 75
W10 5E 80
Blake Ct. N21 5E 22
NW6 3J 81
(off Malvern Rd.)
SE16 5H 103
(off Stubbs Dr.)
Blakeden Dr. KT10: Clay 6A 162
Blake Gdns. SW6 1K 117
Blake Hall Cres. E11 1J 69
Blake Hall Rd. E11 7J 51
Blakehall Rd. SM5: Cars 6D 166
Blake Ho. E14 2C 104
(off Admirals Way)
SE1 1J 19 (3A 102)
SE8 6C 104
(off New King St.)
Blake M. TW9: Kew 1G 115
Blakemore Gdns. SW13 6D 98
Blakemore Rd. CR7: Thor H 5K 155
SW16 3J 137
Blakemore Way DA17: Belv 3E 108
Blakeney Av. BR3: Beck 1B 158
Blakeney Cl. E8 5G 67
N20 1F 31
NW1 7H 65
Blakeney Rd. BR3: Beck 7B 140
Blakenham Rd. SW17 4D 136
Blaker Ct. SE7 7A 106
(not continuous)
Blake Rd. CR0: C'don 2E 168
CR4: Mitc 3C 154
E16 4H 87
N11 7B 32
Blaker Rd. E15 2E 86
Blakes Av. KT3: N Mald 5B 152
Blake's Grn. BR4: W W'ck 1E 170
Blakes La. KT3: N Mald 5B 152
Blakesley Av. W5 6C 78
Blakesley Ho. E12 3E 70
(off Grantham Rd.)
Blakesley Wlk. SW20 2H 153
Blake's Rd. SE15 7E 102
Blakes Ter. KT3: N Mald 5C 152
Blakesware Gdns. N9 7J 23
Blake Twr. EC2 5C 8
(off Fann St.)
Blakewood Cl. TW13: Hanw 4A 130
Blakewood Ct. SE20 7H 139
(off Anerley Pk.)
Blanchard Cl. SE9 3C 142
Blanchard Ho. TW1: Twick 6D 114
(off Clevedon Rd.)
Blanchard Way E8 6G 67
Blanch Cl. SE15 7J 103
Blanchedowne SE5 4D 120
Blanche St. E16 4H 87
Blanchland Rd. SM4: Mord 5K 153
Blandfield Rd. SW12 7E 118
Blandford Av. BR3: Beck 2A 158
TW2: Whitt 1F 131
Blandford Cl. CR0: Bedd 3J 167
N2 4A 46
RM7: Mawney 4H 55
Blandford Ct. N1 7E 66
(off St Peter's Way)
NW6 7F 63
Blandford Cres. E4 7K 25
Blandford Ho. SW8 7K 101
(off Richborne Ter.)
Blandford Rd. BR3: Beck 2J 157
TW11: Tedd 5H 131
UB2: S'hall 4E 94
W4 3A 98
W5 2D 96
Blandford Sq. NW1 4D 4 (4C 82)
Blandford St. W1 7F 5 (6D 82)
Blandford Waye UB4: Yead 6A 76
Bland Ho. SE11 5H 19
Bland St. SE9 4B 124
Blaney Cres. E6 3F 89
Blanmerle Rd. SE9 1F 143
Blann Cl. SE9 6B 124
Blantyre St. SW10 7B 100
Blantyre Twr. SW10 7B 100
(off Worlds End Est.)
Blantyre Wlk. SW10 7B 100
(off Worlds End Est.)
Blashford NW3 7D 64
(off Adelaide Rd.)
Blashford St. SE13 7F 123
Blashill Ct. E14 7E 86
(off Bullivant St.)
Blasker Wlk. E14 5D 104
Blaven Path E16 4H 87
Blawith Rd. HA1: Harr 4J 41
Blaxland Ho. W12 7D 80
(off White City Est.)
Blaydon Cl. HA4: Ruis 7G 39
N17 7C 34
Blaydon Ct. UB5: N'olt 6E 58
Blaydon Wlk. N17 7C 34
Blazer Ct. NW8 2B 4
Bleak Hill La. SE18 6K 107
Bleak Ho. La. W4 5K 97
(off Chiswick High Rd.)
Blean Gro. SE20 7J 139
Bleasdale Av. UB6: G'frd 2A 78
Blechynden Ho. W10 6F 81
(off Kingsdown Cl.)
Blechynden St. W10 7F 81
Bledlow Cl. NW8 4B 4 (4B 82)
SE28 7C 90
Bledlow Ri. UB6: G'frd 2G 77
Bleeding Heart Yd. EC1 6K 7
Blegborough Rd. SW16 6G 137
Blemundsbury WC1 5G 7
(off Dombey St.)
BLENDON 6D 126
Blendon Dr. DA5: Bexl 6D 126
Blendon Path BR1: Broml 7H 141
Blendon Rd. DA5: Bexl 6D 126
Blendon Row SE17 4D 102
(off Orb St.)
Blendon Ter. SE18 5G 107
Blendworth Point SW15 1D 134
Blenheim Av. IG2: Ilf 6E 52
Blenheim Bus. Cen. CR4: Mitc 2D 154
(off London Rd.)
The Blenheim Cen. 3F 113
Blenheim Cl. N21 1H 33
RM7: Mawney 4J 55
SE12 1K 141
SM6: W'gton 7G 167
SW20 3E 152
UB6: G'frd 2H 77
Blenheim Ct. BR2: Broml 4H 159
DA14: Sidc 3H 143
HA3: Kenton 6A 42
IG8: Wfd G 7E 36
N7 6J 65
N19 2J 65
RM13: Rain 2K 91
(off Lowen Rd.)
SE10 5J 105
(off Denham St.)
SE16 1K 103
(off King & Queen Wharf)
SM2: Sutt 6A 166
Blenheim Cres. CR2: S Croy 7C 168
HA4: Ruis 2F 57
W11 7G 81
Blenheim Dr. DA16: Well 1K 125
Blenheim Gdns. HA9: Wemb 3E 60
KT2: King T 7H 133
NW2 6E 62
SM6: W'gton 6G 167
SW2 6K 119
Blenheim Gro. SE15 2G 121
Blenheim Ho. E16 1K 105
(off Constable Av.)
SE18 3G 107
SW3 6D 16
(off Kings Rd.)
TW3: Houn 3E 112
Blenheim Pde. UB10: Hil 4D 74
Blenheim Pk. Rd. CR2: S Croy 7C 168
Blenheim Pas. NW8 2A 82
Blenheim Pl. TW11: Tedd 5K 131
Blenheim Ri. N15 4F 49
Blenheim Rd. BR1: Broml 4C 160
DA15: Sidc 1C 144
E6 3B 88
E15 4G 69
E17 3K 49
EN5: Barn 3A 20
HA2: Harr 6F 41
NW8 2A 82
SE20 7J 139
SM1: Sutt 3J 165
SW20 3E 152
UB5: N'olt 6F 59
W4 3A 98
Blenheim Shop. Cen. 7J 139
Blenheim St. W1 1J 11 (6F 83)
Blenheim Ter. NW8 2A 82
Blenheim Twr. SE14 7A 104
(off Batavia Rd.)
Blenheim Way TW7: Isle 1A 114
Blenkarne Rd. SW11 6D 118
Bleriot Rd. TW5: Hest 7A 94
Blessbury Rd. HA8: Edg 1J 43
Blessington Cl. SE13 3F 123
Blessington Rd. SE13 3F 123
Blessing Way IG11: Bark 3C 90
Bletchingley Cl. CR7: Thor H 4B 156
Bletchley Ct. HA7: Stan 7K 27
(off Hitchin Way)
N1 1E 8
Bletchley St. N1 1D 8 (2D 84)
Bletchmore Cl. UB3: Harl 5F 93
Bletsoe Wlk. N1 2C 84
Blewbury Ho. SE2 2C 108
(not continuous)
Blick Ho. SE16 3J 103
(off Neptune St.)
Blincoe Cl. SW19 2F 135
Bliss Cres. SE13 2D 122
Blissett St. SE10 1E 122
Bliss Ho. EN1: Enf 1B 24
Bliss M. W10 3G 81
Blisworth Cl. UB4: Yead 4C 76
Blisworth Ho. E2 1G 85
(off Whiston Rd.)
Blithbury Rd. RM9: Dag 6B 72
Blithdale Rd. SE2 4A 108
Blithehale Ct. E2 3H 85
(off Withan St.)
Blithfield St. W8 3K 99
Blockley Rd. HA0: Wemb 2B 60
Block Wharf E14 2C 104
(off Cuba St.)
Bloemfontein Av. W12 1D 98
Bloemfontein Rd. W12 7D 80
Bloemfontein Way W12 1D 98
Blomfield Ct. W9 3A 4
(off Maida Vale)
Blomfield Mans. W12 1E 98
(off Stanlake Rd.)
Blomfield Rd. W9 4A 4 (5K 81)
Blomfield St. EC2 6F 9 (5D 84)
Blomfield Vs. W2 5K 81
Blomville Rd. RM8: Dag 3E 72
Blondell Cl. UB7: Harm 2E 174
Blondel St. SW11 2E 118
Blondin Av. W5 4C 96
Blondin Pk. & Nature Area 4B 96
Blondin St. E3 2C 86
Blondin Way SE16 2A 104
Bloomberg Arc. EC4 6D 84
Bloomberg Ct. SW1 4C 18
(off Vauxhall Bri. Rd.)
Bloomburg St. SW1 4B 18 (4H 101)
Bloomfield Ct. E10 3D 68
(off Brisbane Rd.)
N6 6E 46
Bloomfield Cres. IG2: Ilf 6F 53
Bloomfield Ho. E1 5G 85
(off Old Montague St.)
Bloomfield Pl. W1 2K 11
Bloomfield Rd. BR2: Broml 5B 160
KT1: King T 4E 150
N6 6E 46
SE18 6F 107
Bloomfield Ter. SW1 5H 17 (5E 100)
Bloom Gro. SE27 3B 138
Bloomhall Rd. SE19 5D 138
Bloom Ho. E3 2D 86
(off Alameda Pl.)
Bloom Pk. Rd. SW6 7H 99
BLOOMSBURY 5E 6 (5J 83)
Bloomsbury Cl. NW7 7H 29
W5 7F 79
Bloomsbury Ct. HA5: Pinn 3D 40
TW5: Cran 1K 111
WC1 6F 7
Bloomsbury Ho. SW4 6H 119
Bloomsbury Mans. BR1: Broml 1K 159
(off Widmore Rd.)
Bloomsbury M. IG8: Wfd G 6H 37
Bloomsbury Pl. SW18 5A 118
WC1 5F 7 (5J 83)
Bloomsbury Sq. WC1 6F 7 (5J 83)
Bloomsbury St. WC1 6D 6 (5H 83)
Bloomsbury Theatre 3C 6
Bloomsbury Way WC1 6E 6 (5J 83)
Blore Cl. SW8 1H 119
Blore Ct. W1 1C 12
Blore Ho. SW10 7K 99
(off Coleridge Gdns.)
Blossom Av. HA2: Harr 2F 59
Blossom Cl. CR2: S Croy 5F 169
RM9: Dag 1F 91
W5 2E 96
Blossom Ct. SE15 7F 103
(off All Saints Walk)
Blossom Dr. BR6: Orp 2K 173
Blossom La. EN2: Enf 1H 23
Blossom Pl. SE28 3G 107
Blossom St. E1 4H 9 (4E 84)
Blossom Way UB7: W Dray 4C 92
UB10: Hil 7B 56
Blount M. UB10: Uxb 2A 74
Blount St. E14 6A 86
Bloxam Gdns. SE9 5C 124
Bloxhall Rd. E10 1B 68
Bloxham Cres. TW12: Hamp 7D 130
Bloxworth Cl. SM6: W'gton 3G 167
Blucher Rd. SE5 7C 102
Blue Anchor All. TW9: Rich 4E 114
Blue Anchor La. SE16 4G 103
Blue Anchor Yd. E1 2K 15 (7G 85)
Blue Ball Yd. SW1 5A 12 (1G 101)
Bluebell Apts. N4 1C 66
(off Swan La.)
Bluebell Av. E12 5B 70
Bluebell Cl. BR6: Farnb 2G 173
E9 1J 85
RM7: Rush G 2K 73
SE26 4F 139
SM6: W'gton 1F 167
UB5: N'olt 6D 58
Bluebell Ct. NW9 1A 44
(off Heybourne Cres.)
Bluebell Ho. SE16 2A 104
(off Bondin Way)
Bluebell Ter. UB7: W Dray 2B 92
Bluebell Way IG1: Ilf 6F 71
Blueberry Cl. IG8: Wfd G 6D 36
Bluebird Cl. SW20 2E 152
Bluebird Ho. IG11: Bark 3K 89
Bluebird La. RM10: Dag 7G 73
Bluebird Way SE28 2H 107
Blue Boar All. EC3 7J 9
(off Aldgate High St.)
Blue Bldg. SE10 5H 105
(off Glenforth St.)
Blue Ct. N1 1D 84
(off Sherborne St.)
Blue Elephant Theatre 7C 102
(off Bethwin Rd.)
Bluefield Cl. TW12: Hamp 5E 130
Blue Fin Bldg. SE1 4B 14
Bluegate M. E1 7H 85
Bluegates KT17: Ewe 7C 164
Bluehouse Rd. E4 2B 36
Blue Lion Pl. SE1 7G 15 (3E 102)
Blueprint Apts. SW12 7F 119
(off Balham Gro.)
Blue Riband Ind. Est.
CR0: C'don 2B 168
Blues St. E8 6F 67
Blue Water SW18 4K 117
Blumenthal Cl. TW7: Isle 7H 95
Blundell Cl. E8 5G 67
Blundell Rd. HA8: Edg 1K 43
Blundell St. N7 7J 65
Blunden Cl. RM8: Dag 1C 72
Blunden Ct. SW6 7J 99
(off Farm La.)
Blunt Rd. CR2: S Croy 5D 168
Blunts Av. UB7: Sip 7C 92
Blunts Rd. SE9 5E 124
Blurton Rd. E5 4J 67
Blydon Ct. N21 5E 22
(off Chaseville Pk. Rd.)
Blyth Cl. E14 4F 105
TW1: Twick 6K 113
Blyth Ct. BR1: Broml 1H 159
(off Blyth Rd.)
Blythe Cl. SE6 7B 122
BLYTHE HILL 7B 122
Blythe Hill BR5: St P 1K 161
SE6 7B 122
Blythe Hill La. SE6 7B 122
Blythe Hill Pl. SE23 7A 122
Blythe Ho. SE11 7J 19 (6A 102)
Blythe M. W14 3F 99
Blythendale Ho. E2 2G 85
(off Mansford St.)
Blythe Rd. W14 3F 99
Blythe St. E2 3H 85
Blytheswood Pl. SW16 4K 137
Blythe Va. SE6 1B 140
Blyth Hill Pl. SE23 7A 122
(off Brockley Pk.)
Blyth Ho. DA8: Erith 5K 109

188 A-Z Big London

Blyth Rd.—Bowsley Ct.

Blyth Rd. BR1: Broml 1H 159
E17 7B 50
SE28 7C 90
UB3: Hayes 2G 93
Blyth's Wharf E14 7A 86
Blythswood Rd. IG3: Ilf 1A 72
Blyth Wood Pk. BR1: Broml 1H 159
Blythwood Rd. HA5: Pinn 1B 40
N4 7J 47
The BMX Track London 6D 102
Boades M. NW3 4B 64
Boadicea St. N1 1K 83
Boakes Cl. NW9 4J 43
Boardman Av. E4 5J 25
Boardman Cl. EN5: Barn 5B 20
Boardwalk Pl. E14 1E 104
Boarley Ho. *SE17* *4E 102*
(off Massinger St.)
Boars Head Yd. TW8: Bford 7D 96
Boatemah Wlk. *SW9* *2A 120*
(off Peckford Pl.)
Boaters Av. TW8: Bford 7C 96
The Boathouse E14 6C 86
The Boathouse Cen. *W10* *4F 81*
(off Canal Cl.)
Boathouse Wlk. SE15 7F 103
(not continuous)
Boat La. E2 1F 85
Boat Lifter Way SE16 4A 104
Boat Quay E16 7A 88
Boatyard Apts. E14 5D 104
Bob Anker Cl. E13 3J 87
Bobbin Cl. SM6: W'gton 2E 166
SW4 3G 119
Bobby Moore Way IG11: Bark 1G 89
N10 7J 31
The Bob Hope Theatre 6D 124
Bob Marley Way SE24 4A 120
Bockhampton Rd. KT2: King T 7F 133
Bocking St. E8 1H 85
Boddicott Cl. SW19 2G 135
Boddington Gdns. W3 2G 97
Boddington Ho. *SE14* *1J 121*
(off Pomeroy St.)
SW13 *6D 98*
(off Wyatt Dr.)
Bodeney Ho. *SE5* *1E 120*
(off Peckham Rd.)
Boden Ho. *E1* *5K 9*
(off Woodseer St.)
Bodiam Cl. EN1: Enf 2K 23
Bodiam Rd. SW16 7H 137
Bodiam Way NW10 3F 79
Bodicea M. TW4: Houn 6D 112
Bodington Ct. W12 2F 99
Bodium Ct. *E17* *1B 50*
(off Thornbury Way)
Bodleian Ho. SE20 1G 157
Bodley Cl. KT3: N Mald 5A 152
Bodley Mnr. Way SW2 7A 120
Bodley Rd. KT3: N Mald 6K 151
Bodley Way SE17 4C 102
Bodmin Cl. HA2: Harr 3D 58
Bodmin Gro. SM4: Mord 5K 153
Bodmin St. SW18 1J 135
Bodnant Gdns. SW20 3C 152
Bodney Rd. E8 5H 67
Boeing Way UB2: S'hall 3K 93
Boevey Path DA17: Belv 5F 109
Bogart Ct. *E14* *7C 86*
(off Premiere Pl.)
Bogey La. BR6: Downe 7E 172
Bognor Rd. DA16: Well 1D 126
Bohemia Pl. E8 6J 67
Bohn Rd. E1 5A 86
Bohun Gro. EN4: E Barn 6H 21
Boileau Pde. *W5* *6F 79*
(off Boileau Rd.)
Boileau Rd. SW13 7C 98
W5 6F 79
The Boiler Ho. *UB3: Hayes* *2G 93*
(off Material Wlk.)
Boisseau Ho. *E1* *5J 85*
(off Stepney Way)
Bolanachi Bldg. SE16 3F 103
Bolander Gro. SW6 6J 99
Bolden St. SE8 2D 122
Boldero Pl. NW8 4C 4
Bolderwood Way BR4: W W'ck 2D 170
Boldmere Rd. HA5: Eastc 7A 40
Boleyn Av. EN1: Enf 1C 24
Boleyn Cl. E17 4C 50
Boleyn Ct. IG9: Buck H 1D 36
KT8: E Mos *4H 149*
(off Bridge Rd.)
Boleyn Dr. HA4: Ruis 2B 58
KT8: W Mole 3D 148
Boleyn Gdns. BR4: W W'ck 2D 170
RM10: Dag 7J 73
Boleyn Gro. BR4: W W'ck 2E 170
Boleyn Ho. *E16* *1J 105*
(off Southey M.)
Boleyn Rd. E6 2B 88
E7 7J 69
N16 5E 66
Boleyn Way EN5: New Bar 3F 21
Bolina Rd. SE16 5J 103
Bolinder Way E3 3E 86
Bolingbroke Cl. EN4: Cockf 3J 21
Bolingbroke Gro. SW11 4C 118
Bolingbroke Rd. W14 3F 99
Bolingbroke Wlk. SW11 1B 118
Bolingbroke Way UB3: Hayes 1F 93
Bolliger Ct. NW10 4J 79
Bollinder Pl. EC1 1C 8 (3C 84)
Bollo Bri. Rd. W3 3H 97
Bollo La. W3 2H 97
W4 4J 97
Bolney Ga. SW7 7C 10 (2C 100)
Bolney St. SW8 7K 101
Bolney Way TW13: Hanw 3C 130
Bolsover St. W1 4K 5 (4F 83)
Bolstead Rd. CR4: Mitc 1F 155
Bolster Gro. N22 7C 32
Bolt Ct. EC4 6A 84
Bolt Ho. *N1* *1E 84*
(off Phillipp St.)
Boltmore Cl. NW4 3F 45
Bolton Cl. KT9: Chess 6D 162
SE20 2G 157
Bolton Cres. SE5 7B 102
SE11 7A 102
Bolton Dr. SM4: Mord 7A 154
Bolton Gdns. BR1: Broml 6H 141
NW10 2F 81
Bolton Gdns. SW5 5K 99
TW11: Tedd 6A 132
Bolton Gdns. M. SW10 5A 100
Bolton Ho. *SE10* *5G 105*
(off Trafalgar Rd.)
SE11 *4B 102*
(off George Mathers Rd.)
Bolton Pl. *NW8* *1K 81*
(off Bolton Rd.)
Bolton Rd. E15 6H 69
HA1: Harr 4G 41
KT9: Chess 6D 162
N18 5A 34
NW8 1K 81
NW10 1A 80
W4 7J 97
The Boltons HA0: Wemb 4K 59
IG8: Wfd G 4D 36
SW10 5A 100
Boltons Ct. *SW5* *5K 99*
(off Old Brompton Rd.)
Bolton's La. UB3: Harl 1E 110
Boltons Pl. SW5 5A 100
Bolton St. W1 4K 11 (1F 101)
Bolton Studios SW10 5A 100
Bolton Wlk. *N7* *2K 65*
(off Durham Rd.)
Bombay Ct. *SE16* *2J 103*
(off St Marychurch St.)
Bombay St. SE16 4H 103
Bomer Cl. UB7: Sip 7C 92
Bomore Rd. W11 7G 81
Bonar Pl. BR7: Chst 7C 142
Bonar Rd. SE15 7G 103
Bonchester Cl. BR7: Chst 7E 142
Bonchurch Cl. SM2: Sutt 7K 165
Bonchurch Rd. W10 5G 81
W13 1B 96
Bond Cl. DA16: Well 2J 125
UB7: Yiew 6B 74
Bond Ct. EC4 2E 14 (7D 84)
Bondfield Av. UB4: Yead 3J 75
Bondfield Rd. E6 5D 88
Bond Gdns. SM6: W'gton 4G 167
Bond Ho. *NW6* *2H 81*
(off Rupert Rd.)
SE14 *7A 104*
(off Goodwood Rd.)
TW8: Bford 5D 96
Bonding Yd. Wlk. SE16 3A 104
Bond Rd. CR4: Mitc 2C 154
KT6: Surb 2F 163
Bond St. E15 5G 69
W4 4K 97
W5 7D 78
Bondway SW8 7F 19 (6J 101)
Bonesgate Open Space Local Nature Reserve 6G 163
Boneta Rd. SE18 3D 106
Bonfield Rd. SE13 4E 122
Bonham Cl. DA17: Belv 5F 109
Bonham Gdns. RM8: Dag 2D 72
Bonham Ga. *KT12: Walt T* *7H 147*
(off New Zealand Av.)
Bonham Ho. *W11* *1H 99*
(off Boyne Ter. M.)
Bonham Rd. RM8: Dag 2D 72
SW2 5K 119
Bonheur Rd. W4 2K 97
Bonhill St. EC2 4F 9 (4D 84)
Boniface Gdns. HA3: Hrw W 7A 26
Boniface Rd. UB10: Ick 3D 56
Boniface Wlk. HA3: Hrw W 7A 26
Bonington Ho. EN1: Enf 5B 24
Bonita M. SE4 3K 121
Bon Marche M. SE27 4E 138
Bonner Hill Rd. KT1: King T 2F 151
Bonner Rd. E2 2J 85
Bonnersfield Cl. HA1: Harr 6K 41
Bonnersfield La. HA1: Harr 6K 41
(not continuous)
Bonner St. E2 2J 85
Bonnet St. E16 2K 105
Bonneville Gdns. SW4 6G 119
Bonnington Ct. *UB5: N'olt* *2B 76*
(off Gallery Gdns.)
Bonnington Ho. N1 2K 83
Bonnington Sq. SW8 7G 19 (6K 101)
Bonny St. NW1 7G 65
Bonser Rd. TW1: Twick 2K 131
Bonsor Ho. SW8 1G 119
Bonsor St. SE5 7E 102
Bonville Gdns. NW4 4D 44
Bonville Rd. BR1: Broml 5H 141
Bookbinders Cott. Homes N20 3J 31
Bookbinders Ct. *E1* *4H 85*
(off Cudworth St.)
Booker Cl. E14 5B 86
Booker Rd. N18 5B 34
Bookham Ct. CR4: Mitc 3B 154
Book Ho. N1 1C 8 (2C 84)
Book M. WC2 6H 83
Boone Ct. N9 3D 34
Boones Rd. SE13 4G 123
Boone St. SE13 4G 123
Boord St. SE10 3G 105
Boothby Ct. E4 3K 35
Boothby Rd. N19 2H 65
Booth Cl. E9 1H 85
SE28 1B 108
Booth Ct. SE13 3D 122
Booth Dr. TW18: Staines 6A 128
Booth Ho. *TW8: Bford* *7C 96*
(off High St.)
Booth La. EC4 2C 14
Boothman Ho. HA3: Kenton 4D 42
Booth Rd. CR0: C'don 2B 168
E16 2A 106
NW9 2K 43
Booth's Pl. W1 6B 6 (5G 83)
Boot Pde. *HA8: Edg* *6B 28*
(off High St.)
Boot St. N1 2G 9 (3E 84)
Bordars Rd. W7 5J 77
Bordars Wlk. W7 5J 77
Bordeaux Ho. *E15* *5G 69*
(off Luxembourg M.)
Borden Av. EN1: Enf 6J 23
Border Cres. SE26 5H 139
Border Gdns. CR0: C'don 4D 170
Bordergate CR4: Mitc 1D 154
Border Rd. SE26 5H 139
Bordesley Rd. SM4: Mord 5K 153
Bordeston Ct. *TW8: Bford* *7C 96*
(off The Ham)
Bordon Wlk. SW15 7C 116
Boreas Wlk. N1 1B 8
Boreham Av. E16 6J 87
Boreham Cl. E11 1E 68
Boreham Rd. N22 2C 48
Boreman Ho. *SE10* *6E 104*
(off Thames St.)
Borgard Rd. SE18 4D 106
Borkwood Pk. BR6: Orp 4K 173
Borkwood Way BR6: Orp 4J 173
Borland Rd. SE15 4J 121
TW11: Tedd 7B 132
Borley Ct. TW19: Stanw 1A 128
Borneo St. SW15 3E 116
THE BOROUGH 7D 14 (2D 102)
Borough High St. SE1 7D 14 (2C 102)
Borough Hill CR0: Wadd 3B 168
Borough Mkt. SE1 5E 14
Borough Rd. CR4: Mitc 2C 154
KT2: King T 1G 151
SE1 7B 14 (3B 102)
TW7: Isle 1J 113
Borough Sq. SE1 7C 14
Borrett Cl. SE17 5C 102
Borrodaile Rd. SW18 6K 117
Borrowdale *NW1* *2A 6*
(off Robert St.)
Borrowdale Av. HA3: W'stone 2A 42
Borrowdale Cl. IG4: Ilf 4C 52
N2 2A 46
Borrowdale Ct. EN2: Enf 1H 23
Borthwick M. E15 4G 69
Borthwick Rd. E15 4G 69
NW9 6B 44
Borthwick St. SE8 5C 104
Borwick Av. E17 3B 50
Bosanquet Cl. UB8: Cowl 4A 74
Bosbury Rd. SE6 3E 140
Boscastle Rd. NW5 3F 65
Boscobel Cl. BR1: Broml 2D 160
Boscobel Ho. E8 6H 67
Boscobel Pl. SW1 3H 17 (4E 100)
Boscobel St. NW8 4B 4 (4B 82)
Bosco Cl. BR6: Orp 4K 173
Boscombe Av. E10 7F 51
Boscombe Cir. NW9 1K 43
Boscombe Cl. E5 5A 68
Boscombe Gdns. SW16 6J 137
Boscombe Ho. *CR0: C'don* *1D 168*
(off Sydenham Rd.)
Boscombe Rd. KT4: Wor Pk 1E 164
SW17 6E 136
SW19 1K 153
W12 1C 98
Bose Cl. N3 1G 45
Bosgrove E4 2K 35
Boss Ho. *SE1* *6J 15*
(off Boss St.)
Boss St. SE1 6J 15 (2F 103)
Bostall Heath SE2 5C 108
Bostall Hill SE2 5A 108
Bostall La. SE2 4B 108
Bostall Mnr. Way SE2 4B 108
Bostall Pk. Av. DA7: Bex 7E 108
Bostall Rd. BR5: St P 7B 144
Bostock Ho. TW5: Hest 6E 94
Boston Bus. Pk. W7 3J 95
Boston Ct. SE25 4F 157
SM2: Sutt 7A 166
Boston Gdns. TW8: Bford 4A 96
W4 6A 98
W7 4A 96
Boston Gro. HA4: Ruis 6E 38
Boston Ho. *SW5* *4K 99*
(off Collingham Rd.)
BOSTON MANOR 4A 96
Boston Manor House 5B 96
Boston Mnr. Rd. TW8: Bford 4B 96
Boston Pde. W7 3A 96
Boston Pk. Rd. TW8: Bford 5C 96
Boston Pl. NW1 4E 4 (4D 82)
Boston Rd. CR0: C'don 6K 155
E6 3C 88
E17 6C 50
HA8: Edg 7D 28
W7 1J 95
Bostonthorpe Rd. W7 2J 95
Boston Va. W7 4A 96
Bosun Cl. E14 2C 104
Boswell Ct. *KT2: King T* *1F 151*
(off Clifton Rd.)
NW9 *2A 44*
(off Charcot Rd.)
W14 *3F 99*
(off Blythe Rd.)
WC1 5F 7 (5J 83)
Boswell Ho. *WC1* *5F 7*
(off Boswell St.)
Boswell Path UB3: Harl 4H 93
Boswell Rd. CR7: Thor H 4C 156
Boswell St. WC1 5F 7 (5J 83)
Boswood Ct. TW3: Houn 3D 112
Bosworth Cl. E17 1B 50
Bosworth Ho. *W10* *4G 81*
(off Bosworth Rd.)
Bosworth Rd. EN5: New Bar 3D 20
N11 6C 32
RM10: Dag 3G 73
W10 4G 81
Botanic Sq. E14 6G 87
Botany Bay La. BR7: Chst 3G 161
Botany Cl. EN4: E Barn 4H 21
Boteley Cl. E4 2A 36
Botham Cl. HA8: Edg 7D 28
Botha Rd. E13 5K 87
Bothwell Cl. E16 5H 87
Bothwell St. W6 6F 99
Botolph All. EC3 2G 15
Botolph La. EC3 3G 15 (7E 84)
Botsford Rd. SW20 2G 153
Botts M. W2 6J 81
Botwell Comn. Rd. UB3: Hayes 7F 75
Botwell Cres. UB3: Hayes 6G 75
Botwell Green Sports & Leisure Cen. 1H 93
Botwell La. UB3: Hayes 7G 75
Boucher Cl. TW11: Tedd 5K 131
Bouchier Ho. *N2* *2B 46*
(off The Grange)
Boughton Av. BR2: Hayes 7H 159
Boughton Ho. *SE1* *6E 14*
(off Tennis St.)
Boughton Rd. SE28 3J 107
Boulcott St. E1 6K 85
The Boulevard
IG8: Wfd G 6K 37
SW6 1A 118
The Boulevard SW17 2E 136
SW18 4K 117
Boulevard Dr. NW9 2B 44
Boulevard Walkway E1 1K 15 (6G 85)
Boulogne Ho. SE1 7J 15
Boulogne Rd. CR0: C'don 6C 156
Boulter Cl. BR1: Broml 3E 160
Boulter Ho. *SE14* *1J 121*
(off Kender St.)
Boulton Ho. TW8: Bford 5E 96
Boulton Rd. RM8: Dag 2F 72
Boultwood Rd. E6 6D 88
Bounces La. N9 2C 34
Bounces Rd. N9 2C 34
Boundaries Rd. SW12 2D 136
TW13: Felt 1A 130
Boundary Av. E17 7B 50
Boundary Bus. Ct. CR4: Mitc 3B 154
Boundary Cl. EN5: Barn 1C 20
IG3: Ilf 4J 71
KT1: King T 3H 151
SE20 2G 157
UB2: S'hall 5E 94
Boundary Ct. *N18* *6A 34*
(off Snells Pk.)
Boundary Ho. SE5 7C 102
W11 *1F 99*
(off Queensdale Cres.)
Boundary La. E13 3B 88
SE17 6C 102
Boundary Pas. E2 3J 9 (4F 85)
Boundary Rd. DA15: Sidc 5J 125
E13 2A 88
E17 7B 50
HA5: Eastc 7B 40
HA9: Wemb 3E 60
IG11: Bark 2G 89
(The Clarksons)
IG11: Bark 1H 89
(King Edwards Rd.)
N2 1B 46
N9 6D 24
N22 3B 48
NW8 1K 81
SM5: W'gton, Cars 6F 167
SM6: W'gton 6F 167
SW19 6B 136
Boundary Row SE1 6A 14 (2B 102)
Boundary St. E2 2J 9 (3F 85)
Boundary Way CR0: Addtn 5C 170
Boundfield Rd. SE6 3G 141
BOUNDS GREEN 6C 32
Bounds Grn. Ct. *N11* *6C 32*
(off Bounds Grn. Rd.)
Bounds Grn. Ind. Est. N11 6B 32
Bounds Grn. Rd. N11 6B 32
N22 6B 32
Bourbon Ho. SE6 5E 140
Bourbon La. W12 1F 99
Bourbon Rd. SW9 1A 120
Bourchier St. W1 2C 12 (7H 83)
Bourdon Pl. W1 2K 11
Bourdon Rd. SE20 2J 157
Bourdon St. W1 3J 11 (7F 83)
Bourke Cl. NW10 6A 62
SW4 6J 119
Bourlet Cl. W1 6A 6 (5G 83)
Bourn Av. EN4: E Barn 5G 21
N15 4D 48
UB8: Hil 4C 74
Bournbrook Rd. SE3 3B 124
The Bourne N14 1C 32
Bourne Av. HA4: Ruis 5A 58
N14 2D 32
UB3: Harl 3E 92
Bournebrook Gro. RM7: Rush G 6K 55
Bourne Cir. UB3: Harl 3E 92
Bourne Cl. TW7: Isle 3J 113
Bourne Ct. E11 5J 51
HA4: Ruis 5K 57
IG8: Wfd G 3B 52
W4 6J 97
Bourne Dr. CR4: Mitc 2B 154
Bourne Est. EC1 5J 7 (5A 84)
Bourne Gdns. E4 4J 35
Bourne Hall Mus. 7B 164
Bourne Hill N13 2D 32
Bourne Hill Cl. N13 2E 32
Bourne Ho. IG9: Buck H 3G 37
TW15: Ashf 5C 128
Bourne Ind. Pk. DA1: Cray 5K 127
Bourne Mead DA5: Bexl 5K 127
Bournemead Av. UB5: N'olt 2J 75
Bournemead Cl. UB5: N'olt 3J 75
Bournemead Way UB5: N'olt 2K 75
Bourne M. W1 1H 11 (6E 82)
Bournemouth Cl. SE15 2G 121
Bournemouth Rd. SE15 2G 121
SW19 1J 153
Bourne Pde. DA5: Bexl 7H 127
Bourne Pl. W4 5K 97
Bourne Rd. BR2: Broml 4B 160
DA1: Cray 6J 127
DA5: Bexl, Dart 7H 127
E7 3H 69
N8 6J 47
Bournes Ho. *N15* *6E 48*
(off Chisley Rd.)
Bourneside Cres. N14 1C 32
Bourneside Gdns. SE6 5E 140
Bourne St. CR0: C'don 2B 168
SW1 4G 17 (4E 100)
Bourne Ter. W2 5K 81
Bourne Va. BR2: Hayes 1H 171
Bournevale Rd. SW16 4J 137
Bourne Vw. UB6: G'frd 6K 59
Bourne Way BR2: Hayes 2H 171
KT19: Ewe 4J 163
SM1: Sutt 5H 165
Bournewood Rd. SE18 7A 108
Bournville Rd. SE6 7C 122
Bournwell Cl. EN4: Cockf 3J 21
Bourton Cl. UB3: Hayes 1J 93
Bousfield Rd. SE14 2K 121
Boutflower Rd. SW11 4C 118
Boutique Hall SE13 4E 122
Bouton Pl. *N1* *7B 66*
(off Waterloo Ter.)
Bouverie Gdns. HA3: Kenton 6D 42
Bouverie M. N16 2E 66
Bouverie Pl. W2 7B 4 (6B 82)
Bouverie Rd. HA1: Harr 6G 41
N16 2E 66
Bouverie St. EC4 1K 13 (6A 84)
Bouvier Rd. EN3: Enf W 1D 24
Boveney Cl. SE23 6K 121
Boveney Rd. SE23 7K 121
Bovet Ct. *E1* *5A 86*
(off Ocean Est.)
Bovill Rd. SE23 7K 121
Bovingdon Av. HA9: Wemb 6G 61
Bovingdon Cl. N19 2G 65
Bovingdon La. NW9 1A 44
Bovingdon Rd. SW6 1K 117
Bovril Ct. *SW6* *7K 99*
(off Fulham Rd.)
BOW 3B 86
Bowater Cl. NW9 5K 43
SW2 6J 119
Bowater Gdns. TW16: Sun 2A 148
Bowater Ho. *EC1* *4C 8*
(off Golden La. Est.)
Bowater Pl. SE3 7K 105
Bowater Rd. HA9: Wemb 3H 61
SE18 3B 106
Bow Bell Twr. *E3* *1C 86*
(off Pancras Way)
Bow Bri. Est. E3 3D 86
The Bow Brook *E2* *2K 85*
(off Mace St.)
Bow Churchyard EC4 1D 14
BOW COMMON 5C 86
Bow Comn. La. E3 4B 86
Bow Creek Ecology Pk. 6G 87
Bowden Cl. TW14: Bedf 1G 129
Bowden Ho. *E3* *3D 86*
(off Rainhill Way)
Bowden St. SE11 6K 19 (5A 102)
Bowditch SE8 4B 104
Bowdon Rd. E17 7C 50
Bowen Ct. *SE16* *4J 103*
(off Debnams Rd.)
Bowen Dr. SE21 3E 138
Bowen Rd. HA1: Harr 7G 41
Bowen St. E14 6D 86
Bower Av. SE10 1G 123
Bower Cl. RM5: Col R 1K 55
UB5: N'olt 2A 76
Bower Ct. *E4* *1K 35*
(off The Ridgeway)
Bowerdean St. SW6 1K 117
Bowerden Ct. NW10 2D 80
Bowerman Av. SE14 6A 104
Bowerman Ct. *N19* *2H 65*
(off St John's Way)
Bower St. E1 6K 85
Bowers Wlk. E6 6D 88
Bowery Apartments *W12* *7E 80*
(off Fountain Park Way)
Bowery Ct. RM10: Dag 6H 73
Bowes Cl. DA15: Sidc 6B 126
Bowe's Ho. IG11: Bark 7F 71
Bowes-Lyon Hall *E16* *1J 105*
(off Wesley Av.)
BOWES PARK 6D 32
Bowes Rd. N11 5B 32
N13 5B 32
RM8: Dag 4C 72
W3 7A 80
Bow Exchange *E3* *5D 86*
(off Yeo St.)
Bow Fair *E3* *2C 86*
(off Fairfield Rd.)
Bowfell Rd. W6 6E 98
Bowford Av. DA7: Bex 1E 126
Bowhill Cl. SW9 7A 102
Bow Ho. *N1* *1E 84*
(off Wilmer Gdns.)
Bowie Cl. SW4 7H 119
BOW INTERCHANGE 2D 86
Bowland Rd. IG8: Wfd G 6F 37
SW4 4H 119
Bowland Yd. SW1 7F 11
Bow La. EC4 1D 14 (6C 84)
N12 7F 31
SM4: Mord 6G 153
Bowlby Ho. *SE4* *4K 121*
(off Frendsbury Rd.)
Bowl Ct. EC2 4H 9 (4E 84)
Bowles Ct. N12 7H 31
Bowles Rd. SE1 6G 103
Bowley Cl. SE19 6F 139
Bowley Ho. SE16 3G 103
Bowley La. SE19 5F 139
Bowline Ct. SE10 4G 105
TW8: Bford *7C 96*
(off Durham Wharf Dr.)
The Bowling KT12: Walt T 7J 147
Bowling Cl. UB10: Uxb 1B 74
Bowling Grn. Cl. SW15 7D 116
Bowling Grn. Ct. HA9: Wemb 2F 61
Bowling Grn. Ho. *SW10* *7B 100*
(off Riley St.)
Bowling Grn. La. EC1 3K 7 (4A 84)
Bowling Grn. Pl. SE1 6E 14 (2D 102)
Bowling Grn. Row SE18 3D 106
Bowling Grn. St. SE11 7J 19 (6A 102)
Bowling Grn. Wlk. N1 1G 9 (3E 84)
Bow Locks E3 4E 86
Bowls Cl. HA7: Stan 5G 27
Bowman Av. E16 7H 87
Bowman Ho. *N1* *1E 84*
(off Nuttall St.)
Bowman M. SW18 1H 135
Bowman's Bldgs. *NW1* *5C 4*
(off Penfold Pl.)
Bowmans Cl. W13 1B 96
Bowmans Lea SE23 7J 121
Bowmans Mdw. SM6: W'gton 3F 167
Bowman's M. E1 6G 85
N7 3J 65
Bowman's Pl. N7 3J 65
Bowman Trad. Est. NW9 3G 43
Bowmead SE9 2D 142
Bowmore Wlk. NW1 7H 65
Bowness Cl. *E8* *6F 67*
(off Beechwood Rd.)
Bowness Cres. SW15 5A 134
Bowness Dr. TW4: Houn 4C 112
Bowness Ho. *SE15* *7J 103*
(off Hillbeck Cl.)
Bowness Rd. DA7: Bex 2H 127
SE6 7D 122
Bowood Rd. EN3: Enf H 2E 24
SW11 5E 118
Bow River Village *E3* *2E 86*
(off Global App.)
Bow Rd. E3 3B 86
Bowrons Av. HA0: Wemb 7D 60
Bowry Ho. *E14* *5B 86*
(off Wallwood St.)
Bowsley Ct. TW13: Felt 2J 129

A-Z Big London 189

Bowspirit Apts. SE8 7D 104
Bowsprit Point *E14* 3C 104
(off Westferry Rd.)
Bow St. E15 5G 69
WC2 1F 13 (6J 83)
Bowstring Plaza *E3* 3B 86
(off St Clements Av.)
Bow Triangle Bus. Cen. E3 4C 86
(not continuous)
Bowyer Cl. E6 5D 88
Bowyer Ho. *N1* 1E 84
(off Whitmore Est.)
Bowyer Pl. SE5 7C 102
Bowyer Plaza *E3* 3B 86
(off St Clements Av.)
Bowyers Ct. TW1: Isle 4B 114
Bowyer St. SE5 7C 102
Boxall Rd. SE21 6E 120
Boxelder Cl. HA8: Edg 5D 28
Boxgrove Rd. SE2 3C 108
Box La. IG11: Bark 2B 90
Boxley Rd. SM4: Mord 4A 154
Boxley St. E16 1K 105
Boxmoor Ho. *E2* 1G 85
(off Whiston Rd.)
W11 1F 99
(off Queensdale Cres.)
Boxmoor Rd. HA3: Kenton 4B 42
Boxoll Rd. RM9: Dag 4F 73
Box Park 2D 168
Boxted Cl. IG9: Buck H 1H 37
Box Tree Ho. SE8 6A 104
Boxtree La. HA3: Hrw W 1G 41
Boxtree Rd. HA3: Hrw W 7C 26
Boxwood Cl. UB7: W Dray 2B 92
Boxworth Cl. N12 5G 31
Boxworth Gro. N1 1K 83
Boyce Ho. SW16 5G 137
W10 3H 81
(off Bruckner St.)
Boyce Way E13 4J 87
Boycroft Av. NW9 6J 43
Boyd Av. UB1: S'hall 1D 94
Boyd Bldg. *E16* 7G 89
(off Frobisher Yd.)
Boyd Cl. KT2: King T 7G 133
Boydell Ct. NW8 7B 64
(not continuous)
Boyden Ho. E17 3E 50
Boyd Rd. SW19 6B 136
Boyd St. E1 6G 85
Boyd Way SE3 4A 124
Boyfield St. SE1 7B 14 (2B 102)
Boyland Rd. BR1: Broml 5H 141
Boyle Av. HA7: Stan 6F 27
Boyle Cl. UB10: Uxb 2B 74
Boyle Farm Island KT7: T Ditt 6A 150
Boyle Farm Rd. KT7: T Ditt 6A 150
Boyle St. W1 2A 12 (7G 83)
Boyne Av. NW4 4F 45
Boyne Rd. RM10: Dag 3G 73
SE13 3E 122
Boyne Ter. M. W11 1H 99
Boyseland Ct. HA8: Edg 2D 28
Boyson Rd. SE17 6C 102
(not continuous)
Boyson Wlk. SE17 6D 102
Boyton Cl. E1 4J 85
N8 3J 47
Boyton Ho. *NW8* 2B 82
(off Wellington Rd.)
Boyton Rd. N8 3J 47
Brabant Ct. EC3 2G 15
Brabant Rd. N22 2K 47
Brabazon Av. SM6: W'gton 7J 167
Brabazon Ct. *SW1* 5C 18
(off Moreton St.)
Brabazon Rd. TW5: Hest 7A 94
UB5: N'olt 2E 76
Brabazon St. E14 6D 86
Brabner Ho. *E2* 1K 9
(off Wellington Row)
Brabourne Cl. SE19 5E 138
Brabourne Cres. DA7: Bex 6F 109
Brabourne Hgts. NW7 3F 29
Brabourne Ri. BR3: Beck 5E 158
Brabourn Gro. SE15 2J 121
Brabrook Ct. SM6: W'gton 4F 167
Brabstone Ho. UB6: G'frd 2K 77
Bracer Ho. *N1* 2E 84
(off Whitmore Est.)
Bracewell Av. UB6: G'frd 5K 59
Bracewell Rd. W10 5E 80
Bracewood Gdns. CR0: C'don 3F 169
Bracey M. N4 2J 65
Bracey St. N4 2J 65
The Bracken E4 2K 35
Bracken Av. CR0: C'don 3D 170
SW12 6E 118
Brackenbridge Dr. HA4: Ruis 3B 58
Brackenbridge Ho. *HA4: Ruis* 4C 58
(off Brackenhill)
Brackenbury *N4* 1A 66
(off Osborne Rd.)
Brackenbury Gdns. W6 3D 98
Brackenbury Rd. N2 3A 46
W6 3D 98
Bracken Cl. E6 5D 88
TW2: Whitt 7E 112
TW16: Sun 6H 129
Brackendale N21 2E 32
Brackendale Cl. TW3: Houn 1F 113
Brackendene DA2: Wilm 4K 145
Bracken End TW7: Isle 5H 113
Brackenfield Cl. E5 3H 67
Bracken Gdns. SW13 2C 116
Brackenhill HA4: Ruis 4C 58
Bracken Hill Cl. BR1: Broml 1H 159
Bracken Hill La. BR1: Broml 1H 159
Bracken Ho. *E3* 5C 86
(off Devons Rd.)
Bracken Ind. Est. IG6: Ilf 1J 53
Bracken M. E4 1K 35
RM7: Rom 6H 55
Brackens BR3: Beck 7C 140
The Brackens EN1: Enf 7K 23
Brackenwood TW16: Sun 1J 147
Brackenwood Lodge *EN5: New Bar* 4D 20
(off Prospect Rd.)
Brackley Av. SE15 3J 121
Brackley Cl. SM6: W'gton 7J 167
Brackley Ct. *NW8* 3B 4
(off Pollitt Dr.)
Brackley Rd. BR3: Beck 7B 140
W4 5A 98
Brackley Sq. IG8: Wfd G 7G 37
Brackley St. EC1 5D 8 (4C 84)
Brackley Ter. W4 5A 98
Brackley Wlk. HA8: Edg 7C 28
Bracklyn Ct. N1 2D 84
(not continuous)
Bracklyn St. N1 2D 84
Bracknell Cl. N22 1A 48
Bracknell Gdns. NW3 4K 63
Bracknell Ga. NW3 5K 63
Bracknell Way NW3 4K 63
Bracondale Rd. SE2 4A 108
Bradbeer Ho. *E2* 3J 85
(off Cornwall Av.)
Bradbourne Rd. DA5: Bexl 7G 127
Bradbourne St. SW6 2J 117
Bradbury Cl. UB2: S'hall 4D 94
Bradbury M. N16 5E 66
Bradbury St. N16 5E 66
Bradby Ho. *NW8* 2K 81
(off Hamilton Ter.)
Bradby's *HA1: Harr* 1J 59
(off High St.)
Braddock Cl. TW7: Isle 2K 113
Braddon Ct. EN5: Barn 3B 20
Braddon Rd. TW9: Rich 3F 115
Braddyll St. SE10 5G 105
Bradenham Av. DA16: Well 4A 126
Bradenham Cl. SE17 6D 102
Bradenham Rd. HA3: Kenton 4B 42
UB4: Hayes 3G 75
Braden St. W9 4K 81
Bradfield Ct. *NW1* 7F 65
(off Hawley Rd.)
Bradfield Dr. IG11: Bark 5A 72
Bradfield Ho. IG8: Wfd G 6K 37
Bradfield Rd. E16 2J 105
HA4: Ruis 5C 58
Bradford Cl. BR2: Broml 1D 172
N17 6A 34
SE26 4H 139
Bradford Dr. KT19: Ewe 6B 164
Bradford Ho. *W14* 3F 99
(off Spring Va. Ter.)
Bradford Rd. IG1: Ilf 1H 71
W3 2A 98
Bradfords Cl. IG9: Buck H 4G 37
Bradgate Rd. SE6 6D 122
Brading Cres. E11 2K 69
Brading Rd. CR0: C'don 6K 155
SW2 7K 119
Brading Ter. W12 3C 98
Bradiston Rd. W9 3H 81
Bradley Cl. N7 6J 65
Bradley Gdns. W13 6B 78
Bradley Ho. *E3* 3D 86
(off Bromley High St.)
IG8: Wfd G 7D 36
SE16 4J 103
(off Raymouth Rd.)
Bradley M. SW17 1D 136
Bradley Rd. N22 2K 47
SE19 6C 138
Bradley's Cl. N1 2A 84
Bradley Stone Rd. E6 5D 88
Bradman Ho. *NW8* 3A 82
(off Abercorn Pl.)
Bradman Row HA8: Edg 7D 28
Bradmead SW8 7F 101
Bradmore Ct. *EN3: Enf H* 3F 25
(off Enstone Rd.)
Bradmore Pk. Rd. W6 4D 98
Bradshaw Cl. SW19 6J 135
Bradshaw Cotts. *E14* 6A 86
(off Repton St.)
Bradshaw Dr. NW7 7A 30
Bradshawe Waye UB8: Hil 5B 74
Bradshaws Cl. SE25 3G 157
Bradstock Ho. E9 7K 67
Bradstock Rd. E9 6K 67
KT17: Ewe 5C 164
Brad St. SE1 5K 13 (1A 102)
Bradwell Av. RM10: Dag 2G 73
Bradwell Cl. E18 4H 51
Bradwell Ho. *NW6* 1K 81
(off Mortimer Cres.)
Bradwell M. N18 4B 34
Bradwell Rd. IG9: Buck H 1H 37
Bradwell St. E1 3K 85
Brady Ct. RM8: Dag 1D 72
Brady Dr. BR1: Broml 3E 160
Brady Ho. *SW8* 1G 119
(off Corunna Rd.)
Bradymead E6 6E 88
Brady St. E1 4H 85
Braeburn Ct. *BR6: Orp* 2K 173
(off Blossom Dr.)
EN4: E Barn 4G 21
RM13: Rain 2K 91
(off Broadis Way)
Brae Ct. KT2: King T 1G 151
Braemar SW15 6F 117
Braemar Av. CR2: S Croy 7C 168
CR7: Thor H 3A 156
DA7: Bex 4J 127
HA0: Wemb 7D 60
N22 1J 47
NW10 3K 61
SW18 2J 135
SW19 2J 135
Braemar Cl. *SE16* 5H 103
(off Masters Dr.)
Braemar Ct. *SE6* 1H 141
(off Cumberland Pl.)
Braemar Gdns. BR4: W W'ck 1E 170
DA15: Sidc 3H 143
NW9 1K 43
Braemar Ho. *W9* 3A 82
(off Maida Vale)
Braemar Mans. *SW7* 3K 99
(off Cornwall Gdns.)
Braemar Rd. E13 4H 87
KT4: Wor Pk 3D 164
N15 5E 48
TW8: Bford 6D 96
Braeside BR3: Beck 5C 140
Braeside Av. SW19 1G 153
Braeside Cres. DA7: Bex 4J 127
Braeside Rd. SW16 7G 137
Braes St. N1 7B 66
Braesyde Cl. DA17: Belv 4F 109
Brafferton Rd. CR0: C'don 4C 168
Braganza St. SE17 5B 102
Bragg Cl. RM8: Dag 6B 72
Braham Ct. *E2* 4H 85
(off Three Colts La.)
Braham Ho. SE11 6H 19 (5K 101)
Braham St. E1 1K 15 (6F 85)
Braid Av. W3 6A 80
Braid Cl. TW13: Hanw 2D 130
Braidwood Pas. *EC1* 5C 8
(off Aldersgate St.)
Braidwood Rd. SE6 1F 141
Braidwood St. SE1 5G 15 (1E 102)
Brailsford Cl. CR4: Mitc 7C 136
Brailsford Rd. SW2 5A 120
Brainton Av. TW14: Felt 7K 111
Braintree Av. IG4: Ilf 4C 52
Braintree Ho. *E1* 4J 85
(off Malcolm Rd.)
Braintree Rd. HA4: Ruis 4K 57
RM10: Dag 3G 73
Braintree St. E2 3J 85
Braithwaite Av. RM7: Rush G 7J 55
Braithwaite Gdns. HA7: Stan 1C 42
Braithwaite Ho. *E15* 6F 69
(off Forrester Way)
EC1 3E 8
(off Bunhill Row)
Braithwaite Rd. EN3: Brim 3G 25
Braithwaite St. E1 4J 9 (4F 85)
Braithwaite Twr. W2 5B 4
Bramah Grn. *SW9* 1A 120
(off Eythorne Rd.)
Bramah Ho. SW1 6J 17 (5F 101)
Bramah Rd. SW9 1A 120
Bramalea Cl. N6 6E 46
Bramall Cl. E15 5H 69
Bramall Ct. *N7* 6K 65
(off Watkinson Rd.)
Bramber WC1 2E 6
Bramber Ct. TW8: Bford 4E 96
W14 6H 99
(off Bramber Rd.)
Bramber Ho. *KT2: King T* 1E 150
(off Seven Kings Way)
Bramber Rd. N12 5H 31
W14 6H 99
Bramble Acres Cl. SM2: Sutt 7J 165
Bramblebury Rd. SE18 5G 107
Bramble Cl. BR3: Beck 5E 158
CR0: C'don 4C 170
HA7: Stan 7J 27
N15 4G 49
SE19 1D 156
TW17: Shep 3F 147
UB8: Hil 6B 74
Bramble Cft. DA8: Erith 4J 109
Brambledown Cl. BR4: W W'ck 5G 159
Brambledown Rd. CR2: Sande 7E 168
SM5: Cars 7E 166
SM6: W'gton 7E 166
Bramble Gdns. W12 7B 80
Bramble Ho. *E3* 5C 86
(off Devons Rd.)
Bramble La. TW12: Hamp 6D 130
The Brambles SM1: Sutt 2B 166
SW19 5H 135
(off Woodside)
UB7: W Dray 4A 92
Brambles Cl. TW7: Isle 7B 96
Brambles Farm Dr. UB10: Hil 3C 74
Bramblewood Cl. SM5: Cars 1C 166
Brambling Ct. *SE8* 6B 104
(off Abinger Gro.)
The Bramblings E4 4A 36
Bramcote Av. CR4: Mitc 4D 154
Bramcote Ct. *CR4: Mitc* 4D 154
(off Bramcote Av.)
Bramcote Gro. SE16 5J 103
Bramcote Rd. SW15 4D 116
Bramdean Cres. SE12 1J 141
Bramdean Gdns. SE12 1J 141
Bramerton *NW6* 7F 63
(off Willesden La.)
Bramerton Rd. BR3: Beck 3B 158
Bramerton St. SW3 7C 16 (6C 100)
Bramfield Ct. *N4* 2C 66
(off Queen's Dr.)
Bramfield Rd. SW11 6C 118
Bramford Ct. N14 2C 32
Bramford Rd. SW18 4A 118
Bramham Gdns. KT9: Chess 4D 162
SW5 5K 99
Bramhope La. SE7 6K 105
Bramlands Cl. SW11 3C 118
Bramley Av. TW17: Shep 3G 147
Bramley Bank Local Nature Reserve 6J 169
Bramley Cl. BR6: Farnb 1F 173
CR2: S Croy 5C 168
E17 2A 50
HA5: Eastc 3H 39
IG8: Wfd G 7F 37
N14 5A 22
NW7 3F 29
TW2: Whitt 6G 113
UB3: Hayes 7J 75
Bramley Ct. *BR6: Orp* 2K 173
(off Blossom Dr.)
CR4: Mitc 2B 154
DA16: Well 1B 126
E4 1K 35
(off The Ridgeway)
EN4: E Barn 4H 21
RM13: Rain 2K 91
(off Broadis Way)
UB1: S'hall 7G 77
(off Haldane Rd.)
Bramley Cres. IG2: Ilf 6E 52
SW8 7H 101
Bramley Hill CR2: S Croy 5B 168
Bramley Ho. *SW15* 6B 116
(off Tunworth Cres.)
TW4: Houn 4D 112
W10 6F 81
Bramley Hyrst CR2: S Croy 5C 168
Bramley Lodge HA0: Wemb 4D 60
Bramley Pde. N14 4C 22
Bramley Rd. N14 5K 21
SM1: Sutt 5B 166
SM2: Cheam 7F 165
W5 3C 96
W10 6F 81
Bramley Sports Ground 5K 21
Bramley Way BR4: W W'ck 2D 170
TW4: Houn 5D 112
Brampton *WC1* 6G 7
(off Red Lion Sq.)
Brampton Cl. E5 2H 67
Brampton Ct. NW4 4D 44
RM7: Rush G 6K 55
(off Union Rd.)
Brampton Gro. HA3: Kenton 4A 42
HA9: Wemb 1G 61
NW4 4D 44
Brampton Ho. *SE16* 2J 103
(off Albatross Way)
Brampton La. NW4 4E 44
Brampton Pk. Rd. N22 3A 48
Brampton Rd. CR0: C'don 7F 157
DA7: Bex 3D 126
E6 3B 88
N15 5C 48
NW9 4G 43
SE2 6C 108
UB10: Hil 2D 74
Bramshaw Ri. KT3: N Mald 6A 152
Bramshaw Rd. E9 6K 67
Bramshill Gdns. NW5 3F 65
Bramshill Rd. NW10 2B 80
Bramshot Av. SE7 6J 105
Bramshurst *NW8* 1K 81
(off Abbey Rd.)
Bramston Rd. NW10 2C 80
SW17 3A 136
Bramwell Cl. TW16: Sun 2B 148
Bramwell Ho. SE1 3C 102
SW1 6A 18
(off Churchill Gdns.)
Bramwell M. N1 1K 83
Bramwell Way E16 1A 106
Brancaster Dr. NW7 7H 29
Brancaster Ho. *E1* 3K 85
(off Moody St.)
Brancaster Rd. E12 4D 70
IG2: Ilf 6J 53
SW16 3J 137
Brancepeth Gdns. IG9: Buck H 2D 36
Branch Hill NW3 3A 64
Branch Hill Ho. NW3 3K 63
Branch Pl. N1 1D 84
Branch Rd. E14 7A 86
Branch St. SE15 7E 102
Brancker Rd. HA3: Kenton 3D 42
Brancroft Way EN3: Brim 1F 25
Brand Av. UB10: Uxb 2A 74
Brand Cl. N4 1B 66
Brandesbury Sq. IG8: Wfd G 7K 37
Brandlehow Rd. SW15 4H 117
Brandon Ct. E16 4H 87
Brandon Est. SE17 6B 102
Brandon Ho. *BR3: Beck* 5D 140
(off Beckenham Hill Rd.)
Brandon Mans. *W14* 6G 99
(off Queen's Club Gdns.)
Brandon M. EC2 6E 8
SE17 4C 102
Brandon Rd. E17 4E 50
N7 7J 65
SM1: Sutt 4K 165
UB2: S'hall 5D 94
Brandon St. SE17 4C 102
(not continuous)
Brandram M. *SE13* 4G 123
(off Brandram Rd.)
Brandram Rd. SE13 3G 123
Brandrams Wharf SE16 2J 103
Brandreth Ct. HA1: Harr 6K 41
Brandreth Rd. E6 6D 88
SW17 2F 137
The Brandries SM6: Bedd 3H 167
Brands Ho. *NW6* 1H 81
(off Lincoln M.)
Brand St. SE10 7E 104
Brandville Gdns. IG6: Ilf 4F 53
Brandville Rd. UB7: W Dray 2A 92
Brandy Way SM2: Sutt 7J 165
Brangbourne Rd. BR1: Broml 5E 140
Brangton Rd. SE11 6H 19 (5K 101)
Brangwyn Ct. *W14* 3G 99
(off Blythe Rd.)
Brangwyn Cres. SW19 1A 154
Branksea St. SW6 7G 99
Branksome Av. N18 6A 34
Branksome Cl. TW11: Tedd 4H 131
Branksome Ho. *SW8* 7K 101
(off Meadow Rd.)
Branksome Rd. SW2 5J 119
SW19 1J 153
Branksome Way HA3: Kenton 6F 43
KT3: N Mald 1J 151
Branksone Ct. N2 3A 46
Brannigan Way HA8: Edg 4K 27
Bransby Rd. KT9: Chess 6E 162
Branscombe *NW1* 1G 83
(off Plender St.)
Branscombe Ct. BR2: Broml 5H 159
Branscombe Gdns. N21 7F 23
Branscombe St. SE13 3D 122
Bransdale Cl. NW6 1J 81
Bransgrove Rd. HA8: Edg 1F 43
Branston Cres. BR5: Pet W 1H 173
Branstone Rd. TW9: Kew 1F 115
Brants Wlk. W7 4J 77
Brantwood Av. DA8: Erith 7J 109
TW7: Isle 4A 114
Brantwood Cl. E17 3D 50
Brantwood Gdns. EN2: Enf 4D 22
IG4: Ilf 4C 52
Brantwood Ho. *SE5* 7C 102
(off Wyndam Est.)
Brantwood Rd. CR2: S Croy 7C 168
DA7: Bex 2H 127
N17 6B 34
SE24 5C 120
Branxholme Ct. *BR1: Broml* 1H 159
(off Highland Rd.)
Braque Bldg. *SE1* 5C 14
(off Union St.)
Brasenose Dr. SW13 6E 98
Brasher Cl. UB6: G'frd 5H 59
Brassett Point *E15* 1G 87
(off Abbey Rd.)
Brassey Cl. TW14: Felt 1J 129
Brassey Ho. *E14* 4D 104
(off Cahir St.)
Brassey Rd. NW6 6H 63
Brassey Sq. SW11 3E 118
Brassie Av. W3 6A 80
Brass Talley All. SE16 2K 103
Brasted Cl. BR6: Orp 2K 173
DA6: Bex 5D 126
SE26 4J 139
Brasted Lodge BR3: Beck 7C 140
Brathay *NW1* 1B 6
(off Ampthill Est.)
Brathway Rd. SW18 7J 117
Bratley St. E1 4G 85
Bratten Ct. CR0: C'don 6D 156
Braund Av. UB6: G'frd 4F 77
Braundton Av. DA15: Sidc 1K 143
Braunston Dr. UB4: Yead 4C 76
Braunston Ho. HA0: Wemb 1E 78
Bravington Cl. TW17: Shep 5B 146
Bravington Pl. W9 4H 81
Bravington Rd. W9 2H 81
Bravingtons Wlk. *N1* 1F 7
(off York Way)
Brawne Ho. *SE17* 6B 102
(off Brandon Est.)
Braxfield Rd. SE4 4A 122
Braxted Pk. SW16 6K 137
Bray NW3 7C 64
Brayards Rd. SE15 2H 121
Brayards Rd. Est. *SE15* 2H 121
(off Caulfield Rd.)
Braybourne Dr. TW7: Isle 7K 95
Braybrooke Gdns. SE19 7E 138
Braybrook St. W12 5B 80
Brayburne Av. SW4 2G 119
Bray Ct. *E2* 3K 85
(off Meath Cres.)
SW16 5J 137
Braycourt Av. KT12: Walt T 7K 147
Bray Cres. SE16 2K 103
Braydon Rd. N16 1G 67
Bray Dr. E16 7H 87
Brayfield Ter. N1 7A 66
Brayford Sq. E1 6J 85
Bray Pas. E16 7J 87
Bray Pl. SW3 4E 16 (4D 100)
Bray Rd. NW7 6A 30
Brays Gdns. SE6 7D 122
SE13 6E 122
Brayton Gdns. EN2: Enf 4C 22
Braywood Rd. SE9 4H 125
Brazier Cres. UB5: N'olt 4D 76
Brazil Cl. CR0: Bedd 7J 155
Breacher Ho. Apts. IG11: Bark 4A 90
Breach La. RM9: Dag 3G 91
Bread St. EC4 1D 14 (6C 84)
(not continuous)
Breakspear Crematorium 5E 38
Breakspear Ho. UB9: Hare 3A 38
Breakspear M. UB9: Hare 3A 38
Breakspear Rd. HA4: Ruis 7D 38
Breakspear Rd. Nth. UB9: Hare 3A 38
Breakspear Rd. Sth. UB9: Hare 3B 56
UB10: Ick 3B 56
Breakspears Dr.
BR5: St P 7A 144, 1K 161
Breakspears M. SE4 2B 122
Breakspears Rd. SE4 4B 122
(not continuous)
Breakwell Ct. *W10* 4G 81
(off Wornington Rd.)
Bream Cl. N17 4H 49
Bream Gdns. E6 3E 88
Breamore Cl. SW15 1C 134
Breamore Ct. IG3: Ilf 2A 72
Breamore Ho. *SE15* 7G 103
(off Friary Est.)
Breamore Rd. IG3: Ilf 2K 71
Bream's Bldgs. EC4 7J 7 (6A 84)
Bream St. E3 7C 68
Breamwater Gdns. TW10: Ham 3B 132
Brearley Cl. HA8: Edg 7D 28
UB8: Uxb 6A 56
Breasley Cl. SW15 4D 116
Breasy Pl. *NW4* 4D 44
(off Burroughs Gdns.)
Brechin Pl. SW7 4A 100
Brecknock Rd. N7 5H 65
N19 4G 65
Brecknock Rd. Est. N19 4G 65
Breckonmead BR1: Broml 2A 160
Brecon Cl. CR4: Mitc 3J 155
KT4: Wor Pk 2E 164
Brecon Grn. NW9 6A 44
Brecon Ho. *E3* 2B 86
(off Ordell Rd.)
UB5: N'olt 3D 76
(off Taywood Rd.)
W2 6A 82
(off Hallfield Est.)
Brecon Lodge UB7: W Dray 2B 92
Brecon M. N7 5H 65
Brecon Rd. EN3: Pond E 4D 24
W6 6G 99
Brede Cl. E6 3E 88
Bredel Ho. *E14* 5C 86
(off St Paul's Way)
Brede M. E6 3E 88
Bredgar SE13 5D 122
Bredgar Rd. N19 2G 65
Bredhurst Cl. SE20 6J 139
Bredinghurst SE22 7G 121
Bredin Ho. *SW10* 7K 99
(off Coleridge Gdns.)
Bredon Rd. CR0: C'don 7F 157
Bree Ct. NW9 3J 43
Breer St. SW6 3K 117
Breezers Ct. *E1* 7G 85
(off The Highway)
Breezer's Hill E1 7G 85
Bremans Rd. HA2: Harr 2G 59
Bremer M. E17 4D 50
Bremner Rd. SW7 1A 16 (3A 100)
Brenchley Cl. BR2: Broml 6H 159
BR7: Chst 1E 160
Brenchley Gdns. SE23 6J 121
Brenchley Rd. BR5: St P 2K 161
Brenda Rd. SW17 2D 136
Brende Gdns. KT8: W Mole 4F 149
Brendon Av. NW10 4A 62
Brendon Cl. UB3: Harl 7E 92
Brendon Ct. UB2: S'hall 4F 95
Brendon Gdns. HA2: Harr 4F 59
IG2: Ilf 5J 53
Brendon Gro. N2 2A 46
Brendon Rd. RM8: Dag 1F 73
SE9 2H 143
Brendon St. W1 7D 4 (6C 82)
Brendon Vs. N21 1H 33
Brendon Way EN1: Enf 7K 23
Brenley Cl. CR4: Mitc 3E 154
Brenley Gdns. SE9 4B 124
Brenley Ho. *SE1* 6E 14
(off Tennis St.)
Brennand Ct. N19 3G 65
Brent Cl. DA5: Bexl 1E 144
Brentcot Cl. W13 4B 78
Brent Ct. NW11 7F 45
W7 7H 77

Brent Cres.—Broadfield Way

Brent Cres. NW10 ... 2F 79
BRENT CROSS ... 7E 44
Brent Cross Fly-Over NW4 ... 7F 45
Brent Cross Gdns. NW4 ... 6F 45
BRENT CROSS INTERCHANGE ... 6E 44
Brent Cross Shop. Cen. ... 7E 44
Brentfield NW10 ... 7H 61
Brentfield Cl. NW10 ... 6K 61
Brentfield Gdns. NW2 ... 7F 45
Brentfield Ho. NW10 ... 7K 61
Brentfield Rd. NW10 ... 6K 61
BRENTFORD ... 6D 96
Brentford Bus. Cen. TW8: Bford ... 7C 96
Brentford Cl. UB4: Yead ... 4B 76
BRENTFORD END ... 7B 96
Brentford FC ... 6D 96
Brentford Fountain Leisure Cen. ... 5G 97
Brentford Ho. TW1: Twick ... 7B 114
Brent Grn. NW4 ... 5E 44
Brent Grn. Wlk. HA9: Wemb ... 3J 61
Brentham Club ... 3C 78
Brentham Way W5 ... 4D 78
Brent Ho. E9 ... 6J 67
(off Brenthouse Rd.)
Brenthouse Rd. E9 ... 7J 67
Brenthurst Rd. NW10 ... 6B 62
Brent Lea TW8: Bford ... 7C 96
Brentmead Cl. W7 ... 7J 77
Brentmead Gdns. NW10 ... 2F 79
Brentmead Pl. NW11 ... 6F 45
Brent Mus. ... 6D 62
Brent New Ent. Cen. NW10 ... 6B 62
Brenton Ct. E9 ... 5A 68
(off Mabley St.)
Brenton St. E14 ... 6A 86
Brent Pk. Ind. Est. UB2: S'hall ... 3K 93
Brent Pk. Rd. NW4 ... 7D 44
NW9 ... 7D 44
Brent Pl. EN5: Barn ... 5C 20
Brent Reservoir ... 1B 62
Brent Rd. CR2: Sels ... 7H 169
E16 ... 6J 87
SE18 ... 7F 107
TW8: Bford ... 6C 96
UB2: S'hall ... 3A 94
Brent Side TW8: Bford ... 6C 96
Brentside Cl. W13 ... 4A 78
Brentside Executive Cen.
TW8: Bford ... 6B 96
Brent Sth. Shop. Pk. ... 1E 62
Brent St. NW4 ... 4E 44
Brent Ter. NW2 ... 1E 62
(not continuous)
Brent Trad. Cen. NW10 ... 5A 62
Brentvale Av. HA0: Wemb ... 1F 79
UB1: S'hall ... 1H 95
Brent Valley Golf Course ... 7J 77
Brent Vw. Rd. NW9 ... 6C 44
Brentwaters Bus. Pk. TW8: Bford ... 7C 96
Brent Way HA9: Wemb ... 6H 61
N3 ... 6D 30
TW8: Bford ... 7D 96
Brentwick Gdns. TW8: Bford ... 4E 96
Brentwood Cl. SE9 ... 1G 143
Brentwood Ho. SE18 ... 7B 106
(off Portway Gdns.)
Brentwood Lodge NW4 ... 5F 45
(off Holmdale Gdns.)
Brereton Rd. N17 ... 7A 34
Bressay Dr. NW7 ... 7H 29
Bressenden Pl. SW1 ... 1K 17 (3F 101)
Bressey Av. EN1: Enf ... 1B 24
Bressey Gro. E18 ... 2H 51
Bresslaw Ct. E3 ... 5B 86
(off Wager St.)
Breton Highwalk EC2 ... 5D 8
(off Golden La.)
Breton Ho. EC2 ... 5D 8
SE1 ... 7J 15
(off St Saviour's Est.)
Brett Cl. N16 ... 2E 66
UB5: N'olt ... 3B 76
Brett Ct. N9 ... 2D 34
Brettell St. SE17 ... 5D 102
Brettenham Av. E17 ... 1C 50
Brettenham Rd. E17 ... 2C 50
N18 ... 4B 34
Brett Gdns. RM9: Dag ... 7E 72
Brett Ho. Cl. SW15 ... 7F 117
Brettinghurst SE1 ... 5G 103
(off Avondale Sq.)
Brett Pas. E8 ... 5H 67
Brett Rd. E8 ... 5H 67
Brewers Bldgs. EC1 ... 1A 8
(off Rawstorne St.)
Brewers Ct. W2 ... 5A 82
Brewer's Grn. SW1 ... 1C 18
Brewer's Hall Gdn. EC2 ... 6D 8
(off Aldermanbury Sq.)
Brewers La. E20 ... 5D 68
TW9: Rich ... 5D 114
Brewer St. W1 ... 2B 12 (7G 83)
The Brewery EC2 ... 5E 8 (5C 84)
RM1: Rom ... 5K 55
Brewery Cl. HA0: Wemb ... 5A 60
The Brewery Ind. Est. N1 ... 1D 8
(off Wenlock Rd.)
Brewery La. TW1: Twick ... 7K 113
Brewery M. Cen. TW7: Isle ... 3A 114
Brewery Rd. BR2: Broml ... 1C 172
N7 ... 7J 65
SE18 ... 5H 107
Brewery Sq. EC1 ... 3B 8 (4B 84)
SE1 ... 5J 15
Brewery Wlk. RM1: Rom ... 5K 55
Brewhouse La. E1 ... 1H 103
SW15 ... 3G 117
Brewhouse Rd. SE18 ... 4D 106
Brewhouse Wlk. SE16 ... 1A 104
Brewhouse Yd. EC1 ... 3A 8 (4B 84)
Brewin Ter. UB4: Yead ... 5A 76
(off Larch Cres.)
Brewood Rd. RM8: Dag ... 6B 72
Brewster Gdns. W10 ... 5E 80
Brewster Ho. E14 ... 7B 86
(off Three Colt St.)
SE1 ... 4F 103
(off Dunton Rd.)
Brewster Pl. KT1: King T ... 2J 151
Brewster Rd. E10 ... 1D 68
The Breyer Group Stadium ... 3D 68
(shown as Leyton Orient FC)
Brian Rd. RM6: Chad H ... 5C 54
Briant Ho. SE1 ... 2J 19
Briants Cl. HA5: Pinn ... 2D 40
Briant St. SE14 ... 1K 121
Briar Av. SW16 ... 7K 137
Briarbank Rd. W13 ... 6A 78
Briar Cl. IG9: Buck H ... 2G 37
N2 ... 3K 45
N13 ... 3H 33
TW7: Isle ... 5K 113
TW12: Hamp ... 5D 130
Briar Ct. E3 ... 2C 86
(off Morville St.)
SM3: Cheam ... 4E 164
SW15 ... 4D 116
Briar Cres. UB5: N'olt ... 6F 59
Briardale HA8: Edg ... 4E 28
Briardale Gdns. NW3 ... 3J 63
Briarfield Av. N3 ... 2K 45
(not continuous)
Briarfield Cl. DA7: Bex ... 2G 127
Briar Gdns. BR2: Hayes ... 1H 171
Briaris Cl. N17 ... 7C 34
Briar La. BR4: Addtn ... 4D 170
Briar Rd. DA5: Bexl ... 3K 145
HA3: Kenton ... 5C 42
NW2 ... 4E 62
SW16 ... 3J 155
TW2: Twick ... 1J 131
TW17: Shep ... 5B 146
The Briars TW19: Stanw M ... 7B 174
WD23: B Hea ... 1D 26
Briarswood Way BR6: Chels ... 5K 173
Briar Wlk. HA8: Edg ... 7D 28
SW15 ... 4D 116
W10 ... 4G 81
Briar Way UB7: W Dray ... 2C 92
Briar Wood Cl. BR2: Broml ... 2C 172
Briarwood Cl. NW9 ... 6J 43
TW13: Felt ... 4G 129
Briarwood Ct. KT4: Wor Pk ... 1C 164
(off The Avenue)
Briarwood Dr. HA6: Nwood ... 2J 39
Briarwood Rd. KT17: Ewe ... 6C 164
SW4 ... 5H 119
Briary Cl. NW3 ... 7C 64
Briary Ct. DA14: Sidc ... 5B 144
E16 ... 6H 87
Briary Gdns. BR1: Broml ... 5K 141
Briary Gro. HA8: Edg ... 2H 43
Briary La. N9 ... 3A 34
Briary Lodge BR3: Beck ... 1E 158
Brickbarn Cl. SW10 ... 7A 100
(off King's Barn)
Brick Ct. EC4 ... 1J 13 (6A 84)
Brickett Cl. HA4: Ruis ... 5E 38
Brick Farm Cl. TW9: Kew ... 1H 115
Brickfield Cl. E9 ... 6J 67
TW8: Bford ... 7C 96
Brickfield Cotts. BR7: Chst ... 5E 142
SE18 ... 6K 107
Brickfield Farm Gdns.
BR6: Farnb ... 4G 173
Brickfield Ho. N1 ... 1E 84
(off Hertford Rd.)
Brickfield La. UB3: Harl ... 6F 93
Brickfield Rd. CR4: Mitc ... 3C 154
CR7: Thor H ... 1B 156
E3 ... 4D 86
SW4 ... 6H 119
(off Parkfield Rd.)
SW19 ... 4K 135
Brickfields HA2: Harr ... 2H 59
(not continuous)
Brickfields Way UB7: W Dray ... 3B 92
Brick Kiln One SE13 ... 3E 122
(off Station Rd.)
Brick Kiln Two SE13 ... 3E 122
(off Station Rd.)
Brick La. E1 ... 3K 9 (4F 85)
E2 ... 2K 9 (3F 85)
EN1: Enf ... 2C 24
EN3: Enf H ... 2C 24
HA7: Stan ... 7J 27
UB5: N'olt ... 3D 76
Brick Lane Mosque ... 5K 9
Brick Lane Music Hall ... 1B 106
BRICKLAYER'S ARMS ... 4D 102
Bricklayers Arms Distribution Cen.
SE1 ... 4E 102
(not continuous)
Bricklayers St. SE11 ... 4A 102
Brick St. W1 ... 5J 11 (1F 101)
Brickwall La. HA4: Ruis ... 1G 57
Brickwood Cl. SE26 ... 3H 139
Brickwood Rd. CR0: C'don ... 2E 168
Brideale Cl. SE15 ... 6F 103
Bride Ct. EC4 ... 1A 14
Bride La. EC4 ... 1A 14 (6B 84)
Bridel M. N1 ... 1B 84
(off Colebrook Row)
Brides M. N7 ... 6K 65
Brides Pl. N1 ... 7E 66
Bride St. N7 ... 6K 65
Bridewain St. SE1 ... 7J 15 (3F 103)
Bridewell Pl. E1 ... 1H 103
EC4 ... 1A 14 (6B 84)
Bridford M. W1 ... 5K 5 (5F 83)
The Bridge HA3: W'stone ... 4K 41
SW11 ... 7F 101
Bridge App. NW1 ... 7E 64
Bridge Av. W6 ... 4E 98
W7 ... 5H 77
Bridge Av. Mans. W6 ... 5E 98
(off Bridge Av.)
The Bridge Bus. Cen. UB2: S'hall ... 2E 94
Bridge Cl. EN1: Enf ... 2C 24
KT12: Walt T ... 7H 147
TW11: Tedd ... 4K 131
W10 ... 6F 81
Bridge Ct. E10 ... 1B 68
E14 ... 7F 87
(off Newport Av.)
HA2: Harr ... 2G 59
KT12: Walt T ... 7H 147
(off Bridge St.)
Bridge Dr. N13 ... 4E 32
Bridge End E17 ... 1E 50
Bridge End Cl. KT2: King T ... 1G 151
Bridgefield Ho. W2 ... 6K 81
(off Queensway)
Bridgefield Rd. SM1: Sutt ... 6J 165
Bridgefoot SE1 ... 6F 19 (5J 101)
TW16: Sun ... 1H 147
Bridge Gdns.
KT8: E Mos ... 4H 149
N16 ... 4D 66
TW15: Ashf ... 7E 128
Bridge Ga. N21 ... 7H 23
Bridgehill Cl. HA0: Wemb ... 1D 78
Bridge Ho. CR0: C'don ... 3C 168
(off Surrey St.)
E9 ... 6K 67
(off Shepherds La.)
NW3 ... 7E 64
(off Adelaide Rd.)
NW10 ... 2F 81
(off Chamberlayne Rd.)
SE4 ... 4B 122
SM2: Sutt ... 6K 165
(off Bridge Rd.)
SW1 ... 5J 17
(off Ebury Bri.)
UB7: W Dray ... 1A 92
Bridgehouse Ct. SE1 ... 7A 14
(off Blackfriars Rd.)
Bridge Ho. Quay E14 ... 1E 104
Bridgeland Rd. E16 ... 7J 87
Bridgelands Cl. BR3: Beck ... 7B 140
Bridge La. NW11 ... 4G 45
SW11 ... 1C 118
The Bridge Leisure Cen. ... 4B 140
Bridgeman Ho. E9 ... 7J 67
(off Frampton Pk. Rd.)
W14 ... 4H 99
(off Radnor Ter.)
Bridgeman Rd. N1 ... 7K 65
TW11: Tedd ... 6A 132
Bridgeman St. NW8 ... 2C 82
Bridge Mdws. SE14 ... 6K 103
Bridge M. NW10 ... 6A 62
Bridgemount M. N4 ... 7K 47
BRIDGEN ... 7E 126
Bridgend Rd. SW18 ... 4A 118
Bridgenhall Rd. EN1: Enf ... 1A 24
Bridgen Ho. E1 ... 6H 85
(off Nelson St.)
Bridgen Rd. DA5: Bexl ... 7E 126
Bridge Pde. N21 ... 7H 23
(off Ridge Av.)
Bridgepark SW18 ... 5J 117
Bridge Pk. Community Leisure Cen.
... 7H 61
Bridge Pl. CR0: C'don ... 1D 168
SW1 ... 3K 17 (4F 101)
Bridgepoint Lofts E7 ... 7A 70
Bridgepoint Pl. N6 ... 1G 65
(off Hornsey La.)
Bridgeport Pl. E1 ... 1G 103
Bridge Rd. BR3: Beck ... 7B 140
DA7: Bex ... 2E 126
E6 ... 7D 70
E11 ... 6F 51
E15 ... 7F 69
E17 ... 7B 50
HA9: Wemb ... 3G 61
KT8: E Mos ... 4H 149
KT9: Chess ... 5E 162
N9 ... 3B 34
N22 ... 1J 47
NW10 ... 6A 62
SM2: Sutt ... 6K 165
SM6: W'gton ... 5F 167
TW1: Twick ... 6B 114
TW3: Houn, Isle ... 3H 113
TW7: Isle ... 3H 113
UB2: S'hall ... 2D 94
Bridge Rd. Dpt. E15 ... 1G 87
Bridge Row CR0: C'don ... 1D 168
Bridges Av. KT8: E Mos ... 6H 149
Bridges Ct. Rd. SW11 ... 3B 118
Bridges Ho. SE5 ... 7D 102
(off Elmington Est.)
Bridgeside Lodge N1 ... 2C 84
(off Wharf Rd.)
Bridges La. CR0: Bedd ... 4J 167
Bridges Pl. SW6 ... 1H 117
Bridges Rd. HA7: Stan ... 5E 26
SW19 ... 6K 135
Bridges Rd. M. SW19 ... 6K 135
Bridge St. HA5: Pinn ... 3C 40
KT12: Walt T ... 7G 147
SW1 ... 7E 12 (2J 101)
TW9: Rich ... 5D 114
W4 ... 4K 97
Bridges Wharf SW11 ... 3B 118
Bridge Ter. E15 ... 7F 69
Bridge Theatre ... 5J 15
(off Tower Bri. Rd.)
Bridgetown Cl. SE19 ... 5E 138
Bridge Vw. W6 ... 5E 98
Bridge Vw. Ct. SE1 ... 3E 102
(off Grange Rd.)
Bridge Wlk. SE8 ... 6D 104
(off Copperas St.)
Bridgewalk Hgts. SE1 ... 6F 15
(off Weston St.)
Bridgewater Cl. BR7: Chst ... 3J 161
Bridgewater Gdns. HA8: Edg ... 2F 43
Bridgewater Highwalk EC2 ... 5C 8
Bridgewater House E14 ... 6G 87
(off Lookout Lane)
Bridgewater Rd. E15 ... 1E 86
HA0: Wemb ... 6C 60
Bridgewater Sq. EC2 ... 5C 8 (5C 84)
Bridgewater St. EC2 ... 5C 8 (5C 84)
Bridge Way N11 ... 3B 32
NW11 ... 5H 45
TW2: Whitt ... 7G 113
UB10: Ick ... 5D 56
Bridgeway HA0: Wemb ... 7E 60
IG11: Bark ... 7K 71
Bridgeway St. NW1 ... 2G 83
Bridge Wharf E2 ... 2K 85
N1 ... 2K 83
(off Calshot St.)
Bridge Wharf Rd. TW7: Isle ... 3B 114
Bridgewood Cl. SE20 ... 7H 139
Bridgewood Rd. KT4: Wor Pk ... 4C 164
SW16 ... 7H 137
Bridge Yd. SE1 ... 4F 15 (1D 102)
Bridgford St. SW18 ... 3A 136
Bridgman Rd. W4 ... 3J 97
Bridgnorth Ho. SE15 ... 6G 103
(off Friary Est.)
Bridgwater Ho. W2 ... 6A 82
(off Hallfield Est.)
Bridgwater Rd. HA4: Ruis ... 4J 57
Bridle Cl. KT1: King T ... 4D 150
KT19: Ewe ... 5K 163
TW16: Sun ... 3J 147
Bridle La. TW1: Twick ... 6B 114
W1 ... 2B 12 (7G 83)
Bridle M. E1 ... 6G 85
(off Boulevard Walkway)
EN5: Barn ... 4C 20
Bridle Path CR0: Bedd ... 3J 167
The Bridle Path IG8: Wfd G ... 7B 36
Bridlepath Way TW14: Bedf ... 7G 111
Bridle Rd. CR0: C'don ... 3C 170
CR2: Sande ... 7G 169
HA5: Eastc ... 6K 39
KT10: Clay ... 6B 162
Bridle Way BR6: Farnb ... 4G 173
CR0: C'don ... 5C 170
The Bridle Way SM6: W'gton ... 4G 167
Bridlington Rd. N9 ... 7C 24
Bridport SE17 ... 5D 102
(off Cadiz St.)
Bridport Av. RM7: Rom ... 6H 55
Bridport Ho. N1 ... 1D 84
(off Bridport Pl.)
N18 ... 5A 34
(off College Gdns.)
Bridport Pl. N1 ... 1D 84
(not continuous)
Bridport Rd. CR7: Thor H ... 3A 156
N18 ... 5K 33
UB6: G'frd ... 1F 77
Bridport Ter. SW8 ... 1H 119
(off Deeley Rd.)
Bridstow Pl. W2 ... 6J 81
Brief St. SE5 ... 1B 120
Brierfield NW1 ... 1G 83
(off Arlington Rd.)
Brierley CR0: New Ad ... 6D 170
(not continuous)
Brierley Av. N9 ... 1D 34
Brierley Cl. SE25 ... 4G 157
Brierley Ct. W7 ... 7J 77
Brierley Rd. E11 ... 4F 69
SW12 ... 2G 137
Brierly Gdns. E2 ... 2J 85
Brigade Cl. HA2: Harr ... 2H 59
Brigade St. SE3 ... 2H 123
(off Tranquil Va.)
Brigadier Av. EN2: Enf ... 1H 23
Brigadier Hill EN2: Enf ... 1H 23
Brigadier Ho. NW9 ... 2B 44
(off Heritage Av.)
Briggeford Cl. E5 ... 2G 67
Briggs Cl. CR4: Mitc ... 1F 155
Briggs Ho. E2 ... 1K 9
(off Chambord St.)
Bright Cl. DA17: Belv ... 4D 108
Brightfield Rd. SE12 ... 5G 123
Bright Ho. KT1: King T ... 3D 150
(off Kingston Hall Rd.)
Brightling Rd. SE4 ... 6B 122
Brightlingsea Pl. E14 ... 7B 86
Brightman Rd. SW18 ... 1B 136
Brighton Av. E17 ... 5B 50
Brighton Bldgs. SE1 ... 3E 102
(off Tower Bri. Rd.)
Brighton Cl. UB10: Hil ... 7D 56
Brighton Dr. UB5: N'olt ... 6E 58
Brighton Gro. SE14 ... 1A 122
Brighton Ho. SE5 ... 1D 120
(off Camberwell Grn.)
Brighton Rd. CR2: S Croy ... 5C 168
E6 ... 3E 88
(not continuous)
KT6: Surb ... 6C 150
N2 ... 2A 46
N16 ... 4E 66
SM2: Sutt ... 7K 165
Brighton Ter. SW9 ... 4K 119
The Brightside EN3: Enf H ... 1E 24
Brightside Rd. SE13 ... 6F 123
Bright St. E14 ... 5D 86
Brightwell Cl. CR0: C'don ... 1A 168
Brightwell Ct. N7 ... 5K 65
(off Mackenzie Rd.)
Brightwell Cres. SW17 ... 5D 136
Brightwen Gro. HA7: Stan ... 2F 27
Brig M. SE8 ... 6C 104
Brigstock Ho. SE5 ... 2C 120
Brigstock Rd. CR7: Thor H ... 5A 156
DA17: Belv ... 4H 109
Brill Pl. NW1 ... 1D 6 (2H 83)
Brim Hill N2 ... 4A 46
Brimpsfield Cl. SE2 ... 3B 108
(not continuous)
BRIMSDOWN ... 2G 25
Brimsdown Av. EN3: Enf H ... 2F 25
Brimsdown Ho. E3 ... 4D 86
Brimsdown Ind. Est. EN3: Brim ... 1G 25
(Lockfield Av.)
EN3: Brim ... 2G 25
(Stockingswater La.)
Brimstone Ho. E15 ... 7G 69
(off Victoria St.)
Brindle Ga. DA15: Sidc ... 1J 143
Brindlewick Gdns. BR3: Beck ... 6C 140
Brindley Cl. DA7: Bex ... 3H 127
HA0: Wemb ... 7D 60
Brindley Ct. HA7: Stan ... 7J 27
Brindley Ho. W2 ... 5J 81
(off Alfred Rd.)
Brindley St. SE14 ... 1B 122
Brindley Way BR1: Broml ... 5J 141
UB1: S'hall ... 7F 77
Brindwood Rd. E4 ... 3G 35
Brine Ho. E3 ... 2A 86
(off St Stephen's Rd.)
Brinkburn Cl. HA8: Edg ... 3H 43
SE2 ... 4A 108
Brinkburn Gdns. HA8: Edg ... 3G 43
Brinkley KT1: King T ... 2G 151
Brinkley Rd. KT4: Wor Pk ... 2D 164
Brinklow Cres. SE18 ... 7F 107
Brinklow Ho. W2 ... 5K 81
(off Torquay St.)
Brinkworth Rd. IG5: Ilf ... 3C 52
Brinkworth Way E9 ... 6B 68
Brinsdale Rd. NW4 ... 3F 45
Brinsley Ho. E1 ... 6J 85
(off Tarling St.)
Brinsley Rd. HA3: Hrw W ... 2H 41
Brinsworth Cl. TW2: Twick ... 1H 131
Brinsworth Ho. TW2: Twick ... 2H 131
Brinton Wlk. SE1 ... 5A 14
Brion Pl. E14 ... 5E 86
Brisbane Av. SW19 ... 1K 153
Brisbane Ho. W12 ... 7D 80
(off White City Est.)
Brisbane Rd. E10 ... 2D 68
IG1: Ilf ... 7F 53
W13 ... 2A 96
Brisbane St. SE5 ... 7D 102
Briscoe Cl. E11 ... 2H 69
Briscoe M. TW2: Twick ... 2H 131
Briscoe Rd. SW19 ... 6B 136
Briset Rd. SE9 ... 3B 124
Briset St. EC1 ... 5A 8 (4B 84)
Briset Way N7 ... 2K 65
Bristol Av. NW9 ... 1B 44
Bristol Cl. SM6: W'gton ... 7J 167
TW4: Houn ... 7E 112
TW19: Stanw ... 6A 110
Bristol Ct. TW19: Stanw ... 6A 110
Bristol Gdns. SW15 ... 7E 116
W9 ... 4K 81
Bristol Ho. IG11: Bark ... 7A 72
(off Margaret Bondfield Av.)
SE11 ... 2J 19
SW1 ... 5G 17
(off Lwr. Sloane St.)
WC1 ... 5F 7
(off Southampton Row)
Bristol M. W9 ... 4K 81
Bristol Pk. Rd. E17 ... 4A 50
Bristol Rd. E7 ... 6A 70
SM4: Mord ... 5A 154
UB6: G'frd ... 1F 77
Bristol Wlk. NW6 ... 2J 81
(off Alpha Pl.)
Briston Gro. N8 ... 6J 47
Briston M. NW7 ... 7H 29
Bristow Ct. E8 ... 1H 85
(off Triangle Rd.)
Bristowe Cl. SW2 ... 6A 120
Bristow Rd. CR0: Bedd ... 4J 167
DA7: Bex ... 1E 126
SE19 ... 5E 138
TW3: Houn ... 3G 113
Britannia Bldg. N1 ... 1E 8
(off Ebenezer St.)
Britannia Bus. Cen. NW2 ... 4F 63
Britannia Cl. SW4 ... 4H 119
UB5: N'olt ... 3B 76
Britannia Ct. KT2: King T ... 1D 150
(off Skerne Wlk.)
UB7: W Dray ... 3A 92
Britannia Ga. E16 ... 1J 105
BRITANNIA JUNC. ... 1F 83
Britannia La. TW2: Whitt ... 7G 113
Britannia Leisure Cen. ... 1D 84
Britannia Rd. E14 ... 4C 104
IG1: Ilf ... 3F 71
KT5: Surb ... 7F 151
N12 ... 3F 31
SW6 ... 7K 99
Britannia Row N1 ... 1B 84
Britannia St. WC1 ... 1G 7 (3K 83)
Britannia Wlk. N1 ... 1E 8 (2D 84)
(not continuous)
Britannia Way NW10 ... 4H 79
SW6 ... 7K 99
(off Britannia Rd.)
TW19: Stanw ... 7A 110
Britannic Highwalk EC2 ... 6E 8
(off Moor La.)
British Gro. W4 ... 5B 98
British Gro. Nth. W4 ... 5B 98
British Gro. Pas. W4 ... 5B 98
British Gro. Sth. W4 ... 5B 98
British Legion Rd. E4 ... 2C 36
British Library ... 1D 6 (3H 83)
British Mus. ... 6D 6 (5J 83)
British St. E3 ... 3B 86
British Telecom Cen. ... 7C 8
British Wharf Ind. Est. SE14 ... 5K 103
Britley Ho. E14 ... 6B 86
(off Copenhagen Pl.)
Brittain Ct. SE9 ... 1C 142
Brittain Rd. RM8: Dag ... 3E 72
Brittany Ho. EN2: Enf ... 1H 23
Brittany Point SE11 ... 4J 19
Britten Cl. NW11 ... 1K 63
Britten Ct. E15 ... 2F 87
Brittenden Cl. BR6: Chels ... 6K 173
Brittenden Pde. BR6: Chels ... 6K 173
Britten Dr. UB1: S'hall ... 6E 76
Britten Ho. SW3 ... 5D 16
(off Britten St.)
Britten St. SW3 ... 6C 16 (5C 100)
Britten Theatre ... 1A 16
(off Prince Consort Rd.)
Brittidge Rd. NW10 ... 7A 62
Britton Cl. SE6 ... 7F 123
Britton St. EC1 ... 4A 8 (4B 84)
Brixham Cres. HA4: Ruis ... 1J 57
Brixham Gdns. IG3: Ilf ... 5J 71
Brixham Rd. DA16: Well ... 1D 126
Brixham St. E16 ... 1E 106
BRIXTON ... 4K 119
Brixton Hill SW2 ... 7J 119
Brixton Hill Ct. SW2 ... 5K 119
Brixton Hill Pl. SW2 ... 7J 119
Brixton Oval SW2 ... 4A 120
Brixton Recreation Cen. ... 3A 120
(off Brixton Sta. Rd.)
Brixton Rd. SE11 ... 7J 19 (6A 102)
SW9 ... 4A 120
Brixton Sta. Rd. SW9 ... 3A 120
Brixton Water La. SW2 ... 5K 119
Broadacre Cl. UB10: Ick ... 3D 56
Broadash Cl. SW16 ... 3A 138
Broadbent Cl. N6 ... 1F 65
Broadbent St. W1 ... 2J 11 (7F 83)
Broadberry Ct. N18 ... 6C 34
Broadbridge Cl. SE3 ... 7J 105
Broad Comn. Est. N16 ... 1G 67
(off Osbaldeston Rd.)
Broadcoombe CR2: Sels ... 7J 169
Broad Ct. WC2 ... 1F 13 (6J 83)
Broadcroft Av. HA7: Stan ... 2D 42
Broadcroft Rd. BR5: Pet W ... 7H 161
Broadeaves Cl. CR2: S Croy ... 5E 168
Broadfield NW6 ... 6K 63
Broadfield Cl. CR0: Wadd ... 2K 167
NW2 ... 3E 62
Broadfield Ct. HA2: Harr ... 1F 41
(off Broadfields)
WD23: B Hea ... 2D 26
Broadfield La. NW1 ... 7J 65
Broadfield Pde. HA8: Edg ... 3C 28
(off Glengall Rd.)
Broadfield Rd. SE6 ... 7G 123
Broadfields HA2: Harr ... 2F 41
KT8: E Mos ... 6J 149
Broadfields Av. HA8: Edg ... 4C 28
N21 ... 6F 23
Broadfields Hgts. HA8: Edg ... 4C 28
Broadfield Sq. EN1: Enf ... 2C 24
Broadfields Way NW10 ... 5B 62
Broadfield Way IG9: Buck H ... 3F 37

Broadford Ho.—Broom Pk.

Broadford Ho. E1 . . . 4A 86
(off Commodore St.)
Broadgate EC2 . . . 6F 9
Broadgate Circle . . . 6G 9 (5E 84)
Broadgate Circ. EC2 . . . 5G 9 (5E 84)
Broadgate Plaza EC2 . . . 5E 84
Broadgate Rd. E16 . . . 6B 88
Broadgates Av. EN4: Had W . . . 1E 20
Broadgates Ct. SE11 . . . 6K 19
(off Cleaver St.)
Broadgates Rd. SW18 . . . 1B 136
Broadgate Twr. EC2 . . . 4H 9 (4E 84)
BROAD GREEN . . . 7B 156
Broad Grn. Av. CR0: C'don . . . 7B 156
Broadhead Apts. E3 . . . 3B 86
(off St Clements Av.)
Broadhead Strand NW9 . . . 1B 44
Broadheath Dr. BR7: Chst . . . 5D 142
Broadhinton Rd. SW4 . . . 3F 119
Broadhurst Av. HA8: Edg . . . 4C 28
IG3: Ilf . . . 4K 71
Broadhurst Cl. NW6 . . . 6A 64
TW10: Rich . . . 5F 115
Broadhurst Gdns. HA4: Ruis . . . 2A 58
NW6 . . . 6K 63
Broadis Way RM13: Rain . . . 2K 91
Broadlands E17 . . . 3A 50
TW13: Hanw . . . 3E 130
Broadlands Av. EN3: Enf H . . . 3C 24
SW16 . . . 2J 137
TW17: Shep . . . 6E 146
Broadlands Cl. EN3: Enf H . . . 3D 24
N6 . . . 7E 46
SW16 . . . 2J 137
Broadlands Ct. TW9: Kew . . . 7G 97
(off Kew Gdns. Rd.)
Broadlands Lodge N6 . . . 7D 46
Broadlands Rd. BR1: Broml . . . 4K 141
N6 . . . 7D 46
Broadlands Way KT3: N Mald . . . 6B 152
Broad La. EC2 . . . 5G 9 (5E 84)
N8 . . . 5K 47
N15 . . . 4F 49
N17 . . . 4G 49
TW12: Hamp . . . 7D 130
Broad Lawn SE9 . . . 2E 142
Broadlawns Ct. HA3: Hrw W . . . 1K 41
Broadley St. NW8 . . . 5B 4 (5B 82)
Broadley Ter. NW1 . . . 4D 4 (4C 82)
Broadmayne SE17 . . . 5D 102
(off Portland St.)
Broadmead SE6 . . . 3C 140
W14 . . . 4G 99
Broadmead Av. KT4: Wor Pk . . . 7C 152
Broadmead Cen. IG8: Wfd G . . . 7F 37
(off Navestock Cres.)
Broadmead Cl. HA5: Hat E . . . 1C 40
TW12: Hamp . . . 6E 130
Broadmead Ct. IG8: Wfd G . . . 6D 36
Broadmead Rd. IG8: Wfd G . . . 6D 36
(not continuous)
UB4: Yead . . . 4C 76
UB5: N'olt . . . 4C 76
Broad Oak IG8: Wfd G . . . 5E 36
TW16: Sun . . . 6H 129
Broad Oak Cl. E4 . . . 5H 35
Broadoak Ct. SW9 . . . 3A 120
(off Gresham Rd.)
Broadoak Ho. NW6 . . . 1K 81
(off Mortimer Cres.)
Broadoak Rd. DA8: Erith . . . 7K 109
Broadoaks KT6: Surb . . . 2H 163
Broadoaks Way BR2: Broml . . . 5H 159
Broad Pas. W3 . . . 1B 98
Broad Sanctuary SW1 . . . 7D 12 (2H 101)
Broadstone NW1 . . . 7H 65
(off Agar Gro.)
Broadstone Ho. SW8 . . . 7K 101
(off Dorset Rd.)
Broadstone Pl. W1 . . . 6G 5 (5E 82)
Broad St. RM10: Dag . . . 7G 73
TW11: Tedd . . . 6K 131
Broad St. Av. EC2 . . . 6G 9 (5E 84)
Broad St. Mkt. RM10: Dag . . . 7G 73
Broad St. Pl. EC2 . . . 6F 9
Broadview NW9 . . . 6G 43
Broadview Pl. E5 . . . 1J 67
Broadview Rd. SW16 . . . 7H 137
Broad Wlk. N21 . . . 2E 32
NW1 . . . 1H 5 (1E 82)
SE3 . . . 2A 124
TW5: Hest . . . 1B 112
TW9: Kew . . . 7F 97
W1 . . . 3F 11 (7D 82)
Broadwalk E18 . . . 3H 51
HA2: Harr . . . 5E 40
The Broad Wlk. KT8: E Mos . . . 4K 149
W8 . . . 1K 99
The Broadwalk HA6: Nwood . . . 2E 38
Broadwalk Ct. W8 . . . 1J 99
(off Palace Gdns. Ter.)
Broadwalk Ho. EC2 . . . 5G 9
SW7 . . . 2A 100
(off Hyde Pk. Ga.)
Broad Wlk. La. NW11 . . . 7H 45
Broadwalk Shop. Cen.
Edgware . . . 6C 28
Broadwall SE1 . . . 4K 13 (1A 102)
Broadwater Farm Est. N17 . . . 2D 48
Broadwater Gdns. BR6: Farnb . . . 4F 173
Broadwater Rd. N17 . . . 1E 48
SE28 . . . 3H 107
SW17 . . . 4C 136
Broadway DA6: Bex . . . 4E 126
(not continuous)
DA7: Bex . . . 4H 127
E15 . . . 7F 69
IG11: Bark . . . 1G 89
SW1 . . . 7C 12 (3H 101)
W7 . . . 1J 95
W13 . . . 1A 96
The Broadway CR0: Bedd . . . 4J 167
E4 . . . 6A 36
E13 . . . 2K 87
HA2: Harr . . . 2H 59
HA3: W'stone . . . 2J 41
HA6: Nwood . . . 2J 39
HA7: Stan . . . 5H 27
HA9: Wemb . . . 3E 60
IG8: Wfd G . . . 6E 36
KT7: T Ditt . . . 7J 149
N8 . . . 6J 47
N9 . . . 3B 34
N11 . . . 5J 31
N14 . . . 1C 32
(off The Bourne)
The Broadway N22 . . . 2A 48
NW7 . . . 5F 29
RM8: Dag . . . 1F 73
SM1: Sutt . . . 5A 166
SM3: Cheam . . . 6G 165
SW13 . . . 2A 116
SW19 . . . 6H 135
UB1: S'hall . . . 7B 76
UB6: G'frd . . . 4G 77
W3 . . . 2G 97
(off Ridgeway Dr.)
W5 . . . 7D 78
Broadway Arc. W6 . . . 4E 98
(off Hammersmith B'way.)
Broadway Av. CR0: C'don . . . 5D 156
TW1: Twick . . . 6B 114
The Broadway Cen. . . . 4E 98
Broadway Chambers W6 . . . 4E 98
(off Hammersmith B'way.)
Broadway Cl. IG8: Wfd G . . . 6E 36
Broadway Ct. BR3: Beck . . . 3E 158
SW19 . . . 6J 135
Broadway Gdns. CR4: Mitc . . . 4C 154
IG8: Wfd G . . . 6E 36
Broadway Ho. BR1: Broml . . . 5F 141
(off Bromley Rd.)
BR1: Broml . . . 3J 159
(High St.)
E8 . . . 1H 85
(off Ada St.)
Broadway Mans. SW6 . . . 7J 99
(off Fulham Rd.)
Broadway Mkt. E8 . . . 1H 85
(not continuous)
IG6: Ilf . . . 1H 53
(not continuous)
SW17 . . . 4D 136
Broadway Mkt. M. E8 . . . 1G 85
Broadway M. E5 . . . 7F 49
N13 . . . 5E 32
N21 . . . 1G 33
Broadway Pde. E4 . . . 6K 35
(off The Broadway)
HA2: Harr . . . 5F 41
N8 . . . 6J 47
UB3: Hayes . . . 1J 93
Broadway Pl. SW19 . . . 6H 135
Broadway Retail Pk. . . . 4F 63
Broadway Shop. Cen.
Bexleyheath . . . 4G 127
Broadway Shop. Mall
St James's Park . . . 1C 18 (3H 101)
Broadway Sq. DA6: Bex . . . 4G 127
The Broadway Theatre
Barking . . . 1G 89
Catford . . . 7D 122
Broadway Wlk. E14 . . . 2C 104
Broadwell Ct. TW5: Hest . . . 1B 112
(off Springwell Rd.)
Broadwell Pde. NW6 . . . 6K 63
(off Broadhurst Gdns.)
Broadwick St. W1 . . . 2B 12 (7G 83)
Broadwood Av. HA4: Ruis . . . 6F 39
Broadwood Ter. W8 . . . 4H 99
Broad Yd. EC1 . . . 4A 8 (4B 84)
Brocade Cl. SM6: W'gton . . . 2F 167
Brocas Cl. NW3 . . . 7C 64
Brockbridge Ho. SW15 . . . 6B 116
Brockdene Dr. BR2: Kes . . . 4B 172
Brockdish Av. IG11: Bark . . . 5K 71
Brockenhurst KT8: W Mole . . . 5D 148
Brockenhurst Av. KT4: Wor Pk . . . 1A 164
Brockenhurst Gdns. IG1: Ilf . . . 5G 71
NW7 . . . 5F 29
Brockenhurst M. N18 . . . 4B 34
Brockenhurst Rd. CR0: C'don . . . 7H 157
Brockenhurst Way SW16 . . . 2H 155
Brocket Ho. SW8 . . . 2H 119
Brockham Cl. SW19 . . . 5H 135
Brockham Ct. CR2: S Croy . . . 5C 168
Brockham Cres. CR0: New Ad . . . 7F 171
Brockham Dr. IG2: Ilf . . . 6F 53
SW2 . . . 7K 119
Brockham Ho. NW1 . . . 1G 83
(off Bayham Pl.)
SW2 . . . 7K 119
(off Brockham Dr.)
Brockham St. SE1 . . . 7D 14 (3C 102)
Brockhurst Cl. HA7: Stan . . . 6E 26
Brockill Cres. SE4 . . . 4A 122
Brocklebank Ho. E16 . . . 1E 106
(off Glenister St.)
Brocklebank Retail Park . . . 4K 105
Brocklebank Rd. SE7 . . . 4K 105
SW18 . . . 7A 118
Brocklehurst St. SE14 . . . 7K 103
Brocklesby Rd. SE25 . . . 4H 157
BROCKLEY . . . 4K 121
Brockley Av. HA7: Stan . . . 3K 27
Brockley Cl. HA7: Stan . . . 4K 27
Brockley Cres. RM5: Col R . . . 1J 55
Brockley Cross SE4 . . . 3A 122
Brockley Cross Bus. Cen. SE4 . . . 3A 122
Brockley Footpath SE15 . . . 3J 121
(not continuous)
Brockley Gdns. SE4 . . . 2B 122
Brockley Gro. SE4 . . . 5B 122
Brockley Hall Rd. SE4 . . . 5A 122
Brockley Hill HA7: Stan . . . 1H 27
Brockley Jack Theatre . . . 5A 122
Brockley M. SE4 . . . 5A 122
Brockley Pk. SE23 . . . 7A 122
Brockley Ri. SE23 . . . 1A 140
Brockley Rd. SE4 . . . 3B 122
Brockleyside HA7: Stan . . . 4K 27
Brockley Vw. SE23 . . . 7A 122
Brockley Way SE4 . . . 5K 121
Brockman Ri. BR1: Broml . . . 4F 141
Brockmer Ho. E1 . . . 7H 85
(off Crowder St.)
Brock Pl. E3 . . . 4D 86
Brock Rd. E13 . . . 5K 87
Brocks Dr. SM3: Cheam . . . 3G 165
Brockshot Cl. TW8: Bford . . . 5D 96
Brock St. NW1 . . . 3A 6
(off Triton Sq.)
SE15 . . . 3J 121
Brockway Cl. E11 . . . 2G 69
Brockweir E2 . . . 2J 85
(off Cyprus St.)
Brockwell Av. BR3: Beck . . . 5D 158
Brockwell Cl. BR5: St M Cry . . . 5K 161
Brockwell Ct. SW2 . . . 5A 120
Brockwell Ho. SE11 . . . 7H 19
(off Vauxhall St.)
Brockwell Pk. . . . 6B 120
Brockwell Pk. Gdns. SE24 . . . 7A 120
Brockwell Pk. Lido . . . 6B 120
Brockwell Pk. Row SW2 . . . 7A 120
Brockwell Pas. SE24 . . . 6B 120
Brodia Rd. N16 . . . 3D 152
Brodick Ho. E3 . . . 2B 86
(off Saxon Rd.)
Brodie Ho. SE1 . . . 5F 103
(off Cooper's Rd.)
Brodie Rd. E4 . . . 1K 35
EN2: Enf . . . 1H 23
Brodie St. SE1 . . . 5F 103
Brodlove La. E1 . . . 7K 85
Brodrick Gro. SE2 . . . 4B 108
Brodrick Rd. SW17 . . . 2C 136
Brody Ho. E1 . . . 6J 9
(off Strype St.)
Brograve Gdns. BR3: Beck . . . 2D 158
Broken Wharf EC4 . . . 2C 14 (7C 84)
Brokesley St. E3 . . . 3B 86
Broke Wlk. E8 . . . 1F 85
Bromar Rd. SE5 . . . 3E 120
Bromefield HA7: Stan . . . 1C 42
Bromehead St. E1 . . . 6J 85
Bromell's Rd. SW4 . . . 4G 119
Brome Rd. SE9 . . . 3D 124
Bromfelde Rd. SW4 . . . 3H 119
Bromfelde Wlk. SW4 . . . 2H 119
Bromfield Ct. SE16 . . . 3G 103
(off Ben Smith Way)
Bromfield St. N1 . . . 1A 84
Bromhall Rd. RM8: Dag . . . 6B 72
RM9: Dag . . . 6B 72
Bromhead Rd. E1 . . . 6J 85
(off Jubilee St.)
Bromhedge SE9 . . . 3D 142
Bromholm Rd. SE2 . . . 3B 108
Bromleigh Ct. SE23 . . . 2G 139
Bromleigh Ho. SE1 . . . 7J 15
(off St Saviour's Est.)
BROMLEY
BR1 . . . 2J 159
E3 . . . 3D 86
Bromley Av. BR1: Broml . . . 7G 141
Bromley Coll. BR1: Broml . . . 1J 159
BROMLEY COMMON . . . 7C 160
Bromley Comn. BR2: Broml . . . 4A 160
Bromley Cres. BR2: Broml . . . 3H 159
HA4: Ruis . . . 4H 57
Bromley FC . . . 5K 159
Bromley Gdns. BR2: Broml . . . 3H 159
Bromley Golf Course . . . 7C 160
Bromley Gro. BR2: Broml . . . 2F 159
Bromley Hall Rd. E14 . . . 5E 86
Bromley High St. E3 . . . 3D 86
Bromley Hill BR1: Broml . . . 6G 141
Bromley Ho. BR1: Broml . . . 1J 159
(off North St.)
Bromley Ind. Cen. BR1: Broml . . . 3B 160
Bromley La. BR7: Chst . . . 7G 143
Bromley Little Theatre . . . 1J 159
BROMLEY PARK . . . 1G 159
Bromley Pk. BR1: Broml . . . 1H 159
Bromley Pl. W1 . . . 5A 6 (5G 83)
Bromley Rd. BR1: Broml . . . 1D 140
BR2: Broml . . . 2D 158
BR3: Beck . . . 1D 158
BR7: Chst . . . 1F 161
E10 . . . 6D 50
E17 . . . 3C 50
N17 . . . 1G 49
N18 . . . 3J 33
SE6 . . . 1D 140
Bromley St. E1 . . . 5K 85
Bromley Tennis Cen. . . . 3H 173
BROMPTON . . . 2D 16 (3C 100)
Brompton Arc. SW3 . . . 7E 10
Brompton Cemetery . . . 6K 99
Brompton Cl. SE20 . . . 2G 157
TW4: Houn . . . 5D 112
Brompton Cotts. SW10 . . . 6A 100
(off Hollywood Rd.)
Brompton Ct. BR1: Broml . . . 1J 159
(off Tweedy Rd.)
Brompton Gro. N2 . . . 4C 46
Brompton M. N12 . . . 6F 31
Brompton Oratory . . . 2C 16 (3C 100)
Brompton Pk. Cres. SW6 . . . 6K 99
Brompton Pl. SW3 . . . 1D 16 (3C 100)
Brompton Rd. SW1 . . . 3C 16 (4C 100)
SW3 . . . 3C 16 (4C 100)
SW7 . . . 4C 100
Brompton Sq. SW3 . . . 1C 16 (3C 100)
Brompton Ter. SE18 . . . 1D 124
Brompton Vs. SW6 . . . 6J 99
(off Lillie Rd.)
Bromwich Av. N6 . . . 2E 64
Bromyard Av. W3 . . . 7A 80
Bromyard Ho. SE15 . . . 7H 103
(off Commercial Way)
Bromyward Ho. W3 . . . 1B 98
Bron Ct. NW6 . . . 1J 81
BRONDESBURY . . . 7H 63
Brondesbury Ct. NW2 . . . 6F 63
Brondesbury M. NW6 . . . 7J 63
BRONDESBURY PARK . . . 1E 80
Brondesbury Pk. NW2 . . . 6E 62
NW6 . . . 6E 62
Brondesbury Pk. Mans. NW6 . . . 1G 81
(off Salusbury Rd.)
Brondesbury Rd. NW6 . . . 2H 81
Brondesbury Vs. NW6 . . . 2H 81
Bronhill Ter. N17 . . . 1G 49
Bronsart Rd. SW6 . . . 7G 99
Bronson Rd. SW20 . . . 2F 153
Bronte Cl. DA8: Erith . . . 7H 109
E7 . . . 4J 69
IG2: Ilf . . . 4E 52
Bronte Ct. W3 . . . 2G 97
W14 . . . 3F 99
(off Girdler's Rd.)
Bronte Ho. N16 . . . 5E 66
SW4 . . . 7G 119
SW17 . . . 3B 136
(off Grosvenor Way)
Bronti Cl. SE17 . . . 5C 102
Bronwen Ct. NW8 . . . 2A 4
(off Grove End Rd.)
Bronze Age Way DA8: Erith . . . 2H 109
DA17: Belv . . . 2H 109
Bronze St. SE8 . . . 7C 104
Bronze Wlk. W12 . . . 7F 81
Brook Av. HA8: Edg . . . 6C 28
HA9: Wemb . . . 2F 61
RM10: Dag . . . 7H 73
Brookbank Av. W7 . . . 5H 77
Brookbank Rd. SE13 . . . 3C 122
Brook Cl. HA4: Ruis . . . 7G 39
NW7 . . . 7B 30
SW17 . . . 2E 136
SW20 . . . 3D 152
TW19: Stanw . . . 7B 110
W3 . . . 1G 97
Brook Ct. BR3: Beck . . . 1B 158
E11 . . . 3G 69
E17 . . . 3J 35
EC4 . . . 2E 14
(off Laurence Pountney La.)
HA8: Edg . . . 5C 28
IG11: Bark . . . 1K 89
(Sebastian Ct.)
IG11: Bark . . . 2G 89
(Spring Pl.)
SE12 . . . 3A 142
Brook Cres. E4 . . . 4H 35
N9 . . . 4C 34
Brookdale N11 . . . 4B 32
Brookdale Rd. DA5: Bexl . . . 6E 126
E17 . . . 3C 50
SE6 . . . 7D 122
(Catford B'way.)
SE6 . . . 6D 122
(Medusa Rd.)
Brookdales NW11 . . . 4G 45
Brookdene Rd. SE18 . . . 4J 107
Brook Dr. HA1: Harr . . . 4G 41
HA4: Ruis . . . 7G 39
SE11 . . . 2K 19 (3A 102)
Brooke Av. HA2: Harr . . . 3G 59
Brooke Cl. WD23: Bush . . . 1B 26
Brooke Ct. W10 . . . 2G 81
(off Kilburn La.)
Brooke Ho. SE14 . . . 1A 122
WD23: Bush . . . 1B 26
Brookehowse Rd. SE6 . . . 2C 140
Brookend Rd. DA15: Sidc . . . 1J 143
Brooke Rd. E5 . . . 3G 67
E17 . . . 4E 50
N16 . . . 3F 67
Brooke's Ct. EC1 . . . 6J 7 (5A 84)
Brooke's Mkt. EC1 . . . 5K 7
Brooke St. EC1 . . . 6J 7 (5A 84)
Brooke Way WD23: Bush . . . 1B 26
Brookfield N6 . . . 3E 64
Brookfield Av. E17 . . . 4E 50
NW7 . . . 6J 29
SM1: Sutt . . . 4B 166
W5 . . . 4D 78
Brookfield Cl. NW7 . . . 6J 29
Brookfield Ct. N12 . . . 4E 30
UB6: G'frd . . . 3G 77
Brookfield Cres. HA3: Kenton . . . 5E 42
NW7 . . . 6J 29
Brookfield Gdns. KT10: Clay . . . 6A 162
Brookfield Pk. NW5 . . . 3F 65
Brookfield Path IG8: Wfd G . . . 6B 36
Brookfield Rd. E9 . . . 6A 68
N9 . . . 3B 34
W4 . . . 2K 97
Brookfields EN3: Pond E . . . 4E 24
Brookfields Av. CR4: Mitc . . . 5C 154
Brook Gdns. E4 . . . 4J 35
KT2: King T . . . 1J 151
SW13 . . . 3B 116
Brook Ga. W1 . . . 3F 11 (7D 82)
BROOK GREEN . . . 4F 99
Brook Grn. W6 . . . 3F 99
Brook Grn. Flats W14 . . . 3F 99
(off Dunsany Rd.)
Brookhill Cl. EN4: E Barn . . . 5H 21
SE18 . . . 5F 107
Brookhill Rd. EN4: E Barn . . . 5H 21
SE18 . . . 6F 107
Brook Ho. E1 . . . 7G 85
(off Fletcher St.)
W6 . . . 4E 98
(off Shepherd's Bush Rd.)
Brookhouse Gdns. E4 . . . 4B 36
Brook Ho's. NW1 . . . 2G 83
(off Cranleigh St.)
Brook Ind. Est. UB4: Yead . . . 1B 94
Brooking Cl. RM8: Dag . . . 3C 72
Brooking Rd. E7 . . . 5J 69
Brookland Cl. NW11 . . . 4J 45
Brookland Gth. NW11 . . . 4J 45
Brookland Hill NW11 . . . 4K 45
Brookland Ri. NW11 . . . 4J 45
The Brooklands TW7: Isle . . . 1H 113
Brooklands App. RM1: Rom . . . 4K 55
Brooklands Av. DA15: Sidc . . . 2H 143
SW19 . . . 2K 135
Brooklands Cl. RM7: Rom . . . 4K 55
TW16: Sun . . . 1G 147
Brooklands Ct. CR4: Mitc . . . 2B 154
KT1: King T . . . 4D 150
(off Surbiton Rd.)
N21 . . . 5J 23
NW6 . . . 7H 63
Brooklands Dr. UB6: G'frd . . . 1C 78
Brooklands La. RM7: Rom . . . 4K 55
(not continuous)
Brooklands Pk. SE3 . . . 3J 123
Brooklands Pas. SW8 . . . 1H 119
Brooklands Pl. TW12: Hamp H . . . 5F 131
Brooklands Rd. KT7: T Ditt . . . 1A 162
RM7: Rom . . . 4K 55
Brooklands Ter. TW16: Sun . . . 4J 147
Brook La. BR1: Broml . . . 6J 141
DA5: Bexl, Bex . . . 6D 126
SE3 . . . 2K 123
Brook La. Bus. Cen. TW8: Bford . . . 5D 96
Brook La. Nth. TW8: Bford . . . 5D 96
(not continuous)
Brooklea Cl. NW9 . . . 1A 44
Brook Lodge NW11 . . . 5F 45
(off Nth. Circular Rd.)
RM7: Rom . . . 4K 55
(off Brooklands Rd.)
Brooklyn SE20 . . . 7G 139
Brooklyn Av. SE25 . . . 4H 157
Brooklyn Cl. SM5: Cars . . . 2C 166
Brooklyn Ct. W12 . . . 1E 98
(off Frithville Gdns.)
Brooklyn Gro. SE25 . . . 4H 157
Brooklyn Rd. BR2: Broml . . . 5B 160
SE25 . . . 4H 157
Brookman Ho. E3 . . . 2B 86
(off Mostyn Gro.)
Brookmarsh Ind. Est. SE10 . . . 7D 104
Brook Mead KT19: Ewe . . . 6A 164
Brookmead CR0: Bedd . . . 6G 155
Brookmead Av. BR1: Broml . . . 5D 160
Brookmead Ind. Est. CR0: Bedd . . . 6G 155
Brook Mdw. N12 . . . 3E 30
Brook Mdw. Cl. IG8: Wfd G . . . 6B 36
Brookmead Rd. CR0: C'don . . . 6G 155
Brook M. IG7: Chig . . . 3K 37
N13 . . . 5F 33
Brook M. Nth. W2 . . . 2A 10 (7A 82)
Brookmill Rd. SE8 . . . 1C 122
Brook Pde. IG7: Chig . . . 3K 37
Brook Pk. Cl. N21 . . . 5G 23
Brook Pl. EN5: Barn . . . 5D 20
Brook Retail Pk.
South Ruislip . . . 5B 58
Brook Ri. IG7: Chig . . . 3K 37
Brook Rd. CR7: Thor H . . . 4C 156
IG2: Ilf . . . 6J 53
IG9: Buck H, Wfd G . . . 2D 36
KT6: Surb . . . 2E 162
N8 . . . 4J 47
N22 . . . 3K 47
NW2 . . . 2B 62
TW1: Twick . . . 6A 114
Brook Rd. Sth. TW8: Bford . . . 6D 96
Brooks Apts. E3 . . . 5C 86
(off Geoff Cade Way)
Brooks Av. E6 . . . 4D 88
Brooksbank Ho. E9 . . . 6J 67
(off Retreat Pl.)
Brooksbank St. E9 . . . 6J 67
Brooksby Ho. N1 . . . 7A 66
(off Liverpool Rd.)
Brooksby M. N1 . . . 7A 66
Brooksby St. N1 . . . 7A 66
Brooksby's Wlk. E9 . . . 5K 67
Brooks Cl. SE9 . . . 2E 142
Brooks Ct. SW11 . . . 7G 101
Brookscroft E17 . . . 3D 50
Brookscroft Rd. E17 . . . 1D 50
(not continuous)
Brooks Farm . . . 7D 50
Brookshill HA3: Hrw W . . . 5C 26
Brookshill Av. HA3: Hrw W . . . 5C 26
Brookshill Dr. HA3: Hrw W . . . 5C 26
Brookshill Ga. HA3: Hrw W . . . 5C 26
Brookside BR6: Orp . . . 7K 161
EN4: E Barn . . . 6H 21
N21 . . . 6E 22
SM5: Cars . . . 5E 166
UB10: Uxb . . . 7B 56
Brookside Cl. EN5: Barn . . . 6B 20
HA2: Harr . . . 4C 58
HA3: Kenton . . . 5D 42
TW13: Felt . . . 3J 129
Brookside Cres. KT4: Wor Pk . . . 1C 164
Brookside Rd. N9 . . . 4C 34
(not continuous)
N19 . . . 2G 65
NW11 . . . 6G 45
UB4: Yead . . . 7A 76
Brookside Sth. EN4: E Barn . . . 7K 21
Brookside Wlk. N3 . . . 3G 45
Brookside Way CR0: C'don . . . 6K 157
Brooks La. W4 . . . 6G 97
Brooks Lodge N1 . . . 2E 84
Brook's M. W1 . . . 2J 11 (7F 83)
Brook Sq. SE18 . . . 1C 124
Brooks Rd. E13 . . . 1J 87
W4 . . . 5G 97
Brook St. DA8: Erith . . . 5H 109
DA17: Belv, Erith . . . 5H 109
KT1: King T . . . 2E 150
N17 . . . 2F 49
W1 . . . 2H 11 (7F 83)
W2 . . . 2B 10 (7B 82)
Brooksville Av. NW6 . . . 1G 81
Brook Va. DA8: Erith . . . 1H 127
Brook Valley Gdns. EN5: Barn . . . 5C 20
Brookview Ct. EN1: Enf . . . 5K 23
Brookview Rd. SW16 . . . 5G 137
Brookville Rd. SW6 . . . 7H 99
Brook Wlk. HA8: Edg . . . 6E 28
N2 . . . 1B 46
Brook Way IG7: Chig . . . 3K 37
Brookway SE3 . . . 3J 123
Brookwell Ho. E17 . . . 4K 49
Brookwood Av. SW13 . . . 2B 116
Brookwood Cl. BR2: Broml . . . 4H 159
Brookwood Ho. SE1 . . . 7B 14
(off Webber St.)
Brookwood Rd. SW18 . . . 1H 135
TW3: Houn . . . 2F 113
Broom Cl. BR2: Broml . . . 6C 160
TW11: Tedd . . . 7D 132
Broomcroft Av. UB5: N'olt . . . 3A 76
Broome Rd. TW12: Hamp . . . 7D 130
Broome Way SE5 . . . 7D 102
Broomfield E17 . . . 7B 50
NW1 . . . 7E 64
(off Ferdinand St.)
TW16: Sun . . . 1J 147
Broomfield Av. N13 . . . 5E 32
Broomfield Ct. N2 . . . 4C 46
Broomfield Ho. HA7: Stan . . . 3F 27
(off Stanmore Hill)
SE17 . . . 4E 102
(off Massinger St.)
Broomfield La. N13 . . . 4D 32
Broomfield Pl. W13 . . . 1B 96
Broomfield Rd. BR3: Beck . . . 3A 158
DA6: Bex . . . 5G 127
KT5: Surb . . . 1F 163
N13 . . . 5D 32
RM6: Chad H . . . 7D 54
TW9: Kew . . . 1F 115
TW11: Tedd . . . 6C 132
W13 . . . 1B 96
Broomfield St. E14 . . . 5C 86
Broom Gdns. CR0: C'don . . . 3C 170
Broomgrove Gdns. HA8: Edg . . . 1G 43
Broomgrove Rd. SW9 . . . 2K 119
Broomhall Rd. CR2: Sande . . . 7D 168
BROOM HILL . . . 7K 161
Broomhill Ct. IG8: Wfd G . . . 6D 36
Broomhill Ri. DA6: Bex . . . 5G 127
Broomhill Rd. BR6: Orp . . . 7K 161
IG3: Ilf . . . 2A 72
IG8: Wfd G . . . 6D 36
(not continuous)
SW18 . . . 5J 117
Broomhill Wlk. IG8: Wfd G . . . 6C 36
Broomhouse La. SW6 . . . 2J 117
Broomhouse Rd. SW6 . . . 2J 117
Broomloan La. SM1: Sutt . . . 2J 165
Broom Lock TW11: Tedd . . . 6C 132
Broom Mead DA6: Bex . . . 6G 127
Broom Pk. TW11: Tedd . . . 7D 132

Broom Rd.—Burleigh Gdns.

Broom Rd. CR0: C'don 3C 170
TW11: Tedd 5B 132
Broomsleigh Bus. Pk. SE26 5B 140
Broomsleigh St. NW6 5H 63
Broom Water TW11: Tedd 6C 132
Broom Water W. TW11: Tedd 5C 132
Broomwood Cl. CR0: C'don 5K 157
DA5: Bexl 2K 145
Broomwood Rd. SW11 6D 118
Broseley Gro. SE26 5A 140
Brosse Way BR2: Broml 6C 160
Broster Gdns. SE25 3F 157
Brotherstone Wlk. TW9: Kew 1H 115
Brouard Ct. BR1: Broml 3J 159
Brougham Rd. E8 1G 85
W3 6J 79
Brougham St. SW11 2D 118
Brough Cl. KT2: King T 5D 132
SW8 7J 101
Broughton Av. N3 3G 45
TW10: Ham 3B 132
Broughton Ct. W13 7B 78
Broughton Dr. SW9 4A 120
Broughton Gdns. N6 6G 47
Broughton Pl. E17 1B 50
Broughton Rd. BR6: Orp 2H 173
CR7: Thor H 6A 156
SW6 2K 117
W13 7B 78
Broughton Rd. App. SW6 2K 117
Broughton St. SW8 2E 118
Broughton St. Ind. Est. SW11 2E 118
Brouncker Rd. W3 2J 97
Browells La. TW13: Felt 2K 129
(not continuous)
Brown Bear Ct. TW13: Hanw 4B 130
Brown Cl. SM6: W'gton 7J 167
Browne Ho. *SE8* *7C 104*
(off Deptford Chu. St.)
Brownell Pl. W7 2K 95
Brownfield Area E14 6D 86
Brownfield St. E14 6D 86
Browngraves Rd. UB3: Harl 7E 92
Brown Hart Gdns. W1 2H 11 (7E 82)
Brownhill Rd. SE6 7D 122
Browning Apts. *E3* *4B 86*
(off Hamlets Way)
Browning Av. KT4: Wor Pk 1D 164
SM1: Sutt 4C 166
W7 6K 77
Browning Cl. DA16: Well 1J 125
E17 4E 50
RM5: Col R 1F 55
TW12: Hamp 4D 130
W9 4A 4 (4A 82)
Browning Ct. *W14* *6H 99*
(off Turneville Rd.)
Browning Ho. *N16* *4E 66*
(off Shakspeare Wlk.)
SE14 *1A 122*
(off Loring Rd.)
W12 *6E 80*
(off Wood La.)
Browning M. W1 6H 5 (5F 83)
Browning Rd. E11 7H 51
E12 5D 70
EN2: Enf 1J 23
Browning St. SE17 5C 102
Browning Way TW5: Hest 1B 112
Brownlea Gdns. IG3: Ilf 2A 72
Brownlow Cl. EN4: E Barn 5G 21
Brownlow Ct. N2 5A 46
N11 *6D 32*
(off Brownlow Rd.)
Brownlow Ho. *SE16* *2G 103*
(off George Row)
Brownlow M. WC1 4H 7 (4K 83)
Brownlow Rd. CR0: C'don 4E 168
E7 4J 69
E8 1F 85
N3 7E 30
N11 6D 32
NW10 7A 62
W13 1A 96
Brownlow St. WC1 6H 7 (5K 83)
Brownrigg Rd. TW15: Ashf 4C 128
Brown's Bldgs. EC3 1H 15 (6E 84)
Brownsea Wlk. NW7 6A 30
Browns La. NW5 5F 65
Brownspring Dr. SE9 4F 143
Brown's Rd. KT5: Surb 7F 151
Browns Rd. E17 3C 50
Brown St. W1 7E 4 (6D 82)
Brownswell Rd. N2 2B 46
BROWNSWOOD PARK 2B 66
Brownswood Rd. N4 3B 66
Broxash Rd. SW11 6E 118
Broxbourne Av. E18 4K 51
Broxbourne Ho. *E3* *4D 86*
(off Empson St.)
Broxbourne Rd. BR6: Orp 1K 173
E7 3J 69
Broxholme Cl. SE25 4D 156
Broxholme Ho. *SW6* *1K 117*
(off Harwood Rd.)
Broxholm Rd. SE27 3A 138
Broxted Rd. SE6 2B 140
Broxwood Way NW8 1C 82
Bruce Av. TW17: Shep 6E 146
Bruce Castle Ct. *N17* *1F 49*
(off Lordship La.)
Bruce Castle Mus. 1E 48
Bruce Castle Rd. N17 1F 49
Bruce Cl. DA16: Well 1B 126
W10 5F 81
Bruce Ct. DA15: Sidc 4K 143
Bruce Gdns. N20 3J 31
Bruce Gro. N17 1E 48
Bruce Hall M. SW17 4E 136
Bruce Ho. W10 5F 81
Bruce Rd. CR4: Mitc 7E 136
E3 3D 86
EN5: Barn 3B 20
HA3: W'stone 2J 41
NW10 7K 61
SE25 4D 156
Bruckner St. W10 3G 81
Brudenell Rd. SW17 3D 136
Bruffs Mdw. UB5: N'olt 6C 58
Bruford Ct. SE8 6C 104
Bruges Pl. *NW1* *7G 65*
(off Randolph St.)
Brumfield Rd. KT19: Ewe 5J 163
Brummel Cl. DA7: Bex 3J 127
Brumwell Av. SE18 5E 106
Brune Ho. E1 6J 9
Brunei Gallery 5D 6 (5H 83)
Brunel Bldg. W2 6A 4
Brunel Cl. SE19 6F 139
TW5: Cran 7K 93
UB5: N'olt 3D 76
Brunel Ct. HA8: Edg 4A 28
SE16 *2J 103*
(off Canon Beck Rd.)
SW13 *2B 116*
(off Westfields Av.)
Brunel Est. W2 5J 81
Brunel Ho. *BR2: Broml* *6C 160*
(off Wells Vw. Dr.)
E14 *5D 104*
(off Ship Yd.)
RM8: Dag 4A 72
SW10 *7B 100*
(off Cheyne Rd.)
Brunel M. W10 3F 81
Brunel Mus. 2J 103
Brunel Pl. UB1: S'hall 6F 77
Brunel Rd. E17 6A 50
IG8: Wfd G 5J 37
SE16 2J 103
W3 5A 80
Brunel Science Pk. UB8: Cowl 3A 74
Brunel St. E16 6H 87
Brunel University
Indoor Athletics Cen. 3A 74
Sports Pk. 4B 74
Brunel University
Uxbridge Campus 3A 74
Brunel Wlk. N15 5E 48
TW2: Whitt 7E 112
Brune St. E1 6J 9 (5F 85)
Brunlees Ho. *SE1* *3C 102*
(off Bath Ter.)
Brunner Cl. NW11 5K 45
Brunner Ho. SE6 4E 140
Brunner Rd. E17 5A 50
W5 4D 78
Bruno Pl. NW9 2J 61
Brunswick Av. N11 3K 31
Brunswick Cen. 3E 6 (4J 83)
Brunswick Cl. DA6: Bex 4D 126
HA5: Pinn 6C 40
KT7: T Ditt 1A 162
TW2: Twick 3H 131
Brunswick Cl. Est. EC1 2A 8 (3B 84)
Brunswick Ct. *EC1* *2A 8*
(off Tompion St.)
EN4: E Barn 5G 21
SE1 7H 15 (2E 102)
SM1: Sutt 4K 165
SW1 *4D 18*
(off Regency St.)
Brunswick Cres. N11 3K 31
Brunswick Flats *W11* *6J 81*
(off Westbourne Gro.)
Brunswick Gdns. IG6: Ilf 1G 53
W5 4E 78
W8 1J 99
Brunswick Gro. N11 3K 31
Brunswick Ho. *E2* *2F 85*
(off Thurtle Rd.)
N3 1H 45
SE16 *3A 104*
(off Brunswick Quay)
W6 *5E 98*
(off Parrs Way)
Brunswick Ind. Pk. N11 4A 32
Brunswick Mans. *WC1* *3F 7*
(off Handel St.)
Brunswick M. SW16 6H 137
W1 7F 5 (6D 82)
BRUNSWICK PARK 3J 31
Brunswick Pk. SE5 1E 120
Brunswick Pk. Gdns. N11 2K 31
Brunswick Pk. Rd. N11 2K 31
Brunswick Pl. N1 2F 9 (3D 84)
NW1 4H 5 (4E 82)
(not continuous)
SE19 7G 139
Brunswick Quay SE16 3K 103
Brunswick Rd. DA6: Bex 4D 126
E10 1E 68
E14 6E 86
EN3: Enf L 1H 25
KT2: King T 1G 151
N15 5E 48
SM1: Sutt 4K 165
W5 4D 78
Brunswick Sq. N17 6A 34
WC1 3F 7 (4J 83)
(not continuous)
Brunswick St. E17 5E 50
Brunswick Ter. BR3: Beck 1D 158
Brunswick Vs. SE5 1E 120
Brunswick Way N11 4A 32
Brunton Pl. E14 6A 86
Brushfield St. E1 5H 9 (5E 84)
Brushwood Cl. E14 5D 86
Brussels Rd. SW11 4B 118
Bruton Cl. BR7: Chst 7D 142
Bruton La. W1 3K 11 (7F 83)
Bruton Pl. W1 3K 11 (7F 83)
Bruton Rd. SM4: Mord 4A 154
Bruton St. W1 3K 11 (7F 83)
Bruton Way W13 5A 78
Brutus Ct. *SE11* *4B 102*
(off Kennington La.)
Bryan Av. NW10 7D 62
Bryan Cl. TW16: Sun 7J 129
Bryan Ho. NW10 7D 62
SE16 2B 104
Bryan Rd. SE16 2B 104
Bryan's All. SW6 2K 117
Bryanston Av. TW2: Whitt 1F 131
Bryanston Cl. UB2: S'hall 4D 94
Bryanston Ct. W1 7E 4
(not continuous)
Bryanstone Ct. SM1: Sutt 3A 166
Bryanstone Rd. N8 5H 47
Bryanston Mans. *W1* *5E 4*
(off York St.)
Bryanston M. E. W1 6E 4 (5D 82)
Bryanston M. W. W1 6E 4 (5D 82)
Bryanston Pl. W1 6E 4 (5D 82)
Bryanston Sq. W1 6E 4 (6D 82)
Bryanston St. W1 1E 10 (6D 82)
Bryan St. N1 1K 83
Bryant Av. RM10: Dag 7J 73
Bryant Cl. EN5: Barn 5C 20
Bryant Ct. *E2* *1F 85*
(off Whiston Rd.)
W3 1K 97
Bryant Ho. *E3* *2C 86*
(off Thomas Fyre Dr.)
Bryant Rd. UB5: N'olt 3A 76
Bryant St. E2 1F 85
E15 7F 69
Bryantwood Rd. N7 5A 66
Brycedale Cres. N14 4C 32
Bryce Ho. *SE14* *6K 103*
(off John Williams Cl.)
Bryce Rd. RM8: Dag 4C 72
Brydale Ho. *SE16* *4K 103*
(off Rotherhithe New Rd.)
Bryden Cl. SE26 5A 140
Brydges Pl. WC2 3E 12 (7J 83)
Brydges Rd. E15 5F 69
Brydon Wlk. N1 1J 83
Bryer Ct. EC2 5C 8
Bryett Rd. N7 3J 65
Bryher Ct. SE11 5J 19
Brymay Cl. E3 2C 86
Brymcourt W9 2K 81
Brynmaer Rd. SW11 1D 118
Bryn-y-mawr Rd. EN1: Enf 4A 24
Bryony Cl. UB8: Hil 5B 74
Bryony Rd. W12 7C 80
Bryony Way TW16: Sun 6J 129
Bubbling Well Sq. *SW18* *5K 117*
(off Ryland Blvd.)
Buccleugh Ho. E5 7G 49
Buchanan Cl. N21 5E 22
Buchanan Ct. *SE16* *4K 103*
(off Worgan St.)
Buchanan Gdns. NW10 2D 80
Buchan Ho. *W3* *2H 97*
(off Hanbury Rd.)
Buchan Rd. SE15 3J 121
Bucharest Rd. SW18 7A 118
Buckden Cl. N2 4C 46
SE12 6J 123
Buckfast Ct. *W13* *7A 78*
(off Romsey Rd.)
Buckfast Ho. N14 5B 22
Buckfast Rd. SM4: Mord 4K 153
Buckfast St. E2 3G 85
Buck Hill Wlk. W2 3B 10 (7B 82)
Buckhold Rd. SW18 6J 117
Buckhurst Av. SM5: Cars 1C 166
Buckhurst Ct. IG9: Buck H 1G 37
BUCKHURST HILL 2G 37
Buckhurst Hill Ho. IG9: Buck H 2E 36
Buckhurst Ho. N7 5H 65
Buckhurst St. E1 4H 85
E2 4H 85
Buckhurst Way IG9: Buck H 4G 37
Buckingham Arc. WC2 3F 13
Buckingham Av. CR7: Thor H 1A 156
DA16: Well 4J 125
KT8: W Mole 2F 149
N20 7F 21
TW14: Felt 6K 111
UB6: G'frd 1A 78
Buckingham Chambers *SW1* *3B 18*
(off Greencoat Pl.)
Buckingham Cl. BR5: Pet W 7J 161
EN1: Enf 2K 23
TW12: Hamp 5D 130
W5 5C 78
Buckingham Ct. NW4 3C 44
UB5: N'olt 2C 76
W7 *4K 77*
(off Copley Cl.)
W11 *7J 81*
(off Kensington Pk. Rd.)
Buckingham Dr. BR7: Chst 4G 143
Buckingham Gdns. CR7: Thor H 2A 156
HA8: Edg 7K 27
KT8: W Mole 2F 149
Buckingham Ga. SW1 1A 18 (3G 101)
Buckingham Gro. UB10: Hil 2C 74
Buckingham La. SE23 7A 122
Buckingham Mans. *NW6* *5K 63*
(off West End La.)
Buckingham M. N1 6E 66
NW10 2B 80
SW1 1A 18
Buckingham Palace 7K 11 (2F 101)
Buckingham Pal. Rd.
SW1 4J 17 (4F 101)
Buckingham Pde. HA7: Stan 5H 27
Buckingham Pl. SW1 1A 18 (3G 101)
Buckingham Rd. CR4: Mitc 4J 155
E10 3D 68
E11 5A 52
E15 5H 69
E18 1H 51
HA1: Harr 5H 41
HA8: Edg 7A 28
IG1: Ilf 2H 71
KT1: King T 4F 151
N1 6E 66
N22 1J 47
NW10 2B 80
TW10: Ham 2D 132
TW12: Hamp 4D 130
Buckingham St. WC2 4F 13 (7J 83)
Buckingham Way SM6: W'gton 7G 167
Buckland Cl. NW7 4H 29
Buckland Ct. *N1* *2E 84*
(off St John's Est.)
UB10: Ick 2E 56
Buckland Cres. NW3 7B 64
Buckland Ho. *SW1* *5J 17*
(part of Abbots Mnr.)
Buckland Ri. HA5: Pinn 1A 40
Buckland Rd. BR6: Orp 4J 173
E10 2E 68
KT9: Chess 5F 163
Bucklands Rd. TW11: Tedd 6C 132
Buckland St. N1 2D 84
Buckland's Wharf KT1: King T 2D 150
Buckland Wlk. SM4: Mord 4A 154
W3 2J 97
Buckland Way KT4: Wor Pk 1E 164
Buck La. NW9 5K 43
Bucklebury *NW1* *3A 6*
(off Stanhope St.)
Buckleigh Av. SW20 3G 153
Buckleigh Rd. SW16 6H 137
Buckleigh Way SE19 7F 139
Buckler Ct. N7 5K 65
Buckler Gdns. SE9 3D 142
Bucklers All. SW6 6H 99
Bucklersbury EC4 1E 14 (6D 84)
Bucklersbury Pas. EC4 6D 84
Buckler's Way SM5: Cars 3D 166
Buckles Ct. DA17: Belv 4D 108
Buckle St. E1 7K 9 (6F 85)
Buckley Cl. SE23 7H 121
Buckley Ct. NW6 7H 63
SE1 3F 103
Buckley Ho. *W14* *2G 99*
(off Holland Pk. Av.)
Buckley Rd. NW6 7H 63
Buckmaster Cl. *SW9* *3A 120*
(off Stockwell Pk. Rd.)
Buckmaster Ho. N7 4K 65
Buckmaster Rd. SW11 4C 118
Bucknall St. WC2 7D 6 (6J 83)
Bucknall Way BR3: Beck 4D 158
Bucknell Cl. SW2 4K 119
Buckner Rd. SW2 4K 119
Bucknill Ho. *SW1* *5J 17*
(off Ebury Bri. Rd.)
Buckrell Rd. E4 2A 36
Buckridge Ho. *EC1* *5J 7*
(off Portpool La.)
Buckshead Ho. *W2* *5J 81*
(off Gt. Western Rd.)
Buckstone Cl. SE23 6J 121
Buckstone Rd. N18 5B 34
Buck St. NW1 7F 65
Buckters Rents SE16 1A 104
Buckthorne Rd. SE4 5A 122
Buckthorn Ho. *DA15: Sidc* *3K 143*
(off Longlands Rd.)
E15 *3G 87*
(off Manor Rd.)
Buck Wlk. E17 4F 51
Buckwheat Ct. DA18: Erith 3D 108
Budd Cl. N12 4E 30
The Buddhapadipa Temple 4F 135
Buddings Circ. HA9: Wemb 3J 61
Buddleia Ho. TW13: Felt 1J 129
Budd's All. TW1: Twick 5C 114
Bude Cl. E17 5B 50
Budge La. CR4: Mitc 7D 154
Budge's Wlk. W2 3A 10
Budleigh Cres. DA16: Well 1C 126
Budleigh Ho. *SE15* *7G 103*
(off Bird in Bush Rd.)
Budoch Ct. IG3: Ilf 2A 72
Budoch Dr. IG3: Ilf 2A 72
Buer Rd. SW6 2G 117
Bugsby's Way SE7 4H 105
SE10 4H 105
Buick Ho. *E3* *4C 86*
(off Wellington Way)
KT2: King T 2F 151
Building 50 SE18 3G 107
Bulbarrow *NW8* *1K 81*
(off Abbey Rd.)
Bulganak Rd. CR7: Thor H 4C 156
Bulinga St. SW1 4E 18
Bullace Row SE5 1D 120
Bull All. DA16: Well 3B 126
Bullard's Pl. E2 3K 85
Bullbanks Rd. DA17: Belv 4J 109
Bulleid Way SW1 4K 17 (4F 101)
Bullen Ho. *E1* *4H 85*
(off Collingwood St.)
Bullen St. SW11 2C 118
Buller Cl. SE15 7G 103
Buller Rd. CR7: Thor H 2D 156
IG11: Bark 7J 71
N17 2G 49
N22 2A 48
NW10 3F 81
Bullers Cl. DA14: Sidc 5E 144
Bullers Wood Dr. BR7: Chst 7D 142
Bullescroft Rd. HA8: Edg 3B 28
Bullfinch Ho. *NW9* *6B 44*
(off Perryfield Way)
Bullingham Mans. *W8* *2J 99*
(off Pitt St.)
Bull Inn Ct. WC2 3F 13
Bullivant St. E14 7E 86
Bull La. BR7: Chst 7H 143
N18 5K 33
RM10: Dag 3H 73
Bullman Cl. DA7: Bex 3H 127
Bull Rd. E15 2H 87
Bullrush Cl. CR0: C'don 6E 156
SM5: Cars 2C 166
Bull's All. SW14 2K 115
Bulls Bri. Cen. UB3: Hayes 3J 93
Bullsbridge Ind. Est.
UB2: S'hall 4K 93
Bulls Bri. Rd. UB2: S'hall 4A 94
UB3: Hayes 3K 93
Bullsbrook Rd. UB4: Yead 1A 94
Bulls Gdns. SW3 3D 16 (4C 100)
Bulls Head Pas. EC3 1G 15
The Bull Theatre 4C 20
Bull Yd. SE15 1G 121
Bulmer Gdns. HA3: Kenton 7D 42
Bulmer M. W11 7J 81
Bulmer Pl. W11 1J 99
Bulstrode Av. TW3: Houn 2D 112
Bulstrode Gdns. TW3: Houn 3E 112
Bulstrode Pl. W1 6H 5 (5E 82)
Bulstrode Rd. TW3: Houn 3E 112
Bulstrode St. W1 7H 5 (6E 82)
Bulwark Ct. *E14* *4E 104*
(off Parkside Sq.)
Bulwer Ct. E11 1F 69
Bulwer Ct. Rd. E11 1F 69
Bulwer Gdns. EN5: New Bar 4F 21
Bulwer Rd. E11 7F 51
EN5: New Bar 4E 20
N18 4K 33
Bulwer St. W12 1E 98
Bunbury Ho. *SE15* *7G 103*
(off Fenham Rd.)
Bunce's La. IG8: Wfd G 7C 36
Bungalow Rd. SE25 4E 156
The Bungalows E10 6E 50
HA2: Harr 4D 58
IG6: Ilf 1J 53
SM6: W'gton 5F 167
SW16 7F 137
UB4: Yead 4B 76
Bunhill Row EC1 3E 8 (4D 84)
Bunhouse Pl. SW1 5H 17 (5E 100)
Bunkers Hill DA14: Sidc 3B 144
DA17: Belv 4G 109
NW11 7A 46
Bunning Way N7 7J 65
Bunns La. NW7 6F 29
(not continuous)
Bunsen Ho. *E3* *2A 86*
(off Grove Rd.)
Bunsen St. E3 2A 86
Buntingbridge Rd. IG2: Ilf 5H 53
Bunting Cl. CR4: Mitc 5D 154
N9 1E 34
Bunting Ct. NW9 2A 44
Bunting Ho. *UB10: Ick* *2E 56*
(off Coyle Dr.)
Bunton St. SE18 3E 106
Bunwell Ho. *E3* *4B 86*
(off William Whiffin Sq.)
Bunyan Ct. EC2 5C 8
Bunyan Rd. E17 3A 50
Buonaparte M. SW1 5C 18 (5H 101)
Burbage Cl. SE1 3D 102
UB3: Hayes 6F 75
Burbage Ho. *N1* *1D 84*
(off Poole St.)
SE14 *6K 103*
(off Samuel Cl.)
Burbage Rd. SE21 6C 120
SE24 6C 120
Burberry Cl. KT3: N Mald 2A 152
Burbidge Rd. TW17: Shep 4C 146
Burbridge Gdns. UB10: Uxb 2A 74
Burbridge Way N17 2G 49
Burcham Cl. TW12: Hamp 7E 130
Burcham St. E14 6D 86
Burcharbro Rd. SE2 6D 108
Burchell Ct. WD23: Bush 1B 26
Burchell Ho. *SE11* *5H 19*
(off Jonathan St.)
Burchell Rd. E10 1D 68
SE15 1H 121
Burcher Gale Gro. SE15 7F 103
Burchetts Way TW17: Shep 6D 146
Burchett Way RM6: Chad H 6F 55
Burchwall Cl. RM5: Col R 1J 55
Burcote Rd. SW18 7B 118
Burden Cl. TW8: Bford 5C 96
Burden Ho. *SW8* *7J 101*
(off Thorncroft St.)
Burdenshott Av. TW10: Rich 4H 115
Burden Way E11 2K 69
Burder Cl. N1 6E 66
Burder Rd. N1 6E 66
Burdett Av. SW20 1C 152
Burdett Cl. DA14: Sidc 5E 144
W7 1K 95
Burdett M. NW3 6B 64
W2 6K 81
Burdett Rd. CR0: C'don 6D 156
E3 4A 86
E14 4A 86
TW9: Rich 2F 115
Burdetts Rd. RM9: Dag 1F 91
Burdock Cl. CR0: C'don 1K 169
Burdock Rd. N17 3G 49
Burdon La. SM2: Cheam 7G 165
Burdon Pk. SM2: Cheam 7H 165
Bure Ct. EN5: New Bar 5E 20
Burfield Cl. SW17 4B 136
Burford Cl. IG6: Ilf 4G 53
RM8: Dag 3C 72
UB10: Ick 4A 56
Burford Gdns. N13 3E 32
Burford Ho. TW8: Bford 5D 96
Burford Rd. BR1: Broml 4C 160
E6 3C 88
E15 1F 87
KT4: Wor Pk 7B 152
SE6 2B 140
SM1: Sutt 2J 165
TW8: Bford 5E 96
Burford Wlk. SW6 7A 100
Burford Way CR0: New Ad 6E 170
Burford Wharf Apts. *E15* *1F 87*
(off Cam Rd.)
Burges Gro. SW13 7D 98
Burges Rd. E6 7C 70
Burgess Av. NW9 6K 43
Burgess Bus. Pk. SE5 7D 102
Burgess Cl. TW13: Hanw 4C 130
Burgess Ct. E6 7E 70
SE6 7C 122
UB1: S'hall *6F 77*
(off Fleming Rd.)
Burgess Hill NW2 4J 63
Burgess Ho. *SE5* *7C 102*
(off Bethwin Rd.)
Burgess Lofts *SE5* *7C 102*
(off Bethwin Rd.)
Burgess M. SW19 6K 135
Burgess Pk. 6D 102
Burgess Rd. E6 7E 70
E15 4G 69
SM1: Sutt 4K 165
Burgess St. E14 5C 86
Burge St. SE1 3D 102
Burgh House 4B 64
Burghill Rd. SE26 4A 140
Burghley Av. KT3: N Mald 1K 151
Burghley Hall Cl. SW19 1G 135
Burghley Ho. SW19 3G 135
Burghley Pl. CR4: Mitc 5D 154
Burghley Rd. E11 1G 69
N8 3A 48
NW5 4F 65
SW19 4F 135
Burghley Twr. W3 7B 80
Burgh St. N1 2B 84
Burgoine Quay KT1: Hamp W 1D 150
Burgon St. EC4 1B 14 (6B 84)
Burgos Cl. CR0: Wadd 6A 168
Burgos Gro. SE10 1D 122
Burgoyne Ho. *TW8: Bford* *5D 96*
(off Ealing Rd.)
Burgoyne Rd. N4 6B 48
SE25 4F 157
SW9 3K 119
TW16: Sun 6H 129
Burgundy Ct. HA4: Ruis 4A 58
Burgundy Ho. *E20* *5E 68*
(off Liberty Bri. Rd.)
Burgundy Pl. W12 1F 99
Burham Cl. SE20 7J 139
Burhill Gro. HA5: Pinn 2C 40
Burke Cl. SW15 4A 116
Burke Lodge E13 3K 87
Burke St. E16 5H 87
(not continuous)
Burket Cl. UB2: S'hall 4C 94
Burland Rd. SW11 5D 118
Burleigh Av. DA15: Sidc 5K 125
SM6: W'gton 3E 166
Burleigh Cl. RM7: Mawney 4H 55
Burleigh Gdns. N14 1B 32
TW15: Ashf 5E 128

Burleigh Ho.—Cadogan Ct.

Burleigh Ho. SW3 . . . . 7B 16
W10 . . . . 5G 81
(off St Charles Sq.)
WC1 . . . . 2F 7
Burleigh Pde. N14 . . . . 1C 32
Burleigh Pl. SW15 . . . . 5F 117
Burleigh Rd. EN1: Enf 4K 23
SM3: Sutt 1G 165
UB10: Hil 1D 74
Burleigh St. WC2 . . . . 2G 13 (7K 83)
Burleigh Wlk. SE6 . . . . 1E 140
Burleigh Way EN2: Enf 3J 23
Burley Cl. E4 . . . . 5H 35
SW16 . . . . 2H 155
Burley Ho. E1 . . . . 6K 85
(off Chudleigh St.)
Burley Rd. E16 . . . . 6A 88
Burlington Arc. W1 . . . . 3A 12 (7G 83)
Burlington Av.
RM7: Rom 6H 55
TW9: Kew 1G 115
Burlington Cl. BR6: Farnb 2F 173
E6 . . . . 6C 88
HA5: Eastc 3K 39
TW14: Bedf 7F 111
W9 . . . . 4J 81
Burlington Cnr. NW1 . . . . 7G 65
(off Camden Rd.)
Burlington Ct. E1 . . . . 7G 85
(off Cable St.)
Burlington Gdns. RM6: Chad H 7E 54
SW6 . . . . 2G 117
W1 . . . . 3A 12 (7G 83)
W3 . . . . 1J 97
W4 . . . . 5J 97
Burlington Ho. N15 . . . . 6D 48
(off Tewkesbury Rd.)
SE16 . . . . 2K 103
(off Province Dr.)
UB7: W Dray 2B 92
(off Park Lodge Av.)
Burlington La. W4 . . . . 7J 97
Burlington M. SW15 . . . . 5H 117
W3 . . . . 1J 97
Burlington Pl. IG8: Wfd G 3E 36
SW6 . . . . 2G 117
Burlington Ri. EN4: E Barn 1H 31
Burlington Rd. CR7: Thor H 2C 156
EN2: Enf 1J 23
KT3: N Mald 4B 152
N10 . . . . 3E 46
N17 . . . . 1G 49
SW6 . . . . 2G 117
TW7: Isle 1H 113
W4 . . . . 5J 97
Burma M. N16 . . . . 4D 66
Burma Rd. N16 . . . . 4D 66
Burmarsh NW5 . . . . 6E 64
Burmarsh Ct. SE20 . . . . 1J 157
Burma Ter. SE19 . . . . 5E 138
Burmester Rd. SW17 . . . . 3A 136
Burnaby Cres. W4 . . . . 6J 97
Burnaby Gdns. W4 . . . . 6H 97
Burnaby St. SW10 . . . . 7A 100
Burnand Ho. W14 . . . . 3F 99
(off Redan St.)
Burnbrae Cl. N12 . . . . 6E 30
Burnbury Rd. SW12 . . . . 1G 137
Burncroft Av. EN3: Enf H 2D 24
Burndell Way UB4: Yead 5B 76
Burne Jones Ho. W14 . . . . 4G 99
Burnell Av. DA16: Well 2A 126
TW10: Ham 5C 132
Burnell Bldg. NW2 . . . . 2E 62
Burnell Gdns. HA7: Stan 2D 42
Burnell Ho. E20 . . . . 5D 68
(off Peloton Av.)
Burnelli Bldg. SW11 . . . . 7F 101
(off Sopwith Way)
Burnell Rd. SM1: Sutt 4K 165
Burnell Wlk. SE1 . . . . 5F 103
(off Cadet Dr.)
Burnels Av. E6 . . . . 3E 88
Burness Cl. N7 . . . . 6K 65
Burne St. NW1 . . . . 5C 4 (5C 82)
Burnett Cl. E9 . . . . 5J 67
Burnett Ho. SE13 . . . . 2E 122
(off Lewisham Hill)
Burnett Rd. IG6: Ilf 7K 37
Burney Av. KT5: Surb 5F 151
Burney St. SE10 . . . . 7E 104
Burnfoot Av. SW6 . . . . 1G 117
Burnham NW3 . . . . 7C 64
Burnham Av. UB10: Ick 4E 56
Burnham Cl. EN1: Enf 1K 23
HA3: W'stone 4A 42
NW7 . . . . 7H 29
SE1 . . . . 4F 103
Burnham Ct. NW4 . . . . 4E 44
(off Brent St.)
NW6 . . . . 7A 64
(off Fairhazel Gdns.)
W2 . . . . 7K 81
(off Moscow Rd.)
Burnham Cres. E11 . . . . 4A 52
Burnham Dr. KT4: Wor Pk 2F 165
Burnham Est. E2 . . . . 3J 85
(off Burnham St.)
Burnham Gdns. CR0: C'don 7F 157
TW4: Cran 1K 111
UB3: Harl 3F 93
Burnham Rd. DA14: Sidc 2E 144
E4 . . . . 5G 35
RM7: Rom 3K 55
RM9: Dag 7B 72
SM4: Mord 4K 153
Burnham St. E2 . . . . 3J 85
KT2: King T 1G 151
Burnham Way SE26 . . . . 5B 140
W13 . . . . 4B 96
Burnhill Cl. SE15 . . . . 7H 103
Burnhill Ho. EC1 . . . . 2C 8
(off Norman St.)
Burnhill Rd. BR3: Beck 2C 158
Burnley Rd. NW10 . . . . 5B 62
SW9 . . . . 2K 119
Burnsall St. SW3 . . . . 6D 16 (5C 100)
Burns Av. DA15: Sidc 6B 126
RM6: Chad H 7C 54
TW14: Felt 6J 111
UB1: S'hall 7E 76
Burns Cl. DA16: Well 1K 125
E17 . . . . 4E 50
SM5: Cars 7E 166
SW19 . . . . 6B 136
UB4: Hayes 5H 75
Burns Ho. E2 . . . . 3J 85
(off Cornwall Av.)
SE17 . . . . 5B 102
(off Doddington Gro.)
Burnside Av. E4 . . . . 6G 35
Burnside Cl. EN5: New Bar 3D 20
SE16 . . . . 1K 103
TW1: Twick 6A 114
Burnside Ct. SM5: Cars 3E 166
Burnside Cres. HA0: Wemb 1D 78
Burnside Rd. RM8: Dag 2C 72
Burns Rd. HA0: Wemb 2E 78
NW10 . . . . 1B 80
SW11 . . . . 2D 118
W13 . . . . 2B 96
Burns Way TW5: Hest 2B 112
Burnt Ash Hgts. BR1: Broml 5K 141
Burnt Ash Hill SE12 . . . . 6H 123
Burnt Ash La. BR1: Broml 7J 141
Burnt Ash Rd. SE12 . . . . 5H 123
Burnthwaite M. SW6 . . . . 7J 99
(off Burnthwaite Rd.)
Burnthwaite Rd. SW6 . . . . 7H 99
BURNT OAK 1H 43
Burnt Oak Apts. E16 . . . . 6J 87
(off Pacific Rd.)
Burnt Oak B'way. HA8: Edg 7B 28
Burnt Oak Flds. HA8: Edg 1J 43
Burnt Oak La. DA15: Sidc 6A 126
(not continuous)
Burntwood Cl. SW18 . . . . 1C 136
Burntwood Grange Rd.
SW18 . . . . 1B 136
Burntwood La. SW17 . . . . 3A 136
Burntwood Vw. SE19 . . . . 5F 139
Buross St. E1 . . . . 6H 85
Burpham Cl. UB4: Yead 5B 76
Burrage Ct. SE16 . . . . 4K 103
(off Worgan St.)
Burrage Gro. SE18 . . . . 4G 107
Burrage Pl. SE18 . . . . 5F 107
Burrage Rd. SE18 . . . . 5G 107
Burrard Ho. E2 . . . . 2J 85
(off Bishop's Way)
Burrard Rd. E16 . . . . 6K 87
NW6 . . . . 5J 63
Burr Cl. DA7: Bex 3F 127
E1 . . . . 4K 15 (1G 103)
Burreed M. RM13: Rain 2J 91
Burrell Cl. CR0: C'don 6A 158
HA8: Edg 2C 28
Burrell Row BR3: Beck 2C 158
Burrell St. SE1 . . . . 4A 14 (1B 102)
Burrells Wharf Sq. E14 . . . . 5D 104
Burrell Towers E10 . . . . 7C 50
Burrhill Ct. SE16 . . . . 3K 103
(off Worgan St.)
Burritt Rd. KT1: King T 2G 151
The Burroughs NW4 . . . . 4D 44
The Burroughs Club 4D 44
Burroughs Cotts. E14 . . . . 5A 86
(off Halley St.)
Burroughs Gdns. NW4 . . . . 4D 44
Burroughs Pde. NW4 . . . . 4D 44
Burrow Ho. SW9 . . . . 2A 120
(off Stockwell Pk. Rd.)
Burrow Rd. SE22 . . . . 4E 120
Burrows M. SE1 . . . . 6A 14 (2B 102)
Burrows Rd. NW10 . . . . 3E 80
Burrow Wlk. SE21 . . . . 7C 120
Burr Rd. SW18 . . . . 1J 135
Bursar St. SE1 . . . . 5G 15 (1E 102)
Bursdon Cl. DA15: Sidc 2K 143
Bursland Rd. EN3: Pond E 4E 24
Burslem St. E1 . . . . 6G 85
Burstock Rd. SW15 . . . . 4G 117
Burston Rd. SW15 . . . . 5F 117
Burston Vs. SW15 . . . . 5F 117
(off St John's Av.)
Burstow Rd. SW20 . . . . 1G 153
Burtenshaw Rd. KT7: T Ditt 7A 150
Burtley Cl. N4 . . . . 1C 66
Burton Bank N1 . . . . 7D 66
(off Yeate St.)
Burton Cl. CR7: Thor H 3D 156
KT9: Chess 7D 162
Burton Ct. KT7: T Ditt 6A 150
SE20 . . . . 2J 157
SW3 . . . . 5F 17
(not continuous)
Burton Gdns. TW5: Hest 1D 112
Burton Gro. SE17 . . . . 5D 102
Burtonhole Cl. NW7 . . . . 4A 30
Burtonhole La. N12 . . . . 4B 30
NW7 . . . . 5K 29
Burton Ho. SE16 . . . . 2H 103
(off Cherry Gdn. St.)
Burton La. SW9 . . . . 2A 120
(not continuous)
Burton M. SW1 . . . . 4H 17 (4E 100)
Burton Pl. WC1 . . . . 2D 6 (3H 83)
Burton Ridge Ct. E3 . . . . 2B 86
(off Festubert Pl.)
Burton Rd. E18 . . . . 3K 51
KT2: King T 7E 132
NW6 . . . . 7H 63
SW9 . . . . 2B 120
(Akerman Rd.)
SW9 . . . . 2A 120
(Evesham Wlk.)
Burtons Ct. E15 . . . . 7F 69
Burton's Rd. TW12: Hamp H 4F 131
Burton St. WC1 . . . . 2D 6 (3H 83)
Burtonwood Ho. N4 . . . . 7D 48
Burtop Rd. Est. SW17 . . . . 3A 136
Burt Rd. E16 . . . . 1A 106
Burts Wharf DA17: Belv 7J 91
Burtt Ho. N1 . . . . 1G 9
(off Aske St.)
Burtwell La. SE27 . . . . 4D 138
Burwash Ho. SE1 . . . . 7F 15
(off Kipling Est.)
Burwash Rd. SE18 . . . . 5H 107
Burway Cl. CR2: S Croy 6E 168
Burwell KT1: King T 2G 151
(off Excelsior Cl.)
Burwell Av. UB6: G'frd 6J 59
Burwell Cl. E1 . . . . 6H 85
Burwell Rd. E10 . . . . 1A 68
Burwell Wlk. E3 . . . . 4C 86
Burwood Av. BR2: Hayes 2K 171
HA5: Eastc 5K 39
Burwood Cl. KT6: Surb 1G 163
Burwood Ho. SW9 . . . . 4B 120
Burwood Pl. EN4: Had W 1F 21
W2 . . . . 7D 4 (6C 82)
Bury Av. HA4: Ruis 6E 38
UB4: Hayes 2G 75
Bury Cl. SE16 . . . . 1K 103
Bury Ct. EC3 . . . . 7H 9 (6E 84)
Buryfield Ct. SE8 . . . . 4K 103
(off Lower Rd.)
Bury Gro. SM4: Mord 5K 153
Bury Hall Vs. N9 . . . . 7A 24
Bury Pl. WC1 . . . . 6E 6 (5J 83)
Bury Rd. E4 . . . . 1B 36
N22 . . . . 2A 48
RM10: Dag 5H 73
Buryside Cl. IG2: Ilf 4K 53
Bury St. EC3 . . . . 1H 15 (6E 84)
HA4: Ruis 5E 38
N9 . . . . 7A 24
SW1 . . . . 4B 12 (1G 101)
Bury St. W. N9 . . . . 7J 23
Bury Wlk. SW3 . . . . 4C 16 (4C 100)
Busbridge Ho. E14 . . . . 5C 86
(off Brabazon St.)
Busby Ho. SW16 . . . . 4G 137
Busby M. NW5 . . . . 6H 65
Busby Pl. NW5 . . . . 6H 65
Busch Cl. TW7: Isle 1B 114
Bushbaby Cl. SE1 . . . . 3E 102
Bushberry Rd. E9 . . . . 6A 68
Bush Cl. IG2: Ilf 5H 53
Bush Cotts. SW18 . . . . 5J 117
Bush Ct. N14 . . . . 1B 32
W12 . . . . 2F 99
Bushell Cl. SW2 . . . . 2K 137
Bushell Grn. WD23: B Hea 2C 26
Bushell St. E1 . . . . 1G 103
Bushell Way BR7: Chst 5E 142
BUSHEY 1C 26
Bushey Av. BR5: Pet W 7H 161
E18 . . . . 3H 51
Bushey Cl. E4 . . . . 3K 35
UB10: Ick 2C 56
Bushey Ct. SW20 . . . . 3D 152
Bushey Down SW12 . . . . 2F 137
BUSHEY HEATH 1C 26
Bushey Hill Rd. SE5 . . . . 1E 120
Bushey La. SM1: Sutt 4J 165
Bushey Lees DA15: Sidc 6K 125
BUSHEY MEAD 2F 153
Bushey Rd. CR0: C'don 2C 170
E13 . . . . 2A 88
N15 . . . . 6E 48
SM1: Sutt 4J 165
(not continuous)
SW20 . . . . 3D 152
UB3: Harl 4G 93
UB10: Ick 2C 56
Bushey Way BR3: Beck 6F 159
Bush Fair Ct. N14 . . . . 6A 22
Bushfield Cl. HA8: Edg 2C 28
Bushfield Cres. HA8: Edg 2C 28
Bush Gro. HA7: Stan 1D 42
NW9 . . . . 7J 43
Bushgrove Rd. RM8: Dag 4D 72
Bush Hill N21 . . . . 7H 23
Bush Hill Pde. EN1: Enf 7J 23
N9 . . . . 7J 23
BUSH HILL PARK 6A 24
Bush Hill Pk. Golf Course 5H 23
Bush Hill Rd. HA3: Kenton 6F 43
N21 . . . . 6J 23
Bush House 2G 13
Bush Ind. Est. N19 . . . . 3G 65
NW10 . . . . 4K 79
Bush La. EC4 . . . . 2E 14 (7D 84)
Bushmead Cl. N15 . . . . 4F 49
Bushmoor Cres. SE18 . . . . 7F 107
Bushnell Rd. SW17 . . . . 2F 137
Bush Rd. E8 . . . . 1H 85
E11 . . . . 7H 51
IG9: Buck H 4G 37
SE8 . . . . 4K 103
TW9: Kew 6F 97
TW17: Shep 5B 146
Bush Theatre 2E 98
Bushway RM8: Dag 4D 72
Bushwood E11 . . . . 7H 51
Bushwood Dr. SE1 . . . . 4F 103
Bushwood Rd. TW9: Kew 6G 97
Bushy Ct. KT1: Hamp W 1C 150
(off Beverley Rd.)
Bushy Pk. 7H 131
Bushy Pk. Gdns. TW11: Tedd 5H 131
Bushy Pk. Rd. TW11: Tedd 7B 132
(not continuous)
Bushy Rd. TW11: Tedd 6K 131
Business Design Centre 1A 84
(off Upper St.)
Buspace Studios W10 . . . . 4G 81
(off Conlan St.)
Butcher Row E14 . . . . 7K 85
Butchers M. UB3: Hayes 7H 75
(off Hemmen La.)
Butchers Rd. E16 . . . . 6J 87
Bute Av. TW10: Ham 2E 132
Bute Ct. SM6: W'gton 5G 167
Bute Gdns. SM6: W'gton 5G 167
TW10: Ham 1E 132
W6 . . . . 4F 99
Bute Gdns. W. SM6: W'gton 5G 167
Bute M. NW11 . . . . 5K 45
Bute Rd. CR0: C'don 1A 168
IG6: Ilf 5F 53
SM6: W'gton 4G 167
Bute St. SW7 . . . . 3A 16 (4B 100)
Bute Wlk. N1 . . . . 6D 66
Butfield Ho. E9 . . . . 6J 67
(off Stevens Av.)
Butler Av. HA1: Harr 7H 41
Butler Cl. HA8: Edg 2H 43
Butler Ct. HA0: Wemb 4A 60
RM8: Dag 2G 73
(off Gosfield Rd.)
SW11 . . . . 1C 118
(off Hyde La.)
Butler Farm Cl. TW10: Ham 4D 132
Butler Ho. E2 . . . . 3J 85
(off Bacton St.)
E3 . . . . 5B 86
(off Geoffrey Chaucer Way)
E14 . . . . 6B 86
(off Burdett St.)
SW9 . . . . 1B 120
(off Lothian Rd.)
Butler Pl. SW1 . . . . 1C 18 (3H 101)
Butler Rd. HA1: Harr 7G 41
NW10 . . . . 7B 62
RM8: Dag 4B 72
Butlers & Colonial Wharf SE1 . . . . 6K 15
(off Shad Thames)
Butlers Cl. TW4: Houn 3D 112
Butlers Dr. E4 . . . . 1K 25
Butler St. E2 . . . . 3J 85
UB10: Hil 4D 74
Butlers Wharf SE1 . . . . 5K 15 (1F 103)
Butlers Wharf W. SE1 . . . . 5J 15
(off Shad Thames)
Butley Ct. E3 . . . . 2A 86
(off Ford St.)
Buttercup Cl. UB5: N'olt 6D 58
Butterfield Cl. N17 . . . . 6H 33
SE16 . . . . 2H 103
TW1: Twick 6K 113
Butterfields E17 . . . . 5E 50
Butterfield Sq. E6 . . . . 6D 88
Butterfly Apts. SW11 . . . . 4C 118
(off Comyn Rd.)
Butterfly Ct. E6 . . . . 3D 88
N15 . . . . 4E 48
(off Bathurst Sq.)
NW9 . . . . 1A 44
Butterfly La. SE9 . . . . 6F 125
Butterfly Wlk. SE5 . . . . 1D 120
(off Denmark Hill)
Butter Hill SM5: Cars 3E 166
SM6: W'gton 3E 166
Butteridges Cl. RM9: Dag 1F 91
Buttermere NW1 . . . . 1K 5
(off Augustus St.)
Buttermere Cl. E15 . . . . 4F 69
SE1 . . . . 4F 103
SM4: Mord 6F 153
TW14: Felt 1H 129
Buttermere Ct. NW8 . . . . 1B 82
(off Boundary Rd.)
Buttermere Dr. SW15 . . . . 5G 117
Buttermere Ho. E3 . . . . 3B 86
(off Mile End Rd.)
Buttermere Wlk. E8 . . . . 6F 67
Butterwick W6 . . . . 4F 99
Butterworth Gdns. IG8: Wfd G 6D 36
Butterworth Ter. SE17 . . . . 5C 102
(off Sutherland Wlk.)
Buttery M. N14 . . . . 3D 32
Buttesland St. N1 . . . . 1F 9 (3D 84)
Buttfield Cl. RM10: Dag 6H 73
Buttmarsh Cl. SE18 . . . . 5F 107
Button Lodge E17 . . . . 4C 50
Buttonscroft Cl. CR7: Thor H 3C 156
The Butts TW8: Bford 6C 96
TW16: Sun 3A 148
Buttsbury Rd. IG1: Ilf 5G 71
Butts Cotts. TW13: Hanw 3C 130
Butts Cres. TW13: Hanw 3E 130
Buttsmead HA6: Nwood 1A 38
Butts Piece UB5: N'olt 2K 75
Butts Rd. BR1: Broml 5G 141
Buxhall Cres. E9 . . . . 6B 68
Buxted Rd. E8 . . . . 7F 67
N12 . . . . 5H 31
SE22 . . . . 4E 120
Buxton Cl. IG8: Wfd G 6G 37
N9 . . . . 2D 34
Buxton Ct. E11 . . . . 7H 51
N1 . . . . 1D 8
(not continuous)
Buxton Cres. SM3: Cheam 4G 165
Buxton Dr. E11 . . . . 4G 51
KT3: N Mald 2K 151
Buxton Gdns. W3 . . . . 7H 79
Buxton Ho. E11 . . . . 4G 51
Buxton M. SW4 . . . . 2H 119
Buxton Rd. CR7: Thor H 5B 156
DA8: Erith 7K 109
E4 . . . . 1A 36
E6 . . . . 3C 88
E15 . . . . 5G 69
E17 . . . . 4A 50
(not continuous)
IG2: Ilf 6J 53
N19 . . . . 1H 65
NW2 . . . . 6D 62
SW14 . . . . 3A 116
TW15: Ashf 5A 128
Buxton St. E1 . . . . 4K 9 (4G 85)
Buzzard Creek Ind. Est. IG11: Bark 5A 90
Buzz Bingo
Bexleyheath 4H 127
Enfield 4B 24
Feltham 2K 129
Stratford 1F 87
Byam St. SW6 . . . . 2A 118
Byards Ct. SE16 . . . . 4K 103
(off Worgan St.)
Byards Cft. SW16 . . . . 1H 155
Byas Ho. E3 . . . . 3B 86
(off Benworth St.)
Byatt Wlk. TW12: Hamp 6C 130
Bychurch End TW11: Tedd 5K 131
Bycroft Rd. UB1: S'hall 4E 76
Bycroft St. SE20 . . . . 7K 139
Bycullah Av. EN2: Enf 3G 23
Bycullah Rd. EN2: Enf 2G 23
The Bye W3 . . . . 6A 80
Byegrove Rd. SW19 . . . . 6B 136
Byelands Cl. SE16 . . . . 1K 103
The Bye Way HA3: W'stone 1J 41
The Byeway SW14 . . . . 3J 115
Byeways TW2: Twick 3F 131
The Byeways KT5: Surb 5G 151
Byfeld Gdns. SW13 . . . . 1C 116
Byfield Cl. SE16 . . . . 2B 104
Byfield Rd. TW7: Isle 3A 114
Byford Cl. E15 . . . . 7G 69
Byford Ho. EN5: Barn 4A 20
HA2: Harr 1E 58
Bygrove CR0: New Ad 6D 170
Bygrove St. E14 . . . . 6D 86
(not continuous)
Byland Cl. N21 . . . . 7E 22
SE2 . . . . 3B 108
SM4: Mord 7A 154
Byne Rd. SE26 . . . . 6J 139
SM5: Cars 2C 166
Bynes Rd. CR2: S Croy 7D 168
Byng Pl. WC1 . . . . 4D 6 (4H 83)
Byng Rd. EN5: Barn 2A 20
Byng St. E14 . . . . 2C 104
Bynon Av. DA7: Bex 3F 127
Byre Rd. N14 . . . . 6A 22
Byrne Cl. CR0: C'don 6C 156
Byrne Rd. SW12 . . . . 1F 137
Byron Av. E12 . . . . 6C 70
E18 . . . . 3H 51
Byron Av. KT3: N Mald 5C 152
NW9 . . . . 4H 43
SM1: Sutt 4B 166
TW4: Cran 2J 111
Byron Av. E. SM1: Sutt 4B 166
Byron Cl. E8 . . . . 1G 85
KT12: Walt T 7C 148
SE20 . . . . 3H 157
SE26 . . . . 4A 140
SE28 . . . . 1C 108
SW16 . . . . 6J 137
TW12: Hamp 4D 130
Byron Ct. E11 . . . . 4K 51
(off Makepeace Rd.)
EN2: Enf 2G 23
HA1: Harr 6J 41
NW6 . . . . 7A 64
(off Fairfax Rd.)
SE22 . . . . 1G 139
SW3 . . . . 4D 16
(off Elystan St.)
W7 . . . . 4A 96
(off Boston Rd.)
W9 . . . . 4J 81
(off Lanhill Rd.)
WC1 . . . . 3G 7
(off Mecklenburgh Sq.)
Byron Dr. DA8: Erith 7H 109
N2 . . . . 6B 46
Byron Gdns. SM1: Sutt 4B 166
Byron Hill Rd. HA2: Harr 1H 59
Byron Ho. DA1: Cray 5K 127
Byron M. NW3 . . . . 4C 64
W9 . . . . 4J 81
Byron Pde. UB10: Hil 4E 74
Byron Rd. E10 . . . . 1D 68
E17 . . . . 3C 50
HA0: Wemb 2C 60
HA1: Harr 6J 41
HA3: W'stone 2K 41
NW2 . . . . 2D 62
NW7 . . . . 5H 29
W5 . . . . 1F 97
Byron St. E14 . . . . 6E 86
Byron Ter. N9 . . . . 6D 24
SE7 . . . . 7A 106
Byron Way UB4: Hayes 4H 75
UB5: N'olt 3C 76
UB7: W Dray 4B 92
Bysouth Cl. IG5: Ilf 1F 53
N15 . . . . 4D 48
Bythorn St. SW9 . . . . 3K 119
Byton Rd. SW17 . . . . 6D 136
Byward Av. TW14: Felt 6A 112
Byward St. EC3 . . . . 3H 15 (7E 84)
Bywater Ho. SE18 . . . . 3C 106
Bywater Pl. SE16 . . . . 1A 104
Bywater St. SW3 . . . . 5E 16 (5D 100)
The Byway KT19: Ewe 4B 164
SM2: Sutt 7B 166
Bywell Pl. E16 . . . . 5H 87
W1 . . . . 6A 6
Bywood Av. CR0: C'don 6J 157
Byworth Wlk. N19 . . . . 1J 65

C

Cabanel Pl. SE11 . . . . 4H 19 (4A 102)
Cabbell St. NW1 . . . . 6C 4 (5C 82)
Cabinet Ct. NW2 . . . . 3B 62
Cabinet Way E4 . . . . 6G 35
Cable Ct. SE16 . . . . 4A 104
(off Rope St.)
Cable Ho. WC1 . . . . 1J 7
(off Gt. Percy St.)
Cable Pl. SE10 . . . . 1E 122
Cable St. E1 . . . . 7G 85
E16 . . . . 2K 105
Cable Trade Pk. SE7 . . . . 4A 106
Cable Wlk. SE10 . . . . 4G 105
Cabot Cl. CR0: Wadd 3A 168
Cabot Ct. SE16 . . . . 4K 103
(off Worgan St.)
Cabot Sq. E14 . . . . 1C 104
Cabot Way E6 . . . . 1B 88
Cabrail Court E14 . . . . 5A 86
(off Aston Street)
Cab Rd. SE1 . . . . 5H 13
Cabul Rd. SW11 . . . . 2C 118
Caci Ho. W14 . . . . 4H 99
(off Kensington Village)
Cactus Cl. SE15 . . . . 2E 120
Cactus Wlk. W12 . . . . 6B 80
Cadbury Cl. N20 . . . . 1F 31
TW7: Isle 1A 114
TW16: Sun 7G 129
Cadbury Rd. TW16: Sun 7G 129
Cadbury Way SE16 . . . . 3F 103
Caddington Cl. EN4: E Barn 5H 21
Caddington Rd. NW2 . . . . 3G 63
Caddis Cl. HA7: Stan 7E 26
Cadell Cl. E2 . . . . 1K 9 (2F 85)
Cade Rd. SE10 . . . . 1F 123
Cader Rd. SW18 . . . . 6A 118
Cadet Dr. SE1 . . . . 4F 103
Cadet Ho. SE18 . . . . 3F 107
Cadiz Ct. RM10: Dag 7K 73
Cadiz Rd. RM10: Dag 7J 73
Cadiz St. SE17 . . . . 5C 102
Cadley Ter. SE23 . . . . 2J 139
Cadman Cl. SW9 . . . . 7B 102
Cadman Ct. W4 . . . . 5H 97
(off Chaseley Dr.)
Cadmer Cl. KT3: N Mald 4A 152
Cadmium Sq. E2 . . . . 3K 85
(off Palmer's Rd.)
Cadmore Ho. N1 . . . . 7B 66
(off The Sutton Est.)
Cadmus Cl. SW4 . . . . 3H 119
Cadmus Ct. SE16 . . . . 4A 104
(off Seafarer Way)
SW9 . . . . 1A 120
(off Southey Rd.)
Cadnam Lodge E14 . . . . 3E 104
(off Schooner Cl.)
Cadnam Point SW15 . . . . 1D 134
Cadogan Cl. BR3: Beck 1F 159
E9 . . . . 7B 68
HA2: Harr 4F 59
TW11: Tedd 5J 131
Cadogan Ct. E9 . . . . 7B 68
(off Cadogan Ter.)
SM2: Sutt 6K 165
SW3 . . . . 4E 16
(off Draycott Av.)

Canal Wharf—Carnoustie Cl.

Canal Wharf E8 1E 84
(off Kingsland Rd.)
UB6: G'frd 1A 78
Canal Yd. UB2: S'hall 4K 93
Canary Vw. SE10 6D 104
(off Dowells St.)
Canary Wharf Tower 1D 104
Canberra Cl. NW4 3C 44
RM10: Dag 1K 91
Canberra Cres. RM10: Dag 7K 73
Canberra Dr. UB4: N'olt 3A 76
UB5: N'olt 3A 76
Canberra Path E10 7D 50
(off Whitney Rd.)
Canberra Pl. TW9: Rich 3G 115
Canberra Rd. DA7: Bex 6D 108
E6 1D 88
SE7 6A 106
TW6: H'row A 3C 110
W13 1A 96
Canbury Av. KT2: King T 1F 151
Canbury Bus. Cen. KT2: King T 1E 150
Canbury Bus. Pk. KT2: King T 1E 150
(off Canbury Pk. Rd.)
Canbury Ct. KT2: King T 7D 132
Canbury M. SE26 3G 139
Canbury Pk. Rd. KT2: King T 1E 150
Canbury Pas. KT2: King T 1D 150
Cancell Rd. SW9 1A 120
Candahar Rd. SW11 2C 118
Candida Ct. NW1 7F 65
Candid Ho. NW10 3D 80
(off Trenmar Gdns.)
Candle Gro. SE15 3H 121
Candlelight Ct. E15 6H 69
(off Romford Rd.)
Candler M. TW1: Twick 7A 114
Candler St. N15 6D 48
Candle St. E1 5A 86
Candover Cl. UB7: Harm 3E 174
Candover St. W1 6A 6 (5G 83)
Candy St. E3 1B 86
Candy Wharf E3 4A 86
Caney M. NW2 2F 63
Canfield Dr. HA4: Ruis 5K 57
Canfield Gdns. NW6 7K 63
Canfield Ho. N15 6E 48
(off Albert Rd.)
Canfield Pl. NW6 6A 64
Canfield Rd. IG8: Wfd G 7H 37
Canford Av. UB5: N'olt 1D 76
Canford Cl. EN2: Enf 2F 23
Canford Gdns. KT3: N Mald 6A 152
Canford Pl. TW11: Tedd 6C 132
Canford Rd. SW11 5E 118
Canham Gdns. TW4: Houn 7D 112
Canham Rd. SE25 3E 156
W3 2A 98
Canius Ho. CR0: C'don 3C 168
(off Scarbrook Rd.)
Canmore Gdns. SW16 7G 137
CANN HALL 4G 69
Cann Hall Rd. E11 4G 69
Cann Ho. W14 3G 99
(off Russell Rd.)
Canning Cres. N22 1K 47
Canning Cross SE5 2E 120
Canning Ho. W12 7D 80
(off Australia Rd.)
Canning Pas. W8 3A 100
Canning Pl. W8 3A 100
Canning Pl. M. W8 3A 100
(off Canning Pl.)
Canning Rd. CR0: C'don 2F 169
E15 2G 87
E17 4A 50
HA3: W'stone 3J 41
N5 3B 66
Canning Sq. EN1: Enf 1B 24
Cannington Rd. RM9: Dag 6C 72
CANNING TOWN 6H 87
CANNING TOWN 5G 87
Cannizaro Rd. SW19 6E 134
Cannock Ct. E17 2E 50
Cannock Ho. N4 7C 48
Cannonbury Av. HA5: Pinn 6B 40
Cannon Cl. SW20 3E 152
TW12: Hamp 6F 131
Cannon Ct. EC1 3B 8
(off Brewhouse Yd.)
Cannon Dr. E14 7C 86
Cannon Hill N14 3D 32
NW6 5J 63
Cannon Hill La. SW20 5F 153
Cannon Hill M. N14 3D 32
Cannon Ho. SE11 4H 19
Cannon La. HA5: Pinn 5C 40
NW3 3B 64
Cannon Pl. NW3 3B 64
SE7 5C 106
Cannon Retail Pk. 7A 90
Cannon Rd. DA7: Bex 1E 126
N14 3D 32
N17 6A 34
Cannon St. EC4 1C 14 (6C 84)
Cannon St. Rd. E1 6H 85
Cannon Trad. Est. HA9: Wemb 4H 61
Cannon Way KT8: W Mole 4E 148
Cannon Wharf Bus. Cen. SE8 4A 104
(off Pell St.)
Cannon Wharf Development SE8 4A 104
(off Yeoman St.)
Cannon Workshops E14 7C 86
(off Cannon Dr.)
Canoe Wlk. E14 6B 86
Canon All. EC4 1C 14
(off Queen's Head Pas.)
Canon Av. RM6: Chad H 5C 54
Canon Beck Rd. SE16 2J 103
Canonbie Rd. SE23 7J 121
CANONBURY 6C 66
Canonbury Bus. Cen. N1 1C 84
Canonbury Cotts. EN1: Enf 1K 23
Canonbury Ct. N1 7B 66
(off Hawes St.)
Canonbury Cres. N1 7C 66
Canonbury Gro. N1 7C 66
Canonbury Hgts. N1 6D 66
(off Dove Rd.)
Canonbury La. N1 7B 66
Canonbury Pk. Nth. N1 6C 66
Canonbury Pk. Sth. N1 6C 66
Canonbury Pl. N1 6B 66
(not continuous)
Canonbury Rd. EN1: Enf 1K 23
N1 6B 66
Canonbury Sq. N1 7B 66
Canonbury St. N1 7C 66
Canonbury Vs. N1 7B 66
Canon Ho. W10 3H 81
(off Bruckner St.)
Canon Mohan Cl. N14 6K 21
Canon Rd. BR1: Broml 3A 160
Canon Row SW1 7E 12 (2J 101)
(not continuous)
Canon's Cl. N2 7B 46
Canons Cl. CR4: Mitc 4D 154
HA8: Edg 6A 28
Canons Cnr. HA8: Edg 4K 27
Canons Ct. E15 4G 69
HA8: Edg 6A 28
Canons Dr. HA8: Edg 6K 27
Canonsleigh Rd. RM9: Dag 7B 72
Canons Leisure Cen.
Mitcham 4D 154
CANONS PARK 7J 27
Canons Pk. 6J 27
Canons Pk. Cl. HA8: Edg 7K 27
Canons Row HA8: Edg 4K 27
Canon St. N1 1C 84
Canon's Wlk. CR0: C'don 3K 169
Canons Way HA8: Edg 4A 28
Canopus Way TW19: Stanw 7A 110
Canrobert St. E2 2H 85
Cantelowes Rd. NW1 6H 65
Canterbury Av. DA15: Sidc 2B 144
IG1: Ilf 7C 52
Canterbury Cl. BR3: Beck 1D 158
E6 6D 88
KT4: Wor Pk 2F 165
SE5 2C 120
(off Lilford Rd.)
UB6: G'frd 5F 77
Canterbury Ct. CR2: S Croy 7C 168
(off St Augustine's Av.)
NW6 2J 81
(off Canterbury Rd.)
NW9 2A 44
SE5 7A 102
SE12 3K 141
TW15: Ashf 4B 128
Canterbury Cres. SW9 3A 120
Canterbury Gro. SE27 4A 138
Canterbury Hall KT4: Wor Pk 7D 152
Canterbury Ho. CR0: C'don 1D 168
(off Sydenham Rd.)
E3 3D 86
(off Bow Rd.)
IG11: Bark 7A 72
(off Margaret Bondfield Av.)
RM8: Dag 4A 72
(off Academy Way)
SE1 1H 19 (3K 101)
SE8 5C 104
(off Wharf St.)
Canterbury Ind. Pk. SE15 6J 103
Canterbury Pl. SE17 5B 102
Canterbury Rd. CR0: C'don 7K 155
E10 7E 50
HA1: Harr 5F 41
HA2: Harr 5F 41
NW6 2H 81
(Carlton Va.)
NW6 2J 81
(Princess Rd.)
SM4: Mord 7K 153
TW13: Hanw 2C 130
Canterbury Ter. NW6 2J 81
Canter Way E1 1K 15 (6G 85)
Cantium Retail Pk. 6G 103
Cantley Gdns. IG2: Ilf 6G 53
SE19 1F 157
Cantley Rd. W7 3A 96
Canto Ct. EC1 3D 8
(off Old St.)
Canton St. E14 6C 86
Cantrell Rd. E3 4B 86
Cantwell Rd. SE18 7F 107
Canute Gdns. SE16 4K 103
Canvey St. SE1 4C 14 (1C 102)
Canyon Gdn. E3 3B 86
(off St Clements Av.)
Cape Cl. IG11: Bark 7F 71
Cape Henry Ct. E14 7F 87
(off Jamestown Way)
Cape Ho. E8 6F 67
(off Dalston La.)
E16 1K 105
(off Cunningham Av.)
Capel Av. SM6: W'gton 5K 167
Capel Cl. BR2: Broml 1C 172
N20 3F 31
Capel Ct. EC2 1F 15
(off Bartholomew La.)
SE20 1J 157
Capel Cres. HA7: Stan 2F 27
Capel Gdns. HA5: Pinn 4D 40
IG3: Bark, Ilf 4K 71
Capel Ho. E9 7J 67
(off Loddiges Rd.)
Capel Rd. E7 4K 69
E12 4K 69
EN4: E Barn 6H 21
Capener's Cl. SW1 7F 11
Capern Rd. SW18 1A 136
Cape Rd. N17 3G 49
Cape Yd. E1 1G 103
Capital Bus. Cen. CR2: S Croy 7D 168
HA0: Wemb 2D 78
Capital E. Apts. E16 7J 87
(off Western Gateway)
Capital Ho. SW15 5G 117
(off Plaza Gdns.)
Capital Ind. Est. CR4: Mitc 5D 154
DA17: Belv 3H 109
Capital Interchange Way
TW8: Bford 5G 97
Capital Mill Apts. E2 1F 85
(off Whiston Rd.)
Capital Trad. Est. IG11: Bark 2H 89
Capital Wharf E1 1G 103
Capitol Bldg. SW11 6H 101
(off New Union Sq.)
Capitol Ind. Pk. NW9 3J 43
Capitol Wlk. SE23 2J 139
(off London Rd.)
Capitol Way NW9 3J 43
Capland Ho. NW8 3B 4
(off Capland St.)
Capland St. NW8 3B 4 (4B 82)
Caple Ho. SW10 7A 100
(off King's Rd.)
Caple Rd. NW10 2B 80
Capper St. WC1 4B 6 (4G 83)
Caprea Cl. UB4: Yead 5B 76
Capricorn Cen. RM8: Dag 7F 55
Capricorn Ct. HA8: Edg 7B 28
(off Zodiac Cl.)
Capri Ho. E17 2B 50
NW9 3B 44
(off Caversham Rd.)
Capri Rd. CR0: C'don 1F 169
Capstan Cl. RM6: Chad H 6B 54
Capstan Ct. E1 7J 85
(off Wapping Wall)
Capstan Ho. E14 7F 87
(off Clove Cres.)
E14 4E 104
(off Stebondale St.)
Capstan Ride EN2: Enf 2F 23
Capstan Rd. SE8 4B 104
Capstan Sq. E14 2E 104
Capstan Way SE16 1A 104
Capstone Rd. BR1: Broml 4H 141
Captain St. SE18 1C 124
(off Tellson Av.)
Capthorne Av. HA2: Harr 1C 58
Capuchin Cl. HA7: Stan 6G 27
Capulet M. E16 1J 105
Capulet Sq. E3 3D 86
(off Talwin St.)
Capworth St. E10 1C 68
Caradoc Cl. W2 6J 81
Caradoc Evans Cl. N11 5A 32
(off Springfield Rd.)
Caradoc St. SE10 5G 105
Caradon Cl. E11 1G 69
Caradon Way N15 4D 48
Caragh Mews UB2: S'hall 4C 94
Cara Ho. N1 7A 66
(off Liverpool Rd.)
NW9 3J 43
Caramel Ct. E3 2D 86
(off Taylor Pl.)
Caranday Vs. W11 1F 99
(off Norland Rd.)
Carat Ho. E14 5C 86
(off Ursula Gould Way)
Caravel Cl. E14 3C 104
Caravel House E16 2K 105
(off Regalia Close)
Caravelle Gdns. UB5: N'olt 3B 76
Caravel M. SE8 6C 104
Caraway Apts. SE1 6K 15
(off Cayenne Ct.)
Caraway Cl. E13 5K 87
Caraway Hgts. E14 7E 86
(off Poplar High St.)
Caraway Pl. SM6: W'gton 3F 167
Carberry Rd. SE19 6E 138
Carbery Av. W3 2F 97
Carbis Cl. E4 1A 36
Carbis Rd. E14 6B 86
Carbrooke Ho. E9 1J 85
(off Templecombe Rd.)
Carbuncle Pas. N17 2G 49
Carburton St. W1 5K 5 (5F 83)
Cardale St. E14 2E 104
Cardamon Bldg. SE1 5K 15
(off Shad Thames)
Carden Ct. KT8: W Mole 4F 149
Carden Rd. SE15 3H 121
Cardiff Ho. SE15 6G 103
(off Friary Est.)
Cardiff Rd. EN3: Pond E 4C 24
W7 3A 96
Cardiff St. SE18 7J 107
Cardigan Ct. W7 4K 77
(off Copley Cl.)
Cardigan Gdns. IG3: Ilf 2A 72
Cardigan Pl. SE3 2F 123
Cardigan Rd. E3 2B 86
SW13 2C 116
SW19 6A 136
TW10: Rich 6E 114
Cardigan St. SE11 5J 19 (5A 102)
Cardigan Wlk. N1 7C 66
(off Ashby Gro.)
Cardinal Av. KT2: King T 5E 132
SM4: Mord 6G 153
Cardinal Bourne St. SE1 3D 102
Cardinal Cap All. SE1 1C 102
Cardinal Cl. BR7: Chst 1J 161
HA8: Edg 7D 28
KT4: Wor Pk 4C 164
SM4: Mord 6G 153
Cardinal Ct. E1 7G 85
(off Thomas More St.)
Cardinal Cres. KT3: N Mald 2J 151
Cardinal Hinsley Cl. NW10 2C 80
Cardinal Mans. SW1 3A 18
(off Carlisle Pl.)
Cardinal Pl. SW1 1A 18 (3G 101)
(not continuous)
SW15 4F 117
Cardinal Rd. HA4: Ruis 1B 58
TW13: Felt 1K 129
Cardinals Wlk. TW12: Hamp 7G 131
TW16: Sun 6G 129
Cardinals Way N19 1H 65
Cardinal Wlk. SW1 2A 18
Cardinal Way HA3: W'stone 3J 41
Cardine M. SE15 7H 103
Cardington Sq.
TW4: Houn 4B 112
Cardington St. NW1 1B 6 (3G 83)
Cardinham Rd.
BR6: Chels 4K 173
Cardozo Rd. N7 5J 65
Cardrew Av. N12 5G 31
Cardrew Cl. N12 5H 31
Cardrew Ct. N12 5G 31
Cardross Ho. W6 3D 98
(off Cardross St.)
Cardross St. W6 3D 98
Cardwell Rd. N7 4J 65
Cardwell Ter. N7 4J 65
(off Cardwell Rd.)
Career Ct. SE16 2K 103
(off Christopher Cl.)
Carew Cl. N7 2K 65
Carew Ct. RM6: Chad H 6B 54
(off Quarles Pk. Rd.)
SE14 6K 103
(off Samuel Cl.)
SM2: Sutt 7K 165
Carew Manor & Dovecote 3H 167
Carew Mnr. Cotts. SM6: Bedd 3H 167
Carew Rd. CR4: Mitc 2E 154
CR7: Thor H 4B 156
N17 2G 49
SM6: W'gton 6G 167
TW15: Ashf 6E 128
W13 2C 96
Carew St. SE5 2C 120
Carey Ct. DA6: Bex 5H 127
SE5 7C 102
Carey Gdns. SW8 1G 119
Carey La. EC2 7C 8 (6C 84)
Carey Mans. SW1 3C 18
(off Rutherford St.)
Carey Pl. SW1 4C 18 (4H 101)
Carey Rd. RM9: Dag 4E 72
Carey St. WC2 1H 13 (6K 83)
Carey Way HA9: Wemb 4H 61
Carfax Ho. SE20 1G 157
Carfax Pl. SW4 4H 119
Carfax Rd. UB3: Harl 5H 93
Carfree Cl. N1 7A 66
Cargill Rd. SW18 1K 135
Cargo Point TW19: Stanw 6B 110
Cargreen Pl. SE25 4F 157
(off Cargreen Rd.)
Cargreen Rd. SE25 4F 157
Cargrey Ho. HA7: Stan 5H 27
Carholme Rd. SE23 1B 140
Carillon Ct. E1 5G 85
(off Greatorex St.)
W5 7D 78
Carina Ho. E20 5E 68
(off Cheering La.)
Carinthia Ct. SE16 4A 104
(off Plough Way)
Carisbrook N10 2F 47
Carisbrook Cl. EN1: Enf 1A 24
Carisbrooke Av. DA5: Bexl 1D 144
Carisbrooke Cl. HA7: Stan 2D 42
TW4: Houn 7C 112
Carisbrooke Ct. SM2: Cheam 7H 165
UB5: N'olt 1D 76
(off Eskdale Av.)
W1 6H 5
(off Weymouth St.)
W3 2J 97
(off Brouncker Rd.)
Carisbrooke Gdns. SE15 7F 103
Carisbrooke Ho. KT2: King T 1E 150
(off Seven Kings Way)
TW10: Rich 5G 115
UB7: W Dray 2B 92
(off Park Lodge Av.)
Carisbrooke Rd. BR2: Broml 4A 160
CR4: Mitc 4H 155
E17 4A 50
Carker's La. NW5 5F 65
Carlcott Cl. KT12: Walt T 7K 147
Carleton Av. KT8: E Mos 6H 149
SM6: W'gton 7H 167
Carleton Cl. KT10: Esh 7H 149
Carleton Gdns. N19 5G 65
Carleton Ho. NW9 3B 44
(off Boulevard Dr.)
Carleton Rd. N7 5H 65
N19 5H 65
Carleton Vs. NW5 5G 65
Carlile Cl. E3 2B 86
Carlile Ho. SE1 3D 102
(off Tabard St.)
Carlile Pl. TW10: Rich 6F 115
Carlina Gdns. IG8: Wfd G 5E 36
Carlingford Gdns. CR4: Mitc 7D 136
Carlingford Rd. N15 3B 48
NW3 4B 64
SM4: Mord 6F 153
Carlisle Av. EC3 1J 15 (6E 84)
W3 6A 80
Carlisle Cl. HA5: Pinn 7C 40
KT2: King T 1G 151
Carlisle Gdns. HA3: Kenton 7D 42
IG1: Ilf 6C 52
Carlisle Ho. IG1: Ilf 6C 52
Carlisle La. SE1 2H 19 (3K 101)
Carlisle Mans. SW1 3A 18
(off Carlisle Pl.)
Carlisle M. KT2: King T 1G 151
Carlisle Pl. N11 4A 32
SW1 2A 18 (3G 101)
Carlisle Rd. E10 1C 68
N4 7A 48
NW6 1G 81
NW9 3J 43
SM1: Sutt 6H 165
TW12: Hamp 7F 131
Carlisle St. W1 1C 12 (6H 83)
Carlisle Wlk. E8 6F 67
Carlisle Way SW17 5E 136
Carlos Pl. W1 3H 11 (7E 82)
Carlow St. NW1 2G 83
Carlson Ct. SW15 4H 117
Carlton Av. CR2: S Croy 7E 168
HA3: Kenton 5B 42
N14 5C 22
TW14: Felt 6A 112
UB3: Harl 4G 93
Carlton Av. E. HA9: Wemb 2D 60
Carlton Av. W. HA0: Wemb 2B 60
Carlton Cl. HA8: Edg 5B 28
KT9: Chess 6D 162
NW3 2J 63
UB5: N'olt 5G 59
Carlton Ct. IG6: Ilf 3H 53
N3 7D 30
SE20 1H 157
UB8: Cowl 5A 74
W9 2K 81
(off Maida Vale)
Carlton Cres. SM3: Cheam 4G 165
Carlton Dr. IG6: Ilf 3H 53
SW15 5F 117
Carlton Gdns. SW1 5C 12 (1H 101)
W5 6C 78
Carlton Grn. DA14: Sidc 4K 143
Carlton Gro. SE15 1H 121
Carlton Hill NW8 2K 81
Carlton Ho. NW6 2J 81
(off Canterbury Ter.)
SE16 2K 103
(off Wolfe Cres.)
TW3: Houn 6E 112
TW14: Felt 6H 111
Carlton Ho. Ter.
SW1 5C 12 (1H 101)
Carlton Lodge N4 7A 48
(off Carlton Rd.)
Carlton Mans. N16 1F 67
NW6 7J 63
(off West End La.)
W9 3K 81
W14 2G 99
(off Holland Pk. Gdns.)
Carlton M. NW6 5J 63
(off West Cotts.)
Carlton Pde. HA9: Wemb 2E 60
Carlton Pk. Av. SW20 2F 153
Carlton Rd. CR2: S Croy 6D 168
DA8: Erith 6H 109
DA14: Sidc 5K 143
DA16: Well 3B 126
E11 1H 69
E12 4B 70
E17 1A 50
KT3: N Mald 2A 152
KT12: Walt T 7K 147
N4 7A 48
N11 5K 31
SW14 3J 115
TW16: Sun 7H 129
W4 2K 97
W5 7C 78
Carlton Sq. E1 4K 85
(not continuous)
Carlton St. SW1 3C 12 (7H 83)
Carlton Ter. E7 7A 70
E11 5K 51
(not continuous)
N18 3J 33
SE26 3J 139
Carlton Twr. Pl. SW1 1F 17 (3D 100)
Carlton Towers SM5: Cars 3D 166
Carlton Va. NW6 2H 81
Carlton Vs. SW15 5G 117
The Carlton Works SE15 7H 103
(off Asylum Rd.)
Carlwell St. SW17 5C 136
Carlyle Av. BR1: Broml 3B 160
UB1: S'hall 7D 76
Carlyle Cl. KT8: W Mole 2F 149
N2 6A 46
Carlyle Ct. SW6 1K 117
(off Imperial Rd.)
SW10 1A 118
(off Chelsea Harbour Dr.)
Carlyle Gdns. UB1: S'hall 7D 76
Carlyle Ho. KT8: W Mole 5E 148
(off Down St.)
N16 3E 66
SE5 7C 102
(off Bethwin Rd.)
SW3 7B 16
(off Old Church St.)
Carlyle Mans. SW3 7C 16
(off Cheyne Wlk.)
W8 1J 99
(off Kensington Mall)
Carlyle M. E1 4K 85
Carlyle Pl. SW15 4F 117
Carlyle Rd. CR0: C'don 2G 169
E12 4C 70
NW10 1K 79
SE28 7B 90
W5 4C 96
Carlyle's House 7C 16
Carlyle Sq. SW3 6B 16 (5B 100)
Carly M. E2 3G 85
(off Barnet Gro.)
Carlyon Av. HA2: Harr 4D 58
Carlyon Cl. HA0: Wemb 1E 78
Carlyon Rd. HA0: Wemb 2E 78
UB4: Yead 5A 76
(not continuous)
Carlys Cl. BR3: Beck 2K 157
Carmalt Gdns. SW15 4E 116
Carmarthen Ct. W7 4K 77
(off Copley Cl.)
Carmarthen Pl. SE1 6G 15 (2E 102)
Carmel Ct. HA9: Wemb 2H 61
W8 2K 99
(off Holland St.)
Carmelite Cl. HA3: Hrw W 1G 41
Carmelite Rd. HA3: Hrw W 1G 41
Carmelite St. EC4 2K 13 (7A 84)
Carmelite Wlk.
HA3: Hrw W 1G 41
Carmelite Way HA3: Hrw W 2G 41
Carmel Lodge SW6 6J 99
(off Lillie Rd.)
Carmelo M. E1 5K 85
(off Maria Ter.)
Carmel Way TW9: Rich 2H 115
Carmen St. E14 6D 86
Carmichael Cl. HA4: Ruis 4J 57
SW11 3B 118
Carmichael Ct. SW13 2B 116
(off Grove Rd.)
Carmichael Ho. E14 7E 86
(off Poplar High St.)
Carmichael M. SW18 7B 118
Carmichael Rd. SE25 5F 157
Carmine W2 6B 4
Carmine Ct. BR1: Broml 7H 141
Carmine Wharf E14 6B 86
Carminia Rd. SW17 2F 137
Carnaby St. W1 1A 12 (6G 83)
Carnac St. SE27 4D 138
Carnanton Rd. E17 1F 51
Carnarvon Av. EN1: Enf 3A 24
Carnarvon Dr. UB3: Harl 3E 92
Carnarvon Rd. E10 5E 50
E15 6H 69
E18 1H 51
EN5: Barn 3B 20
Carnation Cl. RM7: Rush G 2K 73
Carnation St. SE2 5B 108
Carnbrook M. SE3 3B 124
Carnbrook Rd. SE3 3B 124
Carnecke Gdns. SE9 5C 124
Carnegie Cl. KT6: Surb 2F 163
Carnegie Pl. SW19 3F 135
Carnegie Rd. HA1: Harr 7K 41
Carnegie St. N1 1K 83
Carnell Apts. E14 6B 86
(off St Anne's Row)
Carney Pl. SW9 4A 120
Carnforth Cl. KT19: Ewe 6H 163
Carnforth Rd. SW16 7H 137
(not continuous)
Carnie Lodge SW17 3F 137
Carnival Ho. SE1 6K 15
(off Gainsford St.)
Carnoustie Cl. SE28 6D 90

Carnoustie Dr.—Cecil Mans.

Carnoustie Dr. N1 7K 65
(not continuous)
Carnwath Rd. SW6 3J 117
Caroe Ct. N9 1C 34
Carol Cl. NW4 4F 45
Carolean Cres. SE8 4A 104
Carole Ho. NW1 1D 82
(off Regent's Pk. Rd.)
Carolina Cl. E15 5G 69
Carolina Rd. CR7: Thor H 2B 156
Caroline Cl. CR0: C'don 4E 168
N10 2F 47
SW16 3K 137
TW7: Isle 7H 95
UB7: W Dray 2A 92
W2 7K 81
Caroline Ct. HA7: Stan 6F 27
SE6 4F 141
TW15: Ashf 6D 128
Caroline Gdns. E2 1H 9 (3E 84)
SE15 7H 103
(not continuous)
Caroline Ho. W2 7K 81
(off Bayswater Rd.)
W6 5E 98
(off Queen Caroline St.)
Caroline Pl. SW11 2E 118
UB3: Harl 7G 93
W2 7K 81
Caroline Pl. M. W2 7K 81
Caroline Rd. SW19 7H 135
Caroline St. E1 6K 85
Caroline Ter. SW1 4G 17 (4E 100)
Caroline Wlk. W6 6G 99
(off Lillie Rd.)
Carol St. NW1 1G 83
Caronia Ct. SE16 4A 104
(off Plough Way)
Caro Pl. KT3: N Mald 4B 152
Carpenter Gdns. N21 2G 33
Carpenter Ho. E1 5K 85
(off Trafalgar Gdns.)
E14 5C 86
(off Burgess St.)
NW11 6A 46
Carpenters Arms Apts. SE1 4G 103
(off Welsford St.)
Carpenters Cl. EN5: New Bar 6E 20
Carpenters Ct. BR1: Broml 2B 160
NW1 1G 83
(off Pratt St.)
TW2: Twick 2J 131
Carpenters M. N7 5J 65
Carpenters Pl. SW4 4H 119
Carpenter's Rd. E15 7E 68
E20 6C 68
Carpenter St. W1 3J 11 (7F 83)
Carp Ho. E3 1B 86
(off Old Ford Rd.)
Carradale Ho. E14 6E 86
(off St Leonard's Rd.)
Carrara Cl. SE24 4A 120
SW9 4B 120
Carrara M. E8 6G 67
(off Dalston La.)
Carrara Wharf SW6 3G 117
Carr Cl. HA7: Stan 6F 27
Carre M. SE5 1B 120
(off Calais St.)
Carrera Twr. EC1 1C 8
Carr Gro. SE18 4C 106
Carr Ho. DA1: Cray 5K 127
Carriage Dr. E. SW11 7E 100
Carriage Dr. Nth. SW11 7H 17 (6E 100)
(Carriage Dr. E.)
SW11 7D 100
(The Parade)
Carriage Dr. Sth. SW11 1D 118
(not continuous)
Carriage Dr. W. SW11 7D 100
Carriage Ho. E15 6F 69
(off Leyton Rd.)
N4 2A 66
Carriage M. IG1: Ilf 2G 71
Carriage Pl. N16 3D 66
SW16 5G 137
Carriage St. SE18 3F 107
Carriage Way SE8 7C 104
(off Deptford High St.)
Carrick Cl. TW7: Isle 3A 114
Carrick Ct. E3 3E 86
(off Bolinder Way)
Carrick Dr. IG6: Ilf 1G 53
Carrick Gdns. N17 7K 33
Carrick Ho. N7 6K 65
(off Caledonian Rd.)
SE11 5K 19 (5A 102)
Carrick M. SE8 6C 104
Carrick Sq. TW8: Bford 7C 96
(off Narrowboat Av.)
Carrill Way DA17: Belv 3D 108
Carrington Av. TW3: Houn 5F 113
Carrington Cl. CR0: C'don 7A 158
KT2: King T 5J 133
Carrington Ct. SW11 4C 118
(off Barnard Rd.)
Carrington Gdns. E7 4J 69
Carrington Ho. W1 5J 11
(off Carrington St.)
Carrington Rd. TW10: Rich 4G 115
Carrington Sq. HA3: Hrw W 6B 26
Carrington St. W1 5J 11 (1F 101)
Carrock Ct. RM7: Rush G 6K 55
(off Union Rd.)
Carrol Cl. NW5 4F 65
Carroll Cl. E15 5H 69
Carroll Ho. W2 2A 10
(off Craven Ter.)
Carronade Ct. N7 5K 65
Carronade Pl. SE28 3G 107
Carron Cl. E14 6D 86
Carroun Rd. SW8 7K 101
Carroway La. UB6: G'frd 3H 77
Carrow Rd. RM9: Dag 7B 72
Carr Rd. E17 2B 50
UB5: N'olt 6E 58
Carrs La. N21 5H 23
Carr St. E14 5A 86
CARSHALTON 4E 166
Carshalton Athletic FC 4C 166
CARSHALTON BEECHES 7C 166
Carshalton Boys Sports Coll. Cen.
2C 166
Carshalton Gro. SM1: Sutt 4B 166
CARSHALTON ON THE HILL 7E 166
Carshalton Pk. Rd. SM5: Cars 5D 166
Carshalton Pl. SM5: Cars 5E 166
Carshalton Rd. CR4: Mitc 4E 154
SM1: Sutt 5A 166
SM5: Cars 5A 166
Carslake Rd. SW15 6E 116
Carson Rd. E16 4J 87
EN4: Cockf 4J 21
SE21 2D 138
Carson Ter. W11 1G 99
(off Princes Pl.)
Carstairs Rd. SE6 3E 140
Carston Cl. SE12 5H 123
Carswell Cl. IG4: Ilf 4B 52
Carswell Rd. SE6 7E 122
Carter Cl. EN5: Barn 5B 20
NW9 6K 43
Carter Ct. EC4 1A 14
Carter Dr. RM5: Col R 1H 55
Carteret Ho. W12 7D 80
(off White City Est.)
Carteret St. SW1 7C 12 (2H 101)
Carteret Way SE8 4A 104
Carterhatch La. EN1: Enf 1A 24
Carterhatch Rd. EN3: Enf H 1D 24
Carter Ho. E1 6J 9
Carter La. EC4 1B 14 (6B 84)
Carter Pl. SE17 5C 102
Carter Rd. E13 1K 87
SW19 6B 136
Carters Cl. KT4: Wor Pk 2F 165
NW5 5H 65
(off Torriano Av.)
Carters Hill Cl. SE9 1A 142
Carters La. SE23 2A 140
Carter Sq. E14 6D 86
(off Bowen St.)
Carter St. SE17 6C 102
Carter's Yd. SW18 5J 117
Carthew Rd. W6 3D 98
Carthew Vs. W6 3D 98
Carthusian Ct. EC1 5C 8
(off Carthusian St.)
Carthusian St. EC1 5C 8 (5C 84)
Cartier Circ. E14 1D 104
Carting La. WC2 3F 13 (7J 83)
Cart La. E4 1B 36
Cart Lodge M. CR0: C'don 1E 168
Cartmel NW1 1A 6
(off Harrington St.)
Cartmel Cl. N17 7C 34
Cartmel Ct. UB5: N'olt 6C 58
Cartmel Gdns. SM4: Mord 5A 154
Carton Rd. DA7: Bex 1G 127
Carton Ho. W11 7F 81
(off St Ann's Rd.)
Cartoon Mus. 6A 6 (6G 83)
Cartridge Pl. SE18 3F 107
Cartwright Gdns. WC1 2E 6 (3J 83)
Cartwright Ho. SE1 3C 102
(off County St.)
Cartwright Rd. RM9: Dag 7F 73
Cartwright St. E1 2K 15 (7F 85)
Cartwright Way SW13 7D 98
Carvel Ho. E14 5E 104
(off Manchester Rd.)
Carvell Ho. NW9 3B 44
(off Aerodrome Rd.)
Carver Cl. W4 3J 97
Carver Rd. SE24 6C 120
Carville Cres. TW8: Bford 4E 96
Carville Hall Pk. TW8: Bford 5E 96
(off Claypond La.)
Carville St. N4 2A 66
Cary Av. SE16 4A 104
Cary Rd. E11 4G 69
Carysfort Rd. N8 5H 47
N16 3D 66
Casbeard St. N4 2C 66
Casby Ho. SE16 3G 103
(off Marine St.)
Cascade Av. N10 4G 47
Cascade Cl. IG9: Buck H 2G 37
Cascade Ct. SW11 7F 101
Cascade Rd. IG9: Buck H 2G 37
Cascades Ct. SW19 7H 135
Cascades Twr. E14 1B 104
Casel Ct. HA7: Stan 2F 27
(off Brightwen Gro.)
Casella Rd. SE14 7K 103
Casewick Rd. SE27 5A 138
Casey Av. UB5: N'olt 2D 76
Casey Cl. NW8 2C 4 (3C 82)
Casey Ct. SE14 1K 121
(off Besson St.)
Cashmere Ho. E8 1F 85
(off Pamela St.)
Casia Point E20 7E 68
Casimir Rd. E5 2J 67
Casings Way E3 7C 68
Casino Av. SE24 5C 120
Caspian St. SE5 7D 102
Caspian Wlk. E16 6B 88
Caspian Wharf E3 5D 86
(off Violet Rd.)
Cassander Pl. HA5: Pinn 1C 40
(off Holly Gro.)
Cassandra Cl. UB5: N'olt 4H 59
Casselden Rd. NW10 7K 61
Cassell Ho. SW9 2K 119
(off Stockwell Gdns. Est.)
Cass Ho. E9 6K 67
(off Harrowgate Rd.)
Cassia Ho. E1 6G 85
(off Piazza Wlk.)
Cassidy Rd. SW6 7J 99
(not continuous)
Cassilda Rd. SE2 4A 108
Cassilis Rd. E14 2C 104
TW1: Twick 5B 114
Cassini Apts. E16 6J 87
Cassiobury Av. TW14: Felt 7H 111
Cassiobury Rd. E17 5A 50
Cassland Rd. CR7: Thor H 4D 156
E9 7K 67
Casslee Rd. SE6 7B 122
Cassocks Sq. TW17: Shep 7F 147
Casson Apts. E14 6C 86
(off Upper Nth. St.)
Casson Ho. E1 5K 9
(off Hanbury St.)
Casson Sq. SE1 5H 13 (1K 101)
Casson St. E1 5G 85
Castalia Sq. E14 2E 104
Castellain Mans. W9 4K 81
(off Castellain Rd.)
Castellain Rd. W9 4K 81
Castellane Cl. HA7: Stan 7E 26
Castell Ho. SE8 7C 104
Castello Av. SW15 5E 116
CASTELNAU 6D 98
Castelnau SW13 1C 116
Castelnau Gdns. SW13 6D 98
Castelnau Mans. SW13 6D 98
(off Castelnau)
Castelnau Row SW13 6D 98
Casterbridge NW6 1K 81
(off Abbey Rd.)
W11 6H 81
(off Dartmouth Cl.)
Casterbridge Rd. SE3 3J 123
Casterton St. E8 6H 67
Castile Rd. SE18 4E 106
Castillon Rd. SE6 2G 141
Casting Ho. SE14 6B 104
Castlands Rd. SE6 2B 140
Castleacre W2 1C 10
(off Hyde Pk. Cres.)
Castle Av. E4 5A 36
KT17: Ewe 7D 164
UB7: Yiew 7A 74
Castlebar Ct. W5 5C 78
Castlebar Hill W5 5C 78
Castlebar M. W5 5C 78
Castlebar Pk. W5 5B 78
Castlebar Rd. W5 5C 78
Castle Baynard St. EC4 2B 14 (7B 84)
Castlebrook Cl. SE11 4B 102
Castle Bus. Cen. TW12: Hamp 1F 149
(off Castle M.)
The Castle Cen. 4B 102
The Castle Cinema 5K 67
The Castle Climbing Cen. 2C 66
Castle Cl. BR2: Broml 3G 159
E9 5A 68
SW19 3F 135
TW16: Sun 7G 129
W3 2H 97
Castlecombe Dr. SW19 7F 117
Castlecombe Rd. SE9 4C 142
Castle Ct. EC3 1F 15
(off Birchin La.)
SE26 4A 140
SW15 3G 117
(off Brewhouse La.)
Castleden Ho. NW3 7B 64
(off Hilgrove Rd.)
Castledine Rd. SE20 7H 139
Castle Dr. IG4: Ilf 6C 52
Castleford Av. SE9 1F 143
Castleford Cl. N17 6A 34
Castleford Ct. NW8 3B 4
(off Henderson Dr.)
Castlegate TW9: Rich 3F 115
Castle Green Leisure Cen. 1D 90
Castlehaven Rd. NW1 7F 65
Castle Hgts. RM9: Dag 1B 90
Castle Hill Av. CR0: New Ad 7D 170
Castle Hill Local Nature Reserve
6G 163
Castle Hill Pde. W13 7B 78
(off The Avenue)
Castle Ho. SM2: Sutt 6J 165
SW8 7J 101
(off Sth. Lambeth Rd.)
Castle La. SW1 1B 18 (3G 101)
Castleleigh Ct. EN2: Enf 5J 23
Castlemaine SW11 2D 118
Castlemaine Av. CR2: S Croy 5F 169
KT17: Ewe 7D 164
Castlemain St. E1 5H 85
Castle Mead SE5 7C 102
Castle M. N12 5F 31
NW1 6F 65
SW17 4C 136
TW12: Hamp 1F 149
(not continuous)
Castle Pde. KT17: Ewe 7C 164
Castle Pl. NW1 6F 65
W4 4A 98
Castle Point E13 2A 88
(off Boundary Rd.)
Castlereagh Ho. HA7: Stan 6G 27
Castlereagh St. W1 7E 4 (6D 82)
Castle Rd. EN3: Enf H 1F 25
N12 5F 31
NW1 6F 65
RM9: Dag 1B 90
TW7: Isle 2K 113
UB2: S'hall 3D 94
UB5: N'olt 6F 59
Castle Row W4 5K 97
Castle Sq. SE17 4C 102
Castle St. E6 2A 88
E13 2A 88
KT1: King T 2E 150
Castleton Av. DA7: Bex 1K 127
HA9: Wemb 4E 60
Castleton Cl. CR0: C'don 6A 158
Castleton Gdns. HA9: Wemb 3E 60
Castleton Ho. E14 4E 104
(off Pier St.)
Castleton Rd. CR4: Mitc 4H 155
E17 2F 51
HA4: Ruis 1B 58
IG3: Ilf 1A 72
SE9 4B 142
Castletown Rd. W14 5G 99
Castleview Cl. N4 2C 66
Castleview Gdns. IG1: Ilf 5B 52
Castle Wlk. TW16: Sun 3A 148
Castle Way SW19 3F 135
TW13: Hanw 4A 130
Castle Wharf E14 7G 87
(off Orchard Pl.)
Castlewood Dr. SE9 2D 124
Castlewood Rd. EN4: Cockf 3G 21
N15 6G 49
N16 6G 49
Castle Yd. N6 7E 46
SE1 4B 14 (1B 102)
TW10: Rich 5D 114
Castor La. E14 7D 86
Catalina Ho. E1 1K 15
Catalina Rd. TW6: H'row A 2D 110
Catalpa Ct. SE13 6F 123
Caterham Av. IG5: Ilf 2D 52
Caterham High School Fitness Cen.
2D 52
Caterham Rd. SE13 3F 123
Catesby Ho. E9 7J 67
(off Frampton Pk. Rd.)
Catesby St. SE17 4D 102
CATFORD 7D 122
Catford B'way. SE6 7D 122
CATFORD GYRATORY 7D 122
Catford Hill SE6 1B 140
Catford Island SE6 7D 122
Catford M. SE6 7D 122
Catford Rd. SE6 7C 122
Catford Trad. Est. SE6 2D 140
Cathall Rd. E11 2F 69
Cathay Ho. SE16 2H 103
Cathay St. SE16 2H 103
Cathay Wlk. UB5: N'olt 2E 76
(off Brabazon Rd.)
Cathcart Dr. BR6: Orp 2J 173
Cathcart Hill N19 3G 65
Cathcart Ho. SW10 5A 100
(off Cathcart Rd.)
Cathcart Rd. SW10 6K 99
Cathcart St. NW5 6F 65
Cathedral Lodge EC1 5C 8
(off Aldersgate St.)
Cathedral Mans. SW1 3A 18
(off Vauxhall Bri. Rd.)
Cathedral Piazza SW1 2A 18 (3G 101)
Cathedral St. SE1 4E 14 (1D 102)
Cathedral Wlk. SW1 1A 18 (3G 101)
Catherall Rd. N5 3C 66
Catherine Cl. NW4 4D 44
Catherine Ct. IG2: Ilf 5G 53
N14 5B 22
SW3 7A 16
(off Callow St.)
SW19 5H 135
Catherine Dr. TW9: Rich 4E 114
TW16: Sun 6H 129
Catherine Gdns. TW3: Houn 4H 113
Catherine Griffiths Ct. EC1 3K 7
(off Northampton Rd.)
Catherine Gro. SE10 1D 122
Catherine Ho. E3 2C 86
(off Thomas Fyre Dr.)
N1 1E 84
(off Whitmore Est.)
Catherine Howard Ct. SE9 6H 125
Catherine of Aragon Ct. SE9 6G 125
Catherine Parr Ct. SE9 6H 125
Catherine Pl. HA1: Harr 5K 41
SW1 1A 18 (3G 101)
Catherine Rd. KT6: Surb 5D 150
Catherine St. WC2 2G 13 (7K 83)
Catherine Wheel All. E1 6H 9 (5E 84)
Catherine Wheel Rd. TW8: Bford 7D 96
Catherine Wheel Yd. SW1 5A 12
Catherwood Ct. N1 1E 8
Cat Hill EN4: E Barn 6H 21
Cathles Rd. SW12 6F 119
Cathnor Rd. W12 2D 98
Catkin Cl. E14 6F 87
Catlin Cres. TW17: Shep 5F 147
Catling Cl. SE23 3J 139
Catlin's La. HA5: Eastc 3K 39
Catlin St. SE16 5G 103
Cator La. BR3: Beck 1B 158
Cato Rd. SW4 3H 119
Cator Rd. SE26 6K 139
SM5: Cars 5D 166
Cator St. SE15 7F 103
(Commercial Way)
SE15 6F 103
(Ebley Cl.)
Cato St. W1 6D 4 (5C 82)
Catsey La. WD23: Bush 1B 26
Catsey Woods WD23: Bush 1B 26
Catterick Cl. N11 6K 31
Cattistock Rd. SE9 5C 142
Cattley Cl. EN5: Barn 4B 20
Catton St. WC1 6G 7 (5K 83)
Catwalk Pl. N15 6D 48
Caudwell Ter. SW18 6B 118
Caughley Ho. SE11 2J 19
Caulfield Ct. NW1 7G 65
(off Baynes St.)
Caulfield Gdns. HA5: Pinn 2A 40
Caulfield Rd. E6 1C 88
SE15 2H 121
W3 3J 97
The Causeway KT9: Chess 4E 162
KT10: Clay 7A 162
N2 4C 46
N18 6D 34
SM2: Sutt 7A 166
SM5: Cars 3E 166
SW18 5K 117
SW19 5E 134
TW11: Tedd 6K 131
TW14: Felt, Houn 4J 111
Causeyware Rd. N9 7D 24
Causton Cotts. E14 6A 86
(off Galsworthy Av.)
Causton Ho. SE5 6C 102
SW9 1K 119
Causton Rd. N6 7F 47
Causton Sq. RM10: Dag 7G 73
Causton St. SW1 4D 18 (4H 101)
Cautley Av. SW4 5G 119
Cavalier Cl. RM6: Chad H 4D 54
SM6: W'gton 6G 167
Cavalier Ct. KT5: Surb 6F 151
Cavalier Gdns. UB3: Hayes 6F 75
Cavalier Ter. SE7 6A 106
Cavalry Cres. TW4: Houn 4B 112
Cavalry Gdns. SW15 5H 117
Cavalry Memorial 5G 11
Cavalry Pl. E17 2K 49
Cavalry Sq. SW3 5F 17 (5D 100)
Cavan Pl. HA5: Hat E 1D 40
Cavatina Point SE8 6D 104
(off Coppers St.)
Cavaye Ho. SW10 7A 16
(off Cavaye Pl.)
Cavaye Pl. SW10 6A 16 (5A 100)
Cavell Dr. EN2: Enf 2F 23
Cavell Ho. N1 1E 84
(off Colville Est.)
Cavell Rd. N17 7J 33
Cavell St. E1 5H 85
Cavendish Av. DA8: Erith 6J 109
DA15: Sidc 7A 126
DA16: Well 3K 125
HA1: Harr 4H 59
HA4: Ruis 5K 57
IG8: Wfd G 1K 51
KT3: N Mald 5C 152
N3 2J 45
NW8 1B 4 (2B 82)
W13 5A 78
Cavendish Cl. N18 5C 34
NW6 6H 63
NW8 1B 4 (3B 82)
TW16: Sun 6H 129
UB4: Hayes 5G 75
Cavendish Ct. EC3 7H 9
SE6 1D 140
(off Bromley Rd.)
SM6: W'gton 6F 167
TW16: Sun 6H 129
Cavendish Dr. E11 1F 69
HA8: Edg 6A 28
Cavendish Gdns. IG1: Ilf 1E 70
IG11: Bark 5J 71
RM6: Chad H 5E 54
SW4 6G 119
Cavendish Ho. CR0: C'don 1D 168
(off Tavistock Rd.)
NW8 1B 4
(off Wellington Rd.)
NW9 3B 44
SW1 2D 18
(off Monck St.)
UB7: W Dray 2B 92
(off Park Lodge Av.)
W1 6A 6
(off Mortimer St.)
Cavendish Mans. EC1 4J 7
(off Rosebery Av.)
NW6 5J 63
Cavendish M. Nth. W1 5K 5 (5F 83)
Cavendish M. Sth. W1 6K 5 (5F 83)
Cavendish Pde. SW4 6F 119
(off Clapham Comn. Sth. Side)
TW4: Houn 2C 112
Cavendish Pl. BR1: Broml 4D 160
NW2 6F 63
SW4 5H 119
W1 7K 5 (6F 83)
Cavendish Rd. CR0: C'don 1B 168
E4 6K 35
EN5: Barn 3A 20
KT3: N Mald 4B 152
N4 6B 48
N18 5C 34
NW6 7G 63
SM2: Sutt 7A 166
SW12 6F 119
SW19 7B 136
TW16: Sun 6H 129
W4 1J 115
Cavendish Sq. W1 7K 5 (6F 83)
Cavendish St. N1 2D 84
Cavendish Ter. E3 3B 86
TW13: Felt 2J 129
Cavendish Way BR4: W W'ck 1D 170
Cavenham Gdns. IG1: Ilf 3H 71
Caverleigh Pl. BR1: Broml 2A 160
Caverleigh Way KT4: Wor Pk 1C 164
Cave Rd. E13 3K 87
TW10: Ham 4C 132
Caversham Av. N13 3F 33
SM3: Cheam 2G 165
Caversham Ct. N11 3K 31
(off Brunswick Pk. Rd.)
Caversham Ho. KT1: King T 2E 150
(off Lady Booth Rd.)
N15 4C 48
(off Caversham Rd.)
SE15 6G 103
(off Haymerle Rd.)
Caversham M. SW3 7E 16
Caversham Rd. KT1: King T 2F 151
N15 4C 48
NW5 6G 65
NW9 3C 44
Caversham St. SW3 7E 16 (6D 100)
Caverswall St. W12 6E 80
Caveside Cl. BR7: Chst 1E 160
Cavesson Ho. E20 5E 68
(off Ribbons Wlk.)
Cavour Ho. SE17 5B 102
(off Alberta Est.)
Cawdor Cres. W7 4A 96
Cawdor Wlk. E14 6E 86
Cawnpore St. SE19 5E 138
Cawston Ct. BR1: Broml 7H 141
Cawston M. SW16 5B 138
Caxton Ct. SW11 2C 118
Caxton Gro. E3 3C 86
Caxton Hall SW1 1C 18
Caxton Ho. 7D 12
Caxton M. TW8: Bford 6D 96
Caxton Pl. IG1: Ilf 3E 70
Caxton Rd. N22 2K 47
SW19 5A 136
UB2: S'hall 3B 94
W12 2F 99
The Caxtons SW9 7B 102
(off Langton Rd.)
Caxton St. SW1 1C 18 (3G 101)
Caxton St. Nth. E16 6H 87
Caxton Trad. Est. UB3: Hayes 2G 93
Caxton Wlk. WC2 1D 12 (6H 83)
Cayenne Ct. SE1 6K 15 (2F 103)
Caygill Cl. BR2: Broml 4H 159
Cayley Rd. TW6: H'row A 3D 110
UB2: S'hall 3F 95
Cayton Pl. EC1 2E 8
Cayton Rd. UB6: G'frd 2J 77
Cayton St. EC1 2E 8 (3D 84)
Cazenove Rd. E17 1C 50
N16 2F 67
Cearns Ho. E6 1B 88
Cecil Av. EN1: Enf 4A 24
HA9: Wemb 5F 61
IG11: Bark 7H 71
Cecil Cl. KT9: Chess 4D 162
TW15: Ashf 7E 128
W5 5D 78
Cecil Ct. CR0: C'don 2F 169
EN2: Enf 4J 23
EN5: Barn 3A 20
NW6 7K 63
SW10 6A 100
(off Fawcett St.)
WC2 3E 12 (7J 83)
Cecile Pk. N8 6J 47
Cecil Gro. NW8 1C 82
The Cecil Hepworth Playhouse 7H 147
(off Hepworth Way)
Cecil Ho. E17 1C 50
Cecilia Cl. N2 3A 46
Cecilia Rd. E8 5F 67
Cecil Manning Cl. UB6: G'frd 1A 78
Cecil Mans. SW17 2E 136

Cecil Pk.—The Chantry

Cecil Pk. HA5: Pinn . . . 4C 40
Cecil Pl. CR4: Mitc . . . 5D 154
Cecil Rhodes Ho. NW1 . . . 2H 83
(off Goldington St.)
Cecil Rd. CR0: C'don . . . 6J 155
E11 . . . 3H 69
E13 . . . 1J 87
E17 . . . 1C 50
EN2: Enf . . . 3H 23
HA3: W'stone . . . 3J 41
IG1: Ilf . . . 4F 71
N10 . . . 2F 47
N14 . . . 1B 32
NW9 . . . 3A 44
NW10 . . . 1A 80
RM6: Chad H . . . 7D 54
SM1: Sutt . . . 6H 165
SW19 . . . 7K 135
TW3: Houn . . . 2G 113
TW15: Ashf . . . 7E 128
W3 . . . 5J 79
Cecil Rosen Ct. HA0: Wemb . . . 3B 60
WD23: B Hea . . . 1D 26
Cecil Sharp House . . . 1E 82
(off Gloucester Av.)
Cecil Way BR2: Hayes . . . 1J 171
Cedar Av. DA15: Sidc . . . 7A 126
EN3: Enf H . . . 2D 24
EN4: E Barn . . . 7H 21
HA4: Ruis . . . 5A 58
RM6: Chad H . . . 5E 54
TW2: Whitt . . . 6F 113
UB3: Hayes . . . 6J 75
UB7: Yiew . . . 7B 74
Cedar Cl. BR2: Broml . . . 3C 172
E3 . . . 1B 86
IG1: Ilf . . . 5H 71
IG9: Buck H . . . 2G 37
KT8: E Mos . . . 4J 149
RM7: Rom . . . 4J 55
SE21 . . . 1C 138
SM5: Cars . . . 6D 166
SW15 . . . 4K 133
Cedar Copse BR1: Broml . . . 2D 160
Cedar Ct. E11 . . . 5K 51
E18 . . . 1J 51
N1 . . . 7C 66
N10 . . . 2E 46
N11 . . . 5B 32
N20 . . . 1G 31
SE1 . . . 7G 15
(off Royal Oak Yd.)
SE7 . . . 6A 106
SE9 . . . 6C 124
SE13 . . . 4F 123
SM2: Sutt . . . 6A 166
SW19 . . . 3F 135
TW8: Bford . . . 6C 96
Cedar Cres. BR2: Broml . . . 3C 172
Cedarcroft Rd. KT9: Chess . . . 4F 163
Cedar Dr. HA5: Hat E . . . 6A 26
N2 . . . 4C 46
Cedar Gdns. SM2: Sutt . . . 6A 166
Cedar Grange EN1: Enf . . . 5K 23
Cedar Gro. DA5: Bexl . . . 6D 126
UB1: S'hall . . . 5E 76
W5 . . . 3E 96
Cedar Hgts. NW2 . . . 6H 63
TW10: Ham . . . 1E 132
Cedar Ho. CR0: New Ad . . . 6D 170
E2 . . . 2H 85
(off Mowlem St.)
E14 . . . 2E 104
(off Manchester Rd.)
HA9: Wemb . . . 4G 61
(off Engineers Way)
N22 . . . 1A 48
(off Acacia Rd.)
SE14 . . . 1K 121
SE16 . . . 2K 103
(off Woodland Cres.)
SW6 . . . 2A 118
(off Lensbury Av.)
TW9: Kew . . . 1H 115
TW16: Sun . . . 7H 129
(off Spelthorne Gro.)
UB4: Yead . . . 4A 76
W8 . . . 3K 99
(off Marloes Rd.)
Cedarhurst BR1: Broml . . . 7G 141
Cedarhurst Cotts. DA5: Bexl . . . 7G 127
Cedarhurst Dr. SE9 . . . 5A 124
Cedarland Ter. SW20 . . . 7D 134
Cedar Lawn Av. EN5: Barn . . . 5B 20
Cedar M. SE4 . . . 3B 122
SW15 . . . 5F 117
Cedar Mt. SE9 . . . 1B 142
Cedarne Rd. SW6 . . . 7K 99
Cedar Pk. IG7: Chig . . . 4K 37
Cedar Pk. Gdns. RM6: Chad H . . . 7D 54
SW19 . . . 5D 134
Cedar Pk. Rd. EN2: Enf . . . 1H 23
Cedar Pl. SE7 . . . 5A 106
Cedar Ri. N14 . . . 7K 21
Cedar Rd. BR1: Broml . . . 2A 160
CR0: C'don . . . 2D 168
EN2: Enf . . . 1G 23
KT8: E Mos . . . 4J 149
N17 . . . 1F 49
NW2 . . . 4E 62
RM7: Rom . . . 4J 55
SM2: Sutt . . . 6A 166
TW4: Cran . . . 2A 112
TW11: Tedd . . . 5A 132
TW14: Bedf . . . 1F 129
The Cedars E9 . . . 7K 67
(off Banbury Rd.)
E15 . . . 7H 69
IG9: Buck H . . . 1D 36
SM6: W'gton . . . 4G 167
TW11: Tedd . . . 6K 131
W13 . . . 6C 78
Cedars Av. CR4: Mitc . . . 4E 154
E17 . . . 5C 50
Cedars Cl. NW4 . . . 3F 45
SE13 . . . 3F 123
Cedars Ct. N9 . . . 2K 33
Cedars Dr. UB10: Hil . . . 2B 74
Cedars Ho. E17 . . . 3D 50
Cedarside Apts. NW6 . . . 2H 81
Cedars M. SW4 . . . 4F 119
(not continuous)
Cedars Rd. BR3: Beck . . . 2A 158
CR0: Bedd . . . 3J 167
E15 . . . 6G 69
KT1: Hamp W . . . 1C 150
Cedars Rd. N9 . . . 2B 34
N21 . . . 2G 33
SM4: Mord . . . 4J 153
SW4 . . . 3F 119
SW13 . . . 2C 116
W4 . . . 5J 97
Cedar Ter. TW9: Rich . . . 4E 114
Cedar Tree Gro. SE27 . . . 5B 138
Cedar Vw. KT1: King T . . . 3D 150
(off Milner Rd.)
Cedarville Gdns. SW16 . . . 6K 137
Cedar Way N1 . . . 7H 65
TW16: Sun . . . 7G 129
Cedar Way Ind. Est. N1 . . . 7H 65
Cedarwood Pl. DA14: Sidc . . . 2D 144
Cedra Ct. N16 . . . 1G 67
Cedric Chambers NW8 . . . 3A 4
(off Northwick Cl.)
Cedric Rd. SE9 . . . 3G 143
Celadon Cl. EN3: Enf H . . . 3F 25
Celandine Cl. E14 . . . 5C 86
Celandine Ct. E4 . . . 3J 35
Celandine Dr. E8 . . . 7F 67
SE28 . . . 1B 108
Celandine Gro. N14 . . . 5B 22
Celandine Way E15 . . . 3G 87
Celbridge M. W2 . . . 5K 81
Celebration Av. E20 . . . 5E 68
Celebration Way E4 . . . 6K 35
Celestial Gdns. SE13 . . . 4F 123
Celia Cres. TW15: Ashf . . . 6A 128
Celia Ho. N1 . . . 2E 84
(off Arden Est.)
Celia Rd. N19 . . . 4G 65
Cellini St. SW8 . . . 7H 101
Celtic Av. BR2: Broml . . . 3G 159
Celtic St. E14 . . . 5D 86
Cemetery La. SE7 . . . 6C 106
TW17: Shep . . . 7D 146
Cemetery Rd. E7 . . . 5H 69
N17 . . . 7K 33
SE2 . . . 7B 108
Cemetery Way E4 . . . 3H 35
Cenacle Cl. NW3 . . . 3J 63
Cenotaph . . . 6E 12 (2J 101)
Centaur Ct. TW8: Bford . . . 5E 96
Centaurs Bus. Pk. TW7: Isle . . . 6A 96
Centaur St. SE1 . . . 1H 19 (3K 101)
Centenary Rd. EN3: Brim . . . 4G 25
Centenary Trad. Est. EN3: Brim . . . 3G 25
Centennial Av. WD6: E'tree . . . 1H 27
Centennial Ct. WD6: E'tree . . . 1H 27
Centennial Pk. WD6: E'tree . . . 1H 27
Central Apts. HA9: Wemb . . . 5E 60
Central Arc. TW15: Ashf . . . 4B 128
(off Woodthorpe Rd.)
Central Av. DA16: Well . . . 2K 125
E11 . . . 2F 69
EN1: Enf . . . 2C 24
HA5: Pinn . . . 6D 40
KT8: W Mole . . . 4D 148
N2 . . . 2B 46
N9 . . . 3K 33
SM6: W'gton . . . 5J 167
SW6 . . . 3A 118
SW11 . . . 7D 100
TW3: Houn . . . 4G 113
UB3: Hayes . . . 1H 93
Central Bus. Cen. NW10 . . . 5A 62
Central Cir. NW4 . . . 5D 44
Central Ctyd. EC2 . . . 7H 9
(off Cutlers Gdns.)
Central Criminal Court
Old Bailey . . . 7B 8 (6B 84)
Central Cross Apts. CR0: C'don . . . 4C 168
(off South End)
Centrale Shop. Cen. . . . 2C 168
Central Gdns. SM4: Mord . . . 5K 153
Central Gurdwara (Khalsa Jatha) . . . 1F 99
Central Hill SE19 . . . 5D 138
Central Ho. E15 . . . 2D 86
IG11: Bark . . . 7G 71
Central Lawn RM8: Dag . . . 1E 72
(off Ager Av.)
Central Mall SW18 . . . 6K 117
(within Southside Shop. Cen.)
Central Mans. NW4 . . . 5D 44
(off Watford Way)
Central Mill Apts. E8 . . . 1F 85
(off Samuel St.)
Central Pde. DA15: Sidc . . . 3A 144
E17 . . . 4C 50
EN3: Enf H . . . 2D 24
HA1: Harr . . . 5K 41
IG2: Ilf . . . 6H 53
KT6: Surb . . . 6E 150
KT8: W Mole . . . 4D 148
SE20 . . . 7K 139
(off High St.)
TW5: Hest . . . 7D 94
TW14: Felt . . . 7A 112
UB6: G'frd . . . 3A 78
W3 . . . 2H 97
Central Pk. NW10 . . . 3J 79
Central Pk. Av. RM10: Dag . . . 3H 73
Central Pk. Est. TW4: Houn . . . 5B 112
Central Pk. Rd. E6 . . . 2B 88
Central Pl. SE25 . . . 5G 157
Central Rd. HA0: Wemb . . . 5B 60
KT4: Wor Pk . . . 1C 164
SM4: Mord . . . 6J 153
Central St Giles Piazza WC2 . . . 7E 6
Central St Martins College of Art & Design
Back Hill Site . . . 4K 7
Byam Shaw Campus . . . 2H 65
The Central School of Speech & Drama
. . . 7B 64
Central School Path SW14 . . . 3J 115
Central Sq. HA9: Wemb . . . 5E 60
(off High Rd.)
KT8: W Mole . . . 5D 148
N18 . . . 6D 34
NW11 . . . 6K 45
Central St. EC1 . . . 1C 8 (3C 84)
Central Synagogue . . . 5K 5 (5F 83)
Central Ter. BR3: Beck . . . 3K 157
Central Walkway N19 . . . 4H 65
(off Pleshey Rd.)
Central Way NW10 . . . 3J 79
SE28 . . . 1A 108
SM5: Cars . . . 7C 166
TW14: Felt . . . 5J 111
Central W. UB6: G'frd . . . 4G 77
The Centre KT12: Walt T . . . 7J 147
TW3: Houn . . . 3F 113
TW13: Felt . . . 1K 129
Centre Av. W3 . . . 1K 97
Centre Comn. Rd. BR7: Chst . . . 6G 143
Centre Ct. Shop. Cen. . . . 6H 135
Cen. for Wildlife Gardening Vis. Cen.
. . . 3F 121
Centre Hgts. NW3 . . . 7B 64
(off Finchley Rd.)
Cen. Point SE1 . . . 5G 103
Centrepoint WC2 . . . 7D 6
Cen. Point Ho. WC2 . . . 7D 6
(off St Giles High St.)
Centre Rd. E7 . . . 2J 69
E11 . . . 2J 69
RM10: Dag . . . 2H 91
Centre Square KT1: King T . . . 2E 150
(off Eden Walk Shop. Cen.)
Centre St. E2 . . . 2H 85
Centre Vw. Apts. CR0: C'don . . . 3C 168
(off Whitgift St.)
Centre Way E17 . . . 7K 35
N9 . . . 2D 34
Centreway IG1: Ilf . . . 2G 71
(off High Rd.)
Centreway Apts. IG1: Ilf . . . 2G 71
(off Axon Pl.)
Centric Cl. NW1 . . . 1E 82
Centrillion Point CR0: C'don . . . 4F 169
(off Mason's Av.)
Centro Ct. E6 . . . 4D 88
Centurian Sq. SE18 . . . 1C 124
Centurion Bldg. SW11 . . . 7J 17 (6F 101)
Centurion Cl. N7 . . . 7K 65
Centurion Ct. SE18 . . . 4E 106
SM6: W'gton . . . 2F 167
Centurion Ho. UB3: Hayes . . . 6F 75
Centurion La. E3 . . . 1B 86
Centurion Way DA18: Erith . . . 3F 109
Century Cl. NW4 . . . 5F 45
Century Ct. NW8 . . . 2B 4
Century Ho. HA9: Wemb . . . 2F 61
SW15 . . . 4F 117
Century M. E5 . . . 4J 67
N5 . . . 3B 66
(off Conewood St.)
Century Plaza HA8: Edg . . . 6B 28
(off Station Rd.)
Century Rd. E17 . . . 3A 50
Century Way BR3: Beck . . . 6B 140
Century Yd. SE23 . . . 2J 139
(not continuous)
Cephas Av. E1 . . . 4J 85
Cephas Ho. E1 . . . 4J 85
(off Doveton St.)
Cephas St. E1 . . . 4J 85
Ceres Rd. SE18 . . . 4K 107
Cerise Apts. E3 . . . 1A 86
(off Gunmaker's La.)
Cerise Rd. SE15 . . . 1G 121
Cerne Cl. UB4: Yead . . . 7A 76
Cerne Rd. SM4: Mord . . . 6A 154
Cerney M. W2 . . . 2A 10
Cervantes Ct. W2 . . . 6K 81
W11 . . . 6G 81
(off Rushton M.)
Cervantes Theatre . . . 6B 14 (2B 102)
Cester St. E2 . . . 1G 85
Ceylon Ho. E1 . . . 1K 15
(off Alie St.)
Ceylon Rd. W14 . . . 3F 99
Ceylon Wharf Apts. SE16 . . . 2J 103
(off St Marychurch St.)
CFGS Community Performing Arts &
Sports Cen. . . . 3B 86
Chabot Dr. SE15 . . . 3H 121
Chadacre Av. IG5: Ilf . . . 3D 52
Chadacre Ct. E15 . . . 1J 87
(off Vicars Cl.)
Chadacre Ho. SW9 . . . 4B 120
(off Loughborough Pk.)
Chadacre Rd. KT17: Ewe . . . 6D 164
Chadbourn St. E14 . . . 5D 86
Chadbury Ct. NW7 . . . 1C 44
Chad Cres. N9 . . . 3D 34
Chadd Dr. BR1: Broml . . . 3C 160
Chadd Grn. E13 . . . 1J 87
(not continuous)
Chadston Ho. N1 . . . 7B 66
(off Halton Rd.)
Chadswell WC1 . . . 2F 7
(off Cromer St.)
Chadview Ct. RM6: Chad H . . . 7D 54
Chadville Gdns. RM6: Chad H . . . 5D 54
Chadway RM8: Dag . . . 1C 72
Chadwell Av. RM6: Chad H . . . 7B 54
CHADWELL HEATH . . . 7D 54
Chadwell Heath Ind. Pk.
RM8: Dag . . . 1D 72
Chadwell Heath La.
RM6: Chad H . . . 4B 54
Chadwell Ho. SE17 . . . 5D 102
(off Inville Rd.)
Chadwell La. N8 . . . 3K 47
Chadwell St. EC1 . . . 1K 7 (3A 84)
Chadwick Av. E4 . . . 4A 36
N21 . . . 5E 22
SW19 . . . 6J 135
Chadwick Cl. SW15 . . . 7B 116
TW11: Tedd . . . 6A 132
W7 . . . 5K 77
Chadwick Ct. E14 . . . 6C 86
(off Jonzen Wlk.)
Chadwick Gdns. UB8: Uxb . . . 7A 56
Chadwick M. W4 . . . 6H 97
Chadwick Pl. KT6: Surb . . . 7C 150
Chadwick Rd. E11 . . . 6G 51
IG1: Ilf . . . 3F 71
NW10 . . . 1B 80
SE15 . . . 2F 121
Chadwick St. SW1 . . . 2C 18 (3H 101)
Chadwick Way SE28 . . . 7D 90
Chadwin Rd. E13 . . . 5K 87
Chadworth Ho. EC1 . . . 2C 8
(off Lever St.)
N4 . . . 1C 66
Chaffinch Av. CR0: C'don . . . 6K 157
Chaffinch Bus. Pk. BR3: Beck . . . 4K 157
Chaffinch Cl. CR0: C'don . . . 5K 157
KT6: Surb . . . 3G 163
N9 . . . 1E 34
Chaffinch Rd. BR3: Beck . . . 1A 158
Chafford Way RM6: Chad H . . . 4C 54
Chagford Ho. E3 . . . 3D 86
(off Talwin St.)
Chagford St. NW1 . . . 4E 4 (4D 82)
Chailey Av. EN1: Enf . . . 2A 24
Chailey Cl. TW5: Hest . . . 1B 112
Chailey Ind. Est. UB3: Hayes . . . 2J 93
Chailey St. E5 . . . 3J 67
Chainmakers Ho. E14 . . . 6F 87
(off Blair St.)
Chalbury Wlk. N1 . . . 2K 83
Chalcombe Rd. SE2 . . . 3B 108
Chalcot Cl. SM2: Sutt . . . 7J 165
Chalcot Cres. NW1 . . . 1D 82
Chalcot Gdns. NW3 . . . 6D 64
Chalcot M. SW16 . . . 3J 137
Chalcot Rd. NW1 . . . 7E 64
Chalcot Sq. NW1 . . . 7E 64
(not continuous)
Chalcott Gdns. KT6: Surb . . . 1C 162
Chalcroft Rd. SE13 . . . 5G 123
Chaldon Ct. SE19 . . . 2D 156
Chaldon Path CR7: Thor H . . . 4B 156
Chaldon Rd. SW6 . . . 7G 99
Chale Rd. SW2 . . . 6J 119
Chalet Cl. DA5: Bexl . . . 4K 145
TW15: Ashf . . . 6F 129
Chalet Ct. CR7: Thor H . . . 5C 156
Chalet Est. NW7 . . . 4H 29
Chalfont Av. HA9: Wemb . . . 6H 61
Chalfont Ct. HA1: Harr . . . 6K 41
(off Northwick Pk. Rd.)
NW1 . . . 4F 5
(off Baker St.)
NW9 . . . 3B 44
Chalfont Grn. N9 . . . 3K 33
Chalfont Ho. SE16 . . . 3H 103
(off Keetons Rd.)
Chalfont M. SW19 . . . 1H 135
UB10: Hil . . . 7D 56
Chalfont Rd. N9 . . . 3K 33
SE25 . . . 3F 157
UB3: Hayes . . . 2J 93
Chalfont Wlk. HA5: Pinn . . . 2A 40
Chalfont Way W13 . . . 3B 96
Chalford NW6 . . . 6A 64
(off Finchley Rd.)
Chalford Cl. KT8: W Mole . . . 4E 148
Chalford Rd. SE21 . . . 4D 138
Chalford Wlk. IG8: Wfd G . . . 1B 52
Chalgrove Av. SM4: Mord . . . 5J 153
Chalgrove Cres. IG5: Ilf . . . 2C 52
Chalgrove Gdns. N3 . . . 3G 45
Chalgrove Rd. N17 . . . 1H 49
SM2: Sutt . . . 7B 166
Chalice Cl. SM6: W'gton . . . 6H 167
Chalice Ct. N2 . . . 4C 46
SE19 . . . 6D 138
Chalkenden Cl. SE20 . . . 7H 139
CHALKER'S CORNER . . . 3H 115
CHALK FARM . . . 7E 64
Chalk Farm Pde. NW3 . . . 7E 64
(off Adelaide Rd.)
Chalk Farm Rd. NW1 . . . 7E 64
Chalk Hill Rd. W6 . . . 4F 99
Chalkhill Rd. HA9: Wemb . . . 3H 61
Chalklands HA9: Wemb . . . 3J 61
Chalk La. EN4: Cockf . . . 3J 21
Chalkley Cl. CR4: Mitc . . . 2D 154
Chalkmill Dr. EN1: Enf . . . 3C 24
Chalk Pit Way SM1: Sutt . . . 5A 166
Chalk Rd. E13 . . . 5K 87
Chalkstone Cl. DA16: Well . . . 1A 126
Chalkwell Ho. E1 . . . 6K 85
(off Pitsea St.)
Chalkwell Pk. Av. EN1: Enf . . . 4K 23
Challenge Cl. NW10 . . . 1A 80
Challenge Ct. TW2: Twick . . . 7J 113
Challenger Ho. E14 . . . 7A 86
(off Victory Pl.)
Challenge Rd. TW15: Ashf . . . 3F 129
Challice Way SW2 . . . 1K 137
Challin St. SE20 . . . 1J 157
Challis Ho. SW11 . . . 2D 118
Challis Rd. TW8: Bford . . . 5D 96
Challoner Cl. N2 . . . 2B 46
Challoner Ct. BR2: Broml . . . 2F 159
W14 . . . 5H 99
(off Challoner St.)
Challoner Cres. W14 . . . 5H 99
Challoner Mans. W14 . . . 5H 99
(off Challoner St.)
Challoners Cl. KT8: E Mos . . . 4H 149
Challoner St. W14 . . . 5H 99
Challoner Wlk. E1 . . . 6G 85
(off Christian St.)
Chalmers Ho. E17 . . . 5D 50
Chalmers Rd. TW15: Ashf . . . 5D 128
Chalmers Rd. E. TW15: Ashf . . . 4D 128
Chalmers Wlk. SE17 . . . 6B 102
(off Hillingdon St.)
Chalmers Way TW1: Isle . . . 4B 114
TW14: Felt . . . 5K 111
Chaloner Ct. SE1 . . . 6E 14
Chalsey Rd. SE4 . . . 4B 122
Chalton Dr. N2 . . . 6B 46
Chalton Ho. NW1 . . . 1C 6
(off Chalton St.)
Chalton St. NW1 . . . 1C 6 (2G 83)
(not continuous)
Chamberlain Cl. IG1: Ilf . . . 3G 71
SE28 . . . 3H 107
UB3: Hayes . . . 7H 75
Chamberlain Cotts. SE5 . . . 1D 120
Chamberlain Ct. SE16 . . . 4J 103
(off Silwood St.)
Chamberlain Cres.
BR4: W W'ck . . . 1D 170
Chamberlain Gdns. TW3: Houn . . . 1G 113
Chamberlain Ho. E1 . . . 7J 85
(off Cable St.)
EC2 . . . 3G 9
(off Blackall St.)
NW1 . . . 1D 6
SE1 . . . 7J 13
(off Westminster Bri. Rd.)
Chamberlain La. HA5: Eastc . . . 3J 39
Chamberlain Pl. E17 . . . 3A 50
Chamberlain Rd. N2 . . . 2A 46
W13 . . . 2A 96
Chamberlain St. NW1 . . . 7D 64
Chamberlain Wlk. TW13: Hanw . . . 4C 130
Chamberlain Way HA5: Eastc . . . 3K 39
KT6: Surb . . . 7E 150
Chamberlayne Av. HA9: Wemb . . . 3E 60
Chamberlayne Mans. NW10 . . . 3F 81
(off Chamberlayne Rd.)
Chamberlayne Rd. NW10 . . . 1E 80
Chamberlens Garages W6 . . . 4D 98
(off Dalling Rd.)
The Chambers SW10 . . . 1A 118
(off Chelsea Harbour Dr.)
Chambers Av. DA14: Sidc . . . 6E 144
Chambers Bus. Pk. UB7: Sip . . . 6C 92
Chambers Gdns. N2 . . . 1B 46
Chambers La. NW10 . . . 7D 62
Chambers Pk. Hill SW20 . . . 7D 134
Chambers Pl. CR2: S Croy . . . 7D 168
Chambers Rd. N7 . . . 4J 65
Chambers St. SE16 . . . 2G 103
Chamber St. E1 . . . 2K 15 (7F 85)
Chambers Wlk. HA7: Stan . . . 5G 27
Chambers Wharf SE16 . . . 2G 103
Chambon Pl. W6 . . . 4C 98
Chambord Ho. E2 . . . 2K 9
(off Chambord St.)
Chambord St. E2 . . . 2K 9 (3F 85)
Chamomile Ct. E17 . . . 6C 50
(off Yunus Khan Cl.)
Champa Cl. N17 . . . 2F 49
Champion Cres. SE26 . . . 4A 140
Champion Gro. SE5 . . . 3D 120
Champion Hill SE5 . . . 3D 120
Champion Hill Est. SE5 . . . 3E 120
Champion Hill Stadium . . . 4E 120
Champion Ho. SE7 . . . 6A 106
(off Charlton Rd.)
Champion Pk. SE5 . . . 2D 120
Champion Rd. SE26 . . . 4A 140
Champions Wlk. E20 . . . 5E 68
Champions Way NW4 . . . 1D 44
NW7 . . . 1D 44
Champlain Ho. W12 . . . 7D 80
(off White City Est.)
Champness Cl. E17 . . . 3K 49
SE27 . . . 4D 138
Champness Rd. IG11: Bark . . . 6K 71
Champneys Cl. SM2: Cheam . . . 7H 165
Chancel Ct. W1 . . . 2C 12
(off Old Compton St.)
Chancel Ind. Est. NW10 . . . 5B 62
Chancellor Gdns. CR2: S Croy . . . 7B 168
Chancellor Gro. SE21 . . . 2C 138
Chancellor Ho. E1 . . . 1H 103
(off Green Bank)
SW7 . . . 3A 100
(off Hyde Pk. Ga.)
Chancellor Pas. E14 . . . 1C 104
Chancellor Pl. NW9 . . . 2B 44
Chancellors Cl. BR3: Beck . . . 7C 158
Chancellors Ct. WC1 . . . 5G 7
Chancellor's Rd. W6 . . . 5E 98
Chancellor's St. W6 . . . 5E 98
Chancellors Wharf W6 . . . 5E 98
Chancellor Way RM8: Dag . . . 4A 72
Chancelot Rd. SE2 . . . 4B 108
Chancel St. SE1 . . . 5A 14 (1B 102)
Chancery Bldg. SW11 . . . 7H 101
Chancery Bldgs. E1 . . . 7H 85
(off Lowood St.)
Chancerygate UB7: Yiew . . . 1C 92
Chancerygate Bus. Cen.
HA4: Ruis . . . 4C 58
Chancery Ga. Bus. Pk.
KT6: Surb . . . 2F 163
Chancerygate Ind. Pk.
DA14: Sidc . . . 7D 144
Chancery La. BR3: Beck . . . 2D 158
WC2 . . . 6H 7 (6A 84)
Chancery M. SW17 . . . 2C 136
Chance St. E1 . . . 3J 9 (4F 85)
E2 . . . 3J 9 (4F 85)
Chanctonbury Cl. SE9 . . . 3F 143
Chanctonbury Gdns. SM2: Sutt . . . 7K 165
Chanctonbury Way N12 . . . 4C 30
Chandaria Ct. CR0: C'don . . . 3C 168
(off Church Rd.)
Chandler Av. E16 . . . 5J 87
Chandler Cl. TW12: Hamp . . . 1E 148
Chandler Ct. TW14: Felt . . . 6J 111
Chandler Ho. NW6 . . . 1H 81
(off Willesden La.)
WC1 . . . 4F 7
(off Colonnade)
Chandlers Av. SE10 . . . 2H 105
Chandlers Cl. KT8: W Mole . . . 5F 149
TW14: Felt . . . 7H 111
Chandlers Ct. SE12 . . . 1K 141
Chandlers Dr. DA8: Erith . . . 4K 109
Chandlers M. E14 . . . 2C 104
Chandler St. E1 . . . 1H 103
Chandlers Way SW2 . . . 7A 120
Chandlers Way SE15 . . . 6E 102
The Chandlery SE1 . . . 1K 19
(off Gerridge St.)
Chandlery Ho. E1 . . . 6G 85
(off Gower's Wlk.)
Chandon Lodge SM2: Sutt . . . 7A 166
Chandos Av. E17 . . . 2C 50
N14 . . . 3B 32
N20 . . . 1F 31
W5 . . . 4C 96
Chandos Cl. IG9: Buck H . . . 2E 36
Chandos Ct. HA7: Stan . . . 6G 27
HA8: Edg . . . 7A 28
N14 . . . 2C 32
Chandos Cres. HA8: Edg . . . 7A 28
Chandos Pde. HA8: Edg . . . 7A 28
Chandos Pl. WC2 . . . 3E 12 (7J 83)
Chandos Rd. E15 . . . 5F 69
HA1: Harr . . . 5G 41
HA5: Eastc . . . 7B 40
N2 . . . 2B 46
N17 . . . 2E 48
NW2 . . . 5E 62
NW10 . . . 4A 80
Chandos St. W1 . . . 6K 5 (5F 83)
Chandos Way NW11 . . . 1K 63
Change All. EC3 . . . 1F 15 (6D 84)
Chanin M. NW2 . . . 5E 62
Channel 4 TV . . . 2C 18
Channel Cl. TW5: Hest . . . 1E 112
Channel Ga. Rd. NW10 . . . 3A 80
Channel Ho. E14 . . . 2K 103
(off Water Gdns. Sq.)
Channel Islands Est. N1 . . . 6C 66
Channelsea Ho. E15 . . . 2F 87
Channelsea Path E15 . . . 1F 87
Channelsea Rd. E15 . . . 1F 87
Channon Ct. KT6: Surb . . . 5E 150
(off Maple Rd.)
Chantrelle Ct. SE8 . . . 4A 104
(off Yeoman St.)
Chantress Cl. RM10: Dag . . . 1J 91
Chantrey Ho. SW1 . . . 3K 17
Chantrey Rd. SW9 . . . 3K 119
The Chantry E4 . . . 1K 35
UB8: Hil . . . 3B 74

Chantry Cl. DA14: Sidc 5E 144
EN2: Enf 1H 23
HA3: Kenton 5F 43
SE2 3C 108
TW16: Sun 7J 129
UB7: Yiew 7A 74
W9 4J 81
Chantry Ct. SM5: Cars 3C 166
Chantry Cres. NW10 6B 62
Chantry Ho. KT1: King T 4E 150
Chantry La. BR2: Broml 5B 160
Chantry Pl. HA3: Hrw W 1F 41
Chantry Rd. HA3: Hrw W 1F 41
KT9: Chess 5F 163
Chantry Sq. W8 3K 99
Chantry St. N1 1B 84
Chantry Way CR4: Mitc 3B 154
Chant Sq. E15 7F 69
Chant St. E15 7F 69
(not continuous)
The Chapel SW15 6G 117
Chapel Cl. DA1: Cray 5K 127
NW10 5B 62
Chapel Ct. *E10* *2D 68*
(off Rosedene Ter.)
N2 3C 46
RM7: Rush G *6K 55*
(off Bournebrook Gro.)
SE1 6E 14 (2D 102)
SE18 6A 108
UB3: Hayes 7H 75
CHAPEL END 1D 50
Chapel Farm Rd. SE9 3D 142
Chapel Ga. M. *SW4* *3J 119*
(off Bedford Rd.)
Chapel Ga. Pl. BR7: Chst 6F 143
Chapel Hill DA1: Cray 5K 127
Chapel Ho. St. E14 5D 104
Chapelier Ho. SW18 4J 117
Chapel La. HA5: Pinn 3B 40
RM6: Chad H 7D 54
UB8: Hil 6C 74
Chapel Mkt. N1 2A 84
Chapel M. IG8: Wfd G 6K 37
Chapel Mill Rd. KT1: King T 3F 151
Chapelmount Rd. IG8: Wfd G 6J 37
Chapel of St John the Evangelist *3J 15*
(within The Tower of London)
Chapel of St Peter & St Paul *6F 105*
(within University of Greenwich)
Chapel Pl. EC2 2G 9 (3E 84)
N1 2A 84
N17 7A 34
W1 1J 11 (6F 83)
Chapel Rd. DA7: Bex 4G 127
IG1: Ilf 3E 70
SE27 4B 138
TW1: Twick 7B 114
TW3: Houn 3F 113
W13 1B 96
Chapel Side W2 7K 81
Chapel Stones N17 1F 49
Chapel St. EN2: Enf 3H 23
NW1 6C 4 (5C 82)
SW1 1H 17 (3E 100)
Chapel Vw. CR2: Sels 6J 169
Chapel Wlk. CR0: C'don 2C 168
NW4 4D 44
(not continuous)
Chapel Way N7 3K 65
Chapel Yd. *SW18* *5K 117*
(off Wandsworth High St.)
Chaplin Cl. HA0: Wemb 6D 60
SE1 6K 13 (2A 102)
Chaplin Ct. *E3* *4B 86*
(off Joseph St.)
SE14 *1K 121*
(off Besson St.)
SE17 *6B 102*
(off Royal Rd.)
Chaplin Cres. TW16: Sun 6G 129
Chaplin Ho. *DA14: Sidc* *4A 144*
(off Sidcup High St.)
E17 *4C 50*
(off Hoe St.)
N1 *1D 84*
(off Shepperton Rd.)
W3 *3J 97*
(off All Saints Rd.)
Chaplin Rd. E15 2H 87
HA0: Wemb 6C 60
N17 3F 49
NW2 6C 62
RM9: Dag 7E 72
Chaplin Sq. N12 7G 31
Chapman Cl. UB7: W Dray 3B 92
Chapman Cres. HA3: Kenton 6E 42
Chapman Grn. N22 1A 48
Chapman Ho. *E1* *6H 85*
(off Bigland St.)
NW9 *3B 44*
(off Aerodrome Rd.)
Chapman Pl. N4 2B 66
Chapman Rd. CR0: C'don 1A 168
DA17: Belv 5G 109
E9 6B 68
Chapman's La. DA17: Belv 4D 108
SE2 4C 108
Chapmans Pk. Ind. Est. NW10 6B 62
Chapman Sq. SW19 2F 135
Chapman's Ter. N22 1B 48
Chapman St. E1 7H 85
Chapone Pl. W1 1C 12 (6H 83)
Chapter Chambers *SW1* *4C 18*
(off Chapter St.)
Chapter Cl. UB10: Hil 7B 56
W4 3J 97
Chapter House 1C 14
Chapter Ho. *E2* *4G 85*
(off Dunbridge St.)
Chapter Rd. NW2 5C 62
SE17 5B 102
Chapter St. SW1 4C 18 (4H 101)
Chapter Way SW19 1B 154
TW12: Hamp 4E 130
Chara Pl. W4 6K 97
Charcot Ho. SW15 6B 116
Charcot Rd. NW9 2A 44
Charcroft Ct. *W14* *2F 99*
(off Minford Gdns.)
Charcroft Gdns. EN3: Pond E 4E 24
Chardin Ho. *SW9* *1A 120*
(off Gosling Way)
Chardin Rd. W4 4A 98
Chardmore Rd. N16 1G 67
Chard Rd. TW6: H'row A 2D 110

Chardwell Cl. E6 6D 88
Charecroft Way W14 2F 99
Charfield Ct. *W9* *4K 81*
(off Shirland Rd.)
Charford Rd. E16 5J 87
Chargeable La. E13 4H 87
Chargeable St. E16 4H 87
Chargrove Cl. SE16 2K 103
Charing Cl. BR6: Orp 4K 173
Charing Ct. BR2: Broml 2G 159
Charing Cross SW1 4E 12
Charing Cross Rd. WC2 7D 6 (6H 83)
Charing Cross Sports Club 6F 99
Charing Cross Theatre *4F 13*
(off Villiers St.)
Charing Cross Underground Shop. Cen.
3E 12
Charing Ho. *SE1* *6K 13*
(off Windmill Wlk.)
Chariot Cl. E3 1C 86
Charis Ho. *E3* *3D 86*
(off Grace St.)
Charlbert Ct. *NW8* *2C 82*
(off Charlbert St.)
Charlbert St. NW8 2C 82
Charlbury Av. HA7: Stan 5J 27
Charlbury Gdns. IG3: Ilf 2K 71
Charlbury Gro. W5 6C 78
Charlbury Rd. UB10: Ick 3B 56
Charldane Rd. SE9 3F 143
Charlecote Gro. SE26 3H 139
Charlecote Rd. RM8: Dag 3E 72
Charlemont Rd. E6 4D 88
Charles II Pl. SW3 6E 16 (5D 100)
Charles II St. SW1 4C 12 (1H 101)
Charles Auffray Ho. *E1* *5J 85*
(off Smithy St.)
Charles Babbage Cl. KT9: Chess 7C 162
Charles Baker Pl. SW17 1C 136
Charles Barry Cl. SW4 3G 119
Charles Bradlaugh Ho. *N17* *7C 34*
(off Haynes Cl.)
Charles Burton Ct. *E5* *5A 68*
(off Ashenden Rd.)
Charles Chu. Wlk. IG1: Ilf 6D 52
Charles Cl. DA14: Sidc 4B 144
Charles Clowes Wlk. SW11 7H 101
Charles Cobb Gdns. CR0: Wadd 5A 168
Charles Coveney Rd. SE15 1F 121
Charles Cres. HA1: Harr 7H 41
(not continuous)
The Charles Cryer Studio Theatre
4E 166
Charles Darwin Ho. *E2* *3H 85*
(off Canrobert St.)
E16 *6H 87*
(off Minnie Baldock St.)
Charles Dickens Ho. *E2* *3G 85*
(off Mansford St.)
The Charles Dickens Mus. 4H 7
Charlesfield SE9 3A 142
Charles Flemwell M. E16 1J 105
Charles Gardner Ct. *N1* *1F 9*
(off Haberdasher St.)
Charles Grinling Wlk. SE18 4E 106
Charles Gro. N14 1B 32
Charles Haller St. SW2 7A 120
Charles Harrod Ct. *SW13* *6E 98*
(off Somerville Av.)
Charles Hocking Ho. *W3* *2J 97*
(off Bollo Bri. Rd.)
Charles Ho. *N17* *7A 34*
(off Love La.)
UB2: S'hall 2E 94
W14 4H 99
Charles Lamb Ct. *N1* *2B 84*
(off Gerrard Rd.)
Charles La. NW8 2C 82
Charles Lesser Ho. KT9: Chess 5D 162
Charles Mackenzie Ho. *SE16* *4G 103*
(off Linsey St.)
Charlesmere Gdns. *SE28* *2J 107*
(off Thames Reach)
Charles Nex M. SE21 2C 138
Charles Pl. E4 7K 25, 1A 36
NW1 2B 6 (3G 83)
Charles Rd. E7 7A 70
RM6: Chad H 6D 54
RM10: Dag 6K 73
SW19 1J 153
TW18: Staines 6A 128
W13 6A 78
Charles Rowan Ho. *WC1* *2J 7*
(off Margery St.)
Charles Sevright Way NW7 5A 30
Charles Simmons Ho. *WC1* *2J 7*
(off Margery St.)
Charles Sq. N1 2F 9 (3D 84)
Charles Sq. Est. N1 2F 9
Charles St. CR0: C'don 3C 168
E16 1A 106
EN1: Enf 5A 24
N19 1J 65
SW13 2A 116
TW3: Houn 2D 112
UB10: Hil 4D 74
W1 4J 11 (1F 101)
Charles Talbot M. SE22 1H 139
Charleston Cl. TW13: Felt 3J 129
Charleston St. SE17 4C 102
Charles Townsend Ho. *EC1* *3A 8*
(off Skinner St.)
Charles Uton Ct. E8 4G 67
Charles Whincup Rd. E16 1K 105
Charlesworth Ho. *E14* *6C 86*
(off Dod St.)
Charlesworth Pl. SW13 3A 116
Charleville Cir. SE26 5G 139
Charleville Ct. *W14* *5H 99*
(off Charleville Rd.)
Charleville Mans. *W14* *5G 99*
(off Charleville Rd.)
Charleville M. TW7: Isle 4B 114
Charleville Rd. W14 5G 99
CHARLIE BROWN'S RDBT. 2A 52
Charlie Chaplin Wlk.
SE1 4H 13 (1K 101)
Charlieville Rd. DA8: Erith 7J 109
Charlmont Rd. SW17 6C 136
Charlotte Cl. DA6: Bex 5E 126
IG6: Ilf 1G 53
Charlotte Ct. IG2: Ilf 6E 52
N8 6H 47
SE1 *4E 102*
(off Old Kent Rd.)
W6 4C 98

Charlotte Despard Av. SW11 1E 118
Charlotte Ho. *E16* *1K 105*
(off Fairfax M.)
W6 *5E 98*
(off Queen Caroline St.)
Charlotte M. W1 5B 6 (5G 83)
W10 6F 81
W14 4G 99
Charlotte Pk. Av. BR1: Broml 3C 160
Charlotte Pl. NW9 5J 43
SW1 4A 18 (4G 101)
W1 6B 6 (5G 83)
Charlotte Rd. EC2 2G 9 (3E 84)
RM10: Dag 6H 73
SM6: W'gton 6G 167
SW13 1B 116
Charlotte Row SW4 3G 119
Charlotte Sq. TW10: Rich 6F 115
Charlotte St. W1 5B 6 (5G 83)
Charlotte Ter. N1 1K 83
Charlow Cl. SW6 2A 118
CHARLTON
SE7 7B 106
TW17 3E 146
Charlton Athletic FC 5A 106
Charlton Chu. La. SE7 5A 106
Charlton Cl. UB10: Ick 2D 56
Charlton Ct. E2 1F 85
NW5 5H 65
Charlton Cres. IG11: Bark 2K 89
Charlton Dene SE7 7A 106
Charlton Ga. Bus. Pk. SE7 4A 106
Charlton Ho. TW8: Bford 6E 96
Charlton King's Rd. NW5 5H 65
Charlton La. SE7 4B 106
TW17: Shep 3E 146
(not continuous)
Charlton Lido 7B 106
Charlton Pk. La. SE7 7B 106
Charlton Pk. Rd. SE7 6B 106
Charlton Pl. N1 2B 84
Charlton Riverside Pl. SE7 4K 105
Charlton Rd. HA3: Kenton 4D 42
HA9: Wemb 1F 61
N9 1E 34
NW10 1A 80
SE3 7J 105
SE7 7J 105
TW17: Shep 3E 146
Charlton Ter. SE11 6A 102
Charlton Way SE3 1G 123
Charlwood CR0: Sels 7B 170
Charlwood Cl. HA3: Hrw W 6D 26
Charlwood Ho. *SW1* *4C 18*
(off Vauxhall Bri. Rd.)
TW9: Kew 7H 97
Charlwood Ho's. *WC1* *2F 7*
(off Midhope St.)
Charlwood Pl. SW1 4B 18 (4G 101)
Charlwood Rd. SW15 4F 117
Charlwood St. SW1 6A 18 (5G 101)
(not continuous)
Charlwood Ter. SW15 4F 117
Charmans Ho. *SW8* *7J 101*
(off Wandsworth Rd.)
Charmeuse Ct. *E2* *2H 85*
(off Silk Weaver Way)
Charmian Av. HA7: Stan 3D 42
Charmian Ho. *N1* *1G 9*
(off Crondall St.)
Charmille Av. NW9 1B 44
Charminster Av. SW19 2J 153
Charminster Ct. KT6: Surb 7D 150
Charminster Rd. KT4: Wor Pk 1F 165
SE9 4B 142
Charmouth Ct. TW10: Rich 5F 115
Charmouth Ho. SW8 7K 101
Charmouth Rd. DA16: Well 1C 126
Charnock Ho. *W12* *7D 80*
(off White City Est.)
Charnock Rd. E5 3H 67
Charnwood Av. SW19 2J 153
Charnwood Cl. KT3: N Mald 4A 152
Charnwood Dr. E18 3K 51
Charnwood Gdns. E14 4C 104
Charnwood Pl. N20 3F 31
Charnwood Rd. SE25 5D 156
UB10: Hil 2C 74
Charnwood St. E5 2H 67
Charrington Rd. CR0: C'don 2C 168
Charrington St. NW1 2H 83
(not continuous)
Charsley Rd. SE6 2D 140
Chart Cl. BR2: Broml 1G 159
CR0: C'don 6J 157
CR4: Mitc 4D 154
Charter Av. IG2: Ilf 1H 71
Charter Bldgs. *SE10* *1D 122*
(off Catherine Gro.)
Charter Ct. KT3: N Mald 3A 152
N4 1A 66
N22 1H 47
UB1: S'hall 1E 94
Charter Cres. TW4: Houn 4C 112
Charter Dr. DA5: Bexl 7E 126
Charterhouse 4B 8 (4B 84)
Charter Ho. *SM2: Sutt* *6K 165*
(off Mulgrave Rd.)
WC2 *1F 13*
(off Crown Ct.)
Charterhouse Apts. SW18 4A 118
Charterhouse Av. HA0: Wemb 4C 60
Charterhouse Bldgs. EC1 4B 8 (4C 84)
Charterhouse M. EC1 5B 8 (5B 84)
Charterhouse Museum 5B 8
Charterhouse Rd. BR6: Chels 3K 173
E8 4G 67
Charterhouse Sq. EC1 5B 8 (5B 84)
Charterhouse St. EC1 6K 7 (5A 84)
Charteris Community Sports Cen.
1J 81
Charteris Rd. IG8: Wfd G 7E 36
N4 1A 66
NW6 1H 81
Charter Quay *KT1: King T* *2D 150*
(off Wadbrook St.)
Charter Rd. KT1: King T 3H 151
The Charter Rd. IG8: Wfd G 6B 36
Charters Cl. SE19 5E 138
Charter Sq. KT1: King T 2H 151
Charter Way N3 4H 45
N14 6B 22
Chartes Ho. *SE1* *7H 15*
(off Stevens St.)
Chartfield Av. SW15 5D 116
Chartfield Sq. SW15 5F 117

Chartham Ct. *SW9* *3A 120*
(off Canterbury Cres.)
Chartham Gro. SE27 3B 138
Chartham Ho. *SE1* *7F 15*
(off Weston St.)
Chartham Rd. SE25 3H 157
Chart Hills Cl. SE28 6E 90
Chart Ho. CR4: Mitc 2D 154
E14 *5D 104*
(off Burrells Wharf Sq.)
Chartley Av. HA7: Stan 6E 26
NW2 3A 62
Charton Cl. DA17: Belv 6F 109
Chartres Ct. UB6: G'frd 2H 77
Chartridge *SE17* *6D 102*
(off Westmoreland Rd.)
Chart St. N1 1F 9 (3D 84)
Chartwell Bus. Cen. BR1: Broml 3B 160
Chartwell Cl. CR0: C'don 1D 168
SE9 2H 143
UB6: G'frd 1F 77
Chartwell Ct. EN5: Barn 4B 20
IG8: Wfd G 7C 36
NW2 3C 62
UB3: Hayes 7H 75
Chartwell Dr. BR6: Farnb 5H 173
Chartwell Gdns. SM3: Cheam 4G 165
Chartwell Ho. SW10 1A 118
W11 *1H 99*
(off Ladbroke Rd.)
Chartwell Lodge BR3: Beck 7C 140
Chartwell Pl. HA2: Harr 2H 59
SM3: Cheam 4G 165
Chartwell Way SE20 1H 157
Charville Ct. *HA1: Harr* *6K 41*
(off Gayton Rd.)
SE10 *6F 105*
(off Trafalgar Gro.)
Charville La. UB4: Hayes 3E 74
Charville La. W. UB10: Hil 3D 74
(not continuous)
Charwood SW16 4A 138
The Chase BR1: Broml 3K 159
DA7: Bex 3H 127
E12 4B 70
HA5: Eastc 6A 40
HA5: Pinn 4D 40
HA7: Stan 6F 27
HA8: Edg 1H 43
RM1: Rom 3K 55
RM6: Chad H 6E 54
RM7: Rush G 3K 73
SM6: W'gton 5J 167
SW4 3F 119
SW16 7K 137
SW20 1G 153
TW16: Sun 1K 147
UB10: Ick 5C 56
Chase Bank Ct. *N14* *6B 22*
(off Avenue Rd.)
The Chase Cen. NW10 3K 79
Chase Ct. *SW3* *2E 16*
(off Beaufort Gdns.)
SW20 2G 153
TW7: Isle 2A 114
Chase Ct. Gdns. EN2: Enf 3H 23
Chase Cross Rd. RM5: Col R 1J 55
Chasefield Rd. SW17 4D 136
Chase Gdns. E4 4H 35
TW2: Whitt 7H 113
Chase Grn. EN2: Enf 3H 23
Chase Grn. Av. EN2: Enf 2G 23
Chase Hill EN2: Enf 3H 23
Chase Ho. *NW6* *3J 81*
(off Hansel Rd.)
Chase La. IG2: Ilf 5H 53
IG6: Ilf 5H 53
Chaseley Dr. W4 5H 97
Chaseley St. E14 6A 86
Chasemore Cl. CR4: Mitc 7D 154
Chasemore Gdns. CR0: Wadd 5A 168
Chasemore Ho. *SW6* *7G 99*
(off Williams Cl.)
Chase Ridings EN2: Enf 2F 23
Chase Rd. N14 5B 22
NW10 4K 79
Chase Rd. Trad. Est. NW10 4K 79
CHASE SIDE 1J 23
Chase Side EN2: Enf 3H 23
N14 5K 21
Chase Side Av. EN2: Enf 2H 23
SW20 1G 153
Chase Side Cres. EN2: Enf 1H 23
Chase Side Pl. EN2: Enf 2H 23
Chaseville Pde. N21 5E 22
Chaseville Pk. Rd. N21 5D 22
Chase Way N14 2A 32
Chaseway Lodge *E16* *6J 87*
(off Butchers Rd.)
Chaseways Vs. RM5: Col R 1F 55
Chasewood Av. EN2: Enf 2G 23
Chasewood Ct. NW7 5E 28
Chasewood Pk. HA1: Harr 3K 59
Chaston Pl. *NW5* *5E 64*
(off Grafton Ter.)
Chater Ho. *E2* *3K 85*
(off Roman Rd.)
Chatfield Rd. CR0: C'don 1B 168
SW11 3A 118
Chatham Av. BR2: Hayes 7H 159
Chatham Cl. NW11 5J 45
SE18 3F 107
SM3: Sutt 7H 153
Chatham Ho. *SM6: W'gton* *5F 167*
(off Melbourne Rd.)
Chatham Pl. E9 6J 67
Chatham Rd. E17 3A 50
E18 2H 51
KT1: King T 2G 151
SW11 6D 118
Chatham St. SE17 4D 102
Chatsfield Pl. W5 6E 78
Chats Palace Arts Cen. 5K 67
Chatswood M. DA14: Sidc 4K 143
Chatsworth Av. BR1: Broml 4K 141
DA15: Sidc 1A 144
HA9: Wemb 5F 61
NW4 2E 44
SW20 1G 153
Chatsworth Cl. BR4: W W'ck 2H 171
NW4 2E 44
W4 6J 97
Chatsworth Ct. HA7: Stan 5H 27
SW16 3K 155
W8 *4J 99*
(off Pembroke Rd.)

Chatsworth Cres. TW3: Houn 4H 113
Chatsworth Dr. EN1: Enf 7B 24
Chatsworth Est. E5 4K 67
Chatsworth Gdns. HA2: Harr 1F 59
KT3: N Mald 5B 152
W3 1H 97
Chatsworth Ho. *BR2: Broml* *4J 159*
(off Westmoreland Rd.)
E16 *1K 105*
(off Wesley Av.)
SE1 *5J 15*
(off Duchess Wlk.)
Chatsworth Lodge *W4* *5K 97*
(off Bourne Pl.)
Chatsworth Pde. BR5: Pet W 5G 161
Chatsworth Pl. CR4: Mitc 3D 154
TW11: Tedd 4A 132
Chatsworth Ri. W5 4F 79
Chatsworth Rd. CR0: C'don 4D 168
E5 3J 67
E15 5H 69
NW2 6E 62
SM3: Cheam 5F 165
UB4: Yead 4K 75
W4 6J 97
W5 4F 79
Chatsworth Way SE27 3B 138
CHATTERN HILL 4D 128
Chattern Hill TW15: Ashf 4D 128
Chattern Rd. TW15: Ashf 4E 128
Chatterton Ct. TW9: Kew 2F 115
Chatterton M. *N4* *3B 66*
(off Chatterton Rd.)
Chatterton Rd. BR2: Broml 4B 160
N4 3B 66
Chatto Rd. SW11 5D 118
Chaucer Av. TW4: Cran 2K 111
TW9: Rich 3G 115
UB4: Hayes 5J 75
Chaucer Cl. N11 5B 32
Chaucer Ct. BR2: Broml 5A 160
EN5: New Bar 5E 20
N16 4E 66
SW17 *3B 136*
(off Lanesborough Way)
Chaucer Dr. SE1 4F 103
Chaucer Gdns. *E1* *1K 15*
(off Piazza Wlk.)
SM1: Sutt 3J 165
Chaucer Grn. CR0: C'don 7H 157
Chaucer Ho. EN5: Barn 4A 20
SM1: Sutt *3J 165*
(off Chaucer Gdns.)
SW1 *6A 18*
(off Churchill Gdns.)
Chaucer Mans. *W14* *6G 99*
(off Queen's Club Gdns.)
Chaucer Rd. DA15: Sidc 1C 144
DA16: Well 1J 125
E7 6J 69
E11 6J 51
E17 2E 50
SE24 5A 120
SM1: Sutt 4J 165
TW15: Ashf 4A 128
W3 1J 97
Chaucer Way SW19 6B 136
Chaulden Ho. *EC1* *2F 9*
(off Cranwood St.)
Chauncey Cl. N9 3B 34
Chaundrye Cl. SE9 6D 124
Chauntler Cl. E16 6K 87
Chaville Ct. N11 4K 31
Chaville Way N3 1J 45
Cheadle Ct. *NW8* *3B 4*
(off Henderson Dr.)
Cheadle Ho. *E14* *6B 86*
(off Copenhagen Pl.)
CHEAM 6G 165
Cheam Comn. Rd. KT4: Wor Pk 2D 164
Cheam Leisure Cen. 4F 165
Cheam Mans. SM3: Cheam 7G 165
Cheam Pk. Way SM3: Cheam 6G 165
Cheam Rd. SM1: Sutt 6H 165
SM2: Cheam 7F 165
Cheam St. SE15 3J 121
CHEAM VILLAGE 6G 165
Cheapside EC2 1D 14 (6C 84)
N13 4J 33
N22 3A 48
Cheapside Pas. *EC2* *1C 14*
(off One New Change)
Cheddar Cl. N11 6J 31
Cheddar Waye UB4: Yead 6K 75
Cheddington Ho. *E2* *1G 85*
(off Whiston Rd.)
Cheddington Rd. N18 3K 33
Chedworth Cl. *E16* *6H 87*
(off Wouldham Rd.)
Chedworth Ho. *N15* *4D 48*
(off West Grn. Rd.)
Cheering La. E20 5E 68
The Cheesegrater 1G 15
Cheeseman Cl. TW12: Hamp 6C 130
Cheesemans Ter. W14 5H 99
(not continuous)
Cheffery Ct. TW15: Ashf 6D 128
Cheldon Av. NW7 7A 30
Chelford Rd. BR1: Broml 5F 141
Chelmer Cres. IG11: Bark 2B 90
Chelmer Rd. E9 5K 67
Chelmsford Cl. E6 6D 88
W6 6F 99
Chelmsford Ct. *N14* *7C 22*
(off Chelmsford Rd.)
Chelmsford Gdns. IG1: Ilf 7C 52
Chelmsford Ho. *N7* *4K 65*
(off Holloway Rd.)
Chelmsford Rd. E11 1F 69
E17 6C 50
E18 1H 51
N14 7B 22
Chelmsford Sq. NW10 1E 80
Chelmsine Ct. HA4: Ruis 5E 38
CHELSEA 6D 16 (5C 100)
CHELSEA BRI. 7J 17 (6F 101)
Chelsea Bri. Rd. SW1 5G 17 (5E 100)
Chelsea Bri. Wharf SW11 6F 101
Chelsea Cloisters
SW3 4D 16 (4C 100)
Chelsea Cl. HA8: Edg 2G 43
KT4: Wor Pk 7C 152
NW10 1K 79
TW12: Hamp H 5G 131
Chelsea Ct. *BR1: Broml* *3C 160*
(off Holmdene Ct.)

Chelsea Ct.—Child's St.

Chelsea Ct. SW3 7G 17
(off Embankment Gdns.)
Chelsea Cres. NW2 6H 63
SW10 1A 118
Chelsea Emb. SW3 7D 16 (6C 100)
Chelsea Farm Ho. Studios
SW10 6B 100
(off Cremorne Est.)
Chelsea FC 7K 99
Chelsea Flds. SW19 1B 154
Chelsea Gdns. SM3: Cheam 4G 165
SW1 6H 17 (5E 100)
W13 5K 77
Chelsea Ga. SW1 6H 17
Chelsea Harbour SW10 1A 118
Chelsea Harbour Design Cen.
SW10 1A 118
(off Chelsea Harbour Dr.)
Chelsea Harbour Dr. SW10 1A 118
Chelsea Lodge SW3 7F 17
(off Tite St.)
Chelsea Mnr. Ct. SW3 7D 16 (6C 100)
Chelsea Mnr. Gdns.
SW3 6D 16 (5C 100)
Chelsea Mnr. St. SW3 6D 16 (5C 100)
Chelsea Mnr. Studios SW3 6D 16
(off Flood St.)
Chelsea Pk. Gdns.
SW3 7A 16 (6B 100)
Chelsea Physic Garden 7E 16 (6D 100)
Chelsea Reach Twr. SW10 7B 100
(off Worlds End Est.)
Chelsea Sports Cen. 6D 16 (5C 100)
Chelsea Sq. SW3 5B 16 (5B 100)
Chelsea Studios SW6 7K 99
(off Fulham Rd.)
The Chelsea Theatre 7A 100
Chelsea Towers SW3 7D 16
Chelsea Village SW6 7K 99
(off Fulham Rd.)
Chelsea Vista SW6 1A 118
Chelsea Wharf SW10 7B 100
(off Lots Rd.)
Chelsfield Av. N9 7E 24
Chelsfield Gdns. SE26 3J 139
Chelsfield Grn. N9 7E 24
(not continuous)
Chelsfield Ho. SE17 4E 102
(off Massinger St.)
Chelsfield Point E9 7K 67
(off Penshurst Rd.)
Chelsham Rd. CR2: S Croy 7D 168
SW4 3H 119
Chelsiter Ct. DA14: Sidc 4K 143
Chelston App. HA4: Ruis 2J 57
Chelston Ct. E11 5K 51
Chelston Rd. HA4: Ruis 1J 57
Chelsworth Dr. SE18 6H 107
Cheltenham Av. TW1: Twick 7A 114
Cheltenham Cl. KT3: N Mald 3J 151
UB5: N'olt 6F 59
Cheltenham Ct. HA7: Stan 5H 27
(off Marsh La.)
Cheltenham Gdns. E6 2C 88
Cheltenham Ho. IG8: Wfd G 6K 37
UB3: Harl 3E 92
(off Skipton Dr.)
Cheltenham Pl. HA3: Kenton 4E 42
W3 1H 97
Cheltenham Rd. BR6: Chels 3K 173
E10 6E 50
SE15 4J 121
Cheltenham Ter. SW3 5F 17 (5D 100)
Chelverton Rd. SW15 4F 117
Chelwood N20 2G 31
Chelwood Cl. E4 6J 25
Chelwood Ct. CR2: S Croy 5C 168
SW11 1B 118
(off Westbridge Rd.)
Chelwood Gdns. TW9: Kew 2G 115
Chelwood Gdns. Pas. TW9: Kew 2G 115
Chelwood Ho. W2 1B 10
(off Gloucester Sq.)
Chelwood Wlk. SE4 4A 122
Chenappa Cl. E13 3J 87
Chenduit Way HA7: Stan 5E 26
Cheney Ct. SE23 1K 139
Cheney Row E17 1B 50
Cheneys Rd. E11 3G 69
Cheney St. HA5: Eastc 4A 40
The Chenies BR6: Pet W 6J 161
NW1 2H 83
(off Pancras Rd.)
Chenies Ho. W2 7K 81
(off Moscow Rd.)
W4 7B 98
(off Corney Reach Way)
Chenies M. WC1 4C 6 (4H 83)
Chenies Pl. NW1 2H 83
Chenies St. WC1 5C 6 (5H 83)
Cheniston Gdns. W8 3K 99
Chenla SE13 2D 122
Chenneston Cl. TW16: Sun 1J 147
Cheping Ho. W10 7F 81
(off Shalfleet Dr.)
Chepstow Cl. SW15 5G 117
Chepstow Cnr. W2 6J 81
(off Chepstow Pl.)
Chepstow Ct. W11 7J 81
(off Chepstow Vs.)
Chepstow Cres. IG3: Ilf 6J 53
W11 7J 81
Chepstow Gdns. UB1: S'hall 6D 76
Chepstow Pl. W2 6J 81
Chepstow Ri. CR0: C'don 3E 168
Chepstow Rd. CR0: C'don 3E 168
W2 6J 81
W7 3A 96
Chepstow Vs. W11 7H 81
Chequers IG9: Buck H 1E 36
The Chequers HA5: Pinn 3B 40
Chequers Cl. BR5: St P 4K 161
NW9 3A 44
Chequers Ct. DA17: Belv 4G 109
EC1 4D 8
(off Chequer St.)
Chequers Ho. NW8 3C 4
(off Jerome Cres.)
Chequers La. RM9: Dag 4F 91
(not continuous)
Chequers Pde. N13 5H 33
RM9: Dag 1F 91
SE9 6D 124
(off Eltham High St.)
Chequer St. EC1 4D 8 (4C 84)
(not continuous)
Chequers Way N13 5G 33
Cherbury Cl. SE28 6D 90
Cherbury Ct. N1 2D 84
(off St John's Est.)
Cherbury St. N1 2D 84
Cherchefelle M. HA7: Stan 5G 27
Cherimoya Gdns. KT8: W Mole 3F 149
Cherington Rd. W7 1J 95
Cheriton Av. BR2: Broml 5H 159
IG5: Ilf 2D 52
Cheriton Cl. EN4: Cockf 3J 21
W5 5C 78
Cheriton Ct. SE12 7J 123
SE25 5E 156
Cheriton Dr. SE18 7H 107
Cheriton Lodge HA4: Ruis 1H 57
Cheriton Sq. SW17 2E 136
Cherry Av. UB1: S'hall 1B 94
Cherry Blossom Cl. N13 5G 33
Cherry Cl. E17 5D 50
HA0: Wemb 3D 60
HA4: Ruis 3H 57
NW9 2A 44
SM4: Mord 4G 153
SM5: Cars 2D 166
SW2 7A 120
W5 3D 96
Cherrycot Hill BR6: Farnb 4G 173
Cherrycot Ri. BR6: Farnb 4G 173
Cherry Ct. HA5: Pinn 2B 40
IG6: Ilf 3F 53
W3 1A 98
Cherry Cres. TW8: Bford 7B 96
Cherrydown Av. E4 3G 35
Cherrydown Cl. E4 3H 35
Cherrydown Rd. DA14: Sidc 2D 144
Cherrydown Wlk. RM7: Mawney 2H 55
Cherry Gdn. Ho. SE16 2H 103
(off Cherry Gdn. St.)
Cherry Gdns. RM9: Dag 5F 73
UB5: N'olt 7F 59
Cherry Gdn. St. SE16 2H 103
Cherry Gth. TW8: Bford 5D 96
Cherry Gro. UB3: Hayes 1K 93
UB8: Hil 5D 74
Cherry Hill EN5: New Bar 6E 20
HA3: Hrw W 6E 26
Cherry Hill Gdns. CR0: Wadd 4K 167
Cherrylands Cl. NW9 2J 61
Cherry La. UB7: W Dray 4B 92
Cherry Laurel Wlk. SW2 6K 119
Cherry Orchard SE7 6A 106
UB7: W Dray 2A 92
Cherry Orchard Gdns.
CR0: C'don 1D 168
KT8: W Mole 3D 148
Cherry Orchard Rd. BR2: Broml 2C 172
CR0: C'don 2D 168
KT8: W Mole 3E 148
Cherry Pk. La. E20 7E 68
Cherry Red Records Stadium 3H 151
Cherry Rd. EN3: Enf W 1D 24
Cherry St. RM7: Rom 5K 55
Cherry Tree Av. UB7: Yiew 6B 74
Cherry Tree Cl. E9 1J 85
HA0: Wemb 4A 60
Cherry Tree Ct. NW1 7G 65
(off Camden Rd.)
NW9 4J 43
SE7 6A 106
Cherry Tree Dr. SW16 3J 137
Cherry Tree Hill N2 5C 46
Cherry Tree Ho. N22 7D 32
Cherry Tree Ri. IG9: Buck H 4F 37
Cherry Tree Rd. E15 5G 69
N2 4D 46
Cherry Tree Ter. SE1 7H 15
(off Whites Grounds)
Cherry Tree Wlk. BR3: Beck 4B 158
BR4: W W'ck 4H 171
EC1 4D 8 (4C 84)
Cherry Tree Way E13 4B 88
HA7: Stan 6G 27
Cherry Wlk. BR2: Hayes 1J 171
Cherry Way KT19: Ewe 6K 163
TW17: Shep 4F 147
Cherrywood Cl. E3 3A 86
KT2: King T 7G 133
Cherrywood Ct. TW11: Tedd 5A 132
Cherrywood Dr. SW15 5F 117
Cherrywood La. SM4: Mord 4G 153
Cherrywood Lodge SE13 6F 123
(off Birdwood Av.)
Cherry Wood Way W5 5G 79
Chertsey Bri. Rd. KT16: Chert 7A 146
Chertsey Ct. SW14 3H 115
Chertsey Dr. SM3: Cheam 2G 165
Chertsey Ho. E2 2J 9
(off Arnold Cir.)
CHERTSEY MEADS 7A 146
Chertsey Meads
Local Nature Reserve 7A 146
Chertsey Rd. E11 2F 69
IG1: Ilf 4H 71
TW1: Twick 6K 113
TW2: Twick 2F 131
TW13: Felt 3G 129
TW15: Ashf 7F 129
TW16: Sun 7F 129
TW17: Shep 7A 146
Chertsey St. SW17 5E 136
Chervil Cl. TW13: Felt 3J 129
Chervil M. SE28 1B 108
Cherwell Ct. KT19: Ewe 4J 163
Cherwell Ho. NW8 4B 4
Cherwell M. SW11 4C 118
Cherwell Way HA4: Ruis 6E 38
Cheryls Cl. SW6 1K 117
Cheseman St. SE26 3H 139
Chesfield Rd. KT2: King T 7E 132
Chesham Apts. E4 7J 35
Chesham Av. BR5: Pet W 6F 161
Chesham Cl. NW7 4F 29
RM7: Rom 4K 55
SW1 2G 17
Chesham Cres. SE20 1J 157
Chesham Flats W1 2H 11
(off Brown Hart Gdns.)
Chesham Ho. SE8 1C 122
(off Brookmill Rd.)
Chesham M. SW1 1G 17
Chesham Pl. SW1 2G 17 (3E 100)
(not continuous)
Chesham Rd. KT1: King T 2G 151
SE20 2J 157
SW19 5B 136
Chesham St. NW10 3K 61
SW1 2G 17 (3E 100)
Chesham Ter. W13 2B 96
Cheshire Cl. CR4: Mitc 3J 155
E17 1D 50
SE4 2B 122
Cheshire Ct. EC4 1K 13
(off Fleet St.)
Cheshire Gdns. KT9: Chess 6D 162
Cheshire Ho. N18 4C 34
SM4: Mord 7K 153
Cheshire Rd. N22 7E 32
Cheshire St. E2 3K 9 (4F 85)
Cheshir Ho. NW4 4E 44
Chesholm Rd. N16 3E 66
Cheshunt Ho. NW6 1K 81
(off Mortimer Cres.)
Cheshunt Rd. DA17: Belv 5G 109
E7 6K 69
Chesil Ct. E2 2J 85
SW3 7D 16 (6C 100)
Chesilton Rd. SW6 1H 117
Chesil Way UB4: Hayes 3H 75
Chesley Gdns. E6 2B 88
Chesney Ct. W9 4J 81
(off Shirland Rd.)
Chesney Cres. CR0: New Ad 7E 170
Chesney Ho. SE13 4F 123
(off Mercator Rd.)
Chesney St. SW11 1E 118
Chesnut Gro. N17 3F 49
Chesnut Rd. N17 3F 49
Chesnut Row N3 7D 30
(off Nether St.)
Chessell Cl. CR7: Thor H 4B 156
Chessholme Ct. TW16: Sun 7G 129
(off Scotts Av.)
Chessholme Rd. TW15: Ashf 6E 128
Chessing Ct. N2 3D 46
(off Fortis Grn.)
CHESSINGTON 5E 162
Chessington Av. DA7: Bex 7E 108
N3 3G 45
Chessington Cl. KT19: Ewe 6J 163
Chessington Ct. HA5: Pinn 4D 40
N3 3H 45
(off Charter Way)
Chessington Hall Gdns.
KT9: Chess 7D 162
Chessington Hill Pk. KT9: Chess 5G 163
Chessington Ho. SW8 2H 119
Chessington Lodge N3 3H 45
Chessington Mans. E10 7C 50
E11 7G 51
Chessington Pde. KT9: Chess 6D 162
Chessington Pk. KT9: Chess 4G 163
Chessington Rd. KT17: Ewe 7B 164
KT19: Ewe 6G 163
Chessington Sports Cen. 7D 162
Chessington Trade Pk.
KT9: Chess 4G 163
Chessington Way BR4: W W'ck 2D 170
Chesson Rd. W14 6H 99
Chesswood Way HA5: Pinn 2B 40
Chestbrook Ct. EN1: Enf 5K 23
(off Forsyth Pl.)
Chester Av. TW2: Whitt 1D 130
TW10: Rich 6F 115
Chester Cl. SM1: Sutt 2J 165
SW1 7J 11 (2F 101)
SW13 3D 116
TW10: Rich 6F 115
TW15: Ashf 5F 129
UB8: Hil 6D 74
Chester Cl. Nth. NW1 1K 5 (3F 83)
Chester Cl. Sth. NW1 2K 5 (3F 83)
Chester Cotts. SW1 4G 17
Chester Ct. BR2: Broml 4H 159
(off Durham Rd.)
NW1 1K 5 (3F 83)
(not continuous)
SE5 7D 102
(off Lomond Gro.)
SE8 5K 103
W6 4F 99
(off Wolverton Gdns.)
Chester Cres. E8 5F 67
Chester Dr. HA2: Harr 6D 40
Chesterfield Cl. SE13 2F 123
Chesterfield Ct. KT5: Surb 5E 150
(off Cranes Pk.)
Chesterfield Dr. KT10: Hin W 2A 162
Chesterfield Flats EN5: Barn 5A 20
(off Bells Hill)
Chesterfield Gdns. N4 5B 48
SE10 7F 105
W1 4J 11 (1F 101)
Chesterfield Gro. SE22 5F 121
Chesterfield Hill W1 4J 11 (1F 101)
Chesterfield Ho. W1 4H 11
(off Chesterfield Gdns.)
Chesterfield Lodge N21 7E 22
(off Church Hill)
Chesterfield M. N4 5B 48
TW15: Ashf 4A 128
Chesterfield Rd. E10 6E 50
EN5: Barn 5A 20
KT19: Ewe 7K 163
N3 6D 30
TW15: Ashf 4A 128
W4 6J 97
Chesterfield St. W1 4J 11 (1F 101)
Chesterfield Wlk. SE10 1F 123
Chesterfield Way SE15 7J 103
UB3: Hayes 2J 93
Chesterford Gdns. NW3 4K 63
Chesterford Ho. SE18 1B 124
(off Tellson Av.)
Chesterford Rd. E12 5D 70
Chester Gdns. EN3: Pond E 6C 24
SM4: Mord 6A 154
W13 6B 78
Chester Ga. NW1 2J 5 (3F 83)
Chester Ho. N10 2F 47
SE8 6B 104
SW1 3J 17
(off Eccleston Pl.)
SW9 7A 102
(off Cranmer Rd.)
Chesterman Ct. W4 7A 98
(off Corney Reach Way)
Chester M. E17 2C 50
SW1 1J 17 (3F 101)
Chester Pl. NW1 1J 5 (3F 83)
Chester Rd. DA15: Sidc 5J 125
E7 7B 70
Chester Rd. E11 6K 51
E16 4G 87
E17 5K 49
HA6: Nwood 1H 39
IG3: Ilf 1K 71
IG7: Chig 3K 37
N9 1C 34
N17 3D 48
N19 2F 65
NW1 2H 5 (3E 82)
SW19 6E 134
TW4: Houn 3K 111
TW6: H'row A 5C 110
Chester Row SW1 4G 17 (4E 100)
The Chesters KT3: N Mald 1A 152
Chester Sq. SW1 3H 17 (4E 100)
Chester Sq. M. SW1 2J 17
Chester St. E2 4G 85
SW1 1H 17 (3E 100)
Chester Ter. IG11: Bark 6K 71
NW1 1J 5 (3F 83)
(not continuous)
Chesterton Cl. SW18 5J 117
UB6: G'frd 2F 77
Chesterton Ct. W5 5D 78
Chesterton Dr. TW19: Stanw 1B 128
Chesterton Ho. CR0: C'don 4D 168
(off Heathfield Rd.)
SW11 3B 118
(off Ingrave St.)
W10 5G 81
(off Portobello Rd.)
Chesterton Rd. E13 3J 87
W10 5F 81
Chesterton Sq. W8 4J 99
Chesterton Ter. E13 3J 87
KT1: King T 2G 151
Chester Way SE11 4K 19 (4A 102)
Chesthunte Rd. N17 1C 48
Chestlands Ct. UB10: Hil 6C 56
Chestnut All. SW6 6H 99
Chestnut Apts. E3 2D 86
(off Alameda Pl.)
Chestnut Av. BR4: W W'ck 5G 171
E7 4K 69
HA0: Wemb 5B 60
HA6: Nwood 2H 39
HA8: Edg 6K 27
IG9: Buck H 3G 37
KT8: E Mos 3K 149
KT10: Esh 7H 149
KT19: Ewe 4A 164
N8 5J 47
SW14 3K 115
TW8: Bford 4D 96
TW11: Tedd 2K 149
TW12: Hamp 7E 130
UB7: Yiew 7B 74
Chestnut Av. Nth. E17 4F 51
Chestnut Av. Sth. E17 5E 50
Chestnut Cl. BR6: Chels 5K 173
DA15: Sidc 1A 144
IG9: Buck H 3G 37
N14 5B 22
N16 2D 66
SE6 5E 140
SE14 1B 122
SM5: Cars 1D 166
SW16 4A 138
TW15: Ashf 4D 128
TW16: Sun 6H 129
UB3: Hayes 7G 75
UB7: Harl, Sip 7D 92
Chestnut Ct. CR2: S Croy 4C 168
(off Bramley Hill)
N8 5J 47
SW6 6H 99
TW13: Hanw 5B 130
TW19: Stanw 1A 128
(off Mulberry Av.)
W8 3K 99
(off Abbots Wlk.)
Chestnut Dr. DA7: Bex 3D 126
E11 6J 51
HA3: Hrw W 7E 26
HA5: Pinn 6B 40
Chestnut Gro. CR2: Sels 7H 169
CR4: Mitc 5H 155
DA2: Wilm 4K 145
EN4: E Barn 5J 21
HA0: Wemb 5B 60
KT3: N Mald 3K 151
SE20 7H 139
SW12 7E 118
TW7: Isle 4A 114
W5 3D 96
Chestnut Ho. E3 1B 86
(off Sycamore Av.)
SW15 4B 116
W4 4A 98
(off The Orchard)
Chestnut La. N20 1B 30
Chestnut M. SW14 4J 115
Chestnut Pl. SE26 4F 139
Chestnut Plaza E20 6E 68
(within Westfield Shop. Cen.)
Chestnut Ri. SE18 6H 107
WD23: Bush 1A 26
Chestnut Rd. KT2: King T 7E 132
SE27 3B 138
SW20 2F 153
TW2: Twick 2J 131
TW15: Ashf 4D 128
The Chestnuts BR3: Beck 3K 157
HA5: Hat E 1D 40
N5 4C 66
(off Highbury Grange)
UB10: Uxb 7A 56
Chestnuts Ho. E17 6C 50
(off Hoe St.)
Chestnut Ter. SM1: Sutt 4K 165
Chestnut Wlk. IG8: Wfd G 5D 36
TW17: Shep 4G 147
Chestnut Way TW13: Felt 3K 129
Cheston Av. CR0: C'don 2A 170
Chestwood Gro. UB10: Hil 7B 56
Chesworth Ct. E1 5J 85
(off Fulneck Pl.)
Chettle Cl. SE1 3D 102
(off Spurgeon St.)
Chettle Ct. N8 6A 48
Chetwode Ho. NW8 3C 4
Chetwode Rd. SW17 3D 136
Chetwood Wlk. E6 5C 88
(off Greenwich Cres.)
Chetwynd Av. EN4: E Barn 1J 31
Chetwynd Dr. UB10: Hil 2B 74
Chetwynd Rd. NW5 4F 65
Chetwynd Vs. NW5 4F 65
(off Chetwynd Rd.)
Chevalier Cl. HA7: Stan 4K 27
Cheval Pl. SW7 1D 16 (3C 100)
Cheval St. E14 3C 104
Cheveney Wlk. BR2: Broml 3J 159
Chevening Rd. NW6 2F 81
SE10 5H 105
SE19 6D 138
The Chevenings DA14: Sidc 3C 144
Cheverell Ho. E2 2G 85
(off Pritchard's Rd.)
Cheverton Rd. N19 1H 65
Chevet St. E9 5A 68
Chevington NW2 6H 63
Cheviot N17 7C 34
(off Northumberland Gro.)
Cheviot Cl. DA7: Bex 2K 127
EN1: Enf 2J 23
UB3: Harl 7F 93
Cheviot Ct. SE14 6J 103
(off Avonley Rd.)
UB2: S'hall 4F 95
Cheviot Gdns. NW2 2F 63
SE27 4B 138
Cheviot Ga. NW2 2G 63
Cheviot Ho. E1 6H 85
(off Commercial Rd.)
Cheviot Rd. SE27 5A 138
Cheviot Way IG2: Ilf 4J 53
Chevron Cl. E16 6J 87
Chevy Rd. UB2: S'hall 2G 95
Chewton Rd. E17 4A 50
Cheylesmore Ho. SW1 5J 17
(off Ebury Bri. Rd.)
Cheyne Av. E18 3H 51
TW2: Whitt 1D 130
Cheyne Cl. BR2: Broml 3C 172
NW4 5E 44
Cheyne Ct. SW3 7E 16 (6D 100)
Cheyne Gdns. SW3 7D 16 (6C 100)
Cheyne Hill KT5: Surb 4F 151
Cheyne Ho. SW3 7E 16
(off Chelsea Emb.)
Cheyne M. SW3 7D 16 (6C 100)
Cheyne Pk. Dr. BR4: W W'ck 3E 170
Cheyne Path W7 5K 77
Cheyne Pl. SW3 7E 16 (6D 100)
Cheyne Rd. TW15: Ashf 7F 129
Cheyne Row SW3 7C 16 (6C 100)
Cheyne Wlk. CR0: C'don 2G 169
N21 5G 23
NW4 6E 44
SW3 7C 16 (7B 100)
SW10 7B 100
Cheyneys Av. HA8: Edg 6J 27
Chichele Gdns. CR0: C'don 4E 168
Chichele Rd. NW2 5F 63
Chicheley Gdns. HA3: Hrw W 7B 26
(not continuous)
Chicheley Rd. HA3: Hrw W 7B 26
Chicheley St. SE1 6H 13 (2K 101)
Chichester Av. HA4: Ruis 2F 57
Chichester Cl. E6 6C 88
SE3 7A 106
TW12: Hamp 6D 130
Chichester Ct. HA7: Stan 3E 42
HA8: Edg 6B 28
(off Whitchurch La.)
KT17: Ewe 7B 164
NW1 7G 65
(off Royal Coll. St.)
TW19: Stanw 1A 128
UB5: N'olt 1D 76
Chichester Gdns. IG1: Ilf 7C 52
Chichester Ho. NW6 2J 81
SW9 7A 102
(off Cranmer Rd.)
Chichester Lodge SE10 4J 105
(off Peartree Way)
Chichester M. SE27 4A 138
Chichester Rents WC2 7J 7
Chichester Rd. CR0: C'don 3E 168
E11 3G 69
N9 1B 34
NW6 2J 81
W2 5K 81
Chichester St. SW1 6B 18 (5G 101)
Chichester Way E14 4F 105
TW14: Felt 7A 112
Chickenshed Theatre 5K 21
Chicksand Ho. E1 5K 9
(off Chicksand St.)
Chicksand St. E1 6K 9 (5F 85)
(not continuous)
Chiddingfold N12 3D 30
Chiddingstone SE13 5E 122
Chiddingstone Av. DA7: Bex 7F 109
Chiddingstone St. SW6 2J 117
Chieveley Pde. DA7: Bex 3H 127
Chieveley Rd. DA7: Bex 4H 127
Chignell Pl. W13 1A 96
CHIGWELL 3K 37
Chigwell Ct. E9 6A 68
(off Ballance Rd.)
Chigwell Golf Course 4K 37
Chigwell Hill E1 7H 85
Chigwell Hurst Ct. HA5: Pinn 3B 40
Chigwell Pk. IG7: Chig 4K 37
Chigwell Pk. Dr. IG7: Chig 4K 37
Chigwell Ri. IG7: Chig 2K 37
Chigwell Rd. E18 3K 51
IG8: Wfd G 2A 52
Chilcombe Ho. SW15 7C 116
(off Fontley Way)
Chilcot Cl. E14 6D 86
Chilcott Cl. HA0: Wemb 4C 60
Childebert Rd. SW17 2F 137
Childeric Rd. SE14 7A 104
Childerley KT1: King T 3G 151
(off Burritt Rd.)
Childerley St. SW6 1G 117
The Childers IG8: Wfd G 5J 37
Childers St. SE8 6A 104
Child La. SE10 3H 105
Childs Ct. UB3: Hayes 7J 75
CHILD'S HILL 3H 63
Childs Hill Wlk. NW2 3H 63
(off Cricklewood La.)
Child's La. SE19 6E 138
Child's M. SW5 4J 99
(off Child's Pl.)
Child's Pl. SW5 4J 99
Child's St. SW5 4J 99

Child's Wlk.—Churchyard Row

Child's Wlk. SW5 4J 99
(off Child's St.)
Childs Way NW11 5H 45
Chilham Cl. DA5: Bexl 7F 127
UB6: G'frd 2A 78
Chilham Ho. SE1 3D 102
SE15 6J 103
Chilham Rd. SE9 4C 142
Chilham Way BR2: Hayes 7J 159
Chilianwallah Memorial 7G 17 (6E 100)
Chillerton Rd. SW17 5E 136
Chillingford Ho. SW17 4A 136
Chillington Dr. SW11 4B 118
Chillingworth Gdns.
TW1: Twick 3K 131
Chillingworth Rd. N7 5A 66
Chill La. N1 1H 83
Chilmark Gdns. KT3: N Mald 6C 152
Chilmark Rd. SW16 2H 155
Chiltern Av. TW2: Whitt 1E 130
Chiltern Cl. CR0: C'don 3E 168
DA7: Bex 1K 127
KT4: Wor Pk 1E 164
UB10: Ick 2C 56
Chiltern Ct. BR2: Broml 2C 172
(off Gravel Rd.)
EN5: New Bar 5F 21
HA1: Harr 5H 41
N10 2E 46
NW1 4F 5
(off Baker St.)
SE14 7J 103
(off Avonley Rd.)
UB8: Hil 4D 74
Chiltern Dene EN2: Enf 4E 22
Chiltern Dr. KT5: Surb 6G 151
Chiltern Gdns. BR2: Broml 4H 159
NW2 3F 63
Chiltern Hgts. N1 7K 65
(off Caledonian Rd.)
Chiltern Ho. N9 3B 34
SE17 6D 102
(off Portland St.)
W5 5E 78
W10 5G 81
(off Telford Rd.)
Chiltern Rd. E3 4C 86
HA5: Eastc 5A 40
IG2: Ilf 5J 53
The Chilterns BR1: Broml 2K 159
(off Murray Av.)
Chiltern St. W1 5G 5 (5E 82)
Chiltern Way IG8: Wfd G 3D 36
Chilthorne Cl. SE6 7B 122
Chilton Av. W5 4D 96
Chilton Ct. N22 7D 32
(off Truro Rd.)
Chilton Gro. SE8 4K 103
Chiltonian Ind. Est. SE12 6H 123
Chiltonian M. SE13 5F 123
Chilton Rd. HA8: Edg 6B 28
TW9: Rich 3G 115
The Chiltons E18 2J 51
Chilton St. E2 3K 9 (4F 85)
Chilvers Cl. TW2: Twick 2J 131
Chilver St. SE10 5H 105
Chilworth Ct. SW19 1F 135
Chilworth Gdns. SM1: Sutt 3A 166
Chilworth M. W2 1A 10 (6B 82)
Chilworth Pl. IG11: Bark 4A 90
Chilworth St. W2 1A 10 (6A 82)
Chimes Av. N13 5F 33
Chimes Ho. BR3: Beck 1A 158
Chimes Ter. N8 5J 47
Chimney Ct. E1 1H 103
(off Brewhouse La.)
China Ct. E1 1H 103
(off Asher Way)
China Hall M. SE16 3J 103
China M. SW2 7K 119
CHINA TOWN 2D 12
China Wharf SE1 6K 15 (2G 103)
Chinbrook Cres. SE12 3K 141
Chinbrook Rd. SE12 3K 141
Chinchilla Dr. TW4: Houn 2A 112
The Chine HA0: Wemb 5B 60
N10 4G 47
N21 6G 23
Ching Ct. WC2 1E 12
(off Monmouth St.)
Chingdale Rd. E4 3B 36
CHINGFORD 1K 35
Chingford Av. E4 3H 35
Chingford Golf Course 1B 36
Chingford Golf Range 1H 35
CHINGFORD GREEN 1A 36
CHINGFORD HATCH 4A 36
Chingford Ind. Cen. E4 5F 35
Chingford La. IG8: Wfd G 4B 36
Chingford Leisure Cen. 4K 35
CHINGFORD MOUNT 4H 35
Chingford Mt. Rd. E4 4H 35
Chingford Rd. E4 6H 35
E17 1D 50
Chingley Cl. BR1: Broml 6G 141
Chingstone Ter. E4 1K 35
Ching Way E4 6G 35
(not continuous)
Chinnery Cl. EN1: Enf 1A 24
Chinnock's Wharf E14 7A 86
(off Narrow St.)
Chinnor Cres. UB6: G'frd 2F 77
Chipka St. E14 2E 104
(not continuous)
Chipley St. SE14 6A 104
Chipmunk Gro. UB5: N'olt 3C 76
Chippendale All. UB8: Uxb 7A 56
Chippendale Ho. SW1 6K 17
(off Churchill Gdns.)
Chippendale St. E5 3K 67
Chippendale Waye UB8: Uxb 7A 56
Chippenham KT1: King T 2F 151
(off Excelsior Cl.)
Chippenham Av. HA9: Wemb 5H 61
Chippenham Cl. HA5: Eastc 4H 39
Chippenham Gdns. NW6 3J 81
Chippenham M. W9 4J 81
Chippenham Rd. W9 4J 81
Chipperfield Ho. SW3 5C 16
(off Cale St.)
Chipperfield Rd. BR5: St P 7A 144
(not continuous)
CHIPPING BARNET 4B 20
Chipping Cl. EN5: Barn 3B 20
Chipstead Av. CR7: Thor H 4B 156
Chipstead Cl. SE19 7F 139
SM2: Sutt 7K 165
Chipstead Gdns. NW2 2D 62
Chipstead Rd. TW6: H'row A 3C 110
Chipstead St. SW6 1J 117
Chip St. SW4 3H 119
Chirk Cl. UB4: Yead 4C 76
Chisenhale Rd. E3 2A 86
Chisholm Ct. W6 5C 98
Chisholm Rd. CR0: C'don 2E 168
TW10: Rich 6F 115
Chisledon Wlk. E9 6B 68
(off Osborne Rd.)
CHISLEHURST 6F 143
Chislehurst Av. N12 7F 31
Chislehurst Caves 1E 160
Chislehurst Golf Course 7F 143
Chislehurst Rd. BR1: Broml 2B 160
BR5: Pet W 4J 161
BR6: Orp, Pet W, St M Cry 4J 161
BR7: Chst 2B 160
DA14: Sidc 5A 144
TW10: Rich 5E 114
CHISLEHURST WEST 6E 142
Chislet Cl. BR3: Beck 7C 140
Chisley Rd. N15 6E 48
Chiswell Sq. SE3 2K 123
Chiswell St. EC1 5E 8 (5C 84)
SE5 7D 102
(off Edmund St.)
CHISWICK 5K 97
CHISWICK BRI. 2J 115
Chiswick Cl. CR0: Bedd 3K 167
Chiswick Comn. Rd. W4 4K 97
Chiswick Community Sports Hall 7K 97
Chiswick Ct. HA5: Pinn 3D 40
W4 4H 97
Chiswick High Rd. TW8: Bford 5G 97
W4 5G 97
Chiswick House & Gdns. 6K 97
Chiswick Ho. Grounds W4 6A 98
Chiswick La. W4 5A 98
Chiswick La. Sth. W4 6B 98
Chiswick Lifeboat Station 7B 98
Chiswick Mall W4 6B 98
W6 6B 98
Chiswick Pk. W4 4H 97
Chiswick Pier 7B 98
Chiswick Plaza W4 6J 97
Chiswick Quay W4 1J 115
Chiswick Rd. N9 2B 34
W4 4J 97
CHISWICK RDBT. 5G 97
Chiswick Sq. W4 6A 98
Chiswick Staithe W4 1J 115
Chiswick Ter. W4 4J 97
(off Chiswick High Rd.)
Chiswick Village W4 6G 97
Chiswick Wharf W4 6B 98
Chitterfield Ga. UB7: Sip 7C 92
Chitty's La. RM8: Dag 2D 72
Chitty St. W1 5B 6 (5G 83)
Chivalry Rd. SW11 5C 118
Chivelston SW19 1F 135
Chivenor Gro. KT2: King T 5D 132
Chivers Pas. SW18 5K 117
Chivers Rd. E4 3J 35
Choats Mnr. Way RM9: Dag 2E 90
Choats Rd. IG11: Bark 2C 90
RM9: Dag 2C 90
Chobham Academy Sports Cen. 5E 68
Chobham Gdns. SW19 2F 135
CHOBHAM MANOR 5D 68
Chobham Rd. E15 5F 69
The Chocolate Factory 1 N22 2K 47
(off Clarendon Rd.)
The Chocolate Factory 2 N22 2K 47
(off Coburg Rd.)
Chocolate Studios N1 1E 8
(off Shepherdess Pl.)
Choice Vw. IG1: Ilf 2G 71
(off Axon Pl.)
Cholmeley Cl. N6 7F 47
Cholmeley Cres. N6 7F 47
Cholmeley Lodge N6 1F 65
Cholmeley Pk. N6 1F 65
Cholmley Gdns. NW6 5J 63
Cholmley Rd. KT7: T Ditt 6B 150
Cholmley Ter. KT7: T Ditt 7B 150
(off Portsmouth Rd.)
Cholmley Vs. KT7: T Ditt 6B 150
(off Portsmouth Rd.)
Cholmondeley Av. NW10 2C 80
Cholmondeley Wlk. TW9: Rich 5C 114
Choppin's Ct. E1 1H 103
Chopwell Cl. E15 7F 69
Chorleywood Cres. BR5: St P 2K 161
Choudhury Mans. N1 7J 65
(off Pembroke St.)
Choumert Gro. SE15 2G 121
Choumert M. SE15 2G 121
Choumert Rd. SE15 3F 121
Choumert Sq. SE15 2G 121
Chow Sq. E8 5F 67
Chrislea Cl. TW5: Hest 6D 94
Chrisp Ho. SE10 6G 105
(off Maze Hill)
Chrisp St. E14 5D 86
(not continuous)
Chris Pullen Way N7 6J 65
Christabel Cl. TW7: Isle 3J 113
Christabel Pankhurst Ct. SE5 7D 102
(off Brisbane St.)
Christchurch Av. DA8: Erith 6K 109
HA0: Wemb 6E 60
HA3: Kenton, W'stone 4K 41
N12 6F 31
NW6 1F 81
TW11: Tedd 5A 132
Christchurch Cl. EN2: Enf 2H 23
N12 7G 31
SW19 7B 136
Christ Church Ct. NW10 1A 80
Christchurch Ct. EC4 7B 8
(off Warwick La.)
NW6 7G 63
(off Willesden La.)
UB4: Yead 4A 76
(off Dunedin Way)
Christchurch Flats TW9: Rich 3E 114
Christchurch Gdns. HA3: W'stone 4A 42
Christchurch Grn. HA0: Wemb 6E 60
Christchurch Hill NW3 3B 64
Christchurch Ho. RM8: Dag 5B 72
SW2 1K 137
(off Christchurch Rd.)
Christchurch La. EN5: Barn 2B 20
Christchurch Lodge EN4: Cockf 4J 21
Christchurch Pk. SM2: Sutt 7A 166
Christchurch Pas. EN5: Barn 2B 20
NW3 3A 64
Christchurch Path UB3: Harl 3E 92
Christchurch Pl. SW8 2H 119
Christ Chu. Rd. BR3: Beck 2C 158
KT5: Surb 6F 151
Christchurch Rd. DA15: Sidc 4K 143
IG1: Ilf 1F 71
N8 6J 47
SW2 1K 137
SW14 5H 115
SW19 7B 136
TW6: H'row A 3C 110
Christ Church Spitalfields 5J 9 (5F 85)
Christchurch Sq. E9 1J 85
Christchurch St. SW3 7E 16 (6D 100)
Christchurch Ter. SW3 7E 16
Christchurch Way SE10 5G 105
Christian Ct. SE16 1B 104
Christian Flds. SW16 7A 138
Christian Pl. E1 6G 85
(off Burslem St.)
Christian St. E1 6G 85
Christie Ct. N19 2J 65
Christie Dr. CR0: C'don 5G 157
Christie Gdns. RM6: Chad H 6B 54
Christie Ho. E16 5J 87
(off Hammersley Rd.)
SE10 5H 105
(off Blackwall La.)
W12 6D 80
(off Du Cane Rd.)
Christie Rd. E9 6A 68
Christina Sq. N4 1B 66
Christina St. EC2 3G 9 (4E 84)
Christine Worsley Cl. N21 1G 33
Christopher Av. W7 3A 96
Christopher Bell Twr. E3 2C 86
(off Pancras Way)
Christopher Boones Ct. SE13 4F 123
(off Bessington Rd.)
Christopher Cl. DA15: Sidc 5K 125
SE16 2K 103
Christopher Ct. DA15: Sidc 2A 144
(off Station Rd.)
E1 1K 15
TW15: Ashf 5A 128
Christopher Gdns. RM9: Dag 5D 72
Christopher Pl. N22 7D 32
(off Myddleton Rd.)
NW1 1D 6 (3H 83)
Christopher Rd. UB2: S'hall 4K 93
Christophers M. W11 1G 99
Christopher St. EC2 4F 9 (4D 84)
Chroma Mans. E20 6E 68
(off Penny Brookes St.)
Chronicle Av. NW9 3A 44
Chronicle Twr. N1 1C 8
Chryssell Rd. SW9 7A 102
Chubworthy St. SE14 6A 104
Chudleigh DA14: Sidc 4B 144
Chudleigh Cres. IG3: Ilf 4J 71
Chudleigh Gdns. SM1: Sutt 3A 166
Chudleigh Rd. NW6 7F 63
SE4 5B 122
TW2: Twick 6J 113
Chudleigh St. E1 6K 85
Chudleigh Way HA4: Ruis 1J 57
Chulsa Rd. SE26 5H 139
Chumleigh Gdns. SE5 6E 102
(off Chumleigh St.)
Chumleigh St. SE5 6E 102
Chumleigh Wlk. KT5: Surb 4F 151
Church All. CR0: C'don 1A 168
Church App. SE21 3D 138
Church Av. BR3: Beck 1C 158
DA14: Sidc 5A 144
E4 6A 36
(not continuous)
HA4: Ruis 1F 57
HA5: Pinn 6C 40
NW1 6F 65
SW14 3K 115
UB2: S'hall 3C 94
UB5: N'olt 7D 58
Churchbank E17 4C 50
(off Eastfield Rd.)
Churchbury Cl. EN1: Enf 2K 23
Churchbury La. EN1: Enf 3J 23
Churchbury Rd. EN1: Enf 2K 23
SE9 7B 124
Church Cloisters EC3 3G 15
Church Cl. HA6: Nwood 1H 39
HA8: Edg 5D 28
N20 3H 31
TW3: Houn 2C 112
UB4: Hayes 5F 75
UB7: W Dray 3A 92
W8 2K 99
Church Ct. EC4 6A 84
SE16 2B 104
(off Rotherhithe St.)
TW9: Rich 5D 114
Church Cres. E9 7K 67
N3 1H 45
N10 4F 47
N20 3H 31
Churchcroft Cl. SW12 7E 118
Churchdown BR1: Broml 4G 141
Church Dr. BR4: W W'ck 3G 171
HA2: Harr 6E 40
NW9 1K 61
Church Elm La. RM10: Dag 6G 73
CHURCH END
N3 1H 45
NW10 7A 62
Church End E17 4D 50
NW4 3D 44
Church Entry EC4 1B 14
Church Est. Almshouses
TW9: Rich 4F 115
(off Sheen Rd.)
Church Farm La. SM3: Cheam 6G 165
Church Farm Leisure Cen. 7J 21
Churchfield Av. N12 6G 31
Churchfield Cl. HA2: Harr 4G 41
UB3: Hayes 7H 75
Churchfield Ho. KT12: Walt T 7J 147
W2 4A 4
(off Hall Pl.)
Churchfield Mans. SW6 2H 117
(off New Kings Rd.)
Churchfield Pl. TW17: Shep 7D 146
Churchfield Rd. DA16: Well 3A 126
KT12: Walt T 7J 147
W3 1J 97
W7 2J 95
W13 1B 96
Churchfields E18 1J 51
KT8: W Mole 3E 148
SE10 6E 104
Churchfields Av. TW13: Hanw 3D 130
Churchfields Rd. BR3: Beck 2K 157
Churchfield Way N12 6F 31
Church Gdns. HA0: Wemb 4A 60
W5 2D 96
Church Gth. N19 2H 65
(off St John's Gro.)
Church Ga. SW6 3G 117
Church Grn. SW9 1A 120
UB3: Hayes 6H 75
Church Gro. KT1: Hamp W 1C 150
SE13 5D 122
Church Hill DA1: Cray 4K 127
E17 4C 50
HA1: Harr 1J 59
N21 7E 22
SE18 3D 106
SM5: Cars 5D 166
SW19 5H 135
Church Hill Rd. E17 4D 50
EN4: E Barn 6H 21
KT6: Surb 5E 150
SM3: Cheam 3F 165
Church Hill Wood BR5: St M Cry 5K 161
Church Ho. EC1 3B 8
(off Compton St.)
SW1 1D 18
(off Gt. Smith St.)
Church Hyde SE18 6J 107
Churchill Av. HA3: Kenton 6B 42
UB10: Hil 3D 74
Churchill Cl. TW14: Felt 1H 129
UB10: Hil 3D 74
Churchill Ct. BR6: Farnb 5G 173
HA2: Harr 2F 59
(Eastcote Av.)
HA2: Harr 5F 41
(Montrose Ct.)
HA5: Hat E 1C 40
N4 7A 48
N9 1K 33
SE18 4D 106
UB5: N'olt 5E 58
(off Newmarket Av.)
W5 4F 79
Churchill Gdns. SW1 6A 18
(not continuous)
W3 6G 79
Churchill Gdns. Rd.
SW1 6K 17 (5F 101)
Churchill Lodge IG6: Ilf 4G 53
Churchill Pl. E14 1D 104
HA1: Harr 4J 41
Churchill Rd. CR2: S Croy 7C 168
E16 6A 88
HA8: Edg 6A 28
NW2 6D 62
NW5 4F 65
UB10: Uxb 2A 74
Churchills M. IG8: Wfd G 6C 36
Churchill Ter. E4 4H 35
Churchill Theatre 2J 159
Churchill Wlk. E9 5J 67
Churchill War Rooms 6D 12 (2H 101)
Churchill Way BR1: Broml 2J 159
TW16: Sun 5J 129
Churchlands Way KT4: Wor Pk 2F 165
Church La. BR2: Broml 1C 172
BR7: Chst 1G 161
E11 1G 69
E17 4D 50
EN1: Enf 3J 23
HA3: W'stone 1K 41
HA5: Pinn 3C 40
KT7: T Ditt 6K 149
KT9: Chess 6F 163
N2 3B 46
N8 4K 47
N9 2B 34
N17 1E 48
NW9 6J 43
RM10: Dag 7J 73
SM6: Bedd 3H 167
(not continuous)
SW17 5D 136
SW19 1H 153
TW1: Twick 1A 132
TW10: Ham 1E 132
TW11: Tedd 5K 131
W5 2C 96
Churchley Rd. SE26 4H 139
Church Manorway DA8: Erith 4K 109
DA17: Belv 2J 109
SE2 5A 108
Church Mead SE5 7C 102
(off Camberwell Rd.)
Churchmead Cl. EN4: E Barn 6H 21
Church Mdw. KT6: Surb 2C 162
Churchmead Rd. NW10 6C 62
Churchmore Rd. SW16 1G 155
Church Mt. N2 5B 46
Church Paddock Ct. SM6: Bedd 3H 167
Church Pde. TW15: Ashf 4B 128
Church Pas. EN5: Barn 3B 20
KT6: Surb 5E 150
TW1: Twick 1B 132
Church Path CR0: C'don 2C 168
CR4: Mitc 3C 154
(not continuous)
E11 5J 51
E17 4D 50
N5 5B 66
N12 3F 31
(Woodside La.)
N12 4F 31
(Woodside Pk. Rd.)
N17 7K 33
NW10 7A 62
SM6: Bedd 3H 167
SW14 3K 115
(not continuous)
SW19 2H 153
UB1: S'hall 1E 94
UB2: S'hall 3D 94
(not continuous)
W3 2J 97
(not continuous)
W4 3J 97
Church Pl. CR4: Mitc 3C 154
SW1 3B 12 (7G 83)
UB10: Ick 3E 56
W5 2D 96
Church Ri. KT9: Chess 6F 163
SE23 2K 139
Church Rd. BR2: Broml 2J 159
(Edison Rd.)
BR2: Broml 3G 159
(Hazelwood Ho's.)
BR2: Kes 7B 172
BR6: Farnb 5G 173
CR0: C'don 3C 168
(not continuous)
CR4: Mitc 1B 154
DA7: Bex 2F 127
DA8: Erith 5K 109
DA14: Sidc 4A 144
DA16: Well 2B 126
E10 1C 68
E12 5C 70
E17 2A 50
EN3: Pond E 6D 24
HA6: Nwood 1H 39
HA7: Stan 5G 27
IG2: Ilf 6J 53
IG9: Buck H 1E 36
IG11: Bark 6G 71
KT1: King T 2F 151
KT4: Wor Pk 1A 164
KT6: Surb 1C 162
KT8: E Mos 4H 149
KT10: Clay 7A 162
KT19: Ewe 7K 163
N1 6C 66
N6 6E 46
N17 1E 48
(not continuous)
NW4 4D 44
NW10 7A 62
SE19 1E 156
SM3: Cheam 6G 165
SM6: Bedd 3H 167
SW13 2B 116
SW19 5G 135
(Courthorpe Rd.)
SW19 1B 154
(Reynolds Cl.)
TW5: Cran 5K 93
TW5: Hest 7E 94
TW7: Isle 1H 113
TW9: Rich 4E 114
TW10: Ham 4D 132
TW10: Rich 5E 114
TW11: Tedd 4J 131
TW13: Hanw 5B 130
TW15: Ashf 3B 128
TW17: Shep 7D 146
UB2: S'hall 3D 94
UB3: Hayes 1H 93
UB5: N'olt 2B 76
UB7: W Dray 3A 92
UB8: Cowl 4A 74
W3 1J 97
W7 7H 77
Church Rd. Almshouses E10 2D 68
(off Church Rd.)
Church Rd. Ind. Est. E10 1C 68
Church Row BR7: Chst 1G 161
NW3 4A 64
SW6 7K 99
(off Moore Pk. Rd.)
SW18 5K 117
Church Row M. BR7: Chst 7G 143
Church Sq. TW17: Shep 7D 146
Church St. CR0: C'don 3B 168
E15 1G 87
E16 1F 107
EN2: Enf 3H 23
KT1: King T 2D 150
KT12: Walt T 7J 147
KT17: Ewe 7C 164
N9 7J 23
NW8 5B 4 (5B 82)
RM10: Dag 6H 73
SM1: Sutt 5K 165
TW1: Twick 1A 132
TW7: Isle 3B 114
TW12: Hamp 1G 149
TW16: Sun 3K 147
W2 5B 4 (5B 82)
(not continuous)
W4 6B 98
Church St. Est. NW8 4B 4 (4B 82)
Church St. Nth. E15 1G 87
Church Stretton Rd. TW3: Houn 5G 113
Church Ter. NW4 3D 44
SE13 3G 123
TW10: Rich 5D 114
Church Va. N2 3D 46
SE23 2K 139
Church Vw. TW10: Rich 5E 114
Church Vw. Gro. SE26 6K 139
Churchview Rd. TW2: Twick 1H 131
Church Wlk. EN2: Enf 3J 23
KT7: T Ditt 6K 149
KT12: Walt T 7J 147
(not continuous)
N6 3E 64
N16 3D 66
(not continuous)
NW2 3H 63
NW4 3E 44
NW9 2K 61
SW13 1C 116
SW15 5D 116
SW16 2G 155
SW20 3E 152
TW8: Bford 6C 96
(not continuous)
TW9: Rich 5D 114
UB3: Hayes 6G 75
Churchward Ho. SE17 6B 102
(off Lorrimore Sq.)
W14 5H 99
(off Ivatt Pl.)
Church Way EN4: Cockf 4J 21
HA8: Edg 6B 28
N20 3H 31
Churchway NW1 1D 6 (3H 83)
(not continuous)
Churchwell Path E9 5J 67
Churchwood Gdns. IG8: Wfd G 4D 36
SE23 7J 121
Churchyard Pas. SE5 2D 120
Churchyard Row SE11 4B 102

Churston Av.—Clerics Wlk.

Churston Av. E13 . . . . 1K 87
Churston Cl. SW2 . . . . 1A 138
Churston Dr. SM4: Mord 5F 153
Churston Gdns. N11 . . . . 6B 32
Churston Mans. *WC1* *4H 7*
(off Gray's Inn Rd.)
Churton Pl. SW1 . . . . 4B 18 (4G 101)
W4 . . . . *6H 97*
(off Chiswick Village)
Churton St. SW1 . . . . 4B 18 (4G 101)
Chusan Pl. E14 . . . . 6B 86
Chute Ho. *SW9* *2A 120*
(off Stockwell Pk. Rd.)
Chuter Ede Ho. *SW6* *6H 99*
(off Clem Attlee Ct.)
Chyngton Cl. DA15: Sidc 3K 143
Cibber Rd. SE23 . . . . 2K 139
Cicada Rd. SW18 . . . . 6A 118
Cicely Ct. CR0: Wadd 5A 168
Cicely Ho. *NW8* *2B 82*
(off Cochrane St.)
Cicely Rd. SE15 . . . . 1G 121
Cinderella Path NW11 . . . . 1K 63
Cinderford Way BR1: Broml 4G 141
Ciné Lumière *3A 16*
(off Queensberry Pl.)
Cineworld Cinema
Bexleyheath 4H 127
Chelsea, Fulham Rd. 5A 100
Enfield 4B 24
Feltham 2K 129
Ilford *3F 71*
(off Clements Rd.)
Leicester Sq. *2D 12*
(off Leicester Sq.)
The O2 . . . . *1G 105*
(within The O2)
South Ruislip 4K 57
Wandsworth 5K 117
Wembley 4G 61
West India Quay 7C 86
Wood Green *2A 48*
(within Wood Green Shop. City)
Cinnabar Wharf Central *E1* *1G 103*
(off Wapping High St.)
Cinnabar Wharf E. *E1* *1G 103*
(off Wapping High St.)
Cinnabar Wharf W. *E1* *1G 103*
(off Wapping High St.)
Cinnamon Cl. CR0: C'don 7J 155
SE15 . . . . 7F 103
Cinnamon M. N13 . . . . 2F 33
Cinnamon Row SW11 . . . . 3A 118
Cinnamon St. E1 . . . . 1H 103
Cinnamon Wharf *SE1* *6K 15*
(off Shad Thames)
Cintra Pk. SE19 . . . . 7F 139
Cipher Ct. NW2 . . . . 3C 62
Circa Apts. NW1 . . . . 7E 64
The Circle NW2 . . . . 3A 62
NW7 . . . . 6E 28
SE1 . . . . *6J 15*
(off Queen Elizabeth St.)
Circle Gdns. SW19 . . . . 2J 153
The Circuits HA5: Pinn 4A 40
Circular Rd. N17 . . . . 3F 49
Circular Way SE18 . . . . 6D 106
Circus Lodge NW8 . . . . 1A 4
Circus M. W1 . . . . 5E 4
Circus Pl. EC2 . . . . 6F 9 (5D 84)
Circus Rd. NW8 . . . . 1A 4 (3B 82)
Circus Rd. E. SW11 . . . . 7K 17 (7F 101)
Circus Rd. W. SW11 . . . . 7F 101
Circus St. SE10 . . . . 7E 104
Circus W. SW11 . . . . 7K 17 (6F 101)
Cirencester St. W2 . . . . 5K 81
Cirrus Apts. *E1* *3K 9*
(off Bacon St.)
Cirrus Cl. SM6: W'gton 7J 167
Cissbury Ho. SE26 . . . . 3G 139
Cissbury Ring Nth. N12 . . . . 5C 30
Cissbury Ring Sth. N12 . . . . 5C 30
Cissbury Rd. N15 . . . . 5D 48
Citadel Pl. SE11 . . . . 5G 19 (5K 101)
Citius Apts. *E3* *2C 86*
(off Tredegar La.)
Citius Ct. E4 . . . . 6K 35
Citius Wlk. E20 . . . . 6E 68
Citizen Ho. N7 . . . . 4A 66
Citizen Rd. N7 . . . . 4A 66
Citrine Apts. *E3* *1A 86*
(off Gunmaker's La.)
Citrus Ho. *SE8* *5B 104*
(off Alverton St.)
City Apts. *E1* *7K 9*
(off White Church La.)
City Bus. Cen. SE16 . . . . 3J 103
City Ct. CR0: C'don 7B 156
City Cross Bus. Pk. SE10 . . . . 4G 105
City E. Bldg. *E1* *7H 85*
(off Cable St.)
City Forum EC1 . . . . 1C 8 (3C 84)
City Gdn. Row EC1 . . . . 3C 84
N1 . . . . 1C 8 (2B 84)
City Ga. Ho. *IG2: Ilf* *6E 52*
(off Eastern Av.)
City Gateway *E1* *7G 85*
(off Ensign St.)
City Hall
Southwark 5H 15 (1E 102)
City Harbour *E14* *3D 104*
(off Selsdon Way)
City Hgts. *E8* *1F 85*
(off Kingsland Rd.)
City Ho. BR2: Broml 6C 160
City Island E14 . . . . 6G 87
City Island Way E14 . . . . 6G 87
City Lights Ct. *SE11* *5K 19*
(off Bowden St.)
City Mill Apts. *E8* *1F 85*
(off Lovelace St.)
City Mill River Path E15 . . . . 1E 86
City Nth. E. Twr. *N4* *2A 66*
(off City Nth. Pl.)
City Nth. Pl. N4 . . . . 2A 66
City Nth. W. Twr. N4 . . . . 2A 66
CITY OF LONDON 1E 14 (6D 84)
City of London Almshouses
SW9 . . . . 4K 119
City of London Crematorium 3C 70
City of London Distillery 6B 84
City of London Point *N7* *6H 65*
(off York Way)
City of London Police Mus. 6C 84
City of London Tourist Info. Cen.
. . . . 1C 14 (6C 84)
The City Pavilion
Marks Gate 2F 55
City Pav. *EC1* *5A 8*
(off Britton St.)
City Pl. Ho. *EC2* *6D 8*
(off Basinghall St.)
Citypoint EC2 . . . . 5E 8
City Pride Development E14 . . . . 1C 104
City Rd. EC1 . . . . 1A 8 (2B 84)
City Twr. *EC2* *6E 8*
(off Basinghall St.)
SW8 . . . . 7E 18 (6J 101)
City University London
The Saddlers Sports Cen.
. . . . 3B 8 (4B 84)
City University London
Goswell Pl. 3B 84
Northampton Square Campus
. . . . 2A 8 (3B 84)
City Vw. *IG1: Ilf* *2G 71*
(off Axon Pl.)
Cityview SE7 . . . . 6A 106
City Vw. Apts. *N1* *7C 66*
(off Essex Rd.)
N4 . . . . *7D 48*
(off Devan Gro.)
City Vw. Ct. SE22 . . . . 7G 121
City Wlk. SE1 . . . . 7G 15 (2E 102)
City Wlk. Apts. *EC1* *2C 8*
(off Seward St.)
City Wharf Ho. KT7: T Ditt 6B 150
Civic Way HA4: Ruis 5B 58
IG6: Ilf 4G 53
Civil & Family Court
Barnet 1J 45
Civil Justice Cen.
Central London 4J 5
Clabon M. SW1 . . . . 2E 16 (3D 100)
Clack La. HA4: Ruis 1E 56
Clack St. SE16 . . . . 2J 103
Clacton Rd. E6 . . . . 3B 88
E17 . . . . 6A 50
N17 . . . . 2F 49
Claigmar Gdns. N3 . . . . 1K 45
Claire Ct. HA5: Hat E 1D 40
N12 . . . . 3F 31
NW2 . . . . 6G 63
WD23: B Hea 1C 26
Claire Gdns. HA7: Stan 5H 27
Claire Ho. IG1: Ilf 4F 71
Claire Pl. E14 . . . . 3C 104
Clairvale Rd. TW5: Hest 1B 112
Clairview Rd. SW16 . . . . 5F 137
Clairville Gdns. W7 . . . . 1J 95
Clairville Point *SE23* *3K 139*
(off Dacres Rd.)
Clamp Hill HA7: Stan 4C 26
Clancarty Rd. SW6 . . . . 2J 117
Clandon Cl. KT17: Ewe 6B 164
W3 . . . . 2H 97
Clandon Gdns. N3 . . . . 3J 45
Clandon Ho. *SE1* *7B 14*
(off Webber St.)
Clandon Rd. IG3: Ilf 2J 71
Clandon St. SE8 . . . . 2C 122
Clandon Ter. SW20 . . . . 2F 153
Clanricarde Gdns. W2 . . . . 7J 81
CLAPHAM 4G 119
CLAPHAM COMMON 4H 119
Clapham Comn. Nth. Side SW4 . . . . 4D 118
Clapham Comn. Northside *SW4* *4G 119*
(off Rookery Rd.)
Clapham Comn. Sth. Side SW4 . . . . 6F 119
Clapham Comn. W. Side SW4 . . . . 4D 118
(not continuous)
Clapham Cres. SW4 . . . . 4H 119
Clapham High St. SW4 . . . . 4H 119
CLAPHAM JUNCTION 3C 118
Clapham Leisure Cen. 3H 119
Clapham Mnr. Ct. SW4 . . . . 3G 119
Clapham Mnr. St. SW4 . . . . 3G 119
CLAPHAM PARK 5H 119
Clapham Pk. Est. SW4 . . . . 6H 119
Clapham Pk. Rd. SW4 . . . . 4G 119
Clapham Pk. Ter. *SW2* *5J 119*
(off Lyham Rd.)
Clapham Picturehouse 4G 119
Clapham Rd. SW9 . . . . 3J 119
Clapham Rd. Est. SW4 . . . . 3J 119
Clap La. RM10: Dag, Rush G 2H 73
Claps Ga. La. E6 . . . . 4E 88
Clapton Comn. E5 . . . . 7F 49
(not continuous)
CLAPTON PARK 4K 67
Clapton Pk. Est. E5 . . . . 4K 67
Clapton Pas. E5 . . . . 5J 67
Clapton Sq. E5 . . . . 5J 67
Clapton Ter. E5 . . . . 1G 67
Clapton Way E5 . . . . 4G 67
Clara Grant Ho. *E14* *3C 104*
(off Mellish St.)
Clara Nehab Ho. *NW11* *5H 45*
(off Leeside Cres.)
Clara Pl. SE18 . . . . 4E 106
Clare Cl. N2 . . . . 3A 46
Clare Cnr. SE9 . . . . 7F 125
Clare Ct. *W11* *7G 81*
(off Clarendon Rd.)
WC1 . . . . *2F 7*
(off Judd St.)
Claredale Ho. *E2* *2H 85*
(off Claredale St.)
Claredale St. E2 . . . . 2G 85
Clare Gdns. E7 . . . . 4J 69
IG11: Bark 6K 71
W11 . . . . 6G 81
Clare Ho. E3 . . . . 1B 86
E16 . . . . *7E 88*
(off University Way)
HA8: Edg *2J 43*
(off Burnt Oak B'way.)
SE1 . . . . *5F 103*
(off Cooper's Rd.)
Clare La. N1 . . . . 7C 66
Clare Lawn Av. SW14 . . . . 5K 115
Clare Mkt. WC2 . . . . 1H 13 (6K 83)
Clare M. SW6 . . . . 7K 99
Claremont *TW17: Shep* *6D 146*
(off Laleham Rd.)
Claremont Av. HA3: Kenton 5E 42
KT3: N Mald 5C 152
TW16: Sun 1K 147
Claremont Cl. BR6: Farnb 4E 172
E16 . . . . 1E 106
N1 . . . . 1K 7 (2A 84)
SW2 . . . . 1J 137
Claremont Ct. *E2* *2H 85*
(off Cambridge Heath Rd.)
E2 . . . . *2G 85*
(off Claredale St.)
W2 . . . . *6K 81*
(off Queensway)
W9 . . . . *2H 81*
(off Claremont Rd.)
Claremont Dr. TW17: Shep 6D 146
Claremont Gdns. IG3: Ilf 2J 71
KT6: Surb 5E 150
Claremont Gro. IG8: Wfd G 6F 37
W4 . . . . 7A 98
Claremont Ho. NW9 . . . . 3B 44
SE16 . . . . 2A 104
SM2: Sutt 7K 165
Claremont Pk. N3 . . . . 1G 45
Claremont Pl. KT10: Clay 6A 162
Claremont Rd. BR1: Broml 4C 160
CR0: C'don 1G 169
E7 . . . . 5K 69
E11 . . . . 3F 69
E17 . . . . 2A 50
HA3: W'stone 2J 41
KT6: Surb 5E 150
N6 . . . . 7G 47
NW2 . . . . 7F 45
TW1: Twick 6B 114
TW11: Tedd 5K 131
W9 . . . . 2G 81
W13 . . . . 5A 78
Claremont Sq. N1 . . . . 1J 7 (2A 84)
Claremont St. E16 . . . . 2E 106
N18 . . . . 6B 34
SE10 . . . . 6D 104
Claremont Ter. KT7: T Ditt 7B 150
Claremont Vs. *SE5* *7D 102*
(off Southampton Way)
Claremont Way NW2 . . . . 1E 62
(not continuous)
Claremont Way Ind. Est. NW2 . . . . 1E 62
Clarence Av. BR1: Broml 4C 160
IG2: Ilf 6E 52
KT3: N Mald 2J 151
SW4 . . . . 7H 119
Clarence Cl. EN4: E Barn 5G 21
WD23: B Hea 1E 26
Clarence Ct. NW7 . . . . 6F 29
W6 . . . . *4D 98*
(off Cambridge Gro.)
Clarence Cres. DA14: Sidc 3B 144
SW4 . . . . 6H 119
Clarence Gdns. NW1 . . . . 2K 5 (3F 83)
Clarence Ga. IG8: Ilf, Wfd G 6K 37
Clarence Ga. Gdns. *NW1* *4F 5*
(off Glentworth St.)
Clarence House 6B 12
Clarence Ho. *SE17* *6D 102*
(off Merrow St.)
Clarence La. SW15 . . . . 6A 116
Clarence M. E5 . . . . 5H 67
SE16 . . . . 1K 103
SW12 . . . . 7F 119
Clarence Pk. Cres. HA7: Stan 3D 26
Clarence Pl. E5 . . . . 5H 67
Clarence Rd. BR1: Broml 3B 160
CR0: C'don 7D 156
DA6: Bex 4E 126
DA14: Sidc 3B 144
E5 . . . . 4H 67
E12 . . . . 4A 70
E16 . . . . 4G 87
E17 . . . . 2K 49
EN3: Pond E 5C 24
N15 . . . . 5C 48
N22 . . . . 7D 32
NW6 . . . . 7H 63
SE8 . . . . 6D 104
SE9 . . . . 2C 142
SM1: Sutt 5K 165
SM6: W'gton 5F 167
SW19 . . . . 6K 135
TW9: Kew 1F 115
TW11: Tedd 6K 131
W4 . . . . 5G 97
Clarence St. KT1: King T 2D 150
TW9: Rich 4E 114
UB2: S'hall 3B 94
Clarence Ter. NW1 . . . . 3F 5 (4D 82)
TW3: Houn 4F 113
Clarence Wlk. SW4 . . . . 2J 119
Clarence Way NW1 . . . . 7F 65
Clarenden Pl. DA2: Wilm 5K 145
Clarendon Cl. BR5: St P 3K 161
E9 . . . . 7J 67
W2 . . . . 2C 10 (7C 82)
Clarendon Ct. *BR3: Beck* *1D 158*
(off Albemarle Rd.)
EC1 . . . . 4D 8
NW2 . . . . 7E 62
NW11 . . . . 4H 45
TW5: Cran 1J 111
TW9: Kew 1F 115
W9 . . . . *3A 4*
(off Maida Va.)
Clarendon Cres. TW2: Twick 3H 131
Clarendon Cross W11 . . . . 7G 81
Clarendon Dr. SW15 . . . . 4E 116
Clarendon Flats *W1* *1H 11*
(off Balderton St.)
Clarendon Gdns. HA9: Wemb 3D 60
IG1: Ilf 7D 52
NW4 . . . . 3C 44
W9 . . . . 4A 82
Clarendon Grn. BR5: St P 4K 161
Clarendon Gro. CR4: Mitc 3D 154
NW1 . . . . 1C 6 (3H 83)
Clarendon Ho. *KT2: King T* *1E 150*
(off Cowleaze Rd.)
NW1 . . . . *1B 6*
(off Werrington St.)
W2 . . . . *2C 10*
(off Strathearn Pl.)
Clarendon Lodge *W11* *7G 81*
(off Clarendon Rd.)
Clarendon M. DA5: Bexl 1H 145
W2 . . . . 2C 10 (7C 82)
Clarendon Path BR5: St P 4K 161
(not continuous)
Clarendon Pl. W2 . . . . 2C 10 (7C 82)
Clarendon Ri. SE13 . . . . 4E 122
Clarendon Rd. CR0: C'don 2B 168
E11 . . . . 1F 69
E17 . . . . 6D 50
E18 . . . . 3J 51
HA1: Harr 6J 41
Clarendon Rd. N8 . . . . 3K 47
N15 . . . . 4C 48
N18 . . . . 6B 34
N22 . . . . 2K 47
SM6: W'gton 6G 167
SW19 . . . . 7C 136
TW15: Ashf 4B 128
UB3: Hayes 2H 93
W5 . . . . 3E 78
W11 . . . . 7G 81
Clarendon St. SW1 . . . . 5K 17 (5F 101)
Clarendon Ter. W9 . . . . 3A 4 (4A 82)
Clarendon Wlk. W11 . . . . 6G 81
Clarendon Way BR5: St P 3K 161
BR7: Chst 3K 161
N21 . . . . 6H 23
Clarens St. SE6 . . . . 2B 140
Clare Pl. SW15 . . . . 7B 116
Clare Point *NW2* *1F 63*
(off Whitefield Av.)
Clare Rd. E11 . . . . 6F 51
NW10 . . . . 7C 62
SE14 . . . . 1B 122
TW4: Houn 3D 112
TW19: Stanw 1A 128
UB6: G'frd 6H 59
Clare St. E2 . . . . 2H 85
Claret Gdns. SE25 . . . . 3E 156
Clareville Ct. *SW7* *4A 16*
(off Clareville St.)
Clareville Gro. SW7 . . . . 4A 16 (4A 100)
Clareville Gro. M. SW7 . . . . 4A 16 (4A 100)
Clareville Rd. BR5: Farnb 2G 173
Clareville St. SW7 . . . . 4A 16 (4A 100)
Clare Way DA7: Bex 1E 126
Clarewood Ct. *W1* *6E 4*
(off Seymour Pl.)
Clarewood Wlk. SW9 . . . . 4A 120
Clarges M. W1 . . . . 4J 11 (1F 101)
Clarges St. W1 . . . . 4K 11 (1F 101)
Claribel Rd. SW9 . . . . 2B 120
Clarice Way SM6: W'gton 7J 167
Claridge Ct. SW6 . . . . 2H 117
Claridge Rd. RM8: Dag 1D 72
Clarinet Ct. HA8: Edg 7C 28
Clarion Ho. *E3* *2A 86*
(off Roman Rd.)
SW1 . . . . *5B 18*
(off Moreton Pl.)
W1 . . . . *1C 12*
(off St Anne's Ct.)
Clarissa Ho. *E14* *6D 86*
(off Cordelia St.)
Clarissa Rd. RM6: Chad H 7D 54
Clarissa St. E8 . . . . 1F 85
Clarke Apts. *E3* *4B 86*
(off Heath Pl.)
Clarke Cl. CR0: C'don 6C 156
Clarke Mans. *IG11: Bark* *7K 71*
(off Upney La.)
Clarke M. N9 . . . . 3C 34
Clarke Path N16 . . . . 1G 67
Clarkes Av. KT4: Wor Pk 1F 165
Clarkes Dr. UB8: Hil 5A 74
Clarke's M. W1 . . . . 5H 5 (5E 82)
Clark Gro. IG3: Ilf 4J 71
Clark Ho. *SW10* *7A 100*
(off Coleridge Gdns.)
Clarks Mead WD23: Bush 1B 26
Clarkson Rd. E16 . . . . 6H 87
Clarkson Row *NW1* *2G 83*
(off Mornington Ter.)
The Clarksons IG11: Bark 2G 89
Clarkson St. E2 . . . . 3H 85
Clarks Rd. IG1: Ilf 2H 71
Clark St. E1 . . . . 5H 85
(not continuous)
Clark Way TW5: Hest 7B 94
Clarnico Rd. E20 . . . . 6E 68
Clarson Ho. *SE5* *7B 102*
(off Midnight Av.)
SE8 . . . . 6A 104
Classic Mans. *E9* *7H 67*
(off Wells St.)
Classon Cl. UB7: W Dray 2A 92
Claude Av. NW9 . . . . 1B 44
Claude Rd. E10 . . . . 2E 68
E13 . . . . 1K 87
SE15 . . . . 2H 121
Claude St. E14 . . . . 4C 104
Claudia Jones Ho. N17 . . . . 1C 48
Claudia Jones Way SW2 . . . . 6J 119
Claudia Pl. SW19 . . . . 1G 135
Claudius Cl. HA7: Stan 3J 27
Claughton Rd. E13 . . . . 2A 88
Clauson Av. UB5: N'olt 5F 59
Clavell St. SE10 . . . . 6E 104
Claverdale Rd. SW2 . . . . 7K 119
Clavering Av. SW13 . . . . 6D 98
Clavering Cl. TW1: Twick 4A 132
Clavering Ho. *SE13* *4F 123*
(off Blessington Rd.)
Clavering Pl. SW12 . . . . 6E 118
Clavering Rd. E12 . . . . 1B 70
Claverings Ind. Est. *N9* *2D 34*
(off Centre Way)
Claverley Gro. N3 . . . . 1K 45
Claverley Vs. N3 . . . . 7E 30
Claverton St. SW1 . . . . 6B 18 (5G 101)
Clave St. E1 . . . . 1J 103
Claxton Gro. W6 . . . . 5F 99
Claxton Path *SE4* *4K 121*
(off Coston Wlk.)
Clay Av. CR4: Mitc 2F 155
Claybank Gro. SE13 . . . . 3D 122
Claybourne M. SE19 . . . . 7E 138
Claybridge Rd. SE12 . . . . 4A 142
Claybrook Cl. N2 . . . . 3B 46
Claybrook Rd. W6 . . . . 6F 99
Claybury WD23: Bush 1A 26
Claybury B'way. IG5: Ilf 3C 52
Claybury Hall IG8: Wfd G 7J 37
Claybury M. IG5: Ilf 2D 52
Claybury Rd. IG8: Wfd G 7H 37
Clay Ct. E17 . . . . 3F 51
SE1 . . . . *7G 15*
(off Long La.)
Claydon Dr. CR0: Bedd 4J 167
Claydon Ho. *NW4* *2F 45*
(off Holders Hill Rd.)
SW10 . . . . 1A 118
Claydown M. SE18 . . . . 5E 106
Clayfarm Rd. SE9 . . . . 2G 143
CLAYGATE 7A 162
Claygate Common 7A 162
Claygate Cres. CR0: New Ad 6E 170
Claygate La. KT7: T Ditt 1A 162
KT10: Clay, Hin W 2A 162
Claygate Rd. W13 . . . . 3B 96
CLAYHALL 3C 52
Clayhall Av. IG5: Ilf 3C 52
Clayhall Ct. *E3* *2B 86*
(off St Stephen's Rd.)
Clay Hill EN2: Enf 1K 23
Clayhill KT5: Surb 5G 151
Clayhill Cres. SE9 . . . . 4B 142
Claylands Pl. SW8 . . . . 7A 102
Claylands Rd. SW8 . . . . 7H 19 (6K 101)
Clay La. HA3: Kenton 4D 42
HA8: Edg 2B 28
TW19: Stanw 7B 110
WD23: B Hea 1D 26
Claymill Ho. SE18 . . . . 5G 107
Claymore Cl. SM4: Mord 7J 153
Clay Path E17 . . . . 2C 50
Claypole Ct. *E17* *5C 50*
(off Yunus Khan Cl.)
Claypole Dr. TW5: Hest 1C 112
Claypole Rd. E15 . . . . 2E 86
Clayponds Av. TW8: Bford 4D 96
Clayponds Gdns. W5 . . . . 4D 96
(not continuous)
Clayponds La. TW8: Bford 5E 96
(not continuous)
Clay St. W1 . . . . 6F 5 (5D 82)
Clayton Av. HA0: Wemb 7E 60
Clayton Bus. Cen. UB3: Hayes 2G 93
Clayton Cl. E6 . . . . 6D 88
Clayton Cres. N1 . . . . 1J 83
TW8: Bford 5D 96
Clayton Dr. SE8 . . . . 5A 104
Clayton Fld. NW9 . . . . 7F 29
Clayton Ho. *E9* *7J 67*
(off Frampton Pk. Rd.)
KT7: T Ditt 1B 162
SW13 . . . . *7E 98*
(off Trinity Chu. Rd.)
Clayton M. SE10 . . . . 1F 123
Clayton Rd. KT9: Chess 4C 162
RM7: Rush G 1J 73
SE15 . . . . 1G 121
TW7: Isle 3J 113
UB3: Hayes 2G 93
Clayton St. SE11 . . . . 7J 19 (6A 102)
Clayton Ter. UB4: Yead 5C 76
Claytonville Ter. DA17: Belv 2J 109
Clay Wood Cl. BR6: Orp 7J 161
Clayworth Cl. DA15: Sidc 6B 126
Cleanthus Cl. SE18 . . . . 1F 125
Cleanthus Rd. SE18 . . . . 2F 125
(not continuous)
Clearbrook Way E1 . . . . 6J 85
Clearwater Pl. KT6: Surb 6C 150
Clearwater Ter. W11 . . . . 2F 99
Clearwater Yd. *NW1* *1F 83*
(off Inverness St.)
Clearwell Dr. W9 . . . . 4K 81
Cleave Av. BR6: Chels 6J 173
UB3: Harl 4G 93
Cleaveland Rd. KT6: Surb 5D 150
Cleaverholme Cl. SE25 . . . . 6H 157
Cleaver Ho. *NW3* *7D 64*
(off Adelaide Rd.)
Cleaver Sq. SE11 . . . . 6K 19 (5A 102)
Cleaver St. SE11 . . . . 5K 19 (5A 102)
Cleaves Almshouses *KT2: King T* *2E 150*
(off London Rd.)
Cleeve Ct. TW14: Bedf 1G 129
Cleeve Hill SE23 . . . . 1H 139
Cleeve Ho. *E2* *2H 9*
(off Calvert Av.)
Cleeve Pk. Gdns. DA14: Sidc 2B 144
Cleeve Way SM1: Sutt 1K 165
SW15 . . . . 7B 116
Cleeve Workshops *E2* *2H 9*
(off Boundary Rd.)
Clegg Ho. *SE16* *3J 103*
(off Moodkee St.)
Clegg St. E1 . . . . 1H 103
E13 . . . . 2J 87
Cleland Ho. *E2* *2J 85*
(off Sewardstone Rd.)
Clematis Apts. *E3* *3B 86*
(off Merchant St.)
Clematis Gdns. IG8: Wfd G 5D 36
Clematis St. W12 . . . . 7C 80
Clem Attlee Ct. SW6 . . . . 6H 99
Clem Attlee Pde. *SW6* *6H 99*
(off North End Rd.)
Clemence Rd. RM10: Dag 1J 91
Clemence St. E14 . . . . 5B 86
Clement Av. SW4 . . . . 4H 119
Clement Cl. NW6 . . . . 7E 62
W4 . . . . 4K 97
Clement Danes Ho. W12 . . . . 6D 80
Clement Gdns. UB3: Harl 4G 93
Clementhorpe Rd. RM9: Dag 6C 72
Clement Ho. SE8 . . . . 4A 104
W10 . . . . *5E 80*
(off Dalgarno Gdns.)
Clementina Ct. *E3* *4A 86*
(off Copperfield Rd.)
Clementina Rd. E10 . . . . 1B 68
Clementine Cl. W13 . . . . 2B 96
Clementine Wlk. IG8: Wfd G 7D 36
Clement Rd. BR3: Beck 2K 157
SW19 . . . . 5G 135
Clement's Av. E16 . . . . 7J 87
Clements Cl. N12 . . . . 4E 30
Clements Ct. IG1: Ilf 3F 71
TW4: Houn 4B 112
Clement's Inn WC2 . . . . 1H 13 (6K 83)
Clement's Inn Pas. WC2 . . . . 1H 13
Clements La. EC4 . . . . 2F 15 (7D 84)
IG1: Ilf 3F 71
Clements Pl. TW8: Bford 5D 96
Clements Rd. E6 . . . . 7C 70
IG1: Ilf 3F 71
SE16 . . . . 3G 103
Clemson Ho. E8 . . . . 1F 85
Clendon Way SE18 . . . . 4H 107
Clennam St. SE1 . . . . 6D 14 (2C 102)
Clensham Ct. SM1: Sutt 2J 165
Clensham La. SM1: Sutt 2J 165
Clenston M. W1 . . . . 7E 4 (6D 82)
Cleopatra Cl. HA7: Stan 3J 27
Cleopatra's Needle 3G 13 (7K 83)
Clephane Rd. N1 . . . . 6C 66
Clephane Rd. Nth. N1 . . . . 6C 66
Clere Pl. EC2 . . . . 3F 9 (4D 84)
Clere St. EC2 . . . . 3F 9 (4D 84)
Clerics Wlk. TW17: Shep 7F 147

202 A-Z Big London

Clerkenwell—Colebrook Cl.

CLERKENWELL 4K 7 (4A 84)
Clerkenwell Cl. EC1 3K 7 (4A 84)
(not continuous)
Clerkenwell Ct. *N1* 2B 84
(off Duncan St.)
Clerkenwell Grn. EC1 4K 7 (4A 84)
Clerkenwell Rd. EC1 4J 7 (4A 84)
Clerks Pl. EC3 7G 9 (6E 84)
Clermont Rd. E9 1J 85
Clevedon Cl. N16 3F 67
Clevedon Ct. CR2: S Croy 5E 168
SW11 1C 118
(off Bolingbroke Wlk.)
Clevedon Gdns. TW5: Cran 1K 111
UB3: Harl 3F 93
Clevedon Ho. SM1: Sutt 4A 166
Clevedon Mans. NW5 4E 64
Clevedon Pas. N16 2F 67
Clevedon Rd. KT1: King T 2G 151
SE20 1K 157
TW1: Twick 6D 114
Cleve Ho. NW6 7K 63
Cleveland Av. SW20 2H 153
TW12: Hamp 7D 130
W4 4B 98
Cleveland Cl. W13 5B 78
Cleveland Gdns. KT4: Wor Pk 2A 164
N4 5C 48
NW2 2F 63
SW13 2B 116
W2 6A 82
Cleveland Gro. E1 4J 85
Cleveland Ho. *N2* 2B 46
(off The Grange)
Cleveland Mans. *NW6* 7H 63
(off Willesden La.)
SW9 7A 102
(off Mowll St.)
W9 4J 81
Cleveland M. W1 5A 6 (5G 83)
Cleveland Pk. TW19: Stanw 6A 110
Cleveland Pk. Av. E17 4C 50
Cleveland Pk. Cres. E17 4C 50
Cleveland Pl. SW1 4B 12 (1G 101)
Cleveland Ri. SM4: Mord 7F 153
Cleveland Rd. DA16: Well 2K 125
E18 3J 51
IG1: Ilf 3F 71
KT3: N Mald 4A 152
KT4: Wor Pk 2A 164
N1 7D 66
N9 7C 24
SW13 2B 116
TW7: Isle 4A 114
W4 3J 97
W13 5A 78
Cleveland Row SW1 5A 12 (1G 101)
Cleveland Sq. W2 6A 82
Cleveland St. W1 4K 5 (4F 83)
Cleveland Ter. W2 6A 82
Cleveland Way E1 4J 85
Cleveley Cl. SE7 4B 106
Cleveley Ct. *SE16* 4A 104
(off Ashton Reach)
Cleveley Cres. W5 2E 78
Cleveleys Rd. E5 3H 67
Cleverly Est. W12 1C 98
Cleve Rd. DA14: Sidc 3D 144
NW6 7J 63
Cleves Av. KT17: Ewe 7D 164
Cleves Ho. *E16* 1J 105
(off Southey M.)
Cleves Rd. E6 1B 88
TW10: Ham 3C 132
Cleves Wlk. IG6: Ilf 1G 53
Cleves Way HA4: Ruis 1B 58
TW12: Hamp 7D 130
TW16: Sun 6H 129
Clewer Ct. *E10* 1C 68
(off Leyton Grange Est.)
Clewer Cres. HA3: Hrw W 1H 41
Clewer Ho. *SE2* 2D 108
(off Wolvercote Rd.)
Cley Ho. SE4 4K 121
C&L Golf Course 7K 57
Clichy Est. E1 5J 85
Clichy Ho. *E1* 5J 85
(off Stepney Way)
Clifden M. E5 4K 67
Clifden Rd. E5 5J 67
TW1: Twick 1K 131
TW8: Bford 6D 96
Cliffe Ho. *SE10* 5H 105
(off Blackwall La.)
Cliffe Rd. CR2: S Croy 5D 168
Cliffe Wlk. *SM1: Sutt* 5A 166
(off Greyhound Rd.)
Clifford Av. BR7: Chst 6D 142
IG5: Ilf 1F 53
SM6: W'gton 4G 167
SW14 3H 115
Clifford Cl. UB5: N'olt 1C 76
Clifford Ct. *W2* 5K 81
(off Westbourne Pk. Vs.)
Clifford Dr. SW9 4B 120
Clifford Gdns. NW10 2E 80
UB3: Harl 4G 93
Clifford Gro. TW15: Ashf 4C 128
Clifford Haigh Ho. SW6 7F 99
Clifford Ho. *BR3: Beck* 6D 140
(off Calverley Cl.)
W14 4H 99
(off Edith Vs.)
Clifford Rd. E16 4H 87
E17 2E 50
EN5: New Bar 3E 20
HA0: Wemb 7D 60
N1 1E 84
N9 6D 24
SE25 4G 157
TW4: Houn 3B 112
TW10: Ham 2D 132
Clifford's Inn EC4 1J 13
Clifford's Inn Pas. EC4 1J 13 (6A 84)
Clifford St. W1 3A 12 (7G 83)
Clifford Way NW10 4B 62
Cliff Rd. NW1 6H 65
Cliffsend Ho. *SW9* 1A 120
(off Cowley Rd.)
Cliff Ter. SE8 2C 122
Cliffview Rd. SE13 3C 122
Cliff Vs. NW1 6H 65
Cliff Wlk. E16 5H 87
Clifton Av. E17 3K 49
HA7: Stan 2B 42
HA9: Wemb 6F 61
Clifton Av. N3 1H 45
TW13: Felt 3A 130
W12 1B 98
Clifton Cl. BR6: Farnb 5G 173
Clifton Ct. BR3: Beck 1D 158
IG8: Wfd G 6D 36
KT5: Surb 7F 151
N4 2A 66
NW8 3A 4
SE15 7H 103
TW19: Stanw 6A 110
Clifton Cres. SE15 7H 103
Clifton Est. SE15 1H 121
Clifton Gdns. EN2: Enf 4D 22
N15 6F 49
NW11 6H 45
UB10: Hil 2D 74
W4 4K 97
(not continuous)
W9 4A 82
Clifton Ga. SW10 6A 100
Clifton Gro. E8 6G 67
Clifton Hill NW8 2K 81
Clifton Hill Studios NW8 2A 82
Clifton Ho. *E2* 3J 9
(off Club Row)
E11 2G 69
Clifton M. SE25 4E 156
Clifton Pde. TW13: Felt 3A 130
Clifton Pk. Av. SW20 2E 152
Clifton Pl. SE16 2J 103
SW10 6A 100
(off Hollywood Rd.)
W2 1B 10 (6B 82)
W3 5J 79
Clifton Ri. SE14 7A 104
(not continuous)
Clifton Rd. DA14: Sidc 4J 143
DA16: Well 3C 126
E7 6B 70
E16 5G 87
HA3: Kenton 4F 43
IG2: Ilf 6H 53
KT2: King T 7F 133
N1 6C 66
N3 1A 46
N8 6H 47
N22 1J 47
NW10 2C 80
SE25 4E 156
SM6: W'gton 5F 167
SW19 6F 135
TW7: Isle 2J 113
TW11: Tedd 4J 131
UB2: S'hall 4C 94
UB6: G'frd 4G 77
W9 3A 4 (4A 82)
Clifton St. EC2 4G 9 (4E 84)
Clifton Ter. N4 2A 66
Clifton Vs. W9 5A 82
Cliftonville Ct. SE12 1J 141
Clifton Wlk. *W6* 4D 98
(off King St.)
Clifton Way HA0: Wemb 1E 78
SE15 7H 103
Climsland Ho. SE1 4K 13 (1A 102)
Cline Rd. N11 6B 32
Clinger Ct. *N1* 1E 84
(off Hobbs Pl. Est.)
Clink Prison Mus. 4E 14
Clink St. SE1 4D 14 (1D 102)
Clink Wharf *SE1* 4E 14
(off Clink St.)
Clinton Av. DA16: Well 4A 126
KT8: E Mos 4G 149
Clinton Ho. *KT6: Surb* 7D 150
(off Lovelace Gdns)
Clinton Rd. E3 3A 86
E7 4J 69
N15 4D 48
Clinton Ter. *SE8* 6C 104
(off Watergate St.)
SM1: Sutt 4A 166
Clipper Apts. *SE10* 6E 104
(off Welland St.)
Clipper Cl. SE16 2K 103
Clipper Ho. *E14* 5E 104
(off Manchester Rd.)
Clipper Way SE13 4E 122
Clippesby Cl. KT9: Chess 6F 163
Clipstone M. W1 5A 6 (5G 83)
Clipstone Rd. TW3: Houn 3E 112
Clipstone St. W1 5K 5 (5F 83)
Clissold Cl. N2 3D 46
Clissold Ct. N4 2C 66
Clissold Cres. N16 3D 66
Clissold Leisure Cen. 3D 66
Clissold Rd. N16 3D 66
Clitheroe Av. HA2: Harr 1E 58
Clitheroe Rd. SW9 2J 119
Clitherow Av. W7 3A 96
Clitherow Ct. TW8: Bford 5C 96
Clitherow Pas.
TW8: Bford 5C 96
Clitherow Rd. TW8: Bford 5B 96
Clitterhouse Cres. NW2 1E 62
Clitterhouse Rd. NW2 1E 62
Clive Av. N18 6B 34
Clive Ct. W9 4A 82
Cliveden Cl. N12 4F 31
Cliveden Ho. *E16* 1J 105
(off Fitzwilliam M.)
SW1 3G 17
(off Cliveden Pl.)
Cliveden Pl. SW1 3G 17 (4E 100)
TW17: Shep 6E 146
Cliveden Rd. SW19 1H 153
Clivedon Ct. W13 5B 78
Clivedon Rd. E4 5B 36
Clive Ho. *SE10* 6E 104
(off Haddo St.)
Clive Lloyd Ho. *N15* 5C 48
(off Woodlands Pk. Rd.)
Clive Lodge NW4 6F 45
Clive Pas. SE21 3D 138
Clive Rd. DA17: Belv 4G 109
EN1: Enf 4C 24
SE21 3D 138
SW19 6C 136
TW1: Twick 4K 131
TW14: Felt 6J 111
Clivesdale Dr.
UB3: Hayes 1K 93
Clive Way EN1: Enf 4B 24
Cloak La. EC4 2D 14 (7C 84)
Clochar Ct. NW10 1B 80
Clock Ct. E11 4K 51
Clock Ho. E3 3E 86
E17 4F 51
(off Wood St.)
The Clockhouse SW19 3E 134
Clockhouse Av. IG11: Bark 1G 89
Clockhouse Cl. SW19 2E 134
Clockhouse Ct. BR3: Beck 2A 158
CLOCKHOUSE JUNC. 5E 32
Clockhouse La. RM5: Col R 1H 55
TW14: Bedf 4C 128
TW15: Ashf 4C 128
Clock Ho. Pde. E11 6K 51
Clockhouse Pde. N13 5F 33
Clockhouse Pl. SW15 6G 117
Clock Ho. Rd. BR3: Beck 3A 158
CLOCKHOUSE RDBT. 1D 128
Clock Pde. EN2: Enf 5J 23
Clock Pl. *SE1* 4B 102
(off Newington Butts)
Clock Twr. Ind. Est. TW7: Isle 3K 113
Clock Twr. M. N1 1C 84
SE28 7B 90
W7 1J 95
Clock Twr. Rd. TW7: Isle 3K 113
Clock Vw. Cres. N7 6J 65
(not continuous)
Clockwork Apts. *EC4* 1B 14
(off Ludgate Sq.)
Clockwork M. E5 5K 67
Cloister Cl. TW11: Tedd 5B 132
Cloister Gdns. HA8: Edg 5D 28
SE25 6H 157
Cloister Rd. NW2 3H 63
W3 5J 79
The Cloisters 1E 18
The Cloisters E1 4J 9
SW9 1A 120
Cloisters Av. BR2: Broml 5D 160
Cloisters Bus. Cen. *SW8* 7F 101
(off Battersea Pk. Rd.)
Cloisters Ct. DA7: Bex 3H 127
Cloisters Mall KT1: King T 2E 150
Clonard Way HA5: Hat E 6A 26
Clonbrock Rd. N16 4E 66
Cloncurry St. SW6 2F 117
Clonmel Cl. HA2: Harr 2H 59
Clonmell Rd. N17 3D 48
Clonmel Rd. SW6 7H 99
TW11: Tedd 4H 131
Clonmore St. SW18 1H 135
Cloonmore Av. BR6: Chels 4K 173
Clorane Gdns. NW3 3J 63
The Close BR3: Beck 4A 158
BR5: Pet W 6J 161
CR4: Mitc 4D 154
DA5: Bexl 6G 127
DA14: Sidc 4B 144
E4 7K 35
EN4: E Barn 6J 21
HA0: Wemb 6E 60
HA2: Harr 2G 41
HA5: Eastc 7A 40
HA5: Pinn 7D 40
HA9: Wemb 3J 61
IG2: Ilf 6J 53
KT3: N Mald 2J 151
KT6: Surb 6E 150
N10 2F 47
N14 2C 32
N20 2C 30
RM6: Chad H 6E 54
SE3 2F 123
SE25 6G 157
SM3: Sutt 7H 153
SM5: Cars 7C 166
TW7: Isle 2H 113
TW9: Rich 3H 115
UB10: Hil 1C 74
Cloth Ct. EC1 6B 8
Cloth Fair EC1 6B 8 (5B 84)
Cloth Ho. *EC1* 5C 8
(off Cloth St.)
Clothier St. E1 7H 9 (6E 84)
Cloth St. EC1 5C 8 (5C 84)
Clothworkers Rd. SE18 7H 107
Cloudesdale Rd. SW17 2F 137
Cloudesley Cl. DA14: Sidc 4K 143
Cloudesley Ho. *N1* 1A 84
(off Cloudesley St.)
Cloudesley Mans. *N1* 1A 84
(off Cloudesley Pl.)
Cloudesley Pl. N1 1A 84
Cloudesley Rd. DA7: Bex 1F 127
N1 1A 84
(not continuous)
Cloudesley Sq. N1 1A 84
Cloudesley St. N1 1A 84
Cloud Way TW6: H'row A 3D 110
Clouston Cl. SM6: W'gton 5J 167
Clova Rd. E7 6H 69
Clove Cres. E14 7E 86
Clove Hitch Quay SW11 3A 118
Clovelly Av. NW9 4B 44
UB10: Ick 4E 56
Clovelly Cl. HA5: Eastc 3K 39
UB10: Ick 4E 56
Clovelly Ct. NW2 5E 62
Clovelly Gdns. EN1: Enf 7K 23
RM7: Mawney 1H 55
SE19 1F 157
Clovelly Ho. *W2* 6A 82
(off Hallfield Est.)
Clovelly Rd. DA7: Bex 6E 108
N8 4H 47
TW3: Houn 2E 112
W4 2K 97
W5 2C 96
Clovelly Way BR6: St M Cry 6K 161
E1 6J 85
HA2: Harr 2D 58
Clover Cl. E11 2F 69
Clover Court *E14* 3D 104
(off Watergate Walk)
Cloverdale Ct. SM6: W'gton 6F 167
Cloverdale Gdns. DA15: Sidc 6K 125
Clover M. SW3 7F 17 (6D 100)
Clover Way SM6: W'gton 1E 166
Clove St. E13 4J 87
RM9: Dag 3E 90
Clowders Rd. SE6 3B 140
Clowser Cl. SM1: Sutt 5A 166
Cloysters Grn. E1 1G 103
Cloyster Wood HA8: Edg 7J 27
Club Gdns. Rd. BR2: Hayes 7J 159
The Clubhouse E14 6C 86
Clubhouse La. UB10: Ick 4C 56
Club Row E1 3J 9 (4F 85)
E2 3J 9 (4F 85)
The Clumps TW15: Ashf 4F 129
Clunbury Av. UB2: S'hall 5D 94
Clunbury St. N1 2D 84
Clunie Ho. *SW1* 1F 17
(off Hans Pl.)
Cluny Est. SE1 7G 15 (3E 102)
Cluny M. SW5 4J 99
Cluny Pl. SE1 7G 15 (3E 102)
Cluse Ct. *N1* 2C 84
(off St Peters St.)
Cluster Ho. W3 1B 98
Clutton St. E14 5D 86
Clydach Rd. EN1: Enf 4A 24
Clyde Cir. N15 4E 48
Clyde Ct. *NW1* 2H 83
(off Hampden Cl.)
Clyde Flats *SW6* 7H 99
(off Rylston Rd.)
Clyde Ho. KT2: King T 1D 150
SW18 4J 117
(off Enterprise Way)
Clyde Pl. E10 7D 50
Clyde Rd. CR0: C'don 2F 169
N15 4E 48
(not continuous)
N22 1H 47
SM1: Sutt 5J 165
SM6: W'gton 6G 167
TW19: Stanw 1A 128
Clydesdale EN3: Pond E 4E 24
Clydesdale Av. HA7: Stan 3D 42
Clydesdale Cl. TW7: Isle 3K 113
Clydesdale Ct. N20 1G 31
Clydesdale Gdns. TW10: Rich 4H 115
Clydesdale Ho. *DA18: Erith* 2E 108
(off Kale Rd.)
W11 6H 81
(off Clydesdale Rd.)
Clydesdale Rd. W11 6H 81
Clydesdale Way DA17: Belv 2H 109
Clyde Sq. E14 6B 86
Clyde St. SE8 6B 104
Clyde Ter. SE23 2J 139
Clyde Va. SE23 2J 139
Clyde Way RM1: Rom 1K 55
Clyde Wharf E16 1J 105
Clydon Cl. DA8: Erith 6K 109
Clyfford Rd. HA4: Ruis 4H 57
Clymping Dene TW14: Felt 7K 111
Clynes Ho. *E2* 3K 85
(off Knottisford St.)
RM10: Dag 3G 73
(off Uvedale Rd.)
Clyston St. SW8 2G 119
Coach & Horses Yd.
W1 2K 11 (7G 83)
Coach Ho. La. N5 4B 66
SW19 4F 135
Coach Ho. M. *SE1* 7G 15
(off Long La.)
SE14 2K 121
SE23 6K 121
SM2: Sutt 6K 165
Coachhouse M. SE20 7H 139
Coach Ho. Yd. *NW3* 4A 64
(off Heath St.)
SW18 4K 117
Coachmaker M. *SW4* 3J 119
(off Bedford Rd.)
W4 3K 97
(off Berrymede Rd.)
Coach Yd. M. N19 1J 65
Coalbrookdale Gates 6A 10 (2B 100)
Coaldale Wlk. SE21 7C 120
Coal Drops Yard 1J 83
Coalecroft Rd. SW15 4E 116
Coal Lane SW9 4A 120
Coalmakers Wharf E14 6C 86
Coalport Ho. SE11 2J 19
Coal Post Cl. BR6: Chels 6K 173
Coalstore Ct. E1 5A 86
Coatbridge Ho. *N1* 7K 65
(off Carnoustie Dr.)
Coates Av. SW18 6C 118
Coates Cl. CR7: Thor H 3C 156
Coates Hill Rd. BR1: Broml 2E 160
Coate St. E2 2G 85
Coates Wlk. TW8: Bford 6E 96
Cobalt SE28 2A 108
The Cobalt Bldg. *EC2* 5C 8
(off Bridgewater Sq.)
Cobalt Cl. BR3: Beck 4K 157
NW9 1B 44
Cobalt Ct. HA4: Ruis 4A 58
Cobalt Pl. SW11 1B 118
Cobalt Sq. SW8 7G 19
Cobalt Twr. SE14 6A 104
Cobbett Rd. SE9 3C 124
TW2: Whitt 1E 130
Cobbetts Av. IG4: Ilf 5B 52
Cobbett St. SW8 7K 101
Cobble La. N1 7B 66
Cobble M. N5 3C 66
N6 1E 64
(off Highgate West Hill)
Cobble Path *E17* 5C 50
(off Cedars Av.)
Cobblestone Pl. CR0: C'don 1C 168
Cobblestone Sq. E1 1H 103
Cobbold Ct. *SW1* 3C 18
(off Elverton St.)
Cobbold Ind. Est. NW10 6B 62
Cobbold M. W12 2B 98
Cobbold Rd. E11 3H 69
NW10 6B 62
W12 2A 98
Cobb's Ct. EC4 1B 14
Cobb's Hall *SW6* 6F 99
(off Fulham Pal. Rd.)
Cobb's Rd. TW4: Houn 4D 112
Cobbsthorpe Vs. SE26 4K 139
Cobb St. E1 6J 9 (5F 85)
Cobden Bldgs. *WC1* 1G 7
(off King's Cross Rd.)
Cobden Ct. BR2: Broml 4A 160
Cobden Ho. *E2* 3G 85
(off Nelson Gdns.)
NW1 2G 83
(off Arlington Rd.)
Cobden M. SE26 5H 139
Cobden Rd. BR6: Farnb 4H 173
E11 3G 69
SE25 5G 157
Cobham Av. KT3: N Mald 5C 152
Cobham Cl. BR2: Broml 7C 160
DA15: Sidc 6B 126
EN1: Enf 3B 24
HA8: Edg 2H 43
SM6: W'gton 6J 167
SW11 6C 118
Cobham Ct. CR4: Mitc 2B 154
Cobham M. NW1 7H 65
Cobham Pl. DA6: Bex 5E 126
Cobham Rd. E17 1E 50
IG3: Ilf 2J 71
KT1: King T 2G 151
N22 3B 48
TW5: Hest 7A 94
Cobland Rd. SE12 4A 142
Coborn M. *E3* 3B 86
(off Coborn St.)
Coborn Rd. E3 2B 86
Coborn St. E3 3B 86
Cobourg Rd. SE5 6F 103
Cobourg St. NW1 2B 6 (3G 83)
Cobtree Ct. *UB1: S'hall* 6G 77
(off Fleming Rd.)
Coburg Cl. SW1 3B 18 (4G 101)
Coburg Cres. SW2 1K 137
Coburg Dwellings *E1* 6J 85
(off Hardinge St.)
Coburg Gdns. IG5: Ilf 2B 52
Coburg Rd. N22 3K 47
Cochrane Cl. NW8 1B 4
Cochrane Ct. *E10* 1C 68
(off Leyton Grange Est.)
Cochrane Ho. *E14* 2C 104
(off Admirals Way)
Cochrane M. NW8 2B 82
Cochrane Rd. SW19 7G 135
Cochrane St. NW8 1B 4 (2B 82)
Cockburn Ho. *SW1* 6D 18
(off Aylesford St.)
COCKCROW HILL 1D 162
Cockerell Rd. E17 7A 50
COCKFOSTERS 4J 21
Cockfosters Pde. EN4: Cockf 4K 21
Cockfosters Rd. EN4: Cockf, Had W 1H 21
Cock Hill E1 6H 9 (5E 84)
Cock La. EC1 6A 8 (5B 84)
Cockpit Steps SW1 7C 12
Cockpit Theatre 4C 4
(off Gateforth St.)
Cockpit Yd. WC1 5H 7 (5K 83)
Cocks Cres. KT3: N Mald 4B 152
Cocksett Av. BR6: Chels 6J 173
Cockspur Ct. SW1 4D 12 (1H 101)
Cockspur St. SW1 4D 12 (1H 101)
Cocksure La. DA14: Sidc 3G 145
The Coda Cen. SW6 7G 99
Coda Residences *SW11* 3B 118
(of York Place)
Code Ct. NW2 3C 62
Code St. E1 4K 9
Codicote Ho. *SE8* 4K 103
(off Chilton Gro.)
Codling Cl. E1 1G 103
Codling Way HA0: Wemb 4D 60
Codrington Ct. E1 4H 85
SE16 7A 86
Codrington Hill SE23 7A 122
Codrington M. W11 6G 81
Cody Cl. HA3: Kenton 3D 42
SM6: W'gton 7H 167
Cody Rd. E16 4F 87
Coe Av. SE25 6G 157
Coe's All. EN5: Barn 4B 20
Cofferdam Way SE8 7D 104
Coffey St. SE8 7C 104
Cogan Av. E17 1A 50
Coin St. SE1 4J 13 (1A 102)
(not continuous)
Coity Rd. NW5 6E 64
Cokers La. SE21 1D 138
Coke St. E1 6G 85
Colas M. NW6 1J 81
Colbeck M. SE6 7F 123
SW7 4K 99
Colbeck Rd. HA1: Harr 7G 41
Colberg Pl. N16 7F 49
Colbert *SE5* 1E 120
(off Sceaux Gdns.)
Colborne Cl. KT17: Ewe 6B 164
Colborne Ho. *E14* 7C 86
(off E. India Dock Rd.)
Colborne Way KT4: Wor Pk 3E 164
Colbrook Av. UB3: Harl 3F 93
Colbrook Cl. UB3: Harl 3F 93
Colburn Way SM1: Sutt 3B 166
Colby M. SE19 5E 138
Colby Rd. KT12: Walt T 7J 147
SE19 5E 138
Colchester Av. E12 4D 70
Colchester Dr. HA5: Pinn 5B 40
Colchester Ho. *E3* 1B 86
(off Parnell Rd.)
Colchester Rd. E10 7E 50
E17 6C 50
HA6: Nwood 2J 39
HA8: Edg 7D 28
Colclough Ct. *CR0: C'don* 6C 156
(off Simpson Cl.)
Coldbath Sq. EC1 3J 7 (4A 84)
Coldbath St. SE13 1D 122
COLDBLOW 1J 145
Cold Blow Cres. DA5: Bexl 1K 145
Cold Blow La. SE14 7K 103
(not continuous)
Cold Blows CR4: Mitc 3D 154
Coldershaw Rd. W7 1A 96
W13 1A 96
Coldfall Av. N10 2E 46
Coldham Ct. N22 1B 48
Coldharbour E14 2E 104
Coldharbour Crest SE9 3E 142
Coldharbour Ind. Est. SE5 2C 120
Coldharbour La. SE5 3C 120
SW9 4A 120
UB3: Hayes 1J 93
Coldharbour Leisure Cen. 2D 142
Coldharbour Pl. SE5 2C 120
Coldharbour Rd. CR0: Wadd 5A 168
Coldharbour Way CR0: Wadd 5A 168
Coldstream Gdns. SW18 6H 117
Colebeck M. N1 6B 66
Colebert Av. E1 4J 85
Colebert Ho. *E1* 4J 85
(off Colebert Av.)
Colebrook Cl. NW7 6A 30
SW15 7F 117

Colebrook Ct. SW3 ....4D 16
(off Makins St.)
Colebrooke Av. W13 ....6B 78
Colebrooke Ct. DA14: Sidc ..3B 144
Colebrooke Dr. E11 ....7A 52
Colebrooke Pl. N1 ....1B 84
Colebrooke Ri. BR2: Broml ..2G 159
Colebrooke Row N1 ....2B 84
Colebrook Ho. E14 ....6D 86
(off Ellesmere St.)
SE18 ....7E 106
Colebrook Rd. SW16 ....1J 155
Colebrook Way N11 ....5A 32
Coleby Path SE5 ....7D 102
Colechurch Ho. SE1 ....5G 103
(off Avondale Sq.)
Cole Cl. SE28 ....1B 108
Cole Ct. TW1: Twick 7A 114
Coledale Dr. HA7: Stan 1C 42
Colefax Bldgs. E1 ....6G 85
(off Plumber's Row)
Coleford Rd. SW18 ....5A 118
Cole Gdns. TW5: Cran ..7J 93
Colegrave Rd. E15 ....5F 69
Colegrove Rd. SE15 ....6F 103
Coleherne Ct. SW5 ....5K 99
Coleherne Mans. SW5 ....5K 99
(off Old Brompton Rd.)
Coleherne M. SW10 ....5K 99
Coleherne Rd. SW10 ....5K 99
Colehill Gdns. SW6 ....2G 117
Colehill La. SW6 ....1G 117
Cole Ho. SE1 ....7K 13
(off Baylis Rd.)
Coleman Cl. SE25 ....2G 157
Coleman Ct. SW18 ....7J 117
Coleman Flds. N1 ....1C 84
Coleman Mans. N8 ....7J 47
Coleman Rd. DA17: Belv ..4G 109
RM9: Dag 6E 72
SE5 ....7E 102
Colemans Heath SE9 ....3E 142
Coleman St. EC2 ....7E 8 (6D 84)
Coleman St. Bldgs. EC2 ....7E 8
Colenso Dr. NW7 ....7H 29
Colenso Rd. E5 ....4J 67
IG2: Ilf 1J 71
COLE PARK 6A 114
Cole Pk. Gdns. TW1: Twick ..5A 114
Cole Pk. Rd. TW1: Twick ..6A 114
Cole Pk. Vw. TW1: Twick ..6A 114
Colepits Wood Rd. SE9 ..5H 125
Coleraine Rd. N8 ....3A 48
SE3 ....6H 105
Coleridge Av. E12 ....6C 70
SM1: Sutt 4C 166
Coleridge Cl. SW8 ....2F 119
Coleridge Ct. EN5: New Bar ..5E 20
(off Station Rd.)
N1 ....1C 84
(off Dibden St.)
SW1 ....3C 18
(off Regency St.)
W14 ....3F 99
(off Blythe Rd.)
Coleridge Cres. SL3: Poyle ..4A 174
Coleridge Dr. HA4: Ruis ..6K 39
Coleridge Gdns. NW6 ....7A 64
SW10 ....7K 99
Coleridge Ho. SE17 ....5C 102
(off Browning St.)
SW1 ....6J 18
(off Churchill Gdns.)
Coleridge La. N8 ....6J 47
Coleridge Rd. CR0: C'don ..7J 157
E17 ....4B 50
N4 ....2A 66
N8 ....6H 47
N12 ....5F 31
TW15: Ashf 4A 128
Coleridge Sq. SW10 ....7A 100
(off Coleridge Gdns.)
W13 ....6A 78
Coleridge Wlk. NW11 ....4J 45
Coleridge Way UB4: Hayes ..6J 75
UB7: W Dray 4A 92
Cole Rd. TW1: Twick 6A 114
Colesburg Rd. BR3: Beck ..3B 158
Coles Cres. HA2: Harr 2F 59
Coles Grn. WD23: B Hea ..1B 26
Coles Grn. Ct. NW2 ....2C 62
Coles Grn. Rd. NW2 ....1C 62
Coleshill Flats SW1 ....4H 17
Colestead Rd. TW11: Tedd ..6J 131
Colestown St. SW11 ....2C 118
Cole St. SE1 ....7D 14 (2C 102)
Colesworth Ho. HA8: Edg ..2J 43
(off Burnt Oak B'way.)
Colet Cl. N13 ....6G 33
Colet Ct. W6 ....4F 99
(off Hammersmith Rd.)
Colet Flats E1 ....6A 86
(off Troon St.)
Colet Gdns. W14 ....4F 99
Colet Ho. SE17 ....5B 102
(off Doddington Gro.)
Colette Ct. SE16 ....2K 103
(off Eleanor Cl.)
Coley St. WC1 ....4H 7 (4K 83)
Colfe & Hatcliffe Glebe SE13 ..5D 122
(off Lewisham High St.)
Colfe Rd. SE23 ....1A 140
Colfes Leisure Cen. 6J 123
Colgate Ct. EN5: Barn 5B 20
(off Leecroft Rd.)
Colham Av. UB7: Yiew ..1A 92
COLHAM GREEN 5C 74
Colham Grn. Rd. UB8: Hil ..5C 74
Colham Mill Rd. UB7: W Dray ..2A 92
Colham Rd. UB8: Hil 4B 74
COLHAM RDBT. 6C 74
Colina M. N15 ....5B 48
Colina Rd. N15 ....5B 48
Colin Cl. BR4: W W'ck 3H 171
CR0: C'don 3B 170
NW9 ....4A 44
Colin Ct. SE6 ....7B 122
Colin Cres. NW9 ....4B 44
COLINDALE 3K 43
Colindale Av. NW9 ....3K 43
Colindale Bus. Pk. NW9 ..3J 43
Colindale Gdns. NW9 ....3B 44
Colindale Retail Pk. 4K 43
Colindeep Gdns. NW4 ....4C 44
Colindeep La. NW4 ....3A 44
NW9 ....3A 44

Colin Dr. NW9 ....5B 44
Colinette Rd. SW15 ....4E 116
Colin Gdns. NW9 ....4B 44
Colin Pde. NW9 ....4A 44
Colin Pk. Rd. NW9 ....4A 44
Colin Pond Ct. RM6: Chad H ..4D 54
Colin Rd. NW10 ....6C 62
Colinsdale N1 ....1B 84
(off Camden Wlk.)
Colinton Rd. IG3: Ilf 2B 72
Colin Winter Ho. E1 ....4J 85
(off Nicholas Rd.)
Coliseum Theatre 3E 12
(off St Martin's La.)
Coliston Pas. SW18 ....7J 117
(off Coliston Rd.)
Coliston Rd. SW18 ....7J 117
Collamore Av. SW18 ....1C 136
Collapit Cl. HA1: Harr 6F 41
Collard Pl. NW1 ....7F 65
Collards Almshouses E17 ..5E 50
(off Maynard Rd.)
Collection Pl. NW8 ....1K 81
(off Bolton Pl.)
College App. SE10 ....6E 104
College Av. HA3: Hrw W ..1J 41
College Cl. E9 ....5J 67
HA3: Hrw W 7D 26
N18 ....5A 34
TW2: Twick 1H 131
College Ct. EN3: Pond E ..5D 24
NW3 ....6B 64
(off College Cres.)
SW3 ....6F 17
W5 ....7E 78
W6 ....5E 99
(off Queen Caroline St.)
College Cl. Rd. EN3: Pond E ..5D 24
College Cres. NW3 ....6A 64
College Cross N1 ....7A 66
College Dr. HA4: Ruis 7J 39
KT7: T Ditt 7J 149
College E. E1 ....6K 9 (5F 85)
College Flds. Bus. Cen. SW19 ..1C 154
College Gdns. E4 ....7J 25
EN2: Enf 1J 23
IG4: Ilf 5C 52
KT3: N Mald 5B 152
N18 ....5B 34
SE21 ....1E 138
SW17 ....2C 136
College Grn. SE19 ....7E 138
College Gro. NW1 ....1G 83
College Hall 4C 6 (4H 83)
College Hill EC4 ....2D 14 (7C 84)
College Hill Rd. HA3: Hrw W ..7D 26
College La. NW5 ....4F 65
College Mans. NW6 ....1G 81
(off Salusbury Rd.)
SW1 ....7A 66
(off College Cross)
SW18 ....5K 117
College of Arms 2C 14
College Pde. NW6 ....1G 81
(off Salusbury Rd.)
COLLEGE PARK 3D 80
College Pk. Cl. SE13 ....4F 123
College Pk. Rd. N17 ....6A 34
College Pl. E17 ....4G 51
NW1 ....1G 83
SW10 ....7A 100
College Point E15 ....6H 69
College Rd. BR1: Broml ..1J 159
BR8: Hext 7K 145
CR0: C'don 2D 168
E17 ....5E 50
EN2: Enf 2J 23
HA1: Harr 6J 41
HA3: Hrw W 1J 41
HA9: Wemb 1D 60
N17 ....6A 34
N21 ....2F 33
NW10 ....2E 80
SE19 ....5F 139
SE21 ....7E 120
SW19 ....6B 136
TW7: Isle 1K 113
W13 ....6B 78
COLLEGE RDBT. 3E 150
College Row E9 ....5K 67
(off Homerton Gro.)
College Slip BR1: Broml ..1J 159
College St. EC4 ....2D 14 (7C 84)
College Ter. E3 ....3B 86
N3 ....2H 45
College Vw. SE9 ....1B 142
College Vw. Rd. N17 ....6A 34
College Wlk. KT1: King T ..3E 150
College Way RM8: Dag ..4A 72
TW15: Ashf 4B 128
UB3: Hayes 7J 75
College Yd. NW5 ....4F 65
NW6 ....1G 81
Collendale Rd. E17 ....3K 49
Collent St. E9 ....6J 67
Collerston Ho. SE10 ....5H 105
(off Armitage Rd.)
Colless Rd. N15 ....5F 49
Collett Rd. SE16 ....3G 103
Collett Way UB2: S'hall ..2F 95
Collier Cl. E6 ....7F 89
Collier Dr. HA8: Edg 2G 43
COLLIER ROW 1H 55
Collier Row La. RM5: Col R ..1H 55
Collier Row Rd. RM5: Col R ..1F 55
Colliers Ct. CR0: C'don ..4D 168
(off St Peter's Rd.)
Colliers Shaw BR2: Kes ..4B 172
Colliers Water La. CR7: Thor H ..5A 156
COLLIERS WOOD 7B 136
Colliford Ct. HA8: Edg 4A 28
(off King's Dr.)
Collindale Av. DA8: Erith ..7H 109
DA15: Sidc 1A 144
Collingbourne Rd. W12 ....1D 98
Collingham Gdns. SW5 ..4K 99
Collingham Pl. SW5 ....4K 99
Collingham Rd. SW5 ....4K 99
Collings Cl. N22 ....6E 32
Collington St. SE10 ....5F 105
Collingtree Rd. SE26 ....4J 139

Collingwood Av. KT5: Surb ..1J 163
N10 ....3E 46
Collingwood Cl. SE20 ....1H 157
TW2: Whitt 7E 112
Collingwood Ct. EN5: New Bar ..5E 20
W5 ....5F 79
Collingwood Ho. E1 ....4J 85
(off Darling Row)
SE16 ....2H 103
(off Cherry Gdn. St.)
SW1 ....4B 18
(off Dolphin Sq.)
W1 ....5A 6
(off Clipstone St.)
Collingwood Rd. CR4: Mitc ..3C 154
E17 ....6C 50
N15 ....4E 48
SM1: Sutt 3J 165
UB8: Hil 4D 74
Collingwood St. E1 ....4H 85
Collins Av. HA7: Stan 2E 42
Collins Bldg. NW2 ....6G 63
Collins Ct. E8 ....6G 67
DA14: Ruis 2A 58
Collins Ho. E14 ....7E 86
(off Newby St.)
SE10 ....5H 105
(off Armitage Rd.)
Collinson Ct. SE1 ....7C 14
Collinson Ho. SE15 ....7G 103
(off Peckham Pk. Rd.)
Collinson St. SE1 ....7C 14 (2C 102)
Collinson Wlk. SE1 ....7C 14 (2C 102)
Collins Path TW12: Hamp ..6D 130
Collins Rd. N5 ....4C 66
Collins Sq. SE3 ....2H 123
Collins St. SE3 ....2G 123
(not continuous)
Collin's Yd. N1 ....1B 84
Collinwood Av. EN3: Enf H ..3D 24
Collinwood Gdns. IG5: Ilf ..5D 52
Collis All. TW2: Twick 1J 131
Collison Pl. N16 ....1E 66
Coll's Rd. SE15 ....1G 121
Collyer Av. CR0: Bedd ..4J 167
Collyer Pl. SE15 ....1G 121
Collyer Rd. CR0: Bedd ..4J 167
Colman Cl. HA7: Stan 6G 27
N12 ....6F 31
Colman Pde. EN1: Enf 3K 23
Colman Rd. E16 ....5A 88
Colmans Wharf E14 ....5D 86
(off Morris Rd.)
Colmar Cl. E1 ....4K 85
Colmer Pl. HA3: Hrw W ..7C 26
Colmer Rd. SW16 ....1J 155
Colmore M. SE15 ....1H 121
Colmore Rd. EN3: Pond E ..4D 24
Colnbrook By-Pass SL3: Poyle ..4A 174
Colnbrook Ct. SL3: Poyle ..4A 174
Colnbrook St. SE1 ....3B 102
W7 ....6H 77
Colne Ct. KT19: Ewe 4J 163
Colne Ho. NW8 ....4B 4
(off Penfold St.)
Colne Reach TW19: Stanw M ..7A 174
Colne Rd. E5 ....4A 68
N21 ....7J 23
TW1: Twick 1J 131
TW2: Twick 1J 131
Colne St. E13 ....3J 87
COLNEY HATCH 6J 31
Colney Hatch La. N10 ....6J 31
N11 ....6J 31
Colnmore Ct. E2 ....3K 85
(off Meath Cres.)
Cologne Rd. SW11 ....4B 118
Colomb Ct. BR4: W W'ck ..4G 171
Colombo Centre 5A 14
Colombo Rd. IG1: Ilf 1G 71
Colombo St. SE1 ....5A 14 (1B 102)
Colomb St. SE10 ....5G 105
Colonel's Wlk. EN2: Enf ..3G 23
Colonial Av. TW2: Whitt ..6G 113
Colonial Ct. N7 ....3K 65
Colonial Dr. W4 ....4J 97
Colonial Rd. TW14: Felt ..7G 111
The Colonnade WC1 ....4F 7 (4J 83)
The Colonnade SE1 ....6J 13
(off Waterloo Rd.)
SE8 ....4B 104
Colonnade Gdns. W3 ....1B 98
The Colonnades W2 ....6K 81
The Colonnades Leisure Pk. ..6A 168
Colonnade Wlk. SW1 ....4J 17 (4F 101)
Colony Mans. SW5 ....5K 99
(off Earl's Ct. Rd.)
Colony M. N1 ....5D 66
Colorado Apts. N8 ....3K 47
(off Gt. Amwell La.)
Colorado Bldg. SE13 ....6H 85
(off Deal's Gateway)
Colosseum Apts. E2 ....2K 85
(off Palmers Rd.)
Colosseum Ter. NW1 ....2K 5
Colour Ct. SW1 ....5B 12
Colour Ho. SE1 ....7H 15
(off Bell Yd M.)
Colour House Theatre 1A 154
Colroy Ct. NW11 ....5G 45
Colson Rd. CR0: C'don ..2E 168
Colson Way SW16 ....4G 137
Colstead Ho. E1 ....6H 85
(off Watney Mkt.)
Colsterworth Rd. N15 ....4F 49
(not continuous)
Colston Av. SM5: Cars ..4C 166
Colston Cl. SM5: Cars ..4D 166
Colston Rd. E7 ....6B 70
SW14 ....4J 115
Coltash Ct. EC1 ....3D 8
(off Whitecross St.)
Coltbeck Rd. E28 ....2B 66
Colthurst Cres. N4 ....2C 66
Colthurst Dr. N9 ....3C 34
Coltman Ho. SE10 ....6E 104
(off Welland St.)
Coltman St. E14 ....5A 86
Coltness Cres. SE2 ....5B 108

Colton Gdns. N17 ....3C 48
Colton Rd. HA1: Harr 5J 41
Coltsfoot Dr. UB7: Yiew ..6A 74
Columbas Dr. NW3 ....1B 64
Columbia Av. HA4: Ruis ..1K 57
HA8: Edg 1H 43
KT4: Wor Pk 1B 164
Columbia Gdns. SW6 ....6J 99
(off One Lillie Sq.)
Columbia Gdns. Nth. SW6 ..6J 99
(off Rickett St.)
Columbia Gdns. Sth. SW6 ..6J 99
(off Rickett St.)
Columbia Ho. E3 ....4B 86
(off Hamlets Way)
Columbia Point SE16 ....3J 103
(off Canada Est.)
Columbia Rd. E2 ....1J 9 (3F 85)
E13 ....4H 87
Columbia Rd. Flower Market ..1K 9
(off Columbia Rd.)
Columbia Sq. SW14 ....4J 115
Columbia Wharf EN3: Pond E ..6F 25
Columbine Av. CR2: S Croy ..7B 168
E6 ....5C 88
Columbine Way SE13 ....2E 122
Columbus Ctyd. E14 ....1C 104
Columbus Ct. SE16 ....1J 103
(off Rotherhithe St.)
Colva Wlk. N19 ....2F 65
Colvern Ho. RM7: Rom ..5J 55
Colverson Ho. E1 ....5J 85
(off Lindley St.)
Colvestone Cres. E8 ....5F 67
Colview Ct. SE9 ....1B 142
Colville Est. N1 ....1E 84
Colville Est. W. E2 ....2K 9
Colville Gdns. W11 ....6H 81
(not continuous)
Colville Ho. E2 ....2J 85
(off Waterloo Gdns.)
Colville Ho's. W11 ....6H 81
Colville Mans. E20 ....1J 69
(off Victory Pde.)
Colville M. W11 ....6H 81
Colville Pl. W1 ....6B 6 (5H 83)
Colville Rd. E11 ....3E 68
E17 ....2A 50
N9 ....1C 34
W3 ....3H 97
W11 ....6H 81
Colville Sq. W11 ....6H 81
Colville Ter. W11 ....6H 81
Colvin Cl. SE26 ....5J 139
Colvin Gdns. E4 ....3K 35
E11 ....4K 51
IG6: Ilf 1G 53
Colvin Ho. W10 ....6F 81
(off Kingsdown Cl.)
Colvin Rd. CR7: Thor H ..5A 156
E6 ....7C 70
Colwall Gdns. IG8: Wfd G ..5D 36
Colwell Cres. EN3: Pond E ..5D 24
Colwell Ho. KT12: Walt T ..7H 147
(off Hepworth Way)
Colwell Rd. SE22 ....5F 121
Colwick Cl. N6 ....7H 47
Colwith Rd. W6 ....6E 98
Colwood Gdns. SW19 ....7B 136
Colworth Gro. SE17 ....4C 102
Colworth Rd. CR0: C'don ..1G 169
E11 ....6G 51
Colwyn Av. UB6: G'frd 2K 77
Colwyn Cl. SW16 ....5G 137
Colwyn Cres. TW3: Houn ..1G 113
Colwyn Grn. NW9 ....6A 44
Colwyn Ho. SE1 ....2J 19 (3A 102)
Colwyn Rd. NW2 ....3D 62
Colyer Cl. SE9 ....2F 143
N1 ....2B 84
Colyers Cl. DA8: Erith ..1K 127
Colyers La. DA8: Erith ..1J 127
Colyers Wlk. DA8: Erith ..1K 127
Colyton Cl. DA16: Well ..1D 126
HA0: Wemb 6C 60
Colyton La. SW16 ....5A 138
Colyton Rd. SE22 ....5H 121
Colyton Way N18 ....5B 34
The Combe NW1 ....2K 5 (3F 83)
Combe Av. SE3 ....7H 105
Combedale Rd. SE10 ....5J 105
Combe Ho. W2 ....5J 81
(off Gt. Western Rd.)
Combemartin Rd. SW18 ..7G 117
Combe M. SE3 ....7H 105
Comber Cl. NW2 ....3D 62
Comber Gro. SE5 ....7C 102
Comber Ho. SE5 ....7C 102
Combermere Rd. SM4: Mord ..6K 153
SW9 ....3K 119
Comberton KT1: King T ..2G 151
(off Eureka St.)
Comberton Rd. E5 ....2H 67
Combeside SE18 ....7K 107
Combwell Cres. SE2 ....3A 108
Comedy Store 3C 12
(off Oxendon St.)
Comedy Theatre 3D 12
(off Panton St.)
Comely Bank Rd. E17 ....5E 50
Comeragh M. W14 ....5G 99
Comeragh Rd. W14 ....5G 99
Comer Cres. UB2: S'hall ..2G 95
Comer Ho. EN5: New Bar ..4F 21
Comerford Rd. SE4 ....4A 122
Comet Cl. E12 ....4B 70
Comet Ho. UB3: Harl 7E 92
Comet Pl. SE8 ....7C 104
(not continuous)
Comet Rd. TW19: Stanw ..7A 110
Comet St. SE8 ....7C 104
Comfort St. SE15 ....6E 102
Commander Av. NW9 ....3C 44
Commerce Pk. CR0: Wadd ..2K 167
Commerce Rd. N22 ....1K 47
TW8: Bford 6C 96
Commerce Way CR0: Wadd ..2K 167
Commercial Rd. E1 ....7K 9 (6G 85)
E14 ....6G 86
N18 ....5K 33
Commercial Rd. Ind. Est. N18 ..6A 34
Commercial St. E1 ....4J 9 (4F 85)
Commercial Way NW10 ....2H 79
SE10 ....4H 105
SE15 ....7F 103

Commercial Wharf E8 ....1E 84
(off Kingsland Rd.)
Commerell Pl. SE10 ....5H 105
Commerell St. SE10 ....5G 105
Commodity Quay E1 ....3K 15 (7F 85)
Commodore Ct. SE8 ....1C 122
(off Albyn Rd.)
Commodore Ho. E14 ....7E 86
(off Poplar High St.)
E16 ....2K 105
(off Royal Crest Av.)
SW18 ....3A 118
Commodore St. E1 ....4A 86
The Common E15 ....6G 69
HA7: Stan 2D 26
UB2: S'hall 4A 94
UB7: W Dray 1D 174
W5 ....7E 78
(not continuous)
Commondale SW15 ....2E 116
Commonfield La. SW17 ....5C 136
Common La. KT10: Clay ..7A 162
Common Mile Cl. SW4 ..5H 119
Common Rd. HA7: Stan 4C 26
KT10: Clay 6A 162
SW13 ....3D 116
Commonside BR2: Kes 4A 172
Commonside E. CR4: Mitc ..3E 154
Commonside W. CR4: Mitc ..3D 154
Commonwealth Av. UB3: Hayes ..6F 75
W12 ....7D 80
Commonwealth Memorial Gates ..6J 11 (2F 101)
Commonwealth Rd. N17 ....7B 34
Commonwealth Secretariat ..5B 12
Commonwealth Way SE2 ..5B 108
Community Cl. TW5: Cran ..1K 111
UB10: Ick 3D 56
Community La. N7 ....5H 65
Community Rd. E15 ....5F 69
UB6: G'frd 1G 77
Como Rd. SE23 ....2A 140
Como St. RM7: Rom 5K 55
Compass Bus. Pk. KT9: Chess ..4G 163
Compass Cl. HA8: Edg 4A 28
TW15: Ashf 7E 128
Compass Ct. SE1 ....5J 15
(off Shad Thames)
Compass Hill TW10: Rich ..6D 114
Compass Ho. E1 ....1J 103
(off Raine St.)
SW18 ....4K 117
Compass La. BR1: Broml ..1J 159
(off North St.)
Compass Point E14 ....7B 86
(off Grenade St.)
Compass Theatre 3E 56
Compayne Gdns. NW6 ....7K 63
Compayne Mans. NW6 ....6K 63
(off Fairhazel Gdns.)
Compter Pas. EC2 ....1D 14
Compton Av. E6 ....2B 88
HA0: Wemb 4C 60
N1 ....6B 66
N6 ....7C 46
Compton Cl. E3 ....5C 86
HA8: Edg 7D 28
NW1 ....2K 5
NW11 ....2K 5
SE15 ....7G 103
W13 ....6A 78
Compton Ct. SE19 ....6E 138
SM1: Sutt 4A 166
Compton Cres. KT9: Chess ..5E 162
N17 ....7H 33
UB5: N'olt 1B 76
Compton Ho. E20 ....5D 68
(off Peloton Av.)
SW10 ....1A 118
SW11 ....1C 118
Compton Leisure Cen. 6H 31
Compton Pas. EC1 ....3B 8 (4B 84)
Compton Pl. WC1 ....3E 6 (4J 83)
Compton Ri. HA5: Pinn 5C 40
Compton Rd. CR0: C'don ..1H 169
N1 ....6B 66
N21 ....1G 33
NW10 ....3F 81
SW19 ....6H 135
UB3: Hayes 7G 75
Compton St. EC1 ....3A 8 (4B 84)
Compton Ter. N1 ....6B 66
N4 ....6C 48
N21 ....1F 33
Comredly Cl. EN2: Enf 1G 23
Comus Ho. SE17 ....4E 102
(off Comus Pl.)
Comus Pl. SE17 ....4E 102
Comyn Rd. SW11 ....4C 118
The Comyns WD23: B Hea ..1B 26
Comyns Cl. E16 ....5H 87
Comyns Rd. RM9: Dag ..7G 73
Conant Ho. SE11 ....7K 19
(off St Agnes Pl.)
Conant M. E1 ....7G 85
Concanon Rd. SW2 ....4K 119
Concert Hall App. 5H 13 (1K 101)
SE1 ....5H 13 (1K 101)
Concord Bus. Cen. W3 ....4H 79
Concord Cl. UB5: N'olt 3B 76
Concord Ct. KT1: King T ..3F 151
(off Winery La.)
Concorde Cl. TW3: Houn ..2F 113
UB10: Uxb 2A 74
Concorde Dr. E6 ....5D 88
Concorde Way SE16 ....4K 103
Concord Ho. CR0: C'don ..6B 156
KT3: N Mald 3A 152
N17 ....7A 34
(off Park La.)
Concordia Wharf E14 ....1E 104
(off Coldharbour)
Concord Rd. EN3: Pond E ..5C 24
W3 ....4H 79
Concord Ter. HA2: Harr ..2F 59
(off Coles Cres.)
The Concourse N9 ....2B 34
(within Edmonton Grn. Shop. Cen.)
NW9 ....1B 44
(off Quakers Course)
Condell Rd. SW8 ....1G 119
Conder St. E14 ....6A 86
Condor Ho. E13 ....1J 87
(off Brooks Rd.)

Condor Path—Corfe Twr.

Condor Path *UB5: N'olt* 2E 76
(off Union Rd.)
Condor Way TW6: H'row A 3C 110
Condover Cres. SE18 7F 107
Condray Pl. SW11 7C 100
Conduit Av. SE10 1F 123
Conduit Ct. WC2 2E 12
Conduit La. CR0: C'don 5G 169
CR2: S Croy 5G 169
EN3: Pond E 6F 25
N18 5D 34
Conduit M. SE18 5F 107
W2 1A 10 (6B 82)
Conduit Pas. W2 1A 10
Conduit Pl. W2 1A 10 (6B 82)
Conduit Rd. SE18 5F 107
Conduit St. W1 2K 11 (7F 83)
Conduit Way NW10 7J 61
Conewood St. N5 3B 66
Coney Acre SE21 1C 138
Coneybear Point SE10 4J 105
Coney Burrows E4 2B 36
Coney Gro. UB8: Hil 3C 74
Coneygrove Path *UB5: N'olt* 6C 58
(off Arnold Rd.)
CONEY HALL 3G 171
Coney Hall Pde. BR4: W W'ck 3G 171
Coney Hill Rd. BR4: W W'ck 2G 171
Coney Way SW8 6K 101
Conference Cl. E4 2K 35
Conference Rd. SE2 4C 108
Confluence Plaza *SE13* 3E 122
(off Station Rd.)
Congers Ho. SE8 7C 104
Congleton Gro. SE18 5G 107
Congo Dr. N9 3D 34
Congo Rd. SE18 5H 107
Congress Rd. SE2 4C 108
Congreve Ho. N16 5E 66
Congreve Rd. SE9 3D 124
Congreve St. SE17 4E 102
Congreve Wlk. *E16* 5B 88
(off Fulmer Rd.)
Conical Cnr. EN2: Enf 2H 23
Conifer Cl. BR6: Orp 4H 173
Conifer Ct. *TW15: Ashf* 5B 128
(off The Crescent)
Conifer Gdns. EN1: Enf 6K 23
SM1: Sutt 2K 165
SW16 3K 137
Conifer Ho. *SE4* 4B 122
(off Brockley Rd.)
Conifers Cl. TW11: Tedd 7B 132
Conifer Way HA0: Wemb 3C 60
UB3: Hayes 7J 75
Coniger Rd. SW6 2J 117
Coningham Ct. *SW10* 7A 100
(off King's Rd.)
Coningham M. W12 1C 98
Coningham Rd. W12 2D 98
Coningsby Av. NW9 2A 44
Coningsby Cotts. W5 2D 96
Coningsby Ct. CR4: Mitc 2E 154
Coningsby Gdns. E4 6J 35
Coningsby Rd. CR2: S Croy 7C 168
N4 7B 48
W5 2D 96
Conington Rd. SE13 2D 122
Conisbee Ct. N14 5B 22
Conisborough Cres. SE6 3E 140
Conisbrough *NW1* 1G 83
(off Bayham St.)
Coniscliffe Cl. BR7: Chst 1E 160
Coniscliffe Rd. N13 3H 33
Coniston *NW1* 1A 6
(off Harrington St.)
Coniston Av. DA16: Well 3J 125
IG11: Bark 7J 71
UB6: G'frd 3B 78
Coniston Cl. DA7: Bex 1J 127
DA8: Erith 7K 109
IG11: Bark 7J 71
N20 3F 31
SW13 7B 98
SW20 6F 153
W4 7J 97
Coniston Ct. *NW7* 7B 30
(off Langstone Way)
SE16 2K 103
(off Eleanor Cl.)
SM6: W'gton 4F 167
TW15: Ashf 3A 128
W2 1D 10
(off Kendal St.)
Conistone Way N7 7J 65
Coniston Gdns. HA5: Eastc 4J 39
HA9: Wemb 1C 60
IG4: Ilf 4C 52
N9 1D 34
NW9 5K 43
SM2: Sutt 6B 166
Coniston Ho. *E3* 4B 86
(off Southern Gro.)
SE5 7C 102
(off Wyndham Rd.)
Coniston Rd. BR1: Broml 6G 141
CR0: C'don 7G 157
DA7: Bex 1J 127
N10 2F 47
N17 6B 34
TW2: Whitt 6F 113
Coniston Wlk. E9 5J 67
Coniston Way KT9: Chess 3E 162
Conlan St. W10 4G 81
Conley Rd. NW10 6A 62
Conley St. SE10 5G 105
Connaught Av. E4 7K 25, 1A 36
EN1: Enf 2K 23
EN4: E Barn 1J 31
SW14 3J 115
TW4: Houn 4C 112
TW15: Ashf 4A 128
Connaught Bri. E16 1B 106
Connaught Bus. Cen. CR0: Wadd 6K 167
CR4: Mitc 5D 154
NW9 5B 44
Connaught Cl. E10 2A 68
EN1: Enf 2K 23
SM1: Sutt 2B 166
UB8: Hil 4E 74
W2 1D 10 (6C 82)
The Connaught Club 1C 36
Connaught Ct. *E17* 4D 50
(off Orford Rd.)
W2 1E 10
(off Connaught St.)
Connaught Dr. NW11 4J 45
Connaught Gdns. N10 5F 47
N13 4G 33
SM4: Mord 4A 154
Connaught Hall 3D 6 (4H 83)
Connaught Hgts. *E16* 1B 106
(off Agnes George Wlk.)
UB10: Hil 4E 74
(off Uxbridge Rd.)
Connaught Ho. *NW10* 3D 80
(off Trenmar Gdns.)
W1 3J 11
(off Davies St.)
Connaught La. IG1: Ilf 2G 71
Connaught Lodge *N4* 7A 48
(off Connaught Rd.)
Connaught M. NW3 4C 64
SE18 5E 106
SW6 1G 117
Connaught Pl. W2 2E 10 (7D 82)
Connaught Rd. E4 1B 36
E11 1F 69
E16 1B 106
E17 5C 50
EN5: Barn 6A 20
HA3: W'stone 1K 41
IG1: Ilf 2H 71
KT3: N Mald 4A 152
N4 7A 48
NW10 1A 80
SM1: Sutt 2B 166
TW10: Rich 5F 115
TW11: Tedd 5H 131
W13 7B 78
CONNAUGHT RDBT. 7B 88
(off Victoria Dock Rd.)
Connaught Sq. W2 1D 10 (6D 82)
Connaught St. W2 1D 10 (6C 82)
Connaught Way N13 4G 33
Connaught Works *E3* 1A 86
(off Old Ford Rd.)
Connect La. IG6: Ilf 2G 53
Connell Ct. *SE14* 6K 103
(off Myers La.)
Connell Cres. W5 4F 79
Connersville Way CR0: Wadd 3A 168
Conniffe Ct. SE9 5F 125
Conningham Ct. SE9 5A 124
Connington Cres. E4 3A 36
Connolly Ct. *RM7: Rush G* 6K 55
(off Union Rd.)
Connor Cl. E11 7G 51
IG6: Ilf 1G 53
Connor Ct. SW11 1F 119
Connor Rd. RM9: Dag 4F 73
Connor St. E9 1K 85
Conolly Rd. W7 1J 95
Conrad Ct. *NW9* 2A 44
(off Needleman Cl.)
SE16 4A 104
(off Cary Av.)
Conrad Dr. KT4: Wor Pk 1E 164
Conrad Ho. E8 6G 67
E14 7A 86
(off Victory Pl.)
E16 1K 105
(off Wesley Av.)
N16 5E 66
(off Matthias Rd.)
SW8 7J 101
(off Wyvil Rd.)
Consfield Av. KT3: N Mald 4C 152
Consort Ct. *W8* 3K 99
(off Wright's La.)
Consort Ho. *E14* 5D 104
(off St Davids Sq.)
SW6 2A 118
(off Lensbury Av.)
W2 7K 81
(off Queensway)
Consort Lodge *NW8* 1D 82
(off Prince Albert Rd.)
Consort M. TW7: Isle 5H 113
Consort Rd. SE15 1H 121
Cons St. SE1 6K 13 (2A 102)
Constable Av. E16 1K 105
Constable Cl. N11 5J 31
NW11 6K 45
UB4: Hayes 2E 74
Constable Ct. *SE16* 5H 103
(off Stubbs Dr.)
W4 5H 97
(off Chaseley Dr.)
Constable Cres. N15 5G 49
Constable Gdns. HA8: Edg 1G 43
TW7: Isle 5H 113
Constable Ho. *E14* 2C 104
(off Cassilis Rd.)
NW3 7D 64
UB5: N'olt 2B 76
(off Gallery Gdns.)
Constable M. BR1: Broml 2K 159
RM8: Dag 4B 72
Constable Wlk. SE21 3E 138
Constabulary Cl. UB7: W Dray 3A 92
Constance Allen Ho. *W10* 6F 81
(off Bridge Cl.)
Constance Cl. SW15 4K 133
Constance Cres. BR2: Hayes 7H 159
Constance Rd. CR0: C'don 7B 156
EN1: Enf 6K 23
SM1: Sutt 4A 166
TW2: Whitt 7F 113
Constance St. E16 1C 106
Constant Ho. *E14* 7D 86
(off Harrow La.)
Constantine Ct. *E1* 6G 85
(off Fairclough St.)
Constantine Ho. *NW9* 3B 44
(off Boulevard Dr.)
UB3: Hayes 6F 75
Constantine Pl. UB10: Hil 1B 74
Constantine Rd. NW3 4C 64
Constellation Way
TW6: H'row A 3D 110
Constitution Hill SW1 6J 11 (2F 101)
Constitution Ri. SE18 1E 124
Consul Av. RM9: Dag, Rain 3J 91
RM13: Rain 3J 91
Consul Ho. *E3* 4C 86
(off Wellington Way)
Container City 1 E14 7G 87
Container City 2 E14 7G 87
Contemporary Applied Arts 5B 14
(off Southwark St.)
Content St. SE17 4D 102
Contessa Cl. BR6: Farnb 5J 173
Contrail Way TW6: H'row A 3D 110
Convair Wlk. UB5: N'olt 3B 76
Convent Cl. BR3: Beck 7E 140
EN5: Barn 2C 20
Convent Gdns. W5 4C 96
W11 6G 81
Convent Hill SE19 6C 138
Convent Rd. TW15: Ashf 5D 128
Convent Way UB2: S'hall 4A 94
Conway Cl. BR3: Beck 1A 158
HA7: Stan 6F 27
Conway Cres. RM6: Chad H 6C 54
UB6: G'frd 2J 77
Conway Dr. SM2: Sutt 6K 165
TW15: Ashf 6E 128
UB3: Harl 3E 92
Conway Gdns. CR4: Mitc 4J 155
EN2: Enf 1K 23
HA9: Wemb 7C 42
Conway Gro. W3 5K 79
Conway Ho. *E14* 4C 104
(off Cahir St.)
SW3 6F 17
(off Ormonde Ga.)
Conway M. W1 4A 6
Conway Rd. N14 3D 32
N15 5B 48
NW2 2E 62
SE18 4H 107
SW20 1E 152
TW4: Houn 7D 112
TW13: Hanw 5B 130
Conway St. W1 4A 6 (4G 83)
(not continuous)
Conway Wlk. TW12: Hamp 6D 130
Conybeare NW3 7C 64
Conyers Cl. IG8: Wfd G 6B 36
Conyer's Rd. SW16 5H 137
Conyer St. E3 2A 86
Cooden Cl. BR1: Broml 7K 141
Cook Ct. *SE8* 5A 104
(off Evelyn St.)
SE16 1J 103
(off Rotherhithe St.)
Cooke Cl. SE2 3C 108
Cookes Cl. E11 2H 69
Cookes La. SM3: Cheam 6G 165
Cooke St. IG11: Bark 1G 89
(not continuous)
Cookham Cl. UB2: S'hall 3F 95
Cookham Cres. SE16 2K 103
Cookham Dene Cl. BR7: Chst 1H 161
Cookham Ho. *E2* 3J 9
(off Montclare St.)
Cookham Rd. BR8: Swan 7G 145
Cookhill Rd. SE2 2B 108
Cook Rd. RM9: Dag 1E 90
Cook's Cl. RM5: Col R 1J 55
Cooks Cl. *E14* 1C 104
(off Cabot Sq.)
Cooks Hole Rd. EN2: Enf 1H 23
Cookson Gro. DA8: Erith 7H 109
Cook's Rd. E15 2D 86
Cooks Rd. SE17 6B 102
Coolfin Rd. E16 6J 87
Coolgardie Av. E4 5A 36
IG7: Chig 3K 37
Coolgardie Rd. TW15: Ashf 5E 128
Coolhurst Rd. N8 6H 47
Coolhurst Tennis & Squash Club 6H 47
Cool Oak La. NW9 7A 44
Coomassie Rd. W9 4H 81
COOMBE 7J 133
Coombe Av. CR0: C'don 4E 168
Coombe Bank KT2: King T 1A 152
Coombe Cl. HA8: Edg 2F 43
TW3: Houn 4E 112
Coombe Cnr. N21 1G 33
Coombe Ct. *CR0: C'don* 4D 168
(off Coombe Rd.)
Coombe Cres. TW12: Hamp 7D 130
Coombe Dene *BR2: Broml* 4H 159
(off Cumberland Rd.)
Coombe Dr. HA4: Ruis 1K 57
Coombe End KT2: King T 7K 133
Coombefield Cl. KT3: N Mald 5A 152
Coombe Gdns. KT3: N Mald 4B 152
SW20 2C 152
Coombe Hill Glade KT2: King T 7A 134
Coombe Hill Golf Course 7K 133
Coombe Hill Rd. KT2: King T 7A 134
Coombe Ho. N7 5H 65
Coombe Ho. Chase
KT3: N Mald 1K 151
Coombehurst Cl. EN4: Cockf 2J 21
COOMBE LANE 1B 152
Coombe La. CR0: C'don 5H 169
SW20 1B 152
Coombe La. Flyover SW20 1B 152
Coombe La. W. KT2: King T 1H 151
Coombe Lea BR1: Broml 3C 160
Coombe Lodge SE7 6A 106
Coombe Neville KT2: King T 7K 133
Coombe Pk. KT2: King T 5J 133
Coombe Pl. KT2: King T 5J 133
Coomber Ho. *SW6* 3K 117
(off Wandsworth Bri. Rd.)
Coombe Ridings KT2: King T 5J 133
Coombe Ri. KT2: King T 1J 151
Coombe Rd. CR0: C'don 4D 168
KT2: King T 1G 151
KT3: N Mald 2A 152
N22 2A 48
NW10 3K 61
SE26 4H 139
TW12: Hamp 6D 130
W4 5A 98
W13 3B 96
Coomber Way CR0: Bedd 7H 155
Coombes Rd. RM9: Dag 1F 91
Coombe Wlk. SM1: Sutt 3K 165
Coombewood Dr. RM6: Chad H 6F 55
Coombe Wood Golf Course 7H 133
Coombe Wood
Local Nature Reserve 7B 134
Coombe Wood Rd. KT2: King T 5J 133
Coombrook Ct. *SE16* 2A 104
(off Elgar St.)
Coombs St. N1 1B 8 (2B 84)
Coomer M. SW6 6H 99
Coomer Pl. SW6 6H 99
Coomer Rd. SW6 6H 99
Cooms Wlk. HA8: Edg 1J 43
Coope Ct. *RM7: Rush G* 6K 55
(off Union Rd.)
The Cooperage *SE1* 6J 15
(off Gainsford St.)
SW8 7K 101
(off Regent's Bri. Gdns.)
Cooperage Cl. N17 6A 34
Cooperage Yd. E15 2E 86
Co-operative Ho. SE15 3G 121
Cooper Av. E17 1A 50
Cooper Cl. SE1 7K 13 (2A 102)
Cooper Ct. SE18 6F 107
Cooper Cres. SM5: Cars 3D 166
Cooper Ho. *NW8* 4A 4
(off Lyons Pl.)
SE4 5K 121
(off St Norbert Rd.)
TW4: Houn 3D 112
Cooper Rd. CR0: Wadd 4B 168
NW4 6F 45
NW10 5C 62
Coopersale Cl. IG8: Wfd G 7F 37
Coopersale Rd. E9 5K 67
Coopers Cl. E1 4J 85
RM10: Dag 6H 73
Coopers Ct. *E3* 4B 86
(off Eric St.)
TW7: Isle 2K 113
(off Woodlands Rd.)
W3 1J 97
(off Church Rd.)
Cooper's La. SE12 2K 141
Coopers La. E10 1D 68
E20 5D 68
NW1 2H 83
Coopers Lodge *SE1* 6J 15
(off Tooley St.)
Coopers M. BR3: Beck 2C 158
Cooper's Rd. SE1 5F 103
Coopers Row EC3 2J 15 (7F 85)
Cooper St. E16 5H 87
Coopers Wlk. E15 5G 69
Cooper's Yd. SE19 6E 138
Coopers Yd. *N1* 7B 66
(off Upper St.)
Coote Gdns. RM8: Dag 3F 73
Coote Rd. DA7: Bex 1F 127
RM8: Dag 3F 73
Cope Ho. EC1 2D 8
Copeland Dr. E14 4C 104
Copeland Ho. SE11 2H 19
SW17 4B 136
Copeland Rd. E17 6D 50
SE15 2G 121
Copeman Cl. SE26 5J 139
Copenhagen Ct. *SE8* 4A 104
(off Pell St.)
Copenhagen Gdns. W4 2K 97
Copenhagen Ho. *N1* 1K 83
(off Barnsbury Est.)
Copenhagen Pl. E14 6B 86
(not continuous)
Copenhagen St. N1 1J 83
Cope Pl. W8 3J 99
Copers Cope Rd. BR3: Beck 7B 140
Cope St. SE16 4K 103
Copford Cl. IG8: Wfd G 6H 37
Copford Wlk. *N1* 1C 84
(off Popham St.)
Copgate Path SW16 6K 137
Copinger Wlk. HA8: Edg 1H 43
Copland Av. HA0: Wemb 5D 60
Copland Cl. HA0: Wemb 5C 60
Copland M. HA0: Wemb 6E 60
Copland Rd. HA0: Wemb 6E 60
Copleston M. SE15 2F 121
Copleston Pas. SE5 2F 121
Copleston Rd. SE15 3F 121
Copley Cl. SE17 6C 102
W7 4K 77
Copley Dene BR1: Broml 1B 160
Copley Pk. SW16 6K 137
Copley Rd. HA7: Stan 5H 27
Copley St. E1 5K 85
Coppard Gdns. KT9: Chess 6C 162
Coppelia Rd. SE3 4H 123
Coppen Rd. RM8: Dag 7F 55
Copperas St. SE8 6D 104
Copper Beech Cl. IG5: Ilf 1E 52
Copperbeech Cl. NW3 5B 64
Copper Beeches Ct. TW7: Isle 1H 113
Copper Box Arena 6C 68
Copper Cl. N17 7C 34
SE19 7F 139
Copper Ct. E5 2J 67
Copperdale Rd. UB3: Hayes 2J 93
Copperfield Av. UB8: Hil 5C 74
Copperfield Dr. N15 4F 49
Copperfield Ho. *SE1* 7K 15
(off Wolseley St.)
W1 5H 5
(off Marylebone High St.)
W11 1F 99
(off St Ann's Rd.)
Copperfield M. *E2* 2G 85
(off Claredale St.)
N18 4K 33
Copperfield Rd. E3 4A 86
SE28 6C 90
Copperfields BR3: Beck 1E 158
HA1: Harr 7J 41
TW16: Sun 6H 129
Copperfields Ct. W3 2G 97
Copperfield St. SE1 6B 14 (2B 102)
Copperfield Way BR7: Chst 6G 143
HA5: Pinn 4D 40
Coppergate Cl. BR1: Broml 1K 159
Copper La. N16 4D 66
Copperlight Apts. *SW18* 5J 117
(off Buckhold Rd.)
Coppermead Cl. NW2 3E 62
Copper M. W4 3J 97
Copper Mill Dr. TW7: Isle 2K 113
Coppermill Hgts. *N17* 3H 49
(off Daneland Wlk.)
Copper Mill La. SW17 4A 136
Coppermill La. E17 6J 49
Copper Row SE1 5J 15
Copperwood Pl. SE10 1E 122
The Copperworks *N1* 2J 83
(off Railway St.)
Coppetts Cen. 7J 31
Coppetts Cl. N12 7H 31
Coppetts Rd. N10 7J 31
Coppetts Wood & Glebelands
Local Nature Reserve 6J 31
The Coppice DA5: Bexl 3K 145
EN2: Enf 4G 23
The Coppice *EN5: New Bar* 6E 20
(off Great Nth. Rd.)
TW15: Ashf 6D 128
UB7: Yiew 6A 74
Coppice Cl. BR3: Beck 4D 158
HA4: Ruis 6F 39
HA7: Stan 6E 26
SW20 3E 152
Coppice Dr. SW15 6D 116
Coppice Wlk. N20 3D 30
Coppice Way E18 4H 51
Coppies Gro. N11 4A 32
Copping Cl. CR0: C'don 4E 168
The Coppins CR0: New Ad 6D 170
HA3: Hrw W 6D 26
Coppock Cl. SW11 2C 118
Coppsfield KT8: W Mole 3E 148
The Copse E4 1C 36
N2 3D 46
Copse Av. BR4: W W'ck 2D 170
Copse Cl. HA6: Nwood 2E 38
SE7 6K 105
Copse Glade KT6: Surb 7D 150
COPSE HILL 7C 134
Copse Hill SM2: Sutt 7K 165
SW20 1C 152
Copse Vw. CR2: Sels 7K 169
Copsewood Cl. DA15: Sidc 6K 125
Copse Wood Way HA6: Nwood 1D 38
Coptain Ho. SW18 4J 117
Coptefield Dr. DA17: Belv 3D 108
Copthall Av. EC2 7F 9 (6D 84)
(not continuous)
Copthall Bldgs. EC2 7F 9
Copthall Cl. EC2 7E 8 (6D 84)
Copthall Ct. NW7 7H 29
Copthall Gdns. NW7 7H 29
TW1: Twick 1K 131
Copthall Rd. E. UB10: Ick 2C 56
Copthall Rd. W. UB10: Ick 2C 56
Copthorne Av. BR2: Broml 2D 172
SW12 7H 119
Copthorne Chase TW15: Ashf 4B 128
Copthorne Cl. TW17: Shep 6E 146
Copthorne M. UB3: Harl 4G 93
Coptic St. WC1 6E 6 (5J 83)
Copt Pl. NW7 6B 30
Copwood Cl. N12 4G 31
Coral Apts. *E16* 7J 87
(off Western Gateway)
Coral Cl. RM6: Chad H 3D 54
Coral Ho. *E1* 4A 86
(off Harford St.)
NW10 3G 79
Coraline Cl. UB1: S'hall 3D 76
Coralline Wlk. SE2 3C 108
Coral Mans. *NW6* 1J 81
(off Kilburn High Rd.)
Coral Row SW11 3A 118
Coral St. SE1 7K 13 (2A 102)
Coram Ho. *W4* 5A 98
(off Wood St.)
WC1 3E 6
Coram Mans. *WC1* 4G 7
(off Millman St.)
Coram St. WC1 4E 6 (4J 83)
Coran Cl. N9 7E 24
Corban Rd. TW3: Houn 3E 112
Corbar Cl. EN4: Had W 1G 21
Corbden Cl. SE15 1F 121
Corben M. SW8 2G 119
Corbet Cl. SM6: W'gton 2E 166
Corbet Ct. EC3 1F 15 (6D 84)
Corbet Ho. *N1* 2A 84
(off Barnsbury Est.)
SE5 7C 102
(off Wyndham Rd.)
Corbet Pl. E1 5J 9 (5F 85)
Corbett Av. KT8: E Mos 6H 149
Corbett Ct. SE26 4B 140
Corbett Gro. N22 7D 32
Corbett Ho. *SW10* 6A 100
(off Cathcart Rd.)
Corbett Rd. E11 6A 52
E17 3E 50
Corbetts La. SE16 4J 103
(not continuous)
Corbetts Pas. *SE16* 4J 103
(off Corbetts La.)
Corbetts Wharf *SE16* 2H 103
(off Bermondsey Wall E.)
Corbicum E11 7G 51
Corbidge Ct. SE8 6D 104
Corbiere Ct. SW19 6F 135
Corbiere Ho. *N1* 1D 84
(off De Beauvoir Est.)
Corbin Ho. *E3* 3D 86
(off Bromley High St.)
Corbins La. HA2: Harr 3F 59
Corbould Cl. SM5: Cars 6D 166
Corbridge N17 7C 34
Corbridge Cres. E2 2H 85
Corby Cres. EN2: Enf 4D 22
Corbylands Rd. DA15: Sidc 7J 125
Corbyn St. N4 1J 65
Corby Rd. NW10 2K 79
Corby Way E3 4C 86
Cordage Ho. *E1* 1H 103
(off Cobblestone Sq.)
Cordelia Cl. SE24 4B 120
Cordelia Gdns. TW19: Stanw 7A 110
Cordelia Ho. *N1* 2E 84
(off Arden Est.)
Cordelia Rd. TW19: Stanw 7A 110
Cordelia St. E14 6D 86
Cordell Ho. *N15* 5F 49
(off Newton Rd.)
Cordingley Rd. HA4: Ruis 2F 57
Cording St. E14 5D 86
Cordwainer Ho. E8 1H 85
Cordwainers Ct. *E9* 7J 67
(off St Thomas's Sq.)
Cordwainers Wlk. E13 2J 87
Cord Way E14 3C 104
Cordwell Rd. SE13 5G 123
Corefield Cl. N11 2K 31
Corelli Ct. SE1 4H 103
SW5 4J 99
(off W. Cromwell Rd.)
Corelli Rd. SE3 2C 124
Corfe Av. HA2: Harr 4E 58
Corfe Cl. TW4: Houn 1C 130
UB4: Yead 6A 76
Corfe Ho. *SW8* 7K 101
(off Dorset Rd.)
Corfe Twr. W3 2H 97

Corfield Rd.—Cowper Rd.

Corfield Rd. N21 5E 22
Corfield St. E2 3H 85
Corfton Lodge W5 5E 78
Corfton Rd. W5 6E 78
Coriander Av. E14 6F 87
Coriander Ct. SE1 6K 15
(off Gainsford St.)
Cories Cl. RM8: Dag 2D 72
Corinium Cl. HA9: Wemb 4F 61
Corinne Rd. N19 4G 65
Corinthian Manorway
DA8: Erith 4K 109
Corinthian Rd. DA8: Erith 4K 109
Corinthian Way TW19: Stanw 7A 110
Corkers Path IG1: Ilf 2G 71
Corker Wlk. N7 2K 65
Cork Ho. SW19 4K 135
Corkran Rd. KT6: Surb 7D 150
Corkscrew Hill
BR4: W W'ck 2E 170
Cork Sq. E1 1H 103
Cork St. W1 3A 12 (7G 83)
Cork St. M. W1 3A 12
Cork Tree Ho. SE27 5B 138
(off Lakeview Rd.)
Cork Tree Retail Pk. 5F 35
Cork Tree Way E4 5F 35
Corlett St. NW1 5C 4 (5C 82)
Cormont Rd. SE5 1B 120
Cormorant Cl. E17 7F 35
Cormorant Ct. SE8 6B 104
(off Pilot Cl.)
Cormorant Ho. EN3: Pond E 5E 24
Cormorant Lodge E1 1G 103
(off Thomas More St.)
Cormorant Pl. SM1: Sutt 5H 165
Cormorant Rd. E7 5H 69
Cornbury Ho. SE8 6B 104
(off Evelyn St.)
Cornbury Rd. HA8: Edg 7J 27
Cornel Ho. DA15: Sidc 3A 144
Cornelia Dr. UB4: Yead 4A 76
Cornelia Ho. TW1: Twick 6D 114
(off Denton Rd.)
Cornelia St. N7 6K 65
Cornell Bldg. E1 6G 85
(off Coke St.)
Cornell Cl. DA14: Sidc 6E 144
Cornell Ct. EN3: Enf H 3F 25
Cornell Gdns. EN4: E Barn 5K 21
Cornell Ho. HA2: Harr 3D 58
Cornell Sq. SW8 1H 119
The Corner W5 1E 96
Corner Ct. E2 4H 85
(off Three Colts La.)
Cornercroft SM3: Cheam 5F 165
(off Wickham Av.)
Corner Fielde SW2 1K 137
Corner Grn. SE3 2J 123
Corner Ho. NW6 2K 81
(off Oxford Rd.)
The Corner HOUSE Arts Cen. 1F 163
Corner Ho. St. WC2 4E 12
Corner Mead NW9 7G 29
Cornerside TW15: Ashf 7E 128
Cornerstone Ho. CR0: C'don 7C 156
Corney Reach Way W4 7A 98
Corney Rd. W4 6A 98
Cornfield Cl. UB8: Uxb 2A 74
Cornflower La. CR0: C'don 1K 169
Cornflower Ter. SE22 6H 121
Cornford Cl. BR2: Broml 5J 159
Cornford Gro. SW12 2F 137
Cornhill EC3 1F 15 (6D 84)
Cornick Ho. SE16 3H 103
(off Slippers Pl.)
Cornish Ct. N9 7C 24
Cornish Gro. SE20 1H 157
Cornish Ho. SE17 6B 102
(off Brandon Est.)
TW8: Bford 5F 97
Corn Mill Dr. BR6: Orp 7K 161
Cornmill Ho. RM7: Rom 6J 55
SE8 5C 104
(off Wharf St.)
Cornmill La. SE13 3E 122
Cornmow Dr. NW10 5B 62
Cornshaw Rd. RM8: Dag 1D 72
Cornthwaite Rd. E5 3J 67
Cornwall Av. DA16: Well 3J 125
E2 3J 85
KT10: Clay 7A 162
N3 7D 30
N22 1J 47
UB1: S'hall 5D 76
Cornwall Cl. IG11: Bark 6K 71
Cornwall Ct. HA5: Hat E 1D 40
W7 4K 77
(off Copley Cl.)
Cornwall Cres. W11 6G 81
Cornwall Dr. BR5: St P 7C 144
Cornwall Gdns. NW10 6D 62
SE25 4F 157
SW7 3K 99
Cornwall Gdns. Wlk. SW7 3K 99
Cornwall Gro. W4 5A 98
Cornwall Ho. SW7 3K 99
(off Cornwall Gdns.)
Cornwallis Av. N9 2C 34
SE9 2H 143
Cornwallis Ct. SW8 1J 119
(off Lansdowne Grn.)
Cornwallis Gro. N9 2C 34
Cornwallis Ho. SE16 2H 103
(off Cherry Gdn. St.)
W12 7D 80
(off India Way)
Cornwallis Rd. E17 4K 49
N9 2C 34
N19 2J 65
RM9: Dag 4D 72
SE18 3G 107
(Gunnery Ter.)
SE18 3F 107
(Warren La.)
Cornwallis Sq. N19 2J 65
Cornwallis Wlk. SE9 3D 124
Cornwall Mans. SW10 7A 100
(off Cremorne Rd.)
W8 2K 99
(off Kensington Ct.)
W14 3F 99
(off Blythe Rd.)
Cornwall M. Sth. SW7 3A 100
Cornwall M. W. SW7 3K 99
Cornwall Pl. E4 4J 25
Cornwall Rd. CR0: C'don 2B 168
HA1: Harr 6G 41
HA4: Ruis 3H 57
HA5: Hat E 1D 40
N4 7A 48
N15 5D 48
N18 5B 34
SE1 4J 13 (1A 102)
SM2: Sutt 7H 165
TW1: Twick 7A 114
UB8: Uxb 6A 56
Cornwall Sq. SE11 5K 19
Cornwall St. E1 7H 85
Cornwall Ter. NW1 4F 5 (4D 82)
Cornwall Ter. M. NW1 4F 5
Corn Way E11 3F 69
Cornwell Gdns. E10 7C 50
Cornwood Cl. N2 5B 46
Cornwood Dr. E1 6J 85
Cornworthy Rd. RM8: Dag 5C 72
Corona Bldg. E14 1E 104
(off Blackwall Way)
Corona Rd. SE12 7J 123
Coronation Av. N16 4F 67
Coronation Cl. DA5: Bexl 6D 126
IG6: Ilf 4G 53
Coronation Ct. DA8: Erith 7K 109
E15 6H 69
KT1: King T 4E 150
(off Surbiton Rd.)
W10 5E 80
(off Brewster Gdns.)
Coronation Rd. E13 3A 88
NW10 3G 79
UB3: Harl 4H 93
Coronation Vs. NW10 4H 79
Coronation Wlk. TW2: Whitt 1E 130
Coroner's Court
City of London 2E 14 (7D 84)
North London 4C 20
Poplar 7D 86
(off Poplar High St.)
St Pancras 1H 83
South London 3D 168
(off Barclay Rd.)
Southwark 2D 102
West London 1A 118
Westminster 3D 18 (4H 101)
Coronet Pde. HA0: Wemb 6E 60
Coronet St. N1 2G 9 (3E 84)
Corporate Dr. TW13: Felt 3K 129
Corporate Ho. HA3: Hrw W 1H 41
Corporation Av. TW4: Houn 4C 112
Corporation Row EC1 3K 7 (4A 84)
Corporation St. E15 2G 87
N7 5J 65
Corrance Rd. SW2 4J 119
Corri Av. N14 4C 32
Corrib Ct. N13 3E 32
Corrib Dr. SM1: Sutt 5C 166
Corrigan Cl. NW4 3E 44
Corringham Ct. NW11 7J 45
Corringham Ho. E1 6K 85
(off Pitsea St.)
Corringham Rd. HA9: Wemb 2G 61
NW11 7J 45
Corringway NW11 7K 45
W5 4G 79
Corris Grn. NW9 5A 44
Corry Dr. SW9 4B 120
Corry Ho. E14 7D 86
(off Wade's Pl.)
Corsair Cl. TW19: Stanw 7A 110
Corsair Ho. E16 2A 106
(off Starboard Way)
Corsair Rd. TW19: Stanw 7A 110
Corscombe Cl. KT2: King T 5J 133
Corsehill St. SW16 6G 137
Corsellis Sq. TW1: Isle 4B 114
(off Varley Dr.)
Corsham St. N1 2F 9 (3D 84)
Corsica St. N5 6B 66
Corsley Way E9 6B 68
Cortayne Ct. TW2: Twick 2J 131
Cortayne Rd. SW6 2H 117
Cortis Rd. SW15 6D 116
Cortis Ter. SW15 6D 116
Cortland Cl. IG8: Wfd G 1A 52
Corunna Rd. SW8 1G 119
Corunna Ter. SW8 1G 119
Corvette Sq. SE10 6F 105
Corwell Gdns. UB8: Hil 6E 74
Corwell La. UB8: Hil 6E 74
Coryton Path W9 4H 81
(off Ashmore Rd.)
Cosbycote Av. SE24 5C 120
Cosdach Av. SM6: W'gton 7H 167
Cosedge Cres. CR0: Wadd 5A 168
Cosgrove Cl. N21 2H 33
UB4: Yead 4B 76
Cosgrove Ho. E2 1G 85
(off Whiston Rd.)
HA0: Wemb 1E 78
(off Hatton Rd.)
Cosmo Pl. WC1 5F 7 (5J 83)
Cosmopolitan Ct. EN1: Enf 5B 24
Cosmopolitan Way
TW6: H'row A 3D 110
Cosmur Cl. W12 3B 98
Cossall Wlk. SE15 2H 121
Cossar M. SW2 5A 120
Cosser St. SE1 1J 19 (3A 102)
Costa St. SE15 2G 121
Costemonger Bldg. SE16 3F 103
(off Arts La.)
Coster Av. N4 1C 66
Costons Av. UB6: G'frd 3H 77
Costons La. UB6: G'frd 3H 77
(not continuous)
Coston Wlk. SE4 4K 121
Cosway Mans. NW1 5D 4
(off Shroton St.)
Cosway St. NW1 5D 4 (5C 82)
Cotall St. E14 5C 86
Coteford Cl. HA5: Eastc 5J 39
Coteford St. SW17 4D 136
Cotelands CR0: C'don 3E 168
Cotesbach Rd. E5 3J 67
Cotes Ho. NW8 4C 4
(off Broadley St.)
Cotesmore Gdns. RM8: Dag 4C 72
Cotford Rd. CR7: Thor H 4C 156
Cotham St. SE17 4C 102
Cotherstone Ct. E2 4H 85
(off Three Colts La.)
Cotherstone Rd. SW2 1K 137
Cotleigh Av. DA5: Bexl 2D 144
Cotleigh Rd. NW6 7J 63
RM7: Rom 6K 55
Cotman Cl. NW11 6A 46
SW15 6F 117
Cotman Gdns. HA8: Edg 2G 43
Cotman Ho. NW8 2C 82
(off Townshend Est.)
UB5: N'olt 2B 76
(off Academy Gdns.)
Cotman M. RM8: Dag 5C 72
(off Highgrove Rd.)
Cotmans Cl. UB3: Hayes 1J 93
Coton Dr. UB10: Ick 3E 56
Coton Rd. DA16: Well 3A 126
Cotsford Av. KT3: N Mald 5J 151
Cotswold Cl. DA7: Bex 2K 127
KT2: King T 6J 133
KT10: Hin W 2A 162
N11 4K 31
Cotswold Ct. EC1 3C 8
UB6: G'frd 2K 77
(off Hodder Dr.)
Cotswold Gdns. E6 3B 88
IG2: Ilf 7H 53
NW2 2F 63
Cotswold Ga. NW2 1G 63
Cotswold Grn. EN2: Enf 4E 22
Cotswold M. SW11 1B 118
Cotswold Ri. BR6: St M Cry 6K 161
Cotswold Rd. TW12: Hamp 5E 130
Cotswold St. SE27 4B 138
Cotswold Way EN2: Enf 3E 22
KT4: Wor Pk 2E 164
Cottage Av. BR2: Broml 1C 172
Cottage Cl. E1 4J 85
(off Mile End Rd.)
HA2: Harr 2H 59
HA4: Ruis 1F 57
Cottage Fld. Cl. DA14: Sidc 1C 144
Cottage Grn. SE5 7D 102
Cottage Gro. KT6: Surb 6D 150
SW9 3J 119
Cottage Pl. SW3 1C 16 (3C 100)
Cottage Rd. KT19: Ewe 7K 163
N7 5K 65
(not continuous)
The Cottages UB10: Ick 2A 56
Cottage St. E14 7D 86
Cottage Wlk. N16 3F 67
Cottenham Dr. NW9 3B 44
SW20 7D 134
Cottenham Pde. SW20 2D 152
COTTENHAM PARK 1D 152
Cottenham Pk. Rd. SW20 1C 152
(not continuous)
Cottenham Pl. SW20 7D 134
Cottenham Rd. E17 4B 50
Cotterill Rd. KT6: Surb 2E 162
Cottesbrook St. SE14 7A 104
Cottesloe Ho. NW8 3C 4
Cottesloe M. SE1 1K 19
(off Emery St.)
Cottesmore Av. IG5: Ilf 2E 52
Cottesmore Ct. W8 3K 99
(off Stanford Rd.)
Cottesmore Gdns. W8 3K 99
Cottesmore Ho. UB10: Ick 2E 56
Cottimore Av. KT12: Walt T 7K 147
Cottimore Cres. KT12: Walt T 7K 147
Cottimore La. KT12: Walt T 7K 147
Cottimore Ter. KT12: Walt T 7K 147
Cottingham Chase HA4: Ruis 3J 57
Cottingham Rd. SE20 7K 139
SW8 7K 101
Cottington Rd. TW13: Hanw 4B 130
Cottington St. SE11 5K 19 (5A 102)
Cottle Way SE16 2H 103
(off Paradise St.)
Cotton Apts. E1 5K 85
(off Killick Way)
Cotton Av. W3 6K 79
Cotton Cl. CR4: Mitc 3C 154
E11 2G 69
RM9: Dag 7C 72
Cottongrass Cl. CR0: C'don 1K 169
Cottonham Cl. N12 5G 31
Cotton Hill BR1: Broml 4E 140
Cotton Ho. SW2 7J 119
Cotton Row SW11 3A 118
Cottons App. RM7: Rom 5K 55
Cottons Cen. SE1 4G 15 (1E 102)
Cottons Ct. RM7: Rom 5K 55
Cotton's Gdns. E2 1H 9 (3E 84)
Cottons La. SE1 4F 15 (1D 102)
Cotton St. E14 7E 86
Cotton Way SM6: W'gton 2E 166
Cottonworks Ho. N7 3K 65
(off Seven Sisters Rd.)
Cottrell Ct. SE10 4H 105
(off Hop St.)
Cottrill Gdns. E8 6H 67
Cotts Cl. W7 5K 77
Couchmore Av. IG5: Ilf 2D 52
Coulgate St. SE4 3A 122
Coulson Cl. RM8: Dag 1C 72
Coulson St. SW3 5E 16 (5D 100)
Coulter Cl. UB4: Yead 4C 76
Coulter Rd. W6 3D 98
Coulthurst Ct. SW16 7J 137
(off Heybridge Av.)
Councillor St. SE5 7C 102
Counter Ct. SE1 5E 14
(off Borough High St.)
Counter Ho. E1 7G 85
Counters Ct. W14 3G 99
(off Holland Rd.)
Counter St. SE1 5G 15 (1E 102)
Countess Rd. NW5 5G 65
Countisbury Av. EN1: Enf 7A 24
Country Way TW13: Hanw 6K 129
County Court
Brentford 6D 96
Bromley 1J 159
Central London 4J 5
Clerkenwell & Shoreditch
3C 8 (4C 84)
Croydon 2D 168
Edmonton 6B 34
Kingston upon Thames 2D 150
Uxbridge 5H 75
Wandsworth 5G 117
West London 5F 99
(off Talgarth Rd.)
Willesden 2B 80
County Gdns. TW7: Isle 4H 113
County Ga. EN5: New Bar 6E 20
SE9 3G 143
The County Ground
Beckenham 6C 140
County Gro. SE5 1C 120
County Hall Apts. SE1 6G 13
County Hall (Former) 6G 13
(off Westminster Bri. Rd.)
County Ho. BR3: Beck 1A 158
SW9 1A 120
(off Brixton Rd.)
County Pde. TW8: Bford 7D 96
County Rd. CR7: Thor H 2B 156
E6 5F 89
County St. SE1 3C 102
Coupland Pl. SE18 5G 107
Courage Stadium 5K 159
Courcy Rd. N8 3A 48
Courier Rd. RM9: Dag 4J 91
Courland Gro. SW8 1H 119
Courland St. SW8 1H 119
The Course SE9 3E 142
The Court HA4: Ruis 4C 58
Court Annexe 7D 14 (2C 102)
Courtauld Cl. SE28 1A 108
Courtauld Gallery 2G 13
Courtauld Ho. E2 1G 85
(off Goldsmiths Row)
The Courtauld Institute of Art 7K 83
(off Strand)
Courtauld Rd. N19 1J 65
Court Av. DA17: Belv 5F 109
Court Cl. HA3: Kenton 3E 42
NW8 7B 64
(off Boydell Ct.)
SM6: W'gton 7H 167
TW2: Twick 3F 131
Court Cl. Av. TW2: Twick 3F 131
Court Cres. KT9: Chess 5D 162
Court Downs Rd. BR3: Beck 2D 158
Court Dr. CR0: Wadd 4K 167
HA7: Stan 4K 27
SM1: Sutt 4C 166
UB10: Hil 1B 74
Courtenay Av. HA3: Hrw W 7B 26
N6 7C 46
SM2: Sutt 7J 165
Courtenay Dr. BR3: Beck 2F 159
Courtenay Gdns. HA3: Hrw W 2G 41
Courtenay Ho. CR0: C'don 7C 156
(off Oakfield Rd.)
Courtenay M. E17 5A 50
Courtenay Pl. E17 5A 50
Courtenay Rd. E11 3H 69
E17 4K 49
HA9: Wemb 3D 60
KT4: Wor Pk 3E 164
SE20 6K 139
Courtenay Sq. SE11 6J 19 (5A 102)
Courtenay St. SE11 5J 19 (5A 102)
Courtens M. HA7: Stan 7H 27
Court Farm Av. KT19: Ewe 5K 163
Court Farm La. UB5: N'olt 7E 58
Court Farm Rd. SE9 2B 142
UB5: N'olt 7E 58
Courtfield W5 5C 78
Courtfield Av. HA1: Harr 5K 41
Courtfield Cres. HA1: Harr 5K 41
Courtfield Gdns. HA4: Ruis 2H 57
SW5 4K 99
W13 6A 78
Courtfield Ho. EC1 5J 7
(off Baldwins Gdns.)
Courtfield M. SW5 4A 100
Courtfield Ri. BR4: W W'ck 3F 171
Courtfield Rd. SW7 4A 100
TW15: Ashf 6D 128
Court Gdns. N1 6A 66
N7 6A 66
Courtgate Cl. NW7 6G 29
Courthill Rd. SE13 4E 122
Courthope Ho. SE16 3J 103
(off Lower Rd.)
SW8 7J 101
(off Hartington Rd.)
Courthope Rd. NW3 4D 64
SW19 5G 135
UB6: G'frd 2H 77
Courthope Vs. SW19 7G 135
The Courthouse SW1 2D 18
(off Horseferry Rd.)
Courthouse Gdns. N3 6D 30
Courthouse La. N16 4F 67
Courthouse Rd. N12 6E 30
Courthouse Way SW18 5K 117
Courtland Av. E4 2C 36
IG1: Ilf 2D 70
NW7 3E 28
SW16 7K 137
Courtland Gro. SE28 6D 90
Courtland Ho. SE20 1G 157
Courtland Rd. E6 1C 88
Courtlands KT12: Walt T 7J 147
TW10: Rich 5G 115
Courtlands Av. BR2: Hayes 1G 171
SE12 5K 123
TW9: Kew 2H 115
TW12: Hamp 6D 130
Courtlands Cl. HA4: Ruis 7H 39
Courtlands Dr. KT19: Ewe 6A 164
Courtlands Rd. KT5: Surb 7G 151
Court La. SE21 6E 120
Court La. Gdns. SE21 7E 120
Courtleet Dr. DA8: Erith 1H 127
Courtleigh NW11 5H 45
Courtleigh Gdns. NW11 4G 45
Court Lodge DA17: Belv 5G 109
SW1 4G 17
(off Sloane Sq.)
Courtman Rd. N17 7H 33
Court Mead UB5: N'olt 3D 76
Courtmead Cl. SE24 6C 120
Court M. SE13 6G 123
Courtnell St. W2 6J 81
Courtney Cl. SE19 6E 138
Courtney Ct. N7 5A 66
Courtney Cres. SM5: Cars 7D 166
Courtney Ho. NW4 3E 44
(off Mulberry Cl.)
W14 3G 99
(off Russell Rd.)
Courtney Pl. CR0: Wadd 3A 168
Courtney Rd. CR0: Wadd 3A 168
N7 5A 66
SW19 7C 136
TW6: H'row A 3C 110
Courtney Way TW6: H'row A 2C 110
Court Pde. HA0: Wemb 3B 60
Courtrai Rd. SE23 6A 122
Court Rd. SE9 6D 124
SE25 2F 157
UB2: S'hall 4D 94
UB10: Ick 5D 56
Ct. Royal SW15 5G 117
Courtside N8 6H 47
SE26 3H 139
Court St. BR1: Broml 2J 159
E1 5H 85
Courtville Ho. W10 3G 81
(off Third Av.)
Court Way NW9 4A 44
TW2: Twick 7K 113
W3 5J 79
Courtway IG6: Ilf 3G 53
IG8: Wfd G 5F 37
Courtwood La. CR0: Sels 7B 170
Court Yd. SE9 6D 124
Courtyard SW3 5E 16
(off Smith St.)
The Courtyard BR2: Kes 6C 172
E2 1K 9
(off Ezra St.)
EC3 1F 15
(within Royal Exchange)
N1 7K 65
NW1 7E 64
SE14 1K 121
(off Besson St.)
SW3 7B 16
(off Trident Pl.)
Courtyard Apts. E1 3K 9
(off Sclater St.)
Courtyard Ho. SW6 2A 118
(off Lensbury Av.)
Courtyard M. BR5: St P 7A 144
Courtyard Theatre 2G 9 (3E 84)
Cousin La. EC4 3E 14 (7D 84)
Cousins Cl. UB7: Yiew 7A 74
Couthurst Rd. SE3 6K 105
Coutts Av. KT9: Chess 5E 162
Coutt's Cres. NW5 3E 64
Couzens Ho. E3 5B 86
(off Weatherley Cl.)
Coval Gdns. SW14 4H 115
Coval La. SW14 4H 115
Coval Pas. SW14 4J 115
Coval Rd. SW14 4H 115
Covelees Wall E6 6E 88
Covell Ct. EN2: Enf 1E 22
(off The Ridgeway)
SE8 7C 104
COVENT GARDEN 2F 13 (7J 83)
Covent Gdn. WC2 2F 13 (7J 83)
Covent Garden Piazza WC2 2F 13
Coventry Cl. E6 6D 88
NW6 2J 81
Coventry Hall SW16 5J 137
Coventry Rd. E1 4H 85
E2 4H 85
IG1: Ilf 2F 71
SE25 4G 157
Coventry St. W1 3C 12 (7H 83)
Coverack Cl. CR0: C'don 7A 158
N14 6B 22
Coverdale Cl. HA7: Stan 5G 27
Coverdale Gdns. CR0: C'don 3F 169
Coverdale Rd. N11 6K 31
NW2 7F 63
W12 2D 98
The Coverdales IG11: Bark 2H 89
Coverham Ho. SE4 4K 121
(off Billingford Cl.)
Coverley Cl. E1 5G 85
Coverley Point SE11 4G 19
The Covert BR6: Pet W 6J 161
HA6: Nwood 1E 38
SE19 7F 139
(off Fox Hill)
Coverton Rd. SW17 5C 136
Covert Way EN4: Had W 2F 21
Covet Wood Cl. BR5: St M Cry 6K 161
Covey Cl. SW19 2K 153
Covey Rd. KT4: Wor Pk 2F 165
Covington Gdns. SW16 7B 138
Covington Way SW16 6K 137
(not continuous)
Cowan Cl. E6 5C 88
Cowbridge La. IG11: Bark 7F 71
Cowbridge Rd. HA3: Kenton 4F 43
Cowcross St. EC1 5A 8 (5B 84)
Cowdenbeath Path N1 1K 83
Cowden Rd. BR6: Orp 7K 161
Cowden St. SE6 4C 140
Cowdray Rd. UB10: Hil 1E 74
Cowdrey Cl. EN1: Enf 2K 23
Cowdrey M. SE6 4C 140
Cowdrey Rd. SW19 5K 135
Cowen Av. HA2: Harr 2H 59
Cowgate Rd. UB6: G'frd 3H 77
Cowick Rd. SW17 4D 136
Cowings Mead UB5: N'olt 6C 58
Cowland Av. EN3: Pond E 4D 24
Cow La. UB6: G'frd 2H 77
Cow Leaze E6 6E 88
Cowleaze Rd. KT2: King T 1E 150
COWLEY 4A 74
Cowley La. E11 3G 69
COWLEY PEACHEY 6A 74
Cowley Pl. NW4 5E 44
Cowley Rd. E11 5K 51
IG1: Ilf 7D 52
SW9 1A 120
(not continuous)
SW14 3A 116
W3 1B 98
Cowley St. SW1 1E 18 (3J 101)
Cowling Cl. W11 1G 99
Cowper Av. E6 7C 70
SM1: Sutt 4B 166
Cowper Cl. BR2: Broml 4B 160
DA16: Well 5A 126
Cowper Gdns. N14 6A 22
SM6: W'gton 6G 167
Cowper Ho. SE17 5C 102
(off Browning St.)
SW1 6C 18
(off Aylesford St.)
Cowper Rd. BR2: Broml 4B 160
DA17: Belv 4G 109
KT2: King T 5F 133
N14 1A 32
N16 5E 66

206 A-Z Big London

Cowper Rd.—Croft Av.

Cowper Rd. N18 . . . 5B 34
SW19 . . . 6A 136
W3 . . . 1K 97
W7 . . . 7K 77
Cowper's Ct. *EC3* . . . *1F 15*
(off Birchin La.)
Cowper St. EC2 . . . 3F 9 (4D 84)
Cowper Ter. W10 . . . 5F 81
Cowslip Cl. UB10: Uxb . . . 7A 56
Cowslip Rd. E18 . . . 2K 51
Cowthorpe Rd. SW8 . . . 1H 119
Cox Ct. EN4: E Barn . . . 4H 21
Coxe Pl. HA3: W'stone . . . 4A 42
Cox Ho. *W6* . . . *6G 99*
(off Field Rd.)
Cox La. KT9: Chess . . . 4F 163
KT19: Ewe . . . 5H 163
(not continuous)
Coxmount Rd. SE7 . . . 5B 106
Coxs Av. TW17: Shep . . . 3G 147
Coxson Way SE1 . . . 7J 15 (2F 103)
Cox's Wlk. SE21 . . . 1G 139
Coxwell Blvd. NW9 . . . 7G 29
Coxwell Rd. SE18 . . . 5H 107
SE19 . . . 7E 138
Coxwold Path KT9: Chess . . . 7E 162
Coyle Dr. UB10: Ick . . . 2E 56
Crabbs Cft. Cl. BR6: Farnb . . . 5G 173
Crab Hill BR3: Beck . . . 7F 141
Crabtree Av. HA0: Wemb . . . 2E 78
RM6: Chad H . . . 4D 54
Crabtree Cl. E2 . . . 2F 85
Crabtree Ct. EN5: New Bar . . . 4E 20
Crabtree Hall *SW6* . . . *7E 98*
(off Crabtree La.)
Crabtree La. SW6 . . . 7E 98
(not continuous)
Crabtree Manorway Nth.
DA17: Belv, Erith . . . 2J 109
Crabtree Manorway Sth.
DA17: Belv . . . 3J 109
Crabtree Pl. W1 . . . 6C 6 (5G 83)
Crabtree Wlk. CR0: C'don . . . 1G 169
Crace St. NW1 . . . 1C 6 (3H 83)
Craddock Rd. EN1: Enf . . . 3A 24
Craddock St. NW5 . . . 6E 64
Cradford Ho. Nth. E2 . . . 3K 85
Cradford Ho. Sth. E2 . . . 3K 85
Cradley Rd. SE9 . . . 1H 143
Crafts Council & Gallery . . . 2A 84
Cragie Ho. *SE1* . . . *4F 103*
(off Balaclava Rd.)
Craig Dr. UB8: Hil . . . 6D 74
Craigen Av. CR0: C'don . . . 1H 169
Craigen Gdns. IG3: Ilf . . . 4J 71
Craigerne Rd. SE3 . . . 7K 105
Craig Gdns. E18 . . . 2H 51
Craigholm SE18 . . . 2E 124
Craig Ho. *E17* . . . *4C 50*
(off High St.)
Craigmore Ct. HA6: Nwood . . . 1G 39
Craigmuir Pk. HA0: Wemb . . . 1F 79
Craignair Rd. SW2 . . . 7A 120
Craignish Av. SW16 . . . 2K 155
Craig Pk. Rd. N18 . . . 4C 34
Craig Rd. TW10: Ham . . . 4C 132
Craig's Ct. SW1 . . . 4E 12 (1J 101)
Craigton Rd. SE9 . . . 4D 124
Craigweil Cl. HA7: Stan . . . 5J 27
Craigweil Dr. HA7: Stan . . . 5J 27
Craigwell Av. TW13: Felt . . . 3J 129
Craik Ct. *NW6* . . . *2H 81*
(off Carlton Vale)
Crail Row SE17 . . . 4D 102
Crales Ho. SE18 . . . 3C 106
Cramer St. W1 . . . 6H 5 (5E 82)
Crammond Cl. W6 . . . 6G 99
Cramond Ct. TW14: Bedf . . . 1G 129
Cramonde Ct. DA16: Well . . . 2A 126
Crampton Ho. SW8 . . . 1G 119
Crampton Rd. SE20 . . . 6J 139
Crampton St. SE17 . . . 4C 102
Cranberry Cl. NW7 . . . 6G 29
UB5: N'olt . . . 2B 76
Cranberry Ent. Pk. *N17* . . . *7A 34*
(off White Hart La.)
Cranberry La. E16 . . . 4G 87
Cranborne Av. KT6: Surb . . . 3G 163
UB2: S'hall . . . 4E 94
Cranborne Rd. IG11: Bark . . . 1H 89
Cranborne Waye UB4: Yead . . . 6K 75
(not continuous)
Cranbourn All. *WC2* . . . *2D 12*
(off Cranbourn St.)
Cranbourne *NW1* . . . *7H 65*
(off Agar Gro.)
Cranbourne Av. E11 . . . 4K 51
Cranbourne Cl. SW16 . . . 3J 155
Cranbourne Ct. *SW11* . . . *7C 100*
(off Albert Bri. Rd.)
Cranbourne Dr. HA5: Pinn . . . 5B 40
Cranbourne Gdns. IG6: Ilf . . . 3G 53
NW11 . . . 5G 45
Cranbourne Rd. E12 . . . 5C 70
E15 . . . 4E 68
HA6: Nwood . . . 3H 39
N10 . . . 2F 47
Cranbourn Ho. *SE16* . . . *2H 103*
(off Marigold St.)
Cranbourn Pas. SE16 . . . 2H 103
Cranbourn St. WC2 . . . 2D 12 (7H 83)
CRANBROOK . . . 1D 70
Cranbrook *NW1* . . . *1G 83*
(off Camden St.)
Cranbrook Castle Tennis Club . . . 7D 52
Cranbrook Cl. BR2: Hayes . . . 6J 159
Cranbrook Ct. CR2: S Croy . . . 5E 168
TW8: Bford . . . 6C 96
Cranbrook Dr. KT10: Esh . . . 7G 149
TW2: Whitt . . . 1F 131
Cranbrook Est. E2 . . . 2K 85
Cranbrook La. N11 . . . 4A 32
Cranbrook M. E17 . . . 5B 50
Cranbrook Pk. N22 . . . 1A 48
Cranbrook Ri. IG1: Ilf . . . 6D 52
Cranbrook Rd. CR7: Thor H . . . 2C 156
DA7: Bex . . . 1F 127
EN4: E Barn . . . 6G 21
IG1: Ilf . . . 7E 52
IG2: Ilf . . . 6E 52
IG6: Ilf . . . 5E 52
SE8 . . . 1C 122
SW19 . . . 7G 135
TW4: Houn . . . 4D 112
W4 . . . 5A 98
Cranbrook St. E2 . . . 2K 85
Cranbury Rd. SW6 . . . 2K 117
Crandley Ct. SE8 . . . 4A 104
(not continuous)
Crane Av. TW7: Isle . . . 5A 114
W3 . . . 7J 79
Cranebank . . . 2J 111
Cranebank M. TW1: Twick . . . 4A 114
Cranebrook TW2: Twick . . . 2G 131
Crane Cl. HA2: Harr . . . 3G 59
RM10: Dag . . . 6G 73
Crane Ct. EC4 . . . 6A 84
KT19: Ewe . . . 4J 163
SW14 . . . 4J 115
Craneford Cl. TW2: Twick . . . 7K 113
Craneford Way TW2: Twick . . . 7J 113
Crane Gdns. UB3: Harl . . . 4H 93
Crane Gro. N7 . . . 6A 66
Crane Hgts. *N17* . . . *3H 49*
(off Waterside Way)
Crane Ho. *E3* . . . *2A 86*
(off Roman Rd.)
SE15 . . . 1F 121
TW13: Hanw . . . 3E 130
Crane Lodge Rd. TW5: Cran . . . 6K 93
Crane Mead SE16 . . . 5J 103
Crane Mead Ct.
TW1: Twick . . . 7K 113
Crane Pk. Island Nature Reserve
. . . 2D 130
Crane Pk. Rd. TW2: Whitt . . . 2F 131
Crane Rd. TW2: Twick . . . 1J 131
TW19: Stanw . . . 6C 110
Cranesbill Cl. NW9 . . . 3K 43
SW16 . . . 2H 155
Cranes Dr. KT5: Surb . . . 4E 150
Cranes Pk. KT5: Surb . . . 4E 150
Cranes Pk. Av. KT5: Surb . . . 4E 150
Cranes Pk. Cres. KT5: Surb . . . 4F 151
Crane St. SE10 . . . 5F 105
SE15 . . . 1F 121
Craneswater UB3: Harl . . . 7H 93
Craneswater Pk. UB2: S'hall . . . 5D 94
Crane Way TW2: Whitt . . . 7G 113
Cranfield Cl. SE27 . . . 3C 138
Cranfield Ct. W1 . . . 6D 4
Cranfield Dr. NW9 . . . 7F 29
Cranfield Ho. WC1 . . . 5E 6
Cranfield Rd. SE4 . . . 3B 122
Cranfield Rd. E. SM5: Cars . . . 7E 166
Cranfield Rd. W. SM5: Cars . . . 7E 166
Cranfield Row SE1 . . . 1K 19
Cranfield Wlk. SE3 . . . 3K 123
CRANFORD . . . 7J 93
Cranford Av. N13 . . . 5D 32
TW19: Stanw . . . 7A 110
Cranford Cl. SW20 . . . 7D 134
TW19: Stanw . . . 7A 110
Cranford Community College
Sports Cen. . . . 6K 93
Cranford Cotts. *E1* . . . *7K 85*
(off Cranford St.)
Cranford Dr. UB3: Harl . . . 4H 93
Cranford La. TW5: Cran, Hest . . . 7K 93
TW6: H'row A . . . 1H 111
(Bath Rd.)
TW6: H'row A . . . 3H 111
(Elmdon Rd.)
UB3: Cran, Harl . . . 6F 93
Cranford M. BR2: Broml . . . 5C 160
Cranford Pk. Rd. UB3: Harl . . . 4H 93
Cranford St. E1 . . . 7K 85
Cranford Way N8 . . . 4K 47
Cranhurst Rd. NW2 . . . 5E 62
Cranleigh *W11* . . . *1H 99*
(off Ladbroke Rd.)
Cranleigh Cl. BR6: Chels . . . 3K 173
DA5: Bexl . . . 6H 127
SE20 . . . 2H 157
Cranleigh Ct. CR4: Mitc . . . 3B 154
TW9: Rich . . . 3G 115
UB1: S'hall . . . 6D 76
Cranleigh Gdns. HA3: Kenton . . . 5E 42
IG11: Bark . . . 7H 71
KT2: King T . . . 6F 133
N21 . . . 5F 23
SE25 . . . 3E 156
SM1: Sutt . . . 2K 165
UB1: S'hall . . . 6D 76
Cranleigh Gdns. Ind. Est.
UB1: S'hall . . . 6D 76
Cranleigh Ho's. *NW1* . . . *2G 83*
(off Cranleigh St.)
Cranleigh M. SW11 . . . 2C 118
Cranleigh Rd. N15 . . . 5C 48
SW19 . . . 3J 153
TW13: Felt . . . 4H 129
Cranleigh St. NW1 . . . 2G 83
Cranley Dene Ct. N10 . . . 4F 47
Cranley Dr. HA4: Ruis . . . 2H 57
IG2: Ilf . . . 7G 53
CRANLEY GARDENS . . . 4F 47
Cranley Gdns. N10 . . . 4F 47
N13 . . . 3E 32
SM6: W'gton . . . 7G 167
SW7 . . . 5A 16 (5A 100)
Cranley M. SW7 . . . 5A 16 (5A 100)
Cranley Pde. *SE9* . . . *4C 142*
(off Beaconsfield Rd.)
Cranley Pl. SW7 . . . 4A 16 (4B 100)
Cranley Rd. E13 . . . 5K 87
IG2: Ilf . . . 6G 53
Cranmer Av. W13 . . . 3B 96
Cranmer Cl. HA4: Ruis . . . 1B 58
HA7: Stan . . . 7H 27
SM4: Mord . . . 6F 153
Cranmer Ct. N3 . . . 2G 45
SW3 . . . 4D 16 (4C 100)
SW4 . . . 3H 119
TW12: Hamp H . . . 5F 131
Cranmere Ct. EN2: Enf . . . 2F 23
Cranmer Farm Cl. CR4: Mitc . . . 4D 154
Cranmer Gdns. RM10: Dag . . . 4J 73
Cranmer Ho. *SW9* . . . *7A 102*
(off Cranmer Rd.)
SW11 . . . *1C 118*
(off Surrey La. Est.)
Cranmer Rd. CR0: C'don . . . 3B 168
CR4: Mitc . . . 4D 154
E7 . . . 4K 69
HA8: Edg . . . 3C 28
KT2: King T . . . 5E 132
SW9 . . . 7A 102
TW12: Hamp H . . . 5F 131
UB3: Hayes . . . 6F 75
Cranmer Ter. SW17 . . . 5B 136
Cranmore Av. TW7: Isle . . . 7G 95
Cranmore Rd. BR1: Broml . . . 3H 141
BR7: Chst . . . 5D 142
Cranmore Way N10 . . . 4G 47
Cranston Cl. TW3: Houn . . . 2C 112
UB10: Ick . . . 2F 57
Cranston Est. N1 . . . 2D 84
Cranston Gdns. E4 . . . 6J 35
Cranston Rd. SE23 . . . 1A 140
Cranswick Rd. SE16 . . . 5H 103
Crantock Rd. SE6 . . . 2D 140
Cranwell Cl. E3 . . . 4D 86
Cranwell Gro. TW17: Shep . . . 4B 146
Cranwell Rd. TW6: H'row A . . . 2D 110
Cranwich Av. N21 . . . 7J 23
Cranwich Rd. N16 . . . 7D 48
Cranwood Ct. EC1 . . . 2F 9
Cranwood St. EC1 . . . 2E 8 (3D 84)
Cranworth Cres. E4 . . . 1A 36
Cranworth Gdns. SW9 . . . 1A 120
Craster Rd. SW2 . . . 7K 119
Crathie Rd. SE12 . . . 6K 123
Cravan Av. TW13: Felt . . . 2J 129
Craven Av. UB1: S'hall . . . 5D 76
W5 . . . 7C 78
Craven Cl. N16 . . . 7G 49
UB4: Hayes . . . 6J 75
Craven Cottage . . . 2F 117
Craven Ct. NW10 . . . 1A 80
RM6: Chad H . . . 6E 54
Craven Gdns. IG6: Ilf . . . 2H 53
IG11: Bark . . . 2J 89
SW19 . . . 5J 135
Craven Hill W2 . . . 7A 82
Craven Hill Gdns. W2 . . . 7A 82
(not continuous)
Craven Hill M. W2 . . . 7A 82
Craven Ho. *N2* . . . *2B 46*
(off High Rd. E. Finchley)
Craven Lodge *SW6* . . . *1F 117*
(off Harbord St.)
W2 . . . *7A 82*
(off Craven Hill)
Craven M. SW11 . . . 3E 118
Craven Pk. NW10 . . . 1K 79
Craven Pk. M. NW10 . . . 7A 62
Craven Pk. Rd. N15 . . . 6F 49
NW10 . . . 1A 80
Craven Pas. *WC2* . . . *4E 12*
(off Craven St.)
Craven Rd. CR0: C'don . . . 1H 169
KT2: King T . . . 1F 151
NW10 . . . 1K 79
W2 . . . 1A 10 (7A 82)
W5 . . . 7C 78
Craven St. WC2 . . . 4E 12 (1J 101)
Craven Ter. W2 . . . 2A 10 (7A 82)
Craven Wlk. N16 . . . 7G 49
Crawford Av. HA0: Wemb . . . 5D 60
Crawford Bldgs. *W1* . . . *6D 4*
(off Homer St.)
Crawford Cl. TW7: Isle . . . 2J 113
Crawford Ct. *NW9* . . . *3A 44*
(off Charcot Rd.)
Crawford Est. SE5 . . . 2C 120
Crawford Gdns. N13 . . . 3G 33
UB5: N'olt . . . 3D 76
Crawford Mans. *W1* . . . *6D 4*
(off Crawford St.)
Crawford M. SW20 . . . 7D 134
W1 . . . 6E 4 (5D 82)
Crawford Pas. EC1 . . . 4K 7 (4A 84)
Crawford Pl. W1 . . . 7D 4 (6C 82)
Crawford Rd. SE5 . . . 1C 120
Crawford St. NW10 . . . 7K 61
W1 . . . 6E 4 (5C 82)
Crawley Rd. E10 . . . 1D 68
EN1: Enf . . . 7K 23
N22 . . . 2C 48
Crawshay Rd. SW9 . . . 1A 120
Crawthew Gro. SE22 . . . 4F 121
Craybrooke Rd. DA14: Sidc . . . 4B 144
Craybury End SE9 . . . 2G 143
Crayfields Bus. Pk. BR5: St P . . . 7C 144
CRAYFORD . . . 5K 127
Crayford Cl. E6 . . . 6C 88
Crayford Ct. *W3* . . . *3J 97*
(off Bollo Bri. Rd.)
Crayford Ho. *SE1* . . . *7F 15*
(off Long La.)
Crayford M. N7 . . . 4J 65
Crayford Rd. N7 . . . 4H 65
Cray Ho. *NW8* . . . *5B 4*
(off Penfold St.)
Crayke Hill KT9: Chess . . . 7E 162
Crayle Ho. *EC1* . . . *3B 8*
(off Malta St.)
Crayleigh Ter. DA14: Sidc . . . 6C 144
Crayonne Cl. TW16: Sun . . . 1G 147
Cray Rd. DA14: Sidc . . . 6C 144
DA17: Belv . . . 6G 109
Cray Valley Rd. BR5: St M Cry . . . 5K 161
Cray Wanderers FC . . . 5K 159
Crayzee Barn . . . 2F 145
Crealock Gro. IG8: Wfd G . . . 5C 36
Crealock St. SW18 . . . 6K 117
Creasy Est. SE1 . . . 3E 102
Creative Ho. *SW8* . . . *7F 101*
(off Prince of Wales Dr.)
Creative Rd. SE8 . . . 7D 104
Crebor St. SE22 . . . 6G 121
Crecy Ct. *SE11* . . . *5J 19*
(off Hotspur St.)
Credenhall Dr. BR2: Broml . . . 1D 172
Credenhill Ho. SE15 . . . 7H 103
Credenhill St. SW16 . . . 6G 137
Crediton Hgts. *NW10* . . . *1F 81*
(off Okehampton Rd.)
Crediton Hill NW6 . . . 5K 63
Crediton Rd. E16 . . . 6J 87
NW10 . . . 1F 81
Crediton Way KT10: Clay . . . 5A 162
Credon Rd. E13 . . . 2A 88
SE16 . . . 5H 103
Creechurch La. EC3 . . . 1H 15 (6E 84)
(not continuous)
Creechurch Pl. EC3 . . . 1H 15
Creed Ct. E1 . . . 3A 86
EC4 . . . 1B 14
Creed La. EC4 . . . 1B 14 (6B 84)
Creed Pas. *SE10* . . . *5G 105*
(off Hoskins St.)
The Creek TW16: Sun . . . 5J 147
Creek Cotts. *KT8: E Mos* . . . *4J 149*
(off Creek Rd.)
Creek Ho. *W14* . . . *3G 99*
(off Russell Rd.)
CREEKMOUTH . . . 4K 89
Creekmouth Ind. Pk. IG11: Bark . . . 4K 89
Creek Rd. IG11: Bark . . . 3K 89
KT8: E Mos . . . 4J 149
SE8 . . . 6C 104
SE10 . . . 6C 104
Creekside SE8 . . . 7D 104
Creekside Foyer *SE8* . . . *6D 104*
(off Stowage)
Creek Way RM13: Rain . . . 5K 91
Creeland Gro. SE6 . . . 1B 140
Crefeld Cl. W6 . . . 6G 99
Creffield Rd. W3 . . . 7F 79
W5 . . . 7F 79
Creighton Av. E6 . . . 2B 88
N2 . . . 3C 46
N10 . . . 3C 46
Creighton Cl. W12 . . . 7C 80
Creighton Rd. N17 . . . 7K 33
NW6 . . . 2F 81
W5 . . . 3D 96
Cremer Bus. Cen. *E2* . . . *1J 9*
(off Cremer St.)
Cremer Ho. *SE8* . . . *7C 104*
(off Deptford Chu. St.)
Cremer St. E2 . . . 1J 9 (2F 85)
Cremorne Est. SW10 . . . 6B 100
(not continuous)
Cremorne Riverside Cen. . . . 7B 100
Cremorne Rd. SW10 . . . 7A 100
Creon Ct. *SW9* . . . *7A 102*
(off Caldwell St.)
Crescent EC3 . . . 2J 15 (7F 85)
The Crescent BR3: Beck . . . 1C 158
BR4: W W'ck . . . 6G 159
CR0: C'don . . . 5D 156
DA5: Bexl . . . 7C 126
DA14: Sidc . . . 4K 143
E17 . . . 6A 50
EN5: New Bar . . . 2E 20
HA0: Wemb . . . 2B 60
HA2: Harr . . . 1G 59
IG2: Ilf . . . 6E 52
KT3: N Mald . . . 3J 151
KT6: Surb . . . 5E 150
KT8: W Mole . . . 4E 148
N11 . . . 4J 31
NW2 . . . 3D 62
SE8 . . . *1C 122*
(off Seager Pl.)
SM1: Sutt . . . 5B 166
SW13 . . . 2B 116
SW19 . . . 3J 135
TW15: Ashf . . . 5B 128
TW17: Shep . . . 7H 147
UB1: S'hall . . . 2D 94
UB3: Harl . . . 7E 92
W3 . . . 6A 80
W12 . . . 1E 98
Crescent Arc. *SE10* . . . *6E 104*
(off Creek Rd.)
Crescent Ct. KT6: Surb . . . 5D 150
SW4 . . . *5H 119*
(off Park Hill)
Crescent Ct. Bus. Cen. E16 . . . 4F 87
Crescent Dr. BR5: Pet W . . . 5F 161
Crescent E. EN4: Had W . . . 1F 21
Crescent Gdns. HA4: Ruis . . . 7K 39
SW19 . . . 3J 135
Crescent Gro. CR4: Mitc . . . 4C 154
SW4 . . . 4G 119
Crescent Ho. *EC1* . . . *4C 8*
(off Golden La. Est.)
SE13 . . . 2D 122
Crescent La. SW4 . . . 4G 119
Crescent Mans. *SW3* . . . *4C 16*
(off Fulham Rd.)
W11 . . . *7G 81*
(off Elgin Cres.)
Crescent M. N22 . . . 1J 47
Crescent Pde. UB10: Hil . . . 3C 74
Crescent Pl. SW3 . . . 3D 16 (4C 100)
Crescent Ri. EN4: E Barn . . . 5H 21
N3 . . . 1H 45
N22 . . . 1H 47
Crescent Rd. BR1: Broml . . . 7J 141
BR3: Beck . . . 2D 158
DA15: Sidc . . . 3K 143
E4 . . . 1B 36
E6 . . . 1A 88
E10 . . . 2D 68
E13 . . . 1J 87
E18 . . . 1A 52
EN2: Enf . . . 4G 23
EN4: E Barn . . . 4G 21
KT2: King T . . . 7G 133
N3 . . . 1H 45
N8 . . . 6H 47
N9 . . . 1B 34
N11 . . . 4J 31
N15 . . . 3B 48
N22 . . . 1H 47
RM10: Dag . . . 3H 73
SE18 . . . 5F 107
SW20 . . . 1F 153
TW17: Shep . . . 5F 146
Crescent Row EC1 . . . 4C 8 (4C 84)
Crescent Stables SW15 . . . 5G 117
Crescent St. N1 . . . 7K 65
Cres. Way BR6: Orp . . . 5J 173
N12 . . . 6H 31
SE4 . . . 3C 122
SW16 . . . 6K 137
Crescent W. EN4: Had W . . . 1F 21
Crescent Wood Rd. SE26 . . . 3G 139
Cresford Rd. SW6 . . . 1K 117
Crespigny Rd. NW4 . . . 6D 44
Cressage Cl. UB1: S'hall . . . 4E 76
Cressage Ho. *TW8: Bford* . . . *6E 96*
(off Ealing Rd.)
Cressal Ho. *E14* . . . *3C 104*
(off Tiller Rd.)
Cresset Ho. E9 . . . 6J 67
Cresset Rd. E9 . . . 6J 67
Cresset St. SW4 . . . 3H 119
Cressfield Cl. NW5 . . . 5E 64
Cressida Rd. N19 . . . 1G 65
Cressingham Gro. SM1: Sutt . . . 4A 166
Cressingham Rd. HA8: Edg . . . 6E 28
SE13 . . . 3E 122
Cressington Cl. N16 . . . 5E 66
Cress M. BR1: Broml . . . 5F 141
Cresswell Gdns. SW5 . . . 5A 100
Cresswell Ho. HA9: Wemb . . . 3E 60
TW19: Stanw . . . *6A 110*
(off Douglas Rd.)
Cresswell Pk. SE3 . . . 3H 123
Cresswell Pl. SW10 . . . 5A 100
Cresswell Rd. SE25 . . . 4G 157
TW1: Twick . . . 6D 114
TW13: Hanw . . . 3C 130
Cresswell Way N21 . . . 7F 23
Cressy Ct. E1 . . . 5J 85
W6 . . . 3D 98
Cressy Ho. SW15 . . . 3D 116
Cressy Ho's. *E1* . . . *5J 85*
(off Hannibal Rd.)
Cressy Pl. E1 . . . 5J 85
Cressy Rd. NW3 . . . 5D 64
The Crest KT5: Surb . . . 5G 151
N13 . . . 4F 33
NW4 . . . 5E 44
Cresta Ct. W5 . . . 4F 79
Cresta Ho. *E3* . . . *4C 86*
(off Dimson Cres.)
NW3 . . . *7B 64*
(off Finchley Rd.)
Crestbrook Av. N13 . . . 3G 33
Crestbrook Pl. *N13* . . . *3G 33*
(off Green Lanes)
Crest Ct. NW4 . . . 5E 44
Crest Dr. EN3: Enf W . . . 1D 24
Crested Ct. NW9 . . . 7B 44
Crestfield St. WC1 . . . 1F 7 (3J 83)
Crest Gdns. HA4: Ruis . . . 3A 58
Creston House *SW11* . . . *3B 118*
(off Gartons Way)
Creston Way KT4: Wor Pk . . . 1F 165
Crest Rd. BR2: Hayes . . . 7H 159
CR2: Sels . . . 7H 169
NW2 . . . 2B 62
Crest Vw. HA5: Pinn . . . 4B 40
Crest Vw. Dr. BR5: Pet W . . . 5F 161
Crest Wlk. E18 . . . 2A 52
Crestway SW15 . . . 6C 116
Crestwood Way
TW4: Houn . . . 5C 112
Creswell Dr. BR3: Beck . . . 5D 158
Creswick Ct. W3 . . . 7H 79
Creswick Rd. W3 . . . 7H 79
Creswick Wlk. E3 . . . 3C 86
NW11 . . . 4H 45
Creton St. SE18 . . . 3E 106
Creukhorne Rd. NW10 . . . 7A 62
Crewdson Rd. SW9 . . . 7A 102
Crewe Pl. NW10 . . . 3B 80
Crewkerne Ct. *SW11* . . . *1B 118*
(off Bolingbroke Wlk.)
Crews St. E14 . . . 4C 104
Crewys Rd. NW2 . . . 2H 63
SE15 . . . 2H 121
Crichton Av. SM6: Bedd . . . 5H 167
Crichton Ho. DA14: Sidc . . . 6D 144
Crichton Rd. SM5: Cars . . . 6D 166
Crichton St. SW8 . . . 2G 119
Crick Ct. *IG11: Bark* . . . *2G 89*
(off Spring Pl.)
Cricketers Arms Rd. EN2: Enf . . . 2H 23
Cricketers Cl. DA8: Erith . . . 5K 109
KT9: Chess . . . 4D 162
N14 . . . 7B 22
Cricketers Ct. *SE11* . . . *4B 102*
(off Kennington La.)
Cricketers M. SW18 . . . 5K 117
Cricketers Ter. SM5: Cars . . . 3C 166
Cricketers Wlk. SE26 . . . 5J 139
Cricketfield Rd. E5 . . . 4H 67
Cricket Grn. CR4: Mitc . . . 3D 154
Cricket Ground Rd.
BR7: Chst . . . 1F 161
Cricket La. BR3: Beck . . . 6A 140
TW12: Hamp H . . . 6G 131
Cricklade Av. SW2 . . . 2J 137
Cricklefield Pl. IG1: Ilf . . . 2J 71
CRICKLEWOOD . . . 4F 63
Cricklewood B'way. NW2 . . . 3E 62
Cricklewood La. NW2 . . . 4F 63
Cridland St. E15 . . . 1H 87
Crieff Ct. TW11: Tedd . . . 7C 132
Crieff Rd. SW18 . . . 6A 118
Criffel Av. SW2 . . . 2H 137
Crimscott St. SE1 . . . 3E 102
Crimsworth Rd. SW8 . . . 1H 119
Crinan St. N1 . . . 2J 83
Cringle St. SW11 . . . 7G 101
Crinoline M. E1 . . . 6J 9 (5F 85)
Cripplegate St. EC2 . . . 5D 8 (5C 84)
Cripps Cl. IG6: Ilf . . . 3G 53
Cripps Grn. UB4: Yead . . . 4K 75
Crispe Ho. IG11: Bark . . . 2H 89
N1 . . . *1K 83*
(off Barnsbury Est.)
Crispen Rd. TW13: Hanw . . . 4C 130
Crispian Cl. NW10 . . . 4A 62
Crispin Cl. CR0: Bedd . . . 2J 167
Crispin Ct. SE17 . . . 4E 102
Crispin Cres. CR0: Bedd . . . 3H 167
Crispin Ind. Cen. N18 . . . 5D 34
Crispin Lodge N11 . . . 5J 31
Crispin M. NW11 . . . 5H 45
Crispin Pl. E1 . . . 5J 9 (5F 85)
Crispin Rd. HA8: Edg . . . 6D 28
Crispin St. E1 . . . 6J 9 (5F 85)
Crispin Way UB8: Hil . . . 4B 74
Crisp Rd. W6 . . . 5E 98
Cristie Ct. E16 . . . 4H 87
Cristowe Rd. SW6 . . . 2H 117
Criterion Bldgs. *KT7: T Ditt* . . . *7B 150*
(off Portsmouth Rd.)
Criterion Ct. *E8* . . . *7F 67*
(off Middleton Rd.)
Criterion M. N19 . . . 2H 65
SE24 . . . *5B 120*
(off Shakespeare Rd.)
Criterion Theatre . . . 3C 12
(off Piccadilly Cir.)
CRITTALLS CORNER . . . 7C 144
Crockerton Rd. SW17 . . . 2D 136
Crockham Way SE9 . . . 4E 142
Crocus Cl. CR0: C'don . . . 1K 169
Crocus Fld. EN5: Barn . . . 6C 20
The Croft CR0: C'don . . . 3F 169
E4 . . . 2B 36
EN5: Barn . . . 4B 20
HA0: Wemb . . . 5C 60
HA4: Ruis . . . 4A 58
HA5: Pinn . . . 7D 40
HA8: Edg . . . 7C 28
NW10 . . . 2B 80
TW5: Hest . . . 6C 94
W5 . . . 5E 78
Croft Av. BR4: W W'ck . . . 1E 170

Croft Cl.—Culross Cl.

Croft Cl. BR7: Chst 5D 142
DA17: Belv 5F 109
NW7 3F 29
UB3: Harl 7E 92
UB10: Hil 7C 56
Croft Ct. HA4: Ruis 1H 57
SE13 6E 122
SM1: Sutt 2B 166
Croftdown Rd. NW5 3E 64
Croft End Cl. KT9: Chess 3F 163
Crofters Cl. TW7: Isle 5H 113
Crofters Ct. SE8 4A 104
(off Croft St.)
Crofters Mead CR0: Sels 7B 170
Crofters Way NW1 1H 83
Croft Gdns. HA4: Ruis 1H 57
W7 2A 96
Croft Ho. E17 4D 50
NW9 2B 44
W10 3G 81
(off Third Av.)
Croft Lodge Cl. IG8: Wfd G 6E 36
Croft M. N12 3F 31
CROFTON 2G 173
Crofton Albion Sports Ground 4J 123
Crofton Av. BR6: Farnb 2G 173
DA5: Bexl 7D 126
W4 7J 97
Croftongate Way SE4 5A 122
Crofton Gro. E4 4A 36
Crofton Ho. SW3 7C 16
(off Old Church St.)
Crofton La.
BR5: Farnb, Orp, Pet W 2H 173
BR6: Pet W 7H 161
CROFTON PARK 5B 122
Crofton Pk. Rd. SE4 6B 122
Crofton Rd. BR6: Farnb, Orp 3E 172
E13 4K 87
SE5 1E 120
Crofton Roman Villa 2J 173
Crofton Ter. E5 5A 68
TW9: Rich 4F 115
Crofton Way EN2: Enf 2F 23
EN5: New Bar 6E 20
Croft Rd. BR1: Broml 6J 141
EN3: Enf H 1F 25
SM1: Sutt 5C 166
SW16 1A 156
SW19 7A 136
The Crofts TW17: Shep 4G 147
Crofts Ho. E2 2G 85
(off Teale St.)
The Croftside SE25 3G 157
Crofts La. N22 7F 33
Crofts Rd. HA1: Harr 6A 42
Crofts St. E1 3K 15 (7G 85)
Croft St. SE8 4A 104
Crofts Vs. HA1: Harr 6A 42
Cft. Way DA15: Sidc 3J 143
TW10: Ham 3B 132
Croftway NW3 4J 63
Crogsland Rd. NW1 7E 64
Croham Cl. CR2: S Croy 7E 168
Croham Hurst Golf Course 6F 169
Croham Mnr. Rd. CR2: S Croy 7E 168
Croham Mt. CR2: S Croy 7E 168
Croham Pk. Av. CR2: S Croy 5E 168
Croham Rd. CR2: S Croy 5D 168
Croham Valley Rd. CR2: Sels 6G 169
Croindene Rd. SW16 1J 155
Crokesley Ho. HA8: Edg 2J 43
(off Burnt Oak B'way.)
Cromartie Rd. N19 7H 47
Cromarty Ct. SW2 5K 119
Cromarty Ho. E1 5A 86
(off Ben Jonson Rd.)
Cromarty Rd. HA8: Edg 2C 28
Cromberdale Ct. N17 1G 49
(off Spencer Rd.)
Crombie Cl. IG4: Ilf 5D 52
Crombie M. SW11 2C 118
Crombie Rd. DA15: Sidc 1H 143
Crome Ho. UB5: N'olt 2C 76
(off Parkfield Dr.)
Cromer Cl. UB8: Hil 6E 74
Cromer Hyde SM4: Mord 5K 153
Crome Rd. NW10 6A 62
Cromer Pl. BR6: Orp 1J 173
Cromer Rd. E10 7F 51
EN5: New Bar 4F 21
IG8: Wfd G 4D 36
N17 2G 49
RM6: Chad H 6E 54
RM7: Rom 6K 55
SE25 3H 157
SW17 6E 136
TW6: H'row A 2C 110
Cromer St. WC1 2E 6 (3J 83)
Cromer Ter. E8 5G 67
RM6: Chad H 5B 54
Cromer Vs. Rd. SW18 6H 117
Cromford Cl. BR6: Orp 3J 173
Cromford Path E5 4K 67
Cromford Rd. SW18 5J 117
Cromford Way KT3: N Mald 1K 151
Cromie Cl. N13 3F 33
Cromlix Cl. BR7: Chst 2F 161
Crompton Ct. BR2: Broml 3J 159
(off St Mark's Sq.)
SW3 3C 16 (4C 100)
Crompton Ho. SE1 3C 102
(off County St.)
W2 4A 4
(off Hall Pl.)
Crompton Pl. EN3: Enf L 1H 25
Crompton St. W2 4A 4 (4B 82)
Cromwell Av. BR2: Broml 4K 159
KT3: N Mald 5B 152
N6 1F 65
W6 5D 98
Cromwell Cen. IG11: Bark 3A 90
NW10 3K 79
The Cromwell Cen. RM8: Dag 7F 55
(off Coppen Rd.)
Cromwell Cl. BR2: Broml 4K 159
E1 1G 103
KT12: Walt T 7K 147
N2 4B 46
W3 1J 97
(not continuous)
W4 5H 97
(off Harvard Rd.)
Cromwell Ct. EN3: Pond E 5E 24
Cromwell Cres. SW5 4J 99
Cromwell Gdns. SW7 2B 16 (3B 100)
Cromwell Gro. W6 3E 98
Cromwell Highwalk EC2 5D 8
Cromwell Ho. CR0: C'don 3B 168
SW11 1E 118
(off Charlotte Despard Av.)
Cromwell Ind. Est. E10 1A 68
Cromwell Lodge DA6: Bex 5E 126
E1 4J 85
(off Cleveland Gro.)
IG11: Bark 5J 71
Cromwell Mans. SW5 4J 99
(off Cromwell Rd.)
Cromwell M. SW7 3B 16 (4B 100)
Cromwell Pl. EC2 5D 8
(off Silk St.)
N6 1F 65
SW7 3B 16 (4B 100)
SW14 3J 115
Cromwell Rd. BR3: Beck 2A 158
CR0: C'don 7D 156
E7 7A 70
E17 5E 50
HA0: Wemb 2E 78
KT2: King T 1E 150
KT4: Wor Pk 3K 163
N3 1A 46
N10 7K 31
(not continuous)
SW5 4J 99
SW7 3A 16 (4J 99)
SW9 1A 120
SW19 5J 135
TW3: Houn 4E 112
TW11: Tedd 6A 132
TW13: Felt 1K 129
UB3: Hayes 6F 75
Cromwell St. TW3: Houn 4E 112
Cromwell Twr. EC2 5D 8
Cromwell Trad. Cen. IG11: Bark 3J 89
Crondace Rd. SW6 1J 117
Crondall Ct. N1 1F 9
Crondall Ho. SW15 7C 116
Crondall St. N1 1F 9 (2D 84)
Crone Ct. NW6 2H 81
(off Denmark Rd.)
Cronin St. SE15 7F 103
CROOKED BILLET 1C 50
Crooked Billet SW19 6E 134
Crooked Billet Yd. E2 1H 9
Crooked Usage N3 3G 45
Crooke Rd. SE8 5A 104
Crookham Rd. SW6 1H 117
Crook Log DA6: Bex 3D 126
Crook Log Leisure Cen. 3D 126
Crookston Rd. SE9 3E 124
Croombs Rd. E16 5A 88
Croom's Hill SE10 7E 104
Croom's Hill Gro. SE10 7E 104
Cropley Ct. N1 2D 84
(off Cropley St.)
Cropley St. N1 1E 8 (2D 84)
Croppath Rd. RM10: Dag 4G 73
Cropthorne Ct. W9 3A 82
Crosbie Ho. E17 3E 50
(off Prospect Hill)
Crosby Cl. TW13: Hanw 3C 130
Crosby Ct. SE1 6E 14 (2D 102)
Crosby Gdns. UB8: Uxb 7A 56
Crosby Ho. BR1: Broml 2J 159
(off Elmfield Rd.)
E7 6J 69
E14 3E 104
(off Manchester Rd.)
Crosby Rd. E7 6J 69
RM10: Dag 2H 91
Crosby Row SE1 7E 14 (2D 102)
Crosby Sq. EC3 1G 15 (6E 84)
Crosby Wlk. E8 6F 67
SW2 7A 120
Crosby Way SW2 7A 120
Crosier Cl. SE3 1C 124
Crosier Rd. UB10: Ick 4E 56
Crosier Way HA4: Ruis 3G 57
Crosland Pl. SW11 3E 118
Cross Av. SE10 6F 105
Crossbones Graveyard 5D 14
(off Redcross Way)
Crossbow Ho. N1 1E 84
(off Whitmore Est.)
W13 1B 96
(off Sherwood Cl.)
Crossbrook Rd. SE3 2C 124
Cross Cl. SE15 2H 121
Cross Ct. SE28 7B 90
(off Titmuss Av.)
Cross Deep TW1: Twick 2K 131
Cross Deep Gdns. TW1: Twick 2K 131
Crossfield Ct. W10 6F 81
(off Cambridge Gdns.)
Crossfield Ho. W11 7G 81
(off Mary Pl.)
Crossfield Rd. N17 3C 48
NW3 6B 64
Crossfield St. SE8 7C 104
(not continuous)
Crossford St. SW9 2K 119
Cross Ga. HA8: Edg 3B 28
Crossgate UB6: G'frd 6B 60
Crossharbour Plaza E14 3D 104
Cross Keys Cl. N9 2B 34
W1 6H 5 (5E 82)
Cross Keys Sq. EC1 6C 8
(off Little Britain)
Cross Lances Rd. TW3: Houn 4F 113
Crossland Rd. CR7: Thor H 6B 156
Crosslands Av. UB2: S'hall 5D 94
W5 1F 97
Crosslands Pde. UB2: S'hall 5E 94
Crosslands Rd. KT19: Ewe 6K 163
Cross La. DA5: Bexl 6F 127
EC3 3G 15 (7E 84)
(not continuous)
N8 3K 47
(not continuous)
Crossleigh Ct. SE14 7B 104
(off New Cross Rd.)
Crosslet St. SE17 4D 102
Crosslet Va. SE10 1D 122
Crossley St. N7 6A 66
Crossmead SE9 1D 142
Crossmead Av. UB6: G'frd 3E 76
Crossmount Ho. SE5 7C 102
(off Bowyer St.)
Crossness Footpath DA18: Erith 1F 109
Crossness La. SE2 7E 90
Crossness Nature Reserve 1G 109
The Crossness Pumping Station 6F 91
Crossness Rd. IG11: Bark 3K 89
Crosspoint Ho. SE8 7C 104
(off Watson's St.)
Crossrail Pl. E14 1D 104
Crossrail Wlk. E14 1D 104
Cross Rd. BR2: Broml 2C 172
CR0: C'don 1D 168
DA14: Sidc 4B 144
E4 1A 36
EN1: Enf 4K 23
HA1: Harr 4H 41
HA2: Harr 3F 59
HA3: W'stone 2A 42
IG8: Wfd G 6J 37
KT2: King T 7F 133
N11 5A 32
N22 7F 33
RM6: Chad H 7C 54
RM7: Mawney 4G 55
SE5 2E 120
SM1: Sutt 5B 166
SW19 7J 135
TW13: Hanw 4C 130
Cross St. N1 1B 84
N18 5B 34
SE5 3D 120
SW13 2A 116
TW12: Hamp H 5G 131
Crossthwaite Av. SE5 4D 120
Crosstrees Ho. E14 3C 104
(off Cassilis Rd.)
Crosswall EC3 2J 15 (7F 85)
Cross Way NW10 7C 62
Crossway BR5: Pet W 4H 161
EN1: Enf 7K 23
HA4: Ruis 4A 58
HA5: Pinn 2K 39
IG8: Wfd G 4F 37
N12 6G 31
N16 5E 66
NW9 4B 44
RM8: Dag 3C 72
SE28 6B 90
SW20 4E 152
UB3: Hayes 1J 93
W13 4A 78
The Cross Way HA3: W'stone 2J 41
The Crossway N22 7G 33
SE9 2B 142
UB10: Hil 2B 74
Crossway Ct. SE4 2A 122
Crossway Pde. N22 7G 33
(off The Crossway)
Crossways CR2: Sels 7A 170
N21 6H 23
SM2: Sutt 7B 166
TW16: Sun 7H 129
The Crossways HA9: Wemb 2G 61
KT5: Surb 1H 163
TW5: Hest 7D 94
Crossways Rd. BR3: Beck 4C 158
CR4: Mitc 3F 155
Crossways Ter. E5 4J 67
Crosswell Cl. TW17: Shep 2E 146
Croston St. E8 1G 85
Crothall Cl. N13 3E 32
Crouch Av. IG11: Bark 2B 90
Crouch Cl. BR3: Beck 6C 140
Crouch Cft. SE9 3E 142
CROUCH END 7H 47
Crouch End Hill N8 7H 47
Crouch Hall Ct. N19 1J 65
Crouch Hall Rd. N8 6H 47
Crouch Hill N4 6J 47
N8 6J 47
Crouchman's Cl. SE26 3F 139
Crouch Rd. NW10 7K 61
Crowborough Rd. SW17 6E 136
Crowden Way SE28 7C 90
Crowder Cl. N12 1A 46
Crowder St. E1 7H 85
Crowfield Ho. N5 4C 66
Crowfoot Cl. E9 5B 68
SE28 1J 107
Crowhurst Cl. SW9 2A 120
Crowhurst Ho. SW9 2K 119
(off Aytoun Rd.)
Crowland Av. UB3: Harl 4G 93
Crowland Gdns. N14 7D 22
Crowland Ho. NW8 1A 82
(off Springfield Rd.)
Crowland Rd. CR7: Thor H 4D 156
N15 5F 49
CROWLANDS 7H 55
Crowlands Av. RM7: Rom 6H 55
Crowlands Heath Golf Course 1H 73
Crowland Ter. N1 7D 66
Crowland Wlk. SM4: Mord 6K 153
Crow La. RM7: Rush G 7F 55
Crowley Cres. CR0: Wadd 5A 168
Crowley M. SW16 3G 155
Crowline Wlk. N1 6C 66
Crowmarsh Gdns. SE23 7J 121
Crown All. SE9 6D 124
(off Court Yd.)
Crown Apts. HA4: Ruis 1J 57
Crown Arc. KT1: King T 2D 150
Crownbourne Ct. SM1: Sutt 4K 165
(off St Nicholas Way)
Crown Bldgs. E4 1K 35
Crown Cl. E3 1C 86
IG9: Buck H 1E 36
KT12: Walt T 7A 148
N22 1A 48
NW6 6K 63
NW7 2G 29
UB3: Hayes 2H 93
Crown Cl. Bus. Cen. E3 1C 86
(off Crown Cl.)
Crown Cotts. RM5: Col R 1G 55
Crown Court
Blackfriars 6B 14 (2B 102)
Croydon 2D 168
Harrow 3H 41
Inner London 7C 14 (3C 102)
Isleworth 1J 113
Kingston upon Thames 3D 150
Snaresbrook 5H 51
Southwark 4G 15 (1E 102)
Wood Green 1A 48
Woolwich 2J 107
Crown Ct. EC2 1D 14
N10 7K 31
NW8 2D 4
(off Park Rd.)
Crown Ct. SE12 6K 123
WC2 1F 13 (6J 83)
Crown Dale SE19 6B 138
(not continuous)
Crowndale Ct. NW1 2H 83
(off Crowndale Rd.)
Crowndale Pl. E17 2E 50
Crowndale Rd. NW1 2G 83
Crown Dr. RM7: Rush G 6K 55
Crownfield Av. IG2: Ilf 6J 53
Crownfield Rd. E15 4F 69
Crowngate Ho. E3 2B 86
(off Hereford Rd.)
Crown Grn. M. HA9: Wemb 2E 60
Crown Hill CR0: C'don 2C 168
Crownhill Rd. IG8: Wfd G 7H 37
NW10 1B 80
Crown Ho. KT3: N Mald 3J 151
NW10 2G 79
Crown La. BR2: Broml 5B 160
BR7: Chst 1G 161
N14 1B 32
SM4: Mord 4J 153
SW16 5A 138
Crown La. Gdns. SW16 5A 138
Crown La. Spur BR2: Broml 6B 160
Crown Lodge SW3 4D 16
Crown Mdw. Ct. BR2: Broml 6C 160
Crownmead Way RM7: Mawney 4H 55
Crown M. E1 5K 85
(off White Horse La.)
E13 1A 88
TW13: Felt 1K 129
W6 4C 98
Crown Mill CR4: Mitc 5C 154
Crown Office Row EC4 2J 13 (7A 84)
Crown Pde. N14 1B 32
SM4: Mord 3J 153
Crown Pas. KT1: King T 2D 150
(off Church St.)
SW1 5B 12 (1G 101)
Crown Pl. EC2 5G 9 (5E 84)
NW5 6F 65
SE16 5H 103
Crown Point SE19 6B 138
Crown Point Pde. SE19 6B 138
(off Crown Dale)
Crown Reach SW1 6D 18 (5H 101)
Crown Rd. EN1: Enf 3B 24
HA4: Ruis 5B 58
(not continuous)
IG6: Ilf 6G 53
KT3: N Mald 1J 151
N10 7K 31
SM1: Sutt 4K 165
SM4: Mord 4K 153
TW1: Twick 6B 114
Crown Sq. SE1 5H 15
Crownstone Ct. SW2 5A 120
Crownstone Rd. SW2 5A 120
Crown St. HA2: Harr 1H 59
RM10: Dag 6J 73
(not continuous)
SE5 7C 102
W3 1H 97
Crown Ter. N14 1C 32
(off Crown La.)
TW9: Rich 4F 115
Crown Trad. Cen. UB3: Hayes 2G 93
Crowntree Cl. TW7: Isle 6K 95
Crown Wlk. HA9: Wemb 3F 61
Crown Way UB7: Yiew 1B 92
Crown Wharf E14 1E 104
(off Coldharbour)
SE8 5B 104
(off Grove St.)
Crown Woods La. SE18 2F 125
Crown Woods Way SE9 5H 125
Crown Yd. E2 2H 85
SW6 2J 117
TW3: Houn 3G 113
Crowshott Av. HA7: Stan 2C 42
Crows Rd. E3 3F 87
IG11: Bark 6F 71
Crowther Av. TW8: Bford 4E 96
Crowther Cl. SW6 6H 99
(off Bucklers All.)
Crowther Rd. SE25 5G 157
Crowthorne Cl. SW18 7H 117
Crowthorne Rd. W10 6F 81
Croxall Ho. KT12: Walt T 6A 148
Croxden Cl. HA8: Edg 3G 43
Croxden Wlk. SM4: Mord 6A 154
Croxford Gdns. N22 7G 33
Croxford Way RM7: Rush G 1K 73
Croxley Grn. BR5: St P 7B 144
Croxley Rd. W9 3H 81
Croxted Cl. SE21 7C 120
Croxted M. SE24 6C 120
Croxted Rd. SE21 7C 120
SE24 7C 120
Croxteth Ho. SW8 2H 119
Croyde Av. UB3: Harl 4G 93
UB6: G'frd 3G 77
Croyde Cl. DA15: Sidc 7H 125
CROYDON 2C 168
Croydon N17 2D 48
(off Gloucester Rd.)
Croydon Airport Ind. Est.
CR0: Wadd 6K 167
Croydon Airport Vis. Cen. 6A 168
Croydon Clocktower 3C 168
(off Katharine St.)
Croydon Crematorium 5K 155
The Croydon Flyover CR0: C'don 4B 168
Croydon Gro. CR0: C'don 1B 168
Croydon Ho. SE1 6K 13
(off Wootton St.)
Croydon Rd. BR2: Hayes, Kes 3G 171
BR3: Beck 4K 157
BR4: Hayes, W W'ck 3G 171
CR0: Bedd, Wadd 4F 167
CR0: C'don 4E 154
CR4: Mitc 4E 154
E13 4H 87
SE20 2H 157
SM6: Bedd, W'gton 4F 167
TW6: H'row A 2D 110
Croydon Rd. Ind. Est.
BR3: Beck 4K 157
Croydon Sailing Club 2F 157
Croydon Sports Arena 5J 157
Croydon Valley Trade Pk.
CR0: Bedd 7J 155
(off Therapia La.)
Croyland Rd. N9 1B 34
Croylands Dr. KT6: Surb 7E 150
Croysdale Av. TW16: Sun 3J 147
Crozier Ho. SW8 7K 101
(off Wilkinson St.)
Crozier Ter. E9 5K 67
(not continuous)
Crucible Cl. RM6: Chad H 6B 54
Crucifix La. SE1 6H 15 (2E 102)
Cruden Ho. E3 2B 86
(off Vernon Rd.)
SE17 6B 102
(off Brandon Est.)
Cruden St. N1 1B 84
Cruikshank Ho. NW8 2C 82
(off Townshend Rd.)
Cruikshank Rd. E15 4G 69
Cruikshank St. WC1 1J 7 (3A 84)
Crummock Gdns. NW9 5A 44
Crumpsall St. SE2 4C 108
Crundale Av. NW9 5G 43
Crunden Rd. CR2: S Croy 7D 168
Crusader Gdns. CR0: C'don 3E 168
Crusader Ind. Est. N4 6C 48
Crusoe M. N16 2D 66
Crusoe Rd. CR4: Mitc 7D 136
DA8: Erith 5K 109
Crutched Friars EC3 2H 15 (7E 84)
Crutchley Rd. SE6 2G 141
The Crypt 1D 120
The Crystal 7J 87
Crystal Ct. E8 1H 85
N14 5B 22
SE19 5F 139
(off College Rd.)
Crystal Ho. SE18 5K 107
CRYSTAL PALACE 6F 139
Crystal Palace Athletics Stadium
6G 139
Crystal Pal. Caravan Club Site 5G 139
Crystal Palace Dinosaurs 6G 139
Crystal Palace FC 4E 156
Crystal Palace Indoor Bowling Club
1H 157
Crystal Palace Mus. 6F 139
Crystal Palace National Sports Cen.
5G 139
Crystal Palace Pde. SE19 6F 139
Crystal Palace Pk. 5G 139
Crystal Palace Pk. Farm 6G 139
Crystal Palace Pk. Rd. SE26 5G 139
Crystal Palace Rd. SE22 6F 121
Crystal Palace Sta. Rd. SE19 6G 139
Crystal Pl. KT4: Wor Pk 2D 164
Crystal Ter. SE19 6D 138
Crystal Vw. Ct. BR1: Broml 4F 141
Crystal Way HA1: Harr 5K 41
RM8: Dag 1C 72
Crystal Wharf N1 2B 84
Cuba Dr. EN3: Enf H 2D 24
Cuba St. E14 2C 104
The Cube
North East London Gymnastic Club
4D 66
Cube Ho. SE16 3F 103
Cubitt Apts. SW11 3A 118
(off Chatfield Rd.)
Cubitt Bldg. SW1 7J 17 (5F 101)
Cubitt Ct. NW1 1A 6
(off Park Village E.)
Cubitt Ho. SW4 6G 119
Cubitt Sq. UB2: S'hall 1G 95
Cubitt Steps E14 1C 104
Cubitt St. WC1 2H 7 (3K 83)
Cubitt Ter. SW4 3G 119
CUBITT TOWN 4E 104
Cuckoo Av. W7 4J 77
Cuckoo Dene W7 5H 77
Cuckoo Hall La. N9 7D 24
Cuckoo Hall Rd. N9 7D 24
Cuckoo Hill HA5: Eastc, Pinn 3A 40
Cuckoo Hill Dr. HA5: Pinn 3A 40
Cuckoo Hill Rd. HA5: Pinn 4A 40
Cuckoo La. W7 7J 77
Cuckoo Pound TW17: Shep 5G 147
Cudas Cl. KT19: Ewe 4B 164
Cuddington Av. KT4: Wor Pk 3B 164
Cudham La. Nth. BR6: Downe 7J 173
Cudham St. SE6 7E 122
Cudweed Court E14 3D 104
(off Watergate Walk)
Cudworth Ho. SW8 1G 119
Cudworth St. E1 4H 85
Cuff Cres. SE9 6B 124
Cuffley Ho. W10 5E 80
(off Sutton Way)
Cuff Point E2 1J 9
(off Columbia Rd.)
Culand Ho. SE17 4E 102
(off Congreve St.)
Culford Gdns. SW3 4F 17 (4D 100)
Culford Gro. N1 6E 66
Culford Mans. SW3 4F 17
(off Culford Gdns.)
Culford M. N1 6E 66
Culford Rd. N1 7E 66
Culford Ter. N1 6E 66
(off Balls Pond Rd.)
Culgaith Gdns. EN2: Enf 4D 22
Culham Ho. E2 2J 9
(off Palissy St.)
W2 5J 81
(off Gt. Western Rd.)
Cullen Way NW10 4J 79
Culling Rd. DA17: Belv 3J 109
SE16 3J 103
Cullington Cl. HA3: W'stone 4A 42
Cullingworth Rd. NW10 5C 62
Culloden Cl. SE7 6K 105
SE16 5G 103
Culloden Ho. SE14 7A 104
(off Batavia Rd.)
Culloden Rd. EN2: Enf 2G 23
Cullum St. EC3 2G 15 (7E 84)
Cullum Welch Ct. N1 1F 9
(off Haberdasher St.)
Cullum Welch Ho. EC1 4C 8
(off Golden La. Est.)
Culmington Pde. W13 1C 96
(off Uxbridge Rd.)
Culmington Rd. CR2: S Croy 7C 168
W13 1C 96
Culmore Rd. SE15 7H 103
Culmstock Rd. SW11 5E 118
Culpepper Cl. N18 5C 34
Culpepper Ct. SE11 3J 19
Culross Cl. N15 4C 48

208 A-Z Big London

Culross Ho.—Daplyn St.

Culross Ho. W10 6F 81
(off Bridge Cl.)
Culross St. W1 3G 11 (7E 82)
Culsac Rd. KT6: Surb 2E 162
Culverden Rd. SW12 2G 137
Culver Gro. HA7: Stan 2C 42
Culverhouse WC1 6G 7
(off Red Lion Sq.)
Culverhouse Gdns. SW16 3K 137
Culverlands Cl. HA7: Stan 4G 27
Culverley Rd. SE6 1D 140
Culvers Av. SM5: Cars 2D 166
Culvers Retreat SM5: Cars 1D 166
Culverstone Cl. BR2: Broml 6H 159
Culvers Way SM5: Cars 2D 166
Culvert Dr. E3 3E 86
Culvert Pl. SW11 2E 118
Culvert Rd. N15 5E 48
(not continuous)
SW11 2D 118
Culworth Ho. NW8 2C 82
(off Allitsen Rd.)
Culworth St. NW8 2C 82
Culzean Cl. SE27 3B 138
Cumberland Av. DA16: Well 3J 125
NW10 3H 79
Cumberland Basin 1E 82
Cumberland Basin NW1 1E 82
Cumberland Bus. Pk. NW10 3H 79
Cumberland Cl. E8 6F 67
IG6: Ilf 1G 53
SW20 7F 135
TW1: Twick 6B 114
Cumberland Ct. CR0: C'don 1D 168
DA16: Well 2J 125
HA1: Harr 3J 41
(off Princes Dr.)
SW1 5K 17
(off Cumberland St.)
W1 1F 11
(off Gt. Cumberland Pl.)
Cumberland Cres. W14 4G 99
(not continuous)
Cumberland Dr. DA7: Bex 7E 108
KT9: Chess 3E 162
KT10: Hin W 2A 162
Cumberland Gdns. NW4 2G 45
WC1 1J 7 (3A 84)
Cumberland Ga. W1 2E 10 (7D 82)
Cumberland Ho. E16 1J 105
(off Wesley Av.)
KT2: King T 7H 133
N9 1D 34
(off Cumberland Rd.)
SE28 2G 107
W8 2K 99
(off Kensington Ct.)
Cumberland Mans. W1 7E 4
Cumberland Mkt. NW1 1K 5 (3F 83)
Cumberland M. SE11 6K 19 (5A 102)
Cumberland Mills Sq. E14 5F 105
Cumberland Pk. NW10 3C 80
W3 7J 79
Cumberland Pl. NW1 1J 5 (3F 83)
SE6 1H 141
TW16: Sun 4J 147
Cumberland Rd. BR2: Broml 4G 159
E12 4B 70
E13 5K 87
E17 2A 50
HA1: Harr 5F 41
HA7: Stan 3J 43
N9 1D 34
N22 2K 47
SE25 6H 157
SW13 1B 116
TW9: Kew 7G 97
TW15: Ashf 3A 128
W3 7J 79
W7 2K 95
Cumberland St. SW1 5K 17 (5F 101)
Cumberland Ter. NW1 1J 5 (2F 83)
Cumberland Ter. M. NW1 1J 5
(not continuous)
Cumberland Vs. W3 7J 79
(off Cumberland Rd.)
Cumberland Wharf SE16 2J 103
(off Rotherhithe St.)
Cumberlow Av. SE25 3F 157
Cumbernauld Gdns.
TW16: Sun 5H 129
Cumberton Rd. N17 1D 48
Cumbrae Gdns. KT6: Surb 2D 162
Cumbrian Gdns. NW2 2F 63
Cumbrian Way UB8: Uxb 7A 56
Cumming St. N1 1H 7 (2K 83)
Cumnor Cl. SW9 2K 119
(off Robsart St.)
Cumnor Gdns. KT17: Ewe 6C 164
Cumnor Rd. SM2: Sutt 6A 166
Cunard Ct. HA7: Stan 2F 27
(off Brightwen Gro.)
Cunard Cres. N21 6J 23
Cunard Pl. EC3 1H 15 (6E 84)
Cunard Rd. NW10 3K 79
Cunard Wlk. SE16 4K 103
Cundy Rd. E16 6A 88
Cundy St. SW1 4H 17 (4E 100)
Cuneo Mews NW7 5B 30
Cunliffe Pde. KT19: Ewe 4B 164
Cunliffe Rd. KT19: Ewe 4B 164
Cunliffe St. SW16 6G 137
Cunningham Av. E16 2K 105
Cunningham Cl. BR4: W W'ck 2D 170
RM6: Chad H 5C 54
Cunningham Ct. E10 3D 68
(off Oliver Rd.)
W9 4A 4
(off Maida Vale)
Cunningham Dr. UB10: Ick 2E 56
Cunningham Ho. SE5 7D 102
(off Elmington Est.)
Cunningham Pk. HA1: Harr 5G 41
Cunningham Pl. NW8 3A 4 (4B 82)
Cunningham Rd. N15 4G 49
Cunnington St. W4 3J 97
Cupar Rd. SW11 1E 118
Cupola Cl. BR1: Broml 5K 141
Cureton St. SW1 4D 18 (4H 101)
Curfew Ho. IG11: Bark 1G 89
The Curfew Tower 1G 89
Curie Ct. HA1: Harr 7B 42
Curie Gdns. NW9 2A 44
Curlew Cl. SE28 7D 90
Curlew Ct. KT6: Surb 3G 163
W13 4K 77
Curlew Ho. EN3: Pond E 5E 24
SE4 4A 122
(off St Norbert Rd.)
SE15 1F 121
Curlew St. SE1 6K 15 (2F 103)
SE18 1C 124
(off Tellson Av.)
Curlew Way UB4: Yead 5B 76
Curness St. SE13 4E 122
Curnick's La. SE27 4C 138
Curran Av. DA15: Sidc 5K 125
SM6: W'gton 3E 166
Curran Ho. SW3 4C 16
(off Lucan Pl.)
Currey Rd. UB6: G'frd 6H 59
Curricle St. W3 1A 98
Currie Hill Cl. SW19 4H 135
Curry Ri. NW7 6A 30
Cursitor St. EC4 7J 7 (6A 84)
Curtain Pl. EC2 3H 9 (3E 84)
Curtain Rd. EC2 2H 9 (4E 84)
Curthwaite Gdns. EN2: Enf 4C 22
Curtis & Staub Health Club
Golders Green 7H 45
Curtis Dr. W3 6K 79
Curtis Fld. Rd. SW16 4K 137
Curtis Ho. SE17 5D 102
(off Morecambe St.)
Curtis La. HA0: Wemb 6E 60
Curtis Rd. KT19: Ewe 4J 163
TW4: Houn 7D 112
Curtiss Ho. NW9 3B 44
Curtis St. SE1 4F 103
Curtis Way SE1 4F 103
SE28 7B 90
Curtlington Ho. HA8: Edg 2J 43
(off Burnt Oak B'way.)
The Curve W12 7C 80
Curwen Av. E7 4K 69
Curwen Rd. W12 2C 98
Curzon Av. EN3: Pond E 5E 24
HA7: Stan 1A 42
Curzon Cinema
Bloomsbury 4F 7 (4J 83)
Mayfair 5J 11
(off Curzon St.)
Richmond 5D 114
Soho 2D 12
(off Shaftesbury Av.)
Victoria 1B 18
(off Victoria St.)
Curzon Cl. BR6: Orp 4H 173
Curzon Ct. SW6 1A 118
(off Imperial Rd.)
Curzon Cres. IG11: Bark 2K 89
NW10 7A 62
Curzon Ga. W1 5H 11 (1E 100)
Curzon Pl. HA5: Eastc 5A 40
Curzon Rd. CR7: Thor H 6A 156
N10 2F 47
W5 4B 78
Curzon Sq. W1 5H 11 (1E 100)
Curzon St. W1 5H 11 (1E 100)
Cusack Cl. TW1: Tedd 4K 131
Custance Ho. N1 1E 8
(off Provost St.)
Custance St. N1 1E 8 (3D 84)
CUSTOM HOUSE 6A 88
Custom Ho. EC3 3G 15 (7E 84)
Custom Ho. Reach SE16 2B 104
Custom Ho. Wlk. EC3 3G 15 (7E 84)
The Cut SE1 6K 13 (2A 102)
Cutbush Ho. N7 5H 65
Cutcombe Rd. SE5 2C 120
Cuthberga Cl. IG11: Bark 7G 71
Cuthbert Bell Twr. E3 2C 86
(off Pancras Way)
Cuthbert Gdns. SE25 3E 156
Cuthbert Harrowing Ho. EC1 4C 8
(off Golden La. Est.)
Cuthbert Ho. W2 5A 4
(off Hall Pl.)
Cuthbert Rd. CR0: C'don 2B 168
E17 3E 50
N18 5B 34
Cuthbert St. W2 5A 4 (5B 82)
Cuthill Wlk. SE5 1D 120
Cutlers Gdns. EC2 6H 9 (5E 84)
Cutlers Gdns. Arc. EC2 7H 9
(off Devonshire Sq.)
Cutlers Sq. E14 4C 104
Cutlers Ter. N1 6E 66
(off Balls Pond Rd.)
Cutler St. E1 7H 9 (6E 84)
Cutter Ho. DA8: Erith 4K 109
E16 2K 105
(off Admiralty Av.)
Cutter La. SE10 2G 105
Cutthroat All. TW10: Ham 2C 132
Cutty Sark 6E 104
Cutty Sark Gdns. SE10 6E 104
(off King William Wlk.)
Cutty Sark Hall SE10 6E 104
(off Welland St.)
Cuxton BR5: Pet W 5G 161
Cuxton Cl. DA6: Bex 5E 126
Cuxton Ho. SE17 5E 102
(off Mina Rd.)
Cyan Apts. E3 1A 86
(off Gunmaker's La.)
Cyclamen Cl. TW12: Hamp 6E 130
Cyclamen Way KT19: Ewe 5J 163
Cyclops M. E14 4C 104
Cygnet Av. TW14: Felt 7A 112
Cygnet Cl. NW10 5K 61
Cygnet Ho. CR0: C'don 1D 168
SE15 6G 103
SW3 6D 16
(off King's Rd.)
Cygnet Ho. Nth. E14 6D 86
(off Chrisp St.)
Cygnet Ho. Sth. E14 6D 86
(off Chrisp St.)
The Cygnets TW13: Hanw 4C 130
Cygnet St. E1 3K 9 (4F 85)
Cygnet Way UB4: Yead 5B 76
Cygnus Bus. Cen. NW10 5B 62
Cymbeline Ct. HA1: Harr 6K 41
Cynthia St. N1 1H 7 (2K 83)
Cyntra Pl. E8 7H 67
Cypress Av. TW2: Whitt 7G 113
Cypress Cl. E5 2G 67
KT19: Eps 7K 163
Cypress Ct. NW9 4G 43
(off Alpine Rd.)
SM1: Sutt 5J 165
Cypress Gdns. SE4 5A 122
Cypress Ho. SE14 1K 121
SE16 2K 103
(off Woodland Cres.)
Cypress Pl. W1 4B 6 (4G 83)
Cypress Rd. HA3: Hrw W 2H 41
SE25 2E 156
Cypress Tree Cl. DA15: Sidc 1K 143
CYPRUS 7E 88
Cyprus Av. N3 2H 45
Cyprus Cl. N4 6B 48
Cyprus Gdns. N3 2G 45
Cyprus Pl. E2 2J 85
E6 7E 88
Cyprus Rd. N3 2H 45
N9 2A 34
Cyprus St. E2 2J 85
(not continuous)
Cyrena Rd. SE22 6F 121
Cyril Lodge DA14: Sidc 4A 144
Cyril Mans. SW11 1D 118
Cyril Rd. BR6: Orp 7K 161
DA7: Bex 2E 126
Cyrus Fld. St. SE10 4G 105
Cyrus Ho. EC1 3B 8
Cyrus St. EC1 3B 8
Cyrus Ter. UB10: Ick 3E 56
(off Pentland Way)
Czar St. SE8 6C 104

D

Dabbs Hill La. UB5: N'olt 6D 58
(not continuous)
Dabbs La. EC1 4K 7
(off Farringdon Rd.)
Dabin Cres. SE10 1E 122
Dacca St. SE8 6B 104
Dace Rd. E3 1C 86
Dacre Av. IG5: Ilf 2E 52
Dacre Cl. UB6: G'frd 2F 77
Dacre Gdns. SE13 4G 123
Dacre Ho. SW3 7B 16
Dacre Pk. SE13 3G 123
Dacre Pl. SE13 3G 123
Dacre Rd. CR0: C'don 7J 155
E11 1H 69
E13 1K 87
Dacres Est. SE23 3K 139
Dacres Ho. SW4 3F 119
Dacres Rd. SE23 2K 139
Dacre St. SW1 1C 18 (3H 101)
Dade Way UB2: S'hall 5D 94
Daerwood Cl.
BR2: Broml 1D 172
Daffodil Cl. CR0: C'don 1K 169
Daffodil Gdns. IG1: Ilf 5F 71
Daffodil Pl. TW12: Hamp 6E 130
Daffodil St. W12 7B 80
Dafforne Rd. SW17 3E 136
Da Gama Pl. E14 5C 104
DAGENHAM 6G 73
Dagenham & Redbridge FC 5H 73
Dagenham Av. RM9: Dag 1E 90
(not continuous)
Dagenham Pk. Leisure Cen. 7G 73
Dagenham Rd. E10 1B 68
RM7: Rush G 7K 55
RM10: Dag 4J 73
RM13: Rain 7K 73
Dagmar Av. HA9: Wemb 4F 61
Dagmar Ct. E14 3E 104
Dagmar Gdns. NW10 2F 81
Dagmar M. UB2: S'hall 3C 94
(off Dagmar Rd.)
Dagmar Pas. N1 1B 84
(off Cross St.)
Dagmar Rd. KT2: King T 1F 151
N4 7A 48
N15 4D 48
N22 1H 47
RM10: Dag 7J 73
SE5 1E 120
SE25 5E 156
UB2: S'hall 3C 94
Dagmar Ter. N1 1B 84
Dagnall Pk. SE25 6E 156
Dagnall Rd. SE25 5E 156
Dagnall St. SW11 2D 118
Dagnan Rd. SW12 7F 119
Dagobert Ho. E1 5J 85
(off Smithy St.)
Dagonet Gdns. BR1: Broml 3J 141
Dagonet Rd. BR1: Broml 3J 141
Dahlia Gdns. CR4: Mitc 4H 155
IG1: Ilf 6F 71
Dahlia Rd. SE2 4B 108
Dahomey Rd. SW16 6G 137
Daimler Ho. E3 4C 86
(off Wellington Way)
Daimler Way SM6: W'gton 7J 167
Dain Ct. W8 4J 99
(off Lexham Gdns.)
Daines Cl. E12 3D 70
Dainford Cl. BR1: Broml 5F 141
Dainton Cl. BR1: Broml 1K 159
Dainton Ho. W2 5J 81
(off Gt. Western Rd.)
Daintry Cl. HA3: W'stone 4A 42
Daintry Way E9 6B 68
Dairsie Ct. BR1: Broml 1A 160
Dairsie Rd. SE9 3E 124
Dairy Cl. BR1: Broml 7K 141
CR7: Thor H 2C 156
NW10 1C 80
SW6 1J 117
UB6: G'frd 2H 77
Dairy Farm Pl. SE15 1J 121
Dairy La. SE18 4D 106
Dairyman Cl. NW2 3F 63
Dairy M. N2 4C 46
RM6: Chad H 7D 54
SW9 3J 119
Dairy Wlk. SW19 4G 135
Daisy Cl. CR0: C'don 1K 169
NW9 2J 61
Daisy Dobbings Wlk. N19 7J 47
(off Jessie Blythe La.)
Daisy La. SW6 3J 117
Daisy Rd. E16 4G 87
E18 2K 51
Dakin Pl. E1 5A 86
Dakota Bldg. SE13 1D 122
(off Deal's Gateway)
Dakota Cl. SM6: W'gton 7K 167
Dakota Gdns. E6 4C 88
UB5: N'olt 3C 76
Dakota Ho. CR7: Thor H 6B 156
Dalberg Rd. SW2 4A 120
(not continuous)
Dalberg Way SE2 3D 108
Dalby Rd. SW18 4A 118
Dalbys Cres. N17 6K 33
Dalby St. NW5 6F 65
Dalcross Rd. TW4: Houn 2C 112
The Dale BR2: Kes 4B 172
Dale Av. HA8: Edg 1F 43
TW4: Houn 3C 112
Dalebury Pl. TW5: Hest 5E 94
Dalebury Rd. SW17 2D 136
Dale Cl. E4 3K 35
EN5: New Bar 6E 20
HA5: Pinn 1K 39
SE3 3J 123
Dale Ct. EN2: Enf 1H 23
KT2: King T 7F 133
(off York Rd.)
Dale Dr. UB4: Hayes 4H 75
Dalefield IG9: Buck H 1F 37
(off Roebuck La.)
Dale Gdns. IG8: Wfd G 4E 36
Dale Grn. Rd. N11 3A 32
Dale Gro. N12 5F 31
Daleham Dr. UB8: Hil 6D 74
Daleham Gdns. NW3 5B 64
Daleham M. NW3 6B 64
Dalehead NW1 1A 6
(off Hampstead Rd.)
Dale Ho. N1 1E 84
(off Halcomb St.)
NW8 1A 82
(off Boundary Rd.)
SE4 4A 122
Dale Lodge N6 6G 47
Dalemain M. E16 1J 105
Dale Pk. Av. SM5: Cars 2D 166
Dale Pk. Rd. SE19 1C 156
Dale Rd. KT12: Walt T 7H 147
NW5 5E 64
SE17 6B 102
SM1: Sutt 4H 165
TW16: Sun 7H 129
UB6: G'frd 5F 77
Dale Row W11 6G 81
Daleside Rd. KT19: Ewe 6K 163
SW16 5F 137
Dale St. W4 5A 98
Dale Vw. Av. E4 2K 35
Dale Vw. Cres. E4 2K 35
Dale Vw. Gdns. E4 3A 36
Daleview Rd. N15 6E 48
Dalewood Gdns. KT4: Wor Pk 2D 164
Dale Wood Rd. BR6: Orp 7J 161
Daleworth Cl. BR3: Beck 6C 140
Daley Ho. W12 6D 80
Daley St. E9 6K 67
Daley Thompson Way SW8 2F 119
Dalgarno Gdns. W10 5E 80
Dalgarno Way W10 4E 80
Dalgleish St. E14 6A 86
Daling Way E3 1A 86
Dalkeith Ct. SW1 3D 18
(off Vincent St.)
Dalkeith Gro. HA7: Stan 5J 27
Dalkeith Ho. SW9 1B 120
(off Lothian Rd.)
Dalkeith Rd. IG1: Ilf 3G 71
SE21 1C 138
Dallas Rd. NW4 7C 44
SE26 3H 139
SM3: Cheam 6G 165
W5 5F 79
Dallas Ter. UB3: Harl 3H 93
Dallega Cl. UB3: Hayes 7F 75
Dallinger Rd. SE12 6H 123
Dalling Rd. W6 4D 98
Dallington Sq. EC1 3B 8
(off Dallington St.)
Dallington St. EC1 3B 8 (4B 84)
Dallin Rd. DA6: Bex 4D 126
SE18 7F 107
Dalmain Rd. SE23 1K 139
Dalmally Rd. CR0: C'don 7F 157
Dalmany Pas. CR0: C'don 7F 157
Dalmeny Av. N7 4H 65
SW16 2A 156
Dalmeny Cl. HA0: Wemb 6C 60
Dalmeny Cres. TW3: Houn 4H 113
Dalmeny Rd. DA8: Erith 1H 127
EN5: New Bar 6F 21
KT4: Wor Pk 3D 164
N7 3H 65
(not continuous)
SM5: Cars 7E 166
Dalmeyer Rd. NW10 6B 62
Dalmore Rd. SE21 2C 138
Dalo Lodge E3 5C 86
(off Gale St.)
Dalrymple Cl. N14 7C 22
Dalrymple Rd. SE4 4A 122
DALSTON 6F 67
Dalston Gdns. HA7: Stan 1E 42
Dalston La. E8 6F 67
Dalston Sq. E8 6F 67
(not continuous)
Dalton Av. CR4: Mitc 2C 154
Dalton Cl. BR6: Orp 3J 173
UB4: Hayes 4F 75
Dalton Ho. E3 2A 86
(off Ford St.)
HA7: Stan 5F 27
SE14 6K 103
(off John Williams Cl.)
SW1 5J 17
(off Ebury Bri. Rd.)
Dalton Ho. Apts. IG11: Bark 4A 90
Dalton Rd. HA3: W'stone 2H 41
Dalton St. SE27 3B 138
Dalwood St. SE5 1E 120
Daly Dr. BR1: Broml 3E 160
Dalyell Rd. SW9 3K 119
Damascene Wlk. SE21 1C 138
Damask Ct. SM1: Sutt 1K 165
Damask Cres. E16 4G 87
Damer Ter. SW10 7A 100
Dames Rd. E7 3J 69
Dame St. N1 2C 84
Damien Ct. E1 6H 85
(off Damien St.)
Damien St. E1 6H 85
Damon Cl. DA14: Sidc 3B 144
Damory Ho. SE16 4H 103
(off Abbeyfield Est.)
Damsel Ho. SE4 3A 122
(off Dragonfly Pl.)
Damsel Wlk. NW9 6C 44
(off Perryfield Way)
Damson Dr. UB3: Hayes 7J 75
Damson Way SM5: Cars 7D 166
Damsonwood Rd. UB2: S'hall 3E 94
Danbrook Rd. SW16 1J 155
Danbury Cl. RM6: Chad H 3D 54
Danbury Mans. IG11: Bark 7F 71
(off Whiting Av.)
Danbury M. SM6: W'gton 4F 167
Danbury St. N1 2B 84
Danbury Way IG8: Wfd G 6F 37
Danby Ct. EN2: Enf 3H 23
Danby Ho. E9 7J 67
(off Frampton Pk. Rd.)
W10 3G 81
(off Bruckner St.)
Danby St. SE15 3F 121
Dance Ho. SE4 5K 121
(off St Norbert Rd.)
Dancer Rd. SW6 1H 117
TW9: Rich 3G 115
Dancers Way SE8 6D 104
Dance Sq. EC1 2C 8 (3C 84)
Dan Ct. NW10 3G 79
Dandelion Court E14 3D 104
(off Watergate Walk)
Dandridge Cl. SE10 5H 105
Dandridge Ho. E1 5J 9
(off Lamb St.)
Danebury CR0: New Ad 6E 170
Danebury Av. SW15 6A 116
Daneby Rd. SE6 3D 140
Dane Cl. BR6: Farnb 5H 173
DA5: Bexl 7G 127
Danecourt Gdns. CR0: C'don 3F 169
Danecroft Rd. SE24 5C 120
Danehill Wlk. DA14: Sidc 3A 144
Danehurst TW8: Bford 7C 96
Danehurst Gdns. IG4: Ilf 5C 52
Danehurst St. SW6 1G 117
Daneland EN4: E Barn 6J 21
Daneland Wlk. N17 3H 49
Danemead Gro. UB5: N'olt 5F 59
Danemere St. SW15 3E 116
Dane Pl. E3 2A 86
Dane Rd. IG1: Ilf 5G 71
N18 3D 34
SW19 1A 154
TW15: Ashf 6E 128
UB1: S'hall 7C 76
W13 1C 96
Danesbury Rd. TW13: Felt 1K 129
Danescombe SE12 1J 141
Danes Ct. HA9: Wemb 3H 61
NW8 1D 82
(off St Edmund's Ter.)
Danescourt Cres. SM1: Sutt 2A 166
Danescroft NW4 5F 45
Danescroft Av. NW4 5F 45
Danescroft Gdns. NW4 5F 45
Danesdale Rd. E9 6A 68
Danesfield SE5 6E 102
(off Albany Rd.)
Danes Ga. HA1: Harr 3J 41
Danes Ho. W10 5E 80
(off Sutton Way)
Danes Rd. RM7: Rush G 7J 55
Dane St. WC1 6G 7 (5K 83)
Daneswood Av. SE6 3E 140
Dane's Yd. E15 2E 86
Danethorpe Rd. HA0: Wemb 6D 60
Danetree Cl. KT19: Ewe 7J 163
Danetree Rd. KT19: Ewe 7J 163
Danette Gdns. RM10: Dag 2G 73
Daneville Rd. SE5 1D 120
Danewood Dr. N2 7B 46
Dangan Rd. E11 6J 51
Daniel Bolt Cl. E14 5D 86
Daniel Cl. N18 4D 34
SW17 6C 136
TW4: Houn 7D 112
Daniel Ct. BR3: Beck 7C 140
(off Brackley Rd.)
NW9 1A 44
Daniel Gdns. SE15 7F 103
Daniell Ho. N1 2D 84
(off Cranston Est.)
Daniell Way CR0: Wadd 1J 167
Daniel Pl. NW4 7D 44
Daniel Rd. W5 7F 79
Daniels Rd. SE15 3J 121
Danleigh Ct. N14 7C 22
Dan Leno Wlk. SW6 7K 99
Dan Mason Dr. W4 2J 115
Dannatt Cl. N20 2G 31
DANNY FISZMAN BRI. 4A 66
Dansey Pl. W1 2C 12
Dansington Rd. DA16: Well 4A 126
Danson Cres. DA16: Well 3B 126
Danson House 4C 126
DANSON INTERCHANGE 5C 126
Danson La. DA16: Well 4B 126
Danson Mead DA16: Well 3C 126
Danson Pk. 5C 126
Danson Pk. Watersports Cen. 4C 126
Danson Rd. DA5: Bexl, Bex 6C 126
DA6: Bex 5D 126
SE17 5B 102
Danson Underpass DA15: Sidc 6C 126
Dante Pl. SE11 4B 102
Dante Rd. SE11 4B 102
Danube Apts. N8 3K 47
(off Gt. Amwell La.)
Danube Cl. N9 3D 34
Danube Ct. SE15 7F 103
(off Daniel Gdns.)
Danube St. SW3 5D 16 (5C 100)
Danvers Av. SW11 4C 118
Danvers Ho. E1 6G 85
(off Christian St.)
Danvers Rd. N8 4H 47
Danvers St. SW3 7B 16 (6B 100)
Dao Ct. E13 1K 87
Da Palma Ct. SW6 6J 99
(off Anselm Rd.)
Daphne Ct. KT4: Wor Pk 2A 164
Daphne Gdns. E4 3K 35
Daphne Ho. N22 1A 48
(off Acacia Rd.)
Daphne St. SW18 6A 118
Daplyn St. E1 5K 9 (5G 85)

Dara Ho.—The Den

Dara Ho. NW9 ... 3K 43
Darbishire Pl. E1 ... 2K 15
D'Arblay St. W1 ... 1B 12 (6G 83)
Darby Cres. TW16: Sun ... 2A 148
Darby Gdns. TW16: Sun ... 2A 148
Darcies M. N8 ... 6J 47
Darcy Av. SM6: W'gton ... 4G 167
Darcy Cl. N20 ... 2G 31
D'Arcy Dr. HA3: Kenton ... 4D 42
D'Arcy Gdns. HA3: Kenton ... 4D 42
Darcy Gdns. RM9: Dag ... 1F 91
Darcy Ho. E8 ... 1H 85
(off London Flds. E. Side)
RM9: Dag ... 1G 91
D'Arcy Pl. BR2: Broml ... 4J 159
D'Arcy Rd. SM3: Cheam ... 4F 165
Darcy Rd. SW16 ... 2J 155
TW7: Isle ... 1A 114
Dare Gdns. RM8: Dag ... 3E 72
Darell Rd. TW9: Rich ... 3G 115
Darent Ho. BR1: Broml ... 5F 141
NW8 ... 5B 4
(off Church St. Est.)
Darenth Rd. DA16: Well ... 1A 126
N16 ... 7F 49
Darfield NW1 ... 1G 83
(off Bayham St.)
Darfield Rd. SE4 ... 5B 122
Darfield Way W10 ... 6F 81
Darfur St. SW15 ... 3F 117
Dargate Cl. SE19 ... 7F 139
Darien Rd. SW11 ... 3B 118
Daring Ho. E3 ... 2A 86
(off Roman Rd.)
Dark Ho. Wlk. EC3 ... 3F 15 (7D 84)
Darlands Dr. EN5: Barn ... 5A 20
Darlan Rd. SW6 ... 7H 99
Darlaston Rd. SW19 ... 7F 135
Darley Cl. CR0: C'don ... 6A 158
Darley Dr. KT3: N Mald ... 2K 151
Darley Gdns. SM4: Mord ... 6A 154
Darley Ho. SE11 ... 6G 19
Darley Rd. N9 ... 1A 34
SW11 ... 6D 118
Darling Ho. TW1: Twick ... 6D 114
Darling Rd. SE4 ... 3C 122
Darling Row E1 ... 4H 85
Darlington Ct. SE6 ... 1H 141
Darlington Ho. SW8 ... 7H 101
(off Hemans St.)
Darlington Rd. SE27 ... 5B 138
Darmaine Cl. CR2: S Croy ... 7C 168
Darnall Ho. SE10 ... 1E 122
(off Royal Hill)
Darnaway Pl. E14 ... 5E 86
(off Aberfeldy St.)
Darnay Apts. E15 ... 6F 69
Darndale Cl. E17 ... 2B 50
Darnley Cl. DA15: Sidc ... 5K 125
Darnley Ho. E14 ... 6A 86
(off Camdenhurst St.)
Darnley Rd. E9 ... 6J 67
IG8: Wfd G ... 1J 51
Darnley Ter. W11 ... 1F 99
Darrell Charles Ct. UB8: Uxb ... 7A 56
Darrell Rd. SE22 ... 5G 121
Darren Cl. N4 ... 7K 47
Darren Ct. N7 ... 4J 65
Darrick Wood Rd. BR6: Orp ... 2H 173
Darrick Wood Sports Cen. ... 3G 173
Darrick Wood Swimming Pool ... 3G 173
Darris Cl. UB4: Yead ... 4C 76
Darsley Dr. SW8 ... 1H 119
Dartford Av. N9 ... 6D 24
Dartford By-Pass DA5: Bexl ... 7K 127
Dartford Gdns. RM6: Chad H ... 5B 54
Dartford Ho. SE1 ... 4F 103
(off Longfield Est.)
Dartford Rd. DA5: Bexl ... 1J 145
Dartford St. SE17 ... 6C 102
Dartington NW1 ... 1G 83
(off Plender St.)
Dartington Ho. SW8 ... 2H 119
(off Union Gro.)
W2 ... 5K 81
(off Senior St.)
Dartle Ct. SE16 ... 2G 103
(off Scott Lidgett Cres.)
Dartmoor Wlk. E14 ... 4C 104
(off Severnake Cl.)
Dartmouth Cl. W11 ... 6H 81
Dartmouth Ct. SE10 ... 1E 122
Dartmouth Gro. SE10 ... 1E 122
Dartmouth Hill SE10 ... 1E 122
Dartmouth Ho. KT2: King T ... 1E 150
(off Seven Kings Way)
SE10 ... 1D 122
(off Catherine Gro.)
DARTMOUTH PARK ... 3F 65
Dartmouth Pk. Av. NW5 ... 3F 65
Dartmouth Pk. Hill N19 ... 1F 65
NW5 ... 1F 65
Dartmouth Pk. Rd. NW5 ... 4F 65
Dartmouth Pl. SE23 ... 2J 139
W4 ... 6A 98
Dartmouth Rd. BR2: Hayes ... 7J 159
HA4: Ruis ... 3J 57
NW2 ... 6F 63
NW4 ... 6C 44
SE23 ... 3H 139
SE26 ... 3H 139
Dartmouth Row SE10 ... 2E 122
Dartmouth St. SW1 ... 7D 12 (2H 101)
Dartmouth Ter. SE10 ... 1F 123
Dartnell Rd. CR0: C'don ... 7F 157
Darton Ct. W3 ... 1J 97
Dartrey Twr. SW10 ... 7A 100
(off Worlds End Est.)
Dartrey Wlk. SW10 ... 7A 100
Dart St. W10 ... 3G 81
Darvell Ho. SE17 ... 5D 102
(off Inville Rd.)
Darville Rd. N16 ... 3F 67
Darwell Cl. E6 ... 2E 88
Darwell M. E6 ... 2E 88
Darwen Pl. E2 ... 2H 85
Darwin Cl. BR6: Farnb ... 5H 173
N11 ... 3A 32
Darwin Ct. CR2: S Croy ... 5B 168
(off Warham Rd.)
E13 ... 3K 87
NW1 ... 1F 83
(not continuous)
SE17 ... 4D 102
(off Barlow St.)
Darwin Dr. UB1: S'hall ... 6F 77
Darwin Ho. SE20 ... 1G 157
SW1 ... 7A 18
Darwin Rd. DA16: Well ... 3K 125
N22 ... 1B 48
W5 ... 5C 96
Darwin St. SE17 ... 4D 102
(not continuous)
Darwood Ct. NW6 ... 7A 64
(off Belsize Rd.)
Daryngton Dr. UB6: G'frd ... 2H 77
Daryngton Ho. SE1 ... 7F 15
(off Hankey Pl.)
SW8 ... 7J 101
(off Hartington Rd.)
Dashwood Cl. DA6: Bex ... 5G 127
Dashwood Rd. N8 ... 6K 47
Dashwood Studios SE17 ... 4C 102
(off Walworth Rd.)
Dassett Rd. SE27 ... 5B 138
Data Point Bus. Cen. E16 ... 4F 87
Datchelor Pl. SE5 ... 1D 120
Datchet Ho. E2 ... 2J 9
(off Virginia Rd.)
NW1 ... 1K 5
(off Augustus St.)
Datchet Rd. SE6 ... 2B 140
Datchworth Ct. EN1: Enf ... 5K 23
Datchworth Ho. N1 ... 7B 66
(off The Sutton Est.)
Date St. SE17 ... 5D 102
Daubeney Gdns. N17 ... 7H 33
Daubeney Pl. TW12: Hamp ... 1G 149
(off High St.)
Daubeney Rd. E5 ... 4A 68
N17 ... 7H 33
Daubeney Twr. SE8 ... 5B 104
(off Bowditch)
Dault Rd. SW18 ... 6A 118
Dauncey Ho. SE1 ... 7A 14
Dave Adams Ho. E3 ... 2B 86
(off Norman Gro.)
Davema Cl. BR7: Chst ... 1E 160
Davenant Ho. E1 ... 5G 85
(off Old Montague St.)
Davenant Pl. SE26 ... 5H 139
Davenant Rd. CR0: C'don ... 4B 168
N19 ... 2H 65
Davenant St. E1 ... 5G 85
Davenport Cen. IG11: Bark ... 1B 90
Davenport Cl. TW11: Tedd ... 6A 132
Davenport Ct. CR0: C'don ... 7B 156
Davenport Ho. SE11 ... 3J 19
(off Walnut Tree Wlk.)
UB7: W Dray ... 2B 92
Davenport Lodge TW5: Hest ... 7C 94
Davenport Rd. DA14: Sidc ... 2E 144
SE6 ... 6D 122
Daventer Dr. HA7: Stan ... 7E 26
Daventry Av. E17 ... 6C 50
Daventry Cl. SL3: Poyle ... 4A 174
Daventry St. NW1 ... 5C 4 (5C 82)
Daver Ct. SW3 ... 5D 16 (5C 100)
W5 ... 4D 78
Davern Cl. SE10 ... 4H 105
Davey Cl. N7 ... 6K 65
N13 ... 5E 32
Davey Gdns. IG11: Bark ... 4A 90
Davey Rd. E9 ... 7C 68
Davey's Ct. WC2 ... 2E 12
Davey St. SE15 ... 6F 103
David Av. UB6: G'frd ... 3J 77
David Cl. UB3: Harl ... 7G 93
David Coffer Ct. DA17: Belv ... 4H 109
David Ct. E14 ... 5D 86
(off Hillary M.)
N20 ... 3F 31
Davidge Ho. SE1 ... 7K 13
(off Coral St.)
Davidge St. SE1 ... 7A 14 (2B 102)
David Hewitt Ho. E3 ... 5D 86
(off Watts Gro.)
David Ho. DA15: Sidc ... 3A 144
SW8 ... 7J 101
(off Wyvil Rd.)
David Lean Cinema ... 3D 168
(within Fairfield Halls)
David Lee Point E15 ... 1G 87
(off Leather Gdns.)
David Lloyd Leisure
Barnet ... 7G 31
Beckenham ... 4B 158
Cheam ... 7F 165
Chigwell ... 1J 37
Enfield ... 2B 24
Fulham ... 7J 99
(within Fulham Broadway Shop. Cen.)
Hampton ... 3E 130
Heston ... 5A 94
Kidbrooke ... 4K 123
Kingston upon Thames ... 2E 150
(within The Rotunda Cen.)
Purley ... 6K 167
Raynes Park ... 4F 153
Sidcup ... 5C 144
Sudbury Hill ... 5H 59
David M. SE10 ... 7E 104
W1 ... 5F 5 (5D 82)
David Rd. RM8: Dag ... 2E 72
SL3: Poyle ... 5A 174
Davidson Gdns. SW8 ... 7J 101
Davidson La. HA1: Harr ... 7K 41
Davidson Rd. CR0: C'don ... 1E 168
Davidson Terraces E7 ... 5K 69
(off Claremont Rd.)
David's Rd. SE23 ... 1J 139
David St. E15 ... 6F 69
David Twigg Cl.
KT2: King T ... 1E 150
David Weir Leisure Cen. ... 7B 154
David Wildman La. NW7 ... 6B 30
Davies Cl. CR0: C'don ... 6G 157
Davies La. E11 ... 2G 69
Davies M. W1 ... 2J 11 (7F 83)
Davies St. W1 ... 1J 11 (6F 83)
Davies Wlk. TW7: Isle ... 1H 113
Da Vinci Ct. SE16 ... 5H 103
(off Rossetti Rd.)
Da Vinci Lodge SE10 ... 3H 105
(off W. Parkside)
Da Vinci Torre SE13 ... 3D 122
(off Loampit Va.)
Davington Gdns. RM8: Dag ... 5B 72
Davington Rd. RM8: Dag ... 5B 72
Davinia Cl. IG8: Wfd G ... 6J 37
Davis Ho. W12 ... 7D 80
(off White City Est.)
Davis Rd. KT9: Chess ... 4G 163
W3 ... 1B 98
Davis Rd. Ind. Pk. KT9: Chess ... 4G 163
Davis St. E13 ... 2K 87
Davisville Rd. W12 ... 2C 98
Davis Way DA14: Sidc ... 6E 144
Davmor Ct. TW8: Bford ... 5C 96
Dawburn Pl. TW5: Hest ... 7B 94
Dawes Av. TW7: Isle ... 5A 114
Dawes Cl. UB10: Uxb ... 2A 74
Dawes Ho. SE17 ... 4D 102
(off Orb St.)
Dawe's Rd. UB10: Uxb ... 2A 74
Dawes Rd. SW6 ... 7G 99
Dawes St. SE17 ... 5D 102
Dawkins Ct. SE1 ... 3D 102
Dawley Av. UB8: Hil ... 5E 74
Dawley Pde. UB3: Hayes ... 7E 74
Dawley Pk. UB3: Hayes ... 2F 93
Dawley Rd. UB3: Harl, Hayes ... 7E 74
Dawlish Av. N13 ... 4D 32
SW18 ... 2K 135
UB6: G'frd ... 2A 78
Dawlish Dr. HA4: Ruis ... 2J 57
HA5: Pinn ... 5C 40
IG3: Ilf ... 4J 71
Dawlish Rd. E10 ... 1E 68
N17 ... 3G 49
NW2 ... 6F 63
Dawnay Gdns. SW18 ... 2B 136
Dawnay Rd. SW18 ... 2A 136
Dawn Cl. TW4: Houn ... 3C 112
Dawn Cres. E15 ... 1F 87
Dawpool Rd. NW2 ... 2B 62
Daws Hill E4 ... 2K 25
Daws La. NW7 ... 5G 29
Dawson Av. IG11: Bark ... 7K 71
Dawson Cl. SE18 ... 4G 107
UB3: Hayes ... 5F 75
Dawson Ct. W3 ... 3J 97
(off Palmerston Rd.)
Dawson Gdns. IG11: Bark ... 7K 71
Dawson Ho. E2 ... 3J 85
(off Sceptre Rd.)
Dawson Pl. W2 ... 7J 81
Dawson Rd. KT1: King T ... 3F 151
NW2 ... 5E 62
Dawson St. E2 ... 1K 9 (2F 85)
Dawson Ter. N9 ... 7D 24
Dax Ct. TW16: Sun ... 3A 148
Daybrook Rd. SW19 ... 2K 153
Day Dr. RM8: Dag ... 1D 72
Day Ho. SE5 ... 7C 102
(off Bethwin Rd.)
Daylesford Av. SW15 ... 4C 116
Daymer Gdns. HA5: Eastc ... 4K 39
Daynor Ho. NW6 ... 1J 81
(off Quex Ho.)
Daysbrook Rd. SW2 ... 1K 137
Days La. DA15: Sidc ... 7J 125
Dayton Gro. SE15 ... 1J 121
Deaconess Ct. N15 ... 4F 49
(off Tottenham Grn. E.)
The Deacon Est. E4 ... 6G 35
Deacon Ho. SE11 ... 4H 19
(off Black Prince Rd.)
Deacon M. N1 ... 7D 66
Deacon Rd. KT2: King T ... 1F 151
NW2 ... 5C 62
Deacons Cl. HA5: Pinn ... 2K 39
Deacons Ct. TW1: Twick ... 2K 131
Deacons Leas BR6: Orp ... 4H 173
Deacon's Ri. N2 ... 5B 46
Deacons Ter. N1 ... 6C 66
(off Harecourt Rd.)
Deacons Wlk. TW12: Hamp ... 4E 130
Deacon Way IG8: Wfd G ... 7J 37
Deal Ct. NW9 ... 2B 44
(off Hazel Cl.)
UB1: S'hall ... 6G 77
(off Haldane Rd.)
Deal Ho. SE15 ... 6K 103
(off Lovelinch La.)
SE17 ... 5E 102
(off Mina Rd.)
Deal M. W5 ... 4D 96
Deal Porters Wlk. SE16 ... 2K 103
Deal Porters Way SE16 ... 3J 103
Deal Rd. SW17 ... 6E 136
Deal's Gateway SE10 ... 1C 122
SE13 ... 1C 122
Deal St. E1 ... 5G 85
Dealtry Rd. SW15 ... 4E 116
Deal Wlk. SW9 ... 7A 102
Dean Abbott Ho. SW1 ... 3C 18
(off Vincent St.)
Dean Bradley St. SW1 ... 2E 18 (3J 101)
Dean Cl. E9 ... 5J 67
SE16 ... 1K 103
UB10: Hil ... 7B 56
Dean Ct. HA0: Wemb ... 3B 60
HA8: Edg ... 6D 28
RM7: Rom ... 5K 55
SW8 ... 7J 101
(off Thorncroft St.)
W3 ... 6K 79
Deancross St. E1 ... 6J 85
Dean Dr. HA7: Stan ... 2E 42
Deane Av. HA4: Ruis ... 5A 58
Deane Ct. HA6: Nwood ... 1G 39
Deane Cft. Rd. HA5: Eastc ... 6A 40
Deanery Cl. N2 ... 4C 46
Deanery M. W1 ... 4H 11
Deanery Rd. E15 ... 6G 69
Deanery St. W1 ... 4H 11 (1E 100)
Deane Way HA4: Ruis ... 6K 39
Dean Farrar St. SW1 ... 1D 18 (3H 101)
Deanfield Gdns.
CR0: C'don ... 4D 168
Dean Gdns. E17 ... 4F 51
Deanhill Ct. SW14 ... 4H 115
Deanhill Rd. SW14 ... 4H 115
Dean Ho. E1 ... 6J 85
(off Tarling St.)
SE14 ... 7A 104
(off New Cross Rd.)
Dean Path RM8: Bark ... 4A 72
Dean Rd. CR0: C'don ... 4D 168
NW2 ... 6E 62
SE28 ... 1A 108
TW3: Houn ... 5F 113
TW12: Hamp ... 5E 130
Dean Ryle St. SW1 ... 3E 18 (4J 101)
Deansbrook Cl. HA8: Edg ... 7D 28
Deansbrook Rd. HA8: Edg ... 7C 28
Dean's Bldgs. SE17 ... 4D 102
Deans Cl. CR0: C'don ... 3F 169
HA8: Edg ... 6D 28
W4 ... 6H 97
Dean's Ct. EC4 ... 1B 14 (6B 84)
Deanscroft Av. NW9 ... 1J 61
Deans Dr. HA8: Edg ... 5E 28
N13 ... 6G 33
Deans Ga. Cl. SE23 ... 3K 139
Deanshanger Ho. SE8 ... 4K 103
(off Chilton Gro.)
Deans La. HA8: Edg ... 6D 28
W4 ... 6H 97
(off Deans Cl.)
Dean's M. W1 ... 7K 5 (6F 83)
Deans Rd. SM1: Sutt ... 3K 165
W7 ... 1K 95
Dean Stanley St. SW1 ... 2E 18 (3J 101)
Deanston Wharf E16 ... 2K 105
(not continuous)
Dean St. E7 ... 5J 69
W1 ... 7C 6 (6H 83)
Deans Way HA8: Edg ... 5D 28
Deansway N2 ... 4B 46
N9 ... 3K 33
Deanswood N11 ... 6C 32
Dean's Yd. SW1 ... 1D 18 (3H 101)
Dean Trench St. SW1 ... 2E 18 (3J 101)
Dean Wlk. HA8: Edg ... 6D 28
Dean Way UB2: S'hall ... 2F 95
Dearne Cl. HA7: Stan ... 5F 27
De'Arn Gdns. CR4: Mitc ... 3C 154
Dearsley Ho. RM13: Rain ... 2K 91
Dearsley Rd. EN1: Enf ... 3B 24
Deauville Cl. E14 ... 6F 87
Deauville Ct. SE16 ... 2K 103
(off Eleanor Cl.)
SW4 ... 6G 119
De Barowe M. N5 ... 4B 66
Debdale Ho. E2 ... 1G 85
(off Whiston Rd.)
Debden N17 ... 2D 48
(off Gloucester Rd.)
Debden Cl. IG8: Wfd G ... 7G 37
KT2: King T ... 5D 132
NW9 ... 1A 44
Debden Pl. UB10: Uxb ... 1A 74
De Beauvoir Ct. N1 ... 7D 66
(off Northchurch Rd.)
De Beauvoir Cres. N1 ... 1E 84
De Beauvoir Est. N1 ... 1E 84
De Beauvoir Pl. N1 ... 6E 66
De Beauvoir Rd. N1 ... 1E 84
De Beauvoir Sq. N1 ... 7E 66
DE BEAUVOIR TOWN ... 1E 84
De Beauvoir Wharf N1 ... 1E 84
(off Hertford Rd.)
Debenham Ct. E8 ... 1G 85
(off Pownall Rd.)
Debham Ct. NW2 ... 3E 62
Deblin Dr. UB10: Uxb ... 2A 74
Debnams Rd. SE16 ... 4J 103
De Bohun Av. N14 ... 6A 22
Deborah Cl. TW7: Isle ... 1J 113
Deborah Ct. E18 ... 3K 51
(off Victoria Rd.)
Deborah Cres. HA4: Ruis ... 7F 39
Deborah Lodge HA8: Edg ... 1H 43
Debrabant Cl. DA8: Erith ... 6K 109
De Brome Rd. TW13: Felt ... 1A 130
De Bruin Ct. E14 ... 5E 104
(off Ferry St.)
Deburgh Rd. SW19 ... 7A 136
Debussy NW9 ... 2B 44
Decapod St. E15 ... 5F 69
Decima St. SE1 ... 7G 15 (3E 102)
Decima Studios SE1 ... 7G 15
(off Decima St.)
Decimus Cl. CR7: Thor H ... 4D 156
Deck Cl. SE16 ... 1K 103
De Coubertin St. E20 ... 6E 68
Decoy Av. NW11 ... 5G 45
De Crespigny Pk. SE5 ... 2D 120
Dee Ct. W7 ... 6H 77
(off Hobbayne Rd.)
Dee Ho. KT2: King T ... 1D 150
(off May Bate Av.)
Deeley Rd. SW8 ... 1H 119
Deena Cl. W3 ... 6F 79
Deen City Farm ... 2A 154
Deepak Ho. SW17 ... 4C 136
Deepdale SW19 ... 4F 135
Deepdale Av. BR2: Broml ... 4H 159
Deepdale Cl. N11 ... 6K 31
Deepdale Ct. CR2: S Croy ... 4D 168
(off Birdhurst Av.)
Deep Dene W5 ... 4F 79
Deepdene Av. CR0: C'don ... 3F 169
Deepdene Cl. E11 ... 4J 51
Deepdene Ct. BR2: Broml ... 3G 159
N21 ... 6G 23
Deepdene Gdns. SW2 ... 7K 119
Deepdene Mans. SW6 ... 1H 117
(off Rostrevor Rd.)
Deepdene Point SE23 ... 3K 139
Deepdene Rd. DA16: Well ... 3A 126
SE5 ... 4D 120
Deepwell Cl. TW7: Isle ... 1A 114
Deepwood La. UB6: G'frd ... 3H 77
Deerbrook Rd. SE24 ... 1B 138
Deerdale Rd. SE24 ... 4C 120
Deerfield Cl. NW9 ... 5B 44
Deerfield Cotts. NW9 ... 5B 44
Deerhurst Cl. TW13: Felt ... 4K 129
Deerhurst Ct. CR0: C'don ... 1B 168
(off Parson's Mead)
Deerhurst Cres. TW12: Hamp H ... 5G 131
Deerhurst Ho. SE15 ... 6G 103
(off Haymerle Rd.)
Deerhurst Rd. NW2 ... 6F 63
SW16 ... 5K 137
Deering Ho. SE3 ... 4A 124
Deerings Dr. HA5: Eastc ... 5J 39
Deerleap Gro. E4 ... 5J 25
Dee Rd. TW9: Rich ... 4F 115
Deer Pk. Cl. KT2: King T ... 7H 133
Deer Pk. Gdns. CR4: Mitc ... 4B 154
Deer Pk. Rd. SW19 ... 2K 153
Deer Pk. Way BR4: W W'ck ... 2H 171
Deeside Rd. SW17 ... 3B 136
Dee St. E14 ... 6E 86
Defence Cl. SE28 ... 1J 107
Defiance Wlk. SE18 ... 3D 106
Defiant Way SM6: W'gton ... 7J 167
Defoe Av. TW9: Kew ... 7G 97
Defoe Cl. SE16 ... 2B 104
SW17 ... 6C 136
Defoe Ho. EC2 ... 5D 8
Defoe Pl. EC2 ... 5C 8
(off Beech St.)
SW17 ... 4D 136
Defoe Rd. N16 ... 3E 66
De Frene Rd. SE26 ... 4K 139
Degema Rd. BR7: Chst ... 5F 143
Dehar Cres. NW9 ... 7B 44
Dehavilland Cl. UB5: N'olt ... 3B 76
De Havilland Ct. N17 ... 3H 49
De Havilland Dr. SE18 ... 6F 107
De Havilland Rd. HA8: Edg ... 2G 43
TW5: Hest ... 7A 94
Dehavilland Studios E5 ... 2J 67
(off Theydon Rd.)
De Havilland Way TW19: Stanw ... 6A 110
Dekker Cl. RM5: Col R ... 1G 55
Dekker Ho. SE5 ... 7D 102
(off Elmington Est.)
Dekker Rd. SE21 ... 6E 120
Dekota HA9: Wemb ... 4G 61
(off Engineers Way)
Delacourt Rd. SE3 ... 7K 105
Delafield Ho. E1 ... 6G 85
(off Christian St.)
Delafield Rd. SE7 ... 5K 105
Delaford Rd. SE16 ... 5H 103
Delaford St. SW6 ... 7G 99
Delahay Ho. SW3 ... 7E 16
(off Chelsea Emb.)
Delamare Ct. SE6 ... 3D 140
Delamare Cres. CR0: C'don ... 6J 157
Delamere Ct. E17 ... 2E 50
Delamere Gdns. NW7 ... 6E 28
Delamere Rd. SW20 ... 1F 153
UB4: Yead ... 7B 76
W5 ... 2E 96
Delamere St. W2 ... 5K 81
Delamere Ter. W2 ... 5K 81
Delancey Pas. NW1 ... 1F 83
(off Delancey St.)
Delancey St. NW1 ... 1F 83
Delancey Studios NW1 ... 1F 83
Delany Ho. SE10 ... 6E 104
(off Thames St.)
Delarch Ho. SE1 ... 7A 14
De Laune St. SE17 ... 6K 19 (5B 102)
Delaware Mans. W9 ... 4K 81
(off Delaware Rd.)
Delaware Rd. W9 ... 4K 81
Delawyk Cres. SE24 ... 6C 120
Delcombe Av. KT4: Wor Pk ... 1E 164
Delderfield Ho. RM1: Rom ... 2K 55
(off Portnoi Cl.)
Delft Ho. KT2: King T ... 7F 133
(off Acre Rd.)
Delft Way SE22 ... 5E 120
Delhi Rd. EN1: Enf ... 7A 24
Delhi St. N1 ... 1J 83
Delia St. SW18 ... 7K 117
Delisle Rd. SE28 ... 1J 107
Delius Gro. E15 ... 2F 87
The Dell DA5: Bexl ... 1K 145
HA0: Wemb ... 5B 60
HA5: Pinn ... 2B 40
IG8: Wfd G ... 3E 36
SE2 ... 5A 108
SE19 ... 1F 157
TW8: Bford ... 6C 96
TW14: Felt ... 7K 111
Della Path E5 ... 3G 67
Dellbow Rd. TW14: Felt ... 5K 111
Dell Cl. E15 ... 1F 87
IG8: Wfd G ... 3E 36
SM6: W'gton ... 4G 167
Dell Farm Rd. HA4: Ruis ... 5F 39
Dellfield Cl. BR3: Beck ... 1E 158
Dell La. KT17: Ewe ... 5C 164
Dellors Cl. EN5: Barn ... 5A 20
Dellow Cl. IG2: Ilf ... 7H 53
Dellow Ho. E1 ... 7H 85
(off Dellow St.)
Dellow St. E1 ... 7H 85
Dell Rd. KT17: Ewe ... 6C 164
UB7: W Dray ... 4B 92
Dells Cl. E4 ... 7J 25
TW11: Tedd ... 6K 131
Dell's M. SW1 ... 4B 18
Dell Wlk. KT3: N Mald ... 2A 152
Dell Way W13 ... 6C 78
Dellwood Gdns. IG5: Ilf ... 3E 52
Delmare Cl. SW9 ... 4K 119
Delme Cres. SE3 ... 2K 123
Delmerend Ho. SW3 ... 5C 16
(off Cale St.)
Delmey Cl. CR0: C'don ... 3F 169
Deloraine Ho. SE8 ... 1C 122
Delorme St. W6 ... 6F 99
Delroy Ct. N20 ... 7F 21
Delta Bldg. E14 ... 6E 86
(off Ashton St.)
The Delta Bldg. RM7: Rush G ... 6K 55
Delta Cen. HA0: Wemb ... 1F 79
Delta Cl. KT4: Wor Pk ... 3B 164
Delta Ct. NW2 ... 2C 62
SE8 ... 6A 104
(off Trundleys Rd.)
Delta Gro. UB5: N'olt ... 3B 76
Delta Ho. N1 ... 1E 8
(off Nile St.)
Delta Mews NW7 ... 5B 30
Delta Pk. SW18 ... 4K 117
Delta Pk. Ind. Est. EN3: Brim ... 3G 25
Delta Point CR0: C'don ... 1C 168
(off Wellesley Rd.)
E2 ... 3G 85
(off Delta St.)
Delta Rd. KT4: Wor Pk ... 3A 164
Delta St. E2 ... 3G 85
De Luci Rd. DA8: Erith ... 5J 109
De Lucy St. SE2 ... 4B 108
Delvan Cl. SE18 ... 7E 106
Delvers Mead RM10: Dag ... 4J 73
Delverton Ho. SE17 ... 5B 102
(off Delverton Rd.)
Delverton Rd. SE17 ... 5B 102
Delvino Rd. SW6 ... 1J 117
Demesne Rd. SM6: W'gton ... 4H 167
Demeta Cl. HA9: Wemb ... 3J 61
De Montfort Pde. SW16 ... 3J 137
De Montfort Rd. SW16 ... 3J 137
De Morgan Rd. SW6 ... 3K 117
Dempsey Ct. SE6 ... 7C 122
Dempster Cl. KT6: Surb ... 1C 162
Dempster Rd. SW18 ... 5A 118
The Den ... 5J 103

210 A-Z Big London

Denbar Pde.—The Dingle

Denbar Pde. RM7: Rom . . . 4J 55
Denberry Dr. DA14: Sidc . . . 3B 144
Denbigh Cl. BR7: Chst . . . 6D 142
HA4: Ruis . . . 2H 57
SM1: Sutt . . . 5H 165
UB1: S'hall . . . 6D 76
W11 . . . 7H 81
Denbigh Ct. E6 . . . 3B 88
W7 . . . 5K 77
(off Copley Cl.)
Denbigh Dr. UB3: Harl . . . 2E 92
Denbigh Gdns. TW10: Rich . . . 5F 115
Denbigh Ho. SW1 . . . 1F 17
(off Hans Pl.)
W11 . . . 7H 81
(off Westbourne Gro.)
Denbigh M. SW1 . . . 4A 18
Denbigh Pl. SW1 . . . 5A 18 (5G 101)
Denbigh Rd. E6 . . . 3B 88
TW3: Houn . . . 2F 113
UB1: S'hall . . . 6D 76
W11 . . . 7H 81
W13 . . . 7B 78
Denbigh St. SW1 . . . 4A 18 (4G 101)
(not continuous)
Denbigh Ter. W11 . . . 7H 81
Denbridge Rd. BR1: Broml . . . 2D 160
Denbury Ho. E3 . . . 3D 86
(off Talwin St.)
Denby Ct. SE11 . . . 3H 19
Dence Ho. E2 . . . 2K 9
(off Turin St.)
Denchworth Ho. SW9 . . . 2A 120
Dencliffe TW15: Ashf . . . 5C 128
Den Cl. BR3: Beck . . . 3F 159
The Dencora Cen. EN3: Brim . . . 3F 25
The Dene CR0: C'don . . . 4K 169
HA9: Wemb . . . 4E 60
KT8: W Mole . . . 5D 148
W13 . . . 5B 78
Dene Av. DA15: Sidc . . . 7B 126
TW3: Houn . . . 3D 112
Dene Cl. BR2: Hayes . . . 1H 171
DA2: Wilm . . . 4K 145
E10 . . . 2D 68
KT4: Wor Pk . . . 2B 164
SE4 . . . 3A 122
Dene Ct. CR2: S Croy . . . 5C 168
(off Warham Rd.)
W5 . . . 5C 78
Denecroft Cres. UB10: Hil . . . 1D 74
Dene Gdns. HA7: Stan . . . 5H 27
KT7: T Ditt . . . 2A 162
Dene Ho. N14 . . . 7C 22
Denehurst Gdns. IG8: Wfd G . . . 4E 36
NW4 . . . 6E 44
TW2: Twick . . . 7H 113
TW10: Rich . . . 4G 115
W3 . . . 1H 97
Dene Rd. IG9: Buck H . . . 1G 37
N11 . . . 1J 31
Denesmead SE24 . . . 5C 120
Denewood EN5: New Bar . . . 5F 21
Denewood Rd. N6 . . . 6D 46
Denford St. SE10 . . . 5H 105
(off Glenforth St.)
Dengie Wlk. N1 . . . 1C 84
(off Basire St.)
Denham Cl. DA16: Well . . . 3C 126
Denham Ct. NW6 . . . 7A 64
(off Fairfax Rd.)
SE26 . . . 3H 139
(off Kirkdale)
UB1: S'hall . . . 7G 77
(off Baird Av.)
Denham Cres. CR4: Mitc . . . 4D 154
Denham Dr. IG2: Ilf . . . 6G 53
Denham Ho. UB7: W Dray . . . 2B 92
(off Park Lodge Av.)
W12 . . . 7D 80
(off White City Est.)
Denham Rd. N20 . . . 3J 31
TW14: Felt . . . 7A 112
Denham St. SE10 . . . 5J 105
Denham Way IG11: Bark . . . 1J 89
Denholme Rd. W9 . . . 3H 81
Denison Cl. N2 . . . 3A 46
Denison Ho. E14 . . . 3D 104
Denison Rd. SW19 . . . 6B 136
TW13: Felt . . . 4H 129
W5 . . . 4C 78
Deniston Av. DA5: Bexl . . . 1E 144
Denis Way SW4 . . . 3H 119
Denland Ho. SW8 . . . 7K 101
(off Dorset Rd.)
Denleigh Gdns. KT7: T Ditt . . . 6J 149
N21 . . . 1F 33
Denman Av. UB2: S'hall . . . 1H 95
Denman Dr. KT10: Clay . . . 5A 162
NW11 . . . 5J 45
TW15: Ashf . . . 6D 128
Denman Dr. Nth. NW11 . . . 5J 45
Denman Dr. Sth. NW11 . . . 5J 45
Denman Ho. N16 . . . 2E 66
Denman Pl. W1 . . . 2C 12
Denman Rd. SE15 . . . 1F 121
Denman St. W1 . . . 3C 12 (7H 83)
Denmark Av. SW19 . . . 7G 135
Denmark Ct. SM4: Mord . . . 6J 153
Denmark Gdns. SM5: Cars . . . 3D 166
Denmark Gro. N1 . . . 2A 84
DENMARK HILL . . . 3C 120
Denmark Hill SE5 . . . 1D 120
Denmark Hill Dr. NW9 . . . 3C 44
Denmark Hill Est. SE5 . . . 4D 120
Denmark Ho. SE7 . . . 4C 106
Denmark Mans. SE5 . . . 2C 120
(off Coldharbour La.)
Denmark Path SE25 . . . 5H 157
Denmark Pl. E3 . . . 3C 86
WC2 . . . 7D 6 (6H 83)
Denmark Rd. BR1: Broml . . . 1K 159
KT1: King T . . . 3E 150
N8 . . . 4A 48
NW6 . . . 2H 81
SE5 . . . 1C 120
SE25 . . . 5G 157
SM5: Cars . . . 3D 166
SW19 . . . 6F 135
TW2: Twick . . . 3H 131
W13 . . . 7B 78
Denmark St. E11 . . . 3G 69
E13 . . . 5K 87
N17 . . . 1H 49
WC2 . . . 7D 6 (6H 83)
Denmark Ter. N2 . . . 3D 46
Denmark Wlk. SE27 . . . 4C 138
Denmead Ho. SW15 . . . 6B 116
Denmead Rd. CR0: C'don . . . 1B 168
Denmore Ct. SM6: W'gton . . . 5F 167
Dennan Rd. KT6: Surb . . . 1F 163
Dennard Way BR6: Farnb . . . 4F 173
Denner Rd. E4 . . . 2H 35
Denne Ter. E8 . . . 1F 85
Dennett Rd. CR0: C'don . . . 1A 168
Dennett's Gro. SE14 . . . 2K 121
Dennett's Rd. SE14 . . . 1J 121
Denning Av. CR0: Wadd . . . 4A 168
Denning Cl. NW8 . . . 1A 4 (3A 82)
TW12: Hamp . . . 5D 130
Denning M. SW12 . . . 6E 118
Denning Point E1 . . . 7K 9
(off Commercial St.)
Denning Rd. NW3 . . . 4B 64
Dennington Cl. E5 . . . 2J 67
Dennington Pk. Rd. NW6 . . . 6J 63
The Denningtons
KT4: Wor Pk . . . 2A 164
Dennis Av. HA9: Wemb . . . 5F 61
Dennis Cl. TW15: Ashf . . . 7F 129
Dennis Gdns. HA7: Stan . . . 5H 27
Dennis Ho. E3 . . . 2B 86
(off Roman Rd.)
SM1: Sutt . . . 4K 165
Dennis La. HA7: Stan . . . 3G 27
Dennison Point E15 . . . 7E 68
Dennis Pde. N14 . . . 1C 32
Dennis Pk. Cres. SW20 . . . 1G 153
Dennis Reeve Cl. CR4: Mitc . . . 1D 154
Dennis Rd. KT8: E Mos . . . 4G 149
Dennis Severs' House . . . 5H 9 (5E 84)
Dennis Way SW4 . . . 3H 119
Denny Cl. E6 . . . 5C 88
Denny Cres. SE11 . . . 5K 19 (5A 102)
Denny Gdns. RM9: Dag . . . 7B 72
Denny Rd. N9 . . . 1C 34
Denny St. SE11 . . . 5K 19 (5A 102)
Den Rd. BR2: Broml . . . 3F 159
Densham Ho. NW8 . . . 1B 4
(off Cochrane St.)
Densham Rd. E15 . . . 1G 87
Densole Cl. BR3: Beck . . . 1A 158
Denstone Ho. SE15 . . . 6G 103
(off Haymerle Rd.)
Densworth Gro. N9 . . . 2D 34
Dent Ho. SE17 . . . 4E 102
(off Peacock St.)
Denton NW1 . . . 6E 64
Denton Ho. N1 . . . 7B 66
(off Halton Rd.)
Denton Rd. DA5: Bexl . . . 2K 145
DA16: Well . . . 7C 108
N8 . . . 5K 47
N18 . . . 4K 33
TW1: Twick . . . 6D 114
Denton St. SW18 . . . 6K 117
Denton Ter. DA5: Bexl . . . 2K 145
Denton Way E5 . . . 3K 67
Dents Rd. SW11 . . . 6D 118
Denver Cl. BR6: Pet W . . . 6J 161
Denver Rd. N16 . . . 7E 48
Denwood SE23 . . . 3K 139
Denyer St. SW3 . . . 4D 16 (4C 100)
Denys Ho. EC1 . . . 5J 7
(off Bourne Est.)
Denziloe Av. UB10: Hil . . . 3D 74
Denzil Rd. NW10 . . . 5B 62
Deodar Rd. SW15 . . . 4G 117
Deodora Cl. N20 . . . 3H 31
Department for Business,
Energy & Industrial Strategy
. . . 1D 18 (3H 101)
Department for Communities . . . 1A 18
Department for Education . . . 1D 18
Department for Energy & Climate Change
. . . 5E 12
Department for Transport
. . . 3D 18 (4H 101)
Department for Work & Pensions . . . 7D 12
Department of Environment
Parks Department . . . 1J 5 (3E 82)
De Pass Gdns. IG11: Bark . . . 4A 90
Depot App. NW2 . . . 4F 63
NW10: Wemb . . . 6G 61
Depot Rd. TW3: Houn . . . 3H 113
W12 . . . 7E 80
Depot St. SE5 . . . 6D 102
DEPTFORD . . . 7C 104
Deptford Bri. SE8 . . . 1C 122
Deptford B'way. SE8 . . . 1C 122
Deptford Bus. Pk. SE15 . . . 6J 103
Deptford Chu. St. SE8 . . . 6C 104
Deptford Ferry Rd. E14 . . . 4C 104
Deptford Grn. SE8 . . . 6C 104
Deptford High St. SE8 . . . 6C 104
Deptford Pk. Bus. Cen. SE8 . . . 5A 104
Deptford Strand SE8 . . . 4B 104
Deptford Trad. Est. SE8 . . . 5A 104
Deptford Wharf SE8 . . . 4B 104
De Quincey Ho. SW1 . . . 6A 18
(off Lupus St.)
De Quincey M. E16 . . . 1J 105
De Quincey Rd. N17 . . . 1D 48
Derby Av. HA3: Hrw W . . . 1H 41
N12 . . . 5F 31
RM7: Rom . . . 6J 55
Derby Ga. SW1 . . . 6E 12 (2J 101)
(not continuous)
Derby Hill SE23 . . . 2J 139
Derby Hill Cres. SE23 . . . 2J 139
Derby Ho. HA5: Pinn . . . 2B 40
SE11 . . . 3J 19
Derby Lodge N3 . . . 2H 45
WC1 . . . 1G 7
(off Britannia St.)
Derby Rd. CR0: C'don . . . 1B 168
E7 . . . 7B 70
E9 . . . 1K 85
E18 . . . 1H 51
EN3: Pond E . . . 5C 24
KT5: Surb . . . 1G 163
N18 . . . 5D 34
SM1: Sutt . . . 6H 165
SW14 . . . 4H 115
SW19 . . . 7J 135
TW3: Houn . . . 4F 113
UB6: G'frd . . . 1F 77
Derby Rd. Ind. Est. TW3: Houn . . . 4F 113
Derbyshire St. E2 . . . 3G 85
(not continuous)
Derby St. W1 . . . 5H 11 (1E 100)
Dere Cl. SW6 . . . 1G 117
Dereham Ho. SE4 . . . 4K 121
(off Frendsbury Rd.)
Dereham Pl. EC2 . . . 2H 9 (3E 84)
Dereham Rd. IG11: Bark . . . 5K 71
Derek Av. HA9: Wemb . . . 7H 61
KT19: Ewe . . . 6G 163
SM6: W'gton . . . 4F 167
Derek Cl. KT19: Ewe . . . 5H 163
Derek Walcott Cl. SE24 . . . 5B 120
Dericote St. E8 . . . 1H 85
Deridene Cl. TW19: Stanw . . . 6A 110
Derifall Cl. E6 . . . 5D 88
Dering Pl. CR0: C'don . . . 4C 168
Dering Rd. CR0: C'don . . . 4C 168
Dering St. W1 . . . 1K 11 (6F 83)
Dering Yd. W1 . . . 1K 11 (6F 83)
Derinton Rd. SW17 . . . 4D 136
Derley Rd. UB2: S'hall . . . 3A 94
Dermody Gdns. SE13 . . . 5F 123
Dermody Rd. SE13 . . . 5F 123
Derny Av. E20 . . . 5D 68
Deronda Rd. SE24 . . . 1B 138
Deroy Cl. SM5: Cars . . . 6D 166
Derrick Gdns. SE7 . . . 3A 106
Derrick Rd. BR3: Beck . . . 3B 158
Derrycombe Ho. W2 . . . 5J 81
(off Gt. Western Rd.)
Derry Ho. NW8 . . . 4B 4
(off Church St. Est.)
Derry M. N19 . . . 2J 65
Derry Rd. CR0: Bedd . . . 3J 167
Derry St. W8 . . . 2K 99
Dersingham Av. E12 . . . 4D 70
Dersingham Rd. NW2 . . . 3G 63
Derwent NW1 . . . 2A 6
(off Robert St.)
Derwent Av. EN4: E Barn . . . 1J 31
N18 . . . 5J 33
NW7 . . . 6E 28
NW9 . . . 5A 44
SW15 . . . 4A 134
UB10: Ick . . . 2C 56
Derwent Cl. TW14: Felt . . . 1H 129
Derwent Ct. SE16 . . . 2K 103
(off Eleanor Cl.)
Derwent Cres. DA7: Bex . . . 2G 127
HA7: Stan . . . 2C 42
N20 . . . 3F 31
Derwent Dr. BR5: Pet W . . . 7H 161
UB4: Hayes . . . 5G 75
Derwent Gdns. HA9: Wemb . . . 7C 42
IG4: Ilf . . . 4C 52
Derwent Gro. SE22 . . . 4F 121
Derwent Ho. E3 . . . 4B 86
(off Southern Gro.)
KT2: King T . . . 1D 150
(off May Bate Av.)
SW7 . . . 3A 16
(off Cromwell Rd.)
Derwent Lodge KT4: Wor Pk . . . 2D 164
TW7: Isle . . . 2H 113
Derwent Point EC1 . . . 1A 8
(off Goswell Rd.)
Derwent Ri. NW9 . . . 6A 44
Derwent Rd. N13 . . . 4E 32
SE20 . . . 2G 157
SW20 . . . 6F 153
TW2: Whitt . . . 6F 113
UB1: S'hall . . . 6D 76
W5 . . . 3C 96
Derwent St. SE10 . . . 5G 105
Derwent Wlk. SM6: W'gton . . . 7F 167
Derwentwater Rd. W3 . . . 1J 97
Derwent Yd. W5 . . . 3C 96
(off Derwent Rd.)
De Salis Rd. UB10: Hil . . . 4E 74
Des Barres Ct. SE10 . . . 3J 105
(off Peartree Way)
Desborough Cl. TW17: Shep . . . 7C 146
W2 . . . 5K 81
Desborough Ho. W14 . . . 6H 99
(off North End Rd.)
Desborough Sailing Club . . . 7D 146
Desborough St. W2 . . . 5K 81
(off Cirencester St.)
Desenfans Rd. SE21 . . . 6E 120
Desford Rd. E16 . . . 4G 87
Desford Way TW15: Ashf . . . 2B 128
Design Museum . . . 3H 99
Desmond Ho. EN4: E Barn . . . 6H 21
Desmond St. SE14 . . . 6A 104
Desmond Tutu Dr. SE23 . . . 1B 140
Despard Rd. N19 . . . 1G 65
Desvignes Dr. SE13 . . . 6F 123
Dethick Ct. E3 . . . 1A 86
Detling Ho. SE17 . . . 4E 102
(off Congreve St.)
Detling Rd. BR1: Broml . . . 5J 141
DA8: Erith . . . 7K 109
Detmold Rd. E5 . . . 2J 67
Dettingen Pl. IG11: Bark . . . 2B 90
Devalls Cl. E6 . . . 7F 89
Devana End SM5: Cars . . . 3D 166
Devane Way SE27 . . . 3B 138
Devan Gro. N4 . . . 7D 48
Devas Rd. SW20 . . . 1E 152
Devas St. E3 . . . 4D 86
Devenay Rd. E15 . . . 7H 69
Devenish Rd. SE2 . . . 2A 108
Deventer Cres. SE22 . . . 5E 120
Deveraux Cl. BR3: Beck . . . 5E 158
De Vere Cl. SM6: W'gton . . . 7J 167
De Vere Cotts. W8 . . . 3A 100
(off Canning Pl.)
De Vere Gdns. IG1: Ilf . . . 2D 70
W8 . . . 2A 100
Deverell St. SE1 . . . 3D 102
De Vere M. W8 . . . 3A 100
(off Canning Pl.)
Devereux Ct. WC2 . . . 1J 13
Devereux La. SW13 . . . 7D 98
Devereux Rd. SW11 . . . 6D 118
Deveron Way RM1: Rom . . . 1K 55
Devey Cl. KT2: King T . . . 7B 134
Devitt Ho. E14 . . . 7D 86
(off Wade's Pl.)
Devizes St. N1 . . . 1D 84
Devon Av. TW2: Twick . . . 1G 131
Devon Cl. IG9: Buck H . . . 2E 36
N17 . . . 3F 49
UB6: G'frd . . . 1C 78
Devon Ct. TW12: Hamp . . . 7E 130
W7 . . . 5K 77
(off Copley Cl.)
Devoncroft Gdns. TW1: Twick . . . 7A 114
Devon Gdns. N4 . . . 6B 48
Devon Ho. E17 . . . 2B 50
N1 . . . 2B 84
(off Upper St.)
Devonhurst Pl. W4 . . . 5K 97
Devonia Gdns. N18 . . . 6H 33
Devonia Rd. N1 . . . 2B 84
Devon Mans. HA3: Kenton . . . 5C 42
(off Woodcock Hill)
SE1 . . . 6J 15
(off Tooley St.)
Devon Pde. HA3: Kenton . . . 5C 42
Devonport W2 . . . 1C 10 (6C 82)
Devonport Gdns. IG1: Ilf . . . 6D 52
Devonport Ho. W2 . . . 5J 81
(off Gt. Western Rd.)
Devonport M. W12 . . . 2D 98
Devonport Rd. W12 . . . 1D 98
(not continuous)
Devonport St. E1 . . . 6J 85
Devon Ri. N2 . . . 4B 46
Devon Rd. IG11: Bark . . . 1J 89
SM2: Cheam . . . 7G 165
Devons Est. E3 . . . 3D 86
Devonshire Av. SM2: Sutt . . . 7A 166
Devonshire Cl. E15 . . . 4G 69
N13 . . . 3F 33
W1 . . . 5J 5 (5F 83)
Devonshire Ct. E1 . . . 3J 85
(off Bancroft Rd.)
HA5: Hat E . . . 1D 40
(off Devonshire Rd.)
N17 . . . 6H 33
TW13: Felt . . . 2K 129
WC1 . . . 5F 7
(off Boswell St.)
Devonshire Cres. NW7 . . . 7A 30
Devonshire Dr. KT6: Surb . . . 1D 162
SE10 . . . 7D 104
Devonshire Gdns. N17 . . . 6H 33
N21 . . . 7H 23
W4 . . . 7J 97
Devonshire Gro. SE15 . . . 6H 103
Devonshire Hall E9 . . . 6J 67
(off Frampton Pk. Rd.)
Devonshire Hill La. N17 . . . 6G 33
Devonshire Ho. E14 . . . 4C 104
(off Westferry Rd.)
IG8: Wfd G . . . 7K 37
NW6 . . . 6H 63
(off Kilburn High Rd.)
SE1 . . . 3C 102
(off Bath Ter.)
SM2: Sutt . . . 7A 166
SW1 . . . 5D 18
(off Lindsay Sq.)
SW15 . . . 5F 117
W2 . . . 5B 4
(off Adpar St.)
Devonshire Ho. Bus. Cen.
BR2: Broml . . . 4K 159
(off Devonshire Sq.)
Devonshire M. N13 . . . 4F 33
SW10 . . . 7A 16
(off Park Wlk.)
W4 . . . 5A 98
Devonshire M. Nth. W1 . . . 5J 5 (5F 83)
Devonshire M. Sth. W1 . . . 5J 5 (5F 83)
Devonshire M. W. W1 . . . 4H 5 (4E 82)
Devonshire Pas. W4 . . . 5A 98
Devonshire Pl. NW2 . . . 3J 63
W1 . . . 4H 5 (4E 82)
W8 . . . 3K 99
Devonshire Pl. M. W1 . . . 4H 5 (5E 82)
Devonshire Point TW15: Ashf . . . 3E 128
Devonshire Rd. BR6: Orp . . . 7K 161
CR0: C'don . . . 7D 156
DA6: Bex . . . 4E 126
E16 . . . 6K 87
E17 . . . 6C 50
HA1: Harr . . . 6H 41
HA5: Eastc . . . 6A 40
HA5: Hat E . . . 1D 40
IG2: Ilf . . . 7J 53
N9 . . . 1D 34
N13 . . . 4E 32
N17 . . . 6H 33
NW7 . . . 7A 30
SE9 . . . 2C 142
SE23 . . . 1J 139
SM2: Sutt . . . 7A 166
SM5: Cars . . . 4E 166
SW19 . . . 7C 136
TW13: Hanw . . . 3C 130
UB1: S'hall . . . 5E 76
W4 . . . 5A 98
W5 . . . 3C 96
Devonshire Road Nature Reserve
. . . 7K 121
Devonshire Road Nature Reserve
Vis. Cen. . . . 7K 121
Devonshire Row EC2 . . . 6H 9 (5E 84)
Devonshire Row M. W1 . . . 4K 5
Devonshire Sq. BR2: Broml . . . 4K 159
EC2 . . . 6H 9 (6E 84)
Devonshire St. W1 . . . 5H 5 (5E 82)
W4 . . . 5A 98
Devonshire Ter. W2 . . . 6A 82
Devonshire Way CR0: C'don . . . 2A 170
UB4: Yead . . . 6K 75
Devons Rd. E3 . . . 3D 86
Devon St. SE15 . . . 6H 103
Devon Way KT9: Chess . . . 5C 162
KT19: Ewe . . . 5H 163
UB10: Hil . . . 2B 74
Devon Waye TW5: Hest . . . 7D 94
De Walden Ho. NW8 . . . 2C 82
(off Allitsen Rd.)
De Walden St. W1 . . . 6H 5 (5E 82)
Dewar St. SE15 . . . 3G 121
Dewberry Gdns. E6 . . . 5C 88
Dewberry St. E14 . . . 5E 86
Dewey Ct. BR1: Broml . . . 3J 159
Dewey La. SW2 . . . 6A 120
(off Tulse Hill)
Dewey Rd. N1 . . . 2A 84
RM10: Dag . . . 6H 73
Dewey St. SW17 . . . 5D 136
Dewhurst Ct. TW3: Houn . . . 4E 112
Dewhurst Rd. W14 . . . 3F 99
Dewsbury Cl. HA5: Pinn . . . 6C 40
Dewsbury Ct. W4 . . . 4J 97
Dewsbury Gdns. KT4: Wor Pk . . . 3C 164
Dewsbury Rd. NW10 . . . 5C 62
Dewsbury Ter. NW1 . . . 1F 83
Dews Farm Sand Pits Nature Reserve
. . . 6A 38
De Wyndsor Ct. SE16 . . . 3G 103
(off Jamaica Rd.)
Dexter Apts. SE15 . . . 1H 121
(off Queen's Rd.)
Dexter Ho. DA18: Erith . . . 3E 108
(off Kale Rd.)
Dexter Rd. EN5: Barn . . . 6A 20
Deyncourt Rd. N17 . . . 1C 48
Deynecourt Gdns. E11 . . . 4A 52
D'Eynsford Rd. SE5 . . . 1D 120
Dhonau Ho. SE1 . . . 4F 103
(off Longfield Est.)
Diadem Ct. W1 . . . 7C 6
The Dial Wlk. W8 . . . 2K 99
Diameter Rd. BR5: Pet W . . . 7F 161
Diamond Cl. RM8: Dag . . . 1C 72
Diamond Est. SW17 . . . 3C 136
Diamond Gdns. E3 . . . 5B 86
Diamond Ho. E3 . . . 2A 86
(off Roman Rd.)
Diamond Jubilee Way SM5: Cars . . . 7D 166
Diamond Rd. HA4: Ruis . . . 4B 58
Diamond St. NW10 . . . 7K 61
SE15 . . . 7E 102
Diamond Ter. SE10 . . . 1E 122
Diamond Way SE8 . . . 6C 104
Diana Cl. DA14: Sidc . . . 2E 144
E18 . . . 1K 51
SE8 . . . 6B 104
Diana Gdns. KT6: Surb . . . 2F 163
Diana Ho. SW13 . . . 1B 116
Diana, Princess of Wales Memorial
Fountain . . . 6C 10 (2C 100)
Diana, Princess of Wales Memorial
Playground . . . 1K 99
Diana, Princess of Wales Memorial Wlk.
Kensington Gdns. . . . 1K 99
Diana Rd. E17 . . . 3B 50
Dianne Ct. SE12 . . . 1J 141
Dianne Way EN4: E Barn . . . 4H 21
Dianthus Cl. SE2 . . . 5B 108
Dibden Ho. SE5 . . . 7E 102
Dibden St. N1 . . . 1C 84
Dibdin Cl. SM1: Sutt . . . 3J 165
Dibdin Ho. W9 . . . 2K 81
Dibdin Rd. SM1: Sutt . . . 3J 165
Dibdin Row SE1 . . . 1K 19 (3A 102)
Dicey Av. NW2 . . . 4E 62
Dickens Av. N3 . . . 1A 46
UB8: Hil . . . 6D 74
Dickens Cl. DA8: Erith . . . 7H 109
TW10: Ham . . . 2E 132
UB3: Harl . . . 4G 93
Dickens Ct. E11 . . . 4J 51
(off Makepeace Rd.)
SW17 . . . 3B 136
(off Grosvenor Way)
Dickens Dr. BR7: Chst . . . 6G 143
Dickens Est. SE1 . . . 2G 103
SE16 . . . 3G 103
Dickens Ho. NW6 . . . 3J 81
(off Malvern Rd.)
NW8 . . . 3B 4
SE17 . . . 5B 102
(off Doddington Gro.)
SE19 . . . 7E 138
WC1 . . . 3E 6
Dickens La. N18 . . . 5K 33
Dickens M. EC1 . . . 5A 8
(off Turnmill St.)
Dickenson Cl. N9 . . . 1B 34
Dickenson Rd. N8 . . . 7J 47
TW13: Hanw . . . 5A 130
Dickenson's La. SE25 . . . 6G 157
Dickensons La. SE25 . . . 5G 157
(not continuous)
Dickensons Pl. SE25 . . . 6G 157
Dickens Pl. SL3: Poyle . . . 4A 174
Dickens Ri. IG7: Chig . . . 3K 37
Dickens Rd. E6 . . . 2B 88
Dickens Sq. SE1 . . . 7D 14 (3C 102)
Dickens St. SW8 . . . 2F 119
Dickenswood Cl. SE19 . . . 7B 138
Dickerage La. KT3: N Mald . . . 3J 151
Dickerage Rd. KT1: King T . . . 1J 151
KT3: N Mald . . . 1J 151
Dickinson Ct. EC1 . . . 3B 8
(off Brewhouse Yd.)
Dicksee Ho. NW8 . . . 4A 4
(off Lyons Pl.)
Dickson Fold HA5: Pinn . . . 4B 40
Dickson Ho. E1 . . . 6H 85
(off Philpot St.)
N1 . . . 7A 66
(off Drummond Way)
Dickson Rd. SE9 . . . 3C 124
Dick Turpin Way TW14: Felt . . . 4H 111
Didsbury Cl. E6 . . . 1D 88
Dieppe Cl. W14 . . . 5H 99
Digby Bus. Cen. E9 . . . 6K 67
(off Digby Rd.)
Digby Cres. N4 . . . 2C 66
Digby Gdns. RM10: Dag . . . 1G 91
Digby Mans. W6 . . . 5D 98
(off Hammersmith Bri. Rd.)
Digby Pl. CR0: C'don . . . 3F 169
Digby Rd. E9 . . . 6K 67
IG11: Bark . . . 7K 71
Digby St. E2 . . . 3J 85
Digby Stuart College
Roehampton University . . . 5C 116
Diggon St. E1 . . . 5K 85
Dighton Ct. SE5 . . . 6C 102
Dighton Rd. SW18 . . . 5A 118
Dignum St. N1 . . . 2A 84
Digswell St. N7 . . . 6A 66
Dilhorne Cl. SE12 . . . 3K 141
Dilke St. SW3 . . . 7F 17 (6D 100)
Dillmount Dr. KT12: Walt T . . . 5A 148
Dilloway La. UB2: S'hall . . . 2C 94
Dillwyn Cl. SE26 . . . 4A 140
Dilston Cl. UB5: N'olt . . . 3A 76
Dilston Gro. SE16 . . . 4J 103
Dilton Gdns. SW15 . . . 1C 134
Dilwyn Ct. E17 . . . 2A 50
Dimes Pl. W6 . . . 4D 98
Dimmock Dr. UB6: G'frd . . . 5H 59
Dimond Cl. E7 . . . 4J 69
Dimsdale Dr. EN1: Enf . . . 7B 24
NW9 . . . 1J 61
Dimsdale Hgts. E1 . . . 6H 85
(off Spencer Way)
Dimsdale Wlk. E13 . . . 2J 87
Dimson Cres. E3 . . . 3C 86
Dinerman Ct. NW8 . . . 1A 82
The Dingle UB10: Hil . . . 3D 74

Dingle Gdns.—Downalong

Dingle Gdns. E14 .... 7C 86
Dingle Rd. TW15: Ashf 5D 128
Dingles Ct. HA5: Pinn 1B 40
Dingley La. SW16 .... 2H 137
Dingley Pl. EC1 .... 1D 8 (3C 84)
Dingley Rd. EC1 .... 2C 8 (3C 84)
Dingwall Av. CR0: C'don 2C 168
Dingwall Gdns. NW11 .... 6J 45
Dingwall Rd. CR0: C'don 1D 168
SM5: Cars 7D 166
SW18 .... 7A 118
Dinmont Est. E2 .... 2G 85
Dinmont Ho. *E2* *2G 85*
(off Pritchard's Rd.)
Dinmont St. E2 .... 2H 85
Dinmore Ho. *E9* *1J 85*
(off Templecombe Rd.)
Dinnington Ho. *E1* *4H 85*
(off Coventry Rd.)
Dinosaur Escape Adventure Golf 1A 76
Dinsdale Gdns. EN5: New Bar 5E 20
SE25 .... 5E 156
Dinsdale Rd. SE3 .... 6H 105
Dinsmore Rd. SW12 .... 7F 119
Dinton Ho. *NW8* *3C 4*
(off Lilestone St.)
Dinton Rd. KT2: King T 7F 133
SW19 .... 6B 136
Diploma Av. N2 .... 4C 46
Diploma Ct. N2 .... 4C 46
Diprose Lodge SW17 .... 4B 136
Dirleton Rd. E15 .... 1H 87
Dirty La. SE1 .... 1C 102
Disbrowe Rd. W6 .... 6G 99
Discover
Stratford 7F 69
Discover Greenwich Visitor Cen.
.... 6E 104
Discovery Bus. Pk. *SE16* *3G 103*
(off St James's Rd.)
The Discovery Centre
Becton 3G 89
Discovery Dock Apts. E. *E14* *2D 104*
(off Sth. Quay Sq.)
Discovery Dock Apts. W. *E14* *2D 104*
(off Sth. Quay Sq.)
Discovery Ho. *E14* *7E 86*
(off Newby Pl.)
Discovery Twr. *E16* *6H 87*
(off Minnie Baldock St.)
Discovery Wlk. E1 .... 1H 103
Dishforth La. NW9 .... 7F 29
Disley Ct. *UB1: S'hall* *6F 77*
(off Howard Rd.)
Disney Pl. SE1 .... 6D 14 (2C 102)
Disney St. SE1 .... 6D 14 (2C 102)
Dison Cl. EN3: Enf H 1E 24
Dispensary La. E8 .... 5H 67
Disraeli Cl. SE28 .... 1C 108
W4 .... 3K 97
Disraeli Gdns. SW15 .... 4H 117
Disraeli Rd. E7 .... 6J 69
NW10 .... 2K 79
SW15 .... 4G 117
W5 .... 1D 96
Diss St. E2 .... 1J 9 (3F 85)
Distaff La. EC4 .... 2C 14 (7C 84)
Distel Apts. *SE10* *4G 105*
(off Telegraph Av.)
Distillery La. W6 .... 5E 98
Distillery Rd. W6 .... 5E 98
Distillery Twr. SE8 .... 1C 122
Distillery Wlk. TW8: Bford 6E 96
Distillery Wharf W6 .... 6E 98
Distin St. SE11 .... 4J 19 (4A 102)
District Rd. HA0: Wemb 5B 60
Ditch All. SE13 .... 1D 122
Ditchburn St. E14 .... 7E 86
Ditchfield Rd. UB4: Yead 4C 76
Ditchley Ct. *W7* *5K 77*
(off Templeman Rd.)
Dittisham Rd. SE9 .... 4C 142
Ditton Cl. KT7: T Ditt 7A 150
Dittoncroft Cl. CR0: C'don 4E 168
Ditton Grange Cl. KT6: Surb 1D 162
Ditton Grange Dr. KT6: Surb 1D 162
Ditton Hill KT6: Surb 1C 162
Ditton Hill Rd. KT6: Surb 1C 162
Ditton Lawn KT7: T Ditt 1A 162
Ditton Pl. SE20 .... 1H 157
Ditton Reach KT7: T Ditt 6B 150
Ditton Rd. DA6: Bex 5D 126
KT6: Surb 2D 162
UB2: S'hall 5D 94
Diversity Av. RM13: Rain 2K 91
Divine Way UB3: Hayes 6F 75
Divis Way *SW15* *6D 116*
(off Dover Pk. Dr.)
Dixie Ct. SE6 .... 6C 122
Dixon Butler M. W9 .... 4J 81
Dixon Clark Ct. N1 .... 6B 66
Dixon Cl. E6 .... 6D 88
Dixon Ho. *W10* *6F 81*
(off Darfield Way)
Dixon Pl. BR4: W W'ck 1D 170
Dixon Rd. SE14 .... 1A 122
SE25 .... 3E 156
Dixon's All. SE16 .... 2H 103
Dixon Way NW10 .... 7A 62
Dobbin Cl. HA3: Kenton 2A 42
Dobell Rd. SE9 .... 5D 124
Dobree Av. NW10 .... 7D 62
Dobson Cl. NW6 .... 7B 64
Dobson Ho. *SE14* *6K 103*
(off John Williams Cl.)
Dobson Wlk. SE5 .... 7D 102
Doby Ct. EC4 .... 2D 14
The Dock E1 .... 7H 85
Dock Cotts. *E1* *7J 85*
(off The Highway)
Dockers Tanner Rd. E14 .... 3C 104
Dockett Eddy KT16: Chert 7A 146
Dockett Eddy La. TW17: Shep 7B 146
Dockett Moorings KT16: Chert 7A 146
Dockhead SE1 .... 7K 15 (2F 103)
Dockhead Wharf *SE1* *7K 15*
(off Shad Thames)
Dock Hill Av. SE16 .... 1K 103
Docklands Ct. *E14* *6B 86*
(off Wharf La.)
The Docklands Equestrian Cen. 4E 88
Docklands Sailing & Watersports Cen.
.... 3C 104
Dockland St. E16 .... 1E 106
(not continuous)
Dockley Rd. SE16 .... 3G 103
Dockley Rd. Ind. Est. *SE16* *3G 103*
(off Dockley Rd.)
Dock Mdw. Reach W7 .... 3J 95
Dock Offices *SE16* *3J 103*
(off Surrey Quays Rd.)
Dock Rd. E16 .... 7H 87
IG11: Bark 2G 89
TW8: Bford 7D 96
Dockside Ct. E5 .... 2J 67
Dockside Rd. E16 .... 7B 88
Dock St. E1 .... 7G 85
Dockweed Court *E14* *3D 104*
(off Watergate Walk)
Dockwell Cl. TW14: Felt 4J 111
Dockwell's Ind. Est. TW14: Felt 5K 111
Dockyard La. E14 .... 2D 104
Dr Johnson Av. SW17 .... 3F 137
Dr Johnson's House *1K 13*
(off Pemberton Row)
Doctors Cl. SE26 .... 5J 139
Docura Ho. N7 .... 2K 65
Docwra's Bldgs. N1 .... 6E 66
Dodbrooke Rd. SE27 .... 3A 138
Dodd Ho. *SE16* *4H 103*
(off Rennie Est.)
Doddington Gro. SE17 .... 6B 102
Doddington Pl. SE17 .... 6B 102
Dodds Ho. *SE10* *3J 105*
(off Peartree Way)
Dodsley Pl. N9 .... 3D 34
Dodson St. SE1 .... 7K 13 (2A 102)
Dod St. E14 .... 6B 86
Doebury Wlk. *SE18* *7A 108*
(off Prestwood Cl.)
Doel Cl. SW19 .... 7A 136
Dog & Duck Yd. WC1 .... 5H 7
Doggett Rd. SE6 .... 7C 122
Doggetts Ct. EN4: E Barn 5H 21
Doghurst Av. UB3: Harl 7D 92
Doghurst Dr. UB7: Sip 7D 92
Dog Kennel Hill SE22 .... 3E 120
Dog Kennel Hill Est. *SE22* *3E 120*
(off Albrighton Rd.)
Dog La. NW10 .... 4A 62
Doherty Rd. E13 .... 4J 87
Dokal Ind. Est. UB2: S'hall 2C 94
Dolben Ct. *SW1* *4D 18*
(off Montaigne Cl.)
Dolben St. SE1 .... 5A 14 (1B 102)
(not continuous)
Dolby Rd. SW6 .... 2H 117
Dolland Ho. SE11 .... 6H 19
Dolland St. SE11 .... 6H 19 (5K 101)
Dollar Bay Pl. E14 .... 2E 104
Dollary Pde. *KT1: King T* *3H 151*
(off Kingston Rd.)
Dolliffe Cl. CR4: Mitc 2C 154
Dollis Av. N3 .... 1H 45
Dollis Brook Wlk. EN5: Barn 6B 20
Dollis Cres. HA4: Ruis 1A 58
Dolliscroft NW7 .... 7B 30
DOLLIS HILL 2D 62
Dollis Hill Av. NW2 .... 3D 62
Dollis Hill Est. NW2 .... 3C 62
Dollis Hill La. NW2 .... 4B 62
Dollis M. N3 .... 1J 45
Dollis Pk. N3 .... 1H 45
Dollis Rd. N3 .... 7B 30
NW7 .... 7B 30
Dollis Valley Dr. EN5: Barn 6C 20
Dollis Valley Way EN5: Barn 6C 20
Dolman Cl. N3 .... 2A 46
Dolman Rd. W4 .... 4K 97
Dolman St. SW4 .... 4K 119
Dolomite Ct. HA4: Ruis 4A 58
Dolphin Cl. KT6: Surb 5D 150
SE16 .... 2K 103
SE28 .... 6D 90
Dolphin Ct. NW11 .... 6G 45
Dolphin Ct. TW16: Sun 1G 147
Dolphin Ho. *SW6* *2A 118*
(off Lensbury Av.)
SW18 .... 4K 117
TW16: Sun *1G 147*
(off Windmill Rd.)
Dolphin La. E14 .... 7D 86
Dolphin Rd. TW16: Sun 1G 147
UB5: N'olt 2D 76
Dolphin Rd. Nth. TW16: Sun 1G 147
Dolphin Rd. Sth. TW16: Sun 1G 147
Dolphin Rd. W. TW16: Sun 1G 147
Dolphin Sq. SW1 .... 6B 18 (5G 101)
W4 .... 7A 98
Dolphin St. KT1: King T 2E 150
Dolphin Twr. *SE8* *6B 104*
(off Abinger Gro.)
Dombey Ho. *SE1* *7K 15*
(off Wolseley St.)
W11 .... *1F 99*
(off St Ann's Rd.)
Dombey St. WC1 .... 5G 7 (5K 83)
(not continuous)
Domecq Ho. *EC1* *3B 8*
(off Dallington St.)
Dome Hill Pk. SE26 .... 4F 139
Domelton Ho. *SW18* *6K 117*
(off Iron Mill Rd.)
Domett Cl. SE5 .... 4D 120
Domfe Pl. E5 .... 4J 67
Domingo St. EC1 .... 3C 8 (4C 84)
Dominica Cl. E13 .... 2B 88
Dominion Apartments E17 .... 5B 50
Dominion Bus. Pk. N9 .... 2E 34
The Dominion Cen. UB2: S'hall 2C 94
Dominion Cl. TW3: Houn 2H 113
Dominion Ct. *E8* *7F 67*
(off Middleton Rd.)
Dominion Dr. SE16 .... 2K 103
Dominion Ho. *E14* *5D 104*
(off St Davids Sq.)
EC1 .... *6C 8*
(off Bartholomew Cl.)
Dominion Ind. Est. *UB2: S'hall* *2C 94*
(off Feather Rd.)
Dominion Pde. HA1: Harr 5K 41
Dominion Rd. CR0: C'don 7F 157
UB2: S'hall 2C 94
Dominion St. EC2 .... 5F 9 (5D 84)
Dominion Theatre *7D 6*
(off Tottenham Ct. Rd.)
Dominion Wlk. *E14* *7F 87*
(off Fairmont Av.)
Domonic Dr. SE9 .... 4F 143
Domville Cl. N20 .... 2G 31
Domville Ct. *SE17* *5E 102*
(off Bagshott St.)
Donald Dr. RM6: Chad H 5C 54
Donald Hunter Ho. *E7* *5K 69*
(off Woodgrange Rd.)
Donald Rd. CR0: C'don 7A 156
E13 .... 1K 87
Donaldson Rd. NW6 .... 1H 81
SE18 .... 1E 124
Donald Woods Gdns. KT5: Surb 2H 163
Donato Dr. SE15 .... 6E 102
Doncaster Dr. UB5: N'olt 5D 58
Doncaster Gdns. N4 .... 6C 48
UB5: N'olt 5D 58
Doncaster Rd. N9 .... 7C 24
Donegal Ho. *E1* *4H 85*
(off Cambridge Heath Rd.)
Donegal St. N1 .... 2K 83
Doneraile Ho. *SW1* *5J 17*
(off Ebury Bri. Rd.)
Doneraile St. SW6 .... 2F 117
Dongola Rd. E1 .... 5A 86
E13 .... 3K 87
N17 .... 3E 48
Dongola Rd. W. E13 .... 3K 87
Don Gratton Ho. *E1* *5G 85*
(off Old Montague St.)
Donington Av. IG2: Ilf 5G 53
IG6: Ilf 5G 53
Donkey All. SE22 .... 7G 121
Donkey La. EN1: Enf 2B 24
UB7: W Dray 1D 174
Donkin Ho. *SE16* *4H 103*
(off Rennie Est.)
Donmar Warehouse Theatre *1E 12*
(off Earlham St.)
Donnatt's Rd. SE14 .... 1B 122
Donne Ct. SE24 .... 6C 120
Donnefield Av. HA8: Edg 7K 27
Donne Ho. *E14* *6C 86*
(off Dod St.)
SE14 .... *6K 103*
(off Samuel Cl.)
Donnelly Ct. *SW6* *7G 99*
(off Dawes Rd.)
Donnelly Ho. *SE1* *1J 19*
(off McAuley Cl.)
Donne Pl. CR4: Mitc 4F 155
SW3 .... 3D 16 (4C 100)
Donne Rd. RM8: Dag 2C 72
Donnington Ct. *NW1* *7F 65*
(off Castlehaven Rd.)
NW10 .... *7D 62*
(off Donnington Rd.)
Donnington Mans. *NW10* *1E 80*
(off Donnington Rd.)
Donnington Rd. HA3: Kenton 5D 42
KT4: Wor Pk 2C 164
NW10 .... 7D 62
Donnybrook Ct. *E3* *1B 86*
(off Old Ford Rd.)
Donnybrook Rd. SW16 .... 7G 137
Donoghue Bus. Pk. NW2 .... 3F 63
Donoghue Cotts. *E14* *5A 86*
(off Galsworthy Av.)
Donoghue Ct. *E3* *4D 86*
(off Barry Blandford Way)
Donovan Av. N10 .... 2F 47
Donovan Ct. *SW10* *6A 16*
(off Drayton Gdns.)
Donovan Ho. *E1* *7J 85*
(off Cable St.)
Donovan Pl. N21 .... 5E 22
Don Phelan Cl. SE5 .... 1D 120
Dons Ct. *BR1: Broml* *1H 159*
(off London Rd.)
Doone Cl. TW11: Tedd 6A 132
Doon St. SE1 .... 5J 13 (1A 102)
Dora Ho. *E14* *6B 86*
(off Rhodeswell Rd.)
W11 .... *7F 81*
(off St Ann's Rd.)
Doral Way SM5: Cars 5D 166
Doran Ct. E6 .... 2D 88
Dorando Cl. W12 .... 7D 80
Doran Gro. SE18 .... 7J 107
Doran Mnr. *N2* *5D 46*
(off Great Nth. Rd.)
Doran Wlk. E15 .... 7E 68
Dora Rd. SW19 .... 5J 135
Dora St. E14 .... 6B 86
Dora Way SW9 .... 2A 120
Dorchester Av. DA5: Bexl 1D 144
HA2: Harr 6G 41
N13 .... 4H 33
Dorchester Cl. BR5: St P 7B 144
KT10: Hin W 2A 162
UB5: N'olt 5F 59
Dorchester Ct. *E18* *1H 51*
(off Buckingham Rd.)
N1 .... *7E 66*
(off Englefield Rd.)
N10 .... 3F 47
N14 .... 7A 22
NW2 .... 3F 63
SE24 .... 5C 120
SW1 .... *2F 17*
(off Sloane St.)
Dorchester Dr. SE24 .... 5C 120
TW14: Bedf 6G 111
Dorchester Gdns. E4 .... 4H 35
NW11 .... 4J 45
Dorchester Gro. W4 .... 5A 98
Dorchester Ho. TW9: Kew 7H 97
Dorchester M. KT3: N Mald 4K 151
TW1: Twick 6C 114
Dorchester Rd.
KT4: Wor Pk 1E 164
SM4: Mord 7K 153
UB5: N'olt 5F 59
Dorchester Ter. *NW2* *3F 63*
(off Needham Ter.)
Dorchester Way HA3: Kenton 6F 43
Dorchester Waye UB4: Yead 6K 75
(not continuous)
Dorcis Av. DA7: Bex 2E 126
Dordrecht Rd. W3 .... 1A 98
Dore Av. E12 .... 5E 70
Doreen Av. NW9 .... 1K 61
Doreen Capstan Ho. *E11* *3G 69*
(off Apollo Pl.)
Dore Gdns. SM4: Mord 7K 153
Dorell Cl. UB1: S'hall 5D 76
Dorey Ho. *TW8: Bford* *7C 96*
(off High St.)
Dorfman Theatre *4H 13*
(within National Theatre)
Doria Rd. SW6 .... 2H 117
Doric Ho. *E2* *2K 85*
(off Mace St.)
Doric Way NW1 .... 1C 6 (3H 83)
Dorie M. *N12* *4E 30*
(off Ashbourne Cl.)
Dorien Rd. SW20 .... 2F 153
Doris Ashby Cl. UB6: G'frd 1A 78
Doris Av. DA8: Erith 1J 127
Doris Emmerton Ct. SW11 .... 4A 118
Doris Rd. E7 .... 7J 69
TW15: Ashf 6F 129
Dorking Cl. KT4: Wor Pk 2F 165
SE8 .... 6B 104
Dorking Ct. *N17* *1G 49*
(off Hampden La.)
Dorking Ho. SE1 .... 3D 102
Dorlcote Rd. SW18 .... 7C 118
Dorly Cl. TW17: Shep 5G 147
Dorman Pl. N9 .... 2B 34
Dormans Cl. HA6: Nwood 1F 39
Dorman Wlk. NW10 .... 5K 61
Dorman Way NW8 .... 1B 82
Dorma Trad. Pk. E10 .... 1K 67
Dormay St. SW18 .... 5K 117
Dormer Cl. E15 .... 6H 69
EN5: Barn 5A 20
Dormer's Av. UB1: S'hall 6E 76
Dormers Ri. UB1: S'hall 7F 77
DORMER'S WELLS 6E 76
Dormer's Wells La. UB1: S'hall 6E 76
Dormers Wells Leisure Cen. 6F 77
Dormstone Ho. *SE17* *4E 102*
(off Congreve St.)
Dormywood HA4: Ruis 5H 39
Dornberg Cl. SE3 .... 7J 105
Dornberg Rd. SE3 .... 7K 105
Dorncliffe Rd. SW6 .... 2G 117
Dorney NW3 .... 7C 64
Dorney Ri. BR5: St M Cry 4K 161
Dorney Way TW4: Houn 5C 112
Dornfell St. NW6 .... 5H 63
Dornoch Ho. *E3* *2B 86*
(off Anglo Rd.)
Dornton Rd. CR2: S Croy 5D 168
SW12 .... 2F 137
Dorothy Av. HA0: Wemb 7E 60
Dorothy Evans Cl. DA7: Bex 4H 127
Dorothy Gdns. RM8: Dag 4B 72
Dorothy Pettingell Ho. *SM1: Sutt* *3K 165*
(off Vermont Rd.)
Dorothy Rd. SW11 .... 3D 118
Dorothy Smith La. N17 .... 7J 33
Dorrell Pl. SW9 .... 3A 120
Dorrien Wlk. SW16 .... 2H 137
Dorrington Cl. IG11: Bark 7A 72
Dorrington Ct. SE25 .... 2E 156
Dorrington Point *E3* *3D 86*
(off Bromley High St.)
Dorrington St. EC1 .... 5J 7 (5A 84)
Dorrington Way BR3: Beck 5E 158
Dorrit Ho. *W11* *1F 99*
(off St Ann's Rd.)
Dorrit M. N18 .... 5K 33
Dorrit St. SE1 .... 6D 14 (2C 102)
Dorrit Way BR7: Chst 6G 143
Dorryn Ct. SE26 .... 5K 139
Dors Cl. NW9 .... 1K 61
Dorset Av. DA16: Well 4K 125
RM1: Rom 4K 55
UB2: S'hall 4E 94
UB4: Hayes 3G 75
Dorset Bldgs. EC4 .... 1A 14 (6B 84)
Dorset Cl. KT9: Chess 4D 162
NW1 .... 5E 4 (5D 82)
UB4: Hayes 3G 75
Dorset Ct. HA6: Nwood 1H 39
N1 .... *7E 66*
(off Hertford Rd.)
UB5: N'olt 3C 76
W7 .... *5K 77*
(off Copley Cl.)
Dorset Dr. HA8: Edg 6A 28
Dorset Gdns. CR4: Mitc 4K 155
HA0: Wemb 5C 60
Dorset Ho. *NW1* *5F 5*
(off Gloucester Pl.)
Dorset Mans. *SW6* *6F 99*
(off Lillie Rd.)
Dorset M. N3 .... 1J 45
SW1 .... 1J 17 (3F 101)
Dorset Pl. E15 .... 6F 69
Dorset Ri. EC4 .... 1A 14 (6B 84)
Dorset Rd. BR3: Beck 3K 157
CR4: Mitc 2C 154
E7 .... 7A 70
HA1: Harr 6G 41
N15 .... 4D 48
N22 .... 1J 47
SE9 .... 2C 142
SW8 .... 7J 101
SW19 .... 1J 153
TW15: Ashf 3A 128
W5 .... 3C 96
Dorset Sq. NW1 .... 4E 4 (4D 82)
Dorset St. W1 .... 6F 5 (5D 82)
Dorset Way TW2: Twick 1H 131
UB10: Hil 2B 74
Dorset Waye TW5: Hest 7D 94
Dorset Wharf *W6* *7E 98*
(off Rainville Rd.)
Dorsey Ho. *N1* *6B 66*
(off Canonbury Rd.)
Dorton Cl. SE15 .... 7E 102
Dorton Vs. UB7: Sip 7C 92
Dorville Cres. W6 .... 3D 98
Dorville Rd. SE12 .... 5H 123
Dothill Rd. SE18 .... 7G 107
Douai Gro. TW12: Hamp 1G 149
Doughty Ct. *E1* *1H 103*
(off Prusom St.)
Doughty Ho. *SW10* *6A 100*
(off Netherton Gro.)
Doughty M. WC1 .... 4G 7 (4K 83)
Doughty St. WC1 .... 3G 7 (4K 83)
Douglas Av. E17 .... 1B 50
HA0: Wemb 7E 60
KT3: N Mald 4D 152
Douglas Bader Ho. TW7: Isle 3H 113
Douglas Cl. HA7: Stan 5F 27
IG6: Ilf 7K 37
SM6: W'gton 6J 167
Douglas Ct. *KT1: King T* *4E 150*
(off Geneva Rd.)
N3 .... 2K 45
NW6 .... *7J 63*
(off Quex Rd.)
Douglas Cres. UB4: Yead 4A 76
Douglas Dr. CR0: C'don 3C 170
Douglas Eyre Sports Cen. 5K 49
Douglas Ho. KT6: Surb 1F 163
Douglas Johnstone Ho. *SW6* *6H 99*
(off Clem Attlee Ct.)
Douglas Mans. TW3: Houn 3F 113
Douglas M. NW2 .... 3G 63
Douglas Path *E14* *5E 104*
(off Manchester Rd.)
Douglas Rd. DA16: Well 1B 126
E4 .... 1B 36
E16 .... 5J 87
IG3: Ilf 7A 54
KT1: King T 2H 151
KT6: Surb 2F 163
N1 .... 7C 66
N22 .... 1A 48
NW6 .... 1H 81
TW3: Houn 3F 113
TW19: Stanw 6A 110
Douglas Rd. Nth. N1 .... 6C 66
Douglas Rd. Sth. N1 .... 6C 66
Douglas Robinson Ct. *SW16* *7J 137*
(off Streatham High Rd.)
Douglas Sq. SM4: Mord 6J 153
Douglas St. SW1 .... 4C 18 (4H 101)
Douglas Ter. E17 .... 1B 50
Douglas Waite Ho. NW6 .... 7J 63
Douglas Way SE8 .... 7B 104
(Stanley St.)
SE8 .... 7C 104
(Watsons St.)
Doulton Ho. SE11 .... 2H 19
Doulton M. NW6 .... 6K 63
Dounesforth Gdns. SW18 .... 1K 135
Douro Pl. W8 .... 3K 99
Douro St. E3 .... 2C 86
Douthwaite Sq. E1 .... 1G 103
Dove App. E6 .... 5C 88
Dove Cl. NW7 .... 7G 29
SM6: W'gton 7K 167
UB5: N'olt 4B 76
Dove Commercial Cen. NW5 .... 5G 65
Dovecot Cl. HA5: Eastc 5A 40
Dovecote Av. N22 .... 3A 48
Dovecote Gdns. SW14 .... 3K 115
Dovecote Ho. *SE16* *2K 103*
(off Water Gdns. Sq.)
Dovecote M. UB9: Hare 3A 38
Dove Ct. TW19: Stanw 7A 110
Dovedale Av. HA3: Kenton 6C 42
IG5: Ilf 2E 52
Dovedale Bus. Est. *SE15* *2G 121*
(off Blenheim Gro.)
Dovedale Cl. DA16: Well 2A 126
Dovedale Ri. CR4: Mitc 7D 136
Dovedale Rd. SE22 .... 5H 121
Dovedon Cl. N14 .... 2D 32
Dovehouse Ct. *UB5: N'olt* *3B 76*
(off Delta Gro.)
Dove Ho. Gdns. E4 .... 2H 35
Dovehouse Mead IG11: Bark 2H 89
Dovehouse St. SW3 .... 5B 16 (5B 100)
Dove M. SW5 .... 4A 100
Dove Pk. HA5: Hat E 1E 40
Dover Cl. NW2 .... 2F 63
RM5: Col R 2J 55
Dover Ct. *EC1* *3A 8*
(off St John St.)
N1 .... *7D 66*
(off Southgate Rd.)
Dovercourt Av. CR7: Thor H 5A 156
Dovercourt Est. N1 .... 6D 66
Dovercourt Gdns. HA7: Stan 5K 27
Dovercourt La. SM1: Sutt 3A 166
Dovercourt Rd. SE22 .... 6E 120
Doverfield Rd. SW2 .... 7J 119
Dover Flats SE1 .... 4E 102
Dover Gdns. SM5: Cars 3D 166
Dover Ho. N18 .... 5A 34
SE15 .... 6J 103
Dover Ho. Rd. SW15 .... 4C 116
Doveridge Gdns. N13 .... 4G 33
Dove Rd. N1 .... 6D 66
Dove Row E2 .... 1G 85
Dover Pk. Dr. SW15 .... 6D 116
Dover Patrol SE3 .... 2K 123
Dover Rd. E12 .... 2A 70
N9 .... 2D 34
RM6: Chad H 6E 54
SE19 .... 6D 138
Dover St. W1 .... 3K 11 (7F 83)
Dover Ter. *TW9: Rich* *2F 115*
(off Sandycombe Rd.)
Dover Yd. W1 .... 4A 12
Doves Cl. BR2: Broml 2C 172
Doves Yd. N1 .... 1A 84
Dovet Ct. SW9 .... 1K 119
Doveton Ho. *E1* *4J 85*
(off Doveton St.)
Doveton Rd. CR2: S Croy 5D 168
Doveton St. E1 .... 4J 85
Dove Wlk. SW1 .... 5G 17 (5E 100)
Dovey Lodge *N1* *7A 66*
(off Bewdley St.)
Dovoll Ct. *SE16* *3G 103*
(off Old Jamaica Rd.)
Dowanhill Rd. SE6 .... 1F 141
Dowd Cl. N11 .... 2K 31
Dowdeswell Cl. SW15 .... 4A 116
Dowding Dr. SE9 .... 5A 124
Dowding Ho. *N6* *7E 46*
(off Hillcrest)
Dowding Pl. HA7: Stan 6F 27
Dowding Rd. UB10: Uxb 7B 56
Dowdney Cl. NW5 .... 5G 65
Dowe Ho. SE3 .... 3G 123
Dowells St. SE10 .... 6D 104
Dower Av. SM6: W'gton 7F 167
Dower Ct. *SE16* *4J 103*
(off Silwood Rd.)
Dowes Ho. SW16 .... 3J 137
Dowgate Hill EC4 .... 2E 14 (7D 84)
Dowland St. W10 .... 3G 81
Dowlas St. SE5 .... 7E 102
Dowler Ct. KT2: King T 1E 150
Dowler Ho. *E1* *6G 85*
(off Burslem St.)
Dowlerville Rd. BR6: Chels 6K 173
Dowletts Rd. RM8: Dag 1E 72
Dowling Ho. DA17: Belv 3F 109
Dowman Cl. SW19 .... 7K 135
Downage NW4 .... 3E 44
(not continuous)
Downalong WD23: B Hea 1C 26

212 A-Z Big London

Downbank Av.—Dunedin M.

Downbank Av. DA7: Bex 1K 127
Down Barns Rd. HA4: Ruis 3B 58
Downbarton Ho. *SW9* 1A 120
(off Gosling Way)
Downbury M. SW18 5J 117
Down Cl. UB5: N'olt 2K 75
Downderry Rd. BR1: Broml 3F 141
Downe Cl. DA16: Well 7C 108
Downend SE18 7F 107
Downend Ct. *SE15* 6E 102
(off Bibury Cl.)
Downe Rd. BR2: Kes 7C 172
CR4: Mitc 2D 154
Downer's Cott. SW4 4G 119
Downesbury *NW3* 6D 64
(off Steele's Rd.)
Downes Cl. TW1: Twick 6B 114
Downes Ct. N21 1F 33
Downes Ho. *CR0: Wadd* 4B 168
(off Violet La.)
Downe Ter. TW10: Rich 6E 114
Downey Ho. *E1* 4K 85
(off Globe Rd.)
Downfield KT4: Wor Pk 1B 164
Downfield Cl. W9 4K 81
Down Hall Rd. KT2: King T 1D 150
DOWNHAM 5F 141
Downham Cl. RM5: Col R 1G 55
Downham Ct. *N1* 7D 66
(off Downham Rd.)
Downham Ent. Cen. SE6 2H 141
Downham Health & Leisure Cen. 4H 141
Downham La. BR1: Broml 5F 141
Downham Rd. N1 7D 66
Downham Way BR1: Broml 5F 141
Downham Wharf *N1* 1E 84
(off Downham Rd.)
Downhills Av. N17 3D 48
Downhills Pk. Rd. N17 3C 48
Downhills Way N17 3C 48
Downhurst Av. NW7 5E 28
Downhurst Ct. NW4 3E 44
Downie Wlk. *SE18* 5F 107
(off Brumwell Av.)
Downing Cl. HA2: Harr 3G 41
Downing Ct. *WC1* 4F 7
(off Grenville St.)
Downing Dr. UB6: G'frd 1H 77
Downing Ho. *W10* 6F 81
(off Cambridge Gdns.)
Downing Rd. RM9: Dag 7F 73
Downings E6 6E 88
Downing St. SW1 6E 12 (2J 101)
Downland Cl. N20 1F 31
Downland Ct. E11 2G 69
Downleys Cl. SE9 2C 142
Downman Rd. SE9 3C 124
Down Pl. W6 4D 98
Down Rd. TW11: Tedd 6B 132
The Downs SW20 7F 135
Downs Av. BR7: Chst 5D 142
HA5: Pinn 6C 40
Downs Bri. Rd. BR3: Beck 1F 159
Downs Ct. UB6: G'frd 3A 78
Downs Ct. Pde. *E8* 5H 67
(off Amhurst Rd.)
Downsell Rd. E15 4E 68
Downsfield Rd. E17 6A 50
Downshall Av. IG3: Ilf 6J 53
Downs Hill BR3: Beck 7F 141
Downshire Hill NW3 4B 64
Downside TW1: Twick 3K 131
TW16: Sun 1J 147
Downside Cl. SW19 6A 136
Downside Cres. NW3 5C 64
W13 4A 78
Downside Rd. SM2: Sutt 6B 166
Downside Wlk. *TW8: Bford* 6D 96
(off Windmill Rd.)
UB5: N'olt 3D 76
Downs La. E5 4H 67
Downs Pk. Rd. E5 5F 67
E8 5F 67
Downs Rd. BR3: Beck 2D 158
CR7: Thor H 1C 156
E5 4G 67
EN1: Enf 4K 23
Down St. KT8: W Mole 5E 148
W1 5J 11 (1F 101)
Down St. M. W1 5J 11 (1F 101)
Downs Vw. TW7: Isle 1K 113
Downsview Gdns. SE19 7B 138
Downsview Rd. SE19 7C 138
Downsway BR6: Orp 5J 173
The Downsway SM2: Sutt 7A 166
Downton Av. SW2 2J 137
Downtown Rd. SE16 2A 104
Down Way UB5: N'olt 3K 75
Downy Ho. W3 1A 98
Dowrey St. N1 1A 84
Dowsett Rd. N17 2F 49
Dowson Cl. SE5 4D 120
Dowson Ho. *E1* 6K 85
(off Bower St.)
Doyce St. SE1 6C 14 (2C 102)
Doyle Gdns. NW10 1C 80
Doyle Ho. *SW13* 7E 98
(off Trinity Chu. Rd.)
Doyle Rd. SE25 4G 157
D'Oyley St. SW1 3G 17 (4E 100)
Doynton St. N19 2F 65
Draco Ga. SW15 3E 116
Draco St. SE17 6C 102
Dragmore St. SW4 6H 119
Dragonfly Cl. E13 3K 87
KT5: Surb 1J 163
Dragonfly Ct. *NW9* 1A 44
(off Heybourne Cres.)
Dragonfly Pl. SE4 3A 122
Dragon Rd. SE15 6E 102
Dragons Way EN5: Barn 5C 20
Dragon Yd. WC1 7F 7 (6J 83)
Dragoon Rd. SE8 5B 104
Dragor Rd. NW10 4J 79
Drake Cl. IG11: Bark 4K 90
SE16 2K 103
Drake Ct. *KT5: Surb* 4E 150
(off Cranes Pk. Av.)
SE1 7C 14
(off Swan St.)
SE19 5F 139
W12 2E 98
(off Scott's Rd.)
Drake Cres. SE28 6C 90
Drakefell Rd. SE4 2K 121
SE14 2K 121
Drakefield Rd. SW17 3E 136
Drake Hall *E16* 1K 105
(off Wesley Av.)
Drake Ho. *E1* 5J 85
(off Stepney Way)
E14 7A 86
(off Victory Pl.)
SW1 7C 18
(off Dolphin Sq.)
Drakeland Ho. *W9* 4H 81
(off Fernhead Rd.)
Drakeley Ct. N5 4B 66
Drake M. BR2: Broml 4A 160
Drake Rd. CR0: C'don 7K 155
CR4: Mitc 6E 154
HA2: Harr 2D 58
KT9: Chess 5G 163
SE4 3C 122
The Drakes SE8 6C 104
Drakes Ct. SE23 1J 139
Drakes Ctyd. NW6 7H 63
Drakes Dr. HA6: Nwood 1D 38
Drake St. EN2: Enf 1J 23
WC1 6G 7 (5K 83)
Drakes Wlk. E6 1D 88
Drakewood Rd. SW16 7H 137
Draper Cl. DA17: Belv 4F 109
TW7: Isle 2H 113
Draper Ct. BR1: Broml 4C 160
Draper Ho. *SE1* 4B 102
(off Newington Butts)
Draper Pl. *N1* 1B 84
(off Dagmar Ter.)
Drapers Almshouses *E3* 3D 86
(off Rainhill Way)
Drapers Cott. Homes NW7 4G 29
(not continuous)
Draper's Ct. *SW11* 1E 118
(off Battersea Pk. Rd.)
Drapers Gdns. EC2 7F 9 (6D 84)
Drapers Rd. E15 4F 69
EN2: Enf 2G 23
N17 3F 49
Drapers Yd. *SW18* 5K 117
(off Ryland Blvd.)
Drappers Way SE16 4G 103
Draven Cl. BR2: Hayes 7H 159
Drawdock Rd. SE10 2F 105
Drawell Cl. SE18 5J 107
Drax Av. SW20 7C 134
Draxmont SW19 6G 135
Draycot Rd. E11 6K 51
KT6: Surb 1G 163
Draycott Av. HA3: Kenton 6B 42
SW3 3D 16 (4C 100)
Draycott Cl. HA3: Kenton 6B 42
NW2 3F 63
SE5 7D 102
(not continuous)
Draycott Ct. *SW11* 1C 118
(off Westbridge Rd.)
Draycott M. *SW6* 2H 117
(off Laurel Bank Gdns.)
Draycott Pl. SW3 4E 16 (4D 100)
Draycott Ter. SW3 4F 17 (4D 100)
Dray Ct. *HA0: Wemb* 5A 60
(off Brewery Cl.)
Drayford Cl. W9 4H 81
Dray Gdns. SW2 5K 119
Draymans M. SE15 2F 121
Draymans Way TW7: Isle 3K 113
Drayside M. UB2: S'hall 2D 94
Drayson M. W8 2J 99
Drayton Av. BR6: Farnb 1F 173
W13 7A 78
Drayton Bri. Rd. W7 7K 77
W13 7K 77
Drayton Cl. IG1: Ilf 1H 71
TW4: Houn 5D 112
Drayton Ct. UB7: W Dray 4B 92
Drayton Gdns. N21 7G 23
SW10 6A 16 (5A 100)
UB7: W Dray 2A 92
W13 7A 78
Drayton Grn. W13 7A 78
Drayton Grn. Rd. W13 7B 78
Drayton Gro. W13 7A 78
Drayton Ho. E11 1F 69
SE5 7D 102
(off Elmington Rd.)
Drayton Pk. N5 4A 66
Drayton Pk. M. N5 5A 66
Drayton Rd. CR0: C'don 2B 168
E11 1F 69
N17 2E 48
NW10 1B 80
W13 7A 78
Drayton Waye HA3: Kenton 6B 42
Dray Wlk. E1 4K 9 (4F 85)
Dreadnought Cl. SW19 2B 154
Dreadnought St. SE10 3G 105
Dreadnought Wlk. SE10 6D 104
Drenon Sq. UB3: Hayes 7H 75
Dresden Cl. NW6 6K 63
Dresden Ho. SE11 3H 19
SW11 2E 118
(off Dagnall St.)
Dresden Rd. N19 1G 65
Dressington Av. SE4 6C 122
Drewery Ct. SE3 3G 123
Drewett Ho. *E1* 6G 85
(off Christian St.)
Drew Gdns. UB6: G'frd 6K 59
Drew Ho. SE8 5C 104
SW16 3J 137
Drew Rd. E16 1B 106
(not continuous)
Drewstead La. SW16 2H 137
Drewstead Rd. SW16 2H 137
Drey Ct. *KT4: Wor Pk* 2C 164
(off The Avenue)
Driffield Ct. *NW9* 1A 44
(off Pageant Av.)
Driffield Rd. E3 2A 86
The Drift BR2: Broml 3B 172
Drift Ct. E16 7F 89
The Driftway CR4: Mitc 1E 154
Driftway Ho. *E3* 2B 86
(off Stafford Rd.)
Drinkwater Ho. *SE5* 7D 102
(off Picton St.)
Drinkwater Rd. HA2: Harr 2F 59
The Drive BR3: Beck 2C 158
BR4: W W'ck 7F 159
BR6: Orp 2K 173
BR7: Chst 3K 161
The Drive CR7: Thor H 4D 156
DA5: Bexl 6C 126
DA8: Erith 7H 109
DA14: Sidc 3B 144
E4 1A 36
E17 3D 50
E18 4J 51
EN2: Enf 1J 23
EN5: Barn 3B 20
EN5: New Bar 6F 21
HA2: Harr 7E 40
HA6: Nwood 2G 39
HA8: Edg 5B 28
HA9: Wemb 2J 61
IG1: Ilf 6C 52
IG9: Buck H 1F 37
IG11: Bark 7K 71
KT2: King T 7J 133
KT6: Surb 7E 150
KT10: Esh 7G 149
KT19: Ewe 6B 164
N3 7D 30
N6 5D 46
N7 6K 65
(not continuous)
N11 6B 32
NW10 1B 80
NW11 7G 45
RM5: Col R 1J 55
SM4: Mord 5A 154
SW6 2G 117
SW20 7E 134
TW3: Houn 2H 113
TW7: Isle 2H 113
TW14: Felt 7A 112
TW15: Ashf 7F 129
UB10: Ick 4A 56
W3 6J 79
Drive Ct. HA8: Edg 5B 28
Drive Mans. *SW6* 2G 117
(off Fulham Rd.)
Droitwich Cl. SE26 3G 139
Dromey Gdns. HA3: Hrw W 7E 26
Dromore Rd. SW15 6G 117
Dronfield Gdns. RM8: Dag 5C 72
Dron Ho. *E1* 5J 85
(off Adelina Gro.)
Droop St. W10 3F 81
Drovers Ct. *KT1: King T* 2E 150
(off Fairfield E.)
Drovers Pl. SE15 7J 103
Drovers Rd. CR2: S Croy 5D 168
Drovers Way N7 6J 65
Druce Rd. SE21 6E 120
Druid St. SE1 6H 15 (2E 102)
(not continuous)
Druids Way BR2: Broml 4F 159
Drumaline Ridge KT4: Wor Pk 2A 164
Drum Ct. *N1* 7J 65
(off Gifford St.)
Drummer Stagpole M. NW7 5B 30
Drummond Av. RM7: Rom 4K 55
Drummond Ct. N12 7H 31
W3 3J 97
(off Palmerston Rd.)
Drummond Cres. NW1 1C 6 (3H 83)
Drummond Dr. HA7: Stan 7E 26
Drummond Ga. SW1 5D 18 (5H 101)
Drummond Ho. *E2* 2G 85
(off Goldsmiths Row)
N2 2A 46
(off Font Hills)
Drummond Pl. TW1: Twick 7B 114
Drummond Rd. CR0: C'don 2C 168
E11 6A 52
RM7: Rom 4K 55
SE16 3H 103
The Drummonds IG9: Buck H 2E 36
Drummonds Pl. TW9: Rich 4E 114
Drummond St. NW1 3A 6 (4G 83)
Drummond Way N1 7A 66
Druries *HA1: Harr* 1J 59
(off High St.)
Drury Cl. SW15 6C 116
Drury Cres. CR0: Wadd 2A 168
Drury Ho. SW8 1G 119
Drury La. WC2 7F 7 (6J 83)
Drury Lane Theatre Royal 2G 13
(off Catherine St.)
Drury Rd. HA1: Harr 7G 41
Drury Way NW10 5K 61
Drury Way Ind. Est. NW10 5J 61
Dryad St. SW15 3F 117
Dryburgh Gdns. NW9 3G 43
Dryburgh Ho. *SW1* 5K 17
(part of Abbots Mnr.)
Dryburgh Rd. SW15 3D 116
Dryden Av. W7 6K 77
Dryden Bldg. *E1* 6G 85
(off Commercial Rd.)
Dryden Cl. SW4 5H 119
Dryden Ct. SE11 4K 19 (4A 102)
Dryden Mans. *W14* 6G 99
(off Queen's Club Gdns.)
Dryden Rd. DA16: Well 1K 125
EN1: Enf 6K 23
HA3: W'stone 1K 41
SW19 6A 136
Dryden St. WC2 1F 13 (6J 83)
Dryfield Cl. NW10 6J 61
Dryfield Rd. HA8: Edg 6D 28
Dryfield Wlk. SE8 6C 104
Dryhill Rd. DA17: Belv 6F 109
Dryland Av. BR6: Orp 4K 173
Drylands Rd. N8 6J 47
Drysdale Av. E4 7J 25
Drysdale Dwellings *E8* 5F 67
(off Dunn St.)
Drysdale Pl. N1 1H 9 (3E 84)
Drysdale St. N1 1H 9 (3E 84)
Dublin Av. E8 1G 85
Dublin Ct. *HA2: Harr* 2H 59
(off Northolt Rd.)
Du Burstow Ter. W7 2J 95
Ducaine Apts. *E3* 3B 86
(off Merchant St.)
Ducal St. E2 2K 9 (3F 85)
Du Cane Cl. W12 6E 80
Du Cane Ct. SW17 1E 136
Du Cane Rd. W12 6B 80
Ducavel Ho. SW2 1K 137
Duchess Cl. N11 5A 32
SM1: Sutt 4A 166
Duchess Cres. HA7: Stan 3E 26
Duchess Dr. E13 4K 87
Duchess Gro. IG9: Buck H 2E 36
Duchess M. W1 6K 5 (5F 83)
W3 1G 97
Duchess of Bedford Ho. *W8* 2J 99
(off Duchess of Bedford's Wlk.)
Duchess of Bedford's Wlk. W8 2J 99
Duchess St. W1 6K 5 (5F 83)
Duchess Theatre 2G 13
(off Catherine St.)
Duchess Wlk. SE1 5J 15 (1F 103)
Duchy Rd. EN4: Had W 1G 21
Duchy St. SE1 4K 13 (1A 102)
(not continuous)
Ducie St. SW4 4K 119
Duckett M. N4 6B 48
Duckett Rd. N4 6B 48
Duckett's Apts. *E3* 7B 68
(off Wick La.)
Duckett St. E1 4K 85
Duckham Ct. *E14* 4D 104
(off Nauticus Wlk.)
Duck La. W1 1C 12
Duck Lees La. EN3: Pond E 4F 25
Duck's Hill Rd. HA4: Ruis 2D 38
HA6: Nwood 1D 38
DUCKS ISLAND 6A 20
Ducks Wlk. TW1: Twick 5C 114
Du Cros Dr. HA7: Stan 6J 27
Du Cros Rd. W3 1A 98
DUDDEN HILL 5D 62
Dudden Hill La. NW10 4B 62
Dudden Hill Pde. NW10 4B 62
Duddington Cl. SE9 4B 142
Dudley Av. HA3: Kenton 3C 42
Dudley Ct. NW11 4H 45
W1 1E 10
(off Up. Berkeley St.)
WC2 7E 6 (6J 83)
Dudley Dr. HA4: Ruis 5K 57
SM4: Mord 1G 165
Dudley Gdns. HA2: Harr 1H 59
W13 2B 96
Dudley M. SW2 6A 120
Dudley Pl. TW19: Stanw 6B 110
UB3: Harl 4F 93
Dudley Rd. E17 2C 50
HA2: Harr 2G 59
IG1: Ilf 4F 71
KT1: King T 3F 151
KT12: Walt T 6J 147
N3 2K 45
NW6 2G 81
SW19 6J 135
TW9: Rich 2F 115
TW14: Bedf 1E 128
TW15: Ashf 5B 128
UB2: S'hall 2B 94
Dudley St. W2 6A 4 (5B 82)
Dudlington Rd. E5 2J 67
Dudmaston M. SW3 5B 16
Dudrich Cl. N11 6J 31
Dudrich M. EN2: Enf 1F 23
SE22 5F 121
Dudsbury Rd. DA14: Sidc 6B 144
Dudset La. TW5: Cran 1J 111
Duett Ct. TW5: Hest 7C 94
Duffell Ho. SE11 6H 19
Dufferin Av. EC1 4E 8
Dufferin Ct. *EC1* 4E 8
(off Dufferin St.)
Dufferin St. EC1 4D 8 (4C 84)
Duffield Cl. HA1: Harr 5K 41
Duffield Dr. N15 4F 49
Duff St. E14 6D 86
Dufour's Pl. W1 1B 12 (6G 83)
Dufton Dwellings *E15* 4G 69
(off High Rd. Leyton)
Dugard Way SE11 4B 102
Dugdale Cen. 4J 23
Dugdale Ct. *NW10* 3D 80
(off Harrow Rd.)
Duggan Dr. BR7: Chst 6C 142
Dugolly Av. HA9: Wemb 3H 61
Dujardin M. EN3: Pond E 6E 24
Duke Ct. TW3: Houn 4D 112
Duke Gdns. IG6: Ilf 4H 53
Duke Humphrey Rd. SE3 1G 123
Duke of Cambridge Cl.
TW2: Whitt 6H 113
Duke of Clarence Ct. *SE17* 5C 102
(off Manor Pl.)
Duke of Edinburgh Rd.
SM1: Sutt 2B 166
Duke of Wellington Av. SE18 3F 107
Duke of Wellington Pl.
SW1 6H 11 (2E 100)
Duke of York Column 5D 12 (1H 101)
Duke of York Sq. SW3 4F 17 (5D 100)
Duke of York's Theatre 3E 12
(off St Martin's La.)
Duke of York St. SW1 4B 12 (1G 101)
Duke Rd. IG6: Ilf 4H 53
W4 5K 97
Duke's Av. HA8: Edg 6A 28
N10 3F 47
W4 5K 97
Dukes Av. HA1: Harr 4J 41
HA2: Harr 6D 40
KT2: King T 4C 132
KT3: N Mald 3A 152
N3 1K 45
TW4: Houn 4C 112
TW10: Ham 4C 132
UB5: N'olt 7C 58
Dukes Cl. TW12: Hamp 5D 130
TW15: Ashf 4E 128
Dukes Ct. E6 1E 88
(not continuous)
SE13 2E 122
SW14 2K 115
W2 7K 81
(off Moscow Rd.)
Dukes Ga. W4 4J 97
Dukes Grn. Av. TW14: Felt 5J 111
Dukes Head Pas. TW12: Hamp 7G 131
Duke's Head Yd. N6 1F 65
Duke Shore Wharf E14 7B 86
Duke's Ho. *SW1* 3D 18
(off Vincent St.)
Dukes La. W8 2K 99
Duke's La. Chambers *W8* 2K 99
(off Dukes La.)
Duke's La. Mans. *W8* 2K 99
(off Dukes La.)
Dukes Lodge *W8* 1H 99
(off Holland Wlk.)
Dukes Meadow Golf & Tennis 2K 115
Duke's Meadow Golf Course 2K 115
Duke's Meadows 2K 115
Duke's M. W1 7H 5
Dukes M. N10 3F 47
Dukes Orchard DA5: Bexl 1J 145
Duke's Pas. E17 4E 50
Duke's Pl. EC3 1H 15 (6E 84)
Dukes Point *N6* 1F 65
(off Dukes Head Yd.)
Dukes Ride UB10: Ick 4A 56
Duke's Rd. WC1 2D 6 (3H 83)
Dukes Rd. E6 1E 88
W3 4G 79
Dukesthorpe Rd. SE26 4K 139
Duke St. SM1: Sutt 4B 166
TW9: Rich 4D 114
W1 7H 5 (6E 82)
Duke St. Hill SE1 4F 15 (1D 102)
Duke St. Mans. *W1* 1H 11
(off Duke St.)
Duke St. St James's SW1 4B 12 (1G 101)
Dukes Way BR4: W W'ck 3G 171
HA9: Wemb 5E 60
Duke's Yd. W1 2H 11 (7E 82)
Dulas St. N4 1K 65
Dulford St. W11 7G 81
Dulka Rd. SW11 5D 118
Dulverton *NW1* 1G 83
(off Royal College St.)
Dulverton Mans. WC1 4H 7
Dulverton Rd. HA4: Ruis 1J 57
SE9 2G 143
DULWICH 2E 138
Dulwich & Sydenham Hill Golf Course 2F 139
Dulwich Bus. Cen. SE23 1K 139
Dulwich Comn. SE21 1E 138
SE22 1E 138
Dulwich Hamlet FC 4E 120
Dulwich Lawn Cl. SE22 5F 121
Dulwich Leisure Cen. 4G 121
The Dulwich Oaks SE21 3F 139
Dulwich Picture Gallery 7D 120
Dulwich Ri. Gdns. SE22 5F 121
Dulwich Rd. SE24 5A 120
Dulwich Upper Wood Nature Pk. 5F 139
DULWICH VILLAGE 7E 120
Dulwich Village SE21 6D 120
Dulwich Wood Av. SE19 4E 138
Dulwich Wood Pk. SE19 4E 138
Dumain Ct. *SE11* 4B 102
(off Opal St.)
Dumbarton Ct. SW2 6J 119
Dumbarton Rd. SW2 6J 119
Dumbleton Cl. KT1: King T 1H 151
Dumbreck Rd. SE9 4D 124
Dumont Rd. N16 3E 66
Dumpton Pl. NW1 7E 64
Dumsey Eyot KT16: Chert 7A 146
Dunally Pk. TW17: Shep 7F 147
Dunbar Av. BR3: Beck 4A 158
RM10: Dag 3G 73
SW16 2A 156
Dunbar Cl. UB4: Hayes 5K 75
Dunbar Ct. *BR2: Broml* 3H 159
(off Durham Rd.)
SM1: Sutt 5B 166
Dunbar Gdns. RM10: Dag 5G 73
Dunbar Rd. E7 6J 69
KT3: N Mald 4J 151
N22 1A 48
Dunbar St. SE27 3C 138
Dunbar Twr. *E8* 6F 67
(off Dalston Sq.)
Dunbar Wharf *E14* 7B 86
(off Narrow St.)
Dunblane Cl. HA8: Edg 2C 28
Dunblane Rd. SE9 3C 124
Dunboe Pl. TW17: Shep 7E 146
Dunboyne Rd. NW3 5D 64
Dunbridge Ho. SW15 6B 116
Dunbridge St. E2 4G 85
Duncan Cl. EN5: New Bar 4F 21
Duncan Ct. *E14* 5E 86
(off Teviot St.)
N21 1G 33
Duncan Gro. W3 6A 80
Duncan Ho. E15 1F 87
NW3 7D 64
(off Fellows Rd.)
SW1 6B 18
(off Dolphin Sq.)
Duncannon Ho. *SW1* 6D 18
(off Lindsay Sq.)
Duncannon St. WC2 3E 12 (7J 83)
Duncan Rd. E8 1H 85
TW9: Rich 4E 114
Duncan St. N1 2B 84
Duncan Ter. N1 2B 84
(not continuous)
Dunch St. E1 6H 85
Dunchurch Ho. RM10: Dag 7G 73
Duncombe Hill SE23 7A 122
Duncombe Rd. N19 1H 65
Duncrievie Rd. SE13 6F 123
Duncroft SE18 7J 107
Dundalk Ho. *E1* 6J 85
(off Clark St.)
Dundalk Rd. SE4 3A 122
Dundas Ct. *SE10* 6D 104
(off Dowells St.)
Dundas Gdns. KT8: W Mole 3F 149
Dundas Ho. *E2* 2J 85
(off Bishop's Way)
Dundas Rd. SE15 2J 121
SW9 1A 120
Dundee Ct. *E1* 1H 103
(off Wapping High St.)
SE1 7G 15
(off Long La.)
Dundee Ho. *W9* 3A 82
(off Maida Vale)
Dundee Rd. E13 2K 87
SE25 5H 157
Dundee St. E1 1H 103
Dundee Way EN3: Brim 3F 25
Dundee Wharf E14 7B 86
Dundela Gdns. KT4: Wor Pk 4D 164
Dundonald Cl. E6 6C 88
Dundonald Rd. NW10 1F 81
SW19 7G 135
Dundry Ho. SE26 3G 139
Dunedin Ho. *E16* 1D 106
(off Manwood St.)
Dunedin M. SW2 1J 137

Dunedin Rd.—E. Row

Dunedin Rd. E10 . . . 4E 68
IG1: Ilf . . . 1G 71
Dunedin Way UB4: Yead . . . 4A 76
Dunelm Gro. SE27 . . . 3C 138
Dunelm St. E1 . . . 6K 85
Dunfield Gdns. SE6 . . . 5D 140
Dunfield Rd. SE6 . . . 5D 140
(not continuous)
Dunford Ct. HA5: Hat E . . . 1D 40
Dunford Rd. N7 . . . 4K 65
Dungannon Ho. *SW6* . . . 7J 99
(off Vanston Pl.)
Dungarvan Av. SW15 . . . 4C 116
Dunheved Cl. CR7: Thor H . . . 6A 156
Dunheved Rd. Nth. CR7: Thor H . . . 6A 156
Dunheved Rd. Sth. CR7: Thor H . . . 6A 156
Dunheved Rd. W. CR7: Thor H . . . 6A 156
Dunhill Point SW15 . . . 1C 134
Dunholme Grn. N9 . . . 3A 34
Dunholme La. N9 . . . 3A 34
Dunholme Rd. N9 . . . 3A 34
Dunkeld Rd. RM8: Dag . . . 2B 72
SE25 . . . 4D 156
Dunkery Rd. SE9 . . . 4B 142
Dunkirk Ho. SE1 . . . 2D 102
Dunkirk St. SE27 . . . 4C 138
Dunlace Rd. E5 . . . 4J 67
Dunleary Cl. TW4: Houn . . . 7D 112
Dunley Dr. CR0: New Ad . . . 7D 170
Dunlin Ho. *SE16* . . . 4K 103
(off Tawny Way)
Dunloe Av. N17 . . . 3D 48
Dunloe Ct. E2 . . . 2F 85
Dunloe St. E2 . . . 2F 85
Dunlop Pl. SE16 . . . 3F 103
Dunmore Point *E2* . . . 2J 9
(off Gascoigne Pl.)
Dunmore Rd. NW6 . . . 1G 81
SW20 . . . 1E 152
Dunmow Cl. RM6: Chad H . . . 5C 54
TW13: Hanw . . . 3C 130
Dunmow Ho. *SE11* . . . 5H 19
(off Newburn St.)
Dunmow Rd. E15 . . . 4F 69
Dunmow Wlk. *N1* . . . 1C 84
(off Popham St.)
Dunnage Cres. SE16 . . . 4A 104
(not continuous)
Dunnell Cl. TW16: Sun . . . 1J 147
Dunnett Ho. *E3* . . . 2B 86
(off Vernon Rd.)
Dunnico Ho. *SE17* . . . 5E 102
(off East St.)
Dunn Mead NW9 . . . 7G 29
Dunnock Cl. N9 . . . 1E 34
Dunnock Dr. HA7: Stan . . . 5E 26
Dunnock Ho. NW9 . . . 6B 44
Dunnock M. E5 . . . 3G 67
Dunnock Rd. E6 . . . 6C 88
Dunn's Pas. WC1 . . . 7F 7
Dunn St. E8 . . . 5F 67
Dunollie Pl. NW5 . . . 5G 65
Dunollie Rd. NW5 . . . 5G 65
Dunoon Gdns. SE23 . . . 7K 121
Dunoon Ho. *N1* . . . 1K 83
(off Bemerton Est.)
Dunoon Rd. SE23 . . . 7J 121
Dunoran Home BR1: Broml . . . 1C 160
Dunraven Dr. EN2: Enf . . . 2F 23
Dunraven Rd. W12 . . . 1C 98
Dunraven St. W1 . . . 2F 11 (7D 82)
Dunsany Rd. W14 . . . 3F 99
Dunsfold Ct. *SM2: Sutt* . . . 7K 165
(off Blackbush Cl.)
Dunsfold Way CR0: New Ad . . . 7D 170
Dunsford Way SW15 . . . 6D 116
Dunsmore Cl. UB4: Yead . . . 4B 76
Dunsmore Rd. KT12: Walt T . . . 6K 147
Dunsmure Rd. N16 . . . 1E 66
Dunspring La. IG5: Ilf . . . 2F 53
Dunstable M. W1 . . . 5H 5 (5E 82)
Dunstable Rd. KT8: W Mole . . . 4D 148
TW9: Rich . . . 4E 114
Dunstall Rd. SW20 . . . 6D 134
Dunstall Way KT8: W Mole . . . 3F 149
Dunstall Welling Est. DA16: Well . . . 2B 126
Dunstan Cl. N2 . . . 3A 46
Dunstan Glade BR5: Pet W . . . 6H 161
Dunstan Gro. SE20 . . . 7H 139
Dunstan Ho's. *E1* . . . 5J 85
(off Stepney Grn.)
Dunstan M. EN1: Enf . . . 3K 23
Dunstan Rd. NW11 . . . 1H 63
Dunstan's Gro. SE22 . . . 6H 121
Dunstan's Rd. SE22 . . . 7G 121
Dunster Av. SM4: Mord . . . 1F 165
Dunster Cl. EN5: Barn . . . 4A 20
RM5: Col R . . . 1J 55
Dunster Ct. EC3 . . . 2H 15 (7E 84)
Dunster Dr. NW9 . . . 1J 61
Dunster Gdns. NW6 . . . 7H 63
Dunster Ho. SE6 . . . 3E 140
Dunsterville Way SE1 . . . 7F 15 (2D 102)
Dunster Way HA2: Harr . . . 3C 58
SM6: W'gton . . . 1E 166
Dunstone Ct. SE6 . . . 7C 122
Dunston Rd. E8 . . . 1F 85
SW11 . . . 2E 118
Dunston St. E8 . . . 1E 84
Dunton Cl. KT6: Surb . . . 1E 162
Dunton Ct. SE23 . . . 2H 139
Dunton Rd. E10 . . . 7D 50
RM1: Rom . . . 4K 55
SE1 . . . 5F 103
Duntshill Rd. SW18 . . . 1K 135
Dunvegan Cl. KT8: W Mole . . . 4E 148
Dunvegan Rd. SE9 . . . 4D 124
Dunwich Ct. *RM6: Chad H* . . . 5B 54
(off Glandford Way)
Dunwich Rd. DA7: Bex . . . 1F 127
Dunworth M. W11 . . . 6H 81
Duplex Ride SW1 . . . 7F 11 (2D 100)
Dupont Rd. SW20 . . . 2F 153
Duppas Av. CR0: Wadd . . . 4B 168
Duppas Cl. TW17: Shep . . . 5F 147
Duppas Ct. *CR0: C'don* . . . 3B 168
(off Duppas Hill Ter.)
Duppas Hill La. CR0: C'don . . . 4B 168
Duppas Hill Rd. CR0: Wadd . . . 4A 168
Duppas Hill Ter. CR0: C'don . . . 3B 168
Duppas Rd. CR0: Wadd . . . 3A 168
Dupree Rd. SE7 . . . 5K 105
Dura Den Cl. BR3: Beck . . . 7D 140
Durand Gdns. SW9 . . . 1K 119
Durands Wlk. SE16 . . . 2B 104
Durand Way NW10 . . . 7J 61
Durants Pk. . . . 3D 24
Durants Pk. Av. EN3: Pond E . . . 4E 24
Durants Rd. EN3: Pond E . . . 4D 24
Durant St. E2 . . . 2G 85
Durban Ct. E7 . . . 7B 70
Durban Gdns. RM10: Dag . . . 7J 73
Durban Ho. *W12* . . . 7D 80
(off White City Est.)
Durban Rd. BR3: Beck . . . 2B 158
E15 . . . 3G 87
E17 . . . 1B 50
IG2: Ilf . . . 1J 71
N17 . . . 6K 33
SE27 . . . 4C 138
Durbin Rd. KT9: Chess . . . 4E 162
Durdan Cotts. *UB1: S'hall* . . . 6D 76
(off Denbigh Rd.)
Durdans Ho. *NW1* . . . 7F 65
(off Farrier St.)
Durdans Rd. UB1: S'hall . . . 6D 76
Durell Gdns. RM9: Dag . . . 5D 72
Durell Ho. *SE16* . . . 2K 103
(off Wolfe Cres.)
Durell Rd. RM9: Dag . . . 5D 72
Durfey Pl. SE5 . . . 7D 102
Durford Cres. SW15 . . . 1D 134
Durham Av. BR2: Broml . . . 4H 159
IG8: Buck H, Wfd G . . . 5G 37
TW5: Hest . . . 5D 94
Durham Cl. SW20 . . . 2D 152
Durham Ct. *NW6* . . . 2J 81
(off Kilburn Pk. Rd.)
TW11: Tedd . . . 4J 131
Durham Hill BR1: Broml . . . 4H 141
Durham Ho. BR2: Broml . . . 4G 159
IG11: Bark . . . 7A 72
(off Margaret Bondfield Av.)
NW8 . . . 2D 4
(off Lorne Cl.)
RM10: Dag . . . 5J 73
Durham Ho. St. WC2 . . . 3F 13
Durham Pl. IG1: Ilf . . . 4G 71
SW3 . . . 6E 16 (5D 100)
Durham Ri. SE18 . . . 5G 107
Durham Rd. BR2: Broml . . . 3H 159
DA14: Sidc . . . 5B 144
E12 . . . 4B 70
E16 . . . 4G 87
HA1: Harr . . . 5F 41
N2 . . . 3C 46
N7 . . . 2K 65
N9 . . . 2B 34
RM10: Dag . . . 5J 73
SW20 . . . 1D 152
TW14: Felt . . . 7A 112
W5 . . . 3D 96
Durham Row E1 . . . 5A 86
Durham St. SE11 . . . 6G 19 (5K 101)
Durham Ter. W2 . . . 6K 81
Durham Wharf Dr. TW8: Bford . . . 7C 96
Durham Yd. E2 . . . 3H 85
Durley Av. HA5: Pinn . . . 7C 40
Durley Rd. N16 . . . 7E 48
Durlston Rd. E5 . . . 2G 67
KT2: King T . . . 6E 132
Durnford Ho. SE6 . . . 3E 140
Durnford St. N15 . . . 5E 48
SE10 . . . 6E 104
Durning Rd. SE19 . . . 5D 138
Durnsford Av. SW19 . . . 2J 135
Durnsford Ct. *EN3: Enf H* . . . 3F 25
(off Enstone Rd.)
Durnsford Rd. N11 . . . 1H 47
SW19 . . . 2J 135
Durrant Ct. HA3: Hrw W . . . 2J 41
Durrant Ho. *EC1* . . . 5E 8
(off Chiswell St.)
Durrant Way BR6: Farnb . . . 5H 173
Durrell Rd. SW6 . . . 1H 117
Durrell Way TW17: Shep . . . 6F 147
Durrels Ho. *W14* . . . 4H 99
(off Warwick Gdns.)
Durrington Av. SW20 . . . 7E 134
Durrington Pk. Rd. SW20 . . . 1E 152
Durrington Rd. E5 . . . 4A 68
Durrington Twr. SW8 . . . 2G 119
Durrisdeer Ho. *NW2* . . . 4H 63
(off Lyndale)
Dursley Cl. SE3 . . . 2A 124
Dursley Gdns. SE3 . . . 1B 124
Dursley Rd. SE3 . . . 2A 124
Durward Ho. *W8* . . . 2K 99
(off Kensington Ct.)
Durward St. E1 . . . 5H 85
Durweston M. W1 . . . 5F 5
Durweston St. W1 . . . 6F 5 (5D 82)
Dury Falls Ct. RM5: Col R . . . 2J 55
Dury Rd. EN5: Barn . . . 1C 20
Dutch Barn Cl.
TW19: Stanw . . . 6A 110
Dutch Gdns. KT2: King T . . . 6H 133
Dutch Yd. SW18 . . . 5J 117
Dutton St. SE10 . . . 1E 122
Duval Ho. *N19* . . . 2H 65
(off Ashbrook Rd.)
SW11 . . . 3C 118
Duxberry Av. TW13: Felt . . . 3A 130
Duxberry Cl. BR2: Broml . . . 5C 160
Duxford Ho. *SE2* . . . 2D 108
(off Wolvercote Rd.)
DW Fitness
Waldorf Hotel . . . 2G 13
Dyas Rd. TW16: Sun . . . 1J 147
Dye Ho. La. E3 . . . 1C 86
Dyer Ho. TW12: Hamp . . . 1F 149
Dyer's Bldgs. EC1 . . . 6J 7 (5A 84)
Dyers Hall Rd. E11 . . . 1G 69
Dyers Hall Rd. Sth. E11 . . . 2F 69
Dyers La. SW15 . . . 4D 116
Dykes Way BR2: Broml . . . 3H 159
Dykewood Cl. DA5: Bexl . . . 3K 145
Dylan Rd. DA17: Belv . . . 3G 109
SE24 . . . 4B 120
Dylways SE5 . . . 4D 120
Dymchurch Cl. BR6: Orp . . . 4J 173
IG5: Ilf . . . 2E 52
Dymes Path SW19 . . . 2F 135
Dymock St. SW6 . . . 3K 117
Dyneley Rd. SE12 . . . 3A 142
Dyne Rd. NW6 . . . 7G 63
Dynevor Rd. N16 . . . 3E 66
TW10: Rich . . . 5E 114
Dynham Rd. NW6 . . . 7J 63
Dyott St. WC1 . . . 7D 6 (6H 83)
Dysart Av. KT2: King T . . . 5C 132
Dysart St. EC2 . . . 4G 9 (4D 84)
Dyson Ct. HA0: Wemb . . . 4A 60
NW2 . . . 1E 62
Dyson Dr. UB10: Uxb . . . 1A 74
Dyson Ho. *SE10* . . . 5H 105
(off Blackwall La.)
Dyson Rd. E11 . . . 6G 51
E15 . . . 6H 69
Dysons Rd. N18 . . . 5C 34

E

Eade Rd. N4 . . . 7C 48
Eagans Cl. N2 . . . 3B 46
Eagle Av. RM6: Chad H . . . 6E 54
Eagle Cl. EN3: Pond E . . . 4D 24
SE16 . . . 5J 103
SM6: W'gton . . . 6J 167
Eagle Ct. E11 . . . 4J 51
EC1 . . . 5A 8 (5B 84)
Eagle Dr. NW9 . . . 2A 44
Eagle Dwellings *EC1* . . . 1D 8
(off City Rd.)
Eagle Hgts. SW11 . . . 3C 118
Eagle Hill SE19 . . . 6D 138
Eagle Ho. *E1* . . . 4H 85
(off Headlam St.)
EC1 . . . 2E 8
(off City Rd.)
N1 . . . 2D 84
(off Eagle Wharf Rd.)
Eagle Ho. M. SW4 . . . 5G 119
Eagle La. E11 . . . 4J 51
Eagle Lodge NW11 . . . 7H 45
Eagle Mans. *N16* . . . 5F 67
(off Salcombe Rd.)
Eagle M. N1 . . . 6E 66
Eagle Pl. SW1 . . . 3B 12
SW7 . . . 5A 100
Eagle Point *EC1* . . . 2E 8
(off City Rd.)
Eagle Rd. HA0: Wemb . . . 7D 60
TW6: H'row A . . . 3H 111
Eaglesfield Rd. SE18 . . . 1F 125
Eagle St. WC1 . . . 6G 7 (5K 83)
Eagle Ter. IG8: Wfd G . . . 7E 36
Eagle Trad. Est. CR4: Mitc . . . 6D 154
Eagle Wharf Ct. *SE1* . . . 5J 15
(off Lafone St.)
Eagle Wharf E. *E14* . . . 7A 86
(off Narrow St.)
Eagle Wharf Rd. N1 . . . 2C 84
Eagle Wharf W. *E14* . . . 7A 86
(off Narrow St.)
Eagle Works E. E1 . . . 4K 9
Eagle Works W. E1 . . . 4J 9
Eagling Cl. E3 . . . 3C 86
Ealdham Sq. SE9 . . . 4A 124
EALING . . . 7D 78
Ealing B'way. Cen. . . . 7D 78
EALING COMMON . . . 7F 79
Ealing Golf Course . . . 3B 78
Ealing Grn. W5 . . . 1D 96
Ealing Lawn Tennis Club &
Indoor Tennis Cen. . . . 7F 79
Ealing Pk. Gdns. W5 . . . 4C 96
Ealing Pk. Mans. *W5* . . . 3D 96
(off Sth. Ealing Rd.)
Ealing Rd. HA0: Wemb . . . 6E 60
TW8: Bford . . . 5D 96
UB5: N'olt . . . 1E 76
Ealing Squash & Fitness Club . . . 6E 78
Ealing Studios . . . 1D 96
Ealing Village W5 . . . 6E 78
Eamont Cl. HA4: Ruis . . . 7D 38
Eamont Ct. *NW8* . . . 2C 82
(off Eamont St.)
Eamont St. NW8 . . . 2C 82
Eardley Cres. SW5 . . . 5J 99
Eardley Point *SE18* . . . 4F 107
(off Wilmount St.)
Eardley Rd. DA17: Belv . . . 5G 109
SW16 . . . 5G 137
Earhart Ho. *NW9* . . . 3C 44
(off East Dr.)
Earhart Way TW6: Cran, H'row A . . . 3J 111
Earl Cl. N11 . . . 5A 32
Earldom Rd. SW15 . . . 4E 116
Earle Gdns. KT2: King T . . . 7E 132
Earle Ho. *SW1* . . . 4D 18
(off Montaigne Cl.)
Earlham Ct. E11 . . . 7H 51
Earlham Gro. E7 . . . 5H 69
N22 . . . 7E 32
Earlham St. WC2 . . . 1D 12 (6J 83)
Earl Ho. *NW1* . . . 4D 4
(off Lisson Gro.)
Earlom Ho. *WC1* . . . 2J 7
(off Margery St.)
Earl Ri. SE18 . . . 5H 107
Earl Rd. SW14 . . . 4J 115
Earlsbury Gdns. HA8: Edg . . . 4B 28
EARL'S COURT . . . 4K 99
Earl's Ct. Gdns. SW5 . . . 4K 99
Earl's Ct. Rd. SW5 . . . 3J 99
W8 . . . 3J 99
Earl's Ct. Sq. SW5 . . . 5K 99
Earls Cres. HA1: Harr . . . 4J 41
Earlsdown Ho. IG11: Bark . . . 2H 89
Earlsferry Way N1 . . . 7J 65
(not continuous)
EARLSFIELD . . . 1A 136
Earlsfield Ho. *KT2: King T* . . . 1D 150
(off Seven Kings Way)
Earlsfield Rd. SW18 . . . 1A 136
Earlshall Rd. SE9 . . . 4D 124
Earls Ho. TW9: Kew . . . 7H 97
Earlsmead HA2: Harr . . . 4D 58
Earlsmead Rd. N15 . . . 5F 49
NW10 . . . 3E 80
Earlsmead Stadium . . . 4D 58
Earls Ter. W8 . . . 3H 99
Earlsthorpe M. SW12 . . . 6E 118
Earlsthorpe Rd. SE26 . . . 4K 139
Earlstoke St. EC1 . . . 1A 8 (3B 84)
Earlston Gro. E9 . . . 1H 85
Earl St. EC2 . . . 5G 9 (5D 84)
Earl's Wlk. RM8: Dag . . . 4B 72
Earls Wlk. W8 . . . 3J 99
Earls Way *SE1* . . . 5J 15
(off Queen Elizabeth St.)
Earlswood Av. CR7: Thor H . . . 5A 156
Earlswood Cl. SE10 . . . 6G 105
Earlswood Gdns. IG5: Ilf . . . 3E 52
Earlswood St. SE10 . . . 5G 105
Early M. NW1 . . . 1F 83
Early Rivers Ho. *E20* . . . 5E 68
(off Ellis Way)
Earnshaw Ho. *EC1* . . . 2B 8
(off Percival St.)
Earnshaw St. WC2 . . . 7D 6 (6H 83)
Earsby St. W14 . . . 4G 99
(not continuous)
Easby Cres. SM4: Mord . . . 6K 153
Easebourne Rd. RM8: Dag . . . 5C 72
Easedale Ho. TW7: Isle . . . 5K 113
Eashing Point *SW15* . . . 1D 134
(off Wanborough Dr.)
Easleys M. W1 . . . 7H 5 (6E 82)
East 10 Ent. Pk. E10 . . . 1A 68
EAST ACTON . . . 7B 80
E. Acton Arc. W3 . . . 6A 80
E. Acton Ct. W3 . . . 7A 80
E. Acton La. W3 . . . 1A 98
E. Arbour St. E1 . . . 6K 85
East Av. E12 . . . 7C 70
E17 . . . 4D 50
SM6: W'gton . . . 5K 167
UB1: S'hall . . . 7D 76
UB3: Hayes . . . 1H 93
E. Bank N16 . . . 7E 48
Eastbank Cl. E17 . . . 5D 50
Eastbank Rd. TW12: Hamp H . . . 5G 131
EAST BARNET . . . 6H 21
E. Barnet Rd. EN4: E Barn . . . 4G 21
E. Bay La. E20 . . . 5C 68
E. Beckton District Cen. . . . 5D 88
EAST BEDFONT . . . 7G 111
E. Block *SE1* . . . 6H 13
(off York Rd.)
Eastbourne Av. W3 . . . 6K 79
Eastbourne Gdns. SW14 . . . 3J 115
Eastbourne M. W2 . . . 7A 4 (6A 82)
Eastbourne Rd. E6 . . . 3E 88
(not continuous)
E15 . . . 1G 87
N15 . . . 6E 48
SW17 . . . 6E 136
TW8: Bford . . . 5C 96
TW13: Felt . . . 2B 130
W4 . . . 6J 97
Eastbourne Ter. W2 . . . 7A 4 (6A 82)
Eastbournia Av. N9 . . . 3C 34
Eastbrook Av. N9 . . . 7D 24
RM10: Dag . . . 4J 73
Eastbrook Cl. RM10: Dag . . . 4J 73
Eastbrook Dr. RM7: Rush G . . . 3K 73
Eastbrookend Country Pk. . . . 3K 73
Eastbrook Rd. SE3 . . . 1K 123
Eastbury Av. EN1: Enf . . . 1A 24
IG11: Bark . . . 1J 89
Eastbury Ct. *EN5: New Bar* . . . 5F 21
(off Lyonsdown Rd.)
IG11: Bark . . . 1J 89
Eastbury Gro. W4 . . . 5A 98
Eastbury Manor House . . . 1K 89
Eastbury Rd. BR5: Pet W . . . 6H 161
E6 . . . 4E 88
KT2: King T . . . 7E 132
RM7: Rom . . . 6K 55
Eastbury Sq. IG11: Bark . . . 1K 89
Eastbury Ter. E1 . . . 4K 85
E. Carriage Ho. *SE18* . . . 3F 107
(off Royal Carriage M.)
Eastcastle St. W1 . . . 7A 6 (6G 83)
Eastcheap EC3 . . . 2G 15 (7E 84)
E. Churchfield Rd. W3 . . . 1K 97
Eastchurch Rd. TW6: H'row A . . . 2G 111
East Cl. EN4: Cockf . . . 4K 21
UB6: G'frd . . . 2G 77
W5 . . . 4G 79
Eastcombe Av. SE7 . . . 6K 105
EASTCOTE . . . 7K 39
Eastcote BR6: Orp . . . 1K 173
Eastcote Av. HA2: Harr . . . 2F 59
KT8: W Mole . . . 5D 148
UB6: G'frd . . . 5A 60
Eastcote Hockey & Badminton Club . . . 6H 39
Eastcote Ind. Est. HA4: Ruis . . . 7A 40
Eastcote La. HA2: Harr . . . 4C 58
UB5: N'olt . . . 5D 58
(not continuous)
Eastcote La. Nth. UB5: N'olt . . . 6D 58
Eastcote Pl. HA5: Eastc . . . 6K 39
Eastcote Rd. DA16: Well . . . 2H 125
HA2: Harr . . . 3G 59
HA4: Ruis . . . 7G 39
HA5: Pinn . . . 5B 40
Eastcote St. SW9 . . . 2K 119
Eastcote Vw. HA5: Pinn . . . 4A 40
EASTCOTE VILLAGE . . . 5K 39
Eastcott Cl. KT2: King T . . . 5J 133
East Ct. HA0: Wemb . . . 2C 60
East Cres. EN1: Enf . . . 5A 24
N11 . . . 4J 31
East Cft. Ho. HA2: Harr . . . 2G 59
Eastcroft Rd. KT19: Ewe . . . 7A 164
E. Cross Route E9 . . . 5B 68
(Crowfoot Cl.)
E9 . . . 7B 68
(Wansbeck Rd.)
Eastdown Ct. SE13 . . . 4F 123
Eastdown Ho. E8 . . . 4G 67
Eastdown Pk. SE13 . . . 4F 123
East Dr. NW9 . . . 3C 44
SM5: Cars . . . 7C 166
E. Duck Lees La. EN3: Pond E . . . 4F 25
EAST DULWICH . . . 4F 121
East Dulwich Est. *SE22* . . . 3E 120
(off Albrighton Rd.)
E. Dulwich Gro. SE22 . . . 5E 120
E. Dulwich Rd. SE15 . . . 4F 121
SE22 . . . 4F 121
(not continuous)
E. End Farm HA5: Pinn . . . 3D 40
E. End Rd. N2 . . . 3K 45
N3 . . . 2J 45
E. End Way HA5: Pinn . . . 3C 40
East Entrance RM10: Dag . . . 2H 91
Eastern App. IG11: Bark . . . 1A 90
Eastern Av. E11 . . . 6K 51
HA5: Pinn . . . 7B 40
IG2: Ilf . . . 6F 53
IG4: Ilf . . . 6C 52
RM6: Chad H . . . 4A 54
Eastern Av. E. RM1: Rom . . . 3K 55
Eastern Av. Retail Pk. . . . 4J 55
Eastern Av. W. RM1: Rom . . . 4E 54
RM6: Chad H . . . 4E 54
RM7: Chad H, Mawney, Rom
. . . 4E 54
Eastern Bus. Pk. TW6: H'row A . . . 2G 111
Eastern Ct. *E15* . . . 6G 69
(off Gt. Eastern Rd.)
Eastern Gateway E16 . . . 7A 88
Eastern Ho. *E2* . . . 3H 85
(off Bethnal Grn. Rd.)
Eastern Ind. Est. DA18: Erith . . . 2G 109
Eastern Perimeter Rd.
TW6: H'row A . . . 2H 111
Eastern Quay Apts. *E16* . . . 1K 105
(off Portsmouth M.)
Eastern Rd. E13 . . . 2K 87
E17 . . . 5E 50
N2 . . . 3D 46
N22 . . . 1J 47
SE4 . . . 4C 122
EASTERN RDBT. . . . 2G 71
Easternville Gdns. IG2: Ilf . . . 6G 53
Eastern Way DA17: Belv . . . 2A 108
DA18: Erith . . . 2A 108
SE2 . . . 2A 108
SE28 . . . 2A 108
E. Ferry Rd. E14 . . . 4D 104
Eastfield Gdns. RM10: Dag . . . 4G 73
Eastfield Rd. E17 . . . 4C 50
EN3: Enf W . . . 1E 24
N8 . . . 3J 47
RM9: Dag . . . 4F 73
RM10: Dag . . . 4F 73
Eastfields HA5: Eastc . . . 5A 40
Eastfields Av. SW18 . . . 4J 117
Eastfields Rd. CR4: Mitc . . . 2E 154
W3 . . . 5J 79
Eastfield St. E14 . . . 5A 86
EAST FINCHLEY . . . 4C 46
East Gdns. SW17 . . . 6C 136
Eastgate Bus. Pk. E10 . . . 1A 68
Eastgate Cl. SE28 . . . 6D 90
Eastglade HA5: Pinn . . . 3D 40
East Gro. SE17 . . . 4C 102
EAST HAM . . . 2D 88
East Ham & Barking By-Pass
IG11: Bark . . . 2H 89
Eastham Cl. EN5: Barn . . . 5B 20
East Ham Ind. Est. E6 . . . 4C 88
East Ham Leisure Cen. . . . 1D 88
East Ham Mnr. Way E6 . . . 6E 88
East Ham Nature Reserve . . . 4D 88
East Ham Nature Reserve Vis. Cen.
. . . 4D 88
E. Handyside Canopy . . . 1J 83
E. Harding St. EC4 . . . 7K 7 (6A 84)
E. Heath Rd. NW3 . . . 3A 64
E. Hill HA9: Wemb . . . 2G 61
SW18 . . . 5K 117
Eastholm NW11 . . . 4K 45
East Holme DA8: Erith . . . 1K 127
Eastholme UB3: Hayes . . . 1J 93
E. India Bldgs. *E14* . . . 7C 86
(off Saltwell St.)
E. India Ct. *SE16* . . . 2J 103
(off St Marychurch St.)
East India Dock Basin
Local Nature Reserve . . . 7G 87
E. India Dock Ho. E14 . . . 6E 86
E. India Dock Rd. E14 . . . 6C 86
E. India Way CR0: C'don . . . 1F 169
Eastlake Ho. NW8 . . . 4B 4
Eastlake Rd. SE5 . . . 2C 120
Eastlands Cres. SE21 . . . 6F 121
East La. HA0: Wemb . . . 3B 60
HA9: Wemb . . . 3B 60
KT1: King T . . . 3D 150
SE16 . . . 2G 103
(Chambers St.)
SE16 . . . 2G 103
(Scott Lidgett Cres.)
East La. Bus. Pk. HA9: Wemb . . . 2D 60
Eastlea M. E16 . . . 4G 87
Eastleigh Av. HA2: Harr . . . 2F 59
Eastleigh Cl. NW2 . . . 3A 62
SM2: Sutt . . . 7K 165
Eastleigh Rd. DA7: Bex . . . 3J 127
E17 . . . 2B 50
Eastleigh Wlk. SW15 . . . 7C 116
Eastleigh Way TW14: Felt . . . 1J 129
E. Lodge *E16* . . . 1J 105
(off Wesley Av.)
E. London Crematorium . . . 3H 87
East London Gymnastic Cen. . . . 6D 88
E. London Markazi Mosque . . . 7G 85
E. London Mosque . . . 5G 85
Eastman Ho. SW4 . . . 6G 119
Eastman Rd. W3 . . . 2K 97
E. Mead HA4: Ruis . . . 3B 58
Eastmead Av. UB6: G'frd . . . 3F 77
Eastmead Cl. BR1: Broml . . . 2C 160
Eastmearn Rd. SE21 . . . 2C 138
EAST MOLESEY . . . 4H 149
Eastmoor Pl. SE7 . . . 3B 106
Eastmoor St. SE7 . . . 3B 106
East Mt. St. E1 . . . 5H 85
(not continuous)
Eastney Rd. CR0: C'don . . . 1B 168
Eastney St. SE10 . . . 5F 105
Eastnor Rd. SE9 . . . 1G 143
Eastone Apts. *E1* . . . 6K 9
(off Lolesworth Cl.)
Easton St. WC1 . . . 3J 7 (4A 84)
East Pk. Cl. RM6: Chad H . . . 5E 54
E. Parkside SE10 . . . 2G 105
E. Park Wlk. E20 . . . 5E 68
East Pas. EC1 . . . 5C 8
East Pl. SE27 . . . 4C 138
E. Point SE1 . . . 5G 103
E. Pole Cotts. N14 . . . 4C 22
E. Poultry Av. EC1 . . . 6A 8 (5B 84)
East Ramp TW6: H'row A . . . 1D 110
East Rd. DA16: Well . . . 2B 126
E15 . . . 1J 87
EN3: Enf W . . . 1E 24
EN4: E Barn . . . 1K 31
HA1: Harr . . . 7B 42
HA8: Edg . . . 1H 43
KT2: King T . . . 1E 150
N1 . . . 2E 8 (3D 84)
RM6: Chad H . . . 5E 54
RM7: Rush G . . . 7K 55
SW3 . . . 6G 17 (5E 100)
SW19 . . . 6A 136
TW14: Bedf . . . 7F 111
UB7: W Dray . . . 4B 92
E. Rochester Way DA5: Bexl . . . 6F 127
DA15: Sidc . . . 5J 125
E. Row E11 . . . 6J 51
W10 . . . 4G 81

214 A-Z Big London

Eastry Av.—Eldertree Pl.

Eastry Av. BR2: Hayes 6H 159
Eastry Ho. SW8 7J 101
(off Hartington Rd.)
W11 7G 81
(off Walmer Rd.)
Eastry Rd. DA8: Erith 7G 109
EAST SHEEN 4J 115
E. Sheen Av. SW14 5K 115
East Shop. Cen. 7K 69
E. Side W12 2E 98
(off Shepherd's Bush Mkt.)
Eastside Halls SW7 1B 16
(off Prince's Gdns.)
Eastside M. E3 2C 86
(off Morville St.)
Eastside Rd. NW11 4H 45
E. Smithfield E1 3K 15 (7F 85)
E. Stand N5 3B 66
East St. BR1: Broml 2J 159
DA7: Bex 4G 127
IG11: Bark 1G 89
SE17 5C 102
(not continuous)
E. Surrey Gro. SE15 7F 103
E. Tenter St. E1 1K 15 (6F 85)
East Ter. DA15: Sidc 1J 143
E. Thamesmead Bus. Pk.
DA18: Erith 2F 109
East Twr. E14 2D 104
(off Pan Peninsula Sq.)
SW10 7B 100
East Towers HA5: Pinn 5B 40
East Va. W3 1B 98
East Vw. E4 5K 35
EN5: Barn 2C 20
Eastview Av. SE18 7J 107
EAST VILLAGE 5E 68
Eastville Av. NW11 6H 45
East Wlk. EN4: E Barn 7K 21
UB3: Hayes 1J 93
E. Way BR2: Hayes 7J 159
CR0: C'don 2A 170
E11 5K 51
HA4: Ruis 1J 57
UB3: Hayes 1J 93
Eastway E9 6B 68
(not continuous)
SM4: Mord 5F 153
SM6: W'gton 4G 167
Eastway Cres. HA2: Harr 2F 59
Eastwell Cl. BR3: Beck 7A 140
Eastwell Ho. SE1 7F 15
E. Wick E20 5C 68
EAST WICKHAM 1C 126
East Wintergarden 1D 104
(off Bank St.)
Eastwood Cl. E18 2J 51
N7 5A 66
N17 7C 34
Eastwood Ho. E3 5C 86
(off Bow Comn. La.)
Eastwood Rd. E18 2J 51
IG3: Ilf 1A 72
N10 2E 46
UB7: W Dray 2C 92
East Woodside DA5: Bexl 7E 126
Eastwood St. SW16 6G 137
easyGym
Fulham 6H 99
Eatington Rd. E10 5F 51
Eaton Cl. HA7: Stan 4G 27
SW1 4G 17 (4E 100)
Eaton Ct. E18 2J 51
HA8: Edg 4B 28
Eaton Dr. KT2: King T 7G 133
RM5: Col R 1H 55
SW9 4B 120
Eaton Gdns. RM9: Dag 7E 72
Eaton Ga. SW1 3G 17 (4E 100)
Eaton Ho. E14 7B 86
(off Westferry Cir.)
SW11 1B 118
Eaton La. SW1 2K 17 (3F 101)
Eaton Mans. SW1 4G 17
(off Bourne St.)
Eaton M. Nth. SW1 3G 17 (4E 100)
Eaton M. Sth. SW1 3H 17 (4E 100)
Eaton M. W. SW1 3H 17 (4E 100)
Eaton Pk. Rd. N13 2F 33
Eaton Pl. SW1 2G 17 (4E 100)
Eaton Ri. E11 5A 52
W5 5D 78
Eaton Rd. DA14: Sidc 2D 144
EN1: Enf 4K 23
NW4 5E 44
SM2: Sutt 6B 166
TW3: Houn 4H 113
Eaton Row SW1 2J 17 (3F 101)
Eatons Mead E4 2H 35
Eaton Sq. SW1 3G 17 (4E 100)
Eaton Ter. E3 3A 86
SW1 3G 17 (4E 100)
Eaton Ter. M. SW1 3G 17
Eatonville Rd. SW17 2D 136
Eatonville Vs. SW17 2D 136
Ebb Ct. E16 7G 89
Ebbett Ct. W3 5K 79
Ebbisham Dr. SW8 7G 19 (6K 101)
Ebbisham Rd. KT4: Wor Pk 2E 164
Ebbsfleet Rd. NW2 5G 63
Ebdon Way SE3 3K 123
Ebenezer Ho. SE11 4K 19 (4B 102)
Ebenezer Mussel Ho. E2 2J 85
(off Patriot Sq.)
Ebenezer St. N1 1E 8 (3D 84)
Ebenezer Wlk. SW16 1G 155
Ebley Cl. SE15 6F 103
Ebner St. SW18 5K 117
Ebony Cres. EN4: E Barn 5K 21
Ebony Ho. E2 3G 85
(off Buckfast St.)
Ebor Cotts. SW15 3A 134
Ebor St. E1 3J 9 (4F 85)
Ebrington Rd. HA3: Kenton 6D 42
Ebsworth St. SE23 7K 121
Eburne Rd. N7 3J 65
Ebury Bri. SW1 5J 17 (5F 101)
Ebury Bri. Est. SW1 5J 17 (5F 101)
Ebury Bri. Rd. SW1 6H 17 (5E 100)
Ebury Cl. BR2: Kes 3C 172
Ebury M. N5 3C 66
SE27 3B 138
SW1 3J 17 (4F 101)
Ebury M. E. SW1 2J 17 (3F 101)
Ebury Sq. SW1 4H 17 (4E 100)
Ebury St. SW1 4H 17 (4E 100)
Ecclesbourne Apts. N1 7D 66
(off Ecclesbourne Rd.)
Ecclesbourne Cl. N13 5F 33
Ecclesbourne Gdns. N13 5F 33
Ecclesbourne Rd. CR7: Thor H 5C 156
N1 7C 66
Eccleshill BR2: Broml 4H 159
(off Durham Rd.)
Eccles Rd. SW11 4D 118
Eccleston Bri. SW1 3K 17 (4F 101)
Eccleston Cl. BR6: Orp 1H 173
EN4: Cockf 4J 21
Eccleston Cres. RM6: Chad H 7B 54
Ecclestone Ct. HA9: Wemb 5E 60
Ecclestone M. HA9: Wemb 5E 60
Ecclestone Pl. HA9: Wemb 5F 61
Eccleston Ho. SW2 6A 120
Eccleston M. SW1 2H 17 (3E 100)
Eccleston Pl. SW1 3J 17 (4F 101)
Eccleston Rd. W13 7A 78
Eccleston Sq. SW1 4K 17 (4F 101)
(not continuous)
Eccleston Sq. M. SW1 4A 18 (4F 101)
Eccleston St. SW1 2J 17 (3F 101)
Eccleston Yard SW1 3J 17
Echelforde Dr. TW15: Ashf 4C 128
Echo Ct. E16 2A 106
(off Admiralty Av.)
Echo Hgts. E4 1J 35
Eckford St. N1 2A 84
Eckington Cl. SE14 7K 103
Eckington Ho. N15 6D 48
(off Fladbury Rd.)
Eckington La. SE14 7K 103
Eckstein Rd. SW11 4C 118
Eclipse Bldg. N1 6A 66
(off Laycock St.)
Eclipse Ho. N22 2K 47
(off Station Rd.)
Eclipse Rd. E13 5K 87
Ecology Cen. & Arts Pavilion 3A 86
Eco Va. SE23 6H 121
Ector Rd. SE6 2G 141
Edam Ct. DA15: Sidc 3A 144
Edans Ct. W12 2B 98
Edbrooke Rd. W9 4J 81
Eddington Ct. E16 6H 87
(off Silvertown Sq.)
Eddinton Cl. CR0: New Ad 6E 170
Eddisbury Ho. SE26 3G 139
Eddiscombe Rd. SW6 2H 117
Eddy Cl. RM7: Rom 6H 55
Eddystone Rd. SE4 5A 122
Eddystone Twr. SE8 5A 104
Eddystone Wlk. TW19: Stanw 7A 110
Ede Cl. TW3: Houn 3D 112
Edeleny Cl. N2 3A 46
Eden Apts. E14 4E 104
(off Glengarnock Av.)
Edenbridge Cl. SE16 5H 103
(off Masters Dr.)
Edenbridge Rd. E9 7K 67
EN1: Enf 6K 23
Eden Cl. DA5: Bexl 4K 145
HA0: Wemb 1D 78
NW3 2J 63
W8 3J 99
Eden Ct. IG6: Ilf 1H 53
Edencourt Rd. SW16 6F 137
Edendale W3 7H 79
Edendale Rd. DA7: Bex 1K 127
Edenfield Gdns. KT4: Wor Pk 3B 164
Eden Gro. E17 5D 50
N7 5K 65
NW10 6D 62
Edenham Way W10 4H 81
Eden Ho. NW8 4C 4
(off Church St.)
SE8 7C 104
(off Deptford High St.)
SE16 2K 103
(off Water Gdns. Sq.)
Edenhurst Av. SW6 3H 117
Eden Lodge NW6 7F 63
Eden M. SW17 3A 136
EDEN PARK 5C 158
Eden Pk. Av. BR3: Beck 4A 158
Eden Rd. BR3: Beck 4A 158
CR0: C'don 4D 168
DA5: Bexl 4J 145
E17 5D 50
SE27 4B 138
Edensor Gdns. W4 7A 98
Edensor Rd. W4 7A 98
Eden St. KT1: King T 2D 150
Edenvale Cl. CR4: Mitc 7E 136
Edenvale Rd. CR4: Mitc 7E 136
Edenvale St. SW6 2A 118
Eden Wlk. KT1: King T 2E 150
Eden Walk Shopping Centre 2E 150
Eden Way BR3: Beck 5B 158
E3 1B 86
Ederline Av. SW16 3K 155
Edgar Ct. KT3: N Mald 2A 152
Edgar Ho. E9 5A 68
(off Homerton Rd.)
E11 7J 51
SW8 7J 101
(off Wyvil Rd.)
Edgar Kail Way SE22 4E 120
Edgarley Ter. SW6 1G 117
Edgar Myles Ho. E16 5H 87
(off Ordnance Rd.)
Edgar Rd. E3 3D 86
RM6: Chad H 7D 54
TW4: Houn 7D 112
UB7: Yiew 7A 74
Edgar Wallace Cl. SE15 7E 102
Edgar Wright Ct. SW6 7H 99
(off Dawes Rd.)
Edgcott Ho. W10 5E 80
(off Sutton Way)
The Edge
Finsbury 7C 48
The Edge SE8 7B 104
(off Glenville Gro.)
Edge Apts. E15 7F 69
Edgeborough Way BR1: Broml 7B 142
Edgebury BR7: Chst 4F 143
Edgebury Wlk. BR7: Chst 4G 143
The Edge Bus. Cen. NW2 2D 62
Edgecombe Ho. SE5 2E 120
SW19 1G 135
Edgecoombe CR2: Sels 7J 169
Edgecoombe Cl. KT2: King T 7K 133
Edgecote Cl. W3 1J 97
Edgecot Gro. N15 5E 48
Edgecumbe Av. NW9 1B 44
Edgefield Av. IG11: Bark 7K 71
Edgefield Cl. BR3: Beck 6C 140
Edgefield Ct. IG11: Bark 7K 71
(off Edgefield Av.)
Edge Hill SE18 6F 107
SW19 7F 135
Edge Hill Av. N3 4J 45
Edge Hill Ct. DA14: Sidc 4K 143
SW19 7F 135
Edgehill Gdns. RM10: Dag 4G 73
Edgehill Ho. SW9 2B 120
Edgehill Rd. BR7: Chst 3G 143
CR4: Mitc 1F 155
W13 5C 78
Edgeley La. SW4 3H 119
Edgeley Rd. SW4 3H 119
Edgel St. SW18 4K 117
Edge Point Cl. SE27 5B 138
Edge St. W8 1J 99
Edgewood Dr. BR6: Chels 5K 173
Edgewood Grn. CR0: C'don 1K 169
Edgeworth Av. NW4 5C 44
Edgeworth Cl. NW4 5C 44
Edgeworth Ct. EN4: Cockf 4H 21
(off Fordham Rd.)
Edgeworth Cres. NW4 5C 44
Edgeworth Ho. NW8 1A 82
(off Boundary Rd.)
Edgeworth Rd. EN4: Cockf 4H 21
SE9 4A 124
The Edge Youth Cen. 4J 163
Edgington Rd. SW16 6H 137
Edgington Way DA14: Sidc 7C 144
Edgson Ho. SW1 5J 17
(off Ebury Bri. Rd.)
EDGWARE 6B 28
EDGWARE BURY 1A 28
Edgwarebury Gdns.
HA8: Edg 5B 28
Edgwarebury La. HA8: Edg 1A 28
(not continuous)
WD6: E'tree 1A 28
Edgware Ct. HA8: Edg 6B 28
Edgware Rd. NW2 1D 62
NW9 2J 43
W2 4A 4 (4B 82)
Edgware Way HA8: Edg 4A 28
NW7 4A 28
WD6: E'tree 1J 27
Edicule Sq. E3 3A 86
Edinburgh Cl. E2 2J 85
HA5: Pinn 7B 40
UB10: Ick 4D 56
Edinburgh Ct. DA8: Erith 7K 109
KT1: King T 3E 150
(off Watersplash Cl.)
SE16 1K 103
(off Rotherhithe St.)
SW20 5F 153
Edinburgh Dr. UB10: Ick 4D 56
Edinburgh Ga. SW1 7E 10 (2D 100)
Edinburgh Ho. NW4 3E 44
W9 3K 81
(off Maida Vale)
Edinburgh Rd. E13 2K 87
E17 5C 50
N18 5B 34
SM1: Sutt 2A 166
W7 2K 95
Edington NW5 6E 64
Edington Rd. EN3: Enf H 2D 24
SE2 3B 108
Edison Bldg. E14 2C 104
Edison Cl. E17 5C 50
UB7: W Dray 2B 92
Edison Ct. CR0: C'don 7B 156
(off Campbell Rd.)
SE10 3H 105
(off Schoolbank Rd.)
W3 2A 98
Edison Dr. HA9: Wemb 3E 60
UB1: S'hall 6F 77
Edison Gro. SE18 7K 107
Edison Hgts. E1 3K 9
(off Cygnet St.)
Edison Ho. HA9: Wemb 3J 61
(off Barnhill Rd.)
SE1 4D 102
(off New Kent Rd.)
Edison M. SW18 6K 117
Edison Rd. BR2: Broml 2J 159
DA16: Well 1K 125
EN3: Brim 2G 25
N8 6H 47
Edis St. NW1 1E 82
Ediswan Way EN3: Pond E 5D 24
Editha Mans. SW10 6A 100
(off Edith Gro.)
Edith Brinson Ho. E14 6F 87
(off Oban St.)
Edith Cavell Cl. N19 7J 47
Edith Cavell Ho. E14 6D 86
(off Sturry St.)
Edith Cavell Way SE18 1C 124
Edith Gdns. KT5: Surb 7H 151
Edith Gro. SW10 6A 100
Edith Ho. W6 5E 98
(off Queen Caroline St.)
Edithna St. SW9 3J 119
Edith Nesbit Wlk. SE9 5D 124
Edith Neville Cotts. NW1 1C 6
(off Drummond Cres.)
Edith Ramsay Ho. E1 5A 86
(off Duckett St.)
Edith Rd. E6 7B 70
E15 5F 69
N11 7C 32
RM6: Chad H 6C 54
SE25 5D 156
SW19 6K 135
W14 4G 99
Edith Row SW6 1K 117
Edith St. E2 2G 85
Edith Summerskill Ho. SW6 7H 99
(off Clem Attlee Ct.)
Edith Ter. SW10 7A 100
Edith Vs. W14 4H 99
Edith Yd. SW10 7A 100
Edmansons Cl. N17 1F 49
Edmeston Cl. E9 6A 68
Edmond Ct. SE14 1J 121
Edmonds Ct. KT8: W Mole 5F 149
Edmonscote W13 5A 78
EDMONTON 3B 34
Edmonton Ct. SE16 3J 103
(off Canada Est.)
Edmonton Grn. Shop. Cen. 2B 34
Edmonton Leisure Cen. 3B 34
Edmund Gro. TW13: Hanw 2D 130
Edmund Halley Way SE10 2G 105
Edmund Ho. SE17 6B 102
Edmund Hurst Dr. E6 5F 89
Edmund Rd. CR4: Mitc 3C 154
DA16: Well 3A 126
Edmundsbury Ct. Est. SW9 4K 119
Edmunds Cl. UB4: Yead 5A 76
Edmund St. SE5 7D 102
Edmunds Wlk. N2 4C 46
Ednam Ho. SE15 6G 103
(off Haymerle Rd.)
Edna Rd. SW20 2F 153
Edna St. SW11 1C 118
Edred Ho. E9 4A 68
(off Lindisfarne Way)
Edrich Ho. SW4 1J 119
Edric Ho. SW1 3D 18
(off Page St.)
Edrick Rd. HA8: Edg 6D 28
Edrick Wlk. HA8: Edg 6D 28
Edric Rd. SE14 7K 103
Edridge Rd. CR0: C'don 3C 168
Education Sq. E1 6G 85
(off Alder St.)
Edward VII Mans. NW10 3F 81
(off Chamberlayne Rd.)
Edward Alderton Theatre 3D 126
Edward Av. E4 6J 35
SM4: Mord 5B 154
Edward Bond Ho. WC1 2F 7
(off Cromer St.)
Edward Clifford Ho. SE17 4D 102
(off Elsted St.)
Edward Cl. N9 7A 24
NW2 4F 63
TW12: Hamp H 5G 131
Edward Ct. E16 5J 87
Edward Dodd Ct. N1 1F 9
(off Chart St.)
Edward Edward's Ho. SE1 5A 14
Edwardes Pl. W8 3H 99
Edwardes Sq. W8 3H 99
Edward Gro. EN4: E Barn 5G 21
Edward Heylin Ct. E15 2D 86
(off High St.)
Edward Heylyn Ho. E3 2C 86
(off Thomas Fyre Dr.)
Edward Ho. SE11 5H 19
W2 4A 4
(off Hall Pl.)
Edward Kennedy Ho. W10 4G 81
(off Wornington Rd.)
Edward Mann Cl. E. E1 6K 85
(off Pitsea St.)
Edward Mann Cl. W. E1 6K 85
(off Pitsea St.)
Edward M. NW1 1K 5 (3F 83)
Edward Mills Way E14 6C 86
Edward Pl. SE8 6B 104
Edward Rd. BR1: Broml 7K 141
BR7: Chst 5F 143
CR0: C'don 7E 156
E17 4K 49
EN4: E Barn 5G 21
HA2: Harr 3G 41
RM6: Chad H 6D 54
SE20 7K 139
TW12: Hamp H 5G 131
TW14: Felt 5F 111
UB5: N'olt 2A 76
Edward's Av. HA4: Ruis 6K 57
Edwards Cl. KT4: Wor Pk 2F 165
Edward's Cotts. N1 6B 66
Edwards Ct. CR0: C'don 4E 168
(off South Pk. Hill Rd.)
Edwards Dr. N11 7C 32
Edward's La. N16 2E 66
Edwards Mans. IG11: Bark 7K 71
(off Upney La.)
Edwards M. N1 7B 66
W1 1G 11 (6E 82)
Edwards Pas. E1 5J 85
(off Trinity Grn.)
Edward Sq. N1 1K 83
SE16 1A 104
Edwards Rd. DA17: Belv 4G 109
Edward St. E16 4J 87
(not continuous)
SE8 6B 104
SE14 7A 104
Edwards Way SE4 5C 122
Edwards Yd. HA0: Wemb 1E 78
Edward Temme Av. E15 7H 69
Edward Tyler Rd. SE12 2A 142
Edward Way TW15: Ashf 2B 128
Edwina Gdns. IG4: Ilf 5C 52
Edwin Arnold Ct. DA14: Sidc 4K 143
Edwin Av. E6 2E 88
(not continuous)
Edwin Cl. DA7: Bex 6F 109
Edwin Hall Pl. SE13 6F 123
Edwin Ho. SE15 7G 103
Edwin Pl. CR0: C'don 1E 168
(off Cross Rd.)
Edwin Rd. HA8: Edg 6E 28
TW1: Twick 1K 131
TW2: Twick 1J 131
Edwin's Mead E9 4A 68
Edwin Stray Ho. TW13: Hanw 2E 130
Edwin St. E1 4J 85
E16 5J 87
Edwin Ware Ct. HA5: Pinn 2A 40
Edwy Ho. E9 4B 68
(off Homerton Rd.)
Edwyn Cl. EN5: Barn 6A 20
Edwyn Ho. SW18 6K 117
(off Neville Gill Cl.)
Eel Brook Cl. SW6 1K 117
Eel Pie Island TW1: Twick 1A 132
Effie Pl. SW6 7J 99
Effie Rd. SW6 7J 99
Effingham Cl. SM2: Sutt 7K 165
Effingham Lodge KT1: King T 4D 150
Effingham Rd. CR0: C'don 7K 155
KT6: Surb 7B 150
N8 5A 48
SE12 5G 123
Effort St. SW17 5C 136
Effra Cl. SW19 6K 135
Effra Ct. SW2 5K 119
(off Brixton Hill)
Effra Pde. SW2 5A 120
Effra Rd. SW2 4A 120
SW19 6K 135
Effra Rd. Retail Pk. 5A 120
Egan Way UB3: Hayes 7G 75
Egbert Ho. E9 5A 68
(off Homerton Rd.)
Egbert St. NW1 1E 82
Egbury Ho. SW15 6B 116
(off Tangley Gro.)
Egeremont Rd. SE13 2D 122
Egerton Cl. DA17: Belv 5J 109
HA5: Eastc 4J 39
Egerton Ct. E11 7F 51
Egerton Cres. SW3 3D 16 (4C 100)
Egerton Dr. SE10 1D 122
TW7: Isle 3B 114
Egerton Gdns. IG3: Ilf 3K 71
NW4 4D 44
NW10 1E 80
SW3 2C 16 (4C 100)
W13 6B 78
Egerton Gdns. M.
SW3 2D 16 (3C 100)
Egerton Pl. SW3 2D 16 (3C 100)
Egerton Rd. HA0: Wemb 7F 61
KT3: N Mald 4B 152
N16 7F 49
SE25 3E 156
TW2: Twick 1J 113
Egerton Ter. SW3 2D 16 (3C 100)
Egerton Way UB3: Harl 7D 92
Eggardon Ct. UB5: N'olt 6F 59
Egham Cl. SM3: Cheam 2G 165
SW19 2G 135
Egham Cres. SM3: Cheam 3G 165
Egham Rd. E13 5K 87
Eglantine Rd. SW18 5A 118
Egleston Rd. SM4: Mord 6K 153
Egleton Ho. SW15 7C 116
Eglington Ct. SE17 6C 102
Eglington Rd. E4 7K 25
Eglinton Hill SE18 6F 107
Eglinton Rd. SE18 6E 106
Egliston M. SW15 3E 116
Egliston Rd. SW15 3E 116
Eglon M. NW1 7D 64
Egmont Av. KT6: Surb 1F 163
Egmont Ct. KT12: Walt T 7K 147
(off Egmont Rd.)
Egmont M. KT19: Ewe 4K 163
Egmont Rd. KT3: N Mald 4B 152
KT6: Surb 1F 163
KT12: Walt T 7K 147
SM2: Sutt 7A 166
Egmont St. SE14 7K 103
Egremont Ho. E20 5E 68
(off Medals Way)
SE13 2D 122
(off Russett Way)
Egremont Rd. SE27 3A 138
Egret Hgts. N17 3H 49
(off Waterside Way)
Egret Ho. SE16 4K 103
(off Tawny Way)
Egret Way UB4: Yead 5B 76
Eider Cl. E7 5H 69
UB4: Yead 5B 76
Eider Ct. SE8 6B 104
(off Pilot Cl.)
Eighteenth Rd. CR4: Mitc 4J 155
Eighth Av. E12 4D 70
UB3: Hayes 1J 93
Eileen Lenton Ct. N15 4F 49
(off Tottenham Grn. E.)
Eileen Rd. SE25 5D 156
Eindhoven Cl. SM5: Cars 1E 166
Einstein Ho. HA9: Wemb 3J 61
Eisenhower Dr. E6 5C 88
Ekarro Ho. SW8 1J 119
(off Guildford Rd.)
Elaine Gro. NW5 5E 64
Elam Cl. SE5 2B 120
Elam St. SE5 2B 120
Elan Ct. E1 5H 85
Eland Pl. CR0: Wadd 3B 168
Eland Rd. CR0: Wadd 3B 168
SW11 3D 118
Elba Pl. SE17 4C 102
Elberon Av. CR0: Bedd 6G 155
Elbe St. SW6 2A 118
Elborough Rd. SE25 5G 157
Elborough St. SW18 1J 135
Elbourne Ct. SE16 3K 103
(off Worgan St.)
Elbourne Trad. Est. DA17: Belv 3H 109
Elbourn Ho. SW3 5C 16
(off Cale St.)
Elbow Mdw. SL3: Poyle 4A 174
Elbury Dr. E16 6J 87
Elcho St. SW11 7C 100
Elcot Av. SE15 7H 103
Elden Ho. SW3 3C 16
(off Sloane Av.)
Eldenwall Ind. Est. RM8: Dag 1F 73
Elder Av. N8 5J 47
Elderberry Gro. SE27 4C 138
Elderberry Rd. W5 2E 96
Elderberry Way E6 3D 88
Elder Cl. DA15: Sidc 1K 143
N20 2E 30
UB7: Yiew 7A 74
Elder Ct. WD23: B Hea 2D 26
Elderfield Ho. E14 7C 86
(off Pennyfields)
Elderfield Pl. SW17 4F 137
Elderfield Rd. E5 4K 67
Elderfield Wlk. E11 5K 51
Elderflower Way E15 7G 69
Elder Gdns. SE27 5C 138
Elder Ho. E15 3G 87
(off Manor Rd.)
KT1: King T 1D 150
(off Water La.)
SE16 3A 104
Elder Oak Cl. SE20 1H 157
Elder Oak Ct. SE20 1H 157
(off Anerley Rd.)
Elder Pl. CR2: S Croy 6B 168
Elder Rd. SE27 5C 138
Elderslie Cl. BR3: Beck 5C 158
Elderslie Rd. SE9 5E 124
Elder St. E1 5J 9 (4F 85)
(not continuous)
Elderton Rd. SE26 4A 140
Eldertree Pl. CR4: Mitc 1G 155

Eldertree Way CR4: Mitc ... 1G 155
Elder Wlk. N1 ... 1B 84
(off Popham St.)
SE13 ... 3E 122
Elderwood Pl. SE27 ... 5C 138
Eldon Av. CR0: C'don ... 2J 169
TW5: Hest ... 7E 94
Eldon Ct. NW6 ... 1J 81
Eldon Gro. NW3 ... 5B 64
Eldon Ho. NW9 ... 3C 44
(off East Dr.)
Eldon Pk. SE25 ... 4H 157
Eldon Rd. E17 ... 4B 50
N9 ... 1D 34
N22 ... 1B 48
W8 ... 3K 99
Eldons Pas. E1 ... 7G 85
(off Cable St.)
Eldon St. EC2 ... 6F 9 (5D 84)
Eldon Way NW10 ... 3H 79
Eldred Rd. IG11: Bark ... 1J 89
Eldrick Ct. TW14: Bedf ... 1F 129
Eldridge Cl. TW14: Felt ... 1J 129
Eldridge Ct. RM10: Dag ... 6H 73
SE16 ... 3G 103
Eleanor Cl. N15 ... 3F 49
SE16 ... 2K 103
Eleanor Ct. E2 ... 1G 85
(off Whiston Rd.)
Eleanor Cres. NW7 ... 5A 30
Eleanor Gdns. EN5: Barn ... 5A 20
RM8: Dag ... 2F 73
Eleanor Gro. SW13 ... 3A 116
UB10: Ick ... 3D 56
Eleanor Ho. W6 ... 5E 98
(off Queen Caroline St.)
Eleanor Rathbone Ho. N6 ... 7H 47
(off Avenue Rd.)
Eleanor Rd. E8 ... 6H 67
E15 ... 6H 69
N11 ... 6D 32
SW9 ... 1A 120
Eleanor St. E3 ... 3C 86
Eleanor Wlk. SE18 ... 4C 106
Electra Av. TW6: H'row A ... 3H 111
Electra Bus. Pk. E16 ... 5F 87
Electric Av. SW9 ... 4A 120
Electric Cinema
Portobello ... 6H 81
Shoreditch ... 4F 85
(off Club Row)
The Electric Empire SE14 ... 1K 121
(off New Cross Rd.)
Electric Ho. E3 ... 3C 86
(off Bow Rd.)
Electric La. SW9 ... 4A 120
(not continuous)
Electric Pde. E18 ... 2J 51
(off George La.)
IG3: Ilf ... 2J 71
KT6: Surb ... 6D 150
Elektron Twr. E14 ... 7F 87
Eleonora Ter. SM1: Sutt ... 5A 166
(off Lind Rd.)
ELEPHANT & CASTLE ... 3B 102
Elephant & Castle SE1 ... 4B 102
Elephant La. SE16 ... 2J 103
Elephant Pk. Development SE17 ... 4C 102
Elephant Rd. SE17 ... 4C 102
Elers Rd. UB3: Harl ... 4F 93
W13 ... 2C 96
Eley Rd. N18 ... 4E 34
Eley Rd. Retail Pk. ... 5D 34
Eleys Est. N18 ... 4E 34
(not continuous)
Elfindale Rd. SE24 ... 5C 120
Elfin Gro. TW11: Tedd ... 5K 131
Elfin Oak ... 1K 99
Elford Cl. SE3 ... 4A 124
Elford M. SW4 ... 5G 119
Elfort Rd. N5 ... 4A 66
Elfrida Cl. IG8: Wfd G ... 7D 36
Elfrida Cres. SE6 ... 4C 140
Elf Row E1 ... 7J 85
Elfwine Rd. W7 ... 5J 77
Elgal Cl. BR6: Farnb ... 5F 173
Elgar N8 ... 3J 47
(off Boyton Cl.)
Elgar Av. KT5: Surb ... 1G 163
NW10 ... 6K 61
(not continuous)
SW16 ... 3J 155
W5 ... 2E 96
Elgar Cl. E13 ... 2A 88
IG9: Buck H ... 2G 37
SE8 ... 7C 104
UB10: Ick ... 2C 56
Elgar Ct. NW6 ... 3J 81
W14 ... 3G 99
(off Blythe Rd.)
Elgar Ho. NW6 ... 7A 64
(off Fairfax Rd.)
SW1 ... 6K 17
(off Churchill Gdns.)
Elgar St. SE16 ... 3A 104
Elgin Av. HA3: Kenton ... 2B 42
TW15: Ashf ... 6E 128
W9 ... 4H 81
W12 ... 2C 98
Elgin Cl. W12 ... 2D 98
Elgin Ct. CR2: S Croy ... 4C 168
(off Bramley Hill)
W9 ... 4K 81
Elgin Cres. TW6: H'row A ... 2G 111
W11 ... 7G 81
Elgin Dr. HA6: Nwood ... 1G 39
Elgin Est. W9 ... 4J 81
(off Elgin Av.)
Elgin Ho. E14 ... 6D 86
(off Ricardo St.)
RM6: Chad H ... 6F 55
(off High Rd.)
Elgin Mans. W9 ... 3K 81
Elgin M. W11 ... 6G 81
Elgin M. Nth. W9 ... 3K 81
Elgin M. Sth. W9 ... 3K 81
Elgin Rd. CR0: C'don ... 2F 169
IG3: Ilf ... 1J 71
N22 ... 2G 47
SM1: Sutt ... 3A 166
SM6: W'gton ... 6G 167
Elgood Cl. W11 ... 7G 81
Elgood Ho. NW8 ... 2B 82
(off Wellington Rd.)
SE1 ... 7E 14
(off Tabard St.)
Elham Cl. BR1: Broml ... 7B 142
Elham Ho. E5 ... 5H 67
Elia M. N1 ... 1A 8 (2B 84)
Elias Pl. SW8 ... 6A 102
Elia St. N1 ... 1B 8 (2B 84)
Elibank Rd. SE9 ... 4D 124
Elim Est. SE1 ... 7G 15 (3E 102)
Elim St. SE1 ... 7G 15 (3D 102)
(not continuous)
Elim Way E13 ... 3H 87
Eliot Bank SE23 ... 2H 139
Eliot Cotts. SE3 ... 2G 123
Eliot Ct. SW18 ... 6K 117
Eliot Dr. HA2: Harr ... 2F 59
Eliot Gdns. SW15 ... 4C 116
Eliot Hill SE13 ... 2E 122
Eliot M. NW8 ... 2A 82
Eliot Pk. SE13 ... 2E 122
Eliot Pl. SE3 ... 2G 123
Eliot Rd. RM9: Dag ... 4D 72
Eliot Va. SE3 ... 2F 123
Elis David Almshouses
CR0: C'don ... 3B 168
Elis Way E20 ... 5E 68
Elizabethan Cl. TW19: Stanw ... 7A 110
Elizabethan Way
TW19: Stanw ... 7A 110
Elizabeth Av. EN2: Enf ... 3G 23
IG1: Ilf ... 2H 71
N1 ... 1C 84
TW18: Staines ... 7A 128
Elizabeth Barnes Ct. SW6 ... 2K 117
(off Marinefield Rd.)
Elizabeth Bates Ct. E1 ... 5J 85
(off Fulneck Pl.)
Elizabeth Blackwell Ho. N22 ... 1A 48
(off Progress Way)
Elizabeth Blount Ct. E14 ... 6A 86
(off Carr St.)
Elizabeth Bri. SW1 ... 4J 17 (4F 101)
Elizabeth Cl. E14 ... 6D 86
EN5: Barn ... 3A 20
RM7: Mawney ... 1H 55
SM1: Sutt ... 4H 165
W9 ... 4A 82
Elizabeth Clyde Cl. N15 ... 4E 48
Elizabeth Cotts. TW9: Kew ... 1F 115
Elizabeth Ct. BR1: Broml ... 1H 159
(off Highland Rd.)
CR0: C'don ... 3E 168
(off The Avenue)
E4 ... 5G 35
E10 ... 7D 50
IG8: Wfd G ... 7F 37
KT2: King T ... 1E 150
NW1 ... 3D 4
SW1 ... 2D 18
SW10 ... 6B 100
(off Milman's St.)
TW11: Tedd ... 5J 131
TW16: Sun ... 3A 148
(off Elizabeth Gdns.)
Elizabeth Croll Ho. WC1 ... 1H 7
(off Penton Ri.)
Elizabeth Fry Apts. IG11: Bark ... 7G 71
(off Kings Rd.)
Elizabeth Fry Ho. UB3: Harl ... 4H 93
Elizabeth Fry M. E8 ... 7H 67
Elizabeth Fry Pl. SE18 ... 1C 124
Elizabeth Gdns. HA7: Stan ... 6H 27
TW7: Isle ... 4A 114
TW16: Sun ... 3A 148
W3 ... 1B 98
Elizabeth Garrett Anderson Ho.
DA17: Belv ... 3G 109
(off Ambrooke Rd.)
Elizabeth Ho. E3 ... 3D 86
(off St Leonard's St.)
SE11 ... 4K 19
(off Reedworth St.)
SM3: Cheam ... 6G 165
(off Park La.)
W6 ... 5E 98
(off Queen Caroline St.)
Elizabeth Ind. Est. SE14 ... 6K 103
Elizabeth M. E2 ... 2G 85
(off Kay St.)
E10 ... 1E 68
HA1: Harr ... 6J 41
NW3 ... 6C 64
Elizabeth Newcomen Ho. SE1 ... 6E 14
(off Newcomen St.)
Elizabeth Pl. N15 ... 4D 48
Elizabeth Ride N9 ... 7C 24
Elizabeth Rd. E6 ... 1B 88
N15 ... 5E 48
Elizabeth Sq. SE16 ... 7A 86
(off Sovereign Cres.)
Elizabeth St. SW1 ... 3H 17 (4E 100)
Elizabeth Ter. SE9 ... 6D 124
Elizabeth Way SE19 ... 7D 138
TW13: Hanw ... 4A 130
Elkanette M. N20 ... 2F 31
Elkington Point SE11 ... 4J 19
Elkington Rd. E13 ... 4K 87
Elkstone Rd. W10 ... 5H 81
Ella Cl. BR3: Beck ... 2C 158
Ellacott M. SW16 ... 2H 137
Ellaline Rd. W6 ... 6F 99
Ella M. NW3 ... 4D 64
Ellanby Cres. N18 ... 4C 34
Elland Cl. EN5: New Bar ... 5G 21
Elland Ho. E14 ... 6B 86
(off Copenhagen Pl.)
Elland Rd. SE15 ... 4J 121
Ella Rd. N8 ... 7J 47
Ellement Cl. HA5: Pinn ... 5B 40
Ellena Ct. N14 ... 3D 32
(off Conway Rd.)
Ellenborough Ho. W12 ... 7D 80
(off White City Est.)
Ellenborough Pl. SW15 ... 4C 116
Ellenborough Rd. DA14: Sidc ... 5D 144
N22 ... 1C 48
Ellenbridge Way CR2: Sande ... 7E 168
Ellen Cl. BR1: Broml ... 3B 160
Ellen Ct. E4 ... 1K 35
(off The Ridgeway)
N9 ... 2D 34
Ellen Julia Ct. E1 ... 6J 85
(off James Voller Way)
Ellen Phillips La. E2 ... 2G 85
Ellen St. E1 ... 6G 85
Ellen Terry Ct. NW1 ... 7F 65
(off Farrier St.)
Ellen Webb Dr. HA3: W'stone ... 3J 41
Ellen Wilkinson Ho. E2 ... 3K 85
(off Usk St.)
RM10: Dag ... 3G 73
SW6 ... 6H 99
(off Clem Attlee Ct.)
Elleray Rd. TW11: Tedd ... 6K 131
Ellerby St. SW6 ... 1F 117
Ellerdale Cl. NW3 ... 4A 64
Ellerdale Rd. NW3 ... 5A 64
Ellerdale St. SE13 ... 4D 122
Ellerdine Rd. TW3: Houn ... 4G 113
Ellerker Gdns. TW10: Rich ... 6E 114
Ellerman Av. TW2: Whitt ... 1D 130
Ellerslie Gdns. NW10 ... 1C 80
Ellerslie Rd. W12 ... 1D 98
Ellerslie Sq. Ind. Est. SW2 ... 5J 119
Ellerton Gdns. RM9: Dag ... 7C 72
Ellerton Lodge N3 ... 2J 45
Ellerton Rd. KT6: Surb ... 2F 163
RM9: Dag ... 7C 72
SW13 ... 1C 116
SW18 ... 1B 136
SW20 ... 7C 134
Ellery Ho. SE17 ... 4D 102
Ellery Rd. SE19 ... 7D 138
Ellery St. SE15 ... 2H 121
Ellesmere Av. BR3: Beck ... 2E 158
NW7 ... 3E 28
Ellesmere Cl. E11 ... 5H 51
HA4: Ruis ... 7E 38
Ellesmere Ct. SE12 ... 1J 141
W4 ... 5K 97
Ellesmere Gdns. IG4: Ilf ... 5C 52
Ellesmere Gro. EN5: Barn ... 5C 20
Ellesmere Ho. SW10 ... 6A 100
(off Fulham Rd.)
Ellesmere Mans. NW6 ... 6A 64
(off Canfield Gdns.)
Ellesmere Rd. E3 ... 2A 86
NW10 ... 5C 62
TW1: Twick ... 6C 114
UB6: G'frd ... 4G 77
W4 ... 6K 97
Ellesmere St. E14 ... 6D 86
Ellie M. E13 ... 2A 88
TW15: Ashf ... 2A 128
Ellingfort Rd. E8 ... 7H 67
Ellingham Rd. E15 ... 4F 69
KT9: Chess ... 6D 162
W12 ... 2C 98
Ellington Ct. N14 ... 2C 32
Ellington Ho. SE1 ... 3C 102
SE18 ... 7E 106
Ellington Rd. N10 ... 4F 47
TW3: Houn ... 2F 113
TW13: Felt ... 4H 129
Ellington St. N7 ... 6A 66
Elliot Cl. E15 ... 7G 69
IG8: Wfd G ... 6G 37
Elliot Ho. SW17 ... 3B 136
(off Grosvenor Way)
W1 ... 6D 4
(off Cato St.)
Elliot Rd. NW4 ... 6D 44
Elliott Av. HA4: Ruis ... 2K 57
Elliott Cl. HA9: Wemb ... 3F 61
Elliott Gdns. TW17: Shep ... 4C 146
Elliott Rd. BR2: Broml ... 4B 160
CR7: Thor H ... 4B 156
HA7: Stan ... 6F 27
SW9 ... 1B 120
W4 ... 4A 98
Elliott's Pl. N1 ... 1B 84
Elliott Sq. NW3 ... 7C 64
Elliotts Row SE11 ... 4B 102
Ellis Av. RM8: Dag ... 1E 72
Ellis Cl. HA4: Eastc ... 6J 39
HA8: Edg ... 6F 29
NW10 ... 6D 62
SE9 ... 2G 143
Elliscombe Mt. SE7 ... 6A 106
Elliscombe Rd. SE7 ... 6A 106
Ellis Ct. E1 ... 6J 85
(off James Voller Way)
W7 ... 5K 77
Ellisfield Dr. SW15 ... 7C 116
Ellis Franklin Ct. NW8 ... 2A 82
(off Abbey Rd.)
Ellis Ho. SE17 ... 5D 102
(off Brandon St.)
Ellison Apts. E3 ... 3C 86
(off Merchant St.)
Ellison Gdns. UB2: S'hall ... 4D 94
Ellison Ho. SE13 ... 2D 122
(off Lewisham Rd.)
Ellison Rd. DA15: Sidc ... 1H 143
SW13 ... 2B 116
SW16 ... 7H 137
Ellis Rd. CR4: Mitc ... 6D 154
UB2: S'hall ... 1G 95
Ellis St. SW1 ... 3F 17 (4E 100)
Ellis Ter. SE11 ... 7A 102
Elliston Ho. SE18 ... 4E 106
(off Wellington St.)
Ellora Rd. SW16 ... 5H 137
Ellswood Ct. KT6: Surb ... 7D 150
Ellsworth St. E2 ... 3H 85
Ellwood Ct. W9 ... 4K 81
(off Clearwell Dr.)
Elmar Rd. N15 ... 4D 48
Elm Av. HA4: Ruis ... 1J 57
TW19: Stanw ... 2A 128
W5 ... 1E 96
Elmbank N14 ... 7D 22
Elmbank Av. EN5: Barn ... 4A 20
Elm Bank Dr. BR1: Broml ... 2B 160
Elm Bank Gdns. SW13 ... 2A 116
Elmbank Way W7 ... 5H 77
Elmbourne Dr. DA17: Belv ... 4H 109
Elmbourne Rd. SW17 ... 3F 137
Elmbridge Av. KT5: Surb ... 5H 151
Elmbridge Cl. HA4: Ruis ... 6J 39
Elmbridge Dr. HA4: Ruis ... 5H 39
Elmbridge Wlk. E8 ... 7G 67
Elmbridge Xcel Leisure Complex
... 5K 147
Elmbridge Xcel Sports Hub ... 5K 147
Elmbrook Cl. TW16: Sun ... 1K 147
Elmbrook Gdns. SE9 ... 4C 124
Elmbrook Rd. SM1: Sutt ... 4H 165
Elm Cl. CR2: S Croy ... 6E 168
E11 ... 6K 51
HA2: Harr ... 6F 41
IG9: Buck H ... 2G 37
KT5: Surb ... 7J 151
N19 ... 2G 65
Elm Cl. NW4 ... 5F 45
RM7: Mawney ... 1H 55
SM5: Cars ... 1D 166
SW20 ... 4E 152
TW2: Twick ... 2F 131
UB3: Hayes ... 6J 75
Elmcote HA5: Pinn ... 2B 40
Elm Cotts. CR4: Mitc ... 2D 154
Elm Ct. CR4: Mitc ... 2D 154
EC4 ... 1J 13
EN4: E Barn ... 6H 21
KT8: W Mole ... 4F 149
SE1 ... 7G 15
(off Royal Oak Yd.)
SE13 ... 3F 123
SW9 ... 1A 120
(off Cranworth Gdns.)
TW16: Sun ... 7H 129
(off Grangewood Dr.)
W9 ... 5J 81
(off Admiral Wlk.)
Elmcourt Rd. SE27 ... 2B 138
Elm Cres. KT2: King T ... 1E 150
W5 ... 1E 96
Elmcroft N6 ... 7G 47
N8 ... 5K 47
Elmcroft Av. DA15: Sidc ... 7K 125
E11 ... 5K 51
N9 ... 6C 24
NW11 ... 7H 45
Elmcroft Cl. E11 ... 4K 51
KT9: Chess ... 3E 162
TW14: Felt ... 6H 111
W5 ... 6D 78
Elmcroft Cres. HA2: Harr ... 3E 40
NW11 ... 7G 45
Elmcroft Dr. KT9: Chess ... 3E 162
TW15: Ashf ... 5C 128
Elmcroft Gdns. NW9 ... 4G 43
Elmcroft St. E5 ... 4J 67
Elmcroft Ter. UB8: Hil ... 6C 74
Elmdale Rd. N13 ... 5E 32
Elmdene KT5: Surb ... 1J 163
Elmdene Cl. BR3: Beck ... 6B 158
Elmdene Rd. SE18 ... 5F 107
Elmdon Rd. TW4: Houn ... 2B 112
TW6: H'row A ... 3H 111
Elm Dr. HA2: Harr ... 6F 41
TW16: Sun ... 2A 148
Elmer Cl. EN2: Enf ... 3E 22
Elmer Gdns. HA8: Edg ... 7C 28
TW7: Isle ... 3H 113
Elmer Ho. NW8 ... 5C 4
(off Penfold St.)
Elmer Rd. SE6 ... 7E 122
Elmers Dr. TW11: Tedd ... 6B 132
ELMERS END ... 4A 158
Elmers End Rd. BR3: Beck ... 2J 157
SE20 ... 2J 157
Elmerside Rd. BR3: Beck ... 4A 158
Elmers Lodge BR3: Beck ... 4K 157
Elmers Rd. SE25 ... 7G 157
Elmfield HA1: Harr ... 7K 41
Elmfield Av. CR4: Mitc ... 1E 154
N8 ... 5J 47
TW11: Tedd ... 5K 131
Elmfield Cl. HA1: Harr ... 2J 59
Elmfield Ct. DA16: Well ... 1B 126
Elmfield Ho. N2 ... 2B 46
(off The Grange)
NW8 ... 2K 81
(off Carlton Hill)
W9 ... 4J 81
(off Goldney Rd.)
Elmfield Pk. BR1: Broml ... 3J 159
Elmfield Rd. BR1: Broml ... 2J 159
E4 ... 2K 35
E17 ... 6K 49
N2 ... 3B 46
SW17 ... 2E 136
UB2: S'hall ... 3C 94
Elmfield Way CR2: Sande ... 7F 169
W9 ... 5J 81
Elm Friars Wlk. NW1 ... 7H 65
Elm Gdns. CR4: Mitc ... 4H 155
KT10: Clay ... 6A 162
N2 ... 3A 46
Elmgate Av. TW13: Felt ... 3K 129
Elmgate Gdns. HA8: Edg ... 5D 28
Elm Grn. W3 ... 6A 80
Elmgreen Cl. E15 ... 1G 87
Elm Gro. BR6: Orp ... 1K 173
DA8: Erith ... 7K 109
HA2: Harr ... 7E 40
IG8: Wfd G ... 5C 36
KT2: King T ... 1E 150
N8 ... 6J 47
NW2 ... 4F 63
SE15 ... 2F 121
SM1: Sutt ... 4K 165
SW19 ... 7G 135
UB7: Yiew ... 7B 74
Elmgrove Cres. HA1: Harr ... 5K 41
Elmgrove Gdns. HA1: Harr ... 5A 42
Elm Gro. Pde. SM6: W'gton ... 3E 166
Elmgrove Point SE18 ... 4H 107
Elm Gro. Rd. SW13 ... 1C 116
W5 ... 2E 96
Elmgrove Rd. CR0: C'don ... 7H 157
HA1: Harr ... 5K 41
Elm Hall Gdns. E11 ... 5K 51
(not continuous)
Elm Ho. E3 ... 1B 86
(off Sycamore Av.)
E14 ... 2E 104
(off E. Ferry Rd.)
KT2: King T ... 7F 133
(off Elm Rd.)
W10 ... 4G 81
(off Briar Wlk.)
Elmhurst DA17: Belv ... 6E 108
Elmhurst Av. CR4: Mitc ... 7F 137
N2 ... 3B 46
Elmhurst Ct. CR0: C'don ... 4D 168
Elmhurst Dr. E18 ... 2J 51
Elmhurst Lodge SM2: Sutt ... 7A 166
Elmhurst Mans. SW4 ... 3H 119
Elmhurst Rd. E7 ... 7K 69
N17 ... 2F 49
SE9 ... 2C 142
Elmhurst St. SW4 ... 3H 119
Elmington Cl. DA5: Bexl ... 6H 127
Elmington Est. SE5 ... 7D 102
Elmington Rd. SE5 ... 7D 102
Elmira St. SE13 ... 3D 122
Elm La. SE6 ... 2B 140
Elm Lawn Cl. UB8: Uxb ... 7A 56
Elmlea Dr. UB3: Hayes ... 5G 75
Elm Lea Trad. Est. N17 ... 6C 34
Elmlee Cl. BR7: Chst ... 6D 142
Elmley Cl. E6 ... 5C 88
Elmley St. SE18 ... 5H 107
(not continuous)
Elm Lodge SW6 ... 1E 116
Elmore Cl. HA0: Wemb ... 2E 78
HA3: Kenton ... 2B 42
Elmore Dr. HA3: Kenton ... 2B 42
Elmore Ho. N1 ... 7D 66
(off Elmore St.)
SW9 ... 2B 120
Elmore Rd. E11 ... 3E 68
EN3: Enf W ... 1E 24
Elmore St. N1 ... 7C 66
Elm Pde. DA14: Sidc ... 4A 144
Elm Pk. HA7: Stan ... 5G 27
SW2 ... 6K 119
Elm Pk. Av. N15 ... 5F 49
Elm Pk. Chambers SW10 ... 6A 16
(off Fulham Rd.)
Elm Pk. Ct. HA5: Pinn ... 3A 40
Elm Pk. Gdns. NW4 ... 5F 45
SW10 ... 6A 16 (5B 100)
Elm Pk. Ho. SW10 ... 6A 16 (5B 100)
Elm Pk. La. SW3 ... 6A 16 (5B 100)
Elm Pk. Mans. SW10 ... 7A 16 (6A 100)
Elm Pk. Rd. E10 ... 1A 68
HA5: Pinn ... 2A 40
N3 ... 7C 30
N21 ... 7H 23
SE25 ... 3F 157
SW3 ... 7A 16 (6B 100)
Elm Pas. EN5: Barn ... 4C 20
Elm Pl. SW7 ... 5A 16 (5B 100)
TW15: Ashf ... 5C 128
Elm Quay Ct. SW11 ... 7C 18 (6H 101)
Elm Rd. BR3: Beck ... 2B 158
BR6: Chels ... 7K 173
CR7: Thor H ... 4D 156
DA14: Sidc ... 4A 144
E7 ... 6H 69
E11 ... 2F 69
E17 ... 5E 50
EN5: Barn ... 4C 20
HA9: Wemb ... 5E 60
KT2: King T ... 1F 151
KT3: N Mald ... 2K 151
KT9: Chess ... 4E 162
KT17: Ewe ... 6B 164
N22 ... 1B 48
RM7: Mawney ... 2H 55
SM6: W'gton ... 1E 166
SW14 ... 3J 115
TW14: Bedf ... 1F 129
Elm Rd. W. SM3: Sutt ... 7H 153
Elm Row NW3 ... 3A 64
The Elms CR0: C'don ... 1C 168
(off Tavistock Rd.)
E12 ... 6B 70
KT10: Clay ... 7A 162
SW13 ... 3B 116
TW15: Ashf ... 5C 128
Elms Av. N10 ... 3F 47
NW4 ... 5F 45
Elmscott Gdns. N21 ... 6H 23
Elmscott Rd. BR1: Broml ... 5G 141
Elms Ct. HA0: Wemb ... 4A 60
Elms Cres. SW4 ... 6G 119
Elmsdale Rd. E17 ... 4B 50
Elms Gdns. HA0: Wemb ... 4A 60
RM9: Dag ... 4F 73
Elmshaw Rd. SW15 ... 5C 116
Elmshurst Cres. N2 ... 4B 46
Elmside CR0: New Ad ... 6D 170
Elmside Rd. HA9: Wemb ... 3G 61
Elms La. HA0: Wemb ... 3A 60
Elmsleigh Av. HA3: Kenton ... 4B 42
Elmsleigh Ct. SM1: Sutt ... 3K 165
Elmsleigh Ho. TW2: Twick ... 2H 131
(off Staines Rd.)
Elmsleigh Rd. TW2: Twick ... 2H 131
Elmslie Cl. IG8: Wfd G ... 6J 37
Elmslie Point E3 ... 5B 86
(off Leopold St.)
Elms M. W2 ... 2A 10 (7B 82)
Elms Pk. Av. HA0: Wemb ... 4A 60
Elms Rd. HA3: Hrw W ... 7D 26
SW4 ... 5G 119
ELMSTEAD ... 6D 142
Elmstead Av. BR7: Chst ... 5D 142
HA9: Wemb ... 1E 60
Elmstead Cl. KT19: Ewe ... 5A 164
N20 ... 2D 30
Elmstead Gdns. KT4: Wor Pk ... 3C 164
Elmstead Glade BR7: Chst ... 6D 142
Elmstead La. BR7: Chst ... 7C 142
Elmstead Rd. DA8: Erith ... 1K 127
IG3: Ilf ... 2J 71
Elmsted Cres. DA16: Well ... 6C 108
Elmstone Rd. SW6 ... 1J 117
Elm St. WC1 ... 4H 7 (4K 83)
Elmsway TW15: Ashf ... 5C 128
Elmsworth Av. TW3: Houn ... 2F 113
Elm Ter. HA3: Hrw W ... 1H 41
NW2 ... 3J 63
NW3 ... 4C 64
SE9 ... 6E 124
Elmton Ct. NW8 ... 3A 4
(off Cunningham Pl.)
Elm Tree Av. KT10: Esh ... 7H 149
Elm Tree Cl. NW8 ... 1A 4 (3B 82)
TW15: Ashf ... 5D 128
UB5: N'olt ... 2D 76
Elm Tree Ct. NW8 ... 1A 4
SE7 ... 6A 106
Elm Tree Rd. NW8 ... 1A 4 (3B 82)
Elmtree Rd. TW11: Tedd ... 4J 131
Elm Vw. Ct. UB2: S'hall ... 4E 94
Elm Vw. Ho. UB3: Harl ... 4F 93
Elm Wlk. BR6: Farnb ... 3D 172
NW3 ... 2J 63
SW20 ... 4E 152
Elm Way KT4: Wor Pk ... 3E 164
KT19: Ewe ... 5K 163
N11 ... 6K 31
NW10 ... 4A 62
Elmwood Av. HA3: Kenton ... 5A 42
N13 ... 5D 32
TW13: Felt, Hanw ... 2J 129
Elmwood Cl. KT17: Ewe ... 7C 164
SM6: W'gton ... 2F 167
Elmwood Ct. E10 ... 1C 68
(off Goldsmith Rd.)

Elmwood Ct.—Essendine Rd.

Elmwood Ct. HA0: Wemb 3A 60
SW11 1F 119
Elmwood Cres. NW9 4J 43
Elmwood Dr. DA5: Bexl 7E 126
KT17: Ewe 6C 164
Elmwood Gdns. W7 6J 77
Elmwood Ho. NW10 2D 80
(off All Souls Av.)
Elmwood Rd. CR0: C'don 7B 156
CR4: Mitc 3D 154
SE24 5D 120
W4 6J 97
Elmworth Gro. SE21 2D 138
Elnathan M. W9 4K 81
Elphinstone Ct. SW16 6J 137
Elphinstone Rd. E17 2B 50
Elphinstone St. N5 4B 66
Elrington Rd. E8 6G 67
IG8: Wfd G 5D 36
Elsa Cotts. E14 5A 86
(off Halley St.)
Elsa Ct. BR3: Beck 1B 158
Elsa Rd. DA16: Well 2B 126
Elsa St. E1 5A 86
Elsdale St. E9 6J 67
Elsden M. E2 2J 85
Elsden Rd. N17 1F 49
Elsenham Rd. E12 5E 70
Elsenham St. SW18 1H 135
Elsham Rd. E11 3G 69
W14 2G 99
Elsham Ter. W14 3G 99
(off Elsham Rd.)
Elsiedene Rd. N21 7H 23
Elsie La. Ct. W2 5J 81
(off Westbourne Pk. Vs.)
Elsiemaud Rd. SE4 5B 122
Elsie Rd. SE22 4F 121
Elsinore Av. TW19: Stanw 7A 110
Elsinore Gdns. NW2 3G 63
Elsinore Ho. N1 1A 84
(off Denmark Gro.)
SE5 2C 120
(off Denmark Rd.)
SE7 4C 106
W6 5F 99
(off Fulham Pal. Rd.)
Elsinore Rd. SE23 1A 140
Elsinore Way TW9: Rich 3H 115
Elsley Ct. HA9: Wemb 6H 61
Elsley Rd. SW11 3D 118
Elspeth Rd. HA0: Wemb 5E 60
SW11 4D 118
Elsrick Av. SM4: Mord 5J 153
Elstan Way CR0: C'don 7A 158
Elstar Ct. RM13: Rain 2K 91
(off Lowen Rd.)
Elstead Ct. SM3: Sutt 1G 165
Elstead Ho. SW2 7K 119
(off Redlands Way)
Elsted St. SE17 4D 102
Elstow Cl. HA4: Ruis 7B 40
SE9 5D 124
(not continuous)
Elstow Gdns. RM9: Dag 1E 90
Elstow Grange NW6 7F 63
Elstow Rd. RM9: Dag 1E 90
Elstree Gdns. DA17: Belv 4E 108
IG1: Ilf 5G 71
N9 1C 34
Elstree Hill BR1: Broml 7G 141
Elstree Hill Sth. WD6: E'tree 1H 27
Elstree Rd. WD23: B Hea 1C 26
Elswick Rd. SE13 2D 122
Elswick St. SW6 2A 118
Elsworth Cl. TW14: Bedf 1G 129
Elsworthy KT7: T Ditt 6J 149
Elsworthy Ct. NW3 7D 64
(off Primrose Hill Rd.)
Elsworthy Ri. NW3 7C 64
Elsworthy Rd. NW3 1C 82
Elsworthy Ter. NW3 7C 64
Elsynge Rd. SW18 5B 118
ELTHAM 6D 124
Eltham Cen. 5E 124
Eltham Crematorium 4H 125
Eltham Grn. SE9 5B 124
Eltham Grn. Rd. SE9 4A 124
Eltham High St. SE9 6D 124
Eltham Hill SE9 5B 124
Eltham Palace & Gdns. 7C 124
Eltham Pal. Rd. SE9 6A 124
ELTHAM PARK 4E 124
Eltham Pk. Gdns. SE9 4E 124
Eltham Rd. SE9 5H 123
SE12 5H 123
Eltham Warren Golf Course 5F 125
Elthiron Rd. SW6 1J 117
Elthorne Av. W7 2K 95
Elthorne Ct. TW13: Felt 1A 130
ELTHORNE HEIGHTS 5J 77
Elthorne Pk. Rd. W7 2K 95
Elthorne Rd. N19 2H 65
NW9 7K 43
Elthorne Sports Cen. 3K 95
Elthorne Way NW9 6K 43
Elthruda Rd. SE13 6F 123
Eltisley Rd. IG1: Ilf 4F 71
Elton Av. EN5: Barn 5C 20
HA0: Wemb 5B 60
UB6: G'frd 6J 59
Elton Cl. KT1: Hamp W 7C 132
Elton Ho. E3 1B 86
(off Candy St.)
Elton Pl. N16 5E 66
Elton Rd. KT2: King T 1F 151
Eltringham St. SW18 4A 118
Eluna Apts. E1 7H 85
(off Wapping La.)
Elvaston M. SW7 2A 16 (3A 100)
Elvaston Pl. SW7 2A 16 (3A 100)
Elveden Ho. SE24 5B 120
Elveden Pl. NW10 2G 79
Elveden Rd. NW10 2G 79
Elvedon Rd. TW13: Felt 3H 129
Elvendon Rd. N13 6D 32
Elven M. SE15 1J 121
Elver Gdns. E2 3G 85
Elverson Rd. SE8 2D 122
Elverton St. SW1 3C 18 (4H 101)
Elvin Ct. NW9 7J 43
Elvin Gardens HA9: Wemb 4G 61
Elvington Grn. BR2: Broml 5H 159
Elvington La. NW9 1A 44
Elvino Rd. SE26 5A 140
Elvis Rd. NW2 6E 62
Elwill Way BR3: Beck 4E 158
Elwin St. E2 1K 9 (3G 85)
Elwood Cl. EN5: New Bar 4F 21
Elwood St. N5 3B 66
Elworth Ho. SW8 7K 101
(off Oval Pl.)
Elwyn Gdns. SE12 7J 123
Ely Cl. KT3: N Mald 2B 152
Ely Ct. EC1 6K 7
KT1: King T 2G 151
Ely Gdns. IG1: Ilf 7C 52
RM10: Dag 3J 73
Ely Ho. SE15 7G 103
(off Friary Est.)
Elyne Rd. N4 6A 48
Ely Pl. EC1 6K 7 (5A 84)
IG8: Wfd G 6K 37
SW8 7K 101
Ely Rd. CR0: C'don 5D 156
E10 6E 50
TW4: Houn 3A 112
TW6: H'row A 2H 111
(off Esher Cres.)
Elysian Av. BR5: St M Cry 6K 161
Elysian M. N7 6K 65
Elysian Pl. CR2: S Croy 7C 168
Elysium Apts. E1 4J 85
(off Theven St.)
Elysium Pl. SW6 2H 117
(off Elysium St.)
Elysium St. SW6 2H 117
Elystan Bus. Cen. UB4: Yead 7A 76
Elystan Cl. SM6: W'gton 7G 167
Elystan Ho. SW3 4C 16
(off Elystan St.)
Elystan Pl. SW3 5D 16 (5C 100)
Elystan St. SW3 4C 16 (4C 100)
Elystan Wlk. N1 1A 84
Ely's Yd. E1 5K 9 (5F 85)
Emanuel Av. W3 6J 79
Emanuel Dr. TW12: Hamp 5D 130
Emanuel Ho. SW1 3H 101
Embankment SW15 2F 117
The Embankment TW1: Twick 1A 132
Embankment Galleries 2H 13
(within Somerset House)
Embankment Gdns.
SW3 7F 17 (6D 100)
Embankment Pier WC2 4F 13 (1J 101)
Embankment Pl. WC2 4F 13 (1J 101)
Embassy Apts. SE5 2C 120
(off Coldharbour La.)
Embassy Ct. DA14: Sidc 3B 144
DA16: Well 3B 126
E2 4H 85
(off Brady St.)
N11 6C 32
(off Bounds Grn. Rd.)
NW8 1B 4
SM6: W'gton 6F 167
W5 7F 79
Embassy Gdns. BR3: Beck 1B 158
Embassy Ho. NW6 7K 63
Embassy Lodge N3 2H 45
(off Cyprus Rd.)
Embassy of United States of America
7D 18 (6H 101)
Embassy Theatre 7B 64
Embassy Way SW11 6H 101
Emba St. SE16 2G 103
Ember Cl. BR5: Pet W 7G 161
Ember Ct. NW9 2B 44
Embercourt Rd. KT7: T Ditt 6J 149
Ember Farm Av. KT8: E Mos 6H 149
Ember Farm Way KT8: E Mos 6H 149
Ember Gdns. KT7: T Ditt 7J 149
Ember La. KT8: E Mos 7H 149
KT10: Esh 7H 149
Emberton SE5 6E 102
(off Albany Rd.)
Emberton Ct. EC1 2A 8
(off Tompion St.)
Embleton Rd. SE13 4D 122
Embleton Wlk. TW12: Hamp 5D 130
Embroidery World Bus. Cen.
IG8: Wfd G 2B 52
Embry Cl. HA7: Stan 4F 27
Embry Dr. HA7: Stan 7F 27
Embry Rd. SE9 4A 124
Embry Way HA7: Stan 5F 27
Emden Cl. UB7: W Dray 2C 92
Emden St. SW6 1K 117
Emerald Cl. E16 6B 88
Emerald Ct. HA4: Ruis 4A 58
Emerald Gdns. RM8: Dag 1G 73
Emerald Rd. NW10 1K 79
Emerald Sq. SW15 5C 116
UB2: S'hall 3B 94
Emerald St. WC1 5G 7 (5K 83)
Emerson Apts. N8 3K 47
Emerson Gdns. HA3: Kenton 6F 43
Emerson M. KT3: N Mald 4A 152
Emerson Rd. IG1: Ilf 7E 52
Emerson St. SE1 4C 14 (1C 102)
Emerton Cl. DA6: Bex 4E 126
Emery Hill St. SW1 2B 18 (3G 101)
Emery St. SE1 1K 19 (3A 102)
Emery Walker Trust 5C 98
(off Hammersmith Ter.)
Emes Rd. DA8: Erith 7J 109
Emilia Cl. EN3: Pond E 5C 24
Emily Bowes Ct. N17 3H 49
Emily Ct. SE1 7C 14
(off Sudrey St.)
Emily Duncan Pl. E7 4K 69
Emily Ho. W10 4G 81
(off Kensal Rd.)
Emily St. E16 6H 87
(off Jude St.)
Emirates Stadium 4A 66
Emlyn Gdns. W12 2A 98
Emlyn Rd. W12 2A 98
Emma Ho. RM1: Rom 4K 55
Emmanuel Ct. E10 7D 50
Emmanuel Ho. SE11 4J 19 (4A 102)
Emmanuel Rd. HA6: Nwood 1H 39
SW12 1G 137
Emma Rd. E13 2H 87
Emma St. E2 2H 85
Emmaus Way IG7: Chig 5K 37
Emmeline Ct. KT12: Walt T 7A 148
Emminster NW6 1K 81
(off Abbey Rd.)
Emmott Av. IG6: Ilf 5G 53
Emmott Cl. E1 4A 86
NW11 6A 46
Emms Pas. KT1: King T 2D 150
Emperor Ho. E20 5E 68
(off Napa Cl.)
SE4 3A 122
(off Dragonfly Pl.)
Emperor's Ga. SW7 3A 100
Empingham Ho. SE8 4K 103
(off Chilton Gro.)
Empire Av. N18 5H 33
Empire Cinema
Haymarket 3C 12
(off Haymarket)
Sutton 5K 165
Walthamstow 4C 50
Empire Cl. SE7 6K 105
Empire Ct. HA9: Wemb 3H 61
Empire Ho. N18 6J 33
SW7 2C 16
Empire M. SW16 5J 137
Empire Pde. HA9: Wemb 3G 61
N18 6J 33
Empire Reach SE10 6D 104
(off Dowells St.)
Empire Rd. UB6: G'frd 1B 78
Empire Sq. N7 3J 65
SE1 7E 14
(off Tabard St.)
SE20 7K 139
(off High St.)
Empire Sq. E. SE1 7E 14
Empire Sq. Sth. SE1 7E 14
Empire Sq. W. SE1 7E 14
Empire Way HA9: Wemb 4F 61
Empire Wharf E3 1A 86
(off Old Ford Rd.)
Empire Wharf Rd. E14 4F 105
Empress App. SW6 5J 99
Empress Av. E4 7J 35
E12 2A 70
IG1: Ilf 2D 70
IG8: Wfd G 7C 36
Empress Dr. BR7: Chst 6F 143
Empress M. SE5 2C 120
Empress Pde. E4 7H 35
Empress Pl. SW6 5J 99
Empress State Bldg. SW6 5J 99
Empress St. SE17 6C 102
Empson St. E3 4D 86
Emsworth Cl. N9 1D 34
Emsworth Ct. SW16 3J 137
Emsworth Rd. IG6: Ilf 2F 53
Emsworth St. SW2 2K 137
EMT Ho. E6 5E 88
Emu Rd. SW8 2F 119
Enard Ho. E3 2B 86
(off Cardigan Rd.)
Ena Rd. SW16 3J 155
Enbrook St. W10 3G 81
The Enclave SW13 2B 116
Enclave Ct. EC1 3B 8
(off Dallington St.)
Endale Cl. SM5: Cars 2D 166
Endeavour Ho. E14 2C 104
(off Cuba St.)
SE16 4A 104
(off Ashton Reach)
Endeavour Sq. E20 7E 68
Endeavour Way CR0: Bedd 7J 155
IG11: Bark 2A 90
SW19 4K 135
Endell St. WC2 7E 6 (6J 83)
Enderby St. SE10 5F 105
Enderley Cl. HA3: Hrw W 2J 41
Enderley Rd. HA3: Hrw W 1J 41
Enders Cl. EN2: Enf 1F 23
Endersleigh Gdns. NW4 4C 44
Endlebury Rd. E4 2K 35
Endlesham Rd. SW12 7E 118
Endsleigh Ct. WC1 3D 6
Endsleigh Gdns. IG1: Ilf 2D 70
KT6: Surb 6C 150
WC1 3C 6 (4H 83)
Endsleigh Ind. Est. UB2: S'hall 4C 94
Endsleigh Pl. WC1 3D 6 (4H 83)
Endsleigh Rd. UB2: S'hall 4C 94
W13 7A 78
Endsleigh St. WC1 3D 6 (4H 83)
Endway KT5: Surb 7H 151
Endwell Rd. SE4 2A 122
Endymion Rd. N4 7A 48
SW2 6K 119
Energen Cl. NW10 6A 62
énergie Fitness
Old Street 4D 84
The Energy Cen. N1 1G 9
(off Bowling Grn. Wlk.)
ENFIELD 3J 23
Enfield Bus. Cen. EN3: Enf H 2D 24
Enfield Cloisters N1 1G 9
(off Fanshaw St.)
Enfield Golf Course 4G 23
ENFIELD HIGHWAY 3D 24
Enfield Ho. SW9 2J 119
(off Stockwell Rd.)
ENFIELD ISLAND VILLAGE 1H 25
ENFIELD LOCK 1G 25
Enfield Lock EN3: Enf L 1H 25
Enfield Mus. 4J 23
(off London Rd.)
Enfield Retail Pk. 3B 24
Enfield Rd. EN2: Enf 4C 22
N1 7E 66
TW6: H'row A 2G 111
TW8: Bford 5D 96
W3 2H 97
ENFIELD ROAD RDBT. 2G 111
ENFIELD TOWN 4J 23
Enfield Town FC 2A 24
Enfield Wlk. TW8: Bford 5D 96
ENFIELD WASH 1F 25
Enford St. W1 5E 4 (5D 82)
Engadine Cl. CR0: C'don 3F 169
Engadine St. SW18 1H 135
Engate St. SE13 4E 122
Engel Pk. NW7 6K 29
Engine Ct. SW1 5B 12
(off Ambassador's Ct.)
Engineer Cl. SE18 6E 106
Engineers Row SE18 4E 106
(off Woolwich New Rd.)
Engineers Way HA9: Wemb 4G 61
Engineers Wharf UB5: N'olt 4D 76
England's La. NW3 6D 64
England Way KT3: N Mald 4H 151
Englefield NW1 2A 6
(off Clarence Gdns.)
Englefield Cl. BR5: St M Cry 5K 161
CR0: C'don 6C 156
EN2: Enf 2F 23
Englefield Cres. BR5: St M Cry 4K 161
Englefield Path BR5: St M Cry 4K 161
Englefield Rd. N1 7D 66
Engleheart Dr. TW14: Felt 6H 111
Engleheart Rd. SE6 7D 122
Englewood Rd. SW12 6F 119
English Grounds SE1 5G 15 (1E 102)
English St. E3 4B 86
Enid St. SE16 7K 15 (3F 103)
Enmore Av. SE25 5G 157
Enmore Gdns. SW14 5K 115
Enmore Rd. SE25 5G 157
SW15 4E 116
UB1: S'hall 4E 76
Ennerdale NW1 1A 6
(off Varndell St.)
Ennerdale Av. HA7: Stan 3C 42
Ennerdale Cl. SM1: Sutt 4H 165
TW14: Felt 1H 129
Ennerdale Ct. E11 7J 51
(off Cambridge Rd.)
Ennerdale Dr. NW9 5A 44
Ennerdale Gdns. HA9: Wemb 1C 60
Ennerdale Ho. E3 4B 86
Ennerdale Rd. DA7: Bex 1G 127
TW9: Kew, Rich 2F 115
Ennersdale Rd. SE13 5F 123
Ennis Ho. E14 6D 86
(off Vesey Path)
Ennismore Av. UB6: G'frd 6J 59
W4 4B 98
Ennismore Gdns. KT7: T Ditt 6J 149
SW7 7C 10 (2C 100)
Ennismore Gdns. M.
SW7 1C 16 (3C 100)
Ennismore M. SW7 7C 10 (3C 100)
Ennismore St. SW7 1C 16 (3C 100)
Ennis Rd. N4 1A 66
SE18 6G 107
Ennor Ct. SM3: Cheam 4E 164
Ensbury Ho. SW8 7K 101
(off Carroun Rd.)
Ensham Ho. SW17 5D 136
Ensign Cl. TW6: H'row A 3G 111
TW19: Stanw 1A 128
Ensign Dr. N13 3H 33
Ensign Ho. E14 2C 104
(off Admirals Way)
NW9 3C 44
(off East Dr.)
SW18 3A 118
Ensign St. E1 7G 85
SE3 4K 123
Ensign Way SM6: W'gton 7J 167
TW19: Stanw 1A 128
Enslin Rd. SE9 6E 124
Ensor M. SW7 5A 16 (5B 100)
Enstone Rd. EN3: Enf H 3F 25
UB10: Ick 3B 56
Enterprise Bus. Pk. E14 2D 104
The Enterprise Cen. BR3: Beck 5A 140
(off Cricket La.)
Enterprise Cl. CR0: C'don 1A 168
Enterprise Ho. E4 7K 25
E9 7J 67
(off Tudor Gro.)
E14 5D 104
(off St Davids Sq.)
IG11: Bark 3K 89
KT12: Walt T 7K 147
Enterprise Ind. Est. SE16 5J 103
Enterprise Row N15 5F 49
Enterprise Trad. Est. UB2: S'hall 2F 95
Enterprise Way NW10 3B 80
SW18 4J 117
TW11: Tedd 6K 131
Enterprize Way SE8 4B 104
Entertainment Av. SE10 1G 105
Envoy Av. TW6: H'row A 3H 111
Envoy Ho. NW9 3C 44
(off East Dr.)
ENVOY RDBT. 3H 111
Epcot M. NW10 3F 81
Epirus M. SW6 7J 99
Epirus Rd. SW6 7H 99
Epping Cl. E14 4C 104
RM7: Mawney 3H 55
Epping Glade E4 6K 25
Epping New Rd. IG9: Buck H 3D 36
Epping Pl. N1 6A 66
Epping Way E4 6J 25
Epple Rd. SW6 1H 117
Epsom Cl. DA7: Bex 3H 127
UB5: N'olt 5D 58
Epsom Rd. CR0: Wadd 4A 168
E10 6E 50
IG3: Ilf 6K 53
SM3: Sutt 7H 153
SM4: Mord 7H 153
Epsom Sq. TW6: H'row A 2H 111
Epstein Ct. N1 1B 84
(off Gaskin St.)
Epstein Rd. SE28 1A 108
Epstein Sq. E14 6C 86
(off Upper Nth. St.)
Epworth Rd. TW7: Isle 7B 96
Epworth St. EC2 4F 9 (4D 84)
Equana Apts. SE8 5A 104
(off Evelyn St.)
Equiano Ho. SW9 1K 119
(off Lett Rd.)
Equinox Ct. IG2: Ilf 5F 53
Equinox Ho. IG11: Bark 6G 71
(off Wakering Rd.)
Equinox Sq. E14 6D 86
Equity M. W5 1D 96
Equity Sq. E2 2K 9
(off Shacklewell St.)
Erasmus St. SW1 4D 18 (4H 101)
Erconwald St. W12 6B 80
Erebus Dr. SE28 3G 107
Eresby Dr. BR3: Beck 1C 170
Eresby Ho. SW7 7D 10
(off Rutland Ga.)
Eresby Pl. NW6 7J 63
Erica Gdns. CR0: C'don 3D 170
Erica Ho. N22 1A 48
(off Acacia Rd.)
SE4 3B 122
Erica St. W12 7C 80
Eric Clarke La. IG11: Bark 4F 89
Eric Cl. E7 4J 69
Ericcson Cl. SW18 5J 117
Eric Fletcher Ct. N1 7C 66
(off Essex Rd.)
Erickson Gdns. BR2: Broml 6C 160
Eric Liddell Sports Cen. 2B 142
Eric Rd. E7 4J 69
NW10 6B 62
RM6: Chad H 7D 54
Eric Shipman Ter. E13 4J 87
(off Balaam St.)
Ericson Ho. SE13 4F 123
(off Blessington Rd.)
Eric St. E3 4B 86
(not continuous)
Eric Wilkins Ho. SE1 5G 103
(off Old Kent Rd.)
Eridge Rd. W4 3K 97
Erin Cl. BR1: Broml 7G 141
IG3: Ilf 6A 54
SW6 7J 99
Erin Ct. NW2 6E 62
Erindale SE18 6H 107
Erindale Ter. SE18 6H 107
Erin M. N22 1B 48
Erin's Vs. SE14 1K 121
(off New Cross Rd.)
ERITH 5K 109
Erith Cres. RM5: Col R 1J 55
Erith Quarry DA8: Erith 6J 109
Erith Rd. DA7: Bex 4H 127
DA8: Erith 5G 109
(Picardy Rd.)
DA8: Erith 4H 127
(Watling St.)
DA17: Belv, Erith 5G 109
Erith School Community Sports Cen.
7J 109
Erlanger Rd. SE14 1K 121
Erlesmere Gdns. W13 3A 96
Erlich Cotts. E1 5J 85
(off Sidney St.)
Ermine Cl. TW4: Houn 2A 112
Ermine Ho. E3 1B 86
(off Parnell Rd.)
N17 7A 34
(off Moselle St.)
Ermine M. E2 1F 85
Ermine Rd. N15 6F 49
SE13 4D 122
Ermine Side EN1: Enf 5B 24
Ermington Rd. SE9 2G 143
Ernald Av. E6 2C 88
Erncroft Way TW1: Twick 6K 113
Ernest Av. SE27 4B 138
Ernest Cl. BR3: Beck 5C 158
Ernest Cotts. KT17: Ewe 7B 164
Ernest Gdns. W4 6H 97
Ernest Gro. BR3: Beck 5B 158
Ernest Harriss Ho. W9 4J 81
(off Elgin Av.)
Ernest Rd. KT1: King T 2H 151
Ernest Shackleton Lodge
SE10 4G 105
(off Christchurch Way)
Ernest Sq. KT1: King T 2H 151
Ernest St. E1 4K 85
Ernle Rd. SW20 7D 134
Ernshaw Pl. SW15 5G 117
Ernst Bldg. SE1 5C 14
(off Union St.)
Eros 3C 12 (7H 83)
Eros Ho. Shops SE6 7D 122
(off Brownhill Rd.)
Erpingham Rd. SW15 3E 116
Erridge Rd. SW19 2J 153
Errington Rd. W9 4H 81
Errol Gdns. KT3: N Mald 4C 152
UB4: Yead 4K 75
Errol St. EC1 4D 8 (4C 84)
Erskine Cl. SM1: Sutt 3C 166
Erskine Cres. N17 4H 49
Erskine Hill NW11 4J 45
Erskine Ho. SW1 6A 18
(off Churchill Gdns.)
Erskine M. NW3 7D 64
(off Erskine Rd.)
Erskine Rd. E17 4B 50
NW3 7D 64
SM1: Sutt 4B 166
Erwin Ho. NW9 3C 44
(off Commander Av.)
Erwood Rd. SE7 5C 106
Esam Way SW16 5A 138
Escot Rd. TW16: Sun 7G 129
Escott Gdns. SE9 4C 142
Escreet Gro. SE18 4E 106
Esher Av. KT12: Walt T 7J 147
RM7: Rom 6J 55
SM3: Cheam 3F 165
Esher Cl. DA5: Bexl 1E 144
Esher Cres. TW6: H'row A 2H 111
Esher Gdns. SW19 2F 135
Esher M. CR4: Mitc 3E 154
Esher Rd. IG3: Ilf 3J 71
KT8: E Mos 6H 149
Eskdale NW1 1A 6
(off Stanhope St.)
Eskdale Av. UB5: N'olt 1D 76
Eskdale Cl. HA9: Wemb 2D 60
Eskdale Rd. DA7: Bex 2G 127
Esker Pl. E2 2H 85
Esk Ho. E3 4B 86
(off British St.)
Eskmont Ridge SE19 7D 138
Esk Rd. E13 4J 87
Esk Way RM1: Rom 1K 55
Esmar Cres. NW9 7C 44
Esmat Cl. E11 5K 51
Esmeralda Rd. SE1 4G 103
Esmond Ct. W8 3K 99
(off Thackeray St.)
Esmond Gdns. W4 4K 97
Esmond Rd. NW6 1H 81
W4 4K 97
Esmond St. SW15 4G 117
Esparto St. SW18 7K 117
Esprit Ct. E1 6J 9
(off Brune St.)
Esquiline La. CR4: Mitc 3F 155
Essan Ho. W5 5B 78
Essence E3 2B 86
(off Cardigan Rd.)
Essence Ct. HA9: Wemb 2F 61
Essenden Rd. CR2: S Croy 7E 168
DA17: Belv 5G 109
Essendine Mans. W9 3J 81
Essendine Rd. W9 3J 81

A-Z Big London 217

Fairfield W.—Felix Mnr.

Fairfield W. KT1: King T 2E 150
Fairfoot Rd. E3 4C 86
Fairford SE6 1C 140
Fairford Av. CR0: C'don 5K 157
DA7: Bex 1K 127
Fairford Cl. CR0: C'don 5A 158
Fairford Ct. SM2: Sutt 7K 165
Fairford Gdns. KT4: Wor Pk 2B 164
Fairford Ho. SE11 4K 19 (4A 102)
Fairgreen EN4: Cockf 3J 21
Fairgreen Ct. EN4: Cockf 3J 21
Fairgreen E. EN4: Cockf 3J 21
Fairgreen Rd. CR7: Thor H 5B 156
Fairhall Ct. KT5: Surb 7F 151
Fairhaven Av. CR0: C'don 6K 157
Fairhaven Ct. CR2: S Croy 5C 168
(off Warham Rd.)
Fairhazel Gdns. NW6 6K 63
Fairhazel Mans. NW6 7A 64
(off Fairhazel Gdns.)
Fairholme TW14: Bedf 7F 111
Fairholme Cl. N3 4G 45
Fairholme Cres. UB4: Hayes 4H 75
Fairholme Gdns. N3 3G 45
Fairholme Rd. CR0: C'don 7A 156
HA1: Harr 5K 41
IG1: Ilf 7D 52
SM1: Sutt 6H 165
TW15: Ashf 5A 128
W14 5G 99
Fairholt Cl. N16 1E 66
Fairholt Rd. N16 1D 66
Fairholt St. SW7 1D 16 (3C 100)
Fairland Ho. BR2: Broml 4K 159
Fairland Rd. E15 6H 69
Fairlands Av. CR7: Thor H 4K 155
IG9: Buck H 2D 36
SM1: Sutt 2J 165
Fairlands Ct. SE9 6E 124
Fairlawn KT2: King T 6J 133
SE7 7A 106
Fairlawn Av. DA7: Bex 2D 126
N2 4C 46
W4 4J 97
Fairlawn Cl. KT2: King T 6J 133
KT10: Clay 6A 162
N14 6B 22
TW13: Hanw 4D 130
Fairlawn Ct. SE7 7A 106
(not continuous)
W4 4J 97
Fairlawn Dr. IG8: Wfd G 7D 36
Fairlawnes SM6: W'gton 5F 167
Fairlawn Gdns. UB1: S'hall 7D 76
Fairlawn Gro. W4 4J 97
Fairlawn Mans. SE14 1K 121
Fairlawn Pk. SE26 5A 140
Fairlawn Rd. SW19 7H 135
Fairlawns HA5: Pinn 2B 40
TW1: Twick 6C 114
TW16: Sun 3J 147
Fairlead Ho. E14 3C 104
(off Alpha Gro.)
Fairleads Ho. E17 4K 49
(off Wickford Way)
Fairlea Pl. W5 4C 78
Fairlie Ct. E3 3D 86
(off Stroudley Wlk.)
Fairlie Gdns. SE23 7J 121
Fairlight TW12: Hamp H 5F 131
Fairlight Av. E4 2A 36
IG8: Wfd G 6D 36
NW10 2A 80
Fairlight Cl. E4 2A 36
KT4: Wor Pk 4E 164
Fairlight Ct. NW10 2A 80
UB6: G'frd 2G 77
Fairlight Rd. SW17 4B 136
Fairline Ct. BR3: Beck 2E 158
FAIRLOP 1J 53
Fairlop Ct. E11 1F 69
Fairlop Gdns. IG6: Ilf 1G 53
Fairlop Outdoor Activity Cen. 1K 53
Fairlop Rd. E11 7F 51
IG6: Ilf 2G 53
Fairlop Waters Country Pk. 2K 53
Fairlop Waters Golf Course 1J 53
Fairmark Dr. UB10: Hil 6C 56
Fairmead BR1: Broml 4D 160
KT5: Surb 1H 163
Fairmead Cl. BR1: Broml 4D 160
KT3: N Mald 3K 151
TW5: Hest 7B 94
Fairmead Ct. TW9: Rich 2H 115
Fairmead Cres. HA8: Edg 3D 28
Fairmead Gdns. IG4: Ilf 5C 52
Fairmead Ho. E9 4A 68
Fairmead Rd. CR0: C'don 7K 155
N19 3H 65
Fairmile Av. SW16 5H 137
Fairmile Ho. TW11: Tedd 4A 132
Fairmont Av. E14 1F 105
Fairmont Cl. DA17: Belv 5F 109
Fairmont Ho. E3 4C 86
(off Wellington Way)
SE16 2K 103
(off Needleman St.)
Fairmont M. NW2 2J 63
Fairmount Rd. SW2 6K 119
Fairoak Cl. BR5: Pet W 7F 161
Fairoak Dr. SE9 5H 125
Fairoak Gdns. RM1: Rom 2K 55
Fair Oak Pl. IG6: Ilf 2G 53
Fairseat Cl. WD23: B Hea 2D 26
Fairstead Lodge IG8: Wfd G 6D 36
(off Snakes La. W.)
Fairstead Wlk. N1 1C 84
(off Popham St.)
Fair St. SE1 6H 15 (2E 102)
TW3: Houn 3G 113
Fairthorne Vs. SE7 5J 105
(off Felltram Way)
Fairthorn Rd. SE7 5J 105
Fairview HA4: Ruis 4A 58
Fairview Av. HA0: Wemb 6D 60
Fairview Cl. E17 1A 50
SE26 5A 140
Fairview Ct. NW4 2F 45
TW15: Ashf 5C 128
Fairview Cres. HA2: Harr 1E 58
Fairview Dr. BR6: Orp 4H 173
TW17: Shep 5B 146
Fairview Est. NW10 3J 79
Fairview Gdns. IG8: Wfd G 1K 51
Fairview Ho. SW2 7K 119
Fairview Ind. Pk. RM13: Rain 5K 91
Fairview Pl. SW2 7K 119
Fairview Rd. EN2: Enf 1F 23
N15 5F 49
SM1: Sutt 5B 166
SW16 1K 155
Fairview Vs. E4 7H 35
Fairview Way HA8: Edg 4B 28
Fairwall Ho. SE5 1E 120
Fairwater Av. DA16: Well 4A 126
Fairwater Dr. TW17: Shep 5E 146
Fairwater Ho. E16 2K 105
(off Bonnet St.)
TW11: Tedd 4A 132
Fairway BR5: Pet W 5H 161
DA6: Bex 5E 126
IG8: Wfd G 5F 37
SW20 3E 152
The Fairway BR1: Broml 5D 160
EN5: New Bar 6E 20
HA0: Wemb 3B 60
HA4: Ruis 4A 58
KT3: N Mald 1K 151
KT8: W Mole 3F 149
N13 3H 33
N14 6A 22
NW7 3E 28
UB5: N'olt 6G 59
UB10: Hil 3B 74
W3 6A 80
Fairway Av. NW9 3H 43
Fairway Cl. CR0: C'don 5A 158
KT10: Surb 3B 162
KT19: Ewe 4J 163
NW11 7A 46
TW4: Houn 5A 112
(Amberley Way)
TW4: Houn 5B 112
(Islay Gdns.)
Fairway Ct. E3 3E 86
(off Culvert Dr.)
EN5: New Bar 6E 20
NW7 3E 28
SE16 2K 103
(off Christopher Cl.)
Fairway Dr. SE28 6D 90
UB6: G'frd 7F 59
Fairway Gdns. BR3: Beck 6F 159
IG1: Ilf 5G 71
Fairways E17 4E 50
HA7: Stan 2E 42
TW7: Isle 1H 113
TW11: Tedd 7D 132
TW15: Ashf 6D 128
Fairways Bus. Pk. E10 2A 68
Fairway Trad. Est.
TW4: Houn 5A 112
Fairweather Cl. DA16: Well 5A 126
N15 4E 48
Fairweather Ct. N13 3E 32
Fairweather Ho. N7 4J 65
Fairweather Rd. N16 6G 49
Fairwyn Rd. SE26 4A 140
Faith Ct. E3 2C 86
(off Lefevre Wlk.)
SE1 5F 103
(off Cooper's Rd.)
Faith M. E12 4B 70
Fakenham Cl. NW7 7H 29
UB5: N'olt 6D 58
Fakruddin St. E1 4G 85
Falcon WC1 5F 7
(off Old Gloucester St.)
Falcon Av. BR1: Broml 4C 160
Falconberg M. W1 7D 6 (6H 83)
Falcon Cl. HA6: Nwood 1G 39
W4 6J 97
Falcon Ct. E18 3K 51
(off Albert Rd.)
EC4 1K 13 (6A 84)
EN5: New Bar 4F 21
HA4: Ruis 2G 57
N1 1B 8
(off City Gdn. Row)
Falcon Cres. EN3: Pond E 5E 24
Falcondal Ct. NW10 3G 79
Falcon Dr. TW19: Stanw 6A 110
Falconer Ct. N17 7H 33
(off Compton Cres.)
Falconer Wlk. N7 2K 65
Falconet Ct. E1 1H 103
(off Wapping High St.)
Falcon Gro. SW11 3C 118
Falcon Highwalk EC2 6C 8
Falcon Ho. BR1: Broml 1H 159
E14 5D 104
(off St Davids Sq.)
NW6 1K 81
(off Springfield Wlk.)
SW5 5K 99
(off Old Brompton Rd.)
Falcon La. SW11 3C 118
Falcon Lodge W9 5J 81
(off Admiral Wlk.)
Falcon Park Community Sports Centre
2D 118
Falcon Pk. Ind. Est. NW10 4A 62
Falcon Point SE1 3B 14 (7B 84)
Falcon Rd. EN3: Pond E 5E 24
SW11 2C 118
TW12: Hamp 7D 130
Falconry Ct. KT1: King T 3E 150
(off Fairfield Sth.)
Falcon St. E13 4J 87
Falcon Ter. SW11 3C 118
Falcon Way E11 4J 51
E14 4D 104
HA3: Kenton 5E 42
NW9 2A 44
TW14: Felt 5K 111
TW16: Sun 2G 147
Falcon Wharf SW11 2B 118
FALCONWOOD 2H 125
FALCONWOOD 4H 125
Falconwood Av. DA16: Well 2H 125
Falconwood Ct. SE3 2H 123
(off Montpelier Row)
Falconwood Pde. DA16: Well 4J 125
Falconwood Rd. CR0: Sels 7B 170
Falcourt Cl. SM1: Sutt 5K 165
Falkirk Ct. SE16 1K 103
(off Rotherhithe St.)
Falkirk Ho. W9 2K 81
(off Maida Vale)
Falkirk St. N1 1H 9 (2E 84)
Falkland Av. N3 7D 30
N11 4A 32
Falkland Ho. SE6 4E 140
W8 3K 99
W14 5H 99
(off Edith Vs.)
Falkland Pk. Av. SE25 3E 156
Falkland Pl. NW5 5G 65
Falkland Rd. EN5: Barn 2B 20
N8 4A 48
NW5 5G 65
Fallaize Av. IG1: Ilf 4F 71
Falling La. UB7: Yiew 7A 74
Falloden Way NW11 4J 45
Fallodon Ho. W11 5H 81
(off Tavistock Cres.)
FALLOW CORNER 7F 31
Fallow Ct. SE16 5G 103
(off Argyle Way)
Fallow Ct. Av. N12 7F 31
Fallowfield HA7: Stan 4F 27
Fallowfield Ct. HA7: Stan 3F 27
Fallowfields Dr. N12 6H 31
Fallowhurst Path N3 7F 31
Fallow Pl. TW11: Tedd 5J 131
Fallows Cl. N2 2B 46
Fallsbrook Rd. SW16 6F 137
Falman Cl. N9 1B 34
Falmer Rd. E17 3D 50
EN1: Enf 4K 23
N15 5C 48
Falmouth Av. E4 5A 36
Falmouth Cl. N22 7E 32
SE12 5H 123
Falmouth Gdns. IG4: Ilf 4B 52
Falmouth Ho. HA5: Hat E 1D 40
KT2: King T 1D 150
(off Skerne Rd.)
SE11 5K 19
(off Seaton Cl.)
W2 2C 10
(off Clarendon Pl.)
Falmouth Rd. SE1 7E 14 (3C 102)
Falmouth St. E15 5F 69
Falmouth Wlk. SW15 6C 116
Falmouth Way E17 5B 50
Falstaff Bldg. E1 7H 85
(off Cannon St. Rd.)
Falstaff Cl. DA1: Cray 7K 127
Falstaff Ct. SE11 4B 102
(off Opal St.)
Falstaff Ho. N1 1G 9
(off Regan Way)
Falstaff M. TW12: Hamp H 5H 131
(off High St.)
Fambridge Cl. SE26 4B 140
Fambridge Ct. RM7: Rom 5K 55
(off Marks Rd.)
Fambridge Rd. RM8: Dag 1G 73
Family Court
East London 1C 104
West London 6J 111
Fancourt M. BR1: Broml 3E 160
Fane St. W14 6H 99
The Fan Mus. 7E 104
Fann St. EC1 4C 8 (4C 84)
EC2 4C 8 (4C 84)
(not continuous)
Fanshawe Av. IG11: Bark 6G 71
Fanshawe Cres. RM9: Dag 5E 72
Fanshawe Rd. TW10: Ham 4C 132
Fanshaw St. N1 1G 9 (3E 84)
THE FANTAIL 3D 172
Fantail Cl. SE28 6C 90
Fanthorpe St. SW15 3E 116
Faraday Av. DA14: Sidc 2A 144
Faraday Cl. N7 6K 65
Faraday Ho. E14 7B 86
(off Brightlingsea Pl.)
HA9: Wemb 3J 61
SE1 7E 14
(off Cole St.)
SW11 7K 17 (6F 101)
Faraday Lodge SE10 3H 105
Faraday Mans. W14 6G 99
(off Queen's Club Gdns.)
The Faraday Mus. 3A 12 (7G 83)
Faraday Pl. KT8: W Mole 4E 148
Faraday Rd. DA16: Well 3A 126
E15 6H 69
KT8: W Mole 4E 148
SW19 6J 135
UB1: S'hall 7F 77
W3 7J 79
W10 5G 81
Faraday Way CR0: Wadd 1K 167
SE18 3B 106
Fareham Rd. TW14: Felt 7A 112
Farewell Pl. CR4: Mitc 1C 154
Fari Ct. E17 4C 50
(off Tower M.)
Faringdon Av. BR2: Broml 7E 160
Faringford Rd. E15 7G 69
Farjeon Ho. NW6 7B 64
(off Hilgrove Rd.)
Farjeon Rd. SE3 1B 124
Farleigh Av. BR2: Hayes 7H 159
Farleigh Ct. CR2: S Croy 5C 168
Farleigh Ho. N1 7B 66
(off Halton Rd.)
Farleigh Pl. N16 4F 67
Farleigh Rd. N16 4F 67
Farley Ct. NW1 4G 5
(off Allsop Pl.)
W14 3H 99
Farley Dr. IG3: Ilf 1J 71
Farley Ho. SE26 3H 139
Farley M. SE6 7E 122
Farley Pl. SE25 4G 157
Farley Rd. CR2: Sels 7H 169
SE6 7D 122
Farlington Pl. SW15 7D 116
Farlow Rd. SW15 3F 117
Farlton Rd. SW18 1K 135
Farman Gro. UB5: N'olt 3B 76
Farman Ter. HA3: Kenton 4D 42
Farm Av. HA0: Wemb 6C 60
HA2: Harr 7D 40
NW2 3G 63
SW16 4J 137
Farmborough Cl. HA1: Harr 7H 41
Farm Cl.
BR4: W W'ck 3H 171
IG9: Buck H 3F 37
RM10: Dag 7J 73
SM2: Sutt 7B 166
SW6 7J 99
TW17: Shep 7C 146
Farm Cl. UB1: S'hall 7F 77
UB10: Ick 2D 56
Farmcote Rd. SE12 1J 141
Farm Ct. NW4 3C 44
Farmdale Rd. SE10 5J 105
SM5: Cars 7C 166
Farm Dr. CR0: C'don 2B 170
Farm End HA6: Nwood 1D 38
Farmer Rd. E10 1D 68
Farmer's Rd. SE5 7B 102
Farmer St. W8 1J 99
Farmfield Rd. BR1: Broml 5G 141
Farm Ho. Ct. NW7 7H 29
Farmhouse Rd. SW16 7G 137
Farmilo Rd. E17 7B 50
Farmington Av. SM1: Sutt 3B 166
Farmlands EN2: Enf 1F 23
HA5: Eastc 4J 39
The Farmlands UB5: N'olt 6D 58
Farmland Wlk. BR7: Chst 5F 143
Farm La. CR0: C'don 2B 170
N14 7A 22
SW6 6J 99
Farmleigh N14 7B 22
Farmleigh Ho. SW9 5B 120
Farm M. CR4: Mitc 2F 155
Farm Pl. W8 1J 99
Farm Rd. HA8: Edg 6C 28
N21 1H 33
NW10 1K 79
SM2: Sutt 7B 166
SM4: Mord 5K 153
TW4: Houn 1C 130
Farmstead Ct. SM6: W'gton 5F 167
(off Melbourne Rd.)
Farmstead Rd. HA3: Hrw W 1H 41
SE6 4D 140
Farm St. W1 3J 11 (7F 83)
Farm Va. DA5: Bexl 6H 127
Farm Wlk. NW11 5H 45
Farm Way IG9: Buck H 4F 37
KT4: Wor Pk 3E 164
Farmway RM8: Dag 3C 72
Farnaby Ho. W10 3H 81
(off Bruckner St.)
Farnaby Rd. BR1: Broml 7F 141
BR2: Broml 7F 141
SE9 4A 124
Farnan Av. E17 2C 50
Farnan Lodge SW16 5J 137
Farnan Rd. SW16 5J 137
FARNBOROUGH 5G 173
Farnborough Av. CR2: Sels 7K 169
E17 3A 50
Farnborough Cl. HA9: Wemb 2H 61
Farnborough Comn. BR6: Farnb 3D 172
Farnborough Cres. BR2: Hayes 1H 171
CR2: Sels 7A 170
Farnborough Hill
BR6: Chels, Farnb 5H 173
Farnborough Ho. SW15 1C 134
Farnborough Way
BR6: Chels, Farnb 5G 173
Farncombe St. SE16 2G 103
Farndale Av. N13 2G 33
Farndale Ct. SE18 7C 106
Farndale Cres. UB6: G'frd 3G 77
Farndale Ho. NW6 1K 81
(off Kilburn Vale)
Farnell M. SW5 5K 99
Farnell Pl. W3 7H 79
Farnell Rd. TW7: Isle 3H 113
Farnfield Ct. CR2: S Croy 5B 168
Farnham Cl. N20 7F 21
Farnham Ct. SM3: Cheam 6G 165
UB1: S'hall 7G 77
(off Redcroft Rd.)
Farnham Gdns. SW20 2D 152
Farnham Ho. NW1 4D 4
SE1 5C 14
(off Union St.)
Farnham Pl. SE1 5B 14 (1B 102)
Farnham Rd. DA16: Well 2C 126
IG3: Ilf 7K 53
Farnham Royal SE11 6H 19 (5K 101)
Farningham Ct. SW16 7H 137
Farningham Ho. N4 7D 48
Farningham Rd. N17 7B 34
Farnley Ho. SW8 2H 119
Farnley Rd. E4 1B 36
SE25 4D 156
Farnsworth Ct. SE10 3H 105
(off West Parkside)
Farnsworth Dr. HA8: Edg 4K 27
Farnworth Ho. E14 4F 105
(off Manchester Rd.)
Faro Cl. BR1: Broml 2E 160
Faroe Rd. W14 3F 99
Farorna Wlk. EN2: Enf 1F 23
Farquhar Rd. SE19 5F 139
SW19 3J 135
Farquharson Rd. CR0: C'don 1C 168
Farrance Rd. RM6: Chad H 7E 54
Farrance St. E14 6C 86
Farrans Ct. HA3: Kenton 7B 42
Farrant Av. N22 2A 48
Farrant Cl. BR6: Chels 7K 173
Farr Av. IG11: Bark 2A 90
Farrell Ho. E1 6J 85
(off Ronald St.)
Farren Rd. SE23 2A 140
Farrer Ct. TW1: Twick 7D 114
Farrer Ho. SE8 7C 104
Farrer M. N8 4G 47
Farrer Rd. HA3: Kenton 5E 42
N8 4G 47
Farrer's Pl. CR0: C'don 4K 169
Farrier Cl. BR1: Broml 3B 160
TW16: Sun 4J 147
UB8: Hil 6C 74
Farrier Ct. E1 5K 85
(off White Horse La.)
RM13: Rain 2K 91
(off Lowen Rd.)
Farrier Pl. SM1: Sutt 3K 165
Farrier Rd. UB5: N'olt 2E 76
Farriers Ho. EC1 4D 8
(off Errol St.)
Farriers M. SE15 3J 121
SW9 4A 120
Farrier St. NW1 7F 65
Farriers Yd. W6 5F 99
(off Smiths Sq.)
Farrier Wlk. SW10 6A 100
Farringdon Ho. TW9: Kew 7H 97
UB7: W Dray 2B 92
Farringdon La. EC1 4K 7 (4A 84)
Farringdon Rd. EC1 3J 7 (4A 84)
Farringdon St. EC4 6A 8 (5B 84)
Farrington Ct. BR1: Broml 2K 159
(off Widmore Rd.)
Farrington Pl. BR7: Chst 7H 143
Farrins Rents SE16 1A 104
Farrow Ho. NW9 3C 44
Farrow La. SE14 7J 103
Farrow Pl. SE16 3A 104
Farr Rd. EN2: Enf 1J 23
Farsby Ho. Apts. IG11: Bark 4A 90
(off Manwell La.)
Farthingale Wlk. E15 7F 69
Farthing All. SE1 7K 15 (2G 103)
Farthing Barn La. BR6: Downe 7E 172
Farthing Ct. NW7 7B 30
Farthing Flds. E1 1H 103
The Farthings KT2: King T 1G 151
Farthings Cl. E4 3B 36
HA5: Eastc 6K 39
FARTHING STREET 7D 172
Farthing St. BR6: Downe 7D 172
Farwell Rd. DA14: Sidc 4B 144
Farwig La. BR1: Broml 1H 159
Fashion & Textile Mus. 6H 15 (2E 102)
Fashion St. E1 6K 9 (5F 85)
Fashoda Rd. BR2: Broml 4B 160
Fassett Rd. E8 6G 67
KT1: King T 4E 150
Fassett Sq. E8 6G 67
Fathom Ct. E16 7F 89
(off Basin App.)
Fauconberg Ct. W4 6J 97
(off Fauconberg Rd.)
Fauconberg Rd. W4 6J 97
Faulkner Cl. RM8: Dag 7D 54
Faulkner Ho. BR7: Chst 7H 143
W6 6E 98
Faulkner M. E17 1A 50
Faulkners All. EC1 5A 8 (5B 84)
Faulkner St. SE14 1J 121
Fauna Cl. HA7: Stan 4J 27
RM6: Chad H 6C 54
Faunce Ho. SE17 6B 102
(off Doddington Gro.)
Faunce St. SE17 5B 102
Favart Rd. SW6 1J 117
Faversham Av. E4 1B 36
EN1: Enf 6J 23
Faversham Ho. NW1 1G 83
(off Bayham Pl.)
SE17 5E 102
(off Kinglake St.)
Faversham Rd. BR3: Beck 2B 158
SE6 7B 122
SM4: Mord 6K 153
Fawcett Cl. SW11 2B 118
SW16 5A 138
Fawcett Ct. SW10 6A 100
(off Fawcett St.)
Fawcett Est. E5 1G 67
Fawcett Rd. CR0: C'don 3C 168
NW10 7B 62
Fawcett St. SW10 6A 100
Fawe Pk. M. SW15 4H 117
Fawe Pk. Rd. SW15 4H 117
Fawe St. E14 5D 86
Fawkham Ho. SE1 4F 103
(off Longfield Est.)
Fawley Lodge E14 4F 105
(off Millennium Dr.)
Fawley Rd. NW6 5K 63
Fawnbrake Av. SE24 5B 120
Fawn Hgts. IG9: Buck H 2E 36
(off Stag La.)
Fawn Rd. E13 2A 88
Fawns Mnr. Cl. TW14: Bedf 1E 128
Fawns Mnr. Rd. TW14: Bedf 1F 129
Fawood Av. NW10 7J 61
Faygate Cres. DA6: Bex 5G 127
Faygate Rd. SW2 2K 137
Fayland Av. SW16 5G 137
Fazeley Ct. W9 5J 81
(off Elmfield Way)
Fazeley Ho. UB5: N'olt 3D 76
(off Taywood Rd.)
Fearnley Cres. TW12: Hamp 5C 130
Fearnley Ho. SE5 2E 120
Fearns Ho. W13 1A 96
Fearon St. SE10 5J 105
Featherbed La. CR0: Sels 7B 170
Feather M. E1 5G 85
Feathers Pl. SE10 6F 105
Featherstone Av. SE23 2H 139
Featherstone Ct. UB2: S'hall 3B 94
Featherstone Ho. UB4: Yead 5A 76
Featherstone Ind. Est.
UB2: S'hall 3C 94
(off Feather Rd.)
Featherstone Rd. NW7 6J 29
UB2: S'hall 3C 94
Featherstone Sports Cen. 4B 94
Featherstone St. EC1 3E 8 (4D 84)
Featherstone Ter. UB2: S'hall 3C 94
Featley Rd. SW9 3B 120
Federal Rd. UB6: G'frd 1C 78
Federation Rd. SE2 4B 108
Fee Farm Rd. KT10: Clay 7A 162
Feeny Cl. NW10 4B 62
Felbridge Av. HA7: Stan 1A 42
Felbridge Cl. SM2: Sutt 7K 165
SW16 4A 138
Felbridge Ct. TW13: Felt 1K 129
(off High St.)
UB3: Harl 6F 93
Felbridge Ho. SE22 3E 120
Felbrigge Rd. IG3: Ilf 2K 71
Felday Rd. SE13 6D 122
Felden Cl. HA5: Hat E 1C 40
Felden St. SW6 1H 117
Feldman Cl. N16 1G 67
Feldspar Ct. EN3: Enf H 3F 25
(off Enstone Rd.)
Feldspar M. N13 5G 33
Felgate M. W6 4D 98
Felhampton Rd. SE9 2F 143
Felhurst Cres. RM10: Dag 4H 73
Feline Ct. EN4: E Barn 6H 21
Felix Av. N8 6J 47
Felix Ct. E17 5D 50
NW9 2A 44
Felix Ho. E16 7E 88
(off University Way)
Felix La. TW17: Shep 6G 147
Felix Mnr. BR7: Chst 6J 143

A-Z Big London 219

Felix Neubergh Ho.—Fir Tree Pl.

Felix Neubergh Ho. EN1: Enf .4K 23
Felix Pl. SW2 .5A 120
(off Talma Rd.)
Felix Point E14 .6C 86
(off Upper Nth. St.)
Felix Rd. KT12: Walt T .6J 147
W13 .7A 78
Felixstowe Ct. E16 .1F 107
Felixstowe Rd. N9 .3B 34
N17 .3F 49
NW10 .3D 80
SE2 .3B 108
Felix St. E2 .2H 85
Fellbrigg Rd. SE22 .5F 121
Fellbrigg St. E1 .4H 85
Fellbrook TW10: Ham .3B 132
Fellmongers Path SE1 .7J 15
Fellmongers Yd. CR0: C'don .3C 168
Fellowes Cl. UB4: Yead .4B 76
Fellowes Rd. SM5: Cars .3C 166
Fellows Ct. E2 .1J 9 (2F 85)
(not continuous)
Fellowship Cl. RM8: Dag .4A 72
Fellowship Ho. E6 .2C 88
(off St Bartholomew's Rd.)
Fellows Rd. NW3 .7B 64
Fell Rd. CR0: C'don .3C 168
Felltram M. SE7 .5J 105
Felltram Way SE7 .5J 105
Fell Wlk. HA8: Edg .1J 43
Felmersham Cl. SW4 .4J 119
Felmingham Rd. SE20 .2J 157
Felnex Av. SM6: W'gton .2E 166
Felnex Trad. Est. NW10 .2K 79
SM6: W'gton .2E 166
Felsberg Rd. SW2 .6J 119
Fels Cl. RM10: Dag .3H 73
Fels Farm Av. RM10: Dag .3J 73
Felsham Rd. SW15 .3E 116
Felspar Cl. SE18 .5K 107
Felstead Av. IG5: Ilf .1E 52
Felstead Cl. N13 .5F 33
Felstead Gdns. E14 .5E 104
Felstead Rd. E9 .6B 68
E11 .7J 51
Felstead St. E9 .6B 68
Felstead Wharf E14 .5E 104
Felsted Rd. E16 .6B 88
FELTHAM .1K 129
Feltham Av. KT8: E Mos .4J 149
Felthambrook Ind. Est.
TW13: Felt .3K 129
Felthambrook Way TW13: Felt .3K 129
Feltham Bus. Complex TW13: Felt .2K 129
Feltham Corporate Cen.
TW13: Felt .3K 129
FELTHAMHILL .5H 129
Feltham Hill Rd. TW15: Ashf .5C 128
Feltham Rd. CR4: Mitc .2D 154
TW15: Ashf .4C 128
Felton Cl. BR5: Pet W .6F 161
Felton Gdns. IG11: Bark .1J 89
Felton Hall Ho. SE16 .7K 15
Felton Ho. N1 .1D 84
(off Colville Est.)
Felton Lea DA14: Sidc .5K 143
Felton Rd. IG11: Bark .2J 89
W13 .2C 96
Felton St. N1 .1D 84
Fencepiece Rd. IG6: Chig, Ilf .1G 53
Fenchurch Av. EC3 .1G 15 (6E 84)
Fenchurch Bldgs. EC3 .1H 15 (6E 84)
Fenchurch Ho. EC3 .1J 15
(off Minories)
Fenchurch M. E3 .5B 86
(off St Paul's Way)
Fenchurch Pl. EC3 .2H 15 (6E 84)
Fenchurch St. EC3 .2G 15 (7E 84)
Fen Ct. EC3 .2G 15 (6E 84)
Fendall Rd. KT19: Ewe .5J 163
Fendall St. SE1 .3E 102
(not continuous)
Fendt Cl. E16 .6H 87
Fendyke Rd. DA17: Belv .4D 108
Fenelon Pl. W14 .4H 99
Fengate Cl. KT9: Chess .6D 162
Fen Gro. DA15: Sidc .5K 125
Fenham Rd. SE15 .7G 103
Fenland Ho. E5 .2J 67
Fen La. SW13 .1D 116
Fenman Ct. N17 .1H 49
Fenman Gdns. IG3: Ilf .1B 72
Fenn Cl. BR1: Broml .6J 141
Fennel Apts. SE1 .5J 15
(off Cayenne Ct.)
Fennel Cl. CR0: C'don .1K 169
E16 .4G 87
Fennells Mead KT17: Ewe .7B 164
Fennell St. SE18 .6E 106
Fenner Cl. SE16 .4H 103
Fenner Ho. E1 .1H 103
(off Watts St.)
Fenner Sq. SW11 .3B 118
Fenn Ho. TW7: Isle .1B 114
Fennings Rd. SW4 .6H 119
Fenning St. SE1 .6G 15 (2E 102)
Fenn St. E9 .5K 67
Fenstanton N4 .1K 65
(off Marquis Rd.)
Fenstanton Av. N12 .6G 31
Fen St. E16 .7H 87
Fenswood Cl. DA5: Bexl .6G 127
Fentiman Rd. SW8 .7F 19 (6J 101)
Fentiman Way HA2: Harr .2F 59
Fenton Cl. BR7: Chst .5D 142
E8 .6F 67
SW9 .2K 119
Fenton House .3A 64
(off Hampstead Gro.)
Fenton Ho. SE14 .7A 104
TW5: Hest .6E 94
Fenton Pde. SE10 .5H 105
(off Woolwich Rd.)
Fenton Rd. HA2: Harr .3G 41
N17 .7H 33
Fentons Av. E13 .3K 87
Fenton St. E1 .6H 85
Fenwick Cl. SE18 .6E 106
Fenwick Gro. SE15 .3G 121
Fenwick Ho. EC1 .5B 84
(off Little Britain)
Fenwick Pl. CR2: S Croy .7B 168
SW9 .3J 119
Fenwick Rd. SE15 .3G 121
Ferby Ct. DA14: Sidc .4K 143
(off Main Rd.)
Ferdinand Ct. SE6 .7C 122
(off Adenmore Rd.)
Ferdinand Dr. SE15 .7E 102
Ferdinand Ho. NW1 .7E 64
(off Ferdinand Pl.)
Ferdinand Magellan Court E16 .2K 105
(Ferdinand Magellan Court)
Ferdinand Pl. NW1 .7E 64
Ferdinand St. NW1 .7E 64
Ferguson Av. KT5: Surb .5F 151
Ferguson Cl. BR2: Broml .3F 159
E14 .4C 104
Ferguson Dr. W3 .6K 79
Fergus Rd. N5 .5B 66
Fergusson M. SW4 .2J 119
Fergus St. SE10 .3J 105
Ferial Ct. SE15 .7G 103
(off Fenham Rd.)
Fermain Ct. E. N1 .1E 84
(off Hertford Rd.)
Fermain Ct. Nth. N1 .1E 84
(off De Beauvoir Est.)
Fermain Ct. W. N1 .1E 84
(off De Beauvoir Est.)
Ferme Pk. Rd. N4 .5J 47
N8 .5J 47
Fermor Rd. SE23 .1A 140
Fermoy Ho. W9 .4H 81
(off Fermoy Rd.)
Fermoy Rd. UB6: G'frd .4F 77
W9 .4H 81
(not continuous)
Fern Av. CR4: Mitc .4H 155
Fernbank IG9: Buck H .1E 36
Fernbank Av. HA0: Wemb .4K 59
KT12: Walt T .7C 148
Fernbank M. SW12 .6G 119
Fernbrook Av. DA15: Sidc .5J 125
Fernbrook Cres. SE13 .6G 123
(off Leahurst Rd.)
Fernbrook Dr. HA2: Harr .7F 41
Fernbrook Rd. SE13 .5G 123
Ferncliff Rd. E8 .5G 67
Fern Cl. N1 .2E 84
Fern Ct. DA7: Bex .4G 127
RM7: Rom .5K 55
SE14 .2K 121
Ferncroft Av. HA4: Ruis .2A 58
N12 .6J 31
NW3 .3J 63
Ferndale BR1: Broml .2A 160
Ferndale Av. E17 .5F 51
TW4: Houn .3C 112
Ferndale Cl. DA7: Bex .1E 126
Ferndale Community Sports Cen. .3K 119
Ferndale Cres. SM5: Cars .1D 166
Ferndale Rd. E7 .7K 69
E11 .2G 69
N15 .6F 49
RM5: Col R .2J 55
SE25 .5H 157
SW4 .4J 119
SW9 .4J 119
TW15: Ashf .5A 128
Ferndale St. E6 .7F 89
Ferndale Ter. HA1: Harr .4K 41
Ferndale Way BR6: Farnb .5H 173
Ferndell Av. DA5: Bexl .3K 145
Fern Dene W13 .5B 78
Ferndene Rd. SE24 .4C 120
Fernden Way RM7: Rom .6H 55
Ferndown HA6: Nwood .2J 39
NW1 .7H 65
(off Camley St.)
Ferndown Av. BR6: Orp .1H 173
Ferndown Cl. HA5: Pinn .1C 40
SM2: Sutt .6B 166
Ferndown Ct. UB1: S'hall .6G 77
(off Haldane Rd.)
Ferndown Lodge E14 .3E 104
(off Manchester Rd.)
Ferndown Rd. SE9 .7B 124
Ferney Meade Way TW7: Isle .2A 114
Ferney Rd. EN4: E Barn .7K 21
Fern Gro. TW14: Felt .7K 111
Fernhall Dr. IG4: Ilf .5B 52
Fernham Rd. CR7: Thor H .3C 156
Fernhead Rd. W9 .3H 81
Fernheath Way DA2: Wilm .5K 145
Fernhill Ct. E17 .2F 51
Fernhill Gdns. KT2: King T .5D 132
Fern Hill Pl. BR6: Farnb .5G 173
Fernhill St. E16 .1D 106
Fernholme Rd. SE15 .5K 121
Fernhurst Gdns. HA8: Edg .6B 28
Fernhurst Rd. CR0: C'don .7H 157
SW6 .1G 117
TW15: Ashf .4E 128
Fern La. TW5: Hest .5D 94
Fernlea Rd. CR4: Mitc .2E 154
SW12 .1F 137
Fernleigh Cl. CR0: Wadd .4A 168
W9 .3H 81
Fernleigh Ct. HA2: Harr .2F 41
HA9: Wemb .2E 60
RM7: Rom .5J 55
Fernleigh Rd. N21 .2F 33
Fernly Cl. HA5: Eastc .2C 154
Fernsbury St. WC1 .2J 7 (3A 84)
Fernshaw Cl. SW10 .6A 100
Fernshaw Mans. SW10 .6A 100
(off Fernshaw Rd.)
Fernshaw Rd. SW10 .6A 100
Fernside IG9: Buck H .1E 36
KT7: T Ditt .1B 162
NW11 .2J 63
Fernside Av. NW7 .3E 28
TW13: Felt .4K 129
Fernside Ct. NW4 .2F 45
Fernside Rd. SW12 .1D 136
Ferns Rd. E15 .6H 69
Fern St. E3 .4C 86
Fernthorpe Rd. SW16 .6G 137
Ferntower Rd. N5 .5D 66
Fern Wlk. SE16 .5G 103
TW15: Ashf .5A 128
Fernways IG1: Ilf .4F 71
Fernwood SW19 .1H 135
Fernwood Av. HA0: Wemb .6C 60
SW16 .4H 137
Fernwood Cl. BR1: Broml .2A 160
Fernwood Ct. N14 .7B 22
Fernwood Cres. N20 .3J 31
Fernwood Pl. KT10: Hin W .2A 162
Ferny Hill EN4: Had W .1J 21
Ferranti Cl. SE18 .3B 106
Ferraro Cl. TW5: Hest .6E 94
Ferrers Av. SM6: Bedd .4H 167
UB7: W Dray .2A 92
Ferrers Rd. SW16 .5H 137
Ferrestone Rd. N8 .4K 47
Ferrey M. SW9 .2A 120
Ferriby Cl. N1 .7A 66
Ferrie Cl. NW9 .1B 44
Ferrier Ind. Est. SW18 .4K 117
(off Ferrier St.)
Ferrier Point E16 .5J 87
(off Forty Acre La.)
Ferrier St. SW18 .4K 117
Ferring Cl. HA2: Harr .1G 59
Ferrings SE21 .3E 138
Ferris Av. CR0: C'don .3B 170
Ferris Rd. SE22 .4G 121
Ferron Rd. E5 .3H 67
Ferrybridge Ho. SE11 .2H 19
Ferrydale Lodge NW4 .4E 44
(off Parson St.)
Ferry Ho. E5 .1H 67
(off Harrington Hill)
Ferry Island Retail Pk. .3G 49
Ferry La. N17 .4G 49
SW13 .6B 98
TW8: Bford .6E 96
TW9: Kew .6F 97
TW17: Shep .7C 146
Ferryman's Quay SW6 .2A 118
Ferrymead Av. UB6: G'frd .3E 76
Ferrymead Dr. UB6: G'frd .2E 76
Ferrymead Gdns.
UB6: G'frd .2G 77
Ferrymoor TW10: Ham .3B 132
Ferry Pl. SE18 .3E 106
Ferry Quays TW8: Bford .6E 96
(Ferry La.)
TW8: Bford .7D 96
(off Point Wharf La.)
Ferry Rd. KT7: T Ditt .6B 150
KT8: W Mole .3E 148
SW13 .7C 98
TW1: Twick .1B 132
TW11: Tedd .5B 132
Ferry Sq. TW8: Bford .7E 96
Ferry St. E14 .5E 104
Ferry Wharf TW8: Bford .7E 96
Festing Rd. SW15 .3F 117
Festival Cl. DA5: Bexl .1D 144
UB10: Hil .1D 74
Festival Ct. E8 .7F 67
(off Holly St.)
SM1: Sutt .7K 153
Festival Wlk. SM5: Cars .4D 166
Festival Way E4 .6K 35
Festive Mans. E20 .5E 68
(off Napa Cl.)
Festive Wlk. SW15 .2F 117
Festoon Way E16 .7B 88
Festubert Pl. E3 .2B 86
Festuca Ho. E20 .5E 68
(off Mirabelle Gdns.)
Fetherstone Ct. RM6: Chad H .6F 55
(off High Rd.)
Fetherton Ct. IG11: Bark .2G 89
(off Spring Pl.)
Fetter La. EC4 .1K 13 (6A 84)
Fetter La. Apts. EC4 .1J 13
(off Fetter La.)
Fettes Ho. NW8 .2B 82
(off Wellington Rd.)
Fettle Ct. SE14 .6A 104
(off Moulding La.)
Fews Lodge RM6: Chad H .4D 54
Ffinch St. SE8 .7C 104
Fiador Apts. SE10 .4G 105
(off Telegraph Av.)
Fidelis Ho. E1 .6J 9
(off Gun St.)
Fidgeon Cl. BR1: Broml .3E 160
Field Cl. BR1: Broml .2A 160
E4 .6J 35
HA4: Ruis .1E 56
IG9: Buck H .3F 37
KT8: W Mole .5F 149
KT9: Chess .5C 162
NW2 .2C 62
TW4: Cran .1K 111
UB3: Harl .7E 92
UB10: Ick .3D 56
FIELDCOMMON .7D 148
Fieldcommon La. KT12: Walt T .7C 148
Field Ct. SW19 .3J 135
WC1 .6H 7 (5K 83)
Field End HA4: Ruis .6A 58
UB5: N'olt .6B 58
Fieldend TW1: Twick .4K 131
Fld. End Rd. HA4: Ruis .5K 39
HA5: Eastc .5K 39
Fieldend Rd. SW16 .1G 155
Fielder Apts. E3 .4B 86
(off Heath Pl.)
Fielders Cl. EN1: Enf .4K 23
HA2: Harr .1G 59
Fielders Cres. IG11: Bark .4C 90
Fieldfare Rd. SE28 .7C 90
Fieldgate La. CR4: Mitc .2C 154
Fieldgate Mans. E1 .5G 85
(off Fieldgate St.)
Fieldgate St. E1 .5G 85
Field Ho. NW6 .3F 81
(off Harvist Rd.)
SM4: Mord .5K 153
(off School Ga. Dr.)
Fieldhouse Cl. E18 .1J 51
Fieldhouse Rd. SW12 .1G 137
Fielding Av. TW2: Twick .3G 131
Fielding Ct. WC2 .1E 12
(off Earlham St.)
Fielding Ho. NW8 .1A 82
(off Ainsworth Way)
W4 .6A 98
(off Devonshire Rd.)
Fielding La. BR2: Broml .4A 160
Fielding M. SW13 .6D 98
Fielding Rd. W4 .3K 97
W14 .3F 99
The Fieldings SE23 .1J 139
Fielding St. SE17 .6C 102
Fielding Ter. W5 .7F 79
Fielding Wlk. W13 .3B 96
Field La. TW8: Bford .7C 96
TW11: Tedd .5A 132
Fld. Maple M. RM5: Col R .1G 55
Field Mead NW7 .7F 29
NW9 .7F 29
Fieldpark Gdns. CR0: C'don .1A 170
Field Pl. KT3: N Mald .6B 152
SW19 .1B 154
Field Point E7 .4J 69
Field Rd. E7 .4H 69
N17 .3D 48
TW14: Felt .6K 111
W6 .5G 99
Fieldsend Rd. SM3: Cheam .5G 165
Fields Est. E8 .7G 67
Fieldside Cl. BR6: Farnb .4G 173
Fieldside Rd. BR1: Broml .5F 141
Fields Pk. Cres. RM6: Chad H .5D 54
Field St. WC1 .1G 7 (3K 83)
Fields Wlk. SW11 .7F 101
Fieldsway Ho. N5 .5A 66
Field Vw. TW13: Felt .4F 129
Fieldview SW18 .1B 136
Field Vw. Cl. RM7: Mawney .3G 55
Fieldview Cotts. N14 .2C 32
(off Balaams La.)
Field Way HA4: Ruis .1E 56
NW10 .7J 61
UB6: G'frd .1F 77
Fieldway BR5: Pet W .6H 161
CR0: New Ad .7D 170
RM8: Dag .3C 72
Fieldway Cres. N5 .5A 66
Fiennes Cl. RM8: Dag .1C 72
Fiesta Dr. RM9: Dag .4J 91
Fifehead Cl. TW15: Ashf .6A 128
Fife Rd. E16 .5J 87
KT1: King T .2E 150
N22 .7G 33
SW14 .5J 115
Fife Ter. N1 .2K 83
Fifield Path SE23 .3K 139
Fifth Av. E12 .4D 70
UB3: Hayes .1H 93
W10 .3G 81
Fifth Cross Rd. TW2: Twick .2H 131
Fifth Way HA9: Wemb .4H 61
Figges Rd. CR4: Mitc .7E 136
Fight for Peace Academy .1E 106
Fig Tree Cl. NW10 .1A 80
Figure Ct. SW3 .6F 17
Filament Wlk. SW18 .5J 117
(off Spectrum Way)
Filanco Ct. W7 .1K 95
Filby Cl. DA8: Erith .7K 109
Filby Rd. KT9: Chess .6F 163
Filey Av. N16 .1G 67
Filey Cl. SM2: Sutt .7A 166
Filey Waye HA4: Ruis .2J 57
Filigree Ct. SE16 .1B 104
Fillebrook Av. EN1: Enf .2K 23
Fillebrook Rd. E11 .1F 69
Filmer Chambers SW6 .1G 117
(off Filmer Rd.)
Filmer Ho. SW6 .1H 117
(off Filmer Rd.)
Filmer M. SW6 .1H 117
Filmer Rd. SW6 .1G 117
Filston Rd. DA8: Erith .5J 109
Filton Cl. NW9 .1A 44
Filton Ct. SE14 .7J 103
(off Farrow La.)
Finborough Ho. SW10 .6A 100
(off Finborough Rd.)
Finborough Rd. SW10 .5K 99
SW17 .6D 136
The Finborough Theatre .6K 99
(off Finborough Rd.)
Finchale Rd. SE2 .3A 108
Fincham Cl. UB10: Ick .3E 56
Finch Av. SE27 .4D 138
Finch Cl. EN5: Barn .5D 20
NW10 .6K 61
Finch Ct. DA14: Sidc .3B 144
Finchdean Ho. SW15 .7B 116
Finch Dr. TW14: Felt .7B 112
Finch Gdns. E4 .5H 35
Finch Ho. E3 .1B 86
(off Jasmine Sq.)
SE8 .7D 104
(off Bronze St.)
Finchingfield Av. IG8: Wfd G .7F 37
Finch La. EC3 .1F 15 (6D 84)
FINCHLEY .1J 45
Finchley Ct. N3 .6E 30
Finchley Golf Course .6C 30
Finchley Ind. Est. N12 .4F 31
Finchley La. NW4 .4E 44
Finchley Lido Leisure Cen. .7G 31
Finchley Manor Club .1H 45
Finchley Pk. N12 .4F 31
Finchley Pl. NW8 .2B 82
Finchley Rd. NW2 .4H 45
NW3 .4H 45
NW8 .1B 82
NW11 .4H 45
Finchley Way N3 .7D 30
Finch Lodge W9 .5J 81
(off Admiral Wlk.)
Finch M. SE15 .1F 121
Finch's Ct. E14 .7D 86
Finch's Ct. M. E14 .7D 86
(off Finch's Ct.)
Finden Rd. E7 .5A 70
Findhorn Av. UB4: Yead .5K 75
Findhorn St. E14 .6E 86
Findlay Ho. E3 .3C 86
(off Trevithick Way)
Findon Cl. HA2: Harr .3F 59
SW18 .6J 117
Findon Rd. N9 .1C 34
W12 .2C 98
Fine Bush La. UB9: Hare .6D 38
Fingal St. SE10 .5H 105
Fingest Ho. NW8 .3C 4
(off Lilestone St.)
Finians Cl. UB10: Uxb .7B 56
Finland Rd. SE4 .3A 122
Finland St. SE16 .3A 104
Finlays Cl. KT9: Chess .5G 163
Finlay St. SW6 .1F 117
Finley Ct. SE5 .7C 102
(off Redcar St.)
Finmere Ho. N4 .7C 48
Finnemore Ho. N1 .1C 84
(off Britannia Row)
Finney La. TW7: Isle .1A 114
Finn Ho. N1 .1F 9
(off Bevenden St.)
Finnis St. E2 .3H 85
Finnymore Rd. RM9: Dag .7E 72
FINSBURY .3C 8 (3A 84)
Finsbury Av. EC2 .6F 9 (5D 84)
Finsbury Av. Sq. EC2 .5G 9 (5E 84)
Finsbury Cir. EC2 .6F 9 (5D 84)
Finsbury Cotts. N22 .7D 32
Finsbury Est. EC1 .2K 7 (3A 84)
Finsbury Ho. N22 .1J 47
Finsbury Leisure Cen. .3C 8 (3C 84)
Finsbury Mkt. EC2 .4G 9 (4E 84)
(not continuous)
FINSBURY PARK .1A 66
Finsbury Pk. Av. N4 .6C 48
Finsbury Pk. Rd. N4 .2B 66
Finsbury Pavement EC2 .5F 9 (5D 84)
Finsbury Rd. N22 .7E 32
(not continuous)
Finsbury Sq. EC2 .4F 9 (4D 84)
Finsbury St. EC2 .5E 8 (5D 84)
Finsbury Way DA5: Bexl .6F 127
Finsen Rd. SE5 .4C 120
Finstock Rd. W10 .6F 81
Finucane Ct. TW9: Rich .3F 115
(off Lwr. Mortlake Rd.)
Finucane Ri. WD23: B Hea .2B 26
Finwhale Ho. E14 .3D 104
(off Glengall Gro.)
Fiona Ct. EN2: Enf .3G 23
NW6 .2J 81
Firbank Cl. E16 .5B 88
EN2: Enf .4H 23
Firbank Rd. SE15 .2H 121
Fir Cl. KT12: Walt T .7J 147
Fircroft Gdns. HA1: Harr .3J 59
Fircroft Rd. KT9: Chess .4F 163
SW17 .2D 136
Fir Dene BR6: Farnb .3D 172
Firdene KT5: Surb .1J 163
Fire Bell All. KT6: Surb .6E 150
Firecrest Dr. NW3 .3K 63
Firefly Cl. UB3: Hayes .7H 75
UB5: N'olt .3B 76
Firefly Gdns. E6 .4C 88
Firehorn Ho. E15 .3G 87
(off Teasel Way)
Firemans Flats N22 .7D 32
Fire Station All. EN5: Barn .3B 20
Fire Station M. BR3: Beck .1C 158
Fire Station Square SE1 .5H 15
Firestone Ho. TW8: Bford .5E 96
Firethorn Cl. HA8: Edg .4D 28
Firewatch Ct. E1 .5A 86
(off Candle St.)
Fir Gro. KT3: N Mald .6B 152
Firgrove Ct. SE6 .7C 122
Fir Gro. Rd. SW9 .2A 120
Firhill Rd. SE6 .4C 140
Fir Ho. W10 .4G 81
(off Droop St.)
Firle Ho. W10 .5E 80
(off Sutton Way)
Firman Cl. KT3: N Mald .4A 152
Firmans Ct. E17 .4F 51
Fir Rd. SM3: Sutt .1H 165
TW13: Hanw .5B 130
The Firs DA5: Bexl .1K 145
DA15: Sidc .2K 143
E6 .7C 70
HA8: Edg .4E 28
(off Stoneyfields La.)
IG8: Wfd G .7J 37
N20 .1G 31
SE26 .5H 139
(Border Rd.)
SE26 .5J 139
(Waverley Ct.)
W5 .5D 78
Firs Av. N10 .3E 46
N11 .6J 31
SW14 .4J 115
Firsby Av. CR0: C'don .1K 169
Firsby Rd. N16 .1G 67
Firs Cl. CR4: Mitc .2F 155
N10 .4E 46
SE23 .7A 122
Firscroft N13 .3H 33
Firs Dr. TW5: Cran .7K 93
Firs Ho. N22 .1A 48
(off Acacia Rd.)
Firside Gro. DA15: Sidc .1K 143
Firs La. N13 .3H 33
N21 .7H 23
Firs Pk. Av. N21 .1J 33
Firs Pk. Gdns. N21 .1H 33
First Av. DA7: Bex .7C 108
E12 .4C 70
E13 .3J 87
E17 .5C 50
EN1: Enf .5A 24
HA9: Wemb .2D 60
KT8: W Mole .4D 148
KT12: Walt T .6K 147
KT19: Ewe .7A 164
N18 .4D 34
NW4 .4E 44
RM6: Chad H .5C 54
RM10: Dag .2H 91
SW14 .3A 116
UB3: Hayes .1H 93
W3 .1B 98
W10 .4H 81
First Central Bus. Pk. NW10 .3F 79
First Cl. KT8: W Mole .3G 149
First Cross Rd. TW2: Twick .2J 131
First Dr. NW10 .7J 61
First St. SW3 .3D 16 (4C 100)
First Way HA9: Wemb .4H 61
Firstway SW20 .2E 152
Firs Wlk. IG8: Wfd G .5D 36
Firswood Av. KT19: Ewe .5A 164
Firth Gdns. SW6 .1G 117
Firth Ho. E2 .3G 85
(off Turin St.)
Fir Tree Av. UB7: W Dray .3C 92
Firtree Av. CR4: Mitc .2E 154
Fir Tree Cl. BR6: Chels .5K 173
KT19: Ewe .4B 164
RM1: Rom .3K 55
SW16 .5G 137
W5 .6E 78
Fir Tree Gdns. CR0: C'don .4C 170
Fir Tree Gro. SM5: Cars .7D 166
Firtree Ho. SE13 .7F 123
(off Birdwood Av.)
Fir Tree Pl. TW15: Ashf .5C 128

Fir Tree Rd.—Forest Vw.

Fir Tree Rd. TW4: Houn 4C 112
Fir Trees Cl. SE16 . . . . . 1A 104
Fir Tree Wlk. EN1: Enf 3J 23
RM10: Dag 3J 73
Fir Wlk. SM3: Cheam 6F 165
Fisher Cl. CR0: C'don 1F 169
E9 . . . . . 5K 67
SE16 . . . . . 1K 103
UB6: G'frd 3E 76
Fisher Ho. E1 . . . . . 7J 85
(off Cable St.)
N1 . . . . . 1A 84
(off Barnsbury Est.)
Fisherman Cl. TW10: Ham 4B 132
Fishermans Dr. SE16 . . . . . 2K 103
Fisherman's Pl. W4 . . . . . 6B 98
Fisherman's Wlk. E14 . . . . . 1C 104
Fishermans Wlk. SE28 . . . . . 2J 107
Fisher Rd. HA3: W'stone 2K 41
Fisher's Cl. SW16 . . . . . 3H 137
Fishers Ct. SE14 . . . . . 1K 121
Fishersdene KT10: Clay 7A 162
Fisher's La. W4 . . . . . 4K 97
Fisher St. E16 . . . . . 5J 87
WC1 . . . . . 6G 7 (5K 83)
Fishers Way DA17: Belv 1J 109
HA0: Wemb 5B 60
Fishers Wood Gro. BR2: Broml 7C 160
Fisherton St. NW8 . . . . . 4A 4 (4B 82)
Fishguard Way E16 . . . . . 1F 107
Fishmongers Hall Wharf EC4 . . . . . 3E 14
Fishponds Rd. BR2: Kes 5B 172
SW17 . . . . . 4C 136
Fish St. Hill EC3 . . . . . 3F 15 (7D 84)
Fish Wharf EC3 . . . . . 3F 15 (7D 84)
Fisk Cl. TW16: Sun 6H 129
Fiske Ct. IG11: Bark 2H 89
N17 . . . . . 1G 49
SM2: Sutt 7A 166
Fitch Ct. SW2 . . . . . 5A 120
Fitness4Less
Canning Town 5H 87
Sutton 6J 165
Fitness First
Angel 1A 8 (2B 84)
Baker Street 6F 5 (5D 82)
Beckenham 6C 140
Berkeley Square 3K 11 (7F 83)
Brixton 3A 120
Camden 1F 83
Clapham Junction 4C 118
Covent Garden 3F 13
(off Bedford St.)
Fetter Lane 1K 13
(off Fetter La.)
Gracechurch Street 2F 15
(off Gracechurch St.)
Great Marlborough Street 1A 12
Hammersmith 4E 98
Harringay 6B 48
(off Arena Shop. Pk.)
Highbury 3B 66
High Holborn 6G 7
(off High Holborn)
Ilford 2G 71
Kilburn 1H 81
Kingly Street 2A 12
Leyton Mills 3E 68
London Bridge 5F 15
(off London Bri. St.)
London Bridge, Cottons 4F 15
(off Tooley St.)
Paternoster Square 7B 8
Queen Victoria Street 2C 14
(off Queen Victoria St.)
Streatham 2J 137
Thomas More Square 7G 85
(off Thomas More Sq.)
Tooting Bec 3E 136
Fittleton Gdns. E3 . . . . . 4D 86
Fitzalan Rd. N3 . . . . . 3G 45
Fitzalan St. SE11 . . . . . 3H 19 (4A 102)
Fitzclarence Ho. W11 . . . . . 2G 99
(off Holland Park Av.)
Fitzgeorge Av. KT3: N Mald 1K 151
W14 . . . . . 4G 99
Fitzgerald Av. SW14 . . . . . 3A 116
Fitzgerald Ct. E10 . . . . . 1D 68
(off Leyton Grange Est.)
Fitzgerald Ho. E14 . . . . . 6D 86
(off E. India Dock Rd.)
SW9 . . . . . 2A 120
SW17 . . . . . 3B 136
UB3: Hayes 1K 93
Fitzgerald Rd. E11 . . . . . 5J 51
KT7: T Ditt 6A 150
SW14 . . . . . 3K 115
Fitzhardinge Ho. W1 . . . . . 7G 5
(off Portman Sq.)
Fitzhardinge St. W1 . . . . . 7G 5 (6E 82)
Fitzherbert Cl. IG8: Ilf, Wfd G 1C 52
Fitzherbert Wlk. UB1: S'hall 2H 95
Fitzhugh Gro. SW18 . . . . . 6B 118
Fitzjames Av. CR0: C'don 2G 169
W14 . . . . . 4G 99
Fitzjohn Av. EN5: Barn 5B 20
Fitzjohn's Av. NW3 . . . . . 4A 64
Fitzmaurice Ho. SE16 . . . . . 4H 103
(off Rennie Est.)
Fitzmaurice Pl. W1 . . . . . 4K 11 (1F 101)
Fitzneal St. W12 . . . . . 6B 80
Fitzpatrick Rd. SW9 . . . . . 1B 120
FITZROVIA 5K 5
Fitzrovia Apts. W1 . . . . . 4K 5
(off Bolsover St.)
FITZROY BRI. 1E 82
Fitzroy Bus. Pk. BR5: St P 7D 144
Fitzroy Cl. N6 . . . . . 1D 64
Fitzroy Ct. CR0: C'don 7D 156
N6 . . . . . 6G 47
W1 . . . . . 4B 6
Fitzroy Cres. W4 . . . . . 7K 97
Fitzroy Gdns. SE19 . . . . . 7E 138
Fitzroy Ho. E14 . . . . . 5B 86
(off Wallwood St.)
SE1 . . . . . 5F 103
(off Cooper's Rd.)
Fitzroy House Mus. 4A 6 (4G 83)
Fitzroy M. W1 . . . . . 4A 6
Fitzroy Pk. N6 . . . . . 1D 64
Fitzroy Rd. NW1 . . . . . 1E 82
Fitzroy Sq. W1 . . . . . 4A 6 (4G 83)
Fitzroy St. W1 . . . . . 4A 6 (4G 83)
(not continuous)
Fitzroy Yd. NW1 . . . . . 1E 82
Fitzstephen Rd. RM8: Dag 5B 72
Fitzwarren Gdns. N19 . . . . . 1G 65
Fitzwilliam Av. TW9: Rich 2F 115
Fitzwilliam Cl. N20 . . . . . 1K 31
Fitzwilliam Hgts. SE23 . . . . . 2J 139
Fitzwilliam Ho. TW9: Rich 4D 114
Fitzwilliam M. E16 . . . . . 1J 105
Fitzwilliam Rd. SW4 . . . . . 3G 119
Fitz Wygram Cl. TW12: Hamp H . . . 5G 131
Five Acre NW9 . . . . . 2B 44
Fiveacre Cl. CR7: Thor H 6A 156
Five Arches Bus. Pk. DA14: Sidc . . . 5D 144
Five Bell All. E14 . . . . . 6B 86
(off Three Colt St.)
Five Elms BR2: Hayes 3K 171
Five Elms Rd. BR2: Hayes 3K 171
RM9: Dag 3F 73
Five Oaks M. BR1: Broml 3J 141
Fives Ct. SE11 . . . . . 3B 102
FIVEWAYS 2F 143
Five Ways Bus. Cen. TW13: Felt . . . 3K 129
FIVEWAYS CORNER
(Croydon) 4A 168
(Hendon) 1C 44
Fiveways Rd. SW9 . . . . . 2A 120
Fixie Bldg. E17 . . . . . 5B 50
(off Track St.)
Flack Ct. E10 . . . . . 7D 50
Fladbury Rd. N15 . . . . . 6D 48
Fladgate Rd. E11 . . . . . 6G 51
Flag Cl. CR0: C'don 1K 169
Flagon Ct. CR0: C'don 4C 168
(off St Andrew's Rd.)
Flagship Ho. E16 . . . . . 2K 105
(off Royal Crest Av.)
Flag Wlk. HA5: Eastc 6J 39
Flambard Rd. HA1: Harr 6A 42
Flamborough Ho. SE15 . . . . . 1G 121
(off Clayton Rd.)
Flamborough Rd. HA4: Ruis 3J 57
Flamborough St. E14 . . . . . 6A 86
Flamborough Wlk. E14 . . . . . 6A 86
(off Flamborough St.)
Flamingo Ct. SE8 . . . . . 7C 104
(off Hamilton St.)
SE17 . . . . . 5C 102
(off Crampton St.)
Flamingo Gdns. UB5: N'olt 3C 76
Flamstead Gdns. RM9: Dag 7C 72
Flamstead Ho. SW3 . . . . . 5C 16
(off Cale St.)
Flamstead Rd. RM9: Dag 7C 72
Flamsted Av. HA9: Wemb 6G 61
Flamsteed Rd. SE7 . . . . . 5C 106
Flanaghan Apts. E3 . . . . . 4B 86
(off Portia Way)
Flanchford Rd. W12 . . . . . 3B 98
Flanders Ct. E17 . . . . . 7A 50
Flanders Cres. SW17 . . . . . 7D 136
Flanders Mans. W4 . . . . . 4B 98
Flanders Rd. E6 . . . . . 2D 88
W4 . . . . . 4A 98
Flanders Way E9 . . . . . 6K 67
Flandrian Cl. EN3: Enf L 1J 25
Flank St. E1 . . . . . 7G 85
Flannery Ct. SE16 . . . . . 3H 103
Flansham Ho. E14 . . . . . 6B 86
(off Clemence St.)
Flask Wlk. NW3 . . . . . 4A 64
Flatford Ho. SE6 . . . . . 4E 140
Flather Cl. SW16 . . . . . 5G 137
Flat Iron Sq. SE1 . . . . . 5D 14
(off Southwark Bri. Rd.)
Flatiron Yd. SE1 . . . . . 5D 14
(off Ayres St.)
Flavell M. SE10 . . . . . 5G 105
Flaxen Cl. E4 . . . . . 3J 35
Flaxen Rd. E4 . . . . . 3J 35
Flaxley Ho. SW1 . . . . . 5J 17
(part of Abbots Mnr.)
Flaxley Rd. SM4: Mord 7K 153
Flaxman Ct. DA17: Belv 5G 109
(off Hoddesdon Rd.)
W1 . . . . . 1C 12 (6H 83)
WC1 . . . . . 2D 6
(off Flaxman Ter.)
Flaxman Ho. SE1 . . . . . 3B 102
(off London Rd.)
W4 . . . . . 5A 98
(off Devonshire St.)
Flaxman Rd. SE5 . . . . . 3B 120
Flaxman Sports Cen. 2C 120
Flaxman Ter. WC1 . . . . . 2D 6 (3H 83)
Flaxton Rd. SE18 . . . . . 7H 107
Flecker Cl. HA7: Stan 5E 26
Flecker Ho. SE5 . . . . . 7D 102
(off Lomond Gro.)
Fleece Dr. N9 . . . . . 4B 34
Fleece Rd. KT6: Surb 1C 162
Fleece Wlk. N7 . . . . . 6J 65
Fleeming Cl. E17 . . . . . 2B 50
Fleeming Rd. E17 . . . . . 2B 50
Fleetbank Ho. EC4 . . . . . 1K 13
(off Salisbury Sq.)
Fleet Cl. HA4: Ruis 6E 38
KT8: W Mole 5D 148
Fleetfield WC1 . . . . . 1F 7
(off Birkenhead St.)
Fleet Ho. E14 . . . . . 7A 86
(off Victory Pl.)
Fleet La. KT8: W Mole 6D 148
Fleet Pl. EC4 . . . . . 7A 8 (6B 84)
Fleet Rd. IG11: Bark 1F 89
NW3 . . . . . 5C 64
Fleetside KT8: W Mole 5D 148
Fleet Sq. WC1 . . . . . 2H 7 (3K 83)
Fleet St. EC4 . . . . . 1J 13 (6A 84)
Fleetway WC1 . . . . . 1F 7
(off Birkenhead St.)
Fleetway W. UB6: G'frd 2B 78
Fleetwood Cl. CR0: C'don 3F 169
E16 . . . . . 5B 88
KT9: Chess 7D 162
Fleetwood Ct. E6 . . . . . 5D 88
(off Evelyn Dennington Rd.)
TW19: Stanw 6A 110
(off Douglas Rd.)
Fleetwood Rd. KT1: King T 3H 151
NW10 . . . . . 5C 62
Fleetwood Sq. KT1: King T 3H 151
Fleetwood St. N16 . . . . . 2E 66
Fleming N8 . . . . . 3J 47
(off Boyton Cl.)
Fleming Cl. SW10 . . . . . 6A 4, 5H 13, 6A 16
W9 . . . . . 4J 81
Fleming Ct. CR0: Wadd 5A 168
W2 . . . . . 5A 4
Fleming Dr. N21 . . . . . 5E 22
Fleming Ho. HA9: Wemb 3J 61
(off Barnhill Rd.)
N4 . . . . . 1C 66
SE16 . . . . . 2G 103
(off George Row)
SW17 . . . . . 3B 136
Fleming Lodge W9 . . . . . 5J 81
(off Admiral Wlk.)
Fleming Mead CR4: Mitc 7C 136
Fleming Rd. SE17 . . . . . 6B 102
UB1: S'hall 6F 77
Fleming Wlk. NW9 . . . . . 3A 44
Fleming Way SE28 . . . . . 7D 90
TW7: Isle 4K 113
Flemming Av. HA4: Ruis 1K 57
Flempton Rd. E10 . . . . . 1A 68
Fletcher Bldgs. WC2 . . . . . 1F 13
(off Martlett Ct.)
Fletcher Cl. E6 . . . . . 6F 89
Fletcher Ct. NW9 . . . . . 3A 44
Fletcher Ho. N1 . . . . . 1E 84
(off Nuttall St.)
SE15 . . . . . 7J 103
(off Clifton Way)
Fletcher La. E10 . . . . . 7E 50
Fletcher Path SE8 . . . . . 7C 104
Fletcher Rd. W4 . . . . . 3J 97
Fletchers Cl. BR2: Broml 4K 159
Fletcher St. E1 . . . . . 7G 85
Fletching Apts. E3 . . . . . 4B 86
(off Siyah Gdn.)
Fletching Rd. E5 . . . . . 3J 67
SE7 . . . . . 6A 106
Fletton Rd. N11 . . . . . 7D 32
Fleur de Lis St. E1 . . . . . 4H 9 (4F 85)
Fleur Gates SW19 . . . . . 7F 117
Flexmere Gdns. N17 . . . . . 1D 48
Flexmere Rd. N17 . . . . . 1D 48
Flight App. NW9 . . . . . 2B 44
Flight Ho. N1 . . . . . 1E 84
(off Phillipp St.)
Flimwell Cl. BR1: Broml 5G 141
Flinders Ho. E1 . . . . . 1H 103
(off Green Bank)
Flint Cl. BR6: Chels 6K 173
CR0: C'don 6K 155
E15 . . . . . 7H 69
Flintlock Cl. E1 . . . . . 6H 85
TW19: Stanw M 7B 174
Flintmill Cres. SE3 . . . . . 2C 124
Flinton St. SE17 . . . . . 5E 102
Flint St. SE17 . . . . . 4D 102
Flip Out
Brent Cross 1D 62
East Ham 1C 88
Wandsworth 1K 135
Flitcroft St. WC2 . . . . . 1D 12 (6H 83)
Flitton Ho. N1 . . . . . 7B 66
(off The Sutton Est.)
Floathaven Cl. SE28 . . . . . 1A 108
Flock Mill Pl. SW18 . . . . . 1K 135
Flockton St. SE16 . . . . . 2G 103
Flodden Rd. SE5 . . . . . 1C 120
Flood La. TW1: Twick 1A 132
Flood Pas. SE18 . . . . . 3C 106
Flood St. SW3 . . . . . 6D 16 (5C 100)
Flood Wlk. SW3 . . . . . 7D 16 (6C 100)
Flora Cl. E14 . . . . . 6D 86
HA7: Stan 3K 27
Flora Gdns. RM6: Chad H 6C 54
W6 . . . . . 4D 98
(off Albion Gdns.)
Flora Ho. E3 . . . . . 1C 86
(off Garrison Rd.)
Floral Ct. WC2 . . . . . 2F 13 (7J 83)
Floral Pl. N1 . . . . . 5D 66
Floral St. WC2 . . . . . 2E 12 (7J 83)
Flora St. DA17: Belv 5F 109
Florence Av. EN2: Enf 3H 23
SM4: Mord 5A 154
Florence Cantwell Wlk. N19 . . . . . 7J 47
(off Jessie Blythe La.)
Florence Cl. KT2: King T 5F 133
KT12: Walt T 7K 147
Florence Ct. E11 . . . . . 4K 51
N1 . . . . . 7B 66
(off Florence St.)
SW19 . . . . . 6G 135
W9 . . . . . 3A 82
(off Maida Vale)
Florence Dr. EN2: Enf 3H 23
Florence Elson Cl. E12 . . . . . 4E 70
Florence Gdns. RM6: Chad H 7C 54
W4 . . . . . 6J 97
Florence Ho. KT2: King T 7F 133
(off Florence Rd)
SE16 . . . . . 5H 103
(off Rotherhithe New Rd.)
W11 . . . . . 7F 81
(off St Ann's Rd.)
Florence Mans. NW4 . . . . . 5D 44
(off Vivian Av.)
SW6 . . . . . 1H 117
(off Rostrevor Rd.)
Florence Nightingale Mus. 7G 13 (2K 101)
Florence Rd. BR1: Broml 1J 159
BR3: Beck 2A 158
CR2: Sande 7D 168
E6 . . . . . 1A 88
E13 . . . . . 2J 87
KT2: King T 7F 133
KT12: Walt T 7K 147
N4 . . . . . 7K 47
(not continuous)
SE2 . . . . . 4C 108
SE14 . . . . . 1B 122
SW19 . . . . . 6K 135
TW13: Felt 1K 129
UB2: S'hall 4B 94
W4 . . . . . 3K 97
W5 . . . . . 7E 78
Florence Root Ho. IG4: Ilf 5C 52
Florence Sq. E3 . . . . . 4D 86
Florence St. E16 . . . . . 4H 87
N1 . . . . . 7B 66
NW4 . . . . . 4E 44
Florence Ter. SE14 . . . . . 1B 122
SW15 . . . . . 3A 134
Florence Way SW12 . . . . . 1D 136
Florey Lodge W9 . . . . . 5J 81
(off Admiral Wlk.)
Florey Sq. N21 . . . . . 5E 22
Florfield Pas. E8 . . . . . 6H 67
(off Reading La.)
Florfield Rd. E8 . . . . . 6H 67
Florian SE5 . . . . . 1E 120
Florian Av. SM1: Sutt 4B 166
Florian Ct. E16 . . . . . 5J 87
(off Hastings Rd.)
Florian Rd. SW15 . . . . . 4G 117
Florida Cl. WD23: B Hea 2C 26
Florida Ct. BR2: Broml 4H 159
(off Westmoreland Rd.)
Florida Rd. CR7: Thor H 1B 156
Florida St. E2 . . . . . 3G 85
Florin Ct. EC1 . . . . . 5C 8
N18 . . . . . 4K 33
SE1 . . . . . 7J 15
(off Tanner St.)
Floris Pl. SW4 . . . . . 3G 119
Floriston Av. UB10: Hil 7E 56
Floriston Cl. HA7: Stan 1B 42
Floriston Ct. UB5: N'olt 5F 59
Floriston Gdns. HA7: Stan 1B 42
Florys Ct. SW19 . . . . . 1G 135
Floss St. SW15 . . . . . 2E 116
Flotilla Ho. E16 . . . . . 2K 105
(off Cable St.)
SW18 . . . . . 3A 118
Flounder Ho. SE8 . . . . . 7D 104
(off Creative Rd.)
Flower & Dean Wlk. E1 . . . . . 6K 9 (5F 85)
Flowerdown Ct. HA4: Eastc 6J 39
(off Lidgould Gro.)
Flower La. NW7 . . . . . 5G 29
Flower M. NW11 . . . . . 6G 45
Flower Pot Cl. N15 . . . . . 6F 49
Flowers Av. HA4: Eastc, Ruis 6J 39
Flowers Cl. NW2 . . . . . 3C 62
Flowersmead SW17 . . . . . 2E 136
Flowers M. N19 . . . . . 2G 65
The Flower Wlk. SW7 . . . . . 6A 10 (2A 100)
Floyd Rd. SE7 . . . . . 5A 106
Floyer Cl. TW10: Rich 5F 115
Fludyer St. SE13 . . . . . 4G 123
Flutemakers M. SW4 . . . . . 5H 119
Flying Angel Ho. E16 . . . . . 7K 87
(off Victoria Dock Rd.)
Flynn Ct. E14 . . . . . 7C 86
(off Garford St.)
Foley Ho. E1 . . . . . 6J 85
(off Tarling St.)
Foley St. W1 . . . . . 6A 6 (5G 83)
Folgate St. E1 . . . . . 5H 9 (5E 84)
(not continuous)
Foliot Ho. N1 . . . . . 2K 83
(off Priory Grn. Est.)
Foliot St. W12 . . . . . 6B 80
Folkestone Ct. UB5: N'olt 5F 59
(off Newmarket Av.)
Folkestone Ho. SE17 . . . . . 5E 102
(off Upnor Way)
Folkestone Rd. E6 . . . . . 2E 88
E17 . . . . . 4D 50
N18 . . . . . 4B 34
Folkingham La. NW9 . . . . . 1K 43
Folkington Cnr. N12 . . . . . 5C 30
Folland NW9 . . . . . 2B 44
(off Hundred Acre)
Follett Ho. SW10 . . . . . 7B 100
(off Worlds End Est.)
Follett St. E14 . . . . . 6E 86
Follingham Ct. N1 . . . . . 1H 9
(off Drysdale Pl.)
Folly Brook & Darland's Lake
Nature Reserve 3B 30
Folly La. E4 . . . . . 6G 35
E17 . . . . . 1A 50
Folly M. W11 . . . . . 6H 81
Folly Wall E14 . . . . . 2E 104
Fonda Ct. E14 . . . . . 7C 86
(off Premiere Pl.)
Fondant Ct. E3 . . . . . 2D 86
(off Taylor Pl.)
Fontaine Ho. E17 . . . . . 4C 50
(off Hoe St.)
Fontaine Rd. SW16 . . . . . 7K 137
Fontarabia Rd. SW11 . . . . . 4E 118
Fontayne Av. RM1: Rom 2K 55
Fontenelle SE5 . . . . . 1E 120
Fontenoy Ho. SE11 . . . . . 4B 102
(off Kennington La.)
Fontenoy Rd. SW12 . . . . . 2F 137
Fonteyne Gdns. IG8: Wfd G 2B 52
Fonthill Cl. SE20 . . . . . 2G 157
Fonthill Ho. SW1 . . . . . 5K 17
(part of Abbots Mnr.)
W14 . . . . . 3G 99
(off Russell Rd.)
Fonthill M. N4 . . . . . 2K 65
Fonthill Rd. N4 . . . . . 1K 65
Font Hills N2 . . . . . 2A 46
Fontley Way SW15 . . . . . 7C 116
Fontmell Cl. TW15: Ashf 5C 128
Fontmell Pk. TW15: Ashf 5B 128
Fontwell Cl. HA3: Hrw W 7D 26
UB5: N'olt 6E 58
Fontwell Dr. BR2: Broml 5E 160
Football La. HA1: Harr 1K 59
The Footpath SW15 . . . . . 6C 116
FOOTS CRAY 6C 144
Foots Cray High St. DA14: Sidc 6C 144
Foots Cray La. DA14: Sidc 1C 144
Foots Cray Meadows 4D 144
Footscray Rd. SE9 . . . . . 6E 124
Forber Ho. E2 . . . . . 3J 85
(off Cornwall Av.)
Forbes Cl. NW2 . . . . . 3C 62
Forbes Ho. E7 . . . . . 5A 70
(off Romford Rd.)
W4 . . . . . 5G 97
(off Stonehill Rd.)
Forbes St. E1 . . . . . 6G 85
Forbes Way HA4: Ruis 2K 57
Forburg Rd. N16 . . . . . 1G 67
Forbury Rd. SE13 . . . . . 3G 123
Fordbridge Ct. TW15: Ashf 6A 128
Fordbridge Pk. TW16: Sun 6H 147
Fordbridge Rd. TW15: Ashf 6A 128
TW16: Sun 6G 147
TW17: Shep 6G 147
FORDBRIDGE RDBT. 6A 128
Ford Cl. CR7: Thor H 5B 156
E3 . . . . . 2A 86
HA1: Harr 7H 41
TW15: Ashf 6A 128
TW17: Shep 4C 146
Forde Av. BR1: Broml 3A 160
Fordel Rd. SE6 . . . . . 1E 140
Ford End IG8: Wfd G 6E 36
Fordgate Bus. Pk. DA17: Belv 2J 109
Fordham KT1: King T 2G 151
(off Excelsior Cl.)
Fordham Cl. EN4: Cockf 3H 21
KT4: Wor Pk 1D 164
Fordham Ho. SE14 . . . . . 7A 104
(off Angus St.)
Fordham Rd. EN4: Cockf 3G 21
Fordham St. E1 . . . . . 6G 85
Fordhook Av. W5 . . . . . 1F 97
Ford Ho. EN5: New Bar 5E 20
Fordie Ho. SW1 . . . . . 2F 17
(off Sloane St.)
Ford Ind. Pk. RM9: Dag 4H 91
Fordingley Rd. W9 . . . . . 3H 81
Fordington Ho. SE26 . . . . . 3G 139
Fordington Rd. N6 . . . . . 5D 46
Ford Lodge RM7: Rom 4K 55
Fordmill Rd. SE6 . . . . . 2C 140
Ford Rd. E3 . . . . . 2B 86
RM9: Dag 7F 73
RM10: Dag 7F 73
TW15: Ashf 4B 128
Fords Gro. N21 . . . . . 1H 33
Fords Pk. Rd. E16 . . . . . 5J 87
Fords Pl. HA6: Nwood 2J 39
Ford Sq. E1 . . . . . 5H 85
Ford St. E3 . . . . . 1A 86
E16 . . . . . 6H 87
Fordview Ind. Est. RM13: Rain 3K 91
Fordwich Cl. BR6: Orp 7K 161
Fordwych Rd. NW2 . . . . . 4G 63
Fordyce Rd. SE13 . . . . . 6E 122
Fordyke Rd. RM8: Dag 2F 73
Foreign St. SE5 . . . . . 2B 120
Foreland Ct. NW4 . . . . . 1F 45
Foreland Ho. W11 . . . . . 7G 81
(off Walmer Rd.)
Foreland St. SE18 . . . . . 4H 107
Forelle Way SM5: Cars 7D 166
Foreman Ct. TW1: Twick 1K 131
Foreman Ho. SE4 . . . . . 4K 121
(off Billingford Cl.)
Foreshore SE8 . . . . . 4B 104
The Forest E11 . . . . . 4G 51
Forest App. E4 . . . . . 1B 36
IG8: Wfd G 7D 36
Forest Av. E4 . . . . . 1B 36
IG7: Chig 5K 37
Forest Bus. Pk. E10 . . . . . 7K 49
Forest Cl. BR7: Chst 1E 160
E11 . . . . . 5J 51
IG8: Wfd G 3E 36
N10 . . . . . 1F 47
NW6 . . . . . 7G 63
Forest Ct. E4 . . . . . 1C 36
E11 . . . . . 4G 51
N12 . . . . . 5E 30
Forest Cft. SE23 . . . . . 2H 139
FORESTDALE 7B 170
Forestdale N14 . . . . . 4C 32
The Forestdale Cen. 7B 170
Forest Dene Ct. SM2: Sutt 6A 166
Forest Dr. BR2: Kes 4C 172
BR3: Beck 7B 158
E12 . . . . . 3B 70
IG8: Wfd G 7A 36
TW16: Sun 7H 129
Forest Dr. E. E11 . . . . . 7F 51
Forest Dr. W. E11 . . . . . 7E 50
Forest Edge IG9: Buck H 4F 37
Forester Ho. E14 . . . . . 7A 86
(off Victory Pl.)
Forester Rd. SE15 . . . . . 3H 121
Foresters Cl. SM6: W'gton 7H 167
Foresters Cres. DA7: Bex 4H 127
Foresters Dr. E17 . . . . . 4F 51
SM6: W'gton 7H 167
Forest Gdns. N17 . . . . . 2F 49
FOREST GATE 5J 69
Forest Ga. NW9 . . . . . 4A 44
Forest Gate Learning Zone 4J 69
(off Woodford Rd.)
Forest Ga. Retreat E7 . . . . . 5J 69
(off Odessa Rd.)
Forest Glade E4 . . . . . 4B 36
E11 . . . . . 6G 51
Forest Gro. E8 . . . . . 6F 67
Forest Hgts. IG9: Buck H 2D 36
FOREST HILL 2J 139
Forest Hill Bus. Cen. SE23 . . . . . 2J 139
(off Clyde Va.)
Forest Hill Ind. Est. SE23 . . . . . 2J 139
Forest Hill Pools 2J 139
Forest Hill Rd. SE22 . . . . . 5H 121
SE23 . . . . . 5H 121
Forest Hill School Sports Cen. 3K 139
Forestholme Cl. SE23 . . . . . 2J 139
Forest Ind. Pk. IG6: Ilf 1J 53
Forest La. E7 . . . . . 5G 69
E15 . . . . . 5G 69
IG7: Chig 5K 37
Forest Lodge SE23 . . . . . 3J 139
(off Dartmouth Rd.)
Forest Mt. Rd. IG8: Wfd G 7A 36
Forest Point E7 . . . . . 5K 69
(off Windsor Rd.)
Fore St. EC2 . . . . . 6D 8 (5C 84)
HA5: Eastc 4H 39
N9 . . . . . 4B 34
N18 . . . . . 6A 34
Fore St. Av. EC2 . . . . . 6E 8 (5D 84)
Forest Ridge BR2: Kes 4C 172
BR3: Beck 3C 158
Forest Ri. E17 . . . . . 3F 51
Forest Rd. E7 . . . . . 4J 69
E8 . . . . . 6F 67
E11 . . . . . 7F 51
E17 . . . . . 4A 50
IG6: Chig, Ilf 2H 53
IG8: Wfd G 3D 36
N9 . . . . . 1C 34
N17 . . . . . 4J 49
RM7: Mawney 3H 55
SM3: Sutt 1J 165
TW9: Kew 7G 97
TW13: Felt 2A 130
Forest Side E4 . . . . . 1C 36
E7 . . . . . 4K 69
IG9: Buck H 1F 37
KT4: Wor Pk 1B 164
Forest St. E7 . . . . . 5J 69
Forest Ter. IG7: Chig 5K 37
Forest Trad. Est. E17 . . . . . 3K 49
Forest Vw. E4 . . . . . 7K 25, 1B 36
E11 . . . . . 7H 51

A-Z Big London 221

Forest Vw. Av.—Freston Pk.

Forest Vw. Av. E10 5F 51
Forest Vw. Rd. E12 4C 70
E17 1E 50
Forest Wlk. N10 1F 47
Forest Way BR5: St M Cry 5K 161
DA15: Sidc 7H 125
IG8: Wfd G 4E 36
N19 2G 65
Forfar Rd. N22 1B 48
SW11 1E 118
Forge Cl. BR2: Hayes 1J 171
UB3: Harl 6F 93
Forge Cotts. W5 1D 96
Forge Dr. KT10: Clay 7A 162
Forge La. HA6: Nwood 1G 39
SM3: Cheam 7G 165
TW10: Ham 1E 132
TW13: Hanw 5C 130
TW16: Sun 3J 147
Forge M. CR0: Addtn 5C 170
TW16: Sun 3J 147
(off Forge La.)
Forge Pl. NW1 6E 64
Forge Sq. E14 4D 104
Forlong Path UB5: N'olt 6C 58
(off Cowings Mead)
Forman Pl. N16 4F 67
The Formation E16 2F 107
(off Woolwich Mnr. Way)
Formby Av. HA7: Stan 3C 42
Formby Ct. N7 5A 66
(off Morgan Rd.)
Formosa Ho. E1 4A 86
(off Ernest St.)
Formosa St. W9 4K 81
Formunt Cl. E16 5H 87
Forres Gdns. NW11 6J 45
Forrester Path SE26 4J 139
Forresters Apts. IG11: Bark 7G 71
(off Linton Rd.)
Forrester Way E15 6F 69
Forrest Gdns. SW16 3K 155
Forris Av. UB3: Hayes 1H 93
Forset Ct. W2 7D 4
(off Edgware Rd.)
Forset St. W1 7D 4 (6C 82)
(not continuous)
Forstal Cl. BR2: Broml 3J 159
Forster Cl. IG8: Wfd G 7A 36
Forster Ho. BR1: Broml 4F 141
SW17 3B 136
(off Grosvenor Way)
Forster Rd. BR3: Beck 3A 158
E17 6A 50
N17 3F 49
SW2 7J 119
Forsters Cl. RM6: Chad H 6F 55
Forsters Way UB4: Yead 6K 75
Forston Apartments SW11 4C 118
(off Monarch Square)
Forston St. N1 2C 84
Forsyte Cres. SE19 1E 156
Forsyte Ho. SW3 6D 16
Forsythe Shades Ct. BR3: Beck 1E 158
Forsyth Gdns. SE17 6B 102
Forsyth Ho. E9 7J 67
(off Frampton Pk. Rd.)
SW1 5B 18
(off Tachbrook St.)
Forsythia Cl. IG1: Ilf 5F 71
Forsyth Pl. EN1: Enf 5K 23
Forterie Gdns. IG3: Bark, Ilf 3A 72
Fortescue Av. E8 7H 67
TW2: Twick 3G 131
Fortescue Rd. HA8: Edg 1K 43
SW19 7B 136
Fortess Gro. NW5 5G 65
Fortess Rd. NW5 5F 65
Fortess Wlk. NW5 5F 65
Fortess Yd. NW5 4F 65
Forte St. SE18 1C 124
(off Tellson Av.)
Forthbridge Rd. SW11 4E 118
Forth Ho. E3 2B 86
(off Tredegar Rd.)
Fortis Cl. E16 6A 88
Fortis Ct. N10 3E 46
FORTIS GREEN 4D 46
Fortis Grn. N2 4C 46
N10 4C 46
Fortis Grn. Av. N2 3D 46
Fortis Grn. Rd. N10 3E 46
Fortismere Av. N10 3E 46
Fortius Apts. E3 2C 86
(off Tredegar La.)
Fortius Wlk. E20 6E 68
Fortnam Rd. N19 2H 65
Fortnum's Acre HA7: Stan 6E 26
Fort Rd. SE1 4F 103
UB5: N'olt 7E 58
Fortrose Cl. E14 6F 87
Fortrose Gdns. SW2 1J 137
(not continuous)
Fort St. E1 6H 9 (5E 84)
E16 1K 105
Fortuna Cl. N7 6K 65
Fortuna Ho. E20 5D 68
(off Scarlet Cl.)
Fortune Av. HA8: Edg 1H 43
Fortune Ct. E8 7F 67
(off Queensbridge Rd.)
IG11: Bark 2C 90
Fortune Ga. Rd. NW10 1A 80
FORTUNE GREEN 5J 63
Fortune Grn. Rd. NW6 4J 63
Fortune Ho. EC1 4D 8
(off Fortune St.)
SE11 4J 19
Fortune Pl. SE1 5F 103
Fortunes Mead UB5: N'olt 6C 58
Fortune St. EC1 4D 8 (4C 84)
Fortunes Wlk. E20 5E 68
Fortune Theatre 1F 13
(off Russell St.)
Fortune Wlk. SE28 3H 107
(off Broadwater Rd.)
Fortune Way NW10 3C 80
Forty Acre La. E16 5J 87
Forty Av. HA9: Wemb 3F 61
Forty Cl. HA9: Wemb 3F 61
Forty Footpath SW14 3J 115
Forty Foot Way SE9 7G 125
FORTY HILL 1K 23
Forty Hill EN2: Enf 1K 23
Forty La. HA9: Wemb 2H 61
The Forum KT8: W Mole 4F 149
Forum Cl. E3 1C 86
Forum Ho. HA9: Wemb 4G 61
Forum Magnum Sq. SE1 6H 13
(off York Rd.)
Forumside HA8: Edg 6B 28
Forum Way HA8: Edg 6B 28
Forval Cl. CR4: Mitc 5D 154
The Forward Bus. Cen. E16 4F 87
Forward Dr. HA3: W'stone 4K 41
Fosbrooke Ho. SW8 7J 101
(off Davidson Gdns.)
Fosbury M. W2 7K 81
Foscote Ct. W9 4J 81
(off Amberley Rd.)
Foscote M. W9 4J 81
Foscote Rd. NW4 6D 44
Foskett Ho. N2 2B 46
(off The Grange)
Foskett M. E8 5F 67
Foskett Rd. SW6 2H 117
Foss Av. CR0: Wadd 5A 168
Fossdene Rd. SE7 5K 105
Fossdyke Cl. UB4: Yead 5C 76
Fosset Lodge DA7: Bex 1J 127
Fosse Way W13 5A 78
Foss Ho. NW8 2K 81
(off Carlton Hill)
Fossil Ct. SE1 7G 15
(off Long La.)
Fossil Rd. SE13 3C 122
Fossington Rd. DA17: Belv 4D 108
Foss Rd. SW17 4B 136
Fossway RM8: Dag 2C 72
Foster Ct. E16 7H 87
(off Tarling Rd.)
NW1 7G 65
(off Royal College St.)
NW4 4E 44
Foster Ho. SE14 1B 122
Foster La. EC2 7C 8 (6C 84)
Foster Rd. E13 4J 87
W3 7A 80
W4 5K 97
Fosters Cl. BR7: Chst 5D 142
E18 1K 51
Foster St. NW4 4E 44
Foster's Way SW18 1K 135
Foster Wlk. NW4 4E 44
Fothergill Cl. E13 2J 87
Fothergill Dr. N21 5D 22
Fotheringham Rd. EN1: Enf 4A 24
(not continuous)
Foubert's Pl. W1 1A 12 (6G 83)
Foulden Rd. N16 4F 67
Foulden Ter. N16 4F 67
Foulis Ter. SW7 5B 16 (5B 100)
Foulser Rd. SW17 3D 136
Foulsham Rd. CR7: Thor H 3C 156
Foundation Pl. SE9 5E 124
(off Archery Rd.)
Founder Cl. E6 6F 89
Founders Cl. UB5: N'olt 3D 76
Founders Ct. EC2 7E 8
Founders Gdns. SE19 7C 138
Founders Ho. SW1 6C 18
(off Aylesford St.)
Foundling Ct. WC1 3E 6
(off Brunswick Cen.)
The Foundling Mus. 3F 7
The Foundry EC2 2H 9
(off Dereham Pl.)
Foundry Cl. SE16 1A 104
Foundry Ho. E14 5D 86
(off Morris Rd.)
E15 6F 69
(off Forrester Way)
SW8 1F 119
(off Lockington Rd.)
Foundry M. E17 3E 50
NW1 3B 6 (4G 83)
SW13 2B 116
TW3: Houn 4F 113
Foundry Pl. E1 5J 85
(off Jubilee St.)
SW18 7K 117
Fountain Cl. E5 4H 67
SE18 5F 107
UB8: Hil 5E 74
Fountain Ct. DA15: Sidc 6B 126
EC4 2J 13 (7A 84)
SE23 2K 139
SW1 4J 17
(off Buckingham Pal. Rd.)
W11 2F 99
(off Clearwater Ter.)
Fountain Dr. SE19 4F 139
SM5: Cars 7D 166
Fountain Grn. Sq. SE16 2G 103
Fountain Ho. CR4: Mitc 2D 154
E2 3J 9
(off Redchurch St.)
NW6 7G 63
SE16 2G 103
(off Bermondsey Wall E.)
SW6 2A 118
W1 4G 11
(off Park St.)
Fountain M. N5 4C 66
(off Highbury Grange)
NW3 6D 64
Fountain Park Way W12 7E 80
Fountain Pl. SW9 1A 120
Fountain Rd. CR7: Thor H 3C 156
SW17 5B 136
FOUNTAIN RDBT. 4A 152
The Fountains N3 7E 30
(off Ballards La.)
Fountains Av. TW13: Hanw 3D 130
Fountains Cl. TW13: Hanw 2D 130
(not continuous)
Fountains Cres. N14 7D 22
Fountain Sq. SW1 3K 17 (4F 101)
Fountayne Bus. Cen. N15 4G 49
Fountayne Rd. N15 4G 49
N16 2G 67
Fount St. SW8 7H 101
Fouracre NW1 2A 6
(off Stanhope St.)
Fouracre Path SE25 6E 156
Four Acres N12 3E 30
Fouracres EN3: Enf H 1F 25
Four Casson Sq. SE1 5H 13 (1K 101)
Fourland Wlk. HA8: Edg 6D 28
Fournier St. E1 5J 9 (5F 85)
Fourscore Mans. E8 7G 67
(off Shrubland Rd.)
Four Seasons Cl. E3 2C 86
Four Seasons Cres. SM3: Sutt 2H 165
Four Seasons Ter. UB7: W Dray 2C 92
Four Sq. Ct. TW3: Houn 6E 112
Fourth Av. E12 4D 70
RM7: Rush G 1K 73
UB3: Hayes 1H 93
W10 4G 81
Fourth Cross Rd. TW2: Twick 2H 131
Fourth Way HA9: Wemb 4J 61
The Four Wents E4 1A 36
Fovant Ct. SW8 2G 119
Fowey Av. IG4: Ilf 5B 52
Fowey Cl. E1 1H 103
Fowey Ho. SE11 5K 19
Fowey Pl. SM2: Sutt 7J 165
Fowler Cl. SW11 3B 118
Fowler Ho. N15 5D 48
(off South Gro.)
Fowler Rd. CR4: Mitc 2E 154
E7 4J 69
N1 1B 84
Fowlers Cl. DA14: Sidc 5E 144
Fowlers M. N19 2G 65
(off Holloway Rd.)
Fowler's Wlk. W5 4D 78
Fowler Way UB10: Uxb 2A 74
Fownes St. SW11 3C 118
Fox & Knot St. EC1 5B 8
Foxberry Rd. SE4 3A 122
Foxborough Gdns. SE4 5C 122
Foxbourne Rd. SW17 2E 136
Foxbury Av. BR7: Chst 6H 143
Foxbury Cl. BR1: Broml 6K 141
Foxbury Rd. BR1: Broml 6J 141
Fox Cl. BR6: Chels 5K 173
E1 4J 85
E16 5J 87
Foxcombe CR0: New Ad 6D 170
(not continuous)
Foxcombe Cl. E6 2B 88
Foxcombe Rd. SW15 1C 134
Foxcote SE5 5E 102
Foxcroft WC1 1H 7
(off Penton Ri.)
Foxcroft Rd. SE18 1F 125
Foxdene Cl. E18 3K 51
Foxearth Spur CR2: Sels 7J 169
Foxes Dale BR2: Broml 3F 159
SE3 3J 123
Foxfield NW1 1F 83
(off Arlington Rd.)
Foxfield Rd. BR6: Orp 2H 173
Foxglove Cl. DA15: Sidc 6A 126
N9 1D 34
UB1: S'hall 7C 76
UB7: W Dray 2B 92
Foxglove Ct. E3 2C 86
(off Four Seasons Cl.)
HA0: Wemb 2E 78
Foxglove Gdns. E11 4A 52
Foxglove La. KT9: Chess 4G 163
Foxglove Path SE28 1J 107
(off Martins Pl.)
Foxglove Rd. RM7: Rush G 2K 73
Foxglove St. W12 7B 80
Foxglove Way SM6: W'gton 1F 167
Fox Gro. KT12: Walt T 7K 147
Foxgrove N14 3D 32
Foxgrove Av. BR3: Beck 7D 140
Foxgrove Rd. BR3: Beck 7D 140
Foxham Rd. N19 3H 65
Fox Hill SE19 7F 139
Fox Hill Gdns. SE19 7F 139
Foxhole Rd. SE9 5C 124
Fox Hollow Cl. SE18 5J 107
Fox Hollow Dr. DA7: Bex 3D 126
Foxholt Gdns. NW10 7J 61
Foxhome Cl. BR7: Chst 6E 142
Fox Ho. Rd. DA17: Belv 5H 109
(not continuous)
Foxlands Cres. RM10: Dag 5J 73
Foxlands La. RM10: Dag 5K 73
Foxlands Rd. RM10: Dag 5J 73
Fox La. BR2: Kes 5K 171
N13 2E 32
W5 4E 78
Foxleas Ct. BR1: Broml 7G 141
Foxlees HA0: Wemb 4A 60
Foxley Cl. E8 5G 67
Foxley Ct. SM2: Sutt 7A 166
Foxley Ho. E3 3D 86
(off Bow Rd.)
Foxley Mews N20 2G 31
Foxley Rd. CR7: Thor H 4B 156
SW9 7A 102
Foxley Sq. SW9 7B 102
Foxmead Cl. EN2: Enf 3E 22
Foxmore St. SW11 1D 118
Fox Rd. E16 5H 87
Fox's Path CR4: Mitc 2C 154
Fox's Yd. E2 3K 9
Foxton Gro. CR4: Mitc 2B 154
Foxton Ho. E16 2E 106
(off Albert Rd.)
Foxton M. TW10: Rich 6E 114
Foxton Way SM3: Sutt 1J 165
Foxwarren KT10: Clay 7A 162
Foxwell M. SE4 3A 122
Foxwell St. SE4 3A 122
Foxwood Cl. NW7 4F 29
TW13: Felt 3K 129
Foxwood Grn. Cl. EN1: Enf 6K 23
Fox Wood Nature Reserve 4E 78
Foxwood Rd. SE3 4H 123
Foyle Rd. N17 1G 49
SE3 6H 105
Framfield Cl. N12 3D 30
Framfield Ct. EN1: Enf 6K 23
(off Queen Anne's Gdns.)
Framfield Rd. CR4: Mitc 7E 136
N5 5B 66
W7 6J 77
Framlingham Cl. E5 2J 67
Framlingham Ct. RM6: Chad H 5B 54
(off Norwich Cres.)
Framlingham Cres. SE9 4C 142
Frampton NW1 7H 65
(off Wrotham Rd.)
Frampton Cl. IG6: Ilf 4H 53
SM2: Sutt 7J 165
Frampton Ct. W3 2J 97
(off Avenue Rd.)
Frampton Ho. NW8 4B 4
(off Frampton St.)
Frampton Pk. Est. E9 7J 67
Frampton Pk. Rd. E9 6J 67
Frampton Rd. TW4: Houn 5C 112
Frampton St. NW8 4B 4 (4B 82)
Frampton Ter. SE9 3F 143
Francemary Rd. SE4 5C 122
Frances Ct. E17 6C 50
SE25 3F 157
Frances Rd. E4 6H 35
Frances St. SE18 3D 106
Frances Wharf E14 6B 86
Franche Ct. Rd. SW17 3A 136
Francis & Dick James Ct. NW7 7B 30
Francis Av. DA7: Bex 2G 127
IG1: Ilf 2H 71
TW13: Felt 3J 129
Francis Bacon Ct. SE16 4H 103
(off Galleywall Rd.)
Francis Barber Cl. SW16 5K 137
Francis Bentley M. SW4 3G 119
Franciscan Rd. SW17 5D 136
Francis Chichester Way SW11 1E 118
Francis Cl. E14 4F 105
KT19: Ewe 4K 163
TW17: Shep 4C 146
Francis Ct. EC1 5A 8
KT5: Surb 4E 150
(off Cranes Pk. Av.)
NW7 5G 29
(off Watford Way)
SE14 6K 103
(off Myers La.)
Francis Gro. SW19 6H 135
Francis Harvey Way SE8 1B 122
Francis Ho. N1 1E 84
(off Colville Est.)
SW10 7K 99
(off Coleridge Gdns.)
SW18 4A 118
(off Eltringham St.)
Francis M. SE12 7J 123
Francis Pl. N6 7F 47
(off Shepherd's Cl.)
Francis Rd. CR0: C'don 7B 156
E10 1E 68
HA1: Harr 5A 42
HA5: Eastc 5A 40
IG1: Ilf 2H 71
N2 4D 46
SM6: W'gton 6G 167
TW4: Houn 2B 112
UB6: G'frd 2B 78
Francis St. E15 5G 69
IG1: Ilf 2H 71
SW1 3A 18 (4G 101)
Francis Ter. N19 3G 65
Francis Ter. M. N19 3G 65
Francis Wlk. N1 1K 83
Franck House EC1 2B 8
(off Goswell Road)
Francklyn Gdns. HA8: Edg 3B 28
Franco Av. NW9 1B 44
Franconia Rd. SW4 5H 119
Frank Bailey Wlk. E12 6E 70
Frank Beswick Ho. SW6 6H 99
(off Clem Attlee Ct.)
Frank Burton Cl. SE7 5K 105
Frank Dixon Cl. SE21 7E 120
Frank Dixon Way SE21 1E 138
Frankfurt Rd. SE24 5C 120
Frank Godley Ct. DA14: Sidc 5B 144
Frankham Ho. SE8 7C 104
(off Frankham St.)
Frankham St. SE8 7C 104
Frank Ho. SW8 7J 101
(off Wyvil Rd.)
Frankland Cl. IG8: Wfd G 5F 37
SE16 3H 103
Frankland Rd. E4 5H 35
SW7 2A 16 (3B 100)
Franklin Bldg. E14 2C 104
Franklin Cl. KT1: King T 3G 151
N20 7F 21
SE13 1D 122
SE27 3B 138
Franklin Cotts. HA7: Stan 4G 27
Franklin Cres. CR4: Mitc 4G 155
Franklin Ho. BR2: Broml 3G 159
E1 1H 103
(off Watts St.)
E14 6F 87
(off E. India Dock Rd.)
NW6 3J 81
(off Carlton Va.)
Franklin Ind. Est. SE20 1J 157
(off Franklin Rd.)
Franklin Pas. SE9 3C 124
Franklin Pl. SE13 1D 122
Franklin Rd. DA7: Bex 1E 126
SE20 7J 139
Franklins M. HA2: Harr 2G 59
Franklin Sq. W14 5H 99
Franklin's Row SW3 5F 17 (5D 100)
Franklin St. E3 3D 86
N15 6E 48
Franklin Way CR0: Wadd 7J 155
Franklyn Rd. KT12: Walt T 6J 147
NW10 6B 62
Frank M. SE1 4H 103
Franks Av. KT3: N Mald 4J 151
Frank Soskice Ho. SW6 6H 99
(off Clem Attlee Ct.)
Frank St. E13 4J 87
Frankswood Av. BR5: Pet W 5F 161
UB7: Yiew 6B 74
Frank Towell Ct. TW14: Felt 7J 111
Frank Whipple Pl. E14 6A 86
(off Repton St.)
Frank Whymark Ho. SE16 2J 103
(off Rupack St.)
Franlaw Cres. N13 4H 33
Fransfield Gro. SE26 3H 139
Frans Hals Ct. E14 3F 105
Franshams WD23: B Hea 2D 26
(off Hartsbourne Rd.)
Frant Cl. SE20 7J 139
Franthorne Way SE6 2D 140
Frant Rd. CR7: Thor H 5B 156
Fraserburgh Ho. E3 2B 86
(off Vernon Rd.)
Fraser Cl. DA5: Bexl 1J 145
E6 6C 88
Fraser Ct. E14 5E 104
(off Ferry St.)
SE1 7D 14
SW11 1C 118
(off Surrey La. Est.)
Fraser Ho. TW8: Bford 5F 97
Fraser Rd. DA8: Erith 5K 109
E17 5D 50
N9 3C 34
UB6: G'frd 1B 78
Fraser St. W4 5A 98
Frating Cres. IG8: Wfd G 6E 36
Frazer Av. HA4: Ruis 5A 58
Frazer Nash Cl. TW7: Isle 1K 113
Frazier St. SE1 7J 13 (2A 102)
Frean St. SE16 3G 103
Frearson Ho. WC1 1H 7
(off Penton Ri.)
Freda Corbett Cl. SE15 7G 103
Freda St. SE16 7K 15 (3G 103)
Frederica Ct. SW2 1B 138
Frederica Rd. E4 1A 36
Frederica St. N7 7K 65
Frederick Charrington Ho. E1 4J 85
(off Wickford St.)
Frederick Cl. SM1: Sutt 4H 165
W2 2D 10 (7D 82)
Frederick Ct. SW3 4F 17
(off Duke of York Sq.)
Frederick Cres. EN3: Enf H 2D 24
SW9 7B 102
Frederick Dobson Ho. W11 7G 81
(off Cowling Cl.)
Frederick Gdns. CR0: C'don 6B 156
SM1: Sutt 5H 165
Frederick Ho. SE18 4C 106
(off Pett St.)
Frederick Pl. N8 6H 47
(off Crouch Hall Rd.)
SE18 5F 107
Frederick Rd. RM13: Rain 2K 91
SE17 6B 102
SM1: Sutt 5H 165
Frederick's Pl. EC2 1E 14 (6D 84)
Fredericks Pl. N12 4F 31
Frederick Sq. SE16 7A 86
(off Sovereign Cres.)
Frederick's Row EC1 1A 8 (3B 84)
Frederick St. WC1 2G 7 (3K 83)
Frederick Ter. E8 7F 67
Frederick Vs. W7 1J 95
(off Lwr. Boston Rd.)
Frederic M. SW1 7F 11
Frederic St. E17 5A 50
Fredora Av. UB4: Hayes 4H 75
Fred Styles Ho. SE7 6A 106
Fred Tibble Ct. RM9: Dag 4E 72
Fred White Wlk. N7 6J 65
Freedom Cl. E17 4A 50
Freedom Rd. N17 2D 48
Freedom St. SW11 2D 118
Freegrove Rd. N7 5J 65
(not continuous)
Freehold Ind. Cen. TW4: Houn 5A 112
Freeland Ct. DA15: Sidc 3A 144
Freeland Pk. NW4 2G 45
Freeland Rd. W5 7F 79
Freelands Av. CR2: Sels 7K 169
Freelands Gro. BR1: Broml 1K 159
Freelands Rd. BR1: Broml 1K 159
Freeling Ho. NW8 1B 82
(off Dorman Way)
Freeling St. N1 7K 65
(Carnoustie Dr.)
N1 7J 65
(Pembroke St.)
Freeman Cl. TW17: Shep 4G 147
UB5: N'olt 7C 58
Freeman Ct. N7 3J 65
SW16 2J 155
Freeman Dr. KT8: W Mole 3D 148
Freeman Ho. SE11 4B 102
(off George Mathers Rd.)
Freeman Rd. SM4: Mord 5B 154
Freemans La. UB3: Hayes 7G 75
Freemantle Av.
EN3: Pond E 5E 24
Freemantle St. SE17 5E 102
Freeman Wlk. SE9 5A 124
Freemasons' Hall 7F 7
Freemasons Pl. CR0: C'don 1E 168
(off Freemasons Rd.)
Freemasons Rd. CR0: C'don 1E 168
E16 5K 87
Freesia Cl. BR6: Chels 5K 173
Freethorpe Cl. SE19 7D 138
Free Trade Wharf E1 7K 85
Freezeland Way UB10: Hil 6D 56
Freight La. N1 7H 65
Freightliners City Farm 6A 66
Freke Rd. SW11 3E 118
Fremantle Ho. E1 4H 85
(off Somerford St.)
Fremantle Rd. DA17: Belv 4G 109
IG6: Ilf 2F 53
Fremantle Way UB3: Hayes 7H 75
Fremont St. E9 1H 85
(not continuous)
French Horn Yd. WC1 6G 7
French Ordinary Ct. EC3 2H 15
French Pl. E1 2H 9 (3E 84)
French St. TW16: Sun 2A 148
Frendsbury Rd. SE4 4A 122
Frensham Cl. UB1: S'hall 4D 76
Frensham Ct. SW19 3A 154
Frensham Dr. CR0: New Ad 7E 170
SW15 3B 134
Frensham Rd. SE9 2H 143
Frensham St. SE15 6G 103
Frere St. SW11 2C 118
Fresham Ho. BR2: Broml 3H 159
(off Durham Rd.)
Freshfield Av. E8 7F 67
Freshfield Cl. SE13 4F 123
Freshfield Dr. N14 7A 22
Freshfields CR0: C'don 1B 170
Freshford St. SW18 3A 136
Fresh Mill La. UB1: S'hall 4E 76
Freshwater Cl. SW17 7E 136
Freshwater Ct. UB1: S'hall 3E 76
W1 6D 4
(off Crawford St.)
Freshwater Rd. RM8: Dag 1D 72
SW17 6E 136
Freshwell Av. RM6: Chad H 4C 54
Fresh Wharf Est. IG11: Bark 2F 89
Fresh Wharf Rd. IG11: Bark 1F 89
Freshwood Cl. BR3: Beck 1D 158
Freshwood Way SM6: W'gton 7F 167
Freston Gdns. EN4: Cockf 5K 21
Freston Pk. N3 2H 45

Freston Rd.—Garden Ho.

Freston Rd. W10 7F 81
W11 7F 81
Freswick Ho. SE8 4A 104
(off Chilton Gro.)
Freta Rd. DA6: Bex 5F 127
Freud Mus. 6A 64
Frewell Ho. EC1 5J 7
(off Bourne Est.)
Frewin Rd. SW18 1B 136
Friar M. SE27 3B 138
Friar Rd. BR5: St M Cry 5K 161
EN2: Enf 1F 23
UB4: Yead 4B 76
Friars Av. N20 3H 31
SW15 3B 134
Friars Cl. E4 3K 35
IG1: Ilf 1H 71
SE1 5B 14
UB5: N'olt 3B 76
Friars Ct. E17 1B 50
RM7: Rush G 6K 55
SM6: W'gton 4F 167
Friars Gdns. W3 6K 79
Friarsgate NW10 2H 79
Friars Ga. Cl. IG8: Wfd G 4D 36
Friars La. TW9: Rich 5D 114
Friars Mead E14 3E 104
Friars M. SE9 5E 124
Friars Mt. Ho. E2 2J 9
(off Rochelle St.)
Friars Pl. La. W3 7K 79
Friars Rd. E6 1B 88
Friars Stile Pl. TW10: Rich 6E 114
Friars Stile Rd. TW10: Rich 6E 114
Friar St. EC4 1B 14 (6B 84)
Friars Wlk. N14 7A 22
SE2 5D 108
Friars Way W3 6K 79
Friars Wood CR0: Sels 7A 170
Friary Cl. N12 5H 31
Friary Ct. SW1 5B 12
Friary Est. SE15 6G 103
(not continuous)
Friary La. IG8: Wfd G 4D 36
Friary Pk. W3 6K 79
Friary Pk. Ct. W3 6J 79
Friary Rd. N12 4G 31
N20 4G 31
SE15 7G 103
W3 6J 79
Friary Way N12 4H 31
FRIDAY HILL 2B 36
Friday Hill E4 2B 36
Friday Hill E. E4 3B 36
Friday Hill W. E4 2B 36
Friday Rd. CR4: Mitc 7D 136
DA8: Erith 5K 109
Friday St. EC4 2C 14 (7C 84)
Frideswide Pl. NW5 5G 65
Friendly Pl. SE13 1D 122
Friendly St. SE8 2C 122
Friendly St. M. SE8 2C 122
Friendship Ho. SE1 7B 14
(off Belvedere Pl.)
Friendship Wlk. UB5: N'olt 3B 76
Friendship Way E15 1E 86
Friends Rd. CR0: C'don 3D 168
Friend St. EC1 1A 8 (3B 84)
FRIERN BARNET 5J 31
Friern Barnet La. N11 2G 31
N20 2G 31
Friern Barnet Rd. N11 5J 31
Friern Bri. Retail Pk. 6A 32
Friern Ct. N20 3G 31
Friern Mt. Dr. N20 7F 21
Friern Pk. N12 5F 31
Friern Rd. SE22 7G 121
(not continuous)
Friern Watch Av. N12 4F 31
Frigate Ho. E14 4E 104
(off Stebondale St.)
Frigate M. SE8 6C 104
Frimley Av. SM6: W'gton 5J 167
Frimley Cl. CR0: New Ad 7E 170
SW19 2G 135
Frimley Ct. DA14: Sidc 5C 144
Frimley Cres. CR0: New Ad 7E 170
Frimley Gdns. CR4: Mitc 3C 154
Frimley Rd. IG3: Ilf 3J 71
KT9: Chess 5D 162
Frimley St. E1 4K 85
(off Frimley Way)
Frimley Way E1 4K 85
Fringewood Cl. HA6: Nwood 1D 38
Frinstead Ho. W10 7F 81
(off Freston Rd.)
Frinsted Rd. DA8: Erith 7K 109
Frinton Ct. W13 5B 78
(off Hardwick Grn.)
Frinton Dr. IG8: Wfd G 7A 36
Frinton M. IG2: Ilf 6E 52
Frinton Rd. DA14: Sidc 2E 144
E6 3B 88
N15 6E 48
SW17 6E 136
Friston St. SW6 2K 117
Friswell Pl. DA6: Bex 4G 127
Fritham Cl. KT3: N Mald 6A 152
Frith Ct. NW7 7B 30
Frith Ho. NW8 4B 4
(off Frampton St.)
Frith La. NW7 7B 30
Frith Rd. CR0: C'don 2C 168
E11 4E 68
Frith St. W1 1C 12 (6H 83)
Frithville Ct. W12 1E 98
(off Frithville Gdns.)
Frithville Gdns. W12 1E 98
Frizlands La. RM10: Dag 2H 73
Frobisher Cl. HA5: Pinn 7B 40
Frobisher Ct. NW9 2A 44
SE8 5A 104
(off Evelyn St.)
SE10 6F 105
(off Old Woolwich Rd.)
SE23 2H 139
SM3: Cheam 7G 165
W12 2E 98
(off Lime Gro.)
Frobisher Cres. EC2 5D 8
(off Silk St.)
TW19: Stanw 7A 110
Frobisher Gdns. E10 7D 50
TW19: Stanw 7A 110
Frobisher Ho. E1 1H 103
(off Watts St.)
Frobisher Ho. SW1 7C 18
(off Dolphin Sq.)
Frobisher M. EN2: Enf 4J 23
Frobisher Pas. E14 1C 104
Frobisher Pl. SE15 1J 121
Frobisher Rd. E6 6D 88
N8 4A 48
Frobisher St. SE10 6G 105
Frobisher Yd. E16 7G 89
Froebel College 6B 116
Frog La. RM13: Rain 6K 91
Frogley Rd. SE22 4F 121
Frogmore SW18 5J 117
Frogmore Av. UB4: Hayes 4G 75
Frogmore Cl. SM3: Cheam 3F 165
Frogmore Ct. UB2: S'hall 4D 94
Frogmore Gdns. SM3: Cheam 4G 165
UB4: Hayes 4G 75
Frogmore Ind. Est. N5 5C 66
NW10 3J 79
UB3: Hayes 2G 93
Frognal NW3 4A 64
Frognal Av. DA14: Sidc 6A 144
HA1: Harr 4K 41
Frognal Cl. NW3 5A 64
FROGNAL CORNER 6K 143
Frognal Ct. NW3 6A 64
Frognal Gdns. NW3 4A 64
Frognal La. NW3 5K 63
Frognal Pde. NW3 6A 64
Frognal Pl. DA14: Sidc 6A 144
Frognal Ri. NW3 3A 64
Frognal Way NW3 4A 64
Frogwell Cl. N15 6D 48
Froissart Rd. SE9 5B 124
Frome Ho. SE15 4H 121
Frome Rd. N22 3B 48
Frome St. N1 2C 84
Fromondes Rd. SM3: Cheam 5G 165
Fromows Cnr. W4 5J 97
Frontenac NW10 7D 62
Frontier Works N17 6K 33
Frost Ct. NW9 2A 44
(off Salk Cl.)
Frostic Wlk. E1 6K 9 (5G 85)
Froude St. SW8 2F 119
Fruen Rd. TW14: Felt 7H 111
Fryatt Rd. N17 7J 33
(not continuous)
Fryday Gro. M. SW12 7G 119
(off Weir Rd.)
Frye Ct. E3 3B 86
(off Benworth St.)
Frye Ho. E20 6E 68
(off Penny Brookes St.)
Fryent Cl. NW9 6G 43
Fryent Country Park 7G 43
Fryent Cres. NW9 6A 44
Fryent Flds. NW9 6A 44
Fryent Gro. NW9 6A 44
Fryent Way NW9 5G 43
Fryers Vw. SE4 4K 121
(off Frendsbury Rd.)
Fry Ho. E6 7A 70
Frying Pan All. E1 6J 9
Fry La. HA8: Edg 4A 28
Fry Rd. E6 7B 70
NW10 1B 80
Frys Ct. SE10 6E 104
(off Durnford St.)
Fryston Av. CR0: C'don 2G 169
Fuchsia Cl. RM7: Rush G 2K 73
Fuchsia St. SE2 5B 108
Fulbeck Dr. NW9 1A 44
Fulbeck Ho. N7 6K 65
(off Sutterton St.)
Fulbeck Rd. N19 4G 65
Fulbeck Wlk. HA8: Edg 2C 28
Fulbeck Way HA2: Harr 2G 41
Fulbourn KT1: King T 2G 151
(off Eureka Rd.)
Fulbourne Rd. E17 1E 50
Fulbourne St. E1 5H 85
Fulbrook M. N19 4G 65
Fulcher Ho. N1 1E 84
(off Colville Est.)
SE8 5B 104
Fulford Ho. KT19: Ewe 7K 163
Fulford Rd. KT19: Ewe 7K 163
Fulford St. SE16 2H 103
FULHAM 1G 117
FULHAM BROADWAY 7J 99
Fulham B'way. SW6 7J 99
Fulham B'way. Shop. Cen. 7J 99
Fulham Bus. Exchange SW6 1A 118
(off The Boulevard)
Fulham Cl. UB10: Hil 4E 74
Fulham Ct. SW6 1J 117
Fulham FC 1F 117
Fulham High St. SW6 2G 117
Fulham Island SW6 7J 99
(off Farm La.)
Fulham Palace 2G 117
Fulham Pal. Rd. SW6 5E 98
W6 5E 98
Fulham Pk. Gdns. SW6 2H 117
Fulham Pk. Rd. SW6 2H 117
Fulham Pools
Virgin Active 6G 99
Fulham Rd. SW3 7A 16 (7K 99)
SW6 2G 117
(not continuous)
SW10 7A 16 (7K 99)
Fullbrooks Av. KT4: Wor Pk 1B 164
Fuller Cl. BR6: Chels 5K 173
E2 4G 85
(off Cheshire St.)
WD23: Bush 1C 26
Fuller Ct. N8 5H 47
Fuller Rd. RM8: Dag 3B 72
Fullers Av. IG8: Wfd G 7C 36
KT6: Surb 2F 163
Fullers Cl. RM5: Col R 1J 55
Fuller's Griffin Brewery 6B 98
Fullers La. RM5: Col R 1J 55
Fullers Rd. E18 7C 36
Fuller St. NW4 4E 44
Fullers Way Nth. KT6: Surb 3F 163
Fullers Way Sth. KT9: Chess 4E 162
Fuller's Wood CR0: C'don 5C 170
Fullerton Av. RM8: Dag 1E 72
Fullerton Ct. TW11: Tedd 6A 132
Fullerton Rd. CR0: C'don 7F 157
SM5: Cars 7C 166
SW18 5K 117
Fuller Way UB3: Harl 5H 93
Fullwell Av. IG5: Ilf 1D 52
IG6: Ilf 1F 53
FULLWELL CROSS 2G 53
FULLWELL CROSS 2H 53
Fullwell Cross Leisure Cen. 2G 53
Fullwell Pde. IG5: Ilf 1E 52
Fullwood's M. N1 1F 9 (3D 84)
Fulmar Cl. KT5: Surb 6F 151
Fulmar Ho. SE16 4K 103
(off Tawny Way)
Fulmead St. SW6 1K 117
Fulmer Cl. TW12: Hamp 5C 130
Fulmer Ho. NW8 4D 4
(off Mallory St.)
UB8: Uxb 6A 56
Fulmer Rd. E16 5B 88
Fulmer Way W13 3B 96
Fulneck Pl. E1 4J 85
Fulready Rd. E10 5F 51
Fulstone Cl. TW4: Houn 4D 112
Fulthorp Rd. SE3 2H 123
Fulton M. W2 7A 82
Fulton Rd. HA9: Wemb 3G 61
FULWELL 4H 131
Fulwell Ct. IG5: Ilf 1E 52
UB1: S'hall 7G 77
(off Baird Av.)
Fulwell Golf Course 4H 131
Fulwell Pk. Av. TW2: Twick 2F 131
Fulwell Rd. TW11: Tedd 4H 131
Fulwood Av. HA0: Wemb 2F 79
Fulwood Cl. UB3: Hayes 6H 75
Fulwood Ct. HA3: Kenton 6A 42
Fulwood Gdns. TW1: Twick 6K 113
Fulwood Pl. WC1 6H 7 (5K 83)
Fulwood Wlk. SW19 1G 135
Funky Footprints Nature Reserve
6C 146
Furber St. W6 3D 98
Furham Feild HA5: Hat E 7A 26
Furley Ho. SE15 7G 103
(off Peckham Pk. Rd.)
Furley Rd. SE15 7G 103
Furlong Av. CR4: Mitc 3C 154
Furlong Cl. CR0: C'don 1H 169
SM6: W'gton 1F 167
Furlong Rd. N7 6A 66
Furlow Ho. NW9 3C 44
Furmage St. SW18 7K 117
Furneaux Av. SE27 5B 138
Furness Ho. SW1 5J 17
(part of Abbots Mnr.)
Furness Rd. HA2: Harr 7F 41
NW10 2C 80
SM4: Mord 6K 153
SW6 2K 117
Furnival Ct. E3 2C 86
(off Four Seasons Cl.)
Furnival Mans. W1 6A 6
(off Wells St.)
Furnival St. EC4 7J 7 (6A 84)
Furrow Ho. E4 6K 35
Furrow La. E9 5J 67
Fursby Av. N3 6D 30
Fursecroft W1 7E 4
Furtherfield Cl. CR0: C'don 6A 156
Further Grn. Rd. SE6 7G 123
FURZEDOWN 5F 137
Furzedown Dr. SW17 5F 137
Furzedown Recreation Cen. 5F 137
Furzedown Rd. SW17 5F 137
Furze Farm Cl. RM6: Chad H 2E 54
Furzefield Cl. BR7: Chst 6F 143
Furzefield Rd. SE3 6K 105
Furzeground Way UB11: Stock P 1E 92
Furzeham Rd. UB7: W Dray 2A 92
Furze Rd. CR7: Thor H 3C 156
Furze St. E3 5C 86
Furzewood TW16: Sun 1J 147
The Fusilier Museum 7F 85
Fusiliers Way TW4: Houn 3A 112
(not continuous)
Fusion Apts. SE14 6A 104
(off Moulding La.)
Fye Foot La. EC4 2C 14
(off Queen Victoria St.)
Fyfe Apts. N8 3K 47
Fyfe Way BR1: Broml 2J 159
Fyfield N4 2A 66
(off Six Acres Est.)
Fyfield Cl. BR2: Broml 4F 159
Fyfield Ct. E7 6J 69
Fyfield Ho. E6 1C 88
(off Ron Leighton Way)
Fyfield Rd. E17 3F 51
EN1: Enf 3K 23
IG8: Wfd G 7F 37
SW9 3A 120
Fynes St. SW1 3C 18 (4H 101)

G

Gable Cl. HA5: Hat E 1E 40
Gable Ct. SE26 4H 139
Gable M. BR2: Broml 2C 172
The Gables BR1: Broml 7K 141
HA9: Wemb 3G 61
IG11: Bark 6G 71
N10 3E 46
(off Fortis Grn.)
Gables Av. TW15: Ashf 5B 128
Gables Cl. SE5 1E 120
SE12 1J 141
Gables Lodge EN4: Had W 1F 21
Gabriel Cl. TW13: Hanw 4C 130
Gabriel Ct. E1 5A 86
(off Elsa Street)
NW9 2A 44
Gabriel Ho. N1 1B 84
(off Islington Grn.)
SE11 3G 19 (4K 101)
SE16 3B 104
(off Odessa St.)
Gabrielle Cl. HA9: Wemb 3F 61
Gabrielle Ct. NW3 6B 64
Gabriel M. NW2 2H 63
Gabriel's M. BR3: Beck 1K 157
Gabriel St. SE23 7K 121
Gabriels Wharf SE1 4J 13 (1A 102)
Gad Cl. E13 3K 87
Gaddesden Av. HA9: Wemb 6F 61
Gaddesden Ho. EC1 2F 9
(off Cranwood St.)
Gadebridge Ho. SW3 5C 16
(off Cale St.)
Gade Cl. UB3: Hayes 1K 93
Gadesden Rd. KT19: Ewe 6J 163
Gadsbury Cl. NW9 6B 44
Gadsden Ho. W10 4G 81
(off Hazlewood Cres.)
Gadwall Cl. E16 6K 87
Gadwall Ho. NW9 6C 44
(off Perryfield Way)
Gadwall Way SE28 2H 107
Gage Brown Ho. W10 6F 81
(off Bridge Cl.)
Gage M. CR2: S Croy 5B 168
Gage Rd. E16 5G 87
Gage St. WC1 5F 7 (5J 83)
Gainford Ho. E2 3H 85
(off Ellsworth St.)
Gainford St. N1 1A 84
Gainsboro Gdns. UB6: G'frd 5J 59
Gainsborough Av. E12 5E 70
Gainsborough Cl. BR3: Beck 7C 140
KT10: Esh 7J 149
Gainsborough Ct. BR2: Broml 4A 160
KT19: Ewe 6B 164
N12 5E 30
SE16 5H 103
(off Stubbs Dr.)
SE21 2E 138
W4 5H 97
(off Chaseley Dr.)
W12 2E 98
Gainsborough Gdns. HA8: Edg 2F 43
NW3 3B 64
NW11 7H 45
TW7: Isle 5H 113
Gainsborough Ho. E14 2C 104
(off Cassilis Rd.)
E14 7A 86
(off Victory Pl.)
EN1: Enf 5B 24
RM8: Dag 4B 72
(off Longbridge Rd.)
SW1 4D 18
(off Erasmus St.)
Gainsborough Lodge HA1: Harr 5K 41
(off Hindes Rd.)
Gainsborough Mans. W14 6G 99
(off Queen's Club Gdns.)
Gainsborough M. SE26 3H 139
Gainsborough Rd. E11 7G 51
E15 3G 87
IG8: Wfd G 6H 37
KT3: N Mald 6K 151
N12 5E 30
RM8: Dag 4B 72
TW9: Rich 2F 115
UB4: Hayes 2E 74
W4 4B 98
Gainsborough Sq. DA6: Bex 3D 126
Gainsborough St. E9 6B 68
Gainsborough Studios E. N1 1D 84
(off Poole St.)
Gainsborough Studios Nth. N1 1D 84
(off Poole St.)
Gainsborough Studios Sth. N1 1D 84
(off Poole St.)
Gainsborough Studios W. N1 1D 84
(off Poole St.)
Gainsborough Ter. SM2: Sutt 7H 165
(off Belmont Ri.)
Gainsborough Twr. UB5: N'olt 2B 76
(off Academy Gdns.)
Gainsfield Ct. E11 3G 69
Gainsford Rd. E17 4B 50
Gainsford St. SE1 6J 15 (2F 103)
Gairloch Ho. NW1 7H 65
(off Stratford Vs.)
Gairloch Rd. SE5 2E 120
Gaisford St. NW5 6G 65
Gaitskell Ct. SW11 2C 118
Gaitskell Ho. E6 1B 88
E17 3D 50
SE17 6E 102
(off Villa St.)
Gaitskell Rd. SE9 1G 143
Gaitskell Way SE1 6C 14
(off Weller St.)
Gala Bingo
Surrey Quays 3K 103
Tooting 5C 136
Gala Ct. CR7: Thor H 5A 156
Galahad M. E3 2B 86
Galahad Rd. BR1: Broml 4J 141
N9 3B 34
Galata Rd. SW13 7C 98
Galatea Sq. SE15 3H 121
Galaxy Bldg. E14 4C 104
(off Crews St.)
Galaxy Ho. EC2 3F 9
(off Leonard St.)
Galba Ct. TW8: Bford 7D 96
Galbraith St. E14 3E 104
Galdana Av. EN5: New Bar 3F 21
Galeborough Av. IG8: Wfd G 7A 36
Gale Cl. CR4: Mitc 3B 154
TW12: Hamp 6C 130
Galena Arches W6 4D 98
(off Galena Rd.)
Galena Hgts. E20 6E 68
(off Mirabelle Gdns.)
Galena Ho. SE18 5K 107
(off Grosmont Rd.)
Galena Rd. W6 4D 98
Galen Pl. WC1 6F 7 (5J 83)
Galesbury Rd. SW18 6A 118
Gales Gdns. E2 3H 85
Gale St. E3 5C 86
RM9: Dag 5C 72
Gales Way IG8: Wfd G 7H 37
Galgate Cl. SW19 1F 135
Gallants Farm Rd. EN4: E Barn 7H 21
Galleon Cl. DA8: Erith 4K 109
SE16 2K 103
Galleon Ho. E14 4E 104
(off Glengarnock Av.)
Galleons Dr. IG11: Bark 3A 90
Galleons Vw. E14 2E 104
Galleria Ct. SE15 6F 103
The Galleria Shop. Mall 2J 51
The Galleries NW8 1A 4
(off Abbey Rd.)
The Gallery 1G 89
(off Clockhouse Av.)
The Gallery E20 6E 68
(within Westfield Shop. Cen.)
SE14 7B 104
(off New Cross Rd.)
Gallery Apts. E1 6J 85
(off Commercial Rd.)
SE1 7G 15
(off Lamb Wlk.)
The Gallery at London Glassblowing
6G 15
Gallery By The Pool 3J 103
Gallery Ct. E17 2E 50
(off Fulbourne Rd.)
SE1 7E 14
(off Pilgrimage St.)
SW10 6A 100
(off Gunter Gro.)
Gallery Gdns. UB5: N'olt 2B 76
Gallery Ho. E8 6H 67
(off Hackney Gro.)
Gallery Rd. SE21 1D 138
The Galley E16 7F 89
Galleymead Rd. SL3: Poyle 4A 174
Galleywall Rd. SE16 4H 103
Galleywall Rd. Trad. Est. SE16 4H 103
Galleywood Ho. W10 5E 80
(off Sutton Way)
Galliard Cl. N9 6D 24
Galliard Ct. N9 6B 24
Galliard Rd. N9 1B 34
Gallia Rd. N5 5B 66
Gallica Ct. SM1: Sutt 1K 165
Gallions Cl. IG11: Bark 3A 90
Gallions Reach Shop. Pk. E6 5G 89
Gallions Rd. E16 7F 89
SE7 4K 105
(not continuous)
GALLIONS RDBT. 7F 89
Gallions Vw. Rd. SE28 2J 107
Gallipoli Pl. RM9: Dag 1B 90
Gallon Cl. SE7 4A 106
The Gallop CR2: Sels 7H 169
SM2: Sutt 7B 166
Gallosson Rd. SE18 4J 107
Galloway Path CR0: C'don 4D 168
Galloway Rd. W12 1C 98
Gallus Cl. N21 6E 22
Gallus Sq. SE3 3K 123
Galpins Rd. CR7: Thor H 5J 155
Galsworthy Av. E14 6A 86
RM6: Chad H 7B 54
Galsworthy Cl. NW2 4G 63
SE28 1B 108
Galsworthy Cres. SE3 7A 106
Galsworthy Ho. W11 6G 81
(off Elgin Cres.)
Galsworthy Rd. KT2: King T 7H 133
NW2 4G 63
Galsworthy Ter. N16 3D 66
Galton Ct. NW9 3A 44
(off Joslin Av.)
Galton St. W10 3G 81
Galva Cl. EN4: Cockf 4K 21
Galvani Way CR0: Wadd 1K 167
Galveston Ho. E1 4A 86
(off Harford St.)
Galveston Rd. SW15 5H 117
Galway Cl. SE16 5H 103
(off Masters Dr.)
Galway Ho. E1 5K 85
(off White Horse La.)
EC1 2D 8
Galway St. EC1 2D 8 (3C 84)
Gambado
Beckenham 6C 140
Chelsea 1A 118
(off Station Ct.)
Gambetta St. SW8 2F 119
Gambia St. SE1 5B 14 (1B 102)
Gambier Ho. EC1 2D 8
(off Mora St.)
Gambole Rd. SW17 4C 136
Games Rd. EN4: Cockf 3H 21
Gamlen Rd. SW15 4F 117
Gamma Ct. CR0: C'don 1D 168
(off Sydenham Rd.)
Gamuel Cl. E17 6C 50
Gander Grn. Cres. TW12: Hamp 1E 148
Gander Grn. La. SM1: Sutt 3H 165
SM3: Cheam 2G 165
Gandhi Cl. E17 6C 50
Gandolfi St. SE15 6E 102
Ganley Ct. SW11 3B 118
(off Winstanley Est.)
Ganton St. W1 2A 12 (7G 83)
GANTS HILL 6E 52
GANTS HILL 6E 52
Gantshill Cres. IG2: Ilf 5E 52
Gap Rd. SW19 5J 135
Garage Rd. W3 6G 79
Garand Ct. N7 5K 65
Garbett Ho. SE17 6B 102
(off Doddington Gro.)
Garbutt Pl. W1 5H 5 (5E 82)
Garda Ho. SE10 4G 105
(off Cable Wlk.)
Garden Av. CR4: Mitc 7F 137
DA7: Bex 3F 127
Garden City HA8: Edg 6B 28
Garden Cl. E4 5H 35
HA4: Ruis 2G 57
KT3: N Mald 4A 152
SE12 3K 141
SM6: W'gton 5J 167
SW15 7E 116
TW12: Hamp 5D 130
TW15: Ashf 6E 128
UB5: N'olt 1C 76
Garden Ct. CR0: C'don 2F 169
EC4 2J 13
HA7: Stan 5H 27
N12 5E 30
NW8 1A 4
(off Garden Rd.)
TW9: Kew 1F 115
TW12: Hamp 5D 130
W4 3J 97
W11 7G 81
(off Clarendon Rd.)
Gardener Gro. TW13: Hanw 2D 130
Gardeners Cl. N11 2K 31
SE9 3C 142
Gardeners Rd. CR0: C'don 1B 168
The Garden Halls WC1 2E 6 (3J 83)
Garden Ho. N2 2B 46
(off The Grange)
NW6 2K 81
(off Oxford Rd.)
SW7 3K 99
(off Cornwall Gdns.)

A-Z Big London 223

The Garden Ho's.—Gibson Gdns.

The Garden Ho's. W6 6F 99
(off Bothwell St.)
Gardenia Rd. BR1: Broml 3E 160
EN1: Enf 6K 23
Gardenia Way IG8: Wfd G 6D 36
Garden La. BR1: Broml 6K 141
SW2 1K 137
Garden M. SE10 4G 105
W2 7J 81
The Garden Mus. 2G 19 (3K 101)
Garden Pl. E8 1F 85
Garden Rd. BR1: Broml 7K 141
KT12: Walt T 6K 147
NW8 1A 4 (3A 82)
SE20 1J 157
TW9: Rich 3G 115
Garden Row SE1 3B 102
Garden Royal SW15 6F 117
The Gardens BR3: Beck 1E 158
E5 7F 49
HA1: Harr 6G 41
HA5: Pinn 6D 40
N8 4J 47
(not continuous)
SE22 4G 121
TW14: Felt 5F 111
Garden Sq. SW1 6H 17 (5E 100)
Garden St. E1 5K 85
Garden Ter. SW1 5C 18 (5H 101)
SW7 7D 10
Garden Wlk. BR3: Beck 1B 158
EC2 2G 9 (3E 84)
Gdn. Way NW10 6J 61
Gardiner Av. NW2 5E 62
Gardiner Cl. EN3: Pond E 6E 24
RM8: Dag 4D 72
Gardiner Ct. CR2: S Croy 6D 168
Gardiner Ho. SW11 1C 118
Gardner Cl. E11 6K 51
Gardner Ct. EC1 3A 8
(off Brewery Sq.)
N5 4C 66
Gardner Ho. TW13: Hanw 2D 130
UB1: S'hall 7B 76
(off The Broadway)
Gardner Ind. Est. BR3: Beck 5B 140
Gardner Pl. TW14: Felt 6K 111
Gardner Rd. E13 4K 87
Gardners La. EC4 2C 14 (7C 84)
Gardnor Rd. NW3 4B 64
Gard St. EC1 1B 8 (3B 84)
Garendon Gdns.
SM4: Mord 7K 153
Garendon Rd. SM4: Mord 7K 153
Garenne Ct. E4 1K 35
Gareth Cl. KT4: Wor Pk 2F 165
Gareth Ct. SW16 3H 137
Gareth Dr. N9 2B 34
Gareth Gro. BR1: Broml 4J 141
Garfield EN2: Enf 5J 23
(off London Rd.)
Garfield Ct. NW6 7G 63
(off Willesden La.)
Garfield M. SW11 3E 118
Garfield Rd. E4 1A 36
E13 4H 87
EN3: Pond E 4D 24
SW11 3E 118
SW19 5A 136
TW1: Twick 1A 132
Garford St. E14 7C 86
Garganey Ct. NW10 6K 61
(off Elgar Av.)
Garganey Wlk. SE28 7C 90
Garibaldi St. SE18 4J 107
Garland Cl. SE1 3C 102
Garland Ct. E14 7C 86
(off Premiere Pl.)
SE17 4C 102
(off Wansey St.)
Garland Dr. TW3: Houn 2G 113
Garland Ho. KT2: King T 1E 150
(off Skerne Rd.)
UB7: W Dray 2B 92
Garland Rd. HA7: Stan 1E 42
SE18 7H 107
Garlands Ct. CR0: C'don 4D 168
(off Chatsworth Rd.)
Garlands Ho. NW8 2A 82
(off Carlton Hill)
Garlands La. HA1: Harr 1K 59
Garlick Hill EC4 2D 14 (7C 84)
Garlies Rd. SE23 3A 140
Garlinge Ho. SW9 1A 120
(off Gosling Way)
Garlinge Rd. NW2 6H 63
Garman Cl. N18 5J 33
Garman Rd. N17 7C 34
(not continuous)
Garnault M. EC1 2K 7
Garnault Pl. EC1 2K 7 (3A 84)
Garnault Rd. EN1: Enf 1A 24
Garner Cl. RM8: Dag 1D 72
Garner Ct. TW19: Stanw 6A 110
(off Douglas Rd.)
Garner Rd. E17 1E 50
Garner St. E2 2G 85
Garnet Ho. E1 1J 103
(off Garnet St.)
Garnet Pl. UB7: Yiew 1A 92
Garnet Rd. CR7: Thor H 4C 156
NW10 6A 62
Garnet St. E1 7J 85
Garnett Cl. SE9 3D 124
Garnett Rd. NW3 5D 64
Garnett Way E17 1A 50
(off McEntee Av.)
Garnet Wlk. E6 5C 88
Garnham Cl. N16 2F 67
Garnham St. N16 2F 67
Garnies Cl. SE15 7F 103
Garrad's Rd. SW16 3H 137
Garrard Cl. BR7: Chst 5F 143
DA7: Bex 3G 127
Garrard Wlk. NW10 6A 62
Garratt Cl. CR0: Bedd 4J 167
CR7: Thor H 2C 156
Garratt Ct. SW18 7K 117
Garratt La. SW17 6K 117
SW18 6K 117
Garratt Rd. HA8: Edg 7B 28
Garratts Rd. WD23: Bush 1B 26
Garratt Ter. SW17 4C 136
Garraway Ct. SW13 7E 98
(off Wyatt Dr.)
Garrett Cl. W3 5K 79
Garrett Ho. SE1 6A 14
(off Burrows M.)
Garrett St. EC1 3D 8 (4C 84)
Garrick Av. NW11 6G 45
Garrick Cl. SW18 4A 118
TW9: Rich 5D 114
W5 4E 78
Garrick Ct. E8 7F 67
(off Jacaranda Gro.)
Garrick Cres. CR0: C'don 2E 168
Garrick Dr. NW4 2E 44
SE28 3H 107
Garrick Gdns. KT8: W Mole 3E 148
Garrick Ho. KT1: King T 4E 150
(off Surbiton Rd.)
W1 5J 11
W4 6A 98
Garrick Ind. Cen. NW9 5B 44
Garrick Pk. NW4 2F 45
Garrick Rd. NW9 6B 44
TW9: Rich 2G 115
UB6: G'frd 4F 77
Garricks Ho. KT1: King T 2D 150
(off Wadbrook St.)
Garrick St. WC2 2E 12 (7J 83)
Garrick Theatre 3E 12
(off Charing Cross Rd.)
Garrick Way NW4 4F 45
Garrick Yd. WC2 2E 12
Garrison Cl. SE18 7E 106
TW4: Houn 5D 112
Garrison La. KT9: Chess 7D 162
Garrison Rd. E3 1C 86
Garrison Sq.
SW1 5H 17 (5E 100)
Garrowsfield EN5: Barn 6C 20
Garry Way RM1: Rom 1K 55
Garsdale Cl. N11 6K 31
Garsdale Ter. W14 5H 99
(off Aisgill Av.)
Garside Cl. SE28 3H 107
TW12: Hamp 6F 131
Garside Ct. TW11: Hamp W 1C 150
Garsington M. SE4 3B 122
Garson Ho. W2 2A 10
(off Gloucester Ter.)
Garston Ho. N1 7B 66
(off The Sutton Est.)
Garter Way SE16 2K 103
The Garth HA3: Kenton 6F 43
TW12: Hamp H 6F 131
Garth Cl. HA4: Ruis 1B 58
KT2: King T 5F 133
SM4: Mord 7F 153
Garth Ct. HA1: Harr 6K 41
(off Northwick Pk. Rd.)
W4 5K 97
Garth Ho. NW2 2H 63
Garth M. W5 4E 78
Garthorne Rd. SE23 7K 121
Garthorne Road Nature Reserve 7K 121
Garth Rd. KT2: King T 5F 133
NW2 2H 63
SM4: Mord 6E 152
W4 5K 97
The Garth Rd. Ind. Cen.
SM4: Mord 1F 165
Garthside TW10: Ham 5E 132
Garthway N12 6H 31
Gartmoor Gdns. SW19 1H 135
Gartmore Rd. IG3: Ilf 2K 71
Garton Pl. SW18 6A 118
Gartons Cl. EN3: Pond E 4D 24
Gartons Way SW11 3A 118
Garvary Rd. E16 6K 87
Garway Ct. E3 2C 86
(off Matilda Gdns.)
Garway Rd. W2 6K 81
Garwood Cl. N17 1H 49
Gascoigne Cl. N17 1F 49
Gascoigne Gdns. IG8: Wfd G 7B 36
Gascoigne Pl. E2 1J 9 (3F 85)
(not continuous)
Gascoigne Rd. CR0: New Ad 7F 171
IG11: Bark 1G 89
Gascony Av. NW6 7J 63
Gascony Pl. W12 1F 99
Gascoyne Ho. E9 7A 68
Gascoyne Rd. E9 7K 67
Gaselee St. E14 1E 104
(off Baffin Way)
Gasholder Pk. 1H 83
Gaskarth Rd. HA8: Edg 1J 43
SW12 6F 119
Gaskell Ct. SE20 7K 139
Gaskell Rd. N6 6D 46
Gaskell St. SW4 2J 119
Gaskin St. N1 1B 84
Gaspar Cl. SW5 4K 99
Gaspar M. SW5 4K 99
Gassiot Rd. SW17 4D 136
Gassiot Way SM1: Sutt 3B 166
Gasson Ho. SE14 6K 103
(off John Williams Cl.)
Gastein Rd. W6 6F 99
Gastigny Ho. EC1 2D 8
Gaston Bell Cl. TW9: Rich 3F 115
Gaston Bri. Rd. TW17: Shep 6F 147
Gaston Rd. CR4: Mitc 3E 154
Gaston Way TW17: Shep 5F 147
Gataker Ho. SE16 3H 103
(off Slippers Pl.)
Gataker St. SE16 3H 103
Gatcombe Ct. BR3: Beck 7C 140
Gatcombe Ho. SE22 3E 120
Gatcombe M. W5 7F 79
Gatcombe Rd. E16 1J 105
N19 3H 65
Gatcombe Way EN4: Cockf 3J 21
Gateacre Ct. DA14: Sidc 4B 144
The Gate Cen. TW8: Bford 7A 96
Gate Cinema 1J 99
(off Notting Hill Ga.)
The Gatefold Bldg. UB3: Hayes 3G 93
Gateforth St. NW8 4C 4 (4C 82)
Gate Hill Ct. W11 1H 99
(off Ladbroke Ter.)
Gate Ho. E3 1A 86
(off Gunmakers La.)
N1 7D 66
(off Ufton Rd.)
NW6 2K 81
(off Oxford Rd.)
Gatehouse Cl. KT2: King T 7J 133
Gatehouse Sq. SE1 4D 14
Gateley Ho. SE4 4K 121
(off Coston Wlk.)
Gateley Rd. SW9 3K 119
Gate Lodge W9 5J 81
(off Admiral Wlk.)
Gately Ct. SE15 7F 103
Gate M. SW7 7D 10
Gater Dr. EN2: Enf 1J 23
Gatesborough St. EC2 3G 9 (4E 84)
Gates Cnr. Cl. E18 1J 51
Gates Ct. SE17 5C 102
Gatesden WC1 2G 7 (3J 83)
Gates Grn. Rd. BR2: Kes 3H 171
BR4: W W'ck 3H 171
Gateside Rd. SW17 3D 136
Gatestone Ct. SE19 6E 138
(off Central Hill)
Gatestone Rd. SE19 6E 138
Gate St. WC2 7G 7 (6K 83)
The Gate Theatre 1J 99
(off Pembridge Rd.)
Gateway SE17 6C 102
Gateway Apartments E17 5C 50
Gateway Arc. N1 2B 84
(off Upper St.)
Gateway Bus. Cen. SE26 6A 140
SE28 3H 107
Gateway Ct. IG2: Ilf 6E 52
(off Parham Dr.)
Gateway Ho. IG11: Bark 1G 89
Gateway Ind. Est. NW10 3B 80
Gateway M. E8 5F 67
N11 6B 32
Gateway Retail Pk. 4F 89
Gateway Rd. E10 3D 68
Gateways KT6: Surb 5E 150
(off Surbiton Hill Rd.)
The Gateways SW3 4D 16 (4C 100)
TW9: Rich 4D 114
(off Park La.)
Gateways Ct. SM6: W'gton 5F 167
Gateway Sq. N18 6D 34
Gatfield Gro. TW13: Hanw 2E 130
Gatfield Ho. TW13: Hanw 2D 130
Gathorne Rd. N22 2A 48
Gathorne St. E2 2K 85
Gatley Av. KT19: Ewe 5H 163
Gatliff Cl. SW1 6H 17
Gatliff Rd. SW1 6J 17 (5F 101)
Gatling Rd. SE2 5A 108
Gatonby St. SE15 1F 121
Gatting Cl. HA8: Edg 7D 28
Gatting Way UB8: Uxb 6A 56
Gattis Wharf N1 2J 83
(off New Wharf Rd.)
Gatton Cl. SM2: Sutt 7K 165
Gatton Rd. SW17 4C 136
Gattons Way DA14: Sidc 4F 145
Gatward Cl. N21 6G 23
Gatward Grn. N9 2A 34
Gatwick Ho. E14 6B 86
(off Clemence St.)
Gatwick Rd. SW18 7H 117
Gauden Cl. SW4 3H 119
Gauden Rd. SW4 2H 119
Gaudi Apts. N8 3K 47
(off Gt. Amwell La.)
Gaugin Ct. SE16 5H 103
(off Stubbs Dr.)
Gaugin Sq. E1 7G 85
Gaumont Pl. SW2 2J 137
Gaumont Ter. W12 2E 98
(off Lime Gro.)
Gaumont Twr. E8 6F 67
(off Dalston Sq.)
Gauntlet NW9 2B 44
(off Five Acre)
Gauntlet Cl. UB5: N'olt 7C 58
Gauntlett Ct. HA0: Wemb 5B 60
Gauntlett Rd. SM1: Sutt 5B 166
Gaunt St. SE1 3C 102
Gautrey Rd. SE15 2J 121
Gautrey Sq. E6 6D 88
Gavel St. SE17 4D 102
Gaverick M. E14 4C 104
Gavestone Cres. SE12 7A 124
Gavestone Rd. SE12 7K 123
Gaviller Pl. E5 4H 67
Gavina Cl. SM4: Mord 5C 154
Gavin Ho. SE18 4J 107
Gawain Wlk. N9 3B 34
Gawber St. E2 3J 85
Gawsworth Cl. E15 5H 69
Gawthorne Ct. E3 2C 86
Gay Cl. NW2 5D 62
Gaydon Ho. W2 5K 81
(off Bourne Ter.)
Gaydon La. NW9 1A 44
Gayfere Pl. SE25 2E 156
(off Grange Hill)
Gayfere Rd. IG5: Ilf 3D 52
KT17: Ewe 5C 164
Gayfere St. SW1 2E 18 (3J 101)
Gayford Rd. W12 2B 98
Gay Gdns. RM10: Dag 4J 73
Gay Ho. N16 5E 66
Gayhurst SE17 6D 102
(off Hopwood Rd.)
Gayhurst Ct. UB5: N'olt 3A 76
Gayhurst Ho. NW8 3C 4
(off Mallory St.)
Gayhurst Rd. E8 7G 67
Gaylor Rd. UB5: N'olt 5D 58
Gaymead NW8 1K 81
(off Abbey Rd.)
Gaynesford Rd. SE23 2K 139
SM5: Cars 7D 166
Gaynes Hill Rd. IG8: Wfd G 6H 37
Gay Rd. E15 2F 87
Gaysham Av. IG2: Ilf 5E 52
Gaysham Hall IG5: Ilf 3F 53
Gaysley Ho. SE11 4J 19
Gay St. SW15 3F 117
Gayton HA1: Harr 7J 41
(off Grove Hill)
Gayton Ct. HA1: Harr 6K 41
Gayton Cres. NW3 4B 64
Gayton Ho. E3 4C 86
(off Chiltern Rd.)
Gayton Rd. HA1: Harr 6K 41
NW3 4B 64
SE2 3C 108
Gayville Rd. SW11 6D 118
Gaywood Cl. SW2 1K 137
Gaywood Rd. E17 3C 50
Gaywood St. SE1 3B 102
Gaza St. SE17 5B 102
Gazelle Ho. E15 6G 69
Gean Ct. E11 4F 69
N11 6B 32
(off Cline Rd.)
Geariesville Gdns. IG6: Ilf 4F 53
Gearing Cl. SW17 4E 136
Geary Rd. NW10 5C 62
Geary St. N7 5K 65
Geddes Pl. DA6: Bex 4G 127
(off Arnsberg Way)
Gedeney Rd. N17 1C 48
Gedling Ct. SE1 7K 15
(off Sweeney Cres.)
Gedling Pl. SE1 7K 15 (3F 103)
Geere Rd. E15 1H 87
Gees Ct. W1 1H 11 (6E 82)
Gee St. EC1 3C 8 (4C 84)
Geffery's Ct. SE9 3C 142
Geffrye Ct. N1 2E 84
Geffrye Est. N1 2E 84
Geffrye Mus. 1J 9 (2F 85)
Geffrye St. E2 1J 9 (2F 85)
Geldart Rd. SE15 7H 103
Geldeston Rd. E5 2G 67
Gellatly Rd. SE14 2J 121
Gell Cl. UB10: Ick 3B 56
Gelsthorpe Rd. RM5: Col R 1H 55
Gem Ct. SE10 7D 104
(off Merryweather Pl.)
Gemini Apts. E1 3K 9
(off Sclater St.)
Gemini Bus. Cen. E16 4F 87
Gemini Bus. Est. SE14 5K 103
Gemini Bus. Pk. E6 5F 89
Gemini Ct. E1 7G 85
(off Vaughan Way)
Gemini Gro. UB5: N'olt 3C 76
Gemini Ho. E3 1C 86
(off Garrison Rd.)
Gemini Pl. TW15: Ashf 6G 129
Genas Cl. IG6: Ilf 1F 53
General Gordon Pl. SE18 4F 107
General Gordon Sq. SE18 4F 107
(off Woolwich New Rd.)
General Wolfe Rd. SE10 1F 123
Genesis Bus. Pk. NW10 2H 79
Genesis Cl. TW19: Stanw 1B 128
Genesta Rd. SE18 6F 107
Geneva Cl. TW17: Shep 2G 147
Geneva Ct. NW9 5B 44
Geneva Dr. SW9 4A 120
Geneva Gdns. RM6: Chad H 5E 54
Geneva Rd. CR7: Thor H 5C 156
KT1: King T 4E 150
Genever Cl. E4 5H 35
Genista Rd. N18 5C 34
Genoa Av. SW15 5E 116
Genoa Ho. E1 4K 85
(off Ernest St.)
SW18 3A 118
Genoa Rd. SE20 1J 157
Genotin Rd. EN1: Enf 3J 23
Genotin Ter. EN1: Enf 3J 23
Gentlemans Row EN2: Enf 3H 23
Gentry Gdns. E13 4J 87
Geoff Cade Way E3 5B 86
Geoffrey Chaucer Way E3 5B 86
Geoffrey Cl. SE5 2C 120
Geoffrey Ct. SE4 2B 122
Geoffrey Gdns. E6 2C 88
Geoffrey Ho. SE1 7F 15
(off Pardoner St.)
Geoffrey Jones Ct. NW10 1C 80
Geoffrey Rd. SE4 3B 122
George V Av. HA5: Pinn 2D 40
George V Cl. HA5: Pinn 3E 40
George V Way UB6: G'frd 1B 78
George Beard Rd. SE8 4B 104
George Belt Ho. E2 3K 85
(off Smart St.)
George Comberton Wlk. E12 5E 70
George Ct. TW15: Ashf 4B 128
(off Church Rd.)
UB3: Hayes 5H 75
WC2 3F 13
George Cres. N10 7K 31
George Davies Lodge IG6: Ilf 5G 53
(off Veronique Gdns.)
George Downing Est. N16 2F 67
George Eliot Ho. SE17 5C 102
(off Thrush St.)
SW1 4B 18
(off Vauxhall Bri. Rd.)
George Elliston Ho. SE1 5G 103
(off Old Kent Rd.)
George Eyre Ho. NW8 2B 82
(off Cochrane St.)
George Furness Ho. NW10 6D 62
(off Grange Rd.)
George Gange Way HA3: W'stone 3J 41
George Gillett Ct. EC1 3D 8
George Groves Rd. SE20 1G 157
George Hilsdon Ct. E14 6A 86
(off Repton St.)
George Ho. NW6 2H 81
(off Albert Rd.)
George Hudson Twr. E15 2D 86
(off High St.)
George Inn Yd. SE1 5E 14 (1D 102)
George La. BR2: Hayes 1K 171
E18 2J 51
SE6 6D 122
SE13 6D 122
George Lansbury Ho. E3 3B 86
(off Bow Rd.)
N22 1A 48
(off Progress Way)
NW10 7A 62
George Leybourne Ho. E1 7G 85
(off Fletcher St.)
George Lindgren Ho. SW6 7H 99
(off Clem Attlee Ct.)
George Loveless Ho. E2 1K 9
(off Diss St.)
George Lowe Ct. W2 5K 81
(off Bourne Ter.)
George Mathers Rd. SE11 4B 102
George M. EN2: Enf 3J 23
NW1 2B 6
SW9 2A 120
George Padmore Ho. E8 1G 85
(off Brougham Rd.)
George Peabody Ct. NW1 5C 4
(off Burne St.)
George Peabody St. E13 2A 88
George Pl. N17 3E 48
George Potter Ho. SW11 2B 118
(off George Potter Way)
George Potter Way SW11 2B 118
George Rd. E4 6H 35
KT2: King T 7H 133
KT3: N Mald 4B 152
George Row SE16 2G 103
George Scott Ho. E1 6K 85
(off W. Arbour St.)
George Sq. SW19 3J 153
George's Rd. N7 5K 65
George's Sq. SW6 6H 99
(off North End Rd.)
George St. CR0: C'don 2C 168
E16 6H 87
IG11: Bark 7G 71
TW3: Houn 2D 112
TW9: Rich 5D 114
UB2: S'hall 4C 94
W1 7E 4 (6D 82)
W7 1J 95
Georgetown Cl. SE19 5E 138
Georgette Pl. SE10 7E 104
George Vale Ho. E2 2G 85
(off Mansford St.)
George Vw. Ho. SW18 1K 135
(off Knaresborough Dr.)
Georgeville Gdns. IG6: Ilf 4F 53
George Walter Ct. SE16 4J 103
(off Millender Wlk.)
George Wyver Cl. SW19 7G 117
George Yd. EC3 1F 15 (6D 84)
W1 2H 11 (7E 82)
Georgia Ct. SE16 3G 103
(off Priter Rd.)
Georgiana St. NW1 1G 83
Georgian Cl. BR2: Hayes 1K 171
HA7: Stan 7F 27
UB10: Ick 4A 56
Georgian Ct. CR0: C'don 1D 168
(off Cross Rd.)
E9 1J 85
EN5: New Bar 4F 21
HA9: Wemb 6G 61
N3 1H 45
NW4 5D 44
SW16 4J 137
Georgian Ho. E16 1J 105
(off Capulet M.)
N1 1E 84
(off Hertford Rd.)
Georgian Way HA1: Harr 2H 59
Georgia Rd. CR7: Thor H 1B 156
KT3: N Mald 4J 151
Georgina Gdns. E2 1K 9 (3F 85)
Geotgette Ct. SW18 5K 117
(off Courthouse Way)
Geraint Rd. BR1: Broml 4J 141
Geraldine Rd. SW18 5A 118
W4 6G 97
Geraldine St. SE11 2K 19 (3B 102)
Gerald M. SW1 3H 17
Gerald Pl. E8 6F 67
(off Dalston Sq.)
Gerald Rd. E16 4H 87
RM8: Dag 1F 73
SW1 3H 17 (4E 100)
Gerard Av. TW4: Houn 7E 112
Gerard Gdns. RM13: Rain 2K 91
Gerard Pl. E9 7K 67
Gerard Rd. HA1: Harr 6A 42
SW13 1B 116
Gerards Cl. SE16 5J 103
Gerards Pl. SW4 4H 119
Gerda Rd. SE9 2G 143
Germander Way E15 3G 87
Gernigan Ho. SW18 6B 118
Gernon Rd. E3 2A 86
Geron Way NW2 1D 62
Gerrard Gdns. HA5: Eastc 5J 39
Gerrard Ho. SE14 7J 103
(off Briant St.)
Gerrard Pl. W1 2D 12 (7H 83)
Gerrard Rd. N1 2B 84
Gerrards Cl. N14 5B 22
Gerrards Ct. W5 3D 96
Gerrard St. W1 2D 12 (7H 83)
Gerrard Way SE3 4A 124
Gerridge Ct. SE1 1K 19
(off Gerridge St.)
Gerridge St. SE1 1K 19 (3A 102)
Gerry Raffles Sq. E15 6F 69
Gertrude Rd. DA17: Belv 4G 109
Gertrude St. SW10 7A 16 (6A 100)
Gervase Cl. HA9: Wemb 3J 61
Gervase Rd. HA8: Edg 1J 43
Gervase St. SE15 7H 103
Gervis Ct. TW7: Isle 7G 95
Ghent St. SE6 2C 140
Ghent Way E8 6F 67
The Gherkin 1H 15
Giant Arches Rd. SE24 7C 120
Giant Tree Hill WD23: B Hea 1C 26
Gibbfield Cl. RM6: Chad H 3E 54
Gibbings Ho. SE1 7B 14
(off King James St.)
Gibbins Rd. E15 7E 68
Gibbon Ho. NW8 4B 4
(off Fisherton St.)
Gibbon Rd. KT2: King T 1E 150
SE15 2J 121
W3 7A 80
Gibbons M. NW11 5H 45
Gibbon's Rents SE1 5G 15
Gibbons Rd. NW10 6A 62
Gibbon Wlk. SW15 4C 116
Gibbs Av. SE19 5D 138
Gibbs Cl. SE19 6D 138
Gibbs Grn. HA8: Edg 4D 28
W14 5H 99
(not continuous)
Gibbs Ho. BR1: Broml 1H 159
(off Longfield)
Gibbs La. E2 2G 85
Gibb's Rd. N18 4D 34
Gibbs Sq. SE19 5D 138
Gibney Ter. BR1: Broml 4H 141
Gibraltar Wlk. E2 2K 9
Gibson Cl. E1 4J 85
KT9: Chess 5C 162
N21 6F 23
TW7: Isle 3J 113
Gibson Ct. SE9 5A 124
Gibson Gdns. N16 2F 67

224 A-Z Big London

Gibson Ho.—Globe Rd.

Gibson Ho. SM1: Sutt 4J 165
Gibson M. TW1: Twick 6C 114
Gibson Rd. RM8: Dag 1C 72
SE11 4H 19 (4K 101)
SM1: Sutt 5K 165
UB10: Ick 4B 56
Gibsons Hill SW16 7A 138
(not continuous)
Gibsons Pl. TW8: Bford 6D 96
(off Sidney Gdns.)
Gibson Sq. N1 1A 84
Gibson Sq. Gdns. 1A 84
(off Gibson Sq.)
Gibson St. SE10 5G 105
Gideon Cl. DA17: Belv 4H 109
HA8: Edg 6B 28
Gideon M. W5 2D 96
Gideon Rd. SW11 3E 118
Gielgud Theatre 2C 12
(off Shaftesbury Av.)
Giesbach Rd. N19 2H 65
Giffard Rd. N18 6K 33
Giffin Sq. Mkt. 7C 104
(off Giffin St.)
Giffin St. SE8 7C 104
Gifford Gdns. W7 5H 77
Gifford Ho. SE10 5F 105
(off Eastney St.)
SW1 6A 18
(off Churchill Gdns.)
Gifford Rd. NW10 7A 62
Gifford St. N1 7J 65
Gift La. E15 1G 87
GIGGSHILL 7A 150
Giggs Hill BR5: St P 2K 161
Giggs Hill Gdns. KT7: T Ditt 1A 162
Giggs Hill Rd. KT7: T Ditt 7A 150
GILBERT BRI. 5D 8
(off Wood St.)
Gilbert Cl. SE18 1D 124
SW19 1K 153
(off Morden Rd.)
Gilbert Ct. W5 6F 79
(off Green Va.)
Gilbert Gro. HA8: Edg 1K 43
Gilbert Ho. E2 3K 85
(off Usk St.)
E17 3E 50
EC2 5D 8
SE8 6C 104
SW1 6K 17
(off Churchill Gdns.)
SW8 7J 101
(off Wyvil Rd.)
SW13 7D 98
(off Trinity Chu. Rd.)
Gilbert Pl. WC1 6E 6 (5J 83)
Gilbert Rd. BR1: Broml 7J 141
DA17: Belv 3G 109
HA5: Pinn 4B 40
SE11 4K 19 (4A 102)
SW19 7A 136
UB9: Hare 2A 38
Gilbert Scott Bldg. SW15 6G 117
Gilbert Scott Cl. HA0: Wemb 5D 60
Gilbert Scott Ho. W14 4H 99
(off Warwick La.)
Gilbert Sheldon Ho. W2 5B 4
(off Edgware Rd.)
Gilbertson Ho. E14 3C 104
(off Mellish St.)
Gilbert St. E15 4G 69
TW3: Houn 3G 113
W1 1H 11 (6E 82)
Gilbert Way CR0: Wadd 2K 167
Gilbert White Cl. UB6: G'frd 1A 78
Gilbey Cl. UB10: Ick 4D 56
Gilbey Ho. NW1 7F 65
Gilbey Rd. SW17 4C 136
Gilbeys Yd. NW1 7E 64
Gilbourne Rd. SE18 6K 107
Gilby Ho. E9 6K 67
Gilda Av. EN3: Pond E 5F 25
Gilda Ct. NW7 1C 44
Gilda Cres. N16 1G 67
Gildea Cl. HA5: Hat E 1E 40
Gildea St. W1 6K 5 (5F 83)
Gilden Cres. NW5 5E 64
Gildersome St. SE18 6E 106
Gilders Rd. KT9: Chess 7F 163
Giles Coppice SE19 4F 139
Giles Cres. UB10: Uxb 1B 74
(off St Andrews Rd.)
Giles Ho. E15 6F 69
(off Forrester Way)
W11 6J 81
(off Westbourne Gro.)
Gilesmead SE5 1D 120
Gilford Ho. IG1: Ilf 2F 71
(off Clements Rd.)
Gilfrid Cl. UB8: Hil 6D 74
Gilkes Cres. SE21 6E 120
Gilkes Pl. SE21 6E 120
Gillan Ct. SE12 3K 141
Gillan Grn. WD23: B Hea 2B 26
Gillards M. E17 4C 50
Gillards Way E17 4C 50
Gill Av. E16 6J 87
Gillender St. E3 4E 86
E14 4E 86
Gillespie Pk. Local Nature Reserve
3A 66
Gillespie Rd. N5 3A 66
Gillett Av. E6 2C 88
GILLETTE CORNER 7A 96
Gillett Ho. N8 3J 47
(off Campsfield Rd.)
Gillett Pl. N16 5E 66
Gillett Rd. CR7: Thor H 4D 156
Gillett Sq. N16 5E 66
(off Gillett St.)
Gillett St. N16 5E 66
Gillfoot NW1 1A 6
(off Hampstead Rd.)
Gillham Ter. N17 6B 34
Gillian Ho. HA3: Hrw W 6D 26
Gillian Lynne Theatre 7F 7
(off Parker St.)
Gillian Pk. Rd. SM3: Sutt 1H 165
Gillian St. SE13 5D 122
Gillies Ho. NW6 7B 64
(off Hilgrove Rd.)
Gillies St. NW5 5E 64
Gilling Ct. NW3 6C 64
Gillingham M. SW1 3A 18 (4G 101)
Gillingham Rd. NW2 3G 63
Gillingham Row SW1 3A 18 (4G 101)
Gillingham St. SW1 3A 18 (4G 101)
Gillings Ct. EN5: Barn 4B 20
(off Wood St.)
Gillison Wlk. SE16 3H 103
Gillis Sq. SW15 6C 116
Gillman Dr. E15 1H 87
Gillman Ho. E2 2G 85
(off Pritchard's Rd.)
Gillray Ho. SW10 6B 100
(off Ann La.)
Gill St. E14 6B 86
Gillum Cl. EN4: E Barn 1J 31
Gilman Ho. N1 7A 66
(off Drummond Way)
Gilmore Cl. UB10: Ick 3C 56
Gilmore Ct. N11 5J 31
Gilmore Cres. TW15: Ashf 5C 128
Gilmore Rd. SE13 4F 123
Gilmour Ho. NW9 2C 44
Gilpin Av. SW14 4K 115
Gilpin Cl. CR4: Mitc 2C 154
W2 5A 4
(off Porteus Rd.)
Gilpin Cres. N18 5A 34
TW2: Whitt 7F 113
Gilpin Rd. E5 4A 68
Gilpin Way UB3: Harl 7F 93
Gilray Ho. W2 2A 10
(off Gloucester Ter.)
Gilsland Pl. CR7: Thor H 4D 156
Gilsland Rd. CR7: Thor H 4D 156
Gilson Pl. N10 7J 31
Gilstead Rd. SW6 2K 117
Gilston Rd. SW10 7A 16 (5A 100)
Gilton Rd. SE6 3G 141
Giltspur St. EC1 7B 8 (6B 84)
Gilwell Cl. E4 4J 25
Gilwell La. E4 4K 25
(not continuous)
GILWELL PARK 4K 25
Gilwell Pk. E4 3K 25
Ginger Apts. SE1 6K 15
(off Cayenne Ct.)
Ginsburg Yd. NW3 4A 64
Gippeswyck Cl. HA5: Pinn 1B 40
Gipsy Hill SE19 4E 138
Gipsy La. SW15 3D 116
Gipsy Rd. DA16: Well 7D 108
SE27 4C 138
Gipsy Rd. Gdns. SE27 4C 138
Giralda Cl. E16 5B 88
Giraud St. E14 6D 86
Girdler's Rd. W14 4F 99
Girdlestone Wlk. N19 2G 65
Girdwood Rd. SW18 7G 117
Girling Ho. N1 1E 84
(off Colville Est.)
Girling Way TW14: Felt 3J 111
Gironde Rd. SW6 7H 99
Girtin Ho. UB5: N'olt 2B 76
(off Academy Gdns.)
Girton Av. NW9 3G 43
Girton Cl. UB5: N'olt 6G 59
Girton Gdns. CR0: C'don 3C 170
Girton Rd. SE26 5K 139
UB5: N'olt 6G 59
Girton Vs. W10 6F 81
Gisbourne Cl. SM6: Bedd 3H 167
Gisburn Ho. SE15 6G 103
(off Friary Est.)
Gisburn Rd. N8 4K 47
Gissing Wlk. N1 7A 66
Gittens Cl. BR1: Broml 4H 141
Given Wilson Wlk. E13 2H 87
Giverny Ho. SE16 2K 103
(off Water Gdns. Sq.)
Glacier Ho. SW11 7H 101
(off Ponton Rd.)
Glacier Pl. E2 2H 85
(off Clare St.)
Glacier Way HA0: Wemb 2D 78
Gladbeck Way EN2: Enf 4G 23
Gladding Rd. E12 4B 70
The Glade BR1: Broml 2B 160
BR4: W W'ck 3D 170
CR0: C'don 5K 157
E8 6G 67
EN2: Enf 3F 23
IG5: Ilf 1D 52
IG8: Wfd G 3E 36
KT17: Ewe 6C 164
N12 3G 31
N21 6E 22
SE7 7A 106
SM2: Cheam 7G 165
W12 2D 98
(off Coningham Rd.)
Glade Apts. E14 4E 104
(off Stebondale St.)
Glade Cl. KT6: Surb 2D 162
Glade Ct. IG5: Ilf 1D 52
Glade Gdns. CR0: C'don 7A 158
Glade La. UB2: S'hall 2F 95
Glade Path SE1 2B 102
(off Blackfriars Rd.)
The Glades 2J 159
The Glades KT6: Surb 7E 150
Gladeside CR0: C'don 6K 157
N21 6E 22
Gladeside Cl. KT9: Chess 7D 162
Gladesmore Community School &
Sports Cen. 5G 49
Gladesmore Rd. N15 6F 49
Glades Pl. BR1: Broml 2J 159
Gladeswood Rd.
DA17: Belv 4H 109
Glade Wlk. E20 6D 68
Gladiator St. SE23 7A 122
Glading Ter. N16 3F 67
Gladioli Cl. TW12: Hamp 6E 130
Gladsaxe Ho. SM1: Sutt 4K 165
Gladsdale Dr. HA5: Pinn 4J 39
Gladsmuir Rd. EN5: Barn 2B 20
N19 1G 65
Gladstone Av. E12 7C 70
N22 2A 48
TW2: Twick 1H 131
TW14: Felt 6J 111
Gladstone Ct. NW6 7A 64
(off Fairfax Rd.)
SW1 4D 18
(off Regency St.)
Gladstone Ct. Bus. Cen. SW8 1F 119
(off Pagden St.)
Gladstone Gdns. TW3: Houn 1G 113
Gladstone Ho. CR4: Mitc 2D 154
E14 6C 86
(off E. India Dock Rd.)
Gladstone M. N22 2A 48
NW6 7H 63
(off Cavendish Rd.)
SE20 7J 139
Gladstone Pde. NW2 2E 62
Gladstone Pk. Gdns. NW2 4D 62
Gladstone Pl. E3 2B 86
EN5: Barn 4A 20
KT8: E Mos 5J 149
Gladstone Rd. BR6: Farnb 5G 173
CR0: C'don 7D 156
IG9: Buck H 1F 37
KT1: King T 3G 151
KT6: Surb 2D 162
SW19 7J 135
UB2: S'hall 2C 94
W4 3K 97
Gladstone St. SE1 3B 102
Gladstone Ter. SE27 5C 138
(off Bentons La.)
SW8 1F 119
Gladstone Way HA3: W'stone 3J 41
Gladwell Rd. BR1: Broml 6J 141
N8 6K 47
Gladwin Ho. NW1 1B 6
(off Werrington St.)
Gladwyn Rd. SW15 3F 117
Gladys Ct. BR1: Broml 2H 141
Gladys Dimson Ho. E7 5H 69
Gladys Rd. NW6 7J 63
Glaisher St. SE8 6C 104
Glamis Ct. W3 2H 97
Glamis Cres. UB3: Harl 3E 92
Glamis Pl. E1 7J 85
Glamis Rd. E1 7J 85
Glamis Way UB5: N'olt 6G 59
Glamorgan Cl. CR4: Mitc 3J 155
Glamorgan Ct. W7 5K 77
(off Copley Cl.)
Glamorgan Rd. KT1: Hamp W 7C 132
Glandford Way RM6: Chad H 5B 54
Glanfield Rd. BR3: Beck 4B 158
Glanleam Rd. HA7: Stan 4J 27
Glanville M. HA7: Stan 5F 27
Glanville Rd. BR2: Broml 3K 159
SW2 5J 119
Glasbrook Av. TW2: Whitt 1D 130
Glasbrook Rd. SE9 7B 124
Glaserton Rd. N16 7E 48
Glasford St. SW17 6D 136
Glasfryn Ct. HA2: Harr 2H 59
(off Roxeth Hill)
Glasfryn Ho. HA2: Harr 2H 59
(off Roxeth Hill)
Glasgow Ho. W9 2K 81
(off Maida Vale)
Glasgow Rd. E13 2K 87
N18 5C 34
Glasgow Ter. SW1 6A 18 (5G 101)
Glasier Ct. E15 7G 69
Glaskin M. E9 6A 68
Glass Blowers Ho. E14 6F 87
(off Valencia Cl.)
The Glass Bldg. NW1 1F 83
(off Jamestown Rd.)
Glasse Cl. W13 7A 78
Glass Foundry Yd. E13 5K 87
(off Denmark St.)
Glasshill St. SE1 6B 14 (2B 102)
Glass Ho. WC2 1E 12
(off Shaftesbury Av.)
The Glass Ho. SE1 7G 15
(off Royal Oak Yd.)
Glasshouse Cl. UB8: Hil 5D 74
Glasshouse Flds. E1 7K 85
(not continuous)
Glasshouse Gdns. E20 7E 68
Glasshouse Gdns. Development
E20 7D 68
Glasshouse St. W1 3B 12 (7G 83)
Glasshouse Wlk. SE11 5F 19 (5J 101)
Glasshouse Yd. EC1 4C 8 (4C 84)
Glasslyn Rd. N8 5H 47
Glassmill La. BR2: Broml 2H 159
Glass Mill Leisure Cen. 3E 122
Glass St. E2 4H 85
Glassworks Studios E2 1H 9
(off Basing Pl.)
Glass Yd. SE18 3E 106
Glastonbury Av. IG8: Wfd G 7G 37
Glastonbury Ct. SE14 7J 103
(off Farrow La.)
Glastonbury Ho. SE12 5H 123
(off Wantage Rd.)
SW1 5J 17
(part of Abbots Mnr.)
Glastonbury Pl. E1 6J 85
Glastonbury Rd. N9 1B 34
SM4: Mord 7J 153
Glastonbury St. NW6 5H 63
Glaston Ct. W5 1D 96
(off Grange Rd.)
Glaucus St. E3 5D 86
Glazbury Rd. W14 4G 99
Glazebrook Cl. SE21 2D 138
Glazebrook Rd. TW11: Tedd 7K 131
The Glebe BR7: Chst 1G 161
KT4: Wor Pk 1B 164
SE3 3G 123
SW16 4H 137
UB7: W Dray 4B 92
Glebe Av. CR4: Mitc 2C 154
EN2: Enf 3G 23
HA3: Kenton 4E 42
HA4: Ruis 6K 57
IG8: Wfd G 6D 36
UB10: Ick 3E 56
Glebe Cl. UB10: Ick 4E 56
W4 5A 98
Glebe Cotts. TW13: Hanw 3E 130
(off Twickenham Rd.)
Glebe Ct. CR4: Mitc 3D 154
E3 3D 86
(off Rainhill Way)
HA7: Stan 5H 27
N13 3F 33
SE3 3G 123
W5 1D 96
W7 7H 77
Glebe Cres. HA3: Kenton 3E 42
NW4 4E 44
Glebe Farm Bus. Pk. BR2: Kes 7B 172
Glebe Gdns. KT3: N Mald 7A 152
Glebe Ho. SE16 3H 103
(off Slippers Pl.)
Glebe Ho. Dr. BR2: Hayes 1K 171
Glebe Hyrst SE19 4E 138
Glebe Knoll BR2: Broml 2H 159
Glebeland Gdns. TW17: Shep 6E 146
Glebelands E10 2D 68
KT8: W Mole 5F 149
Glebelands Av. E18 2J 51
IG2: Ilf 7H 53
Glebelands Cl. N12 1B 46
SE5 3E 120
Glebelands Rd. TW14: Felt 1J 129
Glebe La. HA3: Kenton 4E 42
Glebe M. DA15: Sidc 6K 125
Glebe Path CR4: Mitc 3D 154
Glebe Pl. SW3 7C 16 (6C 100)
Glebe Rd. BR1: Broml 1J 159
E8 7F 67
HA7: Stan 5H 27
N3 1A 46
N8 4K 47
NW10 6C 62
RM10: Dag 6H 73
SM2: Cheam 7G 165
SM5: Cars 6D 166
SW13 2C 116
UB3: Hayes 1H 93
Glebe Side TW1: Twick 6K 113
Glebe Sq. CR4: Mitc 3D 154
Glebe St. W4 5A 98
Glebe Ter. W4 5A 98
Glebe Way BR4: W W'ck 2E 170
IG8: Wfd G 5F 37
TW13: Hanw 3E 130
Gledhow Gdns. SW5 4A 100
Gledstanes Rd. W14 5G 99
Gledwood Av. UB4: Hayes 5H 75
Gledwood Ct. UB4: Hayes 5H 75
Gledwood Cres. UB4: Hayes 5H 75
Gledwood Dr. UB4: Hayes 5H 75
Gledwood Gdns. UB4: Hayes 5H 75
Gleed Av. WD23: B Hea 2C 26
Gleeson Dr. BR6: Chels 5K 173
Glegg Pl. SW15 4F 117
The Glen BR2: Broml 2G 159
BR6: Farnb 3D 172
CR0: C'don 3K 169
EN2: Enf 4G 23
HA5: Eastc 5K 39
HA5: Pinn 7C 40
HA9: Wemb 4E 60
UB2: S'hall 5D 94
Glenaffric Av. E14 4E 104
Glen Albyn Rd. SW19 2F 135
Glenallan Ho. W14 4H 99
(off North End Cres.)
Glenalla Rd. HA4: Ruis 7H 39
Glenalmond Ho. TW15: Ashf 3A 128
Glenalmond Rd. HA3: Kenton 4E 42
Glenalvon Way SE18 4C 106
Glena Mt. SM1: Sutt 4A 166
Glenarm Rd. E5 4J 67
Glen Av. TW15: Ashf 4C 128
Glenavon Cl. KT10: Clay 6A 162
Glenavon Ct. KT4: Wor Pk 2D 164
Glenavon Lodge BR3: Beck 7C 140
Glenavon Rd. E15 7G 69
Glenbarr Cl. SE9 3F 125
Glenbow Rd. BR1: Broml 6G 141
Glenbrook Nth. EN2: Enf 4E 22
Glenbrook Rd. NW6 5J 63
Glenbrook Sth. EN2: Enf 4E 22
Glenbuck Ct. KT6: Surb 6E 150
Glenbuck Rd. KT6: Surb 6D 150
Glenburnie Rd. SW17 3D 136
Glencairn Dr. W5 4C 78
Glencairne Cl. E16 5B 88
Glencairn Rd. SW16 1J 155
Glencar Ct. SE19 6B 138
Glen Cl. TW17: Shep 4C 146
Glencoe Av. IG2: Ilf 7H 53
Glencoe Dr. RM10: Dag 4G 73
Glencoe Mans. SW9 7A 102
(off Mowll St.)
Glencoe Rd. UB4: Yead 5B 76
Glen Ct. BR1: Broml 7H 141
(off Bromley Av.)
DA15: Sidc 4A 144
Glen Cres. IG8: Wfd G 6E 36
Glendale Av. HA8: Edg 4A 28
N22 7F 33
RM6: Chad H 7C 54
Glendale Cl. SE9 3E 124
Glendale Dr. SW19 5H 135
Glendale Gdns. HA9: Wemb 1D 60
Glendale M. BR3: Beck 1D 158
Glendale Rd. DA8: Erith 4J 109
Glendale Way SE28 7C 90
Glendall St. SW9 4K 119
Glendarvon St. SW15 3F 117
Glendevon Cl. HA8: Edg 3C 28
Glendish Rd. N17 1H 49
Glendor Gdns. NW7 4E 28
Glendower Gdns. SW14 3K 115
Glendower Pl. SW7 3A 16 (4B 100)
Glendower Rd. E4 1A 36
SW14 3K 115
Glendown Ho. E8 5H 67
Glendown Rd. SE2 5G 108
Glendun Ct. W3 7A 80
Glendun Rd. W3 7A 80
Gleneagle M. SW16 5H 137
Gleneagle Rd. SW16 5H 137
Gleneagles HA7: Stan 7G 27
W13 5B 78
(off Malvern Way)
Gleneagles Cl. BR6: Orp 1H 173
SE16 5H 103
Gleneagles Grn. BR6: Orp 1H 173
Gleneagles Twr. UB1: S'hall 6G 77
(off Fleming Rd.)
Gleneldon M. SW16 4J 137
Gleneldon Rd. SW16 4J 137
Glenelg Rd. SW2 5J 119
Glenesk Rd. SE9 3E 124
Glenfarg Rd. SE6 1E 140
Glenfield Cres. HA4: Ruis 7F 39
Glenfield Rd. SW12 1G 137
TW15: Ashf 6D 128
W13 2B 96
Glenfield Ter. W13 2B 96
Glenfinlas Way SE5 7B 102
Glenforth St. SE10 5H 105
Glengall Bus. Cen. SE15 6F 103
Glengall Gro. E14 3D 104
Glengall Pas. NW6 1J 81
(off Priory Pk. Rd.)
Glengall Rd. DA7: Bex 3E 126
HA8: Edg 3C 28
IG8: Wfd G 6D 36
NW6 1H 81
SE15 5F 103
Glengall Ter. SE15 6F 103
Glen Gdns. CR0: Wadd 3A 168
Glengariff Mans. SW9 7A 102
(off Sth. Island Pl.)
Glengarnock Av. E14 4E 104
Glengarry Rd. SE22 5E 120
Glenham Dr. IG2: Ilf 5F 53
Glenhead Cl. SE9 3F 125
Glenhill Cl. N3 2J 45
Glen Ho. E16 1E 106
(off Storey St.)
Glenhouse Rd. SE9 5E 124
Glenhurst BR3: Beck 1E 158
Glenhurst Av. DA5: Bexl 1F 145
HA4: Ruis 7E 38
NW5 4E 64
Glenhurst Ct. SE19 5F 139
Glenhurst Ri. SE19 7C 138
Glenhurst Rd. N12 5G 31
TW8: Bford 6C 96
Glenilla Rd. NW3 6C 64
Glenister Gdns. UB3: Hayes 2K 93
Glenister Ho. UB3: Hayes 1K 93
(off Avondale Dr.)
Glenister Pk. Rd. SW16 7H 137
Glenister Rd. SE10 5H 105
Glenister St. E16 1E 106
Glenkerry Ho. E14 6E 86
(off Burcham St.)
Glenlea Rd. SE9 5D 124
Glenloch Rd. EN3: Enf H 2D 24
NW3 6C 64
Glenluce Rd. SE3 6J 105
Glenlyon Rd. SE9 5E 124
Glenmead IG9: Buck H 1F 37
Glenmere Av. NW7 7H 29
Glenmere Row SE12 6J 123
Glen M. E17 5B 50
Glenmill TW12: Hamp 5D 130
Glenmore Lawns W13 6A 78
Glenmore Lodge BR3: Beck 1D 158
Glenmore Pde. HA0: Wemb 1E 78
Glenmore Rd. DA16: Well 7K 107
NW3 6C 64
Glenmore Way IG11: Bark 2A 90
Glenmount Path SE18 5G 107
Glennie Ct. SE22 1G 139
Glennie Rd. SE27 3A 138
Glenny Rd. IG11: Bark 6G 71
Glenorchy Cl. UB4: Yead 5C 76
Glenpark Ct. W13 7A 78
Glenparke Rd. E7 6K 69
Glenridding NW1 1B 6
(off Ampthill Est.)
Glen Ri. IG8: Wfd G 6E 36
Glen Rd. E13 4A 88
E17 5B 50
KT9: Chess 4F 163
Glen Rd. End SM6: W'gton 7F 167
Glenrosa St. SW6 2A 118
Glenrose Ct. DA14: Sidc 5B 144
SE1 7G 15
(off Long La.)
Glenroy St. W12 6E 80
Glensdale Rd. SE4 3B 122
Glenshaw Mans. SW9 7A 102
(off Brixton Rd.)
Glenshiel Rd. SE9 5E 124
Glentanner Way SW17 3B 136
Glen Ter. E14 2E 104
(off Manchester Rd.)
Glentham Gdns. SW13 6D 98
Glentham Rd. SW13 6C 98
Glenthorne Av. CR0: C'don 1H 169
Glenthorne Cl. SM3: Sutt 1J 165
UB10: Hil 3C 74
Glenthorne Gdns. IG6: Ilf 3E 52
SM3: Sutt 1J 165
Glenthorne M. W6 4D 98
Glenthorne Rd. E17 5A 50
KT1: King T 4F 151
N11 5J 31
W6 4D 98
Glenthorpe Av. SW15 4C 116
Glenthorpe Gdns. HA7: Stan 3E 26
Glenthorpe Rd. SM4: Mord 5F 153
Glenton M. SE15 2J 121
Glenton Rd. SE13 4G 123
Glentrammon Av. BR6: Chels 6K 173
Glentrammon Cl. BR6: Chels 5K 173
Glentrammon Gdns. BR6: Chels 6K 173
Glentrammon Rd. BR6: Chels 6K 173
Glentworth St. NW1 4F 5 (4D 82)
Glenure Rd. SE9 5E 124
Glenvern Ct. TW7: Isle 2A 114
(off White Lodge Cl.)
Glenview SE2 6D 108
Glenview Rd. BR1: Broml 2B 160
Glenville Av. EN2: Enf 1H 23
Glenville Gro. SE8 7B 104
Glenville M. SW18 7K 117
Glenville M. Ind. Est. SW18 7J 117
Glenville Rd. KT2: King T 1G 151
Glen Wlk. TW7: Isle 5H 113
(not continuous)
Glenwood Av. NW9 1A 62
Glenwood Cl. HA1: Harr 5K 41
Glenwood Ct. DA14: Sidc 4A 144
E18 3J 51
Glenwood Gdns. IG2: Ilf 5E 52
Glenwood Gro. NW9 1J 61
Glenwood Rd. KT17: Ewe 6C 164
N15 5B 48
NW7 3F 29
SE6 1B 140
TW3: Houn 3H 113
Glenwood Way CR0: C'don 6K 157
Glenworth Av. E14 4F 105
Gliddon Dr. E5 4H 67
Gliddon Rd. W14 4G 99
Glimpsing Grn. DA18: Erith 3E 108
Glisson Rd. UB10: Hil 2C 74
Global App. E3 2E 86
Globe Apts. SE8 6B 104
(off Evelyn St.)
Globe Ho. E14 6G 87
Globe Pond Rd. SE16 1A 104
Globe Rd. E1 3J 85
E2 3J 85

Globe Rd.—Grace's Rd.

Globe Rd. E15 5H 69
IG8: Wfd G 6F 37
Globe St. SE1 7E 14 (3D 102)
Globe Ter. E2 3J 85
GLOBE TOWN 3K 85
Globe Town Mkt. 3K 85
Globe Vw. EC4 2C 14
(off High Timber St.)
Globe Wharf SE16 7K 85
Globe Yd. W1 1J 11
Glossop Rd. CR2: Sande 7D 168
Gloster Ridley Ct. E14 6B 86
(off St Anne's Row)
Gloster Rd. KT3: N Mald 4A 152
Gloucester W14 4H 99
(off Kensington Village)
Gloucester Arc. SW7 4A 100
Gloucester Av. DA15: Sidc 2J 143
DA16: Well 4K 125
NW1 7E 64
Gloucester Cir. SE10 7E 104
Gloucester Cl. KT7: T Ditt 1A 162
NW10 7K 61
Gloucester Ct. CR4: Mitc 5J 155
EC3 3H 15 (7E 84)
HA1: Harr 3J 41
NW11 7H 45
(off Golders Grn. Rd.)
SE1 5F 103
(off Rolls Rd.)
SE1 7B 14
(Swan St.)
SE22 1G 139
TW9: Kew 7G 97
W7 5K 77
(off Copley Cl.)
Gloucester Cres. NW1 1F 83
TW18: Staines 6A 128
Gloucester Dr. N4 2B 66
NW11 4J 45
Gloucester Gdns. EN4: Cockf 4K 21
IG1: Ilf 7C 52
NW11 7H 45
SM1: Sutt 2K 165
W2 6A 82
Gloucester Ga. NW1 2F 83
(not continuous)
GLOUCESTER GA. BRI. 1F 83
(off Gloucester Gate)
Gloucester Ga. M. NW1 2F 83
Gloucester Gro. HA8: Edg 1K 43
Gloucester Ho. E16 1J 105
(off Gatcombe Rd.)
NW6 2J 81
(off Cambridge Rd.)
SW9 7A 102
TW10: Rich 5G 115
Gloucester M. E10 7C 50
W2 1A 10 (6A 82)
Gloucester M. W. W2 6A 82
Gloucester Pde. DA15: Sidc 5A 126
UB3: Harl 3E 92
Gloucester Pk. Apts. SW7 4A 100
(off Ashburn Pl.)
Gloucester Pl. NW1 4E 4 (4D 82)
W1 4E 4 (4D 82)
Gloucester Pl. M. W1 6F 5 (5D 82)
Gloucester Rd. CR0: C'don 1D 168
DA17: Belv 5F 109
E10 7C 50
E11 5K 51
E12 3D 70
E17 2K 49
EN2: Enf 1H 23
EN5: New Bar 5E 20
HA1: Harr 5F 41
KT1: King T 2G 151
N17 2D 48
N18 5A 34
SW7 4A 16 (3A 100)
TW2: Twick 1G 131
TW4: Houn 4C 112
TW9: Kew 7G 97
TW11: Tedd 5J 131
TW12: Hamp 7F 131
TW13: Felt 1A 130
W3 2J 97
W5 2C 96
Gloucester Sq. E2 1G 85
W2 1B 10 (6B 82)
(not continuous)
Gloucester St. SW1 6A 18 (5G 101)
Gloucester Ter. N14 1C 32
(off Crown La.)
W2 1A 10 (6K 81)
Gloucester Wlk. W8 2J 99
Gloucester Way EC1 2K 7 (3A 84)
Glover Cl. SE2 4C 108
Glover Dr. N18 6D 34
Glover Ho. NW6 7A 64
(off Harben Rd.)
SE15 4H 121
Glover Rd. HA5: Pinn 6B 40
Glovers Gro. HA4: Ruis 7D 38
Gloxinia Wlk. TW12: Hamp 6E 130
Glycena Rd. SW11 3D 118
Glyn Av. EN4: E Barn 4G 21
Glyn Cl. SE25 2E 156
Glyn Ct. HA7: Stan 6G 27
SW16 3A 138
Glyndale Grange SM2: Sutt 6K 165
Glyndebourne Ct. UB5: N'olt 3A 76
(off Canberra Dr.)
Glyndebourne Pk. BR6: Farnb 2F 173
Glynde M. SW3 2D 16
Glynde Reach WC1 2F 7
Glynde Rd. DA7: Bex 3D 126
Glynde St. SE4 6B 122
Glyndon Rd. SE18 4G 107
(not continuous)
Glyn Dr. DA14: Sidc 4B 144
Glynfield Rd. NW10 7A 62
Glyn Mans. W14 4G 99
(off Hammersmith Rd.)
Glynne Rd. N22 2A 48
Glyn Rd. E5 4K 67
EN3: Pond E 4D 24
KT4: Wor Pk 2F 165
Glyn St. SE11 6G 19 (5K 101)
Glynswood Pl. HA6: Nwood 1D 38
Glynwood Ct. SE23 2J 139
Goals Soccer Cen.
Bexleyheath 3F 127
Chingford 6H 35
Dagenham 1D 90
Eltham 6A 124
Goals Soccer Cen.
Gillette Corner 6K 95
Hayes 1A 94
Heathrow 4E 92
Ruislip 5B 58
Sutton 3F 165
Tolworth 2J 163
Wimbledon 3C 152
Go Ape!
Alexandra Palace 2H 47
Battersea Park 1D 118
Trent Park 3K 21
Goater's All. SW6 7H 99
(off Dawes Rd.)
GOAT HO. BRI. 3G 157
Goat La. EN1: Enf 1A 24
Goat Rd. CR4: Cars, Mitc 7D 154
Goat Wharf TW8: Bford 6E 96
Gobions Av. RM5: Col R 1K 55
Goby Ho. SE8 7D 104
(off Creative Rd.)
Godalming Av. SM6: W'gton 5J 167
Godalming Rd. E14 5D 86
Godbold Rd. E15 4G 87
Goddard Cl. TW17: Shep 3B 146
Goddard Ct. HA3: Kenton 2A 42
Goddard Ho. SE11 4B 102
(off George Mathers Rd.)
Goddard Pl. N19 3G 65
Goddard Rd. BR3: Beck 4K 157
Goddards Way IG1: Ilf 1H 71
Goddarts Ho. E17 3C 50
Goddington La. BR6: Chels 3K 173
Godfree Ct. SE1 6E 14
(off Long La.)
Godfrey Av. TW2: Whitt 7H 113
UB5: N'olt 1C 76
Godfrey Hill SE18 4C 106
Godfrey Ho. EC1 2E 8
Godfrey Pl. E2 2J 9
(off Austin St.)
Godfrey Rd. SE18 4D 106
Godfrey St. E15 2E 86
SW3 5D 16 (5C 100)
Godfrey Way TW4: Houn 7C 112
Goding St. SE11 5F 19 (5J 101)
Godley Cl. SE14 1J 121
Godley Rd. SW18 1B 136
Godliman St. EC4 1B 14 (6B 84)
Godman Rd. SE15 2H 121
Godolphin Cl. N13 6G 33
Godolphin Ho. NW3 7C 64
(off Fellows Rd.)
Godolphin Pl. W3 7K 79
Godolphin Rd. W12 1D 98
(not continuous)
Godric Cres. CR0: New Ad 7F 171
Godson Rd. CR0: Wadd 3A 168
Godson St. N1 2A 84
Godson Yd. NW6 3J 81
Godstone Ho. SE1 7F 15
(off Pardoner St.)
Godstone Rd. SM1: Sutt 4A 166
TW1: Twick 6B 114
Godstow Rd. SE2 2B 108
Godward Sq. E1 4K 85
Godwin Cl. E4 1K 25
KT19: Ewe 6J 163
N1 2C 84
Godwin Ct. NW1 2G 83
(off Chalton St.)
Godwin Ho. E2 2F 85
(off Thurtle Rd.)
SE1 5J 15
(off Still Wlk.)
Godwin Rd. BR2: Broml 3A 160
E7 4K 69
Goffers Rd. SE3 1G 123
Goffs Rd. TW15: Ashf 6F 129
Goidel Cl. SM6: Bedd 4H 167
Golborne Gdns. W10 4G 81
(not continuous)
Golborne M. W10 5G 81
Golborne Rd. W10 5G 81
Golda Cl. EN5: Barn 6A 20
Golda Ct. N3 2H 45
Goldbeaters Gro. HA8: Edg 6F 29
Goldbeaters Ho. W1 1D 12
(off Manette St.)
Goldcliff Cl. SM4: Mord 7J 153
Goldcrest Cl. E16 5B 88
SE28 7C 90
Goldcrest M. N16 3G 67
W5 5D 78
Goldcrest Way CR0: New Ad 7F 171
WD23: Bush 1B 26
Golden Anchor House SE10 3J 105
(off Latimer Square)
Golden Bus. Pk. E10 1A 68
Golden Ct. EN4: E Barn 4H 21
TW7: Isle 2H 113
TW9: Rich 5D 114
Golden Cres. UB3: Hayes 1H 93
Golden Cross M. W11 6H 81
(off Portobello Rd.)
Golden Hinde 4E 14 (1D 102)
Golden Hind Pl. SE8 4B 104
(off Grove St.)
GOLDEN JUBILEE BRIDGES 5G 13
Golden La. BR4: W W'ck 3E 170
EC1 3C 8 (4C 84)
Golden La. Campus EC1 4C 8
Golden La. Est. EC1 4C 8 (4C 84)
Golden Lane Sport & Fitness Centre 4C 8
Golden Mnr. W7 7J 77
Golden M. SE20 1J 157
Golden Mile Ho. TW8: Bford 5E 96
(off Clayponds La.)
Golden Pde. E17 3E 50
(off Wood St.)
Golden Plover Cl. E16 6J 87
Golden Sq. W1 2B 12 (7G 83)
Golden Yd. NW3 4A 64
(off Holly Mt.)
Golders Cl. HA8: Edg 5C 28
Golders Ct. NW11 7H 45
Golders Gdns. NW11 7G 45
GOLDERS GREEN 6G 45
Golders Grn. Crematorium 7J 45
Golders Grn. Cres. NW11 7H 45
Golders Grn. Rd. NW11 6G 45
Golderslea NW11 1J 63
Golders Mnr. Dr. NW11 6F 45
Golders Pk. Cl. NW11 1J 63
Golders Ri. NW4 5F 45
Golders Way NW11 7H 45
Golderton NW4 4D 44
(off Prince of Wales Cl.)
Goldfinch Ct. E3 2C 86
(off Four Seasons Cl.)
Goldfinch Rd. SE28 3H 107
Goldhawk Ho. NW9 2C 44
Goldhawk M. W12 2D 98
Goldhawk Rd. W6 4B 98
W12 4B 98
Goldhaze Cl. IG8: Wfd G 7F 37
Gold Hill HA8: Edg 6E 28
Goldhurst Ho. W6 6E 98
Goldhurst Mans. NW6 6A 64
(off Goldhurst Ter.)
Goldhurst Ter. NW6 7K 63
Goldie Ho. N19 7H 47
Golding Cl. KT9: Chess 6C 162
N18 6J 33
Golding Ct. IG1: Ilf 3E 70
Golding Ho. NW9 2C 44
Golding St. E1 6G 85
(not continuous)
Golding Ter. E1 6G 85
(off Rope Wlk. Gdns.)
SW11 2E 118
Goldington Bldgs. NW1 1H 83
(off Royal College St.)
Goldington Cres. NW1 2H 83
Goldington St. NW1 2H 83
Gold La. HA8: Edg 6E 28
Goldman Cl. E2 3K 9 (4G 85)
Goldney Rd. W9 4J 81
Goldrill Dr. N11 2K 31
Goldsboro' Rd. SW8 1H 119
Goldsborough Cres. E4 2J 35
Goldsborough Ho. E14 5D 104
(off St Davids Sq.)
Goldsdown Cl. EN3: Enf H 2F 25
Goldsdown Rd. EN3: Enf H 2E 24
Goldsmid St. SE18 5J 107
Goldsmith Av. E12 6C 70
NW9 5A 44
RM7: Rush G 7G 55
W3 7K 79
Goldsmith Cl. HA2: Harr 1E 58
Goldsmith Ct. WC2 7F 7
(off Stukeley St.)
Goldsmith Est. SE15 1G 121
Goldsmith La. NW9 4H 43
Goldsmith Rd. E10 1C 68
E17 2K 49
N11 5J 31
SE15 1G 121
W3 1K 97
Goldsmith's Bldgs. W3 1K 97
Goldsmiths Cl. W3 1K 97
Goldsmiths College 1A 122
Goldsmith's Pl. NW6 1K 81
(off Springfield La.)
Goldsmith's Row E2 2G 85
Goldsmith's Sq. E2 2G 85
Goldsmith St. EC2 7D 8 (6C 84)
Goldsworthy Gdns. SE16 5J 103
Goldthorpe NW1 1G 83
(off Camden St.)
Goldwell Ho. SE22 3E 120
(off Quorn Rd.)
Goldwell Rd. CR7: Thor H 4K 155
Goldwin Cl. SE14 1J 121
Goldwing Cl. E16 6J 87
Golf Cl. CR7: Thor H 1A 156
HA7: Stan 7H 27
Golf Club Dr. KT2: King T 7K 133
Golfe Rd. IG1: Ilf 3H 71
Golf Kingdom
Barking 5F 55
Golf Rd. BR1: Broml 3E 160
W5 6F 79
Golf Side TW2: Twick 3H 131
Golfside Cl. KT3: N Mald 2A 152
N20 3H 31
Gollogly Ter. SE7 5A 106
Gomer Gdns. TW11: Tedd 6A 132
Gomer Pl. TW11: Tedd 6A 132
Gomm Rd. SE16 3J 103
Gomshall Av. SM6: W'gton 5J 167
Gondar Gdns. NW6 5H 63
Gonson St. SE8 6D 104
Gonston Cl. SW19 2G 135
Gonville Cres. UB5: N'olt 6F 59
Gonville Rd. CR7: Thor H 5K 155
Gonville St. SW6 3G 117
Gooch Ho. E5 3H 67
EC1 5J 7
(off Portpool La.)
SW11 7H 101
(off Malthouse Rd.)
Goodall Ho. SE4 4K 121
Goodall Rd. E11 3E 68
Goodchild Rd. N4 1C 66
Gooden Ct. HA1: Harr 3J 59
Goodenough Rd. SW19 7H 135
Goodey Rd. IG11: Bark 7K 71
Goodfaith Ho. E14 7D 86
(off Simpson's Rd.)
Goodge Pl. W1 6B 6 (5G 83)
Goodge St. W1 6B 6 (5G 83)
Goodhall Cl. HA7: Stan 6F 27
Goodhall St. NW10 3B 80
(not continuous)
Goodhart Pl. E14 7A 86
Goodhart Way BR4: W W'ck 7G 159
Goodhew Rd. CR0: C'don 6G 157
Goodhope Ho. E14 7D 86
(off Poplar High St.)
Gooding Cl. KT3: N Mald 4J 151
Goodinge Cl. N7 6J 65
Goodinge Rd. N7 6J 65
Gooding Ho. SE7 5A 106
Goodman Cres. CR0: C'don 6B 156
SW2 2J 137
Goodman Rd. E10 7E 50
Goodman's Ct. E1 2J 15 (7F 85)
Goodmans Ct. HA0: Wemb 4D 60
Goodman's Stile E1 6G 85
Goodmans Yd. E1 2J 15 (7F 85)
GOODMAYES 2A 72
Goodmayes Av. IG3: Ilf 1A 72
Goodmayes La. IG3: Ilf 4A 72
Goodmayes Lodge RM8: Dag 4A 72
Goodmayes Retail Pk. 1B 72
Goodmayes Rd. IG3: Ilf 1A 72
Goodrich Ct. W10 6F 81
Goodrich Ho. E2 2J 85
(off Sewardstone Rd.)
Goodrich Rd. SE22 6F 121
Goodridge Ho. E4 7K 35
Goodson Ho. SM4: Mord 7A 154
(off Green La.)
Goodson Rd. NW10 7A 62
Goodspeed Ho. E14 7D 86
(off Simpson's Rd.)
Goods Way N1 2J 83
Goodway Gdns. E14 6F 87
Goodwill Dr. HA2: Harr 1E 58
Goodwill Ho. E14 7D 86
(off Simpson's Rd.)
Goodwin Cl. CR4: Mitc 3B 154
SE16 3F 103
Goodwin Ct. EN4: E Barn 6H 21
N8 3J 47
(off Campsbourne Rd.)
SW19 7C 136
Goodwin Dr. DA14: Sidc 3D 144
Goodwin Gdns. CR0: Wadd 6B 168
Goodwin Ho. N9 1D 34
Goodwin Rd. CR0: Wadd 5B 168
N9 1E 34
W12 2C 98
Goodwins Ct. WC2 2E 12 (7J 83)
Goodwin St. N4 2A 66
Goodwood Apts. E4 7J 35
Goodwood Cl. HA7: Stan 5H 27
SM4: Mord 4J 153
Goodwood Ct. W1 5K 5
(off Devonshire St.)
Goodwood Dr. UB5: N'olt 6E 58
Goodwood Ho. SE14 7A 104
(off Goodwood Rd.)
Goodwood Pde. BR3: Beck 4A 158
Goodwood Rd. SE14 7A 104
Goodwyn Av. NW7 5F 29
Goodwyns Va. N10 1E 46
Goodyear Ho. N2 2B 46
(off The Grange)
Goodyear Pl. SE5 6C 102
Goodyer Ho. SW1 5C 18
(off Tachbrook St.)
Goodyers Gdns. NW4 5F 45
Goosander Way SE28 3H 107
Gooseacre La. HA3: Kenton 5D 42
Goose Grn. Trad. Est. SE22 4F 121
Gooseley La. E6 3E 88
(Claps Ga. La.)
E6 3E 88
(Folkestone Rd.)
Goosens Cl. SM1: Sutt 5A 166
Goose Sq. E6 6D 88
Gophir La. EC4 2E 14 (7D 84)
Gopsall St. N1 1D 84
Gordian Apts. SE10 4G 105
(off Cable Wlk.)
Gordon Av. E4 6B 36
HA7: Stan 7E 26
SW14 4A 116
TW1: Twick 5A 114
Gordonbrock Rd. SE4 5C 122
Gordon Cl. E17 6C 50
N19 1G 65
Gordon Cotts. W8 2K 99
(off Dukes La.)
Gordon Ct. HA8: Edg 5A 28
Gordon Cres. CR0: C'don 1E 168
UB3: Hayes 4J 93
Gordondale Rd. SW19 2J 135
Gordon Dr. TW17: Shep 7F 147
Gordon Gdns. HA8: Edg 2H 43
Gordon Gro. SE5 2B 120
Gordon Hill EN2: Enf 1H 23
Gordon Ho. E1 7J 85
(off Glamis Rd.)
SW1 2B 18
(off Greencoat Pl.)
W5 3E 78
Gordon Ho. Rd. NW5 4E 64
Gordon Mans. W14 3F 99
(off Addison Gdns.)
WC1 4C 6
(off Torrington Pl.)
Gordon Pl. W8 2J 99
Gordon Rd. BR3: Beck 3B 158
DA15: Sidc 5J 125
DA17: Belv 4J 109
E4 1B 36
E11 6J 51
E15 4E 68
E18 1K 51
EN2: Enf 1H 23
HA3: W'stone 3J 41
IG1: Ilf 3H 71
IG11: Bark 1J 89
KT2: King T 1F 151
KT5: Surb 7F 151
N3 7C 30
N9 2C 34
N11 7C 32
RM6: Chad H 6F 55
SE15 2H 121
SM5: Cars 6D 166
TW3: Houn 4G 113
TW9: Rich 2F 115
TW15: Ashf 3A 128
TW17: Shep 6F 147
UB2: S'hall 4C 94
UB7: Yiew 7A 74
W4 6H 97
W5 7B 78
W13 7B 78
Gordon Sq. WC1 3C 6 (4H 83)
Gordon St. E13 3J 87
WC1 3C 6 (4H 83)
Gordon Way BR1: Broml 1J 159
EN5: Barn 4C 20
Gore Ct. NW9 5G 43
Gorefield Ho. NW6 2J 81
(off Gorefield Pl.)
Gorefield Pl. NW6 2J 81
Gore Ho. N1 7A 66
(off Drummond Way)
Gore Rd. E9 1J 85
SW20 2E 152
GORESBROOK INTERCHANGE 2F 91
Goresbrook Rd. RM9: Dag 1B 90
Gore St. SW7 3A 100
Gorham Ho. SE16 2K 103
(off Wolfe Cres.)
Gorham Pl. W11 7G 81
Goring Cl. RM5: Col R 1J 55
Goring Gdns. RM8: Dag 4C 72
Goring Rd. N11 6D 32
RM10: Dag 6K 73
Goring St. EC3 7H 9
Goring Way UB6: G'frd 2G 77
Gorleston Rd. N15 5D 48
Gorleston St. W14 4G 99
(not continuous)
Gorman Rd. SE18 4D 106
Gorringe Pk. Av. CR4: Mitc 7D 136
Gorse Cl. E16 6J 87
Gorsefield Ho. E14 7C 86
(off E. India Dock Rd.)
Gorse Ri. SW17 5E 136
Gorse Rd. CR0: C'don 4C 170
Gorse Wlk. UB7: Yiew 6A 74
Gorseway RM7: Rush G 1K 73, 2K 73
Gorst Rd. NW10 4J 79
SW11 6D 118
Gorsuch Pl. E2 1J 9 (3F 85)
Gorsuch St. E2 1J 9 (2F 85)
Gosberton Rd. SW12 1D 136
Gosbury Hill KT9: Chess 4E 162
Gosfield Rd. RM8: Dag 2G 73
Gosfield St. W1 6A 6 (5G 83)
Gosford Gdns. IG4: Ilf 5D 52
Gosford Ho. E3 2B 86
(off Tredegar Rd.)
Goshawk Ct. NW9 7B 44
Goshawk Gdns. UB4: Hayes 3G 75
Goslett Yd. WC2 1D 12 (6H 83)
Gosling Cl. UB6: G'frd 3E 76
Gosling Ho. E1 7J 85
(off Sutton St.)
Gosling Way SW9 1A 120
Gospatrick Rd. N17 7H 33
GOSPEL OAK 4E 64
Gosport Rd. E17 5B 50
Gosport Wlk. N17 4H 49
Gossage Rd. SE18 5H 107
UB10: Uxb 7B 56
Gossamer Gdns. E2 2H 85
Gosse Ct. N1 1E 84
(off Downham Rd.)
Gosset St. E2 1K 9 (3F 85)
Gosshill Rd. BR7: Chst 2E 160
Gossington Cl. BR7: Chst 4F 143
Gosterwood St. SE8 6A 104
Gostling Rd. TW2: Whitt 1E 130
Goston Gdns. CR7: Thor H 3A 156
Goston Ga. SW8 1K 119
(off Hampson Way)
Goswell Pl. EC1 2B 8
Goswell Rd. EC1 1A 8 (2B 84)
Gothenburg Ct. SE8 4A 104
(off Bailey St.)
Gothic Cotts. EN2: Enf 2H 23
(off Chase Grn. Av.)
Gothic Ct. SE5 7C 102
(off Wyndham Rd.)
UB3: Harl 6F 93
Gothic Rd. TW2: Twick 2H 131
Gottfried M. NW5 4G 65
Goudhurst Rd. BR1: Broml 5G 141
Gough Ho. KT1: King T 2E 150
(off Eden St.)
N1 1B 84
(off Windsor St.)
Gough Rd. E15 4H 69
EN1: Enf 2C 24
Gough Sq. EC4 1K 13 (6A 84)
Gough St. WC1 3H 7 (4K 83)
Gough Wlk. E14 6C 86
Goulden Ho. SW11 2C 118
Goulden Ho. App. SW11 2C 118
Goulding Gdns. CR7: Thor H 2C 156
Gouldman Ho. E1 4J 85
(off Wyllen Cl.)
Gould Rd. TW2: Twick 1J 131
TW14: Felt 7G 111
GOULDS GREEN 5D 74
Gould's Grn. UB8: Hil 7D 74
Gould Ter. E8 5H 67
Gould Way HA8: Edg 7C 28
Goulston St. E1 7J 9 (6F 85)
Goulton Rd. E5 4H 67
Gourley Pl. N15 5E 48
Gourley St. N15 5E 48
Gourock Rd. SE9 5E 124
Govan St. E2 1G 85
Gover Ct. SW4 2J 119
Govett Av. TW17: Shep 5E 146
Govier Cl. E15 7G 69
Gowan Av. SW6 1G 117
Gowan Ho. E2 2K 9
(off Chambord St.)
Gowan Rd. NW10 6D 62
Gower Cl. SW4 6G 119
Gower Ct. WC1 3C 6 (4H 83)
Gower Ho. E17 3D 50
SE17 5C 102
(off Morecambe St.)
Gower M. WC1 6D 6 (5H 83)
Gower M. Mans. WC1 5D 6
(off Gower M.)
Gower Pl. WC1 3B 6 (4H 83)
Gower Rd. E7 6J 69
TW7: Isle 6K 95
Gower St. WC1 3B 6 (4G 83)
Gower's Wlk. E1 6G 85
Gowland Pl. BR3: Beck 2B 158
Gowlett Rd. SE15 3G 121
Gowlland Cl. CR0: C'don 7G 157
Gowrie Rd. SW11 3E 118
Graburn Way KT8: E Mos 3H 149
Grace Av. DA7: Bex 2F 127
Grace Bus. Cen. CR4: Mitc 6D 154
Gracechurch St. EC3 2F 15 (7D 84)
Grace Cl. HA8: Edg 7D 28
SE9 3B 142
Grace Ct. CR0: C'don 3B 168
(off Waddon Rd.)
SM2: Sutt 7K 165
Gracedale Rd. SW16 5F 137
Gracefield Gdns. SW16 3J 137
Gracehill E1 5J 85
(off Hannibal Rd.)
Grace Ho. SE11 7H 19
Grace Jones Cl. E8 6G 67
Grace M. BR3: Beck 6C 140
SE20 2J 157
(off Marlow Rd.)
Grace Path SE26 4J 139
Grace Pl. E3 3D 86
Grace Rd. CR0: C'don 6C 156
Graces All. E1 7G 85
Grace's M. SE5 2D 120
Graces M. NW8 2A 82
Grace's Rd. SE5 2E 120

Grace St.—Greenaway Ho.

Grace St. E3 3D 86
The Gradient SE26 4G 139
Graduate Pl. SE1 7F 15
Graeme Rd. EN1: Enf 2J 23
Graemesdyke Av. SW14 3H 115
Grafton Chambers *NW1* *2D 6*
(off Grafton Pl.)
Grafton Cl. KT4: Wor Pk 3A 164
TW4: Houn 1C 130
W13 6A 78
Grafton Ct. TW14: Bedf 1F 129
Grafton Cres. NW1 6F 65
Grafton Gdns. N4 6C 48
RM8: Dag 2E 72
Grafton Ho. *E3* *3C 86*
(off Wellington Way)
SE8 5B 104
Grafton M. W1 4A 6 (4G 83)
Grafton Pk. Rd. KT4: Wor Pk 2A 164
Grafton Pl. NW1 2D 6 (3H 83)
Grafton Rd. CR0: C'don 1A 168
EN2: Enf 3E 22
HA1: Harr 5G 41
KT3: N Mald 3A 152
KT4: Wor Pk 3K 163
NW5 5E 64
RM8: Dag 2E 72
W3 7J 79
The Graftons NW2 3J 63
Grafton Sq. SW4 3G 119
Grafton St. W1 3K 11 (7F 83)
Grafton Ter. NW5 5D 64
Grafton Way KT8: W Mole 4D 148
W1 4A 6 (4G 83)
(not continuous)
WC1 4A 6 (4G 83)
Grafton Yd. NW5 6F 65
Graham Av. CR4: Mitc 1E 154
W13 2B 96
Graham Cl. CR0: C'don 2C 170
Graham Ct. *SE14* *6K 103*
(off Myers La.)
UB5: N'olt 5C 58
GRAHAME PARK 1A 44
Grahame Pk. Way NW7 7G 29
NW9 2B 44
Grahame White Ho. HA3: Kenton 3D 42
Graham Gdns. KT6: Surb 1E 162
Graham Ho. *N9* *1D 34*
(off Cumberland Rd.)
Graham Lodge NW4 6D 44
Graham Mans. *IG11: Bark* *7A 72*
(off Lansbury Av.)
Graham Rd. CR4: Mitc 1E 154
DA6: Bex 4F 127
E8 6G 67
E13 4J 87
HA3: W'stone 3J 41
N15 3B 48
NW4 6D 44
SW19 7H 135
TW12: Hamp H 4E 130
W4 3K 97
Graham St. N1 1B 8 (2B 84)
Graham Ter. *DA15: Sidc* *6B 126*
(off Westerham Dr.)
SW1 4G 17 (4E 100)
Grail Rd. SE6 2G 141
Grainger Cl. UB5: N'olt 5F 59
Grainger Ct. SE5 7C 102
Grainger Rd. N22 1C 48
TW7: Isle 2K 113
The Grainstore E16 7J 87
Gramer Cl. E11 2F 69
Gramophone La. UB3: Hayes 2G 93
Grampian Cl. BR6: St M Cry 6K 161
SM2: Sutt 7A 166
UB3: Harl 7F 93
Grampian Gdns. NW2 1G 63
The Grampians *W6* *2F 99*
(off Shepherd's Bush Rd.)
Gramsci Way SE6 3D 140
Granada St. SW17 5D 136
Granard Av. SW15 5D 116
Granard Bus. Cen. NW7 6F 29
Granard Ho. E9 6K 67
Granard Rd. SW12 7D 118
Granary Cl. N9 7D 24
Granary Ct. *E15* *6F 69*
(off Millstone Cl.)
Granary Mans. SE28 2G 107
Granary Rd. E1 4H 85
Granary Sq. N1 1J 83
Granary St. NW1 1H 83
Granby Pl. *SE1* *7J 13*
(off Lwr. Marsh)
Granby Rd. SE9 2D 124
Granby St. E2 3K 9 (4G 85)
(not continuous)
Granby Ter. NW1 1A 6 (2G 83)
Grand Arc. N12 5F 31
Grand Av. EC1 5B 8 (5B 84)
(not continuous)
HA9: Wemb 5G 61
KT5: Surb 5H 151
N10 4E 46
Grand Av. E. HA9: Wemb 5H 61
Grand Canal Apts. *N1* *1E 84*
(off De Beauvoir Cres.)
Grand Canal Av. SE16 4A 104
Grand Courts RM8: Dag 3E 72
Grand Depot Rd. SE18 5E 106
Grand Dr. SW20 2E 152
UB2: S'hall 2G 95
Granden Rd. SW16 2J 155
Grandfield Ct. W4 6K 97
Grandison Rd. KT4: Wor Pk 2E 164
SW11 5D 118
Grand Junc. Wharf E2 3K 85
N1 2C 84
Grand Pde. HA9: Wemb 2G 61
KT6: Surb 1G 163
N4 5B 48
SW14 *4J 115*
(off Up. Richmond Rd. W.)
Grand Pde. M. SW15 5G 117
Grand Regent Twr. *E2* *3K 85*
(off Palmer's Rd.)
Grandstand Way UB5: N'olt 5D 58
Grand Twr. *SW15* *5G 117*
(off Plaza Gdns.)
Grand Union Cen. *W10* *4F 81*
(off West Row)
Grand Union Cl. W9 5H 81
Grand Union Cres. E8 1G 85
Grand Union Ent. Pk. UB2: S'hall 3E 94
Grand Union Hgts. HA0: Wemb 1D 78
Grand Union Ho. *N1* *1E 84*
(off Hertford Rd.)
Grand Union Ind. Est. NW10 2H 79
Grand Union Village UB5: N'olt 3D 76
Grand Union Wlk. *NW1* *7F 65*
(off Kentish Town Rd.)
Grand Union Way UB2: S'hall 2E 94
Grand Vitesse Ind. Cen. *SE1* *5B 14*
(off Gt. Suffolk St.)
Grand Wlk. E1 4A 86
Granfield St. SW11 1B 118
The Grange CR0: C'don 2B 170
E17 *5A 50*
(off Lynmouth Rd.)
HA0: Wemb 7G 61
KT3: N Mald 5B 152
KT4: Wor Pk 4K 163
N2 2B 46
N20 1F 31
(Grangeview Rd.)
N20 1G 31
(Oxford Gdns.)
SE1 3F 103
SW19 6F 135
W3 2H 97
W4 5H 97
W13 5C 78
W14 4H 99
Grange Av. EN4: E Barn 1H 31
HA7: Stan 2B 42
IG8: Wfd G 6D 36
N12 5F 31
N20 7B 20
SE25 2E 156
TW2: Twick 2J 131
Grangecliffe Gdns. SE25 2E 156
Grange Cl. DA15: Sidc 3A 144
HA8: Edg 5D 28
IG8: Wfd G 7D 36
KT8: W Mole 4F 149
TW5: Hest 6D 94
UB3: Hayes 5G 75
Grange Ct. HA1: Harr 4K 59
HA5: Pinn 3C 40
NW10 *3A 62*
(off Neasden La.)
SM2: Sutt 7K 165
SM6: W'gton 3F 167
TW17: Shep 4C 146
UB5: N'olt 2A 76
WC2 1H 13 (6K 83)
Grangecourt Rd. N16 1E 66
Grange Cres. SE28 6C 90
Grangedale Cl. HA6: Nwood 1G 39
Grange Dr. BR7: Chst 6C 142
Grange Farm Cl. HA2: Harr 2G 59
Grangefield *NW1* *7H 65*
(off Marquis Rd.)
Grange Gdns. HA5: Pinn 3C 40
N14 1C 32
NW3 3K 63
SE25 2E 156
Grange Gro. N1 6C 66
Grange Hill HA8: Edg 5D 28
SE25 2E 156
Grangehill Pl. SE9 3D 124
Grangehill Rd. SE9 4D 124
Grange Ho. NW10 7D 62
SE1 3F 103
Grange La. SE21 2F 139
Grange Lodge SW19 6F 135
Grange Mans. KT17: Ewe 7B 164
Grange M. N21 6G 23
TW13: Felt 4J 129
Grangemill Rd. SE6 3C 140
Grangemill Way SE6 2C 140
GRANGE PARK 6G 23
Grange Pk. W5 1E 96
Grange Pk. Av. N21 6H 23
Grange Pk. Pl. SW20 7D 134
Grange Pk. Rd. CR7: Thor H 4D 156
E10 1D 68
Grange Pl. NW6 7J 63
Grange Rd. BR6: Orp 2H 173
CR2: S Croy 7C 168
CR7: Thor H 4D 156
E10 1C 68
E13 3H 87
E17 5A 50
(not continuous)
HA1: Harr 5A 42
HA2: Harr 2H 59
HA8: Edg 6E 28
IG1: Ilf 4F 71
KT1: King T 3E 150
KT8: W Mole 4F 149
KT9: Chess 4E 162
N6 6E 46
N17 6B 34
N18 6B 34
NW10 6D 62
SE1 3E 102
SE19 4D 156
SE25 4D 156
SM2: Sutt 7J 165
SW13 1C 116
UB1: S'hall 2C 94
UB3: Hayes 6G 75
W4 5H 97
W5 1D 96
Grange St. N1 1D 84
Grange Va. SM2: Sutt 7K 165
Grange Vw. Rd. N20 1F 31
Grange Wlk. SE1 3E 102
Grange Wlk. M. *SE1* *3E 102*
(off Grange Wlk.)
Grangeway IG8: Wfd G 4F 37
N12 4E 30
NW6 7J 63
The Grangeway N21 6G 23
Grangeway Gdns. IG4: Ilf 5C 52
Grangewood DA5: Bexl 1F 145
Grangewood Cl. HA5: Eastc 5J 39
Grangewood Dr. TW16: Sun 7H 129
Grangewood La. BR3: Beck 6B 140
Grangewood St. E6 1B 88
Grangewood Ter. SE25 2D 156
Grange Yd. SE1 3F 103
Granham Gdns. N9 2A 34
Granite Apts. E15 6G 69
SE10 5G 105
Granite St. SE18 5K 107
Granleigh Rd. E11 2G 69
Gransden Av. E8 7H 67
Gransden Ho. SE8 5B 104
Gransden Rd. W12 2B 98
Grant Av. KT12: Walt T 5A 148
Grantbridge St. N1 2B 84
Grantchester *KT1: King T* *2G 151*
(off St Peters Rd.)
Grantchester Cl. HA1: Harr 3K 59
Grant Cl. DA17: Belv 5F 109
N14 7B 22
N17 2E 48
TW17: Shep 6D 146
Grant Ct. *E4* *1K 35*
(off The Ridgeway)
NW9 *2B 44*
(off Hazel Cl.)
Grantham Cl. HA8: Edg 3K 27
Grantham Ct. KT2: King T 5D 132
RM6: Chad H 7F 55
SE16 *2K 103*
(off Eleanor Cl.)
Grantham Gdns. RM6: Chad H 6F 55
Grantham Ho. E14 6G 87
SE15 *6G 103*
(off Friary Est.)
TW16: Sun 7G 129
UB5: N'olt *3D 76*
(off Taywood Rd.)
Grantham Pl. W1 5J 11 (1F 101)
Grantham Rd. E12 4E 70
SW9 2J 119
W4 7A 98
Grant Ho. *E17* *4C 50*
(off High St.)
SW9 *1K 119*
(off Liberty St.)
Grantley Ho. *SE14* *6K 103*
(off Myers La.)
Grantley Rd. TW4: Cran 2A 112
Grantley St. E1 3K 85
Grant Mus. of Zoology 4C 6 (4H 83)
Grantock Rd. E17 1F 51
Granton Rd. DA14: Sidc 6C 144
IG3: Ilf 1A 72
SW16 1G 155
Grant Pl. CR0: C'don 1F 169
Grant Rd. CR0: C'don 1F 169
HA3: W'stone 3K 41
SW11 4B 118
Grants Cl. NW7 7K 29
Grants Quay Wharf EC3 3F 15 (7D 84)
Grant St. E13 3J 87
N1 2A 84
Grant Ter. *N16* *7G 49*
(off Castlewood Rd.)
Grantully Rd. W9 3K 81
Grant Way TW7: Isle 6A 96
Granville Arc. SW9 4A 120
Granville Av. N9 3D 34
TW3: Houn 5E 112
TW13: Felt 2J 129
Granville Cl. CR0: C'don 2E 168
Granville Ct. N1 1E 84
N4 6K 47
SE14 *7A 104*
(off Nynehead St.)
Granville Gdns. SW16 1K 155
W5 1F 97
Granville Gro. SE13 3E 122
Granville Ho. *E14* *6C 86*
(off E. India Dock Rd.)
Granville Mans. *W12* *2E 98*
(off Shepherd's Bush Grn.)
Granville M. DA14: Sidc 4A 144
Granville Pk. SE13 3E 122
Granville Pl. HA5: Pinn 3B 40
N12 7F 31
SW6 7K 99
W1 1G 11 (6E 82)
Granville Point NW2 2H 63
Granville Rd. DA14: Sidc 4A 144
DA16: Well 3C 126
E17 6D 50
E18 2K 51
EN5: Barn 4A 20
IG1: Ilf 1F 71
N4 6K 47
N12 7F 31
N13 6E 32
N22 1B 48
NW2 2H 63
NW6 2J 81
(not continuous)
SW18 7H 117
SW19 7J 135
UB3: Harl 4H 93
UB10: Hil 6D 56
Granville Sq. SE15 7E 102
WC1 2H 7 (3K 83)
Granville St. WC1 2H 7 (3K 83)
Granwood Ct. TW7: Isle 1J 113
Grape St. WC2 7E 6 (6J 83)
The Graphite Apts. *N1* *1E 8*
(off Provost St.)
Graphite Point *E2* *3K 85*
(off Palmer's Rd.)
Graphite Sq. SE11 5G 19 (5K 101)
Grapsome Cl. KT9: Chess 7C 162
Grasdene Rd. SE18 7A 108
Grasgarth Cl. W3 7J 79
Grasmere *NW1* *2K 5*
(off Osnaburgh St.)
Grasmere Av. BR6: Farnb 3F 173
HA4: Ruis 7E 38
HA9: Wemb 7E 42
SW15 4K 133
SW19 3J 153
TW3: Houn 6F 113
W3 7K 79
Grasmere Cl. TW14: Felt 1H 129
Grasmere Ct. N22 6E 32
SE26 5G 139
SM2: Sutt 6A 166
SW13 *6C 98*
(off Verdun Rd.)
Grasmere Gdns. BR6: Farnb 3F 173
HA3: W'stone 2A 42
IG4: Ilf 5D 52
Grasmere Point *SE15* *7J 103*
(off Old Kent Rd.)
Grasmere Rd. BR1: Broml 1H 159
BR6: Farnb 3F 173
DA7: Bex 1K 127
E13 2J 87
N10 1F 47
N17 6B 34
SE25 6H 157
SW16 5J 137
Grasshaven Way SE28 1K 107
(not continuous)
Grassington Cl. N11 6K 31
Grassington Rd. DA14: Sidc 4A 144
Grassmount SE23 2H 139
Grass Pk. N3 1H 45
Grassway SM6: W'gton 4G 167
Grasvenor Av. EN5: Barn 5D 20
Gratton Rd. W14 3G 99
Gratton Ter. NW2 3F 63
Gravel Hill CR0: Addtn 6K 169
DA6: Bex 4H 127
N3 2H 45
UB8: Uxb 5A 56
Gravel Hill Cl. DA6: Bex 5H 127
Gravel La. E1 7J 9 (6F 85)
Gravel Pit La. SE9 5F 125
Gravel Pit Way BR6: Orp 2K 173
Gravel Rd. BR2: Broml 3C 172
TW2: Twick 1J 131
Gravelwood Cl. BR7: Chst 3G 143
Gravely Ho. *SE8* *4A 104*
(off Chilton Gro.)
Gravenel Gdns. *SW17* *5C 136*
(off Nutwell St.)
Graveney Gro. SE20 7J 139
Graveney Rd. SW17 4C 136
Gravesend Rd. W12 7C 80
Gravesham Way BR3: Beck 7B 158
Gray Av. RM8: Dag 1F 73
Gray Ct. E1 5A 86
HA5: Pinn 4C 40
Grayham Cres. KT3: N Mald 4K 151
Grayham Rd. KT3: N Mald 4K 151
Gray Ho. *SE17* *5C 102*
(off King & Queen St.)
Grayland Cl. BR1: Broml 1B 160
Grayling Cl. E16 4G 87
Grayling Ct. *W5* *1D 96*
(off Grange Rd.)
Grayling Rd. N16 2D 66
Grayling Sq. *E2* *3G 85*
(off Nelson Gdns.)
Grayscroft Rd. SW16 7H 137
Grays Farm Rd. BR5: St P 7B 144
Grayshott Rd. SW11 2E 118
Gray's Inn 5H 7 (5K 83)
Gray's Inn Bldgs. *EC1* *4J 7*
(off Rosebery Av.)
Gray's Inn Pl. WC1 6H 7 (5K 83)
Gray's Inn Rd. WC1 1F 7 (3J 83)
Gray's Inn Sq. WC1 5J 7 (5K 83)
Grays La. TW15: Ashf 4D 128
Grayson Ho. EC1 2D 8
Grays Rd. UB10: Uxb 7A 56
Grays Ter. E7 6A 70
Grayston Ho. SE3 2K 123
Gray St. SE1 7K 13 (2A 102)
Grayswood Gdns. SW20 2D 152
Grayswood Point SW15 1C 134
Gray's Yd. W1 1H 11
Graywood Ct. N12 7F 31
Grazebrook Rd. N16 2D 66
Grazeley Cl. DA6: Bex 5J 127
Grazeley Ct. SE19 5E 138
Gt. Acre Ct. SW4 4H 119
Gt. Amwell La. N8 3K 47
Gt. Arthur Ho. *EC1* *4C 8*
(off Golden La. Est.)
Gt. Bell All. EC2 7E 8 (6D 84)
Great Benty UB7: W Dray 4A 92
Gt. Brownings SE21 4F 139
Gt. Bushey Dr. N20 1E 30
Gt. Cambridge Ind. Est. EN1: Enf 5C 24
GREAT CAMBRIDGE JUNC. 4J 33
Gt. Cambridge Rd. EN1: Enf 4J 33
N9 4J 33
N17 5J 33
N18 4J 33
Gt. Castle St. W1 7K 5 (6F 83)
Gt. Central Av. HA4: Ruis 5A 58
Gt. Central St. NW1 5E 4 (5D 82)
Gt. Central Way HA9: Wemb 4J 61
NW10 5A 62
Gt. Chapel St. W1 7C 6 (6H 83)
Gt. Chart St. SW11 4B 118
Gt. Chertsey Rd. TW2: Twick 3D 130
TW13: Hanw, Twick 3D 130
W4 1J 115
(not continuous)
Gt. Church La. W6 4F 99
Gt. College St. SW1 1E 18 (3J 101)
Great Cft. *WC1* *2F 7*
(off Cromer St.)
Gt. Cross Av. SE10 7F 105
Gt. Cumberland M. W1 1E 10 (6D 82)
Gt. Cumberland Pl. W1 7E 4 (6D 82)
Gt. Dover St. SE1 7D 14 (2C 102)
Greatdown Rd. W7 4K 77
Gt. Eastern Ent. Cen. E14 2D 104
Gt. Eastern Mkt. *6E 68*
(within Westfield Shop. Cen.)
Gt. Eastern Rd. E15 7F 69
Gt. Eastern St. EC2 2G 9 (3E 84)
Gt. Eastern Wlk. EC2 6H 9
Gt. Eastern Wharf SW11 7C 100
Gt. Elms Rd. BR2: Broml 4A 160
Greater London Ho. *NW1* *2G 83*
(off Hampstead Rd.)
Great Fld. NW9 1A 44
Greatfield NW5 5G 65
Greatfield Av. E6 4D 88
Greatfield Cl. N19 4G 65
SE4 4C 122
Greatfields Dr. UB8: Hil 5C 74
Greatfields Rd. IG11: Bark 1H 89
Gt. Fleete Way IG11: Bark 2C 90
Gt. Galley Cl. IG11: Bark 3B 90
Gt. Gatton Cl. CR0: C'don 7A 158
Gt. George St. SW1 7D 12 (2H 101)
Gt. Guildford Bus. Sq.
SE1 5C 14 (1C 102)
Gt. Guildford St. SE1 4C 14 (1C 102)
Great Hall *SW11* *1E 118*
(off Battersea Pk. Rd.)
Greatham Wlk. SW15 1C 134
Gt. Harry Dr. SE9 3E 142
Gt. James St. WC1 5G 7 (5K 83)
Gt. Marlborough St.
W1 1A 12 (6G 83)
Gt. Maze Pond SE1 6F 15 (2D 102)
Gt. Mill Apts. *E2* *1F 85*
(off Whiston Rd.)
Gt. Minster Ho. *SW1* *3D 18*
(off Marsham St.)
Gt. Newport St. WC2 2E 12 (7J 83)
Gt. New St. *EC4* *7K 7*
(off New Fetter La.)
Great Nth. Leisure Pk. N12 7G 31
Great Nth. Rd. EN5: Barn 1C 20, 2C 20
EN5: New Bar 5D 20
N2 5C 46
N6 5C 46
Great Nth. Way NW4 2D 44
Greatorex Ho. *E1* *5G 85*
(off Greatorex St.)
Greatorex St. E1 5G 85
Gt. Ormond St. WC1 5F 7 (5J 83)
Gt. Owl Rd. IG7: Chig 3K 37
Great Pk. Cl. UB10: Hil 7C 56
Gt. Percy St. WC1 1H 7 (3K 83)
Gt. Peter St. SW1 2C 18 (3H 101)
Gt. Portland St. W1 4K 5 (4F 83)
Gt. Pulteney St. W1 2B 12 (7G 83)
Gt. Queen St. WC2 1F 13 (6J 83)
Gt. Russell Mans. *WC1* *6E 6*
(off Gt. Russell St.)
Gt. Russell St. WC1 7D 6 (6H 83)
Gt. St Helen's EC3 7G 9 (6E 84)
Gt. St Thomas Apostle
EC4 2D 14 (7C 84)
Gt. Scotland Yd. SW1 5E 12 (1J 101)
Gt. Smith St. SW1 1D 18 (3H 101)
Great Sth. W. Rd. TW4: Houn 4H 111
TW14: Bedf, Felt 7E 110
Great Spilmans SE22 5E 120
Great Strand NW9 1B 44
Gt. Suffolk St. SE1 5B 14 (1B 102)
Gt. Sutton St. EC1 4B 8 (4B 84)
Gt. Swan All. EC2 7E 8 (6D 84)
Great Thrift BR5: Pet W 4G 161
Gt. Titchfield St. W1 4K 5 (4F 83)
Gt. Tower St. EC3 2G 15 (7E 84)
Gt. Trinity La. EC4 2D 14 (7C 84)
Gt. Turnstile WC1 6H 7 (5K 83)
Gt. Turnstile Ho. *WC1* *6H 7*
(off Great Turnstile)
Gt. Western Ind. Pk. UB2: S'hall 2F 95
Gt. Western Rd. W2 5H 81
W9 5H 81
W11 5H 81
Gt. West Rd. TW5: Hest 2B 112
TW7: Bford, Isle 2B 112
TW8: Bford 2B 112
W4 5H 97
(Cedars Rd.)
W4 6B 98
(Dorchester Gro.)
W6 6B 98
Great W. Trad. Est. TW8: Bford 6B 96
Gt. Winchester St. EC2 7F 9 (6D 84)
Gt. Windmill St. W1 2C 12 (7H 83)
Greatwood BR7: Chst 7E 142
Gt. Yd. SE1 6H 15
Greaves Cl. IG11: Bark 7H 71
Greaves Cotts. *E14* *5A 86*
(off Maroon St.)
Greaves Pl. SW17 4C 136
Greaves Twr. *SW10* *7A 100*
(off Worlds End Est.)
Grebe Av. UB4: Yead 6B 76
Grebe Cl. E7 5H 69
E17 7F 35
IG11: Bark 4A 90
Grebe Ct. *E14* *2E 104*
(off River Barge Cl.)
SE8 *6B 104*
(off Dorking Cl.)
SM1: Sutt 5H 165
Grebe Ter. KT1: King T 3E 150
Grecian Cres. SE19 6B 138
Greek Ct. W1 1D 12 (6H 83)
Greek St. W1 1D 12 (6H 83)
The Green BR1: Broml 3J 141
(not continuous)
BR2: Hayes 7J 159
BR5: St P 7B 144
CR0: Sels 7B 170
DA7: Bex 1G 127
DA14: Sidc 4A 144
DA16: Well 4J 125
E4 1K 35
E11 6K 51
E15 6G 69
HA0: Wemb 2A 60
IG8: Wfd G 5D 36
IG9: Buck H 1E 36
KT3: N Mald 3K 151
N9 2B 34
N14 2C 32
N17 6H 33
N21 7F 23
SM1: Sutt 3K 165
SM4: Mord 4G 153
SM5: Cars 4E 166
SM6: W'gton 2E 166
SW14 3J 115
SW19 5F 135
TW2: Twick 1J 131
TW5: Hest 6E 94
TW9: Rich 5D 114
TW13: Felt 2K 129
TW17: Shep 4G 147
UB2: S'hall 3C 94
UB7: W Dray 3A 92
UB10: Ick 2E 56
W3 6A 80
W5 1D 96
Greenacre Cl. EN5: Barn 1C 20
UB5: N'olt 5D 58
Greenacre Gdns. E17 4E 50
Greenacre Pl. SM6: W'gton 2E 167
Green Acres CR0: C'don 3F 169
DA14: Sidc 4A 144
Greenacres N3 2H 45
SE9 6E 124
WD23: B Hea 2C 26
Greenacres Av. UB10: Ick 3B 56
Greenacres Cl. BR6: Farnb 4G 173
Greenacres Dr. HA7: Stan 6G 27
Greenacres Ho. *SW18* *1K 135*
(off Knaresborough Dr.)
Greenacre Sq. SE16 2K 103
Greenacre Wlk. N14 3C 32
Greenan Ct. *E2* *3K 85*
(off Meath Cres.)
Grn. Arbour Ct. EC1 7A 8
Green Av. NW7 4E 28
W13 3B 96
Greenaway Gdns. NW3 4K 63
Greenaway Ho. *NW8* *1A 82*
(off Boundary Rd.)

A-Z Big London 227

Greenaway Ho.—Grosvenor Pk. Rd.

Greenaway Ho. WC1 2J 7
(off Fernsbury St.)
Greenaway Ter. TW19: Stanw 1A 128
(off Victory Cl.)
Green Bank E1 1H 103
N12 4E 30
Greenbank Av. HA0: Wemb 5A 60
Greenbank Cl. E4 2K 35
Greenbank Ct. TW7: Isle 2K 113
(off Lanadron Cl.)
Greenbank Cres. NW4 4G 45
Greenbank Lodge BR7: Chst 2E 160
(off Forest Cl.)
Greenbanks HA1: Harr 4J 59
Greenbanks Cl. SE13 3D 122
Greenbay Rd. SE7 7B 106
Greenberry St. NW8 1C 4 (2C 82)
Greenbrook Av. EN4: Had W 1F 21
Green Cl. BR2: Broml 3G 159
NW9 6J 43
NW11 7A 46
SM5: Cars 2D 166
TW13: Hanw 5C 130
Greencoat Mans. SW1 2B 18
(off Greencoat Row)
Greencoat Pl. SW1 3B 18 (4G 101)
Greencoat Row SW1 2B 18 (3G 101)
Green Ct. TW16: Sun 6H 129
Greencourt Av. CR0: C'don 2H 169
HA8: Edg 1H 43
Greencourt Gdns. CR0: C'don 1H 169
Greencourt Ho. E1 4K 85
(off Mile End Rd.)
Greencourt Rd. BR5: Pet W 5H 161
Greencrest Pl. NW2 3C 62
Greencroft HA8: Edg 5D 28
Greencroft Av. HA4: Ruis 2A 58
Greencroft Cl. E6 5B 88
Greencroft Gdns. EN1: Enf 3K 23
NW6 7K 63
Greencroft Rd. TW5: Hest 1D 112
Green Dale SE5 4D 120
SE22 5E 120
Greendale NW7 4F 29
Grn. Dale Cl. SE22 5E 120
Grn. Dragon Ct. SE1 4E 14
Grn. Dragon Ho. CR0: C'don 3C 168
(off High St.)
WC2 7F 7
(off Stukeley St.)
Grn. Dragon La. N21 6F 23
TW8: Bford 5E 96
Grn. Dragon Yd. E1 6K 9 (5G 85)
Green Dr. UB1: S'hall 1E 94
Greene Ct. SE14 6K 103
(off Samuel Cl.)
Greene Ho. SE1 3D 102
(off Burbage Cl.)
Green End KT9: Chess 4E 162
N21 2G 33
Greenend Rd. W4 2A 98
Greener Ct. CR0: C'don 6C 156
(off Goodman Cres.)
Greener Ho. SW4 3H 119
Grn. Farm Cl. BR6: Chels 5K 173
Greenfell Mans. SE8 6D 104
Green Ferry Way E17 4K 49
Greenfield Av. KT5: Surb 7H 151
Greenfield Ct. SE9 3C 142
Greenfield Dr. BR1: Broml 2A 160
N2 4D 46
Greenfield Gdns. BR5: Pet W 7H 161
NW2 2G 63
RM9: Dag 1D 90
Greenfield Ho. SW19 1F 135
Greenfield Pl. UB3: Hayes 7H 75
Greenfield Rd. DA2: Wilm 5K 145
E1 5G 85
N15 5E 48
RM9: Dag 1C 90
Greenfields UB1: S'hall 6E 76
Greenfield Way HA2: Harr 3F 41
GREENFORD 3E 76
Greenford Av. UB1: S'hall 7D 76
W7 4J 77
Greenford Bus. Cen. UB6: G'frd 7H 59
Greenford Gdns. UB6: G'frd 3F 77
GREENFORD GREEN 6J 59
Greenford Ind. Est. UB6: G'frd 7F 59
Greenford Pk. UB6: G'frd 7H 59
Greenford Rd. HA1: Harr 2H 77
SM1: Sutt 4K 165
(not continuous)
UB1: S'hall 7G 77
UB6: G'frd 2H 77
GREENFORD RDBT. 2H 77
Greenford Sports Cen. 3E 76
Green Gdns. BR6: Farnb 5G 173
Greengate UB6: G'frd 6B 60
Greengate Lodge E13 2K 87
(off Hollybush St.)
Greengate Pde. IG2: Ilf 6H 53
Greengate St. E13 2K 87
Greenhalgh Wlk. N2 4A 46
Greenham Cl. SE1 7J 13 (2A 102)
Greenham Cres. E4 6G 35
Greenham Ho. E9 1J 85
(off Templecombe Rd.)
TW7: Isle 3H 113
Greenham Rd. N10 2E 46
Greenhaven Dr. SE28 6B 90
Green Hedges TW1: Twick 5C 114
Greenheys Cl. HA6: Nwood 1G 39
Greenheys Dr. E18 3H 51
GREENHILL 5J 41
Greenhill HA9: Wemb 2H 61
IG9: Buck H 1F 37
NW3 4B 64
SE18 5D 106
SM1: Sutt 2A 166
Greenhill Ct. EN5: New Bar 5E 20
SE18 5D 106
Greenhill Gdns. UB5: N'olt 2D 76
Greenhill Gro. E12 4C 70
Greenhill Pde. EN5: New Bar 5E 20
Greenhill Pk. EN5: New Bar 5E 20
NW10 1A 80
Greenhill Rd. HA1: Harr 6J 41
NW10 1A 80
Greenhill's Rents EC1 5A 8 (5B 84)
Greenhills Ter. N1 6D 66
Greenhill Ter. SE18 5D 106
UB5: N'olt 2D 76
Greenhill Way HA1: Harr 6J 41
HA9: Wemb 2H 61
Greenhithe Cl. DA15: Sidc 7J 125
Greenholm Rd. SE9 5F 125
Green Hundred Rd. SE15 6G 103
Greenhurst Rd. SE27 5A 138
Greening St. SE2 4C 108
Greenland Cres. UB2: S'hall 3A 94
Greenland Ho. E1 4A 86
(off Ernest St.)
Greenland M. SE8 5K 103
Greenland Pl. NW1 1F 83
Greenland Quay SE16 4K 103
Greenland Rd. EN5: Barn 6A 20
NW1 1G 83
Greenlands KT19: Ewe 5H 163
Greenlands La. NW4 1D 44
Greenland St. NW1 1F 83
Greenland Way CR0: Bedd 7H 155
Green La. BR7: Chst 1F 143
CR7: Thor H 7K 137
HA1: Harr 3J 59
HA7: Stan 4G 27
HA8: Edg 4A 28
(not continuous)
IG1: Ilf 2H 71
IG3: Ilf 2H 71
KT3: N Mald 5J 151
KT4: Wor Pk 1C 164
KT8: W Mole 5F 149
KT9: Chess 7D 162
NW4 4F 45
RM8: Dag 2H 71
SE9 1F 143
SE20 7K 139
SM4: Mord 6J 153
(Central Rd.)
SM4: Mord 7E 152
(Lwr. Morden La.)
SW16 7K 137
TW4: Houn 3K 111
TW13: Hanw 5C 130
TW16: Sun 7H 129
TW17: Shep 6E 146
UB8: Hil 5E 74
W7 2J 95
Green La. Bus. Pk. SE9 2E 142
Green La. Cotts. HA7: Stan 4G 27
Green La. Gdns. CR7: Thor H 2C 156
Green Lanes KT19: Ewe 7A 164
N4 1C 66
N8 3B 48
N13 6E 32
N15 3B 48
N16 1C 66
N21 3F 33
Grn. Lanes Wlk. N4 1C 66
Greenlaw Ct. W5 6D 78
(off Mount Pk. Rd.)
Greenlaw Gdns. KT3: N Mald 7B 152
Greenlawn La. TW8: Bford 4D 96
Green Lawns HA4: Ruis 1A 58
Greenlawns N12 6E 30
Greenlaw St. SE18 3E 106
Green Leaf Av. SM6: Bedd 4H 167
Greenleaf Cl. SW2 7A 120
Greenleafe Dr. IG6: Ilf 3F 53
Greenleaf Rd. E6 1A 88
E17 3B 50
Greenleaf Way HA3: W'stone 3K 41
Greenlea Pk. SW19 7B 136
Green Leas KT1: King T 3E 150
(off Mill St.)
TW16: Sun 6H 129
Green Leas Cl. TW16: Sun 6H 129
Greenleaves Ct. TW15: Ashf 6D 128
Greenlink Wlk. TW9: Kew 1H 115
Green Man Gdns. W13 7A 78
Green Man La. TW14: Felt 4J 111
(not continuous)
W13 7A 78
Green Man Pas. W13 7B 78
(not continuous)
GREEN MAN RDBT. 7H 51
Greenman St. N1 7C 66
Greenmead DA18: Erith 3E 108
Greenmead Cl. SE25 5G 157
Green M. N1 3D 84
Green Moor Link N21 7G 23
Greenmoor Rd. EN3: Enf H 2D 24
Greenoak Pl. EN4: Cockf 2J 21
Green Oaks UB2: S'hall 4B 94
Greenoak Way SW19 4F 135
Greenock Rd. SW16 1H 155
W3 3H 97
Greeno Cres. TW17: Shep 5C 146
Green Pde. TW3: Houn 5F 113
Green Pk. 6K 11 (2F 101)
Greenpark Ct. HA0: Wemb 7C 60
Green Pk. Way UB6: G'frd 7J 59
Green Pl. SE10 2G 105
Green Point E15 6G 69
Grn. Pond Cl. E17 3B 50
Grn. Pond Rd. E17 3A 50
Green Rd. N14 6A 22
N20 3F 31
Green Rd. Nth. EN3: Pond E 4F 25
Greenrod Pl. TW8: Bford 5E 96
(off Clayponds La.)
Greenroof Way SE10 3H 105
Green's Ct. W1 2C 12
W11 1H 99
(off Lansdowne M.)
Green's End SE18 4F 107
Greenshank Cl. E17 7F 35
Greenshank Ho. NW9 6B 44
Greenshaw School Sports Cen. 2A 166
Greenshields Ind. Est. E16 2J 105
Greenside DA5: Bexl 1E 144
RM8: Dag 1C 72
Greenside Cl. N20 2G 31
SE6 2F 141
Greenside Rd. CR0: C'don 7A 156
W12 3C 98
Greenslade Rd. IG11: Bark 7H 71
Greenstead Av. IG8: Wfd G 7F 37
Greenstead Cl. IG8: Wfd G 6F 37
Greenstead Gdns. IG8: Wfd G 6F 37
SW15 5D 116
Greensted Rd. IG10: Lough 1H 37
Greenstone M. E11 6J 51
Green St. E7 6K 69
E13 6K 69
EN3: Brim, Enf H 2D 24
TW16: Sun 1J 147
W1 2G 11 (7E 82)
GREEN STREET GREEN 6K 173
Greenstreet Hill SE14 2K 121
Green Ter. EC1 2K 7 (3A 84)
Green Va. DA6: Bex 5D 126
W5 6F 79
Greenvale Rd. SE9 4D 124
Green Verges HA7: Stan 7J 27
Green Vw. KT9: Chess 7F 163
Greenview Av. BR3: Beck 6A 158
CR0: C'don 6A 158
Greenview Cl. W3 1A 98
Greenview Ct. TW15: Ashf 4B 128
Greenview Dr. SW20 3E 152
Green Wlk. HA4: Ruis 1H 57
IG8: Wfd G 6H 37
IG10: Lough 1H 37
NW4 5F 45
SE1 3E 102
TW12: Hamp 6D 130
UB2: S'hall 5E 94
The Green Wlk. E4 1A 36
Green Way BR2: Broml 6C 160
SE9 5B 124
TW16: Sun 4J 147
Greenway BR7: Chst 5E 142
E3 1C 86
E6 4E 88
HA3: Kenton 5E 42
HA5: Pinn 2K 39
IG8: Wfd G 5F 37
N14 2D 32
N20 2D 30
RM8: Dag 2C 72
SM6: W'gton 4G 167
SW20 4E 152
UB4: Yead 3J 75
The Greenway HA3: W'stone 1J 41
HA5: Pinn 6D 40
NW9 2K 43
TW4: Houn 4D 112
UB8: Uxb 2A 74
UB10: Ick 2D 56
Greenway Av. E17 4F 51
Greenway Cl. N4 2C 66
N11 6K 31
N15 4F 49
N20 2D 30
NW9 2K 43
Greenway Ct. IG1: Ilf 1E 70
Greenway Gdns. CR0: C'don 3B 170
HA3: W'stone 2J 41
NW9 2K 43
UB6: G'frd 3E 76
Greenways BR3: Beck 3C 158
The Greenways TW1: Twick 6A 114
Greenways Dr. TW4: Houn 4C 112
Greenwell St. W1 4K 5 (4F 83)
GREENWICH 7E 104
Greenwich Bus. Pk. SE10 7D 104
The Greenwich Cen. 5H 105
(off Lambarde Sq.)
Greenwich Chu. St. SE10 6E 104
Greenwich Ct. E1 6H 85
(off Cavell St.)
Greenwich Cres. E6 5C 88
GREENWICH FOOT TUNNEL 5E 104
Greenwich Hgts. SE18 7C 106
Greenwich High Rd. SE10 1D 122
Greenwich Ho. SE13 6F 123
Greenwich Mkt. SE10 6E 104
GREENWICH MILLENNIUM VILLAGE 3H 105
Greenwich Pk. 7F 105
Greenwich Pk. St. SE10 6F 105
Greenwich Peninsula Ecology Pk. 3J 105
Greenwich Peninsula Golf Driving Range 2F 105
Greenwich Picturehouse 7E 104
Greenwich Quay SE8 6D 104
Greenwich Shop. Pk. 4K 105
Greenwich Sth. St. SE10 1D 122
Greenwich Theatre 7E 104
Greenwich Tourist Information Centre 6E 104
Greenwich Vw. Pl. E14 3D 104
Greenwich Yacht Club 3J 105
Greenwood NW5 5G 65
(off Osney Cres.)
Greenwood Av. EN3: Enf H 2F 25
RM10: Dag 4H 73
Greenwood Bus. Cen.
CR0: C'don 7F 157
Greenwood Cl. BR5: Pet W 6J 161
DA15: Sidc 2A 144
KT7: T Ditt 1A 162
SM4: Mord 4G 153
UB3: Hayes 1J 93
WD23: B Hea 1D 26
Greenwood Dr. E4 5A 36
Greenwood Gdns. IG6: Ilf 1G 53
N13 3G 33
Greenwood Ho. EC1 2J 7
(off Rosebery Av.)
N22 1K 47
SE4 4K 121
Greenwood La. TW12: Hamp H 5F 131
Greenwood Mans. IG11: Bark 7A 72
(off Lansbury Av.)
Greenwood Pk. KT2: King T 7A 134
Greenwood Pl. NW5 5F 65
Greenwood Rd. CR0: C'don 7B 156
CR4: Mitc 3H 155
DA5: Bexl 4K 145
E8 6G 67
E13 2H 87
KT7: T Ditt 1A 162
TW7: Isle 3K 113
The Greenwoods HA2: Harr 3G 59
Greenwood Ter. NW10 1K 79
Greenwood Theatre 2D 102
Grn. Wrythe Cres. SM5: Cars 1C 166
Grn. Wrythe La. SM5: Cars 6B 154
Green Yd. WC1 3H 7 (4K 83)
The Green Yd. EC3 1G 15
Greer Rd. HA3: Hrw W 1G 41
Greet Ho. SE1 7K 13
Greet St. SE1 5K 13 (1A 102)
Greg Cl. E10 6E 50
Gregor M. SE3 7J 105
Gregory Cl. BR2: Broml 4G 159
Gregory Cres. SE9 7B 124
Gregory Pl. W8 2K 99
Gregory Rd. RM6: Chad H 4D 54
UB2: S'hall 3E 94
Grehan M. SE14 7B 104
Greig Cl. N8 5J 47
Greig Ter. SE17 6B 102
Grenaby Av. CR0: C'don 7D 156
Grenaby Rd. CR0: C'don 7D 156
Grenada Ho. E14 7B 86
(off Limehouse C'way.)
Grenada Rd. SE7 7A 106
Grenade St. E14 7B 86
Grenadier St. E16 1E 106
Grena Gdns. TW9: Rich 4F 115
Grenard Cl. SE15 7G 103
Grena Rd. TW9: Rich 4F 115
Grendon Gdns. HA9: Wemb 2G 61
Grendon Ho. E9 7J 67
(off Shore Pl.)
N1 2K 83
(off Calshot St.)
Grendon Lodge HA8: Edg 2D 28
Grendon St. NW8 3C 4 (4C 82)
Grenfell Ct. E3 4D 86
(off Barry Blandford Way)
NW7 6J 29
Grenfell Gdns. HA3: Kenton 7E 42
IG3: Ilf 5K 53
Grenfell Ho. SE5 7C 102
Grenfell Rd. CR4: Mitc 6D 136
W11 7F 81
Grenfell Wlk. W11 7F 81
Grenier Apts. SE15 7H 103
Grennell Cl. SM1: Sutt 2B 166
Grennell Rd. SM1: Sutt 2A 166
Grenoble Gdns. N13 6F 33
Grenville Cl. KT5: Surb 1J 163
N3 1G 45
Grenville Ct. W13 5B 78
Grenville Gdns. IG8: Wfd G 1A 52
Grenville Ho. E3 2A 86
(off Arbery Rd.)
SE8 6C 104
(off New King St.)
SW1 7C 18
(off Dolphin Sq.)
Grenville M. N19 1J 65
SW7 4A 100
TW12: Hamp H 5F 131
Grenville Pl. NW7 5E 28
SW7 3A 100
Grenville Rd. N19 1J 65
Grenville St. WC1 4F 7 (4J 83)
Gresham Av. N20 4J 31
Gresham Cl. DA5: Bexl 6E 126
EN2: Enf 3H 23
Gresham Dr. RM6: Chad H 5B 54
Gresham Gdns. NW11 1G 63
Gresham Lodge E17 5D 50
Gresham Pl. E3 5C 86
N19 2H 65
Gresham Rd. BR3: Beck 2A 158
E6 2D 88
E16 6K 87
HA8: Edg 6A 28
NW10 5K 61
SE25 4G 157
SW9 3A 120
TW3: Houn 1G 113
TW12: Hamp 6E 130
UB10: Hil 2D 74
Gresham St. EC2 7C 8 (6C 84)
Gresham Way SW19 3K 135
Gresham Way Ind. Est. SW19 3K 135
(off Gresham Way)
Gresley Cl. E17 6A 50
N15 4D 48
Gresley Rd. N19 1G 65
Gressenhall Rd. SW18 6H 117
Gresse St. W1 6C 6 (6H 83)
Gresswell Cl. DA14: Sidc 3A 144
Greswell St. SW6 1F 117
Gretton Ho. E2 3J 85
(off Globe Rd.)
Gretton Rd. N17 7A 34
Greville Cl. TW1: Twick 7B 114
Greville Ct. E5 3H 67
(off Napoleon Rd.)
HA1: Harr 4J 59
Greville Hall NW6 2K 81
Greville Ho. SW1 1G 17
(off Kinnerton St.)
Greville Lodge E13 1K 87
HA8: Edg 4C 28
(off Broadhurst Av.)
N12 5E 30
Greville M. NW6 1K 81
(off Greville Rd.)
Greville Pl. NW6 2K 81
Greville Rd. E17 4E 50
NW6 2K 81
TW10: Rich 6F 115
Greville St. EC1 6J 7 (5A 84)
(not continuous)
Grey Cl. NW11 6A 46
Greycoat Gdns. SW1 2C 18
(off Greycoat St.)
Greycoat Pl. SW1 2C 18 (3H 101)
Greycoat St. SW1 2C 18 (3H 101)
Greycot Rd. BR3: Beck 5C 140
Grey Eagle St. E1 4K 9 (4F 85)
Greyfell Cl. HA7: Stan 5G 27
Greyfriars SE26 3G 139
(off Wells Pk. Rd.)
Greyfriars Pas. EC1 7B 8 (6B 84)
Greyhound Ct. WC2 2H 13 (7K 83)
Greyhound Hill NW4 3C 44
Greyhound La. SW16 6H 137
Greyhound Mans. W6 6G 99
(off Greyhound Rd.)
Greyhound Rd. N17 3E 48
NW10 3D 80
SM1: Sutt 6A 166
W6 6F 99
W14 6F 99
Greyhound Ter. SW16 1G 155
Grey Ho. W12 7D 80
(off White City Est.)
Greyladies Gdns. SE10 2E 122
Greys Pk. Cl. BR2: Kes 5B 172
Greystead Rd. SE23 7J 121
Greystoke Av. HA5: Pinn 3E 40
Greystoke Ct. W5 4E 78
Greystoke Dr. HA4: Ruis 6D 38
Greystoke Gdns. EN2: Enf 4C 22
W5 4E 78
Greystoke Ho. SE15 6G 103
(off Peckham Pk. Rd.)
W5 4E 78
Greystoke Lodge W5 4F 79
(off Hanger La.)
Greystoke Pk. Ter. W5 3D 78
Greystoke Pl. EC4 7J 7 (6A 84)
Greystone Gdns. HA3: Kenton 6C 42
IG6: Ilf 2G 53
Greyswood St. SW16 6F 137
Greyt Turner Ho. W12 6C 80
Grierson Ho. SW16 4G 137
Grierson Rd. SE23 7K 121
Griffen Ct. BR3: Beck 1D 158
Griffin Cen. TW14: Felt 5K 111
The Griffin Cen. KT1: King T 2D 150
(off Market Pl.)
Griffin Cl. NW10 5D 62
Griffin Ct. TW8: Bford 6E 96
W4 5B 98
Griffin Ho. CR0: C'don 7B 156
E14 6D 86
(off Ricardo St.)
N1 1E 84
(off Halcomb St.)
W6 4F 99
(off Hammersmith Rd.)
Griffin Mnr. Way SE28 3H 107
Griffin M. SW12 1G 137
Griffin Pk. 6D 96
Griffin Rd. N17 2E 48
SE18 5H 107
Griffins Cl. N21 7J 23
Griffin Way TW16: Sun 2J 147
Griffith Cl. E17 1F 51
RM8: Dag 7C 54
Griffiths Cl. KT4: Wor Pk 2D 164
Griffiths Rd. SW19 7J 135
Griggs App. IG1: Ilf 2G 71
Griggs Cl. IG3: Ilf 4J 71
Griggs Ct. SE1 3E 102
(off Grigg's Pl.)
Grigg's Pl. SE1 3E 102
Griggs Rd. E10 6E 50
Grilse Cl. N9 4C 34
Grimaldi Ho. N1 2K 83
(off Calshot St.)
Grimsby Gro. E16 2F 107
Grimsby St. E2 4K 9 (4F 85)
Grim's Ditch 5A 26
Grim's Dyke Golf Course 5A 26
Grimsdyke Rd. HA5: Hat E 1D 40
Grimsel Path SE5 7B 102
Grimshaw Cl. N6 7E 46
Grimston Rd. SW6 2H 117
Grimthorpe Ho. EC1 3A 8
Grimwade Av. CR0: C'don 3G 169
Grimwade Cl. SE15 3J 121
Grimwood Rd. TW1: Twick 7K 113
Grindall Cl. CR0: Wadd 4B 168
Grindall Ho. E1 4H 85
(off Darling Row)
Grindal St. SE1 7J 13 (2A 102)
Grindleford Av. N11 2K 31
Grindley Gdns. CR0: C'don 6F 157
Grindley Ho. E3 5B 86
(off Leopold St.)
Grinling Pl. SE8 6C 104
Grinstead Rd. SE8 5A 104
Grisedale NW1 1A 6
(off Cumberland Mkt.)
Grittleton Av. HA9: Wemb 6H 61
Grittleton Rd. W9 4J 81
Grizedale Ter. SE23 2H 139
Grocer's Hall Ct. EC2 1E 14 (6D 84)
Grocer's Hall Gdns. EC2 1E 14
Grogan Cl. TW12: Hamp 6D 130
Groombridge Cl. DA16: Well 5A 126
Groombridge Ho. SE17 5E 102
(off Upnor Way)
Groombridge Rd. E9 7K 67
Groom Cl. BR2: Broml 4K 159
Groom Cres. SW18 7B 118
Groome Ho. SE11 4H 19 (4K 101)
Groomfield Cl. SW17 4E 136
Groom Pl. SW1 1H 17 (3E 100)
Grooms Dr. HA5: Eastc 5J 39
Grosmont Rd. SE18 5K 107
Grosse Way SW15 6D 116
Grosvenor Av. HA2: Harr 6F 41
N5 5C 66
SM5: Cars 6D 166
SW14 3A 116
TW10: Rich 5E 114
UB4: Hayes 2H 75
Grosvenor Cotts. SW1 3G 17 (4E 100)
Grosvenor Ct. E10 1D 68
E14 6B 86
(off Wharf La.)
N14 7B 22
NW6 1F 81
NW7 5E 28
(off Hale La.)
SE5 6C 102
SM2: Sutt 6K 165
SM4: Mord 4J 153
TW11: Tedd 6A 132
W3 1G 97
W5 7E 78
(off The Grove)
W14 3F 99
(off Irving Rd.)
Grosvenor Ct. Mans. W2 1E 10
(off Edgware Rd.)
Grosvenor Cres. NW9 4G 43
SW1 7H 11 (2E 100)
UB10: Hil 7D 56
Grosvenor Cres. M. SW1 7G 11 (2E 100)
Grosvenor Est. SW1 3D 18 (4H 101)
Grosvenor Gdns. E6 3B 88
IG8: Wfd G 6D 36
KT2: King T 6D 132
N10 3G 47
N14 4C 22
NW2 6E 62
NW11 6H 45
SM6: W'gton 7G 167
SW1 1J 17 (3F 101)
SW14 3A 116
Grosvenor Gdns. M. E. SW1 1K 17
Grosvenor Gdns. M. Nth. SW1 2J 17
Grosvenor Gdns. M. Sth. SW1 2K 17
Grosvenor Ga. W1 3G 11 (7E 82)
Grosvenor Hill SW19 6G 135
W1 2J 11 (7F 83)
Grosvenor Hill Ct. W1 2J 11
(off Bourdon St.)
Grosvenor Ho. SM1: Sutt 5K 165
(off West St.)
Grosvenor Pde. W5 1G 97
(off Uxbridge Rd.)
Grosvenor Pk. SE5 7C 102
Grosvenor Pk. Rd. E17 5C 50

Grosvenor Pl.—Half Moon Ct.

Grosvenor Pl. SW1 ... 7H 11 (2E 100)
Grosvenor Ri. E. E17 ... 5D 50
Grosvenor Rd. BR4: W W'ck ... 1D 170
BR5: St M Cry ... 6J 161
DA6: Bex ... 5D 126
DA17: Belv ... 6G 109
E6 ... 1B 88
E7 ... 6K 69
E10 ... 1E 68
E11 ... 5K 51
IG1: Ilf ... 3G 71
N3 ... 7C 30
N9 ... 1C 34
N10 ... 1F 47
RM7: Rush G ... 7K 55
RM8: Dag ... 1F 73
SE25 ... 4F 157
SM6: W'gton ... 6F 167
SW1 ... 7J 17 (6F 101)
TW1: Twick ... 1A 132
TW3: Houn ... 3D 112
TW8: Bford ... 6D 96
TW10: Rich ... 5E 114
UB2: S'hall ... 3D 94
W4 ... 5H 97
W7 ... 1A 96
Grosvenor Sq. W1 ... 2H 11 (7E 82)
Grosvenor St. W1 ... 2J 11 (7F 83)
Grosvenor Studios *SW1* ... *3G 17*
(off Eaton Ter.)
Grosvenor Ter. SE5 ... 7C 102
Grosvenor Va. HA4: Ruis ... 2H 57
Grosvenor Vale Stadium ... 2H 57
Grosvenor Way E5 ... 2J 67
SW17 ... 3B 136
Grosvenor Wharf Rd. E14 ... 4F 105
Grotes Bldgs. SE3 ... 2G 123
Grote's Pl. SE3 ... 2G 123
Groton Rd. SW18 ... 2K 135
Grotto Ct. SE1 ... 6B 14 (2B 102)
Grotto Pas. W1 ... 5H 5 (5E 82)
Grotto Rd. TW1: Twick ... 2K 131
THE GROVE ... 1G 139
The Grove BR4: W W'ck ... 3D 170
DA6: Bex ... 4D 126
DA14: Sidc ... 5E 144
E15 ... 6G 69
EN2: Enf ... 2F 23
HA1: Harr ... 7J 41
HA7: Stan ... 2F 27
HA8: Edg ... 4C 28
KT12: Walt T ... 7K 147
N3 ... 1J 45
N4 ... 7K 47
N6 ... 1E 64
N8 ... 5H 47
N13 ... 4F 33
(not continuous)
NW9 ... 5K 43
NW11 ... 7G 45
TW1: Twick ... 6B 114
TW7: Isle ... 1J 113
TW11: Tedd ... 4A 132
UB6: G'frd ... 6G 77
UB10: Ick ... 5C 56
W5 ... 1D 96
Grove Av. HA5: Pinn ... 4C 40
N3 ... 7D 30
N10 ... 2G 47
SM1: Sutt ... 6J 165
TW1: Twick ... 1K 131
W7 ... 7J 77
Grovebury Cl. DA8: Erith ... 6K 109
Grovebury Ct. DA6: Bex ... 5H 127
N14 ... 7C 22
Grovebury Rd. SE2 ... 2B 108
Grove Cl. BR2: Hayes ... 2J 171
KT1: King T ... 4F 151
N14 ... 7B 22
SE23 ... 1A 140
TW13: Hanw ... 4C 130
UB10: Ick ... 5C 56
Grove Cotts. SW3 ... 7D 16
W4 ... 6A 98
Grove Ct. *EN5: Barn* ... *3C 20*
(off Hadley Ridge)
KT1: King T ... *3E 150*
(off Grove Cres.)
KT8: E Mos ... 5H 149
NW8 ... 1A 4
SE15 ... *7E 102*
(off Peckham Rd.)
SW10 ... *6A 16*
(off Drayton Gdns.)
TW3: Houn ... 4E 112
W5 ... 1E 96
Grove Cres. E18 ... 2H 51
KT1: King T ... 3E 150
KT12: Walt T ... 7K 147
NW9 ... 4J 43
TW13: Hanw ... 4C 130
Grove Cres. Rd. E15 ... 6F 69
Grovedale Rd. N19 ... 2H 65
Grove Dwellings E1 ... 5J 85
Grove End E18 ... 2H 51
NW5 ... 4F 65
Grove End Gdns. NW8 ... 2B 82
Grove End Ho. NW8 ... 2A 4
Grove End La. KT10: Esh ... 7H 149
Grove End Rd. NW8 ... 1A 4 (2B 82)
Grove Farm Retail Pk. ... 7C 54
Grovefield *N11* ... *4A 32*
(off Coppies Gro.)
Grove Footpath KT5: Surb ... 4E 150
Grove Gdns. EN3: Enf W ... 1E 24
NW4 ... 5C 44
NW8 ... 2D 4 (3C 82)
RM10: Dag ... 3J 73
TW10: Rich ... 6F 115
TW11: Tedd ... 4A 132
Grove Grn. Rd. E11 ... 3E 68
Grove Hall Ct. *E3* ... *2C 86*
(off Jebb St.)
NW8 ... 1A 4 (3A 82)
Grove Hill E18 ... 2H 51
HA1: Harr ... 7J 41
Grovehill Ct. BR1: Broml ... 6H 141
Grove Hill Rd. HA1: Harr ... 7K 41
SE5 ... 3E 120
Grove Ho. N3 ... 3F 45
SW3 ... *7D 16*
(off Chelsea Mnr. St.)
Grove Ho. Rd. N8 ... 4J 47
Groveland Av. SW16 ... 7K 137
Groveland Ct. EC4 ... 1D 14
Groveland Rd. BR3: Beck ... 3B 158
Grovelands *KT1: King T* ... *4D 150*
(off Palace Rd.)
KT8: W Mole ... 4E 148
Grovelands Cl. HA2: Harr ... 3F 59
SE5 ... 2E 120
Grovelands Ct. N14 ... 7C 22
Grovelands Rd. BR5: St P ... 7A 144
N13 ... 4E 32
N15 ... 6G 49
Groveland Way KT3: N Mald ... 5J 151
Grove La. KT1: King T ... 4E 150
SE5 ... 1D 120
UB8: Hil ... 4B 74
Grove La. Ter. SE5 ... 2D 120
Groveley Rd. TW13: Felt ... 5H 129
TW16: Sun ... 5G 129
Grove Mans. *W6* ... *2E 98*
(off Hammersmith Gro.)
Grove M. W6 ... 3E 98
Grove Mill Pl. SM5: Cars ... 3E 166
The Grove Nature Reserve ... 4B 74
GROVE PARK
SE12 ... 3K 141
W4 ... 1J 115
Grove Pk. E11 ... 6K 51
NW9 ... 4J 43
SE5 ... 2E 120
Grove Pk. Av. E4 ... 7J 35
GROVE PK. BRI. ... 7J 97
Grove Pk. Gdns. W4 ... 7H 97
Grove Pk. M. W4 ... 7J 97
Grove Pk. Nature Reserve ... 1H 141
Grove Pk. Rd. N15 ... 4E 48
SE9 ... 3A 142
W4 ... 7H 97
Grove Pk. Ter. W4 ... 7H 97
Grove Pas. E2 ... 2H 85
Grove Pl. IG11: Bark ... 7G 71
NW3 ... 3B 64
SE9 ... 6D 124
SW12 ... 7F 119
W3 ... 1J 97
Grover Ct. SE13 ... 2D 122
Grover Ho. SE11 ... 6H 19 (5K 101)
Grove Rd. CR4: Mitc ... 3E 154
(not continuous)
CR7: Thor H ... 4A 156
DA7: Bex ... 4J 127
DA17: Belv ... 6F 109
E3 ... 1K 85
E4 ... 4K 35
E11 ... 7H 51
E17 ... 6D 50
E18 ... 2H 51
EN4: Cockf ... 3H 21
HA5: Pinn ... 5D 40
HA8: Edg ... 6B 28
KT6: Surb ... 5D 150
KT8: E Mos ... 4H 149
N11 ... 5A 32
N12 ... 5G 31
N15 ... 5E 48
NW2 ... 6E 62
RM6: Chad H ... 7B 54
SM1: Sutt ... 6J 165
SW13 ... 2B 116
SW19 ... 7A 136
TW2: Twick ... 3H 131
TW3: Houn ... 5F 113
TW7: Isle ... 1J 113
TW8: Bford ... 5C 96
TW10: Rich ... 6F 115
TW17: Shep ... 6E 146
UB8: Uxb ... 7A 56
W3 ... 1J 97
W5 ... 7D 78
Groveside Cl. SM5: Cars ... 2C 166
W3 ... 5G 79
Groveside Ct. SW11 ... 2B 118
Groveside Rd. E4 ... 2B 36
Grovestile Waye TW14: Bedf ... 7F 111
Grove St. N18 ... 5A 34
SE8 ... 4B 104
Grove Ter. NW5 ... 3F 65
TW11: Tedd ... 4A 132
UB1: S'hall ... 7E 76
Grove Ter. M. NW5 ... 3F 65
Grove Va. BR7: Chst ... 6E 142
SE22 ... 4F 121
Grove Vs. E14 ... 7D 86
Grove Way HA9: Wemb ... 5H 61
KT10: Esh ... 7G 149
UB8: Uxb ... 7A 56
Groveway RM8: Dag ... 3D 72
SW9 ... 1K 119
Grovewood TW9: Kew ... 1G 115
Grove Wood Cl. BR1: Broml ... 3E 160
Grovewood Pl. IG8: Wfd G ... 6J 37
Grummant Rd. SE15 ... 1F 121
Grundy St. E14 ... 6D 86
Gruneisen Rd. N3 ... 7E 30
Grunwick Cl. NW2 ... 5C 62
Gtec Ho. *E15* ... *2F 87*
(off Canning Rd.)
Guardhouse Way NW7 ... 5A 30
Guardian Apts. *E3* ... *4B 86*
(off Kevtar Gdn.)
Guardian Av. NW9 ... 3A 44
Guardian Ct. SE12 ... 5G 123
Guards Memorial ... 5D 12 (1H 101)
The Guards' Mus. ... 7B 12 (2G 101)
Gubyon Av. SE24 ... 5B 120
Guerin Sq. E3 ... 3B 86
Guernsey Cl. TW5: Hest ... 7E 94
Guernsey Gro. SE24 ... 7C 120
Guernsey Ho. *EN3: Enf W* ... *1E 24*
(off Eastfield Rd.)
N1 ... *6C 66*
(off Channel Island Est.)
Guernsey Rd. E11 ... 1F 69
Guglielmo Marconi M. E3 ... 2B 86
Guibal Rd. SE12 ... 7K 123
Guildersfield Rd. SW16 ... 7J 137
Guildford Av. TW13: Felt ... 2H 129
Guildford Ct. *SW8* ... *7J 101*
(off Guildford Rd.)
Guildford Gro. SE10 ... 1D 122
Guildford Rd. CR0: C'don ... 6D 156
E6 ... 6D 88
E17 ... 1E 50
IG3: Ilf ... 2J 71
SW8 ... 1J 119
Guildford Way SM6: W'gton ... 5J 167
Guildhall ... 7E 8
Guildhall Art Gallery ... *7E 8*
(off Aldermanbury)
Guildhall Bldgs. EC2 ... 7E 8
Guildhall College ... 6H 85
Guildhall Offices EC2 ... 7D 8
Guildhall Yd. EC2 ... 7D 8 (6C 84)
Guildhouse St. SW1 ... 3A 18 (4G 101)
Guildown Av. N12 ... 4E 30
Guild Rd. SE7 ... 6B 106
Guildsway E17 ... 1B 50
Guilford Av. KT5: Surb ... 5F 151
Guilford Pl. WC1 ... 4G 7 (4K 83)
Guilford St. WC1 ... 4E 6 (4J 83)
Guilfoyle NW9 ... 2B 44
Guillemot Ct. *SE8* ... *6B 104*
(off Alexandra Cl.)
Guillemot Pl. N22 ... 2K 47
Guinea Ct. *E1* ... *7G 85*
(off Royal Mint St.)
Guinea Point *E14* ... *6A 86*
(off Repton St.)
Guinness Cl. E9 ... 7A 68
UB3: Harl ... 3F 93
Guinness Ct. CR0: C'don ... 2F 169
E1 ... 1J 15
EC1 ... 2D 8
SE1 ... 6G 15
SW3 ... 4E 16 (4D 100)
Guinness Sq. SE1 ... 4E 102
Guinness Trust *SW3* ... *4E 16*
(off Cadogan St.)
Guinness Trust Bldgs. SE11 ... 5B 102
W6 ... *5E 98*
(off Fulham Pal. Rd.)
The Guinness Trust Est. N16 ... 1E 66
Guion Rd. SW6 ... 2H 117
Gulland Wlk. *N1* ... *6C 66*
(off Church Rd.)
Gullane Ho. *E3* ... *2B 86*
(off Shetland Rd.)
Gulliver Cl. UB5: N'olt ... 1D 76
Gulliver Rd. DA15: Sidc ... 2H 143
Gulliver's Ho. EC1 ... 4C 8
Gulliver St. SE16 ... 3A 104
Gullivers Wlk. SE8 ... 4B 104
Gulston Wlk. SW3 ... 4F 17
Gumleigh Rd. W5 ... 4C 96
Gumley Gdns. TW7: Isle ... 3A 114
Gumping Rd. BR5: Farnb ... 2G 173
Gundulf St. SE11 ... 4A 102
Gundulph Rd. BR2: Broml ... 3A 160
Gun Ho. *E1* ... *1H 103*
(off Wapping High St.)
Gunmakers La. E3 ... 1A 86
Gun M. IG9: Buck H ... 4G 37
Gunnel Ct. *E3* ... *3E 86*
(off Bolinder Way)
Gunnell Cl. CR0: C'don ... 6G 157
SE25 ... *6G 157*
(off Backley Gdns.)
SE26 ... 4G 139
Gunner La. SE18 ... 5E 106
GUNNERSBURY ... 5H 97
Gunnersbury Av. W3 ... 1F 97
W4 ... 1F 97
W5 ... 1F 97
Gunnersbury Cl. W4 ... 5H 97
Gunnersbury Ct. W3 ... 2H 97
Gunnersbury Cres. W3 ... 2G 97
Gunnersbury Dr. W5 ... 2F 97
Gunnersbury Gdns. W3 ... 2G 97
Gunnersbury La. W3 ... 3G 97
Gunnersbury Mnr. W5 ... 1F 97
Gunnersbury M. W4 ... 5H 97
GUNNERSBURY PARK ... 3G 97
Gunnersbury Pk. Mus. ... 3G 97
Gunnersbury Triangle Nature Reserve ... 4J 97
Gunners Gro. E4 ... 3K 35
Gunners Rd. SW18 ... 2B 136
Gunnery Ter. SE18 ... 3G 107
Gunning St. SE18 ... 4J 107
Gunpowder Sq. *EC4* ... *7K 7*
(off E. Harding St.)
Gunstor Rd. N16 ... 4E 66
Gun St. E1 ... 6J 9 (5F 85)
Gunter Gro. HA8: Edg ... 1K 43
SW10 ... 6A 100
Gunter Hall Studios *SW10* ... *6A 100*
(off Gunter Gro.)
Gunterstone Rd. W14 ... 4G 99
Gunthorpe St. E1 ... 6K 9 (5F 85)
Gunton M. SE13 ... 5F 123
Gunton Rd. E5 ... 3H 67
SW17 ... 6E 136
Gunwhale Cl. SE16 ... 1K 103
Gun Wharf *E1* ... *1J 103*
(off Wapping High St.)
Gunyard M. SE18 ... 7C 106
Gurdon Ho. *E14* ... *6C 86*
(off Dod St.)
Gurdon Rd. SE7 ... 5J 105
Gurdwara Sri Guru Singh Sabha
Southall ... 3C 94
Gurnard Cl. UB7: Yiew ... 7A 74
Gurnell Gro. W13 ... 4K 77
Gurnell Leisure Cen. ... 3K 77
Gurney Cl. E15 ... 5G 69
E17 ... 1K 49
IG11: Bark ... 6F 71
Gurney Cres. CR0: C'don ... 1K 167
Gurney Dr. N2 ... 4A 46
Gurney Ho. *E2* ... *2G 85*
(off Goldsmiths Row)
UB3: Harl ... 5G 93
Gurney Rd. E15 ... 5G 69
SM5: Cars ... 4E 166
SW6 ... 3A 118
UB5: N'olt ... 3K 75
Gutenberg Ct. *SE1* ... *3F 103*
(off Grange Rd.)
Guthridge Cl. E14 ... 5C 86
Guthrie Ct. SE1 ... 7K 13
Guthrie St. SW3 ... 5C 16 (5B 100)
Gutter La. EC2 ... 7C 8 (6C 84)
Guyatt Gdns. CR4: Mitc ... 2E 154
Guy Barnett Gro. SE3 ... 3J 123
Guy Rd. SM6: Bedd ... 3H 167
Guyscliff Rd. SE13 ... 5E 122
Guys Retreat IG9: Buck H ... 1F 37
Guy St. SE1 ... 6F 15 (2D 102)
Guy Townsley Sq. E3 ... 5D 86
Gwalior Ho. N14 ... 6B 22
Gwalior Rd. SW15 ... 4F 117
Gwendolen Av. SW15 ... 4F 117
Gwendolen Cl. SW15 ... 5F 117
Gwendolen Ho. *TW19: Stanw* ... *1A 128*
(off Yeoman Dr.)
Gwendoline Av. E13 ... 1K 87
Gwendwr Rd. W14 ... 5G 99
Gweneth Cotts. HA8: Edg ... 6B 28
Gwen Morris Ho. SE5 ... 7C 102
Gwent Ct. *SE16* ... *1K 103*
(off Rotherhithe St.)
Gwillim Cl. DA15: Sidc ... 5A 126
Gwilym Maries Ho. *E2* ... *3H 85*
(off Blythe St.)
Gwydor Rd. BR3: Beck ... 3K 157
Gwydyr Rd. BR2: Broml ... 3H 159
Gwyn Cl. SW6 ... 7A 100
Gwynne Av. CR0: C'don ... 7K 157
Gwynne Cl. W4 ... 6B 98
Gwynne Ho. *E1* ... *5H 85*
(off Turner St.)
SW1 ... *5G 17*
(off Lwr. Sloane St.)
WC1 ... *2J 7*
(off Lloyd Baker St.)
Gwynne Pk. Av. IG8: Wfd G ... 6J 37
Gwynne Pl. WC1 ... 2H 7 (3K 83)
Gwynne Rd. SW11 ... 2B 118
Gylcote Cl. SE5 ... 4D 120
Gyles Pk. HA7: Stan ... 1C 42
Gyllyngdune Gdns. IG3: Ilf ... 2K 71
The Gym
Bloomsbury ... 4E 6 (4J 83)
Holborn Circus ... 6K 7
Hounslow ... 3F 113
Kingsbury ... 5G 43
London Monument ... 7D 84
Walworth Road ... 5C 102
The Gymnasium N1 ... 2J 83
GYPSY CORNER ... 5K 79

H

Haarlem Rd. W14 ... 3F 99
Haberdasher Est. N1 ... 1F 9 (3D 84)
Haberdasher Pl. N1 ... 1F 9 (3D 84)
Haberdashers Ct. SE14 ... 3K 121
Haberdasher St. N1 ... 1F 9 (3D 84)
Habitat Cl. SE15 ... 2H 121
Habitat Sq. *SE10* ... *3H 105*
(off Teal St.)
Haccombe Rd. SW19 ... 6A 136
HACKBRIDGE ... 1E 166
Hackbridge Pk. Gdns.
SM5: Cars ... 2D 166
Hackbridge Rd. SM6: W'gton ... 2E 166
Hackford Rd. SW9 ... 1K 119
Hackford Wlk. SW9 ... 1A 120
Hackington Cres. BR3: Beck ... 6C 140
HACKNEY ... 6H 67
Hackney City Farm ... 2G 85
Hackney Empire Theatre ... 6H 67
Hackney Fashion Hub E9 ... 6J 67
Hackney Gro. E8 ... 6H 67
Hackney Marshes Cen. ... 4B 68
Hackney Mus. ... 6H 67
Hackney Picturehouse ... *6H 67*
(off Mare St.)
Hackney Rd. E2 ... 2J 9 (3F 85)
Hackney University Technical College ... 1H 9 (3E 84)
HACKNEY WICK ... 6B 68
HACKNEY WICK ... 6A 68
Hackworth Point *E3* ... *3D 86*
(off Rainhill Way)
Hacon Sq. *E8* ... *7H 67*
(off Mare St.)
Hadar Cl. N20 ... 1D 30
Hadden Rd. SE28 ... 3J 107
Hadden Way UB6: G'frd ... 6H 59
Haddington Rd. BR1: Broml ... 3F 141
Haddo Ho. *SE10* ... *6D 104*
(off Haddo St.)
Haddon Cl. EN1: Enf ... 6B 24
KT3: N Mald ... 5B 152
Haddon Ct. NW4 ... 3E 44
W3 ... 7B 80
Haddonfield SE8 ... 4K 103
Haddon Gro. DA15: Sidc ... 7K 125
Haddon Rd. SM1: Sutt ... 4K 165
(not continuous)
Haddo St. SE10 ... 6D 104
Haden Ct. N4 ... 2A 66
Haden La. N11 ... 4B 32
Hadfield Cl. UB1: S'hall ... 3D 76
Hadfield Ho. *E1* ... *6G 85*
(off Ellen St.)
Hadleigh Cl. E1 ... 4J 85
HA2: Harr ... 4E 58
SW20 ... 2H 153
Hadleigh Ct. E4 ... 1B 36
NW2 ... 6E 62
Hadleigh Ho. *E1* ... *4J 85*
(off Hadleigh Cl.)
Hadleigh Lodge *IG8: Wfd G* ... *6D 36*
(off Snakes La. W.)
Hadleigh Rd. N9 ... 7C 24
Hadleigh St. E2 ... 3J 85
Hadleigh Wlk. E6 ... 6C 88
HADLEY ... 3C 20
Hadley Cl. N21 ... 6F 23
Hadley Comn.
EN5: Barn, New Bar ... 2D 20
Hadley Ct. EN5: New Bar ... 3E 20
N16 ... 1G 67
SL3: Poyle ... *4A 174*
(off Coleridge Cres.)
Hadley Gdns. UB2: S'hall ... 5D 94
W4 ... 5K 97
Hadley Grn. EN5: Barn ... 2C 20
Hadley Grn. Rd. EN5: Barn ... 2C 20
Hadley Grn. W. EN5: Barn ... 2C 20
Hadley Gro. EN5: Barn ... 2B 20
Hadley Highstone EN5: Barn ... 1C 20
Hadley M. EN5: Barn ... 3C 20
Hadley Pde. *EN5: Barn* ... *3B 20*
(off High St.)
Hadley Ridge EN5: Barn ... 3C 20
Hadley Rd. CR4: Mitc ... 4H 155
DA17: Belv ... 4F 109
EN2: Enf ... 1A 22
EN4: Had W ... 1K 21
EN5: New Bar ... 2E 20
Hadley St. NW1 ... 6F 65
(not continuous)
Hadley Way N21 ... 6F 23
HADLEY WOOD ... 1F 21
Hadley Wood Golf Course ... 1H 21
Hadley Wood Lawn Tennis Club ... 1F 21
Hadley Wood Nature Reserve ... 2F 21
Hadley Wood Rd. EN4: Cockf ... 2F 21
EN5: Cockf, New Bar ... 2F 21
Hadlow Ho. *SE17* ... *5E 102*
(off Kinglake Est.)
Hadlow Pl. SE19 ... 7G 139
Hadlow Rd. DA14: Sidc ... 4A 144
DA16: Well ... 7C 108
Hadrian Cl. *E3* ... *1C 86*
(off Garrison Rd.)
TW19: Stanw ... 7A 110
Hadrian Ct. SM2: Sutt ... 7K 165
Hadrian Est. E2 ... 2G 85
Hadrian M. CR4: Mitc ... 3F 155
N7 ... 7K 65
Hadrians Ride EN1: Enf ... 5A 24
Hadrian St. SE10 ... 5G 105
Hadrian Way TW19: Stanw ... 7A 110
(not continuous)
Hadstock Ho. *NW1* ... *1D 6*
(off Ossulston St.)
Hadyn Pk. Ct. *W12* ... *2C 98*
(off Curwen Rd.)
Hadyn Pk. Rd. W12 ... 2C 98
Hafer Rd. SW11 ... 4D 118
Hafton Rd. SE6 ... 1G 141
Haggard Rd. TW1: Twick ... 7B 114
Hagger Ct. E17 ... 3F 51
HAGGERSTON ... 7F 67
Haggerston Rd. E8 ... 7F 67
Haggerston Studios *E8* ... *1F 85*
(off Kingsland Rd.)
Hague St. E2 ... 3G 85
Ha Ha Rd. SE18 ... 6D 106
Haider Cl. NW2 ... 2F 63
Haig Ho. *E2* ... *1K 9*
(off Shipton St.)
Haig Pl. SM4: Mord ... 6J 153
Haig Rd. HA7: Stan ... 5H 27
UB8: Hil ... 5D 74
Haig Rd. E. E13 ... 3A 88
Haig Rd. W. E13 ... 3A 88
Haigville Gdns. IG6: Ilf ... 4F 53
Hailes Cl. CR0: Bedd ... 2H 167
SW19 ... 6A 136
Haileybury Av. EN1: Enf ... 6A 24
Hailey Rd. DA18: Erith ... 2G 109
Hailey Rd. Bus. Pk. DA18: Erith ... 2G 109
Hailing M. *BR2: Broml* ... *3K 159*
(off Wendover Rd.)
Hailsham Av. SW2 ... 2K 137
Hailsham Cl. KT6: Surb ... 7D 150
Hailsham Dr. HA1: Harr ... 3H 41
Hailsham Ho. *NW8* ... *4C 4*
(off Salisbury St.)
Hailsham Rd. SW17 ... 6E 136
Hailsham Ter. N18 ... 5J 33
Haimo Rd. SE9 ... 5B 124
Hainault Bri. Pde. *IG1: Ilf* ... *2F 71*
(off Hainault St.)
Hainault Ct. *E17* ... *4F 51*
(off Forest Ri.)
Hainault Gore RM6: Chad H ... 5E 54
Hainault Rd. E11 ... 1E 68
RM5: Col R, Rom ... 2J 55
RM6: Chad H ... 1B 54
(Forest Rd.)
RM6: Chad H ... 6F 55
(Sylvan Av.)
Hainault St. IG1: Ilf ... 2G 71
SE9 ... 1F 143
Haines Cl. N1 ... 7E 66
Haines Ho. *SW11* ... *7H 101*
(off Ponton Rd.)
Haines St. SW11 ... 7G 101
Haines Wlk. SM4: Mord ... 7K 153
Hainford Cl. SE4 ... 4K 121
Haining Cl. W4 ... 5G 97
Hainthorpe Rd. SE27 ... 3B 138
Hainton Cl. E1 ... 6H 85
Halberd M. E5 ... 2H 67
Halbutt Gdns. RM9: Dag ... 3F 73
Halbutt St. RM9: Dag ... 4F 73
Halcomb St. N1 ... 1E 84
Halcot Av. DA6: Bex ... 5H 127
Halcrow St. E1 ... 5H 85
Halcyon *EN1: Enf* ... *5K 23*
(off Private Rd.)
Halcyon Cl. SW13 ... 3C 116
Halcyon Wharf *E1* ... *1G 103*
(off Hermitage Wall)
Haldane Cl. N10 ... 7A 32
Haldane Pl. SW18 ... 1K 135
Haldane Rd. E6 ... 3B 88
SE28 ... 7D 90
SW6 ... 7H 99
UB1: S'hall ... 7G 77
Haldan Rd. E4 ... 6K 35
Haldon Rd. SW18 ... 6H 117
THE HALE ... 5E 28
The Hale E4 ... 7A 36
N17 ... 3G 49
Hale Cl. BR6: Farnb ... 4G 173
E4 ... 3K 35
HA8: Edg ... 5D 28
Hale Ct. HA8: Edg ... 5D 28
Hale Dr. NW7 ... 6D 28
HALE END ... 6B 36
Hale End Cl. HA4: Ruis ... 6J 39
Hale End Rd. E4 ... 5A 36
E17 ... 1E 50
IG8: Wfd G ... 7A 36
Halefield Rd. N17 ... 1H 49
Hale Gdns. N17 ... 4G 49
W3 ... 1G 97
Hale Gro. Gdns. NW7 ... 5F 29
Hale Ho. *SW1* ... *5D 18*
(off Lindsay Sq.)
Hale La. HA8: Edg ... 5C 28
NW7 ... 5E 28
Hale Path SE27 ... 4B 138
Hale Rd. E6 ... 4C 88
N17 ... 3G 49
Halesowen Rd. SM4: Mord ... 7K 153
Hales Prior *N1* ... *1G 7*
(off Calshot St.)
Hales St. SE8 ... 7C 104
Hale St. E14 ... 7D 86
Halesworth Cl. E5 ... 2J 67
Halesworth Rd. SE13 ... 3D 122
Hale Wlk. W7 ... 5J 77
Haley Rd. NW4 ... 6E 44
Half Acre HA7: Stan ... 5H 27
TW8: Bford ... 6D 96
Half Acre Rd. W7 ... 1J 95
Half Moon Ct. CR0: C'don ... 7B 156
EC1 ... 6C 8

A-Z Big London 229

Half Moon Cres.—Hanwell

Half Moon Cres. N1 2K 83
(not continuous)
Half Moon La. SE24 6C 120
Half Moon Pas. E1 1K 15 (6F 85)
(not continuous)
Half Moon St. W1 4K 11 (1F 101)
Halford Cl. HA8: Edg 2H 43
Halford Pl. W7 1K 95
Halford Rd. E10 5F 51
SW6 6J 99
TW10: Rich 5E 114
UB10: Ick 4C 56
Halfway St. DA15: Sidc 7H 125
Haliburton Rd. TW1: Twick 5A 114
Haliday Ho. *N1* *6D 66*
(off Mildmay St.)
Haliday Wlk. N1 6D 66
Halidon Cl. E9 5J 67
Halifax NW9 2B 44
Halifax Cl. TW11: Tedd 6J 131
Halifax Rd. EN2: Enf 2H 23
UB6: G'frd 1F 77
Halifax St. SE26 3H 139
Halifield Dr. DA17: Belv 3E 108
Haling Down Pas. CR8: Purl 7C 168
Haling Gro. CR2: S Croy 7C 168
Haling Pk. Gdns. CR2: S Croy 6B 168
Haling Pk. Rd. CR2: S Croy 5B 168
Haling Rd. CR2: S Croy 6D 168
Haliwell Ho. *NW6* *1K 81*
(off Mortimer Cres.)
Halkett Ho. *E2* *1J 85*
(off Waterloo Gdns.)
Halkin Arc. SW1 1F 17 (3D 100)
Halkin M. SW1 1G 17 (3E 100)
Halkin Pl. SW1 1G 17 (3E 100)
Halkin St. SW1 7H 11 (2E 100)
The Hall SE3 3J 123
Hallam Cl. BR7: Chst 5D 142
Hallam Ct. *W1* *5K 5*
(off Hallam St.)
Hallam Gdns. HA5: Hat E 1C 40
Hallam Ho. *SW1* *6B 18*
(off Churchill Gdns.)
Hallam M. W1 5K 5 (5F 83)
Hallam Rd. N15 4B 48
SW13 3D 116
Hallam St. W1 4K 5 (5F 83)
Hallane Ho. SE27 5C 138
Hall Apts. *E3* *5B 86*
(off Geoff Cade Way)
Hall Cl. W5 5E 78
Hall Ct. TW11: Tedd 5K 131
Hall Dr. SE26 5J 139
W7 6J 77
Halley Gdns. SE13 4F 123
Halley Ho. *E2* *2G 85*
(off Pritchards Rd.)
SE10 *5H 105*
(off Armitage Rd.)
Halley Rd. E7 6A 70
E12 6A 70
Halley St. E14 5A 86
Hall Farm Cl. HA7: Stan 4G 27
Hall Farm Dr. TW2: Whitt 7H 113
Hallfield Est. W2 6A 82
(not continuous)
Hall Gdns. E4 4G 35
Hall Ga. NW8 1A 4 (3B 82)
The Halliards KT12: Walt T 6J 147
Halliday Ho. *E1* *6G 85*
(off Christian St.)
Halliday Sq. UB2: S'hall 1H 95
Halliford Cl. TW17: Shep 4F 147
Halliford Rd. TW16: Sun 5G 147
TW17: Shep 5G 147
Halliford St. N1 7C 66
Hallingbury Ct. E17 3D 50
Halling Ho. *SE1* *7F 15*
(off Long La.)
Hallings Wharf Studios E15 1F 87
Hallington Ct. *HA8: Edg* *4A 28*
(off Brannigan Way)
Halliwell Ct. SE22 5G 121
Halliwell Rd. SW2 6K 119
Halliwick Ct. Pde. *N12* *6J 31*
(off Woodhouse Rd.)
Halliwick Rd. N10 1E 46
HALL LANE 5E 34
Hall La. E4 5F 35
NW4 1C 44
UB3: Harl 7F 93
Hallmark Ho. *E14* *5C 86*
(off Ursula Gould Way)
Hallmark Trad. Est. HA9: Wemb 4J 61
Hallmead Rd. SM1: Sutt 3K 165
Hall Oak Wlk. NW6 6H 63
Hallowell Av. CR0: Bedd 4J 167
Hallowell Cl. CR4: Mitc 3E 154
Hallowell Gdns. CR7: Thor H 2C 156
Hallowell Rd. HA6: Nwood 1G 39
Hallowfield Way CR4: Mitc 3B 154
Hallows Gro. TW16: Sun 5H 129
Hall Pl. W2 4A 4 (4B 82)
(not continuous)
Hall Place & Gdns. 6J 127
Hall Pl. Cres. DA5: Bexl 5J 127
Hall Place Sports Pavilion 6J 127
Hall Rd. E6 1D 88
E15 4F 69
NW8 1A 4 (3A 82)
RM6: Chad H 6C 54
SM6: W'gton 7F 167
TW7: Isle 5H 113
Hallside Rd. EN1: Enf 1A 24
Halls Ter. UB10: Hil 4D 74
Hall St. EC1 1B 8 (3B 84)
N12 5F 31
Hallsville Rd. E16 6H 87
Hallswelle Pde. NW11 5H 45
Hallswelle Rd. NW11 5H 45
Hall Twr. W2 5B 4
Hall Vw. SE9 2B 142
Hallywell Cres. E6 5D 88
Halo E15 1E 86
Halons Rd. SE9 7E 124
Halpin Building *SE10* *3J 105*
(off Rennie Street)
Halpin Pl. SE17 4D 102
Halsbrook Rd. SE3 3A 124
Halsbury Cl. HA7: Stan 4G 27
Halsbury Ct. HA7: Stan 5G 27
Halsbury Ho. *N7* *4K 65*
(off Biddestone Rd.)
Halsbury Rd. W12 1D 98
Halsbury Rd. E. UB5: N'olt 4G 59
Halsbury Rd. W. UB5: N'olt 5F 59
Halsend UB3: Hayes 1K 93
Halsey Ho. *WC1* *6G 7*
(off Red Lion Sq.)
Halsey M. SW3 3E 16 (4D 100)
Halsey St. SW3 3E 16 (4D 100)
Halsham Cres. IG11: Bark 5K 71
Halsmere Rd. SE5 1B 120
Halstead Cl. CR0: C'don 3C 168
Halstead Ct. E17 7B 50
N1 *1F 9*
(off Murray Gro.)
Halstead Gdns. N21 1J 33
Halstead Rd. E11 5J 51
EN1: Enf 4K 23
N21 1H 33
Halston Cl. SW11 6D 118
Halstow Rd. NW10 3F 81
SE10 5J 105
Halsway UB3: Hayes 1J 93
Halton Cl. N11 6J 31
Halton Ct. SE3 3K 123
Halton Cross St. N1 1B 84
Halton Ho. *N1* *7B 66*
(off Halton Rd.)
Halton Mans. N1 7B 66
Halton Pl. N1 1C 84
Halton Rd. N1 7B 66
Halt Robin La. DA17: Belv 4H 109
Halt Robin Rd. DA17: Belv 4G 109
(not continuous)
Halyard Ho. *E14* *3E 104*
(off Manchester Rd.)
Halyard Pl. E16 2K 105
Halyard St. RM9: Dag 4E 90
HAM 3C 132
The Ham TW8: Bford 7C 96
Hamara Ghar E13 1A 88
Hambalt Rd. SW4 5G 119
Hamble Cl. HA4: Ruis 2G 57
Hambledon *SE17* *6D 102*
(off Villa St.)
Hambledon Cl. UB8: Hil 4D 74
Hambledon Ct. SE22 4E 120
W5 7E 78
Hambledon Gdns. SE25 3F 157
Hambledon Pl. SE21 1E 138
Hambledon Rd. SW18 7H 117
Hambledown Rd. DA15: Sidc 7H 125
Hamble Dr. UB3: Hayes 7H 75
Hamblehyrst BR3: Beck 2D 158
Hamble St. SW6 3K 117
Hambleton Cl. KT4: Wor Pk 2E 164
Hamble Wlk. *UB5: N'olt* *2E 76*
(off Brabazon Rd.)
Hambley Ho. *SE16* *4H 103*
(off Camilla Rd.)
Hamblin Ho. *UB1: S'hall* *7C 76*
(off The Broadway)
Hambridge Way SW2 7A 120
Hambro Av. BR2: Hayes 1J 171
Hambrook Rd. SE25 3H 157
Hambro Rd. SW16 6H 137
Hambrough Ho. UB4: Yead 5A 76
Hambrough Rd. UB1: S'hall 1C 94
Ham Cl. TW10: Ham 3C 132
(not continuous)
Ham Common 4E 132
Ham Comn. TW10: Ham 3D 132
Ham Ct. NW9 2A 44
Ham Cft. Cl. TW13: Felt 3J 129
Hamden Cres. RM10: Dag 3H 73
Hamel Cl. HA3: Kenton 4D 42
Hamella Ho. *E9* *5A 68*
(off Sadler Pl.)
Hameway E6 3E 88
Ham Farm Rd. TW10: Ham 4D 132
Ham Flds. TW10: Ham 3B 132
Hamfrith Rd. E15 6H 69
Ham Ga. Av. TW10: Ham 3D 132
Ham House & Garden 1C 132
Hamilton Av. IG6: Ilf 4F 53
KT6: Surb 2G 163
N9 7B 24
RM1: Rom 2K 55
SM3: Cheam 2G 165
Hamilton Cl. EN4: Cockf 4H 21
HA7: Stan 2D 26
N17 3F 49
NW8 2A 4 (3B 82)
SE16 2A 104
TW11: Tedd 6B 132
TW13: Felt 5H 129
Hamilton Ct. CR0: C'don 1G 169
SE6 1H 141
SW15 3G 117
TW3: Houn *4F 113*
(off Hanworth Rd.)
W5 7E 78
W9 *3A 82*
(off Maida Vale)
Hamilton Cres. HA2: Harr 3D 58
N13 4F 33
TW3: Houn 5F 113
Hamilton Gdns. NW8 1A 4 (3A 82)
Hamilton Hall *NW8* *2A 82*
(off Hamilton Ter.)
Hamilton Ho. *E3* *3B 86*
(off British St.)
E14 *5D 104*
(off St Davids Sq.)
E14 *7B 86*
(off Victory Pl.)
NW8 1A 4
W4 6A 98
W8 *2K 99*
(off Vicarage Ga.)
Hamilton La. N5 4B 66
Hamilton Lodge *E1* *4J 85*
(off Cleveland Gro.)
Hamilton M. SW18 1J 135
SW19 7J 135
W1 6J 11 (2F 101)
Hamilton Pde. TW13: Felt 4H 129
Hamilton Pk. N5 4B 66
Hamilton Pk. W. N5 4B 66
Hamilton Pl. N19 3H 65
TW16: Sun 7K 129
W1 5H 11 (1E 100)
Hamilton Rd. CR7: Thor H 3D 156
DA7: Bex 2E 126
DA15: Sidc 4A 144
E15 3G 87
E17 2A 50
EN4: Cockf 4H 21
HA1: Harr 5J 41
Hamilton Rd. IG1: Ilf 4F 71
N2 3A 46
N9 7B 24
NW10 5C 62
NW11 7F 45
SE27 4D 138
SW19 7K 135
TW2: Twick 1J 131
TW8: Bford 6D 96
TW13: Felt 4H 129
UB1: S'hall 1D 94
UB3: Hayes 7K 75
W4 2A 98
W5 7E 78
Hamilton Rd. Ind. Est. SE27 4D 138
Hamilton Rd. M. SW19 7K 135
Hamilton Sq. N12 6G 31
SE1 6F 15 (2D 102)
Hamilton St. SE8 6C 104
Hamilton Ter. NW8 2A 4 (2K 81)
Hamilton Way N3 6D 30
N13 4G 33
SM6: W'gton 7H 167
Ham Lands Nature Reserve 2A 132
Hamlea Cl. SE12 5J 123
The Hamlet SE5 3D 120
Hamlet Cl. RM5: Col R 1G 55
SE6 7D 122
SE13 4G 123
Hamlet Ct. *E3* *3C 86*
(off Tomlin's Gro.)
EN1: Enf 5K 23
SE11 *5B 102*
(off Opal St.)
W6 4C 98
Hamlet Gdns. W6 4C 98
Hamlet Ind. Est. E9 7C 68
Hamlet Intl. Ind. Est. DA8: Erith 5K 109
Hamlet Lodge UB10: Hil 6D 56
Hamlet M. SE21 1D 138
Hamleton Ter. *RM9: Dag* *7C 72*
(off Flamstead Rd.)
Hamlet Rd. RM5: Col R 1G 55
SE19 7F 139
Hamlet Sq. NW2 3G 63
Hamlets Way E3 4B 86
Hamlet Way SE1 6F 15 (2D 102)
Hamlin Cres. HA5: Eastc 5A 40
Hamlyn Cl. HA8: Edg 3K 27
Hamlyn Gdns. SE19 7E 138
Hamlyn Ho. TW13: Felt 1K 129
Hammelton Ct. *BR1: Broml* *1H 159*
(off London Rd.)
Hammelton Rd. BR1: Broml 1H 159
Hammerfield Ho. *SW3* *5D 16*
(off Cale St.)
Hammers La. NW7 5H 29
Hammersley Ho. *SE14* *7J 103*
(off Pomeroy St.)
Hammersley Rd. E16 5J 87
HAMMERSMITH 4E 98
Hammersmith Apollo 5E 98
HAMMERSMITH BRI. 6D 98
Hammersmith Bri. Rd. W6 5E 98
HAMMERSMITH BROADWAY 4E 98
Hammersmith B'way. W6 4E 98
Hammersmith Emb. W6 6E 98
Hammersmith Fitness & Squash Cen. *4F 99*
(off Chalk Hill Rd.)
HAMMERSMITH FLYOVER 5E 98
Hammersmith Flyover W6 5E 98
Hammersmith Gro. W6 2E 98
Hammersmith Information Centre *4E 98*
(within The Broadway Cen.)
Hammersmith Rd. W6 4F 99
W14 4F 99
Hammersmith Ter. W6 5C 98
Hammet Cl. UB4: Yead 5B 76
Hammett St. EC3 2J 15 (7F 85)
Hammond Av. CR4: Mitc 2F 155
Hammond Cl. EN5: Barn 5B 20
TW12: Hamp 1E 148
UB6: G'frd 5H 59
Hammond Ct. *E10* *2D 68*
(off Leyton Grange Est.)
SE11 *5J 19*
(off Hotspur St.)
Hammond Ho. *E14* *3C 104*
(off Tiller Rd.)
SE14 *7J 103*
(off Lubbock St.)
Hammond Lodge *W9* *5J 81*
(off Admiral Wlk.)
Hammond Rd. EN1: Enf 2C 24
UB2: S'hall 3C 94
Hammonds Cl. RM8: Dag 3C 72
Hammond St. NW5 6G 65
Hammond Way SE28 7B 90
Hamond Cl. CR2: S Croy 7B 168
Hamonde Cl. HA8: Edg 2C 28
Hamond Sq. N1 2E 84
Ham Pk. Rd. E7 7H 69
E15 7H 69
Hampden Av. BR3: Beck 2A 158
Hampden Cl. NW1 2H 83
Hampden Ct. N10 7K 31
Hampden Gurney St.
W1 1E 10 (6D 82)
Hampden Ho. *SW9* *2A 120*
(off Overton Rd.)
Hampden La. N17 1F 49
Hampden Rd. BR3: Beck 2A 158
HA3: Hrw W 1G 41
KT1: King T 3G 151
N8 4A 48
N10 7K 31
N17 1G 49
N19 2H 65
RM5: Col R 1H 55
Hampden Sq. N14 1A 32
Hampden Way N14 1A 32
Hampshire Cl. N18 5C 34
Hampshire Hog La. W6 5D 98
Hampshire Rd. N22 7E 32
Hampshire St. NW5 6H 65
Hampson Way SW8 1K 119
HAMPSTEAD 4B 64
Hampstead Av. IG8: Wfd G 7K 37
Hampstead Cl. SE28 1B 108
Hampstead Gdns. NW11 6J 45
RM6: Chad H 5B 54
HAMPSTEAD GARDEN SUBURB 5A 46
Hampstead Ga. NW3 5A 64
Hampstead Golf Course 7B 46
Hampstead Grn. NW3 5C 64
Hampstead Gro. NW3 3A 64
Hampstead Heath 2B 64
Hampstead Hgts. N2 3A 46
Hampstead High St. NW3 4B 64
Hampstead Hill Gdns. NW3 4B 64
Hampstead Ho. *NW1* *2A 6*
(off William Rd.)
Hampstead La. N6 1B 64
NW3 1B 64
Hampstead Lodge *NW1* *5C 4*
(off Bell St.)
Hampstead M. BR3: Beck 4D 158
Hampstead Mus. *4B 64*
(off New End Sq.)
Hampstead Rd. NW1 1A 6 (2G 83)
Hampstead Sq. NW3 3A 64
Hampstead Theatre 7B 64
Hampstead Wlk. E3 1B 86
Hampstead Way NW11 5H 45
Hampstead W. NW6 6J 63
HAMPTON 1F 149
Hampton & Richmond Borough FC 1F 149
Hampton Bus. Pk. TW13: Hanw 3C 130
Hampton Cl. N11 5A 32
NW6 3J 81
SW20 7E 134
HAMPTON COURT 4J 149
HAMPTON COURT 3J 149
Hampton Ct. N1 6B 66
N22 1G 47
SE14 *7A 104*
(off Batavia Rd.)
SE16 *7K 85*
(off King & Queen Wharf)
Hampton Ct. Av. KT8: E Mos 6H 149
HAMPTON CT. BRI. 4J 149
Hampton Ct. Cres. KT8: E Mos 3H 149
Hampton Ct. Est. KT7: T Ditt 4J 149
Hampton Ct. M. *KT8: E Mos* *4J 149*
(off Feltham Av.)
Hampton Court Palace 4K 149
Hampton Court Palace Golf Course 5C 150
Hampton Ct. Pde. KT8: E Mos 4J 149
Hampton Ct. Rd. KT1: Hamp W 3K 149
KT8: E Mos 3K 149
TW12: E Mos, Hamp 2G 149
Hampton Ct. Way KT7: T Ditt 7J 149
KT8: E Mos 7J 149
Hampton Golf Course 3E 130
Hampton Grange BR1: Broml 7A 142
HAMPTON HILL 5G 131
Hampton Hill Bus. Pk.
TW12: Hamp H *5G 131*
(off High St.)
Hampton Hill Theatre 5G 131
Hampton Ho. *DA7: Bex* *2H 127*
(off Erith Rd.)
SW8 *7G 101*
(off Ascalon St.)
Hampton La. TW13: Hanw 4C 130
Hampton M. EN3: Enf H 3D 24
NW10 3K 79
WD23: B Hea 1B 26
Hampton Open Air Pool 7G 131
Hampton Ri. HA3: Kenton 6E 42
Hampton Rd. CR0: C'don 6C 156
E4 5G 35
E7 5K 69
E11 1F 69
HA7: Stan 3D 26
IG1: Ilf 4G 71
KT4: Wor Pk 2C 164
TW2: Twick 3H 131
TW11: Tedd 5H 131
TW12: Hamp H 5H 131
Hampton Rd. E. TW13: Hanw 4D 130
Hampton Rd. Ind. Pk.
CR0: C'don 6C 156
Hampton Rd. W. TW13: Hanw 3C 130
Hampton Sports & Fitness Cen. 5E 130
Hampton St. SE1 4C 102
SE17 4B 102
HAMPTON WICK 1C 150
Hampton Youth Project (Sports Hall) 6D 130
Ham Ridings TW10: Ham 5F 133
Hamshades Cl. DA15: Sidc 3K 143
Hamston Ho. *W8* *3K 99*
(off Kensington Ct. Pl.)
Ham St. TW10: Ham 1B 132
Ham Vw. CR0: C'don 6A 158
Ham Yd. W1 2C 12 (7H 83)
Hanah Ct. SW19 7F 135
Hanameel St. E16 1K 105
Hana M. E5 4H 67
Hanbury Cl. NW4 3E 44
Hanbury Ct. HA1: Harr 6K 41
Hanbury Dr. E11 7H 51
N21 5E 22
Hanbury Ho. *E1* *5G 85*
(off Hanbury St.)
SW8 *7J 101*
(off Regent's Bri. Gdns.)
Hanbury M. CR0: C'don 1A 170
N1 1C 84
Hanbury Rd. N17 2H 49
W3 2H 97
Hanbury St. E1 5K 9 (5F 85)
Hanbury Wlk. DA5: Bexl 3K 145
Hancock Nunn Ho. *NW3* *6D 64*
(off Fellows Rd.)
Hancock Rd. E3 3E 86
SE19 6D 138
Handa Wlk. N1 6D 66
Hand Axe Yd. WC1 3J 83
Hand Ct. WC1 6H 7 (5K 83)
Handcroft Rd. CR0: C'don 7B 156
Handel & Hendrix in London *2J 11*
(off Brook St.)
Handel Bus. Cen. SW8 7E 18 (6J 101)
Handel Cl. HA8: Edg 6A 28
Handel Mans. SW13 7E 98
WC1 *3F 7*
(off Handel St.)
Handel Pde. *HA8: Edg* *7B 28*
(off Whitchurch La.)
Handel Pl. NW10 6K 61
Handel St. WC1 3E 6 (4J 83)
Handel Way HA8: Edg 7B 28
Handen Rd. SE12 5G 123
Handforth Rd. IG1: Ilf 3F 71
SW9 7A 102
Handley Dr. SE3 3K 123
Handley Gro. NW2 3F 63
Handley Page Rd. IG11: Bark 4A 90
SM6: W'gton 7K 167
Handley Rd. E9 7J 67
Handowe Cl. NW4 4C 44
Handside Cl. KT4: Wor Pk 1F 165
Hands Wlk. E16 6J 87
Handsworth Av. E4 6A 36
Handsworth Rd. N17 3D 48
Handtrough Way IG11: Bark 2F 89
Handyside St. N1 1H 83
Hanford Cl. SW18 1J 135
Hanford Row SW19 6E 134
Hanger Ct. W5 4F 79
Hanger Grn. W5 4G 79
HANGER HILL 4F 79
HANGER LANE 3E 78
Hanger La. W5 2E 78
Hanger Va. La. W5 6F 79
(not continuous)
Hanger Vw. Way W3 6G 79
Hanging Sword All. EC4 1K 13
Hankey Ho. *SE1* *7F 15*
(off Hankey Pl.)
Hankey Pl. SE1 7F 15 (2D 102)
Hankins Ho. *SE10* *3J 105*
(off Peartree Way)
Hankins La. NW7 2F 29
Hanley Gdns. N4 1K 65
Hanley Pl. BR3: Beck 7C 140
Hanley Rd. N4 1J 65
Hanmer Wlk. N7 2K 65
Hannaford Wlk. E3 4D 86
Hannah Barlow Ho. SW8 1K 119
Hannah Bldg. *E1* *6H 85*
(off Watney St.)
Hannah Cl. BR3: Beck 3E 158
NW10 4J 61
Hannah Ct. E15 2H 87
Hannah Mary Way SE1 4G 103
Hannah M. SM6: W'gton 7G 167
Hannay Ho. SW15 6G 117
Hannay La. N8 7H 47
Hannay Wlk. SW16 2H 137
Hannell Rd. SW6 7G 99
Hannen Rd. SE27 3B 138
Hannibal Rd. E1 5J 85
TW19: Stanw 7A 110
Hannibal Way CR0: Wadd 5K 167
Hannington Rd. SW4 3F 119
Hano Cl. SM6: W'gton 7H 167
Hanover Av. E16 1J 105
TW13: Felt 1J 129
Hanover Circ. UB3: Hayes 6E 74
Hanover Cl. SM3: Cheam 4G 165
TW9: Kew 7G 97
TW15: Ashf 4A 128
Hanover Ct. *E8* *1F 85*
(off Stean St.)
HA4: Ruis 3J 57
NW9 3A 44
SE19 *7G 139*
(off Anerley Rd.)
SW15 4B 116
W12 *1C 98*
(off Uxbridge Rd.)
Hanover Dr. BR7: Chst 4G 143
Hanover Flats *W1* *2H 11*
(off Binney St.)
Hanover Gdns. IG6: Ilf 1G 53
SE11 6A 102
Hanover Ga. NW1 2D 4 (3C 82)
Hanover Ga. Mans. NW1 3D 4 (4C 82)
Hanover Ho. *E14* *1B 104*
(off Westferry Cir.)
NW8 *2C 82*
(off St John's Wood High St.)
SE16 *2K 103*
(off Dominion Dr.)
SW9 3A 120
Hanover Mans. *SW2* *5A 120*
(off Barnwell Rd.)
Hanover Mead NW11 5G 45
Hanover Pk. SE15 1G 121
Hanover Pl. E3 3B 86
WC2 1F 13 (6J 83)
Hanover Rd. N15 4F 49
NW10 7E 62
SW19 7A 136
Hanover Sq. W1 1K 11 (6F 83)
Hanover Steps W2 1D 10
Hanover St. CR0: C'don 3B 168
W1 1K 11 (6F 83)
Hanover Ter. NW1 2E 4 (3D 82)
TW7: Isle 1A 114
Hanover Ter. M. NW1 2D 4 (3C 82)
Hanover Trad. Est. N7 5J 65
Hanover Way DA6: Bex 3D 126
Hanover W. Ind. Est. NW10 3K 79
Hanover Yd. *N1* *2C 84*
(off Noel Rd.)
Hansa Cl. UB2: S'hall 3A 94
Hansard M. W14 2F 99
Hansart Way EN2: Enf 1F 23
Hanscomb M. SW4 4G 119
Hans Ct. SW3 1E 16
Hans Cres. SW1 1E 16 (3D 100)
Hanseatic Wlk. EC4 3E 14
Hanselin Cl. HA7: Stan 5E 26
Hansel Rd. NW6 3J 81
Hansen Dr. N21 5E 22
Hanshaw Dr. HA8: Edg 1K 43
Hansler Ct. *SW19* *1G 135*
(off Princes Way)
Hansler Gro. KT8: E Mos 4H 149
Hansler Rd. SE22 5F 121
Hansol Rd. DA6: Bex 5E 126
Hansom M. SE11 5H 19 (5K 101)
Hansom Ter. *BR1: Broml* *1K 159*
(off Freelands Gro.)
Hanson Cl. BR3: Beck 6D 140
SW12 7F 119
SW14 3J 115
UB7: W Dray 3B 92
Hanson Ct. E17 6D 50
Hanson Gdns. UB1: S'hall 2C 94
Hanson Ho. *E1* *7G 85*
(off Pinchin St.)
Hanson St. W1 5A 6 (5G 83)
Hans Pl. SW1 1F 17 (3D 100)
Hans Rd. SW3 1E 16 (3D 100)
Hans St. SW1 2F 17 (3D 100)
Hanway Pl. W1 7C 6 (6H 83)
Hanway Rd. W7 6H 77
Hanway St. W1 7C 6 (6H 83)
HANWELL 1K 95

230 A-Z Big London

Hanwell Ho.—Harvey Ho.

Hanwell Ho. W2 ... 5J 81
(off Gt. Western Rd.)
HANWORTH ... 4B 130
Hanworth Air Pk. Leisure Cen. ... 2B 130
Hanworth Ho. SE5 ... 7B 102
Hanworth Rd. TW3: Houn ... 1C 130
TW4: Houn ... 1C 130
TW12: Hamp ... 4D 130
TW13: Felt ... 1K 129
TW16: Sun ... 7J 129
(not continuous)
Hanworth Ter. TW3: Houn ... 4F 113
Hanworth Trad. Est.
TW13: Hanw ... 3C 130
Hapgood Cl. UB6: G'frd ... 5H 59
Harad's Pl. E1 ... 7G 85
Harbans Ct. SL3: Poyle ... 4A 174
Harben Pde. NW3 ... 7A 64
(off Finchley Rd.)
Harben Rd. NW6 ... 7A 64
Harberson Rd. E15 ... 1H 87
SW12 ... 1F 137
Harberton Rd. N19 ... 1G 65
Harbet Rd. E4 ... 5F 35
N18 ... 5F 35
W2 ... 6B 4 (5B 82)
Harbex Cl. DA5: Bexl ... 7H 127
Harbinger Rd. E14 ... 4D 104
Harbledown Ho. SE1 ... 7E 14
(off Manciple St.)
Harbledown Rd. SW6 ... 1J 117
Harbord Cl. SE5 ... 2D 120
Harbord Ho. SE16 ... 4K 103
(off Cope St.)
Harbord St. SW6 ... 1F 117
Harborough Av. DA15: Sidc ... 7J 125
Harborough Ho. UB5: N'olt ... 3D 76
(off Taywood Rd.)
Harborough Rd. SW16 ... 4K 137
Harbour Av. SW10 ... 1A 118
Harbour Cl. CR4: Mitc ... 1E 154
Harbour Club
Chelsea ... 2A 118
Kensington ... 4K 99
(off Point West)
Notting Hill ... 5J 81
Harbour Exchange Sq. E14 ... 2D 104
Harbour Quay E14 ... 1E 104
Harbour Reach SW6 ... 1A 118
Harbour Rd. SE5 ... 3C 120
Harbourside Ct. SE8 ... 4A 104
(off Plough Way)
Harbour Way E14 ... 2C 104
Harbour Yd. SW10 ... 1A 118
Harbridge Av. SW15 ... 7B 116
Harbury Rd. SM5: Cars ... 7C 166
Harbut Rd. SW11 ... 4B 118
Harbutt Rd. HA9: Wemb ... 4G 61
Harcombe Rd. N16 ... 3E 66
Harcourt Av. DA15: Sidc ... 6C 126
E12 ... 4D 70
HA8: Edg ... 3D 28
SM6: W'gton ... 4F 167
Harcourt Bldgs. EC4 ... 2J 13
Harcourt Cl. TW7: Isle ... 3A 114
Harcourt Fld. SM6: W'gton ... 4F 167
Harcourt Ho. W1 ... 7J 5
Harcourt Lodge SM6: W'gton ... 4F 167
Harcourt Rd. CR7: Thor H ... 6K 155
DA6: Bex ... 4E 126
E15 ... 2H 87
N22 ... 1H 47
SE4 ... 3B 122
SM6: W'gton ... 4F 167
SW19 ... 7J 135
Harcourt St. W1 ... 6D 4 (5C 82)
Harcourt Ter. SW10 ... 5K 99
Hardcastle Cl. CR0: C'don ... 6G 157
Hardcastle Ho. SE14 ... 1A 122
(off Loring Rd.)
Hardcourts Cl. BR4: W W'ck ... 3D 170
Hardegray Cl. SM2: Sutt ... 7J 165
Hardel Ri. SW2 ... 1B 138
Hardel Wlk. SW2 ... 7A 120
Harden Ct. SE7 ... 4C 106
Harden Ho. SE5 ... 2E 120
Harden's Manorway SE7 ... 3B 106
(not continuous)
Harders Rd. SE15 ... 2H 121
Hardess St. SE24 ... 3C 120
Hardie Cl. NW10 ... 5K 61
Hardie Rd. RM10: Dag ... 3J 73
Harding Cl. CR0: C'don ... 3F 169
SE17 ... 6C 102
Harding Dr. RM8: Dag ... 1E 72
Hardinge Cl. UB8: Hil ... 5D 74
Hardinge Cres. SE18 ... 3G 107
Hardinge La. E1 ... 6J 85
(not continuous)
Hardinge Rd. N18 ... 6K 33
NW10 ... 1D 80
Hardinge St. E1 ... 7J 85
(Johnson St.)
E1 ... 6J 85
(Steel's La.)
Harding Ho. SW13 ... 6D 98
(off Wyatt Dr.)
UB3: Hayes ... 6K 75
Harding Rd. DA7: Bex ... 2F 127
Harding's Cl. KT2: King T ... 1F 151
Hardings La. SE20 ... 6K 139
Hardington NW1 ... 7E 64
(off Belmont St.)
Hardman Rd. KT2: King T ... 2E 150
SE7 ... 5K 105
Hardwick Cl. HA7: Stan ... 5H 27
Hardwick Ct. DA8: Erith ... 6K 109
Hardwicke Av. TW5: Hest ... 1E 112
Hardwicke M. WC1 ... 2H 7
Hardwicke Rd. N13 ... 6D 32
TW10: Ham ... 4C 132
W4 ... 4K 97
Hardwicke St. IG11: Bark ... 1G 89
Hardwick Grn. W13 ... 5B 78
Hardwick Ho. NW8 ... 3D 4
(off Lilestone St.)
Hardwick Pl. SW16 ... 7G 137
Hardwicks Sq. SW18 ... 5J 117
Hardwick St. EC1 ... 2K 7 (3A 84)
Hardwidge St. SE1 ... 6G 15 (2E 102)
Hardy Av. E16 ... 1J 105
HA4: Ruis ... 5K 57
Hardy Cl. EN5: Barn ... 6B 20
HA5: Pinn ... 7B 40
SE16 ... 2K 103
Hardy Cotts. SE10 ... 6F 105
Hardy Ho. SW4 ... 7G 119
SW17 ... 3B 136
(off Grosvenor Way)
SW18 ... 7K 117
Hardying Ho. E17 ... 4A 50
Hardy Pas. N22 ... 1K 47
Hardy Rd. E4 ... 6G 35
SE3 ... 7H 105
SW19 ... 7K 135
Hardy's M. KT8: E Mos ... 4J 149
Hardy Way EN2: Enf ... 1F 23
Hare & Billet Rd. SE3 ... 1F 123
Harebell Dr. E6 ... 5E 88
Harecastle Cl. UB4: Yead ... 4C 76
Hare Ct. EC4 ... 1J 13
Harecourt Rd. N1 ... 6C 66
Harecroft La. UB10: Ick ... 3E 56
Haredale Ho. SE16 ... 2G 103
(off East La.)
Haredale Rd. SE24 ... 4C 120
Haredon Cl. SE23 ... 7K 121
HAREFIELD ... 1A 38
Harefield Cl. EN2: Enf ... 1F 23
Harefield Grn. NW7 ... 6K 29
Harefield M. SE4 ... 3B 122
Harefield Rd. DA14: Sidc ... 3D 144
N8 ... 5H 47
SE4 ... 3B 122
SW16 ... 7K 137
UB8: Uxb ... 5A 56
Hare Marsh E2 ... 4G 85
Harepit Cl. CR2: S Croy ... 7B 168
Hare Pl. EC4 ... 1K 13
(off Fleet St.)
Hare Row E2 ... 2H 85
Haresfield Rd. RM10: Dag ... 6G 73
Hare St. SE18 ... 3E 106
Hare Wlk. N1 ... 2E 84
(not continuous)
Harewood Av. NW1 ... 4D 4 (4C 82)
NW7 ... 6B 30
UB5: N'olt ... 7D 58
Harewood Cl. UB5: N'olt ... 7D 58
Harewood Dr. IG5: Ilf ... 2D 52
Harewood Pl. W1 ... 1K 11 (6F 83)
Harewood Rd. CR2: S Croy ... 6E 168
SW19 ... 6C 136
TW7: Isle ... 7K 95
Harewood Row NW1 ... 5D 4 (5C 82)
Harewood Ter. UB2: S'hall ... 4D 94
Harfield Gdns. SE5 ... 3E 120
Harfield Rd. TW16: Sun ... 2B 148
Harfleur Ct. SE11 ... 4B 102
(off Opal St.)
Harford Cl. E4 ... 7J 25
Harford Ho. SE5 ... 6C 102
(off Bethwin Rd.)
W11 ... 5H 81
Harford M. N19 ... 3H 65
Harford Rd. E4 ... 7J 25
Harford St. E1 ... 4A 86
Harford Wlk. N2 ... 4B 46
Harfst Way BR8: Swan ... 7J 145
Hargood Cl. HA3: Kenton ... 6E 42
Hargood Rd. SE3 ... 1A 124
Hargrave Mans. N19 ... 2H 65
Hargrave Pk. N19 ... 2G 65
Hargrave Pl. N7 ... 5H 65
Hargrave Rd. N19 ... 2G 65
Hargraves Ho. W12 ... 7D 80
(off White City Est.)
Hargreaves Ct. E3 ... 3E 86
(off Bolinder Way)
Hargwyne St. SW9 ... 3K 119
Hari Cl. UB5: N'olt ... 5F 59
Haringey Independent Cinema ... 4C 48
Haringey Pk. N8 ... 6J 47
Haringey Pas. N8 ... 4A 48
Haringey Rd. N8 ... 4J 47
Harington Ter. N9 ... 3J 33
N18 ... 3J 33
Harkett Cl. HA3: W'stone ... 2K 41
Harkett Ct. HA3: W'stone ... 2K 41
Harkness Ct. SM1: Sutt ... 1K 165
(off Cleeve Way)
Harkness Ho. E1 ... 6G 85
(off Christian St.)
Harland Av. CR0: C'don ... 3F 169
DA15: Sidc ... 3H 143
Harland Cl. SW19 ... 3K 153
Harland Rd. SE12 ... 7J 123
Harlands Gro. BR6: Farnb ... 4F 173
Harlech Gdns. HA5: Pinn ... 7B 40
TW5: Hest ... 6A 94
Harlech Rd. N14 ... 3D 32
Harlech Twr. W3 ... 2J 97
Harlequin Av. TW8: Bford ... 6A 96
Harlequin Cl.
IG11: Bark ... 4A 90
TW7: Isle ... 5J 113
UB4: Yead ... 5B 76
Harlequin Ct. E1 ... 7G 85
(off Thomas More St.)
NW10 ... 6K 61
(off Mitchellbrook Way)
W5 ... 7C 78
Harlequin FC ... 7J 113
Harlequin Ho. DA18: Erith ... 3E 108
(off Kale Rd.)
Harlequin Rd. TW11: Tedd ... 7B 132
Harlescott Rd. SE15 ... 4K 121
HARLESDEN ... 2B 80
Harlesden Gdns. NW10 ... 1B 80
Harlesden La. NW10 ... 1C 80
Harlesden Plaza NW10 ... 2B 80
Harlesden Rd. NW10 ... 1C 80
Harleston Cl. E5 ... 2J 67
Harley Cl. HA0: Wemb ... 6D 60
Harley Ct. E11 ... 7J 51
HA1: Harr ... 4H 41
N20 ... 3F 31
Harley Cres. HA1: Harr ... 4H 41
Harleyford BR1: Broml ... 1K 159
Harleyford Ct. SE11 ... 7G 19
Harleyford Mnr. W3 ... 1J 97
(off Edgecote Cl.)
Harleyford Rd. SE11 ... 7G 19 (6K 101)
Harleyford St. SE11 ... 7J 19 (6A 102)
Harley Gdns. BR6: Orp ... 4J 173
SW10 ... 5A 100
Harley Gro. E3 ... 3B 86
Harley Ho. E11 ... 7F 51
E14 ... 6B 86
(off Frances Wharf)
NW1 ... 4H 5
Harley Pl. W1 ... 6J 5 (5F 83)
Harley Rd. HA1: Harr ... 4H 41
NW3 ... 7B 64
NW10 ... 2A 80
Harley St. W1 ... 4J 5 (4F 83)
Harley Vs. NW10 ... 2A 80
Harlie Ct. SE6 ... 6C 122
Harling Ct. SW11 ... 2D 118
Harlinger St. SE18 ... 3C 106
HARLINGTON ... 6F 93
Harlington Cl. UB3: Harl ... 7E 92
HARLINGTON CORNER ... 1F 111
Harlington Rd. DA7: Bex ... 3E 126
UB8: Hil ... 3C 74
Harlington Rd. E. TW13: Felt ... 7K 111
TW14: Felt ... 7K 111
Harlington Rd. W. TW14: Felt ... 6K 111
The Harlington Sports Cen. ... 4F 93
(off Pinkwell La.)
Harlington Young People's Cen. ... 4F 93
Harlow Mans. IG11: Bark ... 7F 71
(off Whiting Av.)
Harlow Rd. N13 ... 3J 33
Harlyn Dr. HA5: Eastc ... 3K 39
Harlynwood SE5 ... 7C 102
(off Wyndham Rd.)
Harman Av. IG8: Wfd G ... 6C 36
Harman Cl. E4 ... 4A 36
NW2 ... 3G 63
SE1 ... 5G 103
Harman Dr. DA15: Sidc ... 6K 125
NW2 ... 3G 63
Harman Ri. IG3: Ilf ... 4J 71
Harman Rd. EN1: Enf ... 5A 24
HARMONDSWORTH ... 2E 174
Harmondsworth La.
UB7: Harm, Sip ... 6A 92
Harmondsworth Moor Waterside ... 2C 174
Harmondsworth Moor Waterside
Vis. Cen. ... 2C 174
Harmondsworth Rd. UB7: W Dray ... 5A 92
Harmon Ho. SE8 ... 4B 104
Harmont Ho. W1 ... 6J 5
(off Harley St.)
Harmony Apts. BR1: Broml ... 2J 159
(off High St.)
Harmony Cl. NW11 ... 5G 45
(not continuous)
SM6: W'gton ... 7J 167
Harmony Pl. SE1 ... 5F 103
SE8 ... 6D 104
(off Dancers Way)
Harmony Ter. HA2: Harr ... 1F 59
Harmony Way BR1: Broml ... 2J 159
NW4 ... 4E 44
Harmood Gro. NW1 ... 7F 65
Harmood Ho. NW1 ... 7F 65
(off Harmood St.)
Harmood Pl. NW1 ... 7F 65
Harmood St. NW1 ... 6F 65
Harmsworth M. SE11 ... 2K 19 (3B 102)
Harmsworth St. SE17 ... 6K 19 (5B 102)
Harmsworth Way N20 ... 1C 30
Harold Av. DA17: Belv ... 5F 109
UB3: Hayes ... 3H 93
Harold Ct. SE16 ... 2K 103
(off Christopher Cl.)
Harold Est. SE1 ... 3E 102
Harold Gibbons Ct. SE7 ... 6A 106
Harold Ho. E2 ... 2K 85
(off Mace St.)
Harold Laski Ho. EC1 ... 2B 8
(off Percival St.)
Harold Maddison Ho. SE17 ... 5B 102
(off Penton Pl.)
Harold Mugford Ter. E6 ... 6E 88
(off Pearl Cl.)
Harold Pinter Theatre ... 3C 12
(off Panton St.)
Harold Pl. SE11 ... 6J 19 (5A 102)
Harold Rd. E4 ... 4K 35
E11 ... 1G 69
E13 ... 1K 87
IG8: Wfd G ... 1J 51
N8 ... 5K 47
N15 ... 5F 49
NW10 ... 3K 79
SE19 ... 7D 138
SM1: Sutt ... 4B 166
Haroldstone Rd. E17 ... 5K 49
Harold Wilson Ho. SE28 ... 1B 108
SW6 ... 6H 99
(off Clem Attlee Ct.)
Harp All. EC4 ... 7A 8 (6B 84)
The Harp Bus. Cen. NW2 ... 2C 62
Harpenden Rd. E12 ... 2A 70
SE27 ... 3B 138
Harpenmead Point NW2 ... 2H 63
Harper Cl. N14 ... 5B 22
Harper Ho. SW9 ... 3B 120
Harper M. SW17 ... 3A 136
Harper Rd. E6 ... 6D 88
SE1 ... 7C 14 (3C 102)
Harper's Yd. N17 ... 1F 49
Harpers Yd. TW7: Isle ... 2J 113
(off Rennels Way)
Harp Island Cl. NW10 ... 2K 61
Harp La. EC3 ... 3G 15 (7E 84)
Harpley Sq. E1 ... 4K 85
Harpour Rd. IG11: Bark ... 6G 71
Harp Rd. W7 ... 4K 77
Harpsden St. SW11 ... 1E 118
Harpur M. WC1 ... 5G 7 (5K 83)
Harpur St. WC1 ... 5G 7 (5K 83)
Harraden Rd. SE3 ... 1A 124
Harrier Av. E11 ... 6K 51
The Harrier Cen. ... 6K 163
Harrier Ct. TW4: Houn ... 3C 112
Harrier M. SE28 ... 2H 107
Harrier Rd. NW9 ... 2A 44
Harriers Cl. W5 ... 7E 78
Harrier Way E6 ... 5D 88
Harries Rd. UB4: Yead ... 4A 76
Harriet Cl. E8 ... 1G 85
Harriet Ct. SE14 ... 7J 103
(off Pomeroy St.)
Harriet Gdns. CR0: C'don ... 2G 169
Harriet Ho. SW6 ... 7K 99
(off Wandon Rd.)
Harriet M. DA16: Well ... 2B 126
Harriet St. SW1 ... 7F 11 (2D 100)
Harriet Tubman Cl. SW2 ... 7K 119
Harriet Wlk. SW1 ... 7F 11 (2D 100)
Harriet Way WD23: Bush ... 1C 26
HARRINGAY ... 5B 48
Harringay Gdns. N8 ... 4B 48
Harringay Rd. N15 ... 5B 48
(not continuous)
Harrington Cl. CR0: Bedd ... 2J 167
NW10 ... 3K 61
Harrington Ct. CR0: C'don ... 2D 168
SW7 ... 3B 16
(off Harrington Rd.)
W10 ... 3H 81
Harrington Gdns. SW7 ... 4K 99
Harrington Hill E5 ... 1H 67
Harrington Ho. NW1 ... 1A 6
(off Harrington St.)
UB10: Ick ... 4D 56
Harrington Rd. E11 ... 1G 69
SE25 ... 4G 157
SW7 ... 3A 16 (4B 100)
Harrington Sq. NW1 ... 2G 83
Harrington St. NW1 ... 1A 6 (2G 83)
(not continuous)
Harrington Way SE18 ... 3B 106
Harriott Cl. SE10 ... 4H 105
Harriott Ho. E1 ... 5J 85
(off Jamaica St.)
Harris Bldgs. E1 ... 6G 85
(off Burslem St.)
Harris Cl. EN2: Enf ... 1G 23
N11 ... 5J 31
TW3: Houn ... 1E 112
Harris Ct. HA9: Wemb ... 3F 61
Harris Ho. E3 ... 3C 86
(off Alfred St.)
E11 ... 1G 69
SW9 ... 3A 120
(off St James's Cres.)
Harris Lodge SE6 ... 1E 140
Harrison Cl. N20 ... 1H 31
RM7: Mawney ... 3G 55
Harrison Ct. E18 ... 1J 51
(off Queen Mary Av.)
Harrison Dr. BR1: Broml ... 4E 160
Harrison Ho. E1 ... 6H 85
SE17 ... 5D 102
(off Brandon St.)
Harrison Rd. NW10 ... 1K 79
RM10: Dag ... 6H 73
Harrisons Ct. SE14 ... 6K 103
(off Myers La.)
Harrison's Ri. CR0: Wadd ... 3B 168
Harrison St. WC1 ... 2F 7 (3J 83)
Harrison Way TW17: Shep ... 5D 146
Harris Rd. DA7: Bex ... 1E 126
RM9: Dag ... 5F 73
Harris Sports Cen. ... 5J 121
Harris St. E17 ... 7B 50
SE5 ... 7D 102
Harris Way TW16: Sun ... 1G 147
Harrod Ct. NW9 ... 4J 43
Harrods ... 1E 16 (3D 100)
Harrogate Ct. N11 ... 6K 31
SE12 ... 7J 123
SE26 ... 3G 139
(off Droitwich Cl.)
Harrold Ho. NW3 ... 7B 64
Harrold Rd. RM8: Dag ... 5B 72
Harrovian Bus. Village HA1: Harr ... 7J 41
HARROW ... 6J 41
Harrow Arts Cen. ... 7A 26
Harrow Av. EN1: Enf ... 6A 24
Harroway Rd. SW11 ... 2B 118
Harrow Borough FC ... 4D 58
Harrowby Ho. W1 ... 7E 4
(off Harrowby St.)
Harrowby St. W1 ... 7D 4 (6C 82)
Harrow Central Mosque ... 4K 41
Harrow Cl. KT9: Chess ... 7D 162
Harrow Club W10 ... 7F 81
Harrowdene Cl. HA0: Wemb ... 4D 60
Harrowdene Gdns. TW11: Tedd ... 6A 132
Harrowdene Rd. HA0: Wemb ... 3D 60
Harrow Dr. N9 ... 1A 34
Harrowes Meade HA8: Edg ... 3B 28
Harrow Flds. Gdns. HA1: Harr ... 3J 59
Harrow Gdns. KT8: E Mos ... 3H 149
Harrowgate Ho. E9 ... 6K 67
Harrowgate Rd. E9 ... 6A 68
Harrow Grn. E11 ... 3G 69
Harrow High School Sports Cen. ... 6A 42
Harrow Hill Golf Course ... 7K 41
Harrow La. E14 ... 7D 86
Harrow Leisure Cen. ... 3K 41
Harrow Lodge NW8 ... 3A 4
(off Northwick Ter.)
Harrow Mnr. Way SE28 ... 7C 90
Harrow Manorway SE2 ... 1C 108
Harrow Mus. ... 3G 41
HARROW ON THE HILL ... 1J 59
Harrow Pk. HA1: Harr ... 3K 59
Harrow Pl. E1 ... 7H 9 (6E 84)
HARROW ROAD ... 7H 61
Harrow Rd. E6 ... 1C 88
E11 ... 3G 69
HA0: Wemb ... 4K 59
HA9: Wemb ... 5G 61
IG1: Ilf ... 4G 71
IG11: Bark ... 1J 89
NW10 ... 3D 80
SM5: Cars ... 6C 166
TW14: Bedf ... 2C 128
W2 ... 6A 4 (5A 82)
(not continuous)
W9 ... 4F 81
W10 ... 4G 81
HARROW RD. BRI. ... 5A 82
Harrow School Golf Course ... 2K 59
Harrow Sports Hall ... 7A 42
Harrow St. NW1 ... 5D 4
Harrow Vw. HA1: Harr ... 2G 41
HA2: Harr ... 2G 41
UB3: Hayes ... 6J 75
UB10: Hil ... 3E 74
Harrow Vw. Rd. W5 ... 4B 78
Harrow Vw. W. HA2: Harr ... 2G 41
Harrow Way TW17: Shep ... 2E 146
HARROW WEALD ... 1J 41
Harrow Weald Lawn Tennis Club ... 1J 41
Harrow Weald Pk. HA3: Hrw W ... 6C 26
Harry Cl. CR0: C'don ... 6C 156
Harry Cole Ct. SE17 ... 5D 102
(off Thurlow St.)
Harry Day M. SE27 ... 3C 138
Harry Hinkins Ho. SE17 ... 5C 102
(off Bronti Cl.)
Harry Lambourn Ho. SE15 ... 7H 103
(off Gervase St.)
Harry Zeital Way E5 ... 2J 67
Harston Wlk. E3 ... 4D 86
Hartcliff Ct. W7 ... 2K 95
Hart Cl. CR0: C'don ... 3B 168
Hart Ct. E6 ... 7E 70
Harte Rd. TW3: Houn ... 2D 112
Hartfield Av. UB5: N'olt ... 2K 75
Hartfield Cres. BR4: W W'ck ... 3J 171
SW19 ... 7H 135
Hartfield Gro. SE20 ... 1J 157
Hartfield Ho. UB5: N'olt ... 2K 75
(off Hartfield Av.)
Hartfield Rd. BR4: W W'ck ... 4J 171
KT9: Chess ... 5D 162
SW19 ... 7H 135
Hartfield Ter. E3 ... 2C 86
Hartford Av. HA3: Kenton ... 3A 42
Hartford Rd. DA5: Bexl ... 6G 127
KT19: Ewe ... 6H 163
Hart Gro. UB1: S'hall ... 5E 76
W5 ... 1G 97
Hart Gro. Ct. W5 ... 1G 97
Hartham Cl. N7 ... 5J 65
TW7: Isle ... 1A 114
Hartham Rd. N7 ... 5J 65
N17 ... 2F 49
TW7: Isle ... 1K 113
Harting Rd. SE9 ... 3C 142
Hartington Cl. BR6: Farnb ... 5G 173
HA1: Harr ... 4J 59
Hartington Ct. SW8 ... 1J 119
W4 ... 7H 97
Hartington Ho. SW1 ... 5D 18
(off Drummond Ga.)
Hartington Rd. E16 ... 6K 87
E17 ... 6A 50
SW8 ... 1J 119
TW1: Twick ... 7B 114
UB2: S'hall ... 3C 94
W4 ... 7H 97
W13 ... 7B 78
Hartismere Rd. SW6 ... 7H 99
Hartlake Rd. E9 ... 6K 67
Hartland NW1 ... 1G 83
(off Royal College St.)
Hartland Cl. HA8: Edg ... 2B 28
N21 ... 6H 23
Hartland Ct. N11 ... 5J 31
(off Hartland Rd.)
Hartland Dr. HA4: Ruis ... 3K 57
HA8: Edg ... 2B 28
Hartland Rd. E15 ... 7H 69
N11 ... 5J 31
NW1 ... 7F 65
NW6 ... 2H 81
SM4: Mord ... 7J 153
TW7: Isle ... 3A 114
TW12: Hamp H ... 4F 131
The Hartlands TW5: Cran ... 6K 93
Hartlands Cl. DA5: Bexl ... 6F 127
Hartland Way CR0: C'don ... 3A 170
SM4: Mord ... 7H 153
Hartlepool Ct. E16 ... 1F 107
Hartley Av. E6 ... 1C 88
NW7 ... 5G 29
Hartley Cl. BR1: Broml ... 2D 160
NW7 ... 5G 29
Hartley Ho. SE1 ... 4F 103
(off Longfield Est.)
Hartley Rd. CR0: C'don ... 7C 156
DA16: Well ... 7C 108
E11 ... 1H 69
Hartley St. E2 ... 3J 85
(not continuous)
Hart Lodge EN5: Barn ... 3B 20
Hartmann Rd. E16 ... 1B 106
Hartnoll St. N7 ... 5K 65
Harton Cl. BR1: Broml ... 1B 160
Harton Lodge SE8 ... 1C 122
(off Harton St.)
Harton Rd. N9 ... 2C 34
Harton St. SE8 ... 1C 122
Hartop Point SW6 ... 7G 99
(off Pellant Rd.)
Hartsbourne Av. WD23: B Hea ... 2B 26
Hartsbourne Cl. WD23: B Hea ... 2C 26
Hartsbourne Country Club & Golf Course
... 2B 26
Hartsbourne Ct. UB1: S'hall ... 6G 77
(off Fleming Rd.)
Hartsbourne Pk. WD23: B Hea ... 2D 26
Hartsbourne Rd. WD23: B Hea ... 2C 26
Harts Gro. IG8: Wfd G ... 5D 36
Hartshill Cl. UB10: Hil ... 7D 56
Hartshorn All. EC3 ... 1H 15
Hartshorn Gdns. E6 ... 4E 88
Hart's La. SE14 ... 1A 122
Harts La. IG11: Bark ... 6F 71
Hartslock Dr. SE2 ... 2D 108
Hartsmead Rd. SE9 ... 2D 142
Hart Sq. SM4: Mord ... 6J 153
Hart St. EC3 ... 2H 15 (7E 84)
Hartsway EN3: Pond E ... 4D 24
Hartswood Gdns. W12 ... 3B 98
Hartswood Grn.
WD23: B Hea ... 2C 26
Hartswood Rd. W12 ... 2B 98
Hartsworth Cl. E13 ... 2H 87
Hartville Rd. SE18 ... 4J 107
Hartwell Cl. SW2 ... 1K 137
Hartwell Dr. E4 ... 6K 35
Hartwell Ho. SE7 ... 5K 105
(off Troughton Rd.)
Hartwell St. E8 ... 6F 67
Harvard Ct. NW6 ... 5K 63
Harvard Hill W4 ... 6H 97
Harvard Ho. SE17 ... 6B 102
(off Doddington Gro.)
Harvard La. W4 ... 5J 97
Harvard Rd. SE13 ... 5E 122
TW7: Isle ... 1J 113
W4 ... 5H 97
Harvel Cl. BR5: St P ... 3K 161
Harvel Cres. SE2 ... 5D 108
Harvest Bank Rd. BR4: W W'ck ... 3H 171
Harvest Ct. RM13: Rain ... 2K 91
(off Broadis Way)
TW17: Shep ... 4C 146
Harvesters Cl. TW7: Isle ... 5H 113
Harvest La. KT7: T Ditt ... 6A 150
Harvest Rd. TW13: Felt ... 4J 129
Harvey Cl. NW9 ... 2A 44
Harvey Ct. E17 ... 5C 50
Harvey Dr. TW12: Hamp ... 1F 149
Harvey Gdns. E11 ... 1H 69
SE7 ... 5A 106
Harvey Ho. E1 ... 4H 85
(off Brady St.)

Harvey Ho.—Hazel M.

Harvey Ho. *N1* 1D 84
(off Colville Est.)
RM6: Chad H 4D 54
SW1 6D 18
(off Aylesford St.)
TW8: Bford 5E 96
Harvey Lodge *W9* 5J 81
(off Admiral Wlk.)
Harvey M. *N8* 5K 47
(off Harvey Rd.)
Harvey Rd. E11 1G 69
IG1: Ilf 5F 71
KT12: Walt T 7H 147
N8 5K 47
SE5 1D 120
(not continuous)
TW4: Houn 7D 112
UB5: N'olt 7A 58
UB10: Hil 2C 74
Harvey's Bldgs. WC2 3F 13 (7J 83)
Harveys La. RM7: Rush G 2K 73
Harvey St. N1 1D 84
Harvil Ct. *NW9* 3A 44
(off Mornington Cl.)
Harvill Rd. DA14: Sidc 5E 144
Harvil Rd. UB9: Hare 6A 38
UB10: Ick 6A 38
Harvington Wlk. E8 7G 67
Harvist Est. N7 4A 66
Harvist Rd. NW6 2F 81
Harwell Cl. HA4: Ruis 1F 57
Harwell Pas. N2 4D 46
Harwicke Ho. *E3* 3D 86
(off Bow Rd.)
Harwood Av. BR1: Broml 2K 159
CR4: Mitc 3C 154
Harwood Cl. HA0: Wemb 4D 60
N12 6H 31
Harwood Ct. *N1* 1D 84
(off Colville Est.)
SW15 4E 116
Harwood Dr. UB10: Hil 1B 74
Harwood M. SW6 7J 99
Harwood Point SE16 2B 104
Harwood Rd. SW6 7J 99
Harwoods Yd. N21 7F 23
Harwood Ter. SW6 1K 117
Hascombe Ter. *SE5* 2D 120
(off Love Wlk.)
Haselbury Rd. N9 4K 33
N18 4K 33
Haseley End SE23 7J 121
Haselrigge Rd. SW4 4H 119
Haseltine Rd. SE26 4B 140
Haselwood Dr. EN2: Enf 4G 23
Haskard Rd. RM9: Dag 4D 72
Hasker St. SW3 3D 16 (4C 100)
Haslam Av. SM3: Sutt 1G 165
Haslam Cl. N1 7A 66
UB10: Ick 2E 56
Haslam Ct. N11 4A 32
Haslam Ho. *N1* 7C 66
(off Canonbury Rd.)
Haslam St. SE15 7F 103
Haslemere Av. CR4: Mitc 2B 154
EN4: E Barn 1J 31
NW4 6F 45
SW18 2K 135
TW5: Cran 2A 112
W7 3A 96
W13 3A 96
Haslemere Bus. Cen. EN1: Enf 4C 24
Haslemere Cl. SM6: W'gton 5J 167
TW12: Hamp 5D 130
Haslemere Gdns. N3 3H 45
The Haslemere Heathrow Est.
TW4: Cran 2K 111
Haslemere Ind. Est. SW18 2K 135
Haslemere Rd. CR7: Thor H 5B 156
DA7: Bex 2F 127
IG3: Ilf 2K 71
N8 7H 47
N21 2G 33
Hasler Cl. SE28 7B 90
Haslers Wharf *E3* 1A 86
(off Old Ford Rd.)
Haslett Rd. TW17: Shep 2G 147
Hasluck Gdns. EN5: New Bar 6E 20
Hassard St. E2 1K 9 (2F 85)
Hassendean Rd. SE3 7K 105
Hassett Rd. E9 6K 67
Hassocks Cl. SE26 3H 139
Hassocks Rd. SW16 1H 155
Hassock Wood BR2: Kes 4B 172
Hassop Rd. NW2 4F 63
Hassop Wlk. SE9 4C 142
Hasted Rd. SE7 5B 106
Haste Hill Golf Course 2G 39
Hastings Av. IG6: Ilf 4G 53
Hastings Cl. EN5: New Bar 4F 21
HA0: Wemb 4C 60
SE15 7G 103
Hastings Ct. TW11: Tedd 5H 131
Hastings Dr. KT6: Surb 6C 150
Hastings Ho. EN3: Enf H 2D 24
SE18 4D 106
(off Mulgrave Rd.)
W12 7D 80
(off White City Est.)
W13 7B 78
WC1 2E 6
(off Hastings St.)
Hastings Pl. *CR0: C'don* 1F 169
(off Hastings Rd.)
Hastings Rd. BR2: Broml 1C 172
CR0: C'don 1F 169
E16 5J 87
N11 5B 32
N17 3D 48
W13 7B 78
Hastings St. SE18 3G 107
WC1 2E 6 (3J 83)
Hastingwood Ct. E17 5D 50
Hastoe Cl. UB4: Yead 4C 76
Hasty Cl. CR4: Mitc 1F 155
Hat & Mitre Ct. EC1 4B 8
The Hatch EN3: Enf H 1E 24
Hatcham Mews Bus. Cen.
SE14 1K 121
(off Hatcham Pk. Rd.)
Hatcham Pk. M. SE14 1K 121
Hatcham Pk. Rd. SE14 1K 121
Hatcham Rd. SE15 6J 103
Hatchard Rd. N19 2H 65
Hatchcroft NW4 3D 44
HATCH END 7A 26
Hatch End Lawn Tennis Club 6A 26
Hatch End Swimming Pool 7A 26
Hatchers M. SE1 7H 15
Hatchett Rd. TW14: Bedf 1E 128
Hatchfield Ho. *N15* 6E 48
(off Albert Rd.)
Hatch Gro. RM6: Chad H 4E 54
Hatch La. E4 4A 36
UB7: Harm 3E 174
Hatch Pl. KT2: King T 5F 133
Hatch Rd. SW16 2J 155
Hatch Side IG7: Chig 5K 37
Hatchwood Cl. IG8: Wfd G 4C 36
Hatcliffe Almshouses *SE10* 5G 105
(off Tuskar St.)
Hatcliffe Cl. SE3 3H 123
Hatcliffe St. SE10 5H 105
Hatfield Cl. CR4: Mitc 4B 154
Hatfield Mead SM4: Mord 5J 153
Hatfield Cl. IG6: Ilf 3F 53
SE14 7K 103
Hatfield Ct. SE3 7J 105
UB5: N'olt 3A 76
(off Canberra Dr.)
Hatfield Ho. EC1 4C 8
SE10 7D 104
Hatfield M. RM9: Dag 7E 72
Hatfield Rd. E15 5G 69
RM9: Dag 6E 72
W4 2K 97
W13 1A 96
Hatfields SE1 4K 13 (1A 102)
Hathaway Cl. BR2: Broml 1D 172
HA4: Ruis 4H 57
HA7: Stan 5F 27
Hathaway Cres. E12 6D 70
Hathaway Gdns. RM6: Chad H 5D 54
W13 5K 77
Hathaway Ho. N1 2E 84
Hathaway Rd. CR0: C'don 7B 156
Hatherleigh Cl. KT9: Chess 5D 162
NW7 6A 30
SM4: Mord 4J 153
Hatherleigh Rd. HA4: Ruis 2J 57
Hatherley Ct. *W2* 6K 81
(off Hatherley Gro.)
Hatherley Cres. DA14: Sidc 2A 144
Hatherley Gdns. E6 3B 88
N8 6J 47
Hatherley Gro. W2 6K 81
Hatherley Ho. E17 4C 50
Hatherley M. E17 4C 50
Hatherley Rd. DA14: Sidc 4A 144
E17 4B 50
TW9: Kew 1F 115
Hatherley St. SW1 4B 18 (4G 101)
Hathern Gdns. SE9 4E 142
Hatherop Rd. TW12: Hamp 7D 130
Hathersage Ct. N1 5D 66
Hathorne Cl. SE15 2H 121
Hathway St. SE14 2K 121
Hathway Ter. *SE14* 2K 121
(off Hathway St.)
Hatley Av. IG6: Ilf 4G 53
Hatley Cl. N11 5J 31
Hatley Rd. N4 2K 65
Hatteraick St. SE16 2J 103
Hattersfield Cl. DA17: Belv 4F 109
HATTON 4H 111
Hatton Cl. SE18 7H 107
HATTON CROSS 4H 111
Hatton Cross Cen.
TW6: H'row A 3H 111
Hatton Gdn. EC1 5K 7 (5A 84)
Hatton Gdns. CR4: Mitc 5D 154
Hatton Grn. TW14: Felt 4J 111
Hatton Gro. UB7: W Dray 2A 92
Hatton Ho. *E1* 7G 85
(off Hindmarsh Cl.)
KT1: King T 2F 151
(off Victoria Rd.)
Hatton Pl. EC1 5K 7 (5A 84)
Hatton Rd. CR0: C'don 1A 168
HA0: Wemb 1E 78
TW14: Bedf, Felt 7E 110
Hatton Rd. Sth. TW14: Felt 4H 111
Hatton Row NW8 4B 4
Hatton St. NW8 4B 4 (4B 82)
Hatton Wlk. EN2: Enf 3J 23
Hatton Wall EC1 5K 7 (5A 84)
Haughmond N12 4E 30
Haunch of Venison Yd. W1 1J 11 (6F 83)
Hauteville Ct. Gdns. *W6* 3B 98
(off South Side)
Havana Rd. SW19 2J 135
Havanna Dr. NW11 5G 45
Havannah St. E14 2C 104
Havant Rd. E17 3E 50
Havelock Cl. W12 7D 80
Havelock Ct. *UB2: S'hall* 3D 94
(off Havelock Rd.)
Havelock Ho. *SE1* 4F 103
(off Fort Rd.)
SE23 1J 139
Havelock Pl. HA1: Harr 6J 41
Havelock Rd. BR2: Broml 4A 160
CR0: C'don 2F 169
DA17: Belv 4F 109
HA3: W'stone 3J 41
N17 2G 49
SW19 5A 136
UB2: S'hall 3C 94
Havelock St. IG1: Ilf 2F 71
N1 1J 83
Havelock Ter. SW8 1F 119
Havelock Ter. Arches *SW8* 1F 119
(off Havelock Ter.)
Havelock Wlk. SE23 1J 139
The Haven TW9: Rich 3G 115
TW16: Sun 7J 129
Haven Cl. DA14: Sidc 6C 144
SE9 3D 142
SW19 3F 135
UB4: Hayes 4G 75
Haven Ct. BR3: Beck 2E 158
KT5: Surb 6F 151
Haven Grn. W5 6D 78
Haven Grn. Ct. W5 6D 78
Havenhurst Ri. EN2: Enf 2F 23
Haven La. W5 6E 78
Haven Lodge *EN1: Enf* 6K 23
(off Village Rd.)
SE18 4F 107
(off Vincent Rd.)
Haven M. E3 5B 86
N1 7A 66
Haven Pl. W5 7D 78
Havenpool *NW8* 1K 81
(off Abbey Rd.)
Haven Rd. TW15: Ashf 4D 128
Haven St. NW1 7F 65
Haven Way SE1 3F 103
Havenwood HA9: Wemb 3H 61
Haverfield Gdns. TW9: Kew 7G 97
Haverfield Rd. E3 3A 86
Haverford Way HA8: Edg 1F 43
Haverhill Rd. E4 1K 35
SW12 1G 137
Havering *NW1* 7F 65
(off Castlehaven Rd.)
Havering Dr. RM1: Rom 4K 55
Havering Gdns. RM6: Chad H 5C 54
Havering Mus. 5K 55
Havering Rd. RM1: Rom 3K 55
Havering St. E1 6K 85
Havering Way IG11: Bark 3B 90
Haversham Cl. TW1: Twick 6D 114
Haversham Ct. UB6: G'frd 6K 59
Haversham Pl. N6 2D 64
Haverstock Cl. HA1: Harr 7G 41
Haverstock Hill NW3 5C 64
Haverstock Pl. *N1* 1B 8
(off Haverstock St.)
Haverstock Rd. NW5 5E 64
Haverstock St. N1 1B 8 (2B 84)
Haverthwaite Rd. BR6: Orp 2H 173
Havilland M. W12 2D 98
Havil St. SE5 7E 102
Havisham Apts. *E15* 6F 69
(off Grove Cres. Rd.)
Havisham Ho. SE16 2G 103
Havisham Pl. SE19 7B 138
Hawarden Gro. SE24 7C 120
Hawarden Hill NW2 3C 62
Hawarden Rd. E17 4K 49
Hawbridge Rd. E11 1F 69
Hawbush Cl. RM6: Ilf 4B 54
Hawes Ho. E17 4K 49
Hawes La. BR4: W W'ck 1E 170
Hawes Rd. BR1: Broml 1K 159
(not continuous)
N18 6C 34
Hawes St. N1 7B 66
Haweswater Ho. TW7: Isle 5K 113
Hawfinch Ho. NW9 7B 44
Hawgood St. E3 5C 86
Hawkdene E4 6J 25
Hawke Ct. *UB4: Yead* 4A 76
(off Perth Av.)
Hawke Ho. *E1* 4K 85
(off Ernest St.)
Hawke Pk. Rd. N22 3B 48
Hawke Pl. SE16 2K 103
Hawker *NW9* 1B 44
(off Everglade Strand)
Hawker Ct. *E3* 3E 86
(off Bolinder Way)
KT1: King T 2F 151
(off Church Rd.)
Hawke Rd. SE19 6D 138
Hawker Pl. E17 2E 50
Hawker Rd. CR0: Wadd 6A 168
Hawkesbury Rd. SW15 5D 116
Hawkesfield Rd. SE23 2A 140
Hawkesley Cl. TW1: Twick 4A 132
Hawkes Rd. CR4: Mitc 1D 154
TW14: Felt 7J 111
Hawkesworth Cl. HA6: Nwood 1G 39
Hawkes Yd. KT7: T Ditt 6K 149
Hawke Twr. SE14 6A 104
Hawkewood Rd. TW16: Sun 3J 147
Hawkfield Ct. TW7: Isle 2J 113
Hawkhurst Gdns. KT9: Chess 4E 162
Hawkhurst Rd. SW16 1H 155
Hawkhurst Way
BR4: W W'ck 2D 170
KT3: N Mald 5K 151
Hawkinge *N17* 2D 48
(off Gloucester Rd.)
Hawkins Cl. HA1: Harr 7H 41
NW7 5E 28
Hawkins Ct. SE18 4C 106
Hawkins Ho. *SE8* 6C 104
(off New King St.)
SW1 7B 18
(off Dolphin Sq.)
Hawkins Rd. NW10 7A 62
TW11: Tedd 6B 132
Hawkins Ter. SE7 5C 106
Hawkins Way SE6 5C 140
Hawkley Gdns. SE27 2B 138
Hawkridge Cl. RM6: Chad H 6C 54
Hawksbrook La. BR3: Beck 6D 158
Hawkshaw Cl. SW2 7J 119
Hawkshead NW1 1A 6
Hawkshead Cl. BR1: Broml 7G 141
Hawkshead Rd. NW10 7B 62
W4 2A 98
Hawkslade Rd. SE15 5K 121
Hawksley Rd. N16 3E 66
Hawks M. SE10 7E 104
Hawksmoor Cl. E6 6C 88
SE18 5J 107
Hawksmoor Gro. BR2: Broml 6B 160
Hawksmoor M. E1 7H 85
Hawksmoor Pl. *E2* 3K 9
(off Cheshire St.)
Hawksmoor St. W6 6F 99
Hawksmouth E4 7K 25
Hawks Pas. *KT1: King T* 2F 151
(off London Rd.)
Hawks Rd. KT1: King T 2F 151
Hawkstone Rd. SE16 4J 103
Hawksworth Ho. BR1: Broml 2J 159
Hawkwell Ct. E4 3K 35
Hawkwell Ho. RM8: Dag 1G 73
Hawkwell Wlk. *N1* 1C 84
(off Maldon Cl.)
Hawkwood Cres. E4 6J 25
Hawkwood La. BR7: Chst 1G 161
Hawkwood Mt. E5 1H 67
Hawlands Dr. HA5: Pinn 7C 40
Hawley Cl. TW12: Hamp 6D 130
Hawley Cres. NW1 7F 65
Hawley M. NW1 7F 65
Hawley Rd. N18 5E 34
NW1 7F 65
(not continuous)
Hawley St. NW1 7F 65
Hawley Way TW15: Ashf 5C 128
Hawstead Rd. SE6 6D 122
Hawsted IG9: Buck H 1E 36
Hawthorn Av. CR7: Thor H 1B 156
E3 1B 86
N13 5D 32
The Hawthorn Cen. HA1: Harr 5K 41
Hawthorn Cl. BR5: Pet W 6H 161
TW5: Cran 7K 93
TW12: Hamp 5E 130
Hawthorn Cotts. *DA16: Well* 3A 126
(off Hook La.)
Hawthorn Ct. *HA5: Pinn* 2A 40
(off Rickmansworth Rd.)
TW9: Kew 1H 115
TW15: Ashf 7E 128
Hawthorn Cres. IG5: Ilf 1D 52
SW17 5E 136
Hawthornden Cl. N12 6H 31
Hawthorndene Cl. BR2: Hayes 2H 171
Hawthorndene Rd. BR2: Hayes 2H 171
Hawthorn Dr. BR4: W W'ck 4G 171
HA2: Harr 6E 40
Hawthorne Av. CR4: Mitc 2B 154
HA3: Kenton 6A 42
HA4: Ruis 6K 39
SM5: Cars 7E 166
Hawthorne Cl. BR1: Broml 3D 160
N1 6E 66
SM1: Sutt 2A 166
Hawthorne Ct. HA6: Nwood 2J 39
W5 1E 96
Hawthorne Cres. SE10 5H 105
UB7: W Dray 2B 92
Hawthorne Gro. NW9 7J 43
Hawthorne Ho. N15 5G 49
SW1 6B 18
(off Churchill Gdns.)
Hawthorne M. UB6: G'frd 6G 77
Hawthorne Pl. UB3: Hayes 7H 75
Hawthorne Rd. BR1: Broml 3C 160
E17 3C 50
N18 6A 34
Hawthorne Way N9 2A 34
Hawthorn Farm Av. UB5: N'olt 1C 76
Hawthorn Gdns. W5 3D 96
Hawthorn Gro. EN2: Enf 1J 23
SE20 7H 139
Hawthorn Hatch TW8: Bford 7B 96
Hawthorn Ho. *E15* 6F 69
(off Forrester Way)
SE16 2A 104
(off Blondin Way)
Hawthorn M. NW7 1G 45
Hawthorn Pl. DA8: Erith 5J 109
Hawthorn Rd. DA6: Bex 4F 127
IG9: Buck H 4G 37
N8 3H 47
NW10 7C 62
SM1: Sutt 6C 166
SM6: W'gton 7F 167
TW8: Bford 7B 96
TW13: Felt 1J 129
Hawthorns *CR2: S Croy* 4C 168
(off Bramley Hill)
IG8: Wfd G 3D 36
The Hawthorns KT17: Ewe 7B 164
SL3: Poyle 4A 174
Hawthorn Ter. DA15: Sidc 5K 125
Hawthorn Wlk. W10 4G 81
Hawthorn Way TW17: Shep 4F 147
Hawtrey Av. UB5: N'olt 2B 76
Hawtrey Dr. HA4: Ruis 7J 39
Hawtrey Rd. NW3 7C 64
Haxted Rd. BR1: Broml 1K 159
Hay Cl. E15 7G 69
Haycroft Gdns. NW10 1C 80
Haycroft Rd. KT6: Surb 2D 162
SW2 5J 119
Hay Currie St. E14 6D 86
Hayday Rd. E16 5J 87
(not continuous)
Hayden Ct. TW13: Felt 4G 129
Hayden Piper Ho. *SW3* 7E 16
(off Caversham St.)
Haydens M. W3 6J 79
Hayden's Pl. W11 6H 81
Hayden Twr. SW8 7H 101
Hayden Way RM5: Col R 2J 55
Haydock Av. UB5: N'olt 6E 58
Haydock Grn. UB5: N'olt 6E 58
Haydock Grn. Flats *UB5: N'olt* 6E 58
(off Haydock Grn.)
Haydon Cl. EN1: Enf 6K 23
NW9 4J 43
Haydon Ct. NW9 4J 43
Haydon Dr. HA5: Eastc 4J 39
Haydon Pk. Rd. SW19 5J 135
Haydon Rd. RM8: Dag 2C 72
Haydons Rd. SW19 5K 135
Haydon St. EC3 2J 15 (7F 85)
Haydon Wlk. E1 1K 15 (6F 85)
Haydon Way SW11 4B 118
Hay Dr. CR4: Mitc 2C 154
HAYES
BR2 1J 171
UB3 6G 75
Hayes & Yeading United FC 1A 94
Hayes Bri. Retail Pk. 7A 76
Hayes Chase BR4: W W'ck 6F 159
Hayes Cl. BR2: Hayes 2J 171
Hayes Ct. BR2: Hayes 3J 171
HA0: Wemb 1E 78
SE5 7C 102
(off Camberwell New Rd.)
SW2 1J 137
Hayes Cres. NW11 5H 45
SM3: Cheam 4F 165
HAYES END 4F 75
Hayes End Cl. UB4: Hayes 4F 75
Hayes End Dr. UB4: Hayes 4F 75
Hayes End Rd. UB4: Hayes 4F 75
Hayesens Ho. SW17 4A 136
Hayesford Pk. Dr. BR2: Broml 5H 159
Hayes Gdn. BR2: Hayes 2J 171
Hayes Gro. SE22 3F 121
Hayes Hill BR2: Hayes 1G 171
Hayes Hill Rd. BR2: Hayes 1H 171
Hayes La. BR2: Broml, Hayes 5K 159
BR3: Beck 3E 158
Hayes Mead Rd. BR2: Hayes 1G 171
Hayes Metro Cen. UB4: Yead 7A 76
Hayes M. SE8 1B 122
Hayes Pk. Lodge UB4: Hayes 4F 75
Hayes Pl. NW1 4D 4 (4C 82)
Hayes Rd. BR2: Broml 4J 159
UB2: S'hall 4K 93
Hayes St. BR2: Hayes 1K 171
HAYES TOWN 2H 93
Hayes Way BR3: Beck 4E 158
Hayes Wood Av. BR2: Hayes 1K 171
Hayfield Pas. E1 4J 85
Hayfield Yd. E1 4J 85
Haygarth Pl. SW19 5F 135
Haygreen Cl. KT2: King T 6H 133
Hay Hill W1 3K 11 (7F 83)
Hayhurst Ct. *N1* 1B 84
(off Dibden St.)
Hayland Cl. NW9 4K 43
Haylands Ct. TW8: Bford 6C 96
Hay La. NW9 4J 43
Hayles Bldgs. *SE11* 4B 102
(off Elliotts Row)
Hayles St. SE11 4B 102
Haylett Gdns. KT1: King T 4D 150
Hayling Av. TW13: Felt 3J 129
Hayling Cl. N16 5E 66
Hayling Ct. SM3: Cheam 4E 164
Hayling Way HA8: Edg 4A 28
Haymaker Cl. UB10: Uxb 7B 56
Hayman Cres. UB4: Hayes 2F 75
Haymans Point SE11 5G 19 (4K 101)
Hayman St. N1 7B 66
Haymarket SW1 3C 12 (7H 83)
Haymarket Arc. SW1 3C 12
Haymarket Ct. *E8* 7F 67
(off Jacaranda Gro.)
Haymarket Theatre Royal 3D 12
(off Haymarket)
Haymer Gdns. KT4: Wor Pk 3C 164
Haymerle Ho. *SE15* 6G 103
(off Haymerle Rd.)
Haymerle Rd. SE15 6G 103
Hay M. NW3 6D 64
Haymill Cl. UB6: G'frd 3K 77
Hayne Ho. *W11* 1G 99
(off Penzance Pl.)
Hayne Rd. BR3: Beck 2B 158
Haynes Cl. N11 3K 31
N17 7C 34
SE3 3G 123
Haynes Dr. N9 3C 34
Haynes La. SE19 6E 138
Haynes Rd. HA0: Wemb 7E 60
Hayne St. EC1 5B 8 (5B 84)
Haynt Wlk. SW20 3G 153
Hayre Dr. UB2: S'hall 5C 94
Hay's Ct. *SE16* 2J 103
(off Rotherhithe St.)
Hay's Galleria SE1 4G 15 (1E 102)
Hays La. SE1 4G 15 (1E 102)
Haysleigh Gdns. SE20 2G 157
Hay's M. W1 4J 11 (1F 101)
Haysoms Cl. RM1: Rom 4K 55
Haystall Cl. UB4: Hayes 2G 75
Hay St. E2 1G 85
Hayter Ct. E11 2K 69
Hayter Rd. SW2 5J 119
Hayton Cl. E8 6F 67
Hayward Cl. DA1: Cray 5K 127
SW19 7K 135
Hayward Ct. *SW9* 2J 119
(off Studley Rd.)
Hayward Gallery 5H 13 (1K 101)
Hayward Gdns. SW15 6E 116
Hayward Ho. *N1* 2A 84
(off Penton St.)
Hayward M. SE4 5B 122
Hayward Rd. KT7: T Ditt 7K 149
N20 2F 31
Haywards Cl. RM6: Chad H 5B 54
Hayward's Pl. EC1 3A 8 (4B 84)
Haywood Cl. HA5: Pinn 2B 40
Haywood Lodge *N11* 6D 32
(off York Rd.)
Haywood Ri. BR6: Orp 5J 173
Haywood Rd. BR2: Broml 4B 160
Hazel Av. UB7: W Dray 3C 92
Hazel Bank SE25 2E 156
Hazelbank KT5: Surb 1J 163
Hazelbank Rd. SE6 2F 141
Hazelbourne Rd. SW12 6F 119
Hazelbury Cl. SW19 2J 153
Hazelbury Grn. N9 3K 33
Hazelbury La. N9 3K 33
Hazel Cl. CR0: C'don 7K 157
CR4: Mitc 4H 155
N13 3J 33
N19 2G 65
NW9 2A 44
SE15 2G 121
(off Bournemouth Cl.)
TW2: Whitt 7G 113
TW8: Bford 7B 96
Hazel Ct. W5 7E 78
Hazelcroft HA5: Hat E 6A 26
Hazelcroft Cl. UB10: Hil 7B 56
Hazeldean Rd. NW10 7K 61
Hazeldene Dr. HA5: Pinn 3A 40
Hazeldene Gdns. UB10: Hil 1E 74
Hazeldene Rd. DA16: Well 2C 126
IG3: Ilf 2B 72
Hazeldon Rd. SE4 5A 122
Hazeleigh Gdns. IG8: Wfd G 5H 37
Hazel Gdns. HA8: Edg 4C 28
Hazelgreen Cl. N21 1G 33
Hazel Gro. BR6: Farnb 2F 173
EN1: Enf 6B 24
HA0: Wemb 1E 78
RM6: Chad H 3E 54
SE26 4K 139
TW13: Felt 1J 129
Hazel Ho. *E3* 1B 86
(off Barge La.)
Hazelhurst BR3: Beck 1F 159
Hazelhurst Ct. *SE6* 5E 140
(off Beckenham Hill Rd.)
Hazelhurst Rd. SW17 4A 136
Hazel La. IG6: Ilf 6K 37
SE10 5H 105
TW10: Ham 2E 132
Hazell Cres. RM5: Col R 1H 55
Hazellville Rd. N19 7H 47
Hazelmere Cl. TW14: Felt 6G 111
UB5: N'olt 2D 76
Hazelmere Ct. SW2 1K 137
Hazelmere Dr. UB5: N'olt 2D 76
Hazelmere Rd. BR5: Pet W 4G 161
NW6 1H 81
UB5: N'olt 2D 76
Hazelmere Wlk. UB5: N'olt 2D 76
(not continuous)
Hazelmere Way BR2: Hayes 6J 159
Hazel M. *N22* 3A 48
(off High Rd.)

Column 1

Hazel Rd. E15 . . . . .5G 69
NW10 . . . . .3D 80
(not continuous)
Hazeltree La. UB5: N'olt 3C 76
Hazel Wlk. BR2: Broml 6E 160
Hazel Way E4 . . . . .6G 35
SE1 . . . . .4F 103
Hazelwood Av. SM4: Mord 4K 153
Hazelwood Cl. W5 . . . . .2E 96
Hazelwood Cl. KT6: Surb 6E 150
N13 . . . . .4F 33
(off Hazelwood La.)
NW10 . . . . .3A 62
Hazelwood Cres. N13 . . . . .4F 33
Hazelwood Dr. HA5: Pinn 2K 39
TW16: Sun 3J 147
Hazelwood Ho. SE8 . . . . .4A 104
TW16: Sun 1J 147
Hazelwood Ho's. BR2: Broml . . .3G 159
Hazelwood La. N13 . . . . .4F 33
Hazelwood Rd. E17 . . . . .5A 50
EN1: Enf 6A 24
Hazelwood Sports Club 7H 23
Hazlebury Rd. SW6 . . . . .2K 117
Hazledean Rd. CR0: C'don 2D 168
Hazledene Rd. W4 . . . . .6J 97
Hazlemere Gdns. KT4: Wor Pk . . .1C 164
Hazlewell Rd. SW15 . . . . .5E 116
Hazlewood Cl. E5 . . . . .3A 68
HA2: Harr 4F 41
Hazlewood Cres. W10 . . . . .4G 81
Hazlewood M. SW9 . . . . .3J 119
Hazlewood Twr. W10 . . . . .4G 81
(off Golborne Gdns.)
Hazlitt Cl. TW13: Hanw 4C 130
Hazlitt M. W14 . . . . .3G 99
Hazlitt Rd. W14 . . . . .3G 99
Heacham Av. UB10: Ick 3E 56
Headbourne Ho. E17 . . . . .3A 50
(off Sutherland Rd.)
SE1 . . . . .7F 15 (3D 102)
Headcorn Pl. CR7: Thor H 4K 155
Headcorn Rd. BR1: Broml 5H 141
CR7: Thor H 4K 155
N17 . . . . .7A 34
Headfort Pl. SW1 . . . . .7H 11 (2E 100)
Headingley Dr. BR3: Beck 6C 140
Headington Ct. CR0: C'don 4C 168
(off Tanfield Rd.)
Headington Rd. SW18 . . . . . . .2A 136
Headlam Rd. SW4 . . . . .6H 119
(not continuous)
Headlam St. E1 . . . . .4H 85
Headley App. IG2: Ilf 5F 53
Headley Av. SM6: W'gton 5K 167
Headley Cl. KT19: Ewe 6G 163
Headley Ct. SE26 . . . . .5J 139
Headley Dr. CR0: New Ad 7D 170
IG2: Ilf 6F 53
Headley M. SW18 . . . . .5K 117
Head's M. W11 . . . . .6J 81
HEADSTONE 4G 41
Headstone Dr. HA1: Harr 3H 41
HA3: W'stone 3J 41
Headstone Gdns. HA2: Harr 4G 41
Headstone La. HA2: Harr 4E 40
HA3: Hrw W 7A 26
Headstone Manor 3G 41
Headstone Pde. HA1: Harr 4H 41
Headstone Rd. HA1: Harr 5J 41
Head St. E1 . . . . .6K 85
(not continuous)
Headway Cl. TW10: Ham 4C 132
Headway Gdns. E17 . . . . .1C 50
Heald St. SE14 . . . . .1C 122
Healey Ho. E3 . . . . .4C 86
(off Wellington Way)
SW9 . . . . .7A 102
Healey St. NW1 . . . . .6F 65
Healey Ct. EN5: Barn 6A 20
Healy Dr. BR6: Orp 4K 173
Hearne Rd. W4 . . . . .6G 97
Hearn Pl. SW16 . . . . .4A 138
Hearn Ri. UB5: N'olt 1B 76
Hearn's Bldgs. SE17 . . . . .4D 102
Hearnshaw St. E14 . . . . .6A 86
Hearn St. EC2 . . . . . . .4H 9 (4E 84)
Hearnville Rd. SW12 . . . . .1E 136
The Heart KT12: Walt T 7J 147
The Heath W7 . . . . .1J 95
Heatham Pk. TW2: Twick 7K 113
Heath Av. DA7: Bex 6D 108
WD23: B Hea 1D 26
Heath Brow NW3 . . . . .3A 64
Heath Bus. Cen.
TW3: Houn 4G 113
Heath Cl. CR2: S Croy 6B 168
NW11 . . . . .7K 45
UB3: Harl 7F 93
W5 . . . . .4F 79
Heathcock Ct. WC2 . . . . .3F 13
(off Exchange Ct.)
Heathcote Av. IG5: Ilf 2D 52
Heathcote Ct. IG5: Ilf 1D 52
(not continuous)
Heathcote Ga. SW6 . . . . .3J 117
Heathcote Gro. E4 . . . . .3K 35
Heathcote Rd. TW1: Twick 6B 114
Heathcote St. WC1 . . . . .3G 7 (4K 83)
Heath Ct. CR0: C'don 4C 168
(off Heathfield Rd.)
SE9 . . . . .1G 143
TW4: Houn 4D 112
UB8: Uxb 7A 56
Heath Cft. NW11 . . . . .1K 63
Heathcroft W5 . . . . .4F 79
Heathcroft Av. TW16: Sun 7H 129
Heathcroft Gdns. E17 . . . . .1F 51
Heathdale Av. TW4: Houn 3C 112
Heathdene DA17: Belv 4H 109
Heathdene Rd. SM6: W'gton . . .7F 167
SW16 . . . . .7K 137
Heath Dr. NW3 . . . . .4K 63
SM2: Sutt 7A 166
SW20 . . . . .4E 152
Heathedge SE26 . . . . .2H 139
Heath End Rd. DA5: Bexl 1K 145
Heather Av. RM1: Rom 2K 55
Heatherbank BR7: Chst 2E 160
SE9 . . . . .2D 124
Heather Cl. E6 . . . . .6E 88
N7 . . . . .3K 65
RM1: Rom 1K 55
SE13 . . . . .7F 123
SW8 . . . . .3F 119

Column 2

Heather Cl. TW7: Isle 5H 113
TW12: Hamp 1D 148
UB8: Hil 5B 74
Heatherdale Cl. KT2: King T 6G 133
Heatherdene Cl. CR4: Mitc 4B 154
N12 . . . . .7F 31
Heather Dr. EN2: Enf 2G 23
RM1: Rom 2K 55
Heather Gdns. NW11 . . . . .6G 45
RM1: Rom 2K 55
SM2: Sutt 6J 165
Heather Glen RM1: Rom 2K 55
Heather Ho. E14 . . . . .6E 86
(off Dee St.)
Heatherlands TW16: Sun 6J 129
Heather La. UB7: Yiew 6A 74
Heatherlea Gro. KT4: Wor Pk . . .1D 164
Heatherley Ct. E5 . . . . .3G 67
Heatherley Dr. IG5: Ilf 3C 52
Heather Pk. Dr. HA0: Wemb 7G 61
Heather Pk. Pde. HA0: Wemb . . .7G 61
(off Heather Pk. Dr.)
Heather Rd. E4 . . . . .6G 35
NW2 . . . . .2B 62
SE12 . . . . .2J 141
The Heathers TW19: Stanw 7B 110
Heatherset Gdns. SW16 . . . . . .7K 137
Heatherside Rd. DA14: Sidc 3C 144
KT19: Ewe 7K 163
Heather Wlk. HA8: Edg 5C 28
TW2: Whitt 7E 112
(off Stephenson Rd.)
W10 . . . . .4G 81
Heather Way CR2: Sels 7K 169
HA7: Stan 6E 26
RM1: Rom 2K 55
Heatherwood Cl. E12 . . . . .2A 70
Heatherwood Dr. UB4: Hayes . . .2F 75
Heathfield BR7: Chst 6G 143
E4 . . . . .3K 35
Heathfield Av. SW18 . . . . .7B 118
Heathfield Cl. BR2: Kes 5A 172
E16 . . . . .5B 88
Heathfield Ct. E3 . . . . .2C 86
(off Tredegar Rd.)
SE14 . . . . .7J 103
SE20 . . . . .7J 139
TW15: Ashf 3A 128
W4 . . . . .5K 97
Heathfield Gdns. CR0: C'don . . .4D 168
NW11 . . . . .6F 45
SE3 . . . . .2G 123
(off Baizdon Rd.)
SW18 . . . . .6B 118
W4 . . . . .5J 97
Heathfield Ho. SE3 . . . . .2G 123
Heathfield La. BR7: Chst 6G 143
Heathfield Nth. TW2: Twick 7J 113
Heathfield Pk. NW2 . . . . .6E 62
Heathfield Pk. Dr. RM6: Chad H . .5B 54
Heathfield Ri. HA4: Ruis 7E 38
Heathfield Rd. BR1: Broml 7H 141
BR2: Kes 5A 172
CR0: C'don 4D 168
DA6: Bex 4F 127
SW18 . . . . .6A 118
W3 . . . . .2H 97
Heathfields Ct. TW4: Houn 5C 112
Heathfield Sth. TW2: Twick 7K 113
Heathfield Sq. SW18 . . . . .7B 118
Heathfield Ter. SE18 . . . . .6J 107
W4 . . . . .5J 97
Heathfield Va. CR2: Sels 7K 169
Heath Gdns. TW1: Twick 1K 131
Heathgate NW11 . . . . .6K 45
Heathgate Pl. NW3 . . . . .5D 64
Heath Gro. SE20 . . . . .7J 139
TW16: Sun 7H 129
Heath Ho. DA15: Sidc 4K 143
Heathhurst Rd. CR2: Sande 7E 168
Heathland Rd. N16 . . . . .1E 66
Heathlands Cl. TW1: Twick 2K 131
TW16: Sun 2J 147
Heathlands Way TW4: Houn 5C 112
Heath La. SE3 . . . . .2F 123
(not continuous)
Heathlee Rd. SE3 . . . . .4H 123
Heath End BR7: Chst 6G 143
Heath Lodge WD23: B Hea 1D 26
Heath Mead SW19 . . . . .3F 135
Heath Pk. Dr. BR1: Broml 3C 160
Heath Pas. NW3 . . . . .2K 63
Heath Pl. E3 . . . . .4B 86
Heathpool Ct. E1 . . . . .4H 85
Heath Ri. BR2: Hayes 6H 159
SW15 . . . . .6F 117
Heath Rd. CR7: Thor H 3C 156
DA5: Bexl 1J 145
HA1: Harr 7G 41
RM6: Chad H 7D 54
SW8 . . . . .2F 119
TW1: Twick 1K 131
TW2: Twick 1K 131
TW3: Houn, Isle 4F 113
TW7: Isle 4F 113
UB10: Hil 4E 74
Heath Royal SW15 . . . . .6F 117
Heaths Cl. EN1: Enf 2K 23
Heath Side BR5: Pet W 1G 173
NW3 . . . . .4B 64
Heathside DA7: Bex 1E 126
TW4: Houn 7D 112
Heathside Cl. IG2: Ilf 5H 53
Heathstan Rd. W12 . . . . .6C 80

Column 3

Heath St. NW3 . . . . .4A 64
Heath Ter. RM6: Chad H 7D 54
Heath Vw. N2 . . . . .4A 46
Heathview NW5 . . . . .4E 64
Heath Vw. Cl. N2 . . . . .4A 46
Heathview Dr. SE2 . . . . .6D 108
Heathview Gdns. SW15 . . . . . . .7E 116
Heathview Rd. CR7: Thor H 4A 156
Heath Vs. NW3 . . . . .3B 64
SE18 . . . . .5K 107
Heathwall St. SW11 . . . . .3D 118
HEATHWAY 1G 91
Heath Way DA8: Erith 1J 127
IG8: Wfd G 5F 37
RM9: Dag 3F 73
RM10: Dag 3F 73
SE3 . . . . .7J 105
UB2: S'hall 4B 94
Heathway Ct. NW3 . . . . .2J 63
Heathway Ind. Est. RM10: Dag . . .4H 73
Heathwood Ct. SW12 . . . . .4C 106
Heathwood Point SE23 . . . . . . .3K 139
Heathwood Wlk. DA5: Bexl 1K 145
Heaton Cl. E4 . . . . .3K 35
Heaton Ho. SW10 . . . . .6A 100
(off Fulham Rd.)
Heaton Rd. CR4: Mitc 7E 136
SE15 . . . . .2H 121
Heaven Tree Cl. N1 . . . . .6C 66
Heaver Rd. SW11 . . . . .3B 118
Heavitree Cl. SE18 . . . . .5H 107
Heavitree Rd. SE18 . . . . .5H 107
(not continuous)
Hebden Ct. E2 . . . . .1F 85
SW8 . . . . .7H 101
Hebden Ter. N17 . . . . .6K 33
Hebdon Rd. SW17 . . . . .3C 136
Heber Mans. W14 . . . . .6G 99
(off Queen's Club Gdns.)
Heber Rd. NW2 . . . . .5F 63
SE22 . . . . .6F 121
Hebrides Ct. E1 . . . . .6A 86
(off Ocean Est.)
Hebron Rd. W6 . . . . .3E 98
Hecham Cl. E17 . . . . .2A 50
Heckfield Pl. SW6 . . . . .7J 99
Heckford St. SE18 . . . . .5J 107
Heckford Ho. E14 . . . . .6D 86
(off Grundy St.)
Heckford St. E1 . . . . .7K 85
Heckford St. Bus. Cen. E1 . . . . .7K 85
(off Heckford St.)
Hector NW9 . . . . .1B 44
(off Five Acre)
Hector Cl. N9 . . . . .2B 34
Hector Ct. SW9 . . . . .7A 102
(off Caldwell St.)
Hector Ho. E2 . . . . .2H 85
(off Old Bethnal Grn. Rd.)
Hector St. SE18 . . . . .4J 107
Heddington Gro. N7 . . . . .5K 65
Heddon Cl. TW7: Isle 4A 114
Heddon Ct. Av. EN4: Cockf 5J 21
Heddon Ct. Pde. EN4: Cockf 5K 21
Heddon Rd. EN4: Cockf 5J 21
Heddon St. W1 . . . . . . .2A 12 (7G 83)
Hedera Pl. KT9: Chess 4D 112
Hedgegate Ct. W11 . . . . .6H 81
(off Powis Sq.)
Hedge Hill EN2: Enf 1G 23
Hedge La. N13 . . . . .3G 33
Hedgeley IG4: Ilf 4D 52
Hedgemans Rd. RM9: Dag 7D 72
Hedgemans Way RM9: Dag 6E 72
Hedgerley Gdns. UB6: G'frd 2G 77
Hedgerow La. EN5: Barn 1D 88
(off Nelson St.)
Hedgers Gro. E9 . . . . .6A 68
Hedger St. SE11 . . . . .4B 102
Hedgers Cl. TW14: Felt 6K 111
Hedge Wlk. SE6 . . . . .5D 140
Hedgewood Gdns. IG5: Ilf 5E 52
Hedgley M. SE12 . . . . .5H 123
Hedingham Cl. N1 . . . . .7C 66
Hedingham Ho. KT2: King T 1F 151
(off Royal Quarter)
Hedingham Rd. RM8: Dag 5B 72
Hedley Cl. RM1: Rom 5K 55
Hedley Ho. E14 . . . . .3E 104
(off Stewart St.)
Hedley Rd. TW2: Whitt 7E 112
Hedley Row N5 . . . . .5D 66
Hedsor Ho. E2 . . . . .3J 9
(off Ligonier St.)
Heenan Cl. IG11: Bark 6G 71
Heene Rd. EN2: Enf 1J 23
Heer M. E2 . . . . .2G 85
(off Hackney Rd.)
Hega Ho. E14 . . . . .5E 86
(off Ullin St.)
Heidegger Cres. SW13 . . . . . . .7D 98
Heigham Rd. E6 . . . . .7C 70
Heighton Gdns. CR0: Wadd 5B 168
The Heights BR3: Beck 7E 140
(not continuous)
SE7 . . . . .5A 106
UB5: N'olt 5D 58
Heights Cl. SW20 . . . . .7D 134
Heiron St. SE17 . . . . .6B 102
Helby Rd. SW4 . . . . .6H 119
Heldar Ct. SE1 . . . . . .7F 15 (2D 102)
Heldar Gro. SE1 . . . . .7H 123
Helder St. CR2: S Croy 6D 168
Heldmann Cl. TW3: Houn 4H 113
Helegan Cl. BR6: Chels 4K 173
Helena Cl. SW19 . . . . .7F 117
Helena Cl. NW6 . . . . .7K 63
(off Compayne Gdns.)
W5 . . . . .5D 78
Helena Pl. E9 . . . . .1H 85
Helena Rd. E13 . . . . .2H 87
E17 . . . . .5C 50
NW10 . . . . .5D 62
W5 . . . . .5D 78
Helena Sq. SE16 . . . . .7A 86
(off Sovereign Cres.)
Helen Cl. KT8: W Mole 4F 149
N2 . . . . .3A 46
Helen Gladstone Ho. SE1 . . . . . .6A 14
(off Surrey Row)
Helen Ho. E2 . . . . .2H 85
(off Old Bethnal Grn. Rd.)

Column 4

Helen Peele Cotts. SE16 . . . . . . .3J 103
(off Lower Rd.)
Helenslea Av. NW11 . . . . .1J 63
Helen's Pl. E2 . . . . .3J 85
Helen St. SE18 . . . . .4F 107
Helen Taylor Ho. SE16 . . . . .3G 103
(off Evelyn Lowe Est.)
Helford Cl. HA4: Ruis 2J 57
Helgiford Gdns. TW16: Sun 7G 129
Heligan Ho. SE16 . . . . .2K 103
(off Water Gdns. Sq.)
The Helios 7E 80
Helios Rd. SM6: W'gton 1E 166
Helios Way EN5: Barn 5C 20
Helix Ct. W11 . . . . .1F 99
(off Swanscombe St.)
Helix Gdns. SW2 . . . . .6K 119
Helix Rd. SW2 . . . . .6K 119
Hellings St. E1 . . . . .1G 103
Helix Ter. SW19 . . . . .2F 135
Helme Cl. SW19 . . . . .5H 135
Helmet Row EC1 . . . . .2D 8 (4C 84)
Helmore Rd. IG11: Bark 7K 71
Helmsdale Apartments SW11 . . .4C 118
(off Monarch Square)
Helmsdale Cl. UB4: Yead 4C 76
Helmsdale Ho. NW6 . . . . .2K 81
(off Carlton Vale)
Helmsdale Rd. SW16 . . . . .1H 155
Helmsley Pl. E8 . . . . .7H 67
Helmsley St. E8 . . . . .7H 67
Helperby Rd. NW10 . . . . .7A 62
Helsby Ct. NW8 . . . . .3A 4
(off Pollitt Dr.)
Helsinki Sq. SE16 . . . . .3A 104
Helston NW1 . . . . .1G 83
(off Camden St.)
Helston Ct. N15 . . . . .5E 48
(off Culvert Rd.)
Helston Ho. SE11 . . . . .5K 19
(off Kennings Way)
Helvetia St. SE6 . . . . .2B 140
Helwys Ct. E4 . . . . .6J 35
Hemans St. SW8 . . . . .7H 101
Hemans St. Est. SW8 . . . . .7J 101
Hemberton Rd. SW9 . . . . .3J 119
Hemery Rd. UB6: G'frd 5H 59
Hemingford Cl. N12 . . . . .5G 31
Hemingford Rd. N1 . . . . .1K 83
SM3: Cheam 4E 164
Heming Rd. HA8: Edg 7C 28
Hemington Av. N11 . . . . .5J 31
Hemingway Cl. NW5 . . . . .4E 64
Hemlock Cl. SW16 . . . . .2G 155
Hemlock Ho. SE16 . . . . .3A 104
Hemlock Rd. W12 . . . . .7B 80
(not continuous)
Hemmen La. UB3: Hayes 6H 75
Hemming Cl. TW12: Hamp 1E 148
Hemmings Cl. DA14: Sidc 2B 144
Hemmings Mead KT19: Ewe 6J 163
Hempstead Cl. IG9: Buck H 2D 36
Hempstead Rd. E17 . . . . .3F 51
Hemp Wlk. SE17 . . . . .4D 102
Hemsby Rd. KT9: Chess 6F 163
Hemstal Rd. NW6 . . . . .7J 63
Hemsted Rd. DA8: Erith 7K 109
Hemswell Dr. NW9 . . . . .1A 44
Hemsworth Ct. N1 . . . . .2E 84
Hemsworth St. N1 . . . . .2E 84
Hemus Pl. SW3 . . . . .6D 16 (5C 100)
Hen & Chicken Ct. EC4 . . . . . . .1J 13
(off Fleet St.)
Hen & Chickens Theatre 6B 66
(off St Paul's Rd.)
Henchman St. W12 . . . . .6B 80
Hendale Av. NW4 . . . . .3D 44
Henderson Cl. NW10 . . . . .6J 61
Henderson Ct. N12 . . . . .4E 30
NW3 . . . . .5B 64
(off Fitzjohn's Av.)
SE14 . . . . .6K 103
(off Myers La.)
Henderson Dr. NW8 . . . . .3A 4 (4B 82)
DA8: Erith 3G 73
Henderson Ho. RM10: Dag 3B 72
(off Kershaw Rd.)
Henderson Rd. CR0: C'don 6D 156
E7 . . . . .6A 70
N9 . . . . .1C 34
SW18 . . . . .7C 118
UB4: Yead 3J 75
Hendfield Ct. SM6: W'gton 6F 167
Hendham Rd. SW17 . . . . .2C 136
HENDON 4E 44
Hendon Av. N3 . . . . .1G 45
Hendon Crematorium 1F 45
Hendon FC 4D 58
Hendon Golf Course 7K 29
Hendon Hall Ct. NW4 . . . . .3F 45
Hendon Ho. NW4 . . . . .5F 45
Hendon La. N3 . . . . .3G 45
Hendon Leisure Cen. 4F 45
Hendon Lodge NW4 . . . . .3D 44
Hendon Pk. Mans. NW4 . . . . . . .5E 44
Hendon Pk. Row NW11 . . . . . . .6H 45
Hendon Rd. N9 . . . . .2B 34
Hendon St. SE10 . . . . .3H 105
Hendon Ter. TW15: Ashf 6F 129
Hendon Way NW2 . . . . .1F 63
NW4 . . . . .6D 44
Hendon Wood La. NW7 . . . . . . .1G 29
Hendre Ho. SE1 . . . . .4E 102
(off Hendre Rd.)
Hendre Rd. SE1 . . . . .4E 102
Hendren Cl. UB6: G'frd 5H 59
Hendre Rd. SE1 . . . . .4E 102
Hendrick Av. SW12 . . . . .7D 118
Heneage La. EC3 . . . . .1H 15 (6E 84)
Heneage Pl. EC3 . . . . .1H 15 (6E 84)
Heneage St. E1 . . . . . .5K 9 (5F 85)
Henfield Cl. DA5: Bexl 6G 109
N19 . . . . .1G 65
Henfield Rd. SW19 . . . . .1H 153
Hengelo Gdns. CR4: Mitc 4B 154
Hengest Av. KT10: Surb 3G 162
Hengist Rd. DA8: Erith 7H 109
SE12 . . . . .7K 123
Hengist Way BR2: Broml 4G 159
SM6: W'gton 7J 167
Hengrave Rd. SE23 . . . . .6J 121
Hengrove Ct. DA5: Bexl 1E 144
Hengrove Cres. TW15: Ashf 3A 128
Henham Ct. RM5: Col R 1J 55

Column 5

Henley Av. SM3: Cheam 3G 165
Henley Cl. SE16 . . . . .2J 103
(off St Marychurch St.)
TW7: Isle 1K 113
UB6: G'frd 2G 77
Henley Ct. N14 . . . . .7B 22
NW2 . . . . .6F 63
Henley Dr. KT2: King T 7B 134
SE1 . . . . .4F 103
Henley Gdns. HA5: Eastc 3K 39
RM6: Chad H 5E 54
Henley Hgts. N1 . . . . .7K 65
(off Caledonian Rd.)
Henley Ho. E2 . . . . .3K 9
(off Swanfield St.)
Henley Prior N1 . . . . .1G 7
(off Affleck St.)
Henley Rd. E16 . . . . .2D 106
IG1: Ilf 4G 71
N18 . . . . .4K 33
NW10 . . . . .1E 80
Henley St. SW11 . . . . .2E 118
Henley Way TW13: Hanw 5B 130
Henlow Pl. TW10: Ham 2D 132
HENLYS CORNER 4H 45
HENLYS RDBT. 2A 112
Hennel Cl. SE23 . . . . .3J 139
Hennessy M. RM8: Dag 1E 72
Hennessy Ct. E10 . . . . .6E 50
Hennessy Rd. N9 . . . . .2D 34
Henniker Gdns. E6 . . . . .3B 88
Henniker M. SW3 . . . . . .7A 16 (6B 100)
Henniker Point E15 . . . . .5G 69
(off Leytonstone Rd.)
Henniker Rd. E15 . . . . .5F 69
Henningham Rd. N17 . . . . .1D 48
Henning St. SW11 . . . . .1C 118
Henrietta Barnet Wlk. NW11 . . . .6J 45
Henrietta Cl. SE8 . . . . .6C 104
Henrietta Ct. TW1: Twick 7C 114
(off Richmond Rd.)
Henrietta Gdns. N21 . . . . .1F 33
Henrietta Ho. N15 . . . . .6E 48
(off St Ann's Rd.)
W6 . . . . .5E 98
(off Queen Caroline St.)
Henrietta M. WC1 . . . . . .3F 7 (4J 83)
Henrietta Pl. W1 . . . . . .1J 11 (6F 83)
Henrietta St. WC2 . . . . .2F 13 (7J 83)
Henriques St. E1 . . . . .6G 85
Henry Addlington Cl. E6 . . . . . . .5F 89
Henry Chester Bldg. SW15 . . . . .2E 116
Henry Cl. EN2: Enf 1K 23
Henry Cooper Way SE9 . . . . . . .3B 142
Henry Ct. HA7: Stan 7J 27
Henry Darlot Dr. NW7 . . . . .6A 30
Henry Dickens Ct. W11 . . . . . . .7F 81
Henry Doulton Dr. SW17 . . . . . .4E 136
(not continuous)
Henry Hatch Ct. SM2: Sutt 7A 166
Henry Ho. SE1 . . . . . . .5J 13 (1A 102)
SW8 . . . . .7J 101
(off Wyvil Rd.)
Henry Hudson Apts. SE10 . . . . .5G 105
(off Banning St.)
Henry Jackson Rd. SW15 . . . . . .3F 117
Henry Macaulay Av.
KT2: King T 1D 150
Henry Moore Ct. SW3 . . . .6C 16 (5C 100)
Henry Peters Dr. TW11: Tedd . . .5J 131
(off Somerset Gdns.)
Henry Purcell Ho. E16 . . . . .1K 105
(off Evelyn Rd.)
Henry Rd. E6 . . . . .2C 88
EN4: E Barn 5G 21
N4 . . . . .1C 66
SW9 . . . . .1A 120
Henrys Av. IG8: Wfd G 5C 36
Henryson Rd. SE4 . . . . .5C 122
Henry St. BR1: Broml 1K 159
Henry's Wlk. IG6: Ilf 1H 53
Henry Tate M. SW16 . . . . .5K 137
Henry Tudor Ct. SE9 . . . . .7G 125
Henry Wise Ho. SW1 . . . . .4B 18
(off Vauxhall Bri. Rd.)
Hensford Gdns. SE26 . . . . .4H 139
Henshall Point E3 . . . . .3D 86
(off Bromley High St.)
Henshall St. N1 . . . . .6D 66
Henshawe Rd. RM8: Dag 3D 72
Henshaw St. SE17 . . . . .4D 102
Henslowe Rd. SE22 . . . . .5G 121
Henslow Ho. SE15 . . . . .7G 103
(off Peckham Pk. Rd.)
Henson Av. NW2 . . . . .5E 62
Henson Cl. BR6: Farnb 2F 173
Henson Path HA3: Kenton 3D 42
Henson Pl. UB5: N'olt 1A 76
Henson Rd. RM8: Dag 1E 72
Henstridge Pl. NW8 . . . . .1C 82
Henty Cl. SW11 . . . . .7C 100
Henty Wlk. SW15 . . . . .5D 116
Henville Rd. BR1: Broml 1K 159
Henwick Rd. SE9 . . . . .3B 124
Henwood Side IG8: Wfd G 6J 37
Hepburn Gdns. BR2: Hayes 1G 171
Hepburn M. SW11 . . . . .5D 118
Hepburn Pl. W3 . . . . .7H 79
Hepdon M. SW17 . . . . .5B 136
Hepple Cl. TW7: Isle 2B 114
Hepplestone Cl. SW15 . . . . . . .6D 116
Hepscott Rd. E9 . . . . .6C 68
Hepworth Ct. N1 . . . . .1B 84
(off Gaskin St.)
NW3 . . . . .5C 64
SM3: Sutt 1J 165
SW1 . . . . .6J 17 (5F 101)
Hepworth Gdns. IG11: Bark 5A 72
Hepworth Rd. SW16 . . . . .7J 137
Hepworth Way
KT12: Walt T 7H 147
Hera Av. EN5: Barn 3C 20
Heracles NW9 . . . . .1B 44
(off Five Acre)
Hera Ct. E14 . . . . .4C 104
(off Homer Dr.)
Herald Gdns. SM6: W'gton 2F 167
Herald's Pl. SE11 . . . . . .3K 19 (4B 102)
Herald St. E2 . . . . .4H 85
Herbal Hill EC1 . . . . . .4K 7 (4A 84)
Herbal Hill Gdns. EC1 . . . . .4K 7
(off Herbal Hill)
Herbal Pl. EC1 . . . . .4K 7
Herbert Cres. KT5: Surb 6F 151
(off Fulmar Cl.)
Herbert Cres. SW1 . . . . .1F 17 (3D 100)

Herbert Gdns.—Highstone Ct.

Herbert Gdns. NW10 2D 80
RM6: Chad H 7D 54
W4 6H 97
Herbert Ho. E1 7J 9
(off Old Castle St.)
Herbert M. SW2 6A 120
Herbert Morrison Ho. SW6 6H 99
(off Clem Attlee Ct.)
Herbert Pl. SE18 6F 107
TW7: Isle 2H 113
Herbert Rd. BR2: Broml 5B 160
DA7: Bex 2E 126
E12 4C 70
E17 7B 50
IG3: Ilf 2J 71
KT1: King T 3F 151
N11 7D 32
N15 5F 49
NW9 6C 44
SE18 7E 106
(not continuous)
SW19 7H 135
(not continuous)
UB1: S'hall 1D 94
Herbert St. E13 2J 87
NW5 6E 64
Herbrand Est. WC1 3E 6 (4J 83)
Herbrand St. WC1 3E 6 (4J 83)
Hercies Rd. UB10: Hil 7B 56
Hercules Ct. SE14 6A 104
Hercules Ho. E14 6G 87
Hercules Pl. N7 3J 65
(not continuous)
Hercules Rd. SE1 2H 19 (3K 101)
Hercules St. N7 3J 65
Hercules Wharf E14 7G 87
(off Orchard Pl.)
Hercules Yd. N7 3J 65
Here E. E20 5C 68
Hereford Av. EN4: E Barn 1J 31
Hereford Bldgs. SW3 7B 16
(off Old Church St.)
Hereford Ct. HA1: Harr 4J 41
SM2: Sutt 7J 165
W7 5K 77
(off Copley Cl.)
Hereford Gdns. HA5: Pinn 5C 40
IG1: Ilf 7C 52
SE13 5G 123
TW2: Twick 1G 131
Hereford Ho. N18 5C 34
(off Cameron Cl.)
NW6 2J 81
(off Carlton Vale)
SW3 1D 16
(off Ovington Gdns.)
SW10 7K 99
(off Fulham Rd.)
Hereford Mans. W2 6J 81
(off Hereford Rd.)
Hereford M. W2 6J 81
Hereford Pl. SE14 7B 104
Hereford Retreat SE15 7G 103
Hereford Rd. E3 2B 86
E11 5K 51
TW13: Felt 1A 130
W2 6J 81
W3 7H 79
W5 3C 96
Hereford Sq. SW7 4A 100
Hereford St. E2 4G 85
Hereford Way KT9: Chess 5C 162
Herent Dr. IG5: Ilf 4C 52
Herent Gdns. IG5: Ilf 4D 52
Hereward Gdns. N13 5F 33
Hereward Rd. SW17 4D 136
Herga Ct. HA1: Harr 3J 59
Herga Rd. HA3: W'stone 4K 41
Heriot Av. E4 2H 35
Heriot Rd. NW4 5E 44
Heriots Cl. HA7: Stan 4F 27
Heritage Av. NW9 3B 44
Heritage Cl. SW9 3B 120
TW16: Sun 1J 147
Heritage Ct. SE8 5K 103
Heritage Hill BR2: Kes 5A 172
Heritage La. NW6 6J 63
Heritage Pl. SW18 1A 136
TW8: Bford 5F 97
(off Heritage Wlk.)
Heritage Vw. HA1: Harr 3K 59
Heritage Wlk. TW8: Bford 5F 97
(off Kew Bri. Rd.)
Herlwyn Av. HA4: Ruis 2G 57
Herlwyn Gdns. SW17 4D 136
Her Majesty's Theatre 4C 12
(off Haymarket)
Herm Cl. TW7: Isle 7G 95
Hermes Cl. EN5: Barn 5C 20
W9 4J 81
Hermes Ct. SW2 6K 119
SW9 1A 120
(off Southey Rd.)
Hermes St. N1 1J 7 (2A 84)
Hermes Wlk. UB5: N'olt 2E 76
Herm Ho. EN3: Enf W 1E 24
N1 6C 66
(off Clifton Rd.)
Hermiston Av. N8 5J 47
The Hermitage KT1: King T 4D 150
SE13 2E 122
SE23 1J 139
SW13 1B 116
TW10: Rich 5E 114
TW13: Felt 3H 129
UB8: Uxb 6A 56
Hermitage Cl. E18 4H 51
EN2: Enf 2G 23
KT10: Clay 6A 162
SE2 3C 108
TW17: Shep 4C 146
Hermitage Ct. E1 1G 103
(off Knighten St.)
E18 4J 51
NW2 3J 63
Hermitage Gdns. NW2 3J 63
SE19 7C 138
Hermitage Grn. SW16 1J 155
Hermitage Ho. N1 2B 84
(off Gerrard Rd.)
Hermitage La. CR0: C'don 7G 157
N18 5J 33
NW2 3J 63
SE25 6G 157
SW16 7K 137
Hermitage Moorings E1 1G 103
Hermitage Path SW16 1J 155
Hermitage Rd. N4 7B 48
N15 7B 48
SE19 7C 138
Hermitage Row E8 5G 67
Hermitage St. W2 6A 4 (5B 82)
Hermitage Vs. SW6 6J 99
(off Lillie Rd.)
Hermitage Wlk. E18 4H 51
Hermitage Wall E1 1G 103
Hermitage Waterside E1 1G 103
(off Thomas More St.)
Hermitage Way HA7: Stan 1A 42
Hermit Pl. NW6 1K 81
Hermit Rd. E16 5H 87
Hermit St. EC1 1A 8 (3B 84)
Hermon Gro. UB3: Hayes 1J 93
Hermon Hill E11 5J 51
E18 5J 51
Herndon Rd. SW18 5A 118
Herne Cl. NW10 5K 61
UB3: Hayes 6H 75
WD23: Bush 1C 26
Herne Ct. WD23: Bush 1B 26
HERNE HILL 5C 120
Herne Hill SE24 6C 120
Herne Hill Ho. SE24 6B 120
(off Railton Rd.)
Herne Hill Rd. SE24 3C 120
Herne Hill Velodrome 6D 120
Herne M. N18 4B 34
Herne Pl. SE24 5B 120
Herne Rd. KT6: Surb 2D 162
Heron Cl. E17 2B 50
IG9: Buck H 1D 36
NW10 6A 62
SM1: Sutt 5H 165
WD23: Bush 1C 26
Heron Ct. BR2: Broml 4A 160
E14 3E 104
(off New Union Cl.)
HA4: Ruis 2F 57
KT1: King T 3E 150
NW9 2A 44
TW19: Stanw 1A 128
Heron Cres. DA14: Sidc 3J 143
Herondale Av. SW18 1B 136
Heron Dr. N4 2C 66
Herongate N1 1C 84
(off Ridgewell Cl.)
Herongate Rd. E12 2A 70
Heron Hill DA17: Belv 5F 109
Heron Ho. DA14: Sidc 3B 144
E3 1B 86
(off Sycamore Av.)
E6 7C 70
NW8 1C 4
(off Newcourt St.)
SW11 7C 100
(off Searles Cl.)
W13 4A 78
Heron Ind. Est. E15 2D 86
Heron Mead EN3: Enf L 1H 25
Heron M. IG1: Ilf 2F 71
Heron Pl. E16 1A 106
(off Bramwell Way)
SE16 1A 104
W1 7H 5
(off Thayer St.)
Heron Quay E14 1C 104
Heron Rd. CR0: C'don 2E 168
SE24 4C 120
TW1: Twick 4A 114
The Herons E11 6H 51
Heronsforde W13 6C 78
Heronsgate HA8: Edg 5B 28
Heron's Lea N6 6D 46
Heronslea Dr. HA7: Stan 5K 27
Heron's Pl. TW7: Isle 3B 114
Heron Sq. TW9: Rich 5D 114
Herons Ri. EN4: E Barn 4H 21
Heron Tower 7H 9
Heron Trad. Est. W3 5H 79
Heron Vw. TW8: Bford 7C 96
(off Commerce Rd.)
Heron Way SM6: W'gton 7H 167
TW14: Felt 4J 111
Heronway IG8: Wfd G 4F 37
Herrick Ct. W3 3J 97
(off Bollo Bri. Rd.)
Herrick Ho. N16 4D 66
(off Howard Rd.)
SE5 7D 102
(off Elmington Est.)
Herrick Rd. N5 3C 66
Herrick St. SW1 4D 18 (4H 101)
Herries St. W10 2G 81
Herringham Rd. SE7 3A 106
Herron Ct. BR2: Broml 4H 159
Herrongate Cl. EN1: Enf 2A 24
Hersant Cl. NW10 1C 80
Herschell M. SE5 3C 120
Herschell Rd. SE23 7A 122
Hersham Cl. SW15 7C 116
Hershell Ct. SW14 4H 115
Hertford Av. SW14 5K 115
Hertford Cl. EN4: Cockf 3G 21
Hertford Ct. E6 3D 88
N13 3F 33
Hertford Ho. UB5: N'olt 4D 76
Hertford Lock Ho. E3 1B 86
(off Parnell Rd.)
Hertford Pl. W1 4B 6 (4G 83)
Hertford Rd.
EN3: Enf H, Enf W 3D 24
EN4: Cockf 3F 21
IG2: Ilf 6J 53
IG11: Bark 7E 70
N1 1E 84
(not continuous)
N2 3C 46
N9 2C 34
Hertford St. W1 5J 11 (1F 101)
Hertford Wlk. DA17: Belv 5G 109
Hertford Way CR4: Mitc 4J 155
Hertford Wharf N1 1E 84
(off Hertford Rd.)
Hertslet Rd. N7 3K 65
Hertsmere Rd. E14 1C 104
Hertswood Ct. EN5: Barn 4B 20
Hervey Cl. N3 1J 45
Hervey Pk. Rd. E17 4A 50
Hervey Rd. SE3 1K 123
Hervey Way N3 1J 45
Hesa Rd. UB3: Hayes 6J 75
Hesewall Cl. SW4 2G 119
Hesketh Pl. W11 7G 81
Hesketh Rd. E7 3J 69
Heslop Rd. SW12 1D 136
Hesper M. SW5 4K 99
Hesperus Cres. E14 4D 104
Hessel Rd. W13 2A 96
Hessel St. E1 6H 85
Hestercombe Av. SW6 2G 117
Hesterman Way CR0: Wadd 1K 167
Hester Rd. N18 5B 34
SW11 7C 100
Hester Ter. TW9: Rich 3G 115
Hestia Ho. SE1 7G 15
HESTON 7E 94
Heston Av. TW5: Hest 6C 94
The Heston Cen.
TW5: Cran 5A 94
Heston Community Sports Hall 7E 94
Heston Grange TW5: Hest 6D 94
Heston Grange La.
TW5: Hest 6D 94
Heston Ho. SE8 1C 122
Heston Ind. Mall TW5: Hest 7D 94
Heston Phoenix Distribution Pk.
TW5: Hest 6A 94
Heston Pool 6D 94
Heston Rd. TW5: Hest 6E 94
HESTON SERVICE AREA 6B 94
Heston St. SE14 1C 122
Hetherington Rd. SW4 4J 119
TW17: Shep 2E 146
Hetherington Way UB10: Ick 4A 56
Hethpool Ho. W2 4A 4
Hetley Gdns. SE19 7F 139
Hetley Rd. W12 1D 98
Heton Gdns. NW4 4D 44
Hevelius Cl. SE10 5H 105
Hever Cft. SE9 4E 142
Hever Gdns. BR1: Broml 2E 160
Heverham Rd. SE18 4J 107
Hever Ho. SE15 6K 103
(off Lovelinch Cl.)
Hever Pl. KT8: E Mos 3G 149
Heversham Ho. SE15 6J 103
Heversham Rd. DA7: Bex 2G 127
Hevingham Dr. RM6: Chad H 5C 54
Hevingham Vw. SE26 5H 139
Hewens Rd. UB4: Hil 4E 74
UB10: Hil 4E 74
Hewer St. W10 5F 81
Hewett Cl. HA7: Stan 4G 27
Hewett Rd. RM8: Dag 5D 72
Hewetts Quay IG11: Bark 1F 89
Hewett St. EC2 4H 9 (4E 84)
Hewish Rd. N18 4K 33
Hewison St. E3 2B 86
Hewitt Av. N22 2B 48
Hewitt Cl. CR0: C'don 3C 170
Hewitt Rd. N8 5A 48
Hewlett Ho. SW8 7F 101
(off Havelock Ter.)
Hewlett Rd. E3 2A 86
Hewson Way SE17 4C 102
The Hexagon N6 1D 64
Hexagon Bus. Cen.
UB4: Yead 7A 76
Hexal Rd. SE6 3G 141
Hexham Gdns. TW7: Isle 7A 96
Hexham Rd. EN5: New Bar 4E 20
SE27 2C 138
SM4: Mord 1K 165
Heybourne Cres. NW9 1A 44
Heybourne Rd. N17 7C 34
Heybridge NW1 6F 65
(off Lewis St.)
Heybridge Av. SW16 7J 137
Heybridge Dr. IG6: Ilf 2H 53
Heybridge Way E10 7A 50
Heydon Ct. BR4: W W'ck 2G 171
(off Deer Pk. Way)
Heydon Ho. SE14 1J 121
(off Kender St.)
Heyford Av. SW8 7J 101
SW20 3H 153
Heyford Rd. CR4: Mitc 2C 154
Heyford Ter. SW8 7J 101
(off Old Sth. Lambeth Rd.)
Heygate St. SE17 4C 102
Heylyn Sq. E3 3B 86
Heynes Rd. RM8: Dag 4C 72
Heysham La. NW3 3K 63
Heysham Rd. N15 6D 48
Heythorp St. SW18 1H 135
Heythrop Dr. UB10: Ick 4B 56
Heywood Av. NW9 1A 44
Heywood Ct. HA7: Stan 5H 27
Heywood Ho. SE14 6K 103
(off Myers La.)
Heyworth Rd. E5 4H 67
E15 5H 69
Hibbert Ho. E14 3C 104
(off Tiller Rd.)
Hibbert Rd. E17 7B 50
HA3: W'stone 2K 41
Hibbert St. SW11 3B 118
Hibernia Gdns. TW3: Houn 4E 112
Hibernia Point SE2 2D 108
(off Wolvercote Rd.)
Hibernia Rd. TW3: Houn 4E 112
Hibiscus Cl. HA8: Edg 4D 28
Hibiscus Ho. E17 3D 50
TW13: Felt 1G 129
Hibiscus Lodge E15 7G 69
(off Glenavon Rd.)
Hichisson Rd. SE15 5J 121
Hicken Rd. SW2 5K 119
Hickes Ho. NW6 7B 64
Hickey's Almshouses
TW9: Rich 4F 115
Hickin Cl. SE7 4B 106
Hickin St. E14 3E 104
Hickleton NW1 1G 83
(off Camden St.)
Hickling Ho. SE16 3H 103
(off Slippers Pl.)
Hickling Rd. IG1: Ilf 5F 71
Hickman Av. E4 6K 35
Hickman Cl. E16 5B 88
Hickman Rd. RM6: Chad H 7C 54
Hickman Wlk. SE18 5E 106
(off Brumwell Av.)
Hickmore Wlk. SW4 3H 119
Hickory Cl. N9 7B 24
Hicks Av. UB6: G'frd 3H 77
Hicks Bolton Ho. NW6 2H 81
(off Denmark Ho.)
Hicks Cl. SW11 3C 118
Hicks Ct. RM10: Dag 3H 73
Hicks Gallery 5J 135
Hicks Ho. SE16 3G 103
(off Spa Rd.)
Hicks St. SE8 5A 104
Hidcote Apts. SW11 4C 118
(off Danvers Av.)
Hidcote Gdns. SW20 3D 152
Hidden Cl. KT8: W Mole 4G 149
Hide E6 6E 88
Hide Pl. SW1 4C 18 (4H 101)
Hider Ct. SE3 7A 106
Hide Rd. HA1: Harr 4G 41
Hides St. N7 6K 65
Hide Twr. SW1 4C 18
(off Regency St.)
Hierro Ct. E1 5A 86
(off Ocean Est.)
Higgins Ho. N1 1E 84
(off Colville Est.)
Higginson Ho. NW3 7D 64
(off Fellows Rd.)
Higgins Wlk. TW12: Hamp 6C 130
(off Abbott Cl.)
Higgs Ind. Est. SE24 3B 120
High Acres EN2: Enf 3G 23
HIGHAM HILL 2A 50
Higham Hill Rd. E17 1A 50
Higham M. UB5: N'olt 4D 76
Higham Path E17 3A 50
Higham Pl. E17 3A 50
Higham Rd. IG8: Wfd G 6D 36
N17 3D 48
The Highams E17 1E 50
Highams Ct. E4 3K 35
Highams Lodge Bus. Cen. E17 3K 49
HIGHAMS PARK 6A 36
Higham Sta. Av. E4 6H 35
Higham St. E17 3A 50
High Ashton KT2: King T 7H 133
Highbanks Cl. DA16: Well 7B 108
Highbanks Rd. HA5: Hat E 6A 26
Highbank Way N8 6A 48
HIGH BARNET 2A 20
Highbarrow Rd. CR0: C'don 1G 169
High Beech CR2: S Croy 7E 168
N21 6E 22
High Beeches DA14: Sidc 5E 144
High Birch Ct. EN4: E Barn 4H 21
(off Park Rd.)
High Bri. SE10 5F 105
Highbridge Ct. SE14 7J 103
(off Farrow La.)
Highbridge Rd. IG11: Bark 1F 89
High Bri. Wharf SE10 5F 105
(off High Bri.)
Highbrook Rd. SE3 3B 124
High Broom Cres.
BR4: W W'ck 7D 158
HIGHBURY 4B 66
Highbury Av. CR7: Thor H 2A 156
Highbury Cl. BR4: W W'ck 2D 170
KT3: N Mald 4J 151
HIGHBURY CORNER 6B 66
Highbury Cres. N5 5B 66
Highbury Est. N5 5C 66
Highbury Gdns. IG3: Ilf 2J 71
N7 5A 66
Highbury Grange N5 4C 66
Highbury Gro. N5 5B 66
Highbury Gro. Ct. N5 6C 66
Highbury Hill N5 3A 66
Highbury Leisure Centre 6B 66
Highbury Mans. N1 7B 66
(off Upper St.)
Highbury New Pk. N5 5C 66
Highbury Pk. N5 3B 66
Highbury Pl. N5 6B 66
Highbury Quad. N5 3C 66
Highbury Rd. SW19 5G 135
Highbury Sq. N14 1B 32
Highbury Stadium Sq. N5 3B 66
Highbury Sta. Rd. N1 6A 66
Highbury Ter. N5 5B 66
Highbury Ter. M. N5 5B 66
High Cedar Dr. SW20 7E 134
Highclere Rd. KT3: N Mald 3K 151
Highclere St. SE26 4A 140
Highcliffe W13 5B 78
(off Clivedon Ct.)
Highcliffe Dr. SW15 6B 116
Highcliffe Gdns. IG4: Ilf 5C 52
Highcombe SE7 6K 105
Highcombe Cl. SE9 1B 142
High Coombe Pl. KT2: King T 6K 133
Highcroft NW9 5A 44
Highcroft Av. HA0: Wemb 7G 61
Highcroft Est. N19 7J 47
Highcroft Gdns. NW11 6H 45
Highcroft Rd. N19 7J 47
The High Cross Cen. N15 4G 49
High Cross Rd. N17 3G 49
Highcross Way SW15 1C 134
Highdaun Dr. SW16 4K 155
Highdown KT4: Wor Pk 2A 164
Highdown Rd. SW15 6D 116
High Dr. KT3: N Mald 1J 151
High Elms IG8: Wfd G 5D 36
High Elms Country Pk. 7H 173
High Elms Golf Course 7G 173
High Elms Rd. BR6: Downe 7G 173
Highfield WD23: B Hea 1D 26
Highfield Av. BR6: Chels 5K 173
DA8: Erith 6H 109
HA5: Pinn 5D 40
HA9: Wemb 3F 61
NW9 5J 43
NW11 7F 45
UB6: G'frd 5J 59
Highfield Cl. HA6: Nwood 1G 39
KT6: Surb 2D 162
N22 1A 48
NW9 5J 43
SE13 6F 123
Highfield Ct. N14 6B 22
NW11 6G 45
Highfield Cres. HA6: Nwood 1G 39
Highfield Dr. BR2: Broml 4G 159
BR4: W W'ck 2D 170
KT19: Ewe 6B 164
UB10: Ick 4A 56
Highfield Gdns. NW11 6G 45
Highfield Hill SE19 7D 138
Highfield M. NW6 7K 63
(off Compayne Gdns.)
Highfield Rd. BR1: Broml 4D 160
BR7: Chst 3K 161
DA6: Bex 5F 127
HA6: Nwood 1G 39
IG8: Wfd G 7H 37
KT5: Surb 7J 151
KT12: Walt T 7J 147
N21 2G 33
NW11 6G 45
SM1: Sutt 5C 166
TW7: Isle 1K 113
TW13: Felt 2J 129
TW16: Sun 5H 147
W3 5H 79
Highfields SM1: Sutt 2J 165
Highfields Gro. N6 1D 64
High Foleys KT10: Clay 7B 162
High Gables BR2: Broml 2G 159
HIGHGATE 6E 46
Highgate Av. N6 7F 47
Highgate Cemetery 1E 64
Highgate Cl. N6 7E 46
Highgate Edge N2 5C 46
Highgate Golf Course 6C 46
Highgate Hgts. N6 6G 47
Highgate High St. N6 1E 64
Highgate Hill N6 1F 65
N19 1F 65
Highgate Ho. SE26 3G 139
Highgate Rd. NW5 3E 64
Highgate Spinney N8 6H 47
Highgate Wlk. SE23 2J 139
Highgate W. Hill N6 1E 64
High Gro. BR1: Broml 1B 160
SE18 7H 107
Highgrove Cl. BR7: Chst 1C 160
N11 5K 31
Highgrove Ct. BR3: Beck 7C 140
SM1: Sutt 6J 165
Highgrove Ho. HA4: Ruis 6J 39
Highgrove M. SM5: Cars 3D 166
Highgrove Pool & Fitness Cen. 6J 39
Highgrove Rd. RM8: Dag 5C 72
Highgrove Ter. E4 2A 36
Highgrove Way HA4: Ruis 6J 39
High Hill Est. E5 1H 67
High Hill Ferry E5 1H 67
High Holborn WC1 7E 6 (6J 83)
High Ho. M. N16 2E 66
Highland Av. RM10: Dag 3J 73
W7 6J 77
Highland Cotts. SM6: W'gton 4G 167
Highland Ct. BR1: Broml 1H 159
E18 1K 51
Highland Cft. BR3: Beck 5D 140
Highland Dr. WD23: Bush 1A 26
Highland Pk. TW13: Felt 4H 129
Highland Rd. BR1: Broml 1H 159
BR2: Broml 1H 159
DA6: Bex 5G 127
HA6: Nwood 2H 39
SE19 6E 138
Highlands N20 2G 31
The Highlands EN5: New Bar 4D 20
HA8: Edg 2H 43
Highlands Av. N21 5E 22
W3 7J 79
Highlands Cl. N4 7J 47
TW3: Houn 1F 113
Highlands Ct. SE19 6E 138
Highlands Gdns. IG1: Ilf 1D 70
Highlands Heath SW15 7E 116
Highlands Rd. EN5: New Bar 5D 20
Highland St. E15 2D 86
HIGHLANDS VILLAGE 5E 22
Highland Ter. SE13 3D 122
(off Algernon Rd.)
Highland Vw. Pk. Homes 1D 174
High La. W7 5H 77
Highlawn Hall HA1: Harr 3J 59
Highlea Cl. NW9 7F 29
High Level Dr. SE26 4G 139
Highlever Rd. W10 5E 80
High Mead BR4: W W'ck 2F 171
HA1: Harr 5J 41
Highmead SE18 7K 107
Highmead Cres. HA0: Wemb 7F 61
High Mdw. Cl. HA5: Eastc 4A 40
Highmeadow Cres. NW9 5K 43
High Meads Rd. E16 6B 88
Highmore Rd. SE3 7G 105
High Mt. NW4 6C 44
High Oaks EN2: Enf 1E 22
The High Pde. SW16 3J 137
High Pk. Av. TW9: Kew 1G 115
High Pk. Rd. TW9: Kew 1G 115
High Path SW19 1K 153
High Point N6 7E 46
SE9 3F 143
High Ridge N10 1F 47
High Rd. E18 1J 51
HA0: Wemb 5D 60
HA3: Hrw W 7D 26
HA5: Eastc 6J 39
HA9: Wemb 5D 60
IG1: Ilf 3F 71
(not continuous)
IG3: Ilf 1K 71
IG7: Chig 5K 37
IG9: Buck H 2E 36
N11 5A 32
N15 4F 49
N17 2F 49
N22 7E 32
NW10 6A 62
RM6: Chad H 7D 54
UB4: Hayes 5G 75
UB10: Ick 3D 56
WD23: B Hea 1C 26
High Rd. E. Finchley N2 1B 46
High Rd. Leyton E10 6D 50
E15 2D 68
High Rd. Leytonstone E11 3G 69
E15 4G 69
High Rd. Nth. Finchley N12 3F 31
(not continuous)
High Rd. Whetstone N20 7F 21
High Rd. Woodford Grn. E18 1J 51
IG8: Wfd G 6C 36
High Sheldon N6 6D 46
Highshore Rd. SE15 2F 121
(not continuous)
Highstead Cres. DA8: Erith 1K 127
Highstone Av. E11 6J 51
Highstone Ct. E11 6H 51
(off New Wanstead)

Highstone Mans. *NW1* 7G **65**
(*off Camden Rd.*)
High St. BR1: Broml 2J **159**
(not continuous)
BR3: Beck 2C **158**
BR4: W W'ck 1D **170**
BR6: Chels 7K **173**
BR6: Farnb 5F **173**
BR6: Orp 2K **173**
BR7: Chst 6F **143**
CR0: C'don 3C **168**
CR7: Thor H 4C **156**
E11 5J **51**
E13 2J **87**
E15 2E **86**
E17 5A **50**
EN3: Pond E 6D **24**
EN5: Barn 3B **20**
HA1: Harr 1J **59**
HA3: Hrw W, W'stone 2J **41**
HA4: Ruis 7G **39**
HA5: Pinn 3C **40**
HA6: Nwood 1H **39**
HA8: Edg 6B **28**
HA9: Wemb 4F **61**
IG6: Ilf 3G **53**
KT1: Hamp W 1C **150**
KT1: King T 3D **150**
KT3: N Mald 4A **152**
KT7: T Ditt 6A **150**
KT8: W Mole 4E **148**
KT12: Walt T 7J **147**
KT17: Ewe 7B **164**
N8 4J **47**
N14 1C **32**
NW7 5J **29**
RM1: Rom 5K **55**
SE20 6J **139**
SE25 4F **157**
SM1: Sutt 4K **165**
SM3: Cheam 6G **165**
SM5: Cars 5E **166**
SW19 5F **135**
TW2: Whitt 7G **113**
TW3: Houn 3F **113**
TW5: Cran 1J **111**
TW8: Bford 7C **96**
TW11: Tedd 5K **131**
TW12: Hamp, Hamp H 1G **149**
TW13: Felt 3H **129**
TW17: Shep 6D **146**
TW19: Stanw 6A **110**
UB1: S'hall 1D **94**
UB3: Harl 6F **93**
UB7: Harm 2E **174**
UB7: Yiew 7A **74**
UB8: Uxb 1A **74**
W3 1H **97**
W5 1D **96**
High St. Colliers Wood SW19 7B **136**
High St. Harlesden NW10 2B **80**
High St. M. SW19 5G **135**
High St. Nth. E6 1C **88**
E12 5C **70**
High St. Sth. E6 2D **88**
High Timber St. EC4 2C **14** (7C **84**)
High Tor Cl. BR1: Broml 7K **141**
High Tor Vw. SE28 1J **107**
High Trees CR0: C'don 1A **170**
EN4: E Barn 5H **21**
N20 3F **31**
SW2 1A **138**
Hightrees Ct. W7 7J **77**
Hightrees Ho. SW12 6E **118**
High Vw. HA5: Pinn 4A **40**
Highview N6 6G **47**
NW7 3E **28**
UB5: N'olt 3C **76**
Highview Av. HA8: Edg 4D **28**
SM6: W'gton 5K **167**
High Vw. Cl. SE19 2F **157**
High Vw. Ct. HA3: Hrw W 7D **26**
Highview Gdns. HA8: Edg 4D **28**
N3 3G **45**
N11 5B **32**
Highview Ho.
RM6: Chad H 4E **54**
Highview Lodge *EN2: Enf* 3G **23**
(*off The Ridgeway*)
High Vw. Pde. IG4: Ilf 5D **52**
High Vw. Rd. E18 2H **51**
SE19 6D **138**
Highview Rd. DA14: Sidc 4B **144**
W13 5A **78**
The Highway E1 7G **85**
HA7: Stan 1K **41**
SM2: Sutt 7A **166**
The Highway Trad. Cen. *E1* 7K **85**
(*off Heckford St.*)
Highwood BR2: Broml 3F **159**
Highwood Av. N12 4F **31**
Highwood Cl. BR6: Farnb 2G **173**
SE22 1G **139**
Highwood Ct. EN5: New Bar 5D **20**
N12 3F **31**
Highwood Dr. BR6: Farnb 2G **173**
Highwood Gdns. IG5: Ilf 5D **52**
Highwood Gro. NW7 5E **28**
HIGHWOOD HILL 3G **29**
Highwood Hill NW7 2G **29**
Highwood Rd. N19 3J **65**
High Worple HA2: Harr 7D **40**
Highworth Rd. N11 6C **32**
Highworth St. NW1 5D **4**
Hi-Gloss Cen. SE8 5A **104**
Hilary Av. CR4: Mitc 3E **154**
Hilary Cl. DA8: Erith 1H **127**
SW6 7K **99**
Hilary Dennis Ct. E11 4J **51**
Hilary M. SE1 2C **102**
Hilary Rd. W12 6B **80**
(not continuous)
Hilberry Ct. WD23: Bush 1A **26**
Hilbert Rd. SM3: Cheam 3F **165**
Hilborough Cl. SW19 7A **136**
Hilborough Ct. E8 7F **67**
Hilborough Way BR6: Farnb 5H **173**
Hilda Ct. KT6: Surb 7D **150**
Hilda Lockert Wlk. *SW9* 2B **120**
(*off Loughborough Rd.*)
Hilda Rd. E6 7B **70**
E16 4G **87**
UB2: S'hall 2G **95**
Hilda Ter. SW9 2A **120**
Hilda Va. Cl. BR6: Farnb 4F **173**
Hilda Va. Rd. BR6: Farnb 4E **172**
Hildenborough Gdns.
BR1: Broml 6G **141**
Hildenborough Ho. *BR3: Beck* 7B **140**
(*off Bethersden Cl.*)
Hildenlea Pl. BR2: Broml 2F **159**
Hilderley Ho. *KT1: King T* 3F **151**
(*off Winery La.*)
Hildreth St. SW12 1F **137**
Hildreth St. M. SW12 1F **137**
Hildyard Rd. SW6 6J **99**
Hiley Rd. NW10 3E **80**
Hilgrove Rd. NW6 7A **64**
Hiliary Gdns. HA7: Stan 2C **42**
Hillary *N8* 3J **47**
(*off Boyton Cl.*)
Hillary Ct. *W12* 2E **98**
(*off Titmuss St.*)
Hillary Cres. KT12: Walt T 7A **148**
Hillary Dr. TW7: Isle 5K **113**
Hillary M. E14 5D **86**
Hillary Ri. EN5: New Bar 4D **20**
Hillary Rd. UB2: S'hall 3E **94**
Hillbeck Cl. SE15 7J **103**
(not continuous)
Hillbeck Way UB6: G'frd 1H **77**
Hillborne Cl. UB3: Harl 5J **93**
Hillboro Ct. E11 7F **51**
Hillbrook Rd. SW17 3D **136**
Hill Brow BR1: Broml 1B **160**
Hillbrow KT3: N Mald 3B **152**
Hillbrow Cl. DA5: Bexl 4K **145**
Hillbrow Rd. BR1: Broml 7G **141**
Hillbury Av. HA3: Kenton 5B **42**
Hillbury Rd. SW17 3F **137**
Hill Cl. BR7: Chst 5F **143**
HA1: Harr 3J **59**
HA7: Stan 4G **27**
NW2 3D **62**
NW11 6J **45**
Hillcote Av. SW16 7A **138**
Hill Ct. EN4: E Barn 4H **21**
UB5: N'olt 5E **58**
W5 4F **79**
Hillcourt Av. N12 6E **30**
Hillcourt Est. N16 1D **66**
Hillcourt Rd. SE22 6H **121**
Hill Cres. DA5: Bexl 1J **145**
HA1: Harr 5A **42**
KT4: Wor Pk 2E **164**
KT5: Surb 5F **151**
N20 2E **30**
Hill Crest DA15: Sidc 7A **126**
KT6: Surb 7E **150**
Hillcrest N6 7E **46**
N21 7F **23**
SE24 4D **120**
W11 7H **81**
(*off St John's Gdns.*)
Hillcrest Av. HA5: Pinn 4B **40**
HA8: Edg 4C **28**
NW11 5H **45**
Hillcrest Cl. BR3: Beck 6B **158**
SE26 4G **139**
Hillcrest Ct. RM5: Col R 1K **55**
SM2: Sutt 6B **166**
(*off Eaton Rd.*)
Hillcrest Gdns. KT10: Hin W 3A **162**
N3 4G **45**
NW2 3C **62**
Hillcrest Rd. BR1: Broml 5J **141**
BR6: Chels 2K **173**
E17 2F **51**
E18 2H **51**
W3 1H **97**
W5 5E **78**
Hillcrest Vw. BR3: Beck 6B **158**
Hillcroft Av. HA5: Pinn 6D **40**
Hillcroft Cres. HA4: Ruis 3B **58**
HA9: Wemb 4F **61**
W5 6D **78**
Hillcroft Rd. E6 5F **89**
Hillcroome Rd. SM2: Sutt 6B **166**
Hillcross Av. SM4: Mord 6F **153**
Hilldale Rd. SM1: Sutt 4H **165**
Hilldown Ct. SW16 7J **137**
Hilldown Rd. BR2: Hayes 1G **171**
SW16 7J **137**
Hill Dr. NW9 1J **61**
SW16 3K **155**
Hilldrop Cres. N7 5H **65**
Hilldrop Est. N7 5H **65**
(not continuous)
Hilldrop La. N7 5H **65**
Hilldrop Rd. BR1: Broml 6K **141**
N7 5H **65**
Hill End BR6: Orp 2K **173**
Hillend SE18 1E **124**
Hillend Green NW7 4K **29**
Hillersden Ho. *SW1* 5J **17**
(*off Ebury Bri. Rd.*)
Hillersdon Av. HA8: Edg 5A **28**
SW13 2C **116**
Hillery Cl. SE17 4D **102**
Hill Farm Cotts. HA4: Ruis 7E **38**
Hill Farm Rd. UB10: Ick 4F **57**
W10 5E **80**
Hillfield Av. HA0: Wemb 7E **60**
N8 5J **47**
NW9 5A **44**
SM4: Mord 6C **154**
Hillfield Cl. HA2: Harr 4G **41**
Hillfield Ct. NW3 5C **64**
Hillfield Ho. N5 5C **66**
Hillfield M. N8 4K **47**
Hillfield Pde. SM4: Mord 6B **154**
Hillfield Pk. N10 4F **47**
N21 2F **33**
Hillfield Pk. M. N10 4F **47**
Hill Fld. Rd. TW12: Hamp 7D **130**
Hillfield Rd. NW6 5H **63**
Hillfoot Av. RM5: Col R 1J **55**
Hillfoot Rd. RM5: Col R 1J **55**
Hillgate Pl. SW12 7F **119**
W8 1J **99**
Hillgate St. W8 1J **99**
Hill Ga. Wlk. N6 6G **47**
Hill Gro. RM1: Rom 3K **55**
TW13: Hanw 2D **130**
Hill Ho. BR2: Broml 3H **159**
E5 1H **67**
(*off Harrington Hill*)
N19 2G **65**
(*off Highgate Hill*)
SE28 1H **107**
Hill Ho. Apts. *N1* 1H **7**
(*off Pentonville Rd.*)
Hill Ho. Av. HA7: Stan 7E **26**
Hill Ho. Cl. N21 7F **23**
Hill Ho. Dr. TW12: Hamp 1E **148**
Hill Ho. M. BR2: Broml 2H **159**
Hill Ho. Rd. SW16 5K **137**
Hilliard Ho. *E1* 1H **103**
(*off Prusom St.*)
Hilliard Rd. HA6: Nwood 1H **39**
Hilliards Ct. E1 1J **103**
Hillier Cl. EN5: New Bar 6E **20**
Hillier Gdns. CR0: Wadd 5A **168**
Hillier Ho. *NW1* 7H **65**
(*off Camden Sq.*)
Hillier Lodge TW11: Tedd 5H **131**
Hillier Pl. KT9: Chess 6D **162**
Hillier Rd. SW11 6D **118**
Hilliers Av. UB8: Hil 3C **74**
Hilliers La. CR0: Bedd 3J **167**
HILLINGDON 3C **74**
Hillingdon Athletic Club 5F **39**
Hillingdon Athletics Stadium 6A **56**
Hillingdon Av. TW19: Stanw 1A **128**
HILLINGDON CIRCUS 6D **56**
Hillingdon Ct.
HA3: Kenton 4D **42**
Hillingdon Cycle Circuit 1A **94**
Hillingdon Golf Course 2B **74**
HILLINGDON HEATH 4D **74**
Hillingdon Hill UB10: Hil 2A **74**
Hillingdon Pde. *UB10: Hil* 4D **74**
(*off Uxbridge Rd.*)
Hillingdon Rd. DA7: Bex 2J **127**
UB8: Uxb 1A **74**
UB10: Uxb 1A **74**
Hillingdon Sports & Leisure Complex
6A **56**
Hillingdon St. SE17 6B **102**
Hillington Gdns. IG8: Wfd G 2B **52**
Hill La. HA4: Ruis 1E **56**
Hillman Cl. UB8: Uxb 5A **56**
Hillman Dr. W10 4E **80**
Hillman St. E8 6H **67**
Hillmarton Rd. N7 5J **65**
Hillmarton Ter. *N7* 5J **65**
(*off Hillmarton Rd.*)
Hillmead Dr. SW9 4B **120**
Hillmore Ct. *SE13* 3F **123**
(*off Belmont Hill*)
Hillmore Gro. SE26 5A **140**
Hill Path SW16 5K **137**
Hillreach SE18 5D **106**
Hill Ri. HA4: Ruis 1E **56**
KT10: Hin W 2B **162**
N9 6C **24**
NW11 4K **45**
SE23 1H **139**
TW10: Rich 5D **114**
UB6: G'frd 7G **59**
Hillrise KT12: Walt T 7H **147**
Hillrise Mans. *N19* 7J **47**
(*off Warltersville Rd.*)
Hillrise Rd. N19 7J **47**
Hill Rd. CR4: Mitc 1F **155**
HA0: Wemb 3B **60**
HA1: Harr 5A **42**
HA5: Pinn 5C **40**
N10 1D **46**
NW8 2A **82**
SM1: Sutt 5K **165**
SM5: Cars 6C **166**
Hillsboro' Rd. SE22 5E **120**
Hillsborough Ct. *NW6* 1K **81**
(*off Mortimer Cres.*)
Hillsgrove Cl. DA16: Well 7C **108**
HILLSIDE 4J **109**
Hillside DA8: Erith 4J **109**
EN5: New Bar 5F **21**
N8 6H **47**
NW5 3E **64**
NW9 4K **43**
NW10 7J **61**
SE10 7F **105**
(*off Croom's Hill*)
SW19 6F **135**
Hillside Av. HA9: Wemb 4F **61**
IG8: Wfd G 6F **37**
N11 6J **31**
SE10 1E **122**
Hillside Cl. IG8: Wfd G 5F **37**
NW8 2K **81**
SM4: Mord 4G **153**
Hillside Cres. HA2: Harr 1G **59**
HA6: Nwood 1J **39**
Hillside Dr. HA8: Edg 6B **28**
Hillside Gdns. E17 3F **51**
EN5: Barn 4B **20**
HA3: Kenton 7E **42**
HA6: Nwood 1J **39**
HA8: Edg 4A **28**
N6 6F **47**
N11 6B **32**
SM6: W'gton 7G **167**
SW2 2A **138**
Hillside Gro. N14 7C **22**
NW7 7H **29**
Hillside Ho. *CR0: Wadd* 4B **168**
(*off Duppas Av.*)
Hillside La. BR2: Hayes 2H **171**
(not continuous)
Hillside Mans. EN5: Barn 4C **20**
Hillside Pas. SW2 2K **137**
Hillside Ri. HA6: Nwood 1J **39**
Hillside Rd. BR2: Broml 3H **159**
CR0: Wadd 5B **168**
HA5: Pinn 1K **39**
HA6: Nwood 1J **39**
KT5: Surb 4F **151**
N15 7E **48**
SM2: Sutt 7H **165**
SW2 2K **137**
UB1: S'hall 4E **76**
W5 5E **78**
Hills La. HA6: Nwood 1G **39**
Hillsleigh Rd. W8 1H **99**
Hills M. W5 7E **78**
Hills Pl. W1 1A **12** (6G **83**)
Hills Rd. IG9: Buck H 1E **36**
Hillstone Ct. *E3* 4D **86**
(*off Empson St.*)
Hillstowe St. E5 3J **67**
Hill St. TW9: Rich 5D **114**
W1 4H **11** (1E **100**)
Hill Top NW11 4K **45**
SM3: Sutt 7H **153**
SM4: Mord 6J **153**
Hilltop E17 3D **50**
Hilltop Av. NW10 7J **61**
(not continuous)
Hill Top Cl. IG8: Wfd G 6J **37**
Hilltop Ct. *NW8* 7A **64**
(*off Alexandra Rd.*)
Hilltop Gdns. BR6: Orp 2J **173**
NW4 2D **44**
Hilltop Ho. N6 7H **47**
Hilltop Rd. NW6 7J **63**
Hill Top Vw. IG8: Wfd G 6J **37**
Hilltop Way HA7: Stan 3F **27**
Hill Vw. *NW3* 1D **82**
(*off Ainger Rd.*)
Hillview SW20 7D **134**
Hillview Av. HA3: Kenton 5E **42**
Hillview Cl. HA9: Wemb 2F **61**
Hillview Cres. BR6: Orp 1J **173**
IG1: Ilf 6D **52**
Hill Vw. Dr. DA16: Well 2J **125**
SE28 1J **107**
Hill Vw. Gdns. NW9 5K **43**
Hillview Gdns. HA2: Harr 3E **40**
NW4 4F **45**
Hill Vw. Rd. KT10: Clay 7A **162**
TW1: Twick 6A **114**
Hillview Rd. BR6: Orp 1K **173**
BR7: Chst 5E **142**
HA5: Hat E 1D **40**
NW7 4B **30**
SM1: Sutt 3A **166**
Hillway N6 2E **64**
NW9 1A **62**
Hill-Wood Ho. *NW1* 1B **6**
(*off Polygon Rd.*)
Hillworth BR3: Beck 2D **158**
Hillworth Rd. SW2 7A **120**
Hillyard Ho. SW9 1A **120**
Hillyard Pl. SW20 7D **134**
Hillyard Rd. W7 5J **77**
Hillyard St. SW9 1A **120**
Hillyfield E17 2A **50**
Hillyfield Cl. E9 5A **68**
Hilly Flds. Cres. SE4 3C **122**
SE13 3C **122**
Hilsea Point SW15 1D **134**
Hilsea St. E5 4J **67**
Hilton Av. N12 5G **31**
Hilton Ho. SE4 4K **121**
W13 6C **78**
Hilversum Cres. SE22 5E **120**
Himalaya Palace Cinema 1D **94**
Himley Rd. SW17 5C **136**
Hinchinbrook Ho. *NW6* 1K **81**
(*off Mortimer Cres.*)
Hinchley Cl. KT10: Hin W 4A **162**
Hinchley Dr. KT10: Hin W 3A **162**
Hinchley Mnr. KT10: Hin W 3A **162**
Hinchley Way KT10: Hin W 3A **162**
HINCHLEY WOOD 3A **162**
Hinckley Rd. SE15 4G **121**
Hind Ct. EC4 1K **13** (6A **84**)
Hind Cres. DA8: Erith 6K **109**
Hinde Ho. *W1* 7H **5**
(*off Hinde St.*)
Hinde M. W1 7H **5**
Hindes Rd. HA1: Harr 5H **41**
Hinde St. W1 7H **5** (6E **82**)
Hind Gro. E14 6C **86**
Hindhead Cl. N16 1E **66**
UB8: Hil 5D **74**
Hindhead Gdns. UB5: N'olt 1C **76**
Hindhead Point SW15 1D **134**
Hindhead Way SM6: W'gton 5J **167**
Hind Ho. N7 4A **66**
SE14 6K **103**
(*off Myers La.*)
Hindle Ho. E8 5F **67**
Hindlip Ho. SW8 1H **119**
Hindmans Rd. SE22 5G **121**
Hindmans Way RM9: Dag 4F **91**
Hindmarsh Cl. E1 7G **85**
Hindon Ct. SW1 3A **18**
Hindrey Rd. E5 5H **67**
Hindsley's Pl. SE23 2J **139**
Hinkler Rd. HA3: Kenton 3D **42**
Hinksey Path SE2 2D **108**
Hinstock *NW6* 1K **81**
(*off Belsize Rd.*)
Hinstock Rd. SE18 6G **107**
Hinton Av. TW4: Houn 4B **112**
Hinton Cl. SE9 1C **142**
Hinton Ct. *E10* 2D **68**
(*off Leyton Grange Est.*)
Hinton Rd. N18 4K **33**
SE24 3C **120**
SM6: W'gton 6G **167**
SW9 3B **120**
Hippisley Ct. TW7: Isle 3K **113**
Hippodrome M. W11 7G **81**
Hippodrome Pl. W11 7G **81**
Hiroshima Prom. SE7 3A **106**
Hirst Ct. SW1 7J **17** (6F **101**)
Hirst Cres. HA9: Wemb 3E **60**
Hitcham Rd. E17 7B **50**
Hitchcock Cl. TW17: Shep 3B **146**
Hitchcock La. E20 6E **68**
Hitchin La. HA7: Stan 7J **27**
Hitchin Rd. HA7: Stan 7K **27**
Hitchin Sq. E3 2A **86**
Hitch St. RM9: Dag 3E **90**
Hithe Gro. SE16 3J **103**
Hitherbroom Rd. UB3: Hayes 1J **93**
Hither Farm Rd. SE3 3A **124**
Hitherfield Rd. RM8: Dag 2E **72**
SW16 2K **137**
HITHER GREEN 6F **123**
Hither Green Crematorium 2H **141**
Hither Grn. La. SE13 5E **122**
Hithermoor Rd. TW19: Stanw M 7B **174**
Hitherwell Dr. HA3: Hrw W 1H **41**
Hitherwood Ct. *NW9* 2A **44**
(*off Charcot Rd.*)
Hitherwood Dr. SE19 4F **139**
Hittard Ct. *SE17* 6D **102**
(*off Red Lion Row*)
The Hive 1E **42**
Hive Cl. WD23: B Hea 2C **26**
The Hive Football & Fitness Cen. 1E **42**
Hive Rd. WD23: B Hea 2C **26**
HMP Belmarsh 2J **107**
HMP Brixton 6J **119**
HMP Isis 2K **107**
HMP Pentonville 6K **65**
HMP Thameside 3J **107**
HMP Wandsworth 7B **118**
HMP Wormwood Scrubs 6C **80**
HMS Belfast 4G **15** (1E **102**)
HMYOI Feltham 3F **129**
Hoadly Ho. *SE1* 5C **14**
(*off Union St.*)
Hoadly Rd. SW16 3H **137**
Hobart Cl. N20 2H **31**
UB4: Yead 4B **76**
Hobart Ct. *CR2: S Croy* 5D **168**
(*off South Pk. Hill Rd.*)
IG8: Wfd G 4C **36**
Hobart Dr. UB4: Yead 4B **76**
Hobart Gdns. CR7: Thor H 3D **156**
Hobart La. UB4: Yead 4B **76**
Hobart Pl. SW1 1J **17** (3F **101**)
TW10: Rich 7F **115**
Hobart Rd. IG6: Ilf 2G **53**
KT4: Wor Pk 3D **164**
RM9: Dag 4D **72**
UB4: Yead 4B **76**
Hobbayne Rd. W7 6H **77**
Hobbes Wlk. SW15 5D **116**
Hobbs Ct. *SE1* 6K **15**
(*off Mill St.*)
Hobbs Grn. N2 3A **46**
Hobbs M. IG3: Ilf 2K **71**
Hobbs Pl. N1 1E **84**
Hobbs Pl. Est. *N1* 2E **84**
(*off Hobbs Pl.*)
Hobbs Rd. SE27 4C **138**
Hobby Ho. SE1 4H **103**
Hobby St. EN3: Pond E 5E **24**
Hobday St. E14 6D **86**
Hobhouse Ct. *SW1* 3D **12**
(*off Suffolk St.*)
Hobill Wlk. KT5: Surb 6F **151**
Hoblands End BR7: Chst 6J **143**
Hobson's Pl. E1 5G **85**
Hobury St. SW10 7A **16** (6A **100**)
Hocker St. E2 2J **9** (3F **85**)
Hockett Cl. *SE8* 4B **104**
(*off Grove St.*)
Hockington Ct. EN5: New Bar 4E **20**
Hockley Av. E6 2C **88**
Hockley Ct. E18 1J **51**
Hockley M. IG11: Bark 3J **89**
Hockliffe Ho. *W10* 5E **80**
(*off Sutton Way*)
Hockney Ct. *SE16* 5H **103**
(*off Rossetti Rd.*)
Hocroft Av. NW2 3H **63**
Hocroft Ct. NW2 3H **63**
Hocroft Rd. NW2 4H **63**
Hocroft Wlk. NW2 3H **63**
Hodder Dr. UB6: G'frd 2K **77**
Hoddesdon Rd. DA17: Belv 5G **109**
Hodes Row NW3 4E **64**
Hodford Rd. NW11 1H **63**
Hodgkin Cl. SE28 7D **90**
Hodgkin Ct. *SE5* 7D **102**
(*off Dobson Wlk.*)
Hodgkins M. HA7: Stan 5G **27**
Hodister Cl. SE5 7C **102**
Hodnet Gro. SE16 4K **103**
Hodson Cl. HA2: Harr 3D **58**
Hoecroft Ct. *EN3: Enf W* 1D **24**
(*off Hoe La.*)
Hoe La. EN1: Enf 1B **24**
EN3: Enf W 1C **24**
Hoe St. E17 4C **50**
Hoever Ho. SE6 4E **140**
Hoey Ct. *E3* 4D **86**
(*off Barry Blandford Way*)
Hoffmann Gdns. CR2: Sels 7H **169**
Hoffman Sq. N1 1F **9**
Hoffmans Rd. E17 3K **49**
Hofland Rd. W14 3G **99**
Hogan M. W2 5A **4** (5A **82**)
Hogan Way E5 2G **67**
Hogarth Av. TW15: Ashf 6E **128**
Hogarth Bus. Pk. W4 6A **98**
Hogarth Cl. E16 5B **88**
W5 5F **78**
Hogarth Ct. *E1* 6G **85**
(*off Batty St.*)
NW1 7G **65**
(*off St Pancras Way*)
SE19 4F **139**
TW5: Hest 7C **94**
Hogarth Cres. CR0: C'don 7C **156**
SW19 1B **154**
Hogarth Gdns. TW5: Hest 7E **94**
The Hogarth Health Club 4B **98**
Hogarth Hill NW11 4H **45**
Hogarth Ho. *EC1* 6C **8**
(*off Bartholomew Cl.*)
SW1 4D **18**
(*off Erasmus St.*)
UB5: N'olt 2B **76**
(*off Gallery Gdns.*)
Hogarth Ind. Est. NW10 4C **80**
Hogarth La. W4 6A **98**
Hogarth Pl. *SW5* 4K **99**
(*off Hogarth Rd.*)
Hogarth Rd. HA8: Edg 2G **43**
RM8: Dag 5B **72**
SW5 4K **99**
HOGARTH RDBT. 6A **98**
Hogarth's House 6A **98**
(*off Hogarth La.*)
Hogarth Way TW12: Hamp 1G **149**
Hog Hill Rd. RM5: Col R 1F **55**
Hogsmill Ho. *KT1: King T* 3F **151**
(*off Vineyard Cl.*)
Hogsmill La. KT1: King T 3F **151**
Hogsmill Local Nature Reserve 5H **163**
Hogsmill Wlk. *KT1: King T* 3E **150**
(*off Penrhyn Rd.*)
Hogsmill Way KT19: Ewe 5J **163**
Holbeach Cl. NW9 1A **44**
Holbeach Gdns. DA15: Sidc 6J **125**
Holbeach M. SW12 1F **137**
Holbeach Rd. SE6 7C **122**
Holbeck Rd. W13 1B **96**
Holbeck Row SE15 7G **103**
Holbein Ho. *SW1* 5G **17**
(*off Holbein M.*)
Holbein M. SW1 5G **17** (5E **100**)
Holbein Pl. SW1 4G **17** (4E **100**)
Holbein Ter. *RM8: Dag* 4C **72**
(*off Marlborough Rd.*)
Holberton Gdns. NW10 3D **80**
HOLBORN 7F **7** (6J **83**)
Holborn EC1 6J **7** (5A **84**)
Holborn Bars *EC1* 6J **7**
(*off Holborn*)
Holborn Cir. EC1 6K **7** (5A **84**)

Holborn Cl.—Hop Ct.

Holborn Cl. NW7 4G 29
Holborn Ho. W12 6D 80
Holborn Pl. WC1 6G 7 (5K 83)
Holborn Rd. E13 4K 87
Holborn Viaduct EC1 6K 7 (5B 84)
Holborn Way CR4: Mitc 2D 154
Holbrook Cl. EN1: Enf 1A 24
N19 1F 65
Holbrooke Ct. N7 4J 65
Holbrooke Pl. TW10: Rich 5D 114
Holbrook Ho. BR7: Chst 1H 161
Holbrook La. BR7: Chst 7H 143
Holbrook Rd. E15 2H 87
Holbrook Way BR2: Broml 6D 160
Holburne Cl. SE3 1A 124
Holburne Gdns. SE3 1B 124
Holburne Rd. SE3 1A 124
Holcombe Hill NW7 3H 29
Holcombe Ho. *SW9* 3J 119
(off Landor Rd.)
Holcombe Pl. *SE4* 3A 122
(off St Asaph Rd.)
Holcombe Rd. IG1: Ilf 7E 52
N17 3F 49
Holcombe St. W6 4D 98
Holcote Cl. DA17: Belv 3E 108
Holcroft Ct. W1 5A 6
Holcroft Ho. SW11 3B 118
Holcroft Rd. E9 7J 67
Holden Av. N12 5E 30
NW9 1J 61
Holdenby Rd. SE4 5A 122
Holden Cl. RM8: Dag 3B 72
Holden Ho. *N1* 1C 84
(off Prebend St.)
SE8 7C 104
Holdenhurst Av. N12 7F 31
Holden Point *E15* 6F 69
(off Waddington St.)
Holden Rd. N12 5E 30
Holden St. SW11 2E 118
Holder Cl. N3 7E 30
Holdernesse Cl. TW7: Isle 1A 114
Holdernesse Rd. SW17 3D 136
Holderness Ho. SE5 3E 120
Holderness Way SE27 5B 138
HOLDERS HILL 2F 45
Holder's Hill Av. NW4 2F 45
HOLDERS HILL CIR. 7B 30
Holders Hill Cres. NW4 2F 45
Holders Hill Dr. NW4 3F 45
Holder's Hill Gdns. NW4 2G 45
Holders Hill Pde. NW7 1G 45
Holders Hill Rd. NW4 2F 45
NW7 2F 45
Holford Ho. *SE16* 4H 103
(off Camilla Rd.)
WC1 1H 7
(off Gt. Percy St.)
Holford M. WC1 1J 7
Holford Pl. WC1 1H 7 (3K 83)
Holford Rd. NW3 3A 64
Holford St. WC1 1J 7 (3K 83)
Holford Way SW15 6C 116
Holford Yd. *WC1* 1J 7
(off Cruikshank St.)
Holgate Av. SW11 3B 118
Holgate Gdns. RM10: Dag 6G 73
Holgate Rd. RM10: Dag 5G 73
Holgate St. SE7 3B 106
Holinser Ter. W5 1D 96
Hollam Ho. N8 4K 47
Holland Av. SM2: Sutt 7J 165
SW20 1B 152
Holland Cl. BR2: Hayes 2H 171
EN5: New Bar 7G 21
HA7: Stan 5G 27
RM7: Rom 5J 55
Holland Ct. *E17* 4E 50
(off Evelyn Rd.)
KT6: Surb 7D 150
NW7 6H 29
Holland Dr. SE23 3A 140
Holland Dwellings *WC2* 7F 7
(off Newton St.)
Holland Gdns. SE9: Sidc 1H 143
TW8: Bford 6E 96
W14 3G 99
Hollandgreen Pl. W8 3J 99
Holland Gro. SW9 7A 102
Holland Ho. E4 4K 35
NW10 2D 80
(off Holland Rd.)
HOLLAND PARK 1H 99
Holland Pk. 2H 99
Holland Pk. W11 1G 99
Holland Pk. Av. IG3: Ilf 6J 53
W11 2G 99
Holland Pk. Ct. *W14* 2G 99
(off Holland Pk. Gdns.)
Holland Pk. Gdns. W14 2G 99
Holland Pk. Mans. *W14* 1G 99
(off Holland Pk. Gdns.)
Holland Pk. M. W11 1G 99
Holland Pk. Rd. W14 3H 99
HOLLAND PARK RDBT. 2F 99
Holland Pk. Tennis Ground 1G 99
Holland Pk. Ter. *W11* 1G 99
(off Portland Rd.)
Holland Pk. Theatre (Open Air) 2H 99
Holland Pas. *N1* 1C 84
(off Basire St.)
Holland Pl. *W8* 2K 99
(off Kensington Chu. St.)
Holland Pl. Chambers *W8* 2K 99
(off Holland Pl.)
Holland Ri. Ho. *SW9* 7K 101
(off Clapham Rd.)
Holland Rd. E6 1D 88
E15 3G 87
HA0: Wemb 6D 60
NW10 1C 80
SE25 5G 157
W14 2F 99
The Hollands KT4: Wor Pk 1B 164
TW13: Hanw 4B 130
Holland St. SE1 4B 14 (1B 102)
W8 2J 99
Holland Vs. Rd. W14 2G 99
Holland Wlk. HA7: Stan 5F 27
N19 1H 65
(off Calverley Gro.)
N19 1H 65
(Up. Holloway)
W8 1H 99
Holland Way BR2: Hayes 2H 171
Hollar Rd. N16 3F 67
Hollen St. W1 7C 6 (6H 83)
Holles Cl. TW12: Hamp 6E 130
Holles Ho. SW9 2A 120
Holles St. W1 7K 5 (6F 83)
Holley Rd. W3 2A 98
Hollickwood Av. N12 6J 31
Holliday Sq. *SW11* 3B 118
(off Fowler Cl.)
Hollidge Way RM10: Dag 7H 73
The Hollies *E11* 5J 51
(off New Wanstead)
HA3: W'stone 4A 42
N20 1G 31
Hollies Av. DA15: Sidc 2K 143
Hollies Cl. SW16 6A 138
TW1: Twick 2K 131
Hollies End NW7 5J 29
Hollies Rd. W5 4C 96
Hollies Way SW12 7E 118
Holligrave Rd. BR1: Broml 1J 159
Hollingbourne Av. DA7: Bex 1F 127
Hollingbourne Gdns. W13 5B 78
Hollingbourne Rd. SE24 5C 120
Hollingsworth Ct. KT6: Surb 7D 150
Hollingsworth Rd. CR0: C'don 6H 169
Hollington Ct. BR7: Chst 6F 143
Hollington Cres. KT3: N Mald 6B 152
Hollington Rd. E6 3D 88
N17 2G 49
Hollingworth Cl. KT8: W Mole 4D 148
Hollingworth Rd. BR5: Pet W 6F 161
Hollins Ho. N7 4J 65
Hollisfield *WC1* 2F 7
(off Cromer St.)
Hollister Ho. *NW6* 3J 81
(off Kilburn Pk. Rd.)
Hollman Gdns. SW16 6B 138
The Hollow IG8: Wfd G 4C 36
HOLLOWAY 3J 65
Holloway Cl. UB7: Harm 5A 92
Holloway Ho. *NW2* 3E 62
(off Stoll Cl.)
Holloway La.
UB7: Harm, W Dray 2E 174
Holloway Rd. E6 3D 88
E11 3F 69
N7 4K 65
N19 2H 65
Holloway St. TW3: Houn 3F 113
Hollowfield Wlk. UB5: N'olt 6C 58
The Hollows TW8: Bford 6F 97
Holly Av. HA7: Stan 2E 42
KT12: Walt T 7B 148
Hollybank Cl. TW12: Hamp 5E 130
Hollyberry La. NW3 4A 64
Hollybrake Cl. BR7: Chst 7H 143
Hollybush Cl. E11 5J 51
HA3: Hrw W 1J 41
Hollybush Gdns. E2 3H 85
Holly Bush Hill NW3 4A 64
Hollybush Hill E11 6H 51
Hollybush Ho. E2 3H 85
Holly Bush La. TW12: Hamp 7D 130
Hollybush Pl. E2 3H 85
Hollybush Rd. KT2: King T 5E 132
Holly Bush Steps *NW3* 4A 64
(off Holly Mt.)
Hollybush St. E13 3K 87
Holly Bush Va. NW3 4A 64
Hollybush Wlk. SW9 4B 120
Holly Cl. BR3: Beck 4E 158
IG9: Buck H 3G 37
KT19: Eps 7K 163
SM6: W'gton 7F 167
TW13: Hanw 5C 130
TW16: Sun 3K 147
Holly Cott. M. UB8: Hil 5C 74
Holly Ct. *DA14: Sidc* 4B 144
(off Sidcup Hill)
N15 4E 48
SE10 3H 105
SM2: Sutt 7J 165
Holly Cres. BR3: Beck 5B 158
IG8: Wfd G 7A 36
Hollycroft Av. HA9: Wemb 2F 61
NW3 3J 63
Hollycroft Cl. CR2: S Croy 5E 168
UB7: Sip 6C 92
Hollycroft Gdns. UB7: Sip 6C 92
Hollydale Cl. UB5: N'olt 4F 59
Hollydale Dr. BR2: Broml 3D 172
Hollydale Rd. SE15 1J 121
Hollydene *BR2: Broml* 1H 159
(off Beckenham La.)
SE13 6F 123
SE15 1H 121
Hollydown Way E11 3F 69
Holly Dr. E4 7J 25
Holly Farm Rd. UB2: S'hall 5C 94
Hollyfield Av. N11 5J 31
Hollyfield Rd. KT5: Surb 7F 151
Holly Gdns. DA7: Bex 4J 127
UB7: W Dray 2B 92
Holly Gro. HA5: Pinn 1C 40
NW9 7J 43
SE15 2F 121
Hollygrove WD23: Bush 1C 26
Hollygrove Cl. TW3: Houn 4D 112
Holly Hedge Ter. SE13 5F 123
Holly Hill N21 6E 22
NW3 4A 64
Holly Hill Rd. DA8: Erith 5H 109
DA17: Belv, Erith 5H 109
Holly Ho. TW8: Bford 6C 96
W10 4G 81
(off Hawthorn Wlk.)
Holly La. IG3: Ilf 2A 72
Holly Lodge HA1: Harr 5H 41
W8 2J 99
(off Thornwood Gdns.)
Holly Lodge Gdns. N6 2E 64
Holly Lodge Mans. N6 2E 64
Hollymead SM5: Cars 3D 166
Holly M. SW10 6A 16 (5A 100)
Holly Mt. NW3 4A 64
Hollymount Cl. SE10 1E 122
Holly Pde. *TW13: Felt* 3H 129
(off High St.)
Holly Pk. N3 3H 45
N4 7J 47
(not continuous)
Holly Pk. Est. N4 7K 47
Holly Pk. Gdns. N3 3J 45
Holly Pk. Rd. N11 5K 31
W7 1K 95
Holly Pl. *NW3* 4A 64
(off Holly Berry La.)
Holly Rd. E11 7H 51
TW1: Twick 1K 131
TW3: Houn 4F 113
TW12: Hamp H 6G 131
W4 4K 97
Holly St. E8 7F 67
Holly Ter. N6 1E 64
Holly Tree Cl. SW19 1F 135
Holly Tree Cres. SM5: Cars 1D 166
Holly Tree Ho. *SE4* 3B 122
(off Brockley Rd.)
Hollytree Pde. *DA14: Sidc* 6C 144
(off Sidcup Hill)
Hollyview Cl. NW4 6C 44
Holly Village N6 2F 65
Holly Vs. *W6* 3D 98
(off Wellesley Av.)
Holly Wlk. EN2: Enf 3H 23
NW3 4A 64
Holly Way CR4: Mitc 4H 155
Hollywood Bowl
Dagenham 1E 90
Finchley 7G 31
The O2 1G 105
Surrey Quays 3K 103
Tolworth 2H 163
Hollywood Ct. *SW10* 6A 100
(off Hollywood Rd.)
W5 7F 79
Hollywood Gdns. UB4: Yead 6K 75
Hollywood M. SW10 6A 100
Hollywood Rd. E4 5F 35
SW10 6A 100
Hollywood Way IG8: Wfd G 7A 36
Holman Ct. KT17: Ewe 7C 164
Holman Rd. UB2: S'hall 1H 95
Holman Ho. *E2* 3K 85
(off Roman Rd.)
Holman Hunt Ho. *W6* 5G 99
(off Field Rd.)
Holman Rd. KT19: Ewe 5J 163
SW11 2B 118
Holmbank Dr. TW17: Shep 4G 147
Holmbridge Gdns. EN3: Pond E 4E 24
Holmbrook *NW1* 2G 83
(off Eversholt St.)
Holmbrook Dr. NW4 5F 45
Holmbury Ct. CR2: S Croy 5E 168
SW17 3D 136
SW19 7C 136
Holmbury Gdns. UB3: Hayes 1H 93
Holmbury Gro. CR0: Sels 7B 170
Holmbury Ho. SE24 5B 120
Holmbury Mnr. DA14: Sidc 4A 144
Holmbury Pk. BR1: Broml 7C 142
Holmbury Vw. E5 1H 67
Holmbush Rd. SW15 6G 117
Holmcote Gdns. N5 5C 66
Holm Ct. SE12 3K 141
Holmcroft Ho. E17 4D 50
Holmcroft Way BR2: Broml 5D 160
Holmdale Gdns. NW4 5F 45
Holmdale Rd. BR7: Chst 5G 143
NW6 5J 63
Holmdale Ter. N15 6E 48
Holmdene N12 5E 30
Holmdene Av. HA2: Harr 3F 41
NW7 6H 29
SE24 5C 120
Holmdene Cl. BR3: Beck 2E 158
Holmdene Ct. BR1: Broml 3C 160
Holmead Rd. SW6 7K 99
Holmebury Cl. WD23: B Hea 2D 26
Holme Ct. TW7: Isle 3A 114
Holmefield Ho. *W10* 4G 81
(off Hazlewood Cres.)
Holme Ho. *SE15* 7H 103
(off Studholme St.)
Holme Lacey Rd. SE12 6H 123
Holmeoak Av. RM13: Rain 2K 91
Holme Rd. E6 1C 88
Holmes Av. E17 3B 50
Holmes Cl. SE22 4G 121
Holmesdale Av. SW14 3H 115
Holmesdale Cl. SE25 3F 157
Holmesdale Ho. *NW6* 1J 81
(off Kilburn Vale)
Holmesdale Rd. CR0: C'don 5D 156
DA7: Bex 2D 126
N6 7F 47
SE25 5D 156
TW9: Kew 1F 115
TW11: Tedd 7C 132
Holmesley Rd. SE23 6A 122
Holmes Pl. SW10 6A 100
Holmes Rd. NW5 5F 65
SW19 7A 136
TW1: Twick 2K 131
Holmes Ter. SE1 6J 13
Holmeswood SM2: Sutt 6K 165
Holmeswood Ct. N22 2A 48
Holme Way HA7: Stan 6E 26
Holmewood Gdns. SW2 7K 119
Holmewood Rd. SE25 3E 156
SW2 7K 119
Holmfield Av. NW4 5F 45
Holmfield Ct. NW3 5C 64
Holm Gro. UB10: Hil 7C 56
Holmhurst SE13 6F 123
Holmhurst Rd. DA17: Belv 5H 109
Holmlea Ct. *CR0: C'don* 4D 168
(off Chatsworth Rd.)
Holmleigh Ct. EN3: Pond E 4D 24
Holmleigh Rd. N16 1E 66
Holmleigh Rd. Est. N16 1E 66
Holm Oak Cl. SW15 6H 117
Holm Oak M. SW4 5J 119
Holmoaks Ho. BR3: Beck 2E 158
Holmsdale Ho. *E14* 7D 86
(off Poplar High St.)
N11 4A 32
(off Coppies Gro.)
Holmshaw Cl. SE26 4A 140
Holmside Rd. SW12 6E 118
Holmsley Cl. KT3: N Mald 6B 152
Holmsley Ho. *SW15* 7B 116
(off Tangley Gro.)
Holmstall Av. HA8: Edg 3J 43
Holmstall Pde. HA8: Edg 2J 43
Holmstead Ct. CR2: S Croy 5D 168
Holm Wlk. SE3 2J 123
Holmwood Cl. HA2: Harr 3G 41
SM2: Cheam 7F 165
UB5: N'olt 6F 59
Holmwood Gdns. N3 2J 45
SM6: W'gton 6F 167
Holmwood Gro. NW7 5E 28
Holmwood Rd. IG3: Ilf 2J 71
KT9: Chess 5D 162
SM2: Cheam 7E 164
Holmwood Vs. SE7 5J 105
Holne Chase N2 6A 46
SM4: Mord 6H 153
Holness Rd. E15 6H 69
The Holocaust Memorial Garden 6F 11 (2D 100)
Holroyd Rd. KT10: Clay 7A 162
SW15 4E 116
Holsgrove Ho. W3 1A 98
Holst Ct. *SE1* 1J 19
(off Kennington Rd.)
Holstein Way DA18: Erith 3D 108
Holst Ho. *W12* 6D 80
(off Du Cane Rd.)
Holst Mans. SW13 6E 98
Holstock Rd. IG1: Ilf 2G 71
Holst Rd. W3 5J 79
Holsworth Cl. HA2: Harr 5G 41
Holsworthy Ho. *E3* 3D 86
(off Talwin St.)
Holsworthy Sq. WC1 4H 7
Holsworthy Way KT9: Chess 5C 162
The Holt SM4: Mord 4J 153
SM6: W'gton 4G 167
Holt Cl. BR7: Chst 5D 142
DA14: Sidc 4E 144
N10 4E 46
SE28 7B 90
Holt Ct. *SE10* 6E 104
(off Horseferry Pl.)
Holt Ho. SW2 6A 120
Holton St. E1 4K 85
Holt Rd. E16 1C 106
HA0: Wemb 3B 60
Holtwhite Av. EN2: Enf 2H 23
Holtwhite's Hill EN2: Enf 1G 23
Holwell Pl. HA5: Pinn 4C 40
Holwood Est. BR2: Kes 6C 172
Holwood Pk. Av.
BR6: Farnb 4D 172
Holwood Pl. SW4 4H 119
Holybourne Av. SW15 7C 116
Holycross Cl. SM4: Mord 7J 153
Holyhead Cl. E6 5D 88
Holyhead Ct. *KT1: King T* 4D 150
(off Anglesea Rd.)
Holyoake Ct. SE16 2B 104
Holyoake Ho. W5 4C 78
Holyoake Wlk. N2 3A 46
W5 4C 78
Holyoak Rd. SE11 4B 102
Holyport Rd. SW6 7F 99
Holyrood Av. HA2: Harr 4C 58
Holyrood Ct. *NW1* 1F 83
(off Gloucester Av.)
Holyrood Gdns. HA8: Edg 3H 43
Holyrood M. E16 1J 105
Holyrood Rd. EN5: New Bar 6G 21
Holyrood St. SE1 5G 15 (1E 102)
Holywell Cen. *EC2* 3G 9
(off Phipp St.)
Holywell Cl. BR6: Chels 4K 173
SE3 6J 105
SE16 5H 103
TW19: Stanw 1A 128
Holywell La. EC2 3H 9 (4E 84)
Holywell Row EC2 4G 9 (4E 84)
Holywell Way TW19: Stanw 1A 128
Homan Ct. N12 4G 31
Homebush Ho. E4 7J 25
Homecedars Ho.
WD23: B Hea 1C 26
Home Cl. SM5: Cars 2D 166
UB5: N'olt 3D 76
Home Ct. KT6: Surb 5D 150
Homecroft Rd. N22 1C 48
SE26 5J 139
Home Farm Cl. KT7: T Ditt 7K 149
TW17: Shep 4G 147
Homefarm Rd. W7 6J 77
Homefield SM4: Mord 4J 153
Homefield Av. IG2: Ilf 5J 53
Homefield Cl. NW10 6J 61
UB4: Yead 4B 76
Homefield Gdns. CR4: Mitc 2A 154
N2 3B 46
Homefield Ho. SE23 3J 139
Homefield M. BR3: Beck 1C 158
Homefield Pk. SM1: Sutt 6K 165
Homefield Pl. CR0: C'don 2F 169
Homefield Rd. BR1: Broml 1A 160
HA0: Wemb 4A 60
HA8: Edg 6E 28
KT12: Walt T 7C 148
SW19 6F 135
W4 5B 98
Homefield St. N1 1G 9 (2E 84)
Homefirs Ho. HA9: Wemb 3F 61
Home Gdns. RM10: Dag 3J 73
Homeheather Ho. IG4: Ilf 5D 52
Homeland Dr. SM2: Sutt 7K 165
Homelands Dr. SE19 7E 138
Home Lea BR6: Chels 5K 173
Homeleigh Ct. SW16 3J 137
Homeleigh Rd. SE15 5K 121
Home Mead HA7: Stan 1C 42
Home Mdw. M. SE22 5G 121
Homemead Rd.
BR2: Broml 5D 160
CR0: C'don 6G 155
Home Pk. KT1: E Mos 5B 150
Home Pk. Ct. *KT1: King T* 4D 150
(off Palace Rd.)
Home Pk. Pde. *KT1: Hamp W* 2D 150
(off High St.)
Home Pk. Rd. SW19 4H 135
Home Pk. Ter. *KT1: Hamp W* 2D 150
(off Hampton Ct. Rd.)
Home Pk. Wlk. KT1: King T 5D 150
Homer Cl. DA7: Bex 1J 127
Homer Dr. E14 4C 104
Home Rd. SW11 2C 118
Homer Rd. CR0: C'don 6K 155
E9 6A 68
Homer Row W1 6D 4 (5C 82)
Homersham Rd.
KT1: King T 2G 151
Homer St. W1 6D 4 (5C 82)
HOMERTON 5K 67
Homerton Gro. E9 5K 67
Homerton High St. E9 5K 67
Homerton Rd. E9 5A 68
Homerton Row E9 5J 67
Homerton Ter. E9 6J 67
(not continuous)
Homesdale Cl. E11 5J 51
Homesdale Rd. BR1: Broml 4A 160
BR2: Broml 4A 160
BR5: Pet W 7J 161
Homesfield NW11 5J 45
Homestall Rd. SE22 5J 121
Homestead Ct. EN5: New Bar 5D 20
Homestead Paddock N14 5A 22
Homestead Pk. NW2 3B 62
Homestead Rd. RM8: Dag 2F 73
SW6 7H 99
The Homesteads N11 4A 32
Homevale Cl. BR2: Hayes 7H 159
Homewalk Ho. SE26 4H 139
Homewaters Av. TW16: Sun 1H 147
Homewillow Cl. N21 6G 23
Homewood Cl. TW12: Hamp 6D 130
Homewood Cres. BR7: Chst 6J 143
Homewoods SW12 7G 119
Homildon Ho. SE26 3G 139
Honduras St. EC1 3C 8 (4C 84)
Honeybourne Rd. NW6 5K 63
Honeybourne Way
BR5: Pet W 1H 173
Honeybrook Rd. SW12 7G 119
Honey Cl. RM10: Dag 6H 73
Honeycroft Hill UB10: Uxb 7A 56
Honeyden Rd. DA14: Sidc 6E 144
Honeyfield M. SE23 3K 139
Honeyghan Ct. *SE17* 5E 102
(off Sedan Way)
Honey Hill UB10: Uxb 7B 56
Honey La. EC2 1D 14
Honey La. Ho. *SW10* 6K 99
(off Finborough Rd.)
Honeyman Cl. NW6 7F 63
Honeymead *N8* 3J 47
(off Campsfield Rd.)
Honey M. RM7: Rom 5J 55
SE27 4C 138
(off Norwood High St.)
Honeypot Bus. Cen. HA7: Stan 1E 42
Honeypot Cl. NW9 4F 43
Honeypot La. HA7: Stan 7J 27
NW9 1D 42
Honeysett Rd. N17 2F 49
Honeysuckle Cl. UB1: S'hall 7C 76
Honeysuckle Ct. IG1: Ilf 6F 71
IG9: Buck H 3G 37
Honeysuckle Gdns.
CR0: C'don 7K 157
E17 3C 50
Honeysuckle La. N22 2C 48
Honeywell Rd. SW11 6D 118
Honeywood Ho. *SE15* 1G 121
(off Goldsmith Rd.)
Honeywood Mus. 5D 166
Honeywood Rd. NW10 2B 80
TW7: Isle 4A 114
Honeywood Wlk. SM5: Cars 4D 166
Honister Cl. HA7: Stan 1B 42
Honister Gdns. HA7: Stan 7G 27
Honister Pl. HA7: Stan 1B 42
Honiton Gdns. NW7 7A 30
SE15 2J 121
(off Gibbon Rd.)
Honiton Ho. EN3: Pond E 3E 24
Honiton Rd. DA16: Well 2K 125
NW6 2H 81
RM7: Rom 6K 55
Honley Rd. SE6 7D 122
Honnor Gdns. TW7: Isle 2H 113
HONOR OAK 6J 121
Honor Oak Crematorium 5K 121
HONOR OAK PARK 7A 122
Honor Oak Pk. SE23 6J 121
Honor Oak Ri. SE23 6J 121
Honor Oak Rd. SE23 1J 139
Honour Gdns. RM8: Dag 4A 72
Honour Lea Av. E20 5D 68
Hood Av. N14 6A 22
SW14 5J 115
Hood Cl. CR0: C'don 1B 168
Hoodcote Gdns. N21 7G 23
Hood Ct. EC4 1K 13
Hood Ho. *SE5* 7D 102
(off Elmington Est.)
SW1 6C 18
(off Dolphin Sq.)
Hood Point *SE16* 2B 104
(off Rotherhithe St.)
Hood Rd. SW20 7B 134
Hood Wlk. RM7: Mawney 1H 55
HOOK 4D 162
The Hook EN5: New Bar 6G 21
Hooke Ct. *SE10* 1E 122
(off Winforton St.)
Hooke Ho. *E3* 2A 86
(off Gernon Rd.)
Hookers Rd. E17 3K 49
Hook Farm Rd. BR2: Broml 5B 160
Hookham Ct. SW8 1H 119
Hooking Grn. HA2: Harr 5F 41
HOOK JUNC. 3E 162
Hook La. DA16: Well 4K 125
Hook Ri. Nth. KT6: Surb 3E 162
Hook Ri. Sth. KT6: Surb 3E 162
Hook Ri. Sth. Ind. Pk.
KT6: Surb 3F 163
Hook Rd. KT6: Surb 2E 162
KT9: Chess 5D 162
KT19: Eps, Ewe 7J 163
Hooks Cl. SE15 1H 121
Hooks Hall Dr. RM10: Dag 3J 73
Hookstone Way IG8: Wfd G 7G 37
Hook Wlk. HA8: Edg 6D 28
Hool Cl. NW9 5J 43
Hooper Dr. UB8: Hil 5D 74
Hooper Ho. TW15: Ashf 3A 128
Hooper Rd. E16 6J 87
Hooper's Ct. SW3 7E 10 (2D 100)
Hooper's M. W3 1J 97
Hoopers M. WD23: Bush 1A 26
Hooper Sq. *E1* 6G 85
(off Hooper St.)
Hooper St. E1 6G 85
Hoopers Yd. *NW6* 1H 81
(off Kimberley Rd.)
Hoop La. NW11 7H 45
Hop Ct. *HA0: Wemb* 5A 60
(off Brewery Cl.)

Hope Cl.—Hurleston Ho.

Hope Cl. IG8: Wfd G 6F 37
N1 6C 66
NW4 2E 44
RM6: Chad H 4D 54
SE12 3K 141
SM1: Sutt 5A 166
TW8: Bford 5E 96
Hope Ct. *NW10* 3F 81
(off Chamberlayne Rd.)
SE1 5G 103
(off Avocet Cl.)
Hopedale Rd. SE7 6K 105
Hopefield Av. NW6 2G 81
Hope Gdns. W3 2H 97
Hope Ho. *CR0: C'don* 4E 168
(off Steep Hill)
Hope La. SE9 2F 143
Hope Pk. BR1: Broml 7H 141
Hopes Cl. TW5: Hest 6E 94
Hope Sq. EC2 6G 9
Hope St. E14 6G 87
SW11 3B 118
Hopetown St. E1 6K 9 (5F 85)
Hopewell St. SE5 7D 102
Hopewell Yd. *SE5* 7D 102
(off Hopewell St.)
Hope Wharf SE16 2J 103
Hop Gdns. WC2 3E 12 (7J 83)
Hopgood St. W12 1E 98
Hopground Ho. *E20* 6E 68
(off De Coubertin St.)
Hopkins Cl. N10 7K 31
Hopkins Ho. *E14* 6C 86
(off Canton St.)
Hopkins M. E15 1H 87
Hopkinsons Pl. NW1 1E 82
Hopkins Rd. E10 7D 50
Hopkins St. W1 1B 12 (6G 83)
Hoppers Rd. N13 2F 33
N21 2F 33
Hoppett Rd. E4 2B 36
Hopping La. N1 6B 66
Hoppingwood Av. KT3: N Mald 3A 152
Hoppner Rd. UB4: Hayes 2F 75
Hopps Ct. *NW9* 2A 44
(off Salk Cl.)
Hops Ho. *E17* 5B 50
(off Old Brewery Way)
Hop St. SE10 4H 105
Hopton Ct. BR2: Hayes 1K 171
Hopton Gdns. KT3: N Mald 6C 152
Hopton Rd. SE18 3F 107
SW16 5J 137
Hopton's Gdns. SE1 4B 14
Hopton St. SE1 3A 14 (7B 84)
Hoptree Cl. N12 5E 30
Hopwood Cl. SW17 3A 136
Hopwood Rd. SE17 6D 102
Hopwood Wlk. E8 7G 67
Horace Av. RM7: Rush G 1J 73
Horace Bldg. SW11 7F 101
Horace Jones Ho. *SE1* 5J 15
(off Duchess Wlk.)
Horace Rd. E7 4K 69
IG6: Ilf 3G 53
KT1: King T 3F 151
Horatio Ct. *SE16* 1J 103
(off Rotherhithe St.)
Horatio Ho. *E2* 2F 85
(off Horatio St.)
W6 5F 99
(off Fulham Pal. Rd.)
Horatio Pl. *E14* 1E 104
(off Managers St.)
SW19 1J 153
Horatio St. E2 2F 85
Horatius Way CR0: Wadd 5K 167
Horbury Cres. W11 7J 81
Horbury M. W11 7H 81
Horder Rd. SW6 1G 117
Hordle Prom. Sth. *SE15* 7F 103
(off Quarley Way)
Horizon Bldg. *E14* 7C 86
(off Hertsmere Rd.)
Horizon Bus. Cen. *N9* 2E 34
(off Goodwin Rd.)
Horizon Ct. *SM2: Cheam* 7G 165
(off Up. Mulgrave Rd.)
Horizon Ho. *SW18* 3A 118
(off Juniper Dr.)
Horizon Ind. Est. SE15 6G 103
Horle Wlk. SE5 2B 120
Horley Cl. DA6: Bex 5G 127
Horley Rd. SE9 4C 142
Hormead Rd. W9 4H 81
Hornbeam Cl. IG1: Ilf 5H 71
IG9: Buck H 3G 37
IG11: Bark 3A 90
NW7 3G 29
SE11 3J 19 (4A 102)
UB5: N'olt 5D 58
Hornbeam Cres. TW8: Bford 7B 96
Hornbeam Gdns. KT3: N Mald 6C 152
Hornbeam Gro. E4 3B 36
Hornbeam Ho. IG9: Buck H 3H 37
Hornbeam La. DA7: Bex 2J 127
Hornbeam Rd. IG9: Buck H 3G 37
UB4: Yead 5A 76
Hornbeam Sq. E3 1B 86
Hornbeams Ri. N11 6K 31
Hornbeam Ter. SM5: Cars 1C 166
Hornbeam Wlk. TW10: Rich 2F 133
Hornbeam Way BR2: Broml 6E 160
Hornbean Ho. *E15* 3G 87
(off Manor Rd.)
Hornblower Cl. SE16 3A 104
Hornbuckle Cl. HA2: Harr 2H 59
Hornby Cl. NW3 7B 64
Hornby Ct. NW10 6B 62
Hornby Ho. SE11 7J 19
Horncastle Cl. SE12 7J 123
Horncastle Rd. SE12 7J 123
Hornchurch *N17* 2D 48
(off Gloucester Rd.)
Hornchurch Cl. KT2: King T 4D 132
Horndean Cl. SW15 1C 134
Horndon Cl. RM5: Col R 1J 55
Horndon Grn. RM5: Col R 1J 55
Horndon Rd. RM5: Col R 1J 55
Horner Ho. *N1* 1E 84
(off Nuttall St.)
Horner La. CR4: Mitc 2B 154
Horne Rd. TW17: Shep 4C 146
Horner Sq. *E1* 5J 9
(within Old Spitalfields Mkt.)
Hornet Way E6 5H 89
Horne Way SW15 2E 116
Hornfair Rd. SE7 6A 106
Horniman Dr. SE23 1H 139
Horniman Gdns. 1H 139
Horniman Mus. 1H 139
Horning Cl. SE9 4C 142
Horn La. IG8: Wfd G 6D 36
SE10 5J 105
(not continuous)
W3 7J 79
(not continuous)
Horn Link Way SE10 4J 105
HORN PARK 5K 123
Horn Pk. Cl. SE12 5K 123
Horn Pk. La. SE12 5K 123
Hornscroft Cl. IG11: Bark 7J 71
Horns End Pl. HA5: Eastc 4A 40
HORNSEY 4J 47
Hornsey Cricket Club 5H 47
Hornsey La. N6 1F 65
Hornsey La. Est. N19 7H 47
Hornsey La. Gdns. N6 7G 47
Hornsey Pk. Rd. N8 3K 47
Hornsey Ri. N19 7H 47
Hornsey Ri. Gdns. N19 7H 47
Hornsey Rd. N7 1J 65
N19 1J 65
Hornsey St. N7 5K 65
HORNSEY VALE 5K 47
Hornshay St. SE15 6J 103
Horns Rd. IG2: Ilf 5G 53
IG6: Ilf 4H 53
Hornton Ct. *W8* 2J 99
(off Kensington High St.)
Hornton Pl. W8 2K 99
Hornton St. W8 2J 99
Horsa Rd. DA8: Erith 7H 109
SE12 7A 124
Horse & Dolphin Yd. W1 2D 12
Horsebridge Cl. RM9: Dag 1E 90
Horsecroft Rd. HA8: Edg 7E 28
Horse Fair KT1: King T 2D 150
Horseferry Pl. SE10 6E 104
Horseferry Rd. E14 7A 86
SW1 2C 18 (3H 101)
Horseferry Rd. Est. SW1 2C 18
Horse Guards Av. SW1 5E 12 (1J 101)
Horse Guards Parade 5E 12 (1H 101)
Horse Guards Rd.
SW1 5D 12 (1H 101)
Horse Leaze E6 6E 88
Horseley Ct. E1 5A 86
Horsell Rd. BR5: St P 7B 144
N5 5A 66
(not continuous)
Horselydown La. SE1 6J 15 (2F 103)
Horselydown Mans. *SE1* 6J 15
(off Lafone St.)
Horsemongers M. SE1 7D 14
Horsenden Av. UB6: G'frd 5K 59
Horsenden Cres. UB6: G'frd 5K 59
Horsenden Hill Footgolf Cen. 6A 60
Horsenden Hill Golf Course 7A 60
Horsenden La. Nth. UB6: G'frd 6J 59
Horsenden La. Sth. UB6: G'frd 1A 78
Horse Ride SW1 5C 12 (1G 101)
Horseshoe Cl. E14 5E 104
NW2 2D 62
Horseshoe Ct. *EC1* 3B 8
(off Brewhouse Yd.)
Horse Shoe Cres. UB5: N'olt 2E 76
Horse Shoe Dr. UB8: Hil 6C 74
Horse Shoe Grn. SM1: Sutt 2K 165
Horseshoe La. EN2: Enf 3H 23
N20 1A 30
Horseshoe M. SW2 4J 119
Horseshoe Wharf *SE1* 4E 14
(off Clink St.)
Horse Yd. *N1* 1B 84
(off Essex Rd.)
Horsfeld Gdns. SE9 5C 124
Horsfeld Rd. SE9 5B 124
Horsfield Ho. *N1* 7C 66
(off Northampton St.)
Horsford Rd. SW2 5K 119
Horsham Av. N12 5H 31
Horsham Ct. *N17* 1G 49
(off Lansdowne Rd.)
Horsham Rd. DA6: Bex 5G 127
TW14: Bedf 6E 110
Horsley Ct. *SW1* 4D 18
(off Vincent St.)
Horsley Dr. CR0: New Ad 7E 170
KT2: King T 5D 132
Horsley Rd. BR1: Broml 1K 159
E4 2K 35
Horsley St. SE17 6D 102
Horsman Ho. *SE5* 6C 102
(off Bethwin Rd.)
Horsman St. SE5 6C 102
Horsmonden Cl. BR6: Orp 7K 161
Horsmonden Rd. SE4 5B 122
Horsnell Close SE5 7D 102
Hortensia Ho. *SW10* 7A 100
(off Gunter Gro.)
Hortensia Rd. SW10 7A 100
Horticultural Pl. W4 5K 97
Horton Av. NW2 4G 63
Horton Bri. Rd. UB7: Yiew 1B 92
Horton Cl. UB7: Yiew 1C 92
Horton Country Pk.
Local Nature Reserve 7G 163
Horton Halls SW17 3B 136
Horton Ho. SE15 6J 103
SW8 7K 101
W6 5G 99
(off Field Rd.)
Horton Ind. Pk. UB7: Yiew 1B 92
Horton La. KT19: Eps 7H 163
Horton Pde. UB7: Yiew 1A 92
Horton Pk. Golf Course 7J 163
Horton Rd. E8 6H 67
SL3: Poyle 6A 174
TW19: Stanw M 7A 174
UB7: Yiew 1A 92
UB11: Stock P 1A 92
Horton Rd. Ind. Est. UB7: Yiew 1B 92
Horton Way CR0: C'don 5K 157
Hortus Rd. E4 2K 35
UB2: S'hall 2D 94
Horwood Ho. *E2* 3H 85
(off Pott St.)
NW8 3D 4
(off Paveley St.)
Hosack Rd. SW17 2E 136
Hoser Av. SE12 2J 141
Hosier La. EC1 6A 8 (5B 84)
Hoskins Cl. E16 6A 88
UB3: Harl 5H 93
Hoskins St. SE10 5F 105
Hospital Bri. Rd.
TW2: Twick, Whitt 7F 113
HOSPITAL BRIDGE RDBT. 2F 131
Hospital Rd. E9 5K 67
E11 5F 51
TW3: Houn 3E 112
Hospital Way SE13 7F 123
Hotham Cl. KT8: W Mole 3E 148
Hotham Rd. SW15 3E 116
SW19 7A 136
Hotham Rd. M. SW19 7A 136
Hotham St. E15 1G 87
Hothfield Pl. SE16 3J 103
Hotspur Ind. Est. N17 6C 34
Hotspur Rd. UB5: N'olt 2E 76
Hotspur St. SE11 5J 19 (4A 102)
Houblon Rd. TW10: Rich 5E 114
Houghton Cl. E8 6F 67
TW12: Hamp 6C 130
Houghton Ct. *EC1* 4C 8
(off Glasshouse Yd.)
Houghton Rd. N15 4F 49
Houghton Sq. *SW9* 2J 119
(off Clapham Rd.)
Houghton St. WC2 1H 13 (6K 83)
(not continuous)
Houlder Cres. CR0: Wadd 6B 168
Houlton Ho. *SW3* 5E 16
(off Walpole St.)
Houlton Pl. *E3* 4B 86
(off Hamlets Way)
Houndsden Rd. N21 6E 22
Houndsditch EC3 7H 9 (6E 84)
Houndsfield Rd. N9 7C 24
HOUNSLOW 3F 113
Hounslow & District Indoor Bowls Club
2D 112
Hounslow Av. TW3: Houn 5F 113
Hounslow Bus. Pk. TW3: Houn 4E 112
Hounslow Cen. TW3: Houn 3F 113
Hounslow Gdns. TW3: Houn 5F 113
Hounslow Heath
Local Nature Reserve 6C 112
Hounslow Rd. TW2: Whitt 6F 113
TW13: Hanw 4B 130
TW14: Felt 1K 129
Hounslow Urban Farm 5J 111
HOUNSLOW WEST 3C 112
The Household Cavalry Mus.
5D 12 (1H 101)
The House Mill 3E 86
House of Illustration 1J 83
Houses of Parliament 1F 19 (3J 101)
Houston Bus. Pk. UB4: Yead 1A 94
Houston Pl. KT10: Esh 7J 149
Houston Rd. KT6: Surb 6B 150
SE23 2A 140
Houstoun Ct. TW5: Hest 7D 94
Hove Av. E17 5B 50
Hoveden Rd. NW2 5G 63
Hove Gdns. SM1: Sutt 1K 165
Hove St. *SE15* 7J 103
(off Culmore Rd.)
Hoveton Rd. SE28 6C 90
Hoveton Way IG6: Ilf 1F 53
Howard Av. DA5: Bexl 1C 144
Howard Bldg. SW11 7J 17 (6F 101)
Howard Cl. N11 2K 31
NW2 4G 63
TW12: Hamp 7G 131
TW16: Sun 6H 129
W3 6H 79
WD23: B Hea 1D 26
Howard Ct. IG11: Bark 1H 89
Howard Ho. *E16* 1K 105
(off Wesley Av.)
SE8 6B 104
(off Evelyn St.)
SW1 6B 18
(off Dolphin Sq.)
SW9 3B 120
(off Barrington Rd.)
W1 4K 5
(off Cleveland St.)
Howard M. N5 4B 66
Howard Rd. BR1: Broml 7J 141
E6 2D 88
E11 3G 69
E17 3C 50
HA7: Stan 1D 42
IG1: Ilf 4F 71
IG11: Bark 1H 89
KT3: N Mald 3A 152
KT5: Surb 6F 151
N15 6E 48
N16 4D 66
NW2 4F 63
SE20 1J 157
SE25 5G 157
TW7: Isle 3K 113
UB1: S'hall 6F 77
Howards Cl. HA5: Pinn 2K 39
Howards Crest Cl. BR3: Beck 2E 158
Howard's La. SW15 4D 116
Howards Rd. E13 3J 87
Howard St. KT7: T Ditt 7B 150
Howard Wlk. N2 4A 46
Howard Way EN5: Barn 5A 20
Howarth Rd. SE2 5A 108
Howberry Cl. HA8: Edg 6J 27
Howberry Rd. CR7: Thor H 1D 156
HA7: Stan 6J 27
HA8: Edg 6J 27
Howbury Rd. SE15 3J 121
Howcroft Cres. N3 7D 30
Howcroft Ho. *E3* 3B 86
(off Benworth St.)
Howcroft La. UB6: G'frd 3H 77
Howden Cl. SE28 7D 90
Howden Rd. SE25 2F 157
Howden St. SE15 3G 121
Howe Cl. RM7: Mawney 1G 55
Howell Cl. RM6: Chad H 5D 54
Howell Ct. E10 7D 50
Howell Wlk. SE1 4B 102
Howerd Way SE18 1C 124
(not continuous)
Howes Cl. N3 3J 45
Howeth Ct. *N11* 6J 31
(off Ribblesdale Av.)
Howfield Pl. N17 3F 49
Howgate Rd. SW14 3K 115
Howick Pl. SW1 2B 18 (3G 101)
Howie St. SW11 7C 100
Howitt Cl. N16 4E 66
NW3 6C 64
Howitt Rd. NW3 6C 64
Howland Est. SE16 3J 103
Howland Ho. SW16 3J 137
Howland M. E. W1 5B 6 (5G 83)
Howland St. W1 5A 6 (5G 83)
Howland Way SE16 2A 104
Howlett Apts. *N1* 7J 65
(off Caledonian Rd.)
Howletts La. HA4: Ruis 5E 38
Howlett's Rd. SE24 6C 120
Howley Pl. W2 5A 4 (5A 82)
Howley Rd. CR0: C'don 3B 168
Howsman Rd. SW13 6C 98
Howson Rd. SE4 4A 122
Howson Ter. TW10: Rich 6E 114
How's St. E2 2F 85
Howton Pl. WD23: B Hea 1C 26
HOXTON 2E 84
Hoxton Hall Theatre 2E 84
(off Hoxton St.)
Hoxton Mkt. N1 2G 9
Hoxton Sq. N1 2G 9 (3E 84)
Hoxton St. N1 2H 9 (1E 84)
Hoylake Cres. UB10: Ick 2C 56
Hoylake Gdns. CR4: Mitc 3G 155
HA4: Ruis 1K 57
Hoylake Rd. W3 6A 80
Hoyland Cl. SE15 7H 103
Hoyle Rd. SW17 5C 136
Hoy St. E16 6H 87
HQS Wellington 3J 13
The Hub
Westminster 1F 5 (2D 82)
Hubbard Ct. IG10: Lough 1H 37
Hubbard Dr. KT9: Chess 6D 162
Hubbard Ho. *SW10* 7B 100
(off World's End Pas.)
Hubbard Rd. SE27 4C 138
Hubbards Cl. UB8: Hil 6D 74
Hubbard St. E15 1G 87
Hubbinet Ind. Est. RM7: Mawney 3J 55
Huberd Ho. *SE1* 7F 15
(off Mancipie St.)
Hubert Gro. SW9 3J 119
Hubert Ho. *NW8* 4C 4
(off Ashbridge St.)
Hubert Rd. E6 3B 88
Hucknall Ct. *NW8* 3A 4
(off Cunningham Pl.)
Huddart St. E3 5B 86
(not continuous)
Huddleston Cl. E2 2J 85
Huddlestone Rd. E7 4H 69
NW2 6D 62
Huddleston Rd. N7 3G 65
Hudson *NW9* 1B 44
(off Five Acre)
Hudson Apts. N8 3K 47
Hudson Bldg. *E1* 6K 9
(off Chicksand St.)
Hudson Cl. E15 1J 87
W12 7D 80
Hudson Ct. *E14* 5C 104
(off Maritime Quay)
Hudson Gdns. BR6: Chels 6K 173
Hudson Ho. *SW10* 7A 100
(off Hortensia Rd.)
W11 6G 81
(off Ladbroke Gro.)
Hudson Pl. SE18 5G 107
Hudson Rd. DA7: Bex 2F 127
UB3: Harl 6F 93
Hudson's Pl. SW1 3A 18 (4F 101)
Hudson Way E16 7G 89
N9 3D 34
NW2 3F 63
Hugero Point SE10 3J 105
Huggin Ct. EC4 2D 14
Huggin Hill EC4 2C 14 (7C 84)
Huggins Ho. *E3* 3C 86
(off Alfred St.)
Huggins Pl. SW2 1K 137
Hughan Rd. E15 5F 69
Hugh Astor Ct. *SE1* 7B 14
(off Keyworth St.)
Hugh Clark Ho. *W13* 1A 96
(off Singapore Rd.)
Hugh Cubitt Ho. *N1* 2K 83
(off Collier St.)
Hugh Dalton Av. SW6 6H 99
Hughenden Av. HA3: Kenton 5B 42
Hughenden Gdns. UB5: N'olt 3A 76
(not continuous)
Hughenden Ho. NW8 3C 4
Hughenden Rd. KT4: Wor Pk 7C 152
Hughendon EN5: New Bar 4E 20
Hughendon Ct. *UB3: Hayes* 7H 75
(off Chamberlain Cl.)
Hughendon Ter. E15 4E 68
Hughes Cl. N12 5F 31
Hughes Ct. N7 5H 65
Hughes Ho. *E2* 3J 85
(off Sceptre Ro.)
E3 3C 86
(off Trevithick Way)
SE5 1C 120
(off Flodden Rd.)
SE8 6C 104
(off Benbow St.)
SE17 4B 102
(off Peacock St.)
Hughes Mans. E1 4G 85
Hughes Rd. TW15: Ashf 7E 128
UB3: Hayes 7K 75
Hughes Ter. *SW9* 3B 120
(off Styles Gdns.)
Hughes Wlk. CR0: C'don 7C 156
Hugh Gaitskell Cl. SW6 6H 99
Hugh Gaitskell Ho. N16 2F 67
Hugh Herland Ho. KT1: King T 3E 150
Hugh M. SW1 4K 17 (4F 101)
Hugh Platt Ho. *E2* 2H 85
(off Patriot Sq.)
Hugh St. SW1 4K 17 (4F 101)
Hugo Ho. *SW1* 1F 17
(off Sloane St.)
Hugon Rd. SW6 3K 117
Hugo Rd. N19 4G 65
Huguenot Dr. N13 5F 33
Huguenot Pl. E1 5K 9 (5F 85)
SW18 5A 118
Huguenot Sq. SE15 3H 121
Hullbridge M. N1 1D 84
Hull Cl. SE16 2K 103
Hull Pl. E16 1G 107
Hull St. EC1 2C 8 (3C 84)
Hulme Pl. SE1 7D 14 (2C 102)
Hulse Av. IG11: Bark 6H 71
RM7: Mawney 1H 55
Hulse Ter. IG1: Ilf 6G 71
Hult Intl. Studios *E1* 6G 85
(off Alder St.)
Hult Twr. *E1* 6G 85
(off Alder St.)
Hulverston Cl. SM2: Sutt 7K 165
Humber Cl. UB7: W Dray 1A 92
Humber Ct. *W7* 6H 77
(off Hobbayne Rd.)
Humber Dr. W10 4F 81
Humber Rd. NW2 2D 62
SE3 6H 105
Humberstone Rd. E13 3A 88
Humberton Cl. E9 5A 68
Humber Trad. Est. NW2 2D 62
Humbolt Rd. W6 6G 99
Hume Ct. *N1* 7B 66
(off Hawes St.)
Hume Ho. *W11* 1F 99
(off Queensdale Cres.)
Humes Av. W7 3J 95
Hume Ter. E16 5K 87
Hume Way HA4: Ruis 6J 39
Humphrey Cl. IG5: Ilf 1D 52
Humphrey St. SE1 5F 103
Humphries Cl. RM9: Dag 4F 73
Humphry Repton Way
HA9: Wemb 4G 61
Hundred Acre NW9 2B 44
Hungerdown E4 1K 35
Hungerford Ho. *SW1* 7B 18
(off Churchill Gdns.)
Hungerford La. WC2 4F 13
(not continuous)
Hungerford Rd. N7 6H 65
Hungerford St. E1 6H 85
Hunsdon Cl. RM9: Dag 6E 72
Hunsdon Rd. SE14 7K 103
Hunslett St. E2 3J 85
Hunstanton Ho. *NW1* 5D 4
(off Cosway St.)
Hunston Rd. SM4: Mord 1K 165
Hunt Cl. W11 1F 99
Hunt Ct. N14 7A 22
RM7: Rush G 6K 55
(off Union Rd.)
UB5: N'olt 2B 76
(off Gallery Gdns.)
Hunter Cl. SE1 3D 102
SM6: W'gton 7J 167
SW12 1E 136
Hunter Ho. *SE1* 7B 14
(off King James St.)
SW5 5J 99
(off Old Brompton Rd.)
SW8 7H 101
(off Fount St.)
TW13: Felt 1J 129
(off Hazel Gro.)
WC1 3F 7
(off Hunter St.)
Hunterian Mus. 1H 13 (6K 83)
Hunter Lodge *W9* 5J 81
(off Admiral Wlk.)
Hunter Rd. CR7: Thor H 3D 156
IG1: Ilf 5F 71
SW20 1E 152
Hunters Cl. DA5: Bexl 3K 145
Hunters Ct. TW9: Rich 5D 114
Hunters Gro. BR6: Farnb 4G 173
HA3: Kenton 4C 42
UB3: Hayes 1J 93
Hunters Hall Rd. RM10: Dag 4G 73
Hunters Hill HA4: Ruis 3A 58
Hunters Mdw. SE19 4E 138
Hunter's Rd. KT9: Chess 3E 162
Hunters Sq. RM10: Dag 4G 73
Hunter St. WC1 3F 7 (4J 83)
Hunter's Way CR0: C'don 4E 168
Hunters Way EN2: Enf 1F 23
Hunter Wlk. E13 2J 87
Huntingdon Cl. CR4: Mitc 3J 155
UB5: N'olt 6E 58
Huntingdon Gdns. KT4: Wor Pk 3E 164
W4 7J 97
Huntingdon Rd. N2 3C 46
N9 2D 34
Huntingdon St. E16 6H 87
N1 7K 65
Huntingfield CR0: Sels 7B 170
Huntingfield Rd. SW15 4C 116
Hunting Ga. Cl. EN2: Enf 3F 23
Hunting Ga. Dr. KT9: Chess 7E 162
Hunting Ga. M. SM1: Sutt 3K 165
TW2: Twick 1J 131
Hunting Pl. TW5: Hest 6D 94
Huntings Farm IG1: Ilf 2J 71
Huntings Rd. RM10: Dag 6G 73
Huntington Cl. DA5: Bexl 1H 145
Huntington Ho. *SW11* 7F 101
(off Palmer Rd.)
Huntley Cl. SE10 5G 105
TW19: Stanw 7A 110
Huntley St. WC1 4B 6 (4G 83)
Huntley Way SW20 2C 152
Huntloe Ho. *SE14* 1J 121
(off Kender St.)
Huntly Dr. N3 6D 30
Huntly Rd. SE25 4E 156
Hunton St. E1 4K 9 (5G 85)
Hunt Rd. UB2: S'hall 3E 94
Hunt's Cl. SE3 2J 123
Hunt's Ct. WC2 3D 12 (7H 83)
Huntshaw Ho. *E3* 3D 86
(off Devons Rd.)
Hunts La. E15 2E 86
Huntsmans Cl. TW13: Felt 4K 129
Huntsman St. SE17 4E 102
Hunts Mead EN3: Enf H 3E 24
Hunts Mead Cl. BR7: Chst 7D 142
Huntsmoor Rd. KT19: Ewe 5K 163
Huntspill St. SW17 3A 136
Hunts Slip Rd. SE21 3E 138
Huntsworth M. NW1 3E 4 (4D 82)
Hurdwick Ho. *NW1* 2G 83
(off Harrington Sq.)
Hurdwick Pl. *NW1* 2G 83
(off Hampstead Rd.)
Hurleston Ho. SE8 5B 104

Hurley Ct. SW17 ... 6E 136
(off Mitcham Rd.)
W5 ... 6C 78
Hurley Cres. SE16 ... 2K 103
Hurley Ho. SE11 ... 4K 19 (4B 102)
UB7: W Dray ... 2B 92
(off Park Lodge Av.)
Hurley Rd. UB6: G'frd ... 6F 77
HURLINGHAM ... 3K 117
Hurlingham Bus. Pk. SW6 ... 3J 117
The Hurlingham Club ... 3J 117
Hurlingham Ct. SW6 ... 3H 117
Hurlingham Gdns. SW6 ... 3H 117
Hurlingham Pk. ... 2H 117
Hurlingham Retail Pk. ... 3K 117
Hurlingham Rd. DA7: Bex ... 7F 109
SW6 ... 2H 117
Hurlingham Sq. SW6 ... 3J 117
Hurlingham Yacht Club ... 3G 117
Hurlock St. N5 ... 3B 66
Hurlstone Rd. SE25 ... 5E 156
Hurn Ct. TW4: Houn ... 2B 112
Hurn Ct. Rd. TW4: Houn ... 2B 112
Huron Cl. BR6: Chels ... 6J 173
Huron Rd. SW17 ... 2E 136
Hurrell Dr. HA2: Harr ... 3G 41
Hurren Cl. SE3 ... 3G 123
Hurricane Rd. SM6: W'gton ... 7J 167
Hurricane Trad. Cen. NW9 ... 1C 44
Hurry Cl. E15 ... 7G 69
Hurst Av. E4 ... 4H 35
N6 ... 6G 47
Hurstbourne KT10: Clay ... 6A 162
Hurstbourne Gdns. IG11: Bark ... 6J 71
Hurstbourne Ho. SW15 ... 6B 116
(off Tangley Gro.)
Hurstbourne Rd. SE23 ... 1A 140
Hurst Cl. BR2: Hayes ... 1H 171
E4 ... 3H 35
KT9: Chess ... 5G 163
NW11 ... 6K 45
UB5: N'olt ... 6D 58
Hurstcombe IG9: Buck H ... 2D 36
Hurst Ct. DA15: Sidc ... 2A 144
E6 ... 5B 88
(off Tollgate Rd.)
IG8: Wfd G ... 6E 36
(off Snakes La. W.)
Hurstcourt Rd. SM1: Sutt ... 2K 165
Hurstdene Av. BR2: Hayes ... 1H 171
Hurstdene Gdns. N15 ... 7E 48
Hurstfield BR2: Broml ... 5J 159
Hurstfield Cres. UB4: Hayes ... 4G 75
Hurstfield Rd. KT8: W Mole ... 3E 148
Hurst Gro. KT12: Walt T ... 7H 147
Hurst Ho. WC1 ... 1H 7
(off Penton Ri.)
Hurst La. KT8: E Mos ... 4G 149
SE2 ... 5D 108
Hurst La. Est. SE2 ... 5D 108
Hurstleigh Gdns. IG5: Ilf ... 1D 52
Hurstmead Ct. HA8: Edg ... 4C 28
HURST PARK ... 2G 149
Hurst Pl. HA6: Nwood ... 1D 38
Hurst Pool ... 3F 149
Hurst Ri. EN5: New Bar ... 3D 20
Hurst Rd. CR0: C'don ... 5D 168
DA5: Bexl ... 1D 144
DA8: Erith ... 1J 127
DA15: Bexl, Sidc ... 2A 144
E17 ... 3D 50
IG9: Buck H ... 1G 37
KT8: W Mole, E Mos ... 3F 149
KT12: Walt T ... 5A 148
N21 ... 1F 33
Hurst Springs DA5: Bexl ... 1E 144
Hurst St. SE24 ... 6B 120
Hurstview Grange
CR2: S Croy ... 7B 168
Hurst Vw. Rd. CR2: S Croy ... 7E 168
Hurst Way CR2: S Croy ... 6E 168
Hurstway Rd. W11 ... 7F 81
(off Hurstway Wlk.)
Hurstway Wlk. W11 ... 7F 81
Hurstwood Av. DA5: Bexl ... 1E 144
E18 ... 4K 51
Hurstwood Ct. N12 ... 6H 31
NW11 ... 4H 45
(off Finchley Rd.)
Hurstwood Dr. BR1: Broml ... 3D 160
Hurstwood Rd. NW11 ... 4G 45
Hurtwood Rd.
KT12: Walt T ... 7D 148
Husborne Ho. SE8 ... 4A 104
(off Chilton Gro.)
Huson Cl. NW3 ... 7C 64
Hussain Cl. HA1: Harr ... 4K 59
Hussars Cl. TW4: Houn ... 3C 112
Husseywell Cres. BR2: Hayes ... 1J 171
Hutchings St. E14 ... 2C 104
Hutchings Wlk. NW11 ... 4K 45
Hutchings Wharf E14 ... 2C 104
(off Hutchings St.)
Hutchins Cl. E15 ... 7E 68
Hutchinson Ct. RM6: Chad H ... 4D 54
Hutchinson Ho. NW3 ... 7D 64
SE14 ... 7J 103
Hutchinson Ter. HA9: Wemb ... 3D 60
Hutchins Rd. SE28 ... 7A 90
Hutton Cl. IG8: Wfd G ... 6E 36
UB6: G'frd ... 5H 59
Hutton Ct. N4 ... 1K 65
(off Victoria Rd.)
N9 ... 7D 24
(off Tramway Av.)
W5 ... 5B 78
Hutton Gdns. HA3: Hrw W ... 7B 26
Hutton Gro. N12 ... 5E 30
Hutton La. HA3: Hrw W ... 7B 26
Hutton M. SW15 ... 5D 116
Hutton Row HA8: Edg ... 7D 28
Hutton St. EC4 ... 2K 13 (6B 84)
Hutton Wlk. HA3: Hrw W ... 7B 26
Huxbear St. SE4 ... 5B 122
Huxley Cl. UB5: N'olt ... 2C 76
UB8: Cowl ... 4A 74
Huxley Dr. RM6: Chad H ... 7B 54
Huxley Gdns. NW10 ... 3F 79
Huxley Ho. NW8 ... 4B 4
(off Fisherton St.)
Huxley Pde. N18 ... 5J 33
Huxley Pl. N13 ... 3G 33
Huxley Rd. DA16: Well ... 3K 125
E10 ... 2E 68
N18 ... 4J 33
Huxley Sayze N18 ... 5J 33
Huxley Sth. N18 ... 5J 33
Huxley St. W10 ... 3G 81
Hyacinth Cl. IG1: Ilf ... 6F 71
TW12: Hamp ... 6E 130
Hyacinth Dr. UB10: Uxb ... 7A 56
Hyacinth Ho. E17 ... 3D 50
(off Vine St.)
Hyacinth Rd. SW15 ... 1C 134
Hybrid Ho. W3 ... 1A 98
THE HYDE ... 5B 44
The Hyde NW9 ... 4A 44
(not continuous)
Hyde Cl. E13 ... 2J 87
EN5: Barn ... 3C 20
TW15: Ashf ... 6G 129
Hyde Ct. N20 ... 3G 31
Hyde Cres. NW9 ... 5A 44
Hyde Est. Rd. NW9 ... 5B 44
Hyde Farm M. SW12 ... 1H 137
Hydefield Cl. N21 ... 1J 33
Hydefield Ct. N9 ... 2K 33
Hyde Ho. E3 ... 5C 86
(off Furze St.)
TW3: Houn ... 3G 113
UB8: Uxb ... 6A 56
W13 ... 1A 96
(off Singapore Rd.)
The Hyde Ind. Est. NW9 ... 5B 44
Hyde La. SW11 ... 1C 118
Hyde Pk. ... 4D 10 (1D 100)
Hyde Pk. Av. N21 ... 2H 33
Hyde Park Barracks ... 7D 10
HYDE PARK CORNER ... 2F 101
Hyde Pk. Cnr. W1 ... 6H 11 (2E 100)
Hyde Pk. Cres. W2 ... 1C 10 (6C 82)
Hyde Pk. Gdns. N21 ... 2H 33
W2 ... 2B 10 (7B 82)
(not continuous)
Hyde Pk. Gdns. M. W2 ... 2B 10 (7B 82)
Hyde Pk. Ga. SW7 ... 2A 100
(not continuous)
Hyde Pk. Ga. M. SW7 ... 2A 100
Hyde Pk. Mans. NW1 ... 6C 4
(off Cabbell St.)
Hyde Pk. Pl. W2 ... 2D 10 (7C 82)
Hyde Pk. Sq. W2 ... 1C 10 (6C 82)
Hyde Pk. Sq. M. W2 ... 1C 10
Hyde Pk. St. W2 ... 1C 10 (6C 82)
Hyde Pk. Towers W2 ... 7A 82
Hyderabad Way E15 ... 7G 69
Hyde Rd. DA7: Bex ... 2F 127
N1 ... 1E 84
TW10: Rich ... 5F 115
Hydeside Gdns. N9 ... 2A 34
Hyde's Pl. N1 ... 7B 66
Hyde St. SE8 ... 6C 104
Hyde Ter. TW15: Ashf ... 6G 129
Hydethorpe Av. N9 ... 2A 34
Hydethorpe Rd. SW12 ... 1G 137
Hyde Va. SE10 ... 7E 104
Hyde Wlk. SM4: Mord ... 7J 153
Hyde Way N9 ... 2A 34
UB3: Harl ... 4H 93
Hydon Ct. N11 ... 5J 31
The Hydra Bldg. EC1 ... 2K 7
Hylands Rd. E17 ... 2F 51
Hylton St. SE18 ... 4K 107
Hyndewood SE23 ... 3K 139
Hyndman Ho. RM10: Dag ... 3G 73
(off Kershaw Rd.)
Hyndman St. SE15 ... 6H 103
Hynton Rd. RM8: Dag ... 2C 72
Hyperion Ct. E16 ... 5J 87
(off Robertson Rd.)
Hyperion Ho. E3 ... 2A 86
(off Arbery Rd.)
SW2 ... 6K 119
Hyrstdene CR2: S Croy ... 4B 168
Hyson Rd. SE16 ... 5H 103
Hythe Av. DA7: Bex ... 7E 108
Hythe Cl. N18 ... 4B 34
Hythe Ho. SE16 ... 2J 103
(off Swan Rd.)
W6 ... 4E 98
(off Shepherd's Bush Rd.)
Hythe Rd. CR7: Thor H ... 2D 156
KT6: Surb ... 6E 150
NW10 ... 3B 80
Hythe Rd. Ind. Est. NW10 ... 3C 80

I

Ian Bowater Ct. N1 ... 1F 9
(off East Rd.)
Ian Ct. SE23 ... 2J 139
Ian Sq. EN3: Enf H ... 1E 24
Ibberton Ho. SW8 ... 7K 101
(off Meadow Rd.)
W14 ... 3G 99
(off Russell Rd.)
Ibbotson Av. E16 ... 6H 87
Ibbott St. E1 ... 4J 85
Iberia Ho. N19 ... 7H 47
Iberian Av. SM6: Bedd ... 4H 167
Ibex Ho. E15 ... 5G 69
(off Forest La.)
Ibis Ct. BR3: Beck ... 1F 159
(off Albemarle Rd.)
SE8 ... 6B 104
(off Edward Pl.)
Ibis La. W4 ... 1J 115
Ibis Way UB4: Yead ... 6B 76
Ibrox Ct. IG9: Buck H ... 2F 37
Ibscott Cl. RM10: Dag ... 6J 73
Ibsley Gdns. SW15 ... 1C 134
Ibsley Way EN4: Cockf ... 5H 21
ICA Cinema ... 4D 12
(within ICA)
Icarus Ho. E3 ... 3B 86
(off British St.)
ICA Theatre ... 4D 12
(within ICA)
Iceland Rd. E3 ... 1C 86
Iceland Wharf SE16 ... 4A 104
Iceni Ct. E3 ... 1B 86
(off Parnell Rd.)
IG9: Buck H ... 1E 36
Ice Wharf N1 ... 2J 83
Ice Wharf Marina N1 ... 2J 83
(off New Wharf Rd.)
The Ice Works NW1 ... 7F 65
(off Jamestown Rd.)
Ickburgh Est. E5 ... 2H 67
Ickburgh Rd. E5 ... 3H 67
ICKENHAM ... 3D 56
Ickenham Cl. HA4: Ruis ... 2F 57
Ickenham Grn. UB10: Ick ... 1D 56
Ickenham Rd. HA4: Ruis ... 2E 56
Ickleton Rd. SE9 ... 4C 142
Icknield Dr. IG2: Ilf ... 5F 53
Icknield Ho. SW3 ... 5D 16
(off Cale St.)
Ickworth Pk. Rd. E17 ... 4A 50
Icon Apts. SE1 ... 7G 15
(off Cluny Pl.)
Icona Point E15 ... 1E 86
(off Warton Rd.)
Icon College of Technology & Management
... 6G 85
(off Adler St.)
Iconia Ho. BR2: Broml ... 4A 160
Idaho Bldg. SE13 ... 1D 122
(off Deal's Gateway)
Ida Rd. N15 ... 4D 48
Ida St. E14 ... 6E 86
(not continuous)
Ide Mans. E1 ... 7K 85
(off Cable St.)
Iden Cl. BR2: Broml ... 3G 159
Idlecombe Rd. SW17 ... 6E 136
Idmiston Rd. E15 ... 4H 69
KT4: Wor Pk ... 7B 152
SE27 ... 3C 138
Idmiston Sq. KT4: Wor Pk ... 7B 152
Idol La. EC3 ... 3G 15 (7E 84)
Idonia St. SE8 ... 7C 104
Iffley Cl. UB8: Uxb ... 7A 56
Iffley Rd. W6 ... 3D 98
Ifield Ho. SE17 ... 5E 102
(off Madron St.)
Ifield Rd. SW10 ... 6K 99
Ifor Evans Pl. E1 ... 4K 85
Ightham Ho. BR3: Beck ... 7B 140
(off Bethersden Cl.)
SE17 ... 4E 102
(off Beckway St.)
Ightham Rd. DA8: Erith ... 7G 109
Ikon Ho. E1 ... 7J 85
(off Devonport St.)
Ilbert St. W10 ... 3F 81
Ilchester Gdns. W2 ... 7K 81
Ilchester Mans. W8 ... 3J 99
(off Abingdon Rd.)
Ilchester Pl. W14 ... 3H 99
Ilchester Rd. RM8: Dag ... 5B 72
Ildersly Gro. SE21 ... 2D 138
Ilderton Rd. SE15 ... 5J 103
SE16 ... 5J 103
Ilderton Wharf SE15 ... 6J 103
(off Rollins St.)
Ilex Cl. TW16: Sun ... 2A 148
Ilex Rd. NW10 ... 6B 62
Ilex Way SW16 ... 5A 138
ILFORD ... 3F 71
Ilford Bldg. IG1: Ilf ... 3E 70
Ilford Golf Course ... 1D 70
Ilford Hill IG1: Ilf ... 3E 70
Ilford Ho. N1 ... 6D 66
(off Dove Rd.)
Ilford La. IG1: Ilf ... 3F 71
Ilford Sports Club ... 2J 71
Ilfracombe Flats SE1 ... 6D 14
(off Marshalsea Rd.)
Ilfracombe Gdns. RM6: Chad H ... 7B 54
Ilfracombe Rd. BR1: Broml ... 3H 141
Iliffe St. SE17 ... 5B 102
Iliffe Yd. SE17 ... 5B 102
(off Crampton St.)
Ilkeston Ct. E5 ... 4K 67
(off Overbury St.)
Ilkley Cl. SE19 ... 6D 138
Ilkley Rd. E16 ... 5A 88
Illingworth Cl. CR4: Mitc ... 3B 154
Illingworth Way EN1: Enf ... 5K 23
Illumina Ho. SW18 ... 5J 117
(off Broomhill Rd.)
Ilmington Rd. HA3: Kenton ... 6D 42
Ilminster Gdns. SW11 ... 4C 118
Ilsley Ct. SW8 ... 2G 119
Image Ct. RM7: Rush G ... 6K 55
Images IG2: Ilf ... 6E 52
Imani Mans. SW11 ... 2B 118
IMAX (BFI) ... 5J 13 (1A 102)
Imber Cl. N14 ... 7B 22
Imber Court ... 7H 149
Imber Cross KT7: T Ditt ... 6K 149
Imber Gro. KT10: Esh ... 7H 149
Imber Pk. Rd. KT10: Esh ... 7H 149
Imber St. N1 ... 1D 84
Impact Bus. Pk. UB6: G'frd ... 2B 78
Impact Ct. SE20 ... 2H 157
Impact Ho. CR0: C'don ... 3C 168
Imperial Av. N16 ... 4E 66
Imperial Cl. HA2: Harr ... 6E 40
NW2 ... 5D 62
Imperial College London
Charing Cross Campus ... 6F 99
Chelsea & Westminster Campus
... 6A 100
(within Chelsea & Westminster Hospital)
Hamersmith Campus ... 6C 80
Royal Brompton Campus,
Emmanuel Kaye ... 6C 16
Guy Scadding Bldg. ... 5C 16
St Mary's Campus ... 7B 4
Sth. Kensington Campus
... 1A 16 (3B 100)
Ennismore Gdns. M. ... 1B 16
Kensington Gore ... 1A 16 (3B 100)
Imperial Coll. Rd.
SW7 ... 2A 16 (3B 100)
Imperial Ct. HA2: Harr ... 7E 40
N6 ... 6G 47
N20 ... 3F 31
NW8 ... 2C 82
(off Prince Albert Rd.)
SE11 ... 6J 19 (5A 102)
Imperial Cres. SW6 ... 2A 118
Imperial Dr. HA2: Harr ... 3E 58
Imperial Gdns. CR4: Mitc ... 3F 155
Imperial Gro.
EN4: Had W ... 1E 20
Imperial Hgts. E18 ... 1J 51
(off Queen Mary Av.)
Imperial Ho. E3 ... 3A 86
(off Grove Rd.)
E14 ... 7B 86
(off Victory Pl.)
Imperial M. E6 ... 2B 88
SW9 ... 4K 119
(off Brighton Ter.)
Imperial Pl. BR7: Chst ... 1E 160
Imperial Rd. N22 ... 7D 32
SW6 ... 1K 117
TW14: Felt ... 7G 111
Imperial Sq. SW6 ... 1K 117
Imperial St. E3 ... 3E 86
Imperial War Mus. London
All Saints Annexe ... 3K 19
(off Austral St.)
Main Museum ... 2K 19 (3A 102)
Imperial Way BR7: Chst ... 3G 143
CR0: Wadd ... 6K 167
HA3: Kenton ... 6E 42
Imperial Wharf E2 ... 2H 85
(off Darwen Pl.)
SW6 ... 2A 118
Imperium Ho. E1 ... 6H 85
(off Cannon St. Rd.)
Imre Cl. W12 ... 1D 98
Inca Dr. SE9 ... 7F 125
Inca Ter. N15 ... 3B 48
Inchmery Rd. SE6 ... 2D 140
Inchwood BR4: Addtn ... 4D 170
Independence Ho. SW19 ... 1B 154
(off Chapter Way)
Independent Ind. Est. UB7: Yiew ... 1A 92
Independent Pl. E8 ... 5F 67
Independents Rd. SE3 ... 3H 123
Inderwick Rd. N8 ... 5K 47
Indescon Ct. E14 ... 2D 104
Indescon Sq. E14 ... 2C 104
India Gdns. UB5: N'olt ... 7A 58
India House ... 2G 13
(off Aldwych)
Indiana Bldg. SE13 ... 1C 122
(off Deal's Gateway)
India Pl. WC2 ... 2G 13
India St. EC3 ... 1J 15 (6F 85)
India Way SW15 ... 6C 116
W12 ... 7D 80
indigo at the O2 ... 1G 105
Indigo M. E14 ... 7E 86
N16 ... 3D 66
Indigo Wlk. N2 ... 4D 46
N6 ... 4D 46
Indus Ct. SE15 ... 7F 103
(off Amstel Ct.)
Indus Rd. SE7 ... 7A 106
Infirmary Ct. SW3 ... 7F 17
Inforum M. SE15 ... 7G 103
Infrastructure Way IG11: Bark ... 3D 90
Ingal Rd. E13 ... 4J 87
Ingate Pl. SW8 ... 1F 119
Ingatestone Rd. E12 ... 1A 70
IG8: Wfd G ... 7E 36
SE25 ... 4H 157
Ingelow Ho. W8 ... 2K 99
(off Holland St.)
Ingelow Rd. SW8 ... 2F 119
Ingersoll Rd. EN3: Enf W ... 1D 24
W12 ... 1D 98
Ingestre Pl. W1 ... 1B 12 (6G 83)
Ingestre Rd. E7 ... 4J 69
NW5 ... 4F 65
Ingham Cl. CR2: Sels ... 7K 169
Ingham Rd. CR2: Sels ... 7J 169
NW6 ... 4J 63
Inglebert St. EC1 ... 1J 7 (3A 84)
Ingleborough St. SW9 ... 2A 120
Ingleby Dr. HA1: Harr ... 3H 59
Ingleby Rd. IG1: Ilf ... 1F 71
N7 ... 3J 65
RM10: Dag ... 6H 73
Ingleby Way BR7: Chst ... 5E 142
SM6: W'gton ... 7H 167
Ingle Cl. HA5: Pinn ... 3C 40
Ingledene Cl. NW4 ... 6C 44
Ingledew Rd. SE18 ... 5H 107
Inglefield Sq. E1 ... 1H 103
(off Prusom St.)
Inglehurst Gdns. IG4: Ilf ... 5D 52
Inglemere Rd. CR4: Mitc ... 7D 136
SE23 ... 3K 139
Ingle M. EC1 ... 1J 7 (3A 84)
Inglesham Wlk. E9 ... 6B 68
Ingleside SL3: Poyle ... 4A 174
Ingleside Cl. BR3: Beck ... 7C 140
Ingleside Gro. SE3 ... 6H 105
Inglethorpe St. SW6 ... 1F 117
Ingleton Av. DA16: Well ... 5A 126
Ingleton Rd. N18 ... 6B 34
SM5: Cars ... 7C 166
Ingleton St. SW9 ... 2A 120
Ingleway N12 ... 6G 31
Inglewood BR7: Chst ... 6H 143
CR0: Sels ... 7A 170
Inglewood Cl. E14 ... 4C 104
Inglewood Copse
BR1: Broml ... 2C 160
Inglewood Ct. BR1: Broml ... 7G 141
Inglewood M. KT6: Surb ... 1G 163
SE27 ... 5C 138
(off Elder Rd.)
Inglewood Rd. DA7: Bex ... 4K 127
NW6 ... 5J 63
Inglis Barracks NW7 ... 6A 30
Inglis Rd. CR0: C'don ... 1F 169
W5 ... 7F 79
Inglis St. SE5 ... 1B 120
Inglis Way NW7 ... 6A 30
Ingoldisthorpe Gro. SE15 ... 6F 103
Ingot Twr. E14 ... 5C 86
(off Ursula Gould Way)
Ingram Av. NW11 ... 7A 46
Ingram Cl. HA7: Stan ... 5H 27
SE11 ... 3H 19 (4K 101)
Ingram Ct. CR0: C'don ... 1B 168
Ingram Ho. E3 ... 1A 86
Ingram Rd. CR7: Thor H ... 1C 156
N2 ... 4C 46
Ingram Way UB6: G'frd ... 1H 77
Ingrave Rd. RM1: Rom ... 4K 55
Ingrave St. SW11 ... 3B 118
Ingrebourne Apts. SW6 ... 3K 117
Ingrebourne Ct. E4 ... 3J 35
Ingrebourne Ho. BR1: Broml ... 5F 141
(off Brangbourne Rd.)
NW8 ... 5B 4
(off Broadley St.)
Ingress St. W4 ... 5A 98
Inigo Jones Rd. SE7 ... 7C 106
Inigo Pl. WC2 ... 2E 12
Ink Bldg. W10 ... 5F 81
Inkerman Rd. NW5 ... 6F 65
Inkerman Ter. W8 ... 3J 99
(off Allen St.)
Inks Grn. E4 ... 5K 35
Inkster Ho. SW11 ... 3C 118
Inkwell Cl. N12 ... 3F 31
Ink Works Ct. SE1 ... 7H 15
(off Bell Yd. M.)
Inman Rd. NW10 ... 1A 80
SW18 ... 7A 118
Inmans Row IG8: Wfd G ... 4D 36
Inner Circ. NW1 ... 2G 5 (3E 82)
Inner Ct. SW3 ... 7C 16 (6C 100)
Innerd Ct. CR0: C'don ... 6C 156
(off Harry Cl.)
Inner Pk. Rd. SW19 ... 1F 135
Inner Ring E.
TW6: H'row A ... 3D 110
Inner Ring W.
TW6: H'row A ... 3C 110
Inner Temple La. EC4 ... 1J 13
Innes Cl. SW20 ... 2G 153
Innes Gdns. SW15 ... 6D 116
Innes St. SE15 ... 7E 102
Innes Yd. CR0: C'don ... 3C 168
Innis Ho. SE17 ... 5E 102
(off East St.)
Inniskilling Rd. E13 ... 2A 88
Innova Ct. CR0: C'don ... 1E 168
Innova Pas. E1 ... 3J 9
(off Sclater St.)
The Innovation Cen. E14 ... 2E 104
(off Marsh Wall)
Innovation Cl. HA0: Wemb ... 1E 78
Inns of Court & City Yeomanry Mus.
... 6H 7 (5K 83)
Insignia Point E20 ... 5E 68
Inskip Cl. E10 ... 2D 68
Inskip Rd. RM8: Dag ... 1D 72
Insley Ho. E3 ... 3D 86
(off Bow Rd.)
The Institute for Arts in
Therapy & Education ... 1B 84
(off Britannia Row)
Institute of Archaeology Collections
... 4H 83
Institute of Commonwealth Studies
... 5D 6
Institute of Contemporary Arts (ICA)
... 5D 12
Institute of Germanic & Romance Studies
... 5D 6
Institute of Ophthalmology ... 2E 8
(off Peerless St.)
The Institute of Psychoanalysis ... 4J 81
(off Elgin Av.)
Institute Pl. E8 ... 5H 67
Instituto Cervantes ... 1J 13
(off Devereux Ct.)
Integer Gdns. E11 ... 7F 51
The Interchange NW1 ... 7F 65
(off Camden Lock Pl.)
Interface Ho. TW3: Houn ... 3E 112
(off Staines Rd.)
Intl. Av. TW5: Cran ... 5A 94
Intl. Bus. Pk. E15 ... 1F 87
Intl. Hall ... 4F 7
Intl. Ho. E1 ... 3K 15
(off St Katharine's Way)
TW8: Bford ... 5E 96
(off Gt. West Rd.)
THE INTERNATIONAL QUARTER ... 6E 68
Intl. Sq. E20 ... 6E 68
(within Westfield Shop. Cen.)
Intl. Trad. Est. UB2: S'hall ... 3K 93
Intl. Way E20 ... 6E 68
TW16: Sun ... 1G 147
Inverary Pl. SE18 ... 6H 107
Inver Cl. E5 ... 2J 67
Inverclyde Gdns. RM6: Chad H ... 4C 54
(not continuous)
Inver Ct. W2 ... 6K 81
W6 ... 3C 98
Inveresk Gdns. KT4: Wor Pk ... 3C 164
Inverforth Cl. NW3 ... 2A 64
Inverforth Rd. N11 ... 5A 32
Invergarry Ho. NW6 ... 2K 81
(off Carlton Vale)
Inverine Rd. SE7 ... 5K 105
Invermead Cl. W6 ... 3C 98
Invermore Pl. SE18 ... 4G 107
Inverness Av. EN1: Enf ... 1J 23
Inverness Ct. SE6 ... 1H 141
Inverness Gdns. W8 ... 1K 99
Inverness M. E16 ... 1G 107
W2 ... 7K 81
Inverness Pl. W2 ... 7K 81
Inverness Rd. KT4: Wor Pk ... 1F 165
N18 ... 5C 34
TW3: Houn ... 4D 112
UB2: S'hall ... 4C 94
Inverness St. NW1 ... 1F 83
Inverness Ter. W2 ... 6K 81
Inverton Rd. SE15 ... 4K 121
The Invicta Cen.
IG11: Bark ... 1A 90
Invicta Cl. BR7: Chst ... 5E 142
E3 ... 5C 86
TW14: Felt ... 1H 129
Invicta Gro. UB5: N'olt ... 3D 76
Invicta Pde. DA14: Sidc ... 4B 144
Invicta Plaza SE1 ... 4A 14 (1B 102)
Invicta Rd. SE3 ... 7J 105
Inville Rd. SE17 ... 5D 102
(not continuous)
Inville Wlk. SE17 ... 5D 102
Invito IG2: Ilf ... 6E 52
Inwen Ct. SE8 ... 5A 104
(not continuous)
Inwood Av. TW3: Houn ... 3G 113
Inwood Bus. Pk. TW3: Houn ... 4F 113
Inwood Cl. CR0: C'don ... 2A 170
Inwood Ct. NW1 ... 7G 65
(off Rochester Sq.)
Inwood Ho. N1 ... 1B 84
(off Elliott's Pl.)
Inwood Rd. TW3: Houn ... 4F 113
Inworth St. SW11 ... 2C 118
Inworth Wlk. N1 ... 1C 84
(off Popham St.)
IO Centre SE18 ... 3G 107
(not continuous)
Iona Cl. SE6 ... 7C 122
SM4: Mord ... 7K 153
Ion Ct. E2 ... 2G 85
Ionian Bldg. E14 ... 7A 86
(off Narrow St.)
Ionian Ho. E1 ... 4K 85
(off Duckett St.)

Ion Sq.—Jesmond Av.

Ion Sq. E2 .... 2G 85
IO Trade Cen. CR0: Bedd 4K 167
Ipsden Bldgs. SE1 .... 5K 13
Ipswich Rd. SW17 .... 6E 136
Ira Ct. SE27 .... 2B 138
Ireland Cl. E6 .... 5D 88
Ireland Pl. N22 .... 7D 32
Ireland Yd. EC4 .... 1B 14 (6B 84)
Irene M. W7 .... 1K 95
(off Uxbridge Rd.)
Irene Rd. BR6: Orp 7K 161
SW6 .... 1J 117
Ireton Cl. N10 .... 7K 31
Ireton Ho. SW15 .... 5G 117
(off Stamford Sq.)
Ireton St. E3 .... 4C 86
Iris Av. DA5: Bexl 5E 126
Iris Cl. CR0: C'don 1K 169
E6 .... 5C 88
KT6: Surb 7F 151
N14 .... 7C 22
Iris Ct. SE14 .... 1J 121
(off Briant St.)
Iris Cres. DA7: Bex 6F 109
Iris Gdns. KT7: T Ditt 7J 149
Iris M. TW4: Houn 6E 112
Iris Rd. KT19: Ewe 5H 163
Iris Wlk. HA8: Edg 4D 28
Iris Way E4 .... 6G 35
Irkdale Av. EN1: Enf 1A 24
Iron Bri. Cl. NW10 .... 5A 62
Ironbridge Cl. UB2: S'hall 1G 95
Iron Bri. Ho. NW1 .... 7D 64
Iron Bri. Rd. Nth.
UB11: Stock P 2C 92
Iron Bri. Rd. Sth.
UB7: W Dray 2C 92
Iron Mill Pl. SW18 .... 6K 117
Iron Mill Rd. SW18 .... 6K 117
Ironmonger La. EC2 .... 1D 14 (6C 84)
Ironmonger Pas. EC1 .... 2D 8
(off Ironmonger Row)
Ironmonger Row EC1 .... 2D 8 (3C 84)
Ironmonger Row Baths 2C 8
Ironmongers Pl. E14 .... 4C 104
Ironside Cl. SE16 .... 2K 103
Ironside Ct.
CR2: S Croy 6D 168
TW11: Hamp W 1C 150
Ironside Ho. E9 .... 4A 68
Irons Way RM5: Col R 1J 55
Iron Works E3 .... 1C 86
The Ironworks N1 .... 2J 83
(off Albion Wlk.)
Ironworks Way E13 .... 2B 88
Irvine Av. HA3: Kenton 3A 42
Irvine Cl. E14 .... 5D 86
N20 .... 2H 31
Irvine Ct. W1 .... 4B 6
(off Whitfield St.)
Irvine Ho. N7 .... 6K 65
(off Caledonian Rd.)
Irvine Way BR6: Orp 7K 161
Irving Av. UB5: N'olt 1B 76
Irving Gro. SW9 .... 2K 119
Irving Ho. SE17 .... 5B 102
(off Doddington Gro.)
Irving Mans. W14 .... 6G 99
(off Queen's Club Gdns.)
Irving M. N1 .... 6C 66
Irving Rd. W14 .... 3F 99
Irving St. WC2 .... 3D 12 (7H 83)
Irving Way NW9 .... 5C 44
Irwell Ct. W7 .... 6H 77
(off Hobbayne Rd.)
Irwell Est. SE16 .... 3J 103
Irwin Av. SE18 .... 7J 107
Irwin Cl. NW7 .... 5B 30
UB10: Ick 3C 56
Irwin Gdns. NW10 .... 1D 80
Isaac Way SE1 .... 6D 14
(off Sanctuary St.)
Isabel Hill Cl. TW12: Hamp 1F 149
Isabella Cl. N14 .... 7B 22
Isabella Ct. TW10: Rich 6F 115
(off Kingsmead)
Isabella Dr. BR6: Farnb 4G 173
Isabella Ho. SE11 .... 5K 19
W6 .... 5E 98
(off Queen Caroline St.)
Isabella M. N1 .... 6E 66
Isabella Pl. KT2: King T 5F 133
Isabella Plantation Garden 3H 133
Isabella Rd. E9 .... 5J 67
Isabella St. SE1 .... 5A 14 (1B 102)
Isabel St. SW9 .... 1K 119
Isambard M. E14 .... 3E 104
Isambard Pl. SE16 .... 1J 103
Isel Way SE22 .... 5E 120
Isham Rd. SW16 .... 2J 155
Isis Cl. HA4: Ruis 6E 38
SW15 .... 4E 116
Isis Ct. W4 .... 7H 97
Isis Ho. N18 .... 6A 34
NW8 .... 4B 4
(off Church St. Est.)
SE20 .... 7G 139
Isis St. SW18 .... 2A 136
The Island KT7: T Ditt 6A 150
UB7: Lford 3D 174
Island Apts. N1 .... 1C 84
Island Barn Reservoir Sailing Club
.... 6F 149
Island Farm Av. KT8: W Mole 5D 148
Island Farm Rd.
KT8: W Mole 5D 148
Island Ho. E3 .... 3E 86
Island Rd. CR4: Mitc 7D 136
SE16 .... 4K 103
Island Row E14 .... 6B 86
Isla Rd. SE18 .... 6G 107
Islay Gdns. TW4: Houn 5B 112
Islay Wlk. N1 .... 6C 66
(off Douglas Rd. Sth.)
Isleden Ho. N1 .... 1C 84
(off Prebend St.)
Isledon Rd. N7 .... 3A 66
ISLEDON VILLAGE 3A 66
Islehurst Cl. BR7: Chst 1E 160
ISLE OF DOGS 2D 104
ISLEWORTH 3A 114
Isleworth Ait Nature Reserve 3B 114
Isleworth Bus. Complex
TW7: Isle 2K 113
Isleworth Prom. TW1: Twick 4B 114
Isleworth Recreation Cen. 4K 113
Isley Ct. E14 .... 4E 86
(off Teviot St.)
SW8 .... 2G 119
ISLINGTON 7B 66
Islington Bus. Cen. N1 .... 1C 84
(off Coleman Flds.)
Islington Crematorium 1D 46
The Islington Ecology Cen. 3A 66
Islington Grn. N1 .... 1B 84
(not continuous)
Islington High St. N1 .... 2A 84
(not continuous)
Islington Mus. 2A 8 (3B 84)
Islington Pk. M. N1 .... 7B 66
Islington Pk. St. N1 .... 7A 66
Islington Pl. N1 .... 1A 84
Islington Sq. N1 .... 1B 84
Islington Tennis Cen. 6J 65
Islip Gdns. HA8: Edg 7E 28
UB5: N'olt 7C 58
Islip Mnr. Rd. UB5: N'olt 7C 58
Islip St. NW5 .... 5G 65
Ismailia Rd. E7 .... 7K 69
Ismaili Cen. 3B 16
Isobel Ho. HA1: Harr 5K 41
Isobel Pl. N15 .... 4F 49
Isola Ct. N1 .... 1C 84
(off Popham Rd.)
Isom Cl. E13 .... 3K 87
Issa Rd. TW3: Houn 4D 112
Issigonis Ho. W3 .... 1B 98
(off Cowley Rd.)
Istra Ho. E20 .... 5E 68
(off Logan Cl.)
Itaska Cotts. WD23: B Hea 1D 26
Ithell Ct. HA0: Wemb 5D 60
Ivanhoe Cl. UB8: Cowl 5A 74
Ivanhoe Dr.
HA3: Kenton 3A 42
Ivanhoe Ho. E3 .... 2A 86
(off Grove Rd.)
Ivanhoe Rd. SE5 .... 3F 121
TW4: Houn 3B 112
Ivaro Cl. RM5: Col R 1J 55
Ivatt Pl. W14 .... 5H 99
Ivatt Way N17 .... 3B 48
Iveagh Av. NW10 .... 2G 79
Iveagh Cl. E9 .... 1K 85
HA6: Nwood 1D 38
NW10 .... 2G 79
Iveagh Ct. BR3: Beck 3E 158
E1 .... 1J 15
Iveagh Ho. SW9 .... 2B 120
SW10 .... 7A 100
(off King's Rd.)
Iveagh Ter. NW10 .... 2G 79
(off Iveagh Av.)
Ivedon Rd. DA16: Well 2C 126
Ive Farm Cl. E10 .... 2C 68
Ive Farm La. E10 .... 2C 68
Iveley Rd. SW4 .... 2G 119
Ivere Dr. EN5: New Bar 6E 20
Iver Ho. N1 .... 1E 84
(off Halcomb St.)
Iverhurst Cl. DA6: Bex 5D 126
Iverna Ct. W8 .... 3J 99
Iverna Gdns. TW14: Felt 5F 111
W8 .... 3J 99
Iverson Rd. NW6 .... 6H 63
Ivers Way CR0: New Ad 7D 170
Ives Rd. E16 .... 5G 87
Ives St. SW3 .... 3D 16 (4C 100)
Ivestor Ter. SE23 .... 7J 121
Ivimey St. E2 .... 3G 85
Ivinghoe Cl. EN1: Enf 1K 23
Ivinghoe Ho. N7 .... 5H 65
Ivinghoe Rd.
RM8: Dag 5B 72
Ivo Pl. N19 .... 3H 65
Ivor Ct. N8 .... 6J 47
NW1 .... 3E 4
(off Gloucester Pl.)
Ivor Gro. SE9 .... 1F 143
The Ivories N1 .... 7C 66
(off Northampton St.)
Ivor Pl. NW1 .... 4E 4 (4D 82)
Ivor St. NW1 .... 7G 65
Ivory Ct. E18 .... 1J 51
TW13: Felt 1J 129
Ivorydown BR1: Broml 4J 141
Ivory Ho. E1 .... 3K 15 (1F 103)
Ivory Pl. W11 .... 7G 81
(off Treadgold St.)
Ivory Sq. SW11 .... 3A 118
Ivybridge Cl. TW1: Twick 7A 114
UB8: Uxb 3A 74
Ivybridge Ct. BR7: Chst 1E 160
(off Old Hill)
NW1 .... 7F 65
(off Lewis St.)
Ivybridge La. WC2 .... 3F 13 (7J 83)
Ivy Bri. Retail Pk. 5K 113
Ivychurch Cl. SE20 .... 7J 139
Ivychurch La. SE17 .... 5F 103
Ivy Cl. HA2: Harr 4D 58
HA5: Eastc 7A 40
TW16: Sun 2A 148
Ivy Cotts. E14 .... 7E 86
UB10: Hil 3C 74
Ivy Ct. SE16 .... 5G 103
(off Argyle Way)
Ivy Cres. W4 .... 4J 97
Ivydale Rd. SE15 .... 3K 121
SM5: Cars 2D 166
Ivyday Gro. SW16 .... 3K 137
Ivydene KT8: W Mole 5D 148
Ivydene Cl. SM1: Sutt 4A 166
Ivy Ho. Ct. IG9: Buck H 2F 37
(off Queen's Rd.)
Ivy Gdns. CR4: Mitc 3H 155
N8 .... 6J 47
Ivy Ho. Rd. UB10: Ick 3D 56
Ivyhouse Rd. RM9: Dag 6D 72
Ivy La. TW4: Houn 4D 112
Ivy Lodge W11 .... 1J 99
(off Notting Hill Ga.)
Ivymount Rd. SE27 .... 3A 138
Ivy Rd. E16 .... 6J 87
E17 .... 6C 50
KT6: Surb 1G 163
N14 .... 7B 22
NW2 .... 4E 62
SE4 .... 4B 122
SW17 .... 5C 136
TW3: Houn 4F 113
Ivy St. N1 .... 2E 84
Ivy Wlk. HA6: Nwood 1G 39
RM9: Dag 6E 72
Ixworth Pl. SW3 .... 5C 16 (5C 100)
Izane Rd. DA6: Bex 4F 127

J

Jacana Ct. E1 .... 3K 15
(off Star Pl.)
Jacaranda Cl. KT3: N Mald 3A 152
Jacaranda Gro. E8 .... 7F 67
Jackass La. BR2: Kes 5K 171
Jack Barnett Way N22 .... 2K 47
Jack Clow Rd. E15 .... 2G 87
Jack Cook Ho. IG11: Bark 7F 71
Jack Cornwell St. E12 .... 4E 70
Jack Dash Way E6 .... 4C 88
Jack Dimmer Cl. SW16 .... 2G 155
Jackets La. HA6: Nwood 1D 38
Jack Goodchild Way
KT1: King T 3H 151
Jack Jones Way RM9: Dag 1F 91
Jacklin Grn. IG8: Wfd G 4D 36
Jackman Ho. E1 .... 1H 103
(off Watts St.)
Jackman M. NW2 .... 3A 62
Jackman St. E8 .... 1H 85
Jacks Farm Way E4 .... 6K 35
Jackson & Joseph Bldg. E1 .... 5K 9
(off Princelet St.)
Jackson Cl. E9 .... 7J 67
UB10: Uxb 7A 56
Jackson Ct. E7 .... 6K 69
Jackson Ho. N11 .... 5B 32
Jackson Rd. BR2: Broml 2D 172
EN4: E Barn 6H 21
IG11: Bark 1H 89
N7 .... 4K 65
UB10: Uxb 7A 56
Jacksons La. N6 .... 7E 46
Jacksons Lane Theatre 6F 47
(off Archway Rd.)
Jacksons Pl. CR0: C'don 1D 168
Jackson St. SE18 .... 6E 106
Jackson's Way CR0: C'don 3C 170
Jackson Way UB2: S'hall 2F 95
Jacks Pl. E1 .... 5J 9
(off Corbet Pl.)
Jack the Ripper Mus. 7G 85
Jack Walker Ct. N5 .... 4B 66
Jacob Ho. DA18: Erith 2D 108
(off Kale Rd.)
Jacobin Lodge N7 .... 5J 65
Jacob Mans. E1 .... 6H 85
(off Commercial Rd.)
Jacob M. HA7: Stan 2F 27
Jacobs Cl. RM10: Dag 4H 73
Jacobs Ct. E1 .... 6G 85
(off Plumber's Row)
Jacobs Ho. E13 .... 3A 88
(off New City Rd.)
Jacobs Island Ho. SE16 .... 3F 103
(off Spa Rd.)
Jacobs M. SW15 .... 4G 117
Jacob St. SE1 .... 6K 15 (2G 103)
Jacob's Well M. W1 .... 6H 5 (5E 82)
Jacotts Ho. W10 .... 4E 80
(off Sutton Way)
Jacquard Ct. SW18 .... 5K 117
(off Courthouse Way)
Jacqueline Cl. UB5: N'olt 1C 76
Jacqueline Creft Ter. N6 .... 6E 46
(off Grange Rd.)
Jacqueline Ho. NW1 .... 1D 82
(off Regent's Pk. Rd.)
Jacqueline Vs. E17 .... 5E 50
(off Shernhall St.)
Jade Cl. E16 .... 6B 88
NW2 .... 7F 45
RM8: Dag 1C 72
Jade Ter. NW6 .... 7A 64
Jaffe Rd. IG1: Ilf 1H 71
Jaffray Pl. SE27 .... 4B 138
Jaffray Rd. BR2: Broml 4B 160
Jaggard Way SW12 .... 7D 118
Jagger Ho. SW11 .... 1D 118
(off Rosenau Rd.)
Jago Cl. SE18 .... 6G 107
Jago Wlk. SE5 .... 7D 102
Jake Russell Wlk. E16 .... 7A 88
Jamaica Rd. CR7: Thor H 7B 156
SE1 .... 7K 15 (2F 103)
SE16 .... 7K 15 (2F 103)
Jamaica St. E1 .... 6J 85
James Allens School Swimming Pool
.... 5E 120
James Anderson Ct. E2 .... 2E 84
(off Kingsland Rd.)
James Av. NW2 .... 5E 62
RM8: Dag 1F 73
James Bedford Cl. HA5: Pinn 2A 40
James Boswell Cl. SW16 .... 4K 137
James Brine Ho. E2 .... 1K 9
(off Ravenscroft St.)
James Campbell Ho. E2 .... 2J 85
(off Old Ford Rd.)
James Clavell Sq. SE18 .... 3F 107
James Cl. E13 .... 2J 87
NW11 .... 6G 45
James Collins Cl. W9 .... 4H 81
James Ct. HA6: Nwood 1H 39
N1 .... 1C 84
(off Raynor Pl.)
NW9 .... 2A 44
UB5: N'olt 2C 76
(off Church Rd.)
James Docherty Ho. E2 .... 2H 85
(off Patriot Sq.)
James Dudson Ct. NW10 .... 7J 61
James Est. CR4: Mitc 2D 154
James Gdns. N22 .... 7G 33
James Hammett Ho. E2 .... 1K 9
(off Ravenscroft St.)
James Hill Ho. W10 .... 4G 81
(off Kensal Rd.)
James Ho. E1 .... 4A 86
(off Solebay St.)
SE16 .... 2K 103
(off Wolfe Cres.)
SW8 .... 7J 101
(off Wyvil Rd.)
W10 .... 4G 81
James Joyce Wlk. SE24 .... 4B 120
James La. E10 .... 7E 50
E11 .... 7F 51
James Leal Cen.
Woodford 5G 37
James Lighthill Ho. WC1 .... 1H 7
(off Penton Ri.)
James Lind Ho. SE8 .... 4B 104
(off Grove St.)
James Middleton Ho. E2 .... 3H 85
(off Middleton St.)
James Morgan M. N1 .... 1C 84
James Newman Ct. SE9 .... 3E 142
Jameson Cl. W3 .... 2J 97
Jameson Ct. E2 .... 2J 85
(off Russia La.)
Jameson Ho. SE11 .... 5G 19
(off Glasshouse Wlk.)
Jameson Lodge N6 .... 6G 47
Jameson St. W8 .... 1J 99
James Pl. N17 .... 1F 49
James Riley Point E15 .... 1E 86
(off Carpenters Rd.)
James's Cotts. TW9: Kew 7G 97
James Stewart Ho. NW6 .... 7H 63
James St. EN1: Enf 5A 24
IG11: Bark 7G 71
TW3: Houn 3H 113
W1 .... 1H 11 (6E 82)
WC2 .... 1F 13 (7J 83)
James Stroud Ho. SE17 .... 5C 102
(off Walworth Pl.)
James Ter. SW14 .... 3K 115
(off Church Path)
Jameston Lodge HA4: Ruis 1H 57
Jamestown Rd. NW1 .... 1F 83
Jamestown Way E14 .... 7F 87
James Voller Way E1 .... 6J 85
James Yd. E4 .... 6A 36
The Jam Factory SE1 .... 3E 102
(off Green Wlk.)
Jamieson Ho. TW4: Houn 6D 112
Jamilah Ho. E16 .... 7E 88
(off University Way)
Jamuna Cl. E14 .... 5A 86
Jane Austen Hall E16 .... 1K 105
(off Wesley Av.)
Jane Austen Ho. SW1 .... 6A 18
(off Churchill Gdns.)
Jane Seymour Ct. SE9 .... 7H 125
Jane St. E1 .... 6H 85
Janet Adegoke Swimming Pool 7C 80
Janet St. E14 .... 3C 104
Janeway Pl. SE16 .... 2H 103
Janeway St. SE16 .... 2G 103
Janice M. IG1: Ilf 2F 71
Jansen Wlk. SW11 .... 3B 118
Janson Cl. E15 .... 5G 69
NW10 .... 3A 62
Janson Rd. E15 .... 5G 69
Jansons Rd. N15 .... 3E 48
Japan Cres. N4 .... 7K 47
Japan Rd. RM6: Chad H 6D 54
Jaquard Ct. E2 .... 2J 85
(off Bishop's Way)
Jardine Rd. E1 .... 7K 85
Jarman Ho. E1 .... 5J 85
(off Jubilee St.)
SE16 .... 4K 103
(off Hawkstone Rd.)
Jarret Ho. E3 .... 3C 86
(off Bow Rd.)
Jarrett Cl. SW2 .... 1B 138
Jarrow Cl. SM4: Mord 5K 153
Jarrow Rd. N17 .... 4H 49
RM6: Chad H 6C 54
SE16 .... 4J 103
Jarrow Way E9 .... 4B 68
Jarvis Cl. EN5: Barn 5A 20
IG11: Bark 1H 89
Jarvis Ho. SE15 .... 1G 121
(off Goldsmith Rd.)
Jarvis Rd. CR2: S Croy 6D 168
SE22 .... 4E 120
Jashoda Ho. SE18 .... 5E 106
(off Connaught M.)
Jasmin Cl. HA6: Nwood 1H 39
Jasmin Ct. SE12 .... 6J 123
Jasmine Cl. BR6: Farnb 2F 173
IG1: Ilf 5F 71
UB1: S'hall 7C 76
Jasmine Ct. SW19 .... 5J 135
Jasmine Gdns. CR0: C'don 3D 170
HA2: Harr 2E 58
Jasmine Gro. SE20 .... 1H 157
Jasmine Ho. SW18 .... 3A 118
Jasmine Rd. RM7: Rush G 2K 73
Jasmine Sq. E3 .... 1B 86
(off Hawthorn Av.)
Jasmine Ter. UB7: W Dray 2C 92
Jasmine Way
KT8: E Mos 4J 149
Jasmin Lodge SE16 .... 5H 103
(off Sherwood Gdns.)
Jasmin Rd. KT19: Ewe 5H 163
Jason Ct. SW9 .... 1A 120
(off Southey Rd.)
W1 .... 7H 5
Jason Wlk. SE9 .... 4E 142
Jasper Av. W7 .... 2K 95
Jasper Cl. EN3: Enf W 1D 24
Jasper Pas. SE19 .... 6F 139
Jasper Rd. E16 .... 6B 88
SE19 .... 5F 139
Jasper Wlk. N1 .... 3D 84
Java Ho. E14 .... 6G 87
Java Wharf SE1 .... 6K 15
(off Shad Thames)
Javelin Ct. HA7: Stan 5G 27
(off William Dr.)
Javelin Way UB5: N'olt 3B 76
Jaycroft EN2: Enf 1F 23
Jay Gdns. BR7: Chst 4D 142
Jay Ho. E3 .... 1B 86
(off Hawthorn Av.)
Jay M. SM5: Cars 3D 166
SW7 .... 7A 10 (2A 100)
Jays St. N1 .... 1K 83
Jazzfern Ter. HA0: Wemb 5A 60
Jean Batten Cl.
SM6: W'gton 7K 167
The Jean Brown Indoor Arena 1H 53
Jean Darling Ho. SW10 .... 6B 100
(off Milman's St.)
Jean Ho. SW17 .... 5C 136
Jeanne Court E14 .... 5A 86
(off Pechora Way)
Jean Pardies Ho. E1 .... 5J 85
(off Jubilee St.)
Jebb Av. SW2 .... 6J 119
(not continuous)
Jebb St. E3 .... 2C 86
Jedburgh Rd. E13 .... 3A 88
Jedburgh St. SW11 .... 4E 118
Jeddo M. W12 .... 2B 98
Jeddo Rd. W12 .... 2B 98
Jeeyas Apts. E16 .... 5H 87
Jefferson Bldg. E14 .... 2C 104
Jefferson Cl. IG2: Ilf 5F 53
W13 .... 3B 96
Jefferson Ho. TW8: Bford 6E 96
UB7: W Dray 2B 92
(off Park Lodge Av.)
Jefferson Pl. BR2: Broml 6B 160
Jefferson Plaza E3 .... 4E 86
(off Hannaford Wlk.)
Jefferson Wlk. SE18 .... 6E 106
Jeffrey Row SE12 .... 5K 123
Jeffrey's Pl. NW1 .... 7G 65
Jeffreys Rd. EN3: Brim 4F 25
SW4 .... 2J 119
Jeffrey's St. NW1 .... 7G 65
Jeffreys Wlk. SW4 .... 2J 119
Jeffs Cl. TW12: Hamp 6F 131
Jeffs Rd. SM1: Sutt 4H 165
Jeger Av. E2 .... 1F 85
Jeken Rd. SE9 .... 4A 124
Jelf Rd. SW2 .... 5A 120
Jelico Point SE16 .... 2B 104
(off Rotherhithe St.)
Jellicoe Gdns. HA7: Stan 6E 26
Jellicoe Ho. E2 .... 2G 85
(off Ropley St.)
Jellicoe Rd. E13 .... 4J 87
N17 .... 7J 33
Jemma Knowles Cl. SW2 .... 1A 138
(off Tulse Hill)
Jemmett Cl. KT2: King T 1H 151
Jemotts Ct. SE14 .... 6K 103
(off Myers La.)
Jem Paterson Ct. HA1: Harr 4J 59
Jengar Cl. SM1: Sutt 4K 165
Jenkins La. IG11: Bark 2G 89
Jenkinson Ho. E2 .... 3K 85
(off Usk St.)
Jenkins Rd. E13 .... 4K 87
Jenner Av. W3 .... 5K 79
Jenner Cl. DA14: Sidc 4A 144
Jenner Ct. N21 .... 5D 22
(off Pennington Dr.)
Jenner Ho. WC1 .... 3F 7
(off Hunter St.)
Jenner Pl. SW13 .... 6D 98
Jenner Rd. N16 .... 3F 67
Jennett Rd. CR0: Wadd 3A 168
Jennifer Ho. E14 .... 6E 86
SE11 .... 4K 19
(off Reedworth St.)
Jennifer Rd. BR1: Broml 3H 141
Jenningsbury Ho. SW3 .... 5D 16
(off Cale St.)
Jennings Cl. KT6: Surb 7C 150
RM8: Dag 1E 72
Jennings Ho. SE10 .... 5F 105
(off Old Woolwich Rd.)
Jennings Rd. SE22 .... 6F 121
Jennings Way EN5: Barn 3A 20
Jenningtree Way DA17: Belv 2J 109
Jenny Hammond Cl. E11 .... 3H 69
Jensen Ho. E3 .... 4C 86
(off Wellington Way)
Jenson Hgts. N1 .... 7K 65
(off Caledonian Rd.)
Jenson Way SE19 .... 7F 139
Jenton Av. DA7: Bex 1E 126
Jephson Ct. SW4 .... 2J 119
Jephson Ho. SE17 .... 6B 102
(off Doddington Gro.)
Jephson Rd. E7 .... 7A 70
Jephson St. SE5 .... 1D 120
Jephtha Rd. SW18 .... 6J 117
Jeppos La. CR4: Mitc 4D 154
Jepson Ho. SW6 .... 1K 117
(off Pearscroft Rd.)
Jerdan Ho. SW6 .... 7J 99
(off North End Rd.)
Jerdan Pl. SW6 .... 7J 99
Jeremiah St. E14 .... 6D 86
Jeremy Bentham Ho. E2 .... 3G 85
(off Mansford St.)
Jeremy's Grn. N18 .... 4C 34
Jermyn St. SW1 .... 4A 12 (1G 101)
Jermyn Street Theatre 3C 12
(off Jermyn St.)
Jernigham Av. IG5: Ilf 2F 53
Jerningham Ct. SE14 .... 1A 122
Jerningham Rd. SE14 .... 2A 122
Jerome Cres. NW8 .... 3C 4 (4C 82)
Jerome Ho. KT1: Hamp W 2D 150
(off Old Bridge St.)
NW1 .... 5D 4
(off Lisson Gro.)
SW7 .... 3A 16
(off Glendower Pl.)
Jerome Pl. KT1: King T 2D 150
(off Wadbrook St.)
Jerome St. E1 .... 5J 9 (4F 85)
Jerome Twr. W3 .... 2H 97
Jerrard St. SE13 .... 3D 122
Jerrold St. N1 .... 1H 9 (2E 84)
Jersey Av. HA7: Stan 2B 42
Jersey Dr. BR5: Pet W 6H 161
Jersey Ho. EN3: Enf W 1E 24
(off Eastfield Rd.)
N1 .... 6C 66
(off Jersey Rd.)
Jersey Rd. E11 .... 1F 69
E16 .... 6A 88
IG1: Ilf 4F 71
N1 .... 6C 66
SW17 .... 6F 137
TW3: Houn 1F 113
TW5: Hest, Isle 1F 113
TW7: Isle 7H 95
W7 .... 2A 96
Jersey St. E2 .... 3H 85
Jerusalem Pas. EC1 .... 4A 8 (4B 84)
Jervis Ct. RM10: Dag 6H 73
SE10 .... 1E 122
(off Blissett St.)
W1 .... 1K 11
Jervis Rd. SW6 .... 6H 99
Jerviston Gdns. SW16 .... 6A 138
Jerwood Space Art Gallery 6C 14
Jesmond Av. HA9: Wemb 6F 61

Jesmond Cl.—Keilder Cl.

Jesmond Cl. CR4: Mitc 3F 155
Jesmond Dene NW3 6A 64
Jesmond Rd. CR0: C'don 7F 157
Jesmond Way HA7: Stan 5K 27
Jessam Av. E5 1H 67
Jessamine Rd. W7 1K 95
Jessel Ho. SW1 3D 18
(off Page St.)
WC1 2E 6
(off Judd St.)
Jessel Mans. W14 6G 99
(off Queen's Club Gdns.)
Jesse Rd. E10 1E 68
Jessett Cl. DA8: Erith 4K 109
Jessica Rd. SW18 6A 118
Jessie Blythe La. N19 7J 47
Jessie Duffett Ho. SE5 7C 102
(off Pitman St.)
Jessie Wood Ct. SW9 7A 102
(off Caldwell St.)
Jessiman Ter. TW17: Shep 5C 146
Jesson Ho. SE17 4D 102
(off Orb St.)
Jessop Av. UB2: S'hall 4D 94
Jessop Ct. N1 2B 84
Jessop Ho. W4 4K 97
(off Kirton Cl.)
Jessop Lodge CR0: C'don 2C 168
(off Tamworth Rd.)
Jessop Pl. W7 3J 95
Jessop Rd. SE24 4B 120
Jessop Sq. E14 1C 104
Jessops Way CR0: Bedd, Mitc 6G 155
Jessup Cl. SE18 4G 107
Jetstar Way UB5: N'olt 3C 76
Jevington Way SE12 1K 141
Jevons Ho. NW8 7B 64
(off Hilgrove Rd.)
Jewel Rd. E17 3C 50
Jewel Sq. E1 7H 85
Jewel Tower 1E 18
(off College M.)
Jewish Mus. 1F 83
Jewry St. EC3 1J 15 (6F 85)
Jew's Row SW18 4K 117
Jews' Wlk. SE26 4H 139
Jeymer Av. NW2 5D 62
Jeymer Dr. UB6: G'frd 1F 77
(not continuous)
Jeypore Rd. SW18 7A 118
Jeypore Rd. Pas. SW18 6A 118
Jhumat Pl. IG1: Ilf 3E 70
(off Roden St.)
Jigger Mast Ho. SE18 3E 106
Jillian Cl. TW12: Hamp 7E 130
Jim Bradley Cl. SE18 4E 106
Jim Griffiths Ho. SW6 6H 99
(off Clem Attlee Ct.)
Jim Veal Dr. N7 6J 65
Joan Cres. SE9 7B 124
Joan Gdns. RM8: Dag 2E 72
Joanna Ho. W6 5E 98
(off Queen Caroline St.)
Joan Rd. RM8: Dag 2E 72
Joan St. SE1 5A 14 (1B 102)
Job Drain Pl. IG11: Bark 2A 90
Jocelin Ho. N1 1K 83
(off Barnsbury Est.)
Jocelyn Rd. TW9: Rich 3E 114
Jocelyn St. SE15 1G 121
Jockey's Flds. WC1 5H 7 (5K 83)
Jodane St. SE8 4B 104
Jodrell Cl. TW7: Isle 1A 114
Jodrell Rd. E3 1B 86
Joe Hunte Ct. SE27 5B 138
Joel St. HA5: Eastc 3J 39
HA6: Nwood 2J 39
Johanna St. SE1 7J 13 (2A 102)
John Adams Ct. N9 2A 34
John Adam St. WC2 3F 13 (7J 83)
John Aird Ct. W2 5A 4
(not continuous)
John Archer Way SW18 6B 118
John Ashby Cl. SW2 6J 119
John Austin Cl. KT2: King T 1F 151
John Baird Ct. SE26 4J 139
John Barker Ct. NW6 7G 63
John Barnes Wlk. E15 6H 69
John Bell Twr. E. E3 2C 86
(off Pancras Way)
John Bell Twr. W. E3 2C 86
(off Pancras Way)
John Betts' Ho. W12 3B 98
John Bond Ho. E3 2B 86
(off Wright's Rd.)
John Bowles Ct. E1 7K 85
(off Schoolhouse La.)
John Bradshaw Rd. N14 1C 32
John Brent Ho. SE8 4K 103
(off Haddonfield)
John Buck Ho. NW10 1B 80
John Bull Pl. W4 4H 97
John Burns Dr. IG11: Bark 7J 71
John Campbell Rd. N16 5E 66
John Carpenter St. EC4 2A 14 (7B 84)
John Cartwright Ho. E2 3H 85
(off Old Bethnal Grn. Rd.)
John Crane St. SE17 6D 102
John Donne Way SE10 7D 104
(off Norman Rd.)
John Drinkwater Cl. E11 7H 51
John Fearon Wlk. W10 3G 81
(off Dart St.)
John Fielden Ho. E2 3H 85
(off Canrobert St.)
John Fisher St. E1 2K 15 (7G 85)
John Goddard Way TW13: Felt 2K 129
John Gooch Dr. EN2: Enf 1G 23
John Harrison Way SE10 3H 105
John Horner M. N1 2C 84
John Hunter Av. SW17 3C 136
John Islip St. SW1 5D 18 (4H 101)
John Kaye Ct. TW17: Shep 5C 146
John Keats Ho. N22 7E 32
John Keats Lodge EN2: Enf 1J 23
John Kennedy Ct. N1 6D 66
(off Newington Grn. Rd.)
John Kennedy Ho. SE16 4K 103
(off Rotherhithe Old Rd.)
John Knight Lodge SW6 7J 99
John Lamb Ct. HA3: W'stone 1J 41
John McDonald Ho. E14 3E 104
(off Glengall Gro.)
John McKenna Wlk. SE16 3G 103
John Masefield Ho. N15 6D 48
(off Fladbury Rd.)
John Maurice Cl. SE17 4D 102
John Nash M. E14 6A 86
(off Commercial Rd.)
John Newton Ct. DA16: Well 3B 126
Johnny Andrews Ho. E1 6K 85
(off Boulcott St.)
John Orwell Sports Cen. 1H 103
John Parker Cl. RM10: Dag 7H 73
John Parker Sq. SW11 3B 118
John Parry Ct. N1 2E 84
(off Hare Wlk.)
John Penn Ho. SE14 7B 104
(off Amersham Va.)
John Penn St. SE13 1D 122
John Penry Ho. SE1 5G 103
(off Marlborough Gro.)
John Perrin Pl. HA3: Kenton 7E 42
John Prince's St. W1 7K 5 (6F 83)
John Pritchard Ho. E1 4G 85
(off Buxton St.)
John Ratcliffe Ho. NW6 3J 81
(off Chippenham Gdns.)
John Rennie Wlk. E1 7H 85
John Riley Ho. E3 5B 86
(off Geoffrey Chaucer Way)
John Roll Way SE16 3G 103
John Ruskin St. SE5 7B 102
John's Av. NW4 4E 44
John Sayer Cl. IG11: Bark 3K 89
John's Cl. TW15: Ashf 4E 128
John Scurr Ho. E14 6A 86
(off Ratcliffe La.)
John Sessions Sq. E1 7K 9
(off Alie St.)
John Silkin La. SE8 5K 103
John's La. SM4: Mord 5A 154
John's M. WC1 4H 7 (4K 83)
John Smith Av. SW6 7H 99
John Smith M. E14 7F 87
Johnson Cl. E8 1G 85
Johnson Ct. SE9 4A 124
Johnson Ho. E2 3G 85
(off Roberta St.)
NW1 2G 83
(off Cranleigh St.)
NW3 7D 64
(off Adelaide Rd.)
SW1 4H 17
(off Cundy St.)
SW8 7H 101
(off Wandsworth Rd.)
W8 2J 99
(off Campden Hill)
Johnson Lock Ct. E1 5A 86
Johnson Lodge W9 5J 81
(off Admiral Wlk.)
Johnson Mans. W14 6G 99
(off Queen's Club Gdns.)
Johnson Rd. BR2: Broml 5B 160
CR0: C'don 7D 156
NW10 1K 79
TW5: Hest 7A 94
Johnsons Cl. SM5: Cars 2D 166
Johnson's Ct. EC4 6A 84
Johnsons Dr. TW12: Hamp 1G 149
Johnsons Ind. Est. UB3: Hayes 2H 93
Johnson's Pl. SW1 6A 18 (5G 101)
Johnson St. E1 7J 85
UB2: S'hall 3A 94
Johnsons Way NW10 4H 79
John Spencer Sq. N1 6B 66
John's Pl. E1 6H 85
John's Ter. CR0: C'don 1E 168
Johnston Cl. SW9 1K 119
Johnston Ct. E10 3D 68
Johnstone Ho. SE13 3F 123
(off Belmont Hill)
Johnstone Rd. E6 3D 88
Johnston Rd. IG8: Wfd G 6D 36
Johnston Ter. NW2 3F 63
John Strachey Ho. SW6 6H 99
(off Clem Attlee Ct.)
John St. E15 1H 87
EN1: Enf 5A 24
SE25 4G 157
TW3: Houn 2C 112
WC1 4H 7 (4K 83)
John Strype Ct. E10 1D 68
John Trundle Ct. EC2 5C 8
John Trundle Highwalk EC2 5C 8
(off Aldersgate St.)
John Tucker Ho. E14 3C 104
(off Mellish St.)
John Watkin Cl. KT19: Eps 7H 163
John Wesley Cl. E6 3D 88
John Wesley Ct. TW1: Twick 1A 132
John Wesley Highwalk EC2 6C 8
(off Aldersgate St.)
John Wetherby Ct. E15 2D 86
(off High St.)
John Wetherby Ct. E. E15 2D 86
(off High St.)
John Wetherby Ct. W. E15 2D 86
(off High St.)
John Wheatley Ho. SW6 6H 99
(off Clem Attlee Ct.)
John Williams Cl. KT2: King T 1D 150
SE14 6K 103
John Wilson St. SE18 3E 106
John Woolley Cl. SE13 4G 123
Joiners Arms Yd. SE5 1D 120
Joiners M. E11 3G 69
Joiners Pl. N5 4D 66
Joiner St. SE1 5F 15 (1D 102)
Joiners Yd. N1 1F 7
(off Caledonia St.)
Jolles Ho. E3 3D 86
(off Bromley High St.)
Jolly M. SW16 2G 155
Jollys La. HA2: Harr 1H 59
UB4: Yead 5B 76
Jonathan St. SE11 5G 19 (5K 101)
Jones Ho. E14 6F 87
(off Blair St.)
Jones M. SW15 4G 117
Jones Rd. E13 4K 87
Jones St. W1 3J 11 (7F 83)
Jones Wlk. TW10: Rich 6F 115
Jonquil Gdns. TW12: Hamp 6E 130
Jonson Cl. CR4: Mitc 4F 155
UB4: Hayes 5J 75
Jonson Ho. SE1 3D 102
(off Burbage Cl.)
Jonzen Wlk. E14 6C 86
Jordan Cl. HA2: Harr 3D 58
Jordan Ct. SW15 4F 117
Jordan Ho. N1 1D 84
(off Colville Est.)
SE4 4K 121
(off St Norbert Rd.)
Jordan Rd. UB6: G'frd 1B 78
Jordans Cl. RM10: Dag 4H 73
TW7: Isle 1J 113
Jordans Ho. NW8 3C 4
(off Capland St.)
Jordans M. TW2: Twick 2J 131
Joscoyne Ho. E1 6H 85
(off Philpot St.)
Joseph Av. W3 6K 79
Joseph Cl. N4 2B 66
Joseph Conrad Ho. SW1 4B 18
(off Tachbrook St.)
Joseph Ct. N16 6E 48
(off Amhurst Pk.)
Joseph Hardcastle Cl. SE14 7K 103
Josephine Av. SW2 5K 119
Joseph Irwin Ho. E14 7B 86
(off Gill St.)
Joseph Lister Ct. E7 7J 69
Joseph M. N7 6A 66
(off Westbourne Rd.)
SE15 5K 121
Joseph Powell Cl. SW12 6G 119
Joseph Priestley Ho. E2 3H 85
(off Canrobert St.)
Joseph Ray Rd. E11 2G 69
Joseph St. E3 4B 86
Joseph Trotter Cl. EC1 2K 7
Joshua Cl. CR2: S Croy 7B 168
N10 7A 32
Joshua Pedley M. E3 2C 86
Joshua St. E14 6E 86
Josiah Dr. UB10: Ick 2E 56
Joslin Av. NW9 3A 44
Joslings Cl. W12 7C 80
Joslyn Cl. EN3: Enf L 1H 25
Jossiline Ct. E3 2A 86
(off Ford St.)
Joubert Mans. SW3 5D 16
(off Jubilee Pl.)
Joubert St. SW11 2D 118
Jowett St. SE15 7F 103
Jowitt Ho. E2 3K 85
(off Morpeth St.)
Joyce Av. N18 5A 34
Joyce Butler Ho. N22 1K 47
Joyce Dawson Way SE28 7A 90
Joyce Latimore Ct. N9 3C 34
(off Colthurst Dr.)
Joyce Page Cl. SE7 6B 106
Joyce Wlk. SW2 6A 120
JOYDENS WOOD 4K 145
Joydens Wood 4H 145
Joydens Wood Rd. DA5: Bexl 4K 145
Joydon Dr. RM6: Chad H 6B 54
Joyners Cl. RM9: Dag 4F 73
Joy of Life Fountain 1E 100
Joystone Ct. EN4: E Barn 4H 21
(off Park Rd.)
Jubb Powell Ho. N15 6E 48
The Jubilee SE10 7D 104
Jubilee Av. E4 6K 35
RM7: Rom 5H 55
TW2: Whitt 1G 131
Jubilee Bldgs. NW8 1B 82
Jubilee Cl. HA5: Pinn 2A 40
KT1: Hamp W 1C 150
NW9 6K 43
NW10 2A 80
RM7: Rom 5H 55
Jubilee Country Pk. 4F 161
Jubilee Country Pk.
Local Nature Reserve 5F 161
Jubilee Ct. BR4: W W'ck 1E 170
E16 6H 87
(off Silvertown Sq.)
E18 1J 51
HA3: Kenton 7E 42
N10 3E 46
SE10 6D 104
(off Dowells St.)
TW3: Houn 3F 113
(off Bristow Rd.)
Jubilee Cres. E14 3E 104
N9 1B 34
Jubilee Dr. HA4: Ruis 4B 58
Jubilee Gdns. UB1: S'hall 5E 76
Jubilee Hall Gym 2F 13
(within Jubilee Hall)
Jubilee Hgts. SE10 1E 122
(off Parkside Av.)
Jubilee Ho. HA7: Stan 5J 27
SE11 4K 19
(off Reedworth St.)
WC1 3G 7
Jubilee La. W5 6E 78
Jubilee Mans. E1 6J 85
(off Jubilee St.)
Jubilee Mkt. 2F 13
(off Covent Gdn.)
Jubilee Mkt. IG8: Wfd G 6F 37
WC2 2F 13
Jubilee Pde. IG8: Wfd G 6F 37
Jubilee Pl. SW3 5D 16 (5C 100)
Jubilee Pl. Shop. Mall 1D 104
(off Bank St.)
Jubilee Rd. SM3: Cheam 7F 165
UB6: G'frd 1B 78
Jubilee St. E1 6J 85
Jubilee Vs. KT10: Esh 7H 149
Jubilee Walkway SE1 3B 14 (7B 84)
Jubilee Way DA14: Sidc 2A 144
KT9: Chess 4G 163
SW19 1K 153
TW14: Felt 1J 129
Jubilee Way Training Track 3H 163
Jubilee Yd. SE1 6J 15
Judd Apts. N8 3K 47
(off Gt. Amwell La.)
Judd St. WC1 2E 6 (3J 83)
Jude St. E16 6H 87
Judge Heath La. UB3: Hayes 6E 74
UB8: Hil 6E 74
Judges Wlk. NW3 3A 64
Juer St. SW11 7C 100
Juett Lodge SE10 4J 105
(off Peartree Way)
Jules Thorn Av. EN1: Enf 4B 24
Julia Ct. E17 5D 50
Julia Gdns. IG11: Bark 2D 90
Julia Garfield M. E16 1K 105
(not continuous)
Juliana Cl. N2 2A 46
Julian Av. W3 7H 79
Julian Cl. EN5: New Bar 3E 20
Julian Ct. NW1 7G 65
(off Rochester Sq.)
Julian Hill HA1: Harr 2J 59
Julian Ho. SE21 4E 138
Julian Pl. E14 5D 104
Julian Taylor Path SE23 2H 139
Julia Scurr St. E3 5C 86
Julia St. NW5 4E 64
Julien Rd. W5 3C 96
Juliet Ho. N1 2E 84
(off Arden Est.)
Juliette Rd. E13 2J 87
Julius Caesar Way HA7: Stan 3J 27
Julius Ho. E14 6F 87
(off E. India Dock Rd.)
Julius Nyerere Cl. N1 1K 83
(off Copenhagen St.)
Junction App. SE13 3E 122
SW11 3C 118
Junction M. W2 7C 4 (6C 82)
Junction Pl. W2 7B 4
Junction Rd. CR2: S Croy 5D 168
E13 2K 87
HA1: Harr 6H 41
(not continuous)
N9 1B 34
N17 3G 49
N19 4G 65
TW8: Bford 4C 96
TW15: Ashf 5E 128
W5 4C 96
Junction Rd. E. RM6: Chad H 7E 54
Junction Rd. W. RM6: Chad H 7E 54
The Junction Shop. Cen. 4C 118
Jungle Falls Adventure Golf 4B 22
Juniper Cl. EN5: Barn 5A 20
HA2: Harr 2F 59
HA9: Wemb 5G 61
KT9: Chess 5F 163
TW13: Felt 3K 129
Juniper Ct. HA3: Hrw W 1K 41
HA6: Nwood 1J 39
KT8: W Mole 4F 149
RM6: Chad H 6B 54
TW3: Houn 4F 113
(off Grove Rd.)
W8 3K 99
(off St Mary's Pl.)
Juniper Cres. NW1 7E 64
Juniper Dr. SW18 4A 118
Juniper Gdns. SW16 1G 155
TW16: Sun 6H 129
Juniper Ho. SE14 7J 103
TW9: Kew 1H 115
W10 4G 81
(off Fourth Av.)
Juniper La. E6 5C 88
Juniper Rd. IG1: Ilf 3E 70
Juniper St. E1 7J 85
Juniper Way UB3: Hayes 7F 75
Juno Ct. SW9 7A 102
(off Caldwell St.)
Juno Ent. Cen. SE14 6K 103
Juno Ho. E3 1C 86
(off Garrison Rd.)
Juno Way SE14 6K 103
Juno Way Ind. Est. SE14 6K 103
Jupiter Ct. E3 2C 86
(off Four Seasons Cl.)
SW9 7A 102
(off Caldwell St.)
UB5: N'olt 3B 76
(off Seaspirite Cl.)
Jupiter Hgts. UB10: Uxb 1B 74
Jupiter Ho. E14 5D 104
(off St Davids Sq.)
E16 6H 87
(off Turner St.)
HA2: Harr 1E 58
Jupiter Way N7 6K 65
Jupp Rd. E15 7F 69
Jupp Rd. W. E15 1F 87
Jura Ho. SE16 4K 103
(off Plough Way)
Jurassic Encounter 3C 152
Jurston Ct. SE1 7K 13
Justice Apts. E1 6K 85
(off Aylward St.)
Justice Wlk. SW3 7C 16 (6C 100)
Justin Cl. TW8: Bford 7D 96
Justines Pl. E2 3K 85
Justin Pl. N22 7E 32
Justin Plaza CR4: Mitc 4C 154
Justin Rd. E4 6G 35
Jute La. EN3: Brim 2F 25
Jutland Cl. N19 1J 65
Jutland Ho. SE5 2C 120
SE18 4C 106
(off Prospect Va.)
Jutland Rd. E13 4J 87
SE6 7E 122
Jutsums Av. RM7: Rom 6H 55
Jutsums Ct. RM7: Rom 6H 55
Jutsums La.
RM7: Rom, Rush G 6H 55
Juxon Cl. HA3: Hrw W 1F 41
Juxon Ho. EC4 1B 14
(off St Paul's Chyd.)
Juxon St. SE11 3H 19 (4K 101)
JVC Bus. Pk. NW2 1C 62

K

Kaduna Cl. HA5: Eastc 5J 39
Kaine Pl. CR0: C'don 7A 158
Kaleidoscope Ho. E20 5E 68
(off Mirabelle Gdns.)
Kale Rd. DA18: Erith 2D 108
Kambala Rd. SW11 3B 118
Kamen Ho. SE1 5G 15
(off Magdalen St.)
Kamrans Pl. HA8: Edg 2F 43
Kane Ct. SE10 4J 105
(off Peartree Way)
Kangley Bri. Rd. SE26 6B 140
Kangley Bus. Cen. SE26 5B 140
Kaplan Dr. N21 5E 22
Kapuvar Cl. SE15 2G 121
Karachi Ho. E15 6G 69
(off Well St.)
Kara Way NW2 4F 63
Karen Ct. BR1: Broml 1H 159
Karen Ter. E11 2H 69
Karenza Ct. HA9: Wemb 7C 42
Kariba Cl. N9 3D 34
Karim M. E17 4A 50
Karma Way HA2: Harr 1E 58
Karner Ho. E20 5D 68
(off Logan Cl.)
Karoline Gdns. UB6: G'frd 2H 77
Kashgar Rd. SE18 4K 107
Kashmir Rd. SE7 7B 106
Kassala Rd. SW11 1D 118
Katella Trad. Est.
IG11: Bark 3J 89
Katharine Ho. CR0: C'don 3C 168
(off Katharine St.)
Katharine St. CR0: C'don 3C 168
Katherine Bell Twr. E3 2C 86
(off Pancras Way)
Katherine Cl. N4 3C 48
NW7 7K 29
SE16 1K 103
Katherine Ct. SE23 1H 139
Katherine Gdns. SE9 4B 124
Katherine Ho. W10 4G 81
(off Portobello Rd.)
Katherine Rd. E6 5A 70
E7 5A 70
TW1: Twick 1A 132
Katherine Sq. W11 1G 99
Kathleen Av. HA0: Wemb 7E 60
W3 5J 79
Kathleen Godfree Ct. SW19 6J 135
Kathleen Rd. SW11 3D 118
Katial House EC1 1B 8
(off Goswell Road)
Kavan Gdns. TW5: Cran 7J 93
Kavsan Pl. TW5: Cran 7J 93
Kayani Av. N4 1C 66
Kayani Ho. E16 6K 87
(off Burrard Rd.)
Kayemoor Rd. SM2: Sutt 6B 166
Kay Rd. SW9 2J 119
Kays Ter. E18 1H 51
Kay St. DA16: Well 1B 126
E2 2G 85
E15 7F 69
(off New Mount St.)
Kean Cres. RM8: Dag 1E 72
Kean Ho. SE17 6B 102
TW1: Twick 6D 114
(off Arosa Rd.)
Kean St. WC2 1G 13 (6K 83)
Keatley Grn. E4 6G 35
Keats CR0: C'don 1C 168
(off Saffron Central Sq.)
Keats Apts. E3 4B 86
(off Wraxall Rd.)
Keats Av. E16 1K 105
Keats Cl. E11 5K 51
EN3: Pond E 5E 24
NW3 4C 64
SE1 4F 103
SE7 7A 106
SW19 6B 136
UB4: Hayes 5J 75
Keats Est. N16 2F 67
(off Kyverdale Rd.)
Keats Gro. NW3 4C 64
Keats House 4C 64
Keats Ho. E2 3J 85
(off Roman Rd.)
HA2: Harr 2J 59
SE5 7C 102
(off Elmington Est.)
SW1 7K 17
Keats Pde. N9 2B 34
(off Church St.)
Keats Pl. EC2 6E 8
(off Moorfields)
Keats Rd. DA16: Well 1J 125
DA17: Belv 3J 109
E10 7D 50
Keats Way CR0: C'don 6J 157
UB6: G'frd 5F 77
UB7: W Dray 4B 92
Kebbell Ter. E7 5K 69
(off Claremont Rd.)
Keble Cl. KT4: Wor Pk 1B 164
UB5: N'olt 5G 59
Keble Pl. SW13 6D 98
Keble St. SW17 4A 136
Kebony Cl. UB7: W Dray 2C 92
Kechill Gdns. BR2: Hayes 7J 159
Kedeston Ct. SM1: Sutt 1K 165
Kedge Ho. E14 3C 104
(off Tiller Rd.)
Kedleston Dr. BR5: St M Cry 5K 161
Kedleston Wlk. E2 3H 85
Kedyngton Ho. HA8: Edg 2J 43
(off Burnt Oak B'way.)
Keeble Cl. SE18 6F 107
Keedonwood Rd. BR1: Broml 5G 141
Keel Cl. IG11: Bark 2C 90
N18 6K 33
SE16 1K 103
Keel Ct. E14 7F 87
(off Newport Av.)
Keele Ho. RM8: Dag 4A 72
Keeley Rd. CR0: C'don 2C 168
Keeley St. WC2 1G 13 (6K 83)
Keeling Ho. E2 2H 85
(off Claredale St.)
Keeling Rd. SE9 5B 124
Keelson Ho. E14 3C 104
(off Mellish St.)
Keely Cl. EN4: E Barn 5H 21
Keemor Cl. SE18 7E 106
Keens Cl. SW16 5H 137
Keens Rd. CR0: C'don 4C 168
Keen's Yd. N1 6B 66
The Keep KT2: King T 6F 133
SE3 2J 123
Keepers Ct. CR2: S Croy 5C 168
(off Warham Rd.)
Keepers M. TW11: Tedd 6C 132
Keepier Wharf E14 7K 85
(off Narrow St.)
Keeping Ct. BR2: Broml 3J 159
(off St Mark's Sq.)
Keeton's Rd. SE16 3H 103
(not continuous)
Keevil Dr. SW19 7F 117
Keibs Way SE17 5E 102
Keighley Cl. N7 5J 65
Keightley Dr. SE9 1G 143
Keilder Cl. UB10: Hil 2C 74

Keildon Rd.—Keswick Cl.

Keildon Rd. SW11 . . . . .4D 118
Keiller Ho. E16 . . . . .1D 106
(off Kennard St.)
The Keir SW19 . . . . .5E 134
Keir Hardie Est. E5 . . . . .1H 67
Keir Hardie Ho. N19 . . . . .7H 47
NW10 . . . . .7B 62
W6 . . . . .6F 99
(off Fulham Pal. Rd.)
Keir Hardie Way IG11: Bark 7A 72
UB4: Yead 3J 75
Keirin Rd. E20 . . . . .5D 68
Keith Connor Cl. SW8 . . . . .3F 119
Keith Gro. W12 . . . . .2C 98
Keith Ho. NW6 . . . . .2K 81
(off Carlton Vale)
SW8 . . . . .7J 101
(off Wheatsheaf La.)
Keith Pk. Rd. UB10: Uxb 7B 56
Keith Rd. E17 . . . . .1B 50
IG11: Bark 2H 89
UB3: Hayes 3G 93
Kelbrook Rd. SE3 . . . . .2C 124
Kelby Ho. N7 . . . . .6K 65
(off Sutterton St.)
Kelby Path SE9 . . . . .3F 143
Kelceda Cl. NW2 . . . . .2C 62
Kelday Hgts. E1 . . . . .6H 85
(off Spencer Way)
Kelf Gro. UB3: Hayes 6H 75
Kelfield Ct. W10 . . . . .6F 81
Kelfield Gdns. W10 . . . . .6E 80
Kelfield M. W10 . . . . .6F 81
Kelland Cl. N8 . . . . .5H 47
Kelland Rd. E13 . . . . .4J 87
Kellaway Rd. SE3 . . . . .2B 124
Keller Cres. E12 . . . . .4B 70
Kellerton Rd. SE13 . . . . .5G 123
Kellet Ho's. WC1 . . . . .2F 7
(off Tankerton St.)
Kellett Ho. N1 . . . . .1E 84
(off Colville Est.)
Kellett Rd. SW2 . . . . .4A 120
Kelling Gdns. CR0: C'don 7B 156
Kellino St. SW17 . . . . .4D 136
Kellner Rd. SE28 . . . . .3K 107
Kellogg Twr. UB6: G'frd 5J 59
Kellow Ho. SE1 . . . . .6E 14
(off Tennis St.)
Kell St. SE1 . . . . .7B 14 (3B 102)
Kelly Av. SE15 . . . . .7F 103
Kelly Cl. NW10 . . . . .3K 61
TW17: Shep 2G 147
Kelly Ct. E14 . . . . .7C 86
(off Garford St.)
Kelly M. W9 . . . . .5H 81
Kelly St. NW1 . . . . .6F 65
Kelly Ter. E17 . . . . .4C 50
Kelly Way RM6: Chad H 5E 54
Kelman Cl. SW4 . . . . .2H 119
Kelmore Gro. SE22 . . . . .4G 121
Kelmscott Cl. E17 . . . . .1B 50
Kelmscott Gdns. W12 . . . . .3C 98
Kelmscott House 5D 98
Kelmscott Rd. SW11 . . . . .5C 118
Kelross Pas. N5 . . . . .4C 66
Kelross Rd. N5 . . . . .4C 66
Kelsall Cl. SE3 . . . . .2K 123
Kelsall M. TW9: Kew 1H 115
Kelsey Cl. KT9: Chess 7D 162
Kelsey Ga. BR3: Beck 2D 158
Kelsey La. BR3: Beck 2C 158
Kelsey Pk. Av. BR3: Beck 2D 158
Kelsey Pk. Rd. BR3: Beck 2C 158
Kelsey Sq. BR3: Beck 2C 158
Kelsey St. E2 . . . . .4G 85
Kelsey Way BR3: Beck 3C 158
Kelson Ho. E14 . . . . .3E 104
E16 . . . . .2K 105
Kelso Pl. W8 . . . . .3K 99
Kelso Rd. SM5: Cars 7A 154
Kelston Rd. IG6: Ilf 2F 53
Kelvedon Cl. KT2: King T 6G 133
Kelvedon Ho. SW8 . . . . .1J 119
Kelvedon Rd. SW6 . . . . .7H 99
Kelvedon Way IG8: Wfd G 6J 37
Kelvin Av. N13 . . . . .6E 32
TW11: Tedd 6J 131
Kelvinbrook KT8: W Mole 3F 149
Kelvin Cl. KT19: Ewe 6G 163
Kelvin Ct. SE20 . . . . .1H 157
TW7: Isle 2J 113
W11 . . . . .7J 81
(off Kensington Pk. Rd.)
Kelvin Cres. HA3: Hrw W 7D 26
Kelvin Dr. TW1: Twick 6B 114
Kelvin Gdns. CR0: Wadd 7J 155
UB1: S'hall 6E 76
Kelvin Gro. KT9: Chess 3D 162
SE26 . . . . .3H 139
Kelvington Cl. CR0: C'don 7A 158
Kelvington Rd. SE15 . . . . .5K 121
Kelvin Ho. SE26 . . . . .4B 140
(off Worsley Bri. Rd.)
Kelvin Ind. Est. UB6: G'frd 7F 59
Kelvin Pde. BR6: Orp 1J 173
Kelvin Rd. DA16: Well 3A 126
N5 . . . . .4C 66
Kelway Ho. W14 . . . . .5H 99
Kember St. N1 . . . . .7K 65
Kemble Dr. BR2: Broml 3C 172
Kemble Ho. SW9 . . . . .3B 120
(off Barrington Rd.)
Kemble Rd. CR0: Wadd 3B 168
N17 . . . . .1G 49
SE23 . . . . .1K 139
Kemble St. WC2 . . . . .1G 13 (6K 83)
Kemerton Rd. BR3: Beck 2D 158
CR0: C'don 7F 157
SE5 . . . . .3C 120
Kemey's St. E9 . . . . .5A 68
Kemmel Rd. RM9: Dag 1B 90
Kemnal Rd. BR7: Chst 4H 143
Kemp NW9 .1B 44
(off Quakers Course)
Kemp Ct. SW8 . . . . .7J 101
(off Hartington Rd.)
Kempe Ho. SE1 . . . . .3D 102
(off Burbage Cl.)
Kempe Rd. NW6 . . . . .2F 81
Kemp Gdns. CR0: C'don 6C 156
Kemp Ho. E2 . . . . .2K 85
(off Sewardstone Rd.)
E6 . . . . .6E 70
W1 . . . . .2C 12
(off Berwick St.)
Kempis Way SE22 . . . . .5E 120
Kemplay Rd. NW3 . . . . .4B 64
Kemp Rd. RM8: Dag 1D 72
Kemps Ct. W1 . . . . .1B 12
(off Hopkins St.)
Kemps Dr. E14 . . . . .7C 86
HA6: Nwood 1H 39
Kempsford Gdns. SW5 . . . . .5J 99
Kempsford Rd. SE11 . . . . . .4K 19 (4B 102)
(not continuous)
Kemps Gdns. SE13 . . . . .5E 122
Kempshott Rd. SW16 . . . . .7H 137
Kempson Rd. SW6 . . . . .1J 117
Kempthorne Rd. SE8 . . . . .4B 104
Kempton Av. TW16: Sun 1K 147
UB5: N'olt 6E 58
Kempton Cl. DA8: Erith 6J 109
UB10: Ick 4E 56
Kempton Ct. E1 . . . . .5H 85
TW16: Sun 1K 147
Kempton Ga. Bus. Cen.
TW12: Hamp 1D 148
Kempton Ho. N1 . . . . .1E 84
(off Hoxton St.)
Kempton Nature Reserve 6B 130
Kempton Pk. Racecourse 7K 129
Kempton Rd. E6 . . . . .1D 88
The Kemptons TW15: Ashf 2C 128
Kempton Wlk. CR0: C'don 6A 158
Kempt St. SE18 . . . . .6E 106
Kemsing Cl. BR2: Hayes 2H 171
CR7: Thor H 4C 156
DA5: Bexl 7E 126
Kemsing Ho. SE1 . . . . .7F 15
(off Long La.)
Kemsing Rd. SE10 . . . . .5J 105
Kemsley SE13 . . . . .5D 122
Kemsley Ct. W13 . . . . .1C 96
Kenbrook Ho. NW5 . . . . .5G 65
W14 . . . . .3H 99
Kenbury Cl. UB10: Ick 3C 56
Kenbury Gdns. SE5 . . . . .2C 120
Kenbury Mans. SE5 . . . . .2C 120
(off Kenbury St.)
Kenbury St. SE5 . . . . .2C 120
Kenchester Cl. SW8 . . . . .7J 101
Kencot Way DA18: Erith 2F 109
Kendal NW1 .1K 5
(off Augustus St.)
Kendal Av. IG11: Bark 1J 89
N18 . . . . .4J 33
W3 . . . . .4G 79
Kendal Cl. IG8: Wfd G 2C 36
N20 . . . . .2H 31
SW9 . . . . .7B 102
TW14: Felt 1H 129
UB4: Hayes 2G 75
Kendal Ct. W3 . . . . .5G 79
Kendale Rd. BR1: Broml 5G 141
Kendal Gdns. N18 . . . . .4J 33
SM1: Sutt 2A 166
Kendal Ho. E9 . . . . .1J 85
N1 . . . . .2K 83
(off Priory Grn. Est.)
SE20 . . . . .2G 157
(off Derwent Rd.)
Kendall Av. BR3: Beck 2A 158
CR2: Sande 7D 168
Kendall Ct. DA15: Sidc 3A 144
SW19 . . . . .6B 136
Kendall Ho. W14 . . . . .4H 99
(off Warwick La.)
Kendall Lodge BR1: Broml 1K 159
(off Willow Tree Wlk.)
Kendall Mnr. HA6: Nwood 1D 38
Kendall Pl. W1 . . . . .6G 5 (5E 82)
Kendall Rd. BR3: Beck 2A 158
SE18 . . . . .1C 124
TW7: Isle 2A 114
Kendalmere Cl. N10 . . . . .1F 47
Kendal Pde. N18 . . . . .4J 33
Kendal Pl. SW15 . . . . .5H 117
Kendal Rd. NW10 . . . . .4C 62
Kendal Steps W2 . . . . .1D 10
Kendal St. W2 . . . . .1D 10 (6C 82)
Kender Est. SE14 . . . . .1J 121
(off Queen's Rd.)
Kender St. SE14 . . . . .7J 103
Kendoa Rd. SW4 . . . . .4H 119
Kendon Cl. E11 . . . . .5K 51
Kendon Ho. E15 . . . . .7F 69
(off Bryant St.)
Kendra Hall Rd. CR2: S Croy 7B 168
Kendrey Gdns.
TW2: Whitt 7J 113
Kendrick Ct. SE15 . . . . .1H 121
(off Colmore M.)
Kendrick M. SW7 . . . . .3A 16 (4B 100)
Kendrick Pl. SW7 . . . . .4A 16 (4B 100)
Kenelm Cl. HA1: Harr 3A 60
Kenerne Dr. EN5: Barn 5B 20
KEN FRIAR BRI. 4A 66
Kenilford Rd. SW12 . . . . .7F 119
Kenilworth Av. E17 . . . . .2C 50
HA2: Harr 4D 58
SW19 . . . . .5J 135
Kenilworth Ct. SW15 . . . . .3G 117
(off Lwr. Richmond Rd.)
Kenilworth Cres. EN1: Enf 1K 23
Kenilworth Gdns. IG3: Ilf 2K 71
SE18 . . . . .2F 125
UB1: S'hall 3D 76
UB4: Hayes 5H 75
Kenilworth Rd. BR5: Pet W 6G 161
E3 . . . . .2A 86
HA8: Edg 3D 28
KT17: Ewe 5C 164
NW6 . . . . .1H 81
SE20 . . . . .1K 157
TW15: Ashf 3A 128
W5 . . . . .1E 96
Kenley N17 . . . . .2D 48
(off Gloucester Rd.)
Kenley Av. NW9 . . . . .1A 44
Kenley Cl. BR7: Chst 3J 161
DA5: Bexl 7G 127
EN4: E Barn 4H 21
Kenley Gdns. CR7: Thor H 4B 156
Kenley Pl. UB10: Uxb 1A 74
Kenley Rd. KT1: King T 2J 151
SW19 . . . . .2J 153
TW1: Twick 6B 114
Kenley Wlk. SM3: Cheam 4F 165
W11 . . . . .7G 81
Kenlor Rd. SW17 . . . . .5B 136
Kenmare Cl. UB10: Ick 2F 57
Kenmare Dr. CR4: Mitc 7D 136
N17 . . . . .2F 49
Kenmare Gdns. N13 . . . . .4H 33
Kenmare Rd. CR7: Thor H 6A 156
Kenmere Gdns. HA0: Wemb 1G 79
Kenmere Rd. DA16: Well 2C 126
Kenmont Gdns. NW10 . . . . .3D 80
(not continuous)
Kenmore Av.
HA3: Kenton, W'stone 4A 42
Kenmore Cl. TW9: Kew 7G 97
Kenmore Ct. NW6 . . . . .7K 63
(off Acol Rd.)
Kenmore Cres. UB4: Hayes 3H 75
Kenmore Gdns. HA8: Edg 2H 43
Kenmore Rd. HA3: Kenton 3D 42
Kenmure Rd. E8 . . . . .5H 67
Kenmure Yd. E8 . . . . .5H 67
Kennacraig Cl. E16 . . . . .1J 105
Kennard Ho. SW11 . . . . .2E 118
Kennard Rd. E15 . . . . .7F 69
N11 . . . . .5J 31
Kennard St. E16 . . . . .1D 106
SW11 . . . . .1E 118
Kennedy Av. EN3: Pond E 6D 24
Kennedy Cl. BR5: Pet W 1H 173
CR4: Mitc 1E 154
E13 . . . . .2J 87
Kennedy Ct. TW15: Ashf 5E 128
WD23: B Hea 2C 26
Kennedy Cox Ho. E16 . . . . .5H 87
(off Burke St.)
Kennedy Ho. SE11 . . . . .5G 19
(off Vauxhall Wlk.)
Kennedy Path W7 . . . . .4K 77
Kennedy Rd. IG11: Bark 1J 89
W7 . . . . .5J 77
Kennedy Wlk. SE17 . . . . .4D 102
(off Elsted St.)
Kennet Cl. E17 . . . . .3F 51
SW11 . . . . .4B 118
Kennet Ct. W9 . . . . .5J 81
(off Elmfield Way)
Kenneth Av. IG1: Ilf 4F 71
Kenneth Campbell Ho. NW8 . . . . .3B 4
(off Orchardson St.)
Kenneth Chambers Ct.
IG8: Wfd G 6H 37
Kenneth Ct. SE11 . . . . . . .3K 19 (4A 102)
Kenneth Cres. NW2 . . . . .5D 62
Kenneth Gdns. HA7: Stan 6F 27
Kenneth More Rd. IG1: Ilf 3F 71
Kenneth More Theatre 3F 71
Kennet Ho. NW8 . . . . .4B 4
(off Church St. Est.)
SW18 . . . . .4J 117
(off Enterprise Way)
Kenneth Rd. RM6: Chad H 7D 54
Kenneth Robbins Ho. N17 . . . . .7C 34
Kenneth Way W5 . . . . .7F 79
Kenneth Younger Ho. SW6 . . . . .6H 99
(off Clem Attlee Ct.)
Kennet Rd. TW7: Isle 3K 113
W9 . . . . .4H 81
Kennet Sq. CR4: Mitc 1C 154
Kennet St. E1 . . . . .1G 103
Kennett Ct. W4 . . . . .7H 97
Kennett Dr. UB4: Yead 5C 76
Kennet Wharf La. EC4 . . . . .3D 14 (7C 84)
KENNINGHALL 5D 34
Kenninghall Rd. E5 . . . . .3G 67
N18 . . . . .5D 34
Kenning Ho. N1 . . . . .1E 84
(off Colville Est.)
Kenning St. SE16 . . . . .2J 103
Kennings Way SE11 . . . . . .5K 19 (5A 102)
Kenning Ter. N1 . . . . .1E 84
KENNINGTON 7K 19 (6A 102)
Kennington Grn. SE11 . . . . .6J 19 (5A 102)
Kennington La. SE11 . . . . .6G 19 (5K 101)
KENNINGTON OVAL 6A 102
Kennington Oval SE11 . . . .7H 19 (6K 101)
Kennington Pal. Ct.
SE11 . . . . .5J 19
Kennington Pk. Gdns.
SE11 . . . . .7K 19 (6B 102)
Kennington Pk. Ho. SE11 . . . . .6K 19
Kennington Pk. Pl.
SE11 . . . . .7K 19 (6A 102)
Kennington Pk. Rd.
SE11 . . . . .7K 19 (6A 102)
Kennington Rd. SE1 . . . . . . .1J 19 (3A 102)
SE11 . . . . .1J 19 (3A 102)
Kennistoun Ho. NW5 . . . . .5G 65
Kennoldes SE21 . . . . .2D 138
(off Croxted Rd.)
Kenny Dr. SM5: Cars 7E 166
Kennyland Ct. NW4 . . . . .6D 44
(off Hendon Way)
Kenrick Pl. W1 . . . . .6G 5 (5E 82)
KENSAL GREEN 3E 80
Kensal Ho. W10 . . . . .4F 81
(off Ladbroke Gro.)
KENSAL RISE 2F 81
Kensal Rd. W10 . . . . .4G 81
KENSAL TOWN 4G 81
Kensal Wharf W10 . . . . .4F 81
KENSINGTON 3J 99
Kensington Arc. W8 . . . . .2K 99
(off Kensington High St.)
Kensington Av. CR7: Thor H 1A 156
E12 . . . . .6C 70
Kensington Bus. Cen. SW3 . . . . . . .1D 16
Kensington Cen. W14 . . . . .4G 99
(not continuous)
Kensington Chu. Ct. W8 . . . . .2K 99
Kensington Chu. St. W8 . . . . .1J 99
Kensington Chu. Wlk. W8 . . . . .2K 99
(not continuous)
Kensington Cl. N11 . . . . .6K 31
Kensington Ct. SE16 . . . . .1K 103
(off King & Queen Wharf)
W8 . . . . .2K 99
Kensington Ct. Gdns. W8 . . . . .3K 99
(off Kensington Ct. Pl.)
Kensington Ct. Mans. W8 . . . . .2K 99
(off Kensington Ct.)
Kensington Ct. M. W8 . . . . .3K 99
(off Kensington Ct. Pl.)
Kensington Ct. Pl. W8 . . . . .3K 99
Kensington Dr.
IG8: Wfd G 2B 52
Kensington Gdns. 4A 10 (1A 100)
Kensington Gdns. IG1: Ilf 2D 70
KT1: King T 3D 150
Kensington Gdns. Sq. W2 . . . . .6K 81
Kensington Ga. W8 . . . . .3A 100
Kensington Gore SW7 . . . . .7A 10 (2A 100)
Kensington Hall Gdns. W14 . . . . .5H 99
Kensington Hgts. HA1: Harr 6K 41
(off Sheepcote Rd.)
W8 . . . . .1J 99
Kensington High St. W8 . . . . .3H 99
W14 . . . . .3H 99
Kensington Ho. IG8: Wfd G 7K 37
SW11 . . . . .7F 101
(off Palmer Rd.)
UB7: W Dray 2B 92
(off Park Lodge Av.)
W8 . . . . .2K 99
(off Kensington Ct.)
W14 . . . . .2F 99
Kensington Leisure Cen. 7G 81
Kensington Mall W8 . . . . .1J 99
Kensington Mans. SW5 . . . . .5J 99
(off Trebovir Rd.)
Kensington Palace 1K 99
Kensington Pal. Gdns. W8 . . . . .1K 99
Kensington Pk. Gdns. W11 . . . . .7H 81
Kensington Pk. M. W11 . . . . .6H 81
Kensington Pk. Rd. W11 . . . . .6H 81
Kensington Pl. W8 . . . . .1J 99
Kensington Rd. RM7: Rom 6J 55
SW7 . . . . .2A 100
UB5: N'olt 3E 76
W8 . . . . .2K 99
Kensington Sq. W8 . . . . .3K 99
Kensington Ter. CR2: S Croy 7D 168
Kensington Village W14 . . . . .4H 99
Kensington W. W14 . . . . .4G 99
Kensworth Ho. EC1 . . . . .2F 9
(off Cranwood St.)
Kent Av. DA16: Well 5K 125
RM9: Dag 4G 91
W13 . . . . .5B 78
Kent Bldg. E14 . . . . .6G 87
Kent Cl. BR6: Chels 6J 173
CR4: Mitc 4J 155
Kent Ct. E2 .2F 85
NW9 . . . . .2A 44
Kent Dr. EN4: Cockf 4K 21
TW11: Tedd 5J 131
Kentford Way UB5: N'olt 1C 76
Kent Gdns. HA4: Ruis 6J 39
W13 . . . . .5B 78
Kent Ga. Way CR0: Addtn 6B 170
Kent Ho. SE1 . . . . .5F 103
SW1 . . . . .5C 18
(off Aylesford St.)
W4 . . . . .5A 98
(off Devonshire St.)
W8 . . . . .2K 99
(off Kensington Ct.)
W11 . . . . .1H 99
(off Boyne Ter. M.)
Kent Ho. La. BR3: Beck 6A 140
Kent Ho. Rd. BR3: Beck 1K 157
SE26 . . . . .5A 140
Kent House Station Approach
BR3: Beck 1A 158
Kentish Bldgs. SE1 . . . . . . .5E 14 (2D 102)
Kentish Pl. SE2 . . . . .3A 108
Kentish Rd. DA17: Belv 4G 109
KENTISH TOWN 5F 65
Kentish Town Ind. Est.
NW5 . . . . .5F 65
Kentish Town Rd. NW1 . . . . .7F 65
NW5 . . . . .7F 65
Kentish Town Sports Cen. 6F 65
Kentish Way BR1: Broml 2K 159
BR2: Broml 2K 159
Kentlea Rd. SE28 . . . . .2J 107
Kentmere Ho. SE15 . . . . .6J 103
Kentmere Mans. W5 . . . . .4B 78
Kentmere Rd. SE18 . . . . .4J 107
KENTON 5C 42
Kenton Av. HA1: Harr 7K 41
TW16: Sun 2B 148
UB1: S'hall 7E 76
Kenton Ct. HA3: Kenton 6B 42
SE26 . . . . .4A 140
(off Adamsrill Rd.)
TW1: Twick 6D 114
W14 . . . . .3H 99
Kentone Ct. SE25 . . . . .4H 157
Kenton Gdns. HA3: Kenton 5C 42
Kenton Ho. E1 . . . . .4J 85
(off Mantus Cl.)
Kentonian Cl. HA3: Kenton 5B 42
Kenton La.
HA3: Hrw W, Kenton, W'stone
. . . . .6E 26
Kenton Pk. Av. HA3: Kenton 5D 42
Kenton Pk. Cl. HA3: Kenton 4C 42
Kenton Pk. Cres.
HA3: Kenton 4D 42
Kenton Pk. Mans. HA3: Kenton 5C 42
(off Kenton Rd.)
Kenton Pk. Pde. HA3: Kenton 5C 42
Kenton Pk. Rd. HA3: Kenton 4C 42
Kenton Rd. E9 . . . . .6K 67
HA1: Harr 7K 41
HA3: Kenton 6A 42
Kenton St. WC1 . . . . .3E 6 (4J 83)
Kenton Way UB4: Hayes 3G 75
Kent Pk. Ind. Est. SE15 . . . . .6H 103
Kent Pas. NW1 . . . . .3E 4 (4D 82)
Kent Rd.
BR4: W W'ck 1D 170
KT1: King T 3D 150
KT8: E Mos 4G 149
N21 . . . . .1J 33
RM10: Dag 5H 73
TW9: Kew 7G 97
W4 . . . . .3J 97
Kent's Pas. TW12: Hamp 1D 148
Kent St. E2 .2F 85
E13 . . . . .3A 88
Kent Ter. NW1 . . . . .2D 4 (3C 82)
Kent Vw. Gdns. IG3: Ilf 2J 71
Kent Wlk. SW9 . . . . .4B 120
Kent Way KT6: Surb 3E 162
Kentwell Cl. SE4 . . . . .4A 122
Kent Wharf SE8 . . . . .7D 104
(off Creekside)
Kentwode Grn. SW13 . . . . .7C 98
Kent Yd. SW7 . . . . .7D 10 (2C 100)
Kenver Av. N12 . . . . .6G 31
Kenward Rd. SE9 . . . . .5A 124
Kenward Way SW11 . . . . .2E 118
Ken Way HA9: Wemb 3J 61
Kenway RM5: Col R 2J 55
Kenway Rd. SW5 . . . . .4K 99
Ken Wilson Ho. E2 . . . . .2G 85
(off Pritchards Rd.)
Kenwood Av. N14 . . . . .5C 22
Kenwood Cl. NW3 . . . . .1B 64
UB7: Sip .6C 92
Kenwood Ct. NW9 . . . . .4J 43
(off Elmwood Cres.)
Kenwood Dr. BR3: Beck 2E 158
Kenwood Gdns. E18 . . . . .3K 51
IG2: Ilf 5E 52
IG5: Ilf 4E 52
Kenwood House 1C 64
Kenwood Ho. SW9 . . . . .4B 120
Kenwood Pl. N6 . . . . .1D 64
Kenwood Rd. N6 . . . . .6D 46
N9 . . . . .1B 34
Kenworthy Rd. E9 . . . . .5A 68
Kenwrick Ho. N1 . . . . .1K 83
(off Barnsbury Est.)
Kenwyn Dr. NW2 . . . . .2A 62
Kenwyn Lodge N2 . . . . .4D 46
Kenwyn Rd. SW4 . . . . .4H 119
SW20 . . . . .1E 152
Kenya Rd. SE7 . . . . .7B 106
Kenyngton Ct. TW16: Sun 5J 129
Kenyngton Dr. TW16: Sun 5J 129
Kenyngton Pl.
HA3: Kenton 5C 42
Kenyon Ho. SE5 . . . . .7C 102
(off Camberwell Rd.)
Kenyon Mans. W14 . . . . .6G 99
(off Queen's Club Gdns.)
Kenyon St. SW6 . . . . .1F 117
Keogh Rd. E15 . . . . .6G 69
Kepler Ho. SE10 . . . . .5H 105
(off Armitage Rd.)
Kepler Rd. SW4 . . . . .4J 119
Keppel Ho. SE8 . . . . .5B 104
SW3 . . . . .4C 16
(off Elystan St.)
Keppel Rd. E6 . . . . .7D 70
RM9: Dag 4E 72
Keppel Row SE1 . . . . .5C 14 (1C 102)
Keppel St. WC1 . . . . .5D 6 (5H 83)
Kepplestone M.
BR3: Beck 2E 158
Kerbela St. E2 . . . . .3K 9 (4G 85)
Kerbey St. E14 . . . . .6D 86
Kerfield Cres. SE5 . . . . .1D 120
Kerfield Pl. SE5 . . . . .1D 120
Kerlin Vw. SW16 . . . . .2G 155
Kerr Cl. CR2: Sels 7A 170
Kerridge Ct. N1 . . . . .6E 66
(off Balls Pond Rd.)
Kerrier Ho. SW10 . . . . .7A 100
(off Stadium St.)
Kerrington Ct. W10 . . . . .4G 81
(off Wornington Rd.)
W12 . . . . .2E 98
(off Uxbridge Rd.)
Kerris Ho. SE11 . . . . .5K 19
(off Tavy Cl.)
Kerrison Pl. W5 . . . . .1D 96
Kerrison Rd. E15 . . . . .1F 87
SW11 . . . . .3C 118
W5 . . . . .1D 96
Kerrison Vs. W5 . . . . .1D 96
Kerry Av. HA7: Stan 4H 27
Kerry Cl. E16 . . . . .6K 87
N13 . . . . .2E 32
Kerry Ct. HA7: Stan 4J 27
Kerry Ho. E1 . . . . .6J 85
(off Sidney St.)
Kerry Path SE14 . . . . .6B 104
Kerry Rd. SE14 . . . . .6B 104
Kerscott Ho. E3 . . . . .3D 86
(off Rainhill Way)
Kersey Gdns. SE9 . . . . .4C 142
Kersfield Ho. SW15 . . . . .6F 117
Kersfield Rd. SW15 . . . . .6F 117
Kershaw Cl. SW18 . . . . .6B 118
Kershaw Rd. RM10: Dag 3G 73
Kersley M. SW11 . . . . .1D 118
Kersley Rd. N16 . . . . .2E 66
Kersley St. SW11 . . . . .2D 118
Kerstin Cl. UB3: Hayes 7H 75
Kerswell Cl. N15 . . . . .5E 48
Kerwick Cl. N7 . . . . .7J 65
Keslake Mans. NW10 . . . . .2F 81
(off Station Ter.)
Keslake Rd. NW6 . . . . .2F 81
Kessock Cl. N17 . . . . .5H 49
Kestlake Rd. DA5: Bexl 6C 126
KESTON 5A 172
Keston Av. BR2: Kes 5A 172
Keston Cl. DA16: Well 7C 108
N18 . . . . .3J 33
Keston Ct. DA5: Bexl 7F 127
KT5: Surb 5F 151
(off Cranes Pk.)
Keston Gdns. BR2: Kes 4A 172
Keston Ho. SE17 . . . . .5E 102
(off Kinglake Est.)
KESTON MARK 4C 172
KESTON MARK 3C 172
Keston Pk. Cl. BR2: Kes 3D 172
Keston Rd. CR7: Thor H 6A 156
N17 . . . . .3D 48
SE15 . . . . .3G 121
Keston Windmill 5B 172
Kestrel Av. E6 . . . . .5C 88
SE24 . . . . .5B 120
Kestrel Cl. KT2: King T 4D 132
NW9 . . . . .2A 44
NW10 . . . . .5K 61
Kestrel Ct. CR2: S Croy 6C 168
E3 . . . . .2C 86
(off Four Seasons Cl.)
E17 . . . . .2K 49
HA4: Ruis 2G 57
SM6: W'gton 5G 167
Kestrel Ho. EC1 . . . . .1C 8
(off Pickard St.)
EN3: Pond E 5F 25
SE10 . . . . .1E 122
(off Parkside Av.)
Kestrel Pl. SE14 . . . . .6A 104
Kestrel Way CR0: New Ad 7F 171
UB3: Hayes 2F 93
Keswick Av. SW15 . . . . .5A 134
SW19 . . . . .2J 153
TW17: Shep 3G 147
Keswick B'way. SW15 . . . . .5H 117
(off Up. Richmond Rd.)
Keswick Cl. SM1: Sutt 4A 166

Keswick Ct.—Kingsmead

Keswick Ct. BR2: Broml 4H 159
SE6 1H 141
SE13 5D 122
Keswick Gdns. HA4: Ruis 6F 39
HA9: Wemb 4E 60
IG4: Ilf 4C 52
Keswick Ho. SE5 2C 120
Keswick M. W5 1E 96
Keswick Rd. BR4: W W'ck 2G 171
BR6: Orp 1K 173
DA7: Bex 1G 127
SW15 5G 117
TW2: Whitt 6G 113
Ketch St. IG11: Bark 1H 89
Kettering Ct. CR7: Thor H 4C 156
Kettering St. SW16 6G 137
Kett Gdns. SW2 5K 119
Kettlebaston Rd. E10 1B 68
Kettleby Ho. *SW9* 3B 120
(off Barrington Rd.)
Kettlewell Cl. N11 6K 31
Ketton Ho. *W10* 4E 80
(off Sutton Way)
Kevan Ct. E17 4C 50
Kevan Ho. SE5 7C 102
Kevelioc Rd. N17 1C 48
Kevin Cl. TW4: Houn 2B 112
Kevington Cl. BR5: St P 4K 161
Kevington Dr. BR5: St P 4K 161
BR7: Chst 4K 161
Kevtar Gdn. E3 3B 86
KEW 1G 115
KEW BRIDGE 6G 97
Kew Bri. Arches TW9: Kew 6G 97
Kew Bri. Ct. W4 5G 97
Kew Bri. Distribution Cen.
TW8: Bford 5F 97
KEW BRIDGE JUNCTION 5F 97
Kew Bri. Rd. TW8: Bford 6F 97
Kew Ct. KT2: King T 1E 150
Kew Cres. SM3: Cheam 3G 165
Kew Foot Rd. TW9: Rich 4E 114
Kew Gdns. 7E 96
Kew Gdns. Rd. TW9: Kew 7F 97
KEW GREEN 7G 97
Kew Grn. TW9: Kew 6F 97
Kew Mdw. Path TW9: Kew 2J 115
(Clifford Av.)
TW9: Kew 1H 115
(Magnolia Ct.)
Kew Palace 7E 96
Kew Retail Pk.
Kew 1H 115
Kew Riverside Pk. TW9: Kew 7H 97
Kew Rd. TW9: Kew, Rich 6G 97
Key Cl. E1 4J 85
Keyes Ho. *SW1* 6C 18
(off Dolphin Sq.)
Keyes Rd. NW2 5F 63
Keyham Ho. *W2* 5J 81
(off Westbourne Pk. Rd.)
Key Ho. SE11 7K 19 (6A 102)
Keymer Pl. E14 6B 86
Keymer Rd. SW2 2K 137
Keynes Cl. N2 4D 46
Keynes Ct. *SE28* 7B 90
(off Attlee Rd.)
Keynsham Av. IG8: Wfd G 4B 36
Keynsham Gdns. SE9 5C 124
Keynsham Rd. SE9 5B 124
SM4: Mord 1K 165
Keynsham Wlk. SM4: Mord 1K 165
Keys Ct. *CR0: C'don* 3D 168
(off Beech Ho. Rd.)
Keyse Rd. SE1 3F 103
Keysham Av. TW5: Cran 1J 111
Keystone Cres. N1 1F 7 (2J 83)
Key W. Ct. IG7: Chig 4K 37
Keywood Dr. TW16: Sun 6J 129
Keyworth Cl. E5 4A 68
Keyworth Pl. SE1 7B 14
Keyworth St. SE1 7B 14 (3B 102)
Kezia M. SE8 5A 104
Kezia St. SE8 5A 104
Khalsa Ct. N22 1B 48
Khama Rd. SW17 4C 136
Khartoum Rd. E13 3K 87
IG1: Ilf 5F 71
SW17 4B 136
Khyber Rd. SW11 2C 118
The Kia Oval 7H 19 (6K 101)
Kibble Cl. RM6: Chad H 7C 54
Kibworth St. SW8 7K 101
Kidabulous 1G 147
KIDBROOKE 2K 123
Kidbrooke Est. SE3 3A 124
Kidbrooke Gdns. SE3 2J 123
Kidbrooke Green Nature Reserve
3A 124
Kidbrooke Gro. SE3 1J 123
Kidbrooke La. SE9 4C 124
Kidbrooke Pk. Cl. SE3 1K 123
Kidbrooke Pk. Rd. SE3 1K 123
Kidbrooke Way SE3 2K 123
Kidderminster Pl. CR0: C'don 1B 168
Kidderminster Rd. CR0: C'don 1B 168
Kidderpore Av. NW3 4J 63
Kidderpore Gdns. NW3 4J 63
Kidd Pl. SE7 5C 106
Kidspace
Croydon 6A 168
Kiebs Way SE17 5D 102
Kiffen St. EC2 3F 9 (4D 84)
Kilberry Cl. TW7: Isle 1H 113
Kilbrennan Ho. *E14* 6E 86
(off Findhorn St.)
KILBURN 2H 81
Kilburn Bri. NW6 1J 81
Kilburn Ga. NW6 2K 81
Kilburn High Rd. NW6 7H 63
Kilburn Ho. *NW6* 2H 81
(off Malvern Pl.)
Kilburn La. W9 3F 81
W10 3F 81
Kilburn Pk. Rd. NW6 3J 81
Kilburn Pl. NW6 1J 81
Kilburn Priory NW6 1K 81
Kilburn Sq. NW6 1J 81
Kilburn Va. NW6 1K 81
Kilburn Va. Est. *NW6* 1K 81
(off Kilburn Vale)
Kilby Ct. *SE10* 3H 105
(off Greenroof Way)
Kildare Cl. HA4: Ruis 1A 58
Kildare Ct. *W2* 6J 81
(off Kildare Ter.)
Kildare Gdns. W2 6J 81
Kildare Rd. E16 5J 87
Kildare Ter. W2 6J 81
Kildare Wlk. E14 6C 86
Kildoran Rd. SW2 5J 119
Kildowan Rd. IG3: Ilf 1A 72
Kilgour Rd. SE23 6A 122
Kilkie St. SW6 2A 118
Killarney Rd. SW18 6A 118
Killburns Mill Cl. SM6: W'gton 2F 167
Killearn Rd. SE6 1F 141
Killester Gdns. KT4: Wor Pk 4D 164
Killick Ho. SM1: Sutt 4J 165
Killick M. SM3: Cheam 6G 165
Killick St. N1 1G 7 (2K 83)
Killick Way E1 5K 85
Killieser Av. SW2 2J 137
Killigarth Ct. DA14: Sidc 4A 144
Killigrew Ho. TW16: Sun 7G 129
Killip Cl. E16 6H 87
Killoran Ho. *E14* 3E 104
(off Galbraith St.)
Killowen Av. UB5: N'olt 5G 59
Killowen Rd. E9 6K 67
Killyon Rd. SW8 2G 119
Killyon Ter. SW8 2G 119
Kilmaine Rd. SW6 7G 99
Kilmarnock Gdns. RM8: Dag 3C 72
Kilmarsh Rd. W6 4E 98
Kilmartin Av. SW16 3A 156
Kilmartin Rd. IG3: Ilf 2A 72
Kilmington Rd. SW13 6C 98
Kilmiston Av. TW17: Shep 6E 146
Kilmiston Ho. TW17: Shep 6E 146
Kilmore Ho. *E14* 6D 86
(off Vesey Path)
Kilmorey Gdns. TW1: Twick 5B 114
Kilmorey Rd. TW1: Twick 4B 114
Kilmorie Rd. SE23 1A 140
Kilmuir Ho. *SW1* 4H 17
(off Bury St.)
Kiln Cinema 7H 63
Kiln Cl. UB3: Harl 6F 93
Kiln Ct. *E14* 7B 86
(off Newell St.)
Kilner Ho. *E16* 5K 87
(off Freemasons Rd.)
SE11 7J 19
Kilner St. E14 5C 86
Kiln Ho. *E1* 5K 85
(off Duckett St.)
UB2: S'hall 3E 94
(off Lockwood Rd.)
Kiln M. SW17 5B 136
Kiln Pl. NW5 5E 64
Kilnside KT10: Clay 7A 162
Kiln Theatre 7H 63
Kilpatrick Way UB4: Yead 5C 76
Kilravock St. W10 3G 81
Kilronan W3 6K 79
Kilross Rd. TW14: Bedf 1F 129
Kilsby Wlk. RM9: Dag 6B 72
Kilsha Rd. KT12: Walt T 6A 148
Kimbell Gdns. SW6 1G 117
Kimbell Pl. SE3 4A 124
Kimber Ct. *SE1* 7G 15
(off Long La.)
Kimberley Av. E6 2C 88
IG2: Ilf 7H 53
RM7: Rom 6J 55
SE15 2H 121
Kimberley Ct. *NW6* 1G 81
(off Kimberley Rd.)
Kimberley Dr. DA14: Sidc 2D 144
Kimberley Gdns. EN1: Enf 3A 24
N4 5B 48
Kimberley Ga. BR1: Broml 7G 141
Kimberley Ho. *E14* 3E 104
(off Galbraith St.)
Kimberley Rd. BR3: Beck 2K 157
CR0: C'don 6B 156
E4 1B 36
E11 2F 69
E16 4H 87
E17 1A 50
N17 2G 49
N18 6C 34
NW6 1G 81
SW9 2J 119
Kimberley Wlk. KT12: Walt T 7K 147
Kimberley Way E4 1B 36
Kimber Pl. TW4: Houn 7D 112
(Conway Rd.)
TW4: Houn 4D 112
(Marryat Cl.)
Kimber Rd. SW18 7J 117
Kimble Cres. WD23: Bush 1B 26
Kimble Ho. NW8 3D 4
Kimble Rd. SW19 6B 136
Kimbolton Cl. SE12 6H 123
Kimbolton Ct. *SW3* 4C 16
(off Fulham Rd.)
Kimbolton Row *SW3* 4C 16
(off Fulham Rd.)
Kimmeridge Gdns. SE9 4C 142
Kimmeridge Rd. SE9 4C 142
Kimmins Ct. *SE16* 7K 15
(off Old Jamaica Rd.)
Kimpton Ho. SW15 7C 116
Kimpton Ind. Est. SM3: Sutt 2H 165
Kimpton Link Bus. Cen.
SM3: Sutt 2H 165
Kimpton Pk. Way SM1: Sutt 2G 165
SM3: Sutt 2G 165
Kimpton Rd. SE5 1D 120
SM3: Sutt 2H 165
Kimpton Trade & Bus. Cen.
SM3: Sutt 2H 165
Kinburn St. SE16 2K 103
Kincaid Rd. SE15 7H 103
Kincardine Gdns. *W9* 4J 81
(off Harrow Rd.)
Kincha Lodge *KT2: King T* 1F 151
(off Elm Rd.)
Kinch Gro. HA9: Wemb 7F 43
Kinder Cl. SE28 7D 90
Kinder Ho. *N1* 2D 84
(off Cranston Est.)
Kindersley Ho. *E1* 6G 85
(off Pinchin St.)
Kinder St. E1 6H 85
Kinderton Cl. N14 1B 32
Kinefold Ho. *N7* 6J 65
(off York Way Est.)
Kinesis Gym & Fitness Cen. 4C 124
(off Well Hall Rd.)
Kinfauns Rd. IG3: Ilf 1A 72
SW2 2A 138
King Alfred Av. SE6 4C 140
(not continuous)
King & Queen Cl. SE9 4C 142
King & Queen St. SE17 5C 102
King & Queen Wharf SE16 7K 85
King Arthur Cl. SE15 7J 103
KING CHARLES I ISLAND 4E 12
King Charles Ct. *SE17* 6B 102
(off Royal Rd.)
King Charles Cres. KT5: Surb 7F 151
King Charles Ho. *SW6* 7K 99
(off Wandon Rd.)
King Charles Rd. KT5: Surb 5F 151
King Charles's Ct. *SE10* 6E 104
(off Park Row)
King Charles St. SW1 6D 12 (2H 101)
King Charles Ter. *E1* 7H 85
(off Sovereign Cl.)
King Charles Wlk. SW19 1G 135
King Ct. E10 7D 50
Kingcup Cl. CR0: C'don 7K 157
King David La. E1 7J 85
Kingdom St. W2 5A 82
Kingdon Ho. *E14* 3E 104
(off Galbraith St.)
Kingdon Rd. NW6 6J 63
King Edward Bldg. *EC1* 7B 8
(off King Edward St.)
King Edward Ct. *HA9: Wemb* 5E 60
(off Elm Rd.)
King Edward Dr. KT9: Chess 3E 162
King Edward Mans. *E8* 1H 85
(off Mare St.)
King Edward M. SW13 1C 116
King Edward Rd. E10 1E 68
E17 3A 50
EN5: New Bar 4D 20
King Edward's Gdns. W3 1G 97
King Edwards Gro. TW11: Tedd 6B 132
King Edwards Mans. *SW6* 7J 99
(off Fulham Rd.)
King Edward's Pl. W3 1G 97
King Edward's Rd. E9 1H 85
EN3: Pond E 4E 24
HA4: Ruis 1F 57
N9 7C 24
King Edwards Rd. IG11: Bark 1H 89
King Edward St. EC1 7C 8 (6C 84)
King Edward the Third M.
SE16 2H 103
King Edward Wlk. SE1 1K 19 (3A 102)
Kingfield Rd. W5 4D 78
Kingfield St. E14 4E 104
Kingfisher Av. E11 6K 51
Kingfisher Cl. HA3: Hrw W 7E 26
HA6: Nwood 1D 38
SE28 7C 90
Kingfisher Ct. *CR0: C'don* 3C 168
(off Wandle Rd.)
E14 2E 104
(off River Barge Cl.)
EN2: Enf 1E 22
KT8: E Mos 4J 149
SE1 7D 14
(off Swan St.)
SM1: Sutt 5H 165
SW19 2F 135
TW3: Houn 5F 113
TW7: Isle 2H 113
Kingfisher Dr. TW10: Ham 4B 132
Kingfisher Hgts. *E16* 1A 106
(off Bramwell Way)
N17 3H 49
(off Waterside Way)
Kingfisher Ho. SW18 3A 118
W14 3H 99
(off Melbury Rd.)
Kingfisher Leisure Cen.
Kingston upon Thames 2E 150
Kingfisher M. SE13 4D 122
Kingfisher Pl. N22 2K 47
Kingfisher Sq. *SE8* 6B 104
(off Clyde St.)
Kingfisher St. E6 5C 88
Kingfisher Wlk. NW9 2A 44
Kingfisher Way BR3: Beck 5K 157
NW10 6K 61
King Frederick IX Twr. SE16 3B 104
King Gdns. CR0: Wadd 5B 168
King George IV Ct. *SE17* 5D 102
(off Dawes St.)
King George VI Av. CR4: Mitc 4D 154
King George VI Memorial
5C 12 (1H 101)
King George Av. E16 6A 88
IG2: Ilf 5H 53
King George Cl. RM7: Mawney 3J 55
TW16: Sun 5G 129
King George Cres.
HA0: Wemb 5D 60
King George M. SW17 5D 136
King George Sailing Club 6J 25
King George's Dr. UB1: S'hall 5D 76
King George's Field 3G 163
King George Sq. TW10: Rich 6F 115
King George's Trad. Est.
KT9: Chess 4G 163
King George St. SE10 7E 104
King George Way E4 4J 25
Kingham Cl. SW18 7A 118
W11 2G 99
King Harolds Way
DA7: Belv, Bex 7D 108
DA17: Belv 7D 108
King Henry Lodge E4 4H 35
King Henry M. BR6: Chels 5K 173
HA2: Harr 1J 59
King Henry's Dr. CR0: New Ad 7D 170
King Henry's Reach W6 6E 98
King Henry's Rd. KT1: King T 3H 151
NW3 7C 64
King Henry's Stairs E1 1H 103
King Henry St. N16 5E 66
King Henry's Wlk. N1 6E 66
King Henry Ter. *E1* 7H 85
(off Sovereign Cl.)
Kinghorn St. EC1 6C 8 (5C 84)
King Ho. W12 6D 80
Kingisholt Ct. *NW10* 3F 81
(off Wellington Rd.)
King James Ct. SE1 7B 14
King James St. SE1 7B 14 (2B 102)
King John Ct. EC2 3H 9 (4E 84)
King John St. E1 5K 85
King John's Wlk. SE9 7C 124
Kinglake Est. SE17 5E 102
Kinglake St. SE17 5E 102
(not continuous)
Kinglet Cl. E7 6J 69
Kingly Ct. W1 2B 12
Kingly St. W1 1A 12 (6G 83)
Kingsand Rd. SE12 2J 141
Kings Arbour UB2: S'hall 5C 94
King's Arms All.
TW8: Bford 6D 96
Kings Arms Ct. E1 5G 85
King's Arms Yd. SW18 5K 117
Kings Arms Yd. EC2 7E 8 (6D 84)
Kingsash Dr. UB4: Yead 4C 76
King's Av. IG8: Wfd G 6E 36
IG9: Buck H 6E 36
(The Broadway)
IG9: Buck H 2G 37
(Langfords)
N10 3E 46
SM5: Cars 7C 166
TW16: Sun 5H 129
UB6: G'frd 5F 77
Kings Av. BR1: Broml 6H 141
KT3: N Mald 4A 152
N21 1G 33
RM6: Chad H 6F 55
SW4 1H 137
SW12 1H 137
TW3: Houn 1F 113
W5 6D 78
King's Bench St. SE1 6B 14 (2B 102)
King's Bench Wlk.
EC4 1K 13 (6A 84)
King's Blvd. N1 2J 83
Kingsbridge Av. W3 2F 97
Kingsbridge Ct. *E14* 3C 104
(off Dockers Tanner Rd.)
NW1 7F 65
(off Castlehaven Rd.)
Kingsbridge Cres. UB1: S'hall 5D 76
Kingsbridge Dr. NW7 7A 30
Kingsbridge Rd. IG11: Bark 2H 89
KT12: Walt T 7K 147
SM4: Mord 6F 153
UB2: S'hall 4D 94
W10 6E 80
Kingsbridge Way UB4: Hayes 3G 75
Kingsbridge Wharf IG11: Bark 3J 89
KINGSBURY 5H 43
Kingsbury Circ. NW9 5G 43
KINGSBURY GREEN 6K 43
Kingsbury Rd. N1 6E 66
NW9 5G 43
Kingsbury Ter. N1 6E 66
Kingsbury Trad. Est. NW9 6K 43
Kings Chase KT8: E Mos 3G 149
Kings Chase Vw. EN2: Enf 2F 23
Kingsclere Cl. SW15 7C 116
Kingsclere Ct. N12 5H 31
Kingsclere Pl. EN2: Enf 2H 23
Kingscliffe Gdns. SW19 1H 135
King's Cl. DA1: Cray 4K 127
NW4 4F 45
Kings Cl. E10 7D 50
KT7: T Ditt 6A 150
KT12: Walt T 7K 147
TW18: Staines 7A 128
The King's Club 6E 134
Kings Coll. Ct. NW3 7C 64
King's College London
Denmark Hill Campus 2D 120
Guy's Campus 5E 14
(within Guy's Hospital)
Institute of Psychiatry,
De Crespigny Park 2D 120
Maughan Library 7J 7 (6A 84)
St Thomas' Campus -
Lambeth Pal. Rd. 2F 19
St Thomas' House 1G 19
Strand Campus 2H 13 (7K 83)
Waterloo Campus 5J 13 (1A 102)
King's Coll. Rd. NW3 7C 64
Kings Coll. Rd. HA4: Ruis 6H 39
King's College School of
Medicine & Dentistry 2C 120
Kingscote Rd. CR0: C'don 7H 157
KT3: N Mald 3K 151
W4 3K 97
Kingscote St. EC4 2A 14 (7B 84)
King's Ct. E13 1K 87
SE1 6B 14 (2B 102)
Kings Ct. HA9: Wemb 2H 61
IG9: Buck H 2G 37
N7 7K 65
(off Caledonian Rd.)
NW8 1D 82
(off Prince Albert Rd.)
W6 4C 98
Kings Ct. Mans. *SW6* 1H 117
(off Fulham Rd.)
Kings Ct. M. KT8: E Mos 5H 149
Kings Ct. Nth. SW3 6C 16 (5C 100)
Kingscourt Rd. SW16 3H 137
Kings Ct. Sth. SW3 6C 16
King's Cres. N4 3C 66
Kings Cres. Est. N4 2C 66
Kingscroft SW4 6J 119
Kingscroft Rd. NW2 6H 63
KING'S CROSS 2J 83
King's Cross Bri. N1 1F 7
King's Cross Rd. WC1 1G 7 (3K 83)
King's Cross Sq. *N1* 1E 6
(off Euston Rd.)
Kingsdale Gdns. W11 1F 99
Kingsdale Rd. SE18 7K 107
SE20 7K 139
Kingsdown Av. CR2: S Croy 7C 168
W3 7A 80
W13 2B 96
Kingsdown Cl. *SE16* 5H 103
(off Masters Dr.)
W10 6F 81
Kingsdowne Rd. KT6: Surb 7E 150
Kingsdown Ho. E8 5G 67
Kingsdown Point SW2 2A 138
Kingsdown Rd. E11 3G 69
N19 2J 65
SM3: Cheam 5G 165
Kingsdown Way BR2: Hayes 7J 159
King's Dr. HA8: Edg 4A 28
Kings Dr. HA9: Wemb 2H 61
KT5: Surb 7G 151
KT7: T Ditt 7B 150
TW11: Tedd 5H 131
Kingsend HA4: Ruis 1F 57
Kingsend Ct. HA4: Ruis 1G 57
Kings Farm E17 1D 50
Kings Farm Av. TW10: Rich 4G 115
Kingsfield Av. HA2: Harr 4F 41
Kingsfield Ho. SE9 3B 142
Kingsfield Rd. HA1: Harr 7H 41
Kingsfield Ter. HA1: Harr 7H 41
Kingsford St. NW5 5D 64
Kingsford Way E6 5D 88
King's Gdns. NW6 7J 63
Kings Gdns. IG1: Ilf 1H 71
KT12: Walt T 7K 147
Kings Gth. M. SE23 2J 139
Kingsgate HA9: Wemb 3J 61
Kingsgate Av. N3 3J 45
Kingsgate Bus. Cen.
KT2: King T 1E 150
(off Kingsgate Rd.)
Kingsgate Cl. DA7: Bex 1E 126
Kingsgate Est. N1 6E 66
Kingsgate Ho. SW9 1A 120
Kingsgate Mans. *WC1* 6G 7
(off Red Lion Sq.)
Kings Ga. M. *N8* 5K 47
(off Spencer Rd.)
Kingsgate Pde. SW1 2B 18
Kingsgate Pl. NW6 7J 63
Kingsgate Rd. KT1: King T 1E 150
KT2: King T 1E 150
NW6 7J 63
Kings Ga. Wlk. *SW1* 1B 18
(off Victoria St.)
Kings Grange HA4: Ruis 1H 57
Kingsground SE9 7B 124
King's Gro. SE15 7H 103
(not continuous)
Kingsgrove Cl. DA14: Sidc 4K 143
Kings Hall Leisure Cen. 5J 67
Kings Hall M. SE13 3E 122
Kings Hall Rd. BR3: Beck 7A 140
Kings Head Hill E4 7J 25
Kingshead Ho. NW7 4J 29
Kings Head Pas. *SW4* 4H 119
(off Clapham Pk. Rd.)
Kings Head Theatre 1B 84
(off Upper St.)
King's Head Yd. SE1 5E 14 (1D 102)
King's Highway SE18 6J 107
Kingshill Av. HA3: Kenton 4B 42
KT4: Wor Pk 7C 152
UB4: Hayes, Yead 3G 75
UB5: N'olt 3G 75
Kingshill Ct. UB4: Hayes 3J 75
Kingshill Ct. EN5: Barn 4B 20
Kingshill Dr. HA3: Kenton 2B 42
Kingshold Rd. E9 7J 67
Kingsholm Gdns. SE9 4B 124
King's Ho. *SW10* 7A 16
(off King's Rd.)
Kings Ho. *SW8* 7J 101
(off Sth. Lambeth Rd.)
King's Ho. Studios *SW10* 7A 16
(off Lamont Rd. Pas.)
Kingshurst Rd. SE12 7J 123
Kingside SE18 3C 106
Kings Keep BR2: Broml 2G 159
KT1: King T 4E 150
SW15 5F 117
KINGSLAND 6E 66
Kingsland NW8 1C 82
Kingsland Basin 1E 84
Kingsland Grn. E8 6E 66
Kingsland High St. E8 6F 67
Kingsland Pas. E8 6E 66
Kingsland Rd. E2 2H 9 (3E 84)
E8 3E 84
E13 3A 88
Kingsland Shop. Cen. 6F 67
Kings La. SM1: Sutt 6B 166
Kingslawn Cl. SW15 5D 116
Kingslee Ct. SM2: Sutt 7K 165
Kingsleigh Cl. TW8: Bford 6D 96
Kingsleigh Pl. CR4: Mitc 3D 154
Kingsleigh Wlk.
BR2: Broml 4H 159
Kingsley Av. SM1: Sutt 4B 166
TW3: Houn 2G 113
UB1: S'hall 7E 76
W13 5A 78
Kingsley Cl. N2 5A 46
RM10: Dag 4H 73
Kingsley Ct. DA6: Bex 4G 127
HA8: Edg 3C 28
KT4: Wor Pk 2B 164
(off The Avenue)
NW2 6D 62
Kingsley Dr. KT4: Wor Pk 2B 164
Kingsley Flats *SE1* 4E 102
(off Old Kent Rd.)
Kingsley Gdns. E4 5H 35
Kingsley Ho. *SW3* 6B 100
(off Beaufort St.)
W14 4G 99
(off Avonmore Pl.)
Kingsley Mans. *W14* 6G 99
(off Greyhound Rd.)
Kingsley M. BR7: Chst 6F 143
E1 7H 85
W8 3K 99
Kingsley Pl. N6 7E 46
Kingsley Rd. BR6: Chels 7K 173
CR0: C'don 1A 168
E7 7J 69
E17 2E 50
HA2: Harr 4G 59
HA5: Pinn 4D 40
IG6: Ilf 1G 53
N13 4F 33
NW6 1H 81
SW19 5K 135
TW3: Houn 1F 113
Kingsley St. SW11 3D 118
Kingsley Way N2 5A 46
Kingsley Wood Dr. SE9 3D 142
Kings Lodge *HA4: Ruis* 1G 57
(off Pembroke Rd.)
N12 6F 31
Kingslyn Cres. SE19 1E 156
Kings Mall W6 4E 98
Kingsman Pde. SE18 3D 106
Kings Mans. *SW3* 7C 16
(off Lawrence St.)
Kingsman St. SE18 3D 106
Kingsmead EN5: New Bar 4D 20
TW10: Rich 6F 115

242 A-Z Big London

Laburnum Cres.—Langland Cres.

Laburnum Cres. TW16: Sun 1K 147
Laburnum Gdns. CR0: C'don 7K 157
N21 2H 33
Laburnum Gro. HA4: Ruis 6F 39
KT3: N Mald 2K 151
N21 2H 33
NW9 7J 43
TW3: Houn 4D 112
UB1: S'hall 4D 76
Laburnum Ho. BR2: Broml 1F 159
RM10: Dag 2G 73
Laburnum La. E2 2F 85
Laburnum Lodge N3 2H 45
Laburnum Pl. SE9 5E 124
Laburnum Rd. CR4: Mitc 2E 154
SW19 7A 136
UB3: Harl 4H 93
The Laburnums E6 4C 88
Laburnum St. E2 1F 85
Laburnum Way BR2: Broml 7E 160
TW19: Stanw 1B 128
Labyrinth Twr. *E8* *6F 67*
(off Dalston Sq.)
Lacebark Cl. DA15: Sidc 7K 125
Lace Cl. SM6: W'gton 2F 167
Lace Ct. *E1* *5K 85*
(off Master's St.)
Lacewing Cl. E13 3J 87
Lacey Cl. N9 2B 34
Lacey Dr. HA8: Edg 4K 27
RM8: Dag 3C 72
TW12: Hamp 1D 148
Lacey Gro. UB10: Uxb 2A 74
Lacey M. E3 2C 86
Lacine Ct. *SE16* *2K 103*
(off Christopher Cl.)
Lackington St. EC2 5F 9 (5D 84)
Lackland Ho. *SE1* *5F 103*
(off Rowcross St.)
Lacland Ho. *SW10* *7B 100*
(off Worlds End Est.)
Lacock Cl. SW19 6A 136
Lacock Ct. W13 1A 96
Lacon Ho. *WC1* *5G 7*
(off Theobald's Rd.)
Lacon Rd. SE22 4G 121
Lacrosse Way SW16 1H 155
Lacy Rd. SW15 4F 117
Ladas Rd. SE27 4C 138
Ladbroke Ct. E1 6F 85
Ladbroke Cres. W11 6G 81
Ladbroke Gdns. W11 7H 81
Ladbroke Gro. W10 4F 81
W11 4F 81
Ladbroke Gro. Ho. *W11* *7H 81*
(off Ladbroke Gro.)
Ladbroke Grove Memorial 4F 81
Ladbroke M. W11 1G 99
Ladbroke Rd. EN1: Enf 6A 24
W11 1H 99
Ladbroke Sq. W11 7H 81
Ladbroke Ter. W11 7H 81
Ladbroke Wlk. W11 1H 99
Ladbrook Cl. BR1: Broml 6G 141
HA5: Pinn 5D 40
Ladbrooke Cres. DA14: Sidc 3D 144
Ladbrook Rd. SE25 4D 156
Ladderstile Ride KT2: King T 5H 133
Ladderswood Way N11 5B 32
Ladlands SE22 7G 121
Lady Anne Ct. *E18* *1J 51*
(off Queen Mary Av.)
Lady Aylesford Av. HA7: Stan 5F 27
Lady Booth Rd. KT1: King T 2E 150
Lady Craig Ct. UB8: Hil 5D 74
Ladycroft Gdns. BR6: Farnb 5G 173
Ladycroft Rd. SE13 3D 122
Ladycroft Wlk. HA7: Stan 1D 42
Ladycroft Way BR6: Farnb 5G 173
Lady Dock Path SE16 2A 104
Lady Elizabeth Ho. SW14 3J 115
Ladyfern Ho. *E3* *5C 86*
(off Gail St.)
Lady Florence Ctyd. *SE8* *7C 104*
(off Reginald Sq.)
Lady Forsdyke Way KT19: Eps 7G 163
Ladygate La. HA4: Ruis 6D 38
Lady Harewood Way KT19: Eps 7G 163
Lady Hay KT4: Wor Pk 2B 164
Lady Jane Ct. *KT2: King T* *2F 151*
(off Cambridge Rd.)
Lady Margaret Ho. *SE17* *6D 102*
(off Queen's Row)
Lady Margaret Rd. N19 4G 65
NW5 5G 65
UB1: S'hall 7D 76
Lady May Ho. *SE5* *7C 102*
(off Pitman St.)
Lady Micos Almshouses *E1* *6J 85*
(off Aylward St.)
Lady Sarah Cohen Ho. *N11* *6J 31*
(off Asher Loftus Way)
Lady Shaw Ct. N13 2E 32
Ladyship Ter. SE22 7G 121
Ladysmith Av. E6 2C 88
IG2: Ilf 7J 53
Ladysmith Cl. NW7 7H 29
Ladysmith Rd. E16 3H 87
EN1: Enf 3K 23
(not continuous)
HA3: W'stone 2J 41
N17 2G 49
N18 5C 34
SE9 6E 124
Lady Somerset Rd. NW5 4F 65
LADYWELL 5D 122
Ladywell Arena
(Running Track) 6C 122
Ladywell Cl. SE4 5C 122
Ladywell Hgts. SE4 6B 122
Ladywell Rd. SE13 5C 122
Ladywell St. E15 1H 87
Ladywell Water Twr. SE4 5C 122
Ladywood Av. BR5: Pet W 5J 161
Ladywood Rd. KT6: Surb 2G 163
Lafone Av. TW13: Felt 2A 130
Lafone St. SE1 6J 15 (2F 103)
Lagado M. SE16 1K 103
Lagare Apts. *SE1* *6B 14*
(off Surrey Row)
Lagonda Ho. *E3* *4C 86*
(off Tidworth Rd.)
Lagonier Ho. *EC1* *2D 8*
(off Ironmonger Row)
Laidlaw Dr. N21 5E 22
Laing Dean UB5: N'olt 1A 76
Laing Ho. SE5 7C 102
Laings Av. CR4: Mitc 2D 154
Lainlock Pl.
TW3: Houn 1F 113
Lainson St. SW18 7J 117
Lairdale Cl. SE21 1C 138
Laird Ho. *SE5* *7C 102*
(off Redcar St.)
Lairs Cl. N7 5J 65
Lait Ho. BR3: Beck 1D 158
Laitwood Rd. SW12 1F 137
Lakanal *SE5* *1E 120*
(off Sceaux Gdns.)
The Lake WD23: B Hea 1C 26
Lake Av. BR1: Broml 6J 141
Lake Bus. Cen. N17 7B 34
Lake Cl. RM8: Dag 3D 72
SW19 5H 135
Lakedale Ct. IG11: Bark 4B 90
Lakedale Rd. SE18 6J 107
Lake Dr. WD23: B Hea 2C 26
Lake Farm Country Pk. 1G 93
Lakefield Cl. SE20 7H 139
Lakefield Rd. N22 2B 48
Lake Gdns. RM10: Dag 5G 73
SM6: W'gton 3F 167
TW10: Ham 2B 132
Lakehall Gdns.
CR7: Thor H 5B 156
Lakehall Rd. CR7: Thor H 5B 156
Lake Ho. *SE1* *7C 14*
(off Southwark Bri. Rd.)
Lake Ho. Rd. E11 3J 69
Lakehurst Rd. KT19: Ewe 5A 164
Lakeland Cl. HA3: Hrw W 6C 26
Lakenham Pl. E3 4B 86
Lakenheath N14 5B 22
Laker Ct. SW4 1J 119
Laker Ho. E16 2K 105
Laker Ind. Est. BR3: Beck 5A 140
Lake Rd. CR0: C'don 2B 170
E10 7D 50
RM6: Chad H 4D 54
RM9: Dag 3H 91
SW19 5H 135
Laker Pl. SW15 6G 117
Lakeside BR3: Beck 3D 158
EN2: Enf 4C 22
KT2: King T 7H 133
KT19: Ewe 6A 164
N3 2K 45
SM6: W'gton 4F 167
W13 6C 78
Lakeside Av. IG4: Ilf 4B 52
SE28 1A 108
Lakeside Cl. DA15: Sidc 5C 126
HA4: Ruis 4F 39
SE25 2G 157
Lakeside Ct. N4 2C 66
Lakeside Cres. EN4: E Barn 5J 21
Lakeside Dr. BR2: Broml 3C 172
NW10 3F 79
Lakeside Ind. Est. SL3: Coln 2B 174
Lakeside Rd. N13 4E 32
SL0: Rich P 3A 174
SL3: Coln, Rich P 3A 174
W14 3F 99
Lakeside Ter. EC2 5D 8
Lakeside Way HA9: Wemb 4G 61
Lakes Rd. BR2: Kes 5A 172
Lakeswood Rd. BR5: Pet W 6F 161
Lake Vw. HA8: Edg 5A 28
Lakeview Ct. SE28 7B 90
Lake Vw. Est. E3 2A 86
Lakeview Rd. DA16: Well 4B 126
SE27 5A 138
Lake Vw. Ter. *N18* *4A 34*
(off Sweet Briar Wlk.)
Lakin Cl. SM5: Cars 4E 166
Lakis Cl. NW3 4A 64
Laleham Av. NW7 3E 28
Laleham Ct. SM1: Sutt 5A 166
Laleham Ho. *E2* *3J 9*
(off Camlet St.)
Laleham Rd. SE6 7E 122
TW17: Shep 4B 146
Lalor St. SW6 2G 117
Lambarde Av. SE9 4E 142
Lambarde Sq. SE10 5H 105
Lambard Ho. *SE10* *7E 104*
(off Langdale Rd.)
Lamb Cl. UB5: N'olt 3C 76
Lamb Ct. *E14* *7A 86*
(off Narrow St.)
Lamberhurst Ho. SE15 6J 103
Lamberhurst Rd. RM8: Dag 1F 73
SE27 4A 138
Lambert Av. TW9: Rich 3G 115
Lambert Ct. *DA8: Erith* *6J 109*
(off Park Cres.)
Lambert Ho. *SW11* *3B 118*
(off Gartons Way)
Lambert Jones M. EC2 5C 8
Lambert Lodge *TW8: Bford* *5D 96*
(off Layton Rd.)
Lambert M. *N12* *5F 31*
(off Lambert Way)
Lambert Rd. E16 6K 87
N12 5G 31
SW2 5J 119
Lambert's Pl. CR0: C'don 1D 168
Lamberts Rd. KT5: Surb 5E 150
Lambert St. N1 7A 66
Lambert Wlk. HA9: Wemb 3E 60
Lambert Way N12 5F 31
LAMBETH 3G 19 (3K 101)
Lambeth Bri. SW1 3F 19 (4J 101)
Lambeth Crematorium 4A 136
Lambeth High St.
SE1 4G 19 (4K 101)
Lambeth Hill EC4 2C 14 (7C 84)
Lambeth Palace 2G 19 (3K 101)
Lambeth Pal. Rd. SE1 2G 19 (3K 101)
Lambeth Rd. CR0: C'don 7A 156
SE1 3G 19 (4K 101)
SE11 3G 19 (4K 101)
Lambeth Towers SE11 2J 19
Lambeth Wlk. SE11 4H 19 (4K 101)
(not continuous)
Lambfold Ho. *N7* *6J 65*
(off North Rd.)
Lamb Ho. *SE5* *7C 102*
(off Elmington Est.)
SE10 *6E 104*
(off Haddo St.)
Lambkins M. E17 4E 50
Lamb La. E8 7H 67
Lamble St. NW5 5E 64
Lambley Rd. RM9: Dag 6B 72
Lambolle Pl. NW3 6C 64
Lambolle Rd. NW3 6C 64
Lamborne Pl. UB10: Ick 3D 56
Lambourn Cl. CR2: S Croy 7B 168
NW5 4G 65
W7 2K 95
Lambourne Av. SW19 4H 135
Lambourne Ct. IG8: Wfd G 7F 37
Lambourne Gdns. E4 2H 35
EN1: Enf 2A 24
IG11: Bark 7K 71
Lambourne Gro. SE16 5K 103
Lambourne Ho. *NW8* *5B 4*
(off Broadley St.)
SE20 1G 157
Lambourne Pl. SE3 1K 123
Lambourne Rd. E11 7E 50
IG3: Ilf 2J 71
IG11: Bark 7J 71
Lambourn Gro.
KT1: King T 2H 151
Lambourn Rd. SW4 3F 119
Lambrook Ho. SE15 1G 121
Lambrook Ter. SW6 1G 117
Lamb's Bldgs. EC1 4E 8 (4D 84)
Lamb's Cl. N9 2B 34
Lamb's Conduit Pas.
WC1 5G 7 (5K 83)
Lamb's Conduit St. WC1 4G 7 (4K 83)
(not continuous)
Lambscroft Av. SE9 3A 142
Lambs Mdw. IG8: Wfd G 2B 52
Lamb's M. N1 1B 84
Lambs Pas. EC1 5E 8 (4D 84)
Lambs Ter. N9 2J 33
Lamb St. E1 5J 9 (5F 85)
Lamb's Wlk. EN2: Enf 2H 23
Lambton M. *N19* *1J 65*
(off Lambton Rd.)
Lambton Pl. W11 7H 81
Lambton Rd. N19 1J 65
SW20 1E 152
Lamb Wlk. SE1 7G 15 (2E 102)
Lamerock Rd. BR1: Broml 4H 141
Lamerton Rd. IG6: Ilf 2F 53
Lamerton St. SE8 6C 104
Lamford Cl. N17 7J 33
Lamington St. W6 4D 98
Lamlash St. SE11 4B 102
Lamley Ho. *SE10* *7D 104*
(off Ashburnham Pl.)
Lammas Av. CR4: Mitc 2E 154
Lammas Grn. SE26 3H 139
Lammas Pk. Gdns. W5 1C 96
Lammas Pk. Rd. W5 2D 96
Lammas Rd. E9 7K 67
E10 2A 68
TW10: Ham 4C 132
Lammermoor Rd. SW12 7F 119
Lamont Rd.
SW10 7A 16 (6B 100)
Lamont Rd. Pas. SW10 7A 16
LAMORBEY 1K 143
Lamorbey Cl. DA15: Sidc 1K 143
Lamorbey Pk. 1B 144
Lamorna Cl. BR6: Orp 7K 161
E17 2E 50
Lamorna Gro. HA7: Stan 1D 42
Lampard Gro. N16 1F 67
Lampern Sq. E2 3G 85
Lampeter Cl. NW9 6A 44
Lampeter Sq. W6 6G 99
Lamplighter Cl. E1 4J 85
Lampmead Rd. SE12 5H 123
Lamp Office Ct. WC1 4G 7
Lamport Cl. SE18 4D 106
LAMPTON 1F 113
Lampton Av. TW3: Houn 1F 113
Lampton Ct. TW3: Houn 1F 113
Lampton Ho. Cl. SW19 4F 135
Lampton Pk. Rd.
TW3: Houn 2F 113
Lampton Rd. TW3: Houn 2F 113
Lanacre Av. NW9 1K 43
Lanadron Cl. TW7: Isle 2K 113
Lanain Ct. SE12 7H 123
Lanark Cl. W5 5C 78
Lanark Ct. *UB5: N'olt* *5E 58*
(off Newmarket Av.)
Lanark Ho. *SE1* *5G 103*
(off Old Kent Rd.)
Lanark Mans. *W9* *4A 82*
(off Lanark Rd.)
W12 *2E 98*
(off Pennard Rd.)
Lanark M. W9 3A 82
Lanark Pl. W9 3A 4 (4A 82)
Lanark Rd. W9 2K 81
Lanark Sq. E14 3D 104
Lanata Wlk. *UB4: Yead* *4B 76*
(off Alba Cl.)
Lanbury Rd. SE15 4K 121
Lancashire Ct. W1 2K 11 (7F 83)
Lancaster Av. CR4: Mitc 5J 155
E18 4K 51
EN4: Had W 1F 21
IG11: Bark 7J 71
SE27 2B 138
SW19 5F 135
Lancaster Cl. BR2: Broml 4H 159
KT2: King T 5D 132
N1 7E 66
N17 7B 34
NW9 7G 29
TW15: Ashf 4A 128
TW19: Stanw 6A 110
W2 *7K 81*
(off St Petersburgh Pl.)
Lancaster Cotts. TW10: Rich 6E 114
Lancaster Ct. KT12: Walt T 7J 147
SE27 2B 138
SM2: Sutt *7J 165*
(off Mulgrave Rd.)
SW6 7H 99
TW19: Stanw 1A 128
W2 *2A 10*
(off Lancaster Ga.)
Lancaster Dr. E14 1E 104
NW3 6C 64
Lancaster Gdns. BR1: Broml 5C 160
KT2: King T 5D 132
SW19 5G 135
W13 2B 96
Lancaster Ga. W2 2A 10 (7A 82)
Lancaster Gro. NW3 6B 64
Lancaster Hall *E16* *1J 105*
(off Wesley Av.)
Lancaster House 6A 12
Lancaster Ho. E11 2H 69
EN2: Enf 1J 23
RM8: Dag 4B 72
TW7: Isle 7K 95
Lancaster Lodge *W11* *6G 81*
(off Lancaster Rd.)
Lancaster M. SW18 5K 117
TW10: Rich 6E 114
W2 2A 10 (7A 82)
Lancaster Pk. TW10: Rich 5E 114
Lancaster Pl. IG1: Ilf 5G 71
SW19 5F 135
TW1: Twick 6A 114
TW4: Houn 2A 112
WC2 2G 13 (7K 83)
Lancaster Rd. E7 7J 69
E11 2G 69
E17 2K 49
EN2: Enf 1J 23
EN4: E Barn 5G 21
HA2: Harr 5E 40
N4 7K 47
N11 6C 32
N18 5A 34
NW10 5C 62
SE25 2F 157
SW19 5F 135
UB1: S'hall 7C 76
UB5: N'olt 6G 59
W11 6G 81
Lancaster Rd. Ind. Est.
EN4: E Barn 5G 21
Lancaster Stables NW3 6C 64
Lancaster St. SE1 7A 14 (2B 102)
Lancaster Ter. W2 2A 10 (7B 82)
Lancaster Wlk.
UB3: Hayes 6E 74
W2 3A 10 (1A 100)
Lancaster Way KT4: Wor Pk 7D 152
Lancastrian Rd.
SM6: W'gton 7J 167
Lancefield Ho. SE15 4H 121
Lancefield St. W10 3H 81
Lancell St. N16 2E 66
Lancelot Av. HA0: Wemb 4D 60
Lancelot Cres. HA0: Wemb 4D 60
Lancelot Gdns. EN4: E Barn 7K 21
Lancelot Pl. SW7 7E 10 (2D 100)
Lancelot Rd. DA16: Well 4A 126
HA0: Wemb 4D 60
Lance Rd. HA1: Harr 7G 41
Lancer Sq. *W8* *2K 99*
(off Kensington Chu. St.)
Lancey Cl. SE7 4C 106
Lanchester Ct. *W2* *1E 10*
(off Seymour St.)
Lanchester Rd. N6 5D 46
Lanchester Way SE14 1J 121
Lancing Gdns. N9 1A 34
Lancing Ho. *CR0: C'don* *4D 168*
(off Coombe Rd.)
Lancing Rd. CR0: C'don 7K 155
IG2: Ilf 6H 53
TW13: Felt 2H 129
W13 7B 78
Lancing St. NW1 2C 6 (3H 83)
Lancresse Ct. *N1* *1E 84*
(off De Beauvoir Est.)
Landale Ho. *SE16* *3J 103*
(off Lower Rd.)
Landau Apts. SW6 6J 99
Landau Ct. *CR2: S Croy* *5C 168*
(off Warham Rd.)
Landcroft Rd. SE22 5F 121
Landells Rd. SE22 6F 121
Landford Rd. SW15 3E 116
Landgrove Rd. SW19 5J 135
Landing Waiters Ho. *E14* *6F 87*
(off New Village Av.)
Landin Ho. *E14* *6C 86*
(off Thomas Rd.)
Landleys Fld. *N7* *5H 65*
(off Long Mdw.)
Landmann Ho. *SE16* *4H 103*
(off Rennie Est.)
Landmann Point SE10 3J 105
Landmann Way SE14 5K 103
Landmark Arts Cen. 5B 132
Landmark Commercial Cen.
N18 6K 33
Landmark East Twr. *E14* *2C 104*
(off Marsh Wall)
Landmark Hgts. E5 4A 68
Landmark Ho. *W6* *5E 98*
(off Hammersmith Bri. Rd.)
Landmark Pl. UB10: Hil 2D 74
Landmark Sq. E14 2C 104
Landmark West Twr. *E14* *2C 104*
(off Marsh Wall)
Landon Pl. SW1 1E 16 (3D 100)
Landon's Cl. E14 1E 104
Landon Wlk. E14 7D 86
Landon Way TW15: Ashf 6D 128
Landor Ho. *SE5* *7D 102*
(off Elmington Est.)
W2 *5J 81*
(off Westbourne Pk. Rd.)
Landor Rd. SW9 3J 119
Landor Space 3J 119
Landor Wlk. W12 2C 98
Landra Gdns. N21 6G 23
Landrake *NW1* *1G 83*
(off Plender St.)
Landridge Dr. EN1: Enf 1C 24
Landridge Rd. SW6 2H 117
Landrock Rd. N8 6J 47
Landscape Rd. IG8: Wfd G 7E 36
Landsdown Cl. EN5: New Bar 4F 21
Landsdowne Ct. *N19* *1J 65*
(off Fairbridge Rd.)
Landseer Av. E12 5E 70
Landseer Cl. HA8: Edg 2G 43
SW19 1A 154
Landseer Ct. UB4: Hayes 2F 75
Landseer Ho. *NW8* *3B 4*
(off Frampton St.)
SW1 *4D 18*
(off Herrick St.)
SW11 1E 118
UB5: N'olt *5J 59*
(off Parkfield Dr.)
Landseer Rd. EN1: Enf 5B 24
KT3: N Mald 7K 151
N19 3J 65
(not continuous)
SM1: Sutt 6J 165
Landstead Rd. SE18 7H 107
Landulph Ho. *SE11* *5K 19*
(off Kennings Way)
Landward Ct. *W1* *7D 4*
(off Harrowby St.)
The Lane NW8 2A 82
SE3 3J 123
Lane Cl. NW2 3D 62
La. End DA7: Bex 3H 127
SW15 6F 117
Lane Gdns. WD23: B Hea 1D 26
Lane M. E12 3D 70
Lanercost Cl. SW2 2A 138
Lanercost Gdns. N14 7D 22
Lanercost Rd. SW2 2A 138
Lanesborough Ct. *N1* *1G 9*
(off Fanshaw St.)
Lanesborough Pl. SW1 6H 11
Lanesborough Way SW17 3B 136
Laneside BR7: Chst 5F 143
HA8: Edg 5D 28
Laneside Av. RM8: Dag 7F 55
Laneway SW15 5D 116
Laney Ho. *EC1* *5J 7*
(off Leather La.)
Lanfranc Ct. HA1: Harr 3K 59
Lanfranc Rd. E3 2A 86
Lanfrey Pl. W14 5H 99
Langan Ho. *E14* *6B 86*
(off Keymer Pl.)
Langbourne Av. N6 2E 64
Langbourne Ct. E17 6A 50
Langbourne Mans. N6 2E 64
Langbourne Pl. E14 5D 104
Langbourne Way
KT10: Clay 6A 162
Langbrook Rd. SE3 3B 124
Langcroft Cl. SM5: Cars 3D 166
Langdale *NW1* *1A 6*
(off Stanhope St.)
Langdale Av. CR4: Mitc 3D 154
Langdale Cl. BR6: Farnb 3F 173
RM8: Dag 1C 72
SE17 6C 102
SW14 4H 115
Langdale Cres. DA7: Bex 7G 109
Langdale Dr. UB4: Hayes 2G 75
Langdale Gdns. UB6: G'frd 3B 78
Langdale Ho. *SW1* *6A 18*
(off Churchill Gdns.)
Langdale Pde. CR4: Mitc 3D 154
Langdale Rd. CR7: Thor H 4A 156
SE10 7E 104
Langdale St. E1 6H 85
Langdon Ct. *EC1* *1B 8*
(off City Rd.)
NW10 1A 80
Langdon Cres. E6 2E 88
Langdon Dr. NW9 1J 61
Langdon Ho. *E14* *6E 86*
(off Ida St.)
Langdon Pk. TW11: Tedd 7C 132
Langdon Pk. Rd. N6 7G 47
Langdon Pl. SW14 3J 115
Langdon Rd. BR2: Broml 3K 159
E6 1E 88
SM4: Mord 5A 154
Langdons Ct. UB2: S'hall 3E 94
Langdon Shaw DA14: Sidc 5K 143
Langdon Wlk. SM4: Mord 5A 154
Langdon Way SE1 4G 103
Langford Cl. E8 5G 67
N15 6E 48
NW8 2A 82
W3 2H 97
Langford Ct. *NW8* *2A 82*
(off Abbey Rd.)
Langford Cres. EN4: Cockf 4J 21
Langford Grn. SE5 3E 120
Langford Ho. SE8 6C 104
Langford M. N1 7A 66
SW11 *4B 118*
(off St John's Hill)
Langford Pl. DA14: Sidc 3A 144
NW8 2A 82
Langford Rd. EN4: Cockf 4J 21
IG8: Wfd G 6F 37
SW6 2K 117
Langfords IG9: Buck H 2G 37
Langham Cl. BR2: Broml 2C 172
N15 *3B 48*
(off Langham Rd.)
Langham Ct. HA4: Ruis 5K 57
NW4 5F 45
SW20 2E 152
Langham Dr. RM6: Chad H 6B 54
Langham Gdns.
HA0: Wemb 2C 60
HA8: Edg 7D 28
N21 5F 23
TW10: Ham 4C 132
W13 7B 78
Langham Ho. *E15* *6F 69*
(off Forrester Way)
Langham Ho. Cl. TW10: Ham 4D 132
Langham Mans. *SW5* *5K 99*
(off Earl's Ct. Sq.)
Langham Pk. Pl. BR2: Broml 4H 159
Langham Pl. N15 3B 48
W1 6K 5 (5F 83)
W4 6A 98
Langham Rd. HA8: Edg 6D 28
N15 3B 48
SW20 1E 152
TW11: Tedd 5B 132
Langham St. W1 6K 5 (5F 83)
Langhedge Cl. N18 6A 34
Langhedge La. N18 6A 34
Langhedge La. Ind. Est.
N18 6A 34
Langholm Cl. SW12 7H 119
Langholme WD23: Bush 1B 26
Langhorn Dr. TW2: Twick 7J 113
Langhorne Ct. *NW8* *7B 64*
(off Dorman Way)
Langhorne Rd. RM10: Dag 7G 73
Langhorne St. SE18 7D 106
Lang Ho. *SW8* *7J 101*
(off Hartington Rd.)
TW19: Stanw 1A 128
Langland Cres. HA7: Stan 2D 42

Langland Dr.—Laxton Ct.

Langland Dr. HA5: Pinn 1C 40
Langland Gdns. CR0: C'don 2B 170
NW3 5K 63
Langland Ho. *SE5* *7D 102*
(off Edmund St.)
Langler Rd. NW10 2E 80
Langley Av. HA4: Ruis 2K 57
KT4: Wor Pk 1F 165
KT6: Surb 1D 162
Langley Ct. WC2 2E 12 (7J 83)
Langley Cres. E11 7A 52
HA8: Edg 3D 28
RM9: Dag 7C 72
UB3: Harl 7H 93
Langley Dr. E11 7K 51
W3 2H 97
Langley Gdns. BR2: Broml 4A 160
BR5: Pet W 6F 161
RM9: Dag 7D 72
Langley Gro. KT3: N Mald 2A 152
Langley Ho. *W2* *5J 81*
(off Alfred Rd.)
Langley La. SW8 7F 19 (6K 101)
Langley Mans. SW8 7F 19
Langley M. RM9: Dag 7D 72
Langley Pk. NW7 6F 29
Langley Pk. Golf Course 6F 159
Langley Pk. Rd. SM1: Sutt 5A 166
SM2: Sutt 5A 166
Langley Pk. Sports Cen. 6E 158
Langley Rd. BR3: Beck 4A 158
DA16: Well 6C 108
KT6: Surb 7E 150
SW19 1H 153
TW7: Isle 2K 113
Langley Row EN5: Barn 1C 20
Langley St. WC2 1E 12 (6J 83)
Langley Way BR4: W W'ck 1F 171
Langmead Dr.
WD23: B Hea 1D 26
Langmead Ho. *E3* *3D 86*
(off Bruce Rd.)
Langmead St. SE27 4B 138
Langmore Ct. DA6: Bex 3D 126
Langmore Ho. *E1* *6G 85*
(off Stutfield St.)
Langport Ct. KT12: Walt T 7A 148
Langport Ho. SW9 2B 120
Langridge M. TW12: Hamp 6D 130
Langroyd Rd. SW17 2D 136
Langside Av. SW15 4C 116
Langside Cres. N14 3C 32
Langstone Mews UB1: S'hall 1E 94
Langstone Way NW7 7A 30
Langston Hughes Cl. SE24 4B 120
Lang St. E1 4J 85
Langthorn Ct. EC2 7E 8 (6D 84)
Langthorne Ct. BR1: Broml 4E 140
Langthorne Ho. *E3* *3B 86*
(off Merchant St.)
UB3: Harl 4G 93
Langthorne Rd. E11 3E 68
(not continuous)
Langthorne St. SW6 7F 99
Langton Av. E6 3E 88
N20 7F 21
Langton Cl. WC1 3H 7 (4K 83)
Langton Ho. SE11 3H 19
Langton Pl. SW18 1J 135
Langton Ri. SE23 7H 121
Langton Rd. HA3: Hrw W 7B 26
KT8: W Mole 4G 149
NW2 3E 62
SW9 7B 102
Langton St. SW10 6A 100
Langton Way CR0: C'don 3E 168
SE3 1H 123
Langtry Ct. TW7: Isle 2K 113
Langtry Ho. *KT2: King T* *1G 151*
(off London Rd.)
Langtry Pl. SW6 6J 99
Langtry Rd. NW8 1K 81
UB5: N'olt 2B 76
Langtry Wlk. NW8 1K 81
Langwood Chase TW11: Tedd 6C 132
Langworth Dr. UB4: Yead 6K 75
Lanhill Rd. W9 4J 81
Lanier Rd. SE13 6F 123
Lanigan Dr. TW3: Houn 5F 113
Lankaster Gdns. N2 1B 46
Lankers Dr. HA2: Harr 6D 40
Lankton Cl. BR3: Beck 1E 158
Lannock Rd. UB3: Hayes 1H 93
Lannoy Point *SW6* *7G 99*
(off Pellant Rd.)
Lannoy Rd. SE9 1G 143
Lanrick Rd. E14 6F 87
Lanridge Rd. SE2 3D 108
Lansbury Av. IG11: Bark 7A 72
N18 5J 33
RM6: Chad H 5E 54
TW14: Felt 6K 111
Lansbury Cl. NW10 5J 61
Lansbury Ct. *SE28* *7B 90*
(off Saunders Way)
Lansbury Dr. UB4: Hayes 2G 75
Lansbury Est. E14 6D 86
Lansbury Gdns. E14 6F 87
Lansbury Rd. EN3: Enf H 1E 24
Lansbury Way N18 5K 33
Lanscombe Wlk. SW8 1J 119
Lansdell Ho. SW2 6A 120
Lansdell Rd. CR4: Mitc 2E 154
Lansdowne Av. BR6: Farnb 1F 173
DA7: Bex 7D 108
Lansdowne Cl. KT6: Surb 2H 163
SW20 7F 135
TW1: Twick 1K 131
Lansdowne Ct. IG5: Ilf 3C 52
KT4: Wor Pk 2C 164
W11 *7G 81*
(off Lansdowne Ri.)
Lansdowne Cres. W11 7G 81
Lansdowne Dr. E8 6G 67
Lansdowne Gdns. SW8 1J 119
Lansdowne Grn. SW8 1J 119
Lansdowne Gro. NW10 4A 62
Lansdowne Hill SE27 3B 138
Lansdowne Ho. *W11* *1H 99*
(off Ladbroke Rd.)
Lansdowne La. SE7 6B 106
Lansdowne M. SE7 5B 106
W11 1H 99
Lansdowne Pl. SE1 3D 102
SE19 7F 139
Lansdowne Ri. W11 7G 81
Lansdowne Rd. BR1: Broml 7J 141
CR0: C'don 2D 168
E4 2H 35
E11 2H 69
E17 6C 50
E18 3J 51
HA1: Harr 7J 41
HA7: Stan 6H 27
IG3: Ilf 1K 71
KT19: Ewe 7J 163
N3 7D 30
N10 2G 47
N17 1F 49
SW20 7E 134
TW3: Houn 3F 113
UB8: Hil 6E 74
W11 7G 81
Lansdowne Row W1 4K 11 (1F 101)
Lansdowne Ter. WC1 4F 7 (4J 83)
Lansdowne Wlk. W11 1H 99
Lansdowne Way SW8 1H 119
Lansdowne Wood Cl. SE27 3B 138
Lansdowne Workshops SE7 5A 106
Lansdown Rd. DA14: Sidc 3B 144
E7 7A 70
Lansfield Av. N18 4B 34
Lanson Apts. SW11 7F 101
Lantan Hgts. E20 7E 68
Lantern *SE1* *6C 14*
(off Lant St.)
Lantern Cl. BR6: Farnb 4F 173
HA0: Wemb 5D 60
SW15 4C 116
Lantern Ho. *UB3: Harl* *3E 92*
(off Nine Acres Cl.)
Lanterns Way E14 2C 104
Lantern Way UB7: W Dray 2A 92
Lant Ho. *SE1* *7C 14*
(off Toulmin St.)
Lantry Ct. W3 1H 97
Lant St. SE1 6C 14 (2C 102)
Lanvanor Rd. SE15 2J 121
Lanward Apts. *N1* *7K 65*
(off Caledonian Rd.)
Lanyard Ho. SE8 4B 104
Lapford Cl. W9 4H 81
Lapis Cl. NW10 3G 79
Lapis M. E15 1E 86
Lapponum Wlk. UB4: Yead 4B 76
Lapse Wood Wlk. SE23 1H 139
Lapstone Gdns. HA3: Kenton 6C 42
Lapwing Ct. KT6: Surb 3G 163
SE1 *7D 14*
(off Swan St.)
Lapwing Ter. E7 5B 70
Lapwing Twr. *SE8* *6B 104*
(off Taylor Cl.)
Lapwing Way UB4: Yead 6B 76
Lapworth *N11* *4A 32*
(off Coppies Gro.)
Lapworth Ct. *W2* *5K 81*
(off Delamere Ter.)
Lara Cl. KT9: Chess 7E 162
SE13 6E 122
Larbert Rd. SW16 7G 137
Larch Av. W3 1A 98
Larch Cl. E13 4K 87
N11 7K 31
N19 2G 65
SE8 6B 104
SW12 2F 137
Larch Ct. *SE1* *3J 105*
(off Royal Oak Yd.)
W9 *5J 81*
(off Admiral Wlk.)
Larch Cres. KT19: Ewe 6H 163
UB4: Yead 4A 76
Larch Dene BR6: Farnb 2E 172
Larch Dr. W4 5G 97
The Larches N13 3H 33
UB10: Hil 3D 74
Larches Av. SW14 4K 115
Larch Grn. NW9 1A 44
Larch Gro. DA15: Sidc 1K 143
Larch Ho. BR2: Broml 1G 159
SE16 *2J 103*
(off Ainsty Est.)
UB4: Yead 5A 76
W10 *4G 81*
(off Rowan Wlk.)
Larch Rd. E10 2C 68
NW2 4E 62
Larch Tree Way CR0: C'don 3C 170
Larchvale Ct. SM2: Sutt 7K 165
Larch Way BR2: Broml 1E 172
Larchwood Ho. *UB7: W Dray* *2B 92*
(off Park Lodge Av.)
Larchwood Rd. SE9 2F 143
Larcombe Cl. CR0: C'don 4F 169
Larcombe Ct. *SM2: Sutt* *7K 165*
(off Worcester Rd.)
Larcom St. SE17 4C 102
Larden Rd. W3 1A 98
Largewood Av. KT6: Surb 2G 163
Lariat Apts. *SE10* *4G 105*
(off Cable Wlk.)
Larissa St. SE17 5D 102
Larkbere Rd. SE26 4A 140
Lark Ct. *NW9* *1A 44*
(off Lanacre Av.)
Larken Cl. WD23: Bush 1B 26
Larken Dr. WD23: Bush 1B 26
Larkfield Av. HA3: Kenton 3B 42
Larkfield Cl. BR2: Hayes 2H 171
Larkfield Rd. DA14: Sidc 3K 143
TW9: Rich 4E 114
Larkhall La. SW4 2H 119
Larkhall Ri. SW4 3G 119
(not continuous)
Larkham Cl. TW13: Felt 3G 129
Lark Row E2 1J 85
Larksfield Gro. EN1: Enf 1C 24
Larks Gro. IG11: Bark 7J 71
Larkshall Ct. RM7: Mawney 2J 55
Larkshall Cres. E4 4K 35
Larkshall Rd. E4 5K 35
Larkspur Cl. E6 5C 88
HA4: Ruis 7E 38
N17 1B 48
NW9 5H 43
Larkspur Gro. HA8: Edg 4D 28
Larkspur Lodge DA14: Sidc 3B 144
Larkspur Way KT19: Ewe 5J 163
Larkswood Ct. E4 5A 36
Larkswood Ri. HA5: Eastc 4A 40
Larkswood Rd. E4 4H 35
Lark Way SM5: Cars 7C 154
Larkway Cl. NW9 4K 43
Larkwood Av. SE10 1E 122
Larnach Rd. W6 6F 99
Larne Rd. HA4: Ruis 7H 39
Larpent Av. SW15 5E 116
Larson Wlk. E14 3C 104
Larwood Cl. UB6: G'frd 5H 59
Lascar Cl. TW3: Houn 3D 112
Lascar Wharf Bldg. *E14* *6A 86*
(off Parnham St.)
Lascelles Av. HA1: Harr 7H 41
Lascelles Cl. E11 2F 69
Lascelles Ho. NW1 4D 4
Lascotts Rd. N22 6E 32
Laseron Ho. *N15* *4F 49*
(off Tottenham Grn. E.)
Laserquest
Romford 2F 55
Las Palmas Est. TW17: Shep 7E 146
Lassa Rd. SE9 5C 124
Lassell St. SE10 5F 105
Lasseter Pl. SE3 6H 105
Latchett Rd. E18 1K 51
Latchingdon Ct. E17 4K 49
Latchingdon Gdns. IG8: Wfd G 6H 37
Latchmere Cl. TW10: Ham 5E 132
Latchmere La. KT2: King T 6F 133
TW10: Ham 6F 133
Latchmere Leisure Cen. 2D 118
Latchmere Pas. SW11 2C 118
Latchmere Pl. TW15: Ashf 2A 128
Latchmere Rd. KT2: King T 7E 132
SW11 2D 118
Latchmere St. SW11 2D 118
Lateward Rd. TW8: Bford 6D 96
Latham Cl. E6 5C 88
TW1: Twick 7A 114
Latham Ct. *N11* *6D 32*
(off Brownlow Rd.)
SW5 *4J 99*
(off W. Cromwell Rd.)
UB5: N'olt *3B 76*
(off Delta Gro.)
Latham Ho. *E1* *6K 85*
(off Chudleigh St.)
Latham Rd. DA6: Bex 5G 127
TW1: Twick 7K 113
Latham's Way CR0: Wadd 1K 167
Lathkill Cl. EN1: Enf 7B 24
Lathkill Ct. BR3: Beck 1B 158
Lathom Rd. E6 7C 70
Latimer Av. E6 1D 88
Latimer Cl. HA5: Pinn 1A 40
KT4: Wor Pk 4D 164
Latimer Ct. *BR2: Broml* *4H 159*
(off Durham Rd.)
Latimer Gdns. HA5: Pinn 1A 40
Latimer Ho. E9 6K 67
W11 *7H 81*
(off Kensington Pk. Rd.)
Latimer Ind. Est. W10 6E 80
Latimer Pl. W10 6E 80
Latimer Rd. CR0: C'don 3B 168
E7 4K 69
EN5: New Bar 3E 20
N15 6E 48
SW19 6K 135
TW11: Tedd 5K 131
W10 5E 80
(not continuous)
Latimer Square SE10 3J 105
Latitude Apts. *CR0: C'don* *3D 168*
(off Fairfield Rd.)
Latitude Ct. E16 7G 89
Latitude Ho. *NW1* *1F 83*
(off Oval Rd.)
Latona Ct. *SW9* *7A 102*
(off Caldwell St.)
Latona Rd. SE15 6G 103
La Tourne Gdns.
BR6: Farnb 3G 173
Lattimer Pl. W4 7A 98
Latton Cl. KT12: Walt T 7C 148
Latvia Ct. *SE17* *5C 102*
(off Macleod St.)
Latymer Ct. W6 4F 99
Latymer Gdns. N3 2G 45
Latymer Rd. N9 1A 34
Latymer Way N9 2K 33
Laubin Cl. TW1: Twick 4B 114
Lauder Cl. UB5: N'olt 2B 76
Lauder Ct. N14 7D 22
Lauderdale Dr. TW10: Ham 3D 132
Lauderdale House 1F 65
Lauderdale Ho. *SW9* *1A 120*
(off Gosling Way)
Lauderdale House Community Arts Cen.
1F 65
(within Lauderdale House)
Lauderdale Mans. *W9* *3K 81*
(off Lauderdale Rd.)
Lauderdale Pde. W9 4K 81
Lauderdale Pl. *EC2* *5C 8*
(off Beech St.)
Lauderdale Rd. W9 3K 81
Lauderdale Twr. EC2 5C 8
Laud St. CR0: C'don 3C 168
SE11 5G 19 (5K 101)
Laugan Wlk. SE17 5C 102
Laughton Rd. UB5: N'olt 1B 76
Launcelot Rd. BR1: Broml 4J 141
Launcelot St. SE1 7J 13 (2A 102)
Launceston Gdns.
UB6: G'frd 1C 78
Launceston Pl. W8 3A 100
Launceston Rd. UB6: G'frd 1C 78
Launch St. E14 3E 104
Launders Ga. W3 2H 97
Laundress La. N16 3G 67
Laundry Cl. CR0: C'don 7D 156
Laundry La. N1 1C 84
Laundry M. SE23 7A 122
Laundry Rd. W6 6G 99
Launton Dr. DA6: Bex 4D 126
Laura Cl. E11 5A 52
EN1: Enf 5K 23
Lauradale Rd. N2 4D 46
Laura Pl. E5 4J 67
Laura Ter. N4 2B 66
Laurel Apts. *SE17* *4E 102*
(off Townsend St.)
Laurel Av. TW1: Twick 1K 131
Laurel Bank N12 4F 31
Laurel Bank Gdns. SW6 2H 117
Laurel Bank Rd. EN2: Enf 1H 23
Laurel Bank Vs. *W7* *2J 95*
(off Lwr. Boston Rd.)
Laurel Cl. DA14: Sidc 3A 144
N19 2G 65
SW17 5C 136
Laurel Ct. *CR2: S Croy* *4E 168*
(off South Pk. Hill Rd.)
HA0: Wemb 2E 78
SE1 *3D 102*
(off Garland Cl.)
Laurel Cres. CR0: C'don 3C 170
RM7: Rush G 1K 73
Laurel Dr. N21 7F 23
Laurel Gdns. BR1: Broml 4C 160
E4 7J 25
NW7 3E 28
TW4: Houn 4C 112
TW15: Ashf 5E 128
W7 1J 95
Laurel Gro. SE20 7J 139
SE26 4K 139
Laurel Ho. BR2: Broml 1G 159
E3 *1B 86*
(off Hornbeam Sq.)
SE8 6B 104
Laurel La. UB7: W Dray 4A 92
Laurel Mnr. SM2: Sutt 7A 166
Laurel M. *SE5* *3C 120*
(off Harbour Rd.)
Laurel Pk. HA3: Hrw W 7E 26
Laurel Rd. SW13 2C 116
SW20 1D 152
TW12: Hamp H 5H 131
The Laurels BR1: Broml 1K 159
BR2: Broml 4J 159
IG9: Buck H 1F 37
NW10 1D 80
SW9 *7B 102*
(off Langton Rd.)
WD23: B Hea 2D 26
Laurel St. E8 6F 67
Laurel Vw. N12 3E 30
Laurel Way E18 4H 51
N20 3D 30
Laurence Calvert Cl. IG11: Bark 2J 89
Laurence Ct. E10 7D 50
W11 *7G 81*
(off Lansdowne Rd.)
Laurence M. W12 2C 98
Laurence Pountney Hill
EC4 2E 14 (7D 84)
Laurence Pountney La.
EC4 2E 14 (7D 84)
Laurenson Rd. TW3: Houn 3G 113
Laurie Gro. SE14 1A 122
Laurie Ho. *SE1* *3B 102*
(off St George's Rd.)
W8 *1J 99*
(off Airlie Gdns.)
Laurie Rd. W7 5J 77
Laurier Rd. CR0: C'don 7F 157
NW5 3F 65
Laurimel Cl. HA7: Stan 6G 27
Laurino Pl. WD23: B Hea 2B 26
Lauriston Ho. *E9* *7J 67*
(off Lauriston Rd.)
Lauriston Rd. E9 7J 67
SW19 6F 135
Lausanne Rd. N8 4A 48
SE15 1J 121
Laval Ho. *TW8: Bford* *5E 96*
(off Ealing Rd.)
Lavell St. N16 4D 66
Lavender Av. CR4: Mitc 1C 154
KT4: Wor Pk 3E 164
NW9 1J 61
Lavender Cl. BR2: Broml 6C 160
E4 4H 35
SM5: Cars 4F 167
SW3 7B 16 (6B 100)
Lavender Ct. KT8: W Mole 3F 149
SM2: Sutt 7A 166
TW14: Felt 6K 111
Lavender Gdns. EN2: Enf 1G 23
HA3: Hrw W 6D 26
SW11 4D 118
Lavender Gro. CR4: Mitc 1C 154
E8 7G 67
Lavender Hill EN2: Enf 1F 23
SW11 4C 118
Lavender Ho. *SE16* *1K 103*
(off Rotherhithe St.)
TW9: Kew 1H 115
Lavender M. TW12: Hamp H 6G 131
Lavender Pl. IG1: Ilf 5F 71
Lavender Pond Nature Pk. 1A 104
Lavender Ri. UB7: W Dray 2C 92
Lavender Rd. CR0: C'don 6K 155
EN2: Enf 1J 23
KT19: Ewe 5H 163
SE16 1A 104
SM1: Sutt 4B 166
SM5: Cars 4E 166
SW11 3B 118
UB8: Hil 5B 74
Lavender Sq. *SW9* *1K 119*
(off Printers Rd.)
Lavender St. E15 6G 69
Lavender Sweep SW11 4D 118
Lavender Ter. SW11 3C 118
Lavender Va. SM6: W'gton 6H 167
Lavender Wlk. CR4: Mitc 3E 154
SW11 4D 118
Lavender Way CR0: C'don 6K 157
Lavendon Ho. *NW8* *3D 4*
(off Paveley St.)
Lavengro Rd. SE27 2C 138
Lavenham Rd. SW18 2H 135
Lavernock Rd. DA7: Bex 2G 127
Lavers Rd. N16 3E 66
Laverstoke Gdns. SW15 7B 116
Laverton M. SW5 4K 99
Laverton Pl. SW5 4K 99
Lavette Ho. *E3* *3C 86*
(off Rainhill Way)
Lavidge Rd. SE9 2C 142
Lavina Gro. N1 2K 83
Lavington Cl. E9 6B 68
Lavington Rd. CR0: Bedd 3K 167
W13 1B 96
Lavington St. SE1 5B 14 (1B 102)
Lavisham Ho. BR1: Broml 5K 141
Lawdons Gdns. CR0: Wadd 4B 168
Lawes Ho. *W10* *3H 81*
(off Lancefield St.)
Lawes Way IG11: Bark 3K 89
Lawford Rd. N1 7E 66
NW5 6G 65
W4 7J 97
Lawfords Wharf *NW1* *7G 65*
(off Lyme St.)
Law Ho. IG11: Bark 2A 90
Lawless Ho. *E14* *7E 86*
(off Bazely St.)
Lawless St. E14 7D 86
Lawley Ho. TW1: Twick 6D 114
Lawley Rd. N14 7A 22
Lawley St. E5 4J 67
Lawlor Cl. TW16: Sun 1K 147
The Lawn UB2: S'hall 5E 94
Lawn Cl. BR1: Broml 6K 141
HA4: Ruis 3H 57
KT3: N Mald 2A 152
N9 7A 24
Lawn Cres. TW9: Kew 2G 115
Lawn Farm Gro. RM6: Chad H 4E 54
Lawnfield Ct. *NW6* *7F 63*
(off Coverdale Rd.)
Lawn Gdns. W7 1J 95
Lawn Ho. Cl. E14 2E 104
Lawn La. SW8 7F 19 (6K 101)
Lawn Rd. BR3: Beck 7B 140
NW3 5D 64
The Lawns DA14: Sidc 4B 144
E4 5H 35
HA5: Hat E 7A 26
SE3 3H 123
SE19 1D 156
SM2: Cheam 7G 165
SW19 5H 135
Lawns Ct. HA9: Wemb 2F 61
Lawnside SE3 4H 123
Lawns Way RM5: Col R 1J 55
Lawnswood EN5: Barn 5B 20
Lawn Ter. SE3 3G 123
Lawn Va. HA5: Pinn 2C 40
Lawrence Av. E12 4E 70
E17 1K 49
KT3: N Mald 6K 151
N13 4G 33
NW7 4F 29
NW10 1K 79
Lawrence Bldgs. N16 3F 67
Lawrence Campe Cl. N20 3G 31
Lawrence Cl. E3 3C 86
N15 4E 48
W12 7D 80
Lawrence Ct. N10 3G 47
N16 *3F 67*
(off Smalley Rd. Est.)
NW7 5F 29
SE6 6C 122
W3 *3J 97*
(off Stanley Rd.)
Lawrence Cres. HA8: Edg 2G 43
RM10: Dag 3H 73
Lawrence Dr. UB10: Ick 4E 56
Lawrence Est. TW4: Houn 4A 112
Lawrence Gdns. NW7 3G 29
Lawrence Gro. UB10: Uxb 2A 74
Lawrence Hill E4 2H 35
Lawrence Ho. *NW1* *7F 65*
(off Hawley Cres.)
SW1 *4D 18*
(off Cureton St.)
Lawrence La. EC2 7D 8 (6C 84)
Lawrence Mans. *SW3* *7C 16*
(off Lordship Pl.)
Lawrence M. SW8 7J 101
SW15 4E 116
Lawrence Pde. *TW7: Isle* *3B 114*
(off Lower Sq.)
Lawrence Pl. *N1* *1J 83*
(off Brydon Wlk.)
Lawrence Rd. BR4: W W'ck 4J 171
DA8: Erith 7H 109
E6 1C 88
E13 1K 87
HA5: Pinn 6B 40
N15 4E 48
N18 4C 34
(not continuous)
SE25 4F 157
TW4: Houn 4A 112
TW10: Ham 4C 132
TW12: Hamp 7D 130
UB4: Hayes 2E 74
W5 4D 96
Lawrence St. E16 5H 87
NW7 5G 29
SW3 7C 16 (6C 100)
Lawrence Trad. Est. SE10 4G 105
Lawrence Way NW10 3J 61
Lawrence Weaver Cl.
SM4: Mord 6J 153
Lawrence Yd. N15 4E 48
Lawrie Ho. *SW19* *5K 135*
(off Durnsford Rd.)
Lawrie Pk. Av. SE26 5H 139
Lawrie Pk. Cres. SE26 5H 139
Lawrie Pk. Gdns. SE26 4H 139
Lawrie Pk. Rd. SE26 6H 139
Laws Cl. SE25 4D 156
Lawson Cl. E16 5A 88
IG1: Ilf 5H 71
SW19 3F 135
Lawson Ct. KT6: Surb 7D 150
N4 *1K 65*
(off Lorne Rd.)
N11 *6B 32*
(off Ring Way)
Lawson Gdns. HA5: Eastc 3K 39
Lawson Ho. *SE18* *6E 106*
(off Nightingale Pl.)
W12 *7D 80*
(off White City Est.)
Lawson Rd. EN3: Enf H 1D 24
UB1: S'hall 4E 76
Lawson Ter. SE15 4J 121
Law St. SE1 3D 102
Lawton Rd. E3 3A 86
(not continuous)
E10 1E 68
EN4: Cockf 3G 21
Laxcon Cl. NW10 5K 61
Laxey Rd. BR6: Chels 6K 173
Laxfield Ct. *E8* *1G 85*
(off Pownall Rd.)
Laxford Ho. *SW1* *4H 17*
(off Cundy St.)
Laxley Cl. SE5 7B 102
Laxton Ct. CR7: Thor H 4C 156

A-Z Big London 245

Laxton Pl.—Lewisham St.

Laxton Pl. NW1 . . . . 3K 5 (4F 83)
Layard Rd. CR7: Thor H 2D 156
EN1: Enf 1A 24
SE16 . . . . 4H 103
Layard Sq. SE16 . . . . 4H 103
Laybourne Ho. *E14* *2C 104*
(off Admirals Way)
Laybrook Lodge E18 . . . . 4H 51
Laycock St. N1 . . . . 6A 66
Layer Gdns. W3 . . . . 7G 79
Layfield Cl. NW4 . . . . 7D 44
Layfield Cres. NW4 . . . . 7D 44
Layfield Ho. *SE10* *5J 105*
(off Kemsing Rd.)
Layfield Rd. NW4 . . . . 7D 44
Layhams Rd. BR2: Kes 4G 171
BR4: W W'ck 4G 171
Laymarsh Cl. DA17: Belv 3F 109
Laymead Cl. UB5: N'olt 6C 58
Laystall Ct. *WC1* *4J 7*
(off Mt. Pleasant)
Laystall St. EC1 . . . . 4J 7 (4A 84)
Layton Ct. TW8: Bford 5D 96
Layton Cres. CR0: Wadd 5A 168
Layton Pl. TW9: Kew 1G 115
Layton Rd. TW3: Houn 4F 113
TW8: Bford 5D 96
Layton's La. TW16: Sun 2H 147
Layzell Wlk. SE9 . . . . 1B 142
Lazar Wlk. N7 . . . . 2K 65
Lazenby Ct. WC2 . . . . 2E 12
Leabank Cl. HA1: Harr 3J 59
Leabank Sq. E9 . . . . 6C 68
Leabank Vw. N15 . . . . 6G 49
Lea Bon Ct. *E15* *1H 87*
(off Plaistow Gro.)
Leabourne Rd. N16 . . . . 7G 49
LEA BRIDGE 3K 67
Lea Bri. Ind. Cen. E10 . . . . 1A 68
Lea Bri. Rd. E5 . . . . 3J 67
E10 . . . . 7C 50
E17 . . . . 5F 51
Lea Cl. TW2: Whitt 7D 112
Lea Ct. E4 . . . . 2K 35
E13 . . . . 3J 87
N15 . . . . 4G 49
Lea Cres. HA4: Ruis 4H 57
Leacroft Av. SW12 . . . . 7D 118
Leacroft Cl. N21 . . . . 2G 33
UB7: Yiew 6A 74
Leadale Av. E4 . . . . 2H 35
Leadale Rd. N15 . . . . 6G 49
N16 . . . . 6G 49
Leadbeaters Cl. N11 . . . . 5J 31
Leadbetter Ct. *NW10* *7K 61*
(off Melville Rd.)
Leadenhall Mkt. 1G 15 (6E 84)
Leadenhall Pl. EC3 . . . . 1G 15 (6E 84)
Leadenhall St. EC3 . . . . 1G 15 (6E 84)
Leadenham Ct. E3 . . . . 4C 86
Leader Av. E12 . . . . 5E 70
The Leadings HA9: Wemb 3J 61
Leadmill La. E20 . . . . 4D 68
Leaf Cl. HA6: Nwood 1F 39
KT7: T Ditt 5J 149
Leaf Gro. SE27 . . . . 5A 138
Leaf Ho. *HA1: Harr* *5K 41*
(off Catherine Pl.)
Leafield Cl. SW16 . . . . 6B 138
Leafield La. DA14: Sidc 3F 145
Leafield Rd. SM1: Sutt 2J 165
SW20 . . . . 3H 153
Leaf Wlk. N7 . . . . 4H 65
Leafy Gro. BR2: Kes 5A 172
Leafy Oak Rd. SE12 . . . . 4A 142
Leafy Way CR0: C'don 2F 169
Lea Gdns. HA9: Wemb 4F 61
Leagrave St. E5 . . . . 3J 67
Lea Hall Gdns. E10 . . . . 1C 68
Lea Hall Rd. E10 . . . . 1C 68
Leaholme Way HA4: Ruis 6E 38
Lea Ho. *NW8* *4C 4*
(off Salisbury St.)
Leahurst Rd. SE13 . . . . 5F 123
LEA INTERCHANGE 5C 68
Leake Ct. SE1 . . . . 7H 13 (2K 101)
Leake St. SE1 . . . . 6H 13 (2K 101)
(not continuous)
Lealand Rd. N15 . . . . 6F 49
Leamington Av. BR1: Broml 5A 142
BR6: Orp 4J 173
E17 . . . . 5C 50
SM4: Mord 4G 153
Leamington Cl. BR1: Broml 4A 142
E12 . . . . 5C 70
TW3: Houn 5G 113
Leamington Ct. SE3 . . . . 6G 105
Leamington Cres.
HA2: Harr 3C 58
Leamington Gdns. IG3: Ilf 2K 71
Leamington Ho. HA8: Edg 5A 28
W11 . . . . *5H 81*
(off Tavistock Rd.)
Leamington Pk. W3 . . . . 5K 79
Leamington Pl. UB4: Hayes 4H 75
Leamington Rd. UB2: S'hall 4B 94
Leamington Rd. Vs. W11 . . . . 5H 81
Leamore Ct. E2 . . . . 3K 85
Leamore St. W6 . . . . 4E 98
LEAMOUTH 7G 87
Leamouth Rd. E6 . . . . 5C 88
E14 . . . . 6F 87
Leander Ct. *E9* *7K 67*
(off Lauriston Rd.)
KT6: Surb 7D 150
NW9 . . . . 1A 44
SE8 . . . . 1C 122
Leander Rd. CR7: Thor H 4K 155
SW2 . . . . 6K 119
UB5: N'olt 2E 76
Lea Pk. Trad. Est. E10 . . . . 7B 50
Learner Dr. HA2: Harr 2E 58
Lea Rd. BR3: Beck 2C 158
EN2: Enf 1J 23
UB2: S'hall 4C 94
Learoyd Gdns. E6 . . . . 7E 88
Leary Ho. SE11 . . . . 5K 101
Leas Cl. KT9: Chess 7F 163
Leas Dale SE9 . . . . 3E 142
Leas Grn. BR7: Chst 6K 143
Leaside Av. N10 . . . . 3E 46
Leaside Bus. Cen. EN3: Brim 2G 25
Leaside Ct. UB10: Hil 3D 74
Leaside Mans. *N10* *3E 46*
(off Fortis Grn.)
Leaside Rd. E5 . . . . 1J 67
Leasowes Rd. E10 . . . . 1C 68
Lea Sq. E3 . . . . 1B 86
Leatherbottle Grn. DA18: Erith 3F 109
Leather Bottle La.
DA17: Belv 4E 108
Leather Cl. CR4: Mitc 2E 154
Leatherdale St. E1 . . . . 3K 85
Leather Gdns. E15 . . . . 1G 87
Leatherhead Cl. N16 . . . . 1F 67
Leatherhead Rd. KT9: Chess 7D 162
Leather La. EC1 . . . . 5J 7 (5A 84)
(not continuous)
The Leather Mkt. SE1 . . . . 7G 15
Leathermarket Ct.
SE1 . . . . 7G 15 (2E 102)
Leathermarket St.
SE1 . . . . 7G 15 (2E 102)
Leather Pl. *SE1* *3E 102*
(off Crimscott St.)
Leather Rd. SE16 . . . . 4K 103
Leathersellers Cl. *EN5: Barn* *3B 20*
(off The Avenue)
Leather St. E1 . . . . 7K 85
Leathsail Rd. HA2: Harr 3F 59
Leathwaite Rd. SW11 . . . . 4D 118
Leathwell Rd. SE8 . . . . 2D 122
Lea Va. DA1: Cray 4K 127
Lea Valley Bus. Pk. E10 . . . . 2A 68
Lea Valley Rd. E4 . . . . 5F 25
EN3: Pond E 5F 25
Lea Valley Trad. Est. N18 . . . . 6E 34
Lea Valley Viaduct N18 . . . . 5E 34
Leaveland Cl. BR3: Beck 4C 158
Leaver Gdns. UB6: G'frd 2H 77
Leavesden Rd. HA7: Stan 6F 27
Leaves Grn. Rd. BR2: Kes 7B 172
Lea Vw. Ho. E5 . . . . 1H 67
Leaway E10 . . . . 1K 67
Lebanon Av. TW13: Hanw 5B 130
Lebanon Ct. TW1: Twick 7B 114
Lebanon Gdns. SW18 . . . . 6J 117
Lebanon Pk. TW1: Twick 7B 114
Lebanon Rd. CR0: C'don 1E 168
SW18 . . . . 5J 117
Leben Ct. SM1: Sutt 6A 166
Lebus Ho. *NW8* *1C 4*
(off Cochrane St.)
Lebus St. N17 . . . . 3H 49
Le Chateau *CR0: C'don* *3D 168*
(off Chatsworth Rd.)
Lechmere App. IG8: Wfd G 2A 52
Lechmere Av. IG8: Wfd G 2B 52
Lechmere Rd. NW2 . . . . 6D 62
Leckford Rd. SW18 . . . . 2A 136
Leckhampton Pl. SW2 . . . . 7A 120
Leckwith Av. DA7: Bex 6E 108
Lecky St. SW7 . . . . 5A 16 (5B 100)
Leconfield Av. SW13 . . . . 3B 116
Leconfield Ho. SE5 . . . . 4E 120
Leconfield Rd. N5 . . . . 4D 66
Leda Av. EN3: Enf W 1E 24
Leda Ct. *SW9* *7A 102*
(off Caldwell St.)
Ledam Ho. *EC1* *5J 7*
(off Bourne Est.)
Leda Rd. SE18 . . . . 3D 106
Ledbury Ho. SE22 . . . . 3E 120
W11 . . . . *6H 81*
(off Colville Rd.)
Ledbury M. Nth. W11 . . . . 7J 81
Ledbury M. W. W11 . . . . 7J 81
Ledbury Pl. CR0: C'don 4C 168
Ledbury Rd. CR0: C'don 4D 168
W11 . . . . 6H 81
Ledbury St. SE15 . . . . 7G 103
Ledger M. E17 . . . . 6C 50
Ledrington Rd. SE19 . . . . 6G 139
Ledway Dr. HA9: Wemb 7F 43
LEE 6J 123
Lee Av. RM6: Chad H 6E 54
Lee Bri. SE13 . . . . 3E 122
Leechcroft Av. DA15: Sidc 5K 125
Leechcroft Rd. SM6: W'gton 3E 166
Lee Chu. St. SE13 . . . . 4G 123
Lee Cl. E17 . . . . 1K 49
EN5: New Bar 4F 21
Lee Conservancy Rd. E9 . . . . 5B 68
Lee Ct. *E3* *4E 86*
(off Navigation Rd.)
SE13 . . . . *4F 123*
(off Lee High Rd.)
Leecroft Rd. EN5: Barn 5B 20
Leeds Ct. *EC1* *3A 8*
(off St John St.)
Leeds Pl. N4 . . . . 1K 65
Leeds Rd. IG1: Ilf 1H 71
Leeds St. N18 . . . . 5B 34
Leefern Rd. W12 . . . . 2C 98
Leegate SE12 . . . . 5H 123
LEE GREEN 5H 123
Lee Gro. IG7: Chig 2K 37
Lee High Rd. SE12 . . . . 3E 122
SE13 . . . . 3E 122
Leeke St. WC1 . . . . 1G 7 (3K 83)
Leeland Rd. W13 . . . . 1A 96
Leeland Ter. W13 . . . . 1A 96
Leeland Way NW10 . . . . 4B 62
Lee M. BR3: Beck 3A 158
Leemount Ho. NW4 . . . . 4F 45
Lee Pk. SE3 . . . . 4H 123
Lee Pk. Way N9 . . . . 4E 34
N18 . . . . 4E 34
Leerdam Dr. E14 . . . . 3E 104
Lee Rd. EN1: Enf 6B 24
NW7 . . . . 7A 30
SE3 . . . . 3H 123
SW19 . . . . 1K 153
UB6: G'frd 1C 78
The Lees CR0: C'don 2B 170
Lees Av. HA6: Nwood 1H 39
Lees Ct. *W1* *2G 11*
(off Lees Pl.)
Lees Ho. *SE17* *5D 102*
(off Inville Rd.)
Leeside EN5: Barn 5B 20
Leeside Ct. *SE16* *1K 103*
(off Rotherhithe St.)
Leeside Cres. NW11 . . . . 6G 45
Leeside Ind. Est. N17 . . . . 7D 34
Leeside Rd. N17 . . . . 6C 34
Leeside Works N17 . . . . 7D 34
Leeson Ho. TW1: Twick 7B 114
Leeson Rd. SE24 . . . . 4A 120
Leesons Hill BR5: St P 3J 161
BR7: Chst 3J 161
Leeson's Way BR5: St P 2K 161
Lees Pde. UB10: Hil 4D 74
Lees Pl. W1 . . . . 2G 11 (7E 82)
Lees Rd. UB8: Hil 4D 74
Lee St. E8 . . . . 1F 85
Lee Ter. SE3 . . . . 3G 123
SE13 . . . . 3G 123
Lee Valley Athletics Cen. 1E 34
Lee Valley Golf Course 7F 25
Lee Valley Hockey & Tennis Cen.
. . . . 4D 68
Lee Valley Ice Cen. 2K 67
Lee Valley Pk. 7E 34
Lee Valley Technopark N17 . . . . 3G 49
Lee Valley VeloPark 5D 68
Leeve Ho. *W10* *3H 81*
(off Lancefield St.)
Lee Vw. EN2: Enf 1G 23
Leeward Ct. E1 . . . . 1G 103
SE8 . . . . *4A 104*
(off Yeoman St.)
Leeward Gdns. SW19 . . . . 5G 135
Leeward Ho. *N1* *1E 84*
(off Halcomb St.)
Leeway SE8 . . . . 5B 104
Leeway Cl. HA5: Hat E 1D 40
The Leeways SM3: Cheam 6G 165
Leewood Cl. SE12 . . . . 6J 123
Lefa Bus. & Ind. Pk.
DA14: Sidc 6D 144
Lefevre Wlk. E3 . . . . 2C 86
Leff Ho. NW6 . . . . 1G 81
Lefroy Ho. *SE1* *7C 14*
(off Southwark Bri. Rd.)
Lefroy Rd. W12 . . . . 2B 98
Left Side *N14* *1C 32*
(off Stationе Pde.)
Legacy Bldg. SW11 . . . . 6H 101
Legacy Wharf E15 . . . . 2D 86
Legard Rd. N5 . . . . 3B 66
Legatt Rd. SE9 . . . . 5B 124
Leggatt Rd. E15 . . . . 2E 86
Legge St. SE13 . . . . 5E 122
Leghorn Rd. NW10 . . . . 2B 80
SE18 . . . . 5H 107
Legion Cl. N1 . . . . 7A 66
Legion Ct. SM4: Mord 6J 153
Legion Rd. UB6: G'frd 1G 77
Legion Ter. E3 . . . . 1B 86
Legion Way N12 . . . . 7H 31
Leg O'Mutton Reservoir
Local Nature Reserve 7B 98
Legon Av. RM7: Rush G 1J 73
Legrace Av. TW4: Houn 2B 112
Leicester Av. CR4: Mitc 4J 155
Leicester Cl. KT4: Wor Pk 4E 164
Leicester Ct. *TW1: Twick* *6D 114*
(off Clevedon Rd.)
W9 . . . . *5J 81*
(off Elmfield Way)
WC2 . . . . 2D 12
Leicester Flds. 3D 12
Leicester Gdns. IG3: Ilf 7J 53
Leicester Ho. *N18* *5C 34*
(off Cavendish Cl.)
SW9 . . . . *3B 120*
(off Loughborough Rd.)
Leicester M. N2 . . . . 3C 46
Leicester Pl. WC2 . . . . 2D 12 (7H 83)
Leicester Rd. CR0: C'don 7E 156
E11 . . . . 5K 51
EN5: New Bar 5E 20
N2 . . . . 3C 46
NW10 . . . . 7K 61
Leicester Sq. WC2 . . . . 3D 12 (7H 83)
Leicester Square Theatre *2D 12*
(off Leicester Pl.)
Leicester St. WC2 . . . . 2D 12 (7H 83)
The Leigh KT2: King T 7A 134
Leigham Av. SW16 . . . . 3J 137
Leigham Cl. SW16 . . . . 3K 137
Leigham Ct. SM6: W'gton 6G 167
Leigham Ct. Rd. SW16 . . . . 2J 137
Leigham Dr. TW7: Isle 7J 95
Leigham Hall Pde. *SW16* *3J 137*
(off Streatham High Rd.)
Leigham Va. SW2 . . . . 3K 137
SW16 . . . . 3K 137
Leigh Av. IG4: Ilf 4B 52
Leigh Cl. KT3: N Mald 4J 151
Leigh Cl. Ind. Est. KT3: N Mald . . . 4K 151
Leigh Ct. HA2: Harr 1J 59
W14 . . . . *4H 99*
(off Avonmore Pl.)
Leigh Cres. CR0: New Ad 7D 170
Leigh Gdns. NW10 . . . . 2E 80
Leigh Hunt Dr. N14 . . . . 1C 32
Leigh Orchard Cl. SW16 . . . . 3K 137
Leigh Pl. DA16: Well 2A 126
EC1 . . . . 5J 7 (5A 84)
TW13: Felt 1A 130
Leigh Rd. E6 . . . . 6E 70
E10 . . . . 7E 50
N5 . . . . 4B 66
TW3: Houn 4H 113
Leigh St. WC1 . . . . 2E 6 (3J 83)
Leighton Av. E12 . . . . 5E 70
HA5: Pinn 3C 40
Leighton Cl. HA8: Edg 2G 43
Leighton Cres. NW5 . . . . 5G 65
Leighton Gdns. CR0: C'don 1B 168
NW10 . . . . 2D 80
Leighton Gro. NW5 . . . . 5G 65
Leighton Ho. *SW1* *4D 18*
(off Herrick St.)
Leighton House Mus. 3H 99
Leighton Mans. *W14* *6G 99*
(off Greyhound Rd.)
Leighton Pl. NW5 . . . . 5G 65
Leighton Rd. EN1: Enf 5A 24
HA3: Hrw W 2H 41
NW5 . . . . 5G 65
W13 . . . . 2A 96
Leighton St. CR0: C'don 1B 168
Leila Parnell Pl. SE7 . . . . 6A 106
Leinster Av. SW14 . . . . 3J 115
Leinster Gdns. W2 . . . . 6A 82
Leinster M. EN5: Barn 3B 20
W2 . . . . 7A 82
Leinster Pl. W2 . . . . 6A 82
Leinster Rd. N10 . . . . 4F 47
Leinster Sq. W2 . . . . 6J 81
(not continuous)
Leinster Ter. W2 . . . . 7A 82
Leirum St. N1 . . . . 1K 83
Leisure Way N12 . . . . 7G 31
Leisure W. 2K 129
Leitch Ho. *NW8* *7B 64*
(off Hilgrove Rd.)
Leith Cl. NW9 . . . . 1K 61
Leithcote Gdns. SW16 . . . . 4K 137
Leithcote Path SW16 . . . . 3K 137
Leith Hill BR5: St P 1K 161
Leith Hill Grn. BR5: St P 1K 161
Leith Mans. *W9* *3K 81*
(off Grantully Rd.)
Leith Rd. N22 . . . . 1B 48
Leith Towers SM2: Sutt 7K 165
Leith Yd. *NW6* *1J 81*
(off Quex Rd.)
Lela Av. TW4: Houn 2A 112
Lelitia Cl. E8 . . . . 1G 85
Lely Ho. *UB5: N'olt* *2B 76*
(off Academy Gdns.)
Leman St. E1 . . . . 7K 9 (6F 85)
Le Mare Ter. E3 . . . . 5C 86
Lemark Cl. HA7: Stan 6H 27
Le May Av. SE12 . . . . 3K 141
Lemmon Rd. SE10 . . . . 6G 105
Lemna Rd. E11 . . . . 7H 51
Le Moal Ho. *E1* *5J 85*
(off Stepney Way)
Lemonade Bldg. *IG11: Bark* *7G 71*
(off Ripple Rd.)
Lemon Gro. TW13: Felt 1J 129
Lemon Tree Ho. *E3* *3B 86*
(off Bow Rd.)
Lemonwell Dr. SE9 . . . . 5G 125
Lemsford Cl. N15 . . . . 6G 49
Lemsford Ct. N4 . . . . 2C 66
Lemuel St. SW18 . . . . 6A 118
Lena Cres. N9 . . . . 2D 34
Lena Gdns. W6 . . . . 3E 98
Lena Kennedy Cl. E4 . . . . 6K 35
Lenanton Steps *E14* *2C 104*
(off Manilla St.)
Len Bishop Ct. *E1* *7K 85*
(off Schoolhouse La.)
Len Clifton Ho. *SE18* *4D 106*
(off Cambridge Barracks Rd.)
Lendal Ter. SW4 . . . . 3H 119
Lendy Pl. TW16: Sun 4J 147
Lenelby Rd. KT6: Surb 1G 163
Len Freeman Pl. SW6 . . . . 6H 99
Lenham Ho. *SE1* *7F 15*
(off Staple St.)
Lenham Rd. CR7: Thor H 2D 156
DA7: Bex 6F 109
SE12 . . . . 4H 123
SM1: Sutt 4K 165
Lennard Av. BR4: W W'ck 2G 171
Lennard Cl. BR4: W W'ck 2G 171
Lennard Rd. BR2: Broml 1D 172
BR3: Beck 6K 139
CR0: C'don 1C 168
SE20 . . . . 6K 139
Lennon Rd. NW2 . . . . 5E 62
Lennox Gdns. CR0: Wadd 4B 168
IG1: Ilf 1D 70
NW10 . . . . 4B 62
SW1 . . . . 2E 16 (3D 100)
Lennox Gdns. M. SW1 . . . . 2E 16 (3D 100)
Lennox Ho. *DA17: Belv* *3G 109*
(off Ambrooke Rd.)
TW1: Twick *6D 114*
(off Clevedon Rd.)
Lennox Rd. E17 . . . . 6B 50
N4 . . . . 2K 65
SW9 . . . . 1B 120
Lenor Cl. DA6: Bex 4E 126
Lensbury Av. SW6 . . . . 2A 118
Lensbury Way SE2 . . . . 3C 108
Lens Rd. E7 . . . . 7A 70
Len Taylor Cl. UB4: Hayes 4G 75
Lenthall Ho. *SW1* *6B 18*
(off Churchill Gdns.)
Lenthall Rd. E8 . . . . 7G 67
Lenthorp Rd. SE10 . . . . 4H 105
Lentmead Rd. BR1: Broml 3H 141
Lenton Path SE18 . . . . 6H 107
Lenton Ri. TW9: Rich 3E 114
Lenton St. SE18 . . . . 4H 107
Lenton Ter. N4 . . . . 2A 66
Len Williams Ct. NW6 . . . . 2J 81
Leo Ct. TW8: Bford 7D 96
Leof Cres. SE6 . . . . 5D 140
Leominster Rd.
SM4: Mord 6A 154
Leominster Wlk.
SM4: Mord 6A 154
Leonard Av. RM7: Rush G 1K 73
SM4: Mord 5A 154
Leonard Cir. EC2 . . . . 3F 9 (4D 84)
Leonard Ct. HA3: Hrw W 1J 41
W8 . . . . 3J 99
WC1 . . . . 3D 6 (4H 83)
Leonard Pl. N16 . . . . 4E 66
Leonard Rd. E4 . . . . 6H 35
E7 . . . . 4J 69
N9 . . . . 3A 34
SW16 . . . . 1G 155
UB2: S'hall 3B 94
Leonard Robbins Path *SE28* *7B 90*
(off Tawney Rd.)
Leonard St. E16 . . . . 1C 106
EC2 . . . . 3F 9 (4D 84)
Leon Ho. CR0: C'don 3C 168
Leonora Ho. *W9* *4A 82*
(off Lanark Rd.)
Leonora Tyson M. SE21 . . . . 2D 138
Leontine Cl. SE15 . . . . 7G 103
Leopards Ct. EC1 . . . . 5J 7
Leopold Av. SW19 . . . . 5H 135
Leopold Bldgs. *E2* *1J 9*
(off Columbia Rd.)
Leopold M. E9 . . . . 1J 85
Leopold Rd. E17 . . . . 5C 50
N2 . . . . 3B 46
N18 . . . . 5C 34
NW10 . . . . 7A 62
SW19 . . . . 4H 135
W5 . . . . 1F 97
Leopold St. E3 . . . . 5B 86
Leopold Ter. SW19 . . . . 5H 135
Leo St. SE15 . . . . 7H 103
Leo Yd. EC1 . . . . 4B 8
Leppoc Rd. SW4 . . . . 5H 119
Leroy St. SE1 . . . . 4E 102
Lerry Cl. W14 . . . . 6H 99
Lerwick Ct. EN1: Enf 5K 23
Lescombe Cl. SE23 . . . . 3A 140
Lescombe Rd. SE23 . . . . 3A 140
Lescot Pl. BR2: Broml 6C 160
Lesley Cl. DA5: Bexl 7H 127
Lesley Ct. *SW1* *2C 18*
(off Strutton Ground)
Leslie Foster Cl. IG11: Bark 2K 89
Leslie Gdns. SM2: Sutt 6J 165
Leslie Gro. CR0: C'don 1E 168
Leslie Gro. Pl. CR0: C'don 1E 168
Leslie Ho. *SW8* *7J 101*
(off Wheatsheaf La.)
Leslie Pk. Rd. CR0: C'don 1E 168
Leslie Prince Ct. SE5 . . . . 7D 102
Leslie Rd. E11 . . . . 4E 68
E16 . . . . 6K 87
N2 . . . . 3B 46
Leslie Smith Sq. SE18 . . . . 6E 106
Lesnes Abbey 4D 108
Lesnes Abbey Woods 4D 108
Lesney Av. E20 . . . . 5C 68
Lesney Farm Est. DA8: Erith 7K 109
Lesney Pk. DA8: Erith 6K 109
Lesney Pk. Rd. DA8: Erith 6K 109
Lessar Av. SW4 . . . . 6G 119
Lessingham Av. IG5: Ilf 3E 52
SW17 . . . . 4D 136
Lessing St. SE23 . . . . 7A 122
Lessington Av. RM7: Rom 6J 55
Lessness Av. DA7: Bex 7D 108
LESSNESS HEATH 5G 109
Lessness Pk. DA17: Belv 5F 109
Lessness Rd. DA17: Belv 6G 109
SM4: Mord 6A 154
Lester Av. E15 . . . . 4G 87
Lester Ct. *E3* *3D 86*
(off Bruce Rd.)
Lestock Cl. *SE25* *3G 157*
(off Manor Rd.)
Leswin Pl. N16 . . . . 3F 67
Leswin Rd. N16 . . . . 3F 67
Letchford Gdns. NW10 . . . . 3C 80
Letchford Ho. *E3* *2C 86*
(off Thomas Fyre Dr.)
Letchford M. NW10 . . . . 3C 80
Letchford Ter. HA3: Hrw W 1F 41
Letchmore Ho. *W10* *4E 80*
(off Sutton Way)
Letchworth Av. TW14: Felt 7H 111
Letchworth Cl. BR2: Broml 5J 159
Letchworth Dr. BR2: Broml 5J 159
Letchworth Rd. HA7: Stan 7K 27
Letchworth St. SW17 . . . . 4D 136
Lethbridge Cl. SE10 . . . . 1E 122
Letterstone Rd. SW6 . . . . 7H 99
Lettice St. SW6 . . . . 1H 117
Lett Rd. E15 . . . . 7F 69
SW9 . . . . 1K 119
Lettsom St. SE5 . . . . 2E 120
Lettsom Wlk. E13 . . . . 2J 87
Leucha Rd. E17 . . . . 5A 50
Levana Cl. SW19 . . . . 1G 135
Levant Ho. *E1* *4K 85*
(off Ernest St.)
Levehurst Ho. SE27 . . . . 5C 138
Levendale Rd. SE23 . . . . 2A 140
Levenhurst Way SW4 . . . . 2J 119
Leven Rd. E14 . . . . 5E 86
Leven Way UB3: Hayes 6G 75
Leverett St. SW3 . . . . 3D 16 (4C 100)
Leverholme Gdns. SE9 . . . . 4E 142
Leverington Pl. N1 . . . . 2F 9 (3D 84)
Leverson St. SW16 . . . . 6G 137
Leverstock Ho. *SW3* *5D 16*
(off Cale St.)
Lever St. EC1 . . . . 2B 8 (3B 84)
Leverton Cl. N22 . . . . 1K 47
Leverton Pl. NW5 . . . . 5G 65
Leverton St. NW5 . . . . 5G 65
The Levett Buildging *EC1* *5B 84*
(off Little Britain)
Levett Gdns. IG3: Ilf 4K 71
Levett Rd. IG11: Bark 6J 71
Levett Square TW9: Kew 7H 97
Levine Gdns. IG11: Bark 2D 90
Levison Way N19 . . . . 1H 65
Levita Ho. NW1 . . . . 1D 6
(not continuous)
Levyne Ct. *EC1* *3J 7*
(off Pine St.)
Lewen Cl. CR0: C'don 1D 168
Lewes Cl. UB5: N'olt 6E 58
Lewes Ct. *CR4: Mitc* *3D 154*
(off Chatsworth Pl.)
Lewesdon Cl. SW19 . . . . 1F 135
Lewes Ho. *SE1* *6H 15*
(off Druid St.)
SE15 . . . . *6G 103*
(off Friary Est.)
Lewes Rd. BR1: Broml 2B 160
N12 . . . . 5H 31
Leweston Pl. N16 . . . . 7F 49
Lew Evans Ho. SE22 . . . . 5G 121
Lewey Ho. *E3* *4B 86*
(off Joseph St.)
Lewgars Av. NW9 . . . . 6J 43
Lewing Cl. BR6: Orp 1J 173
Lewington Apts. *SE16* *4J 103*
(off Alpine Rd.)
Lewington Cen. *SE16* *4J 103*
(off Alpine Rd.)
Lewin Rd. DA6: Bex 4E 126
SW14 . . . . 3K 115
SW16 . . . . 6H 137
Lewin Ter. TW14: Bedf 7F 111
Lewis Av. E17 . . . . 1C 50
Lewis Cl. N14 . . . . 7B 22
Lewis Ct. *SE16* *5H 103*
(off Stubbs Dr.)
Lewis Cres. NW10 . . . . 5K 61
Lewis Cubitt Pk. 1J 83
Lewis Cubitt Sq. N1 . . . . 1J 83
Lewis Cubitt Wlk. N1 . . . . 1J 83
Lewis Gdns. N2 . . . . 2B 46
N16 . . . . 6F 49
Lewis Gro. SE13 . . . . 3E 122
LEWISHAM 3E 122
Lewisham Cen. 4E 122
Lewisham Hgts. SE23 . . . . 1J 139
Lewisham High St. SE13 . . . . 3E 122
(not continuous)
Lewisham Hill SE13 . . . . 2E 122
Lewisham Indoor Bowls Cen. 5B 140
Lewisham Lions Cen. 5J 103
Lewisham Model Mkt. *4E 122*
(off Lewisham High St.)
Lewisham Pk. SE13 . . . . 5E 122
Lewisham Rd. SE13 . . . . 1D 122
Lewisham St. SW1 . . . . 7D 12 (2H 101)

Lewisham Way—Links Rd.

Lewisham Way SE4 1B 122
SE14 1B 122
Lewis Ho. *E14* 1E 104
(off Coldharbour)
N1 6B 66
(off Canonbury Rd.)
Lewis M. BR7: Chst 5D 142
Lewis Pl. E8 5G 67
Lewis Rd. CR4: Mitc 2B 154
DA14: Sidc 3C 144
DA16: Well 3C 126
SM1: Sutt 4K 165
TW10: Rich 5D 114
UB1: S'hall 2C 94
Lewis Silkin Ho. *SE15* 6J 103
(off Lovelinch Cl.)
Lewis Sports & Leisure Cen. 1F 157
Lewis St. NW1 6F 65
(not continuous)
Lewiston Cl. KT4: Wor Pk 7D 152
Lewis Way RM10: Dag 6H 73
Lexden Dr. RM6: Chad H 6B 54
Lexden Rd. CR4: Mitc 4H 155
W3 7H 79
Lexham Gdns. W8 4J 99
Lexham Gdns. M. W8 3K 99
Lexham Ho. *W8* 4K 99
(off Lexham Gdns.)
Lexham M. W8 4J 99
Lexham Wlk. W8 3K 99
Lexington Apts. EC1 3F 9 (4D 84)
Lexington Bldg. E3 2C 86
Lexington Ho. *UB7: W Dray* 2B 92
(off Park Lodge Av.)
Lexington Pl. KT1: Hamp W 7D 132
Lexington St. W1 2B 12 (7G 83)
Lexington Way
EN5: Barn 4A 20
Lexton Gdns. SW12 1H 137
Leyborne Av. W13 2B 96
Leyborne Pk. TW9: Kew 1G 115
Leybourne Cl. BR2: Broml 6J 159
Leybourne Ho. *E14* 6B 86
(off Dod St.)
SE15 6J 103
Leybourne Rd. E11 1H 69
NW1 7F 65
NW9 5G 43
UB10: Hil 1E 74
Leybourne St. NW1 7F 65
Leybridge Ct. SE12 5J 123
Leyburn Cl. E17 4D 50
Leyburn Gdns. CR0: C'don 2E 168
Leyburn Gro. N18 6B 34
Leyburn Rd. N18 6B 34
Leydenhatch La.
BR8: Swan 7J 145
Leyden Mans. N19 7J 47
Leyden St. E1 6J 9 (5F 85)
Leydon Cl. SE16 1K 103
Leyes Rd. E16 6B 88
Leyfield KT4: Wor Pk 1A 164
Ley Ho. *SE1* 7C 14
(off Scovell Rd.)
Leyland Av. EN3: Enf H 2F 25
Leyland Court *SE15* 7F 103
(off Shield Street)
Leyland Gdns. IG8: Wfd G 5F 37
Leyland Ho. *E14* 7D 86
(off Hale St.)
Leyland Rd. SE12 5J 123
Leylands SW18 6H 117
Leylands La.
TW19: Stanw M 7A 174
(not continuous)
Leylang Rd. SE14 7K 103
The Leys HA3: Kenton 6F 43
N2 4A 46
Leys Av. RM10: Dag 1J 91
Leys Cl. HA1: Harr 5H 41
RM10: Dag 7J 73
Leys Ct. SW9 2A 120
Leysdown Av. DA7: Bex 4J 127
Leysdown Ho. *SE17* 5E 102
(off Madron St.)
Leysdown Rd. SE9 2C 142
Leysfield Rd. W12 3C 98
Leys Gdns. EN4: Cockf 5K 21
Leyspring Rd. E11 1H 69
Leys Rd. E. EN3: Enf H 1F 25
Leys Rd. W. EN3: Enf H 1F 25
Leys Sq. N3 1K 45
Ley St. IG1: Ilf 2F 71
IG2: Ilf 2G 71
Leyswood Dr. IG2: Ilf 5J 53
Leythe Rd. W3 2J 97
LEYTON 2E 68
Leyton Bus. Cen. E10 2C 68
Leyton Ct. SE23 1J 139
Leyton Grange E10 1C 68
Leyton Grn. Rd. E10 6E 50
Leyton Grn. Twr. *E10* 6E 50
(off Leyton Grn. Rd.)
Leyton Ho. *E2* 2J 9
(off Calvert Av.)
Leyton Ind. Village E10 7K 49
Leyton Leisure Cen. 7E 50
Leyton Link Est. E10 7A 50
Leyton Mills E10 3E 68
Leyton Orient FC 3D 68
Leyton Pk. Rd. E10 4E 68
Leyton Rd. E15 5E 68
SW19 7A 136
LEYTONSTONE 1G 69
Leytonstone Ho. *E11* 7H 51
(off Hanbury Dr.)
Leytonstone Leisure Cen. 2G 69
Leytonstone Rd. E15 6G 69
Leyton Way E11 7G 51
Leywick St. E15 2G 87
Lezayre Rd. BR6: Chels 6K 173
Lianne Gro. SE9 3A 142
Liardet St. SE14 6A 104
Libari Mans. *E20* 5E 68
(off Victory Pde.)
Liberal Jewish Synagogue
2B 4 (3B 82)
Liberia Rd. N5 6B 66
Liberty Av. SW19 1B 154
Liberty Bri. Rd. E15 5E 68
E20 5E 68
Liberty Cen. HA0: Wemb 1F 79
Liberty Cl. KT4: Wor Pk 1E 164
N18 4A 34
Liberty Ct. BR1: Broml 3B 160
IG11: Bark 2B 90
Liberty Ho. *CR7: Thor H* 5A 156
(off Thornton Rd.)
E1 7G 85
(off Ensign St.)
E13 2J 87
Liberty M. N22 1B 48
SW12 6F 119
Liberty Point *CR0: C'don* 7G 157
(off Blackhorse La.)
Liberty St. SW9 1K 119
Libra Mans. *E3* 2B 86
(off Libra Rd.)
Libra Rd. E3 1B 86
E13 2J 87
The Library & Mus. of Freemasonry
7F 7
(in Freemasons' Hall)
Library Ct. N17 3F 49
Library Mans. *W12* 2E 98
(off Pennard Rd.)
Library M. TW12: Hamp H 6G 131
Library Pde. *NW10* 1A 80
(off Craven Pk. Rd.)
Library Pl. E1 7H 85
Library Sq. E1 4A 86
Library St. SE1 7A 14 (2B 102)
Library Way TW2: Whitt 7G 113
Libro Ct. E4 4H 35
Lichfield Cl. EN4: Cockf 3J 21
Lichfield Ct. *KT6: Surb* 5E 150
(off Claremont Rd.)
TW9: Rich 5E 114
Lichfield Gdns. TW9: Rich 4E 114
Lichfield Gro. N3 1J 45
Lichfield La. TW2: Whitt 1G 131
Lichfield Rd. E3 3A 86
E6 3B 88
HA6: Nwood 3J 39
IG8: Wfd G 4B 36
N9 2B 34
NW2 4G 63
RM8: Dag 4B 72
TW4: Houn 3A 112
TW9: Kew 1F 115
Lichfield Ter. *TW9: Rich* 5E 114
(off Sheen Rd.)
Lichlade Cl. BR6: Orp 4K 173
Lickey Ho. *W14* 6H 99
(off North End Rd.)
Lidcote Gdns. SW9 2K 119
Liddall Way UB7: Yiew 1B 92
Liddell Cl. HA3: Kenton 3D 42
Liddell Gdns. NW10 2E 80
Liddell Pl. NW6 6J 63
Liddell Rd. NW6 6J 63
Liddiard Ho. *W11* 7G 81
(off Lansdowne Rd.)
Lidding Rd. HA3: Kenton 5D 42
Liddington Rd. E15 1H 87
Liddon Rd. BR1: Broml 3A 160
E13 3K 87
Liden Cl. E17 7B 50
Lidfield Rd. N16 4D 66
Lidgate Rd. SE15 7F 103
Lidgould Gro. HA4: Ruis 6J 39
Lidiard Rd. SW18 2A 136
Lidlington Pl. NW1 2G 83
Lido Sq. N17 2D 48
Lidyard Rd. N19 1G 65
Lifeboat Station
Chiswick 7B 98
The Lifestyle Club @ Charlton 7B 106
Liffler Rd. SE18 5J 107
Liffords Pl. SW13 2B 116
Lifford St. SW15 4F 117
Lightcliffe Rd. N13 4F 33
Lighterage Ct. TW8: Bford 6E 96
Lighter Cl. SE16 4A 104
Lighterman Ho. E14 7E 86
Lighterman M. E1 6K 85
Lighterman Point *E14* 6F 87
(off New Village Av.)
Lightermans Rd. E14 2C 104
Lightermans Wlk. SW18 4J 117
Lightfoot Rd. N8 5J 47
Lightfoot Vs. *N1* 7A 66
(off Augustas La.)
Light Horse Ct. SW3 6G 17
The Lighthouse 7C 102
Lighthouse Apts. *E1* 6J 85
(off Commercial Rd.)
Lighthouse View SE10 1G 105
Lightley Cl. HA0: Wemb 1E 78
Ligonier St. E2 3J 9 (4F 85)
Lilac Cl. E4 6G 35
Lilac Ct. E13 1A 88
TW11: Tedd 4K 131
Lilac Gdns. CR0: C'don 3C 170
RM7: Rush G 1K 73
UB3: Hayes 6G 75
W5 3D 96
Lilac Ho. SE4 3C 122
Lilac La. E2 3K 85
Lilac M. *N22* 3A 48
(off High Rd.)
Lilac Pl. SE11 4G 19 (4K 101)
UB7: Yiew 1A 92
Lilac St. W12 7C 80
Lilah M. BR2: Broml 2G 159
Lilburne Gdns. SE9 5C 124
Lilburne Rd. SE9 5C 124
Lilburne Wlk. NW10 6J 61
Lile Cres. W7 5J 77
Lilestone Ho. *NW8* 3B 4
(off Frampton St.)
Lilestone St. NW8 3C 4 (4C 82)
Lilford Ho. SE5 2C 120
Lilford Rd. SE5 2B 120
Lilian Barker Cl. SE12 5J 123
Lilian Board Way UB6: G'frd 5H 59
Lilian Cl. N16 3E 66
Lilian Gdns. IG8: Wfd G 1K 51
Lilian Knowles Ho. *E1* 6J 9
(off Crispin St.)
Lilian Rd. SW16 1G 155
Lilium M. E10 7C 50
Lillechurch Rd. RM8: Dag 6B 72
Lilleshall Rd. SM4: Mord 6B 154
Lilley Cl. E1 1G 103
Lilley La. NW7 5E 28
Lillian Av. W3 2G 97
Lillian Rd. SW13 6C 98
Lillie Bri. Dpt. *W14* 5H 99
(off Aisgill Av.)
Lillie Mans. *SW6* 6G 99
(off Lillie Rd.)
Lillie Rd. SW6 6G 99
Lillie Road Fitness Cen. 7F 99
Lillieshall Rd. SW4 3F 119
Lillie Sq. SW6 6J 99
Lillie Yd. SW6 6J 99
Lillington Ho. N7 4A 66
Lillington Gdns. Est. SW1 4B 18
Lilliput Av. UB5: N'olt 1C 76
Lilliput Ct. SE12 5K 123
Lilliput Rd. E15 1G 87
RM7: Rush G 7K 55
Lily Cl. HA5: Pinn 2A 40
W14 4F 99
Lily Gdns. HA0: Wemb 2C 78
Lily M. SE11 4B 102
Lily Nichols Ho. *E16* 1B 106
(off Connaught Rd.)
Lily Pl. EC1 5K 7 (5A 84)
Lily Rd. E17 6C 50
Lilyville Rd. SW6 1H 117
Lily Way N13 5D 32
Limasol St. SE16 3F 103
Limborough Ho. *E14* 5C 86
(off Thomas Rd.)
Limbourne Av. RM8: Dag 7F 55
Limburg Rd. SW11 4C 118
Lime Av. UB7: Yiew 7B 74
Limeburner La. EC4 1A 14 (6B 84)
Lime Cl. BR1: Broml 4C 160
E1 1G 103
HA3: W'stone 2A 42
HA5: Eastc 3H 39
IG9: Buck H 2G 37
RM7: Rom 4J 55
SM5: Cars 2D 166
Lime Ct. CR4: Mitc 2B 154
E11 2G 69
(off Trinity Cl.)
E17 5E 50
HA1: Harr 6K 41
(off Gayton Rd.)
HA4: Ruis 7K 39
SE9 2F 143
Lime Cres. TW16: Sun 2A 148
Limecroft Cl. KT19: Ewe 7K 163
Limedene Cl. HA5: Pinn 1B 40
Lime Gro. BR6: Farnb 2F 173
DA15: Sidc 6K 125
E4 6G 35
HA4: Ruis 6K 39
KT3: N Mald 3K 151
N20 1C 30
TW1: Twick 6K 113
UB3: Hayes 7F 75
W12 2E 98
Limeharbour E14 3D 104
LIMEHOUSE 6B 86
Lime Ho. TW9: Kew 1H 115
Limehouse C'way. E14 7B 86
Lime Ho. Ct. *E14* 6B 86
(off Wharf La.)
Limehouse Ct. E14 6C 86
Limehouse Cut *E14* 5D 86
(off Morris Rd.)
Limehouse Flds. Est. E14 5A 86
Limehouse Link E14 6A 86
Limehouse Lodge *E5* 2J 67
(off Harry Zeital Way)
Lime Kiln Dr. SE7 6K 105
Limekiln Pl. SE19 7F 139
Limekiln Wharf E14 7B 86
Limelight Ho. *SE11* 4B 102
(off Dugard Way)
Lime Lodge *TW16: Sun* 7H 129
(off Forest Dr.)
Lime Quay E14 7E 86
Limerick Cl. SW12 7G 119
Limerick M. N2 3C 46
Lime Rd. TW9: Rich 4F 115
Lime Row DA18: Erith 3F 109
Limerston St. SW10 7A 16 (6A 100)
The Limes BR2: Broml 2C 172
KT8: W Mole 4F 149
SW18 6J 117
W2 7J 81
Limes Av. CR0: Wadd 3A 168
E11 4K 51
N12 4F 31
NW7 6F 29
NW11 7G 45
SE20 7H 139
SM5: Cars 1D 166
SW13 2B 116
The Limes Av. N11 5A 32
Limes Cl. N11 5A 32
TW15: Ashf 5C 128
Limes Ct. BR3: Beck 2D 158
NW6 7G 63
(off Brondesbury Pk.)
Limesdale Gdns. HA8: Edg 2J 43
Limes Fld. Rd. SW13 3A 116
Limesford Rd. SE15 4K 121
Limes Gdns. SW18 6J 117
Limes Gro. SE13 4E 122
Limes Pl. CR0: C'don 7D 156
Limes Rd. BR3: Beck 2D 158
CR0: C'don 7D 156
Limes Row BR6: Farnb 5F 173
Limestone Wlk. DA18: Erith 2D 108
Lime St. E17 4A 50
EC3 2G 15 (7E 84)
Lime St. Pas. EC3 1G 15 (6E 84)
Lime St. Sq. EC3 1G 15 (6E 84)
Limes Wlk. SE15 4J 121
W5 2D 96
Lime Ter. W7 7J 77
Lime Tree Av. KT7: T Ditt 7H 149
KT10: Esh 7H 149
Lime Tree Cl. E18 4A 52
Limetree Cl. SW2 1K 137
Lime Tree Ct. CR2: S Croy 6C 168
E3 5C 86
(off Whitehorn St.)
SE17 5C 102
(off Walworth Rd.)
Lime Tree Gro. CR0: C'don 3B 170
Lime Tree Pl. CR4: Mitc 1F 155
Lime Tree Rd. TW5: Hest 1F 113
Limetree Ter. DA16: Well 3A 126
SE6 1B 140
Lime Tree Wlk. BR4: W W'ck 4H 171
EN2: Enf 1H 23
WD23: B Hea 1D 26
Limetree Wlk. SW17 5E 136
Lime View Apts. *E14* 6A 86
(off Commerical Rd.)
Lime Wlk. E15 1G 87
KT8: E Mos 4K 149
Limewood Cl. BR3: Beck 5E 158
E17 4B 50
W13 6B 78
Limewood Ct. IG4: Ilf 5D 52
Limewood M. *SE20* 7G 139
(off Lullington Rd.)
Limewood Rd. DA8: Erith 7J 109
Limpsfield Av. CR7: Thor H 5K 155
SW19 2F 135
Limscott Ho. *E3* 3D 86
(off Bruce Rd.)
Linacre Cl. SE15 3H 121
Linacre Ct. W6 5F 99
Linacre Rd. NW2 6D 62
Linale Ho. N1 1E 8
Linberry Wlk. SE8 4B 104
Linchmere Rd. SE12 7H 123
Lincoln Apartments *W12* 7E 80
(off Fountain Park Way)
Lincoln Av. N14 3B 32
RM7: Rush G 2K 73
SW19 3F 135
TW2: Twick 2G 131
Lincoln Cl. HA2: Harr 5D 40
SE25 6G 157
UB6: G'frd 1G 77
Lincoln Ct. *CR2: S Croy* 5C 168
(off Warham Rd.)
IG2: Ilf 6G 53
N16 7D 48
SE12 3K 141
Lincoln Cres. EN1: Enf 5K 23
Lincoln Gdns. IG1: Ilf 7C 52
Lincoln Grn. Rd. BR5: St M Cry 5K 161
Lincoln Ho. SE5 7A 102
SW3 2D 100
TW8: Bford 5D 96
(off Ealing Rd.)
Lincoln M. N15 4C 48
NW6 1H 81
SE21 2D 138
Lincoln Pde. HA9: Wemb 1E 60
N2 3C 46
(off Lincoln Rd.)
Lincoln Plaza *E14* 2D 104
(off Lightermans Rd.)
Lincoln Rd. CR4: Mitc 5J 155
DA14: Sidc 5B 144
E7 6B 70
E13 4K 87
E18 1J 51
EN1: Enf 4K 23
EN3: Pond E 5B 24
HA0: Wemb 6D 60
HA2: Harr 5D 40
HA6: Nwood 3H 39
KT3: N Mald 3J 151
KT4: Wor Pk 1D 164
N2 3C 46
SE25 3H 157
TW13: Hanw 3D 130
The Lincolns NW7 3G 29
Lincoln's Inn Flds. WC2 7G 7 (6K 83)
Lincoln's Inn Hall 7H 7 (6K 83)
Lincoln St. E11 2G 69
SW3 4E 16 (4D 100)
Lincoln Ter. SM2: Sutt 7J 165
Lincoln Way EN1: Enf 5C 24
TW16: Sun 1G 147
Lincombe Rd. BR1: Broml 3H 141
Lindal Ct. E18 1H 51
Lindal Cres. EN2: Enf 4D 22
Lindale Cl. IG4: Ilf 5D 52
The Lindales *N17* 6B 34
(off Grasmere Rd.)
Lindal Rd. SE4 5B 122
Lindbergh Rd. SM6: W'gton 7J 167
Linden Av. CR7: Thor H 4B 156
EN1: Enf 1B 24
HA4: Ruis 1J 57
HA9: Wemb 5F 61
NW10 2F 81
TW3: Houn 5F 113
Linden Cl. HA4: Ruis 1J 57
HA7: Stan 5G 27
KT7: T Ditt 7K 149
N14 6B 22
Linden Ct. DA14: Sidc 4J 143
SE20 7H 139
(off Anerley Pk.)
W12 1E 98
Linden Cres. IG8: Wfd G 6E 36
KT1: King T 2F 151
UB6: G'frd 6K 59
Lindenfield BR7: Chst 2F 161
Linden Gdns. EN1: Enf 1B 24
W2 7J 81
W4 5A 98
Linden Gro. KT3: N Mald 3A 152
SE15 3H 121
SE26 6J 139
TW11: Tedd 5K 131
Linden Ho. *SE8* 6B 104
(off Abinger Gro.)
TW12: Hamp 6E 130
Linden Lawns HA9: Wemb 4F 61
Linden Lea N2 5A 46
Linden Leas BR4: W W'ck 2F 171
Linden Mans. *N6* 1F 65
(off Hornsey La.)
Linden M. N1 5D 66
W2 7J 81
Linden Pl. CR4: Mitc 4C 154
Linden Rd. N10 4F 47
N11 2J 31
N15 4C 48
TW12: Hamp 7E 130
The Lindens CR0: New Ad 6E 170
E17 4D 50
(off Prospect Hill)
N12 5G 31
W4 1J 115
Linden St. RM7: Rom 4K 55
Linden Wlk. N19 2G 65
Linden Way N14 6B 22
TW17: Shep 5E 146
Linder's Field Local Nature Reserve
1G 37
Lindeth Cl. HA7: Stan 6G 27
Lindfield Gdns. NW3 5K 63
Lindfield Rd. CR0: C'don 6F 157
W5 4C 78
Lindfield St. E14 6C 86
Lindhill Cl. EN3: Enf H 2E 24
Lindholme Ct. *NW9* 1A 44
(off Pageant Av.)
Lindie Gdns. UB8: Uxb 7A 56
Lindisfarne Ct. HA8: Edg 4A 28
Lindisfarne Rd. RM8: Dag 3C 72
SW20 7C 134
Lindisfarne Way E9 4A 68
Lindley Ct. KT1: Hamp W 1C 150
Lindley Est. SE15 7G 103
Lindley Ho. *E1* 5J 85
(off Lindley St.)
SE15 7G 103
(off Peckham Pk. Rd.)
Lindley Pl. TW9: Kew 1G 115
Lindley Rd. E10 2E 68
Lindley St. E1 5J 85
Lindop Ho. *E1* 4A 86
(off Mile End Rd.)
Lindore Rd. SW11 4D 118
Lindores Rd. SM5: Cars 7A 154
Lindo St. SE15 2J 121
Lind Rd. SM1: Sutt 5A 166
Lindrop St. SW6 2A 118
Lindsay Cl. KT9: Chess 7E 162
TW19: Stanw 5A 110
Lindsay Ct. *CR0: C'don* 4D 168
(off Eden Rd.)
SE13 3D 122
(off Loampit Va.)
SW11 1B 118
(off Battersea High St.)
Lindsay Dr. HA3: Kenton 6E 42
TW17: Shep 6F 147
Lindsay Ho. *SW7* 3A 100
(off Gloucester Rd.)
Lindsay Rd. KT4: Wor Pk 2D 164
TW12: Hamp H 4F 131
Lindsay Sq. SW1 5D 18 (5H 101)
Lindsell St. SE10 1E 122
Lindsey Cl. BR1: Broml 3B 160
CR4: Mitc 4J 155
Lindsey Ct. *N13* 3F 33
(off Green Lanes)
Lindsey Gdns. TW14: Bedf 7F 111
Lindsey Ho. W5 4D 96
Lindsey M. N1 7C 66
Lindsey Rd. RM8: Dag 4C 72
Lindsey St. EC1 5B 8 (5B 84)
Lind St. SE8 2C 122
Lindum Rd. TW11: Tedd 7C 132
Lindway SE27 5B 138
Lindwood Cl. E6 6D 88
Linear Pk. 6H 101
The Linen Ho. W10 2G 81
Linen M. W12 2B 98
Liner Ho. E16 2A 106
Linfield *WC1* 2G 7
(off Sidmouth St.)
Linfield Cl. NW4 3E 44
Linford Christie Stadium 5C 80
Linford Ho. *E2* 1G 85
(off Whiston Rd.)
E16 5J 87
(off Hammersley Rd.)
Linford Rd. E17 3E 50
Linford St. SW8 1G 119
Linford St. Bus. Est. *SW8* 1G 119
(off Linford St.)
Lingard Av. NW9 1A 44
Lingard Ho. *E14* 3E 104
(off Marshfield St.)
Lingards Rd. SE13 4E 122
Lingey Cl. DA15: Sidc 2K 143
Lingfield Apts. E4 7J 35
Lingfield Av. KT1: King T 4E 150
Lingfield Cl. EN1: Enf 6K 23
HA6: Nwood 1G 39
Lingfield Ct. UB5: N'olt 2E 76
Lingfield Cres. SE9 4H 125
Lingfield Gdns. N9 7C 24
Lingfield Ho. SE1 7B 14
Lingfield Rd. KT4: Wor Pk 3E 164
SW19 5F 135
Lingham Ct. SW9 2J 119
Lingham St. SW9 2J 119
Lingholm Way EN5: Barn 5A 20
Ling Rd. DA8: Erith 6J 109
E16 5J 87
Lingrove Gdns.
IG9: Buck H 2E 36
Lings Coppice SE21 2D 138
Lingwell Rd. SW17 3C 136
Lingwood DA7: Bex 2H 127
Lingwood Ct. *N2* 3C 46
(off Norfolk Cl.)
Lingwood Gdns. TW7: Isle 7J 95
Lingwood Rd. E5 7G 49
Linhope St. NW1 3E 4 (4D 82)
The Link EN3: Enf H 1F 25
HA0: Wemb 1C 60
HA5: Eastc 7A 40
NW2 1C 62
SE9 3E 142
(off William Barefoot Dr.)
UB5: N'olt 5D 58
W3 6H 79
Linkenholt Mans. *W6* 4B 98
(off Stamford Brook Av.)
Linkfield BR2: Hayes 6J 159
KT8: W Mole 3F 149
Linkfield Rd. TW7: Isle 2K 113
Link Ho. E3 3D 86
W10 6F 81
(off Kingsdown Cl.)
Link La. SM6: W'gton 6H 167
Linklea Cl. NW9 7F 29
Link Rd. E1 2K 15 (7G 85)
N11 4K 31
RM9: Dag 2H 91
SM6: W'gton 1E 166
TW14: Felt 7H 111
The Links E17 4A 50
Links Av. SM4: Mord 4J 153
Linkscroft Av. TW15: Ashf 6D 128
Links Dr. N20 1D 30
Links Gdns. SW16 7A 138
Linkside KT3: N Mald 2A 152
N12 6D 30
Linkside Cl. EN2: Enf 3E 22
Linkside Gdns. EN2: Enf 3E 22
Links Rd. BR4: W W'ck 1E 170
IG8: Wfd G 5D 36
NW2 2B 62
SW17 6E 136
TW15: Ashf 5A 128
W3 6G 79

Links Side—London M.

Links Side EN2: Enf 3E 22
Link St. E9 .6J 67
Links Vw. N3 . . . . .7C 30
Linksview N2 . . . . .5D 46
(off Great Nth. Rd.)
Links Vw. Cl. HA7: Stan 7F 27
Linksview Ct. TW12: Hamp H 4H 131
Links Vw. Rd. CR0: C'don 3C 170
TW12: Hamp H 5G 131
Links Way BR3: Beck 6C 158
Linksway HA6: Nwood 1E 38
NW4 . . . . .2F 45
Links Yd. E1 . . . . .5K 9
Link Way BR2: Broml 7C 160
HA5: Pinn 1B 40
TW10: Ham 2B 132
Linkway N4 . . . . .7C 48
RM8: Dag 4C 72
SW20 . . . . .3D 152
The Linkway EN5: Barn 6E 20
Linkwood Wlk. NW1 . . . . .7H 65
Linley Ct. SM1: Sutt 4A 166
Linley Cres. RM7: Mawney 3H 55
Linley Rd. N17 . . . . .2E 48
Linnell Cl. NW11 . . . . .6K 45
Linnell Dr. NW11 . . . . .6K 45
Linnell Ho. E1 . . . . .5J 9
(off Folgate St.)
NW8 . . . . .1A 82
(off Ainsworth Way)
Linnell Rd. N18 . . . . .5B 34
SE5 . . . . .2E 120
Linnet Cl. N9 . . . . .1E 34
SE28 . . . . .7C 90
WD23: Bush 1B 26
Linnet Ct. SW15 . . . . .6E 116
Linnet M. SW12 . . . . .7E 118
Linnett Cl. E4 . . . . .4K 35
Linom Rd. SW4 . . . . .4J 119
Linscott Rd. E5 . . . . .4J 67
Linsdell Rd. IG11: Bark 1G 89
Linsey Ct. E10 . . . . .1C 68
(off Grange Rd.)
Linsey St. SE16 . . . . .4G 103
(not continuous)
Linslade Cl. HA5: Eastc 4K 39
TW4: Houn 5C 112
Linslade Ho. E2 . . . . .1G 85
NW8 . . . . .3D 4
(off Paveley St.)
Linslade Rd. BR6: Chels 6K 173
Linstead St. NW6 . . . . .7J 63
Linstead Way SW18 . . . . .7G 117
Linsted Ct. SE9 . . . . .6J 125
Lintaine Cl. W6 . . . . .6G 99
Linthorpe Av. HA0: Wemb 6C 60
Linthorpe Rd. EN4: Cockf 3H 21
N16 . . . . .7E 48
Linton Cl. CR4: Mitc 7D 154
DA16: Well 1B 126
SE7 . . . . .5A 106
Linton Ct. NW1 . . . . .7G 65
(off Agar Gro.)
RM1: Rom 2K 55
Linton Gdns. E6 . . . . .6C 88
Linton Gro. SE27 . . . . .5B 138
Linton Ho. E3 . . . . .5C 86
(off St Paul's Way)
Linton Rd. IG11: Bark 7G 71
Linton St. N1 . . . . .1C 84
(not continuous)
Lintott Ct. TW19: Stanw 6A 110
Linver Rd. SW6 . . . . .2J 117
Linwood Cl. SE5 . . . . .2F 121
Linwood Cres. EN1: Enf 1B 24
Linzee Rd. N8 . . . . .4J 47
Lion Apts. SE16 . . . . .5H 103
(off Rotherhithe New Rd.)
Lion Av. TW1: Twick 1K 131
Lion Cl. SE4 . . . . .6C 122
TW17: Shep 3A 146
Lion Ct. E1 .7K 85
(off The Highway)
N1 . . . . .1K 83
(off Copenhagen St.)
SE1 . . . . .5G 15
(off Magdalen St.)
Lionel Gdns. SE9 . . . . .5B 124
Lionel Mans. W14 . . . . .3F 99
(off Haarlem Rd.)
Lionel M. W10 . . . . .5G 81
Lionel Rd. SE9 . . . . .5B 124
Lionel Rd. Nth. TW8: Bford 3E 96
Lionel Rd. Sth. TW8: Bford 5F 97
Liongate Ent. Pk.
CR4: Mitc 4B 154
Lion Ga. Gdns. TW9: Rich 3F 115
Lion Ga. M. SW18 . . . . .7J 117
Liongate M. KT8: E Mos 3K 149
Lion Head Ct. CR0: C'don 4C 168
(off St Andrew's Rd.)
Lion Mills E2 . . . . .2G 85
Lion Pk. Av. KT9: Chess 4G 163
Lion Rd. CR0: C'don 5C 156
DA6: Bex 4E 126
E6 . . . . .5D 88
N9 . . . . .2B 34
TW1: Twick 1K 131
Lions Cl. SE9 . . . . .3A 142
Lion Way TW8: Bford 7D 96
Lion Wharf Rd. TW7: Isle 3B 114
Lion Yd. SW4 . . . . .4H 119
Liphook Cres. SE23 . . . . .7J 121
Lipton Cl. SE28 . . . . .7C 90
Lipton Rd. E1 . . . . .6K 85
Lisbon Av. TW2: Twick 2G 131
Lisbon Cl. E17 . . . . .2B 50
Lisburne Rd. NW3 . . . . .4D 64
Lisford St. SE15 . . . . .1F 121
Lisgar Ter. W14 . . . . .4H 99
Liskeard Cl. BR7: Chst 6G 143
Liskeard Gdns. SE3 . . . . .1J 123
Liskeard Ho. SE11 . . . . .5K 19
(off Kennings Way)
Lisle Cl. SW17 . . . . .4F 137
Lisle Ct. NW2 . . . . .3G 63
Lisle St. WC2 . . . . .2D 12 (7H 83)
Lismore SW19 . . . . .5H 135
(off Woodside)
Lismore Boulevard NW9 . . . . .3B 44
Lismore Cir. NW5 . . . . .5E 64
Lismore Cl. TW7: Isle 2A 114
Lismore Rd. CR2: S Croy 6E 168
N17 . . . . .3D 48
Lismore Wlk. N1 . . . . .6C 66
(off Clephane Rd. Nth.)
Lissant Cl. KT6: Surb 7D 150
Lisselton Ho. NW4 . . . . .4F 45
(off Belle Vue Est.)
Lissenden Gdns. NW5 . . . . .4E 64
(not continuous)
Lissenden Mans. NW5 . . . . .4E 64
Lisson Grn. Est. NW8 . . . . .3C 4
(off Tresham Cres.)
LISSON GROVE 5B 4 (5C 82)
Lisson Gro. NW1 . . . . .3B 4 (4B 82)
NW8 . . . . .3B 4 (4B 82)
Lisson Ho. NW1 . . . . .5C 4
(off Lisson St.)
Lisson St. NW1 . . . . .5C 4 (5C 82)
Lister Cl. CR4: Mitc 1C 154
W3 . . . . .5K 79
Lister Ct. HA1: Harr 7B 42
N16 . . . . .2E 66
NW9 . . . . .2A 44
Lister Gdns. N18 . . . . .5H 33
Listergate Ct. SW15 . . . . .4E 116
Lister Ho. E1 . . . . .5G 85
(off Lomas St.)
HA9: Wemb 3J 61
(off Barnhill Rd.)
UB3: Harl 4G 93
Lister Lodge W9 . . . . .5J 81
(off Admiral Wlk.)
Lister Rd. E11 . . . . .1G 69
Lister Wlk. SE28 . . . . .7D 90
Liston Rd. N17 . . . . .1G 49
SW4 . . . . .3G 119
Liston Way IG8: Wfd G 7F 37
Listowel Cl. SW9 . . . . .7A 102
Listowel Rd. RM10: Dag 3G 73
Listria Pk. N16 . . . . .2E 66
Litcham Ho. E1 . . . . .3K 85
(off Longnor Rd.)
Litchfield Av. E15 . . . . .6G 69
SM4: Mord 7H 153
Litchfield Ct. E17 . . . . .6C 50
Litchfield Gdns. NW10 . . . . .6C 62
Litchfield Rd. SM1: Sutt 4A 166
Litchfield St. WC2 . . . . .2D 12 (7H 83)
Litchfield Way NW11 . . . . .5K 45
Lithgow's Rd.
TW6: H'row A 4G 111
Lithos Rd. NW3 . . . . .6K 63
Litten Nature Reserve 3G 77
Lit. Acre BR3: Beck 3C 158
Lit. Albany St. NW1 . . . . .3K 5
Little Angel Theatre 1B 84
(off Dagmar Ter.)
Lit. Argyll St. W1 . . . . .1A 12 (6G 83)
Lit. Benty UB7: W Dray 1E 174
Lit. Birches DA15: Sidc 2J 143
The Lit. Boltons SW5 . . . . .5K 99
SW10 . . . . .5K 99
Lit. Bornes SE21 . . . . .4E 138
Littlebourne SE13 . . . . .7G 123
Littlebourne Ho. SE17 . . . . .5E 102
(off Upnor Way)
Lit. Brights Rd. DA17: Belv 2H 109
Lit. Britain EC1 . . . . .6B 8 (5B 84)
Littlebrook Cl. CR0: C'don 6K 157
Lit. Brownings SE23 . . . . .2H 139
Littlebury Rd. SW4 . . . . .3H 119
Lit. Bury St. N9 . . . . .1J 33
Lit. Bushey La. WD23: Bush 1C 26
Lit. Cedars N12 . . . . .4F 31
Lit. Chelsea Ho. SW10 . . . . .6A 100
(off Edith Gro.)
Lit. Chester St. SW1 . . . . . . .1J 17 (3F 101)
Lit. Cloisters SW1 . . . . . . .1E 18 (3J 101)
Lit. College La. EC4 . . . . .2E 14
(off College St.)
Lit. College St. SW1 . . . . . .1E 18 (3J 101)
Littlecombe SE7 . . . . .6K 105
Littlecombe Cl. SW15 . . . . .6F 117
Little Comn. HA7: Stan 3F 27
Littlecote Cl. SW19 . . . . .7G 117
Littlecote Pl. HA5: Hat E 1C 40
Lit. Cottage Pl. SE10 . . . . .7D 104
Little Ct. BR4: W W'ck 2G 171
Littlecroft SE9 . . . . .3E 124
Littledale SE2 . . . . .6A 108
Lit. Dean's Yd. SW1 . . . . .1E 18
Lit. Dimocks SW12 . . . . .2F 137
Lit. Dorrit Ct. SE1 . . . . .6D 14 (2C 102)
LITTLE EALING 3D 96
Lit. Ealing La. W5 . . . . .4C 96
Lit. Edward St. NW1 . . . . .1K 5 (3F 83)
Lit. Elms UB3: Harl 7F 93
Lit. Essex St. WC2 . . . . .2J 13
Lit. Ferry Rd. TW1: Twick 1B 132
Littlefield Cl. KT1: King T 2E 150
N19 . . . . .4G 65
Littlefield Ho. KT1: King T 2E 150
(off Littlefield Cl.)
Littlefield Rd. HA8: Edg 7D 28
Lit. Friday Rd. E4 . . . . .2B 36
Lit. Gearies IG6: Ilf 4F 53
Lit. George St. SW1 . . . . . . .7E 12 (2J 101)
Lit. Grange UB6: G'frd 3A 78
Little Grn. TW9: Rich 4D 114
Lit. Green St. NW5 . . . . .4F 65
Littlegrove EN4: E Barn 6H 21
Lit. Halliards KT12: Walt T 6J 147
LITTLE HEATH 5B 54
Lit. Heath RM6: Chad H 4B 54
SE7 . . . . .6C 106
Lit. Heath Rd. DA7: Bex 1F 127
Littleheath Rd. CR2: Sels 7H 169
Little Holland House 7D 166
Lit. Holt E11 . . . . .5J 51
LITTLE ILFORD 5D 70
Lit. Ilford La. E12 . . . . .4D 70
Littlejohn Rd. W7 . . . . .6K 77
Lit. Larkins EN5: Barn 6B 20
Lit. London Cl. UB8: Hil 5D 74
Lit. London Ct. SE1 . . . . .7K 15
(off Wolseley St.)
Lit. Marlborough St. W1 . . . . .1A 12
Littlemede SE9 . . . . .3D 142
Littlemoor Rd. IG1: Ilf 3H 71
Littlemore Rd. SE2 . . . . .2A 108
Lit. Moss La. HA5: Pinn 2C 40
Lit. Newport St. WC2 . . . . . .2D 12 (7H 83)
Lit. New St. EC4 . . . . .7K 7 (6A 84)
Lit. Oaks Cl. TW17: Shep 4B 146
Lit. Orchard Cl. HA5: Pinn 2C 40
Lit. Park Dr. TW13: Felt 2C 130
Lit. Park Gdns. EN2: Enf 3H 23
Lit. Pluckett's Way IG9: Buck H 1G 37
Lit. Portland St. W1 . . . . .7K 5 (6G 83)
Lit. Potters WD23: Bush 1C 26
Lit. Queen's Rd. TW11: Tedd 6K 131
Lit. Redlands BR1: Broml 2C 160
Little Rd. UB3: Hayes 2H 93
Littlers Cl. SW19 . . . . .1B 154
Lit. Russell St. WC1 . . . . . . .6E 6 (5J 83)
Lit. St James's St.
SW1 . . . . .5A 12 (1G 101)
Lit. St Leonard's SW14 . . . . .3J 115
Lit. Sanctuary SW1 . . . . . . .7D 12 (2H 101)
Lit. Smith St. SW1 . . . . .1D 18 (3H 101)
Lit. Somerset St. E1 . . . . .1J 15 (6F 85)
Lit. South St. SE5 . . . . .1E 120
LITTLE STANMORE 7A 28
Littlestone Cl. BR3: Beck 6C 140
Lit. Strand NW9 . . . . .2B 44
Lit. Thames Wlk. SE8 . . . . .6D 104
(off Dancers Way)
Lit. Thrift BR5: Pet W 4G 161
Lit. Titchfield St. W1 . . . . .6A 6 (5G 83)
LITTLETON 3C 146
Littleton Av. E4 . . . . .1C 36
LITTLETON COMMON 7E 128
Littleton Cres. HA1: Harr 2K 59
Littleton Ho. SW1 . . . . .6A 18
(off Lupus St.)
Littleton La. TW17: Shep 7A 146
Littleton Rd. HA1: Harr 2K 59
TW15: Ashf 7E 128
Littleton St. SW18 . . . . .2A 136
Lit. Trinity La. EC4 . . . . .2D 14 (7C 84)
Lit. Turnstile WC1 . . . . .6G 7 (5K 83)
LITTLE VENICE 5A 82
Little Venice Sports Cen. 5A 4 (5B 82)
Littlewood SE13 . . . . .6E 122
Littlewood Cl. W13 . . . . .3B 96
Lit. Wood St. KT1: King T 2D 150
Littleworth Bus. Cen.
DA5: Bexl 1H 145
Livermere Ct. E8 . . . . .1F 85
(off Queensbridge Rd.)
Livermere Rd. E8 . . . . .1F 85
Liverpool Gro. SE17 . . . . .5C 102
Liverpool Rd. CR7: Thor H 3C 156
E10 . . . . .6E 50
E16 . . . . .5G 87
KT2: King T 7G 133
N1 . . . . .5A 66
N7 . . . . .5A 66
W5 . . . . .2D 96
Liverpool St. EC2 . . . . .6G 9 (5E 84)
Livery Stables Cl. BR2: Broml 3B 172
Livesey Cl. KT1: King T 3F 151
SE28 . . . . .3G 107
Livesey Pl. SE15 . . . . .6G 103
Livingstone Ct. E10 . . . . .6E 50
EN5: Barn 2B 20
(off Church La.)
HA3: W'stone 3K 41
Livingstone Ho. NW10 . . . . .7K 61
SE5 . . . . .7C 102
(off Wyndham Rd.)
Livingstone Lodge W9 . . . . .5J 81
(off Admiral Wlk.)
Livingstone Mans. W14 . . . . .6G 99
(off Queen's Club Gdns.)
Livingstone Pl. E14 . . . . .5E 104
Livingstone Rd. CR7: Thor H 2C 156
E17 . . . . .6D 50
N13 . . . . .6D 32
SW11 . . . . .3B 118
TW3: Houn 4G 113
UB1: S'hall 7B 76
LivingWell Health Club
London Heathrow Hilton 6E 110
Wembley .4G 61
Livonia St. W1 . . . . .1B 12 (6G 83)
Lizard St. EC1 . . . . .2D 8 (3C 84)
Lizban St. SE3 . . . . .7K 105
Lizmans Ter. W8 . . . . .3J 99
(off Earl's Ct. Rd.)
Llandovery Ho. E14 . . . . .2E 104
(off Chipka St.)
Llanelly Rd. NW2 . . . . .2H 63
Llanover Rd. HA9: Wemb 3D 60
SE18 . . . . .6E 106
Llanthony Rd. SM4: Mord 5B 154
Llanvanor Rd. NW2 . . . . .2H 63
Llewellyn Ct. SE20 . . . . .1J 157
Llewellyn Mans. W14 . . . . .4G 99
(off Hammersmith Rd.)
Llewellyn St. SE16 . . . . .2G 103
Lloyd Av. SW16 . . . . .1J 155
Lloyd Baker St. WC1 . . . . .2H 7 (3K 83)
(not continuous)
Lloyd Ct. HA5: Pinn 5B 40
SW11 . . . . .2D 118
(off Roydon Cl.)
Lloyd Ho. BR3: Beck 6D 140
CR0: C'don 1D 168
(off Tavistock Rd.)
Lloyd M. EN3: Enf L 1H 25
Lloyd Pk. 2C 50
Lloyd Pk. Av. CR0: C'don 4F 169
Lloyd Pk. Ho. E17 . . . . .3C 50
Lloyd Rd. E6 . . . . .1D 88
E17 . . . . .4K 49
KT4: Wor Pk 3E 164
RM9: Dag 7F 73
Lloyd's Av. EC3 . . . . .1H 15 (6E 84)
Lloyd's Building 1G 15 (6E 84)
Lloyd's Pl. SE3 . . . . .2G 123
Lloyd Sq. WC1 . . . . .1J 7 (3A 84)
Lloyd's Row EC1 . . . . .2K 7 (3A 84)
Lloyd St. WC1 . . . . .1J 7 (3A 84)
Lloyds Way BR3: Beck 5A 158
Lloyds Wharf SE1 . . . . .6K 15
Lloyd Thomas Ct. N22 . . . . .7E 32
Lloyd Vs. E6 . . . . .4C 88
SE4 . . . . .2C 122
Loampit Hill SE13 . . . . .2C 122
Loampit Rd. DA8: Erith 6J 109
LOAMPIT VALE 3E 122
Loampit Va. SE13 . . . . .3D 122
Loanda Cl. E8 . . . . .1F 85
Loats Rd. SW2 . . . . .6J 119
Lobelia Cl. E6 . . . . .5C 88
Locarno Ct. SW16 . . . . .5G 137
Locarno Rd. UB6: G'frd 4H 77
W3 . . . . .1J 97
Lochaber Rd. SE13 . . . . .4G 123
Lochaline St. W6 . . . . .6E 98
Lochan Cl. UB4: Yead 4C 76
Loch Cres. HA8: Edg 4A 28
Lochinvar St. SW12 . . . . .7F 119
Lochleven Ho. N2 . . . . .2B 46
(off The Grange)
Lochmere Cl. DA8: Erith 6H 109
Lochmore Ho. SW1 . . . . .4H 17
(off Cundy St.)
Lochnagar St. E14 . . . . .5E 86
Lockbridge Ct. W9 . . . . .5J 81
(off Woodfield Rd.)
The Lock Bldg. E15 . . . . .2E 86
Lock Chase SE3 . . . . .3G 123
Lock Cl. UB2: S'hall 2G 95
Lock Cotts. UB1: S'hall 2H 95
Lock Ct. E5 .2K 67
Locke Hgts. N1 . . . . .7K 65
(off Caledonian Rd.)
Locke Ho. SW8 . . . . .1G 119
(off Wadhurst Rd.)
Lockes End E17 . . . . .4E 50
Lockesfield Pl. E14 . . . . .5D 104
Lockesley Dr. BR5: St M Cry 6K 161
Lockesley Sq. KT6: Surb 6D 150
Locket Rd. HA3: W'stone 3J 41
Locket Rd. M. HA3: W'stone 2J 41
Lockfield Av. EN3: Brim 2F 25
Lockgate Cl. E9 . . . . .5B 68
Lockhart Cl. EN3: Pond E 5C 24
N7 . . . . .6K 65
Lockhart St. E3 . . . . .4B 86
The Lockhouse NW1 . . . . .1E 82
Lockhurst St. E5 . . . . .4K 67
Lockie Pl. SE25 . . . . .3G 157
Lockier Wlk. HA9: Wemb 3D 60
Lockington Rd. SW8 . . . . .1F 119
Lock Keepers Hgts. SE16 . . . . .3K 103
(off Brunswick Quay)
Lockmead Rd. N15 . . . . .6G 49
SE13 . . . . .3E 122
Lock M. NW1 . . . . .6H 65
(off Northpoint Sq.)
Lock Mill Apts. E2 . . . . .1F 85
(off Whiston Rd.)
Lock Rd. TW10: Ham 4C 132
LOCKSBOTTOM 3E 172
Locksfields SE17 . . . . .4D 102
(off Catesby St.)
Lockside E14 . . . . .7A 86
(off Narrow St.)
Lock Side Way E16 . . . . .7G 89
Locks La. CR4: Mitc 1E 154
Locksley Est. E14 . . . . .6B 86
Locksley Ho. E15 . . . . .6F 69
(off Forrester Way)
Locksley St. E14 . . . . .5B 86
Locksmeade Rd. TW10: Ham 4C 132
Locksons Cl. E14 . . . . .5D 86
Lockswood Cl. EN4: Cockf 4J 21
Lockton St. W10 . . . . .7F 81
(off Bramley Rd.)
Lock Vw. Ct. E14 . . . . .7A 86
(off Narrow St.)
Lockwell Rd. RM10: Dag 3G 73
Lockwood Cl. SE26 . . . . .4K 139
Lockwood Ho. E5 . . . . .2J 67
SE11 . . . . .7J 19 (6A 102)
Lockwood Ind. Pk. N17 . . . . .3H 49
Lockwood Pl. E4 . . . . .6H 35
Lockwood Rd. UB2: S'hall 3E 94
Lockwood Sq. SE16 . . . . .3H 103
Lockwood Way E17 . . . . .2K 49
KT9: Chess 5G 163
Lockworks Ho. E17 . . . . .4K 49
(off Wickford Way)
Lockyer Est. SE1 . . . . .7F 15
(not continuous)
Lockyer Ho. SE10 . . . . .5H 105
(off Armitage Rd.)
SW8 . . . . .7H 101
(off Wandsworth Rd.)
SW15 . . . . .3F 117
Lockyer M. EN3: Enf L 1J 25
Lockyer St. SE1 . . . . .7F 15 (2D 102)
Locomotive Dr.
TW14: Felt 1J 129
Locton Grn. E3 . . . . .1B 86
Loddiges Ho. E9 . . . . .7J 67
Loddiges Rd. E9 . . . . .7J 67
Loddon Ho. NW8 . . . . .4B 4
(off Church St. Est.)
Loder St. SE15 . . . . .7J 103
The Lodge W12 . . . . .2F 99
(off Richmond Way)
Lodge Av. CR0: Wadd 3A 168
HA3: Kenton 4E 42
RM8: Dag 6B 72
RM9: Dag 1A 90
SW14 . . . . .3A 116
LODGE AVENUE FLYOVER JUNC.
. . . . .1A 90
Lodge Cl. HA8: Edg 6A 28
N18 . . . . .5H 33
SM6: W'gton 1E 166
TW7: Isle 1B 114
Lodge Ct. HA0: Wemb 5E 60
(off Station Gro.)
Lodge Dr. N13 . . . . .4F 33
Lodge Gdns. BR3: Beck 5B 158
Lodge Hill DA16: Well 7B 108
IG4: Ilf .4C 52
SE2 . . . . .7B 108
Lodgehill Pk. Cl. HA2: Harr 2F 59
Lodge La. CR0: New Ad 6C 170
DA5: Bexl 6D 126
N12 . . . . .5F 31
RM5: Col R 1G 55
Lodge M. N5 . . . . .4C 66
Lodge Pl. SM1: Sutt 5K 165
Lodge Rd. BR1: Broml 7A 142
CR0: C'don 6B 156
NW4 . . . . .4E 44
NW8 . . . . .2B 4 (3B 82)
SM6: W'gton 5F 167
Lodge Vs. IG8: Wfd G 6C 36
Lodge Way TW15: Ashf 2A 128
TW17: Shep 2E 146
Lodore Gdns. NW9 . . . . .5A 44
Lodore Grn. UB10: Ick 3A 56
Lodore St. E14 . . . . .6E 86
The Loft W12 . . . . .1F 99
Loft Ho. E1 .7J 85
(off Middlesex St.)
Lofthouse Pl. KT9: Chess 6C 162
Loftie St. SE16 . . . . .2G 103
Lofting Ho. N1 . . . . .7A 66
(off Liverpool Rd.)
Lofting Rd. N1 . . . . .7K 65
Lofts on the Park E9 . . . . .6K 67
(off Cassland Rd.)
Loftus Road 1D 98
Loftus Rd. IG11: Bark 6G 71
W12 . . . . .1D 98
Loftus Vs. W12 . . . . .1D 98
(off Loftus Rd.)
Logan Cl. E20 . . . . .5E 68
EN3: Enf H 1E 24
TW4: Houn 3D 112
Logan M. RM1: Rom 5K 55
W8 . . . . .4J 99
Logan Pl. W8 . . . . .4J 99
Logan Rd. HA9: Wemb 2D 60
N9 . . . . .2C 34
The Log Cabin 3C 96
(off Northfield Av.)
Loggetts SE21 . . . . .2E 138
Logs Hill BR1: Broml 7C 142
BR7: Chst 7C 142
Logs Hill Cl. BR7: Chst 1C 160
Lohmann Ho. SE11 . . . . .7J 19
Lois Dr. TW17: Shep 5D 146
Lolesworth Cl. E1 . . . . .6J 9 (5F 85)
Lolland Ho. SE7 . . . . .4C 106
Lollard St. SE11 . . . . .3H 19 (4K 101)
(not continuous)
Loman St. SE1 . . . . .6B 14 (2B 102)
Lomas Cl. CR0: New Ad 7E 170
Lomas Dr. E8 . . . . .7F 67
Lomas St. E1 . . . . .5G 85
Lombard Av. EN3: Enf H 1D 24
IG3: Ilf 1J 71
Lombard Bus. Pk. CR0: C'don 7K 155
SW19 . . . . .2K 153
Lombard Ct. EC3 . . . . .2F 15 (7D 84)
RM7: Rom 4J 55
W3 . . . . .1H 97
Lombard La. EC4 . . . . .1K 13 (6A 84)
Lombard Pl. E3 . . . . .2A 86
Lombard Rd. N11 . . . . .5A 32
SW11 . . . . .2B 118
SW19 . . . . .2K 153
LOMBARD RDBT. 7K 155
Lombard St. EC3 . . . . .1F 15 (6D 84)
Lombard Trad. Est. SE7 . . . . .4K 105
Lombard Wall SE7 . . . . .3K 105
Lombard Wharf SW11 . . . . .2B 118
Lombardy Cl. IG6: Ilf 7K 37
Lombardy Pl. W2 . . . . .7K 81
Lombardy Retail Pk. 7K 75
Lomond Cl. HA0: Wemb 7F 61
N15 . . . . .5E 48
Lomond Gdns. CR2: Sels 7A 170
Lomond Gro. SE5 . . . . .7D 102
Lomond Ho. SE5 . . . . .7D 102
Loncroft Rd. SE5 . . . . .6F 103
Londesborough Rd. N16 . . . . .4E 66
Londinium Twr. E1 . . . . .2K 15
(off W. Tenter St.)
LONDON 4E 12 (1J 101)
London Aquatics Cen.
Queen Elizabeth Olympic Pk.
. . . . .7E 68
London Bri. EC4 . . . . .3F 15 (7D 84)
SE1 . . . . .4F 15 (1D 102)
London Bridge Experience 4F 15
(off Tooley St.)
London Bri. St. SE1 . . . . . .5F 15 (1D 102)
London Bri. Wlk. SE1 . . . . .4F 15
(off Duke St. Hill)
London Broncos RLFC 1E 42
London Buddhist Cen. 3J 85
(off Roman Rd.)
London Business School 3E 4 (4D 82)
London Canal Mus. 2J 83
London Central Markets 6A 8
London Central Mosque 2D 4 (3C 82)
London City College 5J 13
(off Waterloo Rd.)
London Coliseum 3E 12
(off St Martin's La.)
The London College of Fashion
John Prince's St. 7K 5 (6F 83)
Mare St. .7J 67
Londonderry Pde. DA8: Erith 7K 109
London Designer Outlet
HA9: Wemb 4G 61
London Dock E1 . . . . .7G 85
London Dungeon 6G 13 (2K 101)
London E. Leisure Pk.
RM9: Dag 1E 90
London Eye 6G 13 (2K 101)
London Fazal Mosque 7H 117
London Flds. East Side E8 . . . . .7H 67
London Fields Lido 7H 67
London Flds. West Side E8 . . . . .7G 67
London Film Mus. 2F 13
London Fruit Exchange E1 . . . . .6J 9
(off Brushfield St.)
LONDON GATEWAY SERVICE AREA
. . . . .1D 28
London Group Bus. Pk. NW2 . . . . .1B 62
London Ho. EC1 . . . . .6C 8
(off Aldersgate St.)
NW8 . . . . .2C 82
(off Avenue Rd.)
WC1 . . . . .3G 7 (4K 83)
The London Ind. Pk. E6 . . . . .5F 89
(not continuous)
London Information Centre 7H 83
(off Leicester Sq.)
London International Gallery of
Children's Art 1F 65
(within Waterlow Pk. Cen.)
London Irish RFC 3H 147
London La. BR1: Broml 7H 141
E8 . . . . .7H 67
London Marathon Community Track
. . . . .1D 86
London Master Bakers Almshouses
E10 . . . . .6D 50
London Mercantile Court
. . . . .7J 7 (6A 84)
London Metropolitan Archives
. . . . .3K 7
London Metropolitan University
London City Campus,
Calcutta House & Goulston St.
. . . . .7K 9 (6F 85)
Central House 7K 9
Commercial Rd. 6G 85
Moorgate .6E 8
North London Campus,
Eden Grove 5K 65
Stapleton House 5K 65
Tower Bldg. & Graduate Cen.
. . . . .5A 66
London M. W2 . . . . .7B 4 (6B 82)

248 A-Z Big London

London Mill Apts.—Lowther Dr.

London Mill Apts. E2 1F 85
(off Whiston Rd.)
London Mithraeum 1E 14
London Motorcycle Mus. 3G 77
London Oxford St. Youth Hostel 1A 12
(off Noel St.)
The London Palace 4C 102
(within Elephant & Castle Shopping Centre)
London Palladium 1A 12
(off Argyll St.)
London Pavilion 3C 12
(off Piccadilly Circus)
London Plane Ho. E15 3G 87
(off Teasel Way)
London Regatta Cen. 7B 88
London Rd. BR1: Broml 7H 141
CR0: C'don 7B 156
CR4: Mitc 5C 154
(Brookfields Av.)
CR4: Mitc 7E 154
(Mill Grn. Rd.)
CR7: Thor H 1K 155
DA1: Bexl, Cray 5K 127
E13 2J 87
EN2: Enf 3J 23
HA1: Harr 2J 59
HA7: Stan 5H 27
HA9: Wemb 5E 60
IG11: Bark 7F 71
KT2: King T 2F 151
KT17: Ewe 7B 164
RM6: Chad H 6G 55
RM7: Chad H, Rom 6G 55
SE1 7A 14 (3B 102)
SE23 1H 139
SM3: Cheam 3F 165
SM4: Mord 5J 153
SM6: W'gton 4F 167
SW16 1K 155
SW17 7D 136
TW1: Twick 7A 114
TW3: Houn 3G 113
TW7: Bford, Isle 2K 113
TW7: Isle, Twick 5A 114
TW8: Bford 2K 113
TW14: Bedf 2A 128
TW15: Ashf 2A 128
LONDON ROAD RDBT. 6A 114
London School of Economics & Political Science 1G 13 (6K 83)
London Scottish FC 3D 114
London Scottish Golf Course 3D 134
London Shootfighters Gym 4G 79
London South Bank University
Keyworth St. 7B 14 (3B 102)
London Rd. 7A 14
Southwark Campus 7B 14 (3B 102)
London South Bank University Technopark 3B 102
(off London Rd.)
London's Roman Amphitheatre 7E 8
(off Aldermanbury)
London Stadium
Queen Elizabeth Olympic Pk. 7D 68
London Stile W4 5G 97
London Stock Exchange 7C 8
London St. EC3 2H 15 (7E 84)
W2 7A 4 (6B 82)
The London Telecom Tower 5A 6 (5G 83)
London Ter. E2 2G 85
London Transport Mus. 2F 13 (7J 83)
London Transport Mus. Depot 2G 97
London Trocadero 2C 12 (7H 83)
London Underwriting Cen. 2H 15
London Wall EC2 6D 8 (5C 84)
London Wall Bldgs. EC2 6F 9
London Wall Pl. EC2 6D 8
London Wetland Cen. 1D 116
London Wetland Cen. Vis. Cen. 1D 116
London Wharf E2 1H 85
(off Wharf Pl.)
London Zoo 2E 82
LONESOME 1G 155
Lonesome Cvn. Site 1F 155
Lonesome Way SW16 1F 155
Long Acre WC2 2E 12 (7J 83)
Long Acre Ct. W13 5A 78
Longacre Pl. SM5: Cars 6E 166
Longacre Rd. E17 1F 51
Longbeach Rd. SW11 3D 118
Longberrys NW2 3H 63
Longboat Row UB1: S'hall 6D 76
Longbow Apts. E3 4B 86
(off St Clements Av.)
Longbow Ho. EC1 5E 8
(off Chiswell St.)
Longbridge Ho. E16 7F 89
(off University Way)
RM8: Dag 4B 72
(off Longbridge Rd.)
Longbridge Rd. IG11: Bark 6H 71
RM8: Dag 6H 71
Longbridge Way SE13 5E 122
Longcourt M. E11 4A 52
Longcroft SE9 3D 142
Longcrofte Rd. HA8: Edg 7J 27
Long Deacon Rd. E4 1B 36
LONG DITTON 1C 162
Longdon Wood BR2: Kes 3C 172
Longdown Rd. SE6 4C 140
Long Dr. HA4: Ruis 5A 58
UB6: G'frd 1F 77
UB7: W Dray 2A 92
W3 6A 80
Long Elmes HA3: Hrw W 1F 41
Longfellow Rd. E17 6B 50
KT4: Wor Pk 2C 164
Longfellow Way SE1 4F 103
Long Fld. NW9 7F 29
Longfield BR1: Broml 1H 159
Longfield Av. E17 4A 50
HA9: Wemb 1E 60
NW7 7H 29
SM6: W'gton 1E 166
W5 7C 78
Longfield Cres. SE26 3J 139
Longfield Dr. CR4: Mitc 1C 154
SW14 5H 115
Longfield Est. SE1 4F 103
Longfield Ho. E17 5B 50
W5 7C 78
Longfield Rd. W5 6C 78
Longfield St. SW18 7J 117
Longfield Wlk. W5 6C 78
LONGFORD 4C 174
Longford Av. TW14: Felt 6G 111
TW19: Stanw 1A 128
UB1: S'hall 7F 77
LONGFORD CIR. 4C 174
Longford Cl. TW12: Hamp H 4E 130
TW13: Hanw 3C 130
UB4: Yead 7B 76
Longford Ct. E5 4K 67
(off Pedro St.)
KT19: Ewe 4J 163
NW4 4F 45
TW12: Hamp H 6F 131
UB1: S'hall 1E 94
(off Uxbridge Rd.)
Longford Gdns. SM1: Sutt 3A 166
UB4: Yead 7B 76
Longford Ho. BR1: Broml 5F 141
(off Brangbourne Rd.)
E1 6J 85
(off Jubilee St.)
TW12: Hamp H 4E 130
Longford Ind. Est.
TW12: Hamp 6F 131
LONGFORDMOOR 4B 174
Longford Rd. TW2: Whitt 1E 130
Longford St. NW1 3K 5 (4F 83)
Longford Wlk. SW2 7A 120
Longford Way TW19: Stanw 1A 128
Longhayes Av. RM6: Chad H 4D 54
Longhayes Ct. RM6: Chad H 4D 54
Longheath Gdns.
CR0: C'don 5J 157
Longhedge Ho. SE26 4G 139
(off High Level Dr.)
Long Hedges TW3: Houn 2E 112
Longhedge St. SW11 2E 118
Longhill Rd. SE6 2F 141
Longhook Gdns. UB5: N'olt 2J 75
Longhope Cl. SE15 6E 102
Longhurst Ho. W10 3H 81
(off Lancefield St.)
Longhurst Rd. CR0: C'don 6H 157
SE13 5F 123
Longitude Apts. CR0: C'don 2D 168
(off Addiscombe Gro.)
Longland Ct. E9 5A 68
(off Mabley St.)
SE1 5G 103
Longland Dr. N20 3E 30
LONGLANDS 3G 143
Longlands Ct. CR4: Mitc 1E 154
DA15: Sidc 2K 143
W11 7H 81
Longlands Pk. Cres.
DA15: Sidc 3J 143
Longlands Rd. DA15: Sidc 3J 143
Long La. CR0: C'don 6J 157
DA7: Bex 7D 108
EC1 6B 8 (5B 84)
N2 7E 30
N3 7E 30
SE1 7E 14 (2D 102)
TW19: Stanw 2B 128
UB10: Hil, Ick 3C 74
Longleat Ho. SW1 5C 18
(off Rampayne St.)
Longleat Rd. EN1: Enf 5K 23
Longleat Way TW14: Bedf 7F 111
Longleigh Ho. SE5 1E 120
(off Peckham Rd.)
Longleigh La. DA7: Bex 6C 108
SE2 6C 108
Long Lents Ho. NW10 1K 79
(off Shrewsbury Rd.)
Longley Av. HA0: Wemb 1F 79
Longley Ct. SW8 1J 119
Longley Rd. CR0: C'don 7B 156
HA1: Harr 5G 41
SW17 6C 136
Long Leys E4 6J 35
Longley St. SE1 4G 103
Longley Way NW2 3E 62
Longman Ho. E2 2K 85
(off Mace St.)
E8 1F 85
(off Haggerston Rd.)
Longmans M. SW20 2G 153
Long Mark Rd. E16 5B 88
Longmarsh La. SE28 1J 107
Long Mead NW9 1B 44
Longmead BR7: Chst 2E 160
Longmead Dr. DA14: Sidc 2D 144
Longmead Ho. SE27 5C 138
Long Mdw. NW5 5H 65
Long Mdw. Cl. BR4: W W'ck 7E 158
Longmeadow Rd.
DA15: Sidc 1J 143
Longmead Rd. KT7: T Ditt 7J 149
SW17 5D 136
UB3: Hayes 7H 75
Long Mill SE10 1D 122
(off Greenwich High Rd.)
Longmoore St. SW1 4A 18 (4G 101)
Longmoor Point SW15 1D 134
(off Norley Va.)
Longmore Av. EN4: E Barn 6F 21
EN5: New Bar 6F 21
Longmore Gdns. Est. SW1 4A 18
Longnor Est. E1 3K 85
Longnor Rd. E1 3K 85
Long Pond Rd. SE3 1G 123
Longreach Ct. IG11: Bark 2H 89
Long Reach Rd. IG11: Bark 4K 89
Longridge Ho. SE1 3C 102
Longridge La. UB1: S'hall 6F 77
Longridge Rd. IG11: Bark 7G 71
SW5 4J 99
Long Ridges N2 3E 46
(off Fortis Grn.)
Long Rd. SW4 4F 119
Long's Ct. WC2 3D 12
Longs Ct. TW9: Rich 4F 115
Longshaw Rd. E4 3A 36
Longshore SE8 4B 104
Longshott Ct. SW5 4J 99
(off W. Cromwell Rd.)
Longstaff Cres. SW18 6J 117
Longstaff Rd. SW18 6J 117
Longstone Av. NW10 7B 62
Longstone Ct. SE1 7E 14
(off Gt. Dover St.)
Longstone Rd. SW17 5F 137
Long St. E2 1J 9 (3F 85)
Longthornton Rd. SW16 2G 155
Longthorpe Ct. W6 4C 98
Longton Av. SE26 4G 139
Longton Gro. SE26 4H 139
Longview Vs. RM5: Col R 1F 55
Longview Way RM5: Col R 1K 55
Longville Rd. SE11 4B 102
Long Wlk. KT3: N Mald 3J 151
SE1 3E 102
SE18 6F 107
SW13 2A 116
Longwalk Rd. UB11: Stock P 1D 92
Long Wall E15 3F 87
Longwater Ho. KT1: King T 3D 150
(off Portsmouth Rd.)
Longwood Bus. Pk. TW16: Sun 5H 147
Longwood Dr. SW15 6C 116
Longwood Gdns. IG5: Ilf 4D 52
IG6: Ilf 4D 52
Longworth Cl. SE28 6D 90
Long Yd. WC1 4G 7 (4K 83)
The Loning NW9 4A 44
Lonsdale Av. E6 4B 88
HA9: Wemb 5E 60
RM7: Rom 6J 55
Lonsdale Cl. E6 4C 88
HA5: Hat E 1C 40
HA8: Edg 5A 28
SE9 3B 142
UB8: Hil 5E 74
Lonsdale Ct. KT6: Surb 7D 150
Lonsdale Cres. IG2: Ilf 6F 53
Lonsdale Dr. EN2: Enf 4C 22
Lonsdale Dr. Nth. EN2: Enf 5D 22
Lonsdale Gdns. CR7: Thor H 4K 155
Lonsdale Ho. W11 6H 81
(off Lonsdale Rd.)
Lonsdale M. TW9: Kew 1G 115
W11 6H 81
(off Colville M.)
Lonsdale Pl. N1 7A 66
Lonsdale Rd. DA7: Bex 2F 127
E11 6H 51
NW6 2H 81
SE25 4H 157
SW13 6C 98
UB2: S'hall 3B 94
W4 4B 98
W11 6H 81
Lonsdale Road Reservoir Local Nature Reserve 7B 98
Lonsdale Sq. N1 7A 66
Lonsdale Yd. W11 7J 81
Loobert Rd. N15 3E 48
Looe Gdns. IG6: Ilf 3F 53
Lookout Lane E14 6G 87
Loop Ct. SE10 4G 105
(off Telegraph Av.)
Loop Rd. BR7: Chst 6G 143
Lopen Rd. N18 4K 33
Lopez Ho. SW9 3J 119
Lorac Ct. SM2: Sutt 7J 165
Loraine Cl. EN3: Pond E 5D 24
Loraine Cotts. N7 4K 65
Loraine Ct. BR7: Chst 5F 143
Loraine Ho. SM6: W'gton 4F 167
Loraine Rd. N7 4K 65
W4 6H 97
Lord Admiral's Vw. SE18 4D 106
(off Frances St.)
Lord Amory Way E14 2E 104
Lord Av. IG5: Ilf 4D 52
Lord Chancellor Wlk.
KT2: King T 1J 151
Lord Ct. IG5: Ilf 4D 52
Lordell Pl. SW19 6E 134
Lorden Wlk. E2 2K 9 (3G 85)
Lord Gdns. IG5: Ilf 4D 52
Lord Graham M. N18 5B 34
Lord Hills Bri. W2 5K 81
Lord Hills Rd. W2 5K 81
Lord Holland La. SW9 2A 120
Lord Kensington Ho. W14 4H 99
(off Radnor Ter.)
Lord Knyvetts Ct. TW19: Stanw 6A 110
Lord Napier Pl. W6 5C 98
Lord Nth. St. SW1 2E 18 (3J 101)
Lord Roberts M. SW6 7K 99
Lord Robert's Ter. SE18 5E 106
Lord's 2B 4 (3B 82)
Lords Cl. SE21 2C 138
TW13: Hanw 2C 130
Lordship Gro. N16 2D 66
Lordship La. N17 1D 48
N22 2A 48
SE22 4F 121
Lordship La. Est. SE21 7G 121
Lordship Pk. N16 2C 66
Lordship Pk. M. N16 2C 66
Lordship Pl. SW3 7C 16 (6C 100)
Lordship Rd. N16 1D 66
UB5: N'olt 7C 58
Lordship Ter. N16 2D 66
Lordsmead Rd. N17 1E 48
Lord St. E16 1C 106
Lords Vw. NW8 2C 4 (3B 82)
(not continuous)
Lordswood Cl. DA6: Bex 5E 126
Lord Warwick St. SE18 3D 106
Loreburn Ho. N7 4K 65
Lorenzo Ho. IG3: Ilf 6A 54
Lorenzo St. WC1 1G 7 (3K 83)
Loretto Gdns. HA3: Kenton 4E 42
Lorian Cl. N12 4E 30
Lorimer Row BR2: Broml 6B 160
Loring Rd. N20 2H 31
SE14 1A 122
TW7: Isle 2K 113
Loris Rd. W6 3E 98
Lorn Ct. SW9 2A 120
Lorne Av. CR0: C'don 7K 157
Lorne Cl. NW8 2D 4 (3C 82)
Lorne Gdns. CR0: C'don 7K 157
E11 4A 52
W11 2F 99
Lorne Ho. E1 5A 86
(off Ben Jonson Rd.)
Lorne Rd. E7 4K 69
E17 5C 50
HA3: W'stone 2K 41
N4 1K 65
TW10: Rich 5F 115
Lorne Ter. N3 2H 45
Lorn Rd. SW9 2K 119
Lorraine Ct. NW1 7F 65
Lorraine Pk. HA3: Hrw W 7D 26
Lorrimore Rd. SE17 6B 102
Lorrimore Sq. SE17 6B 102
Lorton Ho. NW6 1J 81
(off Kilburn Vale)
Lost Theatre 1H 119
Lothair Rd. W5 2D 96
Lothair Rd. Nth. N4 6B 48
Lothair Rd. Sth. N4 7A 48
Lothair St. SW11 3C 118
Lothbury EC2 7E 8 (6D 84)
Lothian Av. UB4: Yead 5K 75
Lothian Cl. HA0: Wemb 3A 60
Lothian Rd. SW9 1B 120
Lothrop St. W10 3G 81
Lots Rd. SW10 7A 100
Lotus Cl. SE21 3D 138
Lotus M. N19 2J 65
Loubet St. SW17 6D 136
Loudoun Av. IG6: Ilf 5F 53
Loudoun Rd. NW8 1A 82
Loudwater Cl. TW16: Sun 4J 147
Loudwater Rd. TW16: Sun 4J 147
Loughborough Est. SW9 3B 120
Loughborough Ho. RM8: Dag 4A 72
(off Academy Way)
Loughborough Pk. SW9 4B 120
Loughborough Rd. SW9 2A 120
Loughborough St.
SE11 5H 19 (5K 101)
Lough Rd. N7 5K 65
Loughton Way IG9: Buck H 1G 37
Louisa Cl. E9 1K 85
Louisa Ct. TW2: Twick 2J 131
Louisa Gdns. E1 4K 85
Louisa Ho. IG3: Ilf 6A 54
Louisa Oakes Cl. E4 4G 35
Louisa St. E1 4K 85
Louise Aumonier Wlk. N19 7J 47
(off Jessie Blythe La.)
Louise Bennett Cl. SE24 4B 120
Louise Ct. E11 5K 51
N22 1A 48
Louise De Marillac Ho. E1 5J 85
(off Smithy St.)
Louise Rd. E15 6G 69
Louise White Ho. N19 1H 65
Louis Gdns. BR7: Chst 4D 142
Louis M. N10 1F 47
Louisville Rd. SW17 3E 136
Lourdes Cl. SE13 3F 123
Lousada Lodge N14 6B 22
(off Avenue Rd.)
Louvaine Rd. SW11 4B 118
Lovage App. E6 5C 88
Lovat Cl. E14 6B 86
NW2 3B 62
Lovat La. EC3 2G 15 (7E 84)
Lovatt Cl. HA8: Edg 6C 28
Lovatt Ct. SW12 1F 137
Lovatt Dr. HA4: Ruis 5J 39
Lovat Wlk. TW5: Hest 7C 94
Loveday Rd. W13 2B 96
Lovegrove St. SE1 5G 103
Lovegrove Wlk. E14 1E 104
Lovegrove Way N20 2G 31
Lovejoy Ct. SE11 6A 102
(off Pownell Ter.)
Lovekyn Cl. KT2: King T 2E 150
Lovelace Av. BR2: Broml 6E 160
Lovelace Gdns. IG11: Bark 4A 72
KT6: Surb 7D 150
Lovelace Grn. SE9 3D 124
Lovelace Ho. W13 7B 78
Lovelace Rd. EN4: E Barn 7H 21
KT6: Surb 7C 150
SE21 2C 138
Lovelace St. E8 1F 85
Lovelace Vs. KT7: T Ditt 7B 150
(off Portsmouth Rd.)
Loveland Ct. SE1 7K 15
(off Jamaica Rd.)
Loveland Mans. IG11: Bark 7K 71
(off Upney La.)
Love La. BR1: Broml 3K 159
CR4: Mitc 3C 154
(not continuous)
DA5: Bexl 6F 127
EC2 7D 8 (6C 84)
HA5: Pinn 2B 40
IG8: Wfd G 5J 37
KT6: Surb 2C 162
N17 7A 34
SE18 4F 107
SE25 3H 157
SM1: Sutt 6H 165
SM3: Cheam, Sutt 6G 165
SM4: Mord 7J 153
Lovel Av. DA16: Well 2A 126
Lovelinch Cl. SE15 6J 103
Lovell Ho. E8 1G 85
(off Shrubland Rd.)
Lovell Pl. SE16 3A 104
Lovell Rd. TW10: Ham 3C 132
UB1: S'hall 6F 77
Loveridge M. NW6 6H 63
Loveridge Rd. NW6 6H 63
Lovers Wlk. N3 7D 30
NW7 6C 30
SE10 6F 105
Lovers' Wlk. W1 4G 11 (1E 100)
Lovett Dr. SM5: Cars 7A 154
Lovett's Pl. SW18 4K 117
Lovett Way NW10 5J 61
Love Wlk. SE5 2D 120
Lovibond La. SE10 7D 104
(off Norman Rd.)
Lovibonds Av. BR6: Farnb 4F 173
UB7: Yiew 6B 74
Lowbrook Rd. IG1: Ilf 4F 71
Low Cross Wood La. SE21 3F 139
Lowdell Cl. UB7: Yiew 6A 74
Lowden Rd. N9 1C 34
SE24 4B 120
UB1: S'hall 7C 76
Lowder Ho. E1 1H 103
(off Wapping La.)
Lowe Av. E16 5J 87
Lowell Ho. SE5 7C 102
(off Wyndham Est.)
Lowell St. E14 6A 86
Lowen Rd. RM13: Rain 2K 91
Lwr. Addiscombe Rd.
CR0: C'don 1E 168
Lwr. Addison Gdns. W14 2G 99
Lwr. Ash Est. TW17: Shep 6H 147
Lwr. Belgrave St. SW1 2J 17 (3F 101)
Lwr. Boston Rd. W7 1J 95
Lwr. Broad St. RM10: Dag 1G 91
Lower Camden BR7: Chst 7D 142
Lwr. Church St. CR0: C'don 2B 168
LOWER CLAPTON 4H 67
Lwr. Clapton Rd. E5 3H 67
Lwr. Clarendon Wlk. W11 6G 81
(off Clarendon Rd.)
Lwr. Common Sth. SW15 3D 116
Lwr. Coombe St. CR0: C'don 4C 168
Lwr. Downs Rd. SW20 1F 153
Lwr. Drayton Pl. CR0: C'don 2B 168
LOWER EDMONTON 2B 34
LOWER FELTHAM 3J 129
Lower Fosters NW4 5E 44
(off New Brent St.)
Lwr. George St. TW9: Rich 5D 114
Lwr. Gravel Rd. BR2: Broml 1C 172
Lower Grn. Gdns.
KT4: Wor Pk 1C 164
Lower Grn. W. CR4: Mitc 3C 154
Lwr. Grosvenor Pl.
SW1 1K 17 (3F 101)
Lower Gro. Rd. TW10: Rich 6F 115
LOWER HALLIFORD 7F 147
Lwr. Hall La. E4 5F 35
(not continuous)
Lwr. Hampton Rd. TW16: Sun 3A 148
Lwr. Ham Rd. KT2: King T 5D 132
LOWER HOLLOWAY 5K 65
Lwr. Hook Bus. Pk.
BR6: Downe 7D 172
Lwr. James St. W1 2B 12 (7G 83)
Lwr. John St. W1 2B 12 (7G 83)
Lwr. Kenwood Av. EN2: Enf 5D 22
Lwr. King's Rd. KT2: King T 1E 150
Lwr. Lea Crossing E14 7G 87
E16 7G 87
Lwr. Maidstone Rd. N11 6B 32
Lwr. Mall W6 5D 98
Lwr. Mardyke Av. RM13: Rain 2J 91
Lwr. Marsh SE1 7J 13 (2A 102)
Lwr. Marsh La. KT1: King T 4F 151
Lwr. Merton Ri. NW3 7C 64
Lower Mill KT17: Ewe 7B 164
Lwr. Morden La. SM4: Mord 6E 152
Lwr. Mortlake Rd.
TW9: Rich 4E 114
Lwr. New Change Pas. EC4 1D 14
(off One New Change)
Lower Pk. Rd. DA17: Belv 4G 109
N11 5B 32
Lwr. Park Trad. Est. NW10 4J 79
LOWER PLACE 2J 79
Lower Pl. Bus. Cen. NW10 2K 79
(off Steele Rd.)
Lwr. Queen's Rd. IG9: Buck H 2G 37
Lwr. Richmond Rd. SW14 3G 115
SW15 3D 116
TW9: Rich 3G 115
Lower Rd. DA8: Erith 3H 109
DA17: Belv 3H 109
HA2: Harr 1H 59
SE1 6J 13 (2A 102)
SE8 4K 103
SE16 2J 103
(not continuous)
SM1: Sutt 4A 166
Lwr. Robert St. WC2 3F 13
(off Robert St.)
Lwr. Sand Hills KT6: Surb 7C 150
Lwr. Sloane St. SW1 4G 17 (4E 100)
Lower Sq. TW7: Isle 3B 114
The Lower Sq. SM1: Sutt 5K 165
(off St Nicholas Way)
Lwr. Stable St. N1 1J 83
(off Stable Street)
Lower Strand NW9 2B 44
Lwr. Sunbury Rd. TW12: Hamp 2D 148
LOWER SYDENHAM 4K 139
Lwr. Sydenham Ind. Est. SE26 5B 140
Lwr. Teddington Rd.
KT1: Hamp W 1D 150
Lower Ter. NW3 3A 64
SE27 5B 138
(off Woodcote Pl.)
Lwr. Thames St. EC3 3F 15 (7D 84)
Lowerwood Ct. W11 6G 81
(off Westbourne Pk. Rd.)
Lwr. Wood Rd. KT10: Clay 6B 162
Lowestoft Cl. E5 2J 67
(off Theydon Rd.)
Lowestoft M. E16 2F 107
Loweswater Cl. HA9: Wemb 2D 60
Loweswater Ho. E3 4B 86
Lowfield Rd. NW6 7J 63
W3 6H 79
Low Hall Cl. E4 7J 25
Low Hall La. E17 6A 50
Low Hall Mnr. Bus. Cen. E17 6A 50
Lowick Rd. HA1: Harr 4J 41
Lowlands Gdns. RM7: Rom 6H 55
Lowlands Rd. HA1: Harr 6J 41
HA5: Eastc 7A 40
Lowman Rd. N7 4K 65
Lownde M. SW16 2J 137
Lowndes Cl. SW1 2H 17 (3E 100)
Lowndes Ct. SW1 1F 17 (3D 100)
W1 1A 12
(off Carnaby St.)
Lowndes Lodge SW1 1F 17
(off Cadogan Pl.)
Lowndes M. SW16 2J 137
Lowndes Pl. SW1 2G 17 (3E 100)
Lowndes Sq. SW1 7F 11 (2D 100)
Lowndes St. SW1 1F 17 (3E 100)
Lownds Ct. BR1: Broml 2J 159
Lowood Ct. SE19 5F 139
(off Farquhar Rd.)
Lowood Ho. E1 7J 85
(off Bewley St.)
Lowood St. E1 7H 85
Lowry Cl. DA8: Erith 4K 109
Lowry Ct. SE16 5H 103
(off Stubbs Dr.)
Lowry Cres. CR4: Mitc 2C 154
Lowry Ho. E14 2C 104
(off Cassilis Rd.)
N17 1F 49
(off Pembury Rd.)
W3 3J 97
(off Palmerston Rd.)
Lowry Rd. RM8: Dag 5B 72
Lowshoe La. RM5: Col R 1G 55
Lowswood Cl. HA6: Nwood 1E 38
Lowther Dr. EN2: Enf 4D 22

A-Z Big London 249

Lowther Hill SE23 7A 122
Lowther Ho. *SW1* 6B 18
(off Churchill Gdns.)
Lowther Rd. E17 2A 50
HA7: Stan 3F 43
KT2: King T 1F 151
N7 5A 66
SW13 1B 116
Lowth Rd. SE5 1C 120
LOXFORD 5G 71
Loxford Av. E6 2B 88
Loxford Gdns. N5 4B 66
Loxford La. IG1: Ilf 5G 71
IG3: Ilf 5G 71
Loxford Rd. IG11: Bark 6F 71
Loxford Ter. IG11: Bark 6G 71
Loxham Rd. E4 7J 35
Loxham St. WC1 2F 7 (3J 83)
Loxley Cl. SE26 5K 139
Loxley Ho. HA9: Wemb 3E 60
Loxley Rd.
SW18 1B 136
TW12: Hamp 4D 130
Loxton Rd. SE23 1K 139
Loxwood Cl. TW14: Bedf 1F 129
Loxwood Rd. N17 3E 48
LSO St Lukes 3D 8
(off Old St.)
Lubbock Ho. *E14* 7D 86
(off Poplar High St.)
Lubbock Rd. BR7: Chst 7D 142
Lubbock St. SE14 7J 103
Lucan Ho. *N1* 1D 84
(off Colville Est.)
Lucan Pl. SW3 4C 16 (4C 100)
Lucan Rd. EN5: Barn 3B 20
Lucas Av. E13 1K 87
HA2: Harr 2E 58
Lucas Cl. NW10 7C 62
Lucas Ct. SE26 5A 140
SW11 1E 118
Lucas Gdns. N2 2A 46
Lucas Ho. *SW10* 7K 99
(off Coleridge Gdns.)
WC1 2E 6
(off Tonbridge St.)
Lucas Rd. SE20 6J 139
Lucas Sq. NW11 6J 45
Lucas St. SE8 1C 122
Lucent Ho. *SW18* 5J 117
(off Hardwicks Sq.)
Lucerne Cl. N13 3D 32
Lucerne Ct. DA18: Erith 3E 108
Lucerne Gro. E17 4F 51
Lucerne M. W8 1J 99
Lucerne Rd. BR6: Orp 1K 173
CR7: Thor H 5B 156
N5 4B 66
Lucey Rd. SE16 3G 103
Lucey Way SE16 3G 103
Lucia Hgts. *E20* 5E 68
(off Logan Cl.)
Lucie Av. TW15: Ashf 6D 128
Lucien Rd. SW17 4E 136
SW19 2K 135
Lucinda Ct. E17 2K 49
EN1: Enf 4K 23
Lucknow St. SE18 7J 107
Lucorn Cl. SE12 6H 123
Luctons Av. IG9: Buck H 1F 37
Lucy Brown Ho. SE1 5D 14
Lucy Cres. W3 5J 79
Lucy Gdns. RM8: Dag 3F 73
Luddesdon Rd.
DA8: Erith 7G 109
Ludford Cl. CR0: Wadd 3B 168
Ludgate B'way.
EC4 1A 14 (6B 84)
Ludgate Cir. EC4 1A 14 (6B 84)
Ludgate Hill EC4 1A 14 (6B 84)
Ludgate Sq. EC4 1B 14 (6B 84)
Ludham NW5 5D 64
Ludham Cl. IG6: Ilf 1G 53
SE28 6C 90
Ludlow Cl. BR2: Broml 3J 159
HA2: Harr 4D 58
Ludlow Ct. W3 2J 97
Ludlow Rd. TW13: Felt 4J 129
W5 4C 78
Ludlow St. EC1 3C 8 (4C 84)
Ludlow Way N2 4A 46
Ludovick Wlk. SW15 4A 116
Ludwell Ho. *W14* 3G 99
(off Russell Rd.)
Ludwick M. SE14 7A 104
Luff Ct. *E3* 5C 86
(off Shelmerdine Cl.)
Luffield Rd. SE2 3B 108
Luffman Rd. SE12 3K 141
Lugard Ho. *W12* 1D 98
(off Bloemfontein Rd.)
Lugard Rd. SE15 2H 121
Lugg App. E12 3E 70
Luke Allsopp Sq. RM10: Dag 3H 73
Luke Ho. *E1* 6H 85
(off Tillman St.)
Lukes Cl. NW2 2C 62
Luke St. EC2 3G 9 (4E 84)
Lukin Cres. E4 3A 36
Lukin St. E1 6J 85
Luli Ct. SE14 6B 104
Lullingstone Cl. BR5: St P 7B 144
Lullingstone Cres.
BR5: St P 7A 144
Lullingstone Ho. *SE15* 6J 103
(off Lovelinch Cl.)
Lullingstone La. SE13 6F 123
Lullingstone Rd.
DA17: Belv 6F 109
Lullington Gth. BR1: Broml 7G 141
N12 5C 30
Lullington Rd. RM9: Dag 7E 72
SE20 7G 139
Lulot Gdns. N19 2F 65
Lulsgate M. E3 4B 86
Lulworth *NW1* 7H 65
(off Wrotham Rd.)
SE17 5D 102
(off Portland St.)
Lulworth Av. HA9: Wemb 7C 42
TW5: Hest 1F 113
Lulworth Cl. HA2: Harr 3D 58
Lulworth Ct. *N1* 7E 66
(off St Peter's Way)
Lulworth Cres. CR4: Mitc 2C 154
Lulworth Dr. HA5: Pinn 6B 40
Lulworth Gdns. HA2: Harr 2C 58
Lulworth Ho. SW8 7K 101
Lulworth Rd. DA16: Well 2K 125
SE9 2C 142
SE15 2H 121
Lulworth Waye
UB4: Yead 6K 75
Lumen Rd. HA9: Wemb 2D 60
Lumiere Apts. SW11 4B 118
The Lumiere Bldg. *E7* 5B 70
(off Romford Rd.)
Lumiere Ct. SW17 2E 136
Lumina Bldgs. *E14* 1E 104
(off Prestons Rd.)
Lumina Bus. Pk. EN1: Enf 5B 24
Lumina Loft Apts. *SE1* 7H 15
(off Tower Bri. Rd.)
Lumina Way EN1: Enf 5B 24
Luminosity Ct. W13 7B 78
Lumley Cl.
DA17: Belv 5G 109
Lumley Ct. WC2 3F 13 (7J 83)
Lumley Flats *SW1* 5G 17
(off Holbein Pl.)
Lumley Gdns. SM3: Cheam 5G 165
Lumley Rd.
SM3: Cheam 5G 165
Lumley St. W1 1H 11 (6E 82)
Lumsdon *NW8* 1K 81
(off Abbey Rd.)
Luna Ho. SE16 2G 103
Lunan Ho. *E3* 2B 86
(off Shetland Rd.)
Lunaria Ho. *E20* 5E 68
(off Elis Way)
Luna Rd. CR7: Thor H 3C 156
Lund Point E15 1E 86
Lundy Dr. UB3: Harl 4G 93
Lundy Wlk. N1 6C 66
Lunham Rd. SE19 6E 138
Luntley Pl. *E1* 6K 9
(off Chicksand St.)
Lupin Cl. CR0: C'don 1K 169
RM7: Rush G 2K 73
SW2 2B 138
UB7: W Dray 1E 174
Lupin Cres. IG1: Ilf 6F 71
Lupin M. E17 3E 50
Lupino Ct. SE11 3H 19 (4K 101)
Lupin Point SE1 7K 15
Lupton Cl. SE12 3K 141
Lupton St. NW5 4G 65
(not continuous)
Lupus St. SW1 6K 17 (5F 101)
Luralda Wharf E14 5F 105
Lurgan Av. W6 6F 99
Lurline Gdns. SW11 1E 118
Luscombe Ct.
BR2: Broml 2G 159
Luscombe Way SW8 7J 101
Lushington Ho.
KT12: Walt T 6A 148
Lushington Rd. NW10 2D 80
SE6 4D 140
Lushington Ter. E8 5G 67
Lutea Ho. *SM2: Sutt* 7A 166
(off Walnut M.)
Luther Cl. HA8: Edg 2D 28
Luther King Cl. E17 6B 50
Luther M. TW11: Tedd 5K 131
Luther Rd. TW11: Tedd 5K 131
Luton Ho. *E13* 4J 87
(off Luton Rd.)
Luton Pl. SE10 7E 104
Luton Rd. DA14: Sidc 3C 144
E13 4J 87
E17 3B 50
Luton St. NW8 4B 4 (4B 82)
Lutton Ter. *NW3* 4A 64
(off Lakis Cl.)
Luttrell Av. SW15 5D 116
Lutwyche M. SE6 2B 140
Lutwyche Rd. SE6 2B 140
Lutyens Ho. *SW1* 6A 18
(off Churchill Gdns.)
Lux Apts. *SW18* 5J 117
(off Broomhill Rd.)
Luxborough Ho. *W1* 5G 5
(off Luxborough St.)
Luxborough La. IG7: Chig 3H 37
Luxborough St. W1 5G 5 (5E 82)
Luxborough Twr. W1 5G 5
The Lux Bldg.
RM7: Rush G 6K 55
Luxembourg M. E15 5G 69
Luxemburg Gdns. W6 4F 99
Luxfield Rd. SE9 1C 142
Luxford St. SE16 4K 103
Luxmore St. SE4 1B 122
Luxor St. SE5 3C 120
Lyall Av. SE21 4E 138
Lyall M. SW1 2G 17 (3E 100)
Lyall M. W. SW1 2G 17 (3E 100)
Lyall St. SW1 2G 17 (3E 100)
Lyal Rd. E3 2A 86
Lycett Pl. W12 2C 98
Lyceum Theatre 2G 13
Lychgate Ct. N12 5G 31
Lychgate Mnr.
HA1: Harr 7J 41
Lych Ga. Wlk. UB3: Hayes 7H 75
(not continuous)
Lyconby Gdns. CR0: C'don 7A 158
Lydd Cl. DA14: Sidc 3J 143
Lydden Ct. SE9 6J 125
Lydden Gro. SW18 7K 117
Lydden Rd. SW18 7K 117
Lydd Rd. DA7: Bex 7F 109
Lydeard Rd. E6 7D 70
Lydford *NW1* 1G 83
(off Royal College St.)
Lydford Cl. *N16* 5E 66
(off Pellerin Rd.)
Lydford Rd. N15 5D 48
NW2 6E 62
W9 4H 81
Lydhurst Av. SW2 2K 137
Lydia Ct. *KT1: King T* 3E 150
(off Grove Cres.)
N12 6F 31
Lydney Cl. SW19 2G 135
Lydon Rd. SW4 3G 119
Lydstep Rd. BR7: Chst 4E 142
Lyell St. E14 6G 87
Lyford Rd. SW18 7B 118
Lyford St. SE7 4C 106
Lygon Ho. *E2* 1K 9
(off Gosset St.)
SW6 1G 117
(off Fulham Pal. Rd.)
Lygon Pl. SW1 2J 17 (3F 101)
Lyham Cl. SW2 6J 119
Lyham Rd. SW2 5J 119
Lyle Cl. CR4: Mitc 7E 154
Lyle Ct. SM4: Mord 6B 154
Lyly Ho. *SE1* 3D 102
(off Burbage Cl.)
Lyme Farm Rd. SE12 4J 123
Lyme Gro. E9 7J 67
Lyme Gro. Ho. *E9* 7J 67
(off Lyme Gro.)
Lymer Av. SE19 5F 139
Lyme Rd. DA16: Well 1B 126
Lymescote Gdns.
SM1: Sutt 2J 165
Lyme St. NW1 7G 65
Lyme Ter. NW1 7G 65
Lyminge Cl. DA14: Sidc 4K 143
Lyminge Gdns. SW18 1C 136
Lymington Av. N22 2A 48
Lymington Cl. E6 5D 88
SW16 2H 155
Lymington Ct. SM1: Sutt 3K 165
Lymington Dr. HA4: Ruis 2F 57
Lymington Gdns.
KT19: Ewe 5B 164
Lymington Lodge *E14* 3F 105
(off Schooner Cl.)
Lymington Rd. NW6 6K 63
RM8: Dag 1D 72
Lyminster Cl. UB4: Yead 5C 76
Lympne *N17* 2D 48
(off Gloucester Rd.)
Lympstone Gdns. SE15 7G 103
Lynbridge Gdns. N13 4G 33
Lynbrook Cl.
RM13: Rain 2K 91
Lynbrook Gro. SE15 7E 102
Lynch Cl. SE3 2H 123
Lynchen Cl. TW5: Cran 1K 111
Lynch Wlk. *SE8* 6B 104
(off Prince St.)
Lyncott Cres. SW4 4F 119
Lyncourt SE3 2F 123
Lyncroft Av. HA5: Pinn 5C 40
Lyncroft Gdns. NW6 5J 63
TW3: Houn 5G 113
W13 2C 96
Lyncroft Mans. NW6 5J 63
Lyndale KT7: T Ditt 7J 149
NW2 4H 63
Lyndale Av. NW2 3H 63
Lyndale Cl. SE3 6H 105
Lyndean Ind. Est. SE2 3C 108
Lynde Ho. KT12: Walt T 6A 148
SW4 3H 119
Lynden Ho. *E1* 3K 85
(off Westfield Way)
Lynden Hyrst CR0: C'don 2F 169
Lyndhurst Av. HA5: Pinn 1K 39
KT5: Surb 1H 163
N12 6J 31
NW7 6F 29
SW16 2H 155
TW2: Whitt 1D 130
TW16: Sun 3J 147
UB1: S'hall 1F 95
Lyndhurst Cl. BR6: Farnb 4F 173
CR0: C'don 3F 169
DA7: Bex 3H 127
NW10 3K 61
Lyndhurst Ct. E18 1J 51
NW8 1B 82
(off Finchley Rd.)
SM2: Sutt 7J 165
(off Grange Rd.)
Lyndhurst Dr. E10 7E 50
KT3: N Mald 7A 152
Lyndhurst Gdns. EN1: Enf 4K 23
HA5: Pinn 1K 39
IG2: Ilf 6H 53
IG11: Bark 6J 71
N3 1G 45
NW3 5B 64
Lyndhurst Gro. SE15 2E 120
Lyndhurst Lodge *E14* 4F 105
(off Millennium Dr.)
Lyndhurst Ri. IG7: Chig 4K 37
Lyndhurst Rd. CR7: Thor H 4A 156
DA7: Bex 3H 127
E4 7K 35
N18 4B 34
N22 6F 33
NW3 5B 64
UB6: G'frd 4F 77
Lyndhurst Sq. SE15 1F 121
Lyndhurst Ter. NW3 5B 64
Lyndhurst Way SE15 1F 121
SM2: Sutt 7J 165
Lyndon Av. DA15: Sidc 5K 125
SM6: W'gton 3E 166
Lyndon Ho. *E18* 1J 51
(off Queen Mary Av.)
Lyndon Rd. DA17: Belv 4G 109
Lyndon Yd. SW17 4A 136
Lyne Cres. E17 1B 50
Lynegrove Av.
TW15: Ashf 5E 128
Lyneham Dr. NW9 1A 44
Lyneham Wlk. E5 5A 68
HA5: Eastc 3H 39
Lynette Av. SW4 6F 119
Lynford Cl. HA8: Edg 1J 43
Lynford Ct. *CR0: C'don* 4E 168
(off Coombe Rd.)
Lynford French Ho. *SE17* 5C 102
(off Thrush St.)
Lynford Gdns. HA8: Edg 3C 28
IG3: Ilf 2K 71
Lynford Ter. N9 1A 34
Lynhurst Cres. UB10: Hil 7E 56
Lynhurst Rd. UB10: Hil 7E 56
Lynmere Rd. DA16: Well 2B 126
Lyn M. E3 3B 86
N16 4E 66
Lynmouth Av. EN1: Enf 6A 24
SM4: Mord 6F 153
Lynmouth Av. Gdns. 1F 165
Lynmouth Dr. HA4: Ruis 2K 57
Lynmouth Gdns.
TW5: Hest 7B 94
UB6: G'frd 1B 78
Lynmouth Rd. E17 6A 50
N2 3D 46
N16 1G 67
UB6: G'frd 1B 78
Lynn Cl. HA3: Hrw W 2H 41
TW15: Ashf 5F 129
Lynne Cl. BR6: Chels 6K 173
SE23 7B 122
Lynne Ct. *CR2: S Croy* 4E 168
(off Birdhurst Rd.)
NW6 7K 63
(off Priory Rd.)
Lynnett Ct. *E9* 6A 68
(off Annis Rd.)
Lynnett Rd. RM8: Dag 2D 72
Lynne Way UB5: N'olt 2B 76
Lynn Ho. *SE15* 6H 103
(off Friary Est.)
Lynn M. E11 2G 69
Lynn Rd. E11 2G 69
IG2: Ilf 7H 53
SW12 7F 119
Lynn St. EN2: Enf 1J 23
Lynscott Way CR2: S Croy 7B 168
Lynstead Ct. BR3: Beck 2A 158
Lynsted Cl. BR1: Broml 2A 160
DA6: Bex 5H 127
Lynsted Gdns. SE9 4B 124
Lynton Av. N12 4G 31
NW9 4B 44
RM7: Mawney 1G 55
W13 6A 78
Lynton Cl. KT9: Chess 4E 162
NW10 5A 62
TW7: Isle 4K 113
Lynton Cres. IG2: Ilf 6F 53
Lynton Est. SE1 4G 103
Lynton Gdns. EN1: Enf 7K 23
N11 6C 32
Lynton Grange N2 3D 46
Lynton Ho. *IG1: Ilf* 2G 71
(off High Rd.)
W2 6A 82
(off Hallfield Est.)
Lynton Mans. *SE1* 1J 19
(off Westminster Bri. Rd.)
Lynton Mead N20 3D 30
Lynton Rd. CR0: C'don 6A 156
E4 5J 35
HA2: Harr 2C 58
KT3: N Mald 5K 151
N8 5H 47
(not continuous)
NW6 2H 81
SE1 4F 103
W3 7G 79
Lynton Ter. W3 6J 79
Lynton Wlk. UB4: Hayes 3G 75
Lynwood Cl. E18 1A 52
HA2: Harr 3C 58
Lynwood Ct. KT1: King T 2H 151
Lynwood Dr. HA6: Nwood 1H 39
KT4: Wor Pk 2C 164
Lynwood Gdns. CR0: Wadd 4K 167
UB1: S'hall 6D 76
Lynwood Gro. BR6: Orp 7J 161
N21 1F 33
Lynwood Rd. KT7: T Ditt 2A 162
SW17 3D 136
W5 3D 78
Lynx Way E16 7B 88
Lyon Bus. Pk. IG11: Bark 2J 89
Lyon Ct. HA4: Ruis 1H 57
Lyon Ho. *NW8* 4C 4
(off Broadley St.)
Lyon Ind. Est. NW2 2D 62
Lyon Meade HA7: Stan 1C 42
Lyon Pk. Av. HA0: Wemb 6E 60
(not continuous)
Lyon Rd. HA1: Harr 6K 41
SW19 1A 154
LYONSDOWN 5F 21
Lyonsdown Av.
EN5: New Bar 6F 21
Lyonsdown Rd.
EN5: New Bar 6F 21
Lyons Pl. HA7: Stan 3D 26
NW8 4A 4 (4B 82)
Lyon St. N1 7K 65
Lyons Wlk. W14 4G 99
Lyon Way UB6: G'frd 1J 77
Lyoth Rd. BR5: Farnb 2G 173
Lyric Ct. *E8* 7F 67
(off Holly St.)
Lyric Dr. UB6: G'frd 4F 77
Lyric M. SE26 4J 139
Lyric Rd. SW13 1B 116
Lyric Sq. *W6* 4E 98
(off King St.)
Lyric Theatre
Hammersmith 4E 98
Westminster 2C 12
(off Shaftesbury Av.)
Lysander NW9 1B 44
Lysander Gdns. KT6: Surb 6F 151
Lysander Gro. N19 1H 65
Lysander Ho. *E2* 2H 85
(off Temple St.)
Lysander M. N19 1G 65
Lysander Rd. CR0: Wadd 6K 167
HA4: Ruis 2F 57
Lysander Way BR6: Farnb 3G 173
Lysia Ct. *SW6* 7F 99
(off Lysia St.)
Lysias Rd. SW12 6F 119
Lysia St. SW6 7F 99
Lysons Wlk. SW15 4C 116
Lytchet Rd. BR1: Broml 7J 141
Lytchet Way EN3: Enf H 1D 24
Lytchgate Cl.
CR2: S Croy 7E 168
Lytcott Dr. KT8: W Mole 3D 148
Lytcott Gro. SE22 5E 120
Lytham Cl. SE28 6E 90
Lytham Gro. W5 3F 79
Lytham St. SE17 5D 102
Lyttelton Cl. NW3 7C 64
Lyttelton Ct. N2 5A 46
Lyttelton Ho. *E9* 7J 67
(off Well St.)
Lyttelton Rd. E10 3D 68
N2 5A 46
Lyttelton Theatre 4H 13
(within National Theatre)
Lyttleton Ct. *UB4: Yead* 4A 76
(off Dunedin Way)
Lyttleton Rd. N8 3A 48
Lytton Av. EN3: Enf L 1F 25
N13 2F 33
Lytton Cl. N2 6B 46
UB5: N'olt 7D 58
Lytton Ct. *WC1* 6F 7
(off Barter St.)
Lytton Gdns. SM6: Bedd 4H 167
Lytton Gro. SW15 5F 117
Lytton Rd. E11 7G 51
EN5: New Bar 4F 21
HA5: Pinn 1C 40
Lytton Strachey Path SE28 7B 90
Lytton Ter. E12 6D 70
Lyveden Rd. SE3 7K 105
SW17 6D 136

M

Mabbett Ho. *SE18* 6E 106
(off Nightingale Pl.)
Mabel Evetts Ct. UB3: Hayes 7K 75
Maberley Cres. SE19 7G 139
Maberley Rd. BR3: Beck 3K 157
SE19 1F 157
Mabledon Pl. WC1 2D 6 (3H 83)
Mablethorpe Rd. SW6 7G 99
Mabley St. E9 5A 68
Mablin Lodge IG9: Buck H 1F 37
McAdam Dr. EN2: Enf 2G 23
McAllister Gro.
IG11: Bark 3A 90
Macaret Cl. N20 7E 20
Macarthur Cl. DA8: Erith 5K 109
E7 6J 69
HA9: Wemb 6H 61
Macarthur Ter. SE7 6B 106
Macartney Ho. *SE10* 7F 105
(off Chesterfield Wlk.)
SW9 1A 120
(off Gosling Way)
Macaulay Ct. SW4 3F 119
Macaulay Rd. E6 2B 88
SW4 3F 119
Macaulay Sq. SW4 4F 119
Macaulay Wlk. *SW9* 1K 119
(off Lett Rd.)
Macaulay Way SE28 1B 108
McAuley Cl. SE1 1J 19 (3A 102)
SE9 5F 125
Macauley Ho. *W10* 5G 81
(off Portobello Rd.)
Macauley M. SE13 2E 122
McAusland Ho. *E3* 2B 86
(off Wright's Rd.)
Macbean St. SE18 3F 107
Macbeth Ho. N1 2E 84
Macbeth St. W6 5D 98
McBride Ho. *E3* 2B 86
(off Libra Rd.)
McCabe Ct. *E16* 5H 87
(off Barking Rd.)
McCall Cl. SW4 2J 119
McCall Cres. SE7 5C 106
McCall Ho. N7 4J 65
McCarthy Rd. TW13: Hanw 5B 130
Macclesfield Apts. *N1* 1D 84
(off Branch Pl.)
Macclesfield Ho. *EC1* 2C 8
(off Central St.)
Macclesfield Rd. EC1 1C 8 (3C 84)
SE25 5J 157
Macclesfield St. W1 2D 12 (7H 83)
McCoid Way SE1 7C 14 (2C 102)
McCrone M. NW3 6B 64
McCullum Rd. E3 1B 86
McDermott Cl. SW11 3C 118
McDermott Rd. SE15 3G 121
Macdonald Av. RM10: Dag 3H 73
Macdonald Ho. *SW11* 2E 118
(off Dagnall St.)
McDonald Ho. *NW6* 3J 81
(off Malvern Rd.)
Macdonald Rd. E7 4J 69
E17 2E 50
(not continuous)
N11 5J 31
N19 2G 65
McDonough Cl. KT9: Chess 4E 162
McDougall Ct. TW9: Rich 2G 115
McDowall Cl. E16 5H 87
McDowall Rd. SE5 1C 120
Macduff Rd. SW11 1E 118
Mace Cl. E1 1H 103
Mace Ho. TW7: Isle 1B 114
McEntee Av. E17 1A 50
Mace St. E2 2K 85
McEwan Ho. *E3* 2B 86
(off Roman Rd.)
McEwen Way *E15* 1F 87
(off Rokeby St.)
Macey Ho. SW11 1C 118
Macey St. *SE10* 6E 104
(off Thames St.)
McFadden Ct. *E10* 3D 68
(off Buckingham Rd.)
Macfarland Gro. SE15 7E 102
Macfarlane La. TW7: Isle 6K 95
Macfarlane Rd. W12 1E 98
Macfarren Pl. NW1 4H 5 (4E 82)
Macfarron Ho. *W10* 3G 81
(off Parry Rd.)
McGlashon Ho. *E1* 4K 9
(off Hunton St.)
McGrath Rd. E15 5H 69
McGregor Ct. N1 1H 9
Macgregor Rd. E16 5A 88
McGregor Rd. W11 6H 81
Machell Rd. SE15 3J 121
McIndoe Ct. *N1* 1D 84
(off Sherborne St.)
McIntosh Cl. RM1: Rom 3K 55
SM6: W'gton 7J 167
Macintosh Ho. *W1* 5H 5
(off Beaumont St.)
McIntosh Ho. *SE16* 4J 103
(off Millender Wlk.)
SE20 1G 157
McIntosh Rd. RM1: Rom 3K 55
McIntyre Ct. *SE18* 4C 106
(off Prospect Va.)
Mackay Ho. *W12* 7D 80
(off White City Est.)
Mackay Rd. SW4 3F 119
McKay Rd. SW20 7D 134

McKeever Ho.—Manor Cl.

McKeever Ho. E16 5J 87
(off Hammersley Rd.)
McKellar Cl. WD23: B Hea 2B 26
McKenna Ho. E3 2B 86
(off Wright's Rd.)
Mackennal St. NW8 2C 82
Mackenzie Cl. W12 7D 80
Mackenzie Ho. N8 4J 47
(off Pembroke Rd.)
NW2 3C 62
Mackenzie Rd. BR3: Beck 2J 157
N7 6K 65
Mackenzie Wlk. E14 1C 104
McKerrell Rd. SE15 1G 121
Mackeson Rd. NW3 4D 64
Mackie Rd. SW2 7A 120
McKillop Way DA14: Sidc 7C 144
Mackintosh La. E9 5K 67
Mackintosh St.
BR2: Broml 6B 160
Macklin St. WC2 7F 7 (6J 83)
Mackonochie Ho. EC1 5J 7
(off Baldwins Gdns.)
Mackrow Wlk. E14 7E 86
Mack's Rd. SE16 4G 103
Mackworth Ho. NW1 1A 6
(off Augustus St.)
Mackworth St. NW1 1A 6 (3G 83)
McLaren Ho. SE1 7A 14
(off St Georges Cir.)
Maclaren M. SW15 4E 116
Maclean Rd. SE23 6A 122
McLeod Ct. SE22 1G 139
Macleod Rd. N21 5D 22
McLeod Rd. SE2 4B 108
McLeod's M. SW7 4K 99
Macleod St. SE17 5C 102
Maclise Ho. SW1 4E 18
(off Marsham St.)
Maclise Rd. W14 3G 99
Macmillan Ct. HA2: Harr 1E 58
UB6: G'frd 4H 77
Macmillan Ho. NW8 2D 4
(off Lorne Cl.)
McMillan Ho. SE4 3A 122
(off Arica Rd.)
SE14 1A 122
McMillan St. SE8 6C 104
McMillan Student Village
SE8 6C 104
Macmillan Way SW17 4F 137
McNair Rd. UB2: S'hall 3F 95
Macnamara Ho. SW10 7B 100
(off Worlds End Est.)
McNeil Rd. SE5 2E 120
McNicol Dr. NW10 2J 79
Macoma Rd. SE18 6H 107
Macoma Ter. SE18 6H 107
Maconochies Rd. E14 5D 104
MacOwan Theatre 4J 99
Macquarie Way E14 4D 104
McRae La. CR4: Mitc 7D 154
Macready Ho. W1 6E 4
(off Crawford St.)
Macready Pl. N7 4J 65
(not continuous)
Mcready Rd. N20 2G 31
Macrea Ho. E3 3B 86
(off Bow Rd.)
Macroom Ho. W9 3H 81
(off Macroom Rd.)
Macroom Rd. W9 3H 81
Macs Ho. E17 3D 50
Mac's Pl. EC4 7J 7
Madame Tussaud's 4G 5 (4E 82)
Mada Rd. BR6: Farnb 3F 173
Maddams St. E3 4D 86
Madderfields Ct. N11 1H 47
Maddison Cl. N2 2A 46
TW11: Tedd 6K 131
Maddison Ct. E16 5J 87
(off Hastings Rd.)
Maddocks Cl. DA14: Sidc 5E 144
Maddocks Ho. E1 7H 85
(off Cornwall St.)
Maddock Way SE17 6B 102
Maddox St. W1 2K 11 (7F 83)
Madeira Av. BR1: Broml 7G 141
Madeira Gro.
IG8: Wfd G 6F 37
Madeira Rd. CR4: Mitc 4D 154
E11 1F 69
N13 4G 33
SW16 5J 137
Madeira St. E14 5D 86
Madeira Twr. SW11 7H 101
Madeleine Cl.
RM6: Chad H 6C 54
Madeleine Ct. HA7: Stan 7K 27
(off Letchworth Rd.)
Madeley Rd. W5 6D 78
Madeline Gro. IG1: Ilf 5H 71
Madeline Rd. SE20 7G 139
Madge Gill Way E6 1C 88
(off High St. Nth.)
Madge Hill W7 7J 77
Madinah Rd. E8 6G 67
The Madison SE1 6E 14
(off Long La.)
Madison Bldg. SE10 1D 122
(off Blackheath Rd.)
Madison Cl. SM2: Sutt 7B 166
Madison Ct. RM10: Dag 6H 73
Madison Cres. DA7: Bex 7C 108
Madison Gdns.
BR2: Broml 3H 159
DA7: Bex 7C 108
Madison Ho. E14 7B 86
(off Victory Pl.)
Madison Way E20 5D 68
Madoc Cl. NW2 2J 63
Madras Pl. N7 6A 66
Madras Rd. IG1: Ilf 4F 71
Madrid Rd. SW13 1C 116
Madrigal La. SE5 7B 102
Madron St. SE17 5E 102
Mafeking Av. E6 2C 88
IG2: Ilf 7H 53
TW8: Bford 6E 96
Mafeking Rd. E16 4H 87
EN1: Enf 3A 24
N17 2G 49
Magazine Ga. W2 4D 10 (1C 100)
Magdala Av. N19 2G 65
Magdala Rd. CR2: S Croy 7D 168
TW7: Isle 3A 114
Magdalene Cl. SE15 2H 121
Magdalene Gdns. E6 4E 88
N20 1J 31
Magdalene Rd.
TW17: Shep 4B 146
Magdalen Ho. E16 1K 105
(off Keats Av.)
Magdalen M. NW3 6A 64
(off Frognal)
Magdalen Pas. E1 2K 15 (7F 85)
Magdalen Rd. SW18 1A 136
Magdalen St. SE1 5G 15 (1E 102)
Magee St. SE11 7J 19 (6A 102)
Magellan Blvd. E16 7G 89
Magellan Ct. NW10 7K 61
(off Brentfield Rd.)
Magellan Ho. E1 4K 85
(off Ernest St.)
Magellan Pl. E14 4C 104
Magic Circle 3B 6
(off Stephenson Way)
Magistrates' Court
Barkingside 3G 53
Belmarsh 2J 107
Bexley 4G 127
Bromley 1H 159
City of London 1E 14
Croydon 3D 168
Ealing 1A 96
(off Green Man La.)
Hendon 6B 44
Highbury Corner 6A 66
Lavender Hill 3D 118
Stratford 7F 69
Thames 3C 86
Westminster 5D 4 (5C 82)
Willesden 6B 62
Wimbledon 6J 135
Magna Sq. SW14 3J 115
(off Moore Cl.)
Magnaville Rd. WD23: B Hea 1D 26
Magnet Rd. HA9: Wemb 2D 60
Magnin Cl. E8 1G 85
Magnolia Cl. E10 2C 68
KT2: King T 6H 133
Magnolia Ct. HA3: Kenton 7F 43
SM2: Sutt 7J 165
(off Grange Rd.)
SM6: W'gton 5F 167
TW9: Kew 1H 115
TW13: Felt 1J 129
(off Plum Cl.)
UB5: N'olt 4C 76
UB10: Hil 6D 56
Magnolia Gdns. E10 2C 68
HA8: Edg 4D 28
Magnolia Ho. SE8 6B 104
(off Evelyn St.)
TW16: Sun 7H 129
Magnolia Lodge E4 3J 35
W8 3K 99
(off St Mary's Ga.)
Magnolia Pl. HA2: Harr 2H 41
SW4 5J 119
W5 5D 78
Magnolia Rd. W4 6H 97
Magnolia St. UB7: W Dray 4A 92
Magnolia Way KT19: Ewe 5J 163
Magnolia Wharf W4 6G 97
Magpie All. EC4 1K 13 (6A 84)
Magpie Cl. E7 5H 69
EN1: Enf 1B 24
NW9 2A 44
Magpie Hall Cl. BR2: Broml 6C 160
Magpie Hall La. BR2: Broml 5D 160
Magpie Hall Rd.
WD23: B Hea 2D 26
Magpie Ho. E3 1B 86
(off Sycamore Av.)
Magpie Pl. SE14 6A 104
Magri Wlk. E1 5J 85
Maguire Apts. E3 5B 86
(off Geoff Cade Way)
Maguire Dr. TW10: Ham 4C 132
Maguire St. SE1 6K 15 (2F 103)
Maha Bldg. E3 3C 86
(off Merchant St.)
Mahatma Gandhi Ind. Est.
SE24 4B 120
Mahlon Av. HA4: Ruis 5K 57
(not continuous)
Mahogany Cl. SE16 1A 104
Mahon Cl. EN1: Enf 1A 24
Mahoney Ho. SE14 1B 122
(off Heald St.)
Maibeth Gdns. BR3: Beck 4A 158
Maida Av. E4 7J 25
W2 4A 4 (5A 82)
MAIDA HILL 4H 81
Maida Rd. DA17: Belv 3G 109
MAIDA VALE 4K 81
Maida Va. W9 3A 4 (2K 81)
Maida Way E4 7J 25
Maiden Erlegh Av.
DA5: Bexl 1E 144
Maiden La. NW1 7H 65
SE1 5D 14 (1C 102)
WC2 3F 13 (7J 83)
Maiden Pl. NW5 3G 65
Maiden Rd. E15 7G 69
Maidenstone Hill SE10 1E 122
Maids of Honour Row
TW9: Rich 5D 114
Maidstone Av. RM5: Col R 2J 55
Maidstone Bldgs. M.
SE1 5D 14 (1C 102)
Maidstone Ho. E14 6D 86
(off Carmen St.)
Maidstone Rd.
DA14: Sidc, Swan 6D 144
N11 6B 32
Mailcoach Yd. E2 1H 9 (3E 84)
Main Av. EN1: Enf 5A 24
Main Dr. HA9: Wemb 3D 60
Main Mill SE10 7D 104
(off Greenwich High St.)
Mainridge Rd. BR7: Chst 4E 142
Main Rd. DA14: Sidc 3H 143
Main St. TW13: Hanw 5B 130
Mainwaring Ct.
CR4: Mitc 2E 154
Mais Ho. SE26 2H 139
Maismore St. SE15 6G 103
The Maisonettes
SM1: Sutt 5H 165
Maison Ho. N20 1F 31
Maitland Cl. SE10 7D 104
TW4: Houn 3D 112
Maitland Ct. W2 2A 10
(off Lancaster Ter.)
Maitland Ho. E2 2J 85
(off Waterloo Gdns.)
SW1 7A 18
(off Churchill Gdns.)
Maitland Pk. Est. NW3 6D 64
Maitland Pk. Rd. NW3 6D 64
Maitland Pk. Vs. NW3 6D 64
Maitland Pl. E5 4H 67
Maitland Rd. E15 6H 69
SE26 6K 139
Maitland Yd. W13 1A 96
Maize Row E14 7B 86
Majendie Rd. SE18 5H 107
Majestic Way CR4: Mitc 2D 154
Major Cl. SW9 3B 120
Major Draper St. SE18 3F 107
Major Rd. E15 5F 69
SE16 3G 103
Makepeace Av. N6 2E 64
Makepeace Mans. N6 2E 64
Makepeace Rd. E11 4J 51
UB5: N'olt 2C 76
Makers' Yd. E20 6C 68
Makinen Ho.
IG9: Buck H 1F 37
Makins St. SW3 4D 16 (4C 100)
Malabar Ct. W12 7D 80
(off India Way)
Malabar St. E14 2C 104
Malam Ct. SE11 4J 19 (4A 102)
Malam Gdns. E14 7D 86
Malbrook Rd. SW15 4D 116
Malcolm Cl. SE20 7J 139
Malcolm Ct. E7 6H 69
HA7: Stan 5H 27
NW4 6C 44
Malcolm Cres. NW4 6C 44
Malcolm Dr. KT6: Surb 1E 162
Malcolm Ho. N1 2E 84
(off Arden Est.)
Malcolm Pl. E2 4J 85
Malcolm Rd. E1 4J 85
SE20 7J 139
SE25 6G 157
SW19 6G 135
UB10: Ick 4B 56
Malcolm Sargent Ho. E16 1K 105
(off Evelyn Rd.)
Malcolmson Ho. SW1 6C 18
(off Aylesford St.)
Malcolms Way N14 5B 22
Malcolm Way E11 5J 51
Malden Av. SE25 4H 157
UB6: G'frd 5J 59
Malden Ct. KT3: N Mald 3D 152
N4 6C 48
Malden Cres. NW1 6E 64
Malden Golf Course 2A 152
MALDEN GREEN 1C 164
Malden Grn. Av.
KT4: Wor Pk 1B 164
Malden Grn. M.
KT4: Wor Pk 1C 164
Malden Hill KT3: N Mald 3B 152
Malden Hill Gdns.
KT3: N Mald 3B 152
MALDEN JUNC. 5B 152
Malden Pk. KT3: N Mald 6B 152
Malden Pl. NW5 5E 64
Malden Rd. KT3: N Mald 5A 152
KT4: Wor Pk 6B 152
NW5 5D 64
SM3: Cheam 4F 165
Malden Way KT3: N Mald 6K 151
Maldon & District Society of
Model Engineers 1A 162
Maldon Cl. E15 5G 69
N1 1C 84
SE5 3E 120
Maldon Ct. E6 1E 88
SM6: W'gton 5G 167
Maldon Rd. N9 3A 34
RM7: Rush G 7J 55
SM6: W'gton 5F 167
W3 7J 79
Maldon Wlk. IG8: Wfd G 6F 37
Malet Pl. WC1 4C 6 (4H 83)
Malet St. WC1 4C 6 (4H 83)
Maley Av. SE27 2B 138
Malford Ct. E18 2J 51
Malford Gro. E18 4H 51
Malfort Rd. SE5 3E 120
Malham Cl. N11 6K 31
Malham Rd. SE23 1K 139
Malham Rd. Ind. Est.
SE23 1K 139
Malham Ter. N18 5C 34
Malibu Ct. SE26 3H 139
The Mall BR1: Broml 3J 159
CR0: C'don 2C 168
DA6: Bex 4G 127
E15 7F 69
HA3: Kenton 6F 43
KT6: Surb 5D 150
N14 3D 32
RM10: Dag 6G 73
SW1 6B 12 (2G 101)
SW14 5J 115
TW8: Bford 6D 96
W5 7E 78
Mallams M. SW9 3B 120
Mallard Cl. E9 6B 68
EN5: New Bar 6G 21
NW6 2J 81
TW2: Whitt 7E 112
W7 2J 95
Mallard Ct. E17 3F 51
Mallard Ho. NW8 2C 82
(off Bridgeman St.)
SW6 1A 118
(off Station Ct.)
Mallard Path SE28 3H 107
Mallard Pl. N22 2K 47
TW1: Twick 3A 132
Mallard Point E3 3D 86
(off Rainhill Way)
Mallards E11 7J 51
(off Blake Hall Rd.)
Mallards Rd. IG8: Wfd G 7E 36
IG11: Bark 4A 90
Mallard Wlk. BR3: Beck 5K 157
DA14: Sidc 6C 144
Mallard Way NW9 7J 43
SM6: W'gton 7G 167
Mall Chambers W8 1J 99
(off Kensington Mall)
Mallet Dr. UB5: N'olt 5D 58
Mallet Rd. SE13 6F 123
Mall Galleries 4D 12
Malling SE13 5D 122
Malling Cl. CR0: C'don 6J 157
Malling Gdns. SM4: Mord 6A 154
Malling Way BR2: Hayes 7H 159
Mallinson Rd. CR0: Bedd 3H 167
SW11 5C 118
Mallinson Sports Cen. 7D 46
Mallon Gdns. E1 7K 9
(off Commercial St.)
Mallord St. SW3 7B 16 (6B 100)
Mallory Bldgs. EC1 4A 8
(off St John St.)
Mallory Cl. E14 5D 86
SE4 4A 122
Mallory Ct. N17 6A 34
(off Cannon Rd.)
SE12 7K 123
Mallory Gdns. EN4: E Barn 7K 21
Mallory St. NW8 3D 4 (4C 82)
Mallory Way SE3 4K 123
Mallow Cl. CR0: C'don 1K 169
Mallow Mead NW7 7B 30
The Mallows UB10: Ick 3D 56
Mallow St. EC1 3E 8 (4D 84)
Mall Rd. W6 5D 98
Mall Vs. W6 5D 98
(off Mall Rd.)
Malmains Cl. BR3: Beck 4F 159
Malmains Way BR3: Beck 4E 158
Malmesbury E2 2J 85
(off Cyprus St.)
Malmesbury Cl. HA5: Eastc 4H 39
Malmesbury Rd. E3 3B 86
E16 5G 87
E18 1H 51
SM4: Mord 7A 154
Malmesbury Ter. E16 5H 87
Malmo Twr. SE8 4A 104
Malmsey Ho. SE11 5H 19 (5K 101)
Malmsmead Ho. E9 5B 68
(off Homerton Rd.)
Malory Cl. BR3: Beck 2A 158
Malpas Dr. HA5: Pinn 5B 40
Malpas Rd. E8 5H 67
RM9: Dag 6D 72
SE4 2B 122
Malswick Ct. SE15 7E 102
(off Tower Mill Rd.)
Malta Rd. E10 1C 68
Malta St. EC1 3A 8 (4B 84)
Maltby Cl. BR6: Orp 1K 173
Maltby Dr. EN1: Enf 1C 24
Maltby Ho. SE1 7J 15
(off Maltby St.)
SE3 4A 124
Maltby Rd. KT9: Chess 6G 163
Maltby St. SE1 7J 15 (2F 103)
Malt Ho. E17 5B 50
(off Old Brewery Way)
Malthouse Ct. TW8: Bford 6E 96
(off High St.)
Malthouse Dr. TW13: Hanw 5B 130
W4 6B 98
Malthouse Pas. SW13 2B 116
(off Clevelands Gdns.)
Malthouse Rd. SW11 7H 101
Malthus Path SE28 1C 108
Malting Ho. E14 7B 86
(off Oak La.)
The Maltings BR6: Orp 1K 173
W4 5G 97
(off Spring Gro.)
Maltings Cl. E3 3E 86
SW13 2B 116
Maltings Lodge W4 6A 98
(off Corney Reach Way)
Maltings M. DA15: Sidc 3A 144
Maltings Pl. SE1 7H 15
SW6 1K 117
Malting Way TW7: Isle 3K 113
Malton M. SE18 6J 107
W10 6G 81
Malton Rd. W10 6G 81
Malton St. SE18 6J 107
Maltravers St. WC2 2H 13 (7K 83)
Malt St. SE1 6G 103
Malva Cl. SW18 5K 117
Malvern Av. DA7: Bex 7E 108
E4 7A 36
HA2: Harr 3C 58
Malvern Cl. CR4: Mitc 3G 155
KT6: Surb 1E 162
SE20 2G 157
UB10: Ick 2C 56
W10 5H 81
Malvern Ct. SM2: Sutt 7J 165
SW7 3B 16
W12 2C 98
(off Hadyn Pk. Rd.)
Malvern Dr. IG3: Bark, Ilf 4K 71
IG8: Wfd G 5F 37
TW13: Hanw 5B 130
Malvern Gdns. HA3: Kenton 4E 42
NW2 2G 63
Malvern Ho. N16 1F 67
SE17 5C 102
(off Liverpool Gro.)
Malvern M. NW6 3J 81
Malvern Pl. NW6 3H 81
Malvern Rd. CR7: Thor H 4A 156
E6 1C 88
E8 7G 67
E11 2G 69
KT6: Surb 2E 162
N8 3K 47
N17 3G 49
NW6 2H 81
(not continuous)
TW12: Hamp 7E 130
UB3: Harl 7G 93
Malvern Ter. N1 1A 84
N9 1A 34
Malvern Way W13 5B 78
Malwood Rd. SW12 6F 119
The Malyons TW17: Shep 6F 147
Malyons Rd. SE13 6D 122
Malyons Ter. SE13 5D 122
Managers St. E14 1E 104
Manatee Pl. SM6: Bedd 3H 167
Manaton Cl. SE15 3H 121
Manaton Cres. UB1: S'hall 6E 76
Manbey Gro. E15 6G 69
Manbey M. E15 6G 69
Manbey Pk. Rd. E15 6G 69
Manbey Rd. E15 6G 69
Manbey St. E15 6G 69
Manbre Rd. W6 6E 98
Manbrough Av. E6 3D 88
Manby Wlk. E17 5A 50
Manchester Ct. E16 6K 87
(off Garvary Rd.)
Manchester Dr. W10 4G 81
Manchester Gro. E14 5E 104
Manchester Ho. SE17 5C 102
(off East St.)
Manchester M. W1 6G 5
Manchester Rd. CR7: Thor H 3C 156
E14 5E 104
N15 6D 48
Manchester Sq. W1 7G 5 (6E 82)
Manchester St. W1 6G 5 (5E 82)
Manchester Way RM10: Dag 4H 73
Manchuria Rd. SW11 6E 118
Manciple St. SE1 7E 14 (2D 102)
Mancroft Ct. NW8 1B 82
(off St John's Wood Pk.)
Mandalay Rd. SW4 5G 119
Mandara Pl. SE8 4A 104
(off Yeoman St.)
Mandarin Ct. NW10 6K 61
(off Mitchellbrook Way)
SE8 6B 104
Mandarin St. E14 7C 86
Mandarin Way UB4: Yead 6B 76
Mandarin Wharf N1 1E 84
(off De Beauvoir Cres.)
Mandela Cl. NW10 7J 61
W12 7D 80
Mandela Ho. E2 2J 9
(off Virginia Rd.)
SE5 2B 120
Mandela Rd. E16 6J 87
Mandela St. NW1 1G 83
SW9 7A 102
(not continuous)
Mandela Way SE1 4E 102
Mandeley M. E11 1H 69
Mandel Ho. SW18 4J 117
Manderley W14 3H 99
(off Oakwood La.)
Mandeville Cl. SE3 7H 105
SW20 7G 135
Mandeville Ct. E4 5F 35
Mandeville Dr. KT6: Surb 1D 162
Mandeville Ho. SE1 5F 103
(off Rolls Rd.)
SW4 5G 119
Mandeville M. SW4 4J 119
Mandeville Pl. W1 7H 5 (6E 82)
Mandeville Rd. N14 2A 32
TW7: Isle 2A 114
TW17: Shep 5C 146
UB5: N'olt 7E 58
Mandeville St. E5 3A 68
Mandrake Rd. SW17 3D 136
Mandrake Way E15 7G 69
Mandrell Rd. SW2 5J 119
Manesty Ct. N14 7C 22
(off Ivy Rd.)
Manet Gdns. W3 7A 80
Manette St. W1 1D 12 (6H 83)
Manfred Rd. SW15 5H 117
Manger Rd. N7 6J 65
Mangold Way DA18: Erith 3D 108
Manhattan Bldg. E3 2C 86
Manhattan Bus. Pk. W5 3E 78
Manhattan Loft Gdns.
E20 6E 68
Manilla Ct. RM6: Chad H 6B 54
(off Quarles Pk. Rd.)
Manilla St. E14 2C 104
Manilla Wlk. SE10 4G 105
Manister Rd. SE2 3A 108
Manitoba Ct. SE16 2J 103
(off Canada Est.)
Manitoba Gdns. BR6: Chels 6K 173
Manley Ct. N16 3F 67
Manley Ho. SE11 5J 19 (4A 102)
Manley St. NW1 1E 82
Manna Ho. E20 6E 68
(off Glade Wlk.)
Mannan Ho. E3 2B 86
(off Roman Rd.)
Mann Cl. CR0: C'don 3C 168
Manneby Prior N1 1H 7
(off Cumming St.)
Mannequin Ho. E17 3K 49
Manning Ct. SE28 1B 108
(off Titmuss Av.)
Manningford Cl. EC1 1A 8 (3B 84)
Manning Gdns. CR0: C'don 7H 157
HA3: Kenton 7D 42
Manning Ho. W11 6G 81
(off Westbourne Pk. Rd.)
Manning Pl. TW10: Rich 6F 115
Manning Rd. E17 5A 50
RM10: Dag 6G 73
Manningtree Cl. SW19 1G 135
Manningtree Rd. HA4: Ruis 4K 57
Manningtree St. E1 6G 85
Mannin Rd. RM6: Chad H 7B 54
Mannock Cl. NW9 3K 43
Mannock M. E18 1A 52
Mannock Rd. N22 3B 48
Mann's Cl. TW7: Isle 5K 113
Manns Rd. HA8: Edg 6B 28
Manns Ter. SE27 3C 138
Manny Shinwell Ho. SW6 6H 99
(off Clem Attlee Ct.)
Manoel Rd. TW2: Twick 2G 131
The Manor IG8: Wfd G 7K 37
Manor Av. SE4 2B 122
TW4: Houn 3B 112
UB5: N'olt 7D 58
Manorbrook SE3 4J 123
MANOR CIRCUS 3G 115
Manor Cl. DA1: Cray 4K 127
E17 1A 50
EN5: Barn 4B 20
HA4: Ruis 1H 57
KT4: Wor Pk 1A 164
NW7 5E 28
NW9 5H 43
RM10: Dag 6K 73
SE28 7C 90

A-Z Big London 251

Manor Cotts.—Mkt. Way

Manor Cotts. HA6: Nwood 1H 39
N2 2A 46
(off Manor Cotts. App.)
Manor Cotts. App. N2 2A 46
Manor Ct. BR4: W W'ck 1D 170
DA7: Bex 4H 127
E4 1B 36
E10 1D 68
HA1: Harr 6K 41
HA9: Wemb 5E 60
IG11: Bark 7K 71
KT2: King T 1G 151
KT8: W Mole 4E 148
N2 5D 46
N14 2C 32
N20 3J 31
(off York Way)
SM5: Cars 3E 166
SW2 5K 119
SW3 6D 16
(off Hemus Pl.)
SW6 1K 117
SW16 3J 137
TW2: Twick 2G 131
W3 4G 97
Manor Ct. Rd. W7 7J 77
Manor Cres. KT5: Surb 6G 151
Manor Dene SE28 6C 90
Manordene Cl. KT7: T Ditt 1A 162
Manordene Rd. SE28 6C 90
Manor Dr. HA9: Wemb 4F 61
KT5: Surb 6F 151
KT10: Hin W 2A 162
KT19: Ewe 6A 164
N14 1A 32
N20 4J 31
NW7 5E 28
TW13: Hanw 5B 130
TW16: Sun 2J 147
The Manor Dr. KT4: Wor Pk 1A 164
Manor Dr. Nth.
KT3: N Mald 7K 151
KT4: Wor Pk 1A 164
Manor Est. SE16 4H 103
Manor Farm 7G 39
Mnr. Farm Av. TW17: Shep 6D 146
Mnr. Farm Cl.
KT4: Wor Pk 1A 164
Mnr. Farm Ct. E6 3D 88
Mnr. Farm Dr. E4 3B 36
Mnr. Farm Rd.
HA0: Wemb 2D 78
SW16 2A 156
Manorfield Cl. N19 4G 65
(off Fulbrook M.)
Manor Flds. SW15 6F 117
Manorfields Cl. BR7: Chst 3K 161
Manor Gdns. CR2: S Croy 6F 169
HA4: Ruis 5A 58
N7 3J 65
SW4 2G 119
(off Larkhall Ri.)
SW20 2H 153
TW9: Rich 4F 115
TW12: Hamp 7F 131
TW16: Sun 1J 147
W3 4G 97
W4 5A 98
Manor Ga. UB5: N'olt 7C 58
Manorgate Rd. KT2: King T 1G 151
Manor Gro. BR3: Beck 2D 158
SE15 6J 103
TW9: Rich 4G 115
Mnr. Hall Av. NW4 2F 45
Mnr. Hall Dr. NW4 2F 45
Manorhall Gdns. E10 1C 68
MANOR HOUSE 7D 48
MANOR HOUSE 7C 48
Manor Ho. NW1 5D 4
(off Lisson Gro.)
UB2: S'hall 3C 94
Manor Ho. Ct. TW17: Shep 7D 146
W9 4A 82
(off Warrington Gdns.)
Manor Ho. Dr. HA6: Nwood 1D 38
NW6 7F 63
Manor Ho. Est. HA7: Stan 6G 27
Manor Ho. Gdn. E11 6K 51
Manor Ho. Way
TW7: Isle 3B 114
Manor La.
SE12 5G 123
SE13 5G 123
SM1: Sutt 5A 166
TW13: Felt 2J 129
TW16: Sun 2J 147
UB3: Harl 6F 93
Manor La. Ter. SE13 4G 123
Manor Lodge NW6 7F 63
(off Willesden La.)
Manor M. NW6 2J 81
(off Cambridge Av.)
SE4 2B 122
Manor Mt. SE23 1J 139
Manor Pde. HA1: Harr 6K 41
N16 2F 67
NW10 2B 80
(off High St. Harlesden)
MANOR PARK 4B 70
Manor Pk. BR7: Chst 2H 161
SE13 4F 123
TW9: Rich 4F 115
TW13: Felt 2H 129
Manor Pk. Cl. BR4: W W'ck 1D 170
Manor Pk. Crematorium 4A 70
Manor Pk. Cres. HA8: Edg 6B 28
Manor Pk. Dr. HA2: Harr 3F 41
Manor Pk. Gdns.
HA8: Edg 5B 28
Manor Pk. Pde. SE13 4F 123
(off Lee High Rd.)
Manor Pk. Rd. BR4: W W'ck 1D 170
BR7: Chst 1G 161
E12 4B 70
(not continuous)
N2 3A 46
NW10 1B 80
SM1: Sutt 5A 166
Manor Pl. BR1: Broml 1C 160
BR7: Chst 2H 161
CR4: Mitc 3G 155
KT12: Walt T 7H 147
(not continuous)
SE17 5B 102
SM1: Sutt 4K 165
TW14: Felt 1J 129
Manor Rd. BR3: Beck 2D 158
BR4: W W'ck 2D 170
CR4: Mitc 4G 155
DA1: Cray 4K 127
DA5: Bexl 1H 145
DA15: Sidc 3K 143
E10 7C 50
E15 2G 87
E16 2G 87
E17 2A 50
EN2: Enf 2H 23
EN5: Barn 4B 20
HA1: Harr 6A 42
HA4: Ruis 1F 57
IG7: Chig 6J 37
IG8: Wfd G 6J 37
IG11: Bark 6K 71
KT8: E Mos 4H 149
KT12: Walt T 7H 147
N16 2D 66
N17 1G 49
N22 6D 32
RM6: Chad H 6D 54
RM10: Dag 6J 73
SE25 4G 157
SM2: Cheam 7H 165
SM6: W'gton 4F 167
SW20 2H 153
TW2: Twick 2G 131
TW9: Rich 4G 115
TW11: Tedd 5A 132
(not continuous)
TW15: Ashf 5B 128
UB3: Hayes 6J 75
W13 7A 78
Manor Rd. Ho. HA1: Harr 6A 42
Manor Rd. Nth. KT7: T Ditt 3A 162
KT10: Hin W, T Ditt
3A 162, 3A 162
SM6: W'gton 4F 167
Manorside EN5: Barn 4B 20
Manorside Cl. SE2 4C 108
Manor Sq. RM8: Dag 2C 72
Manor Va. TW8: Bford 5C 96
Manor Vw. N3 2K 45
Mnr. Way BR2: Broml 6C 160
BR3: Beck 2C 158
BR5: Pet W 4G 161
CR2: S Croy 6E 168
CR4: Mitc 3G 155
DA5: Bexl 1G 145
DA7: Bex 3K 127
E4 4A 36
HA2: Harr 4F 41
HA4: Ruis 7G 39
KT4: Wor Pk 1A 164
NW9 4A 44
RM13: Rain 4K 91
SE3 4H 123
SE23 7J 121
UB2: S'hall 4B 94
Manorway EN1: Enf 7K 23
IG8: Wfd G 5F 37
The Manor Way SM6: W'gton 4F 167
Manor Way Bus. Cen.
RM13: Rain 5K 91
Manor Waye UB8: Uxb 1A 74
Manpreet Ct. E12 5D 70
Manresa Rd. SW3 6C 16 (5C 100)
Mansard Beeches SW17 5E 136
Mansard Cl. HA5: Pinn 3B 40
Mansbridge Ho. SW8 1F 119
(off Patcham Ter.)
Manse Cl. UB3: Harl 6F 93
Mansel Gro. E17 1C 50
Mansell Rd. UB6: G'frd 5F 77
W3 2K 97
Mansell St. E1 1K 15 (6F 85)
Mansel Rd. SW19 6G 135
Manser Ct. RM13: Rain 3K 91
Mansergh Cl. SE18 7C 106
Manse Rd. N16 3F 67
Manser Rd. RM13: Rain 3K 91
Mansfield Av. EN4: E Barn 6J 21
HA4: Ruis 1K 57
N15 4D 48
Mansfield Cl. N9 6B 24
Mansfield Ct. E2 1F 85
(off Whiston Rd.)
SE15 7F 103
(off Sumner Rd.)
Mansfield Dr. UB4: Hayes 4G 75
Mansfield Hgts. N2 5C 46
Mansfield Hill E4 7J 25
Mansfield Ho. N1 1E 84
(off Halcomb St.)
Mansfield M. W1 6J 5 (5F 83)
Mansfield Pl. CR2: S Croy 6D 168
NW3 4A 64
Mansfield Rd. CR2: S Croy 6D 168
E11 6K 51
E17 4B 50
IG1: Ilf 2E 70
KT9: Chess 5C 162
NW3 5D 64
W3 4H 79
Mansfield St. W1 6J 5 (5F 83)
Mansford St. E2 2G 85
Manship Rd. CR4: Mitc 7E 136
Mansion Cl. SW9 1A 120
(not continuous)
Mansion Gdns. NW3 3K 63
Mansion House
London 1E 14 (6D 84)
Mansion Ho. Dr. HA7: Stan 2D 26
Mansion Ho. Pl. EC4 1E 14 (6D 84)
Mansion Ho. St. EC4 1E 14
Mansion Lock Ho. NW1 7F 65
(off Hawley Cres.)
The Mansions SW5 5K 99
(Earl's Ct. Rd.)
SW5 5K 99
(off Old Brompton Rd.)
Mansion Vw. E15 1F 87
(off High St.)
Manson Ho. N1 7A 66
(off Drummond Way)
Manson M. SW7 4A 16 (4B 100)
Manson Pl. SW7 4A 16 (4B 100)
Mansted Gdns. RM6: Chad H 7C 54
Manston N17 2D 48
(off Adams Rd.)
NW1 7G 65
(off Agar Gro.)
Manston Av. UB2: S'hall 4E 94
Manston Cl. SE20 1J 157
Manston Ct. E17 1B 50
Manstone Rd. NW2 5G 63
Manston Gro. KT2: King T 5D 132
Manston Ho. W14 3G 99
(off Russell Rd.)
Manthorpe Rd. SE18 5G 107
Mantilla Rd. SW17 4E 136
Mantle Ct. SW18 6K 117
(off Mapleton Rd.)
Mantle Rd. SE4 3A 122
Mantlet Cl. SW16 7G 137
Mantle Way E15 7G 69
Manton Av. W7 2K 95
Manton Cl. UB3: Hayes 7G 75
Manton Rd. EN3: Enf L 1H 25
SE2 4A 108
Manton Way EN3: Enf L 1J 25
Mantua St. SW11 3B 118
Mantus Cl. E1 4J 85
Mantus Rd. E1 4J 85
Manuka Cl. W7 1A 96
Manuka Hgts. E20 5E 68
(off Napa Cl.)
Manus Way N20 2F 31
Manville Gdns. SW17 3F 137
Manville Rd. SW17 2E 136
Manwell La. IG11: Bark 4A 90
Manwood Rd. SE4 5B 122
Manwood St. E16 1D 106
Manygate La. TW17: Shep 7E 146
Manygate Pk. TW17: Shep 6F 147
(off Mitre Cl.)
Manygates SW12 2F 137
Mapesbury Ct. NW2 5G 63
Mapesbury M. NW4 6C 44
Mapesbury Rd. NW2 7G 63
Mapeshill Pl. NW2 6E 62
Mapes Ho. NW6 7G 63
Mape St. E2 4H 85
(not continuous)
Maple Av. E4 5G 35
HA2: Harr 2F 59
UB7: Yiew 7A 74
W3 1A 98
Maple Cl. BR5: Pet W 5H 161
CR4: Mitc 1F 155
HA4: Ruis 6K 39
IG9: Buck H 3G 37
N3 6D 30
N16 6G 49
SW4 6H 119
TW12: Hamp 6D 130
UB4: Yead 3B 76
Maple Ct. CR0: C'don 4C 168
(off Lwr. Coombe St.)
CR0: C'don 4C 168
(off The Waldrons)
E3 2C 86
(off Four Seasons Cl.)
E6 5E 88
KT3: N Mald 3K 151
SE6 1D 140
TW15: Ashf 7F 129
Maple Cres. DA15: Sidc 6A 126
Maplecroft Cl. E6 6B 88
Mapledale Av. CR0: C'don 2G 169
Mapledene BR7: Chst 6G 143
Mapledene Est. E8 7G 67
Mapledene Rd. E8 7F 67
Maple Gdns. HA8: Edg 7F 29
TW19: Stanw 2A 128
Maple Gro. NW9 7J 43
TW8: Bford 7B 96
UB1: S'hall 5D 76
W5 3D 96
Maple Gro. Bus. Cen.
TW4: Houn 4A 112
Maple Ho. E17 3D 50
HA9: Wemb 4G 61
(off Empire Way)
KT1: King T 5E 150
(off Maple Rd.)
N19 3G 65
SE8 7B 104
(off Idonia St.)
TW9: Kew 1H 115
Maplehurst BR2: Broml 2G 159
Maplehurst Cl. KT1: King T 4E 150
Maple Ind. Est. TW13: Felt 3J 129
Maple Leaf Dr. DA15: Sidc 1K 143
Mapleleafe Gdns. IG6: Ilf 3F 53
Maple Leaf Sq. SE16 2K 103
Maple Lodge W8 3K 99
(off Abbots Wlk.)
Maple M. NW6 2K 81
SE16 2K 103
SW16 5K 137
Maple Pl. N17 7B 34
UB7: Yiew 1A 92
W1 5B 6 (4G 83)
Maple Rd. E11 6G 51
KT6: Surb 6D 150
SE20 1H 157
UB4: Yead 3A 76
The Maples KT1: Hamp W 7C 132
KT10: Clay 7A 162
Maples Pl. E1 5H 85
Maplestead Rd. RM9: Dag 1B 90
SW2 7K 119
Maple St. E2 2H 85
RM7: Rom 4J 55
W1 5A 6 (5G 83)
Maplethorpe Rd.
CR7: Thor H 4A 156
Mapleton Cl. BR2: Broml 6J 159
Mapleton Cres. EN3: Enf W 1D 24
SW18 6K 117
Mapleton Rd. E4 3K 35
EN1: Enf 2C 24
SW18 6J 117
(not continuous)
Maple Tree Pl. SE3 1C 124
Maple Wlk. W10 3F 81
Maple Way SE16 2A 104
TW13: Felt 3J 129
Maplewood Apts. N4 7C 48
(off Katherine Cl.)
Maplewood Ct. TW15: Ashf 4A 128
Maplin Cl. N21 6E 22
Maplin Ho. SE2 2D 108
(off Wolvercote Rd.)
Maplin Rd. E16 6J 87
Maplin St. E3 3B 86
Mapperley Cl. E11 6H 51
Mapperley Dr. IG8: Wfd G 7B 36
Marabou Cl. E12 5C 70
Mara Ho. E20 5D 68
(off Victory Pde.)
Maran Way DA18: Erith 2D 108
Maraschino Apartment
CR0: C'don 1D 168
(off Cherry Orchard Rd.)
Marathon Ho. NW1 5E 4
(off Marylebone Rd.)
Marathon Way SE28 2K 107
Marbaix Gdns. TW7: Isle 1H 113
Marban Rd. W9 3H 81
Marble Arch 2F 11
MARBLE ARCH 7D 82
Marble Arch W1 2E 10 (7D 82)
Marble Arch Apts. W1 7E 4
(off Harrowby St.)
Marble Cl. W3 1H 97
Marble Dr. NW2 1F 63
Marble Hill Cl. TW1: Twick 7B 114
Marble Hill Gdns.
TW1: Twick 7B 114
Marble Hill House 7C 114
Marble Ho. SE18 5K 107
W9 4H 81
Marble Quay E1 4K 15 (1G 103)
Marbles Ho. SE5 6C 102
(off Grosvenor Ter.)
Marbrook Ct. SE12 3A 142
Marcella Rd. SW9 2A 120
Marcellina Way BR6: Orp 3J 173
March NW9 1B 44
(off Long Mead)
Marchant Cl. NW7 6F 29
Marchant Ho. N1 1E 84
(off Halcomb St.)
Marchant Rd. E11 2F 69
Marchant St. SE14 6A 104
Marchbank Rd. W14 6H 99
March Ct. SW15 4D 116
Marchmont Gdns. TW10: Rich 5F 115
Marchmont Rd.
SM6: W'gton 7G 167
TW10: Rich 5F 115
Marchmont St. WC1 3E 6 (4J 83)
March Rd. TW1: Twick 7A 114
Marchside Cl. TW5: Hest 1B 112
Marchwood Cl. SE5 7E 102
Marchwood Cres. W5 6C 78
Marcia Ct. SE1 4E 102
(off Marcia Rd.)
Marcia Rd. SE1 4E 102
Marcilly Rd. SW18 5B 118
Marco Dr. HA5: Hat E 1D 40
Marcon Ct. E8 5H 67
(off Amhurst Rd.)
Marconi Pl. N11 4A 32
Marconi Rd. E10 1C 68
Marconi Way UB1: S'hall 6F 77
Marcon Pl. E8 6H 67
Marco Rd. W6 3E 98
Marcourt Lawns W5 4E 78
Marcus Ct. E15 1G 87
Marcus Garvey M. SE22 6H 121
Marcus Garvey Way SE24 4A 120
Marcus St. E15 1H 87
SW18 6K 117
Marcus Ter. SW18 6K 117
Mardale Ct. NW7 7H 29
Mardale Dr. NW9 5K 43
Mardell Rd. CR0: C'don 5K 157
Marden Av. BR2: Hayes 6J 159
Marden Cres. CR0: C'don 6K 155
DA5: Bexl 5J 127
Marden Ho. E8 5H 67
Marden Rd. CR0: C'don 6K 155
N17 2E 48
Marden Sq. SE16 3H 103
Marder Rd. W13 2A 96
Mardyke Cl. RM13: Rain 2J 91
Mardyke Ho. SE17 4D 102
(off Mason St.)
Marechal Niel Av. DA15: Sidc 3H 143
Marechal Niel Pde.
DA14: Sidc 3H 143
(off Main Rd.)
Maresby Ho. E4 2J 35
Maresfield CR0: C'don 3E 168
Maresfield Gdns. NW3 5A 64
Mare St. E8 5H 67
Marfleet Cl. SM5: Cars 2C 166
Margaret Av. E4 6J 25
Margaret Bondfield Av.
IG11: Bark 7A 72
Margaret Bondfield Ho. E3 2A 86
(off Driffield Rd.)
Margaret Ct. EN4: E Barn 4G 21
W1 7A 6
Margaret Gardner Dr. SE9 2D 142
Margaret Herbison Ho. SW6 6H 99
(off Clem Attlee Ct.)
Margaret Ho. W6 5E 98
(off Queen Caroline St.)
Margaret Ingram Cl. SW6 6H 99
Margaret Lockwood Cl.
KT1: King T 4F 151
Margaret McMillan Ho. E16 6A 88
Margaret Rd. DA5: Bexl 6D 126
E11 6G 51
EN4: E Barn 4G 21
N16 1F 67
Margaret Rutherford Pl.
SW12 1G 137
Margarets Ct. HA8: Edg 5C 28
Margaret St. W1 7K 5 (6F 83)
Margaretta Ter. SW3 7C 16 (6C 100)
Margaretting Rd. E12 1A 70
Margaret Way IG4: Ilf 6C 52
Margaret White Ho. NW1 1D 6
(off Chalton St.)
Margate Rd. SW2 5J 119
Margerie Ct. E2 2H 85
(off Esker Pl.)
Margery Fry Ct. N7 3J 65
Margery Pk. Rd. E7 6J 69
Margery Rd. RM8: Dag 3D 72
Margery St. WC1 2J 7 (3A 84)
Margery Ter. E7 6J 69
(off Margery Pk. Rd.)
Margin Dr. SW19 5F 135
Margravine Gdns. W6 5F 99
Margravine Rd. W6 5F 99
Marham Dr. NW9 1A 44
Marham Gdns. SM4: Mord 6A 154
SW18 1C 136
Mar Ho. NW9 3K 43
Maria Cl. SE1 4H 103
Maria Ct. SE25 2E 156
Marian Cl. UB4: Yead 4B 76
Marian Ct. E9 5J 67
SM1: Sutt 5K 165
Marian Gdns. BR1: Broml 7A 142
Marianne Cl. SE5 1E 120
Marianne North Gallery 2F 115
Marian Pl. E2 2H 85
Marian Rd. SW16 1G 155
Marian St. E2 2H 85
Marian Way NW10 7B 62
Maria Ter. E1 5K 85
Maria Theresa Cl.
KT3: N Mald 5K 151
Maribor SE10 7E 104
(off Burney St.)
Maricas Av. HA3: Hrw W 1H 41
Marie Curie SE5 1F 121
Marie Lloyd Gdns. N19 7J 47
Marie Lloyd Ho. N1 1E 8
(off Murray Gro.)
Marie Lloyd Wlk. E8 6F 67
Marien Ct. E4 5A 36
Mariette Way SM6: W'gton 7J 167
Marigold All. SE1 3A 14 (7B 84)
Marigold Cl. UB1: S'hall 7C 76
Marigold Rd. N17 7D 34
Marigold St. SE16 2H 103
Marigold Way CR0: C'don 1K 169
Marina App. UB4: Yead 5C 76
Marina Av. KT3: N Mald 5D 152
Marina Cl. BR2: Broml 3J 159
Marina Ct. E3 3B 86
(off Alfred St.)
Marina Dr. DA16: Well 2J 125
Marina Gdns. RM7: Rom 5J 55
Marina One N1 2J 83
(off New Wharf Rd.)
Marina Pl. KT1: Hamp W 1D 150
Marina Point E14 3D 104
(off Lanark Sq.)
SW6 2A 118
Marina Way TW11: Tedd 7D 132
Marine Ct. E11 2G 69
Marine Dr. IG11: Bark 4A 90
SE18 4D 106
Marinefield Rd. SW6 2K 117
Marinel Ho. SE5 7C 102
Mariner Bus. Cen. CR0: Wadd 5A 168
Mariner Gdns. TW10: Ham 3C 132
Mariner Rd. E12 4E 70
Mariners Cl. EN4: E Barn 5G 21
Mariners M. E14 4F 105
Mariners Pl. SE16 4A 104
(off Plough Way)
Marine St. SE16 3G 103
Marine Twr. SE8 6B 104
(off Abinger Gro.)
Marion Av. TW17: Shep 5D 146
Marion Gro. IG8: Wfd G 5B 36
Marion Ho. NW1 1D 82
(off Regent's Pk. Rd.)
Marion M. SE21 3D 138
Marion Rd. CR7: Thor H 5C 156
NW7 5H 29
Marischal Rd. SE13 3F 123
Maritime Ho. SE18 4F 107
Maritime Quay E14 5C 104
Maritime St. E3 4B 86
SE16 3K 103
Marius Mans. SW17 2E 136
Marius Rd. SW17 2E 136
Marjorie Gro. SW11 4D 118
Marjorie M. E1 6K 85
Mark Av. E4 6J 25
Mark Cl. DA7: Bex 1E 126
UB1: S'hall 7F 77
Marke Cl. BR2: Kes 4C 172
The Market SM1: Sutt 1A 166
SM5: Cars 1A 166
Market App. W12 2E 98
Market Chambers EN2: Enf 3J 23
(off Church St.)
Market Ct. W1 7A 6
Market Dr. W4 7A 98
Market Entrance SW8 7G 101
Market Est. N7 6J 65
Market Hall N22 2A 48
Market Hill SE18 3E 106
Market La. HA8: Edg 1J 43
W12 2E 98
Market Link RM1: Rom 4K 55
Market M. W1 5J 11 (1F 101)
Market Pde. BR1: Broml 1J 159
(off East St.)
DA14: Sidc 4B 144
E10 6E 50
(off High Rd. Leyton)
E17 3B 50
(off Higham Hill Rd.)
N9 2B 34
(off Winchester Rd.)
N16 1G 67
(off Oldhill St.)
SE25 4G 157
TW13: Hanw 3C 130
Market Pav. E10 3C 68
Market Pl. DA6: Bex 4G 127
EN2: Enf 3J 23
KT1: King T 2D 150
N2 3B 46
SE16 4G 103
(not continuous)
TW8: Bford 7C 96
UB1: S'hall 1D 94
W1 7A 6 (6G 83)
W3 1J 97
The Market Pl. NW11 4A 46
Market Rd. N7 6J 65
TW9: Rich 3G 115
Market Row SW9 4A 120
Market Sq. BR1: Broml 2J 159
(not continuous)
E14 6D 86
KT1: King T 2D 150
(off Market Pl.)
The Market Square N9 2C 34
(within Edmonton Grn. Shop. Cen.)
Market St. E1 5J 9 (5F 85)
E6 2D 88
SE18 4E 106
Market Ter. TW8: Bford 6E 96
(off Albany Rd.)
Market Trad. Est. UB2: S'hall 4K 93
Mkt. Way E14 6D 86
HA0: Wemb 5E 60

252 A-Z Big London

Market Yd. SE8 7C 104
Market Yd. M. SE1 7G 15 (2E 102)
Markfield Beam Engine & Mus. 5G 49
Markfield Gdns. E4 7J 25
Markfield Rd. N15 4G 49
Markham Ho. RM10: Dag 3G 73
(off Uvedale Rd.)
Markham Pl. SW3 5E 16 (5D 100)
Markham Sq. SW3 5E 16 (5D 100)
Markham St. SE17 5E 102
SW3 5D 16 (5C 100)
Markhole Cl. TW12: Hamp 7D 130
Mark Ho. E2 2K 85
(off Sewardstone Rd.)
Markhouse Av. E17 6A 50
Markhouse Pas. E17 6B 50
(off Downsfield Rd.)
Markhouse Rd. E17 6B 50
Markland Ho. W10 7F 81
(off Darfield Way)
Mark La. EC3 2H 15 (7E 84)
Mark Lodge EN4: Cockf 4H 21
(off Edgeworth Rd.)
Markmanor Av. E17 7A 50
Mark Rd. N22 2B 48
Marksbury Av. TW9: Rich 3G 115
MARKS GATE 1E 54
Mark Sq. EC2 3G 9 (4E 84)
Marks Rd. RM7: Rom 5J 55
(not continuous)
Markstone Ho. SE1 7A 14
(off Lancaster St.)
Mark St. E15 7G 69
EC2 3G 9 (4E 84)
Mark Twain Dr. NW2 4D 62
Mark Wade Cl. E12 1B 70
Markway TW16: Sun 2A 148
Markwell Cl. SE26 4H 139
Markyate Ho. W10 4E 80
(off Sutton Way)
Markyate Rd. RM8: Dag 5B 72
Marland Ho. SW1 1F 17
(off Sloane St.)
Marlands Rd. IG5: Ilf 3C 52
Marlborough SW19 1F 135
(off Inner Pk. Rd.)
W9 3A 82
(off Maida Vale)
Marlborough Av. E8 1G 85
(not continuous)
HA4: Ruis 6E 38
HA8: Edg 3C 28
N14 3B 32
Marlborough Cl. BR6: Orp 6K 161
N20 3J 31
SE17 4C 102
SW19 6C 136
Marlborough Ct. CR2: S Croy 4E 168
(off Birdhurst Rd.)
EN1: Enf 5K 23
HA1: Harr 4H 41
HA6: Nwood 1H 39
IG9: Buck H 2F 37
N17 1G 49
(off Kemble Rd.)
SM6: W'gton 7G 167
W1 1B 12
(off Carnaby St.)
W8 4J 99
(off Pembroke Rd.)
Marlborough Cres. UB3: Harl 7F 93
W4 3K 97
Marlborough Dr. IG5: Ilf 3C 52
Marlborough Flats SW3 3D 16
Marlborough Gdns.
KT6: Surb 7D 150
N20 3J 31
Marlborough Ga. Ho. W2 2A 10
(off Elms M.)
Marlborough Gro. SE1 5G 103
Marlborough Hill HA1: Harr 4H 41
NW8 2A 82
Marlborough House 5B 12 (1G 101)
Marlborough Ho. E16 1J 105
(off Hardy Av.)
UB7: W Dray 2B 92
(off Park Lodge Av.)
Marlborough La. SE7 6A 106
Marlborough Lodge NW8 2A 82
(off Hamilton Ter.)
Marlborough Mans. NW6 5K 63
(off Canon Hill)
Marlborough M. SW2 4K 119
Marlborough Pde. UB10: Hil 4D 74
Marlborough Pk. Av.
DA15: Sidc 7A 126
Marlborough Pl. NW8 2A 82
Marlborough Rd. BR2: Broml 4A 160
CR2: S Croy 7C 168
DA7: Bex 3D 126
E4 6J 35
E7 7A 70
E15 4G 69
E18 2J 51
N9 1B 34
N19 2H 65
N22 7D 32
RM7: Mawney 4G 55
RM8: Dag 4B 72
SE18 3F 107
SE28 3G 107
SM1: Sutt 3J 165
SW1 5B 12 (1G 101)
SW19 6C 136
TW7: Isle 1B 114
TW10: Rich 6F 115
TW12: Hamp 6E 130
TW13: Felt 2B 130
TW15: Ashf 5A 128
UB2: S'hall 3A 94
UB10: Hil 4D 74
W4 5J 97
W5 2D 96
Marlborough St.
SW3 4C 16 (4C 100)
Marlborough Yd. N19 2H 65
Marlbury NW8 1K 81
(off Abbey Rd.)
Marler Rd. SE23 1A 140
Marley Av. DA7: Bex 6D 108
Marley Cl. N15 4B 48
UB6: G'frd 3E 76
Marley Ho. E16 7F 89
(off University Way)
W11 7F 81
(off St Ann's Rd.)
Marley St. SE16 4K 103
Marley Wlk. NW2 5E 62
Marl Fld. Cl. KT4: Wor Pk 1C 164
Marlin Cl. TW16: Sun 6G 129
Marling Ct. TW12: Hamp 6D 130
Marlingdene Cl.
TW12: Hamp 6E 130
MARLING PARK 7D 130
Marlings Cl. BR7: Chst 4J 161
Marlings Pk. Av. BR7: Chst 4J 161
Marlin Pk. TW14: Felt 5K 111
Marlins Cl. SM1: Sutt 5A 166
Marloes Cl. HA0: Wemb 4D 60
Marloes Rd. W8 3K 99
Marlow Cl. SE20 3H 157
Marlow Ct. N14 7B 22
NW6 7F 63
NW9 3B 44
Marlow Cres. TW1: Twick 6K 113
Marlow Dr. SM3: Cheam 2F 165
Marlowe Cl. BR7: Chst 6H 143
IG6: Ilf 1G 53
Marlowe Ct. SE19 5F 139
SW3 4D 16
(off Petyward)
Marlowe Gdns. SE9 6E 124
Marlowe Ho. IG8: Wfd G 7K 37
KT1: King T 4D 150
(off Portsmouth Rd.)
Marlowe Path SE8 6C 104
Marlowe Rd. E17 4E 50
The Marlowes DA1: Cray 4K 127
NW8 1B 82
Marlowe Sq. CR4: Mitc 4G 155
Marlowe Way CR0: Bedd 2J 167
Marlow Gdns. UB3: Harl 3F 93
Marlow Ho. E2 2J 9
(off Calvert Av.)
KT5: Surb 5E 150
(off Cranes Pk.)
SE1 7J 15
(off Abbey St.)
TW11: Tedd 4A 132
W2 6K 81
(off Hallfield Est.)
Marlow Rd. E6 3D 88
RM8: Dag 1E 72
SE20 3H 157
UB2: S'hall 3D 94
Marlow Way SE16 2K 103
Marlow Workshops E2 2J 9
(off Virginia Rd.)
Marl Rd. SW18 4A 118
Marlston NW1 2K 5
Marlton St. SE10 5H 105
Marlu Ct. SE14 1K 121
(off Hatcham Pk. M.)
Marlu Ho. SE14 1K 121
(off Hatcham Pk. M.)
Marlwood Cl. DA15: Sidc 2J 143
Marmadon Rd. SE18 4K 107
Marmara Apts. E16 7J 87
(off Western Gateway)
Marmion App. E4 4H 35
Marmion Av. E4 4G 35
Marmion Cl. E4 4G 35
Marmion M. SW11 3E 118
Marmion Rd. SW11 4E 118
Marmont Rd. SE15 1G 121
Marmora Rd. SE22 6J 121
Marmot Rd. TW4: Houn 3B 112
Marne Av. DA16: Well 3A 126
N11 4A 32
Marnell Way TW4: Houn 3B 112
Marne Rd. RM9: Dag 1B 90
Marner Point E3 4E 86
Marne St. W10 3G 81
Marney Rd. SW11 4E 118
Marnfield Cres. SW2 1A 138
Marnham Av. NW2 4G 63
Marnham Ct. HA0: Wemb 5C 60
Marnham Cres. UB6: G'frd 3F 77
Marnock Ho. SE17 5D 102
(off Brandon St.)
Marnock Rd. SE4 5B 122
Maroon St. E14 5A 86
Maroons Way SE6 5C 140
Marqueen Ct. W8 2K 99
(off Kensington Chu. St.)
Marqueen Towers SW16 7K 137
Marquess Hgts. E18 1K 51
Marquess Rd. N1 6D 66
Marquis Cl. HA0: Wemb 7F 61
Marquis Ct. IG11: Bark 5J 71
KT1: King T 4D 150
(off Anglesea Rd.)
N4 1K 65
(off Marquis Rd.)
TW19: Stanw 1A 128
Marquis Rd. N4 1K 65
N22 6E 32
NW1 6H 65
Marrabon Cl. DA15: Sidc 1A 144
Marrick Cl. SW15 4C 116
Marrick Ho. NW6 1K 81
(off Mortimer Cres.)
Marriett Ho. SE6 4E 140
Marrilyne Av. EN3: Enf L 1G 25
Marriner Ct. UB3: Hayes 7G 75
(off Barra Hall Rd.)
Marriott Cl. TW14: Felt 6F 111
Marriott Rd. E15 1G 87
EN5: Barn 3A 20
N4 1K 65
N10 1D 46
Marriotts Cl. NW9 6B 44
Marryat Cl. TW4: Houn 4D 112
Marryat Ho. SW1 6A 18
(off Churchill Gdns.)
Marryat Pl. SW19 4G 135
Marryat Rd. SW19 5F 135
Marryat Sq. SW6 1G 117
Marsala Rd. SE13 4D 122
Marsalis Ho. E3 3C 86
(off Rainhill Way)
Marsault Ct. TW9: Rich 4E 114
(off Kew Foot Rd.)
Marsden Rd. N9 2C 34
SE15 3F 121
Marsden St. NW5 6E 64
Marsden Way BR6: Orp 4K 173
Marshall Bldg. W2 6A 4
(off Hermitage St.)
Marshall Cl. HA1: Harr 7H 41
SW18 6A 118
TW4: Houn 5D 112
Marshall Ct. NW6 7F 63
(off Coverdale Rd.)
SE20 7H 139
(off Anerley Pk.)
Marshall Dr. UB4: Hayes 5H 75
Marshall Est. NW7 4H 29
Marshall Ho. N1 2D 84
(off Cranston Est.)
SE1 3E 102
(off Page's Wlk.)
SE17 5D 102
(off East St.)
Marshall Path SE28 7B 90
Marshall Rd. E10 3D 68
N17 1D 48
Marshalls Cl. N11 4A 32
Marshalls Dr. RM1: Rom 3K 55
Marshalls Gro. SE18 4C 106
Marshall's Pl. SE16 3F 103
Marshall's Rd. SM1: Sutt 4K 165
Marshalls Rd.
RM7: Rom 4K 55
Marshall St. NW10 7K 61
W1 1B 12 (6G 83)
Marshall Street Leisure Cen. 1B 12 (6G 83)
Marshalsea Rd.
SE1 6D 14 (2C 102)
Marsham Cl. BR7: Chst 5F 143
Marsham Ct. SW1 3D 18 (4H 101)
Marsham St. SW1 2D 18 (3H 101)
Marsh Av. CR4: Mitc 2D 154
Marshbrook Cl. SE3 3B 124
The Marsh Cen. E1 7K 9
(off Whitechapel High St.)
Marsh Cl. NW7 3G 29
Marsh Ct. E8 6G 67
SE17 5D 102
(off Thurlow St.)
SW19 1A 154
Marsh Dr. NW9 6B 44
Marsh Farm Rd. TW2: Twick 1K 131
Marshfield St. E14 3E 104
Marshgate Bus. Cen. E15 1E 86
Marshgate La. E15 1D 86
E20 7C 68
Marshgate Path SE28 3G 107
Marsh Grn. Rd.
RM10: Dag 1G 91
Marsh Hall HA9: Wemb 3F 61
Marsh Hill E9 5A 68
Marsh Ho. SW1 6D 18
(off Aylesford St.)
SW8 1G 119
Marsh La. E10 2B 68
HA7: Stan 5H 27
N17 7C 34
NW7 3F 29
Marsh Rd. HA0: Wemb 3D 78
HA5: Pinn 4C 40
Marshside Cl. N9 1D 34
Marsh St. E14 4D 104
Marsh Wall E14 1C 104
Marsh Way RM13: Rain 3K 91
Marshwood Apartments SW11 4C 118
(off Eckstein Road)
Marshwood Ho. NW6 1J 81
(off Kilburn Vale)
Marsland Cl. SE17 5B 102
Marsom Ho. N1 1E 8
(off Provost St.)
Marston Av. KT9: Chess 6E 162
RM10: Dag 2G 73
Marston Cl. NW6 7A 64
RM10: Dag 3G 73
Marston Ho. SW9 2A 120
Marston Rd. IG5: Ilf 1C 52
TW11: Tedd 5B 132
Marston Way SE19 7B 138
Marsworth Av. HA5: Pinn 1B 40
Marsworth Cl. UB4: Yead 5C 76
Marsworth Ho. E2 1G 85
(off Whiston Rd.)
HA0: Wemb 1E 78
Martaban Rd. N16 2F 67
Martara M. SE17 5C 102
Marta Rose Ct. SE20 2H 157
(off Wadhurst Cl.)
Martello St. E8 7H 67
Martello Ter. E8 7H 67
Martell Rd. SE21 3D 138
Martel Pl. E8 6F 67
Marten Rd. E17 2C 50
Martens Av. DA7: Bex 4H 127
Martens Cl. DA7: Bex 4J 127
Martham Cl. IG6: Ilf 1F 53
SE28 7D 90
Martha Rd. E15 6G 69
Martha's Bldgs. EC1 3E 8 (4D 84)
Martha St. E1 6J 85
Marthorne Cres.
HA3: Hrw W 2H 41
Martin Bowes Rd. SE9 3D 124
Martinbridge Trad. Est.
EN1: Enf 5B 24
Martin Cl. N9 1E 34
UB10: Uxb 2A 74
Martin Ct. CR2: S Croy 5E 168
(off Birdhurst Rd.)
E14 2E 104
(off River Barge Cl.)
Martin Cres. CR0: C'don 1A 168
Martindale SW14 5J 115
Martindale Av. BR6: Chels 5K 173
E16 7J 87
Martindale Ho. E14 7D 86
(off Poplar High St.)
Martin Dale Ind. Est. EN1: Enf 3C 24
Martindale Rd. SW12 7F 119
TW4: Houn 3C 112
Martin Dene DA6: Bex 5F 127
Martin Dr. UB5: N'olt 5D 58
Martineau Dr.
TW1: Twick 4B 114
Martineau Est. E1 7J 85
Martineau Ho. SW1 6A 18
(off Churchill Gdns.)
Martineau M. N5 4B 66
Martineau Rd. N5 4B 66
Martineau Sq. E1 7G 85
Martingale Cl. TW16: Sun 4J 147
Martingale Ho. E1 1H 103
(off Raine St.)
Martingales Cl. TW10: Ham 3D 132
Martin Gdns. RM8: Dag 4C 72
Martin Gro. SM4: Mord 3J 153
Martin Ho. E3 1B 86
(off Old Ford Rd.)
SE1 3C 102
SW8 7J 101
(off Wyvil Rd.)
Martin Kinggett Gdns. RM9: Dag 1E 90
Martin La. EC4 2F 15 (7D 84)
(not continuous)
Martin Ri. DA6: Bex 5F 127
Martin Rd. RM8: Dag 4C 72
The Martins HA9: Wemb 3F 61
SE26 5H 139
Martins Cl. BR4: W W'ck 1F 171
Martin's Mt. EN5: New Bar 4D 20
Martins Pl. SE28 1J 107
Martin's Rd. BR2: Broml 2G 159
Martin St. SE28 1J 107
Martins Wlk. N10 1E 46
N22 3A 48
SE28 1J 107
Martin Way SM4: Mord 2F 153
SW20 2F 153
Martlesham N17 2E 48
(off Adams Rd.)
Martlesham Wlk. NW9 2A 44
Martlet Gro. UB5: N'olt 3B 76
Martlett Ct. WC2 1F 13 (6J 83)
Martley Dr. IG2: Ilf 5F 53
Martock Cl. HA3: W'stone 4A 42
Martock Gdns. N11 5J 31
Marton Cl. SE6 3C 140
Marton Rd. N16 2E 66
Martynside NW9 1B 44
Martys Yd. NW3 4B 64
Marula Ho. E1 6G 85
(off Boulevard Walkway)
Marvell Av. UB4: Hayes 5J 75
Marvell Ct. RM6: Chad H 6B 54
(off Quarles Pk. Rd.)
Marvell Ho. SE5 7D 102
(off Camberwell Rd.)
Marvels Cl. SE12 2K 141
Marvels La. SE12 2K 141
Marville Rd. SW6 7H 99
Marvin St. E8 6H 67
Marwell Cl. BR4: W W'ck 2H 171
Marwood Cl. DA16: Well 3B 126
Marwood Dr. NW7 7A 30
Marwood Square N10 4E 46
Mary Adelaide Cl. SW15 4A 134
Mary Ann Gdns. SE8 6C 104
Maryatt Av. HA2: Harr 2F 59
Marybank SE18 4D 106
Mary Bayly Ho. W11 1G 99
(off Wilsham St.)
Mary Boast Wlk. SE5 2D 120
Mary Cl. HA7: Stan 4F 43
Mary Datchelor Cl. SE5 1D 120
Mary Datchelor Ho. SE5 1D 120
(off Grove La.)
Maryfield Cl. DA5: Bexl 3K 145
Mary Flux Ct. SW5 5K 99
(off Bramham Gdns.)
Mary Grn. NW8 1K 81
Mary Holben Ho. SW16 5G 137
Mary Ho. W6 5E 98
(off Queen Caroline St.)
Mary Jones Ct. E14 7C 86
(off Garford St.)
Maryland Ind. Est. E15 5G 69
Maryland Pk. E15 5G 69
(not continuous)
Maryland Point E15 6G 69
(off The Grove)
Maryland Rd. CR7: Thor H 1B 156
E15 5F 69
N22 6E 32
Maryland Sq. E15 5G 69
Marylands Rd. W9 4J 81
(not continuous)
Maryland St. E15 5F 69
Maryland Wlk. N1 1C 84
(off Popham St.)
Maryland Way TW16: Sun 2J 147
Mary Lawrenson Pl. SE3 7J 105
MARYLEBONE 5H 5 (5E 82)
Marylebone Cricket Club 2B 4
MARYLEBONE FLYOVER 5C 82
Marylebone Fly-Over
W2 6B 4 (5B 82)
Marylebone Gdns.
TW9: Rich 4G 115
Marylebone High St. W1 5H 5 (5E 82)
Marylebone La. W1 6H 5 (5E 82)
Marylebone M. W1 6J 5 (5F 83)
Marylebone Pas. W1 7B 6 (6G 83)
Marylebone Rd. NW1 5D 4 (5C 82)
Marylebone St. W1 6H 5 (5E 82)
Mary Le Bow Way E3 5D 86
Marylee Way SE11 4H 19 (4K 101)
Mary Macarthur Ho. E2 3K 85
(off Warley St.)
RM10: Dag 3G 73
(off Wythenshawe Rd.)
W6 6G 99
Mary Neuner Rd. N8 3K 47
N22 3K 47
Maryon Gro. SE7 4C 106
Maryon Ho. NW6 7A 64
(off Goldhurst Ter.)
Maryon M. NW3 4C 64
Maryon Rd. SE7 4C 106
SE18 4C 106
Mary Peters Dr. UB6: G'frd 5H 59
Mary Pl. W11 7G 81
Mary Rose Cl. TW12: Hamp 1E 148
Mary Rose Mall E6 5D 88
Mary Rose Sq. SE16 4A 104
(off Cary Av.)
Maryrose Way N20 1G 31
Marys Ct. NW1 3D 4
Mary Seacole Cl. E8 1F 85
Mary Seacole Ho. W6 3C 98
(off Invermead Cl.)
Mary Smith Ct. SW5 4J 99
(off Trebovir Rd.)
Marysmith Ho. SW1 5D 18
(off Cureton St.)
Mary's Ter. TW1: Twick 7A 114
Mary St. E16 5H 87
N1 1C 84
Mary Ter. NW1 1F 83
Maryville DA16: Well 2K 125
Mary Wallace Theatre 1A 132
Mary Wharrie Ho. NW3 7D 64
(off Fellows Rd.)
Marzell Ho. W14 5H 99
(off North End Rd.)
Marzena Ct. TW3: Houn 6G 113
Masbro' Rd. W14 3F 99
Mascalls Ct. SE7 6A 106
Mascalls Rd. SE7 6A 106
Mascotte Rd. SW15 4F 117
Mascotts Cl. NW2 3D 62
Masefield Av. HA7: Stan 5E 26
UB1: S'hall 7E 76
Masefield Ct. EN5: New Bar 4F 21
KT6: Surb 7D 150
Masefield Cres. N14 5B 22
Masefield Gdns. E6 4E 88
Masefield Ho. NW6 3J 81
(off Stafford Rd.)
Masefield La. UB4: Yead 4K 75
Masefield Rd. TW12: Hamp 4D 130
Masefield Vw. BR6: Farnb 3G 173
Masefield Way TW19: Stanw 1B 128
Masey M. SW2 5A 120
Masham Ho. DA18: Erith 2D 108
(off Kale Rd.)
Mashie Rd. W3 6A 80
Mashiters Hill RM1: Rom 1K 55
Masjid La. E14 5B 86
Maskall Cl. SW2 1A 138
Maskani Wlk. SW16 7G 137
Maskell Rd. SW17 3A 136
Maskelyne Cl. SW11 1C 118
Mason Cl. DA7: Bex 3H 127
E16 7J 87
SE16 5G 103
SW20 1F 153
TW12: Hamp 1D 148
Mason Ho. E9 7J 67
(off Frampton Pk. Rd.)
SE1 4G 103
(off Simms Rd.)
Mason Rd. IG8: Wfd G 4B 36
SM1: Sutt 5K 165
Masonry Ho. SE14 1K 121
(off Fishers Ct.)
Mason's Arms M. W1 1K 11 (6F 83)
Mason's Av. CR0: C'don 3C 168
EC2 7E 8 (6D 84)
Masons Av. HA3: W'stone 4K 41
Masons Grn. La. W3 4G 79
W5 4G 79
Masons Hill BR1: Broml 3J 159
BR2: Broml 3K 159
SE18 4F 107
Masons Pl. CR4: Mitc 1D 154
EC1 1B 8 (3C 84)
Mason St. SE17 4D 102
Mason's Yd. SW1 4B 12 (1G 101)
SW19 5F 135
Masons Yd. EC1 1B 8 (3B 84)
Massey Cl. N11 5A 32
Massey Ct. E6 1A 88
(off Florence Rd.)
Massie Rd. E8 6G 67
Massingberd Way SW17 4F 137
Massinger St. SE17 4E 102
Massingham St. E1 4K 85
Masson Av. HA4: Ruis 6A 58
Masson Ho. TW8: Bford 6F 97
The Mast E16 7G 89
Mast Ct. SE16 4A 104
(off Boat Lifter Way)
Master Gunner Pl. SE18 7C 106
Masterhead Ho. E16 2K 105
(off Royal Crest Av.)
Masterman Ho. SE5 7D 102
(off Elmington Est.)
Masterman Rd. E6 3C 88
Masters Cl. SW16 6G 137
Masters Dr. SE16 5H 103
Masters Lodge E1 6J 85
(off Johnson St.)
Masters St. E1 5K 85
Mast Ho. Ter. E14 4C 104
(not continuous)
Mastmaker Ct. E14 2C 104
Mastmaker Rd. E14 2C 104
Mast Quay SE18 3D 106
Mast St. IG11: Bark 1H 89
MASWELL PARK 5G 113
Maswell Pk. Cres.
TW3: Houn 5G 113
Maswell Pk. Rd. TW3: Houn 5F 113
Matcham Ct. TW1: Twick 6D 114
(off Clevedon Rd.)
Matcham Rd. E11 3G 69
Match Ct. E3 2C 86
(off Blondin St.)
Matching Ct. E3 3B 86
(off Merchant St.)
Matchless Dr. SE18 7E 106
The Material Store UB3: Hayes 3G 93
(off Material Wlk.)
Material Wlk. UB3: Hayes 2G 93
Matfield Cl. BR2: Broml 5J 159
Matfield Rd. DA17: Belv 6G 109
Matha Ct. BR1: Broml 1A 160
Matham Gro. SE22 4F 121
Matham Rd. KT8: E Mos 5H 149
Matheson Lang Ho. SE1 7J 13
Matheson Rd. W14 4H 99
Mathews Av. E6 2E 88
Mathews Pk. Av. E15 6H 69
Mathews Yd. WC2 1E 12 (6J 83)
Mathieson Ct. SE1 7B 14
(off King James St.)
Mathison Ho. SW10 7A 100
(off Coleridge Gdns.)
Matilda Cl. SE19 7D 138
Matilda Gdns. E3 2C 86
Matilda Ho. E1 1G 103
(off St Katherine's Way)
Matilda St. N1 1K 83
Matisse Ct. EC1 3E 8
Matisse Rd. TW3: Houn 3F 113
Matlock Cl. EN5: Barn 5A 20
SE24 4C 120
Matlock Ct. NW8 2A 82
(off Abbey Rd.)
SE5 4D 120
W11 7J 81
(off Kensington Pk. Rd.)
Matlock Cres. SM3: Cheam 4G 165
Matlock Gdns. SM3: Cheam 4G 165
Matlock Ho. E15 6F 69
(off Forrester Way)
Matlock Pl. SM3: Cheam 4G 165
Matlock Rd. E10 6E 50

Matlock St. E14 6A 86
Matlock Way KT3: N Mald 1K 151
Maton Ho. *SW6* 7H 99
(off Estcourt Rd.)
Matrimony Pl. SW8 2G 119
Matson Ct. IG8: Wfd G 7B 36
Matson Ho. SE16 3H 103
Matthew Cl. W10 4F 81
Matthew Ct. CR4: Mitc 5H 155
E17 3E 50
Matthew Parker St.
SW1 7D 12 (2H 101)
Matthews Cl. HA9: Wemb 3G 61
Matthews Ho. *E14* 5C 86
(off Burgess St.)
Matthews Rd. UB6: G'frd 5H 59
Matthews St. SW11 2D 118
Matthews Wlk. *E17* 1C 50
(off Chingford Rd.)
Matthews Yd. *CR0: C'don* 3C 168
(off Surrey St.)
Matthias Apts. *N1* 7D 66
(off Northchurch Rd.)
Matthias Ct. TW10: Rich 5E 114
Matthias Rd. N16 5E 66
Mattison Rd. N4 6A 48
Mattock La. W5 1B 96
W13 1B 96
Maud Cashmore Way SE18 3D 106
Maud Chadburn Pl. SW4 6F 119
Maude Ho. *E2* 2G 85
(off Ropley St.)
Maude Rd. E17 5A 50
SE5 1E 120
Maudesville Cottages W7 1J 95
Maude Ter. E17 5A 50
Maud Gdns. E13 1H 87
IG11: Bark 2K 89
Maudlins Grn. E1 4K 15 (1G 103)
Maud Rd. E10 3E 68
E13 2H 87
Maudslay Rd. SE9 3D 124
Maudsley Ho. TW8: Bford 5E 96
Maud St. E16 5H 87
Maud Wilkes Cl. NW5 5G 65
Maugham Way W3 3J 97
Mauleverer Rd. SW2 5J 119
Maundeby Wlk. NW10 6A 62
Maunder Rd. W7 1K 95
Maunsel St. SW1 3C 18 (4H 101)
Maureen Campbell Ct.
TW17: Shep 5D 146
(off Harrison Way)
Maureen Ct. BR3: Beck 2J 157
Maurer Ct. SE10 3H 105
Mauretania Bldg. *E1* 7K 85
(off Jardine Rd.)
Maurice Av. N22 2B 48
Maurice Browne Av. NW7 6A 30
Maurice Ct. E1 3K 85
N22 1K 47
TW8: Bford 7D 96
Maurice Drummond Ho. *SE10* 1D 122
(off Catherine Gro.)
Maurice St. W12 6D 80
Maurice Wlk. NW11 4A 46
Maurier Cl. UB5: N'olt 1A 76
Mauritius Rd. SE10 4G 105
Maury Rd. N16 2G 67
Mauveine Gdns. TW3: Houn 4E 112
Mavelstone Cl. BR1: Broml 1C 160
Mavelstone Rd. BR1: Broml 1B 160
Maverton Rd. E3 1C 86
Mavery Ct. *BR1: Broml* 7H 141
(off Bromley Av.)
Mavis Av. KT19: Ewe 5A 164
Mavis Cl. KT19: Ewe 5A 164
Mavis Wlk. *E6* 5C 88
(off Greenwich Cres.)
Mavor Ho. *N1* 1K 83
(off Barnsbury Est.)
Mawbey Ho. SE1 5G 103
Mawbey Pl. SE1 5F 103
Mawbey Rd. SE1 5F 103
Mawbey St. SW8 7J 101
Mawdley Ho. SE1 7A 14
MAWNEY 3H 55
Mawney Cl. RM7: Mawney 2H 55
Mawney Rd. RM7: Mawney, Rom 2H 55
Mawson Cl. SW20 2G 153
Mawson Ct. *N1* 1D 84
(off Gopsall St.)
Mawson Ho. *EC1* 5J 7
(off Baldwins Gdns.)
Mawson La. W4 6B 98
Maxden Ct. SE15 3F 121
Maxey Gdns. RM9: Dag 4E 72
Maxey Rd. RM9: Dag 4E 72
SE18 4G 107
Maxfield Cl. N20 7F 21
Maxilla Wlk. W10 6F 81
Maxim Apts. *BR2: Broml* 4K 159
(off Tiger La.)
Maximfeldt Rd. DA8: Erith 5K 109
Maxim Rd. DA8: Erith 4K 109
N21 6F 23
Maxted Pk. HA1: Harr 7J 41
Maxted Rd. SE15 3F 121
Maxwell Cl. CR0: Wadd 1J 167
UB3: Hayes 7J 75
Maxwell Ct. SE22 1G 139
SW4 5H 119
Maxwell Gdns. BR6: Orp 3K 173
Maxwell Rd. DA16: Well 3K 125
HA6: Nwood 1F 39
RM7: Rush G 6K 55
SW6 7K 99
TW15: Ashf 6E 128
UB7: W Dray 4B 92
Maxwelton Av. NW7 5E 28
Maxwelton Cl. NW7 5E 28
Maya Angelou Ct. E4 4K 35
Maya Apts. *E20* 5E 68
(off Victory Pde.)
Maya Cl. SE15 2H 121
Mayall Cl. EN3: Enf L 1H 25
Mayall Rd. SE24 5B 120
Maya Pl. N11 7C 32
Maya Rd. N2 4A 46
Maybank Av. E18 2K 51
HA0: Wemb 5K 59
Maybank Gdns. HA5: Eastc 5J 39
Maybank Rd. E18 1K 51
May Bate Av. KT2: King T 1D 150
Maybells Commercial Est.
IG11: Bark 2D 90
Mayberry Ct. *BR3: Beck* 7B 140
(off Copers Cope Rd.)
Mayberry Pl. KT5: Surb 7F 151
Maybourne Cl. SE26 6H 139
Maybury Cl. BR5: Pet W 5F 161
EN1: Enf 1C 24
Maybury Ct. *CR2: S Croy* 5B 168
(off Haling Pk. Rd.)
HA1: Harr 6H 41
W1 6H 5
(off Marylebone St.)
Maybury Gdns. NW10 6D 62
Maybury M. N6 7G 47
Maybury Rd. E13 4A 88
IG11: Bark 2K 89
Maybury St. SW17 5C 136
Maychurch Cl. HA7: Stan 7J 27
May Cl. KT9: Chess 6F 163
May Ct. *SW19* 1A 154
(off Pincott Rd.)
Maycroft HA5: Pinn 2K 39
Maycross Av. SM4: Mord 4H 153
Mayday Gdns. SE3 2C 124
Mayday Rd. CR7: Thor H 6B 156
Maydeb Ct. RM6: Chad H 6F 55
Maydew Ho. *SE16* 4J 103
(off Abbeyfield Est.)
Maydwell Ho. *E14* 5C 86
(off Thomas Rd.)
Mayerne Rd. SE9 5B 124
Mayesbrook Pk. Arena 5A 72
Mayesbrook Rd. IG3: Ilf 3A 72
IG11: Bark 1K 89
RM8: Dag 3A 72
Mayes Cl. CR0: New Ad 7F 171
Mayesford Rd. RM6: Chad H 7C 54
Mayes Rd. N22 2K 47
Mayeswood Rd. SE12 4A 142
MAYFAIR 3J 11 (7F 83)
Mayfair Av. DA7: Bex 1D 126
IG1: Ilf 2D 70
KT4: Wor Pk 1C 164
RM6: Chad H 6D 54
TW2: Whitt 7G 113
Mayfair Cl. BR3: Beck 1D 158
KT6: Surb 1E 162
Mayfair Ct. HA8: Edg 5A 28
Mayfair Gdns. IG8: Wfd G 7D 36
N17 6H 33
Mayfair M. *NW1* 7D 64
(off Regents Pk. Rd.)
SW12 1F 137
Mayfair Pl. W1 4K 11 (1F 101)
Mayfair Row W1 1F 101
Mayfair Ter. N14 7C 22
Mayfield DA7: Bex 3F 127
Mayfield Av. BR6: Orp 1K 173
HA3: Kenton 5B 42
IG8: Wfd G 6D 36
N12 4F 31
N14 2C 32
W4 4A 98
W13 3B 96
Mayfield Cl. E8 6F 67
KT7: T Ditt 1B 162
SE20 1H 157
SW4 5H 119
TW15: Ashf 6D 128
UB10: Hil 3D 74
Mayfield Cres. CR7: Thor H 4K 155
N9 6C 24
Mayfield Dr. HA5: Pinn 4D 40
Mayfield Gdns. NW4 6F 45
W7 6H 77
Mayfield Ho. *E2* 2H 85
(off Cambridge Heath Rd.)
Mayfield Mans. SW15 5H 117
Mayfield Rd. BR1: Broml 5C 160
CR2: Sande 7D 168
CR7: Thor H 4K 155
DA17: Belv 4J 109
E4 2K 35
E8 7F 67
E13 4H 87
E17 2A 50
EN3: Enf H 2E 24
N8 5K 47
RM8: Dag 1C 72
SM2: Sutt 6B 166
SW19 1H 153
W3 7H 79
W12 2A 98
Mayfield Rd. Flats N8 6K 47
Mayfields HA9: Wemb 2G 61
Mayfields Cl. HA9: Wemb 2G 61
Mayfield Vs. DA14: Sidc 6C 144
Mayflower Cl. HA4: Ruis 6E 38
SE16 4K 103
Mayflower Ho. *E14* 2C 104
(off Westferry Rd.)
IG11: Bark 1H 89
(off Westbury Rd.)
Mayflower Rd. SW9 3J 119
Mayflower St. SE16 2J 103
Mayfly Cl. HA5: Eastc 7A 40
Mayfly Gdns. UB5: N'olt 3B 76
Mayford NW1 2G 83
(not continuous)
Mayford Cl. BR3: Beck 3K 157
SW12 7D 118
Mayford Rd. SW12 7D 118
May Gdns. HA0: Wemb 3C 78
Maygood Ho. *N1* 2K 83
(off Maygood St.)
Maygood St. N1 2A 84
Maygrove Rd. NW6 6H 63
Mayhew Cl. E4 3H 35
Mayhew Ct. SE5 4D 120
Mayhill Ct. *SE15* 7E 102
(off Tower Mill Rd.)
Mayhill Rd. EN5: Barn 6B 20
SE7 6K 105
May Ho. *E3* 2C 86
(off Thomas Fyre Dr.)
Mayland Mans. *IG11: Bark* 7F 71
(off Whiting Av.)
Maylands Dr. DA14: Sidc 3D 144
UB8: Uxb 6A 56
Maylands Ho. *SW3* 4D 16
(off Cale St.)
May La. HA3: Kenton 7F 43
Maylie Ho. *SE16* 2H 103
(off Marigold St.)
Maynard Cl. N15 5E 48
SW6 7K 99
Maynard Path E17 5E 50
Maynard Rd. E17 5E 50
Maynards Quay E1 7J 85
Mayne Ct. SE26 5H 139
Maynooth Gdns. SM5: Cars 7D 154
Mayo Ct. W13 3B 96
Mayo Ho. *E1* 5J 85
(off Lindley St.)
Mayola Rd. E5 4J 67
Mayo Rd. CR0: C'don 5D 156
KT12: Walt T 7J 147
NW10 6A 62
The Mayor's & City of London Court
7E 8
Mayow Rd. SE23 4K 139
SE26 4K 139
Mayplace Cl. DA7: Bex 3H 127
Mayplace La. SE18 6F 107
(not continuous)
Mayplace Rd. E. DA1: Cray 3J 127
DA7: Bex 3H 127
Mayplace Rd. W. DA7: Bex 4G 127
MAYPOLE 1K 145
Maypole Ct. *UB2: S'hall* 2D 94
(off Merrick Rd.)
May Rd. E4 6H 35
E13 2J 87
TW2: Twick 1J 131
Mayroyd Av. KT6: Surb 2G 163
May's Bldgs. M. SE10 7E 104
May's Ct. SE10 7F 105
Mays Ct. WC2 3E 12 (7J 83)
Mays Hill Rd. BR2: Broml 2G 159
Mays La. EN5: Ark, Barn 6A 20, 1H 29
Maysoule Rd. SW11 4B 118
Mays Rd. TW11: Tedd 5H 131
Mayston M. *SE10* 5J 105
(off Ormiston Rd.)
May St. W14 5H 99
(Kelway Ho.)
W14 5H 99
(Orchard Sq.)
Mayswood Gdns. RM10: Dag 6J 73
Maythorne Cotts. SE13 5F 123
Mayton St. N7 3K 65
Maytree Cl. HA8: Edg 3D 28
Maytree Ct. CR4: Mitc 3E 154
UB5: N'olt 3C 76
Maytree Gdns. W5 2D 96
May Tree Ho. *SE4* 3B 122
(off Wickham Rd.)
Maytree La. HA7: Stan 7F 27
Maytree Wlk. SW2 2A 138
Mayville Est. N16 5E 66
Mayville Rd. E11 2G 69
(not continuous)
IG1: Ilf 5F 71
May Wlk. E13 2K 87
Mayward Ho. *SE5* 1E 120
(off Peckham Rd.)
Maywood Cl. BR3: Beck 7D 140
May Wynne Ho. *E16* 7K 87
(off Murray Sq.)
Mazal Ct. KT8: W Mole 4F 149
Maze Hill SE3 7H 105
SE10 6G 105
Maze Hill Lodge *SE10* 6F 105
(off Park Vista)
Mazenod Av. NW6 7J 63
Maze Rd. TW9: Kew 7G 97
MCC Cricket Mus. & Tours 2A 4 (3B 82)
The Mead BR3: Beck 1E 158
BR4: W W'ck 1F 171
N2 2A 46
SM6: W'gton 6H 167
UB10: Ick 2C 56
W13 5B 78
Meadbank Studios *SW11* 7C 100
(off Parkgate Rd.)
Mead Cl. HA3: Hrw W 1H 41
NW1 6E 64
Mead Ct. NW9 5J 43
Mead Cres. E4 4K 35
SM1: Sutt 3C 166
Meadcroft Rd. SE11 7K 19 (6B 102)
(not continuous)
SE17 6B 102
Meade Cl. W4 6G 97
Meade Ho. *E14* 6G 87
(off Lyell St.)
Meade M. *SW1* 5D 18
(off Causton St.)
Meader Ct. SE14 7K 103
Mead Fld. HA2: Harr 3D 58
Meadfield HA8: Edg 2C 28
(not continuous)
Meadfield Grn. HA8: Edg 2C 28
Meadfoot Rd. SW16 7G 137
Meadgate Av. IG8: Wfd G 5H 37
Mead Gro. RM6: Chad H 3D 54
Mead Ho. *W11* 1H 99
(off Ladbroke Rd.)
Mead Ho. La. UB4: Hayes 4F 75
Meadhurst Club 5H 129
Meadhurst Pk. TW16: Sun 6G 129
Meadlands Dr. TW10: Ham 2D 132
Mead Lodge W4 2K 97
The Meadow BR7: Chst 6G 143
N10 3E 46
Meadow Av. CR0: C'don 6K 157
Mdw. Bank N21 6E 22
Meadowbank KT5: Surb 6F 151
NW3 7D 64
SE3 3H 123
Meadowbank Cl. SW6 7E 98
TW7: Isle 1J 113
Meadowbank Gdns. TW5: Cran 1J 111
Meadowbank Rd. NW9 7K 43
Meadowbridge Ct. *CR0: C'don* 5D 156
(off Princess Rd.)
Meadowbrook Cl. SL3: Poyle 4A 174
Meadowbrook Ct. TW7: Isle 3J 113
Meadow Cl. BR7: Chst 5F 143
DA6: Bex 5F 127
E4 1J 35
E9 6B 68
EN3: Enf W 1F 25
EN5: Barn 6C 20
HA4: Ruis 6H 39
IG11: Bark 7A 72
KT10: Hin W 3A 162
SE6 5C 140
SM1: Sutt 2A 166
SW20 4E 152
TW4: Houn 6E 112
TW10: Ham 1E 132
UB5: N'olt 2E 76
Meadow Ct. *E16* 1A 106
(off Booth Rd.)
N1 2E 84
TW3: Houn 6F 113
Meadowcourt Rd. SE3 4H 123
Meadowcroft BR1: Broml 3D 160
W4 5G 97
(off Brooks Rd.)
Meadowcroft Cl. E10 7D 50
N13 2F 33
Meadowcroft M. *E1* 7G 85
(off Cable St.)
SE6 6D 122
Meadowcroft Rd. N13 2F 33
Meadow Dr. N10 3F 47
NW4 2E 44
Meadowford Cl. SE28 7A 90
Meadow Gdns. HA8: Edg 6C 28
Meadow Gth. NW10 6J 61
Meadow Ga. HA2: Harr 3F 59
Meadowgate Cl. NW7 5G 29
Meadow Hill
KT3: N Mald 6A 152
Meadow La. SE12 3K 141
Meadowlark Ho. NW9 7B 44
Meadowlea Cl. UB7: Harm 2E 174
Meadow M. SW8 6K 101
Meadow Pl. SW8 7J 101
W4 7A 98
Meadow Rd. BR2: Broml 2G 159
HA5: Pinn 4B 40
IG11: Bark 7K 71
RM7: Rush G 1J 73
RM9: Dag 6F 73
SM1: Sutt 4C 166
SW8 7H 19 (7K 101)
SW19 7A 136
TW13: Felt 2C 130
TW15: Ashf 5F 129
UB1: S'hall 7D 76
Meadow Row SE1 3C 102
The Meadows E4 4A 36
Meadows Cl. E10 2C 68
Meadows Ct. DA14: Sidc 6B 144
Meadows End TW16: Sun 1J 147
Meadowside SE3 4A 124
SE9 4A 124
TW1: Twick 7D 114
Meadow Stile CR0: C'don 3C 168
Mdws. Way SE4 3A 122
Meadowsweet Cl. E16 5B 88
SW20 4E 152
Meadow Vw. DA15: Sidc 7B 126
HA1: Harr 1J 59
TW19: Stanw M 7A 174
Meadow Vw. Rd.
CR7: Thor H 5B 156
SW20 4E 152
UB4: Hayes 4F 75
Meadowview Rd. DA5: Bexl 6E 126
KT19: Ewe 7A 164
SE6 5B 140
Meadow Wlk. E18 4J 51
KT17: Ewe 7B 164
KT19: Ewe 6A 164
RM9: Dag 6F 73
SM6: W'gton 3F 167
Mdw. Way BR6: Farnb 3E 172
HA4: Ruis 6K 39
HA9: Wemb 4D 60
KT9: Chess 5E 162
NW9 5K 43
The Meadow Way
HA3: Hrw W 1J 41
Meadow Waye TW5: Hest 6C 94
Meadow Works
EN5: New Bar 6E 20
Mead Path SW17 4A 136
Mead Pl. CR0: C'don 1C 168
E9 6J 67
Mead Plat NW10 6J 61
Mead Rd. BR7: Chst 6G 143
HA8: Edg 6B 28
TW10: Ham 3C 132
Mead Row SE1 1J 19 (3A 102)
The Meads
HA8: Edg 6E 28
SM3: Cheam 3G 165
SM4: Mord 5C 154
UB8: Cowl 4A 74
Meads Ct. E15 6H 69
Meadside Cl. BR3: Beck 1A 158
Meads La. IG3: Ilf 7J 53
Meads Rd. EN3: Enf H 1F 25
N22 2B 48
Mead Ter. HA9: Wemb 4D 60
Meadvale Rd. CR0: C'don 7F 157
W5 4B 78
Mead Way BR2: Hayes 6H 159
CR0: C'don 2A 170
HA4: Ruis 6F 39
Meadway BR3: Beck 1E 158
EN5: Barn, New Bar 4D 20
IG3: Bark, Ilf 4J 71
IG8: Wfd G 5F 37
KT5: Surb 1J 163
N14 2C 32
NW11 6J 45
SW20 4E 152
TW2: Twick 1H 131
TW15: Ashf 4C 128
The Meadway IG9: Buck H 1G 37
SE3 2F 123
Meadway Cl. EN5: Barn 4D 20
HA5: Hat E 6A 26
NW11 6K 45
Meadway Ct. RM8: Dag 2F 73
TW11: Tedd 5C 132
W5 4F 79
Meadway Gdns. HA4: Ruis 6F 39
Meadway Ga. NW11 6J 45
Meaford Way SE20 7H 139
Meakin Est. SE1 3E 102
Meander Ho. *E20* 5D 68
(off Logan Cl.)
Meanley Rd. E12 4C 70
Meard St. W1 1C 12 (6H 83)
(not continuous)
Mears Cl. *E1* 5G 85
(off Settles St.)
Meath Cres. E2 3K 85
Meath Ho. *SE24* 6B 120
(off Dulwich Rd.)
Meath Rd. E15 2H 87
IG1: Ilf 3G 71
Meath St. SW11 1F 119
Mecca Bingo
Camden 1F 83
(off Arlington Rd.)
Catford 7D 122
Croydon 2C 168
Dagenham 1E 90
Hayes 6J 75
Morden 7A 154
Wood Green 2A 48
(off Lordship La.)
Mecklenburgh Pl. WC1 3G 7 (4K 83)
Mecklenburgh Sq.
WC1 3G 7 (4K 83)
Mecklenburgh St. WC1 3G 7 (4K 83)
Medals Way E20 5E 68
Medburn St. NW1 2H 83
Medcroft Gdns. SW14 4J 115
Medebourne Cl. SE3 3J 123
Mede Ho. *BR1: Broml* 5K 141
(off Pike Cl.)
Medesenge Way N13 6G 33
Medfield St. SW15 7C 116
Medhurst Cl. E3 2A 86
(not continuous)
Medhurst Dr. BR1: Broml 5G 141
Median Rd. E5 5J 67
Medici Cl. IG3: Ilf 6A 54
(not continuous)
Medina Gro. N7 3A 66
Medina Pl. E14 5C 86
Medina Rd. N7 3A 66
Medland Cl. SM6: W'gton 1E 166
Medland Ho. E14 7A 86
Medlar Cl. UB5: N'olt 2B 76
Medlar Ho. DA15: Sidc 3A 144
Medlar St. SE5 1C 120
Medley Rd. NW6 6J 63
Medora Rd. RM7: Rom 4K 55
SW2 7K 119
Medusa Rd. SE6 6D 122
Medway Bldgs. *E3* 2A 86
(off Medway Rd.)
Medway Cl. CR0: C'don 6J 157
IG1: Ilf 5G 71
RM7: Mawney 1H 55
Medway Ct. NW11 6K 45
WC1 2E 6
(off Judd St.)
Medway Dr. UB6: G'frd 2K 77
Medway Gdns. HA0: Wemb 4A 60
Medway Ho. KT2: King T 1D 150
NW8 4C 4
(off Penfold St.)
SE1 7F 15
(off Hankey Pl.)
Medway M. E3 2A 86
Medway Pde. UB6: G'frd 2K 77
Medway Rd. E3 2A 86
Medway St. SW1 2D 18 (3H 101)
Medwin St. SW4 4K 119
Meerbrook Rd. SE3 3A 124
Meeson Rd. E15 7H 69
Meeson St. E5 4A 68
Meeson's Wharf E15 2E 86
Meeting Fld. Path E9 6J 67
Meeting Ho. All. E1 1H 103
Meeting Ho. La. SE15 1H 121
Megan Ct. *SE14* 7J 103
(off Pomeroy St.)
Megelish M. UB1: S'hall 3E 76
Mehetabel Rd. E9 5J 67
Meister Cl. IG1: Ilf 1H 71
Melancholy Wlk. TW10: Ham 2C 132
Melanda Cl. BR7: Chst 5D 142
Melanie Cl. DA7: Bex 1E 126
Melba Way SE13 1D 122
Melbourne Av. HA5: Pinn 3F 41
N13 6E 32
W13 1A 96
Melbourne Cl. BR6: Orp 7J 161
SE20 7G 139
SM6: W'gton 5G 167
UB10: Ick 4C 56
Melbourne Ct. *E5* 4A 68
(off Daubeney Rd.)
N10 7A 32
W9 4A 82
(off Randolph Av.)
Melbourne Gdns. RM6: Chad H 5E 54
Melbourne Gro. SE22 4E 120
Melbourne Ho. UB4: Yead 4A 76
W8 1J 99
(off Kensington Pl.)
Melbourne Mans. *W14* 6G 99
(off Musard Rd.)
Melbourne M. SE6 7E 122
SW9 1A 120
Melbourne Pl. WC2 1H 13 (6K 83)
Melbourne Rd. E6 2D 88
E10 7D 50
E17 4A 50
IG1: Ilf 1F 71
SM6: W'gton 5F 167
SW19 1J 153
TW11: Tedd 6C 132
Melbourne Sq. SW9 1A 120
Melbourne Ter. *SW6* 7K 99
(off Moore Pk. Rd.)
Melbourne Way EN1: Enf 6A 24
Melbourne Yd. SE19 6E 138
Melbray M. SW6 2H 117
Melbreak Ho. SE22 3E 120
Melbury Av. UB2: S'hall 3F 95
Melbury Cl. BR7: Chst 6C 142
KT10: Clay 6B 162
Melbury Ct. W8 3H 99
Melbury Dr. SE5 7E 102
Melbury Gdns. SW20 1D 152
Melbury Ho. *SW8* 7K 101
(off Richborne Ter.)
Melbury Rd. HA3: Kenton 5F 43
W14 3H 99
Melchester *W11* 6H 81
(off Ledbury Rd.)
Melchester Ho. *N19* 3H 65
(off Wedmore St.)
Melcombe Ct. *NW1* 5E 4
(off Melcombe Pl.)
Melcombe Gdns. HA3: Kenton 6F 43
Melcombe Ho. *SW8* 7K 101
(off Dorset Rd.)
Melcombe Pl. NW1 5E 4 (5D 82)
Melcombe Regis Ct. *W1* 6H 5
(off Weymouth St.)
Melcombe St. NW1 4F 5 (4D 82)
Meldex Cl. NW7 6K 29

Meldon Cl.—Middle Way

Meldon Cl. SW6 . . . . 1K 117
Meldone Cl. KT5: Surb 7H 151
Meldrum Rd. IG3: Ilf 2A 72
Melfield Gdns. SE6 . . . . 4E 140
Melford Av. IG11: Bark 6J 71
Melford Cl. KT9: Chess 5F 163
Melford Ct. SE1 . . . . 3E 102
(off Fendall St.)
SE22 . . . . 1G 139
(not continuous)
Melford Pas. SE22 . . . . 7G 121
Melford Rd. E6 . . . . 4D 88
E11 . . . . 2G 69
E17 . . . . 4A 50
IG1: Ilf 2H 71
SE22 . . . . 7G 121
Melfort Av. CR7: Thor H 3B 156
Melfort Rd. CR7: Thor H 3B 156
Melgund Rd. N5 . . . . 5A 66
Melina Cl. UB3: Hayes 5F 75
Melina Ct. NW8 . . . . 2A 4
SW15 . . . . 3C 116
Melina Pl. NW8 . . . . 2A 4 (3B 82)
Melina Rd. W12 . . . . 2D 98
Melior Ct. N6 . . . . 6G 47
Melior Pl. SE1 . . . . 6G 15 (2E 102)
Melior St. SE1 . . . . 6G 15 (2E 102)
Meliot Rd. SE6 . . . . 2F 141
Meller Cl. CR0: Bedd 3J 167
Meller Ho. E20 . . . . 6E 68
(off Champions Wlk.)
Mellifont Cl. SM5: Cars 7B 154
Melling Dr. EN1: Enf 1B 24
Melling St. SE18 . . . . 6J 107
Mellish Cl. IG11: Bark 1K 89
N20 . . . . 2G 31
Mellish Flats E10 . . . . 7C 50
Mellish Gdns. IG8: Wfd G 5D 36
Mellish Ho. E1 . . . . 6H 85
(off Varden St.)
Mellish Ind. Est. SE18 . . . . 3B 106
Mellish St. E14 . . . . 3C 104
Mellison Rd. SW17 . . . . 5C 136
Melliss Av. TW9: Kew 1H 115
Mellitus St. W12 . . . . 5B 80
Mellor Cl. KT12: Walt T 7D 148
Mellow La. E. UB4: Hayes 3E 74
Mellow La. W. UB10: Hil 3E 74
Mellows Rd. IG5: Ilf 3D 52
SM6: W'gton 5H 167
Mells Cres. SE9 . . . . 4D 142
Mell St. SE10 . . . . 5G 105
Melody La. N5 . . . . 5C 66
Melody Rd. SW18 . . . . 5A 118
Melon Pl. W8 . . . . 2J 99
Melon Rd. E11 . . . . 3G 69
SE15 . . . . 1G 121
Melrose Av. CR4: Mitc 7F 137
DA1: Cray 7K 127
N22 . . . . 1B 48
NW2 . . . . 5D 62
SW16 . . . . 3K 155
SW19 . . . . 2H 135
TW2: Whitt 7F 113
UB6: G'frd 2F 77
Melrose Cl. SE12 . . . . 1J 141
UB4: Hayes 5J 75
UB6: G'frd 2F 77
Melrose Ct. W13 . . . . 1A 96
(off Williams Rd.)
Melrose Cres. BR6: Orp 4H 173
Melrose Dr. UB1: S'hall 1E 94
Melrose Gdns. HA8: Edg 3H 43
KT3: N Mald 3K 151
W6 . . . . 3E 98
Melrose Ho. NW6 . . . . 3J 81
(off Carlton Vale)
SW1 . . . . 5J 17
(part of Abbots Mnr.)
Melrose Rd. HA5: Pinn 4D 40
SW13 . . . . 2B 116
SW18 . . . . 6H 117
SW19 . . . . 2J 153
W3 . . . . 3J 97
Melrose Ter. W6 . . . . 3E 98
Melrose Tudor SM6: W'gton 5J 167
(off Plough La.)
Melsa Rd. SM4: Mord 6A 154
Melthorne Dr. HA4: Ruis 3A 58
Melthorpe Gdns. SE3 . . . . 1C 124
Melton Cl. HA4: Ruis 1A 58
Melton Ct. SM2: Sutt 7A 166
SW7 . . . . 4B 16 (4B 100)
Melton St. NW1 . . . . 2B 6 (3G 83)
Melville Av. CR2: S Croy 5F 169
SW20 . . . . 7C 134
UB6: G'frd 5K 59
Melville Cl. UB10: Ick 2F 57
Melville Ct. SE8 . . . . 4A 104
W4 . . . . 5G 97
(off Haining Cl.)
W12 . . . . 3D 98
(off Goldhawk Rd.)
Melville Gdns. N13 . . . . 5G 33
Melville Ho. EN5: New Bar 5G 21
Melville Pl. N1 . . . . 7C 66
Melville Rd. DA14: Sidc 2C 144
E17 . . . . 3B 50
NW10 . . . . 7K 61
RM5: Col R 1H 55
SW13 . . . . 1C 116
Melville Vs. Rd. W3 . . . . 1J 97
Melvin Rd. SE20 . . . . 1J 157
Melwood Ho. E1 . . . . 6H 85
(off Watney Mkt.)
Melyn Cl. N7 . . . . 4G 65
Memel Ct. EC1 . . . . 4C 8
Memel St. EC1 . . . . 4C 8 (4C 84)
Memess Path SE18 . . . . 6E 106
Memorial Av. E15 . . . . 3G 87
Memorial Cl. TW5: Hest 6D 94
Memorial Hgts. IG2: Ilf 6H 53
Menai Pl. E3 . . . . 2C 86
(off Blondin St.)
Menard Ct. EC1 . . . . 2D 8
(off Galway St.)
Mendez Way SW15 . . . . 6C 116
Mendham Ho. SE1 . . . . 7G 15
(off Cluny Pl.)
Mendip Cl. KT4: Wor Pk 1E 164
SE26 . . . . 4J 139
UB3: Harl 7F 93
Mendip Ct. SE14 . . . . 6J 103
(off Avonley Rd.)
SW11 . . . . 3A 118
Mendip Dr. NW2 . . . . 2G 63
Mendip Ho. N9 . . . . 2B 34
(within Edmonton Grn. Shop. Cen.)
Mendip Ho's. E2 . . . . 3J 85
(off Welwyn St.)
Mendip Rd. DA7: Bex 1K 127
IG2: Ilf 5J 53
SW11 . . . . 3A 118
Mendora Rd. SW6 . . . . 7G 99
Menelik Rd. NW2 . . . . 4G 63
Menier Chocolate Factory 5D 14
(off Southwark St.)
Menlo Gdns. SE19 . . . . 7D 138
Menlo Lodge N13 . . . . 3E 32
(off Crothall Cl.)
Menon Dr. N9 . . . . 3C 34
Menotti St. E2 . . . . 4G 85
Menteath Ho. E14 . . . . 6C 86
(off Dod St.)
Mentmore Cl. HA3: Kenton 6C 42
Mentmore Ter. E8 . . . . 7H 67
Mentone Mans. SW10 . . . . 7K 99
(off Fulham Rd.)
Meon Ct. TW7: Isle 2J 113
Meon Rd. W3 . . . . 2J 97
Meopham Rd. CR4: Mitc 1G 155
Mepham Cres.
HA3: Hrw W 7B 26
Mepham Gdns.
HA3: Hrw W 7B 26
Mepham St. SE1 . . . . 5H 13 (1A 102)
Mera Dr. DA7: Bex 4G 127
Meranti Ho. E1 . . . . 6G 85
(off Goodman's Stile)
Merantun Way SW19 . . . . 1K 153
Merbury Cl. SE13 . . . . 5E 122
SE28 . . . . 1H 107
Merbury Rd. SE28 . . . . 1H 107
Mercator Pl. E14 . . . . 5C 104
Mercator Rd. SE13 . . . . 4F 123
Mercer Bldg. EC2 . . . . 3H 9
(off New Inn Yd.)
Mercer Cl. KT7: T Ditt 7K 149
Mercer Ct. E1 . . . . 5A 86
Mercer Ho. SW1 . . . . 5J 17
(off Ebury Bri. Rd.)
SW8 . . . . 1F 119
(off Gladstone Ter.)
Merceron Ho's. E2 . . . . 3J 85
(off Globe Rd.)
Merceron St. E1 . . . . 4H 85
Mercer Pl. HA5: Pinn 2A 40
Mercers Cl. SE10 . . . . 4H 105
Mercer's Cotts. E1 . . . . 6A 86
(off White Horse Rd.)
Mercers M. N19 . . . . 3H 65
Mercers Pl. W6 . . . . 4F 99
Mercers Rd. N19 . . . . 3H 65
(not continuous)
Mercer St. WC2 . . . . 1E 12 (6J 83)
Mercer Wlk. WC2 . . . . 1E 12
(off Mercer St.)
Merchant Cl. KT19: Ewe 5K 163
Merchant Ct. E1 . . . . 1J 103
(off Wapping Wall)
Merchant Ho. E14 . . . . 3D 104
(off Selsdon Way)
Merchant Ind. Ter. NW10 . . . . 4J 79
Merchant Navy Memorial
. . . . 3H 15 (7F 85)
Merchants Cl. SE25 . . . . 4G 157
Merchants Ho. E14 . . . . 6F 87
(off New Village Av.)
E15 . . . . 6F 69
(off Forrester Way)
SE10 . . . . 5F 105
(off Collington St.)
Merchants Lodge E17 . . . . 4C 50
(off Westbury Rd.)
Merchant Sq. W2 . . . . 6B 4
Merchant Square East W2 . . . . 6B 4
Merchant Square West W2 . . . . 6B 4
Merchants Row SE10 . . . . 5F 105
(off Hoskins St.)
Merchant St. E3 . . . . 3B 86
Merchiston Rd. SE6 . . . . 2F 141
Merchland Rd. SE9 . . . . 1G 143
Mercia Gro. SE13 . . . . 4E 122
Mercia Ho. SE5 . . . . 2C 120
(off Denmark Rd.)
TW15: Ashf 1E 146
Mercier Ct. E16 . . . . 1A 106
(off Starboard Way)
Mercier Rd. SW15 . . . . 5G 117
Mercury NW9 . . . . 1B 44
(off Quakers Course)
Mercury Cen. TW14: Felt 5J 111
Mercury Ct. E14 . . . . 4C 104
(off Homer Dr.)
SW9 . . . . 1A 120
(off Southey Rd.)
Mercury Ho. E3 . . . . 1C 86
(off Garrison Rd.)
E16 . . . . 6H 87
(off Jude St.)
TW8: Bford 6C 96
(off Glenhurst Rd.)
W5 . . . . 4F 79
Mercury Rd. TW8: Bford 6C 96
Mercury Way SE14 . . . . 6K 103
Mercy Ter. SE13 . . . . 5D 122
Merebank La. CR0: Wadd 5K 167
Mere Cl. BR6: Farnb 2E 172
SW15 . . . . 7F 117
Meredith Av. NW2 . . . . 5E 62
Meredith Cl. HA5: Pinn 1B 40
Meredith Ho. N16 . . . . 5E 66
Meredith M. SE4 . . . . 4B 122
Meredith St. E13 . . . . 3J 87
EC1 . . . . 2A 8 (3B 84)
Meredith Wlk. RM8: Dag 1E 72
(off Ellis Av.)
Meredyth Rd. SW13 . . . . 2C 116
Mere End CR0: C'don 7K 157
Mere Rd. SE2 . . . . 2D 108
TW17: Shep 6D 146
Mereside BR6: Farnb 2E 172
Mereside Pk. TW15: Ashf 4E 128
Meretone Cl. SE4 . . . . 4A 122
Mereton Mans. SE8 . . . . 1C 122
(off Brookmill Rd.)
Merevale Cres. SM4: Mord 6A 154
Mereway Rd. TW2: Twick 1H 131
Merewood Cl. BR1: Broml 2E 160
Merewood Gdns.
CR0: C'don 7K 157
Merewood Rd. DA7: Bex 2J 127
Mereworth Cl. BR2: Broml 5H 159
Mereworth Dr. SE18 . . . . 7F 107
Mereworth Ho. SE15 . . . . 6J 103
Merganser Ct. E1 . . . . 3K 15
(off Star Pl.)
SE8 . . . . 6B 104
(off Edward St.)
Merganser Gdns. SE28 . . . . 3H 107
Meriden Cl. BR1: Broml 7B 142
IG6: Ilf 1G 53
Meriden Ct. SW3 . . . . 6C 16
Meriden Ho. N1 . . . . 1E 84
(off Wilmer Gdns.)
Merideth Ct. KT1: King T 2F 151
Meridia Ct. E15 . . . . 1E 86
(off Biggerstaff Rd.)
Meridian Bus. Pk. EN3: Pond E 6F 25
Meridian Cl. NW7 . . . . 4E 28
Meridian Ct. SE15 . . . . 7H 103
(off Gervase St.)
SE16 . . . . 2G 103
(off East La.)
UB4: Yead 4A 76
Meridian Ga. E14 . . . . 2D 104
Meridian Ho. NW1 . . . . 7G 65
(off Baynes St.)
SE10 . . . . 4G 105
(off Azof St.)
SE10 . . . . 7E 104
(off Royal Hill)
SW18 . . . . 4A 118
(off Juniper Dr.)
Meridian Pl. E14 . . . . 2D 104
Meridian Point SE8 . . . . 6D 104
Meridian Rd. SE7 . . . . 7B 106
Meridian Sq. E15 . . . . 7F 69
Meridian Trad. Est. SE7 . . . . 4K 105
Meridian Wlk. N17 . . . . 6K 33
Meridian Water Development
N18 . . . . 6E 34
Meridian Way EN3: Pond E 4D 34
N9 . . . . 4D 34
N18 . . . . 5D 34
Merifield Rd. SE9 . . . . 4A 124
Merino Cl. E11 . . . . 4A 52
SM6: W'gton 2E 166
Merino Ct. EC1 . . . . 2D 8
(off Lever St.)
Merino Pl. DA15: Sidc 6A 126
Merioneth Ct. W7 . . . . 5K 77
(off Copley Cl.)
Merita Ho. E1 . . . . 1G 103
(off Nesham St.)
Merivale Rd. HA1: Harr 7G 41
SW15 . . . . 4G 117
Merle Mans. E20 . . . . 6E 68
(off Glade Wlk.)
Merlewood Dr. BR7: Chst 1D 160
Merley Ct. NW9 . . . . 1J 61
Merlin NW9 . . . . 1B 44
(off Near Acre)
Merlin Cl. CR0: C'don 4E 168
CR4: Mitc 3C 154
SM6: W'gton 6K 167
UB5: N'olt 3A 76
Merlin Ct. BR2: Broml 3H 159
HA4: Ruis 2F 57
HA7: Stan 5G 27
(off William Dr.)
SE3 . . . . 4K 123
Merlin Cres. HA8: Edg 1F 43
Merlin Gdns. BR1: Broml 3J 141
Merling Cl. KT9: Chess 5C 162
Merlin Gro. BR3: Beck 4B 158
Merlin Hgts. N17 . . . . 3H 49
(off Daneland Wlk.)
Merlin Ho. EN3: Pond E 5E 24
Merlin Rd. DA16: Well 4A 126
E12 . . . . 2B 70
Merlin Rd. Nth. DA16: Well 4A 126
Merlins Av. HA2: Harr 3D 58
Merlins Ct. WC1 . . . . 2J 7
(off Margery St.)
Merlin St. WC1 . . . . 2J 7 (3A 84)
Mermaid Ct. E8 . . . . 7F 67
(off Celandine Dr.)
SE1 . . . . 6E 14 (2D 102)
SE16 . . . . 1B 104
Mermaid Ho. E14 . . . . 7E 86
(off Bazely St.)
Mermaid Twr. SE8 . . . . 6B 104
(off Abinger Gro.)
Meroe Ct. N16 . . . . 2E 66
Mero Way NW7 . . . . 7B 30
Merredene St. SW2 . . . . 6K 119
Merriam Av. E9 . . . . 6B 68
Merriam Cl. E4 . . . . 5K 35
Merrick Rd. UB2: S'hall 2D 94
Merrick Sq. SE1 . . . . 7E 14 (3D 102)
Merridene N21 . . . . 6G 23
Merrielands Cres. RM9: Dag 2F 91
Merrielands Retail Pk. 1F 91
Merrilands Rd.
KT4: Wor Pk 1E 164
Merrilees Rd. DA15: Sidc 7J 125
Merrilyn Cl. KT10: Clay 6A 162
Merriman Rd. SE3 . . . . 1A 124
Merrington Rd. SW6 . . . . 6J 99
Merrion Av. HA7: Stan 5J 27
Merrion Ct. HA4: Ruis 1H 57
(off Pembroke Rd.)
Merritt Gdns. KT9: Chess 6C 162
Merritt Rd. SE4 . . . . 5B 122
Merrivale N14 . . . . 6C 22
NW1 . . . . 1G 83
(off Camden St.)
Merrivale Av. IG4: Ilf 4B 52
Merrivale M. HA8: Edg 1J 43
Merrow Bldgs. SE1 . . . . 6B 14
(off Rushworth St.)
Merrow Ct. CR4: Mitc 2B 154
Merrow Rd. SM2: Cheam 7F 165
Merrow St. SE17 . . . . 5D 102
Merrow Wlk. SE17 . . . . 5D 102
Merrow Way CR0: New Ad 6E 170
Merrydown Way BR7: Chst 1C 160
Merryfield SE3 . . . . 2H 123
Merryfield Ct. SW11 . . . . 2D 118
Merryfield Gdns. HA7: Stan 5H 27
Merryfield Ho. SE9 . . . . 3A 142
(off Grove Pk. Rd.)
Merryfields UB8: Uxb 2A 74
Merryfields Way SE6 . . . . 7D 122
MERRY HILL 1A 26
Merryhill Cl. E4 . . . . 7J 25
Merry Hill Mt. WD23: Bush 1A 26
Merry Hill Rd. WD23: Bush 1A 26
Merryhills Ct. N14 . . . . 5B 22
Merryhills Dr. EN2: Enf 4C 22
Merryweather Ct.
KT3: N Mald 5A 152
N19 . . . . 3G 65
Merryweather Pl. SE10 . . . . 7D 104
Mersea Ho. IG11: Bark 6F 71
Mersey Ct. KT2: King T 1D 150
(off Samuel Gray Gdns.)
Mersey Rd. E17 . . . . 3B 50
Mersey Wlk. UB5: N'olt 2E 76
Mersham Dr. NW9 . . . . 5G 43
Mersham Pl. CR7: Thor H 2D 156
(off Livingstone Rd.)
SE20 . . . . 1H 157
Mersham Rd. CR7: Thor H 3D 156
Merten Rd. RM6: Chad H 7E 54
Merthyr Ter. SW13 . . . . 6D 98
MERTON 7A 136
Merton Abbey Mills SW19 . . . . 1A 154
Merton Av. UB5: N'olt 5G 59
UB10: Hil 7D 56
W4 . . . . 4B 98
Merton Ct. DA16: Well 2B 126
IG1: Ilf 6C 52
Merton Gdns. BR5: Pet W 5F 161
Merton Hall Gdns. SW20 . . . . 1G 153
Merton Hall Rd. SW19 . . . . 7G 135
Merton High St. SW19 . . . . 7K 135
Merton Ind. Pk. SW19 . . . . 1K 153
Merton La. N6 . . . . 2D 64
Merton Lodge EN5: New Bar 5F 21
Merton Mans. SW20 . . . . 2F 153
MERTON PARK 2J 153
Merton Pk. Pde. SW19 . . . . 1H 153
Merton Pl. SW19 . . . . 1A 154
(off Nelson Gro. Rd.)
Merton Ri. NW3 . . . . 7C 64
Merton Rd. E17 . . . . 5E 50
EN2: Enf 1J 23
HA2: Harr 1G 59
IG3: Ilf 7K 53
IG11: Bark 7K 71
SE25 . . . . 5G 157
SW18 . . . . 6J 117
SW19 . . . . 7K 135
Merton's Intergenerational Cen.
. . . . 2F 155
Merton Way KT8: W Mole 4F 149
UB10: Hil 7D 56
Mertoun Ter. W1 . . . . 7E 4
(off Seymour Pl.)
Merttins Rd. SE15 . . . . 5K 121
Meru Cl. NW5 . . . . 4E 64
Mervan Rd. SW2 . . . . 4A 120
Mervyn Av. SE9 . . . . 3G 143
Mervyn Rd. TW17: Shep 7E 146
W13 . . . . 3A 96
Messaline Av. W3 . . . . 6J 79
Messenger Ct. SE16 . . . . 3G 103
(off Spa Rd.)
Messent Rd. SE9 . . . . 5A 124
Messeter Pl. SE9 . . . . 6E 124
Messina Av. NW6 . . . . 7J 63
Messina Way RM9: Dag 2F 91
Messiter Ho. N1 . . . . 1K 83
(off Barnsbury Est.)
Messom M. TW1: Twick 1A 132
Metcalfe Ct. SE10 . . . . 3H 105
Metcalf Rd. TW15: Ashf 5D 128
Metcalf Wlk. TW13: Hanw 4C 130
Meteor St. SW11 . . . . 4E 118
Meteor Way SM6: W'gton 7J 167
Methley St. SE11 . . . . 6K 19 (5A 102)
Methuen Cl. HA8: Edg 7B 28
Methuen Pk. N10 . . . . 3F 47
Methuen Rd. DA6: Bex 4F 127
DA17: Belv 4H 109
HA8: Edg 7B 28
Methven Ct. N9 . . . . 3B 34
(off The Broadway)
Methwold Rd. W10 . . . . 5F 81
Metro Bus. Cen. SE26 . . . . 6B 140
Metro Central Hgts. SE1 . . . . 3C 102
(off Newington C'way.)
Metro Golf Cen. 7K 29
Metro Ind. Cen. TW7: Isle 2J 113
Metropolis SE11 . . . . 3B 102
(off Oswin St.)
Metropolis Plaza E3 . . . . 4A 86
(off Copperfield Rd.)
Metropolitan Bldg. SW10 . . . . 7A 100
Metropolitan Bus. Cen. N1 . . . . 7E 66
(off Enfield Rd.)
The Metropolitan Cen.
UB6: G'frd 1F 77
Metropolitan Cl. E14 . . . . 5C 86
Metropolitan Cres. SW4 . . . . 5H 119
Metropolitan Ho.
TW8: Bford 6F 97
Metropolitan Police FC 6H 149
Metropolitan Sta. Bldgs. W6 . . . . 4E 98
(off Beadon Rd.)
Metropolitan Wharf E1 . . . . 1J 103
Metro Trad. Est. HA9: Wemb 4H 61
The Mews DA14: Sidc 4A 144
IG4: Ilf 5B 52
N1 . . . . 1C 84
N8 . . . . 3A 48
RM1: Rom 4K 55
TW1: Twick 6B 114
TW12: Hamp H 6G 131
Mews Pl. IG8: Wfd G 4D 36
Mews St. E1 . . . . 4K 15 (1G 103)
Mexborough NW1 . . . . 1G 83
Mexfield Rd. SW15 . . . . 5H 117
Meyer Grn. EN1: Enf 1B 24
Meyer Rd. DA8: Erith 6K 109
Meymott St. SE1 . . . . 5A 14 (1B 102)
Meynell Cres. E9 . . . . 7K 67
Meynell Gdns. E9 . . . . 7K 67
Meynell Rd. E9 . . . . 7K 67
Meyrick Ho. E14 . . . . 5C 86
(off Burgess St.)
Meyrick Rd. NW10 . . . . 6C 62
SW11 . . . . 3B 118
MFA Bowl
Lewisham 3E 122
Miah Ter. E1 . . . . 1G 103
Miall Wlk. SE26 . . . . 4A 140
Mia M. N13 . . . . 5F 33
Mica Ho. N1 . . . . 7A 66
Micawber Av. UB8: Hil 4C 74
Micawber Ct. N1 . . . . 1D 8
(off Windsor Ter.)
Micawber Ho. SE16 . . . . 2G 103
(off Llewellyn St.)
Micawber St. N1 . . . . 1D 8 (3C 84)
Michael Cliffe Ho. EC1 . . . . 2A 8
Michael Cl. E3 . . . . 4B 86
The Michael Edwards Studio Theatre
. . . . 6E 104
(within Cutty Sark)
Michael Faraday Ho. SE17 . . . . 5E 102
(off Beaconsfield Rd.)
Michael Gaynor Cl. W7 . . . . 1K 95
Michael Haines Ho. SW9 . . . . 7A 102
(off Sth. Island Pl.)
Michael Manley Ind. Est. SW8 . . . . 1G 119
Michaelmas Cl. SW20 . . . . 3E 152
Michael Rd. E11 . . . . 1G 69
SE25 . . . . 3E 156
SW6 . . . . 1K 117
Michael Robbins Way NW7 . . . . 5B 30
Michaels Cl. SE13 . . . . 4G 123
Michael Stewart Ho. SW6 . . . . 6H 99
(off Clem Attlee Ct.)
Michelangelo Ct. SE16 . . . . 5H 103
(off Stubbs Dr.)
Micheldever Rd. SE12 . . . . 6G 123
Michelham Gdns.
TW1: Twick 3K 131
Michelle Ct. BR1: Broml 1H 159
(off Blyth Rd.)
N12 . . . . 5F 31
W3 . . . . 7K 79
Michelsdale Dr. TW9: Rich 4E 114
Michelson Ho. SE11 . . . . 4H 19
Michel's Row TW9: Rich 4E 114
(off Michelsdale Dr.)
Michel Wlk. SE18 . . . . 5F 107
Michigan Av. E12 . . . . 4D 70
Michigan Bldg. E14 . . . . 1F 105
(off Biscayne Av.)
Michigan Ho. E14 . . . . 3C 104
Michleham Down N12 . . . . 4C 30
Mickledore NW1 . . . . 1B 6
(off Ampthill Est.)
Mickleham Cl. BR5: St P 2K 161
Mickleham Gdns.
SM3: Cheam 6G 165
Mickleham Rd. BR5: St P 1K 161
Mickleham Way
CR0: New Ad 7F 171
Micklethwaite Rd. SW6 . . . . 6J 99
Mickleton Ho. W2 . . . . 5J 81
(off Westbourne Pk. Rd.)
Midas Bus. Cen. RM10: Dag 4H 73
Midas Metropolitan Ind. Est.
SM4: Mord 7E 152
MID BECKTON 5D 88
Midcroft HA4: Ruis 1G 57
Middle Dartrey Wlk. SW10 . . . . 7A 100
(off Worlds End Est.)
Middle Dene NW7 . . . . 3E 28
Middlefield NW8 . . . . 1B 82
Middlefielde W13 . . . . 5B 78
Middlefield Gdns. IG2: Ilf 6F 53
Middle Grn. Cl. KT5: Surb 6F 151
Middleham Gdns. N18 . . . . 6B 34
Middleham Rd. N18 . . . . 6B 34
Middle La. N8 . . . . 5J 47
TW11: Tedd 6K 131
Middle La. M. N8 . . . . 5J 47
Middle Mill Halls of Residence
KT1: King T 3F 151
Middle New St. EC4 . . . . 7K 7
(off Pemberton Row)
Middle Pk. Av. SE9 . . . . 6B 124
Middle Path HA2: Harr 1H 59
Middle Rd. E13 . . . . 2J 87
EN4: E Barn 6H 21
HA2: Harr 2H 59
SW16 . . . . 2H 155
Middle Row W10 . . . . 4G 81
Middlesborough Rd. N18 . . . . 6B 34
The Middlesex Bldg. E1 . . . . 6H 9
(off Artillery La.)
Middlesex Bus. Cen. UB2: S'hall 2E 94
Middlesex CCC 1B 4 (3B 82)
Middlesex Cl. UB1: S'hall 4F 77
Middlesex Ct. HA1: Harr 5K 41
TW8: Bford 5C 96
(off Glenhurst Rd.)
W4 . . . . 4B 98
Middlesex Filter Beds Nature Reserve
. . . . 3K 67
Middlesex Guildhall 7E 12
(off Lit. George St.)
Middlesex Ho. HA0: Wemb 1D 78
Middlesex Pas. EC1 . . . . 6B 8
Middlesex Pl. E9 . . . . 6J 67
(off Elsdale St.)
Middlesex Rd. CR4: Mitc 5J 155
Middlesex St. E1 . . . . 6H 9 (5E 84)
Middlesex University
Archway Campus 1G 65
Hendon Campus 4D 44
Middlesex Wharf E5 . . . . 2J 67
Middle St. CR0: C'don 2C 168
(not continuous)
EC1 . . . . 5C 8 (5C 84)
Middle Temple Hall 7A 84
Middle Temple La.
EC4 . . . . 1J 13 (6A 84)
Middleton Av. DA14: Sidc 6B 144
E4 . . . . 4G 35
UB6: G'frd 2H 77
Middleton Cl. E4 . . . . 3G 35
Middleton Dr. HA5: Eastc 3J 39
SE16 . . . . 2K 103
Middleton Gdns. IG2: Ilf 6F 53
Middleton Gro. IG11: Bark 3A 90
N7 . . . . 5J 65
Middleton Ho. E8 . . . . 7G 67
SE1 . . . . 3D 102
(off Burbage Cl.)
SW1 . . . . 4D 18
(off Causton St.)
Middleton M. N7 . . . . 5J 65
Middleton Pl. W1 . . . . 6A 6
Middleton Rd. E8 . . . . 7F 67
NW11 . . . . 7J 45
SM4: Mord, Cars 6K 153
SM5: Cars 6A 154
UB3: Hayes 5F 75
Middleton St. E2 . . . . 3H 85
Middleton Way SE13 . . . . 4F 123
Middle Way DA18: Erith 3E 108
SW16 . . . . 2H 155
UB4: Yead 4A 76

Middleway—Mocatta Ho.

Middleway NW11 . . . . . 5K 45
The Middle Way HA3: W'stone 2K 41
Middle Yd. SE1 . . . . . 4G 15 (1E 102)
Midfield Av. DA7: Bex 3J 127
Midfield Pde. DA7: Bex 3J 127
Midfield Way BR5: St P 7A 144
Midford Ho. NW4 . . . . . 4E 44
(off Belle Vue Est.)
Midford Pl. W1 . . . . . 4B 6 (4G 83)
Midholm HA9: Wemb 1G 61
NW11 . . . . . 4K 45
Midholm Cl. NW11 . . . . . 4K 45
Midholm Rd. CR0: C'don 2A 170
Midhope Ho. WC1 . . . . . 2F 7
(off Midhope St.)
Midhope St. WC1 . . . . . 2F 7 (3J 83)
Midhurst SE26 . . . . . 6J 139
Midhurst Av. CR0: C'don 7A 156
N10 . . . . . 3E 46
Midhurst Gdns. UB10: Hil 1E 74
Midhurst Hill DA6: Bex 6G 127
Midhurst Ho. E14 . . . . . 6B 86
(off Salmon La.)
Midhurst Pde. N10 . . . . . 3E 46
(off Fortis Grn.)
Midhurst Rd. W13 . . . . . 2A 96
Midhurst Way E5 . . . . . 4G 67
Midland Goods Shed N1 . . . . . 1J 83
(off Handyside St.)
Midland Pde. NW6 . . . . . 6K 63
Midland Pl. E14 . . . . . 5E 104
Midland Rd. E10 . . . . . 7E 50
NW1 . . . . . 1D 6 (2H 83)
Midland Ter. NW2 . . . . . 3F 63
NW10 . . . . . 4A 80
Midleton Rd. KT3: N Mald 3J 151
Midlothian Rd. E3 . . . . . 4B 86
(off Burdett Rd.)
Midmoor Rd. SW12 . . . . . 1G 137
SW19 . . . . . 1F 153
Midnight Av. SE5 . . . . . 7B 102
Midship Cl. SE16 . . . . . 1K 103
Midship Point E14 . . . . . 2C 104
(off The Quarterdeck)
Midstrath Rd. NW10 . . . . . 4A 62
Midsummer Av. TW4: Houn 4D 112
Midway SM3: Sutt 7H 153
Midway Ho. EC1 . . . . . 1A 8
Midwinter Cl. DA16: Well 3A 126
Midwood Cl. NW2 . . . . . 3D 62
Miers Cl. E6 . . . . . 1E 88
Mighell Av. IG4: Ilf 5B 52
Mikardo Ct. E14 . . . . . 7E 86
(off Poplar High St.)
Milan Ct. N11 . . . . . 1H 47
Milan Rd. UB1: S'hall 2D 94
Milborne Gro. SW10 . . . . . 6A 16 (5A 100)
Milborne St. E9 . . . . . 6J 67
Milborough Cres. SE12 . . . . . 6G 123
Milbourne Ho. KT1: King T 1G 151
(off Coombe Rd.)
Milbourne Pl. KT19: Ewe 4K 163
Milburn Dr. UB7: Yiew 7A 74
Milcote St. SE1 . . . . . 7A 14 (2B 102)
Mildenhall Rd. E5 . . . . . 4J 67
Mildmay Av. N1 . . . . . 6D 66
Mildmay Gro. Nth. N1 . . . . . 5D 66
Mildmay Gro. Sth. N1 . . . . . 5D 66
Mildmay Pk. N1 . . . . . 5D 66
Mildmay Pl. N16 . . . . . 5E 66
Mildmay Rd. IG1: Ilf 3F 71
N1 . . . . . 5D 66
RM7: Rom 5J 55
Mildmay St. N1 . . . . . 6D 66
Mildred Av. UB3: Harl 4F 93
UB5: N'olt 5F 59
Mildred Ct. CR0: C'don 1G 169
Mildred Rd. DA8: Erith 5K 109
Mildrose Ct. NW6 . . . . . 3J 81
(off Malvern M.)
Mildura Ct. N8 . . . . . 4K 47
MILE END 4B 86
The Mile End E17 . . . . . 1K 49
Mile End Climbing Wall 3A 86
Mile End Pk. 2A 86
Mile End Pk. Leisure Cen. 5A 86
Mile End Pl. E1 . . . . . 4K 85
Mile End Rd. E1 . . . . . 5J 85
E3 . . . . . 5J 85
Mile End Stadium 5B 86
Miles Bldgs. NW1 . . . . . 5C 4
(off Penfold Pl.)
Miles Cl. SE28 . . . . . 1H 107
Miles Ct. CR0: C'don 2B 168
(off Cuthbert Rd.)
E1 . . . . . 6H 85
(off Tillman St.)
Miles Dr. SE28 . . . . . 1J 107
Miles Ho. SE10 . . . . . 5G 105
(off Tuskar St.)
Miles Lodge E15 . . . . . 5F 69
(off Colegrave Rd.)
HA1: Harr 5H 41
Milespit Hill NW7 . . . . . 5J 29
Miles Pl. KT5: Surb 4F 151
NW8 . . . . . 5B 4
Miles Rd. CR4: Mitc 3C 154
N8 . . . . . 3J 47
Miles St. SW8 . . . . . 7E 18 (6J 101)
(not continuous)
Milestone Cl. N9 . . . . . 2B 34
SM2: Sutt 6B 166
Milestone Ct. E10 . . . . . 7D 50
MILESTONE GREEN 4J 115
Milestone Ho. KT1: King T 3D 150
(off Surbiton Rd.)
Milestone Rd. SE19 . . . . . 6F 139
Miles Way N20 . . . . . 2H 31
Milfoil St. W12 . . . . . 7C 80
Milford Cl. SE2 . . . . . 6E 108
Milford Ct. UB1: S'hall 1E 94
Milford Gdns. CR0: C'don 5J 157
HA0: Wemb 4D 60
HA8: Edg 7B 28
Milford Gro. SM1: Sutt 4A 166
Milford La. WC2 . . . . . 2H 13 (7A 84)
Milford M. SW16 . . . . . 3K 137
Milford Rd. UB1: S'hall 7E 76
W13 . . . . . 1B 96
Milford Towers SE6 . . . . . 7D 122
Milk St. BR1: Broml 6K 141
E16 . . . . . 1F 107
EC2 . . . . . 7D 8 (6C 84)
Milkwell Gdns. IG8: Wfd G 7E 36
Milkwell Yd. SE5 . . . . . 1C 120
Milkwood Rd. SE24 . . . . . 5B 120
Milk Yd. E1 . . . . . 7J 85
Millais Av. E12 . . . . . 5E 70
Millais Ct. UB5: N'olt 2B 76
(off Academy Gdns.)
Millais Cres. KT19: Ewe 5A 164
Millais Gdns. HA8: Edg 2G 43
Millais Ho. SW1 . . . . . 4E 18
(off Marsham St.)
Millais Rd. E11 . . . . . 4E 68
EN1: Enf 5A 24
KT3: N Mald 7A 152
Millais Way KT19: Ewe 4J 163
Millard Cl. N16 . . . . . 5E 66
Millard Rd. SE8 . . . . . 5B 104
Millard Ter. RM10: Dag 6G 73
Millbank SM6: W'gton 5H 167
SW1 . . . . . 2E 18 (3J 101)
Millbank Ct. SW1 . . . . . 3E 18
Millbank Twr. SW1 . . . . . 4E 18 (4J 101)
Millbank Way SE12 . . . . . 5J 123
Millbourne Rd.
TW13: Hanw 4C 130
Mill Bridge EN5: Barn 6C 20
Millbroke M. IG8: Wfd G 6B 36
Millbrook Av.
DA16: Well 4H 125
Millbrooke Ct. SW15 . . . . . 5G 117
(off Keswick Rd.)
Millbrook Gdns. RM6: Chad H 6F 55
Millbrook Ho. SE15 . . . . . 6G 103
(off Peckham Pk. Rd.)
Millbrook Pk. NW7 . . . . . 6B 30
Millbrook Pas. SW9 . . . . . 3B 120
Millbrook Pl. NW1 . . . . . 2G 83
(off Hampstead Rd.)
Millbrook Rd. N9 . . . . . 1C 34
SW9 . . . . . 3B 120
Mill Cl. NW7 . . . . . 1G 45
SM5: Cars 2E 166
Mill Cnr. EN5: Barn 1C 20
Mill Ct. E5 . . . . . 2J 67
E10 . . . . . 3E 68
SE28 . . . . . 7B 90
(off Titmuss Av.)
Millcroft Ho. SE6 . . . . . 4E 140
(off Melfield Gdns.)
Mill Dr. HA4: Ruis 7F 39
Millender Wlk. SE16 . . . . . 4J 103
(off New Rotherhithe Rd.)
MILLENNIUM BRIDGE
. . . . . 3C 14 (7C 84)
Millennium Bri. Ho. EC4 . . . . . 2C 14
(off Up. Thames St.)
Millennium Bus. Cen. NW2 . . . . . 2D 62
The Millennium Cen. 4K 73
Millennium Cl. E16 . . . . . 6K 87
Millennium Dr. E14 . . . . . 4F 105
Millennium Ho. E17 . . . . . 5K 49
SW15 . . . . . 5G 117
(off Plaza Gdns.)
Millennium Pl. E2 . . . . . 2H 85
Millennium Sq. SE1 . . . . . 6K 15 (2F 103)
Millennium Way SE10 . . . . . 2G 105
Miller Av. EN3: Enf L 1H 25
Miller Cl. BR1: Broml 5K 141
CR4: Mitc 7D 154
HA5: Pinn 2A 40
RM5: Col R 1G 55
Miller Ct. DA7: Bex 3J 127
Miller Ho. E1 . . . . . 5K 85
(off Shandy St.)
W10 . . . . . 4H 81
(off Harrow Rd.)
Miller Rd. CR0: C'don 1K 167
SW19 . . . . . 6B 136
Miller's Av. E8 . . . . . 5F 67
Millers Cl. NW7 . . . . . 4H 29
Millers Ct. HA0: Wemb 2E 78
(off Vicars Bri. Cl.)
Millers Grn. Cl. EN2: Enf 3G 23
Miller's House Visitor Centre 3E 86
(off Three Mill La.)
Millers Mdw. Cl. SE3 . . . . . 4H 123
Millers Row E20 . . . . . 5D 68
Miller's Ter. E8 . . . . . 5F 67
Miller St. NW1 . . . . . 2G 83
(not continuous)
Millers Way W6 . . . . . 2E 98
Millers Wharf Ho. E1 . . . . . 5K 15
(off St Katherine's Way)
Millers Yd. N3 . . . . . 1K 45
Miller Wlk. SE1 . . . . . 5K 13 (1A 102)
Milles Sq. SW9 . . . . . 4A 120
Millet Rd. UB6: G'frd 2F 77
Mill Farm Av. TW16: Sun 7G 129
Mill Farm Bus. Pk.
TW4: Houn 7C 112
Mill Farm Cl. HA5: Pinn 2A 40
Mill Farm Cres.
TW4: Houn 1C 130
Millfield KT1: King T 3F 151
N4 . . . . . 2A 66
TW16: Sun 1F 147
Millfield Av. E17 . . . . . 1A 50
Millfield La. N6 . . . . . 1C 64
Millfield Pl. N6 . . . . . 2E 64
Millfield Rd. HA8: Edg 2J 43
TW4: Houn 1C 130
Millfields Rd. E5 . . . . . 4J 67
Millfield Theatre 4J 33
Mill Gdns. SE26 . . . . . 3H 139
Mill Grn. CR4: Mitc 7E 154
Mill Grn. Bus. Pk.
CR4: Mitc 7E 154
Mill Grn. Rd. CR4: Mitc 7D 154
Millgrove St. SW11 . . . . . 1E 118
Millharbour E14 . . . . . 2D 104
Millhaven Cl. RM6: Chad H 6B 54
MILL HILL 5F 29
Mill Hill SW13 . . . . . 2C 116
MILL HILL CIR. 5G 29
Mill Hill Cir. NW7 . . . . . 5G 29
Mill Hill Golf Course 2F 29
Mill Hill Gro. W3 . . . . . 1J 97
Mill Hill Ind. Est. NW7 . . . . . 6G 29
Mill Hill Old Railway Nature Reserve
. . . . . 6D 28
Mill Hill Rd. SW13 . . . . . 2C 116
W3 . . . . . 2H 97
Mill Hill School Sports Cen. 4H 29
Mill Hill Ter. W3 . . . . . 1H 97
Mill Ho. IG8: Wfd G 5C 36
Millhouse Pl. SE27 . . . . . 4B 138
Millicent Fawcett Ct. N17 . . . . . 1F 49
Millicent Gro. N13 . . . . . 5G 33
Millicent Preston Ho. IG11: Bark 1H 89
(off Ripple Rd.)
Millicent Rd. E10 . . . . . 1B 68
Milligan St. E14 . . . . . 7B 86
Milliner Ho. SW10 . . . . . 7A 100
(off Hortensia Rd.)
Milliners Ho. SE1 . . . . . 7H 15
(off Bermondsey St.)
SW18 . . . . . 4J 117
Milling Rd. HA8: Edg 7E 28
Millington Ho. N16 . . . . . 3D 66
Millington Rd. UB3: Harl 3G 93
Mill La. CR0: Wadd 3K 167
E4 . . . . . 3J 25
IG8: Wfd G 5C 36
KT17: Ewe 7B 164
NW6 . . . . . 5H 63
RM6: Chad H 6E 54
SE8 . . . . . 1C 122
(off Deptford Bri.)
SE18 . . . . . 5E 106
SM5: Cars 4D 166
Mill La. Trad. Est.
CR0: Wadd 3K 167
Millman Ct. WC1 . . . . . 4G 7
(off Millman St.)
Millman M. WC1 . . . . . 4G 7 (4K 83)
Millman Pl. WC1 . . . . . 4G 7
(off Millman St.)
Millman Rd. E16 . . . . . 7D 88
Millman St. WC1 . . . . . 4G 7 (4K 83)
Millmark Gro. SE14 . . . . . 2A 122
Millmarsh La. EN3: Brim 2F 25
Millmead Ind. Cen. N17 . . . . . 2H 49
Mill Mead Rd. N17 . . . . . 3H 49
MILL MEADS 2F 87
Mill Pl. BR7: Chst 1E 160
E14 . . . . . 6A 86
KT1: King T 3F 151
Mill Plat TW7: Isle 2A 114
(not continuous)
Mill Plat Av. TW7: Isle 2A 114
Mill Pond Cl. SW8 . . . . . 7H 101
Millpond Est. SE16 . . . . . 2H 103
Millpond Pl. SM5: Cars 3E 166
Mill Ridge HA8: Edg 5A 28
Mill River Trad. Est.
EN3: Pond E 3F 25
Mill Rd. DA8: Erith 7J 109
E16 . . . . . 1K 105
IG1: Ilf 3E 70
SW19 . . . . . 7A 136
TW2: Twick 2G 131
Mill Row DA5: Bexl 1H 145
N1 . . . . . 1E 84
Mills Cl. UB10: Hil 2C 74
Mills Ct. EC2 . . . . . 3G 9
Mills Gro. E14 . . . . . 6E 86
NW4 . . . . . 3F 45
Millshott Cl. SW6 . . . . . 1E 116
Mills Ho. SW8 . . . . . 1G 119
(off Thessaly Rd.)
Millside SM5: Cars 2D 166
Millside Pl. TW7: Isle 2B 114
Millson Cl. N20 . . . . . 2G 31
Mills Row W4 . . . . . 4K 97
Millstone Cl. E15 . . . . . 6F 69
Millstream Cl. N13 . . . . . 5F 33
Millstream Ho. SE16 . . . . . 2H 103
(off Jamaica Rd.)
Millstream Rd. SE1 . . . . . 7J 15 (2F 103)
Mill St. KT1: King T 3E 150
SE1 . . . . . 7K 15 (2F 103)
W1 . . . . . 2A 12 (7F 83)
Mills Yd. SW6 . . . . . 3K 117
The Mill Trad. Est. NW10 . . . . . 3J 79
Mill Va. BR2: Broml 2H 159
Mill Vw. Cl. KT17: Ewe 7B 164
Mill Vw. Gdns.
CR0: C'don 3K 169
MILLWALL 4D 104
Millwall Dock Rd. E14 . . . . . 3C 104
Millwall FC 5J 103
Millwall Pk. 4E 104
Mill Way TW14: Felt 5K 111
Millway NW7 . . . . . 4F 29
Millway Gdns. UB5: N'olt 6D 58
Millwood Rd. TW3: Houn 5G 113
Millwood St. W10 . . . . . 5G 81
Mill Yd. E1 . . . . . 7G 85
Mill Yd. Ind. Est.
HA8: Edg 1H 43
Milman Cl. HA5: Pinn 3B 40
Milman Rd. NW6 . . . . . 2F 81
Milman's Ho. SW10 . . . . . 6B 100
(off Milman's St.)
Milman's St. SW10 . . . . . 6B 100
Milne Ct. E18 . . . . . 1J 51
Milne Gdns. SE9 . . . . . 5C 124
Milne Ho. SE18 . . . . . 4D 106
(off Ogilby St.)
Milner Ct. SE15 . . . . . 7F 103
(off Colegrove Rd.)
Milner Dr. TW2: Whitt 7H 113
Milner Pl. N1 . . . . . 1A 84
SE1 . . . . . 6H 13 (2K 101)
SM5: Cars 4E 166
Milner Rd. CR7: Thor H 3D 156
E15 . . . . . 3G 87
KT1: King T 3D 150
RM8: Dag 2C 72
SM4: Mord 5B 154
SW19 . . . . . 1K 153
Milner Sq. N1 . . . . . 7B 66
Milner St. SW3 . . . . . 3E 16 (4D 100)
Milner Wlk. SE9 . . . . . 2H 143
Milnthorpe Rd. W4 . . . . . 6K 97
Milo Gdns. SE22 . . . . . 6F 121
Milo Rd. SE22 . . . . . 6F 121
Milrood Ho. E1 . . . . . 5K 85
(off Stepney Grn.)
Milroy Wlk. SE1 . . . . . 4A 14 (1B 102)
Milsom Rd. W14 . . . . . 3F 99
Milstead Ho. E5 . . . . . 5H 67
Milton Av. CR0: C'don 7D 156
E6 . . . . . 7B 70
EN5: Barn 5C 20
N6 . . . . . 7G 47
NW9 . . . . . 3J 43
NW10 . . . . . 1J 79
SM1: Sutt 3B 166
Milton Cl. N2 . . . . . 5A 46
SE1 . . . . . 4F 103
SM1: Sutt 3B 166
UB4: Hayes 6J 75
Milton Ct. E17 . . . . . 4C 50
EC2 . . . . . 5E 8 (5D 84)
RM6: Chad H 7C 54
SE14 . . . . . 6B 104
(not continuous)
SW18 . . . . . 5J 117
TW2: Twick 3J 131
UB10: Ick 3D 56
Milton Court Concert Hall 5E 8
(off Milton Ct.)
Milton Ct. Rd. SE14 . . . . . 6A 104
Milton Cres. IG2: Ilf 7F 53
Milton Dr. TW17: Shep 4A 146
Milton Gdn. Est. N16 . . . . . 4D 66
Milton Gdns. TW19: Stanw 1B 128
Milton Gro. N11 . . . . . 5B 32
N16 . . . . . 4D 66
Milton Ho. E2 . . . . . 3J 85
(off Roman Rd.)
E17 . . . . . 4C 50
SE5 . . . . . 7D 102
(off Elmington Est.)
SM1: Sutt 3J 165
Milton Lodge DA14: Sidc 4A 144
TW1: Twick 7K 113
Milton Mans. W14 . . . . . 6G 99
(off Queen's Club Gdns.)
Milton Pk. N6 . . . . . 7G 47
Milton Rd. CR0: C'don 7D 156
CR4: Mitc 7E 136
DA16: Well 1K 125
DA17: Belv 4G 109
E17 . . . . . 4C 50
HA1: Harr 4J 41
N6 . . . . . 7G 47
N15 . . . . . 4B 48
NW7 . . . . . 5H 29
NW9 . . . . . 7C 44
SE24 . . . . . 5B 120
SM1: Sutt 3J 165
SM6: W'gton 6G 167
SW14 . . . . . 3K 115
SW19 . . . . . 6A 136
TW12: Hamp 7E 130
UB10: Ick 4D 56
W3 . . . . . 1K 97
W7 . . . . . 7K 77
Milton St. EC2 . . . . . 5E 8 (5D 84)
Milton Way UB7: W Dray 4B 92
Milverton Dr. UB10: Ick 4E 56
Milverton Gdns. IG3: Ilf 2K 71
Milverton Ho. SE6 . . . . . 3A 140
Milverton Pl. BR1: Broml 5A 142
Milverton Rd. NW6 . . . . . 7E 62
Milverton St. SE11 . . . . . 6K 19 (5A 102)
Milverton Way SE9 . . . . . 4E 142
Milward St. E1 . . . . . 5H 85
Milward Wlk. SE18 . . . . . 6E 106
Mimosa Ho. E20 . . . . . 5E 68
(off Liberty Bri. Rd.)
UB4: Yead 5A 76
Mimosa Lodge NW10 . . . . . 5B 62
Mimosa Rd. UB4: Yead 5A 76
Mimosa St. SW6 . . . . . 1H 117
Minard Rd. SE6 . . . . . 7G 123
Mina Rd. SE17 . . . . . 5E 102
SW19 . . . . . 1J 153
Mina Ter. N9 . . . . . 7B 24
Minchenden Ct. N14 . . . . . 2C 32
Minchenden Cres. N14 . . . . . 3B 32
Minchin Ho. E14 . . . . . 6C 86
(off Dod St.)
Mincing La. EC3 . . . . . 2G 15 (7E 84)
Minden Gdns. IG11: Bark 3B 90
Minden Rd. SE20 . . . . . 1H 157
SM3: Sutt 2G 165
Minehead Rd. HA2: Harr 3E 58
SW16 . . . . . 5K 137
Mineral Cl. EN5: Barn 6A 20
Mineral St. SE18 . . . . . 4J 107
Minera M. SW1 . . . . . 3G 17 (4E 100)
Minerva Cl. DA14: Sidc 3J 143
SW9 . . . . . 7A 102
TW19: Stanw M 7B 174
Minerva Ct. EC1 . . . . . 4K 7
(off Bowling Grn. La.)
Minerva Lodge N7 . . . . . 6K 65
Minerva Rd. E4 . . . . . 7J 35
KT1: King T 2F 151
NW10 . . . . . 4J 79
Minerva St. E2 . . . . . 2H 85
Minerva Wlk. EC1 . . . . . 7B 8 (6B 84)
Minerva Way EN5: Barn 5C 20
Minet Av. NW10 . . . . . 2A 80
Minet Country Pk. 2A 94
Minet Dr. UB3: Hayes 1J 93
Minet Gdns. NW10 . . . . . 2A 80
UB3: Hayes 1K 93
Minet Rd. SW9 . . . . . 2B 120
Minford Gdns. W14 . . . . . 2F 99
Minford Ho. W14 . . . . . 2F 99
(off Minford Gdns.)
Mingard Wlk. N7 . . . . . 2K 65
Ming St. E14 . . . . . 7C 86
Minimax Cl. TW14: Felt 6J 111
Minima Yacht Club 3D 150
(off High St.)
Ministry Way SE9 . . . . . 2D 142
Miniver Pl. EC4 . . . . . 2D 14
Mink Ct. TW4: Houn 2A 112
Minnie Baldock St. E16 . . . . . 6H 87
Minniedale KT5: Surb 5F 151
Minnow St. SE17 . . . . . 4E 102
Minnow Wlk. SE17 . . . . . 4E 102
Minories EC3 . . . . . 1J 15 (6F 85)
Minotaur Dr. EN5: Barn 5C 20
Minshaw Ct. DA14: Sidc 4K 143
Minshill St. SW8 . . . . . 1H 119
Minshull Pl. BR3: Beck 7C 140
Minson Rd. E9 . . . . . 1K 85
Minstead Gdns. SW15 . . . . . 7B 116
Minstead Way KT3: N Mald 6A 152
Minster Av. SM1: Sutt 2J 165
Minster Ct. EC3 . . . . . 2H 15
W5 . . . . . 4E 78
Minster Dr. CR0: C'don 4E 168
Minster Gdns. KT8: W Mole 4D 148
Minsterley Av. TW17: Shep 4G 147
Minster Pavement EC3 . . . . . 2H 15
(off Mincing La.)
Minster Rd. BR1: Broml 7K 141
NW2 . . . . . 5G 63
Minster Wlk. N8 . . . . . 4J 47
Minstrel Gdns. KT5: Surb 4F 151
Mint Bus. Pk. E16 . . . . . 5K 87
Mint Cl. UB10: Hil 3D 74
Mintern Cl. N13 . . . . . 3G 33
Minterne Av. UB2: S'hall 4E 94
Minterne Rd. HA3: Kenton 5F 43
Minterne Waye UB4: Yead 6A 76
Mintern St. N1 . . . . . 2D 84
Minter Rd. IG11: Bark 4A 90
Minton Apts. SW8 . . . . . 7J 101
Minton Ho. SE11 . . . . . 3J 19
Minton M. NW6 . . . . . 6K 63
Mint Rd. SM6: W'gton 4F 167
Mint St. E2 . . . . . 4H 85
(off Three Colts La.)
SE1 . . . . . 6C 14 (2C 102)
Mint Wlk. CR0: C'don 3C 168
Mirabelle Gdns. E20 . . . . . 5E 68
Mirabel Rd. SW6 . . . . . 7H 99
Mira Ho. E20 . . . . . 5E 68
(off Prize Wlk.)
Miranda Cl. E1 . . . . . 5J 85
Miranda Ct. W3 . . . . . 6F 79
Miranda Ho. N1 . . . . . 1G 9
(off Crondall St.)
Miranda Rd. N19 . . . . . 1G 65
Mirfield St. SE7 . . . . . 4B 106
Miriam Rd. SE18 . . . . . 5J 107
Mirravale Trad. Est. RM8: Dag 7E 54
Mirren Cl. HA2: Harr 4D 58
Mirror Path SE9 . . . . . 3A 142
Misbourne Rd. UB10: Hil 1C 74
Missenden SE17 . . . . . 5D 102
(off Roland Way)
Missenden Cl. TW14: Felt 1H 129
Missenden Gdns. SM4: Mord 6A 154
Missenden Ho. NW8 . . . . . 3C 4
The Mission E14 . . . . . 6B 86
(off Commercial Rd.)
Mission Gro. E17 . . . . . 5A 50
Mission Pl. SE15 . . . . . 1G 121
Mission Sq. TW8: Bford 6E 96
Missouri Ct. HA5: Eastc 6A 40
Misletoe Cl. CR0: C'don 1K 169
Mistral SE5 . . . . . 1E 120
Misty's Fld. KT12: Walt T 7A 148
Mitali Pas. E1 . . . . . 6G 85
MITCHAM 3D 154
Mitcham Gdn. Village
CR4: Mitc 5E 154
Mitcham Golf Course 5E 154
Mitcham Ho. SE5 . . . . . 1C 120
Mitcham Ind. Est. CR4: Mitc 1E 154
Mitcham La. SW16 . . . . . 6G 137
Mitcham Pk. CR4: Mitc 4C 154
Mitcham Rd. CR0: C'don 6J 155
E6 . . . . . 3C 88
IG3: Ilf 7K 53
SW17 . . . . . 5D 136
Mitchell NW9 . . . . . 1B 44
(off Quakers Course)
Mitchellbrook Way NW10 . . . . . 6K 61
Mitchell Cl. DA17: Belv 3J 109
RM8: Dag 3C 72
SE2 . . . . . 4C 108
Mitchell Ho. N1 . . . . . 7B 66
(off College Cross)
W12 . . . . . 7D 80
(off White City Est.)
Mitchell Rd. BR6: Orp 4K 173
N13 . . . . . 5H 33
Mitchell's Pl. SE21 . . . . . 6E 120
(off Aysgarth Rd.)
Mitchell St. EC1 . . . . . 3C 8 (4C 84)
(not continuous)
Mitchell Wlk. E6 . . . . . 5C 88
(off Allhallows Rd.)
E6 . . . . . 5D 88
(Elmley Cl.)
Mitchell Way BR1: Broml 1J 159
NW10 . . . . . 6J 61
Mitchison Ct. TW16: Sun 1J 147
(off Downside)
Mitchison Rd. N1 . . . . . 6D 66
Mitchley Rd. N17 . . . . . 3G 49
Mitford Bldgs. SW6 . . . . . 7J 99
(off Dawes Rd.)
Mitford Cl. KT9: Chess 6C 162
Mitford Rd. N19 . . . . . 2J 65
The Mitre E14 . . . . . 7B 86
Mitre Av. E17 . . . . . 3C 50
Mitre Bri. Ind. Pk. W10 . . . . . 4D 80
(not continuous)
Mitre Cl. BR2: Broml 2H 159
SM2: Sutt 7A 166
TW17: Shep 6F 147
Mitre Ho. SW3 . . . . . 5E 16
(off King's Rd.)
Mitre Pas. EC3 . . . . . 1H 15
(off Mitre Sq.)
SE10 . . . . . 2G 105
Mitre Rd. E15 . . . . . 2G 87
SE1 . . . . . 6K 13 (2A 102)
Mitre Sq. EC3 . . . . . 1H 15 (6E 84)
Mitre St. EC3 . . . . . 1H 15 (6E 84)
Mitre Way W10 . . . . . 4D 80
Mitre Yd. SW3 . . . . . 3D 16 (4C 100)
Mitten Ho. SE8 . . . . . 7D 104
(off Creative Rd.)
Mizen Ct. E14 . . . . . 2C 104
(off Alpha Gro.)
Mizzen Mast Ho. SE18 . . . . . 3D 106
Mizzen St. IG11: Bark 1H 89
The Moat KT3: N Mald 1A 152
Moat Cl. BR6: Chels 6K 173
Moat Ct. DA15: Sidc 3K 143
SE9 . . . . . 6D 124
Moat Cres. N3 . . . . . 3K 45
Moat Cft. DA16: Well 3C 126
Moat Dr. E13 . . . . . 2A 88
HA1: Harr 4G 41
HA4: Ruis 7G 39
Moat Farm Rd. UB5: N'olt 6D 58
Moatfield NW6 . . . . . 7G 63
Moatlands Ho. WC1 . . . . . 2F 7
(off Cromer St.)
Moat La. KT8: E Mos 3K 149
The Moat Lodge HA2: Harr 2J 59
Moat Pl. SW9 . . . . . 3K 119
W3 . . . . . 6H 79
Moat Side EN3: Pond E 4E 24
TW13: Hanw 4A 130
Moberly Rd. SW4 . . . . . 7H 119
Moberly Sports Cen. 3F 81
Mobil Ct. WC2 . . . . . 1H 13
(off Clement's Inn)
MOBY DICK 4E 54
Mocatta Ho. E1 . . . . . 4H 85
(off Brady St.)

Mocha Ct.—Mornington Cl.

Mocha Ct. E3 2D 86
(off Taylor Pl.)
MoDA 2B 44
Modbury Gdns. NW5 6E 64
Modder Pl. SW15 4F 117
Model Cotts. SW14 4J 115
W13 2B 96
Model Farm Cl. SE9 3C 142
Modena Ho. E14 6G 87
(off Lyell St.)
Modern Ct. EC4 7A 8
Modling Ho. E2 2K 85
(off Mace St.)
Moelwyn N7 5H 65
Moelyn M. HA1: Harr 5A 42
Moffat Ct. SW19 5J 135
Moffat Ho. SE5 7C 102
Moffat Rd. CR7: Thor H 2C 156
N13 6D 32
SW17 4D 136
Mogden La. TW7: Isle 5K 113
Mogul Bldg. E15 5E 68
(off Property Row)
Mohammedi Pk. UB5: N'olt 1E 76
Mohawk Ho. E3 2A 86
(off Gernon Rd.)
Mohmmad Khan Rd. E11 1H 69
Moineau NW9 1B 44
(off Long Mead)
Moira Cl. N17 2E 48
Moira Ho. SW9 1A 120
(off Gosling Way)
Moira Rd. SE9 4D 124
Mokswell Ct. N10 1E 46
Molasses Ho. SW11 3A 118
(off Clove Hitch Quay)
Molasses Row SW11 3A 118
Mole Abbey Gdns.
KT8: W Mole 3F 149
Mole Ct. KT19: Ewe 4J 163
Mole Ho. NW8 4B 4
(off Church St. Est.)
Molember Ct. KT8: E Mos 4J 149
Molember Rd. KT8: E Mos 5J 149
Mole Pl. KT8: W Mole 4F 149
Molescroft SE9 3G 143
Molesey Av. KT8: W Mole 5D 148
Molesey Dr. SM3: Cheam 2G 165
Molesey Heath Local Nature Reserve
6E 148
Molesey Pk. Av. KT8: W Mole 5F 149
Molesey Pk. Cl. KT8: E Mos 5G 149
Molesey Pk. Rd.
KT8: W Mole, E Mos 5F 149
Molesey Rd. KT8: W Mole 5C 148
KT12: Walt T 7C 148
Molesford Rd. SW6 1J 117
Molesham Cl. KT8: W Mole 3F 149
Molesham Way KT8: W Mole 3F 149
Molesworth Ho. SE17 6B 102
(off Brandon Est.)
Molesworth St. SE13 4E 122
Moliner Ct. BR3: Beck 7C 140
Mollis Ho. E3 5C 86
(off Gale St.)
Mollison Av.
EN3: Brim, Enf L, Enf W, Pond E
4F 25
Mollison Dr. SM6: W'gton 7H 167
Mollison Sq. SM6: W'gton 7H 167
(off Mollison Dr.)
Mollison Way HA8: Edg 2F 43
Molly Huggins Cl. SW12 7G 119
Molten Ct. SE14 6B 104
(off Moulding La.)
Molton Ho. N1 1K 83
(off Barnsbury Est.)
Molyneux Dr. SW17 4F 137
Molyneux St. W1 6D 4 (5C 82)
Monarch Cl. BR4: W W'ck 4H 171
TW14: Felt 7G 111
Monarch Ct. HA7: Stan 7J 27
(off Howard Rd.)
N2 5B 46
Monarch Dr. E16 5B 88
UB3: Hayes 7H 75
Monarch Ho. W8 3J 99
(off Kensington High St.)
Monarch M. E17 6D 50
SW16 5A 138
Monarch Pde. CR4: Mitc 2D 154
Monarch Pl. IG9: Buck H 2F 37
Monarch Point SW6 2A 118
Monarch Rd. DA17: Belv 3G 109
Monarch Sq. SW11 4C 118
Monarchs Way HA4: Ruis 1F 57
Monarch Way IG2: Ilf 6H 53
Mona Rd. SE15 2J 121
Monastery Gdns. EN2: Enf 2J 23
Mona St. E16 5H 87
Monaveen Gdns.
KT8: W Mole 3F 149
Monck Ho. SE1 7D 14
(off Cole St.)
Moncks Row SW18 6H 117
Monck St. SW1 2D 18 (3H 101)
Monckton Ct. W14 3H 99
(off Strangways Ter.)
Monclar Rd. SE5 4D 120
Moncorvo Cl. SW7 7C 10 (2C 100)
Moncrieff Cl. E6 6C 88
Moncrieff Pl. SE15 2G 121
Moncrieff St. SE15 2G 121
Monday All. N16 2F 67
(off High St.)
Mondial Way UB3: Harl 7E 92
Mondragon Ho. SW8 1J 119
(off Guildford Rd.)
Monega Rd. E7 6A 70
E12 6A 70
Monet Ct. SE16 5H 103
(off Stubbs Dr.)
Moneyer Ho. N1 1E 8
(off Provost St.)
Money La. UB7: W Dray 3A 92
Mongers Almshouses E9 7K 67
(off Church Cres.)
Monica Ct. EN1: Enf 5K 23
Monica James Ho. DA14: Sidc 3A 144
Monica Shaw Ct. NW1 1D 6
(off Purchese St.)
Monier Rd. E3 7C 68
Monivea Rd. BR3: Beck 7B 140
Monk Ct. W12 1C 98
Monk Dr. E16 7J 87
MONKEN HADLEY 2C 20
Monkfrith Av. N14 6A 22
Monkfrith Cl. N14 7A 22
Monkfrith Way N14 7K 21
Monkham's Av. IG8: Wfd G 5E 36
Monkham's Dr. IG8: Wfd G 5E 36
Monkham's La. IG8: Wfd G 5D 36
IG9: Buck H 3E 36
Monkleigh Rd. SM4: Mord 3G 153
Monks Av. EN5: New Bar 6F 21
KT8: W Mole 5D 148
Monks Cl. EN2: Enf 2H 23
HA2: Harr 2F 59
HA4: Ruis 4B 58
SE2 4D 108
Monks Cres. KT12: Walt T 7K 147
Monksdene Gdns.
SM1: Sutt 3K 165
Monks Dr. W3 5G 79
Monksfarm Pl. SE2 2B 108
MONKS ORCHARD 7A 158
Monks Orchard Rd. BR3: Beck 1C 170
Monks Pk. HA9: Wemb 6H 61
Monks Pk. Gdns.
HA9: Wemb 7H 61
Monks Rd. EN2: Enf 2G 23
Monk St. SE18 4E 106
Monks Way BR3: Beck 6C 158
BR5: Farnb 1G 173
NW11 4H 45
UB7: Harm 6A 92
Monkswood Gdns. IG5: Ilf 3E 52
Monkton Ho. E5 5H 67
SE16 2K 103
(off Wolfe Cres.)
Monkton Rd. DA16: Well 2K 125
Monkton St. SE11 3K 19 (4A 102)
Monkville Av. NW11 4H 45
Monkville Pde. NW11 4H 45
Monkwell Sq. EC2 6D 8 (5C 84)
Monmouth Av. E18 3K 51
KT1: Hamp W 7C 132
Monmouth Cl. CR4: Mitc 4J 155
DA16: Well 4A 126
W4 3J 97
Monmouth Ct. W7 5K 77
(off Copley Cl.)
Monmouth Gro. TW8: Bford 4E 96
Monmouth Pl. W2 6K 81
(off Monmouth Rd.)
Monmouth Rd. E6 3D 88
N9 2C 34
RM9: Dag 5F 73
UB3: Harl 4G 93
W2 6J 81
Monmouth St. WC2 1E 12 (6J 83)
Monnery Rd. N19 3G 65
Monnow Rd. SE1 5G 103
Mono La. TW13: Felt 2K 129
Monolulu Ct. SE17 5D 102
(off East St.)
Monoux Almshouses E17 4D 50
Monoux Gro. E17 1C 50
Monro Ct. E16 4H 87
Monroe Cres. EN1: Enf 1C 24
Monroe Dr. SW14 5H 115
Monroe Ho. NW8 2D 4
(off Lorne Cl.)
Monro Gdns. HA3: Hrw W 7D 26
Monro Way E5 4G 67
Monsell Ct. N4 3B 66
Monsell Rd. N4 3A 66
Monsey Pl. E1 4A 86
Monson Rd. NW10 2C 80
SE14 7K 103
Mons Way BR2: Broml 6C 160
Montacute Rd. CR0: New Ad 7E 170
SE6 7B 122
SM4: Mord 6B 154
WD23: B Hea 1E 26
Montagu Ct. W1 6F 5
(off Montagu Pl.)
Montagu Cres. N18 4C 34
Montague Av. SE4 4B 122
W7 1K 95
Montague Cl. EN5: Barn 4C 20
KT12: Walt T 7K 147
SE1 4E 14 (1D 102)
Montague Ct. DA15: Sidc 3A 144
N7 7A 66
(off St Clements St.)
Montague Gdns. W3 7G 79
Montague Ho. E16 1K 105
(off Wesley Av.)
IG3: Ilf 1A 72
N1 1E 84
(off Halcomb St.)
Montague M. E3 3B 86
(off Tredegar Ter.)
SE20 6J 139
Montague Pas. UB8: Uxb 7A 56
Montague Pl. WC1 5D 6 (5H 83)
Montague Rd. CR0: C'don 1B 168
E8 5G 67
E11 2H 69
N8 5K 47
N15 4G 49
SW19 7K 135
TW3: Houn 3F 113
TW10: Rich 6E 114
UB2: S'hall 4C 94
UB8: Uxb 7A 56
W7 1K 95
W13 6B 78
Montague Sq. SE15 7J 103
Montague St. EC1 6C 8 (5C 84)
WC1 5E 6 (5J 83)
Montague Ter. BR2: Broml 4H 159
Montague Walks
HA0: Wemb 1F 79
Montague Waye UB2: S'hall 3C 94
Montagu Gdns. N18 4C 34
SM6: W'gton 4G 167
Montagu Ind. Est. N18 4D 34
Montagu Mans. W1 5F 5 (5D 82)
Montagu M. Nth. W1 6F 5 (5D 82)
Montagu M. Sth. W1 7F 5 (6D 82)
Montagu M. W. W1 7F 5 (6D 82)
Montagu Pl. W1 6E 4 (5D 82)
Montagu Rd. N9 3E 34
N18 5C 34
NW4 6C 44
Montagu Row W1 6F 5 (5D 82)
Montagu Sq. W1 6F 5 (5D 82)
Montagu St. W1 7F 5 (6D 82)
Montaigne Cl. SW1 4D 18 (4H 101)
Montalt Rd. IG8: Wfd G 4C 36
Montana HA9: Wemb 4G 61
(off Exhibition Way)
Montana Bldg. SE13 1D 122
(off Deal's Gateway)
Montana Gdns. SE26 5B 140
SM1: Sutt 5A 166
Montana Rd. SW17 3E 136
SW20 1E 152
Montanaro Ct. N1 1C 84
(off Coleman Flds.)
Montbelle Rd. SE9 3F 143
Montcalm Cl. BR2: Hayes 6J 159
UB4: Yead 3K 75
Montcalm Ho. E14 4B 104
Montcalm Rd. SE7 7B 106
Montclare St. E2 3J 9 (4F 85)
Monteagle Av. IG11: Bark 6G 71
Monteagle Ct. N1 2E 84
Monteagle Way E5 3G 67
SE15 3H 121
Montefiore Ct. N16 1F 67
Montefiore St. SW8 2F 119
Montego Cl. SE24 4A 120
Montem Rd. KT3: N Mald 4A 152
SE23 7B 122
Montem St. N4 1K 65
Montenotte Rd. N8 5G 47
Monterey Apts. N15 5D 48
Monterey Cl. DA5: Bexl 2J 145
NW7 5F 29
(off The Broadway)
UB10: Hil 7C 56
Monterey Studios W10 2G 81
Montesole Ct. HA5: Pinn 2A 40
Montevetro SW11 1B 118
Montfichet Rd. E20 7E 68
Montford Pl. E15 2E 86
SE11 6J 19 (5A 102)
Montford Rd. TW16: Sun 4J 147
Montfort Ho. E2 3J 85
(off Victoria Pk. Sq.)
E14 3E 104
(off Galbraith St.)
Montfort Pl. SW19 1F 135
Montgolfier Wlk. UB5: N'olt 3C 76
Montgomerie M. SE23 7J 121
Montgomery Cl. CR4: Mitc 4J 155
DA15: Sidc 6K 125
Montgomery Ct. CR2: S Croy 5E 168
(off Birdhurst Rd.)
W4 7J 97
Montgomery Gdns. SM2: Sutt 7B 166
Montgomery Ho. UB5: N'olt 3D 76
(off Taywood Rd.)
W2 6A 4
(off Harrow Rd.)
Montgomery Lodge E1 4J 85
(off Cleveland Gro.)
Montgomery Rd. HA8: Edg 6A 28
W4 4J 97
Montgomery Sq. E14 1D 104
Montgomery St. E14 1D 104
Montholme Rd. SW11 6D 118
Monthope Rd. E1 6K 9 (5G 85)
Montolieu Gdns. SW15 5D 116
Montpelier Av. DA5: Bexl 7D 126
W5 5C 78
Montpelier Cl. UB10: Hil 1C 74
Montpelier Ct. BR2: Broml 4H 159
(off Westmoreland Rd.)
W5 5D 78
Montpelier Gdns. E6 3B 88
RM6: Chad H 7C 54
Montpelier Gro. NW5 5G 65
Montpelier M. SW7 1D 16 (3C 100)
Montpelier Pl. E1 6J 85
SW7 1D 16 (3C 100)
Montpelier Ri. HA9: Wemb 1D 60
NW11 7G 45
(not continuous)
Montpelier Rd. N3 1A 46
SE15 1H 121
SM1: Sutt 4A 166
W5 5D 78
Montpelier Row SE3 2H 123
TW1: Twick 7C 114
Montpelier Sq. SW7 7D 10 (2C 100)
Montpelier St. SW7 1D 16 (3C 100)
Montpelier Ter. SW7 7D 10 (2C 100)
Montpelier Va. SE3 2H 123
Montpelier Wlk. SW7 1D 16 (3C 100)
Montpelier Way NW11 7G 45
Montpellier Ct. KT12: Walt T 6J 147
Montrave Rd. SE20 6J 139
Montreal Ho. SE16 2K 103
(off Maple M.)
UB4: Yead 3K 75
(off Ayles Rd.)
Montreal Pl. WC2 2G 13 (7K 83)
Montreal Rd. IG1: Ilf 7G 53
Montrell Rd. SW2 1J 137
Montrose Av. DA15: Sidc 7A 126
DA16: Well 3H 125
HA8: Edg 2J 43
NW6 2G 81
TW2: Whitt 7F 113
Montrose Cl. DA16: Well 3K 125
IG8: Wfd G 4D 36
TW15: Ashf 6E 128
Montrose Ct. HA1: Harr 5F 41
NW9 2J 43
NW11 4H 45
SE6 2H 141
SW7 7B 10 (2B 100)
Montrose Cres. HA0: Wemb 6E 60
N12 6F 31
Montrose Gdns. CR4: Mitc 2D 154
SM1: Sutt 2K 165
Montrose Ho. E14 3C 104
SW1 7H 11
(off Montrose Pl.)
Montrose Pl. SW1 7H 11 (2E 100)
Montrose Rd. HA3: W'stone 2J 41
TW14: Bedf 6F 111
Montrose Wlk. HA7: Stan 6G 27
Montrose Way SE23 1K 139
Montserrat Av. IG8: Wfd G 7A 36
Montserrat Cl. SE19 5D 138
Montserrat Rd. SW15 4G 117
The Monument 3F 15 (7D 84)
Monument Gdns. SE13 5E 122
Monument St. EC3 2F 15 (7D 84)
Monument Way N15 3F 49
N17 3F 49
Monza St. E1 7J 85
Moodkee St. SE16 3J 103
Moody Rd. SE15 1F 121
Moody St. E1 3K 85
Moon Ct. SE12 4J 123
Moon Ho. HA1: Harr 4J 41
Moon La. EN5: Barn 3C 20
Moonlight Dr. SE23 7H 121
Moonraker Point SE1 6B 14
(off Pocock St.)
Moon St. N1 1B 84
Moorcroft HA8: Edg 1H 43
Moorcroft Gdns. BR2: Broml 5C 160
Moorcroft La. UB8: Hil 5C 74
Moorcroft Rd. SW16 3J 137
Moorcroft Way HA5: Pinn 5C 40
Moordown SE18 7F 107
Moore Cl. CR4: Mitc 2F 155
SW14 3J 115
Moore Ct. HA0: Wemb 6E 60
HA7: Stan 1D 42
N1 1B 84
(off Gaskin St.)
Moore Cres. RM9: Dag 1B 90
Moorefield Rd. N17 2F 49
Moorehead Way SE3 3J 123
Moore Ho. E1 7J 85
(off Cable St.)
E2 3J 85
(off Roman Rd.)
E14 2C 104
N8 4J 47
(off Pembroke Rd.)
SE10 5H 105
(off Armitage Rd.)
SW1 6J 17
Mooreland Rd. BR1: Broml 7H 141
Moore Pk. Rd. SW6 7J 99
Moore Rd. SE19 6C 138
Moore St. SW3 3E 16 (4D 100)
Moore Wlk. E7 4J 69
Moore Way SM2: Sutt 7J 165
Moorey Cl. E15 1H 87
Moorfield Av. W5 4D 78
Moorfield Rd. EN3: Enf H 1D 24
KT9: Chess 5E 162
UB8: Cowl 6A 74
Moorfields EC2 6E 8 (5D 84)
Moorfields Highwalk EC2 6E 8
(off New Union St.)
Moorgate EC2 7E 8 (6D 84)
Moorgate Pl. EC2 7E 8
Moorgreen Ho. EC1 1A 8
Moorhen Dr. NW9 6B 44
Moorhen Ho. E3 1B 86
(off Old Ford Rd.)
Moorhouse NW9 1B 44
Moorhouse Rd. HA3: Kenton 3D 42
W2 6J 81
The Moorings E16 5A 88
(off Prince Regent La.)
Moorings Ho. TW8: Bford 7C 96
MOOR JUNC. 3C 174
Moorland Cl. RM5: Col R 1H 55
TW2: Whitt 7E 112
Moorland Rd. SW9 4B 120
UB7: Harm 2D 174
Moorlands UB5: N'olt 1C 76
Moorlands Av. NW7 6J 29
Moor La. EC2 6E 8 (5D 84)
(not continuous)
KT9: Chess 4E 162
UB7: Harm 2D 174
Moormead Dr. KT19: Ewe 5A 164
Moor Mead Rd. TW1: Twick 6A 114
Moor Pk. Gdns. KT2: King T 7A 134
Moor Pl. EC2 6E 8 (5D 84)
Moorside Rd. BR1: Broml 3G 141
Moor St. W1 1D 12 (6H 83)
Moot Ct. NW9 5G 43
Moran Ho. E1 1H 103
(off Wapping La.)
Morant Pl. N22 1K 47
Morant St. E14 7C 86
Mora Rd. NW2 4E 62
Mora St. EC1 2D 8 (3C 84)
Morat St. SW9 1K 119
Moravian Cl. SW10 7A 16 (6B 100)
Moravian Pl. SW10 6B 100
Moravian St. E2 2J 85
Moray Av. UB3: Hayes 1H 93
Moray Cl. HA8: Edg 2C 28
RM1: Rom 1K 55
Moray Ct. CR2: S Croy 5C 168
(off Warham Rd.)
Moray Ho. E1 4A 86
(off Harford St.)
Moray M. N7 2K 65
Moray Rd. N4 2K 65
Moray Way RM1: Rom 1K 55
Mordaunt Gdns. RM9: Dag 7E 72
Mordaunt Ho. NW10 1K 79
(off Stracey Rd.)
Mordaunt Rd. NW10 1K 79
Mordaunt St. SW9 3K 119
MORDEN 3K 153
Morden Ct. SM4: Mord 4K 153
Morden Ct. Pde. SM4: Mord 4K 153
Morden Gdns. CR4: Mitc 4B 154
UB6: G'frd 5K 59
Morden Hall Pk. 3A 154
Morden Hall Rd. SM4: Mord 3K 153
Morden Hill SE13 2E 122
Morden Ho. SM4: Mord 4J 153
Morden La. SE13 2E 122
Morden Leisure Centre 5H 153
MORDEN PARK 6G 153
Morden Rd. CR4: Mitc 4A 154
RM6: Chad H 7E 54
SE3 2J 123
SM4: Mord 4A 154
SW19 1K 153
Morden Rd. M. SE3 2J 123
Morden St. SE13 1D 122
Morden Way SM3: Sutt 7J 153
Morden Wharf SE10 3G 105
(off Morden Wharf Rd.)
Morden Wharf Rd. SE10 3G 105
Mordern Ho. NW1 3D 4
Mordon Rd. IG3: Ilf 7K 53
Morea M. N5 5C 66
Morecambe Cl. E1 5K 85
Morecambe Gdns. HA7: Stan 4J 27
Morecambe St. SE17 4C 102
Morecambe Ter. N18 4J 33
(off Gt. Cambridge Rd.)
More Cl. E16 6H 87
W14 4F 99
Morecoombe Cl. KT2: King T 7H 133
More Copper Ho. SE1 5G 15
(off Magdalen St.)
Moree Way N18 4B 34
Moreland Cotts. E3 2C 86
(off Fairfield Rd.)
Moreland Ct. NW2 3J 63
Moreland St. EC1 1B 8 (3B 84)
Moreland Way E4 3J 35
Morella Rd. SW12 7D 118
Morell Cl. EN5: New Bar 3F 21
Morello Av. UB8: Hil 5D 74
Morel M. RM8: Dag 1D 72
More London Pl.
SE1 5G 15 (1E 102)
(not continuous)
More London Riverside
SE1 5H 15 (1E 102)
(not continuous)
Moremead Rd. SE6 4B 140
Morena St. SE6 7D 122
Moreno Ho. E2 2H 85
(off Esker Pl.)
Moresby Av. KT5: Surb 7H 151
Moresby Rd. E5 1H 67
Moresby Wlk. SW8 2G 119
More's Gdn. SW3 7B 16
Moreton Av. TW7: Isle 1J 113
Moreton Cl. E5 2H 67
N15 6D 48
NW7 6K 29
SW1 5B 18
Moreton Gdns. IG8: Wfd G 5H 37
Moreton Ho. SE16 3H 103
Moreton Pl.
SW1 5B 18 (5G 101)
Moreton Rd. CR2: S Croy 5D 168
KT4: Wor Pk 2C 164
N15 6D 48
Moretons HA1: Harr 1J 59
Moreton St.
SW1 5B 18 (5G 101)
Moreton Ter. SW1 5B 18 (5G 101)
Moreton Ter. M. Nth.
SW1 5B 18 (5G 101)
Moreton Ter. M. Sth.
SW1 5B 18 (5G 101)
Moreton Twr. W3 1H 97
Morford Cl. HA4: Ruis 7K 39
Morford Way HA4: Ruis 7K 39
Morgan Av. E17 4F 51
Morgan Cl. RM10: Dag 7G 73
Morgan Ct. SM5: Cars 4D 166
TW15: Ashf 5D 128
Morgan Cres. RM8: Dag 1E 72
Morgan Ho. SW1 4B 18
(off Vauxhall Bri. Rd.)
SW8 1G 119
(off Wadhurst Rd.)
Morgan Mans. N7 5A 66
(off Morgan Rd.)
Morgan Rd. BR1: Broml 7J 141
N7 5A 66
W10 5H 81
Morgan's La. UB3: Hayes 5F 75
Morgans La. SE1 5G 15
(off Tooley St.)
Morgan St. E3 3A 86
(not continuous)
E16 5H 87
Morgan Wlk. BR3: Beck 4D 158
Morgan Way IG8: Wfd G 6H 37
Moriarty Cl. BR1: Broml 4E 160
Moriatry Cl. N7 4J 65
Morie St. SW18 5K 117
Morieux Rd. E10 1B 68
Moring Rd. SW17 4E 136
Morkyns Wlk. SE21 3E 138
Morland Av. CR0: C'don 1E 168
Morland Cl. CR4: Mitc 3C 154
NW11 1K 63
TW12: Hamp 5D 130
Morland Ct. W12 2D 98
(off Coningham Rd.)
Morland Est. E8 7G 67
Morland Gdns. NW10 7K 61
UB1: S'hall 1F 95
Morland Ho. NW1 1B 6
(off Werrington St.)
NW6 1J 81
SW1 3E 18
(off Marsham St.)
W11 6G 81
(off Lancaster Rd.)
Morland M. N1 7A 66
Morland Pl. N15 4E 48
Morland Rd. CR0: C'don 1E 168
E17 5K 49
HA3: Kenton 5E 42
IG1: Ilf 2F 71
RM10: Dag 7G 73
SE20 6K 139
SM1: Sutt 5A 166
Morley Av. E4 7A 36
N18 4B 34
N22 2A 48
Morley Cl. BR6: Farnb 2F 173
Morley Ct. BR2: Broml 4H 159
E4 5G 35
Morley Cres. HA4: Ruis 2A 58
HA8: Edg 2D 28
Morley Cres. E. HA7: Stan 2C 42
Morley Cres. W. HA7: Stan 3C 42
Morley Hill EN2: Enf 1J 23
Morley Ho. SE15 7F 103
(off Commercial Way)
Morley Rd. BR7: Chst 1G 161
E10 1E 68
E15 2H 87
IG11: Bark 1H 89
RM6: Chad H 5E 54
SE13 4E 122
SM3: Sutt 1H 165
TW1: Twick 6D 114
Morley St. SE1 1K 19 (3A 102)
Morna Rd. SE5 2C 120
Morning La. E9 6J 67
Morningside Rd.
KT4: Wor Pk 2E 164
Mornington Av. BR1: Broml 3A 160
IG1: Ilf 7E 52
W14 4H 99
Mornington Av. Mans. W14 4H 99
(off Mornington Av.)
Mornington Cl. IG8: Wfd G 4D 36
NW9 3A 44

A-Z Big London 257

Mornigton Ct.—Musway Hill B'way

Mornington Ct. DA5: Bexl 1K 145
NW1 2G 83
(off Mornington Cres.)
Mornington Cres. NW1 2G 83
TW5: Cran 1K 111
Mornington Gro. E3 3C 86
Mornington M. SE5 1C 120
Mornington Pl. NW1 2G 83
SE8 7B 104
(off Mornington Rd.)
Mornington Rd. E4 7K 25, 1A 36
E11 7H 51
IG8: Wfd G 4C 36
SE8 7B 104
TW15: Ashf 5E 128
UB6: G'frd 5F 77
Mornington St. NW1 2F 83
Mornington Ter. NW1 1F 83
Mornington Wlk. TW10: Ham 4C 132
Moro Apts. E14 6C 86
(off New Festival Av.)
Morocco St. SE1 7G 15 (2E 102)
Morocco Wharf E1 1H 103
(off Wapping High St.)
Morpeth Gro. E9 1K 85
Morpeth Mans. SW1 2A 18
(off Morpeth Ter.)
Morpeth Rd. E9 1K 85
Morpeth St. E2 3J 85
Morpeth Ter. SW1 2A 18 (3G 101)
Morpeth Wlk. N17 7C 34
Morphou Rd. NW7 6B 30
Morrab Gdns. IG3: Ilf 3K 71
Morrel Ct. E2 2G 85
(off Goldsmiths Row)
Morrells Yd. SE11 5K 19
(off Cleaver St.)
Morris Av. E12 5D 70
UB8: Uxb 6A 56
Morris Blitz Ct. N16 4F 67
Morris Cl. BR6: Orp 3J 173
CR0: C'don 5A 158
Morris Ct. E4 3J 35
Morris Dr. DA17: Erith 4J 109
Morris Gdns. SW18 7J 117
Morris Ho. E2 3J 85
(off Roman Rd.)
NW8 4C 4
(off Salisbury St.)
W3 2B 98
Morrish Rd. SW2 7J 119
Morris M. SW19 5A 136
Morrison Av. E4 6H 35
N17 3E 48
Morrison Bldgs. Nth. E1 6G 85
(off Commercial Rd.)
Morrison Ct. EN5: Barn 4B 20
(off Manor Way)
N12 7H 31
SW1 1D 18
(off Gt. Smith St.)
Morrison Ho. SW2 1A 138
(off Tulse Hill)
Morrison Rd. IG11: Bark 2E 90
RM9: Bark, Dag 2E 90
SW9 2A 120
UB4: Yead 3K 75
Morrison St. SW11 3E 118
Morris Pl. N4 2A 66
Morris Rd. E14 5D 86
E15 4G 69
RM8: Dag 2F 73
TW7: Isle 3K 113
Morriss Ho. SE16 2H 103
(off Cherry Gdn. St.)
Morris St. E1 6H 85
Morritt Ho. HA0: Wemb 5D 60
(off Talbot Rd.)
Morse Cl. E13 3J 87
Morshead Mans. W9 3J 81
(off Morshead Rd.)
Morshead Rd. W9 3J 81
Morson Rd. EN3: Pond E 6F 25
Morston Gdns. SE9 4D 142
Mortain Ho. SE16 4H 103
(off Roseberry St.)
Morten Cl. SW4 6H 119
Morteyne Rd. N17 1D 48
Mortgramit Sq. SE18 3E 106
Mortham St. E15 1G 87
Mortimer Cl. NW2 2H 63
SW16 2H 137
Mortimer Ct. NW8 1A 4
(off Abbey Rd.)
Mortimer Cres. KT4: Wor Pk 3K 163
NW6 1K 81
Mortimer Dr. EN1: Enf 5K 23
Mortimer Est. NW6 1K 81
(off Mortimer Pl.)
Mortimer Ho. W11 1F 99
W14 4G 99
(off North End Rd.)
Mortimer Mkt. WC1 4B 6 (4G 83)
Mortimer Pl. NW6 1K 81
Mortimer Rd. CR4: Mitc 1D 154
DA8: Erith 6K 109
E6 3D 88
N1 7E 66
(not continuous)
NW10 3E 80
W13 6C 78
Mortimer Sq. W11 7F 81
Mortimer St. W1 7K 5 (6G 83)
Mortimer Ter. NW5 4F 65
MORTLAKE 3K 115
Mortlake Cl. CR0: Bedd 3J 167
Mortlake Crematorium 2H 115
Mortlake Dr. CR4: Mitc 1C 154
Mortlake High St. SW14 3K 115
Mortlake Rd. E16 6K 87
IG1: Ilf 4G 71
TW9: Kew, Rich 7G 97
Mortlake Ter. TW9: Kew 7G 97
(off Mortlake Rd.)
Mortlock Cl. SE15 1H 121
Mortlock Ct. E7 4B 70
Morton Apts. E16 7G 89
(off Lock Side Way)
Morton Cl. E1 6J 85
SM6: W'gton 7K 167
UB8: Hil 4B 74
Morton Ct. UB5: N'olt 5G 59
Morton Cres. N14 4C 32
Morton Gdns. SM6: W'gton 5G 167
Morton Ho. SE17 6B 102
Morton M. SW5 4K 99
Morton Pl. SE1 2J 19 (3A 102)
Morton Rd. E15 7H 69
N1 7C 66
SM4: Mord 5B 154
Morton Way N14 3B 32
Morvale Cl. DA17: Belv 4F 109
Morval Rd. SW2 5A 120
Morven Rd. SW17 3D 136
Morville Ho. SW18 6B 118
(off Fitzhugh Gro.)
Morville St. E3 2C 86
Morwell St. WC1 6C 6 (5H 83)
Moscow Mans. SW5 4J 99
(off Cromwell Rd.)
Moscow Pl. W2 7K 81
Moscow Rd. W2 7J 81
Mosedale NW1 2K 5
(off Cumberland Mkt.)
Moseley Row SE10 4H 105
Moselle Av. N22 2A 48
Moselle Cl. N8 3K 47
Moselle Ho. N17 7A 34
(off William St.)
Moselle Pl. N17 7A 34
Moselle St. N17 7A 34
Mosque Ter. E1 5G 85
(off Whitechapel Rd.)
Mosque Twr. E1 5G 85
(off Fieldgate St.)
E3 2A 86
(off Ford St.)
Mosquito Cl. SM6: W'gton 7J 167
Mossborough Cl. N12 6E 30
Mossbury Rd. SW11 3C 118
Moss Cl. E1 5G 85
HA5: Pinn 2D 40
N9 1B 34
Mossdown Cl. DA17: Belv 4G 109
Mossford Ct. IG6: Ilf 3F 53
Mossford Grn. IG6: Ilf 3F 53
Mossford La. IG6: Ilf 2F 53
Mossford St. E3 4B 86
Moss Gdns. CR2: Sels 7K 169
TW13: Felt 2J 129
Moss Hall Ct. N12 6E 30
Moss Hall Cres. N12 6E 30
Moss Hall Gro. N12 6E 30
Mossington Gdns. SE16 4J 103
Moss La. HA5: Pinn 1C 40
Mosslea Rd. BR2: Broml 5B 160
BR6: Farnb 3G 173
SE20 6J 139
(not continuous)
Mossop St. SW3 3D 16 (4C 100)
Moss Rd. RM10: Dag 7G 73
Mossville Gdns. SM4: Mord 3H 153
Mosswell Ho. N10 1E 46
Moston Cl. UB3: Harl 5H 93
Mostyn Av. HA9: Wemb 5F 61
Mostyn Gdns. NW10 3F 81
Mostyn Gro. E3 2C 86
Mostyn Rd. HA8: Edg 7F 29
SW9 1A 120
SW19 1H 153
Mosul Way BR2: Broml 6C 160
Motcomb St. SW1 1G 17 (3E 100)
Moth Cl. SM6: W'gton 7J 167
Mothers Sq. E5 4H 67
Motley Av. EC2 4G 9
MOTSPUR PARK 6C 152
Motspur Pk. KT3: N Mald 6B 152
MOTTINGHAM 2C 142
Mottingham Gdns. SE9 1B 142
Mottingham La. SE9 1A 142
SE12 1A 142
Mottingham Rd. N9 6E 24
SE9 2C 142
Mottisfont Rd. SE2 3A 108
Mottistone Gro. SM2: Sutt 7K 165
Motts La. RM8: Dag 2F 73
Mott St. E4 1K 25
Moulding La. SE14 6A 104
Moules Ct. SE5 7C 102
Moulins Rd. E9 7J 67
Moulsford Ho. N7 5H 65
W2 5J 81
(off Westbourne Pk. Rd.)
Moulton Av. TW3: Houn 2C 112
The Mound SE9 3E 142
Moundfield Rd. N16 6G 49
Mounsey Ho. W10 3G 81
(off Third Av.)
The Mount BR1: Broml 1C 160
CR2: S Croy 5C 168
(off Warham Rd.)
DA6: Bex 5H 127
E5 2H 67
(not continuous)
HA9: Wemb 2H 61
KT3: N Mald 3B 152
KT4: Wor Pk 4D 164
N20 2F 31
NW3 3A 64
UB5: N'olt 5F 59
W3 1J 97
W8 1J 99
(off Bedford Gdns.)
Mountacre Cl. SE26 4F 139
Mt. Adon Pk. SE22 7G 121
Mountague Pl. E14 7E 86
Mountain Ho. SE11 4H 19 (4K 101)
Mt. Angelus Rd. SW15 7B 116
Mt. Ararat Rd.
TW10: Rich 5E 114
Mt. Arlington BR2: Broml 2G 159
(off Park Hill Rd.)
Mt. Ash Rd. SE26 3H 139
Mount Av. E4 3H 35
UB1: S'hall 6E 76
W5 5C 78
Mountbatten Cl. SE18 6J 107
SE19 5E 138
Mountbatten Ct. IG9: Buck H 2G 37
SE16 1J 103
(off Rotherhithe St.)
Mountbatten Gdns. BR3: Beck 4A 158
Mountbatten Ho. N6 7E 46
(off Hillcrest)
Mountbatten M. SW18 7A 118
Mountbel Rd. HA7: Stan 1A 42
Mt. Carmel Chambers W8 2J 99
(off Dukes La.)
Mount Cl. BR1: Broml 1C 160
EN4: Cockf 4K 21
SM5: Cars 7E 166
W5 5C 78
Mountcombe Cl. KT6: Surb 7E 150
Mount Ct. BR4: W W'ck 2G 171
SW15 3G 117
Mt. Culver Av. DA14: Sidc 6D 144
Mount Dr. DA6: Bex 5E 126
HA2: Harr 5D 40
HA9: Wemb 2J 61
Mountearl Gdns. SW16 3K 137
Mt. Eaton Ct. W5 5C 78
(off Mount Av.)
Mt. Echo Av. E4 2J 35
Mt. Echo Dr. E4 1J 35
Mt. Ephraim La. SW16 3H 137
Mt. Ephraim Rd. SW16 3H 137
Mount Felix KT12: Walt T 7H 147
Mountfield Cl. SE6 7F 123
Mountfield Rd. E6 2E 88
N3 3H 45
W5 6D 78
Mountfield Ter. SE6 7F 123
Mountford Mans. SW11 1E 118
(off Battersea Pk. Rd.)
Mountfort Cres. N1 7A 66
Mountfort Ho. N1 7A 66
(off Barnsbury Sq.)
Mountfort Ter. N1 7A 66
Mount Gdns. SE26 3H 139
Mount Gro. HA8: Edg 3D 28
Mountgrove Rd. N5 3B 66
Mount Holme KT7: T Ditt 7B 150
Mounthurst Rd. BR2: Hayes 7H 159
Mountington Pk. Cl.
HA3: Kenton 6D 42
Mountjoy Cl. EC2 6D 8
(off Monkwell Sq.)
SE2 2B 108
Mountjoy Ho. EC2 6C 8
Mount Lodge N6 6G 47
Mount M. TW12: Hamp 1F 149
Mount Mills EC1 2B 8 (3B 84)
Mt. Nod Rd. SW16 3K 137
Mt. Olive Ct. W7 2J 95
Mount Pde. EN4: Cockf 4H 21
Mount Pk. SM5: Cars 7E 166
Mount Pk. Av. CR2: S Croy 7B 168
HA1: Harr 2H 59
Mount Pk. Cres. W5 6D 78
Mount Pk. Rd. HA1: Harr 3H 59
HA5: Eastc 5J 39
W5 5D 78
Mount Pl. W3 1H 97
Mt. Pleasant EN4: Cockf 4H 21
HA0: Wemb 1E 78
HA4: Ruis 2A 58
IG1: Ilf 5G 71
SE27 4C 138
WC1 4J 7 (4A 84)
Mt. Pleasant Cotts. N14 7C 22
(off The Wells)
Mt. Pleasant Cres. N4 1K 65
Mt. Pleasant Hill E5 2H 67
Mt. Pleasant La. E5 1H 67
Mt. Pleasant M. N4 1K 65
(off Mt. Pleasant Cres.)
Mt. Pleasant Pl. SE18 4H 107
Mt. Pleasant Rd. E17 2A 50
KT3: N Mald 3J 151
N17 2E 48
NW10 7E 62
SE13 6D 122
W5 4C 78
Mt. Pleasant Vs. N4 7K 47
Mt. Pleasant Wlk. DA5: Bexl 5J 127
Mount Rd. CR4: Mitc 2B 154
DA6: Bex 5D 126
EN4: E Barn 5H 21
KT3: N Mald 3K 151
KT9: Chess 5F 163
NW2 3D 62
NW4 6C 44
RM8: Dag 1F 73
SE19 6D 138
SW19 2J 135
TW13: Hanw 3C 130
UB3: Hayes 2J 93
Mount Row W1 3J 11 (7F 83)
Mountsfield Ct. SE13 6F 123
Mountsfield Ho. SE10 1E 122
(off Primrose Way)
Mountside HA7: Stan 1A 42
Mounts Pond Rd. SE3 2F 123
(not continuous)
The Mount Sq. NW3 3A 64
Mt. Stewart Av. HA3: Kenton 7D 42
Mount St. W1 3G 11 (7E 82)
Mount St. M. W1 3J 11 (7F 83)
Mountstuart Ct.
TW11: Hamp W 1B 150
Mount Ter. E1 5H 85
Mount Vernon NW3 4A 64
Mount Vw. EN2: Enf 1E 22
NW7 3E 28
UB2: S'hall 4B 94
W5 4D 78
Mountview Cl. NW11 1K 63
Mountview Ct. N8 4B 48
Mount Vw. Rd. E4 7K 25, 1A 36
KT10: Clay 7B 162
N4 7J 47
NW9 5K 43
Mountview Rd.
BR6: Orp, St M Cry 7K 161
(not continuous)
Mount Vs. SE27 3B 138
Mount Way SM5: Cars 7E 166
Mountwood KT8: W Mole 3F 149
MOVERS LANE 2J 89
Movers La. IG11: Bark 1H 89
Mowat Ct. KT4: Wor Pk 2B 164
(off The Avenue)
Mowatt Cl. N19 1H 65
Mowbray Ct. N22 1A 48
SE19 7F 139
Mowbray Gdns. UB5: N'olt 1E 76
Mowbray Ho. N2 2B 46
(off The Grange)
Mowbray Pde. HA8: Edg 4B 28
Mowbray Rd.
EN5: New Bar 5F 21
HA8: Edg 4B 28
NW6 7G 63
SE19 1F 157
TW10: Ham 3C 132
Mowbrays Cl. RM5: Col R 1J 55
Mowbrays Rd. RM5: Col R 2J 55
Mowlem St. E2 2H 85
Mowlem Trad. Est. N17 7D 34
Mowll St. SW9 7A 102
Moxon Cl. E13 2H 87
Moxon Pl. UB10: Uxb 1B 74
Moxon St. EN5: Barn 3C 20
W1 6G 5 (5E 82)
Moye Cl. E2 2G 85
Moyers Rd. E10 7E 50
Moy La. SE18 5F 107
Moylan Rd. W6 6G 99
Moyle Ho. DA17: Belv 2H 109
SW1 6B 18
(off Churchill Gdns.)
Moyne Ho. SW9 5B 120
Moyne Pl. NW10 2G 79
Moynihan Dr. N21 5D 22
Moys Cl. CR0: C'don 6J 155
Moyser Rd. SW16 5F 137
Mozart St. W10 3H 81
Mozart Ter. SW1 4H 17 (4E 100)
MTV Europe 7F 65
Muchelney Rd. SM4: Mord 6A 154
Mudchute Park & Farm 4E 104
Mudlarks Blvd. SE10 3H 105
Mudlarks Way SE10 3J 105
Muggeridge Cl.
CR2: S Croy 5D 168
Muggeridge Rd.
RM10: Dag 4H 73
Muirdown Av. SW14 4K 115
Muir Dr. SW18 6C 118
Muirfield W3 6A 80
Muirfield Cl. SE16 5H 103
Muirfield Cres. E14 3D 104
Muirhead Quay IG11: Bark 2G 89
Muirkirk Rd. SE6 1E 140
Muir Rd. E5 3G 67
Muir St. E16 1C 106
(not continuous)
Mulberry Apts. N4 1C 66
(off Coster Av.)
Mulberry Av. TW19: Stanw 1A 128
Mulberry Cl. E4 2H 35
EN4: E Barn 4G 21
N8 5J 47
NW3 4B 64
NW4 3E 44
SE7 6B 106
SE22 5G 121
SW3 6B 100
(off Beaufort St.)
SW16 4G 137
TW13: Felt 3K 129
UB5: N'olt 2C 76
Mulberry Ct. DA1: Cray 5K 127
E11 4F 69
(off Langthorne Rd.)
EC1 2B 8
(off Tompion St.)
IG11: Bark 6K 71
KT6: Surb 7D 150
N2 3C 46
(off Bedford Rd.)
SW3 7B 16 (6B 100)
(not continuous)
TW1: Twick 3K 131
W9 3H 81
(off Ashmore Rd.)
Mulberry Cres. TW8: Bford 7B 96
UB7: W Dray 2C 92
Mulberry Ho. BR2: Broml 1G 159
E2 3J 85
(off Victoria Pk. Sq.)
SE8 6B 104
SE10 1E 122
(off Parkside Av.)
Mulberry Housing Co-operative
SE1 4K 13
Mulberry La. CR0: C'don 1F 169
Mulberry M. SE14 1B 122
SM6: W'gton 6G 167
Mulberry Pde. UB7: W Dray 3C 92
Mulberry Pl. E14 7E 86
(off Clove Cres.)
HA2: Harr 2H 41
SE9 4B 124
W6 5C 98
Mulberry Rd. E8 7F 67
Mulberry St. E1 6G 85
Mulberry Tree M. W4 2J 97
Mulberry Trees TW17: Shep 7F 147
Mulberry Wlk. SW3 7B 16 (6B 100)
Mulberry Way DA17: Belv 2J 109
E18 2K 51
IG6: Ilf 4G 53
Mulgrave Ct. SM2: Sutt 6K 165
(off Mulgrave Rd.)
Mulgrave Rd. CR0: C'don 3D 168
HA1: Harr 2A 60
NW10 4B 62
SE18 4D 106
SM2: Sutt 7H 165
SW6 6H 99
W5 3D 78
Mulholland Cl. CR4: Mitc 2F 155
Mulkern Rd. N19 1H 65
(not continuous)
Mullards Cl. CR4: Mitc 1D 166
Mullen Twr. WC1 4J 7
(off Mt. Pleasant)
Mullet Gdns. E2 3G 85
Mulletsfield WC1 2F 7
(off Cromer St.)
Mull Ho. E3 2B 86
(off Stafford Rd.)
Mulligans Apts. NW6 7J 63
(off Kilburn High Rd.)
Mullins Path SW14 3K 115
Mullins Pl. SW4 7J 119
Mullion Cl. HA3: Hrw W 1F 41
Mull Wlk. N1 6C 66
(off Clephane Rd.)
Mulready Ho. SW1 4E 18
(off Marsham St.)
Mulready St. NW8 4C 4 (4C 82)
Multi Way W3 2A 98
Multon Ho. E9 7J 67
Multon Rd. SW18 7B 118
Mulvaney Way SE1 7F 15 (2D 102)
(not continuous)
Mumford Mills SE10 1D 122
(off Greenwich High Rd.)
Mumford Rd. SE24 5B 120
Muncaster Cl. TW15: Ashf 4C 128
Muncaster Rd. SW11 5D 118
TW15: Ashf 5D 128
Muncies M. SE6 2E 140
Mundania Ct. SE22 6H 121
Mundania Rd. SE22 6H 121
Munday Ho. SE1 3D 102
(off Burbage Cl.)
Munday Rd. E16 7J 87
Munden Ho. E3 3D 86
(off Bromley High St.)
Munden St. W14 4G 99
Mundford Rd. E5 2J 67
Mundon Gdns. IG1: Ilf 1H 71
Mund St. W14 5H 99
Mundy Ho. W10 3G 81
(off Dart St.)
Mundy St. N1 1G 9 (3E 84)
Mungo Pk. Cl.
WD23: B Hea 2B 26
Munkenbeck Bldg. W2 6A 4
(off Hermitage St.)
Munnery Way BR6: Farnb 3E 172
Munnings Gdns. TW7: Isle 5H 113
Munnings Ho. E16 1K 105
(off Portsmouth M.)
Munro Dr. N11 6B 32
Munro Ho. SE1 7J 13 (2A 102)
Munro M. W10 5G 81
(not continuous)
Munro Ter. SW10 7B 100
Munslow Gdns. SM1: Sutt 4B 166
Munster Av. TW4: Houn 5C 112
Munster Ct. SW6 2H 117
TW11: Tedd 6C 132
Munster Gdns. N13 4G 33
Munster M. SW6 7G 99
Munster Rd. SW6 7G 99
TW11: Tedd 6B 132
Munster Sq. NW1 2K 5 (3F 83)
Munster Ter. E13 3A 88
Munton Rd. SE17 4C 102
Muratori Ho. WC1 2J 7
(off Margery St.)
Murchison Av. DA5: Bexl 1D 144
Murchison Ho. W10 5G 81
(off Ladbroke Gro.)
Murchison Rd. E10 2E 68
Murdoch Ho. SE16 3J 103
(off Moodkee St.)
Murdock Cl. E16 6H 87
Murdock St. SE15 6H 103
Murfett Cl. SW19 2G 135
Muriel St. N1 2K 83
(not continuous)
Murillo Rd. SE13 4F 123
Muro Ct. SE1 7B 14
(off Milcote St.)
Murphy Ho. SE1 7B 14
(off Borough Rd.)
Murphy St. SE1 7J 13 (2A 102)
Murrain Rd. N4 2C 66
Murray Av. BR1: Broml 3K 159
TW3: Houn 5F 113
Murray Cl. SE28 1J 107
Murray Ct. E3 5B 86
(off Geoff Cade Way)
HA1: Harr 6K 41
TW2: Twick 2H 131
W7 2J 95
Murray Cres. HA5: Pinn 1B 40
Murray Gro. N1 1D 8 (2C 84)
Murray Ho. SE18 4D 106
(off Rideout St.)
Murray M. NW1 7H 65
Murray Rd. HA6: Nwood 1G 39
SW19 6F 135
TW10: Ham 2B 132
W5 4C 96
Murray Sq. E16 6J 87
Murray St. NW1 7G 65
Murrays Yd. SE18 4F 107
Murray Ter. NW3 4A 64
W5 4D 96
Mursell Est. SW8 1K 119
Musard Rd. W6 6G 99
W14 6G 99
Musbury St. E1 6J 85
Muscal W6 6G 99
(off Field Rd.)
Muscatel Pl. SE5 1E 120
Muschamp Rd. SE15 3F 121
SM5: Cars 2C 166
Muscott Ho. E2 1G 85
(off Whiston Rd.)
Muscovy Ho. DA18: Erith 2E 108
(off Kale Rd.)
Muscovy St. EC3 2H 15 (7E 84)
Museum Chambers WC1 6E 6
(off Bury Pl.)
Museum Ho. E2 3J 85
(off Burnham St.)
Museum La. SW7 2B 16 (3B 100)
Museum Mans. WC1 6E 6
(off Gt. Russell St.)
Mus. of Brands, Packaging & Advertising 6G 81
(off Lancaster Rd.)
Mus. of Comedy 6E 6
Mus. of Croydon 3C 168
(off High St.)
Mus. of Domestic Design & Architecture 2B 44
Mus. of London 6C 8 (5C 84)
Mus. of London Docklands 7C 86
Mus. of Richmond 5D 114
Mus. of The Order of St John 4B 84
Mus. of Water & Steam 5F 97
Mus. of Wimbledon 6G 135
Museum Pas. E2 3J 85
Museum St. WC1 6E 6 (5J 83)
Mus. Way W3 2G 97
Musgrave Cl. EN4: Had W 1F 21
Musgrave Ct. SW11 1C 118
Musgrave Cres. SW6 7J 99
Musgrave Rd. TW7: Isle 1K 113
Musgrove Rd. SE14 1K 121
The Musical Mus. 6E 96
Musjid Rd. SW11 2B 118
Musket Cl. EN4: E Barn 6G 21
Musquash Way TW4: Houn 2A 112
Mustang Ho. N1 6B 66
(off Canonbury Rd.)
Muston Rd. E5 2H 67
Mustow Pl. SW6 2H 117
Muswell Av. N10 1F 47
MUSWELL HILL 3F 47
Muswell Hill N10 3F 47
Muswell Hill B'way. N10 3F 47

258 A-Z Big London

Muswell Hill Golf Course—New College Pde.

Muswell Hill Golf Course ... 1G 47
Muswell Hill Pl. N10 ... 4F 47
Muswell Hill Rd. N6 ... 6E 46
N10 ... 6E 46
Muswell M. N10 ... 3F 47
Muswell Rd. N10 ... 3F 47
Mutrix Rd. NW6 ... 1J 81
Mutton Pl. NW1 ... 6E 64
Muybridge Rd.
KT3: N Mald ... 2J 151
Muybridge Yd. KT5: Surb ... 7F 151
Myatt Rd. SW9 ... 1B 120
Myatts Fld. Sth. SW9 ... 2A 120
Mycenae Rd. SE3 ... 7J 105
Myddelton Av. EN1: Enf ... 1K 23
Myddelton Cl. EN1: Enf ... 1A 24
Myddelton Gdns. N21 ... 7H 23
Myddelton Pk. N20 ... 3G 31
Myddelton Pas. EC1 ... 1K 7 (3A 84)
Myddelton Rd. N8 ... 4J 47
(not continuous)
Myddelton Sq. EC1 ... 1K 7 (3A 84)
Myddelton St. EC1 ... 2K 7 (3A 84)
Myddleton Av. N4 ... 2C 66
Myddleton Cl. HA7: Stan ... 2F 27
Myddleton Ho. N1 ... 1J 7
Myddleton M. N22 ... 7D 32
Myddleton Rd. N22 ... 7D 32
Myers Ho. *SE5* ... *7C 102*
(off Bethwin Rd.)
Myers La. SE14 ... 6K 103
Myers Wlk. E14 ... 1E 104
Myles Ct. *SE16* ... *3J 103*
(off Neptune St.)
Mylis Cl. SE26 ... 4H 139
Mylius Cl. SE14 ... 7J 103
Mylne Cl. W6 ... 5C 98
Mylne St. EC1 ... 1J 7 (3A 84)
Myra St. SE2 ... 4A 108
Myrdle Ct. *E1* ... *6G 85*
(off Myrdle St.)
Myrdle St. E1 ... 5G 85
Myrna Cl. SW19 ... 7C 136
Myron Pl. SE13 ... 3E 122
Myrtle Av. HA4: Ruis ... 7J 39
TW14: Felt ... 5G 111
Myrtleberry Cl. *E8* ... *6F 67*
(off Beechwood Rd.)
Myrtle Cl. EN4: E Barn ... 1J 31
UB7: W Dray ... 3B 92
UB8: Hil ... 5B 74
Myrtledene Rd. SE2 ... 5A 108
Myrtle Gdns. W7 ... 1J 95
Myrtle Gro. EN2: Enf ... 1J 23
KT3: N Mald ... 2J 151
Myrtle Rd. CR0: C'don ... 3C 170
E6 ... 1D 88
E17 ... 6A 50
IG1: Ilf ... 2F 71
N13 ... 3H 33
SM1: Sutt ... 5A 166
TW3: Houn ... 2G 113
TW12: Hamp H ... 6G 131
W3 ... 1J 97
Myrtle Wlk. N1 ... 1G 9 (2E 84)
Mysore Rd. SW11 ... 3D 118
Myton Rd. SE21 ... 3D 138
Mytton Ho. *SW8* ... *7K 101*
(off St Stephens Ter.)

N

N1 Shop. Cen. ... 2A 84
Nacton Ct. *RM6: Chad H* ... *5C 54*
(off Hevingham Dr.)
Nadine Ct. SM6: W'gton ... 7G 167
Nadine St. SE7 ... 5A 106
Nagasaki Wlk. SE7 ... 3K 105
Nagle Cl. E17 ... 2F 51
NAG'S HEAD ... 3J 65
Nags Head Ct. EC1 ... 4D 8
Nags Head La. DA16: Well ... 3B 126
Nags Head Rd.
EN3: Pond E ... 4D 24
Nags Head Shop. Cen. ... 4K 65
Nainby Ho. SE11 ... 4J 19
Nairne Gro. SE24 ... 5D 120
Nairn Rd. HA4: Ruis ... 6A 58
Nairn St. E14 ... 5E 86
Naldera Gdns. SE3 ... 6J 105
Nallhead Rd.
TW13: Hanw ... 5A 130
Nalton Ho. *NW6* ... *7A 64*
(off Belsize Rd.)
Namba Roy Cl. SW16 ... 4K 137
Namco Funscape
Romford ... 6K 55
Namton Dr. CR7: Thor H ... 4K 155
Nan Clark's La. NW7 ... 2F 29
Nankin St. E14 ... 6C 86
Nansen Ho. *NW10* ... *7K 61*
(off Stonebridge Pk.)
Nansen Rd. SW11 ... 3E 118
Nansen Village N12 ... 4E 30
Nant Ct. NW2 ... 2H 63
Nantes Cl. SW18 ... 4A 118
Nantes Pas. E1 ... 5J 9 (5F 85)
Nant Rd. NW2 ... 2H 63
Nant St. E2 ... 3H 85
Naomi St. SE8 ... 4A 104
Naoroji St. WC1 ... 2J 7 (3A 84)
Napa Cl. E20 ... 5E 68
Napier NW9 ... 1B 44
Napier Av. E14 ... 5C 104
SW6 ... 3H 117
Napier Cl. SE8 ... 7B 104
UB7: W Dray ... 3B 92
W14 ... 3G 99
Napier Ct. *BR2: Broml* ... *4K 159*
(off Napier Rd.)
N1 ... *2D 84*
(off Cropley St.)
SE12 ... 3K 141
SW6 ... *3H 117*
(off Ranelagh Gdns.)
UB4: Yead ... *4A 76*
(off Dunedin Way)
Napier Gro. N1 ... 2C 84
Napier Ho. *E3* ... *3C 86*
(off Campbell Rd.)
SE17 ... *6B 102*
(off Cooks Rd.)
W3 ... 1A 98
Napier Lodge TW15: Ashf ... 6F 129
Napier Pl. W14 ... 3H 99
Napier Rd. BR2: Broml ... 4K 159
CR2: S Croy ... 7D 168
DA17: Belv ... 4F 109
E6 ... 1E 88
E11 ... 4G 69
E15 ... 2G 87
(not continuous)
EN3: Pond E ... 5E 24
HA0: Wemb ... 6D 60
N17 ... 3E 48
NW10 ... 3D 80
SE25 ... 4H 157
TW7: Isle ... 4A 114
TW15: Ashf ... 7F 129
W14 ... 3H 99
Napier St. *SE8* ... *7B 104*
(off Napier Cl.)
Napier Ter. N1 ... 7B 66
Napier Wlk. TW15: Ashf ... 7F 129
Napoleon La. SE18 ... 7D 106
Napoleon Rd. E5 ... 3H 67
TW1: Twick ... 7B 114
Napton Cl. UB4: Yead ... 4C 76
Nara SE13 ... 2D 122
Narbonne Av. SW4 ... 5G 119
Narborough Cl. UB10: Ick ... 2E 56
Narborough St. SW6 ... 2K 117
Narcissus Rd. NW6 ... 5J 63
Nardini *NW9* ... *1B 44*
(off Long Mead)
Naresby Fold HA7: Stan ... 6H 27
Nares Cl. TW19: Stanw ... 1A 128
Narev Dr. EN4: E Barn ... 5H 21
Narford Rd. E5 ... 3G 67
Narrowboat Av. TW8: Bford ... 7C 96
Narrow Boat Cl. SE28 ... 2H 107
Narrow St. E14 ... 7A 86
W3 ... 1H 97
Narrow Way BR2: Broml ... 6C 160
Narvic Ho. SE5 ... 2C 120
Narwhal Inuit Art Gallery ... 5K 97
Nascot St. W12 ... 6E 80
Naseby Cl. NW6 ... 7A 64
TW7: Isle ... 1J 113
Naseby Ct. DA14: Sidc ... 4K 143
Naseby Rd. IG5: Ilf ... 1D 52
RM10: Dag ... 3G 73
SE19 ... 6D 138
NASH ... 6J 171
Nash Cl. SM1: Sutt ... 3B 166
Nash Ct. HA3: Kenton ... 6E 42
Nashe Ho. *SE1* ... *3D 102*
(off Burbage Cl.)
Nash Grn. BR1: Broml ... 6J 141
Nash Ho. *E14* ... *2C 104*
(off Alpha Gro.)
E17 ... 3D 50
NW1 ... *2F 83*
(off Park Village E.)
SW1 ... *6K 17*
(off Lupus St.)
Nash La. BR2: Kes ... 7J 171
Nash Pl. E14 ... 1D 104
Nash Rd. N9 ... 2D 34
RM6: Chad H ... 5D 54
SE4 ... 4A 122
Nash St. NW1 ... 1K 5 (3F 83)
Nash Way HA3: Kenton ... 6B 42
Nasmyth St. W6 ... 3D 98
Nassau Path SE28 ... 1C 108
Nassau Rd. SW13 ... 1B 116
Nassau St. W1 ... 6A 6 (5G 83)
Nassington Rd. NW3 ... 4D 64
Natalie Cl. TW14: Bedf ... 7F 111
Natalie M. N22 ... 6D 32
TW2: Twick ... 3H 131
Natal Rd. CR7: Thor H ... 3D 156
IG1: Ilf ... 4F 71
N11 ... 6D 32
SW16 ... 6H 137
Natasha M. SE15 ... 4J 121
Nathan Ct. *N9* ... *7D 24*
(off Causeyware Rd.)
Nathan Ho. *SE11* ... *4K 19*
(off Reedworth St.)
Nathaniel Cl. E1 ... 6K 9 (5F 85)
Nathaniel Ct. E17 ... 7A 50
Nathans Rd. HA0: Wemb ... 1C 60
Nathan Way SE28 ... 4J 107
The National Archives ... 7H 97
National Army Mus. ... 7F 17 (6D 100)
National Gallery ... 3D 12 (7H 83)
National Maritime Mus. ... 6F 105
National Portrait Gallery ... 3D 12
National Tennis Cen. ... 5A 116
National Ter. *SE16* ... *2H 103*
(off Bermondsey Wall E.)
National Theatre ... 4H 13 (1A 102)
National Works TW4: Houn ... 3D 112
Nation Way E4 ... 1K 35
Natural History Mus. ... 2A 16 (3B 100)
Nature Gdn. ... *5J 103*
(off Bramcote Gro.)
Nautical Dr. E16 ... 2K 105
Nautical Ho. *SW18* ... *4A 118*
(off Juniper Dr.)
Nauticus Wlk. E14 ... 4D 104
The Nautilus Bldg. *EC1* ... *1K 7*
(off Myddelton Pas.)
Naval Ho. *E14* ... *7F 87*
(off Quixley St.)
SE18 ... 3F 107
Naval Row E14 ... 7E 86
Naval Wlk. *BR1: Broml* ... *2J 159*
(off High St.)
Navarino Gro. E8 ... 6G 67
Navarino Mans. E8 ... 6G 67
Navarino Rd. E8 ... 6G 67
Navarre Rd. E6 ... 2C 88
SW9 ... 1B 120
Navarre St. E2 ... 3J 9 (4F 85)
Navenby Wlk. E3 ... 4C 86
Navestock Cl. E4 ... 3K 35
Navestock Cres. IG8: Wfd G ... 7F 37
Navigation Ct. E16 ... 7G 89
Navigation Dr.
EN3: Enf L ... 1H 25
Navigation Ho. *SE16* ... *4A 104*
(off Grand Canal Av.)
Navigation Rd. E3 ... 4E 86
Navigator Dr. UB2: S'hall ... 2G 95
Navigator Pk. UB2: S'hall ... 4A 94
Navigator Sq. N19 ... 2G 65
Navy St. SW4 ... 3H 119
Naxos Bldg. E14 ... 2B 104
Nayim Pl. E8 ... 5H 67
Nayland Ho. SE6 ... 4E 140
Naylor Bldg. E. *E1* ... *6G 85*
(off Assam St.)
Naylor Bldg. W. *E1* ... *6G 85*
(off Adler St.)
Naylor Gro. EN3: Pond E ... 5E 24
Naylor Ho. *SE17* ... *4D 102*
(off Flint St.)
W10 ... *3G 81*
(off Dart St.)
Naylor Rd. N20 ... 2F 31
SE15 ... 7H 103
Nazareth Gdns. SE15 ... 2H 121
Nazrul St. E2 ... 1J 9 (3F 85)
NCR Bus. Cen. NW10 ... 5A 62
Neagle Ho. *NW2* ... *3E 62*
(off Stoll Cl.)
Neal Av. UB1: S'hall ... 4D 76
Neal Cl. HA6: Nwood ... 1J 39
Nealden St. SW9 ... 3K 119
Neale Cl. N2 ... 3A 46
Neale Ct. RM9: Dag ... 6B 72
Neal St. SE10 ... 3H 105
WC2 ... 1E 12 (6J 83)
Neal's Yd. WC2 ... 1E 12 (6J 83)
Neap Ct. *E3* ... *4E 86*
(off Navigation Rd.)
Near Acre NW9 ... 1B 44
NEASDEN ... 3A 62
Neasden Cl. NW10 ... 5A 62
NEASDEN JUNC. ... 4A 62
Neasden La. NW10 ... 3A 62
Neasden La. Nth. NW10 ... 3K 61
Neasham Rd. RM8: Dag ... 5B 72
Neate Ho. *SW1* ... *6B 18*
(off Lupus St.)
Neate St. SE5 ... 6E 102
Neath Gdns. SM4: Mord ... 6A 154
Neathouse Pl.
SW1 ... 3A 18 (4G 101)
Neats Acre HA4: Ruis ... 7F 39
Neatscourt Rd. E6 ... 5B 88
Nebraska Bldg. *SE13* ... *1D 122*
(off Deal's Gateway)
Nebraska St. SE1 ... 7E 14 (2D 102)
Nebula Ct. *E13* ... *2J 87*
(off Umbriel Pl.)
Neckinger SE16 ... 7K 15 (3F 103)
Neckinger Est. SE16 ... 3F 103
Neckinger St. SE1 ... 7K 15 (2F 103)
Nectarine Way SE13 ... 2D 122
Needham Ho. SE11 ... 4J 19
Needham Rd. W11 ... 6J 81
Needham Ter. NW2 ... 3F 63
Needleman Cl. NW9 ... 2A 44
Needleman St. SE16 ... 2K 103
Needwood Ho. N4 ... 1C 66
Neela Cl. UB10: Ick ... 4D 56
Neeld Cres. HA9: Wemb ... 5G 61
NW4 ... 5D 44
Neeld Pde. HA9: Wemb ... 5F 61
Neeld Pl. W9 ... 5H 81
Neil Cl. TW15: Ashf ... 5E 128
Neil Wates Cres. SW2 ... 1A 138
Nelgarde Rd. SE6 ... 7C 122
Nella Rd. W6 ... 6F 99
Nelldale Rd. SE16 ... 4J 103
Nellgrove Rd. UB10: Hil ... 4D 74
Nell Gwynn Av. TW17: Shep ... 6F 147
Nell Gwynn Ho.
SW3 ... 4D 16 (4C 100)
Nellie Cressall Way E3 ... 5B 86
Nello James Gdns. SE27 ... 4D 138
Nelson Arc. *SE10* ... *6E 104*
(off Nelson Rd.)
Nelson Cl. CR0: C'don ... 1B 168
KT12: Walt T ... 7K 147
NW6 ... 3J 81
RM7: Mawney ... 1H 55
TW14: Felt ... 1H 129
UB10: Hil ... 3D 74
Nelson Ct. *SE16* ... *1J 103*
(off Brunel Rd.)
Nelson Gdns. E2 ... 3G 85
TW3: Houn ... 6E 112
Nelson Gro. Rd. SW19 ... 1K 153
Nelson Ho. *SW1* ... *7B 18*
(off Dolphin Sq.)
Nelson La. UB10: Hil ... 3D 74
Nelson Mandela Cl. N10 ... 2E 46
Nelson Mandela Ho.
N16 ... 2G 67
Nelson Mandela Rd. SE3 ... 3A 124
Nelson Pas. EC1 ... 1D 8 (3C 84)
Nelson Pl. N1 ... 1B 8 (2B 84)
Nelson Rd. BR2: Broml ... 4A 160
DA14: Sidc ... 4A 144
DA17: Belv ... 5F 109
E4 ... 6J 35
E11 ... 4J 51
EN3: Pond E ... 6E 24
HA1: Harr ... 1H 59
HA7: Stan ... 6H 27
KT3: N Mald ... 5K 151
N8 ... 5K 47
N9 ... 2C 34
N15 ... 4E 48
SE10 ... 6E 104
SW19 ... 7K 135
TW2: Whitt ... 7F 113
TW3: Houn ... 6E 112
TW6: H'row A ... 1B 110
TW15: Ashf ... 5A 128
UB10: Hil ... 3D 74
Nelson Rd. M. *SW19* ... *7K 135*
(off Nelson Rd.)
Nelson's Column ... 4E 12 (1J 101)
Nelson Sq. SE1 ... 6A 14 (2B 102)
Nelson's Row SW4 ... 4H 119
Nelson St. E1 ... 6H 85
E6 ... 2D 88
(not continuous)
E16 ... 6H 87
Nelsons Yd. *NW1* ... *2G 83*
(off Mornington Cres.)
Nelson Ter. N1 ... 1B 8 (2B 84)
Nelson Trad. Est. SW19 ... 1K 153
Nelson Wlk. E3 ... 4D 86
KT19: Eps ... 7G 163
SE16 ... 1A 104
Nemoure Rd. W3 ... 7J 79
Nemus Apts. SE8 ... 4K 103
Nene Gdns. TW13: Hanw ... 3D 130
Nene Rd. TW6: H'row A ... 1D 110
NENE ROAD RDBT. ... 1D 110
Nepaul Rd. SW11 ... 2C 118
Nepean St. SW15 ... 6C 116
Neptune Ct. *E14* ... *4C 104*
(off Homer Dr.)
E16 ... *5J 87*
(off Hammersley Rd.)
Neptune Development SE8 ... 5A 104
Neptune Ho. *E3* ... *1C 86*
(off Garrison Rd.)
SE16 ... *3J 103*
(off Moodkee St.)
Neptune Rd. HA1: Harr ... 6H 41
TW6: H'row A ... 1F 111
Neptune St. SE16 ... 3J 103
Neptune Wlk. DA8: Erith ... 4K 109
Nero Ct. TW8: Bford ... 7D 96
Nero Ho. *E20* ... *6E 68*
(off Anthems Way)
Neroli Ho. *E1* ... *1K 15*
(off Blvd. Walkway)
Nesbit Ct. *SE17* ... *6B 102*
(off Cook's Rd.)
Nesbit Rd. SE9 ... 4B 124
Nesbitt Cl. SE3 ... 3G 123
Nesbitts All. EN5: Barn ... 3C 20
Nesbitt Sq. SE19 ... 7E 138
Nesham Ho. *N1* ... *1E 84*
(off Hoxton St.)
Nesham St. E1 ... 7G 85
Ness St. SE16 ... 3G 103
Nesta Rd. IG8: Wfd G ... 6B 36
Nestles Av. UB3: Hayes ... 3H 93
Nestor Av. N21 ... 6G 23
Nestor Ho. *E2* ... *2H 85*
(off Old Bethnal Grn. Rd.)
Netheravon Rd. W4 ... 4B 98
W7 ... 1K 95
Netheravon Rd. Sth. W4 ... 5B 98
Netherbury Rd. W5 ... 3D 96
Netherby Gdns. EN2: Enf ... 4D 22
Netherby Rd. SE23 ... 7J 121
Nether Cl. N3 ... 7D 30
Nethercott Ho. *E3* ... *3D 86*
(off Bruce Rd.)
Nethercourt Av. N3 ... 6D 30
Netherfield Gdns. IG11: Bark ... 6H 71
Netherfield Rd. N12 ... 5E 30
SW17 ... 3E 136
Netherford Rd. SW4 ... 2G 119
Netherhall Gdns. NW3 ... 6A 64
Netherhall Way NW3 ... 5A 64
Netherheys Dr. CR2: S Croy ... 7B 168
Netherlands Rd.
EN5: New Bar ... 6G 21
Netherleigh Cl. N6 ... 1F 65
Nether St. N3 ... 7D 30
N12 ... 5F 31
(not continuous)
Netherton Gro. SW10 ... 6A 100
Netherton Rd. N15 ... 6D 48
TW1: Twick ... 5A 114
Netherwood N2 ... 2B 46
Netherwood Pl. *W14* ... *3F 99*
(off Netherwood Rd.)
Netherwood Rd. W14 ... 3F 99
Netherwood St. NW6 ... 7H 63
Nethewode Ct. *DA17: Belv* ... *3H 109*
(off Lower Pk. Rd.)
Netley *SE5* ... *1E 120*
(off Redbridge Gdns.)
Netley Cl. CR0: New Ad ... 7E 170
SM3: Cheam ... 5F 165
Netley Dr. KT12: Walt T ... 7D 148
Netley Gdns. SM4: Mord ... 7A 154
Netley Rd. E17 ... 5B 50
IG2: Ilf ... 5H 53
SM4: Mord ... 7A 154
TW8: Bford ... 6E 96
Netley St. NW1 ... 2A 6 (3G 83)
Nettlecombe *NW1* ... *7H 65*
(off Agar Gro.)
Nettleden Av. HA9: Wemb ... 6G 61
Nettleden Ho. *SW3* ... *4D 16*
(off Cale St.)
Nettlefold Pl. SE27 ... 3B 138
Nettlefold Wlk. KT12: Walt T ... 7H 147
Nettlestead Cl. BR3: Beck ... 7B 140
Nettleton Ct. *EC2* ... *6C 8*
(off London Wall)
Nettleton Rd. SE14 ... 1K 121
TW6: H'row A ... 1D 110
UB10: Ick ... 4B 56
Nettlewood Rd. SW16 ... 7H 137
Neuchatel Rd. SE6 ... 2B 140
Neutron Twr. E14 ... 7F 87
Nevada Bldg. *SE10* ... *1D 122*
(off Blackheath Rd.)
Nevada Cl. KT3: N Mald ... 4J 151
Nevada St. SE10 ... 6E 104
Nevern Mans. *SW5* ... *5J 99*
(off Warwick Rd.)
Nevern Pl. SW5 ... 4J 99
Nevern Rd. SW5 ... 4J 99
Nevern Sq. SW5 ... 4J 99
Nevil Ho. *SW9* ... *2B 120*
(off Loughborough Est.)
Nevill Ct. *SW10* ... *7A 100*
(off Edith Ter.)
Neville Av. KT3: N Mald ... 1K 151
Neville Cl. DA15: Sidc ... 4K 143
E11 ... 3H 69
NW1 ... 2H 83
NW6 ... 2H 81
SE15 ... 1G 121
TW3: Houn ... 2F 113
W3 ... 2J 97
Neville Ct. NW8 ... 1A 4
Neville Dr. N2 ... 6A 46
Neville Gdns. RM8: Dag ... 3D 72
Neville Gill Cl. SW18 ... 6J 117
Neville Ho. N11 ... 4K 31
N22 ... *1K 47*
(off Neville Pl.)
NW6 ... *2H 81*
(off Denmark Rd.)
Neville Ho. Yd. KT1: King T ... 2E 150
Neville Pl. N22 ... 1K 47
Neville Rd. CR0: C'don ... 7D 156
E7 ... 7J 69
IG6: Ilf ... 1G 53
KT1: King T ... 2G 151
NW6 ... 2H 81
RM8: Dag ... 3D 72
TW10: Ham ... 3C 132
W5 ... 4D 78
Nevilles Ct. NW2 ... 3C 62
Neville St. SW7 ... 5A 16 (5B 100)
Neville Ter. SW7 ... 5A 16 (5B 100)
Neville Wlk. SM5: Cars ... 7C 154
Nevill La. EC4 ... 7K 7
Nevill Rd. N16 ... 4E 66
Nevin Dr. E4 ... 1J 35
Nevin Ho. UB3: Harl ... 3E 92
Nevinson Cl. SW18 ... 6B 118
Nevis Cl. E13 ... 2K 87
Nevis Rd. SW17 ... 2E 136
Nevitt Ho. *N1* ... *2D 84*
(off Cranston Est.)
New Acres Rd. SE28 ... 2J 107
NEW ADDINGTON ... 7F 171
Newall Cl. UB10: Uxb ... 1B 74
Newall Ho. *SE1* ... *3C 102*
(off Bath Ter.)
Newall Rd. TW6: H'row A ... 1E 110
Newark Cres. NW10 ... 3K 79
Newark Ho. SW9 ... 2B 120
Newark Knok E6 ... 6E 88
Newark Rd. CR2: S Croy ... 6D 168
Newark St. E1 ... 5H 85
(not continuous)
Newark Way NW4 ... 4C 44
New Ash Cl. N2 ... 3B 46
New Atlas Wharf *E14* ... *3C 104*
(off Arnhem Pl.)
New Baltic Wharf *SE8* ... *5A 104*
(off Evelyn St.)
New Barn Cl. SM6: W'gton ... 6K 167
NEW BARNET ... 4G 21
New Barn Rd. BR8: Swan ... 7K 145
New Barns Av. CR4: Mitc ... 4H 155
New Barn St. E13 ... 4J 87
New Barns Way IG7: Chig ... 3K 37
Newbeck Ct. BR3: Beck ... 7B 140
NEW BECKENHAM ... 6B 140
New Bentham Ct. *N1* ... *7C 66*
(off Ecclesbourne Rd.)
Newberry M. SW4 ... 4J 119
Newbery Ho. *N1* ... *7C 66*
(off Northampton St.)
Newbold Cotts. E1 ... 6J 85
Newbolt Av. SM3: Cheam ... 5E 164
Newbolt Ho. *SE17* ... *5D 102*
(off Brandon St.)
Newbolt Rd. HA7: Stan ... 5E 26
New Bond St. W1 ... 1J 11 (6F 83)
Newborough Grn.
KT3: N Mald ... 4K 151
New Brent St. NW4 ... 5E 44
Newbridge Point *SE23* ... *3K 139*
(off Windrush La.)
New Bri. St. EC4 ... 1A 14 (6B 84)
New Broad St. EC2 ... 6G 9 (5E 84)
New Broadway
TW12: Hamp H ... 5H 131
UB10: Hil ... 3D 74
W5 ... 7D 78
New Broadway Bldgs. W5 ... 7D 78
Newburgh Rd. W3 ... 1J 97
Newburgh St. W1 ... 1B 12 (6G 83)
New Burlington M.
W1 ... 2A 12 (7G 83)
New Burlington Pl.
W1 ... 2A 12 (7G 83)
New Burlington St.
W1 ... 2A 12 (7G 83)
Newburn Ho. *SE11* ... *5H 19*
(off Newburn St.)
Newburn St. SE11 ... 5H 19 (5K 101)
Newbury Cl. RM10: Dag ... 2G 73
UB5: N'olt ... 6D 58
Newbury Ct. DA14: Sidc ... 4K 143
E5 ... *5A 68*
(off Daubeney Rd.)
Newbury Gdns. KT19: Ewe ... 4B 164
Newbury Ho. N22 ... 1J 47
SW9 ... 2B 120
W2 ... *6K 81*
(off Hallfield Est.)
Newbury M. NW5 ... 6E 64
NEWBURY PARK ... 5H 53
Newbury Rd. BR2: Broml ... 3J 159
E4 ... 6K 35
IG2: Ilf ... 6J 53
TW6: H'row A ... 1B 110
Newbury St. EC1 ... 6C 8 (5C 84)
Newbury Way UB5: N'olt ... 6C 58
The New Bus. Cen. NW10 ... 3B 80
New Butt La. SE8 ... 7C 104
New Butt La. Nth. *SE8* ... *7C 104*
(off Hales St.)
Newby *NW1* ... *2A 6*
(off Robert St.)
Newby Cl. EN1: Enf ... 2K 23
Newby Ho. *E14* ... *7E 86*
(off Newby Pl.)
Newby Pl. E14 ... 7E 86
Newby St. SW8 ... 3F 119
New Caledonian Mkt. ... 7H 15
(off Bermondsey Sq.)
New Caledonian Wharf SE16 ... 3B 104
Newcastle Cl. EC4 ... 7A 8 (6B 84)
Newcastle Ct. *EC4* ... *2D 14*
(off College Hill)
Newcastle Ho. *W1* ... *5G 5*
(off Luxborough St.)
Newcastle Pl. W2 ... 5B 4 (5B 82)
Newcastle Row EC1 ... 4K 7 (4A 84)
New Cavendish St. W1 ... 6H 5 (5E 82)
New Century Ho. *E16* ... *6H 87*
(off Jude St.)
New Change EC4 ... 1C 14 (6C 84)
New Change Pas. *EC4* ... *1C 14*
(off New Change)
New Chapel Sq. TW13: Felt ... 1K 129
New Charles St.
EC1 ... 1B 8 (3B 84)
NEW CHARLTON ... 4A 106
New Chiswick Pool ... 7A 98
New Church Rd. SE5 ... 7C 102
(not continuous)
New City Rd. E13 ... 3A 88
New Claremont Apts. *SE1* ... *4F 103*
(off Setchell Rd.)
New Clocktower Pl. N7 ... 6J 65
New Cl. SW19 ... 3A 154
TW13: Hanw ... 5C 130
New Colebrooke Ct. SM5: Cars ... 7D 166
New College Ct. *NW3* ... *6A 64*
(off College Cres.)
New College M. N1 ... 7A 66
New College Pde. *NW3* ... *6B 64*
(off Finchley Rd.)

A-Z Big London 259

Newcombe Gdns. SW16 . . . . .4J 137
TW4: Houn 4D 112
Newcombe Ho. E5 . . . . .3H 67
Newcombe Pk. HA0: Wemb 1F 79
NW7 . . . . .5F 29
Newcombe Ri. UB7: Yiew 6A 74
Newcombe St. W8 . . . . .1J 99
Newcomen Rd. E11 . . . . .3H 69
SW11 . . . . .3B 118
Newcomen St. SE1 . . . . . . .6E 14 (2D 102)
New Compton St. WC2 . . . . .1D 12 (6H 83)
New Concordia Wharf
SE1 . . . . .6K 15 (2G 103)
New Ct. EC4 . . . . .2J 13
UB5: N'olt 5F 59
Newcourt Ho. *E2* *3H 85*
(off Pott St.)
Newcourt St. NW8 . . . . .1C 4 (2C 82)
New Covent Garden Market 7H 101
New Crane Pl. E1 . . . . .1J 103
New Crane Wharf *E1* *1J 103*
(off New Crane Pl.)
New Cres. Yd. NW10 . . . . .2B 80
Newcroft Cl. UB8: Hil 5B 74
Newcroft Ho. *CR0: C'don* *2F 169*
(off Homefield Pl.)
NEW CROSS 7B 104
NEW CROSS 1B 122
NEW CROSS GATE 1K 121
NEW CROSS GATE 1K 121
New Cross Rd. SE14 . . . . .7J 103
Newdales Cl. N9 . . . . .2B 34
Newdene Av. UB5: N'olt 2B 76
Newdigate Ho. *E14* *6B 86*
(off Norbiton Rd.)
New Diorama Theatre 4F 83
New Drum St. *E1* *7K 9*
(off Buckle St.)
Newell St. E14 . . . . .6B 86
NEW ELTHAM 2G 143
New End NW3 . . . . .3A 64
New End Sq. NW3 . . . . .4B 64
New England Ind. Est.
IG11: Bark 2G 89
Newent Cl. SE15 . . . . .7E 102
SM5: Cars 1D 166
New Era Est. *N1* *1E 84*
(off Halcomb St.)
New Era Ho. *N1* *1E 84*
(off Halcomb St.)
New Farm Av. BR2: Broml 4J 159
New Farm La. HA6: Nwood 1G 39
New Ferry App. SE18 . . . . .3E 106
New Festival Av. E14 . . . . .6C 86
New Fetter La.
EC4 . . . . .7K 7 (6A 84)
Newfield Cl. TW12: Hamp 1E 148
Newfield Ri. NW2 . . . . .3C 62
New Forest La. IG7: Chig 6K 37
Newgale Gdns. HA8: Edg 1F 43
New Gdn. Dr. UB7: W Dray 2A 92
Newgate CR0: C'don 1C 168
Newgate Cl. TW13: Hanw 2C 130
Newgate St. E4 . . . . .3B 36
(not continuous)
EC1 . . . . .7B 8 (6B 84)
New Globe Wlk. SE1 . . . . .4C 14 (1C 102)
New Goulston St. E1 . . . . .7J 9 (6F 85)
New Grn. Pl. SE19 . . . . .6E 138
New Gun Wharf *E3* *1A 86*
(off Gunmaker's La.)
Newhall Ct. *N1* *1C 84*
(off Popham Rd.)
Newham Academy of Music 1C 88
Newham City Farm 6B 88
Newham Dockside E16 . . . . .7C 88
Newham Leisure Cen. 4A 88
Newham's Row
SE1 . . . . .7H 15 (3E 102)
Newham Way E6 . . . . .5A 88
E16 . . . . .5H 87
Newhaven Cl. UB3: Harl 4H 93
Newhaven Cres. TW15: Ashf 5F 129
Newhaven Gdns. SE9 . . . . .4B 124
Newhaven La. E16 . . . . .4H 87
Newhaven Rd. SE25 . . . . .5D 156
New Heston Rd. TW5: Hest 7D 94
New Hope Ct. NW10 . . . . .3D 80
New Horizons Ct.
TW8: Bford 6A 96
Newhouse Av. RM6: Chad H 3D 54
Newhouse Cl. KT3: N Mald 7A 152
Newhouse Wlk. SM4: Mord 7A 154
Newick Cl. DA5: Bexl 6H 127
Newick Rd. E5 . . . . .4H 67
Newing Grn. BR1: Broml 7B 142
NEWINGTON 3C 102
Newington Barrow Way N7 . . . . .3K 65
Newington Butts SE1 . . . . .4B 102
SE11 . . . . .4B 102
Newington C'way. SE1 . . . .7C 14 (3B 102)
Newington Ct. *N16* *4C 66*
(off Green Lanes)
Newington Ct. Bus. Cen. SE1 . . . . . .7C 14
Newington Grn. N1 . . . . .5D 66
N16 . . . . .5D 66
Newington Grn. Community Gdns.
. . . .*5D 66*
(off Newington Grn.)
Newington Grn. Mans. N16 . . . . .5D 66
Newington Grn. Rd. N1 . . . . .6D 66
Newington Ind. Est. SE17 . . . . .4B 102
New Inn B'way. EC2 . . . . .3H 9 (4E 84)
New Inn Pas. WC2 . . . . .1H 13
New Inn Sq. EC2 . . . . .3H 9
New Inn St. EC2 . . . . .3H 9 (4E 84)
New Inn Yd. EC2 . . . . .3H 9 (4E 84)
New Jubilee Ct. IG8: Wfd G 7D 36
New Jubilee Wharf *E1* *1J 103*
(off Wapping Wall)
New Kelvin Av. TW11: Tedd 6J 131
New Kent Rd. SE1 . . . . .3C 102
New Kings Rd. SW6 . . . . .2H 117
New King St. SE8 . . . . .6C 104
Newland Ct. EC1 . . . . .2E 8
HA9: Wemb 2G 61
Newland Dr. EN1: Enf 1C 24
Newland Gdns. W13 . . . . .2A 96
Newland Ho. *N8* *3J 47*
(off Newland Rd.)
SE14 . . . .*6K 103*
(off John Williams Cl.)
Newland Rd. N8 . . . . .3J 47
NEWLANDS
HA8 . . . . .3K 27
SE23 . . . . .5K 121
Newlands HA1: Harr 1J 59
NW1 . . . .*1A 6*
(off Harrington St.)
The Newlands KT7: T Ditt 7J 149
SM6: W'gton 7G 167
Newlands Av. KT7: T Ditt 7J 149
Newlands Cl. HA0: Wemb 6C 60
HA8: Edg 3K 27
UB2: S'hall 5C 94
Newlands Ct. SE9 . . . . .6E 124
Newlands Dr. SL3: Poyle 6A 174
Newlands Pk. SE26 . . . . .6J 139
Newlands Pl. EN5: Barn 5A 20
Newlands Quay E1 . . . . .7J 85
Newlands Rd. IG8: Wfd G 2C 36
SW16 . . . . .2J 155
Newland St. E16 . . . . .1C 106
Newlands Way KT9: Chess 5C 162
Newlands Woods
CR0: Sels 7B 170
Newling Cl. E6 . . . . .6D 88
New London Performing Arts Cen.
. . . . .4F 47
New London St. EC3 . . . . .2H 15
New Lydenburg Commercial Est.
SE7 . . . . .3A 106
New Lydenburg St. SE7 . . . . .3A 106
Newlyn *NW1* *1G 83*
(off Plender St.)
Newlyn Cl. BR6: Chels 4K 173
UB8: Hil 5C 74
Newlyn Gdns. HA2: Harr 7D 40
Newlyn Ho. HA5: Hat E 1D 40
Newlyn Rd. DA16: Well 2K 125
EN5: Barn 4C 20
N17 . . . . .1F 49
NEW MALDEN 4A 152
Newman Cl. NW10 . . . . .6D 62
SE26 . . . . .4J 139
Newman Ct. *BR1: Broml* *1J 159*
(off North St.)
TW15: Ashf 6D 128
Newman Ho. SE1 . . . . .3B 102
Newman Pas.
W1 . . . . .6B 6 (5G 83)
Newman Rd. BR1: Broml 1J 159
CR0: C'don 1K 167
E13 . . . . .3K 87
E17 . . . . .5K 49
UB3: Hayes 7K 75
Newman Rd. Ind. Est.
CR0: C'don 7K 155
Newman's Ct. EC3 . . . . .1F 15
Newmans La. KT6: Surb 6D 150
Newman's Row WC2 . . . . .6H 7 (5K 83)
Newman St. W1 . . . . .6B 6 (5G 83)
Newman's Way
EN4: Had W 1F 21
Newmarket Av. UB5: N'olt 5E 58
Newmarket Grn. SE9 . . . . .7B 124
Newmarsh Rd. SE28 . . . . .1K 107
Newmill Ho. E3 . . . . .4E 86
New Mill Rd. SW11 . . . . .6H 101
Newminster Rd. SM4: Mord 6A 154
New Mossford Way IG6: Ilf 4G 53
New Mt. St. E15 . . . . .7F 69
Newnes Path SW15 . . . . .4D 116
Newnham Av. HA4: Ruis 1A 58
Newnham Cl. CR7: Thor H 2C 156
UB5: N'olt 6G 59
Newnham Gdns. UB5: N'olt 6G 59
Newnham Grn. *N22* *1A 48*
(off Highfield Cl.)
Newnham Lodge *DA17: Belv* *5G 109*
(off Erith Rd.)
Newnham M. N22 . . . . .7F 33
Newnham Rd. N22 . . . . .1K 47
Newnhams Cl. BR1: Broml 3D 160
Newnham Ter.
SE1 . . . . .1J 19 (3A 102)
Newnham Way HA3: Kenton 5E 42
New Nth. Pl. EC2 . . . . .3G 9 (4E 84)
New Nth. Rd. IG6: Ilf 1G 53
N1 . . . . .1F 9 (7C 66)
New Nth. St. WC1 . . . . .5G 7 (5K 83)
Newnton Cl. N4 . . . . .7D 48
New Oak Rd. N2 . . . . .2A 46
New Orleans Wlk. N19 . . . . .7H 47
New Oxford St. WC1 . . . . .7D 6 (6H 83)
New Pde. TW15: Ashf 4B 128
UB7: Yiew 1A 92
New Paragon Wlk. SE17 . . . . .4D 102
New Pk. Av. N13 . . . . .3H 33
New Pk. Cl. UB5: N'olt 6C 58
New Pk. Est. N18 . . . . .5D 34
New Pk. Ho. N13 . . . . .4E 32
New Pk. Pde. *SW2* *7J 119*
(off New Pk. Rd.)
New Pk. Rd. SW2 . . . . .1H 137
TW15: Ashf 5E 128
New Pl. CR0: Addtn 6C 170
New Pl. Sq. SE16 . . . . .3H 103
New Plaistow Rd. E15 . . . . .1G 87
New Pond Pde. HA4: Ruis 3J 57
Newport Av. E13 . . . . .4K 87
E14 . . . . .7F 87
Newport Ct. WC2 . . . . .2D 12 (7H 83)
Newport Ho. *E3* *3A 86*
(off Strahan Rd.)
Newport Lodge *EN1: Enf* *5K 23*
(off Village Rd.)
Newport Pl. WC2 . . . . .2D 12 (7H 83)
Newport Rd. E10 . . . . .2E 68
E17 . . . . .4A 50
SW13 . . . . .1C 116
TW6: H'row A 1C 110
UB4: Hayes 5F 75
W3 . . . . .2J 97
Newport St. SE11 . . . . .4G 19 (4K 101)
Newport Street Gallery . . .3H 19 (4K 101)
New Priory Ct. *NW6* *7J 63*
(off Mazenod Av.)
New Providence Wharf E14 . . . . .1F 105
Newquay Cres. HA2: Harr 2C 58
Newquay Ho.
SE11 . . . . .5J 19 (5A 102)
Newquay Rd. SE6 . . . . .2D 140
New Quebec St. W1 . . . . . . .1F 11 (6D 82)
New Ride SW7 . . . . .6C 10 (2C 100)
New River Av. N8 . . . . .3K 47
New River Ct. N5 . . . . .4C 66
New River Cres. N13 . . . . .4G 33
New River Head EC1 . . . . . . .1K 7 (3A 84)
New River Sports & Fitness Cen. . . .7G 33
New River Wlk. N1 . . . . .6C 66
(not continuous)
New River Way N4 . . . . .7D 48
New Rd. CR4: Mitc 1D 166
DA16: Well 2B 126
E1 . . . . .5H 85
E4 . . . . .4J 35
HA1: Harr 4K 59
IG3: Ilf .2J 71
KT2: King T 7G 133
KT8: W Mole 4E 148
N8 . . . . .5J 47
N9 . . . . .2C 34
N17 . . . . .1F 49
N22 . . . . .1C 48
NW7 . . . . .7B 30
RM9: Dag 2G 91
RM10: Dag 2G 91
RM13: Rain 2G 91
SE2 . . . . .4D 108
TW3: Houn 4F 113
TW8: Bford 6D 96
TW10: Ham 4C 132
TW13: Hanw 5C 130
TW14: Bedf 6F 111
TW14: Felt 1K 129
TW17: Shep 3C 146
UB3: Harl 7E 92
UB8: Hil 4E 74
New Rd. Hill BR2: Kes 7C 172
BR6: Downe 7C 172
New Rochford St. NW5 . . . . .5D 64
New Row NW2 . . . . .3E 62
WC2 . . . . .2E 12 (7J 83)
Newry Rd. TW1: Twick 5A 114
Newsam Av. N15 . . . . .5D 48
New Scotland Yard 6F 13
Newsholme Dr. N21 . . . . .5E 22
NEW SOUTHGATE 5A 32
New Southgate Crematorium 3A 32
New Southgate Ind. Est. N11 . . . . . .5B 32
New Spitalfields Mkt. E10 . . . . .3C 68
New Spring Gdns. Wlk.
SE11 . . . . .6F 19 (5J 101)
New Sq. TW14: Bedf 1E 128
WC2 . . . . .7J 7 (6A 84)
New Sq. Pk. TW14: Bedf 1E 128
New Sq. Pas. WC2 . . . . .7J 7
Newstead Av. BR6: Orp 3H 173
Newstead Cl. N12 . . . . .6H 31
Newstead Ct. UB5: N'olt 3C 76
Newstead Ho. *N1* *2A 84*
(off Tolpuddle St.)
Newstead Rd. SE12 . . . . .7H 123
Newstead Wlk. SM5: Cars 7A 154
Newstead Way SW19 . . . . .4F 135
New St. EC2 . . . . .6H 9 (5E 84)
New St. Hill BR1: Broml 5K 141
New St. Sq. EC4 . . . . .7K 7 (6A 84)
(not continuous)
Newton Av. N10 . . . . .1E 46
W3 . . . . .2J 97
Newton Cl. E17 . . . . .6A 50
HA2: Harr 2E 58
Newton Ct. E3 . . . . .5C 86
NW6 . . . .*7A 64*
(off Fairfax Rd.)
SW17 . . . .*3B 136*
(off Grosvenor Way)
W8 . . . .*2J 99*
(off Kensington Chu. St.)
Newton Gro. W4 . . . . .4A 98
Newton Ho. *E1* *7H 85*
(off Cornwall St.)
E17 . . . .*3D 50*
(off Prospect Hill)
EN3: Enf H 3E 24
NW8 . . . .*1K 81*
(off Abbey Rd.)
SE20 . . . . .7K 139
Newton Ind. Est. RM6: Chad H 4D 54
Newton Lodge *SE10* *3H 105*
(off Teal St.)
Newton Mans. *W14* *6G 99*
(off Queen's Club Gdns.)
Newton Pk. Pl. BR7: Chst 7D 142
Newton Pl. E14 . . . . .4C 104
Newton Rd. DA16: Well 3A 126
E15 . . . . .5F 69
HA0: Wemb 7F 61
HA3: Hrw W 2J 41
N15 . . . . .5G 49
NW2 . . . . .4E 62
SW19 . . . . .7G 135
TW7: Isle 2K 113
W2 . . . . .6K 81
Newton St. WC2 . . . . .7F 7 (6J 83)
Newton's Yd. SW18 . . . . .5J 117
Newton Ter. BR2: Broml 6B 160
Newton Wlk. HA8: Edg 1H 43
Newton Way N18 . . . . .5H 33
New Tower Bldgs. E1 . . . . .1H 103
Newtown St. SW11 . . . . .1F 119
New Trinity Rd. N2 . . . . .3B 46
New Turnstile WC1 . . . . .6G 7
New Union Cl. E14 . . . . .3E 104
New Union Sq. SW11 . . . . .6H 101
New Union St. EC2 . . . . .6E 8 (5D 84)
New Village Av. E14 . . . . .6F 87
New Wanstead E11 . . . . .6H 51
New Warren La. SE18 . . . . .3F 107
New Way Rd. NW9 . . . . .4A 44
New West End Synagogue *7K 81*
(off St Petersburgh Pl.)
New Wharf Rd. N1 . . . . .2J 83
New Willow Ho. *E13* *2J 87*
(off Plaistow Rd.)
NEWYEARS GREEN 7B 38
New Years Grn. La. UB9: Hare 6A 38
New Zealand Av. KT12: Walt T 7H 147
New Zealand Way W12 . . . . .7D 80
Nexus Apts. *BR1: Broml* *3K 159*
(off Elmfield Rd.)
Nexus Cl. TW14: Felt 5J 111
Nexus Ct. E11 . . . . .1G 69
NW6 . . . . .3J 81
Niagara Av. W5 . . . . .4C 96
Niagara Cl. N1 . . . . .2C 84
Niagra Ct. *SE16* *3J 103*
(off Canada Est.)
Nibthwaite Rd. HA1: Harr 5J 41
Nice Bus. Pk. SE15 . . . . .6H 103
Nicholas Cl. UB6: G'frd 2F 77
Nicholas Ct. E13 . . . . .3K 87
N7 . . . . .5K 65
SE12 . . . . .1J 141
W4 . . . .*6A 98*
(off Corney Reach Way)
Nicholas Gdns. W5 . . . . .2D 96
Nicholas La. EC4 . . . . .2F 15 (7D 84)
(not continuous)
Nicholas M. W4 . . . . .6A 98
Nicholas Pas. EC4 . . . . .2F 15
Nicholas Rd. CR0: Bedd 4J 167
E1 . . . . .4J 85
RM8: Dag 2F 73
W11 . . . . .7F 81
Nicholas Stacey Ho. *SE7* *5K 105*
(off Frank Burton Cl.)
Nicholas Way HA6: Nwood 1E 38
Nicholay Rd. N19 . . . . .1H 65
(not continuous)
Nichol Cl. N14 . . . . .1C 32
Nicholes Rd. TW3: Houn 4E 112
Nichol La. BR1: Broml 7J 141
Nicholl Ho. N4 . . . . .1C 66
Nicholls Av. UB8: Hil 4C 74
Nichollsfield Wlk. N7 . . . . .5K 65
Nicholls M. SW16 . . . . .4J 137
Nicholls Point *E15* *1J 87*
(off Park Gro.)
Nicholl St. E2 . . . . .1G 85
Nichols Cl. KT9: Chess 6C 162
N4 . . . .*1A 66*
(off Osborne Rd.)
Nichols Ct. E2 . . . . .2F 85
Nichols Grn. W5 . . . . .5E 78
Nicholson Ct. E17 . . . . .4K 49
N17 . . . . .3F 49
Nicholson Ho. SE17 . . . . .5D 102
Nicholson M. KT1: King T 4E 150
Nicholson Rd. CR0: C'don 1F 169
Nicholson Sq. *E3* *3E 86*
(off Bolinder Way)
Nicholson St. SE1 . . . . .5A 14 (1B 102)
Nicholson Wlk. UB10: Uxb 1A 74
Nickelby Apts. *E15* *6F 69*
(off Grove Cres. Rd.)
Nickelby Cl. SE28 . . . . .6C 90
Nickleby Cl. UB8: Hil 6D 74
Nickleby Ho. *SE16* *7K 15*
(off Parkers Row)
W11 . . . .*1F 99*
(off St Ann's Rd.)
Nickols Wlk. SW18 . . . . .4K 117
Nicola Cl. CR2: S Croy 6C 168
HA3: Hrw W 2H 41
Nicola Ter. DA7: Bex 1E 126
Nicol Cl. TW1: Twick 6B 114
Nicoll Cir. NW7 . . . . .6B 30
Nicoll Ct. N10 . . . . .7A 32
NW10 . . . . .1A 80
Nicoll Pl. NW4 . . . . .6D 44
Nicoll Rd. NW10 . . . . .1A 80
Nicolson NW9 . . . . .1A 44
Nicolson Dr. WD23: B Hea 1B 26
Nicosia Rd. SW18 . . . . .7C 118
Niederwald Rd. SE26 . . . . .4A 140
Nield Rd. UB3: Hayes 2H 93
Nigel Cl. UB5: N'olt 1C 76
Nigel Ct. N3 . . . . .7E 30
Nigel Fisher Way KT9: Chess 7C 162
Nigel Ho. *EC1* *5J 7*
(off Portpool La.)
Nigel M. IG1: Ilf 4F 71
Nigel Playfair Av. W6 . . . . .4D 98
Nigel Rd. E7 . . . . .5A 70
SE15 . . . . .3G 121
Nigeria Rd. SE7 . . . . .7A 106
Nighthawk NW9 . . . . .1B 44
Nightingale Av. E4 . . . . .5B 36
HA1: Harr 7B 42
Nightingale Cl. E4 . . . . .4A 36
HA5: Eastc 5A 40
SM5: Cars 2E 166
W4 . . . . .6J 97
Nightingale Ct. BR2: Broml 2G 159
E14 . . . .*2E 104*
(off Ovex Cl.)
HA1: Harr 6K 41
N4 . . . .*2K 65*
(off Tollington Pk.)
SM1: Sutt 5A 166
Nightingale Dr. KT19: Ewe 6H 163
Nightingale Gro. SE13 . . . . .5F 123
Nightingale Hgts. SE18 . . . . .6F 107
Nightingale Ho. *E1* *1G 103*
(off Thomas More St.)
E2 . . . .*1E 84*
(off Kingsland Rd.)
NW8 . . . .*4C 4*
(off Samford St.)
SE18 . . . .*5E 106*
(off Connaught M.)
UB7: W Dray 2B 92
W12 . . . .*6E 80*
(off Du Cane Rd.)
Nightingale La. BR1: Broml 2A 160
E11 . . . . .4K 51
N8 . . . . .4J 47
SW4 . . . . .7D 118
SW12 . . . . .7D 118
TW10: Rich 7E 114
Nightingale Lodge *W9* *5J 81*
(off Admiral Wlk.)
Nightingale M. E3 . . . . .2K 85
E11 . . . . .5J 51
KT1: King T *3D 150*
(off South La.)
SE11 . . . . .3K 19 (4B 102)
Nightingale Pl. SE18 . . . . .6E 106
SW10 . . . . .7A 16 (6A 100)
Nightingale Rd. BR5: Pet W 6G 161
E5 . . . . .3H 67
KT8: W Mole 5F 149
KT12: Walt T 7A 148
N1 . . . . .6C 66
N9 . . . . .6D 24
N22 . . . . .1J 47
NW10 . . . . .2B 80
SM5: Cars 3D 166
TW12: Hamp 5E 130
W7 . . . . .1K 95
The Nightingales TW19: Stanw 1B 128
Nightingale Sq. SW12 . . . . .7E 118
Nightingale Va. SE18 . . . . .6E 106
Nightingale Wlk. N1 . . . . .6C 66
SW4 . . . . .6F 119
Nightingale Way E6 . . . . .5C 88
Nihill Pl. CR0: C'don 1F 169
Nile Cl. N16 . . . . .3F 67
Nile Dr. N9 . . . . .2D 34
Nile Ho. *N1* *1E 8*
(off Nile St.)
Nile Path SE18 . . . . .6E 106
Nile Rd. E13 . . . . .2A 88
Nile St. N1 . . . . .1D 8 (3C 84)
Nile Ter. SE15 . . . . .5F 103
Nimegen Way SE22 . . . . .5E 120
Nimmo Dr. WD23: B Hea 1C 26
Nimrod NW9 . . . . .1A 44
Nimrod Cl. UB5: N'olt 3B 76
Nimrod Ho. *E16* *5K 87*
(off Vanguard Cl.)
Nimrod Pas. N1 . . . . .6E 66
Nimrod Rd. SW16 . . . . .6F 137
Nina Mackay Cl. E15 . . . . .1G 87
Nine Acres Cl. E12 . . . . .5C 70
UB3: Harl 3E 92
NINE ELMS 7G 101
Nine Elms Cl. TW14: Felt 1H 129
Nine Elms La. SW8 . . . . .6G 101
SW11 . . . . .7C 18 (7G 101)
Nineteenth Rd. CR4: Mitc 4J 155
Ninhams Wood BR6: Farnb 4E 172
Ninth Av. UB3: Hayes 7J 75
Nipper All. *KT1: King T* *2E 150*
(off Clarence St.)
Nipponzan Myohoji Peace Pagoda
. . . . .6D 100
Nisbet Ho. E9 . . . . .5K 67
Nisbett Wlk. DA14: Sidc 4A 144
Nita Ct. SE12 . . . . .1J 141
Nithdale Rd. SE18 . . . . .7F 107
Nithsdale Gro. UB10: Ick 3E 56
Niton Cl. EN5: Barn 6A 20
Niton Rd. TW9: Rich 3G 115
Niton St. SW6 . . . . .7F 99
Niveda Cl. W12 . . . . .2C 98
Noah Cl. EN3: Enf W 1D 24
Noah's Yd. N1 . . . . .2J 83
Nobel Cl. NW9 . . . . .2K 43
Nobel Dr. UB3: Harl 1F 111
Nobel Ho. SE5 . . . . .2C 120
Nobel Rd. N18 . . . . .4D 34
Noble Cnr. TW5: Hest 1E 112
Noble Ct. CR4: Mitc 2B 154
E1 . . . . .7H 85
Noblefield Hgts. N2 . . . . .5C 46
Noble M. *N16* *3D 66*
(off Albion Rd.)
Noble St. EC2 . . . . .7C 8 (6C 84)
Noble Yd. *N1* *1B 84*
(off Camden Pas.)
Nocavia Ho. *SW6* *2A 118*
(off Townmead Rd.)
Noel NW9 . . . . .1A 44
Noel Ct. CR0: C'don 7D 156
TW4: Houn 3D 112
Noel Coward Ho. *SW1* *4B 18*
(off Vauxhall Bri. Rd.)
Noel Coward Theatre *2E 12*
(off St Martin's La.)
Noel Ho. *NW6* *7B 64*
(off Harben Rd.)
NOEL PARK .2B 48
Noel Pk. Rd. N22 . . . . .2A 48
Noel Rd. E6 . . . . .4C 88
N1 . . . . .2B 84
W3 . . . . .7G 79
Noel Sq. RM8: Dag 4C 72
TW11: Tedd 5K 131
Noel St. W1 . . . . .1B 12 (6G 83)
Noel Ter. DA14: Sidc 4B 144
SE23 . . . . .2J 139
Noko W10 .3F 81
Nolands Cl. RM5: Col R 2J 55
Nolan Mans. *E20* *5D 68*
(off Honour Lea Av.)
Nolan Way E5 . . . . .4G 67
Noll Ho. *N7* *2K 65*
(off Tomlins Wlk.)
Nolton Pl. HA8: Edg 1F 43
Nonsuch Ho. *SW19* *1B 154*
(off Chapter Way)
Nonsuch Pl. *SM3: Cheam* *7F 165*
(off Ewell Rd.)
Nonsuch Wlk. SM2: Cheam 7F 165
Nook Apts. *E1* *1K 15*
(off Scarborough St.)
Nora Gdns. NW4 . . . . .4F 45
Nora Leverton Ct. *NW1* *7G 65*
(off Randolph St.)
NORBITON 2G 151
Norbiton Av. KT1: King T 1G 151
Norbiton Comn. Rd.
KT1: King T 3H 151
Norbiton Hall KT2: King T 2F 151
Norbiton Ho. *NW1* *1G 83*
(off Camden St.)
Norbiton Rd. E14 . . . . .6B 86
Norbreck Gdns. NW10 . . . . .3F 79
Norbreck Pde. NW10 . . . . .3E 78
Norbroke St. W12 . . . . .7B 80
Norburn St. W10 . . . . .5G 81
NORBURY .1K 155
Norbury Av. CR7: Thor H 1K 155
SW16 . . . . .1K 155
TW3: Houn 4H 113
Norbury Cl. SW16 . . . . .1A 156
Norbury Ct. Rd. SW16 . . . . .3J 155
Norbury Cres. SW16 . . . . .1K 155
Norbury Cross SW16 . . . . .3J 155
Norbury Gdns.
RM6: Chad H 5D 54
Norbury Gro. NW7 . . . . .3F 29
Norbury Hill SW16 . . . . .7A 138
Norbury Ri. SW16 . . . . .3J 155
Norbury Rd. CR7: Thor H 2C 156
E4 . . . . .5H 35
TW13: Felt 3H 129
Norbury Trad. Est. SW16 . . . . .2K 155
Norcombe Gdns. HA3: Kenton 6C 42
Norcombe Ho. *N19* *3H 65*
(off Wedmore St.)
Norcott Cl. UB4: Yead 4A 76
Norcott Rd. N16 . . . . .2G 67
Norcroft Gdns. SE22 . . . . .7G 121
Norcutt Rd. TW2: Twick 1J 131
Nordenfeldt Rd. DA8: Erith 5K 109
Norden Ho. *E2* *3H 85*
(off Pott St.)
Norfield Rd. DA2: Wilm 4J 145
Norfolk Apts. E4 . . . . .7J 35
Norfolk Av. N13 . . . . .6G 33
N15 . . . . .6F 49
Norfolk Cl. EN4: Cockf 4K 21
N2 . . . . .3C 46
N13 . . . . .6G 33
TW1: Twick 6B 114

Norfolk Ct.—Notley St.

Norfolk Ct. EN5: Barn 4B 20
RM6: Chad H 5B 54
(off Norwich Cres.)
Norfolk Cres. DA15: Sidc 7J 125
W2 7C 4 (6C 82)
Norfolk Gdns. DA7: Bex 1F 127
Norfolk Ho. BR2: Broml 4H 159
(off Westmoreland Rd.)
EC4 2C 14
SE8 1C 122
(off Brookmill Rd.)
SE20 1J 157
SW1 3D 18
(off Page St.)
Norfolk Ho. Rd. SW16 3H 137
Norfolk Mans. SW11 1D 118
(off Prince of Wales Dr.)
Norfolk M. W10 5G 81
(off Blagrove Rd.)
Norfolk Pl. DA16: Well 2A 126
W2 7B 4 (6B 82)
(not continuous)
Norfolk Rd. CR7: Thor H 3C 156
E6 1D 88
E17 2K 49
EN3: Pond E 6C 24
EN5: New Bar 3D 20
HA1: Harr 5F 41
IG3: Ilf 1J 71
IG11: Bark 7J 71
NW8 1B 82
NW10 7A 62
RM7: Rom 6J 55
RM10: Dag 5H 73
SW19 7C 136
TW13: Felt 1A 130
UB8: Uxb 6A 56
Norfolk Row SE1 3G 19 (4K 101)
Norfolk Sq. W2 1B 10 (6B 82)
Norfolk Sq. M. W2 1B 10
Norfolk St. E7 5J 69
Norfolk Ter. W6 5G 99
Norgrove St. SW12 7E 118
Norhyrst Av. SE25 3F 157
Norland Ho. W11 1F 99
(off Queensdale Cres.)
Norland Pl. W11 1G 99
Norland Rd. W11 1F 99
(not continuous)
Norlands Cres. BR7: Chst 1F 161
Norland Sq. W11 1G 99
Norland Sq. Mans. W11 1G 99
(off Norland Sq.)
Norlem Ct. SE8 4A 104
(off Seafarer Way)
Norley Va. SW15 1C 134
Norlington Rd. E10 1E 68
E11 1E 68
Norman Av. N22 1B 48
TW1: Twick 7C 114
TW13: Hanw 2C 130
UB1: S'hall 7C 76
Norman Butler Ho. W10 4G 81
(off Ladbroke Gro.)
Normanby Cl. SW15 5H 117
Normanby Rd. NW10 4B 62
Norman Cl. BR6: Farnb 3G 173
N22 1C 48
RM5: Col R 1H 55
Norman Ct. IG2: Ilf 7H 53
N3 1J 45
(off Nether St.)
N4 7A 48
NW10 7C 62
W13 1B 96
(off Kirkfield Cl.)
Norman Cres. HA5: Pinn 1A 40
TW5: Hest 7B 94
Normand Gdns. W14 6G 99
(off Greyhound Rd.)
Normand Mans. W14 6G 99
(off Normand M.)
Normand M. W14 6G 99
Normand Rd. W14 6H 99
Normandy Av. EN5: Barn 5C 20
Normandy Cl. SE26 3A 140
Normandy Dr. UB3: Hayes 6E 74
Normandy Ho. E14 2E 104
(off Plevna St.)
EN2: Enf 1H 23
Normandy Pl. W12 1F 99
Normandy Rd. SW9 1A 120
Normandy Ter. E16 6K 87
Normandy Way DA8: Erith 1K 127
Norman Gro. E3 2A 86
The Norman Hay Trad. Est.
UB7: Sip 7B 92
Norman Ho. SE1 7H 15
(off Riley Rd.)
SW8 7J 101
(off Wyvil Rd.)
TW13: Hanw 2D 130
(off Watermill Way)
Normanhurst TW15: Ashf 5C 128
Normanhurst Av. DA7: Bex 1D 126
Normanhurst Dr.
TW1: Twick 5A 114
Normanhurst Rd. SW2 2K 137
Norman Leddy Memorial Gdns.
6H 75
Norman Pk. Athletics Track 6K 159
Norman Rd. CR7: Thor H 5B 156
DA17: Belv 3H 109
(not continuous)
E6 4D 88
E11 2F 69
IG1: Ilf 5F 71
N15 5F 49
SE10 7D 104
SM1: Sutt 5J 165
SW19 7A 136
TW15: Ashf 6F 129
Norman's Cl. NW10 6K 61
Normans Cl. UB8: Hil 5B 74
Normansfield Av.
TW11: Tedd 7C 132
Normanshire Dr. E4 4H 35
Norman's Mead NW10 6K 61
Norman St. EC1 2D 8 (3C 84)
Norman Ter. NW6 5H 63
Normanton Av. SW19 2J 135
Normanton Ct. CR2: S Croy 5E 168
(off Croham Rd.)
Normanton Pk. E4 2B 36
Normanton Rd. CR2: S Croy 5E 168
Normanton St. SE23 2K 139
Norman Way N14 2D 32
W3 5H 79
Normington Cl. SW16 5A 138
Norrice Lea N2 5B 46
Norris NW9 1B 44
(off Withers Mead)
Norris Ho. E9 1J 85
(off Handley Rd.)
N1 1E 84
(off Colville Est.)
SE8 5B 104
(off Grove St.)
TW7: Isle 2A 114
Norris St. SW1 3C 12 (7H 83)
Norroy Rd. SW15 4F 117
Norry's Cl. EN4: Cockf 4J 21
Norry's Rd. EN4: Cockf 4J 21
Norseman Cl. IG3: Ilf 1B 72
Norseman Way UB6: G'frd 1F 77
Norstead Pl. SW15 2C 134
Nth. Access Rd. E17 6K 49
North Acre NW9 1A 44
NORTH ACTON 4K 79
Nth. Acton Bus. Pk. W3 5K 79
Nth. Acton Rd. NW10 2K 79
Northall Rd. DA7: Bex 2J 127
Northampton Gro. N1 5D 66
Northampton Pk. N1 6C 66
Northampton Rd.
CR0: C'don 2G 169
EC1 3K 7 (4A 84)
EN3: Pond E 4F 25
Northampton Row EC1 3K 7
Northampton Sq. EC1 2A 8 (3B 84)
Northampton St. N1 7C 66
Northanger Rd. SW16 6J 137
Nth. Audley St. W1 1G 11 (7E 82)
North Av. HA2: Harr 6F 41
N18 4B 34
SM5: Cars 7E 166
TW9: Kew 1G 115
UB1: S'hall 7D 76
UB3: Hayes 7J 75
W13 5B 78
Northaw Ho. W10 4E 80
(off Sutton Way)
Nth. Bank NW8 2C 4 (3C 82)
Northbank Rd. E17 2E 50
NORTH BECKTON 5D 88
Nth. Birkbeck Rd. E11 3F 69
Nth. Block SE1 6H 13
(off Chicheley St.)
Northborough Rd. SW16 3H 155
Northbourne BR2: Hayes 7J 159
Northbourne Rd. SW4 5H 119
Northbrook Dr.
HA6: Nwood 1G 39
Northbrook Rd. CR0: C'don 5D 156
EN5: Barn 6A 20
IG1: Ilf 2E 70
N22 7D 32
SE13 5G 123
Northburgh St. EC1 4B 8 (4B 84)
Northbury Cl. IG11: Bark 7G 71
Nth. Carriage Dr. W2 2C 10
NORTH CHEAM 3E 164
Northchurch SE17 5D 102
(not continuous)
Northchurch Ho. E2 1G 85
(off Whiston Rd.)
Northchurch Rd. HA9: Wemb 6G 61
N1 7D 66
(not continuous)
Northchurch Ter. N1 7E 66
Nth. Circular Rd. E4 6G 35
E12 3E 70
E18 2H 51
IG1: Ilf 2D 70
IG11: Bark 2D 70
N3 4H 45
N12 4H 45
N13 5F 33
NW2 3A 62
NW4 7E 44
NW10 2F 79
NW11 7E 44
Northcliffe Cl. KT4: Wor Pk 3A 164
Northcliffe Dr. N20 1C 30
North Cl. DA6: Bex 4D 126
RM10: Dag 1G 91
SM4: Mord 4G 153
TW14: Bedf 6F 111
The Nth. Colonnade E14 1C 104
(not continuous)
North Comn. Rd. UB8: Uxb 5A 56
W5 7E 78
Northcote HA5: Pinn 2A 40
Northcote Av. KT5: Surb 7H 151
TW7: Isle 5A 114
UB1: S'hall 7C 76
W5 7E 78
Northcote Rd. CR0: C'don 6D 156
DA14: Sidc 4J 143
E17 4A 50
KT3: N Mald 3J 151
NW10 7A 62
SW11 5C 118
TW1: Twick 5A 114
Northcott Av. N22 1J 47
Nth. Countess Rd. E17 2B 50
North Ct. BR1: Broml 1K 159
(off Palace Gro.)
SE24 3B 120
SW1 2E 18
(off Gt. Peter St.)
W1 5B 6 (5G 83)
NORTH CRAY 5E 144
Nth. Cray Rd. DA5: Bexl 1H 145
DA14: Sidc 6E 144
North Cray Woods 4D 144
North Cres. E16 4F 87
N3 2H 45
WC1 5C 6 (5H 83)
Northcroft Ct. W12 2C 98
Northcroft Rd. KT19: Ewe 7A 164
W13 2B 96
Nth. Crofts SE23 1H 139
Northcroft Ter. W13 2B 96
Nth. Cross Rd. IG6: Ilf 4G 53
SE22 5F 121
Northdale Ct. SE25 3F 157
North Dene NW7 3E 28
TW3: Houn 1F 113
Northdene Gdns. N15 6F 49
Northdown Cl. HA4: Ruis 3H 57
Northdown Gdns. IG2: Ilf 5J 53
Northdown Rd. DA16: Well 2B 126
Northdown St. N1 1G 7 (2J 83)
North Dr. BR3: Beck 4D 158
BR6: Orp 4J 173
HA4: Ruis 7G 39
SW16 4G 137
TW3: Houn 2G 113
Nth. E. Surrey Crematorium 6E 152
NORTH END 2A 64
Nth. End CR0: C'don 2C 168
IG9: Buck H 1F 37
NW3 2A 64
Nth. End Av. NW3 2A 64
Nth. End Cres. W14 4H 99
Nth. End Ho. W14 4G 99
Nth. End La. BR6: Downe 7F 173
Nth. End Pde. W14 4G 99
(off North End Rd.)
Nth. End Rd. HA9: Wemb 3G 61
NW11 1J 63
SW6 4G 99
W14 4G 99
Nth. End Way NW3 2A 64
Northern Av. N9 2K 33
Northernhay Wlk. SM4: Mord 4G 153
Northern Hgts. N8 7H 47
(off Crescent Rd.)
Northern Perimeter Rd.
TW6: H'row A 1D 110
Northern Perimeter Rd. (W.)
TW6: H'row A 4E 174
Northern Rd. E13 2K 87
Northesk Ho. E1 4H 85
(off Tent St.)
Nth. Eyot Gdns. W6 5B 98
Northey St. E14 7A 86
NORTH FELTHAM 6K 111
Nth. Feltham Trad. Est.
TW14: Felt 5K 111
Northfield Av. HA5: Pinn 4B 40
W5 1B 96
W13 1B 96
Northfield Cl. BR1: Broml 1C 160
UB3: Harl 3H 93
Northfield Cres. SM3: Cheam 4G 165
Northfield Gdns.
RM9: Dag 4F 73
Northfield Ho. SE15 6G 103
Northfield Pde. UB3: Harl 3G 93
Northfield Pk. UB3: Harl 3H 93
Northfield Path RM9: Dag 4F 73
Northfield Recreation Ground
W5 4B 96
Northfield Rd. E6 7D 70
EN3: Pond E 5C 24
EN4: Cockf 3H 21
N16 7E 48
RM9: Dag 4F 73
TW5: Hest 6B 94
W13 2B 96
NORTHFIELDS 3B 96
Northfields SW18 4J 117
Northfields Ind. Est.
HA0: Wemb 1G 79
Northfields Prospect Bus. Cen.
SW18 4J 117
Northfields Rd. W3 5H 79
NORTH FINCHLEY 5F 31
Northfleet Ho. SE1 6E 14
(off Tennis St.)
Northflock St. SE16 2G 103
Nth. Flower Wlk. W2 3A 10
North Gdn. E14 1B 104
North Gdns. SW19 7B 136
North Ga. NW8 1C 4
Northgate HA6: Nwood 1E 38
Northgate Bus. Cen. EN1: Enf 3C 24
Northgate Ct. SW9 3A 120
Northgate Dr. NW9 6A 44
Northgate Ho. E14 7C 86
(off E. India Dock Rd.)
Northgate Ind. Pk. RM5: Col R 1F 55
Northgate Rd. IG11: Bark 3C 90
North Gates N12 1A 46
(off Bow La.)
The Nth. Glade DA5: Bexl 7F 127
Nth. Gower St. NW1 2B 6 (3G 83)
North Grn. NW9 7F 29
North Gro. N6 7E 46
N15 5D 48
NORTH HARROW 5F 41
Nth. Hatton Rd. TW6: H'row A 1F 111
Nth. Hill N6 6D 46
North Hill Av. N6 6E 46
NORTH HILLINGDON 7E 56
North Ho. SE8 5B 104
Nth. Hyde Gdns.
UB3: Harl, Hayes 4J 93
Nth. Hyde La. TW5: Hest 5C 94
UB2: S'hall 5B 94
Nth. Hyde Rd.
UB3: Harl, Hayes 3G 93
Nth. Hyde Wharf UB2: S'hall 4A 94
Northiam N12 4D 30
(not continuous)
WC1 2F 7
(off Cromer St.)
Northiam St. E9 1H 85
Northington St. WC1 4H 7 (4K 83)
NORTH KENSINGTON 5E 80
Northlands Av. BR6: Orp 4J 173
Northlands St. SE5 2C 120
North La. TW11: Tedd 6K 131
Northleigh Ho. E3 3D 86
(off Powis Rd.)
Nth. Lodge E16 1K 105
(off Wesley Av.)
EN5: New Bar 5F 21
Nth. Lodge Cl. SW15 5F 117
Nth. London Bus. Pk. N11 2K 31
Nth. Mall N9 2C 34
(within Edmonton Grn. Shop. Cen.)
SW18 5K 117
(off Southside Shop. Cen.)
North M. WC1 4H 7 (4K 83)
North Middlesex Golf Course 3G 31
Nth. Mill Apts. E8 1F 85
(off Lovelace St.)
North Mt. N20 2F 31
(off High Rd.)
Northolm HA8: Edg 4E 28
Northolme Gdns. HA8: Edg 1G 43
Northolme Ri. BR6: Orp 2J 173
Northolme Rd. N5 4C 66
NORTHOLT 7E 58
Northolt N17 2E 48
(off Griffin Rd.)
Northolt Av. HA4: Ruis 5K 57
Northolt Gdns. UB6: G'frd 5K 59
Northolt Golf Course 2C 76
Northolt Leisure Cen. 6E 58
Northolt Rd. HA2: Harr 4F 59
TW6: H'row A 1A 110
(not continuous)
Northolt Trad. Est. UB5: N'olt 7F 59
Northover BR1: Broml 3H 141
North Pde. HA8: Edg 2G 43
KT9: Chess 5F 163
UB1: S'hall 6E 76
(off North Rd.)
North Pk. SE9 6D 124
North Pas. SW18 5J 117
North Pl. CR4: Mitc 7D 136
TW11: Tedd 6K 131
North Point N8 5K 47
Northpoint Cl. SM1: Sutt 3A 166
Northpoint Ho. N1 6D 66
(off Essex Rd.)
Northpoint Sq. NW1 6H 65
Nth. Pole La. BR2: Kes 6H 171
Nth. Pole Rd. W10 5E 80
Northport St. N1 1D 84
North Quay Pl. E14 7D 86
Nth. Ride W2 3C 10 (7C 82)
Nth. Ri. W2 1D 10 (6C 82)
North Rd. BR1: Broml 1K 159
BR4: W W'ck 1D 170
DA17: Belv 3H 109
HA1: Harr 7A 42
HA8: Edg 1H 43
IG3: Ilf 2J 71
KT6: Surb 6D 150
N6 7E 46
N7 6J 65
N9 1C 34
RM6: Chad H 5E 54
SE18 4J 107
SW19 6A 136
TW8: Bford 6E 96
TW9: Kew, Rich 3G 115
TW14: Bedf 6F 111
UB1: S'hall 6E 76
UB3: Hayes 5F 75
UB7: W Dray 3B 92
W5 3D 96
Northrop Rd. TW6: H'row A 1G 111
Nth. Row W1 2F 11 (7D 82)
Nth. Row Bldgs. W1 2G 11
(off North Row)
Nth. Several SE3 2F 123
NORTH SHEEN 3G 115
Northside Rd. BR1: Broml 1J 159
Northside Studios E8 1H 85
(off Andrew's Rd.)
Nth. Side Wandsworth Comn.
SW18 5B 118
Northspur Rd. SM1: Sutt 3J 165
North Sq. N9 2C 34
(off New Rd.)
NW11 5J 45
Nth. Stand N5 3B 66
Northstead Rd. SW2 2A 138
North St. BR1: Broml 1J 159
DA7: Bex 4G 127
E13 2K 87
IG11: Bark 6F 71
NW4 5E 44
RM1: Rom 3K 55
RM5: Rom 3K 55
SM5: Cars 3D 166
SW4 3G 119
TW7: Isle 3A 114
North St. Pas. E13 2K 87
Nth. Tenter St. E1 1K 15 (6F 85)
North Ter. SW3 2C 16 (3C 100)
WC2 4E 12
Northumberland All.
EC3 1H 15 (6E 84)
(not continuous)
Northumberland Av.
DA16: Well 4H 125
E12 1A 70
EN1: Enf 1C 24
TW7: Isle 1K 113
WC2 4E 12 (1J 101)
Northumberland Cl.
DA8: Erith 7J 109
TW19: Stanw 6A 110
Northumberland Cres.
TW14: Felt 6G 111
Northumberland Gdns.
BR1: Broml 4E 160
CR4: Mitc 5H 155
N9 3A 34
TW7: Isle 7A 96
Northumberland Gro. N17 7C 34
NORTHUMBERLAND HEATH 7J 109
Northumberland Ho.
IG8: Wfd G 7K 37
SW1 4E 12
(off Northumberland Av.)
Northumberland Pk. DA8: Erith 7J 109
N17 7A 34
Northumberland Pk. Ind. Est.
N17 7C 34
Northumberland Pk. School Sports Cen.
7B 34
Northumberland Pl.
TW10: Rich 5D 114
W2 6J 81
Northumberland Rd. E6 6C 88
E17 7C 50
EN5: New Bar 6F 21
HA2: Harr 5D 40
Northumberland St.
WC2 4E 12 (1J 101)
Northumberland Way
DA8: Erith 1J 127
Northumbria St. E14 6C 86
Nth. Verbena Gdns. W6 5C 98
North Vw. HA5: Eastc 7A 40
SW19 5E 134
W5 4C 78
North Vw. Cvn. Site 1A 54
Northview Cres. NW10 4B 62
North Vw. Dr. IG8: Wfd G 2B 52
Northview Pde. N7 3J 65
North Vw. Rd. N8 4H 47
North Vs. NW1 6H 65
North Wlk. CR0: New Ad 6D 170
(not continuous)
Northwall Rd. E20 5C 68
Nth. Way HA5: Pinn 4B 40
N9 2E 34
N11 6B 32
NW9 3H 43
UB10: Uxb 7A 56
Northway NW11 5K 45
SM4: Mord 3G 153
SM6: W'gton 4G 167
Northway Cir. NW7 4E 28
Northway Ct. NW7 4F 29
Northway Cres. NW7 4E 28
Northway Gdns. 5K 45
Northway Ho. N20 1F 31
Northway Rd. CR0: C'don 6F 157
SE5 3C 120
Northways NW3 7B 64
(off College Cres.)
Northways Pde. NW3 7B 64
(off College Cres.)
Northweald La. KT2: King T 5D 132
NORTH WEMBLEY 3D 60
Northwest Pl. N1 2A 84
Nth. Wharf E14 1E 104
(off Coldharbour)
Nth. Wharf Rd. W2 6A 4 (5B 82)
Northwick Av. HA3: Kenton 6A 42
Northwick Circ.
HA3: Kenton 6C 42
Northwick Cl. HA1: Harr 1B 60
NW8 3A 4 (4B 82)
Northwick Ho. NW8 3A 4
Northwick Pk. Playgolf 1A 60
Northwick Pk. Rd.
HA1: Harr 6K 41
NORTHWICK PARK RDBT. 7A 42
Northwick Rd.
HA0: Wemb 1D 78
Northwick Ter. NW8 3A 4 (4B 82)
Northwick Wlk. HA1: Harr 7K 41
Northwold Dr. HA5: Pinn 2A 40
Northwold Rd. E5 2F 67
N16 2F 67
NORTHWOOD 1H 39
The Northwood Club 2H 39
Nth. Wood Ct. SE25 3G 157
Northwood Est. E5 2G 67
Northwood Gdns. IG5: Ilf 4E 52
N12 5G 31
UB6: G'frd 5K 59
Northwood Golf Course 1F 39
Northwood Hall N6 7G 47
NORTHWOOD HILLS 2J 39
NORTHWOOD HILLS CIR. 1J 39
Northwood Ho. KT2: King T 2G 151
(off Coombe Rd.)
SE27 4D 138
Northwood Pl. DA18: Erith 3F 109
Northwood Rd.
CR7: Thor H 2B 156
N6 7F 47
SE23 1B 140
SM5: Cars 6E 166
TW6: H'row A 4E 174
UB9: Hare 1A 38
Northwood Way HA6: Nwood 1J 39
SE19 6D 138
UB9: Hare 1A 38
NORTH WOOLWICH 2E 106
Nth. Woolwich Rd. E16 1H 105
Nth. Worple Way SW14 3K 115
Norton Av. KT5: Surb 7H 151
Norton Cl. E4 5H 35
EN1: Enf 2C 24
Norton Ct. BR3: Beck 1B 158
Norton Folgate E1 5H 9 (5E 84)
Norton Folgate Ho. E1 5J 9
(off Puma Ct.)
Norton Gdns. SW16 2J 155
Norton Ho. E1 6H 85
(off Bigland St.)
E2 2K 85
(off Mace St.)
SW1 2D 18
(off Arneway St.)
SW9 2K 119
(off Aytoun Rd.)
Norton Rd. E10 1B 68
HA0: Wemb 6D 60
RM10: Dag 6K 73
Norval Grn. SW9 2A 120
Norval Rd. HA0: Wemb 2B 60
Norway Ga. SE16 3A 104
Norway Ho. N1 1E 84
(off Hertford Rd.)
Norway Pl. E14 6B 86
Norway St. SE10 6D 104
Norway Wharf E14 6B 86
Norwegian War Memorial
5D 10 (1C 100)
Norwich Cres. RM6: Chad H 5B 54
Norwich Ho. E14 6D 86
(off Cordelia St.)
Norwich M. IG3: Ilf 1A 72
Norwich Pl. DA6: Bex 4G 127
Norwich Rd. CR7: Thor H 3C 156
E7 5J 69
HA6: Nwood 3H 39
UB6: G'frd 1F 77
Norwich St. EC4 7J 7 (6A 84)
Norwich Wlk. HA8: Edg 7D 28
NORWOOD 6E 138
Norwood Av. HA0: Wemb 1F 79
RM7: Rush G 7K 55
Norwood Cl. NW2 3G 63
TW2: Twick 2H 131
UB2: S'hall 4E 94
Norwood Dr. HA2: Harr 6D 40
Norwood Gdns.
UB2: S'hall 4D 94
UB4: Yead 4A 76
NORWOOD GREEN 4D 94
Norwood Grn. Rd.
UB2: S'hall 4E 94
Norwood High St. SE27 3B 138
Norwood Ho. E14 7D 86
(off Poplar High St.)
NORWOOD NEW TOWN 6C 138
Norwood Pk. Rd. SE27 5C 138
Norwood Rd. SE24 1B 138
SE27 2B 138
TW5: Hest 6A 94
UB2: S'hall 3C 94
Norwood Ter. UB2: S'hall 4F 95
Notley Pl. SW4 7J 119
Notley St. SE5 7D 102

Notson Rd.—Occupation Rd.

Notson Rd. SE25 4H 157
Notting Barn Rd. W10 4F 81
Nottingdale Sq. W11 1G 99
Nottingham Av. E16 5A 88
Nottingham Ct. WC2 1E 12 (6J 83)
Nottingham Ho. WC2 1E 12
(off Shorts Gdns.)
Nottingham Pl. W1 4G 5 (5E 82)
Nottingham Rd. CR2: S Croy 4C 168
E10 6E 50
SW17 1D 136
TW7: Isle 2K 113
Nottingham St. W1 5G 5 (5E 82)
Nottingham Ter. NW1 4G 5
NOTTING HILL 7H 81
Notting Hill Ga. W11 1J 99
Nottingwood Ho. W11 7G 81
(off Clarendon Rd.)
Nova Bldg. E14 4C 104
Nova Ct. E. E14 1E 104
(off Yabsley St.)
Nova Ct. W. E14 1E 104
(off Yabsley St.)
Nova M. SM3: Sutt 1G 165
Novar Cl. BR6: Orp 7K 161
Nova Rd. CR0: C'don 1B 168
Novar Rd. SE9 1G 143
Novello Ct. N1 1C 84
(off Dibden St.)
Novello St. SW6 1J 117
Novello Theatre 2G 13
(off Aldwych)
Novem Ho. E1 6K 9
(off Chicksand St.)
Nowell Rd. SW13 6C 98
Nower Ct. HA5: Pinn 4D 40
Nower Hill HA5: Pinn 4D 40
Noyna Rd. SW17 3D 136
Nubia Way
BR1: Broml 3G 141
Nucleus Apts. SW15 7F 117
(off W. Hill)
Nuding Cl. SE13 3C 122
Nuffield Ct. TW5: Hest 7D 94
Nuffield Health
Baker Street 2J 23
Battersea 2D 118
(within Latchmere Leisure Cen.)
Bloomsbury 3G 7
(off Mecklenburgh Pl.)
Bromley 5K 159
Cannon Street 3E 14
Cheam 7G 165
Chingford 4K 35
Chislehurst 5J 143
Covent Garden 1F 13
(off Endell St.)
Ealing 7D 78
(within Ealing Broadway Cen.)
Friern Barnet 5K 31
Fulham 1F 117
Hendon 5E 44
Ilford 3F 71
(off Clements Rd.)
Islington 1B 84
Kingston upon Thames,
Richmond Rd. 1E 150
Merton Abbey 1B 154
(off Watermill Way)
Norbury 2K 155
Paddington 5A 82
Purley Way 6A 168
Romford 5K 55
Stockley Park 7E 74
Sunbury 1J 147
Surbiton 6C 150
Surrey Street 3C 168
(off Surrey St.)
Sydney Rd. 4J 23
Twickenham 7J 113
Wandsworth 7K 117
Wandsworth,
Southside Shop. Cen. 5J 117
Willesden Green 7E 62
Wimbledon 6H 135
Nuffield Lodge N6 6G 47
W9 5J 81
(off Admiral Wlk.)
Nugent Rd. N19 1J 65
SE25 3F 157
Nugents Ct. HA5: Pinn 1C 40
Nugent's Pk. HA5: Hat E 1C 40
Nugent Ter. NW8 2A 82
Numa Ct. TW8: Bford 7D 96
No. 1 St. SE18 3F 107
No. One EC1 4D 8 (4C 84)
Nun Ct. EC2 7E 8
Nuneaton Rd. RM9: Dag 7E 72
NUNHEAD 3H 121
Nunhead Cemetery
Local Nature Reserve 4J 121
Nunhead Cres. SE15 3H 121
Nunhead Est. SE15 4H 121
Nunhead Grn. SE15 3H 121
Nunhead Gro. SE15 3H 121
Nunhead La. SE15 3H 121
Nunhead Pas. SE15 3G 121
Nunnington Cl. SE9 3C 142
Nunns Rd. EN2: Enf 2H 23
Nupton Dr. EN5: Barn 6A 20
Nurse Cl. HA8: Edg 1J 43
Nursery App. N12 6H 31
Nursery Av. CR0: C'don 2K 169
DA7: Bex 3F 127
N3 2A 46
Nursery Cl. BR6: Orp 7K 161
CR0: C'don 2K 169
EN3: Enf H 1E 24
IG8: Wfd G 5E 36
RM6: Chad H 6D 54
SE4 2B 122
SW15 4F 117
TW14: Felt 7K 111
(not continuous)
Nursery Ct. N17 7A 34
W13 5A 78
Nursery Gdns. BR7: Chst 6F 143
EN3: Enf H 1E 24
TW4: Houn 5D 112
TW12: Hamp 4D 130
TW16: Sun 2H 147
Nursery La. E2 1F 85
E7 6J 69
UB8: Cowl 4A 74
W10 5E 80
Nurserymans Rd. N11 2K 31
Nursery Rd. CR4: Mitc 3C 154
CR7: Thor H 4D 156
E9 6J 67
HA5: Pinn 3A 40
N2 1B 46
N14 7B 22
SM1: Sutt 4A 166
SW9 4K 119
SW19 7G 135
(Elm Gro.)
SW19 2K 153
(Parkleigh Rd.)
TW16: Sun 2G 147
Nursery Row EN5: Barn 3B 20
SE17 4D 102
Nursery St. N17 7A 34
Nursery Wlk. NW4 3E 44
RM7: Rush G 7K 55
Nursery Waye UB8: Uxb 1A 74
Nurstead Rd. DA8: Erith 7G 109
Nutbourne St. W10 3G 81
Nutbrook St. SE15 3G 121
Nutbrowne Rd. RM9: Dag 1F 91
Nutcroft Rd. SE15 7H 103
Nutfield Cl. N18 6B 34
SM5: Cars 3C 166
Nutfield Ct. BR1: Broml 3J 159
Nutfield Gdns. IG3: Ilf 2K 71
UB5: N'olt 2A 76
Nutfield Rd. CR7: Thor H 4B 156
E15 4E 68
NW2 3C 62
SE22 4F 121
Nutfield Way BR6: Farnb 2F 173
Nutford Pl. W1 7D 4 (6D 82)
Nuthatch Cl. TW19: Stanw 1B 128
Nuthatch Gdns. SE28 2H 107
(not continuous)
Nuthatch M. IG5: Ilf 1D 52
Nuthatch Row KT10: Clay 6A 162
Nuthurst Av. SW2 2K 137
Nutkin Wlk. UB8: Uxb 7A 56
Nutley Ter. NW3 6A 64
Nutmead Cl. DA5: Bexl 1J 145
Nutmeg Cl. E16 4G 87
Nutmeg La. E14 6F 87
Nuttall St. N1 2E 84
Nutter La. E11 6A 52
Nutt Gro. HA8: Edg 2J 27
Nutt St. SE15 7F 103
Nutty La. TW17: Shep 3E 146
Nutwell St. SW17 5C 136
Nuxley Rd. DA17: Belv 6F 109
Nyanza St. SE18 6H 107
Nye Bevan Est. E5 3K 67
Nye Bevan Ho. SW6 7H 99
(off St Thomas's Way)
Nyland Ct. SE8 4A 104
(off Naomi St.)
Nylands Av. TW9: Kew 1G 115
Nymans Gdns. SW20 3D 152
Nynehead St. SE14 7A 104
Nyon Gro. SE6 2B 140
Nyssa Cl. IG8: Wfd G 6J 37
Nyton Cl. N19 1J 65

O

The O2 1G 105
O2 Brixton Academy 3A 120
O2 Cen. 6A 64
O2 Forum Kentish Town 5F 65
O2 Shepherd's Bush Empire Theatre
2E 98
Oak Apple Ct. SE12 1J 141
Oak Av. CR0: C'don 1C 170
EN2: Enf 1E 22
N8 4J 47
N10 7A 32
N17 7J 33
TW5: Hest 7B 94
TW12: Hamp 5C 130
UB7: W Dray 3C 92
UB10: Ick 2D 56
Oak Avenue
Local Nature Reserve 5C 130
Oak Bank CR0: New Ad 6E 170
Oakbank Av. KT12: Walt T 7D 148
Oakbank Gro. SE24 4C 120
Oakbark Ho. TW8: Bford 7C 96
(off High St.)
Oakbrook Cl. BR1: Broml 4K 141
Oakbury Rd. SW6 2K 117
Oak Cl. N14 7A 22
SM1: Sutt 2A 166
Oakcombe Cl. KT3: N Mald 1A 152
Oak Cott. Cl. SE6 1H 141
Oak Cotts. W7 2J 95
Oak Ct. SE15 7F 103
(off Sumner Rd.)
Oak Cres. E16 5G 87
Oakcroft Bus. Cen. KT9: Chess 4F 163
Oakcroft Cl. HA5: Pinn 2K 39
Oakcroft Rd. KT9: Chess 4F 163
SE13 2F 123
Oakcroft Vs. KT9: Chess 4F 163
Oakdale N14 1A 32
Oakdale Av. HA3: Kenton 5E 42
HA6: Nwood 2J 39
Oakdale Cl. E4 5K 35
Oakdale Gdns. E4 5K 35
Oakdale Rd. E7 7K 69
E11 2F 69
E18 2K 51
KT19: Ewe 7K 163
N4 6C 48
SE15 3J 121
SW16 5J 137
Oakdale Way CR4: Mitc 7E 154
Oak Dene W13 5B 78
Oakdene SE15 1H 121
Oakdene Av. BR7: Chst 5E 142
DA8: Erith 6J 109
KT7: T Ditt 1A 162
Oakdene Cl. HA5: Hat E 1D 40
Oakdene Dr. KT5: Surb 7J 151
Oakdene M. SM3: Sutt 1H 165
Oakdene Pk. N3 7C 30
Oakdene Rd. BR5: St M Cry 5K 161
UB10: Hil 2D 74
Oakden St. SE11 3K 19 (4A 102)
Oake Ct. SW15 5G 117
Oakeford Ho. W14 3G 99
(off Russell Rd.)
Oakenholt Ho. SE2 1D 108
Oakenshaw Cl. KT6: Surb 7E 150
Oakes Cl. E6 6D 88
Oakeshott Av. N6 2E 64
Oakes M. E14 5E 86
(off Nairn St.)
Oakey La. SE1 1J 19 (3A 102)
Oakfield E4 5J 35
Oakfield Av. HA3: Kenton 3B 42
Oakfield Cen. HA4: Ruis 6H 39
KT3: N Mald 5B 152
Oakfield Ct. N8 7J 47
NW2 7F 45
Oakfield Gdns. BR3: Beck 5D 158
N18 4K 33
SE19 5E 138
(not continuous)
SM5: Cars 1C 166
UB6: G'frd 4H 77
Oakfield Ho. E3 5C 86
(off Gale St.)
Oakfield La. BR2: Kes 4A 172
Oakfield Lodge IG1: Ilf 3F 71
(off Albert Rd.)
Oakfield Rd. CR0: C'don 1C 168
E6 1C 88
E17 2A 50
IG1: Ilf 3F 71
N3 1K 45
N4 6A 48
N14 2D 32
SE20 7H 139
SW19 3F 135
TW15: Ashf 5D 128
Oakfield Rd. Ind. Est. SE20 7H 139
Oakfields Rd. NW11 6G 45
Oakfield St. SW10 6A 100
Oakford Rd. NW5 4G 65
Oak Gdns. CR0: C'don 2C 170
HA8: Edg 2J 43
Oak Glade HA6: Nwood 1D 38
Oak Gro. BR4: W W'ck 1E 170
HA4: Ruis 7K 39
NW2 4G 63
TW16: Sun 7K 129
Oak Gro. Rd. SE20 1J 157
Oakhall Ct. E11 6K 51
TW16: Sun 5H 129
Oakhall Dr. TW16: Sun 5H 129
Oak Hall Rd. E11 6K 51
Oakham Cl. EN4: Cockf 3J 21
SE6 2B 140
Oakham Dr. BR2: Broml 4H 159
Oakham Ho. W10 4E 80
(off Sutton Way)
Oakhampton Rd. NW7 7A 30
Oak Hill IG8: Wfd G 7A 36
KT6: Surb 7E 150
Oakhill KT10: Clay 6A 162
Oakhill Av. HA5: Pinn 2C 40
NW3 4K 63
Oak Hill Cl. IG8: Wfd G 7A 36
Oak Hill Ct. IG8: Wfd G 7A 36
Oakhill Ct. SE23 6J 121
SW19 7F 135
Oak Hill Cres. IG8: Wfd G 7A 36
KT6: Surb 7E 150
Oakhill Dr. KT6: Surb 7E 150
Oak Hill Gdns. IG8: Wfd G 1G 51
Oak Hill Gro. KT6: Surb 6E 150
Oak Hill Pk. NW3 4K 63
Oak Hill Pk. M. NW3 4A 64
Oak Hill Path KT6: Surb 6E 150
Oakhill Pl. SW15 5J 117
Oak Hill Rd. KT6: Surb 6E 150
Oakhill Rd. BR3: Beck 2E 158
BR6: Orp 1K 173
SM1: Sutt 3K 165
SW15 5H 117
SW16 1K 155
Oak Hill Way NW3 4K 63
(not continuous)
Oak Hill Woods Nature Reserve 6J 21
Oak Ho. E14 2E 104
(off Stewart St.)
N2 2B 46
RM7: Rom 5K 55
TW9: Kew 1H 115
W10 4G 81
(off Sycamore Wlk.)
Oakhouse Rd. DA6: Bex 5G 127
Oakhurst Av. DA7: Bex 7E 108
EN4: E Barn 7H 21
Oakhurst Cl. BR7: Chst 1D 160
E17 4G 51
IG6: Ilf 1G 53
KT2: King T 6F 133
TW11: Tedd 5J 131
Oakhurst Ct. E17 4G 51
(off Woodford New Rd.)
Oakhurst Gdns. DA7: Bex 7E 108
E4 1C 36
E17 4G 51
Oakhurst Gro. SE22 4G 121
Oakhurst Rd. KT19: Ewe 6J 163
Oakington Av. HA2: Harr 7E 40
HA9: Wemb 3F 61
UB3: Harl 4F 93
Oakington Cl. TW16: Sun 2A 148
Oakington Ct. EN2: Enf 2G 23
Oakington Dr. TW16: Sun 2A 148
Oakington Mnr. Dr.
HA9: Wemb 5G 61
Oakington Rd. W9 4J 81
Oakington Way N8 7J 47
Oakland Pl. IG9: Buck H 2D 36
Oakland Quay E14 3D 104
Oakland Rd. E15 4F 69
Oaklands BR3: Beck 1D 158
N21 2E 32
W13 5A 78
Oaklands Av. BR4: W W'ck 3D 170
CR7: Thor H 4A 156
DA15: Sidc 7K 125
KT10: Esh 7H 149
N9 6C 24
TW7: Isle 6K 95
Oaklands Cl. BR5: Pet W 6J 161
DA6: Bex 5F 127
HA0: Wemb 5D 60
KT9: Chess 4C 162
Oaklands Ct. HA0: Wemb 5D 60
NW10 1A 80
(off Nicoll Rd.)
SE20 7J 139
(off Chestnut Gro.)
Oaklands Dr. TW2: Whitt 7G 113
Oaklands Est. SW4 6G 119
Oaklands Gro. W12 1C 98
Oaklands M. NW2 4F 63
(off Oaklands Rd.)
Oaklands Pk. Av. IG1: Ilf 2G 71
Oaklands Pas. NW2 4F 63
(off Oaklands Rd.)
Oaklands Pl. SW4 4G 119
Oaklands Rd. BR1: Broml 7G 141
DA6: Bex 5F 127
N20 7C 20
NW2 4F 63
SW14 3K 115
W7 2K 95
(not continuous)
W13 2K 95
Oaklands Way SM6: W'gton 7H 167
Oakland Way KT19: Ewe 6A 164
Oak La. E14 7B 86
IG8: Wfd G 4C 36
N2 2B 46
N11 6C 32
TW1: Twick 7A 114
TW7: Isle 4J 113
Oakleafe Gdns. IG6: Ilf 3F 53
Oaklea Lodge IG3: Ilf 3A 72
Oaklea Pas. KT1: King T 3D 150
Oakleigh Av. HA8: Edg 2H 43
KT6: Surb 1G 163
N20 2G 31
Oakleigh Cl. N20 3J 31
Oakleigh Ct. EN4: E Barn 6H 21
HA8: Edg 2J 43
N1 1E 8
UB1: S'hall 1D 94
Oakleigh Cres. N20 2H 31
Oakleigh Gdns. BR6: Orp 4J 173
HA8: Edg 5A 28
N20 1F 31
Oakleigh M. N20 1F 31
OAKLEIGH PARK 1F 31
Oakleigh Pk. Av. BR7: Chst 1E 160
Oakleigh Pk. Lawn Tennis & Squash Club
2G 31
Oakleigh Pk. Nth. N20 1G 31
Oakleigh Pk. Sth. N20 7H 21
Oakleigh Rd. UB10: Hil 7E 56
Oakleigh Rd. Nth. N20 2G 31
Oakleigh Rd. Sth. N11 3K 31
Oakleigh Way CR4: Mitc 1F 155
KT6: Surb 1G 163
Oakley Av. CR0: Bedd 4K 167
IG11: Bark 7K 71
W5 7G 79
Oakley Cl. E4 3K 35
E6 6C 88
TW7: Isle 1H 113
W7 7J 77
Oakley Ct. CR4: Mitc 7E 154
Oakley Cres. EC1 2B 84
Oakley Dr. BR2: Broml 3C 172
SE9 1H 143
SE13 6F 123
Oakley Gdns. N8 5K 47
SW3 7D 16 (6C 100)
Oakley Grange HA1: Harr 2H 59
Oakley Ho. SE11 4J 19
(off Hotspur St.)
SW1 2F 17 (4D 100)
W5 7G 79
Oakley M. EN2: Enf 2F 23
Oakley Pk. DA5: Bexl 7C 126
Oakley Pl. SE1 5F 103
Oakley Rd. BR2: Broml 3C 172
HA1: Harr 6J 41
N1 7D 66
SE25 5H 157
Oakley Sq. NW1 2G 83
Oakley St. SW3 7C 16 (6C 100)
Oakley Studios SW3 7C 16
(off Up. Cheyne Row)
Oakley Wlk. W6 6F 99
Oakley Yd. E2 3K 9 (4F 85)
Oak Lock M. W4 5A 98
Oak Lodge E11 6J 51
SM1: Sutt 4A 166
TW16: Sun 7H 129
(off Forest Dr.)
W8 3K 99
(off Chantry Sq.)
Oak Lodge Cl. HA7: Stan 5H 27
Oak Lodge Dr. BR4: W W'ck 7D 158
Oaklodge Way NW7 5G 29
Oakman Ho. SW19 1F 135
Oakmead Av. BR2: Hayes 6J 159
Oakmead Ct. HA7: Stan 3H 27
Oakmeade HA5: Hat E 6A 26
Oakmead Gdns. HA8: Edg 4E 28
Oakmead Pl. CR4: Mitc 1C 154
Oakmead Rd. CR0: C'don 6H 155
SW12 1E 136
Oakmede EN5: Barn 4A 20
Oakmere Rd. SE2 6A 108
Oakmont Pl. BR6: Orp 1H 173
Oak Pk. Gdns. SW19 1F 135
Oak Pk. M. N16 3F 67
Oak Pl. SW18 5K 117
Oakridge Dr. N2 3B 46
Oakridge La. BR1: Broml 5F 141
Oakridge Rd. BR1: Broml 4F 141
Oak Ri. IG9: Buck H 3G 37
Oak Rd. BR6: Chels 7K 173
DA8: Erith 7J 109
KT3: N Mald 2K 151
W5 7D 78
Oak Row SW16 2G 155
The Oaks BR2: Broml 6E 160
EN2: Enf 3G 23
HA4: Ruis 7F 39
IG8: Wfd G 6B 36
N12 4E 30
NW6 7F 63
(off Brondesbury Pk.)
NW10 7D 62
SE18 5G 107
SM4: Mord 4G 153
TW13: Felt 2B 130
UB4: Hayes 2E 74
Oaks Av. KT4: Wor Pk 3D 164
RM5: Col R 2J 55
SE19 5E 138
TW13: Felt 2C 130
The Oaks Cvn. Pk. 3C 162
Oaksford Av. SE26 3H 139
Oaks Gro. E4 2B 36
Oakshade Rd. BR1: Broml 4F 141
Oakshaw Rd. SW18 7K 117
Oakshott Ct. NW1 1C 6 (2H 83)
(not continuous)
Oakside Ct. IG6: Ilf 2H 53
Oakside Ter. NW10 3K 61
Oaks La. CR0: C'don 3H 169
IG2: Ilf 5J 53
Oaks Pavilion M. SE19 5E 138
Oak Sq. SW9 2K 119
Oaks Rd. CR0: C'don 5H 169
TW19: Stanw 5A 110
Oak St. RM7: Rom 5J 55
Oaks Way KT6: Surb 1D 162
SM5: Cars 7D 166
Oakthorpe Ct. N13 5H 33
Oakthorpe Est. N13 5H 33
Oakthorpe Rd. N13 5F 33
Oaktree Av. N13 3G 33
Oak Tree Cl. HA7: Stan 7H 27
KT19: Ewe 6H 163
W5 6C 78
Oak Tree Ct. UB5: N'olt 2A 76
W3 7H 79
Oak Tree Dell NW9 5J 43
Oak Tree Dr. N20 1E 30
Oak Tree Gdns. BR1: Broml 5K 141
Oaktree Gdns. SE9 3F 143
Oaktree Gro. IG1: Ilf 5H 71
Oak Tree Ho. W9 4J 81
(off Shirland Rd.)
Oak Tree M. NW2 6C 62
Oak Tree Rd. NW8 2B 4 (3C 82)
Oakview Apts. SM1: Sutt 4B 166
Oakview Gdns. N2 4B 46
Oakview Gro. CR0: C'don 1A 170
Oakview Lodge NW11 7H 45
(off Beechcroft Av.)
Oakview Rd. SE6 5D 140
Oak Village NW5 4E 64
Oak Vs. NW11 6H 45
(off Hendon Pk. Row)
Oakville Ho. SE16 2K 103
(off Dominion Dr.)
Oak Wlk. SM6: W'gton 1E 166
(off Helios Rd.)
Oak Way CR0: C'don 6K 157
N14 7A 22
TW14: Felt 1G 129
W3 1A 98
Oakway BR2: Broml 2F 159
SW20 4E 152
Oakway Cl. DA5: Bexl 6E 126
Oakways SE9 6F 125
OAKWOOD 4C 22
Oakwood SM6: W'gton 7F 167
Oakwood Av. BR2: Broml 3K 159
BR3: Beck 2E 158
CR4: Mitc 2B 154
N14 7C 22
UB1: S'hall 7E 76
Oakwood Bus. Pk. NW10 4K 79
Oakwood Cl. BR7: Chst 6D 142
IG8: Wfd G 6H 37
N14 6B 22
SE13 6F 123
Oakwood Ct. E6 1C 88
HA1: Harr 6H 41
W14 3H 99
Oakwood Cres. N21 6D 22
UB6: G'frd 6A 60
Oakwood Dr. DA7: Bex 4J 127
HA8: Edg 6D 28
SE19 6D 138
Oakwood Gdns. BR6: Farnb 2G 173
IG3: Ilf 2K 71
SM1: Sutt 2J 165
Oakwood Ho. E9 6J 67
(off Frampton Pk. Rd.)
Oakwood La. W14 3H 99
Oakwood Lodge N14 6B 22
(off Avenue Rd.)
Oakwood Mans. W14 3H 99
(off Oakwood Ct.)
Oakwood Pde. N14 5B 22
Oakwood Pk. Rd. N14 7C 22
Oakwood Pl. CR0: C'don 6A 156
Oakwood Rd. BR6: Farnb 2G 173
CR0: C'don 6A 156
HA5: Pinn 2K 39
NW11 4J 45
SW20 1C 152
Oakwood Vw. N14 6C 22
Oakworth Rd. W10 5E 80
Oarsman Pl. KT8: E Mos 4J 149
The Oasis BR1: Broml 2A 160
Oasis Academy Sports Hall 1E 24
Oasis Sports Cen. 7E 6 (6J 83)
Oast Ct. E14 7B 86
(off Newell St.)
Oast Lodge W4 7A 98
(off Corney Reach Way)
Oates Cl. BR2: Broml 3F 159
Oatfield Ho. N15 6E 48
(off Perry Ct.)
Oatfield Rd. BR6: Orp 1K 173
Oatland Ri. E17 2A 50
Oatlands Dr. KT13: Weyb 7G 147
Oatlands Rd. EN3: Enf H 1D 24
Oat La. EC2 7C 8 (6C 84)
Oatwell Ho. SW3 4D 16
(off Cale St.)
Oban Cl. E13 4A 88
Oban Ho. E14 6F 87
(off Oban St.)
IG11: Bark 2H 89
Oban Rd. E13 3A 88
SE25 4D 156
Oban St. E14 6F 87
Oberon Ct. E6 7B 70
Oberon Ho. N1 2E 84
(off Arden Est.)
Oberon Way TW17: Shep 3A 146
Oberstein Rd. SW11 4B 118
Oborne Cl. SE24 5B 120
O'Brien Ho. E2 3K 85
(off Roman Rd.)
Observatory Gdns. W8 2J 99
Observatory M. E14 4F 105
Observatory Rd. SW7 2A 16 (3B 100)
SW14 4J 115
Observer Cl. NW9 3A 44
Occupation La. SE18 1F 125
W5 4D 96
Occupation Rd. KT19: Ewe 7K 163
SE17 5C 102
W13 2B 96

Ocean Est.—Orbital Cen.

Ocean Est. E1 ... 5A 86
(Ben Jonson Rd.)
E1 ... 4K 85
(Ernest St.)
Oceanis Apts. E16 ... 7J 87
(off Seagull La.)
Ocean St. E1 ... 5K 85
Ocean Wharf E14 ... 2B 104
Ockbrook E1 ... 5J 85
(off Hannibal Rd.)
Ockendon M. N1 ... 6D 66
Ockendon Rd. N1 ... 6D 66
Ockham Bldg. SE16 ... 3F 103
(off Arts La.)
Ockham Dr. BR5: St P ... 7A 144
UB6: G'frd ... 7G 59
Ockley Ct. DA14: Sidc ... 3J 143
SM1: Sutt ... 4A 166
Ockley Rd. CR0: C'don ... 7K 155
SW16 ... 4J 137
The Octagon SW10 ... 7K 99
(off Coleridge Gdns.)
Octagon Arc. EC2 ... 6G 9 (5E 84)
Octagon Ct. SE16 ... 1K 103
(off Rotherhithe St.)
Octavia Cl. CR4: Mitc ... 5C 154
Octavia Ho. SW1 ... 2C 18
(off Medway St.)
W10 ... 4G 81
Octavia M. W9 ... 4H 81
Octavia Rd. TW7: Isle ... 3J 113
Octavia St. SW11 ... 1C 118
Octavia Way SE28 ... 7B 90
Octavius St. SE8 ... 7C 104
October Pl. NW4 ... 3F 45
Odard Rd. KT8: W Mole ... 4E 148
Oddmark Ho. IG11: Bark ... 2H 89
Odelia Ct. E15 ... 1E 86
(off Biggerstaff Rd.)
Odell Cl. IG11: Bark ... 6K 71
Odell Ho. E14 ... 6C 86
(off New Festival Av.)
Odell Wlk. SE13 ... 3E 122
The Odeon IG11: Bark ... 7H 71
Odeon Cinema
Beckenham ... 2C 158
Camden Town ... 1F 83
(off Parkway)
Covent Gdn. ... 1D 12
(off Shaftesbury Av.)
Edmonton ... 7E 24
Greenwich ... 4H 105
Haymarket, Panton St. ... 3D 12
(off Panton St.)
Holloway ... 3J 65
IMAX (BFI) ... 5J 13 (1A 102)
Kingston upon Thames ... 2E 150
(within The Rotunda Cen.)
Leicester Sq. ... 3D 12
(off Leicester Sq.)
Putney ... 3G 117
Richmond upon Thames,
Hill Street ... 5D 114
Red Lion Street ... 5D 114
South Woodford ... 2J 51
Streatham ... 3J 137
Surrey Quays ... 3K 103
Swiss Cottage ... 7B 64
Tottenham Ct. Rd. ... 6C 6
(off Tottenham Ct. Rd.)
Uxbridge ... 7A 56
Whiteleys ... 6K 81
Wimbledon ... 6H 135
Odeon Ct. E16 ... 5J 87
NW10 ... 1A 80
(off St Albans Rd.)
Odeon Pde. N7 ... 3J 65
(off Holloway Rd.)
SE9 ... 4C 124
(off Well Hall Rd.)
UB6: G'frd ... 6B 60
(off Allendale Rd.)
Odessa Rd. E7 ... 3H 69
NW10 ... 2C 80
Odessa St. SE16 ... 2B 104
Odessa Wharf SE16 ... 3B 104
(off Odessa St.)
Odessey Ho. E15 ... 6F 69
(off Leyton Rd.)
Odette Duval Ho. E1 ... 5J 85
(off Stepney Way)
Odger St. SW11 ... 2D 118
Odhams Wlk. WC2 ... 1F 13 (6J 83)
Odin Ho. SE5 ... 2C 120
O'Donnell Ct. WC1 ... 3F 7 (4J 83)
O'Driscoll Ho. W12 ... 6D 80
Odyssey Bus. Pk. HA4: Ruis ... 5K 57
Offa's Mead E9 ... 4B 68
Offenbach Ho. E2 ... 2K 85
(off Mace St.)
Offenham Rd. SE9 ... 4D 142
SW9 ... 1A 120
Offers Ct. KT1: King T ... 3F 151
Offerton Rd. SW4 ... 3G 119
Offham Ho. SE17 ... 4E 102
(off Beckway St.)
Offham Slope N12 ... 5C 30
Offley Pl. TW7: Isle ... 2H 113
Offley Rd. SW9 ... 7A 102
Offord Cl. N17 ... 6B 34
Offord Rd. N1 ... 7K 65
Offord St. N1 ... 7K 65
Ogden Ho. TW13: Hanw ... 3C 130
Ogilby St. SE18 ... 4D 106
Ogilvie Ho. E1 ... 6K 85
(off Stepney C'way.)
Oglander Rd. SE15 ... 4F 121
Ogle St. W1 ... 5A 6 (5G 83)
Oglethorpe Rd. RM10: Dag ... 3F 73
O'Gorman Ho. SW10 ... 7A 100
(off King's Rd.)
O'Grady Ho. E17 ... 3D 50
Ohio Bldg. SE13 ... 1D 122
(off Deal's Gateway)
Ohio Rd. E13 ... 4H 87
Oil Mill La. W6 ... 5C 98
Okeburn Rd. SW17 ... 5E 136
Okehampton Cl. N12 ... 5G 31
Okehampton Cres. DA16: Well ... 1B 126
Okehampton Rd. NW10 ... 1E 80
Olaf Ct. W8 ... 2J 99
(off Kensington Chu. St.)
Olaf St. W11 ... 7F 81
Old Abbey La. SE16 ... 3F 103
(off Vauban St.)
Oldacre M. SW12 ... 7E 118
The Old Aeroworks NW8 ... 4B 4
(off Hatton St.)
Old Bailey ... 7B 8 (6B 84)
Old Bailey EC4 ... 1B 14 (6B 84)
Old Barge Ho. All. SE1 ... 3K 13
Old Barn Cl. SM2: Cheam ... 7G 165
Old Barn Way DA7: Bex ... 3K 127
Old Barracks W8 ... 2K 99
Old Barrack Yd. SW1 ... 7G 11 (2E 100)
(not continuous)
Old Barrowfield E15 ... 1G 87
Old Bellgate Pl. E14 ... 3C 104
Oldberry Rd. HA8: Edg ... 6E 28
Old Bethnal Grn. Rd. E2 ... 3G 85
OLD BEXLEY ... 7H 127
Old Bexley Bus. Pk.
DA5: Bexl ... 7H 127
Old Bexley La.
DA5: Bexl, Dart ... 2K 145
Old Billingsgate Mkt. EC3 ... 3F 15
Old Billingsgate Wlk.
EC3 ... 3G 15 (7E 84)
Old Bond St. W1 ... 3A 12 (7G 83)
Oldborough Rd. HA0: Wemb ... 3C 60
OLD BRENTFORD ... 7D 96
Old Brewer's Yd. WC2 ... 1E 12 (6J 83)
Old Brewery M. NW3 ... 4B 64
Old Brewery Way E17 ... 5B 50
Old Bri. Cl. UB5: N'olt ... 2E 76
Old Bridge St.
KT1: Hamp W ... 2D 150
Old Broad St. EC2 ... 7F 9 (6D 84)
Old Bromley Rd. BR1: Broml ... 5F 141
Old Brompton Rd. SW5 ... 5J 99
SW7 ... 4A 16 (5J 99)
Old Bldgs. WC2 ... 7J 7
Old Burlington St. W1 ... 2A 12 (7G 83)
Oldbury Ct. E9 ... 5A 68
(off Mabley St.)
Oldbury Ho. W2 ... 5K 81
(off Harrow Rd.)
Oldbury Pl. W1 ... 5H 5 (5E 82)
Oldbury Rd. EN1: Enf ... 2B 24
Old Canal M. SE15 ... 5F 103
(off Trafalgar Av.)
Old Castle St. E1 ... 7J 9 (6F 85)
Old Cavendish St. W1 ... 7J 5 (6F 83)
Old Change Ct. EC4 ... 1C 14
Old Chapel Pl. SW9 ... 2A 120
Old Charlton Rd.
TW17: Shep ... 5E 146
Old Chelsea M. SW3 ... 7C 16 (6C 100)
Old Chiswick Yd. W4 ... 6A 98
(off Pumping Sta. Rd.)
Old Church Ct. N11 ... 5A 32
Oldchurch Gdns.
RM7: Rush G ... 7K 55
Old Church La. HA7: Stan ... 5G 27
NW9 ... 3K 61
UB6: G'frd ... 3A 78
Oldchurch Ri. RM7: Rush G ... 7K 55
Old Church Rd. E1 ... 6K 85
E4 ... 4H 35
Oldchurch Rd. RM7: Rush G ... 7K 55
Old Church St.
SW3 ... 6B 16 (5B 100)
Old Claygate La.
KT10: Clay ... 6A 162
Old Clem Sq. SE18 ... 6E 106
(off Woolwich Comn.)
Old Coal Yd. SE28 ... 4H 107
Old College Ct. DA17: Belv ... 5H 109
Old Compton St. W1 ... 2C 12 (7H 83)
Old Cople La. SE19 ... 5F 139
Old Cote Dr. TW5: Hest ... 6E 94
Old Ct. Ho. W8 ... 2K 99
(off Old Court Pl.)
Old Ct. Pl. W8 ... 2K 99
The Old Ctyd. BR1: Broml ... 1K 159
Old Curiosity Shop ... 7G 7
(off Portsmouth St.)
Old Dairy N15 ... 6E 48
Old Dairy Gro. UB2: S'hall ... 5E 94
Old Dairy La. HA4: Ruis ... 4K 57
Old Dairy M. NW5 ... 6F 65
SW4 ... 4J 119
(off Tintern St.)
SW12 ... 1E 136
Old Dairy Sq. N21 ... 7F 23
(off Wade Hill)
Old Deer Pk. ... 2C 114
Old Deer Pk. Gdns. TW9: Rich ... 3E 114
Old Devonshire Rd. SW12 ... 7F 119
Old Dock Cl. TW9: Kew ... 6G 97
Old Dover Rd. SE3 ... 7J 105
Oldegate Ho. E6 ... 7B 70
Old Farm Av. DA15: Sidc ... 1H 143
N14 ... 7B 22
SW12 ... 6E 118
Old Farm Cl. SW17 ... 2C 136
TW4: Houn ... 4D 112
Old Farm La. SW19 ... 5K 135
Old Farm Pas. TW12: Hamp ... 1G 149
Old Farm Rd. N2 ... 1B 46
TW12: Hamp ... 6D 130
UB7: W Dray ... 2A 92
Old Farm Rd. E. DA15: Sidc ... 2A 144
Old Farm Rd. W. DA15: Sidc ... 2K 143
Oldfield Cl. BR1: Broml ... 4D 160
HA7: Stan ... 5F 27
UB6: G'frd ... 5J 59
Oldfield Ct. KT5: Surb ... 4F 151
(off Cranes Pk. Cres.)
Oldfield Farm Gdns. UB6: G'frd ... 1H 77
Oldfield Gro. SE16 ... 4K 103
Oldfield Ho. W4 ... 5A 98
(off Devonshire Rd.)
Oldfield La. Nth. UB6: G'frd ... 2H 77
Oldfield La. Sth. UB6: G'frd ... 4G 77
Oldfield M. N6 ... 7G 47
Oldfield Rd. BR1: Broml ... 4D 160
DA7: Bex ... 2E 126
N16 ... 3E 66
NW10 ... 7B 62
SW19 ... 6G 135
TW12: Hamp ... 1D 148
W3 ... 2B 98
Oldfields Cir. UB5: N'olt ... 6G 59
Oldfields Rd. SM1: Sutt ... 3H 165
The Old Fire Station SE18 ... 7F 107
Old Fish St. Hill EC4 ... 2C 14
(off Queen Victoria St.)
Old Fleet La. EC4 ... 7A 8 (6B 84)
Old Fold Cl. EN5: Barn ... 1C 20
Old Fold La. EN5: Barn ... 1C 20
Old Fold Manor Golf Course ... 1B 20
Old Fold Vw. EN5: Barn ... 3A 20
OLD FORD ... 1B 86
OLD FORD ... 1C 86
Old Ford Rd. E2 ... 3J 85
E3 ... 2A 86
Old Ford Trading Cen. E3 ... 1C 86
(off Maverton Rd.)
Old Forge Cl. HA7: Stan ... 4F 27
Old Forge Cres. TW17: Shep ... 6D 146
Old Forge M. W12 ... 2D 98
Old Forge Rd. EN1: Enf ... 1A 24
N19 ... 2H 65
Old Forge Way DA14: Sidc ... 4B 144
Old Gloucester St.
WC1 ... 5F 7 (5J 83)
The Old Goods Yd. W2 ... 5A 82
Old Hall Cl. HA5: Pinn ... 1C 40
Old Hall Dr. HA5: Pinn ... 1C 40
Oldham Ter. W3 ... 1J 97
(not continuous)
Old Hatch Mnr. HA4: Ruis ... 7H 39
Old Highwayman Pl. SW15 ... 1D 134
Old Hill BR6: Downe ... 6H 173
BR7: Chst ... 1E 160
Oldhill St. N16 ... 1G 67
Old Homesdale Rd.
BR2: Broml ... 4A 160
Old Hospital Cl. SW12 ... 1D 136
Old Ho. Cl. SW19 ... 5G 135
Old Ho. Gdns. TW1: Twick ... 6C 114
Old Howlett's La. HA4: Ruis ... 6F 39
OLD ISLEWORTH ... 3B 114
Old Jamaica Bus. Est.
SE16 ... 7K 15 (3F 103)
Old Jamaica Rd. SE16 ... 7K 15 (3G 103)
Old James St. SE15 ... 3H 121
Old Jewry EC2 ... 1E 14 (6D 84)
Old Kenton La. NW9 ... 5H 43
Old Kent Rd. SE1 ... 4E 102
SE15 ... 4E 102
Old Kingston Rd. KT4: Wor Pk ... 2J 163
The Old Laundry BR7: Chst ... 1G 161
Old Library Ct. HA4: Ruis ... 2J 57
Old Library Ho. E3 ... 2A 86
(off Roman Rd.)
Old Lodge Pl. TW1: Twick ... 6B 114
Old Lodge Way HA7: Stan ... 5F 27
Old London Rd.
DA14: Sidc, Swan ... 7G 145
KT2: King T ... 2E 150
Old Lyonian Sports Club ... 5G 41
Old Maidstone Rd.
DA14: Sidc ... 7F 145
OLD MALDEN ... 1A 164
Old Malden La. KT4: Wor Pk ... 2K 163
Old Mnr. Ct. NW8 ... 2A 82
Old Mnr. Dr. TW7: Isle ... 6G 113
Old Mnr. Ho. M. TW17: Shep ... 3C 146
Old Mnr. Rd. UB2: S'hall ... 4B 94
Old Mnr. Way BR7: Chst ... 5D 142
DA7: Bex ... 2K 127
Old Manor Yd. SW5 ... 4K 99
Old Mkt. Ct. SM1: Sutt ... 4K 165
Old Mkt. Sq. E2 ... 1J 9 (3F 85)
Old Marylebone Rd.
NW1 ... 6D 4 (5C 82)
Oldmead Ho. RM10: Dag ... 6H 73
Old M. HA1: Harr ... 5J 41
Old Mill Ct. E18 ... 3A 52
Old Mill Pl. RM7: Rom ... 6K 55
Old Mill Rd. SE18 ... 6H 107
Old Mitre Ct. EC4 ... 1K 13 (6A 84)
Old Montague St. E1 ... 6K 9 (5G 85)
Old Nichol St. E2 ... 3J 9 (4F 85)
Old North St. WC1 ... 5G 7
Old Nursery Ct. E2 ... 2F 85
(off Dawson St.)
Old Nursery Pl. TW15: Ashf ... 5D 128
Old Oak Cl. KT9: Chess ... 4F 163
OLD OAK COMMON ... 5A 80
Old Oak Comn. La. NW10 ... 5A 80
W3 ... 5A 80
Old Oak La. NW10 ... 3A 80
Old Oak Rd. W3 ... 7B 80
The Old Operating Theatre Mus. &
Herb Garret ... 5F 15
Old Orchard TW16: Sun ... 2A 148
The Old Orchard NW3 ... 4D 64
Old Orchard Cl. EN4: Had W ... 1G 21
UB8: Hil ... 6C 74
Old Palace La. TW9: Rich ... 5C 114
Old Palace Rd. CR0: C'don ... 3B 168
Old Palace Ter. TW9: Rich ... 5D 114
Old Palace Yd.
SW1 ... 1E 18 (3J 101)
TW9: Rich ... 5C 114
Old Paradise St. SE11 ... 3G 19 (4K 101)
Old Pk. Av. EN2: Enf ... 4H 23
SW12 ... 6E 118
Old Pk. Gro. EN2: Enf ... 4H 23
Old Pk. La. W1 ... 5J 11 (1F 101)
Old Pk. M. TW5: Hest ... 7D 94
Old Pk. Ridings N21 ... 6G 23
Old Pk. Rd. EN2: Enf ... 3G 23
N13 ... 4E 32
SE2 ... 5A 108
Old Pk. Rd. Sth. EN2: Enf ... 4G 23
Old Pk. Vw. EN2: Enf ... 3F 23
Old Pearson St. SE10 ... 7D 104
Old Perry St. BR7: Chst ... 6J 143
Old Police Station M. SE20 ... 7K 139
The Old Police Stn. SW17 ... 2D 136
Old Post Office La. SE3 ... 3K 123
Old Post Office Wlk. KT6: Surb ... 6D 150
(off Victoria Rd.)
Old Pound Cl. TW7: Isle ... 1A 114
Old Pye St. SW1 ... 1C 18 (3H 101)
Old Pye St. Est. SW1 ... 2C 18
(off Old Pye St.)
Old Quebec St. W1 ... 1F 11 (6D 82)
Old Queen St. SW1 ... 7D 12 (2H 101)
Old Rectory Gdns. HA8: Edg ... 6B 28
Old Redding HA3: Hrw W ... 5A 26
Old Red Lion Theatre ... 1K 7
(off St John St.)
Oldridge Rd. SW12 ... 7E 118
Old Rd. DA1: Cray ... 5K 127
EN3: Enf H ... 1D 24
SE13 ... 4G 123
Old Rope Wlk. TW16: Sun ... 3K 147
Old Royal Free Pl. N1 ... 1A 84
Old Royal Free Sq. N1 ... 1A 84
Old Royal Naval College ... 5F 105
Old Ruislip Rd. UB5: N'olt ... 2A 76
The Old School WC1 ... 5H 7
(off Princeton St.)
Old School Cl. BR3: Beck ... 2K 157
SE10 ... 3G 105
SW19 ... 2J 153
Old School Ct. N17 ... 3F 49
Old School Cres. E7 ... 6J 69
Old School Pl. CR0: Wadd ... 4A 168
Old School Rd. UB8: Hil ... 4B 74
Old Schools La. KT17: Ewe ... 7B 164
Old School Sq. E14 ... 6C 86
(off Pelling St.)
KT7: T Ditt ... 6K 149
Old School Ter.
SM3: Cheam ... 7F 165
Old Seacoal La. EC4 ... 7A 8 (6B 84)
The Old Sessions Ho.
EC1 ... 4A 8 (4B 84)
Old Slade La. SL0: Rich P ... 1A 174
SL3: Coln ... 1A 174
Old Sth. Cl. HA5: Pinn ... 1B 40
Old Sth. Lambeth Rd. SW8 ... 7J 101
Old Speech Room Gallery ... 1J 59
Old Spitalfields Market
... 5J 9 (5F 85)
Old Sq. WC2 ... 7J 7 (6K 83)
Old Stable M. N5 ... 3C 66
Old Stable Row SE18 ... 4E 106
(off Woolwich New Rd.)
Old Stables Ct. SE5 ... 1C 120
(off Camberwell New Rd.)
Old Station Gdns. TW11: Tedd ... 6A 132
(off Victoria Rd.)
Old Station Ho. SE17 ... 5C 102
Old Station Rd. UB3: Harl ... 3H 93
Old Station Way SW4 ... 3H 119
(Off Voltaire Road)
The Old Station Yd. E17 ... 4E 50
Oldstead Rd. BR1: Broml ... 4E 140
Old Stn. Way SW4 ... 3H 119
(off Voltaire Rd.)
Old Stockley Rd. UB7: W Dray ... 2D 92
OLD STREET ... 3F 9 (4D 84)
Old St. E13 ... 2K 87
EC1 ... 3C 8 (4C 84)
Old St. Yd. EC1 ... 3E 8
Old Studio Cl. CR0: C'don ... 7D 156
Old Sungate Cotts.
RM5: Col R ... 1F 55
Old Sun Wharf E14 ... 7A 86
(off Narrow St.)
Old Swan Wharf SW11 ... 1B 118
Old Swan Yd. SM5: Cars ... 4D 166
Old Theatre Ct. SE1 ... 4D 14
Old Town CR0: C'don ... 3B 168
SW4 ... 3G 119
Old Town Hall Apts. SE16 ... 3F 103
Old Tramyard SE18 ... 4J 107
Old Twelve Cl. W7 ... 4J 77
The Old Vic Theatre ... 6K 13
The Old Vinyl Factory
UB3: Hayes ... 2G 93
Old Watercress Wlk. SM5: Cars ... 4E 166
Old Willow Cl. E3 ... 3C 86
Old Woolwich Rd. SE10 ... 6F 105
Old York Rd. SW18 ... 5K 117
Oleander Cl. BR6: Farnb ... 5H 173
Oleander Ho. SE15 ... 5F 103
O'Leary Sq. E1 ... 5J 85
Olga St. E3 ... 2A 86
Olinda Rd. N16 ... 6F 49
Oliphant St. E14 ... 7E 86
(off Bullivant St.)
W10 ... 3F 81
Olive Blythe Ho. W10 ... 4G 81
(off Ladbroke Gro.)
Olive Ct. E5 ... 2J 67
(off Woodmill Rd.)
N1 ... 1A 84
(off Liverpool Rd.)
Olive Gro. N15 ... 4C 48
Olive Haines Lodge SW15 ... 5H 117
Olive Ho. EC1 ... 3K 7
(off Bowling Grn. La.)
Oliver Av. SE25 ... 3F 157
Oliver Bus. Pk. NW10 ... 2J 79
Oliver Cl. W4 ... 6H 97
Oliver Ct. SE18 ... 4G 107
Oliver Gdns. E6 ... 5C 88
Oliver Goldsmith Est. SE15 ... 1G 121
Oliver Gro. SE25 ... 4F 157
Oliver Ho. SE14 ... 7B 104
(off New Cross Rd.)
SE16 ... 2G 103
(off George Row)
SW8 ... 7J 101
(off Wyvil Rd.)
Oliver M. SE15 ... 2G 121
Olive Rd. E13 ... 3A 88
NW2 ... 4D 62
SW19 ... 7A 136
W5 ... 3D 96
Oliver Rd. E10 ... 2D 68
E17 ... 5E 50
KT3: N Mald ... 2J 151
NW10 ... 2J 79
SM1: Sutt ... 4B 166
Olivers Row N8 ... 6J 47
Olivers Wharf E1 ... 1H 103
(off Wapping High St.)
Olivers Yd. EC1 ... 3F 9 (4D 84)
Olive St. RM7: Rom ... 5K 55
Olive Tree Ho. SE15 ... 6J 103
(off Sharratt St.)
Olivette St. SW15 ... 3F 117
Olive Waite Ho. NW6 ... 7J 63
Olivia Ct. CR0: C'don ... 7C 156
(off Whitehorse Rd.)
EN2: Enf ... 1H 23
(off Chase Side)
Olivia M. HA3: Hrw W ... 7D 26
Olivier Theatre ... 4H 13
(within National Theatre)
Ollerton Grn. E3 ... 1B 86
Ollerton Rd. N11 ... 5C 32
Olley Cl. SM6: W'gton ... 7J 167
Ollgar Cl. W12 ... 1B 98
Olliffe St. E14 ... 3E 104
Olmar St. SE1 ... 6G 103
Olmstead Cl. N10 ... 4E 46
Olney Ho. NW8 ... 3D 4
(off Tresham Cres.)
Olney Rd. SE17 ... 6B 102
(not continuous)
Olron Cres. DA6: Bex ... 5D 126
Olven Rd. SE18 ... 6G 107
Olveston Wlk. SM5: Cars ... 6B 154
Olwen M. HA5: Pinn ... 2B 40
Olyffe Av. DA16: Well ... 1A 126
Olyffe Dr. BR3: Beck ... 1E 158
Olympia ... 3G 99
Olympia Ind. Est. N22 ... 3K 47
Olympia M. W2 ... 7K 81
Olympian Ct. E3 ... 2C 86
(off Wick La.)
E14 ... 4C 104
(off Homer Dr.)
Olympian Way SE10 ... 1G 105
(not continuous)
Olympia Way W14 ... 3G 99
Olympic Ho. N16 ... 4F 67
Olympic M. SW18 ... 5A 118
Olympic Pk. Av. E20 ... 5D 68
Olympic Way HA9: Wemb ... 3G 61
UB6: G'frd ... 1G 77
Olympus Gro. N22 ... 1A 48
Olympus Sq. E5 ... 3G 67
O'Mahoney Ct. SW17 ... 3A 136
Oman Av. NW2 ... 4E 62
Oman Way E14 ... 6A 86
O'Meara St. SE1 ... 5D 14 (1C 102)
Omega Cl. E14 ... 3D 104
Omega Ct. RM7: Rom ... 5K 55
Omega Ho. SW10 ... 7A 100
(off King's Rd.)
Omega Pl. N1 ... 1F 7
Omega St. SE14 ... 1C 122
Omega Works E3 ... 7C 68
Ommaney Rd. SE14 ... 1K 121
Omnibus Ho. N22 ... 2A 48
(off Lordship La.)
Omnibus Way E17 ... 2C 50
Omnium Ct. WC1 ... 5G 7
(off Princeton St.)
Ondine Rd. SE15 ... 4F 121
One Blackfriars SE1 ... 4A 14
One Casson Sq. SE1 ... 5H 13
(off Casson Sq.)
Onedin Ct. E1 ... 7G 85
(off Ensign St.)
Onega Ga. SE16 ... 3A 104
One Hyde Pk. SW1 ... 7E 10 (2D 100)
O'Neill Ho. NW8 ... 1B 4
(off Cochrane St.)
O'Neill Path SE18 ... 6E 106
One Lillie Sq. SW6 ... 6J 99
One New Change ... 1C 14 (6C 84)
One Owen St. EC1 ... 1A 8
(off Goswell St.)
One Southbank Pl. SE1 ... 6H 13
(off York Rd.)
One The Elephant SE1 ... 4B 102
(off Brook Dr.)
One Tree Cl. SE23 ... 6J 121
One Tree Hill
Local Nature Reserve ... 6J 121
Ongar Cl. RM6: Chad H ... 5C 54
Ongar Rd. SW6 ... 6J 99
Onra Rd. E17 ... 7C 50
Onslow Av. TW10: Rich ... 5E 114
Onslow Cl. E4 ... 2K 35
KT7: T Ditt ... 7J 149
W10 ... 3H 81
Onslow Ct. SW10 ... 6A 16
Onslow Cres. BR7: Chst ... 1F 161
SW7 ... 4B 16 (4B 100)
Onslow Dr. DA14: Sidc ... 2D 144
Onslow Gdns. E18 ... 3K 51
KT7: T Ditt ... 7J 149
N10 ... 5F 47
N21 ... 5F 23
SM6: W'gton ... 6G 167
SW7 ... 4A 16 (4B 100)
Onslow Ho. KT2: King T ... 1F 151
(off Acre Rd.)
Onslow M. E. SW7 ... 4A 16 (4B 100)
Onslow M. W. SW7 ... 4A 16 (4B 100)
Onslow Pde. N14 ... 1A 32
Onslow Rd. CR0: C'don ... 7K 155
KT3: N Mald ... 4C 152
TW10: Rich ... 5E 114
Onslow Sq. SW7 ... 3B 16 (4B 100)
Onslow St. EC1 ... 4K 7 (4A 84)
Onslow Way KT7: T Ditt ... 7J 149
Ontario Point SE16 ... 2J 103
(off Surrey Quays Rd.)
Ontario St. SE1 ... 3B 102
Ontario Twr. E14 ... 7F 87
Ontario Way E14 ... 7C 86
(not continuous)
Onyx M. E15 ... 6H 69
Opal Apts. W2 ... 6J 81
(off Hereford Rd.)
Opal Cl. E16 ... 6B 88
Opal Ct. E15 ... 1E 86
Opal M. IG1: Ilf ... 2F 71
NW6 ... 1H 81
Opal St. SE11 ... 5K 19 (5B 102)
Open Air Stage ... 1C 64
Openshaw Rd. SE2 ... 4B 108
Openview SW18 ... 1A 136
Opera Ct. N19 ... 3H 65
(off Wedmore St.)
Ophelia Gdns. NW2 ... 3G 63
Ophelia Ho. W6 ... 5F 99
(off Fulham Pal. Rd.)
Ophir Ter. SE15 ... 1G 121
Opie Ho. NW8 ... 2C 82
(off Townshend Est.)
Opossum Way TW4: Houn ... 3A 112
Oppenheim Rd. SE13 ... 2E 122
Oppidan Apts. NW6 ... 7J 63
(off Netherwood St.)
Oppidans Rd. NW3 ... 7D 64
Opulens Pl. HA6: Nwood ... 1E 38
Orange Ct. La.
BR6: Downe ... 7E 172
Orange Gro. E11 ... 3G 69
Orange Hill Rd. HA8: Edg ... 7D 28
Orange Pl. SE16 ... 3J 103
The Orangery TW10: Ham ... 2C 132
The Orangery Gallery ... 2H 99
Orangery La. SE9 ... 5D 124
Orange St. WC2 ... 3D 12 (7H 83)
Orange Tree Ct. SE5 ... 7E 102
(off Havil St.)
Orange Tree Theatre ... 4E 114
Orange Yd. W1 ... 1D 12
Oransay Rd. N1 ... 6C 66
Oratory La. SW3 ... 5B 16 (5B 100)
Orbain Rd. SW6 ... 7G 99
Orbel St. SW11 ... 1C 118
Orbis Wharf SW11 ... 3B 118
Orbital Cen. IG8: Wfd G ... 2B 52

A-Z Big London 263

Orb St.—Oxford & Cambridge Mans.

Orb St. SE17 4D 102
The Orchard KT17: Ewe 7B 164
N14 5A 22
N20 1E 30
N21 6J 23
NW11 5J 45
SE3 2F 123
TW3: Houn 2G 113
W4 4K 97
W5 5D 78
(off Montpelier Rd.)
Orchard Av. CR0: C'don 2A 170
CR4: Mitc 1E 166
DA17: Belv 6E 108
KT3: N Mald 2A 152
KT7: T Ditt 1A 162
N3 3J 45
N14 6B 22
N20 2G 31
TW5: Hest 7C 94
TW14: Felt 5F 111
TW15: Ashf 6E 128
UB1: S'hall 1D 94
Orchard Bus. Cen. SE26 5B 140
Orchard Cl. DA7: Bex 1E 126
E4 4H 35
E11 4K 51
HA0: Wemb 1E 78
HA4: Ruis 7E 38
HA8: Edg 6K 27
KT6: Surb 1B 162
KT12: Walt T 7K 147
KT19: Ewe 6H 163
N1 7C 66
NW2 3C 62
SE23 6J 121
SW20 4E 152
TW15: Ashf 6E 128
UB5: N'olt 6G 59
W10 5H 81
WD23: B Hea 1C 26
Orchard Cotts. KT2: King T 1F 151
UB3: Hayes 2G 93
Orchard Ct. E10 1D 68
EN5: New Bar 3E 20
HA8: Edg 5A 28
KT4: Wor Pk 1C 164
KT12: Walt T 7H 147
(off Bridge St.)
N14 6B 22
SE26 4B 140
SM6: W'gton 5F 167
TW2: Twick 2H 131
TW7: Isle 1H 113
UB7: Lford 3D 174
UB8: Uxb 2A 74
(off The Greenway)
W1 7G 5
(off Fitzhardinge St.)
Orchard Cres. EN1: Enf 1A 24
HA8: Edg 5D 28
Orchard Dr. HA8: Edg 5A 28
SE3 2F 123
TW17: Shep 3G 147
Orchard Farm Av. KT8: E Mos 6H 149
Orchard Gdns. KT9: Chess 4E 162
SM1: Sutt 5J 165
Orchard Ga. KT10: Esh 7H 149
NW9 4A 44
UB6: G'frd 6B 60
Orchard Grn. BR6: Orp 2J 173
Orchard Gro. BR6: Orp 2K 173
CR0: C'don 7A 158
HA3: Kenton 5F 43
HA8: Edg 1G 43
SE20 7G 139
Orchard Hill DA1: Cray 5K 127
SE13 2D 122
SM5: Cars 5D 166
Orchard Ho. SE5 1C 120
(off County Gro.)
SE16 3J 103
SW6 7H 99
(off Varna Rd.)
W12 1C 98
Orchard La. IG8: Wfd G 4F 37
KT8: E Mos 6H 149
SW20 1D 152
Orchardleigh Av. EN3: Enf H 2D 24
Orchard Mead Ho. NW2 2J 63
Orchardmede N21 6J 23
Orchard M. N1 7D 66
N6 7F 47
SW17 3A 136
Orchard Pl. BR2: Kes 7A 172
E5 5H 67
E14 7G 87
(not continuous)
N17 7A 34
W4 4A 98
Orchard Ri. CR0: C'don 1A 170
HA5: Eastc 3H 39
KT2: King T 1J 151
TW10: Rich 4H 115
Orchard Ri. E. DA15: Sidc 5K 125
Orchard Ri. W. DA15: Sidc 5J 125
Orchard Rd. BR1: Broml 1A 160
BR6: Farnb 5F 173
CR4: Mitc 1E 166
DA14: Sidc 4J 143
DA16: Well 3B 126
DA17: Belv 4G 109
EN3: Pond E 5D 24
EN5: Barn 4C 20
KT1: King T 2E 150
KT9: Chess 4E 162
N6 7F 47
RM7: Mawney 1H 55
RM10: Dag 1G 91
SE3 2G 123
SE18 4H 107
SM1: Sutt 5J 165
TW1: Twick 5A 114
TW4: Houn 5D 112
TW8: Bford 6C 96
TW9: Rich 3G 115
TW12: Hamp 7D 130
TW13: Felt 1J 129
TW16: Sun 7K 129
UB3: Hayes 7J 75
Orchardson Ho. NW8 4A 4
Orchardson St. NW8 4A 4 (4B 82)
Orchard Sq. SW1 5H 17 (5E 100)
W14 5H 99
Orchard St. E17 4A 50
W1 1G 11 (6E 82)
Orchard Studios W6 4F 99
(off Brook Grn.)
Orchard Ter. EN1: Enf 6B 24
NW10 4B 62
Orchard Vs. DA14: Sidc 6C 144
Orchard Wlk. KT2: King T 1G 151
(off Gordon Rd.)
Orchard Way BR3: Beck 7C 158
(Monks Orchard Rd.)
BR3: Beck 1A 170
(Orchard Av.)
CR0: C'don 1A 170
EN1: Enf 3K 23
SM1: Sutt 4B 166
TW15: Ashf 2B 128
Orchard Waye UB8: Uxb 2A 74
Orchard Wharf E14 7G 87
(off Orchard Pl.)
Orchestra Ct. HA8: Edg 7C 28
Orchid Cl. E6 5C 88
KT9: Chess 7C 162
SE13 5F 123
UB1: S'hall 7C 76
Orchid Ct. HA9: Wemb 2E 60
Orchid Gdns. TW3: Houn 4D 112
Orchid Grange N14 7B 22
Orchid M. NW10 1K 79
Orchid Rd. N14 7B 22
Orchid St. W12 7C 80
Orde NW9 1B 44
Orde Hall St. WC1 4G 7 (4K 83)
Ordell Ct. E3 2B 86
(off Ordell Rd.)
Ordell Rd. E3 2B 86
Ordnance Cl. TW13: Felt 2J 129
Ordnance Cres. SE10 2G 105
Ordnance Dock Pl. UB2: S'hall 4B 94
Ordnance Hill NW8 1B 82
Ordnance M. NW8 2B 82
Ordnance Rd. E16 5H 87
SE18 6E 106
Oregano Cl. UB7: Yiew 6A 74
Oregano Dr. E14 6F 87
Oregon Av. E12 4D 70
Oregon Bldg. SE13 1D 122
(off Deal's Gateway)
Oregon Cl. KT3: N Mald 4J 151
Oregon M. W5 5C 78
Oregon Sq. BR6: Orp 1H 173
Oreilly St. SE1 4F 103
(off Willow Wlk.)
Orestes M. NW6 5J 63
Orford Ct. HA7: Stan 6H 27
SE27 2B 138
Orford Gdns. TW1: Twick 2K 131
Orford Rd. E17 5C 50
E18 3K 51
SE6 3D 140
ORGAN CROSSROADS 7C 164
Organ La. E4 2K 35
Oriana Ho. E10 2D 68
(off Grange Pk. Rd.)
E14 7B 86
(off Victory Pl.)
Oriel Cl. CR4: Mitc 4H 155
Oriel Ct. CR0: C'don 1D 168
NW3 4A 64
Oriel Dr. SW13 6E 98
Oriel Gdns. IG5: Ilf 3D 52
Oriel Ho. NW6 1J 81
(off Priory Pk. Rd.)
RM7: Rom 6K 55
Oriel M. E18 2J 51
Oriel Pl. NW3 4A 64
(off Heath St.)
Oriel Rd. E9 6K 67
Oriel Way UB5: N'olt 7F 59
Oriens M. E20 5E 68
Oriental Rd. E16 1B 106
Oriental St. E14 7C 86
(off Pennyfields)
Orient Ho. SW6 1A 118
(off Station Ct.)
Orient Ind. Pk. E10 2C 68
Orient St. SE11 4B 102
Orient Way E5 3K 67
E10 1A 68
Orient Wharf E1 1H 103
(off Wapping High St.)
Origin Bus. Pk. NW10 3G 79
Oriole Way SE28 7B 90
Orion E14 4C 104
(off Crews St.)
Orion Bus. Cen. SE14 5K 103
The Orion Cen. CR0: Bedd 2J 167
Orion Ho. E1 4H 85
(off Coventry Rd.)
Orion M. SM4: Mord 4J 153
Orion Pk. RM9: Dag 2F 91
Orion Rd. N11 7K 31
Orissa Rd. SE18 5J 107
Orkney Ct. E1 5A 86
(off Ocean Est.)
Orkney Ho. N1 1K 83
(off Bemerton Est.)
Orkney St. SW11 2E 118
Orlando Rd. SW4 3G 119
Orleans Ct. TW1: Twick 7B 114
Orleans House Gallery 1B 132
Orleans Pk. School Sports Cen.
7B 114
Orleans Rd. SE19 6D 138
TW1: Twick 7B 114
Orleston M. N7 6A 66
Orleston Rd. N7 6A 66
Orley Ct. HA1: Harr 4K 59
Orley Farm Rd. HA1: Harr 3J 59
Orlop St. SE10 5G 105
Ormanton Rd. SE26 4G 139
Orme Ct. W2 7K 81
Orme Ct. M. W2 7K 81
(off Orme La.)
Orme Ho. E8 1F 85
Orme La. W2 7K 81
Ormeley Rd. SW12 1F 137
Orme Rd. KT1: King T 2H 151
SM1: Sutt 6K 165
Ormerod Gdns. CR4: Mitc 2E 154
Ormesby Cl. SE28 7D 90
Ormesby Way HA3: Kenton 6F 43
Orme Sq. W2 7K 81
Ormiston Gro. W12 1D 98
Ormiston Rd. SE10 5J 105
Ormond Av. TW10: Rich 5D 114
TW12: Hamp 1F 149
Ormond Cl. WC1 5F 7 (5J 83)
Ormond Cres. TW12: Hamp 1F 149
Ormond Dr. TW12: Hamp 7F 131
Ormonde Av. BR6: Farnb 2G 173
Ormonde Ct. NW8 1D 82
(off St Edmund's Cl.)
SW15 4E 116
Ormonde Ga. SW3 6F 17 (5D 100)
(not continuous)
Ormonde Mans. WC1 5F 7
(off Southampton Row)
Ormonde Pl. SW1 4G 17 (4E 100)
Ormonde Ri.
IG9: Buck H 1F 37
Ormonde Rd. SW14 3J 115
Ormonde Ter. NW8 1D 82
Ormond Ho. N16 2D 66
Ormond M. WC1 4F 7 (4J 83)
Ormond Rd. N19 1J 65
TW10: Rich 5D 114
Ormond Yd. SW1 4B 12 (1G 101)
Ormrod Ct. W11 6G 81
(off Westbourne Pk. Rd.)
Ormsby SM2: Sutt 7K 165
Ormsby Gdns. UB6: G'frd 2G 77
Ormsby Lodge W4 3A 98
Ormsby Pl. N16 3F 67
Ormsby Point SE18 4F 107
(off Vincent Rd.)
Ormsby St. E2 2F 85
Ormside St. SE15 6J 103
Ornan Rd. NW3 5C 64
Orpen Ho. SW5 4J 99
(off Trebovir Rd.)
Orpen Wlk. N16 3E 66
Orpheus Ho. W10 4H 81
(off Harrow Rd.)
Orpheus St. SE5 1D 120
ORPINGTON 1K 173
Orpington Gdns. N18 3K 33
Orpington Golf Cen. 7E 144
Orpington Mans. N21 1G 33
Orpington Rd. BR7: Chst 3J 161
N21 1G 33
Orpwood Cl. TW12: Hamp 6D 130
Orsett M. W2 6K 81
(not continuous)
Orsett St. SE11 5H 19 (5K 101)
Orsett Ter. IG8: Wfd G 7F 37
W2 6K 81
Orsman Rd. N1 1E 84
Orton Gro. EN1: Enf 1B 24
Orton Pl. SW19 7K 135
Orton St. E1 1G 103
Orville Rd. SW11 2B 118
Orwell Cl. RM13: Rain 5K 91
UB3: Hayes 7G 75
Orwell Ct. E8 1G 85
(off Pownall Rd.)
N5 4C 66
SE13 3D 122
SW17 3B 136
(off Grosvenor Way)
Orwell Rd. E13 2A 88
Osbaldeston Rd. N16 2G 67
Osberton Rd. SE12 5J 123
Osbert St. SW1 4C 18 (4H 101)
Osborn Cl. E8 1G 85
Osborne Av. TW19: Stanw 1A 128
Osborne Cl. BR3: Beck 4A 158
EN4: Cockf 3J 21
TW13: Hanw 5B 130
Osborne Ct. E10 7D 50
HA2: Harr 4F 41
W5 5E 78
Osborne Gdns. CR7: Thor H 2C 156
Osborne Gro. E17 4B 50
Osborne Ho. E16 1J 105
(off Wesley Av.)
Osborne M. E17 4B 50
Osborne Pl. SM1: Sutt 5B 166
Osborne Rd. CR7: Thor H 2C 156
DA17: Belv 5F 109
E7 5K 69
E9 6B 68
E10 2D 68
EN3: Enf H 2F 25
IG9: Buck H 1E 36
KT2: King T 7E 132
KT12: Walt T 7J 147
N4 1A 66
N13 3F 33
NW2 6D 62
RM9: Dag 5F 73
TW3: Houn 3D 112
UB1: S'hall 6G 77
W3 3H 97
Osborne Sq. RM9: Dag 4F 73
Osborne Ter. SW17 5D 136
(off Church La.)
Osborne Way KT9: Chess 5F 163
Osborn Gdns. NW7 7A 30
Osborn La. SE23 7A 122
Osborn St. E1 6K 9 (5F 85)
Osborn Ter. SE3 4H 123
(not continuous)
Osbourne Ho. IG8: Wfd G 7K 37
TW2: Twick 2G 131
Oscar Ct. SE16 2A 104
Oscar Faber Pl. N1 7E 66
Oscar St. SE8 2C 122
(not continuous)
Oseney Cres. NW5 5G 65
Osgood Av. BR6: Chels 5K 173
Osgood Gdns. BR6: Chels 5K 173
OSIDGE 1A 32
Osidge La. N14 1K 31
Osier Cl. BR6: Farnb 4F 173
Osier Ct. E1 4K 85
(off Osier St.)
RM7: Rom 6K 55
TW8: Bford 6E 96
(off Ealing Rd.)
Osier Cres. N10 1D 46
Osier Ho. SE16 3A 104
Osier La. SE10 3H 105
Osier M. W4 6A 98
Osiers Ct. KT1: King T 1D 150
(off Steadfast Rd.)
Osiers Rd. SW18 4J 117
Osiers Twr. SW18 4J 117
(off Enterprise Way)
Osier St. E1 4J 85
Osier Way CR4: Mitc 5D 154
E10 3D 68
Oslac Rd. SE6 5D 140
Oslo Ct. NW8 2C 82
(off Prince Albert Rd.)
Oslo Ho. E9 6B 68
(off Felstead St.)
SE5 2C 120
(off Carew St.)
Oslo Sq. SE16 3A 104
Oslo Twr. SE8 4A 104
(off Naomi St.)
Osman Cl. N15 6D 48
Osmani Youth Cen. 5G 85
Osman Rd. N9 3C 34
W6 3E 98
Osmington Ho. SW8 7K 101
(off Dorset Rd.)
Osmond Cl. HA2: Harr 2G 59
Osmond Gdns. SM6: W'gton 5G 167
Osmunda Ct. E1 6G 85
(off Myrdle St.)
Osmund St. W12 5B 80
Osnaburgh St. NW1 4K 5 (4F 83)
(Euston Rd.)
NW1 2K 5
(Robert St.)
Osnaburgh Ter. NW1 3K 5 (4F 83)
Osney Ho. SE2 2D 108
Osney Wlk. SM5: Cars 6B 154
Osprey NW9 1B 44
Osprey Cl. BR2: Broml 1C 172
E6 5C 88
E11 4J 51
E17 7F 35
SM1: Sutt 5H 165
UB7: W Dray 2A 92
Osprey Ct. BR3: Beck 7C 140
CR0: C'don 3C 168
(off Innes Yd.)
E1 3K 15
(off Star Pl.)
Osprey Est. SE16 4K 103
Osprey Ho. E14 7A 86
(off Victory Pl.)
SE1 5H 103
(off Lynton Rd.)
Osprey La. HA2: Harr 2F 59
Osprey M. EN3: Pond E 5D 24
Ospringe Cl. SE20 7J 139
Ospringe Ct. SE9 6H 125
Ospringe Ho. SE1 6K 13
(off Wootton St.)
Ospringe Rd. NW5 4G 65
Osram Ct. W6 3E 98
Osram Rd. HA9: Wemb 3D 60
Osric Path N1 2E 84
Ossel Ct. SE10 4G 105
Ossian M. N4 7K 47
Ossian Rd. N4 7K 47
OSSIE GARVIN RDBT. 7K 75
Ossington Bldgs.
W1 5G 5 (5E 82)
Ossington Cl. W2 7J 81
Ossington St. W2 7J 81
Ossory Rd. SE1 6G 103
Ossulston St. NW1 1D 6 (2H 83)
Ossulton Pl. N2 3A 46
Ossulton Way N2 4A 46
Ostade Rd. SW2 7K 119
Ostell Cres. EN3: Enf L 1H 25
Ostend Pl. SE1 4C 102
Osten M. SW7 3K 99
OSTERLEY 7H 95
Osterley Av. TW7: Isle 7H 95
Osterley Cl. BR5: St P 1K 161
Osterley Ct. TW7: Isle 1H 113
UB5: N'olt 3A 76
(off Canberra Dr.)
Osterley Cres. TW7: Isle 1J 113
Osterley Gdns. CR7: Thor H 2C 156
UB2: S'hall 2G 95
Osterley Ho. E14 6D 86
(off Giraud St.)
Osterley La. TW7: Isle 4G 95
UB2: S'hall 5E 94
Osterley Lodge TW7: Isle 7J 95
(off Church Rd.)
Osterley Pk. 6G 95
Osterley Pk. & House 6G 95
Osterley Pk. Rd.
UB2: S'hall 3D 94
Osterley Pk. Vw. Rd. W7 2J 95
Osterley Rd. N16 4E 66
TW7: Isle 7J 95
Osterley Sports & Athletics Cen. 7J 95
Osterley Sports Club 3G 95
Osterley Views
UB2: S'hall 2H 95
Oster Ter. E17 5K 49
Ostlers Dr. TW15: Ashf 5E 128
Ostliffe Rd. N13 5H 33
Oswald Bldg. SW11 6F 101
Oswald Rd. UB1: S'hall 1C 94
Oswald's Mead E9 4A 68
Oswald St. E5 3K 67
Oswald Ter. NW2 3E 62
Osward CR0: Sels 7B 170
(not continuous)
Osward Pl. N9 2C 34
Osward Rd. SW17 2D 136
Oswell Ho. E1 1H 103
(off Farthing Flds.)
Oswin St. SE11 4B 102
Oswyth Rd. SE5 2E 120
Otford Cl. BR1: Broml 3E 160
DA5: Bexl 6H 127
SE20 1J 157
Otford Cres. SE4 6B 122
Otford Ho. SE1 7F 15
(off Staple St.)
SE15 6J 103
(off Lovelinch Cl.)
Othello Cl. SE11 5K 19 (5B 102)
The Other Place Theatre 1A 18
(off Palace St.)
Otho Ct. TW8: Bford 7D 96
Otley App. IG2: Ilf 6F 53
Otley Dr. IG2: Ilf 5F 53
Otley Ho. N5 3A 66
Otley Rd. E16 6A 88
Otley Ter. E5 3K 67
Ottawa Gdns. RM10: Dag 7K 73
Ottawa Ho. SE16 2J 103
(off Province Dr.)
UB4: Yead 3K 75
(off Ayles Rd.)
Ottaway St. E5 3G 67
Otterbourne Rd. CR0: C'don 2C 168
E4 3A 36
Otterburn Gdns. TW7: Isle 7A 96
Otterburn Ho. SE5 7C 102
(off Sultan St.)
Otterburn St. SW17 6D 136
Otter Cl. E15 1E 86
Otterden Cl. BR6: Orp 3J 173
Otterden St. SE6 4C 140
Otterden Ter. SE1 4F 103
(off Lynton Rd.)
Otter Dr. SM5: Cars 1D 166
Otterfield Rd. UB7: Yiew 7A 74
Otter Rd. UB6: G'frd 4G 77
Otter Way UB7: Yiew 1A 92
Ottley Dr. SE3 4A 124
Otto Cl. SE26 3H 139
Otto Dr. UB2: S'hall 3E 94
Otto St. SE17 6B 102
Ott's Yd. N19 4G 65
(off Southcote Rd.)
Otway Gdns. WD23: Bush 1D 26
Oulton Cl. E5 2J 67
SE28 6C 90
Oulton Cres. IG11: Bark 5K 71
Oulton Rd. N15 5D 48
Our Lady's Cl. SE19 6D 138
Ouseley Rd. SW12 1D 136
Outer Circ.
NW1 1D 4, 1J 5 (2C 82)
Outgate Rd. NW10 7B 62
Outram Pl. N1 1J 83
Outram Rd. CR0: C'don 2F 169
E6 1C 88
N22 1H 47
Outwich St. EC3 7H 9
Outwood Ho. SW2 7K 119
(off Deepdene Gdns.)
The Oval
Surrey CCC 7H 19 (6K 101)
The Oval DA15: Sidc 7A 126
E2 2H 85
Oval Ct. HA8: Edg 7D 28
Ovalhouse 6A 102
Oval Ho. CR0: C'don 1E 168
(off Oval Rd.)
Oval Mans. SE11 7H 19 (6K 101)
Oval Pl. SW8 7K 101
Oval Rd. CR0: C'don 2D 168
NW1 1F 83
Oval Rd. Nth. RM10: Dag 1H 91
Oval Rd. Sth. RM10: Dag 2H 91
Oval Way SE11 6H 19 (5K 101)
Ovanna M. N1 6E 66
Overbrae BR3: Beck 6C 140
Overbrook Wlk. HA8: Edg 7B 28
(not continuous)
Overbury Av. BR3: Beck 3D 158
Overbury Rd. N15 6D 48
Overbury St. E5 4K 67
Overcliff Rd. SE13 3C 122
Overcourt Cl. DA15: Sidc 6B 126
Overdale Av. KT3: N Mald 2J 151
Overdale Rd. W5 3C 96
Overdown Rd. SE6 4C 140
Overhill Rd. SE22 7G 121
Overhill Way BR3: Beck 5F 159
Overlea Rd. E5 7G 49
Overmead DA15: Sidc 7H 125
Oversley Ho. W2 5J 81
(off Alfred Rd.)
Overstand Cl. BR3: Beck 5C 158
Overstone Gdns.
CR0: C'don 7B 158
Overstone Ho. E14 6C 86
(off E. India Dock Rd.)
Overstone Rd. W6 3E 98
Overstrand Mans. SW11 1D 118
Overton Cl. NW10 6J 61
TW7: Isle 1K 113
Overton Ct. E11 7J 51
SM2: Sutt 7J 165
Overton Dr. E11 7J 51
RM6: Chad H 7C 54
Overton Ho. SW15 7B 116
(off Tangley Gro.)
Overton Rd. E10 1A 68
N14 5D 22
SE2 3C 108
SM2: Sutt 6J 165
SW9 2A 120
Overton Rd. E. SE2 3D 108
Overton's Yd.
CR0: C'don 3C 168
Overy Ho. SE1 7A 14 (2B 102)
Ovesdon Av. HA2: Harr 1D 58
Ovett Cl. SE19 6E 138
Ovex Cl. E14 2E 104
Ovington Ct. SW3 2D 16
(off Brompton Rd.)
Ovington Gdns. SW3 2D 16 (3C 100)
Ovington M. SW3 2D 16
Ovington Sq. SW3 2D 16 (3C 100)
Ovington St. SW3 3D 16 (4C 100)
Owen Cl. CR0: C'don 6D 156
SE28 1C 108
TW16: Sun 1G 147
UB5: N'olt 6C 58
(Arnold Rd.)
UB5: N'olt 3K 75
(Attlee Rd.)
Owen Gdns. IG8: Wfd G 6H 37
Owen Ho. TW1: Twick 7B 114
TW14: Felt 7J 111
Owenite St. SE2 4B 108
Owen Mans. W14 6G 99
(off Queen's Club Gdns.)
Owen Rd. N13 5H 33
UB4: Yead 3K 75
Owens M. E11 2G 69
Owen's Row EC1 1A 8 (3B 84)
Owen St. EC1 1A 8 (2B 84)
Owens Way SE23 7A 122
Owen Wlk. SE20 1G 157
Owen Way NW10 6J 61
Owgan Cl. SE5 7D 102
Oxberry Av. SW6 2G 117
Oxborough Ho. SW18 4A 118
(off Eltringham St.)
Oxendon St. SW1 3C 12 (7H 83)
Oxenford St. SE15 3F 121
Oxenham Ho. SE8 6C 104
(off Benbow St.)
Oxenholme NW1 1A 6
(off Hampstead Rd.)
Oxenpark Av. HA9: Wemb 7E 42
Oxestall's Rd. SE8 5A 104
Oxford & Cambridge Mans. NW1 6D 4
(off Old Marylebone Rd.)

Oxford Av.—Parker Bldg.

Oxford Av. N14 1B 32
SW20 2G 153
TW5: Hest 5E 94
UB3: Harl 7H 93
Oxford Cir. W1 1A 12
Oxford Cir. Av. W1 1A 12 (6G 83)
Oxford Cl. CR4: Mitc 3G 155
N9 2C 34
TW15: Ashf 7E 128
Oxford Ct. EC4 2E 14
KT6: Surb 5E 150
(off Avenue Elmers)
TW13: Hanw 4B 130
W3 6G 79
W4 5H 97
W7 5K 77
(off Copley Cl.)
W9 5J 81
(off Elmfield Way)
Oxford Cres. KT3: N Mald 6K 151
Oxford Dr. HA4: Ruis 2A 58
SE1 5G 15 (1E 102)
Oxford Gdns. N20 1G 31
N21 7H 23
W4 5G 97
W10 6E 80
Oxford Ga. W6 4F 99
Oxford Ho. *BR2: Broml* 6B 160
(off Wells Vw. Dr.)
E3 5B 86
(off William Whiffin Sq.)
NW6 2J 81
(off Oxford Rd.)
RM8: Dag 4A 72
Oxford M. DA5: Bexl 7G 127
Oxford Pl. *NW10* 3K 61
(off Press Rd.)
Oxford Rd. DA14: Sidc 5B 144
E15 6F 69
(not continuous)
EN3: Pond E 5C 24
HA1: Harr 6G 41
HA3: W'stone 3K 41
IG1: Ilf 5G 71
IG8: Wfd G 5G 37
N4 1A 66
N9 2C 34
NW6 2J 81
SE19 6D 138
SM5: Cars 6C 166
SM6: W'gton 5G 167
SW15 4G 117
TW11: Tedd 5H 131
W5 7D 78
Oxford Rd. Nth. W4 5H 97
Oxford Rd. Sth. W4 5G 97
Oxford Row TW16: Sun 3A 148
Oxford Sq. W2 1D 10 (6C 82)
Oxford St. W1 1G 11 (6E 82)
Oxford Ter. *NW6* 2K 81
(off Oxford Rd.)
Oxford Wlk. UB1: S'hall 1D 94
Oxford Way TW13: Hanw 4B 130
Oxgate Cen. NW2 2D 62
Oxgate Ct. NW2 2C 62
Oxgate Ct. Pde. NW2 2C 62
Oxgate Gdns. NW2 3D 62
Oxgate La. NW2 2D 62
Oxgate Pde. NW2 2C 62
Oxhawth Cres.
BR2: Broml 5E 160
Oxhey La. HA3: Hrw W 5A 26
HA5: Hat E 5A 26
Oxleas E6 6F 89
Oxleas Cl. DA16: Well 2H 125
Oxleay Rd. HA2: Harr 1E 58
Oxleigh Cl. KT3: N Mald 5A 152
Oxley Cl. SE1 5F 103
Oxley Sq. *E3* 4D 86
(off Truman Wlk.)
Oxleys Rd. NW2 3D 62
Oxlip Cl. CR0: C'don 1K 169
Oxlow La. RM9: Dag 4F 73
RM10: Dag 4F 73
Oxonian St. SE22 4F 121
Oxo Tower Wharf 3K 13 (7A 84)
Oxted Cl. CR4: Mitc 3B 154
Oxtoby Way SW16 1H 155
The Oxygen E16 7J 87
OYO Bus. Units
DA17: Belv 2J 109
RM9: Dag 4F 91
Oystercatcher Cl. E16 6K 87
Oyster Cl. EN5: Barn 6B 20
Oyster Ct. *SE17* 4C 102
(off Crampton St.)
Oystergate Wlk. EC4 3E 14
Oyster M. E7 6B 70
Oyster Row E1 6J 85
Oyster Wharf SW11 2B 118
Ozolins Way E16 6J 87

P

Pablo Neruda Cl. SE24 4B 120
Pace Pl. E1 6H 85
Pacific Bldg. *E15* 5F 69
(off Property Row)
Pacific Cl. TW14: Felt 1H 129
Pacific Ct. E1 5J 85
Pacific Ho. *E1* 4K 85
(off Ernest St.)
Pacific M. SW9 4A 120
Pacific Rd. E16 6J 87
Pacific Wharf SE16 1K 103
Packenham Ho. *E2* 1K 9
(off Wellington Row)
W10 7F 81
(off Shalfleet Dr.)
Packham Ct. KT4: Wor Pk 3E 164
Packington Rd. W3 3J 97
Packington Sq. N1 1C 84
(not continuous)
Packington St. N1 1B 84
Packmores Rd. SE9 5H 125
Packwell Pl.
TW5: Hest 6A 94
Padbury *SE17* 5E 102
(off Bagshot St.)
Padbury Cl. TW14: Bedf 1F 129
Padbury Ct. E2 2K 9 (3F 85)
Padbury Ho. *NW8* 3D 4
(off Tresham Cres.)
Padbury Oaks UB7: Lford 4C 174
Padcroft Rd. UB7: Yiew 1A 92
Paddenswick Rd. W6 3C 98
PADDINGTON 7A 4 (6B 82)
Paddington Cl. UB4: Yead 4B 76
Paddington Ct. *W7* 5K 77
(off Copley Cl.)
Paddington Gdns. W2 6A 4 (5B 82)
Paddington Grn.
W2 5A 4 (5B 82)
Paddington Sports Club 4K 81
Paddington St. W1 5G 5 (5E 82)
The Paddock N10 3E 46
NW9 5G 43
UB10: Ick 4D 56
Paddock Cl. BR6: Farnb 4F 173
KT4: Wor Pk 1A 164
SE3 2J 123
SE26 4K 139
UB5: N'olt 2E 76
Paddock Gdns. SE19 6E 138
Paddock Lodge *EN1: Enf* 5K 23
(off Village Rd.)
Paddock Mobile Home Pk. 7C 172
Paddock Rd. DA6: Bex 4E 126
HA4: Ruis 3B 58
NW2 3C 62
The Paddocks CR0: Addtn 6C 170
EN4: Cockf 3J 21
HA9: Wemb 2H 61
W5 3D 96
(off Popes La.)
Paddocks Cl. HA2: Harr 4F 59
Paddocks Grn. NW9 1H 61
Paddock Way BR7: Chst 7H 143
SW15 7E 116
Padelford La. HA7: Stan 2F 27
Padfield Ct. HA9: Wemb 3F 61
Padfield Rd. SE5 3C 120
Padley Cl. KT9: Chess 5F 163
Padnall Ct. RM6: Chad H 3D 54
Padnall Rd. RM6: Chad H 3D 54
Padstone Ho. *E3* 3D 86
(off Talwin St.)
Padstow Cl. BR6: Chels 4K 173
Padstow Ho. *E14* 7B 86
(off Three Colt St.)
Padstow Rd. EN2: Enf 1G 23
Padstow Wlk. TW14: Felt 1H 129
Padua Rd. SE20 1J 157
Pagden St. SW8 1F 119
Pageant Av. NW9 1K 43
Pageant Cres. SE16 1A 104
Pageantmaster Ct. EC4 1A 14
Pageant Wlk. CR0: C'don 3E 168
Page Av. HA9: Wemb 3J 61
Page Cl. HA3: Kenton 6F 43
RM9: Dag 5E 72
TW12: Hamp 6C 130
Page Ct. NW7 7J 29
Page Cres. CR0: Wadd 5B 168
Page Grn. Rd. N15 5G 49
Page Grn. Ter. N15 5F 49
Page Heath La.
BR1: Broml 3B 160
Page Heath Vs.
BR1: Broml 3B 160
Page High *N22* 2A 48
(off Lymington Av.)
Page Ho. *SE10* 6E 104
(off Welland St.)
Pagehurst Rd. CR0: C'don 7H 157
Page Mdw. NW7 7J 29
Page M. SW11 2E 118
Page Rd. TW14: Bedf 6F 111
Pages Hill N10 2E 46
Pages La. N10 2E 46
Page St. NW7 1C 44
SW1 3D 18 (4H 101)
Page's Wlk. SE1 4E 102
Pages Yd. W4 6B 98
Paget Av. SM1: Sutt 3B 166
Paget Cl.
TW12: Hamp H 4H 131
Paget Gdns. BR7: Chst 1F 161
Paget Ho. *E2* 2J 85
(off Bishop's Way)
Paget La. TW7: Isle 3H 113
Paget Pl. KT2: King T 6J 133
KT7: T Ditt 1A 162
Paget Ri. SE18 6E 106
Paget Rd. IG1: Ilf 4F 71
N16 1D 66
UB10: Hil 4E 74
Paget St. EC1 1A 8 (3B 84)
Paget Ter. SE18 6F 107
Pagham Ho. *W10* 4E 80
(off Sutton Way)
Pagin Ho. *N15* 5E 48
(off Braemar Rd.)
Pagitts Gro. EN4: Had W 1E 20
Pagnell St. SE14 7B 104
Pagoda Av. TW9: Rich 3F 115
Pagoda Gdns. SE3 2F 123
Pagoda Gro. SE27 2C 138
Paignton Rd. HA4: Ruis 3J 57
N15 6E 48
Paines Cl. HA5: Pinn 3C 40
Paines La. HA5: Pinn 1C 40
Pain's Cl. CR4: Mitc 2F 155
Painsthorpe Rd. N16 3E 66
Painted Hall 6F 105
Painters M. SE16 4G 103
Painters Rd. IG2: Ilf 3K 53
Paisley Rd. N22 1B 48
SM5: Cars 1B 166
Paisley Ter. SM5: Cars 7B 154
Pakefield M. SW2 1K 137
Pakeman Ho. *SE1* 6B 14
(off Surrey Row)
Pakeman St. N7 3K 65
Pakenham Cl. SW12 1E 136
Pakenham St.
WC1 2H 7 (3K 83)
Pakington Ho. *SW9* 2J 119
(off Stockwell Gdns. Est.)
Palace Arts Way HA9: Wemb 4G 61
Palace Av. W8 2K 99
Palace Cl. E9 6B 68
Palace Ct. *BR1: Broml* 1K 159
(off Palace Gro.)
HA3: Kenton 6E 42
NW3 5K 63
W2 7K 81
(not continuous)
Palace Ct. Gdns. N10 3G 47
Palace Exchange 4J 23
Palace Gdns. IG9: Buck H 1G 37
Palace Gdns. M. W8 1K 99
Palace Gdns. Shop. Cen. 4J 23
Palace Gdns. Ter. W8 1J 99
Palace Ga. W8 2A 100
Palace Gates M. *N8* 4J 47
(off The Campsbourne)
Palace Gates Rd. N22 1H 47
Palace Grn. CR0: Sels 7B 170
W8 1K 99
Palace Gro. BR1: Broml 1K 159
SE19 7F 139
Palace Mans. *KT1: King T* 4D 150
(off Palace Rd.)
W14 4G 99
(off Hammersmith Rd.)
Palace M. E17 4B 50
SW1 4H 17
SW6 7H 99
Palace Pde. E17 4B 50
Palace Pl. SW1 1A 18 (3G 101)
Palace Pl. Mans. *W8* 2K 99
(off Kensington Ct.)
Palace Rd. BR1: Broml 1K 159
HA4: Ruis 4C 58
KT1: King T 4D 150
KT8: E Mos 3G 149
N8 5H 47
(not continuous)
N11 7D 32
SE19 7F 139
SW2 1K 137
Palace Sq. SE19 7F 139
Palace St. SW1 1A 18 (3G 101)
Palace Superbowl 4C 102
(within Elephant & Castle Shop. Cen.)
Palace Theatre 1D 12
(off Shaftesbury Av.)
Palace Vw. BR1: Broml 3K 159
(not continuous)
CR0: C'don 4B 170
SE12 2J 141
Palace Vw. Rd. E4 5J 35
Pal. Wharf *W6* 7E 98
(off Rainville Rd.)
Palamos Rd. E10 1C 68
Palatine Av. N16 4E 66
Palatine Rd. N16 4E 66
Palazzo Apts. *N1* 7E 66
(off Ardleigh Rd.)
Palemead Cl. SW6 1F 117
Palermo Rd. NW10 2C 80
Palestine Gro. SW19 1B 154
Palestra Ho. *SE1* 5A 14
(off Blackfriars Rd.)
Palewell Comn. Dr. SW14 5K 115
Palewell Pk. SW14 5K 115
Palfrey Pl. SW8 7K 101
Palgrave Av. UB1: S'hall 7E 76
Palgrave Ct.
TW11: Hamp W 7C 132
Palgrave Gdns. NW1 3D 4 (4C 82)
Palgrave Ho. *SE5* 7C 102
(off Wyndham Est.)
TW2: Whitt 7G 113
Palgrave Rd. W12 3B 98
Palissy St. E2 2J 9 (3F 85)
(not continuous)
Palladian Gdns. W4 6A 98
Palladino Ho. *SW17* 5C 136
(off Laurel Cl.)
Palladio Ct. *SW18* 6K 117
(off Mapleton Cres.)
Palladium Ct. *E8* 7F 67
(off Queensbridge Rd.)
Pallant Ho. *SE1* 3D 102
(off Tabard St.)
Pallant Way BR6: Farnb 3E 172
Pallet Way SE18 1C 124
Palliser Ct. *W14* 5G 99
(off Palliser Rd.)
Palliser Ho. *E1* 4K 85
(off Ernest St.)
SE10 6F 105
(off Trafalgar Rd.)
Palliser Rd. W14 5G 99
Pallister Ter. SW15 3B 134
Pall Mall SW1 5B 12 (1G 101)
Pall Mall E. SW1 4D 12 (1H 101)
Pall Mall Pl. SW1 5B 12
Palmadium Cl. N13 3F 33
Palmar Cres.
DA7: Bex 3G 127
Palmar Rd. DA7: Bex 2G 127
Palm Av. DA14: Sidc 6D 144
Palm Cl. E10 3D 68
Palm Ct. *SE15* 7F 103
(off Garnies Cl.)
Palmeira Rd. DA7: Bex 3D 126
Palmer Av. SM3: Cheam 4E 164
Palmer Cl. BR4: W W'ck 3F 171
TW5: Hest 1E 112
UB5: N'olt 6C 58
Palmer Cres. KT1: King T 3E 150
Palmer Dr. BR1: Broml 4F 161
Palmer Gdns. EN5: Barn 5A 20
Palmer Ho. *SE14* 7K 103
(off Lubbock St.)
Palmer Pl. N7 5A 66
Palmer Rd. E13 4K 87
RM8: Dag 1D 72
SW11 7F 101
Palmer's Ct. *N11* 5B 32
(off Palmer's Rd.)
PALMERS GREEN 3F 33
Palmers Gro. KT8: W Mole 4E 148
Palmers La. EN1: Enf 1C 24
EN3: Enf H 1C 24
Palmer's Rd. E2 2K 85
N11 5B 32
Palmers Rd. SW14 3J 115
SW16 2K 155
Palmerston Cen.
HA3: W'stone 3K 41
Palmerston Ct. *E3* 2K 85
(off Old Ford Rd.)
IG9: Buck H 1F 37
KT6: Surb 7D 150
Palmerston Cres. N13 5E 32
SE18 6G 107
Palmerston Gro. SW19 7J 135
Palmerston Ho. *SE1* 7J 13
(off Westminster Bri. Rd.)
W8 1J 99
(off Kensington Pl.)
Palmerston Mans. *W14* 6G 99
(off Queen's Club Gdns.)
Palmerston Rd. BR6: Farnb 4G 173
CR0: C'don 5D 156
E7 6K 69
E17 3B 50
HA3: W'stone 3J 41
IG9: Buck H 2E 36
N22 7E 32
NW6 7H 63
(not continuous)
SM1: Sutt 5A 166
SM5: Cars 4D 166
SW14 4J 115
SW19 7J 135
TW2: Twick 6J 113
TW3: Houn 1G 113
W3 3J 97
Palmerston Way SW8 7F 101
Palmer St. SW1 1C 18 (3H 101)
(not continuous)
Palmers Wharf *KT1: King T* 2D 150
(off Emms Pas.)
Palm Gro. W5 3E 96
Palm Rd. RM7: Rom 5J 55
Palomino Cl. UB4: Hayes 2F 75
Palyn Ho. *EC1* 2D 8
(off Radnor St.)
Pamela Ct. N12 6E 30
Pamela Gdns. HA5: Eastc 5K 39
Pamela St. E8 1F 85
Pampisford Rd. CR2: S Croy 7B 168
Pams Way KT19: Ewe 5K 163
Panama Ho. *E1* 5K 85
(off Beaumont Sq.)
Panavia Ct. NW9 2B 44
Pancras La. EC4 1E 14 (6C 84)
Pancras Rd. N1 1E 6 (2J 83)
NW1 2H 83
Pancras Sq. N1 2J 83
Pancras Square Leisure Cen. 2J 83
Pancras Way E3 2C 86
Pandangle Ho. *E8* 1F 85
(off Kingsland Rd.)
Pandian Way NW1 6H 65
Pandora Ct. *E16* 5J 87
(off Robertson Rd.)
Pandora Rd. NW6 6J 63
Panfield M. IG2: Ilf 6E 52
Panfield Rd. SE2 3A 108
Pangbourne *NW1* 2A 6
(off Stanhope St.)
Pangbourne Av. W10 5E 80
Pangbourne Dr. HA7: Stan 5J 27
Panhard Pl. UB1: S'hall 7F 77
Pank Av. EN5: New Bar 5F 21
Pankhurst Av. E3 5D 86
E16 1K 105
Pankhurst Cl. SE14 7K 103
TW7: Isle 3K 113
Pankhurst Ho. W12 6D 80
Pankhurst Rd. KT12: Walt T 7A 148
Panmuir Rd. SW20 1D 152
Panmure Cl. N5 4B 66
Panmure Ct. SE26 3H 139
UB1: S'hall 6G 77
(off Osborne Rd.)
Panmure Rd. SE26 3H 139
Pannells Ct. TW5: Hest 6E 94
Panorama Ct. N6 6G 47
Panoramic Twr. *E14* 6D 86
(off Burcham St.)
Pan Peninsula Sq. E14 2D 104
Pansy Gdns. W12 7C 80
Panther Dr. NW10 5K 61
The Pantiles BR1: Broml 3C 160
DA7: Bex 7F 109
NW11 4H 45
WD23: B Hea 1C 26
Pantiles Cl. N13 5G 33
Panton Cl. CR0: C'don 1B 168
Panton St. SW1 3C 12 (7H 83)
Panyer All. *EC1* 7C 8
(off Newgate St.)
Panyers Gdns. RM10: Dag 3H 73
Paper Bldgs. EC4 2K 13
Papermill Cl. SM5: Cars 4E 166
Papermill Pl. E17 2A 50
Paper Mill Wharf E14 7A 86
Papillons Wlk. SE3 2J 123
Papworth Gdns. N7 5K 65
Papworth Way SW2 7A 120
Papyrus Ho. N1 1C 8
Parabola Ct. KT8: E Mos 4G 149
The Parade CR0: C'don 6J 155
KT2: King T 2E 150
(off London Rd.)
KT4: Wor Pk 4B 164
N4 1A 66
SE4 2B 122
(off Up. Brockley Rd.)
SE26 3H 139
(off Wells Pk. Rd.)
SM1: Sutt 3H 165
SM5: Cars 5D 166
(off Beynon Rd.)
SW11 7D 100
TW12: Hamp H 5H 131
TW16: Sun 7H 129
UB6: G'frd 5B 60
Parade Gdns. E4 7J 35
Parade Ground Path SE18 7D 106
Parade Mans. NW4 5D 44
Parade M. SE27 2B 138
Paradise Gdns. W6 4D 98
Paradise Pas. N7 5A 66
Paradise Path SE28 1A 108
Paradise Pl. SE18 4C 106
Paradise Rd. SW4 2J 119
TW9: Rich 5D 114
Paradise Row E2 3H 85
Paradise St. SE16 2H 103
Paradise Wlk. SW3 7F 17 (6D 100)
Paragon *TW8: Bford* 5C 96
(off Boston Pk. Rd.)
The Paragon SE3 2H 123
Paragon Cl. E16 6J 87
Paragon Gro. KT5: Surb 6F 151
Paragon M. SE1 4D 102
SW8 6K 101
Paragon Pl. KT5: Surb 6F 151
SE3 2H 123
Paragon Rd. E9 6J 67
Paramount Bldg. *EC1* 3A 8
(off St John St.)
Paramount Ct. WC1 4B 6
Parbury Ri. KT9: Chess 6E 162
Parbury Rd. SE23 6A 122
Parchment Cl. CR4: Mitc 7E 154
Parchmore Rd. CR7: Thor H 2B 156
Parchmore Way CR7: Thor H 2B 156
Pardoe Rd. E10 7D 50
Pardoner Ho. *SE1* 3D 102
(off Pardoner St.)
Pardoner St. SE1 7F 15 (3D 102)
(not continuous)
Pardon St. EC1 3B 8 (4B 84)
Parent Shop. Mall 2J 51
(off Marlborough Rd.)
Parfett St. E1 5G 85
(not continuous)
Parfitt Cl. NW3 1A 64
Parfrey St. W6 6E 98
Pargraves Ct. HA9: Wemb 2G 61
Parham Dr. IG2: Ilf 6F 53
Parham Way N10 2G 47
Paris Corte *SE13* 3D 122
(off Loampit Va.)
Paris Gdn. SE1 4A 14 (1B 102)
Parish Ct. KT6: Surb 5E 150
Parish Ga. Dr. DA15: Sidc 6J 125
Parish La. SE20 6K 139
Parish M. SE20 7K 139
Paris Ho. *E2* 2H 85
(off Old Bethnal Grn. Rd.)
Parish Wharf Pl. SE18 4C 106
Parison Cl. TW9: Rich 3G 115
The Park DA14: Sidc 5A 144
HA1: Harr 1J 59
N6 6E 46
NW11 1K 63
SE23 1J 139
SM5: Cars 5D 166
W5 1D 96
Park App. DA16: Well 4B 126
SE16 3H 103
Park Av. BR1: Broml 6H 141
BR4: W W'ck 2E 170
BR6: Chels 2K 173
BR6: Farnb 3D 172
CR4: Mitc 7F 137
E6 1E 88
E15 6G 69
EN1: Enf 5J 23
HA4: Ruis 6F 39
IG1: Ilf 1E 70
IG8: Wfd G 5E 36
IG11: Bark 6G 71
N3 1K 45
N13 3F 33
N18 4B 34
N22 2J 47
NW2 5D 62
NW10 2F 79
(Brent Cres., not continuous)
NW10 5D 62
(Park Av. Nth.)
NW11 1K 63
SM5: Cars 6E 166
SW14 4K 115
TW3: Houn 6F 113
TW17: Shep 3G 147
UB1: S'hall 2D 94
Park Av. E. KT17: Ewe 6C 164
Park Av. M. CR4: Mitc 7F 137
Park Av. Nth. N8 3H 47
NW10 5D 62
Park Av. Rd. N17 7C 34
Park Av. Sth. N8 4H 47
Park Av. W. KT17: Ewe 6C 164
Park Central SE17 4C 102
Park Central Bldg. E3 2C 86
Park Chase HA9: Wemb 4F 61
Park Cl. E9 1J 85
HA3: Hrw W 1J 41
KT2: King T 1G 151
N12 3G 31
NW2 3D 62
NW10 3F 79
SM5: Cars 6D 166
SW1 7E 10 (2D 100)
TW3: Houn 5G 113
TW12: Hamp 1G 149
W4 6K 97
W14 3H 99
The Park Club
Acton 1A 98
Park Ct. *CR2: S Croy* 5C 168
(off Warham Rd.)
E4 2K 35
E17 5D 50
HA3: Kenton 7E 42
HA9: Wemb 5E 60
KT1: Hamp W 1C 150
KT3: N Mald 4K 151
N11 7C 32
N17 7B 34
SE21 3C 138
SE26 6H 139
SM6: W'gton 5J 167
SW11 1F 119
UB8: Uxb 1A 74
W6 4C 98
Park Cres. DA8: Erith 6J 109
EN2: Enf 4J 23
HA3: Hrw W 1J 41
N3 7F 31
TW2: Twick 1H 131
W1 4J 5 (4F 83)
Park Cres. M. E. W1 4K 5 (4F 83)
Park Cres. M. W. W1 4J 5 (4F 83)
Park Cres. Rd. DA8: Erith 6K 109
Park Cft. HA8: Edg 1J 43
Parkcroft Rd. SE12 7H 123
Parkdale N11 6C 32
Parkdale Cres.
KT4: Wor Pk 3K 163
Parkdale Rd. SE18 5J 107
Park Dr. HA2: Harr 7E 40
HA3: Hrw W 6C 26
N21 6H 23
NW11 1K 63
RM1: Rom 4K 55
RM10: Dag 3J 73
SE7 6C 106
SW14 5K 115
W3 3G 97
Park Dwellings NW3 5D 64
Park E. Bldg. *E3* 2C 86
(off Fairfield Rd.)
Park End BR1: Broml 1H 159
NW3 4C 64
Parker Bldg. *SE16* 7K 15
(off Old Jamaica Rd.)

A-Z Big London 265

Parker Cl.—Paul Ct.

Parker Cl. E16 1C 106
SM5: Cars 6D 166
Parker Ct. *N1* *1C 84*
(off Basire St.)
Parker Ho. *E14* *2C 104*
(off Admirals Way)
Parker M. WC2 7F 7 (6J 83)
Parke Rd. SW13 1C 116
TW16: Sun 4J 147
Parker Rd. CR0: C'don 4C 168
Parkers Row SE1 7K 15 (2G 103)
Parker St. E16 1C 106
WC2 7F 7 (6J 83)
Parkes St. E20 6C 68
Park Farm Cl. HA5: Eastc 5K 39
N2 3A 46
Park Farm Ct. UB3: Hayes 7G 75
Park Farm Rd. BR1: Broml 1B 160
KT2: King T 7E 132
Parkfield TW7: Isle 1J 113
Parkfield Av. HA2: Harr 2G 41
SW14 4A 116
TW13: Felt 3J 129
UB5: N'olt 2B 76
UB10: Hil 3D 74
Parkfield Cl. HA8: Edg 6C 28
UB5: N'olt 2C 76
Parkfield Ct. *SE14* *1B 122*
(off Parkfield Rd.)
Parkfield Cres. HA2: Harr 2G 41
HA4: Ruis 2C 58
TW13: Felt 3J 129
Parkfield Dr. UB5: N'olt 2B 76
Parkfield Gdns. HA2: Harr 3F 41
Parkfield Ho. HA2: Harr 1F 41
Parkfield Ind. Est. SW11 2E 118
Parkfield Pde. TW13: Felt 3J 129
Parkfield Rd. HA2: Harr 3G 59
NW10 7D 62
SE14 1B 122
SW4 6H 119
(not continuous)
TW13: Felt 3J 129
UB5: N'olt 2C 76
UB10: Ick 2D 56
Parkfields CR0: C'don 1B 170
SW15 4E 116
Parkfields Av. NW9 1K 61
SW20 1D 152
Parkfields Cl. SM5: Cars 4E 166
Parkfields Rd. KT2: King T 5F 133
Parkfield St. N1 2A 84
Parkfield Way BR2: Broml 6D 160
Park Gdns. DA8: Erith 4K 109
E10 1C 68
KT2: King T 5F 133
NW9 3H 43
Park Ga. N2 3B 46
N21 7E 22
W5 5D 78
Parkgate *N1* *1D 84*
(off Southgate Rd.)
SE3 3H 123
Parkgate Av. EN4: Had W 1F 21
Parkgate Cl. KT2: King T 6H 133
Park Ga. Ct. TW12: Hamp H 6G 131
Parkgate Cres. EN4: Had W 1F 21
Parkgate Gdns. SW14 5K 115
Parkgate M. N6 7G 47
Parkgate Rd. SM6: W'gton 5E 166
SW11 7C 100
Park Gates HA2: Harr 4E 58
Park Gro. BR1: Broml 1K 159
DA7: Bex 4J 127
E15 1J 87
HA8: Edg 5A 28
N11 7C 32
Park Gro. Rd. E11 2G 69
Park Hall *SE10* *7F 105*
(off Croom's Hill)
Park Hall Rd. N2 4C 46
SE21 3C 138
Park Hall Trad. Est. SE21 3C 138
Parkham Ct. BR2: Broml 2G 159
Parkham St. SW11 1C 118
Park Hgts. Ct. *E14* *6B 86*
(off Wharf La.)
Park Hill BR1: Broml 4C 160
SE23 2H 139
SM5: Cars 6C 166
SW4 5H 119
TW10: Rich 6F 115
W5 5D 78
Park Hill Cl. SM5: Cars 5C 166
Park Hill Ct. SW17 3D 136
Park Hill M. CR2: S Croy 5D 168
Park Hill Ri. CR0: C'don 2E 168
Park Hill Rd. BR2: Broml 2G 159
CR0: C'don 2E 168
SM6: W'gton 7F 167
Parkhill Rd. DA5: Bexl 7F 127
DA14: Sidc 3H 143
DA15: Sidc 3H 143
E4 1K 35
NW3 5D 64
Parkhill Wlk. NW3 5D 64
Parkholme Rd. E8 6G 67
Park Ho. *E9* *7J 67*
(off Shore Rd.)
N21 7E 22
SE5 *1D 120*
(off Camberwell Grn.)
W1 1G 11
Park Ho. Gdns. TW1: Twick 5C 114
Park Ho. Pas. N6 7E 46
Parkhouse St. SE5 7D 102
Parkhurst Ct. N7 4J 65
Parkhurst Gdns. DA5: Bexl 7G 127
Parkhurst Rd. DA5: Bexl 7G 127
E12 4E 70
E17 4A 50
N7 4J 65
N11 5K 31
N17 2G 49
N22 6E 32
SM1: Sutt 4B 166
Parkinson Ct. *N1* *2F 9*
(off Charles Sq. Est.)
Parkinson Ho. *E9* *7J 67*
(off Frampton Pk. Rd.)
SW1 *5C 18*
(off Tachbrook St.)
Parkland Ct. *E15* *5G 69*
(off Maryland Pk.)
W14 *2G 99*
(off Holland Pk. Av.)
Parkland Gdns. SW19 1F 135
Parkland Gro. TW15: Ashf 3C 128
Parkland Mead BR1: Broml 3F 161
(not continuous)
Parkland M. BR7: Chst 7H 143
Parkland Rd. IG8: Wfd G 7E 36
N22 2K 47
TW15: Ashf 4C 128
Parklands KT5: Surb 5F 151
N6 7F 47
Parklands Cl. EN4: Had W 1G 21
IG2: Ilf 7G 53
SW14 5J 115
Parklands Ct. TW5: Hest 2B 112
Parklands Dr. N3 3G 45
Parklands Gro. TW7: Isle 1K 113
Parklands Pde. *TW5: Hest* *2B 112*
(off Parklands Ct.)
Parklands Rd. SW16 5F 137
Parklands Way KT4: Wor Pk 2A 164
Parkland Wlk. Local Nature Reserve 7J 47
Park La. CR0: C'don 3D 168
E15 1F 87
HA2: Harr 3F 59
HA7: Stan 3F 27
HA9: Wemb 5E 60
N9 3K 33
(not continuous)
N17 7A 34
(not continuous)
RM6: Chad H 6D 54
SM3: Cheam 6G 165
SM5: Cars 4E 166
SM6: W'gton 5E 166
TW5: Cran 7J 93
TW9: Rich 4D 114
TW11: Tedd 6K 131
UB4: Hayes 5G 75
W1 2F 11 (7D 82)
Park La. Cl. N17 7B 34
Park La. Mans. *CR0: C'don* *3D 168*
(off Park La.)
PARK LANGLEY 4E 158
The Parklangley Club 4E 158
Parklangley Tennis Club 4E 158
Parklea Cl. NW9 1A 44
Park Lee Ct. N16 7E 48
Parkleigh Rd. SW19 2K 153
Parkleys TW10: Ham 4D 132
Parkleys Pde.
TW10: Ham 4D 132
Park Lodge NW8 7B 64
W14 *3H 99*
(off Melbury Rd.)
Park Lodge Av. UB7: W Dray 2B 92
Park Lofts *SW2* *5J 119*
(off Lyham Rd.)
Park Lorne *NW8* *2D 4*
(off Park Rd.)
Park Mnr. *SM2: Sutt* *7A 166*
(off Christchurch Pk.)
Park Mans. NW4 5D 44
NW8 *2C 82*
(off Allitsen Rd.)
SW1 *7E 10*
(off Knightsbridge)
SW8 7F 19 (6J 101)
SW11 *1D 118*
(off Prince of Wales Dr.)
Park Mead DA15: Sidc 5B 126
HA2: Harr 3F 59
Parkmead SW15 6D 116
Parkmead Cl. CR0: C'don 6K 157
Parkmead Gdns. NW7 6G 29
Park M. BR7: Chst 6F 143
N8 6J 47
SE10 5H 105
SE24 7C 120
TW19: Stanw 7B 110
W10 2G 81
Parkmore Cl. IG8: Wfd G 4D 36
Park Pde. NW10 2B 80
UB3: Hayes 6G 75
W3 3G 97
Park Piazza SE13 6F 123
Park Pl. *BR1: Broml* *1K 159*
(off Park Rd.)
E14 1C 104
HA9: Wemb 4F 61
N1 *7D 66*
(off Downham Rd.)
SW1 5A 12 (1G 101)
TW12: Hamp H 6G 131
W3 4G 97
W5 1D 96
Park Pl. Dr. W3 3G 97
Park Pl. Vs. W2 5A 4 (5A 82)
Park Ridings N8 3A 48
Park Ri. HA3: Hrw W 1J 41
SE23 1A 140
Park Ri. Rd. SE23 1A 140
Park Rd. BR1: Broml 1K 159
BR3: Beck 7B 140
BR7: Chst 6F 143
E6 1A 88
E10 1C 68
E12 1K 69
E15 1J 87
E17 5B 50
EN4: E Barn 4G 21
EN5: Barn 4C 20
HA0: Wemb 6E 60
IG1: Ilf 3H 71
KT1: Hamp W 1C 150
KT2: King T 5F 133
KT3: N Mald 4K 151
KT5: Surb 6F 151
KT8: E Mos 4G 149
N2 3B 46
N8 4G 47
N11 7C 32
N14 1C 32
N15 4B 48
N18 4B 34
NW1 2D 4 (4D 82)
NW4 7C 44
NW8 2D 4 (3C 82)
NW9 7K 43
NW10 1A 80
SE25 4E 156
SM3: Cheam 6G 165
SM6: W'gton 5F 167
(Clifton Rd.)
SM6: W'gton 2F 167
(Elmwood Cl.)
Park Rd. SW19 6B 136
TW1: Twick 6C 114
TW3: Houn 5F 113
TW7: Isle 1B 114
TW10: Rich 6F 115
TW11: Tedd 6K 131
TW12: Hamp H 4F 131
TW13: Hanw 4B 130
TW15: Ashf 5D 128
TW16: Sun 7K 129
UB4: Hayes 5G 75
UB8: Uxb 1A 74
W4 7J 97
W7 7K 77
Park Rd. E. UB10: Uxb 2A 74
W3 2H 97
Park Rd. Ho. KT2: King T 7G 133
Park Rd. Nth. W3 2H 97
W4 5K 97
Park Rd. Pools & Fitness 5H 47
Park Row SE10 6F 105
PARK ROYAL 3H 79
Park Royal NW10 3G 79
PARK ROYAL JUNC. 1G 79
Park Royal Metro Cen.
NW10 4H 79
Park Royal Rd. NW10 3J 79
W3 3J 79
Park St James *NW8* *1D 82*
(off St James's Ter. M.)
Parkshot TW9: Rich 4D 114
Park Side NW2 3C 62
Parkside DA14: Sidc 2B 144
IG9: Buck H 2E 36
N3 1K 45
NW7 6H 29
SE3 7H 105
SM3: Cheam 6G 165
SW1 6F 11
SW19 3F 135
TW12: Hamp H 5H 131
UB3: Hayes 7G 75
W3 1A 98
W5 7E 78
Parkside Av. BR1: Broml 4C 160
DA7: Bex 2K 127
RM1: Rom 3K 55
SE10 1E 122
SW19 5F 135
Parkside Bus. Est. SE8 6A 104
(not continuous)
Parkside Cl. SE20 7J 139
Parkside Ct. *E11* *6J 51*
(off Wanstead Pl.)
E16 *2A 106*
(off Booth Rd.)
N22 6E 32
Parkside Cres. KT5: Surb 6J 151
N7 3A 66
Parkside Cross DA7: Bex 2K 127
Parkside Dr. HA8: Edg 3B 28
Parkside Est. E9 1J 85
(not continuous)
Parkside Gdns. EN4: E Barn 1J 31
SW19 4F 135
Parkside Ho. RM10: Dag 3J 73
Parkside Lodge DA17: Belv 5J 109
Parkside Rd. DA17: Belv 4H 109
SW11 1E 118
TW3: Houn 5F 113
Parkside Sq. E14 4E 104
SE10 1E 122
Parkside Ter. *BR6: Farnb* *3F 173*
(off Willow Wlk.)
N18 4J 33
Parkside Way HA2: Harr 4F 41
Parks Info. Cen. 4D 10 (1C 100)
Park Sth. *SW11* *1E 118*
(off Austin Rd.)
Park Sq. E. NW1 3J 5 (4F 83)
Park Sq. M. NW1 4J 5 (4F 83)
Park Sq. W. NW1 3J 5 (4F 83)
Parkstead Rd. SW15 5C 116
Park Steps W2 2D 10
Parkstone Av. N18 6A 34
Parkstone Rd. E17 3E 50
SE15 2G 121
Park St. CR0: C'don 2C 168
SE1 4C 14 (1C 102)
SW6 1A 118
TW11: Tedd 6J 131
W1 2G 11 (7E 82)
Park Ter. EN3: Enf H 1F 25
KT4: Wor Pk 1C 164
SE3 1A 124
SM5: Cars 3C 166
Park Theatre 2A 66
Parkthorne Cl. HA2: Harr 6F 41
Parkthorne Dr. HA2: Harr 6E 40
Parkthorne Rd. SW12 7H 119
Park Towers *W1* *5J 11*
(off Brick St.)
Park Vw. HA5: Hat E 1D 40
HA9: Wemb 5H 61
IG7: Chig 3H 37
KT3: N Mald 3B 152
N5 4C 66
N21 7E 22
RM6: Chad H 6D 54
SE8 *5K 103*
(off Trundleys Rd.)
UB7: Yiew 7A 74
W3 5J 79
Parkview *UB6: G'frd* *3A 78*
(off Perivale La.)
Park View Academy Sports Cen. 4C 48
Park Vw. Apts. *SE16* *3H 103*
(off Banyard Rd.)
Parkview Apts. *E14* *6D 86*
(off Chrisp St.)
Parkview Cl. SM5: Cars 7D 166
Park Vw. Ct. E3 5C 86
N12 4H 31
SE12 3A 142
SE20 1H 157
Parkview Ct. HA3: Hrw W 7D 26
IG2: Ilf 6J 53
SW6 2G 117
SW18 6J 117
Park Vw. Cres. N11 4A 32
Parkview Cres. KT4: Wor Pk 7E 152
Park Vw. Dr. CR4: Mitc 2B 154
Park Vw. Est. E2 2K 85
Park Vw. Gdns. IG4: Ilf 4D 52
N22 1A 48
NW4 5E 44
Park Vw. Ho. E4 5H 35
SE24 *6B 120*
(off Hurst St.)
Parkview Ho. N9 7C 24
Park Vw. Mans. *E20* *5D 68*
(off Olympic Pk. Av.)
N4 6B 48
Park Vw. M. SW9 2K 119
Park View Road 3C 126
Park Vw. Rd. DA16: Well 3C 126
N3 1K 45
N17 3G 49
NW10 4B 62
UB1: S'hall 1E 94
UB8: Hil 6B 74
W5 5E 78
Parkview Rd. CR0: C'don 1G 169
SE9 1F 143
Park Village E. NW1 1K 5 (2F 83)
Park Village W. NW1 2F 83
Park Vs. RM6: Chad H 6D 54
Parkville Rd. SW6 7H 99
Park Vista SE10 6F 105
Park Wlk. N6 7E 46
SE10 7F 105
SW10 7A 16 (6A 100)
Park Way EN2: Enf 2F 23
HA4: Ruis 1J 57
HA8: Edg 1H 43
KT8: W Mole 3F 149
N20 4J 31
NW11 5G 45
TW14: Felt 7K 111
W3 3G 97
Parkway DA18: Erith 3E 108
IG3: Ilf 3K 71
IG8: Wfd G 5F 37
N14 2D 32
NW1 1F 83
SW20 4F 153
UB10: Hil 7C 56
The Parkway TW5: Cran 5J 93
Park Way Ct. HA4: Ruis 1H 57
Parkway Cres. E15 5E 68
Parkway Trad. Est. TW5: Hest 6A 94
Park W. W2 7D 4
Park W. Bldg. E3 2C 86
Park W. Pl. W2 7D 4 (6C 82)
Park Wharf *SE8* *5A 104*
(off Evelyn St.)
Parkwood BR3: Beck 7C 140
N20 3K 31
NW8 *1D 82*
(off St Edmund's Ter.)
Parkwood Av. KT10: Esh 7G 149
Park Wood Ct. HA4: Ruis 4E 38
Parkwood Flats N20 3J 31
Parkwood Gro. TW16: Sun 3J 147
Parkwood M. N6 6F 47
Parkwood Rd. DA5: Bexl 7F 127
SW19 5H 135
TW7: Isle 1K 113
Parliament Ct. E1 6H 9
Parliament Hill 3D 64
Parliament Hill NW3 4C 64
Parliament Hill Fields 3E 64
Parliament Hill Lido 4E 64
Parliament Hill Mans.
NW5 4E 64
Parliament M. SW14 2J 115
Parliament Sq. SW1 7E 12 (2J 101)
Parliament St. SW1 6E 12 (2J 101)
Parliament Vw. SE1 3G 19 (4K 101)
Parma Cres. SW11 4D 118
Parmiter St. E2 2H 85
Parmoor Ct. EC1 3C 8
Parndon Ho. IG10: Lough 1H 37
Parnell Cl. HA8: Edg 4C 28
W12 3D 98
Parnell Ho. WC1 6D 6 (5H 83)
Parnelli Ho. *N1* *6B 66*
(off Canonbury Rd.)
Parnell Rd. E3 1B 86
Parnell Way HA3: Stan 1B 42
Parnham Cl. BR1: Broml 3F 161
Parnham St. E14 6A 86
(not continuous)
Parolles Rd. N19 1G 65
Paroma Rd. DA17: Belv 4G 109
Parr Cl. N9 4C 34
N18 4C 34
Parr Ct. *N1* *2D 84*
(off New North Rd.)
TW13: Hanw 4A 130
Parr Ho. *E16* *1K 105*
(off Beaulieu Av.)
Parrington Ho. SW4 6H 119
Parr Rd. E6 1B 88
HA7: Stan 1D 42
Parrs Cl. CR2: Sande 7D 168
Parrs Pl. TW12: Hamp 7E 130
Parr St. N1 2D 84
Parrs Way W6 6E 98
Parry Av. E6 6D 88
Parry Cl. KT17: Ewe 7D 164
Parry Ho. *E1* *1H 103*
(off Green Bank)
Parry Pl. SE18 4F 107
Parry Rd. SE25 3E 156
W10 3G 81
Parry St. SW8 7F 19 (6J 101)
Parsifal Rd. NW6 5J 63
Parsley Gdns. CR0: C'don 1K 169
Parsloes Av. RM9: Dag 4D 72
Parsonage Cl. UB3: Hayes 6H 75
Parsonage Gdns. EN2: Enf 2H 23
Parsonage La. DA14: Sidc 4F 145
EN1: Enf 2H 23
EN2: Enf 2H 23
Parsonage Manorway
DA17: Belv 6G 109
Parsonage St. E14 4E 104
Parsons Cl. SM1: Sutt 3K 165
Parson's Cres. HA8: Edg 3B 28
Parsons Ga. M. SW6 2J 117
PARSONS GREEN 2H 117
Parson's Grn. SW6 1J 117
Parson's Grn. La. SW6 1J 117
Parson's Gro. HA8: Edg 3B 28
Parsons Hill *SE18* *3E 106*
(off Powis St.)
Parsons Ho. W2 4A 4
Parsons Lodge *NW6* *7K 63*
(off Priory Rd.)
Parson's Mead CR0: C'don 1B 168
Parsons Mead KT8: E Mos 3G 149
Parsons M. SW18 5A 118
Parson's Rd. E13 2A 88
Parson St. NW4 4E 44
Parthenia Dr. TW7: Isle 3A 114
Parthenia Rd. SW6 1J 117
Partingdale La. NW7 5A 30
Partington Cl. N19 1H 65
Partridge Cl. E16 5B 88
EN5: Barn 6A 20
HA7: Stan 4K 27
UB10: Uxb 1B 74
WD23: Bush 1B 26
Partridge Ct. EC1 3A 8
Partridge Dr. BR6: Farnb 3G 173
Partridge Grn. SE9 3E 142
Partridge Ho. *E3* *2B 86*
(off Stafford Rd.)
Partridge Rd. DA14: Sidc 3J 143
TW12: Hamp 6D 130
Partridge Sq. E6 5C 88
Partridge Way N22 1J 47
Pasadena Cl. UB3: Hayes 2J 93
Pasadena Cl. Trad. Est.
UB3: Hayes 2K 93
Pascall Ho. *SE17* *6C 102*
(off Draco St.)
Pascal M. SE19 7G 139
Pascal Rd. UB1: S'hall 6F 77
Pascal St. SW8 7H 101
Pascoe Rd. SE13 5F 123
Pasley Cl. SE17 5B 102
Pasquier Rd. E17 3A 50
The Passage TW9: Rich 5E 114
Passey Pl. SE9 6D 124
Passfield Dr. E14 5D 86
Passfield Hall *WC1* *3D 6*
(off Endsleigh Pl.)
Passfield Path SE28 7B 90
Passfields SE6 3D 140
W14 *5H 99*
(off Star Rd.)
Passing All. EC1 4B 8
Passingham Ho. TW5: Hest 6E 94
Passmore Ct. *E14* *6C 86*
(off New Festival Av.)
Passmore Edwards Ho. N11 6C 32
Passmore Gdns. N11 6C 32
Passmore Ho. *E2* *1F 85*
(off Kingsland Rd.)
Passmore St. SW1 5G 17 (5E 100)
Pastel Ct. *E15* *5K 85*
(off Shandy St.)
Pasteur Cl. NW9 2A 44
Pasteur Ct. HA1: Harr 1B 60
Pasteur Gdns. N18 5G 33
Paston Cl. E5 3K 67
SM6: W'gton 3G 167
Paston Cres. SE12 7K 123
Pastor Ct. N6 6G 47
Pastor St. SE11 4B 102
Pasture Cl. HA0: Wemb 3B 60
Pasture Rd. HA0: Wemb 2B 60
RM9: Dag 5F 73
SE6 1H 141
The Pastures N20 1C 30
Pastures Mead UB10: Hil 6C 56
Pastures Path E11 1H 69
Patcham Ter. SW8 1F 119
Patch Cl. UB10: Uxb 1B 74
Patching Way UB4: Yead 5C 76
Patent Ho. *E14* *5D 86*
(off Morris Rd.)
Paternoster La. EC4 1B 14 (6B 84)
Paternoster Row EC4 1C 14 (6C 84)
Paternoster Sq. EC4 1B 14 (6B 84)
Paterson Ct. EC1 2E 8
Pater St. W8 3J 99
Pates Mnr. Dr. TW14: Bedf 7F 111
The Path SW19 1K 153
Pathfield Rd. SW16 6H 137
Patience Rd. SW11 2C 118
Patina Mans. *E20* *5E 68*
(off Mirabelle Gdns.)
Patio Cl. SW4 6H 119
Patmore Est. SW8 1G 119
Patmore Ho. N16 5E 66
Patmore St. SW8 1G 119
Patmos Lodge *SW9* *1B 120*
(off Elliott Rd.)
Patmos Rd. SW9 7B 102
Paton Cl. E3 3C 86
Paton Ho. *SW9* *2K 119*
(off Stockwell Rd.)
Paton St. EC1 2C 8 (3C 84)
Patricia Ct. BR7: Chst 1H 161
DA16: Well 7B 108
Patrick Coman Ho. *EC1* *2A 8*
(off St John St.)
Patrick Connolly Gdns. E3 3D 86
Patrick Ct. *SE1* *7B 14*
(off Webber St.)
Patrick Cres. RM8: Dag 1E 72
Patrick Pas. SW11 2C 118
Patrick Rd. E13 3A 88
Patriot Sq. E2 2H 85
Patrol Pl. SE6 6D 122
Patroni Ct. *E15* *3G 87*
(off Durban Rd.)
Pat Shaw Ho. *E1* *4K 85*
(off Globe Rd.)
Patshull Pl. NW5 6G 65
Patshull Rd. NW5 6G 65
Patten All. TW10: Rich 5D 114
Pattenden Rd. SE6 1B 140
Patten Ho. N4 1C 66
Patten Rd. SW18 7C 118
Patterdale *NW1* *2K 5*
(off Osnaburgh St.)
Patterdale Cl. BR1: Broml 6H 141
Patterdale Rd. SE15 7J 103
Pattern Ho. EC1 3A 8 (4B 84)
Patterson Ct. SE19 7F 139
Patterson Rd. SE19 6F 139
Pattina Wlk. *SE16* *1A 104*
(off Silver Wlk.)
Pattison Ho. *E1* *6K 85*
(off Wellesley St.)
SE1 *6D 14*
(off Redcross Way)
Pattison Rd. NW2 3J 63
Pattison Wlk. SE18 5G 107
Paul Byrne Ho. N2 3A 46
Paul Cl. E15 1G 87
Paul Ct. *N18* *4B 34*
(off Fairfield Rd.)
RM7: Rom 5J 55

Paul Daisley Ct.—Penny La.

Paul Daisley Ct. NW6 7G 63
(off Christchurch Av.)
Paulet Rd. SE5 2B 120
Paulet Way NW10 7A 62
Paul Gdns. CR0: C'don 2F 169
Paulhan Rd. HA3: Kenton 4D 42
Paul Ho. W10 4G 81
(off Ladbroke Gro.)
Paulin Dr. N21 7F 23
Pauline Cres.
TW2: Whitt 1G 131
Pauline Ho. E1 5G 85
(off Old Montague St.)
Paul Julius Cl. E14 7F 87
Paul Robeson Cl. E6 3E 88
Paul Robeson Ho. WC1 1H 7
(off Penton Ri.)
The Paul Robeson Theatre 3F 113
Paul St. E15 1G 87
EC2 4F 9 (4D 84)
Paul's Wlk. EC4 2B 14 (7C 84)
Paultons Ho. SW3 7B 16
(off Paultons Sq.)
Paultons Sq. SW3 7B 16 (6B 100)
Paultons St.
SW3 7B 16 (6B 100)
Pauntley St. N19 1G 65
Pavan Ct. E2 3J 85
(off Sceptre Rd.)
Paved Ct. TW9: Rich 5D 114
Paveley Ct. NW7 7B 30
(off Langstone Way)
Paveley Dr. SW11 7C 100
Paveley Ho. N1 2K 83
(off Priory Grn. Est.)
Paveley St. NW8 2C 4 (3C 82)
The Pavement E11 1E 68
(off Hainault Rd.)
SW4 4G 119
SW19 6H 135
(off Worple Rd.)
TW7: Isle 3A 114
(off South St.)
TW11: Tedd 7B 132
W5 3E 96
Pavement M.
RM6: Chad H 7D 54
Pavement Sq. CR0: C'don 1G 169
Pavers Way E3 2K 85
Pavet Cl. RM10: Dag 6H 73
The Pavilion SW8 7H 101
Pavilion Apts. NW8 2B 4 (3B 82)
Pavilion Ct. NW6 3J 81
(off Stafford Rd.)
Pavilion La. BR3: Beck 6B 140
Pavilion Leisure Cen. 2J 159
Pavilion Lodge
HA2: Harr 1H 59
Pavilion M. N3 3J 45
Pavilion Pde. W12 6E 80
(off Wood La.)
Pavilion Rd. IG1: Ilf 7D 52
SW1 7F 11 (3D 100)
SW3 1F 17 (4D 100)
TW11: Tedd 7K 131
The Pavilion Sports & Fitness Club
3G 149
Pavilion Sq. SW17 3D 136
Pavilion St. E13 2A 88
SW1 2F 17 (3D 100)
Pavilion Ter. IG2: Ilf 5J 53
W12 6E 80
(off Wood La.)
Pavilion Wlk. E10 2C 68
Pavilion Way HA4: Ruis 2A 58
HA8: Edg 7C 28
SE10 2G 105
Pavillion Ho. SE16 2K 103
(off Water Gdns. Sq.)
Pavillion M. N4 2K 65
(off Tollington Pl.)
Pawleyne Cl. SE20 7J 139
Pawsey Cl. E13 1K 87
Pawsons Rd.
CR0: C'don 6C 156
Paxfold HA7: Stan 5J 27
Paxford Rd. HA0: Wemb 2B 60
Paxton Cl. KT12: Walt T 7A 148
TW9: Kew 2F 115
Paxton Ct. CR4: Mitc 2D 154
(off Armfield Cres.)
N7 6A 66
(off Westbourne Rd.)
SE12 3A 142
SE26 4A 140
(off Adamsrill Rd.)
Paxton Ho. SE17 5D 102
(off Morecambe St.)
SE25 4F 157
Paxton M. SE19 7E 138
(off Westow St.)
Paxton Pl. SE27 4E 138
Paxton Point SE10 7D 104
Paxton Rd. BR1: Broml 7J 141
SE23 3A 140
W4 6A 98
Paxton Ter. SW1 7K 17 (6F 101)
Paymal Ho. E1 5J 85
(off Stepney Way)
Payne Cl. IG11: Bark 7J 71
Payne Ho. N1 1K 83
(off Barnsbury Est.)
Paynell Ct. SE3 3G 123
Payne Rd. E3 2D 86
Paynesfield Av. SW14 3K 115
Paynesfield Rd.
WD23: B Hea 1E 26
Payne St. SE8 7B 104
Paynes Wlk. W6 6G 99
Payzes Gdns.
IG8: Wfd G 6C 36
Peaberry Ct. NW4 3C 44
Peabody Av. SW1 5J 17 (5F 101)
Peabody Bldgs. E1 7G 85
(off John Fisher St.)
EC1 4D 8
(off Banner St.)
SW3 7C 16
Peabody Cl. CR0: C'don 1J 169
SE10 1D 122
SW1 7K 17 (5F 101)
Peabody Cotts. N17 1E 48
Peabody Ct. EC1 4D 8
(off Roscoe St.)
SE5 1D 120
(off Kimpton Rd.)
Peabody Est. E1 7K 85
(off Brodlove La.)
E2 2H 85
(off Minerva St.)
EC1 4D 8
(off Dufferin St.)
EC1 4K 7
(off Farringdon La.)
N1 1C 84
SE1 5K 13 (1A 102)
(Duchy St.)
SE1 6D 14
(Marshalsea Rd.)
SE1 5C 14 (1C 102)
(Southwark St.)
SE5 1D 120
(off Camberwell Grn.)
SE24 7B 120
SW1 3B 18
SW3 7D 16 (6C 100)
SW6 6J 99
(off Lillie Rd.)
SW11 4C 118
W6 5E 98
W10 5E 80
Peabody Hill SE21 1B 138
Peabody Ho. N1 1C 84
(off Greenman St.)
Peabody Sq. N1 1C 84
(off Peabody Est.)
SE1 7A 14 (2B 102)
(not continuous)
Peabody Ter. EC1 4K 7
(off Farringdon La.)
Peabody Twr. EC1 4D 8
(off Golden La.)
Peabody Trust SE17 4D 102
Peabody Yd. N1 1C 84
Peace Cl. N14 5A 22
SE25 4E 156
UB6: G'frd 1H 77
Peace Ct. SE1 5G 103
(off Harmony Pl.)
Peace Gro. HA9: Wemb 3H 61
Peace St. SE18 6E 106
Peaches Cl. SM2: Cheam 7G 165
Peachey Ho. SW18 4A 118
(off Eltringham St.)
Peachey La. UB8: Cowl 5A 74
Peach Gro. E11 3F 69
Peach Rd. TW13: Felt 1J 129
W10 3F 81
Peach Tree Av. UB7: Yiew 6B 74
Peachtree Cl. EN1: Enf 2B 24
IG6: Ilf 1F 53
Peachum Rd. SE3 6H 105
Peachwalk M. E3 2K 85
Peachy Cl. HA8: Edg 6B 28
Peacock Av. TW14: Bedf 1F 129
Peacock Cl. E4 7G 35
NW7 5B 30
RM8: Dag 1C 72
Peacock Ho. SE5 1E 120
(off St Giles Rd.)
Peacock Ind. Est. N17 7A 34
Peacock Pl. N1 6A 66
Peacock St. SE17 4B 102
Peacock Theatre 1G 13
(off Portugal St.)
Peacock Wlk. N6 7F 47
Peacock Yd. SE17 5B 102
(off Iliffe St.)
The Peak SE26 3J 139
Peaketon Av. IG4: Ilf 4B 52
Peak Hill SE26 4J 139
Peak Hill Av. SE26 4J 139
Peak Hill Gdns. SE26 4J 139
Peal Gdns. W13 4A 78
Peall Rd. CR0: C'don 6K 155
Peall Rd. Ind. Est.
CR0: C'don 6K 155
Pearce Cl. CR4: Mitc 2E 154
Pearcefield Av. SE23 1J 139
Pearce Ho. SW1 4D 18
(off Causton St.)
Pear Cl. NW9 4K 43
SE14 7A 104
Pear Ct. SE15 7F 103
(off Thruxton Way)
Pearcroft Rd. E11 2F 69
Peardon St. SW8 2F 119
Peareswood Gdns. HA7: Stan 1D 42
Pearfield Rd. SE23 3A 140
Pearing Cl. KT4: Wor Pk 2F 165
Pearl Cl. CR7: Thor H 2D 156
E6 6E 88
NW2 7F 45
Pearl Rd. E17 3C 50
Pearl St. E1 1H 103
Pearmain Cl. TW17: Shep 5D 146
Pearmain Ct. W6 3D 98
(off Vinery Way)
Pearman St. SE1 1K 19 (3A 102)
Pear Pl. SE1 6J 13 (2A 102)
Pear Rd. E11 3F 69
Pears Av. TW17: Shep 3G 147
Pearscroft Ct. SW6 1K 117
Pearscroft Rd. SW6 1K 117
Pearse St. SE15 6E 102
Pearson Cl. EN5: New Bar 3E 20
SE5 1C 120
(off Camberwell New Rd.)
Pearson M. SW4 3H 119
(off Edgeley Rd.)
Pearson's Av. SE14 1C 122
Pearson Sq. W1 6B 6 (5G 83)
Pearson St. E2 2F 85
Pearson Way CR4: Mitc 1E 154
Pears Rd. TW3: Houn 3G 113
Peartree SE26 5A 140
Pear Tree Av. UB7: Yiew 6B 74
Peartree Av. SW17 3A 136
Pear Tree Cl. BR2: Broml 5B 160
CR4: Mitc 2C 154
E2 1F 85
KT9: Chess 5G 163
KT19: Eps 7K 163
Peartree Cl. DA8: Erith 1K 127
Pear Tree Ct. E18 1K 51
EC1 4K 7 (4A 84)
SE26 3B 140
Peartree Gdns. RM7: Mawney 2H 55
RM8: Dag 4B 72
Pear Tree Ho. SE4 3B 122
Pear Tree La. RM13: Rain 2K 91
Peartree La. E1 7J 85
Pear Tree Rd. TW15: Ashf 5E 128
Peartree Rd. EN1: Enf 3K 23
Peartrees UB7: Yiew 7A 74
Pear Tree St. EC1 3B 8 (4C 84)
Peartree Way SE10 4J 105
Peary Ho. NW10 7K 61
Peary Pl. E2 3J 85
Peasmead Ter. E4 4K 35
Peatfield Cl. DA15: Sidc 3J 143
Pebble Way W3 1H 97
(off Steyne Rd.)
Pebworth Rd. HA1: Harr 2A 60
Pechora Way E14 5A 86
Peckarmans Wood SE26 3G 139
Peckett Sq. N5 4C 66
Peckford Pl. SW9 2A 120
PECKHAM 1G 121
Peckham Gro. SE15 7E 102
Peckham High St. SE15 1G 121
Peckham Hill St. SE15 7G 103
Peckham Pk. Rd. SE15 7G 103
Peckhamplex 2G 121
Peckham Pulse Leisure Cen. 1G 121
Peckham Rd. SE5 1E 120
SE15 1E 120
Peckham Rye SE15 3G 121
SE22 4G 121
Peckham Sq. SE15 1G 121
Pecks Yd. E1 5J 9
(off Hanbury St.)
Peckwater St. NW5 5G 65
Pedlar's Wlk. N7 5K 65
Pedley Rd. RM8: Dag 1C 72
Pedley St. E1 4G 85
Pedro St. E5 3K 67
Pedworth Gdns. SE16 4J 103
Peebles Ct. UB1: S'hall 6G 77
(off Haldane Rd.)
Peebles Ho. NW6 2K 81
(off Carlton Vale)
Peek Cres. SW19 5F 135
Peel Cl. E4 2J 35
N9 3B 34
Peel Dr. IG5: Ilf 3C 52
NW9 3B 44
Peel Gro. E2 2J 85
Peel Pas. W8 1J 99
Peel Pl. IG5: Ilf 2C 52
SE18 1D 124
SW6 6J 99
Peel Pct. NW6 2J 81
Peel Rd. BR6: Farnb 5G 173
E18 1H 51
HA3: W'stone 3K 41
HA9: Wemb 3D 60
Peel Square NW9 3C 44
Peel St. W8 1J 99
Peel Way UB8: Hil 5A 74
Peerglow Est. EN3: Pond E 5D 24
Peerless St. EC1 2E 8 (3D 84)
Pegamoid Rd. N18 3D 34
Pegasus Cl. N16 4D 66
Pegasus Ct. KT1: King T 3D 150
N21 7H 23
NW10 3D 80
(off Trenmar Gdns.)
TW8: Bford 5F 97
W3 6J 79
(off Horn La.)
Pegasus Ho. E1 4K 85
(off Beaumont Sq.)
E13 3K 87
Pegasus Pl. SE11 7J 19 (6A 102)
SW6 1J 117
Pegasus Rd. CR0: Wadd 6A 168
Pegasus Way N11 6A 32
Peggotty Way UB8: Hil 6D 74
Pegg Rd. TW5: Hest 7B 94
Pegler Sq. SE3 3K 123
Pegley Gdns. SE12 2J 141
Pegswood Ct. E1 7G 85
(off Cable St.)
Pegwell St. SE18 7J 107
Pekin Cl. E14 6C 86
(off Pekin St.)
Pekin St. E14 6C 86
Pelabon Ho. TW1: Twick 6D 114
(off Clevedon Rd.)
Peldon Cl. IG8: Wfd G 7F 37
Peldon Ct. TW9: Rich 4F 115
Peldon Pas. TW10: Rich 4F 115
Peldon Wlk. N1 1B 84
(off Popham St.)
Pelham Av. IG11: Bark 1K 89
Pelham Cl. SE5 3E 120
Pelham Cotts. DA5: Bexl 1H 145
Pelham Ct. DA14: Sidc 2A 144
SW3 4C 16
(off Fulham Rd.)
Pelham Cres. SW7 4C 16 (4C 100)
Pelham Ho. SW1 2D 18
(off Gt. Peter St.)
W14 4H 99
(off Mornington Av.)
Pelham Pl. SW7 4C 16 (4C 100)
W13 4K 77
Pelham Rd. BR3: Beck 2J 157
DA7: Bex 3G 127
E18 3K 51
IG1: Ilf 2H 71
N15 4F 49
N22 2A 48
SW19 7J 135
Pelham St. SW7 3B 16 (4B 100)
Pelican Dr. HA2: Harr 2F 59
Pelican Est. SE15 1F 121
Pelican Ho. SE5 1F 121
SE8 4B 104
Pelican Pas. E1 4J 85
Pelican Wlk. SW9 4B 120
Pelican Wharf E1 1J 103
(off Wapping Wall)
Pelier St. SE17 6C 102
Pelinore Rd. SE6 2G 141
Pella Ho. SE11 5H 19 (5K 101)
Pellant Rd. SW6 7G 99
Pellatt Gro. N22 1A 48
Pellatt Rd. HA9: Wemb 2D 60
SE22 5F 121
Pellerin Rd. N16 5E 66
Pellew Ho. E1 4H 85
(off Somerford St.)
Pellings Cl. BR2: Broml 3G 159
Pelling St. E14 6C 86
Pellipar Cl. N13 3F 33
Pellipar Gdns. SE18 5D 106
Pellipar Rd. SE18 5D 106
Pellow Cl. EN5: Barn 6C 20
Pell St. SE8 4A 104
Pelly Rd. E13 1J 87
(not continuous)
Peloton Av. E20 5D 68
Pelter St. E2 1J 9 (3F 85)
Pelton Rd. SE10 5G 105
Pembar Av. E17 3A 50
Pemberley Chase KT19: Ewe 5H 163
Pemberley Cl. KT19: Ewe 5H 163
Pemberley Ho. KT19: Ewe 5H 163
(off Pemberley Chase)
Pember Rd. NW10 3F 81
Pemberton Cl. TW19: Stanw 1A 128
Pemberton Ct. E1 3K 85
(off Portelet Rd.)
EN1: Enf 3K 23
Pemberton Gdns. N19 3G 65
RM6: Chad H 5E 54
Pemberton Ho. SE26 4G 139
(off High Level Dr.)
Pemberton Pl. E8 7H 67
Pemberton Rd. KT8: E Mos 4G 149
N4 5A 48
Pemberton Row EC4 7K 7 (6A 84)
Pemberton Ter. N19 3G 65
Pembridge Av. TW2: Whitt 1D 130
Pembridge Cres. W11 7J 81
Pembridge Gdns. W2 7J 81
Pembridge M. W11 7J 81
Pembridge Pl. SW15 5J 117
W2 7J 81
Pembridge Rd. W11 7J 81
Pembridge Sq. W2 7J 81
Pembridge Studios W11 7J 81
(off Pembridge Vs.)
Pembridge Vs. W2 7J 81
W11 7J 81
Pembroke W14 4H 99
(off Kensington Village)
Pembroke Av. EN1: Enf 1C 24
HA3: Kenton 3A 42
HA5: Pinn 1B 58
KT5: Surb 5H 151
N1 1J 83
Pembroke Bldgs. NW10 3C 80
Pembroke Bus. Cen.
BR8: Swan 7K 145
The Pembroke Cen. HA4: Ruis 1H 57
Pembroke Cl. SW1 7H 11 (2E 100)
Pembroke Cotts. W8 3J 99
(off Pembroke Sq.)
Pembroke Ct. W7 6K 77
(off Copley Cl.)
W8 3J 99
(off Sth. Edwardes Sq.)
Pembroke Gdns. HA4: Ruis 1H 57
RM10: Dag 3H 73
SW14 4H 115
W8 4H 99
Pembroke Gdns. Cl. W8 3J 99
Pembroke Hall NW4 3E 44
(off Mulberry Cl.)
Pembroke Ho. RM8: Dag 5A 72
SW1 2G 17
(off Chesham St.)
W2 6K 81
(off Hallfield Est.)
W3 2J 97
(off Park Rd. E.)
Pembroke Lodge HA7: Stan 6J 27
Pembroke Mans. NW6 6A 64
(off Canfield Gdns.)
Pembroke M. E3 3A 86
N10 1E 46
W8 3J 99
Pembroke Pde. DA8: Erith 5J 109
Pembroke Pl. HA8: Edg 7B 28
TW7: Isle 2J 113
W8 3J 99
Pembroke Rd. BR1: Broml 2A 160
CR4: Mitc 2E 154
DA8: Erith 5J 109
E6 5D 88
E17 5D 50
HA4: Ruis 1G 57
HA9: Wemb 3D 60
IG3: Ilf 1K 71
N8 4J 47
N10 1E 46
N13 3H 33
N15 5F 49
SE25 4E 156
UB6: G'frd 4F 77
W8 4H 99
Pembroke Sq. W8 3J 99
Pembroke St. N1 7J 65
(not continuous)
Pembroke Studios W8 3H 99
Pembroke Ter. NW8 1B 82
(off Queen's Ter.)
Pembroke Vs. TW9: Rich 4D 114
W8 4J 99
Pembroke Wlk. W8 4J 99
Pembroke Way UB3: Harl 3E 92
Pembrook M. SW11 4B 118
Pembry Cl. SW9 1A 120
Pembury Av. KT4: Wor Pk 1C 164
Pembury Cl. BR2: Hayes 7H 159
E5 5H 67
Pembury Ct. UB3: Harl 6F 93
Pembury Cres. DA14: Sidc 2E 144
Pembury Pl. E5 5H 67
Pembury Rd. DA7: Bex 7E 108
E5 5H 67
N17 1F 49
SE25 4G 157
Pemdevon Rd. CR0: C'don 7A 156
Pemell Cl. E1 4J 85
Pemell Ho. E1 4J 85
(off Pemell Cl.)
Pemerich Cl. UB3: Harl 5H 93
Pempath Pl. HA9: Wemb 2D 60
Penally Pl. N1 1D 84
Penang Ho. E1 1H 103
(off Prusom St.)
Penang St. E1 1H 103
Penard Rd. UB2: S'hall 3F 95
Penarth Cen. SE15 6J 103
Penarth Ct. SM2: Sutt 7A 166
Penarth St. SE15 6J 103
Penberth Rd. SE6 2E 140
Penbury Rd. UB2: S'hall 4D 94
Pencombe M. W11 7H 81
Pencraig Way SE15 6H 103
Pendall Cl. EN4: E Barn 4H 21
Penda Rd. DA8: Erith 7H 109
Pendarves Rd. SW20 1E 152
Penda's Mead E9 4A 68
Pendell Av. UB3: Harl 7H 93
Pendennis Ho. SE8 4A 104
Pendennis Rd. N17 3D 48
SW16 4J 137
Penderel Rd. TW3: Houn 5E 112
Penderry Ri. SE6 2F 141
Penderyn Way N7 4H 65
Pendlebury Ct. KT5: Surb 4E 150
(off Cranes Pk.)
Pendle Ct. UB10: Hil 1D 74
Pendle Ho. SE26 3G 139
Pendle Rd. SW16 6F 137
Pendlestone Rd. E17 5D 50
Pendlewood Cl. W5 5C 78
Pendley Ho. E2 1G 85
(off Whiston Rd.)
Pendolino Way NW10 7G 61
Pendragon Rd. BR1: Broml 3H 141
Pendragon Wlk. NW9 6A 44
Pendrell Ho. WC2 1D 12
(off New Compton St.)
Pendrell Rd. SE4 2A 122
Pendrell St. SE18 6H 107
Pendula Dr. UB4: Yead 4B 76
Pendulum M. E8 5F 67
Penerley Rd. SE6 1D 140
Penfield Ct. NW9 3A 44
(off Tanner Cl.)
Penfield Lodge W9 5J 81
(off Admiral Wlk.)
Penfields Ho. N7 6J 65
(off York Way Est.)
Penfold Cl. CR0: Wadd 3A 168
Penfold La. DA5: Bexl 2D 144
(not continuous)
Penfold Pl. NW1 5C 4 (5C 82)
Penfold Rd. N9 1E 34
Penfold St. NW1 4B 4 (4B 82)
NW8 4B 4 (4B 82)
Penford Gdns. SE9 3B 124
Penford St. SE5 2B 120
Pengarth Rd. DA5: Bexl 5D 126
PENGE 7J 139
Penge Ho. SW11 3B 118
Penge La. SE20 7J 139
Pengelly Apts. E14 5D 104
(off Bartlett M.)
Penge Rd. E13 1A 88
SE20 3G 157
SE25 3G 157
Penhale Cl. BR6: Chels 4K 173
Penhall Rd. SE7 4B 106
Penhill Rd. DA5: Bexl 6C 126
Penhurst Mans. SW6 1H 117
(off Rostrevor Rd.)
Penhurst Pl. SE1 1H 19
Penhurst Rd. IG6: Ilf 1F 53
Penifather La.
UB6: G'frd 3H 77
Peninsula Apts. N1 1C 84
(off Basire St.)
W2 6C 4
(off Praed St.)
Peninsula Ct. E14 3D 104
(off E. Ferry Rd.)
N1 1C 84
(off Basire St.)
Peninsula Hgts. SE1 5F 19 (5J 101)
Peninsular Cl. NW7 5B 30
TW14: Felt 6F 111
Peninsular Pk. 4J 105
Peninsular Pk. Rd. SE7 4J 105
Peninsula Sq. SE10 2G 105
Penistone Rd. SW16 7J 137
Penketh Dr. HA1: Harr 3H 59
Penley Ct. WC2 2H 13 (7K 83)
Penmayne Ho. SE11 5K 19
(off Kennings Way)
Penmon Rd. SE2 3A 108
Pennack Rd. SE15 6F 103
Penn Almshouses SE10 1E 122
(off Greenwich Sth. St.)
Pennant M. W8 4K 99
Pennant Ter. E17 2B 50
Pennard Mans. W12 2E 98
(off Goldhawk Rd.)
Pennard Rd. W12 2E 98
The Pennards TW16: Sun 3A 148
Penn Cl. HA3: Kenton 4C 42
UB6: G'frd 2F 77
Penn Ct. NW9 3K 43
Penner Cl. SW19 2G 135
Penners Gdns. KT6: Surb 7E 150
Pennethorne Cl. E9 1J 85
Pennethorne Ho. SW11 3B 118
Pennethorne Rd. SE15 7H 103
Penn Gdns. BR7: Chst 2F 161
RM5: Col R 1G 55
Penn Ho. NW8 4C 4
(off Mallory St.)
Pennine Dr. NW2 2F 63
Pennine Ho. N9 3B 34
(off Plevna Rd.)
Pennine La. NW2 2G 63
Pennine Pde. NW2 2G 63
Pennine Way DA7: Bex 1K 127
UB3: Harl 7F 93
Pennington Cl. SE27 4D 138
Pennington Ct. SE16 1A 104
Pennington Dr. N21 5D 22
Pennington Lodge KT5: Surb 5E 150
(off Cranes Dr.)
Pennington St. E1 7H 85
Pennington Way SE12 2K 141
Penniston Cl. N17 2C 48
Penniwell Cl. HA8: Edg 4A 28
Penn La. DA5: Bexl 5D 126
Penn Rd. N7 5J 65
Penn St. N1 1D 84
Penny Brookes St. E20 6E 68
Penny Cl. E4 3B 36
Pennycroft CR0: Sels 7A 170
Penny Farthing M.
TW12: Hamp H 6G 131
Pennyfather La. EN2: Enf 3H 23
Pennyfields E14 7C 86
(not continuous)
Penny Flds. Ho. SE8 1B 122
(off Francis Harvey Way)
Pennyford Ct. NW8 3A 4
(off St John's Wood Rd.)
Penny La. TW17: Shep 7G 147

Pietra Lara Bldg.—Pooley Dr.

Pietra Lara Bldg. EC1 ... 3C 8
(off Pear Tree St.)
Pigeon La. TW12: Hamp ... 4E 130
Piggott Ho. E2 ... 2K 85
(off Sewardstone Rd.)
Pigott St. E14 ... 6C 86
Pike Cl. BR1: Broml ... 5K 141
UB10: Uxb ... 1B 74
Pike Cres. TW15: Ashf ... 4B 128
Pikemans Ct. SW5 ... 4J 99
(off W. Cromwell Rd.)
Pike Rd. NW7 ... 4E 28
Pike's End HA5: Eastc ... 4K 39
Pikestone Cl. UB4: Yead ... 4C 76
Pikethorne SE23 ... 2K 139
Pilgrimage St. SE1 ... 7E 14 (2D 102)
Pilgrim Cl. SM4: Mord ... 7K 153
Pilgrim Hill SE27 ... 4C 138
Pilgrim Ho. SE1 ... 3D 102
(off Tabard St.)
SE16 ... 2J 103
(off Brunel Rd.)
Pilgrims Cloisters SE5 ... 7E 102
(off Sedgmoor Pl.)
Pilgrims Cl. N13 ... 4E 32
UB5: N'olt ... 5G 59
Pilgrims Cnr. NW6 ... 2J 81
(off Chichester Rd.)
Pilgrims Ct. EN1: Enf ... 2J 23
Pilgrim's La. NW3 ... 4B 64
Pilgrims M. E14 ... 7G 87
Pilgrim's Pl. NW3 ... 4B 64
Pilgrims Ri. EN4: E Barn ... 5H 21
Pilgrim St. EC4 ... 1A 14 (6B 84)
Pilgrim's Way HA9: Wemb ... 1H 61
Pilgrims Way CR2: S Croy ... 6F 169
E6 ... 1C 88
N19 ... 1H 65
Pilkington Rd. BR6: Farnb ... 3G 173
SE15 ... 2H 121
Pill Box Studios E2 ... 4H 85
(off Coventry Rd.)
Pillfold Ho. SE11 ... 3G 19
(off Old Paradise St.)
Pillions La. UB4: Hayes ... 4F 75
Pilot Cl. SE8 ... 6B 104
Pilot Ind. Cen. NW10 ... 4K 79
Pilot Wlk. SE10 ... 2H 105
Pilsdon Cl. SW19 ... 1F 135
The Pilton Est. CR0: C'don ... 2B 168
Pilton Gdns. SM4: Mord ... 6K 153
Pilton Pl. SE17 ... 5C 102
Pimento Ct. W5 ... 3D 96
PIMLICO ... 6B 18 (5G 101)
Pimlico Ho. SW1 ... 5J 17
(off Ebury Bri. Rd.)
Pimlico Rd. SW1 ... 5G 17 (5E 100)
Pimlico Sq. SW1 ... 5G 17 (5E 100)
Pimlico Wlk. N1 ... 1G 9
Pimp Hall Nature Reserve ... 2A 36
Pinchbeck Rd. BR6: Chels ... 6K 173
Pinchin & Johnsons Yd. E1 ... 7G 85
(off Pinchin St.)
Pinchin St. E1 ... 7G 85
Pincombe Ho. SE17 ... 5D 102
(off Orb St.)
Pincott Pl. SE4 ... 3K 121
Pincott Rd. DA6: Bex ... 5G 127
SW19 ... 7A 136
Pindar St. EC2 ... 5G 9 (5E 84)
Pindock M. W9 ... 4K 81
Pindoria M. E1 ... 4J 9
Pineapple Ct. SW1 ... 1B 18
Pine Av. BR4: W W'ck ... 1D 170
E15 ... 5F 69
Pine Cl. E10 ... 2D 68
HA7: Stan ... 4G 27
N14 ... 7B 22
N19 ... 2G 65
SE20 ... 1J 157
Pine Coombe CR0: C'don ... 4K 169
Pine Ct. N21 ... 5E 22
UB5: N'olt ... 4C 76
Pinecrest Gdns. BR6: Farnb ... 4F 173
Pinecroft Ct. DA16: Well ... 7A 108
Pinecroft Cres. EN5: Barn ... 4B 20
Pinedene SE15 ... 1H 121
Pinefield Cl. E14 ... 7C 86
Pine Gdns. HA4: Ruis ... 1K 57
KT5: Surb ... 6G 151
Pine Glade BR6: Farnb ... 4D 172
Pine Gro. N4 ... 2J 65
N20 ... 1C 30
SW19 ... 5H 135
Pine Ho. E3 ... 1A 86
(off Barge La.)
SE16 ... 2J 103
(off Ainsty Est.)
W10 ... 4G 81
(off Droop St.)
Pinehurst Ct. W11 ... 6H 81
(off Colville Gdns.)
Pinehurst Wlk. BR6: Orp ... 1H 173
Pinelands Cl. SE3 ... 7H 105
Pinemartin Cl. NW2 ... 3E 62
Pine M. NW10 ... 2F 81
(off Clifford Gdns.)
Pine Needle La. HA6: Nwood ... 1H 39
Pine Pl. UB4: Hayes ... 4H 75
Pine Ridge SM5: Cars ... 7E 166
Pineridge Ct. EN5: Barn ... 4A 20
Pine Rd. N11 ... 2K 31
NW2 ... 4E 62
The Pines IG8: Wfd G ... 3C 36
KT9: Chess ... 3E 162
N14 ... 5B 22
SE19 ... 6B 138
TW16: Sun ... 3J 147
Pines Rd. BR1: Broml ... 2C 160
Pine St. EC1 ... 3K 7 (4A 84)
Pine Tree Cl. TW2: Whitt ... 7F 113
TW5: Cran ... 1K 111
Pine Tree Lodge BR2: Broml ... 4H 159
Pine Trees Dr. UB10: Ick ... 4A 56
Pine Tree Way SE13 ... 3D 122
Pineview Ct. E4 ... 1K 35
Pine Wlk. KT5: Surb ... 6G 151
Pine Wood TW16: Sun ... 1J 147
Pinewood Av. DA15: Sidc ... 1J 143
HA5: Hat E ... 6A 26
UB8: Hil ... 6B 74
Pinewood Cl. BR6: Orp ... 1H 173
CR0: C'don ... 3A 170
HA5: Hat E ... 6A 26
Pinewood Ct. EN2: Enf ... 3G 23
SW4 ... 6H 119
Pinewood Dr. BR6: Orp ... 5J 173
Pinewood Gdns. TW11: Tedd ... 5B 132
Pinewood Gro. W5 ... 6C 78
Pinewood Lodge
WD23: B Hea ... 1C 26
Pinewood Pl. DA2: Wilm ... 2K 145
KT19: Ewe ... 4K 163
Pinewood Rd. BR2: Broml ... 4J 159
SE2 ... 6D 108
TW13: Felt ... 3K 129
Pinfold Rd. SW16 ... 4J 137
Pinglestone Cl. UB7: Harm ... 7A 92
Pinkcoat Cl. TW13: Felt ... 3K 129
Pinkerton Pl. SW16 ... 4H 137
Pinkham Mans. W4 ... 5G 97
Pinkham Way N11 ... 7K 31
Pinkwell Av. UB3: Harl ... 4F 93
Pinkwell La. UB3: Harl ... 4E 92
Pinley Gdns. RM9: Dag ... 1B 90
Pinnace Ho. E14 ... 3E 104
(off Manchester Rd.)
The Pinnacle ... 1G 15
The Pinnacle RM6: Chad H ... 6E 54
(off High Rd.)
Pinnacle Apts. CR0: C'don ... 1C 168
(off Saffron Central Sq.)
Pinnacle Cl. N10 ... 3F 47
Pinnacle Hill DA7: Bex ... 4H 127
Pinnacle Hill Nth. DA7: Bex ... 4H 127
Pinnacle Ho. EN1: Enf ... 3K 23
(off Colman Pde.)
NW9 ... 2B 44
(off Heritage Av.)
SW18 ... 4A 118
Pinnacle Pl. HA7: Stan ... 4G 27
Pinnacle Way E14 ... 6A 86
(off Commercial Rd.)
Pinnata Cl. EN2: Enf ... 1H 23
Pinnell Rd. SE9 ... 4B 124
PINNER ... 4C 40
Pinner Ct. HA5: Pinn ... 4E 40
NW8 ... 3A 4
PINNER GREEN ... 2A 40
Pinner Grn. HA5: Pinn ... 2A 40
Pinner Gro. HA5: Pinn ... 5C 40
Pinner Hill Farm HA5: Pinn ... 1K 39
Pinner Hill Golf Course ... 1A 40
Pinner Hill Rd. HA5: Pinn ... 1K 39
Pinner Pk. ... 1E 40
Pinner Pk. HA5: Pinn ... 2C 40
Pinner Pk. Av. HA2: Harr ... 3F 41
Pinner Pk. Gdns. HA2: Harr ... 2G 41
Pinner Rd. HA1: Harr ... 4E 40
HA2: Harr ... 4E 40
HA5: Pinn ... 4D 40
HA6: Nwood, Pinn ... 1H 39
Pinners Cl. SM5: Cars ... 2C 166
Pinner Vw. HA1: Harr ... 4G 41
HA2: Harr ... 4G 41
PINNERWOOD PARK ... 1A 40
Pinn Way HA4: Ruis ... 7F 39
Pintail Cl. E6 ... 5C 88
Pintail Ct. SE8 ... 6B 104
(off Pilot Cl.)
Pintail Rd. IG8: Wfd G ... 7E 36
Pintail Way UB4: Yead ... 5B 76
Pinter Ho. SW9 ... 2J 119
(off Grantham Rd.)
Pintle Pl. E3 ... 3E 86
Pinto Twr. SW8 ... 7J 101
Pinto Way SE3 ... 4K 123
The Pioneer Cen. SE15 ... 1J 121
Pioneer Cl. E14 ... 5D 86
Pioneer Ct. E16 ... 5J 87
(off Hammersley Rd.)
Pioneer Ho. WC1 ... 1G 7
(off Britannia St.)
Pioneer Pl. CR0: Sels ... 7C 170
Pioneer Point IG1: Ilf ... 3F 71
Pioneers Ind. Pk. CR0: Bedd ... 1J 167
Pioneer St. SE15 ... 1G 121
Pioneer Way W12 ... 6D 80
The Piper Bldg. SW6 ... 3K 117
Piper Cl. N7 ... 6K 65
Piper Rd. KT1: King T ... 3G 151
Piper's Gdns. CR0: C'don ... 7A 158
Pipers Grn. NW9 ... 5J 43
Pipers Grn. La. HA8: Edg ... 3K 27
(not continuous)
Pipers Ho. SE10 ... 5F 105
(off Collington St.)
Piper Way IG1: Ilf ... 1H 71
Pipewell Rd. SM5: Cars ... 6C 154
Pipit Dr. SW15 ... 6E 116
Pippenhall SE9 ... 6F 125
Pippin Cl. CR0: C'don ... 1B 170
NW2 ... 3C 62
TW13: Hanw ... 3D 130
Pippin Ct. SW8 ... 7G 19
(off Vauxhall Gro.)
Pippin Ho. W10 ... 7F 81
(off Freston Rd.)
Pippin Mans. E20 ... 5E 68
(off Mirabelle Gdns.)
Pippins Cl. UB7: W Dray ... 3A 92
Pippins Ct. TW15: Ashf ... 6D 128
Pique M. E1 ... 7K 85
(off Glasshouse Flds.)
Piquet Rd. SE20 ... 2J 157
Pirbright Cres. CR0: New Ad ... 6E 170
Pirbright Rd. SW18 ... 1H 135
Pirie Cl. SE5 ... 3D 120
Pirie St. E16 ... 1K 105
Pirin Ct. E4 ... 4H 35
Pisces Ct. HA8: Edg ... 7B 28
Pissaro Ho. N1 ... 7A 66
(off Augustas La.)
Pitcairn Cl. RM7: Mawney ... 4G 55
Pitcairn Ho. E9 ... 7J 67
Pitcairn Rd. CR4: Mitc ... 7D 136
Pitcairn's Path HA2: Harr ... 3G 59
Pitcher La. TW15: Ashf ... 4B 128
Pitchford St. E15 ... 7F 69
Pitfield Cres. SE28 ... 1A 108
Pitfield Est. N1 ... 1G 9 (3E 84)
Pitfield St. N1 ... 1G 9 (3E 84)
Pitfield Way EN3: Enf H ... 1D 24
NW10 ... 6J 61
Pitfold Cl. SE12 ... 6K 123
Pitfold Rd. SE12 ... 6J 123
Pitlake CR0: C'don ... 2B 168
Pitlochry Ho. SE27 ... 2B 138
(off Elmcourt Rd.)
Pitman Bldg. SE16 ... 7K 15
(off Old Jamaica Rd.)
Pitman Ho. SE8 ... 1C 122
Pitman St. SE5 ... 7C 102
Pitmaston Ho. SE13 ... 2E 122
(off Lewisham Rd.)
Pitmaston Rd. SE13 ... 2E 122
Pitsea Pl. E1 ... 6K 85
Pitsea St. E1 ... 6K 85
Pitshanger La. W5 ... 4B 78
Pitshanger Manor House & Gallery ... 1D 96
Pitt Cres. SW19 ... 4K 135
Pittman Gdns. IG1: Ilf ... 5G 71
Pitt Rd. BR6: Farnb ... 4G 173
CR0: C'don ... 5C 156
CR7: Thor H ... 5C 156
Pitt's Head M. W1 ... 5H 11 (1E 100)
Pittsmead Av. BR2: Hayes ... 7J 159
Pitt St. W8 ... 2J 99
Pittville Gdns. SE25 ... 3G 157
Pitwell M. E8 ... 6G 67
Pixfield Ct. BR2: Broml ... 2H 159
(off Beckenham La.)
Pixley St. E14 ... 6B 86
Pixton Way CR0: Sels ... 7A 170
The Place ... 3H 83
The Place SE1 ... 5F 15 (1D 102)
Place Farm Av. BR6: Orp ... 1H 173
Plaisterers Highwalk EC2 ... 6C 8
(off London Wall)
PLAISTOW
BR1 ... 7J 141
E13 ... 2J 87
Plaistow Gro. BR1: Broml ... 7K 141
E15 ... 1H 87
Plaistow La. BR1: Broml ... 7J 141
Plaistow Pk. Rd. E13 ... 2K 87
(not continuous)
Plaistow Rd. E13 ... 1H 87
E15 ... 1H 87
Plaistow Wharf E16 ... 2J 105
Plamer Ct. NW9 ... 2A 44
Plane Ho. BR2: Broml ... 2G 159
Plane St. SE26 ... 3H 139
Planetree Ct. W6 ... 4F 99
(off Brook Grn.)
Plane Tree Cres. TW13: Felt ... 3K 129
Plane Tree Ho. SE8 ... 6A 104
(off Etta St.)
W8 ... 2H 99
(off Duchess of Bedford's Wlk.)
Plane Tree Wlk. N2 ... 3C 46
SE19 ... 6E 138
Plantagenet Cl. KT4: Wor Pk ... 4K 163
Plantagenet Gdns. RM6: Chad H ... 7D 54
Plantagenet Ho. SE18 ... 3D 106
(off Leda Rd.)
Plantagenet Pl. RM6: Chad H ... 7D 54
Plantagenet Rd. EN5: New Bar ... 4F 21
Plantain Gdns. E11 ... 3F 69
(off Hollydown Way)
Plantain Pl. SE1 ... 6E 14 (2D 102)
The Plantation SE3 ... 2J 123
Plantation Cl. SW4 ... 5J 119
Plantation La. EC3 ... 2G 15
Plantation Pl. EC3 ... 2G 15
Plantation Wharf SW11 ... 3A 118
Plants & People Exhibition ... 7F 97
Plasel Ct. E13 ... 1K 87
(off Pawsey Cl.)
PLASHET ... 6C 70
Plashet Gro. E6 ... 1A 88
Plashet Rd. E13 ... 1J 87
Plassy Rd. SE6 ... 7D 122
Plate Ho. E14 ... 5D 104
(off Burrells Wharf Sq.)
Platform Theatre ... 1J 83
Platina St. EC2 ... 3F 9
Platinum Ct. E1 ... 4J 85
(off Cephas Av.)
RM7: Mawney ... 3H 55
Platinum M. N15 ... 5F 49
Plato Rd. SW2 ... 4J 119
The Platt SW15 ... 3F 117
Platt Halls NW9 ... 2B 44
Platt's Eyot TW12: Hamp ... 2E 148
Platt's La. NW3 ... 4J 63
Platts Rd. EN3: Enf H ... 1D 24
Platt St. NW1 ... 2H 83
Plawsfield Rd. BR3: Beck ... 1K 157
Plaxdale Ho. SE17 ... 4E 102
(off Congreve St.)
Plaxtol Cl. BR1: Broml ... 1A 160
Plaxtol Rd. DA8: Erith ... 7G 109
Plaxton Ct. E11 ... 3H 69
Playfair Ho. E14 ... 6C 86
(off Saracen St.)
Playfair Mans. W14 ... 6G 99
(off Queen's Club Gdns.)
Playfair St. W6 ... 5E 98
Playfield Av. RM5: Col R ... 1J 55
Playfield Cres. SE22 ... 5F 121
Playfield Rd. HA8: Edg ... 2J 43
Playford Rd. N4 ... 2K 65
(not continuous)
Playgreen Way SE6 ... 3C 140
Playground Cl. BR3: Beck ... 2K 157
Playground Gdns. E2 ... 2J 9
(off Rochelle St.)
Playhouse Ct. SE1 ... 6C 14
(off Southwark Bri. Rd.)
Playhouse Theatre ... 4F 13
(off Northumberland Av.)
Playhouse Yd. EC4 ... 1A 14 (6B 84)
Plaza Bus. Cen.
EN3: Brim ... 2G 25
Plaza Gdns. SW15 ... 5G 117
Plaza Hgts. E10 ... 3E 68
Plaza Pde. HA0: Wemb ... 6E 60
(off Ealing Rd.)
NW6 ... 2K 81
Plaza Wlk. NW9 ... 3J 43
The Pleasance SW15 ... 4D 116
Pleasance Rd. SW15 ... 5D 116
Pleasance Theatre ... 6J 65
(off Carpenters M.)
Pleasant Gro. CR0: C'don ... 3B 170
Pleasant Pl. N1 ... 7B 66
Pleasant Row NW1 ... 1F 83
Pleasant Vw. Pl. BR6: Farnb ... 5F 173
Pleasant Way HA0: Wemb ... 2C 78
Pleasaunce Mans. SE10 ... 5J 105
(off Halstow Rd.)
Plender Ct. NW1 ... 1G 83
(off College Pl.)
Plender St. NW1 ... 1G 83
Pleshey Rd. N7 ... 4H 65
Plesman Way SM6: W'gton ... 7J 167
Plessey Bldg. E14 ... 6C 86
(off Dod St.)
Plevna Cres. N15 ... 6E 48
Plevna Rd. N9 ... 3B 34
TW12: Hamp ... 1G 149
Plevna St. E14 ... 3E 104
Pleydell Av. SE19 ... 7F 139
W6 ... 4B 98
Pleydell Ct. EC4 ... 1K 13
(off Pleydell St.)
Pleydell Est. EC1 ... 2D 8
Pleydell Gdns. SE19 ... 6F 139
(off Anerley Hill)
Pleydell Ho. EC4 ... 1K 13
(off Pleydell St.)
Pleydell St. EC4 ... 1K 13
Plimley Pl. W12 ... 2F 99
(off Shepherd's Bush Pl.)
Plimsoll Cl. E14 ... 6D 86
Plimsoll Rd. N4 ... 3A 66
Plough Cl. NW10 ... 3D 80
Plough Ct. EC3 ... 2F 15 (7D 84)
RM13: Rain ... 2K 91
(off Broadis Way)
Plough Farm Cl. HA4: Ruis ... 6F 39
Plough La. CR8: Purl ... 7J 167
SE22 ... 6F 121
SM6: Bedd ... 4J 167
SW17 ... 5K 135
SW19 ... 5K 135
TW11: Tedd ... 5A 132
Plough La. Cl. SM6: Bedd ... 5J 167
Ploughmans Cl. NW1 ... 1H 83
Ploughmans End TW7: Isle ... 5H 113
Plough M. SW11 ... 4B 118
Plough Pl. EC4 ... 7K 7 (6A 84)
Plough Rd. KT19: Ewe ... 7K 163
SW11 ... 3B 118
Plough St. E1 ... 7K 9
Plough Ter. SW11 ... 4B 118
Plough Way SE16 ... 4K 103
Plough Yd. EC2 ... 4H 9 (4E 84)
Plover Ho. SW9 ... 7A 102
(off Brixton Rd.)
Plover Way SE16 ... 3A 104
UB4: Yead ... 6B 76
Plowden Bldgs. EC4 ... 2J 13
Plowman Cl. N18 ... 5J 33
Plowman Way RM8: Dag ... 1C 72
Plumber's Row E1 ... 5G 85
Plumbridge St. SE10 ... 1E 122
Plum Cl. TW13: Felt ... 1J 129
Plume Ho. SE10 ... 6D 104
(off Creek Rd.)
Plum Gth. TW8: Bford ... 4D 96
Plum La. RM13: Rain ... 2K 91
SE18 ... 7F 107
Plummer La. CR4: Mitc ... 2D 154
Plummer Rd. SW4 ... 7H 119
Plumpton Cl. UB5: N'olt ... 6E 58
Plumpton Way SM5: Cars ... 3C 166
PLUMSTEAD ... 4J 107
PLUMSTEAD COMMON ... 6F 107
Plumstead Comn. Rd. SE18 ... 6F 107
Plumstead High St. SE18 ... 4H 107
Plumstead Rd. SE18 ... 4F 107
(not continuous)
Plumtree Cl. RM10: Dag ... 6H 73
SM6: W'gton ... 7H 167
Plumtree Ct. EC4 ... 7A 8 (6B 84)
Plum Tree M. SW16 ... 6J 137
Plymen Ho. KT8: W Mole ... 5E 148
Plymouth Ct. KT5: Surb ... 4E 150
(off Cranes Pk. Av.)
Plymouth Ho. IG11: Bark ... 7A 72
(off Margaret Bondfield Av.)
SE10 ... 1D 122
(off Devonshire Dr.)
Plymouth Rd. BR1: Broml ... 1K 159
E16 ... 5J 87
Plymouth Ter. NW2 ... 6E 62
(off Sidmouth Rd.)
Plymouth Wharf E14 ... 4F 105
Plympton Av. NW6 ... 7H 63
Plympton Cl. DA17: Belv ... 3E 108
Plympton Pl. NW8 ... 4C 4 (4C 82)
Plympton Rd. NW6 ... 7H 63
Plympton St. NW8 ... 4C 4 (4C 82)
Plymstock Rd. DA16: Well ... 7C 108
Pocklington Cl. NW9 ... 2A 44
W12 ... 3C 98
(off Ashchurch Pk. Vs.)
Pocklington Ct. SW15 ... 1C 134
Pocklington Lodge W12 ... 3C 98
Pocock Av. UB7: W Dray ... 3B 92
Pocock St. SE1 ... 6A 14 (2B 102)
Podmore Rd. SW18 ... 4A 118
Poet Ct. E1 ... 5K 85
(off Shandy St.)
Poets Ct. SE25 ... 4G 157
W3 ... 1J 97
Poet's Rd. N5 ... 5D 66
Poets Way HA1: Harr ... 4J 41
The Point E17 ... 4C 50
(off Tower M.)
HA4: Ruis ... 4J 57
W2 ... 6A 4
Pointalls Cl. N3 ... 2A 46
Point Cl. SE10 ... 1E 122
Pointer Cl. SE28 ... 6D 90
Pointers Cl. E14 ... 5D 104
Pointers Cotts. TW10: Ham ... 2C 132
Point Hill SE10 ... 7E 104
Point Pl. HA9: Wemb ... 7H 61
Point Pleasant SW18 ... 4J 117
Point Ter. E7 ... 5K 69
(off Claremont Rd.)
Point W. SW7 ... 4K 99
Point Wharf TW8: Bford ... 7E 96
Point Wharf La. TW8: Bford ... 7D 96
Poland St. W1 ... 1B 12 (6G 83)
Polar Pk. UB7: Harm ... 7B 92
Poldo Ho. SE10 ... 4G 105
(off Cable Wlk.)
Polebrook Rd. SE3 ... 3A 124
Pole Cat All. BR2: Hayes ... 2H 171
Polecroft La. SE6 ... 2B 140
The Polehamptons
TW12: Hamp ... 7G 131
Pole Hill Rd. E4 ... 7K 25
UB4: Hayes ... 4D 74
UB10: Hil ... 4D 74
Polesden Gdns. SW20 ... 2D 152
Polesworth Ho. W2 ... 5J 81
(off Alfred Rd.)
Polesworth Rd. RM9: Dag ... 7D 72
Police Sta. La. WD23: Bush ... 1A 26
POLISH WAR MEMORIAL ... 7A 58
Polka Theatre for Children ... 6K 135
Pollard Cl. E16 ... 7J 87
N7 ... 4K 65
Pollard Ho. KT4: Wor Pk ... 4E 164
N1 ... 1G 7
(off Northdown St.)
SE16 ... 3F 103
(off Spa Rd.)
Pollard Rd. N20 ... 2H 31
SM4: Mord ... 5B 154
Pollard Row E2 ... 3G 85
Pollards Cres. SW16 ... 3J 155
Pollards Hill E. SW16 ... 3K 155
Pollards Hill Nth. SW16 ... 3J 155
Pollards Hill Sth. SW16 ... 3J 155
Pollards Hill W. SW16 ... 3K 155
Pollard St. E2 ... 3G 85
Pollards Wood Rd. SW16 ... 3J 155
Pollard Wlk. DA14: Sidc ... 6C 144
Pollen St. W1 ... 1A 12 (6G 83)
Pollitt Dr. NW8 ... 3B 4 (4B 82)
Pollock Ho. W10 ... 4G 81
(off Kensal Rd.)
Pollock's Toy Mus. ... 5B 6 (5G 83)
Polo M. BR7: Chst ... 5H 143
Polperro Cl. BR6: St M Cry ... 6K 161
Polperro Ho. W2 ... 5J 81
(off Westbourne Pk. Rd.)
Polperro M. SE11 ... 3K 19 (4B 102)
Polsted Rd. SE6 ... 7B 122
Polthorne Est. SE18 ... 4H 107
(off Polthorne Gro.)
Polthorne Gro. SE18 ... 4G 107
Polworth Rd. SW16 ... 5J 137
Polychrome Ct. SE1 ... 7A 14
(off Waterloo Rd.)
Polydamas Cl. E3 ... 2C 86
The Polygon NW8 ... 1B 82
(off Avenue Rd.)
SW4 ... 4G 119
Polygon Bus. Cen. SL3: Poyle ... 5A 174
Polygon Rd. NW1 ... 1C 6 (2H 83)
(not continuous)
Polytechnic St. SE18 ... 4E 106
Pomell Way E1 ... 7K 9 (6F 85)
Pomeroy Cl. TW1: Twick ... 4B 114
Pomeroy Ho. E2 ... 2K 85
(off St James's Av.)
W11 ... 6G 81
(off Lancaster Rd.)
Pomeroy St. SE14 ... 7J 103
Pomfret Pl. E14 ... 7E 86
(off Bullivant St.)
Pomfret Rd. SE5 ... 3B 120
Pomoja La. N19 ... 2J 65
Pomona Ho. SE8 ... 4A 104
(off Evelyn St.)
Pompadour Way IG11: Bark ... 2B 90
Pond Cl. N12 ... 6H 31
SE3 ... 2J 123
Pond Cott. La. BR4: W W'ck ... 1C 170
Pond Cotts. SE21 ... 1E 138
PONDERS END ... 5D 24
Ponders End Ind. Est.
EN3: Pond E ... 5F 25
Ponder St. N7 ... 7K 65
Pond Farm Est. E5 ... 3J 67
Pondfield Ho. SE27 ... 5C 138
Pondfield Rd. BR2: Hayes ... 1G 171
BR6: Farnb ... 3F 173
RM10: Dag ... 5H 73
Pond Grn. HA4: Ruis ... 2G 57
Pond Hill Gdns.
SM3: Cheam ... 6G 165
Pond Ho. HA7: Stan ... 6G 27
SW3 ... 4C 16 (4C 100)
Pond Lees Cl.
RM10: Dag ... 7K 73
Pond Mead SE21 ... 6D 120
Pond Path BR7: Chst ... 6F 143
Pond Pl. SW3 ... 4C 16 (4C 100)
Pond Rd. E15 ... 2G 87
SE3 ... 2H 123
Pondside Av. KT4: Wor Pk ... 1E 164
Pondside Cl. UB3: Harl ... 6F 93
Pond Sq. N6 ... 1E 64
Pond St. NW3 ... 5C 64
Pond Way TW11: Tedd ... 6C 132
Pondwood Ri. BR6: Orp ... 7J 161
Ponler St. E1 ... 6H 85
Ponsard Rd. NW10 ... 3D 80
Ponsford St. E9 ... 6J 67
Ponsonby Ho. E2 ... 2J 85
(off Bishop's Way)
Ponsonby Pl. SW1 ... 5D 18 (5H 101)
Ponsonby Rd. SW15 ... 7D 116
Ponsonby Ter. SW1 ... 5D 18 (5H 101)
Ponsonby Vs. E2 ... 2J 85
(off Lark Row)
Pontefract Ct. UB5: N'olt ... 5F 59
(off Newmarket Av.)
Pontefract Rd. BR1: Broml ... 5H 141
Pontes Av. TW3: Houn ... 4D 112
Pontifex Apts. SE1 ... 4E 14
(off Stoney St.)
Ponton Rd. SW11 ... 7C 18 (6H 101)
Pontoon Reach E16 ... 1B 106
Pont St. SW1 ... 2E 16 (3D 100)
Pont St. M. SW1 ... 2E 16 (3D 100)
Pontypool Pl. SE1 ... 6A 14 (2B 102)
Pooja Ct. NW1 ... 7G 65
(off Agar Gro.)
Pool Cl. BR3: Beck ... 5C 140
KT8: W Mole ... 5D 148
Pool Ct. SE6 ... 2C 140
Poole Cl. HA4: Ruis ... 2G 57
Poole Ct. N1 ... 7E 66
(off St Peter's Way)
TW4: Houn ... 2C 112
Poole Ct. Rd. TW4: Houn ... 2C 112
Poole Ho. SE11 ... 2H 19
Poole La. TW19: Stanw ... 7B 110
POOL END ... 5C 146
Pool End Cl. TW17: Shep ... 5C 146
Poole Rd. E9 ... 6K 67
KT19: Ewe ... 6K 163
Pooles Bldgs. WC1 ... 4J 7
Pooles Cotts. TW10: Ham ... 2D 132
Pooles La. RM9: Dag ... 2E 90
SW10 ... 7A 100
Pooles Pk. N4 ... 2A 66
Poole St. N1 ... 1D 84
Poole Way UB4: Hayes ... 3G 75
Pooley Dr. SW14 ... 3J 115

A-Z Big London 269

Pooley Ho.—Prince Charles Dr.

Pooley Ho. E1 ... 3K 85
E18 ... 1J 51
Pool Ho. NW8 ... 5C 4
(off Penfold St.)
Poolmans St. SE16 ... 2K 103
Pool Rd. HA1: Harr ... 7H 41
KT8: W Mole ... 5D 148
Poolsford Rd. NW9 ... 4A 44
Poolside Manor ... 1H 45
Pools on the Pk. ... 4D 114
Pool St. E20 ... 7E 68
Poonah St. E1 ... 6J 85
Pope Cl. SW19 ... 6B 136
TW14: Felt ... 1H 129
Pope Ho. SE5 ... 7D 102
(off Elmington Est.)
SE16 ... 4H 103
(off Manor Est.)
Pope Rd. BR2: Broml ... 5B 160
Popes Av. TW2: Twick ... 2J 131
Popes Ct. TW2: Twick ... 2J 131
Popes Dr. N3 ... 1J 45
Popes Gro. CR0: C'don ... 3B 170
TW1: Twick ... 2K 131
TW2: Twick ... 2K 131
Pope's Head All. EC3 ... 1F 15 (6D 84)
Popes La. W5 ... 3D 96
Pope's Rd. SW9 ... 3A 120
Pope St. SE1 ... 7H 15 (2E 102)
Popham Cl. TW13: Hanw ... 3D 130
Popham Gdns. TW9: Rich ... 3G 115
Popham Rd. N1 ... 1C 84
Popham St. N1 ... 1B 84
(not continuous)
Pop in Commercial Cen.
HA9: Wemb ... 5H 61
Popinjays Row SM3: Cheam ... 5F 165
(off Netley Cl.)
POPLAR ... 7D 86
Poplar Av. BR6: Farnb ... 2F 173
CR4: Mitc ... 1D 154
UB2: S'hall ... 3F 95
UB7: Yiew ... 7B 74
Poplar Baths Leisure Cen. ... 7D 86
Poplar Bath St. E14 ... 6D 86
Poplar Bus. Pk. E14 ... 7E 86
Poplar Cl. E9 ... 5B 68
HA5: Pinn ... 1B 40
SL3: Poyle ... 4A 174
Poplar Ct. SW19 ... 5J 135
TW1: Twick ... 6C 114
UB5: N'olt ... 2A 76
Poplar Cres. KT19: Ewe ... 6J 163
Poplar Farm Cl. KT19: Ewe ... 6J 163
Poplar Gdns. KT3: N Mald ... 2K 151
Poplar Gro. HA9: Wemb ... 3J 61
KT3: N Mald ... 2K 151
N11 ... 6K 31
W6 ... 2E 98
Poplar High St. E14 ... 7D 86
Poplar Ho. SE4 ... 4B 122
(off Wickham Rd.)
SE16 ... 2K 103
(off Woodland Cres.)
Poplar M. W12 ... 1E 98
Poplar Mt. DA17: Belv ... 4H 109
Poplar Pl. SE28 ... 7C 90
UB3: Hayes ... 7J 75
W2 ... 7K 81
Poplar Rd. KT10: Surb ... 3B 162
SE24 ... 4C 120
SM3: Sutt ... 1H 165
SW19 ... 2J 153
TW15: Ashf ... 5E 128
Poplar Rd. Sth. SW19 ... 3J 153
The Poplars N14 ... 5A 22
Poplars Av. NW2 ... 6E 62
Poplars Cl. HA4: Ruis ... 1G 57
Poplars Rd. E17 ... 6D 50
Poplar St. RM7: Rom ... 4J 55
Poplar Vw. HA9: Wemb ... 2D 60
Poplar Wlk. CR0: C'don ... 2C 168
SE24 ... 3C 120
(not continuous)
Poplar Way IG6: Ilf ... 4G 53
TW13: Felt ... 3J 129
Poppins Cl. KT12: Walt T ... 5A 148
Poppins Ct. EC4 ... 1A 14 (6B 84)
Poppleton Rd. E11 ... 6G 51
Poppy Cl. DA17: Belv ... 3H 109
EN5: New Bar ... 6F 21
SM6: W'gton ... 1E 166
UB5: N'olt ... 6D 58
UB7: W Dray ... 3B 92
Poppy Dr. EN3: Pond E ... 4C 24
Poppy La. CR0: C'don ... 7J 157
Poppy M. SE22 ... 5G 121
Poppy Pl. SE13 ... 6F 123
Porchester Cl. SE5 ... 4C 120
Porchester Ct. W2 ... 7K 81
(off Porchester Gdns.)
Porchester Gdns. W2 ... 7K 81
Porchester Gdns. M. W2 ... 6K 81
Porchester Ga. W2 ... 7K 81
(off Bayswater Rd.)
Porchester Ho. E1 ... 6H 85
(off Philpot St.)
Porchester Leisure Cen. ... 6K 81
Porchester Mead
BR3: Beck ... 6D 140
Porchester Pl. W2 ... 1D 10 (6C 82)
Porchester Rd.
KT1: King T ... 2H 151
W2 ... 6K 81
Porchester Sq. W2 ... 6K 81
Porchester Sq. M. W2 ... 6K 81
Porchester Ter. W2 ... 7A 82
Porchester Ter. Nth. W2 ... 6K 81
Porch Way N20 ... 3J 31
Porcupine Cl. SE9 ... 2C 142
Porden Rd. SW2 ... 4K 119
Porlock Av. HA2: Harr ... 1G 59
Porlock Ho. SE26 ... 3G 139
Porlock Rd. EN1: Enf ... 7A 24
Porlock St. SE1 ... 6F 15 (2D 102)
Porrington Ct. BR7: Chst ... 1D 160
Portal Cl. HA4: Ruis ... 4J 57
SE27 ... 3A 138
UB10: Uxb ... 7A 56
Portal Way W3 ... 5K 79
Portbury Cl. SE15 ... 1G 121
Port Cres. E13 ... 4K 87
Portcullis Ho. SW1 ... 7E 12
Portcullis Lodge Rd. EN1: Enf ... 3J 23
Port East Apts. E14 ... 7C 86
(off Hertsmere Rd.)
Portelet Ct. N1 ... 1E 84
(off De Beauvoir Est.)
Portelet Rd. E1 ... 3K 85
Porten Ho's. W14 ... 3G 99
(off Porten Rd.)
Porten Rd. W14 ... 3G 99
Porter Rd. E6 ... 6D 88
Porters & Walters Almshouses
N22 ... 7E 32
(off Nightingale Rd.)
Porters Av. RM8: Dag ... 6B 72
RM9: Dag ... 6B 72
The Porters Lodge SW10 ... 7A 100
(off Coleridge Gdns.)
Porters M. RM9: Dag ... 6B 72
Porter Sq. N19 ... 1J 65
Porter St. SE1 ... 4D 14 (1C 102)
W1 ... 5F 5 (5D 82)
Porters Wlk. E1 ... 7H 85
Porters Way N12 ... 6H 31
UB7: W Dray ... 3B 92
Porteus Pl. SW4 ... 3G 119
Porteus Rd. W2 ... 5A 4 (5A 82)
Portfleet Pl. N1 ... 1E 84
(off De Beauvoir Rd.)
Portgate Cl. W9 ... 4H 81
Porthallow Cl. BR6: Chels ... 4K 173
Porthcawe Rd. SE26 ... 4A 140
Porthkerry Av. DA16: Well ... 4A 126
Port Ho. E14 ... 5D 104
(off Burrells Wharf Sq.)
Portia Ct. IG11: Bark ... 7A 72
SE11 ... 5B 102
(off Opal St.)
Portia Way E3 ... 4B 86
The Porticos SW3 ... 7A 16
Portinscale Rd. SW15 ... 5G 117
Portishead Ho. W2 ... 5J 81
(off Westbourne Pk. Rd.)
Portland Av. DA15: Sidc ... 6A 126
KT3: N Mald ... 7B 152
N16 ... 7F 49
Portland Cl. KT4: Wor Pk ... 7D 152
RM6: Chad H ... 5E 54
Portland Commercial Est.
IG11: Bark ... 2C 90
Portland Cotts. CR0: Bedd ... 7H 155
Portland Ct. N1 ... 7E 66
(off St Peter's Way)
SE1 ... 7E 14
(off Gt. Dover St.)
SE14 ... 6A 104
(off Whitcher Cl.)
Portland Cres. HA7: Stan ... 2D 42
SE9 ... 2C 142
TW13: Felt ... 4F 129
UB6: G'frd ... 4F 77
Portland Dr. EN2: Enf ... 1K 23
Portland Gdns. N4 ... 6B 48
RM6: Chad H ... 5D 54
Portland Gro. SW8 ... 1K 119
Portland Ho. SW1 ... 1A 18
SW15 ... 5F 117
Portland Mans. W14 ... 4H 99
(off Addison Bri. Pl.)
Portland M. W1 ... 1B 12 (6G 83)
Portland Pl. SE25 ... 4G 157
(off Sth. Norwood Hill)
W1 ... 4J 5 (5F 83)
Portland Ri. N4 ... 1B 66
(not continuous)
Portland Rd. BR1: Broml ... 4A 142
CR4: Mitc ... 2C 154
KT1: King T ... 3E 150
N15 ... 4F 49
SE9 ... 2C 142
SE25 ... 4G 157
TW15: Ashf ... 3A 128
UB2: S'hall ... 3D 94
UB4: Hayes ... 3G 75
W11 ... 7G 81
Portland Sq. E1 ... 1H 103
Portland St. SE17 ... 5D 102
Portland Ter. HA8: Edg ... 7B 28
TW9: Rich ... 4D 114
Portland Wlk. SE17 ... 6D 102
Portman Av. SW14 ... 3K 115
Portman Cl. DA5: Bexl ... 1K 145
DA7: Bex ... 3E 126
W1 ... 7F 5 (6D 82)
Portman Dr. IG8: Wfd G ... 2B 52
Portman Gdns. NW9 ... 2K 43
UB10: Hil ... 7C 56
Portman Ga. NW1 ... 4D 4 (4C 82)
Portman Mans. W1 ... 5F 5
(off Chiltern St.)
Portman M. Sth. W1 ... 1G 11 (6E 82)
Portman Pl. E2 ... 3J 85
Portman Rd. KT1: King T ... 2F 151
Portman Sq. W1 ... 7G 5 (6E 82)
Portman St. W1 ... 1G 11 (6E 82)
Portman Towers W1 ... 7F 5 (6D 82)
Portmeadow Wlk. SE2 ... 2D 108
Portmeers Cl. E17 ... 6B 50
Portnall Ho. W9 ... 3H 81
(off Portnall Rd.)
Portnall Rd. W9 ... 2H 81
Portnoi Cl. RM1: Rom ... 2K 55
Portobello Ct. W11 ... 6H 81
Portobello Grn. W10 ... 5G 81
(off Portobello Rd.)
Portobello Ho. BR2: Broml ... 6B 160
Portobello Lofts W10 ... 4G 81
(off Kensal Rd.)
Portobello Mkt. ... 6H 81
Portobello M. W11 ... 7J 81
Portobello Rd. W10 ... 5G 81
W11 ... 6H 81
Portobello Road Market ... 7H 81
(off Portobello Rd.)
Porton Ct. KT6: Surb ... 6C 150
Portpool La. EC1 ... 5J 7 (5A 84)
Portree Cl. N22 ... 6F 32
Portree St. E14 ... 6F 87
Portrush Ct. UB1: S'hall ... 6G 77
(off Whitecote Rd.)
Portsdown HA8: Edg ... 5B 28
Portsdown Av. NW11 ... 6H 45
Portsdown M. NW11 ... 6H 45
Portsea Hall W2 ... 1D 10
(off Portsea Pl.)
Portsea M. W2 ... 1D 10
Portsea Pl. W2 ... 1D 10 (6C 82)
Portslade Rd. SW8 ... 2G 119
Portsmouth Av. KT7: T Ditt ... 7A 150
Portsmouth M. E16 ... 1K 105
Portsmouth Rd. KT1: King T ... 7A 150
KT6: Surb ... 7A 150
KT7: T Ditt ... 1A 162
SW15 ... 7D 116
Portsmouth St. WC2 ... 1G 13 (6K 83)
Portsoken Pav. EC3 ... 1J 15
(off Aldgate Sq.)
Portsoken St. E1 ... 2J 15 (7F 85)
Portswood Pl. SW15 ... 6B 116
Portugal Gdns. TW2: Twick ... 2G 131
Portugal St. WC2 ... 1G 13 (6K 83)
Portway E15 ... 1H 87
Portway Gdns. SE18 ... 7B 106
Pory Ho. SE11 ... 4H 19 (4K 101)
Poseidon Ct. E14 ... 4C 104
(off Homer Dr.)
POSK ... 4C 98
(off King St.)
Postal Cl. DA5: Bexl ... 7H 127
The Postal Mus. ... 3H 7 (4K 83)
The Postern EC2 ... 6D 8
Postern Grn. EN2: Enf ... 2F 23
Post La. TW2: Twick ... 1H 131
Postmark Development
EC1 ... 3H 7 (4K 83)
Postmasters Lodge HA5: Pinn ... 7C 40
Postmill Cl. CR0: C'don ... 3J 169
Post Office App. E7 ... 5K 69
Post Office Ct. EC3 ... 1F 15
(off King William St.)
Post Office Way SW11 ... 7H 101
Post Rd. UB2: S'hall ... 3F 95
Postway M. IG1: Ilf ... 3F 71
(not continuous)
Potager Pl. CR0: Bedd ... 3H 167
Potier St. SE1 ... 3D 102
Potter Cl. CR4: Mitc ... 2F 155
SE2 ... 5A 108
SE15 ... 7E 102
Potter Ho. E1 ... 5K 85
(off Beaufort Gdns.)
The Potteries EN5: Barn ... 5D 20
Potterne Cl. SW19 ... 7F 117
Potters Cl. CR0: C'don ... 1A 170
Potters Ct. SM1: Sutt ... 6H 165
(off Rosebery Rd.)
Pottersfield EN1: Enf ... 4K 23
(off Lincoln Rd.)
Potters Flds. SE1 ... 5H 15 (1E 102)
Potters Gro. KT3: N Mald ... 4J 151
Potters Hgts. Cl. HA5: Pinn ... 1K 39
Potter's La. SW16 ... 6H 137
Potters La. EN5: New Bar ... 4D 20
Potters Lodge E14 ... 5E 104
(off Ferry St.)
Potter's Rd. EN5: New Bar ... 4E 20
Potters Rd. SW6 ... 2A 118
UB2: S'hall ... 3E 94
Potters Row E20 ... 5D 68
(off Keirin Rd.)
Potter St. HA5: Pinn ... 1K 39
HA6: Nwood ... 1J 39
Potter St. Hill HA5: Pinn ... 1K 39
Pottery Café ... 1H 117
(off Fulham Rd.)
Pottery Cl. SE25 ... 3G 157
Pottery Ga. N11 ... 6K 31
Pottery La. W11 ... 1G 99
Pottery M. SW6 ... 2H 117
Pottery Rd. DA5: Bexl ... 2J 145
TW8: Bford ... 6E 96
Pottery St. SE16 ... 2H 103
Pott St. E2 ... 3H 85
Poulett Gdns. TW1: Twick ... 1A 132
Poulett Rd. E6 ... 2D 88
Poulter Pk. ... 6C 154
Poulters Wood BR2: Kes ... 5B 172
Poulton Av. SM1: Sutt ... 3B 166
Poulton Cl. E8 ... 6H 67
Poulton Ho. W3 ... 5K 79
(off Victoria Rd.)
Poultry EC2 ... 1E 14 (6D 84)
Pound Cl. BR6: Orp ... 2H 173
KT6: Surb ... 1C 162
Pound Ct. Dr. BR6: Orp ... 2H 173
Pound Farm Cl.
KT10: Esh ... 7G 149
Pound Grn. DA5: Bexl ... 7G 127
Pound La. NW10 ... 6C 62
Pound Pk. Rd. SE7 ... 4B 106
Pound Path E3 ... 2K 85
(off Stoneway Wlk.)
Pound Pl. SE9 ... 6E 124
Pound St. SM5: Cars ... 5D 166
Pound Way BR7: Chst ... 7G 143
Pountney Rd. SW11 ... 3E 118
POVEREST ... 4K 161
Poverest Rd. BR5: St M Cry ... 5K 161
Povey Ho. SE17 ... 4E 102
(off Beckway St.)
Powder Mill La. TW2: Whitt ... 7D 112
Powell Cl. HA8: Edg ... 6A 28
KT9: Chess ... 5D 162
Powell Ct. CR2: S Croy ... 4B 168
(off Bramley Hill)
E17 ... 3D 50
Powell Dr. E4 ... 4J 25
Powell Gdns. RM10: Dag ... 4G 73
Powell Ho. EN1: Enf ... 4K 23
(off Dunstan M.)
W2 ... 2A 10
(off Gloucester Ter.)
Powell Rd. E5 ... 3H 67
IG9: Buck H ... 1F 37
Powell's Wlk. W4 ... 6A 98
Powergate Bus. Pk. NW10 ... 3K 79
The Powerhouse ... 2G 93
Powerhouse La. UB3: Hayes ... 2G 93
Powerleague
Battersea ... 7G 101
Colney Hatch ... 7K 31
Croydon ... 6K 167
Ilford ... 1K 53
Mill Hill ... 7J 29
Newham ... 3G 89
Tottenham ... 6C 34
Wembley ... 4G 61
Power Rd. W4 ... 4G 97
Powers Ct. TW1: Twick ... 7D 114
Powerscroft Rd. DA14: Sidc ... 6C 144
(not continuous)
E5 ... 4J 67
Powis Ct. W11 ... 6H 81
(off Powis Gdns.)
WD23: B Hea ... 1C 26
(off Rutherford Way)
Powis Gdns. NW11 ... 7H 45
W11 ... 6H 81
Powis Ho. WC2 ... 7F 7
(off Macklin St.)
Powis M. W11 ... 6H 81
Powis Pl. WC1 ... 4F 7 (4J 83)
Powis Rd. E3 ... 3D 86
Powis Sq. W11 ... 6H 81
(not continuous)
Powis St. SE18 ... 3E 106
Powis Ter. W11 ... 6H 81
Powlesland Ct. E1 ... 6A 86
(off White Horse Rd.)
Powlett Ho. NW1 ... 6F 65
(off Powlett Pl.)
Powlett Pl. NW1 ... 7E 64
Pownall Gdns. TW3: Houn ... 4F 113
Pownall Rd. E8 ... 1F 85
TW3: Houn ... 4F 113
Pownell Ter. SE11 ... 6A 102
Pownsett Ter. IG1: Ilf ... 5G 71
Powster Rd. BR1: Broml ... 5J 141
Powys Cl. DA7: Bex ... 6D 108
Powys Ct. N11 ... 5D 32
Powys La. N13 ... 4D 32
N14 ... 4D 32
POYLE ... 4A 174
Poyle Ind. Est. SL3: Poyle ... 6A 174
Poyle New Cotts.
SL3: Poyle ... 5A 174
Poyle Technical Cen.
SL3: Poyle ... 5A 174
Poyle Trad. Est. SL3: Poyle ... 6A 174
Poynders Ct. SW4 ... 6G 119
Poynders Gdns. SW4 ... 7G 119
Poynders Pde. SW4 ... 6H 119
Poynders Rd. SW4 ... 6G 119
The Poynings SL0: Rich P ... 1A 174
Poynings Rd. N19 ... 3G 65
Poynings Way N12 ... 5D 30
Poyntell Cres. BR7: Chst ... 1H 161
Poynter Ct. UB5: N'olt ... 2B 76
(off Gallery Gdns.)
Poynter Ho. NW8 ... 3A 4
(off Fisherton St.)
W11 ... 1F 99
(off Queensdale Cres.)
Poynter Rd. EN1: Enf ... 5B 24
Poynton Rd. N17 ... 2G 49
Poyntz Rd. SW11 ... 2D 118
Poyser St. E2 ... 2H 85
Prado Path TW1: Twick ... 1K 131
(off Laurel Av.)
Praed M. W2 ... 7B 4 (6B 82)
Praed St. W2 ... 1A 10 (6B 82)
Pragel St. E13 ... 2A 88
Pragnell Rd. SE12 ... 2K 141
Prague Pl. SW2 ... 5J 119
Prah Rd. N4 ... 2A 66
Prairie Bldg. E15 ... 5F 69
(off Property Row)
Prairie St. SW8 ... 2E 118
Praline Ct. E3 ... 2D 86
(off Taylor Pl.)
Pratt M. NW1 ... 1G 83
Pratts Pas. KT1: King T ... 2E 150
Pratt St. NW1 ... 1G 83
Pratt Wlk. SE11 ... 3H 19 (4K 101)
Prayle Gro. NW2 ... 1F 63
Preachers Ct. EC1 ... 5B 8
(off Charterhouse Sq.)
Prebend Gdns. W4 ... 4B 98
W6 ... 4B 98
(not continuous)
Prebend Mans. W4 ... 4B 98
(off Chiswick High Rd.)
Prebend St. N1 ... 1C 84
The Precinct N1 ... 1C 84
Precinct Rd. UB3: Hayes ... 7J 75
The Precincts SM4: Mord ... 6J 153
Premier Cnr. W9 ... 2H 81
Premier Ct. EN3: Enf W ... 1D 24
Premiere Pl. E14 ... 7B 86
Premier Ho. N1 ... 7B 66
(off Waterloo Ter.)
Premier Pk. NW10 ... 1H 79
(not continuous)
Premier Pk. Rd. NW10 ... 2H 79
Premier Pl. SW15 ... 4G 117
Prendergast Rd. SE3 ... 3G 123
Prentice Ct. SW19 ... 5H 135
Prentis Rd. SW16 ... 4H 137
Prentiss Ct. SE7 ... 4B 106
Presburg Rd. KT3: N Mald ... 5A 152
Presburg St. E5 ... 3K 67
Prescelly Pl. HA8: Edg ... 1F 43
Prescot St. E1 ... 2K 15 (7F 85)
Prescott Av. BR5: Pet W ... 6F 161
Prescott Cl. SW16 ... 7J 137
Prescott Ho. SE17 ... 6B 102
(off Hillingdon St.)
Prescott Pl. SW4 ... 3H 119
Presentation M. SW2 ... 2K 137
Preshaw Cres. CR4: Mitc ... 3C 154
President Dr. E1 ... 1H 103
President Ho. EC1 ... 2B 8 (3B 84)
President Quay E1 ... 4K 15
President St. EC1 ... 1C 8
Prespa Cl. N9 ... 2D 34
Press Ct. SE1 ... 5G 103
Press Ho. BR5: Pet W ... 5G 161
E1 ... 5K 85
(off Trafalgar Gdns.)
NW10 ... 3A 62
Pressing La. UB3: Hayes ... 3G 93
Press Rd. NW10 ... 3K 61
Prestage Way E14 ... 7E 86
Prestbury Rd. E7 ... 7A 70
Prestbury Sq. SE9 ... 4D 142
Prested Rd. SW11 ... 4C 118
Prestige Ho. N20 ... 1F 31
(off Acton Wlk.)
Prestige Way NW4 ... 5E 44
PRESTON ... 1E 60
Preston Av. E4 ... 6A 36
Preston Cl. SE1 ... 4E 102
TW2: Twick ... 3J 131
Preston Ct. DA14: Sidc ... 4K 143
(off The Crescent)
EN5: New Bar ... 4F 21
Preston Dr. DA7: Bex ... 1D 126
E11 ... 5A 52
KT19: Ewe ... 6A 164
Preston Gdns. IG1: Ilf ... 6C 52
NW10 ... 6B 62
Preston Hill HA3: Kenton ... 7E 42
Preston Ho. RM10: Dag ... 3G 73
(off Uvedale Rd.)
SE1 ... 4E 102
(off Preston Cl.)
SE1 ... 7J 15
(off St Saviour's Est.)
Preston Pl. NW2 ... 6C 62
TW10: Rich ... 5E 114
Preston Rd. E11 ... 6G 51
HA3: Kenton ... 1E 60
HA9: Wemb ... 1E 60
SE19 ... 6B 138
SW20 ... 7B 134
TW17: Shep ... 5C 146
Preston's Rd. E14 ... 7E 86
Prestons Rd. BR2: Hayes ... 3J 171
Preston St. E2 ... 2K 85
Preston Waye HA3: Kenton ... 1E 60
Prestwich Ter. SW4 ... 5G 119
Prestwick Cl. UB2: S'hall ... 5C 94
Prestwick Ct. UB1: S'hall ... 7G 77
(off Baird Av.)
Prestwood Av. HA3: Kenton ... 4B 42
Prestwood Cl. HA3: Kenton ... 4B 42
SE18 ... 6A 108
Prestwood Gdns. CR0: C'don ... 7C 156
Prestwood Ho. SE16 ... 3H 103
(off Drummond Rd.)
Prestwood St. N1 ... 1D 8 (2C 84)
Pretoria Av. E17 ... 4A 50
Pretoria Cres. E4 ... 1K 35
Pretoria Rd. E4 ... 1K 35
E11 ... 1F 69
E16 ... 4H 87
IG1: Ilf ... 5F 71
N17 ... 7A 34
RM7: Rom ... 4J 55
SW16 ... 6F 137
Pretoria Rd. Nth. N18 ... 6A 34
Prevost Rd. N11 ... 2K 31
Priam Ho. E2 ... 2H 85
(off Old Bethnal Grn. Rd.)
Price Cl. SW17 ... 3D 136
Price Ho. N1 ... 1C 84
(off Britannia Row)
Price Rd. CR0: Wadd ... 5B 168
Prices Cl. NW7 ... 6B 30
Price's Ct. SW11 ... 3B 118
Price's M. N1 ... 1K 83
Price's St. SE1 ... 5B 14 (1B 102)
Price Way TW12: Hamp ... 6C 130
Prichard Ct. N7 ... 5K 65
Prichard Ho. SE11 ... 4J 19
(off Kennington Rd.)
Pricklers Hill EN5: New Bar ... 6E 20
Prickley Wood BR2: Hayes ... 1H 171
Priddy's Yd. CR0: C'don ... 2C 168
Prideaux Ho. WC1 ... 1H 7
(off Prideaux Pl.)
Prideaux Pl. W3 ... 7K 79
WC1 ... 1H 7 (3K 83)
Prideaux Rd. SW9 ... 3J 119
Pridham Rd. CR7: Thor H ... 4D 156
Priest Cl. TW12: Hamp ... 4E 130
Priestfield Rd. SE23 ... 3A 140
Priestlands Pk. Rd. DA15: Sidc ... 3K 143
Priestley Cl. N16 ... 7F 49
Priestley Gdns. RM6: Chad H ... 6B 54
Priestley Ho. EC1 ... 3D 8
(off Old St.)
HA9: Wemb ... 3J 61
(off Barnhill Rd.)
Priestley Rd. CR4: Mitc ... 2E 154
Priestley Way E17 ... 3K 49
NW2 ... 1C 62
Priestman Point E3 ... 3D 86
(off Rainhill Way)
Priest Pk. Av. HA2: Harr ... 2E 58
Priests Av. RM1: Rom ... 2K 55
Priests Bri. SW14 ... 3A 116
SW15 ... 3A 116
Priest's Ct. EC2 ... 7C 8
Prima Rd. SW9 ... 7A 102
Prime Meridian Line ... 7F 105
Prime Meridian Wlk. E14 ... 7F 87
Primeplace M. CR7: Thor H ... 2C 156
Primezone M. N8 ... 6J 47
Primrose Av. EN2: Enf ... 1J 23
RM6: Chad H ... 7B 54
Primrose Cl. E3 ... 2C 86
HA2: Harr ... 3D 58
N3 ... 2K 45
SE6 ... 5E 140
SM6: W'gton ... 7F 155
Primrose Ct. NW8 ... 2D 82
(off Prince Albert Rd.)
SW12 ... 7H 119
Primrose Gdns. HA4: Ruis ... 5A 58
NW3 ... 6C 64
WD23: Bush ... 1A 26
PRIMROSE HILL ... 1E 82
Primrose Hill EC4 ... 1K 13 (6A 84)
Primrose Hill Ct. NW3 ... 7D 64
Primrose Hill Rd. NW3 ... 7D 64
Primrose Hill Studios NW1 ... 1E 82
Primrose Ho. SE15 ... 1G 121
(off Peckham Hill St.)
SE16 ... 2A 104
(off Blondin Way)
Primrose La. CR0: C'don ... 1J 169
Primrose Mans. SW11 ... 1E 118
Primrose M. NW1 ... 7D 64
(off Sharpleshall St.)
SE3 ... 7J 105
Primrose Pl. TW7: Isle ... 2K 113
Primrose Rd. E10 ... 1D 68
E18 ... 2K 51
Primrose Sq. E9 ... 7J 67
Primrose St. EC2 ... 5G 9 (5E 84)
Primrose Wlk. KT17: Ewe ... 7B 164
SE14 ... 7A 104
Primrose Way HA0: Wemb ... 2D 78
SE10 ... 2E 122
Primula St. W12 ... 6C 80
Prince Albert Ct. NW8 ... 1D 82
(off Prince Albert Rd.)
TW16: Sun ... 7H 129
Prince Albert Mews SW11 ... 7C 100
Prince Albert Rd.
NW1 ... 1C 4 (3C 82)
NW8 ... 1C 4 (3C 82)
Prince Arthur M. NW3 ... 4A 64
Prince Arthur Rd. NW3 ... 5A 64
Prince Charles Cinema ... 2D 12
(off Leicester Pl.)
Prince Charles Dr. NW4 ... 7E 44

Prince Charles Rd.—Pymmes Gdns. Sth.

Prince Charles Rd. SE3 ... 2H 123
Prince Charles Way
SM6: W'gton ... 3F 167
Prince Consort Dr. BR7: Chst ... 1H 161
Prince Consort Rd.
SW7 ... 1A 16 (3A 100)
Princedale Rd. W11 ... 1G 99
Prince Edward Mans. *W2* ... *7J 81*
(off Moscow Rd.)
Prince Edward Rd. E9 ... 6B 68
Prince Edward Theatre ... *1D 12*
(off Old Compton St.)
Prince George Av. N14 ... 5C 22
Prince George Rd. N16 ... 4E 66
Prince George's Av. SW20 ... 2E 152
Prince George's Rd. SW19 ... 1B 154
Prince Henry Rd. SE7 ... 7B 106
Prince Imperial Rd.
BR7: Chst ... 1F 161
SE18 ... 1D 124
Prince John Rd. SE9 ... 5C 124
Princelet St. E1 ... 5K 9 (5F 85)
Prince of Orange Ct. *SE16* ... *3J 103*
(off Lower Rd.)
Prince of Orange La. SE10 ... 7E 104
Prince of Wales Cl. NW4 ... 4D 44
Prince of Wales Dr. SW8 ... 7F 101
SW11 ... 1C 118
Prince of Wales Mans.
SW11 ... 1E 118
Prince of Wales Pas. NW1 ... 2A 6
Prince of Wales Rd. E16 ... 6A 88
NW5 ... 6E 64
SE3 ... 2H 123
SM1: Sutt ... 2B 166
Prince of Wales Ter. W4 ... 5A 98
W8 ... 2K 99
Prince of Wales Theatre ... *3C 12*
(off Coventry St.)
Prince Regent Ct. *NW8* ... *2C 82*
(off Avenue Rd.)
SE16 ... *7A 86*
(off Edward Sq.)
Prince Regent La. E13 ... 3K 87
E16 ... 3K 87
Prince Regent M. NW1 ... 2A 6
Prince Regent Rd.
TW3: Houn ... 3F 113
Prince Rd. SE25 ... 5E 156
Prince Rupert Rd. SE9 ... 4D 124
Princes Arc. SW1 ... 4B 12
Prince's Av. UB6: G'frd ... 6F 77
Princes Av. BR5: Pet W ... 5J 161
IG8: Wfd G ... 4E 36
KT6: Surb ... 1G 163
N3 ... 1J 45
N10 ... 3F 47
N13 ... 5F 33
N22 ... 1H 47
NW9 ... 4G 43
SM5: Cars ... 7D 166
W3 ... 3G 97
Princes Cir. WC2 ... 7E 6 (6J 83)
Prince's Cl. TW11: Tedd ... 4H 131
Princes Cl. DA14: Sidc ... 3D 144
HA8: Edg ... 5B 28
N4 ... 1B 66
NW9 ... 4G 43
SW4 ... 3G 119
Prince's Ct. SE16 ... 3B 104
SW3 ... *1E 16*
(off Brompton Rd.)
Princes Ct. HA9: Wemb ... 5E 60
Princes Ct. Bus. Cen. E1 ... 7H 85
Princes Dr. HA1: Harr ... 3J 41
Prince's Gdns. SW7 ... 1B 16 (3B 100)
Princes Gdns. W3 ... 5G 79
W5 ... 4C 78
Prince's Ga. SW7 ... 7B 10 (2B 100)
(not continuous)
Prince's Ga. Ct. SW7 ... 7B 10 (2B 100)
Prince's Ga. M. SW7 ... 1B 16 (3B 100)
Princes Ho. W11 ... 7H 81
Princes La. N10 ... 3F 47
Prince's M. W2 ... 7K 81
Princes M. TW3: Houn ... 4E 112
W6 ... *5D 98*
(off Down Pl.)
Princes Pde. *NW11* ... *6G 45*
(off Golders Grn. Rd.)
Princes Pk. Av. NW11 ... 6G 45
UB3: Hayes ... 7F 75
Princes Pk. Circ. UB3: Hayes ... 7F 75
Princes Pk. Cl. UB3: Hayes ... 7F 75
Princes Pk. La. UB3: Hayes ... 7F 75
Princes Pk. Pde. UB3: Hayes ... 7F 75
Princes Pl. SW1 ... 4B 12
W11 ... 1G 99
Prince's Plain BR2: Broml ... 7C 160
Prince's Ri. SE13 ... 2E 122
Princes Riverside Rd.
SE16 ... 1K 103
Prince's Rd. SW19 ... 6J 135
TW11: Tedd ... 4H 131
Princes Rd. IG6: Ilf ... 4H 53
IG9: Buck H ... 2F 37
KT2: King T ... 7G 133
N18 ... 4D 34
SE20 ... 6K 139
SW14 ... 3K 115
TW9: Kew ... 1F 115
TW10: Rich ... 5F 115
TW13: Felt ... 2H 129
TW15: Ashf ... 5B 128
W13 ... 1B 96
Princessa Ct. EN2: Enf ... 5J 23
Princess Alice Ho. W10 ... 4E 80
Princess Alice Way SE28 ... 2H 107
Princess Av. HA9: Wemb ... 2E 60
Princess Cl. SE28 ... 6D 90
Princess Ct. *KT1: King T* ... *3F 151*
(off Horace Rd.)
N6 ... 7G 47
NW6 ... *6K 63*
(off Compayne Gdns.)
W1 ... *6E 4*
(off Bryanston Pl.)
W2 ... *7K 81*
(off Queensway)
Princess Cres. N4 ... 2B 66
Princess La. HA4: Ruis ... 1G 57
Princess Louise Bldg. *SE8* ... *7C 104*
(off Hales St.)
Princess Louise Cl. W2 ... 5B 4 (5B 82)
Princess Louise Wlk. W10 ... 5F 81
Princess Mary Ho. *SW1* ... *3D 18*
(off Vincent St.)
Princess May Rd. N16 ... 4E 66
Princess M. KT1: King T ... 3F 151
NW3 ... 5B 64
Princess Pde. BR6: Farnb ... 3E 172
RM10: Dag ... 2G 91
Princess Pk. Mnr. N11 ... 5K 31
Princes Sq. W2 ... 7K 81
(not continuous)
Princess Rd. CR0: C'don ... 6C 156
NW1 ... 1E 82
NW6 ... 2J 81
Princess St. SE1 ... 3B 102
Prince's St. EC2 ... 1E 14 (6D 84)
Princes St. DA7: Bex ... 3F 127
N17 ... 6K 33
SM1: Sutt ... 4B 166
TW9: Rich ... 4E 114
W1 ... 1K 11 (6F 83)
Princes Ter. E13 ... 1K 87
Prince's Twr. *SE16* ... *2J 103*
(off Elephant La.)
Prince St. SE8 ... 6B 104
Princes Way
BR4: W W'ck ... 4H 171
CR0: Wadd ... 5K 167
HA4: Ruis ... 4C 58
IG9: Buck H ... 2F 37
SW19 ... 7F 117
W3 ... 3G 97
Prince's Yd. W11 ... 1G 99
Princethorpe Ho. *W2* ... *5K 81*
(off Woodchester Sq.)
Princethorpe Rd. SE26 ... 4K 139
Princeton Ct. SW15 ... 3F 117
Princeton M. KT2: King T ... 1G 151
Princeton St.
WC1 ... 6G 7 (5K 83)
Prince William Ct. *T*
W15: Ashf ... *5B 128*
(off Clarendon Rd.)
Principal Cl. N14 ... 1B 32
Principal Pl. EC2 ... 4H 9
Principal Sq. E9 ... 5K 67
Pringle Gdns. SW16 ... 4G 137
(not continuous)
Printers Inn Ct. EC4 ... 6A 84
Printers M. E3 ... 1A 86
Printers Rd. SW9 ... 1K 119
Printer St. EC4 ... 7K 7 (6A 84)
Printing Ho. La. UB3: Hayes ... 2G 93
Printing Ho. Yd. E2 ... 1H 9 (3E 84)
Printon Ho. *E14* ... *5B 86*
(off Wallwood St.)
The Print Room ... *6J 81*
(off Hereford Rd.)
Print Room at the Coronet ... *1J 99*
(off Notting Hill Ga.)
Print Village SE15 ... 2F 121
Printwork Apts. *SE1* ... *7G 15*
(off Long La.)
SE5 ... *2C 120*
(off Coldharbour La.)
Priolo Rd. SE7 ... 5A 106
Prior Av. SM2: Sutt ... 7C 166
Prior Bolton St. N1 ... 6B 66
Prior Ct. KT8: W Mole ... 5D 148
Prioress Ho. *E3* ... *3D 86*
(off Bromley High St.)
Prioress Rd. SE27 ... 3B 138
Prioress St. SE1 ... 3E 102
Prior Rd. IG1: Ilf ... 3E 70
The Priors NW3 ... 3B 64
Priors Cft. E17 ... 2A 50
Priors Farm La. UB5: N'olt ... 6C 58
Priors Fld. UB5: N'olt ... 6C 58
Priors Gdns. HA4: Ruis ... 5A 58
Priors Mead EN1: Enf ... 1K 23
Prior St. SE10 ... 7E 104
Priors Wood KT10: Hin W ... 2A 162
The Priory CR0: Wadd ... 4A 168
N8 ... 4H 47
SE3 ... 4H 123
The Priory Apts. SE6 ... 1D 140
Priory Av. BR5: Pet W ... 6H 161
E4 ... 3G 35
E17 ... 5C 50
HA0: Wemb ... 4K 59
N8 ... 4H 47
SM3: Cheam ... 4F 165
W4 ... 4A 98
Priory Cl. BR3: Beck ... 3A 158
BR7: Chst ... 1D 160
E4 ... 3G 35
E18 ... 1J 51
HA0: Wemb ... 4K 59
HA4: Ruis ... 1H 57
HA7: Stan ... 3E 26
N3 ... 1H 45
N14 ... 5A 22
N20 ... 1C 30
SW19 ... 1K 153
TW12: Hamp ... 1D 148
TW16: Sun ... 7J 129
UB3: Hayes ... 7K 75
Priory Ct. E6 ... 1A 88
E9 ... 5K 67
E17 ... 2B 50
EC4 ... *1B 14*
(off Pilgrim St.)
HA0: Wemb ... 2E 78
KT1: King T ... *3E 150*
(off Denmark Rd.)
KT17: Ewe ... 7B 164
SM3: Cheam ... 4G 165
SW8 ... 1H 119
TW3: Houn ... 3F 113
WD23: Bush ... *1B 26*
(off Sparrows Herne)
Priory Ct. Est. E17 ... 2B 50
Priory Cres. HA0: Wemb ... 3A 60
SE19 ... 7C 138
SM3: Cheam ... 4F 165
Priory Dr. HA7: Stan ... 3E 26
SE2 ... 5D 108
Priory Fld. Dr. HA8: Edg ... 4C 28
Priory Gdns. HA0: Wemb ... 4A 60
N6 ... 6F 47
NW10 ... 3C 80
SE25 ... 4F 157
SW13 ... 3B 116
TW12: Hamp ... 7D 130
TW15: Ashf ... 5F 129
W4 ... 4A 98
W5 ... 3E 78
Priory Grange *N2* ... *3D 46*
(off Fortis Grn.)
Priory Grn. N1 ... 2K 83
Priory Grn. Est. N1 ... 2K 83
Priory Gro. EN5: Barn ... 5D 20
SW8 ... 1J 119
Priory Hgts. *N1* ... *2K 83*
(off Wynford Rd.)
Priory Hill HA0: Wemb ... 4A 60
Priory Ho. *E1* ... *5J 9*
(off Folgate St.)
EC1 ... *3A 8*
(off Sans Wlk.)
SW1 ... *5C 18*
(off Rampayne St.)
Priory La. KT8: W Mole ... 4F 149
SW15 ... 6A 116
Priory Leas SE9 ... 1C 142
Priory Lodge *W4* ... *5G 97*
(off Kew Bri. Ct.)
Priory Mans. *SW10* ... *5A 100*
(off Drayton Gdns.)
Priory M. SW8 ... 1J 119
Priory Pk. HA8: Edg ... 4C 28
SE3 ... 3H 123
Priory Pk. Rd. HA0: Wemb ... 4A 60
NW6 ... 1H 81
Priory Retail Pk. ... 7B 136
Priory Rd. CR0: C'don ... 7A 156
E6 ... 1B 88
IG11: Bark ... 7H 71
KT9: Chess ... 3E 162
N8 ... 4G 47
NW6 ... 1K 81
SM3: Cheam ... 4F 165
SW19 ... 7B 136
TW3: Houn ... 5G 113
TW9: Kew ... 6G 97
TW12: Hamp ... 7D 130
W4 ... 3K 97
Priory St. E3 ... 3D 86
Priory Ter. NW6 ... 1K 81
TW16: Sun ... 7J 129
Priory Vw. WD23: B Hea ... 1D 26
Priory Vs. *N11* ... *6J 31*
(off Colney Hatch La.)
Priory Wlk. SW10 ... 5A 100
TW16: Sun ... 7J 129
Priory Way HA2: Harr ... 4F 41
UB2: S'hall ... 3B 94
UB7: Harm ... 6A 92
Priscilla Cl. N15 ... 5C 48
Pritchard Ho. *E2* ... *2H 85*
(off Ada Pl.)
Pritchard's Rd. E2 ... 1G 85
Priter Rd. SE16 ... 3G 103
Priter Rd. Hostel *SE16* ... *3G 103*
(off Dockley Rd.)
Priter Way SE16 ... 3G 103
Private Rd. EN1: Enf ... 5J 23
Prize Wlk. E20 ... 5E 68
Probert Rd. SW2 ... 5A 120
Probyn Ho. *SW1* ... *3D 18*
(off Page St.)
Probyn Rd. SW2 ... 2B 138
Procter Ho. *SE1* ... *5G 103*
(off Avondale Sq.)
SE5 ... *7D 102*
(off Picton St.)
Procter St. WC1 ... 6G 7 (5K 83)
Proctor Cl. CR4: Mitc ... 1E 154
Proctors Cl. TW14: Felt ... 1J 129
Progress Bus. Pk. CR0: Wadd ... 2K 167
The Progress Cen. EN3: Pond E ... 3E 24
Progress Way CR0: Wadd ... 2K 167
EN1: Enf ... 5B 24
N22 ... 1A 48
Project Pk. E16 ... 4F 87
Project Rd. IG11: Bark ... 4B 90
Prologis Pk. CR0: Bedd ... 7H 155
E3 ... 4E 86
TW4: Houn ... 4A 112
The Promenade HA8: Edg ... 5B 28
W4 ... 2A 116
Promenade App. Rd. W4 ... 7A 98
Propeller Cres. CR0: Wadd ... 5A 168
Propeller Way NW4 ... 3C 44
Prospect Cl. DA17: Belv ... 4G 109
HA4: Ruis ... 7B 40
SE26 ... 4H 139
TW3: Houn ... 1D 112
Prospect Cotts. SW18 ... 4J 117
Prospect Cres. TW2: Whitt ... 6G 113
Prospect Hill E17 ... 4D 50
Prospect Ho. *E3* ... *3C 86*
(off Campbell Rd.)
E17 ... *3E 50*
(off Prospect Hill)
N1 ... *2A 84*
(off Donegal St.)
SE1 ... *3B 102*
(off Gaywood St.)
SE16 ... *3G 103*
(off Frean St.)
SW19 ... *1B 154*
(off Chapter Way)
W10 ... *6F 81*
(off Bridge Cl.)
Prospect Pl. BR2: Broml ... 3K 159
E1 ... 1J 103
(not continuous)
N2 ... 4B 46
N7 ... 4J 65
N17 ... 7K 33
NW2 ... 3H 63
NW3 ... 4A 64
RM5: Col R ... 2J 55
SE8 ... *6B 104*
(off Evelyn St.)
SW11 ... 7F 101
SW20 ... 7D 134
W4 ... 5K 97
Prospect Quay *SW18* ... *4J 117*
(off Lightermans Wlk.)
Prospect Ring N2 ... 3B 46
Prospect Rd. EN5: New Bar ... 4D 20
IG8: Wfd G ... 6F 37
KT6: Surb ... 6C 150
NW2 ... 3H 63
Prospect Row E15 ... 5E 68
Prospect Row Ho's. *E15* ... *5E 68*
(off Property Row)
Prospect St. SE16 ... 3H 103
Prospectus Pl. CR2: S Croy ... 6C 168
Prospect Va. SE18 ... 4C 106
Prospect Wharf E1 ... 7J 85
Prospero Ho. *E1* ... *2J 15*
(off Portsoken St.)
Prospero Rd. N19 ... 1H 65
Protea Cl. E16 ... 4H 87
Protea Pl. *E9* ... *7J 67*
(off Lyme Gro.)
Protheroe Ho. N17 ... 3F 49
Prothero Gdns. NW4 ... 5D 44
Prothero Ho. *NW10* ... *7K 61*
(off Fawood Av.)
Prothero Rd. SW6 ... 7G 99
Proton Twr. E14 ... 7F 87
Proud Ho. *E1* ... *6H 85*
(off Amazon St.)
Prout Gro. NW10 ... 4A 62
Prout Rd. E5 ... 3H 67
Provence St. N1 ... 2C 84
Providence Av. HA2: Harr ... 1E 58
Providence Cl. E9 ... 1K 85
Providence Ct. W1 ... 2H 11 (7E 82)
Providence Ho. *E14* ... *6B 86*
(off Three Colt St.)
Providence La. UB3: Harl ... 7F 93
Providence Pl. N1 ... 1B 84
RM5: Col R ... 1F 55
SE10 ... 5G 105
Providence Rd. UB7: Yiew ... 1A 92
Providence Row *N1* ... *2K 83*
(off Pentonville Rd.)
Providence Row Cl. E2 ... 3H 85
Providence Sq. SE1 ... 6K 15 (2G 103)
Providence Twr. *E14* ... *7F 87*
(off Fairmont Av.)
SE16 ... *2G 103*
(off Bermondsey Wall W.)
Providence Yd. *E2* ... *1K 9*
(off Ezra St.)
Provident Ind. Est. UB3: Hayes ... 2J 93
Province Dr. SE16 ... 2J 103
Province Sq. *E14* ... *1E 104*
(off Blackwall Way)
Provincial Ter. SE20 ... 7K 139
Provost Ct. *NW3* ... *6D 64*
(off Eton Rd.)
Provost Est. N1 ... 1E 8
Provost Rd. NW3 ... 7D 64
Provost St. N1 ... 1E 8 (2D 84)
Provost Way RM8: Dag ... 4A 72
Prowse Av. WD23: B Hea ... 1B 26
Prowse Ct. *N18* ... *5B 34*
(off Lord Graham M.)
Prowse Pl. NW1 ... 7G 65
Pryers Path HA1: Harr ... 7B 42
Prudence La. BR6: Farnb ... 4E 172
Pruden Cl. N14 ... 2B 32
Prudent Pas. EC2 ... 7D 8
Prusom's Island *E1* ... *1J 103*
(off Wapping High St.)
Prusom St. E1 ... 1H 103
Pryce Ho. *E3* ... *3C 86*
(off Campbell Rd.)
Puccinia Ct. *TW19: Stanw* ... *1A 128*
(off Yeoman Dr.)
Pucknells Cl. BR8: Swan ... 7J 145
Pudding La. EC3 ... 3F 15 (7D 84)
Pudding Mill La. E15 ... 1D 86
Puddle Dock EC4 ... 2A 14 (7B 84)
(not continuous)
Puffin Cl. BR3: Beck ... 5K 157
IG11: Bark ... 3B 90
Pugin Cl. SW19 ... 4K 135
Pugin Ct. *N1* ... *7A 66*
(off Liverpool Rd.)
Pulborough Rd. SW18 ... 7H 117
Pulborough Way TW4: Houn ... 4A 112
Pulford Rd. N15 ... 6D 48
Pulham Av. N2 ... 4A 46
Pulham Ho. *SW8* ... *7K 101*
(off Dorset Rd.)
Pullen's Bldgs. *SE17* ... *5B 102*
(off Iliffe St.)
Puller Rd. EN5: Barn ... 2B 20
Pulleyns Av. E6 ... 3C 88
Pullman Ct. SW2 ... 1J 137
Pullman Gdns. SW15 ... 6E 116
Pullman M. SE12 ... 3K 141
Pullman Pl. SE9 ... 5C 124
Pulross Rd. SW9 ... 3K 119
Pulse Apts. *NW6* ... *5K 63*
(off Lymington Rd.)
Pulse Ct. RM7: Rush G ... 6K 55
Pulsford Close TW1: Twick ... 7K 113
Pulteney Cl. E3 ... 1B 86
TW7: Isle ... 3A 114
Pulteney Gdns. E18 ... 3J 51
Pulteney Rd. E18 ... 3K 51
Pulteney Ter. N1 ... 1K 83
(not continuous)
Pulton Ho. *SE4* ... *4A 122*
(off Turnham Rd.)
Pulton Pl. SW6 ... 7J 99
Puma Ct. E1 ... 5J 9 (5F 85)
Pump All. TW8: Bford ... 7D 96
Pump Cl. UB5: N'olt ... 2E 76
Pump Ct. EC4 ... 1J 13 (6A 84)
The Pumphouse N8 ... 4K 47
Pump Ho. Cl. BR2: Broml ... 2G 159
SE16 ... 2J 103
Pump Ho. Cres. TW8: Bford ... 5E 96
Pump House Gallery ... 7E 100
Pump Ho. La. SW11 ... 7G 101
Pump Ho. M. *E1* ... *7G 85*
(off Hooper St.)
Pumping Ho. *E14* ... *7F 87*
(off Naval Row)
Pumping Station Rd. W4 ... 7A 98
Pump La. SE14 ... 7J 103
UB3: Hayes ... 2J 93
Pump Pail Nth. CR0: C'don ... 3C 168
Pump Pail Sth. CR0: C'don ... 3C 168
Punchard Cres. EN3: Enf L ... 1J 25
Punderson's Gdns. E2 ... 3H 85
Punjab La. UB1: S'hall ... 1D 94
Purbeck Av. KT3: N Mald ... 6B 152
Purbeck Dr. NW2 ... 2F 63
Purbeck Gdns. SE26 ... 5B 140
Purbeck Ho. *SW8* ... *7K 101*
(off Bolney St.)
Purbrook Est. SE1 ... 7H 15 (2E 102)
Purbrook St. SE1 ... 7H 15 (3E 102)
Purcell Cres. SW6 ... 7F 99
Purcell Ho. EN1: Enf ... 1B 24
SW10 ... *6B 100*
(off Milman's St.)
Purcell Mans. *W14* ... *6G 99*
(off Queen's Club Gdns.)
Purcell M. NW10 ... 7A 62
Purcell Rd. UB6: G'frd ... 5F 77
Purcell Room ... *4H 13*
(in Southbank Cen.)
Purcells Av. HA8: Edg ... 5B 28
Purcell St. N1 ... 2E 84
Purchese St. NW1 ... 1D 6 (2H 83)
Purday Ho. *W10* ... *3G 81*
(off Bruckner St.)
Purdon Ho. *SE15* ... *1G 121*
(off Oliver Goldsmith Est.)
Purdy Ct. KT4: Wor Pk ... 2C 164
Purdy St. E3 ... 4D 86
PureGym
Aldgate ... 7J 9
Bayswater ... *7K 81*
(off Moscow Pl.)
Canary Wharf ... 7C 86
Croydon ... *2C 168*
(off Crown Hill)
East India Dock ... *7E 86*
(off Clove Cres.)
Edgware ... 6B 28
Finchley ... 2K 45
Hallam St. ... *5K 5*
(off Hallam St.)
Hammersmith Palais ... 4E 98
Holborn ... *5G 7*
(off Theobald's Rd.)
Limehouse ... 6A 86
London Wall ... 6E 8
Marylebone, Balcombe St.
... 5E 4 (5D 82)
Muswell Hill ... 4F 47
New Barnet ... 4G 21
Northolt ... 1E 76
Piccadilly ... *4C 12*
(off Regent St.)
Putney ... 4G 117
St Pauls ... *6C 8*
(off Little Britain)
Southgate ... 1C 32
South Kensington
... 3C 16 (4C 100)
Sydenham ... 4J 139
Tower Hill ... 2J 15
Wembley ... 5E 60
Purelake M. *SE13* ... *3F 123*
(off Marischal Rd.)
Purkis Cl. UB8: Hil ... 7E 74
Purland Cl. RM8: Dag ... 1F 73
Purland Rd. SE28 ... 2K 107
(not continuous)
Purleigh Av. IG8: Wfd G ... 6H 37
Purley Av. NW2 ... 2G 63
Purley Cl. IG5: Ilf ... 2E 52
Purley Pl. N1 ... 7B 66
Purley Rd. CR2: S Croy ... 7D 168
N9 ... 3K 33
Purley Vw. Ter. *CR2: S Croy* ... *7D 168*
(off Sanderstead Rd.)
Purley Way CR0: C'don, Wadd ... 7K 155
The Purley Way Cen. ... 2A 168
Purley Way Cres. CR0: C'don ... 7K 155
Purneys Rd. SE9 ... 4B 124
Purrett Rd. SE18 ... 5K 107
Purser Ho. SW2 ... 6A 120
Pursers Cross Rd. SW6 ... 1H 117
Pursewardens Cl. W13 ... 1C 96
Pursley Rd. NW7 ... 7J 29
Purves Rd. NW10 ... 3D 80
Purvis Ho. CR0: C'don ... 7D 156
Pusey Ho. *E14* ... *6C 86*
(off Saracen St.)
Puteaux Ho. *E2* ... *2K 85*
(off Mace St.)
PUTNEY ... 4F 117
Putney Arts Theatre ... 4F 117
PUTNEY BRI. ... 3G 117
Putney Bri. App. SW6 ... 3G 117
Putney Bri. Rd. SW15 ... 4G 117
SW18 ... 4G 117
Putney Comn. SW15 ... 3E 116
Putney Exchange (Shop. Cen.) ... 4F 117
Putney Gdns. RM6: Chad H ... 5B 54
PUTNEY HEATH ... 6E 116
Putney Heath SW15 ... 7D 116
Putney Heath La. SW15 ... 6F 117
Putney High St. SW15 ... 4F 117
Putney Hill SW15 ... 7F 117
(not continuous)
Putney Leisure Cen. ... 4E 116
Putney Pk. Av. SW15 ... 4C 116
Putney Pk. La. SW15 ... 4D 116
(not continuous)
PUTNEY VALE ... 3C 134
Putney Va. Crematorium ... 2D 134
Putney Wharf SW15 ... 3G 117
Putt in the Pk. ... 4H 117
Pycroft Way N9 ... 4A 34
Pyecombe Cnr. N12 ... 4C 30
Pylbrook Rd. SM1: Sutt ... 3J 165
Pylon Way CR0: Bedd ... 1J 167
Pym Cl. EN4: E Barn ... 5G 21
Pymers Mead SE21 ... 1C 138
Pymmes Brook Dr. EN4: E Barn ... 4H 21
Pymmes Brook Ho. N10 ... 7K 31
Pymmes Cl. N13 ... 5E 32
N17 ... 1H 49
Pymmes Gdns. Nth. N9 ... 3A 34
Pymmes Gdns. Sth. N9 ... 3A 34

A-Z Big London 271

Pymmes Grn. Rd.—Radley's La.

Pymmes Grn. Rd. N11 4A 32
Pymmes Rd. N13 6D 32
Pynchester Cl. UB10: Ick 2C 56
Pyne Rd. KT6: Surb 1G 163
Pyne Ter. SW19 1G 135
(off Windlesham Gro.)
Pynfolds SE16 2H 103
Pynham Cl. SE2 3B 108
Pynnacles Cl. HA7: Stan 5G 27
Pynnersmead SE24 5C 120
Pyramid Ct. KT1: King T 2F 151
(off Cambridge Rd.)
Pyramid Ho. TW4: Houn 2C 112
Pyrford Ho. SW9 4B 120
Pyrland Rd. N5 5D 66
TW10: Rich 6F 115
Pyrmont Gro. SE27 3B 138
Pyrmont Rd. W4 6G 97
Pytchley Cres. SE19 6C 138
Pytchley Rd. SE22 3E 120

Q

The Q Bldg. E15 6G 69
(off The Grove)
QPR Training Academy & Sports Complex 3H 95
Quad Ct. SE1 3E 102
(off Grigg's Pl.)
The Quadrangle E15 6G 69
SE24 5C 120
SW6 7G 99
SW10 1A 118
W2 7C 4 (6C 82)
Quadrangle Cl. SE1 4E 102
Quadrangle M. HA7: Stan 7H 27
The Quadrant DA7: Bex 7D 108
HA2: Harr 3H 41
HA8: Edg 6B 28
(off Manor Pk. Cres.)
SM2: Sutt 6A 166
SW20 1G 153
TW9: Rich 4D 114
W10 3F 81
Quadrant Arc. W1 3B 12
Quadrant Bus. Cen. NW6 1G 81
Quadrant Cl. NW4 5D 44
Quadrant Ct. HA9: Wemb 4F 61
Quadrant Gro. NW5 5D 64
Quadrant Ho. E1 7G 85
(off Nesham St.)
E15 3G 87
(off Durban Rd.)
SE1 4A 14
Quadrant Rd. CR7: Thor H 4B 156
TW9: Rich 4D 114
Quadrant Wlk. E14 3D 104
(off Lanterns Way)
Quad Rd. HA9: Wemb 3D 60
Quaggy Wlk. SE3 4J 123
Quain Mans. W14 6G 99
(off Queen's Club Gdns.)
Quainton St. NW10 3K 61
Quaker Ct. E1 4J 9
(off Quaker St.)
EC1 3E 8
Quaker La. UB2: S'hall 3E 94
Quakers Course NW9 1B 44
Quakers La. TW7: Isle 7A 96
Quakers Pl. E7 5B 70
Quaker St. E1 4J 9 (4F 85)
Quakers Wlk. N21 5J 23
Quality Ct. WC2 7J 7
Quant Bldg. E17 4C 50
Quantock Cl. UB3: Harl 7F 93
Quantock Dr. KT4: Wor Pk 2E 164
Quantock Gdns. NW2 2F 63
Quantock Ho. N16 1F 67
Quantock M. SE15 2G 121
Quantum Ct. E1 7J 85
(off King David La.)
Quarles Pk. Rd. RM6: Chad H 6B 54
Quarrendon St. SW6 2J 117
Quarr Rd. SM5: Cars 6B 154
Quarry Pk. Rd. SM1: Sutt 6H 165
Quarry Ri. SM1: Sutt 6H 165
Quarry Rd. SW18 6A 118
The Quarterdeck E14 2C 104
Quarter Ho. SW18 4A 118
Quartermaster La. NW7 5B 30
Quarters Apts. CR0: C'don 2D 168
(off Wellesley Rd.)
Quartz Apts. SE14 6A 104
(off Moulding La.)
Quartz Ho. HA2: Harr 1E 58
Quastel Ho. SE1 7E 14
(off Long La.)
Quatre Ports E4 5A 36
Quay Ho. E14 2C 104
(off Admirals Way)
Quayle Cres. N20 2F 31
Quay Rd. IG11: Bark 1F 89
Quayside Cotts. E1 4K 15
(off Mews St.)
Quayside Ct. SE16 1K 103
(off Abbotshade Rd.)
Quayside Ho. E14 1B 104
E16 6H 87
(off Tarling Rd.)
TW8: Bford 6F 97
W10 4G 81
Quayside Wlk. KT1: King T 2D 150
(off Wadbrook St.)
Quay Vw. Apts. E14 3C 104
(off Arden Cres.)
Quebec M. W1 1F 11 (6D 82)
Quebec Rd. IG1: Ilf 7F 53
IG2: Ilf 7F 53
UB4: Yead 6A 76
Quebec Way SE16 2K 103
Quebec Wharf E8 1E 84
(off Kingsland Rd.)
E14 6B 86
Quedgeley Ct. SE15 6F 103
(off Ebley Cl.)
Queen Adelaide Ct. SE20 6J 139
Queen Adelaide Rd. SE20 6J 139
Queen Alexandra Mans. WC1 2E 6
(off Bidborough St.)
Queen Alexandra's Ct. SW19 5H 135
Queen Anne Alcove 3A 10
Queen Anne Av. BR2: Broml 3H 159
Queen Anne Ga. DA7: Bex 3D 126
Queen Anne Ho. E16 1J 105
(off Hardy Av.)
Queen Anne M. W1 6K 5 (5F 83)
Queen Anne Rd. E9 6K 67
Queen Anne's Cl. TW2: Twick 3H 131
Queen Anne's Ct. SE10 5F 105
(off Park Row)
Queen Anne's Gdns. CR4: Mitc 3D 154
EN1: Enf 6K 23
W4 3A 98
W5 2E 96
Queen Anne's Ga.
SW1 7C 12 (2H 101)
Queen Anne's Gro. EN1: Enf 7J 23
W4 3A 98
W5 2E 96
Queen Anne's Pl. EN1: Enf 6K 23
Queen Annes Sq. SE1 4G 103
(off Monnow Rd.)
Queen Anne St. W1 7J 5 (6F 83)
Queen Anne's Wlk. WC1 4F 7
Queen Anne Ter. E1 7H 85
(off Sovereign Cl.)
Queenborough Gdns. BR7: Chst 6H 143
IG2: Ilf 4E 52
Queen Caroline's Temple 5A 10 (1B 100)
Queen Caroline St. W6 5E 98
Queen Catherine Ho. SW6 7K 99
(off Wandon Rd.)
Queen Charlotte's Cottage 2D 114
Queen Ct. WC1 4F 7
(off Queen Sq.)
Queen Elizabeth II Stadium 2A 24
Queen Elizabeth Bldgs. EC4 2J 13
Queen Elizabeth Ct. EN5: Barn 3D 20
Queen Elizabeth Gdns.
SM4: Mord 4J 153
Queen Elizabeth Hall 4H 13 (1K 101)
Queen Elizabeth Ho. SW12 7E 118
Queen Elizabeth Leisure Cen. 4C 20
Queen Elizabeth II Conference Cen. 7D 12 (2H 101)
Queen Elizabeth Olympic Pk. 7D 68
Queen Elizabeth Rd. E17 3A 50
KT2: King T 2F 151
Queen Elizabeth's Cl. N16 2D 66
Queen Elizabeth's Coll. SE10 7E 104
Queen Elizabeth's Dr.
CR0: New Ad 7F 171
N14 1D 32
Queen Elizabeth's Hunting Lodge 1C 36
Queen Elizabeth St.
SE1 6J 15 (2E 102)
Queen Elizabeth's Wlk. N16 1D 66
SM6: Bedd 4H 167
Queen Elizabeth Wlk. SW13 1C 116
Queenhithe EC4 2D 14 (7C 84)
Queen Isabella Way EC1 7B 8
Queen Margaret Flats E2 3H 85
(off St Jude's Rd.)
Queen Margaret's Gro. N1 5E 66
Queen Mary Av. E18 1J 51
SM4: Mord 5F 153
Queen Mary Cl. KT6: Surb 3G 163
Queen Mary Ct. TW19: Stanw 1A 128
Queen Mary Ho. E16 1K 105
(off Wesley Av.)
E18 1K 51
Queen Mary Rd. SE19 6B 138
TW17: Shep 2E 146
Queen Mary's Av. SM5: Cars 7D 166
Queen Marys Bldgs. SW1 3B 18
(off Stillington St.)
Queen Mary's Ct. SE10 6F 105
(off Park Row)
Queen Mary's Ho. SW15 6C 116
Queen Mary University of London
Charterhouse Sq. 4B 8 (4B 84)
Lincoln's Inn Flds. Campus 7G 7
(off Remnant St.)
Mile End Campus 4A 86
W. Smithfield Campus 6B 8
Queen Mother Memorial 5C 12
The Queen Mother Sports Cen. 3A 18
Queen of Denmark Ct. SE16 3B 104
Queens Acre SM3: Cheam 7F 165
Queen's Av. UB6: G'frd 6F 77
Queens Av. HA7: Stan 3C 42
IG8: Wfd G 5E 36
N3 7F 31
N10 3E 46
N20 2G 31
N21 1G 33
TW13: Hanw 4A 130
Queensberry Ho. TW9: Rich 5C 114
Queensberry M. W.
SW7 3A 16 (4B 100)
Queensberry Pl. E12 5B 70
SW7 3A 16 (4B 100)
TW9: Rich 5D 114
(off Friars La.)
Queensberry Way
SW7 3A 16 (4B 100)
Queensborough Ct. N3 4H 45
(off Tillingbourne Gdns.)
Queensborough M. W2 7A 82
Queensborough Pas. W2 7A 82
(off Queensborough M.)
Queensborough Studios W2 7A 82
(off Queensborough M.)
Queensborough Ter. W2 7K 81
Queensbridge Ct. E2 1F 85
(off Queensbridge Rd.)
Queensbridge Pk. TW7: Isle 5J 113
Queensbridge Rd. E2 6F 67
E8 6F 67
Queensbridge Sports & Community Cen. 7F 67
QUEENSBURY 3E 42
Queensbury Circ. Pde.
HA3: Kenton 3E 42
HA7: Kenton 3E 42
Queensbury Rd. HA0: Wemb 2F 79
NW9 7K 43
Queensbury Sta. Pde. HA8: Edg 3F 43
Queensbury St. N1 7C 66
Queen's Cir. SW11 7F 101
Queens Cl. HA8: Edg 5B 28
SM6: W'gton 5F 167
Queen's Club Gdns. W14 6G 99
The Queen's Club
(Tennis Courts) 5G 99
Queens Club Ter. W14 6H 99
(off Normand Rd.)
Queen's Ct. NW8 2B 82
(off Queen's Ter.)
Queens Ct. CR2: S Croy 5C 168
(off Warham Rd.)
CR7: Thor H 5A 156
E11 7G 51
HA3: Kenton 2B 42
IG9: Buck H 2G 37
NW6 5K 63
NW11 5H 45
SE16 7K 15
SE23 2J 139
TW10: Rich 6F 115
W2 7K 81
(off Queensway)
Queenscourt HA9: Wemb 4E 60
Queen's Cres. NW5 6E 64
TW10: Rich 5F 115
Queenscroft Rd. SE9 5B 124
Queensdale Cres. W11 1F 99
(not continuous)
Queensdale Pl. W11 1G 99
Queensdale Rd. W11 1F 99
Queensdale Wlk. W11 1G 99
The Queen's Diamond Jubilee Galleries 1E 18 (3J 101)
Queensdown Rd. E5 4H 67
Queen's Dr. KT5: Surb 7G 151
KT7: T Ditt 6A 150
N4 2B 66
Queens Dr. E10 7C 50
W3 6F 79
W5 6F 79
Queen's Elm Pde. SW3 5B 16
(off Old Church St.)
Queen's Elm Sq. SW3 6B 16 (5B 100)
Queensferry Wlk. N17 4H 49
Queensfield Ct. SM3: Cheam 4E 164
Queen's Gallery 7K 11 (2F 101)
Queen's Gdns. NW4 5E 44
RM13: Rain 2K 91
TW5: Hest 1C 112
W2 7A 82
W5 4C 78
Queen's Ga. SW7 7A 10 (2A 100)
Queensgate Ct. N12 5E 30
Queen's Ga. Gdns. SW7 3A 100
Queens Ga. Gdns. BR7: Chst 1H 161
SW15 4D 116
Queensgate Ho. E3 2B 86
(off Hereford Rd.)
Queen's Ga. M. SW7 3A 100
Queensgate M. BR3: Beck 1A 158
Queen's Ga. Pl. SW7 3A 100
Queensgate Pl. NW6 7J 63
Queen's Ga. Pl. M.
SW7 2A 16 (3A 100)
Queen's Ga. Ter. SW7 1A 16 (3A 100)
Queens Ga. Vs. E9 7A 68
Queens Gro. NW8 1B 82
Queens Gro. Rd. E4 1A 36
Queen's Gro. Studios NW8 1B 82
Queen's Head Pas. EC4 7C 8 (6C 84)
Queen's Head St. N1 1B 84
Queen's Head Yd. SE1 5E 14
The Queen's House 6F 105
(within National Maritime Mus.)
Queens Ho. SE17 6D 102
(off Merrow St.)
SW8 7J 101
(off Sth. Lambeth Rd.)
TW11: Tedd 6K 131
W2 7K 81
(off Queensway)
Queenshurst Sq. KT2: King T 1E 150
Queen's Ice & Bowl 7K 81
Queen's Keep TW1: Twick 6C 114
Queensland Av. N18 6H 33
SW19 1K 153
Queensland Cl. E17 2B 50
Queensland Ho. E16 1E 106
(off Rymill St.)
Queensland Rd. N7 4A 66
Queens La. N10 3F 47
Queen's Mans. W6 4F 99
(off Brook Grn.)
Queen's Mkt. E13 1A 88
Queens Mead HA8: Edg 6A 28
Queensmead NW8 1B 82
Queens Mead Rd. BR2: Broml 2H 159
Queensmead Sports Cen. 5B 58
Queensmere Cl. SW19 2F 135
Queensmere Ct. SW13 7B 98
Queensmere Rd. SW19 2F 135
Queen's M. W2 7K 81
Queensmill Rd. SW6 7F 99
Queen's Pde. N11 5J 31
(off Friern Barnet Rd.)
NW2 6E 62
(off Willesden La.)
Queens Pde. N8 4B 48
NW4 5E 44
(off Queens Rd.)
W5 6F 79
Queen's Pde. Cl. N11 5J 31
QUEENS PARK 2G 81
Queens Pk. Ct. W10 3F 81
Queen's Pk. Gdns. TW13: Felt 3H 129
Queen's Pk. Rangers FC 1D 98
Queens Pas. BR7: Chst 6F 143
Queens Pl. SM4: Mord 4J 153
Queen's Prom.
KT1: King T, Surb 4D 150
Queen Sq. WC1 4F 7 (4J 83)
Queen Sq. Pl. WC1 4F 7
Queen's Quay EC4 2C 14
(off Up. Thames St.)
Queens Reach KT1: King T 2D 150
KT8: E Mos 4J 149
Queens Ride SW13 3C 116
Queens Ri. TW10: Rich 6F 115
Queen's Rd. CR4: Mitc 3B 154
DA16: Well 2B 126
E17 6B 50
EN1: Enf 4K 23
IG9: Buck H 2E 36
KT7: T Ditt 5K 149
SE14 1H 121
SE15 1H 121
SW14 3K 115
TW3: Houn 3F 113
TW10: Rich 7F 115
TW11: Tedd 6K 131
TW12: Hamp H 4F 131
TW13: Felt 1K 129
W5 6E 78
Queens Rd. BR1: Broml 2J 159
BR3: Beck 2A 158
BR7: Chst 6F 143
CR0: C'don 6B 156
E11 7F 51
E13 1K 87
EN5: Barn 3A 20
IG11: Bark 6G 71
KT2: King T 7G 133
KT3: N Mald 4B 152
N3 1A 46
N9 3C 34
N11 7D 32
NW4 5E 44
SM4: Mord 4J 153
SM6: W'gton 5F 167
SW19 6H 135
TW1: Twick 1A 132
UB2: S'hall 2B 94
UB3: Hayes 6G 75
UB7: W Dray 2B 92
Queens Rd. Est. EN5: Barn 3A 20
Queens Rd. W. E13 2J 87
Queen's Row SE17 6D 102
Queens St. TW15: Ashf 4B 128
Queen's Ter. E13 1K 87
NW8 1B 82
Queens Ter. E1 4J 85
(off Cephas St.)
KT7: T Ditt 6A 150
(off Queens Dr.)
TW7: Isle 4A 114
Queen's Ter. Cotts. W7 2J 95
Queen's Theatre 2C 12
(off Shaftesbury Av.)
Queensthorpe M. SE26 4K 139
Queensthorpe Rd. SE26 4K 139
Queen's Tower 1A 16
(within Imperial College London)
Queenstown M. SW8 2F 119
Queenstown Rd. SW8 1F 119
SW11 7J 17 (6F 101)
Queen St. CR0: C'don 4C 168
DA7: Bex 3F 127
EC4 2D 14 (7C 84)
(not continuous)
N17 6K 33
RM7: Rom 6K 55
W1 4J 11 (1F 101)
Queen St. Pl. EC4 2D 14 (7C 84)
Queensville Rd. SW12 7H 119
Queen's Wlk. N5 5B 66
SW1 5A 12 (1G 101)
TW15: Ashf 4A 128
W5 4C 78
Queens Wlk. E4 1A 36
HA1: Harr 4J 41
HA4: Ruis 2A 58
NW9 2J 61
The Queen's Wlk. SE1 4H 13 (1K 101)
Queens Wlk. Ter. HA4: Ruis 3A 58
Queen's Way NW4 5E 44
Queens Way TW13: Hanw 4A 130
Queensway BR4: W W'ck 3G 171
BR5: Pet W 5G 161
CR0: Wadd 6K 167
EN3: Pond E 4C 24
TW16: Sun 2K 147
W2 6K 81
Queensway Bus. Cen.
EN3: Pond E 4C 24
Queensway Ind. Est.
EN3: Pond E 4D 24
Queensway M. SE6 4E 140
(off Whitefoot La.)
Queenswell Av. N20 3H 31
Queenswood Av. CR7: Thor H 5A 156
E17 1E 50
SM6: Bedd 4H 167
TW3: Houn 2D 112
TW12: Hamp 6F 131
Queenswood Ct. KT2: King T 1G 151
SE27 4D 138
SW4 5J 119
Queenswood Gdns. E11 1K 69
Queenswood Pk. N3 2G 45
Queens Wood Rd. N10 6F 47
Queenswood Rd. DA15: Sidc 5K 125
SE23 3K 139
Queen's Yd. WC1 4B 6 (5G 83)
Queens Yd. E9 6C 68
QUEEN VICTORIA 4F 165
Queen Victoria Av. HA0: Wemb 7D 60
Queen Victoria Memorial 7A 12 (2G 101)
Queen Victoria Seaman's Rest
E14 6D 86
(off E. India Dock Rd.)
Queen Victoria Statue 1K 99
Queen Victoria St. EC4 2A 14 (7B 84)
Queen Victoria Ter. E1 7H 85
(off Sovereign Cl.)
Quemerford Rd. N7 5K 65
Quendon Ho. W10 4E 80
(off Sutton Way)
Quenington Ct. SE15 6F 103
Quentin Ho. SE1 6A 14
(off Chaplin Cl.)
Quentin Pl. SE13 3G 123
Quentin Rd. SE13 3G 123
Quernmore Cl. BR1: Broml 6J 141
Quernmore Rd. BR1: Broml 6J 141
N4 6A 48
Querrin St. SW6 2A 118
The Quest W11 7G 81
(off Clarendon Rd.)
Quested Ct. E8 5H 67
(off Brett Rd.)
The Questors Theatre 7C 78
Quex Ct. NW6 1K 81
(off West End La.)
Quex M. NW6 1J 81
Quex Rd. NW6 1J 81
Quiberon Ct. E13 1J 87
(off Pelly Rd.)
TW16: Sun 3J 147
Quick Rd. W4 5A 98
Quicks Rd. SW19 7K 135
Quick St. N1 2B 84
Quick St. M. N1 2B 84
Quickswood NW3 7C 64
Quiet Nook BR2: Hayes 3B 172
Quill Ho. E2 3K 9
(off Cheshire St.)
Quill La. SW15 4F 117
Quill St. N4 3A 66
W5 3E 78
Quilp St. SE1 6C 14 (2C 102)
(not continuous)
Quilters Pl. SE9 1G 143
Quilter St. E2 1K 9 (3G 85)
SE18 5K 107
Quilting Ct. SE16 2K 103
(off Garter Way)
Quince Ho. SE13 2D 122
(off Quince Rd.)
Quince Rd. SE13 2D 122
Quinn Cl. E2 2J 85
Quinnell Cl. SE18 5K 107
Quinta Dr. EN5: Barn 5A 20
Quintain Ho. KT1: King T 2D 150
(off Wood St.)
The Quintet KT12: Walt T 7J 147
Quintin Av. SW20 1H 153
Quintin Cl. HA5: Eastc 4K 39
Quinton Cl. BR3: Beck 3E 158
SM6: W'gton 4F 167
TW5: Cran 7K 93
Quinton Ct. SE16 4A 104
(off Plough Way)
Quinton Ho. SW8 7J 101
(off Wyvil Rd.)
Quinton Rd. KT7: T Ditt 1A 162
Quinton St. SW18 2A 136
Quixley St. E14 7F 87
Quorn Rd. SE22 4E 120

R

Rabbit Row W8 1J 99
Rabbits Rd. E12 4C 70
Rabournmead Dr. UB5: N'olt 5C 58
Raby Rd. KT3: N Mald 4K 151
Raby St. E14 6A 86
Raccoon Way TW4: Houn 2A 112
Rachel Cl. IG6: Ilf 3H 53
Racine SE5 1E 120
(off Sceaux Gdns.)
Rackham Cl. DA16: Well 2B 126
Rackham M. SW16 6G 137
Rackstraw Ho. NW3 7D 64
Racton Rd. SW6 6J 99
RADA
Chenies St. 5C 6
(off Chenies St.)
Gower St. 5C 6
RADA Studios 5C 6
(off Chenies St.)
Radbourne Av. W5 4C 96
Radbourne Cl. E5 4K 67
Radbourne Ct. HA3: Kenton 6B 42
Radbourne Cres. E17 2F 51
Radbourne Rd. SW12 7G 119
Radcliff Ct. E3 4B 86
(off Joseph St.)
Radcliffe Av. EN2: Enf 1H 23
NW10 2C 80
Radcliffe Gdns. SM5: Cars 7C 166
Radcliffe Ho. SE16 4H 103
(off Anchor St.)
SE20 1G 157
Radcliffe M. TW12: Hamp H 5G 131
Radcliffe Path SW8 2F 119
Radcliffe Rd. CR0: C'don 2F 169
HA3: W'stone 2A 42
N21 1G 33
SE1 3E 102
Radcliffe Sq. SW15 6F 117
Radcliffe Way UB5: N'olt 3B 76
Radcot Point SE23 3K 139
Radcot St. SE11 6K 19 (5A 102)
Raddington Rd. W10 5G 81
Raddon Twr. E8 6F 67
(off Dalston Sq.)
Radfield Way DA15: Sidc 7H 125
Radford Ct. SE15 7H 103
(off Old Kent Rd.)
Radford Est. NW10 3A 80
Radford Ho. E14 5D 86
(off St Leonard's Rd.)
N7 5K 65
Radford Rd. SE13 6E 122
Radford Way IG11: Bark 3K 89
Radio La. RM8: Dag 3B 72
Radipole Rd. SW6 1H 117
Radisson Ct. SE1 7G 15
(off Long La.)
Radius Apts. N1 1G 7
(off Omega Pl.)
Radius Pk. TW14: Felt 4H 111
Radland Rd. E16 6H 87
Radleigh Pl. BR3: Beck 6C 140
Radlet Av. SE26 3H 139
Radlett Cl. E7 6H 69
Radlett Pl. NW8 1C 82
Radley Av. IG3: Bark, Ilf 4A 72
Radley Cl. TW14: Felt 1H 129
Radley Ct. SE16 2K 103
Radley Gdns. HA3: Kenton 4E 42
Radley Ho. NW1 3E 4
(off Gloucester Pl.)
SE2 2D 108
(off Wolvercote Rd.)
Radley M. W8 3J 99
Radley Rd. N17 2E 48
Radley's La. E18 2J 51

272 A-Z Big London

Radleys Mead—Rayne Ho.

Radleys Mead RM10: Dag 6H 73
Radley Sq. E5 2J 67
Radley Ter. E16 5H 87
(off Hermit Rd.)
Radlix Rd. E10 1C 68
Radnor Av. DA16: Well 5B 126
HA1: Harr 5J 41
Radnor Cl. BR7: Chst 6J 143
CR4: Mitc 4J 155
Radnor Ct. HA3: Hrw W 1K 41
W7 6K 77
(off Copley Cl.)
Radnor Cres. IG4: Ilf 5D 52
SE18 7A 108
Radnor Gdns. EN1: Enf 1K 23
TW1: Twick 2K 131
Radnor Gro. UB10: Hil 2C 74
Radnor Ho. EC1 2D 8
(off Radnor St.)
SW16 2K 155
Radnor Lodge W2 1B 10
(off Sussex Pl.)
Radnor M. W2 1B 10 (6B 82)
Radnor Pl. W2 1C 10 (6C 82)
Radnor Rd. HA1: Harr 5H 41
NW6 1G 81
SE15 7G 103
TW1: Twick 1K 131
Radnor St. EC1 2D 8 (3C 84)
Radnor Ter. SM2: Sutt 7J 165
W14 4H 99
Radnor Wlk. CR0: C'don 6A 158
E14 4C 104
(off Barnsdale Av.)
SW3 6D 16 (5C 100)
Radnor Way NW10 4H 79
Radstock Av. HA3: Kenton 3A 42
Radstock Cl. N11 6K 31
Radstock St. SW11 7C 100
(not continuous)
Radway Ho. W2 5J 81
(off Alfred Rd.)
Raeburn Av. KT5: Surb 1H 163
Raeburn Cl. KT1: Hamp W 7D 132
NW11 6A 46
Raeburn Ho. UB5: N'olt 2B 76
(off Academy Gdns.)
Raeburn Rd. DA15: Sidc 6J 125
HA8: Edg 1G 43
UB4: Hayes 2F 75
Raeburn St. SW2 4J 119
RAF Bomber Command Memorial
6J 11 (2F 101)
Raffles Ho. NW4 4D 44
Rafford Way BR1: Broml 2K 159
RAF Mus. London 2C 44
RAF Uxbridge, Battle of Britain Bunker
1B 74
Ragged School Mus. 5A 86
Raggleswood BR7: Chst 1E 160
Raglan Cl. TW4: Houn 5D 112
Raglan Ct. CR2: S Croy 5B 168
E17 5E 50
HA9: Wemb 4F 61
SE12 5J 123
Raglan Rd. BR2: Broml 4A 160
DA17: Belv 4F 109
E17 5E 50
EN1: Enf 7A 24
SE18 5G 107
Raglan St. NW5 6F 65
Raglan Ter. HA2: Harr 4F 59
Raglan Way UB5: N'olt 6G 59
Ragley Cl. W3 2J 97
Ragwort Ct. SE26 5H 139
Rahere Ct. E1 4A 86
(off Toby La.)
Raider Cl. RM7: Mawney 1G 55
Railey M. NW5 5G 65
Railshead Rd. TW1: Isle 4B 114
TW7: Isle 4B 114
Railton Rd. SE24 4A 120
Railway App. HA1: Harr 4K 41
HA3: Harr 4K 41
N4 6A 48
RM7: Rush G 6K 55
SE1 5F 15 (1D 102)
SM6: W'gton 5F 167
TW1: Twick 7A 114
Railway Arches E1 6K 85
(off Barnardo St.)
E1 7H 85
(off Chapman St.)
E2 1J 9
(off Cremer St.)
E2 2F 85
(off Geffrye St.)
E2 1F 85
(off Laburnum St.)
E3 4B 86
(off Cantrell Rd.)
E7 4J 69
(off Winchelsea Rd.)
E8 7H 67
(off Martello Ter.)
E8 7H 67
(off Mentmore Ter.)
E10 1E 68
E11 1F 69
(off Grove Grn. Rd.)
E16 1J 105
W6 3E 98
W12 2E 98
(off Shepherd's Bush Mkt.)
Railway Av. SE16 2J 103
(not continuous)
Railway Children Wlk.
BR1: Broml 2J 141
Railway Cotts. E15 2G 87
(off Baker's Row)
SW19 4K 135
W6 2E 98
(off Sulgrave Rd.)
Railway Fields Local Nature Reserve
6B 48
Railway Gro. SE14 7B 104
Railway M. W10 6G 81
Railway Pas. TW11: Tedd 6A 132
Railway Pl. DA17: Belv 3G 109
Railway Ri. SE22 4E 120
Railway Rd. TW11: Tedd 4J 131
Railway Side SW13 3A 116
Railway Sidings Rd. SE16 3G 103
Railway Sta. Bri. E7 5K 69
Railway St. N1 2J 83
RM6: Chad H 7C 54
Railway Ter. E17 1E 50
SE13 5D 122
TW13: Felt 1J 129
Railway Wharf KT1: King T 1D 150
(off Thames Side)
Rainbird Cl. HA0: Wemb 2C 78
Rainborough Cl. NW10 6J 61
Rainbow Av. E14 5D 104
Rainbow Ct. SE14 6A 104
(off Chipley St.)
Rainbow Ind. Est. SW20 2D 152
UB7: Yiew 7A 74
Rainbow Quay SE16 3A 104
(not continuous)
Rainbow St. SE5 7E 102
Raine Gdns. IG8: Wfd G 4D 36
Rainer Apartment CR0: C'don 1D 168
(off Cherry Orchard Rd.)
Raines Ct. N16 2F 67
Raine St. E1 1H 103
Rainham Cl. SE9 6J 125
SW11 6C 118
Rainham Ho. NW1 1G 83
(off Bayham Pl.)
Rainham Rd. NW10 3E 80
Rainham Rd. Nth. RM10: Dag 2G 73
Rainham Rd. Sth. RM10: Dag 4H 73
Rainhill Way E3 3C 86
(not continuous)
Rainsborough Av. SE8 4A 104
Rainsborough Ho. SW15 5G 117
(off Stamford Sq.)
Rainsborough Sq. SW6 6J 99
Rainsford Cl. HA7: Stan 5H 27
Rainsford Rd. NW10 3G 79
Rainsford St. W2 7C 4 (6C 82)
Rainton Rd. SE7 5J 105
Rainville Rd. W6 6E 98
Raisins Hill HA5: Eastc 3A 40
Raith Av. N14 3C 32
Rajsee Apts. E2 3G 85
(off Bethnal Grn. Rd.)
Raleana Rd. E14 1E 104
Raleigh Av. SM6: Bedd 4H 167
UB4: Yead 5K 75
Raleigh Cl. HA4: Ruis 2H 57
HA5: Pinn 7B 40
NW4 5E 44
Raleigh Ct. BR3: Beck 1D 158
SE8 5A 104
(off Evelyn St.)
SE16 1K 103
(off Clarence M.)
SM6: W'gton 6F 167
W12 2E 98
(off Scott's Rd.)
W13 5B 78
Raleigh Dr. KT5: Surb 1J 163
N20 3H 31
Raleigh Gdns. CR4: Mitc 3D 154
(not continuous)
SW2 6K 119
Raleigh Ho. BR1: Broml 1J 159
(off Hammelton Rd.)
CR0: C'don 7K 155
(off Mitcham Rd.)
E14 2D 104
(off Admirals Way)
SW1 7C 18
(off Dolphin Sq.)
Raleigh M. BR6: Chels 5K 173
N1 1B 84
(off Packington St.)
Raleigh Rd. EN2: Enf 4J 23
N8 4A 48
SE20 7K 139
TW9: Rich 3F 115
TW13: Felt 3H 129
UB2: S'hall 5C 94
Raleigh St. N1 1B 84
Raleigh Way N14 1C 32
TW13: Hanw 5A 130
Rale La. E4 1A 36
Rally Bldg. E17 5B 50
Ralph Bayer Ct. E3 5C 86
(off Geoff Cade Way)
Ralph Brook Ct. N1 1F 9
(off Chart St.)
Ralph Ct. W2 6K 81
(off Queensway)
Ralph Perring Ct. BR3: Beck 4C 158
Ralston St.
SW3 6E 16 (5D 100)
Ramac Ind. Est. SE7 4K 105
Rama Cl. SW16 7J 137
Rama Ct. HA1: Harr 2J 59
Ramac Way SE7 4K 105
Rama La. SE19 7F 139
Ramar Ho. E1 5G 85
(off Hanbury St.)
Rambert 4J 13
(off Upper Ground)
Rambler Cl. SW16 4G 137
Rame Cl. SW17 5E 136
Ramilles Cl. SW2 6J 119
Ramillies Pl. W1 1A 12 (6G 83)
Ramillies Rd. DA15: Sidc 6B 126
NW7 2F 29
W4 4K 97
Ramillies St. W1 1A 12 (6G 83)
Ramones Ter. CR4: Mitc 4J 155
(off Yorkshire Rd.)
Rampart St. E1 6H 85
Ram Pas. KT1: King T 2D 150
Rampayne St. SW1 5C 18 (5H 101)
Ram Pl. E9 6J 67
Rampton Cl. E4 3H 35
Ram Quarter SW18 5K 117
Ramsay Ho. NW8 2C 82
(off Townshend Est.)
Ramsay M. SW3 7C 16 (6C 100)
Ramsay Rd. E7 4G 69
W3 3J 97
Ramscroft Cl. N9 7K 23
Ramsdale Rd. SW17 5E 136
Ramsden Dr. RM5: Col R 1G 55
Ramsden Rd. DA8: Erith 7K 109
N11 5J 31
SW12 6E 118
Ramsey Cl. NW9 6B 44
UB6: G'frd 5H 59
Ramsey Ct. CR0: C'don 2B 168
(off Church St.)
Ramsey Ho. SW9 7A 102
Ramsey Rd. CR7: Thor H 6K 155
Ramsey St. E2 4G 85
Ramsey Wlk. N1 6D 66
Ramsey Way N14 7B 22
Ramsfort Ho. SE16 4H 103
(off Camilla Rd.)
Ramsgate Cl. E16 1K 105
Ramsgate St. E8 6F 67
Ramsgill App. IG2: Ilf 4K 53
Ramsgill Dr. IG2: Ilf 5K 53
Rams Gro. RM6: Chad H 4E 54
Ram St. SW18 5K 117
Ram Twr. SW18 5K 117
Ramulis Dr. UB4: Yead 4B 76
Ramuswood Av. BR6: Chels 5J 173
Rancliffe Gdns. SE9 4C 124
Rancliffe Rd. E6 2C 88
Randall Av. NW2 2A 62
Randall Cl. DA8: Erith 6J 109
SW11 1C 118
Randall Ct. NW7 7H 29
Randall Pl. SE10 7E 104
Randall Rd. SE11 4G 19 (5K 101)
Randall Row SE11 4G 19 (4K 101)
Randalls Rents SE16 3B 104
(off Gulliver St.)
Randell's Rd. N1 1J 83
Randisbourne Gdns. SE6 3D 140
Randle Rd. TW10: Ham 4C 132
Randlesdown Rd. SE6 4C 140
(not continuous)
Randolph App. E16 6A 88
Randolph Av. W9 4A 4 (2K 81)
Randolph Cl. DA7: Bex 3J 127
KT2: King T 5J 133
Randolph Ct. NW8 1A 82
Randolph Cres. W9 4A 82
Randolph Gdns. NW6 2K 81
Randolph Gro. RM6: Chad H 5C 54
Randolph M. W9 4A 82
Randolph Rd. BR2: Broml 1D 172
E17 5D 50
UB1: S'hall 2D 94
W9 4A 82
Randolph St. NW1 7G 65
Randon Cl. HA2: Harr 2F 41
Ranelagh Av. SW6 3H 117
SW13 2C 116
Ranelagh Bri. W2 5K 81
Ranelagh Cl. HA8: Edg 4B 28
Ranelagh Cotts. SW1 5J 17
(off Ebury Bri. Rd.)
Ranelagh Dr. HA8: Edg 4B 28
TW1: Twick 4B 114
Ranelagh Gdns. E11 5A 52
IG1: Ilf 1D 70
SW6 3G 117
(not continuous)
W4 7J 97
W6 4B 98
Ranelagh Gdns. Mans. SW6 3G 117
(off Ranelagh Gdns.)
Ranelagh Gro. SW1 5H 17 (5E 100)
Ranelagh Ho. SW3 5E 16
(off Elystan Pl.)
Ranelagh M. W5 2D 96
Ranelagh Pl. KT3: N Mald 5A 152
Ranelagh Rd. E6 1E 88
E11 4G 69
E15 2G 87
HA0: Wemb 6D 60
N17 3E 48
N22 1K 47
NW10 2B 80
SW1 6B 18 (5G 101)
UB1: S'hall 1B 94
W5 2D 96
Ranfurly Rd. SM1: Sutt 2J 165
Rangbourne Ho. N7 5J 65
Rangefield Rd. BR1: Broml 5G 141
Rangemoor Rd. N15 5F 49
Ranger's House 1F 123
Ranger's Rd. E4 1B 36
Rangers Sq. SE10 1F 123
Range Way TW17: Shep 7C 146
Rangeworth Pl. DA15: Sidc 3K 143
Rangoon St. EC3 1J 15
Rankin Cl. NW9 3A 44
Rankine Ho. SE1 3C 102
(off Bath Ter.)
Ranleigh Gdns. DA7: Bex 7F 109
Ranmere St. SW12 1F 137
Ranmoor Cl. HA1: Harr 4H 41
Ranmoor Gdns. HA1: Harr 4H 41
Ranmore Av. CR0: C'don 3F 169
Ranmore Ct. KT6: Surb 5D 150
Ranmore Path BR5: St M Cry 4K 161
Ranmore Rd. SM2: Cheam 7F 165
Rannoch Cl. HA8: Edg 2C 28
Rannoch Rd. W6 6E 98
Rannock Av. NW9 7K 43
Ransome's Dock Bus. Cen.
SW11 7C 100
Ransom Rd. SE7 4A 106
Ranston St. NW1 5C 4 (5C 82)
Ranulf Rd. NW2 4H 63
Ranwell Cl. E3 1B 86
Ranwell Ho. E3 1B 86
(off Ranwell Cl.)
Ranworth Rd. N9 2D 34
Ranyard Cl. KT9: Chess 3F 163
Raphael Cl. KT1: King T 4D 150
Raphael Ct. SE16 5H 103
(off Stubbs Dr.)
Raphael Dr. KT7: T Ditt 7K 149
Raphael Ho. IG1: Ilf 2G 71
Raphael St. SW7 7E 10 (2D 100)
Raphen Apts. E3 2A 86
(off Medway Rd.)
Rapley Ho. E2 2K 9
(off Turin St.)
Raquel Ct. SE1 6G 15
(off Snowfields)
Rashleigh Ct. SW8 2F 119
Rashleigh Ho. WC1 2E 6
(off Thanet St.)
Rashleigh St. SW8 2F 119
(off Peardon St.)
Rasper Rd. N20 2F 31
Rastell Av. SW2 2H 137
RATCLIFF 5A 86
Ratcliffe Cl. SE12 7J 123
Ratcliffe Ct. SE1 7D 14
(off Gt. Dover St.)
Ratcliffe Cross St. E1 6K 85
Ratcliffe Ho. E14 6A 86
(off Barnes St.)
Ratcliffe La. E14 6A 86
Ratcliffe Orchard E1 7K 85
Ratcliff Rd. E7 5A 70
Rathbone Ho. E16 6H 87
(off Rathbone St.)
NW6 1J 81
Rathbone Mkt. E16 5H 87
Rathbone Pl. W1 6C 6 (5H 83)
Rathbone Sq. CR0: C'don 4C 168
W1 7C 6 (6G 83)
Rathbone St. E16 6H 87
W1 6B 6 (5G 83)
Rathcoole Av. N8 5K 47
Rathcoole Gdns. N8 5K 47
Rathfern Rd. SE6 1B 140
Rathgar Av. W13 1B 96
Rathgar Cl. N3 2H 45
Rathgar Rd. SW9 3B 120
Rathmell Dr. SW4 6H 119
Rathmore Rd. SE7 5K 105
Rathnew Ct. E2 3K 85
(off Meath Cres.)
Rathore Cl. RM6: Chad H 5D 54
Rattray Ct. SE6 2H 141
Rattray Rd. SW2 4A 120
Raul Rd. SE15 2G 121
Raveley St. NW5 4G 65
(not continuous)
Ravel Ho. SW11 3B 118
(off York Place)
Raven Cl. NW9 2A 44
RM7: Rush G 7G 55
Ravendale Rd. TW16: Sun 2H 147
Ravenet St. SW8 1F 119
SW11 1F 119
(not continuous)
Ravenfield Rd. SW17 3D 136
Ravenhill Rd. E13 2A 88
Raven Ho. SE16 4K 103
(off Tawny Way)
Ravenings Pde. IG3: Ilf 1A 72
Ravenna Rd. SW15 5F 117
Ravenor Ct. UB6: G'frd 4F 77
Ravenor Pk. Rd. UB6: G'frd 3F 77
Raven Rd. E18 2A 52
Raven Row E1 5H 85
Raven Row Contemporary Art Cen.
5F 85
Ravensbourne Apts. SW6 3A 118
(off Central Av.)
Ravensbourne Av. BR2: Broml 7F 141
BR3: Beck 7F 141
TW19: Stanw 1A 128
Ravensbourne Ct. SE6 7C 122
Ravensbourne Gdns. IG5: Ilf 1E 52
W13 5B 78
Ravensbourne Ho. BR1: Broml 5F 141
E15 6F 69
(off Forrester Way)
NW8 5C 4
(off Broadley St.)
Ravensbourne Mans. SE8 6C 104
(off Berthon St.)
Ravensbourne Pk. SE6 7C 122
Ravensbourne Pk. Cres. SE6 7B 122
Ravensbourne Pl. SE8 1C 122
SE13 2D 122
Ravensbourne Rd. BR1: Broml 3J 159
SE6 7B 122
TW1: Twick 6C 114
Ravensbourne Ter.
TW19: Stanw 1A 128
Ravensbury Av. SM4: Mord 5A 154
Ravensbury Ct. CR4: Mitc 4B 154
(off Ravensbury Gro.)
Ravensbury Gro. CR4: Mitc 4B 154
Ravensbury La. CR4: Mitc 4B 154
Ravensbury Path CR4: Mitc 4B 154
Ravensbury Rd. BR5: St P 3K 161
SW18 2K 135
Ravensbury Ter. SW18 2K 135
Ravenscar NW1 1G 83
(off Bayham St.)
Ravenscar Rd. BR1: Broml 4G 141
KT6: Surb 2F 163
Ravens Cl. BR2: Broml 2H 159
EN1: Enf 2K 23
KT6: Surb 6D 150
Ravens Ct. KT1: King T 5D 150
(off Uxbridge Rd.)
Ravenscourt TW16: Sun 1H 147
Ravenscourt Av. W6 4C 98
Ravenscourt Cl. HA4: Ruis 7E 38
Ravenscourt Gdns. W6 4C 98
Ravenscourt Pk. EN5: Barn 4A 20
W6 3C 98
Ravenscourt Pk. Mans. W6 3D 98
(off Paddenswick Rd.)
Ravenscourt Pl. W6 4D 98
Ravenscourt Rd. W6 4D 98
Ravenscourt Sq. W6 3C 98
Ravenscraig Rd. N11 4B 32
Ravenscroft Av. HA9: Wemb 1E 60
NW11 7H 45
(not continuous)
Ravenscroft Cl. E16 5J 87
Ravenscroft Cotts. EN5: New Bar 4D 20
Ravenscroft Cres. SE9 3D 142
Ravenscroft Pk. EN5: Barn 3A 20
Ravenscroft Rd. BR3: Beck 2J 157
E16 5J 87
W4 4J 97
Ravenscroft St. E2 1K 9 (2F 85)
Ravensdale Av. N12 4F 31
Ravensdale Gdns. SE19 7D 138
TW4: Houn 3C 112
Ravensdale Ind. Est. N16 6G 49
Ravensdale Mans. N8 6J 47
(off Haringey Pk.)
Ravensdale Rd. N16 7F 49
TW4: Houn 3C 112
Ravens Dene BR7: Chst 5D 142
Ravensdon St. SE11 6K 19 (5A 102)
Ravensfield Cl. RM9: Dag 4D 72
Ravensfield Gdns.
KT19: Ewe 5A 164
Ravens Ga. M. BR2: Broml 2G 159
Ravenshaw St. NW6 5H 63
Ravenshill BR7: Chst 1F 161
Ravenshurst Av. NW4 4E 44
Ravenside KT1: King T 5D 150
(off Portsmouth Rd.)
Ravenside Cl. N18 5E 34
Ravenside Retail Pk.
London 5E 34
Ravenslea Rd. SW12 7D 118
Ravensleigh Gdns.
BR1: Broml 5K 141
Ravensmead Rd. BR2: Broml 7F 141
Ravensmede Way W4 4B 98
Ravens M. SE12 5J 123
Ravenstone SE17 5E 102
Ravenstone Rd. N8 3A 48
NW9 6B 44
Ravenstone St. SW12 1E 136
Ravens Wlk. E20 6D 68
Ravens Way SE12 5J 123
Ravenswood DA5: Bexl 1E 144
Ravenswood Av. BR4: W W'ck 1E 170
KT6: Surb 2F 163
Ravenswood Ct. KT2: King T 6H 133
W3 3J 97
(off Bassington Rd.)
Ravenswood Cres.
BR4: W W'ck 1E 170
HA2: Harr 2D 58
Ravenswood Gdns. TW7: Isle 1J 113
Ravenswood Ind. Est. E17 4E 50
Ravenswood Rd. CR0: Wadd 3B 168
E17 4E 50
SW12 7F 119
Ravensworth Ct. SW6 7J 99
(off Fulham Rd.)
Ravensworth Rd. NW10 3D 80
SE9 3D 142
Raven Wharf SE1 6J 15
(off Lafone St.)
Ravey St. EC2 3G 9 (4E 84)
Ravine Gro. SE18 6J 107
Ravine Way SW11 6H 101
Rav Pinter Cl. N16 7E 48
Rawchester Cl. SW18 1H 135
Rawlings Cl. BR3: Beck 5E 158
BR6: Chels 5K 173
Rawlings Cres.
HA9: Wemb 3H 61
Rawlings St. SW3 3E 16 (4D 100)
Rawlins Cl. CR2: Sels 7B 170
N3 3G 45
Rawlinson Ct. NW2 7E 44
Rawlinson Ho. SE13 4F 123
(off Mercator Rd.)
Rawlinson Ter. N17 3F 49
Rawnsley Av. CR4: Mitc 5B 154
Rawreth Wlk. N1 1C 84
(off Basire St.)
Rawson St. SW11 1E 118
(not continuous)
Rawsthorne Cl. E16 1D 106
Rawsthorne Ct. TW4: Houn 4D 112
Rawstone Wlk. E13 2J 87
Rawstorne Pl. EC1 1A 8 (3B 84)
Rawstorne St. EC1 1A 8 (3B 84)
(not continuous)
Raybell Ct. TW7: Isle 2K 113
Rayburne Ct. IG9: Buck H 1F 37
W14 3G 99
Ray Cl. KT9: Chess 6C 162
Raydean Rd. EN5: New Bar 5E 20
Raydons Gdns. RM9: Dag 5E 72
Raydons Rd. RM9: Dag 5E 72
Raydon St. N19 2F 65
Rayfield Cl. BR2: Broml 6C 160
Rayford Av. SE12 7H 123
Ray Gdns. HA7: Stan 5G 27
IG11: Bark 2A 90
Ray Gunter Ho. SE17 5B 102
(off Marsland Cl.)
Ray Ho. N1 1E 84
(off Colville Est.)
W10 6F 81
(off Cambridge Gdns.)
Rayleas Cl. SE18 1F 125
Rayleigh Av. TW11: Tedd 6J 131
Rayleigh Cl. N13 3J 33
Rayleigh Ct. KT1: King T 2G 151
N22 1C 48
Rayleigh Ri. CR2: S Croy 6E 168
Rayleigh Rd. E16 1K 105
IG8: Wfd G 6F 37
N13 3H 33
SW19 1H 153
Ray Lodge Rd. IG8: Wfd G 6F 37
Ray Massey Way E6 1C 88
(off High St. Nth.)
Raymead Av. CR7: Thor H 5A 156
Raymede Towers W10 5F 81
(off Treverton St.)
Raymere Gdns. SE18 7H 107
Raymond Av. E18 3H 51
W13 3A 96
Raymond Bldgs. WC1 5H 7 (5K 83)
Raymond Chadburn Ho. E7 4K 69
Raymond Cl. SE26 5J 139
SL3: Poyle 4A 174
Raymond Ct. N10 7A 32
Raymond Postgate Ct. SE28 7B 90
Raymond Rd. BR3: Beck 4A 158
E13 1A 88
IG2: Ilf 7H 53
SW19 6G 135
Raymond Way KT10: Clay 6A 162
Raymouth Rd. SE16 4H 103
Raynald Ho. SW16 3J 137
Rayne Ct. E18 4H 51
Rayne Ho. SW12 6E 118
W9 4K 81
(off Delaware Rd.)

A-Z Big London 273

Rayner Cl.—Renforth St.

Rayner Cl. SM5: Cars 5D 166
Rayner Ct. W12 2E 98
(off Bamborough Gdns.)
Rayners Cl. HA0: Wemb 5D 60
Rayners Cres. UB5: N'olt 3K 75
Rayners Gdns.
UB5: N'olt 2K 75
RAYNERS LANE 1D 58
Rayners La. HA2: Harr 1E 58
HA5: Pinn 5D 40
Rayners Rd. SW15 5G 117
Rayners Ter. E14 6A 86
(off Carr St.)
Rayner Towers E10 7C 50
(off Albany Rd.)
Raynes Av. E11 7A 52
RAYNES PARK 4E 152
RAYNES PK. BRI. 2E 152
Raynes Pk. School Sports Cen.
3D 152
Raynham W2 7D 4
(off Norfolk Cres.)
Raynham Av. N18 6B 34
Raynham Ho. E1 4K 85
(off Harpley Sq.)
Raynham Rd. N18 5B 34
W6 4D 98
Raynham Ter. N18 5B 34
Raynor Cl. UB1: S'hall 1D 94
Raynor Pl. N1 7C 66
Raynton Cl. HA2: Harr 1C 58
UB4: Hayes 4H 75
Raynton Dr. UB4: Hayes 4H 75
Rayon Cl. SM6: W'gton 2E 166
Ray Rd. KT8: W Mole 5F 149
Rays Av. N18 4D 34
Rays Rd. BR4: W W'ck 7E 158
N18 4D 34
Ray St. EC1 4K 7 (4A 84)
RAY ST. BRI. 4K 7
Ray Wlk. N7 2K 65
Raywood Cl. UB3: Harl 7E 92
Raywood Mans. E20 6E 68
(off West Pk. Wlk.)
Razia M. E12 5D 70
Reachview Cl. NW1 7G 65
Read Cl. KT7: T Ditt 7A 150
Read Ct. E17 6C 50
Reade Ct. W3 3J 97
(off Stanley Rd.)
Reader Ho. SE5 1C 120
(off Badsworth Rd.)
Read Ho. SE11 7J 19
SE20 7H 139
(off Anerley Pk.)
Reading Cl. SE22 6G 121
Reading Ho. SE15 6G 103
(off Friary Est.)
W2 6A 82
(off Hallfield Est.)
Reading La. E8 6H 67
Reading Rd. SM1: Sutt 5A 166
UB5: N'olt 5F 59
Readman Ct. SE20 1H 157
Reads Cl. IG1: Ilf 3F 71
Ream Apts. SE23 2J 139
(off Clyde Ter.)
Reapers Cl. NW1 1H 83
Reapers Way TW7: Isle 5H 113
Reardon Ct. N21 2G 33
Reardon Ho. E1 1H 103
(off Reardon St.)
Reardon Path E1 1H 103
(not continuous)
Reardon St. E1 1H 103
Reaston St. SE14 7K 103
Rebecca Ct. DA14: Sidc 4B 144
Rebecca Ho. E3 4B 86
(off Brokesley St.)
N12 4E 30
(off Woodside Pk. Rd.)
Reckitt Rd. W4 5A 98
Record St. SE15 6J 103
Record Wlk. UB3: Hayes 2G 93
Recovery St. SW17 5C 136
Recreation Av. RM7: Rom 5J 55
Recreation Rd. BR2: Broml 2H 159
DA15: Sidc 3J 143
SE26 4K 139
UB2: S'hall 4C 94
Recreation Way CR4: Mitc 3H 155
Rector St. N1 1C 84
Rectory Bus. Cen.
DA14: Sidc 4B 144
Rectory Chambers SW3 7C 16
(off Old Church St.)
Rectory Cl. DA14: Sidc 4B 144
E4 3H 35
HA7: Stan 5G 27
KT6: Surb 1C 162
N3 1H 45
SW20 3E 152
TW17: Shep 3C 146
Rectory Ct. E18 1H 51
SM6: W'gton 4G 167
TW13: Felt 4A 130
Rectory Cres. E11 6A 52
(not continuous)
Rectory Farm 1A 112
Rectory Farm Rd. EN2: Enf 1E 22
(not continuous)
Rectory Field 7K 105
Rectory Fld. Cres. SE7 7A 106
Rectory Gdns. BR3: Beck 1C 158
(off Rectory Rd.)
N8 4J 47
SW4 3G 119
UB5: N'olt 1D 76
Rectory Grn. BR3: Beck 1B 158
Rectory Gro. CR0: C'don 2B 168
SW4 3G 119
TW12: Hamp 4D 130
Rectory La. DA14: Sidc 4B 144
HA7: Stan 5G 27
HA8: Edg 6B 28
KT6: Surb 1B 162
SM6: W'gton 4G 167
SW17 6E 136
Rectory Orchard SW19 4G 135
Rectory Pk. Av. UB5: N'olt 3D 76
Rectory Pl. SE18 4E 106
Rectory Rd. BR2: Kes 7B 172
BR3: Beck 1C 158
E12 5D 70
E17 4D 50
N16 2F 67
RM10: Dag 6H 73
SM1: Sutt 3J 165
SW13 2C 116
TW4: Cran 2A 112
UB2: S'hall 3D 94
UB3: Hayes 6J 75
W3 1H 97
Rectory Sq. E1 5K 85
Rectory Way UB10: Ick 2D 56
Reculver Ho. SE15 6J 103
(off Lovelinch Cl.)
Reculver M. N18 4B 34
Reculver Rd. SE16 5K 103
Red Anchor Cl. SW3 6B 100
Redan Pl. W2 6K 81
Redan St. W14 3F 99
Redan Ter. SE5 2B 120
Red Barracks Rd. SE18 4D 106
Redberry Gro. SE26 3J 139
Redbourne Av. N3 1J 45
Redbourne Dr. SE28 6D 90
(not continuous)
Redbourne Ho. E14 6B 86
(off Norbiton Rd.)
Redbourn Ho. W10 4E 80
(off Sutton Way)
REDBRIDGE 6C 52
Redbridge Ent. Cen. IG1: Ilf 2G 71
Redbridge Foyer IG1: Ilf 2G 71
(off Sylvan Rd.)
Redbridge Gdns. SE5 7E 102
Redbridge Ho. E16 7F 89
(off University Way)
Redbridge La. E. IG4: Ilf 6B 52
Redbridge La. W. E11 6K 51
REDBRIDGE RDBT. 6B 52
Redbridge Sports & Leisure Cen.
1H 53
Redburn Ind. Est. EN3: Pond E 6E 24
Redburn St. SW3 7E 16 (6D 100)
Redcar Cl. UB5: N'olt 5F 59
Redcar St. SE5 7C 102
Redcastle Cl. E1 7J 85
Red Cedars Rd. BR6: Orp 7J 161
Redchurch St. E2 3J 9 (4F 85)
Redcliffe Cl. SW5 5K 99
(off Old Brompton Rd.)
Redcliffe Ct. E5 3H 67
(off Napoleon Rd.)
Redcliffe Gdns. IG1: Ilf 1E 70
SW5 5K 99
SW10 5K 99
W4 7H 97
Redcliffe M. SW10 5K 99
Redcliffe Pl. SW10 6A 100
Redcliffe Rd. SW10 5A 100
Redcliffe Sq. SW10 5K 99
Redcliffe St. SW10 6K 99
Redclose Av. SM4: Mord 5J 153
Redclyffe Rd. E6 1A 88
Redclyf Ho. E1 4J 85
(off Cephas St.)
Redcourt CR0: C'don 3E 168
Red Cow La. EC1 3C 8 (4C 84)
Redcroft Rd. UB1: S'hall 7G 77
Red Cross Cotts. SE1 6D 14
(off Ayres St.)
Redcross Way SE1 6D 14 (2C 102)
Redding Ho. SE18 3C 106
The Reddings NW7 3G 29
Reddings Cl. NW7 4G 29
Reddins Rd. SE15 6G 103
Reddons Rd. BR3: Beck 7A 140
Redenham Ho. SW15 7C 116
(off Ellisfield Dr.)
Rede Pl. W2 6J 81
Redesdale Gdns. TW7: Isle 7A 96
Redesdale St. SW3 7D 16 (6C 100)
Redfern Av. TW4: Houn 7E 112
Redfern Ho. E13 1H 87
(off Redriffe Rd.)
NW8 1B 82
(off Dorman Way)
Redfern Rd. NW10 7A 62
SE6 7E 122
Redfield La. SW5 4J 99
Redfield M. SW5 4K 99
Redford Av. CR7: Thor H 4K 155
SM6: W'gton 6J 167
Redford Cl. TW13: Felt 2H 129
Redford Wlk. N1 1C 84
(off Popham St.)
Redgate Dr. BR2: Hayes 2K 171
Redgate Ter. SW15 6F 117
Redgrave Cl. CR0: C'don 6F 157
Redgrave Rd. SW15 3F 117
Redgrave Ter. E2 3G 85
(off Derbyshire St.)
Red Hill BR7: Chst 5F 143
Redhill Ct. SW2 2A 138
Redhill Dr. HA8: Edg 2H 43
Redhill St. NW1 1K 5 (2F 83)
Red House 4E 126
Red Ho. La. DA6: Bex 4D 126
Redhouse Rd. CR0: C'don 6H 155
Red Ho. Sq. N1 7C 66
Redif Ho. RM10: Dag 4H 73
Redington Gdns. NW3 4K 63
Redington Ho. N1 2K 83
(off Priory Grn. Est.)
Redington Rd. NW3 3K 63
Redknap Ho. TW10: Ham 3C 132
Redland Gdns. KT8: W Mole 4D 148
Redlands N15 4D 48
TW11: Tedd 6A 132
The Redlands BR3: Beck 2D 158
Redlands Ct. BR1: Broml 7H 141
Redlands Rd. EN3: Enf H 1F 25
Redlands Way SW2 7K 119
Red La. KT10: Clay 6A 162
Redleaf Cl. DA17: Belv 6G 109
Redleaves Av. TW15: Ashf 6D 128
Redlees Cl. TW7: Isle 4A 114
Red Leys UB8: Uxb 7A 56
Red Lion Bus. Pk.
KT6: Surb 3F 163
Red Lion Cl. SE17 6D 102
(off Red Lion Row)
Red Lion Ct. EC4 1K 13 (6A 84)
SE1 4D 14 (1C 102)
TW3: Houn 3F 113
(off Alexandra Rd.)
Red Lion Hill N2 2B 46
(not continuous)
Red Lion La. SE18 7E 106
Red Lion Pde. HA5: Pinn 3C 40
Red Lion Pl. SE18 1E 124
Red Lion Rd. KT6: Surb 2F 163
Red Lion Row SE17 6C 102
Red Lion Sq. SW18 5J 117
WC1 6G 7 (5K 83)
Red Lion St. TW9: Rich 5D 114
WC1 5G 7 (5K 83)
Red Lion Wlk. TW3: Houn 3F 113
(off High St.)
Red Lion Yd. W1 4H 11
Red Lodge BR4: W W'ck 1E 170
Red Lodge Cres. DA5: Bexl 3K 145
Red Lodge Rd. BR4: W W'ck 1E 170
DA5: Bexl 3K 145
Redlynch Ct. W14 2G 99
(off Addison Cres.)
Redlynch Ho. SW9 1A 120
(off Gosling Way)
Redman Cl. UB5: N'olt 2A 76
Redman Ho. EC1 5J 7
(off Bourne Est.)
SE1 7D 14
(off Borough High St.)
Redman's Rd. E1 5J 85
Redmead La. E1 1G 103
Redmead Rd. UB3: Harl 4G 93
Redmill Ho. E1 4H 85
(off Headlam St.)
Redmond Ho. N1 1K 83
(off Barnsbury Est.)
Redmore Rd. W6 4D 98
Red Oak Cl. BR6: Farnb 3F 173
CR0: C'don 2C 170
Redo Ho. E12 5E 70
(off Dore Av.)
Red Path E9 6A 68
Redpath Way SE10 2G 105
Red Pl. W1 2G 11 (7E 82)
Redpoll Way DA18: Erith 3D 108
Red Post Hill SE21 4D 120
SE24 4D 120
Red Post Ho. E6 7B 70
Redriffe Rd. E13 1H 87
Redriff Est. SE16 3B 104
Redriff Rd. RM7: Mawney 2H 55
SE16 4K 103
Redroofs Cl. BR3: Beck 1D 158
Redrose Trad. Cen.
EN4: E Barn 5G 21
RED ROVER 4C 116
Redrup Ho. SE14 6K 103
(off John Williams Cl.)
Redruth Cl. N22 7E 32
Redruth Gdns. KT10: Clay 7A 162
Redruth Ho. SM2: Sutt 7K 165
Redruth Rd. E9 1J 85
Redsan Cl. CR2: S Croy 7D 168
Redshank Ho. SE1 5F 103
(off Avocet Cl.)
Red Sq. N16 3D 66
Redstart Cl. E6 5C 88
SE14 7A 104
Redstart Mans. IG1: Ilf 3E 70
(off Mill Rd.)
Redston Rd. N8 4H 47
Redvers Rd. N22 2A 48
Redvers St. N1 1H 9 (3E 84)
Redwald Rd. E5 4K 67
Redway Dr. TW2: Whitt 7G 113
Redwing Ct. SE1 7D 14
(off Swan St.)
Redwing M. SE5 2C 120
Redwing Path SE28 2H 107
Redwing Rd. SM6: W'gton 7J 167
Redwood Cl. DA15: Sidc 1A 144
E3 2C 86
N14 7C 22
SE16 1A 104
UB10: Hil 2D 74
Redwood Ct. KT6: Surb 7D 150
N19 7H 47
NW6 7G 63
UB5: N'olt 3C 76
Redwood Est. TW5: Cran 6K 93
Redwood Gdns. E4 6J 25
Redwood Gro. W5 3B 96
Redwood Ho. EC1 2C 8
(off Bollinder Pl.)
HA9: Wemb 4G 61
(off Empire Way)
Redwood Mans. W8 3K 99
(off Chantry Sq.)
Redwood M. SW4 3F 119
TW15: Ashf 7F 129
(off Staines Rd. W.)
Redwoods SW15 1C 134
Redwoods Cl. IG9: Buck H 2E 36
Redwood Wlk. KT6: Surb 1D 162
Redwood Way EN5: Barn 5A 20
Reece M. SW7 3A 16 (4B 100)
Reed Av. BR6: Orp 3J 173
Reed Cl. E16 5J 87
SE12 5J 123
Reede Gdns. RM10: Dag 5H 73
Reede Rd. RM10: Dag 6G 73
Reede Way RM10: Dag 6H 73
Reedham Cl. N17 4H 49
Reedham St. SE15 2G 121
Reedholm Vs. N16 4D 66
Reed Ho. SW19 4K 135
Reed Pl. SW4 4H 119
Reed Rd. N17 2F 49
Reedsfield Cl. TW15: Ashf 3D 128
Reedsfield Rd. TW15: Ashf 4D 128
Reed's Pl. NW1 7G 65
Reedworth St. SE11 4K 19 (4A 102)
Reef Ho. E14 3E 104
(off Manchester St.)
Reef St. RM9: Dag 3E 90
Reenglass Rd. HA7: Stan 4J 27
Rees Dr. HA7: Stan 4K 27
Rees Gdns. CR0: C'don 6F 157
Reesland Cl. E12 6E 70
Rees St. N1 1C 84
Reeves Farm Cl. NW9 6A 44
Reeves Av. NW9 7K 43
Reeves Cnr. CR0: C'don 2B 168
Reeves Ho. SE1 7J 13
(off Baylis Rd.)
Reeves M. W1 3G 11 (7E 82)
Reeves Rd. E3 4D 86
SE18 6F 107
Reference Ho. NW9 3B 44
The Reflection E16 2F 107
(off Woolwich Mnr. Way)
Reflection Ho. E2 4G 85
(off Cheshire St.)
Reflex Apts. BR2: Broml 4K 159
(off Wheeler Pl.)
Reform Row N17 2F 49
Reform St. SW11 2D 118
Regal Bldg. W10 3F 81
Regal Cl. E1 5G 85
W5 5D 78
Regal Ct. CR4: Mitc 3D 154
N18 5A 34
NW6 2H 81
(off Malvern Rd.)
SW6 7J 99
(off Dawes Rd.)
Regal Cres. SM6: W'gton 3F 167
Regal Dr. N11 5A 32
Regal Ho. IG2: Ilf 6H 53
The Regal Ho. SW6 2A 118
Regalia Cl. E16 2K 105
Regalia Point E2 3K 85
(off Palmer's Rd.)
Regal La. NW1 1E 82
Regal Pl. E3 3B 86
SW6 7K 99
Regal Row SE15 1J 121
Regal Way HA3: Kenton 6E 42
Regal Wharf Apts. N1 1E 84
(off De Beauvoir Cres.)
Regan Ho. N18 6A 34
Regan Way N1 1G 9 (2E 84)
Regatta Ho. TW11: Tedd 4A 132
Regatta La. W6 6E 98
Regatta Point E14 2C 104
(off Westferry Rd.)
TW8: Bford 6F 97
Regency Cl. TW12: Hamp 5D 130
W5 6E 78
Regency Ct. BR2: Broml 6B 160
E3 2B 86
(off Norman Gro.)
E9 1J 85
(off Park Cl.)
E18 2J 51
EN1: Enf 5J 23
HA7: Stan 7J 27
(off Unwin Way)
SE8 7B 104
(off Glenville Gro.)
SM1: Sutt 4A 166
TW11: Tedd 6B 132
Regency Cres. NW4 2F 45
Regency Dr. HA4: Ruis 1G 57
Regency Gdns. KT12: Walt T 7A 148
Regency Ho. E16 1J 105
(off Pepys Cres.)
N3 2H 45
SW1 3D 18
(off Regency St.)
SW6 1A 118
(off The Boulevard)
Regency Lawn NW5 3F 65
Regency Lodge IG9: Buck H 2G 37
NW3 7B 64
(off Adelaide Rd.)
Regency M. BR3: Beck 1E 158
NW10 6C 62
SW9 7B 102
TW7: Isle 5J 113
Regency Pde. NW3 7B 64
(off Finchley Rd.)
Regency Pl. SW1 3D 18 (4H 101)
Regency St. NW10 4A 80
SW1 3D 18 (4H 101)
Regency Ter. SW7 5A 16
Regency Wlk. CR0: C'don 6B 158
TW10: Rich 5E 114
(off The Vineyard)
Regency Way DA6: Bex 3D 126
Regeneration House 1J 83
Regeneration Rd. SE16 4K 103
Regent Av. UB10: Hil 7D 56
Regent Bus. Cen.
UB3: Hayes 2K 93
Regent Cl. HA3: Kenton 6E 42
N12 5F 31
TW4: Cran 1K 111
Regent Ct. N3 7E 30
N20 2G 31
NW6 7H 63
(off Cavendish Rd.)
NW8 2C 4
W6 3D 98
(off Vinery Way)
W8 3K 99
(off Wright's La.)
Regent Gdns. IG3: Ilf 7A 54
Regent Ho. W14 4G 99
(off Windsor Way)
Regent Pde. SM2: Sutt 6A 166
Regent Pl. CR0: C'don 1F 169
SW19 5A 136
W1 2B 12 (7G 83)
Regent Rd. KT5: Surb 5F 151
SE24 6B 120
Regents Av. N13 5F 33
Regent's Bri. Gdns. SW8 7J 101
Regents Canal Ho. E14 6A 86
(off Commercial Rd.)
Regents Cl. CR2: S Croy 6E 168
HA8: Edg 4K 27
UB4: Hayes 5H 75
Regents Ct. BR1: Broml 7H 141
E8 1G 85
HA5: Pinn 2B 40
KT2: King T 1E 150
(off Sopwith Way)
Regents Dr. BR2: Kes 5B 172
IG8: Wfd G 6K 37
Regents Ga. Ho. E14 7A 86
(off Horseferry Rd.)
Regents Ho. E3 5C 86
(off Bow Common La.)
Regents M. NW8 2A 82
REGENT'S PARK 2K 5 (3F 83)
Regent's Pk. 1F 5 (2D 82)
Regent's Pk. Barracks 1K 5
Regents Pk. Est. NW1 1A 6
Regent's Pk. Gdns. M. NW1 1D 82
Regent's Pk. Ho. NW8 2D 4
(off Park Rd.)
Regent's Pk. Open Air Theatre
2G 5 (3E 82)
Regent's Pk. Rd. NW1 7D 64
(not continuous)
Regents Pk. Rd. N3 3H 45
Regent's Pk. Ter. NW1 1F 83
Regent's Pl. SE3 2J 123
Regents Pl. NW1 3A 6 (4G 83)
Regent's Pl. Plaza NW1 4G 83
Regents Plaza NW6 2K 81
(off Kilburn High Rd.)
Regent Sq. DA17: Belv 4H 109
E3 3D 86
WC1 2F 7 (3J 83)
Regent's Row E8 1G 85
Regents Studios E8 1H 85
Regent St. NW10 3F 81
SW1 3C 12 (7H 83)
W1 7K 5 (6F 83)
W4 5G 97
Regent Street Cinema 7K 5 (6F 83)
Regent's University London
3F 5 (4D 82)
Regents Wharf E2 1H 85
(off Wharf Pl.)
N1 2K 83
Regent Ter. SW8 6J 101
Regiment Hill NW7 6B 30
Regina Cl. EN5: Barn 3A 20
Regina Ho. SE20 1K 157
Reginald Ellingworth St.
RM9: Dag 1B 90
Reginald Pl. SE8 7C 104
(off Deptford High St.)
Reginald Rd. E7 7J 69
HA6: Nwood 1H 39
SE8 7C 104
Reginald Sorenson Ho. E11 7F 51
Reginald Sq. SE8 7C 104
Regina Point SE16 3J 103
(off Canada Est.)
Regina Rd. N4 1K 65
SE25 3G 157
UB2: S'hall 4C 94
W13 1A 96
Regina Ter. W13 1B 96
Regis Ct. CR4: Mitc 1C 154
N8 4K 47
NW1 5E 4
(off Melcombe Pl.)
Regis Ho. W1 5H 5
(off Beaumont St.)
Regis Pl. SW2 4K 119
Regis Rd. NW5 5F 65
Regnart Bldgs. NW1 3B 6
Regnas Ho. E15 6H 69
(off Carnarvon Rd.)
Regnolruf Ct. KT12: Walt T 7J 147
Regnum Apts. E1 4J 9
(off Wheler St.)
Reid Bldg. E3 4B 86
(off Eric St.)
Reid Cl. HA5: Eastc 4J 39
UB3: Hayes 6G 75
Reidhaven Rd. SE18 4J 107
Reigate Av. SM1: Sutt 1J 165
Reigate Rd. BR1: Broml 3H 141
IG3: Ilf 2K 71
Reigate Way SM6: W'gton 5J 167
Reighton Rd. E5 3G 67
Reindeer Cl. E13 1J 87
Reinickendorf Av. SE9 6G 125
Reis Pl. N15 4F 49
(off Blenheim Ri.)
Reizel Cl. N16 1F 67
Relay Rd. W12 7F 81
Relf Rd. SE15 3G 121
Reliance Arc. SW9 4A 120
Reliance Wharf N1 1E 84
Relko Gdns. SM1: Sutt 5B 166
Relton M. SW7 1D 16 (3C 100)
Rembrandt Cl. E14 3F 105
SW1 4G 17
Rembrandt Ct. KT19: Ewe 6B 164
SE16 5H 103
(off Stubbs Dr.)
Rembrandt Rd. HA8: Edg 2G 43
SE13 4G 123
Reminder La. SE10 3H 105
(not continuous)
Remington Rd. E6 6C 88
N15 6D 48
Remington St. N1 1B 8 (2B 84)
Remnant St. WC2 7G 7 (6K 83)
Remsted Ho. NW6 1K 81
(off Mortimer Cres.)
The Remus Bldg. EC1 2K 7
(off Hardwick St.)
Remus Rd. E3 7C 68
Renaissance Ct. SM1: Sutt 1A 166
TW3: Houn 3G 113
(off Prince Regent Rd.)
Renaissance Sq. W4 6A 98
Renaissance Wlk. SE10 3H 105
(off Teal St.)
Renbold Ho. SE10 1E 122
(off Blissett St.)
Rendalls HA1: Harr 1J 59
(off Grove Hill)
Rendel Apts. E16 7G 89
(off Lock Side Way)
Rendle Cl. CR0: C'don 5F 157
Rendle Ho. W10 4G 81
(off Wornington Rd.)
Rendlesham Rd. E5 4G 67
EN2: Enf 1G 23
Renforth St. SE16 3J 103

274 A-Z Big London

Renfree Way—Riverbank Rd.

Renfree Way TW17: Shep 7C 146
Renfrew Cl. E6 7E 88
Renfrew Ct. TW4: Houn 2C 112
Renfrew Ho. E17 2B 50
NW6 2K 81
(off Carlton Vale)
Renfrew Rd. KT2: King T 7H 133
SE11 3K 19 (4B 102)
TW4: Houn 2B 112
Renmuir St. SW17 6D 136
Rennell St. SE13 3E 122
Rennels Way TW7: Isle 2J 113
Renness Rd. E17 3A 50
Rennets Cl. SE9 5J 125
Rennets Wood Rd. SE9 5H 125
Rennie Cotts. E1 4J 85
(off Pemell Cl.)
Rennie Ct. EN3: Enf L 1H 25
SE1 4A 14
Rennie Est. SE16 4H 103
Rennie Ho. SE1 3C 102
(off Bath Ter.)
Rennie St. SE1 4A 14 (1B 102)
(not continuous)
SE10 3J 105
Renoir Ct. SE16 5H 103
(off Stubbs Dr.)
The Renovation E16 2F 107
(off Woolwich Mnr. Way)
Renown Cl. CR0: C'don 1B 168
RM7: Mawney 1G 55
Rensburg Rd. E17 5K 49
Renshaw Cl. DA17: Belv 6F 109
SE6 7C 122
Renters Av. NW4 6E 44
Renton Cl. SW2 6K 119
Renwick Dr. BR2: Broml 6B 160
Renwick Ind. Est.
IG11: Bark 2B 90
Renwick Rd. IG11: Bark 4B 90
Repens Way UB4: Yead 4B 76
Rephidim St. SE1 3E 102
Replingham Rd. SW18 1H 135
Reporton Rd. SW6 7G 99
Repository Rd. SE18 6D 106
Repton Av. HA0: Wemb 4C 60
UB3: Harl 4F 93
Repton Cl. SM5: Cars 5C 166
Repton Ct. BR1: Broml 6B 142
BR3: Beck 1D 158
Repton Gro. IG5: Ilf 1D 52
Repton Ho. E4 6K 35
E16 2K 105
(off Royal Crest Av.)
SW1 4B 18
(off Charlwood St.)
REPTON PARK 7K 37
Repton Rd. BR6: Chels 3K 173
HA3: Kenton 4F 43
Repton St. E14 6A 86
Repulse Cl. RM5: Col R 1G 55
Reservoir Cl. CR7: Thor H 3D 156
Reservoir Rd. HA4: Ruis 4E 38
N14 5B 22
SE4 2A 122
Reservoir Studios E1 6K 85
(off Cable St.)
Reservoir Way NW10 7C 62
Resham Cl. UB2: S'hall 3A 94
Residence Twr. N4 2C 48
(off Goodchild Rd.)
Resolution Plaza E1 7K 9
Resolution Wlk. SE18 3D 106
Resolution Way SE8 7C 104
(off Deptford High St.)
Restell Cl. SE3 6G 105
Restmor Way SM6: W'gton 2E 166
Reston Pl. SW7 2A 100
Restons Cres. SE9 6H 125
Restoration Sq. SW11 1B 118
Restormel Cl. TW3: Houn 5E 112
Restormel Ho. SE11 4J 19
Retcar Pl. N19 2F 65
Retford St. N1 1H 9 (2E 84)
Retingham Way E4 2J 35
Retles Ct. HA1: Harr 7J 41
The Retreat CR7: Thor H 4D 156
HA2: Harr 7E 40
KT4: Wor Pk 2D 164
KT5: Surb 6F 151
NW9 5K 43
SW14 3A 116
Retreat Cl. HA3: Kenton 5C 42
Retreat Ho. E9 6J 67
The Retreat Mobile Home Pk. 2D 36
Retreat Pl. E9 6J 67
Retreat Rd. TW9: Rich 5D 114
Reubens Ct. W4 5H 97
(off Chaseley Dr.)
Reuters Plaza E14 1D 104
(off The South Colonnade)
Reveley Sq. SE16 2A 104
Revell Ri. SE18 6K 107
Revell Rd. KT1: King T 2H 151
SM1: Sutt 6H 165
Revelon Rd. SE4 4A 122
Revelstoke Rd. SW18 2H 135
Reventlow Rd. SE9 1G 143
Reverdy Rd. SE1 4G 103
Reverend Cl. HA2: Harr 3F 59
Revesby Rd. SM5: Cars 6B 154
Review Lodge RM10: Dag 1H 91
Review Rd. NW2 2B 62
RM10: Dag 1H 91
Revolution Karting 5B 86
Rewell St. SW6 7A 100
Rewley Rd. SM5: Cars 6B 154
Rex Av. TW15: Ashf 6C 128
Rex Cl. RM5: Col R 1H 55
Rex Pl. W1 3H 11 (7E 82)
Reydon Av. E11 5A 52
Reynard Cl. BR1: Broml 3E 160
SE4 3A 122
Reynard Dr. SE19 7F 139
Reynard Pl. SE14 6A 104
Reynardson Rd. N17 7H 33
Reynard Way TW8: Bford 5C 96
Reynolah Gdns. SE7 5K 105
Reynolds Av. E12 5E 70
KT9: Chess 7E 162
RM6: Chad H 7C 54
Reynolds Cl. NW11 7K 45
SM5: Cars 1D 166
SW19 1B 154
Reynolds Ct. RM6: Chad H 3D 54
Reynolds Dr. HA8: Edg 3F 43
Reynolds Ho. E2 2J 85
(off Approach Rd.)
NW8 2B 82
(off Wellington Rd.)
SW1 4D 18
(off Erasmus St.)
Reynolds Pl. SE3 7K 105
TW10: Rich 6F 115
Reynolds Rd. KT3: N Mald 7K 151
SE15 4J 121
UB4: Yead 4A 76
W4 3J 97
Reynolds Sports Cen. 2G 97
Reynolds Way CR0: C'don 4E 168
Rheidol M. N1 2C 84
Rheidol Ter. N1 1C 84
Rheingold Way SM6: W'gton 7J 167
Rhein Ho. N8 3J 47
(off Campsfield Rd.)
Rheola Cl. N17 1F 49
Rhoda St. E2 3K 9 (4F 85)
Rhodes Av. N22 1G 47
Rhodes Ho. N1 1E 8
(off Provost St.)
Rhodesia Rd. E11 2F 69
SW9 2J 119
Rhodes Moorhouse Ct.
SM4: Mord 6J 153
Rhodes St. N7 5K 65
Rhodeswell Rd. E14 5A 86
(not continuous)
Rhodium Ct. E14 5C 86
(off Thomas Rd.)
Rhodrons Av. KT9: Chess 5E 162
Rhondda Gro. E3 3A 86
RHS Lawrence Hall 2C 18 (3H 101)
RHS Lindley Hall 3C 18
Rhyl Rd. UB6: G'frd 2K 77
Rhyl St. NW5 6E 64
Rhys Av. N11 7C 32
Rialto Rd. CR4: Mitc 2E 154
Ribble Cl. IG8: Wfd G 6F 37
Ribblesdale Av. N11 6K 31
UB5: N'olt 6F 59
Ribblesdale Ho. NW6 1J 81
(off Kilburn Vale)
Ribblesdale Rd. N8 4K 47
SW16 6F 137
Ribbon Dance M. SE5 1D 120
Ribbons Wlk. E20 5E 68
Ribchester Av. UB6: G'frd 3K 77
Ribston Cl. BR2: Broml 1D 172
Ricardo Path SE28 1C 108
Ricardo St. E14 6D 86
Ricards Rd. SW19 5H 135
Riccall Ct. NW9 1A 44
(off Pageant Av.)
Rice Pde. BR5: Pet W 5H 161
Riceyman Ho. WC1 2J 7
(off Lloyd Baker St.)
Richard Anderson Ct. SE14 7K 103
(off Monson Rd.)
Richard Burbidge Mans. SW13 6E 98
(off Brasenose Dr.)
Richard Burton Ct. IG9: Buck H 2F 37
(off Palmerston Rd.)
Richard Challoner Sports Cen. 7K 151
Richard Cl. SE18 4C 106
Richard Fell Ho. E12 4E 70
(off Walton Rd.)
Richard Fielden Ho. E1 3A 86
Richard Ho. SE16 4J 103
(off Silwood St.)
Richard Ho. Dr. E16 6B 88
Richard Neale Ho. E1 7H 85
(off Cornwall St.)
Richard Neve Ho. SE18 4J 107
(off Plumstead High St.)
The Richard Robert Residence
E15 6F 69
(off Salway Rd.)
Richard Ryan Pl. RM9: Dag 1E 90
Richards Av. RM7: Rom 6J 55
Richards Cl. HA1: Harr 5A 42
UB3: Harl 6F 93
UB10: Hil 7C 74
WD23: Bush 1B 26
Richards Fld. KT19: Ewe 7K 163
Richard Sharples Ct.
SM2: Sutt 7A 166
Richardson Cl. E8 1F 85
Richardson Ct. SW4 2J 119
(off Studley Rd.)
Richardson Gdns. RM10: Dag 6H 73
Richardson Rd. E15 2G 87
Richardson's M. W1 4A 6
Richard's Pl. SW3 3D 16 (4C 100)
Richards Pl. E17 3C 50
Richard St. E1 6H 85
Richard Tress Way E3 4B 86
Richbell WC1 5F 7
(off Boswell St.)
Richbell Pl. WC1 5G 7 (5K 83)
Richborne Ter. SW8 7K 101
Richborough Ho. SE15 6J 103
(off Sharratt St.)
Richborough Rd. NW2 4G 63
Richbourne Ct. W1 7D 4
(off Harrowby St.)
Richens Cl. TW3: Houn 2H 113
Riches Rd. IG1: Ilf 2G 71
Richfield Rd. WD23: Bush 1B 26
Richford Ga. W6 3E 98
Richford Rd. E15 1H 87
Richford St. W6 2E 98
Rich Ind. Est. SE1 4E 102
SE15 6H 103
Richland Ho. SE15 1G 121
(off Goldsmith Rd.)
Richlands Av. KT17: Ewe 4C 164
Rich La. SW5 5K 99
Richman Ho. SE8 5B 104
(off Grove St.)
Richmix Sq. E1 3K 9
(off Bethnal Grn. Rd.)
RICHMOND 5D 114
Richmond, The American International
University in London
Kensington Campus,
Ansdell Street 3K 99
(off Ansdell St.)
St Albans Grove 3K 99
Young Street 2K 99
Richmond Hill Campus 7E 114
Richmond & London Scottish RUFC
3D 114
Richmond Athletic Ground 3D 114
Richmond Av. E4 5A 36
N1 1K 83
NW10 6E 62
SW20 1G 153
TW14: Felt 6G 111
UB10: Hil 6D 56
RICHMOND BRI. 6D 114
Richmond Bldgs. W1 1C 12 (6H 83)
RICHMOND CIRCUS 4E 114
Richmond Cl. E17 6B 50
Richmond Cotts. W14 4G 99
(off Hammersmith Rd.)
Richmond Ct. CR4: Mitc 3B 154
E8 7H 67
(off Mare St.)
HA9: Wemb 3F 61
N11 6K 31
(off Pickering Gdns.)
NW6 7F 63
(off Willesden La.)
SW1 7F 11
(off Sloane St.)
W14 4G 99
(off Hammersmith Rd.)
Richmond Cres. E4 5A 36
N1 1K 83
N9 1B 34
Richmond Cricket Ground 3E 114
Richmond Dr. IG8: Wfd G 7K 37
TW17: Shep 6F 147
Richmond FC 3D 114
Richmond Gdns. HA3: Hrw W 7E 26
NW4 5C 44
Richmond Golf Course
Surrey 2E 132
Richmond Grn. CR0: Bedd 3J 167
Richmond Gro. KT5: Surb 6F 151
N1 7B 66
(not continuous)
Richmond Hill TW10: Rich 6E 114
Richmond Hill Ct. TW10: Rich 6E 114
Richmond Ho. E3 5C 86
(off Bow Common La.)
NW1 1K 5
(off Park Village E.)
SE17 5D 102
(off Portland St.)
Richmond Mans. SW5 5K 99
(off Old Brompton Rd.)
TW1: Twick 6D 114
Richmond M. SE6 1D 140
TW11: Tedd 5K 131
W1 1C 12 (6H 83)
Richmond Olympus Gym & Squash Club
Richmond 4D 114
Richmond Pde. TW1: Twick 6C 114
(off Richmond Rd.)
Richmond Pk. 1G 133
Richmond Pk. Golf Course 7A 116
Richmond Pk. Rd. KT2: King T 1E 150
SW14 5J 115
Richmond Pl. SE18 4G 107
Richmond Rd. CR0: Bedd 3J 167
CR7: Thor H 3B 156
E4 1A 36
E7 5K 69
E8 7F 67
E11 2F 69
EN5: New Bar 5E 20
IG1: Ilf 3G 71
KT2: King T 5D 132
N2 2A 46
N11 6D 32
N15 6E 48
SW20 1D 152
TW1: Twick 7B 114
TW7: Isle 3A 114
W5 2E 96
Richmond St. E13 2J 87
Richmond Ter. SW1 6E 12 (2J 101)
Richmond Theatre 4D 114
Richmond Way E11 2J 69
W12 2F 99
W14 3F 99
Richmount Gdns. SE3 3J 123
Rich St. E14 7B 86
Rickard Cl. NW4 4D 44
SW2 1A 138
Rickards Cl. KT6: Surb 2E 162
Rickett St. SW6 6J 99
Rickman Ho. E1 3J 85
(off Rickman St.)
Rickman St. E1 4J 85
Rickmansworth Rd. HA5: Pinn 2K 39
HA6: Nwood 1F 39
Rick Roberts Way E15 1E 86
Rickthorne Rd. N19 2J 65
Rickyard Path SE9 4C 124
Riddell Ct. SE5 5F 103
(off Albany Rd.)
Ridding La. UB6: G'frd 5K 59
Riddons Rd. SE12 3A 142
The Ride EN3: Pond E 3D 24
TW8: Bford 5B 96
Rideout St. SE18 4D 106
Rider Cl. DA15: Sidc 6J 125
Riders Twr. E17 5B 50
(off Track St.)
Rideway Dr. W3 3G 97
Ridgdale St. E3 2D 86
The Ridge BR6: Orp 2H 173
DA5: Bexl 7F 127
EN5: Barn 5C 20
KT5: Surb 5G 151
TW2: Whitt 7H 113
Ridge Av. N21 7H 23
Ridgebrook Rd. SE3 3B 124
Ridge Cl. NW4 2F 45
NW9 4K 43
SE28 2H 107
Ridge Ct. SE22 7G 121
Ridge Crest EN2: Enf 1E 22
Ridgecroft Cl. DA5: Bexl 1J 145
Ridge Hill NW11 1G 63
Ridgemead Cl. N14 2D 32
Ridgemont Gdns. HA8: Edg 4D 28
Ridgemount Av. CR0: C'don 1K 169
Ridgemount Cl. SE20 7H 139
Ridgemount Gdns. EN2: Enf 3G 23
Ridge Rd. CR4: Mitc 7F 137
N8 6K 47
N21 1H 33
NW2 3H 63
SM3: Sutt 1G 165
(not continuous)
Ridges Yd. CR0: C'don 3B 168
Ridgeview Cl. EN5: Barn 6A 20
Ridgeview Rd. N20 3E 30
Ridge Way SE19 6E 138
TW13: Hanw 3C 130
Ridgeway BR2: Hayes 2J 171
IG8: Wfd G 4F 37
The Ridgeway CR0: Wadd 3K 167
E4 2J 35
EN2: Enf 1E 22
HA2: Harr 5D 40
(not continuous)
HA3: Kenton 6C 42
HA4: Ruis 7J 39
HA7: Stan 6H 27
KT12: Walt T 7H 147
N3 7E 30
N11 4J 31
N14 2D 32
NW7 3H 29
NW9 4K 43
NW11 7G 45
W3 3G 97
Ridgeway Av. EN4: E Barn 6J 21
Ridgeway Cres. BR6: Orp 3J 173
Ridgeway Cres. Gdns.
BR6: Orp 2J 173
Ridgeway Dr. BR1: Broml 4K 141
Ridgeway E. DA15: Sidc 5K 125
Ridgeway Gdns. IG4: Ilf 5C 52
N6 7G 47
Ridgeway Rd. TW7: Isle 7J 95
Ridgeway Rd. Nth. TW7: Isle 6J 95
Ridgeway Wlk. UB5: N'olt 6C 58
(off Cowings Mead)
Ridgeway W. DA15: Sidc 5J 125
Ridgewell Cl. N1 1C 84
RM10: Dag 1H 91
SE26 4B 140
Ridgmount Gdns. WC1 5C 6 (5H 83)
Ridgmount Pl. WC1 5C 6 (5H 83)
Ridgmount Rd. SW18 5K 117
Ridgmount St. WC1 5C 6 (5H 83)
Ridgway SW19 7E 134
TW10: Rich 6E 114
The Ridgway SM2: Sutt 7B 166
Ridgway Ct. SW19 6F 135
Ridgway Gdns. SW19 7F 135
Ridgway Pl. SW19 6G 135
Ridgway Rd. SW9 3B 120
Ridgwell Rd. E16 5A 88
The Riding NW11 7H 45
Riding Ho. St. W1 6K 5 (5F 83)
The Ridings E11 5J 51
EN4: E Barn 7G 21
KT5: Surb 5G 151
KT17: Ewe 7B 164
TW16: Sun 1J 147
W5 4F 79
Ridings Av. N21 4G 23
Ridings Cl. N6 7G 47
Ridings La. UB4: Hayes 2F 75
Ridler Rd. EN1: Enf 1K 23
Ridley Av. W13 3B 96
Ridley Cl. IG11: Bark 7K 71
Ridley Ct. SW16 6J 137
Ridley Ho. SW1 2D 18
(off Monck St.)
Ridley Rd. BR2: Broml 3H 159
DA16: Well 1B 126
E7 4A 70
E8 5F 67
NW10 2C 80
SW19 7K 135
Ridsdale Rd. SE20 7H 139
Riefield Rd. SE9 4G 125
Riesco Dr. CR0: C'don 6J 169
Riffel Rd. NW2 5E 62
Rifle St. E14 5D 86
Riga M. E1 7K 9
Rigault Rd. SW6 2G 117
Rigby Cl. CR0: Wadd 3A 168
Rigby La. UB3: Hayes 2E 92
Rigby M. IG1: Ilf 2E 70
Rigden St. E14 6D 86
Rigeley Rd. NW10 3C 80
Rigg App. E10 1K 67
Rigge Pl. SW4 4H 119
Riggindale Rd. SW16 5H 137
Riley Ho. E3 4C 86
(off Ireton St.)
SW10 7B 100
(off Riley St.)
Riley Rd. EN3: Enf W 1D 24
SE1 7H 15 (3F 103)
Riley St. SW10 6B 100
Rill Ct. IG11: Bark 2G 89
(off Spring Pl.)
Rill Ho. SE5 7D 102
(off Harris St.)
Rill La. HA8: Edg 6E 28
Rima Ho. SW3 7A 16
(off Callow St.)
Rinaldo Rd. SW12 7F 119
The Ring SW7 7B 10 (2B 100)
W2 2C 10 (7B 82)
Ring Cl. BR1: Broml 7K 141
Ring Ct. SE1 6A 14
(off The Cut)
Ringcroft St. N7 5A 66
Ringcross Youth Cen. 5K 65
(off Lough Rd.)
Ringers Ct. BR1: Broml 3J 159
(off Ringers Rd.)
Ringers Rd. BR1: Broml 3J 159
Ringford Rd. SW18 5H 117
Ring Ho. E1 7J 85
(off Sage St.)
Ringles Ct. E6 1D 88
Ringlet Cl. E16 5K 87
Ringlewell Cl. EN1: Enf 2C 24
Ringmer Av. SW6 1G 117
Ringmer Gdns. N19 2J 65
Ringmer Pl. N21 5J 23
Ringmer Way BR1: Broml 5C 160
Ringmore Ri. SE23 7H 121
Ringmore Vw. SE23 7H 121
Ring Rd. W12 1E 98
(not continuous)
Ringsfield Ho. SE17 5C 102
(off Bronti Cl.)
Ringside Ct. SE28 1C 108
Ringslade Rd. N22 2K 47
Ringstead Rd. SE6 7D 122
SM1: Sutt 4B 166
Ring Way N11 6B 32
Ringway UB2: S'hall 5B 94
Ringwold Cl. BR3: Beck 7A 140
Ringwood Av. CR0: C'don 7J 155
N2 2D 46
Ringwood Cl. HA5: Pinn 3A 40
Ringwood Gdns. E14 4C 104
SW15 1C 134
Ringwood Rd. E17 6B 50
Ringwood Way N21 1G 33
TW12: Hamp H 4E 130
Rio Cinema 5E 66
(off Kingsland High St.)
Ripley Bldgs. SE1 6B 14
(off Rushworth St.)
Ripley Cl. BR1: Broml 5D 160
CR0: New Ad 6E 170
Ripley Ct. CR4: Mitc 2B 154
Ripley Gdns. SM1: Sutt 4A 166
(not continuous)
SW14 3K 115
Ripley Ho. SW1 7A 18
(off Churchill Gdns.)
Ripley M. E11 6G 51
Ripley Rd. DA17: Belv 4G 109
E16 6A 88
EN2: Enf 1H 23
IG3: Ilf 2K 71
TW12: Hamp 7E 130
Ripley Vs. W5 6C 78
Ripon Cl. UB5: N'olt 5E 58
Ripon Ct. N11 6K 31
(off Ribblesdale Av.)
Ripon Gdns. IG1: Ilf 6C 52
KT9: Chess 5D 162
Ripon Rd. N9 7C 24
N17 3D 48
SE18 6F 107
Rippersley Rd. DA16: Well 1A 126
The Ripple Nature Reserve 3B 90
Ripple Rd. IG11: Bark, Dag 7G 71
RM9: Dag 1B 90
RIPPLESIDE 1B 90
Rippleside Commercial Est.
IG11: Bark 2C 90
Ripplevale Gro. N1 7K 65
Rippolson Rd. SE18 5K 107
Ripston Rd. TW15: Ashf 5F 129
Risborough Cl. N10 3F 47
Risborough Dr.
KT4: Wor Pk 7C 152
Risborough Ho. NW8 3D 4
(off Mallory St.)
Risborough St. SE1 6B 14 (2B 102)
Risdon Ho. SE16 2J 103
(off Risdon St.)
Risdon St. SE16 3J 103
The Rise DA5: Bexl 7C 126
E11 5J 51
HA8: Edg 5C 28
IG9: Buck H 1G 37
N13 4F 33
NW7 6G 29
NW10 4K 61
UB6: G'frd 5A 60
UB10: Hil 2B 74
Risedale Rd. DA7: Bex 3J 127
Riseholme Ct. E9 6B 68
Riseldine Rd. SE23 6A 122
RISE PARK 2K 55
Rise Pk. Pde. RM1: Rom 2K 55
Risinghill St. N1 2K 83
Risingholme Cl. HA3: Hrw W 1J 41
WD23: Bush 1A 26
Risingholme Rd. HA3: Hrw W 2J 41
The Risings E17 4F 51
Rising Sun Ct. EC1 5B 8
Risley Av. N17 1C 48
Risley Cl. SM4: Mord 5K 153
Rita Rd. SW8 6J 101
Ritches Rd. N15 5C 48
Ritchie Ho. E14 6F 87
(off Blair St.)
N19 1H 65
SE16 3J 103
(off Howland Est.)
Ritchie Rd. CR0: C'don 6H 157
Ritchie St. N1 2A 84
Ritchings Av. E17 4A 50
Ritherdon Rd. SW17 2E 136
Ritson Ho. N1 1K 83
(off Barnsbury Est.)
Ritson Rd. E8 6G 67
Ritter St. SE18 6E 106
Ritz Pde. W5 4F 79
Ritzy Picturehouse 4A 120
(off Coldharbour La.)
The Riva Bldg. SE13 4F 123
Rivaz Pl. E9 6J 67
Riven Ct. W2 6K 81
(off Inverness Ter.)
Rivenhall Gdns. E18 4H 51
River App. HA8: Edg 1J 43
RIVER ASH ESTATE 7H 147
River Av. KT7: T Ditt 7A 150
N13 3G 33
River Av. Ind. Est. N13 5F 33
River Bank KT7: T Ditt 5K 149
KT8: E Mos 3J 149
N21 7H 23
TW12: Hamp 3E 148
Riverbank Rd. BR1: Broml 3J 141

A-Z Big London 275

Riverbank Way—Roman Ct.

Riverbank Way SM6: W'gton 1E 166
TW8: Bford 6C 96
River Barge Cl. E14 2E 104
River Brent Bus. Pk. W7 3J 95
River Cl. E11 6A 52
HA4: Ruis 6H 39
UB2: S'hall 2G 95
River Ct. KT6: Surb 5D 150
(off Portsmouth Rd.)
SE1 3A 14 (7B 84)
TW17: Shep 7E 146
Rivercourt Rd. W6 4D 98
River Crane Way TW13: Hanw 2D 130
(off Watermill Way)
Riverdale SE13 4E 122
Riverdale Cl. IG11: Bark 4B 90
Riverdale Ct. N21 5J 23
Riverdale Dr. SW18 1K 135
Riverdale Gdns. TW1: Twick 6C 114
Riverdale Ho. SE13 4E 122
Riverdale Rd. DA5: Bexl 7F 127
DA8: Erith 5H 109
SE18 5K 107
TW1: Twick 6C 114
TW13: Hanw 4C 130
Riverdale Shop. Cen. 3E 122
Riverdene HA8: Edg 3D 28
Riverdene Rd. IG1: Ilf 3E 70
Riverfleet WC1 1F 7
(off Birkenhead St.)
Riverford Ho. W2 5J 81
(off Westbourne Pk. Rd.)
River Front EN1: Enf 3K 23
River Gdns. SM5: Cars 2E 166
TW14: Felt 5K 111
River Gdns. Bus. Cen.
TW14: Felt 5K 111
River Gdns. Wlk. SE10 5G 105
River Gro. Pk. BR3: Beck 1B 158
Riverhead Cl. E17 2K 49
River Hgts. E15 1E 86
N17 1F 49
Riverhill KT4: Wor Pk 2K 163
Riverhill M. KT4: Wor Pk 3K 163
Riverhill Mobile Home Pk. 2K 163
Riverholme Dr. KT19: Ewe 7K 163
Riverhope Mans. SE18 3C 106
River Ho. SE26 3H 139
Riverhouse Barn 7H 147
River La. TW10: Ham 7D 114
Riverleigh Ct. E4 5G 35
Riverlight Quay SW11 7B 18 (6G 101)
River Lodge SW1 7B 18
(off Grosvenor Rd.)
Rivermead KT1: King T 5D 150
KT8: E Mos 3G 149
Rivermead Cl. TW11: Tedd 5B 132
Rivermead Ct. SW6 3H 117
Rivermead Ho. E9 5A 68
TW16: Sun 3A 148
(off Thames St.)
Rivermead Rd. N18 6E 34
Rivermeads Av. TW2: Twick 3E 130
River Mill One SE13 3E 122
(off Station Rd.)
River Mill Two SE13 3E 122
(off Station Rd.)
River Mt. KT12: Walt T 7H 147
Rivernook Cl. KT12: Walt T 5A 148
River Pk. Gdns. BR2: Broml 7F 141
River Pk. Rd. N22 2K 47
River Pl. N1 7C 66
River Reach TW11: Tedd 5C 132
River Rd. IG9: Buck H 1H 37
IG11: Bark 2J 89
River Rd. Bus. Pk. IG11: Bark 3K 89
Rivers Apts. N17 6A 34
(off Cannon Rd.)
Riversdale Gdns. N22 1A 48
Riversdale Rd. KT7: T Ditt 5A 150
N5 3B 66
RM5: Col R 1H 55
Riversfield Rd. EN1: Enf 3K 23
Rivers Ho. TW7: Isle 4B 114
(off Richmond Rd.)
TW8: Bford 5G 97
(off Aitman Dr.)
Riverside E3 1C 86
NW4 7D 44
SE7 3K 105
SW11 7C 100
TW1: Twick 1B 132
TW9: Rich 5D 114
TW10: Rich 5D 114
TW16: Sun 2B 148
TW17: Shep 7G 147
W6 6E 98
WC1 1F 7
(off Birkenhead St.)
The Riverside KT8: E Mos 3H 149
Riverside Apts. N4 7D 48
(off Goodchild Rd.)
N13 5E 32
Riverside Arts Cen. 3A 148
Riverside Av. KT8: E Mos 5H 149
Riverside Bus. Cen. SW18 1K 135
Riverside Bus. Pk. SW19 1A 154
Riverside Cl. E5 1J 67
KT1: King T 4D 150
RM1: Rom 4K 55
SM6: W'gton 3F 167
W7 4J 77
Riverside Cotts. IG11: Bark 2H 89
Riverside Ct. E4 6H 25
SE3 4H 123
SW8 7D 18 (6H 101)
TW7: Isle 2K 113
(off Woodlands Rd.)
TW14: Felt 7G 111
Riverside Dr. CR4: Mitc 5C 154
NW11 6G 45
TW10: Ham 3B 132
W4 7K 97
Riverside Gdns. EN2: Enf 2H 23
HA0: Wemb 2E 78
N3 3G 45
W6 5D 98
Riverside Ho. N1 7C 66
(off Canonbury St.)
Riverside Ind. Est. EN3: Pond E 6F 25
IG11: Bark 3A 90
Riverside Mans. E1 1J 103
(off Milk Yd.)
Riverside M. CR0: Bedd 3J 167
Riverside Pl. N11 3B 32
TW19: Stanw 6A 110
Riverside Rd. DA14: Sidc 3E 144
E15 2E 86
N15 6G 49
SW17 4K 135
TW19: Stanw 5A 110
Riverside Sq. N18 6E 34
Riverside Studios 5E 98
Riverside Twr. SW6 2A 118
(off The Boulevard)
Riverside Vs. KT6: Surb 6C 150
Riverside Wlk. BR4: W W'ck 1D 170
EN5: Barn 6A 20
(not continuous)
KT1: King T 3D 150
N12 6D 30
(not continuous)
TW7: Isle 3J 113
Riverside Wharf E3 1C 86
Riverside Works IG11: Bark 7F 71
Riverside Yd. SW17 4A 136
Riverstone Cl. HA2: Harr 1H 59
Riverstone Ct. KT2: King T 1F 151
River St. EC1 1J 7 (3A 84)
River St. M. EC1 1J 7
River Ter. WC2 3G 13
River Thames Vis. Cen. 6D 114
Riverton Cl. W9 3H 81
River Twr. SW8 7E 18 (6J 101)
River Vw. EN2: Enf 3H 23
Riverview Ct. E14 3B 104
River Vw. Gdns. TW1: Twick 2K 131
Riverview Gdns. SW13 6D 98
Riverview Gro. W4 6H 97
River Vw. Hgts. SE16 2G 103
(off Bermondsey Wall W.)
River Vw. M. CR0: Bedd 3J 167
Riverview Pk. SE6 2C 140
Riverview Rd. KT19: Ewe 4J 163
W4 7H 97
Riverview Wlk. SE6 3B 140
River Wlk. E4 7K 35
KT12: Walt T 6J 147
W6 7E 98
(not continuous)
Riverwalk SW1 5J 101
Riverwalk Apts. SW6 3A 118
(off Central Av.)
Riverwalk Bus. Pk. EN3: Brim 4G 25
Riverwalk Rd. EN3: Brim 4G 25
River Way BR3: Beck 1C 170
KT19: Ewe 5K 163
SE10 3H 105
TW2: Twick 2F 131
Riverway N13 5F 33
River Wharf Bus. Pk.
DA17: Belv 1K 109
Riverwood La. BR7: Chst 1H 161
Rivet Ho. SE1 5F 103
(off Cooper's Rd.)
Riviera Ct. E1 1G 103
(off St Katharine's Way)
Rivington Av. IG8: Wfd G 2B 52
Rivington Ct. NW10 1C 80
RM10: Dag 6H 73
Rivington Cres. NW7 7G 29
Rivington Pl. EC2 2H 9 (3E 84)
Rivington St. EC2 2G 9 (3E 84)
Rivington Wlk. E8 1G 85
Rivulet Apts. N4 7D 48
Rivulet Rd. N17 7H 33
Rixon Ho. SE18 6F 107
Rixon St. N7 3A 66
Rixsen Rd. E12 5C 70
Roach Rd. E3 7C 68
Roads Pl. N19 2J 65
Roan Gdns. CR4: Mitc 1D 154
Roan St. SE10 6E 104
Robarts Cl. HA5: Eastc 5K 39
Robbins Hall EN3: Pond E 6E 24
Robb Rd. HA7: Stan 6F 27
Robert Adam St. W1 7G 5 (6E 82)
Roberta St. E2 3G 85
Robert Bell Ho. SE16 4G 103
(off Rouel Rd.)
Robert Burns Ho. N17 7C 34
(off Northumberland Pk.)
Robert Burns M. SE24 5B 120
Robert Clack Leisure Cen. 1G 73
Robert Cl. W9 4A 4 (4A 82)
Robert Ct. SE15 2G 121
Robert Dashwood Way
SE17 4C 102
Robert Gentry Ho. W14 5G 99
(off Gledstanes Rd.)
Robert Jones Ho. SE16 4G 103
(off Rouel Rd.)
Robert Keen Cl. SE15 1G 121
Robert Lewis Ho. IG11: Bark 4B 90
Robert Lowe Cl. SE14 7K 103
Robert Morton Ho. NW8 7A 64
Roberton Dr. BR1: Broml 1A 160
Robert Owen Ho. E2 1K 9
(off Baroness Rd.)
N22 1A 48
(off Progress Way)
SW6 1F 117
Robert Runcie Ct. SW2 4K 119
Roberts All. W5 2D 96
Robertsbridge Rd. SM5: Cars 1A 166
Roberts Cl. CR7: Thor H 3D 156
IG11: Bark 6G 71
(off Tanner St.)
SE9 1H 143
SE16 2K 103
SM3: Cheam 7F 165
UB7: Yiew 1A 92
Roberts Ct. KT9: Chess 5D 162
N1 1B 84
(off Essex Rd.)
NW10 6A 62
SE20 1J 157
(off Maple Rd.)
Roberts M. SW1 1G 17 (3E 100)
Robertson Gro. SW17 5C 136
Robertson Rd. E16 5J 87
Robertson St. SW8 3F 119
Roberts Pl. EC1 3K 7 (4A 84)
RM10: Dag 6G 73
Robert Sq. SE13 4E 122
Roberts Rd. DA17: Belv 5G 109
E17 1D 50
Robert St. CR0: C'don 3C 168
E16 1F 107
NW1 2K 5 (3F 83)
SE18 5H 107
(not continuous)
WC2 3F 13 (7J 83)
Robert Sutton Ho. E1 6J 85
(off Tarling St.)
Robeson St. E3 5B 86
Robina Cl. DA6: Bex 4D 126
HA6: Nwood 1H 39
Robin Cl. NW7 3F 29
RM5: Col R 1K 55
TW12: Hamp 5C 130
Robin Ct. E14 2E 104
SE16 4G 103
SM6: W'gton 5G 167
Robin Cres. E6 5B 88
Robin Gro. HA3: Kenton 6F 43
N6 2E 64
TW8: Bford 6C 96
Robin Hill Dr. BR7: Chst 6C 142
ROBIN HOOD 3A 134
Robinhood Cl. CR4: Mitc 3G 155
Robin Hood Ct. EC4 7K 7
(off Shoe La.)
Robin Hood Dr. HA3: Hrw W 7E 26
Robin Hood Gdns. E14 7E 86
(off Woolmore St.)
Robin Hood Grn. BR5: St M Cry 5K 161
Robin Hood La. DA6: Bex 5E 126
E14 7E 86
SM1: Sutt 5J 165
SW15 3A 134
Robinhood La. CR4: Mitc 3G 155
Robin Hood Rd. SW19 5C 134
Robin Hood Way SW15 3A 134
SW20 3A 134
UB6: G'frd 6K 59
Robin Ho. NW8 2C 82
(off Newcourt St.)
Robin Howard Dance Theatre
(The Place) 2D 6
(off Duke's Rd.)
Robinia Cl. SE20 1G 157
(off Sycamore Gro.)
Robinia Cres. E10 2D 68
Robinia Ho. SE16 2A 104
(off Blondin Way)
Robin La. NW4 3F 45
Robin's Ct. BR3: Beck 2F 159
Robins Ct. CR2: S Croy 4E 168
(off Birdhurst Rd.)
SE12 3A 142
Robinscroft M. SE10 1E 122
Robins Gro. BR4: W W'ck 3J 171
Robinson Cl. E11 3G 69
EN2: Enf 3H 23
Robinson Ct. CR7: Thor H 6B 156
N1 1B 84
(off St Mary's Path)
TW9: Rich 4F 115
Robinson Cres. WD23: B Hea 1B 26
Robinson Ho. E14 5C 86
(off Selsey St.)
W10 6F 81
(off Bramley Rd.)
Robinson Rd. E2 2J 85
RM10: Dag 4G 73
SE1 4A 14 (1B 102)
SW17 6C 136
Robinson's Cl. W13 5A 78
Robinson St. SW3 7E 16 (6D 100)
Robinson Way SE14 7K 103
Robinswood Gdns. E17 1B 50
Robinswood M. N5 5B 66
Robinwood Gro. UB8: Hil 4B 74
Robinwood Pl. SW15 4K 133
Robsart St. SW9 2K 119
Robson Av. NW10 7C 62
Robson Cl. E6 6C 88
EN2: Enf 2G 23
Robson Rd. SE27 3C 138
Roby Ho. EC1 3C 8
(off Mitchell St.)
Roca Ct. E11 5J 51
Rocastle Rd. SE4 5A 122
Roch Av. HA8: Edg 2F 43
Rochdale Rd. E17 7C 50
SE2 5B 108
Rochdale Way SE8 7C 104
(not continuous)
Roche Ho. E14 7B 86
(off Beccles St.)
Rochelle Cl. SW11 4B 118
Rochelle St. E2 2J 9 (3F 85)
(not continuous)
Rochemont Wlk. E8 1G 85
(off Pownell Rd.)
Roche Rd. SW16 1K 155
Rochester Av. BR1: Broml 2K 159
E13 1A 88
TW13: Felt 2H 129
Rochester Cl. DA15: Sidc 6B 126
EN1: Enf 1K 23
SW16 7J 137
Rochester Ct. E2 4H 85
(off Wilmot St.)
NW1 7G 65
(off Rochester Sq.)
Rochester Dr. DA5: Bexl 6F 127
HA5: Pinn 5B 40
Rochester Gdns. CR0: C'don 3E 168
IG1: Ilf 7D 52
Rochester Ho. SE1 7F 15
(off Manciple St.)
SE15 6J 103
(off Sharratt St.)
Rochester M. NW1 7G 65
W5 4C 96
Rochester Pde. TW13: Felt 2J 129
Rochester Pl. NW1 6G 65
Rochester Rd. HA6: Nwood 3H 39
NW1 6G 65
SM5: Cars 4D 166
Rochester Row SW1 3B 18 (4G 101)
Rochester Sq. NW1 7G 65
Rochester St. SW1 2C 18 (3H 101)
Rochester Ter. NW1 6G 65
Rochester Wlk. SE1 4E 14 (1D 102)
Rochester Way DA1: Dart 7K 127
SE3 1K 123
SE9 3D 124
Rochester Way Relief Rd. SE3 1K 123
Roche Wlk. SM5: Cars 6B 154
Rochford N17 2E 48
(off Griffin Rd.)
Rochford Av. RM6: Chad H 5C 54
Rochford Cl. E6 2B 88
Rochford Wlk. E8 7G 67
Rochford Way CR0: C'don 6J 155
Rochfort Ho. SE8 5B 104
Rock Av. SW14 3K 115
Rockbourne M. SE23 1K 139
Rockbourne Rd. SE23 1K 139
Rock Cl. CR4: Mitc 2B 154
Rockell's Pl. SE22 6H 121
Rockfield Ho. NW4 4F 45
(off Belle Vue Est.)
SE10 6E 104
(off Welland St.)
Rockford Av. UB6: G'frd 2A 78
Rock Gdns. RM10: Dag 5H 73
Rock Gro. Way SE16 4G 103
(not continuous)
Rockhall Rd. NW2 4F 63
Rockhall Way NW2 3F 63
Rockhampton Cl. SE27 4A 138
Rockhampton Rd. CR2: S Croy 6E 168
SE27 4A 138
Rock Hill SE26 4F 139
(not continuous)
Rockingham Cl. SW15 4B 116
Rockingham St. SE1 3C 102
Rockland Rd. SW15 4G 117
Rocklands Dr. CR2: S Croy 6D 168
HA7: Stan 2B 42
Rockley Ct. W14 2F 99
(off Rockley Rd.)
Rockley Rd. W14 2F 99
Rockmount Rd. SE18 5K 107
SE19 6D 138
Rocks La. SW13 1C 116
Rock St. N4 2A 66
Rockware Av. UB6: G'frd 1H 77
Rockware Av. Bus. Cen.
UB6: G'frd 1H 77
Rockwell Gdns. SE19 5E 138
Rockwell Rd. RM10: Dag 5H 73
Rockwood Pl. W12 2E 98
Rocliffe St. N1 2B 84
Rocombe Cres. SE23 7J 121
Rocque Ho. SW6 7H 99
(off Estcourt Rd.)
Rocque La. SE3 3H 123
Rodale Mans. SW18 6K 117
Rodborough Ct. W9 4J 81
(off Hermes Cl.)
Rodborough Rd. NW11 1J 63
Rodd Est. TW17: Shep 5E 146
Roden Ct. N6 7H 47
Roden Gdns. CR0: C'don 6E 156
Rodenhurst Rd. SW4 6G 119
Roden St. IG1: Ilf 3E 70
N7 3K 65
Roden Way IG1: Ilf 3E 70
(off Roden St.)
Roderick Ho. SE16 4J 103
(off Raymouth Rd.)
Roderick Rd. NW3 4D 64
Rodgers Ho. SW4 7H 119
(off Clapham Pk. Est.)
Rodin Ct. N1 1B 84
(off Essex Rd.)
Roding Av. IG8: Wfd G 6H 37
Roding Ho. N1 1A 84
(off Barnsbury Est.)
Roding La. IG7: Chig 2K 37
IG9: Buck H 1G 37
Roding La. Nth. IG8: Wfd G 6H 37
Roding La. Sth. IG4: Ilf, Wfd G 4B 52
(not continuous)
IG8: Wfd G 4B 52
Roding M. E1 1G 103
Roding Rd. E5 4K 67
E6 5F 89
The Rodings IG8: Wfd G 6F 37
Roding Trad. Est. IG11: Bark 7F 71
Roding Valley Meadows Nature Reserve 1K 37
Roding Vw. IG9: Buck H 1G 37
Rodmarton St. W1 6F 5 (5D 82)
Rodmell WC1 2F 7
(off Regent Sq.)
Rodmell Cl. UB4: Yead 4C 76
Rodmell Slope N12 5C 30
Rodmere St. SE10 5G 105
Rodmill La. SW2 7J 119
Rodney Cl. CR0: C'don 1B 168
HA5: Pinn 7C 40
KT3: N Mald 5A 152
Rodney Ct. EN5: Barn 3C 20
W9 3A 4 (4A 82)
Rodney Gdns. BR4: W W'ck 4J 171
HA5: Eastc 5K 39
Rodney Ho. E14 4D 104
(off Cahir St.)
N1 2K 83
(off Donegal St.)
SW1 6B 18
(off Dolphin Sq.)
W11 7J 81
(off Pembridge Cres.)
Rodney Pl. E17 2A 50
SE17 4C 102
SW19 1A 154
Rodney Point SE16 2B 104
(off Rotherhithe St.)
Rodney Rd. CR4: Mitc 3C 154
E11 4K 51
KT3: N Mald 5A 152
SE17 4C 102
(not continuous)
TW2: Whitt 6E 112
Rodney St. N1 1H 7 (2K 83)
Rodney Way RM7: Mawney 1H 55
SL3: Poyle 4A 174
Rodway Rd. BR1: Broml 1K 159
SW15 7C 116
Rodwell Cl. HA4: Ruis 1A 58
Rodwell Pl. HA8: Edg 6B 28
Rodwell Rd. SE22 6F 121
Roe NW9 7G 29
Roebourne Way E16 1E 106
Roebuck Cl. N17 6A 34
TW13: Felt 4K 129
Roebuck Hgts. IG9: Buck H 1F 37
Roebuck La. IG9: Buck H 1F 37
Roebuck Rd. KT9: Chess 5G 163
Roedean Av. EN3: Enf H 1D 24
Roedean Cl. EN3: Enf H 1D 24
Roedean Cres. SW15 6A 116
Roe End NW9 4J 43
ROE GREEN 4J 43
Roe Grn. NW9 5J 43
ROEHAMPTON 7C 116
Roehampton Cl. SW15 4C 116
Roehampton Dr. BR7: Chst 6G 143
Roehampton Ga. SW15 6A 116
Roehampton Golf Course 4B 116
Roehampton High St. SW15 7C 116
Roehampton Ho. RM8: Dag 5A 72
ROEHAMPTON LANE 1D 134
Roehampton La. SW15 4C 116
Roehampton Sport & Fitness Cen. 7C 116
Roehampton University
Digby Stuart College 5C 116
Main Site 5C 116
Southlands College 5C 116
Whitelands Site 7C 116
Roehampton Va. SW15 3B 134
Roe La. NW9 4H 43
Roesel Pl. BR5: Pet W 5F 161
Roe Way SM6: W'gton 6J 167
Roffe Gdns. RM8: Dag 1E 72
Roffey St. E14 2E 104
Roffo Ct. SE17 6D 102
(off Boundary La.)
Rogan Ho. SW8 1F 119
(off St Joseph's St.)
Rogate Ho. E5 3G 67
Roger Dowley Ct. E2 2J 85
Roger Harriss Almshouses E15 1H 87
(off Gift La.)
Roger Reede's Almshouses
RM1: Rom 4K 55
Rogers Ct. E14 7C 86
(off Premiere Pl.)
Rogers Est. E2 3J 85
(not continuous)
Rogers Gdns. RM10: Dag 5G 73
Roger's Ho. RM10: Dag 3G 73
Rogers Ho. SW1 3D 18
(off Page St.)
Rogers Rd. E16 6H 87
RM10: Dag 5G 73
SW17 4B 136
Rogers Ruff HA6: Nwood 1E 38
Roger St. WC1 4H 7 (4K 83)
Rogers Wlk. N12 3E 30
Rohere Ho. EC1 1C 8 (3C 84)
Rojack Rd. SE23 1K 139
Rokeby Gdns. IG8: Wfd G 1J 51
Rokeby Ho. SW12 7F 119
(off Lochinvar St.)
WC1 4G 7
(off Lamb's Conduit St.)
Rokeby Pl. SW20 7D 134
Rokeby Rd. HA1: Harr 3H 41
SE4 2B 122
Rokeby St. E15 1F 87
Rokell Ho. BR3: Beck 5D 140
(off Beckenham Hill Rd.)
Roker Pk. Av. UB10: Ick 4A 56
Rokesby Cl. DA16: Well 2H 125
Rokesby Pl. HA0: Wemb 5D 60
Rokesly Av. N8 5J 47
Rokewood Apts. BR3: Beck 1C 158
Roland Gdns. SW7 5A 16 (5A 100)
SW10 5A 100
Roland Ho. SW7 5A 16
(off Old Brompton Rd.)
Roland Mans. SW7 5A 100
(off Old Brompton Rd.)
Roland M. E1 5K 85
Roland Rd. E17 4F 51
Roland Way KT4: Wor Pk 2B 164
SE17 5D 102
SW7 5A 16 (5A 100)
Roles Gro. RM6: Chad H 4D 54
Rolfe Cl. EN4: E Barn 4H 21
Rolfe Ter. SE18 5F 107
Rolinsden Way BR2: Kes 5B 172
Rolland Ho. W7 5J 77
Rollerbowl 2F 55
Rollesby Rd. KT9: Chess 6G 163
Rollesby Way SE28 6C 90
Rolleston Av. BR5: Pet W 6F 161
Rolleston Cl. BR5: Pet W 7F 161
Rolleston Rd. CR2: S Croy 7D 168
Roll Gdns. IG2: Ilf 5E 52
Rolling Mills M. E14 6A 86
Rollins Ho. SE15 6J 103
(off Rollins St.)
Rollins St. SE15 6J 103
Rollit Cres. TW3: Houn 5E 112
Rollit St. N7 5A 66
Rolls Bldgs. EC4 7J 7 (6A 84)
Rollscourt Av. SE24 5C 120
Rolls Pk. Av. E4 5H 35
Rolls Pk. Rd. E4 5J 35
Rolls Pas. EC4 7J 7
Rolls Rd. SE1 5F 103
Rolls Royce Cl. SM6: W'gton 7J 167
Rolt St. SE8 6A 104
(not continuous)
Rolvenden Gdns. BR1: Broml 7B 142
Rolvenden Pl. N17 1G 49
Roma Corte SE13 3D 122
(off Elmira St.)
Romana Ct. CR0: C'don 2F 169
Roman Apts. E8 7H 67
(off Silesia Bldgs.)
Roman Cl. RM13: Rain 2K 91
TW14: Felt 5A 112
W3 2H 97
Roman Ct. N7 6K 65

Romanfield Rd.—Roundtable Rd.

Romanfield Rd. SW2 ... 7K 119
Roman Ho. EC2 ... 6D 8
RM13: Rain ... 2K 91
Romanhurst Av. BR2: Broml ... 4G 159
Romanhurst Gdns.
BR2: Broml ... 4G 159
Roman Ind. Est. CR0: C'don ... 7E 156
Roman Ri. SE19 ... 6D 138
Roman Rd. E2 ... 3J 85
E3 ... 2A 86
E6 ... 4B 88
IG1: Ilf ... 6F 71
N10 ... 7A 32
NW2 ... 3E 62
(Edgware Rd.)
NW2 ... 3E 62
(Temple Rd.)
W4 ... 4A 98
Roman Rd. Mkt. ... 1B 86
(off Roman Rd.)
Roman Sq. SE28 ... 1A 108
Roman Way CR0: C'don ... 2B 168
EN1: Enf ... 5A 24
N7 ... 6K 65
SE15 ... 7J 103
Roman Way Ind. Est. N7 ... 7K 65
(off Roman Way)
Romany Gdns. E17 ... 1A 50
SM3: Sutt ... 7J 153
Romany Ri. BR5: Farnb ... 1G 173
Roma Read Cl. SW15 ... 7D 116
Roma Rd. E17 ... 3A 50
Romayne Ho. SW4 ... 3H 119
Romberg Rd. SW17 ... 3E 136
Romborough Gdns. SE13 ... 5E 122
Romborough Way SE13 ... 5E 122
Romero Cl. SW9 ... 3K 119
Romeyn Rd. SW16 ... 3K 137
ROMFORD ... 5K 55
Romford Greyhound Stadium ... 6J 55
Romford Rd. E7 ... 6G 69
E12 ... 5A 70
E15 ... 6G 69
RM5: Col R ... 1E 54
Romford St. E1 ... 5G 85
Romilly Ho. W11 ... 7G 81
(off Wilsham St.)
Romilly Rd. N4 ... 2B 66
Romilly St. W1 ... 2D 12 (7H 83)
Romily Ct. SW6 ... 2H 117
Rommany Rd. SE27 ... 4D 138
(not continuous)
Romney Cl. HA2: Harr ... 7E 40
KT9: Chess ... 4E 162
N17 ... 1H 49
NW11 ... 1A 64
SE14 ... 7J 103
TW15: Ashf ... 5E 128
Romney Ct. NW3 ... 6C 64
UB5: N'olt ... 2B 76
(off Parkfield Dr.)
W12 ... 2F 99
(off Shepherd's Bush Grn.)
Romney Dr. BR1: Broml ... 7B 142
HA2: Harr ... 7E 40
Romney Gdns. DA7: Bex ... 1F 127
Romney Ho. SW1 ... 2E 18
(off Marsham St.)
Romney M. W1 ... 5G 5 (5E 82)
Romney Pde. UB4: Hayes ... 2F 75
Romney Rd. KT3: N Mald ... 6K 151
SE10 ... 6F 105
UB4: Hayes ... 2F 75
Romney Row NW2 ... 2F 63
(off Brent Ter.)
Romney St. SW1 ... 2E 18 (3J 101)
Romola Rd. SE24 ... 1B 138
Romsey Cl. BR6: Farnb ... 4F 173
Romsey Gdns. RM9: Dag ... 1D 90
Romsey Rd. RM9: Dag ... 1D 90
W13 ... 7A 78
Romside Pl. RM7: Rom ... 4K 55
Romulus Ct. TW8: Bford ... 7D 96
Ronald Av. E15 ... 3G 87
Ronald Buckingham Ct.
SE16 ... 2J 103
(off Kenning St.)
Ronald Cl. BR3: Beck ... 4B 158
Ronald Ct. EN5: New Bar ... 3E 20
Ronaldshay N4 ... 7A 48
Ronalds Rd. BR1: Broml ... 1J 159
N5 ... 5A 66
(not continuous)
Ronaldstone Rd. DA15: Sidc ... 6J 125
Ronald St. E1 ... 6J 85
Rona Rd. NW3 ... 4E 64
Ronart St. HA3: W'stone ... 3K 41
Rona Wlk. N1 ... 6D 66
Rondel Ct. DA5: Bexl ... 6E 126
Rondu Rd. NW2 ... 5G 63
Ronelean Rd. KT6: Surb ... 2F 163
Ron Grn. Ct. DA8: Erith ... 6K 109
Ron Leighton Way E6 ... 1C 88
Ronnie La. E12 ... 4E 70
(not continuous)
Ron Todd Cl. RM10: Dag ... 1G 91
Ronver Rd. SE12 ... 7H 123
Rood La. EC3 ... 2G 15 (7E 84)
The Roof Ter. Apts. EC1 ... 4B 8
(off Gt. Sutton St.)
Rookby Ct. N21 ... 2G 33
Rook Cl. HA9: Wemb ... 3H 61
Rookeries Cl. TW13: Felt ... 3K 129
Rookery Cl. NW9 ... 5B 44
Rookery Ct. E10 ... 3D 68
Rookery Cres. RM10: Dag ... 7H 73
Rookery Dr. BR7: Chst ... 1E 160
Rookery La. BR2: Broml ... 6B 160
Rookery Rd. SW4 ... 4G 119
Rookery Way NW9 ... 5B 44
Rooke Way SE10 ... 5H 105
Rookfield Av. N10 ... 4G 47
Rookfield Cl. N10 ... 4G 47
Rooksmead Rd.
TW16: Sun ... 2H 147
Rooks Ter. UB7: W Dray ... 2A 92
Rookstone Rd. SW17 ... 5D 136
Rook Wlk. E6 ... 6B 88
Rookwood Av.
KT3: N Mald ... 4C 152
SM6: Bedd ... 4H 167
Rookwood Gdns. E4 ... 2C 36
Rookwood Ho. IG11: Bark ... 2H 89
Rookwood Rd. N16 ... 7F 49
Rookwood Way E3 ... 7C 68
Roosevelt Memorial ... 2H 11 (7E 82)
Roosevelt Way RM10: Dag ... 6K 73
Rootes Dr. W10 ... 5F 81
Ropemaker Rd. SE16 ... 2A 104
Ropemaker's Flds. E14 ... 7B 86
Ropemaker St.
EC2 ... 5E 8 (5D 84)
Roper Cres. TW16: Sun ... 1J 147
Roper La. SE1 ... 7H 15 (2E 102)
Ropers Av. E4 ... 5J 35
Ropers Orchard SW3 ... 6C 100
(off Danvers St.)
Roper St. SE9 ... 5D 124
Ropers Wlk. SW2 ... 7A 120
Roper Way CR4: Mitc ... 2E 154
Ropery Bus. Pk. SE7 ... 4A 106
Ropery St. E3 ... 4B 86
Rope St. SE16 ... 4A 104
Rope Ter. E16 ... 2K 105
Rope Wlk. TW16: Sun ... 3A 148
Ropewalk Gdns. E1 ... 6G 85
Ropewalk M. E8 ... 7G 67
The Ropeworks IG11: Bark ... 1G 89
Ropley St. E2 ... 2G 85
Rosa Alba M. N5 ... 4C 66
Rosa Av. TW15: Ashf ... 4C 128
Rosalind Ct. IG11: Bark ... 7A 72
(off Meadow Rd.)
Rosalind Ho. N1 ... 2E 84
(off Arden Est.)
Rosaline Rd. SW6 ... 7G 99
Rosaline Ter. SW6 ... 7G 99
(off Rosaline Rd.)
Rosa M. E17 ... 3B 50
Rosamond St. SE26 ... 3H 139
Rosamund Cl.
CR2: S Croy ... 4D 168
Rosamun St. UB2: S'hall ... 4C 94
Rosa Parks Ho. SE17 ... 4C 102
(off Munton Rd.)
Rosary Cl. TW3: Houn ... 2C 112
Rosary Gdns. SW7 ... 4A 100
TW15: Ashf ... 4D 128
Rosaville Rd. SW6 ... 7H 99
Roscoe St. EC1 ... 4D 8 (4C 84)
(not continuous)
Roscoe St. Est. EC1 ... 4D 8 (4C 84)
Roscoff Cl. HA8: Edg ... 1J 43
Rosea Apts. SW11 ... 4C 118
(off Danvers Av.)
Roseacre Cl. SM1: Sutt ... 2A 166
TW17: Shep ... 5C 146
W13 ... 5B 78
Roseacre Rd. DA16: Well ... 3B 126
Rose All. EC2 ... 6H 9
(off Bishopsgate)
SE1 ... 4D 14 (1C 102)
Rose & Crown Ct. EC2 ... 7D 8
Rose & Crown M. TW7: Isle ... 1A 114
Rose & Crown Yd.
SW1 ... 4B 12 (1G 101)
Rose Apts. SE11 ... 7K 19
Roseary Cl. UB7: W Dray ... 4A 92
Rose Av. CR4: Mitc ... 1D 154
E18 ... 2K 51
SM4: Mord ... 5A 154
Rosebank SE20 ... 7H 139
SW6 ... 7E 98
W3 ... 6K 79
Rosebank Av. HA0: Wemb ... 4K 59
Rosebank Cl. N12 ... 5H 31
TW11: Tedd ... 6A 132
Rosebank Gdns. E3 ... 2B 86
W3 ... 6K 79
Rosebank Gdns. Nth. E3 ... 2B 86
Rosebank Gro. E17 ... 3B 50
Rosebank Rd. E17 ... 6D 50
W7 ... 2J 95
Rosebank Vs. E17 ... 4C 50
Rosebank Wlk. NW1 ... 7H 65
SE18 ... 4C 106
Rosebank Way W3 ... 6K 79
Rose Bates Dr. NW9 ... 4G 43
Rosebay Dr. N17 ... 2F 49
Rosebay Ho. E3 ... 5C 86
(off Hawgood St.)
Roseberry Dr. HA8: Edg ... 2C 28
Roseberry Gdns. BR6: Orp ... 3J 173
N4 ... 6B 48
Roseberry Mans. N1 ... 1J 83
(off Tapper Wlk.)
Roseberry M. SW2 ... 6J 119
Roseberry Pl. E8 ... 6F 67
Roseberry St. SE16 ... 4H 103
Rosebery Av. CR7: Thor H ... 2C 156
DA15: Sidc ... 7J 125
E12 ... 6C 70
EC1 ... 4J 7 (4A 84)
HA2: Harr ... 4C 58
KT3: N Mald ... 2B 152
N17 ... 2G 49
Rosebery Cl. SM4: Mord ... 6F 153
Rosebery Ct. EC1 ... 3J 7
(off Rosebery Av.)
W1 ... 4J 11
(off Charles St.)
Rosebery Gdns. N8 ... 5J 47
SM1: Sutt ... 4K 165
W13 ... 6A 78
Rosebery Ho. E2 ... 2J 85
(off Sewardstone Rd.)
Rosebery Ind. Pk. N17 ... 2H 49
Rosebery M. N10 ... 2G 47
Rosebery Pl. NW7 ... 7G 29
Rosebery Rd. KT1: King T ... 2H 151
N10 ... 2G 47
SM1: Sutt ... 6H 165
SW2 ... 6J 119
TW3: Houn ... 5G 113
WD23: Bush ... 1A 26
Rosebery Sq. EC1 ... 4J 7
KT1: King T ... 2H 151
Rosebine Av. TW2: Twick ... 7H 113
Rosebury Rd. SW6 ... 2K 117
Rosebury Sq. IG8: Wfd G ... 7K 37
Rosebury Va. HA4: Ruis ... 2J 57
Rose Bush Ct. NW3 ... 5D 64
Rose Ct. E1 ... 6K 9
E8 ... 7F 67
(off Richmond Rd.)
HA0: Wemb ... 2E 78
(off Vicars Bri. Cl.)
HA2: Harr ... 2G 59
N1 ... 1B 84
(off Collin's Yd.)
SE8 ... 4K 103
Rosecourt Rd. CR0: C'don ... 6K 155
Rosecrest Ct. N15 ... 4F 49
Rosecroft N14 ... 2D 32
Rosecroft Av. NW3 ... 3J 63
Rosecroft Gdns. NW2 ... 3C 62
TW2: Twick ... 1H 131
Rosecroft Rd. UB1: S'hall ... 4E 76
Rosecroft Wlk. HA0: Wemb ... 5D 60
HA5: Pinn ... 5B 40
Rose Dale BR6: Farnb ... 2F 173
Rosedale Av. UB3: Hayes ... 5F 75
Rosedale Cl. HA7: Stan ... 6G 27
SE2 ... 3B 108
W7 ... 2K 95
Rosedale Ct. HA1: Harr ... 4K 59
N5 ... 4B 66
Rosedale Dr. RM9: Dag ... 7B 72
Rosedale Gdns. RM9: Dag ... 7B 72
Rosedale Ho. N16 ... 1D 66
Rosedale Pl. CR0: C'don ... 7K 157
Rosedale Rd. E7 ... 5A 70
KT17: Ewe ... 5C 164
RM1: Rom ... 2J 55
RM9: Dag ... 7B 72
TW9: Rich ... 3E 114
Rosedale Ter. W6 ... 3D 98
(off Dalling Rd.)
Rosedene NW6 ... 1F 81
Rosedene Av. CR0: C'don ... 7J 155
SM4: Mord ... 5J 153
SW16 ... 3K 137
UB6: G'frd ... 3E 76
Rosedene Ct. HA4: Ruis ... 1G 57
Rosedene Gdns. IG2: Ilf ... 4E 52
Rosedene Ter. E10 ... 2D 68
Rosedew Rd. W6 ... 6F 99
Rose End KT4: Wor Pk ... 1F 165
Rosefield Cl. SM5: Cars ... 5C 166
Rosefield Gdns. E14 ... 7C 86
Roseford Ct. W12 ... 2F 99
(off Shepherd's Bush Grn.)
Rose Gdn. Cl. HA8: Edg ... 6K 27
Rose Gdns. TW13: Felt ... 2J 129
UB1: S'hall ... 4E 76
W5 ... 3D 96
Rosegate Ho. E3 ... 2B 86
(off Hereford Rd.)
Rose Glen NW9 ... 4K 43
RM7: Rush G ... 1K 73
Rosehart M. W11 ... 6J 81
Rose Hatch Av. RM6: Chad H ... 3D 54
Roseheath Rd. TW4: Houn ... 5D 112
ROSEHILL ... 7A 154
Rose Hill SM1: Sutt ... 2K 165
Rosehill KT10: Clay ... 6A 162
TW12: Hamp ... 1E 148
Rosehill Av. SM1: Sutt ... 1A 166
Rosehill Ct. SM4: Mord ... 7A 154
(off St Helier Av.)
Rosehill Ct. Pde. SM4: Mord ... 7A 154
(off St Helier Av.)
Rosehill Gdns. SM1: Sutt ... 2K 165
UB6: G'frd ... 5K 59
Rose Hill Pk. W. SM1: Sutt ... 1A 166
Rosehill Rd. SW18 ... 6A 118
ROSE HILL RDBT. ... 7A 154
Rose Joan M. NW6 ... 4J 63
Rosekey Ct. SE8 ... 7B 104
(off Baildon St.)
Roseland Cl. N17 ... 7J 33
Rose La. RM6: Chad H ... 3D 54
Rose Lawn WD23: B Hea ... 1B 26
Roseleigh Av. N5 ... 4B 66
Roseleigh Cl. TW1: Twick ... 6D 114
Rose Lipman Bldg. ... 1E 84
Rosemary Av. EN2: Enf ... 1K 23
KT8: W Mole ... 3E 148
N3 ... 2K 45
N9 ... 1C 34
TW4: Houn ... 2B 112
Rosemary Branch Theatre ... 1D 84
(off Rosemary St.)
Rosemary Cl. CR0: C'don ... 6J 155
UB8: Hil ... 5C 74
Rosemary Ct. SE8 ... 6B 104
(off Dorking Cl.)
SE15 ... 7E 102
Rosemary Dr. E14 ... 6F 87
IG4: Ilf ... 5B 52
Rosemary Gdns. KT9: Chess ... 4E 162
RM8: Dag ... 1F 73
SW14 ... 3J 115
Rosemary Ho. N1 ... 1D 84
(off Colville Est.)
NW10 ... 1D 80
(off Uffington Rd.)
Rosemary La. SW14 ... 3J 115
Rosemary Rd. DA16: Well ... 1K 125
SE15 ... 7F 103
SW17 ... 3A 136
Rosemary St. N1 ... 1D 84
Rosemary Works N1 ... 1D 84
(off Branch Pl.)
Rosemead Av. CR4: Mitc ... 3G 155
HA9: Wemb ... 5E 60
TW13: Felt ... 2H 129
Rosemead Cl. KT6: Surb ... 1G 163
Rosemere Pl. BR2: Broml ... 4G 159
Rose M. N18 ... 4C 34
Rosemont Av. N12 ... 6F 31
Rosemont Ct. W3 ... 1H 97
(off Rosemont Rd.)
Rosemont Rd. HA0: Wemb ... 1E 78
KT3: N Mald ... 3J 151
NW3 ... 6A 64
TW10: Rich ... 6E 114
W3 ... 7H 79
Rosemoor Ho. W13 ... 1A 96
(off Broadway)
Rosemoor St. SW3 ... 4E 16 (4D 100)
Rosemount SM6: W'gton ... 6G 167
(off Clarendon Rd.)
Rosemount Cl. IG8: Wfd G ... 6J 37
Rosemount Dr. BR1: Broml ... 4D 160
Rosemount Point SE23 ... 3K 139
Rosemount Rd. W13 ... 6A 78
Rosenau Cres. SW11 ... 1D 118
Rosenau Rd. SW11 ... 1C 118
Rosenburg Rd. W3 ... 2H 97
Rosendale Rd. SE21 ... 7C 120
SE24 ... 7C 120
Roseneath Av. N21 ... 1G 33
Roseneath Pl. SW16 ... 4K 137
(off Curtis Fld. Rd.)
Roseneath Rd. SW11 ... 6E 118
Roseneath Wlk. EN1: Enf ... 4K 23
Rosen's Wlk. HA8: Edg ... 3C 28
Rosenthal Rd. SE6 ... 6D 122
Rosenthorpe Rd. SE15 ... 5K 121
Rose Pk. Cl. UB4: Yead ... 5A 76
Rosepark Ct. IG5: Ilf ... 2D 52
Rose Pl. N8 ... 6J 47
Rose Playhouse ... 4D 14
(off Park St.)
Roserton St. E14 ... 2E 104
The Rosery CR0: C'don ... 6K 157
The Roses IG8: Wfd G ... 7C 36
Rose Sq. SW3 ... 5B 16 (5B 100)
Rose Stapleton Ter. SE1 ... 3E 102
(off Page's Wlk.)
Rose St. EC4 ... 7B 8 (6B 84)
WC2 ... 2E 12 (7J 83)
(not continuous)
Rose Theatre
Kingston ... 2D 150
Sidcup ... 1B 144
Rosethorn Cl. SW12 ... 7H 119
Rose Tree M. IG8: Wfd G ... 6H 37
Rosetree Pl. TW12: Hamp ... 7E 130
Rosetta Cl. SW8 ... 7J 101
(off Kenchester Cl.)
Rosetta Ct. SE19 ... 7E 138
Rosetti Ter. RM8: Dag ... 4B 72
(off Marlborough Rd.)
Roseveare Rd. SE12 ... 4A 142
Roseville N21 ... 1F 33
(off The Green)
Roseville Av. TW3: Houn ... 5E 112
Roseville Rd. UB3: Harl ... 5J 93
Rosevine Rd. SW20 ... 1E 152
Rose Wlk. BR4: W W'ck ... 2E 170
KT5: Surb ... 5H 151
Rose Way HA8: Edg ... 5D 28
SE12 ... 5J 123
Roseway SE21 ... 6D 120
Rosewell Cl. SE20 ... 7H 139
Rosewood KT7: T Ditt ... 2A 162
Rosewood Av. UB6: G'frd ... 5A 60
Rosewood Cl. DA14: Sidc ... 3C 144
Rosewood Ct. BR1: Broml ... 1A 160
E11 ... 4F 69
KT2: King T ... 7G 133
RM6: Chad H ... 5C 54
Rosewood Dr. TW17: Shep ... 5B 146
Rosewood Gdns. SE13 ... 2E 122
Rosewood Gro. SM1: Sutt ... 2A 166
Rosewood Ho.
SW8 ... 7G 19 (6K 101)
Rosewood Sq. W12 ... 6C 80
Rosher Cl. E15 ... 7F 69
Roshni Ho. SW17 ... 6C 136
Rosina St. E9 ... 6K 67
Rosing Apts. BR2: Broml ... 4A 160
(off Homesdale Rd.)
Roskeen Ct. SW20 ... 7E 134
Roskell Rd. SW15 ... 3F 117
Rosler Bldg. SE1 ... 5C 14
(off Ewer St.)
Roslin Ho. E1 ... 7K 85
(off Brodlove La.)
Roslin Rd. W3 ... 3H 97
Roslin Way BR1: Broml ... 5J 141
Roslyn Cl. CR4: Mitc ... 2B 154
Roslyn Rd. N15 ... 5D 48
Rosmead Rd. W11 ... 7G 81
Rosoman Pl. EC1 ... 3K 7 (4A 84)
Rosoman St. EC1 ... 2K 7 (3A 84)
Rossall Cres. NW10 ... 3F 79
Ross Apts. E16 ... 7J 87
(off Seagull La.)
Ross Av. RM8: Dag ... 1F 73
Ross Cl. HA3: Hrw W ... 7B 26
UB3: Harl ... 4F 93
UB5: N'olt ... 4H 59
Ross Ct. E5 ... 4H 67
(off Napoleon Rd.)
NW9 ... 3A 44
SW15 ... 7F 117
W13 ... 5B 78
(off Cleveland Rd.)
Rosscourt Mans. SW1 ... 1A 18
(off Buckingham Pal. Rd.)
Rossdale SM1: Sutt ... 5C 166
Rossdale Dr. N9 ... 6D 24
NW9 ... 1J 61
Rossdale Rd. SW15 ... 4E 116
Rosse Gdns. SE13 ... 6F 123
Rosse M. SE3 ... 1K 123
Rossendale St. E5 ... 2H 67
Rossendale Way NW1 ... 7G 65
Rossetti CR0: C'don ... 1C 168
(off Saffron Central Sq.)
Rossetti Ct. WC1 ... 5C 6
(off Ridgmount Pl.)
Rossetti Gdn. Mans. SW3 ... 7E 16
Rossetti Ho. SW1 ... 4D 18
(off Erasmus St.)
Rossetti M. NW8 ... 1B 82
Rossetti Rd. SE16 ... 5H 103
Rossetti Studios SW3 ... 7D 16
(off Flood St.)
Ross Haven Pl. HA6: Nwood ... 1H 39
Ross Ho. E1 ... 1H 103
(off Prusom St.)
Rossignol Gdns. SM5: Cars ... 2E 166
Rossindel Rd. TW3: Houn ... 5E 112
Rossington Cl. EN1: Enf ... 1C 24
Rossington St. E5 ... 2G 67
Rossiter Cl. SE19 ... 7C 138
Rossiter Flds. EN5: Barn ... 6B 20
Rossiter Gro. SW9 ... 3A 120
Rossiter Rd. SW12 ... 1F 137
Rossland Cl. DA6: Bex ... 5H 127
Rosslyn Av. E4 ... 2C 36
EN4: E Barn ... 6H 21
RM8: Dag ... 7F 55
SW13 ... 3A 116
TW14: Felt ... 6J 111
Rosslyn Cl. BR4: W W'ck ... 3H 171
TW16: Sun ... 6G 129
UB3: Hayes ... 5F 75
Rosslyn Cres. HA1: Harr ... 4K 41
HA9: Wemb ... 4E 60
Rosslyn Gdns. HA9: Wemb ... 3E 60
Rosslyn Hill NW3 ... 4B 64
Rosslyn Mans. NW6 ... 7A 64
(off Goldhurst Ter.)
Rosslyn M. NW3 ... 4B 64
Rosslyn Pk. M. NW3 ... 5B 64
Rosslyn Rd. E17 ... 4E 50
IG11: Bark ... 7H 71
TW1: Twick ... 6C 114
Rossmore Cl. EN3: Pond E ... 4E 24
NW1 ... 4D 4
(off Rossmore Rd.)
Rossmore Ct. NW1 ... 3E 4 (4D 82)
Rossmore Rd. NW1 ... 4D 4 (4C 82)
Ross Pde. SM6: W'gton ... 6F 167
Ross Rd. SE25 ... 3D 156
SM6: W'gton ... 5G 167
TW2: Whitt ... 1F 131
Ross Wlk. SE27 ... 3D 138
Ross Way E14 ... 6A 86
SE9 ... 3C 124
Rosswood Gdns. SM6: W'gton ... 6G 167
Rostella Rd. SW17 ... 4B 136
Rostrevor Av. N15 ... 6F 49
Rostrevor Gdns. UB2: S'hall ... 5C 94
UB3: Hayes ... 1G 93
Rostrevor Mans. SW6 ... 1H 117
(off Rostrevor Rd.)
Rostrevor M. SW6 ... 1H 117
Rostrevor Rd. SW6 ... 1H 117
SW19 ... 5J 135
Roswell Apts. E3 ... 5B 86
(off Joseph St.)
Rotary St. SE1 ... 7A 14 (3B 102)
Rothay NW1 ... 1K 5
(off Albany St.)
Rothbury Cotts. SE10 ... 4G 105
(off Maritius Rd.)
Rothbury Gdns. TW7: Isle ... 7A 96
Rothbury Rd. E9 ... 7B 68
Rothbury Wlk. N17 ... 7B 34
Rotheley Ho. E9 ... 7J 67
(off Balcorne St.)
Rotherfield Ct. N1 ... 7D 66
(off Rotherfield St.)
Rotherfield Rd. SM5: Cars ... 4E 166
Rotherfield St. N1 ... 7C 66
Rotherham Wlk. SE1 ... 5A 14
Rotherhill Av. SW16 ... 6H 137
ROTHERHITHE ... 2J 103
Rotherhithe Bus. Est. SE16 ... 4H 103
Rotherhithe New Rd. SE16 ... 5H 103
Rotherhithe Old Rd. SE16 ... 4K 103
Rotherhithe Sands Film Studios
... 2J 103
(off Tunnel Rd.)
Rotherhithe St. SE16 ... 2J 103
ROTHERHITHE TUNNEL ... 1K 103
Rother Ho. SE15 ... 4H 121
Rotherwick Hill W5 ... 4F 79
Rotherwick Ho. E1 ... 7G 85
(off Thomas More St.)
Rotherwick Rd. NW11 ... 7J 45
Rotherwood Cl. SW20 ... 1G 153
Rotherwood Rd. SW15 ... 3F 117
Rothery St. N1 ... 1B 84
(off St Marys Path)
Rothery Ter. SW9 ... 7B 102
(off Foxley Rd.)
Rothesay Av. SW20 ... 2G 153
TW10: Rich ... 4H 115
UB6: G'frd ... 6G 59
(not continuous)
Rothesay Ct. SE6 ... 2H 141
(off Cumberland Pl.)
SE11 ... 7J 19
SE12 ... 3K 141
Rothesay Rd. SE25 ... 4D 156
Rothley Ct. NW8 ... 3A 4
(off St John's Wood Rd.)
Rothsay Rd. E7 ... 7A 70
Rothsay St. SE1 ... 3E 102
Rothsay Wlk. E14 ... 4C 104
(off Charnwood Gdns.)
Rothschild Ho. TW8: Bford ... 6F 97
Rothschild Rd. W4 ... 4J 97
Rothschild St. SE27 ... 4B 138
Roth Wlk. N7 ... 2K 65
Rothwell Ct. HA1: Harr ... 5K 41
Rothwell Gdns. RM9: Dag ... 7C 72
Rothwell Ho. TW5: Hest ... 6E 94
Rothwell Rd. RM9: Dag ... 1C 90
Rothwell St. NW1 ... 1D 82
Rotten Row NW3 ... 1A 64
SW7 ... 6B 10 (2B 100)
Rotterdam Dr. E14 ... 3E 104
The Rotunda RM7: Rom ... 5K 55
(off Yew Tree Gdns.)
SW10 ... 7A 100
The Rotunda Cen. ... 2E 150
Rotunda Ct. BR1: Broml ... 5K 141
(off Burnt Ash La.)
Rouel Rd. SE16 ... 4G 103
Rougemont Av. SM4: Mord ... 6J 153
Roundabout Ho. HA6: Nwood ... 1J 39
Roundacre SW19 ... 2F 135
Roundaway Rd. IG5: Ilf ... 1D 52
Roundel Cl. SE4 ... 4B 122
Round Gro. CR0: C'don ... 7K 157
Roundhay Cl. SE23 ... 2K 139
Roundhedge Way EN2: Enf ... 1E 22
Round Hill SE26 ... 2J 139
(not continuous)
Roundhill Dr. EN2: Enf ... 4E 22
The Roundhouse ... 7E 64
Roundhouse La. E20 ... 6E 68
(off International Way)
ROUNDSHAW ... 7J 167
Roundshaw Downs
Local Nature Reserve ... 7K 167
Roundtable Rd. BR1: Broml ... 3H 141

Roundtree Rd.—Rusper Rd.

Roundtree Rd. HA0: Wemb ... 5B 60
The Roundway KT10: Clay ... 6A 162
N17 ... 1C 48
Roundways HA4: Ruis ... 3H 57
Roundwood BR7: Chst ... 2F 161
Roundwood Av. UB11: Stock P ... 1E 92
Roundwood Cl. HA4: Ruis ... 7F 39
Roundwood Ct. E2 ... 3K 85
Roundwood Rd. NW10 ... 6B 62
Rounton Rd. E3 ... 4C 86
Roupell Ho. KT2: King T ... 7F 133
(off Florence Rd.)
Roupell Rd. SW2 ... 1K 137
Roupell St. SE1 ... 5K 13 (1A 102)
Rousden St. NW1 ... 7G 65
Rouse Gdns. SE21 ... 4E 138
Rous Rd. IG9: Buck H ... 1H 37
Routemaster Cl. E13 ... 3K 87
Routh Ct. TW14: Bedf ... 1F 129
Routh Rd. SW18 ... 7C 118
Routh St. E6 ... 5D 88
Rover Ho. N1 ... 1E 84
(off Whitmore Est.)
Rowallan Rd. SW6 ... 7G 99
Rowallen Pde. RM8: Dag ... 1C 72
Rowan N10 ... 2F 47
Rowan Av. E4 ... 6G 35
NW9 ... 7G 29
Rowan Cl. HA0: Wemb ... 3A 60
HA7: Stan ... 6E 26
IG1: Ilf ... 5H 71
KT3: N Mald ... 2A 152
SW16 ... 1G 155
W5 ... 2E 96
Rowan Ct. E13 ... 2K 87
(off High St.)
SE15 ... 7F 103
(off Garnies Cl.)
SW11 ... 6D 118
Rowan Cres. SW16 ... 1G 155
Rowan Dr. NW9 ... 3C 44
Rowan Gdns. CR0: C'don ... 3F 169
Rowan Ho. BR2: Broml ... 2G 159
DA14: Sidc ... 3K 143
E3 ... 1B 86
(off Hornbeam Sq.)
IG1: Ilf ... 5H 71
SE16 ... 2K 103
(off Woodland Cres.)
Rowan Lodge W8 ... 3K 99
(off Chantry Sq.)
Rowan Pl. UB3: Hayes ... 7H 75
Rowan Rd. DA7: Bex ... 3E 126
SW16 ... 2G 155
TW8: Bford ... 7B 96
UB7: W Dray ... 4A 92
W6 ... 4F 99
The Rowans N13 ... 3G 33
TW16: Sun ... 5H 129
Rowans Tenpin ... 2A 66
Rowan Ter. SW19 ... 7G 135
W6 ... 4F 99
Rowantree Cl. N21 ... 1J 33
Rowantree Rd. EN2: Enf ... 2G 23
N21 ... 1J 33
Rowan Wlk. BR2: Broml ... 3D 172
EN5: New Bar ... 5E 20
N2 ... 5A 46
N19 ... 2G 65
W10 ... 4G 81
Rowan Way RM6: Chad H ... 3C 54
Rowanwood Av. DA15: Sidc ... 1A 144
Rowanwood M. EN2: Enf ... 2G 23
Rowben Cl. N20 ... 1E 30
Rowberry Cl. SW6 ... 7E 98
Rowcross St. SE1 ... 5F 103
Rowdell Rd. UB5: N'olt ... 1E 76
Rowden Pde. E4 ... 6H 35
(off Chingford Rd.)
Rowden Pk. Gdns. E4 ... 7H 35
Rowden Rd. BR3: Beck ... 1A 158
E4 ... 6J 35
KT19: Ewe ... 4H 163
Rowditch La. SW11 ... 2E 118
Rowdon Av. NW10 ... 7D 62
Rowdown Cres. CR0: New Ad ... 7F 171
Rowdowns Rd. RM9: Dag ... 1F 91
Rowe Gdns. IG11: Bark ... 2K 89
Rowe Ho. E9 ... 6J 67
Rowe La. E9 ... 5J 67
Rowena Cres. SW11 ... 2C 118
Rowenhurst Mans. NW6 ... 6A 64
(off Canfield Gdns.)
Rowe Wlk. HA2: Harr ... 3E 58
Rowfant Rd. SW17 ... 1E 136
Rowhill Rd. E5 ... 4H 67
Rowington Cl. W2 ... 5K 81
Rowland Av. HA3: Kenton ... 3C 42
Rowland Ct. E16 ... 4H 87
Rowland Gro. SE26 ... 3H 139
(not continuous)
Rowland Hill Almshouses
TW15: Ashf ... 5C 128
(off Feltham Hill Rd.)
Rowland Hill Av. N17 ... 7H 33
Rowland Hill Ho. SE1 ... 6A 14 (2B 102)
Rowland Hill St. NW3 ... 5C 64
Rowlands Av. HA5: Hat E ... 5A 26
Rowlands Cl. N6 ... 6E 46
NW7 ... 7H 29
Rowlands Rd. RM8: Dag ... 2F 73
Rowland Way SW19 ... 1K 153
TW15: Ashf ... 7F 129
Rowley Av. DA15: Sidc ... 7B 126
Rowley Cl. HA0: Wemb ... 7F 61
Rowley Ct. EN1: Enf ... 5K 23
(off Wellington Rd.)
Rowley Gdns. N4 ... 7C 48
Rowley Ho. SE8 ... 5C 104
(off Watergate St.)
Rowley Ind. Pk. W3 ... 3H 97
Rowley Rd. N15 ... 5C 48
Rowley Way NW8 ... 1K 81
Rowlheys Pl. UB7: W Dray ... 3A 92
Rowlls Rd. KT1: King T ... 3F 151
Rowney Gdns. RM9: Dag ... 6C 72
Rowney Rd. RM9: Dag ... 6B 72
Rowntree Clifford Cl. E13 ... 4J 87
Rowntree Cl. NW6 ... 6J 63
Rowntree M. E17 ... 1B 50
Rowntree Path SE28 ... 1B 108
Rowntree Rd. TW2: Twick ... 1J 131
Rowse Cl. E15 ... 1E 86
Rowsley Av. NW4 ... 3E 44
Rowstock Gdns. N7 ... 5H 65
Rowton Rd. SE18 ... 7G 107
Roxborough Av. HA1: Harr ... 7H 41
TW7: Isle ... 7K 95
Roxborough Hgts. HA1: Harr ... 6J 41
(off College Rd.)
Roxborough Pk. HA1: Harr ... 7J 41
Roxborough Rd. HA1: Harr ... 5H 41
Roxbourne Cl. UB5: N'olt ... 6B 58
Roxbourne Pk. Miniature Railway
... 2B 58
Roxburghe Mans. W8 ... 2K 99
(off Kensington Ct.)
Roxburgh Pl. BR1: Broml ... 1C 160
Roxburgh Rd. SE27 ... 5B 138
Roxburn Way HA4: Ruis ... 3H 57
Roxby Pl. SW6 ... 6J 99
ROXETH ... 2H 59
Roxeth Ct. TW15: Ashf ... 5C 128
Roxeth Grn. Av. HA2: Harr ... 3F 59
UB5: N'olt ... 5E 58
Roxeth Gro. HA2: Harr ... 4F 59
Roxeth Hill HA2: Harr ... 2H 59
Roxford Cl. TW17: Shep ... 5G 147
Roxford Ho. E3 ... 4D 86
(off Devas St.)
Roxley Rd. SE13 ... 6D 122
Roxton Gdns. CR0: Addtn ... 5C 170
Roxwell NW1 ... 6F 65
(off Hartland Rd.)
Roxwell Rd. IG11: Bark ... 2A 90
W12 ... 2C 98
Roxwell Trad. Pk. E10 ... 7A 50
Roxwell Way IG8: Wfd G ... 7F 37
Roxy Av. RM6: Chad H ... 7C 54
Royal Academy of Arts
(Burlington House) ... 3A 12 (7G 83)
Royal Academy of Music ... 4H 5 (4E 82)
Royal Academy of Music Mus. ... 4H 5
(off York Ga.)
Royal Academy Schools ... 7G 83
Royal Air Force Memorial ... 1J 101
Royal Albert Hall ... 7A 10 (2B 100)
ROYAL ALBERT RDBT. ... 7C 88
(on Royal Albert Way)
Royal Albert Way E16 ... 7B 88
Royal Anglian Way RM8: Dag ... 1E 72
Royal Arc. W1 ... 3A 12
Royal Archer SE14 ... 7K 103
(off Egmont St.)
ROYAL ARSENAL WEST ... 3F 107
Royal Av. KT4: Wor Pk ... 2A 164
SW3 ... 5E 16 (5D 100)
Royal Av. Ho. SW3 ... 5E 16
(off Royal Av.)
Royal Ballet School ... 1F 13
(off Floral St.)
Royal Belgrave Ho. SW1 ... 4K 17
(off Hugh St.)
Royal Blackheath Golf Course ... 7D 124
Royal Botanic Gdns.
Kew ... 1E 114
Royal Brass Foundry ... 3F 107
Royal Carriage M. SE18 ... 3F 107
Royal Cir. SE27 ... 3A 138
Royal Cl. BR6: Farnb ... 4F 173
IG3: Ilf ... 7A 54
KT4: Wor Pk ... 2A 164
N16 ... 1E 66
SE8 ... 6B 104
SW19 ... 3F 135
UB8: Hil ... 6B 74
Royal College of Art
Battersea ... 7C 100
(off Parkgate Rd.)
Kensington ... 7A 10 (2B 100)
Royal College of Music
... 1A 16 (3B 100)
Royal College of Nursing ... 7K 5
(off Dean's M.)
Royal College of Obstetricians
& Gynaecologists ... 3E 4 (4D 82)
Royal College of Physicians ... 3K 5
Royal College of Physicians Mus.
... 3K 5 (4F 83)
Royal College of Surgeons ... 7H 7
Royal Coll. St. NW1 ... 7G 65
Royal Connaught Apts. E16 ... 1B 106
(off Connaught Rd.)
Royal Ct. EC3 ... 1F 15
(off Cornhill)
EN1: Enf ... 6K 23
HA4: Ruis ... 6J 39
SE9 ... 1D 142
SE16 ... 3B 104
Royal Courts of Justice ... 1H 13
Royal Court Theatre ... 4G 17
(off Sloane Sq.)
Royal Cres. HA4: Ruis ... 4C 58
IG2: Ilf ... 6H 53
W11 ... 1F 99
Royal Cres. M. W11 ... 1F 99
Royal Crest Av. E16 ... 2K 105
Royal Docks Rd. E6 ... 6F 89
IG11: Bark ... 6F 89
Royal Dr. N11 ... 5K 31
(not continuous)
Royal Duchess M. SW12 ... 7F 119
Royale Leisure Pk. W3 ... 4G 79
Royal Engineers Way NW7 ... 6B 30
Royal Epping Forest
Golf Course ... 6K 25
Royal Exchange ... 1F 15 (6D 84)
Royal Exchange Av. EC3 ... 1F 15
Royal Exchange Bldgs. EC3 ... 1F 15
Royal Festival Hall ... 5H 13 (1K 101)
Royal Gdns. W7 ... 3A 96
Royal Geographical Society ... 7A 10
Royal George M. SE5 ... 4D 120
Royal Herbert Pavilions SE18 ... 1D 124
Royal Hill SE10 ... 7E 104
Royal Hill Ct. SE10 ... 7E 104
(off Greenwich High St.)
Royal Holloway (University of London)
Gower Street ... 5D 6
Royal Hospital Chelsea ... 5E 100
Royal Hospital Chelsea Great Hall
... 6F 17 (5D 100)
Royal Hospital Chelsea Mus.
... 6G 17 (5E 100)
Royal Hospital Rd.
SW3 ... 7E 16 (6D 100)
Royal Institution ... 3A 12 (7G 83)
Royal La. UB7: Yiew ... 5B 74
UB8: Hil ... 5B 74
Royal Langford Apts. NW6 ... 2K 81
(off Greville Rd.)
Royal London Bldgs. SE15 ... 6H 103
(off Old Kent Rd.)
The Royal London Est. N17 ... 6C 34
Royal London Hospital Archives & Mus.
... 5H 85
(off Newark St.)
Royal London Ind. Est. NW10 ... 2K 79
The Royal Mews ... 1K 17 (2F 101)
Royal M.
KT8: E Mos ... 3J 149
SW1 ... 1K 17 (3F 101)
Royal Mid-Surrey Golf Course ... 3D 114
Royal Mint Ct. EC3 ... 3K 15 (7F 85)
Royal Mint Pl. E1 ... 2K 15 (7G 85)
Royal Mint St. E1 ... 2K 15 (7G 85)
Royal Naval Pl. SE14 ... 7B 104
Royal Oak Ct. N1 ... 1G 9
(off Pitfield St.)
Royal Oak M. TW11: Tedd ... 5A 132
Royal Oak Pl. SE22 ... 6H 121
Royal Oak Rd. DA6: Bex ... 5F 127
(not continuous)
E8 ... 6H 67
Royal Oak Yd. SE1 ... 7G 15 (2E 102)
Royal Observatory Greenwich ... 7G 105
Royal Opera Arc. SW1 ... 4C 12 (1H 101)
Royal Opera House ... 1F 13 (6J 83)
Royal Orchard Cl. SW18 ... 7G 117
Royal Pde. BR7: Chst ... 7G 143
RM10: Dag ... 6H 73
SE3 ... 2H 123
SW6 ... 7G 99
TW9: Kew ... 1G 115
(off Station App.)
W5 ... 3E 78
Royal Pde. M. BR7: Chst ... 7G 143
(off Royal Pde.)
SE3 ... 2H 123
(off Royal Pde.)
Royal Pl. SE10 ... 7E 104
Royal Quarter KT2: King T ... 1E 150
Royal Quay Rd. E16 ... 7F 89
Royal Rd. DA14: Sidc ... 3D 144
E16 ... 6B 88
SE17 ... 6B 102
TW11: Tedd ... 5H 131
Royal Route HA9: Wemb ... 4F 61
Royal St. SE1 ... 1H 19 (3K 101)
Royal Thames Wlk.
KT7: T Ditt ... 1A 162
Royal Twr. Lodge E1 ... 3K 15
(off Cartwright St.)
Royalty Mans. W1 ... 1C 12
(off Meard St.)
Royalty M. W1 ... 1C 12 (6H 83)
Royalty Studios W11 ... 6G 81
(off Lancaster Rd.)
Royal Veterinary College
Camden Town ... 1H 83
Royal Victoria Dock E16 ... 7K 87
Royal Victoria Gdns. SE16 ... 4A 104
(off Whiting Way)
Royal Victoria Patriotic Bldg.
SW18 ... 6B 118
Royal Victoria Pl. E16 ... 1K 105
Royal Victoria Sq. E16 ... 7K 87
Royal Victor Pl. E3 ... 2K 85
Royal Wlk. SM6: W'gton ... 2F 167
Royal Westminster Lodge
SW1 ... 3C 18
(off Elverton St.)
Royal Wharf E16 ... 2K 105
Royal Wharf Wlk. E16 ... 2K 105
Royal Wimbledon Golf Course ... 5D 134
Royce Av. NW9 ... 2C 44
Roycraft Av. IG11: Bark ... 2K 89
Roycraft Ho. IG11: Bark ... 2K 89
Roycroft Cl. E18 ... 1K 51
SW2 ... 1A 138
Roydene Rd. SE18 ... 6J 107
Roydon Cl. IG10: Lough ... 1H 37
SW11 ... 2D 118
Roy Gdns. IG2: Ilf ... 4J 53
Roy Gro. TW12: Hamp ... 6F 131
Royle Bldg. N1 ... 2C 84
(off Wenlock Rd.)
Royle Cres. W13 ... 4A 78
Royley Ho. EC1 ... 3D 8
(off Old St.)
Roymount Ct. TW2: Twick ... 3J 131
Roy Rd. HA6: Nwood ... 1H 39
Roy Sq. E14 ... 7A 86
Royston Av. E4 ... 5H 35
SM1: Sutt ... 3B 166
SM6: Bedd ... 4H 167
Royston Cl. KT12: Walt T ... 7J 147
TW5: Cran ... 1K 111
Royston Ct. E13 ... 1J 87
(off Stopford Rd.)
SE24 ... 6C 120
TW9: Kew ... 1F 115
W8 ... 1J 99
(off Kensington Chu. St.)
Royston Gdns. IG1: Ilf ... 6B 52
Royston Ho. N11 ... 4J 31
SE15 ... 6H 103
(off Friary Est.)
Royston Pde. IG1: Ilf ... 6B 52
Royston Pk. Rd. HA5: Hat E ... 5A 26
Royston Rd. SE20 ... 1K 157
TW10: Rich ... 5E 114
The Roystons KT5: Surb ... 5H 151
Royston St. E2 ... 2J 85
Rozel Ct. N1 ... 1E 84
Rozel Rd. SW4 ... 3G 119
Rozel Ter. CR0: C'don ... 3C 168
(off Church Rd.)
RQ33 SW18 ... 4J 117
Rubastic Rd. UB2: S'hall ... 3A 94
Rubens Gdns. SE22 ... 7G 121
(off Lordship La.)
Rubens Pl. SW4 ... 4J 119
Rubens Rd. UB5: N'olt ... 2A 76
Rubens St. SE6 ... 2B 140
Rubicon Ct. N1 ... 1J 83
Ruby Cl. E5 ... 3K 67
Ruby Ct. E15 ... 1E 86
(off Warton Rd.)
RM8: Dag ... 1G 73
(off Emerald Gdns.)
Ruby Mews N13 ... 5D 32
Ruby Rd. E17 ... 3C 50
Ruby St. NW10 ... 1J 79
SE15 ... 6H 103
Ruby Triangle SE15 ... 6H 103
Ruby Way NW9 ... 1B 44
Ruckholt Cl. E10 ... 3D 68
Ruckholt Rd. E10 ... 4C 68
Ruckledge Av. NW10 ... 2B 80
Rudall Cres. NW3 ... 4B 64
Rudbeck Ho. SE15 ... 7G 103
(off Peckham Pk. Rd.)
Ruddington Cl. E5 ... 4A 68
Ruddock Cl. HA8: Edg ... 7D 28
Ruddstreet Cl. SE18 ... 4F 107
Ruddy Way NW7 ... 6G 29
Rudge Ho. SE16 ... 3G 103
(off Jamaica Rd.)
Rudgwick Ct. SE18 ... 4C 106
(off Woodville St.)
Rudgwick Ter. NW8 ... 1C 82
Rudland Rd. DA7: Bex ... 3H 127
Rudloe Rd. SW12 ... 7G 119
Rudolf Pl. SW8 ... 7F 19 (6J 101)
Rudolph Rd. E13 ... 2H 87
NW6 ... 2J 81
Rudstone Ho. E3 ... 3D 86
(off Bromley High St.)
Rudyard Ct. SE1 ... 7F 15
(off Long La.)
Rudyard Gro. NW7 ... 6D 28
Ruegg Ho. SE18 ... 6E 106
(off Woolwich Comn.)
The Ruffetts CR2: Sels ... 7H 169
Ruffetts Cl. CR2: Sels ... 7H 169
Ruffle Cl. UB7: W Dray ... 2A 92
Rufford Cl. HA3: Kenton ... 6A 42
Rufford St. N1 ... 1J 83
Rufford St. M. N1 ... 7J 65
Rufford Twr. W3 ... 1H 97
Rufforth Ct. NW9 ... 1A 44
(off Pageant Av.)
Rufus Bus. Cen. SW18 ... 2K 135
Rufus Cl. HA4: Ruis ... 3C 58
Rufus Ho. SE1 ... 7K 15
(off St Saviour's Est.)
Rufus St. N1 ... 2G 9 (3E 84)
Rugby Av. HA0: Wemb ... 5B 60
N9 ... 1A 34
UB6: G'frd ... 6H 59
Rugby Cl. HA1: Harr ... 4J 41
Rugby Gdns. RM9: Dag ... 6C 72
Rugby Mans. W14 ... 4G 99
(off Bishop King's Rd.)
Rugby Rd. NW9 ... 4H 43
RM9: Dag ... 7B 72
TW1: Twick ... 5J 113
W4 ... 2A 98
Rugby St. WC1 ... 4G 7 (4K 83)
Rugg St. E14 ... 7C 86
Rugless Ho. E14 ... 2E 104
(off E. Ferry Rd.)
Rugmere NW1 ... 7E 64
(off Ferdinand St.)
RUISLIP ... 1G 57
Ruislip Cl. UB6: G'frd ... 4F 77
RUISLIP COMMON ... 4E 38
Ruislip Ct. HA4: Ruis ... 2H 57
RUISLIP GARDENS ... 3J 57
Ruislip Golf Course ... 2E 56
Ruislip Lido ... 4F 39
Ruislip Lido Railway ... 4F 39
Ruislip Lido Woodlands Cen. ... 4F 39
RUISLIP MANOR ... 2J 57
Ruislip Rd. UB5: N'olt ... 1A 76
UB6: G'frd ... 3E 76
Ruislip Rd. E. UB6: G'frd ... 4H 77
W7 ... 4J 77
W13 ... 4H 77
Ruislip Social Club ... 2H 57
(off Cranley Dr.)
Ruislip St. SW17 ... 4D 136
Ruislip Woods ... 3E 38
Rumball Ho. SE5 ... 7E 102
(off Harris St.)
Rumbold Rd. SW6 ... 7K 99
Rum Cl. E1 ... 7J 85
Rumford Ho. SE1 ... 3C 102
(off Tiverton St.)
Rumsey Cl. TW12: Hamp ... 6D 130
Rumsey M. N4 ... 3B 66
Rumsey Rd. SW9 ... 3K 119
Runacres Ct. SE17 ... 5C 102
Runbury Circ. NW9 ... 2K 61
Runcie Ct. IG6: Ilf ... 4H 53
Runcorn Cl. N17 ... 4H 49
Runcorn Pl. W11 ... 7G 81
Rundell Cres. NW4 ... 5D 44
Rundell Twr. SW8 ... 1K 119
Runes Cl. CR4: Mitc ... 4B 154
Runnel Ct. IG11: Bark ... 2G 89
(off Spring Pl.)
Runnelfield HA1: Harr ... 3J 59
Running Horse Yd.
TW8: Bford ... 6E 96
Runnymede SW19 ... 1A 154
Runnymede Cl. TW2: Whitt ... 6F 113
Runnymede Ct.
SM6: W'gton ... 6F 167
SW15 ... 1C 134
Runnymede Cres. SW16 ... 1H 155
Runnymede Gdns.
TW2: Whitt ... 6F 113
UB6: G'frd ... 2J 77
Runnymede Ho. E9 ... 4A 68
Runnymede Rd. TW2: Whitt ... 6F 113
The Runway HA4: Ruis ... 5K 57
Runway Cl. NW9 ... 2B 44
Rupack St. SE16 ... 2J 103
Rupert Av. HA9: Wemb ... 5E 60
Rupert Ct. KT8: W Mole ... 4E 148
(off St Peter's Rd.)
W1 ... 2C 12 (7H 83)
Rupert Gdns. SW9 ... 2B 120
Rupert Ho. SE11 ... 4K 19 (4A 102)
SW5 ... 4J 99
(off Nevern Sq.)
Rupert Rd. N19 ... 3H 65
(not continuous)
NW6 ... 2H 81
W4 ... 3A 98
Rupert St. W1 ... 2C 12 (7H 83)
Rural Way SW16 ... 7F 137
Rusbridge Cl. E8 ... 5G 67
Ruscoe Rd. E16 ... 6H 87
Ruscombe NW1 ... 1F 83
(off Delancey St.)
Ruscombe Way TW14: Felt ... 7H 111
Ruscus Rd. E17 ... 1C 50
The Rush SW19 ... 1H 153
(off Watery La.)
Rusham Rd. SW12 ... 6D 118
Rushbridge Cl.
CR0: C'don ... 6C 156
Rushbrook Cres. E17 ... 1B 50
Rushbrook Rd. SE9 ... 2G 143
Rushbury Ct.
TW12: Hamp ... 1E 148
Rush Comn. M. SW2 ... 7K 119
Rushcroft Rd. E4 ... 7J 35
SW2 ... 4A 120
Rushcutters Ct. SE16 ... 4A 104
(off Boat Lifter Way)
Rushden Cl. SE19 ... 7D 138
Rushdene SE2 ... 3D 108
(not continuous)
Rushdene Av. EN4: E Barn ... 7H 21
Rushdene Cl. UB5: N'olt ... 2A 76
Rushdene Cres. UB5: N'olt ... 2K 75
Rushdene Rd. HA5: Eastc ... 6B 40
Rushden Gdns. IG5: Ilf ... 2E 52
NW7 ... 6K 29
Rushen Wlk. SM5: Cars ... 1B 166
Rushett Cl. KT7: T Ditt ... 1B 162
Rushett Rd. KT7: T Ditt ... 7B 150
Rushey Cl. KT3: N Mald ... 4K 151
Rushey Grn. SE6 ... 7D 122
Rushey Hill EN2: Enf ... 4E 22
Rushey Mead SE4 ... 5C 122
Rushford Rd. SE4 ... 6B 122
RUSH GREEN ... 1K 73
Rush Grn. Gdns.
RM7: Rush G ... 1J 73
Rush Grn. Rd. RM7: Rush G ... 1H 73
Rushgrove Av. NW9 ... 5A 44
Rushgrove Ct. NW9 ... 5A 44
Rushgrove Pde. NW9 ... 5A 44
Rushgrove St. SE18 ... 4D 106
Rush Hill M. SW11 ... 3E 118
(off Rush Hill Rd.)
Rush Hill Rd. SW11 ... 3E 118
Rushley Cl. BR2: Kes ... 4B 172
Rushmead E2 ... 3H 85
TW10: Ham ... 3B 132
Rushmead Cl. CR0: C'don ... 4F 169
HA8: Edg ... 2C 28
Rushmere Ct. KT4: Wor Pk ... 2C 164
Rushmere Pl. SW19 ... 5F 135
Rushmon Pl. SM3: Cheam ... 6G 165
Rushmon Vs. KT3: N Mald ... 4B 152
Rushmoor Cl. HA5: Eastc ... 4K 39
Rushmore Cl. BR1: Broml ... 3C 160
Rushmore Cres. E5 ... 4K 67
Rushmore Ho. SW15 ... 7C 116
W14 ... 3G 99
(off Russell Rd.)
Rushmore Rd. E5 ... 4J 67
(not continuous)
Rusholme Av. RM10: Dag ... 3G 73
Rusholme Gro. SE19 ... 5E 138
Rusholme Rd. SW15 ... 6F 117
Rushout Av. HA3: Kenton ... 6B 42
Rushton Ho. SW8 ... 2H 119
Rushton St. N1 ... 2D 84
Rushton Wlk. E3 ... 4B 86
(off Hamlets Way)
Rushworth St. SE1 ... 6B 14 (2B 102)
Rushy Mdw. La.
SM5: Cars ... 2C 166
Ruskin Av. DA16: Well ... 2A 126
E12 ... 6C 70
TW9: Kew ... 7G 97
TW14: Felt ... 6H 111
Ruskin Cl. NW11 ... 6K 45
Ruskin Ct. N21 ... 7E 22
SE5 ... 3D 120
(off Champion Hill)
Ruskin Dr. BR6: Orp ... 3J 173
DA16: Well ... 3A 126
KT4: Wor Pk ... 2D 164
Ruskin Gdns. HA3: Kenton ... 5F 43
W5 ... 4D 78
Ruskin Gro. DA16: Well ... 2A 126
Ruskin Ho. CR2: S Croy ... 5D 168
(off Selsdon Rd.)
SW1 ... 4D 18
(off Herrick St.)
Ruskin Mans. W14 ... 6G 99
(off Queen's Club Gdns.)
Ruskin Pde. CR2: S Croy ... 5D 168
(off Selsdon Rd.)
HA8: Edg ... 4A 28
Ruskin Pk. Ho. SE5 ... 3D 120
Ruskin Rd. CR0: C'don ... 2B 168
DA17: Belv ... 4G 109
N17 ... 1F 49
SM5: Cars ... 5D 166
TW7: Isle ... 3K 113
UB1: S'hall ... 7C 76
Ruskin Sq. CR0: C'don ... 2D 168
Ruskin Wlk. BR2: Broml ... 6D 160
N9 ... 2B 34
SE24 ... 5C 120
Ruskin Way SW19 ... 1B 154
Rusland Av. BR6: Orp ... 3H 173
Rusland Hgts. HA1: Harr ... 4J 41
Rusland Pk. Rd. HA1: Harr ... 4J 41
Rusper Cl. HA7: Stan ... 4H 27
NW2 ... 3E 62
Rusper Ct. SW9 ... 2J 119
(off Clapham Rd.)
Rusper Rd. N17 ... 3C 48
N22 ... 2B 48
RM9: Dag ... 6C 72

278 A-Z Big London

Russell Av.—St Clement's Ct.

Russell Av. N22 .... 2A 48
Russell Chambers WC1 .... 6F 7
(off Bury Pl.)
Russell Cl. BR3: Beck 3E 158
DA7: Bex 4G 127
HA4: Ruis 2A 58
NW10 .... 7J 61
SE7 .... 7A 106
W4 .... 6B 98
Russell Ct. E10 .... 7D 50
EN5: New Bar 4F 21
N14 .... 6C 22
SE15 .... 2H 121
(off Heaton Rd.)
SM6: W'gton 5G 167
(off Ross Rd.)
SW1 .... 5B 12
SW16 .... 5K 137
WC1 .... 4E 6
Russell Flint Ho. E16 .... 1K 105
(off Pankhurst Av.)
Russell Gdns. IG2: Ilf 7H 53
N20 .... 2H 31
NW11 .... 6G 45
TW10: Ham 2C 132
UB7: Sip 5C 92
W14 .... 3G 99
Russell Gdns. M. W14 .... 2G 99
Russell Gro. NW7 .... 5F 29
SW9 .... 7A 102
Russell Ho. BR2: Broml 6C 160
(off Wells Vw. Dr.)
E14 .... 6C 86
(off Saracen St.)
SW1 .... 5A 18
(off Cambridge St.)
Russell Kerr Cl. W4 .... 7J 97
Russell La. N20 .... 2H 31
Russell Lodge E4 .... 2K 35
SE1 .... 3D 102
(off Spurgeon St.)
Russell Mans. WC1 .... 5F 7
(off Southampton Row)
Russell Mead HA3: Hrw W 1K 41
Russell Pde. NW11 .... 6G 45
(off Golders Grn. Rd.)
Russell Pl. NW3 .... 5C 64
SE16 .... 3A 104
SM2: Sutt 7K 165
Russell Rd. CR4: Mitc 3C 154
E4 .... 4G 35
E10 .... 6D 50
E16 .... 6J 87
E17 .... 3B 50
EN1: Enf 1A 24
IG9: Buck H 1E 36
KT12: Walt T 6J 147
N8 .... 6H 47
N13 .... 6E 32
N15 .... 5E 48
N20 .... 2H 31
NW9 .... 6B 44
SW19 .... 7J 135
TW2: Twick 6K 113
TW17: Shep 7E 146
UB5: N'olt 5G 59
W14 .... 3G 99
Russell's Footpath SW16 .... 5J 137
Russell Sq. WC1 .... 4E 6 (5J 83)
Russell Sq. Mans. WC1 .... 5F 7
(off Southampton Row)
Russell St. WC2 .... 2F 13 (7J 83)
Russell's Wharf Flats W10 .... 4H 81
Russell Wlk. TW10: Rich 6F 115
Russell Way SM1: Sutt 5K 165
Russell Yd. SW15 .... 4G 117
Russet Av. TW17: Shep 3G 147
Russet Cl. UB10: Hil 4E 74
Russet Cres. N7 .... 5K 65
Russet Dr. CR0: C'don 1A 170
Russets Cl. E4 .... 4A 36
Russett Way SE13 .... 2D 122
Russia Dock Rd. SE16 .... 1A 104
Russia La. E2 .... 2J 85
Russia Row EC2 .... 1D 14 (6C 84)
Russia Wlk. SE16 .... 2A 104
Russington Rd.
TW17: Shep 6F 147
Rusthall Av. W4 .... 4K 97
Rusthall Cl. CR0: C'don 6J 157
Rustic Av. SW16 .... 7F 137
Rustic Pl. HA0: Wemb 4D 60
Rustic Wlk. E16 .... 6K 87
(off Lambert Rd.)
Rustington Wlk. SM4: Mord 7H 153
Ruston Av. KT5: Surb 7H 151
Ruston Gdns. N14 .... 6K 21
Ruston M. W11 .... 6G 81
Ruston Rd. SE18 .... 3C 106
Ruston St. E3 .... 1B 86
Rust Sq. SE5 .... 7D 102
Rutford Rd. SW16 .... 5J 137
Ruth Cl. HA7: Stan 4F 43
Ruth Ct. E3 .... 2A 86
Rutherford Cl. SM2: Sutt 6B 166
UB8: Hil 4B 74
Rutherford Ho. E1 .... 4H 85
(off Brady St.)
HA9: Wemb 3J 61
(off Barnhill Rd.)
SW11 .... 2D 118
(off Battersea Pk. Rd.)
Rutherford St. SW1 .... 3C 18 (4H 101)
Rutherford Twr. UB1: S'hall 6F 77
Rutherford Way
HA9: Wemb 3G 61
WD23: B Hea 1C 26
Rutherglen Rd. SE2 .... 6A 108
Rutherwyke Cl.
KT17: Ewe 6C 164
Ruth Ho. W10 .... 4G 81
(off Kensal Rd.)
Ruthin Cl. NW9 .... 6A 44
Ruthin Rd. SE3 .... 6J 105
Ruthven St. E9 .... 1K 85
Rutland Av. DA15: Sidc 7A 126
Rutland Cl.
DA5: Bexl 2D 144
KT9: Chess 6F 163
SW14 .... 3H 115
SW19 .... 7C 136
Rutland Ct. BR7: Chst 1E 160
EN3: Pond E 5C 24
KT1: King T 4D 150
(off Palace Rd.)
SE5 .... 4D 120
SE9 .... 2G 143
SW7 .... 7D 10
W3 .... 6G 79
Rutland Dr. SM4: Mord 6H 153
TW10: Ham 1D 132
Rutland Gdns. CR0: C'don 4E 168
N4 .... 6B 48
RM8: Dag 5C 72
SW7 .... 7D 10 (2C 100)
W13 .... 5A 78
Rutland Gdns. M.
SW7 .... 7D 10 (2C 100)
Rutland Ga. BR2: Broml 4H 159
DA17: Belv 5H 109
SW7 .... 7D 10 (2C 100)
Rutland Ga. M. SW7 .... 7C 10
Rutland Gro. W6 .... 5D 98
Rutland Ho. NW10 .... 3C 80
UB5: N'olt 6E 58
(off The Farmlands)
W8 .... 3K 99
(off Marloes Rd.)
Rutland M. NW8 .... 1K 81
Rutland M. E. SW7 .... 1C 16
Rutland M. Sth. SW7 .... 1C 16
Rutland M. W. SW7 .... 1C 16
Rutland Pk. NW2 .... 6E 62
SE6 .... 2B 140
Rutland Pk. Gdns. NW2 .... 6E 62
(off Rutland Pk.)
Rutland Pk. Mans. NW2 .... 6E 62
Rutland Pl. EC1 .... 5B 8 (4B 84)
WD23: B Hea 1C 26
Rutland Rd. E7 .... 7B 70
E9 .... 1K 85
E11 .... 5K 51
E17 .... 6C 50
HA1: Harr 6G 41
IG1: Ilf 3F 71
SW19 .... 7C 136
TW2: Twick 2H 131
UB1: S'hall 5E 76
UB3: Harl 4F 93
Rutland St. SW7 .... 1D 16 (3C 100)
Rutland Wlk. SE6 .... 2B 140
Rutley Cl. SE17 .... 6B 102
Rutlish Rd. SW19 .... 1J 153
Rutter Gdns. CR4: Mitc 4A 154
Rutters Cl. UB7: W Dray 2C 92
The Rutts WD23: B Hea 1C 26
Rutt's Ter. SE14 .... 1K 121
Ruvigny Gdns. SW15 .... 3F 117
Ruxbury Ct. TW15: Ashf 3A 128
RUXLEY 7D 144
Ruxley Cl. DA14: Sidc 6D 144
KT19: Ewe 5H 163
Ruxley Cnr. Ind. Est.
DA14: Sidc 6D 144
Ruxley Ct. KT19: Ewe 5J 163
Ruxley Cres. KT10: Clay 6B 162
Ruxley Gdns. TW17: Shep 5E 146
Ruxley La. KT19: Ewe 6H 163
Ruxley M. KT19: Ewe 5H 163
Ruxley Pk. Golf Course 7D 144
Ruxley Ridge KT10: Clay 7A 162
Ruxley Towers KT10: Clay 7A 162
Ryalls Ct. N20 .... 3J 31
Ryan Cl. HA4: Ruis 1K 57
SE3 .... 4A 124
Ryan Ct. RM7: Rom 6J 55
SW16 .... 7J 137
Ryan Dr. TW8: Bford 6A 96
Ryarsh Cres. BR6: Orp 4J 173
Rycott Path SE22 .... 7G 121
Rycroft Way N17 .... 3F 49
Ryculff Sq. SE3 .... 2H 123
Rydal Cl. NW4 .... 1G 45
Rydal Ct. HA8: Edg 5A 28
HA9: Wemb 7F 43
Rydal Cres. UB6: G'frd 3B 78
Rydal Dr. BR4: W W'ck 2G 171
DA7: Bex 1G 127
Rydal Gdns. HA9: Wemb 1C 60
NW9 .... 5A 44
SW15 .... 5A 134
TW3: Houn 6F 113
Rydal Mt. BR2: Broml 4H 159
Rydal Rd. SW16 .... 4H 137
Rydal Water NW1 .... 2A 6 (3G 83)
Rydal Way EN3: Pond E 6D 24
HA4: Ruis 4A 58
Ryde Ho. NW6 .... 1J 81
(off Priory Pk. Rd.)
Rydens Ho. SE9 .... 3A 142
Rydens Rd. KT12: Walt T 7C 148
Ryde Pl. TW1: Twick 6D 114
Ryder Av. E10 .... 7D 50
Ryder Cl. BR1: Broml 5K 141
Ryder Ct. E10 .... 2D 68
SW1 .... 4B 12
Ryder Dr. SE16 .... 5H 103
Ryder Ho. E1 .... 4J 85
(off Colebert Av.)
Ryder M. E9 .... 5J 67
Ryder's Ter. NW8 .... 2A 82
Ryder St. SW1 .... 4B 12 (1G 101)
Ryde Va. Rd. SW12 .... 2G 137
Rydon M. SW19 .... 7E 134
Rydons Cl. SE9 .... 3C 124
Rydon St. N1 .... 1C 84
Rydston Cl. N7 .... 7J 65
The Rye N14 .... 7C 22
Rye Cl. DA5: Bexl 6H 127
Ryecotes Mead SE21 .... 1E 138
Ryecroft Av. IG5: Ilf 2F 53
TW2: Whitt 7F 113
Ryecroft Rd. BR5: Pet W 6H 161
SE13 .... 5E 122
SW16 .... 6A 138
Ryecroft St. SW6 .... 1K 117
Ryedale SE22 .... 6H 121
Ryefield Av. UB10: Hil 7D 56
Ryefield Ct. HA6: Nwood 2J 39
Ryefield Cres. HA6: Nwood 2J 39
Ryefield Pde. HA6: Nwood 2J 39
(off Joel St.)
Ryefield Path SW15 .... 1C 134
Ryefield Rd. SE19 .... 6C 138
Ryegates SE15 .... 2H 121
(off Caulfield Rd.)
Rye Hill Pk. SE15 .... 4J 121
Rye Ho. SE16 .... 2J 103
(off Swan Rd.)
SW1 .... 5J 17
(off Ebury Bri. Rd.)
Ryeland Blvd. SW18 .... 5K 117
Ryeland Cl. UB7: Yiew 6A 74
Ryelands Cres. SE12 .... 6A 124
Rye La. SE15 .... 1G 121
Rye Mans. E20 .... 5E 68
(off Napa Cl.)
Rye Pas. SE15 .... 3G 121
Rye Rd. SE15 .... 4K 121
Rye Wlk. SW15 .... 5F 117
Rye Way HA8: Edg 6A 28
Ryfold Rd. SW19 .... 3J 135
Ryhope Rd. N11 .... 4A 32
Ryland Cl. TW13: Felt 4H 129
Rylandes Rd. NW2 .... 3C 62
Ryland Rd. NW5 .... 6F 65
Rylett Cres. W12 .... 2B 98
Rylett Rd. W12 .... 2B 98
Rylston Rd. N13 .... 3J 33
SW6 .... 6H 99
Rymer Rd. CR0: C'don 7E 156
Rymer St. SE24 .... 6B 120
Rymill St. E16 .... 1E 106
Rysbrack St. SW3 .... 1E 16 (3D 100)
Rythe Bank Cl. KT7: T Ditt 7B 150
Rythe Cl. KT9: Chess 7C 162
Rythe Ct. KT7: T Ditt 7A 150

S

Saatchi Gallery 5F 17 (5D 100)
Sabah Ct. TW15: Ashf 4C 128
Sabella Ct. E3 .... 2B 86
Sabine Rd. SW11 .... 3D 118
Sable Cl. TW4: Houn 3A 112
Sable Ho. E20 .... 5D 68
(off Scarlet Cl.)
Sable St. N1 .... 7B 66
Sach Rd. E5 .... 2H 67
Sackett Rd. IG11: Bark 4A 90
Sackville Av. BR2: Hayes 1J 171
Sackville Cl. HA2: Harr 3H 59
Sackville Gdns. IG1: Ilf 1D 70
Sackville Ho. SW16 .... 3J 137
Sackville Rd. SM2: Sutt 7J 165
Sackville St. W1 .... 3B 12 (7G 83)
Saddleback La. W7 .... 3J 95
Saddlebrook Pk. TW16: Sun 7G 129
Saddle M. CR0: C'don 7C 156
Saddlers Cl. HA5: Hat E 6A 26
Saddlers Ho. E17 .... 5B 50
(off Track St.)
E20 .... 5E 68
(off Ribbons Wlk.)
Saddlers M. HA0: Wemb 4K 59
KT1: Hamp W 1C 150
SW8 .... 1J 119
Saddlers Pl. TW3: Houn 3G 113
Saddlescombe Way N12 .... 5D 30
Saddle Yd. W1 .... 4J 11 (1F 101)
Sadler Cl. CR4: Mitc 2D 154
Sadler Hgts. N1 .... 7K 65
(off Caledonian Rd.)
Sadler Ho. E3 .... 3D 86
(off Bromley High St.)
EC1 .... 1K 7
(off Spa Grn. Est.)
Sadler Pl. E9 .... 5A 68
Sadlers Ct. SE1 .... 7G 15
Sadlers Ga. M. SW15 .... 3E 116
Sadlers Ride KT8: W Mole 2G 149
Sadler's Wells Theatre 1K 7 (3A 84)
Safara Ho. SE5 .... 1E 120
(off Dalwood St.)
Safari Cinema 5K 41
Saffron Av. E14 .... 7F 87
Saffron Central Sq. CR0: C'don 1C 168
Saffron Cl. CR0: C'don 6J 155
NW11 .... 6H 45
Saffron Ct. E15 .... 5G 69
(off Maryland Pk.)
TW14: Bedf 7E 110
Saffron Hill EC1 .... 5K 7 (5A 84)
Saffron Ho. SM2: Sutt 7K 165
TW9: Kew 1H 115
Saffron M. SW19 .... 7G 135
Saffron Rd. RM5: Col R 2K 55
Saffron St. EC1 .... 5K 7 (5A 84)
Saffron Way KT6: Surb 1D 162
Saffron Wharf SE1 .... 6K 15
(off Shad Thames)
Sage Cl. E6 .... 5D 88
Sage M. SE22 .... 5F 121
Sage St. E1 .... 7J 85
Sage Way WC1 .... 2G 7
Sage Yd. KT6: Surb 1F 163
Sahara Ct. UB1: S'hall 7C 76
Saigasso Cl. E16 .... 6B 88
Sailacre Ho. SE10 .... 5H 105
Sail Ct. E14 .... 7F 87
(off Newport Av.)
Sailmakers Ct. SW6 .... 3A 118
Sailors Ho. E14 .... 6F 87
(off Deauville Cl.)
Sail St. SE11 .... 3H 19 (4K 101)
Saimet NW9 .... 7G 29
(off Wiggins Mead)
Sainfoin Rd. SW17 .... 2E 136
Sainsbury Rd. SE19 .... 5E 138
Sainsbury Wing 3D 12
(within National Gallery)
St Agatha's Dr. KT2: King T 6F 133
St Agatha's Gro. SM5: Cars 1D 166
St Agnes Cl. E9 .... 1J 85
St Agnes Ho. E3 .... 2C 86
(off Ordell Rd.)
St Agnes Pl. SE11 .... 7K 19 (6B 102)
St Agnes Quad. SE11 .... 6A 102
St Agnes Well EC1 .... 3F 9
St Aidans Ct. IG11: Bark 2B 90
St Aidan's Rd. SE22 .... 6H 121
W13 .... 2B 96
St Alban's Av. E6 .... 3D 88
W4 .... 4K 97
St Albans Av. TW13: Hanw 5B 130
St Albans Cl. NW11 .... 1J 63
St Albans Ct. EC2 .... 6D 8
St Alban's Cres. IG8: Wfd G 7D 36
N22 .... 1A 48
St Albans Farm TW14: Houn 5A 112
St Alban's Gdns. TW11: Tedd 5A 132
St Alban's Gro. SM5: Cars 7C 154
W8 .... 3K 99
St Alban's La. NW11 .... 1J 63
St Albans Mans. W8 .... 3K 99
(off Kensington Ct. Pl.)
St Albans Pl. N1 .... 1B 84
St Alban's Rd. IG8: Wfd G 7D 36
KT2: King T 6E 132
SM1: Sutt 4H 165
St Albans Rd. EN5: Barn 1A 20
IG3: Ilf 1K 71
NW5 .... 3E 64
NW10 .... 1A 80
St Alban's St. SW1 .... 3C 12 (7H 83)
St Albans Studios W8 .... 3K 99
(off St Albans Gro.)
St Albans Ter. W6 .... 6G 99
St Albans Vs. NW5 .... 3E 64
St Alfege Pas. SE10 .... 6E 104
St Alfege Rd. SE7 .... 6B 106
St Alphage Ct. NW9 .... 3K 43
St Alphage Gdn. EC2 .... 6D 8 (5C 84)
St Alphage Highwalk EC2 .... 6D 8
St Alphage Wlk. HA8: Edg 2J 43
St Alphege Rd. N9 .... 7D 24
St Alphonsus Rd. SW4 .... 4G 119
St Amunds Cl. SE6 .... 4C 140
St Andrew's Av. HA0: Wemb 4A 60
St Andrews Chambers W1 .... 6B 6
(off Wells St.)
St Andrew's Cl. HA4: Ruis 2B 58
HA7: Stan 2C 42
N12 .... 4F 31
NW2 .... 3D 62
TW7: Isle 1J 113
TW17: Shep 4F 147
St Andrews Cl. KT7: T Ditt 1B 162
SE16 .... 5H 103
SE28 .... 6D 90
SW19 .... 6K 135
St Andrew's Ct. SW18 .... 2A 136
St Andrews Ct. E17 .... 2A 50
SM1: Sutt 3C 166
St Andrews Dr. HA7: Stan 1C 42
St Andrew's Gro. N16 .... 1D 66
St Andrew's Hill EC4 .... 2B 14 (6B 84)
(not continuous)
St Andrews Ho. RM8: Dag 4A 72
SE16 .... 3H 103
(off Southwark Pk. Rd.)
St Andrews Mans. W1 .... 6G 5
(off Dorset St.)
W14 .... 6G 99
(off St Andrew's Rd.)
St Andrew's M. N16 .... 1E 66
SE3 .... 7J 105
St Andrews M. SW12 .... 1H 137
St Andrew's Pl. NW1 .... 3K 5 (4F 83)
St Andrew's Rd. CR0: C'don 4C 168
DA14: Sidc 3D 144
E11 .... 6G 51
E13 .... 3K 87
E17 .... 2K 49
EN1: Enf 3J 23
IG1: Ilf 7D 52
KT6: Surb 6D 150
N9 .... 7D 24
NW9 .... 1K 61
NW10 .... 6D 62
NW11 .... 6H 45
RM7: Rom 6K 55
SM5: Cars 3C 166
UB10: Uxb 1A 74
W3 .... 7A 80
W14 .... 6G 99
St Andrews Rd. W7 .... 2J 95
St Andrew's Sq. KT6: Surb 6D 150
St Andrews Sq. W11 .... 6G 81
St Andrew's Twr. UB1: S'hall 7G 77
(off Baird Av.)
St Andrew St. EC4 .... 6K 7 (5A 84)
St Andrews Way E3 .... 4D 86
St Andrew's Wharf SE1 .... 2F 103
St Anna Rd. EN5: Barn 5A 20
St Anne's Cl. N6 .... 3E 64
St Anne's Ct. BR4: W W'ck 4G 171
NW6 .... 1G 81
W1 .... 1C 12 (6H 83)
St Anne's Flats NW1 .... 1C 6
(off Doric Way)
St Anne's Gdns. NW10 .... 3F 79
St Annes M. SW20 .... 7F 135
St Anne's Pas. E14 .... 6B 86
St Anne's Rd. E11 .... 2F 69
HA0: Wemb 5D 60
St Anne's Row E14 .... 6B 86
St Anne's Trad. Est. E14 .... 6B 86
(off St Anne's Row)
St Anne St. E14 .... 6B 86
St Ann's IG11: Bark 1G 89
St Ann's Ct. NW4 .... 3D 44
St Ann's Cres. SW18 .... 6K 117
St Ann's Gdns. NW5 .... 6E 64
St Ann's Hill SW18 .... 5K 117
St Ann's Ho. WC1 .... 2J 7
(off Margery St.)
St Ann's La. SW1 .... 2D 18 (3H 101)
St Ann's Pk. Rd. SW18 .... 6A 118
St Ann's Pas. SW13 .... 3A 116
St Ann's Rd. HA1: Harr 6J 41
IG11: Bark 1G 89
N9 .... 2A 34
N15 .... 5B 48
SW13 .... 2B 116
W11 .... 7F 81
St Ann's Shop. Cen. 6J 41
St Ann's St. SW1 .... 1D 18 (3H 101)
St Ann's Ter. NW8 .... 2B 82
St Ann's Vs. W11 .... 1F 99
St Ann's Way CR2: S Croy 6B 168
St Anselms Ct. SW16 .... 5J 137
St Anselm's Pl. W1 .... 2J 11 (7F 83)
St Anselm's Rd. UB3: Hayes 2H 93
St Anthony's Av. IG8: Wfd G 6F 37
St Anthony's Cl. E1 .... 1G 103
E9 .... 6B 68
(off Wallis Rd.)
SW17 .... 2C 136
St Anthony's Ct. BR6: Farnb 2F 173
SW17 .... 2E 136
St Anthony's Flats NW1 .... 2H 83
(off Aldenham St.)
St Anthony's Way TW14: Felt 4H 111
St Antony's Rd. E7 .... 7K 69
St Arvan's Cl. CR0: C'don 3E 168
St Asaph Rd. SE4 .... 3K 121
St Aubins Ct. N1 .... 1D 84
St Aubyn's Av. SW19 .... 5H 135
TW3: Houn 5E 112
St Aubyn's Cl. BR6: Orp 3K 173
St Aubyn's Gdns. BR6: Orp 2K 173
St Aubyn's Rd. SE19 .... 6F 139
St Audrey Av. DA7: Bex 2G 127
St Augustine's Av. BR2: Broml 5C 160
CR2: S Croy 6C 168
HA9: Wemb 3E 60
W5 .... 2E 78
St Augustine's Ct. SE1 .... 5H 103
(off Lynton Rd.)
St Augustine's Ho. NW1 .... 1C 6
(off Werrington St.)
St Augustine's Mans. SW1 .... 4B 18
(off Bloomburg St.)
St Augustine's Path N5 .... 4C 66
St Augustine's Rd. DA17: Belv 4F 109
NW1 .... 7H 65
St Augustine's Sports Cen. 2J 81
St Austell Cl. HA8: Edg 2F 43
St Austell Rd. SE13 .... 2E 122
St Awdry's Rd. IG11: Bark 7H 71
St Awdry's Wlk. IG11: Bark 7G 71
St Barnabas Cl. BR3: Beck 2E 158
SE22 .... 5E 120
St Barnabas Ct. HA3: Hrw W 1G 41
St Barnabas Gdns. KT8: W Mole 5E 148
St Barnabas M. SW1 .... 5H 17
St Barnabas Rd. CR4: Mitc 7E 136
E17 .... 6C 50
IG8: Wfd G 1K 51
SM1: Sutt 5B 166
St Barnabas St. SW1 .... 5H 17 (5E 100)
St Barnabas Ter. E9 .... 5K 67
St Barnabas Vs. SW8 .... 1J 119
St Bartholomew's Cl. SE26 .... 4H 139
St Bartholomew's Ct. E6 .... 2C 88
(off St Bartholomew's Rd.)
St Bartholomew's Hospital Mus. 6B 8
St Bartholomew's Rd. E6 .... 2D 88
St Benedict's Cl. SW17 .... 5E 136
St Benet's Cl. SW17 .... 2C 136
St Benet's Gro. SM5: Cars 7A 154
St Benet's Pl. EC3 .... 2F 15 (7D 84)
St Bernards CR0: C'don 3E 168
St Bernard's Cl. SE27 .... 4D 138
St Bernards Ho. E14 .... 3E 104
(off Galbraith St.)
St Bernard's Rd. E6 .... 1B 88
St Blaise Av. BR1: Broml 2K 159
St Botolph Row EC3 .... 1J 15 (6F 85)
St Botolphs E1 .... 7J 9
(off St Botolph St.)
St Botolph St. EC3 .... 7J 9 (6F 85)
St Brelades Ct. N1 .... 1E 84
St Bride's Av. EC4 .... 1A 14
HA8: Edg 1F 43
St Bride's Church 1A 14 (6B 84)
St Brides Cl. DA18: Erith 2D 108
St Bride's Crypt Mus. 1A 14
(off Fleet St.)
St Bride's Ho. E3 .... 2C 86
(off Ordell Rd.)
St Bride's Pas. EC4 .... 1A 14
St Bride St. EC4 .... 7A 8 (6B 84)
St Catherine's Apts. E3 .... 3D 86
(off Bow Rd.)
St Catherine's Cl. SW17 .... 2C 136
SW20 .... 5E 152
St Catherines Cl. KT9: Chess 6D 162
St Catherine's Ct. W4 .... 3A 98
St Catherines Ct. TW13: Felt 1J 129
St Catherine's Dr. SE14 .... 2K 121
St Catherine's Farm Ct.
HA4: Ruis 6E 38
St Catherines M.
SW3 .... 3E 16 (4D 100)
St Catherine's Rd. E4 .... 2H 35
HA4: Ruis 6F 39
St Cecilia Pl. SE3 .... 5J 105
St Cecilia's Cl. SM3: Sutt 1G 165
St Chads Cl. KT6: Surb 7C 150
St Chad's Gdns.
RM6: Chad H 7E 54
St Chad's Pl. WC1 .... 1F 7 (3J 83)
St Chad's Rd. RM6: Chad H 7E 54
St Chad's St. WC1 .... 1F 7 (3J 83)
(not continuous)
St Charles Pl. W10 .... 5G 81
St Charles Sq. W10 .... 5F 81
St Chloe's Ho. E3 .... 2C 86
(off Ordell Rd.)
St Christopher Rd. UB8: Cowl 6A 74
St Christopher's Cl.
TW7: Isle 1J 113
St Christophers Dr. UB3: Hayes 7K 75
St Christophers Gdns.
CR7: Thor H 3A 156
St Christopher's Ho. NW1 .... 2G 83
(off Bridgeway St.)
St Christopher's M.
SM6: W'gton 5G 167
St Christopher's Pl. W1 .... 7H 5 (6E 82)
St Clair Cl. IG5: Ilf 2D 52
St Clair Dr. KT4: Wor Pk 3D 164
St Clair Ho. E3 .... 3B 86
(off British St.)
St Clair Rd. E13 .... 2K 87
St Clair's Rd. CR0: C'don 2E 168
St Clare Bus. Pk.
TW12: Hamp H 6G 131
St Clare St. EC3 .... 1J 15 (6F 85)
St Clements Av. E3 .... 3B 86
St Clement's Ct. EC4 .... 2F 15
N7 .... 6A 66

St Clements Ct. SE14 6K 103
(off Myers La.)
W11 7F 81
(off Stoneleigh St.)
St Clement's Development E3 3B 86
St Clement's Hgts. SE26 4G 139
St Clements Ho. E1 6J 9
(off Leyden St.)
St Clement's La. WC2 1G 13 (6K 83)
St Clements Mans. SW6 6F 99
(off Lillie Rd.)
St Clements St. N7 6A 66
St Clements Yd. SE22 4F 121
St Cloud Rd. SE27 4C 138
St Columba's Ct. E15 4G 69
(off Janson Rd.)
St Columbas Ho. E17 4D 50
St Columb's Ho. W10 5G 81
(off Blagrove Rd.)
St Crispin's Cl. NW3 4C 64
UB1: S'hall 6D 76
St Cross St. EC1 5K 7 (5A 84)
St Cuthbert's Rd. NW2 6H 63
St Cuthberts Rd. N13 6F 33
St Cyprian's St. SW17 4D 136
St David's Cl. BR4: W W'ck 7D 158
HA9: Wemb 3J 61
St Davids Cl. SE16 5H 103
(off Masters Dr.)
St David's Ct. BR1: Broml 3F 161
E17 3E 50
St Davids Ct. TW15: Ashf 2B 128
St David's Dr. HA8: Edg 1F 43
St Davids M. E3 3A 86
(off Morgan St.)
E18 1J 51
St David's Pl. NW4 7D 44
St Davids Sq. E14 5D 104
St Denis Rd. SE27 4D 138
St Dionis Rd. SW6 2H 117
St Domingo Ho. SE18 3D 106
(off Leda Rd.)
St Donatt's Rd. SE14 1B 122
ST DUNSTAN'S 6H 165
St Dunstan's All. EC3 2G 15
St Dunstans Av. W3 7K 79
St Dunstan's Ct. UB3: Harl 5H 93
St Dunstan's Ct. EC4 1K 13 (6A 84)
St Dunstan's Enterprises 1C 140
St Dunstan's Gdns. W3 7K 79
St Dunstan's Hill SM1: Sutt 5G 165
St Dunstans Hill EC3 3G 15 (7E 84)
St Dunstan's Ho. WC2 1J 13
(off Chancery La.)
St Dunstan's La. BR3: Beck 6E 158
EC3 3G 15 (7E 84)
St Dunstans M. E1 5A 86
(off White Horse Rd.)
St Dunstan's Rd. E7 6K 69
SE25 4F 157
TW4: Cran 2K 111
(not continuous)
TW13: Felt 3H 129
W6 5F 99
W7 2J 95
St Edmund's Av. HA4: Ruis 6F 39
St Edmund's Cl. NW8 1D 82
SW17 2C 136
St Edmunds Cl. DA18: Erith 2D 108
St Edmund's Ct. NW8 1D 82
(off St Edmund's Ter.)
St Edmunds Ct. CR0: C'don 2B 168
St Edmunds Dr. HA7: Stan 1A 42
St Edmund's La. TW2: Whitt 7F 113
St Edmund's Rd. IG1: Ilf 6D 52
N9 7B 24
St Edmunds Sq. SW13 6E 98
St Edmund's Ter. NW8 1C 82
St Edward's Cl. NW11 6J 45
St Edwards Ct. NW11 6J 45
St Edwards Way RM1: Rom 5K 55
St Egberts Way E4 1K 35
St Elmo Rd. W12 1B 98
St Elmos Rd. SE16 2A 104
St Erkenwald M. IG11: Bark 1H 89
St Erkenwald Rd. IG11: Bark 1H 89
St Ermin's Hill SW1 1C 18
St Ervan's Rd. W10 5H 81
St Eugene Ct. NW6 1G 81
(off Salusbury Rd.)
St Faith's Cl. EN2: Enf 1H 23
St Faith's Rd. SE21 1B 138
St Fidelis Rd. DA8: Erith 4K 109
St Fillans Rd. SE6 1E 140
St Francis Cl. BR5: Pet W 6J 161
St Francis' Ho. NW1 2H 83
(off Bridgeway St.)
St Francis Pl. SW12 6F 119
St Francis Rd. DA8: Erith 4K 109
SE22 4E 120
St Francis Way IG1: Ilf 4H 71
St Frideswide's M. E14 6E 86
St Gabriel's Cl. E11 2K 69
E14 5D 86
St Gabriels Ct. N11 7C 32
St Gabriels Mnr. SE5 1B 120
(off Cormont Rd.)
St Gabriels Rd. NW2 5F 63
St Gabriel Wlk. SE1 4B 102
(off Elephant & Castle)
St George's Av. E7 7K 69
N7 4H 65
NW9 4K 43
UB1: S'hall 7D 76
W5 2D 96
St George's Bldgs. SE1 3B 102
(off St George's Rd.)
St George's Cir. SE1 7A 14 (3B 102)
St George's Cl. HA0: Wemb 3A 60
NW11 6H 45
SW8 1G 119
St Georges Cl. SE28 6D 90
St George's Ct. E6 4D 88
SE1 3B 102
(off Garden Row)
SW1 5A 18
(off St George's Dr.)
SW3 3C 16
(off Brompton Rd.)
SW7 3A 100
SW15 4H 117
St Georges Ct. E17 5F 51
EC4 7A 8 (6B 84)
HA3: Kenton 6A 42
(off Kenton Rd.)
St George's Dr. SW1 4K 17 (4F 101)
UB10: Ick 3B 56
ST GEORGE'S FIELD 7C 82
St George's Flds. W2 1D 10 (6C 82)
St George's Gdns. KT6: Surb 2H 163
St George's Gro. SW17 3B 136
St George's Ho. NW1 2H 83
(off Bridgeway St.)
St Georges Ho. SW11 1E 118
(off Charlotte Despard Av.)
St George's Ind. Est.
KT2: King T 5D 132
N22 7G 33
St George's La. EC3 2F 15
St George's Leisure Cen. 7H 85
St George's Mans. SW1 5D 18
(off Causton St.)
St George's M. NW1 7D 64
SE1 1K 19
SE8 4B 104
St Georges Pde. SE6 2B 140
(off Perry Hill)
St George's Pl. TW1: Twick 1A 132
St George's Rd. BR1: Broml 2D 160
BR3: Beck 1D 158
BR5: Pet W 6H 161
CR4: Mitc 3F 155
DA14: Sidc 6D 144
E7 7K 69
E10 3E 68
EN1: Enf 1A 24
IG1: Ilf 7D 52
KT2: King T 7G 133
N13 3E 32
NW11 6H 45
RM9: Dag 5E 72
SE1 1K 19 (3A 102)
SM6: W'gton 5F 167
SW19 7H 135
(not continuous)
TW1: Twick 5B 114
TW13: Hanw 4B 130
W4 2K 97
W7 1K 95
St Georges Rd. TW9: Rich 3F 115
St George's Rd. W. BR1: Broml 1C 160
St George's Shop. & Leisure Cen.
6J 41
St George's Sq. E7 7K 69
KT3: N Mald 3A 152
SE8 4B 104
(not continuous)
SW1 5C 18 (5H 101)
St Georges Sq. E14 7A 86
St George's Sq. M.
SW1 6C 18 (5H 101)
St George's Ter. E6 3C 88
(off Masterman Rd.)
NW1 7D 64
SE15 7G 103
(off Peckham Hill St.)
St George St. W1 1K 11 (7F 83)
St George's University of London
5B 136
St George's Wlk. CR0: C'don 3C 168
St George's Way SE15 6E 102
St George's Wharf SE1 6K 15
(off Shad Thames)
St George Wharf SW8 7E 18 (6J 101)
St Gerards Cl. SW4 5G 119
St German's Pl. SE3 1J 123
St German's Rd. SE23 1A 140
St Giles Av. RM10: Dag 7H 73
UB10: Ick 4E 56
St Giles Churchyard EC2 6D 8 (5C 84)
St Giles Cir. W1 7D 6 (6H 83)
St Giles Cl. BR6: Farnb 5H 173
RM10: Dag 7H 73
TW5: Hest 7C 94
St Giles High St. WC2 7D 6 (6H 83)
St Giles Ho. EN5: New Bar 4F 21
SE5 1E 120
St Giles Pas. WC2 1D 12
St Giles Rd. SE5 7E 102
St Giles Sq. WC2 7D 6 (6H 83)
St Giles Ter. EC2 6D 8
(off Wood St.)
St Giles Twr. SE5 1E 120
(off Gables Cl.)
St Gilles Ho. E2 2K 85
(off Mace St.)
St Gothard Rd. SE27 4D 138
(not continuous)
St Gregory Cl. HA4: Ruis 4A 58
St Helena Ho. WC1 2J 7
(off Margery St.)
St Helena Rd. SE16 4K 103
St Helena St. WC1 2J 7 (3A 84)
St Helena Ter. TW9: Rich 5D 114
St Helens KT7: T Ditt 7K 149
St Helen's Cl. KT4: Wor Pk 1C 164
St Helens Cl. UB8: Cowl 5A 74
St Helen's Cres. SW16 1K 155
St Helen's Gdns. W10 5F 81
St Helen's Pl. EC3 7G 9 (6E 84)
St Helens Pl. E10 7A 50
St Helen's Rd. DA18: Erith 2D 108
IG1: Ilf 6D 52
SW16 1K 155
W13 1B 96
ST HELIER 7C 154
St Helier Av. SM4: Mord 7A 154
St Helier Ct. N1 1E 84
(off De Beauvoir Est.)
SE16 2K 103
(off Poolmans St.)
St Helier's Av. TW3: Houn 5E 112
St Helier's Rd. E10 6E 50
St Henera's Ct. BR1: Broml 3E 160
(off Brady Dr.)
St Hilary's Ct. BR1: Broml 3F 161
St Hilda's Av. TW15: Ashf 5A 128
St Hilda's Cl. NW6 7F 63
SW17 2C 136
St Hilda's Rd. SW13 6D 98
St Hilda's Wharf E1 1J 103
(off Wapping High St.)
St Hubert's Ho. E14 3C 104
(off Janet St.)
St Hughes Cl. SW17 2C 136
St Hugh's Rd. SE20 1H 157
St Ives Pl. E14 5E 86
St Ivian Ct. N10 2E 46
St James Apts. E17 5A 50
(off Pretoria Av.)
St James Av. N20 3H 31
SM1: Sutt 5J 165
W13 1A 96
St James Cl. EN4: E Barn 4G 21
HA4: Ruis 2A 58
KT3: N Mald 5B 152
N20 3H 31
St James Ct. CR0: C'don 7B 156
E2 3G 85
(off Bethnal Grn. Rd.)
E12 2A 70
SE3 1K 123
St James' Ct. SW1 1B 18 (3G 101)
St James Gdns. RM6: Chad H 4B 54
St James' Gdns. HA0: Wemb 7D 60
St James Ga. IG9: Buck H 1F 37
St James Gro. SW11 2D 118
St James Hall N1 1C 84
(off Prebend St.)
St James Ind. M. SE1 5G 103
St James Mans. SE1 1J 19
(off McAuley Cl.)
St James' Mans. NW6 7J 63
(off West End La.)
St James M. E14 3E 104
E17 5A 50
St James Path E17 5A 50
St James Residences W1 2C 12
(off Brewer St.)
St James Rd. CR4: Mitc 7E 136
SM1: Sutt 5J 165
SM5: Cars 3C 166
St James' Rd. E15 5H 69
KT6: Surb 6D 150
N9 2C 34
ST JAMES'S 4B 12 (1H 101)
St James's SE14 1A 122
St James's App. EC2 4G 9 (4E 84)
St James's Av. BR3: Beck 3A 158
E2 2J 85
TW12: Hamp H 5G 131
St James's Chambers SW1 4B 12
(off Jermyn St.)
St James's Cl. NW8 1D 82
(off St James's Ter. M.)
SE18 5G 107
SW17 2D 136
St James's Cotts. TW9: Rich 5D 114
St James's Ct. HA1: Harr 6A 42
KT1: King T 3E 150
N18 5B 34
(off Fore St.)
St James's Cres. SW9 3A 120
St James's Dr. SW12 1D 136
SW17 1D 136
St James's Gdns. W11 1G 99
(not continuous)
St James's Ho. SE1 4G 103
(off Strathnairn St.)
St James's La. N10 4F 47
St James's Mkt. SW1 3C 12 (7H 83)
St James's Palace 6B 12 (2G 101)
St James's Pk. 6C 12 (2H 101)
St James's Pk. CR0: C'don 7C 156
St James's Pas. EC3 1H 15
St James's Pl. SW1 5A 12 (1G 101)
St James's Rd. CR0: C'don 7B 156
KT1: King T 2D 150
SE1 6G 103
SE16 3G 103
TW12: Hamp H 5F 131
St James's Sq. SW1 4B 12 (1G 101)
St James's St. E17 5A 50
SW1 4A 12 (1G 101)
St James's Ter. NW8 1D 82
(off Prince Albert Rd.)
St James's Ter. M. NW8 1D 82
St James St. W6 5E 98
St James's Wlk. EC1 3A 8 (4B 84)
St James Ter. SW12 1E 136
St James Way DA14: Sidc 5E 144
St Jeromes Gro. UB3: Hayes 6E 74
St Joan's Ho. NW1 1C 6
(off Phoenix Rd.)
St Joan's Rd. N9 2A 34
St John Fisher Rd.
DA18: Erith 3D 108
ST JOHNS 2C 122
St John's Av. N11 5J 31
NW10 1B 80
SW15 5F 117
St Johns Chu. Rd. E9 5J 67
St John's Cl. HA9: Wemb 5E 60
N20 3F 31
(off Rasper Rd.)
SW6 7J 99
St Johns Cl. N14 6B 22
St John's Cotts. SE20 7J 139
St John's Ct. DA8: Erith 4K 109
E1 1H 103
(off Scandrett St.)
HA1: Harr 6K 41
HA6: Nwood 1G 39
(off Murray Rd.)
IG9: Buck H 1E 36
KT1: King T 4E 150
(off Beaufort Rd.)
N4 2B 66
SE13 2E 122
TW7: Isle 2K 113
W6 4D 98
(off Glenthorne Rd.)
St Johns Ct. SW10 7A 100
(off Ashburnham Rd.)
St John's Cres. SW9 3A 120
St Johns Dr. SW18 1K 135
St John's Est. N1 2D 84
SE1 6J 15
St John's Gdns. W11 7G 81
St John's Gate 4A 8
St John's Gro. N19 2G 65
SW13 2B 116
TW9: Rich 4E 114
St John's Hill SW11 5B 118
St John's Hill Gro. SW11 4B 118
St John's Ho. E14 4E 104
(off Pier St.)
St Johns Ho. SE17 6D 102
(off Lytham St.)
St John's La. EC1 4A 8 (4B 84)
St John's Lodge NW3 7C 64
(off King Henry's Rd.)
St John's Mans. EC1 1A 8
(off St John St.)
St John's M. KT1: Hamp W 2C 150
W11 6J 81
St John Smith Square 2E 18
St John's Pde. W13 1B 96
St Johns Pde. DA14: Sidc 4A 144
(off Sidcup High St.)
St John's Pk. SE3 7H 105
St John's Pk. Mans. N19 3G 65
St John's Pas. SW19 6G 135
St John's Path EC1 4A 8
St Johns Pathway SE23 1J 139
St John's Pl. EC1 4A 8 (4B 84)
St John's Rd. BR5: Pet W 6H 161
CR0: C'don 3B 168
DA8: Erith 5K 109
DA14: Sidc 4B 144
(not continuous)
DA16: Well 3B 126
E4 4J 35
E6 1C 88
E16 6J 87
E17 2D 50
HA1: Harr 6K 41
HA9: Wemb 4D 60
IG2: Ilf 7H 53
IG11: Bark 1J 89
KT1: Hamp W 2C 150
KT3: N Mald 3J 151
KT8: E Mos 4H 149
N15 6E 48
NW11 6H 45
SE20 6J 139
SM1: Sutt 2K 165
SM5: Cars 3C 166
SW11 4C 118
SW19 7G 135
TW7: Isle 3K 113
TW9: Rich 4E 114
TW13: Hanw 4C 130
UB2: S'hall 3C 94
St John's Sq. EC1 4A 8 (4B 84)
St John's Ter. E7 6K 69
SE18 6G 107
SW15 3A 134
(off Kingston Va.)
W10 4F 81
St John St. EC1 1K 7 (2A 84)
St John's Va. SE8 2C 122
St John's Vs. N11 5J 31
(off Friern Barnet Rd.)
N19 2H 65
W8 3K 99
(off St Mary's Pl.)
St John's Way N19 2G 65
ST JOHN'S WOOD 1A 4 (2B 82)
St John's Wood Ct. NW8 2B 4
St John's Wood High St.
NW8 1C 4 (2B 82)
St John's Wood Pk. NW8 1B 82
St John's Wood Rd. NW8 3A 4 (4B 82)
St John's Wood Ter. NW8 2B 82
St Josephs Almshouses W6 4F 99
(off Brook Grn.)
St Joseph's Cl. BR6: Orp 4K 173
W10 5G 81
St Joseph's College Sports Cen.
6B 138
St Joseph's Cotts. SW3 4E 16
(off Cadagon St.)
St Josephs Ct. SE2 6D 108
SE7 6K 105
St Joseph's Dr. UB1: S'hall 1C 94
St Joseph's Flats NW1 1C 6
(off Drummond Cres.)
St Joseph's Gro. NW4 4D 44
St Joseph's Ho. W6 4F 99
(off Brook Grn.)
St Joseph's Rd. N9 7C 24
St Joseph's St. SW8 1F 119
St Joseph's Va. SE3 3F 123
St Judes Cl. IG8: Wfd G 7H 37
St Jude's Rd. E2 2H 85
St Jude St. N16 5E 66
St Julian's Cl. SW16 4A 138
St Julian's Farm Rd. SE27 4A 138
St Julian's Rd. NW6 1J 81
St Katharine Docks 3K 15
St Katharine's Pct. NW1 2F 83
St Katharine's Way E1 4K 15 (1F 103)
(not continuous)
St Katharine's Yacht Haven 1F 103
(off St Katharine's Way)
St Katherine's Rd. DA18: Erith 2D 108
St Katherine's Row EC3 2H 15
St Katherines Wlk. W11 1F 99
St Keverne Rd. SE9 4C 142
St Kilda Rd. BR6: Orp 1K 173
W13 1A 96
St Kilda's Rd. HA1: Harr 6J 41
N16 1D 66
St Kitts Ter. SE19 5E 138
St Laurence Cl. NW6 1F 81
St Lawrence Bus. Cen.
TW13: Felt 2K 129
St Lawrence Cl. HA8: Edg 7A 28
St Lawrence Cotts. E14 1E 104
(off St Lawrence St.)
St Lawrence Ct. N1 7D 66
St Lawrence Dr. HA5: Eastc 5K 39
St Lawrence Ho. SE1 7H 15
(off Purbrook St.)
St Lawrence St. E14 1E 104
St Lawrence Ter. W10 5G 81
St Lawrence Way SW9 1A 120
St Leger Ct. NW6 7F 63
(off Coverdale Rd.)
St Leonard M. N1 2E 84
(off Hoxton St.)
St Leonard's Av. E4 6A 36
HA3: Kenton 5C 42
St Leonard's Cl. DA16: Well 3A 126
St Leonard's Ct. N1 1F 9
St Leonards Ct. SW14 3J 115
St Leonard's Gdns. IG1: Ilf 5G 71
TW5: Hest 7C 94
St Leonard's Ri. BR6: Orp 4J 173
St Leonard's Rd. CR0: Wadd 3B 168
E14 5D 86
(not continuous)
KT6: Surb 5D 150
KT7: T Ditt 6A 150
KT10: Clay 6A 162
NW10 4K 79
SW14 3H 115
W13 7C 78
(not continuous)
St Leonards Sq. KT6: Surb 5D 150
NW5 6E 64
St Leonard's St. E3 3D 86
St Leonard's Studios SW3 6E 16
(off Smith St.)
St Leonard's Ter. SW3 6E 16 (5D 100)
St Leonard's Wlk. SW16 7K 137
St Loo Av. SW3 7D 16 (6C 100)
St Loo Ct. SW3 7D 16
(off St Loo Av.)
St Louis Rd. SE27 4D 138
St Loy's Rd. N17 2E 48
St Lucia Dr. E15 1H 87
St Luke Cl. UB8: Cowl 6A 74
ST LUKE'S 3D 8 (4C 84)
St Luke's Av. EN2: Enf 1J 23
IG1: Ilf 5F 71
SW4 4H 119
St Luke's Cl. EC1 3D 8 (4C 84)
SE25 6H 157
St Lukes Ct. E10 7D 50
(off Capworth St.)
W11 6H 81
(off St Luke's Rd.)
St Luke's Est. EC1 2E 8 (3D 84)
St Luke's M. W11 6H 81
St Lukes M. E14 2C 104
(off Strafford St.)
St Luke's Pas. KT2: King T 1F 151
St Luke's Path IG1: Ilf 5F 71
St Luke's Rd. UB10: Uxb 1A 74
W11 5H 81
St Luke's Sq. E16 6H 87
St Luke's St. SW3 5D 16 (5C 100)
St Luke's Yd. W9 2H 81
(not continuous)
St Malo Av. N9 3D 34
ST MARGARETS 6B 114
St Margaret's IG11: Bark 1H 89
KT2: King T 5J 133
St Margaret's Av. DA15: Sidc 3H 143
HA2: Harr 3G 59
N15 4B 48
N20 1F 31
SM3: Cheam 3G 165
TW15: Ashf 5D 128
St Margarets Av. UB8: Hil 4C 74
St Margarets Bus. Cen.
TW1: Twick 6B 114
St Margarets Cl. EC2 6D 84
St Margaret's Ct. N11 4K 31
St Margarets Ct. SE1 5D 14 (1C 102)
SW15 4D 116
St Margaret's Cres. SW15 5D 116
St Margaret's Dr. TW1: Twick 5B 114
St Margaret's Gro. E11 3H 69
SE18 6G 107
TW1: Twick 6A 114
St Margaret's Ho. NW1 1C 6
(off Polygon Rd.)
St Margaret's La. W8 3K 99
St Margaret's M. KT2: King T 5J 133
St Margarets Pas. SE13 3G 123
(not continuous)
St Margarets Path SE18 5G 107
St Margaret's Rd. E12 2A 70
HA4: Ruis 6F 39
HA8: Edg 5C 28
N17 3E 48
NW10 3E 80
W7 2J 95
St Margarets Rd. BR3: Beck 4K 157
SE4 4B 122
(not continuous)
TW1: Twick 6B 114
TW7: Isle, Twick 6A 114
ST MARGARETS RDBT. 6B 114
St Margaret's Sports Cen. 1A 26
St Margaret's Ter. SE18 5G 107
St Margaret St. SW1 7E 12 (2J 101)
St Mark's Cl. EN5: New Bar 3E 20
SE10 7E 104
W11 6G 81
St Marks Cl. HA1: Harr 7B 42
SW6 1J 117
St Marks Ct. NW8 2A 82
(off Abercorn Pl.)
W7 2J 95
(off Lwr. Boston Rd.)
St Mark's Cres. NW1 1E 82
St Mark's Ga. E9 7B 68
St Mark's Gro. SW10 7K 99
St Mark's Hill KT6: Surb 6E 150
St Marks Ho. SE17 6D 102
(off Lytham St.)
St Marks Ind. Est. E16 1B 106
St Mark's Pl. RM10: Dag 6G 73
SW19 6H 135
W11 6G 81
St Mark's Ri. E8 5F 67
St Mark's Rd. BR2: Broml 3J 159
SE25 4G 157
TW11: Tedd 7B 132
W5 1F 97
W7 2J 95
W10 6F 81
W11 6G 81
St Marks Rd. CR4: Mitc 2D 154
EN1: Enf 6A 24
St Mark's Sq. BR2: Broml 3J 159
NW1 1E 82
St Mark St. E1 1K 15 (6F 85)
St Mark's Vs. N4 2K 65
(off Moray Rd.)
St Martin Cl. UB8: Cowl 6A 74

St Martin-in-the-Fields Church—Samira Cl.

St Martin-in-the-Fields Church . . . 3E 12
St Martin-in-the-Fields Chu. Pth. WC2 . . . 3E 12 (off St Martin's Pl.)
St Martin's Almshouses NW1 . . . 1G 83
St Martin's App. HA4: Ruis . . . 7G 39
St Martin's Av. E6 . . . 2B 88
St Martin's Cl. DA18: Erith . . . 2D 108
EN1: Enf . . . 1C 24
NW1 . . . 1G 83
St Martin's Ct. EC4 . . . 7C 8 (off Newgate St.)
WC2 . . . 2E 12 (7J 83)
St Martins Ct. N1 . . . 1E 84 (off De Beauvoir Est.)
St Martin's Ctyd. WC2 . . . 2E 12 (off Up. St Martin's La.)
St Martins Est. SW2 . . . 1A 138
St Martin's Ho. NW1 . . . 1C 6 (off Polygon Rd.)
St Martin's La. BR3: Beck . . . 5D 158
WC2 . . . 2E 12 (7J 83)
St Martin's Le-Grand EC1 . . . 7C 8 (6C 84)
St Martin's Pl. WC2 . . . 3E 12 (7J 83)
St Martin's Rd. N9 . . . 2C 34
SW9 . . . 2K 119
St Martin's St. WC2 . . . 3D 12 (7H 83) (not continuous)
St Martin's Theatre . . . 2E 12 (off West St.)
St Martins Way SW17 . . . 3A 136
St Mary Abbot's Ct. W14 . . . 3H 99 (off Warwick Gdns.)
St Mary Abbot's Pl. W8 . . . 3H 99
St Mary Abbot's Ter. W14 . . . 3H 99
St Mary at Hill EC3 . . . 3G 15 (7E 84)
St Mary Av. SM6: W'gton . . . 3E 166
St Mary Axe EC3 . . . 1G 15 (6E 84)
St Marychurch St. SE16 . . . 2J 103
St Mary Graces Ct. E1 . . . 3K 15 (7F 85)
St Marylebone Cl. NW10 . . . 1A 80
St Marylebone Crematorium . . . 3K 45
St Mary le-Park Ct. SW11 . . . 7C 100 (off Parkgate Rd.)
St Mary Magdalene Cres. SE18 . . . 3E 106
St Mary Magdalene Gdns. N7 . . . 4A 66
St Mary Newington Cl. SE17 . . . 5E 102 (off Surrey Sq.)
St Mary Rd. E17 . . . 4C 50
St Mary's IG11: Bark . . . 1H 89
St Mary's App. E12 . . . 5D 70
St Mary's Av. BR2: Broml . . . 3G 159
E11 . . . 7K 51
N3 . . . 2G 45
TW11: Tedd . . . 6K 131
St Mary's Av. Central UB2: S'hall . . . 4F 95
St Mary's Av. Nth. UB2: S'hall . . . 4F 95
St Mary's Av. Sth. UB2: S'hall . . . 4F 95
St Mary's Cl. KT9: Chess . . . 7F 163
KT17: Ewe . . . 7B 164
N17 . . . 1G 49
TW16: Sun . . . 4J 147
St Mary's Community Gdn. . . . 2F 85 (off Appleby St.)
St Mary's Copse KT4: Wor Pk . . . 2A 164
St Mary's Ct. E3 . . . 3D 86 (off Bow Rd.)
E6 . . . 4D 88
KT3: N Mald . . . 3A 152
SE7 . . . 7B 106
SM6: W'gton . . . 4G 167
W5 . . . 2D 96
W6 . . . 3B 98
St Mary's Cres. NW4 . . . 3D 44
TW7: Isle . . . 7H 95
UB3: Hayes . . . 7H 75
St Mary's Dr. TW14: Bedf . . . 7E 110
St Mary's Est. SE16 . . . 2J 103 (off Elephant La.)
St Mary's Flats NW1 . . . 1C 6 (off Drummond Cres.)
St Mary's Gdns. SE11 . . . 3K 19 (4A 102)
St Mary's Ga. W8 . . . 3K 99
St Mary's Grn. N2 . . . 2A 46
St Mary's Gro. N1 . . . 6B 66
SW13 . . . 3D 116
TW9: Rich . . . 4F 115
W4 . . . 6H 97
St Mary's Ho. N1 . . . 1B 84 (off St Mary's Path)
St Mary's Mans. W2 . . . 5A 4 (5B 82)
St Mary's M. NW6 . . . 7K 63
St Marys M. TW10: Ham . . . 2C 132
St Mary's Path N1 . . . 1B 84
St Mary's Pl. SE9 . . . 6E 124
W5 . . . 2D 96
W8 . . . 3K 99
St Mary's Rd. DA5: Bexl . . . 1J 145
E10 . . . 3E 68
E13 . . . 2K 87
EN4: E Barn . . . 7J 21
IG1: Ilf . . . 2G 71
KT4: Wor Pk . . . 2A 164
KT6: Surb . . . 7C 150 (St Chads Cl.)
KT6: Surb . . . 6D 150 (Victoria Rd.)
KT8: E Mos . . . 5H 149
N8 . . . 4J 47
N9 . . . 1C 34 (not continuous)
NW10 . . . 1A 80
NW11 . . . 7G 45
SE15 . . . 1J 121
SE25 . . . 3E 156
SW19 . . . 5G 135
UB3: Hayes . . . 7H 75
St Marys Rd. W5 . . . 2D 96
St Mary's Sq. W2 . . . 5A 4 (5B 82)
W5 . . . 2D 96
St Mary's Ter. W2 . . . 5A 4 (5B 82)
St Mary's Twr. EC1 . . . 4D 8 (off Fortune St.)
St Mary St. SE18 . . . 4D 106
St Mary's University College . . . 3K 131
St Mary's University College Sports Cen. . . . 4K 131
St Mary's Vw. HA3: Kenton . . . 5C 42
St Mary's Wlk. SE11 . . . 3K 19 (4A 102)
UB3: Hayes . . . 7H 75
St Mary's Way IG7: Chig . . . 5K 37
St Matthew Cl. UB8: Cowl . . . 6A 74
St Matthew's Av. KT6: Surb . . . 1E 162
St Matthew's Ct. TW15: Ashf . . . 4C 128 (off Feltham Rd.)
St Matthews Ct. E10 . . . 7D 50
N10 . . . 2E 46
SE1 . . . 3C 102 (off Meadow Row)
St Matthew's Dr. BR1: Broml . . . 3D 160
St Matthews Ho. SE17 . . . 6D 102 (off Phelp St.)
St Matthew's Lodge NW1 . . . 2G 83 (off Oakley Sq.)
St Matthew's Rd. SW2 . . . 4K 119
W5 . . . 1E 96
St Matthew's Row E2 . . . 3G 85
St Matthew St. SW1 . . . 2C 18 (3H 101)
St Matthias Cl. NW9 . . . 5B 44
St Maur Rd. SW6 . . . 1H 117
St Meddens BR7: Chst . . . 7H 143
St Mellion Cl. SE28 . . . 6D 90
St Merryn Cl. SE18 . . . 7H 107
St Merryn Ct. BR3: Beck . . . 7C 140
St Michael's All. EC3 . . . 1F 15 (6D 84)
St Michael's Av. HA9: Wemb . . . 6G 61
N9 . . . 7D 24
St Michael's Cl. BR1: Broml . . . 3C 160
DA18: Erith . . . 2D 108
KT4: Wor Pk . . . 2B 164
N3 . . . 2H 45
N12 . . . 5H 31
St Michaels Cl. E16 . . . 5B 88
St Michael's Ct. CR0: C'don . . . 1C 168 (off Poplar Wlk.)
SE1 . . . 7D 14 (off Trinity St.)
St Michaels Ct. E14 . . . 5E 86 (off St Leonard's Rd.)
St Michael's Cres. HA5: Pinn . . . 6C 40
St Michael's Flats NW1 . . . 1C 6 (off Aldenham St.)
St Michael's Gdns. W10 . . . 5G 81
St Michael's M. SW1 . . . 4G 17 (4E 100)
St Michael's Ri. DA16: Well . . . 1B 126
St Michael's Rd. CR0: C'don . . . 1C 168
DA16: Well . . . 3B 126
NW2 . . . 4E 62
SM6: W'gton . . . 6G 167
SW9 . . . 2K 119
TW15: Ashf . . . 5C 128
St Michael's St. W2 . . . 7B 4 (6B 82)
St Michael's Ter. N22 . . . 1J 47
St Michaels Ter. N6 . . . 1E 64 (off South Gro.)
St Mildred's Ct. EC2 . . . 1E 14 (6D 84)
St Mildreds Rd. SE6 . . . 7G 123
SE12 . . . 7G 123
St Mirren Ct. EN5: New Bar . . . 5F 21
St Nicholas Cen. . . . 5K 165
St Nicholas Cl. UB8: Cowl . . . 6A 74
St Nicholas Ct. KT1: King T . . . 4E 150 (off Surbiton Rd.)
St Nicholas Dr. TW17: Shep . . . 7C 146
St Nicholas' Flats NW1 . . . 1C 6 (off Werrington St.)
St Nicholas Glebe SW17 . . . 5E 136
St Nicholas Ho. SE8 . . . 6C 104 (off Deptford Grn.)
St Nicholas M. KT7: T Ditt . . . 6K 149
St Nicholas Rd. KT7: T Ditt . . . 6K 149
SE18 . . . 5K 107
SM1: Sutt . . . 5K 165
St Nicholas St. SE8 . . . 1B 122
St Nicholas Way SM1: Sutt . . . 4K 165
St Nicolas La. BR7: Chst . . . 1C 160
St Ninian's Ct. N20 . . . 3J 31
St Norbert Grn. SE4 . . . 4A 122
St Norbert Rd. SE4 . . . 5K 121
St Olaf Ho. SE1 . . . 4F 15
St Olaf's Rd. SW6 . . . 7G 99
St Olaf Stairs SE1 . . . 4F 15
St Olave's Ct. EC2 . . . 1E 14 (6D 84)
St Olave's Est. SE1 . . . 6H 15 (2E 102)
St Olave's Gdns. SE11 . . . 3J 19 (4A 102)
St Olaves Ho. SE11 . . . 3J 19 (off Walnut Tree Wlk.)
St Olave's Mans. SE11 . . . 3J 19
St Olave's Rd. E6 . . . 1E 88
St Olaves Wlk. SW16 . . . 2G 155
St Olav's Sq. SE16 . . . 2J 103
St Onge Pde. EN1: Enf . . . 3J 23 (off Southbury Rd.)
St Oswald's Pl. SE11 . . . 6G 19 (5K 101)
St Oswald's Rd. SW16 . . . 1B 156
St Oswalds Studios SW6 . . . 6J 99 (off Sedlescombe Rd.)
St Oswulf St. SW1 . . . 4D 18 (4H 101)
St Owen Ho. SE1 . . . 3E 102 (off St Saviour's Est.)
ST PANCRAS . . . 2F 7 (3J 83)
St Pancras Commercial Cen. NW1 . . . 1G 83 (off Pratt St.)
St Pancras Ct. N2 . . . 2B 46
St Pancras Gardens . . . 2H 83
St Pancras Gdns. NW1 . . . 2H 83 (off Pancras Rd.)
St Pancras Way NW1 . . . 7G 65
St Patrick's Ct. IG8: Wfd G . . . 7B 36
St Paul Cl. UB8: Cowl . . . 5A 74
St Paulinus Ct. DA1: Cray . . . 4K 127 (off Manor Rd.)
St Paul's All. EC4 . . . 1B 14 (off St Paul's Chyd.)
St Paul's Av. HA3: Kenton . . . 4F 43
NW2 . . . 6E 62
SE16 . . . 1K 103
St Paul's Bldgs. EC1 . . . 3B 8 (off Dallington St.)
St Paul's Cathedral . . . 1B 14 (6C 84)
St Paul's Churchyard EC4 . . . 1B 14 (6B 84)
St Paul's Cl. KT9: Chess . . . 4D 162
SM5: Cars . . . 1C 166
TW3: Houn . . . 2C 112
TW15: Ashf . . . 5E 128
UB3: Harl . . . 5F 93
W5 . . . 2F 97
St Pauls Cl. SE7 . . . 5B 106
St Paul's Ct. TW4: Houn . . . 3C 112
St Pauls Ct. SW4 . . . 5H 119
St Pauls Ctyd. SE8 . . . 7C 104 (off Crossfield St.)
ST PAUL'S CRAY . . . 2K 161
St Paul's Cray Rd. BR7: Chst . . . 1H 161
St Paul's Cres. NW1 . . . 7H 65 (not continuous)
St Paul's Dr. E15 . . . 5F 69
St Pauls Ho. SE8 . . . 7C 104 (off Market Yd.)
St Paul's M. NW1 . . . 7H 65
St Paul's Pl. N1 . . . 6D 66
St Paul's Ri. N13 . . . 6G 33
St Paul's Rd. CR7: Thor H . . . 3C 156
DA8: Erith . . . 7J 109
IG11: Bark . . . 1G 89
N1 . . . 6B 66
N17 . . . 7B 34
TW8: Bford . . . 6D 96
TW9: Rich . . . 3F 115
St Paul's Shrubbery N1 . . . 6D 66
St Paul's Sq. BR2: Broml . . . 2H 159
St Paul's Studios W14 . . . 5G 99 (off Talgarth Rd.)
St Pauls Ter. SE17 . . . 6B 102
St Paul St. N1 . . . 1C 84 (not continuous)
St Pauls Vw. Apts. EC1 . . . 2J 7 (off Amwell St.)
St Paul's Wlk. KT2: King T . . . 7G 133
St Paul's Way E3 . . . 5B 86
N3 . . . 7E 30
St Paul's Wood Hill BR5: St P . . . 2J 161
St Peter's All. EC3 . . . 1F 15 (off Gracechurch St.)
St Peter's Av. E2 . . . 2G 85
E17 . . . 4G 51
N18 . . . 4B 34
St Petersburgh M. W2 . . . 7K 81
St Petersburgh Pl. W2 . . . 7K 81
St Peter's Cen. E1 . . . 1H 103 (off Reardon St.)
St Peter's Chu. Ct. N1 . . . 1B 84 (off St Peter's St.)
St Peter's Cl. BR7: Chst . . . 7H 143
E2 . . . 2G 85
HA4: Ruis . . . 2B 58
IG2: Ilf . . . 4J 53
SW17 . . . 2C 136
St Peters Cl. WD23: B Hea . . . 1C 26
St Peter's Ct. NW4 . . . 5E 44
WC1 . . . 2F 7 (off Seaford St.)
St Peters Ct. E1 . . . 4J 85 (off Cephas St.)
KT8: W Mole . . . 4E 148
SE12 . . . 5H 123
St Peter's Gdns. SE27 . . . 3A 138
St Peter's Gro. W6 . . . 4C 98
St Peter's Ho. WC1 . . . 2F 7 (off Regent Sq.)
St Peters Ho. SE17 . . . 6D 102
St Peters M. N4 . . . 5B 48
N8 . . . 5A 48
St Peter's Path E17 . . . 3G 51
St Peters Pl. W9 . . . 4K 81
St Peter's Rd. CR0: C'don . . . 4D 168
KT1: King T . . . 2G 151
KT8: W Mole . . . 4E 148
N9 . . . 1C 34
TW1: Twick . . . 5B 114
UB1: S'hall . . . 5E 76
W6 . . . 5C 98
St Peters Rd. UB8: Cowl . . . 5A 74
St Peter's Sq. E2 . . . 2G 85
W6 . . . 4B 98
St Peter's St. CR2: S Croy . . . 5D 168
N1 . . . 1B 84
St Peter's St. M. N1 . . . 2B 84 (off St Peters St.)
St Peter's Ter. SW6 . . . 7H 99
St Peter's Vs. W6 . . . 4C 98
St Peter's Way N1 . . . 7E 66
W5 . . . 5D 78
St Peters Way UB3: Harl . . . 5F 93
St Peter's Wharf W4 . . . 5C 98
St Philip Ho. WC1 . . . 2J 7 (off Lloyd Baker St.)
St Philip's Av. KT4: Wor Pk . . . 2D 164
St Philip's Ga. KT4: Wor Pk . . . 2D 164
St Philip Sq. SW8 . . . 2F 119
St Philip's Rd. E8 . . . 6G 67
St Philips Rd. KT6: Surb . . . 6D 150
St Philip St. SW8 . . . 2F 119
St Philip's Way N1 . . . 1C 84
St Quentin Ho. SW18 . . . 6B 118
St Quentin Rd. DA16: Well . . . 3K 125
St Quintin Av. W10 . . . 5E 80
St Quintin Gdns. W10 . . . 5E 80
St Quintin Ho. W10 . . . 5F 81 (off Princess Louise Wlk.)
St Quintin Rd. E13 . . . 3K 87
St Quintin Vw. W10 . . . 5E 80
St Raphael's Way NW10 . . . 5J 61
St Regis Cl. N10 . . . 2F 47
St Regis Hgts. NW3 . . . 3K 63
St Richard's Ho. NW1 . . . 1C 6 (off Eversholt St.)
St Ronan's Cl. EN4: Had W . . . 1G 21
St Ronan's Cres. IG8: Wfd G . . . 7D 36
St Rule St. SW8 . . . 2G 119
St Saviours Ct. HA1: Harr . . . 5J 41
N22 . . . 2H 47
St Saviour's Est. SE1 . . . 7J 15 (2F 103)
St Saviour's Rd. CR0: C'don . . . 6B 156
SW2 . . . 5K 119
St Saviour's Wharf SE1 . . . 6K 15 (off Mill St.)
SE1 . . . 6K 15 (off Shad Thames)
Saints Cl. SE27 . . . 4B 138
Saints Dr. E7 . . . 5B 70
St Silas Pl. NW5 . . . 6E 64
St Simon's Av. SW15 . . . 5E 116
Saints M. CR4: Mitc . . . 3C 154
St Stephen's Av. E17 . . . 5E 50
W12 . . . 1D 98 (not continuous)
W13 . . . 6B 78
St Stephen's Cl. E17 . . . 5D 50
NW8 . . . 1C 82
UB1: S'hall . . . 5E 76
St Stephens Cl. NW5 . . . 5D 64 (off Malden Rd.)
St Stephen's Ct. EN1: Enf . . . 6K 23 (off Park Av.)
St Stephens Ct. N8 . . . 6K 47
W13 . . . 6B 78
St Stephen's Cres. CR7: Thor H . . . 3A 156
W2 . . . 6J 81
St Stephen's Gdns. SW15 . . . 5H 117
TW1: Twick . . . 6C 114
W2 . . . 6J 81 (not continuous)
St Stephens Gro. SE13 . . . 3E 122
St Stephens Ho. SE17 . . . 6D 102 (off Lytham St.)
St Stephen's M. W2 . . . 5J 81
St Stephens Pde. E7 . . . 7A 70
St Stephen's Pas. TW1: Twick . . . 6C 114
St Stephen's Rd. E3 . . . 1A 86
E6 . . . 7A 70
E17 . . . 5D 50
EN5: Barn . . . 5A 20
TW3: Houn . . . 6E 112
UB7: Yiew . . . 1A 92
W13 . . . 6B 78
St Stephen's Row EC4 . . . 1E 14
St Stephen's Ter. SW8 . . . 7K 101
St Stephen's Wlk. SW7 . . . 4A 100 (off Southwell Gdns.)
St Swithins La. EC4 . . . 2E 14 (7D 84)
St Swithun's Rd. SE13 . . . 6F 123
St Theresa's Cl. E9 . . . 4C 68
St Theresa's Rd. TW14: Felt . . . 4H 111
St Thomas Cl. KT6: Surb . . . 1F 163
St Thomas Ct. DA5: Bexl . . . 7G 127
E10 . . . 7D 50 (off Lake Rd.)
HA5: Pinn . . . 1C 40
NW1 . . . 7G 65 (off Wrotham Rd.)
St Thomas Dr. BR5: Farnb . . . 1G 173
St Thomas' Dr. HA5: Pinn . . . 1C 40
St Thomas Gdns. IG1: Ilf . . . 6G 71
St Thomas Ho. E1 . . . 6K 85 (off W. Arbour St.)
St Thomas M. SW18 . . . 5J 117
St Thomas Rd. DA17: Belv . . . 2J 109
E16 . . . 6J 87
N14 . . . 7C 22
W4 . . . 6J 97
St Thomas's Gdns. NW5 . . . 6E 64
St Thomas's M. SE7 . . . 4C 106
St Thomas's Pl. E9 . . . 7J 67
St Thomas's Rd. N4 . . . 2A 66
NW10 . . . 1A 80
St Thomas's Sq. E9 . . . 7J 67
St Thomas St. SE1 . . . 5F 15 (1D 102)
St Thomas's Way SW6 . . . 7H 99
St Timothys M. BR1: Broml . . . 1K 159
St Ursula Gro. HA5: Pinn . . . 5B 40
St Ursula Rd. UB1: S'hall . . . 6E 76
St Valery Pl. TW5: Hest . . . 7B 94
St Vincent Cl. SE27 . . . 5B 138
St Vincent De Paul Ho. E1 . . . 5J 85 (off Jubilee St.)
St Vincent Ho. SE1 . . . 3F 103 (off St Saviour's Est.)
St Vincent Rd. TW2: Whitt . . . 6G 113
St Vincent's La. NW7 . . . 4K 29
St Vincent St. W1 . . . 6H 5 (5E 82)
St Wilfrid's Cl. EN4: E Barn . . . 5H 21
St Wilfrid's Rd. EN4: E Barn . . . 5G 21
St Williams Ct. N1 . . . 7J 65
St Winefride's Av. E12 . . . 5D 70
St Winifred's Rd. TW11: Tedd . . . 6B 132
Sakura Dr. N22 . . . 1H 47
Salamanca Pl. IG11: Bark . . . 2B 90
SE1 . . . 4G 19 (4K 101)
Salamanca Sq. SE1 . . . 4G 19 (off Salamanca Pl.)
Salamanca St. SE1 . . . 4G 19 (4K 101)
SE11 . . . 4G 19 (4K 101)
Salamander Cl. KT2: King T . . . 5C 132
Salamander Quay KT1: Hamp W . . . 1D 150
Salcombe Ct. E14 . . . 5E 86 (off St Ives Pl.)
Salcombe Dr. RM6: Chad H . . . 6F 55
SM4: Mord . . . 1F 165
Salcombe Gdns. NW7 . . . 6K 29
Salcombe Rd. E17 . . . 7B 50
N16 . . . 5E 66
TW15: Ashf . . . 3A 128
Salcombe Vs. TW10: Rich . . . 5E 114
Salcombe Way HA4: Ruis . . . 2J 57
UB4: Hayes . . . 3F 75
Salcott Rd. CR0: Bedd . . . 3J 167
SW11 . . . 5C 118
Salehurst Cl. HA3: Kenton . . . 5E 42
Salehurst Rd. SE4 . . . 6B 122
Salem Pl. CR0: C'don . . . 3C 168
Salem Rd. W2 . . . 7K 81
Salento Cl. N3 . . . 7D 30
Sale Pl. W2 . . . 6C 4 (5C 82)
Sale St. E2 . . . 4G 85
Salford Ho. E14 . . . 4E 104 (off Seyssel St.)
Salford Rd. SW2 . . . 1H 137
Salhouse Cl. SE28 . . . 6C 90
Salisbury Av. IG11: Bark . . . 7H 71
N3 . . . 3H 45
SM1: Sutt . . . 6H 165
Salisbury Cl. KT4: Wor Pk . . . 3B 164
SE17 . . . 4D 102
Salisbury Ct. E9 . . . 5A 68 (off Mabley St.)
EC4 . . . 1A 14 (6B 84)
EN2: Enf . . . 4J 23 (off London Rd.)
SE16 . . . 3G 103 (off Stork's Rd.)
SM5: Cars . . . 5D 166
UB5: N'olt . . . 5F 59 (off Newmarket Av.)
Salisbury Gdns. IG9: Buck H . . . 2G 37
SW19 . . . 7G 135
Salisbury Hall Gdns. E4 . . . 6H 35
Salisbury Ho. E14 . . . 6D 86 (off Hobday St.)
EC2 . . . 6F 9 (off London Wall)
HA7: Stan . . . 6F 27
N1 . . . 1B 84 (off St Mary's Path)
SM6: W'gton . . . 5F 167
SW1 . . . 5D 18 (off Drummond Ga.)
SW9 . . . 7A 102 (off Cranmer Rd.)
Salisbury Mans. N15 . . . 5B 48
Salisbury M. SW6 . . . 7H 99
Salisbury Pas. SW6 . . . 7H 99 (off Dawes Rd.)
Salisbury Pavement SW6 . . . 7H 99 (off Dawes Rd.)
Salisbury Pl. SW9 . . . 7B 102
W1 . . . 5E 4 (5D 82)
Salisbury Prom. N8 . . . 5B 48
Salisbury Rd. BR2: Broml . . . 5C 160
DA5: Bexl . . . 1G 145
E4 . . . 3H 35
E7 . . . 6J 69
E10 . . . 2E 68
E12 . . . 5B 70
E17 . . . 5E 50
EN5: Barn . . . 3B 20
HA1: Harr . . . 5H 41
HA5: Eastc . . . 4J 39
IG3: Ilf . . . 2J 71
KT3: N Mald . . . 3K 151
KT4: Wor Pk . . . 4K 163
N4 . . . 5B 48
N22 . . . 1B 48
RM10: Dag . . . 6H 73
SE25 . . . 6G 157
SM5: Cars . . . 6D 166
SW19 . . . 7G 135
TW4: Houn . . . 3A 112
TW6: H'row A . . . 6E 110 (not continuous)
TW9: Rich . . . 4E 114
TW13: Felt . . . 1A 130
UB2: S'hall . . . 4C 94
W13 . . . 2B 96
Salisbury Sq. EC4 . . . 1K 13 (6A 84)
Salisbury St. NW8 . . . 4C 4 (4C 82)
W3 . . . 2J 97
Salisbury Ter. SE15 . . . 3J 121
Salisbury Wlk. N19 . . . 2G 65
Salix Cl. TW16: Sun . . . 7K 129
Salix Ct. N3 . . . 6D 30
Salix La. IG8: Wfd G . . . 1C 52
Salk Cl. NW9 . . . 2A 44
Salliesfield TW2: Whitt . . . 6H 113
Sally Murray Cl. E12 . . . 4E 70
Salmen Rd. E13 . . . 2H 87
Salmond Cl. HA7: Stan . . . 6F 27
Salmon La. E14 . . . 6A 86
Salmon M. NW6 . . . 5J 63
Salmon Rd. DA17: Belv . . . 5G 109
Salmons Rd. KT9: Chess . . . 6E 162
N9 . . . 1B 34
Salmon St. E14 . . . 6B 86
NW9 . . . 1H 61
Salomons Rd. E13 . . . 5A 88
Salop Rd. E17 . . . 6K 49
Salsabil Apts. E3 . . . 4B 86
Saltash Cl. SM1: Sutt . . . 4H 165
Saltash Rd. DA16: Well . . . 1C 126
IG6: Ilf . . . 1H 53
Saltcoats Rd. W4 . . . 2A 98
Saltcroft Cl. HA9: Wemb . . . 1H 61
Saltdene N4 . . . 1K 65
Salter Cl. HA2: Harr . . . 4D 58
Salterford Rd. SW17 . . . 6E 136
Saltern Ct. IG11: Bark . . . 3B 90 (off Galleons Dr.)
Salter Rd. SE16 . . . 1K 103
Salters Ct. EC4 . . . 1D 14
Salter's Hall Ct. EC4 . . . 2E 14
Salter's Hill SE19 . . . 5D 138
Salters Rd. E17 . . . 4F 51
W10 . . . 4F 81
Salters Row N1 . . . 6D 66 (off Tilney Gdns.)
Salter St. E14 . . . 7B 86 (not continuous)
NW10 . . . 3C 80
Salterton Rd. N7 . . . 3K 65
Salt Hill Cl. UB8: Uxb . . . 5A 56
Salting St. IG11: Bark . . . 1H 89
Saltley Cl. E6 . . . 6C 88
Salton Cl. N3 . . . 2J 45
Salton Sq. E14 . . . 6B 86
Saltoun Rd. SW2 . . . 4A 120
Saltram Cl. N15 . . . 4F 49
Saltram Cres. W9 . . . 3H 81
Saltwell St. E14 . . . 7C 86
Saltwood Gro. SE17 . . . 5D 102
Saltwood Ho. SE15 . . . 6J 103 (off Lovelinch Cl.)
Salusbury Rd. NW6 . . . 1G 81
Salus Ct. CR0: C'don . . . 4C 168 (off Parker Rd.)
Salutation Rd. SE10 . . . 4G 105
Salvador SW17 . . . 5D 136
Salvia Gdns. UB6: G'frd . . . 2A 78
Salvin Rd. SW15 . . . 3F 117
Salway Cl. IG8: Wfd G . . . 7D 36
Salway Pl. E15 . . . 6F 69
Salway Rd. E15 . . . 6F 69
Samantha Cl. E17 . . . 7B 50
Samaras Mans. E20 . . . 5E 68 (off Liberty Bri. Rd.)
Sam Bartram Cl. SE7 . . . 5A 106
The Sambourne Family Home . . . 3J 99 (off Stafford Ter.)
Sambroke Sq. EN4: E Barn . . . 4G 21
Sambrooke Ct. EN1: Enf . . . 6K 23
Sambrook Ho. E1 . . . 5J 85 (off Jubilee St.)
SE11 . . . 4J 19
Sambruck M. SE6 . . . 1D 140
Samels Ct. W6 . . . 5C 98
Samford Ho. N1 . . . 1A 84 (off Barnsbury Est.)
Samford St. NW8 . . . 4C 4 (4B 82)
Samira Cl. E17 . . . 6C 50

A-Z Big London 281

Sam King Wlk.—Schooner Rd.

Sam King Wlk. SE5 ....7D 102
(off Edmund St.)
Sam Manners Ho. SE10 ....5G 105
(off Tuskar St.)
Sam March Ho. E14 ....6F 87
(off Blair St.)
Sammi Ct. CR7: Thor H 4C 156
Samos Rd. SE20 ....2H 157
Samphire Hgts. E20 ....5E 68
(off Napa Cl.)
Sampson Av. EN5: Barn 5A 20
Sampson Cl. DA17: Belv 3D 108
Sampson Ct.
TW17: Shep 5E 146
Sampson Ho. SE1 ....4A 14 (1B 102)
Sampson St. E1 ....1G 103
Samson St. E13 ....2A 88
Samuda Est. E14 ....3E 104
Samuel Cl. E8 ....1F 85
HA7: Stan 2F 27
SE14 ....6K 103
SE18 ....4C 106
Samuel Ct. N1 ....2G 9
(off Pitfield St.)
Samuel Ferguson Pl.
IG11: Bark 2K 89
Samuel Gray Gdns.
KT2: King T 1D 150
Samuel Johnson Cl. SW16 ....4K 137
Samuel Jones Ct. SE15 ....7E 102
Samuel Lewis Bldgs. N1 ....6A 66
Samuel Lewis Trust Dwellings
E8 ....5G 67
(off Amhurst Rd.)
N16 ....6E 48
SW3 ....4C 16 (4C 100)
SW6 ....7J 99
(off Vanston Pl.)
W14 ....4H 99
(off Lisgar Ter.)
Samuel Lewis Trust Est. SE5 ....1C 120
(off Warner Rd.)
Samuel Richardson Ho. W14 ....4H 99
(off North End Cres.)
Samuel's Cl. W6 ....4E 98
Samuelson Pl. TW7: Isle 2J 113
Samuel St. E8 ....1F 85
SE15 ....7F 103
SE18 ....4D 106
Samuel Wallis Lodge SE3 ....3H 123
(off Banning St.)
SE10 ....4G 105
(off Banning St.)
Sanchia Ct. E2 ....3G 85
(off Wellington Row)
Sancroft Cl. NW2 ....3D 62
Sancroft Ho. SE11 ....5H 19
Sancroft Rd. HA3: W'stone 2K 41
Sancroft St. SE11 ....5H 19 (5K 101)
The Sanctuary DA5: Bexl 6D 126
SM4: Mord 6J 153
SW1 ....1D 18
Sanctuary M. E8 ....6F 67
Sanctuary Rd. TW6: H'row A 6C 110
Sanctuary St. SE1 ....6D 14 (2C 102)
Sandale Cl. N16 ....3D 66
Sandall Cl. W5 ....4E 78
Sandall Ho. E3 ....2A 86
Sandall Rd. NW5 ....6G 65
W5 ....4E 78
Sandal Rd. KT3: N Mald 5K 151
N18 ....5B 34
Sandal St. E15 ....1G 87
Sandalwood Cl. E1 ....4A 86
Sandalwood Dr. HA4: Ruis 7E 38
Sandalwood Ho. DA15: Sidc 2K 143
Sandalwood Mans. W8 ....3K 99
(off Stone Hall Gdns.)
Sandalwood Rd. TW13: Felt 3K 129
Sandbach Pl. SE18 ....4G 107
Sandbanks TW14: Felt 1G 129
Sandbourne NW8 ....1K 81
(off Abbey Rd.)
W11 ....6J 81
(off Dartmouth Cl.)
Sandbourne Av. SW19 ....2K 153
Sandbourne Rd. SE4 ....2A 122
Sandbrook Cl. NW7 ....6E 28
Sandbrook Rd. N16 ....3E 66
Sandby Ct. NW10 ....3D 80
(off Plough Cl.)
Sandby Grn. SE9 ....3C 124
Sandby Ho. NW6 ....1J 81
Sandcliff Rd. DA8: Erith 4K 109
Sandcroft Cl. N13 ....6G 33
Sandell's Av. TW15: Ashf 4E 128
Sandell St. SE1 ....6J 13 (2A 102)
Sanderling Ct. SE8 ....6B 104
(off Abinger Gro.)
SE28 ....7C 90
Sanderling Lodge E1 ....3K 15
(off Star Pl.)
Sanders Cl. TW12: Hamp H 5G 131
Sanders Ho. WC1 ....1J 7
(off Gt. Percy St.)
Sanders La. NW7 ....7K 29
(Bittacy Ri.)
NW7 ....7A 30
(Grants Cl.)
TW4: Houn 5D 112
Sanderson Bldg. NW2 ....2E 62
Sanderson Cl. NW5 ....4F 65
Sanderson Ho. E16 ....5J 87
(off Hammersley Rd.)
SE8 ....5B 104
(off Grove St.)
Sandersons La. W4 ....5K 97
(off Chiswick High Rd.)
Sanderson Sq. BR1: Broml 3E 160
Sanderstead Av. NW2 ....2G 63
Sanderstead Cl. SW12 ....7G 119
Sanderstead Rd.
CR2: Sande, S Croy 7D 168
E10 ....1A 68
Sanders Way N19 ....1H 65
Sandes Ct. CR7: Thor H 3C 156
Sandfield WC1 ....2F 7
(off Cromer St.)
Sandfield Gdns. CR7: Thor H 3B 156
Sandfield Pas. CR7: Thor H 3C 156
Sandfield Pl. CR7: Thor H 3C 156
Sandfield Rd. CR7: Thor H 3B 156
Sandford Av. N22 ....1C 48
Sandford Cl. E6 ....4D 88
Sandford Ct. EN5: New Bar 3E 20
N16 ....1E 66
Sandford Rd. BR2: Broml 3J 159
DA7: Bex 4E 126
E6 ....3C 88
Sandford St. SW6 ....7K 99
Sandgate Cl. RM7: Rush G 7J 55
Sandgate Ho. E5 ....5H 67
W5 ....5C 78
Sandgate La. SW18 ....1C 136
Sandgate Rd. DA16: Well 7C 108
Sandgate St. SE15 ....6H 103
Sandgate Trad. Est. SE15 ....6H 103
(off Sandgate St.)
Sandham Ct. SW4 ....1J 119
Sandham Point SE18 ....4F 107
(off Vincent Rd.)
Sandhills SM6: Bedd 4H 167
The Sandhills SW10 ....7A 16
(off Limerston St.)
Sandhills Mdw. TW17: Shep 7E 146
Sandhurst Av. HA2: Harr 6F 41
KT5: Surb 7H 151
Sandhurst Cl. CR2: Sande 7E 168
NW9 ....3G 43
Sandhurst Ct. SW2 ....4J 119
Sandhurst Dr. IG3: Bark, Ilf 4K 71
Sandhurst Ho. E1 ....5J 85
(off Wolsy St.)
E17 ....1B 50
(off Robinswood Gdns.)
Sandhurst Mkt. SE6 ....1E 140
(off Sandhurst Rd.)
Sandhurst Rd. BR6: Chels 3K 173
DA5: Bexl 5D 126
DA15: Sidc 3K 143
N9 ....6D 24
NW9 ....3G 43
SE6 ....1F 141
Sandhurst Way CR2: Sande 7E 168
Sandifer Dr. NW2 ....3F 63
Sandiford Rd. SM3: Sutt 2H 165
Sandiland Cres.
BR2: Hayes 2H 171
Sandilands CR0: C'don 2G 169
Sandilands Rd. SW6 ....1K 117
Sandison St. SE15 ....3G 121
Sandland St. WC1 ....6H 7 (5K 83)
Sandling Ri. SE9 ....3E 142
The Sandlings N22 ....2A 48
Sandlings Cl. SE15 ....2H 121
Sandmartin Way
SM6: W'gton 1E 166
Sandmere Rd. SW4 ....4J 119
Sandon Cl. KT10: Esh 7H 149
Sandover Ho. SE16 ....3G 103
(off Spa Rd.)
Sandow Cres. UB3: Hayes 3H 93
Sandown Av. RM10: Dag 6J 73
Sandown Cl. TW5: Cran 1J 111
Sandown Ct. HA7: Stan 5H 27
RM10: Dag 6J 73
(off Sandown Av.)
SE26 ....3H 139
SM2: Sutt 7K 165
Sandown Dr. SM5: Cars 7E 166
Sandown Rd. SE25 ....5H 157
Sandown Way UB5: N'olt 6C 58
Sandpiper Cl. E17 ....7E 34
SE16 ....2B 104
Sandpiper Ct. E1 ....7G 85
(off Thomas More St.)
E14 ....3E 104
(off New Union Cl.)
SE8 ....6C 104
(off Edward Pl.)
Sandpiper Dr. HA2: Harr 2F 59
Sandpiper Rd. SM1: Sutt 5H 165
Sandpiper Ter. IG5: Ilf 3F 53
Sandpit Pl. SE7 ....5C 106
Sandpit Rd. BR1: Broml 5G 141
Sandpits Rd. CR0: C'don 4K 169
TW10: Ham 2D 132
Sandra Cl. N22 ....1C 48
TW3: Houn 5F 113
Sandra Ct. CR4: Mitc 6D 136
Sandra Ho. KT8: E Mos 5H 149
Sandridge Cl. HA1: Harr 4J 41
Sandridge St. N19 ....2G 65
Sandringham Av. SW20 ....1G 153
Sandringham Bldgs. SE17 ....4D 102
(off Balfour St.)
Sandringham Cl. EN1: Enf 2K 23
IG6: Ilf 3G 53
SW19 ....1F 135
Sandringham Ct. DA15: Sidc 6K 125
KT2: King T 1E 150
(off Skerne Wlk.)
SE16 ....1K 103
(off King & Queen Wharf)
UB10: Hil 4E 74
W1 ....1B 12
(off Dufour's Pl.)
W9 ....3A 82
(off Maida Vale)
Sandringham Cres. HA2: Harr 2E 58
Sandringham Dr.
DA2: Wilm 2K 145
DA16: Well 2J 125
TW15: Ashf 4A 128
Sandringham Flats WC2 ....2D 12
(off Charing Cross Rd.)
Sandringham Gdns. IG6: Ilf 3G 53
KT8: W Mole 4E 148
N8 ....6J 47
N12 ....6G 31
TW5: Cran 1J 111
Sandringham Ho. SE1 ....1E 102
(off Potters Flds.)
W14 ....4G 99
(off Windsor Way)
Sandringham M. TW12: Hamp 1D 148
W5 ....7D 78
Sandringham Rd. BR1: Broml 5J 141
CR7: Thor H 5C 156
E7 ....5A 70
E8 ....5F 67
E10 ....6F 51
Sandringham Rd. IG11: Bark 5K 71
KT4: Wor Pk 3C 164
N22 ....3C 48
NW2 ....6D 62
NW11 ....7G 45
TW6: H'row A 5A 110
UB5: N'olt 7E 58
Sandrock Pl. CR0: C'don 4K 169
Sandrock Rd. SE13 ....3C 122
SANDS END 1A 118
Sand's End La. SW6 ....1K 117
Sandstone La. E16 ....7K 87
Sandstone Pl. N19 ....2F 65
Sandstone Rd. SE12 ....2K 141
Sands Way IG8: Wfd G 6J 37
Sandtoft Rd. SE7 ....6K 105
Sandwell Cres. NW6 ....6J 63
Sandwich Ho. SE16 ....2J 103
(off Swan Rd.)
WC1 ....2E 6
(off Sandwich St.)
Sandwich St. WC1 ....2E 6 (3J 83)
Sandwick Cl. NW7 ....7H 29
Sandy Bury BR6: Orp 3H 173
Sandycombe Rd.
TW9: Kew, Rich 3F 115
TW14: Felt 1J 129
Sandycoombe Rd. TW1: Twick 6C 114
Sandycroft SE2 ....6A 108
Sandy Dr. TW14: Felt 1G 129
Sandy Hill Av. SE18 ....5F 107
Sandy Hill Rd. SE18 ....5F 107
SM6: W'gton 7G 167
Sandyhill Rd. IG1: Ilf 4F 71
Sandy Ho. IG11: Bark 4A 90
Sandy La. BR5: St P 7D 144
BR6: Orp 7K 161
CR4: Mitc 1E 154
DA14: Sidc 7D 144
HA3: Kenton 6F 43
KT1: Hamp W 7A 132
KT12: Walt T 6K 147
SM2: Cheam 7G 165
SM6: W'gton 6H 167
TW10: Ham 2C 132
TW11: Hamp W, Tedd 7A 132
Sandy La. Nth. SM6: W'gton 6H 167
Sandy La. Sth. SM6: W'gton 7G 167
Sandymount Av. HA7: Stan 5H 27
Sandy Ridge BR7: Chst 6E 142
Sandy Rd. DA8: Erith 5J 109
NW3 ....2K 63
Sandys Row E1 ....6H 9 (5E 84)
Sandy Way CR0: C'don 3B 170
KT12: Walt T 7H 147
Sanford La. N16 ....3F 67
Sanford St. SE14 ....6A 104
Sanford Ter. N16 ....3F 67
Sanford Wlk. N16 ....2F 67
SE14 ....6A 104
Sangam Cl. UB2: S'hall 3C 94
Sanger Av. KT9: Chess 5E 162
Sangley Rd. SE6 ....7D 122
SE25 ....4E 156
Sangora Rd. SW11 ....4B 118
Sankey Ho. E2 ....2J 85
(off St James's Av.)
Sansom Rd. E11 ....2H 69
Sansom St. SE5 ....1D 120
Sans Wlk. EC1 ....3K 7 (4A 84)
Santa Maria Ct. E1 ....5A 86
(off Ocean Est.)
Sant Ho. SE17 ....4C 102
(off Browning St.)
Santiago Ct. E1 ....5A 86
(off Ocean Est.)
Santina Apartment CR0: C'don 1D 168
(off Cherry Orchard Rd.)
Santley Ho. SE1 ....7K 13 (2A 102)
Santley St. SW4 ....4K 119
Santos Rd. SW18 ....5J 117
The Santway HA7: Stan 5D 26
Sapcote Trad. Cen. NW10 ....6B 62
Saperton Wlk. SE11 ....3H 19
Saphire Ct. E15 ....1E 86
(off Warton Rd.)
Saphora Cl. BR6: Farnb 5H 173
Sapperton Ct. EC1 ....3C 8
Sapperton Ho. W2 ....5J 81
(off Westbourne Pk. Rd.)
Sapphire Cl. E6 ....6E 88
RM8: Dag 1C 72
Sapphire Ct. E1 ....7G 85
(off Cable St.)
Sapphire Rd. NW10 ....7J 61
SE8 ....4A 104
Saracen Cl. CR0: C'don 6D 156
Saracens FC 7K 29
Saracens Head Yd. EC3 ....1J 15
Saracen St. E14 ....6C 86
Sarah Ct. UB5: N'olt 1D 76
Sarah Ho. E1 ....6H 85
(off Commercial Rd.)
Sarah Swift Ho. SE1 ....6F 15
(off Kipling St.)
Sara La. Ct. N1 ....2E 84
(off Stanway St.)
Saratoga Rd. E5 ....4J 67
Sara Turnbull Ho. SE18 ....4D 106
Saravia Ct. SE13 ....6G 123
Sardinia St. WC2 ....1G 13 (6K 83)
Sarita Cl. HA3: Hrw W 2H 41
Sarjant Path SW19 ....2F 135
(off Blincoe Cl.)
Sarjeant Ct. BR4: W W'ck 2F 171
(off Bencurtis Pk.)
Sark Cl. TW5: Hest 7E 94
Sark Ho. EN3: Enf W 1E 24
Sark Twr. SE28 ....2G 107
Sark Wlk. E16 ....6K 87
Sarnes Ct. N11 ....4A 32
(off Oakleigh Rd. Sth.)
Sarnesfield Ho. SE15 ....6H 103
(off Pencraig Way)
Sarnesfield Rd. EN2: Enf 4J 23
Sarratt Ho. W10 ....5E 80
(off Sutton Way)
Sarre Rd. NW2 ....5H 63
Sarsen Av. TW3: Houn 2E 112
Sarsfeld Rd. SW12 ....2D 136
Sarsfield Rd. UB6: G'frd 2B 78
Sartor Rd. SE15 ....4K 121
Sarum Ho. W11 ....7H 81
(off Portobello Rd.)
Sarum Ter. E3 ....4B 86
Saskia M. SE15 ....2H 121
Sassoon NW9 ....1B 44
Satanita Cl. E16 ....6B 88
Satchell Mead NW9 ....1B 44
Satchwell Rd. E2 ....2K 9 (3G 85)
Satchwell St. E2 ....2K 9 (3G 85)
Satin Ho. E1 ....1K 15
Sattar M. N16 ....3D 66
Saturn Ho. E3 ....1C 86
(off Garrison Rd.)
E15 ....1F 87
(off High St.)
Sauls Grn. E11 ....3G 69
Saundby La. SE3 ....4K 123
Saunders Apts. E3 ....3C 86
(off Marchant St.)
Saunders Cl. E14 ....7B 86
(off Limehouse C'way.)
IG1: Ilf 1H 71
Saunders Ho. SE16 ....2K 103
(off Quebec Way)
Saunders Ness Rd. E14 ....5E 104
Saunders Rd. SE18 ....5K 107
UB10: Uxb 7B 56
Saunders St. SE11 ....3J 19 (4A 102)
Saunders Way SE28 ....7B 90
Saunderton Rd. HA0: Wemb 5B 60
Saunton Av. UB3: Harl 7H 93
Saunton Ct. UB1: S'hall 7G 77
(off Haldane Rd.)
Savage Gdns. E6 ....6D 88
EC3 ....2H 15 (7E 84)
(not continuous)
Savannah Cl. SE15 ....7F 103
Savera Cl. UB2: S'hall 3A 94
Savernake Ct. HA7: Stan 6G 27
Savernake Ho. N4 ....7C 48
Savernake Rd. N9 ....6B 24
NW3 ....4D 64
Savery Dr. KT6: Surb 7B 150
Savile Cl. KT3: N Mald 5A 152
KT7: T Ditt 7K 149
Savile Gdns. CR0: C'don 2F 169
Savile Row W1 ....2A 12 (7G 83)
Saville Cres. TW15: Ashf 6F 129
Saville Rd. E16 ....1C 106
RM6: Chad H 6F 55
TW1: Twick 1K 131
W4 ....3K 97
Saville Row BR2: Hayes 1H 171
EN3: Enf H 2E 24
Savill Gdns. SW20 ....3C 152
Savill Ho. E16 ....1F 107
(off Robert St.)
SW4 ....6H 119
Savill Row IG8: Wfd G 6C 36
Savin Lodge SM2: Sutt 7A 166
(off Walnut M.)
Savona Cl. SW19 ....7F 135
Savona Ho. SW8 ....7G 101
(off Savona St.)
Savona St. SW8 ....7G 101
Savoy Av. UB3: Harl 5G 93
Savoy Bldgs. WC2 ....3G 13
Savoy Chapel 3G 13
SAVOY CIRCUS 7B 80
Savoy Cl. E15 ....1G 87
HA8: Edg 5B 28
Savoy Ct. HA2: Harr 5F 41
NW3 ....3A 64
SW5 ....4J 99
(off Cromwell Rd.)
WC2 ....3F 13 (7K 83)
Savoy Hill WC2 ....3G 13 (7K 83)
Savoy M. SW9 ....3J 119
Savoy Pde. EN1: Enf 3K 23
Savoy Pl. W12 ....1F 99
WC2 ....3F 13 (7J 83)
Savoy Row WC2 ....2G 13
Savoy Steps WC2 ....3G 13
Savoy St. WC2 ....3G 13 (7K 83)
Savoy Theatre 3F 13
(off Strand)
Savoy Way WC2 ....3G 13
Sawbill Cl. UB4: Yead 5B 76
Sawkins Cl. SW19 ....2G 135
Sawley Rd. W12 ....1C 98
Saw Mill Way N16 ....6G 49
Sawmill Yd. E3 ....1A 86
Sawtry Cl. SM5: Cars 7C 154
Sawyer Cl. N9 ....2B 34
Sawyer Ct. NW10 ....7K 61
Sawyers Apartments SW11 ....4C 118
(off Danvers Avenue)
Sawyers Cl. RM10: Dag 6J 73
Sawyer's Hill TW10: Rich 7F 115
Sawyers Lawn W13 ....6A 78
Sawyer St. SE1 ....6C 14 (2C 102)
Saxby Rd. SW2 ....7J 119
Saxham Rd. IG11: Bark 2J 89
Saxlingham Rd. E4 ....3A 36
Saxon Av. TW13: Hanw 2C 130
Saxonbury Av. TW16: Sun 3K 147
Saxonbury Cl. CR4: Mitc 3B 154
Saxonbury Ct. N7 ....5J 65
Saxonbury Gdns. KT6: Surb 1C 162
Saxon Bus. Cen. SW19 ....2A 154
Saxon Chase N8 ....6K 47
Saxon Cl. E17 ....7C 50
KT6: Surb 6D 150
UB8: Hil 5B 74
Saxon Ct. N1 ....1J 83
Saxon Dr. W3 ....6G 79
Saxonfield Cl. SW2 ....7K 119
Saxon Gdns. UB1: S'hall 7C 76
Saxon Hall W2 ....7K 81
(off Palace Ct.)
Saxon Ho. E1 ....6K 9
(off Thrawl St.)
KT1: King T 4F 151
SM6: W'gton 1E 166
(off London Rd.)
TW13: Hanw 2D 130
Saxon Lea Ct. E3 ....2B 86
(off Saxon Rd.)
Saxon Lodge CR0: C'don 1C 168
(off Tavistock Rd.)
Saxon Rd. BR1: Broml 7H 141
E3 ....2B 86
E6 ....4D 88
HA9: Wemb 3J 61
IG1: Ilf 6F 71
KT2: King T 1E 150
N22 ....1B 48
SE25 ....5D 156
TW15: Ashf 6F 129
UB1: S'hall 7C 76
Saxon Ter. SE6 ....2B 140
Saxon Wlk. DA14: Sidc 6C 144
Saxon Way N14 ....6C 22
UB7: Harm 2D 174
Saxon Way Ind. Est.
UB7: Harm 2D 174
Saxony Pde. UB3: Hayes 5E 74
Saxton Cl. SE13 ....3F 123
Saxton Pl. KT8: W Mole 4D 148
Sayers Ct. W5 ....2D 96
Sayers Ho. N2 ....2B 46
(off The Grange)
Sayer St. SE17 ....4C 102
Sayer's Wlk. TW10: Rich 7F 115
Sayesbury La. N18 ....5B 34
Sayes Ct. SE8 ....6B 104
Sayes Ct. St. SE8 ....6B 104
Scadbury Pk. 7K 143
Scads Hill Cl. BR6: Pet W 6K 161
Scafell NW1 ....1A 6
(off Stanhope St.)
Scala 1F 7
Scala St. W1 ....5B 6 (5G 83)
Scales Rd. N17 ....3F 49
The Scalpel 1G 15
Scampston M. W10 ....6F 81
Scandrett St. E1 ....1H 103
Scarab Cl. E16 ....7H 87
Scarba Wlk. N1 ....6D 66
(off Essex Rd.)
Scarborough Rd. E11 ....1F 69
N4 ....7A 48
N9 ....7D 24
TW6: H'row A 6E 110
Scarborough St. E1 ....1K 15 (6F 85)
Scarbrook Rd. CR0: C'don 3C 168
Scarle Rd. HA0: Wemb 6D 60
Scarlet Cl. E20 ....5D 68
Scarlet Rd. SE6 ....3G 141
Scarlette Mnr. Way SW2 ....7A 120
Scarlet Wlk. EN3: Pond E 5E 24
Scarsbrook Rd. SE3 ....3B 124
Scarsdale Pl. W8 ....3K 99
Scarsdale Rd. HA2: Harr 3G 59
Scarsdale Studios W8 ....3J 99
(off Stratford Rd.)
Scarsdale Vs. W8 ....3J 99
Scarth Rd. SW13 ....3B 116
Scawen Cl. SM5: Cars 4E 166
Scawen Rd. SE8 ....5A 104
Scawfell St. E2 ....2F 85
Scaynes Link N12 ....4D 30
Sceaux Gdns. SE5 ....1E 120
Scena Way SE5 ....7C 102
Sceptre Ct. EC3 ....3K 15
(off Tower Hill)
Sceptre Ho. E1 ....4J 85
(off Malcolm Rd.)
Sceptre Rd. E2 ....3J 85
Schafer Ho. NW1 ....2A 6 (3G 83)
Schofield Wlk. SE3 ....7J 105
Scholars Cl. EN5: Barn 4B 20
Scholars Ho. NW6 ....1J 81
(off Glengall Rd.)
Scholars Pl. N16 ....3E 66
Scholars Rd. E4 ....1A 36
SW12 ....1G 137
Scholars Vw. KT7: T Ditt 7J 149
Scholars Way RM8: Dag 4A 72
Scholefield Rd. N19 ....2H 65
Scholey Ho. SW11 ....3C 118
Schomberg Ho. SW1 ....3D 18
(off Page St.)
Schonfeld Sq. N16 ....2D 66
School All. TW1: Twick 1A 132
School App. E2 ....1H 9
UB4: Hayes 4H 75
Schoolbank Rd. SE10 ....3H 105
Schoolbell M. E3 ....2A 86
Schoolgate Dr. SM4: Mord 5K 153
School Ho. SE1 ....4E 102
(off Page's Wlk.)
School Ho. La. NW7 ....6B 30
TW11: Tedd 7B 132
Schoolhouse La. E1 ....7K 85
Schoolhouse Yd. SE18 ....5F 107
School La. DA16: Well 3B 126
HA5: Pinn 4C 40
KT1: Hamp W 1C 150
KT6: Surb 1F 163
SE23 ....2H 139
TW17: Shep 6D 146
WD23: Bush 1A 26
School M. E1 ....7H 85
(off Hawksmoor M.)
School Nook E20 ....2K 67
School of Oriental & African Studies
Vernon Sq. Campus 1H 7 (3K 83)
The School of Pharmacy 3F 7
School Pas. KT1: King T 2F 151
UB1: S'hall 7D 76
School Rd. BR7: Chst 1G 161
E12 ....4D 70
KT1: Hamp W 1C 150
KT8: E Mos 4H 149
NW10 ....4K 79
RM10: Dag 1G 91
TW3: Houn 3G 113
TW12: Hamp H 6G 131
TW15: Ashf 6D 128
UB7: Harm 2E 174
School Rd. Av. TW12: Hamp H 6G 131
SCHOOL ROAD JUNC. 7D 128
School Sq. SE10 ....3H 105
School Wlk. TW16: Sun 4H 147
School Way N12 ....6G 31
RM8: Dag 3C 72
Schooner Cl. E14 ....3F 105
IG11: Bark 3B 90
SE16 ....2K 103
Schooner Rd. E16 ....2K 105

Schubert Rd.—Shaftesbury Circ.

Schubert Rd. SW15 5H 117
Schurlock Pl. TW2: Twick 2J 131
Schwartz Wharf E9 7C 68
Science Mus. 2B 16 (3B 100)
Sclater St. E1 3J 9 (4F 85)
Scoble Pl. N16 4F 67
Scoles Cres. SW2 1B 138
The Scoop 5H 15 (1E 102)
Scope Way KT1: King T 4E 150
The Score Complex
Leyton 3D 68
Scoresby St. SE1 5A 14 (1B 102)
Scorton Av. UB6: G'frd 2A 78
Scorton Ho. N1 2E 84
(off Whitmore Est.)
Scotch Comn. W13 5A 78
SCOTCH HOUSE 2D 100
Scoter Cl. IG8: Wfd G 7E 36
Scoter Ct. SE8 6B 104
(off Abinger Gro.)
Scot Gro. HA5: Pinn 1B 40
Scotia Bldg. E1 7K 85
(off Jardine Rd.)
Scotia Ct. SE16 2J 103
(off Canada Est.)
Scotia Rd. SW2 7A 120
Scotland Grn. N17 2F 49
Scotland Grn. Rd. EN3: Pond E 5E 24
Scotland Grn. Rd. Nth.
EN3: Pond E 4E 24
Scotland Pl. SW1 5E 12 (1J 101)
Scotland Rd. IG9: Buck H 1F 37
Scotney Cl. BR6: Farnb 4E 172
Scotney Ho. E9 6J 67
Scots Cl. TW19: Stanw 1A 128
Scotsdale Cl. BR5: Pet W 4J 161
SM3: Cheam 7G 165
Scotsdale Rd. SE12 5K 123
Scotson Ho. SE11 4J 19
Scotswood St. EC1 3K 7 (4A 84)
Scotswood Wlk. N17 7B 34
Scott Av. SW15 6G 117
Scott Cl. KT19: Ewe 5J 163
SW16 1K 155
UB7: W Dray 4B 92
Scott Ct. W3 2K 97
Scott Cres. HA2: Harr 1F 59
Scott Ellis Gdns. NW8 2A 4 (3B 82)
Scottes La. RM8: Dag 1D 72
Scott Farm Cl. KT7: T Ditt 1B 162
Scott Gdns. TW5: Hest 7B 94
Scott Ho. DA17: Belv 5F 109
E13 2J 87
(off Queens Rd. W.)
E14 2C 104
(off Admirals Way)
N7 6K 65
(off Caledonian Rd.)
N18 5B 34
(off Woolmer Rd.)
NW8 4C 4
(off Broadley St.)
NW10 7K 61
(off Stonebridge Pk.)
SE8 5B 104
(off Grove St.)
Scott Lidgett Cres. SE16 2G 103
Scott Rd. HA8: Edg 2H 43
Scott Russell Pl. E14 5D 104
Scotts Av. BR2: Broml 2F 159
TW16: Sun 7G 129
Scotts Ct. W12 2E 98
(off Scott's Rd.)
Scotts Dr. TW12: Hamp 7F 131
Scotts Farm Rd. KT19: Ewe 6J 163
Scott's La. BR2: Broml 3F 159
Scotts Pas. SE18 4F 107
Scott's Rd. E10 1E 68
UB2: S'hall 3A 94
W12 2D 98
Scotts Rd. BR1: Broml 7J 141
Scott's Sufferance Wharf SE1 7K 15
Scotts Ter. SE9 2C 142
Scott St. E1 4H 85
Scotts Way TW16: Sun 7G 129
Scott's Yd. EC4 2E 14 (7D 84)
Scott Trimmer Way TW3: Houn 2C 112
Scottwell Dr. NW9 5B 44
Scoulding Ho. E14 3C 104
(off Mellish St.)
Scoulding Rd. E16 6J 87
Scouler St. E14 7E 86
Scout App. NW10 4A 62
Scout La. SW4 3G 119
Scout Pk. 7C 32
Scout Way NW7 4E 28
Scovell Cres. SE1 7C 14
Scovell Rd. SE1 7C 14 (2C 102)
Scrattons Farm Eco-Park 2E 90
Scrattons Ter. IG11: Bark 2D 90
Screenworks N5 5C 66
Scrimgeour Pl. N4 1C 66
Scriven Ct. E8 1F 85
Scriven St. E8 1F 85
Scrooby St. SE6 6D 122
Scrope Ho. EC1 5J 7
(off Bourne Est.)
Scrubs La. NW10 3C 80
W10 3C 80
Scrutton Cl. SW12 7H 119
Scrutton St. EC2 4G 9 (4E 84)
Scudamore La. NW9 4J 43
Sculpture Ho. E1 5K 85
(off Duckett St.)
Scutari Rd. SE22 5J 121
Scylla Cres. TW6: H'row A 7D 110
(not continuous)
Scylla Rd. SE15 3G 121
(not continuous)
TW6: H'row A 6D 110
Seaborne Wharf E3 5C 86
(off Invicta Cl.)
Seabright St. E2 3H 85
Seabrook Dr. BR4: W W'ck 2G 171
Seabrook Gdns. RM7: Rush G 7G 55
Seabrook Rd. RM8: Dag 3D 72
Seaburn Cl. RM13: Rain 2K 91
Seacole Cl. W3 6K 79
Seacole Lodge N21 5E 22
(off Pennington Dr.)
Sea Containers Ho. SE1 3K 13
Seacon Twr. E14 2B 104
Seacourt Rd. SE2 2D 108
Seafarer Way SE16 4A 104
Seafield Rd. N11 4C 32
Seaford Cl. HA4: Ruis 1F 57
Seaford Ho. SE16 2J 103
(off Swan Rd.)
Seaford Rd. E17 3D 50
EN1: Enf 4K 23
N15 5D 48
TW6: H'row A 5A 110
W13 1B 96
Seaford St. WC1 2F 7 (3J 83)
Seaforth Av. KT3: N Mald 5D 152
Seaforth Cres. N5 5C 66
Seaforth Gdns. IG8: Wfd G 5F 37
KT19: Ewe 4B 164
N21 7E 22
Seaforth Pl. SW1 1B 18
Seager Pl. SE8 1C 122
(off Deptford Bri.)
Seagrave Cl. E1 5K 85
Seagrave Lodge SW6 6J 99
(off Seagrave Rd.)
Seagrave Rd. SW6 6J 99
Seagry Rd. E11 7J 51
Seagull Cl. IG11: Bark 3A 90
Seagull La. E16 7J 87
Seahorse Sailing Club 2K 61
Sealand Rd. TW6: H'row A 6C 110
Sealand Wlk. UB5: N'olt 3B 76
Seal Ho. SE1 7F 15
(off Weston St.)
Sea Life
London 6G 13 (2K 101)
Seal St. E8 4F 67
Searle Ho. NW8 1C 82
(off Cecil Gro.)
SW11 1E 118
(off Macduff Rd.)
Searle Pl. N4 1K 65
Searles Cl. SW11 7C 100
Searles Dr. E6 5F 89
Searles Rd. SE1 4D 102
Searson Ho. SE17 4B 102
(off Canterbury Pl.)
Sears St. SE5 7D 102
Seasalter Ho. SW9 1A 120
(off Gosling Way)
Seasons Cl. W7 1K 95
Seasons Ho. E20 6E 68
(off Mirabelle Gdns.)
Seasprite Cl. UB5: N'olt 3B 76
Seaton Av. IG3: Ilf 5K 71
Seaton Cl. E13 4J 87
SE11 5K 19 (5A 102)
SW15 1D 134
TW2: Whitt 6H 113
Seaton Dr. TW15: Ashf 2A 128
Seaton Gdns. HA4: Ruis 3H 57
Seaton Point E5 4G 67
Seaton Rd. CR4: Mitc 2C 154
DA16: Well 7C 108
HA0: Wemb 2E 78
TW2: Whitt 6G 113
UB3: Harl 4F 93
Seaton Sq. NW7 7A 30
Seaton St. N18 5B 34
Seawall Ct. IG11: Bark 2G 89
(off Dock Rd.)
Sebastian Ct. IG11: Bark 1K 89
Sebastian Ho. N1 1G 9
(off Hoxton St.)
Sebastian St. EC1 2B 8 (3B 84)
Sebastopol Rd. N9 4B 34
Sebbon St. N1 7B 66
Sebergham Gro. NW7 7H 29
Sebert Rd. E7 5K 69
Sebright Ho. E2 2G 85
(off Coate St.)
Sebright Pas. E2 2G 85
Sebright Rd. EN5: Barn 2A 20
Secker Cres. HA3: Hrw W 1G 41
Secker Ho. SW9 2B 120
(off Loughborough Est.)
Secker St. SE1 5J 13 (1A 102)
Second Av. E12 4C 70
E13 3J 87
E17 5C 50
EN1: Enf 5A 24
HA9: Wemb 2D 60
KT12: Walt T 6K 147
N18 4D 34
NW4 4F 45
RM6: Chad H 5C 54
RM10: Dag 2H 91
SW14 3A 116
UB3: Hayes 1H 93
W3 1B 98
W10 4G 81
Second Cl. KT8: W Mole 4G 149
Second Cross Rd. TW2: Twick 2J 131
Second Way HA9: Wemb 4H 61
Sedan Way SE17 5E 102
Sedcombe Cl. DA14: Sidc 4B 144
Sedcote Rd. EN3: Pond E 5D 24
Sedding St. SW1 3G 17 (4E 100)
Sedding Studios SW1 3G 17
(off Sedding St.)
Seddon Highwalk EC2 5C 8
(off Aldersgate St.)
Seddon Ho. EC2 5C 8
Seddon Rd. SM4: Mord 5B 154
Seddon St. WC1 2H 7 (3K 83)
Sedgebrook Rd. SE3 2B 124
Sedgecombe Av. HA3: Kenton 5C 42
Sedgefield Ct. UB5: N'olt 5F 59
(off Newmarket Av.)
Sedgeford Rd. W12 1B 98
Sedge Gdns. IG11: Bark 3A 90
Sedgehill Rd. SE6 4C 140
Sedgemere Av. N2 3A 46
Sedgemere Rd. SE2 3C 108
Sedgemoor Dr. RM10: Dag 4G 73
Sedge Rd. N17 7D 34
Sedgeway SE6 1H 141
Sedgewood Cl. BR2: Hayes 7H 159
Sedgmoor Pl. SE5 7E 102
Sedgwick Av. UB10: Hil 7D 56
Sedgwick Ho. E3 5C 86
(off Gale St.)
Sedgwick Rd. E10 2E 68
Sedgwick St. E9 5K 67
Sedleigh Rd. SW18 6H 117
Sedlescombe Rd. SW6 6J 99
Sedley Cl. EN1: Enf 1C 24
Sedley Ct. SE26 2H 139
Sedley Ho. SE11 5H 19
(off Newburn St.)
Sedley Pl. W1 1J 11 (6F 83)
Sedona Ho. E20 6D 68
(off Victory Pde.)
Sedum Cl. NW9 5H 43
Sedum M. EN2: Enf 3F 23
Seeley Dr. SE21 4E 138
Seelig Av. NW9 7C 44
Seely Rd. SW17 6E 136
Seetha Ho. IG1: Ilf 2H 71
(off High Rd.)
Seething La. EC3 2H 15 (7E 84)
SEETHING WELLS 6C 150
Seething Wells La. KT6: Surb 6C 150
Sefton Av. HA3: Hrw W 2H 41
NW7 5E 28
Sefton Cl. BR5: St M Cry 4K 161
Sefton Ct. EN2: Enf 2G 23
TW3: Houn 1F 113
Sefton Rd. BR5: St M Cry 4K 161
CR0: C'don 1G 169
Sefton St. SW15 3E 116
Segal Cl. SE23 7A 122
Sekforde St. EC1 4A 8 (4B 84)
Sekhon Ter. TW13: Hanw 3E 130
Selah Dr. BR8: Swan 7J 145
Selan Gdns. UB4: Yead 5K 75
Selbie Av. NW10 5B 62
Selborne Av. DA5: Bexl 1E 144
E12 4E 70
Selborne Gdns. NW4 4C 44
UB6: G'frd 2A 78
Selborne Rd. CR0: C'don 3E 168
DA14: Sidc 4B 144
E17 5B 50
IG1: Ilf 2E 70
KT3: N Mald 2A 152
N14 3D 32
N22 1K 47
SE5 2D 120
Selborne Wlk. E17 5B 50
Selborne Wlk. Shop. Cen. 5B 50
Selbourne Av. KT6: Surb 2F 163
Selbourne Ho. SE1 7E 14
The Selby Cen. 6K 33
Selby Chase HA4: Ruis 2K 57
Selby Cl. BR7: Chst 6E 142
E6 5C 88
KT9: Chess 7E 162
Selby Gdns. UB1: S'hall 4E 76
Selby Grn. SM5: Cars 7C 154
Selby Rd. E11 3G 69
E13 5K 87
N17 7K 33
SE20 2G 157
SM5: Cars 7C 154
TW15: Ashf 6E 128
W5 4B 78
Selby Sq. W10 3G 81
(off Dowland St.)
Selby St. E1 4G 85
Selcroft Ho. SE10 5H 105
(off Glenister Rd.)
Selden Ho. SE15 2J 121
(off Selden Rd.)
Selden Rd. SE15 2J 121
Selden Wlk. N7 2K 65
Seldon Ho. SW1 6A 18
(off Churchill Gdns.)
SW8 7G 101
(off Stewart's Rd.)
Selfridges 1H 11
SELHURST 6E 156
Selhurst Cl. SW19 1F 135
Selhurst New Rd. SE25 6E 156
Selhurst Pk. 4E 156
Selhurst Pl. SE25 6E 156
Selhurst Rd. N9 3J 33
SE25 6E 156
Selig Ct. NW11 7G 45
Selina Ho. NW8 3B 4
(off Frampton St.)
Selinas La. RM8: Dag 7E 54
Selkirk Ho. N1 1K 83
(off Bingfield St.)
Selkirk Rd. SW17 4C 136
TW2: Twick 2G 131
Sellers Hall Cl. N3 7D 30
Sellincourt Rd. SW17 5C 136
Sellindge Cl. BR3: Beck 7B 140
Sellons Av. NW10 1B 80
Sellwood Dr. EN5: Barn 6A 20
Selman Ho. E9 6A 68
SELSDON 7J 169
Selsdon Av. CR2: S Croy 6D 168
Selsdon Cl. KT6: Surb 5E 150
RM5: Col R 1J 55
Selsdon Pk. Rd. CR0: Sels 7K 169
CR2: Sels 7K 169
Selsdon Rd. CR2: S Croy 5D 168
E11 7J 51
E13 1A 88
NW2 2B 62
SE27 3A 138
Selsdon Way E14 3D 104
Selsea Pl. N16 5E 66
Selsey WC1 2F 7
(off Tavistock Pl.)
Selsey Cres. DA16: Well 1D 126
Selsey St. E14 5C 86
Selvage La. NW7 5E 28
Selway Cl. HA5: Eastc 4K 39
Selway Ho. SW8 1J 119
(off Sth. Lambeth Rd.)
Selwood Pl. SW7 5A 16 (5B 100)
Selwood Rd. CR0: C'don 2H 169
KT9: Chess 4D 162
SM3: Sutt 1H 165
Selwood St. SW2 7A 120
Selwood Ter. SW7 5A 16 (5B 100)
Selworthy Cl. E11 5J 51
Selworthy Ho. SW11 1B 118
(off Battersea Church Rd.)
Selworthy Rd. SE6 3B 140
Selwyn Av. E4 6K 35
IG3: Ilf 6K 53
TW9: Rich 3E 114
Selwyn Cl. TW4: Houn 4C 112
Selwyn Ct. E17 5C 50
(off Yunus Khan Cl.)
HA8: Edg 7C 28
HA9: Wemb 3J 61
SE3 3H 123
TW10: Rich 5F 115
(off Church Rd.)
Selwyn Cres. DA16: Well 3B 126
Selwyn Rd. E3 2B 86
E13 1K 87
KT3: N Mald 5K 151
NW10 7A 62
Semley Ga. E9 6B 68
(not continuous)
Semley Ho. SW1 4J 17
(off Semley Pl.)
Semley Pl. SW1 4H 17 (4E 100)
Semley Rd. SW16 2J 155
Senate St. SE15 2J 121
Senators Lodge E3 2A 86
(off Roman Rd.)
Senator Wlk. SE28 3H 107
Sendall Ct. SW11 3B 118
(off Winstanley Rd.)
Seneca Rd. CR7: Thor H 4C 156
Sener Ct. CR2: S Croy 6C 168
Senga Rd. SM6: W'gton 1E 166
Senhouse Rd. SM3: Cheam 3F 165
Senior St. W2 5K 81
Senlac Rd. SE12 1K 141
Sennen Rd. EN1: Enf 7A 24
Sennen Wlk. SE9 3C 142
Senrab St. E1 6K 85
Sentamu Cl. SE24 1B 138
Sentinel Bldg. E15 5F 69
(off Property Row)
Sentinel Cl. UB5: N'olt 4C 76
Sentinel Sq. NW4 4E 44
September Ct. UB1: S'hall 1F 95
(off Dormer's Wells La.)
September Way HA7: Stan 6G 27
Septimus Pl. EN1: Enf 5B 24
Sequoia Cl. WD23: B Hea 1C 26
Sequoia Gdns. BR6: Orp 7K 161
Sequoia Pk. HA5: Hat E 6A 26
Serap Ct. CR0: C'don 4D 168
(off Dean Rd.)
Seraph Ct. EC1 1C 8
(off Moreland St.)
Serbin Cl. E10 7E 50
Serenaders Rd. SW9 2A 120
Serenity Apts. E17 5D 50
SW11 4C 118
(off Monarch Sq.)
Serenity Cl. HA2: Harr 2F 59
Seren Pk. Gdns. SE3 6G 105
Sergeant Ind. Est. SW18 6K 117
Serica Ct. SE10 7E 104
Serjeants Inn EC4 1K 13 (6A 84)
Serlby Ct. W14 3H 99
(off Somerset Sq.)
Serle St. WC2 7H 7 (6K 83)
Sermon La. EC4 1C 14
The Serpentine 5D 10 (1C 100)
Serpentine Cl. RM6: Chad H 7C 54
Serpentine Ct. SE16 2K 103
(off Christopher Cl.)
Serpentine Gallery 6A 10 (2B 100)
The Serpentine Lido 1C 100
Serpentine Rd. W2 5C 10 (1C 100)
Serpentine Sackler Gallery
4B 10 (1B 100)
Serviden Dr. BR1: Broml 1B 160
Servite Ho. BR3: Beck 1B 158
KT4: Wor Pk 2B 164
(off The Avenue)
N14 5A 22
(off Bramley Rd.)
Servius Ct. TW8: Bford 7D 96
Setchell Rd. SE1 4F 103
Setchell Way SE1 4F 103
Seth St. SE16 2J 103
Seton Gdns. RM9: Dag 7C 72
Settle Point E13 2J 87
Settlers Ct. E14 7F 87
Settles St. E1 5G 85
Settrington Rd. SW6 2K 117
Seven Acres SM5: Cars 2C 166
Seven Dials WC2 1E 12 (6J 83)
Seven Dials Ct. WC2 1E 12
(off Shorts Gdns.)
Sevenex Pde. HA9: Wemb 5E 60
Seven Islands Leisure Cen. 3J 103
SEVEN KINGS 1K 71
Seven Kings Rd. IG3: Ilf 1J 71
Seven Kings Way KT2: King T 1E 150
Sevenoaks Cl. DA7: Bex 4H 127
Sevenoaks Ct. HA6: Nwood 1E 38
Sevenoaks Rd. BR6: Chels, Orp 5K 173
BR6: Prat B 7K 173
SE4 6A 122
Sevenoaks Way BR5: St P 7C 144
DA14: Sidc 7C 144
Seven Sea Gdns. E3 5D 86
Sevenseas Rd. TW6: H'row A 6E 110
SEVEN SISTERS 5F 49
Seven Sisters Rd. N4 2A 66
N7 3K 65
N15 7C 48
Seven Stars Cnr. W12 3C 98
Seven Stars Yd. E1 5K 9
Seventeen SM1: Sutt 6A 166
(off Sutton Ct. Rd.)
Seventh Av. E12 4D 70
UB3: Hayes 1J 93
Seven Ways Pde. IG2: Ilf 5E 52
Severin Ct. SE17 5E 102
(off East St.)
Severnake Cl. E14 4C 104
Severn Av. W10 3G 81
Severn Ct. KT2: King T 1D 150
(off John Williams Cl.)
Severn Dr. KT10: Hin W 2A 162
Severn Ho. SW18 4J 117
(off Enterprise Way)
Severn Way NW10 5B 62
Severus Ho. UB3: Hayes 6F 75
Severus Rd. SW11 4C 118
Seville Ho. E1 1G 103
(off Wapping High St.)
Seville M. N1 7E 66
Seville St. SW1 7F 11 (2D 100)
Sevington Rd. NW4 6D 44
Sevington St. W9 4K 81
Seward Rd. BR3: Beck 2K 157
W7 2A 96
SEWARDSTONE 1K 25
Sewardstone Cl. E4 1K 25
Sewardstone Gdns. E4 5J 25
Sewardstone Rd. E2 2J 85
E4 7J 25
Seward St. EC1 3B 8 (3B 84)
Sewdley St. E5 3K 67
Sewell Rd. SE2 3A 108
Sewell St. E13 3J 87
Sextant Av. E14 4F 105
Sexton Ct. E14 7F 87
(off Newport Av.)
Sextons Ho. SE10 6E 104
(off Bardsley La.)
Seymer Rd. RM1: Rom 3K 55
Seymore M. SE14 7B 104
(off New Cross Rd.)
Seymour Av. KT17: Ewe 7E 164
N17 2G 49
SM4: Mord 7F 153
Seymour Cl. HA5: Hat E 1D 40
KT8: E Mos 5G 149
Seymour Ct. E4 2C 36
KT1: Hamp W 1D 150
N10 2E 46
N21 6E 22
NW2 2D 62
Seymour Dr. BR2: Broml 1D 172
Seymour Gdns. HA4: Ruis 1B 58
IG1: Ilf 1D 70
KT5: Surb 5F 151
SE4 3A 122
TW1: Twick 7B 114
TW13: Hanw 4A 130
Seymour Ho. E16 1J 105
(off De Quincey M.)
NW1 1D 6
(off Churchway)
SM2: Sutt 6K 165
(off Mulgrave Rd.)
WC1 3E 6
(off Tavistock Pl.)
Seymour Leisure Cen. 6E 4 (5D 82)
Seymour M. W1 7G 5 (6E 82)
Seymour Pl. SE25 4H 157
W1 6E 4 (5D 82)
Seymour Rd. CR4: Mitc 7E 154
E4 1J 35
E6 2B 88
E10 1B 68
KT1: Hamp W 1D 150
KT8: W Mole, E Mos 5G 149
N3 7E 30
N8 5A 48
N9 2C 34
SM5: Cars 5E 166
SW18 7H 117
SW19 3F 135
TW12: Hamp H 5G 131
W4 4J 97
Seymour St. SE18 3G 107
W1 1E 10 (6D 82)
W2 1E 10 (6D 82)
Seymour Ter. SE20 1H 157
Seymour Vs. SE20 1H 157
Seymour Wlk. SW10 6A 100
Seymour Way TW16: Sun 7H 129
Seyssel St. E14 4E 104
Shaa Rd. W3 7K 79
Shabana Rd. W12 1D 98
Shacklegate La.
TW11: Tedd 4J 131
Shackleton Cl. SE23 2H 139
Shackleton Ct. E14 5C 104
(off Maritime Quay)
TW19: Stanw 6A 110
(off Whitley Cl.)
W12 2D 98
(off Scott's Rd.)
Shackleton Ho. CR0: Wadd 1K 167
E1 1J 103
(off Prusom St.)
NW10 7K 61
Shackleton Rd. UB1: S'hall 7D 76
Shackleton Way E16 7G 89
SHACKLEWELL 4F 67
Shacklewell Grn. E8 4F 67
Shacklewell Ho. E8 4F 67
Shacklewell La. E8 5F 67
N16 4F 67
Shacklewell Rd. N16 4F 67
Shacklewell Row E8 4F 67
Shacklewell St. E2 2K 9 (3F 85)
Shadbolt Av. E4 5F 35
Shadbolt Cl. KT4: Wor Pk 2B 164
Shad Thames SE1 5J 15 (1F 103)
(Anchor Brewhouse)
SE1 7K 15 (2F 103)
(Jamaica Rd.)
SHADWELL 7H 85
Shadwell Ct. UB5: N'olt 2D 76
Shadwell Dr. UB5: N'olt 3D 76
Shadwell Gdns. E1 7J 85
Shadwell Pierhead E1 7J 85
Shadwell Pl. E1 7J 85
(off Sutton St.)
Shady Bush Cl. WD23: Bush 1B 26
Shaef Way TW11: Tedd 7A 132
Shafter Rd. RM10: Dag 6J 73
Shaftesbury Av. EN3: Enf H 2E 24
EN5: New Bar 4F 21
HA2: Harr 1F 59
HA3: Kenton 5D 42
TW14: Felt 6J 111
UB2: S'hall 4E 94
W1 3C 12 (7H 83)
WC1 7E 6 (6J 83)
WC2 7E 6 (6J 83)
Shaftesbury Barnet Harriers 1E 44
Shaftesbury Cen. W10 4F 81
(off Barlby Rd.)
Shaftesbury Circ. HA2: Harr 1G 59

A-Z Big London 283

Shaftesbury Ct.—The Shire London Golf Course

Shaftesbury Ct. E6 6E 88
(off Sapphire Cl.)
N1 2D 84
(off Shaftesbury St.)
SE1 3D 102
(off Alderney M.)
SE5 4D 120
SW16 3H 137
Shaftesbury Cres.
TW18: Staines 7A 128
Shaftesbury Gdns. NW10 4A 80
Shaftesbury Lodge E14 6D 86
(off Upper Nth. St.)
Shaftesbury M. SW4 5G 119
W8 3J 99
Shaftesbury Pde. HA2: Harr 1G 59
Shaftesbury Pl. EC2 6C 8
(off London Wall)
W14 4H 99
(off Warwick Rd.)
Shaftesbury Point E13 2J 87
(off High St.)
Shaftesbury Rd. BR3: Beck 2B 158
E4 1A 36
E7 7A 70
E10 1C 68
E17 6D 50
N18 6K 33
N19 1J 65
SM5: Cars 7B 154
TW9: Rich 3E 114
Shaftesbury Row SE8 7C 104
(off Speedwell St.)
The Shaftesburys IG11: Bark 2G 89
Shaftesbury St. N1 2C 84
(not continuous)
Shaftesbury Theatre 7E 6
(off Shaftesbury Av.)
Shaftesbury Vs. W8 3J 99
(off Allen St.)
Shaftesbury Way TW2: Twick 3H 131
Shaftesbury Waye
UB4: Yead 5A 76
Shafto M. SW1 2F 17 (3D 100)
Shafton M. E9 1K 85
Shafton Rd. E9 1K 85
Shafts Ct. EC3 1G 15 (6E 84)
Shaftswood Ct. SW17 3D 136
(off Lynwood Rd.)
Shahjalal Ho. E2 2G 85
(off Pritchards Rd.)
Shakespeare Av. N11 5B 32
NW10 1K 79
TW14: Felt 6J 111
UB4: Hayes, Yead 6J 75
(not continuous)
UB4: Yead 4K 75
Shakespeare Cl. HA3: Kenton 7G 43
Shakespeare Ct. EN5: New Bar 3E 20
HA3: Kenton 6F 43
NW6 7A 64
(off Fairfax Rd.)
Shakespeare Cres. E12 6D 70
Shakespeare Dr. HA3: Kenton 6F 43
Shakespeare Gdns. N2 4D 46
Shakespeare Ho. E9 7J 67
(off Lyme Gro.)
N14 2C 32
Shakespeare Rd. DA7: Bex 1E 126
E17 2K 49
N3 1J 45
NW7 4G 29
NW10 1K 79
SE24 5B 120
W3 1J 97
W7 7K 77
Shakespeare's Globe & Exhibition
4C 14 (1C 102)
Shakespeare Twr. EC2 5D 8
Shakespeare Way
TW13: Hanw 4A 130
Shakspeare M. N16 4E 66
Shakspeare Wlk. N16 4E 66
Shalbourne Sq. E9 6B 68
Shalcomb St. SW10 6A 100
Shalden Ho. SW15 6B 116
Shaldon Dr. HA4: Ruis 3A 58
SM4: Mord 5G 153
Shaldon Rd. HA8: Edg 2F 43
Shalfleet Dr. W10 7F 81
Shalford Cl. BR6: Farnb 4G 173
Shalford Ct. N1 2B 84
Shalford Ho. SE1 3D 102
Shalimar Gdns. W3 7J 79
Shalimar Rd. W3 7J 79
Shallons Rd. SE9 4F 143
Shalstone Rd. SW14 3H 115
Shalston Vs. KT6: Surb 6F 151
Shamrock Ho. SE26 4G 139
(off Talisman Sq.)
Shamrock Rd. CR0: C'don 6K 155
Shamrock St. SW4 3H 119
Shamrock Way N14 1A 32
Shandon Rd. SW4 6G 119
Shand St. SE1 6H 15 (2E 102)
Shandy St. E1 5K 85
Shan Ho. WC1 4G 7
(off Millman St.)
Shanklin Ho. E17 2B 50
Shanklin Rd. N8 5H 47
N15 4G 49
Shannon Cl. NW2 3F 63
UB2: S'hall 5B 94
Shannon Commercial Cen.
KT3: N Mald 4C 152
SHANNON CORNER 4C 152
Shannon Cnr. Retail Pk. 4C 152
Shannon Ct. CR0: C'don 1C 168
(off Tavistock Rd.)
N16 3E 66
SE15 7F 103
(off Garnies Cl.)
Shannon Gro. SW9 4K 119
Shannon M. SE3 4H 123
Shannon Pl. NW8 2C 82
Shannon Way
BR3: Beck 6D 140
Shanti Ct. SW18 1J 135
Shap Cres. SM5: Cars 1D 166
Shapland Way N13 5E 32
Shapwick Cl. N11 5J 31
The Shard 5F 15 (1D 102)
Shardcroft Av. SE24 5B 120
Shardeloes Rd. SE4 3B 122
SE14 2B 122
Shard's Sq. SE15 6G 103
Sharland Cl. CR7: Thor H 6A 156
Sharman Ct. DA14: Sidc 4A 144
Sharman Way E3 5D 86
Sharnbrooke Cl.
DA16: Well 3C 126
Sharnbrook Ho. NW14 6J 99
Sharon Cl. KT6: Surb 1C 162
Sharon Ct. CR2: S Croy 5C 168
(off Warham Rd.)
Sharon Gdns. E9 1J 85
Sharon Rd. EN3: Enf H 2F 25
W4 5K 97
Sharpe Cl. W7 5K 77
Sharp Ho. SW8 3F 119
TW1: Twick 6D 114
Sharpleshall St. NW1 7D 64
Sharpley Ct. SE1 6A 14
(off Pocock St.)
Sharpness Cl. UB4: Yead 5C 76
Sharp's La. HA4: Ruis 7F 39
Sharratt St. SE15 6J 103
Sharsted St. SE17 6K 19 (5B 102)
Sharvel La. UB5: N'olt 1J 75
Sharwood WC1 1H 7
(off Penton Ri.)
Shaver's Pl. SW1 3C 12
The Shaw BR7: Chst 7G 143
Shaw Av. IG11: Bark 2E 90
Shawbrooke Rd. SE9 5A 124
Shawbury Cl. NW9 1A 44
Shawbury Rd. SE22 5F 121
Shaw Cl. SE28 1B 108
TW19: Stanw 1A 128
WD23: B Hea 2D 26
Shaw Ct. SM4: Mord 7A 154
Shaw Cres. E14 5A 86
Shaw Dr. KT12: Walt T 7A 148
Shawfield Ct. UB7: W Dray 3A 92
Shawfield Pk. BR1: Broml 2B 160
Shawfield St.
SW3 6D 16 (5C 100)
Shawford Ct. SW15 7C 116
Shawford Rd. KT19: Ewe 6K 163
Shaw Gdns. IG11: Bark 2E 90
Shaw Ho. DA17: Belv 5F 109
E16 1E 106
(off Claremont St.)
Shaw Path BR1: Broml 3H 141
Shaw Pl. N2 3E 46
Shaw Rd. BR1: Broml 3H 141
EN3: Enf H 1E 24
SE22 4E 120
Shaws Cotts. SE23 3A 140
Shaw Sq. E17 1A 50
Shaw Theatre 2D 6 (3H 83)
Shaw Way SM6: W'gton 7J 167
Shead Ct. E1 6H 85
(off James Voller Way)
Shearing Dr. SM5: Cars 7A 154
Shearling Way N7 6J 65
Shearman Rd. SE3 4H 123
THE SHEARS 7G 129
Shears Ct. TW16: Sun 7G 129
Shears La. SW16 7J 137
Shearsmith Ho. E1 7G 85
(off Hindmarsh Cl.)
Shears Way TW16: Sun 1G 147
Shearwater Cl. IG11: Bark 3A 90
Shearwater Ct. E1 3K 15
(off Star Pl.)
SE8 6B 104
(off Abinger Gro.)
Shearwater Dr. NW9 7C 44
Shearwater Rd. SM1: Sutt 5H 165
Shearwater Way UB4: Yead 6B 76
Sheath Cotts. KT7: T Ditt 6B 150
(off Ferry Rd.)
Sheaveshill Av. NW9 4A 44
Sheaveshill Ct. NW9 4K 43
Sheaveshill Pde. NW9 4A 44
(off Sheaveshill Av.)
Sheba Ct. N17 6B 34
(off Altair Cl.)
Sheba Pl. E1 4K 9 (4F 85)
Sheen Comn. Dr. TW10: Rich 4G 115
Sheen Ct. TW10: Rich 4G 115
Sheen Ct. Rd. TW10: Rich 4G 115
Sheendale Rd. TW9: Rich 4F 115
Sheenewood SE26 4H 139
Sheen Ga. Gdns. SW14 4J 115
Sheengate Mans. SW14 4K 115
Sheen Gro. N1 1A 84
Sheen La. SW14 5J 115
Sheen Pk. TW9: Rich 4F 115
Sheen Rd. BR5: St M Cry 4K 161
TW9: Rich 5E 114
TW10: Rich 5E 114
Sheen Way SM6: W'gton 5K 167
Sheen Wood SW14 5J 115
Sheepcote Cl. TW5: Cran 7J 93
Sheepcote La. SW11 2D 118
Sheepcote Rd. HA1: Harr 6K 41
Sheepcotes Rd. RM6: Chad H 4E 54
Sheephouse Way KT3: N Mald 1K 163
Sheep La. E8 1H 85
Sheep Wlk. TW17: Shep 7B 146
Sheep Wlk. M. SW19 6F 135
Sheerness M. E16 2F 107
Sheerwater Rd. E16 5B 88
Sheffield Rd. TW6: H'row A 6E 110
Sheffield Sq. E3 3B 86
Sheffield St. WC2 1G 13 (6K 83)
Sheffield Ter. W8 1J 99
Sheffield Way TW6: H'row A 5F 111
Shelbourne Cl. HA5: Pinn 3D 40
Shelbourne Pl. BR3: Beck 7B 140
Shelbourne Rd. N17 2H 49
Shelburne Dr. TW4: Houn 6E 112
Shelburne Rd. N7 4K 65
Shelbury Cl. DA14: Sidc 3A 144
Shelbury Rd. SE22 5H 121
Sheldon Av. IG5: Ilf 2F 53
N2 6D 46
N6 6D 46
Sheldon Cl. SE12 5K 123
SE20 1H 157
Sheldon Ct. EN5: New Bar 4E 20
RM7: Rush G 6K 55
(off Union Rd.)
SW8 7J 101
(off Lansdowne Grn.)
Sheldon Ho. N1 1E 84
(off Kingsland Rd.)
Sheldon Pl. E2 2G 85
(not continuous)
Sheldon Rd. DA7: Bex 1F 127
N18 4K 33
NW2 4F 63
RM9: Dag 7E 72
Sheldon Sq. W2 6A 4 (5A 82)
Sheldon St. CR0: C'don 3C 168
Sheldrake Cl. E16 1D 106
Sheldrake Ho. SE16 4K 103
(off Tawny Way)
Sheldrake Pl. W8 2J 99
Sheldrick Cl. SW19 2B 154
Shelduck Cl. E15 5H 69
Shelduck Ct. SE8 6B 104
(off Pilot Cl.)
Sheldwich Ter. BR2: Broml 6C 160
Shelford KT1: King T 2G 151
Shelford Pl. N16 3D 66
Shelford Ri. SE19 7F 139
Shelford Rd. EN5: Barn 6A 20
Shelgate Rd. SW11 5C 118
Shell Cl. BR2: Broml 6C 160
Shellduck Cl. NW9 2A 44
Shelley N8 3J 47
(off Boyton Rd.)
Shelley Av. E12 6C 70
UB6: G'frd 3H 77
Shelley Cl. BR6: Orp 3J 173
HA8: Edg 4B 28
SE15 2H 121
UB4: Hayes 5J 75
UB6: G'frd 3H 77
Shelley Ct. E10 7D 50
(off Skelton's La.)
E11 4K 51
(off Makepeace Rd.)
N19 1K 65
SW3 7F 17
(off Tite St.)
Shelley Cres. TW5: Hest 1B 112
UB1: S'hall 6D 76
Shelley Dr. DA16: Well 1J 125
Shelley Gdns. HA0: Wemb 2C 60
Shelley Ho. E2 3J 85
(off Cornwall Av.)
N16 4E 66
SE17 5C 102
(off Browning St.)
SW1 7B 18
(off Churchill Gdns.)
Shelley Lodge EN2: Enf 1J 23
Shelley Pl. N1 1B 84
Shelley Rd. NW10 1K 79
Shelley Way SW19 5B 136
Shellness Rd. E5 5H 67
Shell Rd. SE13 3D 122
Shell Twr. SE1 6H 13
Shellwood Rd. SW11 2D 118
Shelmerdine Cl. E3 5C 86
Shelson Av. TW13: Felt 3H 129
Shelson Pde. TW13: Felt 3H 129
Shelton Rd. SW19 1J 153
Shelton St. WC2 1E 12 (6J 83)
(not continuous)
Shene Ho. EC1 5J 7
(off Bourne Est.)
Shene Sports & Fitness Cen. 4A 116
Shenfield Ho. SE18 1B 124
(off Portway Gdns.)
Shenfield Rd. IG8: Wfd G 7E 36
Shenfield St. N1 1H 9 (2E 84)
(not continuous)
Shenley Av. HA4: Ruis 2H 57
Shenley Rd. SE5 1E 120
TW5: Hest 1C 112
Shenstone W13 1C 96
Shenstone Cl. DA1: Cray 4K 127
Shenstone Ho. SW16 5G 137
Shepheard's Ho. BR7: Chst 1H 161
Shepherd Cl. TW13: Hanw 4C 130
Shepherdess Pl. N1 1D 8 (3C 84)
Shepherdess Wlk. N1 1D 8 (2C 84)
Shepherd Ho. E14 6D 86
(off Annabel Cl.)
E16 7F 89
(off University Way)
Shepherd Mkt. W1 4J 11 (1F 101)
SHEPHERD'S BUSH 2E 98
Shepherd's Bush Empire Theatre
2E 98
Shepherd's Bush Grn. W12 2E 98
Shepherd's Bush Mkt. W12 2E 98
(not continuous)
Shepherd's Bush Pl. W12 2F 99
Shepherd's Bush Rd. W6 4E 98
Shepherd's Cl. BR6: Orp 3K 173
N6 6F 47
Shepherds Cl. HA7: Stan 5F 27
(not continuous)
RM6: Chad H 5D 54
TW17: Shep 6D 146
W1 2G 11
(off Lees Pl.)
Shepherds Ct. W12 2F 99
(off Shepherd's Bush Grn.)
Shepherds Grn. BR7: Chst 7H 143
Shepherd's Hill N6 6F 47
Shepherds La. E9 6K 67
SE28 1J 107
Shepherds Leas SE9 4G 125
Shepherds Path UB5: N'olt 6C 58
(off Arnold Rd.)
Shepherds Pl. W1 2G 11 (7E 82)
Shepherd St. W1 5J 11 (1F 101)
Shepherd's Wlk. NW3 5B 64
Shepherds Wlk. NW2 3D 62
WD23: B Hea 2C 26
Shepherds Way CR2: Sels 7K 169
Shepiston La. UB3: Harl 4D 92
Shepley Cl. SM5: Cars 3E 166
Sheppard Cl. EN1: Enf 1C 24
KT1: King T 4E 150
Sheppard Dr. SE16 5H 103
Sheppard Ho. E2 2G 85
(off Warner Pl.)
SW2 1A 138
Sheppards Coll. BR1: Broml 1J 159
(off London Rd.)
Sheppard St. E16 4H 87
SHEPPERTON 6D 146
Shepperton Bus. Pk.
TW17: Shep 5E 146
Shepperton Ct. TW17: Shep 6D 146
Shepperton Ct. Dr. TW17: Shep 5D 146
Shepperton Film Studios 3B 146
SHEPPERTON GREEN 4C 146
Shepperton Marina
TW17: Shep 6G 147
Shepperton Rd. BR5: Pet W 6G 161
N1 1C 84
TW18: Lale, Shep 4A 146
Sheppey Gdns. RM9: Dag 7C 72
Sheppey Rd. RM9: Dag 7B 72
Shepton Ho's. E2 3J 85
(off Welwyn St.)
Sherard Ct. N7 3J 65
Sherard Ho. E9 7J 67
(off Frampton Pk. Rd.)
Sherard Rd. SE9 5C 124
Sheraton Bus. Cen. UB6: G'frd 2B 78
Sheraton Ho. SW1 7K 17
(off Churchill Gdns.)
Sheraton St. W1 1C 12 (6H 83)
Sherborne NW1 7H 65
(off Agar Gro.)
Sherborne Av. EN3: Enf H 2D 24
UB2: S'hall 4E 94
Sherborne Cl. SL3: Poyle 4A 174
UB4: Yead 6A 76
Sherborne Cres. SM5: Cars 7C 154
Sherborne Gdns. NW9 3G 43
W13 5B 78
Sherborne Ho. SW1 5K 17
(part of Abbots Mnr.)
SW8 7K 101
(off Bolney St.)
Sherborne La. EC4 2E 14 (7D 84)
Sherborne Rd. BR5: St M Cry 4K 161
KT9: Chess 5E 162
SM3: Sutt 2J 165
TW14: Bedf 1F 129
(not continuous)
Sherborne St. N1 1D 84
Sherboro Rd. N15 6F 49
Sherbourne Ct. SM2: Sutt 6A 166
SW5 4K 99
(off Cromwell Rd.)
Sherbourne Gdns. TW17: Shep 7G 147
Sherbourne Pl. HA7: Stan 6F 27
Sherbrooke Cl. DA6: Bex 4G 127
Sherbrooke Ho. E2 2J 85
(off Bonner Rd.)
SW1 2D 18
(off Monck St.)
Sherbrooke Rd. SW6 7G 99
Sherbrooke Ter. SW6 7G 99
(off Sherbrooke Rd.)
Sherbrooke Way KT4: Wor Pk 7D 152
Sherbrook Gdns. N21 7G 23
Sherbrook Ho. SE16 2J 103
(off Albatross Way)
Shere Cl. KT9: Chess 5D 162
Sheredan Rd. E4 5A 36
Shere Ho. SE1 7E 14
Shere Rd. IG2: Ilf 5E 52
Sherfield Cl. KT3: N Mald 4H 151
Sherfield Gdns. SW15 6B 116
Sherfield M. UB3: Hayes 6G 75
Sheridan Bldgs. WC2 1F 13
(off Martlett Ct.)
Sheridan Cl. UB10: Hil 4E 74
Sheridan Ct. CR0: C'don 4E 168
(off Coombe Rd.)
HA1: Harr 6H 41
NW6 7A 64
(off Belsize Rd.)
SW5 4K 99
(off Barkston Gdns.)
TW4: Houn 5C 112
UB5: N'olt 5F 59
W7 7K 77
(off Milton Rd.)
Sheridan Cres. BR7: Chst 2F 161
Sheridan Gdns. HA3: Kenton 6D 42
Sheridan Hgts. E1 6H 85
(off Watney St.)
Sheridan Ho. SE11 4K 19
(off Wincott St.)
Sheridan Lodge BR2: Broml 4A 160
(off Homesdale Rd.)
Sheridan M. E11 6K 51
Sheridan Pl. BR1: Broml 2B 160
SW13 3B 116
TW12: Hamp 1F 149
Sheridan Rd. DA7: Bex 3E 126
DA17: Belv 4G 109
E7 3H 69
E12 5C 70
SW19 1H 153
TW10: Ham 3C 132
Sheridan Ter. UB5: N'olt 5F 59
Sheridan Wlk. NW11 6J 45
SM5: Cars 5D 166
Sheridan Way BR3: Beck 1B 158
Sheriden Pl. HA1: Harr 7J 41
Sheringham NW8 1B 82
Sheringham Av. E12 4D 70
N14 5C 22
RM7: Rom 6J 55
TW2: Whitt 1D 130
Sheringham Ct. TW13: Felt 3J 129
(off Sheringham Av.)
UB3: Hayes 2H 93
Sheringham Dr. IG11: Bark 5K 71
Sheringham Ho. NW1 5C 4
Sheringham Rd. N7 6K 65
SE20 3J 157
Sheringham Twr. UB1: S'hall 7F 77
Sherington Av. HA5: Hat E 7A 26
Sherington Rd. SE7 6K 105
Sherland Rd. TW1: Twick 1K 131
Sherleys Ct. HA4: Ruis 2G 57
Sherlies Av. BR6: Orp 2J 173
Sherlock Cl. SW16 2K 155
Sherlock Ct. NW8 1B 82
(off Dorman Way)
Sherlock Holmes Mus. 4F 5
Sherlock M. W1 5G 5 (5E 82)
Sherman Av. KT12: Walt T 5A 148
Sherman Gdns. RM6: Chad H 6C 54
Sherman Ho. E14 6E 86
(off Dee St.)
UB3: Harl 3E 92
(off Nine Acres Cl.)
Sherman Rd. BR1: Broml 1J 159
Shernhall St. E17 3E 50
Sherrard Rd. E7 6A 70
E12 6A 70
Sherrards Way EN5: Barn 5D 20
Sherren Ho. E1 4J 85
Sherrick Grn. Rd. NW10 5D 62
Sherriff Ct. NW6 6J 63
(off Sherriff Rd.)
Sherriff Rd. NW6 6J 63
Sherringham Av. N17 2G 49
TW13: Felt 3J 129
Sherringham Ct. E16 6H 87
(off Silvertown Sq.)
Sherrington Ct. E16 5H 87
(off Rathbone St.)
Sherrin Rd. E10 4D 68
Sherrock Gdns. NW4 4D 44
Sherry M. IG11: Bark 7H 71
Sherston Ct. SE1 4B 102
(off Newington Butts)
WC1 2J 7
Sherwin Ho. SE11 7J 19
Sherwin Rd. SE14 1K 121
Sherwood KT6: Surb 2D 162
NW6 7G 63
Sherwood Av. E18 3K 51
HA4: Ruis 6G 39
SW16 7H 137
UB4: Yead 4K 75
UB6: G'frd 5J 59
Sherwood Cl. DA5: Bexl 6C 126
E17 2B 50
SW13 3D 116
W13 1B 96
Sherwood Ct. CR2: S Croy 5C 168
(off Nottingham Rd.)
HA2: Harr 2F 59
SW11 3A 118
W1 6E 4
(off Bryanston Pl.)
Sherwood Gdns. E14 4C 104
IG11: Bark 7H 71
SE16 5G 103
Sherwood Pk. Av. DA15: Sidc 7A 126
Sherwood Pk. Rd. CR4: Mitc 4G 155
SM1: Sutt 5J 165
Sherwood Rd. CR0: C'don 7H 157
DA16: Well 2J 125
HA2: Harr 2G 59
IG6: Ilf 4H 53
NW4 3E 44
SW19 7H 135
TW12: Hamp H 5G 131
Sherwood St. N20 3G 31
W1 2B 12 (7G 83)
Sherwood Ter. E16 6A 88
(off Bingley Rd.)
N20 3G 31
Sherwood Way BR4: W W'ck 2E 170
Shetland Ho. DA17: Belv 2H 109
Shetland Rd. E3 2B 86
TW6: H'row A 6E 110
Shield Dr. TW8: Bford 6A 96
Shieldhall St. SE2 4C 108
Shield Rd. TW15: Ashf 4E 128
Shield St. SE15 7F 103
Shifford Path SE23 3K 139
Shillaker Ct. W3 1B 98
Shillibeer Pl. W1 6D 4
Shillingford Cl. NW7 7A 30
Shillingford Ho. E3 3D 86
(off Talwin St.)
Shillingford St. N1 7B 66
Shilling Pl. W7 2A 96
Shillingshaw Lodge E16 6J 87
(off Butchers Rd.)
Shillingstone Ho. W14 3G 99
(off Russell Rd.)
Shinfield St. W12 6E 80
Shinglewell Rd. DA8: Erith 7G 109
Shingly Pl. E4 1K 35
Shinners Cl. SE25 5G 157
Ship All. W4 6G 97
Ship & Mermaid Row
SE1 6F 15 (2D 102)
Shipbuilding Way E13 2B 88
Shipka Rd. SW12 1F 137
Shiplake Ho. E2 2J 9
(off Arnold Cir.)
Ship La. SW14 3J 115
Shipman Rd. E16 6K 87
SE23 2K 139
Ship St. SE8 1C 122
Ship Tavern Pas. EC3 2G 15 (7E 84)
Shipton Cl. RM8: Dag 3D 72
Shipton Ho. E2 1K 9
(off Shipton St.)
Shipton Rd. UB10: Ick 4B 56
Shipton St. E2 1K 9 (2F 85)
Shipwright Rd. SE16 2A 104
Shipwright St. E16 2K 105
Shipwright Yd. SE1 5G 15 (1E 102)
Ship Yd. E14 5D 104
Shirburn Cl. SE23 7J 121
Shirebrook Rd. SE3 3B 124
Shire Ct. DA18: Erith 3D 108
KT17: Ewe 7B 164
Shirehall Cl. NW4 6F 45
Shirehall Gdns. NW4 6F 45
Shirehall La. NW4 6F 45
Shirehall Pk. NW4 5F 45
Shire Horse Way TW7: Isle 3K 113
Shire Ho. E3 3D 86
(off Talwin St.)
EC1 4E 8
(off Lambs Pas.)
Shire La. BR2: Kes 7C 172
BR6: Chels, Downe 7F 173
(not continuous)
The Shire London Golf Course 1A 20

284 A-Z Big London

Shire M.—Skyline Apts.

Shire M. TW2: Whitt 6G 113
Shire Pl. SW18 7A 118
TW8: Bford 7D 96
The Shires TW10: Ham 4E 132
Shirland M. W9 3H 81
Shirland Rd. W9 3H 81
Shirlbutt St. E14 7D 86
SHIRLEY 2K 169
Shirley Av. CR0: C'don 1J 169
DA5: Bexl 7D 126
SM1: Sutt 4B 166
Shirley Chu. Rd. CR0: C'don 3K 169
Shirley Cl. E17 5D 50
TW3: Houn 5G 113
Shirley Ct. SW16 7J 137
Shirley Cres. BR3: Beck 4A 158
Shirley Dr. TW3: Houn 5G 113
Shirley Gdns. IG11: Bark 6J 71
W7 1K 95
Shirley Gro. N9 7D 24
SW11 3E 118
Shirley Hgts. SM6: W'gton 7G 167
Shirley Hills Rd. CR0: C'don 5J 169
Shirley Ho. *SE5* 7D 102
(off Picton St.)
Shirley Ho. Dr. SE7 7A 106
SHIRLEY OAKS 1K 169
Shirley Oaks Rd. CR0: C'don 1K 169
Shirley Pk. CR0: C'don 2J 169
Shirley Pk. Golf Course 2H 169
Shirley Pk. Rd. CR0: C'don 1H 169
Shirley Rd. CR0: C'don 7H 157
DA15: Sidc 3J 143
E15 7G 69
EN2: Enf 3H 23
SM6: W'gton 7G 167
W4 2K 97
The Shirley Sherwood Gallery of Botanical Art 2F 115
Shirley St. E16 6H 87
Shirley Way CR0: C'don 3A 170
Shirley Windmill 3J 169
Shirlock Rd. NW3 4D 64
Shirwell Cl. NW7 7A 30
Shobden Rd. N17 1D 48
Shobroke Cl. NW2 3E 62
Shoebury Rd. E6 7D 70
Shoelands Ct. NW9 3K 43
Shoe La. EC4 7K 7 (6A 84)
Sholto Rd. TW6: H'row A 5B 110
Shona Ho. E13 5A 88
Shooters Av. HA3: Kenton 4C 42
SHOOTERS HILL 1E 124
Shooters Hill DA16: Well 1D 124
SE18 1D 124
Shooters Hill Golf Course 1G 125
Shooters Hill Rd. SE3 1F 123
SE10 1F 123
SE18 1F 123
Shooters Rd. EN2: Enf 1G 23
Shoot Up Hill NW2 5G 63
The Shopping Hall E6 1C 88
Shore Bus. Cen. E9 7J 67
Shore Cl. TW12: Hamp 6C 130
TW14: Felt 7J 111
Shorediche Cl. UB10: Ick 3B 56
SHOREDITCH 1G 9 (3E 84)
Shoreditch Ct. *E8* 7F 67
(off Queensbridge Rd.)
Shoreditch High St. E1 4H 9 (4E 84)
Shoreditch Ho. BR2: Broml 6C 160
N1 2F 9
Shore Gro. TW13: Hanw 2E 130
Shoreham Cl. CR0: C'don 6J 157
DA5: Bexl 1D 144
SW18 5K 117
Shoreham Rd. E.
TW6: H'row A 5A 110
Shoreham Rd. W.
TW6: H'row A 5A 110
Shoreham Way BR2: Hayes 6J 159
Shore Ho. SW8 3F 119
Shore M. *E9* 7J 67
(off Shore Rd.)
Shore Pl. E9 7J 67
Shore Point IG9: Buck H 2E 36
Shore Rd. E9 7J 67
Shore Way *SW9* 2A 120
(off Crowhurst Cl.)
Shorncliffe Rd. SE1 5F 103
Shorndean St. SE6 1E 140
Shorne Cl. DA15: Sidc 6B 126
Shornefield Cl. BR1: Broml 3E 160
Shornells Way SE2 4C 108
Shorrold's Rd. SW6 7H 99
Short Blue Pl. IG11: Bark 7G 71
Shortcroft Rd. KT17: Ewe 7B 164
Shortcrofts Rd. RM9: Dag 6F 73
Shorter St. E1 2J 15 (7F 85)
Shortgate N12 4C 30
Short Hedges TW3: Houn 1E 112
Short Hill HA1: Harr 1J 59
SHORTLANDS 2G 159
Shortlands UB3: Harl 6F 93
W6 4F 99
Shortlands Cl. DA17: Belv 3F 109
N18 3J 33
Shortlands Gdns.
BR2: Broml 2G 159
Shortlands Golf Course 1G 159
Shortlands Gro. BR2: Broml 3F 159
Shortlands Rd. BR2: Broml 3F 159
E10 7D 50
KT2: King T 7F 133
Short La. TW19: Stanw 7B 110
Short Path SE18 6F 107
Short Rd. E11 2G 69
TW6: H'row A 6A 110
W4 6A 98
Shorts Cft. NW9 4H 43
Shorts Gdns. WC2 1E 12 (6J 83)
Shorts Rd. SM5: Cars 4C 166
Short St. *NW4* 4E 44
(off Foster St.)
SE1 6K 13 (2A 102)
Short Wall E15 3E 86
Short Way SE9 3C 124
TW2: Whitt 7G 113
Shortway N12 6H 31
Shotfield SM6: W'gton 6F 167
Shott Cl. SM1: Sutt 5A 166
Shottendane Rd. SW6 1J 117
Shottery Cl. SE9 3C 142
Shottfield Av. SW14 4A 116
Shottsford *W2* 6J 81
(off Talbot Rd.)
Shoulder of Mutton All. E14 7A 86
Shouldham St. W1 6D 4 (5C 82)
Showcase Cinema 3H 89
Showers Way UB3: Hayes 1J 93
Shrapnel Cl. SE18 7C 106
Shrapnel Rd. SE9 3D 124
Shrek's Adventure! 6G 13 (2K 101)
Shrewsbury Av. HA3: Kenton 4E 42
SW14 4J 115
Shrewsbury Cl. KT6: Surb 2E 162
Shrewsbury Ct. EC1 4D 8
Shrewsbury Ho. SW3 7C 16
SW8 7H 19
Shrewsbury La. SE18 1F 125
Shrewsbury M. *W2* 5J 81
(off Chepstow Rd.)
Shrewsbury Rd. BR3: Beck 3A 158
E7 5B 70
N11 6B 32
NW10 1K 79
SM5: Cars 6C 154
TW6: H'row A 6E 110
(not continuous)
W2 6J 81
Shrewsbury St. W10 4E 80
Shrewsbury Wlk. *TW7: Isle* 3A 114
(off Magdala Rd.)
Shrewton Rd. SW17 7D 136
Shri Swaminarayan Mandir
London 6K 61
Shroffold Rd. BR1: Broml 4G 141
Shropshire Cl. CR4: Mitc 4J 155
Shropshire Ct. *W7* 6K 77
(off Copley Cl.)
Shropshire Ho. *N18* 5C 34
(off Cavendish Cl.)
Shropshire Pl. WC1 4C 6 (4G 83)
Shropshire Rd. N22 7E 32
Shroton St. NW1 5D 4 (5C 82)
The Shrubberies E18 2J 51
The Shrubbery E11 5K 51
KT6: Surb 1E 162
Shrubbery Cl. N1 1C 84
Shrubbery Gdns. N21 7G 23
Shrubbery Rd. N9 3B 34
SW16 4J 137
UB1: S'hall 1D 94
Shrubland Gro. KT4: Wor Pk 3E 164
Shrubland Rd. E8 1F 85
E10 7C 50
E17 5C 50
Shrublands Av. CR0: C'don 3C 170
Shrublands Cl. N20 1G 31
SE26 3J 139
Shrubsall Cl. SE9 1C 142
Shuna Wlk. N1 6D 66
Shurland Av. EN4: E Barn 6G 21
Shurland Gdns. SE15 7F 103
Shurlock Dr. BR6: Farnb 4G 173
Shushan Cl. N16 7E 48
Shuters Sq. W14 5H 99
Shuttle Cl. DA15: Sidc 7K 125
Shuttlemead DA5: Bexl 7F 127
Shuttle St. E1 4G 85
Shuttleworth Rd. SW11 2C 118
Siamese M. N3 1J 45
Siani M. N8 4B 48
Sibella Rd. SW4 2H 119
Sibley Cl. BR1: Broml 5C 160
DA6: Bex 5E 126
Sibley Ct. BR2: Broml 2F 159
UB8: Hil 5E 74
Sibley Gro. E12 7C 70
Sibthorpe Rd. SE12 6K 123
Sibthorp Rd. CR4: Mitc 2D 154
Sibton Rd. SM5: Cars 7C 154
Sicilian Av. WC1 6F 7
Sickle Cnr. RM9: Dag 4H 91
Sidbury St. SW6 1G 117
SIDCUP 4A 144
Sidcup By-Pass BR7: Chst 3H 143
Sidcup Family Golf 3G 143
Sidcup Golf Course 1B 144
Sidcup High St. DA14: Sidc 4A 144
Sidcup Hill DA14: Sidc 4B 144
Sidcup Hill Gdns.
DA14: Sidc 5C 144
Sidcup Leisure Cen. 2A 144
Sidcup Place 5A 144
Sidcup Pl. DA14: Sidc 5A 144
Sidcup Rd. SE9 1D 142
SE12 6A 124
Sidcup Technology Cen.
DA14: Sidc 5D 144
Siddeley Dr. TW4: Houn 3C 112
Siddeley Rd. E17 2E 50
Siddons La. NW1 4F 5 (4D 82)
Siddons Rd. CR0: Wadd 3A 168
N17 1G 49
SE23 2A 140
Sidewood Rd. SE9 1H 143
Sidford Ho. SE1 2H 19
Sidford Pl. SE1 2H 19 (3A 102)
Sidgwick Ho. *SW9* 2K 119
(off Stockwell Rd.)
Sidi Ct. N15 3B 48
The Sidings E11 1E 68
The Sidings Apts. E16 2E 106
Sidings M. N7 3A 66
Siding St. E20 1D 86
Sidlaw Ho. N16 1F 67
Sidmouth Av. TW7: Isle 2J 113
Sidmouth Dr. HA4: Ruis 3J 57
Sidmouth Ho. *SE15* 7G 103
(off Lindsey Est.)
W1 7D 4
(off Cato St.)
Sidmouth M. WC1 2G 7 (3K 83)
Sidmouth Pde. NW2 7E 62
Sidmouth Rd. DA16: Well 7C 108
E10 3E 68
NW2 7E 62
Sidmouth St. WC1 2F 7 (3J 83)
Sidney Av. N13 5E 32
Sidney Boyd Ct. NW6 7J 63
Sidney Elson Way E6 2E 88
Sidney Est. E1 6J 85
(Bromhead St.)
E1 5J 85
(Lindley St.)
Sidney Gdns. TW8: Bford 6D 96
Sidney Godley (VC) Ho. *E2* 3J 85
(off Digby St.)
Sidney Gro. EC1 1A 8 (2B 84)
Sidney Ho. *E2* 2K 85
(off Old Ford Rd.)
Sidney Miller Ct. *W3* 1H 97
(off Crown St.)
Sidney Rd. BR3: Beck 2A 158
E7 3J 69
HA2: Harr 3G 41
KT12: Walt T 7J 147
N22 7E 32
SE25 5G 157
SW9 2K 119
TW1: Twick 6A 114
Sidney Sq. E1 5J 85
Sidney St. E1 5H 85
(not continuous)
Sidney Webb Ho. *SE1* 3D 102
(off Tabard St.)
Sidonie Apts. *SW11* 4C 118
(off Danvers Av.)
Sidworth St. E8 7H 67
Siebert Rd. SE3 6J 105
Siege Ho. *E1* 6H 85
(off Sidney St.)
Siemens Brothers Way E16 7J 87
Siemens Rd. SE18 3B 106
Sienna SE28 3A 108
Sienna Alto *SE13* 3E 122
(off Cornmill La.)
Sienna Cl. KT9: Chess 6D 162
Sienna Ho. *E20* 6D 68
(off Victory Pde.)
Sienna Ter. NW2 2C 62
Sigdon Pas. E8 5G 67
Sigdon Rd. E8 5G 67
The Sigers HA5: Eastc 6K 39
Sigmund Freud Statue 6B 64
Signal Ho. *E8* 7H 67
(off Martello Ter.)
SE1 7C 14
(off Gt. Suffolk St.)
Signal Wlk. E4 6K 35
Signmakers Yd. *NW1* 1F 83
(off Delancey St.)
Sigrist Sq. KT2: King T 1E 150
Sikorski Mus. 7B 10 (2B 100)
Silbury Av. CR4: Mitc 1C 154
Silbury Ho. SE26 3G 139
Silbury St. N1 1E 8 (3D 84)
Silchester Ct. CR7: Thor H 4A 156
TW15: Ashf 2A 128
Silchester Rd. W10 6F 81
Silecroft Rd. DA7: Bex 1G 127
Silesia Bldgs. E8 7H 67
Silex St. SE1 7B 14 (2B 102)
Silicon Bus. Cen. UB6: G'frd 2C 78
Silicon M. E3 1C 86
Silicon Way N1 2F 9
Silk Cl. SE12 5J 123
Silk Ct. *E2* 3G 85
(off Squirries St.)
Silkfield Rd. NW9 5A 44
Silk Ho. E1 1K 15
(Leman St.)
E1 5K 85
(off Trafalgar Gdns.)
E2 2F 85
(off How's St.)
NW9 3K 43
Silkin M. SE15 7G 103
Silk M. SE11 5K 19
Silk Mills Pas. SE13 2D 122
Silk Mills Path SE13 2E 122
(not continuous)
Silk Mills Sq. E9 6B 68
Silk Rd. SM6: W'gton 2E 166
Silks Ct. E11 1H 69
Silkstream Pde. HA8: Edg 1J 43
Silkstream Rd. HA8: Edg 1J 43
Silk St. EC2 5D 8 (5C 84)
Silk Weaver Way E2 2H 85
Sillitoe Ho. *N1* 1D 84
(off Colville Est.)
Silsoe Ho. NW1 2F 83
Silsoe Rd. N22 2K 47
Silverbeck Way
TW19: Stanw M 7B 174
Silver Birch Av. E4 5G 35
Silver Birch Cl. DA2: Wilm 4K 145
N11 6K 31
SE6 3B 140
SE28 1A 108
UB10: Ick 4A 56
Silver Birch Gdns. E6 4D 88
Silverbirch Wlk. NW3 6D 64
Silverburn Ho. *SW9* 1B 120
(off Lothian Rd.)
Silvercliffe Gdns. EN4: E Barn 4H 21
Silver Cl. HA3: Hrw W 7C 26
SE14 7A 104
Silver Cres. W4 4H 97
Silverdale EN2: Enf 4D 22
NW1 1A 6
(off Harrington St.)
SE26 4J 139
Silverdale Av. IG2: Ilf 5J 53
The Silverdale Cen. HA0: Wemb 1F 79
Silverdale Cl. SM1: Sutt 4H 165
UB5: N'olt 5D 58
W7 1J 95
Silverdale Ct. EC1 3B 8
Silverdale Dr. SE9 2C 142
TW16: Sun 2K 147
Silverdale Factory Cen.
UB3: Hayes 3J 93
Silverdale Gdns. UB3: Hayes 2J 93
Silverdale Ind. Est. UB3: Hayes 2J 93
Silverdale Rd. BR5: Pet W 4G 161
DA7: Bex 2H 127
E4 6A 36
UB3: Hayes 2H 93
Silverdene *N12* 6E 30
(off Thyra Gro.)
Silvergate KT19: Ewe 5J 163
Silverhall St. TW7: Isle 3A 114
Silverholme Cl. HA3: Kenton 7E 42
Silver Jubilee Way TW4: Cran 2K 111
Silverland St. E16 1D 106
Silver La. BR4: W W'ck 2F 171
Silverleigh Rd. CR7: Thor H 4K 155
Silver Mead E18 1J 51
Silvermere Dr. N18 6E 34
Silvermere Rd. SE6 7D 122
Silver Pl. W1 2B 12 (6G 83)
Silver Rd. SE13 3D 122
W12 7F 81
Silvers *IG9: Buck H* 1F 37
(off Palmerston Rd.)
Silver Spring Cl. DA8: Erith 6H 109
Silverston Way HA7: Stan 6H 27
Silver St. EN1: Enf 3J 23
N18 4J 33
Silverthorn *NW8* 1K 81
(off Abbey Rd.)
Silverthorne Loft Apts. *SE5* 6D 102
(off Albany Rd.)
Silverthorne Rd. SW8 2F 119
Silverthorn Gdns. E4 2H 35
Silverton Rd. W6 6F 99
SILVERTOWN 1A 106
Silvertown Quay Development
E16 1A 106
Silvertown Sq. E16 6H 87
Silvertown Viaduct E16 6H 87
Silvertown Way E16 6G 87
(Clarkson Rd.)
E16 1J 105
(Hanover Av.)
Silvertree La. UB6: G'frd 3H 77
Silver Wlk. SE16 1A 104
Silver Way RM7: Mawney 3H 55
UB10: Hil 2D 74
Silver Wing Ind. Est.
CR0: Wadd 6K 167
Silverwood Cl. BR3: Beck 7C 140
CR0: Sels 7B 170
HA6: Nwood 1E 38
Silverwood Pl. SE10 1E 122
Silverworks Cl. NW9 3K 43
Silvester Ho. *E1* 6H 85
(off Varden St.)
E2 3J 85
(off Sceptre Rd.)
W11 6H 81
(off Basing St.)
Silvester Rd. SE22 5F 121
Silvester St. SE1 7E 14 (2D 102)
Silvocea Way E14 6F 87
Silwood Est. SE16 4J 103
Silwood St. *SE16* 4J 103
(off Rotherhithe New Rd.)
Simkins Cl. SW2 4J 119
Simla Ct. *N7* 7J 65
(off Brewery Rd.)
Simla Ho. *SE1* 7F 15
(off Kipling Est.)
Simmonds Ct. *SW5* 4K 99
(off Earl's Ct. Gdns.)
Simmonds Ho. *TW8: Bford* 5E 96
(off Clayponds La.)
Simmons Cl. KT9: Chess 6C 162
N20 2H 31
Simmons Dr. RM8: Dag 3E 72
Simmons La. E4 2A 36
Simmons Way N20 2H 31
Simms Cl. SM5: Cars 2C 166
Simms Gdns. N2 2A 46
Simms Rd. SE1 4G 103
Simnel Rd. SE12 7K 123
Simon Cl. W11 7H 81
Simon Ct. *W9* 3J 81
(off Saltram Cres.)
Simonds Rd. E10 2C 68
Simone Cl. BR1: Broml 1B 160
Simone Ct. SE26 3J 139
Simons Ct. N16 2F 67
Simons Wlk. E15 5F 69
Simpson Cl. CR0: C'don 5C 156
N21 5D 22
Simpson Dr. W3 6K 79
Simpson Ho. NW8 2D 4 (4C 82)
SE11 6G 19 (5K 101)
Simpson Rd. TW4: Houn 6D 112
TW10: Ham 4C 132
Simpson's Rd. BR1: Broml 3J 159
E14 7D 86
Simpson St. SW11 2C 118
Simpson Way KT6: Surb 6C 150
Simrose Ct. SW18 5J 117
Sim St. N4 2C 66
Sims Wlk. SE3 4H 123
Sinclair Ct. CR0: C'don 2E 168
Sinclair Dr. SM2: Sutt 7K 165
Sinclair Gdns. W14 2F 99
Sinclair Gro. NW11 6F 45
Sinclair Ho. *E15* 6F 69
(off Leyton Rd.)
WC1 2E 6
(off Sandwich St.)
Sinclair Mans. *W12* 2F 99
(off Richmond Way)
Sinclair Pl. SE4 6C 122
Sinclair Rd. E4 5G 35
W14 2F 99
Sinclairs Ho. *E3* 2B 86
(off St Stephen's Rd.)
Sinclare Cl. EN1: Enf 1A 24
Sindercombe M. W12 3C 98
Singapore Rd. W13 1A 96
Singer M. SW4 2J 119
Singer St. EC2 2F 9 (3D 84)
Singleton Cl. CR0: C'don 7C 156
SW17 7D 136
Singleton Rd. RM9: Dag 5F 73
Singleton Scarp N12 5D 30
Sinnott Rd. E17 1K 49
Siobhan Davies Dance Studios 3B 102
(off St George's Rd.)
Sion Ct. TW1: Twick 1B 132
Sion Rd. TW1: Twick 1B 132
Sippets Ct. IG1: Ilf 1H 71
SIPSON 6C 92
Sipson Cl. UB7: Sip 6C 92
Sipson La. UB3: Harl 6C 92
UB7: Sip 6C 92
Sipson Rd. UB7: Sip, W Dray 3B 92
(not continuous)
Sipson Way UB7: Sip 7C 92
Sir Abraham Dawes Cotts.
SW15 4G 117
Sir Alexander Cl. W3 1B 98
Sir Alexander Rd. W3 1B 98
Sir Christopher France Ho.
E1 3A 86
Sir Cyril Black Way SW19 7J 135
Sirdar Rd. CR4: Mitc 6E 136
N22 3B 48
W11 7F 81
Sireen Apts. E3 4B 86
Sir Francis Drake Ct. SE10 5F 105
Sirinham Point SW8 7H 19
Sirius Bldg. *E1* 7K 85
(off Jardine Rd.)
Sirius Ho. *SE16* 4A 104
(off Seafarer Way)
Sir James Black Ho. *SE5* 2D 120
(off Coldharbour La.)
Sir John Kirk Cl. SE5 7C 102
Sir John Lyon Ho. *EC4* 2C 14
(off High Timber St.)
Sir John Morden Wlk. SE3 2J 123
Sir John Soane's Mus. 7G 7 (6K 83)
Sir Nicholas Garrow Ho. *W10* 4G 81
(off Kensal Rd.)
Sir Oswald Stoll Mans. *SW6* 7K 99
(off Fulham Rd.)
Sir Simon Milton Sq.
SW1 2K 17 (3F 101)
SIR STEVE REDGRAVE BRIDGE 7F 89
Sir Walter Raleigh Ct.
SE10 5G 105
Sir William Powell's Almshouses
SW6 2G 117
Sise La. EC4 1E 14 (6D 84)
Siskin Ho. *SE16* 4K 103
(off Tawny Way)
Siskin Pl. UB4: Yead 5A 76
Sisley Rd. IG11: Bark 1J 89
Sispara Gdns. SW18 6H 117
Sissinghurst Cl. BR1: Broml 5G 141
Sissinghurst Ho. *SE15* 6J 103
(off Sharratt St.)
Sissinghurst Rd. CR0: C'don 7G 157
Sissulu Ct. E6 1A 88
Sister Mabel's Way SE15 7G 103
Sisters Av. SW11 3D 118
Sistova Rd. SW12 1F 137
Sisulu Pl. SW9 3A 120
Sitarey Ct. W12 1D 98
Sitka Ho. SE16 2A 104
Sittingbourne Av. EN1: Enf 6J 23
Sitwell Gro. HA7: Stan 5E 26
Siverst Cl. UB5: N'olt 6F 59
Sivill Ho. *E2* 1K 9
(off Columbia Rd.)
Siviter Way RM10: Dag 7H 73
Siward Rd. BR2: Broml 3K 159
N17 1D 48
SW17 3A 136
Six Acres Est. N4 2K 65
Six Bridges Ind. Est. SE1 5G 103
(not continuous)
Sixpenny Ct. IG11: Bark 6G 71
Sixth Av. E12 4D 70
UB3: Hayes 1H 93
W10 3G 81
Sixth Cross Rd. TW2: Twick 3G 131
Siyah Gdn. E3 3B 86
Skardu Rd. NW2 5G 63
Skeena Hill SW18 7G 117
Skeffington Rd. E6 1D 88
Skeffington St. SE18 3G 107
Skeggs Ho. *E14* 3E 104
(off Glengall St.)
Skegness Ho. *N7* 7K 65
(off Sutterton St.)
Skelbrook St. SW18 2A 136
Skelgill Rd. SW15 4H 117
Skelley Rd. E15 7H 69
Skelton Cl. E8 6F 67
Skelton Lodge *SE10* 3J 105
(off Billinghurst Way)
Skelton Rd. E7 6J 69
Skelton's La. E10 7D 50
Skelwith Rd. W6 6E 98
Skenfrith Ho. *SE15* 6H 103
(off Commercial Way)
Skerne Rd. KT2: King T 1D 150
Skerne Wlk. KT2: King T 1D 150
Sketch Apts. *E1* 5K 85
(off Shandy St.)
Sketchley Gdns. SE16 5K 103
Sketty Rd. EN1: Enf 3A 24
Skieasy 2K 115
Skiers St. E15 1G 87
Skiffington Cl. SW2 1A 138
Skillen Lodge HA5: Pinn 1B 40
Skinner Ct. *E3* 4D 86
(off Barry Blandford Way)
Skinner Pl. SW1 4G 17
Skinners Ct. N13 3F 33
Skinners La. EC4 2D 14 (7C 84)
TW5: Hest 1F 113
Skinner's Row SE10 1D 122
Skinner St. EC1 2K 7 (3A 84)
Skip La. UB9: Hare 1A 56
Skipper Ct. IG11: Bark 1G 89
Skipsea Ho. SW18 6C 118
Skipsey Av. E6 3D 88
Skipton Cl. N11 6K 31
Skipton Dr. UB3: Harl 3E 92
Skipton Ho. SE4 4A 122
Skipwith Ho. *EC1* 5J 7
(off Bourne Est.)
Skipworth Rd. E9 1J 85
Skua Ct. *SE8* 6B 104
(off Dorking Cl.)
Skye La. HA8: Edg 4A 28
Sky Gdn. Wlk. *EC3* 2G 15
(off Philpot La.)
Skylark Ct. RM13: Rain 2K 91
SE1 7D 14
(off Swan St.)
SW15 6E 116
Skyline Apts. *N4* 7D 48
(off Devan Gro.)

A-Z Big London 285

Skyline Ct.—South London Theatre

Skyline Ct. CR0: C'don 3D 168
(off Park La.)
SE1 . . . . .3F 103
Skyline Plaza Bldg. E1 . . . . .6G 85
(off Commercial Rd.)
Skylines E14 . . . . .2E 104
Skylines Village E14 . . . . .2E 104
Sky Peals Rd. IG8: Wfd G 7A 36
Skyport Dr. UB7: Harm 3E 174
Sky Studios E16 . . . . .2E 106
Skyvan Cl. TW6: H'row A 5E 110
Skyview Apts. CR0: C'don 2C 168
(off Park St.)
Sky View Tower E15 . . . . .2D 86
(off High Street)
Skyway 14 SL3: Poyle 6A 174
The Slade SE18 . . . . .6J 107
Sladebrook Rd. SE3 . . . . .3B 124
Slade Ct. EN5: New Bar 3E 20
Sladedale Rd. SE18 . . . . .5J 107
Slade Ho. TW4: Houn 6D 112
Sladen Pl. E5 . . . . .4H 67
Slades Cl. EN2: Enf 3F 23
Slades Dr. BR7: Chst 3G 143
Slades Gdns. EN2: Enf 2F 23
Slades Hill EN2: Enf 3F 23
Slades Ri. EN2: Enf 3F 23
Slade Twr. E10 . . . . .2C 68
(off Leyton Grange Est.)
Slade Wlk. SE17 . . . . .6B 102
Slade Way CR4: Mitc 1E 154
Slagrove Pl. SE13 . . . . .5C 122
Slaidburn St. SW10 . . . . .6A 100
Slaithwaite Rd. SE13 . . . . .4E 122
Slaney Ct. NW10 . . . . .7E 62
Slaney Pl. N7 . . . . .5A 66
Slate Ho. E14 . . . . .6B 86
(off Keymer Pl.)
Slater Cl. SE18 . . . . .5E 106
Slater M. SW4 . . . . .3G 119
(off Grafton Sq.)
Slatter NW9 . . . . .7G 29
Slattery Rd. TW13: Felt 1B 130
Sleaford Ho. E3 . . . . .4C 86
(off Fern St.)
Sleaford Ind. Est. SW8 . . . . .7G 101
Sleaford St. SW8 . . . . .7G 101
Sleat Ho. E3 . . . . .2B 86
(off Saxon Rd.)
Sledmere Ct. TW14: Bedf 1G 129
Sleigh Ho. E2 . . . . .3J 85
(off Bacton St.)
The Slide 7D 68
Slievemore Cl. SW4 . . . . .3H 119
Sligo Ho. E1 . . . . .4K 85
(off Beaumont Gro.)
Slindon Ct. N16 . . . . .3F 67
Slingsby Pl. WC2 . . . . .2E 12 (7J 83)
Slippers Pl. SE16 . . . . .3H 103
Slipway Ho. E14 . . . . .5D 104
(off Burrells Wharf Sq.)
Sloane Av. SW3 . . . . .4D 16 (4C 100)
Sloane Av. Mans.
SW3 . . . . .4E 16 (4D 100)
Sloane Ct. TW7: Isle 1J 113
Sloane Ct. E. SW3 . . . . . .5G 17 (5E 100)
Sloane Ct. W. SW3 . . . . . .5G 17 (5E 100)
Sloane Gdns. BR6: Farnb 3G 173
SW1 . . . . .4G 17 (4E 100)
Sloane Ga. Mans. SW1 . . . . .3G 17
(off D'Oyley St.)
Sloane Ho. E9 . . . . .7J 67
(off Loddiges Rd.)
Sloane M. N8 . . . . .5J 47
Sloane Sq. SW1 . . . . . . .4G 17 (4E 100)
Sloane St. SW1 . . . . .7F 11 (2D 100)
Sloane Ter. SW1 . . . . . . .3G 17 (4E 100)
Sloane Ter. Mans. SW1 . . . . .3G 17
(off Sloane Ter.)
Sloane Wlk. CR0: C'don 6B 158
Slocum Cl. SE28 . . . . .7C 90
Slough La. NW9 . . . . .5J 43
Sly St. E1 . . . . .6H 85
Smaldon Cl. UB7: W Dray 3C 92
Smallberry Av. TW7: Isle 2K 113
Smallbrook M. W2 . . . . . . .1A 10 (6B 82)
Smalley Cl. N16 . . . . .3F 67
Smalley Rd. Est. N16 . . . . .3F 67
(off Smalley Cl.)
Smallwood Rd. SW17 . . . . .4B 136
Smarden Cl. DA17: Belv 5G 109
Smarden Gro. SE9 . . . . .4D 142
Smart's Pl. N18 . . . . .5B 34
WC2 . . . . .7F 7 (6J 83)
Smart St. E2 . . . . .3K 85
Smead Way SE13 . . . . .3D 122
Smeaton Cl. KT9: Chess 6D 162
Smeaton Ct. SE1 . . . . .3C 102
Smeaton Rd. IG8: Wfd G 5J 37
SW18 . . . . .7J 117
Smeaton St. E1 . . . . .1H 103
Smedley St. SW4 . . . . .2H 119
SW8 . . . . .2H 119
Smeed Rd. E3 . . . . .7C 68
Smikle Ct. SE14 . . . . .1K 121
(off Hatcham Pk. M.)
Smiles Pl. SE13 . . . . .2E 122
Smith Cl. SE16 . . . . .1K 103
Smithfield Ct. E1 . . . . .7G 85
(off Cable St.)
Smithfield Market 6A 8
Smithfield Sq. N8 . . . . .4J 47
Smithfield St. EC1 . . . . . . .6A 8 (5B 84)
Smith Hill TW8: Bford 6E 96
Smithies Rd. SE2 . . . . .4B 108
Smith's Ct. W1 . . . . .2B 12
Smithson Rd. N17 . . . . .1D 48
Smiths Point E13 . . . . .1J 87
(off Brooks Rd.)
Smith Sq. SW1 . . . . .2E 18 (3J 101)
Smiths Sq. W6 . . . . .5F 99
Smith St. KT5: Surb 6F 151
SW3 . . . . .5E 16 (5D 100)
Smiths Yd. CR0: C'don 3C 168
(off St George's Wlk.)
SW18 . . . . .2A 136
Smith Ter. SW3 . . . . .6E 16 (5D 100)
Smithwood Cl. SW19 . . . . .1G 135
Smithy La. TW3: Houn 3F 113
Smithy St. E1 . . . . .5J 85
Smock Wlk. CR0: C'don 6C 156
Smokehouse Yd. EC1 . . . . .5B 8
(off St John St.)
Smoothfield Ct. TW3: Houn 4E 112
Smugglers Way SW18 . . . . .4K 117
Smugglers Yd. W12 . . . . .1D 98
(off Devonport Rd.)
Smyrk's Rd. SE17 . . . . .5E 102
Smyrna Mans. NW6 . . . . .7J 63
(off Smyrna Rd.)
Smyrna Rd. NW6 . . . . .7J 63
Smythe Cl. N9 . . . . .3B 34
Smythe St. E14 . . . . .7D 86
Snag La. BR6: Prat B 7J 173
Snakes La. N14 . . . . .3A 22
Snakes La. E.
IG8: Buck H, Wfd G 6F 37
Snakes La. W. IG8: Wfd G 5D 36
Snakey La. TW13: Felt 4J 129
SNARESBROOK 5J 51
Snaresbrook Dr. HA7: Stan 4J 27
Snaresbrook Hall E18 . . . . .4J 51
Snaresbrook Ho. E18 . . . . .4H 51
Snaresbrook Rd. E11 . . . . .4G 51
Snarsgate St. W10 . . . . .5E 80
Sneath Av. NW11 . . . . .7H 45
Snells Pk. N18 . . . . .6A 34
Sneyd Rd. NW2 . . . . .4E 62
Snowberry Cl. E15 . . . . .4F 69
EN5: Barn 3C 20
Snowbury Rd. SW6 . . . . .2K 117
Snowden Av. UB10: Hil 2D 74
Snowden St. EC2 . . . . .4G 9 (4E 84)
Snowdon Aviary 1D 82
(in London Zoo)
Snowdon Cres. UB3: Harl 3E 92
Snowdon Dr. NW9 . . . . .6A 44
Snowdon Rd. TW6: H'row A 6E 110
Snowdown Cl. SE20 . . . . .1K 157
Snowdrop Cl. TW12: Hamp 6E 130
Snowdrop Ct. RM13: Rain 2J 91
Snowdrop M. HA5: Pinn 2A 40
Snow Hill EC1 . . . . .6A 8 (5B 84)
Snow Hill Ct. EC1 . . . . . . .7B 8 (6B 84)
Snowman Ho. NW6 . . . . .1K 81
Snowsfields SE1 . . . . . . .6F 15 (2D 102)
Snowshill Rd. E12 . . . . .5C 70
Snowy Fielder Waye
TW7: Isle 2B 114
Soames Pl. EN4: Had W 2E 20
Soames St. SE15 . . . . .3F 121
Soames Wlk. KT3: N Mald 1A 152
Soane Cl. W5 . . . . .2D 96
Soane Ct. NW1 . . . . .7G 65
(off St Pancras Way)
Soane Ho. SE17 . . . . .5D 102
(off Roland Way)
Soane Sq. HA7: Stan 3D 26
Soap Ho. La. TW8: Bford 7E 96
Sobell Leisure Cen. 3K 65
Sobraon Ho. KT2: King T 7F 133
(off Elm Rd.)
Socket La. BR2: Hayes 6K 159
Soda Studios E8 . . . . .1F 85
(off Kingsland Rd.)
SOHO 1C 12 (6G 83)
Soho Ho. W12 . . . . .7E 80
Soho Sq. W1 . . . . .7C 6 (6H 83)
Soho St. W1 . . . . .7C 6 (6H 83)
Soho Theatre 1C 12
(off Dean St.)
Sojourner Truth Cl. E8 . . . . .6H 67
Sola Ct. CR0: C'don 1D 168
(off Sydenham Rd.)
Solander Gdns. E1 . . . . .7H 85
(off Cable St.)
E1 . . . . .7J 85
(The Highway)
Solar Ct. N3 . . . . .7E 30
SE16 . . . . .2G 103
(off Chambers St.)
Solar Ho. E6 . . . . .5E 88
E15 .6G 69
(off Romford Rd.)
Solarium Ct. SE1 . . . . .4F 103
(off Alscot Rd.)
Soldene Ct. N7 . . . . .6K 65
Solebay St. E1 . . . . .4A 86
Solent Ct. SW16 . . . . .2K 155
Solent Ho. E1 . . . . .5A 86
(off Ben Jonson Rd.)
Solent Ri. E13 . . . . .3J 87
Solent Rd. NW6 . . . . .5J 63
Soley M. WC1 . . . . .1J 7 (3A 84)
Solna Av. SW15 . . . . .5E 116
Solna Rd. N21 . . . . .1J 33
Solomon Av. N9 . . . . .4B 34
Solomons Ct. N12 . . . . .7F 31
Solomon's Pas. SE15 . . . . .4H 121
Solomon Way E1 . . . . .5A 86
Solon New Rd. SW4 . . . . .4J 119
Solon New Rd. Est. SW4 . . . . .4J 119
Solon Rd. SW2 . . . . .4J 119
Solway Cl. E8 . . . . .6F 67
(off Queensbridge Rd.)
TW4: Houn 3C 112
Solway Ho. E1 . . . . .4K 85
(off Ernest St.)
Solway Rd. N22 . . . . .1B 48
SE22 . . . . .4G 121
Somaford Gro. EN4: E Barn 6G 21
Somali Rd. NW2 . . . . .5H 63
Sombourne Ho. SW15 . . . . .7C 116
(off Fontley Way)
Somerby Rd. IG11: Bark 7H 71
Somercoates Cl. EN4: Cockf 3H 21
Somer Ct. SW6 . . . . .6J 99
(off Anselm Rd.)
Somerfield Rd. N4 . . . . .2B 66
(not continuous)
Somerfield St. SE16 . . . . .5K 103
Somerford Cl. HA5: Eastc 4J 39
Somerford Gro. N16 . . . . .4F 67
N17 .7B 34
(not continuous)
Somerford Gro. Est. N16 . . . . .4F 67
Somerford St. E1 . . . . .4H 85
Somerford Way SE16 . . . . .2A 104
Somerhill Av. DA15: Sidc 7B 126
Somerhill Rd. DA16: Well 2B 126
Somerleyton Pas. SW9 . . . . .4B 120
Somerleyton Rd. SW9 . . . . .4A 120
Somersby Gdns. IG4: Ilf 5D 52
Somers Cl. NW1 . . . . .2H 83
Somers Cres. W2 . . . . .1C 10 (6C 82)
Somerset Av. DA16: Well 5K 125
KT9: Chess 4D 162
SW20 . . . . .2D 152
Somerset Cl. IG8: Wfd G 1J 51
KT3: N Mald 6A 152
N17 .2D 48
SM3: Wor Pk 4E 164
Somerset Ct. IG9: Buck H 2F 37
NW1 . . . . .1C 6 (2H 83)
TW11: Tedd 5J 131
W7 .6K 77
(off Copley Cl.)
Somerset Est. SW11 . . . . .1B 118
Somerset Gdns. HA0: Wemb 5C 60
N6 . . . . .7E 46
N17 .7K 33
SE13 . . . . .2D 122
SW16 . . . . .3K 155
TW11: Tedd 5J 131
Somerset Hall N17 . . . . .7K 33
Somerset House 2G 13 (7K 83)
Somerset Ho. SW19 . . . . .3F 135
Somerset Lodge TW8: Bford 6D 96
Somerset Rd. E17 . . . . .5C 50
EN5: New Bar 5E 20
HA1: Harr 5G 41
KT1: King T 2F 151
N17 .4F 49
N18 .5A 34
NW4 .4E 44
SW19 . . . . .3F 135
TW8: Bford 6C 96
TW11: Tedd 5J 131
UB1: S'hall 5D 76
W4 . . . . .3K 97
W13 .1B 96
Somerset Sq. W14 . . . . .2G 99
Somerset Waye TW5: Hest 6C 94
Somersham Rd. DA7: Bex 2E 126
Somers Pl. SW2 . . . . .7K 119
Somers Rd. E17 . . . . .4B 50
SW2 .6K 119
Somerston Ho. NW1 . . . . .1G 83
(off St Pancras Way)
SOMERS TOWN 1C 6 (2H 83)
Somers Town Community Sports Cen.
. . . . .2H 83
Somerton Av. TW9: Rich 3H 115
Somerton Ho. WC1 . . . . .2D 6
Somerton Rd. NW2 . . . . .3F 63
SE15 . . . . .4H 121
Somertrees Av. SE12 . . . . .2K 141
Somervell Rd. HA2: Harr 5D 58
Somerville Av. SW13 . . . . .6D 98
Somerville Cl. SW9 . . . . .1K 119
Somerville Point SE16 . . . . .2B 104
Somerville Rd. RM6: Chad H 6C 54
SE20 . . . . .7K 139
Sonderburg Rd. N7 . . . . .2K 65
Sondes St. SE17 . . . . .6D 102
Sonesta Apts. SE15 . . . . .1H 121
Songhurst Cl. CR0: C'don 6K 155
Sonia Ct. HA1: Harr 6K 41
HA8: Edg 7A 28
Sonia Gdns. N12 . . . . .4F 31
NW10 . . . . .4B 62
TW5: Hest 7E 94
Sonning Gdns. TW12: Hamp 6C 130
Sonning Ho. E2 . . . . .2J 9
(off Swanfield St.)
Sonning Rd. SE25 . . . . .6G 157
Soper Cl. E4 . . . . .5G 35
SE23 . . . . .1K 139
Soper M. EN3: Enf L 1H 25
Sophia Cl. N7 . . . . .6K 65
Sophia Ho. W6 . . . . .5E 98
(off Queen Caroline St.)
Sophia Rd. E10 . . . . .1D 68
E16 .6K 87
Sophia Sq. SE16 . . . . .7A 86
(off Sovereign Cres.)
Sophora Ho. SW11 . . . . .7F 101
Soprano Ct. E15 . . . . .1H 87
(off Plaistow Rd.)
Soprano Way KT10: Surb 3B 162
Sopwith NW9 . . . . .7G 29
Sopwith Av. E17 . . . . .4K 49
KT9: Chess 5E 162
Sopwith Cl. KT2: King T 5F 133
Sopwith Rd. TW5: Hest 7A 94
Sopwith Way KT2: King T 1E 150
SW11 . . . . .7J 17 (7F 101)
Sorbus Ct. EN2: Enf 2G 23
Sorensen Ct. E10 . . . . .2D 68
(off Leyton Grange Est.)
Sorrel Cl. SE28 . . . . .1A 108
Sorrel Gdns. E6 . . . . .5C 88
Sorrel La. E14 . . . . .6F 87
Sorrell Cl. SE14 . . . . .7A 104
SW9 .2A 120
Sorrel Mead NW9 . . . . .7C 44
Sorrento Rd. SM1: Sutt 3K 165
Sotheby Rd. N5 . . . . .3B 66
Sotheran Cl. E8 . . . . .1G 85
Sotherby Lodge E2 . . . . .2J 85
(off Sewardstone Rd.)
Sotheron Pl. SW6 . . . . .7K 99
Soudan Rd. SW11 . . . . .1D 118
Souldern Rd. W14 . . . . .3F 99
Soul St. SE6 . . . . .1E 140
Sounding All. E3 . . . . .1C 86
Sth. Access Rd. E17 . . . . .7A 50
Southacre W2 . . . . .1C 10
(off Hyde Pk. Cres.)
Southacre Way HA5: Pinn 1A 40
SOUTH ACTON 2J 97
Sth. Africa Rd. W12 . . . . .1D 98
SOUTHALL 1D 94
Southall Ct. UB1: S'hall 7D 76
Southall Ent. Cen. UB2: S'hall 2E 94
SOUTHALL GREEN 3C 94
Southall La. TW5: Cran 6K 93
UB2: S'hall 6K 93
Southall Pl. SE1 . . . . . . .7E 14 (2D 102)
Southall Sports Cen. 1C 94
Southall Waterside UB1: S'hall 1E 94
Southam Ho. W10 . . . . .4G 81
(off Southam St.)
Southampton Bldgs.
WC2 . . . . .6J 7 (5A 84)
Southampton Gdns. CR4: Mitc 5J 155
Southampton M. E16 . . . . .1K 105
Southampton Pl. WC1 . . . . .6F 7 (5J 83)
Southampton Rd. NW5 . . . . .5D 64
Southampton Rd. E.
TW6: H'row A 6B 110
Southampton Rd. W.
TW6: H'row A 6A 110
Southampton Row WC1 . . . . .5F 7 (5J 83)
Southampton St. WC2 . . . . .2F 13 (7J 83)
Southampton Way SE5 . . . . .7D 102
SE15 . . . . .7E 102
Southam St. W10 . . . . .4G 81
Sth. Audley St. W1 . . . . . .3H 11 (7E 82)
South Av. E4 . . . . .7J 25
SM5: Cars 7E 166
TW9: Kew 2G 115
UB1: S'hall 7D 76
Sth. Av. Gdns. UB1: S'hall 7D 76
Sth. Bank KT6: Surb 6E 150
SE1 . . . . .4G 13 (1K 101)
Southbank KT7: T Ditt 7B 150
Southbank Bus. Cen. SW11 . . . . . . .1D 118
Southbank Cen. 4H 13 (1K 101)
Sth. Bank Ter. KT6: Surb 6E 150
SOUTH BARNET 1K 31
SOUTH BEDDINGTON 6H 167
Sth. Birkbeck Rd. E11 . . . . .3F 69
Sth. Black Lion La. W6 . . . . .5C 98
Sth. Block SE1 . . . . .7G 13
(off Belvedere Rd.)
Sth. Bolton Gdns. SW5 . . . . .5K 99
SOUTHBOROUGH
BR2 .5D 160
KT6 .1E 162
Southborough Cl. KT6: Surb 1D 162
Southborough Ho. SE17 . . . . .5E 102
(off Kinglake Est.)
Southborough La. BR2: Broml 5C 160
Southborough Rd. BR1: Broml 3C 160
E9 . . . . .1K 85
KT6: Surb 1E 162
Southbourne BR2: Hayes 7J 159
Southbourne Av. NW9 . . . . .2J 43
Southbourne Cl. HA5: Pinn 7C 40
Southbourne Ct. NW9 . . . . .2J 43
Southbourne Cres. NW4 . . . . .4G 45
Southbourne Gdns. HA4: Ruis 1K 57
IG1: Ilf 5G 71
SE12 . . . . .5K 123
Southbridge Pl. CR0: C'don 4C 168
Southbridge Rd. CR0: C'don 4C 168
Southbridge Way UB2: S'hall 2C 94
SOUTH BROMLEY 7F 86
Southbrook M. SE12 . . . . .6H 123
Southbrook Rd. SE12 . . . . .6H 123
SW16 . . . . .1J 155
Southbury NW8 . . . . .1A 82
(off Loudoun Rd.)
Southbury Av. EN1: Enf 4B 24
Southbury Leisure Cen. 3B 24
Southbury Rd. EN1: Enf 3K 23
EN3: Pond E 3K 23
Sth. Carriage Dr. SW7 . . . .7B 10 (2B 100)
SOUTH CHINGFORD 5G 35
Southchurch Ct. E6 . . . . .2D 88
(off High St. Sth.)
Southchurch Rd. E6 . . . . .2D 88
South City Ct. SE15 . . . . .7E 102
South Cl. DA6: Bex 4D 126
EN5: Barn 3C 20
HA5: Pinn 7D 40
N6 . . . . .6F 47
RM10: Dag 1G 91
SM4: Mord 6J 153
TW2: Twick 3E 130
UB7: W Dray 3B 92
The Sth. Colonnade E14 . . . . .1C 104
(not continuous)
Southcombe St. W14 . . . . .4G 99
South Comn. Rd. UB8: Uxb 6A 56
Southcote Av. KT5: Surb 7H 151
TW13: Felt 2H 129
Southcote Ri. HA4: Ruis 7F 39
Southcote Rd. E17 . . . . .5K 49
N19 .4G 65
SE25 . . . . .5H 157
Southcott Ho. E3 . . . . .3D 86
(off Devons Rd.)
W9 . . . . .4A 82
(off Clifton Gdns.)
Southcott M. NW8 . . . . .2C 82
Southcott Rd. TW11: Hamp W 1C 150
Sth. Countess Rd. E17 . . . . .3B 50
South Cres. E16 . . . . .4F 87
WC1 . . . . .6C 6 (5H 83)
Sth. Crescent M. WC1 . . . . .4J 83
Southcroft Av. BR4: W W'ck 2E 170
DA16: Well 3J 125
Southcroft Rd. BR6: Orp 3J 173
SW16 . . . . .6E 136
SW17 . . . . .6E 136
Sth. Cross Rd. IG6: Ilf 5G 53
Sth. Croxted Rd. SE21 . . . . .3D 138
SOUTH CROYDON 5D 168
South Croydon Sports Club 5E 168
Southdean Gdns. SW19 . . . . .2H 135
South Dene NW7 . . . . .3E 28
Southdene Ct. N11 . . . . .3A 32
Southdown Av. W7 . . . . .3A 96
Southdown Cres. HA2: Harr 1G 59
IG2: Ilf 5J 53
Southdown Dr. SW20 . . . . .7F 135
Southdown Rd. SM5: Cars 7E 166
SW20 . . . . .1F 153
South Dr. BR6: Orp 5J 173
HA4: Ruis 1G 57
Sth. Ealing Rd. W5 . . . . .2D 96
Sth. Eastern Av. N9 . . . . .3A 34
Sth. Eaton Pl. SW1 . . . . . .3H 17 (4E 100)
Sth. Eden Pk. Rd. BR3: Beck 6D 158
Sth. Edwardes Sq. W8 . . . . .3H 99
SOUTHEND 4F 141
Sth. End CR0: C'don 4C 168
CR2: S Croy 4C 168
W8 . . . . .3K 99
Sth. End Cl. NW3 . . . . .4C 64
Southend Cl. SE9 . . . . .6F 125
Southend Cres. SE9 . . . . .6F 125
Sth. End Grn. NW3 . . . . .4C 64
Southend La. SE6 . . . . .4B 140
SE26 . . . . .4B 140
Sth. End Rd. NW3 . . . . .4C 64
Southend Rd. BR3: Beck 1C 158
E4 . . . . .5F 35
E6 . . . . .7D 70
E17 .1D 50
E18 .1J 51
IG8: Wfd G 2A 52
Sth. End Row W8 . . . . .3K 99
Southern Av. SE25 . . . . .3F 157
TW14: Felt 1J 129
Southern Cotts.
TW19: Stanw M 7B 174
Southerngate Way SE14 . . . . .7A 104
Southern Gro. E3 . . . . .3B 86
Southern Perimeter Rd.
TW6: H'row A, Stanw
. . . . .5A 110, 7C 174
(not continuous)
Southern Pl. HA1: Harr 4K 59
Southern Rd. E13 . . . . .2K 87
N2 . . . . .4D 46
Southern Row W10 . . . . .4G 81
Southern St. N1 . . . . .2K 83
Southern Ter. W12 . . . . .1E 98
Southern Way RM7: Rom 6G 55
SE10 . . . . .4H 105
Southernwood Retail Pk. 5F 103
Southerton Rd. W6 . . . . .4E 98
Sth. Esk Rd. E7 . . . . .6A 70
Southey Ho. SE17 . . . . .5C 102
(off Browning St.)
Southey M. E16 . . . . .1J 105
Southey Rd. N15 . . . . .5E 48
SW9 .1A 120
SW19 . . . . .7J 135
Southey St. SE20 . . . . .7K 139
Southfield EN5: Barn 6A 20
Southfield Cl. UB8: Hil 4C 74
Southfield Cotts. W7 . . . . .2K 95
Southfield Ct. E11 . . . . .3H 69
Southfield Gdns. TW1: Twick 4K 131
Southfield Pk. HA2: Harr 4F 41
Southfield Rd. BR7: Chst 3K 161
EN3: Pond E 6C 24
N17 .2E 48
W4 . . . . .2K 97
SOUTHFIELDS 1H 135
Southfields KT8: E Mos 6J 149
NW4 .3D 44
Southfields Av. TW15: Ashf 6D 128
Southfields Ct. SM1: Sutt 2J 165
Southfields M. SW18 . . . . .6J 117
Southfields Pas. SW18 . . . . .6J 117
Southfields Rd. SW18 . . . . .6J 117
Southfleet NW5 . . . . .6E 64
Southfleet Rd. BR6: Orp 3J 173
South Gdns. HA9: Wemb 2G 61
SE17 . . . . .4C 102
SW19 . . . . .7B 136
SOUTHGATE 1C 32
Southgate Av. TW13: Felt 4F 129
SOUTHGATE CIR. 1C 32
Southgate Ct. N1 . . . . .7D 66
(off Downham Rd.)
Southgate Gro. N1 . . . . .7D 66
Southgate Hockey Cen. 3A 22
Southgate Leisure Cen. 7C 22
Southgate Rd. N1 . . . . .1D 84
Sth. Gipsy Rd. DA16: Well 3D 126
The Sth. Glade DA5: Bexl 1F 145
South Grn. NW9 . . . . .1A 44
(off Parklea Cl.)
South Gro. E17 . . . . .5B 50
N6 . . . . .1E 64
N15 .5D 48
South Gro. Ho. N6 . . . . .1E 64
SOUTH HACKNEY 1K 85
SOUTH HAMPSTEAD 7A 64
SOUTH HARROW 3G 59
Sth. Harrow Ind. Est. HA2: Harr 2G 59
South Herts Golf Course 1D 30
Sth. Hill BR7: Chst 6D 142
HA6: Nwood 1G 39
Sth. Hill Av. HA1: Harr 3G 59
HA2: Harr 3G 59
Sth. Hill Gro. HA1: Harr 4J 59
Sth. Hill Pk. NW3 . . . . .4C 64
Sth. Hill Pk. Gdns. NW3 . . . . .3C 64
Sth. Hill Rd. BR2: Broml 3G 159
Southholme Cl. SE19 . . . . .1E 156
SOUTH HORNCHURCH 2K 91
Southill Ct. BR2: Broml 5H 159
Southill La. HA5: Eastc 4K 39
Southill Rd. BR7: Chst 7C 142
Southill St. E14 . . . . .6D 86
Sth. Island Pl. SW9 . . . . .7K 101
SOUTH KENSINGTON 4B 100
Sth. Kensington Sta. Arc. SW7 . . . .3B 16
(off Pelham St.)
SOUTH LAMBETH 7J 101
Sth. Lambeth Pl. SW8 . . . .7F 19 (6J 101)
Sth. Lambeth Rd. SW8 . . . .7F 19 (6J 101)
Southland Rd. SE18 . . . . .7K 107
Southlands Av. BR6: Orp 4H 173
Southlands College
Roehampton University 5C 116
Southlands Dr. SW19 . . . . .2F 135
Southlands Gro. BR1: Broml 3C 160
Southlands Rd. BR1: Broml 5A 160
BR2: Broml 5A 160
Southland Way TW3: Houn 5H 113
South La. KT1: King T 3D 150
KT3: N Mald 4K 151
South La. W. KT3: N Mald 4K 151
Sth. Lodge E16 . . . . .1K 105
(off Audley Dr.)
NW8 . . . . .1A 4 (2B 82)
SW7 .7D 10
(off Knightsbridge)
TW2: Whitt 6G 113
Sth. Lodge Av. CR4: Mitc 4J 155
Sth. Lodge Cres. EN2: Enf 4C 22
(not continuous)
Sth. Lodge Dr. N14 . . . . .4C 22
Sth. London Crematorium 2G 155
South London Gallery 1E 120
South London Theatre 3B 138
(off Norwood High St.)

286 A-Z Big London

Sth. Mall—Spring Pl.

Sth. Mall N9 3B 34
(off Plevna Rd.)
SW18 6K 117
South Mead KT19: Ewe 7B 164
NW9 1B 44
Southmead Gdns. TW11: Tedd 6A 132
Southmead Rd. SW19 1G 135
Southmere Boating Cen. 2C 108
Southmere Dr. SE2 2D 108
Southmere House E15 2D 86
(off Highland Street)
Sth. Mill Apts. E2 1F 85
(off Hebden St.)
Sth. Molton La. W1 1J 11 (6F 83)
Sth. Molton Rd. E16 6J 87
Sth. Molton St. W1 1J 11 (6F 83)
Southmoor Way E9 6B 68
South Mt. N20 2F 31
(off High Rd.)
SOUTH NORWOOD 4F 157
South Norwood Country Pk. 4J 157
South Norwood Country Pk. Vis. Cen. 4H 157
Sth. Norwood Hill SE25 1E 156
South Norwood Leisure Cen. 5H 157
Sth. Oak Rd. SW16 4K 137
Southold Ri. SE9 3D 142
Southolm St. SW11 1F 119
Southover BR1: Broml 5J 141
N12 3D 30
South Pde. HA8: Edg 2G 43
SM6: W'gton 6G 167
SW3 5B 16 (5B 100)
W4 4K 97
South Pk. Ct. BR3: Beck 7C 140
South Pk. Cres. IG1: Ilf 3H 71
SE6 1G 141
South Pk. Dr. IG3: Ilf 2J 71
IG11: Bark 5J 71
South Pk. Gro. KT3: N Mald 4J 151
South Pk. Hill Rd. CR2: S Croy 5D 168
South Pk. M. SW6 3K 117
South Pk. Rd. IG1: Ilf 3H 71
SW19 6J 135
South Pk. Ter. IG1: Ilf 3J 71
South Pk. Vs. IG3: Ilf 4J 71
Sth. Pk. Way HA4: Ruis 6A 58
South Pl. EC2 5F 9 (5D 84)
EN3: Pond E 5D 24
KT5: Surb 7F 151
South Pl. M. EC2 6F 9 (5D 84)
Southport Rd. SE18 4H 107
Sth. Quay Plaza E14 2D 104
Sth. Quay Sq. E14 2D 104
Southridge Pl. SW20 7F 135
South Ri. SM5: Cars 7C 166
W2 2D 10
Sth. Ri. Way SE18 5H 107
South Rd. HA1: Harr 1A 60
HA8: Edg 1H 43
N9 1B 34
RM6: Chad H 5C 54
(Dunmow Cl.)
RM6: Chad H 6E 54
(Mill La.)
SE23 2K 139
SW19 6A 136
TW2: Twick 3H 131
TW5: Hest 6B 94
TW12: Hamp 6C 130
TW13: Hanw 5B 130
UB1: S'hall 2D 94
UB7: W Dray 3C 92
W5 4D 96
Sth. Row SE3 2H 123
SOUTH RUISLIP 4A 58
Southsea Rd. KT1: King T 4E 150
South Sea St. SE16 3B 104
Sth. Side N15 4F 49
W6 3B 98
Southside N7 4H 65
Southside Cl. UB10: Uxb 7A 56
Southside Comn. SW19 6E 134
Southside Halls SW7 1B 16
(off Prince's Gdns.)
Southside House 6E 134
Southside Ind. Est. SW8 1G 119
(off Havelock Ter.)
Southside Shop. Cen. 6K 117
Southspring DA15: Sidc 7H 125
South Sq. NW11 6K 45
WC1 6J 7 (5A 84)
Sth. Stand N5 4B 66
South St. BR1: Broml 2J 159
EN3: Pond E 5D 24
RM1: Rom 5K 55
RM13: Rain 2J 91
TW7: Isle 3A 114
W1 4H 11 (1E 100)
South St. Studios BR1: Broml 2J 159
(off South St.)
Sth. Tenter St. E1 2K 15 (7F 85)
South Ter. KT6: Surb 6E 150
SW7 3C 16 (4C 100)
SOUTH TOTTENHAM 5F 49
South Va. HA1: Harr 4J 59
SE19 6E 138
Southvale Rd. SE3 2G 123
South Vw. BR1: Broml 2A 160
SW19 6F 135
Southview Av. NW10 5B 62
South Vw. Cl. DA5: Bexl 6F 127
Southview Cl. SW17 5E 136
Southview Ct. SE19 7C 138
Southview Cres. IG2: Ilf 6F 53
South Vw. Dr. E18 3K 51
Southview Gdns. SM6: W'gton 7G 167
Southview Pde. RM13: Rain 3K 91
South Vw. Rd. HA5: Pinn 1K 39
N8 3H 47
Southview Rd. BR1: Broml 4F 141
South Vs. NW1 6H 65
Southville SW8 1H 119
Southville Cl. KT19: Ewe 7K 163
TW14: Bedf, Felt 1G 129
(not continuous)
Southville Cres. TW14: Felt 1G 129
Southville Rd. KT7: T Ditt 7A 150
TW14: Felt 1G 129
South Wlk. BR4: W W'ck 3G 171
UB3: Hayes 5F 75
SOUTHWARK 5A 14 (1B 102)
Southwark Bri. SE1 3D 14 (7C 84)
Southwark Bri. Bus. Cen.
SE1 5D 14
(off Southwark Bri. Rd.)
Southwark Bri. Rd.
SE1 7B 14 (3B 102)
Southwark Cathedral 4E 14 (1D 102)
Southwark Pk. 3H 103
Southwark Pk. Est. SE16 4H 103
(off Southwark Pk. Rd.)
Southwark Pk. Rd. SE16 4F 103
Southwark Pk. Sports Cen. Track 4J 103
Southwark Pk. Sports Complex 4J 103
Southwark Pl. BR1: Broml 3D 160
Southwark Playhouse 3C 102
(off Newington C'way)
Southwark St George's RC Cathedral 1K 19 (3A 102)
Southwark St. SE1 4A 14 (1B 102)
Southwater Cl. BR3: Beck 7D 140
E14 6B 86
Sth. Way CR0: C'don 3A 170
HA2: Harr 4E 40
HA9: Wemb 5G 61
N9 2D 34
N11 6B 32
Southway BR2: Hayes 7J 159
N20 2D 30
NW11 6K 45
SM6: W'gton 4G 167
SW20 5E 152
Southway Cl. W12 2D 98
Southwell Av. UB5: N'olt 6E 58
Southwell Gdns. SW7 4A 100
Southwell Gro. Rd. E11 2G 69
Southwell Ho. SE16 4H 103
(off Anchor St.)
Southwell Rd. CR0: C'don 6A 156
HA3: Kenton 6D 42
SE5 3C 120
Sth. Western Rd. TW1: Twick 6A 114
Sth. W. India Dock Entrance
E14 2E 104
Sth. W. Middlesex Crematorium 1C 130
Southwest Rd. E11 1F 69
Sth. Wharf Rd. W2 7A 4 (6B 82)
Southwick M. W2 7B 4 (6B 82)
Southwick Pl. W2 1C 10 (6C 82)
Southwick St. W2 7C 4 (6C 82)
Southwick Yd. W2 1C 10
SOUTH WIMBLEDON 6K 135
Southwold Dr. IG11: Bark 5A 72
Southwold Mans. W9 3J 81
(off Widley Rd.)
Southwold Rd. DA5: Bexl 6H 127
E5 2H 67
Southwood Av. KT2: King T 1J 151
N6 7F 47
Southwood Cl. BR1: Broml 4D 160
KT4: Wor Pk 1F 165
Southwood Ct. EC1 2A 8
(off Wynyatt St.)
NW11 5K 45
Southwood Dr. KT5: Surb 7J 151
SOUTH WOODFORD 2J 51
Sth. Woodford to Barking Relief Rd.
E11 5B 52
Southwood Gdns. IG2: Ilf 4F 53
KT10: Hin W 3A 162
Southwood Hall N6 6F 47
Southwood Hgts. N6 7F 47
Southwood Ho. W11 7G 81
(off Avondale Pk. Rd.)
Southwood La. N6 7E 46
Southwood Lawn Rd. N6 7E 46
Southwood Mans. N6 6E 46
(off Southwood La.)
Southwood Pk. N6 7E 46
Southwood Rd. SE9 2F 143
SE28 1B 108
Southwood Smith Ho. E2 3H 85
(off Florida St.)
Southwood Smith St. N1 1B 84
Sth. Worple Av. SW14 3A 116
Sth. Worple Way SW14 3K 115
Southwyck Ho. SW9 4B 120
Soval Ct. HA6: Nwood 1F 39
Sovereign Bus. Cen. EN3: Brim 3G 25
Sovereign Cl. E1 7H 85
HA4: Ruis 1G 57
W5 5C 78
Sovereign Ct. CR2: S Croy 5C 168
(off Warham Rd.)
HA6: Nwood 1J 39
HA7: Stan 7J 27
KT8: W Mole 4D 148
TW3: Houn 3E 112
W8 3K 99
(off Wright's La.)
Sovereign Cres. SE16 7A 86
Sovereign Gro. HA0: Wemb 3C 60
Sovereign Ho. E1 4H 85
(off Cambridge Heath Rd.)
SE18 3D 106
(off Leda Rd.)
TW15: Ashf 4A 128
Sovereign M. E2 2F 85
EN4: Cockf 3J 21
Sovereign Pk. NW10 4H 79
Sovereign Pk. Trad. Est.
NW10 4H 79
Sovereign Pl. HA1: Harr 5K 41
Sovereign Rd. IG11: Bark 3C 90
Sowerby Cl. SE9 5D 124
The Spa at Beckenham 1B 158
Spa Bus. Pk. SE16 3G 103
The Space Arts Cen. 4C 104
(off Westferry Rd.)
Space Bus. Pk. NW10 3H 79
Spaces Bus. Cen. SW8 1G 119
Spaces Waye TW14: Felt 5J 111
Spa Cl. SE25 1E 156
Spa Ct. SE16 3G 103
SW16 4K 137
Spafield St. EC1 3J 7 (4A 84)
Spa Grn. Est. EC1 1K 7 (3B 84)
Spa Hill SE19 1D 156
Spalding Cl. HA8: Edg 7F 29
Spalding Ho. SE4 4A 122
Spalding Rd. NW4 7E 44
SW17 5F 137
Spanby Rd. E3 4C 86
Spaniards Cl. NW11 1B 64
Spaniards End NW3 1A 64
Spaniards Rd. NW3 2A 64
Spanish Pl. W1 7H 5 (6E 82)
Spanish Rd. SW18 5A 118
Spanswick Lodge N15 4B 48
Spare St. SE17 4C 102
Sparkbridge Rd. HA1: Harr 4J 41
Sparkes Cl. BR2: Broml 4K 159
Sparkes Cotts. SW1 4G 17
Sparkford Gdns. N11 5K 31
Sparkford Ho. SW11 1B 118
(off Battersea Church Rd.)
Sparks Cl. RM8: Dag 2D 72
TW12: Hamp 6C 130
W3 6K 79
Spa Rd. SE16 3F 103
Sparrick's Row SE1 6F 15 (2D 102)
Sparrow Cl. TW12: Hamp 6C 130
Sparrow Dr. BR5: Farnb 1G 173
Sparrow Farm Dr. TW14: Felt 7A 112
Sparrow Farm Rd.
KT17: Ewe 4C 164
Sparrow Grn. RM10: Dag 3H 73
Sparrow Ho. E1 4J 85
(off Cephas Av.)
Sparrow's Farm Leisure Cen. 7G 125
Sparrows Herne WD23: Bush 1A 26
Sparrows La. SE9 7G 125
Sparrows Way WD23: Bush 1B 26
Sparsholt Cl. IG11: Bark 1J 89
(off St John's Rd.)
Sparsholt Rd. IG11: Bark 1J 89
N19 1K 65
Spartan Cl. SM6: W'gton 7J 167
Sparta St. SE10 1E 122
Speakers' Corner 2F 11 (7D 82)
Speakers Ct. CR0: C'don 1D 168
Speakman Ho. SE4 3A 122
(off Arica Rd.)
Spearman Ho. E14 6C 86
(off Upper Nth. St.)
Spearman St. SE18 6E 106
Spear M. SW5 4J 99
Spearpoint Gdns. IG2: Ilf 5K 53
Spears Rd. N19 1J 65
Speart La. TW5: Hest 7C 94
Spectacle Works E13 3A 88
The Spectrum Bldg. N1 1F 9
(off East Rd.)
Spectrum Pl. SE17 6D 102
(off Lytham St.)
Spectrum Twr. IG1: Ilf 2G 71
(off Hainault St.)
Spectrum Way SW18 5J 117
Spedan Cl. NW3 3A 64
Speechly M. E8 5F 67
Speedbird Way UB7: Harm 3C 174
Speed Highwalk EC2 5D 8
(off Silk St.)
Speed Ho. EC2 5D 8
Speedway Ind. Est. UB3: Hayes 2F 93
Speedwell Ho. N12 4E 30
Speedwell St. SE8 7C 104
Speedy Pl. WC1 2E 6
Speer Rd. KT7: T Ditt 6K 149
Speirs Cl. KT3: N Mald 6B 152
Speirs Gardens RM8: Dag 1E 72
Spekehill SE9 3D 142
Speke Rd. CR7: Thor H 2D 156
Speke's Monument 4A 10 (1A 100)
Speldhurst Cl. BR2: Broml 5H 159
Speldhurst Rd. E9 7K 67
W4 3K 97
Spellbrook Wlk. N1 1C 84
Spelman Ho. E1 6K 9
(off Spelman St.)
Spelman St. E1 5K 9 (5G 85)
(not continuous)
Spelthorne Gro. TW16: Sun 7H 129
Spelthorne La. TW15: Ashf 1E 148
Spence Cl. SE16 2B 104
Spencer Av. N13 6E 32
UB4: Hayes 5J 75
Spencer Cl. BR6: Orp 2J 173
IG8: Wfd G 5F 37
N3 2J 45
NW10 3F 79
Spencer Ct. BR6: Farnb 5G 173
NW8 2A 82
(off Marlborough Pl.)
SW20 1D 152
Spencer Ctyd. N3 2H 45
(off Regents Pk. Rd.)
Spencer Dr. N2 6A 46
Spencer Gdns. SE9 5E 124
SW14 5J 115
Spencer Hill SW19 6G 135
Spencer Hill Rd. SW19 7G 135
Spencer House 5A 12
Spencer Mans. W14 6G 99
(off Queen's Club Gdns.)
Spencer M. SW8 1K 119
(off Lansdowne Way)
W6 6G 99
SPENCER PARK 5B 118
Spencer Pk. KT8: E Mos 5G 149
SW18 5B 118
Spencer Pl. CR0: C'don 7D 156
N1 7B 66
Spencer Ri. NW5 4F 65
Spencer Rd. BR1: Broml 7H 141
CR2: S Croy 5E 168
CR4: Mitc 3E 154
(Commonside E.)
CR4: Mitc 7E 154
(Wood St.)
E6 1B 88
E17 1E 50
HA0: Wemb 2C 60
HA3: W'stone 2J 41
IG3: Ilf 1K 71
KT8: E Mos 4G 149
N8 5K 47
(not continuous)
N11 4A 32
N17 1G 49
Spencer Rd. RM13: Rain 3K 91
SW18 4B 118
SW20 1D 152
TW2: Twick 3J 131
TW7: Isle 1G 113
W3 1J 97
W4 7J 97
Spencer St. EC1 2A 8 (3B 84)
UB2: S'hall 2B 94
Spencer Wlk. NW3 4B 64
SW15 4F 117
Spencer Way E1 6H 85
Spencer Yd. SE3 2H 123
(off Tranquil Va.)
Spenlow Ho. SE16 3G 103
(off Jamaica Rd.)
Spenser Gro. N16 5E 66
Spenser M. SE21 2D 138
Spenser Rd. SE24 5B 120
Spenser St. SW1 1B 18 (3G 101)
Spens Ho. WC1 4G 7
(off Lamb's Conduit St.)
Spensley Wlk. N16 3D 66
Speranza St. SE18 5K 107
Sperling Rd. N17 2E 48
Spert St. E14 7A 86
Speyside N14 6B 22
Spey St. E14 5E 86
Spey Way RM1: Rom 1K 55
Spezia Rd. NW10 2C 80
The Sphere E16 6H 87
(off Hallsville Rd.)
Sphinx Way EN5: Barn 5C 20
Spice Ct. E1 7G 85
Spice Quay Hgts. SE1 5K 15 (1F 103)
Spicer Cl. KT12: Walt T 6A 148
SW9 2B 120
Spicer Ct. EN1: Enf 3K 23
Spice's Yd. CR0: C'don 4C 168
Spigurnell Rd. N17 1D 48
Spikes Bri. Moorings UB4: Yead 7C 76
Spikes Bri. Rd. UB1: S'hall 6C 76
Spindle Cl. SE18 3C 106
Spindle M. BR6: Farnb 4F 173
Spindlewood Gdns. CR0: C'don 4E 168
Spindrift Av. E14 4C 104
Spinel Cl. SE18 5K 107
Spinnaker Cl. IG11: Bark 3B 90
Spinnaker Ct. KT1: Hamp W 1D 150
(off Becketts Pl.)
Spinnaker Ho. E14 2C 104
(off Byng St.)
E16 2K 105
(off Waypoint Way)
SW18 4A 118
(off Juniper Dr.)
Spinnells Rd. HA2: Harr 1D 58
Spinner Ho. E8 1F 85
(off Lovelace St.)
The Spinney DA14: Sidc 5E 144
EN5: New Bar 2E 20
HA0: Wemb 3A 60
HA7: Stan 4K 27
N21 7F 23
SM3: Cheam 4E 164
SW13 7D 98
SW16 3G 137
TW16: Sun 1J 147
Spinney Cl. BR3: Beck 4D 158
KT3: N Mald 5A 152
KT4: Wor Pk 2B 164
UB7: Yiew 7A 74
Spinney Dr. TW14: Bedf 7E 110
Spinney Gdns. RM9: Dag 5E 72
SE19 5F 139
Spinney Oak BR1: Broml 2C 160
The Spinneys BR1: Broml 2D 160
Spinning Wheel Way
SM6: W'gton 2E 166
Spire Ct. BR3: Beck 2D 158
(off Crescent Rd.)
Spire Ho. W2 7A 82
(off Lancaster Ga.)
The Spires Shop. Cen. 3B 20
Spirit Quay E1 1G 103
SPITALFIELDS 5J 9 (5F 85)
Spitalfields City Farm 4G 85
Spital Sq. E1 5H 9 (5E 84)
Spital St. E1 5K 9 (5G 85)
Spital Yd. E1 5H 9 (5E 84)
Spitfire Bldg. N1 2K 83
(off Collier St.)
Spitfire Bus. Pk. CR0: Wadd 6A 168
The Spitfire Est. TW5: Cran 5A 94
Spitfire Rd. SM6: W'gton 7J 167
TW6: H'row A 6E 110
Spitfire Way TW5: Cran 5A 94
Splendour Wlk. SE16 5J 103
(off Verney Rd.)
Spode Ho. SE11 2J 19
Spode Wlk. NW6 5K 63
Spondon Rd. N15 4G 49
Spoonbill Way UB4: Yead 5B 76
Spooner Ho. TW5: Hest 6E 94
Spooners M. W3 1K 97
Spooner Wlk. SM6: W'gton 5J 167
Sporle Ct. SW11 3B 118
Sports Academy (LSBU) 3B 102
(off London Rd.)
Sportsbank St. SE6 7E 122
Sports Direct Fitness
Croydon 7A 168
Epsom 4K 163
SportsDock 7F 89
Sportsman Pl. E2 1G 85
Spottiswood Ct. CR0: C'don 6C 156
(off Harry Cl.)
Spottons Gro. N17 1C 48
Spout Hill CR0: Addtn 5C 170
Spout La. TW19: Stanw M 7B 174
Spout La. Nth. TW19: Stanw M 7C 174
Spratt Hall Rd. E11 6J 51
Spray La. TW2: Whitt 6J 113
Spray St. SE18 4F 107
Spreighton Rd. KT8: W Mole 4F 149
Spriggs Ho. N1 7B 66
(off Canonbury Rd.)
Sprimont Pl. SW3 5E 16 (5D 100)
Springall St. SE15 7H 103
Springalls Wharf SE16 2G 103
(off Bermondsey Wall W.)
Spring Apts. CR0: C'don 2D 168
(off Addiscombe Gro.)
E14 4E 104
(off Stebondale St.)
Springbank N21 6E 22
Springbank Rd. SE13 6F 123
Springbank Wlk. NW1 7H 65
Springbourne Ct. BR3: Beck 1E 158
Spring Bri. M. W5 7D 78
Spring Bri. Rd. W5 7D 78
Spring Cl. EN5: Barn 5A 20
RM8: Dag 1D 72
Springclose La. SM3: Cheam 6G 165
Spring Cnr. TW13: Felt 3J 129
Spring Cotts. KT6: Surb 5D 150
Spring Ct. KT17: Ewe 7B 164
NW6 6H 63
W7 7H 77
Spring Ct. Rd. EN2: Enf 1F 23
Springcroft Av. N2 4D 46
Springdale M. N16 4D 66
Springdale Rd. N16 4D 66
Spring Dr. HA5: Eastc 6J 39
Springer Ct. E3 4E 86
(off Navigation Rd.)
Springett Ho. SW2 5A 120
(off St Matthews Rd.)
Springfield E5 1H 67
SE25 3G 157
WD23: B Hea 1C 26
Springfield Av. N10 3G 47
SW20 3H 153
TW12: Hamp 6F 131
Springfield Cl. HA7: Stan 3F 27
N12 5E 30
Springfield Ct. IG1: Ilf 5F 71
KT1: King T 3E 150
(off Springfield Rd.)
NW3 7C 64
(off Eton Av.)
SM6: W'gton 5F 167
Springfield Dr. IG2: Ilf 5G 53
Springfield Gdns. BR1: Broml 4D 160
BR4: W W'ck 2D 170
E5 1H 67
HA4: Ruis 1K 57
IG8: Wfd G 7F 37
NW9 5K 43
Springfield Gro. SE7 6A 106
TW16: Sun 1H 147
Springfield La. NW6 1K 81
Springfield Mt. NW9 5A 44
Springfield Pde. M. N13 4F 33
Springfield Pk. 2B 136
Springfield Pl. KT3: N Mald 4J 151
Springfield Ri. SE26 3H 139
Springfield Rd. BR1: Broml 4D 160
CR7: Thor H 1C 156
DA7: Bex 4H 127
DA16: Well 3B 126
E4 1B 36
E6 7D 70
E15 3G 87
E17 6B 50
HA1: Harr 6J 41
KT1: King T 3E 150
N11 5A 32
N15 4G 49
NW8 1A 82
SE26 5H 139
SM6: W'gton 5F 167
SW19 5H 135
TW2: Whitt 1E 130
TW11: Tedd 5A 132
TW15: Ashf 5B 128
UB4: Yead 1A 94
W7 1J 95
Springfields EN5: New Bar 5E 20
(off Somerset Rd.)
Springfield Wlk. BR6: Orp 1H 173
(off Place Farm Av.)
NW6 1K 81
Spring Gdns. IG8: Wfd G 7F 37
KT8: W Mole 5F 149
N5 5C 66
RM7: Rom 5J 55
SM6: W'gton 5G 167
SW1 4D 12 (1H 101)
(not continuous)
Spring Gdns. Bus. Pk.
RM7: Rom 6J 55
SPRING GROVE 1J 113
Spring Gro. CR4: Mitc 1E 154
SE19 7F 139
TW12: Hamp 1F 149
W4 5G 97
W7 7J 77
Spring Gro. Cres. TW3: Houn 1G 113
Spring Gro. Rd.
TW3: Houn, Isle 1F 113
TW7: Isle 1F 113
TW10: Rich 5F 115
SpringHealth Leisure Club
Richmond 4D 114
(within Pools on the Pk.)
Spring Hill E5 7G 49
SE26 4J 139
Springhill Cl. SE5 3D 120
Spring Ho. E17 2E 50
(off Fulbourne Rd.)
WC1 2J 7
Springhurst Cl. CR0: C'don 4B 170
Spring Lake HA7: Stan 4G 27
Spring La. E5 7H 49
N10 3E 46
SE25 6H 157
Spring M. KT17: Ewe 7B 164
SE11 5G 19 (5K 101)
TW9: Rich 4E 114
(off Rosedale Rd.)
W1 5F 5 (5D 82)
SPRING PARK 3C 170
Spring Pk. Av. CR0: C'don 2K 169
Spring Pk. Dr. N4 1C 66
Springpark Dr. BR3: Beck 3E 158
Spring Pk. Rd. CR0: C'don 2K 169
Spring Pas. SW15 3F 117
Spring Path NW3 5B 64
Spring Pl. IG11: Bark 2G 89
N3 3J 45
NW5 5F 65

A-Z Big London 287

Springpond Rd.—Statham Gro.

Springpond Rd. RM9: Dag 5E 72
Spring Prom.
UB7: W Dray 2B 92
Springrice Rd. SE13 . . . . 6F 123
Spring Rd. TW13: Felt 3H 129
Springs Cl. TW19: Stanw 1A 128
Spring Shaw Rd.
BR5: St P 7A 144
Spring St. W2 . . . . 1A 10 (6B 82)
Spring Ter. TW9: Rich 5E 114
Spring Tide Cl. SE15 . . . . 1H 121
Spring Va. DA7: Bex 4H 127
Springvale Av.
TW8: Bford 5D 96
Springvale Ter. W14 . . . . 3F 99
Spring Villa Pk. HA8: Edg 7B 28
Spring Villa Rd.
HA8: Edg 7B 28
Spring Wlk. E1 . . . . 5G 85
Springwater WC1 . . . . 5G 7
Springwater Cl. SE18 . . . . 1E 124
Spring Way SE5 . . . . 1C 120
Springway HA1: Harr 7H 41
Springwell Av. NW10 . . . . 1B 80
Springwell Cl. SW16 . . . . 4K 137
Springwell Rd.
SW16 . . . . 4A 138
TW4: Houn 2B 112
TW5: Hest 2B 112
Springwood Cl. E3 . . . . 2C 86
Springwood Ct. *CR2: S Croy* *4E 168*
(off Birdhurst Rd.)
Springwood Cres. HA8: Edg 2C 28
Sproggit Ind. Est.
TW19: Stanw 6B 110
Sprowston M. E7 . . . . 6J 69
Sprowston Rd. E7 . . . . 5J 69
Spruce Ct. W5 . . . . 3E 96
Sprucedale Gdns.
CR0: C'don 4K 169
Spruce Hills Rd. E17 . . . . 2E 50
Spruce Ho. *SE16* *2K 103*
(off Woodland Cres.)
Spruce Pk. BR2: Broml 4H 159
Sprules Rd. SE4 . . . . 2A 122
Spurfield KT8: W Mole 3F 149
Spurgeon Av. SE19 . . . . 1D 156
Spurgeon Rd. SE19 . . . . 1D 156
Spurgeon St. SE1 . . . . 3D 102
Spurling Rd. RM9: Dag 6F 73
SE22 . . . . 4F 121
Spurrell Av. DA5: Bexl 4K 145
Spur Rd. BR6: Orp 2K 173
HA8: Edg 4K 27
N15 . . . . 4D 48
SE1 . . . . 6J 13 (2A 102)
SW1 . . . . 7A 12 (2G 101)
TW7: Isle 7B 96
TW14: Felt 4K 111
Spurstowe Rd. E8 . . . . 6H 67
Spurstowe Ter. E8 . . . . 5G 67
Spurway Pde. *IG2: Ilf* *5D 52*
(off Woodford Av.)
The Square E10 . . . . 3E 68
IG1: Ilf 7E 52
IG8: Wfd G 5D 36
RM8: Dag 1E 72
SM5: Cars 5E 166
TW9: Rich 5D 114
UB2: S'hall 4A 94
UB7: Lford 4C 174
UB11: Stock P 1F 93
W6 . . . . 5E 98
Square of Fame *4G 61*
(off Arena Sq.)
Square Rigger Row SW11 . . . . 3A 118
Squarey St. SW17 . . . . 3A 136
Squire Gdns. *NW8* *2A 4*
(off Grove End Rd.)
The Squires RM7: Rom 6J 55
Squire's Bri. Rd.
TW17: Shep 4B 146
Squires Ct. SW4 . . . . 1J 119
SW19 . . . . 4J 135
Squires La. N3 . . . . 2K 45
Squires Mt. NW3 . . . . 3B 64
Squire's Rd. TW17: Shep 4C 146
Squires Wlk. TW15: Ashf 7F 129
(not continuous)
Squires Way DA2: Wilm 4K 145
Squires Wood Dr.
BR7: Chst 7C 142
Squirrel Cl. TW4: Houn 3A 112
Squirrel M. W13 . . . . 7K 77
The Squirrels
HA5: Pinn 3D 40
SE13 . . . . 3F 123
Squirrels Cl. BR6: Orp 1J 173
N12 . . . . 4F 31
UB10: Hil 7C 56
Squirrels Ct. *KT4: Wor Pk* *2B 164*
(off The Avenue)
Squirrels Drey *BR2: Broml* *2G 159*
(off Park Hill Rd.)
Squirrels Grn. KT4: Wor Pk 2B 164
Squirrel's La.
IG9: Buck H 3G 37
Squirrels Trad. Est.
UB3: Hayes 3H 93
Squirries St. E2 . . . . 3G 85
The SSE Arena Wembley 4G 61
SS Robin 7K 87
Stable Cl. KT2: King T 6F 133
UB5: N'olt 2E 76
Stable Ct. *EC1* *4B 8*
(off Clerkenwell Rd.)
SM6: W'gton 3E 166
Stable La. DA5: Bexl 2H 145
Stable M.
NW5 . . . . 6F 65
SE6 . . . . 1G 141
TW1: Twick 1K 131
Stable Pl. N4 . . . . 2B 66
The Stables IG9: Buck H 1F 37
Stables End BR6: Farnb 3G 173
Stables Gallery & Arts Cen. 3C 62
Stables Lodge *E8* *7H 67*
(off Mare St.)
The Stables Mkt. NW1 . . . . 7F 65
Stables M. SE27 . . . . 5C 138
Stables Row E11 . . . . 5J 51
Stable St. N1 . . . . 1J 83
SE18 . . . . 5F 107
Stables Way SE11 . . . . . . 5J 19 (5A 102)
Stables Yd. SW18 . . . . 6J 117
Stable Vs. BR1: Broml 6B 142
Stable Wlk. *E1* *6G 85*
(off Boulevard Walkway)
N2 . . . . 1B 46
Stable Way W10 . . . . 6E 80
Stable Yd. SW1 . . . . 6A 12
SW15 . . . . 3E 116
The Stableyard SW9 . . . . 2K 119
Stableyard M. TW11: Tedd 6K 131
Stable Yd. Rd. SW1 . . . . 6B 12 (2G 101)
(not continuous)
Staburn Ct. HA8: Edg 2J 43
Stacey Av. N18 . . . . 4D 34
Stacey Cl. E10 . . . . 5F 51
Stacey St. N7 . . . . 3A 66
WC2 . . . . 1D 12 (6H 83)
Stack Ho. *SW1* *4H 17*
(off Cundy St.)
Stackhouse St. SW3 . . . . 1E 16
Stacy Path SE5 . . . . 7E 102
Staddon Cl. BR3: Beck 4A 158
Stadium Bus. Cen.
HA9: Wemb 3H 61
Stadium M. N5 . . . . 3A 66
Stadium Retail Pk. 3G 61
Stadium Rd. SE18 . . . . 7C 106
Stadium Rd. E. NW4 . . . . 7D 44
Stadium St. SW10 . . . . 7A 100
Stadium Way HA9: Wemb 4F 61
Staffa Rd. E10 . . . . 1A 68
Stafford Cl. E17 . . . . 6B 50
(not continuous)
N14 . . . . 5B 22
NW6 . . . . 3J 81
SM3: Cheam 6G 165
Stafford Ct. DA5: Bexl 7F 127
SW8 . . . . 7J 101
W7 . . . . *6K 77*
(off Copley Cl.)
W8 . . . . 3J 99
Stafford Cripps Ho. *E2* *3J 85*
(off Globe Rd.)
SW6 . . . . *6H 99*
(off Clem Attlee Ct.)
Stafford Cross Bus. Pk.
CR0: Wadd 5K 167
Stafford Gdns. CR0: Wadd 5K 167
Stafford Ho. *SE1* *5F 103*
(off Cooper's Rd.)
Stafford Mans. *SW1* *1A 18*
(off Stafford Pl.)
SW4 . . . . 4J 119
SW11 . . . . *7D 100*
(off Albert Bri. Rd.)
W14 . . . . *3F 99*
(off Haarlem Rd.)
Stafford Pl. SW1 . . . . 1A 18 (3G 101)
TW10: Rich 7F 115
Stafford Rd. CR0: Wadd 4A 168
DA14: Sidc 4J 143
E3 . . . . 2B 86
E7 . . . . 7A 70
HA3: Hrw W 7B 26
HA4: Ruis 4H 57
KT3: N Mald 3J 151
NW6 . . . . 3J 81
SM6: W'gton 6G 167
Staffordshire St. SE15 . . . . 1G 121
Stafford St. W1 . . . . 4A 12 (1G 101)
Stafford Ter. W8 . . . . 3J 99
Staff St. EC1 . . . . 2F 9 (3D 84)
Stag Cl. HA8: Edg 2H 43
Stag Ct. *KT2: King T* *1G 151*
(off Coombe Rd.)
STAG LANE 2B 134
Stag La. HA8: Edg 2H 43
IG9: Buck H 2E 36
NW9 . . . . 2H 43
SW15 . . . . 3B 134
Stags Way TW7: Isle 6K 95
Stainbank Rd. CR4: Mitc 3F 155
Stainby Cl. UB7: W Dray 3A 92
Stainby Rd. N15 . . . . 4F 49
Staines Av. SM3: Cheam 2F 165
Staines Rd.
IG1: Ilf 5G 71
TW2: Twick 3E 130
TW3: Houn 3F 113
TW4: Houn 7F 111
TW14: Bedf, Felt 1C 128
Staines Rd. E. TW16: Sun 7J 129
Staines Rd. W.
TW15: Ashf 6D 128
TW16: Sun 6D 128
Staines Wlk. DA14: Sidc 6C 144
Stainford Cl. TW15: Ashf 5F 129
Stainforth Rd. E17 . . . . 4C 50
IG2: Ilf 7H 53
Staining La. EC2 . . . . 7D 8 (6C 84)
Stainmore Cl. BR7: Chst 1H 161
Stainsbury St. E2 . . . . 2J 85
Stainsby Rd. E14 . . . . 6C 86
Stainton Rd. EN3: Enf H 1D 24
SE6 . . . . 6F 123
Staith Ct. *E3* *3E 86*
(off Bolinder Way)
Stalbridge Flats *W1* *1H 11*
(off Lumley St.)
Stalbridge Ho. *NW1* *1A 6*
(off Hampstead Rd.)
Stalbridge St. NW1 . . . . . . 5D 4 (5C 82)
Stalham St. SE16 . . . . 3H 103
Stalham Way IG6: Ilf 1F 53
Stambourne Way
BR4: W W'ck 2E 170
SE19 . . . . 7E 138
Stambourne Woodland Wlk.
SE19 . . . . 7E 138
Stamford Bridge *7K 99*
Stamford Bri. Studios *SW6* *7K 99*
(off Wandon Rd.)
Stamford Brook Arches W6 . . . . . . 4C 98
Stamford Brook Av. W6 . . . . 3B 98
Stamford Brook Gdns. W6 . . . . 3B 98
Stamford Brook Mans. *W6* *4B 98*
(off Goldhawk Rd.)
Stamford Brook Rd. W6 . . . . 3B 98
Stamford Bldgs. *SW8* *7J 101*
(off Meadow Pl.)
Stamford Cl. HA3: Hrw W 7D 26
N15 . . . . 4G 49
NW3 . . . . *3A 64*
(off Heath St.)
UB1: S'hall 7E 76
Stamford Cotts. *SW10* *7K 99*
(off Billing St.)
Stamford Ct. W6 . . . . 4C 98
Stamford Dr. BR2: Broml 4H 159
Stamford Gdns.
RM9: Dag 7C 72
Stamford Ga. SW6 . . . . 7K 99
Stamford Ga. Ho. *SW6* *7K 99*
(off Stamford Ga.)
Stamford Gro. E. N16 . . . . 1G 67
Stamford Gro. W. N16 . . . . 1G 67
STAMFORD HILL 1F 67
Stamford Hill N16 . . . . 2F 67
Stamford Lodge N16 . . . . 7F 49
Stamford Rd. E6 . . . . 1C 88
N1 . . . . 7E 66
N15 . . . . 5G 49
RM9: Dag 1B 90
Stamford Sq. SW15 . . . . 5G 117
Stamford St. SE1 . . . . 5J 13 (1A 102)
Stamp Pl. E2 . . . . 1J 9 (2F 85)
Stanard Cl. N16 . . . . 7E 48
Stanborough Cl.
TW12: Hamp 6D 130
Stanborough Ho. *E3* *4D 86*
(off Empson St.)
Stanborough Pas. E8 . . . . 6F 67
Stanborough Rd.
TW3: Houn 3H 113
Stanbridge Pl. N21 . . . . 2G 33
Stanbridge Rd. SW15 . . . . 3E 116
Stanbrook Rd. SE2 . . . . 2B 108
Stanbury Ct. NW3 . . . . 6D 64
Stanbury Rd. SE15 . . . . 1H 121
(not continuous)
Stancroft NW9 . . . . 5A 44
Standale Gro. HA4: Ruis 5E 38
Standard Ind. Est. E16 . . . . 2D 106
Standard Pl. EC2 . . . . 2H 9
Standard Rd. DA6: Bex 4E 126
DA17: Belv 5G 109
NW10 . . . . 4J 79
TW4: Houn 3C 112
Standcumbe Ct. BR3: Beck 5B 158
Standen Rd. SW18 . . . . 7H 117
Standfield Gdns.
RM10: Dag 6G 73
Standfield Rd. RM10: Dag 5G 73
Standish Ho. *W6* *4C 98*
(off St Peter's Gro.)
Standish Rd. W6 . . . . 4C 98
Standlake Point SE23 . . . . 3K 139
Stane Cl. SW19 . . . . 7K 135
Stane Gro. SW9 . . . . 2J 119
Stanesgate Ho. *SE15* *7G 103*
(off Friary Est.)
Stane Way SE18 . . . . 7B 106
Stanfield Ho. *NW8* *3B 4*
(off Frampton St.)
UB5: N'olt *2B 76*
(off Academy Gdns.)
Stanfield Rd. E3 . . . . 2A 86
Stanford Cl. HA4: Ruis 6E 38
IG8: Wfd G 5H 37
RM7: Rom 6H 55
TW12: Hamp 6D 130
Stanford Ct. SW6 . . . . 1K 117
W8 . . . . *3K 99*
(off Cornwall Gdns.)
Stanford M. E8 . . . . 5G 67
Stanford Pl. SE17 . . . . 4E 102
Stanford Rd. N11 . . . . 5J 31
SW16 . . . . 2H 155
W8 . . . . 3K 99
Stanford St. SW1 . . . . . . 4C 18 (4H 101)
Stanford Way SW16 . . . . 2H 155
Stangate SE1 . . . . 1H 19
Stangate Gdns. HA7: Stan 4G 27
Stangate Lodge N21 . . . . 6E 22
Stanger Rd. SE25 . . . . 4G 157
Stanhill Cotts. DA2: Wilm 7K 145
Stanhope Av. BR2: Hayes 1H 171
HA3: Hrw W 1H 41
N3 . . . . 3H 45
Stanhope Cl. SE16 . . . . 2K 103
Stanhope Gdns. IG1: Ilf 1D 70
N4 . . . . 6B 48
N6 . . . . 6F 47
NW7 . . . . 5G 29
RM8: Dag 3F 73
SW7 . . . . 3A 16 (4A 100)
Stanhope Ga. W1 . . . . 5H 11 (1E 100)
Stanhope Gro. BR3: Beck 5B 158
Stanhope Ho. *N11* *4A 32*
(off Coppies Gro.)
SE8 . . . . *7B 104*
(off Adolphus St.)
Stanhope M. E. SW7 . . . . . 3A 16 (4A 100)
Stanhope M. Sth. SW7 . . . . 4A 100
Stanhope M. W. SW7 . . . . 4A 100
Stanhope Pde. NW1 . . . . 1A 6 (3G 83)
Stanhope Pk. Rd.
UB6: G'frd 4G 77
Stanhope Pl. W2 . . . . 1E 10 (7D 82)
Stanhope Rd. CR0: C'don 3E 168
DA7: Bex 2E 126
DA15: Sidc 4A 144
E17 . . . . 5D 50
EN5: Barn 6A 20
N6 . . . . 6G 47
N12 . . . . 5F 31
RM8: Dag 2F 73
SM5: Cars 7E 166
UB6: G'frd 5G 77
Stanhope Row W1 . . . . 5J 11 (1F 101)
Stanhope St. NW1 . . . . 1A 6 (2G 83)
Stanhope Ter.
TW2: Twick 7K 113
W2 . . . . 2B 10 (7B 82)
Stanier Cl. W14 . . . . 5H 99
Stanier Ho. *SW6* *1A 118*
(off Station Ct.)
Stanlake M. W12 . . . . 1E 98
Stanlake Rd. W12 . . . . 1E 98
Stanlake Vs. W12 . . . . 1E 98
Stanley Av. BR3: Beck 2E 158
HA0: Wemb 7E 60
IG11: Bark 2K 89
KT3: N Mald 5C 152
RM8: Dag 1F 73
UB6: G'frd 1G 77
Stanley Bri. Studios *SW6* *7K 99*
(off King's Rd.)
Stanley Cl. HA0: Wemb 7E 60
SE9 . . . . 1G 143
SW8 . . . . 6K 101
Stanley Cohen Ho. *EC1* *4C 8*
(off Golden La.)
Stanley Ct. SM2: Sutt 7K 165
SM5: Cars 7E 166
W5 . . . . 5C 78
Stanley Cres. W11 . . . . 7H 81
Stanleycroft Cl.
TW7: Isle 1J 113
Stanley Gdns.
CR4: Mitc 6E 136
NW2 . . . . 5E 62
SM6: W'gton 6G 167
W3 . . . . 2A 98
W11 . . . . 7H 81
Stanley Gdns. M. *W11* *7H 81*
(off Kensington Pk. Rd.)
Stanley Gdns. Rd.
TW11: Tedd 5J 131
Stanley Gro. CR0: C'don 6A 156
SW8 . . . . 2E 118
Stanley Holloway Ct. *E16* *6J 87*
(off Coolfin Rd.)
Stanley Ho. *E14* *6C 86*
(off Saracen St.)
SW10 . . . . *7A 100*
(off Coleridge Gdns.)
Stanley Mans. *SW10* *7A 16*
(off Park Wlk.)
Stanley M. *SW10* *7A 100*
(off Coleridge Gdns.)
Stanley Pk. Dr. HA0: Wemb 1F 79
Stanley Pk. Rd.
SM5: Cars 7C 166
SM6: W'gton 6F 167
Stanley Picker Gallery *3E 150*
(off Springfield Rd.)
Stanley Rd. BR2: Broml 4K 159
BR6: Orp 1K 173
CR0: C'don 7A 156
CR4: Mitc 7E 136
DA14: Sidc 3A 144
E4 . . . . 1A 36
E10 . . . . 6D 50
E12 . . . . 5C 70
E18 . . . . 1H 51
EN1: Enf 3K 23
HA2: Harr 2G 59
HA6: Nwood 1J 39
HA9: Wemb 6F 61
IG1: Ilf 2H 71
N2 . . . . 3B 46
N9 . . . . 1A 34
N10 . . . . 7A 32
N11 . . . . 6C 32
N15 . . . . 4B 48
NW9 . . . . 7C 44
SM2: Sutt 6K 165
SM4: Mord 4J 153
SM5: Cars 7E 166
SW14 . . . . 4H 115
SW19 . . . . 6J 135
TW2: Twick 3H 131
TW3: Houn 4G 113
TW11: Tedd 4J 131
TW15: Ashf 5A 128
UB1: S'hall 7C 76
W3 . . . . 3J 97
Stanley Sq. SM5: Cars 7D 166
Stanley St. SE8 . . . . 7B 104
Stanley Studios *SW10* *7A 16*
(off Park Wlk.)
Stanley Ter. DA6: Bex 4G 127
N19 . . . . 2J 65
Stanliff Ho. E14 . . . . 3C 104
Stanmer St. SW11 . . . . 1C 118
STANMORE 5G 27
Stanmore & Edgware Golf Cen.
. . . . 3J 27
Stanmore Common
Local Nature Reserve 2E 26
Stanmore Country Pk. &
Local Nature Reserve 3H 27
Stanmore Gdns.
SM1: Sutt 3A 166
TW9: Rich 3F 115
Stanmore Golf Course 7G 27
Stanmore Hill HA7: Stan 3F 27
Stanmore Lodge
HA7: Stan 4G 27
Stanmore Pl. NW1 . . . . 1F 83
Stanmore Rd.
DA17: Belv 4J 109
E11 . . . . 1H 69
N15 . . . . 4B 48
TW9: Rich 3F 115
Stanmore St. N1 . . . . 1K 83
Stanmore Ter. BR3: Beck 2C 158
Stannard Cotts. *E1* *4J 85*
(off Fox Cl.)
Stannard Ct. SE6 . . . . 1D 140
Stannard Ho. SW19 . . . . 4A 136
Stannard M. *E8* *6G 67*
(off Stannard Rd.)
Stannard Rd. E8 . . . . 6G 67
Stannary Pl. SE11 . . . . . . 6K 19 (5A 102)
Stannary St. SE11 . . . . . . 7K 19 (6A 102)
Stannet Way
SM6: W'gton 4G 167
Stansbury Sq. W10 . . . . 3G 81
Stansfeld Ho. *SE1* *4F 103*
(off Longfield Est.)
Stansfeld Rd. E6 . . . . 5B 88
E16 . . . . 5B 88
Stansfield Rd. SW9 . . . . 3K 119
TW4: Cran 2K 111
Stansgate Rd. RM10: Dag 2G 73
Stanstead *WC1* *2F 7*
(off Tavistock Pl.)
Stanstead Cl. BR2: Broml 5H 159
Stanstead Gro. SE6 . . . . 1B 140
Stanstead Ho. *E3* *4E 86*
(off Devas St.)
Stanstead Mnr. SM1: Sutt 6J 165
Stanstead Rd. E11 . . . . 5K 51
SE6 . . . . 1A 140
SE23 . . . . 1K 139
Stansted Cres. DA5: Bexl 1D 144
Stansted Rd.
TW6: H'row A 6B 110
Stanswood Gdns. SE5 . . . . 7E 102
Stanthorpe Cl. SW16 . . . . 5J 137
Stanthorpe Rd. SW16 . . . . 5J 137
Stanton Av.
TW11: Tedd 6J 131
Stanton Cl.
KT4: Wor Pk 1F 165
KT19: Ewe 5H 163
Stanton Ct. *CR2: S Croy* *5E 168*
(off Birdhurst Ri.)
Stanton Ho. *SE10* *6E 104*
(off Thames St.)
SE16 . . . . *2B 104*
(off Rotherhithe St.)
Stanton Rd. CR0: C'don 7C 156
SE26 . . . . 4B 140
SW13 . . . . 2B 116
SW20 . . . . 1F 153
Stanton Sq. SE26 . . . . 4B 140
Stanton Way SE26 . . . . 4B 140
Stanway Ct. *N1* *1H 9*
(off Shenfield St.)
Stanway Gdns. HA8: Edg 5D 28
W3 . . . . 1G 97
Stanway St. N1 . . . . 2E 84
STANWELL 6A 110
Stanwell Cl. TW19: Stanw 6A 110
Stanwell Moor Rd.
TW19: Staines, Stanw M 7C 174
UB7: Lford 7C 174
Stanwell Rd. TW14: Bedf 7D 110
TW15: Ashf 2A 128
Stanwick Rd. W14 . . . . 4H 99
Stanworth Ct. TW5: Hest 7D 94
Stanworth St. SE1 . . . . 7J 15 (3F 103)
Stanyhurst SE23 . . . . 1A 140
Stapenhill Rd.
HA0: Wemb 3B 60
Staple Cl. DA5: Bexl 3K 145
Staplefield Cl. SW2 . . . . 1J 137
Stapleford *N17* *2E 48*
(off Willan Rd.)
Stapleford Av. IG2: Ilf 5J 53
Stapleford Cl. E4 . . . . 3K 35
KT1: King T 2G 151
SW19 . . . . 7G 117
Stapleford Rd. HA0: Wemb 7D 60
Staplehurst Rd. SE13 . . . . 5F 123
SM5: Cars 7C 166
Staple Inn WC1 . . . . 6J 7
Staple Inn Bldgs. WC1 . . . . . 6J 7 (5A 84)
Staples Cl. SE16 . . . . 1A 104
STAPLES CORNER 1D 62
Staples Cnr. Bus. Pk. NW2 . . . . . . 1D 62
Staples Cnr. Retail Pk. 1D 62
Staples Ho. *E6* *6E 88*
(off Savage Gdns.)
Staple St. SE1 . . . . 7F 15 (2D 102)
Stapleton Gdns.
CR0: Wadd 5A 168
Stapleton Hall Rd. N4 . . . . 1K 65
Stapleton Ho. *E2* *3H 85*
(off Ellsworth St.)
Stapleton Rd. BR6: Orp 4K 173
DA7: Bex 7F 109
SW17 . . . . 3E 136
Stapleton Vs. *N16* *4E 66*
(off Wordsworth Rd.)
Stapley Rd. DA17: Belv 5G 109
Stapylton Rd. EN5: Barn 3B 20
Star All. EC3 . . . . 2H 15
Star & Garter Hill
TW10: Rich 1E 132
Starboard Way E14 . . . . 3C 104
E16 . . . . 1A 106
Starbuck Cl. SE9 . . . . 7E 124
Star Bus. Cen.
RM13: Rain 5K 91
Starch Ho. La. IG6: Ilf 2H 53
Star Cl. EN3: Pond E 6D 24
Starcross St. NW1 . . . . 2B 6 (3G 83)
Starfield Rd. W12 . . . . 2C 98
Star Hill DA1: Cray 5K 127
Star La. E16 . . . . 4G 87
Starley Cl. E17 . . . . 1F 51
Starlight Way
TW6: H'row A 5E 110
Starling Cl.
CR0: C'don 6A 158
HA5: Pinn 3A 40
IG9: Buck H 1D 36
Starling Ho. *NW8* *2C 82*
(off Charlbert St.)
Starling M. KT5: Surb 6F 151
Starling Wlk.
TW12: Hamp 5C 130
Starmans Cl. RM9: Dag 1E 90
Star Path *UB5: N'olt* *2E 76*
(off Brabazon Rd.)
Star Pl. E1 . . . . 3K 15 (7F 85)
Star Rd. TW7: Isle 2H 113
UB10: Hil 4E 74
W14 . . . . 6H 99
Star St. W2 . . . . 7B 4 (6C 82)
Starts Cl. BR6: Farnb 3E 172
Starts Hill Av. BR6: Farnb 4F 173
Starts Hill Rd.
BR6: Farnb 3E 172
Starveall Cl. UB7: W Dray 3B 92
Star Wharf *NW1* *1G 83*
(off St Pancras Way)
Star Yd. WC2 . . . . 7J 7 (6A 84)
State Farm Av. BR6: Farnb 4F 173
Staten Bldg. *E3* *2C 86*
(off Fairfield Rd.)
Staten Gdns. TW1: Twick 1K 131
State Pde. IG6: Ilf 2G 53
Statham Ct. *N19* *3J 65*
(off Alexander Rd.)
Statham Gro. N16 . . . . 4D 66
N18 . . . . 5K 33

Statham Ho.—Stone Pl.

Statham Ho. SW8 1G 119
(off Wadhurst Rd.)
Station App. BR1: Broml 3J 159
(off High St.)
BR2: Hayes 1J 171
BR3: Beck 1C 158
BR4: W W'ck 7E 158
BR6: Orp 2K 173
BR7: Chst 6C 142
(Bennetts Copse)
BR7: Chst 1E 160
(Vale Rd.)
CR2: Sande 7D 168
DA5: Bexl 1G 145
DA7: Bex 2J 127
(Barnehurst Rd.)
DA7: Bex 2E 126
(Percy Rd.)
DA16: Well 2A 126
E4 6A 36
E7 4K 69
E11 5J 51
E17 5C 50
E18 2K 51
EN5: New Bar 4F 21
HA0: Wemb 6B 60
HA1: Harr 7J 41
HA4: Ruis 5K 57
(Mahlon Av.)
HA4: Ruis 1G 57
(Pembroke Rd.)
HA5: Pinn 3C 40
IG8: Wfd G 6E 36
IG9: Buck H 4G 37
KT1: King T 1G 151
KT4: Wor Pk 1C 164
KT17: Ewe 7B 164
KT19: Ewe 5C 164
N11 5A 32
N12 4E 30
N16 2F 67
(off Stamford Hill)
NW1 4F 5 (4D 82)
NW10 3B 80
NW11 7F 45
SE9 2G 143
(Bercta Rd.)
SE9 1D 142
(Crossmead)
SE12 6J 123
(off Burnt Ash Hill)
SE26 5B 140
SM2: Cheam 7G 165
SM5: Cars 4D 166
SW6 3G 117
SW14 3J 115
SW16 6H 137
(Estreham Rd.)
SW16 5H 137
(Gleneagle Rd.)
SW20 2D 152
TW8: Bford 6C 96
(off Sidney Gdns.)
TW9: Kew 1G 115
TW12: Hamp 1E 148
TW15: Ashf 4B 128
TW16: Sun 1J 147
TW17: Shep 5E 146
UB3: Hayes 3H 93
UB6: G'frd 7G 59
UB7: Yiew 1A 92
W7 1J 95
Station App. Nth.
DA15: Sidc 2A 144
Station App. Rd.
SE1 7H 13 (2A 102)
W4 7J 97
Station App. Sth. DA15: Sidc 2A 144
(off Jubilee Way)
Station App. Southside SE9 1D 142
Station Arc. W1 4K 5
(off Gt. Portland St.)
Station Av. KT3: N Mald 3A 152
KT19: Ewe 7A 164
SW9 3B 120
TW9: Kew 1G 115
Station Bldgs. KT1: King T 2E 150
(off Fife Rd.)
Station Chambers E6 7C 70
(off High St. Nth.)
Station Cl. N3 1J 45
N12 4E 30
TW12: Hamp 1F 149
Station Cotts.
BR6: Orp 2K 173
Station Ct. N15 5F 49
SW6 1A 118
Station Cres. HA0: Wemb 6B 60
N15 4D 48
SE3 5J 105
TW15: Ashf 4A 128
Stationer's Hall Ct.
EC4 1B 14 (6B 84)
Station Est. BR3: Beck 3K 157
E18 2K 51
Station Est. Rd. TW14: Felt 1K 129
Station Garage M. SW16 6H 137
Station Gdns. W4 7J 97
Station Gro.
HA0: Wemb 6E 60
Sta. Hill BR2: Hayes 2J 171
Station Ho. SE8 7C 104
(off Deptford High St.)
Station Ho. M. N9 4B 34
Station M. Ter. SE3 5J 105
Station Pde. BR1: Broml 1J 159
(off Tweedy Rd.)
DA15: Sidc 2A 144
E5 3H 67
(off Up. Clapton Rd.)
E6 7C 70
E11 5J 51
E13 1A 88
(off Green St.)
EN4: Cockf 4K 21
HA2: Harr 4F 59
HA3: Kenton 2A 42
HA4: Ruis 2F 57
HA8: Edg 7K 27
IG9: Buck H 4G 37
IG11: Bark 7G 71
Station Pde. N14 1C 32
NW2 6E 62
RM9: Dag 6G 73
SM2: Sutt 6A 166
(off High St.)
SW12 1E 136
TW9: Kew 1G 115
TW14: Felt 1K 129
TW15: Ashf 4B 128
UB5: N'olt 4F 59
(Acock Gro.)
UB5: N'olt 7E 58
(Court Farm Rd.)
W3 6G 79
W4 7J 97
W5 1F 97
Station Pas. E18 2K 51
E20 6J 85
SE15 1J 121
Station Path SW6 3H 117
Station Pl. N4 2A 66
Station Ri. SE27 2B 138
Station Rd. BR1: Broml 1J 159
BR2: Broml 2G 159
BR4: W W'ck 1E 170
BR6: Orp 2K 173
CR0: C'don 1C 168
DA7: Bex 3E 126
DA15: Sidc 2A 144
DA17: Belv 3G 109
E4 1A 36
E7 4J 69
E12 4C 70
E17 6A 50
EN5: New Bar 5E 20
HA1: Harr 4K 41
HA2: Harr 5F 41
HA8: Edg 6B 28
IG1: Ilf 3F 71
IG6: Ilf 3H 53
KT1: Hamp W 1C 150
KT2: King T 1G 151
KT3: N Mald 5D 152
KT7: T Ditt 7K 149
KT9: Chess 5E 162
N3 1J 45
N11 5A 32
N17 3G 49
N19 3G 65
N21 1G 33
N22 2J 47
(not continuous)
NW4 6C 44
NW7 6F 29
NW10 2B 80
RM6: Chad H, Dag 7D 54
SE13 3E 122
SE20 6J 139
SE25 4F 157
SM5: Cars 4D 166
SW13 2B 116
SW19 1A 154
TW1: Twick 1K 131
TW3: Houn 4F 113
TW11: Tedd 6A 132
TW12: Hamp 1E 148
TW15: Ashf 4B 128
TW16: Sun 7J 129
TW17: Shep 5E 146
UB3: Harl, Hayes 4G 93
(not continuous)
UB7: W Dray 2A 92
W5 6F 79
W7 1J 95
Station Rd. Nth. DA17: Belv 3H 109
Station Sq. BR5: Pet W 5G 161
Station St. E15 7F 69
E16 1F 107
Station Ter. NW10 2F 81
SE5 1C 120
Station Vw. UB6: G'frd 1H 77
Station Wlk. W11 7F 81
(off Bramley Rd.)
Station Way IG9: Buck H 4F 37
SE15 2G 121
SE18 3F 107
SM3: Cheam 6G 165
Station Yd. HA4: Ruis 2E 56
TW1: Twick 7A 114
Staton Ct. E10 7D 50
(off Kings Cl.)
Staunton Ho. SE17 4E 102
(off Wansey St.)
Staunton Rd. KT2: King T 6E 132
Staunton St. SE8 6B 104
Stave Hill Ecological Pk. 2A 104
Staveley NW1 1A 6
(off Varndell St.)
Staveley Cl. E9 5J 67
N7 4J 65
SE15 1H 121
Staveley Ct. E11 5J 51
Staveley Gdns. W4 1K 115
Staveley Rd. TW15: Ashf 6F 129
W4 6J 97
Stavers Ho. E3 2B 86
(off Tredegar Rd.)
Staverton Pl. BR1: Broml 4D 160
Staverton Rd. NW2 7E 62
Stave Yd. Rd. SE16 1A 104
Stavordale Lodge W14 3H 99
(off Melbury Rd.)
Stavordale Rd. N5 4B 66
SM5: Cars 7A 154
Stayner's Rd. E1 4K 85
Stayton Rd. SM1: Sutt 3J 165
Stead Cl. BR7: Chst 5E 142
Steadfast Rd.
KT1: King T 1D 150
Steadman Ct. EC1 3D 8
(off Old St.)
Steadman Ho. RM10: Dag 3G 73
(off Uvedale Rd.)
Stead St. SE17 4D 102
Steam Farm La. TW14: Felt 4H 111
Stean St. E8 1F 85
Stebbing Ho. W11 1F 99
(off Queensdale Cres.)
Stebbing Way IG11: Bark 2A 90
Stebondale St. E14 4E 104
Stedham Pl. WC1 7E 6
Stedman Cl. DA5: Bexl 3K 145
UB10: Ick 3C 56
Steedman St. SE17 4C 102
Steeds Rd. N10 1D 46
Steele Ct. TW11: Tedd 7C 132
Steele Ho. E15 2G 87
(off Eve Rd.)
Steele Rd. E11 4G 69
N17 3E 48
NW10 2J 79
TW7: Isle 4A 114
W4 3J 97
Steele's M. Nth. NW3 6D 64
Steele's M. Sth. NW3 6D 64
Steele's Rd. NW3 6D 64
Steele's Studios NW3 6D 64
Steele Wlk. DA8: Erith 7H 109
Steel's La. E1 6J 85
Steelyard Pas. EC4 3E 14
Steen Way SE22 5E 120
Steep Cl. BR6: Chels 6K 173
Steep Hill CR0: C'don 4E 168
SW16 3H 137
Steeple Cl. SW6 2G 117
SW19 5G 135
Steeple Ct. E1 4H 85
Steeplestone Cl. N18 5H 33
Steeple Wlk. N1 1C 84
(off New Nth. Rd.)
Steerforth St. SW18 2A 136
Steering Cl. N9 1D 34
Steers Mead CR4: Mitc 1D 154
Steers Way SE16 2A 104
Stelfox Ho. WC1 1H 7
(off Penton Ri.)
Stella Cl. UB8: Hil 5D 74
Stellar Ho. N17 6A 34
Stella Rd. SW17 6D 136
Stelling Rd. DA8: Erith 7K 109
Stellman Cl. E5 3G 67
Stembridge Rd. SE20 2H 157
Stephan Cl. E8 1G 85
Stephen Cl. BR6: Orp 3J 173
Stephendale Rd. SW6 3K 117
Stephendale Yd. SW6 3K 117
(off Stephendale Rd.)
Stephen Fox Ho. W4 5A 98
(off Chiswick La.)
Stephen Jewers Gdns.
IG11: Bark 7K 71
Stephen M. W1 6C 6 (5H 83)
Stephen Pl. SW4 3G 119
Stephen Rd. DA7: Bex 3J 127
Stephens Ct. E16 4H 87
SE4 3A 122
Stephens Lodge N12 3F 31
(off Woodside La.)
Stephenson Cl. DA16: Well 2A 126
E3 3D 86
Stephenson Ct. SM2: Cheam 7G 165
(off Station App.)
Stephenson Ho. SE1 3C 102
Stephenson Rd. E17 5A 50
TW2: Whitt 7E 112
W7 6K 77
Stephenson St. E16 4G 87
NW10 3A 80
Stephenson Way NW1 3B 6 (4G 83)
Stephen's Rd. E15 1G 87
Stephen St. W1 6C 6 (5H 83)
STEPNEY 5K 85
Stepney C'way. E1 6K 85
Stepney City Apts. E1 5J 85
Stepney City Farm 5K 85
Stepney Cl. CR4: Mitc 1E 154
Stepney Grn. E1 5J 85
Stepney Grn. Ct. E1 5K 85
(off Stepney Grn.)
Stepney High St. E1 5K 85
Stepney Way E1 5H 85
Sterling Av. HA8: Edg 4A 28
Sterling Cl. NW10 7C 62
Sterling Gdns. SE14 6A 104
Sterling Ind. Est.
RM10: Dag 4H 73
Sterling Pl. W5 4E 96
Sterling Rd. DA7: Bex 4H 127
EN2: Enf 1J 23
Sterling St. SW7 1D 16 (3C 100)
Sterling Way N7 6K 65
N18 4J 33
The Sternberg Cen. 3J 45
Stern Cl. IG11: Bark 2C 90
Stern Ct. E3 3E 86
(off Culvert Dr.)
Sterndale Rd. W14 3F 99
Sterne St. W12 2F 99
Sternhall La. SE15 3G 121
Sternhold Av. SW2 2H 137
Sterry Cres. RM10: Dag 5G 73
Sterry Dr. KT7: T Ditt 6J 149
KT19: Ewe 4A 164
Sterry Gdns. RM10: Dag 6G 73
Sterry Rd. IG11: Bark 1K 89
RM10: Dag 4G 73
Sterry St. SE1 7E 14 (2D 102)
Steucers La. SE23 1A 140
Stevannie Ct. DA17: Belv 5F 109
Steve Biko Ct. W10 4F 81
(off St John's Ter.)
Steve Biko La. SE6 4C 140
Steve Biko Lodge E13 2J 87
(off London Rd.)
Steve Biko Rd. N7 3A 66
Steve Biko Way
TW3: Houn 3E 112
Stevedale Rd. DA16: Well 2C 126
Stevedore St. E1 1H 103
Stevenage Rd. E6 6E 70
SW6 7F 99
Stevens Av. E9 6J 67
Stevens Cl. BR3: Beck 6C 140
DA5: Bexl 4K 145
HA5: Eastc 5A 40
TW12: Hamp 6D 130
Stevens Grn. WD23: B Hea 1B 26
Stevens La. KT10: Clay 7A 162
Stevenson Cl. EN5: New Bar 7G 21
Stevenson Ct. CR4: Mitc 3C 154
SE6 2H 141
Stevenson Cres. SE16 5G 103
Stevenson Ho. NW8 1A 82
(off Boundary Rd.)
Stevens Rd. RM8: Dag 2C 72
Stevens St. SE1 7H 15 (3E 102)
Steventon Rd. W12 7B 80
Steward Ho. E3 3C 86
(off Trevithick Way)
Stewards Holte Wlk. N11 4A 32
Steward St. E1 6H 9 (5E 84)
Stewart Av. TW17: Shep 4C 146
Stewart Cl. BR7: Chst 5F 143
NW9 6J 43
TW12: Hamp 6C 130
Stewart Ho. KT1: King T 3F 151
Stewart Quay UB3: Hayes 2G 93
Stewart Rainbird Ho. E12 5E 70
(off Parkhurst Rd.)
Stewart Rd. E15 4F 69
Stewartsby Cl. N18 5H 33
Stewart's Gro. SW3 5B 16 (5B 100)
Stewart's Pl. SW2 6K 119
Stewart's Rd. SW8 7G 101
Stewart St. E14 2E 104
Stew La. EC4 2C 14 (7C 84)
Steyne Horn La. W3 1H 97
Steyne Ho. W3 1J 97
(off Narrow St.)
Steyne Rd. W3 1H 97
Steyning Gro. SE9 4D 142
Steynings Way N12 5D 30
Steyning Way TW4: Houn 4A 112
Steynton Av. DA5: Bexl 2D 144
Stibbington Ho. NW1 2G 83
(off Cranleigh St.)
Stickland Rd. DA17: Belv 4G 109
Stickle Ho. SE8 7D 104
(off Creative Rd.)
Stickleton Cl. UB6: G'frd 3F 77
Stifford Ho. E1 5J 85
(off Stepney Way)
Stilecroft Gdns. HA0: Wemb 3B 60
Stile Hall Gdns. W4 5G 97
Stile Hall Mans. W4 5G 97
(off Wellesley Rd.)
Stile Hall Pde. W4 5G 97
Stileman Ho. E3 5B 86
(off Ackroyd Dr.)
Stile Path TW16: Sun 3J 147
Stiles Cl. BR2: Broml 6D 160
DA8: Erith 5H 109
Stillingfleet Rd. SW13 6C 98
Stillington St. SW1 3B 18 (4G 101)
Stillness Rd. SE23 6A 122
Still Wlk. SE1 5H 15
Stilwell Cl. BR5: St P 7B 144
Stilwell Dr. UB8: Hil 4B 74
STILWELL RDBT. 7C 74
Stipularis Dr. UB4: Yead 4B 76
Stirling Av. HA5: Pinn 1B 58
SM6: W'gton 7J 167
TW17: Shep 3G 147
Stirling Cl. DA14: Sidc 4J 143
SW16 1H 155
Stirling Ct. EC1 3A 8
(off St John St.)
W13 7B 78
Stirling Gro. TW3: Houn 2G 113
Stirling Rd. E13 2K 87
E17 3A 50
HA3: W'stone 3K 41
N17 1G 49
N22 1B 48
SW9 2J 119
TW2: Whitt 7E 112
TW6: H'row A 6B 110
UB3: Hayes 7K 75
W3 3H 97
Stirling Rd. Path E17 3A 50
Stirling Wlk. KT5: Surb 6H 151
Stirling Way CR0: Bedd 7J 155
Stiven Cres. HA2: Harr 3D 58
Stockbeck NW1 1B 6
(off Ampthill Est.)
Stockbridge Ho. SW18 4A 118
(off Eltringham St.)
Stockbury Rd. CR0: C'don 6J 157
Stockdale Rd. RM8: Dag 2F 73
Stockdove Way UB6: G'frd 3K 77
Stocker Gdns. RM9: Dag 7C 72
Stockfield Rd. SW16 3K 137
Stockford Av. NW7 7A 30
Stockholm Apts. NW1 7E 64
(off Chalk Farm Rd.)
Stockholm Ho. E1 7G 85
(off Swedenborg Gdns.)
Stockholm Rd. SE16 5J 103
Stockholm Way E1 1G 103
Stockhurst Cl. SW15 2E 116
Stockingswater La.
EN3: Brim 2G 25
Stockland Rd. RM7: Rom 6K 55
Stockleigh Hall NW8 2C 82
(off Prince Albert Rd.)
Stockley Cl. UB7: W Dray 2D 92
Stockley Country Pk. 7C 74
Stockley Farm Rd.
UB7: W Dray 3D 92
STOCKLEY PARK 1D 92
Stockley Pk. Golf Course 7E 74
Stockley Rd. UB7: W Dray 4D 92
UB8: Hil 6C 74
UB11: Stock P 6C 74
Stock Orchard Cres. N7 5K 65
Stock Orchard St. N7 5K 65
Stockport Rd. SW16 1H 155
Stocksfield Rd. E17 3E 50
Stocks Pl. E14 7B 86
UB10: Hil 1C 74
Stock St. E13 2J 87
Stockton Cl. EN5: New Bar 4F 21
Stockton Ct. SW1 2C 18
(off Greycoat St.)
Stockton Gdns. N17 7H 33
NW7 3F 29
Stockton Ho. E2 3H 85
(off Ellsworth St.)
HA2: Harr 1E 58
Stockton Rd. N17 7H 33
N18 6B 34
STOCKWELL 2K 119
Stockwell Av. SW9 3K 119
Stockwell Cl. BR1: Broml 2K 159
HA8: Edg 2J 43
Stockwell Gdns. SW9 1K 119
Stockwell Gdns. Est. SW9 2J 119
Stockwell Grn. SW9 2K 119
Stockwell Grn. Ct. SW9 2K 119
Stockwell La. SW9 2K 119
Stockwell M. SW9 2K 119
Stockwell Pk. Cres. SW9 2K 119
Stockwell Pk. Est. SW9 2K 119
Stockwell Pk. Rd. SW9 1K 119
Stockwell Pk. Wlk. SW9 3A 120
Stockwell Rd. SW9 2K 119
Stockwell St. SE10 6E 104
Stockwell Ter. SW9 1K 119
Stodart Rd. SE20 1J 157
Stoddart Ho. SW8 7H 19 (6K 101)
Stodmarsh Ho. SW9 1A 120
(off Cowley Rd.)
Stofield Gdns. SE9 3B 142
Stoford Cl. SW19 7G 117
Stokenchurch St. SW6 1K 117
STOKE NEWINGTON 3F 67
Stoke Newington Chu. St. N16 3D 66
Stoke Newington Comn. N16 3F 67
Stoke Newington High St. N16 3F 67
Stoke Newington Rd. N16 5F 67
Stoke Pl. NW10 3B 80
Stoke Rd. KT2: King T 7J 133
Stokesby Rd. KT9: Chess 6F 163
Stokes Cotts. IG6: Ilf 1G 53
Stokes Ct. N2 4C 46
Stokes Field
Local Nature Reserve 2B 162
Stokesley St. W12 6B 80
Stokes M. TW11: Tedd 5A 132
Stokes Rd. CR0: C'don 6K 157
E6 4C 88
Stokley Ct. N8 4J 47
Stoll Cl. NW2 3E 62
Stoms Path SE6 5C 140
(off Maroons Way)
Stonard Rd. N13 3F 33
RM8: Dag 5B 72
Stondon Pk. SE23 6A 122
Stondon Wlk. E6 2B 88
Stonebanks KT12: Walt T 7J 147
STONEBRIDGE 1K 79
Stonebridge Cen. N15 5F 49
Stonebridge Gdns. 1F 85
(off Arbutus St.)
Stonebridge M. SE19 7D 138
Stonebridge Pk. NW10 7K 61
Stonebridge Rd. N15 5F 49
Stonebridge Way HA9: Wemb 6H 61
Stone Bldgs. WC2 6H 7
Stonechat M. SW15 4C 116
Stonechat Sq. E6 5C 88
Stone Cl. RM8: Dag 2F 73
SW4 2G 119
UB7: Yiew 1B 92
Stonecot Cl. SM3: Sutt 1G 165
Stonecot Hill SM3: Sutt 1G 165
Stone Cres. TW14: Felt 7H 111
Stonecroft Rd. DA8: Erith 7J 109
Stonecroft Way CR0: C'don 7J 155
Stonecrop Cl. NW9 3K 43
Stonecutter St. EC4 7A 8 (6B 84)
Stonefield N4 2K 65
Stonefield Cl. DA7: Bex 3G 127
HA4: Ruis 5C 58
Stonefield Mans. N1 1A 84
(off Cloudesley St.)
Stonefield St. N1 1A 84
Stonefield Way HA4: Ruis 4C 58
SE7 7B 106
STONEGROVE 4A 28
Stonegrove HA8: Edg 4K 27
Stone Gro. Ct. HA8: Edg 5A 28
Stonegrove Gdns. HA8: Edg 5K 27
Stone Hall W8 3K 99
(off Stone Hall Gdns.)
Stonehall Av. IG1: Ilf 6C 52
Stone Hall Gdns. W8 3K 99
Stone Hall Pl. W8 3K 99
Stone Hall Rd. N21 7E 22
Stoneham Rd. N11 5B 32
Stonehill Cl. SW14 5K 115
Stonehill Ct. E4 7J 25
STONEHILL GREEN 7J 145
Stonehill Grn. DA2: Wilm 7J 145
Stonehill Rd. SW14 5J 115
W4 5G 97
Stonehills Ct. SE21 3E 138
Stonehill Woods Pk.
DA14: Sidc 6H 145
Stonehorse Rd. EN3: Pond E 5D 24
Stonehouse NW1 1G 83
(off Plender St.)
Stonehouse Ho. W2 5J 81
(off Westbourne Pk. Rd.)
Stone Lake Ind. Pk. SE7 4A 106
Stone Lake Retail Pk. 4A 106
STONELEIGH 5C 164
Stoneleigh Av. EN1: Enf 1C 24
KT4: Wor Pk 4C 164
Stoneleigh B'way. KT17: Ewe 5C 164
Stoneleigh Ct. IG5: Ilf 3C 52
Stoneleigh Cres. KT19: Ewe 5B 164
Stoneleigh M. E3 2A 86
Stoneleigh Pk. Av. CR0: C'don 6K 157
Stoneleigh Pk. Rd.
KT4: Wor Pk 6B 164
KT19: Ewe 6B 164
Stoneleigh Pl. W11 7F 81
Stoneleigh Rd. BR1: Broml 3F 161
IG5: Ilf 3C 52
N17 3F 49
SM5: Cars 7C 154
Stoneleigh St. W11 7F 81
Stoneleigh Ter. N19 2F 65
Stonell's Rd. SW11 6D 118
Stonemason Ct. SE1 7C 14
(off Borough Rd.)
Stonemason Ho. SE14 1K 121
(off Fishers Ct.)
Stonemasons Cl. N15 4D 48
Stonemasons Yd. SW18 7B 118
Stonenest St. N4 1K 65
Stone Pk. Av. BR3: Beck 4C 158
Stone Pl. KT4: Wor Pk 2C 164

A-Z Big London 289

Stone Rd.—Sunbury Ct. Island

Stone Rd. BR2: Broml 5H 159
Stones End St.
SE1 7C 14 (2C 102)
Stonewall E6 5E 88
Stoneway Wlk. E3 2K 85
Stone Well Rd. TW19: Stanw 1A 128
Stonewold Ct. W5 6D 78
Stoney All. SE18 2E 124
Stoneyard La. E14 7D 86
Stoneycroft Cl. SE12 7H 123
Stoneycroft Rd. IG8: Wfd G 6H 37
Stoneydeep TW11: Tedd 4A 132
Stoneydown E17 4A 50
Stoneydown Av. E17 4A 50
Stoneydown Ho. *E17* 4A 50
(off Stoneydown)
Stoneyfields Gdns. HA8: Edg 4E 28
Stoneyfields La. HA8: Edg 5D 28
Stoney La. E1 7H 9 (6F 85)
SE19 6F 139
Stoney St. SE1 4E 14 (1D 102)
Stonhouse St. SW4 4H 119
Stonor Rd. W14 4H 99
Stonycroft Cl. EN3: Enf H 2F 25
Stopes St. SE15 7F 103
Stopford Rd. E13 1J 87
SE17 5B 102
Stopher Ho. *SE1* 7B 14
(off Webber St.)
Storehouse M. E14 7C 86
Storer Dr. DA16: Well 3B 126
Store Rd. E16 2E 106
Storers Quay E14 4F 105
Store St. E15 5F 69
WC1 6C 6 (5H 83)
Storey Cl. UB10: Ick 3E 56
Storey Ct. NW8 2A 4
Storey Ho. *E14* 7D 86
(off Cottage St.)
Storey Rd. E17 4B 50
N6 6D 46
Storey's Ga. SW1 7D 12 (2H 101)
Storey St. E16 1E 106
Stories M. SE5 2E 120
Stories Rd. SE5 3E 120
Stork Rd. E7 6H 69
Storksmead Rd. HA8: Edg 7F 29
Stork's Rd. SE16 3G 103
Stormont Lawn Tennis & Squash Club 5D 46
Stormont Rd. N6 7D 46
SW11 3E 118
Stormont Way KT9: Chess 5C 162
Stormount Dr. UB3: Harl 2E 92
Storrington *WC1* 2F 7
(off Regent Sq.)
Storrington Rd. CR0: C'don 1F 169
Storth Oaks Mead BR7: Chst 5D 142
Story St. N1 7K 65
Stothard Ho. *E1* 4J 85
(off Amiel St.)
Stothard Pl. E1 5H 9 (5E 84)
Stothard St. E1 4J 85
Stott Cl. SW18 6B 118
Stoughton Av. SM3: Cheam 5F 165
Stoughton Cl. SE11 4H 19 (4K 101)
SW15 1C 134
Stour Av. UB2: S'hall 3E 94
Stourcliffe Cl. W1 1E 10 (6D 82)
Stourcliffe St. W1 1E 10 (6D 82)
Stour Cl. BR2: Kes 4A 172
Stourhead Cl. SW19 7F 117
Stourhead Gdns. SW20 3C 152
Stourhead Ho. *SW1* 5C 18
(off Tachbrook St.)
Stour Rd. E3 7C 68
RM10: Dag 2G 73
Stourton Av. TW13: Hanw 4D 130
Stowage SE8 6C 104
Stow Cres. E17 7F 35
Stowe Cres. HA4: Ruis 6D 38
Stowe Gdns. N9 1A 34
Stowe Ho. NW11 6A 46
Stowell Ho. *N8* 4J 47
(off Pembroke Rd.)
Stowe Pl. N15 3E 48
Stowe Rd. W12 2D 98
Stowting Rd. BR6: Orp 4J 173
Stox Mead HA3: Hrw W 1H 41
Stracey Rd. E7 4J 69
NW10 1K 79
Strachan Pl. SW19 6E 134
Stradbroke Dr. IG7: Chig 6K 37
Stradbroke Gro. IG5: Ilf 3C 52
IG9: Buck H 1G 37
Stradbroke Pk. IG7: Chig 6K 37
Stradbroke Rd. N5 4C 66
Stradbrook Cl. HA2: Harr 3D 58
Stradella Rd. SE24 6C 120
Strafford Av. IG5: Ilf 2E 52
Strafford Ho. *SE8* 5B 104
(off Grove St.)
Strafford Rd. EN5: Barn 3B 20
TW1: Twick 7A 114
TW3: Houn 3D 112
W3 2J 97
Strafford St. E14 2C 104
Strahan Rd. E3 3A 86
The Straight UB1: S'hall 2B 94
Straightsmouth SE10 7E 104
Strait Rd. E6 7C 88
Strakers Rd. SE15 4H 121
Strale Ho. *N1* 1E 84
(off Whitmore Est.)
Strand WC2 3F 13 (7J 83)
Strand Ct. SE18 5K 107
Strand Dr. TW9: Kew 7H 97
Strand E. Twr. E15 2E 86
Strandfield Cl. SE18 5J 107
Strand Ho. *BR2: Broml* 6B 160
(off Wells Vw. Dr.)
SE28 1H 107
Strand La. WC2 2H 13 (7K 83)
STRAND ON THE GREEN 6G 97
Strand on the Grn. W4 6G 97
Strand Pl. N18 4K 33
Strand School App. W4 6G 97
Strang Ho. N1 1C 84
Strangways Ter. W14 3H 99
Stranraer Way N1 7J 65
TW6: H'row A 6A 110
Strasburg Rd. SW11 1E 118
Strata *SE1* 4C 102
(off Walworth Rd.)
Strata Ct. KT12: Walt T 7H 147
Strata Rd. DA8: Erith 5J 109
Stratfield Pk. Cl. N21 7G 23
STRATFORD 7F 69
Stratford Av. UB10: Hil 2B 74
The Stratford Cen. 7F 69
Stratford Circus
(Performing Arts Cen.) 6F 69
Stratford Cl. IG11: Bark 7A 72
RM10: Dag 7J 73
Stratford Ct. KT3: N Mald 4K 151
Stratford Eye E15 6F 69
Stratford Gro. SW15 4F 117
Stratford Ho. Av. BR1: Broml 3C 160
STRATFORD NEW TOWN 6F 69
The Stratford Office Village *E15* 7G 69
(off Romford Rd.)
Stratford One E20 6D 68
Stratford Picturehouse 6F 69
Stratford Pl. *E20* 6E 68
(within Westfield Shop. Cen.)
W1 1J 11 (6F 83)
Stratford Rd. CR7: Thor H 4A 156
E13 1H 87
(not continuous)
NW4 4F 45
TW6: H'row A 6D 110
UB2: S'hall 4C 94
UB4: Yead 4K 75
W8 3J 99
Stratford Studios W8 3J 99
Stratford Vs. NW1 7G 65
Stratford Workshops *E15* 1F 87
(off Burford Rd.)
Strathan Cl. SW18 6G 117
Strathaven Rd. SE12 6K 123
Strathblaine Rd. SW11 5B 118
Strathbrook Rd. SW16 7K 137
Strathcona Rd. HA9: Wemb 2D 60
Strathdale SW16 5K 137
Strathdon Dr. SW17 3B 136
Strathearn Av. TW2: Whitt 1F 131
UB3: Harl 7H 93
Strathearn Ho. *W2* 2C 10
(off Strathern Pl.)
Strathearn Pl. W2 1C 10 (6C 82)
Strathearn Rd. SM1: Sutt 5J 165
SW19 5J 135
Stratheden Pde. SE3 7J 105
Stratheden Rd. SE3 1J 123
Strathfield Gdns. IG11: Bark 6H 71
Strathleven Rd. SW2 5J 119
Strathmore Ct. *NW8* 1C 4
(off Park Rd.)
Strathmore Gdns. HA8: Edg 2H 43
N3 1K 45
W8 1J 99
Strathmore Rd. CR0: C'don 7D 156
SW19 3J 135
TW11: Tedd 4J 131
Strathnairn St. SE1 4G 103
(not continuous)
Strathray Gdns. NW3 6C 64
Strath Ter. SW11 4C 118
Strathville Rd. SW18 2J 135
(not continuous)
Strathyre Av. SW16 3A 156
Stratosphere Twr. *E15* 7F 69
(off Gt. Eastern Rd.)
Stratton Cl. DA7: Bex 3E 126
HA8: Edg 6A 28
SW19 2J 153
TW3: Houn 1E 112
Stratton Ct. *HA5: Hat E* 1D 40
(off Devonshire Rd.)
N1 7E 66
(off Hertford Rd.)
Strattondale St. E14 3E 104
Stratton Dr. IG11: Bark 5J 71
Stratton Gdns. UB1: S'hall 6D 76
Stratton Rd. DA7: Bex 3E 126
SW19 2J 153
TW16: Sun 2H 147
Stratton St. W1 4K 11 (1F 101)
Strauss Rd. W4 2K 97
Strawberry Flds. BR6: Farnb 5F 173
STRAWBERRY HILL 3K 131
Strawberry Hill 3K 131
Strawberry Hill KT9: Chess 6D 162
TW1: Twick 3K 131
Strawberry Hill Cl.
TW1: Twick 3K 131
Strawberry Hill Golf Course 3J 131
Strawberry Hill Rd.
TW1: Twick 3K 131
Strawberry La. SM5: Cars 3E 166
Strawberry Ter. N10 1D 46
Strawberry Va. N2 1B 46
TW1: Twick 3A 132
(not continuous)
Streakes Fld. Rd. NW2 2C 62
Streamdale SE2 6B 108
Stream La. HA8: Edg 5C 28
Streamline Ct. *SE22* 1G 139
(off Streamline M.)
Streamline M. SE22 1G 139
Streamside Cl. BR2: Broml 4J 159
N9 1A 34
Streamway DA17: Belv 6G 109
Streatfeild Av. E6 1D 88
Streatfield Rd. HA3: Kenton 3C 42
STREATHAM 3J 137
Streatham Cl. SW16 2J 137
STREATHAM COMMON 6H 137
Streatham Comn. Nth. SW16 5J 137
Streatham Comn. Sth. SW16 6J 137
Streatham Ct. SW16 3J 137
Streatham High Rd. SW16 4J 137
STREATHAM HILL 2J 137
Streatham Hill SW2 2J 137
STREATHAM PARK 5G 137
Streatham Pl. SW2 7J 119
Streatham Rd. CR4: Mitc 1E 154
SW16 1E 154
Streatham St. WC1 7E 6 (6J 83)
STREATHAM VALE 7G 137
Streatham Va. SW16 1G 155
Streathbourne Rd. SW17 2E 136
Streatley Pl. NW3 4A 64
Streatley Rd. NW6 7H 63
The Street *E20* 6E 68
(within Westfield Shop. Cen.)
Streeters La. SM6: Bedd 3H 167
Streetfield M. SE3 3J 123
Streetwater E20 7C 68
Streimer Rd. E15 2E 86
Strelley Way W3 7A 80
Stretton Mans. SE8 5C 104
Stretton Rd. CR0: C'don 7E 156
TW10: Ham 2C 132
Strickland Ct. SE15 3G 121
Strickland Ho. *E2* 2K 9
(off Chambord St.)
Strickland Row SW18 7B 118
Strickland St. SE8 2C 122
Strickland Way BR6: Orp 4K 173
Stride Rd. E13 2H 87
Strimon Cl. N9 2D 34
Stringer Ho. *N1* 1E 84
(off Whitmore Est.)
Strode Cl. N10 7K 31
Strode Rd. E7 4J 69
N17 2E 48
NW10 6C 62
SW6 7G 99
Strome Ho. *NW6* 2K 81
(off Carlton Vale)
Stromness Wlk. W3 1J 97
Strone Rd. E7 6A 70
E12 6A 70
Strone Way UB4: Yead 4C 76
Strongbow Cres. SE9 5D 124
Strongbow Rd. SE9 5D 124
Strongbridge Cl. HA2: Harr 1E 58
Stronsa Rd. W12 2B 98
Strood Av. RM7: Rush G 1K 73
Strood Ho. *SE1* 7F 15
(off Staple St.)
Stroud Cres. SW15 3C 134
Stroudes Cl. KT4: Wor Pk 7A 152
Stroud Fld. UB5: N'olt 6C 58
Stroud Ga. HA2: Harr 4F 59
STROUD GREEN 7K 47
Stroud Grn. Gdns. CR0: C'don 7J 157
Stroud Grn. Rd. N4 1K 65
Stroud Grn. Way CR0: C'don 7H 157
Stroudley Ho. SW8 1G 119
Stroudley Wlk. E3 3D 86
Stroud Rd. SE25 6G 157
SW19 3J 135
Stroud's Cl. RM6: Chad H 5B 54
Stroud Way TW15: Ashf 6D 128
Strouts Pl. E2 1J 9 (3F 85)
Strudwick Ct. *SW4* 1J 119
(off Binfield Rd.)
Strutton Ct. *SW1* 2C 18
(off Gt. Peter St.)
Strutton Ground SW1 1C 18 (3H 101)
Strype St. E1 6J 9 (5F 85)
Stuart Av. BR2: Hayes 1J 171
HA2: Harr 3D 58
KT12: Walt T 7K 147
NW9 7C 44
W5 2F 97
Stuart Cl. UB10: Hil 6C 56
Stuart Ct. *CR0: C'don* 3B 168
(off St John's Rd.)
Stuart Cres. CR0: C'don 3B 170
N22 1K 47
UB3: Hayes 6E 74
Stuart Evans Cl. DA16: Well 3C 126
Stuart Gro. TW11: Tedd 5J 131
Stuart Ho. *E9* 6K 67
(off Queen Anne Rd.)
E16 1K 105
(off Beaulieu Av.)
W14 4G 99
(off Windsor Way)
Stuart Mantle Way DA8: Erith 7K 109
(not continuous)
Stuart Mill Ho. *N1* 1G 7
(off Killick St.)
Stuart Pl. CR4: Mitc 1D 154
Stuart Rd. CR7: Thor H 4C 156
DA16: Well 1B 126
EN4: E Barn 7H 21
HA3: W'stone 3K 41
IG11: Bark 7K 71
NW6 3J 81
SE15 4J 121
SW19 3J 135
TW10: Ham 2B 132
W3 1J 97
Stuart Twr. *W9* 3A 82
(off Maida Vale)
Stubbs Cl. NW9 5J 43
Stubbs Ct. *W4* 5H 97
(off Chaseley Dr.)
Stubbs Dr. SE16 5H 103
Stubbs Ho. *E2* 3K 85
(off Bonner St.)
SW1 4D 18
(off Erasmus St.)
Stubbs M. *RM8: Dag* 4B 72
(off Marlborough Rd.)
Stubbs Point E13 4J 87
Stubbs Way SW19 1B 154
Stucley Pl. NW1 7F 65
Stucley Rd. TW5: Hest 7G 95
Studdridge St. SW6 2J 117
Studd St. N1 1B 84
Studholme Ct. NW3 4J 63
Studholme St. SE15 7H 103
Studio Ct. N15 4F 49
Studio La. W5 1D 96
Studio M. NW4 4E 44
Studio Pl. SW1 7F 11
Studio Plaza 7J 147
The Studios *SW4* 4G 119
(off Crescent La.)
W8 1J 99
(off Edge St.)
Studios Rd. TW17: Shep 3B 146
Studland *SE17* 5D 102
(off Portland St.)
Studland Cl. DA15: Sidc 3K 143
Studland Rd. KT2: King T 6E 132
SE26 5K 139
W7 6H 77
Studland St. W6 4D 98
Studley Av. E4 7A 36
Studley Cl. E5 5A 68
Studley Ct. DA14: Sidc 5B 144
E14 7F 87
(off Jamestown Way)
Studley Dr. IG4: Ilf 6B 52
Studley Est. SW4 1J 119
Studley Grange Rd. W7 2J 95
Studley Rd. E7 6K 69
RM9: Dag 7D 72
SW4 1J 119
Stukeley Rd. E7 7K 69
Stukeley St. WC2 7F 7 (6J 83)
Stumps Hill La. BR3: Beck 6C 140
Stunell Ho. *SE14* 6K 103
(off John Williams Cl.)
Sturdee Ho. *E2* 2G 85
(off Horatio St.)
Sturdy Ho. *E3* 2A 86
(off Gernon Rd.)
Sturdy Rd. SE15 2H 121
Sturge Av. E17 2D 50
Sturgeon Rd. SE17 5C 102
Sturges Fld. BR7: Chst 6H 143
Sturgess Av. NW4 7D 44
Sturge St. SE1 6C 14 (2C 102)
Sturmer Way N7 5K 65
Sturminster *NW1* 7H 65
(off Agar Gro.)
Sturminster Cl. UB4: Yead 6A 76
Sturminster Ho. *SW8* 7K 101
(off Dorset Rd.)
Sturrock Cl. N15 4D 48
Sturry St. E14 6D 86
Sturts Apts. *N1* 1D 84
(off Branch Pl.)
Sturt St. N1 1D 8 (2C 84)
Stutfield St. E1 6G 85
Stuttle Ho. *E1* 4K 9
(off Buxton St.)
Styles Gdns. SW9 3B 120
Styles Ho. SE1 6A 14
Styles Way BR3: Beck 4E 158
Stylus Ho. E1 6J 85
Success Ho. *SE1* 5C 103
(off Cooper's Rd.)
Succession Wlk. E3 7C 68
Sudbourne Rd. SW2 5J 119
Sudbrooke Rd. SW12 6D 118
Sudbrook Gdns.
TW10: Ham 3D 132
Sudbrook La. TW10: Ham 1E 132
SUDBURY 5B 60
Sudbury E6 5E 88
Sudbury Av. HA0: Wemb 3C 60
Sudbury Ct. *SW8* 1H 119
(off Allen Edwards Dr.)
Sudbury Ct. Dr. HA1: Harr 3K 59
Sudbury Ct. Rd. HA1: Harr 3K 59
Sudbury Cres. BR1: Broml 6J 141
HA0: Wemb 5B 60
Sudbury Cft. HA0: Wemb 4K 59
Sudbury Gdns. CR0: C'don 4E 168
Sudbury Golf Course 7C 60
Sudbury Hgts. Av. UB6: G'frd 5K 59
Sudbury Hill HA1: Harr 2J 59
Sudbury Hill Cl. HA0: Wemb 4K 59
Sudbury Ho. SW18 5K 117
Sudbury Rd. IG11: Bark 5K 71
Sudeley Ct. *E17* 1B 50
(off Broughton Pl.)
Sudeley St. N1 2B 84
Sudlow Rd. SW18 5J 117
Sudrey St. SE1 7C 14 (2C 102)
Suez Av. UB6: G'frd 2K 77
Suez Rd. EN3: Brim 4F 25
SUFFIELD HATCH 4K 35
Suffield Ho. *SE17* 5B 102
(off Berryfield Rd.)
Suffield Rd. E4 3J 35
N15 5F 49
SE20 2J 157
Suffolk Ct. E10 7C 50
IG3: Ilf 6J 53
RM6: Chad H 6C 54
Suffolk Ho. *CR0: C'don* 2D 168
(off George St.)
SE20 1K 157
(off Croydon Rd.)
Suffolk La. EC4 2E 14 (7D 84)
Suffolk Pk. Rd. E17 4A 50
Suffolk Pl. SE2 5C 108
SW1 4D 12 (1H 101)
Suffolk Rd. DA14: Sidc 6C 144
E13 3J 87
EN3: Pond E 5C 24
HA2: Harr 6D 40
IG3: Ilf 6J 53
IG11: Bark 7H 71
KT4: Wor Pk 2B 164
N15 5D 48
NW10 7A 62
RM10: Dag 5J 73
SE25 4F 157
SW13 7B 98
Suffolk St. E7 4J 69
SW1 3D 12 (7H 83)
Sugar Bakers Ct. EC3 1H 15
Sugar Ho. *E1* 1K 15
(off Leman St.)
Sugar Ho. Island Development
E15 2E 86
Sugar Ho. La. E15 2E 86
Sugar La. SE16 2G 103
Sugar Loaf Wlk. E2 3J 85
Sugar Quay EC3 3H 15
Sugar Quay Wlk. EC3 3H 15 (7E 84)
Sugden Rd. KT7: T Ditt 1B 162
SW11 3E 118
Sugden Way IG11: Bark 2K 89
Sulby Ho. *SE4* 4A 122
(off Turnham Rd.)
Sulgrave Gdns. W6 2E 98
Sulgrave Rd. W6 3E 98
Sulina Rd. SW2 7J 119
Sulivan Ct. SW6 2J 117
Sulivan Ent. Cen. SW6 3K 117
Sulivan Rd. SW6 3J 117
Sulkin Ho. *E2* 3K 85
(off Knottisford St.)
Sullivan Av. E16 5B 88
Sullivan Cl. KT8: W Mole 3F 149
SW11 3C 118
UB4: Yead 5A 76
Sullivan Ct. *E3* 4B 86
(off Eric St.)
N16 7F 49
SW5 4J 99
(off Earls Ct. Rd.)
Sullivan Cres. UB9: Hare 2A 38
Sullivan Dr. SE9: Sidc 1H 143
Sullivan Ho. *SE11* 4H 19
(off Vauxhall St.)
SW1 7K 17
(off Churchill Gdns.)
Sullivan Rd. SE11 3K 19 (4A 102)
Sullivan Row BR2: Broml 6B 160
Sullivans Reach KT12: Walt T 7H 147
Sultan Ho. *SE1* 5G 103
(off St James's Rd.)
Sultan Rd. E11 4K 51
Sultan St. BR3: Beck 2K 157
SE5 7C 102
Sultan Ter. N22 2A 48
Sumatra Rd. NW6 5J 63
Sumburgh Rd. SW12 6E 118
Sumeria Ct. *SE16* 4J 103
(off Rotherhithe New Rd.)
Summer Av. KT8: E Mos 5J 149
Summerbee Ho. *SW18* 4A 118
(off Eltringham St.)
Summercourt Rd. E1 6J 85
Summer Crossing KT7: T Ditt 5J 149
Summer Dr. UB7: W Dray 2B 92
Summerene Cl. SW16 7G 137
Summerfield *BR1: Broml* 1K 159
(off Freelands Rd.)
Summerfield Av. NW6 2G 81
Summerfield La. KT6: Surb 2D 162
Summerfield Rd. W5 4B 78
Summerfields Av. N12 6H 31
Summerfield St. SE12 7H 123
Summer Gdns. KT8: E Mos 5J 149
UB10: Ick 2E 56
Summer Gro. BR4: W W'ck 2G 171
Summer Hill BR7: Chst 2E 160
Summerhill Cl. BR6: Orp 3J 173
Summerhill Gro. EN1: Enf 6K 23
Summerhill Rd. N15 4D 48
Summerhill Vs. *BR7: Chst* 1E 160
(off Susan Wood)
Summerhill Way CR4: Mitc 1E 154
Summerhouse Av. TW5: Hest 1C 112
Summerhouse Dr.
DA2: Wilm 4K 145
DA5: Bexl, Dart 4K 145
HA7: Stan 5E 26
Summerhouse La. UB7: Harm 2E 174
Summerhouse Rd. N16 2E 66
Summerland Gdns. N10 3F 47
Summerland Grange N10 3F 47
Summerlands Av. W3 7J 79
Summerlands Lodge
BR6: Farnb 4E 172
Summerlee Av. N2 4D 46
Summerlee Gdns. N2 4D 46
Summerley St. SW18 2K 135
Summer Rd. KT7: T Ditt 5J 149
KT8: E Mos 5H 149
(not continuous)
Summersby Rd. N6 6F 47
Summers Cl. HA9: Wemb 1H 61
SM2: Sutt 7J 165
Summerskill Cl. SE15 3H 121
Summerskille Cl. N9 3C 34
Summers La. N12 7G 31
Summers Row N12 6H 31
Summers St. EC1 4J 7 (4A 84)
SUMMERSTOWN 3A 136
Summerstown SW17 3A 136
Summerton Ho. *E16* 2A 106
(off Starboard Way)
Summerton Way SE28 6D 90
Summer Trees TW16: Sun 1K 147
Summerville Gdns. SM1: Sutt 6H 165
Summerwood Rd. TW7: Isle 5K 113
Summit Av. NW9 5K 43
Summit Bus. Pk. TW16: Sun 7J 129
Summit Cl. HA8: Edg 7B 28
N14 2B 32
NW9 4K 43
Summit Ct. NW2 5G 63
Summit Dr. IG8: Wfd G 2B 52
Summit Est. N16 7G 49
Summit Ho. BR4: W W'ck 2E 170
Summit Rd. E17 4D 50
UB5: N'olt 7E 58
Summit Way N14 2A 32
SE19 7E 138
Sumner Av. SE15 1F 121
Sumner Bldgs. SE1 4C 14
Sumner Cl. BR6: Farnb 4G 173
Sumner Ct. SW8 7J 101
Sumner Est. SE15 7F 103
Sumner Gdns. CR0: C'don 1A 168
Sumner Ho. *E3* 5D 86
(off Watts Gro.)
Sumner Pl. SW7 4B 16 (4B 100)
Sumner Pl. M. SW7 4B 16 (4B 100)
Sumner Rd. CR0: C'don 1A 168
HA1: Harr 7G 41
SE15 6F 103
Sumner Rd. Sth. CR0: C'don 1A 168
Sumner St. SE1 4B 14 (1B 102)
Sumpter Cl. NW3 6A 64
Sun All. TW9: Rich 4E 114
Sunbeam Cres. W10 4E 80
Sunbeam Rd. NW10 4J 79
Sunbeam Way NW10 4K 79
Sunbird Wlk. *HA2: Harr* 2F 59
(off Sandpiper Dr.)
SUNBURY 3A 148
Sunbury Av. NW7 5E 28
SW14 4K 115
Sunbury Av. Pas. SW14 4A 116
Sunbury Bus. Cen.
TW16: Sun 1H 147
Sunbury Cl. KT12: Walt T 6J 147
SUNBURY COMMON 7H 129
Sunbury Ct. EN5: Barn 4B 20
Sunbury Ct. Island TW16: Sun 3B 148

Sunbury Ct. M. TW16: Sun 2B 148
Sunbury Ct. Rd. TW16: Sun 2A 148
Sunbury Cres. TW13: Felt 4H 129
SUNBURY CROSS 7J 129
Sunbury Cross Cen.
TW16: Sun 7H 129
The Sunbury Embroidery Gallery
3K 147
Sunbury Gdns. NW7 5E 28
Sunbury Golf Course 4F 147
Sunbury Ho. E2 2J 9
(off Swanfield St.)
SE14 6K 103
(off Myers La.)
TW16: Sun 1G 147
(off Brooklands Cl.)
Sunbury La. KT12: Walt T 6J 147
SW11 1B 118
(not continuous)
Sunbury Leisure Cen. 1H 147
Sunburylock Ait KT12: Walt T 4K 147
Sunbury Pk. Walled Garden 3K 147
Sunbury Rd. SM3: Cheam 3F 165
TW13: Felt 3H 129
Sunbury St. SE18 3D 106
Sunbury Way TW13: Hanw 5A 130
Sunbury Workshops E2 2J 9
(off Swanfield St.)
Sun Ct. E3 4E 86
(off Navigation Rd.)
EC3 1F 15
Suncroft Pl. SE26 3J 139
Sundeala Cl. TW16: Sun 7J 129
(off Hanworth Rd.)
Sunderland Ct. SE22 7G 121
TW19: Stanw 6A 110
(off Whitley Cl.)
Sunderland Ho. W2 5J 81
(off Westbourne Pk. Rd.)
Sunderland Mt. SE23 2K 139
Sunderland Point E16 1G 107
Sunderland Rd. SE23 1K 139
W5 3D 96
Sunderland Ter. W2 6K 81
Sunderland Way E12 2B 70
Sundew Av. W12 7C 80
Sundew Cl. W12 7C 80
Sundew Ct. HA0: Wemb 2E 78
(off Elmore Cl.)
Sundial Av. SE25 3F 157
Sundial Ct. EC1 5E 8
(off Chiswell St.)
Sundorne Rd. SE7 5A 106
Sundown Rd. TW15: Ashf 5E 128
Sundra Wlk. E1 4K 85
SUNDRIDGE 6K 141
Sundridge Av. BR1: Broml 1B 160
BR7: Chst 1B 160
DA16: Well 2H 125
Sundridge Ho. E9 7K 67
(off Church Cres.)
Sundridge Pde. BR1: Broml 7K 141
SUNDRIDGE PARK 7K 141
Sundridge Pk. Golf Course 6K 141
Sundridge Park Mansions
BR1: Broml 6B 142
Sundridge Pl. CR0: C'don 1G 169
Sundridge Rd. CR0: C'don 7F 157
Sunfields Pl. SE3 7K 105
Sunflower Ct. NW2 2H 63
RM13: Rain 2J 91
Sunflower Mews HA7: Stan 5E 26
Sungate Cotts. RM5: Col R 1F 55
Sun Ga. Ho. KT3: N Mald 4B 152
Sunguard Ct. SE1 4A 14 (1B 102)
SUN-IN-THE-SANDS 7K 105
Sunken Rd. CR0: C'don 5J 169
Sunkist Way SM6: W'gton 7J 167
Sunland Av. DA6: Bex 4E 126
Sun La. SE3 7K 105
Sunleigh Rd. HA0: Wemb 1E 78
Sunley Gdns. UB6: G'frd 1A 78
Sun Life Trad. Est.
TW14: Felt 3J 111
Sunlight Cl. SW19 6A 136
Sunlight M. SW6 2K 117
Sunlight Sq. E2 3H 85
Sunmead Rd. TW16: Sun 3J 147
Sunna Gdns. TW16: Sun 2K 147
Sunniholme Ct. CR2: S Croy 5C 168
(off Warham Rd.)
Sunningdale N14 5C 32
W13 5B 78
(off Hardwick Grn.)
Sunningdale Av. HA4: Ruis 1A 58
IG11: Bark 1H 89
TW13: Hanw 2C 130
W3 7A 80
Sunningdale Cl. E6 3D 88
HA7: Stan 6F 27
KT6: Surb 2E 162
SE16 5H 103
SE28 6E 90
Sunningdale Gdns. NW9 5J 43
W8 3J 99
(off Stratford Rd.)
Sunningdale Lodge HA8: Edg 5A 28
(off Stonegrove)
Sunningdale Rd. BR1: Broml 4C 160
SM1: Sutt 3H 165
Sunningfields Cres. NW4 2D 44
Sunningfields Rd. NW4 2D 44
Sunninghill Ct. W3 2J 97
Sunninghill Rd. SE13 2D 122
Sunny Bank SE25 3G 157
Sunny Cres. NW10 7J 61
Sunnycroft Rd. SE25 3G 157
TW3: Houn 2F 113
UB1: S'hall 5E 76
Sunnydale BR6: Farnb 2E 172
Sunnydale Gdns. NW7 6E 28
Sunnydale Rd. SE12 5K 123
Sunnydene Av. E4 5A 36
HA4: Ruis 1J 57
Sunnydene Gdns.
HA0: Wemb 6C 60
Sunnydene St. SE26 4A 140
Sunnyfield NW7 4G 29
Sunnyfield Rd. BR7: Chst 3K 161
Sunny Gdns. Pde. NW4 2D 44
Sunny Gdns. Rd. NW4 2D 44
Sunny Hill NW4 3D 44
Sunnyhill Cl. E5 4A 68
Sunnyhill Rd. SW16 4J 137
Sunnyhurst Cl. SM1: Sutt 3J 165
Sunnymead Av. CR4: Mitc 3H 155
Sunnymead Rd. NW9 7K 43
SW15 5D 116
Sunnymede Av. KT19: Ewe 7A 164
Sunnymede Dr. IG2: Ilf 5F 53
IG6: Ilf 5F 53
Sunny M. NW1 7E 64
Sunny Nook Gdns.
CR2: S Croy 6D 168
Sunny Pl. NW4 4E 44
The Sunny Rd. EN3: Enf H 1E 24
Sunnyside KT12: Walt T 5A 148
NW2 3H 63
SE6 7B 122
(off Blythe Hill)
SW19 6G 135
Sunnyside Dr. E4 7K 25
Sunnyside Ho's. NW2 3H 63
(off Sunnyside)
Sunnyside Pas. SW19 6G 135
Sunnyside Pl. SW19 6G 135
Sunnyside Rd. E10 1C 68
IG1: Ilf 3G 71
N19 7H 47
TW11: Tedd 4H 131
W5 1D 96
Sunnyside Rd. E. N9 3B 34
Sunnyside Rd. Nth. N9 3A 34
Sunnyside Rd. Sth. N9 3A 34
Sunnyside Ter. NW9 3K 43
Sunny Vw. NW9 5K 43
Sunny Way N12 7H 31
Sun Pas. SE16 3G 103
(off Old Jamaica Rd.)
Sunray Av. BR2: Broml 6C 160
KT5: Surb 2H 163
SE24 4D 120
Sunrise Cl. E20 5E 68
TW13: Hanw 3D 130
Sunrise Vw. NW7 6G 29
Sun Rd. W14 5H 99
Sunset Av. E4 1J 35
IG8: Wfd G 4C 36
Sunset Ct. IG8: Wfd G 7F 37
Sunset Gdns. SE25 2F 157
Sunset Lodge NW10 7E 62
(off Hanover Rd.)
Sunset Rd. SE5 4C 120
SE28 1A 108
SW19 5D 134
Sunset Vw. EN5: Barn 2B 20
Sunshine Way CR4: Mitc 2D 154
Sun St. EC2 5F 9 (5D 84)
(Finsbury Sq.)
EC2 5G 9 (5E 84)
(Primrose St.)
Sun St. Pas. EC2 6G 9 (5E 84)
Sun Wlk. E1 3K 15 (7F 85)
Sunwell Cl. SE15 1H 121
Sun Wharf SE8 7D 104
(off Creekside)
Superior Dr. BR6: Chels 6K 173
Supreme Court 2J 101
Supreme Point E16 5J 87
(off Butchers Rd.)
SURBITON 6D 150
Surbiton Ct. KT6: Surb 6C 150
Surbiton Cres. KT1: King T 4E 150
Surbiton Golf Course 4B 162
Surbiton Hall Cl.
KT1: King T 4E 150
Surbiton Hill Pk. KT5: Surb 5F 151
Surbiton Hill Rd. KT6: Surb 4E 150
Surbiton Pde. KT6: Surb 6E 150
Surbiton Plaza KT6: Surb 6D 150
(off St Mary's Rd.)
Surbiton Raceway 3K 163
Surbiton Rd. KT1: King T 4D 150
Surlingham Cl. SE28 7D 90
Surma Cl. E1 4H 85
Surmans Cl. RM9: Dag 1C 90
Surrendale Pl. W9 4J 81
Surrey Canal Rd. SE14 6J 103
Surrey Canal Trade Pk. SE14 6K 103
Surrey Cl. N3 3G 45
Surrey County Cricket Club
7H 19 (6K 101)
Surrey Cres. W4 5G 97
Surrey Docks Farm 2B 104
Surrey Docks Watersports Cen.
3A 104
Surrey Gdns. N4 6C 48
Surrey Gro. SE17 5E 102
SM1: Sutt 3B 166
Surrey Ho. CR0: C'don 3C 168
(off Surrey St.)
SE16 1K 103
(off Rotherhithe St.)
Surrey La. SW11 1C 118
Surrey La. Est. SW11 1C 118
Surrey M. SE27 4E 138
Surrey Mt. SE23 1H 139
Surrey Quays Rd. SE16 3J 103
Surrey Quays Shop. Cen. 3K 103
Surrey Rd. BR4: W W'ck 1D 170
HA1: Harr 5G 41
IG11: Bark 7J 71
RM10: Dag 5H 73
SE15 5K 121
Surrey Row SE1 6A 14 (2B 102)
Surrey Sq. SE17 5E 102
Surrey Steps WC2 2H 13
(off Surrey St.)
Surrey St. CR0: C'don 2C 168
E13 3K 87
WC2 2H 13 (7K 83)
Surrey Ter. SE17 5E 102
Surrey Water Rd. SE16 1K 103
Surridge Ct. SW9 2J 119
(off Clapham Rd.)
Surridge Gdns. SE19 6D 138
Surr St. N7 5J 65
Surry Crescent UB6: G'frd 3E 76
Sury Basin KT2: King T 1E 150
Susan Cl. RM7: Mawney 3J 55
Susan Constant Ct. E14 7F 87
(off Newport Av.)
Susan Lawrence Ho. E3 2A 86
(off Zealand Rd.)
E12 4E 70
(off Walton Rd.)
Susannah St. E14 6D 86
Susan Rd. SE3 2K 123
Susan Wood BR7: Chst 1E 160
Sussex Av. TW7: Isle 3J 113
Sussex Cl. IG4: Ilf 5D 52
KT3: N Mald 4A 152
N19 2J 65
TW1: Twick 6B 114
Sussex Ct. SE10 6E 104
(off Roan St.)
W2 1A 10
(off Spring St.)
Sussex Cres. UB5: N'olt 6E 58
Sussex Gdns. KT9: Chess 6D 162
N4 5C 48
N6 5D 46
W2 2A 10 (7B 82)
Sussex Ga. N6 5D 46
Sussex Ho. NW1 2H 83
(off Chalton St.)
Sussex Lodge W2 1B 10
(off Sussex Pl.)
Sussex Mans. SW7 4A 16
WC2 2F 13
(off Maiden La.)
Sussex M. SE6 7C 122
Sussex M. E. W2 1B 10
Sussex M. W. W2 2B 10 (7B 82)
Sussex Pl. KT3: N Mald 4A 152
NW1 3E 4 (4D 82)
W2 1B 10 (6B 82)
W6 5E 98
Sussex Ring N12 5D 30
Sussex Rd. BR4: W W'ck 1D 170
CR2: S Croy 6D 168
CR4: Mitc 5J 155
DA8: Erith 7H 109
DA14: Sidc 5B 144
E6 1E 88
HA1: Harr 5G 41
KT3: N Mald 4A 152
SM5: Cars 6D 166
UB2: S'hall 3B 94
UB10: Ick 4E 56
Sussex Sq. W2 2B 10 (7B 82)
Sussex St. E13 3K 87
SW1 6K 17 (5F 101)
Sussex Ter. SE20 7J 139
(off Graveney Gro.)
Sussex Way EN4: Cockf 5K 21
N7 2J 65
N19 1H 65
(not continuous)
Sutcliffe Cl. NW11 5K 45
Sutcliffe Ho. UB3: Hayes 6J 75
Sutcliffe Pk. Athletics Track 5A 124
Sutcliffe Rd. DA16: Well 2C 126
SE18 6J 107
Sutherland Av.
BR5: St M Cry 6K 161
DA16: Well 4J 125
TW16: Sun 2H 147
UB3: Hayes 4J 93
W9 4J 81
W13 6B 78
Sutherland Cl. EN5: Barn 4B 20
Sutherland Ct. N16 3D 66
NW9 5H 43
W9 4J 81
(off Marylands Rd.)
Sutherland Dr. SW19 1B 154
Sutherland Gdns.
KT4: Wor Pk 1D 164
SW14 3A 116
TW16: Sun 2H 147
Sutherland Gro. SW18 6G 117
TW11: Tedd 5J 131
Sutherland Ho. IG8: Wfd G 7K 37
W8 3K 99
Sutherland Pl. W2 6J 81
Sutherland Rd. CR0: C'don 7A 156
DA17: Belv 3G 109
E3 2B 86
E17 2K 49
EN3: Pond E 6E 24
N9 1C 34
N17 7B 34
UB1: S'hall 6D 76
W4 6A 98
W13 6A 78
Sutherland Rd. Path E17 3K 49
Sutherland Row
SW1 5K 17 (5F 101)
Sutherland Sq. SE17 5C 102
Sutherland St.
SW1 5J 17 (5F 101)
Sutherland Wlk. SE17 5C 102
Sutlej Rd. SE7 7A 106
Sutterton St. N7 6K 65
SUTTON 5K 165
Sutton Cl. BR3: Beck 1D 158
HA5: Eastc 5J 39
IG10: Lough 1H 37
W4 6J 97
(off Sutton La. Sth.)
Sutton Comn. Rd. SM1: Sutt 7H 153
SM3: Sutt 7H 153
Sutton Ct. KT8: W Mole 5D 148
SE19 7F 139
SM2: Sutt 6A 166
W4 6J 97
W5 1E 96
Sutton Ct. Rd. E13 3A 88
SM1: Sutt 6A 166
UB10: Hil 1D 74
W4 7J 97
Sutton Cres. EN5: Barn 5A 20
Sutton Dene TW3: Houn 1F 113
Sutton Ecology Centre 4D 166
Sutton Est. EC1 2F 9
SW3 5D 16 (5C 100)
W10 5E 80
The Sutton Est. N1 7B 66
Sutton Gdns. CR0: C'don 5F 157
IG11: Bark 1J 89
Sutton Grn. IG11: Bark 1J 89
(off Sutton Rd.)
Sutton Gro. SM1: Sutt 4B 166
Sutton Hall Rd.
TW5: Hest 7E 94
Sutton Hgts. SM2: Sutt 7B 166
Sutton La. EC1 4B 8
(off Gt. Sutton St.)
TW3: Houn 3D 112
Sutton La. Nth. W4 5J 97
Sutton La. Sth. W4 6J 97
Sutton Pde. NW4 4E 44
(off Church Rd.)
Sutton Pk. Rd. SM1: Sutt 6K 165
Sutton Pl. E9 5J 67
Sutton Plaza SM1: Sutt 6A 166
Sutton Rd. E13 4H 87
E17 1K 49
IG11: Bark 2J 89
N10 1E 46
TW5: Hest 1E 112
Sutton Row W1 7D 6 (6H 83)
Suttons Bus. Pk. RM13: Rain 3K 91
Sutton Sports Village 1K 165
Sutton Sq. E9 5J 67
TW5: Hest 1D 112
Sutton St. E1 7J 85
Sutton's Way EC1 4D 8
Suttons Wharf E2 3K 85
Sutton Tennis Academy 1K 165
Sutton United FC 4J 165
Sutton Wlk. SE1 5H 13 (1K 101)
Sutton Way TW5: Hest 1D 112
W10 4E 80
Swaby Rd. SW18 1A 136
Swaffam Ct. RM6: Chad H 6C 54
Swaffham Way N22 7G 33
Swaffield Rd. SW18 7K 117
Swain Cl. SW16 6F 137
Swain Rd. CR7: Thor H 5C 156
Swains Cl. UB7: W Dray 2A 92
Swain's La. N6 1E 64
Swainson Rd. W3 2B 98
Swains Rd. SW17 7D 136
Swain St. NW8 3C 4 (4C 82)
Swakeleys Dr. UB10: Ick 4C 56
Swakeleys Rd. UB10: Ick 4A 56
SWAKELEYS RDBT. 4A 56
Swalecliffe Rd.
DA17: Belv 5H 109
Swaledale Cl. N11 6K 31
Swallands Rd. SE6 3C 140
(not continuous)
Swallow Cl. DA8: Erith 1K 127
SE14 1K 121
WD23: Bush 1B 26
Swallow Ct. HA4: Ruis 1A 58
IG2: Ilf 5F 53
SE1 7D 14
(off Swan St.)
SE12 7J 123
W9 5J 81
(off Admiral Wlk.)
Swallow Dr. NW10 6K 61
UB5: N'olt 2E 76
Swallowfield NW1 2K 5
(off Munster Sq.)
Swallowfield Rd. SE7 5K 105
Swallowfield Way UB3: Hayes 2F 93
Swallow Gdns. SW16 5H 137
Swallow Ho. NW8 2C 82
(off Allitsen Rd.)
Swallow Pk. Cl. KT6: Surb 3F 163
Swallow Pas. W1 1K 11
(off Swallow Pl.)
Swallow Pl. E14 6B 86
(off Newell St.)
W1 1K 11 (6F 83)
Swallows Cl. SM1: Sutt 3J 165
Swallow St. E6 5C 88
W1 3B 12 (7G 83)
Swallowtail Ho. E20 5E 68
(off Sunrise Cl.)
THE SWAN 2E 170
Swanage Ct. N1 7E 66
(off Hertford Rd.)
Swanage Ho. SW8 7K 101
(off Dorset Rd.)
Swanage Rd. E4 7K 35
SW18 6A 118
Swanage Waye UB4: Yead 6A 76
Swan & Pike Rd. EN3: Enf L 1H 25
Swan App. E6 5C 88
Swanbourne Ho. NW8 3C 4
(off Capland St.)
Swanbridge Rd. DA7: Bex 1G 127
The Swan Cen. SW17 3K 135
Swan Cl. CR0: C'don 7E 156
E17 1A 50
KT12: Walt T 7H 147
TW13: Hanw 4C 130
Swan Ct. E1 3K 15
(off Star Pl.)
E14 6B 86
(off Agnes St.)
HA4: Ruis 7F 39
SW3 6D 16 (5C 100)
SW6 7J 99
(off Fulham Rd.)
TW7: Isle 3B 114
(off Swan St.)
Swandon Way SW18 4K 117
Swan Dr. NW9 2A 44
Swanfield St. E2 2J 9 (3F 85)
Swan Ho. E15 7G 69
(off Broadway)
EN3: Pond E 5D 24
N1 7D 66
(off Oakley Rd.)
Swan Island TW1: Twick 3A 132
Swan La. EC4 3F 15 (7D 84)
N4 1C 66
N20 3F 31
Swanley Ho. SE17 5E 102
(off Kinglake Est.)
Swanley Rd. DA16: Well 1C 126
Swan Mead SE1 3E 102
Swan M. CR4: Mitc 1D 154
RM7: Mawney 4H 55
SW6 1H 117
SW9 2K 119
Swann Ct. TW7: Isle 3A 114
(off South St.)
Swanne Ho. SE10 7E 104
(off Gloucester Cir.)
Swannell Way NW2 1F 63
Swan Pas. E1 3K 15
Swan Path KT1: King T 3F 151
Swan Pl. SW13 2B 116
Swan Rd. SE16 2J 103
SE18 3B 106
TW13: Hanw 5C 130
UB1: S'hall 6F 77
UB7: W Dray 2A 92
The Swan Sanctuary 6G 147
Swanscombe Ho. W11 1F 99
(off St Ann's Rd.)
Swanscombe Rd. W4 5A 98
W11 1F 99
Swansea Ct. E16 1F 107
(off Fishguard Way)
Swansea Rd. EN3: Pond E 4D 24
TW14: Felt 6E 110
Swansland Gdns. E17 1A 50
Swansmere Cl.
KT12: Walt T 7A 148
Swan St. SE1 7D 14 (3C 102)
TW7: Isle 3B 114
Swanton Ct. SE13 3D 122
Swanton Gdns. SW19 1F 135
Swanton Rd. DA8: Erith 7G 109
Swan Wlk.
SW3 7E 16 (6D 100)
TW17: Shep 7G 147
Swan Way EN3: Enf H 2E 24
Swanwick Cl. SW15 7B 116
Swan Yd. N1 6B 66
Sward Rd. BR5: St M Cry 6K 161
Swathling Ho. SW15 6B 116
(off Tunworth Cres.)
Swaton Rd. E3 4C 86
Swaylands Rd. DA17: Belv 6G 109
Swaythling Cl. N18 4C 34
Swedeland Ct. E1 6H 9
Swedenborg Gdns. E1 7H 85
Sweden Ga. SE16 3A 104
Swedish Quays SE16 3A 104
(not continuous)
Sweeney Cres. SE1 7K 15 (2F 103)
Sweetbriar Av.
SM5: Cars 1D 166
Sweet Briar Grn. N9 3A 34
Sweet Briar Gro. N9 3A 34
Sweet Briar Wlk. N18 4A 34
Sweetcroft La. UB10: Hil 7B 56
Sweetmans Av. HA5: Pinn 3B 40
Sweets Way N20 2G 31
Swell Ct. E17 6C 50
Swetenham Wlk. SE18 5G 107
Swete St. E13 2J 87
Sweyn Pl. SE3 2J 123
Swift Cen. CR0: Wadd 7K 167
Swift Cl. E17 7F 35
HA2: Harr 2F 59
SE28 7B 90
UB3: Hayes 6H 75
Swift Ct. SM2: Sutt 7K 165
Swift Ho. E3 1B 86
(off Old Ford Rd.)
NW6 2H 81
(off Albert Rd.)
Swift La. SE13 4G 123
Swift Lodge W9 5J 81
(off Admiral Wlk.)
Swift Rd. TW13: Hanw 3C 130
UB2: S'hall 3E 94
Swiftsden Way BR1: Broml 6G 141
Swiftstone Twr. SE10 3J 105
Swift St. SW6 1H 117
Swimmers La. E2 1F 85
Swinbrook Rd. W10 5G 81
Swinburne Ct. SE5 4D 120
(off Basingdon Way)
Swinburne Cres. CR0: C'don 6J 157
Swinburne Ho. E2 3J 85
(off Roman Rd.)
Swinburne Rd. SW15 4C 116
Swinderby Rd. HA0: Wemb 6E 60
Swindon Cl. IG3: Ilf 2J 71
Swindon Rd. TW6: H'row A 5E 110
Swindon St. W12 1D 98
Swinfield Cl. TW13: Hanw 3C 130
Swinford Gdns. SW9 3B 120
Swingate La. SE18 6J 107
Swingfield Ho. E9 1J 85
(off Templecombe Rd.)
Swinley Ho. NW1 1K 5
(off Redhill St.)
Swinnerton St. E9 5A 68
Swinson Ho. N11 5B 32
Swinton Cl. HA9: Wemb 1H 61
Swinton Pl. WC1 1G 7 (3K 83)
Swinton St. WC1 1G 7 (3K 83)
Swires Shaw BR2: Kes 4B 172
SWISS COTTAGE 7B 64
Swiss Cottage Sports Cen. 7B 64
Swiss Ct. W1 3D 12
Swiss Ter. NW6 7B 64
Switch Ho. E14 7F 87
Swithland Gdns. SE9 4E 142
Swyncombe Av. W5 4B 96
Swynford Gdns. NW4 4C 44
Sybil M. N4 6B 48
Sybil Phoenix Cl. SE8 5K 103
Sybil Thorndike Casson Ho.
SW5 5J 99
(off Kramer M.)
Sybourn St. E17 7B 50
Sycamore Av. DA15: Sidc 6K 125
E3 1B 86
UB3: Hayes 7G 75
W5 3D 96
Sycamore Cl. CR2: S Croy 5E 168
E16 4G 87
EN4: E Barn 6G 21
HA8: Edg 4D 28
KT19: Ewe 5H 163
N9 4B 34
SE9 2C 142
SM5: Cars 4D 166
TW13: Felt 3J 129
UB5: N'olt 1C 76
UB7: Yiew 7B 74
W3 1A 98

Sycamore Ct.—Teale St.

Sycamore Ct. DA8: Erith 5K 109
(off Sandcliff Rd.)
E7 6J 69
KT3: N Mald 3A 152
NW6 1J 81
(off Bransdale Cl.)
SE1 7G 15
(off Royal Oak Yd.)
TW4: Houn 4C 112
Sycamore Gdns. CR4: Mitc 2B 154
N15 4F 49
W6 2D 98
Sycamore Gro. KT3: N Mald 3K 151
NW9 7J 43
SE6 6E 122
SE20 1G 157
Sycamore Hill N11 6K 31
Sycamore Ho. BR2: Broml 2G 159
IG9: Buck H 2G 37
N2 2B 46
(off The Grange)
SE16 2K 103
(off Woodland Cres.)
W6 2D 98
Sycamore Lodge BR6: Orp 2K 173
TW16: Sun 7H 129
W8 3K 99
(off Stone Hall Pl.)
Sycamore M. DA8: Erith 5K 109
(off St John's Rd.)
SW4 3G 119
Sycamore Path E17 6D 50
(off Poplars Rd.)
Sycamore Pl. BR1: Broml 3E 160
Sycamore Rd. SW19 6E 134
Sycamore St. EC1 4C 8 (4C 84)
Sycamore Wlk. IG6: Ilf 4G 53
W10 4G 81
Sycamore Way CR7: Thor H 5A 156
TW11: Tedd 6C 132
Sydcote SE21 1C 138
SYDENHAM 4J 139
Sydenham Av. N21 5E 22
SE26 5H 139
Sydenham Cotts. SE12 2A 142
Sydenham Ct. CR0: C'don 1D 168
(off Sydenham Rd.)
Sydenham Hill SE23 1H 139
SE26 4F 139
Sydenham Hill Wood & Cox's Walk
Nature Reserve 2G 139
Sydenham Pk. SE26 3J 139
Sydenham Pk. Mans. SE26 3J 139
(off Sydenham Pk.)
Sydenham Pk. Rd. SE26 3J 139
Sydenham Pl. SE27 3B 138
Sydenham Ri. SE23 2H 139
Sydenham Rd.
CR0: C'don 1C 168
SE26 4J 139
Sydenham Stn. App. SE26 4J 139
Sydmons Ct. SE23 7J 121
Sydner M. N16 4F 67
Sydner Rd. N16 4F 67
Sydney Chapman Way
EN5: Barn 2C 20
Sydney Cl. SW3 4B 16 (4B 100)
Sydney Ct. UB4: Yead 4A 76
Sydney Cres. TW15: Ashf 6D 128
Sydney Gro. NW4 5E 44
Sydney M. SW3 4B 16 (4B 100)
Sydney Pl. SW7 4B 16 (4B 100)
Sydney Rd. DA6: Bex 4D 126
DA14: Sidc 4J 143
E11 6K 51
EN2: Enf 4J 23
IG6: Ilf 2G 53
IG8: Wfd G 4D 36
N8 4A 48
N10 1E 46
SE2 3C 108
SM1: Sutt 4J 165
SW20 2F 153
TW9: Rich 4E 114
TW11: Tedd 5K 131
TW14: Felt 1J 129
W13 1A 96
Sydney Russell Leisure Cen. 5E 72
Sydney St. SW3 5C 16 (5C 100)
Sylva Cotts. SE8 1C 122
Sylvana Cl. UB10: Hil 1B 74
Sylvan Av. N3 2J 45
N22 7E 32
NW7 6F 29
RM6: Chad H 6F 55
Sylvan Ct. N12 3E 30
NW6 1K 81
(off Abbey Rd.)
Sylvan Est. SE19 1F 157
Sylvan Gdns. KT6: Surb 7D 150
Sylvan Gro. NW2 4F 63
SE15 6H 103
Sylvan Hill SE19 1E 156
Sylvan Rd. E7 6K 69
E11 5J 51
E17 5C 50
IG1: Ilf 2G 71
SE19 1F 157
Sylvan Ter. SE15 6H 103
(off Sylvan Gro.)
Sylvan Wlk. BR1: Broml 3D 160
Sylvan Way BR4: W W'ck 4G 171
RM8: Dag 4B 72
Sylverdale Rd. CR0: C'don 3B 168
Sylvester Av. BR7: Chst 6D 142
Sylvester Path E8 6H 67
Sylvester Rd. E8 6H 67
E17 7B 50
HA0: Wemb 5C 60
N2 2A 46
Sylvestrian Leisure Cen. 4G 51
Sylvestrus Cl. KT1: King T 1G 151
Sylvia Ct. HA9: Wemb 7H 61
N1 2D 84
(off Wenlock St.)
Sylvia Gdns. HA9: Wemb 7H 61
Sylvia Pankhurst Ho.
RM10: Dag 3G 73
(off Wythenshawe Rd.)
Sylvia Pankhurst St. E16 6H 87
Symes M. NW1 2G 83
Symington Ho. SE1 3D 102
(off Deverell St.)
Symington M. E9 5K 67
Symister M. N1 2G 9
Symons Cl. SE15 2J 121
Symons St. SW3 4F 17 (4D 100)
Symphony Cl. HA8: Edg 7C 28
Symphony M. W10 3G 81
Syon Ct. E11 5K 51
Syon Ga. Way TW8: Bford 7A 96
Syon House 1C 114
Syon La. TW7: Isle 6J 95
Syon Lodge SE12 7J 123
Syon Pk. 1B 114
Syon Pk. Gdns. TW7: Isle 7K 95
Syringa Ho. SE4 3B 122

T

Tabard Ct. E14 6E 86
(off Lodore St.)
Tabard Gdn. Est. SE1 7E 14 (3D 102)
Tabard Ho. SE1 7F 15
(off Manciple St.)
Tabard St. SE1 6D 14 (2D 102)
Tabard Theatre 4A 98
The Tabernacle 6H 81
(off Powis Sq.)
Tabernacle Av. E13 4J 87
Tabernacle Gdns. E2 2J 9
(off Hackney Rd.)
Tabernacle St. EC2 4F 9 (4D 84)
Tableer Av. SW4 5G 119
Tabley Rd. N7 4J 65
Tabor Ct. SM3: Cheam 6G 165
Tabor Gdns. SM3: Cheam 6H 165
Tabor Gro. SW19 7H 135
Tabor Rd. W6 3D 98
Tachbrook Est. SW1 6C 18 (5H 101)
Tachbrook M. SW1 3A 18 (4G 101)
Tachbrook Rd. TW14: Felt 7H 111
UB2: S'hall 4B 94
UB7: W Dray 1A 92
Tachbrook St. SW1 4B 18 (4G 101)
Tack M. SE4 3C 122
Tadema Ho. NW8 4B 4
Tadema Rd. SW10 7A 100
Tadlow KT1: King T 3G 151
(off Washington Rd.)
Tadmor Cl. TW16: Sun 4H 147
Tadmor St. W12 1F 99
Tadworth Av. KT3: N Mald 4B 152
Tadworth Ho. SE1 7A 14
Tadworth Rd. NW2 2C 62
Taeping St. E14 4D 104
Taffeta Ho. E20 6E 68
(off De Coubertin St.)
Taff Ho. KT2: King T 1D 150
(off Henry Macaulay Av.)
Taffrail Ho. E14 5D 104
(off Burrells Wharf Sq.)
Taffy's How CR4: Mitc 3C 154
Taft Way E3 3D 86
Taggs Ho. KT1: King T 2D 150
(off Market Sq.)
Taggs Island TW12: Hamp 2H 149
Tagore Cl. HA3: W'stone 3K 41
Tagwright Ho. N1 1E 8
(off Westland Pl.)
Tailor Ho. WC1 4F 7
(off Colonnade)
Tailworth St. E1 6K 9
(off Chicksand St.)
Tait Ct. E3 1B 86
(off St Stephen's Rd.)
SW8 1J 119
(off Lansdowne Grn.)
Tait Ho. SE1 5K 13
(off Greet St.)
Tait Rd. CR0: C'don 7E 156
Tait Rd. Ind. Est. CR0: C'don 7E 156
(off Tait Rd.)
Tait St. E1 6H 85
Taj Apts. E1 5K 9
(off Brick La.)
Takeley Cl. RM5: Col R 2K 55
Takhar M. SW11 2C 118
Tala Cl. KT6: Surb 3F 163
Talacre Community Sports Cen. 6E 64
Talacre Rd. NW5 6E 64
Talbot Av. N2 3B 46
Talbot Cl. CR4: Mitc 4G 155
N15 4F 49
Talbot Ct. EC3 2F 15
NW9 3K 61
Talbot Cres. NW4 5C 44
Talbot Gdns. IG3: Ilf 2A 72
Talbot Gro. Ho. W11 6G 81
(off Lancaster Rd.)
Talbot Ho. E14 6D 86
(off Girauld St.)
N7 3A 66
SW11 3B 118
(off York Place)
Talbot Pl. SE3 2G 123
Talbot Rd. CR7: Thor H 4D 156
E6 2E 88
E7 4J 69
HA0: Wemb 6D 60
HA3: W'stone 2K 41
N6 6E 46
N15 4F 49
N22 2G 47
RM9: Dag 6F 73
SE22 4E 120
SM5: Cars 5E 166
TW2: Twick 1J 131
TW7: Isle 4A 114
TW15: Ashf 5A 128
UB2: S'hall 4C 94
W2 6H 81
W11 6H 81
(not continuous)
W13 1A 96
Talbot Sq. W2 1B 10 (6B 82)
Talbot Wlk. NW10 6A 62
W11 6G 81
(off St Mark's Rd.)
Talbot Yd. SE1 5E 14 (1D 102)
Talcott Path SW2 1A 138
Talehangers Cl. DA6: Bex 4D 126
Talfourd Pl. SE15 1F 121
Talfourd Rd. SE15 1F 121
Talgarth Mans. W14 5G 99
(off Talgarth Rd.)
Talgarth Rd. W6 5F 99
W14 5F 99
Talgarth Wlk. NW9 5A 44
Talia Ho. E14 3E 104
(off Manchester Rd.)
Talina Cen. SW6 1A 118
Talisman Cl. IG3: Ilf 1B 72
Talisman Sq. SE26 4G 139
Talisman Way
HA9: Wemb 3F 61
Tallack Cl. HA3: Hrw W 7D 26
Tallack Rd. E10 1B 68
Tall Elms Cl. BR2: Broml 5H 159
Talleyrand Ho. SE5 2C 120
(off Lilford Rd.)
Tallis Cl. E16 6K 87
Tallis Gro. SE7 6K 105
Tallis St. EC4 2K 13 (7A 84)
Tallis Vw. NW10 6K 61
Tallow Cl. RM9: Dag 7D 72
Tallow Rd. TW8: Bford 6C 96
Tall Trees SW16 3K 155
Talma Gdns. TW2: Twick 6J 113
Talmage Cl. SE23 7J 121
Talman Gro. HA7: Stan 6J 27
Talma Rd. SW2 4A 120
Talwin St. E3 3D 86
Tamar Cl. E3 1B 86
Tamar Ho. E14 2E 104
(off Plevna St.)
SE11 5K 19
(off Kennington La.)
Tamarind Ct. SE1 6K 15
W8 3K 99
(off Stone Hall Gdns.)
Tamarind Ho. SE15 7G 103
(off Reddins Rd.)
Tamarind Yd. E1 1G 103
(off Kennet St.)
Tamarisk Sq. W12 7B 80
Tamar Sq. IG8: Wfd G 6E 36
Tamar St. SE7 3C 106
Tamar Way N17 3F 49
Tamesis Gdns. KT4: Wor Pk 2A 164
Tamian Ind. Est. TW4: Houn 4A 112
Tamian Way TW4: Houn 4A 112
Tamworth Av. IG8: Wfd G 6B 36
Tamworth La. CR4: Mitc 2F 155
Tamworth Pk. CR4: Mitc 4F 155
Tamworth Pl. CR0: C'don 2C 168
Tamworth Rd. CR0: C'don 2B 168
Tamworth St. SW6 6J 99
Tancred Rd. N4 6B 48
Tandem Cen. 1B 154
Tandem Ho. E17 5B 50
(off Track St.)
Tandem Way SW19 1B 154
Tandridge Dr. BR6: Orp 1H 173
Tandridge Pl. BR6: Orp 1H 173
Tanfield Av. NW2 4B 62
Tanfield Rd. CR0: C'don 4C 168
Tangerine Ho. SE1 7F 15
(off Long La.)
Tangier Rd. TW10: Rich 4G 115
Tangleberry Cl. BR1: Broml 4D 160
Tangle Tree Cl. N3 2K 45
Tanglewood Cl. CR0: C'don 3J 169
HA7: Stan 2D 26
UB10: Hil 4C 74
Tanglewood Way TW13: Felt 3K 129
Tangley Gro. SW15 6B 116
Tangley Pk. Rd.
TW12: Hamp 6D 130
Tanglyn Av. TW17: Shep 5D 146
Tangmere N17 2D 48
(off Willan Rd.)
WC1 2G 7
(off Sidmouth St.)
Tangmere Cres. UB10: Uxb 1A 74
Tangmere Gdns. UB5: N'olt 2A 76
Tangmere Gro. KT2: King T 5D 132
Tangmere Way NW9 2A 44
Tan Ho. E9 5A 68
(off Sadler Pl.)
Tanhouse Fld. NW5 5H 65
(off Torriano Av.)
Tanhurst Ho. SW2 7K 119
(off Redlands Way)
Tanhurst Wlk. SE2 3D 108
(off Alsike Rd.)
Tankerton Ho's. WC1 2F 7
(off Tankerton St.)
Tankerton Rd. KT6: Surb 2F 163
Tankerton St.
WC1 2F 7 (3J 83)
Tankerton Ter. CR0: C'don 6K 155
Tankerville Ct. TW3: Houn 3G 113
Tankerville Rd. SW16 7H 137
Tankridge Rd. NW2 2D 62
Tanner Cl. NW9 2A 44
Tanner Ho. E1 5K 85
(off White Horse La.)
SE1 7H 15
(off Tanner St.)
The Tanneries E1 4J 85
(off Cephas Av.)
Tanner Point E13 1J 87
(off Pelly Rd.)
Tanners Cl. KT12: Walt T 6K 147
Tanners End La. N18 4K 33
Tanner's Hill SE8 1B 122
Tanners La. IG6: Ilf 3G 53
Tanners M. SE8 1B 122
(off Tanner's Hill)
Tanner St. IG11: Bark 6G 71
SE1 7H 15 (2E 102)
Tanners Yd. E2 2H 85
(off Treadway St.)
The Tannery SE1 3E 102
(Grange Rd.)
SE1 6H 15
(off Black Swan Yd.)
Tannery Cl. BR3: Beck 5K 157
RM10: Dag 3H 73
Tannery Ho. E1 5G 85
(off Deal St.)
Tannery Sq. SE1 3E 102
(off Tannery Way)
Tannery Way SE1 3F 103
Tannington Ter. N5 3B 66
Tannoy Sq. SE27 4D 138
Tannsfeld Rd. SE26 5K 139
Tansley Cl. N7 5H 65
Tanswell St. SE1 7J 13 (2A 102)
Tansy Cl. E6 6E 88
Tantallon Rd. SW12 1E 136
Tant Av. E16 6H 87
Tantony Gro. RM6: Chad H 3D 54
Tanworth Gdns. HA5: Pinn 2K 39
Tanyard Ho. TW8: Bford 7C 96
(off High St.)
Tan Yd. La. DA5: Bexl 7G 127
Tanza Rd. NW3 4D 64
Tapestry Apts. N1 1H 83
Tapestry Bldg. EC2 6H 9
(off New St.)
Tapestry Cl. SM2: Sutt 7K 165
Tapley Cl. E14 6E 86
Tapley Ho. SE1 7K 15
(off Wolseley St.)
Taplow NW3 7B 64
SE17 5D 102
(off Thurlow St.)
Taplow Ct. CR4: Mitc 4C 154
Taplow Ho. E2 2J 9
(off Palissy St.)
Taplow Rd. N13 4H 33
Taplow St. N1 1D 8 (2C 84)
Tapper Wlk. N1 1J 83
Tappesfield Rd. SE15 3J 121
Tapping Cl. KT2: King T 7G 133
Tapp St. E1 4H 85
Tapster St. EN5: Barn 3C 20
Tara Arts Cen. 1K 135
Tara Ct. BR3: Beck 2D 158
Tara Ho. E14 4C 104
(off Deptford Ferry Rd.)
Tara M. N8 6J 47
Taransay Wlk. N1 6D 66
Tarbert M. N15 5E 48
Tarbert Rd. SE22 5E 120
Tarbert Wlk. E1 7J 85
Tarbuck Ho. SE10 4G 105
(off Manilla Wlk.)
Target Cl. TW14: Felt 6G 111
Target Ho. W13 1B 96
(off Sherwood Cl.)
TARGET RDBT. 1D 76
Tariff Cres. SE8 4B 104
Tariff Rd. N17 6B 34
Tarleton Ct. N22 2A 48
Tarleton Gdns. SE23 2H 139
Tarling Cl. DA14: Sidc 3B 144
Tarling Rd. E16 6H 87
N2 2A 46
Tarling St. E1 6H 85
Tarling St. Est. E1 6J 85
Tarmac Way UB7: Harm 3C 174
Tarnbank EN2: Enf 5D 22
Tarnbrook Ct. SW1 4G 17
(off Holbein Pl.)
The Tarns NW1 1A 6
(off Varndell St.)
Tarn St. SE1 3C 102
Tarnwood Pk. SE9 7D 124
Tarplett Ho. SE14 6K 103
(off John Williams Cl.)
Tarquin Ho. SE26 4G 139
(off High Level Dr.)
Tarragon Cl. SE14 7A 104
Tarragon Ct. IG1: Ilf 2J 71
Tarragon Gro. SE26 6K 139
Tarranbrae NW6 7G 63
Tarrant Ho. E2 3J 85
(off Roman Rd.)
W14 3G 99
(off Russell Rd.)
Tarrant Pl. W1 6E 4 (5D 82)
Tarrington Cl. SW16 3H 137
Tartan Ho. E14 6E 86
(off Dee St.)
Tarver Rd. SE17 5B 102
Tarves Way SE10 7D 104
(Lit. Cottage Pl.)
SE10 7D 104
(Norman Rd.)
Taryn Gro. BR1: Broml 3D 160
Tash Pl. N11 5A 32
Tasker Cl. UB3: Harl 7E 92
Tasker Ho. E14 5B 86
(off Wallwood St.)
IG11: Bark 2H 89
Tasker Lodge W8 2J 99
(off Campden Hill)
Tasker Rd. NW3 5D 64
Tasman Ct. E14 4D 104
(off Westferry Rd.)
TW16: Sun 7G 129
Tasman Ho. E1 1H 103
(off Clegg St.)
Tasmania Ter. N18 6H 33
Tasman Rd. SW9 3J 119
Tasman Wlk. E16 6B 88
Tasso Rd. W6 6G 99
Tasso Yd. W6 6G 99
(off Tasso Rd.)
Tatam Rd. NW10 7K 61
Tatchbury Ho. SW15 6B 116
(off Tunworth Cres.)
Tate Apts. E1 6H 85
(off Sly St.)
Tate Britain 4E 18 (4J 101)
Tate Ho. E2 2K 85
(off Mace St.)
Tate Modern 4B 14 (1B 102)
Tate Rd. E16 1D 106
(not continuous)
SM1: Sutt 5J 165
Tatham Pl. NW8 2B 82
Tatnell Rd. SE23 6A 122
Tatsfield Ho. SE1 7F 15
(off Pardoner St.)
Tattersall Cl. SE9 5C 124
Tatton Cl. SM5: W'gton 1E 166
Tatton Cres. N16 7F 49
Tatum St. SE17 4D 102
Tauheed Cl. N4 2C 66
Taunton Av. SW20 2D 152
TW3: Houn 2G 113
Taunton Cl. DA7: Bex 2K 127
SM3: Sutt 1J 165
Taunton Dr. EN2: Enf 3F 23
N2 2A 46
Taunton Ho. W2 6A 82
(off Hallfield Est.)
Taunton M. NW1 4E 4 (4D 82)
Taunton Pl. NW1 3E 4 (4D 82)
Taunton Rd. SE12 5G 123
UB6: G'frd 1F 77
Taunton Way HA7: Stan 2E 42
Tavern Cl. SM5: Cars 7C 154
Tavern Ct. SE1 3C 102
(off New Kent Rd.)
Taverners Cl. W11 1G 99
Taverners Ct. E3 3A 86
(off Grove Rd.)
Taverner Sq. N5 4C 66
Taverners Way E4 1B 36
Tavern La. SW9 2A 120
Tavern Quay SE16 4A 104
Tavistock Av. E17 3K 49
NW7 7A 30
UB6: G'frd 2A 78
Tavistock Cl. N16 5E 66
TW18: Staines 7A 128
Tavistock Ct. CR0: C'don 1D 168
(off Tavistock Rd.)
WC1 3D 6
(off Tavistock Sq.)
WC2 7J 83
(off Tavistock Street)
Tavistock Cres. CR4: Mitc 4J 155
W11 5H 81
(not continuous)
Tavistock Gdns. IG3: Ilf 4J 71
Tavistock Ga. CR0: C'don 1D 168
Tavistock Gro. CR0: C'don 7D 156
Tavistock Ho. IG8: Wfd G 6K 37
WC1 3D 6 (4H 83)
Tavistock M. N19 3J 65
(off Tavistock Ter.)
W11 6H 81
Tavistock Pl. N14 6A 22
WC1 3E 6 (4J 83)
Tavistock Rd. BR2: Broml 4H 159
CR0: C'don 1D 168
DA16: Well 1C 126
E7 4H 69
E15 6H 69
E18 3J 51
HA8: Edg 1G 43
N4 6D 48
NW10 2B 80
SM5: Cars 1B 166
UB7: Yiew 1A 92
UB10: Ick 5F 57
W11 6H 81
(not continuous)
Tavistock Sq. WC1 3D 6 (4H 83)
Tavistock St. WC2 2F 13 (7J 83)
Tavistock Ter. N19 3H 65
Tavistock Twr. SE16 3A 104
Tavistock Wlk. SM5: Cars 1B 166
Tavistock Youth Cen. 2B 80
(off Tavistock Rd.)
Taviton St. WC1 3C 6 (4H 83)
Tavy Bri. SE2 2C 108
Tavy Cl. SE11 5K 19
Tawney Rd. SE28 7B 90
Tawny Cl. TW13: Felt 3J 129
W13 1B 96
Tawny Way SE16 4K 103
Tayben Av. TW2: Twick 6J 113
Tayberry Ho. E20 6D 68
(off Ravens Wlk.)
Taybridge Rd. SW11 3E 118
Tay Bldgs. SE1 7G 15
Tayburn Cl. E14 6E 86
Tay Ct. E2 3K 85
(off Meath Cres.)
SE1 7G 15
(off Decima St.)
Tayfield Cl. UB10: Ick 3F 57
Tay Ho. E3 2B 86
(off St Stephen's Rd.)
Tayler Ct. NW8 1B 82
Taylor Av. TW9: Kew 2H 115
Taylor Cl. BR6: Orp 4K 173
N17 7B 34
SE8 6B 104
TW3: Houn 1G 113
TW12: Hamp H 5G 131
Taylor Ct. SE20 2J 157
(off Elmers End Rd.)
Taylor Ho. E14 7C 86
(off Storehouse M.)
Taylor Pl. E3 2D 86
Taylor Rd. CR4: Mitc 7C 136
SM6: W'gton 5F 167
Taylors Bldgs. SE18 4F 107
Taylors Cl. DA14: Sidc 3K 143
Taylors Ct. TW13: Felt 2J 129
Taylors Grn. W3 6A 80
Taylor's La. SE26 4H 139
Taylors La. EN5: Barn 1C 20
NW10 6A 62
Taylors Mead NW7 5H 29
Taylors Yd. E1 4K 9
(off Brick La.)
Taymount Grange SE23 2J 139
Taymount Ri. SE23 2J 139
Tayport Cl. N1 7J 65
Tayside Ct. SE5 4D 120
Tayside Dr. HA8: Edg 3C 28
Taywood Rd. UB5: N'olt 4D 76
Tazzeta Ho. E20 5E 68
(off Victory Pde.)
Teak Cl. SE16 1A 104
Tealby Ct. N7 6K 65
Teal Cl. E16 5B 88
Teal Ct. E1 3K 15
(off Star Pl.)
NW10 6K 61
SE8 6B 104
(off Taylor Cl.)
SM6: W'gton 5G 167
Teal Dr. HA6: Nwood 1E 38
Teale St. E2 2G 85

Tealing Dr.—Thirlmere Ho.

Tealing Dr. KT19: Ewe 4K 163
Teal Pl. SM1: Sutt 5H 165
Teal St. SE10 3H 105
TeamSport Indoor Karting
Southwark 3H 103
Teamsport Karting
Edmonton 4E 34
Teasel Cl. CR0: C'don 1K 169
Teasel Cres. SE28 1J 107
Teasel Way E15 3G 87
Tea Trade Wharf SE1 6K 15
(off Shad Thames)
Tea Tree Cl. TW15: Ashf 5E 128
Tebworth Rd. N17 7A 34
The Technology Pk. NW9 3A 44
Teck Cl. TW7: Isle 2A 114
Tedder Cl. HA4: Ruis 5J 57
KT9: Chess 5C 162
UB10: Uxb 7B 56
Tedder Rd. CR2: Sels 7J 169
TEDDINGTON 5A 132
Teddington Bus. Pk.
TW11: Tedd 6K 131
(off Station Rd.)
TEDDINGTON LOCK 4B 132
Teddington Lock TW10: Ham 4B 132
Teddington Pk. TW11: Tedd 5K 131
Teddington Pk. Rd.
TW11: Tedd 4K 131
Teddington Pool & Fitness Cen.
5A 132
Teddington Riverside
TW11: Tedd 5B 132
Teddington Sports Cen. 6D 132
Ted Hennem Ho. RM10: Dag 3H 73
Ted Roberts Ho. E2 2H 85
(off Parmiter St.)
Tedworth Gdns. SW3 6E 16 (5D 100)
Tedworth Sq. SW3 6E 16 (5D 100)
The Tee W3 6A 80
Tees Av. UB6: G'frd 2J 77
Tees Ct. W7 6H 77
(off Hanway Rd.)
Teesdale Av. TW7: Isle 1A 114
Teesdale Cl. E2 2G 85
Teesdale Gdns. SE25 2E 156
TW7: Isle 1A 114
Teesdale Rd. E11 6H 51
Teesdale St. E2 2H 85
Teesdale Yd. E2 2H 85
(off Teesdale St.)
Teeswater Ct. DA18: Erith 3D 108
Teevan Cl. CR0: C'don 7G 157
Teevan Rd. CR0: C'don 1G 169
Tegan Cl. SM2: Sutt 7J 165
Teign M. SE9 2C 142
Teignmouth Cl. HA8: Edg 2F 43
SW4 4H 119
Teignmouth Gdns.
UB6: G'frd 2A 78
Teignmouth Pde. UB6: G'frd 2A 78
Teignmouth Rd. DA16: Well 2C 126
NW2 5F 63
Telcon Way SE10 4G 105
Telcote Way HA4: Ruis 7A 40
Telegraph Av. NW9 3A 44
SE10 4G 105
Telegraph Hill NW3 3K 63
Telegraph La. KT10: Clay 4A 162
Telegraph M. IG3: Ilf 1A 72
Telegraph Path BR7: Chst 5F 143
Telegraph Pl. E14 4D 104
Telegraph Rd. SW15 7D 116
Telegraph St. EC2 7E 8 (6D 84)
Telemann Sq. SE3 4K 123
Telephone Pl. SW6 6H 99
Telfer Cl. W3 2J 97
Telfer Ho. EC1 2B 8
Telferscot Rd. SW12 1H 137
Telford Av. SW2 1H 137
Telford Cl. E17 7A 50
SE19 6F 139
Telford Dr. KT12: Walt T 7A 148
Telford Ho. SE1 3C 102
(off Tiverton St.)
Telford Rd. N11 5B 32
NW9 6C 44
SE9 2H 143
TW2: Whitt 7E 112
UB1: S'hall 7F 77
W10 5G 81
Telfords Yd. E1 7G 85
Telford Ter. SW1 7A 18 (6G 101)
Telford Way UB4: Yead 5C 76
W3 5A 80
Telham Rd. E6 2E 88
Tell Gro. SE22 4F 121
Tellson Av. SE18 1B 124
Telscombe Cl. BR6: Orp 2J 173
Temair Ho. SE10 7D 104
(off Tarves Way)
Temeraire Pl. TW8: Bford 5F 97
Temeraire St. SE16 2J 103
Tempelhof Av. NW4 7E 44
Temperley Rd. SW12 7E 118
Templar Ct. NW8 2A 4
RM7: Mawney 4H 55
Templar Dr. SE28 6D 90
Templar Ho. E15 6F 69
(off Leyton Rd.)
HA2: Harr 2G 59
NW2 6H 63
Templar Pl. TW12: Hamp 7E 130
Templars Av. NW11 6H 45
Templars Cres. N3 2J 45
Templars Dr. HA3: Hrw W 6C 26
Templars Ho. E16 7F 89
(off University Way)
Templar St. SE5 2B 120
Temple Av. CR0: C'don 2B 170
EC4 2K 13 (7A 84)
N20 7G 21
RM8: Dag 1G 73
Temple Bar 1J 13 (6A 84)
Temple Bar Gate 1B 14
(off Paternoster Sq.)
Temple Chambers EC4 2K 13
Temple Cl. E11 7G 51
N3 2H 45
SE28 3G 107
Templecombe Rd. E9 1J 85
Templecombe Way SM4: Mord 5G 153
Temple Ct. E1 5K 85
(off Rectory Sq.)
SW8 7J 101
(off Thorncroft St.)
Templecroft TW15: Ashf 6F 129
Temple Dwellings E2 2H 85
(off Temple St.)
TEMPLE FORTUNE 5H 45
Temple Fortune Hill NW11 5J 45
Temple Fortune La. NW11 6H 45
Temple Fortune Pde. NW11 5H 45
Temple Gdns. EC4 2J 13
N21 2G 33
NW11 6H 45
RM8: Dag 3D 72
Temple Gro. EN2: Enf 2G 23
NW11 6J 45
Temple Hall Ct. E4 2A 36
Temple La. EC4 1K 13 (6A 84)
Templeman Rd. W7 5K 77
Temple Mead Cl.
HA7: Stan 6G 27
Templemead Cl. W3 6A 80
Templemead Ho. E9 4A 68
TEMPLE MILLS 4D 68
Temple Mills La. E10 4D 68
E15 5E 68
E20 4E 68
Temple Pde. EN5: New Bar 7G 21
(off Netherlands Rd.)
Temple Pk. UB8: Hil 3C 74
Temple Pl. WC2 2H 13 (7K 83)
Temple Rd. CR0: C'don 4D 168
E6 1C 88
N8 4K 47
NW2 4E 62
TW3: Houn 4F 113
TW9: Rich 2F 115
W4 3J 97
W5 3D 96
Temple Sheen SW14 4J 115
Temple Sheen Rd. SW14 4H 115
Temple St. E2 2H 85
Temple Ter. N22 2A 48
(off Vincent Rd.)
Templeton Av. E4 4H 35
Templeton Cl. N15 6D 48
N16 5E 66
SE19 1D 156
Templeton Ct. EN3: Enf W 1D 24
Templeton Pl. SW5 4J 99
Templeton Rd. N15 6D 48
Temple Way SM1: Sutt 3B 166
Temple W. M. SE11 3B 102
Templewood W13 5B 78
Templewood Av. NW3 3K 63
Templewood Gdns. NW3 3K 63
Templewood Point NW2 2H 63
(off Granville Rd.)
Temple Yd. E2 2H 85
(off Temple St.)
Tempo Ho. UB5: N'olt 3B 76
Tempsford Cl. EN2: Enf 4H 23
Tempsford Ct. HA1: Harr 6K 41
Tempus Apts. EC1 1A 8
(off Goswell Rd.)
Tempus Ct. E18 1J 51
Tempus Wharf SE16 2G 103
(off Bermondsey Wall W.)
Temsford Cl. HA2: Harr 2G 41
Tenbury Cl. E7 5B 70
Tenbury Ct. SW2 1H 137
Tenby Av. HA3: Kenton 2B 42
Tenby Cl. N15 4F 49
RM6: Chad H 6E 54
Tenby Ct. E17 5A 50
Tenby Gdns. UB5: N'olt 6E 58
Tenby Ho. UB3: Harl 3E 92
W2 6A 82
(off Hallfield Est.)
Tenby Mans. W1 5H 5
(off Nottingham St.)
Tenby Rd. DA16: Well 1D 126
E17 5A 50
EN3: Pond E 4D 24
HA8: Edg 1F 43
RM6: Chad H 6E 54
Tench St. E1 1H 103
Tenda Rd. SE16 4H 103
Tendring Way
RM6: Chad H 5C 54
Tenham Av. SW2 1H 137
Tenison Ct. W1 2A 12 (7G 83)
Tenison Way SE1 5J 13
Tenniel Cl. W2 7A 82
Tennis Ct. La. KT8: E Mos 3K 149
Tennison Rd. SE25 4F 157
Tennis St. SE1 6E 14 (2D 102)
Tenniswood Rd.
EN1: Enf 1K 23
Tennyson CR0: C'don 1C 168
Tennyson Av. E11 7J 51
E12 7C 70
KT3: N Mald 5D 152
NW9 3J 43
TW1: Twick 1K 131
Tennyson Cl. DA16: Well 1J 125
EN3: Pond E 5E 24
TW14: Felt 6H 111
Tennyson Ct. NW1 4E 4
(off Dorset Sq.)
Tennyson Ho. DA17: Belv 5F 109
N8 3J 47
(off Boyton Cl.)
SE17 5C 102
(off Browning St.)
Tennyson Mans. SW3 7C 16
(off Lordship Pl.)
W14 6H 99
(off Queen's Club Gdns.)
Tennyson Rd. E10 1D 68
E15 7G 69
E17 6B 50
NW6 1H 81
NW7 5H 29
SE20 7K 139
SW19 6A 136
TW3: Houn 2G 113
TW15: Ashf 5A 128
W7 7K 77
Tennyson St. SW8 2F 119
Tenpin
Acton 4G 79
Bexleyheath 4F 127
Croydon 2K 167
Feltham 2K 129
Kingston upon Thames 2E 150
(within The Rotunda Cen.)
Tensing Rd. UB2: S'hall 3E 94
Tentelow La. UB2: S'hall 3E 94
Tenterden Cl. NW4 3F 45
SE9 4D 142
Tenterden Dr. NW4 3F 45
Tenterden Gdns.
CR0: C'don 7G 157
NW4 3F 45
Tenterden Gro. NW4 3F 45
Tenterden Ho. SE17 5E 102
(off Surrey Gro.)
Tenterden Rd. CR0: C'don 7G 157
N17 7A 34
RM8: Dag 2F 73
Tenterden St. W1 1K 11 (6F 83)
Tenter Ground E1 6J 9 (5F 85)
Tent Peg La. BR5: Pet W 5G 161
Tent St. E1 4H 85
Tenzing Ct. E14 5D 86
(off Hillary M.)
Tequila Wharf E14 6A 86
Tera 40 UB6: G'frd 7G 59
Terborch Way SE22 5E 120
Tercelet Ter. NW3 4A 64
Teredo St. SE16 3K 103
Terence Ct. DA17: Belv 6F 109
(off Nuxley Rd.)
Terence McMillan Stadium 4A 88
Terence Messenger Twr. E10 2D 68
(off Alpine Rd.)
Teresa M. E17 4C 50
Teresa Wlk. N10 5F 47
Terling Cl. E11 3H 69
Terling Ho. W10 5E 80
(off Sutton Way)
Terling Rd. RM8: Dag 2G 73
Terling Wlk. N1 1C 84
(off Popham St.)
TERMINAL 4 RDBT. 6E 110
TERMINAL 5 RDBT. 5C 174
Terminal Ho.
HA7: Stan 5J 27
Terminus Pl. SW1 2K 17 (3F 101)
The Terrace E2 3J 85
(off Old Ford Rd.)
E4 3B 36
(off Newgate St.)
EC4 1K 13
IG8: Wfd G 6D 36
N3 2H 45
NW6 1J 81
SE8 4B 104
(off Longshore)
SE23 7A 122
SW13 2A 116
Terrace Apts. N5 5A 66
Terrace Gdns. SW13 2B 116
Terrace La. TW10: Rich 6E 114
Terrace Rd. E9 7J 67
E13 2J 87
KT12: Walt T 7J 147
The Terraces E2 2G 85
(off Garner St.)
NW8 2B 82
(off Queen's Ter.)
Terrace Wlk. RM9: Dag 5E 72
SW11 7H 17 (7D 100)
Terrano Ho. TW9: Kew 7H 97
Terrapin Rd. SW17 3F 137
Terretts Pl. N1 7B 66
(off Upper St.)
Terrick Rd. N22 1J 47
Terrick St. W12 6D 80
Terrilands HA5: Pinn 3D 40
Territorial Ho. SE11 4K 19
Terront Rd. N15 4C 48
Terry Spinks Pl. E16 5H 87
(off Barking Rd.)
Tersha St. TW9: Rich 4F 115
Tesla Ct. W3 2A 98
Tessa Sanderson Pl. SW8 3F 119
(off Daley Thompson Way)
Tessa Sanderson Way
UB6: G'frd 5H 59
Testerton Rd. W11 7F 81
(off Hurstway Wlk.)
Testerton Wlk. W11 7F 81
Testwood Ct. W7 7J 77
Tetbury Pl. N1 1B 84
Tetcott Rd. SW10 7A 100
(not continuous)
Tetherdown N10 3E 46
Tetty Way BR1: Broml 2J 159
Tevatree Ho. SE1 5G 103
(off Old Kent Rd.)
Teversham La. SW8 1J 119
Teviot Cl. DA16: Well 1B 126
Teviot Est. E14 5D 86
Teviot St. E14 5E 86
Tewkesbury Av.
HA5: Pinn 5C 40
SE23 1H 139
Tewkesbury Cl.
EN4: E Barn 4G 21
N15 6D 48
Tewkesbury Gdns. NW9 3H 43
Tewkesbury Rd. N15 6D 48
SM5: Cars 1B 166
W13 1A 96
Tewkesbury Ter. N11 6B 32
Tewson Rd. SE18 5J 107
Texryte Ho. N1 1D 84
(off Southgate Rd.)
Textile Ho. E1 5K 85
(off Duckett St.)
Teynham Av. EN1: Enf 6J 23
Teynham Ct. BR3: Beck 3D 158
Teynham Grn. BR2: Broml 5J 159
Teynton Ter. N17 1C 48
Thackeray Av. N17 2G 49
Thackeray Cl. SW19 7F 135
TW7: Isle 2A 114
UB8: Hil 6D 74
Thackeray Ct. NW6 7A 64
(off Fairfax Rd.)
SW3 5E 16
(off Elystan Pl.)
W5 6F 79
(off Hanger Va. La.)
W14 3G 99
(off Blythe Rd.)
Thackeray Dr. RM6: Chad H 7A 54
Thackeray Ho. WC1 3E 6
Thackeray Lodge
TW14: Bedf 6F 111
Thackeray M. E8 6G 67
Thackeray Rd. E6 2B 88
SW8 2F 119
Thackeray St. W8 3K 99
Thackery Ct. EC1 5A 8
(off Turnmill St.)
Thackrah Cl. N2 2A 46
(off Simms Gdns.)
Thakeham Cl. SE26 4H 139
Thalia Cl. SE10 6F 105
Thalia Ct. E8 7F 67
(off Albion Dr.)
Thame Rd. SE16 2K 103
Thames Av. KT4: Wor Pk 1E 164
RM9: Dag, Rain 4H 91
SW10 1A 118
UB6: G'frd 2K 77
Thames Bank SW14 2J 115
Thamesbank Pl. SE28 6C 90
Thames Barrier 2B 106
Thames Barrier Ind. Area
SE18 3B 106
(off Faraday Way)
Thames Barrier Info. Cen. 3B 106
Thames Barrier Pk. 2A 106
Thamesbrook SW3 6C 16
Thames Circ. E14 4C 104
Thames Cl. TW12: Hamp 2F 149
Thames Cotts. KT7: T Ditt 6B 150
Thames Ct. KT8: W Mole 2F 149
NW6 2H 81
(off Albert Rd.)
SE15 7F 103
(off Daniel Gdns.)
W7 6J 77
(off Hanway Rd.)
Thames Cres. W4 7A 98
THAMES DITTON 6A 150
Thames Ditton Youth Cen. 7A 150
Thames Dr. HA4: Ruis 6E 38
Thames Exchange Bldg. EC4 3D 14
Thames Eyot TW1: Twick 1A 132
Thamesfield Ct. TW17: Shep 7E 146
Thamesfield M. TW17: Shep 7E 146
Thamesgate Cl. TW10: Ham 4B 132
Thames Gateway RM9: Dag 2F 91
RM13: Rain 2F 91
Thames Gateway Pk.
RM9: Dag 3F 91
Thames Haven KT6: Surb 5D 150
Thames Hgts. SE1 6J 15
(off Gainsford St.)
Thameshill Av. RM5: Col R 2J 55
Thames Ho. EC4 2D 14
(off Queen St. Pl.)
KT1: King T 4D 150
(off Surbiton Rd.)
SW1 4J 101
(off Millbank)
Thameside KT8: W Mole 3F 149
TW11: Tedd 7D 132
Thameside Ind. Est. E16 2B 106
Thameside Pl. KT1: Hamp W 1D 150
Thameside Wlk. SE28 6A 90
Thames Innovation Cen.
DA18: Erith 2F 109
THAMES LOCK 3A 148
THAMESMEAD 1B 108
Thamesmead KT12: Walt T 6J 147
THAMESMEAD CENTRAL 1A 108
THAMESMEAD EAST 2F 109
THAMESMEAD NORTH 6D 90
Thames Mdw. KT8: W Mole 2E 148
TW17: Shep 7F 147
THAMESMEAD SOUTH 2D 108
THAMESMEAD SOUTH WEST 2K 107
THAMESMEAD WEST 3G 107
Thamesmere Dr. SE28 7A 90
Thamesmere Leisure Cen. 7A 90
Thames Path SE10 3J 105
Thames Pl. SW15 3F 117
Thames Point SW6 2A 118
Thamespoint TW11: Tedd 7D 132
Thames Police Mus. 1H 103
Thames Quay E14 2D 104
SW10 1A 118
(off Chelsea Harbour)
Thames Reach KT1: Hamp W 1D 150
SE28 2J 107
W6 6E 98
(off Rainville Rd.)
Thames Rd. E16 1B 106
IG11: Bark 3K 89
W4 6G 97
Thames Rd. Ind. Est. E16 1B 106
Thames Side KT1: King T 1D 150
KT7: T Ditt 6B 150
Thames St. KT1: King T 2D 150
KT12: Walt T 7H 147
SE10 6D 104
TW12: Hamp 1F 149
TW16: Sun 4J 147
Thames Tunnel Mills SE16 2J 103
Thamesvale Cl. TW3: Houn 3E 112
Thames Vw. IG1: Ilf 2G 71
(off Axon Pl.)
Thamesview Bus. Cen.
RM13: Rain 5K 91
Thamesview Ho's.
KT12: Walt T 6J 147
Thames Vw. Lodge IG11: Bark 3J 89
Thames Village W4 1J 115
Thames Wlk. KT12: Walt T 7J 147
(off Manor Rd.)
SW11 7C 100
Thames Wharf Studios W6 6E 98
(off Rainville Rd.)
Thanescroft Gdns. CR0: C'don 3E 168
Thanet Ct. W3 6G 79
Thanet Dr. BR2: Kes 3B 172
Thanet Ho. CR0: C'don 4C 168
(off Coombe Rd.)
WC1 2E 6
(off Thanet St.)
Thanet Lodge NW2 6G 63
(off Mapesbury Rd.)
Thanet Pl. CR0: C'don 4C 168
Thanet Rd. DA5: Bexl 7G 127
Thanet St. WC1 2E 6 (3J 83)
Thanet Wharf SE8 6D 104
(off Copperas St.)
Thane Vs. N7 3K 65
Thane Works N7 3K 65
Thanington Ct. SE9 6J 125
Thant Cl. E10 3D 68
Tharp Rd. SM6: W'gton 5H 167
Thatcham Ct. N20 7F 21
Thatcham Gdns. N20 7F 21
Thatcher Cl. UB7: W Dray 2A 92
Thatchers Way TW7: Isle 5H 113
Thatches Gro. RM6: Chad H 4E 54
Thavie's Inn EC4 7K 7 (6A 84)
Thaxted Ct. N1 1F 9
(off Murray Gro.)
Thaxted Ho. RM10: Dag 7H 73
SE16 4J 103
(off Abbeyfield Est.)
Thaxted Pl. SW20 7F 135
Thaxted Rd. IG9: Buck H 1H 37
SE9 3G 143
Thaxton Pl. E4 1A 36
Thaxton Rd. W14 6H 99
Thayers Farm Rd.
BR3: Beck 1A 158
Thayer St. W1 6H 5 (5E 82)
The Theatre 5C 68
Theatre Bldg. E3 3C 86
(off Paton Cl.)
Theatre Pl. SE8 7C 104
(off Speedwell Ct.)
Theatre-Rites 7A 14
(off Blackfriars Rd.)
Theatre Royal
Drury Lane 2G 13
(off Catherine St.)
Haymarket 3D 12
(off Haymarket)
Stratford East 7F 69
Theatre Sq. E15 6F 69
Theatre St. SW11 3D 118
Theatre Vw. Apts. SE1 6K 13
(off Short St.)
Theatro Technis 1G 83
(off Crowndale Rd.)
Theatro Twr. SE8 6C 104
Theberton St. N1 1A 84
Theed St. SE1 5K 13 (1A 102)
Thelbridge Ho. E3 3D 86
(off Bruce Rd.)
Thelma Gdns. SE3 1B 124
Thelma Gro. TW11: Tedd 6A 132
Theobald Cres. HA3: Hrw W 1G 41
Theobald Rd. CR0: C'don 2B 168
E17 7B 50
Theobalds Av. N12 4F 31
Theobalds Ct. N4 3C 66
Theobald's Rd. WC1 5G 7 (5K 83)
Theobald St. SE1 3D 102
Theodora Way HA5: Eastc 3H 39
Theodor Ct. NW9 2K 43
Theodore Ct. SE13 6F 123
Theodore Rd. SE13 6F 123
Therapia La. CR0: Bedd 7H 155
CR0: C'don 6J 155
Therapia Rd. SE22 6J 121
Theresa Rd. W6 4C 98
Therfield Ct. N4 2C 66
Thermopylae Ga. E14 4D 104
Theseus Wlk. N1 1B 8
Thesiger Rd. SE20 7K 139
Thessaly Ho. SW8 7G 101
(off Thessaly Rd.)
Thessaly Rd. SW8 7G 101
(not continuous)
Thesus Ho. E14 6E 86
(off Blair St.)
Thetford Cl. N13 6G 33
Thetford Gdns. RM9: Dag 7E 72
Thetford Ho. SE1 7J 15
(off St Saviour's Est.)
Thetford Rd. KT3: N Mald 6K 151
RM9: Dag 7D 72
TW15: Ashf 4A 128
Thetis Ter. TW9: Kew 6G 97
Theven St. E1 4J 85
Theydon Gro. IG8: Wfd G 6F 37
Theydon Rd. E5 2J 67
Theydon St. E17 7B 50
The Thicket UB7: Yiew 6A 74
Thicket Cres. SM1: Sutt 4A 166
Thicket Gro. RM9: Dag 6C 72
SE20 7G 139
Thicket Rd. SE20 7G 139
SM1: Sutt 4A 166
Thimble Cres. SM6: W'gton 2E 166
Third Av. E12 4C 70
E13 3J 87
E17 5C 50
EN1: Enf 5A 24
HA9: Wemb 2D 60
RM6: Chad H 6C 54
RM10: Dag 1H 91
UB3: Hayes 1H 93
W3 1B 98
W10 3G 81
Third Cl. KT8: W Mole 4G 149
Third Cross Rd.
TW2: Twick 2H 131
Third Way HA9: Wemb 4H 61
Thirleby Rd. HA8: Edg 1K 43
NW7 5B 30
SW1 2B 18 (3G 101)
Thirlestane Ct. N10 2E 46
Thirlmere NW1 1K 5
(off Cumberland Mkt.)
Thirlmere Av. UB6: G'frd 3C 78
Thirlmere Gdns. HA9: Wemb 1C 60
Thirlmere Ho. N16 4D 66
(off Howard Rd.)
TW7: Isle 5K 113

Thirlmere Ri.—Tirlemont Rd.

Thirlmere Ri. BR1: Broml 6H 141
Thirlmere Rd. DA7: Bex 1J 127
N10 1F 47
SW16 4H 137
Thirsk Cl. UB5: N'olt 6E 58
Thirsk Rd. CR4: Mitc 7E 136
SE25 4D 156
SW11 3E 118
Thirty Casson Sq. *SE1* 5H 13
(off Casson Sq.)
Thirza Ho. *E1* 6J 85
(off Devonport St.)
Thistlebrook SE2 3C 108
Thistlebrook Ind. Est. SE2 3C 108
Thistle Ct. SE12 2J 141
Thistlecroft Gdns.
HA7: Stan 1D 42
Thistledene KT7: T Ditt 6J 149
Thistledene Av. HA2: Harr 3C 58
Thistlefield Cl.
DA5: Bexl 1D 144
Thistle Gro. SW10 6A 16 (5A 100)
Thistle Ho. *E14* 6E 86
(off Dee St.)
Thistlemead BR7: Chst 2F 161
Thistleton Ho. NW9 3B 44
Thistlewaite Rd. E5 3H 67
Thistlewood Cl. N7 2K 65
Thistleworth Cl. TW7: Isle 7H 95
Thistleworth Marine *TW7: Isle* 4B 114
(off Railshead Rd.)
Thistley Cl. N12 6H 31
Thistley Ct. SE8 6D 104
Thomas a Beckett Cl.
HA0: Wemb 4K 59
Thomas Baines Rd. SW11 3B 118
Thomas Barnardo Way IG6: Ilf 3G 53
Thomas Burt Ho. *E2* 3H 85
(off Canrobert St.)
Thomas Coulter House *E16* 2K 105
(off Shipwright Street)
Thomas Ct. IG6: Ilf 4G 53
Thomas Cribb M. E6 6E 88
Thomas Darby Ct. *W11* 6G 81
(off Lancaster Rd.)
Thomas Dean Rd. SE26 4B 140
Thomas Dinwiddy Rd. SE12 2K 141
Thomas Doyle St.
SE1 7A 14 (3B 102)
Thomas Dr. UB8: Uxb 6A 56
Thomas Earle Ho. *W14* 4H 99
(off Warwick La.)
Thomas England Ho. *RM7: Rom* 6K 55
(off Waterloo Gdns.)
Thomas Frye Ct. *E15* 2D 86
(off High St.)
Thomas Fyre Dr. E3 2C 86
Thomas Hardy Ho. N22 7E 32
Thomas Hardy M. SW16 5G 137
Thomas Hewlett Ho.
HA1: Harr 4J 59
Thomas Hollywood Ho. *E2* 2J 85
(off Approach Rd.)
Thomas Ho. SM2: Sutt 7K 165
Thomas Jacomb Pl. E17 4B 50
Thomas Joseph Ho. *SE4* 5K 121
(off St Norbert Rd.)
Thomas La. SE6 7C 122
Thomas Lodge E17 5D 50
Thomas More Highwalk *EC2* 6C 8
(off Aldersgate St.)
Thomas More Ho. EC2 6C 8
HA4: Ruis 1G 57
Thomas More Sq. E1 7G 85
Thomas More St. E1 7G 85
Thomas More Way N2 3A 46
Thomas Neal's Cen. 1E 12 (6J 83)
Thomas Pl. W8 3K 99
Thomas Rd. E14 6B 86
Thomas Rd. Ind. Est. E14 5C 86
(not continuous)
Thomas Spencer Hall of Residence
SE18 4E 106
(off Grand Depot Rd.)
Thomas St. SE18 4F 107
Thomas Tallis Sports Cen. 3K 123
Thomas Twr. *E8* 6F 67
(off Dalston Sq.)
Thomas Turner Path
CR0: C'don 2C 168
(off George St.)
Thomas Wall Cl. SM1: Sutt 5K 165
Thomas Watson Cott. Homes
EN5: Barn 4B 20
(off Leecroft Rd.)
Thompson Av. TW9: Rich 3G 115
Thompson Cl. IG1: Ilf 2G 71
SM3: Sutt 1J 165
Thompson Ho. *SE14* 6K 103
(off John Williams Cl.)
W10 4G 81
(off Wornington Rd.)
Thompson Rd. RM9: Dag 3F 73
SE22 6F 121
TW3: Houn 4F 113
UB10: Uxb 7A 56
Thompson's Av. SE5 7C 102
Thomson Cres. CR0: C'don 1A 168
Thomson Ho. *E14* 6C 86
(off Saracen St.)
SE17 4E 102
(off Tatum St.)
SW1 6D 18
UB1: S'hall 7C 76
(off The Broadway)
Thomson Rd. HA3: W'stone 3J 41
Thonrey Cl. NW9 3B 44
Thorburn Ho. *SW1* 7F 11
(off Kinnerton St.)
Thorburn Sq. SE1 4G 103
Thorburn Way SW19 1B 154
Thoresby St. N1 1D 8 (3C 84)
Thorkhill Gdns.
KT7: T Ditt 1A 162
Thorkhill Rd. KT7: T Ditt 1A 162
Thornaby Gdns. N18 6B 34
Thornaby Ho. *E2* 3H 85
(off Canrobert St.)
Thorn Apts. *E3* 5C 86
(off St Paul's Way)
Thorn Av. WD23: B Hea 1B 26
Thornbill Ho. *SE15* 7G 103
(off Bird in Bush Rd.)
Thornbury *NW4* 4D 44
(off Prince of Wales Cl.)
Thornbury Av. TW7: Isle 7H 95
Thornbury Cl. N16 5E 66
NW7 7A 30
Thornbury Ct. *CR2: S Croy* 5D 168
(off Blunt Rd.)
TW7: Isle 7J 95
W11 7J 81
(off Chepstow Vs.)
Thornbury Lodge EN2: Enf 3G 23
Thornbury Rd. SW2 6J 119
TW7: Isle 7H 95
Thornbury Sq. N6 1G 65
Thornbury Way E17 1B 50
Thornby Rd. E5 3J 67
Thorncliffe Rd. SW2 6J 119
UB2: S'hall 5D 94
Thorn Cl. BR2: Broml 6E 160
UB5: N'olt 3D 76
Thorncombe Rd. SE22 5E 120
Thorncroft Rd. SM1: Sutt 5K 165
Thorncroft St. SW8 7J 101
Thorndean St. SW18 2A 136
Thorndene Av. N11 1K 31
Thorndike Av. UB5: N'olt 1B 76
Thorndike Cl. SW10 7A 100
Thorndike Ho. *SW1* 5C 18
(off Vauxhall Bri. Rd.)
Thorndike Rd. N1 6D 66
Thorndike St. SW1 4C 18 (4H 101)
Thorndon Cl. BR5: St P 2K 161
Thorndon Gdns.
KT19: Ewe 5A 164
Thorndon Rd. BR5: St P 2K 161
Thorne Cl.
DA8: Erith 6H 109
E11 4F 69
E16 6J 87
KT10: Clay 7A 162
TW15: Ashf 7E 128
Thorne Ho. *E2* 3J 85
(off Roman Rd.)
E14 3E 104
(off Launch St.)
Thorneloe Gdns. CR0: Wadd 5A 168
Thorne Pas. SW13 2A 116
Thorne Rd. SW8 7J 101
Thornes Cl. BR3: Beck 3E 158
Thornes Ho. *SW11* 7H 101
(off Ponton Rd.)
Thorne St. SW13 3A 116
Thornet Wood Rd.
BR1: Broml 3E 160
Thornewill Ho. *E1* 7J 85
(off Cable St.)
Thorney Ct. *W8* 2A 100
(off Palace Ga.)
Thorney Cres. SW11 7B 100
Thorneycroft Cl. KT12: Walt T 6A 148
Thorneycroft Rd. N20 2G 31
Thorney Hedge Rd. W4 4H 97
Thorney St. SW1 3E 18 (4J 101)
Thornfield Av. NW7 1G 45
Thornfield Ct. NW7 7B 30
Thornfield Ho. *E14* 7C 86
(off Rosefield Gdns.)
Thornfield Pde. *NW7* 7B 30
(off Holders Hill Rd.)
Thornfield Rd. W12 2D 98
(not continuous)
Thornford Rd. SE13 5E 122
Thorngate Rd. W9 4J 81
Thorngrove Rd. E13 1K 87
Thornham Gro. E15 5F 69
Thornham Ind. Est.
E15 5F 69
Thornham St. SE10 6D 104
Thornhaugh M. WC1 4D 6 (4H 83)
Thornhaugh St. WC1 4D 6 (4H 83)
Thornhill Av. KT6: Surb 2E 162
SE18 7J 107
THORNHILL BRI. 2K 83
(off Caledonian Rd.)
Thornhill Bri. Wharf N1 1K 83
Thornhill Cres. N1 7K 65
Thornhill Gdns. E10 2D 68
IG11: Bark 7J 71
Thornhill Gro. N1 7K 65
Thornhill Ho. *W4* 5A 98
(off Wood St.)
Thornhill Ho's. *N1* 7A 66
(off Thornhill Rd.)
Thornhill M. SW15 4H 117
Thornhill Rd.
CR0: C'don 7C 156
E10 2D 68
KT6: Surb 2E 162
N1 7A 66
UB10: Ick 4B 56
Thornhill Sq. N1 7K 65
Thornhill Way TW17: Shep 5C 146
Thornicroft Ho. *SW9* 2K 119
(off Stockwell Rd.)
Thornlaw Rd. SE27 4A 138
Thornley Cl. N17 7B 34
Thornley Dr. HA2: Harr 2F 59
Thornley Pl. SE10 5G 105
Thornsbeach Rd. SE6 1E 140
Thornsett Pl. SE20 2H 157
Thornsett Rd. SE20 2H 157
SW18 1K 135
Thornsett Ter. *SE20* 2H 157
(off Croydon Rd.)
Thorn Ter. SE15 3J 121
Thornton Av. CR0: C'don 6K 155
SW2 1H 137
UB7: W Dray 3B 92
W4 4A 98
Thornton Cl. UB7: W Dray 3B 92
Thornton Dene BR3: Beck 2C 158
Thornton Gdns. SW12 1H 137
THORNTON HEATH 4C 156
Thornton Heath Leisure Cen. 4C 156
THORNTON HEATH POND 5A 156
Thornton Hill SW19 7G 135
Thornton Ho. *SE17* 4E 102
(off Townsend St.)
Thornton Pl. W1 5F 5 (5D 82)
Thornton Rd. BR1: Broml 5J 141
CR0: C'don 7K 155
CR7: Thor H 7K 155
DA17: Belv 4H 109
E11 2F 69
EN5: Barn 3B 20
IG1: Ilf 4F 71
N18 3D 34
SM5: Cars 1B 166
SW12 7H 119
SW14 4K 115
SW19 6F 135
Thornton Rd. E. SW19 6F 135
Thornton Rd. Ind. Est.
CR0: C'don 6K 155
Thornton Row CR7: Thor H 5A 156
Thornton's Farm Av.
RM7: Rush G 1J 73
Thornton St. E20 7D 68
SW9 2A 120
Thornton Way NW11 5K 45
Thorntree Ct. W5 5E 78
Thorntree Rd. SE7 5B 106
Thornville Gro. CR4: Mitc 2B 154
Thornville St. SE8 1C 122
Thornwell Ct. *W7* 2J 95
(off Lwr. Boston Rd.)
Thornwood Cl. E18 2K 51
Thornwood Gdns. W8 2J 99
Thornwood Ho. IG9: Buck H 1H 37
Thornwood Lodge *W8* 2J 99
(off Thornwood Gdns.)
Thornwood Rd. SE13 5G 123
Thornycroft Ho. *W4* 5A 98
(off Fraser St.)
Thorogood Gdns. E15 5G 69
Thorogood Way RM13: Rain 1K 91
Thorold Ho. *SE1* 6C 14
(off Pepper St.)
Thorold Rd. IG1: Ilf 2F 71
N22 7D 32
Thorparch Rd. SW8 1H 119
Thorpebank Rd. W12 1C 98
Thorpe Cl. BR6: Orp 2J 173
SE26 4K 139
W10 6G 81
Thorpe Ct. EN2: Enf 3G 23
Thorpe Cres. E17 2B 50
Thorpedale Gdns. IG2: Ilf 4E 52
IG6: Ilf 4E 52
Thorpedale Rd. N4 2J 65
Thorpe Hall Rd. E17 1E 50
Thorpe Ho. *N1* 1K 83
(off Barnsbury Est.)
Thorpe Rd. E6 1D 88
E7 4H 69
E17 2E 50
IG11: Bark 7H 71
KT2: King T 7E 132
N15 6E 48
Thorpewood Av. SE26 2H 139
Thorpland Av. UB10: Ick 3E 56
Thorsden Way SE19 5E 138
Thorverton Rd. NW2 3G 63
Thoydon Rd. E3 2A 86
Thrale Rd. SW16 4G 137
Thrale St. SE1 5D 14 (1C 102)
Thrasher Cl. E8 1F 85
Thrawl St. E1 6K 9 (5F 85)
Thrayle Ho. *SW9* 3K 119
(off Benedict Rd.)
Threadgold Ho. *N1* 6D 66
(off Dovercourt Est.)
Threadneedle St. EC2 1F 15 (6D 84)
Threadneedle Wlk. EC2 1F 15
Thread St. SM6: W'gton 2E 166
Three Angels Cl.
SM6: W'gton 5K 167
Three Bridges Bus. Cen.
UB2: S'hall 2G 95
Three Colt Cnr. E2 3K 9
Three Colts La. E2 4H 85
Three Colt St. E14 6B 86
Three Corners DA7: Bex 2H 127
Three Cranes Wlk. EC4 3D 14
Three Cups Yd. WC1 6H 7
Three Kings Yd. W1 2J 11 (7F 83)
Three Meadows M.
HA3: Hrw W 1K 41
Three Mill La. E3 3E 86
Three Mills Studios 3E 86
Three Oak La.
SE1 6J 15 (2F 103)
Three Oaks Cl. UB10: Ick 3B 56
Three Quays EC3 3H 15
Three Quays Wlk. EC3 3H 15 (7E 84)
Threshers Pl. W11 7G 81
Thriffwood SE26 3J 139
Thrigby Rd. KT9: Chess 6F 163
Thring Ho. *SW9* 2K 119
(off Stockwell Rd.)
Throckmorton Rd. E16 6K 87
Throgmorton Av. EC2 7F 9 (6D 84)
(not continuous)
Throgmorton St. EC2 7F 9 (6D 84)
Throwley Cl. SE2 3C 108
(not continuous)
Throwley Rd. SM1: Sutt 5K 165
Throwley Way SM1: Sutt 4K 165
Thrupp Cl. CR4: Mitc 2F 155
Thrush Grn. HA2: Harr 4E 40
Thrush St. SE17 5C 102
Thunderer St. E13 2A 88
Thunderer Wlk. SE18 3F 107
Thurbarn Rd. SE6 5D 140
Thurland Ho. *SE16* 4H 103
(off Camilla Rd.)
Thurland Rd. SE16 3G 103
Thurlby Cl. HA1: Harr 6A 42
IG8: Wfd G 5J 37
Thurlby Cft. *NW4* 3E 44
(off Mulberry Cl.)
Thurlby Rd. HA0: Wemb 6D 60
SE27 4A 138
Thurleigh Av. SW12 6E 118
Thurleigh Ct. SW12 6E 118
Thurleigh Rd. SW12 7D 118
Thurleston Av. SM4: Mord 5G 153
Thurlestone Av. IG3: Bark, Ilf 4K 71
N12 6J 31
Thurlestone Cl. TW17: Shep 6E 146
Thurlestone Ct. *UB1: S'hall* 6F 77
(off Howard Rd.)
Thurlestone Pde. *TW17: Shep* 6E 146
(off High St.)
Thurlestone Rd. SE27 3A 138
Thurloe Cl. SW7 3C 16 (4C 100)
Thurloe Ct. *SW3* 4C 16
(off Fulham Rd.)
Thurloe Pl. SW7 3B 16 (4B 100)
Thurloe Pl. M. SW7 3B 16
Thurloe Sq. SW7 3C 16 (4C 100)
Thurloe St. SW7 3B 16 (4B 100)
Thurlow Cl. E4 6K 35
Thurlow Gdns. HA0: Wemb 5D 60
Thurlow Hill SE21 1C 138
Thurlow Ho. SW16 3J 137
Thurlow Pk. Rd. SE21 2B 138
Thurlow Rd. NW3 5B 64
W7 2A 96
Thurlow St. SE17 5D 102
(not continuous)
Thurlow Ter. NW5 5E 64
Thurlow Wlk. SE17 5E 102
(not continuous)
Thurlstone Rd. HA4: Ruis 3J 57
Thurnby Ct. TW2: Twick 3J 131
Thurnscoe *NW1* 1G 83
(off Pratt St.)
Thursland Rd. DA14: Sidc 5E 144
Thursley Cres. CR0: New Ad 7E 170
Thursley Gdns. SW19 2F 135
Thursley Ho. *SW2* 7K 119
(off Holmewood Gdns.)
Thursley Rd. SE9 3D 142
Thurso Ho. NW6 2K 81
Thurso St. SW17 4B 136
Thurstan Dwellings *WC2* 7F 7
(off Newton St.)
Thurstan Rd. SW20 7D 134
Thurstan St. SW6 1A 118
Thurston Ho. BR3: Beck 6D 140
N1 1K 83
(off Barnsbury Est.)
Thurston Rd. SE13 2D 122
UB1: S'hall 6D 76
Thurtle Rd. E2 1F 85
Thwaite Cl. DA8: Erith 6J 109
Thyer Cl. BR6: Farnb 4G 173
Thyme Cl. SE3 3A 124
Thyme Ct. NW7 1G 45
Thyme Wlk. E5 4K 67
Thyra Gro. N12 6E 30
Tibbatt's Rd. E3 4D 86
Tibbenham Pl. SE6 2C 140
Tibbenham Wlk. E13 2H 87
Tibberton Sq. N1 1C 84
Tibbet's Cl. SW19 1F 135
TIBBET'S CORNER 7F 117
Tibbet's Ride SW15 7F 117
Tiber Cl. E3 1C 86
Tiber Gdns. N1 1J 83
Ticehurst Cl. BR5: St P 7A 144
Ticehurst Rd. SE23 2A 140
Tickford Cl. SE2 2C 108
Tickford Ho. NW8 2C 4 (3C 82)
Tidal Basin Rd. E16 7H 87
(not continuous)
Tidbury Ct. *SW8* 7G 101
(off Stewart's Rd.)
Tide Cl. CR4: Mitc 1E 154
Tideham Ho. SE28 1H 107
Tidelea Twr. SE28 2G 107
Tidemill Sq. SE10 4G 105
Tidemill Way SE8 7C 104
Tidenham Gdns.
CR0: C'don 3E 168
Tideside Ct. SE18 3C 106
Tideslea Path SE28 1H 107
Tideswell Rd. CR0: C'don 3C 170
SW15 4E 116
Tidewaiters Ho. *E14* 6F 87
(off Blair St.)
Tideway Cl. TW10: Ham 4B 132
Tideway Ct. SE16 1K 103
Tideway Ho. *E14* 2C 104
(off Strafford St.)
E17 4K 49
Tideway Wlk. SW11 7B 18 (6G 101)
Tidey St. E3 5C 86
Tidford Rd. DA16: Well 2K 125
Tidlock Ho. SE28 2H 107
Tidworth Rd. E3 4C 86
Tiepigs La. BR2: Hayes 2G 171
BR4: W W'ck 2G 171
Tierney Ct. CR0: C'don 2E 168
Tierney La. W6 6E 98
Tierney Rd. SW2 1J 137
Tiffany Hgts. SW18 7J 117
Tiffin Girls Community Sports Cen.
6E 132
Tiffin Sports Cen. 2F 151
Tiger Cl. IG11: Bark 2B 90
Tiger Ho. *WC1* 2D 6
(off Burton St.)
Tiger La. BR2: Broml 4K 159
Tiger Way E5 4H 67
Tiggap Ho. SE10 4G 105
Tigris Cl. N9 2D 34
Tilbrook Rd. SE3 3A 124
Tilbury Cl. HA5: Hat E 1D 40
SE15 7F 103
Tilbury Ho. *SE14* 6K 103
(off Myers La.)
Tilbury Rd. E6 2D 88
E10 7E 50
Tildesley Rd. SW15 6E 116
Tile Farm Rd. BR6: Orp 3H 173
Tile Ho. *N1* 1J 83
(off Beaconsfield St.)
Tilehurst *NW1* 2K 5
(off Lit. Albany St.)
Tilehurst Point SE2 2C 108
(not continuous)
Tilehurst Rd. SM3: Cheam 5G 165
SW18 1B 136
Tile Kiln La. DA5: Bexl 2J 145
N6 1F 65
N13 5H 33
UB9: Hare 7D 38
Tile Kiln Studios N6 7G 47
Tilemakers Yard SW18 2A 136
Tileyard Rd. N7 7J 65
Tilford Av. CR0: New Ad 7E 170
Tilford Gdns. SW19 1F 135
Tilford Ho. *SW2* 7K 119
(off Holmewood Gdns.)
Tilia Cl. SM1: Sutt 5H 165
Tilia Rd. E5 4H 67
Tilia Wlk. SW9 4B 120
Tiller Ho. *N1* 1E 84
(off Whitmore Est.)
UB2: S'hall 3E 94
(off Lockwood Rd.)
Tiller Leisure Cen. 3C 104
Tiller Rd. E14 3C 104
Tillett Cl. NW10 6J 61
Tillett Sq. SE16 2A 104
Tillett Way E2 3G 85
Tilley Rd. TW13: Felt 1J 129
Tillingbourne Gdns. N3 3H 45
Tillingbourne Grn.
BR5: St M Cry 4K 161, 5K 161
Tillingbourne Way N3 4H 45
Tillingham Way N12 4D 30
Tilling Rd. NW2 1E 62
Tillings Cl. SE5 1C 120
Tilling Way HA9: Wemb 2D 60
Tillman St. E1 6H 85
Tilloch St. N1 7K 65
Tillotson Ct. *SW8* 7H 101
(off Wandsworth Rd.)
Tillotson Rd. HA3: Hrw W 7A 26
IG1: Ilf 7E 52
N9 2A 34
Tilney Ct. EC1 3D 8 (4C 84)
IG9: Buck H 2D 36
Tilney Dr. IG9: Buck H 2D 36
Tilney Gdns. N1 6D 66
Tilney Rd. RM9: Dag 6F 73
UB2: S'hall 4A 94
Tilney St. W1 4H 11 (1E 100)
Tilson Cl. SE5 7E 102
Tilson Gdns. SW2 7J 119
Tilson Ho. SW2 7J 119
Tilson Rd. N17 1G 49
Tilston Bright Sq. SE2 3C 108
Tilston Cl. E11 3H 69
Tiltman Pl. N7 3K 65
Tilton St. SW6 6G 99
The Tiltwood W3 7J 79
Tilt Yd. App. SE9 6D 124
Timber Cl. BR7: Chst 2E 160
Timbercroft KT19: Ewe 4A 164
Timbercroft La. SE18 6J 107
Timberdene NW4 2F 45
Timberdene Av. IG6: Ilf 1G 53
Timberland Cl. SE15 7G 103
Timberland Rd. E1 6H 85
Timberley Ct. DA14: Sidc 5K 143
Timber Mill Way SW4 3H 119
Timber Pond Rd. SE16 1K 103
The Timbers SM3: Cheam 6G 165
Timberslip Dr.
SM6: W'gton 7H 167
Timber St. EC1 3C 8 (4C 84)
Timber Wharf E2 1F 85
Timberwharf Rd. N16 6G 49
Timber Wharves Est. *E14* 4C 104
(off Copeland Dr.)
The Timber Yd. *N1* 2H 9
(off Drysdale St.)
Timberyard M. KT4: Wor Pk 2D 164
Timbrell Pl. SE16 1B 104
Time Sq. E8 5F 67
Times Sq. E1 6G 85
SM1: Sutt 5K 165
Timians Way BR1: Broml 4K 141
Timmins Apts. E2 3K 85
Timms Cl. BR1: Broml 4D 160
Timor Ho. *E1* 4A 86
(off Duckett St.)
Timothy Cl. DA6: Bex 5E 126
SW4 5G 119
Timothy Ho. *DA18: Erith* 2E 108
(off Kale Rd.)
Timothy Pl. KT8: W Mole 5D 148
Timperley Ct. SW19 1G 135
Timsbury Wlk. SW15 1C 134
Tina Ct. SE6 7B 122
Tindal St. SW9 1B 120
Tinderbox All. SW14 3K 115
Tinderbox Ho. *SE8* 7C 104
(off Octavius St.)
Tinniswood Cl. N5 5A 66
Tinsley Cl. SE25 3H 157
Tinsley Rd. E1 5J 85
Tintagel Ct. *EC1* 3A 8
(off St John St.)
Tintagel Cres. SE22 4F 121
Tintagel Dr. HA7: Stan 4J 27
Tintagel Gdns. SE22 4F 121
Tintern Av. NW9 3H 43
Tintern Cl. SW15 5G 117
SW19 6A 136
Tintern Ct. W13 7A 78
Tintern Gdns. N14 7D 22
Tintern Ho. *NW1* 1K 5
(off Augustus St.)
SW1 4J 17
(part of Abbots Mnr.)
Tintern Path *NW9* 6A 44
(off Fryent Gro.)
Tintern Rd. N22 1C 48
SM5: Cars 1B 166
Tintern St. SW4 4J 119
Tintern Way HA2: Harr 1F 59
Tinto Rd. E16 4J 87
Tinworth Ct. *SE17* 6B 102
(off Royal Rd.)
Tinworth St. SE11 5F 19 (5J 101)
Tippett Ct. E6 2D 88
Tippetts Cl. EN2: Enf 1H 23
Tippler Wlk. E15 5F 69
Tipthorpe Rd. SW11 3E 118
Tipton Dr. CR0: C'don 4E 168
Tiptree *NW1* 7F 65
(off Castlehaven Rd.)
Tiptree Cl. E4 3K 35
Tiptree Cres. IG5: Ilf 3E 52
Tiptree Dr. EN2: Enf 4J 23
Tiptree Rd. HA4: Ruis 4K 57
Tirlemont Rd. CR2: S Croy 7C 168

Tirrell Rd.—Tredegar Rd.

Tirrell Rd. CR0: C'don 6C 156
Tisbury Ct. W1 2C 12
Tisbury Rd. SW16 2J 155
Tisdall Ho. SE17 4D 102
(off Barlow St.)
Tisdall Pl. SE17 4D 102
Tissington Ct. SE16 4J 103
Titan Bus. Est. SE8 7C 104
(off Ffinch St.)
Titan Ct. TW8: Bford 5F 97
Titan Ho. E20 5E 68
(off Napa Cl.)
Titanium Point E2 3K 85
(off Palmer's Rd.)
Titchborne Row W2 1D 10 (6C 82)
Titchfield Rd. NW8 1C 82
SM5: Cars 1B 166
Titchfield Wlk. SM5: Cars 7B 154
Titchwell Rd. SW18 1B 136
Tite St. SW3 6E 16 (5D 100)
Tithe Barn Cl. KT2: King T 1F 151
Tithe Barn Way UB5: N'olt 2K 75
Tithe Cl. KT12: Walt T 6K 147
NW7 1C 44
UB4: Hayes 5H 75
Tithe Farm Av. HA2: Harr 3E 58
Tithe Farm Cl. HA2: Harr 3E 58
Tithe Farm Social Club 2E 58
Tithe Wlk. NW7 1C 44
Titian Av. WD23: B Hea 1D 26
Titian Hgts. E20 5D 68
(off Scarlet Cl.)
Titley Cl. E4 5H 35
Titmus Cl. UB8: Hil 6E 74
Titmuss Av. SE28 7B 90
Titmuss St. W12 2E 98
Tivendale N8 3J 47
Tiverton Av. IG5: Ilf 3E 52
Tiverton Cl. CR0: C'don 7F 157
Tiverton Dr. SE9 1G 143
Tiverton Ho. EN3: Enf H 3E 24
Tiverton Rd. HA0: Wemb 2E 78
HA4: Ruis 3J 57
HA8: Edg 2F 43
N15 6D 48
N18 5K 33
NW10 1F 81
TW3: Houn 2G 113
Tiverton St. SE1 3C 102
Tiverton Way KT9: Chess 5D 162
NW7 7A 30
Tivoli Ct. SE16 1B 104
Tivoli Gdns. SE18 4C 106
(not continuous)
Tivoli M. E14 6B 86
Tivoli Rd. N8 5H 47
SE27 5C 138
TW4: Houn 4C 112
Tivoli Way E14 6B 86
Tizzard Gro. SE3 4K 123
Toad La. TW4: Houn 4D 112
Tobacco Dock 7H 85
Tobago St. E14 2C 104
Tobin Cl. NW3 7C 64
Toby Ct. N9 7D 24
(off Tramway Av.)
Toby La. E1 4A 86
Toby Way KT5: Surb 2H 163
Todber Ho. W14 3G 99
(off Russell Rd.)
Todd Ho. N2 2B 46
(off The Grange)
Todds Wlk. N7 2K 65
Todhunter Ter. EN5: New Bar 4D 20
Token Ho. CR0: C'don 3C 168
(off Robert St.)
Tokenhouse Yd. EC2 7E 8 (6D 84)
Token Yd. SW15 4G 117
TOKYNGTON 6H 61
Tokyngton Av. HA9: Wemb 6G 61
Toland Sq. SW15 5C 116
Tolcairn Ct. DA17: Belv 5G 109
Tolcarne Dr. HA5: Eastc 2J 39
Tolchurch W11 6H 81
(off Dartmouth Cl.)
Toley Av. HA9: Wemb 7E 42
Tolhurst Dr. W10 3G 81
Tollard Ho. W14 3H 99
(off Kensington High St.)
Toll Bar Ct. SM2: Sutt 7K 165
Tollbridge Cl. W10 4G 81
Tollesbury Gdns. IG6: Ilf 3H 53
Tollet St. E1 4K 85
Tollgate Ct. CR2: S Croy 5D 168
Tollgate Dr. SE21 2E 138
UB4: Yead 7B 76
Tollgate Gdns. NW6 2K 81
(off Oxford Rd.)
Tollgate Ho. NW6 2K 81
(off Tollgate Gdns.)
Tollgate Lodge BR7: Chst 1E 160
(off Caveside Cl.)
Tollgate Rd. E6 5A 88
E16 5A 88
Tollgate Sq. 5D 88
Tollhouse Way N19 2G 65
Tollington Pk. N4 2K 65
Tollington Pl. N4 2K 65
Tollington Rd. N7 4K 65
Tollington Way N7 3J 65
Tolmers Sq. NW1 3B 6 (4G 83)
(not continuous)
Tolpaide Ho. SE11 4J 19
Tolpuddle Av. E13 1A 88
Tolpuddle St. N1 2A 84
Tolsford Rd. E5 5H 67
Tolson Rd. TW7: Isle 3A 114
Tolverne Rd. SW20 1E 152
TOLWORTH 2H 163
Tolworth B'way. KT6: Surb 1H 163
Tolworth Cl. KT6: Surb 1H 163
Tolworth Gdns.
RM6: Chad H 5D 54
TOLWORTH JUNC.
(TOBY JUG) 2H 163
Tolworth Pde. RM6: Chad H 5E 54
Tolworth Pk. Rd. KT6: Surb 2F 163
Tolworth Recreation Cen. 3F 163
Tolworth Ri. Nth. KT5: Surb 1H 163
Tolworth Ri. Sth. KT5: Surb 2H 163
Tolworth Rd. KT6: Surb 2E 162
Tolworth Twr. KT6: Surb 2H 163
Tomahawk Gdns.
UB5: N'olt 3B 76
Tomblin M. SW16 2G 155
Tom Coombs Cl. SE9 4C 124
Tom Cribb Rd. SE28 3G 107
Tom Groves Cl. E15 5F 69
Tom Hood Cl. E15 5F 69
Tom Jenkinson Rd. E16 1J 105
Tomkyns Ho. SE11 3J 19
Tomline Ho. SE1 5C 14
(off Union St.)
Tomlins All. TW1: Twick 1A 132
Tomlin's Gro. E3 3C 86
Tomlinson Cl. E2 2K 9 (3F 85)
W4 5H 97
Tomlins Orchard IG11: Bark 1G 89
Tomlins Ter. E14 6A 86
Tomlins Wlk. N7 2K 65
Tom Mann Cl. IG11: Bark 1J 89
Tommy Flowers M. NW7 5A 30
Tom Nolan Cl. E15 2G 87
Tompion Ho. EC1 3B 8
(off Percival St.)
Tompion St. EC1 2A 8 (3B 84)
(not continuous)
Tom Smith Cl. SE10 6G 105
Tomson Ho. SE1 7J 15
(off St Saviour's Est.)
Tomswood Ct. IG6: Ilf 1G 53
Tomswood Hill IG6: Ilf 1F 53, 6K 37
Tomswood Rd. IG7: Chig 6K 37
Tom Williams Ho. SW6 6H 99
(off Clem Attlee Ct.)
Tonbridge Cres. HA3: Kenton 4E 42
Tonbridge Ho's. WC1 2E 6
(off Tonbridge St.)
Tonbridge Rd. KT8: W Mole 4D 148
Tonbridge St. WC1 1E 6 (3J 83)
Tonbridge Wlk. WC1 1E 6
Toneborough NW8 1K 81
(off Abbey Rd.)
Tonfield Rd. SM3: Sutt 1H 165
Tonge Cl. BR3: Beck 5C 158
Tonsley Hill SW18 5K 117
Tonsley Pl. SW18 5K 117
Tonsley Rd. SW18 5K 117
Tonsley St. SW18 5K 117
Tonstall Rd. CR4: Mitc 2E 154
Tony Cannell M. E3 3B 86
Tony Law Ho. SE20 1H 157
Tony Rawson Way RM10: Dag 3J 73
Tooke Cl. HA5: Pinn 1C 40
Tookey Cl. HA3: Kenton 7F 43
Took's Ct. EC4 7J 7 (6A 84)
Tooley St. SE1 4F 15 (1D 102)
Toorack Rd. HA3: Hrw W 2H 41
TOOTING 5C 136
TOOTING BEC 3D 136
Tooting Bec Gdns. SW16 4H 137
(not continuous)
Tooting Bec Lido 4G 137
Tooting Bec Rd. SW16 3E 136
SW17 3E 136
Tooting B'way. SW17 5C 136
TOOTING GRAVENEY 6D 136
Tooting Gro. SW17 5C 136
Tooting High St. SW17 6C 136
Tooting Leisure Cen. 4B 136
Tooting Mkt. SW17 4D 136
Tootswood Rd. BR2: Broml 5G 159
Topaz Ct. E11 1G 69
Topaz Wlk. NW2 7F 45
Topcliffe Dr. BR6: Farnb 4H 173
Topham Ho. SE10 7E 104
(off Prior St.)
Topham Sq. N17 1C 48
Topham St. EC1 3J 7 (4A 84)
Topham Yard SW19 1K 153
Top Ho. Ri. E4 7K 25
Topiary Sq. TW9: Rich 3F 115
Topley St. SE9 4A 124
Topmast Point E14 2C 104
Top Pk. BR3: Beck 5G 159
Topp Wlk. NW2 2E 62
Topsfield Cl. N8 5H 47
Topsfield Pde. N8 5J 47
(off Tottenham La.)
Topsfield Rd. N8 5J 47
Topsham Rd. SW17 3D 136
Tora Ct. IG9: Buck H 2F 37
Torbay Ct. NW1 7F 65
Torbay Mans. NW6 1H 81
(off Willesden La.)
Torbay Rd. HA2: Harr 2C 58
NW6 7H 63
Torbay St. NW1 7F 65
Torbitt Way IG2: Ilf 5K 53
Torbridge Cl. HA8: Edg 7K 27
Torbrook Cl. DA5: Bexl 6E 126
Tor Ct. W8 2J 99
Torcross Dr. SE23 2J 139
Torcross Rd. HA4: Ruis 3K 57
Toreno Mansion E20 5D 68
(off Olympic Pk. Av.)
Tor Gdns. W8 2J 99
Tor Gro. SE28 1J 107
Tor Ho. N6 6F 47
Tormead Cl. SM1: Sutt 6J 165
Tormount Rd. SE18 6J 107
Tornay Ho. E9 7J 67
N1 2K 83
(off Priory Grn. Est.)
Toronto Av. E12 4D 70
Toronto Ho. SE16 2K 103
Toronto Rd. IG1: Ilf 1F 71
Torquay Ct. E14 5E 86
(off St Ives Pl.)
Torquay Gdns. IG4: Ilf 4B 52
Torquay St. W2 5K 81
Torrance Cl. SE7 6B 106
Torrens Ct. SE5 3D 120
Torrens Rd. E15 6H 69
SW2 5K 119
Torrens Sq. E15 6H 69
Torrens St. EC1 2A 84
Torrent Lodge SE10 7D 104
(off Merryweather Pl.)
Torres Sq. E14 5C 104
Torre Vista SE13 3E 122
(off Loampit Va.)
Torre Wlk. SM5: Cars 1C 166
Torrey Dr. SW9 2A 120
Torriano Av. NW5 5H 65
Torriano Cotts. NW5 5G 65
Torriano M. NW5 5G 65
Torridge Gdns. SE15 4J 121
Torridge Rd. CR7: Thor H 5B 156
Torridon Ho. NW6 2K 81
(off Randolph Gdns.)
Torridon Rd. SE6 7F 123
SE13 7F 123
Torrington Av. N12 5G 31
Torrington Cl. N12 4G 31
Torrington Ct. SE26 5G 139
(off Crystal Palace Pk. Rd.)
Torrington Dr. HA2: Harr 4F 59
Torrington Gdns. N11 6B 32
UB6: G'frd 1C 78
Torrington Gro. N12 5H 31
Torrington Pk. N12 5F 31
Torrington Pl. E1 1G 103
WC1 5C 6 (5H 83)
Torrington Rd. E18 3J 51
HA4: Ruis 3H 57
RM8: Dag 1F 73
UB6: G'frd 1C 78
Torrington Sq. CR0: C'don 7D 156
WC1 4D 6 (4H 83)
Torrington Way SM4: Mord 6J 153
Tor Rd. DA16: Well 1C 126
Torr Rd. SE20 7K 139
Tortington Ho. SE15 7G 103
(off Friary Est.)
Torver Rd. HA1: Harr 4J 41
Torver Way BR6: Orp 3H 173
Torwood Rd. SW15 5C 116
Tothill Ho. SW1 3D 18
(off Page St.)
Tothill St. SW1 7D 12 (2H 101)
Totnes Rd. DA16: Well 7B 108
Totnes Vs. N11 5B 32
(off Telford Rd.)
Totnes Wlk. N2 4B 46
Tottan Ter. E1 6K 85
Tottenhall NW1 7E 64
(off Ferdinand St.)
Tottenhall Rd. N13 6F 33
TOTTENHAM 2F 49
Tottenham Community Sports Cen.
1F 49
Tottenham Ct. Rd. W1 4B 6 (4G 83)
Tottenham Ent. Cen. N17 2F 49
Tottenham Grn. E. N15 4F 49
(not continuous)
Tottenham Green Pools & Fitness
4F 49
TOTTENHAM HALE 2G 49
TOTTENHAM HALE GYRATORY 4G 49
Tottenham Hale Retail Pk. 4G 49
Tottenham Hotspur FC 7A 34
Tottenham La. N8 6J 47
Tottenham M. W1 5B 6 (5G 83)
Tottenham Rd. N1 6E 66
Tottenham St. W1 6B 6 (5G 83)
Totterdown St. SW17 4D 136
TOTTERIDGE 1C 30
Totteridge Comn. N20 2H 29
Totteridge Fields
Local Nature Reserve 1H 29
Totteridge Grn. N20 2D 30
Totteridge Ho. SW11 2B 118
(off Yelverton Rd.)
Totteridge La. N20 2D 30
Totteridge Village N20 1B 30
Totternhoe Cl. HA3: Kenton 5C 42
Totters Ct. SE17 6D 102
(off Westmorland Rd.)
Totton Rd. CR7: Thor H 3A 156
Toucan Cl. NW10 3G 79
Touchard Ho. N1 2F 9
Toulmin St. SE1 7C 14 (2C 102)
Toulon St. SE5 7C 102
Toulouse Ct. SE16 5H 103
(off Rossetti Rd.)
Tounson Ct. SW1 4D 18
(off Montaigne Cl.)
Tourers Ho. E17 5B 50
(off Track St.)
Tournay Rd. SW6 7H 99
Tours Pas. SW11 4A 118
Toussaint Wlk. SE16 3G 103
Tovil Cl. SE20 2H 157
Tovy Ho. SE1 5G 103
(off Avondale Sq.)
Towcester Rd. E3 4D 86
The Tower SE1 5J 15
(off Potters Flds.)
SW8 7E 18 (6J 101)
TW8: Bford 5D 96
(off Ealing Rd.)
Tower 42 7G 9 (6E 84)
TOWER BRIDGE 5J 15 (1F 103)
Tower Bri. App.
E1 4J 15 (1F 103)
Tower Bri. Bus. Complex
SE16 3G 103
Tower Bri. Bus. Sq. SE16 4H 103
Tower Bridge Exhibition 4J 15
Tower Bri. M. HA1: Harr 4K 59
Tower Bri. Plaza
SE1 5J 15 (1F 103)
Tower Bri. Rd. SE1 7H 15 (3E 102)
Tower Bri. Sq. SE1 6J 15
Tower Bri. Wharf
E1 5K 15 (1G 103)
Tower Bldgs. E1 1H 103
(off Brewhouse La.)
Tower Cl. BR6: Orp 2K 173
NW3 5B 64
SE20 7H 139
Tower Ct. DA17: Belv 4J 109
E5 7F 49
N1 7C 66
(off Canonbury St.)
NW8 2C 82
(off Mackennal St.)
WC2 1E 12
Tower Gdns. KT10: Clay 7A 162
Tower Gdns. Rd. N17 1C 48
Towergate SE1 4E 102
(off Page's Wlk.)
Towergate Cl. UB8: Uxb 5A 56
Towergate Ho. E3 2B 86
(off Ordell Rd.)
Tower Hamlets Rd. E7 4H 69
E17 3C 50
TOWER HILL 7F 85
Twr. Hill EC3 3J 15 (7F 85)
Tower Hill Ct. DA17: Erith 4J 109
(off Tower Ct.)
Tower Hill Memorial 3H 15 (7F 85)
Tower Hill Ter. EC3 3H 15
Tower Ho. E1 5G 85
(off Fieldgate St.)
SE13 3E 122
Tower La. HA9: Wemb 3D 60
Tower Mans. SE1 3F 103
(off Grange Rd.)
Tower M. E5 4A 68
E17 4C 50
Tower Mill Rd. SE15 7E 102
The Tower of London 3J 15 (7F 85)
Tower of London Jewel House
7F 85
Tower of London Welcome Centre
3H 15 (7E 84)
Tower Pier EC3 3H 15 (7E 84)
Tower Pl. EC3 3H 15 (7E 84)
Tower Pl. E. EC3 3H 15
(off Lwr. Thames St.)
Tower Pl. W. EC3 3H 15
(off Lwr. Thames St.)
Tower Point EN2: Enf 4J 23
Tower Ri. TW9: Rich 3E 114
Tower Rd. BR6: Orp 2K 173
DA7: Bex 4G 127
DA17: Belv 4J 109
NW10 7C 62
TW1: Twick 3K 131
Towers Av. UB10: Hil 3E 74
Towers Bus. Pk. HA9: Wemb 4J 61
(off Carey Way)
Towers Ct. UB10: Hil 3E 74
Towers Pl. TW9: Rich 5E 114
Towers Rd. HA5: Pinn 1C 40
UB1: S'hall 4E 76
Tower St. WC2 1E 12 (6J 83)
Tower Ter. N22 2K 47
Tower Vw. CR0: C'don 7A 158
WD23: B Hea 1D 26
Tower Wlk. SE1 4E 102
(off Leroy St.)
Tower Wharf SE1 6J 15
(off Tooley St.)
Tower Workshops SE1 7J 15
Towfield Ct. TW13: Hanw 2D 130
Towfield Rd. TW13: Hanw 2D 130
The Town EN2: Enf 3J 23
Towncourt Cres. BR5: Pet W 5G 161
Towncourt La. BR5: Pet W 6H 161
Town Ct. Path N4 1C 66
Townend Ct. BR1: Broml 1H 159
Town End Pde. KT1: King T 3D 150
(off High St.)
Towney Mead UB5: N'olt 2D 76
Towney Mead Ct. UB5: N'olt 2D 76
Townfield Rd. UB3: Hayes 1H 93
Townfield Sq. UB3: Hayes 7H 75
Town Fld. Way TW7: Isle 2A 114
Town Hall App. N16 4D 66
(off Albion Rd.)
Town Hall App. Rd. N15 4F 49
Town Hall Av. W4 5K 97
Town Hall Rd. SW11 3D 118
Townholm Cres. W7 3K 95
Townhouse M. W12 2D 98
Town La. TW19: Stanw 1A 128
Townley Ct. E15 6H 69
Townley Rd. DA6: Bex 5F 127
SE22 5E 120
Townley St. SE17 5D 102
(not continuous)
Townmead Bus. Cen. SW6 3A 118
Town Mdw. TW8: Bford 6D 96
Town Mdw. Rd. TW8: Bford 7D 96
Townmead Rd. SW6 3K 117
TW9: Kew 2H 115
Town Quay IG11: Bark 1F 89
Town Quay Wharf IG11: Bark 1F 89
Town Rd. N9 2C 34
Townsend Av. N14 4C 32
Townsend Ho. SE1 4G 103
(off Strathnairn St.)
Townsend Ind. Est. NW10 2J 79
Townsend La. NW9 7K 43
Townsend M. SW18 2A 136
Townsend Rd. N15 5F 49
SE3 4A 124
TW15: Ashf 5A 128
UB1: S'hall 1C 94
Townsend St. SE17 4E 102
Townsend Way
HA6: Nwood 1H 39
Townsend Yd. N6 1F 65
Townshend Cl.
DA14: Sidc 6B 144
Townshend Ct. NW8 2C 82
(off Townshend Rd.)
Townshend Est. NW8 2C 82
Townshend Rd. BR7: Chst 5F 143
NW8 1C 82
(not continuous)
TW9: Rich 4F 115
Townshend Ter. TW9: Rich 4F 115
Towns Ho. SW4 3H 119
Townson Av. UB5: N'olt 2J 75
Townson Way UB5: N'olt 2J 75
Town Sq. IG11: Bark 1G 89
(off Clockhouse Av.)
Town Tree Rd. TW15: Ashf 5C 128
Town Wharf TW7: Isle 3B 114
The Towpath SW10 1B 118
Towpath KT12: Walt T 5J 147
TW17: Shep 7B 146
Towpath Rd. N18 6E 34
Towpath Wlk. E9 5B 68
Towpath Way CR0: C'don 6F 157
Towton M. N11 6C 32
Towton Rd. SE27 2C 138
Toye Av. N20 2G 31
Toynbec Cl. BR7: Chst 4F 143
Toynbee Rd. SW20 1G 153
Toynbee St. E1 6J 9 (5F 85)
Toynbee Studios 7K 9
Toyne Way N6 6D 46
Tracey Av. NW2 5E 62
Tracey Bellamy Ct. E14 6A 86
(off Repton St.)
Track St. E17 5B 50
Tracy Ct. HA7: Stan 7H 27
Tracy Ho. E3 3B 86
(off Mile End Rd.)
Trade City Bus. Pk.
TW16: Sun 1G 147
Trade Cl. N13 4F 33
Trader Rd. E6 6F 89
Tradescant Ho. E9 7J 67
(off Frampton Pk. Rd.)
Tradescant Rd. SW8 7J 101
Tradewind Hgts. SE16 1K 103
(off Rotherhithe St.)
Tradewinds Ct. E1 7G 85
Trading Est. Rd. NW10 4J 79
Trafalgar Av.
KT4: Wor Pk 1F 165
N17 6K 33
SE15 5F 103
Trafalgar Bldg. KT2: King T 1D 150
(off Henry Macaulay Av.)
Trafalgar Bus. Cen. IG11: Bark 4K 89
Trafalgar Chambers SW3 5B 16
(off South Pde.)
Trafalgar Cl. SE16 3A 104
Trafalgar Ct. E1 1J 103
(off Wapping Wall)
Trafalgar Gdns. E1 5K 85
W8 3K 99
Trafalgar Gro. SE10 6F 105
Trafalgar Ho. SE17 5C 102
(off Bronti Cl.)
SW18 4A 118
Trafalgar M. E9 6B 68
Trafalgar Pl. E11 4J 51
N18 5B 34
Trafalgar Point N1 7D 66
(off Downham Rd.)
Trafalgar Quarters SE10 6F 105
(off Park Row)
Trafalgar Rd. SE10 6F 105
SW19 7K 135
TW2: Twick 2H 131
Trafalgar Square 4D 12 (1H 101)
Trafalgar Sq. SW1 4D 12 (1H 101)
WC2 4D 12 (1H 101)
Trafalgar St. SE17 5D 102
Trafalgar Studios 4E 12
(off Whitehall)
Trafalgar Ter. HA1: Harr 1J 59
Trafalgar Trad. Est.
EN3: Brim 4F 25
Trafalgar Way CR0: Wadd 2A 168
E14 1E 104
Trafford Ho. N1 2D 84
(off Cranston Est.)
Trafford Rd. CR7: Thor H 5K 155
Trafford Way BR3: Beck 6C 140
Traherne Lodge TW11: Tedd 5K 131
Trahorn Cl. E1 4H 85
Trail St. E17 5B 50
Traitors' Gate 4J 15
Tralee Ct. SE16 5H 103
(off Masters Dr.)
Tram Cl. SE24 3B 120
(off Milkwood Rd.)
The Tramlink SW19 2A 154
The Tramsheds CR0: Bedd 7H 155
Tramway Av. E15 7G 69
N9 7C 24
Tramway Cl. SE20 1J 157
Tramway Ct. E1 5A 86
Tramway Path CR4: Mitc 4C 154
(not continuous)
Tranby M. E9 5K 67
(off Brooksby's Wlk.)
Tranley M. NW3 4C 64
(off Fleet Rd.)
Tranmere Ct. SM2: Sutt 7A 166
Tranmere Rd. N9 7A 24
SW18 2A 136
TW2: Whitt 7F 113
Tranquil La. HA2: Harr 1F 59
Tranquil Pas. SE3 2H 123
(off Montpelier Va.)
Tranquil Va. SE3 2G 123
Transenna Works N1 6B 66
(off Laycock St.)
Transept St. NW1 6D 4 (5C 82)
Transmere Cl. BR5: Pet W 6G 161
Transmere Rd. BR5: Pet W 6G 161
Transom Cl. SE16 4A 104
Transom Sq. E14 5D 104
Transport Av. TW8: Bford 5A 96
Tranton Rd. SE16 3G 103
Trappes Ho. SE16 4H 103
(off Camilla Rd.)
Traps La. KT3: N Mald 1A 152
Traq Motor Racing 6G 155
Travellers Path E6 1B 88
Travellers Way TW4: Cran 2A 112
Travers Cl. E17 1K 49
Travers Ho. SE10 6F 105
(off Trafalgar Gro.)
Travers Rd. N7 3A 66
Trays Hill Cl. N19 7G 47
Treacy Cl. WD23: B Hea 2B 26
Treadgold Ho. W11 7F 81
(off Bomore Rd.)
Treadgold St. W11 7F 81
Treadway St. E2 2H 85
Treasury Cl. SM6: W'gton 5H 167
Treasury M. DA5: Bexl 7H 127
Treasury Pas. SW1 6E 12
Treaty Cen. 3F 113
Treaty St. N1 1K 83
Trebeck St. W1 4J 11 (1F 101)
Trebovir Rd. SW5 5J 99
Treby St. E3 4B 86
Trecastle Way N7 4H 65
Tredegar Ho. E3 3C 86
(off Bow Rd.)
Tredegar M. E3 3B 86
Tredegar Rd. E3 2B 86
N11 7C 32

A-Z Big London 295

Tredagar Sq.—Turners Wood

Tredegar Sq. E3 .3B 86
Tredegar Ter. E3 .3B 86
Trederwen Rd. E8 .1G 85
Tredown Rd. SE26 .5J 139
Tredwell Cl. BR2: Broml .4C 160
SW2 .2K 137
Tredwell Rd. SE27 .4B 138
Treebank Gdns. W7 .7J 77
Tree Cl. TW10: Ham .1D 132
Treen Av. SW13 .3B 116
Tree Rd. E16 .6A 88
Treeside Cl. UB7: W Dray .4A 92
Treeside Pl. N10 .4F 47
Treetop Ct. CR7: Thor H .5C 156
Tree Top M. RM10: Dag .6K 73
Treetop M. NW6 .7G 63
Treetops Cl. SE2 .5E 108
Tree Vw. Cl. SE19 .1E 156
Treewall Gdns.
BR1: Broml .4K 141
Trefgarne Rd. RM10: Dag .2G 73
Trefil Wlk. N7 .4J 65
Trefoil Ho. DA18: Erith .2E 108
(off Kale Rd.)
SE10 .4G 105
Trefoil Rd. SW18 .5A 118
Trefusis Ct. TW5: Cran .1K 111
Tregaron Av. N8 .6J 47
Tregaron Gdns.
KT3: N Mald .4A 152
Tregarvon Rd. SW11 .4E 118
Tregenna Av. HA2: Harr .4E 58
Tregenna Cl. N14 .5B 22
Tregenna Ct. HA2: Harr .4E 58
Tregonwell Ter. SE9 .4F 143
Tregony Rd. BR6: Chels .4K 173
Trego Rd. E9 .7C 68
Tregothnan Rd. SW9 .3J 119
Tregunter Rd. SW10 .6K 99
Trehearn Rd. IG6: Ilf .1H 53
Treherne Ct. SW17 .4E 136
Trehern Rd. SW14 .3K 115
Trehurst St. E5 .5A 68
Trelawney Est. E9 .6J 67
Trelawney Ho. SE1 .5C 14
(off Union St.)
Trelawney Rd. IG6: Ilf .1H 53
Trelawn Rd. E10 .3E 68
SW2 .5A 120
Trelawny Cl. E17 .4D 50
Trellick Twr. W10 .4H 81
(off Golborne Rd.)
Trellis Ho. SW19 .7A 136
Trellis Sq. E3 .3B 86
Treloar Gdns. SE19 .6D 138
Tremadoc Rd. SW4 .4H 119
Tremaine Cl. SE4 .2C 122
Tremaine Rd. SE20 .2H 157
Trematon Bldg. N1 .2J 83
(off Trematon Wlk.)
Trematon Ho. SE11 .5K 19
(off Kennings Way)
Trematon M. N1 .2J 83
Trematon Pl. TW11: Tedd .7C 132
Trematon Wlk. N1 .2J 83
(off Trematon M.)
Tremelo Grn. RM8: Dag .1E 72
Tremlett Gro. N19 .3G 65
Tremlett M. N19 .3G 65
Trenance Gdns. IG3: Ilf .3A 72
Trenchard Av. HA4: Ruis .4K 57
Trenchard Cl. HA7: Stan .6F 27
NW9 .1A 44
Trenchard Ct. NW4 .5C 44
SM4: Mord .6J 153
Trenchard St. SE10 .5F 105
Trenchold St. SW8 .6J 101
Trendell Ho. E14 .6C 86
(off Dod St.)
Trenear Cl. BR6: Chels .4K 173
Trenholme Cl. SE20 .7H 139
Trenholme Rd. SE20 .7H 139
Trenholme Ter. SE20 .7H 139
Trenmar Gdns. NW10 .3D 80
Trent Av. W5 .3C 96
Trent Ct. CR2: S Croy .5C 168
(off Nottingham Rd.)
E11 .5J 51
Trent Gdns. N14 .6A 22
Trentham Ho. W3 .5K 79
Trentham St. SW18 .1J 135
Trent Ho. KT2: King T .1D 150
SE15 .4J 121
TRENT PARK .2A 22
Trent Park .1K 21
Trent Pk. EN4: Cockf .2B 22
Trent Pk. Golf Course .4B 22
Trent Rd. IG9: Buck H .1E 36
SW2 .5K 119
Trent Way KT4: Wor Pk .3E 164
UB4: Hayes .2G 75
Trentwood Side EN2: Enf .3E 22
Treport St. SW18 .7K 117
Tresco Cl. BR1: Broml .6G 141
Trescoe Gdns. HA2: Harr .7C 40
Tresco Gdns. IG3: Ilf .2A 72
Tresco Ho. SE11 .5J 19
Tresco Rd. SE15 .4H 121
Tresham Cres.
NW8 .3D 4 (4C 82)
Tresham Ho. WC1 .5G 7
(off Red Lion Sq.)
Tresham Rd. IG11: Bark .7K 71
Tresham Wlk. E9 .5J 67
Tresidder Ho. SW4 .7H 119
Tresilian Av. N21 .5E 22
Tressell Cl. N1 .7B 66
Tressillian Cres. SE4 .3C 122
Tressillian Rd. SE4 .4B 122
Tress Pl. SE1 .4A 14
Trestis Cl. UB4: Yead .5B 76
Treswell Rd. RM9: Dag .1E 90
Tretawn Gdns. NW7 .4F 29
Tretawn Pk. NW7 .4F 29
Trevanion Rd. W14 .4G 99
Treve Av. HA1: Harr .7H 41
Trevelyan Av. E12 .4D 70
Trevelyan Ct. KT3: N Mald .7A 152
Trevelyan Cres.
HA3: Kenton .7D 42
Trevelyan Gdns. NW10 .1E 80
Trevelyan Ho. E2 .3K 85
(off Morpeth St.)
SE5 .7B 102
(off John Ruskin St.)
Trevelyan Rd. E15 .4H 69
SW17 .5C 136
Trevenna Ho. SE23 .3K 139
(off Dacres Rd.)
Trevera Ct. EN3: Pond E .4F 25
Treveris St.
SE1 .5B 14 (1B 102)
Treversh Ct. BR1: Broml .1G 159
Treverton St. W10 .4F 81
Treverton Towers W10 .5F 81
(off Treverton St.)
Treves Cl. N21 .5E 22
Treves Ho. E1 .4G 85
(off Vallance Rd.)
Treville St. SW15 .7D 116
Treviso Rd. SE23 .2K 139
Trevithick Cl. TW14: Felt .1H 129
Trevithick Ho. SE16 .4H 103
(off Rennie Est.)
Trevithick St. SE8 .6C 104
Trevithick Way E3 .3C 86
Trevone Gdns. HA5: Pinn .6C 40
Trevor Cl. BR2: Hayes .7H 159
EN4: E Barn .6G 21
HA3: Hrw W .7E 26
TW7: Isle .5K 113
UB5: N'olt .2A 76
Trevor Cres. HA4: Ruis .4H 57
Trevor Gdns. HA4: Ruis .4J 57
HA8: Edg .1K 43
UB5: N'olt .2A 76
Trevor Pl. SW7 .7D 10 (2C 100)
Trevor Rd. HA8: Edg .1K 43
IG8: Wfd G .7D 36
SW19 .7G 135
UB3: Hayes .2G 93
Trevor Roper Cl. IG1: Ilf .2D 70
Trevor Sq. SW7 .7E 10 (2D 100)
Trevor St. SW7 .7D 10 (2C 100)
Trevor Wlk. SW7 .7E 10
(off Lancelot Pl.)
Trevose Ho. SE11 .5H 19
(off Orsett St.)
Trevose Rd. E17 .1F 51
Trewenna Dr. KT9: Chess .5D 162
Trewince Rd. SW20 .1E 152
Trewint St. SW18 .2A 136
Trewsbury Ho. SE2 .1D 108
Trewsbury Rd. SE26 .5K 139
Tria Apts. E2 .3G 85
(off Durant St.)
Triandra Way UB4: Yead .5B 76
The Triangle DA15: Sidc .7A 126
(off Burnt Oak La.)
E8 .1H 85
EC1 .3B 8
IG11: Bark .6G 71
KT1: King T .2H 151
N13 .4E 32
The Triangle Bus. Cen.
NW10 .3B 80
Triangle Cen. UB1: S'hall .1H 95
Triangle Ct. E16 .5B 88
SE1 .5D 14
(off Redcross Way)
Triangle Est. SE11 .6J 19
(off Kennington La.)
Triangle Ho. SE1 .6J 15
(off Three Oak La.)
Triangle Pas. EN4: E Barn .4F 21
Triangle Pl. SW4 .4H 119
Triangle Rd. E8 .1H 85
Triangle Way W3 .3G 97
Triangle Works N9 .2E 34
Tribeca Apts. E1 .6K 9
(off Heneage St.)
Trickett Ho. SM2: Sutt .7K 165
Trico Ho. TW8: Bford .5D 96
(off Ealing Rd.)
Tricorn Ho. SE28 .1J 107
Trident Bus. Cen. SW17 .5D 136
Trident Gdns. UB5: N'olt .3B 76
Trident Ho. E14 .6E 86
(off Blair St.)
SE28 .1H 107
TW19: Stanw .7A 110
(off Clare Rd.)
Trident Pl. SW3 .7B 16
(off Old Church St.)
Trident Point HA1: Harr .6H 41
Trident St. SE16 .4K 103
Trident Way UB2: S'hall .3K 93
Trig La. EC4 .2C 14 (7C 84)
Trigon Rd. SW8 .7K 101
Trilby Rd. SE23 .2K 139
Trillo Ct. IG2: Ilf .7J 53
Trimdon NW1 .1G 83
Trimmer Wlk. TW8: Bford .6E 96
Trim St. SE14 .6B 104
Trinder Gdns. N19 .1J 65
Trinder M. SW12 .1E 136
TW11: Tedd .5A 132
Trinder Rd. EN5: Barn .5A 20
N19 .1J 65
Tring Av. HA9: Wemb .6G 61
UB1: S'hall .6D 76
W5 .1F 97
Tring Cl. IG2: Ilf .5H 53
Tring Ct. TW1: Twick .4A 132
Trinidad Gdns. RM10: Dag .7K 73
Trinidad Ho. E14 .7B 86
(off Gill St.)
Trinidad St. E14 .7B 86
Trinity Av. EN1: Enf .6A 24
N2 .3B 46
Trinity Buoy Wharf E14 .7G 87
Trinity Chu. Pas. SW13 .6D 98
Trinity Chu. Rd. SW13 .6D 98
Trinity Chu. Sq. SE1 .7D 14 (3C 102)
Trinity Cl. BR2: Broml .1C 172
CR2: Sande .7E 168
E8 .6F 67
E11 .2G 69
NW3 .4B 64
SE13 .4F 123
SW4 .4G 119
TW4: Houn .4C 112
Trinity Cotts. TW9: Rich .3F 115
Trinity Ct. BR1: Broml .1H 159
(off Highland Rd.)
CR0: C'don .2C 168
EN2: Enf .2H 23
N1 .1E 84
(off Downham Rd.)
N18 .6A 34
NW2 .5E 62
SE7 .4B 106
SE8 .5A 104
(off Evelyn St.)
SE25 .6E 156
SE26 .3J 139
SW9 .3K 119
W2 .6A 82
(off Gloucester Ter.)
W9 .3H 81
(off Croxley Rd.)
WC1 .3G 7
Trinity Cres. SW17 .2D 136
Trinity Dr. UB8: Hil .5E 74
Trinity Gdns. E16 .5H 87
(not continuous)
SW9 .4K 119
Trinity Grn. E1 .4J 85
Trinity Gro. SE10 .1E 122
Trinity Hospital SE10 .5F 105
Trinity Ho. .2J 15
Trinity Ho. RM8: Dag .5B 72
SE1 .3C 102
(off Bath Ter.)
W14 .3H 99
Trinity Laban .6E 104
(within Old Royal Naval College)
Trinity M. E1 .5J 85
(off Redman's Rd.)
SE20 .1H 157
W10 .6F 81
Trinity Pk. E4 .6G 35
Trinity Path SE26 .3J 139
(not continuous)
Trinity Pl. DA6: Bex .4F 127
EC3 .2J 15 (7F 85)
Trinity Ri. SW2 .1A 138
Trinity Rd. IG6: Ilf .3G 53
N2 .3B 46
N22 .7D 32
(not continuous)
SW17 .4A 118
SW18 .4A 118
SW19 .6J 135
TW9: Rich .3F 115
UB1: S'hall .1C 94
Trinity Sq. E14 .6F 69
EC3 .3H 15 (7E 84)
Trinity St. E16 .5H 87
EN2: Enf .2H 23
SE1 .7D 14 (2C 102)
(not continuous)
Trinity Ter. IG9: Lough .1E 36
Trinity Twr. E1 .7G 85
(off Vaughan Way)
E14 .3D 104
Trinity Wlk. NW3 .6A 64
Trinity Way E4 .6G 35
W3 .7A 80
Trio Pl. SE1 .7D 14 (2C 102)
Triptych Ho. SE8 .7C 104
(off Watson's St.)
Triscott Ho. UB3: Hayes .1J 93
Tristan Ct. SE8 .6B 104
(off Dorking Cl.)
Tristan Sq. SE3 .3G 123
Tristram Cl. E17 .3F 51
Tristram Dr. N9 .3B 34
Tristram Rd. BR1: Broml .4H 141
Triton Ct. E16 .5J 87
(off Robertson Rd.)
Triton Ho. E14 .4D 104
(off Cahir St.)
Triton Sq. NW1 .3A 6 (4G 83)
Triton St. NW1 .3K 5 (4F 83)
Tritton Av. CR0: Bedd .4J 167
Tritton Rd. SE21 .3D 138
Triumph Cl. UB3: Harl .1E 110
Triumph Ho. IG11: Bark .3A 90
Triumph Rd. E6 .6D 88
Triumph Trad. Est. N17 .6B 34
Trocette Mans. SE1 .3E 102
(off Bermondsey St.)
Trojan Ct. NW6 .7G 63
Trojan Ind. Est. NW10 .6B 62
Trojan M. SW19 .7J 135
Trojan Way CR0: Wadd .3K 167
Troon Cl. SE16 .5H 103
SE28 .6D 90
Troon Ho. E1 .6A 86
(off White Horse Rd.)
Troon St. E1 .6A 86
Tropical Ct. W10 .3F 81
(off Kilburn La.)
Trosley Rd. DA17: Belv .6G 109
Trossachs Rd. SE22 .5E 120
Trothy Rd. SE1 .4G 103
Trotman Ho. SE14 .1J 121
(off Pomeroy St.)
Trott Rd. N10 .7J 31
Trott St. SW11 .1C 118
Trotwood Ho. SE16 .2H 103
(off Wilson Gro.)
Troubridge Sq. E17 .3E 50
Troughton Rd. SE7 .5K 105
Troutbeck NW1 .2K 5
Troutbeck Rd. SE14 .1A 122
Trout Rd. UB7: Yiew .7A 74
Trouville Rd. SW4 .6G 119
Trowbridge Est. E9 .6B 68
(off Osborne Rd.)
Trowbridge Ho. E9 .6B 68
(off Felstead St.)
Trowbridge Rd. E9 .6B 68
Trowlock Av. TW11: Tedd .6C 132
Trowlock Island TW11: Tedd .6D 132
Trowlock Way TW11: Tedd .6D 132
Troy Ct. SE18 .4F 107
W8 .3J 99
(off Kensington High St.)
Troy Ind. Est. HA1: Harr .5K 41
Troy Rd. SE19 .6D 138
Troy Town SE15 .3G 121
Trubshaw Rd. UB2: S'hall .3F 95
True Lovers Ct. HA6: Nwood .1F 39
Trueman Cl. HA8: Edg .7C 28
Truesdale Rd. E6 .6D 88
Truesdales UB10: Ick .2E 56
truGym
Bromley .1J 159
(off East St.)
Trulock Ct. N17 .7B 34
Trulock Rd. N17 .7B 34
Trumans Rd. N16 .5F 67
Truman Wlk. E3 .4D 86
Trumpers Way W7 .3J 95
Trumpington Rd. E7 .4H 69
Trump St. EC2 .1D 14 (6C 84)
Trundle Ho. SE1 .6C 14
(off Trundle St.)
Trundlers Way WD23: B Hea .1D 26
Trundle St. SE1 .6C 14 (2C 102)
Trundleys Rd. SE8 .5K 103
Trundley's Ter. SE8 .4K 103
Truro Gdns. IG1: Ilf .7C 52
Truro Ho. HA5: Hat E .1D 40
W2 .5J 81
(off Westbourne Pk. Rd.)
Truro Rd. E17 .4B 50
N22 .7D 32
Truro St. NW5 .6E 64
Truro Way UB4: Hayes .3G 75
Truslove Rd. SE27 .5A 138
Trussley Rd. W6 .3E 98
Trust Wlk. SE21 .1B 138
Tryfan Cl. IG4: Ilf .5B 52
Tryon Cres. E9 .1J 85
Tryon St. SW3 .5E 16 (5D 100)
Trystings Cl. KT10: Clay .6A 162
Tuam Rd. SE18 .6H 107
Tubbenden Cl. BR6: Orp .3J 173
Tubbenden Dr. BR6: Orp .4H 173
Tubbenden La. BR6: Orp .4H 173
Tubbenden La. Sth.
BR6: Farnb .5H 173
Tubbs Rd. NW10 .2B 80
Tucana Ct. E1 .3K 9
(off Cygnet St.)
Tucana Hgts. E20 .5E 68
(off Cheering La.)
Tucklow Wlk. SW15 .7B 116
Tudor Av. KT4: Wor Pk .3D 164
TW12: Hamp .7E 130
Tudor Cl. BR7: Chst .1D 160
HA5: Eastc .5J 39
IG7: Chig .4K 37
IG8: Wfd G .5E 36
KT9: Chess .5E 162
N6 .7G 47
NW3 .5C 64
NW7 .6H 29
NW9 .2J 61
SM3: Cheam .5F 165
SM6: W'gton .7G 167
SW2 .6K 119
TW12: Hamp H .5G 131
TW15: Ashf .4A 128
Tudor Ct. DA14: Sidc .3A 144
E17 .7B 50
N1 .6E 66
N22 .7D 32
SE9 .4C 124
SE16 .1K 103
(off Princes Riverside Rd.)
TW11: Tedd .6K 131
TW13: Hanw .4A 130
TW19: Stanw .6A 110
W3 .2G 97
Tudor Ct. Nth. HA9: Wemb .5G 61
Tudor Ct. Sth. HA9: Wemb .5G 61
Tudor Cres. EN2: Enf .1H 23
Tudor Dr. KT2: King T .5D 132
SM4: Mord .6F 153
Tudor Ent. Pk. HA1: Harr .3K 59
HA3: W'stone .3H 41
Tudor Est. NW10 .2H 79
Tudor Gdns. BR4: W W'ck .3E 170
HA3: Hrw W .2H 41
NW9 .2J 61
SW13 .3A 116
TW1: Twick .1K 131
W3 .5G 79
Tudor Gro. E9 .7J 67
N20 .2H 31
Tudor Ho. E9 .7J 67
E16 .1K 105
(off Wesley Av.)
HA5: Pinn .2A 40
(off Pinner Hill Rd.)
SE1 .5J 15
W14 .4F 99
(off Windsor Way)
Tudor M. E17 .4B 50
Tudor Pde. RM6: Chad H .7D 54
SE9 .4C 124
Tudor Park Footgolf .3F 21
Tudor Pl. CR4: Mitc .7C 136
IG9: Buck H .2H 37
SE19 .7F 139
Tudor Rd. BR3: Beck .3E 158
E4 .6J 35
E6 .1A 88
E9 .1H 85
EN5: New Bar .3D 20
HA3: Hrw W, W'stone .2H 41
HA5: Pinn .2A 40
IG11: Bark .1K 89
KT2: King T .7G 133
N9 .7C 24
SE19 .7F 139
SE25 .5H 157
TW3: Houn .4H 113
TW12: Hamp .7E 130
TW15: Ashf .6F 129
UB1: S'hall .7C 76
UB3: Hayes .6F 75
Tudor Sq. UB3: Hayes .5F 75
Tudor Stacks SE24 .4C 120
Tudor St. EC4 .2K 13 (7A 84)
Tudor Wlk. DA5: Bexl .6E 126
Tudor Way BR5: Pet W .6H 161
N14 .1C 32
UB10: Hil .6C 56
W3 .2G 97
Tudor Well Cl. HA7: Stan .5G 27
Tudor Works UB4: Yead .1A 94
Tudway Rd. SE3 .4A 124
Tufnell Ct. E3 .1B 86
(off Old Ford Rd.)
TUFNELL PARK .4G 65
Tufnell Pk. Hall .3G 65
Tufnell Pk. Rd. N7 .4G 65
N19 .4G 65
Tufton Ct. SW1 .2E 18
(off Tufton St.)
Tufton Gdns. KT8: W Mole .2F 149
Tufton Rd. E4 .4H 35
Tufton St. SW1 .1E 18 (3J 101)
Tugboat St. SE28 .2J 107
Tugela Rd. CR0: C'don .6D 156
Tugela St. SE6 .2B 140
Tugmutton Cl. BR6: Farnb .4F 173
Tulett Av. N20 .2G 31
Tulip Cl. CR0: C'don .1K 169
E6 .5D 88
TW12: Hamp .6D 130
UB2: S'hall .2G 95
Tulip Gdns. E4 .3A 36
IG1: Ilf .6F 71
Tullis Ho. E9 .7J 67
(off Frampton Pk. Rd.)
Tull St. CR4: Mitc .7D 154
Tulse Cl. BR3: Beck .3E 158
TULSE HILL .1B 138
Tulse Hill SW2 .6A 120
Tulse Hill Est. SW2 .6A 120
Tulse Ho. SW2 .6A 120
Tulsemere Rd. SE27 .2C 138
Tumbling Bay KT12: Walt T .6J 147
Tummons Gdns. SE25 .2E 156
Tump Ho. SE28 .1J 107
Tunbridge Ho. EC1 .1K 7
Tuncombe Rd. N18 .4K 33
Tunis Rd. W12 .1E 98
Tunley Grn. E14 .5B 86
Tunley Rd. NW10 .1A 80
SW17 .1E 136
Tunmarsh La. E13 .3K 87
Tunnan Leys E6 .6E 88
Tunnel App. E14 .7A 86
SE10 .2G 105
SE16 .2J 103
Tunnel Av. SE10 .2F 105
Tunnel Av. Trad. Est. SE10 .2F 105
Tunnel Gdns. N11 .7B 32
Tunnel Link Rd.
TW6: H'row A .6C 110
Tunnel Rd. SE16 .2J 103
Tunnel Rd. E. TW6: H'row A .1D 110
Tunnel Rd. W. TW6: H'row A .1C 110
Tunstall Cl. BR6: Orp .4J 173
Tunstall Rd. CR0: C'don .1E 168
SW9 .4K 119
Tunstall Wlk. TW8: Bford .6E 96
Tunstock Way DA17: Belv .3E 108
Tunworth Cl. NW9 .6J 43
Tunworth Cres. SW15 .6B 116
Tun Yd. SW8 .2F 119
(off Peardon St.)
Tupelo Rd. E10 .2D 68
Tupman Ho. SE16 .2G 103
(off Scott Lidgett Cres.)
Tuppy St. SE28 .3G 107
Turenne Cl. SW18 .4A 118
Turing St. E20 .7E 68
Turin Rd. N9 .7D 24
Turin St. E2 .2K 9 (3G 85)
Turkey Oak Cl. SE19 .1E 156
Turks Boatyard
KT1: King T .1D 150
Turks Cl. UB8: Hil .3C 74
Turk's Head Yd. EC1 .5A 8 (5B 84)
Turk's Row SW3 .5F 17 (5D 100)
Turle Rd. N4 .2K 65
SW16 .2J 155
Turlewray Cl. N4 .1K 65
Turley Cl. E15 .1G 87
Turnagain La. EC4 .7A 8
Turnage Rd. RM8: Dag .1E 72
Turnant Rd. N17 .1C 48
Turnberry Cl. NW4 .2F 45
SE16 .5H 103
Turnberry Quay E14 .3D 104
Turnberry Way BR6: Orp .1H 173
Turnbull Ho. N1 .1B 84
Turnbury Cl. SE28 .6D 90
Turnchapel M. SW4 .3F 119
Turner Av. CR4: Mitc .1D 154
N15 .4E 48
TW2: Twick .3G 131
Turner Cl. HA0: Wemb .6D 60
NW11 .6K 45
SW9 .7B 102
UB4: Hayes .2E 74
Turner Ct. SE16 .2J 103
(off Albion St.)
Turner Cres. CR0: C'don .6C 156
Turner Dr. NW11 .6K 45
Turner Ho. E14 .2C 104
(off Cassilis Rd.)
NW6 .5A 64
(off Dresden Cl.)
NW8 .2C 82
(off Townshend Est.)
SW1 .4D 18
(off Herrick St.)
TW1: Twick .6D 114
(off Clevedon Rd.)
Turner M. SM2: Sutt .7K 165
Turner Pde. N1 .7A 66
(off Barnsbury Pk.)
Turner Pl. SW11 .5C 118
Turner Rd. E17 .3E 50
HA8: Edg .2E 42
KT3: N Mald .7K 151
Turners Cl. N20 .3J 31
Turners Ct. E15 .4E 68
(off Drapers Rd.)
N15 .5D 48
Turners Mdw. Way BR3: Beck .1B 158
Turners Rd. E3 .5B 86
Turner St. E1 .5H 85
E16 .6H 87
Turners Way CR0: Wadd .2A 168
Turners Wood NW11 .7A 46

Turneville Rd.—Upperton Rd. W.

Turneville Rd. W14 . . . . 6H 99
Turney Rd. SE21 . . . . 7C 120
TURNHAM GREEN 4A 98
Turnham Grn. Ter. W4 . . . . 4A 98
Turnham Grn. Ter. M.
W4 . . . . 4A 98
Turnham Rd. SE4 . . . . 5A 122
Turnmill St. EC1 . . . . 4A 8 (4B 84)
Turnour Ho. E1 . . . . 6H 85
(off Walburgh St.)
Turnpike Cl. DA16: Well 3A 126
SE8 . . . . 7B 104
Turnpike Ct. DA6: Bex 4D 126
Turnpike Ho. EC1 . . . . 2B 8 (3B 84)
Turnpike La. N8 . . . . 4K 47
SM1: Sutt 5A 166
UB10: Uxb 3A 74
Turnpike Link CR0: C'don 2E 168
Turnpike M. N8 . . . . 3A 48
(off Turnpike La.)
Turnpike Pde. N15 . . . . 3B 48
(off Green Lanes)
Turnpike Way TW7: Isle 1A 114
Turnpin La. SE10 . . . . 6E 104
Turnstone Cl. E13 . . . . 3J 87
NW9 . . . . 2A 44
UB10: Ick 5D 56
Turnstone Ho. E1 . . . . 3K 15
(off Star Pl.)
Turpentine La. SW1 . . . . 5K 17 (5F 101)
Turpin Cl. E1 . . . . 7K 85
Turpington Cl. BR2: Broml 7C 160
Turpington La. BR2: Broml 7C 160
Turpin Ho. SW11 . . . . 1F 119
Turpin Rd. TW14: Felt 6H 111
Turpin's La. IG8: Wfd G 5J 37
Turpins Yd. NW2 . . . . 5F 63
SE10 . . . . 7E 104
Turpin Way N19 . . . . 2H 65
SM6: W'gton 7F 167
Turquand St. SE17 . . . . 4C 102
Turret Gro. SW4 . . . . 3G 119
Turton Rd. HA0: Wemb 5E 60
Turville Ho. NW8 . . . . 3C 4
(off Grendon St.)
Turville St. E2 . . . . 3J 9 (4F 85)
Tuscan Ho. E2 . . . . 3J 85
(off Knottisford St.)
Tuscan Rd. SE18 . . . . 5H 107
Tuscany Corte SE13 . . . . 3D 122
(off Loampit Va.)
Tuscany Ho. E17 . . . . 2B 50
IG3: Ilf 6A 54
Tuskar St. SE10 . . . . 6G 105
Tussah Ho. E2 . . . . 2J 85
(off Russia La.)
Tustin Est. SE15 . . . . 6J 103
Tuttlebee La. IG9: Buck H 2D 36
Tuttle Ho. SW1 . . . . 6C 18
(off Aylesford St.)
Tweed Ct. W7 . . . . 6J 77
(off Hanway Rd.)
Tweeddale Gro. UB10: Ick 3E 56
Tweeddale Rd. SM5: Cars 1B 166
Tweed Glen RM1: Rom 1K 55
Tweed Grn. RM1: Rom 1K 55
Tweedmouth Rd. E13 . . . . 2K 87
Tweed Wlk. E14 . . . . 4E 86
Tweed Way RM1: Rom 1K 55
Tweedy Cl. EN1: Enf 5A 24
Tweedy Rd. BR1: Broml 1J 159
Tweezer's All. WC2 . . . . 2J 13
Twelve Acre Ho. E12 . . . . 3E 70
(off Grantham Rd.)
Twelvetrees Bus. Pk. E3 . . . . 4F 87
Twelvetrees Cres. E3 . . . . 4E 86
(not continuous)
Twentyman Cl. IG8: Wfd G 5D 36
TWICKENHAM 1A 132
TWICKENHAM BRI. 5C 114
Twickenham Cl.
CR0: Bedd 3K 167
Twickenham Gdns.
HA3: Hrw W 7D 26
UB6: G'frd 5A 60
Twickenham Mus. 1A 132
(off The Embankment)
Twickenham Rd. E11 . . . . 2E 68
TW7: Isle 5A 114
TW9: Rich 4C 114
TW11: Tedd 4A 132
(not continuous)
TW13: Hanw 3D 130
Twickenham Stadium 6J 113
Twickenham Stoop 7J 113
Twickenham Tourist Information Centre
. . . . 1B 132
(off Church St.)
Twickenham Trad. Est.
TW1: Twick 6K 113
Twig Folly Cl. E2 . . . . 2K 85
Twigg Cl. DA8: Erith 7K 109
Twilley St. SW18 . . . . 7K 117
Twill Way SM6: W'gton 2E 166
Twin Bridges Bus. Pk.
CR2: S Croy 6D 168
Twine Cl. IG11: Bark 3B 90
Twine Ct. E1 . . . . 7J 85
Twineham Grn. N12 . . . . 4D 30
Twine Ter. E3 . . . . 4B 86
(off Ropery St.)
Twining Av. TW2: Twick 3G 131
Twin Tumps Way SE28 . . . . 7A 90
Twisden Rd. NW5 . . . . 4F 65
Twist Ho. SE1 . . . . 3E 102
Twitten Gro. BR1: Broml 3D 160
Two Southbank Pl. SE1 . . . . 6H 13
(off York Rd.)
Twybridge Way NW10 . . . . 7J 61
Twycross M. SE10 . . . . 5G 105
Twyford Abbey Rd. NW10 . . . . 3F 79
Twyford Av. N2 . . . . 3D 46
W3 . . . . 7G 79
Twyford Ct. HA0: Wemb 2E 78
(off Vicars Bri. Cl.)
N10 . . . . 3E 46
Twyford Cres. W3 . . . . 1G 97
Twyford Ho. N5 . . . . 3B 66
N15 . . . . 6E 48
(off Chisley Rd.)
Twyford Pl. WC2 . . . . 7G 7 (6K 83)
Twyford Rd. HA2: Harr 1F 59
IG1: Ilf 5G 71
SM5: Cars 1B 166
Twyford Sports Cen. 1H 97
Twyford St. N1 . . . . 1K 83
Twynholm Mans. SW6 . . . . 7G 99
(off Lillie Rd.)
Tyas Rd. E16 . . . . 4H 87
Tybenham Rd. SW19 . . . . 3J 153
Tyberry Rd. EN3: Enf H 3C 24
Tyburn Ho. NW8 . . . . 3B 4
(off Fisherton St.)
Tyburn La. HA1: Harr 7K 41
Tyburn Tree (site of) 1F 11
Tyburn Way W1 . . . . 2F 11 (7D 82)
Tye La. BR6: Farnb 5G 173
Tyers Est. SE1 . . . . 6G 15
Tyer's Ga. SE1 . . . . 7G 15 (2E 102)
Tyers St. SE11 . . . . 6G 19 (5K 101)
Tyers Ter. SE11 . . . . 6G 19 (5K 101)
Tyeshurst Cl. SE2 . . . . 5E 108
Tygan Ho. SM3: Cheam 6G 165
(off The Broadway)
Tylecroft Rd. SW16 . . . . 2J 155
Tylehurst Gdns. IG1: Ilf 5G 71
Tyler Cl. DA8: Erith 7H 109
E2 . . . . 2F 85
Tyler Ct. SE17 . . . . 4D 102
(off New Paragon Wlk.)
Tyler Rd. UB2: S'hall 3F 95
Tyler's Ct. W1 . . . . 1C 12
Tylers Ct. E17 . . . . 4C 50
(off Westbury Rd.)
HA0: Wemb 2E 78
Tylers Ga. HA3: Kenton 6E 42
Tylers Path SM5: Cars 4D 166
Tyler St. SE10 . . . . 5G 105
(not continuous)
Tylney Av. SE19 . . . . 5F 139
(not continuous)
Tylney Ho. E1 . . . . 6H 85
(off Nelson St.)
Tylney Rd. BR1: Broml 2B 160
E7 . . . . 4A 70
Tynamara KT1: King T 4D 150
(off Portsmouth Rd.)
Tynan Cl. TW14: Felt 1J 129
Tyndale Ct. E9 . . . . 6A 68
(off Brookfield Rd.)
E14 . . . . 5D 104
(off Transom Sq.)
Tyndale Ho. N1 . . . . 7B 66
(off Tyndale La.)
Tyndale La. N1 . . . . 7B 66
Tyndale Mans. N1 . . . . 7B 66
(off Upper St.)
Tyndale Ter. N1 . . . . 7B 66
Tyndall Gdns. E10 . . . . 2E 68
Tyndall Rd. DA16: Well 3K 125
E10 . . . . 2E 68
Tyne Ct. W7 . . . . 6J 77
(off Hanway Rd.)
Tyneham Cl. SW11 . . . . 3E 118
Tyneham Rd. SW11 . . . . 2E 118
Tyne Ho. KT2: King T 1D 150
Tynemouth Cl. E6 . . . . 6F 89
Tynemouth Dr. EN1: Enf 1B 24
Tynemouth Rd. CR4: Mitc 7E 136
N15 . . . . 4F 49
SE18 . . . . 5J 107
Tynemouth St. SW6 . . . . 2A 118
Tyne St. E1 . . . . 7K 9 (6F 85)
Tynne Ct. E14 . . . . 4E 86
(off Teviot St.)
Tynsdale Rd. NW10 . . . . 7A 62
Tynte Ct. E9 . . . . 5A 68
(off Mabley St.)
Tynwald Ho. SE26 . . . . 3G 139
Type St. E2 . . . . 2K 85
Typhoon Way SM6: W'gton 7J 167
Tyrawley Rd. SW6 . . . . 1K 117
Tyre La. NW9 . . . . 4A 44
Tyrell Cl. HA1: Harr 4J 59
Tyrell Ct. SM5: Cars 4D 166
Tyrell Ho. BR3: Beck 5D 140
(off Beckenham Hill Rd.)
Tyrian Pl. E1 . . . . 5G 85
Tyrols Rd. SE23 . . . . 1K 139
Tyrone Rd. E6 . . . . 2D 88
Tyron Way DA14: Sidc 4J 143
Tyrrell Av. DA16: Well 5A 126
Tyrrell Ho. SW1 . . . . 7B 18
(off Churchill Gdns.)
Tyrrell Rd. SE22 . . . . 4G 121
Tyrrell Sq. CR4: Mitc 1C 154
Tyrrel Way NW9 . . . . 7B 44
Tyrwhitt Rd. SE4 . . . . 3C 122
Tysoe St. EC1 . . . . 2K 7 (3A 84)
Tyson Gdns. SE23 . . . . 7J 121
Tyson Rd. SE23 . . . . 7J 121
Tyssen Pas. E8 . . . . 6F 67
Tyssen Rd. N16 . . . . 3F 67
Tyssen St. E8 . . . . 6F 67
N1 . . . . 2E 84
Tytherton E2 . . . . 2J 85
(off Cyprus St.)
Tytherton Rd. N19 . . . . 3H 65

U

UAL (London College of Fashion) 6H 7
Uamvar St. E14 . . . . 5D 86
Uber E17 . . . . 4B 50
Uckfield Gro. CR4: Mitc 7E 136
Udall St. SW1 . . . . 4B 18 (4G 101)
Udimore Ho. W10 . . . . 5E 80
(off Sutton Way)
Udney Pk. Rd. TW11: Tedd 6A 132
Uffington Rd. NW10 . . . . 1C 80
SE27 . . . . 4A 138
Ufford Cl. HA3: Hrw W 7A 26
Ufford Rd. HA3: Hrw W 7A 26
Ufford St. SE1 . . . . 6K 13 (2A 102)
Ufton Ct. UB5: N'olt 3B 76
Ufton Gro. N1 . . . . 7D 66
Ufton Rd. N1 . . . . 7D 66
(not continuous)
Uhura Sq. N16 . . . . 3E 66
Ujima Ct. SW16 . . . . 4J 137
Ullathorne Rd. SW16 . . . . 4G 137
Ulleswater Rd. N14 . . . . 3D 32
Ullin St. E14 . . . . 5E 86
Ullswater E18 . . . . 2J 51
Ullswater Cl. BR1: Broml 7G 141
SW15 . . . . 4K 133
UB4: Hayes 2G 75
Ullswater Ct. HA2: Harr 7E 40
Ullswater Cres. SW15 . . . . 4K 133
Ullswater Ho. SE15 . . . . 6J 103
(off Hillbeck Cl.)
Ullswater Rd. SE27 . . . . 2B 138
SW13 . . . . 7C 98
Ulster Gdns. N13 . . . . 4H 33
Ulster Pl. NW1 . . . . 4J 5 (4F 83)
Ulster Ter. NW1 . . . . 3H 5 (4F 83)
Ulundi Rd. SE3 . . . . 6G 105
Ulva Rd. SW15 . . . . 5F 117
Ulverscroft Rd. SE22 . . . . 5F 121
Ulverstone Rd. SE27 . . . . 2B 138
Ulverston Rd. E17 . . . . 2F 51
Ulysses Rd. NW6 . . . . 5H 63
Umberston St. E1 . . . . 6G 85
Umbria St. SW15 . . . . 6C 116
Umbriel Pl. E13 . . . . 2J 87
Umfreville Rd. N4 . . . . 6B 48
Umpire Vw. HA1: Harr 5G 41
Undercliff Rd. SE13 . . . . 3C 122
UNDERHILL 5D 20
Underhill EN5: Barn 5D 20
Underhill Ct. EN5: Barn 5D 20
Underhill Gdns. W5 . . . . 7C 78
Underhill Ho. E14 . . . . 5C 86
(off Burgess St.)
Underhill Pas. NW1 . . . . 1F 83
(off Camden High St.)
Underhill Rd. SE22 . . . . 5G 121
Underhill St. NW1 . . . . 1F 83
Underne Av. N14 . . . . 2A 32
Undershaft EC3 . . . . 1G 15 (6E 84)
Undershaw Rd.
BR1: Broml 3H 141
The Underwood SE9 . . . . 2D 142
Underwood CR0: New Ad 5E 170
The Underwood Bldg. EC1 . . . . 6C 8
(off Bartholomew Cl.)
Underwood Ct. E10 . . . . 1D 68
(off Leyton Grange Est.)
Underwood Ho.
KT8: W Mole 5E 148
(off Approach Rd.)
W6 . . . . 3D 98
(off Sycamore Gdns.)
Underwood Rd. E1 . . . . 4G 85
E4 . . . . 5J 35
IG8: Wfd G 7F 37
Underwood Row N1 . . . . 1D 8 (3C 84)
Underwood St. N1 . . . . 1D 8 (3C 84)
Undine Rd. E14 . . . . 4D 104
Undine St. SW17 . . . . 5D 136
Uneeda Dr. UB6: G'frd 1H 77
Unex Twr. E15 . . . . 7F 69
(off Station St.)
Unicorn Bldg. E1 . . . . 7K 85
(off Jardine Rd.)
Unicorn Theatre 1E 102
Unicorn Vw. EN5: Barn 6C 20
Unicorn Works N17 . . . . 7D 34
Union Cl. E11 . . . . 4F 69
Union Cotts. E15 . . . . 7G 69
Union Ct. EC2 . . . . 7G 9
SW4 . . . . 2J 119
TW9: Rich 5E 114
W9 . . . . 5J 81
(off Elmfield Way)
Union Dr. E1 . . . . 4A 86
Union Gro. SW8 . . . . 2H 119
Union Ho. CR0: C'don 7C 156
Union La. TW7: Isle 2A 114
Union M. SW4 . . . . 2J 119
Union Mills Apts. E8 . . . . 1F 85
(off Samuel St.)
Union Pk. SE10 . . . . 5H 105
Union Rd. BR2: Broml 5B 160
CR0: C'don 7C 156
E17 . . . . 6B 50
HA0: Wemb 6E 60
N11 . . . . 6C 32
RM7: Rush G 6K 55
SW4 . . . . 2H 119
SW8 . . . . 2H 119
UB5: N'olt 2E 76
Union Sq. N1 . . . . 1C 84
Union St. EN5: Barn 3B 20
KT1: King T 2D 150
SE1 . . . . 5A 14 (1B 102)
Union Theatre 6B 14 (2B 102)
Union Wlk. E2 . . . . 1H 9 (3E 84)
Union Wharf N1 . . . . 1C 84
(Arlington Av.)
N1 . . . . 2C 84
(off Wenlock Rd.)
UB7: Yiew 1A 92
(off Bentinck Rd.)
Union Yd. W1 . . . . 1K 11 (6F 83)
Unitair Cen. TW14: Bedf 6E 110
United Dr. TW14: Felt 7H 111
United Ho. SE16 . . . . 2J 103
(off Brunel Rd.)
Unit Workshops E1 . . . . 6G 85
(off Adler St.)
Unity Cl. CR0: New Ad 7D 170
NW10 . . . . 6C 62
SE19 . . . . 5C 138
Unity Ct. SE1 . . . . 5F 103
(off Fortune Pl.)
Unity M. NW1 . . . . 2H 83
Unity Pl. E17 . . . . 3A 50
Unity Ter. HA2: Harr 1F 59
Unity Trad. Est. IG8: Wfd G 2B 52
Unity Way SE18 . . . . 3B 106
Unity Wharf SE1 . . . . 6K 15
(off Mill St.)
Universal Ho. UB1: S'hall 7C 76
University Cl. NW7 . . . . 7G 29
University College London
Art Mus. 3C 6
(off Gower St.)
Department of Geological
Collections 4C 6
(off Gower St.)
University College London
Bloomsbury Campus
. . . . 3C 6 (4H 83)
The Institute of Cancer Research
. . . . 5A 100
Institute of Neurology 4F 7
(off Queen Sq.)
Slade School of Fine Art 3C 6
(off Gower Ct.)
Wolfson Ho. 2B 6
(off Stephenson Way)
University College
London Medical School
Whittington Hospital Campus
. . . . 2G 65
(within Whittington Hospital)
University Gdns. DA5: Bexl 7F 127
University of East London
Docklands Campus 7E 88
Stratford Campus 6G 69
University of Greenwich
Avery Hill Campus 6G 125
King William Wlk. 6F 105
Maritime Greenwich Campus
. . . . 6E 104
University of London
Birkbeck College 5D 6 (5H 83)
Heythrop College 3K 99
(off Kensington Sq.)
Institutes of Education &
Advanced Legal Studies
. . . . 4D 6 (4H 83)
School of Hygiene &
Tropical Medicine 5D 6
School of Oriental &
African Studies 4D 6
Senate House 5D 6 (5H 83)
Warburg Institute 4D 6 (4H 83)
University of London Observatory
. . . . 6G 29
University of North London
Hornsey Rd. 4A 66
Ladbrooke House 5C 66
North London Campus,
Spring House 6A 66
University of the Arts London
Camberwell College of Arts,
Peckham Rd. 1E 120
Wilson Rd. 1E 120
Chelsea College of Art & Design
. . . . 5D 18 (5H 101)
London College of Communication
. . . . 4B 102
London College of Fashion,
Curtain Rd. 3H 9
Golden La. 4C 8
Mare St. 7J 67
Wimbledon College of Art 1G 153
University of West London
Brentford Campus 5C 96
Ealing Campus,
Grove House 1D 96
St Marys Road 1D 96
Spesom House 7C 78
Vestry Hall 2D 96
Walpole House 7D 78
University of Westminster
Cavendish Campus,
Hanson St. 5A 6 (5G 83)
Lit. Titchfield St. 6A 6
Harrow Campus 7A 42
Marylebone Campus 5G 5 (5E 82)
Regent Campus,
Regent St. 7K 5
Wells St. 7B 6
University Pl. DA8: Erith 7J 109
University Rd. SW19 . . . . 6B 136
University St. WC1 . . . . 4B 6 (4G 83)
University Way E16 . . . . 7E 88
Unwin Av. TW14: Felt 5F 111
Unwin Cl. SE15 . . . . 6G 103
Unwin Ct. N2 . . . . 4C 46
Unwin Mans. W14 . . . . 6H 99
(off Queen's Club Gdns.)
Unwin Rd. SW7 . . . . 1A 16 (3B 100)
TW7: Isle 3J 113
Unwin Way HA7: Stan 7J 27
Up at The O2 . . . . 1G 105
Upbrook M. W2 . . . . 1A 10 (6A 82)
Upcerne Rd. SW10 . . . . 7A 100
Upchurch Cl. SE20 . . . . 7H 139
Upcott Ho. E3 . . . . 3D 86
(off Bruce Rd.)
E9 . . . . 7J 67
(off Frampton Pk. Rd.)
Upcroft Av. HA8: Edg 5D 28
Updale Rd. DA14: Sidc 4K 143
Upfield CR0: C'don 3H 169
Upfield Rd. W7 . . . . 5K 77
Upgrove Mnr. Way SW2 . . . . 7A 120
Uphall Rd. IG1: Ilf 5F 71
Upham Pk. Rd. W4 . . . . 4A 98
Uphill BR2: Broml 4H 159
(off Westmoreland Rd.)
Uphill Dr. NW7 . . . . 5F 29
NW9 . . . . 5J 43
Uphill Gro. NW7 . . . . 4F 29
Uphill Rd. NW7 . . . . 4F 29
Upland M. SE22 . . . . 5G 121
Upland Rd. CR2: S Croy 5D 168
DA7: Bex 3F 127
E13 . . . . 4J 87
SE22 . . . . 5G 121
(not continuous)
SM2: Sutt 7B 166
The Uplands HA4: Ruis 1J 57
Uplands BR3: Beck 2C 158
Uplands Av. E17 . . . . 2K 49
Uplands Bus. Pk. E17 . . . . 3K 49
Uplands Cl. SE18 . . . . 5F 107
SW14 . . . . 5H 115
Uplands Ct. N21 . . . . 7F 23
(off The Green)
Uplands End IG8: Wfd G 7H 37
Uplands Pk. Rd. EN2: Enf 2F 23
Uplands Rd. EN4: E Barn 1K 31
IG8: Wfd G 7H 37
N8 . . . . 5K 47
RM6: Chad H 3D 54
Uplands Way N21 . . . . 5F 23
Upnall Ho. SE15 . . . . 6J 103
Upney La. IG11: Bark 6J 71
Upnor Way SE17 . . . . 5E 102
Uppark Dr. IG2: Ilf 6G 53
Up. Abbey Rd. DA17: Belv 4F 109
Up. Addison Gdns. W14 . . . . 2G 99
Up. Bank St. E14 . . . . 1D 104
(not continuous)
Up. Bardsey Wlk. N1 . . . . 6C 66
(off Douglas Rd. Nth.)
Up. Belgrave St. SW1 . . . . 1H 17 (3E 100)
Up. Berenger Wlk. SW10 . . . . 7B 100
(off Worlds End Est.)
Up. Berkeley St. W1 . . . . 1E 10 (6D 82)
Up. Beulah Hill SE19 . . . . 1E 156
Up. Blantyre Wlk. SW10 . . . . 7B 100
(off Worlds End Est.)
Up. Brighton Rd. KT6: Surb 6D 150
Up. Brockley Rd. SE4 . . . . 3B 122
(not continuous)
Up. Brook St. W1 . . . . 2G 11 (7E 82)
Upper Butts TW8: Bford 6C 96
Up. Caldy Wlk. N1 . . . . 6C 66
(off Caldy Wlk.)
Up. Camelford Wlk. W11 . . . . 6G 81
Up. Cavendish Av. N3 . . . . 3J 45
Up. Cheapside Pas. EC2 . . . . 1C 14
(off Cheapside)
Up. Cheyne Row SW3 . . . . 7C 16 (6C 100)
UPPER CLAPTON 2H 67
Up. Clapton Rd. E5 . . . . 1H 67
Up. Clarendon Wlk. W11 . . . . 6G 81
(off Clarendon Rd.)
Up. Dartrey Wlk. SW10 . . . . 7A 100
(off Worlds End Est.)
Up. Dengie Wlk. N1 . . . . 1C 84
(off Baddow Wlk.)
Up. Dock Wlk. E16 . . . . 7G 89
(off Frobisher Yd.)
UPPER EDMONTON 5B 34
UPPER ELMERS END 5B 158
Up. Elmers End Rd.
BR3: Beck 4A 158
Up. Farm Rd. KT8: W Mole 4D 148
Up. Feilde W1 . . . . 2G 11
(off Park St.)
Upper Fosters NW4 . . . . 4E 44
(off New Brent St.)
Up. Green E. CR4: Mitc 3D 154
Up. Green W. CR4: Mitc 2D 154
(not continuous)
Up. Grosvenor St. W1 . . . . 3G 11 (7E 82)
Up. Grotto Rd. TW1: Twick 2K 131
Up. Ground SE1 . . . . 4J 13 (1A 102)
Upper Gro. SE25 . . . . 4E 156
Up. Grove Rd. DA17: Belv 6F 109
Up. Gulland Wlk. N1 . . . . 7C 66
(off Church Rd.)
UPPER HALLIFORD 4G 147
Up. Halliford By-Pass
TW17: Shep 5G 147
Up. Halliford Grn. TW17: Shep 4G 147
Up. Halliford Rd. TW17: Shep 3G 147
(not continuous)
Up. Hampstead Wlk. NW3 . . . . 4A 64
Up. Ham Rd. KT2: King T 4D 132
TW10: Ham 4D 132
Up. Handa Wlk. N1 . . . . 6D 66
(off Handa Wlk.)
Up. Hawkwell Wlk. N1 . . . . 1C 84
(off Maldon Cl.)
UPPER HOLLOWAY 2G 65
Up. Holly Hill Rd.
DA17: Belv 5H 109
Up. James St. W1 . . . . 2B 12 (7G 83)
Up. John St. W1 . . . . 2B 12 (7G 83)
Up. Lismore Wlk. N1 . . . . 6C 66
(off Clephane Rd.)
Up. Lodge W8 . . . . 1K 99
(off Palace Grn.)
Up. Lodge M. TW12: Hamp H 6H 131
Up. Mall W6 . . . . 5C 98
(not continuous)
Up. Marsh SE1 . . . . 1H 19 (3K 101)
Up. Montagu St. W1 . . . . 5E 4 (5D 82)
Up. Mulgrave Rd.
SM2: Cheam 7G 165
Upper Nth. St. E14 . . . . 5C 86
UPPER NORWOOD 1E 156
Upper Pk. Rd. BR1: Broml 1K 159
DA17: Belv 4H 109
KT2: King T 6G 133
N11 . . . . 5A 32
NW3 . . . . 5D 64
Up. Phillimore Gdns. W8 . . . . 2J 99
Up. Ramsey Wlk. N1 . . . . 6D 66
(off Ramsey Wlk.)
Up. Rawreth Wlk. N1 . . . . 1C 84
(off Basire St.)
Up. Richmond Rd. SW15 . . . . 4B 116
Up. Richmond Rd. W. SW14 . . . . 4G 115
TW10: Rich 4G 115
Upper Rd. E13 . . . . 3J 87
SM6: W'gton 5H 167
UPPER RUXLEY 7G 145
Up. St Martin's La.
WC2 . . . . 2E 12 (7J 83)
Up. Selsdon Rd.
CR2: Sande, Sels 7F 169
Up. Sheridan Rd.
DA17: Belv 4G 109
UPPER SHIRLEY 4K 169
Up. Shirley Rd. CR0: C'don 2J 169
Upper Sq. TW7: Isle 3A 114
Upper St. N1 . . . . 2A 84
Up. Sunbury Rd.
TW12: Hamp 1C 148
Up. Sutton La. TW5: Hest 7E 94
UPPER SYDENHAM 3H 139
Up. Tachbrook St.
SW1 . . . . 3B 18 (4G 101)
Up. Talbot Wlk. W11 . . . . 6G 81
(off Talbot Wlk.)
Up. Teddington Rd.
KT1: Hamp W 7C 132
Upper Ter. NW3 . . . . 3A 64
Up. Thames St. EC4 . . . . 2B 14 (7B 84)
Up. Tollington Pk. N4 . . . . 1A 66
(not continuous)
Upperton Rd. DA14: Sidc 5K 143
Upperton Rd. E. E13 . . . . 3A 88
Upperton Rd. W. E13 . . . . 3A 88

A-Z Big London 297

Upper Tooting—Vicarage Fld. Shop. Cen.

UPPER TOOTING ... 4D 136
Up. Tooting Pk. SW17 ... 2D 136
Up. Tooting Rd. SW17 ... 4D 136
Up. Town Rd. UB6: G'frd ... 4F 77
Up. Tulse Hill SW2 ... 7K 119
Up. Vernon Rd.
SM1: Sutt ... 5B 166
UPPER WALTHAMSTOW ... 4F 51
Up. Walthamstow Rd. E17 ... 4E 50
Up. Whistler Wlk. SW10 ... 7A 100
(off Worlds End Est.)
Up. Wickham La.
DA16: Well ... 7B 108
Up. Wimpole St. W1 ... 5H 5 (5E 82)
Up. Woburn Pl. WC1 ... 2D 6 (3H 83)
Uppingham Av. HA7: Stan ... 1B 42
Upsdell Av. N13 ... 6F 33
Upshire Ho. E17 ... 2B 50
Upstairs at the Gatehouse Theatre
... 1E 64
Upstall St. SE5 ... 1B 120
UPTON
DA6 ... 5D 126
E7 ... 7J 69
Upton Av. E7 ... 7J 69
Upton Cl. DA5: Bexl ... 6F 127
NW2 ... 3G 63
Upton Ct. SE20 ... 7J 139
(off Blean Gro.)
Upton Dene SM2: Sutt ... 7K 165
Upton Gdns. HA3: Kenton ... 5B 42
Upton Hgts. E7 ... 7J 69
Upton Ho. E9 ... 5A 68
(off Ward La.)
Upton La. E7 ... 7J 69
Upton Lodge E7 ... 6J 69
Upton Lodge Cl. WD23: Bush ... 1B 26
UPTON PARK ... 1B 88
Upton Pk. Boleyn Cinema ... 2B 88
Upton Pk. Rd. E7 ... 7K 69
Upton Rd. CR7: Thor H ... 2D 156
DA5: Bexl ... 4E 126
DA6: Bex ... 4E 126
N18 ... 5B 34
SE18 ... 6G 107
TW3: Houn ... 3E 112
Upton Rd. Sth. DA5: Bexl ... 6F 127
Upton Vs. DA6: Bex ... 4E 126
Upway N12 ... 6H 31
Upwey Ho. N1 ... 1E 84
Upwood Rd. SE12 ... 6J 123
SW16 ... 1J 155
Urbanest King's Cross N1 ... 1J 83
Urban M. N4 ... 6B 48
The Urdang ... 2K 7
(off Rosebery Av.)
Urlwin St. SE5 ... 6C 102
Urlwin Wlk. SW9 ... 1A 120
Urmston Dr. SW19 ... 1G 135
Urmston Ho. E14 ... 4E 104
(off Seyssel St.)
Urquhart Ct. BR3: Beck ... 7B 140
Ursa Mans. E20 ... 5E 68
(off Cheering La.)
Ursula Gould Way E14 ... 5C 86
Ursula Lodges DA14: Sidc ... 5B 144
Ursula M. N4 ... 1C 66
Ursula St. SW11 ... 1C 118
Urswick Gdns. RM9: Dag ... 7E 72
Urswick Rd. E9 ... 5J 67
RM9: Dag ... 7D 72
Usborne M. SW8 ... 7K 101
Usher Hall NW4 ... 4D 44
(off The Burroughs)
Usher Rd. E3 ... 1B 86
(not continuous)
Usk Rd. SW11 ... 4A 118
Usk St. E2 ... 3K 85
Utah Bldg. SE13 ... 1D 122
(off Deal's Gateway)
Utopia Village NW1 ... 7E 64
Uvedale Rd. EN2: Enf ... 5J 23
RM10: Dag ... 3G 73
Uverdale Rd. SW10 ... 7A 100
UXBRIDGE ... 1A 74
Uxbridge Ct. KT1: King T ... 5D 150
(off Uxbridge Rd.)
Uxbridge Golf Course ... 2A 56
Uxbridge Lido ... 6A 56
Uxbridge Rd. HA3: Hrw W ... 7A 26
HA5: Hat E, Pinn ... 2A 40
HA7: Stan ... 7A 26
KT1: King T ... 4D 150
TW12: Hamp, Hamp H ... 4E 130
TW13: Felt ... 2A 130
UB1: S'hall ... 1E 94
UB4: Hayes, Yead ... 5G 75
UB10: Hil ... 3C 74
W3 ... 7E 78
W5 ... 7E 78
W7 ... 1K 95
W12 ... 1C 98
W13 ... 1B 96
Uxbridge Rd. Retail Pk. ... 7A 76
Uxbridge St. W8 ... 1J 99
Uxendon Cres. HA9: Wemb ... 1E 60
Uxendon Hill HA9: Wemb ... 1F 61

V

Vaine Ho. E9 ... 6A 68
Vaizeys Wharf SE7 ... 3K 105
Valance Av. E4 ... 1B 36
Valan Leas BR2: Broml ... 3G 159
The Vale CR0: C'don ... 2K 169
HA4: Ruis ... 4A 58
IG8: Wfd G ... 7D 36
N10 ... 1E 46
N14 ... 7C 22
NW11 ... 3F 63
SW3 ... 7A 16 (6B 100)
TW5: Hest ... 6C 94
TW14: Felt ... 6K 111
TW16: Sun ... 6J 129
W3 ... 1K 97
Vale Cl. BR6: Farnb ... 4E 172
N2 ... 3D 46
TW1: Twick ... 3A 132
W9 ... 3A 82
Vale Cotts. SW15 ... 3A 134
Vale Ct. EN5: New Bar ... 4E 20
W3 ... 1B 98
W9 ... 3A 82
Vale Cres. SW15 ... 4A 134
Vale Cft. HA5: Pinn ... 5C 40
Vale Dr. EN5: Barn ... 4C 20
Vale End SE22 ... 4F 121
The Vale Est. W3 ... 1A 98
Vale Farm Sports Cen. ... 4B 60
Vale Gro. N4 ... 7C 48
W3 ... 2K 97
Vale La. W3 ... 5G 79
Vale Lodge SE23 ... 2J 139
Valence Av. RM8: Dag ... 1D 72
Valence Cir. RM8: Dag ... 3D 72
Valence House Mus. ... 3E 72
Valence Rd. DA8: Erith ... 7K 109
Valence Wood Rd.
RM8: Dag ... 3D 72
Valencia Cl. E14 ... 6F 87
Valencia Rd. HA7: Stan ... 4H 27
Valencia Tower EC1 ... 1C 8
(off Bollinder Place)
Valentia Pl. SW9 ... 4A 120
Valentina Av. NW9 ... 2B 44
Valentine Av. DA5: Bexl ... 2E 144
Valentine Ct. SE23 ... 2K 139
(not continuous)
Valentine Ho. E3 ... 1B 86
(off Garrison Rd.)
Valentine Pl. SE1 ... 6A 14 (2B 102)
Valentine Rd. E9 ... 6K 67
HA2: Harr ... 3F 59
Valentine Row SE1 ... 7A 14 (2B 102)
Valentines Mansion & Gdns. ... 7E 52
Valentines Rd. IG1: Ilf ... 1F 71
Valentine's Way RM7: Rush G ... 2K 73
VALE OF HEALTH ... 3A 64
Vale of Health NW3 ... 3B 64
Vale Pde. SW15 ... 3A 134
Valerian Wlk. N11 ... 2K 31
Valerian Way E15 ... 3G 87
Valerie Ct. SM2: Sutt ... 7K 165
WD23: Bush ... 1B 26
Valerio M. N1 ... 6D 66
Vale Ri. NW11 ... 1H 63
Vale Rd. BR1: Broml ... 1E 160
CR4: Mitc ... 3H 155
E7 ... 6K 69
KT4: Wor Pk ... 3B 164
KT19: Ewe ... 4B 164
N4 ... 7C 48
SM1: Sutt ... 4K 165
Vale Rd. Nth. KT6: Surb ... 2E 162
Vale Rd. Sth. KT6: Surb ... 2E 162
Vale Row N5 ... 3B 66
Vale Royal N7 ... 7J 65
Vale Royal Ho. WC2 ... 2D 12
(off Charing Cross Rd.)
Valery Pl. TW12: Hamp ... 7E 130
Valeside Ct. EN5: New Bar ... 4E 20
Vale St. SE27 ... 3D 138
Valeswood Rd. BR1: Broml ... 5H 141
Vale Ter. N4 ... 6C 48
Valetta Gro. E13 ... 2J 87
Valetta Ho. SW11 ... 7F 101
Valetta Rd. W3 ... 2A 98
Valette Ct. N10 ... 4F 47
(off St James's La.)
Valette Ho. E9 ... 6J 67
Valette St. E9 ... 6J 67
Valiant Cl. RM7: Mawney ... 2H 55
UB5: N'olt ... 3B 76
Valiant Ho. E14 ... 2E 104
(off Plevna St.)
SE7 ... 5A 106
Valiant Path NW9 ... 7F 29
Valiant Way E6 ... 5D 88
Vallance Rd. E1 ... 3G 85
E2 ... 3G 85
N22 ... 2G 47
Vallentin Rd. E17 ... 4E 50
The Valley ... 5A 106
Valley Av. N12 ... 4G 31
Valley Cl. HA5: Pinn ... 2K 39
Valley Dr. NW9 ... 6G 43
Valleyfield Rd. SW16 ... 5K 137
Valley Flds. Cres. EN2: Enf ... 2F 23
Valley Gdns. HA0: Wemb ... 7F 61
SW19 ... 7B 136
Valley Gro. SE7 ... 5A 106
Valley Leisure Pk. ... 1J 167
Valleylink Est. EN3: Pond E ... 6F 25
Valley M. TW1: Twick ... 2K 131
Valley Point Ind. Est.
CR0: Bedd ... 7J 155
Valley Rd. BR2: Broml ... 2G 159
BR5: St P ... 7B 144
DA8: Erith ... 4J 109
DA17: Belv ... 4H 109
SW16 ... 5K 137
UB10: Uxb ... 2A 74
Valley Side E4 ... 2H 35
SE7 ... 5B 106
Valley Side Pde. E4 ... 2H 35
Valley Vw. EN5: Barn ... 6B 20
Valley Wlk. CR0: C'don ... 2J 169
Valliere Rd. NW10 ... 3C 80
Valliers Wood Rd.
DA15: Sidc ... 1J 143
Vallings Pl. KT6: Surb ... 7B 150
Vallis Way KT9: Chess ... 4D 162
W13 ... 5A 78
Val McKenzie Av. N7 ... 3A 66
Valmar Rd. SE5 ... 1C 120
Valmar Trad. Est. SE5 ... 1C 120
Valnay St. SW17 ... 5D 136
Valognes Av. E17 ... 1A 50
Valois Ho. SE1 ... 3F 103
(off St Saviour's Est.)
Valonia Gdns. SW18 ... 6H 117
Vambery Rd. SE18 ... 6G 107
Vamey Cl. BR1: Broml ... 3J 159
V&A Mus. of Childhood ... 3J 85
Vanbrugh Cres. UB5: N'olt ... 1A 76
Vanbrugh Castle SE10 ... 6G 105
(off Maze Hill)
Vanbrugh Cl. E16 ... 5B 88
Vanbrugh Ct. SE11 ... 4K 19
Vanbrugh Dr. KT12: Walt T ... 7A 148
Vanbrugh Flds. SE3 ... 6H 105
Vanbrugh Hill SE3 ... 5H 105
SE10 ... 5H 105
Vanbrugh Ho. E9 ... 7J 67
(off Loddiges Rd.)
Vanbrugh M. E15 ... 4G 69
KT12: Walt T ... 7A 148
Vanbrugh Pk. SE3 ... 7H 105
Vanbrugh Pk. Rd. SE3 ... 7H 105
Vanbrugh Pk. Rd. W. SE3 ... 7H 105
Vanbrugh Rd. W4 ... 3K 97
Vanbrugh Ter. SE3 ... 1H 123
Vanburgh Cl. BR6: Orp ... 1J 173
Vanburgh Ho. E1 ... 5J 9
(off Folgate St.)
Vancouver Cl. BR6: Chels ... 4K 173
Vancouver Ho. E1 ... 1H 103
(off Reardon Path)
SE16 ... 2K 103
(off Needleman St.)
Vancouver Mans. HA8: Edg ... 1H 43
Vancouver Rd.
HA8: Edg ... 1H 43
SE23 ... 2A 140
TW10: Ham ... 4C 132
UB4: Yead ... 4K 75
Vanderbilt Rd. SW18 ... 1K 135
Vanderbilt Vs. W12 ... 2F 99
(off Sterne St.)
Vandervell Ct. W3 ... 2A 98
(off Amber Way)
Vanderville Gdns. N2 ... 2B 46
Vandome Cl. E16 ... 6K 87
Vandon Ct. SW1 ... 1B 18
(off Petty France)
Vandon Pas. SW1 ... 1B 18 (3G 101)
Vandon St. SW1 ... 1B 18 (3G 101)
Van Dyck Av. KT3: N Mald ... 7K 151
Vandyke Cl. SW15 ... 7F 117
Vandyke Cross SE9 ... 5C 124
Vandy St. EC2 ... 4G 9 (4E 84)
Vane Cl. HA3: Kenton ... 6F 43
NW3 ... 5B 64
Vanessa Cl. DA17: Belv ... 5G 109
Vanessa Way DA5: Bexl ... 3K 145
Vane St. SW1 ... 3B 18 (4G 101)
Vange Ho. W10 ... 5E 80
(off Sutton Way)
Van Gogh Cl. TW7: Isle ... 3A 114
Van Gogh Ct. E14 ... 3F 105
Vanguard NW9 ... 7F 29
Vanguard Bldg. E14 ... 2B 104
Vanguard Cl. CR0: C'don ... 1B 168
E16 ... 5J 87
RM7: Mawney ... 2G 55
Vanguard Ct. SE5 ... 1E 120
Vanguard Ho. E8 ... 7H 67
Vanguard St. SE8 ... 1C 122
Vanguard Way
SM6: W'gton ... 7J 167
TW6: H'row A ... 2G 111
Vanilla & Sesame Ct. SE1 ... 6K 15
(off Curlew St.)
Vanneck Sq. SW15 ... 5C 116
Vanoc Gdns. BR1: Broml ... 4J 141
Vanquish Cl. TW2: Whitt ... 7E 112
Vansittart Rd. E7 ... 4H 69
Vansittart St. SE14 ... 7A 104
Vanstone Ct. N7 ... 6K 65
(off Blackthorn Av.)
Vanston Pl. SW6 ... 7J 99
Vantage Bldg. UB3: Hayes ... 3H 93
(off Station App.)
Vantage Ct. UB3: Harl ... 7G 93
Vantage M. E14 ... 1E 104
(off Coldharbour)
Vantage Pl. TW14: Felt ... 6J 111
W8 ... 3J 99
Vantage Point BR3: Beck ... 1F 159
(off Albemarle Rd.)
CR2: Sande ... 7D 168
EN5: Barn ... 4C 20
(off Victors Way)
Vantage W. TW8: Bford ... 4F 97
Vantrey Ho. SE11 ... 4J 19
Vant Rd. SW17 ... 5D 136
Varcoe Gdns. UB3: Hayes ... 6F 75
Varcoe Rd. SE16 ... 5H 103
Vardens Rd. SW11 ... 4B 118
Varden St. E1 ... 6H 85
Vardon Cl. W3 ... 6K 79
Varley Dr. TW1: Isle ... 4B 114
Varley Ho. NW6 ... 1J 81
SE1 ... 3C 102
(off County St.)
Varley Pde. NW9 ... 4A 44
Varley Rd. E16 ... 6K 87
Varley Way CR4: Mitc ... 2B 154
Varna Rd. SW6 ... 7G 99
TW12: Hamp ... 1F 149
Varndell St. NW1 ... 1A 6 (3G 83)
Varnishers Yd. N1 ... 1F 7
(off York Way)
Varsity Dr. TW1: Twick ... 5J 113
Varsity Row SW14 ... 2J 115
Vartry Rd. N15 ... 6D 48
Vascroft Est. NW10 ... 4H 79
Vassall Ho. E3 ... 3A 86
(off Antill Rd.)
Vassall Rd. SW9 ... 7A 102
Vat Ho. SW8 ... 7J 101
(off Rita Rd.)
Vauban Est. SE16 ... 3F 103
Vauban St. SE16 ... 3F 103
Vaudeville Theatre ... 3F 13
(off Strand)
Vaughan Almshouses
TW15: Ashf ... 5D 128
(off Feltham Hill Rd.)
Vaughan Av. NW4 ... 5C 44
W6 ... 4B 98
Vaughan Cl. TW12: Hamp ... 6C 130
Vaughan Est. E2 ... 1J 9
Vaughan Gdns. IG1: Ilf ... 7D 52
Vaughan Ho. SE1 ... 6A 14
(off Blackfriars Rd.)
SW4 ... 7G 119
Vaughan Rd. DA16: Well ... 2K 125
E15 ... 6H 69
HA1: Harr ... 6G 41
KT7: T Ditt ... 7B 150
SE5 ... 2C 120
Vaughan St. SE16 ... 2B 104
Vaughan Way E1 ... 7G 85
Vaughan Williams Cl.
SE8 ... 7C 104
Vaughn St. RM8: Dag ... 1E 72
VAUXHALL ... 5H 19 (6J 101)
Vauxhall Bri. SW1 ... 6E 18 (5J 101)
Vauxhall Bri. Rd.
SW1 ... 2A 18 (3G 101)
Vauxhall City Farm ... 6G 19
VAUXHALL CROSS ... 5J 101
Vauxhall Gdns.
CR2: S Croy ... 6C 168
Vauxhall Gro. SW8 ... 7G 19 (6K 101)
Vauxhall St. SE11 ... 5H 19 (5K 101)
Vauxhall Wlk.
SE11 ... 5G 19 (5K 101)
VauxWall East Climbing Centre
... 4K 101
VauxWall West Climbing Centre ... 7F 19
(off Sth. Lambeth Rd.)
Vawdrey Cl. E1 ... 4J 85
Veals Mead CR4: Mitc ... 1C 154
Vectis Gdns. SW17 ... 6F 137
Vectis Rd. SW17 ... 6F 137
Veda Rd. SE13 ... 4C 122
Vega Ho. E20 ... 5E 68
(off Prize Wlk.)
Vega Rd. WD23: Bush ... 1B 26
Veitch Cl. TW14: Felt ... 7H 111
Veldene Way
HA2: Harr ... 3D 58
Velde Way SE22 ... 5E 120
Velletri Ho. E2 ... 2K 85
(off Mace St.)
Vellum Ct. E17 ... 2A 50
Vellum Dr. SM5: Cars ... 3E 166
Velodrome
Queen Elizabeth Olympic Pk.
... 5D 68
Velo Ho. E17 ... 5B 50
(off Track St.)
Velo Pl. E20 ... 5D 68
Velvet Ho. E2 ... 2F 85
(off Whiston Rd.)
Venables Cl. RM10: Dag ... 4H 73
Venables St. NW8 ... 5B 4 (4B 82)
Vencourt Pl. W6 ... 4C 98
The Veneer Bldg. ... 2G 93
Venerable Ho. E3 ... 4B 86
(off Portia Way)
Venetian Ho. E20 ... 6D 68
(off Victory Pde.)
Venetian Rd. SE5 ... 2C 120
Venetia Rd. N4 ... 6B 48
W5 ... 2D 96
Venice Corte SE13 ... 3E 122
(off Elmira St.)
Venice Ct. SE5 ... 7C 102
(off Bowyer St.)
Venice Ho. HA0: Wemb ... 1E 78
Venice Wlk. W2 ... 5A 82
Venner Rd. SE26 ... 6J 139
(not continuous)
Venners Cl. DA7: Bex ... 2K 127
Venn Ho. N1 ... 1K 83
(off Barnsbury Est.)
Venn St. SW4 ... 4G 119
Ventnor Av. HA7: Stan ... 1B 42
Ventnor Dr. N20 ... 3E 30
Ventnor Gdns. IG11: Bark ... 6J 71
Ventnor Rd. SE14 ... 7K 103
SM2: Sutt ... 7K 165
Venture Cl. DA5: Bexl ... 7E 126
Venture Ct. SE1 ... 6K 15
(off Market Yd. M.)
SE12 ... 7J 123
Venture Ho. W10 ... 6F 81
(off Bridge Cl.)
Venue St. E14 ... 5E 86
Venus Ho. E3 ... 1C 86
(off Garrison Rd.)
E14 ... 4C 104
(off Westferry Rd.)
Venus M. CR4: Mitc ... 3C 154
Venus Rd. SE18 ... 3D 106
Vera Av. N21 ... 5F 23
Vera Ct. E3 ... 3D 86
(off Grace Pl.)
Vera Lynn Cl. E7 ... 4J 69
Vera Rd. SW6 ... 1G 117
Verbena Cl. E16 ... 4H 87
UB7: W Dray ... 1E 174
Verbena Gdns. W6 ... 5C 98
Verdant Ct. SE6 ... 7G 123
(off Verdant La.)
Verdant La. SE6 ... 7G 123
Verdayne Av. CR0: C'don ... 2K 169
Verdi Cres. W10 ... 2G 81
Verdon Roe Ct. E4 ... 3J 35
Verdun Rd. SE18 ... 6A 108
SW13 ... 6C 98
Vere Ct. W2 ... 6K 81
(off Westbourne Gdns.)
Vereker Dr. TW16: Sun ... 3J 147
Vereker Rd. W14 ... 5G 99
Vere St. W1 ... 1J 11 (6F 83)
Veridion Way DA18: Erith ... 2F 109
Veritas Ho. DA14: Sidc ... 2A 144
(off Jubilee Way)
Verity Cl. W11 ... 7G 81
Verity Ho. E3 ... 3B 86
(off Merchant St.)
Vermeer Ct. E14 ... 3F 105
Vermeer Gdns. SE15 ... 4J 121
Vermilion Apts. E3 ... 1A 86
(off Gunmaker's La.)
Vermont Cl. EN2: Enf ... 4G 23
Vermont Ho. E17 ... 2B 50
Vermont Rd. SE19 ... 6D 138
SM1: Sutt ... 3K 165
SW18 ... 6K 117
Verna Ho. E20 ... 5E 68
(off Sunrise Cl.)
Verney Gdns. RM9: Dag ... 4E 72
Verney Ho. NW8 ... 3B 4
Verney Rd. RM9: Dag ... 4E 72
(not continuous)
SE16 ... 6G 103
Verney St. NW10 ... 3K 61
Verney Way SE16 ... 5H 103
Vernham Rd. SE18 ... 6G 107
Vernon Av. E12 ... 4D 70
IG8: Wfd G ... 7E 36
SW20 ... 2F 153
Vernon Cl. KT19: Ewe ... 6J 163
TW19: Stanw ... 1A 128
Vernon Ct. HA7: Stan ... 1B 42
NW2 ... 3H 63
W5 ... 7C 78
Vernon Cres. EN4: E Barn ... 6K 21
Vernon Dr. HA7: Stan ... 1A 42
Vernon Ho. SE11 ... 6H 19
WC1 ... 6F 7
(off Vernon Pl.)
Vernon Mans. W14 ... 6H 99
(off Queen's Club Gdns.)
Vernon M. E17 ... 5B 50
W14 ... 4G 99
Vernon Pl. WC1 ... 6F 7 (5J 83)
Vernon Ri. UB6: G'frd ... 5H 59
WC1 ... 1H 7 (3K 83)
Vernon Rd. E3 ... 2B 86
E11 ... 1G 69
E15 ... 7G 69
E17 ... 5B 50
IG3: Ilf ... 1K 71
N8 ... 3A 48
SM1: Sutt ... 5A 166
SW14 ... 3K 115
TW13: Felt ... 2H 129
Vernon Sq. WC1 ... 1H 7 (3K 83)
Vernon St. W14 ... 4G 99
Vernon Yd. W11 ... 7H 81
Veroan Rd. DA7: Bex ... 2E 126
Verona Ct. SE14 ... 6K 103
(off Myers La.)
TW15: Ashf ... 4D 128
W4 ... 5A 98
Verona Dr. KT6: Surb ... 2E 162
Verona Ho. CR4: Mitc ... 3F 155
(off Aventine Av.)
Verona Rd. E7 ... 7J 69
Veronica Gdns. SW16 ... 1G 155
Veronica Ho. E3 ... 3D 86
(off Talwin St.)
SE4 ... 3B 122
Veronica Rd. SW17 ... 2F 137
Veronique Gdns. IG6: Ilf ... 5G 53
Verran Rd. SW12 ... 7F 119
Versailles Rd. SE20 ... 7G 139
Verulam Av. E17 ... 6B 50
Verulam Bldgs. WC1 ... 5H 7
Verulam Ct. NW9 ... 7C 44
UB1: S'hall ... 6G 77
(off Haldane Rd.)
Verulam Ho. W6 ... 2E 98
(off Hammersmith Gro.)
Verulam Rd. UB6: G'frd ... 4E 76
Verulam St. WC1 ... 5J 7 (5A 84)
Vervian Ho. SE15 ... 7G 103
(off Reddins Rd.)
Verwood Dr. EN4: Cockf ... 3J 21
Verwood Ho. SW8 ... 7K 101
(off Cobbett St.)
Verwood Lodge E14 ... 3F 105
(off Manchester Rd.)
Verwood Rd. HA2: Harr ... 2G 41
Veryan Ct. N8 ... 5H 47
Vesage Ct. EC1 ... 6K 7
Vesey Path E14 ... 6D 86
Vespan Rd. W12 ... 2C 98
Vespucci Court E14 ... 5A 86
(off Oman Way)
Vesta Ct. SE1 ... 7G 15
Vesta Ho. E3 ... 1C 86
(off Garrison Rd.)
E20 ... 5E 68
(off Liberty Bri. Rd.)
Vesta Rd. SE4 ... 2A 122
Vestris Rd. SE23 ... 2K 139
Vestry Ct. RM7: Rush G ... 6K 55
SW1 ... 2D 18
(off Monck St.)
Vestry House Mus. ... 4D 50
Vestry M. SE5 ... 1E 120
SW18 ... 5B 118
Vestry Rd. E17 ... 4D 50
SE5 ... 1E 120
Vestry St. N1 ... 1E 8 (3D 84)
Vesuvius Apts. E3 ... 2B 86
(off Centurion La.)
Vevey St. SE6 ... 2B 140
Veysey Gdns. RM10: Dag ... 3G 73
The Viaduct E18 ... 2J 51
N10 ... 4F 47
Viaduct Bldgs. EC1 ... 6K 7 (5A 84)
Viaduct Gdns. SW11 ... 7D 18 (6H 101)
(Ace Way)
SW11 ... 7G 101
(Nine Elms La.)
Viaduct Pl. E2 ... 3H 85
Viaduct Rd. N2 ... 2B 46
Viaduct St. E2 ... 3H 85
Vian St. SE13 ... 3D 122
Viant Ho. NW10 ... 7K 61
(off Fawood Av.)
Vibart Gdns. SW2 ... 7K 119
Vibart Wlk. N1 ... 1J 83
(off Outram Pl.)
Vibeca Apts. E1 ... 6K 9
(off Chicksand St.)
Vibia Cl. TW19: Stanw ... 7A 110
Vicarage Av. SE3 ... 7J 105
Vicarage Cl. DA8: Erith ... 6J 109
HA4: Ruis ... 7F 39
KT4: Wor Pk ... 1A 164
UB5: N'olt ... 7D 58
Vicarage Ct. BR3: Beck ... 3A 158
IG1: Ilf ... 5F 71
TW14: Bedf ... 7E 110
W8 ... 2K 99
Vicarage Cres. SW11 ... 1B 118
Vicarage Dr. BR3: Beck ... 1C 158
IG11: Bark ... 7G 71
SW14 ... 5K 115
Vicarage Farm Ct. TW5: Hest ... 7D 94
Vicarage Farm Rd.
TW3: Houn ... 2C 112
TW5: Hest ... 1C 112
Vicarage Flds. KT12: Walt T ... 6A 148
Vicarage Fld. Shop. Cen. ... 7G 71

Vicarage Gdns.—Voysey Sq.

Vicarage Gdns. CR4: Mitc ... 3C 154
SW14 ... 5J 115
W8 ... 1J 99
Vicarage Ga. W8 ... 1K 99
Vicarage Gro. SE5 ... 1D 120
Vicarage Ho. KT1: King T ... 2F 151
(off Cambridge Rd.)
Vicarage La. E6 ... 3D 88
E15 ... 7G 69
IG1: Ilf ... 1H 71
KT17: Ewe ... 7C 164
(not continuous)
Vicarage M. NW9 ... 2K 61
W4 ... 6A 98
(off Bennett St.)
Vicarage Pde. N15 ... 4C 48
Vicarage Pk. SE18 ... 5G 107
Vicarage Path N8 ... 7J 47
Vicarage Rd.
CR0: Wadd ... 3A 168
DA5: Bexl ... 1H 145
E10 ... 7C 50
E15 ... 7H 69
IG8: Wfd G ... 7H 37
KT1: Hamp W ... 1C 150
KT1: King T ... 2D 150
N17 ... 1G 49
NW4 ... 6C 44
RM10: Dag ... 7H 73
SE18 ... 5G 107
(not continuous)
SM1: Sutt ... 3K 165
SW14 ... 5J 115
TW2: Twick ... 2J 131
TW2: Whitt ... 6G 113
TW11: Tedd ... 5A 132
TW16: Sun ... 5H 129
Vicarage Wlk. KT12: Walt T ... 7J 147
SW11 ... 1B 118
Vicarage Way
HA2: Harr ... 7E 40
NW10 ... 3K 61
Vicars Bri. Cl. HA0: Wemb ... 2E 78
Vicar's Cl. E9 ... 1J 85
Vicars Cl. E15 ... 1J 87
EN1: Enf ... 2K 23
Vicar's Hill SE13 ... 4D 122
Vicars Moor La. N21 ... 7F 23
Vicars Oak Rd.
SE19 ... 6E 138
Vicar's Rd. NW5 ... 5E 64
Vicars Wlk.
RM8: Dag ... 3B 72
Vicary Ho. EC1 ... 6C 8
(off Bartholomew Cl.)
Vicentia Ct. SW11 ... 3A 118
Viceroy Cl. N2 ... 4C 46
(off East End Rd.)
Viceroy Ct. CR0: C'don ... 1D 168
NW8 ... 2C 82
(off Prince Albert Rd.)
Viceroy Pde. N2 ... 4C 46
(off High Rd.)
Viceroy Rd. SW8 ... 1J 119
Vicinity Ho. E14 ... 7C 86
(off Storehouse M.)
Vic Johnson Ho. E3 ... 1B 86
(off Armagh Rd.)
Vickers Cl. SM6: W'gton ... 7K 167
Vickers Ct.
N17 ... 3H 49
SE20 ... 7K 139
TW19: Stanw ... 6A 110
(off Whitley Cl.)
Vickers Rd. DA8: Erith ... 5K 109
Vickers Way
TW4: Houn ... 5C 112
Vickery Ct. EC1 ... 3D 8
(off Mitchell St.)
Vickery's Wharf E14 ... 6C 86
Victor Cazalet Ho. N1 ... 1B 84
(off Gaskin St.)
Victor Gro. HA0: Wemb ... 7E 60
Victor Ho. SE7 ... 6A 106
Victoria & Albert Mus.
... 2B 16 (3B 100)
Victoria Arc. SW1 ... 2K 17
(off Victoria St.)
Victoria Av. E6 ... 1B 88
EC2 ... 6H 9 (5E 84)
EN4: E Barn ... 4G 21
HA9: Wemb ... 6H 61
KT6: Surb ... 6D 150
KT8: W Mole ... 3F 149
N3 ... 1H 45
SM6: W'gton ... 3E 166
TW3: Houn ... 5E 112
UB10: Hil ... 6D 56
Victoria Bldgs. E8 ... 1H 85
(off Mare St.)
Victoria Chambers EC2 ... 3G 9
(off Paul St.)
Victoria Cl. EN4: E Barn ... 4G 21
HA1: Harr ... 6K 41
KT8: W Mole ... 3E 148
SE22 ... 5G 121
UB3: Hayes ... 6F 75
Victoria Colonnade WC1 ... 6F 7
(off Southampton Row)
Victoria Cotts. E1 ... 5G 85
(off Deal St.)
N10 ... 2E 46
TW9: Kew ... 1F 115
Victoria Ct. E18 ... 3K 51
HA7: Stan ... 7J 27
(off Howard Rd.)
HA9: Wemb ... 6G 61
SE1 ... 4E 102
(off Hendre Rd.)
SE26 ... 6J 139
W3 ... 2G 97
Victoria Cres. N15 ... 5E 48
SE19 ... 6E 138
SW19 ... 7H 135
Victoria Dock Rd. E16 ... 7H 87
Victoria Dr. SW19 ... 7F 117
Victoria Emb. EC4 ... 6F 13 (7K 83)
SW1 ... 6F 13 (2J 101)
WC2 ... 6F 13 (2J 101)
Victoria Embankment Gardens
WC2 ... 4F 13
Victoria Gdns. TW5: Hest ... 1C 112
W11 ... 1J 99
Victoria Gro. N12 ... 5G 31
W8 ... 3A 100
Victoria Gro. M. W2 ... 7J 81
Victoria Hall E16 ... 1J 105
(off Wesley Av.)
Victoria Ho. E6 ... 6E 88
HA8: Edg ... 6C 28
SE16 ... 2J 103
(off Surrey Quays Rd.)
SW1 ... 5J 17
(off Ebury Bri. Rd.)
SW1 ... 3B 18
(off Francis St.)
SW8 ... 7J 101
(off Sth. Lambeth Rd.)
Victoria Ind. Est. W3 ... 5A 80
Victoria La.
EN5: Barn ... 4C 20
UB3: Harl ... 5F 93
Victoria Mans. NW10 ... 7D 62
SW8 ... 7J 101
(off Sth. Lambeth Rd.)
W14 ... 6H 99
(off Queen's Club Gdns.)
Victoria M. E8 ... 6G 67
NW6 ... 1J 81
SW4 ... 4F 119
SW18 ... 1A 136
W11 ... 1J 99
Victoria Mills Studios E15 ... 1F 87
(off Burford Rd.)
Victorian Gro. N16 ... 4E 66
Victorian Hgts. SW8 ... 2F 119
(off Thackeray Rd.)
Victorian Rd. N16 ... 3E 66
Victoria Palace Theatre ... 2A 18
(off Victoria St.)
Victoria Pde. SE10 ... 6D 104
TW9: Kew ... 1G 115
(off Sandycombe Rd.)
Victoria Pk. ... 1K 85
Victoria Pk. Ct. E9 ... 7J 67
(off Well St.)
Victoria Pk. Ind. Cen. E9 ... 7C 68
(off Rothbury Rd.)
Victoria Pk. Rd. E9 ... 1J 85
Victoria Pk. Sq. E2 ... 3J 85
Victoria Pk. Studios E9 ... 6J 67
(off Milborne St.)
Victoria Pas. NW8 ... 3B 4
Victoria Pl. TW9: Rich ... 5D 114
Victoria Pl. Shop. Cen. ... 3K 17
Victoria Point E13 ... 2J 87
(off Victoria Rd.)
Victoria Retail Pk.
South Ruislip ... 5B 58
Victoria Ri. NW6 ... 7A 64
(off Hilgrove Rd.)
SW4 ... 3F 119
Victoria Road ... 5H 73
Victoria Rd. BR2: Broml ... 5B 160
BR7: Chst ... 5E 142
CR4: Mitc ... 7C 136
DA6: Bex ... 4G 127
DA8: Erith ... 6K 109
DA15: Sidc ... 3K 143
E4 ... 1B 36
E11 ... 4G 69
E13 ... 2J 87
E17 ... 2E 50
E18 ... 2K 51
EN4: E Barn ... 4G 21
HA4: Ruis ... 1J 57
IG9: Buck H ... 2G 37
IG11: Bark ... 6F 71
KT1: King T ... 2F 151
KT6: Surb ... 6D 150
N4 ... 7K 47
N9 ... 4A 34
N15 ... 4G 49
N18 ... 4A 34
N22 ... 1G 47
NW4 ... 4E 44
NW6 ... 2H 81
NW7 ... 5G 29
NW10 ... 5K 79
RM10: Dag ... 5H 73
SM1: Sutt ... 5B 166
SW14 ... 3K 115
TW1: Twick ... 7B 114
TW11: Tedd ... 6A 132
TW13: Felt ... 1K 129
UB2: S'hall ... 3D 94
W3 ... 5K 79
W5 ... 5B 78
W8 ... 3A 100
WD23: Bush ... 1A 26
Victoria Sq. SW1 ... 1K 17 (3F 101)
Victoria St. DA17: Belv ... 5F 109
E15 ... 7G 69
SW1 ... 2K 17 (3G 101)
Victoria Ter. HA1: Harr ... 1J 59
N4 ... 1A 66
NW10 ... 4B 80
W5 ... 1D 96
Victoria Vs. TW9: Rich ... 3F 115
Victoria Way HA4: Ruis ... 5B 58
SE7 ... 5K 105
Victoria Wharf E2 ... 2K 85
(off Palmers Rd.)
E14 ... 7A 86
SE8 ... 5B 104
(off Dragoon Rd.)
Victoria Works NW2 ... 2D 62
Victoria Yd. E1 ... 6G 85
Victor Rd. HA2: Harr ... 3G 41
NW10 ... 3D 80
SE20 ... 7K 139
TW11: Tedd ... 4J 131
Victors Dr. TW12: Hamp ... 6C 130
Victors Way EN5: Barn ... 3C 20
Victor Vs. N9 ... 3J 33
Victor Wlk. NW9 ... 2A 44
Victor Wharf SE1 ... 4E 14
(off Clink St.)
Victory Av. SM4: Mord ... 5A 154
Victory Bus. Cen.
TW7: Isle ... 4K 113
Victory Cl. TW19: Stanw ... 1A 128
Victory Ct. IG11: Bark ... 4B 90
W9 ... 4J 81
(off Hermes Cl.)
Victory M. UB2: S'hall ... 3C 94
Victory Pde. E20 ... 6D 68
SE18 ... 3F 107
Victory Pk.
HA9: Wemb ... 3D 60
Victory Pl. E14 ... 7A 86
SE17 ... 4D 102
SE19 ... 7E 138
Victory Rd. E11 ... 4J 51
SW19 ... 7A 136
Victory Rd. M. SW19 ... 7A 136
(off Victory Rd.)
Victory Wlk. SE8 ... 1C 122
Victory Way
RM7: Mawney ... 2H 55
SE16 ... 2A 104
TW5: Cran ... 5A 94
Vida Ho. SE8 ... 5K 103
Video Ct. N4 ... 7K 47
Vidler Cl. KT9: Chess ... 6C 162
Vienna Cl. IG5: Ilf ... 2B 52
The View SE2 ... 5E 108
View Cl. HA1: Harr ... 4H 41
N6 ... 7D 46
View Cres. N8 ... 5H 47
Viewfield Cl. HA3: Kenton ... 7E 42
Viewfield Rd.
DA5: Bexl ... 1C 144
SW18 ... 6H 117
Viewland Rd. SE18 ... 5K 107
View Rd. N6 ... 7D 46
The View Tube ... 1D 86
(off Greenway)
Viga Rd. N21 ... 6F 23
Vigers Ct. NW10 ... 3D 80
(off Harrow Rd.)
Vigilant Cl. SE26 ... 4G 139
Vignoles Rd.
RM7: Rush G ... 7G 55
Vigo St. W1 ... 3A 12 (7G 83)
Viking Bus. Cen.
RM7: Rush G ... 7J 55
Viking Cl. E3 ... 2A 86
Viking Ct. SW6 ... 6J 99
Viking Gdns. E6 ... 4C 88
Viking Ho. SE5 ... 2C 120
(off Denmark Rd.)
SE18 ... 4C 106
(off Pett St.)
Viking Pl. E10 ... 1B 68
Viking Rd. UB1: S'hall ... 7C 76
Viking Way DA8: Erith ... 3J 109
Villacourt Rd. SE18 ... 7A 108
The Village ... 1F 99
The Village NW3 ... 2A 64
SE7 ... 6A 106
Village Arc. E4 ... 1A 36
Village Cl. E4 ... 5K 35
NW3 ... 5B 64
(off Belsize La.)
Village Ct. E17 ... 5D 50
(off Eden Rd.)
SE3 ... 3G 123
(off Hurren Cl.)
Village Ctyd. SW11 ... 6F 101
(off Arches La.)
Village Ga. TW17: Shep ... 5D 146
Village Hgts. IG8: Wfd G ... 5C 36
Village M. NW9 ... 2K 61
SW18 ... 1H 135
(off Elsenham St.)
Village Mt. NW3 ... 4A 64
(off Perrins Ct.)
Village Pk. Cl. EN1: Enf ... 6K 23
Village Rd. EN1: Enf ... 5K 23
N3 ... 2G 45
Village Row SM2: Sutt ... 7J 165
Village Way
BR3: Beck ... 2C 158
HA5: Pinn ... 7C 40
IG6: Ilf ... 3G 53
NW10 ... 4K 61
SE21 ... 6D 120
TW15: Ashf ... 4B 128
Village Way E. HA2: Harr ... 7E 40
Villa Rd. SW9 ... 3A 120
Villas on the Heath NW3 ... 3A 64
Villas Rd. SE18 ... 5G 107
Villa St. SE17 ... 5D 102
Villa Wlk. SE17 ... 5D 102
(off Villa St.)
Villiers Av. KT5: Surb ... 5F 151
TW2: Whitt ... 1D 130
Villiers Cl. E10 ... 2C 68
KT5: Surb ... 4F 151
Villiers Ct. SW11 ... 1C 118
(off Battersea Bri. Rd.)
Villiers Gdns. E20 ... 5D 68
Villiers Gro. SM2: Cheam ... 7F 165
Villiers M. NW2 ... 6C 62
Villiers Path KT6: Surb ... 5E 150
Villiers Rd. BR3: Beck ... 2K 157
KT1: King T ... 4F 151
NW2 ... 6C 62
TW7: Isle ... 2J 113
UB1: S'hall ... 1D 94
Villiers St.
WC2 ... 3E 12 (1J 101)
Vimy Cl. TW4: Houn ... 5D 112
Vimy Ridge Ct. E3 ... 2B 86
(off Festubert Pl.)
Vincam Cl. TW2: Whitt ... 7E 112
Vince Ct. N1 ... 2F 9 (3D 84)
Vincennes Est. SE27 ... 4D 138
Vincent Av. KT5: Surb ... 2J 163
Vincent Cl. BR2: Broml ... 4K 159
DA15: Sidc ... 1J 143
EN5: New Bar ... 3E 20
SE16 ... 2A 104
UB7: Sip ... 6C 92
Vincent Ct. HA6: Nwood ... 1H 39
N4 ... 1J 65
NW4 ... 4F 45
SW9 ... 1K 119
W1 ... 7E 4
(off Seymour Pl.)
Vincent Dr. TW17: Shep ... 3G 147
UB10: Uxb ... 1B 74
Vincent Gdns. NW2 ... 3B 62
Vincent Ho. SW1 ... 3D 18
(off Regency St.)
SW1 ... 4C 18
(off Vincent Sq.)
Vincent M. E3 ... 2C 86
Vincent Rd. CR0: C'don ... 7E 156
E4 ... 6A 36
HA0: Wemb ... 7F 61
KT1: King T ... 3G 151
N15 ... 4C 48
N22 ... 2A 48
RM9: Dag ... 7E 72
SE18 ... 4F 107
TW4: Houn ... 2B 112
TW7: Isle ... 1H 113
Vincent Row TW12: Hamp H ... 6G 131
Vincents Path UB5: N'olt ... 6C 58
(off Arnold Rd.)
Vincent Sq. N22 ... 2A 48
SW1 ... 3C 18 (4H 101)
Vincent Sq. Mans. SW1 ... 3B 18
(off Walcott St.)
Vincent St. E16 ... 5H 87
SW1 ... 3C 18 (4H 101)
Vincent's Yd. SW9 ... 1A 120
(off Alphabet M.)
Vincent Ter. N1 ... 2B 84
Vince St. EC1 ... 2F 9 (3D 84)
Vine Cl. E5 ... 4G 67
KT5: Surb ... 6F 151
SM1: Sutt ... 3A 166
TW19: Stanw M ... 7B 174
UB7: W Dray ... 4C 92
Vine Cotts. E1 ... 6J 85
(off Sidney Sq.)
W7 ... 1J 95
Vine Ct. E1 ... 5G 85
HA3: Kenton ... 6E 42
Vinegar All. E17 ... 4D 50
Vine Gdns. IG1: Ilf ... 5G 71
Vinegar St. E1 ... 1H 103
Vinegar Yd. SE1 ... 6G 15 (2E 102)
Vine Gro. UB10: Hil ... 7C 56
Vine Hill EC1 ... 4J 7 (4A 84)
Vine La. SE1 ... 5H 15 (1E 102)
UB10: Hil ... 1B 74
Vine Pl. TW3: Houn ... 4F 113
W5 ... 1E 96
(off St Mark's Rd.)
Viner Cl. KT12: Walt T ... 6A 148
The Vineries EN1: Enf ... 3K 23
N14 ... 6B 22
SE6 ... 1C 140
Vineries Bank NW7 ... 5J 29
Vineries Cl. RM9: Dag ... 6F 73
UB7: Sip ... 6C 92
Vine Rd. BR6: Chels ... 6K 173
E15 ... 7H 69
KT8: E Mos ... 4G 149
SW13 ... 3B 116
Viner Pl. E17 ... 4C 50
The Vinery SW8 ... 7J 101
(off Regent's Bri. Gdns.)
Vinery Way W6 ... 3D 98
Vines Av. N3 ... 1K 45
Vine Sq. W14 ... 5H 99
(off Star Rd.)
Vine St. E17 ... 4D 50
EC3 ... 1J 15 (6F 85)
RM7: Rom ... 4J 55
W1 ... 3B 12 (7G 83)
Vine St. Bri. EC1 ... 4K 7 (4A 84)
The Vineyard TW10: Rich ... 5E 114
Vine Yd. SE1 ... 6D 14
Vineyard Av. NW7 ... 7B 30
Vineyard Cl. KT1: King T ... 3F 151
SE6 ... 1C 140
Vineyard Gro. N3 ... 1K 45
Vineyard Hill Rd. SW19 ... 4H 135
Vineyard M. TW10: Rich ... 5E 114
Vineyard Pas.
TW10: Rich ... 5E 114
Vineyard Path SW14 ... 3K 115
Vineyard Rd. TW13: Felt ... 3J 129
Vineyard Row
KT1: Hamp W ... 1C 150
The Vineyards TW13: Felt ... 3J 129
(off High St.)
TW16: Sun ... 3J 147
Vineyard Wlk. EC1 ... 3J 7 (4A 84)
Viney Bank CR0: Sels ... 7B 170
Viney Rd. SE13 ... 3D 122
Vining St. SW9 ... 4A 120
Vinlake Av. UB10: Ick ... 3B 56
Vinson Cl. BR6: Orp ... 1K 173
Vinson Ho. N1 ... 2D 84
(off Cranston Est.)
Vintage M. E4 ... 4H 35
Vinter Ct. TW17: Shep ... 5C 146
Vintner's Ct. EC4 ... 3D 14 (7C 84)
Vintner's Pl.
EC4 ... 3D 14 (7C 84)
Vintry Ct. SE1 ... 7F 15
(off Porlock St.)
Vintry M. E17 ... 4C 50
Vinyl Pl. UB3: Hayes ... 1F 93
Viola Av. SE2 ... 4B 108
TW14: Felt ... 6A 112
TW19: Stanw ... 1A 128
Viola Sq. W12 ... 7B 80
Violet Av. EN2: Enf ... 1J 23
UB8: Hil ... 5B 74
Violet Cl. E16 ... 4G 87
SE8 ... 6B 104
SM3: Sutt ... 1G 165
SM6: W'gton ... 1E 166
Violet Ct. E15 ... 7G 69
(off Victoria St.)
NW9 ... 1A 44
Violet Gdns. CR0: Wadd ... 5B 168
Violet Hill NW8 ... 2A 82
Violet Hill Ho. NW8 ... 2A 82
(off Violet Hill)
Violet La. CR0: Wadd ... 6B 168
Violet Rd. E3 ... 4D 86
E17 ... 6C 50
E18 ... 2K 51
Violet St. E2 ... 4H 85
Violet Ter. UB8: Hil ... 5C 74
VIP Trading Est. SE7 ... 4A 106
Virgil Pl. W1 ... 6E 4 (5D 82)
Virgil St. SE1 ... 1H 19 (3K 101)
Virgin Active
Aldersgate ... 6C 8
(off Aldersgate St.)
Bank ... 6D 84
Barbican ... 5C 8
(off Aldersgate St.)
Broadgate ... 5G 9
Bromley ... 4B 160
Chelsea ... 6A 100
Chiswick ... 1A 116
Chiswick Pk. ... 4H 97
Cricklewood ... 3G 63
Crouch End ... 5J 47
(off Tottenham La.)
Fulham Pools ... 6G 99
Hammersmith ... 4F 99
(off Hammersmith Rd.)
Islington ... 2B 84
Kensington ... 2K 99
(off Old Court Pl.)
Mansion Ho. ... 2D 14
(off Lit. Trinity La.)
Mayfair ... 2F 11 (6E 82)
Mill Hill East ... 7B 30
Moorgate ... 4E 8 (4D 84)
Notting Hill ... 6G 81
Repton Park ... 7K 37
Smugglers Way ... 4K 117
Strand ... 7J 83
Streatham ... 3J 137
Swiss Cottage ... 6A 64
(within O2 Centre)
Tower Bridge ... 2J 15
(off Haydon St.)
The Twickenham Club ... 6J 113
Walbrook ... 7D 84
West London ... 1A 98
Wimbledon, Worple Rd. ... 6H 135
Virginia Cl. BR2: Broml ... 3G 159
KT3: N Mald ... 4J 151
RM5: Col R ... 1J 55
Virginia Ct. SE16 ... 2K 103
(off Eleanor Cl.)
WC1 ... 3D 6
(off Burton St.)
Virginia Gdns. IG6: Ilf ... 2G 53
Virginia Ho. E14 ... 7E 86
(off Newby Pl.)
TW11: Tedd ... 5B 132
Virginia Rd. CR7: Thor H ... 1B 156
E2 ... 2J 9 (3F 85)
Virginia St. E1 ... 7G 85
Virginia Wlk. SW2 ... 6K 119
Viridian Apts. SW8 ... 7G 101
Visage Apts. NW3 ... 7B 64
(off Winchester Rd.)
Viscount Cl. N11 ... 6A 32
Viscount Ct. W2 ... 6J 81
(off Pembridge Vs.)
Viscount Dr. E6 ... 5D 88
Viscount Gro.
UB5: N'olt ... 3B 76
Viscount M. BR7: Chst ... 6F 143
Viscount Point SW19 ... 7J 135
(off The Broadway)
Viscount Rd. TW19: Stanw ... 1A 128
Viscount St. EC1 ... 4C 8 (4C 84)
Viscount Way
TW6: H'row A ... 4G 111
Vision Ind. Pk. W3 ... 5H 79
The Vista DA14: Sidc ... 5K 143
SE9 ... 6B 124
Vista Av. EN3: Enf H ... 2E 24
Vista Bldg. E3 ... 3B 86
(off Bow Rd.)
SE18 ... 4E 106
Vista Ct. E1 ... 5A 86
(off Ocean Est.)
Vista Dr. IG4: Ilf ... 5B 52
Vista Ho. N4 ... 2A 66
SW19 ... 1B 154
(off Chapter Way)
Vista Way HA3: Kenton ... 6E 42
Vistec Ho. CR0: C'don ... 7B 156
Vita Apts. CR0: C'don ... 2D 168
Vitae Apts. W6 ... 3C 98
Vitali Cl. SW15 ... 6C 116
Vittoria Ho. N1 ... 1K 83
(off High Rd.)
Viveash Cl. UB3: Hayes ... 3H 93
Vivian Av. HA9: Wemb ... 5G 61
NW4 ... 5D 44
Vivian Comma Cl. N4 ... 3B 66
Vivian Ct. N12 ... 5E 30
W9 ... 2K 81
Vivian Gdns. HA9: Wemb ... 5G 61
Vivian Mans. NW4 ... 5D 44
(off Vivian Av.)
Vivian Rd. E3 ... 2A 86
Vivian Sq. SE15 ... 3H 121
Vivian Way N2 ... 5B 46
Vivien Cl. KT9: Chess ... 7E 162
Vivienne Cl. TW1: Twick ... 6D 114
Vixen M. E8 ... 7F 67
(off Haggerston Rd.)
Voce Rd. SE18 ... 7H 107
Voewood Cl. KT3: N Mald ... 6B 152
Vogans Mill SE1 ... 6K 15 (2F 103)
Vogler Ho. E1 ... 7J 85
(off Cable St.)
Vogue Ct. BR1: Broml ... 1K 159
Vollasky Ho. E1 ... 5K 9
(off Daplyn St.)
Volta Cl. N9 ... 3D 34
Voltaire Rd. SW4 ... 3H 119
Voltaire Way UB3: Hayes ... 7G 75
Volt Av. NW10 ... 3K 79
Volta Way CR0: Wadd ... 1K 167
Voluntary Pl. E11 ... 6J 51
Vorley Rd. N19 ... 2G 65
Voss Ct. SW16 ... 6J 137
Voss St. E2 ... 3G 85
Voyager Bus. Est. SE16 ... 3G 103
(off Spa Rd.)
Voyager Ct. E16 ... 5J 87
(off Hammersley Rd.)
Voyagers Cl. SE28 ... 6C 90
Voysey Cl. N3 ... 3G 45
Voysey Sq. E3 ... 4D 86

A-Z Big London 299

Vue Cinema—Warburton Ho.

Vue Cinema
Acton 4G 79
Apollo 3C 12
(off Regent St.)
Bromley 3J 159
Croydon, High St. 3C 168
Croydon, Purley Way 1K 167
Dagenham 1E 90
Finchley Rd. 6A 64
(within O2 Centre)
Fulham Broadway 7J 99
Harrow 6J 41
(within St George's Shop. & Leisure Cen.)
Islington 2A 84
Leicester Square 2D 12
(off Cranbourn St.)
North Finchley 7G 31
Romford 6K 55
Shepherds Bush 2F 99
Stratford City 6E 68
(in Shopping Cen.)
Westfield 1E 98
Wood Green 2A 48
Vulcan Cl. E6 . . . . . 6E 88
Vulcan Ga. EN2: Enf 2F 23
Vulcan Rd. SE4 . . . . . 2B 122
Vulcan Sq. E14 . . . . . 4D 104
Vulcan Ter. SE4 . . . . . 2B 122
Vulcan Way N7 . . . . . 6K 65
SM6: W'gton 7J 167
Vulcan Wharf E15 . . . . . 2D 86
(off Cook's Rd.)
Vulliamy Cl. E4 . . . . . 2A 36
The Vyne DA7: Bex 3H 127
Vyner Rd. W3 . . . . . 7K 79
Vyner St. E2 . . . . . 1H 85
Vyners Way UB10: Ick 5C 56

W

Wadbrook St. KT1: King T 2D 150
Wadding St. SE17 . . . . . 4D 102
Waddington Cl. EN1: Enf 4K 23
Waddington Rd. E15 . . . . . 5F 69
Waddington St. E15 . . . . . 6F 69
Waddington Way SE19 . . . . . 7C 138
WADDON 3A 168
Waddon Cl. CR0: Wadd 3A 168
Waddon Ct. Rd. CR0: Wadd 3A 168
Waddon Leisure Cen. 5A 168
Waddon Marsh Way
CR0: Wadd 1K 167
Waddon New Rd. CR0: C'don 3B 168
Waddon Pk. Av. CR0: Wadd 4A 168
Waddon Rd.
CR0: C'don, Wadd 3A 168
Waddon Way CR0: Wadd 6A 168
Wade Ct. N10 . . . . . 7A 32
Wade Ho. EN1: Enf 5J 23
SE1 . . . . . 7K 15
(off Parkers Row)
Wades Gro. N21 . . . . . 7F 23
Wades Hill N21 . . . . . 6F 23
Wades La. TW11: Tedd 5A 132
Wadeson St. E2 . . . . . 2H 85
Wade's Pl. E14 . . . . . 7D 86
Wadeville Av. RM6: Chad H 6E 54
Wadeville Cl. DA17: Belv 5G 109
Wadham Av. E17 . . . . . 7J 35
Wadham Cl. TW17: Shep 7E 146
Wadham Gdns. NW3 . . . . . 1C 82
UB6: G'frd 6H 59
Wadham Ho. N18 . . . . . 5A 34
Wadham M. SW14 . . . . . 2J 115
Wadham Rd. E17 . . . . . 7J 35
SW15 . . . . . 4G 117
Wadhurst Cl. SE20 . . . . . 2H 157
Wadhurst Rd. SW8 . . . . . 1G 119
W4 . . . . . 3K 97
Wadley Rd. E11 . . . . . 7G 51
Wadsworth Bus. Cen.
UB6: G'frd 2C 78
Wadsworth Cl. EN3: Pond E 5E 24
UB6: G'frd 2C 78
Wadsworth Rd. UB6: G'frd 2B 78
Wager St. E3 . . . . . 4B 86
WAGGONERS RDBT. 1K 111
Waggon La. N17 . . . . . 6B 34
Waggon M. N14 . . . . . 1B 32
Waghorn Rd. E13 . . . . . 1A 88
HA3: Kenton 3D 42
Waghorn St. SE15 . . . . . 3G 121
Wagner M. KT6: Surb 5E 150
(off Avenue Elmers)
Wagner St. SE15 . . . . . 7J 103
Wagstaff Gdns. RM9: Dag 7C 72
Wagtail Cl. EN1: Enf 1C 24
NW9 . . . . . 2A 44
Wagtail Ct. SW15 . . . . . 6E 116
Wagtail Rd. TW6: H'row A 5C 174
Wagtail Wlk. BR3: Beck 5E 158
Waight's Ct. KT2: King T 1E 150
Wainfleet Av. RM5: Col R 2J 55
Wainford Cl. SW19 . . . . . 1F 135
Wainwright Gro. TW7: Isle 4H 113
Wainwright Ho. E1 . . . . . 1J 103
(off Garnet St.)
Waite Davies Rd. SE12 . . . . . 7H 123
Waite Ho. W3 . . . . . 1B 98
Waite St. SE15 . . . . . 6F 103
Waithman St. EC4 . . . . . 1A 14
(off Black Friars La.)
Wakefield Ct. SE26 . . . . . 6J 139
Wakefield Gdns. IG1: Ilf 6C 52
SE19 . . . . . 7E 138
Wakefield Ho. SE15 . . . . . 1G 121
Wakefield M. WC1 . . . . . 2F 7 (3J 83)
Wakefield Rd. N11 . . . . . 5C 32
N15 . . . . . 5F 49
TW10: Rich 5D 114
Wakefield St. E6 . . . . . 1B 88
N18 . . . . . 5B 34
WC1 . . . . . 2F 7 (3J 83)
Wakeford Cl. DA5: Bexl 1D 144
SW4 . . . . . 5G 119
Wakehams Hill HA5: Pinn 3D 40
Wakeham St. N1 . . . . . 6D 66
Wakehurst Rd. SW11 . . . . . 5C 118
Wakeling La. HA0: Wemb 3B 60
Wakeling Rd. W7 . . . . . 5K 77
Wakeling St. E14 . . . . . 6A 86
Wakelin Ho. N1 . . . . . 7B 66
(off Sebbon St.)
Wakelin Rd. E15 . . . . . 2G 87
Wakeman Ho. NW10 . . . . . 3F 81
(off Wakeman Rd.)
Wakeman Rd. NW10 . . . . . 3E 80
Wakemans Hill Av. NW9 . . . . . 5K 43
Wakering Rd. IG11: Bark 6G 71
(not continuous)
Wakerley Cl. E6 . . . . . 6D 88
Wakeup Docklands 7J 87
Wakley St. EC1 . . . . . 1A 8 (3B 84)
Walberswick St. SW8 . . . . . 7J 101
Walbrook EC4 . . . . . 2E 14 (7D 84)
(not continuous)
The Walbrook Bldg. EC4 . . . . . 2E 14
Walbrook Ct. N1 . . . . . 2E 84
(off Hemsworth St.)
Walbrook Ho. N9 . . . . . 2D 34
(off Huntingdon Rd.)
Walbrook Wharf EC4 . . . . . 3D 14
(off Cousin La.)
Walburgh St. E1 . . . . . 6H 85
Walcorde Av. SE17 . . . . . 4C 102
Walcot Gdns. SE11 . . . . . 3J 19
Walcot Rd.
EN3: Brim 2G 25
Walcot Sq. SE11 . . . . . 3K 19 (4A 102)
Walcott St. SW1 . . . . . 3B 18 (4G 101)
Waldair Ct. E16 . . . . . 2F 107
Waldeck Gro. SE27 . . . . . 3B 138
Waldeck Rd. N15 . . . . . 4B 48
SW14 . . . . . 3J 115
W4 . . . . . 6G 97
W13 . . . . . 6B 78
Waldeck Ter. SW14 . . . . . 3J 115
(off Waldeck Rd.)
Waldegrave Ct. IG11: Bark 1H 89
Waldegrave Gdns.
TW1: Twick 2K 131
Waldegrave Pk. TW1: Twick 4K 131
Waldegrave Rd. BR1: Broml 4C 160
N8 . . . . . 3A 48
RM8: Dag 2C 72
SE19 . . . . . 7F 139
TW1: Twick 4K 131
TW11: Tedd 4K 131
W5 . . . . . 7F 79
Waldegrove CR0: C'don 3F 169
Waldemar Av. SW6 . . . . . 1G 117
W13 . . . . . 1C 96
Waldemar Rd. SW19 . . . . . 5J 135
Walden Av. BR7: Chst 4D 142
N13 . . . . . 4H 33
RM13: Rain 2K 91
Walden Cl. DA17: Belv 5F 109
Walden Ct. SW8 . . . . . 1H 119
Walden Gdns. CR7: Thor H 3K 155
Walden Ho. SW1 . . . . . 4H 17
(off Pimlico Rd.)
SW11 . . . . . 1E 118
(off Dagnall St.)
Walden Pde. BR7: Chst 6D 142
(not continuous)
Walden Rd. BR7: Chst 6D 142
N17 . . . . . 1D 48
Waldenshaw Rd. SE23 . . . . . 1J 139
Walden St. E1 . . . . . 6H 85
(not continuous)
Walden Way NW7 . . . . . 6A 30
Waldo Cl. SW4 . . . . . 5G 119
Waldo Ho. NW10 . . . . . 3D 80
(off Waldo Rd.)
Waldo Ind. Est. BR1: Broml 3B 160
Waldo Pl. CR4: Mitc 7C 136
Waldorf Cl. CR2: S Croy 7B 168
Waldo Rd. BR1: Broml 3B 160
NW10 . . . . . 3C 80
Waldram Cres. SE23 . . . . . 1J 139
Waldram Pk. Rd. SE23 . . . . . 1K 139
Waldram Pl. SE23 . . . . . 1J 139
Waldrist Way DA18: Erith 3F 109
Waldron Gdns.
BR2: Broml 3F 159
Waldronhyrst CR2: S Croy 4B 168
Waldron M. SW3 . . . . . 7B 16 (6B 100)
Waldron Rd. HA1: Harr 1J 59
HA2: Harr 1J 59
SW18 . . . . . 3A 136
The Waldrons CR0: C'don 4B 168
Waldrons Path CR2: S Croy 4C 168
Waldrons Yd. HA2: Harr 2H 59
Waldstock Rd. SE28 . . . . . 7A 90
Waleorde Rd. SE17 . . . . . 5C 102
Waleran Cl. HA7: Stan 5E 26
Waleran Rd. SE13 . . . . . 2E 122
Waleran Flats SE1 . . . . . 4E 102
Wales Av. SM5: Cars 5C 166
Wales Cl. SE15 . . . . . 6H 103
Wales Farm Rd. W3 . . . . . 5K 79
Wales Office 5E 12
(off Whitehall)
Waleton Acres SM6: W'gton 6G 167
Waley St. E1 . . . . . 5A 86
Walfield Av. N20 . . . . . 7E 20
Walford Ho. E1 . . . . . 6H 85
Walford Rd. N16 . . . . . 4E 66
Walfrey Gdns. RM9: Dag 7F 73
WALHAM GREEN 1J 117
Walham Grn. Ct. SW6 . . . . . 7K 99
(off Waterford Rd.)
Walham Gro. SW6 . . . . . 7J 99
Walham Ri. SW19 . . . . . 6G 135
Walham Yd. SW6 . . . . . 7J 99
The Walk N13 . . . . . 3F 33
(off Fox La.)
TW16: Sun 7H 129
Waikato Lodge IG9: Buck H 1F 37
Walkden Rd. BR7: Chst 5E 142
Walker Cl. CR0: New Ad 7E 170
N11 . . . . . 4B 32
SE18 . . . . . 4G 107
TW12: Hamp 6D 130
TW14: Felt 7H 111
W7 . . . . . 1J 95
Walker Ho. NW1 . . . . . 1C 6 (2H 83)
SE16 . . . . . 3B 104
(off Redriff Est.)
Walker M. SW2 . . . . . 5A 120
Walker's Ct. W1 . . . . . 2C 12
Walkerscroft Mead SE21 . . . . . 1C 138
Walkers Lodge E14 . . . . . 2E 104
(off Manchester Rd.)
Walkers Pl. SW15 . . . . . 4G 117
The Walkie-Talkie 2G 15
Walkinshaw Ct. N1 . . . . . 7C 66
(off Rotherfield St.)
The Walks N2 . . . . . 3B 46
Walkynscroft SE15 . . . . . 2H 121
(off Caulfield Rd.)
Wallace Bldg. NW8 . . . . . 4B 4
(off Penfold St.)
Wallace Cl. SE28 . . . . . 7D 90
TW17: Shep 4F 147
UB10: Uxb 2A 74
Wallace Collection 7G 5 (6E 82)
Wallace Ct. NW1 . . . . . 6D 4
(off Old Marylebone Rd.)
SE3 . . . . . 4K 123
Wallace Cres. SM5: Cars 5D 166
Wallace Ho. N7 . . . . . 6K 65
(off Caledonian Rd.)
Wallace Rd. N1 . . . . . 6C 66
Wallace Way N19 . . . . . 2H 65
(off St John's Way)
RM1: Rom 1K 55
Wallasey Cres. UB10: Ick 2C 56
Wallbrook Bus. Cen.
TW4: Houn 3K 111
Wallbutton Rd. SE4 . . . . . 2A 122
Wallcote Av. NW2 . . . . . 1F 63
Wall Ct. N4 . . . . . 1K 65
(off Stroud Grn. Rd.)
Walled Gdn. Cl. BR3: Beck 4D 158
Walled Gdn. Ct. HA7: Stan 3D 26
Wallenberg Pl. W1 . . . . . 1F 11
(off Gt. Cumberland Pl.)
WALLEND 1E 88
Wall End Ct. E6 . . . . . 1E 88
(off Wall End Rd.)
Wall End Rd. E6 . . . . . 7E 70
Waller Dr. HA6: Nwood 2J 39
Waller Rd. SE14 . . . . . 1K 121
Wallers Cl. IG8: Wfd G 6J 37
RM9: Dag 1E 90
Waller Way SE10 . . . . . 7D 104
Wallflower St. W12 . . . . . 7B 80
Wallgrave Rd. SW5 . . . . . 4K 99
Wallingford Av. W10 . . . . . 5F 81
WALLINGTON 6F 167
Wallington Cl. HA4: Ruis 6E 38
Wallington Cnr. SM6: W'gton 4F 167
(off Manor Rd. Nth.)
Wallington Ct. SM6: W'gton 6F 167
(off Stanley Pk. Rd.)
WALLINGTON GREEN 4F 167
Wallington Rd. IG3: Ilf 7K 53
Wallington Sq. SM6: W'gton 6F 167
Wallis All. SE1 . . . . . 6D 14
Wallis Cl. SW11 . . . . . 3B 118
Wallis Ho. HA4: Ruis 1F 57
SE14 . . . . . 1A 122
TW8: Bford 5E 96
Wallis M. N8 . . . . . 3A 48
(off Courcy Rd.)
Wallis Rd. E9 . . . . . 6B 68
TW6: H'row A 5C 174
UB1: S'hall 6F 77
Wallis's Cotts. SW2 . . . . . 7J 119
Wallman Pl. N22 . . . . . 1K 47
Wallorton Gdns. SW14 . . . . . 4K 115
The Wallpaper Apts. N1 . . . . . 7A 66
(off Offord Rd.)
Wallside EC2 . . . . . 6D 8
Wall St. N1 . . . . . 6D 66
Wallwood Rd. E11 . . . . . 7F 51
Wallwood St. E14 . . . . . 5B 86
Walmar Cl. EN4: Had W 1G 21
Walmer Cl. BR6: Farnb 4H 173
E4 . . . . . 2J 35
RM7: Mawney 2H 55
Walmer Ct. KT5: Surb 5E 150
(off Cranes Pk.)
Walmer Gdns. W13 . . . . . 2A 96
Walmer Ho. W10 . . . . . 6F 81
(off Bramley Rd.)
Walmer Pl. W1 . . . . . 5E 4
Walmer Rd. W10 . . . . . 6E 80
W11 . . . . . 7G 81
Walmer St. W1 . . . . . 5E 4 (5D 82)
Walmer Ter. SE18 . . . . . 4G 107
Walmgate Rd. UB6: G'frd 1B 78
Walmington Fold N12 . . . . . 6D 30
Walm La. NW2 . . . . . 6E 62
Walney Wlk. N1 . . . . . 6C 66
Walnut Av. UB7: W Dray 3C 92
Walnut Cl. IG6: Ilf 4G 53
SE8 . . . . . 6B 104
SM5: Cars 5D 166
UB3: Hayes 7G 75
Walnut Ct. E17 . . . . . 4E 50
W5 . . . . . 2E 96
W8 . . . . . 3K 99
(off St Mary's Ga.)
Walnut Flds. KT17: Ewe 7B 164
Walnut Gdns. E15 . . . . . 5G 69
Walnut Gro. EN1: Enf 5J 23
Walnut Ho. E3 . . . . . 1B 86
(off Barge La.)
Walnut M. N22 . . . . . 3A 48
(off High Rd.)
SM2: Sutt 7A 166
Walnut Rd. E10 . . . . . 2C 68
Walnut Tree Av. CR4: Mitc 3C 154
(off De'Arn Gdns.)
Walnut Tree Cl. BR7: Chst 1H 161
SW13 . . . . . 1B 116
TW17: Shep 3E 146
UB10: Ick 4A 56
Walnut Tree Cotts. SW19 . . . . . 5G 135
Walnut Tree Ho. SW10 . . . . . 6K 99
(off Tregunter Rd.)
Walnut Tree Rd. RM8: Dag 2E 72
SE10 . . . . . 5G 105
(not continuous)
TW5: Hest 6D 94
TW8: Bford 6E 96
TW17: Shep 2E 146
Walnut Tree Wlk.
SE11 . . . . . 3J 19 (4A 102)
Walnut Way HA4: Ruis 6A 58
IG9: Buck H 3G 37
Walpole Av. TW9: Kew 2F 115
Walpole Cl. W13 . . . . . 2C 96
Walpole Ct. NW6 . . . . . 7A 64
(off Fairfax Rd.)
TW2: Twick 2J 131
W14 . . . . . 3F 99
(off Blythe Rd.)
Walpole Cres. TW11: Tedd 5K 131
Walpole Gdns. TW2: Twick 2J 131
W4 . . . . . 5J 97
Walpole Ho. KT8: W Mole 5E 148
(off Approach Rd.)
SE1 . . . . . 7J 13
(off Westminster Bri. Rd.)
SW15 . . . . . 5G 117
(off Plaza Gdns.)
Walpole Lodge W13 . . . . . 1C 96
Walpole M. NW8 . . . . . 1B 82
SW19 . . . . . 6B 136
Walpole Pl. SE18 . . . . . 4F 107
TW11: Tedd 5K 131
Walpole Rd. BR2: Broml 5B 160
CR0: C'don 2D 168
E6 . . . . . 7A 70
E17 . . . . . 4A 50
E18 . . . . . 1H 51
KT6: Surb 7E 150
N17 . . . . . 2C 48
(not continuous)
SW19 . . . . . 6B 136
TW2: Twick 2J 131
TW11: Tedd 5K 131
Walpole St. SW3 . . . . . 5E 16 (5D 100)
Walrond Av. HA9: Wemb 5E 60
Walsham Cl. N16 . . . . . 1G 67
SE28 . . . . . 7D 90
Walsham Ho. SE14 . . . . . 2K 121
SE17 . . . . . 5D 102
(off Blackwood St.)
Walsham How Cl. E17 . . . . . 5F 51
Walsham Rd. SE14 . . . . . 2K 121
TW14: Felt 7K 111
Walsingham NW8 . . . . . 1B 82
Walsingham Gdns.
KT19: Ewe 4A 164
Walsingham Lodge SW13 . . . . . 1C 116
Walsingham Mans. SW6 . . . . . 7K 99
(off Fulham Rd.)
Walsingham Pk. BR7: Chst 2H 161
Walsingham Pl. SW4 . . . . . 6E 118
Walsingham Rd. CR4: Mitc 5D 154
E5 . . . . . 3G 67
EN2: Enf 4J 23
W13 . . . . . 1A 96
Walsingham Wlk. DA17: Belv 6G 109
Walston Ho. SW1 . . . . . 5C 18
(off Aylesford St.)
Walter Besant Ho. E1 . . . . . 3K 85
(off Bancroft Rd.)
Walter Ct. W3 . . . . . 6J 79
(off Lynton Ter.)
Walter Grn. Ho. SE15 . . . . . 1J 121
(off Lausanne Rd.)
Walter Ho. SW10 . . . . . 7B 100
(off Riley St.)
Walter Hurford Ho. E12 . . . . . 4E 70
(off Grantham Rd.)
Walter Langley Ct. SE16 . . . . . 2J 103
(off Brunel Rd.)
Walter Rodney Cl. E6 . . . . . 6D 70
Walter Savil Twr. E17 . . . . . 6C 50
(off Colchester Rd.)
Walters Cl. SE17 . . . . . 4D 102
(off Brandon St.)
UB3: Hayes 2H 93
Walters Ho. N1 . . . . . 1B 84
(off Essex Rd.)
SE17 . . . . . 6B 102
(off Otto St.)
Walter Sickert Hall N1 . . . . . 1C 8
(off Graham St.)
Walters Rd. EN3: Pond E 4D 24
SE25 . . . . . 4E 156
Walter St. E2 . . . . . 3K 85
KT2: King T 1E 150
Walters Way SE23 . . . . . 6K 121
Walters Yd. BR1: Broml 2J 159
Walter Ter. E1 . . . . . 6K 85
Walterton Rd. W9 . . . . . 4H 81
Walter Wlk. HA8: Edg 6D 28
Waltham Av. NW9 . . . . . 6G 43
UB3: Harl 3E 92
Waltham Dr. HA8: Edg 2G 43
Waltham Forest Feel Good Centre
. . . . . 2D 50
Waltham Ho. NW8 . . . . . 1A 82
Waltham Pk. Way E17 . . . . . 1C 50
Waltham Rd. IG8: Wfd G 6H 37
SM5: Cars 7B 154
UB2: S'hall 3C 94
WALTHAMSTOW 3C 50
Walthamstow Av. E4 . . . . . 6G 35
Walthamstow Bus. Cen. E17 . . . . . 2E 50
Walthamstow Leisure Cen. 6B 50
Walthamstow Marsh Nature Reserve
. . . . . 7H 49
Walthamstow Pumphouse Museum
. . . . . 6A 50
Waltham Way E4 . . . . . 3G 35
Waltheof Av. N17 . . . . . 1D 48
Waltheof Gdns. N17 . . . . . 1D 48
Walton Av. HA2: Harr 5D 58
HA9: Wemb 3H 61
KT3: N Mald 4B 152
SM3: Cheam 3H 165
WALTON BRI. 7G 147
Walton Bri. KT12: Walt T 7G 147
Walton Bri. Rd. TW17: Shep 7G 147
Walton Cl. E4 . . . . . 5H 35
E5 . . . . . 3K 67
(off Orient Way)
HA1: Harr 4H 41
NW2 . . . . . 2D 62
SW8 . . . . . 7J 101
Walton Ct. CR2: S Croy 5C 168
(off Warham Rd.)
EN5: New Bar 5F 21
NW6 . . . . . 7A 64
(off Fairfax Rd.)
Walton Cft. HA1: Harr 4J 59
Walton Dr. HA1: Harr 4H 41
NW10 . . . . . 6K 61
Walton Gdns. HA9: Wemb 2E 60
TW13: Felt 4H 129
W3 . . . . . 5H 79
Walton Grn. CR0: New Ad 7D 170
Walton Ho. E2 . . . . . 3K 9
(off Montclare St.)
E17 . . . . . 3D 50
NW1 . . . . . 3K 5
(off Longford St.)
SW3 . . . . . 2E 16
(off Walton St.)
Walton La.
KT13: Weyb 7F 147, 7G 147
TW17: Shep 7F 147
WALTON-ON-THAMES 7J 147
Walton on Thames
Camping & Cvn. Site 7E 148
Walton Pl. SW3 . . . . . 1E 16 (3D 100)
Walton Rd. DA14: Sidc 2C 144
E12 . . . . . 4E 70
(not continuous)
E13 . . . . . 2A 88
HA1: Harr 4H 41
KT8: W Mole, E Mos 4D 148
KT12: Walt T 5A 148
N15 . . . . . 4F 49
RM5: Col R 1F 55
Walton St. EN2: Enf 1J 23
SW3 . . . . . 3D 16 (4C 100)
Walton Vs. N1 . . . . . 7E 66
(off Downham Rd.)
Walton Way CR4: Mitc 4G 155
W3 . . . . . 5H 79
Walt Whitman Cl. SE24 . . . . . 4B 120
WALWORTH 5C 102
Walworth Pl. SE17 . . . . . 5C 102
Walworth Rd. SE1 . . . . . 4C 102
SE17 . . . . . 4C 102
Walworth Sq. SE17 . . . . . 4C 102
Walwyn Av. BR1: Broml 3B 160
Wanborough Dr. SW15 . . . . . 1D 134
Wanderer Dr. IG11: Bark 3C 90
Wandle Apts. CR2: S Croy 5D 168
Wandle Bank CR0: Bedd 3J 167
SW19 . . . . . 7B 136
Wandle Ct. CR0: Bedd 3J 167
KT19: Ewe 4J 163
Wandle Ct. Gdns. CR0: Bedd 3J 167
Wandle Ho. BR1: Broml 5F 141
NW8 . . . . . 5C 4
(off Penfold St.)
Wandle Industrial Mus. 3D 154
Wandle Meadow Nature Pk. 5A 136
Wandle Pk. 2B 168
The Wandle Pk. Trad. Est.
CR0: C'don 2B 168
Wandle Recreation Cen. 6K 117
Wandle Rd. CR0: Bedd 3J 167
CR0: C'don 3C 168
SM4: Mord 4A 154
SM6: W'gton 3F 167
SW17 . . . . . 2C 136
Wandle Side CR0: Wadd 3K 167
SM6: W'gton 3F 167
Wandle Trad. Est.
CR4: Mitc 7D 154
Wandle Way CR4: Mitc 5D 154
SW18 . . . . . 1K 135
Wandon Rd. SW6 . . . . . 7K 99
WANDSWORTH 5K 117
WANDSWORTH BRI. 3K 117
Wandsworth Bri. Rd. SW6 . . . . . 1K 117
WANDSWORTH COMMON 1D 136
Wandsworth Comn. W. Side
SW18 . . . . . 5A 118
WANDSWORTH GYRATORY 5K 117
Wandsworth High St.
SW18 . . . . . 5J 117
Wandsworth Mus. 5J 117
Wandsworth Plain SW18 . . . . . 5K 117
Wandsworth Rd.
SW8 . . . . . 7E 18 (3F 119)
Wangey Rd. RM6: Chad H 7D 54
Wangford Ho. SW9 . . . . . 4B 120
(off Loughborough Pk.)
Wanless Rd. SE24 . . . . . 3C 120
Wanley Rd. SE5 . . . . . 4D 120
Wanlip Rd. E13 . . . . . 4K 87
Wannock Gdns. IG6: Ilf 1F 53
Wansbeck Ct. EN2: Enf 3G 23
(off Waverley Rd.)
Wansbeck Rd. E9 . . . . . 7B 68
Wansdown Pl. SW6 . . . . . 7K 99
Wansey St. SE17 . . . . . 4C 102
Wansford Rd. IG8: Wfd G 1A 52
WANSTEAD 6K 51
Wanstead Cl. BR1: Broml 2A 160
Wanstead Gdns. IG4: Ilf 6B 52
Wanstead Golf Course 7A 52
Wanstead La. IG1: Ilf 6B 52
Wanstead Leisure Cen. 6A 52
Wanstead Pk. Av. E12 . . . . . 1B 70
Wanstead Pk. Rd. IG1: Ilf 6B 52
Wanstead Pl. E11 . . . . . 6J 51
Wanstead Rd. BR1: Broml 2A 160
Wansunt Rd. DA5: Bexl 1J 145
Wantage Rd. SE12 . . . . . 5H 123
Wantz Rd. RM10: Dag 4H 73
WAPPING 1H 103
Wapping Dock St. E1 . . . . . 1H 103
Wapping High St. E1 . . . . . 1G 103
Wapping La. E1 . . . . . 7H 85
Wapping Wall E1 . . . . . 1J 103
Waratah Dr. BR7: Chst 5D 142
Warbank La. KT2: King T 7B 134
Warbeck Rd. W12 . . . . . 2D 98
Warberry Rd. N22 . . . . . 1K 47
Warboys App. KT2: King T 6H 133
Warboys Cres. E4 . . . . . 5K 35
Warboys Rd. KT2: King T 6H 133
Warburg Ct. NW9 . . . . . 3A 44
(off Mornington Cl.)
Warburton Cl. HA3: Hrw W 6C 26
N1 . . . . . 6E 66
(off Culford Rd.)
Warburton Ct. HA4: Ruis 2J 57
Warburton Ho. E8 . . . . . 1H 85
(off Warburton St.)

Warburton Rd.—Wave Ct.

Warburton Rd. E8 .... 1H 85
TW2: Whitt 1F 131
Warburton St. E8 .... 1H 85
Warburton Ter. E17 .... 2D 50
Wardalls Gro. SE14 .... 7J 103
Wardalls Ho. SE8 .... 6B 104
(off Staunton St.)
Ward Cl. CR2: S Croy 6E 168
DA8: Erith 6K 109
Wardell Cl. NW7 .... 7F 29
Wardell Fld. NW9 .... 1A 44
Wardell Ho. SE10 .... 6E 104
(off Welland St.)
Wardell M. SW4 .... 3F 119
Warden Av. HA2: Harr 1D 58
Warden Rd. NW5 .... 6E 64
Wardens Fld. Cl.
BR6: Chels 6J 173
Wardens Gro. SE1 .... 5C 14 (1C 102)
Ward La. E9 .... 5A 68
Wardle St. E9 .... 5K 67
Wardley St. SW18 .... 7K 117
Wardo Av. SW6 .... 1G 117
Wardour M. W1 .... 1B 12
Wardour St. W1 .... 7B 6 (6G 83)
Ward Point SE11 .... 4J 19 (4A 102)
Ward Rd. E15 .... 1F 87
N19 .... 3G 65
SW19 .... 1A 154
The Wardrobe TW9: Rich 5D 114
(off Old Palace Yd.)
Wardrobe Pl. EC4 .... 1B 14
Wardrobe Ter. EC4 .... 2B 14
Wardroper Ho. SE1 .... 3B 102
(off St George's Rd.)
Wards Rd. IG2: Ilf 7H 53
Wards Wharf App. E16 .... 1B 106
Ware Ct. SM1: Sutt 4H 165
Wareham Cl.
TW3: Houn 4F 113
Wareham Ct. N1 .... 7E 66
(off Hertford Rd.)
Wareham Ho. SW8 .... 7K 101
Warehome M. E13 .... 4J 87
(off Jutland Rd.)
Warehouse Ct. SE18 .... 3F 107
Warehouse Way E16 .... 7K 87
Waremead Rd. IG2: Ilf 5F 53
Warepoint Dr. SE28 .... 2H 107
Warfield Rd. NW10 .... 3F 81
TW12: Hamp 1F 149
TW14: Felt 7G 111
Warfield Yd. NW10 .... 3F 81
(off Warfield Rd.)
Wargrave Av. N15 .... 6F 49
Wargrave Ho. E2 .... 2J 9
(off Navarre St.)
Wargrave Rd. HA2: Harr 3G 59
Warham Rd. CR2: S Croy 5B 168
HA3: W'stone 2K 41
N4 .... 5A 48
Warham St. SE5 .... 7B 102
Waring & Gillow Est. W3 .... 4G 79
Waring Cl. BR6: Chels 6K 173
Waring Dr. BR6: Chels 6K 173
Waring Rd. DA14: Sidc 6C 144
Waring St. SE27 .... 4C 138
Warkworth Gdns. TW7: Isle 7A 96
Warkworth Rd. N17 .... 7J 33
Warland Rd. SE18 .... 7H 107
Warley Av. RM8: Dag 7F 55
UB4: Hayes 6J 75
Warley Cl. E10 .... 1B 68
Warley Rd. IG5: Ilf 1E 52
IG8: Wfd G 7E 36
N9 .... 2D 34
UB4: Hayes 6J 75
Warley St. E2 .... 3K 85
Warlingham Ct. SE13 .... 6E 122
Warlingham Rd.
CR7: Thor H 4B 156
Warlock Rd. W9 .... 4H 81
Warlters Cl. N7 .... 4J 65
Warlters Rd. N7 .... 4J 65
Warltersville Mans. N19 .... 7J 47
Warltersville Rd. N19 .... 7J 47
War Memorial Sports Ground 4C 166
Warmington Cl. E5 .... 3K 67
Warmington Rd. SE24 .... 6C 120
Warmington St. E13 .... 4J 87
Warminster Gdns. SE25 .... 2G 157
Warminster Rd. SE25 .... 2F 157
Warminster Sq. SE25 .... 2G 157
Warminster Way
CR4: Mitc 1F 155
Warmsworth NW1 .... 1G 83
(off Pratt St.)
Warmwell Av. NW9 .... 1A 44
Warndon St. SE16 .... 4K 103
Warneford Rd.
HA3: Kenton 3D 42
TW6: H'row A 5C 174
Warneford St. E9 .... 1H 85
Warne Pl. DA15: Sidc 6B 126
Warner Av. SM3: Cheam 2G 165
Warner Cl. E15 .... 5G 69
NW9 .... 7B 44
TW12: Hamp 5D 130
UB3: Harl 7F 93
Warner Ho. BR3: Beck 6D 140
NW8 .... 3A 82
SE13 .... 2D 122
(off Russett Way)
Warner Pl. E2 .... 2G 85
Warner Rd. BR1: Broml 7H 141
E17 .... 4A 50
N8 .... 4H 47
SE5 .... 1C 120
Warners Cl. IG8: Wfd G 5D 36
Warners La. KT2: King T 4D 132
Warners Path IG8: Wfd G 5D 36
Warner St. EC1 .... 4J 7 (4A 84)
Warner Ter. E14 .... 5D 86
(off Broomfield St.)
Warner Yd. EC1 .... 4J 7
Warnford Ct. EC2 .... 7F 9
(off Throgmorton Av.)
Warnford Ho. SW15 .... 6A 116
(off Tunworth Cres.)
Warnford Ind. Est. UB3: Hayes 2G 93
Warnford Rd. BR6: Chels 5K 173
Warnham WC1 .... 2G 7
(off Sidmouth St.)
Warnham Ct. Rd.
SM5: Cars 7D 166
Warnham Ho. SW2 .... 7K 119
(off Up. Tulse Hill)
Warnham Rd. N12 .... 5H 31
Warple M. W3 .... 2A 98
Warple Way W3 .... 2A 98
The Warren 2A 94
The Warren E12 .... 4C 70
KT4: Wor Pk 4K 163
TW5: Hest 7D 94
UB4: Hayes 6J 75
Warren Av. BR1: Broml 7G 141
BR6: Chels 5K 173
CR2: Sels 7K 169
E10 .... 3E 68
TW10: Rich 4H 115
Warren Cl. DA6: Bex 5G 127
HA9: Wemb 2D 60
N9 .... 7E 24
SE21 .... 7C 120
UB4: Yead 5A 76
Warren Ct. BR3: Beck 7C 140
CR0: C'don 1E 168
N17 .... 3G 49
(off High Cross Rd.)
NW1 .... 3B 6
(off Warren St.)
SE7 .... 6A 106
W5 .... 5C 78
Warren Cres. N9 .... 7A 24
Warren Cutting KT2: King T 7K 133
Warrender Rd. N19 .... 3G 65
Warrender Way HA4: Ruis 7J 39
The Warren Dr. E11 .... 7A 52
Warren Dr. HA4: Ruis 7B 40
UB6: G'frd 4F 77
Warren Dr. Nth. KT5: Surb 1H 163
Warren Dr. Sth. KT5: Surb 1J 163
Warren Farm Cotts.
RM6: Chad H 4F 55
Warren Flds. HA7: Stan 4H 27
Warren Footpath TW1: Twick 1C 132
Warren Gdns. BR6: Chels 5K 173
E15 .... 5F 69
Warren Ho. E3 .... 3D 86
(off Bromley High St.)
N17 .... 3G 49
(off High Cross Rd.)
W14 .... 4H 99
Warren La. HA7: Stan 2F 27
SE18 .... 3F 107
Warren M. W1 .... 4A 6 (4G 83)
Warren Pk. KT2: King T 6J 133
Warren Pk. Rd. SM1: Sutt 6B 166
Warren Pl. E1 .... 6K 85
(off Pitsea St.)
Warren Pond Rd. E4 .... 1C 36
Warren Ri. KT3: N Mald 1K 151
Warren Rd. BR2: Hayes 2J 171
BR6: Chels 5K 173
(not continuous)
CR0: C'don 1E 168
DA6: Bex 5G 127
DA14: Sidc 3C 144
E4 .... 2K 35
E10 .... 3E 68
E11 .... 6A 52
IG6: Ilf 5H 53
KT2: King T 6J 133
NW2 .... 2B 62
SW19 .... 6C 136
TW2: Whitt 6G 113
TW15: Ashf 7G 129
UB10: Ick 4A 56
WD23: B Hea 1B 26
Warren Sports Cen. 5F 55
Warrens Shawe La.
HA8: Edg 2C 28
Warren St. W1 .... 4A 6 (4G 83)
Warren Ter. RM6: Chad H 4D 54
Warren Wlk. SE7 .... 6A 106
Warren Way HA8: Edg 2H 43
Warren Wood Cl.
BR2: Hayes 2H 171
Warriner Dr. N9 .... 3B 34
Warriner Gdns. SW11 .... 1D 118
Warrington Ct. CR0: Wadd 3B 168
(off Warrington Rd.)
Warrington Cres. W9 .... 4A 82
Warrington Gdns. W9 .... 4A 82
(not continuous)
Warrington Rd. CR0: Wadd 3B 168
HA1: Harr 5J 41
RM8: Dag 2D 72
TW10: Rich 5D 114
Warrington Sq. RM8: Dag 2D 72
Warrior Cl. SE28 .... 1H 107
Warrior Ct. SW9 .... 3B 120
(off Coldharbour Rd.)
Warrior Sq. E12 .... 4E 70
Warsaw Cl. HA4: Ruis 6K 57
Warspite Ho. E14 .... 4D 104
(off Cahir St.)
Warspite Rd. SE18 .... 3C 106
Warton Ct. E1 .... 7K 85
(off Cable St.)
W3 .... 3J 97
(off All Saints Rd.)
Warton Ho. E15 .... 1E 86
(off High St.)
Warton Rd. E15 .... 1E 86
Warwall E6 .... 6F 89
Warwark Ct. KT6: Surb 2E 162
Warwick W14 .... 4H 99
(off Kensington Village)
Warwick Av. HA2: Harr 4D 58
HA8: Edg 3C 28
W2 .... 4A 82
W9 .... 4K 81
Warwick Bldg. SW11 .... 6F 101
Warwick Chambers W8 .... 3J 99
(off Pater St.)
Warwick Cl. DA5: Bexl 7F 127
EN4: E Barn 5G 21
TW12: Hamp 7G 131
W8 .... 3H 99
(off Kensington High St.)
WD23: B Hea 1D 26
Warwick Ct. BR2: Broml 2G 159
EC4 .... 1B 14
(off Warwick La.)
EN5: New Bar 5E 20
(off Station Rd.)
HA1: Harr 3J 41
N11 .... 6C 32
UB5: N'olt 5E 58
(off Newmarket Av.)
W7 .... 6J 77
(off Copley Cl.)
WC1 .... 6H 7 (5K 83)
Warwick Cres. UB4: Hayes 4H 75
W2 .... 5A 82
Warwick Dene W5 .... 1F 97
Warwick Dr. SW15 .... 3D 116
Warwick Est. W2 .... 5K 81
Warwick Gdns.
CR7: Thor H 3A 156
EN5: Barn 3C 20
IG1: Ilf 1F 71
KT7: T Ditt 5K 149
N4 .... 5C 48
W14 .... 3H 99
Warwick Gro. E5 .... 1H 67
KT5: Surb 7F 151
Warwick Ho. E16 .... 1J 105
(off Wesley Av.)
KT2: King T 1E 150
(off Acre Rd.)
SW9 .... 2A 120
Warwick Ho. St. SW1 .... 4D 12 (1H 101)
Warwick La. EC4 .... 7B 8 (6B 84)
W14 .... 4H 99
Warwick Lodge TW2: Twick 3F 131
Warwick Mans. SW5 .... 4J 99
(off Cromwell Cres.)
Warwick Pde. HA3: Kenton 2B 42
Warwick Pas. EC4 .... 7B 8
(off Old Bailey)
Warwick Pl. KT7: T Ditt 6A 150
W5 .... 2D 96
W9 .... 5A 82
Warwick Pl. Nth. SW1 .... 4A 18 (4G 101)
Warwick Rd. CR7: Thor H 3A 156
DA14: Sidc 5B 144
DA16: Well 3C 126
E4 .... 5H 35
E11 .... 5K 51
E12 .... 5C 70
E15 .... 6H 69
E17 .... 1B 50
EN5: New Bar 4E 20
KT1: Hamp W 1C 150
KT3: N Mald 3J 151
KT7: T Ditt 5K 149
N11 .... 6C 32
N18 .... 4K 33
SE20 .... 3H 157
SM1: Sutt 4A 166
SW5 .... 4H 99
TW2: Twick 1J 131
TW4: Houn 3K 111
TW15: Ashf 5A 128
UB2: S'hall 3D 94
UB7: W Dray 2A 92
W5 .... 2D 96
W14 .... 4H 99
Warwick Row SW1 .... 1K 17 (3G 101)
Warwickshire Path SE8 .... 7B 104
Warwickshire Rd. N16 .... 4E 66
Warwick Sq. EC4 .... 7B 8 (6B 84)
SW1 .... 5A 18 (5G 101)
(not continuous)
Warwick Sq. M. SW1 .... 4A 18 (4G 101)
Warwick St. W1 .... 2B 12 (7G 83)
Warwick Ter. E17 .... 5F 51
(off Lea Bri. Rd.)
SE18 .... 6H 107
Warwick Way SW1 .... 5J 17 (5F 101)
Warwick Yd. EC1 .... 4D 8 (4C 84)
Wasdale NW1 .... 2K 5
(off Cumberland Mkt.)
Washbourne Ct. N9 .... 2B 34
(off Acton Cl.)
Washbourne Rd. NW10 .... 1K 79
Washington Av. E12 .... 4D 70
Washington Bldg. SE13 .... 1D 122
(off Deal's Gateway)
Washington Cl. E3 .... 3D 86
Washington Ho. E17 .... 2B 50
SW3 .... 7E 10
(off Basil St.)
Washington Rd. E6 .... 7A 70
E18 .... 2H 51
KT1: King T 2G 151
KT4: Wor Pk 2D 164
SW13 .... 7C 98
TW6: H'row A 6D 174
Wasp Rd. TW6: H'row A 5C 174
(off Welland Rd.)
Wastdale Rd. SE23 .... 1K 139
The Watch N12 .... 3H 49
Watchfield Ct. W4 .... 5J 97
Watcombe Cotts.
TW9: Kew 6G 97
Watcombe Pl. SE25 .... 5H 157
Watcombe Rd. SE25 .... 5H 157
Waterbank Ho. SW18 .... 1K 135
(off Knaresborough Dr.)
Waterbank Rd. SE6 .... 3D 140
Waterbeach Rd. RM9: Dag 6C 72
Water Brook La. NW4 .... 5E 44
Watercress Pl. N1 .... 7E 66
Waterdale Rd. SE2 .... 6A 108
Waterden Ct. W11 .... 1G 99
Waterden Rd. E20 .... 5C 68
Waterer Ho. SE6 .... 4E 140
Waterer Ri. SM6: W'gton 6H 167
Waterfall Cl. N14 .... 3B 32
Waterfall Cotts. SW19 .... 6B 136
Waterfall Ho. SW2 .... 5A 120
(off Brixton Water La.)
Waterfall Rd. N11 .... 4A 32
N14 .... 4A 32
SW19 .... 6B 136
Waterfall Ter. SW17 .... 6C 136
Waterfall Wlk. N14 .... 1A 32
Waterfield Cl. DA17: Belv 3G 109
SE28 .... 1B 108
Waterfield Gdns. SE25 .... 4D 156
Waterford Ho. BR1: Broml 1J 159
(off Newman Rd.)
W11 .... 7H 81
(off Kensington Pk. Rd.)
Waterford Point SW8 .... 7J 101
Waterford Rd. SW6 .... 7K 99
Waterford Way NW10 .... 5D 62
Waterfront W6 .... 6E 98
Waterfront Dr. SW10 .... 1A 118
Waterfront Ho. E5 .... 2J 67
(off Harry Zeital Way)
Waterfront Leisure Cen.
Woolwich 3E 106
Waterfront M. N1 .... 2C 84
Waterfront Studios Bus. Cen.
E16 .... 1H 105
(off Dock Rd.)
The Water Gdns. W2 .... 7D 4 (6C 82)
The Watergardens
KT2: King T 6J 133
Water Gdns. HA7: Stan 6G 27
Water Gdns. Sq. SE16 .... 2K 103
Watergate EC4 .... 2A 14 (7B 84)
Watergate St. SE8 .... 6C 104
Watergate Wlk.
WC2 .... 4F 13 (1J 101)
Watergate Wlk.. E14 .... 3D 104
Waterhall Av. E4 .... 4B 36
Waterhall Cl. E17 .... 1K 49
Waterhead NW1 .... 1A 6
(off Varndell St.)
Waterhouse CR0: C'don 1C 168
(off Saffron Central Sq.)
Waterhouse Cl. E16 .... 5B 88
NW3 .... 5B 64
W6 .... 4F 99
Waterhouse Sq. EC1 .... 6J 7 (5A 84)
Wateridge Cl. E14 .... 3C 104
Water La. DA14: Sidc 2F 145
E15 .... 6G 69
EC3 .... 3H 15 (7E 84)
IG3: Ilf 3J 71
KT1: King T 1D 150
N9 .... 1C 34
NW1 .... 7F 65
SE14 .... 7J 103
TW1: Twick 1A 132
TW9: Rich 5D 114
Water Lily Cl. UB2: S'hall 2G 95
Waterline Ho. W2 .... 6B 4
Waterloo Bri.
WC2 .... 3G 13 (7K 83)
Waterloo Cl. E9 .... 5J 67
TW14: Felt 1H 129
Waterloo East Theatre 5K 13
(off Brad St.)
Waterloo Gdns. E2 .... 2J 85
N1 .... 7B 66
RM7: Rom 6K 55
Waterloo Pas. NW6 .... 7H 63
Waterloo Pl. SM5: Cars 3D 166
(off Wrythe Grn.)
SW1 .... 4C 12 (1H 101)
TW9: Rich 4E 114
Waterloo Rd. E6 .... 7A 70
E7 .... 5H 69
E10 .... 7C 50
IG6: Ilf 2G 53
NW2 .... 1C 62
RM7: Rom, Rush G 5K 55
SE1 .... 4H 13 (1K 101)
SM1: Sutt 5B 166
Waterloo Ter. N1 .... 7B 66
The Waterlow Bldg. E3 .... 5B 86
(off Weatherley Cl.)
Waterlow Ct. NW11 .... 7K 45
Waterlow Pk. Cen. 1F 65
Waterlow Rd. N19 .... 1G 65
Waterman Bldg. E14 .... 2B 104
Waterman Ho. E15 .... 6F 69
(off Forrester Way)
Watermans Art Cen.,
Cinema & Theatre 6E 96
Watermans Cl. KT2: King T 7E 132
Watermans Ct. TW8: Bford 6D 96
(off High St.)
Watermans Ho. E14 .... 6F 87
(off New Village Av.)
Watermans M. W5 .... 7E 78
Waterman's Quay SW6 .... 2A 118
Waterman St. SW15 .... 3F 117
Watermans Wlk. SE16 .... 2A 104
Waterman Way E1 .... 1H 103
Watermark Ct. RM6: Chad H 6B 54
(off Quarles Pk. Rd.)
Watermead TW14: Felt 1G 129
Watermead Ho. E9 .... 5A 68
Watermead La. SM5: Cars 7D 154
Watermead Lodge SE16 .... 1K 103
(off Princes Riverside Rd.)
Watermeadow La. SW6 .... 2A 118
Watermead Rd. SE6 .... 4E 140
Watermead Way N17 .... 3J 49
Watermen's Sq. SE20 .... 7J 139
Water M. SE15 .... 4J 121
Watermill Bus. Cen.
EN3: Brim 2G 25
Watermill Cl. TW10: Ham 3C 132
Water Mill Ho.
TW13: Hanw 2E 130
Watermill La. N18 .... 5K 33
Watermill Way SW19 .... 1A 154
TW13: Hanw 2D 130
Watermint Quay N16 .... 7G 49
Water Rd. HA0: Wemb 1F 79
Water's Edge SW6 .... 1E 116
(off Palemead Cl.)
Watersedge KT19: Ewe 4J 163
Watersfield Way HA8: Edg 7J 27
Waters Gdns. RM10: Dag 5G 73
Waterside BR3: Beck 1B 158
E17 .... 6J 49
N1 .... 2C 84
UB7: Harm 3D 174
W2 .... 6A 4
Waterside Apts. N4 .... 1C 66
(off Goodchild Rd.)
Waterside Av. BR3: Beck 5E 158
(off Adamson Way)
Waterside Bus. Cen.
TW7: Isle 4B 114
Waterside Cl. E3 .... 1B 86
HA9: Wemb 3J 61
IG11: Bark 4A 72
KT6: Surb 2E 162
SE16 .... 2G 103
SE28 .... 1K 107
TW17: Shep 1E 146
UB5: N'olt 3D 76
Waterside Ct. SM5: Cars 3E 166
(off Millpond Pl.)
Waterside Dr. KT12: Walt T 5J 147
Waterside Hgts. E16 .... 2A 106
(off Booth Rd.)
Waterside Pl. NW1 .... 1E 82
Waterside Point SW11 .... 7C 100
Waterside Rd. UB2: S'hall 3E 94
Waterside Twr. SW6 .... 2A 118
(off The Boulevard)
Waterside Trad. Cen. W7 .... 3J 95
Waterside Way N17 .... 3H 49
SW17 .... 4A 136
Watersmeet Pl. N4 .... 1C 66
Watersmeet Way SE28 .... 6C 90
Waterson St. E2 .... 1H 9 (3E 84)
Waters Pl. SW15 .... 2E 116
Watersplash Cl. KT1: King T 3E 150
Watersplash La. TW5: Cran 5K 93
UB3: Harl 4J 93
Watersplash Rd. TW17: Shep 5C 146
Watersreach Apts. N4 .... 1C 66
(off Kayani Av.)
Waters Rd. KT1: King T 2H 151
SE6 .... 3G 141
Waters Sq. KT1: King T 3H 151
Water St. WC2 .... 2J 13
Water Twr. Cl. UB8: Uxb 5A 56
Water Twr. Hill CR0: C'don 4D 168
Water Twr. Pl. N1 .... 1A 84
Waterview Cl. DA6: Bex 5D 126
Waterview Dr. SE10 .... 1F 105
Waterview Ho. E14 .... 5A 86
(off Carr St.)
Waterway Av. SE13 .... 3D 122
Waterway Pk. UB3: Hayes 2E 92
Waterways Bus. Cen.
EN3: Enf L 1G 25
Waterworks Cen. 2A 68
WATERWORKS CORNER 1G 51
Waterworks La. E5 .... 2K 67
Waterworks Nature Reserve 2A 68
Waterworks Rd. SW2 .... 6K 119
Waterworks Yd. CR0: C'don 3C 168
(off Charles St.)
Watery La. DA14: Sidc 6B 144
SW19 .... 2H 153
SW20 .... 2H 153
UB3: Harl 5F 93
UB5: N'olt 2A 76
Wates Way CR4: Mitc 6D 154
Wateville Rd. N17 .... 1C 48
Watford By-Pass WD6: E'tree 1G 27
Watford Cl. SW11 .... 1C 118
Watford Rd. E16 .... 5J 87
HA0: Wemb 2A 60
HA1: Harr 7A 42
Watford Way NW4 .... 4C 44
NW7 .... 4F 29
Watkin Rd. HA9: Wemb 3H 61
Watkins Cl. HA6: Nwood 1H 39
Watkins Ho. E14 .... 2E 104
(off Manchester Rd.)
Watkinson Rd. N7 .... 6K 65
Watkins Way RM8: Dag 1E 72
WATLING 7E 28
Watling Av. HA8: Edg 1J 43
Watling Ct. EC4 .... 1D 14
Watling Farm Cl. HA7: Stan 1H 27
Watling Gdns. NW2 .... 6G 63
Watling Ga. NW9 .... 4A 44
Watling Ho. SE1 .... 4C 102
(off New Kent Rd.)
Watlings Cl. CR0: C'don 6A 158
Watling St. DA1: Cray 5K 127
DA6: Bex 4H 127
DA7: Bex 4H 127
EC4 .... 1D 14 (6C 84)
SE15 .... 6E 102
Watlington Gro. SE26 .... 5A 140
Watney Cotts. SW14 .... 3J 115
Watney Mkt. E1 .... 6H 85
Watney Rd. SW14 .... 3J 115
Watney's Rd. CR4: Mitc 5H 155
Watney St. E1 .... 6H 85
Watson Av. E6 .... 7E 70
SM3: Cheam 2G 165
Watson Cl. N16 .... 5D 66
SW19 .... 6C 136
Watson Ct. E3 .... 3C 86
(off Campbell Rd.)
Watson Ho. SW11 .... 7H 101
(off Ponton Rd.)
Watson Pl. SE25 .... 5F 157
Watsons Ho. N1 .... 1E 84
(off Nuttall St.)
Watson's M. W1 .... 6D 4 (5C 82)
Watsons Rd. N22 .... 1K 47
Watsons St. SE8 .... 7C 104
Watson St. E13 .... 2K 87
Watt Ct. W3 .... 2A 98
Watteau Sq. CR0: C'don 1A 168
Wattisfield Rd. E5 .... 3J 67
Watts Apts. SW8 .... 7J 101
(off Cellini St.)
Watts Cl. N15 .... 5E 48
Wattsdown Cl. E13 .... 1J 87
Watts Gro. E3 .... 5C 86
Watts Ho. W10 .... 5G 81
(off Wornington Rd.)
Watts La. BR7: Chst 1F 161
TW11: Tedd 5A 132
Watts M. IG6: Ilf 3H 53
SW16 .... 6H 137
Watts Rd. KT7: T Ditt 7A 150
Watts St. E1 .... 1H 103
SE15 .... 1F 121
Wat Tyler Ho. N8 .... 3J 47
(off Boyton Rd.)
Wat Tyler Rd. SE3 .... 2E 122
SE10 .... 2E 122
Wauthier Cl. N13 .... 5G 33
Wave Ct. RM7: Rush G 6K 55

Wentworth Ct.—Weston Grn. Rd.

Wentworth Ct. SW1 . . . . . .6J 17 (5F 101)
SW18 . . . . . .6K 117
(off Garratt La.)
TW2: Twick 3J 131
W6 . . . . . .6G 99
(off Paynes Wlk.)
Wentworth Cres. SE15 . . . . . .7G 103
UB3: Harl 3F 93
Wentworth Dr. HA5: Eastc 5J 39
TW6: H'row A 5C 174
Wentworth Dwellings *E1* 7J 9
(off Wentworth St.)
Wentworth Flds. UB4: Hayes 2F 75
Wentworth Gdns. N13 . . . . . .3G 33
Wentworth Hill HA9: Wemb 1F 61
Wentworth Ho. IG8: Wfd G 7K 37
Wentworth M. E3 . . . . . .4A 86
W3 . . . . . .6A 80
Wentworth Pk. N3 . . . . . .7D 30
Wentworth Pl. HA7: Stan 6G 27
Wentworth Rd. CR0: C'don 7A 156
E12 . . . . . .4B 70
EN5: Barn 3A 20
NW11 . . . . . .6H 45
UB2: S'hall 4A 94
Wentworth St. E1 . . . . . .7J 9 (6F 85)
Wentworth Way HA5: Pinn 4C 40
Wenvoe Av. DA7: Bex 2H 127
Wepham Cl. UB4: Yead 5B 76
Wernbrook St. SE18 . . . . . .6G 107
Werndee Rd. SE25 . . . . . .4G 157
Werneth Hall Rd. IG5: Ilf 3E 52
Werrington St. NW1 . . . . . .1B 6 (2G 83)
Werter Rd. SW15 . . . . . .4G 117
Wesleyan Pl. NW5 . . . . . .4F 65
Wesley Apts. SW8 . . . . . .1H 119
Wesley Av. E16 . . . . . .1J 105
NW10 . . . . . .3K 79
TW3: Houn 2C 112
Wesley Cl. HA2: Harr 2G 59
KT19: Ewe 5J 163
N7 . . . . . .2K 65
SE17 . . . . . .4B 102
Wesley Ct. SE16 . . . . . .3H 103
Wesley Rd. E10 . . . . . .7E 50
NW10 . . . . . .1J 79
UB3: Hayes 7J 75
Wesley's Chapel 3F 9 (4D 84)
Wesley's House & Mus. of Methodism
. . . . . .3F 9 (4D 84)
Wesley Sq. W11 . . . . . .6G 81
Wesley St. W1 . . . . . .6H 5 (5E 82)
Wessex Av. SW19 . . . . . .3J 153
Wessex Cl. IG3: Ilf 6J 53
KT1: King T 1H 151
Wessex Ct. BR3: Beck 1A 158
EN5: Barn 4A 20
HA9: Wemb 2F 61
TW19: Stanw 6A 110
Wessex Dr. HA5: Hat E 1C 40
Wessex Gdns. NW11 . . . . . .1G 63
Wessex Ho. SE1 . . . . . .5F 103
Wessex La. UB6: G'frd 3H 77
Wessex St. E2 . . . . . .3J 85
Wessex Ter. CR4: Mitc 5C 154
Wessex Wlk. DA2: Wilm 2K 145
Wessex Way NW11 . . . . . .1G 63
Wesson Mead *SE5* 7C 102
(off Camberwell Rd.)
West 12 Shop. Cen. 2F 99
Westacott UB4: Hayes 5G 75
Westacott Cl. N19 . . . . . .1H 65
West Acre HA2: Harr 2J 59
WEST ACTON 6G 79
West App. BR5: Pet W 5G 161
W. Arbour St. E1 . . . . . .6K 85
West Av. E17 . . . . . .4D 50
HA5: Pinn 6D 40
N3 . . . . . .6D 30
NW4 . . . . . .5F 45
SM6: W'gton 5J 167
UB1: S'hall 7D 76
UB3: Hayes 7H 75
West Av. Rd. E17 . . . . . .4C 50
W. Bank EN2: Enf 2H 23
IG11: Bark 1F 89
N16 . . . . . .7E 48
Westbank Rd. TW12: Hamp H 6G 131
WEST BARNES 5D 152
W. Barnes La. KT3: N Mald 3D 152
SW20 . . . . . .3D 152
WEST BECKTON 6B 88
WEST BEDFONT 6B 110
Westbeech Rd. N22 . . . . . .3A 48
Westbere Dr. HA7: Stan 5J 27
Westbere Rd. NW2 . . . . . .4G 63
W. Block *SE1* 7H 13
(off York Rd.)
Westbourne Apts. SW6 . . . . . .3K 117
Westbourne Av.
SM3: Cheam 2G 165
W3 . . . . . .6K 79
Westbourne Bri. W2 . . . . . .5A 82
Westbourne Cl. UB4: Yead 4A 76
Westbourne Ct. W2 . . . . . .5A 82
Westbourne Cres.
W2 . . . . . .2A 10 (7B 82)
Westbourne Cres. M. W2 . . . . . .2A 10
Westbourne Dr. SE23 . . . . . .2K 139
Westbourne Gdns. W2 . . . . . .6K 81
WESTBOURNE GREEN 5J 81
Westbourne Gro. W2 . . . . . .6J 81
W11 . . . . . .7H 81
Westbourne Gro. M. W11 . . . . . .6J 81
Westbourne Gro. Ter. W2 . . . . . .6K 81
Westbourne Ho. *SW1* 5J 17
(off Ebury Bri. Rd.)
TW5: Hest 6E 94
Westbourne Pde. UB10: Hil 4D 74
Westbourne Pk. Pas. *W2* 5J 81
(off Harrow Rd.)
Westbourne Pk. Rd. W2 . . . . . .5J 81
W11 . . . . . .6G 81
Westbourne Pk. Vs. W2 . . . . . .5J 81
Westbourne Pl. N9 . . . . . .3C 34
Westbourne Rd. CR0: C'don 6F 157
DA7: Bex 7D 108
N7 . . . . . .6K 65
SE26 . . . . . .6K 139
TW13: Felt 3H 129
UB8: Hil 4D 74
Westbourne St. W2 . . . . . .2A 10 (7B 82)
Westbourne Ter. *SE23* 2K 139
(off Westbourne Dr.)
W2 . . . . . .1A 10 (6A 82)
Westbourne Ter. M. W2 . . . . . .6A 82
Westbourne Ter. Rd. W2 . . . . . .5K 81
WESTBOURNE TER. RD. BRI.
. . . . . .*5A 82*
(off Westbourne Ter. Rd.)
Westbridge Cl. W12 . . . . . .2C 98
Westbridge Ho. *SW11* 1C 118
(off Westbridge Rd.)
Westbridge Rd. SW11 . . . . . .1B 118
WEST BROMPTON 6A 100
Westbrook Av. TW12: Hamp 7D 130
Westbrook Cl. EN4: Cockf 3G 21
Westbrook Cres. EN4: Cockf 3G 21
Westbrooke Cres. DA16: Well 3C 126
Westbrooke Rd. DA15: Sidc 2H 143
DA16: Well 3B 126
Westbrook Ho. *E2* 3J 85
(off Victoria Pk. Sq.)
Westbrook Rd. CR7: Thor H 1D 156
SE3 . . . . . .1K 123
TW5: Hest 7D 94
Westbrook Sq. EN4: Cockf 3G 21
Westbury Av. HA0: Wemb 7E 60
N22 . . . . . .3B 48
UB1: S'hall 4E 76
Westbury Cl. HA4: Ruis 7J 39
TW17: Shep 6D 146
Westbury Ct. *IG11: Bark* 1H 89
(off Ripple Rd.)
Westbury Gro. N12 . . . . . .6D 30
Westbury Ho. E17 . . . . . .4C 50
W11 . . . . . .5J 81
(off Aldridge Rd. Vs.)
Westbury La. IG9: Buck H 2E 36
Westbury Lodge Cl. HA5: Pinn 3B 40
Westbury Pde. *SW12* 6F 119
(off Balham Hill)
Westbury Pl. TW8: Bford 6D 96
Westbury Rd. BR1: Broml 1B 160
BR3: Beck 3A 158
CR0: C'don 6D 156
E7 . . . . . .6K 69
E17 . . . . . .4B 50
HA0: Wemb 7E 60
IG1: Ilf 2E 70
IG9: Buck H 2F 37
IG11: Bark 1H 89
KT3: N Mald 4K 151
N11 . . . . . .6D 32
N12 . . . . . .6D 30
SE20 . . . . . .1K 157
TW13: Felt 1B 130
W5 . . . . . .6E 78
Westbury Ter. E7 . . . . . .6K 69
Westbush Ct. *W12* 2D 98
(off Goldhawk M.)
W. Cadet Apts. *SE18* 7E 106
(off Langhorne St.)
W. Carriage Dr. W2 . . . . . .3C 10 (7C 82)
(Nth. Ride)
W2 . . . . . .6B 10 (2B 100)
(Rotten Row)
W. Carriage Ho. *SE18* 3F 107
(off Royal Carriage M.)
W. Central St. WC1 . . . . . .7E 6 (6J 83)
West Chantry HA3: Hrw W 1F 41
Westchester Dr. NW4 . . . . . .3F 45
Westcliffe Apts. W2 . . . . . .6B 4 (5B 82)
West Cl. EN4: Cockf 4K 21
HA9: Wemb 1F 61
N9 . . . . . .3A 34
TW12: Hamp 6C 130
TW15: Ashf 4A 128
UB6: G'frd 2G 77
Westcombe Av. CR0: C'don 7J 155
Westcombe Ct. SE3 . . . . . .7H 105
Westcombe Dr. EN5: Barn 5D 20
Westcombe Hill SE3 . . . . . .7J 105
SE10 . . . . . .5J 105
Westcombe Lodge Dr.
UB4: Hayes 5G 75
Westcombe Pk. Rd. SE3 . . . . . .6G 105
West Comn. Rd.
BR2: Hayes, Kes 1J 171
UB8: Uxb 5A 56
Westcoombe Av. SW20 . . . . . .1B 152
Westcote Ri. HA4: Ruis 7E 38
Westcote Rd. SW16 . . . . . .5G 137
West Cotts. NW6 . . . . . .5J 63
Westcott Cl. BR1: Broml 5D 160
CR0: New Ad 7D 170
N15 . . . . . .6F 49
Westcott Cres. W7 . . . . . .6J 77
Westcott Ho. E14 . . . . . .7C 86
Westcott Rd. SE17 . . . . . .6B 102
West Ct. E17 . . . . . .4C 50
HA0: Wemb 2C 60
TW5: Isle 7G 95
Westcroft Cl. EN3: Enf W 1D 24
NW2 . . . . . .4G 63
Westcroft Ct. NW2 . . . . . .4G 63
Westcroft Est. NW2 . . . . . .4G 63
Westcroft Gdns. SM4: Mord 3H 153
Westcroft Leisure Cen. 4E 166
Westcroft Rd. SM5: Cars 4E 166
SM6: W'gton 4E 166
Westcroft Sq. W6 . . . . . .4C 98
Westcroft Way NW2 . . . . . .4G 63
W. Cromwell Rd. SW5 . . . . . .5H 99
W14 . . . . . .5H 99
W. Cross Cen. TW8: Bford 6A 96
W. Cross Route W10 . . . . . .7F 81
W. Cross Way TW8: Bford 6B 96
Westdale Pas. SE18 . . . . . .6F 107
Westdale Rd. SE18 . . . . . .6F 107
Westdean Av. SE12 . . . . . .1K 141
Westdean Cl. SW18 . . . . . .6K 117
West Dene SM3: Cheam 6G 165
Westdene *CR0: C'don* 4D 168
(off Chatsworth Rd.)
Westdown Rd. E15 . . . . . .4E 68
SE6 . . . . . .7C 122
WEST DRAYTON 2A 92
W. Drayton Pk. Av. UB7: W Dray 3A 92
W. Drayton Rd. UB8: Hil 6D 74
West Dr. HA3: Hrw W 6C 26
SM2: Cheam 7F 165
SW16 . . . . . .4G 137
West Dr. Gdns. HA3: Hrw W 6C 26
WEST DULWICH 2D 138
WEST EALING 1B 96
W. Ealing Bus. Cen. W13 . . . . . .7A 78
W. Eaton Pl. SW1 . . . . . .3G 17 (4E 100)
W. Eaton Pl. M. SW1 . . . . . .2G 17
W. Ella Rd. NW10 . . . . . .7A 62
W. Elms Studios SW8 . . . . . .1G 119
WEST END 2B 76
W. End Av. E10 . . . . . .5F 51
HA5: Pinn 4B 40
W. End Cl. NW10 . . . . . .7J 61
W. End Ct. HA5: Pinn 4B 40
NW6 . . . . . .7K 63
W. End Gdns. UB5: N'olt 2A 76
W. End La. EN5: Barn 4A 20
HA5: Pinn 3B 40
NW6 . . . . . .5J 63
(not continuous)
UB3: Harl 7E 92
W. End Quay W2 . . . . . .6B 4
W. End Rd. HA4: Ruis 2G 57
UB1: S'hall 1C 94
UB5: N'olt 7A 58
Westerdale Ct. *N5* 4B 66
(off Hamilton Pk. W.)
Westerdale Rd. SE10 . . . . . .5J 105
Westerfield Rd. N15 . . . . . .5F 49
Westergate W5 . . . . . .5E 78
Westergate Ho. *KT1: King T* 4D 150
(off Portsmouth Rd.)
Westergate Rd. SE2 . . . . . .6E 108
Westerham *NW1* 1G 83
(off Bayham St.)
Westerham Av. N9 . . . . . .3J 33
Westerham Dr. DA15: Sidc 6B 126
Westerham Ho. *SE1* 3D 102
(off Law St.)
Westerham Lodge *BR3: Beck* 7C 140
(off Park Rd.)
Westerham Rd. BR2: Kes 6B 172
E10 . . . . . .7D 50
Westerley Cres. SE26 . . . . . .5B 140
Westerley Ware *TW9: Kew* 6G 97
(off Kew Grn.)
Western Av. HA4: Ruis 6D 56
NW11 . . . . . .6F 45
RM10: Dag 6J 73
UB5: N'olt 7A 58
UB6: G'frd 7A 58
UB10: Hil, Uxb 4A 56
W3 . . . . . .4F 79
W5 . . . . . .4F 79
Western Av. Bus. Pk. W3 . . . . . .4H 79
Western Beach Apts. E16 . . . . . .1J 105
Western Ct. N3 . . . . . .6D 30
NW6 . . . . . .2H 81
W3 . . . . . .6K 79
Western Ctyd. *EC2* 7H 9
(off Cutlers Gdns.)
Western Dr. TW17: Shep 6F 147
Western Gdns. W5 . . . . . .7G 79
Western Gateway E16 . . . . . .7J 87
Western Intl. Mkt.
UB2: S'hall 4K 93
Western La. SW12 . . . . . .7E 118
Western Mans. *EN5: New Bar* 5E 20
(off Great Nth. Rd.)
Western M. W9 . . . . . .4H 81
Western Pde. EN5: New Bar 5D 20
Western Perimeter Rd.
TW6: H'row A, Lford 5C 174
Western Pl. SE16 . . . . . .2J 103
Western Rd. CR4: Mitc 1B 154
E13 . . . . . .2A 88
E17 . . . . . .5E 50
N2 . . . . . .4D 46
N22 . . . . . .2K 47
NW10 . . . . . .4J 79
SM1: Sutt 5J 165
SW9 . . . . . .3A 120
SW19 . . . . . .1B 154
UB2: S'hall 4A 94
W5 . . . . . .7D 78
Western Sq. N18 . . . . . .6D 34
Western Ter. W6 . . . . . .5C 98
Western Transit Shed N1 . . . . . .1J 83
Western Vw. UB3: Hayes 2H 93
Westernville Gdns. IG2: Ilf 7G 53
Western Wlk. *KT1: King T* 2E 150
(off Eden Walk Shop. Cen.)
Western Way EN5: Barn 6D 20
SE28 . . . . . .3H 107
WEST EWELL 7K 163
Westferry Cir. E14 . . . . . .1B 104
Westferry Rd. E14 . . . . . .7B 86
Westfield Av. E20 . . . . . .6D 68
Westfield Cl. EN3: Enf H 3F 25
NW9 . . . . . .3J 43
SM1: Sutt 4H 165
SW10 . . . . . .7A 100
Westfield Ct. *KT6: Surb* 5D 150
(off Portsmouth Rd)
NW10 . . . . . .3F 81
(off Chamberlayne Rd.)
Westfield Dr. HA3: Kenton 4D 42
Westfield Gdns. HA3: Kenton 4D 42
RM6: Chad H 6C 54
Westfield Ho. *SE16* 4K 103
(off Rotherhithe New Rd.)
SW10 . . . . . .7B 100
(off Worlds End Est.)
Westfield La. HA3: Kenton 5D 42
Westfield Pk. HA5: Hat E 1D 40
Westfield Pk. Dr. IG8: Wfd G 6H 37
Westfield Rd. BR3: Beck 2B 158
CR0: C'don 2B 168
CR4: Mitc 2C 154
DA7: Bex 3J 127
KT6: Surb 5D 150
KT12: Walt T 7C 148
NW7 . . . . . .3E 28
RM9: Dag 4E 72
SM1: Sutt 4H 165
W13 . . . . . .1A 96
Westfields SW13 . . . . . .3B 116
Westfields Av. SW13 . . . . . .3A 116
Westfield Shop. Cen.
Stratford City 6E 68
London 1E 98
Westfields Rd. W3 . . . . . .5H 79
Westfield St. SE18 . . . . . .3B 106
Westfield Way E1 . . . . . .3A 86
HA4: Ruis 3G 57
West Gdn. Pl. W2 . . . . . .1D 10 (6C 82)
West Gdns. E1 . . . . . .7H 85
SW17 . . . . . .6C 136
Westgate W5 . . . . . .3E 78
Westgate Apts. *E16* 7J 87
(off Western Gateway)
Westgate Ct. *SE12* 1J 141
(off Burnt Ash Hill)
SW9 . . . . . .3A 120
(off Canterbury Cres.)
Westgate Est. TW14: Bedf 1D 128
Westgate Ho. TW7: Isle 2H 113
TW8: Bford 5D 96
(off Ealing Rd.)
Westgate M. *W10* 4G 81
(off West Row)
Westgate Rd. BR3: Beck 1E 158
SE25 . . . . . .4H 157
Westgate St. E8 . . . . . .1H 85
Westgate Ter. SW10 . . . . . .6K 99
Westglade Ct. HA3: Kenton 5D 42
WEST GREEN 4B 48
West Grn. Pl. UB6: G'frd 1H 77
West Grn. Rd. N15 . . . . . .4B 48
West Gro. IG8: Wfd G 6F 37
SE10 . . . . . .1E 122
SE17 . . . . . .4C 102
Westgrove La. SE10 . . . . . .1E 122
West Gro. Sq. SE17 . . . . . .4C 102
W. Halkin St.
SW1 . . . . . .1G 17 (3E 100)
W. Hallowes SE9 . . . . . .1B 142
W. Hall Rd. TW9: Kew 1H 115
WEST HAM 1H 87
W. Ham La. E15 . . . . . .7F 69
West Ham Pk. E7 . . . . . .7J 69
WEST HAMPSTEAD 6K 63
W. Hampstead M. NW6 . . . . . .6K 63
West Ham Utd FC 1D 86
W. Handyside Canopy N1 . . . . . .1J 83
W. Harding St.
EC4 . . . . . .7K 7 (6A 84)
WEST HARROW 7G 41
W. Hatch Mnr. HA4: Ruis 1H 57
Westhay Gdns. SW14 . . . . . .5H 115
WEST HEATH 6D 108
W. Heath Av. NW11 . . . . . .1J 63
W. Heath Cl. NW3 . . . . . .3J 63
W. Heath Ct. NW11 . . . . . .1J 63
W. Heath Dr. NW11 . . . . . .1J 63
W. Heath Gdns. NW3 . . . . . .2J 63
W. Heath Rd. NW3 . . . . . .2J 63
SE2 . . . . . .6C 108
WEST HENDON 7C 44
W. Hendon B'way. NW9 . . . . . .6B 44
WEST HILL 6H 117
W. Hill CR2: Sande 7E 168
HA2: Harr 2J 59
HA9: Wemb 1F 61
SW15 . . . . . .7F 117
SW18 . . . . . .7F 117
W. Hill Ct. N6 . . . . . .3E 64
Westhill Ct. *W11* 7H 81
(off Denbigh Rd.)
W. Hill Pk. N6 . . . . . .2D 64
(not continuous)
W. Hill Rd. SW18 . . . . . .6H 117
W. Hill Way N20 . . . . . .1E 30
Westholm NW11 . . . . . .4K 45
West Holme DA8: Erith 1J 127
Westholme BR6: Orp 7J 161
Westholme Gdns. HA4: Ruis 1J 57
Westhope Ho. *E2* 4G 85
(off Derbyshire St.)
Westhorne Av. SE9 . . . . . .5B 124
SE12 . . . . . .7J 123
Westhorpe Gdns. NW4 . . . . . .3E 44
Westhorpe Rd. SW15 . . . . . .3E 116
West Ho. IG11: Bark 6F 71
West Ho. Cl. SW19 . . . . . .1G 135
West Ho. Cotts. HA5: Pinn 4B 40
Westhurst Dr. BR7: Chst 5F 143
W. India Av. E14 . . . . . .1C 104
W. India Dock Rd. E14 . . . . . .7B 86
W. India Ho. *E14* 7C 86
(off W. India Dock Rd.)
WEST KENSINGTON 4G 99
W. Kensington Ct. *W14* 5H 99
(off Edith Vs.)
W. Kensington Mans. *W14* 5H 99
(off Beaumont Cres.)
WEST KILBURN 3H 81
Westking Pl. WC1 . . . . . .2G 7 (3K 83)
Westlake *SE16* 4J 103
(off Rotherhithe New Rd.)
Westlake Cl. N13 . . . . . .3F 33
UB4: Yead 4C 76
Westlake Rd. HA9: Wemb 2D 60
Westland Cl. TW19: Stanw 6A 110
Westland Ct. *UB5: N'olt* 3B 76
(off Seasprite Cl.)
Westland Dr. BR2: Hayes 2H 171
Westland Ho. *E16* 1E 106
(off Rymill St.)
Westland Pl. N1 . . . . . .1E 8 (3D 84)
Westlands Cl. UB3: Harl 4J 93
Westlands Ct. KT8: E Mos 4H 149
Westlands Est. UB3: Harl 3G 93
Westlands Ter. SW12 . . . . . .6G 119
West La. SE16 . . . . . .2H 103
Westlea Rd. W7 . . . . . .3A 96
Westleigh Av. SW15 . . . . . .5D 116
Westleigh Ct. *CR2: S Croy* 4E 168
(off Birdhurst Rd.)
E11 . . . . . .5J 51
(off Nightingale La.)
Westleigh Dr. BR1: Broml 1C 160
Westleigh Gdns. HA8: Edg 1G 43
West Links HA0: Wemb 3D 78
Westlinton Cl. NW7 . . . . . .6B 30
W. Lodge *E16* 1J 105
(off Britannia Ga.)
W. Lodge Av. W3 . . . . . .1G 97
W. Lodge Ct. W3 . . . . . .1G 97
W. London Crematorium 4D 80
West London Golf Course 1A 76
W. London Studios *SW6* 7K 99
(off Fulham Rd.)
West London Synagogue
(Reform) 1E 10
(off Up. Berkeley St.)
Westmacott Dr. TW14: Felt 1H 129
Westmacott Ho. *NW8* 4B 4
(off Hatton St.)
W. Mall N9 . . . . . .3B 34
W8 . . . . . .1J 99
(off Kensington Mall)
Westmark Point *SW15* 1D 134
(off Norley Va.)
West Mead HA4: Ruis 4A 58
KT19: Ewe 6A 164
Westmead SW15 . . . . . .6D 116
Westmead Cnr. SM5: Cars 4C 166
Westmead Ct. SE6 . . . . . .6C 122
Westmead Ho. SM1: Sutt 4B 166
Westmead Rd. SM1: Sutt 4B 166
Westmere Dr. NW7 . . . . . .3E 28
W. Mersea Cl. E16 . . . . . .1K 105
West M. N17 . . . . . .7C 34
SW1 . . . . . .4A 18
West Middlesex Golf Course 7G 77
WESTMINSTER 7E 12 (2J 101)
Westminster Abbey 7E 12 (3J 101)
Westminster Abbey Chapter House
. . . . . .1E 18
(within Abbey)
Westminster Abbey Museum 3J 101
Westminster Abbey Pyx Chamber
. . . . . .1E 18
(within Westminster Abbey)
Westminster Av.
CR7: Thor H 2B 156
Westminster Boating Base & Pier
. . . . . .7C 18 (6H 101)
Westminster Bri.
SW1 . . . . . .7F 13 (2J 101)
Westminster Bri. Ho. *SE1* 7A 14
(off Lambeth Rd.)
Westminster Bri. Rd.
SE1 . . . . . .7G 13 (2K 101)
Westminster Bus. Sq. SE11 . . . . . .7H 19
Westminster Cl. IG6: Ilf 2H 53
TW11: Tedd 5A 132
TW14: Felt 1J 129
Westminster Ct. *E11* 6K 51
(off Cambridge Pk.)
NW8 . . . . . .4A 4
(off Aberdeen Pl.)
SE16 . . . . . .1K 103
(off King & Queen Wharf)
Westminster Dr. N13 . . . . . .5D 32
Westminster Gdns. E4 . . . . . .1B 36
IG6: Ilf 2G 53
IG11: Bark 2J 89
SW1 . . . . . .3E 18
(off Vincent St.)
Westminster Hall 7E 12
Westminster Ind. Est.
SE18 . . . . . .3B 106
Westminster Mans. *SW1* 2D 18
(off Gt. Smith St.)
Westminster Pal. Gdns. SW1 . . . . . .2C 18
Westminster RC Cathedral
. . . . . .2A 18 (3G 101)
Westminster Rd. N9 . . . . . .1C 34
SM1: Sutt 2B 166
W7 . . . . . .1J 95
Westmoat Cl. BR3: Beck 7E 140
WEST MOLESEY 4E 148
Westmoor Gdns. EN3: Enf H 2E 24
Westmoor Rd. EN3: Enf H 2E 24
Westmoor St. SE7 . . . . . .3A 106
Westmore Ct. SW15 . . . . . .5G 117
Westmoreland Av.
DA16: Well 3J 125
Westmoreland Dr. SM2: Sutt 7K 165
Westmoreland Ho. *E16* 1J 105
(off Gatcombe Rd.)
NW10 . . . . . .3C 80
Westmoreland Pl. BR1: Broml 3J 159
SW1 . . . . . .6K 17 (5F 101)
W5 . . . . . .5D 78
Westmoreland Rd.
BR1: Broml 5G 159
BR2: Broml 5G 159
NW9 . . . . . .3F 43
SE17 . . . . . .6D 102
(not continuous)
SW13 . . . . . .1B 116
Westmoreland St. W1 . . . . . .6H 5 (5E 82)
Westmoreland Ter. SE20 . . . . . .7H 139
SW1 . . . . . .6K 17 (5F 101)
Westmoreland Wlk. SE17 . . . . . .6D 102
(not continuous)
Westmorland Cl. E12 . . . . . .2B 70
TW1: Twick 6B 114
Westmorland Ct. KT6: Surb 7D 150
Westmorland Rd. E17 . . . . . .6C 50
HA1: Harr 5F 41
Westmorland Way CR4: Mitc 4H 155
Westmount Cen. UB4: Yead 7B 76
Westmount Cl. KT4: Wor Pk 1E 164
Westmount Ct. W5 . . . . . .6F 79
Westmount Rd. SE9 . . . . . .2D 124
WEST NORWOOD 4C 138
West Norwood Crematorium 3C 138
West Oak BR3: Beck 1F 159
Westoe Rd. N9 . . . . . .2C 34
W. Officers Apts. SE18 . . . . . .7E 106
Weston Av. KT7: T Ditt 7J 149
KT8: W Mole 3C 148
Westonbirt Ct. *SE15* 6F 103
(off Ebley Cl.)
Weston Ct. *KT1: King T* 3E 150
(off Grove Cres.)
N4 . . . . . .3C 66
N20 . . . . . .7F 21
(off Farnham Cl.)
Weston Dr. HA7: Stan 1B 42
W. One Ho. *W1* 6A 6
(off Wells St.)
Westone Mans. *IG11: Bark* 7K 71
(off Upney La.)
W. One Shop. Cen. 1H 11
Weston Gdns. TW7: Isle 1J 113
WESTON GREEN 7J 149
Weston Grn. KT7: T Ditt 7J 149
RM9: Dag 4F 73
Weston Grn. Rd. KT7: T Ditt 7J 149

A-Z Big London 303

Weston Gro.—Whiting Way

Weston Gro. BR1: Broml 1H 159
Weston Ho. E9 . . . . .1J 85
(off King Edward's Rd.)
NW6 .7G 63
Weston Pk. KT1: King T 2E 150
KT7: T Ditt 7J 149
N8 . . . . .6J 47
Weston Ri. WC1 . . . . .1H 7 (3K 83)
Weston Rd. BR1: Broml 7H 141
EN2: Enf 2J 23
RM9: Dag 4E 72
W4 . . . . .3J 97
Weston St. SE1 . . . . .7F 15 (2E 102)
(not continuous)
Weston Wlk. E8 . . . . .7H 67
Westover Hill NW3 . . . . .2J 63
Westover Rd. SW18 . . . . .7A 118
Westow Hill SE19 . . . . .6E 138
Westow St. SE19 . . . . .6E 138
West Pk. SE9 . . . . .2C 142
Westpark W5 . . . . .6D 78
West Pk. Av. TW9: Kew 1G 115
West Pk. Cl. RM6: Chad H 5D 54
TW5: Hest 6D 94
West Pk. Rd. TW9: Kew 1G 115
UB2: S'hall 1G 95
W. Parkside SE10 . . . . .2G 105
West Pk. Wlk. E20 . . . . .6E 68
West Pl. SW19 . . . . .5E 134
West Plaza TW15: Ashf 2A 128
W. Point E14 . . . . .7B 86
(off Grenade St.)
SE1 . . . . .5G 103
Westpoint Apts. N8 . . . . .3K 47
W. Point Cl. TW4: Houn 3D 112
(off Grosvenor Rd.)
Westpoint Trad. Est. W3 . . . . .5H 79
Westpole Av. EN4: Cockf 4K 21
Westport Ct. UB4: Yead 4A 76
Westport Rd. E13 . . . . .4K 87
Westport St. E1 . . . . .6K 85
W. Poultry Av. EC1 . . . . . . .6A 8 (5B 84)
W. Quarters W12 . . . . .6C 80
W. Quay SW10 . . . . .1A 118
West Quay Dr. UB4: Yead 5C 76
West Quay Wlk. E14 . . . . .3D 104
West Ramp TW6: H'row A 1C 110
West Reservoir Cen. 1C 66
W. Ridge Gdns. UB6: G'frd 2G 77
West Ri. W2 . . . . .2D 10
West Rd. E15 . . . . .1H 87
EN4: E Barn 1K 31
KT2: King T 1J 151
N17 . . . . .6C 34
RM6: Chad H 6D 54
RM7: Rush G 7K 55
SE1 . . . . .6H 13 (2K 101)
SW3 . . . . .6F 17 (5D 100)
SW4 . . . . .5H 119
TW14: Bedf 6F 111
UB7: W Dray 3B 92
W5 . . . . .5E 78
Westrovia Ct. SW1 . . . . .4C 18
(off Moreton St.)
W. Row W10 . . . . .4G 81
Westrow SW15 . . . . .6E 116
Westrow Dr. IG11: Bark 5A 72
Westrow Gdns. IG3: Ilf 2K 71
WEST RUISLIP 2E 56
W. Ruislip Ct. HA4: Ruis 2F 57
(off Ickenham Rd.)
W. Sheen Va. TW9: Rich 4F 115
Westside N2 . . . . .3D 46
NW4 . . . . .2D 44
Westside Apts. IG1: Ilf 3E 70
(off Roden St.)
W. Side Comn. SW19 . . . . .5E 134
W. Side Ct. TW16: Sun 7G 129
(off Scotts Av.)
Westside Ct. W9 . . . . .4J 81
(off Elgin Av.)
W. Smithfield EC1 . . . . .6A 8 (5B 84)
West Sq. SE11 . . . . . . .2K 19 (3B 102)
W. Stand N5 . . . . .4B 66
West St. BR1: Broml 1J 159
CR0: C'don 4C 168
DA7: Bex 3F 127
DA8: Erith 4K 109
E2 . . . . .2H 85
E11 . . . . .3G 69
E17 . . . . .5D 50
HA1: Harr 1H 59
SM1: Sutt 5K 165
SM5: Cars 3D 166
WC2 . . . . .1D 12 (6H 83)
West St. La. SM5: Cars 4D 166
West St. Pl. CR0: C'don 4C 168
(off West St.)
W. Temple Sheen SW14 . . . . .5H 115
W. Tenter St. E1 . . . . .1K 15 (6F 85)
West Ter. DA15: Sidc 1J 143
W. Thamesmead Bus. Pk.
SE28 .3J 107
(not continuous)
West Twr. E14 . . . . .2D 104
(off Pan Peninsula Sq.)
SW10 . . . . .1B 118
West Towers HA5: Pinn 5B 40
Westvale M. W3 . . . . .2A 98
West Vw. NW4 . . . . .4E 44
TW14: Bedf 7E 110
W. View Apts. N7 . . . . .7J 65
(off York Way)
Westview Cl. NW10 . . . . .5B 62
W7 . . . . .6J 77
W10 . . . . .6E 80
Westview Ct. N20 . . . . .1F 31
Westview Cres. N9 . . . . .7K 23
Westview Dr. IG8: Wfd G 2B 52
Westville Rd. KT7: T Ditt 1A 162
W12 . . . . .2C 98
West Wlk. EN4: E Barn 7K 21
UB3: Hayes 1J 93
W5 . . . . .5E 78
Westward Pde. E14 . . . . .3D 104
(off Pepper St.)
Westward Rd. E4 . . . . .5G 35
(not continuous)
Westward Way HA3: Kenton 6E 42
W. Warwick Pl.
SW1 . . . . .4A 18 (4G 101)
W. Way BR4: W W'ck 6F 159
BR5: Pet W 5H 161
CR0: C'don 2A 170
HA4: Ruis 1H 57
HA5: Pinn 4B 40
HA8: Edg 6C 28
N18 . . . . .4J 33
NW10 . . . . .3K 61
TW5: Hest 1D 112
TW17: Shep 6F 147
Westway SW20 . . . . .3D 152
W10 . . . . .5H 81
W12 . . . . .7B 80
Westway Cl. SW20 . . . . .3D 152
Westway Ct. UB5: N'olt 1E 76
Westway Cross Shopping Park 1J 77
Westway Est. W3 . . . . .5A 80
W. Way Gdns. CR0: C'don 2K 169
Westway Lodge W9 . . . . .5J 81
(off Amberley Rd.)
W. Ways HA6: Nwood 2J 39
Westways KT19: Ewe 4B 164
Westway Sports Cen. 6F 81
Westway Travellers Site W12 . . . . . .7F 81
(off Stable Way)
Westwell M. SW16 . . . . .6J 137
Westwell Rd. SW16 . . . . .6J 137
Westwell Rd. App. SW16 . . . . .6J 137
Westwick KT1: King T 2G 151
(off Chesterton Ter.)
Westwick Gdns. TW4: Cran 2K 111
W14 . . . . .2F 99
WEST WICKHAM 1E 170
West Wickham Leisure Cen. 1E 170
West Wintergarden 1D 104
(off Bank St.)
Westwood Av. HA2: Harr 4F 59
SE19 .1C 156
Westwood Bus. Cen. NW10 . . . . . . .4A 80
Westwood Cl. BR1: Broml 2B 160
HA4: Ruis 6D 38
Westwood Ct. EN1: Enf 6K 23
(off Village Rd.)
HA0: Wemb 4B 60
UB6: G'frd 5H 59
Westwood Gdns. SW13 . . . . .3B 116
Westwood Hill SE26 . . . . .5G 139
Westwood Ho. W12 . . . . .1E 98
(off Wood La.)
Westwood La. DA15: Sidc 5A 126
DA16: Well 3K 125
Westwood M. E3 . . . . .3C 86
(off Addington Rd.)
Westwood Pk. SE23 . . . . .7H 121
Westwood Pk. Trad. Est. W3 . . . . . .5H 79
Westwood Pl. SE26 . . . . .4G 139
Westwood Rd. E16 . . . . .1K 105
IG3: Ilf 1K 71
SW13 . . . . .3B 116
West Woodside DA5: Bexl 7E 126
Wetheral Dr. HA7: Stan 1B 42
Wetherby Cl. UB5: N'olt 6F 59
Wetherby Gdns. SW5 . . . . .4A 100
Wetherby Mans. SW5 . . . . .5K 99
(off Earls Ct. Sq.)
Wetherby M. SW5 . . . . .5K 99
Wetherby Pl. SW7 . . . . .4A 100
Wetherby Rd. EN2: Enf 1H 23
Wetherby Way KT9: Chess 7E 162
Wetherden St. E17 . . . . .7B 50
Wetherell Rd. E9 . . . . .1K 85
Wetherill Rd. N10 . . . . .1E 46
Wevco Wharf SE15 . . . . .6H 103
Wexford Ho. E1 . . . . .5J 85
(off Sidney St.)
Wexford Rd. SW12 . . . . .7D 118
Wexner Bldg. E1 . . . . .6J 9
(off Strype St.)
Weybourne St. SW18 . . . . .2A 136
Weybridge Ct. SE16 . . . . .5H 103
Weybridge Point SW11 . . . . .2D 118
Weybridge Rd. CR7: Thor H 4A 156
Wey Ct. KT19: Ewe 4J 163
Weydown Cl. SW19 . . . . .1G 135
Weyhill Rd. E1 . . . . .6G 85
Wey Ho. NW8 . . . . .4B 4
(off Church St. Est.)
UB5: N'olt 4D 76
(off Taywood Rd.)
Weylands Cl. KT12: Walt T 7D 148
Weylond Rd. RM8: Dag 3F 73
Weyman Rd. SE3 . . . . .1A 124
The Weymarks N17 . . . . .6J 33
Weymouth Av. NW7 . . . . .5F 29
W5 . . . . .3C 96
Weymouth Cl. E6 . . . . .6F 89
Weymouth Ct. E2 . . . . .2F 85
SM2: Sutt 7J 165
Weymouth Ho. BR2: Broml 2H 159
(off Hill Ho. M.)
SW8 .7K 101
(off Bolney St.)
Weymouth M. W1 . . . . .5J 5 (5F 83)
Weymouth Pl. SE2 . . . . .3A 108
Weymouth Rd. UB4: Hayes 3G 75
Weymouth St. W1 . . . . .6H 5 (5E 82)
Weymouth Ter. E2 . . . . .1K 9 (2F 85)
Weymouth Vs. N4 . . . . .2K 65
(off Moray Rd.)
Weymouth Wlk. HA7: Stan 6F 27
Whadcoat St. N4 . . . . .2A 66
Whaddon Ho. SE22 . . . . .3E 120
Whalebone Av. RM6: Chad H 6F 55
Whalebone Ct. EC2 . . . . .7E 8
Whalebone Gro. RM6: Chad H 6F 55
Whalebone La. E15 . . . . .7G 69
Whalebone La. Nth.
RM6: Chad H, Col R 1E 54
Whalebone La. Sth.
RM6: Chad H, Dag 7F 55
RM8: Dag 7F 55
Whales Yd. E15 . . . . .7G 69
(off West Ham La.)
The Wharf EC3 . . . . .4H 15 (1F 103)
Wharfdale Cl. N11 . . . . .6K 31
Wharfdale Rd. N1 . . . . .2J 83
Wharfedale Ct. E5 . . . . .4K 67
Wharfedale Gdns.
CR7: Thor H 4K 155
Wharfedale Ho. NW6 . . . . .1K 81
(off Kilburn Vale)
Wharfedale St. SW10 . . . . .5K 99
Wharfedale Yd. N1 . . . . .2J 83
(off Wharfedale Rd.)
Wharf La. E14 . . . . .6B 86
TW1: Twick 1A 132
Wharf Mill Apts. E2 . . . . .1F 85
(off Laburnum St.)
Wharf Pl. E2 . . . . .1H 85
Wharf Rd. E16 . . . . .1A 106
EN3: Pond E 6F 25
N1 . . . . .1C 8 (2C 84)
(City Rd.)
N1 . . . . .1J 83
(York Way)
Wharf Rd. Ind. Est.
EN3: Pond E 6F 25
Wharfside Point Nth. E14 . . . . .7E 86
(off Poplar High St.)
Wharfside Point Sth. E14 . . . . .7E 86
Wharfside Rd. E16 . . . . .5G 87
Wharf St. E16 . . . . .5G 87
SE8 . . . . .5C 104
Wharf Vw. Ct. E14 . . . . .6E 86
(off Blair St.)
Wharncliffe Dr. UB1: S'hall 1H 95
Wharncliffe Gdns. SE25 . . . . .2E 156
Wharncliffe M. SW4 . . . . .6H 119
Wharncliffe Rd. SE25 . . . . .2E 156
Wharton Cl. NW10 . . . . .6A 62
Wharton Cotts. WC1 . . . . . . .2J 7 (3A 84)
Wharton Ho. E2 . . . . .3K 85
SE1 . . . . .7F 15
Wharton Rd. BR1: Broml 1K 159
Wharton St. WC1 . . . . .2H 7 (3K 83)
Whatcott's Yd. N16 . . . . .4E 66
Whateley Rd. SE20 . . . . .7K 139
SE22 .5F 121
Whatley Av. SW20 . . . . .3F 153
Whatman Ho. E14 . . . . .6B 86
(off Wallwood St.)
Whatman Rd. SE23 . . . . .7K 121
Wheatcroft Ct. SM1: Sutt 1K 165
(off Cleeve Way)
Wheatfield Ho. NW6 . . . . .3J 81
(off Kilburn Pk. Rd.)
Wheatfields E6 . . . . .6F 89
EN3: Enf H 1F 25
Wheatfield Way KT1: King T 2E 150
Wheathill Ho. SE20 . . . . .2H 157
(off Penge Rd.)
Wheathill Rd. SE20 . . . . .3H 157
Wheatland Ho. SE22 . . . . .3E 120
Wheatlands TW5: Hest 6E 94
Wheatlands Rd. SW17 . . . . .3E 136
Wheatley Cl. NW4 . . . . .2C 44
Wheatley Ct. E3 . . . . .3D 86
(off Bruce Rd.)
Wheatley Cres. UB3: Hayes 7J 75
Wheatley Gdns. N9 . . . . .2K 33
Wheatley Ho. SW15 . . . . .7C 116
(off Ellisfield Dr.)
Wheatley Mans. IG11: Bark 7A 72
(off Lansbury Av.)
Wheatley M. KT8: E Mos 4H 149
Wheatley Rd. TW7: Isle 3K 113
Wheatley's Eyot TW16: Sun 5J 147
Wheatley St. W1 . . . . .6H 5 (5E 82)
Wheat Sheaf Cl. E14 . . . . .4D 104
Wheatsheaf Cl. UB5: N'olt 5C 58
Wheatsheaf La. SW6 . . . . .7E 98
SW8 .7J 101
Wheatsheaf Ter. SW6 . . . . .7H 99
Wheatstone Cl. CR4: Mitc 1C 154
Wheatstone Ho. SE1 . . . . .3C 102
(off County St.)
Wheatstone Rd. DA8: Erith 5K 109
Wheeler Cl. IG8: Wfd G 6J 37
Wheeler Gdns. N1 . . . . .1J 83
(off Outram Pl.)
Wheeler Pl. BR2: Broml 4K 159
Wheelers Cross IG11: Bark 2H 89
Wheelers Dr. HA4: Ruis 6E 38
Wheelers Farm Dr. RM10: Dag 3J 73
Wheel Ho. E14 . . . . .5D 104
(off Burrells Wharf Sq.)
E17 . . . . .3K 49
Wheelock Cl. DA8: Erith 7H 109
Wheelwright St. N7 . . . . .7K 65
Whelan Rd. W3 . . . . .3H 97
Whelan Way SM6: Bedd 3H 167
Wheler Ho. E1 . . . . .4J 9
(off Quaker St.)
Wheler St. E1 . . . . .4J 9 (4F 85)
Whellock Rd. W4 . . . . .3A 98
Whenman Av. DA5: Bexl 2J 145
Whernside Cl. SE28 . . . . .7C 90
WHETSTONE 2F 31
Whetstone Cl. N20 . . . . .2G 31
Whetstone Pk. WC2 . . . . . . .7G 7 (6K 83)
Whetstone Rd. SE3 . . . . .2A 124
Whewell Rd. N19 . . . . .2J 65
Whidborne Bldgs. WC1 . . . . .2F 7
(off Whidborne St.)
Whidborne Cl. SE8 . . . . .2C 122
Whidborne St. WC1 . . . . .2F 7 (3J 83)
(not continuous)
Whidbourne M. SW8 . . . . .1H 119
Whimbrel Cl. SE28 . . . . .7C 90
Whimbrel Way UB4: Yead 6B 76
Whinchat Rd. SE28 . . . . .3H 107
Whinfell Cl. SW16 . . . . .5H 137
Whinyates Rd. SE9 . . . . .3C 124
Whippendell Way
BR5: St P 7B 144
Whippingham Ho. E3 . . . . .3B 86
(off Merchant St.)
Whipps Cross E17 . . . . .5F 51
Whipps Cross Ho. E17 . . . . .5F 51
(off Wood St.)
Whipps Cross Rd. E11 . . . . .5F 51
(not continuous)
Whiskin St. EC1 . . . . .2A 8 (3B 84)
Whisperwood Cl.
HA3: Hrw W 1J 41
Whistler Gdns. HA8: Edg 2F 43
Whistler M. RM8: Dag 5B 72
(off Fitzstephen Rd.)
SE15 .7F 103
Whistlers Av. SW11 . . . . .7B 100
Whistlers Gro. DA15: Sidc 7J 125
Whistler St. N5 . . . . .5B 66
Whistler Twr. SW10 . . . . .7A 100
(off Worlds End Est.)
Whistler Wlk. SW10 . . . . .7B 100
Whiston Ho. N1 . . . . .7B 66
(off Richmond Gro.)
Whiston Rd. E2 . . . . .2F 85
Whitacre M. SE11 . . . . . . .6K 19 (5A 102)
Whitakers Lodge EN2: Enf 1J 23
Whitbread Cl. N17 . . . . .1G 49
Whitbread Ho. SW11 . . . . .7H 101
(off Charles Clowes Wlk.)
Whitbread Rd. SE4 . . . . .4A 122
Whitburn Rd. SE13 . . . . .4D 122
Whitby Av. NW10 . . . . .3H 79
Whitby Ct. N7 . . . . .4J 65
Whitby Gdns. NW9 . . . . .3G 43
SM1: Sutt 2B 166
Whitby Ho. NW8 . . . . .1A 82
(off Boundary Rd.)
Whitby Pde. HA4: Ruis 2A 58
Whitby Rd. HA2: Harr 3G 59
HA4: Ruis 3K 57
SE18 .4D 106
SM1: Sutt 2B 166
Whitby St. E1 . . . . .3J 9 (4F 85)
(not continuous)
Whitcher Cl. SE14 . . . . .6A 104
Whitcher Pl. NW1 . . . . .6G 65
Whitchurch Av. HA8: Edg 7A 28
Whitchurch Cl. HA8: Edg 6A 28
Whitchurch Gdns. HA8: Edg 6A 28
Whitchurch Ho. W10 . . . . .6F 81
(off Kingsdown Cl.)
Whitchurch La. HA8: Edg 7J 27
Whitchurch Pde. HA8: Edg 7B 28
Whitchurch Rd. W11 . . . . .7F 81
Whitcomb Ct. WC2 . . . . .3D 12
Whitcombe M. TW9: Kew 1H 115
Whitcomb St. WC2 . . . . . . .3D 12 (7H 83)
Whitcome M. TW9: Kew 1H 115
Whiteadder Way E14 . . . . .4D 104
Whitear Wlk. E15 . . . . .6F 69
Whitebarn La. RM10: Dag 1G 91
Whitebeam Av. BR2: Broml 7E 160
Whitebeam Cl. SW9 . . . . .7K 101
Whitebeam Ho. E15 . . . . .3G 87
(off Teasel Way)
White Bear Pl. NW3 . . . . .4B 64
White Bear Yd. EC1 . . . . .4J 7
(off Clerkenwell Rd.)
White Bri. Av. CR4: Mitc 3B 154
Whitebridge Cl. TW14: Felt 6H 111
White Butts Rd. HA4: Ruis 3B 58
WHITECHAPEL 5G 85
Whitechapel Art Gallery
. . . . .7K 9 (6F 85)
Whitechapel High St.
E1 . . . . .7K 9 (6F 85)
Whitechapel Rd. E1 . . . . . . .7K 9 (5G 85)
Whitechapel Sports Cen. 5H 85
White Church La. E1 . . . . . . .7K 9 (6G 85)
White Church Pas. E1 . . . . .7K 9
(off White Church La.)
WHITE CITY 7D 80
WHITE CITY 6E 80
White City Cl. W12 . . . . .7E 80
White City Est. W12 . . . . .7D 80
White City Rd. W12 . . . . .7E 80
White Collar Factory EC1 . . . . .3E 8
(off Old St. Yd.)
White Conduit St. N1 . . . . .2A 84
Whitecote Rd. UB1: S'hall 6G 77
Whitecroft Cl. BR3: Beck 4F 159
Whitecroft Way BR3: Beck 5E 158
Whitecross Pl. EC2 . . . . .5F 9 (5D 84)
Whitecross St. EC1 . . . . .3D 8 (4C 84)
Whitefield Av. NW2 . . . . .1E 62
Whitefield Cl. SW15 . . . . .6G 117
Whitefoot La. BR1: Broml 4E 140
SE6 . . . . .4E 140
Whitefoot Ter. BR1: Broml 3H 141
Whitefriars Av. HA3: W'stone 2J 41
Whitefriars Ct. N12 . . . . .5G 31
Whitefriars Dr. HA3: Hrw W 2H 41
Whitefriars St. EC4 . . . . . . .1K 13 (6A 84)
Whitefriars Trad. Est.
HA3: W'stone 3H 41
White Gables Ct.
CR2: S Croy 5E 168
White Gdns. RM10: Dag 6G 73
Whitegate Gdns.
HA3: Hrw W 7E 26
White Gates KT7: T Ditt 7A 150
Whitehall 6G 165
Whitehall SW1 . . . . .5E 12 (1J 101)
Whitehall Ct. SW1 . . . . .5F 13 (1J 101)
(not continuous)
Whitehall Cres. KT9: Chess 5D 162
Whitehall Gdns. E4 . . . . .1B 36
SW1 . . . . .5E 12
W3 . . . . .1G 97
W4 . . . . .6H 97
Whitehall La. IG9: Buck H 2D 36
Whitehall Lodge N10 . . . . .2E 46
Whitehall Pk. N19 . . . . .1G 65
Whitehall Pk. Rd. W4 . . . . .6H 97
Whitehall Pl. E7 . . . . .5J 69
SM6: W'gton 4F 167
SW1 . . . . .5E 12 (1J 101)
Whitehall Rd. BR2: Broml 5B 160
CR7: Thor H 5A 156
E4 . . . . .2B 36
HA1: Harr 7J 41
IG8: Wfd G 2B 36
W7 . . . . .2A 96
Whitehall St. N17 . . . . .7A 34
White Hart Av. SE18 . . . . .4K 107
SE28 .4K 107
White Hart Ct. UB3: Harl 6F 93
White Hart Ct. EC2 . . . . .6G 9
White Hart La. N17 . . . . .7H 33
N22 . . . . .1K 47
NW10 .6B 62
RM7: Col R, Mawney 1G 55
SW13 .2A 116
White Hart Rd. SE18 . . . . .4J 107
WHITE HART RDBT. 2B 76
White Hart Slip BR1: Broml 2J 159
White Hart St.
EC4 . . . . .7B 8 (6B 84)
SE11 . . . . .5K 19 (5A 102)
White Hart Triangle SE28 . . . . .2K 107
White Hart Triangle Bus. Pk.
SE28 .2A 108
White Hart Yd. SE1 . . . . . .5E 14 (1D 102)
Whitehaven Cl. BR2: Broml 4J 159
Whitehaven St. NW8 . . . . . . .4C 4 (4C 82)
Whitehead Cl. N18 . . . . .5J 33
SW18 .7A 118
Whiteheads Gro.
SW3 . . . . .4D 16 (4C 100)
White Heart Av. UB8: Hil 5E 74
Whiteheath Av. HA4: Ruis 7E 38
White Heather Ho. WC1 . . . . .2F 7
(off Cromer St.)
White Heron M. TW11: Tedd 6K 131
White Horse All. EC1 . . . . .5A 8
White Horse Apts. N1 . . . . .1A 84
(off Liverpool Rd.)
White Horse Hill BR7: Chst 4E 142
White Horse La. E1 . . . . .5K 85
Whitehorse La. SE25 . . . . .4D 156
White Horse M. EN3: Enf H 2E 24
Whitehorse M. SE1 . . . . . .1K 19 (3A 102)
White Horse Rd. E1 . . . . .6A 86
(not continuous)
E6 . . . . .3D 88
Whitehorse Rd. CR0: C'don 7C 156
CR7: Thor H 7C 156
White Horse St. W1 . . . . . .5K 11 (1F 101)
White Horse Yd. EC2 . . . . . . .7E 8 (6D 84)
The White Ho. NW1 . . . . .3K 5
White Ho. CR0: C'don 4D 168
(off Coombe Rd.)
SW4 .7H 119
(off Clapham Pk. Est.)
SW11 . . . . .1B 118
Whitehouse E10 . . . . .6E 50
(off Leyton Grn. Rd.)
Whitehouse Apts. SE1 . . . . .1K 101
White Ho. Ct. N14 . . . . .2D 32
White Ho. Dr. HA7: Stan 4H 27
IG8: Wfd G 6C 36
White Ho. La. EN2: Enf 1H 23
White Ho. M. E10 . . . . .6E 50
Whitehouse Way N14 . . . . .2A 32
White Kennett St. E1 . . . . . . .7H 9 (6F 85)
Whitelands Cres. SW18 . . . . .7G 117
Whitelands Ho. SW3 . . . . .5F 17
(off Cheltenham Ter.)
Whiteledges W13 . . . . .6C 78
Whitelegg Rd. E13 . . . . .2H 87
Whiteley Rd. SE19 . . . . .5D 138
Whiteleys Cen. 6K 81
Whiteleys Pde. UB10: Hil 4D 74
Whiteley's Way TW13: Hanw 3E 130
White Lion Cen. 2A 84
(off White Lion St.)
White Lion Ct. EC3 . . . . .1G 15
SE15 .6J 103
TW7: Isle 3B 114
White Lion Hill EC4 . . . . . .2B 14 (7B 84)
White Lion St. N1 . . . . .2A 84
White Lodge SE19 . . . . .7B 138
W5 . . . . .5C 78
White Lodge Cl. N2 . . . . .6B 46
SM2: Sutt 7A 166
TW7: Isle 2A 114
White Lodge Ct. TW16: Sun 1A 148
White Lyon Ct. EC2 . . . . .5C 8
Whiteoak Ct. BR7: Chst 6E 142
White Oak Dr. BR3: Beck 2E 158
White Oak Gdns. DA15: Sidc 7K 125
Whiteoaks La. UB6: G'frd 3H 77
White Orchards HA7: Stan 5F 27
N20 . . . . .1C 30
White Post La. E9 . . . . .7B 68
White Post St. SE15 . . . . .7J 103
White Rd. E15 . . . . .7G 69
White Rose Ct. E1 . . . . .6H 9
(off Widegate St.)
Whiterose Trad. Est. EN4: E Barn . . .5G 21
(off Margaret Rd.)
Whites Av. IG2: Ilf 6J 53
Whites Grounds
SE1 . . . . .7H 15 (2E 102)
White's Grounds Est. SE1 . . . . .6H 15
White's Mdw. BR1: Broml 4E 160
White's Row E1 . . . . .6J 9 (5F 85)
Whites Sq. SW4 . . . . .4H 119
Whitestile Rd. TW8: Bford 5C 96
Whitestone Cl. EN4: Had W 1H 21
Whitestone La. NW3 . . . . .3A 64
Whitestone Wlk. NW3 . . . . .3A 64
Whitestone Way CR0: Wadd 2A 168
White Swan M. W4 . . . . .5A 98
Whitethorn Av. UB7: Yiew 7A 74
Whitethorn Gdns.
CR0: C'don 2H 169
EN2: Enf 5J 23
Whitethorn Ho. E1 . . . . .1J 103
(off Prusom St.)
Whitethorn Pas. E3 . . . . .4C 86
(off Whitethorn St.)
Whitethorn Pl. UB7: Yiew 1B 92
Whitethorn St. E3 . . . . .5C 86
The White Tower 7F 85
White Twr. Way E1 . . . . .5A 86
Whitewebbs Way BR5: St P 1K 161
Whitfield Ct. IG1: Ilf 7D 52
SW20 .2F 153
Whitfield Ho. NW8 . . . . .4C 4
(off Salisbury St.)
Whitfield Pl. W1 . . . . .4A 6
Whitfield Rd. DA7: Bex 7F 109
E6 . . . . .7A 70
Whitfield St. W1 . . . . .4A 6 (4G 83)
Whitford Gdns. CR4: Mitc 3D 154
Whitgift Av. CR2: S Croy 5B 168
Whitgift Cen. 2C 168
Whitgift Ct. CR2: S Croy 5C 168
(off Nottingham Rd.)
Whitgift Ho. SE11 . . . . . . .3G 19 (4K 101)
SW11 . . . . .1C 118
Whitgift Sq. CR0: C'don 3C 168
Whitgift St. CR0: C'don 3C 168
SE11 . . . . .3G 19 (4K 101)
Whiting Av. IG11: Bark 7F 71
Whitings IG2: Ilf 5J 53
Whitings Rd. EN5: Barn 5A 20
Whitings Way E6 . . . . .5E 88
Whiting Way SE16 . . . . .4A 104

Whitland Rd.—Willow Way

Whitland Rd. SM5: Cars 1B 166
Whitley Cl. TW19: Stanw 6A 110
Whitley Ho. *SW1* *7B 18*
(off Churchill Gdns.)
Whitley Rd. N17 . . . . .2E 48
Whitlock Dr. SW19 . . . . .7G 117
Whitman Ho. *E2* *3J 85*
(off Cornwall Av.)
Whitman Rd. E3 . . . . .4A 86
Whitmead Cl. CR2: S Croy 6E 168
Whitmore Bldg. *SE16* *3F 103*
(off Arts La.)
Whitmore Cl. N11 . . . . .5A 32
Whitmore Est. N1 . . . . .1E 84
Whitmore Gdns. NW10 . . . . .2E 80
Whitmore Ho. *N1* *1E 84*
(off Whitmore Est.)
Whitmore Rd. BR3: Beck 3B 158
HA1: Harr 7G 41
N1 . . . . .1E 84
Whitnell Way SW15 . . . . .5E 116
(not continuous)
Whitney Av. IG4: Ilf 4B 52
Whitney Rd. E10 . . . . .7D 50
Whitney Wlk. DA14: Sidc 6E 144
Whitstable Cl. BR3: Beck 1B 158
HA4: Ruis 2G 57
Whitstable Ho. *W10* *6F 81*
(off Silchester Rd.)
Whitstable Pl. CR0: C'don 4C 168
Whitstone Av. W7 . . . . .6K 77
Whitstone La. BR3: Beck 5D 158
Whittaker Av. TW9: Rich 5D 114
Whittaker Pl. *TW9: Rich* *5D 114*
(off Whittaker Av.)
Whittaker Rd. E6 . . . . .7A 70
SM3: Sutt 3H 165
Whittaker St. SW1 . . . . . . .4G 17 (4E 100)
Whittaker Way SE1 . . . . .4G 103
Whitta Rd. E12 . . . . .4B 70
Whittell Gdns. SE26 . . . . .3J 139
Whittingham N17 . . . . .7C 34
Whittingham Ct. W4 . . . . .7A 98
Whittingstall Rd. SW6 . . . . .1H 117
Whittington Apts. *E1* *6K 85*
(off E. Arbour St.)
Whittington Av. EC3 . . . . . . .1G 15 (6E 84)
UB4: Hayes 5H 75
Whittington Ct. N2 . . . . .5D 46
Whittington Ho. *N19* *2H 65*
(off Holloway Rd.)
Whittington M. N12 . . . . .4F 31
Whittington Rd. N22 . . . . .7D 32
Whittington Way HA5: Pinn 5C 40
Whittlebury Cl. SM5: Cars 7D 166
Whittlebury M. E. NW1 . . . . .7E 64
Whittlebury M. W. NW1 . . . . .7E 64
Whittle Cl. E17 . . . . .6A 50
UB1: S'hall 6F 77
Whittle Rd. TW5: Hest 7A 94
TW6: H'row A 6C 174
UB2: S'hall 2F 95
Whittlesea Cl. HA3: Hrw W 7B 26
Whittlesea Path HA3: Hrw W 1G 41
Whittlesea Rd. HA3: Hrw W 7B 26
Whittlesey St. SE1 . . . . . .5J 13 (1A 102)
WHITTON 7G 113
Whitton NW3 . . . . .7D 64
Whitton Av. E. UB6: G'frd 5J 59
Whitton Av. W. UB5: N'olt 5F 59
UB6: G'frd 5F 59
Whitton Cl. UB6: G'frd 6B 60
Whitton Dene
TW3: Houn, Isle 5G 113
TW7: Isle 6H 113
Whitton Dr. UB6: G'frd 6A 60
Whitton Mnr. Rd. TW7: Isle 6G 113
Whitton Rd. TW1: Twick 6K 113
TW2: Twick 6J 113
TW3: Houn 4F 113
WHITTON ROAD RDBT. 6K 113
Whitton Sports & Fitness Cen.
. . . . .2F 131
Whitton Wlk. E3 . . . . .3C 86
(not continuous)
Whitton Waye TW3: Houn 6E 112
Whitwell Rd. E13 . . . . .3J 87
Whitworth Ho. SE1 . . . . .3C 102
Whitworth Pl. TW4: Houn 7C 112
Whitworth Rd. SE18 . . . . .7E 106
SE25 .3E 156
Whitworth St. SE10 . . . . .5G 105
Whorlton Rd. SE15 . . . . .3H 121
Whychcote Point *NW2* *1E 62*
(off Whitefield Av.)
Whymark Av. N22 . . . . .3A 48
Whytecroft TW5: Hest 7B 94
Whyte M. SM3: Cheam 7G 165
Whyteville Rd. E7 . . . . .6K 69
Whytlaw Ho. *E3* *5B 86*
(off Baythorne St.)
Wiblin M. NW5 . . . . .4F 65
Wickersley Rd. SW11 . . . . .2E 118
Wickers Oake SE19 . . . . .4F 139
Wicker St. E1 . . . . .6H 85
The Wicket CR0: Addtn 5C 170
Wicket Rd. UB6: G'frd 3A 78
The Wickets TW15: Ashf 4A 128
Wickfield Apts. *E15* *6F 69*
(off Grove Cres. Rd.)
Wickfield Ho. *SE16* *2H 103*
(off Wilson Gro.)
Wickford Ho. *E1* *4J 85*
(off Wickford St.)
Wickford St. E1 . . . . .4J 85
Wickford Way E17 . . . . .4K 49
Wickham Av. CR0: C'don 2A 170
SM3: Cheam 5E 164
Wickham Chase
BR4: W W'ck 1F 171
Wickham Cl. E1 . . . . .5J 85
EN3: Enf H 3C 24
KT3: N Mald 6B 152
Wickham Ct. *KT5: Surb* *5F 151*
(off Cranes Pk.)
Wickham Ct. Rd.
BR4: W W'ck 2E 170
Wickham Cres. BR4: W W'ck 2E 170
Wickham Gdns. SE4 . . . . .3B 122
Wickham Ho. *N1* *1E 84*
(off Halcomb St.)
Wickham La. DA16: Well 5A 108
SE2 . . . . .5A 108
Wickham M. SE4 . . . . .2B 122
Wickham Noakes Ct.
BR3: Beck 1D 158
Wickham Rd. BR3: Beck 2D 158
CR0: C'don 2K 169
E4 . . . . .7K 35
HA3: Hrw W 2H 41
SE4 . . . . .4B 122
Wickham St. DA16: Well 2J 125
SE11 . . . . .5G 19 (5K 101)
Wickham Theatre Cen. 2F 171
Wickham Way BR3: Beck 4E 158
Wick Ho. *KT1: Hamp W* *1D 150*
(off Station Rd.)
Wick La. E3 . . . . .1C 86
Wickliffe Av. N3 . . . . .2G 45
Wickliffe Gdns. HA9: Wemb 2H 61
Wicklow Ho. N16 . . . . .1F 67
Wicklow St. WC1 . . . . .1G 7 (3K 83)
Wick Rd. E9 . . . . .6K 67
TW11: Tedd 7B 132
Wicks Cl. SE9 . . . . .4B 142
Wicksteed Cl. DA5: Bexl 3K 145
Wicksteed Ho. SE1 . . . . .3C 102
TW8: Bford 5F 97
Wicks Way SE19 . . . . .6D 138
Wickway Ct. *SE15* *6F 103*
(off Cator St.)
Wickwood St. SE5 . . . . .2B 120
Widdenham Rd. N7 . . . . .4K 65
Widdicombe Av. HA2: Harr 2C 58
Widdin St. E15 . . . . .7G 69
Widecombe Gdns. IG4: Ilf 4C 52
Widecombe Rd. SE9 . . . . .3C 142
Widecombe Way N2 . . . . .5B 46
Wideford Dr. RM7: Rush G 6K 55
Widegate St. E1 . . . . .6H 9 (5E 84)
Widenham Cl. HA5: Eastc 5A 40
Wide Way CR4: Mitc 3H 155
Widewing Cl. TW11: Tedd 7B 132
Widford *NW1* *6F 65*
(off Lewis St.)
Widford Ho. *N1* *2B 84*
(off Colebrooke Rd.)
Widgeon Cl. E16 . . . . .6K 87
Widgeon Rd. TW6: H'row A 5C 174
Widley Rd. W9 . . . . .3J 81
Widmer Ct. TW3: Houn 2C 112
WIDMORE 3A 160
WIDMORE GREEN 2B 160
Widmore Lodge Rd.
BR1: Broml 2B 160
Widmore Rd. BR1: Broml 2J 159
UB8: Hil 4D 74
Wigan Ho. E5 . . . . .1H 67
Wigeon Path SE28 . . . . .3H 107
Wigeon Way UB4: Yead 6B 76
Wiggins La. TW10: Ham 2C 132
Wiggins Mead NW9 . . . . .7G 29
Wigginton Av.
HA9: Wemb 6H 61
Wight Ho. *KT1: King T* *3D 150*
(off Portsmouth Rd.)
Wightman Rd. N4 . . . . .4A 48
N8 . . . . .4A 48
Wighton M. TW7: Isle 2J 113
Wigley Rd. TW13: Felt 2B 130
Wigmore Hall 7J 5
Wigmore Pl. E17 . . . . .3A 50
W1 . . . . .7J 5 (6F 83)
Wigmore Rd. SM5: Cars 2B 166
Wigmore St. W1 . . . . .7H 5 (6E 82)
Wigmore Wlk. SM5: Cars 2B 166
Wigram Ho. *E14* *7D 86*
(off Wade's Pl.)
Wigram Rd. E11 . . . . .6A 52
Wigram Sq. E17 . . . . .3E 50
Wigston Cl. N18 . . . . .5K 33
Wigston Rd. E13 . . . . .4K 87
Wigton Gdns. HA7: Stan 1E 42
Wigton Pl. SE11 . . . . .6K 19 (5A 102)
Wigton Rd. E17 . . . . .1B 50
Wilberforce Ct. BR2: Kes 7B 172
Wilberforce M. SW4 . . . . .4H 119
Wilberforce Rd. N4 . . . . .2B 66
NW9 . . . . .6C 44
Wilberforce Wlk. E15 . . . . .5G 69
Wilberforce Way SE25 . . . . .4F 157
SW19 .6F 135
Wilbraham Ho. *SW8* *7J 101*
(off Wandsworth Rd.)
Wilbraham Mans. *SW1* *3G 17*
(off Wilbraham Pl.)
Wilbraham Pl. SW1 . . . . . .3F 17 (4D 100)
Wilbrahams Almshouses
EN5: Barn 2C 20
Wilbrooke Pl. SE3 . . . . .1K 123
Wilbury Way N18 . . . . .5J 33
Wilby M. W11 . . . . .1H 99
Wilcox Cl. SW8 . . . . .7J 101
(not continuous)
Wilcox Gdns. TW17: Shep 3A 146
Wilcox Ho. *E3* *5B 86*
(off Ackroyd Dr.)
Wilcox Pl. SW1 . . . . .2B 18 (3G 101)
Wilcox Rd. SM1: Sutt 4K 165
SW8 . . . . .7J 101
TW11: Tedd 4H 131
Wildberry Cl. W7 . . . . .4A 96
Wildbore Ho. *N1* *7A 66*
(off Liverpool Rd.)
Wildcat Rd. *TW6: H'row A* *6C 174*
(off Wayfarer Rd.)
Wild Ct. WC2 . . . . .1G 13 (6K 83)
Wildcroft Gdns. HA8: Edg 6J 27
Wildcroft Mnr. SW15 . . . . .7E 116
Wildcroft Rd. SW15 . . . . .7E 116
Wilde Cl. E8 . . . . .1G 85
Wilde Ho. *W2* *2A 10*
(off Gloucester Ter.)
Wilde Pl. N13 . . . . .6G 33
SW18 .7B 118
Wilder Cl. HA4: Ruis 1K 57
The Wilderness
KT8: W Mole, E Mos 5G 149
TW12: Hamp H 4F 131
Wildernesse Cl. HA8: Edg 4D 28
Wilderness Island
Local Nature Reserve 2E 166
The Wilderness
Local Nature Reserve *7F 101*
(off Queenstown Rd.)
Wilderness M. SW4 . . . . .4F 119
Wilderness Rd. BR7: Chst 7F 143
Wilde Rd. DA8: Erith 7H 109
Wilderton Rd. N16 . . . . .7E 48
Wilder Wlk. *W1* *3B 12*
(off Glasshouse St.)
Wildfell Rd. SE6 . . . . .7D 122
Wild Goose Dr. SE14 . . . . .1J 121
Wild Hatch NW11 . . . . .6J 45
Wild's Rents SE1 . . . . .7G 15 (3E 102)
Wild St. WC2 . . . . .1F 13 (6J 83)
Wildwood Cl. SE12 . . . . .7H 123
Wildwood Gro. NW3 . . . . .1A 64
Wildwood Ri. NW11 . . . . .1A 64
Wildwood Rd. NW11 . . . . .6K 45
Wildwood Ter. NW3 . . . . .1A 64
Wilford Cl. EN2: Enf 3J 23
Wilford Rd. CR0: C'don 6C 156
Wilfred Ct. *N15* *5D 48*
(off South Gro.)
Wilfred Owen Cl. SW19 . . . . .6A 136
Wilfred St. SW1 . . . . .1A 18 (3G 101)
Wilfred Wood Ct. *W6* *4E 98*
(off Samuel's Cl.)
Wilfrid Gdns. W3 . . . . .5J 79
Wilkes Cl. NW7 . . . . .4A 30
Wilkes Rd. TW8: Bford 6E 96
Wilkes St. E1 . . . . .5K 9 (5F 85)
Wilkie Ho. *SW1* *5D 18*
(off Cureton St.)
Wilkins Cl. CR4: Mitc 1C 154
UB3: Harl 5H 93
Wilkins Ho. *SW1* *7A 18*
(off Churchill Gdns.)
Wilkinson Cl. NW2 . . . . .2E 62
UB10: Hil 1D 74
Wilkinson Ct. SW17 . . . . .4B 136
Wilkinson Gdns. SE25 . . . . .1E 156
Wilkinson Ho. *N1* *2D 84*
(off Cranston Est.)
Wilkinson Rd. E16 . . . . .6A 88
Wilkinson St. SW8 . . . . .7K 101
Wilkinson Way W4 . . . . .2K 97
Wilkin St. NW5 . . . . .6E 64
Wilkin St. M. NW5 . . . . .6F 65
Wilks Gdns. CR0: C'don 1A 170
Wilks Pl. N1 . . . . .2E 84
Willan Rd. N17 . . . . .2D 48
Willard St. SW8 . . . . .3F 119
Willcocks Cl. KT9: Chess 3E 162
Willcott Rd. W3 . . . . .1H 97
Will Crooks Gdns. SE9 . . . . .4A 124
Willen Fld. Rd. NW10 . . . . .2J 79
Willenhall Av. EN5: New Bar 6F 21
Willenhall Ct. EN5: New Bar 6F 21
Willenhall Dr. UB3: Hayes 7G 75
Willenhall Rd. SE18 . . . . .5F 107
Willersley Av. BR6: Orp 3H 173
DA15: Sidc 1K 143
Willersley Cl. DA15: Sidc 1K 143
WILLESDEN 6C 62
WILLESDEN GREEN 6E 62
Willesden La. NW2 . . . . .6E 62
NW6 . . . . .6E 62
Willesden Section Ho. *NW6* *7F 63*
(off Willesden La.)
Willesden Sports Cen. 1D 80
Willesden Sports Stadium 1D 80
Willes Rd. NW5 . . . . .6F 65
Willett Cl. BR5: Pet W 6J 161
UB5: N'olt 3A 76
Willett Ho. *E13* *2K 87*
(off Queens Rd. W.)
Willett Pl. CR7: Thor H 5A 156
Willett Rd. CR7: Thor H 5A 156
Willett Way BR5: Pet W 5H 161
William IV St. WC2 . . . . . .3E 12 (7J 83)
William Allen Ho.
HA8: Edg 7A 28
William Ash Cl. RM9: Dag 6B 72
William Banfield Ho. *SW6* *2H 117*
(off Munster Rd.)
William Barefoot Dr. SE9 . . . . .4E 142
William Blake Ho. SW11 . . . . .1C 118
William Bonney Est. SW4 . . . . . . .4H 119
William Booth Ho. *E14* *6C 86*
(off Hind Gro.)
William Booth Rd. SE20 . . . . .1G 157
William Carey Way
HA1: Harr 6J 41
William Caslon Ho. *E2* *2H 85*
(off Patriot Sq.)
William Channing Ho. *E2* *3H 85*
(off Canrobert St.)
William Cl. N2 . . . . .2B 46
RM5: Col R 1J 55
SE7 . . . . .5B 106
SE13 .3E 122
UB2: S'hall 2G 95
William Cobbett Ho. *W8* *3K 99*
(off Scarsdale Pl.)
William Congreve M. N1 . . . . .1C 84
William Cotton Ct. *E14* *5C 86*
(off Selsey St.)
William Ct. NW8 . . . . .3A 82
SE10 . . . .*1D 122*
(off Greenwich High Rd.)
SE25 . . . .*3F 157*
(off Chalfont Rd.)
SW16 . . . .*7K 137*
(off Streatham High Rd.)
W5 . . . . .5C 78
William Covell Cl. EN2: Enf 1E 22
William Dr. HA7: Stan 6F 27
William Dromey Ct. NW6 . . . . .7H 63
William Dunbar Ho. *NW6* *2H 81*
(off Albert Rd.)
William Dyce M. SW16 . . . . .4H 137
William Ellis Way *SE16* *3G 103*
(off St James's Rd.)
William Evans Ho. *SE8* *4K 103*
(off Haddonfield)
William Farm La. SW15 . . . . .3D 116
William Fenn Ho. *E2* *1K 9*
(off Shipton Rd.)
William Foster La. DA16: Well 2A 126
William Fry Ho. *E1* *6K 85*
(off W. Arbour St.)
William Gdns. SW15 . . . . .5D 116
William Gibbs Ct. *SW1* *2C 18*
(off Old Pye St.)
William Gunn Ho. NW3 . . . . .5C 64
William Guy Gdns. E3 . . . . .3D 86
William Harvey Ho. *SW19* *1G 135*
(off Whitlock Dr.)
William Henry Wlk.
SW11 . . . . .7C 18 (6H 101)
William Hope Cl. IG11: Bark 2J 89
William Ho. BR1: Broml 3J 159
William Hunt Mans.
SW13 . . . . .6E 98
William Margrie Cl. SE15 . . . . . . .2G 121
William Marshall Cl. E17 . . . . .6A 50
William M. N1 . . . . .7E 66
SW1 . . . . .7F 11 (2D 100)
William Morley Cl. E6 . . . . .1B 88
William Morris Cl. E17 . . . . .3B 50
William Morris Gallery 3C 50
William Morris Ho. W6 . . . . .6F 99
William Morris Way SW6 . . . . .3A 118
William Murdoch Rd.
E14 . . . . .5F 87
William Owston Ct. *E16* *1C 106*
(off Connaught Rd.)
William Parry House *E16* *2K 105*
(off Shipwright Street)
William Perkin Ct. UB6: G'frd 6J 59
William Pike Ho. *RM7: Rom* *6K 55*
(off Waterloo Gdns.)
William Pl. E3 . . . . .2B 86
William Rathbone Ho. *E2* *3H 85*
(off Florida St.)
William Rd. NW1 . . . . .2A 6 (3G 83)
SM1: Sutt 5A 166
SW19 .7G 135
William Rushbrooke Ho.
SE16 . . . .*4G 103*
(off Rouel Rd.)
Williams Av. E17 . . . . .1B 50
William Saville Ho. *NW6* *2H 81*
(off Denmark Rd.)
William's Bldgs. E2 . . . . .4J 85
Williamsburg Plaza E14 . . . . .7E 86
Williams Cl. N8 . . . . .6H 47
SW6 . . . . .7G 99
Williams Dr. TW3: Houn 4E 112
Williams Gro. KT6: Surb 6C 150
N22 . . . . .1A 48
Williams Ho. *E3* *3C 86*
(off Alfred St.)
E9 . . . .*1H 85*
(off King Edward's Rd.)
NW2 . . . .*3E 62*
(off Stoll Cl.)
SW1 . . . .*4D 18*
(off Montaigne Cl.)
William's La. SW14 . . . . .3J 115
Williams La. SM4: Mord 5A 154
Williams M. SE4 . . . . .6B 122
William Smith Ho. *DA17: Belv* *3G 109*
(off Ambrooke Rd.)
E3 . . . .*3C 86*
(off Ireton St.)
Williamson Cl. SE10 . . . . .5H 105
Williamson Ct. SE17 . . . . .5C 102
Williamson Rd. N4 . . . . .6B 48
Williamson St. N7 . . . . .4J 65
William Sq. *SE16* *7A 86*
(off Sovereign Cres.)
Williams Rd. UB2: S'hall 4C 94
W13 . . . . .1A 96
Williams Ter. CR0: Wadd 6A 168
William St. E10 . . . . .6D 50
IG11: Bark 7G 71
N17 . . . . .7A 34
SM5: Cars 3C 166
SW1 . . . . .7F 11 (2D 100)
Williams Way DA2: Wilm 2K 145
HA0: Wemb 5B 60
William Whiffin Sq. E3 . . . . .4B 86
William Wood Ho. *SE26* *3J 139*
(off Shrublands Cl.)
Willifield Way NW11 . . . . .4H 45
Willingale Cl. IG8: Wfd G 6F 37
Willingdon Rd. N22 . . . . .2B 48
Willingham Cl. NW5 . . . . .5G 65
Willingham Ter. NW5 . . . . .5G 65
Willingham Way
KT1: King T 3G 151
Willington Ct. E5 . . . . .3A 68
Willington Rd. SW9 . . . . .3J 119
Willis Av. SM2: Sutt 6C 166
Willis Ct. BR4: W W'ck 2F 171
CR7: Thor H 6A 156
Willis Ho. *E14* *7D 86*
(off Hale St.)
Willis Rd. CR0: C'don 7C 156
DA8: Erith 4J 109
E15 . . . . .2H 87
Willis St. E14 . . . . .6D 86
Willis Yd. N14 . . . . .7C 22
Will Miles Ct. SW19 . . . . .7A 136
Willmore End SW19 . . . . .1K 153
Willoughby Av.
CR0: Bedd 4K 167
UB10: Uxb 2A 74
Willoughby Dr. RM13: Rain 7K 73
Willoughby Gro. N17 . . . . .7C 34
Willoughby Highwalk *EC2* *6E 8*
(off Moor La.)
Willoughby Ho. *E1* *1H 103*
(off Reardon Path)
EC2 . . . . .5E 8
Willoughby La. BR1: Broml 7K 141
N17 . . . . .6C 34
Willoughby M. N17 . . . . .7C 34
SW4 . . . .*4F 119*
(off Cedars M.)
Willoughby Pk. Rd. N17 . . . . .7C 34
Willoughby Pas. *E14* *1C 104*
(off W. India Av.)
Willoughby Rd. KT2: King T 1F 151
N8 . . . . .3A 48
NW3 . . . . .4B 64
TW1: Twick 5C 114
(not continuous)
The Willoughbys SW14 . . . . .3A 116
Willoughby St. WC1 . . . . .6E 6
Willoughby Way SE7 . . . . .4K 105
Willow Av. DA15: Sidc 6A 126
SW13 .2B 116
UB7: Yiew 7B 74
Willow Bank SW6 . . . . .3G 117
TW10: Ham 3B 132
Willowbank KT7: T Ditt 1A 162
Willowbay Cl. EN5: Barn 6A 20
Willow Bri. Rd. N1 . . . . .6C 66
(not continuous)
Willowbrook TW12: Hamp H 5F 131
Willowbrook Est. SE15 . . . . .7G 103
Willow Brook Rd. SE15 . . . . .7F 103
Willowbrook Rd.
TW19: Stanw 2A 128
UB2: S'hall 3E 94
Willow Bus. Pk. SE26 . . . . .3J 139
Willow Cl. BR2: Broml 5D 160
DA5: Bexl 6F 127
IG9: Buck H 3G 37
SE6 . . . . .1H 141
TW8: Bford 6C 96
Willow Cotts. TW9: Kew 6G 97
TW13: Hanw 3C 130
Willow Ct. *E11* *2G 69*
(off Trinity Cl.)
EC2 . . . . .3G 9 (4E 84)
HA3: Hrw W 1K 41
HA8: Edg 4K 27
N12 . . . . .4E 30
NW6 . . . . .7G 63
SM6: W'gton *7F 167*
(off Willow Rd.)
TW16: Sun *7G 129*
(off Staines Rd. W.)
W4 . . . .*7A 98*
(off Corney Reach Way)
W9 . . . .*5J 81*
(off Admiral Wlk.)
Willowcourt Av. HA3: Kenton 5B 42
Willow Dene HA5: Pinn 2B 40
WD23: B Hea 1D 26
Willowdene N6 . . . . .7D 46
SE15 . . . . .7H 103
Willowdene Cl. TW2: Whitt 7G 113
Willowdene Ct. *N20* *7F 21*
(off High Rd. Whetstone)
Willow Dr. EN5: Barn 4B 20
Willow End KT6: Surb 1E 162
N20 . . . . .2D 30
Willowfields Cl. SE18 . . . . .5J 107
Willow Gdns. HA4: Ruis 2H 57
TW3: Houn 1E 112
Willow Grange DA14: Sidc 3B 144
Willow Grn. NW9 . . . . .1A 44
Willow Gro. BR7: Chst 6E 142
E13 . . . . .2J 87
HA4: Ruis 2H 57
Willowhayne Ct. *KT12: Walt T* *7K 147*
(off Willowhayne Dr.)
Willowhayne Dr. KT12: Walt T 7K 147
Willowhayne Gdns.
KT4: Wor Pk 3E 164
Willow Ho. BR2: Broml 2G 159
SE1 . . . .*4F 103*
(off Curtis St.)
SE4 . . . .*3A 122*
(off Dragonfly Pl.)
W10 . . . .*4F 81*
(off Maple Wlk.)
Willow La. CR4: Mitc 5D 154
SE18 .4D 106
Willow La. Bus. Pk.
CR4: Mitc 6D 154
Willow La. Ind. Est.
CR4: Mitc 6D 154
Willow Lodge RM7: Rom 5K 55
SW6 . . . . .1F 117
TW16: Sun *7H 129*
(off Grangewood Dr.)
Willowmead Cl. W5 . . . . .4D 78
Willow Mt. CR0: C'don 3E 168
Willow Pl. SW1 . . . . .3B 18 (4G 101)
Willow Rd. EN1: Enf 3K 23
KT3: N Mald 4J 151
NW3 . . . . .4B 64
RM6: Chad H 6E 54
SL3: Poyle 5A 174
SM6: W'gton 7F 167
W5 . . . . .2E 96
The Willows BR3: Beck 1C 158
E6 . . . . .7D 70
SE1 . . . . .4E 102
Willows Av. SM4: Mord 5K 153
Willows Cl. HA5: Pinn 2A 40
Willowside Ct. EN2: Enf 3G 23
Willows Ter. *NW10* *2B 80*
(off Rucklidge Av.)
Willow St. E4 . . . . .1A 36
EC2 . . . . .3G 9 (4E 84)
RM7: Rom 4J 55
Willow Tree Cen. 5D 38
Willow Tree Cl. E3 . . . . .1B 86
SW18 .1K 135
UB4: Yead 4A 76
UB5: N'olt 6D 58
Willowtree Cl. UB10: Ick 3E 56
Willow Tree Ct. DA14: Sidc 5A 144
HA0: Wemb 5D 60
Willow Tree La. UB4: Yead 4A 76
WILLOW TREE RDBT. 5B 76
Willow Tree Wlk. BR1: Broml 1K 159
Willowtree Way CR7: Thor H 1A 156
Willow Va. BR7: Chst 6F 143
W12 . . . . .1C 98
Willow Vw. SW19 . . . . .1B 154
Willow Wlk. BR6: Farnb 3F 173
E17 . . . . .5B 50
IG1: Ilf .2F 71
N1 . . . . .2B 84
N2 . . . . .2B 46
N15 . . . . .4B 48
N21 . . . . .6E 22
SE1 . . . . .3E 102
SM3: Sutt 3H 165
Willow Way HA0: Wemb 3A 60
KT19: Ewe 6K 163
N3 . . . . .7E 30
SE26 .3J 139
TW2: Twick 2F 131
TW16: Sun 4J 147
W11 . . . . .7F 81

Willow Wood Cres.—Winter Box Wlk.

Willow Wood Cres. SE25 . . . . .6E 156
Willow Wren Wharf
UB2: S'hall 4K 93
Willrose Cres. SE2 . . . . .5B 108
Willsbridge Ct. SE15 . . . . .6F 103
Wills Cres. TW3: Houn 6F 113
Wills Gro. NW7 . . . . .5H 29
Will Wyatt Ct. N1 . . . . .2E 84
(off Pitfield St.)
Wilman Gro. E8 . . . . .7G 67
Wilmar Cl. UB4: Hayes 4F 75
Wilmar Gdns. BR4: W W'ck 1D 170
Wilmcote Ho. W2 . . . . .5K 81
(off Woodchester Sq.)
Wilment Ct. NW2 . . . . .3E 62
Wilmer Cl. KT2: King T 5F 133
Wilmer Cres.
KT2: King T 5F 133
Wilmer Gdns. N1 . . . . .1E 84
(not continuous)
Wilmer Ho. E3 . . . . .2A 86
(off Daling Way)
Wilmer Lea Cl. E15 . . . . .7F 69
Wilmer Pl. N16 . . . . .2F 67
Wilmer Way N14 . . . . .5C 32
Wilmington Av. W4 . . . . .7K 97
Wilmington Ct. SW16 . . . . .7J 137
Wilmington Gdns.
IG11: Bark 6H 71
Wilmington Sq. WC1 . . . . . . .2J 7 (3A 84)
(not continuous)
Wilmington St. WC1 . . . . . . .2J 7 (3A 84)
Wilmington Ter. SE16 . . . . .4H 103
(off Camilla Rd.)
Wilmot Cl. N2 . . . . .2A 46
SE15 .7G 103
Wilmot Ho. SE11 . . . . .4B 102
(off George Mathers Rd.)
Wilmot Pl. NW1 . . . . .7G 65
(not continuous)
W7 . . . . .1J 95
Wilmot Rd. E10 . . . . .2D 68
N17 . . . . .3D 48
SM5: Cars 5D 166
Wilmot St. E2 . . . . .4H 85
Wilmount St. SE18 . . . . .4F 107
Wilna Rd. SW18 . . . . .7A 118
Wilsham St. W11 . . . . .1F 99
Wilshaw Cl. NW4 . . . . .3C 44
Wilshaw Ho. SE8 . . . . .7C 104
Wilshaw St. SE14 . . . . .1C 122
Wilsmere Dr. HA3: Hrw W 7D 26
UB5: N'olt 6C 58
Wilson Av. CR4: Mitc 7C 136
Wilson Cl. CR2: S Croy 5D 168
HA9: Wemb 7F 43
Wilson Ct. NW9 . . . . .2K 43
RM7: Rush G 6K 55
(off Union Rd.)
SE28 .3G 107
Wilson Dr. HA9: Wemb 7F 43
Wilson Gdns. HA1: Harr 7G 41
Wilson Gro. SE16 . . . . .2H 103
Wilson Ho. NW6 . . . . .7A 64
(off Goldhurst Ter.)
Wilson Rd. E6 . . . . .3B 88
IG1: Ilf 7D 52
KT9: Chess 6F 163
SE5 .1E 120
Wilson's Av. N17 . . . . .2F 49
Wilson's Rd. W6 . . . . .5F 99
Wilson St. E17 . . . . .5E 50
EC2 . . . . .5F 9 (5D 84)
N21 . . . . .7F 23
Wilson Wlk. W4 . . . . .4B 98
(off Prebend Gdns.)
Wilstone Cl. UB4: Yead 4C 76
Wiltern Ct. NW2 . . . . .6G 63
Wilthorne Gdns. RM10: Dag 7H 73
Wilton Av. W4 . . . . .5A 98
Wilton Cl. UB7: Harm 2E 174
Wilton Ct. E1 . . . . .6H 85
(off Cavell St.)
Wilton Cres. SW1 . . . . . .7G 11 (2E 100)
SW19 . . . . .1H 153
Wilton Dr. RM5: Col R 1J 55
Wilton Est. E8 . . . . .6G 67
Wilton Gdns. KT8: W Mole 3E 148
Wilton Gro. KT3: N Mald 6B 152
SW19 . . . . .1H 153
Wilton Ho. CR2: S Croy 5C 168
(off Nottingham Rd.)
Wilton M. E8 . . . . .6H 67
SW1 . . . . .1H 17 (3E 100)
Wilton Pde. TW13: Felt 2J 129
Wilton Pl. E4 . . . . .6A 36
HA1: Harr 6K 41
SW1 . . . . .7G 11 (2E 100)
Wilton Plaza SW1 . . . . .3A 18
(off Wilton Rd.)
Wilton Rd. EN4: Cockf 4J 21
N10 . . . . .2E 46
SE2 .4C 108
SW1 . . . . .2K 17 (3F 101)
SW19 . . . . .7C 136
TW4: Houn 3B 112
Wilton Row SW1 . . . . . . .7G 11 (2E 100)
Wilton's Music Hall 7G 85
(off Graces All.)
Wilton Sq. N1 . . . . .1D 84
Wilton St. SW1 . . . . .1J 17 (3F 101)
Wilton Ter. SW1 . . . . .1G 17 (3E 100)
Wilton Vs. N1 . . . . .1D 84
(off Wilton Sq.)
Wilton Way E8 . . . . .6G 67
Wiltshire Cl. NW7 . . . . .5G 29
SW3 . . . . .3E 16 (4D 100)
Wiltshire Ct. CR2: S Croy 5C 168
IG1: Ilf 6G 71
N4 . . . . .1K 65
(off Marquis Rd.)
Wiltshire Gdns. N4 . . . . .6C 48
TW2: Twick 1G 131
Wiltshire La. HA5: Eastc 3H 39
Wiltshire Rd. BR6: Orp 7K 161
CR7: Thor H 3A 156
SW9 .3A 120
Wiltshire Row N1 . . . . .1D 84
Wilverley Cres. KT3: N Mald 6A 152
Wimbart Rd. SW2 . . . . .7K 119
WIMBLEDON 6G 135
Wimbledon All England Lawn Tennis
& Croquet Club 4G 135
Wimbledon Bri. SW19 . . . . .6H 135
Wimbledon Cl. SW20 . . . . .7F 135
Wimbledon Common 4C 134
Wimbledon Common Golf Course
. . . . .5D 134
Wimbledon Hill Rd. SW19 . . . . . . .6G 135
Wimbledon Lawn Tennis Mus.
. . . . .3G 135
Wimbledon Leisure Cen. 6K 135
WIMBLEDON PARK 3J 135
Wimbledon Pk. Athletics Track
. . . . .2H 135
Wimbledon Pk. Ct. SW19 . . . . . . .1H 135
Wimbledon Pk. Golf Course 3H 135
Wimbledon Pk. Rd. SW18 . . . . . . .2G 135
SW19 . . . . .2G 135
Wimbledon Pk. Side SW19 . . . . . .3F 135
Wimbledon Pk. Watersports Cen.
. . . . .2H 135
Wimbledon Rd. SW17 . . . . .4A 136
Wimbledon Stadium Bus. Cen.
SW17 . . . . .3K 135
Wimbledon Theatre 7J 135
Wimbledon Windmill Mus. 3D 134
Wimbolt St. E2 . . . . .3G 85
Wimborne Av. BR5: St P 4K 161
BR7: Chst 4K 161
UB2: S'hall 4E 94
UB4: Yead 6K 75
Wimborne Cl. IG9: Buck H 2E 36
KT4: Wor Pk 1E 164
SE12 .5H 123
Wimborne Ct. SW12 . . . . .3G 137
UB5: N'olt 6E 58
Wimborne Dr. HA5: Pinn 7B 40
NW9 . . . . .3G 43
Wimborne Gdns. W13 . . . . .5B 78
Wimborne Ho. E16 . . . . .7H 87
(off Victoria Dock Rd.)
NW1 . . . . .4D 4
(off Harewood Av.)
SW8 .7K 101
(off Dorset Rd.)
SW12 . . . . .3G 137
Wimborne Rd. N9 . . . . .2B 34
N17 . . . . .2E 48
Wimborne Way BR3: Beck 3K 157
Wimbourne Ct. N1 . . . . .2D 84
(off Wimbourne St.)
Wimbourne St. N1 . . . . .2D 84
Wimpole Cl. BR2: Broml 4A 160
KT1: King T 2F 151
Wimpole M. W1 . . . . .5J 5 (5F 83)
Wimpole Rd.
UB7: Yiew 1A 92
Wimpole St. W1 . . . . .6J 5 (5F 83)
Wimshurst Cl.
CR0: Wadd 1J 167
Winans Wlk. SW9 . . . . .2A 120
Winant Ho. E14 . . . . .7D 86
(off Simpson's Rd.)
Wincanton Ct. N11 . . . . .6K 31
(off Martock Gdns.)
Wincanton Cres. UB5: N'olt 5E 58
Wincanton Gdns. IG6: Ilf 3F 53
Wincanton Rd. SW18 . . . . .7H 117
Winchcombe Rd. SM5: Cars 7B 154
Winchcomb Gdns. SE9 . . . . .3B 124
Winchelsea Av. DA7: Bex 7F 109
Winchelsea Cl. SW15 . . . . .5F 117
Winchelsea Ho. SE16 . . . . .2J 103
(off Swan Rd.)
Winchelsea Rd. E7 . . . . .3J 69
N17 . . . . .3E 48
NW10 .1K 79
Winchelsey Ri. CR2: S Croy 6F 169
Winchendon Rd. SW6 . . . . .1H 117
TW11: Tedd 4H 131
Winchester Av. NW6 . . . . .1G 81
NW9 . . . . .3G 43
TW5: Hest 6D 94
Winchester Bldgs. SE1 . . . . .6C 14
(off Copperfield St.)
Winchester Cl. BR2: Broml 3H 159
E6 . . . . .6D 88
EN1: Enf 5K 23
KT2: King T 7H 133
SE17 .4B 102
SL3: Poyle 4A 174
Winchester Ct. W8 . . . . .2J 99
(off Vicarage Ga.)
Winchester Dr. HA5: Pinn 5B 40
Winchester Ho. E3 . . . . .3B 86
(off Hamlets Way)
E14 . . . . .6C 86
(off New Festival Av.)
IG11: Bark 7A 72
(off Margaret Bondfield Av.)
SE18 .7B 106
(off Portway Gdns.)
SW3 .7B 16
SW9 .7A 102
W2 . . . . .6A 82
(off Hallfield Est.)
Winchester M. KT4: Wor Pk 2F 165
NW3 . . . . .7B 64
(off Winchester Rd.)
Winchester Palace 4E 14
(off Stoney St.)
Winchester Pk. BR2: Broml 3H 159
Winchester Pl. E8 . . . . .5F 67
N6 . . . . .1F 65
Winchester Rd. BR2: Broml 3H 159
DA7: Bex 2D 126
E4 . . . . .7K 35
HA3: Kenton 4E 42
HA6: Nwood 2H 39
IG1: Ilf 3H 71
KT12: Walt T 7J 147
N6 . . . . .7F 47
N9 . . . . .1A 34
NW3 . . . . .7B 64
TW1: Twick 6B 114
TW13: Hanw 3D 130
UB3: Harl 7G 93
Winchester Sq. SE1 . . . . .4E 14
SE8 . . . . .4B 104
Winchester St. SW1 . . . . .5K 17 (5F 101)
W3 . . . . .1J 97
Winchester Wlk. SE1 . . . . .4E 14 (1D 102)
SW15 . . . . .5H 117
(off Up. Richmond Rd.)
Winchester Wharf SE1 . . . . .4E 14
(off Clink St.)
Winchet Wlk. CR0: C'don 6J 157
Winchfield Cl.
HA3: Kenton 6C 42
Winchfield Ho. SW15 . . . . .6B 116
Winchfield Rd. SE26 . . . . .5A 140
Winch Ho. E14 . . . . .3D 104
(off Tiller Rd.)
SW10 .7A 100
(off King's Rd.)
Winchilsea Cres.
KT8: W Mole 2G 149
Winchilsea Ho. NW8 . . . . .2B 4
(off St John's Wood Rd.)
WINCHMORE HILL 7F 23
Winchmore Hill Rd. N14 . . . . .1C 32
N21 . . . . .1C 32
Winchmore School Sports Cen.
. . . . .2H 33
Winchmore Vs. N21 . . . . .7E 22
(off Winchmore Hill Rd.)
Winchstone Cl. TW17: Shep 4B 146
Winckley Cl. HA3: Kenton 5F 43
Winckworth Ct. N1 . . . . .2F 9
(off Charles Sq. Est.)
Wincott Pde. SE11 . . . . .3K 19
(off Wincott St.)
Wincott St. SE11 . . . . . . .4K 19 (4A 102)
Wincrofts Dr. SE9 . . . . .4H 125
Windall Cl. SE19 . . . . .1G 157
Windborough Rd. SM5: Cars 7E 166
Windermere NW1 . . . . .2K 5
(off Albany St.)
Windermere Av. HA4: Ruis 7A 40
HA9: Kenton, Wemb 7C 42
N3 . . . . .3J 45
NW6 . . . . .1G 81
SW19 . . . . .3K 153
Windermere Cl. BR6: Farnb 3F 173
TW14: Felt 1H 129
TW19: Stanw 1A 128
Windermere Ct. HA9: Wemb 7C 42
SM5: Cars 3E 166
SW13 .6B 98
Windermere Gdns. IG4: Ilf 5C 52
Windermere Gro.
HA9: Wemb 1C 60
Windermere Hall HA8: Edg 5A 28
Windermere Ho. E3 . . . . .4B 86
EN5: New Bar 4E 20
TW7: Isle 5K 113
Windermere Point SE15 . . . . .7J 103
(off Old Kent Rd.)
Windermere Rd. BR4: W W'ck 2G 171
CR0: C'don 1F 169
DA7: Bex 2J 127
N10 . . . . .1F 47
N19 . . . . .2G 65
SW15 . . . . .4A 134
SW16 . . . . .1G 155
UB1: S'hall 5D 76
W5 . . . . .3C 96
Windermere Way UB7: Yiew 1A 92
Winders Rd. SW11 . . . . .2C 118
(not continuous)
Windfield Cl. SE26 . . . . .4K 139
Windham Rd. TW9: Rich 3F 115
Winding Way RM8: Dag 3C 72
Windlass Ho. E16 . . . . .2K 105
(off Schooner Rd.)
Windlass Pl. SE8 . . . . .4A 104
Windlesham Gro. SW19 . . . . .1F 135
Windlesham Ho. SE1 . . . . .5J 15
(off Duchess Wlk.)
Windlesham M.
TW12: Hamp H 6G 131
Windley Cl. SE23 . . . . .2J 139
Windmill WC1 . . . . .5G 7
(off New North St.)
Windmill Av. UB2: S'hall 1G 95
Windmill Bri. Ho. CR0: C'don 1E 168
(off Freemasons Rd.)
Windmill Bus. Village
TW16: Sun 1G 147
Windmill Cl. KT6: Surb 1C 162
SE1 . . . . .4G 103
(off Beatrice Rd.)
SE13 .2E 122
TW16: Sun 7G 129
Windmill Ct. E4 . . . . .2B 36
HA4: Ruis 1J 57
NW2 . . . . .6G 63
W5 . . . . .4C 96
(off Windmill Rd.)
Windmill Dr. BR2: Kes 4A 172
NW2 . . . . .3G 63
SW4 . . . . .5F 119
Windmill Gdns. EN2: Enf 3F 23
Windmill Grn. TW17: Shep 7G 147
Windmill Gro. CR0: C'don 6C 156
Windmill Hill EN2: Enf 3G 23
HA4: Ruis 7H 39
NW3 . . . . .3A 64
Windmill Ho. E14 . . . . .4C 104
SE1 . . . . .5K 13
(off Windmill Wlk.)
Windmill La. E15 . . . . .6F 69
KT6: Surb 6B 150
TW7: Isle 3G 95
UB2: S'hall 1G 95
UB6: G'frd 6G 77
WD23: B Hea 1D 26
Windmill M. W4 . . . . .4A 98
Windmill Pas. W4 . . . . .4A 98
Windmill Pl. UB2: S'hall 1G 95
Windmill Ri. KT2: King T 7H 133
Windmill Rd. CR0: C'don 7C 156
CR4: Mitc 5G 155
N18 . . . . .4J 33
SW18 .6B 118
SW19 . . . . .2D 134
TW8: Bford 4C 96
TW12: Hamp H 5F 131
TW16: Sun 1G 147
W4 . . . . .4A 98
W5 . . . . .4C 96
Windmill Rd. W. TW16: Sun 2G 147
Windmill Row SE11 . . . . . .6J 19 (5A 102)
Windmill St. W1 . . . . .6C 6 (5H 83)
(not continuous)
WD23: B Hea 1D 26
Windmill Ter. TW17: Shep 7G 147
Windmill Wlk.
SE1 . . . . .5K 13 (1A 102)
Windmill Way HA4: Ruis 1H 57
Windmore Cl.
HA0: Wemb 5A 60
Windrose Cl. SE16 . . . . .2K 103
Windrush KT3: N Mald 4H 151
SE28 .1B 108
Windrush Cl. E8 . . . . .7G 67
N17 . . . . .1E 48
SW11 .4B 118
UB10: Ick 4B 56
W4 . . . . .1J 115
Windrush Ho. NW8 . . . . .5B 4
(off Church St. Est.)
Windrush La. SE23 . . . . .3K 139
Windrush Rd. NW10 . . . . .1K 79
Windrush Sq. SW2 . . . . .4A 120
Windsock Cl. SE16 . . . . .4B 104
Windsock Way
TW6: H'row A 5C 174
Windsor Av. E17 . . . . .2A 50
HA8: Edg 4C 28
KT3: N Mald 5J 151
KT8: W Mole 3E 148
SM3: Cheam 3G 165
SW19 . . . . .1A 154
UB10: Hil 1D 74
The Windsor Cen. N1 . . . . .1B 84
(off Windsor St.)
Windsor Cl. BR7: Chst 5F 143
HA2: Harr 3E 58
HA6: Nwood 2J 39
N3 . . . . .2G 45
SE27 .4C 138
TW6: H'row A 6D 174
(off Whittle Rd.)
TW8: Bford 6B 96
Windsor Cotts. SE14 . . . . .7B 104
(off Amersham Gro.)
Windsor Ct. E3 . . . . .2C 86
(off Mostyn Gro.)
HA5: Pinn 3B 40
KT1: King T 4D 150
(off Palace Rd.)
N11 . . . . .5J 31
N14 . . . . .7B 22
NW3 . . . . .4J 63
NW11 .6G 45
(off Golders Grn. Rd.)
SE16 .7K 85
(off King & Queen Wharf)
SW3 .5D 16
(off Jubilee Pl.)
SW11 . . . . .2B 118
TW16: Sun 7J 129
W2 . . . . .7K 81
(off Moscow Rd.)
W10 . . . . .6F 81
(off Bramley Rd.)
WD23: Bush 1B 26
(off Catsey La.)
Windsor Cres. HA2: Harr 3E 58
HA9: Wemb 3H 61
Windsor Dr. BR6: Chels 6K 173
EN4: E Barn 6J 21
Windsor Gdns. CR0: Bedd 3J 167
UB3: Harl 3F 93
W9 . . . . .5J 81
Windsor Gro. SE27 . . . . .4C 138
Windsor Hall E16 . . . . .1K 105
(off Wesley Av.)
Windsor Ho. E2 . . . . .3K 85
(off Knottisford St.)
E20 . . . . .5D 68
(off Peloton Av.)
N1 . . . . .2C 84
NW1 . . . . .1K 5
NW2 . . . . .6G 63
(off Chatsworth Rd.)
SW16 . . . . .2K 155
UB5: N'olt 6E 58
(off The Farmlands)
Windsor M. SE6 . . . . .1E 140
SE23 .1A 140
Windsor Pk. Rd. UB3: Harl 7H 93
Windsor Pl.
SW1 . . . . .3B 18 (3G 101)
Windsor Rd. CR7: Thor H 2B 156
DA6: Bex 4E 126
E4 . . . . .4J 35
E7 . . . . .5K 69
E10 . . . . .2D 68
E11 . . . . .1J 69
EN5: Barn 6A 20
HA3: Hrw W 1G 41
IG1: Ilf 4F 71
KT2: King T 7E 132
KT4: Wor Pk 2C 164
N3 . . . . .2G 45
N7 . . . . .3J 65
N13 . . . . .3F 33
N17 . . . . .2G 49
NW2 . . . . .6D 62
RM8: Dag 3E 72
TW4: Cran 2K 111
TW9: Kew 2F 115
TW11: Tedd 5H 131
TW16: Sun 6J 129
UB2: S'hall 3D 94
W5 . . . . .7E 78
(not continuous)
The Windsors IG9: Buck H 2H 37
Windsor St. N1 . . . . .1B 84
Windsor Ter. N1 . . . . .1D 8 (3C 84)
Windsor Wlk. SE5 . . . . .2D 120
Windsor Way W14 . . . . .4F 99
Windsor Wharf E9 . . . . .5B 68
Windspoint Dr. SE15 . . . . .6H 103
Windus M. N16 . . . . .1F 67
Windus Rd. N16 . . . . .1F 67
Windus Wlk. N16 . . . . .1F 67
Windward Ct. E16 . . . . .7F 89
(off Gallions Rd.)
Windy Ridge BR1: Broml 1C 160
Windy Ridge Cl. SW19 . . . . .5F 135
Wine Cl. E1 . . . . .1J 103
(not continuous)
Wine Office Ct. EC4 . . . . . . .7K 7 (6A 84)
Winery La. KT1: King T 3F 151
Winey Cl. KT9: Chess 7C 162
Winford Ct. SE15 . . . . .1H 121
Winford Ho. E3 . . . . .7B 68
Winford Pde. UB1: S'hall 6F 77
(off Marconi Way)
Winforton St. SE10 . . . . .1E 122
Winfrith Rd. SW18 . . . . .7A 118
Wingate & Finchley FC 7G 31
Wingate Cres. CR0: C'don 6J 155
Wingate Ho. E3 . . . . .3D 86
(off Bruce Rd.)
Wingate Rd. DA14: Sidc 6C 144
IG1: Ilf 5F 71
W6 . . . . .3D 98
Wingate Sq. SW4 . . . . .3G 119
Wingfield Ct. DA15: Sidc 2K 143
E14 . . . . .7F 87
(off Newport Av.)
Wingfield Ho. E2 . . . . .2J 9
(off Virginia Rd.)
Wingfield M. SE15 . . . . .3G 121
Wingfield Rd. E15 . . . . .4G 69
E17 . . . . .5D 50
KT2: King T 6F 133
Wingfield St. SE15 . . . . .3G 121
Wingfield Way HA4: Ruis 5K 57
Wingford Rd. SW2 . . . . .6J 119
Wingmore Rd. SE24 . . . . .3C 120
Wingrad Ho. E1 . . . . .5J 85
(off Jubilee St.)
Wingrave Rd. W6 . . . . .6E 98
Wingreen NW8 . . . . .1K 81
(off Abbey Rd.)
Wingrove E4 . . . . .7H 25
Wingrove Ct. RM7: Rom 5J 55
Wingrove Rd. SE6 . . . . .2G 141
Wings Cl. SM1: Sutt 4J 165
Wings Rd. TW6: H'row A 6C 174
(off Whittle Rd.)
Wing Yip Bus. Cen. NW2 . . . . .2D 62
Winicotte Ho. W2 . . . . .5B 4
(off Paddington Grn.)
Winifred Pl. N12 . . . . .5F 31
Winifred Rd. DA8: Erith 5K 109
RM8: Dag 2E 72
SW19 . . . . .1J 153
TW12: Hamp H 4E 130
Winifred St. E16 . . . . .1D 106
Winifred Ter. EN1: Enf 7A 24
Winkfield Rd. E13 . . . . .2K 87
N22 . . . . .1A 48
Winkley Ct. HA2: Harr 3E 58
N10 . . . . .4F 47
(off St James's La.)
Winkley St. E2 . . . . .2H 85
Winkworth Cotts. E1 . . . . .4J 85
(off Cephas St.)
Winlaton Rd. BR1: Broml 4F 141
Winmill Rd. RM8: Dag 3F 73
Winn Comn. Rd. SE18 . . . . .6J 107
Winnepeg Ho. SE16 . . . . .2J 103
(off Province Dr.)
Winnett St. W1 . . . . .2C 12 (7H 83)
Winningales Ct. IG5: Ilf 2C 52
Winnings Wlk. UB5: N'olt 6C 58
Winnington Cl. N2 . . . . .6B 46
Winnington Ho. SE5 . . . . .7C 102
(off Wyndham Est.)
W10 . . . . .4G 81
(off Southern Row)
Winnington Rd. N2 . . . . .6B 46
Winnipeg Dr. BR6: Chels 6K 173
Winnock Rd. UB7: Yiew 1A 92
Winn Rd. SE12 . . . . .1J 141
Winns Av. E17 . . . . .3B 50
Winns M. N15 . . . . .4E 48
Winns Ter. E17 . . . . .3C 50
Winsbeach E17 . . . . .2F 51
Winscombe Cres. W5 . . . . .4D 78
Winscombe St. N19 . . . . .2F 65
Winscombe Way
HA7: Stan 5F 27
Winsford Rd. SE6 . . . . .3B 140
Winsford Ter. N18 . . . . .5J 33
Winsham Gro. SW11 . . . . .5E 118
Winsham Ho. NW1 . . . . .1D 6
(off Churchway)
Winslade Rd. SW2 . . . . .5J 119
Winslade Way SE6 . . . . .7D 122
Winsland M. W2 . . . . .7A 4 (6B 82)
Winsland St. W2 . . . . .7A 4 (6B 82)
Winsley St. W1 . . . . .7B 6 (6G 83)
Winslow SE17 . . . . .5E 102
Winslow Cl. HA5: Eastc 6K 39
NW10 .3A 62
Winslow Gro. E4 . . . . .2B 36
Winslow Rd. W6 . . . . .6E 98
Winslow Way TW13: Hanw 3B 130
Winsmoor Ct. EN2: Enf 3G 23
WINSOR PARK 5F 89
Winsor Ter. E6 . . . . .5E 88
Winstanley Est. SW11 . . . . .3B 118
Winstanley Rd. SW11 . . . . .3B 118
(not continuous)
Winstead Gdns. RM10: Dag 5J 73
Winston Av. NW9 . . . . .7A 44
Winston Cl. HA3: Hrw W 6E 26
KT8: E Mos 6H 149
RM7: Mawney 4H 55
Winston Ct. BR1: Broml 1K 159
(off Widmore Rd.)
HA3: Hrw W 7A 26
Winston Ho. W13 . . . . .2A 96
(off Balfour Rd.)
WC1 . . . . .3D 6
Winston Rd. N16 . . . . .4D 66
Winston Wlk. W4 . . . . .3K 97
Winston Way IG1: Ilf 3F 71
Winter Av. E6 . . . . .1C 88
Winterborne Av. BR6: Orp 3H 173
Winterbourne Ho. W11 . . . . .7G 81
(off Portland Rd.)
Winterbourne Rd.
CR7: Thor H 4A 156
RM8: Dag 2C 72
SE6 . . . . .1B 140
Winter Box Wlk. TW10: Rich 5F 115

Winterbrook Rd.—Woods Ho.

Winterbrook Rd. SE24 6C 120
Winterburn Cl. N11 6K 31
Winterfold Cl. SW19 2G 135
Winter Gdns. TW11: Tedd 4A 132
Wintergreen Blvd.
UB7: W Dray 2B 92
Wintergreen Cl. E6 5C 88
Winterleys NW6 2H 81
(off Denmark Rd.)
Winter Lodge SE16 5G 103
(off Fern Wlk.)
Winter's Ct. E4 3J 35
Winterslow Ho. SE5 2C 120
(off Flaxman Rd.)
Winterslow Rd. SW9 1B 120
Winters Rd. KT7: T Ditt 7B 150
Winterstoke Gdns. NW7 5H 29
Winterstoke Rd. SE6 1B 140
Winterton Ct. KT1: Hamp W 1D 150
(off Lwr. Teddington Rd.)
SE20 2G 157
Winterton Ho. E1 6J 85
(off Deancross St.)
Winterton Pl. SW10 7A 16 (6A 100)
Winterwell Rd. SW2 5J 119
Winthorpe Rd. SW15 4G 117
Winthrop Ho. W12 7D 80
(off White City Est.)
Winthrop St. E1 5H 85
Winthrop Wlk. HA9: Wemb 3E 60
(off Everard Way)
Winton Av. N11 7B 32
Winton Cl. N9 7E 24
Winton Ct. N1 2K 83
(off Calshot St.)
Winton Gdns. HA8: Edg 7A 28
Winton Rd. BR6: Farnb 4F 173
Winton Way SW16 5A 138
Wireworks Ct. SE1 7C 14
(off Gt. Sufolk St.)
Wirrall Ho. SE26 3G 139
Wirral Wood Cl. BR7: Chst 6E 142
Wirra Rd. TW6: H'row A 5C 174
(off Wayfarer Rd.)
Wisbeach Rd. CR0: C'don 5D 156
Wisbech N4 1K 65
(off Lorne Rd.)
Wisborough Rd. CR2: Sande 7E 168
Wisden Ho. SW8 7H 19 (6K 101)
Wisdom Ct. TW7: Isle 3A 114
(off South St.)
Wisdons Cl. RM10: Dag 1H 73
Wise La. NW7 5H 29
UB7: W Dray 4A 92
Wiseman Rd. E10 2C 68
Wise Rd. E15 1F 87
Wiseton Rd. SW17 1C 136
Wishart Rd. SE3 2B 124
Wishaw Wlk. N13 6D 32
Wisley Ho. SW1 5C 18
(off Rampayne St.)
Wisley Rd. BR5: St P 7A 144
SW11 5E 118
Wistaria Cl. BR6: Farnb 2F 173
Wisteria Apts. E9 6J 67
(off Chatham Pl.)
Wisteria Cl. IG1: Ilf 5F 71
NW7 6G 29
Wisteria Rd. SE13 4F 123
Wistow Ho. E2 1G 85
(off Whiston Rd.)
Witanhurst La. N6 1E 64
Witan St. E2 3H 85
Witchwood Ho. SW9 3A 120
(off Gresham Rd.)
Witham Ct. E10 3D 68
SW17 3D 136
Witham Rd. RM10: Dag 5G 73
SE20 3J 157
TW7: Isle 1H 113
W13 1A 96
Witherby Cl. CR0: C'don 5E 168
Witherington Rd. N5 5A 66
Withers Cl. KT9: Chess 6C 162
Withers Mead NW9 1B 44
Withers Pl. EC1 3D 8 (4C 84)
Witherston Way SE9 2E 142
Withycombe Rd. SW19 7F 117
Withy Ho. E1 4K 85
(off Globe Rd.)
Withy La. HA4: Ruis 5E 38
Withy Mead E4 3A 36
Witley Ct. WC1 4E 6
Witley Cres. CR0: New Ad 6E 170
Witley Gdns. UB2: S'hall 4D 94
Witley Ho. SW2 7J 119
Witley Ind. Est.
UB2: S'hall 4D 94
Witley Point SW15 1D 134
(off Wanborough Dr.)
Witley Rd. N19 2G 65
Witney Cl. UB10: Ick 4B 56
Witney Path SE23 3K 139
Wittenham Way E4 3A 36
Wittering Cl. KT2: King T 5D 132
Wittersham Rd. BR1: Broml 5H 141
Witts Ho. KT1: King T 3F 151
(off Winery La.)
Wivenhoe Cl. SE15 3H 121
Wivenhoe Ct. TW3: Houn 4D 112
Wivenhoe Rd. IG11: Bark 2A 90
Wiverton Rd. SE26 6J 139
Wiverton Twr. E1 7K 9
(off Leman St.)
Wix Rd. RM9: Dag 1D 90
Wix's La. SW4 3F 119
WLA Community Sports Cen. 1C 76
Woburn W13 5B 78
(off Clivedon Ct.)
Woburn Cl. SE28 6D 90
SW19 6A 136
Woburn Ct. CR0: C'don 1C 168
E18 2J 51
SE16 5H 103
(off Masters Dr.)
WC1 4E 6
(off Bernard St.)
Woburn Mans. WC1 5C 6
(off Torrington Pl.)
Woburn M. WC1 4D 6 (4H 83)
Woburn Pl. WC1 4E 6 (4J 83)
Woburn Rd. CR0: C'don 1C 168
SM5: Cars 1C 166
Woburn Sq. WC1 4D 6 (4H 83)
(not continuous)
Woburn Twr. UB5: N'olt 3B 76
(off Broomcroft Av.)
Woburn Wlk. WC1 2D 6 (3H 83)
Wodeham Gdns. E1 5G 85
Wodehouse Av. SE5 1F 121
Woffington Cl. KT1: Hamp W 1C 150
Wogan Ho. W1 6K 5
(off Portland Pl.)
Woking Cl. SW15 4B 116
Wolcot Ho. NW1 1B 6
(off Aldenham St.)
Woldham Pl. BR2: Broml 4A 160
Woldham Rd. BR2: Broml 4A 160
Wolds Dr. BR6: Farnb 4E 172
Wolfe Cl. BR2: Hayes 6J 159
UB4: Yead 3K 75
Wolfe Cres. SE7 5B 106
SE16 2K 103
Wolfe Ho. W12 7D 80
(off White City Est.)
W14 4H 99
Wolferton Rd. E12 4D 70
Wolffe Gdns. E15 6H 69
Wolfington Rd. SE27 4B 138
Wolfram Cl. SE13 5G 123
Wolftencroft Cl. SW11 3C 118
Wollaston Cl. SE1 4C 102
Wollaton Ho. N1 2A 84
(off Batchelor St.)
Wollett Ct. NW1 7G 65
(off St Pancras Way)
Wollstonecraft St. N1 1H 83
Wolmer Cl. HA8: Edg 4B 28
Wolmer Gdns. HA8: Edg 3B 28
Wolseley Av. SW19 2J 135
Wolseley Gdns. W4 6H 97
Wolseley Rd. CR4: Mitc 7E 154
E7 7K 69
HA3: W'stone 3J 41
N8 6H 47
N22 1K 47
RM7: Rush G 7K 55
W4 4J 97
Wolseley St. SE1 7K 15 (2G 103)
Wolsey Av. E6 3E 88
E17 3B 50
KT7: T Ditt 5K 149
Wolsey Cl. KT2: King T 1H 151
KT4: Wor Pk 4C 164
SE2 2C 108
SW20 7D 134
TW3: Houn 4G 113
UB2: S'hall 3G 95
Wolsey Ct. NW6 7A 64
SE9 6D 124
(off Court Rd.)
SW11 1C 118
(off Westbridge Rd.)
Wolsey Cres. CR0: New Ad 7E 170
SM4: Mord 7G 153
Wolsey Dr. KT2: King T 5E 132
KT12: Walt T 7B 148
Wolsey Gro. HA8: Edg 7E 28
Wolsey M. BR6: Chels 5K 173
NW5 6G 65
Wolsey Rd. EN1: Enf 2C 24
KT8: E Mos 4H 149
N1 5D 66
TW12: Hamp H 6F 131
TW15: Ashf 4A 128
TW16: Sun 7H 129
Wolsey St. E1 5J 85
Wolsey Way KT9: Chess 5G 163
Wolstenholme HA7: Stan 5G 27
Wolstonbury N12 5D 30
Wolvercote Rd. SE2 2D 108
Wolverley St. E2 3H 85
Wolverton SE17 5E 102
(not continuous)
Wolverton Av. KT2: King T 1G 151
Wolverton Gdns. W5 7F 79
W6 4F 99
Wolverton Rd. HA7: Stan 6G 27
Wolverton Way N14 5B 22
Wolves La. N13 7F 33
N22 7F 33
Womersley Rd. N8 6K 47
Wonersh Way SM2: Cheam 7F 165
Wonford Cl. KT2: King T 1A 152
Wontner Cl. N1 7C 66
Wontner Rd. SW17 2D 136
Wooburn Cl. UB8: Hil 4D 74
Woodall Av. EN3: Pond E 6E 24
Woodall Cl. E14 7D 86
KT9: Chess 7C 162
Woodall Rd. EN3: Pond E 6E 24
Woodbank Rd.
BR1: Broml 3H 141
Woodbastwick Rd. SE26 5K 139
Woodberry Av. HA2: Harr 4F 41
N21 2F 33
Woodberry Cl. NW7 7A 30
TW16: Sun 6J 129
Woodberry Cres. N10 3F 47
Woodberry Down N4 7C 48
Woodberry Down Est. N4 7C 48
(not continuous)
Woodberry Gdns. N12 6F 31
Woodberry Gro. DA5: Bexl 3K 145
N4 7C 48
N12 6F 31
Woodberry Way E4 7K 25
N12 6F 31
Woodbine Cl. TW2: Twick 2H 131
Woodbine Gro. EN2: Enf 1J 23
SE20 7H 139
Woodbine La. KT4: Wor Pk 3D 164
Woodbine Pl. E11 6J 51
Woodbine Rd. DA15: Sidc 1J 143
Woodbines Av.
KT1: King T 3D 150
Woodbine Ter. E9 6J 67
Woodborough Rd. SW15 4D 116
Woodbourne Av. SW16 3H 137
Woodbourne Cl. SW16 3J 137
Woodbourne Gdns.
SM6: W'gton 7F 167
Woodbridge Cl. N7 2K 65
NW2 3C 62
Woodbridge Ct. IG8: Wfd G 7H 37
Woodbridge Ho. E11 1H 69
Woodbridge Rd. IG11: Bark 5K 71
Woodbridge St. EC1 3A 8 (4B 84)
(not continuous)
Woodbridge Ter. RM6: Chad H 6B 54
Woodbrook Rd. SE2 6A 108
Woodburn Cl. NW4 5F 45
Woodbury Cl. CR0: C'don 2F 169
E11 4K 51
Woodbury Cres. IG5: Ilf 1D 52
Woodbury Gdns. SE12 3K 141
Woodbury Ho. SE26 3G 139
Woodbury Pk. Rd. W13 4B 78
Woodbury Rd. E17 4D 50
Woodbury St. SW17 5C 136
Woodchester Ho. E14 3D 104
(off Selsdon Way)
Woodchester Sq. W2 5K 81
Woodchurch Cl. DA14: Sidc 3H 143
Woodchurch Dr.
BR1: Broml 7B 142
Woodchurch Rd. NW6 7J 63
Wood Cl. E2 4G 85
HA1: Harr 7H 41
NW9 7K 43
Woodclyffe Dr. BR7: Chst 2E 160
Woodcock Cl.
TW6: H'row A 7C 174
Woodcock Ct. HA3: Kenton 7E 42
Woodcock Dell Av.
HA3: Kenton 7D 42
Woodcock Hill HA3: Kenton 5C 42
Woodcock Ho. E14 5C 86
(off Burgess St.)
Woodcocks E16 5A 88
Woodcombe Cres. SE23 1J 139
Woodcote Av. CR7: Thor H 4B 156
NW7 6K 29
SM6: W'gton 7F 167
Woodcote Cl. EN3: Pond E 6D 24
KT2: King T 5F 133
Woodcote Dr. BR6: Orp 1H 173
Woodcote Grn. SM6: W'gton 7G 167
Woodcote Ho. SE8 6B 104
(off Prince St.)
Woodcote M. SM6: W'gton 6F 167
Woodcote Pl. SE27 5B 138
Woodcote Rd. E11 7J 51
SM6: W'gton 6F 167
Woodcote Vs. SE27 5C 138
(off Woodcote Pl.)
Wood Cres. W12 7E 80
Wood Crest SM2: Sutt 7A 166
(off Christchurch Pk.)
Woodcroft N21 1F 33
SE9 3D 142
UB6: G'frd 6A 60
Woodcroft Av. HA7: Stan 1A 42
NW7 6F 29
Woodcroft Cl. SE9 6E 124
Woodcroft Cres. UB10: Hil 1D 74
Woodcroft M. SE8 4A 104
Woodcroft Rd. CR7: Thor H 5B 156
Wood Dr. BR7: Chst 6C 142
Woodedge Cl. E4 1C 36
WOOD END
UB4 5H 75
UB5 5G 59
The Wood End SM6: W'gton 7F 167
Wood End UB3: Hayes 6G 75
Woodend SE19 6C 138
SM1: Sutt 2A 166
Wood End Av. HA2: Harr 4F 59
UB5: N'olt 4F 59
Wood End Cl. UB5: N'olt 5H 59
Wood End Gdns. UB5: N'olt 5G 59
Woodend Gdns. EN2: Enf 4D 22
WOOD END GREEN 5F 75
Wood End Grn. Rd.
UB3: Hayes 5F 75
Wood End La. UB5: N'olt 6F 59
Wood End Rd. HA1: Harr 4H 59
Woodend Rd. E17 2E 50
Wood End Way UB5: N'olt 5G 59
Wooder Gdns. E7 4J 69
Wooderson Cl. SE25 4E 156
Woodfall Av. EN5: Barn 5C 20
Woodfall Rd. N4 2A 66
Woodfall St.
SW3 6E 16 (5D 100)
Wood Farm Cl. HA7: Stan 2G 27
Woodfarrs SE5 4D 120
Wood Fld. NW3 5D 64
Woodfield Av.
HA0: Wemb 3C 60
NW9 4A 44
SM5: Cars 6E 166
SW16 3H 137
W5 4C 78
Woodfield Cl. EN1: Enf 4K 23
SE19 7C 138
Woodfield Cres. W5 4C 78
Woodfield Dr. EN4: E Barn 1K 31
Woodfield Gdns.
KT3: N Mald 5B 152
Woodfield Gro. SW16 3H 137
Woodfield Ho. SE23 3K 139
(off Dacres Rd.)
Woodfield La. SW16 3H 137
Woodfield Pl. W9 4H 81
Woodfield Ri. WD23: Bush 1C 26
Woodfield Rd. TW4: Cran 2K 111
W5 4C 78
W9 5H 81
Woodfield Way N11 7C 32
WOODFORD 6F 37
Woodford Av. IG2: Ilf 5D 52
IG4: Ilf, Wfd G 3B 52
WOODFORD BRIDGE 6H 37
Woodford Bri. Rd. IG4: Ilf 3B 52
Woodford Ct. W12 2F 99
(off Shepherd's Bush Grn.)
Woodford Cres. HA5: Pinn 2K 39
Woodforde Ct. UB3: Harl 5F 93
Woodford Golf Course 5D 36
WOODFORD GREEN 6D 36
Woodford Green Athletics Club
6H 37
Woodford Hall Path E18 1H 51
Woodford Ho. E18 4J 51
Woodford New Rd. E17 4G 51
E18 1G 51
IG8: Wfd G 1G 51
Woodford Pl. HA9: Wemb 1E 60
Woodford Rd. E7 3K 69
E18 4J 51
WOODFORD SIDE 5C 36
Woodford Trad. Est.
IG8: Wfd G 2B 52
WOODFORD WELLS 3E 36
Woodgate Av. KT9: Chess 5D 162
Woodgate Dr. SW16 7H 137
Woodger Rd. W12 2E 98
Woodget Cl. E6 6C 88
Woodgrange Av.
EN1: Enf 6B 24
HA3: Kenton 5C 42
N12 6G 31
W5 1G 97
Woodgrange Cl. HA3: Kenton 5D 42
Woodgrange Gdns. EN1: Enf 6B 24
Woodgrange Ho. W5 1F 97
(off Woodgrange Av.)
Woodgrange Mans.
HA3: Kenton 5D 42
Woodgrange Rd. E7 5K 69
Woodgrange Ter. EN1: Enf 6B 24
WOOD GREEN 2K 47
Wood Grn. Animal Shelter 1B 48
(off Lordship La.)
Wood Grn. Hall N22 2K 47
(off Station Rd.)
Wood Grn. Shop. City 2A 48
Woodhall NW1 2A 6
(off Robert St.)
Woodhall Av. HA5: Pinn 1C 40
SE21 3F 139
Woodhall Cl. UB8: Uxb 5A 56
Woodhall Dr. HA5: Pinn 1B 40
SE21 3F 139
Woodhall Ga. HA5: Pinn 1B 40
Woodhall Ho. SW18 6B 118
Woodham Ct. E18 4H 51
Woodham Rd. SE6 3E 140
Woodhatch Cl. E6 5C 88
Woodhaven Gdns.
IG6: Ilf 4G 53
Woodhayes Rd. SW19 7E 134
Woodhead Dr. BR6: Orp 3J 173
Woodheyes Rd. NW10 5K 61
Woodhill SE18 4C 106
Woodhill Cres.
HA3: Kenton 6D 42
Wood Ho. NW6 2H 81
(off Albert Rd.)
Woodhouse Av. UB6: G'frd 2K 77
Woodhouse Cl. SE22 4G 121
UB3: Harl 3G 93
UB6: G'frd 1K 77
Woodhouse Gro. E12 6C 70
Woodhouse Rd. E11 3H 69
N12 6G 31
Woodhurst Av. BR5: Pet W 6G 161
Woodhurst Rd. SE2 5A 108
W3 7J 79
Woodies La. KT3: N Mald 6K 151
Woodington Cl. SE9 6E 124
Woodknoll Dr. BR7: Chst 1D 160
Woodland App. UB6: G'frd 6A 60
Woodland Cl. IG8: Wfd G 3E 36
KT19: Ewe 6A 164
NW9 6J 43
SE19 6E 138
UB10: Ick 2D 56
Woodland Ct. E11 6J 51
(off New Wanstead)
N7 6J 65
Woodland Cres. SE10 6G 105
SE16 2K 103
Woodland Gdns. N10 5F 47
TW7: Isle 3J 113
Woodland Gro. SE10 5G 105
Woodland Hill SE19 6E 138
Woodland M. SE13 3D 122
(off Loampit Hill)
SW16 3J 137
Woodland Ri. N10 4F 47
UB6: G'frd 6A 60
Woodland Rd. CR7: Thor H 4A 156
E4 1K 35
N11 5A 32
SE19 5E 138
WOODLANDS 3J 113
The Woodlands HA1: Harr 2J 59
HA7: Stan 5G 27
N5 4C 66
N12 6F 31
N14 1A 32
SE13 7F 123
SE19 7C 138
SM6: W'gton 7F 167
SW9 7B 102
(off Langton Rd.)
TW7: Isle 2K 113
Woodlands BR2: Broml 4H 159
DA6: Bex 5H 127
HA2: Harr 4E 40
NW11 5G 45
SW20 4E 152
Woodlands Av. DA15: Sidc 1J 143
E11 1K 69
HA4: Ruis 7A 40
KT3: N Mald 1J 151
KT4: Wor Pk 2B 164
N3 7F 31
RM6: Chad H 7E 54
W3 1H 97
Woodlands Cl. BR1: Broml 2D 160
KT10: Clay 7A 162
NW11 5G 45
Woodlands Ct. BR1: Broml 1H 159
HA1: Harr 5K 41
KT12: Walt T 7K 147
NW10 1F 81
(off Wrentham Av.)
SE23 7H 121
Woodlands Dr. HA7: Stan 6E 26
TW16: Sun 2A 148
Woodlands Gdns. E17 4G 51
Woodlands Ga. SW15 5H 117
(off Woodlands Way)
Woodlands Gro. TW7: Isle 2J 113
Woodlands Hgts. SE3 6H 105
(off Vanburgh Hill)
Woodlands Pde. TW15: Ashf 6E 128
Woodlands Pk. DA5: Bexl 4K 145
Woodlands Pk. Rd. N15 5B 48
SE10 6G 105
(not continuous)
Woodlands Rd. BR1: Broml 2C 160
BR6: Chels 6K 173
DA7: Bex 3E 126
E11 2G 69
E17 3E 50
EN2: Enf 1J 23
HA1: Harr 5K 41
IG1: Ilf 3G 71
KT6: Surb 7D 150
N9 1D 34
SW13 3B 116
TW7: Isle 3H 113
UB1: S'hall 1B 94
Woodlands St. SE13 7F 123
Woodland St. E8 6F 67
Woodlands Way SW15 5H 117
Woodland Ter. SE7 4C 106
Woodland Wlk. BR1: Broml 4F 141
(not continuous)
KT19: Ewe 6G 163
NW3 5C 64
SE10 5G 105
Woodland Way BR4: W W'ck 4D 170
BR5: Pet W 4G 161
CR0: C'don 1A 170
CR4: Mitc 7E 136
IG8: Wfd G 3E 36
KT5: Surb 2H 163
N21 2F 33
NW7 6G 29
SE2 4D 108
SM4: Mord 4H 153
Wood La. HA4: Ruis 1F 57
HA7: Stan 3F 27
IG8: Wfd G 4C 36
N6 6F 47
NW9 7K 43
RM8: Dag 4C 72
RM9: Dag 4C 72
RM10: Dag 2G 73
TW7: Isle 6J 95
W12 6E 80
Wood La. Studios W12 6E 80
Woodlawn Cl. SW15 5H 117
Woodlawn Cres. TW2: Whitt 2F 131
Woodlawn Dr. TW13: Felt 2B 130
Woodlawn Rd. SW6 7F 99
Woodlawns KT19: Ewe 7K 163
Woodlea Dr. BR2: Broml 5G 159
Woodlea Rd. N16 3E 66
Woodleigh E18 1J 51
Woodleigh Av. N12 6H 31
Woodleigh Gdns. SW16 3J 137
Woodley Cl. SW17 7D 136
Woodley La. SM5: Cars 3C 166
Wood Lodge Gdns.
BR1: Broml 7C 142
Wood Lodge La. BR4: W W'ck 3E 170
Woodman M. TW9: Kew 1H 115
Woodman Pde. E16 1E 106
(off Woodman St.)
Woodmans Gro. NW10 5B 62
Woodman's M. W12 5D 80
Woodmansterne Rd. SM5: Cars 7C 166
SW16 7G 137
Woodman St. E16 1E 106
Wood Martyn Ct. BR6: Orp 2K 173
(off Orchard Gro.)
Wood Mead N17 6B 34
Woodmere SE9 1D 142
Woodmere Av. CR0: C'don 7J 157
Woodmere Cl. CR0: C'don 7K 157
SW11 3E 118
Woodmere Ct. N14 7A 22
Woodmere Gdns. CR0: C'don 7K 157
Woodmere Way BR3: Beck 5F 159
Woodmill Cl. SW15 6C 116
Woodmill Rd. E5 2J 67
Woodmill St. SE16 3F 103
Woodnook Rd. SW16 5F 137
Woodpecker Cl. HA3: Hrw W 1K 41
N9 6C 24
WD23: Bush 1B 26
Woodpecker M. SE13 4F 123
(off Freshfield Cl.)
Woodpecker Mt. CR0: Sels 7A 170
Woodpecker Rd. SE14 6A 104
SE28 7C 90
Woodquest Av. SE24 5C 120
Wood Retreat SE18 7H 107
Wood Ride BR5: Pet W 4H 161
EN4: Had W 1G 21
Woodridge Cl. EN2: Enf 1F 23
Woodridings Av. HA5: Hat E 1D 40
Woodridings Cl. HA5: Hat E 1C 40
Woodridings Ct. N22 1H 47
Woodriffe Rd. E11 7F 51
Wood Ri. HA5: Eastc 5J 39
Wood Rd. NW10 7J 61
TW17: Shep 4C 146
Woodrow SE18 4D 106
Woodrow Av. UB4: Hayes 5H 75
Woodrow Cl. UB6: G'frd 7B 60
Woodrow Ct. N17 7C 34
SE5 1C 120
(off Camberwell Sta. Rd.)
Woodrush Cl. SE14 7A 104
Woodrush Way RM6: Chad H 4D 54
The Woods UB10: Ick 4D 56
Wood's Bldgs. E1 5H 85
(off Winthrop St.)
Woods Cl. TW3: Houn 3F 113
(off High St.)
Woodseer St. E1 5K 9 (5F 85)
Woodsford SE17 5D 102
(off Portland St.)
Woodsford Sq. W14 2G 99
Woodshire Rd. RM10: Dag 3H 73
Woods Ho. SW1 6J 17 (5F 101)
SW8 1G 119
(off Wadhurst Rd.)

Woodside—Yarnton Way

WOODSIDE . . . 6G 157
Woodside IG9: Buck H . . . 2F 37
N10 . . . 3E 46
NW11 . . . 5J 45
SW19 . . . 6H 135
Woodside Av. BR7: Chst . . . 5G 143
HA0: Wemb . . . 1E 78
KT10: Esh . . . 7J 149
N6 . . . 5D 46
N10 . . . 5D 46
N12 . . . 4E 30
SE25 . . . 6H 157
Woodside Cl. DA7: Bex . . . 4K 127
HA0: Wemb . . . 1E 78
HA4: Ruis . . . 6F 39
HA7: Stan . . . 5G 27
KT5: Surb . . . 7J 151
Woodside Ct. E12 . . . 1A 70
N12 . . . 4E 30
RM7: Mawney . . . 4G 55
W5 . . . 1E 96
Woodside Ct. Rd. CR0: C'don . . . 7G 157
Woodside Cres. DA15: Sidc . . . 3J 143
Woodside Dr. DA2: Wilm . . . 4K 145
Woodside End HA0: Wemb . . . 1E 78
Woodside Gdns. E4 . . . 6J 35
N17 . . . 2E 48
Woodside Grange Rd. N12 . . . 4E 30
Woodside Grn. SE25 . . . 6G 157
Woodside Gro. N12 . . . 3F 31
Woodside Ho. SW19 . . . 6H 135
Woodside La. DA5: Bexl . . . 6D 126
N12 . . . 3F 31
Woodside M. SE22 . . . 5F 121
Woodside Pde. DA15: Sidc . . . 3J 143
WOODSIDE PARK . . . 4D 30
Woodside Pk. SE25 . . . 6H 157
Woodside Pk. Av. E17 . . . 4F 51
Woodside Pk. Rd. N12 . . . 4E 30
Woodside Pl. HA0: Wemb . . . 1E 78
Woodside Rd. BR1: Broml . . . 5C 160
DA7: Bex . . . 4K 127
DA15: Sidc . . . 3J 143
E13 . . . 4A 88
IG8: Wfd G . . . 4D 36
KT2: King T . . . 7E 132
KT3: N Mald . . . 2K 151
N22 . . . 7E 32
SE25 . . . 6H 157
SM1: Sutt . . . 3A 166
Woodside Way CR0: C'don . . . 6J 157
CR4: Mitc . . . 1F 155
Woods M. W1 . . . 2G 11 (7E 82)
Woodsome Rd. NW5 . . . 3E 64
Woods Pl. SE1 . . . 3E 102
Woodspring Rd. SW19 . . . 2G 135
Woods Rd. SE15 . . . 1H 121
Woodstar Ho. *SE15* . . . *7G 103*
(off Reddins Rd.)
Woodstead Gro. HA8: Edg . . . 6K 27
THE WOODSTOCK . . . 7H 153
Woodstock Av. NW11 . . . 7G 45
SM3: Sutt . . . 7H 153
TW7: Isle . . . 5A 114
UB1: S'hall . . . 3D 76
W13 . . . 3A 96
Woodstock Cl. DA5: Bexl . . . 7F 127
HA7: Stan . . . 2E 42
Woodstock Ct. SE11 . . . 5H 19 (5K 101)
SE12 . . . 6J 123
Woodstock Cres. N9 . . . 6C 24
Woodstock Dr. UB10: Ick . . . 4A 56
Woodstock Gdns. BR3: Beck . . . 1D 158
IG3: Ilf . . . 2A 72
UB4: Hayes . . . 5H 75
Woodstock Grange W5 . . . 1E 96
Woodstock Gro. W12 . . . 2F 99
Woodstock La. KT9: Chess . . . 4B 162
Woodstock La. Nth.
KT6: Surb . . . 2C 162
Woodstock La. Sth.
KT9: Chess . . . 5B 162
KT10: Clay . . . 5B 162
Woodstock M. W1 . . . 6H 5
Woodstock Ri. SM3: Sutt . . . 7H 153
Woodstock Rd. CR0: C'don . . . 3D 168
E7 . . . 7A 70
E17 . . . 2F 51
HA0: Wemb . . . 1F 79
N4 . . . 1A 66
NW11 . . . 7H 45
SM5: Cars . . . 5E 166
W4 . . . 4A 98
Woodstock St. W1 . . . 1J 11 (6F 83)
Woodstock Studios *W12* . . . *2F 99*
(off Woodstock Gro.)
Woodstock Ter. E14 . . . 7D 86
Woodstock Way CR4: Mitc . . . 2F 155
Woodstone Av. KT17: Ewe . . . 5C 164
WOOD STREET . . . 3E 50
Wood St. CR4: Mitc . . . 7E 154
E17 . . . 3E 50
EC2 . . . 7D 8 (6C 84)
(not continuous)
EN5: Barn . . . 4A 20
KT1: King T . . . 2D 150
W4 . . . 5A 98
Woodsyre SE26 . . . 4F 139
Wood Ter. NW2 . . . 3D 62
Woodthorpe Rd. SW15 . . . 4D 116
TW15: Ashf . . . 5A 128
Woodtree Cl. NW4 . . . 2F 45
Wood Va. N10 . . . 5G 47
SE23 . . . 1H 139
Woodvale Av. SE25 . . . 3F 157
Woodvale Ct. *BR1: Broml* . . . *1K 159*
(off Widmore Rd.)
Wood Va. Est. SE23 . . . 7J 121
Woodvale Wlk. SE27 . . . 5C 138
Woodvale Way NW11 . . . 3F 63
Woodview Av. E4 . . . 4K 35
Woodview Cl. BR6: Farnb . . . 2G 173
N4 . . . 7B 48
SW15 . . . 4K 133
Wood Vw. M. RM1: Rom . . . 1K 55
Woodview M. SE19 . . . 1E 156
The Woodville *W5* . . . *6D 78*
(off Woodville Rd.)
Woodville Cl. SE3 . . . 1K 123
SE12 . . . 5J 123
TW11: Tedd . . . 4A 132
Woodville Ct. N14 . . . 5B 22
SE10 . . . *1E 122*
(off Blissett St.)
SE19 . . . 1F 157
Woodville Gdns. HA4: Ruis . . . 7E 38
IG6: Ilf . . . 3F 53
KT6: Surb . . . 7D 150
NW11 . . . 7F 45
W5 . . . 6E 78
Woodville Gro. DA16: Well . . . 3A 126
Woodville Ho. *SE1* . . . *3F 103*
(off St Saviour's Est.)
Woodville Rd. CR7: Thor H . . . 4C 156
E11 . . . 1H 69
E17 . . . 4B 50
E18 . . . 2K 51
EN5: New Bar . . . 3E 20
N16 . . . 5E 66
NW6 . . . 2H 81
NW11 . . . 7F 45
SM4: Mord . . . 4J 153
TW10: Ham . . . 3B 132
W5 . . . 6D 78
Woodville St. SE18 . . . 4C 106
Woodward Av. NW4 . . . 5C 44
Woodward Cl. KT10: Clay . . . 6A 162
Woodwarde Rd. SE22 . . . 6E 120
Woodward Gdns. HA7: Stan . . . 7E 26
RM9: Dag . . . 7C 72
Woodward Rd. RM9: Dag . . . 7B 72
Woodward's Footpath
TW2: Whitt . . . 6G 113
Wood Way BR6: Farnb . . . 2E 172
Woodway Cres. HA1: Harr . . . 6A 42
Woodwell St. SW18 . . . 5A 118
Wood Wharf SE10 . . . 6D 104
Wood Wharf Bus. Pk. E14 . . . 1D 104
Woodyard Cl. NW5 . . . 5E 64
Woodyard La. SE21 . . . 7E 120
Woodyates Rd. SE12 . . . 6J 123
Woolacombe Rd. SE3 . . . 1A 124
Woolacombe Way UB3: Harl . . . 4G 93
Woolcombes Ct. *SE16* . . . *1K 103*
(off Princes Riverside Rd.)
Wooldridge Cl. TW14: Bedf . . . 1E 128
Wooler St. SE17 . . . 5D 102
Woolf Cl. SE28 . . . 1B 108
Woolf M. *WC1* . . . *3D 6*
(off Burton Pl.)
Woolford Ct. *SE5* . . . *2C 120*
(off Coldharbour La.)
Woolgar M. *N16* . . . *5E 66*
(off Gillett St.)
Woollaston Rd. N4 . . . 6B 48
Woolley Ho. *SW9* . . . *3B 120*
(off Loughborough Rd.)
Woollon Ho. *E1* . . . *6J 85*
(off Clark St.)
Woolmead Av. NW9 . . . 7C 44
Woolmer Gdns. N18 . . . 6B 34
Woolmer Rd. N18 . . . 5B 34
Woolmore St. E14 . . . 7E 86
Woolneigh St. SW6 . . . 3K 117
Woolridge Way E9 . . . 7J 67
Wool Rd. SW20 . . . 6D 134
Woolstaplers Way SE16 . . . 3G 103
Woolston Cl. E17 . . . 2K 49
Woolstone Ho. *E2* . . . *1G 85*
(off Whiston Rd.)
Woolstone Rd. SE23 . . . 2A 140
WOOLWICH . . . 3D 106
The Woolwich Cen. . . . *4E 106*
(off Wellington St.)
Woolwich Chu. St. SE18 . . . 3C 106
Woolwich Comn. SE18 . . . 6E 106
Woolwich Comn. Youth Club . . . 6E 106
Woolwich Dockyard Ind. Est.
SE18 . . . 3C 106
Woolwich High St.
SE18 . . . 3E 106
Woolwich Ho. *UB3: Harl* . . . *3E 92*
(off Nine Acres Cl.)
Woolwich Mnr. Way E6 . . . 4D 88
E16 . . . 2F 107
Woolwich New Rd. SE18 . . . 5E 106
Woolwich Rd. DA6: Bex . . . 3G 127
DA7: Bex . . . 3G 127
DA17: Belv . . . 5F 109
SE2 . . . 6D 108
SE7 . . . 5H 105
SE10 . . . 5H 105
Woolwich Trade Pk. SE28 . . . 3H 107
Wooster Gdns. E14 . . . 6F 87
Wooster M. HA2: Harr . . . 3G 41
Wooster Pl. *SE1* . . . *4D 102*
(off Searles Rd.)
Wootton Gro. N3 . . . 1J 45
Wootton St. SE1 . . . 5K 13 (1A 102)
Worbeck Rd. SE20 . . . 2H 157
Worcester Av. N17 . . . 7B 34
Worcester Cl. CR0: C'don . . . 2C 170
CR4: Mitc . . . 2E 154
NW2 . . . 3D 62
SE20 . . . 1G 157
Worcester Ct. HA1: Harr . . . 3J 41
KT4: Wor Pk . . . 3A 164
N12 . . . 5E 30
W7 . . . *6K 77*
(off Copley Cl.)
W9 . . . *5J 81*
(off Elmfield Way)
Worcester Cres. IG8: Wfd G . . . 5E 36
NW7 . . . 3F 29
Worcester Dr. TW15: Ashf . . . 5D 128
W4 . . . 2A 98
Worcester Gdns. IG1: Ilf . . . 7C 52
KT4: Wor Pk . . . 3A 164
SW11 . . . *5D 118*
(off Grandison Rd.)
UB6: G'frd . . . 6H 59
Worcester Ho. *SE11* . . . *2J 19*
(off Kennington Rd.)
SW9 . . . *7A 102*
(off Cranmer Rd.)
W2 . . . *6A 82*
(off Hallfield Est.)
Worcester M. NW6 . . . 6K 63
WORCESTER PARK . . . 1C 164
Worcester Pk. Rd.
KT4: Wor Pk . . . 3K 163
Worcester Point EC1 . . . 3C 84
Worcester Rd. E12 . . . 4D 70
E17 . . . 2K 49
SM2: Sutt . . . 7J 165
SW19 . . . 5H 135
Worcesters Av. EN1: Enf . . . 1B 24
Wordsworth Av. E12 . . . 7C 70
E18 . . . 3H 51
UB6: G'frd . . . 3H 77
Wordsworth Ct. HA1: Harr . . . 7J 41
Wordsworth Dr. SM3: Cheam . . . 4E 164
Wordsworth Ho. *NW6* . . . *3J 81*
(off Stafford Rd.)
SE18 . . . *6E 106*
(off Woolwich Comn.)
Wordsworth Mans. *W14* . . . *6H 99*
(off Queens Club Gdns.)
Wordsworth Pde. N8 . . . 4B 48
Wordsworth Pl. NW5 . . . 5D 64
Wordsworth Rd. DA16: Well . . . 1J 125
N16 . . . 4E 66
SE1 . . . 4F 103
SE20 . . . 7K 139
SM6: W'gton . . . 6G 167
TW12: Hamp . . . 4D 130
Wordsworth Wlk. NW11 . . . 4J 45
Wordsworth Way
UB7: W Dray . . . 4A 92
Worfield St. SW11 . . . 7C 100
Worgan St. SE11 . . . 5G 19 (5K 101)
SE16 . . . 4K 103
Worland Rd. E15 . . . 7G 69
World Bus. Cen.
TW6: H'row A . . . 1E 110
World of Golf Cen.
Croydon . . . 5J 157
New Malden . . . 3C 152
World Rugby Mus. . . . 6J 113
WORLD'S END . . . 3E 22
Worlds End Est. SW10 . . . 7B 100
World's End La. EN2: Enf . . . 5E 22
N21 . . . 5E 22
Worlds End La. BR6: Chels . . . 6K 173
World's End Pas. *SW10* . . . *7B 100*
(off Worlds End Est.)
World's End Pl. *SW10* . . . *7B 100*
(off Worlds End Est.)
Worleys Dr. BR6: Orp . . . 4H 173
Worlidge St. W6 . . . 5E 98
Worlingham Rd. SE22 . . . 4F 121
Wormholt Rd. W12 . . . 7C 80
Wormwood Scrubs Pk. . . . 5B 80
Wormwood St. EC2 . . . 7G 9 (6E 84)
Wornington Rd. W10 . . . 4G 81
(not continuous)
Woronzow Rd. NW8 . . . 1B 82
Worple Av. SW19 . . . 7F 135
TW7: Isle . . . 5A 114
Worple Cl. HA2: Harr . . . 1D 58
Worple Rd. SW19 . . . 2E 152
SW20 . . . 2E 152
TW7: Isle . . . 4A 114
Worple Rd. M. SW19 . . . 6H 135
Worple St. SW14 . . . 3K 115
Worple Way HA2: Harr . . . 1D 58
TW10: Rich . . . 5E 114
Worrall La. UB8: Uxb . . . 7A 56
Worship St. EC2 . . . 4F 9 (4D 84)
(not continuous)
Worslade Rd. SW17 . . . 4B 136
Worsley Bri. Rd. BR3: Beck . . . 7C 140
SE26 . . . 4B 140
Worsley Grange BR7: Chst . . . 6G 143
Worsley Gro. E5 . . . 4G 67
Worsley Ho. SE23 . . . 2J 139
Worsley Rd. E11 . . . 4G 69
Worsopp Dr. SW4 . . . 5G 119
Worth Cl. BR6: Orp . . . 4J 173
Worthfield Cl. KT19: Ewe . . . 7K 163
Worth Gro. SE17 . . . 5D 102
Worthing Cl. E15 . . . 1G 87
Worthing Rd. TW5: Hest . . . 6D 94
Worthington Cl. CR4: Mitc . . . 4F 155
Worthington Ho. *EC1* . . . *1K 7*
(off Myddelton Pas.)
Worthington Rd. KT6: Surb . . . 1F 163
Wortley Rd. CR0: C'don . . . 7A 156
E6 . . . 7B 70
Worton Ct. TW7: Isle . . . 4J 113
Worton Gdns. TW7: Isle . . . 2H 113
Worton Hall Ind. Est.
TW7: Isle . . . 4J 113
Worton Rd. TW7: Isle . . . 4H 113
Worton Way TW3: Houn . . . 2H 113
TW7: Houn, Isle . . . 2H 113
Wotton Ct. *E14* . . . *7F 87*
(off Jamestown Way)
Wotton Rd. NW2 . . . 3E 62
SE8 . . . 6B 104
Wouldham Rd. E16 . . . 6H 87
Wragby Rd. E11 . . . 3G 69
Wrampling Pl. N9 . . . 1B 34
Wrangthorn Wlk. CR0: Wadd . . . 4A 168
Wraxall Rd. *E3* . . . *4B 86*
(off Hamlets Way)
Wray Av. IG5: Ilf . . . 3E 52
Wrayburn Ho. *SE16* . . . *2G 103*
(off Llewellyn St.)
Wray Cres. N4 . . . 2J 65
Wrayfield Rd. SM3: Cheam . . . 3F 165
Wray Rd. SM2: Cheam . . . 7H 165
Wraysbury Cl. TW4: Houn . . . 5C 112
Wrays Way UB4: Hayes . . . 4G 75
Wrekin Rd. SE18 . . . 7G 107
Wren Av. NW2 . . . 4E 62
UB2: S'hall . . . 4D 94
UB10: Uxb . . . 1B 74
Wren Cl. E16 . . . 6H 87
N9 . . . 1E 34
TW6: H'row A . . . 6C 174
Wren Ct. *CR0: C'don* . . . *4D 168*
(off Coombe Rd.)
Wren Cres. WD23: Bush . . . 1B 26
Wren Gdns. RM9: Dag . . . 5D 72
Wren Ho. *E3* . . . *2A 86*
(off Gernon Rd.)
KT1: Hamp W . . . *2D 150*
(off High St.)
SW1 . . . *6C 18*
(off Aylesford St.)
Wren Landing E14 . . . 1C 104
Wren La. HA4: Ruis . . . 6K 39
Wren M. SE11 . . . 4H 19 (4K 101)
SE13 . . . 4G 123
Wrenn Ho. SW13 . . . 6E 98
Wren Path SE28 . . . 3H 107
Wren Rd. DA14: Sidc . . . 4C 144
RM9: Dag . . . 5D 72
SE5 . . . 1D 120
Wren's Av. TW15: Ashf . . . 4E 128
Wren's Pk. Ho. E5 . . . 2H 67
Wren St. WC1 . . . 3H 7 (4K 83)
Wrentham Av. NW10 . . . 2F 81
Wrenthorpe Rd.
BR1: Broml . . . 4G 141
Wren Vw. N6 . . . 7G 47
Wrenwood Way HA5: Eastc . . . 4K 39
Wrexham Rd. E3 . . . 2C 86
Wricklemarsh Rd. SE3 . . . 2K 123
(not continuous)
Wrigglesworth St. SE14 . . . 7K 103
Wright Cl. SE13 . . . 4F 123
Wright Gdns. TW17: Shep . . . 5C 146
Wright Rd. TW5: Hest . . . 7A 94
Wrights All. SW19 . . . 6E 134
Wrights Cl. RM10: Dag . . . 4H 73
Wrights Grn. SW4 . . . 4H 119
Wright's La. W8 . . . 3K 99
Wrights Pl. NW10 . . . 6J 61
Wright's Rd. E3 . . . 2B 86
(not continuous)
Wrights Rd. SE25 . . . 3E 156
Wrights Row SM6: W'gton . . . 4F 167
Wrights Wlk. SW14 . . . 3K 115
Wright Way TW6: H'row A . . . 5C 174
Wrigley Cl. E4 . . . 5A 36
Writtle Ho. NW9 . . . 2B 44
Wrotham Ho. *BR3: Beck* . . . *7B 140*
(off Sellindge Cl.)
SE1 . . . *3D 102*
(off Law St.)
Wrotham Rd. DA16: Well . . . 1C 126
EN5: Barn . . . 2B 20
NW1 . . . 7G 65
W13 . . . 1C 96
Wrottesley Rd. NW10 . . . 2C 80
SE18 . . . 6G 107
Wroughton Rd. SW11 . . . 5D 118
Wroughton Ter. NW4 . . . 4D 44
Wroxall Rd. RM9: Dag . . . 6C 72
Wroxham Gdns. N11 . . . 7C 32
Wroxham Rd. SE28 . . . 7D 90
Wroxham Way IG6: Ilf . . . 1F 53
Wroxton Rd. SE15 . . . 2J 121
THE WRYTHE . . . 3D 166
Wrythe Grn. SM5: Cars . . . 3D 166
Wrythe Grn. Rd. SM5: Cars . . . 3D 166
Wrythe La. SM5: Cars . . . 1A 166
Wulfstan St. W12 . . . 5B 80
Wyatt Cl. SE16 . . . 2B 104
TW13: Felt . . . 1B 130
UB4: Hayes . . . 5J 75
WD23: Bush . . . 1C 26
Wyatt Ct. HA0: Wemb . . . 7E 60
W3 . . . *3J 97*
(off All Saints Rd.)
Wyatt Dr. SW13 . . . 6D 98
Wyatt Ho. *NW8* . . . *4B 4*
(off Frampton St.)
SE3 . . . 2H 123
TW1: Twick . . . 6D 114
Wyatt Pk. Rd. SW2 . . . 2J 137
Wyatt Point SE28 . . . 2G 107
Wyatt Rd. E7 . . . 6J 69
N5 . . . 3C 66
Wyatts La. E17 . . . 3E 50
Wybert St. NW1 . . . 3A 6 (4G 83)
Wyborne Ho. NW10 . . . 7J 61
Wyborne Way NW10 . . . 7J 61
Wyburn Av. EN5: Barn . . . 3C 20
Wychcombe Studios NW3 . . . 6D 64
Wyche Gro. CR2: S Croy . . . 7D 168
Wych Elm Cl. KT2: King T . . . 7F 133
Wych Elm Lodge BR1: Broml . . . 7H 141
Wych Elm Pas. KT2: King T . . . 7F 133
Wycherley Cl. SE3 . . . 7H 105
Wycherley Cres.
EN5: New Bar . . . 6E 20
Wychwood Av. CR7: Thor H . . . 3C 156
HA8: Edg . . . 6J 27
Wychwood Cl. HA8: Edg . . . 6J 27
TW16: Sun . . . 6J 129
Wychwood End N6 . . . 7G 47
Wychwood Gdns. IG5: Ilf . . . 4D 52
Wychwood Way SE19 . . . 6D 138
Wyclif Ct. *EC1* . . . *2A 8*
(off Wyclif St.)
Wycliffe Cl. DA16: Well . . . 1K 125
Wycliffe Rd. SW11 . . . 2E 118
SW19 . . . 6K 135
Wyclif St. EC1 . . . 2A 8 (3B 84)
Wycombe Gdns. NW11 . . . 2J 63
Wycombe Ho. *NW8* . . . *3C 4*
(off Grendon St.)
Wycombe Pl. SW18 . . . 6A 118
Wycombe Rd. HA0: Wemb . . . 1G 79
IG2: Ilf . . . 5D 52
N17 . . . 1G 49
Wycombe Sq. W8 . . . 1H 99
Wydehurst Rd. CR0: C'don . . . 7G 157
Wydell Cl. SM4: Mord . . . 6F 153
Wydeville Mnr. Rd. SE12 . . . 4K 141
Wye Cl. BR6: Orp . . . 7K 161
HA4: Ruis . . . 6E 38
TW15: Ashf . . . 4D 128
Wye Ct. *W13* . . . *5B 78*
(off Malvern Way)
Wyemead Cres. E4 . . . 2B 36
Wye St. SW11 . . . 2B 118
Wyevale Cl. HA5: Eastc . . . 3J 39
Wyfields IG5: Ilf . . . 1F 53
Wyfold Ho. *SE2* . . . *2D 108*
(off Wolvercote Rd.)
Wyfold Rd. SW6 . . . 7G 99
Wyhill Wlk. RM10: Dag . . . 6J 73
Wyke Cl. TW7: Isle . . . 6K 95
Wyke Gdns. W7 . . . 3A 96
Wyke Green Golf Course . . . 6K 95
Wykeham Av. RM9: Dag . . . 6C 72
Wykeham Cl. HA3: W'stone . . . 1K 41
UB7: Sip . . . 6C 92
Wykeham Ct. *NW4* . . . *5E 44*
(off Wykeham Rd.)
Wykeham Grn. RM9: Dag . . . 6C 72
Wykeham Hill HA9: Wemb . . . 1F 61
Wykeham Ho. *SE1* . . . *5C 14*
(off Union St.)
Wykeham Ri. N20 . . . 1B 30
Wykeham Rd. HA3: Kenton . . . 4B 42
NW4 . . . 4E 44
Wyke Rd. E3 . . . 7C 68
SW20 . . . 2E 152
Wylchin Cl. HA5: Eastc . . . 3H 39
Wyldes Cl. NW11 . . . 1A 64
Wyldfield Gdns. N9 . . . 2A 34
Wyld Way HA9: Wemb . . . 6H 61
Wyleu St. SE23 . . . 7A 122
Wyllen Cl. E1 . . . 4J 85
Wymering Mans. *W9* . . . *3J 81*
(off Wymering Rd.)
Wymering Rd. W9 . . . 3J 81
Wymondham Ct. *NW8* . . . *1B 82*
(off Queensmead)
Wymond St. SW15 . . . 3E 116
Wynan Rd. E14 . . . 5D 104
Wynash Gdns. SM5: Cars . . . 5C 166
Wynaud Ct. N22 . . . 6E 32
Wyncham Av. DA15: Sidc . . . 1J 143
Wyncham Ho. *DA15: Sidc* . . . *2A 144*
(off Longlands Rd.)
Wynchgate HA3: Hrw W . . . 7D 26
N14 . . . 1C 32
N21 . . . 1C 32
UB5: N'olt . . . 5C 58
Wyncroft Cl. BR1: Broml . . . 3D 160
Wyndale Av. NW9 . . . 6G 43
Wyndcliff Rd. SE7 . . . 6K 105
Wyndcroft Cl. EN2: Enf . . . 3G 23
Wyndham Apts. SE10 . . . 5G 105
Wyndham Cl. BR6: Farnb . . . 1G 173
SM2: Sutt . . . 7J 165
Wyndham Ct. W7 . . . 4A 96
Wyndham Cres. N19 . . . 3G 65
TW4: Houn . . . 6E 112
Wyndham Deedes Ho. *E2* . . . *2G 85*
(off Hackney Rd.)
Wyndham Est. SE5 . . . 7C 102
Wyndham Ho. *E14* . . . *2D 104*
(off Marsh Wall)
SW1 . . . *4G 17*
(off Sloane Sq.)
Wyndham M. W1 . . . 6E 4 (5D 82)
Wyndham Pl. W1 . . . 6E 4 (5D 82)
Wyndham Rd. E6 . . . 7B 70
EN4: E Barn . . . 1J 31
KT2: King T . . . 7F 133
SE5 . . . 7C 102
W13 . . . 3B 96
Wyndhams Ct. *E8* . . . *7F 67*
(off Celandine Dr.)
Wyndham's Theatre . . . *2E 12*
(off Charing Cross Rd.)
Wyndham St. W1 . . . 5E 4 (5D 82)
Wyndham Yd. W1 . . . 6E 4 (5D 82)
Wyndhurst Cl. CR2: S Croy . . . 7B 168
Wyneham Rd. SE24 . . . 5D 120
Wynell Rd. SE23 . . . 3K 139
Wynford Pl. DA17: Belv . . . 6G 109
Wynford Rd. N1 . . . 2K 83
Wynford Way SE9 . . . 3D 142
Wynlie Gdns. HA5: Pinn . . . 2K 39
Wynn Bri. Cl. IG8: Wfd G . . . 1B 52
Wynndale Rd. E18 . . . 1K 51
Wynne Rd. SW9 . . . 2A 120
Wynn's Av. DA15: Sidc . . . 5K 125
Wynnstay Gdns. W8 . . . 3J 99
Wynter St. SW11 . . . 4A 118
Wynton Gdns. SE25 . . . 5F 157
Wynton Pl. W3 . . . 6H 79
Wynyard Ho. *SE11* . . . *5H 19*
(off Loughborough St.)
Wynyard Ter. SE11 . . . 5H 19 (5K 101)
Wynyatt St. EC1 . . . 2A 8 (3B 84)
Wyre Gro. HA8: Edg . . . 3C 28
UB3: Harl . . . 4J 93
Wyresdale Cres. UB6: G'frd . . . 3K 77
Wyteleaf Cl. HA4: Ruis . . . 6E 38
Wytham Ho. *NW8* . . . *4B 4*
(off Church St. Est.)
Wythburn Ct. *W1* . . . *7E 4*
(off Wythburn Pl.)
Wythburn Pl. W1 . . . 1E 10 (6D 82)
Wythenshawe Rd.
RM10: Dag . . . 3G 73
Wythens Wlk. SE9 . . . 6F 125
Wythes Cl. BR1: Broml . . . 2D 160
Wythes Rd. E16 . . . 1C 106
Wythfield Rd. SE9 . . . 6D 124
Wyvell Cl. CR0: C'don . . . 7K 157
Wyvenhoe Rd. HA2: Harr . . . 4G 59
Wyvern Est. KT3: N Mald . . . 4C 152
Wyvil Rd. SW8 . . . 7J 101
Wyvis St. E14 . . . 5D 86

X

Xylon Ho. KT4: Wor Pk . . . 2D 164

Y

Yabsley St. E14 . . . 1E 104
Yaldham Ho. *SE1* . . . *4E 102*
(off Old Kent Rd.)
Yalding Rd. SE16 . . . 3G 103
Yale Cl. TW4: Houn . . . 5D 112
Yale Ct. NW6 . . . 5K 63
Yarborough Rd. SW19 . . . 1B 154
The Yard *N1* . . . *1F 7*
(off Caledonia Rd.)
Yardley Cl. E4 . . . 5J 25
Yardley Ct. SM3: Cheam . . . 4E 164
Yardley La. E4 . . . 5J 25
Yardley St. WC1 . . . 2J 7 (3A 84)
(not continuous)
Yardmaster Ho. CR0: C'don . . . 1D 168
Yarlington Ct. *N11* . . . *5K 31*
(off Sparkford Gdns.)
Yarmouth Cres. N17 . . . 5H 49
Yarmouth Pl. W1 . . . 5J 11 (1F 101)
Yarnfield Sq. SE15 . . . 1G 121
Yarnton Way DA18: Belv, Erith . . . 3F 109
SE2 . . . 2C 108

HOSPITALS, HOSPICES and selected HEALTHCARE FACILITIES covered by this atlas.

N.B. Where it is not possible to name these facilities on the map,
the reference given is for the road in which they are situated.

ASHFORD HOSPITAL 2A **128**
London Road
ASHFORD
TW15 3AA
Tel: 01784 884488

BARKING HOSPITAL 7K **71**
Upney Lane
BARKING
IG11 9LX
Tel: 020 3644 2301

BARNES HOSPITAL 3A **116**
South Worple Way
LONDON
SW14 8SU
Tel: 020 3513 3663

BARNET HOSPITAL 4A **20**
Wellhouse Lane
BARNET
EN5 3DJ
Tel: 020 8216 4600

BECKENHAM BEACON 2B **158**
379 Croydon Road
BECKENHAM
BR3 3QL
Tel: 01689 863000

BETHLEM ROYAL HOSPITAL 7C **158**
Monks Orchard Road
BECKENHAM
BR3 3BX
Tel: 020 3228 6000

THE BLACKHEATH BMI HOSPITAL 3H **123**
40-42 Lee Terrace
LONDON
SE3 9UD
Tel: 020 8318 7722

**THE BLACKHEATH BMI HOSPITAL
(OUTPATIENT DEPARTMENT)** 3H **123**
Independents Road
LONDON
SE3 9LF
Tel: 020 8297 4500

BMI CAVELL HOSPITAL 2F **23**
Cavell Drive
ENFIELD
EN2 7PR
Tel: 020 8366 2122

BMI CITY MEDICAL 7G **9**
17 St Helen's Place
LONDON
EC3A 6DG
Tel: 0845 123 5380

BMI URGENT CARE CENTRE 3K **59**
The Clementine Hospital
Sudbury Hill
HARROW
HA1 3RX
Tel: 020 8872 3999

BRENT OLDER PEOPLE DAY HOSPITAL 1C **80**
341 Harlesden Road
LONDON
NW10 3RX
Tel: 020 8459 3562

BRIDGEWAYS DAY HOSPITAL 6C **160**
Turpington Lane
BROMLEY
BR2 8JA
Tel: 020 8629 4900

CAMDEN MEWS DAY HOSPITAL 7G **65**
1-5 Camden Mews
LONDON
NW1 9DB
Tel: 020 3317 4740

CASSEL HOSPITAL 4D **132**
1 Ham Common
RICHMOND
TW10 7JF
Tel: 020 8483 2900

CENTRAL MIDDLESEX HOSPITAL 3J **79**
Acton Lane
LONDON
NW10 7NS
Tel: 020 8965 5733

CHARING CROSS HOSPITAL 6F **99**
Fulham Palace Road
LONDON
W6 8RF
Tel: 020 3311 1234

CHASE FARM HOSPITAL 1F **23**
127 The Ridgeway
ENFIELD
EN2 8JL
Tel: 020 8375 2999

CHELSEA & WESTMINSTER HOSPITAL 7A **16** (6A **100**)
369 Fulham Road
LONDON
SW10 9NH
Tel: 020 3315 8000

THE CHILDREN'S HOSPITAL (LEWISHAM) 5D **122**
Lewisham University Hospital
Lewisham High Street
LONDON
SE13 6LH
Tel: 020 8333 3000

CHURCHILL CAMBIAN HOSPITAL 1K **19** (3A **102**)
Barkham Terrace
Lambeth Road
LONDON
SE1 7PW
Tel: 0800 138 1418

CITY & HACKNEY CENTRE FOR MENTAL HEALTH ...5K **67**
Homerton Row
LONDON
E9 6SR
Tel: 020 8510 8117

CLAYPONDS HOSPITAL 4E **96**
Sterling Place
LONDON
W5 4RN
Tel: 020 8560 4011

CLEMENTINE CHURCHILL BMI HOSPITAL 2K **59**
Sudbury Hill
HARROW
HA1 3RX
Tel: 020 8872 3872

THE COBORN CENTRE FOR ADOLESCENT MENTAL HEALTH 4B **88**
Glen Road
LONDON
E13 8SP
Tel: 020 7540 6789

CROMWELL BUPA HOSPITAL 4K **99**
162-178 Cromwell Road
LONDON
SW5 0TU
Tel: 020 7460 2000

CROYDON UNIVERSITY HOSPITAL 6B **156**
530 London Road
THORNTON HEATH
CR7 7YE
Tel: 020 8401 3000

CYGNET HOSPITAL, BECKTON 6E **88**
23 Tunnan Leys
LONDON
E6 6ZB
Tel: 020 7511 2299

CYGNET HOSPITAL, BLACKHEATH 1E **122**
80 Blackheath Hill
LONDON
SE10 8AD
Tel: 020 8694 2111

CYGNET LODGE 6E **122**
44 Lewisham Park
LONDON
SE13 6QZ
Tel: 020 8314 5123

DEMELZA HOSPICE CARE FOR CHILDREN 6D **124**
5 Wensley Close
LONDON
SE9 5AB
Tel: 020 8859 9800

DULWICH COMMUNITY HOSPITAL 4E **120**
East Dulwich Grove
LONDON
SE22 8PT
Tel: 020 3049 8800

EALING CYGNET HOSPITAL 5E **78**
22 Corfton Road
LONDON
W5 2HT
Tel: 020 8991 6699

EALING HOSPITAL 1H **95**
Uxbridge Road
SOUTHALL
UB1 3HW
Tel: 020 8967 5000

EAST HAM CARE CENTRE & DAY HOSPITAL 7B **70**
Shrewsbury Road
LONDON
E7 8QP
Tel: 020 8475 2001

EDGWARE COMMUNITY HOSPITAL 7C **28**
Burnt Oak Broadway
EDGWARE
HA8 0AD
Tel: 020 8952 2381

EDRIDGE ROAD COMMUNITY HEALTH CENTRE 3C **168**
Impact House
2 Edridge Road
CROYDON
CR0 1FE
Tel: 020 3040 0800

ELTHAM COMMUNITY HOSPITAL 6D **124**
Passey Place
LONDON
SE9 5DQ
Tel: 020 3049 0400

ERITH & DISTRICT HOSPITAL 6K **109**
Park Crescent
ERITH
DA8 3EE
Tel: 020 8308 3131

EVELINA CHILDREN'S HOSPITAL 1G **19**
St Thomas' Hospital
Westminster Bridge Road
LONDON
SE1 7EH
Tel: 020 7188 7188

THE FERGUSON CEN. 6A **50**
Low Hall Lane
LONDON
E17 8BE
Tel: 020 8521 5223

FINCHLEY MEMORIAL HOSPITAL 7F **31**
Granville Road
LONDON
N12 0JE
Tel: 020 8349 7500

FITZROY SQUARE HOSPITAL 4A **6** (4G **83**)
1 Fitzroy Square
LONDON
W1T 5HF
Tel: 0333 920 9135

GOODMAYES HOSPITAL 5A **54**
Barley Lane
ILFORD
IG3 8XJ
Tel: 0300 555 1200

GORDON HOSPITAL 4C **18** (4H **101**)
Bloomburg Street
LONDON
SW1V 2RH
Tel: 020 3315 8733

GRAYS COURT COMMUNITY HOSPITAL 7H **73**
John Parker Close
DAGENHAM
RM10 9SR
Tel: 020 3644 2762

GREAT ORMOND STREET HOSPITAL FOR CHILDREN 4F **7** (4J **83**)
Great Ormond Street
LONDON
WC1N 3JH
Tel: 020 7405 9200

GREENWICH & BEXLEY COMMUNITY HOSPICE 5C **108**
185 Bostall Hill
LONDON
SE2 0GB
Tel: 020 8312 2244

GUY'S HOSPITAL 5F **15** (2D **102**)
Great Maze Pond
LONDON
SE1 9RT
Tel: 020 7188 7188

GUY'S NUFFIELD HOUSE 6E **14**
Guy's Hospital
LONDON
SE1 1YR
Tel: 020 7188 5292

HAMMERSMITH HOSPITAL 6C **80**
Du Cane Road
LONDON
W12 0HS
Tel: 020 3313 1000

THE HARLEY STREET CLINIC 5J **5** (5F **83**)
35 Weymouth Street
LONDON
W1G 8BJ
Tel: 020 3553 6106

HARLINGTON HOSPICE 5F **93**
St Peters Way
HAYES
UB3 5AB
Tel: 020 8759 0453

HARROW CYGNET HOSPITAL 2J **59**
London Road
HARROW
HA1 3JL
Tel: 020 8966 7000

HAVEN HOUSE CHILDREN'S HOSPICE 6C **36**
High Road
WOODFORD GREEN
IG8 9LB
Tel: 020 8505 9944

HAYES GROVE PRIORY HOSPITAL 2J **171**
Prestons Road
Hayes
BROMLEY
BR2 7AS
Tel: 020 8462 7722

HENDON BMI HOSPITAL 3E **44**
46-50 Sunny Gardens Road
LONDON
NW4 1RP
Tel: 020 8457 4500

HIGHGATE HOSPITAL 6D **46**
17- 19 View Road
LONDON
N6 4DJ
Tel: 020 8003 4518

HIGHGATE MENTAL HEALTH CENTRE 2F **65**
Dartmouth Park Hill
LONDON
N19 5NX
Tel: 020 7561 4000

HILLINGDON HOSPITAL 5B **74**
Pield Heath Road
UXBRIDGE
UB8 3NN
Tel: 01895 238282

THE HOLLY PRIVATE HOSPITAL 2E **36**
High Road
BUCKHURST HILL
IG9 5HX
Tel: 020 8505 3311

HOMERTON UNIVERSITY HOSPITAL 5K **67**
Homerton Row
LONDON
E9 6SR
Tel: 020 8510 5555

HOSPITAL FOR TROPICAL DISEASES 4B **6**
Mortimer Market
LONDON
WC1E 6JD
Tel: 020 3447 5959

HOSPITAL OF ST JOHN & ST ELIZABETH 2B **82**
60 Grove End Road
LONDON
NW8 9NH
Tel: 020 7806 4000

HUNTERCOMBE HOSPITAL ROEHAMPTON 7C **116**
Holybourne Avenue
LONDON
SW15 4JD
Tel: 020 8780 6155

JOHN HOWARD CENTRE 5A **68**
12 Kenworthy Road
LONDON
E9 5TD
Tel: 020 8510 2003

KING EDWARD VII'S HOSPITAL SISTER AGNES 5H **5** (5E **82**)
5-10 Beaumont Street
LONDON
W1G 6AA
Tel: 020 7486 4411

KING GEORGE HOSPITAL 4A **54**
Barley Lane
ILFORD
IG3 8YB
Tel: 0330 400 4333

KING'S COLLEGE HOSPITAL .2D **120**
Denmark Hill
LONDON
SE5 9RS
Tel: 020 3299 9000

KING'S OAK BMI HOSPITAL .1F **23**
The Ridgeway
ENFIELD
EN2 8SD
Tel: 020 8370 9500

KINGSTON HOSPITAL 1H **151**
Galsworthy Road
KINGSTON UPON THAMES
KT2 7QB
Tel: 020 8546 7711

LAMBETH HOSPITAL 3K **119**
108 Landor Road
LONDON
SW9 9NU
Tel: 020 3228 6000

THE LISTER HOSPITAL 6J **17** (5F **101**)
Chelsea Bridge Road
LONDON
SW1W 8RH
Tel: 020 7730 4345

LONDON BRIDGE HOSPITAL 4F **15** (1D **102**)
27 Tooley Street
LONDON
SE1 2PR
Tel: 020 7407 3100

LONDON CLINIC 4H **5** (4E **82**)
20 Devonshire Place
LONDON
W1G 6BW
Tel: 020 7935 4444

LONDON EYE HOSPITAL 7J **5**
4 Harley Street
LONDON
W1G 9PB
Tel: 020 7060 2602

LONDON INDEPENDENT BMI HOSPITAL 5K **85**
1 Beaumont Square
LONDON
E1 4NL
Tel: 020 7780 2400

LONDON WELBECK HOSPITAL 6J **5**
27 Welbeck Street
LONDON
W1G 8EN
Tel: 020 7224 2242

MARGARET CENTRE (HOSPICE) 6G **51**
Whipps Cross University Hospital
Whipps Cross Road
LONDON
E11 1NR
Tel: 020 8539 5522

MARIE CURIE HOSPICE 5B **64**
11 Lyndhurst Gardens
LONDON
NW3 5NS
Tel: 020 7853 3400

THE MAUDSLEY HOSPITAL .2D **120**
Denmark Hill
LONDON
SE5 8AZ
Tel: 020 3228 6000

MEADOW HOUSE HOSPICE .2H **95**
Uxbridge Road
SOUTHALL
UB1 3HW
Tel: 020 8967 5179

MEMORIAL HOSPITAL 2E **124**
Shooters Hill
LONDON
SE18 3RG
Tel: 020 8836 8500

MILDMAY HOSPITAL 2J **9** (3F **85**)
Austin Street
LONDON
E2 7NB
Tel: 0207 613 6300

MILE END HOSPITAL 4K **85**
Bancroft Road
LONDON
E1 4DG
Tel: 020 3416 5000

MINOR INJURIES UNIT (GUY'S HOSPITAL) 2D **102**
Great Maze Pond
LONDON
SE1 9RT
Tel: 020 7188 3879

MINOR INJURIES UNIT (ROEHAMPTON) 6C **116**
Roehampton Lane
LONDON
SW15 5PN
Tel: 020 8487 6499

MINOR INJURIES UNIT
(ST BARTHOLOMEW'S HOSPITAL) 6B **8** (5B **84**)
West Smithfield
LONDON
EC1A 7BE
Tel: 020 3465 8843

MOLESEY HOSPITAL 5E **148**
High Street
WEST MOLESEY
KT8 2LU
Tel: 020 8941 4481

MOORFIELDS EYE HOSPITAL 2E **8** (3D **84**)
162 City Road
LONDON
EC1V 2PD
Tel: 020 7253 3411

NATIONAL HOSPITAL FOR NEUROLOGY & NEUROSURGERY
. . . . .4F **7** (4J **83**)
Queen Square
LONDON
WC1N 3BG
Tel: 020 3456 7890

NEWHAM CENTRE FOR MENTAL HEALTH 4B **88**
Cherry Tree Way
Glen Road
LONDON
E13 8SP
Tel: 020 7540 4380

NEWHAM UNIVERSITY HOSPITAL 4A **88**
Glen Road
LONDON
E13 8SL
Tel: 020 7476 4000

NEW VICTORIA HOSPITAL .1A **152**
184 Coombe Lane West
KINGSTON UPON THAMES
KT2 7EG
Tel: 020 8949 9000

NHS WALK-IN CENTRE (ASHFORD) 2A **128**
Ashford Hospital
London Road
ASHFORD
TW15 3AA
Tel: 01784 884000

NHS WALK-IN CENTRE (BARKING HOSPITAL) 7K **71**
Upney Lane
BARKING
IG11 9LX
Tel: 020 8924 6262

NHS WALK-IN CENTRE (BELMONT HEALTH CENTRE) 2A **42**
516 Kenton Lane
HARROW
HA3 7LT
Tel: 020 8866 4100

NHS WALK-IN CENTRE (CLAPHAM JUNCTION) 3C **118**
The Junction Health Centre
Arches 5-8, Clapham Junction Station
Grant Road
LONDON
SW11 2NU
Tel: 0333 200 1718

NHS WALK-IN CENTRE (CRICKLEWOOD HEALTH CENTRE) 4F **63**
Britannia Business Centre
Cricklewood Lane
LONDON
NW2 1DZ
Tel: 03000 334335

NHS WALK-IN CENTRE (EARL'S COURT) 4K **99**
Earl's Court Health & Wellbeing Centre
2b Hogarth Road
LONDON
SW5 0PT
Tel: 020 7341 0300

NHS WALK-IN CENTRE (EDGWARE) 7C **28**
Edgware Community Hospital
Burnt Oak Broadway
EDGWARE
HA8 0AD
Tel: 020 8732 6459

NHS WALK-IN CENTRE (FINCHLEY) 7F **31**
Finchley Memorial Hospital
Granville Road
LONDON
N12 0JE
Tel: 020 8349 7470

NHS WALK-IN CENTRE (ISLE OF DOGS) 2C **104**
Barkantine Practice
121 Westferry Road
LONDON
E14 8JH
Tel: 020 7510 4000

NHS WALK-IN CENTRE (PARSONS GREEN) 1J **117**
5-7 Parsons Green
LONDON
SW6 4UL
Tel: 020 8102 4300

NHS WALK-IN CENTRE (PINNER) 3C **40**
Pinn Medical Centre, The
37 Love Lane
PINNER
HA5 3EE
Tel: 020 8866 5766

NHS WALK-IN CENTRE (SOHO) 1C **12**
1 Frith Street
LONDON
W1D 3HZ
Tel: 020 7534 6575

NHS WALK-IN CENTRE (TEDDINGTON) 6J **131**
Teddington Memorial Hospital
Hampton Road
TEDDINGTON
TW11 0JL
Tel: 020 8714 4004

NHS WALK-IN CENTRE (THAMESMEAD) 2J **107**
Thamesmead Health Centre
4-5 Thames Reach
LONDON
SE28 0NY
Tel: 020 8319 5880

NHS WALK-IN CENTRE (WEMBLEY) 6D **60**
116 Chaplin Road
WEMBLEY
HA0 4UZ
Tel: 020 8795 6112

NIGHTINGALE HOSPITAL 5D **4** (5C **82**)
11-19 Lisson Grove
LONDON
NW1 6SH
Tel: 020 7535 7705

NOAH'S ARK CHILDREN'S HOSPICE 4C **20**
Beauchamp Court
10 Victors Way
BARNET
EN5 5TZ
Tel: 020 8449 8877

NORTH LONDON CLINIC 2B **34**
15 Church Street
LONDON
N9 9DY
Tel: 020 8956 1234

NORTH LONDON HOSPICE (FINCHLEY) 3F **31**
47 Woodside Avenue
LONDON
N12 8TT
Tel: 020 8343 8841

NORTH LONDON HOSPICE (WINCHMORE HILL) 3H **33**
110 Barrowell Green
LONDON
N21 3AY
Tel: 020 8343 8841

NORTH LONDON PRIORY HOSPITAL 1D **32**
The Bourne
LONDON
N14 6RA
Tel: 020 8882 8191

NORTH MIDDLESEX UNIVERSITY HOSPITAL 5K **33**
Sterling Way
LONDON
N18 1QX
Tel: 020 8887 2000

NORTHWICK PARK HOSPITAL 7A **42**
Watford Road
HARROW
HA1 3UJ
Tel: 020 8864 3232

OLD BROAD STREET PRIVATE MEDICAL CENTRE 7G *9*
31 Old Broad Street
LONDON
EC2N 1HT
Tel: 020 7496 3522

ORPINGTON HOSPITAL 4K **173**
Sevenoaks Road
ORPINGTON
BR6 9JU
Tel: 01689 863000

PARK ROYAL CENTRE (FOR MENTAL HEALTH) 2J **79**
Central Way
LONDON
NW10 7NS
Tel: 020 8955 4400

PARKSIDE HOSPITAL 3F **135**
53 Parkside
LONDON
SW19 5NX
Tel: 020 8971 8000

PEMBRIDGE PALLIATIVE CARE CENTRE 5F *81*
St Charles Hospital
Exmoor Street
LONDON
W10 6DZ
Tel: 020 8102 5000

PORTLAND HOSPITAL FOR WOMEN & CHILDREN 4K **5** (4F **83**)
205-209 Great Portland Street
LONDON
W1W 5AH
Tel: 020 3131 5755

PRINCESS GRACE HOSPITAL 4G **5** (4E **82**)
42-52 Nottingham Place
LONDON
W1U 5NY
Tel: 020 3130 6833

PRINCESS ROYAL UNIVERSITY HOSPITAL 3E **172**
Farnborough Common
ORPINGTON
BR6 8ND
Tel: 01689 863000

PRIORY HOSPITAL ROEHAMPTON 4B **116**
Priory Lane
LONDON
SW15 5JJ
Tel: 020 8876 8261

QUEEN CHARLOTTE'S & CHELSEA HOSPITAL 6C **80**
Du Cane Road
LONDON
W12 0HS
Tel: 020 3313 1111

QUEEN ELIZABETH HOSPITAL 7C **106**
Stadium Road
LONDON
SE18 4QH
Tel: 020 8836 6000

QUEEN MARY'S HOSPITAL FOR CHILDREN 1A **166**
Wrythe Lane
CARSHALTON
SM5 1AA
Tel: 020 8296 2000

QUEEN MARY'S HOSPITAL, ROEHAMPTON 6C **116**
Roehampton Lane
LONDON
SW15 5PN
Tel: 020 8487 6000

QUEEN MARY'S HOSPITAL, SIDCUP 6A **144**
Frognal Avenue
SIDCUP
DA14 6LT
Tel: 020 8302 2678

QUEEN'S HOSPITAL 7K **55**
Rom Valley Way
ROMFORD
RM7 0AG
Tel: 01708 435000

RICHARD DESMOND CHILDREN'S EYE CENTRE 2E *8*
Moorfields Eye Hospital
3 Peerless Street
LONDON
EC1V 9EZ
Tel: 020 7253 3411

RICHARD HOUSE CHILDREN'S HOSPICE 7B **88**
Richard House Drive
LONDON
E16 3RG
Tel: 020 7511 0222

RICHMOND ROYAL HOSPITAL 3E **114**
Kew Foot Road
RICHMOND
TW9 2TE
Tel: 020 3513 3200

RODING SPIRE HOSPITAL 3B **52**
Roding Lane South
ILFORD
IG4 5PZ
Tel: 020 3131 4324

ROYAL BROMPTON HOSPITAL 5C **16** (5C **100**)
Sydney Street
LONDON
SW3 6NP
Tel: 020 7352 8121

ROYAL BROMPTON HOSPITAL (OUTPATIENTS) ...5B **16** (5B **100**)
Fulham Road
LONDON
SW3 6HP
Tel: 020 7352 8121

ROYAL FREE HOSPITAL 5C **64**
Pond Street
LONDON
NW3 2QG
Tel: 020 7794 0500

ROYAL HOSPITAL FOR NEURO-DISABILITY 6G **117**
West Hill
LONDON
SW15 3SW
Tel: 020 8780 4500

THE ROYAL LONDON HOSPITAL 5H **85**
Whitechapel Road
LONDON
E1 1FR
Tel: 020 3416 5000

ROYAL LONDON HOSPITAL FOR INTEGRATED MEDICINE
....4C **6** (4J **83**)
Great Ormond Street
LONDON
WC1N 3HR
Tel: 020 3456 7890

THE ROYAL MARSDEN HOSPITAL 5B **16** (5B **100**)
Fulham Road
LONDON
SW3 6JJ
Tel: 020 7352 8171

ROYAL NAT. ORTHOPAEDIC HOSPITAL 4K **5** (4F **83**)
45-51 Bolsover Street
LONDON
W1W 5AQ
Tel: 020 3947 0100

ROYAL NAT. ORTHOPAEDIC HOSPITAL 2H **27**
Brockley Hill
STANMORE
HA7 4LP
Tel: 020 8954 2300

ROYAL NATIONAL ENT and EASTMAN DENTAL HOSPITALS
....4C **6** (4H **83**)
Huntley Street
LONDON
WC1E 6DG
Tel: 020 3456 7890

ST ANN'S HOSPITAL 5C **48**
St Ann's Road
LONDON
N15 3TH
Tel: 020 8702 3000

ST ANTHONY'S HOSPITAL 1F **165**
801 London Road
SUTTON
SM3 9DW
Tel: 020 8337 6691

ST BARTHOLOMEW'S HOSPITAL 6B **8** (5B **84**)
West Smithfield
LONDON
EC1A 7BE
Tel: 020 3416 5000

ST BERNARD'S HOSPITAL 2H **95**
Uxbridge Road
SOUTHALL
UB1 3EU
Tel: 020 8354 8354

ST CHARLES HOSPITAL 5F **81**
Exmoor Street
LONDON
W10 6DZ
Tel: 020 8206 7343

ST CHRISTOPHER'S HOSPICE (SYDENHAM) 5J **139**
51-59 Lawrie Park Road
LONDON
SE26 6DZ
Tel: 020 8768 4500

ST CHRISTOPHER'S HOSPISCARE (ORPINGTON) 4K **173**
Tregony Road
ORPINGTON
BR6 9XA
Tel: 01689 825755

ST EBBA'S 7J **163**
Hook Road
EPSOM
KT19 8QJ
Tel: 0300 555 5222

ST GEORGE'S HOSPITAL (TOOTING) 5B **136**
Blackshaw Road
LONDON
SW17 0QT
Tel: 020 8672 1255

ST HELIER HOSPITAL 1A **166**
Wrythe Lane
CARSHALTON
SM5 1AA
Tel: 020 8296 2000

ST JOHN'S HOSPICE 1A *4*
60 Grove End Road
LONDON
NW8 9NH
Tel: 020 7806 4040

ST JOSEPH'S HOSPICE 1H **85**
Mare Street
LONDON
E8 4SA
Tel: 020 8525 6000

ST LUKE'S HEALTHCARE FOR THE CLERGY 4A *6*
14 Fitzroy Square
LONDON
W1T 6HP
Tel: 020 7388 4954

ST LUKE'S HOSPICE 5D **42**
Kenton Road
HARROW
HA3 0YG
Tel: 020 8382 8000

ST MARK'S HOSPITAL (HARROW) 7B **42**
Watford Road
HARROW
HA1 3UJ
Tel: 020 8864 3232

ST MARY'S HOSPITAL 7B **4** (6B **82**)
Praed Street
LONDON
W2 1NY
Tel: 020 7886 6666

ST MICHAEL'S HOSPITAL 1J **23**
Gater Drive
ENFIELD
EN2 0JB
Tel: 020 8375 2894

ST PANCRAS HOSPITAL 1H **83**
4 St Pancras Way
LONDON
NW1 0PE
Tel: 020 3317 3500

ST RAPHAEL'S HOSPICE 2F **165**
London Road
SUTTON
SM3 9DX
Tel: 020 8099 7777

ST THOMAS' HOSPITAL 7G **13** (3K **101**)
Westminster Bridge Road
LONDON
SE1 7EH
Tel: 020 7188 7188

SHIRLEY OAKS BMI HOSPITAL 7J **157**
Poppy Lane
CROYDON
CR9 8AB
Tel: 020 8655 5500

SHOOTING STAR HOUSE, CHILDREN'S HOSPICE 6D **130**
The Avenue
HAMPTON
TW12 3RA
Tel: 020 8783 2000

THE SLOANE BMI HOSPITAL 1F **159**
125 Albemarle Road
BECKENHAM
BR3 5HS
Tel: 020 8466 4000

SPIRE BUSHEY HOSPITAL 1E **26**
Heathbourne Road
Bushey Heath
BUSHEY
WD23 1RD
Tel: 020 3733 5424

SPRINGFIELD UNIVERSITY HOSPITAL 2C **136**
61 Glenburnie Road
LONDON
SW17 7DJ
Tel: 020 3513 5000

TEDDINGTON MEMORIAL HOSPITAL 6J **131**
Hampton Road
TEDDINGTON
TW11 0JL
Tel: 020 8714 4000

THORPE COOMBE HOSPITAL 3E **50**
714 Forest Road
LONDON
E17 3HP
Tel: 0300 555 1247

TOLWORTH HOSPITAL 2G **163**
Red Lion Road
SURBITON
KT6 7QU
Tel: 020 3513 5000

TOWER HAMLETS CENTRE FOR MENTAL HEALTH 4K **85**
Bancroft Road
LONDON
E1 4DG
Tel: 020 8121 5001

TRINITY HOSPICE 4F **119**
30 Clapham Common North Side
LONDON
SW4 0RN
Tel: 020 7787 1000

UCH MACMILLAN CANCER CENTRE 4B **6** (4G **83**)
Huntley Street
LONDON
WC1E 6DH
Tel: 020 3456 7016

UNIVERSITY COLLEGE HOSPITAL 3B **6** (4G **83**)
235 Euston Road
LONDON
NW1 2BU
Tel: 020 3456 7890

UNIVERSITY COLLEGE HOSPITAL 4G **83**
25 Grafton Way
LONDON
WC1E 6DB
Tel: 020 3447 9400

UNIVERSITY COLLEGE HOSPITAL 6J **5** (5E **82**)
16-18 Westmoreland Street
LONDON
W1G 8PH
Tel: 020 3456 7890

UNIVERSITY HOSPITAL, LEWISHAM 5D **122**
Lewisham High Street
LONDON
SE13 6LH
Tel: 020 8333 3000

UPTON CENTRE 4E **126**
14 Upton Road
BEXLEYHEATH
DA6 8LQ
Tel: 020 8301 7900

URGENT CARE CENTRE (ANGEL MEDICAL PRACTICE) 2A **84**
34 Ritchie Street
LONDON
N1 0DG
Tel: 020 7837 1663

URGENT CARE CENTRE (BARNET) 4A **20**
Barnet Hospital
Wellhouse Lane
BARNET
EN5 3DJ
Tel: 020 8216 4600

URGENT CARE CENTRE (BECKENHAM BEACON) 2B **158**
379 Croydon Road
BECKENHAM
BR3 3QL
Tel: 01689 866037

URGENT CARE CENTRE (CARSHALTON) 1B **166**
St Helier Hospital
Wrythe Lane
CARSHALTON
SM5 1AA
Tel: 020 8296 2000

URGENT CARE CENTRE
(CENTRAL MIDDLESEX HOSPITAL) 3J **79**
Acton Lane
LONDON
NW10 7NS
Tel: 0333 999 2575

URGENT CARE CENTRE (CHASE FARM HOSPITAL) 1F **23**
The Ridgeway
ENFIELD
EN2 8JL
Tel: 020 8375 1010

URGENT CARE CENTRE
(CHELSEA & WESTMINSTER HOSPITAL) 6A **100**
369 Fulham Road
LONDON
SW10 9NH
Tel: 020 3315 8000

URGENT CARE CENTRE (EALING) 2H **95**
Ealing Hospital
Uxbridge Road
SOUTHALL
UB1 3HW
Tel: 0333 999 2577

URGENT CARE CENTRE (ERITH & DISTRICT HOSPITAL) 6K **109**
Park Crescent
ERITH
DA8 3EE
Tel: 01322 356116

URGENT CARE CENTRE (FULHAM) 5F **99**
Charing Cross Hospital
Fulham Palace Road
LONDON
W6 8RF
Tel: 020 8846 1005

URGENT CARE CENTRE (HAMMERSMITH HOSPITAL) 6C **80**
Du Cane Road
LONDON
W12 0HS
Tel: 020 8383 4103

URGENT CARE CENTRE (HAMPSTEAD) 5C **64**
Royal Free Hospital
Pond Street
LONDON
NW3 2QG
Tel: 020 7794 0500

URGENT CARE CENTRE (HILLINGDON HOSPITAL) 5B **74**
Hillingdon Hospital
Pield Heath Road
UXBRIDGE
UB8 3NN
Tel: 01895 238282

URGENT CARE CENTRE (HOMERTON UNIVERSITY HOSPITAL) ...5K **67**
Homerton Row
LONDON
E9 6SR
Tel: 020 8510 5555

URGENT CARE CENTRE (KING GEORGE HOSPITAL) 4A **54**
Barley Lane
ILFORD
IG3 8YB
Tel: 020 8983 8000

URGENT CARE CENTRE (NEWHAM) 4A **88**
Newham University Hospital
Glen Road
LONDON
E13 8SL
Tel: 020 7476 4000

URGENT CARE CENTRE
(NORTH MIDDLESEX UNIVERSITY HOSPITAL) 5K **33**
Bridport Road
LONDON
N18 1QX
Tel: 020 8887 2398

URGENT CARE CENTRE
(NORTHWICK PARK HOSPITAL) 7A **42**
Watford Road
HARROW
HA1 3UJ
Tel: 020 8869 3743

URGENT CARE CENTRE
(PRINCESS ROYAL UNIVERSITY HOSPITAL) 4E **172**
Farnborough Common
ORPINGTON
BR6 8ND
Tel: 01689 863050

URGENT CARE CENTRE (QUEEN ELIZABETH HOSPITAL) 6C **106**
Stadium Road
LONDON
SE18 4QH
Tel: 020 8836 6846

URGENT CARE CENTRE (QUEEN'S HOSPITAL) 7K **55**
Rom Valley Way
ROMFORD
RM7 0AG
Tel: 01708 435000

URGENT CARE CENTRE (ST CHARLES CENTRE) 5F **81**
Exmoor Street
LONDON
W10 6DZ
Tel: 020 8102 5111

URGENT CARE CENTRE (ST GEORGE'S HOSPITAL) 5C **136**
Blackshaw Road
LONDON
SW17 0QT
Tel: 020 8672 1255

URGENT CARE CENTRE (ST MARY'S HOSPITAL) 6B **82**
Praed Street
LONDON
W2 1NY
Tel: 020 3312 5757

URGENT CARE CENTRE (SIDCUP) 6A **144**
Queen Mary's Hospital
Frognal Avenue
SIDCUP
DA14 6LT
Tel: 020 8308 5611

URGENT CARE CENTRE (THORNTON HEATH) 6B **156**
Croydon University Hospital
530 London Road
THORNTON HEATH
CR7 7YE
Tel: 020 8401 3000

URGENT CARE CENTRE
(UNIVERSITY COLLEGE HOSPITAL) 3B **6** (4G **83**)
235 Euston Road
LONDON
NW1 2BU
Tel: 020 3456 7890

URGENT CARE CENTRE
(UNIVERSITY HOSPITAL LEWISHAM) 5D **122**
Lewisham High Street
LONDON
SE13 6LH
Tel: 020 8333 3000

URGENT CARE CENTRE
(WEST MIDDLESEX UNIVERSITY HOSPITAL) 2A **114**
Twickenham Road
ISLEWORTH
TW7 6AF
Tel: 020 8560 2121

URGENT CARE CENTRE
(WHIPPS CROSS UNIVERSITY HOSPITAL) 6F **51**
Whipps Cross Road
LONDON
E11 1NR
Tel: 0300 123 0808

URGENT CARE CENTRE (WHITTINGTON HOSPITAL) 2G **65**
Magdala Avenue
LONDON
N19 5NF
Tel: 020 7272 3070

THE WELLINGTON HOSPITAL 1B **4** (3B **82**)
34 Circus Road
LONDON
NW8 9LE
Tel: 020 3733 6667

WESTERN EYE HOSPITAL 5E **4** (5D **82**)
153-173 Marylebone Road
LONDON
NW1 5QH
Tel: 020 7886 6666

WEST MIDDLESEX UNIVERSITY HOSPITAL 2A **114**
Twickenham Road
ISLEWORTH
TW7 6AF
Tel: 020 8560 2121

WEYMOUTH STREET HOSPITAL 5H **5**
42-46 Weymouth Street
LONDON
W1G 6NP
Tel: 020 7935 1200

WHIPPS CROSS UNIVERSITY HOSPITAL 5F **51**
Whipps Cross Road
LONDON
E11 1NR
Tel: 020 8539 5522

WHITTINGTON HOSPITAL 2G **65**
Magdala Avenue
LONDON
N19 5NF
Tel: 020 7272 3070

WILLESDEN CENTRE FOR HEALTH & CARE 7C **62**
Robson Avenue
LONDON
NW10 3RY
Tel: 020 8438 7006

THE WILSON HOSPITAL 4D **154**
Cranmer Road
MITCHAM
CR4 4LD
Tel: 020 8648 3021

WOODBURY UNIT 6G **51**
178 James Lane
LONDON
E11 1NR
Tel: 0300 555 1260

PUBLIC TRANSPORT

with their map square reference

A

Abbey Road (DLR) ... 2G 87
Abbey Wood (Rail & Crossrail) ... 3C 108
Acton Central (Overground) ... 1K 97
Acton Main Line (Rail & Crossrail) ... 6J 79
Acton Town (Underground) ... 2G 97
Addington Bus Station ... 6C 170
Addington Village Stop
(London Tramlink) ... 6C 170
Addiscombe Stop
(London Tramlink) ... 1G 169
Albany Park (Rail) ... 2D 144
Aldgate Bus Station ... 1J 15 (6F 85)
Aldgate East
(Underground) ... 7K 9 (6F 85)
Aldgate
(Underground) ... 1J 15 (6F 85)
Alexandra Palace (Rail) ... 2J 47
All Saints (DLR) ... 7D 86
Alperton (Underground) ... 1D 78
Ampere Way Stop
(London Tramlink) ... 1K 167
Anerley (Rail & Overground) ... 1H 157
Angel (Underground) ... 2A 84
Archway Bus Station ... 2G 65
Archway (Underground) ... 2G 65
Arena Stop
(London Tramlink) ... 5J 157
Arnos Grove (Underground) ... 5B 32
Arsenal (Underground) ... 3A 66
Ashford (Rail) ... 4B 128
Avenue Road Stop
(London Tramlink) ... 2K 157

B

Baker Street (Underground) ... 4F 5 (4D 82)
Balham (Rail & Underground) ... 1F 137
Bankside Pier
(River Bus & Tours) ... 3C 14 (7C 84)
Bank (Underground & DLR) ... 1E 14 (6D 84)
Barbican (Underground) ... 5C 8 (5C 84)
Barking
(Rail, Underground & Overground) ... 7G 71
Barkingside (Underground) ... 3H 53
Barnehurst (Rail) ... 2J 127
Barnes Bridge (Rail) ... 2B 116
Barnes (Rail) ... 3C 116
Barons Court (Underground) ... 5G 99
Battersea Park (Rail) ... 7F 101
Battersea Power Pier
(River Bus) ... 7K 17 (6G 101)
Bayswater (Underground) ... 7K 81
Beckenham Hill (Rail) ... 5E 140
Beckenham Junction
(Rail & London Tramlink) ... 1C 158
Beckenham Road Stop
(London Tramlink) ... 1A 158
Beckton (DLR) ... 5E 88
Beckton Park (DLR) ... 7D 88
Becontree (Underground) ... 6D 72
Beddington Lane Stop
(London Tramlink) ... 6G 155
Belgrave Walk Stop
(London Tramlink) ... 4B 154
Bellingham (Rail) ... 3D 140
Belsize Park (Underground) ... 5C 64
Belvedere (Rail) ... 3H 109
Bermondsey (Underground) ... 3G 103
Berrylands (Rail) ... 4H 151
Bethnal Green (Overground) ... 4H 85
Bethnal Green (Underground) ... 3J 85
Bexleyheath (Rail) ... 2E 126
Bexley (Rail) ... 1G 145
Bickley (Rail) ... 3C 160
Birkbeck (Rail & London Tramlink) ... 3J 157
Blackfriars Millennium Pier
(River Bus) ... 2B 14 (7B 84)
Blackfriars
(Rail & Underground) ... 2A 14 (7B 84)
Blackheath (Rail) ... 3H 123
Blackhorse Lane Stop
(London Tramlink) ... 7G 157
Blackhorse Road
(Underground & Overground) ... 4K 49
Blackwall Basin Moorings ... 1E 104
Blackwall (DLR) ... 7E 86
Bond Street
(Underground & Crossrail) ... 1J 11 (6E 82)
Borough
(Underground) ... 7D 14 (2C 102)
Boston Manor (Underground) ... 4A 96
Bounds Green (Underground) ... 6C 32
Bow Church (DLR) ... 3C 86
Bowes Park (Rail) ... 7D 32
Bow Road (Underground) ... 3C 86
Brent Cross Bus Station ... 7E 44
Brent Cross (Underground) ... 7F 45
Brentford (Rail) ... 6C 96
Brimsdown (Rail) ... 3F 25
Brixton (Rail & Underground) ... 4A 120
Brockley (Rail & Overground) ... 3A 122
Bromley-by-Bow
(Underground) ... 3D 86
Bromley North (Rail) ... 1J 159
Bromley South (Rail) ... 3J 159
Brondesbury (Overground) ... 7H 63
Brondesbury Park
(Overground) ... 1G 81
Bruce Grove (Overground) ... 2F 49
Buckhurst Hill
(Underground) ... 2G 37
Burnt Oak (Underground) ... 1J 43
Bush Hill Park (Overground) ... 6A 24

C

Cable Car ... 2H 105
Cadogan Pier (River Bus) ... 7D 16 (6C 100)
Caledonian Road & Barnsbury
(Overground) ... 7K 65
Caledonian Road (Underground) ... 6K 65
Cambridge Heath (Overground) ... 2H 85
Camden Road (Overground) ... 7G 65
Camden Town (Underground) ... 1F 83
Canada Water Bus Station ... *2J 103*
(off Surrey Quays)
Canada Water
(Underground & Overground) ... 2J 103
Canary Wharf (Crossrail) ... 1D 104
Canary Wharf Pier (River Bus) ... 1B 104
Canary Wharf
(Underground & DLR) ... 1C 104
Canning Town Bus Station ... 6G 87
Canning Town
(Underground & DLR) ... 6G 87
Cannon Street
(Rail & Underground) ... 2E 14 (7D 84)
Canonbury (Overground) ... 5C 66
Canons Park (Underground) ... 7K 27
Carshalton Beeches (Rail) ... 6D 166
Carshalton (Rail) ... 4D 166
Castle Bar Park (Rail) ... 5K 77
Catford Bridge (Rail) ... 7C 122
Catford (Rail) ... 7C 122
Centrale Stop
(London Tramlink) ... 2C 168
Chadwell Heath
(Rail & Crossrail) ... 7D 54
Chalk Farm (Underground) ... 7E 64
Chancery Lane
(Underground) ... 6J 7 (5A 84)
Charing Cross
(Rail & Underground) ... 4E 12 (1J 101)
Charlton (Rail) ... 5A 106
Cheam (Rail) ... 7G 165
Chelsea Harbour Pier (River Bus) ... 1B 118
Chessington North (Rail) ... 5E 162
Chessington South (Rail) ... 7D 162
Chigwell (Underground) ... 3K 37
Chingford Bus Station ... 1B 36
Chingford (Overground) ... 1B 36
Chislehurst (Rail) ... 2E 160
Chiswick Park (Underground) ... 4J 97
Chiswick (Rail) ... 7J 97
Church Street Stop
(London Tramlink) ... 2C 168
City Airport ... 1C 106
City Thameslink (Rail) ... 7A 8 (6B 84)
Clapham Common (Underground) ... 4G 119
Clapham High Street (Overground) ... 3H 119
Clapham Junction
(Rail & Overground) ... 3C 118
Clapham North (Underground) ... 3J 119
Clapham South (Underground) ... 6F 119
Clapton (Overground) ... 2H 67
Clock House (Rail) ... 1A 158
Cockfosters (Underground) ... 4K 21
Colindale (Underground) ... 3A 44
Colliers Wood (Underground) ... 7B 136
Coombe Lane Stop
(London Tramlink) ... 5J 169
Covent Garden
(Underground) ... 2F 13 (7J 83)
Cricklewood (Rail) ... 4F 63
Crofton Park (Rail) ... 5B 122
Cromwell Road Bus Station ... 1E 150
Crossharbour
(Underground & DLR) ... 3D 104
Crouch Hill (Overground) ... 7K 47
Crystal Palace (Rail & Overground) ... 6G 139
Custom House for ExCeL
(DLR & Crossrail) ... 7K 87
Cutty Sark for Maritime Greenwich
(DLR) ... 6E 104
Cyprus (DLR) ... 7E 88

D

Dagenham Dock (Rail) ... 2F 91
Dagenham East (Underground) ... 5J 73
Dagenham Heathway
(Underground) ... 6F 73
Dalston Junction (Overground) ... 6F 67
Dalston Kingsland (Overground) ... 5E 66
Denmark Hill
(Rail & Overground) ... 2D 120
Deptford Bridge (DLR) ... 1C 122
Deptford (Rail) ... 7C 104
Devons Road (DLR) ... 4D 86
Dollis Hill (Underground) ... 5C 62
Doubletree Docklands / Nelson Dock Pier
(River Bus) ... 1B 104
Drayton Green (Rail) ... 6K 77
Drayton Park (Rail) ... 4A 66
Dundonald Road Stop
(London Tramlink) ... 7H 135

E

Ealing Broadway
(Rail, Underground & Crossrail) ... 7D 78
Ealing Common (Underground) ... 1F 97
Earl's Court (Underground) ... 4J 99
Earlsfield (Rail) ... 1A 136
East Acton (Underground) ... 6B 80
East Beckton Bus Station ... 6E 88
Eastcote (Underground) ... 7A 40
East Croydon Bus Station ... 2D 168
East Croydon (Rail & London Tramlink) ... 2D 168
East Dulwich (Rail) ... 4E 120
East Finchley (Underground) ... 4C 46
East Ham (Underground) ... 7C 70
East India (DLR) ... 7F 87
East Putney (Underground) ... 5G 117
Eden Park (Rail) ... 5C 158
Edgware Bus Station ... 6C 28
Edgware Road (Underground) ... 5C 4 (5C 82)
Edgware (Underground) ... 6C 28
Edmonton Bus Station ... 2C 34
Edmonton Green (Overground) ... 2B 34
Elephant & Castle
(Rail & Underground) ... 4C 102
Elmers End (Rail & London Tramlink) ... 4K 157
Elmstead Woods (Rail) ... 6C 142
Eltham (Rail) ... 5D 124
Elverson Road (DLR) ... 2D 122
Embankment Pier
(River Bus & Tours) ... 4G 13 (1J 101)
Embankment
(Underground) ... 4F 13 (1J 101)
Emirates Air Line ... 2H 105
Emirates Greenwich Peninsula ... 2H 105
Emirates Royal Docks ... 7J 87
Enfield Chase (Rail) ... 3H 23
Enfield Town (Overground) ... 3K 23
Erith (Rail) ... 5K 109
Essex Road (Rail) ... 7C 66
Euston (Rail, Underground & Overground)
... 2C 6 (3G 83)
Euston Square (Underground) ... 3B 6 (4G 83)
Ewell West (Rail) ... 7A 164

F

Fairfield Road Bus Station ... 2E 150
Fairlop (Underground) ... 1H 53
Falconwood (Rail) ... 4H 125
Farringdon (Rail, Underground & Crossrail)
... 5A 8 (5B 84)
Feltham (Rail) ... 1K 129
Fenchurch Street (Rail) ... 2J 15 (7F 85)
Festival Pier (River Tours) ... 4G 13 (1K 101)
Fieldway Stop (London Tramlink) ... 7D 170
Finchley Central (Underground) ... 1J 45
Finchley Road & Frognal
(Overground) ... 5A 64
Finchley Road (Underground) ... 6A 64
Finsbury Park Interchange (Bus) ... 2A 66
Finsbury Park (Rail & Underground) ... 2A 66
Forest Gate (Rail & Crossrail) ... 5J 69
Forest Hill (Rail & Overground) ... 2J 139
Fulham Broadway (Underground) ... 7J 99
Fulwell (Rail) ... 4H 131

G

Gallions Reach (DLR) ... 7F 89
Gants Hill (Underground) ... 6E 52
George Street Stop
(London Tramlink) ... 2C 168
Gipsy Hill (Rail) ... 5E 138
Gloucester Road (Underground) ... 4A 100
Golders Green (Underground) ... 1J 63
Goldhawk Road (Underground) ... 2E 98
Goodge Street (Underground) ... 5C 6 (5H 83)
Goodmayes (Rail & Crossrail) ... 1A 72
Gordon Hill (Rail) ... 1G 23
Gospel Oak (Overground) ... 4E 64
Grange Park (Rail) ... 5G 23
Gravel Hill Stop (London Tramlink) ... 6A 170
Great Portland Street
(Underground) ... 4K 5 (4F 83)
Greenford (Rail & Underground) ... 1H 77
Greenland Pier (River Bus) ... 3B 104
Green Line Coach Station ... *4K 17*
(off Bulleid Way)
Green Park (Underground) ... 4K 11 (1F 101)
Greenwich Pier (River Bus & Tours) ... 5E 104
Greenwich (Rail & DLR) ... 7D 104
Grove Park (Rail) ... 3K 141
Gunnersbury
(Underground & Overground) ... 5H 97

H

Hackbridge (Rail) ... 2F 167
Hackney Central (Overground) ... 6H 67
Hackney Downs (Overground) ... 5H 67
Hackney Wick (Overground) ... 6C 68
Hadley Wood (Rail) ... 1F 21
Haggerston (Overground) ... 1F 85
Hammersmith Bus Station ... 4E 98
Hammersmith (Underground) ... 4E 98
Hampstead Heath (Overground) ... 4C 64
Hampstead (Underground) ... 4A 64
Hampton Court (Rail) ... 4J 149
Hampton (Rail) ... 1E 148
Hampton Wick (Rail) ... 1C 150
Hanger Lane (Underground) ... 3E 78
Hanwell (Rail & Crossrail) ... 7J 77
Harlesden
(Underground & Overground) ... 2K 79
Harringay Green Lanes (Overground) ... 6B 48
Harringay (Rail) ... 6A 48
Harrington Road Stop
(London Tramlink) ... 3J 157
Harrow & Wealdstone
(Rail, Underground & Overground) ... 4J 41
Harrow Bus Station ... 6J 41
Harrow-on-the-Hill (Rail & Underground) ... 6J 41
Hatch End (Overground) ... 1E 40
Hatton Cross (Underground) ... 4H 111
Haydons Road (Rail) ... 5A 136
Hayes & Harlington (Rail & Crossrail) ... 3H 93
Hayes (Rail) ... 1J 171
Headstone Lane (Overground) ... 1F 41
Heathrow Airport
Terminals 2, 3 ... 3C 110
Terminal 4 ... 5D 110
Terminal 5 ... 6D 174
Heathrow Central Bus Station ... 3D 110
Heathrow Central (Rail) ... 3C 110
Heathrow Terminals 2 & 3
(Rail, Underground & Crossrail) ... 3C 110
Heathrow Terminal 4 (Rail) ... 6E 110
Heathrow Terminal 4
(Underground & Crossrail) ... 5E 110
Heathrow Terminal 5
(Rail, Underground & Crossrail) ... 6D 174
Hendon Central (Underground) ... 5D 44
Hendon (Rail) ... 6C 44
Herne Hill (Rail) ... 6B 120
Heron Quays (DLR) ... 1C 104
Highams Park (Overground) ... 6A 36
High Barnet (Underground) ... 4D 20
Highbury & Islington
(Rail, Underground & Overground) ... 6B 66
Highgate (Underground) ... 6F 47
High Street Kensington
(Underground) ... 2K 99
Hillingdon (Underground) ... 5D 56
Hither Green (Rail) ... 6G 123
Holborn (Underground) ... 6G 7 (6K 83)
Holland Park (Underground) ... 1H 99
Holloway Road (Underground) ... 5K 65
Homerton (Overground) ... 6K 67
Honor Oak Park
(Rail & Overground) ... 6K 121
Hornbeam Ho. ... 2A 104
Hornsey (Rail) ... 4K 47
Hounslow Central (Underground) ... 3F 113
Hounslow East (Underground) ... 2G 113
Hounslow (Rail) ... 5F 113
Hounslow West (Underground) ... 2C 112
Hoxton (Overground) ... 2F 85
Hyde Park Corner
(Underground) ... 6H 11 (2E 100)

I

Ickenham (Underground) ... 4E 56
Ilford (Overground & Crossrail) ... 3E 70
Imperial Wharf (Overground) ... 1A 118
Island Gardens (DLR) ... 5E 104
Isleworth (Rail) ... 2K 113

J

Jacobs Island Pier ... *2G 103*
(off Bermondsey Wall W.)

K

Kempton Park (Rail) ... 7K 129
Kennington (Underground) ... 5B 102
Kensal Green
(Underground & Overground) ... 3E 80
Kensal Rise (Overground) ... 2F 81
Kensington Olympia
(Rail, Underground & Overground) ... 3G 99
Kent House (Rail) ... 1A 158
Kentish Town (Rail & Underground) ... 5G 65
Kentish Town West (Overground) ... 6F 65
Kenton
(Underground & Overground) ... 6B 42
Kew Bridge (Rail) ... 5F 97
Kew Gardens
(Underground & Overground) ... 1G 115
Kidbrooke (Rail) ... 3K 123
Kilburn High Road (Overground) ... 1K 81
Kilburn Park (Underground) ... 2J 81
Kilburn (Underground) ... 6H 63
King George V (DLR) ... 1E 106
Kingsbury (Underground) ... 5G 43
King's Cross (Rail & Underground) ... 1E 6 (2J 83)
King's Cross St Pancras
(Underground) ... 1E 6 (3J 83)

London's Rail & Tube services

Key to lines and symbols

- Bakerloo
- Central
- Circle
- District — limited service
- Hammersmith & City
- Jubilee
- Metropolitan
- Northern
- Piccadilly
- Victoria
- Waterloo & City
- DLR
- London Overground
- London Trams
- TfL Rail
- Emirates Air Line cable car

- Chiltern Railways
- c2c — limited service
- Gatwick Express
- Great Northern
- Great Western Railway
- Greater Anglia — peak hours only
- Heathrow Express
- London Northwestern Railway
- South Western Railway — peak hours only
- Southeastern — peak hours only
- Southeastern high speed — peak hours and limited service
- Southern
- Thameslink — peak hours only

- ○ Interchange stations
- ⬭ Internal Interchange
- ○•••○ Under a 10 minute walk between stations
- ✈ Airport
- ⛴ Riverboat services
- 🚌 Victoria Coach Station
- Stratford — Station in both fare zones

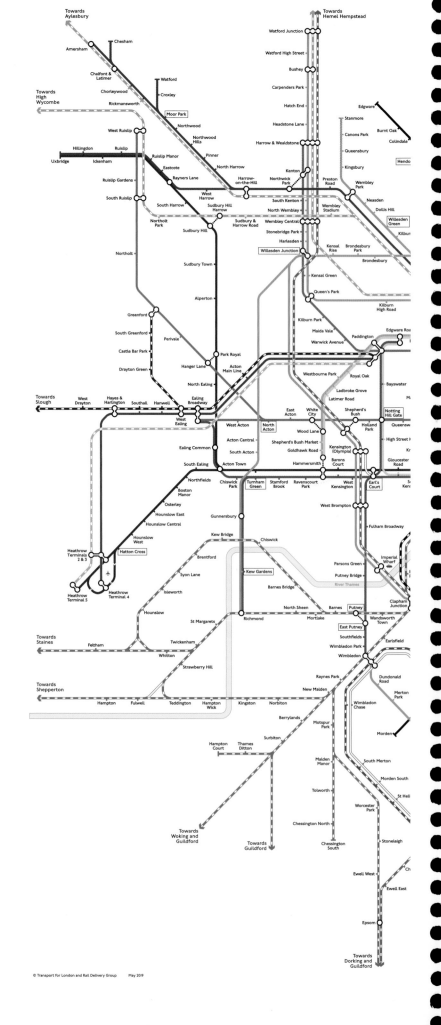

Towards Aylesbury
Towards Hemel Hempstead
Amersham
Chesham
Watford Junction
Watford High Street
Chalfont & Latimer
Watford
Bushey
Chorleywood
Croxley
Carpenders Park
Towards High Wycombe
Rickmansworth
Moor Park
Hatch End
Edgware
Northwood
Headstone Lane
Stanmore
Burnt Oak
West Ruislip
Northwood Hills
Harrow & Wealdstone
Canons Park
Colindale
Pinner
Kenton
Queensbury
Hillingdon
Ruislip
Ruislip Manor
North Harrow
Northwick Park
Preston Road
Kingsbury
Hendon
Uxbridge
Ickenham
Eastcote
Harrow-on-the-Hill
Wembley Park
Ruislip Gardens
Rayners Lane
West Harrow
South Kenton
Neasden
South Ruislip
South Harrow
Sudbury Hill Harrow
North Wembley
Wembley Stadium
Dollis Hill
Willesden Green
Northolt Park
Sudbury & Harrow Road
Stonebridge Park
Kilburn
Sudbury Hill
Harlesden
Kensal Rise
Brondesbury Park
Willesden Junction
Northolt
Sudbury Town
Brondesbury
Kensal Green
Queen's Park
Kilburn High Road
Alperton
Kilburn Park
Maida Vale
Edgware Road
Greenford
Warwick Avenue
Paddington
South Greenford
Perivale
Park Royal
Royal Oak
Bayswater
Castle Bar Park
Hanger Lane
Acton Main Line
Westbourne Park
Ladbroke Grove
Drayton Green
North Ealing
Latimer Road
Notting Hill Gate
Towards Slough
West Drayton
Hayes & Harlington
Southall
Hanwell
Ealing Broadway
East Acton
White City
Shepherd's Bush
Queensw
West Ealing
West Acton
North Acton
Wood Lane
Holland Park
High Street K
Acton Central
Shepherd's Bush Market
Ealing Common
South Acton
Goldhawk Road
Kensington (Olympia)
Gloucester Road
South Ealing
Acton Town
Hammersmith
Barons Court
Northfields
Chiswick Park
Turnham Green
Stamford Brook
Ravenscourt Park
West Kensington
Earl's Court
S Ken
Boston Manor
West Brompton
Osterley
Fulham Broadway
Hounslow East
Gunnersbury
Kew Bridge
Chiswick
Parsons Green
Imperial Wharf
Hounslow Central
Hounslow West
Kew Gardens
Putney Bridge
Heathrow Terminals 2 & 3
Hatton Cross
Brentford
Syon Lane
Barnes Bridge
River Thames
Isleworth
Clapham Junction
Heathrow Terminal 5
Heathrow Terminal 4
Hounslow
North Sheen
Barnes
Putney
St Margarets
Richmond
Mortlake
Wandsworth Town
East Putney
Towards Staines
Feltham
Southfields
Earlsfield
Twickenham
Wimbledon Park
Whitton
Wimbledon
Strawberry Hill
Raynes Park
Dundonald Road
Towards Shepperton
New Malden
Merton Park
Hampton
Fulwell
Teddington
Hampton Wick
Kingston
Norbiton
Wimbledon Chase
Morden
Berrylands
Motspur Park
Hampton Court
Thames Ditton
Surbiton
South Merton
Malden Manor
South Merton
Morden South
Tolworth
St Heli
Worcester Park
Towards Woking and Guildford
Chessington North
Stoneleigh
Towards Guildford
Chessington South
Ewell West
Ch
Ewell East
Epsom
Towards Dorking and Guildford

© Transport for London and Rail Delivery Group   May 2019

tfl.gov.uk

nationalrail.co.uk

316 A-Z Big London

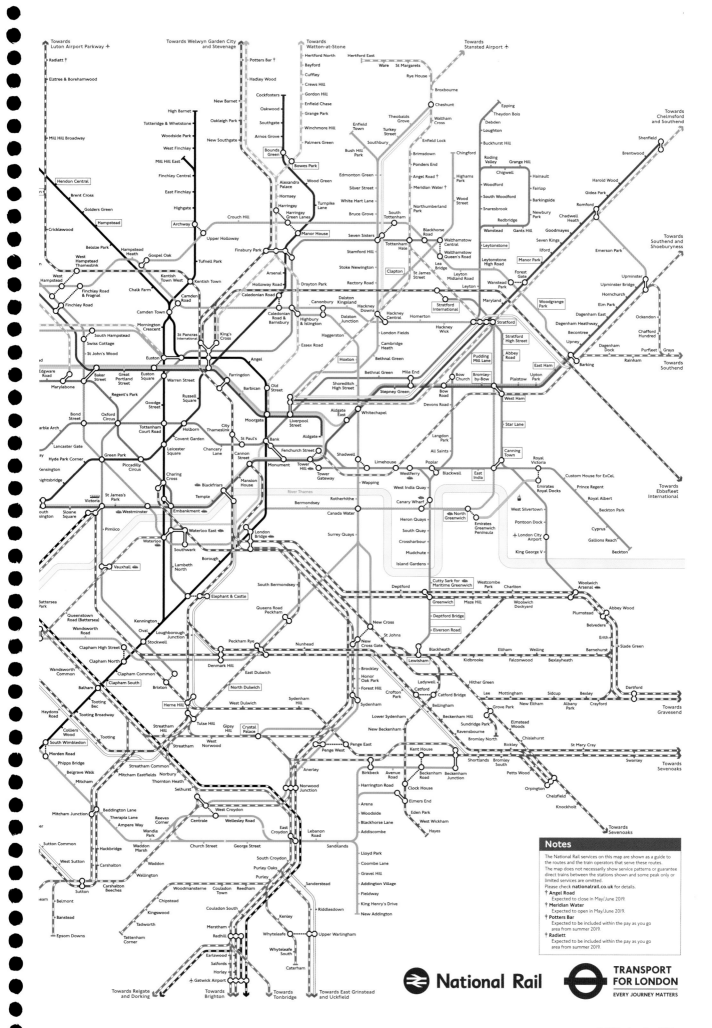

WEST END CINEMAS

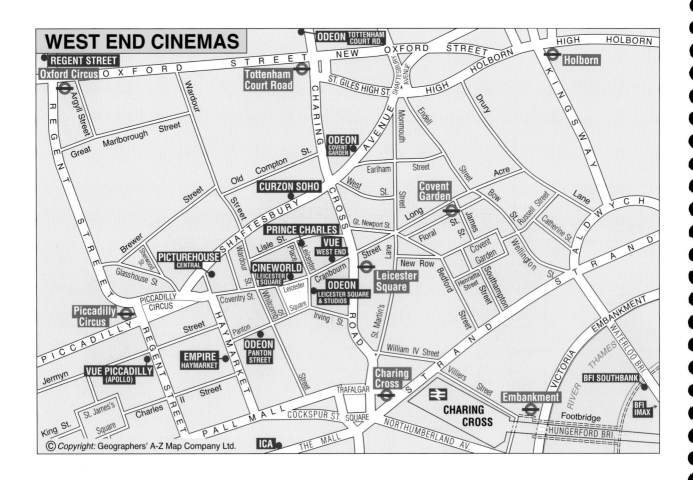

© Copyright: Geographers' A-Z Map Company Ltd.

WEST END THEATRES

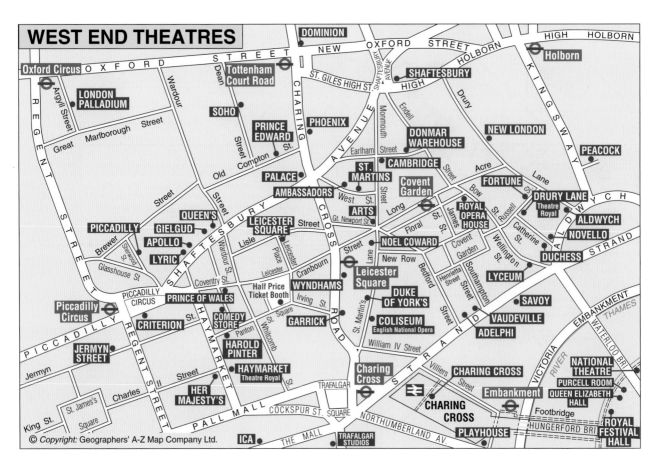

© Copyright: Geographers' A-Z Map Company Ltd.